£ 25.97

PARLIAMENTARY DEBATES

(HANSARD)

SIXTH SERIES—VOLUME 154

HOUSE OF COMMONS

OFFICIAL REPORT

SECOND SESSION OF THE FIFTIETH PARLIAMENT
OF THE UNITED KINGDOM OF GREAT BRITAIN
AND NORTHERN IRELAND
THIRTY-EIGHTH YEAR OF THE REIGN OF
HER MAJESTY QUEEN ELIZABETH II

SESSION 1988-89

COMPRISING PERIOD
6 JUNE—16 JUNE 1989

LONDON
HER MAJESTY'S STATIONERY OFFICE
£68 net

ISBN 0 10 681154 1

HER MAJESTY'S GOVERNMENT

MEMBERS OF THE CABINET

(FORMED BY THE RT. HON. MARGARET THATCHER, MP, JULY 1988)

PRIME MINISTER, FIRST LORD OF THE TREASURY AND MINISTER FOR THE CIVIL SERVICE—
The Rt. Hon. Margaret Thatcher, MP
SECRETARY OF STATE FOR FOREIGN AND COMMONWEALTH AFFAIRS—The Rt. Hon. Sir Geoffrey Howe, QC, MP
CHANCELLOR OF THE EXCHEQUER—The Rt. Hon. Nigel Lawson, MP
LORD CHANCELLOR—The Rt. Hon. The Lord Mackay of Clashfern
SECRETARY OF STATE FOR THE HOME DEPARTMENT—The Rt. Hon. Douglas Hurd, CBE, MP
SECRETARY OF STATE FOR WALES—The Rt. Hon. Peter Walker, MBE, MP
SECRETARY OF STATE FOR DEFENCE—The Rt. Hon. George Younger, TD, MP
SECRETARY OF STATE FOR EMPLOYMENT—The Rt. Hon. Norman Fowler, MP
SECRETARY OF STATE FOR NORTHERN IRELAND—The Rt. Hon. Tom King, MP
SECRETARY OF STATE FOR THE ENVIRONMENT—The Rt. Hon. Nicholas Ridley, MP
SECRETARY OF STATE FOR TRADE AND INDUSTRY AND PRESIDENT OF THE BOARD OF TRADE—
The Rt. Hon. The Lord Young of Graffham
SECRETARY OF STATE FOR EDUCATION AND SCIENCE—The Rt. Hon. Kenneth Baker, MP
SECRETARY OF STATE FOR HEALTH—The Rt. Hon. Kenneth Clarke, QC, MP
MINISTER OF AGRICULTURE, FISHERIES AND FOOD—The Rt. Hon. John MacGregor, OBE, MP
SECRETARY OF STATE FOR SCOTLAND—The Rt. Hon. Malcolm Rifkind, QC, MP
SECRETARY OF STATE FOR TRANSPORT—The Rt. Hon. Paul Channon, MP
SECRETARY OF STATE FOR SOCIAL SECURITY—The Rt. Hon. John Moore, MP
LORD PRESIDENT OF THE COUNCIL AND LEADER OF THE HOUSE OF COMMONS—The Rt. Hon. John Wakeham, MP
LORD PRIVY SEAL AND LEADER OF THE HOUSE OF LORDS—The Rt. Hon. The Lord Belstead
SECRETARY OF STATE FOR ENERGY—The Rt. Hon. Cecil Parkinson, MP
CHIEF SECRETARY TO THE TREASURY—The Rt. Hon. John Major, MP
CHANCELLOR OF THE DUCHY OF LANCASTER AND MINISTER OF TRADE AND INDUSTRY—
The Rt. Hon. Antony Newton, OBE, MP

LAW OFFICERS

ATTORNEY-GENERAL—The Rt. Hon. Sir Patrick Mayhew, QC, MP
LORD ADVOCATE—The Rt. Hon. The Lord Fraser of Carmyllie, QC
SOLICITOR-GENERAL—Sir Nicholas Lyell, QC, MP
SOLICITOR-GENERAL FOR SCOTLAND—Alan Rodger, Esq, QC

MINISTERS NOT IN THE CABINET

PARLIAMENTARY SECRETARY TO THE TREASURY—The Rt. Hon. David Waddington, QC, MP
MINISTER OF STATE, PRIVY COUNCIL OFFICE, (MINISTER FOR THE ARTS)—The Rt. Hon. Richard Luce, MP
MINISTERS OF STATE, FOREIGN AND COMMONWEALTH OFFICE—
The Rt. Hon. Lynda Chalker, MP
The Hon. William Waldegrave, MP
Minister for Overseas Development—Christopher Patten, Esq, MP
The Lord Glenarthur
PAYMASTER GENERAL—The Rt. Hon. Peter Brooke, MP
FINANCIAL SECRETARY TO THE TREASURY—The Rt. Hon. Norman Lamont, MP
MINISTERS OF STATE, HOME OFFICE—
The Rt. Hon. The Earl Ferrers
John Patten, Esq, MP
Tim Renton, Esq, MP
MINISTER OF STATE, WELSH OFFICE—Wyn Roberts, Esq, MP
MINISTERS OF STATE, MINISTRY OF DEFENCE—
Minister of State for Defence Procurement—The Rt. Hon. The Lord Trefgarne
Minister of State for the Armed Forces—The Hon. Archibald Hamilton, MP
MINISTER OF STATE, DEPARTMENT OF EMPLOYMENT—The Rt. Hon. John Cope, MP
MINISTER OF STATE, NORTHERN IRELAND OFFICE—The Rt. Hon. Ian Stewart, RD, MP
MINISTERS OF STATE, DEPARTMENT OF THE ENVIRONMENT—
Minister for Local Government—The Rt. Hon. John Gummer, MP
Minister for Housing, Environment and Countryside—The Earl of Caithness
Minister for Water and Planning—Michael Howard, Esq, QC, MP
MINISTER OF STATE, DEPARTMENT OF TRADE AND INDUSTRY—
Minister for Trade—The Hon. Alan Clark, MP
MINISTER OF STATE, DEPARTMENT OF EDUCATION AND SCIENCE—Mrs. Angela Rumbold, CBE, MP
MINISTER OF STATE, DEPARTMENT OF HEALTH—DAVID MELLOR, ESQ, QC, MP

MINISTERS OF STATE, SCOTTISH OFFICE—
  Ian Lang, Esq, MP
  The Lord Sanderson of Bowden
MINISTER OF STATE, DEPARTMENT OF TRANSPORT—
  Minister for Public Transport—Michael Portillo, Esq, MP
MINISTER OF STATE, DEPARTMENT OF SOCIAL SECURITY—
  Minister for Social Security—Nicholas Scott, Esq, MBE, MP
MINISTER OF STATE, DEPARTMENT OF ENERGY—The Rt. Hon. Peter Morrison, MP

DEPARTMENTS OF STATE AND MINISTERS

Agriculture, Fisheries and Food—
  MINISTER—The Rt. Hon. John MacGregor, OBE, MP
  PARLIAMENTARY SECRETARIES—
  The Baroness Trumpington
  Donald Thompson, Esq, MP
  Richard Ryder, Esq, OBE, MP

Arts and Libraries, Office of—
  MINISTER FOR THE ARTS—The Rt. Hon. Richard Luce, MP

Chancellor of the Duchy of Lancaster and Minister of Trade and Industry—
  The Rt. Hon. Antony Newton, OBE, MP

Civil Service, Office of the Minister for the—
  PRIME MINISTER AND MINISTER FOR THE CIVIL SERVICE—The Rt. Hon. Margaret Thatcher, MP
  MINISTER OF STATE, PRIVY COUNCIL OFFICE (MINISTER FOR THE ARTS)—The Rt. Hon. Richard Luce, MP

Defence—
  SECRETARY OF STATE—The Rt. Hon. George Younger, TD, MP
  MINISTER OF STATE FOR DEFENCE PROCUREMENT—The Rt. Hon. The Lord Trefgarne
  MINISTER OF STATE FOR THE ARMED FORCES—The Hon. Archibald Hamilton, MP
  PARLIAMENTARY UNDER-SECRETARY OF STATE FOR THE ARMED FORCES—Michael Neubert, Esq, MP
  PARLIAMENTARY UNDER-SECRETARY OF STATE FOR DEFENCE PROCUREMENT—The Hon. Tim Sainsbury, MP

Education and Science—
  SECRETARY OF STATE—The Rt. Hon. Kenneth Baker, MP
  MINISTER OF STATE—Mrs. Angela Rumbold, CBE, MP
  PARLIAMENTARY UNDER-SECRETARIES OF STATE—
  John Butcher, Esq, MP
  Robert Jackson, Esq, MP

Employment—
  SECRETARY OF STATE—The Rt. Hon. Norman Fowler, MP
  MINISTER OF STATE—The Rt. Hon. John Cope, MP
  PARLIAMENTARY UNDER-SECRETARIES OF STATE—
  John Lee, Esq, MP
  Patrick Nicholls, Esq, MP

Energy—
  SECRETARY OF STATE—The Rt. Hon. Cecil Parkinson, Esq, MP
  MINISTER OF STATE—The Rt. Hon. Peter Morrison, MP
  PARLIAMENTARY UNDER-SECRETARIES OF STATE—
  Michael Spicer, Esq, MP
  The Baroness Hooper

Environment—
  SECRETARY OF STATE—The Rt. Hon. Nicholas Ridley, MP
  MINISTERS OF STATE—
  Minister for Local Government—The Rt. Hon. John Gummer, MP
  Minister for Housing, Environment and Countryside—The Earl of Caithness
  Minister for Water and Planning—Michael Howard, Esq, QC, MP
  PARLIAMENTARY UNDER-SECRETARIES OF STATE—
  David Trippier, Esq, RD, MP
  Christopher Chope, Esq, OBE, MP
  Mrs. Virginia Bottomley, MP
  The Hon. Colin Moynihan, MP (Minister for Sport)
  The Lord Hesketh

Foreign and Commonwealth Affairs—
  SECRETARY OF STATE—The Rt. Hon. Sir Geoffrey Howe, QC, MP
  MINISTERS OF STATE—
  The Rt. Hon. Lynda Chalker, MP
  The Hon. William Waldegrave, MP
  Minister for Overseas Development—Christopher Patten, Esq, MP
  The Lord Glenarthur
  PARLIAMENTARY UNDER-SECRETARY OF STATE—Timothy Eggar, Esq, MP

Health—
SECRETARY OF STATE FOR HEALTH—The Rt. Hon. Kenneth Clarke, QC, MP
MINISTER OF STATE—
 David Mellor, Esq, QC, MP
PARLIAMENTARY UNDER-SECRETARY OF STATE—
 Roger Freeman, Esq, MP

Home Office—
SECRETARY OF STATE FOR THE HOME DEPARTMENT—The Rt. Hon. Douglas Hurd, CBE, MP
MINISTERS OF STATE—
 The Rt. Hon. The Earl Ferrers
 John Patten, Esq, MP
 Tim Renton, Esq, MP
PARLIAMENTARY UNDER-SECRETARY OF STATE—The Hon. Douglas Hogg, MP

Law Officers' Department—
ATTORNEY-GENERAL—The Rt. Hon. Sir Patrick Mayhew, QC, MP
SOLICITOR-GENERAL—Sir Nicholas Lyell, QC, MP

Lord Advocate's Department—
LORD-ADVOCATE—The Rt. Hon. The Lord Fraser of Carmyllie, QC
SOLICITOR-GENERAL FOR SCOTLAND—Alan Rodger, Esq, QC

Lord Chancellor—
The Rt. Hon. The Lord Mackay of Clashfern

Northern Ireland Office—
SECRETARY OF STATE FOR NORTHERN IRELAND—The Rt. Hon. Tom King, MP
MINISTER OF STATE—The Rt. Hon. Ian Stewart, RD, MP
PARLIAMENTARY UNDER-SECRETARIES OF STATE—
 The Lord Lyell
 Richard Needham, Esq, MP
 Dr. Brian Mawhinney, MP
 Peter Viggers, Esq, MP

Paymaster General—
The Rt. Hon. Peter Brooke, MP

Privy Council Office—
LORD PRESIDENT OF THE COUNCIL AND LEADER OF THE HOUSE OF COMMONS—The Rt. Hon. John Wakeham, MP
LORD PRIVY SEAL AND LEADER OF THE HOUSE OF LORDS—The Rt. Hon. The Lord Belstead
MINISTER OF STATE—The Rt. Hon. Richard Luce, MP

Scottish Office—
SECRETARY OF STATE FOR SCOTLAND—The Rt. Hon. Malcolm Rifkind, QC, MP
MINISTERS OF STATE—
 Ian Lang, Esq, MP
 The Lord Sanderson of Bowden
PARLIAMENTARY UNDER-SECRETARIES OF STATE—
 Lord James Douglas-Hamilton, MP
 Michael Forsyth, Esq, MP

Social Security—
SECRETARY OF STATE FOR SOCIAL SECURITY—The Rt. Hon. John Moore, MP
MINISTER OF STATE—
 Minister for Social Security—Nicholas Scott Esq, MBE, MP
PARLIAMENTARY UNDER-SECRETARIES OF STATE—
 The Lord Skelmersdale
 Peter Lloyd, Esq, MP

Trade and Industry—
SECRETARY OF STATE FOR TRADE AND INDUSTRY AND PRESIDENT OF THE BOARD OF TRADE—
 The Rt. Hon. The Lord Young of Graffham
CHANCELLOR OF THE DUCHY OF LANCASTER AND MINISTER OF TRADE AND INDUSTRY—
 The Rt. Hon. Antony Newton, OBE, MP
MINISTER OF STATE
 Minister for Trade—The Hon. Alan Clark, MP
PARLIAMENTARY UNDER-SECRETARY OF STATE—Robert Atkins, Esq, MP
PARLIAMENTARY UNDER-SECRETARY OF STATE FOR CORPORATE AFFAIRS—The Hon. Francis Maude, MP
PARLIAMENTARY UNDER-SECRETARY OF STATE FOR INDUSTRY AND CONSUMER AFFAIRS—Eric Forth, Esq, MP

Transport—
SECRETARY OF STATE FOR TRANSPORT—The Rt. Hon. Paul Channon, MP
MINISTER OF STATE
Minister for Public Transport—Michael Portillo, Esq, MP
PARLIAMENTARY UNDER-SECRETARIES OF STATE—
Minister for Roads and Traffic—Peter Bottomley, Esq, MP
Minister for Aviation and Shipping—The Lord Brabazon of Tara

Treasury—
PRIME MINISTER, FIRST LORD OF THE TREASURY AND MINISTER FOR THE CIVIL SERVICE—
The Rt. Hon. Margaret Thatcher, MP
CHANCELLOR OF THE EXCHEQUER—The Rt. Hon. Nigel Lawson, MP
CHIEF SECRETARY—The Rt. Hon. John Major, MP
PAYMASTER GENERAL—The Rt. Hon. Peter Brooke, MP
FINANCIAL SECRETARY TO THE TREASURY—The Rt. Hon. Norman Lamont, MP
ECONOMIC SECRETARY—Peter Lilley, Esq, MP
PARLIAMENTARY SECRETARY TO THE TREASURY—The Rt. Hon. David Waddington, QC, MP
LORDS COMMISSIONERS—
David Lightbown, Esq, MP
Kenneth Carlisle, Esq, MP
Alan Howarth, Esq, CBE, MP
David Maclean, Esq, MP
Stephen Dorrell, Esq, MP
ASSISTANT WHIPS—
John Taylor, Esq, MP
David Heathcoat-Amory, Esq, MP
The Hon. Tom Sackville, MP
Michael Fallon, Esq, MP
Sydney Chapman, Esq, MP

Welsh Office—
SECRETARY OF STATE FOR WALES—The Rt. Hon. Peter Walker, MP
MINISTER OF STATE—Wyn Roberts, Esq, MP
PARLIAMENTARY UNDER-SECRETARY OF STATE—Ian Grist, Esq, MP

Her Majesty's Household—
LORD CHAMBERLAIN—The Rt. Hon. The Earl of Airlie, KT, GCVO
LORD STEWARD—The Viscount Ridley, TD
MASTER OF THE HORSE—The Rt. Hon. The Earl of Westmorland, KCVO
TREASURER—David Hunt, Esq, MBE, MP
COMPTROLLER—Tristan Garel-Jones, Esq, MP
VICE-CHAMBERLAIN—Tony Durant, Esq, MP
CAPTAIN OF THE HONOURABLE CORPS OF GENTLEMEN-AT-ARMS—The Rt. Hon. The Lord Denham
CAPTAIN OF THE QUEEN'S BODYGUARD OF THE YEOMEN OF THE GUARD—The Viscount Davidson
LORDS IN WAITING—The Viscount Long, The Earl of Dundee, The Earl of Arran, The Lord Strathclyde, The Lord Henley

---

SECOND CHURCH ESTATES COMMISSIONER, REPRESENTING CHURCH COMMISSIONERS—The Rt. Hon. Michael Alison, MP

HOUSE OF COMMONS

PRINCIPAL OFFICERS AND OFFICIALS

THE SPEAKER—Rt. Hon. Bernard Weatherill, MP

CHAIRMAN OF WAYS AND MEANS—Rt. Hon. Harold Walker, MP

FIRST DEPUTY CHAIRMAN OF WAYS AND MEANS—Sir Paul Dean, MP
SECOND DEPUTY CHAIRMAN OF WAYS AND MEANS—Miss Betty Boothroyd, MP

CHAIRMEN'S PANEL—

Donald Coleman, Esq, MP, Patrick Cormack, Esq, MP, Stan Crowther, Esq, MP, Dame Janet Fookes, MP, Norman Hogg, Esq, MP, Geraint Howells, Esq, MP, John Hunt, Esq, MP, David Knox, Esq, MP, James Lamond, Esq, MP, Michael Latham, Esq, MP, Ted Leadbitter, Esq, MP, Geoffrey Lofthouse, Esq, MP, John McWilliam, Esq, MP, Michael J. Martin, Esq, MP, Sir Anthony Meyer, MP, Michael Morris, Esq, MP, Robert Rhodes James, Esq, MP, Sir Giles Shaw, MP, Sir Michael Shaw, MP, Michael Shersby, Esq, MP, Sir John Stradling Thomas, MP, Nicholas Winterton, Esq, MP

HOUSE OF COMMONS COMMISSION—

Rt. Hon. The Speaker (Chairman), Alan Beith, Esq, MP, Frank Dobson, Esq, MP, Rt. Hon. Sir Barney Hayhoe, MP, Rt. Hon. Peter Shore, MP, Rt. Hon. John Wakeham, MP

SECRETARY OF THE COMMISSION—W. A. Proctor

BOARD OF MANAGEMENT—

C. J. Boulton, CB (Chairman), Sir Victor Le Fanu, KCVO, D. Menhennet, D. Phil., G. A. Roberts, K. S. Morgan, W. J. J. Smillie, FHCIMA, FCFA, ACF

SECRETARY TO THE BOARD OF MANAGEMENT—B. A. Wilson

OFFICE OF THE SPEAKER

SPEAKER'S SECRETARY—P. J. Kitcatt, CB

SPEAKER'S COUNSEL—H. Knorpel, CB, QC, G. E. Gammie, CB, QC

SPEAKER'S CHAPLAIN—Rev. Canon D. C. Gray, TD, PhD

TRAINBEARER—D. J. Lord

DEPUTY TRAINBEARER—P. L. Warwick

HEO (ADMINISTRATION/DIARY)—Mrs. S. Norvell

HEO (ASSISTANT SECRETARY TO THE SPEAKER)—Miss S. Holt

ASSISTANT TO SPEAKER'S COUNSEL—P. Harvey, CB

OFFICE OF THE CHAIRMAN OF WAYS AND MEANS

SECRETARY TO THE CHAIRMAN OF WAYS AND MEANS—R. I. S. Phillips

DEPARTMENT OF THE CLERK OF THE HOUSE

CLERK OF THE HOUSE OF COMMONS—C. J. Boulton, CB

CLERK ASSISTANT—J. F. Sweetman, TD

CLERK OF COMMITTEES—M. T. Ryle

PRINCIPAL CLERKS—
　　H. M. Barclay (Public Bills)
　　D. W. Limon (Table Office)
　　W. R. McKay (Journal Office)
　　C. B. Winnifrith (Select Committees)
　　R. B. Sands (Overseas Office)
　　G. Cubie (Financial Committees)
　　A. J. Hastings (Select Committees)
　　J. R. Rose (Standing Committees)
　　R. J. Willoughby (Private Bills)

DEPUTY PRINCIPAL CLERKS—S. A. L. Panton, M. R. Jack, PhD, D. G. Millar, Mrs. J. Sharpe, Ms. A. Milner-Barry, R. W. G. Wilson, W. A. Proctor, F. A. Cranmer, R. J. Rogers, C. R. M. Ward, PhD, Ms. H. E. Irwin, D. W. N. Doig, A. Sandall, MLitt, D. L. Natzler, E. P. Silk, D. F. Harrison

SENIOR CLERKS—Mrs. S. A. de Ste. Croix, A. R. Kennon, D. W. Robson, L. C. Laurence Smyth, A. R. Gren, S. J. Patrick, D. J. Gerhold, C. J. Poyser, S. J. Priestley, A. H. Doherty, P. A. Evans, R. I. S. Phillips, R. G. James, Miss E. J. Baker, Ms. P. A. Helme, D. R. Lloyd, R. A. Lambert, J. B. Ingram (acting), I. G. Gilbert (acting), J. Darling (acting), J. M. Hope (acting)

CLERK OF SERVICES SUB-COMMITTEES—K. J. Brown

ASSISTANT CLERKS—B. M. Hutton, J. S. Benger, Ms. E. C. Samson, N. P. Walker, M. D. Hamlyn, P. C. Seaward, DPhil, C. G. Lee, C. D. Stanton

SENIOR EXECUTIVE OFFICERS—G. E. Clayton, Miss R. J. Challis, P. G. Moon

HIGHER EXECUTIVE OFFICERS—L. L. Kaye, A. P. Hubner, Miss S. J. Fox, Mrs. P. Fisher, F. McShane, J. D. Whatley, S. D. Barrett, M. Clark, Miss A. M. Loader, Mrs. S. M. Barrett, Miss F. L. Allingham, Mrs. L. M. Nugent, J. A. L. Dresner

SPECIALIST ASSISTANTS—M. P. Hillyard, M. J. Cremin, Ms. A. S. Frost, Dr. L. M. Rosborough, Dr. S. A. Harvey Miss K. Rogers, E. Thompson

EDITORIAL SUPERVISOR OF THE VOTE—G. H. Bright, MBE, DEPUTY—B. Tidball, ASSISTANTS—Miss B. Balcomb, Miss L. Lewis, J. Puricelli, K. B. Wood, P. D. Howlett, Mrs. L. R. Shade

EXAMINERS OF PETITIONS FOR PRIVATE BILLS—R. J. Willoughby, M. G. Pownall

REGISTRAR OF MEMBERS' INTERESTS—A. J. Hastings

TAXING OFFICER—R. J. Willoughby

SUPERINTENDING CLERK—R. A. Broomfield

CHIEF OFFICE CLERKS—M. P. Oxborough, N. P. Wright, Mrs. B. Ward, Miss D. E. Symes, Ms. C. J. D. Quantrell

DEPARTMENT OF THE SERJEANT AT ARMS

SERJEANT AT ARMS—Sir Victor Le Fanu, KCVO

DEPUTY SERJEANT AT ARMS—P. N. W. Jennings

ASSISTANT SERJEANT AT ARMS—M. J. A. Cummins

DEPUTY ASSISTANT SERJEANTS AT ARMS—P. A. J. Wright, J. F. Collins

CLERK IN CHARGE—Miss S. J. Scott Thomson

ASSISTANT CLERK IN CHARGE—Miss P. Penson

ADMISSION ORDER OFFICE—E. D. Palfrey, A. Chipperfield, BEM, Mrs. S. J. Warren

PRINCIPAL DOORKEEPER—G. H. Sargeant

SECOND PRINCIPAL DOORKEEPER—R. T. Warboys

SENIOR DOORKEEPERS—S. E. R. Skinner, R. A. F. Chapman, J. D. Garnett, R. H. Usher, C. Gray, J. C. W. Cooper

HEAD OFFICE KEEPER—W. H. Hazard, MBE

SENIOR OFFICE KEEPERS—M. Bryant, K. R. Kemp, K. R. Dickason

NURSING SISTER—Miss E. Needham

DEPARTMENT OF THE LIBRARY

LIBRARIAN—D. Menhennet, DPhil

DEPUTY LIBRARIAN—D. J. T. Englefield

LIBRARY AND RESEARCH—

ASSISTANT LIBRARIANS (Heads of Division)—G. F. Lock, Miss J. B. Tanfield

DEPUTY ASSISTANT LIBRARIANS (Heads of Section)—S. Z. Young, Mrs. H. R. Coates, Miss P. J. Baines, BLitt, K. G. Cuninghame, Mrs. J. M. Wainwright, FI InfSc, C. C. Pond, PhD, Mrs. C. B. Andrews, R. C. Clements, Mrs. J. M. Lourie

LIBRARY CLERKS, SENIOR—Ms. F. Poole, Mrs. J. M. Fiddick, C. R. Barclay, Mrs. C. M. Gillie, R. J. Ware, DPhil, Ms. D. Gore, PhD, R. J. Twigger, B. K. Winetrobe, T. N. Edmonds, R. J. Cracknell, Miss O. M. Gay, Miss E. M. McInnes, Mrs. G. L. Allen. ASSISTANT—Miss M. Baber, Miss A. J. Cook, PhD, E. J. Fishwick, MPhil, Mrs. K. Greener, Miss P. Strickland, A. J. L. Crompton, Miss V. A. Miller, Ms. M. J. Quiney, Ms. S. C. Penfold, Miss N. R. Donlon, Ms. H. M. Jeffs, J. R. Lunn, PhD, Mrs. P. Carling (temporary)

SENIOR LIBRARY EXECUTIVES—Mrs. S. M. Withers, ALA, Mrs. H. V. Holden, ALA, K. N. H. Parry, ALA, Ms. A. Muir, Miss C. E. Fretten, ALA, Miss I. O. White, ALA (acting)

EDUCATION OFFICER—Mrs. E. R. Stones. ASSISTANT—Mrs. C. C. O'Connor

PROJECT MANAGER, NEW BUILDING—Miss J. Seaton FLA

HIGHER EXECUTIVE OFFICERS—Mrs. P A. Bozdan, S. A. Wise

HIGHER LIBRARY EXECUTIVES—J. A. Prince, MLS, Mrs. P. V. Wiles, Mrs. D. W. Clark, Miss M. H. Fletcher, Mrs. P. E. Cook, ALA, Ms. H. Armstrong, Miss E. J. Jones, ALA, G. Haig, Miss B. Mee, MIInfSc, Miss G. L. Cooper, Mrs. E. H. Riley, ALA, Mrs. F. M. Ward, R. Freebury (acting)

SUPERINTENDING CLERK—J. R. Hutson.

EDITOR, WEEKLY BULLETIN—Miss B. A. Rowlands, ALA

LIBRARY EXECUTIVES—Mrs. M. A. Azim, ALA, Miss S. Holland, A. D. Parker, ALA, Ms. J. B. Hall, ALA, T. C. Holmes, P. E. M. Ward, Ms. F. Whittle, Mrs. J. M. Smith, ALA, Miss J. Lyall, Miss C. E. Jarrett, Ms. Z. A. Smallwood, C. M. Sear (acting)

CHIEF OFFICE CLERKS—D. J. Plowright, Miss N. Harland

EXECUTIVE OFFICERS—P. R. Davis, J. S. Came, D. B. Inns, Mrs. A. J. H. Mara, D. A. Brown, J. P. Brevitt, M. Greenhill (Head Library Attendant)

VOTE OFFICE—

DELIVERER OF THE VOTE—G. R. Russell

DEPUTY DELIVERER OF THE VOTE—H. C. Foster

ASSISTANT DELIVERER OF THE VOTE—O. B. T. Sweeney

HIGHER EXECUTIVE OFFICER—C. D. Lister

SUPERINTENDING CLERKS—Mrs. S. Fuzio, B. G. Underwood, A. J. Ashton (Sales Office)

VOTE OFFICE ASSISTANTS—T. S. Wilson, G. E. Howard, C. P. Williams, P. Hannett

ADMINISTRATION DEPARTMENT

HEAD OF DEPARTMENT—G. A. Roberts

FEES OFFICE—

ACCOUNTANT—J. L. G. Dobson

DEPUTY ACCOUNTANT—A. J. Lewis

SENIOR ASSISTANT ACCOUNTANT—G. P. Brown

ASSISTANT ACCOUNTANTS—A. R. Marskell, M. J. Barram, Miss M. M. McColl, M. Fletcher

SENIOR EXECUTIVE OFFICER—K. E. Walton

HIGHER EXECUTIVE OFFICERS—R. Gunn, M. J. H. Caswell, Mrs. P. D. Page, Mrs. N. Norman, Mrs. G. Crowther, Mrs. P. M. Lowther, Mrs. D. Hill, Miss P. Hurford, Mrs. J. S. Peach

EXECUTIVE OFFICERS—Miss D. E. Johnson, D. M. Allen, Miss L. J. F. Clay, Mrs. D. K. Euesden, D. J. D. Woods, Ms. M. R. Morris, Miss R. Harrison, G. L. Turner, Miss P. R. Mills, Mrs. J. D. Mead, Miss G. Bauman, P. F. Dawson, Miss S. E. Flavell, Miss S. A. Weaver, P. H. Olden, A. D. Rowlands, P. J. S. French

ESTABLISHMENTS OFFICE—

HEAD OF OFFICE—B. A. Wilson

DEPUTY HEAD OF OFFICE—J. A. Robb

SENIOR EXECUTIVE OFFICERS—Mrs. R. A. White, V. H. Stocker

HIGHER EXECUTIVE OFFICER—N.P. Crawley

EXECUTIVE OFFICERS—P. C. Kingsley, R. S. Harrison, Miss J. Bremner, M. Page

COMPUTER OFFICE—

COMPUTER OFFICER—R. S. Morgan, FBCS, FIInfSc

ASSISTANT COMPUTER OFFICERS—Mrs. G. S. P. Smith, Mrs. S. C. White

INTERNAL AUDITOR—A. A. Cameron

STAFF INSPECTOR—R. C. Collins

WELFARE OFFICER—Mrs. A. Mossop

DEPARTMENT OF THE OFFICIAL REPORT

EDITOR—K. S. Morgan

DEPUTY EDITOR—I. D. Church

PRINCIPAL ASSISTANT EDITORS—R. V. Hadlow, J. Gourley, J. Withers, P. Walker

ASSISTANT EDITORS—W. G. Garland, Vee Grainger, J. Ledgerwood, Miss V. A. A. Clarke, Miss H. A. Hales

COMMITTEE SUB-EDITORS—D. Crosswell, Mrs. A. Roberts, Miss L. Sutherland, S. M. Hutchinson, Miss V. A. Widgery, C. Fogarty, Mrs. H. J. G. Natzler, Miss M. Babington, Mrs. A. Street, L. Gilmore, Ms. G. Hardgrave, P. Oglethorpe, P. Hadlow, Miss C. Hanly, M. Watson

REPORTERS—Mrs. E. J. Gregory, Miss J. A. Bradshaw, Miss K. Stewart, Miss E. Morris, Mrs. J. Martin, J. Ransley, Miss J. Goodman, Ms. J. Dall, Mrs. P. Pickford

PRINCIPAL TRANSCRIBER—D. N. Harrington, MBE

DEPUTY PRINCIPAL TRANSCRIBERS—Mrs. M. J. Harding, Miss J. L. Brown

PRINCIPAL HANSARD ASSISTANT—Miss R. Washington

SENIOR HANSARD ASSISTANT—J. Brake

ANNUNCIATOR SUPERINTENDENT—G. Carpenter

REFRESHMENT DEPARTMENT

GENERAL MANAGER—W. J. J. Smillie, FHCIMA, FCFA, ACF

DEPUTY GENERAL MANAGER—E. J. Nash, MCFA

PERSONNEL ADMINISTRATOR—Mrs. S. M. Nicholls, FHCIMA, MIPM

PERSONAL ASSISTANT TO GENERAL MANAGER—Mrs. A. G. Lunn

BANQUETING MANAGER—C. J. Griffiths

CATERING ACCOUNTANT—D. R. W. Wood, FCA

ASSISTANT CATERING ACCOUNTANT—Mrs. B. A. Langley

EXECUTIVE CHEF—I. Gabay

HEAD CELLARMAN—D. Balcombe

HEAD STOREMAN—A. E. Edmond

SHORTHAND WRITER TO THE HOUSE—Mrs. E. M. C. Holland

PARLIAMENTARY WORKS OFFICER (PSA)—B. C. Sewell

HEAD OF SECURITY—Chief Superintendent A. J. Coxon

COMMUNICATIONS MANAGER—Mrs. J. Garbutt

POSTMASTER—J. Arnold

TRANSPORT MANAGER—R. H. Hyde

6 June 1989

THE
PARLIAMENTARY DEBATES

OFFICIAL REPORT

IN THE SECOND SESSION OF THE FIFTIETH PARLIAMENT OF THE
UNITED KINGDOM OF GREAT BRITAIN AND NORTHERN IRELAND
[WHICH OPENED 25 JUNE 1987]

THIRTY-EIGHTH YEAR OF THE REIGN OF
HER MAJESTY QUEEN ELIZABETH II

SIXTH SERIES   **VOLUME 154**

THIRTEENTH VOLUME OF SESSION 1988-89

House of Commons

Tuesday 6 June 1989

The House met at half-past Two o'clock

PRAYERS

[MR. SPEAKER *in the Chair*]

MESSAGES FROM THE QUEEN

DOUBLE TAXATION RELIEF

THE VICE-CHAMBERLAIN OF THE HOUSEHOLD reported Her Majesty's Answer to the Address, as follows:

I have received your Address praying that the Double Taxation Relief (Taxes on the Estates of Deceased Persons and Inheritances and on Gifts) (Sweden) Order 1989 be made in the form of the draft laid before your House.

I will comply with your request.

SUMMER TIME

THE VICE-CHAMBERLAIN OF THE HOUSEHOLD reported Her Majesty's Answer to the Address, as follows:

I have received your Address praying that the Summer Time Order 1989 be made in the form of the draft laid before your House.

I will comply with your request.

PRIVATE BUSINESS

ASSOCIATED BRITISH PORTS (HULL) BILL

ISLE OF WIGHT BILL

TEES (NEWPORT BRIDGE) BILL *[Lords]*

TYNE AND WEAR PASSENGER TRANSPORT BILL

Orders for Third Reading read.
To be read the Third time on Thursday 8 June.

NEW SOUTHGATE CEMETERY AND CREMATORIUM LIMITED BILL

Order for consideration read.
To be considered on Thursday 8 June.

Oral Answers to Questions

EDUCATION AND SCIENCE

Links with Business and Industry

1. **Mr. Cran:** To ask the Secretary of State for Education and Science what resources are made available to local education authorities to ensure that secondary schools are able to develop effective links with businesses.

6. **Mr. Jacques Arnold:** To ask the Secretary of State for Education and Science what steps he is taking to encourage awareness of industry in schools.

The Parliamentary Under-Secretary of State for Education and Science (Mr. John Butcher): Resources are made available for the development of links between schools and business through a number of initiatives involving schools, local education authorities and national organisations. The Department makes direct contributions to particular projects and organisations, publishes and distributes information, and makes funding available to local education authorities for the training of teachers. Industrial and economic awareness are cross-curricular themes in the national curriculum.

Mr. Cran: Does my hon. Friend agree that despite the excellent schemes, some of which are undoubtedly very good, there is a patchiness about the implementation of links between schools and industry so that we are in danger of producing more industrial illiterates than necessary? Against that background, and on the assumption that he agrees with what I say, will my hon. Friend find time to review the implementation of the scheme to see whether there are ways to improve and to even out its performance throughout the United Kingdom in view of the need to attract the best brains into industry?

Mr. Butcher: My hon. Friend, with his great experience in these matters, makes a serious point. We wish to see best practice become common practice, and my hon. Friend's erstwhile colleagues in the Confederation of British Industry are considering how to bring co-ordination to bear on a range of links between education and industry. However, we do not wish to dampen local enthusiasm and dynamism, which appear to be the key to success in these efforts. I am satisfied that there is much enthusiasm, but in the light of the Cadbury report, I appeal to employers to come forward in greater numbers. The schools are ready for the links and wish to see much more contact. Employers should match their enthusiasm.

Mr. Arnold: Will my hon. Friend comment on the development of the technical and vocational education initiative? My constituency of Gravesham has a programme which does a considerable amount to develop the awareness of school students of the opportunities to be found in industry. Surely we should give added emphasis to that area.

Mr. Butcher: When the initiative was first discussed there was some cynicism, which I believe has now all but evaporated. I am delighted that TVEI is being pursued with such enthusiasm, particularly by teachers. It has been a great success. In particular, it seems to "turn on" certain categories of pupil who may find the traditional curriculum less exciting than they would wish. A spend of some £900 million over 10 years shows the kind of cash support that we are prepared to give to this significant breakthrough.

Mr. Flannery: Does the Minister agree that there is a great deal more to education than links with business? Education is for life, and must be broad and tolerant. There is a grave danger—[*Interruption.*] The laughter from Conservative Members suggests that they do not agree with what I am saying, but it is very important. The links with life must be broad, tolerant and educational, not reduced to the distinctly narrow viewpoint of the Conservative party, which is causing such chaos in our education system.

Mr. Butcher: There is no conflict between our traditional desire for the education of the whole man—or the whole person—and the need to establish links with the world of commerce and industry. I put it to the hon. Gentleman that someone who leaves our school system without the basic capability of standing on his or her own feet is not a whole person. Our main priority must be to give people that first capability.

Teachers (Recruitment)

2. **Mr. Arbuthnot:** To ask the Secretary of State for Education and Science what progress his Department is making in promoting teaching as a career.

The Minister of State, Department of Education and Science (Mrs. Angela Rumbold): Our approach, through national publicity and the work of the teaching as a career unit, is creating a positive recruitment climate. This is reflected in the record numbers in recent years applying for

teacher training places, and in the very high response to our recent advertising campaign, to which there were more than 10,000 responses.

Mr. Arbuthnot: Will my hon. Friend confirm that teaching is an extremely important, valuable and good career, but, that while the Government are taking positive steps to encourage people to adopt it others tend to emphasise only the negative aspects? Should they not take note of the words of Walter Ievers, the incoming president of the National Association of Head Teachers, who said recently that negative attitudes were themselves demoralising?

Mrs. Rumbold: I agree. The incoming president of the association was right in saying that negative attitudes do not help the general image of teachers. Conservative Members have a high regard for the teaching profession. We consider it an honourable profession that is executed extraordinarily well by the vast majority of teachers. I am surprised that teachers do not recognise how easily they could regain their authority by showing how competently they are managing the changes in our education system.

Mr. Spearing: Does the Minister agree that in every school, day visits by pupils and particularly longer adventure residential journeys in this country are a valuable means of irrigating learning? Does she accept my view, based on 14 years' experience, that such activities are especially valuable in the case of reluctant pupils, and will she and her right hon. Friend the Secretary of State review the mess-up that they have made and change the rules so that willing teachers can pursue those activities to the benefit of their pupils and of education? More teachers will then stay in our schools, and more will be attracted to teaching—the reverse of the result that the current terrible arrangements are producing.

Mrs. Rumbold: I ask the hon. Gentleman to study carefully the recommendations in the Education Reform Act 1988 on charging for extra-mural activities. Those recommendations allow for all such activities to continue, and indeed follow exactly the changes recommended to the Department—which was not originally minded to make any changes—by local education authorities.

Mr. Kirkhope: Does my hon. Friend agree that there are some difficulties in achieving a balance between teachers wishing to go into one specialty or another? Can she say a word or two about how that imbalance will be remedied?

Mrs. Rumbold: Yes. My right hon. Friend the Secretary of State has taken considerable steps towards ensuring that people are attracted to areas of shortage by means of bursaries, so that they will enter teaching and take it up as a career. That has been very successful. The most recent bursaries offered to those wishing to teach chemistry has resulted in an 8 per cent. increase in the number wishing to enter the profession.

Mr. Straw: The evidence of the recent Gallup poll in the *Daily Telegraph* shows a 40 per cent. drop in support for the Conservative party among teachers since the last general election and that four in 10 of our most experienced teachers wish to leave the profession. Does not that confirm the verdict of the *Daily Express* "that the tolerance of parents—and of voters—" on the Government's education record

"is almost exhausted"?
Why do the Minister and the Secretary of State continue to deny that there is still a serious crisis in respect of our teaching force?

Mrs. Rumbold: The polls to which the hon. Gentleman refers reflect the attitudes of the people who are invited to respond to them. Teachers' actions are reflected by the independent interim advisory committee's report, which reaffirms that the number of people leaving the teaching profession in 1989 is only 1 per cent. of the total.

Mr. Dickens: Does my hon. Friend agree that it is difficult for my right hon. and hon. Friends to take a lecture on teacher recruitment when it was the last Labour Government who, between 1974 and 1979, devalued teachers' pay by as much as 12 per cent.?

Mrs. Rumbold: My hon. Friend is absolutely right. Under the present Government, teachers' pay has increased in the order of 40 per cent.

Student Loans

3. **Mr. Frank Field:** To ask the Secretary of State for Education and Science if he will make a statement on the implementation of his White Paper on student loans.

4. **Mr. Harry Greenway:** To ask the Secretary of State for Education and Science if he will make a statement on the progress of his plans for top-up loans for students.

The Parliamentary Under-Secretary of State for Education and Science (Mr. Robert Jackson): We are continuing to hold constructive discussions with a range of financial institutions about their possible participation in the administration of top-up loans. My right hon. Friend will announce our conclusions in due course.

Mr. Field: As the Government have been collecting information in America, can the Minister tell the House the average size of debt of American students at the end of their courses and the dropout rate, and how both compare with the British scene?

Mr. Jackson: It is not possible to make a comparison with the British scene because we do not yet have student loans, but if the hon. Gentleman studies the White Paper he will find that the figures of comparative indebtedness at the end of the course of study for the different countries which have student loans—as just about every other country does—show that total borrowing by students when our system is fully operational will be considerably less then is already the case in many other countries.

Mr. Greenway: Is my hon. Friend aware that I welcome the fact that there are 266 more students in higher education than there were 10 years ago? *[Interruption.]* Does he agree that they are better provided for in terms of grants than any other students in the world? Will he take note of the advice of Polonius to his son:
"Neither a borrower, nor a lender be"?
What would my hon. Friend's answer have been if Polonius had given him that advice.

Mr. Jackson: My hon. Friend, in his usual modest way, underestimates the Government's contribution to the expansion of higher education. The number of students has increased by 260,000 since we came to office. I will address the serious question put by my hon. Friend the

Member for Ealing, North (Mr. Greenway) about indebtedness in two ways—practically and philosophically. The practical answer is that credit is a fact of life. We know—there is evidence of this in the White Paper—that the use of credit spreads across all classes. We also have evidence from our survey of student income and expenditure of the substantial borrowing that students already incur. The philosophical answer is that is is important for everyone to regard higher education as a form of investment by society on behalf of the economy and of culture. That is the taxpayers' contribution. It is also investment by an individual in his own future. It affords substantial personal benefit, so there should be a reasonable personal contribution to its costs.

Mr. Simon Hughes: Does the Minister admit that he has already failed in the objective set out in the White Paper of finding a cost-effective scheme that the financial institutions will administer? On his own estimate of an initial cost of £120 million, and the scheme not being self-balancing until the end of the century, and given all the reports that the Government will have to find more than £500 million to subsidise the banks, is it not already clear that the loans scheme will cost the country and the Government a fortune?

Mr. Jackson: I admire the hon. Gentleman's keen speculative intelligence. I refer him to the words of the penultimate Liberal Prime Minister, "Wait and see.".

Mr. Haselhurst: Has my hon. Friend considered the particular problems of deaf students and the danger that they will get a lower standard of employment than they deserve and may therefore run into corresponding difficulties in paying off loans which might be higher as a result of their special needs?

Mr. Jackson: I should point out to my hon. Friend a feature of the loans scheme which has been much neglected by commentators upon it. The obligation to repay the loan will be related to income. That should be more than enough to take care of the problem to which my hon. Friend has referred.

Mr. Andrew Smith: Now that I have obtained and today placed in the House of Commons Library the responses that the Government refused to publish in relation to the loans White Paper, will the Minister come clean and admit what his written answer to me on 15 February kept hidden—that those responses are overwhelmingly in opposition to the Government's proposals? Bearing in mind the reports which the Minister has on his desk and which show that it would cost £530 million even to induce the banks to consider operating his scheme, will not even he now concede that these unworkable and profoundly damaging proposals should be dropped, or does he intend to go on being more economical with the truth than he proposes to be with taxpayers' money?

Mr. Jackson: I have here the Labour party's summary of the responses. One third of those responses agreed with the hon. Member for Durham, North (Mr. Radice) in supporting a graduate tax.

Grant-maintained Status

5. **Mr. Pawsey:** To ask the Secretary of State for Education and Science how many inquiries and how many applications have so far been received from schools considering grant-maintained status.

The Secretary of State for Education and Science (Mr. Kenneth Baker): To date, I have approved 15 schools for grant-maintained status. A further 32 schools are currently embarked on the application procedures. Many more schools have expressed an interest.

Mr. Pawsey: I thank my right hon. Friend for his extremely helpful reply, but may I ask whether he is satisfied that we are doing enough to turn those inquiries into grant-maintained schools? Will he take the opportunity to comment on an education policy document issued by the Labour party, which calls for the abolition of grant-maintained schools? Does he agree that such documents should be speedily kebabed?

Mr. Baker: We now have certain proposals from the Labour party which purport to be an education policy. The Opposition want the end of grant-maintained schools. There is no question about that. They do not recognise how popular those schools are with parents and children —*[Interruption.]* Yes, they are popular with parents in Skegness, in Birmingham, in Manchester, in Bolton and throughout the country. The trouble with the Opposition is that when they see something up and running, all they want to do is to abolish it.

Mr. Grocott: Will the Secretary of State confirm that he has repeatedly said that there will be no change in the financial provision for a school once it has achieved grant-maintained status but that he has now said that a further £30,000 handout of taxpayers' money will be given to all grant-maintained schools? Can he assure the House that he will also make £30,000 available to every state school in the country?

Mr. Baker: The basis of the capital funding will be the same for grant-maintained schools as for local education authority maintained schools. The amount to which the hon. Gentleman referred—up to £30,000—is intended to meet early additional expenditure which might fall on the governors of schools in preparing for grant-maintained status. Such expenditure might include advertising for staff, the introduction of financial and administrative systems and other arrangements for taking on their new responsibilities.

Mr. Dunn: Will the Secretary of State confirm yet again that an application for grant-maintained status is a further option available to parents and governors of local schools? Does not that further option which has been made available by the Conservatives compare favourably with the Labour party's policies, which would lead to the abolition of Church schools, grammar schools, secondary modern schools, city technology colleges and the assisted places scheme and would do untold damage to the independent sector? Our policies are about choice, not discussion.

Mr. Baker: I pay tribute to my hon. Friend for his assistance in getting this legislation on the statute book. I confirm entirely what he said. The Labour party wants to destroy all the initiatives that we have taken. It wants to undermine the national curriculum and private schools and destroy CTCs, grammar schools and grant-maintained schools. Its education policy is destruction and abolition.

Language Study

7. **Mr. Livsey:** To ask the Secretary of State for Education and Science if he has any plans to increase the number of foreign languages that are currently listed under schedule 1 of the Education (National Curriculum) (Modern Foreign Language) Order 1989.

Mrs. Rumbold: My right hon. Friend has no such plans.

Mr. Livsey: Why is the Minister denying children the right to learn two languages, and why have the Government prevented the implementation of the Lingua programme in Britain? Is that not proof that the Conservative party is less than wholeheartedly a European party?

Mrs. Rumbold: I think that the hon. Gentleman is under a misapprehension. In Brussels my right hon. Friend the Secretary of State negotiated Britain's participation in a substantial part of the Lingua programme, not least post-16 vocational experience and exchange for students and for teachers who travel to Europe to learn and to extend their teaching practice. Schools are outside the EEC treaty as it was negotiated. Only 40 per cent. of our 16-year-olds are learning a foreign language. Under the national curriculum all children will learn at least one foreign language. We should concentrate on doing that and being able to walk before we run.

Mr. Evennett: Does my hon. Friend agree that progress is being made in the teaching of languages and that under the core curriculum further improvements will be forthcoming? The Lingua proposal is impractical in the present climate.

Mrs. Rumbold: I am afraid that my hon. Friend is right. No one wishes languages to be taught more urgently than we do, which is why my right hon. Friend provided in the national curriculum for all children between 11 and 16 to learn at least one foreign language.

Mr. Fatchett: Does not the Minister realise how complacent she sounds about the state of foreign language teaching? What reason of sovereignty denies our schoolchildren access to the resources that will be provided by the Lingua programme, or is it just the Prime Minister's pride that is denying children the opportunity of modern language teaching, which would enable them to deal better with the Common Market post 1992?

Mrs. Rumbold: As the hon. Gentleman feels so strongly about the matter, it will be interesting to know why the Labour party's proposals exclude a modern foreign language from the core curriculum.

National Curriculum (Primary Schools)

8. **Mrs. Mahon:** to ask the Secretary of State for Education and Science what plans he has to ensure that teachers are fully prepared to implement the national curriculum in primary schools next term.

Mrs. Rumbold: Specific grants are available for £100 million additional expenditure by local education authorities to support introduction of the national curriculum. We have allowed schools two extra closure days for training, and the National Curriculum Council has provided advice and training materials.

Mrs. Mahon: Does the Minister realise and understand the anxiety that primary school teachers feel about the nature and pace of the curriculum change? What plans does she have to provide the extra specialist training and resources necessary so that children with special needs have access to the national curriculum? Would not the Minister be the first to condemn teachers if they acted in such an irresponsible way with such haste?

Mrs. Rumbold: The hon. Lady will be satisfied to know that two extra in-service training days are being provided for primary school teachers in particular to learn about and to update themselves on the national curriculum. In addition, we have made provision for all schools to have the national curriculum documents in their hands in good time, so I hope that all primary school teachers will feel themselves ready. Some provisions will not necessarily apply to children with special needs, but we want such children to study the national curriculum from day one if they can.

Mr. Baldry: Clearly, it is vital that teachers have adequate in-service training to prepare them for the national curriculum, but is there any reason why much of that training should not take place during school holidays so as not to disrupt normal classroom activities?

Mrs. Rumbold: Yes, I tend to agree with my hon. Friend. It is interesting to note that of the 1,265 hours that a teacher is contracted to teach, the average primary school teacher spends 850 hours in lessons. If time is allowed for breaks, assembly and supervision, primary school teachers should still have 130 hours within the allocated time outside school holidays and weekends in which to do additional training.

Ms. Armstrong: I am sure that many primary school teachers will be horrified to hear the Minister's complacency this afternoon. Does she understand primary school teachers' fears that their professional integrity is being undermined by the completely haphazard way in the which the Government have introduced the core curriculum documents? How are teachers seriously to prepare, through training, for the teaching of English in September when the order has not yet been approved by the House? How are they to develop methods of monitoring and to agree ways in which English can be properly taught when the documents will not reach some schools until after the end of the summer term?

Mrs. Rumbold: It is exactly such an attitude that contributes to the demoralisation of teachers. Hearing such statements do not help. Primary school teachers are working extremely hard. Those whom I have met in the schools are looking forward with enthusiasm to the introduction of the national curriculum and are working hard to make their systems work. They appreciate that what they have been doing over the years has now been underwritten by Government action.

City Technology Colleges

9. **Mr. Anthony Coombs:** To ask the Secretary of State for Education and Science what progress has been made with the establishment of city technology colleges.

Mr. Kenneth Baker: The CTC programme is already a great success. Kingshurst opened last year, Nottingham and Teesside will open in September, and Bradford, Dartford, Gateshead and the London school for performing arts and technology will open in 1990. We have public commitments of sponsorship for a further seven colleges and more sponsors will bring us easily up to our target of 20.

Mr. Coombs: Does my right hon. Friend agree that the success of CTCs is based upon their popularity with parents, the motivation of their students and the commitment of their teachers? In evidence of that, does he agree that applications for Solihull's CTC doubled last year, it is now three and a half times over-subscribed and its teachers, despite earning salaries similar to those in the state sector, work a school day that is 25 per cent. longer than average, showing their commitment to the CTC concept and the ethos underlying that?

Mr. Baker: My hon. Friend is correct. The colleges are proving to be popular. Indeed, he underestimates the popularity of the one in Solihull. In the first year, there were some 400 applications to go there, and in the second year, starting in September, there were some 1,200 inquiries from parents who wanted to send their children there. That clearly shows the school's popularity. I confirm that the schools operate for longer hours and take shorter holidays and that students and teachers want to work in them.

Mr. Morley: Are not the funding arrangements for CTCs dramatically different from what was originally planned and is not the contribution from the private sector a shadow of what was originally proposed? Is not the Secretary of State simply buying the schools to save his own face and are not the schools irrelevant in terms of the needs of children in modern education?

Mr. Baker: That is completely wrong. For Kingshurst, the initial contribution was £1 million. That has risen to £2 million, and the school is now on its way to a third million. Taking the programme as a whole, nearly £40 million has now been pledged by British business to this programme, and it will meet its obligations. This is the most successful private industrial fund-raising scheme in the history of education in this country.

Mr. Devlin: Will my right hon. Friend confirm that far from depriving people in schools of much-needed capital investment, the Teesside city technology college is a Government investment which comes on top of a 41 per cent. increase in capital allocation for Cleveland schools this year?

Mr. Baker: I confirm what my hon. Friend says. I do not believe that the CTCs will have a harmful effect on the schools in their surrounding areas. In the case of Solihull and Birmingham, the other schools have already changed their curriculum, have smartened up their whole approach to attracting students and are attracting more students.

Mr. Nellist: Has not the public funding of so-called city technology colleges removed public funding from other colleges of technology in cities, such as Oxford polytechnic? The Secretary of State will be aware—because he received on 12 May a letter from me about this case—that this has led, for example, to a second year geology student, Alexandra Spawls writing to 200 public figures asking each of them to lend her £10 until her course is finished so that she can complete a mandatory six-week solo mapping project on the Isle of Mull and thereby gain her degree, which her grant and help from Oxford polytechnic are insufficient to cover. Instead of fancy back-door privatisation schemes, the right hon. Gentleman should fully fund the existing student population, rather than turning them into beggars.

Mr. Baker: The increase in expenditure for polytechnics this year, in current costs, is nearly 10 per cent., and I have increased the capital allocation for the polytechnic sector this year from £50 million to £84 million.

Mr. Andrew Mitchell: Is my right hon. Friend aware that such is the popularity of Nottingham's forthcoming CTC that I receive regularly letters from my constituents in Gedling complaining that their children do not live within the catchment area of the CTC, and they very much wish that they did?

Mr. Baker: I confirm what my hon. Friend says, and I am sure that the Nottingham CTC will be as popular as the Birmingham CTC. There is now growing demand from towns and cities all over the country to have CTCs, and I suspect that we shall exceed the original target of 20.

Mr. Straw: Is the Secretary of State aware that the proposals to turn the Sylvan school in Croydon and the Haberdashers' Aske girls' school in Lewisham into CTCs are so unpopular with parents that they have voted overwhelmingly against those proposals? Does he appreciate that his refusal to accept conclusively those ballot results will reveal his support for parents' rights to be nothing more than a hollow sham?

Mr. Baker: The answer to the hon. Gentleman's question about Sylvan is that, as he knows, proposals for closure will be coming to me shortly and I shall decide on those proposals on their merits. As for Haberdashers' Aske, the result of the ballot shows that the majority of those voting are in favour of a CTC, and that provides a firm and clear basis on which the governors of the Haberdashers' Aske school may make a decision.

10. **Mr. Simon Hughes:** To ask the Secretary of State for Education and Science what representations he has recently received regarding the establishment of city technology colleges in London and the south-east.

Mr. Kenneth Baker: I am delighted to say that there is tremendous interest in the establishment of CTCs in London and the south-east. As a result, I continue to receive many representations on a number of different possibilities.

Mr. Hughes: Does the Secretary of State concede that there is substantial concern among parents and teachers who might be affected by their school becoming a CTC lest their influence on the future of the school is substantially reduced? For example, Bacon school in Bermondsey, which would be entitled as an over 50-pupil school to have

five elected parents and two elected teachers, would be replaced by a school with one elected parent and one elected teacher. What does the right hon. Gentleman say to the charge that that is entirely inconsistent with the local management of schools, in which I thought be believed?

Mr. Baker: I wish that the hon. Gentleman would make it clear whether or not he supports the Bacon initiative in his locality, despite his repeated support for a national campaign against CTCs. I know that the governors of Bacon school are considering the possibility of moving to a site in docklands with a substantial amount of industrial sponsorship. That seems to be a remarkably attractive option, but I shall of course await the outcome of their deliberations.

Mr. Maples: In correcting the hon. Member for Blackburn (Mr. Straw), my right hon. Friend showed that he is aware that the parents and children of Haberdashers' Aske schools voted by a substantial majority in a joint ballot last week in favour of a proposal to convert to a CTC. Is he aware that this was in the face of concerted and orchestrated opposition by the Labour-controlled Inner London education authority to stop the ballot taking place? As the parents, teachers and governors have now voted in favour of this proposal, will he join me in hoping that the ILEA will now honour the verdict of the majority?

Mr. Baker: I know that this was a hard-fought case and that there was considerable organised opposition to it. But, as I have made clear, the result of that ballot showed that the majority of those voting want a change and that provides a firm and clear basis on which the governors of the school can make a decision. I hope that they will make that decision very quickly indeed.

Careers Education

11. **Mr. Flannery:** To ask the Secretary of State for Education and Science what advice he has given in the current year to secondary schools with regard to careers education.

Mr. Butcher: The Department's publication "National Curriculum—From Policy to Practice", published this year, emphasises the place of careers education and guidance within the whole curriculum. The National Curriculum Council is considering the place of personal and social education—and it sees careers education and guidance as an important part of this—in the same context.

Mr. Flannery: Does the Minister realise that the entire education world in our country believes that the shortage of teachers is now steadily developing to crisis point, such that the Select Committee on Education will be making a report on this shortly? Does he also realise that the morale of teachers is so low owing to constant Government attacks on it that 40 per cent. of them would like to leave the service immediately? What kind of advice will he give to secondary school pupils about entering the teaching profession when the Government have played such havoc with the profession that people want to leave it en masse?

Mr. Butcher: Instead of peddling alarm and despondency the hon. Gentleman will have to await the outcome of a number of studies of this matter. It is not as simple as he states. Indeed, I vigorously deny a number of his assertions. I met careers guidance teachers three weeks ago and discussed their interest in ensuring the place of careers guidance within the national curriculum and was able to reassure them that this would continue.

Deaf Children

12. **Mr. Boyes:** To ask the Secretary of State for Education and Science how many deaf children have a statement of their special educational needs according to the Education Act 1981.

Mr. Butcher: In January 1988 the total number of children in England with a statement of special educational needs under the Education Act 1981 was 138,067. We do not have separate figures for deaf children.

Mr. Boyes: Is the Minister aware of the shortcomings for children with special educational needs of the statement process as spelled out by the National Deaf Children's Society report "A Mockery of Needs"? Is the Minister aware—I am sure he is—that there is a need for extra resources for local authorities to ensure that all children with statements of special educational needs have access to the national curriculum? If he does not give those extra resources quickly to local authorities, will it not be just another example demonstrating that this Government simply do not care about children with special educational needs?

Mr. Butcher: No, Sir, that is not so, whether measured by the amount of effort that has gone into the education of children with special needs and particular disabilities, or in terms of hard cash. In 1979-80 about £249 million was spent on maintained special schools. Our plans this year provide for £630 million at a time when there has been a reduction in the number of pupils in this category of 30,000. So there has been a real increase of 28 per cent. I have read the National Deaf Children's Society document. I stay in contact with this group, mainly through its Coventry branch. I find a lot in the document to support, in particular, the wishes of parents to be more closely involved. Not only I but the Department of Health will be responding shortly.

Mr. Favell: Is my hon. Friend aware that in certain parts of the country, there have been disputes about whether speech therapy is the responsibility of the district health authority or the education authority? Can my hon. Friend update the House on that?

Mr. Butcher: I am aware that over a period of time, the role of speech therapy, both for the overall health of the child and for the educational capability of the child, has exercised the minds of many. I cannot tell my hon. Friend today precisely what the outcome of that considerable discussion will be, but I will write to him as soon as there is a clearer statement to be made.

Mr. Ashley: Now that the pressure on school budgets is so great that it is blighting the lives of deaf children and their future careers, will the Minister accept that it is his job to ensure that local education authorities have both the freedom and the resources to help those children?

Mr. Butcher: I dealt with the very generous provision for those categories of disability in my earlier response. May I also reassure the right hon. Gentleman on a point about which the whole House is concerned—the question

of supporting the teachers themselves in the particular skills required, whether the children are in maintained integrated schools or in special schools. On that front alone, we are providing this year £1·6 million for the training of teachers of children with hearing impairments and in 1990-91, we propose to provide £1·7 million. I hope that the earlier figures that I gave will give the right hon. Gentleman the reassurance that he seeks.

PRIME MINISTER

Engagements

Q1. **Mr. Warren:** To ask the Prime Minister if she will list her official engagements for Tuesday 6 June.

The Prime Minister (Mrs. Margaret Thatcher): This morning I had meetings with ministerial colleagues and others. In addition to my duties in this House, I shall be having further meetings later today. This evening, I hope to have an audience of Her Majesty the Queen.

Mr. Warren: Will my right hon. Friend make known to the Government of China today the utter revulsion of the British people at the killing and unwarranted brutality of Chinese troops in the streets and squares of Beijing and especially at the awful actions taken against the students? Does my right hon. Friend agree that it is impossible for us to continue normal relations with China while this dreadful brutality continues and will she take action on that?

The Prime Minister: I very much agree with my hon. Friend. Everyone who witnessed those scenes on television was afflicted with utter revulsion and outrage at what had happened and at the indiscriminate firing on people who were asking only for democratic rights. It shows that Communism stands ready to impose its will by force on innocent people and we must take that into account in our views on defence. My right hon. and learned Friend the Secretary of State for Foreign and Commonwealth Affairs will be making a statement shortly on the Government's response. I agree with my hon. Friend that, clearly, normal business with the Chinese authorities cannot continue. Our first and greatest concern has to be for the people of Hong Kong, whose confidence will be very badly shaken. Our commitment to a secure future for them is as strong as ever and we shall be looking urgently at what can be done to provide them with some reassurance.

Mr. Kinnock: Does the Prime Minister agree that the memory and meaning of one unarmed young man standing in front of a column of tanks in Beijing yesterday will remain with the British people long after the present leadership in China and what they stand for have been forgotten? Will the Prime Minister make it clear that the orders to commit mass murder given by the old men clinging to power in Beijing are unequivocally and universally condemned by the people of our country? To reinforce that message, will the Prime Minister work with our European partners to bring concerted pressure on the Chinese Government to stop the killing and to respond positively to the call for freedom being made by the people of China?

The Prime Minister: We have made our views very clear. Indeed, the whole civilised world made its views very clear in response to the scenes it saw, as did Mr. Perez de

Cuellar, the Secretary-General of the United Nations. China is, of course, a permanent member of the Security Council. Everyone has expressed outrage, horror and total and utter condemnation, and each country, both separately and jointly with others, is thinking of how best to demonstrate that in practical terms to the Chinese Government.

Mr. John Marshall: During the course of her busy day, will my right hon. Friend examine the recent surveys which show that the postal services have deteriorated? Does she agree that the only way in which to improve the quality of the postal services is by the introduction of greater competition?

The Prime Minister: I am aware of some of the complaints on this matter. I agree that greater competition would be good, and we may have to consider ending the monopoly on the postal letter service, which would bring welcome competition.

Q2. **Mr. George Howarth:** To ask the Prime Minister if she will list her official engagements for Tuesday 6 June.

The Prime Minister: I refer the hon. Gentleman to the reply that I gave some moments ago.

Mr. Howarth: Is the Prime Minister aware that following the recent spate of serious accidents involving dogs the people of Britain expect the Government to take some action? In view of that, will she give serious consideration to the schemes advanced by the Royal Society for the Prevention of Cruelty to Animals and the Association of District Councils?

The Prime Minister: I am aware of the great concern about this matter and of some of the proposals that have been made. Although some of them are undoubtedly very interesting, they would not go to the root of the problem, which is not necessarily a question of identifying the owner of the dog but of trying to persuade people to be very responsible about their ownership.

There are already powers to control dangerous dogs. The Dogs Act 1871 provides that any member of the public can tell the police if he or she believes that any dog is dangerous. A magistrate can then issue an order for any dog to be controlled or destroyed. *[Interruption.]* The question is whether we need to strengthen the legislation and how we catch the people who are not being responsible about owning dogs. It is easier to pose the problem than it is to catch and severely punish the offenders.

Mr. Beaumont-Dark: Does my right hon. Friend accept that in these difficult times with the Chinese problem the people of Hong Kong have every right to feel that the word of a Government who are willing to murder their own people is a word that may well be doubted? Does my right hon. Friend agree that the time has come for Britain at least to give Hong Kong a democratic Government and tell the Chinese Government that if they do not honour that, they will honour nothing, and that we shall not honour any pledges given to them?

The Prime Minister: Under the declaration signed with the Government of China, we are now negotiating the Basic Law and when that is complete, we are steadily introducing an increasing amount of democratic government into Hong Kong, with the view that, by the time 1997 comes, there will be an absolutely smooth changeover,

with full democracy, so that the agreement can be fully implemented—that for 50 years after 1997 the people shall have the same system as they have now, a free democratic system, with substantially the same way of life. Obviously, whatever the declaration says, the confidence of the people of Hong Kong will be very severely jolted at present, for very understandable reasons. Without that agreement, which should bring the people of Hong Kong a much better chance than they would otherwise have, 92 per cent. of the land would automatically revert to the People's Republic of China, without the associated benefits that we have negotiated for the people of Hong Kong.

Mr. Ashdown: The Prime Minister's words of a moment ago will be welcome, but does she realise that, in comparison with the words of President Bush, her muted response immediately following the massacre in Peking will be regarded by many as a matter of shame? Is she aware that, in comparison with the attitude of the Portuguese Government to their citizens in Macau her complete denial of moral responsibility after 1997 for those in Hong Kong who hold British passports will be regarded by many as a matter of dishonour?

The Prime Minister: The statement that I issued said:
"We are all deeply shocked by the news from Peking and appalled by the indiscriminate shooting of unarmed people. It is a reminder that, despite some recent easing of East-West tensions, a very great gulf remains between the democratic and the Communist societies. We view these events in Peking with particular concern because of our responsibility for Hong Kong——

Mr. Ashdown: Concern?

Mr. Speaker: Order.

The Prime Minister: —
"and our obligation—which we share with the Chinese Government under the joint declaration—to safeguard Hong Kong's future stability and prosperity."
There were two more paragraphs which, as I said earlier, said that we were shocked and appalled at such indiscriminate killing.

The right hon. Gentleman stands up and makes a great deal of noise, but is it his only suggestion that we should accept 3·6 million people into this country regardless of the consequences?

Mr. Maxwell-Hyslop: Can my right hon. Friend confirm that the possibility of this problem arising was foreseen more than 20 years ago when we passed the Commonwealth immigration legislation? Would it not be quite heartless to hold out the hope to almost 4 million people that the solution to their problems lies in emigrating to the United Kingdom?

The Prime Minister: Currently 3·5 million people in Hong Kong hold British dependent territory citizens' passports. Since 1945 there have been 1·6 million immigrants to Britain from the New Commonwealth. I cite those figures to show the enormity of the task. Obviously some people, especially those who have worked in certain positions for the British Crown, already have preference in securing British passports.

I agree with my hon. Friend that it would not be right to suggest that 3·5 million people should automatically have the right of abode in this country.

Q3. **Mr. Duffy:** To ask the Prime Minister if she will list her official engagements for Tuesday 6 June.

The Prime Minister: I refer the hon. Gentleman to the reply that I gave some moments ago.

Mr. Duffy: Can the Prime Minister explain why the stock market remains jittery today and why sterling continues to weaken despite higher interest rates, while cuts in prime rates and a mountain of debt fail to weaken the US dollar?

The Prime Minister: The hon. Gentleman is fully aware that at times of great uncertainty, such as is now the case in China, money tends to go into the dollar.

Mr. Rowe: Is my right hon. Friend aware— *[Interruption.]*

Mr. Speaker: Order. Interruptions take up a great deal of time.

Mr. Rowe: Is my right hon. Friend aware that a great many parents of British students in Beijing, of whom I am one, are extremely grateful both to the Foreign Office and to the universities, which have been assiduous in looking after those students? Is it not a source of great pride and great relief that, as far as we know, those students are being lifted out of Beijing? Will my right hon. Friend join me in expressing appreciation to both the Foreign Office and the universities?

The Prime Minister: I gladly pay tribute both to the Foreign Office and to our ambassador in Beijing. There are only between 50 and 60 British students in and around Beijing, all of whom reached the embassy fairly quickly and are being looked after as well as is possible. It is not easy to obtain flights out of Beijing during the present troubles.

Q5. Mr. Fisher: To ask the Prime Minister if she will list her official engagements for Tuesday 6 June.

The Prime Minister: I refer the hon. Gentleman to the reply that I gave some moments ago.

Mr. Fisher: Why will not the Prime Minister reconsider her refusal to do anything to back her condemnation of what is happening in China, or to offer practical help to the people of Hong Kong—including the Hong Kong journalist who was refused sanctuary and help by the British embassy in Beijing? Why is President Bush imposing sanctions but the right hon. Lady doing nothing?

The Prime Minister: There will be a full statement later by my right hon. and learned Friend the Secretary of State for Foreign and Commonwealth Affairs who will indicate in full the measures being taken. Of course, our consul is every bit as anxious to help people who have British dependent territory passports whom we regard as our responsibility but whom the Chinese regard as Chinese. We are as anxious to help them as we are to help our own people who are in Beijing, if we can get to them to help them.

Mr. Stanbrook: Despite what has been properly said about the millions of people involved, is my right hon. Friend aware that when we passed the British Nationality Act 1981 we did not expect the provisions of section 4(5) to allow certain citizens of Hong Kong the right of abode in this country to be used other than sparingly? However, would not we all be surprised to find that after eight years only seven applications out of thousands have been granted? Is there not a case for applying the section more flexibly and thus perhaps bringing some relief to Hong Kong?

The Prime Minister: I agree with my hon. Friend that that section must be applied more flexibly. He will find that we are ready to do so. There is a great deal of difference between that greater flexibility that we are very ready to offer—understandably so—and saying that 3·5 million should have the right of permanent abode in this country.

NATO Summit

3.30 pm

The Prime Minister (Mrs. Margaret Thatcher): With permission, Mr. Speaker, I shall make a statement about the meeting of NATO Heads of State and Government held in Brussels on 29 and 30 May, which I attended together with my right hon. and learned Friend the Foreign and Commonwealth Secretary.

The meeting approved two documents: a declaration to mark NATO's 40th anniversary; and a comprehensive concept for arms control and disarmament. Copies have been placed in the Library.

I will deal first with the declaration. This celebrates NATO's success in withstanding the test of four decades and enabling our countries to enjoy in freedom one of the longest periods of peace and prosperity in their history. It reaffirms NATO's belief in strong defence and a strategy of nuclear deterrence. It confirms that the presence of American conventional and nuclear forces remains vital to the security of Europe.

The declaration endorses NATO's conventional arms control proposals, which call for the elimination of disparities between NATO and the Warsaw pact in tanks, artillery and armoured troop carriers. It also welcomes the initiative announced by President Bush at the summit. For land-based combat aircraft and helicopters, this provides for reduction to equal ceilings at a level 15 per cent. below current Alliance holdings. All the equipment withdrawn is to be destroyed.

The initiative proposes a 20 per cent. cut in combat manpower in United States stationed forces, and a resulting ceiling of 275,000 on United States and Soviet ground and air force personnel stationed outside national territory in the area between the Atlantic and the Urals. This ceiling would require the Soviet Union to reduce its forces in eastern Europe by some 325,000. United States and Soviet forces withdrawn will be demobilised.

The American initiative sets the ambitious goal of trying to accomplish these reductions by 1992 or 1993. In addition, the declaration commends President Bush's "open skies" proposal.

The declaration also sets some very important political aims. At British initiative, it calls upon the Soviet Union and the east European countries to tear down the walls that separate us physically and politically; to ensure that people are not prevented by armed force from crossing the frontiers and boundaries which we share with the eastern countries; to respect in law and practice people's right to determine freely and periodically the nature of the government which they wish to have; and to see to it that their peoples can decide through their elected authorities what form of relations they wish to have with other countries.

I deal next with the comprehensive concept. This asserts a number of very important points: first, NATO's strategy remains one of deterrence. Secondly, conventional defence alone cannot ensure deterrence. Only the nuclear element can confront an aggressor with an unacceptable risk, and thus plays an indispensable role in the current strategy of war prevention.

Thirdly, deterrence therefore requires an appropriate mix of adequate and effective nuclear and conventional forces which will continue to be kept up to date where necessary—that is, a strategy of flexible response.

Fourthly, nuclear forces below the strategic level make an essential contribution to deterrence. Those points match in every respect the Government's views.

The comprehensive concept also deals with the particular role of short-range nuclear forces. This section confirms that land, sea and air-based systems, including ground-based missiles, will continue to be needed in Europe. It challenges the Soviet Union to reduce unilaterally its short-range missiles—in which it has massive superiority—to NATO levels.

It states that introduction and deployment of a follow-on system to the Lance missile will be addressed in 1992. Meanwhile, NATO recognises the value of the continuing research and development work on the follow-on to Lance being done by the United States.

Once agreement has been reached on conventional force reductions and implementation of that agreement is under way, then and only then, the United States is authorised to enter into negotiations to achieve a partial reduction in short-range missiles. But no reductions will be made in NATO's SNF missiles until after the agreement on conventional force reductions has been fully implemented. *[Interruption.]*

Mr. Speaker: Order.

The Prime Minister: Moreover, it is specifically recognised that removal of the imbalance in conventional forces——

An hon. Member: That is not telling the truth.

Mr. Speaker: I heard that remark. Please withdraw it. I ask the hon. Gentleman to withdraw that remark.

Mr. D. N. Campbell-Savours (Workington): Whatever you require, Mr. Speaker.

Mr. Speaker: Order. It was from a sedentary position, and I accept it.

The Prime Minister: Moreover, it is specifically recognised that removal of the imbalance in conventional forces would not obviate the continuing need for short-range missiles. In other words, negotiations will take place only when those strict conditions have been met— and there will be no third zero.

I pay tribute to the contribution of the Secretary-General of NATO, Dr. Woerner, in achieving that excellent result; and also to my right hon. and learned Friend the Foreign and Commonwealth Secretary for his very considerable part in the negotiation of the final documents.

The outcome of the summit is a great success for NATO. We have shown ourselves to be a strong, confident and united alliance, holding the initiative on arms control and challenging the Soviet and east European Governments to give their people the genuine freedom of choice which our own people enjoy. The values which have guided the West for 40 years have been reaffirmed. Our common commitment to a strong defence has been renewed. On NATO's 40th anniversary, this was a very satisfactory outcome for the Alliance and for the United Kingdom.

Mr. Neil Kinnock (Islwyn): I thank the Prime Minister for her statement and specifically welcome, among other things, proposals for the elimination of disparities between NATO and the Warsaw pact countries, and the emphasis given in her statement and in the communiqué to the removal of physical and political barriers between East and West, and rapid progress towards freedom of movement, thought and political and civil rights in the Warsaw pact countries. However, arising from her statement, can the Prime Minister confirm that, when she said that no reductions will be made in NATO's SNF missiles until after the agreement on conventional force reductions has been fully implemented, she did not mean that there would be no negotiations on reductions in missiles until after the conventional force agreement had been completed? *[Interruption.]* In view of the confusion, clarification is necessary.

Will the Prime Minister confirm that her main objectives at last week's NATO summit were, first, to gain a specific commitment to the replacement of the existing Lance missile launchers by new weapon systems with ranges of up to 485 km; secondly, to gain the specific exclusion of all possibility of negotiating short-range nuclear weapons reductions, as she made clear in her statement of 7 May that

"there can be no negotiations";

and, thirdly and consequently, to rule out explicitly any question of a third nuclear zero in central Europe at any time? Will the Prime Minister confirm that she failed to achieve a single one of those objectives?

Will the Prime Minister confirm that, following Secretary of State Baker's visit to Moscow on 11 May, the Russians responded on 23 May by accepting NATO's proposed ceilings on the number of tanks and armoured vehicles, with obvious consequences for reductions in troop levels? Does she agree that it was then very wise of President Bush to lead NATO to accommodate the Soviet proposal that combat aircraft, helicopters and troops should be included in negotiations? Do those proposals and objectives have the right hon. Lady's wholehearted and unremitting support?

In the light of developments over past months, and particularly last week, is it not now obvious that the Prime Minister should change her attitudes to take advantage of changing conditions in the way that the United States, the Federal Republic of Germany and other NATO countries are clearly doing? Is the right hon. Lady prepared to join them in efforts to work to conditions in which, in President Bush's words, Europe can

"forgo the peace of tension for the peace of trust"?

Does the Prime Minister now agree with President Bush that there is a need to go "beyond containment" of the Soviet Union to a situation in which, as freedom and democracy spread in eastern Europe,

"the role of NATO shifts from the main emphasis upon deterrence"?

Is the Prime Minister aware that unless she changes she will ensure that it will be the United States and the Federal Republic of Germany that are, in President Bush's words in Mainz last Wednesday, the "partners in leadership"?

The Prime Minister: I shall read the full extent of what the comprehensive concept says about negotiations on short-range nuclear forces:

"Once implementation of such an agreement is under way"—

Mr. Gerald Kaufman (Manchester, Gorton): But not completed.

The Prime Minister: There is quite a lot to come yet. The comprehensive concept says:

"Once implementation of such an agreement is under way, the United States, in consultation with the Allies concerned, is prepared to enter into negotiations to achieve a partial reduction"—

[Hon. Members: "Read it."] I did—

"of American and Soviet land-based nuclear missile forces of shorter range to equal and verifiable levels. With special reference to the Western proposals on CFE tabled in Vienna, enhanced by the proposals by the United States at the May 1989 Summit, the Allies concerned proceed on the understanding"—

this is the bit that the right hon. Gentleman forgot to observe—

"that negotiated reductions leading to a level below the existing level of their SNF missiles will not be carried out until the results of these negotiations have been implemented."

Negotiations do not start—precisely what I said. *[Interruption.]* Implemented means implemented—yes, fully implemented. No short-range nuclear missile will be taken out until the results of the conventional negotiations have been implemented. Implemented means fully implemented. The comprehensive concept says:

"Reductions of Warsaw Pact SNF systems should be carried out before that date."

On the entire comprehensive concept, it reaffirms all the principles with which we agree but which the Leader of the Opposition rejects. It states that

"for the foreseeable future there is no alternative to the Alliance's strategy for prevention of war."

Deterrence requires

"an appropriate mix of adequate and effective nuclear and conventional forces which will continue to be kept up to date where necessary . . . Only the nuclear element can confront an aggressor with an unacceptable risk."

I am reading directly from the comprehensive concept. It says:

"Nuclear forces below the strategic level will continue to be required."

It states:

"There is . . . a level of forces, both nuclear and conventional, below which the credibility of deterrence cannot be maintained."

It also says that the need for short-range nuclear weapons will not be obviated by anything in the comprehensive concept.

The right hon. Gentleman asked about President Bush's proposal on the reductions of helicopters and aircraft and the amount specified in his proposals. We referred his suggestion, which must be carefully looked at, to a NATO group. France and Great Britain were both deeply concerned that it should not affect dual-capable aircraft which are vital to both our strategies, and are part of the NATO strategy. The proposal will be looked at very carefully by a group in NATO before it goes to the negotiations in Vienna. The right hon. Gentleman will find that, in the light of his recent proposals, he could not possibly have put his signature to the comprehensive concept proposals, which are excellent. They have been agreed by all the allies, and that is the strategy for the foreseeable future. They would be negated by the right hon. Gentleman's Labour policy.

Sir Geoffrey Johnson Smith (Wealden): Will my right hon. Friend accept that Conservative Members unequivocally welcome the statement on the outcome of the summit and warmly congratulate her on her important role in securing a settlement which contributes to the peace of the world and is certainly to the advantage of the West? Can she confirm that, of the 16 countries representing NATO, not one of the eight Socialist Prime Ministers had any reservations about the comprehensive concept and the continuing need for nuclear weapons, unlike the Leader of the Opposition?

The Prime Minister: I agree with my hon. Friend. All the countries at the summit, whether Socialist, Conservative or centre endorsed the comprehensive concept requiring a mix of conventional and nuclear weapons, and also agreed that a mix of nuclear weapons —land, sea and air-based—would be needed for the foreseeable future. All countries absolutely agreed on the concept of flexible response, which must be matched by the requisite weapons. It was a very good summit, but one to which the Labour party could never have acceded.

Mr. James Wallace (Orkney and Shetland): We certainly welcome the initiative taken by President Bush which largely led to the issue of an agreed communiqué. I am sure that the Prime Minister will recognise that that is not the end of the story because clearly there are differences in interpretation. Will she explain why the West German Government maintain that there is a third zero option when she denies it? In one of the many statements after the summit the Prime Minister maintained that our relationship with the United States was paramount. Does she not think that, while affirming the importance of that relationship, it is time to put the development of the European pillar and of our relationship with our European allies as a paramount consideration in our defence and foreign policy?

The Prime Minister: I cannot speak specifically for the Federal Republic of Germany. The Secretary-General of NATO, Dr Woerner, clearly said that the reduction was partial and could not be entire. Paragraph 63 of the comprehensive concept clearly states that the need for short-range nuclear weapons is not obviated. President Bush confirmed that meaning. It is the United States which will have to enter into the partial reduction of those weapons, which belong to it and, when the time comes, the United States will carry out the negotiations. That seems pretty conclusive.

With regard to President Bush's specific proposals for further reductions in conventional armaments, helicopter, aircraft and station forces are being looked at in detail by a committee of NATO. I hope that those considerations will be concluded within a comparatively short time of two months, because there must be a number of detailed considerations before detailed proposals are put on the table in Vienna.

Sir Peter Tapsell (East Lindsey): Does not the sudden and tragic change in the political scene in Beijing underline yet again the need for extreme caution in the handling of these matters, and my right hon. Friend's great wisdom in stressing that point continually in recent weeks?

The Prime Minister: My hon. Friend is absolutely right. What has happened in some part of Russia and—in a much worse way—in China shows that a defence policy can never be based on hope or good intentions; it can be based only on a sure defence. Those who value freedom and democracy will ensure that defences remain certain, and for the foreseeable future that will require a mix of conventional and nuclear weapons, and a mix of nuclear weapons from strategic to short range.

Mr. A. E. P. Duffy (Sheffield, Attercliffe): Is the Prime Minister aware that NATO parliamentarians meeting in the spring session last week warmly welcomed the summit agreement and endorsed the comprehensive concept approach to arms control, but that their discussions reflected differing attitudes to negotiations on short-range nuclear forces? They probably thought that, on balance, the key lay in the Vienna talks on conventional armed forces in Europe—CFE. As so much may hinge on those talks, will the Prime Minister do whatever she can to speed up the timetable?

The Prime Minister: As the hon. Gentleman knows, the negotiations in Vienna on tanks, armoured vehicles and artillery are going very well. Some proposals have been agreed and others have yet to be agreed, but agreement has not yet been reached on the monitoring and verification of the destruction of vehicles. As the hon. Gentleman will realise, that is absolutely vital: there is no earthly good in an agreement that tanks and armoured personnel vehicles shall be destroyed unless there is an adequate verification procedure, without which they might be withdrawn behind the Urals and not actually destroyed. The same goes for helicopters and other aircraft. That, unfortunately, will take some time to negotiate.

As the hon. Gentleman will realise, the question of helicopters and other aircraft must be considered carefully within NATO—because of the dual-capable aircraft and a number of other factors—as must the question of stationed forces. It is thought that the negotiations may not take too long; implementation and verification would of course take much longer. There is no delay, but we want to be certain that verification procedures are adequate so that we can keep our strong defence.

Mr. Alistair Burt (Bury, North): Recalling how both East and West reached their present position on disarmament, should we not pay tribute to the resolve of the British people, who consistently supported a party of nuclear deterrrence—as offered by the Conservatives in the past few general elections—in the teeth of considerable objection from Opposition parties whose policies would never have brought us to our present position? Is there not an element of humbug in the Opposition's cheering of aspects of disarmament policy from the sidelines when their policies would never have allowed us to come anywhere near the position that we have now achieved?

The Prime Minister: I agree wholeheartedly with my hon. Friend. It was the firmness upheld by the Government and our NATO partners that brought the Soviet Union to the negotiating table, which I believe was an aspect of the change in its policies. Without that firmness Communism would be stronger today instead of very much weaker; without it the changes in the Soviet Union could never have come about.

Mr. John Cartwright (Woolwich): The military argument in favour of NATO's land-based short-range nuclear weapons has always been that they were needed to offset the Soviet supremacy in conventional firepower. If, as we all hope, the CFE negotiations will result in the removal of that Soviet threat, why do we need a new generation of SNF missiles in addition to the nuclear artillery and the sea-launched and air-launched nuclear weapons that NATO already deploys in Europe?

The Prime Minister: The hon. Gentleman will find the answer in paragraph 63 of the comprehensive concept. The removal of the imbalance in conventional forces would provide scope for further reductions in the sub-strategic nuclear forces of members of the integrated military structure, although it would not obviate the need for such forces. The hon. Gentleman will find an expansion of that in the comprehensive concept. Short-range nuclear weapons must be available to commanders in the field at all stages so that at any time a potential aggressor could not be certain whether they would be used. That is an essential part of flexible response. *[Interruption.]* I am not preaching to the hon. Gentleman: I would not waste my breath. I am trying to quote from the comprehensive concept.

Sir Eldon Griffiths (Bury St. Edmunds): Can my right hon. Friend say whether the concept of a Europe whole and free embraces the notion of a united Germany? Does she regard that as a stabilising or a destabilising consideration in the future of Europe?

The Prime Minister: The declaration envisages that possibility when it says that the peoples of any particular country should be able to say through their elected representatives—and of course we want democracy in each of them—what its relationship to other countries should be. That idea is embodied in the declaration.

Ms. Clare Short (Birmingham, Ladywood): Does not the Prime Minister understand that the best help we can give to the people of eastern Europe in enhancing democracy and their economic development is to agree to arms reductions on both sides? The right hon. Lady alone in NATO is blocking those processes by pushing for modernisation and opposing the third zero. Her rhetoric belongs to the past. She does not understand the new era that is now possible—a free and united Europe. She is blocking the development of democracy in eastern Europe.

The Prime Minister: The hon. Lady talks nonsense, and she is the prisoner of her own propaganda. It was this Government who, together with our partners in NATO, put on the table in Vienna proposals for very deep cuts in tanks, armoured personnel vehicles and artillery, to bring down their numbers far lower than the Soviet Union ever thought of. We are pursuing those reductions, but we insist on a proper procedure for verifying the destruction of those weapons. To do anything else would be highly dangerous to the future of democracy and freedom in western Europe.

Mr. Nicholas Bennett (Pembroke): Will my right hon. Friend confirm that the Brussels declaration, which reaffirms the necessity for nuclear deterrence, would not in all conscience have been signed by anyone who was a member of CND?

The Prime Minister: Confirmed absolutely.

Mr. Dick Douglas (Dunfermline, West): Will the Prime Minister make clear exactly how she stands on the modernisation of short-range nuclear weapons? Is she really saying that, regardless of what reductions are achieved in conventional weapons, NATO should persist in modernising the remaining short-range weapons that presumably it must have to maintain a flexible response? If that is what the right hon. Lady is saying, is that not to be interpreted as a prophecy of doom—that no matter how

the Soviets use their resources, be they conventional or chemical, NATO's response would have to include retaliation by use of a nuclear deterrent?

The Prime Minister: I repeat that to which 16 nations agreed in the comprehensive concept——

Mr. Douglas: Did you agree?

The Prime Minister: Of course I agreed to it wholeheartedly, on behalf of the Government and people of this country:

"The removal of the imbalance in conventional forces would provide scope for further reductions in sub-strategic nuclear forces . . . though it would not obviate the need for such forces."

Therefore, the need for them remains.

Mr. Douglas: Regardless?

The Prime Minister: Regardless? That is the principle of Alliance security set out in the comprehensive concept. It states also:

"for the foreseeable future there is no alternative to the Alliance's strategy for prevention of war."

Deterrence requires

"an appropriate mix of adequate and effective nuclear and conventional forces which will continue to be kept up to date where necessary."

The concept goes on to refer to short-range nuclear forces also, in paragraph 27:

"The Allies sub-strategic nuclear forces are not designed to compensate for conventional imbalances . . . Their role is to ensure that there are no circumstances in which a potential aggressor might discount the prospect of nuclear retaliation in response to military action. Nulcear forces below the strategic level thus make an essential contribution to deterrence."

Sixteen nations signed up to that agreement—but not the Labour party.

Mr. Andrew MacKay (Berkshire, East): Before she left for Brussels, did my right hon. Friend find time to read the comment of the right hon. Member for Manchester, Gorton (Mr. Kaufman) that she would be alone and totally isolated? In light of the fact that NATO unanimously reaffirmed its commitment to nuclear deterrence, does my right hon. Friend agree that it is the Labour party and the right hon. Member for Gorton who are totally isolated, particularly from their fellow Socialists in Europe, who entirely support nuclear deterrence?

The Prime Minister: Far from being isolated, we were very prominent in negotiating an excellent result. My right hon. and learned Friend the Secretary of State for Foreign and Commonwealth Affairs was particularly prominent in negotiating the final language of the communiqué, especially that concerned with short-range nuclear forces. Altogether it was a very satisfactory conference and result for the United Kingdom and for the Alliance. The Opposition could never have signed that as their policy rejects flexible response and want a third zero—both those options were negated by what we agreed. The Labour party wants to get rid of all nuclear weapons, whereas the NATO summit particularly confirmed the continuing need for a mix of conventional and nuclear weapons. We value democracy and freedom enough to defend it adequately on behalf of the people.

Mr. Stuart Bell (Middlesbrough): Will the Prime Minister enlighten the House? At what stage is she

[*Mr. Stuart Bell*]

prepared to put British land-based aircraft into the negotiations on the reduction of conventional weapons in Europe?

The Prime Minister: We are not prepared to put dual-capable aircraft into the negotiations, for obvious reasons—obvious from what the hon. Gentleman said. The proposal is for a reduction in aircraft of something like 15 per cent., and we are advised that that should not include dual-capable aircraft.

Mr. Roger King (Birmingham, Northfield): My right hon. Friend will be aware that today we celebrate the 45th anniversary of the Anglo-American landings in Normandy to set Europe free. Will she confirm that the Anglo-American partnership within NATO is as strong and united as ever? Does she further agree that the way to freedom in the Eastern bloc is a strong Western democracy?

The Prime Minister: Yes. President Bush reaffirmed once again the United States' commitment to the defence of Europe and its forces to Europe. Of course, Europe would not be free had it not been for the devotion and the forces of the United States. We are eternally grateful for that and for the United States' continuing commitment. The comprehensive concept sets out the need for land-based nuclear missiles from America to be present in Europe.

Mr. Tam Dalyell (Linlithgow): Did the Prime Minister take the opportunity to share with our NATO allies the concerns expressed by one of the Ministers at the Foreign Office about the blackmail of Labour Members of Parliament? Does she share those concerns?

The Prime Minister: The hon. Gentleman will be aware that such thoughts were never mentioned at NATO. He is fully aware of the statement which my right hon. and learned Friend the Secretary of State for Foreign and Commonwealth Affairs published and which the Minister of State, Foreign and Commonwealth Office made quite clear.

Mr. William Cash (Stafford): Will my right hon. Friend note that at about the same time as the NATO summit President Gorbachev announced an increase in spending on defence several times higher than had previously been announced? Does my right hon. Friend agree that against that background we should have looked extremely stupid in NATO and in Britain had we taken the blindest notice of the puny and supine attitude adopted over the years by the Leader of the Opposition and his party?

The Prime Minister: I agree with my hon. Friend. The Warsaw pact countries, particularly the Soviet forces, have immensely increased large numbers of conventional weapons over ours and will continue to do so for a long time to come. Even if a conventional agreement was signed, it would take a long time to get Soviet forces down and verified to the levels we seek, and during that time we should be extremely vulnerable. Even after that, we should need a mix of conventional and nuclear weapons to be a proper deterrent.

Mr. Harry Cohen (Leyton): Will the Prime Minister ever agree to dual-capable aircraft being included in the

negotiations? What does she have against parallel negotiations on conventional and strategic nuclear forces? Is it not time that we stopped nuclear modernisation and gave peace a chance?

The Prime Minister: Reductions in strategic arms by the Soviet Union and United States have recommenced. Discussions on reductions in conventional weapons will go ahead at Vienna, and there will also be talks on reducing chemical weapons. The hon. Gentleman is aware that the Soviet Union has enormous superiority in forces, weaponry and aircraft, which will remain for a long time. Conservative Members are concerned to ensure that we have a proper and effective defence.

Mr. Campbell-Savours: Has Mr. Bush suggested that Tornado be included in the package for negotiation? Do the comments that the Prime Minister made today about modernisation accord with statements made to the West German Parliament by Mr. Kohl?

The Prime Minister: No, President Bush has not suggested that Tornado be included. He has made general proposals and is aware of our view on dual-capable aircraft. Our advice is that they need not be included in the 15 per cent., and that is our understanding. Of course the details are to be worked out—it is vital how they are spread—in a NATO group before they are put on the table at Vienna. Detailed proposals will need to be put on the table. [*Interruption.*] I do not answer for Chancellor Kohl, who is well able to speak for himself. He signed up for the comprehensive concept, and when I challenged everyone assembled at NATO that it did not mean a third zero no one dissented from my view. The Secretary-General of NATO and President Bush said that "partial" means partial, and only partial. Germany signed, in paragraph 63, for the fact that anything in the comprehensive concept does not obviate the need for short-range nuclear weapons. I assume that Germany will keep the word to which she honourably put her name.

Mr. Julian Amery (Brighton, Pavilion): Does my right hon. Friend realise that the far-reaching communiqué that was made soon after the summit is acutely embarrassing to those who have supported CND and unilateralism and to those who have been apologists for Soviet imperialism? When dealing with questions put to her, often by Labour Members, will she continue to practise the Christian virtue of forgiveness?

The Prime Minister: I agree with my right hon. Friend. Sixteen Governments agreed this most far-reaching communiqué, which sets the strategy for the foreseeable future. Precious few Labour Members would agree anything of it.

Mr. Bob Cryer (Bradford, South): Is not the Prime Minister's obsession with modernisation a back-door means of fuelling the arms race? As the Prime Minister has been talking about freedom and democracy, perhaps she will explain to the House what freedom and democracy British people have if nuclear arms are used—she has repeated that she is prepared to use them if necessary—to turn our part of the planet into a radioactive cinder heap?

The Prime Minister: Unless one is prepared to use weapons, they are not, and never could be, a deterrent. I say again that 16 nations across Europe and the other side of the Atlantic—the United States, Canada and the nations of Europe belonging to NATO going way beyond the European Community—signed the treaty, including other Socialist Governments. The Labour party could not sign the document and therefore could not accept the shield and defence of NATO. What a pity Labour Members are such a puny lot.

Mr. Julian Brazier (Canterbury): Does my right hon. Friend agree that one of the most critical reasons for our retention of tactical nuclear weapons is the overwhelming number of chemical weapons that the Soviet Union possesses—approximately one quarter of its forward stocks of ammunition? Does she further agree that those weapons give the Soviet conventional forces an overwhelming advantage, which is further enhanced by their numerical superiority?

The Prime Minister: I agree that the Soviets have colossal superiority in chemical weapons, a point that is dealt with effectively in this year's defence White Paper. In 1991 the older chemical weapons that the United States has stationed in the Federal Republic will be withdrawn and then we shall be without any chemical weapons unless modernised ones are substituted and stationed. In that case, our only response to the use of chemical weapons would be nuclear, and that is an additional reason for keeping nuclear weapons.

Dr. Norman A. Godman (Greenock and Port Glasgow): Why is it so difficult for the right hon. Lady to admit that a major change has taken place in recent times in the special relationship between America and the United Kingdom?

The Prime Minister: The alliance between the United States and Canada and the European partners of NATO is as firm as ever it was, and it is that which makes our defence sure. The major change that has taken place has been in the approach, opinions and views of the Soviet Union, a change that would never have come about but for the firmness of people who share our views on defence.

China

4.10 pm

The Secretary of State for Foreign and Commonwealth Affairs (Sir Geoffrey Howe): With permission, Mr. Speaker, I should like to make a statement about events in China in recent weeks.

During the last few days, units of the Chinese army have been engaged in the violent suppression of peaceful and popular demonstrations in the streets of Peking. The indiscriminate and unprovoked use of military force has caused the death or injury of thousands of students and other innocent civilians.

I am sure that all Members of the House will share the worldwide sense of horror and join in the international condemnation of the slaughter of innocent people.

I summoned the Chinese charge d'affaires yesterday. I told him that the British Government and people were united in condemning the merciless treatment of peaceful demonstrators, and deeply deplored the use of force to suppress the democratic aspirations of the Chinese people. I told him that the British Government looked to the Chinese authorities to fulfil their obligations to Hong Kong in the joint declaration of 1984. I reminded him of the responsibilities of the Chinese Government to ensure the safety of British citizens and Hong Kong residents.

I expressed concern at the maltreatment of British journalists, particularly Michael Fathers of *The Independent* and Johnathan Mirsky of *The Observer*. We have since seen disturbing reports of the ill-treatment of Kate Adie of the BBC.

Our ambassador in Peking and his staff have been working round the clock to ensure the safety of British citizens and Hong Kong residents in Peking and, as far as possible, in other parts of China. The embassy has advised against travel to any part of China. It has also advised those who are concerned about their safety and have no pressing need to remain in China to leave immediately.

Since the cultural revolution there has been a substantial improvement in relations between the United Kingdom and the People's Republic of China as the Chinese Government have sought to broaden their contacts with the international community and to introduce economic and other reforms. Friends of China in this House and around the world must share the hope that sane and balanced government will be swiftly and securely restored in Peking. In present circumstances, however, there can be no question of continuing normal business with the Chinese authorities.

Her Majesty's Government have therefore decided on the following action.

All scheduled ministerial exchanges between Britain and China have been suspended. The visit of the Chinese Minister of Justice, who was due to arrive here tomorrow, has been cancelled. My right hon. Friend the Minister of Agriculture, Fisheries and Food has also cancelled his forthcoming visit to China.

The proposed visit of their Royal Highnesses the Prince and Princess of Wales to China in November clearly cannot take place so long as those responsible for the atrocities over the past weekend remain in control of the Chinese Government.

All high-level military contacts with China have been suspended.

All arms sales to China have been banned.

[*Sir Geoffrey Howe*]

At the same time, the Government are examining how we can respond to any requests for humanitarian assistance from non-governmental organisations.

The whole House will share the Government's special concern about the implications for Hong Kong of what has been happening in Peking. The Government understand and share the grave concern felt by the people of Hong Kong. We have all been deeply impressed by the strength and restraint of their response to what has happened.

Everything that has been accomplished in Hong Kong has been achieved in the unique context of the geography and history of the territory and by the talent and enterprise of its people. All of that underlines the extent to which the future prosperity of Hong Kong must depend on a successful and secure partnership with the Government and people of China. That objective is enshrined in the commitments made by the British Government and the Government of China under the joint declaration. Those commitments were reaffirmed by the charge d'affaires when he called on me yesterday.

But it is self-evident that if we are to have confidence in the commitment of the Chinese Government to their obligations, there must be a stable and responsible Government in Peking. The British Government will stand by their obligations under the joint declaration. The Government and the House look to the Government of the People's Republic of China to live up to that international commitment as well.

The events in Peking must affect the prospects and procedure for implementation of the joint declaration. Consultations about the second draft of the Basic Law for Hong Kong have been suspended. It is also difficult to see how our own contacts with the Chinese Government about the future of Hong Kong can continue in present circumstances.

Meanwhile, I assure the House that we shall be conducting a thorough examination of the programme for advancing and consolidating effective democracy in Hong Kong. We are considering urgently what further steps can be taken to enshrine and protect Hong Kong's freedoms and way of life after 1997.

All of us in this House are acutely conscious of the wish of the people of Hong Kong to secure some form of assurance for themselves and their families. I know that this has been one of the issues studied by the Select Committee on Foreign Affairs.

Some commentators have recommended that a right of abode in this country should be given to the $3\frac{1}{4}$ million people in Hong Kong who hold British nationality. We share the desire of the House to do everything we can to enhance the security of the people of Hong Kong. On that basis, the Government are looking urgently and sympathetically at the scope for flexibility. But the House will appreciate the reason why we could not easily contemplate a massive new immigration commitment which could—and the possibility cannot be disregarded—more than double the ethnic minority population of the United Kingdom.

Our overriding aim must be to do everything possible to secure the continuation of those conditions in Hong Kong that have led to its outstanding success over the last century. I hope the House will send a message to the people of Hong Kong reaffirming our commitment to their secure, stable and prosperous future.

The Chinese people are seeking from their Communist leadership rights and liberties which are taken for granted in the free world. The slaughter in Peking is a tragic setback to the campaign for democracy, but I hope this House will send a united message. China cannot ignore the lessons which are being learned elsewhere in the world. Economic prosperity and personal liberty go hand in hand. People will not for ever tolerate government by repression.

Mr. Gerald Kaufman (Manchester, Gorton): My hon. Friends and I condemn outright and in the strongest terms the abominable massacres which have been perpetrated in Beijing. Those of us who have great feelings of friendship for China and have watched its political and economic progress with hope and satisfaction are particularly appalled at this regression to barbarity. It is impossible for us to return to those attitudes so long as this bloodstained repression continues and until it is clear that those in control of China repudiate it.

The scenes of carnage on our television screens have horrified us all. I pay tribute to the courageous journalists who have reported the events, and in particular to the remarkable Kate Adie of the BBC who has risked her life to get the news to Britain.

We admire the swift and positive action taken by President Bush to demonstrate the anger of the United States.

We support the action which Her Majesty's Government have taken and which the Foreign Secretary has just announced. I wish, though, that as well as suspending arms sales—and of course we support that suspension—he would examine the possibility of cancelling all other exports to China, including exports of vehicles which could be used for repression of the civilian population.

I also ask whether the Foreign Secretary will consult the other Governments of the European Community to ensure that firm and concerted action is taken by the whole Community. I should be grateful if he could tell the House what action the United Kingdom Government are considering taking in the United Nations on this matter.

We have been told—and of course we welcome it—about the action which the Government are taking, so far as they can, to protect and assist British citizens at present in Beijing and any other areas that may be affected. Will our embassy also be accepting its responsibility for the safety of Hong Kong citizens—journalists, business people and others—who may be caught up in these disturbances?

It is essential for the Government to take whatever action is open to them to provide reassurance for the people of Hong Kong. In eight years their colony is due to be incorporated into China, but only if the safety, welfare and governance of Hong Kong remain the sole responsibility of this United Kingdom House of Commons.

As the Foreign Secretary knows, the Opposition recommended that elections to the Hong Kong Legislative Council should take place last year. That was not done. We now ask the Foreign Secretary urgently to consider the possibility of bringing forward the elections scheduled for 1991 if possible to this year, but certainly to no later than next year, and that a higher proportion of the Legislative Council be directly elected. This would be a signal to the people of Hong Kong of our concern for their assured democratic future and to the Government of China that Britain is determined that the terms of the joint declaration be adhered to by them as well as by the United Kingdom.

I suggest to the Foreign Secretary that as soon as possible he should himself go to Hong Kong to discuss the possibility of advancing the election date, as well as to explain to the people and representatives of Hong Kong what he means in his statement today by talking about flexibility regarding the right of abode in this country. I also suggest that the right hon. and learned Gentleman should consider travelling as soon as practicable to Beijing to obtain from the Chinese Government the firmest possible assurances that the joint declaration will be adhered to—*[Interruption.]* I would have thought that that would gain assent from the overwhelming majority in the House.

These are times of turmoil and I do not for a moment suggest that the Government should pretend to be able to do more than they can do. At the same time, whatever can be done must be done, for the sake of the people of Hong Kong and to make it clear to the Government of China that, while China should be welcomed into the wider world community as a great and growing power, that welcome must be conditional upon the Government of China conducting themselves in accordance with the standards of civilisation that they have been trampling on in recent days.

Sir Geoffrey Howe: I am grateful to the right hon. Gentleman for the generally supportive tone of everything that he has had to say because it is clear that on all these matters there is very widespread agreement in the House.

I begin by echoing his tribute to the journalists of the BBC, Independent Television and the newspapers, and indeed to those of other countries. One of the most remarkable features of what has been happening in the last few weeks has been the continued opportunity for the rest of the world to see what has been going on in Peking, and also for Peking to know what has been going on in the rest of China, as a result of the free transmissions of radio from the rest of the world. The openness which has been at least a part of what has taken place in China has played a crucial part in events thus far.

The second question which the right hon. Gentleman raised was about the possibility of extending a prohibition to other exports to China, with particular reference to vehicles. Obviously all such questions must remain under consideration. Our basic principle is to subscribe to the position as outlined by President Bush, that it is important to maintain diplomatic, commercial and other human contacts, so far as is safe and possible, with the people and Government of China in order to try and retain the opportunity for recreating their previous open disposition.

European Community co-operation is under urgent consideration among the 12 countries and the Political Committee is meeting today. Already, the meeting due to take place between the Commission and a Chinese ministerial mission yesterday has been cancelled.

The right hon. Gentleman will have seen that the Secretary-General of the United Nations has expressed his own personal and deep concern about what has happened and has called for the restoration of restraint and moderation in Beijing. However, it is also plain that there

is particular difficulty in pursuing in that organisation questions about human rights affecting one of the permanent members of the Security Council.

I made it plain in my statement that the British embassy has been putting great efforts into protecting and establishing contact with all British nationals and Hong Kong people in Beijing and elsewhere in China, without differentiation.

The right hon. Gentleman raised the matter of representative government in Hong Kong. It is important to recognise that the changes that we have sought to introduce so far in that respect have been those that command the widest possible support in the territory.

Mr. George Foulkes (Carrick, Cumnock and Doon Valley): Matters have changed since then.

Sir Geoffrey Howe: I will come on to that. It is also equally clear that in the light of recent events, opinion in Hong Kong has been evolving—*[Interruption.]* Wait for it. Even before the events of last weekend, the Executive and Legislative Councils called unanimously for full democracy by 2003—*[Interruption.]* That is what they called for. It is right that we should consider, in light of the recommendations of the Select Committee on Foreign Affairs and debates in this House, how we should respond to those views.

I welcome the importance attached by the right hon. Gentleman to the joint declaration. That declaration embodies the substantial principles on which the future of Hong Kong should be built. The crucial point is to secure compliance with that declaration, translated into the Basic Law, as fully and effectively as possible by a responsible Government in Beijing.

I recognise that there is wisdom in trying to find an opportunity to establish contact with ministerial opposite numbers in Beijing as soon as it makes sense to do that. It is equally clear that it would not make sense to try to do so in the present circumstances. The suggestion of a visit to Hong Kong is sensible and I will discuss it with the Governor of Hong Kong in London later this week.

Mr. David Howell (Guildford): After the atrocities and butchery in Peking at the weekend—which my right hon. and learned Friend has rightly condemned, as the world condemns them, in the strongest terms that our language allows—will my right hon. and learned Friend ensure, if and when discussions resume in the joint liaison group about implementing the 1984 treaty, that we seek to make it absolutely clear to the Beijing regime and its officials that if they want to see a stable and prosperous Hong Kong, as they say they do, they must accept and support every measure that we deem necessary to bring that about and to maintain confidence in Hong Kong? Will he also remind the Beijing regime, when discussions begin again, that its obligations to maintain the stability, growth and prosperity of Hong Kong and its people exist not only now and up to 1997, but for 50 years thereafter and in perpetuity?

Sir Geoffrey Howe: I am grateful to my right hon. Friend for the measured wisdom and authority of his remarks. I know that he and his colleagues on the Select Committee have been paying the closest attention to these matters in the important work that they have been doing. It is an important feature of the joint declaration that the Government of the People's Republic of China recognise,

[*Sir Geoffrey Howe*]

without qualification, the responsibility of Her Majesty's Government for the administration of Hong Kong until 1997, which is a responsibility that we shall continue to discharge to the fullest of our ability. It is also important for my right hon. Friend to remind the House and, through the House, the Government of the People's Republic of China of their responsibilities in the years that extend beyond 1997, under the joint declaration for a full span of 50 years, but in practice and aspiration way beyond that into the future.

Mr. Paddy Ashdown (Yeovil): It is probably right, after our initial responses, to wait a few days to see how things develop in China. If democracy were to triumph in what is clearly a developing power struggle, everything would be well, but I am sure that the Foreign Secretary is right to begin to think ahead, in case the worst should happen. Is it not the case that, under the joint declaration, the army that we have seen butchering its fellow citizens on the streets of Peking will be on the streets of Hong Kong in eight years' time? Is it surprising, therefore, that the last vestige of faith that many in Hong Kong had in the joint declaration, has been severely damaged and will have to be patiently rebuilt?

Let me welcome two aspects of the Foreign Secretary's statement. He said that negotiations taking place under the joint declaration will be suspended. Will he use the interim to try to build up international support for the joint declaration, perhaps through the medium of the United Nations? I welcome, too, the Foreign Secretary's flexible attitude to the application of the British Nationality Act. Does he realise that many will be watching closely to see how that develops?

I ask the Foreign Secretary to consider three further steps. First, will he set as the target that he has identified for the development of democracy in Hong Kong the establishment by 1991 of a Legislative Council at least half of whose members have been directly elected? [HON. MEMBERS: "Why half?"] At least half, as a first step, by 1991.

Secondly, when the excellent David Wilson's term as Governor of Hong Kong is up, will the Foreign Secretary consider providing a Hong Kong belonger to take his place—perhaps one elected from the Legislative Council?

Thirdly, does the right hon. and learned Gentleman agree that all free western democracies have a real national interest in ensuring that democracy survives in Hong Kong? Does he agree that there may be a case for the Government considering a conference of the free western democracies to see whether an agreement could be reached whereby they could provide a last-resort sanctuary for the people of Hong Kong, as the ultimate bulwark for the survival of democracy?

Sir Geoffrey Howe: I am impressed by the extent to which the right hon. Gentleman has learnt the case for patience. It is certainly right that we should await developments in Peking, because no one can yet foresee what will happen there, and much depends upon it.

The right hon. Gentleman is also right—I welcome his remarks—to underline the importance of the joint declaration and of securing the effective commitment of the Chinese Government to that declaration.

The right hon. Gentleman drew attention in particular to the need to mobilise international support for the joint declaration. It was for that reason that the declaration was drawn up in the form of an international agreement and registered by both nations simultaneously at the United Nations. For that reason, incidentally, when I presided over the 40th anniversary meeting of the Security Council —with the Chinese Foreign Minister—I drew attention to the importance of the agreement that had been arrived at between us. The then Chinese Foreign Minister endorsed the agreement in the presence of that body. The highest solemnity needs to be attached to that if the Chinese Government are to be reminded of the importance that we attach to the declaration.

The right hon. Gentleman made some suggestions. On the composition of the Legislative Council, I have already made it plain that options and opinions are evolving in Hong Kong as a result of recent events. As soon as a clear view emerges, we shall be considering the best and most effective way to give effect to that. That is one of the matters that I shall wish to discuss when I am able to visit Hong Kong.

It is much too early to consider the replacement of the present Governor of Hong Kong, but the whole House will welcome the tribute that the right hon. Gentleman paid to the quality of Sir David Wilson, who has been bearing a heavy burden in recent weeks.

The right hon. Gentleman referred to the prospect of an international conference on the refuge of last resort. I do not think that that is the right way of handling the matter. It is most important to concentrate not only on aspects of British nationality law but on the best way of restoring confidence in the prospects for Hong Kong.

Sir Peter Blaker (Blackpool, South): Is my right hon. and learned Friend aware that he deserves the support of the whole House for his excellent statement and for the line that the Government have been taking throughout on China and Hong Kong? Will he transmit to the people of Hong Kong the assurance that the House continues to remain deeply interested in their welfare and that they have our continued support?

My right hon. and learned Friend referred to the increased political awareness of the people of Hong Kong in the past few weeks and to the unanimous recommendation of the Executive and Legislative Councils calling for more rapid progress towards direct elections. Is not that a significant resolution? Does it not represent the first statement that gives the point of view of Hong Kong as a whole about the speed of progress towards direct elections—something for which the Basic Law drafting committee has been calling?

Sir Geoffrey Howe: I am grateful for my right hon. Friend's support for my statement. I am sure that the people of Hong Kong will take note of the very widespread support throughout the House for the opinions that I have tried to express. There is a close and continuing interest in this Parliament's discussion of the affairs of Hong Kong, which is a natural reflection of the link between that country and the prospects of democratic government.

I acknowledge the importance of my right hon. Friend's last point. The resolution unanimously arrived at by the Executive and Legislative Councils before the events of last weekend is important and we should take account of it. We should do so on the same basis that we have followed to date, which is to try to identify the basis that commands the widest possible support in the territory and then to commend that to the draftsmen of the Basic Law.

Mr. Andrew Faulds (Warley, East): As the right hon. and learned Gentleman will know, for more than 20 years I have been a proponent of good relations with China and the need to understand political developments in that enormously important country. Will he believe me this afternoon if I say that I share the universal revulsion that has been expressed at the conduct of the geriatric Chinese Government during the last few days? Does he accept that I strongly support the actions that he has adumbrated this afternoon? However, will he reconsider the statement that both he and the Prime Minister have made, that were there to be any lessening of the restraints on British nationals coming to this country from Hong Kong, a flood of 3·5 million people would be battering at the gates of Dover? Would it not be more honest to admit that if the right hon. and learned Gentleman could get his right hon. Friend the Home Secretary to reconsider the issue, it would be a matter of only 10,000 or 15,000 people a year, for six years, from the very limited categories for which, as he knows well, the Hong Kong Commission has been arguing the case for reconsideration? Will he discuss that specific matter with the Home Secretary?

Sir Geoffrey Howe: I acknowledge the force of the hon. Gentleman's opening remarks. All who have watched with growing interest and enthusiasm the emergence of a new-style China during the past 10 years will share the hon. Gentleman's sense of deep grief at what has happened during recent weeks. It is important to note that there are still many people inside China and representing her throughout the rest of the world who also share that sense of grief. It is for that reason that we hope that common sense will be restored to authority in Peking before too long.

The hon. Gentleman rightly drew a distinction between the implied threat of a mass movement of people, which would happen if we tried to deal at once with 3·25 million people, and the alternative, to which I drew attention, of flexibility in the management of individual cases. That matter is certainly a topic for discussion between myself and my right hon. Friend the Home Secretary, and I do not ignore its importance.

Mr. Robert Adley (Christchurch): I share the disgust of the House and the whole of the free world for the unspeakable events in China. Does my right hon. and learned Friend agree that, in reality, our ability to influence what we would all like to happen—that is, the emergence of what he described as a sane and balanced Government in Beijing—is infinitesimal? Would it not, therefore, be wise to avoid giving the present blood-stained leaders any opportunity to continue holding power by playing the xenophobia card?

As regards Hong Kong, will my right hon. and learned Friend repeat what our right hon. Friend the Prime Minister so clearly said, that 1997 is not a date produced out of thin air but the date when our lease ends? The only alternative to an agreement with China is no agreement, an eventuality that would make political boat people out of the whole population of Hong Kong.

Sir Geoffrey Howe: My hon. Friend is right to remind the House—although it needs no reminding—of the inescapable facts of geography and history to which I referred in my statement. One such fact is the expiry of the lease in 1997. It is on that basis that we have secured the support of the House for the achievements of the joint declaration, to which the House attaches importance. My hon. Friend is also right to warn against xenophobia in any aspect of managing a problem of such complexity. I think that he would go too far if he were to believe that the capacity of people outside China to influence the future there should be described as infinitesimal. Of course, the prospect of having influence upon a mass population of 1·25 billion and on the people who seek to govern that country is in one sense very small. Yet, if one thinks of the huge impact of the opinion of the rest of the world as a result of the openness that has come about in recent years, if one thinks of the incredible reality that the leader of the Soviet Union was there only a few weeks ago, being hailed as a champion of democracy, and if one thinks of the changes that have been able to have an impact on that society, my hon. Friend should not despair too much of the ability of the rest of us to make some impact on prospects for the people of China.

Dr. Jeremy Bray (Motherwell, South): Does the Foreign Secretary agree that the great majority of people in China, as they learn the facts, must share the horror of the rest of the world about the events in Beijing and the massacre of citizens and students last Sunday? In those changed circumstances, does the Foreign Secretary agree that the speedy introduction of direct elections for the majority of the members of the Legislative Council in Hong Kong would not only give the people of Hong Kong the best chance of securing their own security but would also be a demonstration to the people of China that it is possible speedily, responsibly and with restraint to introduce democracy?

Sir Geoffrey Howe: I think that the hon. Gentleman has rightly put his finger on one of the most important new factors in the scene, a factor that has already affected the evolution of opinion in Hong Kong, the extent to which the shape of representative institutions in Hong Kong can serve not only as a bulwark for their own freedom but as an example to the Chinese people. It is with that in mind that we shall take account as urgently as would make sense of the evolution of new thinking on the topic within Hong Kong itself.

Mr. Michael Marshall (Arundel): Will my right hon. and learned Friend accept that I regard what he has just said as of particular significance? The question of confidence for the future of the people of Hong Kong is a delicate matter upon which the future, not only of Hong Kong but of many of our own interests and those of China itself, hangs. Will my right hon. and learned Friend therefore take on board the strong feeling that many of us heard over the weekend from all sections of Hong Kong society urging him onwards with the firm commitment, that I believe he is making, to review again the process of democracy so that when the time comes we can really test in the 50-year period the one-country, two-system claim?

Sir Geoffrey Howe: My hon. Friend is more than entitled to remind me of the importance of the opinion and aspirations of the people of Hong Kong. Throughout all the months and years that I have been concerned with the question I have tried as far as possible to display sensitivity

[*Sir Geoffrey Howe*]

to their feelings. During the early and difficult months of negotiation I went to the territory to try to explain to the people and to their representatives how the matter was proceeding. Perhaps no one recognises more than I do the importance of continuing to strengthen that bond of trust between the people and those who represent them, however indirectly, in this Parliament.

Dr. John Marek (Wrexham): Does the Foreign Secretary accept that it was a welcome change to hear him say that he would consult the people of Hong Kong to bring forward democracy as quickly as possible? Will he also accept that the answer to the question whether democracy is wanted in Hong Kong was given not by Legco or by any sampling of opinion but by the people of Hong Kong in the last week, and that there is abundant evidence that the people want democracy to the same extent as the Foreign Secretary of any other hon. Member wants it for the United Kingdom? Will he therefore do his best to make sure that the consultations are as quick and as sharp as possible and that an announcement is made within the next few weeks to reassure the people of Hong Kong on this important matter?

Sir Geoffrey Howe: I do not accept the opening remarks of the hon. Gentleman when he said that it is a welcome change that we have been engaging in consultation with the people of Hong Kong. Throughout we have sought to consult their opinions directly and through their representatives as carefully as possible.

On the second point, the hon. Gentleman is entitled to draw attention to the opinions expressed not only by the members of Legco and the Executive Council but by the people of Hong Kong more directly. He would not be prudent to urge us to jump to a single conclusion on the basis of that, however understandable it may be. We must consider carefully with those who have been governing Hong Kong in recent weeks and months as well as with the people of Hong Kong the right way of responding to the undoubted new needs that exist.

Sir Hal Miller (Bromsgrove): Does my right hon. and learned Friend share my recollection that in the lifetime of the People's Republic of China there have been massive and often violent upheavals every five years, such as the great leap forward, the back to the land campaign and the cultural revolution, leading to loss of confidence in Hong Kong, flight and a search for foreign passports? During that period the Chinese Government, of whatever complexion, still maintained their international agreements. Will my right hon. and learned Friend remind those who are seeking to use the present troubles to propagate their own ideas, whether on passports to this country or on elections in Hong Kong, of that fact and also point out to them that any such proposals must be considered against the overriding need to preserve the peace and prosperity of Hong Kong?

Sir Geoffrey Howe: My hon. Friend, with his close experience of the territory, reminds the House of some important points. Of course, we have to consider all those matters in the light of our experience of the long history of relations between China and the outside world. It is certainly right to remind the House of the frequency with which the Government of China, even in recent circumstances, have emphasised their intention to continue to respect their international agreements. That was one point specifically made to me by the chargé in the exchange of opinion last night. It is important not only to remind the House but for us to remind the Government of the People's Republic of China of their repeated commitment to international obligations.

Mr. Ted Rowlands (Merthyr Tydfil and Rhymney): Despite the problems and the inescapable facts of geography, is it conceivable that there could be effective implementation of agreements with the present leadership, with its bloodstained hands that have been responsible for the death of so many thousands of its own citizens?

Sir Geoffrey Howe: Plainly, so long as the leadership responsible for the events of the last few days, which the whole House has been mourning and condemning, remains in authority the matter will be fraught with a great deal of difficulty. That is why I responded to the right hon. Member for Yeovil (Mr. Ashdown) by emphasising the need for us to see how events unfold. In the long history of China one hopes that the events of the last few weeks may be regarded as only part of a chapter and that a new chapter will begin sooner rather than later.

Mr. Peter Temple-Morris (Leominster): While I in no way advocate the admission of 3·25 million people to this country, may I ask whether my right hon. and learned Friend noticed the evidence to the Select Committee of Lord MacLehose? Dealing with the difficult matter of categories, he said that for many years Governments in this country had used considerable ingenuity to keep people out of the United Kingdom and pointed out that it was perhaps time for them to use a little of that ingenuity to let a few in. How does my right hon. and learned Friend react to that, and how flexible is flexible?

Sir Geoffrey Howe: I am certainly aware of that observation by the noble Lord MacLehose in his evidence to the Select Committee. Of course, it was only part of a more substantial body of evidence. I have drawn attention to the need to recognise the case for flexibility. I think that I would be unwise to be cross-examined by my hon. and learned Friend any further on that at this time.

Mr. Tam Dalyell (Linlithgow): Does the Foreign Secretary accept the analysis that some old men in Peking have, unforgivably, brought in the Manchurian army, some of whose grandfathers were probably the worst and most hated persecutors of the Chinese at the time of the Japanese war? In such circumstances are we wise to say that we should break off all contacts, because there are five or six different Chinas? In particular, what advice would the Foreign Secretary give to the city of Edinburgh with its contacts with Xian where the people probably disapprove, just as much as the House does, of what has happened in Peking?

Sir Geoffrey Howe: The hon. Gentleman has committed himself to some unusually wise observations. He was certainly right to draw attention—as I have tried to do—to the huge diversity of opinion within China, which is why so many of us have expressed the hope with great fervour, although not yet with a great deal of confidence, that the sane, responsible China will prevail. That is why he was right to point out the need to maintain contact and relations of a personal, political and cultural kind with the rest of China. It is in that way that we shall keep the spirit of democracy and the hope for the future alive in that great people.

Sir Philip Goodhart (Beckenham): If the violence and the repression of democratic dissidents continue, is it not plain that another flood of refugees will be heading towards Hong Kong? Are we making any contingency plans to help the colony to deal with that potential flood of asylum seekers?

Sir Geoffrey Howe: My hon. Friend has drawn attention to a hazard that may develop. He will appreciate, of course, the extent to which Hong Kong is already facing very real problems from the number of boat people who for various reasons still arrive there. All I can say at this stage is that any question of refugee status for any individual would have to be considered separately and when it arose.

Mr. Jack Thompson (Wansbeck): I am sure that the Secretary of State is aware that I, along with four other hon. Members, have recently returned from China and Hong Kong. We were in Beijing during the beginnings of the student demonstrations about three weeks ago. I find it, therefore, heartrending to see on television the very same streets that I walked upon now covered with dead bodies, blood and wrecked vehicles.

The discussions that we had with the students in the square at that time clearly indicated that all that the students wanted to do was to talk to the Government. The end result of the Chinese Government not talking to the students or their representatives has been confrontation, chaos, conflict and death. Is not the lesson to be learnt that, when a Government refuse to talk to their people, the end result will be what we have seen on television during the past few days?

In the very brief time we spent in Hong Kong, we discovered that what the people of Hong Kong—I emphasise the people of Hong Kong—clearly desire from the British Government is a very early change over to representative government in Hong Kong. If it were possible for the Government to take that wish into account and to bring the elections forward, that would restore some of the confidence in the people of Hong Kong, which has been greatly shattered in the past few days.

Sir Geoffrey Howe: I understand the extent to which the hon. Member is moved by his recent experience of Peking. We all have recollections of our first contacts with the emergence of proper democratic institutions in that country. He is right to draw attention to the far greater scope for wise government that is available to Governments who engage in dialogue and communication with their people. We fortunately have that kind of relationship through the hon. Gentleman, and through many other hon. Members, with the people of Hong Kong, and we are able to hear and take account of their views. The tragedy of what has happened in Peking is that such an attitude of discussion and non-confrontation appeared to prevail through the early weeks of the extraordinary events there. The horror of the tragedy is that it has only been in the past few days that such profound unwisdom has seized of the minds of those who govern China.

Mr. Timothy Raison (Aylesbury): Does my right hon. and learned Friend accept that, grave though the present

situation is, it would be the greatest mistake to take any hasty steps towards changing the nationality law? Does my right hon. and learned Friend acknowledge that we have a number of years before the transfer of power in which it is quite possible that the situation will improve, as we all hope it will? Will he accept that the worst possible action would be to make concessions that would ultimately prove to be unsustainable?

Sir Geoffrey Howe: My right hon. Friend draws attention to the most important point about that most important argument. We cannot and should not engage in prospective changes in the law upon the footing that they might never need to be implemented. We have to look at the matter in a long perspective with the wisdom that my right hon. Friend has suggested.

Mr. David Winnick (Walsall, North): Following the intervention of my hon. Friend the Member for Wansbeck (Mr. Thompson) should we not first pay particular tribute to all those who have demonstrated continuously, day and night, in the capital of China and in other cities for basic human rights? As we all know, to demonstrate under a dictatorship takes tremendous courage. Is it not a fact that foreign correspondents were constantly asked if the countries from which they came supported what the demonstrators were trying to do? On reflection, perhaps the Foreign Secretary will agree that the democracies—not only that of our country but other democracies—could have spoken out before the bloodshed started over the weekend.

Are there not some people in the Chinese leadership —perhaps, the person who was general secretary of the Communist party until a few days ago, and his predecessor, whose death started the demonstrations, and in the Chinese Communist party at senior levels—who recognise that, just as in eastern Europe and Soviet Union change had to come, so it has to come in China? Stalinism is dead, and all the bullets and all the terror in the world cannot keep Stalinism going.

Sir Geoffrey Howe: The hon. Gentleman is right to draw attention to the fact, as I have already emphasised, that certainly there are voices, and voices at a high level, in the Chinese Government of sanity, democracy and of belief in the kind of standards in which we believe. We must regret the passing of some of those voices, and continue to express the hope that those who remain will prevail in the immense struggles that are no doubt now taking place.

Sir Nicholas Fairbairn (Perth and Kinross): Does my right hon. and learned Friend appreciate that the British people, having watched step by step the enactment of a crime without a name against humanity and liberty in China, are confused, if not infuriated, by the somewhat nonchalant response of the Government and even more of the Opposition, who, had it been a European Government doing something on an infinitesimally smaller scale, would have been up in arms and on the streets? Does my right hon. and learned Friend appreciate that in the meantime it is extraordinary that the Chinese Government should remain a permanent member of the Security Council, which is the alleged protector of human rights?

Sir Geoffrey Howe: My hon. and learned Friend rightly expresses his grave dismay of what has been taking place. However, I must say in the light of his judgment, that I do

[*Sir Geoffrey Howe*]

not regard him as a very well qualified judge of nonchalance. Neither the Government nor, if I may say so, the Opposition, have been disposed to treat the events of recent days with anything other than the utmost seriousness.

Mr. Keith Vaz (Leicester, East): What steps is the British embassy in Beijing taking to contact those British citizens who are resident outside the capital? I have a constituent, a Miss Elaine Sweeney, who is a teacher in the Situhan province in Chengdu. Her parents have been trying to contact her for the past week. I telephoned the Private Office of the Foreign Secretary at the weekend, and, although his official was very helpful and took down the details, the official did not know where the Situhan province was. Will the Foreign Secretary consider allocating additional staff to his Private Office and publishing an inquiry telephone number so that relatives can contact people readily?

Sir Geoffrey Howe: I am grateful to the hon. Gentleman for his tribute to the courtesy of the person to whom he spoke. I apologise for the lack of extensive geographical knowledge, which is understandable in the circumstances. If the hon. Gentleman would like to give me any further details, of course I shall take account of them. The embassy and our consulate in Shanghai are making every possible effort to contact all the known British subjects within China. Almost 500 of the 860 British subjects in China are in Peking and in Shanghai. I shall consider the hon. Gentleman's particular suggestions for more expeditious handling of any other inquiries.

Mr. Nicholas Budgen (Wolverhampton, South-West): Does my right hon. and learned Friend agree that, in spite of our sympathy and concern, our principal obligation is to the people of this country? Does he recognise that the last two major immigrations into this country were not widely welcomed by the indigenous population? Does he agree that if his flexibility led to another major immigration into this country, it would be widely resented and would damage race relations here?

Sir Geoffrey Howe: My hon. Friend is right to draw attention to that factor. That is why in my statement I drew attention to the immense difficulty of contemplating a massive new immigration commitment of the kind involved in any fundamental change. My hon. Friend has underlined the importance of his warning in other contexts as well.

Mr. Frank Field (Birkenhead): Does not hindsight teach that the House was wrong to seek an agreement with China on the future of Hong Kong? Will the right hon. and learned Gentleman tell the House about the Government's fallback position should the changes in the Chinese Government which he has outlined not occur? Will he open international negotiations so that Hong Kong can gain the protection of United Nations trusteeship when it ceases to be a British territory, should the people of Hong Kong wish that?

Sir Geoffrey Howe: I am afraid that, unusually, the hon. Gentleman is drawing the wrong conclusions from hindsight. As I have said already, it would not make sense to ignore the historical and geographical realities that are

implicit in the fact that 92 per cent. of the territory reverts to China in 1997. Any viable future for Hong Kong must be based on co-operation and co-existence with China, not on confrontation. Any attempt to design some alternative to that, dependent upon the goodwill of almost any organisation that the hon. Gentleman cares to name, would be of little, if any, value in the absence of the right relationship with China. That is why I have no doubt about the wisdom of arriving at the joint declaration. I have no doubt about the importance of underlining its significance for the future. Our first task is to restore the substance and confidence that can be placed in it.

Mr. James Couchman (Gillingham): Given China's tendency to isolate itself when it goes through one of these great upheavals, which my hon. Friend the Member for Bromsgrove (Sir H. Miller) mentioned, will my right hon. and learned Friend assure the House that he will maintain relations with the People's Republic at as high a level as possible during these difficult times so that the actions of the British Government in no sense catalyse such a turning inward? Will my right hon. and learned Friend suggest to my right hon. Friend the Leader of the House that at the earliest possible date—certainly before the House rises for the summer recess—a suitable day should be set aside for a debate on Hong Kong?

Sir Geoffrey Howe: I shall draw my hon. Friend's last point to the attention of my right hon. Friend the Leader of the House. In any event, such a debate was in prospect, given the timetable of the Select Committee on Foreign Affairs, which was presided over by my right hon. Friend the Member for Guildford (Mr. Howell).

My hon. Friend's first point is important also. Nothing that we do would be directed towards precipitating any increase in the isolation of the People's Republic of China. That is why we are maintaining our embassy there and other links of the kind suggested by the Opposition. That is why I shall seek any sensible opportunity that presents itself to communicate to those in authority in Peking our anxieties and wishes for the future.

Mr. Pat Wall (Bradford, North): The Foreign Secretary may recall that a year ago I raised with him my opposition to the Basic Law, as it was then put forward, and its lack of provision for democratic elections in Hong Kong. Would not the best tribute to those students and workers who died in the killing streets and squares of Beijing be to announce universal suffrage in Hong Kong immediately, and the holding of elections this year? Is it not tragic that these events have had to occur before the idea of universal suffrage in Hong Kong has been raised? I strongly agree with my right hon. Friend the Leader of the Opposition that what is taking place is a crime against humanity and—speaking as a lifelong anti-Stalinist—a crime against the ideas of Socialism, which comes ill from those in China who claim to defend the Socialist system.

Sir Geoffrey Howe: I shall refrain from making any of the political points that might be made in the face of the hon. Gentleman's closing remarks. I confess that I do not have instant recall of his attitude to these matters 12 months ago. I repeat: we have sought throughout, and will continue, to introduce arrangements for government in Hong Kong along the lines that command the widest possible support in the territory.

Mr. Robert G. Hughes (Harrow, West): Does my right hon. and learned Friend agree that, now that the decrepit leadership of the People's Republic of China has murdered its way to the history books, whatever leadership emerges may welcome faster moves by my right hon. and learned Friend and the Government towards some elements of democracy in Hong Kong? Does he agree that the leaders may welcome it, first, so that they can make a success of the takeover of Hong Kong and, secondly, so that they can be seen by the world to be leading a country in a more decent way than the people from whom they took it over?

Sir Geoffrey Howe: My hon. Friend may well be right, and one must hope so.

Mr. Dave Nellist (Coventry, South-East): Does not the right hon. and learned Gentleman realise that those students and workers who died in their thousands when demonstrating against corruption, bribery, nepotism, the black market and the bureaucratic, Stalinist, one-party dictatorship that rules almost a third of mankind could have expected a little more praise for their heroism, bravery and self-sacrifice? Why does he not declare clear support for the political revolution which is still unfolding in China and honour the martyrs of Tiananmen square by declaring this country's full support for a Socialist workers' democracy in China and for self-determination, free elections and full democracy in Hong Kong?

Sir Geoffrey Howe: As always, the hon. Gentleman brings a unique vision to bear on these matters. In the eyes of the great majority of hon. Members and of the world, the heroism of the people to whom he has rightly paid tribute was exercised in revolt against the logical consequences of the most Socialist country in the world.

Mr. Anthony Beaumont-Dark (Birmingham, Selly Oak): Does my right hon. and learned Friend agree that, in these twilight years of British power in Hong Kong, there will be a need for enlightened and good public servants who are Hong Kong citizens? Does he therefore agree that, at the very least, those who are willing to serve for the next nine years should be given an understanding that, should the same kind of Government prevail, they will be treated properly, mercifully and humanely by the British people and the British Government?

Sir Geoffrey Howe: Those factors are among those that need to be taken into account in appropriate circumstances under section 4(5) of the British Nationality Act 1981.

Mr. Bruce Grocott (The Wrekin): Is not one of the key factors that will ensure that the students and workers have not died in vain the tremendous professional skill of the broadcasters, especially the television journalists, who brought us moving pictures of what happened? Given the unfortunate comments that some of the Foreign Secretary's right hon. Friends have made in the past, will he take this opportunity in particular to congratulate by name Kate Adie, who brought to reporting the facts from China the same standards of integrity and courage that she showed in Tripoli?

Will the right hon. and learned Gentleman talk to the Home Secretary about his plans for broadcasting? Some people fear that, if the present plans go ahead, the quality of the news coverage by British television and broadcasting crews will decline and be threatened. That will be a very bad day for this country.

Sir Geoffrey Howe: Even with the most liberal application of the rules of the House, discussion by me at this stage about the future of British broadcasting policy would be testing the patience of the House a little far.

Dr. Norman A. Godman (Greenock and Port Glasgow): A moment or two ago a Conservative Member warned the Foreign Secretary of the likelihood, if these dreadful circumstances continue, of a huge number of refugees flooding into Hong Kong. What if refugees seek to leave China by way of the sea? What advice has been given to captains of British ships sailing in those waters, about dealing with such refugees? No doubt, their humanitarianism would prompt them to pick up such refugees but where would they be put ashore?

Sir Geoffrey Howe: One must hope that the matter does not escalate on anything like that scale. At the moment, the disturbances, which are grave, have been largely, though not completely, confined to the capital of Peking. Were circumstances to develop as the hon. Gentleman has in mind, sea captains have their own criteria and standards that they apply in similar circumstances.

Passports

5.11 pm

Mr. Dave Nellist (Coventry, South-East): I beg to ask leave to move the Adjournment of the House, under Standing Order No. 20 for the purposes of discussing a specific and important matter that should have urgent consideration, namely

"the crisis in the passport office."

Last week, the patience of the long-suffering staff in the passport offices across the country finally snapped. Before the action, persistent underfunding and management incompetence had led to a backlog of half a million passport applications. That was exacerbated by the applications made in bulk by private agencies which receive preferential treatment. The six offices have had application backlogs of up to 12 weeks. The action started in Liverpool on 30 May, after a secret ballot produced a vote of 87 to 2. Workers said frankly that enough was enough.

The trade unions in the Home Office, principally the Civil and Public Services Association and the National Union of Civil and Public Servants, submitted a claim for 326 extra staff on 24 June 1988. One year later, there are no extra permanent jobs and no improvements in computer systems, despite sources in the management of the passport office saying that both the hardware and software were not up to the job.

On 23 November, I tabled early-day motion 39 and predicted that the increase of more than one million applications since 1979 to a current figure of 2·6 million, which had already led to intolerable delays, backlogs of passengers and holidaymakers and immeasurable pressure being placed on staff, would not be ameliorated by the abuse of casual labour, by overtime or individual work measurement. That early-day motion predicted the chaos which is now ensuing. That warning of six months ago was ignored.

Last week, the National Audit Office issued a report criticising the passport department for its lack of planning and failure to predict the level of applications, or take corrective action on staffing early enough. That is an indictment of the management of the Home Office and a vindication of the trade unions' position.

The crisis is also an indictment of the Government's policy of reducing civil servants and public spending and preparing, through executive agency status, the privatisation of the passport service. Privatisation is irrelevant to the need for more resources to ease the pressures on staff and the public. When negotiations resume tomorrow, an independent review of the computer system, better facilities for staff and public and the full 326 increase in staffing levels are needed. The Government know what the staff and the public want and it is about time that they delivered it.

Mr. Speaker: The hon. Member for Coventry, South-East (Mr. Nellist) asks leave to move the Adjournment of the House under Standing Order No. 20, for the purpose of discussing a specific and important matter that he thinks should have urgent consideration, namely,

"the crisis in the passport office."

As the House knows, I have to take into account the requirements of the order and announce my decision without giving my reasons to the House. I have listened with concern to what the hon. Member has said, but I regret that I do not consider the matter that he has raised is appropriate for discussion under Standing Order No. 20. I cannot therefore submit his application to the House.

Dog Registration

5.15 pm

Mr. Matthew Taylor (Truro): I beg to ask leave to move the Adjournment of the House under Standing Order No. 20 for the purpose of discussing a specific and important matter that should have urgent consideration, namely,
"the need for a dog registration scheme."

The House will have been appalled by the number of savage attacks by Rottweiler dogs on innocent people, including young children, in recent weeks. The matter is urgent because since this April, seven people have been savagely mauled by Rottweiler dogs.

The first victim was Kelly Leech, a little girl of 11 years who died after a horrifying attack by a pair of that breed, which she was taking for a walk. Today's newspapers report yet another assault by a Rottweiler. This latest victim was a man from Luton who needed stitches to his arm. The specific list of vicious calamities makes sickening reading. On 29 May, 5-year-old Jamie Walker from Birmingham was attacked by three Rottweilers and needed 21 stitches. Two days later on May 31, 75-year-old grandmother Mrs. Nellie Williams and her dog were attacked by a Rottweiler while out for a stroll in a Leicester park. The same day a man was bitten by a Rottweiler on Merseyside when he went to pat the dog. Last week a six-month-old baby, Andrew Little, was attacked in his cot by his grandparents' Rottweiler, and another man needed stitches after an attack in Manchester. Today, we have the latest grim instalment of that catalogue of injuries.

Shortly before the recess, I wrote to the Leader of the House who refused to make available Government time to debate dog registration. Given the growing list of tragic attacks, the Government must act now and make time available for an urgent debate on the matter. It is an urgent issue and the Government's unwillingness to act makes it more so. There are more than 500,000 dogs roaming loose in Britain every day. A total of 250,000 dog bites are treated in hopitals each year at a cost of £17 million to the NHS. Stray dogs cause 50,000 road accidents a year, and 10,000 livestock are attacked by dogs, leading to insurance claims of about £1 million a year.

We must find a solution to the problem. First, every dog should have an electronically implanted permanent identification code, or a tattoo, so that it and its owner can be identified. That would, at least, enable a lost dog and its owner to be reunited, and an irresponsible owner to be caught. Rottweilers are proving to be a menace to innocent people. The young and the frail are particularly at the mercy of these animals which have shown that they are capable of turning from family pet to barbarous creature in an instant.

Secondly, a properly funded dog warden scheme is needed to enforce the system, catch the strays and educate dog owners. The Government's unwillingness to act does not match up to public expectations, and I hope that they will act.

Mr. Speaker: The hon. Member for Truro (Mr. Taylor) asked leave to move the Adjournment of the House under Standing Order No. 20, for the purpose of discussing a specific and important matter that he thinks should have urgent consideration, namely,
"the need for a dog registration scheme."

I have listened with care to what the hon. Member has said. As he knows, my sole duty under Standing Order No. 20 is to decide whether the matter should be given priority over business already set down for this evening or tomorrow. I regret that I must give the same answer that I gave to the hon. Member for Coventry, South-East (Mr. Nellist). I regret that I do not consider the matter that he has raised as appropriate for discussion under Standing Order No. 20. I cannot therefore submit his application to the House.

Points of Order

Mr. David Winnick (Walsall, North): On a point of order, Mr. Speaker. May I genuinely apologise for raising a point of order on such a busy day but, of course, if it is not raised today, the first opportunity, I shall be unable to raise it in future.

My right hon. Friend the Member for Manchester, Gorton (Mr. Kaufman) raised a point of order on 26 May with Mr. Deputy Speaker which appears in *Hansard* at columns 1259 and 1260. He referred to a story that had been reported on BBC television the previous evening, 25 May, alleging the connection between the expulsion of Soviet agents from the United Kingdom and possible blackmail attempts on Labour Members.

The actual signing-off headline of the end of the television bulletin said:

"Senior British sources have been giving reasons for the expulsion of Russian spies, who were believed to be involved with middle east terrorists and blackmailing Labour MPs."

The word "possible" had disappeared when the headline was given at the end of the BBC television news. In his point of order, my right hon. Friend said that he had contacted the Foreign Secretary's Office that morning before raising his point of order, but officials there were completely unable to clarify the position.

The following day, the Foreign Secretary responded to a letter from my right hon. Friend the Leader of the Opposition making it perfectly clear that Labour Members were not, in any way, associated with the activities for which Soviet diplomats had been expelled from the United Kingdom. No denial had been made before my right hon. Friend wrote to the Foreign Secretary. The Government knew that the allegations were a tissue of lies and it is surprising that absolutely no statement and no denial was made before my right hon. Friend the Leader of the Opposition wrote to the Foreign Secretary who, I agree, responded immediately.

I understand that it is not a matter for you, Mr. Speaker: I want to make that quite clear. *[Interruption.]* I am on a point of order. Whether the Minister of State, to whom I have given notice of this was misunderstood or misrepresented by the BBC correspondent is of no concern to you, Mr. Speaker, or for that matter to me; I am not interested in that. My point of order simply concerns whether it is right for hon. Members to be subject to baseless allegations, whether or not such lies—and they were lies—originated within the Government.

Although you are not responsible for statements, Mr. Speaker, I beg you to consider the matter. A large number of hon. Members—all belonging to one party—were subject to baseless allegations which the Government knew to be a tissue of lies. Would it not be right and appropriate for the Minister concerned—who is in the Chamber and to whom I have given notice, and who has denied responsibility—to make a statement to the House to clarify the position and to be questioned by hon. Members? He has a duty and responsibility to the House, as a Member of Parliament. He should stand up and make his position clear.

Mr. Speaker: Of course I deprecate any allegations made against any hon. Member of the House, from whatever quarter. I think that what the hon. Gentleman is complaining about is a report on the BBC. That is not a matter for me, and I do not think that I can deal with it.

Mr. Alan Williams (Swansea, West): Further to that point of order, Mr. Speaker. I entirely accept that what was said on the BBC is not directly a matter for you. What is a matter for you is, perhaps, to let the House know whether the Minister who, apparently inadvertently, may have been responsible for the report that was broadcast as a result of a lunchtime conversation with a BBC journalist —as he is present and received warning that the matter was to be raised—will now be honourable enough to ask to be allowed to make a personal statement making clear to the House what he has apparently said outside it.

Mr. Ian Gow (Eastbourne): Further to that point of order, Mr. Speaker. Is it not an astonishing proposition that the Government should make a statement every time allegations are made about members of the Opposition? It is a common experience for all of us to hear allegations against Opposition Members, and indeed against some of my right hon. and hon. Friends. My hon. Friend the Minister, who is in his place, has behaved with complete honour throughout. He issued a full statement on 2 June. The matter was raised in the House on 26 May, the day on which we rose for the recess. Is it not clear that the hon. Member for Walsall, North (Mr. Winnick) is living up to his reputation—that of being, in the words of a former leader of the Labour party, the silliest man in the House?

Mr. Speaker: Order. It is not possible for me to comment on what has been said. I think that we must move on.

Several Hon. Members *rose——*

Mr. Speaker: Order. We have a heavy day ahead of us. There is nothing that I can do about the matter. I cannot be held responsible for conversations with members of the BBC or the press: it is not a point of order for me.

Mr. Tam Dalyell (Linlithgow): On a point of order, Mr. Speaker. You and I were parliamentary colleagues of a Northumberland miner by the name of Will Owen: you may remember him. Will Owen was broken by circumstances which—I choose my words very carefully —turned out subsequently to be rather different from what had been alleged at the time. Will Owen died a broken and, some would say, a disgraced man. I think that all of us, particularly Ministers, must be very careful indeed. The Minister of State probably did not know Will Owen, but he was a friend of mine and of some Conservative Members who privately felt as strongly as I did.

The Minister may recollect that in the case of Will Owen an injustice may have been done. I think that Ministers who were not here during Will Owen's time ought to be very careful about being reported on the subject of events of which they may not have first-hand knowledge. In a sense, Mr. Speaker, you are the custodian of departed colleagues as well. I think that for the protection of one of those colleagues you should at least invite the Minister to make some kind of statement.

Mr. Speaker: Order. I think that we should all be extremely careful about what we say both inside and outside the House.

Mr. Jeremy Corbyn (Islington, North): On a point of order, Mr. Speaker. My point of order relates to a written answer given today by the Minister of State, Home Office about the introduction of visa requirements for people coming to this country from Turkey.

On 26 May there was an Adjournment debate on the position facing Kurdish asylum-seekers. I raised a number of questions with the Minister, as did my hon. Friend the Member for Hackney, South and Shoreditch (Mr. Sedgemore). At no stage in his lengthy reply did the Minister of State say that he had already written to the Turkish Government seeking to lift the provisions of the 1960 agreement between Britain and Turkey to the effect that visas would not be required. He sent the letter to the Turkish Government on 23 May. It is now revealed, on our first day back after a short recess, that the Government are indeed seeking to impose visa restrictions from 23 June on people visiting this country from Turkey. The implications are clearly very serious. Anyone seeking political asylum from Turkey will not be able to come here, as a visa will not be made available. If they try to come here, the airline or other carrier that has brought them can be fined £1,000.

This is a serious matter, Mr. Speaker. It should not creep out in a parliamentary answer; it ought to be the subject of a statement from the Home Secretary so that he can be questioned and opportunities for debate can be provided. I am sure that you agree that it is a serious matter, and we look to you to provide some facility for us to question the Government about their behaviour and, indeed, their treatment of the House in not revealing the information on 26 May, as they could have.

Mr. Speaker: Order. The hon. Gentleman has made his point, and I am sure that it has been heard by those on the Government Front Bench. I have given the hon. Gentleman an opportunity to raise the matter, and no doubt he will have other opportunities.

Mr. Winnick *rose——*

Mr. Speaker: Order. I will not take any more points of order. The hon. Gentleman has made his point, and we have a busy day ahead of us.

Mr. Winnick: On a different point of order, Mr. Speaker.

Mr. Speaker: The hon. Gentleman has had a very good run this afternoon.

BILL PRESENTED

ENVIRONMENTAL CHARTER

Mr. Archy Kirkwood, supported by Mr. Malcolm Bruce, Mr. Richard Livsey, Mr. James Wallace, Mr. Matthew Taylor, Mr. Simon Hughes, Mr. A. J. Beith and Mrs. Ray Michie, presented a Bill to establish local authority ecology working groups for the purpose of adopting an environmental charter to carry out specific measures to protect and enhance the quality of the natural environment; and for connected purposes: And the same was read the First time; and ordered to be read a Second time upon Friday 7 July and to be printed. [Bill 147.]

STATUTORY INSTRUMENTS, &c.

Ordered,

That the draft Restrictive Trade Practices (Sale and Purchase and Share Subscription Agreements) (Goods) Order 1989 be referred to a Standing Committee on Statutory Instruments, &c.

That the draft Restrictive Trade Practices (Services) (Amendment) Order 1989 be referred to a Standing Committee on Statutory Instruments, &c.—*[Mr. Kenneth Carlisle.]*

Agriculture (Control of Nitrates)

5.27 pm

Mr. Roger Knapman (Stroud): I beg to move,

That leave be given to bring in a Bill to restrict the use of nitrogenous fertilisers.

In the late 17th century the satirist Jonathan Swift observed that

"whoever could make two ears of corn or two blades of grass to grow upon a spot of ground where only one grew before, would deserve better of mankind, and do more essential service to his country than the whole race of politicians put together."

I fear that the public perception of politicians may not have changed much in the intervening centuries, but the role of farmers has changed considerably, particularly during the past decade.

As a farmer's son, I would not wish to make any proposals that would penalise agriculture, which is Britain's largest and most successful industry. We can, however, assume that there is a need to curb agricultural production. My right hon. Friend the Minister of Agriculture, Fisheries and Food and his predecessor, my right hon. Friend the Member for Westmorland and Lonsdale (Mr. Jopling) have both introduced packages of measures with that intention. They would, I believe, be the first to pay tribute to the farming community—3 per cent. of our population who produce some 85 per cent. of our temperate foodstuffs and export a substantial amount of food each year.

Ideally, we should try to control production in a way that does not disadvantage farmers or their incomes, and combine it with the environmental advantages that would flow from less intensive farming methods. To date, we have tried controlling production both by quotas on individual commodities and by price restraint. But quotas that deal with one commodity in isolation, such as milk, have a major flaw—because if a farmer cannot produce that commodity, he must produce something else. There is then a greater and growing risk of oversupply of other foodstuffs.

Equally, mild price restraint results in greater production because that is the natural reaction of farmers who wish to preserve their living standards. Above all, there is the dreadful policy of food intervention buying and storage, thereby converting first-quality products into third-quality products, which are sold off at rock bottom prices to those living under Socialist Administrations who know no better and who can afford no better.

The National Economic Development Office's 1987 report entitled "Land Use in the 1990s" suggests that the United Kingdom needs to shed 1·5 million productive hectares or 14 per cent. of our land area by the mid-1990s. However, there is little point taking 14 per cent. of land out of production if the remaining 86 per cent. will be increasingly intensively farmed.

For all those reasons, now is the time to consider supply side control. If we are serious about controlling production, we must look at the means of production. I am pleased to note that the National Farmers Union is seriously considering these suggestions. The means of production are almost wholly good. They include better plant breeding, modern machinery, skilled labour, and most pesticides and fertilisers. However, we must carefully examine the dramatic increase in the use of nitrogenous

[*Mr. Roger Knapman*]

fertilisers; that is, inorganic nitrogen. I quote from the bible on that issue, which is the 1962 edition of "Fream's Elements of Agriculture". It states that

"the effects of nitrogen-containing manures upon plant growth are amongst the most spectacular which can be achieved by manuring, for nitrogen is the food material which is especially responsible for growth, particularly of foliage and stems."

If that was evident in 1962, it is doubly so in 1989 when the reduction in the farm labour force and modern machinery make it more convenient for farmers to apply large quantities of artificial fertilisers than to apply bulky farmyard manure to fields in the traditional and labour-intensive way.

The main contributor to increased production of foodstuffs is nitrogen, which no longer arrives in half-hundredweight bags but usually in 1 tonne sacks. With land valued at about £2,000 per acre, obviously it is to the farmer's advantage to apply additional nitrogen—just 6 lb per hundredweight—substantially to increase plant growth and by that his crop yields.

My Bill provides for the restriction of nitrogen application; that is, a limited number of units per acre with no transfers between farmers but a subsidy to those who do not take up their full allocation. I have already stated that the proposals are advantageous to the farming community, the countryside and the environment. The advantages to farmers are as follows. First, controlling production on a European-wide basis means that supply and demand will be better balanced, which must be in the long-term interests of the industry. Secondly, the farmer will again be able to choose which enterprises best suit his or her farm and pocket. Farmers will be free to adapt to changing circumstances as they see fit.

Thirdly, the proposals favour extensive rather than intensive farming systems, and will inconvenience mainly those who use the largest amounts of nitrogen—especially continuous grain and intensive dairy farmers, who collectively are the worst culprits in respect of overproduction of agricultural products. Even they can easily adapt. The intensive dairy farmer, for example, could purchase additional grass keep in the neighbourhood, which is a logical form of extensification. Finally, my proposals will encourage crop rotations, which are good for the land. Most farmers realise that they are merely custodians of the land for their lifetimes and that the land should always be left in good heart.

The Bill would also bring benefits to the land in general. Nitrogen encourages plant growth, and the fastest growing plants are most encouraged. It logically follows that wild or slow-growing plants become rare where nitrogen is frequently and heavily applied.

An even more topical aspect is the nitrate level in water courses. Nitrate-sensitive areas have already been proposed. The Rothamstead experimental station's aptly entitled report "Keeping the Balance" points out that the amount of nitrogen applied is only one of many factors affecting nitrogen levels in our water supplies and that particular care should be exercised when applications of fertiliser are made in the autumn, for example, when rainfall levels exceed those of evaporation. However, the application rate is a factor, and the public are rightly concerned that high nitrate levels in water supplies can be cancer-inducing—though I understand that that remains to be proved.

An interesting article in *The Times* on 24 November 1988 observed that to treat water intended for drinking in order to remove nitrates would impose unacceptably high costs on the water authorities, which I accept. Prevention is better than a cure, and in most cases the best long-term solution must be to reduce the quantities of nitrates that reach surface and ground water supplies by changing agricultural practices, so that the need for treatment will not arise.

For all those reasons, nitrates should be controlled. We may then be able to do away with the common agricultural policy, and all the fraud, intervention and food storage schemes that together cost far more than any subsidies to farmers. An excellent leader in *The Daily Telegraph* on 13 May headed "Yoke them together" noted that my right hon. Friend the Secretary of State for the Environment requires less intensive farming methods for the benefit of the environment, and that my right hon. Friend the Minister of Agriculture, Fisheries and Food seeks to curb food surpluses. Those aims are mutually compatible, and my Bill should please both my right hon. Friends.

Question put and agreed to.

Bill ordered to be brought in by Mr. Roger Knapman, Mr. Cyril D. Townsend, Dr. Keith Hampson, Mr. James Pawsey, Mr. John Heddle, Mr. David Curry, Mr. William Cash, Mr. Teddy Taylor, Mr. Greg Knight, and Mr. Nicholas Bennett.

AGRICULTURE (CONTROL OF NITRATES)

Mr. Roger Knapman accordingly presented a Bill to restrict the use of nitrogenous fertilisers: And the same was read a First time; and ordered to be read a Second time upon Wednesday 7 June, and to be printed. [Bill 149.]

Orders of the Day

Employment Bill

As amended in the Standing Committee, further considered.

5.36 pm

Mr. Graham Riddick (Colne Valley): On a point of order, Mr. Deputy Speaker. Will you kindly indicate why the two new clauses tabled in my name and that of my hon. Friend the Member for Gainsborough and Horncastle (Mr. Leigh) were not selected. They were designed to close loopholes in earlier employment legislation——

Mr. Deputy Speaker (Mr. Harold Walker): Order. The hon. Gentleman cannot make the speech that he might have made had his clauses been selected. As I understand the hon. Gentleman, he complains that the clauses he tabled were not selected by Mr. Speaker. Is that the case?

Mr. Riddick: Yes, Mr. Deputy Speaker.

Mr. Deputy Speaker: I am sorry, but I cannot help the hon. Gentleman.

Mr. Riddick *rose*——

Mr. Deputy Speaker: Order. The Chair is not required to give reasons for the non-selection of amendments.

Mr. Riddick: I entirely accept your ruling, Mr. Deputy Speaker, but I may point out that the purpose of the Bill, apart from amending the Sex Discrimination Act 1975, is to——

Mr. Deputy Speaker: Order. I have already told the hon. Gentleman that the Chair is not required to give explanations for the non-selection of amendments. The hon. Gentleman cannot debate why his clauses were not selected.

New Clause 12

DISCRIMINATION ON GROUNDS OF AGE

'It shall be unlawful for any person to offer employment at an establishment in the United Kingdom which may discriminate against any person on the grounds that he is older or younger than any other person or persons in:
  (a) any advertisement or other arrangement made to notify prospective employees, or
  (b) the methods of determining who should be offered employment, or
  (c) the terms and conditions on which employment is offered, or
  (d) refusing to offer employment.'.
Brought up, and read the First time.

Mr. Michael Meacher (Oldham, West) *rose*——

Mr. Deputy Speaker: I point out to the hon. Member for Oldham, West (Mr. Meacher) that, as his name is not among those associated with new clause 12, it must be moved formally by an hon. Member who is.

Mr. Gavin Strang (Edinburgh, East): I beg to move, that the clause be read a Second time.

Mr. Deputy Speaker: With this it will be convenient to debate new clause 13—*Discrimination on grounds of unemployment*—

'It shall be unlawful for any person to offer employment at an establishment in the United Kingdom which may discriminate against any person because of current or previous periods of unemployment by:
  (a) the methods of determining who should be offered employment, or
  (b) the terms and conditions on which employment is offered, or
  (c) refusing to offer employment.'.

Mr. Meacher: Age discrimination, which is the topic of new clause 12, is potentially the most wide-ranging form of discrimination in employment. It could affect everyone at some time in their lives. It is obviously in direct defiance of the principle of equality of opportunity which was defined by the Equal Opportunities Commission as follows:
"individuals should be judged as individuals according to their merits and not on the basis of a characteristic ascribed to them arbitrarily because they are members of a group".
That definition would commend itself to both sides of the House and it is clearly breached by discrimination on grounds of age.

There have been two private Members' Bills in Parliament this year to outlaw age discrimination. The Employment (Age Limits) Bill was introduced in the other place and the Employment Age Discrimination Bill was presented to the House by the hon. Member for Isle of Wight (Mr. Field). Neither is likely to succeed without Government support.

The Government seem to have a schizophrenic view of the matter. On one hand, the Under-Secretary of State for Employment said:
"It is both irresponsible and unfair to discriminate without justification on the grounds of age."—[*Official Report,* 15 March 1989; Vol. 149, c. *250.*]
The Opposition very much support that view. On the other hand, in their evidence to the Employment Select Committee on 7 December 1988, the Government refused to take action, stating as their reason:
"it would be neither practical nor beneficial to legislate to prevent age discrimination in employment".
Yet other countries do not take that view and have legislation to prohibit age discrimination.

The United States Age Discrimination in Employment Act has existed for 22 years. That Act, as amended, prohibits age-based employment discrimination against individuals aged 40 and above. Under the Act, it is unlawful for employers to fail or refuse to hire, to dismiss or otherwise discriminate against any individual with respect to compensation, terms, conditions or privileges of employment because of such an individual's age. It is also unlawful for employers to limit, segregate or classify an employee in any way that would deprive the employee of job opportunities or adversely affect employment status because of age. If that can be done in the United States, why can it not be done here?

In Canada, since 1978, when the Canadian Human Rights Act came into effect, it has been unlawful to discriminate in employment on grounds of age. Unlike the American Act, there is no minimum age requirement—the Act prohibits discrimination against all ages.

Furthermore, Britain is a founder member and signatory to the International Labour Organisation—I am well aware that the Government take a fairly flippant and nonchalant view of the ILO, but it is an important international authority. Its older workers recommendation states:
"each member should, with the framework of national policy to promote equality of opportunity and treatment for

[*Mr. Meacher*]

workers, whatever their age . . . take measures for the prevention of discrimination in employment and occupation with regard to older workers".

The problem of age discrimination is not a minor one. In its 1988 study, the EOC found that 27 per cent. of employers specified an age requirement or bar in their vacancy advertisements. In *The Sunday Times,* an average of one third—varying between 17 per cent. and 59 per cent. of all employers—made an age requirement during the sample period. In the Institute of Personnel Management's magazine, 24 per cent. specified an age requirement, although the institute's equal opportunities code specifically advises against age discrimination in employment.

5.45 pm

The most frequent age requirement is as low as 25 to 35 years. That is why it is so serious for older workers. Not many right hon. and hon. Members present in the House would qualify. The EOC found that one quarter of advertisements specified under 45 years while one fifth specified under 35 years and no fewer than 96 per cent. of all job advertisements which specified an age required a person under 45, while nearly two thirds of advertisements required someone under 35. In *The Sunday Times,* half of all advertisements specifying ages required someone under 35. In *Nine to Five,* a London magazine specialising in clerical, secretarial and administrative jobs, almost all advertisements were for people under 35. That is quite serious and arresting for job opportunities for older people.

There are two other disturbing findings in current practice. First, the EOC found that even those employers who claim to be "equal opportunity employers" specified age bars in their advertisements. Secondly, after studying 150 equal opportunity statements, the EOC found that only one third covered age discrimination, although many included other non-statutory forms of discrimination such as class, employment status or sex. Therefore, age discrimination in job recruitment is extensive and unfair. There are many strong age stereotypes which, as we get older, it will no doubt give us some comfort to refute. MORI found that personnel directors and recruitment specialists believe that drive, ambition and health all decline with age, but the empirical evidence does not support those beliefs or other myths about older workers.

A famous study by a researcher called Dr. Gee that was published last year found, first, that age-related declines in productivity, mental efficiency and reaction times are all small. Secondly, many of the small mental losses which occur can be and are compensated by experience. Thirdly, older workers are more satisfied with their job, are less likely to leave an organisation for another job, and have lower rates of absenteeism and accidents at work. Fourthly, there is considerable individual variation in age-related losses which implies that employers should look at differences in individuals rather than age groups. Research has again pointed strongly to the need for action to be taken.

For those reasons, age discrimination, which is so unfair, creates angry and frustrated individuals who find overwhelming difficulty in getting job interviews because of age, and often despite successful interviews, have their applications ruled out on grounds of age. Once unemployed, people's chance of getting a job decline with age, however unfair that might be. That is why it is so important to help them.

Decreases in unemployment in the past two years show that the younger one is, the more likely one is to find a job. Although unemployment fell by 27 per cent. among the under-25s and by just over 11 per cent. among those aged 25 to 44 who had been unemployed for five years or more, it actually increased by 3 per cent. among those aged 45 or over in the past two years. That is very disturbing.

Therefore, there are strong personal and individual reasons for supporting new clause 12. But there are other reasons.

"Because of demographic trends, it is irresponsible to ignore the talents which older workers can contribute to the economy".

I am glad that the Minister was nodding as I was quoting from his Department's evidence to the Employment Select Committee. I strongly agree with those words. As they come from his Department and he agrees with them, I hope that today he will state that he is prepared to take action. Perhaps not surprisingly, strong attempts are being made to use indirect means to prohibit age discrimination when direct means are not available. According to the code of practice of the Equal Opportunities Commission,

"an unjustifiable age limit could constitute unlawful indirect discrimination"

on the ground of sex.

I shall give a further example from a number that have occurred recently to illustrate the problem. In Price *v.* the Civil Service Commission, Ms. Price, who was 36, claimed indirect sex discrimination because the executive officer's post that she had applied for was open only to people under 28. She argued that a considerably smaller proportion of women than men could comply with the age limit because more women were out of the labour market in their twenties having children. Significantly, the tribunal upheld her case.

The statutory authorities are highly sympathetic to complaints about age discrimination in job recruitment. They are prepared to accept arguments based, if necessary, on other criteria to achieve that end. It would clearly be much better if the law openly and directly prohibited discrimination on the grounds of age, which is the purpose of new clause 12, which I strongly commend to the House.

New clause 13 is designed to prevent discrimination against job applicants on the ground of long-term unemployment. I shall cite two surveys that illustrate the problem. The first was of 64 employers, which suggested that while only one in 10 employers would screen out newly unemployed people when recruiting, half would screen out those who had been out of work for a year or more. The second was a postal survey of 456 employers in four different local markets, which was followed up by case studies of 31 employers. It revealed that applicants were likely to be rejected simply because they were long-term unemployed people at least 50 per cent. of the time. The second survey meshes in closely with the conclusion of the first one. Smaller firms were significantly more likely to discriminate than larger ones. Interestingly, there was less discrimination against long-term unemployed people in Preston and Glasgow, where unemployment was more serious and many more jobless people had been out of work for a long time, than in Peterborough and Bournemouth, where unemployment was lower.

A further important finding was that people who had been out of work for a long time tended to use jobcentres or look in newspapers for vacancies and did not have access to specialised or informal job networks, whereby news of vacancies is spread by word of mouth, special notices or journals. We believe that this puts the focus for policy on the quality of information available to the employment service, which receives only about one third of all vacancies. In Sweden, employers are required by law to report nearly all vacancies to the employment services, which allows unemployed people a fairer crack of the whip at all the jobs going and gives the employment services better information about the pattern of vacancies in each local labour market so that it can plan more appropriate training programmes. We believe that that sensible system should be adopted here. The Labour party is committed to a high-quality employment service, and we intend to introduce such a system in Britain.

With or without that change, we are deeply concerned that unemployment has reduced least in the past three years among those who have been unemployed the longest. We strongly believe that there is a role for the law in countering discrimination as well as a role for advice and training of employers to counter prejudice before the problem is overcome and long-term unemployed people, who, we all surely agree, are among the most disadvantaged people in this country, are able to break out of the social and economic trap. That is why new clause 13 is so important, and I strongly urge the Government to accept it.

Mr. James Wallace (Orkney and Shetland): I give general support to the two new clauses.

The recent report of the Select Committee on Employment about employment of the over-50s is useful. Its attention was drawn to the many disadvantages facing the over-50s, not least discrimination against them by people over 50. The report said that many people in public life and companies do not take on jobs of considerable responsibility until they are over 50. Paragraph 10 of the report graphically summed up the problem. It said:

"Age discrimination could quickly wither away if those who have the power to determine employment policies in the private and public sectors bothered to look in the mirror. If they are not too old at 50 neither are others."

There is a home truth in that graphic point.

Hon. Members receive a number of applications for the posts that they advertise. With the best will in the world, it is difficult to overcome certain prejudices when one receives an application from someone aged 45 or 50. One wonders why the applicant is not developing a career structure with the firm that may have been employing him for a number of years. Such prejudice must be overcome.

The suggestion involving employment services being required to ask employers whether an age limit is strictly necessary would go only so far in dealing with the problem. In reply, the Minister may find some technical problem with the drafting of the new clause. Nevertheless, the thrust behind it is appropriate, and only through some form of legislation will age discrimination be tackled.

The hon. Member for Oldham, West (Mr. Meacher) made a telling point when he said that people find out about many jobs only by word of mouth or by a notice being placed on a staff room, works canteen or company notice board. Many jobs are never brought to the attention of people who have been unemployed for a long time.

Long-term unemployed people are discriminated against by the attitudes of many employers when sifting through job applications. They think that if a person has been unemployed a long time he is by definition unemployable and do not offer him the opportunity to present himself at interview and prove his worth. A report of the Campaign for Work said:

"To quote just one study of 250 long term unemployed people in Hull, 80 per cent. of the sample were actively looking for work; nearly half said they were willing to leave Hull if work was offered elsewhere and of those able to take full-time work more than half would be satisfied with take-home pay of less than £100 per week".

It said that that was evidence of considerable motivation among those people.

The fact that people have been unemployed for a long time does not mean that they have lost their motivation. Community programme managers, when there were such people, reported that long-term unemployed people were quickly motivated after only a short time at work. Tragically, many of them never get the opportunity to show their motivation and ability to work. Perhaps employers need to be educated about such innate prejudice by a campaign drawing to their attention the merit and worth of people who are older or have been unemployed for a long time. If such a campaign failed, the fall-back of some statutory powers is equally necessary.

6 pm

Mr. Frank Haynes (Ashfield): I did not expect to be called so early in the debate, Mr. Deputy Speaker. You are very kind.

The Government have created the situation in which we find ourselves and that is why I support new clause 12. The Government have destroyed industry, and, in the wake of that, they have destroyed jobs. I come from a coal-mining area where pits have been closed willy-nilly and people have been put on the dole at the age of 40 and younger, yet job advertisements in the newspapers often have an age limit. That is a shocking state of affairs and the Government must wake up to the fact that they have a responsibility to such people.

I can see that the Minister is listening to what I am saying, just as he listened in Committee when I told him about the situation that the Government had created. We come here to represent our constituents and to tell the Government about the position in our constituencies. What is happening in my constituency is also happening elsewhere, yet the Government try to create jobs by means of low wages.

Many of my constituents want a job but cannot get one. The pits have been closed and they have not been replaced with industry to create new jobs. We have appealed to the Secretaries of State for Energy and for Trade and Industry to use the land that results from a pit closure to give an incentive to industrialists to replace the jobs lost, but they do not want to know. Instead, they blame British Coal, saying that it wants to sell the land for something else. It is time that they put their heads together—or time that we knocked them together—and did something.

The Government should tell British Coal in no uncertain terms what to do with such land to create jobs for people who need them, having been thrown on the dole by the closure of industries resulting from the Government's policies. It is time that the Government woke up and did something. That is why the Opposition have tabled new clause 12. There should be no

[Mr. Frank Haynes]

discrimination against any person on the ground of age. The Government have created this position and it is time that they put things right in the interests of those whom they too are supposed to be representing.

Mr. Greville Janner (Leicester, West): My hon. Friend the Member for Ashfield (Mr. Haynes) is the best possible living argument for the fact that nobody should be discriminated against on the ground of age. It is only in the past few years, in the flowering of his youth, that his voice has developed to its full extent and he has been able to put forward his case with such restraint.

My late father, who some of my hon. Friends will remember, reached his maturity only when he gave up his seat at the age of 78 and went to another place so that I might succeed him. Now that I too am beginning to reach maturity, I recognise the usefulness and importance of the new clause.

I notice that hon. Members on the Government Front Benches have visibly aged since the time that they took up their monstrous task of destroying the employment security of the British people and, in particular, of ruining the law that protects people at work. When they took office they were bright, young and fresh and they were brought in for that reason. We are told that in the coming reshuffle they will be replaced by younger people.

I respectfully suggest that, as we grow older, there are fewer and fewer grounds for accepting discrimination. People should be accepted for what they are and for what they can do, irrespective of sex, race or trade union affiliation, all of which are protected in the sense that it is unlawful to discriminate on those grounds. They should also be protected here, as they are in the United States and Canada, from discrimination on the ground of age.

Discrimination is essential to all those who select for employment or promotion, for training or even for dismissal, but it must be discrimination lawfully exercised. I sit on the Select Committee for Employment and the report, which has been rightly referred to, shows how widespread sex discrimination has become in Britain. It also shows that it is not based on logic or sense. New clause 12 would enable us to get rid of that discrimination as and when we should.

The Select Committee heard evidence of what is happening in Britain. People are retiring earlier and acquiring what one witness called a portfolio of jobs, some paid and some unpaid. In many cases, they are working harder after they have retired than they did before, but it is difficult for them to be accepted for what they are when they are forced out of their jobs by early redundancy when they are older than 35. Today, early retirement in some jobs is beginning at 45 or 52.

It is wrong to discriminate against people on the basis of age and I ask Ministers, in their own interests as well as in the interests of others, to reconsider any opposition to the new clause. The present system is daft. Men are forced to remain at work until they are 65 to obtain a state pension. People are forced out of work when they should not be and they are not permitted to compete on an equal basis because of their age. Discrimination on the grounds of age should be unlawful and this excellent new clause will ban it. I hope that the Government will support it.

Mr. Harry Barnes (Derbyshire, North-East): Those hon. Members who have spoken have correctly stated that the problem is one of discrimination against older people on the ground of age. However new clause 12 says that there should not be discrimination against any person on the grounds that he is older or younger. In some cases young people could be discriminated against because of a particular age bar. That element of new clause 12 may hold some appeal for the Government with their particular philosophy and the idea that there are natural whizz kids around.

However, the serious problem is the one that exists for older people. I am particularly aware of that problem, having acted as a director for access courses. People who study part-time on access courses and then enter full-time education might be out of the job market for a long time. They might spend at least two or three years in part-time education and then, depending which avenue they choose, they might go to university for three years or for five years if they have to attend a preparatory college course.

There are masses of people with great talent and the Government are supposed to be interested in assisting access courses. However, the student loan scheme does nothing to assist them. After such training many people will be able to come back into the job market having acquired new skills in a society that is increasingly subject to technological change which requires new skills. Those people will be older and should not be discriminated against for their own sakes and for the sake of society generally.

Clause 8 will lead to even more discrimination, giving us further grounds for saying that new clauses 12 and 13 are important. They cannot prevent the harmful consequences of the Bill, they can make some minor adjustments to try to improve a desperate situation. For example, measures in clause 8 will lead to more young people being employed and exploited which will in turn affect older people. If we remove the protections which prevent young people from working more than 48 hours a week and allow them to work on Sundays without a day in lieu and to be pushed on to night shifts and remove statutory meal breaks, young people can be considerably exploited by ruthless employers and can be used instead of older skilled people. That can result in youngsters being used to undermine the conditions and wages of older workers.

The Government hold the peculiar view that the decline in the birth rate, leading to fewer youngsters being in the employment market in years to come, will result in young workers having a fantastic bargaining position which will enable them to secure good wages and conditions. Were that to happen, it would have an impact on older workers, because younger workers would be given jobs in preference, especially in view of the changed conditions of which I spoke.

The way in which the YTS has operated makes it clear that schemes of that kind can be used by the Government to exploit young people and thereby undermine the negotiating power of older workers. For all those reasons, the proposed new clauses should be adopted, because they would at least slightly improve an otherwise terrible Bill.

The Parliamentary Under-Secretary of State for Employment (Mr. John Lee): I and—the hon. and learned Member for Leicester, West (Mr. Janner) will be pleased to hear—my youthful ministerial colleagues, have some sympathy with the Opposition's intention in tabling the new clauses, which seek to outlaw discrimination by potential employers on the grounds of a person's age or because he or she is unemployed. The Government firmly believe that employers should recognise the valuable resource represented by applicants, whatever their age or history of unemployment.

It can clearly be wasteful for employers to refuse to consider applicants solely because they have or have not reached a certain age, or because they are unemployed. This is a message we have frequently sought to get across to employers—for example, in our Department's recent White Paper "Employment for the 1990s".

There are barriers of both prejudice and lack of knowledge to overcome. We believe that the best way to overcome these barriers is not by legislation but by encouraging and persuading employers to amend their personnel policies where necessary.

When taking details of vacancies, jobcentres try to persuade employers not to impose often arbitrary and usually unnecessary and pointless age restrictions. That has been longstanding policy, but instructions were strengthened in January of this year to ensure that where an employer insists on an age restriction, the employment service seeks to persuade him to treat it as a preference rather than an absolute requirement. The service will also contact an employer if a recruit becomes available who is suitable in all respects other than age.

Mr. Janner: Is the Minister aware that the efforts which the Department makes in those respects have been failing, are failing and that there is no reason to suppose that they will not continue to fail?

Mr. Lee: I do not agree with the hon. and learned Gentleman. As I shall show, increasingly employers who discriminate are realising the error of their ways, and the changing labour market profile and demographic changes will push them even more in the direction that we wish them to go.

Employers are showing increasing flexibility in this area. For example, Tesco's is already actively recruiting older workers to fill vacancies, and British Telecom is considering taking on and training older recruits to meet its need for skilled engineering staff. A substantial investment is also being made to help older unemployed people get jobs. Longer-term unemployed people up to the age of 60 are able to obtain guidance on ways back to work through the restart programme.

The employment training programme is open to people up to the age of 60 and offers unemployed older workers with out-of-date skills the opportunity to retrain through training packages tailored to their individual needs. Through offering work experience, it also allows them to show prospective employers their abilities.

The job club programme can also offer help to unemployed older workers through training them in how best to present themselves to prospective employers and how to make effective speculative approaches to employers who have not advertised vacancies.

For unemployed people who wish to become self-employed, the enterprise allowance scheme is available up to the age of 64. We have recently announced that a new part-time jobstart scheme for the over 50s is to be piloted in four areas. This will help unemployed older people to get back into the job market by offering them an allowance of £20 a week if they take a part-time job earning up to £2·57 an hour.

The employment service is also taking practical steps through several initiatives to encourage employers to give more consideration to unemployed people in general. For example, in Greenwich the service is carrying out preliminary interviews for vacancies with Texas Homecare. In exchange, Texas has guaranteed to fill half of its vacancies from people who have been unemployed for six months or more. In other areas, companies have run mock interviews at jobclubs which have resulted in members finding jobs with the companies.

6.15 pm

We are taking further positive steps in that area. As hon. Members will know, our Department has recently announced the introduction of the job interview guarantee scheme for unemployed inner-city residents. It will initially be offered in 20 inner-city areas and will be available later this month. It will help not only to prepare long-term unemployed people to re-enter work and increase their opportunities to do so, but to break down employer reticence in considering longer-term unemployed people for such vacancies. It will link the assistance already offered by job clubs and the employment service with new measures. These will include a job preparation course, similar to the current restart course model, but with employers involved in tailoring the course content to meet their specific needs.

"Work trials" will offer unemployed people the chance to demonstrate for a short period their ability to undertake a job with a potential employer while they remain on benefit, allowing employers to reassure themselves about employing people who have been out of work for some time. In return for those services, employers will agree to interview all long-term unemployed people submitted in that way.

It is clear—and ultimately this is far more effective than the new clauses—that demographic trends will put real pressure on employers to consider a much wider range of applicants than they might do at present. Employers will need to give greater consideration to older workers and to unemployed people for their vacancies.

As I have explained, some employers are already taking a sensible lead in doing that. Indeed, it is obvious that that is already happening, as the record falls in unemployment over the last 33 months testify. Employers who fail to improve their personnel practices will learn the hard way that it is in their own economic interests to ensure that they heed the messages that the Government are putting over on these issues.

Question put and negatived.

New Clause 15

EMPLOYMENT OF DISABLED PERSONS

' .—(1) Section 10(2) of the Disabled Persons (Employment) Act 1944 shall be amended as follows—

(2) In paragraph (a) the words ", which shall not be less than 3%," shall be inserted after the words "a standard percentage".'.—[*Mr. Wareing.*]

Brought up, and read the First time.

Mr. Robert N. Wareing (Liverpool, West Derby): I beg to move, That the clause be read a Second time.

Mr. Deputy Speaker: It will be convenient to consider at the same time the following:

New clause 16—*Proceedings under the Disabled Persons (Employment) Act 1944*—

'   .—(1) Section 19 of the Disabled Persons (Employment) Act 1944 shall be amended as follows—

(2) Subsection (1) shall cease to have effect.

(3) In subsection (2) the words "brought by the Minister" shall be inserted after "proceedings for an offence under this Act".'.

New clause 17—*Discrimination on grounds of disability*——

'It shall be unlawful for any person to offer employment at an establishment in the United Kingdom which may unreasonably discriminate against any person on the grounds that they are disabled in—

(a) any advertisement or other arrangement made to notify prospective employees, or

(b) the methods of determining who shall be offered employment, or

(c) the terms and conditions on which employment is offered, or

(d) refusing to offer employment.'

Mr. Wareing: The new clause would enshrine in an Act of Parliament for the first time the 3 per cent. figure often accepted as the quota for disabled people as a percentage of a work force. The Disabled Persons (Employment) Act 1944 mentions only "a standard percentage". That was determined to be 2 per cent. by a statutory rule and order in 1945 and to be 3 per cent. by the Disabled Persons (Standard Percentage) Order No. 1258 of 25 July 1946.

The new clause gives the Government an opportunity to address the problem. Current rumours are giving great concern to organisations representing disabled people and require an answer, for the rumours are that the Government intend to abolish the quota system. No doubt Thatcherite principles will dictate that the quota system is a burden on employers. Compassion plays no part in the race to surrender everything to the hidden and often grotesque hand of the market.

One would have expected the Government to give a lead in ensuring that in their Departments at least 3 per cent. of the work force was disabled. This afternoon I received a written answer to a question that I put to the Prime Minister about the number of registered disabled people employed by the Cabinet Office. I was told:

"There are 16 registered disabled persons employed by the Cabinet Office, which represents approximately 1 per cent. of the total work force, and none at 10 Downing street."

The answer added, ironically:

"The Cabinet Office is an equal opportunities employer". The right hon. Lady could have fooled all of us. Indeed, she will be trying to do that if it is suggested that the Government want to adhere to the 3 per cent. quota.

The number of people who chose to register under the 1984 Act fell from 936,196 in 1950 to 389,273 in 1986. This signifies a complete lack of confidence on the part of disabled people in the adequacy of the existing law and even more in the willingness of the Government fully to apply and implement—to use the Prime Minister's own word—the law as it now stands.

It is rather interesting that more than 1,230,000 people have registered with local authorities as disabled under the Chronically Sick and Disabled Persons Act 1970, which shows that people have more confidence that local authorities may try to provide them with services than in their providing them with suitable employment.

The percentage of employers abiding by the law and meeting the quota fell from 53·2 per cent. in 1965 to 26·8 per cent. in 1986. In 1986, 56 per cent. of employers were not meeting the quota and were being issued with permits by the Minister's Department. It was even true in 1986 that no fewer than 17·2 per cent. of those not meeting the quota had no permit to break the law—I insist, "break the law".

If the Government are considering the quota system in their internal review, as the Minister has told me in answer to a parliamentary question, they should take on board the views of disabled people's organisations. The Royal National Institute for the Deaf says of the quota system:

"despite some calls for its abolition we believe it should be retained, strengthened and enforced."

The Spastics Society, in consulting its members in April this year, found that

"Most favoured the retention of the quota system and the majority of these argued strongly for stricter enforcement and fewer exemptions."

The Government may argue that this is one of those famous burdens on industry. They are not too worried about burdens on the disabled, but they are worried about burdens on industry. However, it is hardly a burden on industry when it can so easily be lifted by Tory Ministers, as has happened in the past five years. In each of the past five years Ministers have issued over 18,000 permits. I should like to know what the criteria are that lead Ministers to exempt so many employers. The law is certainly needed, but it also needs to be applied. This is something else that Tory Governments in particular have failed to do.

Since the 1944 Act, there have been only 10 prosecutions. The last one was in 1975, by my right hon. Friend the Member for Manchester, Wythenshawe (Mr. Morris), I understand. Only one of those prosecutions was during the lifetime of a Tory Government, and that was in 1973. Of the 10 cases that have been heard, two were dismissed and one employer received only an admonition. Fines covering the other seven cases totalled only £434. So there is a case for stiffening the law, and new clause 16 would enable people other than the Minister to take proceedings against employers who deliberately break the law.

New clause 17 is, if anything, the most important of these clauses because for the first time it will enable the House of Commons to vote on the question of discrimination against disabled persons. There have been disgraceful events such as the one on 18 November 1983 when my own private Member's Bill to outlaw all discrimination against disabled people was "unofficially" whipped against by the Government and there was a vote on a closure. This is the first time that we can vote on discrimination against disabled people on matters of employment. Incidentally, by pushing forward the boundaries of equal opportunities, we shall be doing what would have been done had a Labour Government been in office after 1979 because in 1979 my right hon. Friend the Member for Wythenshawe appointed the Committee on Restrictions Against Disabled People, which recommended that Government should take action to outlaw discrimination, particularly in this vital area of employment.

The first seven clauses of this Bill deal inadequately with the question of discrimination on grounds of sex. It is illegal to discriminate on grounds of sex or of ethnic origin or race, but it is still perfectly legal in this country that calls itself civilised for an employer deliberately to discriminate against a person because he or she is disabled. I believe that the time has now come for the abolition of this scourge of disabled people.

The number of disabled people is very great. We know from the report of the Office of Population Censuses and Surveys that 6 million people in our country are disabled. The Royal College of Physicians estimates that approximately one person in 10 is physically disabled and that about 2 million of those people are of working age. Yet only 31 per cent. of disabled people of working age are in paid employment. That is according to the Government's own OPCS survey—and I tell the Minister this because he seemed in some doubt about it some weeks ago.

The degree of unemployment among disabled people is enormous, and the more severe the disability the worse it is, so that 48 per cent. of disabled people in severity category 1 are working but only 2 per cent. in severity category 10 are working. The Royal National Institute for the Deaf has estimated that there are in this country 1·4 million adults of working age with a clinically significant loss of hearing, but that only 50,000 who are profoundly deaf are in the working population. So there is quite clearly a job to be done, and the Opposition believe that the Bill provides the opportunity to do something.

When we look at the question of unemployment among disabled people we find that not only are they discriminated against, not only are they the people who are most likely to be without a job, but they are also the ones who are most likely to be without a job for the longest time. Whereas only 8 per cent. of non-disabled people have been jobless for more than two years, no fewer than 26 per cent. of disabled job seekers have been jobless for more than two years.

The Government's willingness to tackle the problem can be measured by the fact that between 1981 and 1985 they cut the number of disablement resettlement officers by 30 per cent. and reduced the training period of those officers to two weeks—a measly two weeks to train people to do a vital job for a part of the community which has talents that should be taken into account. I believe that far too often society takes more account of the supposed incapabilities of disabled people than of their capabilities.

That discrimination exists there can be no doubt. The Spastics Society survey in 1986 showed that 152 secretarial jobs were applied for and two applications based on two standard letters were sent out for those jobs. Where there was no disability involved, 97 per cent. of the applicants received positive responses. Where a disability was mentioned, only 59 per cent. received positive responses. There is also much anecdotal evidence of which the Minister should be aware, although I doubt whether he is, and should be exploring as the Minister responsible for the disabled.

It is not only an absence of job opportunities but an absence of adequate earnings that faces so many disabled people. The average gross weekly earnings of male full-time workers is £192·40, whereas for disabled male full-time workers the figure is only £156·70. That is 81 per cent. of the average wages of the working population.

6.30 pm

The figures I am quoting are from the OPCS survey —the Government's own survey. When gross weekly earnings are broken down by severity category, the differences are even more stark. For male full-time

employees in severity categories 1 and 2, the level of earnings is only 86 per cent. of that for the average working population. Men who are categorised in group 5 or above receive only 72 per cent. of the average earnings of their non-disabled counterparts. That disparity is seen even when the figures are broken down into hourly rates of pay. For categories 1 and 2, the hourly rate is 90 per cent. of the rate paid to able-bodied workers. For categories 5 and above, the figure is only 74 per cent.

The discrimination in earnings has obvious repercussions on the living standards and lifestyles of disabled people. The cost of disability must be taken into account, as well as the low amounts that so many disabled people receive. Those who are on the lower incomes find that they have to make choices about priorities. The need to spend extra on disability-related items may result in a lower standard of living than that of non-disabled people on the same income level.

It could be argued that our proposal is in line with previous statutory provisions and actually strengthens them. I remind the Minister that the Companies (Directors' Report) (Employment of Disabled Persons) Regulations 1980, administered by the Department of Trade and Industry, require information to be given in directors' reports on what is being done to train, employ and promote the career prospects of disabled employees. It is time to act. The Government should act in combination with the Department of Trade and Industry to strengthen the cause of giving a wider choice to disabled people. After all, this Government talk about freedom and choice, yet the only thing that they seem to give disabled people is sympathy. Disabled people require more than sympathy; they require positive action. Any Government with a semblance of humanity would endorse the new clauses.

The Government's response will be watched carefully by the 6 million disabled people in our country. I hope that the recent report that the Government are planning to axe disability allowances for those who take up employment training is not a precursor of what to expect when it comes to tackling the real problems of disabled people in the labour market. I hope that the House will endorse the new clauses. If it does not, it will be to the detriment of the Government in the near future, who will have to face the wrath of that large minority of the population who are disabled and the wrath of the members of their families.

Mr. Jack Ashley (Stoke-on-Trent, South): I want to speak briefly in support of the new clauses. Throughout the years, various Governments have tried to end the quota system and the argument they use is that persuasion is better than prosecution. The fact that their unemployment figures are so high and that so many disabled people are short of employment makes an absurdity of that claim. We need both persuasion and prosecution. We need to persuade some employers to accept their moral and legal obligations to employ registered disabled people as 3 per cent. of their labour force. We also need to prosecute those who are breaking the law, when persuasion fails. It is essential that we should now do both.

The Government must stop evading the issue and they should ensure that the quota is fully implemented. If you, Mr. Deputy Speaker, break the law by parking your car on a double yellow line, or by stealing cash from a store, you are prosecuted—and rightly so. The same is true of any hon. Member. But employers who break the law by failing

[*Mr. Jack Ashley*]

to fulfil the quota and then by taking on non-disabled workers without a permit are not prosecuted. This Government are condoning law-breaking and that is wholly inexcusable.

There is no substitute for the quota unless the Government are prepared to bring in a levy system. If the Government want to drop the quota, let them bring in a levy system, which imposes a levy on those employers who will not employ disabled people as 3 per cent. of the work force. That is fine. We would then have good employers who employed disabled people as 3 per cent. of their work force and bad employers who would not, but who would pay nevertheless. That is why the Government should either enforce the quota or bring in a levy of 3 per cent. of the payroll, to be paid to the good employers.

The amount of discrimination against disabled people in Britain is appalling. Severely disabled people find that every day of their lives, especially in jobs and in applications for jobs. Unless this Government take action, severely disabled people will continue to suffer abysmal discrimination. As the OPCS report mentioned by my hon. Friend the Member for Liverpool, West Derby (Mr. Wareing) said, we cannot seek to justify any kind of wild discrimination. All we are trying to do is to outlaw unjustified discrimination, as the report of the Committee on Restrictions Against Disabled People pointed out. The best way of tackling discrimination is to outlaw it, as is being done in other countries, such as the United States and Australia, and there is no reason why we should not do that.

Today I wear three hats. I am the chairman of the all-party disablement group. We deplore the failure of employers to fulfil the quota. As chairman of that group, I speak for hon. Members of all parties. We want to keep the quota and we want it to be enforced properly. I also speak as president of the Royal National Institute for the Deaf. That organisation feels deeply about the discrimination against deaf people in employment. I also speak as a disabled person. We resent the discrimination against all kinds of disabled people, we regret it and we ask the Government to act. That is all we are seeking. We do not seek punitive or wild measures, just reasonably firm action to ensure that disabled people get a decent chance of a job.

Mr. Ted Rowlands (Merthyr Tydfil and Rhymney): Disabled people have been the victims of unemployment in the past decade more often than fit people. That is true not only of industry in general, but even of Remploy, the organisation especially devoted to helping provide jobs for disabled people. We have seen stagnation in certain sections there. I represent a part of Remploy which has seen stagnation and reduction. When the Minister replies, I hope that he will tell us how many extra jobs have been created in Remploy for disabled people in the past decade. My right hon. Friend the Member for Stoke-on-Trent, South (Mr. Ashley) was right to demand a categorical assurance from the Minister that the quota system, which the new clauses seek to improve, will not be abolished and is not being threatened by any proposed Government changes.

As my hon. Friend the Member for Liverpool, West Derby (Mr. Wareing) said, we are talking not only about disabled people who are unemployed but about those in employment, who are paid lower wages than other people. There is nothing more degrading for disabled people than being paid poor wages—except, that is, being unemployed.

My hon. Friend said that disabled people were being paid £150 a week, compared with a national average of £190. I remind the House of the wages paid to those in the one organisation that is devoted to offering job opportunities in manufacturing to disabled people. I refer to those in Remploy, who earn £90 a week. The level at which the Government pay income support is £110 a week. The TUC threshold level is £133 a week. The wages of those in Remploy come nowhere near that, let alone the European decency wages of £141 a week. That means that even those employed in the organisation that has been specially devoted to creating and maintaining employment for the disabled are some of the poorest wage earners in the country. Those people deserve a much better deal.

Since 1980, the gap between the income of those in Remploy and those outside it has grown. Remploy workers' wages used to be related to those paid for local government work. In 1980 the difference in wages between those inside Remploy and those outside it was 12p a week; in 1989, the difference is £11 a week. Not only have opportunities stagnated in many sections of Remploy; there is a growing gap between the wages paid to its workers and those paid elsewhere.

I wholeheartedly support the new clause, which would increase the quota. We demand from the Minister a categorical assurance that there is no suggestion that the Government will abolish the quota system—as it has been suggested they will abolish wages councils. At the same time, I underline the point that even those disabled people who are in employment—and particularly in Remploy—are some of the poorest paid workers in the country.

Mr. Lee: The new clauses would affect in various ways the arrangements for ensuring that people with disabilities can obtain and retain suitable employment. Although I am in sympathy with the motives underlying them, they are all of doubtful value as a means of achieving improvements in this very important area.

New clause 15 would make it impossible to lower the standard percentage of registered disabled people under the quota scheme from its current level of 3 per cent. Registration under the Act is voluntary and, as the hon. Member for Liverpool, West Derby (Mr. Wareing) said the number of people who choose to register has declined steadily—from more than 660,000 in 1961 to fewer than 375,000 in 1988. It is therefore now impossible for all employers who fall within the scope of the quota scheme to achieve the 3 per cent. figure. It would be unwise, therefore, not to retain the flexibility to lower the percentage if it were judged that that would increase the quota scheme's effectiveness.

Mr. Haynes: Will the Minister tell the House the percentage of disabled people who work in the Palace of Westminster? Then we shall see whether the Government should be prosecuted.

6.45 pm

Mr. Lee: As the hon. Gentleman would expect, I do not have that figure with me——

Mr. Haynes: The hon. Member should have.

Mr. Lee: —and indeed, it is not my personal ministerial responsibility.

Although I should emphasise that we currently have no plans to do this, it seems to me perfectly possible that, at some time in the future, circumstances might make it appropriate to move to a lower figure.

Mr. Rowlands: I am trying to ascertain what the Minister has just mumbled to us. Was he talking about lowering the quota or actually abolishing it? Will he give us a categorical assurance that the Government do not contemplate abolishing the quota?

Mr. Lee: What I would say is that the quota is one of many items under consideration in the overall review that we are undertaking. That has been made perfectly clear.

New clause 16 would end the current arrangement whereby the power to bring or authorise prosecutions for offences under the Disabled Persons (Employment) Act 1944 is restricted to this Department. It has been the policy of successive Governments, since the Act was first introduced, to bring prosecutions only as a last resort and to pursue a policy of education and persuasion designed to secure and improve the policies and practices of all employers in relation to the employment of people with disabilities. There is no evidence that the current policy on prosecutions has led to a major problem of employers failing to employ people with disabilities. Although 76 per cent. of eligible firms are below the standard percentage, this is largely because of the decline in numbers of registered disabled people. In any event, no offence is committed unless they recruit someone other than a registered disabled person without first obtaining a permit to do so.

Mr. Wallace: I understood the hon. Member for Liverpool, West Derby (Mr. Wareing) to say that the number of registered disabled people had fallen so much because of a lack of confidence in the quota system. To some extent, it is a chicken and egg situation, I suppose, but will the Minister respond to the specific criticism made by the hon. Member for West Derby?

Mr. Lee: As anyone concerned with these matters will concede one of the problems is that we just do not know the size of the market or the size of the problem. That is one of the reasons why my Department is undertaking a major survey whose results we expect to have by the end of the year.

Many employers have other employees who could have registered disabled but who have chosen not to do so. I believe that our policy, backed up, as it is, with practical help to individuals to assist them to overcome problems that they face as a result of their disability, is the best way of securing a genuine commitment among employers to employing people with disabilities.

New clause 17, which seeks to make it unlawful for employers to discriminate against potential employees on the grounds of their disability, is similarly inconsistent with the Government's line. There may be discrimination, although its scale is not clear. The Government believe that encouragement to employers to adopt good practices, combined with practical help in doing so, is the right way forward, and preferable to anti-discrimination measures such as that proposed in the new clause, which would

undoubtedly be difficult and costly to enforce and possibly even counter-productive, making a constructive approach by employers less likely.

The Government remain fully committed to ensuring that people with disabilities are given appropriate help in obtaining and retaining employment. We maintain a wide range of services which provide invaluable assistance to a large number of people with disabilities who are seeking employment or who are already in employment.

We are currently reviewing all our services and have commissioned a major survey of the number and characteristics of people with disabilities. The first draft of the consultative document is being considered by Ministers——

Mr. Ted Leadbitter (Hartlepool): On the subject of that first draft, the Minister has suggested that a degree of flexibility will be required. The law regarding the employment of disabled people passed in 1944 said that not less than 3 per cent. of a given work force should be disabled. The new clause seeks to achieve what was intended then. For 45 years we have had no success in persuading employers to abide by the law. The Department has issued permits of exemption, which shows that the Government have no intention of ensuring that the law is abided by. The first draft has fallen short of what should be the aim, and the Minister has even come here without relevant figures—even those for the disabled employed in the Palace of Westminster or in Government Departments. His sincerity is in question.

Mr. Lee: With respect, the hon. Gentleman's points suggest to us the need for the flexibility that we seek. I reiterate my earlier comment that the whole question of the quota is being looked at in the review that is under way. We shall take the figures to which the hon. Gentleman rightly referred into consideration in the consultative document. We are pledged to publish that document and consult interested parties. Our considered view is that the new clauses would not help the continuing development of appropriate provision.

Mr. Wareing: Will the Minister take the opportunity to tell us what criteria his Department uses in granting permits to allow employers to avoid the quota system?

Mr. Lee: I should have thought that the answer was fairly obvious—the criteria would be the requirements of the particular employer and the numbers of disabled people available for employment in the relevant jobcentre areas. Those would be the dominant considerations, together with any other sensible and realistic evidence. I hope that the Opposition will not press the amendments, but if they do we shall resist them.

Mr. Alfred Morris (Manchester, Wythenshawe): My hon. Friend the Member for Liverpool, West Derby (Mr. Wareing) made a compelling case and I congratulate him on his speech. These are very important matters for disabled people, and their representatives have made it strikingly clear that they want the legislative change sought by the amendments.

My hon. Friend recalled that in 1979, as the then Minister for the Disabled, I set up the Committee on Restrictions Against Disabled People—CORAD—to establish the nature and extent of discrimination and whether legislation was required. Many of the submissions to CORAD stated that

[*Mr. Alfred Morris*]

" . . . cases of discrimination are serious and widespread."
Hundreds of responses gave specific and very disquieting examples. There was discrimination against the disabled then, as there is now, and it is deplorable that the Government's reaction to that committee's report has been so utterly negative.

CORAD strongly recommended legislation to outlaw discrimination against disabled people. It asked for legislation similar to that designed to protect women and ethnic minorities, to prevent
" . . . the unjustifiable withholding, whether intentional or not, of some service, facility or opportunity from a disabled person because of that person's disability."
As well as providing legal protection and redress, legislation would, as both CORAD and my right hon. Friend the Member for Stoke-on-Trent, South (Mr. Ashley) in his speech tonight emphasised, also affect people's attitudes and behaviour through education, persuasion and example.

The Chronically Sick and Disabled Persons Act 1970 already establishes disabled people's rights in important areas such as housing, personal social services and access. CORAD reported the many notable improvements in those and many other areas during the first 10 years of the Act, but there has been scant progress since. This is an opportunity to make progress that would be welcomed by many of the major national organisations of and for disabled people.

The figures for unemployment among disabled job seekers shout of discrimination against them. They suffer from low pay and lack of opportunity. My hon. Friend the Member for West Derby should be congratulated both on the amendments and on his earlier attempt to legislate against discrimination by means of a private Member's Bill. As he said, the House has its first opportunity tonight to vote on discrimination against disabled people. I welcome that opportunity and ask all who wish to show their concern for what people with disabilities are seeking for themselves to support the amendments.

Question put, That the clause be read a Second time:—
The House proceeded to a Division, and Mr. DEPUTY SPEAKER *having directed that the doors be locked*——

Mr. Deputy Speaker (Sir Paul Dean): Order. I direct the doors to be reopened for another two minutes.
Whereupon the doors were unlocked.

Mr. Hugo Summerson (Walthamstow) *(seated and covered)*: On a point of order, Mr. Deputy Speaker. I would be grateful if the timing for the Division could be checked. It appears to me that the Division started at 6.54 pm and that the order to lock the doors was given at 7 pm, thus allowing only six minutes instead of eight minutes to vote.

Mr. Deputy Speaker: Perhaps the hon. Gentleman was not here earlier. There was an error, and I instructed the doors to be locked too early. It was for that reason that I instructed the doors to be unlocked. They are still unlocked.

The House having divided: Ayes 169, Noes 259.

Division No. 221]   **[6.53 pm**

AYES

Allen, Graham
Alton, David
Anderson, Donald
Archer, Rt Hon Peter

Armstrong, Hilary
Ashley, Rt Hon Jack
Ashton, Joe
Barnes, Harry *(Derbyshire NE)*
Barnes, Mrs Rosie *(Greenwich)*
Barron, Kevin
Battle, John
Beckett, Margaret
Beith, A. J.
Bell, Stuart
Benn, Rt Hon Tony
Bennett, A. F. *(D'nt'n & R'dish)*
Bermingham, Gerald
Bidwell, Sydney
Blunkett, David
Boyes, Roland
Bray, Dr Jeremy
Brown, Nicholas *(Newcastle E)*
Bruce, Malcolm *(Gordon)*
Buckley, George J.
Caborn, Richard
Callaghan, Jim
Campbell, Ron *(Blyth Valley)*
Campbell-Savours, D. N.
Canavan, Dennis
Cartwright, John
Clark, Dr David *(S Shields)*
Clarke, Tom *(Monklands W)*
Clay, Bob
Clelland, David
Clwyd, Mrs Ann
Cohen, Harry
Cook, Robin *(Livingston)*
Corbett, Robin
Corbyn, Jeremy
Cousins, Jim
Crowther, Stan
Cryer, Bob
Cunliffe, Lawrence
Dalyell, Tam
Davies, Rt Hon Denzil *(Llanelli)*
Davis, Terry *(B'ham Hodge H'l)*
Dixon, Don
Dobson, Frank
Doran, Frank
Douglas, Dick
Duffy, A. E. P.
Dunwoody, Hon Mrs Gwyneth
Eadie, Alexander
Eastham, Ken
Evans, John *(St Helens N)*
Fatchett, Derek
Faulds, Andrew
Fearn, Ronald
Field, Frank *(Birkenhead)*
Fisher, Mark
Flannery, Martin
Flynn, Paul
Foot, Rt Hon Michael
Foster, Derek
Foulkes, George
Fraser, John
Galbraith, Sam
Garrett, John *(Norwich South)*
George, Bruce
Gilbert, Rt Hon Dr John
Godman, Dr Norman A.
Golding, Mrs Llin
Gould, Bryan
Grant, Bernie *(Tottenham)*
Griffiths, Nigel *(Edinburgh S)*
Griffiths, Win *(Bridgend)*
Grocott, Bruce
Hattersley, Rt Hon Roy
Hinchliffe, David
Hogg, N. *(C'nauld & Kilsyth)*
Howarth, George *(Knowsley N)*
Howells, Geraint
Howells, Dr. Kim *(Pontypridd)*
Hoyle, Doug

Hughes, John *(Coventry NE)*
Hughes, Robert *(Aberdeen N)*
Hughes, Roy *(Newport E)*
Illsley, Eric
Janner, Greville
Jones, Barry *(Alyn & Deeside)*
Jones, Martyn *(Clwyd S W)*
Kennedy, Charles
Kirkwood, Archy
Lamond, James
Leadbitter, Ted
Leighton, Ron
Lewis, Terry
Livsey, Richard
Lofthouse, Geoffrey
Loyden, Eddie
McCartney, Ian
Macdonald, Calum A.
McKay, Allen *(Barnsley West)*
McKelvey, William
Madden, Max
Mahon, Mrs Alice
Marek, Dr John
Marshall, Jim *(Leicester S)*
Meacher, Michael
Meale, Alan
Michael, Alun
Michie, Bill *(Sheffield Heeley)*
Michie, Mrs Ray *(Arg'l & Bute)*
Mitchell, Austin *(G't Grimsby)*
Moonie, Dr Lewis
Morgan, Rhodri
Morley, Elliott
Morris, Rt Hon A. *(W'shawe)*
Morris, Rt Hon J. *(Aberavon)*
Mullin, Chris
Nellist, Dave
Oakes, Rt Hon Gordon
Orme, Rt Hon Stanley
Patchett, Terry
Pike, Peter L.
Powell, Ray *(Ogmore)*
Prescott, John
Quin, Ms Joyce
Randall, Stuart
Redmond, Martin
Rees, Rt Hon Merlyn
Reid, Dr John
Richardson, Jo
Robertson, George
Robinson, Geoffrey
Rogers, Allan
Rooker, Jeff
Rowlands, Ted
Ruddock, Joan
Sedgemore, Brian
Sheerman, Barry
Sheldon, Rt Hon Robert
Short, Clare
Skinner, Dennis
Smith, Andrew *(Oxford E)*
Smith, C. *(Isl'ton & F'bury)*
Smith, Rt Hon J. *(Monk'ds E)*
Snape, Peter
Soley, Clive
Spearing, Nigel
Steinberg, Gerry
Stott, Roger
Strang, Gavin
Straw, Jack
Turner, Dennis
Vaz, Keith
Wall, Pat
Wallace, James
Walley, Joan
Wardell, Gareth *(Gower)*
Wareing, Robert N.
Welsh, Michael *(Doncaster N)*
Wigley, Dafydd
Williams, Rt Hon Alan

Williams, Alan W. *(Carm'then)*
Winnick, David
Wise, Mrs Audrey
Worthington, Tony
Young, David *(Bolton SE)*

Tellers for the Ayes:
Mr. Frank Haynes and
Mr. Allen Adams.

NOES

Adley, Robert
Alexander, Richard
Alison, Rt Hon Michael
Amos, Alan
Arbuthnot, James
Arnold, Jacques *(Gravesham)*
Atkins, Robert
Baker, Rt Hon K. *(Mole Valley)*
Baldry, Tony
Banks, Robert *(Harrogate)*
Batiste, Spencer
Beaumont-Dark, Anthony
Bellingham, Henry
Bendall, Vivian
Bennett, Nicholas *(Pembroke)*
Benyon, W.
Bevan, David Gilroy
Blackburn, Dr John G.
Blaker, Rt Hon Sir Peter
Bonsor, Sir Nicholas
Boscawen, Hon Robert
Boswell, Tim
Bottomley, Peter
Bottomley, Mrs Virginia
Bowden, Gerald *(Dulwich)*
Boyson, Rt Hon Dr Sir Rhodes
Braine, Rt Hon Sir Bernard
Brandon-Bravo, Martin
Brazier, Julian
Bright, Graham
Brown, Michael *(Brigg & Cl't's)*
Bruce, Ian *(Dorset South)*
Buchanan-Smith, Rt Hon Alick
Budgen, Nicholas
Burt, Alistair
Butler, Chris
Butterfill, John
Carlisle, John, *(Luton N)*
Carrington, Matthew
Carttiss, Michael
Cash, William
Chapman, Sydney
Chope, Christopher
Clark, Sir W. *(Croydon S)*
Coombs, Anthony *(Wyre F'rest)*
Cope, Rt Hon John
Cormack, Patrick
Curry, David
Davis, David *(Boothferry)*
Devlin, Tim
Dorrell, Stephen
Douglas-Hamilton, Lord James
Dunn, Bob
Durant, Tony
Evans, David *(Welwyn Hatf'd)*
Evennett, David
Fairbairn, Sir Nicholas
Fallon, Michael
Favell, Tony
Field, Barry *(Isle of Wight)*
Fishburn, John Dudley
Fookes, Dame Janet
Forsyth, Michael *(Stirling)*
Forth, Eric
Fowler, Rt Hon Norman
Franks, Cecil

Freeman, Roger
French, Douglas
Fry, Peter
Gardiner, George
Garel-Jones, Tristan
Gill, Christopher
Glyn, Dr Alan
Goodhart, Sir Philip
Goodson-Wickes, Dr Charles
Gow, Ian
Grant, Sir Anthony *(CambsSW)*
Greenway, Harry *(Ealing N)*
Greenway, John *(Ryedale)*
Gregory, Conal
Griffiths, Sir Eldon *(Bury St E')*
Griffiths, Peter *(Portsmouth N)*
Ground, Patrick
Gummer, Rt Hon John Selwyn
Hague, William
Hamilton, Hon Archie *(Epsom)*
Hamilton, Neil *(Tatton)*
Hampson, Dr Keith
Hanley, Jeremy
Hannam, John
Hargreaves, A. *(B'ham H'll Gr')*
Hargreaves, Ken *(Hyndburn)*
Harris, David
Haselhurst, Alan
Hayward, Robert
Heathcoat-Amory, David
Heddle, John
Heseltine, Rt Hon Michael
Hicks, Mrs Maureen *(Wolv' NE)*
Hicks, Robert *(Cornwall SE)*
Higgins, Rt Hon Terence L.
Hind, Kenneth
Hordern, Sir Peter
Howard, Michael
Howarth, Alan *(Strat'd-on-A)*
Howarth, G. *(Cannock & B'wd)*
Howe, Rt Hon Sir Geoffrey
Howell, Rt Hon David *(G'dford)*
Hughes, Robert G. *(Harrow W)*
Hunt, David *(Wirral W)*
Irvine, Michael
Jack, Michael
Jackson, Robert
Janman, Tim
Johnson Smith, Sir Geoffrey
Jones, Gwilym *(Cardiff N)*
Jopling, Rt Hon Michael
Key, Robert
Kilfedder, James
King, Roger *(B'ham N'thfield)*
Kirkhope, Timothy
Knapman, Roger
Knight, Greg *(Derby North)*
Knight, Dame Jill *(Edgbaston)*
Knowles, Michael
Knox, David
Lamont, Rt Hon Norman
Lang, Ian
Latham, Michael
Lawrence, Ivan
Lee, John *(Pendle)*
Leigh, Edward *(Gainsbor'gh)*

Lennox-Boyd, Hon Mark
Lester, Jim *(Broxtowe)*
Lilley, Peter
Lloyd, Sir Ian *(Havant)*
Lloyd, Peter *(Fareham)*
Lyell, Sir Nicholas
McCrindle, Robert
Macfarlane, Sir Neil
MacGregor, Rt Hon John
MacKay, Andrew *(E Berkshire)*
Maclean, David
McLoughlin, Patrick
McNair-Wilson, Sir Michael
McNair-Wilson, P. *(New Forest)*
Madel, David
Major, Rt Hon John
Maples, John
Marlow, Tony
Marshall, John *(Hendon S)*
Marshall, Michael *(Arundel)*
Martin, David *(Portsmouth S)*
Mates, Michael
Maude, Hon Francis
Maxwell-Hyslop, Robin
Mellor, David
Meyer, Sir Anthony
Miller, Sir Hal
Mills, Iain
Miscampbell, Norman
Mitchell, Andrew *(Gedling)*
Mitchell, Sir David
Moate, Roger
Montgomery, Sir Fergus
Moore, Rt Hon John
Morrison, Sir Charles
Morrison, Rt Hon P *(Chester)*
Moss, Malcolm
Moynihan, Hon Colin
Mudd, David
Nelson, Anthony
Neubert, Michael
Newton, Rt Hon Tony
Nicholls, Patrick
Nicholson, David *(Taunton)*
Nicholson, Emma *(Devon West)*
Norris, Steve
Onslow, Rt Hon Cranley
Page, Richard
Paice, James
Patnick, Irvine
Patten, Chris *(Bath)*
Patten, John *(Oxford W)*
Pattie, Rt Hon Sir Geoffrey
Pawsey, James
Peacock, Mrs Elizabeth
Porter, David *(Waveney)*
Portillo, Michael
Powell, William *(Corby)*
Price, Sir David
Raffan, Keith
Raison, Rt Hon Timothy
Redwood, John
Renton, Tim
Riddick, Graham
Ridley, Rt Hon Nicholas
Ridsdale, Sir Julian

Rifkind, Rt Hon Malcolm
Roberts, Wyn *(Conwy)*
Roe, Mrs Marion
Rost, Peter
Rowe, Andrew
Rumbold, Mrs Angela
Ryder, Richard
Sackville, Hon Tom
Sainsbury, Hon Tim
Sayeed, Jonathan
Shaw, David *(Dover)*
Shepherd, Colin *(Hereford)*
Shepherd, Richard *(Aldridge)*
Shersby, Michael
Sims, Roger
Skeet, Sir Trevor
Smith, Tim *(Beaconsfield)*
Soames, Hon Nicholas
Speller, Tony
Spicer, Michael *(S Worcs)*
Stanbrook, Ivor
Stanley, Rt Hon Sir John
Steen, Anthony
Stevens, Lewis
Stewart, Andy *(Sherwood)*
Stradling Thomas, Sir John
Sumberg, David
Summerson, Hugo
Tapsell, Sir Peter
Taylor, Ian *(Esher)*
Taylor, Teddy *(S'end E)*
Temple-Morris, Peter
Thompson, Patrick *(Norwich N)*
Thorne, Neil
Thornton, Malcolm
Thurnham, Peter
Townend, John *(Bridlington)*
Townsend, Cyril D. *(B'heath)*
Tracey, Richard
Trotter, Neville
Twinn, Dr Ian
Waddington, Rt Hon David
Wakeham, Rt Hon John
Waller, Gary
Ward, John
Wardle, Charles *(Bexhill)*
Warren, Kenneth
Watts, John
Wells, Bowen
Wheeler, John
Widdecombe, Ann
Wiggin, Jerry
Wilshire, David
Winterton, Mrs Ann
Winterton, Nicholas
Wolfson, Mark
Wood, Timothy
Woodcock, Dr. Mike
Yeo, Tim
Young, Sir George *(Acton)*
Younger, Rt Hon George

Tellers for the Noes:
Mr. David Lightbowne and
Mr. Kenneth Carlisle.

Question accordingly negatived.

It being after Seven o'clock, and there being private business set down by direction of THE CHAIRMAN OF WAYS AND MEANS *under Standing Order No. 16 (Time for taking private business), further proceeding stood postponed.*

Redbridge London Borough Council Bill

(By Order)

Order for Second Reading read.

7.8 pm

Mr. Neil Thorne (Ilford, South): I beg to move, That the Bill be now read a Second time.

It is my pleasure to introduce the Second Reading of the Bill. It is said that:

"It would be of public and local advantage to provide for the establishment of a further market in the part of the borough known as Ilford notwithstanding the infringement or non-compliance thereby with any rule of law or enactment:"

Many towns already have local markets but Ilford in the London borough of Redbridge is prevented from doing so because of the existence of other markets nearby. The purpose of the Bill is to give the right to establish a market that most other boroughs already have. In the neighbouring borough of Havering, which includes Romford, in 1247, in the reign of Henry III, a royal writ was issued establishing a market. The council today holds markets everywhere in Romford on every Wednesday throughout the year. Havering council claims the legal fiction of a "lost modern grant", which enables it to hold a market at Romford on Saturdays throughout the year. Havering also holds a statutory Food Act market on Fridays throughout the year at Romford. Thus Havering council holds three markets on premier trading days of the week and, because two of its markets—the Wednesday and Saturday markets—enjoy the benefit of protection under the common law, no other market may be established within a distance of $6\frac{2}{3}$ miles from Romford.

Mr. Dennis Skinner (Bolsover): Is the hon. Gentleman trying to tell us that, as a good old-fashioned Tory, he does not agree with market forces, and that somehow or other he wants those markets protected, or is it that he is a good old-fashioned Tory, but that this knighted Tory, the hon. Member for Upminster (Sir N. Bonsor), is not interested in market forces? I want to get this clear, because this could be a long evening. I want to know which is the Thatcherite and which is the Heathite. Will the hon. Gentleman explain before we go any further?

Mr. Thorne: The hon. Gentleman, as usual, has put his finger on a very interesting point. I assure him that I believe in the free market. My hon. Friend the Member for Upminster (Sir N. Bonsor) will no doubt try to catch your eye, Mr. Deputy Speaker, and explain his position later.

Because the markets on Wednesday and Saturday enjoy the benefit of protection under the common law, no other market may be established within a distance of $6\frac{2}{3}$ miles from Romford. The $6\frac{2}{3}$ miles represent the 13th century jurist Bracton's concept of one third the Roman dieta. The Roman thought was that one could travel 20 miles in a day. Therefore, to travel to a market should take a third of a day, one should spend a third of a day at the market and another third going back, which would allow one to travel $6\frac{2}{3}$ miles in each direction. That is the basis on which this present custom continues.

Ilford lies within the $6\frac{2}{3}$ mile radius and the Ilford town centre, which is the main shopping centre of the Redbridge local authority area, is therefore deprived of its statutory powers by that ancient common law right. It now wishes to establish a market of its own.

In this increasingly sophisticated economy, we find that more and more people expect to shop in a wide variety of shops. They want value, choice and diversity. In order to do that properly, we find that a lot of traders expect to have a market nearby. It was not so long ago that markets tended to be rather scruffy and untidy, but that is now in the past. The majority of markets are high quality, well-designed areas, where one can expect to buy exotic fruits and vegetables at the one end of the spectrum and antiques and craftwork at the other.

Mr. Skinner: What about monocles?

Mr. Thorne: They probably sell those too.

These markets actually encourage conventional retail trade and they are, therefore, welcomed by conventional traders, whereas in the past markets were generally considered to be derogatory and most ordinary traders preferred that they should not be permitted to run side by side with conventional shops.

An efficient and well-run market has become an essential part of any well-developed shopping centre and Redbridge council, having put in a bypass, now wishes to take full advantage of modern shopping methods. A new shopping centre is being developed by the pension funds of some insurance companies. Substantial sums are being invested on behalf of pensioners in that area. Those companies and the shopkeepers locally are very anxious that there should be an open-air market in the Ilford area. The present proposal is that a market shall be permitted within one mile of Ilford town centre.

The traders' association and the local chamber of trade have given this matter full support, and in the past couple of weeks they have been at some pains to obtain signatures to a petition. More than 6,500 people have already signed the petition in favour of such a market.

Mr. Kevin Barron (Rother Valley): How many people from Romford have signed the petition for that market?

Mr. Thorne: I have not examined the petition to see how many people from Romford have signed it, but, if the House allows me to speak later, I shall endeavour to make a rough calculation and tell the hon. Gentleman.

The question of the $6\frac{2}{3}$ miles has already been referred to in a recent case by the Vice-Chancellor of the Chancery Division of the High Court as archaic. I believe that the majority of people would consider such an arbitrary distance now to be quite archaic.

As the hon. Member for Rother Valley (Mr. Barron) has suggested, there may be some people with vested interests who would be against such a proposal and would oppose it, especially those from the Romford area. However, I assure him that that is not universal. Many people in Romford support the opportunity of market facilities being provided in the area. If the hon. Gentleman is interested and looks at a map of the markets in the region, he will see that there is an acute shortage of markets in that part of London. One of the reasons that the London borough of Redbridge is promoting the Bill is to ensure that that to some extent is put right.

Mr. Skinner: Vested interests is a serious matter. The hon. Gentleman has said that about 6,000 have signed in favour of the project. My experience is that, when markets have been proposed—in all parts of the country really—there have been local shopkeepers who have not been very keen on the idea. I know that in Derbyshire there have been several instances where initially—sometimes it has changed—shopkeepers have opposed it. Is the hon. Gentleman telling us that none of the local shopkeepers were saying that they were a bit worried about the market? I would be intrigued if there were none. Will the hon. Gentleman tell us the position of the local shopkeepers?

Mr. Thorne: As I said before, the chamber of trade and the local shopkeepers have indicated that they are in favour. They find that an open-air market, especially one of modest size, encourages trade because it encourages people to come to the local area. Well run markets are an encouragement. The tatty old markets that one used to find in the past, which were upsetting to local shopkeepers, are now out and we can expect shopkeepers in future to view open-air markets in a different light. I am certainly not saying that every single shopkeeper in Ilford is in favour, but I have not had my attention drawn to any who have indicated dissent, whereas I have had confirmation from the chamber of trade and others that they are very much in favour. After all, it was the chamber of trade that set out to raise the petition, and it has now collected 6,500 signatures. That was its own idea. I believe, therefore, that the whole tempo is changing in that regard. I hope that that will be the case in other parts of the country, too, in future.

Some of the objections from Havering are technical and some financial, based on the idea that the Romford market will be damaged by a market in Ilford. Romford market has provision for 600 spaces and 300 traders work there, with an average of two stalls per trader. That substantial market has been in existence for more than 600 years, so it is well-established.

Mr. Martin Redmond (Don Valley): The hon. Gentlman said that there are 600 pitches at Romford. Why are 300 empty? If there is such a demand for market stalls, one would have thought that market traders would be only too pleased to go to Romford market.

Mr. Thorne: Forgive me, but I obviously did not explain myself well. There is provision for 600 stalls at Romford. There are 300 traders and, on average, they have two stalls each. Some have only one and others have three. The proposal for Ilford is to site the market on an existing car park, with provision for between 50 and 60 stalls, and there would be a new multi-storey car park. We are talking about an entirely different scale, perhaps only 10 per cent. of the spaces available at Romford market.

Any problems should be resolved by an opposed Bill Committee, which is the correct place to argue these matters. I suggest that the Bill should be given the general approval of the House and it would be up to members of the opposed Bill Committee to decide whether the arguments were fair and correct.

As to whatever harm would be done to Romford, the Bill promises compensation for losses to the franchise of Romford's market. That is a generous offer. It is strange that a firm such as Sainsbury's can happily open a store within 6 miles of another major store, such as Tesco, and not have to offer compensation, whereas Redbridge is offering compensation to Romford if loss is proved.

Redbridge has received 250 applications for the 60 possible sites, which shows the ready demand that exists.

Mr. Redmond: The hon. Gentleman says that compensation has been put on the table, which means that

compensation will be paid if there is a loss of business. Will he elaborate a little? What is the ceiling and for how many years will the offer be on the table?

Mr. Thorne: Any compensation would have to be agreed by valuers. This aspect would have to be considereed by the opposed Bill Committee because it is technical. It would be necessary for the valuers of the two local authorities to get together to decide on a reasonable and satisfactory formula, and it would be wrong for me to pre-empt what they might decide. The timing would be hammered out by the opposed Bill Committee.

Mr. Redmond: I accept that the valuers would toss around ideas on the amount of money that would be lost. Given my experience, I am always a little sceptical about Bills leaving this place and going into Committee if I am not totally convinced about the merits of the arguments.

Mr. Thorne: I shall consider that matter further and, if given the opportunity, try to respond to it later. The technical details would be hammered out in the opposed Bill Committee, but at this stage I can say that after six months the valuers would establish whether there had been any major change. That would be a reasonable period in which to see whether there had been an adverse effect. The matter would have to be agreed between the valuers and it would be wrong for me to pre-empt their negotiations.

Sir Nicholas Bonsor (Upminster): I shall raise this matter later if I have the good fortune to catch your eye, Mr. Deputy Speaker, but I want to give my hon. Friend the chance to deal with it. Under the Bill a claim must be submitted within three months of the legislation being passed. Is my hon. Friend conceding that the wording is wrong and that the Committee should amend it?

Mr. Thorne: I can confirm that the date is negotiable. I understand that that period has already been proposed by the respective local authorities.

Sir Nicholas Bonsor *indicated dissent.*

Mr. Thorne: If it has not been formally proposed, I can give my hon. Friend that assurance now.

Redbridge is keen to give its shoppers a complete spectrum of shopping facilities. The shopping system has changed considerably in recent years, let alone over the past 600. We should look towards what is required in today's age. When Romford market was first used, a large part was devoted to cattle and sheep trading. I remember that not so long ago livestock occupied a substantial part of the market, but the market has changed. The places that were occupied by cattle pens are now occupied by smart market stalls. Romford market clearly needed to change, and Redbridge wishes to be able to change as well.

Mr. Barron: The hon. Gentleman has made some good points about the period during which the market has been in its position. Given that in 1247 the authorities prevented the market from being put in the place where the hon. Gentleman wishes it to go, has he been in touch with the Crown who issued the writ in the first place to ask Her Majesty whether she believes that her subjects should be treated in the same way now? That point should have been pursued before the Bill was considered by the House.

Mr. Thorne: This is the right and proper forum for deciding the future of a market in Redbridge. That is why the London borough of Redbridge has come to the House to seek approval.

It is important in this day and age, when rents and rates for accommodation are ever on the increase, that we should give people the opportunity to start trading and a market stall is an extremely effective and efficient way of doing so. That opportunity should be available throughout the country so that large numbers of people have the opportunity to start a small business. There is no better way of starting a small shop. The examples of this include British Home Stores and Marks and Spencer, and the many other shops that started as market stalls. We should allow that. I certainly hope that the House will agree and, therefore, give the Bill a Second Reading.

7.30 pm

Mr. Harry Cohen (Leyton): I do not wish to speak at great length. I spoke for two hours 40 minutes on the recent City of London (Various Powers) Bill before I was cut short by a closure. That was the longest speech in the Session so far, and I do not intend to repeat that.

Mr. Skinner: I was present then, and my hon. Friend the Member for Leyton (Mr. Cohen) gave a bravura performance, but there was one weakness. The Secretary of State for the Environment was trying to pinch part of the forest in my hon. Friend's constituency. That was made abundantly clear, but we did not ascertain the amount of land in question. One weakness of my hon. Friend's contribution was that he seemed unable to tell me the kind of trees involved. Could my hon. Friend remedy that today?

Madam Deputy Speaker (Miss Betty Boothroyd): Order. I am sure that the hon. Member for Leyton (Mr. Cohen) will not respond to that intervention. We are concerned only with the market development.

Mr. Cohen: I certainly shall not respond to my hon. Friend's intervention, although trees were involved. In the other debate the Minister for Roads and Traffic suggested that it was scrubland. There are trees all over the place. However, I do not want to go on about trees because we are talking about a market, which is different. In that other debate I was just warming up, but I do not have the opportunity here to get to the substance of what I was on about. My hon. Friend the Member for Bolsover (Mr. Skinner) was right: forest land was being stolen from my constituency.

The two Bills share a common feature and it is the reason why I objected to both of them. I looked at all the private Bills at the beginning of this Session and was concerned about a number, but objected to only two because they had local implications. One was the City of London (Various Powers) Bill to steal my forest land, which has still not been given back, and I shall take that further. The M11 link road scheme also worried me. This Bill worries me because Redbridge has had by far the better deal on roads from the Department of Transport than my borough, Waltham Forest. I am talking not merely about building roads, because we could do without that, but how those roads are built and the environmental effects involved.

In the other debate I suggested that there should be a linear park through Leyton which would provide

environmental beauty to the area instead of the environmental monstrosity of the Department of Transport's plan. Redbridge has the money for roads. The Department of Transport has been biased.

Mr. Vivian Bendall (Ilford, North): Is the hon. Gentleman aware that most of the roads that serve Redbridge were financed by the Greater London council, not the Department of Transport?

Mr. Cohen: The hon. Gentleman makes a super point for me to use later. I hate to give away my speech so early, but one of my arguments is that there should be a strategic planning authority for London, just like the GLC. Clearly, as he has praised the GLC, the hon. Gentleman will come to my support when I make that point. He is obviously saying that the GLC helped with roads in his area, and I am pleased. It also helped in my area, and it was only under the Department of Transport that we had such a rotten deal from the Minister for Roads and Traffic, the husband of the Under-Secretary of State for the Environment.

It is ironic that we have had such a rotten deal on the environment. I have a lot of time for the Under-Secretary. Will she kick her husband in bed one evening and say, "I'm a Minister for the Environment, you are the Minister for Roads, will you give Leyton a bit of a good environment?" I know that a Minister's life is a hard life.

Mr. Skinner: I am not having that.

Mr. Cohen: The Minister for Roads and Transport said that he had visited my area and did not understand the questions asked of him on that visit.

Mr. Skinner: He has a chauffeur-driven car.

Madam Deputy Speaker: Order. I am sure that the hon. Member for Leyton (Mr. Cohen) will come to the question of the market. I should like to hear what he has to say about the scope of the Bill.

Mr. Cohen: This is fundamental to the point that I want to make. Redbridge has received money for roads and has had a better deal from the Department of Transport than has Leyton and Waltham Forest. When the market is built, it will be served by roads; a number of roads are already in place. The source of my objection and deep concern was that the money would go to Redbridge. Perhaps it would not do so immediately because some roads are there already, but, in future, Redbridge might get the roads money that should go to Leyton for a better environment along the M11 link road, which is being used to steal our forest.

Madam Deputy Speaker: Order. The Bill has one objective only—the establishment of a market. It has nothing to do with roads leading from Leyton.

Mr. Cohen: I absolutely agree that it deals with the establishment of a market, but people have to get to a market to shop.

Mr. Skinner: The nub of the matter is that there will have to be roads. The point was well put by the hon. Member for Ilford, South (Mr. Thorne) who said that there used to be a cattle market. Obviously, people then travelled over lanes and fields, but we are not living in that age now and we are talking about markets served by roads. We cannot discuss this properly without considering the general environmental background, which means the infrastructure, roads and everything else, and that could affect my hon. Friend's constituency. All these roads lead to Leyton.

Mr. Cohen: The problem is that the roads lead to Leyton, but when they reach it they do not find the good environment or the greenness that goes with it. Therefore, the Leyton people suffer.

The source of my concern was that the road network around the market for Ilford would be improved and Redbridge would get the money again. That is serious because it has political implications. Certainly, in my area there is a feeling that, when it comes to environmental improvements, Conservative boroughs get the money from the Conservative Government We have only to look at the Channel tunnel to see that Conservative areas have a special deal, while Labour areas are left to rot by the Tory Government. That is political bias, and it is not the way in which markets and the roads around them should be planned.

Mr. Redmond: Strategic planning is, I believe, an important element of how the proposed market fits into the overall picture. Perhaps there should be an authority to look at London as a whole. I remember my hon. Friend speaking one evening in the Chamber about the proposal to move Spitalfields market: he was worried about the loss of character that the move would entail. Markets cannot retain the character that they have possessed for many years if they are moved from one place to another. I do not know London as well as my hon. Friend, but I feel that we should examine the sites of such markets throughout the city.

Let me echo my hon. Friend's remarks to the Minister. Last time we discussed a private Bill we faced someone far less attractive, and it is well worth our while to be here this evening.

Mr. Cohen: I shall not go into the Spitalfields issue tonight, as I have already made my views clear. My hon. Friend is, however, right to say that a strategic planning authority for London is needed to consider the implications of the building of markets and the roads around them. Parliament has not the necessary localised knowledge. This is not Parliament's job; we have plenty of other serious issues to address. Today we have heard statements on China and on the NATO conference, but we should have debated those issues. Those are the real issues for the Parliament of today, rather than the question of some regional market—although it may be important to local people. The market seems to be the cause of an internecine battle between the authorities of Redbridge and Romford which should be sorted out at local level by a strategic planning authority like the old GLC.

Mr. James Arbuthnot (Wanstead and Woodford): I believe that I am the only Member present this evening who was also present for the entire two hours and 40 minutes of the hon. Gentleman's speech on the City of London (Various Powers) Bill. If he really feels that we should not be debating this matter, the solution lies in his hands. I wonder whether his speech this evening will last as long.

The hon. Gentleman expressed concern about the political bias that might be evident. Will he confirm that Labour-controlled Waltham Forest district council has no objection to the Bill?

Mr. Cohen: That was one of the things that put my back up. I objected to the Bill because of the road implications to which I have referred. Like any hon. Member who objects to legislation on such grounds, not knowing all the implications for my constituency—shopping implications, for instance—I expected the promoters to discuss them with me at an early stage. I see that the hon. Member for Ilford, South (Mr. Thorne) is getting het up. Let me be fair: he arranged for the chief executive and the borough solicitor to come and discuss the matter with me last week. It was very late in the day, but I was grateful. Part of the purpose of my speech is to put on record some of the assurances that they gave about the roads not affecting Leyton adversely—or so they claimed.

For months on end, not a word came from the Bill's promoters in response to my legitimate concern expressed in the form of an objection. Then I received a letter of literally three lines from the agent for the borough council, which said, "Why are you objecting? Your council does not object." The hon. Member for Wanstead and Woodford (Mr. Arbuthnot) made the same point. I was deeply insulted. I sent back a very curt postcard saying, "My council does not always speak for Leyton. Members of Parliament have the right to speak for their areas as well." It was rude of the agent not even to bother to find out why I was concerned about the Bill.

In answer to the hon. Gentleman's other point, I certainly do not intend to speak for two hours and 40 minutes this evening. Nevertheless, I have important and legitimate points to make. Leyton, after all, is a neighbour of Redbridge. We have a football team called Leytonstone and Ilford: it used to be called Leytonstone before it merged with Ilford. I fear that you are a little anxious, Madam Deputy Speaker, but one of the team's problems is that it now has no ground and has been thrown out of the league.

Madam Deputy Speaker: Order. Can we get back to markets rather than discussing football teams?

Mr. Cohen: Perhaps the team could play on the ground where the market would be.

Mr. Eric Illsley (Barnsley, Central): My hon. Friend has raised an interesting point. Would the market be held on football match days? That could complicate matters. I hope that my hon. Friend can also tell us whether the recently promoted Leyton Orient could play in the same area.

Mr. Cohen: Leyton Orient play in Brisbane road, Leyton. At the weekend I saw them play magnificently and win promotion to the third division. I should like to place on record my congratulations——

Madam Deputy Speaker: Order. The hon. Gentleman is now straying a long way from the subject. I am sure that he is competent enough to return to the subject of the market at Redbridge.

Mr. Cohen: I mentioned Leytonstone and Ilford merely to show the local connection. The two areas are close enough for the football team to cover both of them.

[*Mr. Cohen*]

A London strategic planning authority would resolve conflicts between areas such as Ilford and Redbridge, and dealing with the question of markets would be one of its functions. I am not a great supporter of ancient charters being cast in iron for ever, such as the one that states that no market should be set up within $6\frac{2}{3}$ miles of another, which was drawn up by Henry III. I think it daft, however, that we have to depend on Parliament for such a provision to be waived. Parliament's time should not be wasted; such disputes should be sorted out by a strategic planning authority.

Mr. Bendall: Is the hon. Gentleman aware that even in the days of the GLC a Bill would have been needed?

Mr. Cohen: Yes, but the conflict would have been sorted out long before now. Because the GLC would have performed that function, we might well have been in a position to scrap the private Bill procedure in such cases and thus save hon. Members' time. Getting rid of that ancient charter could set a precedent in other areas where authorities want to build markets to which the charter would apply. We could be flooded with private Bills aimed at getting round the procedure. There could be an element of corruption. The market is financed by the Prudential and by Norwich Union to the extent of hundreds of millions of pounds. With the involvement of big business in such markets there is scope for corruption through bribing right hon. and hon. Members to push through private Bills, while that procedure operates.

Mr. Andrew F. Bennett (Denton and Reddish): As I understand legislation, compensation will be paid for Romford market as a result of the new market at Redbridge. However, markets compete not only with each other but with shopkeepers. Surely there should be a balance between compensation paid to other markets and to shopkeepers who will lose out by the development of Redbridge market, because shopkeepers pay rates whereas stallholders do not. The private Bill procedure is inappropriate when the matter should form part of strategic shopping plan for the whole of London. The lack of such a plan will cause chaos, with many different shopping centres competing with one another and with resources not being properly used.

Mr. Cohen: My hon. Friend makes an excellent point. A strategic authority would devise such a plan. My hon. Friend is also right about small shopkeepers losing out and not receiving compensation. If they want to make representations under the private Bill procedure, they must incur enormous expense. They may feel that the matter is cut and dried anyway, so there is little point. However, they would have incurred no expense in contacting their GLC councillor or a strategic authority for shops policy.

Under the expensive private Bill procedure, the democratic right to object is being placed beyond the bounds of people who have genuine cause for complaint, and who might receive compensation if they did. Perhaps one should not compare that situation with the recent events in China, which are of course horrendous, but in China too there is a struggle for democracy. The small shopkeepers are crushed not by tanks, thank goodness, but by the expensive and stupid private Bill procedure. It is in that way that their democratic rights are crushed.

Mr. Skinner: My hon. Friend makes an important point about strategic planning and says that we should not hang around here talking about a matter that concerns his constituency and that it should be dealt with by a body such as the old Greater London council. I envisage that under a strategic authority there could be different types of market for different types of area. There could be a flea market in Finchley, a dead sheep market in the Foreign Secretary's constituency, and puppet markets in the constituency of every Cabinet Minister.

Madam Deputy Speaker: Meanwhile, the debate should return to the subject of the market in Redbridge.

Mr Cohen: I recall my hon. Friend's remarkable comments about the Prime Minister cutting jelly babies in half to ensure that customers did not get any extra weight. There have been cuts ever since, but fewer cuts in Tory Redbridge than in Leyton, which has greater need for extra resources, including markets. Again we see the party political bias to which I referred earlier.

My hon. Friend the Member for Don Valley (Mr. Redmond) made a good point concerning Spitalfields market. The local communities make it possible for markets to make big profits. My hon. Friend rightly said that some of those profits should be returned to those local communities. Under the private Bill procedure, that cannot happen. Local communities are being robbed of enjoying an element of the profits that markets make.

The strategic authority, as well as devising better policies for shopping centres and for markets, could devise better policies for roads. Leyton would have had a much better deal over the M11 link road had a strategic authority been involved rather than the Department of Transport. My major concern is that the roads money from that Department will be soaked up in Redbridge market rather than go to Leyton to offset the effects of the road that the Department is blasting through the area.

Mr. Bob Cryer (Bradford, South): As to planning access to markets, one of the problems confronting many local authorities, and one that the Bill may not take into account, is that the European Community is trying to force through, with the agreement of the Minister for Roads and Traffic, 40-tonne lorries instead of the present maximum of 38 tonnes. Clearly, any local authority must consider that serious departure from existing regulations before presenting any Bill to the House in which road access is a factor.

Madam Deputy Speaker: Order. I am sure that the hon. Member for Leyton (Mr. Cohen) will not wish to respond to a matter that is not within the scope of the Bill.

Mr. Cohen: That is perfectly true, Madam Deputy Speaker, except that road access is relevant to many markets. I agree with my hon. Friend that it is horrendous that the Government have again given in to the Common Market and to big business interests. If Redbridge market develops and grows bigger, it may have to be served by larger lorries. In those circumstances, the road network serving the market may not be suitable. Redbridge will then tell the Department of Transport, "Give us the money. The heavy lorries have destroyed the roads around here. We have a market here and we deserve that money." Again, that will put the kibosh on Leyton and on extra money to counter the adverse environmental effects of the new link road. Leyton has already been robbed of its forests by the Government and of money to improve the environment. Now we shall get stuffed up again by 40-tonne lorries because money for new roads will be given only to Redbridge.

Mr. Andrew F. Bennett: Can my hon. Friend say what consultations there have been between the boroughs involved and the police authorities about policing the market? In some areas a substantial volume of goods shoplifted from ordinary shops ends up on market stalls.

Mr. Cohen: I have not received any specific information from the supporters of the Bill, but my hon. Friend makes a fair point and perhaps the Bill's sponsor will be able to answer it. I do not really like the black economy in which street markets operate, but if they can get goods off the back of a lorry, to use the colloquial term, that probably has a beneficial effect because good quality goods can be sold cheap to people who are being hammered by Government policies, by high inflation, and by unemployment. Therefore, I can sympathise with that aspect of the black economy. I detest the other side of the black economy whereby the rich find all the loopholes and rake in millions of pounds.

I am not particularly worried about the black economy. One can get a blooming good bargain in some of the markets in east London. I recommend that my hon. Friend goes down there and gets a few bargains. The other day I came to the House in a suit that cost me only a fiver. It is a wonderful fit. Brick lane market is superb for second-hand clothes.

Mr. Cryer: The next time my hon. Friend buys a suit, will he make sure that it is made in the United Kingdom and that the wool comes from Bradford?

Mr. Cohen: My hon. Friend is right. I am sure that the local markets sell suits made with wool from Bradford. The suit that I bought in Brick lane market for a fiver is a thorn-proof suit. Believe it or not, I saw a Government Minister on "Wogan" and as he sat down he flashed the label of his thorn-proof suit, so I did not know whether my suit once belonged to a Government Minister, but working-class people can get access to thorn-proof suits via markets and the black economy.

My key point concerns the road network. I am very glad that the hon. Member for Ilford, South set up a meeting last week with Mr. Price, the chief executive, and Mr. Bassett, the director of administration and legal services. They were most helpful. They gave me a verbal assurance that no new roads or road improvements are planned.

Mr. Andrew F. Bennett: My hon. Friend should have got it in writing.

Mr. Cohen: I need to be absolutely convinced about that and I hope that the sponsor of the Bill will refer to it. If at any time, even under a Labour Government, Redbridge tried to fool a Labour Government by saying that it had a market and needed money for its roads, it should be on record that the borough has stated that it does not need the money and has not planned any expansion in the road network and that it should not be given priority. Leyton should get priority as the Government have stolen our forest and we have had the worst possible deal from the M11 link road with very poor environmental effect.

Mr. George J. Buckley (Hemsworth): My hon. Friend stressed the necessity of increasing road services to the proposed market. I am not sufficiently local to know whether he is justified in making that point, but if more expenditure is necessary to improve the road services to the site of the market that would generate the need for more car parking to accommodate the increased traffic that will be generated by the establishment of the market. Is my hon. Friend convinced that there is adequate car parking in the locality to accommodate the anticipated increase in traffic?

Mr. Cohen: I am not totally convinced that there will be sufficient car parking space as that will depend on the size of the market. Mr. Price was kind enough to give me a leaflet on Redbridge that refers to the market for Ilford and the Bill. The leaflet states:

"And work has started on a new shopping mall to provide some 100 shops, department store, food court and parking for 1,200 cars. This is due to open in 1991."

I do not know whether 1,200 car parking spaces will be sufficient, but clearly Redbridge has thought about it. The leaflet also talks about the road network and states that:

"the A406—South Woodford to Barking Relief Road—opened in 1987."

So Redbridge already has those flash new roads. That emphasises my point that the money has already gone to Redbridge at the expense of Leyton and it would be quite horrendous if it received any more money.

I want to place it clearly on record that if Redbridge gets the market it should not get any more money for roads and that Leyton should be the first priority ahead of Redbridge. That point has to be rammed in, and that is why I object to the Bill.

Mr. Redmond: I do not know whether my hon. Friend had a meeting at the proposed site with the people whom he mentioned. He spoke about the verbal promise that he received. I would be slightly sceptical about accepting such a promise, as we do not know what the future will hold, especially if the market can expand. I am not quite sure where the site is, but perhaps my hon. Friend can inform me whether future expansion could take place by knocking down a few buildings. There is certainly some demolition taking place at Spitalfields market. The Bill talks about 60 or 80 sites, and I am not sure whether that could be increased to 100, 200 or 300. If the market expands, money will be required to ensure that local services meet the increased capacity. However, I do not know the area and would be grateful if my hon. Friend could help.

Mr. Cohen: There is always a danger of expansion. The Bill deals with the market stalls and, as far as I can see, the site appears to be quite limited. However, the enclosed mall and the food court to which I referred could spread and the parking problem could increase as could the pressure for roads to service the area.

Mr. Cryer: Does my hon. Friend accept that assurances are given by all sorts of people at various times as a matter of convenience to them? One certain way in which those assurances can be made hard and fast is by incorporating a clause or an amendment in the Bill. I wonder whether the chief executive would be prepared to say that he would incorporate into the Bill an amendment to make it a cast-iron guarantee which could be changed only by the Bill being amended in Parliament?

Mr. Cohen: I welcome my hon. Friend's intervention. I am always grateful to hon. Members with much greater experience of such procedures, and the private Bill procedure is certainly archaic. I am very grateful to my hon. Friend for that suggestion; I had not thought of it. I would welcome a clause in the Bill making it clear that the priority for roads money should go not to Redbridge but to Leyton. I hope that the sponsor of the Bill, or even the Minister, will agree to such an amendment because Leyton certainly has had a bad deal.

My hon. Friend the Member for Denton and Reddish (Mr. Bennett) said that I should have got a written assurance from the chief executive about no new roads being needed. Mr. Price came to see me only at the end of last week so there has not been an opportunity for that. Mr. Price has served the London borough of Redbridge for a long time and I take him at his word, and he gave me that assurance and I have put it on record tonight. Mr. Price speaks not for himself but for Redbridge and its honour would also be at stake.

Mr. Andrew F. Bennett: Does my hon. Friend agree that it is an abuse of the private Bill procedure for the promoters not to explore every opportunity to negotiate with anyone who his name down in a block and to give assurances so that there is no need for a debate in the House? Hon. Members would prefer to debate some of the momentous events happening throughout the world rather than give time to private Bills. The tradition in the House is that, wherever possible, the promoters negotiate to avoid the need for a Second Reading debate, which again takes up hon. Members' time, and the possibility of amendments being moved on Third Reading.

Mr. Cohen: I made my objections to the Bill clear at the beginning of the Session, but I do not oppose it as strongly as I opposed the City of London (Various Powers) Bill whereby forest land was stolen and not replaced. I could have gone on all night protesting about that. I am concerned about how the road network will affect Leyton.

Mr. Cryer: Does my hon. Friend accept that sometimes people of integrity give assurances but that one chief executive can be replaced by another? The only way in which an assurance given in perfect faith and utmost honesty will stand the test of time is for it to be written on the face of the Bill. A new chief executive could legitimately say, "Nothing said by a previous office holder can bind me." The promoters should redraw the Bill so that an assurance can appear on the face of it.

Mr. Cohen: I hope that the promoters will take my hon. Friend's point on board. Given the limited time that was available, I could only assume that the chief executive was a man of honour and that he spoke for Redbridge. My only purpose in speaking is to place on record the fact that the chief executive gave me a cast-iron assurance.

Any money for roads should not be given to build a market. There are already prior claims on that money in Leyton, which has been done down by the Government, especially by the husband of the Under-Secretary of State for the Environment. She should be concerned about the environment and should kick him out of bed one evening and say "Leyton should be given the money ahead of Redbridge."

Mr. Redmond: I am a little concerned about the faith that my hon. Friend is placing in the word of the chief executive, who no doubt is an honourable man whose word is his bond. However, chief executives come and go. In a short period, Doncaster has had two chief executives. A new chief executive may argue, "My predecessor should have said this or that." Hon. Members have experience of officers saying things that bind the passage of a Bill. An authority should include in the Bill any undertaking that it gives to an hon. Member.

Mr. Cohen: I bow to my hon. Friend's experience. Under the appalling private Bill procedure, I was consulted very late, but I look to the promoters to include on Third Reading the assurance that was given to me.

Mr. Skinner: That is a bit late.

Mr. Cohen: I know that it is a bit late, but that may be a solution if Redbridge does not want to go to the expense of withdrawing the Bill. I am clearly not in a position to table such a clause.

Mr. Cryer: Redrafting this part of the Bill would be the best way to proceed. It occurred to me while my hon. Friend was making his useful comments that under local government reorganisation—which can occur at any time under this Government, who are reorganising everything in sight to make it more difficult for ordinary people—if something is included in the Bill, which then becomes an Act, any successor organisation is obliged to take over the responsibility of the previous local government authority. An assurance from a chief executive of an authority that has disappeared or merged into another local authority is worthless, no matter how decent or honest the man or woman was who gave it. I urge my hon. Friend to consider the possibility of redrafting this part of the Bill to incorporate the assurance that he was given, because that is the only way it will stand the test of time.

Mr. Cohen: I take my hon. Friend's point, which has thrown me into a dilemma. I was given an assurance in good faith and I am prepared to believe it. Mr. Price is clearly an honourable man, and I merely wanted to get the assurance on the record.

Mr. Illsley: I should like my hon. Friend to bear in mind the example about which Labour Members have been speaking. In 1986, the Government abolished South Yorkshire county council, and any assurances given by it were made worthless. Local authority powers devolved to the district authorities of Doncaster, Sheffield, Rotherham and Barnsley. If that were to happen in London, the district authority might disagree with the policy of the previous authority, thereby scuppering any assurance given to my hon. Friend. Parliament is being asked to approve a Bill to give power to a local authority, but it should incorporate concrete assurances in the Bill.

Mr. Cohen: My hon. Friend has added to my concern. He has experience of assurances becoming worthless.

While my hon. Friend was speaking, I thought of a way round the problem. It would be best if the Minister said, "I am pleased to say to the hon. Member for Leyton that the Government can get round the problem and Parliament can get on and discuss the important issues of the day. We shall give Leyton all the money that it needs for its roads and environment as a result of the M11 link road to prevent any squabbling." After all, we need to improve the environment on that link road. Leyton needs more parks, forests and open space. The Department of

Transport sold some that we had. Many people along that route are about to be made homeless and they deserve to be treated well by the Government.

The way out of the problem would be for Conservatives to help each other. The Government can help Redbridge to get the Bill through without incorporating a new clause if they put up the money for Leyton.

Mr. Skinner: I am a bit worried now. My hon. Friend has been making the point at length that he is a bit worried about undertakings given in a short meeting that he had last week, telling us, I think, that he had serious reservations about the market proposed in the Bill. Is my hon. Friend now saying that if he can get for Leyton what he did not get on the City of London (Various Powers) Bill he is prepared to have another look at the matter? I hope that he will clear up that important matter.

Mr. Cohen: I would not have objected to the Bill if I had thought that Leyton would not be adversely affected. If the money is put up for Leyton's roads and environment, I have no objection if, in a few years' time, a bit more money goes to Redbridge's roads. We shall have had ours in Leyton. I hope that my hon. Friend understands that point.

Mr. Skinner: It sounds mercenary to me.

Mr. Cohen: I can be a bit mercenary when I am fighting for my constituents, especially when they are being done down day after day by the Government. They have to rely on their markets to buy suits for £5, cheap food and towels from the Londonderry hotel. There are towels from the Londonderry hotel in markets throughout Britain and no doubt they will be found in this market.

Mr. Cryer: Many Opposition Members feel that the Government have abused the private Bill procedure by putting forward what is essentially Government legislation in the form of private Bills. For the Minister to intervene and say that a grant will be made to my hon. Friend's constituency, as my hon. Friend is suggesting, would be a further abuse of the private Bill procedure. I hope that my hon. Friend will re-examine the position. The best way to proceed would be to incorporate in the Bill the sort of assurance that he has sought and obtained from the chief executive rather than to rely on the Government intervening with offers of money. As my hon. Friend knows, Goverment money can carry many conditions and difficulties and he might find himself wishing that the Bill had been altered instead.

Mr. Cohen: My hon. Friend is doing a good job in persuading me, but I would take the money for my constituents. If the Minister said that we could have the money for parks and open spaces and for the families who would be made homeless, I would take it, even though my hon. Friend makes excellent constitutional points. The private Bill procedure is bankrupt anyway, and community profits do not go to the community, so I would take the money.

Mr. Skinner: Even if it was in ecus?

Mr. Cohen: Yes, because we have an excellent Member of the European Parliament, Alf Lomas, who might well be able to get them changed on his trips to the Common Market. He does great work in the local area. However, I shall not go further along that route.

I said that I would not speak for long, and I want to start to conclude.

Sir Nicholas Bonsor: Before the hon. Gentleman does so, I may be able to assist him on the procedure that we shall be going through later. I fear that my hon. Friend the Minister is unlikely to give the hon. Gentleman the money that he wants and there is a faint possibility that when we divide later we may fail to throw the Bill out at this stage, regrettable though that will be. However, the private Bill procedure allows Leyton to make representations to the private Bill Committee, when the point that the hon. Gentleman has made so forcefully could be put. At that stage, four of our colleagues will have the right to write that condition into the Bill. Should they do so, Redbridge council will be bound by it. Therefore, the hon. Gentleman should consider inviting his local authority to make representations to the Committee should it be necessary.

Mr. Cohen: I thank the hon. Gentleman for that helpful advice. I shall take it on board and ask my local authority to make those representations. Nevertheless, the Minister should put up the money for Leyton, because it is such a good cause and has been done down so often, and it would ease the Bill's passage.

Another area of concern was that when the M11 link road goes through Leytonstone high road should have the opportunity to be pedestrianised. The Bill relates to part of Redbridge being pedestrianised. Again, Redbridge is getting that first, or rather being the only one to get it, taking priority over Leyton which really needs it.

When the M11 goes through, Leytonstone high road could be pedestrianised, enhancing Leytonstone's shopping opportunities. We do not want Redbridge to have built up its market to such an extent that it stifles Leytonstone at birth and ruins its opportunities for pedestrianisation and the environmental improvements that would flow from that.

Mr. Price and Mr. Bassett of Redbridge referred to the theory of concentric shopping circles. I do not know whether my hon. Friends know about that. Basically, it boils down to some planner drawing a circle around one market and then around another further down the road. Anyone who lives in between the two circles or in the area where the circles overlap might go to either market——

Mr. Skinner: They would get dizzy.

Mr. Cohen: They would spend double the money.

I am not an expert on that new-fangled theory, but I should like Leytonstone to have its shopping facilities improved and to be pedestrianised so that we can draw a nice big circle around Leytonstone and improve the prosperity of my constituency. I would be worried if Redbridge took away that opportunity and ruined Leytonstone's prospects.

Mr. Illsley: My hon. Friend refers to the theory of concentric circles which involves a circle being drawn around one market and then another, leaving an area in between. Does not the royal charter put a protective circle around the market to prevent another market from being placed there? Therefore, is not the concentric circle argument a little confusing?

Mr. Cohen: I recall Mr. Price and Mr. Bassett saying that communications had improved dramatically since the time of Henry III, when the distance to a market was

[*Mr. Cohen*]

thought to involve a third of the day getting there, a third of the day shopping and a third of the day getting home, and I suppose that that comes into the $6\frac{2}{3}$ mile measurement.

We do not want markets springing up in close proximity to each other, with authorities competing unnecessarily and wastefully. The result will be markets going broke. We have seen that happen in other spheres, where local authorities have spent loads of money on advertising simply to compete with each other.

Sir Nicholas Bonsor: I am intrigued by the concentric circle argument. Did Mr. Price tell the hon. Gentleman what he thought about the idea of having concentric circles within one circle? It is proposed that the Ilford circle should occur within the Romford circle. That does not seem to make economic sense.

Mr. Cohen: I agree, and it cannot make sense to have the concentric circles on top of each other. That brings me back to the need for a strategic planning authority, and it brings me to my final point, which is to oppose the idea of having markets virtually on top of each other. In that situation more markets will spring up and they will all go broke.

Mr. Cryer: Does my hon. Friend agree that the original example, dating from 1247, provides an argument for having proper strategic planning? Will my hon. Friend develop the concept of strategic planning, which is essential if we are to make the best use of resources?

Mr. Cohen: I do not want to delay the House by going down that path, remembering that I have been careful strictly to address the issues concerning the market. My hon. Friend makes an important point about strategic planning because it must make sense to optimise resources, otherwise waste results. We do not want many markets in certain areas and none in rural and semi-rural areas, with those living in distant areas having to travel for miles to get their Londonderry hotel towels.

Mr. Barron: If my hon. Friend agrees that the 13th century example mentioned by my hon. Friend the Member for Bradford, South (Mr. Cryer) represented one of the earliest forms of strategic planning, may I ask him to develop the point that it represented wide-ranging foresight on the part of those concerned in relation to housing?

Mr. Cohen: My hon. Friend is right, and the point he makes proves how important it is to have strategic planning in London and elsewhere, including Bradford. Any plan involving shopping areas must have housing in mind. Indeed, transport—not forgetting public transport—roads and all other forms of planning must be taken into account at the same time.

The trouble with the policies of the Government, including their use of the private Bill procedure, is that all of those considerations are the subject of chaos. They are left to market forces. They plan nothing in a co-ordinated way, and that leads to enormous waste.

Mr. Cryer: My hon. Friend might care to reflect on the way in which some authorities will spend large sums of money establishing markets, with good facilities and so on, while others will spend less. If this is left to market forces,

some local authorities will find that their markets become less successful as competitor markets become more profitable. Ratepayers' money will have been spent on facilities, for stallholders and the public, which serve no useful purpose. Indeed, councillors might face being surcharged because of that waste of ratepayers' money.

Mr. Cohen: My hon. Friend makes the point so well that I need not enlarge on it, except to remind the House that part of that expenditure will be on advertising. Once markets are so close—such as Romford and Ilford—that competition is enormous, but local authorities will spend ratepayers' money on advertising, competing against each other, in a chaotic way. The money will, no doubt, go to Saatchi and Saatchi, who will laugh all the way to the bank——

Mr. Barron: And from Saatchi and Saatchi to the Conservative party.

Mr. Cohen: —yes, and on to Tory party funds. That money could have been spent on housing.

Mr. Illsley: I will not delay my hon. Friend because a number of hon. Members wish to take part in the debate, and I hope to have an opportunity later to comment on the royal charter that was awarded to my constituency. The document to which my hon. Friend referred showed that Ilford town centre will have a new shopping mall in addition to a new market. He pointed out that ratepayers' money will be spent on advertising if the market becomes run down.

In my constituency, part of a market was moved to become part of a market complex and shopping centre. The result was that the market competed with the shopping precinct, and the profits of both declined. Eventually the local authority was involved in heavy expense to improve the shopping mall and the market centre simply to re-establish the position that existed prior to the amalgamation. Does my hon. Friend agree that, in the case we are discussing, competition between the market and the shopping complex will lead the authorities into incurring considerable expense?

Mr. Cohen: That is another example of an intervention making the point. I need not add to what my hon. Friend said. It is another reason for having a strategic planning authority.

I shall resume my seat, having spoken about the road network and the need for the money about which we are speaking not to be spent on a market but to come to Leyton for the benefit of the people of the area.

8.38 pm

Sir Nicholas Bonsor (Upminster): The hon. Member for Leyton (Mr. Cohen) will forgive me if I do not follow him down the roads of Leyton. I am grateful for the modest and short intervention that he made in the debate, in which he concisely made important points in favour of his constituency. I have no doubt that those matters will be pursued further if the Bill proceeds to another stage.

I have known my hon. Friend the Member for Ilford, South (Mr. Thorne) for a long time. We have served together on various Select Committees on Defence, and it is sad for me to be against him on this measure. He will forgive me for not being able to vote with him, in the light of the appalling shortcomings of the Bill which he has had the misfortune to present to the House. I say that because the measure is full of flaws in terms of detail and construction.

On the face of it, it is a simple little Bill which appears to be harmless in asking for a market in Ilford. That would be the case if it were something that was taken in a vacuum, but in order to judge the merits of this Bill we have to do two things. First, we have to recognise the background against which it is being brought forward. The Romford market has been operating for something like 742 years and this Bill is in direct abrogation of the rights which the Romford market traders have enjoyed for the whole of that period. Secondly, we have to look at the detail of the Bill to see if in its construction it is a fair Bill and puts its case across adequately.

The key to that can be found in paragraph (2) on page 1, which reads:

"It would be of public and local advantage to provide for the establishment of a further market in the part of the borough known as Ilford notwithstanding the infringement or non-compliance thereby with any rule of law or enactment".

It cannot be very often that a Bill comes before the House announcing at the outset that it intends to flout existing laws and go against existing enactments to the detriment of people other than those for whom the Bill is being promoted. I therefore, to a degree, commend the honesty of the Bill in admitting at the outset that that is its purpose.

Not content with doing that, the Bill is even more explicit in clause 3, which sets out what the Bill is attempting to achieve. It reads:

"The Council may—
(1) establish a market within a distance of one mile from the town hall; and
(2) authorise, on such terms (whether financial or otherwise) as they think fit the establishment by others of a market within a distance of one mile from the town hall;".
So immediately we have a difference between what the Bill is seeking to achieve and that which perhaps its promoters would imagine people to perceive. They are not asking for one market in Ilford; they are asking for the right to set up two markets in competition with the one which exists in Romford.

The Bill goes on in that same clause to say:
"notwithstanding that the holding of such a market would interfere with any rights, powers or privileges enjoyed in respect of a market held by any other person."

That really is extraordinary and it is even more extraordinary because one has to take into account that it is couched in terms which beg the question whether it would interfere with any such rights. And the fact is that it demonstrably and on the face of the Bill is in direct conflict with such rights. I will come back to that point when I examine the terms of the Bill a little more closely.

I would like to take the House through the remaining clauses so that we have a complete picture of what is being put forward tonight.

Mr. Barron: Subsection (2) of clause 3 in fact says that it is asking for the right not to set up other markets owned by a London borough council but to set up markets owned by other people, who normally, as I understand the private Bill procedure, would have to do exactly what this council is doing at the present time—that is, make direct representations to set up a market within the area.

Sir Nicholas Bonsor: The hon. Gentleman makes a very good point and I bow to his great knowledge of the private Bill procedure. It is extraordinary that the Redbridge

borough council should be trying to take upon itself the right to make such appointments not merely to itself, but to others, for their own financial gain, which would normally not be feasible without coming back to the House.

Mr. Barron: Not only that, but they are doing exactly as the hon. Member says without anybody having to come back to the House in future in terms of further developments in that area. It is the House that is losing out and not just the borough council.

Sir Nicholas Bonsor: That is quite right and it is a very important point. The House has to be very careful when allowing powers to be taken from it and delegated to others. I do not believe in delegating such powers without keeping a residual authority within the House to look at again and amend whatever we may see being done under the provisions that we have approved. In this instance we would not have any further power as the House of Commons to take another look at a Redbridge market being set up by that council in a way of which we might thoroughly disapprove, nor would we have any say in who was administering such a market.

Clause 4 deals with compensation. My hon. Friend the Member for Ilford, South has been good enough to admit that this clause is inadequate. None the less, it would be doing the problems less than justice if the House did not look closely at what is proposed. We are not looking here at a draft, a Green Paper, something that has been put to the House for consideration in outline; we are looking at detailed proposals that are being put forward with the recommendation that they should pass into law.

If we pass this now, on Second Reading, we shall have no further powers under the private Bill procedure, unless amendments are made in the private Bill Committee, to look at this again on Report. That is something which is unique to the private Bill procedure, which makes it all the more important that matters are not lightly glossed over. Notwithstanding the undertaking that my hon. Friend has given that this can be looked at later, it may well be that it will not be and that we shall not be able to find an acceptable compromise solution later. There is a danger that if we failed to find such a solution by compromise or by procedures within the private Bill Committee this House, constituted as it is tonight, would not have a further chance of looking at the Bill.

Mr. Barron: The hon. Member makes a very good point. He will know that a private Bill is going through Parliament at the present time which has not just local but national importance because of this very point. The Associated British Ports (No. 2) Bill came back to the House unamended and dozens of hon. Members were very concerned indeed about its implications, yet we do not have the right to amend that Bill.

Sir Nicholas Bonsor: I am sure that the hon. Gentleman will forgive me if I restrict my remarks to what we are considering tonight. Certainly in regard to this Bill there is a danger that this could happen and that gives me grounds for concern.

Under clause 4 it is proposed that:
"If by virtue of the enactment of this Act, the value of the right conferred by statute or by Royal Charter to hold an existing market is diminished, the person in whom that right is vested shall be entitled to compensation from the Council as set out in subsection (2) below or as otherwise agreed with

[*Sir Nicholas Bonsor*]

the Council save that a local authority within the meaning of section 72 of the Act of 1984 shall not be entitled to any compensation in respect of any rights, powers or privileges which they enjoy by reason only of the fact that they have established a market within their own district in the circumstances set out in subsection (3) of section 50 of the Act of 1984."

That is deeply significant in the context of this discussion because, as I will explain a little later, that clause does not cover the circumstances in which Romford market operates. Therefore it does not offer compensation to Romford borough council under its present terms.

Mr. Redmond: What has been said about the Bill being unamended in Committee is very important. The clause to which the hon. Member has referred talks about the local authority within the meaning of section 72 of the 1984 Act. I am sure that the hon. Member is aware that local government is going through tremendous changes and I do not see that stopping within the next couple of years. So any Acts affecting local government can be deleted, amended or whatever, and this will have a direct impact on what is stated in this section.

Sir Nicholas Bonsor: The hon. Gentleman is quite right to be concerned about that. There are procedures whereby such new Bills try to amend or take into account existing legislation to which they refer. One of my more arduous and less enjoyable jobs in the House is to serve on the Committee considering the consolidation of Bills. As the hon. Gentleman knows, that involves looking very closely at new Bills which take into account old legislation and consolidate it. We have to be extremely careful that when that is done no change of law takes place inadvertently through the new wording.

There are procedures whereby the danger that the hon. Member for Don Valley (Mr. Redmond) fears can be averted, but it is a danger that needs to be watched for whenever new legislation is brought forward. The meaning of "the Council" under section 72 of the Food Act 1984, which I confess that I have not read, may or may not be too narrow in terms of those who have the powers to hold local markets. That is another matter to which we should turn our attention if further opportunity arises.

Subsections 4(2) and 4(3) deal with the measure of compensation. Again, I ask the House to pay attention to this because I have strong objections to it. They say:

"(a) The measure of compensation shall be the capitalised value of the estimated loss of income to the claimant from persons trading at his market resulting from the continuance or establishment of a market under this Act.

(b) Compensation under this section shall carry interest from the expiry of six weeks from the date on which the claim is received by the Council.

3. Except as otherwise be agreed by the Council, compensation under this section shall not be payable except upon a claim made in writing to the Council within three months of the commencement of this Act."

I know that my hon. Friend the Member for Ilford, South has admitted that that is an appallingly inadequate time in which compensation can be assessed, but I ask the House to consider how anybody could bring such a proposal before the House in the first place. It shows an appalling lack of regard for those who trade in Romford market and an almost arrogant disregard for the need to give adequate compensation when old, established rights are being taken away. That is certainly not in line with

anything that this Government would like to see done. I very much hope that my hon. Friend the Minister will be able to distance herself from any such proposal, if she wishes to say anything about it now.

The timing of such compensation must be flexible and should be taken from a date at which such damage could conceivably be assessed. To say that the damage can be assessed within three months of the Act being passed, which will be before Redbridge market starts trading anyway, is ludicrous. Even supposing that Redbridge market can manage to start trading in that period, it will take a year or two before the impact of that market is fully felt at Romford. What will my hon. Friend the Member for Ilford, South say later to that, if he has the opportunity, as I hope that he will? What proposal will he be able to make that will adequately cover the point of giving properly assessed compensation at the right time to the council?

It is not, of course, only the council, or primarily the council in many instances, which will be the loser. The losers will be the 300-odd traders who have their market stalls in Romford. They have been established there for a long time and the Bill contains no proposal that compensation should be payable to them.

Mr. Barron: The hon. Gentleman has made the case that I was going to put. It is highly questionable whether the issue of compensation resulting from new retail outlets can be assessed at all, whether it involves a new market or a new shopping mall, which I understand that the town of Ilford will have in the next few years. The whole concept of compensation for the loss of retail trading is not well planned. There have been no major legal judgments on which an assessment could be based. Clause 4 is perhaps a sop, as is the proposal about compensation claims having to be made within three months. That is especially the case under the private Bill procedure. This Bill could go into Committee and two hon. Members could send it back unamended. It would then have to go through with the major defects that the hon. Gentleman has pointed out.

Sir Nicholas Bonsor: That is wholly correct. The Bill could go through with those defects and it would be appalling and unjust if it were to do so. Even if the Bill is amended, it is difficult, I agree, to assess compensation for the loss of retail trade. I am not aware of any great precedents for that, certainly not in the big world outside market trading. There is no previous history of such compensation within market trading because no previous Act has gone against existing rights under part III of the 1984 Act, or any similar rights before that. I may be wrong about that, but, to my knowledge, this matter has not arisen before. Clause 4 is an odd and inadequate clause. As presently drafted, it gives no compensation either to Romford council or to the traders who will lose out and it is, therefore, in the context of the Bill, wholly irrelevant and can be seen only as a red herring.

When I intervened earlier in the speech of the hon. Member for Leyton he said that there had been talk about a compromise on this point. I understand from my local authority that two compromises were offered of which that was one, but that they were offered on wholly unacceptable terms—namely, that the council should undertake not to oppose the Bill on Second Reading. The understanding was that if the Bill was opposed on Second

Reading, the offers of compromise would be withdrawn. Like the hon. Member for Leyton, I am here not as a preacher for my local council, but to represent my constituents. I find it odd, therefore, that Redbridge council should seek to put such terms on any compromise it may seriously have proposed. If it was serious about putting forward a compromise, it should not have been on terms that the local authority should try to gag local members of Parliament and prevent them from properly representing their constituents. That should not be encouraged by this House and should it prove to have been the case we shall have to ensure that it does not happen again. The compensation clause is, therefore, quite irrelevant to the Bill and the House should disregard it when deciding on whether the Bill should go through this stage.

Clause 5 says:

"A market established under this Act shall be deemed to have been established by the Council under Section 50 of the Act of 1984."

I want to make a technical point on that. I may be wrong as I am not a draftsman, but it seems to be an appallingly badly drafted Bill. It makes the claim that a market established under it should be established as follows:

"50.—(1) The council of a district may—

(a) establish a market within their district;

(b) acquire by agreement (but not otherwise), either by purchase or on lease, the whole or any part of an existing market undertaking within their district, and any rights enjoyed by any person within their district in respect of a market and of tolls,

and, in either case, may provide—

(i) a market place with convenient approaches to it;

(ii) a market house and other buildings convenient for the holding of a market.

(2) A market shall not be established in pursuance of this section so as to interfere with any rights, powers or privileges enjoyed within the district in respect of a market by any person, without that person's consent."

That is what section 50 of the 1984 Act says.

How can the promoters of the Bill purport to set up a market under the terms of that Act when in clause 3 of the Bill and elsewhere they propose precisely to set up a market without the consent of the people whose rights will be thus abrogated? This an appallingly bad clause in an appallingly bad Bill, which should be thrown out at this stage. If Redbridge really wants legislation passed, it should bring back a properly drafted Bill and have proper discussions with other concerned local authorities, rather than attempting to obtain such discussions by means that I would consider to be dubious. We could then re-examine the whole question.

Perhaps I may deal with the locus standi of Romford council, the borough of Havering and the three Members of Parliament who represent the area. As my hon. Friend the Member for Ilford, South said, we in Romford have enjoyed our own markets for 742 years, which must make Romford one of the oldest established and most continual trading markets in the country. The market was originally set up under a writ issued by Henry III in 1247, under which he gave the right of a market in the Royal Manor of Havering-atte-Bower, which continues as the Romford market today. That market was the one which meets on Wednesday.

Romford also has the right to hold markets on Fridays and Saturdays. The Saturday market arises from what is called a "lost modern grant". For the benefit of those of my hon. Friends who are not lawyers, and indeed for the benefit of some who are—even as a lawyer, I confess that I had to ask someone exactly what it meant—a "lost modern grant" is, in fact, a lost old grant. No one knows how the right was acquired because it was acquired so long ago and because it has been enjoyed continuously for so long, but the legal fiction is that at some stage someone granted the right. The "lost modern grant" is the basis on which the market is held. The rights of a market held under lost modern grant are as great as those of a market held under original writ. The Friday market is operated by Havering borough in exercise of its powers under part III of the Food Act 1984—on which Ilford and Redbridge so wrongly attempt to base their market operations.

We in Romford have the right to hold markets on three days of the week. That is significant. It means that we are not talking about taking away the rights of market traders who trade in Romford one day of the week and somewhere else the next. We are talking about taking away the rights to an exclusive area which have been enjoyed for a very long time by about 300 traders trading there three days a week. I suspect that those traders base a large part of their livelihood upon their operations in Romford market. The House must think carefully, therefore, before doing anything to undermine the security of their operations in Romford by passing a Bill in direct contravention of the arrangements that have pertained in our area for so long and in direct contravention of anything that has been done in this line before. I am advised that all other new markets set up under the 1984 Act have scrupulously observed the limits and boundaries of other markets that have been operating in the vicinity. We are not talking about following precedent or doing something that is normal in the course of market trading, negotiation and dialogue. We are talking about doing something that has never been done before. One would certainly not guess that from the way in which the Bill has been presented to the House.

I hope that we shall throw the Bill back where it came from and that, in due course, we shall have a chance to negotiate the position with Redbridge and perhaps find some way in which Romford could properly consent to a change in the present structure. If we do not give that consent—if that consent is not forthcoming for proper reasons—it would be wrong for the House to override the rights of the local borough of Havering in this way.

Mr. Barron: The hon. Gentleman says that the Bill should be withdrawn and that the London borough of Redbridge should hold proper discussions. The third paragraph of a letter signed by the chief executive of Redbridge says that major concessions have been discussed between the two local authorities. Does the hon. Gentleman know of any such concessions and, if so, does he know whether his local authority is satisfied with them? The letter seems to suggest that it is.

Sir Nicholas Bonsor: One thing that I certainly do know is that my local authority is not satisfied with the Bill as drafted, nor has it agreed any of the compromises that it was invited to agree. As I said earlier, the terms in which that invitation was expressed were wholly and rightly unacceptable to the local authority, and, indeed, undeliverable by it. Whatever the local authority may have said to me, I would in any case have taken whatever view I considered to be right in the interests of my constituents. I know that there were negotiations and that at some stage

[*Sir Nicholas Bonsor*]

the local authority agreed some of the points, but it certainly did not agree to the Bill in its present form or to the compromises mentioned earlier.

I am concerned that the interests of my constituents, the local traders and those who have enjoyed the facilities of Romford market for so long will be gravely endangered if this Bill is allowed to reach the statute book. I hope that when we vote in about an hour's time the House will take the view that the Bill should not be sent upstairs to Committee.

When I intervened in the speech of the hon. Member for Leyton I said that I was afraid that there would not be any acceptable new clauses or amendments during Committee that would allow the Bill to return to the Floor of the House for further discussion on Report. That must be seriously considered because, unlike the usual procedure for Bills, there will be no further opportunity—other than for the four hon. Members who will consider the Bill upstairs in Committee—to consider possible compromises that would enable those of us who represent the interests of Romford——

Mr. Skinner: If Mr. Speaker accepts a closure motion, even though there are still a number of hon. Members wishing to speak, the hon. Gentleman should have a word with his hon. Friends because two of the four hon. Members who will consider the Bill upstairs will represent the majority—if there is a majority in favour tonight—and it is important that they are distanced from the arguments. Our recent experience of certain private Bills, such as the Associated British Ports (No. 2) Bill, is that hon. Members were not allowed to table amendments on what, under the normal Bill procedure, would have been Report stage.

Neither the hon. Gentleman nor I want the Bill to proceed to its next stage. I am certainly not happy about the private Bill procedure. The hon. Gentleman should use his best endeavours with his hon. Friends, including those in favour of planned, strategic organisation of markets as opposed to market forces—there may not be many of those in the Tory party, but there are certainly more now than there used to be—to ensure that there are two hon. Members on the Committee who will allow justifiable amendments so that the House can have another bite at the cherry on Report.

Sir Nicholas Bonsor: I am sure that the hon. Gentleman will forgive me if I do not follow his general points, although I agree that it is highly desirable that there should be people of an independent mind—and I am sure that there will be—who will properly and closely consider whatever is put before them. As the hon. Gentleman suggested, the judgment of two, three or four Members of Parliament resulting in a final decision is very different from a full discussion in the House with all hon. Members able to make their points on the relevant amendments.

If the Bill proceeds to its next stage, it is important that those appointed to serve on the Committee read what has been said during this debate and take on board the fact that not by any stretch of the imagination could the Bill be said to have the support of those hon. Members present tonight.

I wish to deal with three generalisations that have arisen during the debate. The first is what the catchment area should be around the market. My hon. Friend the Member for Ilford, South informed us that the distance of $6\frac{2}{3}$ miles dates from Roman rule. I know that the market dates from Henry III, but the catchment area obviously dates back a lot further than that. I do not follow the logic of what he tries to persuade us, which is to the effect that because the distance was $6\frac{2}{3}$ miles in the days when people could not get about, it should now be much smaller when people can get about more easily. I would have thought that the logic was the reverse and that, in order to protect the trade and the interests of those who live in the vicinity, such a radius might be extended rather than made smaller.

The second point is about whether it is an unfair restraint of trade for Romford to say that it has had the right for so long and that it should preserve it, never mind the interests of Redbridge. I am prepared to make that point because it can be raised legitimately as an argument against me. I reject the logic of that because we have 300 traders trading in Romford and we cannot sensibly talk about restraint of trade when 300 people are competing with each other.

Sometimes my party gets in a muddle on this. I think that we could draw a parallel between my hon. Friend the Member for Ilford, South and the policy of the Monopolies and Mergers Commission on brewers. It does not seem to be compatible with Conservative philosophy that people who have built up their businesses over many years—200 years in the case of some brewers and by tradition at least 200 years for some of the family interests that have traded regularly at Romford—should lose their business, with no compensation being offered. I was very glad to hear some Opposition Members voicing similar opinions.

Mr. Barron: I do not know whether Opposition Members would go all the way with the hon. Gentleman on compensation for the brewing industry which makes the biggest contribution to Conservative party funds.

Sir Nicholas Bonsor: I understand that that might be a reason for Opposition Members not to go along the same road as me, but I am sure that they would have other and better reasons, were they to take an opposite line. I am sure that they would not allow narrow party political bias to override their natural desire to look after the public interest.

My hon. Friend the Member for Ilford, South referred in his opening remarks to the applications that he has had. He told the House that he has had 240 applications for stalls at Redbridge. [*Interruption.*] That is the very point; the sedentary intervention asks how many of those have come from Romford. I too should like to know that. Perhaps my hon. Friend can tell me how many of the applications are from people who already have stalls in Romford market.

It may be that all that we will do, should the Bill go through, is to move the trade down the road from where it is well established. Even if that does not happen, the historical justification for the laws that have been in force for nearly 800 years is that there is only a limited amount of business to be done in these areas. If we are to have an efficient service in the public interest and if we are to look after consumers and safeguard the livelihood of the traders, we must have safeguards such as exist under the writ of Henry III.

I invite the House to throw the Bill out at this stage. Should there unfortunately be inadequate numbers listening at the moment to hear what the argument is about, I hope that at a later stage hon. Members will read the debate and make their own judgment.

9.13 pm

Ms. Joan Walley (Stoke-on-Trent, North): The longer I listen to the debate, the more convinced I am that the many objections that we have heard to the Bill are justified. We have heard of the many detrimental effects that the Bill would have not just on street traders in Romford but on the local shopkeepers in the communities where markets exist. Such points make Opposition Members very concerned about the Bill. It must also be said that there are strong objections, not least because it sets a precedent. If we really are talking in the absence of total strategic planning, which was a point well highlighted during the earlier stage of the debate, we shall make even more problems for ourselves in local government.

We have heard that there are flaws in the Bill. As a relatively new Member of the House, I do not consider myself as being someone who is as learned in parliamentary procedure as many of my hon. Friends, but, even so, it is clear to me from what has been said that there are flaws. The problems that would ensue, if the Bill went to Committee and we were not able to make amendments to it, should be considered when we vote later.

We have heard from the hon. Member for Ilford, South (Mr. Thorne), in whose constituency the proposed market lies, that it would be to local and public advantage. I would like to ask him to whose local and public advantage he referred. Was he referring to the developers and the large retailers, who will presumably, as a result of market forces, be taking profits from the new development and from the shopping precinct which is being developed, or to the stallholders, and the local people, who will probably find it inconvenient to go into Ilford to shop in the proposed new market? Many comments have been made about the lack of proper provision for highways, for transport and for all the other planning matters that should be taken on board when considering the Bill.

From conversations that I have had with elected members in Redbridge, I know that the planners have not even been able to arrange for bus stops to work properly. I have heard stories of 13 buses stopping at the same bus stop. I do not have any confidence, therefore, that the necessary considerations have been taken on board. Various aspects, especially the fact that there is no strategic planning that could reconcile the conflicting views and pressures, lead the Opposition to oppose the Bill.

Unlike the rest of the country, it must be said that the south-east has never benefited to any great extent from the municipal reforms that provided for the building and operating of so many excellent indoor markets, with all the proper facilities of fair, healthy, hygienic and safe trading. I believe that in our discussions so far on markets, whether indoor or outdoor, we have not shown any concern about the whole infrastructure which goes into supporting a market, such as the cleansing operations. Instead the south-east and even urbanised areas of London have suffered from a crude and opportunistic free-for-all. In what was known as inner London, the late-lamented Greater London council managed to control street trading and similar markets by means of its general powers, which were enforced by the boroughs. In outer London the

historic town centres, of which Kingston and Romford are good examples, had the long-established market rights dating back to time immemorial about which we have heard so much this evening.

We have before us what is in all repects a grubby little Bill, which is designed to upset the pattern of history in the interests—I have to say it—of commercial opportunism.

I understand from the sponsors of the Bill that they have seen fit to allocate £50,000 and £4,000 a month plus expenses for their lobbyists. Their proposal is obviously not so simple and clear-cut as it seems, or as the hon. Members supporting the Bill would have us believe. We were told that the petition had 6,000 signatures. I understand that many people did not institute the petition of their own accord. They signed their names when the major retailers thought that it would be in their commercial interest to get the petition under way.

I take great exception to the comments about tatty old markets which, we have been told, are out of date and have no place in modern market policies. Any former councillor who has been involved in local government knows that the operation of retail markets is not merely a matter of providing some space for a few traders. There are complicated implications for all local shopping facilities —parking, cleansing, hygiene, consumer safety and regulation.

I do not know whether the Minister intends to contribute to the debate. I noted a recent report in *The Independent* of her visit to the Lambeth Walk street market. I am sure that she has had ample opportunity during the Vauxhall by-election campaign to see for herself how the once thriving street market in Lambeth Walk has been laid to waste by developers and the competition of other shopping centres. That factor must be taken on board.

The Bill will allow Redbridge council to set up a market in Ilford or, to be more precise, will allow private interests to do so, with the blessing of their friends on the council. I listened carefully to the hon. Member for Upminster (Sir N. Bonsor) and I wonder whether he has misinterpreted clause 3(2). Is that subsection all about setting up two markets or does it enable the council to invest in the market and then ensure that it is quickly privatised, which means that we are talking about one market? I say that with some trepidation because the council is spilt on this issue.

Anyone who has done his or her homework will know that it is not a matter of bringing before the House a Bill that has the full support of the large Conservative majority on the council. My information is that at least one third of the Conservative councillors do not support it—hardly a portent of success or widespread support within the community. Hon. Members who said that they felt bound to speak on behalf of their constituents should not necessarily be judged by council decisions. I am sorry that there are not a large number of hon. Members present to make it clear that this proposal does not have the 100 per cent. support of the Conservative majority on Redbridge council.

I can, however, well understand why multiple retailers and Ilford developers want the attraction of choice and interest for shoppers in one of those up-market markets about which we have heard. Unfortunately, this is bound to detract from support for small retailers trying to get a

[Ms. Joan Walley]

foothold in the economy. Many people and many small shops near the existing market stand to lose much if the Bill is passed.

The Bill's sponsors need to be alerted to the fact that the demise of small shops will reduce the business rate income —an important point which has not been noted. In inner London and the east end, there are many streets and shops where business income has been greatly reduced. The introduction of a substantial six-day week market in the centre of Ilford is also bound to create a loss of trade, not only to places such as Romford, but to the local shopping centres and markets of Redbridge and its adjoining boroughs.

I have a letter from the National Market Traders Federation. We must take into account the concern that some of us have for those who trade in the Romford markets. The letter states:

"The traders are opposed to new markets, as they have built up their businesses under strict rules and procedures. When they first attended Romford market they had to stand in the casual queue with no certainty of getting a stall. As they progressed up the list by regular attendance they gained a stall every week but not in the same place. After a period of up to eight years on the casual list they finally obtained a regular stall and further service on the market allowed them to transfer to better stalls as they became vacant."

That is the practice by which markets all over the country have become established, and the process by which traders have built up their livelihood. We should think carefully about removing their livelihoods when the clauses in the Bill which deal with compensation are, as the hon. Member for Upminster said, grossly inadequate.

The federation also brought to my attention the fact that

"Romford, in common with other well-run markets, has strict conditions attached to the trader's 'licence' which restricts traders as to what they can sell and they are also required to trade in a responsible manner."

Anyone who is familiar with local markets will be aware of that. I am concerned about the proposal contained in clause 3(2) which could hand over the responsibility of running the markets to private developers.

As the federation states:

"Private operators are not always responsible in the way that they run their markets and do not enforce strict trading practices to protect the shopping public and a 'bad' market at Ilford could reflect badly on the responsible traders at Romford."

That is an important point, which is worth making.

The Bill is not specific about the site of Ilford market. I understand that a site has been earmarked already. I stand to be corrected on that, but I understand that the site is within one mile from the town hall. As usual of late, the site is, at present, a car park. Hon. Members will therefore ask how a loss of parking spaces can be reconciled with the hope, expressed earlier, for an increase in shoppers. We must also question the provisions of other related matters.

I have a copy of a letter from David C. Humble and Company, independent financial advisers, who wrote to the director of land management of Redbridge council, objecting in the strongest possible terms to a planning proposal which is, I understand, currently under consideration and which would take away one existing car park to make way for a large scale office development. The company is expressing concern about the status quo and

the lack of car parking facilities in Ilford. If we are to lose that car park, we should be concerned about the loss of a car park which is to be the very site of the market.

We must also question the provisions for proper food hygiene, refuse storage and disposal, storage of barrows and stores. Anybody who knows anything about street markets, especially if they have been local councillors, knows of the many complaints about street traders who infringe on the amount of space and parking space available and the times when it is possible to deliver to market stalls. Even traders' vehicles will occupy a substantial area of car parking which is, at present, available to shoppers. I wonder whether these detailed items have been taken into account.

We are talking about two issues: whether we are setting a national precedent and whether there are special circumstances in which we should not support the Bill. I submit that the problems that I have mentioned, coupled with the difficult access to the site, constitute a strong case against the Bill.

Opposition Members might be more inclined to support the Bill if it provided for a well-thought-out scheme with some evidence of the strategic planning of which we heard so much from my hon. Friend the Member for Leyton (Mr. Cohen), relevant to shopping in east London and to all the environmental and planning implications. As far as I can see, the Bill merely offers those who live or work in the area the prospect of traffic chaos, dirt, disruption and widespread adverse effects for shoppers as well as established market traders. The Bill —which Redbridge council no doubt sees as a model of late 20th-century enterprise—is no more than a grubby piece of opportunism from the flog-it-off, get-rich-quick school of politics.

Mr. Barron: The free market.

Ms. Walley: The free market, indeed.

I have learnt not to expect any concern for the environment or the health and safety of the public from such people, but in this instance they have exceeded themselves by not even caring about the effects on other traders or the wider interests of shoppers. That is reflected in the number of technical flaws in the Bill.

I am grateful to hon. Members on both sides of the House, and others, who have pointed out to me that the Bill's enactment would represent a major departure from a nationwide policy of many years' standing. Regardless of the position in Redbridge, the Opposition are anxious to avoid the creation of a precedent that would allow the Conservative car park groups to exploit similar opportunities in constituencies all over the country, many of which have excellent retail markets established by people who knew what municipal improvement and initiative really meant. How sad and how significant that, instead of organising strategic planning for London and for councillors who look to the future health and welfare of their boroughs, the House must now spend its time considering a Bill whose sole purpose is to maximise the commercial value of a car park.

9.31 pm

The Parliamentary Under-Secretary of State for the Environment (Mrs. Virginia Bottomley): It may be helpful if I give a brief explanation of the Government's view. It is, of course, for my hon. Friend the Member for Ilford,

South (Mr. Thorne) to respond to the detail of the debate, but it can fairly be said that, whatever the outcome, many of us will wish to take the opportunity of visiting the Romford charter market. A number of hon. Members were not aware that the market is 742 years old. My hon. Friend the Parliamentary Under-Secretary of State for the Armed Forces, the hon. Member for Romford (Mr. Neubert), has been present throughout the debate but, because of his ministerial status, has been unable to participate. No doubt we shall be visiting his constituency to see the market.

Long-established charter rights such as this can be set aside only by Act of Parliament, and it is for Redbridge to persuade Parliament that the powers that it seeks are justified. It is traditional for the Government to take a neutral stance on private Bills, and tonight's Bill is no exception to that rule. The Government have considered its content and have no objections in principle to the powers sought by the council. The Department has raised no observations; we take the view that the issues raised in relation to markets and existing market rights are local matters in which the Government do not wish to intervene.

There is one petition against the Bill, and the petitioner will have an opportunity to present his objections to the Select Committee. The Committee will be in a much better position than we are tonight to examine the issues in detail, and will have the added advantage of hearing expert evidence—not that I wish to suggest that many of tonight's contributions have not been expert in their various ways.

I hope that the Bill will be given a Second Reading and allowed to proceed to Committee in the conventional way for detailed consideration.

9.34 pm

Mr. Martin Redmond (Don Valley): I am grateful to you for calling me, Mr. Speaker. I have been in the Chamber since seven o'clock this evening, apart from nipping out to do some photocopying, and have endured the no-smoking rule that applies in it. I am glad to have this opportunity to speak briefly, because I certainly intend to allow the sponsor of the Bill to answer some of the points raised this evening.

I take exception to a remark made earlier by a Conservative Member who has now left the Chamber to the effect that if one is a Labour Member of Parliament serving a constituency having a Labour-controlled local authority, one should not make any remarks that are contrary to that local authority's wishes—and that the same applies to Conservatives. I have an excellent relationship with my own local authority, but we disagree from time to time on one or two issues.

The Minister stated that the Government have no preference either way but that the Bill should be given a Second Reading, and that anyone who intends opposing it will leave disappointed when the votes are counted. It is obvious from previous debates that private Bills which have the Government's support and which are the subject of Government whipping enjoy a majority vote in favour of them.

The Bill represents the thin end of the wedge. It cannot be considered in isolation. If the Bill receives a Second Reading it will have a domino effect on other markets throughout the country, which will come under fire from people out to make a fast buck and a quick profit—and to hell with long-term planning. Doncaster could find itself in

such a situation. It has a historic market on the site of the old Roman road. I do not doubt for one moment that the existing market at Romford provides similar excellent facilities. Doncaster market offers fresh fruit, vegetables and fish, haberdashery, and other goods. It is protected by the rule that does not permit another market nearer than $6\frac{2}{3}$ miles. If that rule were waived, it would have a tremendous effect on Doncaster market. That is one of the reasons why I am very concerned about getting shot of the royal writ to which the Bill refers.

Under the Bill, the only thing that is certain is that the old royal writ will disappear and that another market will be established nearer than $6\frac{2}{3}$ miles away from Romford. The Bill makes no mention of improved commerce or of any other positive element. It is no use people arguing that the Bill will not have a knock-on effect in other areas, because that will be the case once a precedent is set in this Chamber.

Reference has been made to good strategic planning. If a bad planning decision is made, future generations will have to live with it. There are examples in Yorkshire and in other parts of the country of that happening, where subsequent generations have faced a host of problems as a consequence of someone making an adverse planning decision.

In Doncaster we have an excellent market and an abattoir which serves farmers for miles around. Quite rightly, the local authority seeks to protect the market. There are also other markets outside the $6\frac{2}{3}$ miles. The market at Mexborough is an excellent little market and should certainly be protected. Unfortunately, within our avaricious society many car boot sales have been springing up throughout my area, causing all sorts of problems for local residents becauses the increased traffic does nothing to enhance local villages. The towns in my constituency have suffered many problems due to car boot sales.

I want to allow time for the sponsor of the Bill to respond to the debate, but I should mention briefly the petition which carries 6,500 signatures. A few weeks ago I handed in to 10 Downing street a petition against the poll tax and that had many more signatures, but I do not suppose that the Prime Minister even saw that petition and if she did I am sure that she took no notice of it. The petition to which the hon. Gentleman referred is, therefore, of no concern because the people who signed it want the market and intend to exploit it and profit from it, but no doubt there is also a petition from those who do not want the market within than $6\frac{2}{3}$ miles.

I hope that the House will reject the Bill as it upsets the fundamental principle of the distance of $6\frac{2}{3}$ miles. There is enough greed in society without the House endorsing more greed. I have examined the promotional leaflet that Redbridge council has handed out. There certainly seems to be a large number of car parks. Perhaps Redbridge should have planned more stores and other premises that attract business. The borough council appears to be more concerned with car parks, and perhaps it will have too many car parks without sufficient cars to fill them. That emphasises that good planning is needed to ensure that everything is orderly in future.

The Bill causes great concern. I am not satisfied that certain things will not happen if the Bill is given a Second Reading. I am not quite sure about the safety factor. It would appear from the promotional leaflet that the market stalls will be under a viaduct. The sponsor will probably correct me, but occasionally we get bad weather and I

[*Mr. Martin Redmond*]

would hate to be a customer of one of those stalls when an articulated lorry went over the top of the market. It has been said that the market was hemmed in and that there could be no expansion for the 68 stalls. Although the map does not give all the finer details, if I had a few million pounds and wanted to add another 60, 80 or 100 stalls, I could certainly find room to do so. Therefore, the hon. Member for Upminster (Sir N. Bonsor) who spoke against the Bill had every right to be concerned. We do not want people chasing a cake that is becoming smaller and ending up with no living at all. We have a duty to protect the existing market stalls that are there by royal charter. I hope that the hon. Member for Ilford, South will allay my fears about the possible knock-on effects of the Bill. People outside are waiting to move in to exploit certain circumstances.

Doncaster is a first-class market town. People enjoy visiting it because of its compactness. When I was on the local authority, it used to wish that a certain organisation was in Timbuktu. I must admit that I was a bit of a philistine at that time, but markets have changed, and those that have built up over the centuries have charm and character. No matter how clean and tidy a new market is, it will not have the character and flavour of a centuries-old market. I hope that the hon. Member for Ilford, South will think again and will withdraw the Bill until such time as the points made by hon. Members can be satisfied.

9.45 pm

Mr. Thorne: With the leave of the House, I shall try to answer as many questions as I can. The hon. Member for Leyton (Mr. Cohen) was concerned that the Bill would circumvent the planning process. I reassure him that it must still go through the normal planning procedure.

As the hon. Member for Don Valley (Mr. Redmond) said, the market is partly under a road. It would therefore be quite unsuitable for a football pitch, as was suggested earlier. I shall return to the points made by the hon. Member for Don Valley later.

The strategic plan for Redbridge, which was introduced in 1980, included provision for a market. It was therefore very much on the cards when the Greater London council was in existence. I have no reason to suppose that if that authority had been in existence it would have objected to its promotion now.

Retailers are in favour of the market. I have not been approached by any retailer who is not in favour of it. Local traders and the local chamber of trade were responsible for the petition. It is not a parliamentary petition but merely an expression of support for the Bill. It is not couched in parliamentary terms, so it will not therefore be put in the Bag. I was not a party to it, but if I had been I would have offered certain advice. Local traders and the local chamber of trade did it on their own initiative, and in the time available they did very well.

Rates and competition with shopkeepers were mentioned. These are taken into account by the level of charges for a market stall. Rent for stalls will be paid to the local authority, and this will benefit ratepayers.

Mr. Ian McCartney (Makerfield): The hon. Gentleman makes an interesting point about rents being paid to the local authority. In the foreseeable future, a substantial part of those rents will be used to offset the capital costs of construction and development work. In reality, for a considerable period thereafter, there will be no significant benefit to the ratepayers of the borough.

Mr. Thorne: I do not agree. A shop must be fitted and equipped, and inevitably there is a contribution towards the costs of constructing a market stall. I do not foresee that being a major proportion of the cost. The ratepayers' investment will be well worth while.

The police were consulted. A car park which will take 1,400 cars is now under construction and that will more than make up for the 60 car places which will be displaced by the development.

The hon. Member for Leyton spent a considerable time expressing concern about the availability of funds for roads in his area. He was given an assurance by Mr. Price, the chief executive of the London borough of Redbridge, that there are no plans to spend further money on roads in Ilford town centre in the foreseeable future. Mr. Price cannot bind his successors or the council into the distant future, but there is no question that Ilford town centre will in any way be competing for funds now with the London borough of Waltham Forest for Leyton and Leytonstone.

My hon. Friend the Member for Upminster (Sir N. Bonsor) expressed concern about the number of markets and compensation. I have already given an undertaking that compensation will be calculated six months from the time at which the market is opened, not six months from the Bill being enacted.

Mr. Barron: Is there any legal precedent for people being compensated for the loss of retail trade? Has the relevant clause, on which I have so far been unable to speak, any precedent in law?

Mr. Thorne: Not that I know of. The compensation is payable to the London borough of Havering. It is there to compensate for any effect that there might be on its market, about which it was concerned.

My hon. Friend the Member for Upminster mentioned negotiation between local authorities. As I understand it, there has been a singular lack of negotiation or response to negotiation from his local authority. His remarks this evening have gone further than any previous negotiations in that regard. If the Bill receives its Second Reading tonight, as I hope that it will, there will be an opportunity for further negotiation. That is what should happen before the matter reaches an opposed Bill Committee. I am sure that Redbridge will want to obtain as much agreement as possible.

I have every confidence that the four hon. Members appointed to an opposed Bill Committee would view the matter in an unbiased way. I have served on such Committees myself in the past and I well remember the undertaking that has to be given. I have always been extremely impressed by the way in which Opposition Members have looked at such matters in an impartial way and have done their best, together with Conservative Members, to reach a proper and fair decision.

I have explained in some detail how the figure of $6\frac{2}{3}$ miles was arrived at. The proposed market will be $5\frac{1}{4}$ miles away and that seems to me to be a fair distance. I believe that it will have no effect upon the market in Romford. As I have said, there were 250 applications. A survey has been carried out by some experts, G. L. Hearn and Partners, who expressed the opinion that the effect on Romford market would be negligible, and I believe that that is correct.

I am sorry that the hon. Member for Stoke-on-Trent, North (Ms. Walley) expressed such a negative attitude to the Bill. As I said earlier, it is important to give people an opportunity to start in business. It would be wrong to stop people fulfilling the entirely laudable aim of trading on their own from a market stall when they cannot afford the expense of a shop. Marks and Spencer and British Home Stores started in just that way.

It has been said that the Bill has many flaws. I do not accept that the measure is in any major way different from the majority of Bills that come before the House. Corrections must often be made, and the Committee is the correct place for them to be made.

Reference was made to the question of food hygiene. The stalls will be subject to the same regulations as the stalls that at present exist in the Romford market.

The hon. Member for Don Valley wondered whether petitions were of any value. I disagree with him wholeheartedly on that issue. I believe that petitions have a valuable role to play as an expression of opinion. I am sure that due note was taken of the petition that he presented.

Mr. Redmond: I am pleased to hear that. I hope that when, in the not too distant future, I present another petition, I will be able to count on the hon. Gentleman's support.

Mr. Thorne: As I say, due note is taken of petitions, even though we do not always get the result we would like. I am convinced that it is worth putting in a petition on all occasions as an expression of opinion.

My answer to remarks that were made about the question of greed is that this land is owned by the local authority. Thus, what is proposed will benefit the ratepayers as a whole.

I cannot say what safety factors exist in connection with vehicles crossing the bridge which goes over the railway. That was designed and paid for by the GLC, and I am sure that the GLC looked carefully into the question of safety at the relevant time.

I was asked about the number of people who had signed the Romford petition. I counted over 100 names with addresses in Romford in the time available to me. I regard that as significant. There were a number of others from East Ham and elsewhere.

This is a modest Bill. It proposes a site within one mile of Ilford town centre, which is well built up. Only a small number of sites are available there. A modest number of stalls could be sited on this piece of land. I cannot see how it can be claimed that that would have an adverse effect on Romford market.

I have received a letter from a Mrs. Norris who lives in Romford. It was addressed to the public relations officer of the London borough of Redbridge. She writes:

"Dear Sir, I read in our local paper that Romford market stallholders are going to complain about your wanting to open a market. I feel that these stallholders have got a damned cheek, when I am told that many of them go to other markets on 'no market' day here. You should look into this, and when the Redbridge Bill is read in the House, somebody who is able should have their say for the people of Redbridge and the east London side of Romford. Hope you succeed. Yours truly."

That lady has the right idea. She believes that there should be competition and a full opportunity for people to have the chance of a wide variety of trading. I therefore urge the House to give the Bill a Second reading.

9.58 pm

Mr. Kevin Barron (Rother Valley): I do not wish to delay the House and I must at the outset declare that I do not have a constituency interest in the issue, although I have a passing interest in the number of private Bills that come before the House. My comments will, therefore, go somewhat wider that the subject matter of the Bill.

Mr. Thorne *rose in his place and claimed to move,* That the Question be now put.

Question put, That the Question be now put:—
The House divided: Ayes 174, Noes 92.

Division No. 222]   **[9.59 pm**

AYES

Alexander, Richard
Alison, Rt Hon Michael
Alton, David
Arnold, Jacques (Gravesham)
Ashby, David
Aspinwall, Jack
Atkins, Robert
Baker, Rt Hon K. (Mole Valley)
Beith, A. J.
Bellingham, Henry
Bendall, Vivian
Bennett, Nicholas (Pembroke)
Benyon, W.
Bevan, David Gilroy
Blackburn, Dr John G.
Boscawen, Hon Robert
Boswell, Tim
Bottomley, Peter
Bottomley, Mrs Virginia
Braine, Rt Hon Sir Bernard
Brazier, Julian
Bright, Graham
Brooke, Rt Hon Peter
Bruce, Malcolm (Gordon)
Carlisle, Kenneth (Lincoln)
Carttiss, Michael
Chapman, Sydney
Clark, Sir W. (Croydon S)
Coombs, Anthony (Wyre F'rest)
Cope, Rt Hon John
Cormack, Patrick
Crowther, Stan
Curry, David
Davis, David (Boothferry)
Dorrell, Stephen
Douglas-Hamilton, Lord James
Durant, Tony
Fallon, Michael
Favell, Tony
Fearn, Ronald
Field, Barry (Isle of Wight)
Fishburn, John Dudley
Fookes, Dame Janet
Forth, Eric
Franks, Cecil
Freeman, Roger
French, Douglas
Garel-Jones, Tristan
Gill, Christopher
Glyn, Dr Alan
Gow, Ian
Grant, Sir Anthony (CambsSW)
Greenway, Harry (Ealing N)
Greenway, John (Ryedale)
Gregory, Conal
Griffiths, Sir Eldon (Bury St E')

Griffiths, Peter (Portsmouth N)
Grist, Ian
Ground, Patrick
Gummer, Rt Hon John Selwyn
Hague, William
Hamilton, Hon Archie (Epsom)
Hamilton, Neil (Tatton)
Hampson, Dr Keith
Hannam, John
Hargreaves, Ken (Hyndburn)
Harris, David
Haselhurst, Alan
Hawkins, Christopher
Hayward, Robert
Heathcoat-Amory, David
Heseltine, Rt Hon Michael
Hind, Kenneth
Hordern, Sir Peter
Howard, Michael
Howarth, Alan (Strat'd-on-A)
Howarth, G. (Cannock & B'wd)
Howells, Geraint
Hughes, Robert G. (Harrow W)
Hunt, David (Wirral W)
Irvine, Michael
Jack, Michael
Jackson, Robert
Janman, Tim
Jones, Gwilym (Cardiff N)
Jopling, Rt Hon Michael
Kennedy, Charles
Key, Robert
Kilfedder, James
King, Roger (B'ham N'thfield)
Kirkhope, Timothy
Kirkwood, Archy
Knapman, Roger
Knight, Greg (Derby North)
Knight, Dame Jill (Edgbaston)
Knowles, Michael
Lamont, Rt Hon Norman
Lang, Ian
Lawrence, Ivan
Lee, John (Pendle)
Lightbown, David
Lilley, Peter
Livsey, Richard
Lloyd, Sir Ian (Havant)
Lloyd, Peter (Fareham)
Macfarlane, Sir Neil
MacKay, Andrew (E Berkshire)
Maclean, David
McLoughlin, Patrick
McNair-Wilson, Sir Michael
Major, Rt Hon John
Marshall, John (Hendon S)

Marshall, Michael *(Arundel)*
Maude, Hon Francis
Michie, Mrs Ray *(Arg'l & Bute)*
Mills, Iain
Miscampbell, Norman
Mitchell, Andrew *(Gedling)*
Mitchell, Sir David
Moate, Roger
Montgomery, Sir Fergus
Moore, Rt Hon John
Morrison, Sir Charles
Moss, Malcolm
Moynihan, Hon Colin
Mudd, David
Nicholls, Patrick
Nicholson, David *(Taunton)*
Onslow, Rt Hon Cranley
Page, Richard
Paice, James
Parkinson, Rt Hon Cecil
Patnick, Irvine
Patten, Chris *(Bath)*
Pawsey, James
Peacock, Mrs Elizabeth
Porter, David *(Waveney)*
Portillo, Michael
Price, Sir David
Raison, Rt Hon Timothy
Redwood, John
Riddick, Graham
Roe, Mrs Marion
Rost, Peter
Rumbold, Mrs Angela

Ryder, Richard
Sackville, Hon Tom
Sainsbury, Hon Tim
Shaw, David *(Dover)*
Shepherd, Colin *(Hereford)*
Skeet, Sir Trevor
Speller, Tony
Spicer, Michael *(S Worcs)*
Steel, Rt Hon David
Stradling Thomas, Sir John
Summerson, Hugo
Taylor, Ian *(Esher)*
Taylor, Matthew *(Truro)*
Thompson, Patrick *(Norwich N)*
Thornton, Malcolm
Thurnham, Peter
Townend, John *(Bridlington)*
Trotter, Neville
Twinn, Dr Ian
Waddington, Rt Hon David
Wallace, James
Waller, Gary
Warren, Kenneth
Wheeler, John
Widdecombe, Ann
Wood, Timothy
Woodcock, Dr. Mike
Young, Sir George *(Acton)*
Younger, Rt Hon George

Tellers for the Ayes:
   Mr. James Arbuthnot and
   Mr. Tim Devlin.

NOES

Adams, Allen *(Paisley N)*
Armstrong, Hilary
Barnes, Harry *(Derbyshire NE)*
Barron, Kevin
Battle, John
Bermingham, Gerald
Bidwell, Sydney
Blunkett, David
Bonsor, Sir Nicholas
Brown, Nicholas *(Newcastle E)*
Buckley, George J.
Caborn, Richard
Callaghan, Jim
Campbell-Savours, D. N.
Canavan, Dennis
Carrington, Matthew
Clarke, Tom *(Monklands W)*
Clay, Bob
Clelland, David
Cohen, Harry
Cook, Frank *(Stockton N)*
Cousins, Jim
Cryer, Bob
Cunliffe, Lawrence
Dalyell, Tam
Davies, Rt Hon Denzil *(Llanelli)*
Davis, Terry *(B'ham Hodge H'l)*
Dixon, Don
Duffy, A. E. P.
Eadie, Alexander
Eastham, Ken
Evans, John *(St Helens N)*
Flynn, Paul
Foot, Rt Hon Michael
Foster, Derek
Garrett, John *(Norwich South)*
Godman, Dr Norman A.
Griffiths, Nigel *(Edinburgh S)*
Haynes, Frank
Hinchliffe, David
Home Robertson, John
Howells, Dr. Kim (Pontypridd)
Hughes, John *(Coventry NE)*
Illsley, Eric
Jones, Barry *(Alyn & Deeside)*

Jones, Martyn *(Clwyd S W)*
Lamond, James
Leadbitter, Ted
Lewis, Terry
Loyden, Eddie
Macdonald, Calum A.
McFall, John
McKay, Allen *(Barnsley West)*
Mahon, Mrs Alice
Malins, Humfrey
Marek, Dr John
Martin, David *(Portsmouth S)*
Meacher, Michael
Meale, Alan
Michael, Alun
Michie, Bill *(Sheffield Heeley)*
Miller, Sir Hal
Moonie, Dr Lewis
Nellist, Dave
Neubert, Michael
Norris, Steve
Patchett, Terry
Pike, Peter L.
Powell, Ray *(Ogmore)*
Redmond, Martin
Richardson, Jo
Rogers, Allan
Rowlands, Ted
Skinner, Dennis
Smith, Andrew *(Oxford E)*
Smith, C. *(Isl'ton & F'bury)*
Steinberg, Gerry
Stott, Roger
Strang, Gavin
Taylor, Teddy *(S'end E)*
Turner, Dennis
Vaz, Keith
Walley, Joan
Wardell, Gareth *(Gower)*
Wareing, Robert N.
Welsh, Michael *(Doncaster N)*
Williams, Alan W. *(Carm'then)*
Winnick, David
Winterton, Mrs Ann
Wise, Mrs Audrey

Worthington, Tony
Young, David *(Bolton SE)*

Tellers for the Noes:
   Mr. Richard Shepherd and
   Mr. Ian McCartney.

Question accordingly agreed to.

Question put accordingly, That the Bill be now read a Second time:—

The House divided: Ayes 157, Noes 88.

Division No. 223]   **[10.14 pm**

AYES

Alexander, Richard
Alison, Rt Hon Michael
Alton, David
Arnold, Jacques *(Gravesham)*
Aspinwall, Jack
Atkins, Robert
Baker, Rt Hon K. *(Mole Valley)*
Beith, A. J.
Bellingham, Henry
Bendall, Vivian
Bennett, Nicholas *(Pembroke)*
Bevan, David Gilroy
Blackburn, Dr John G.
Boscawen, Hon Robert
Boswell, Tim
Bottomley, Peter
Bottomley, Mrs Virginia
Braine, Rt Hon Sir Bernard
Brazier, Julian
Bright, Graham
Brooke, Rt Hon Peter
Bruce, Malcolm *(Gordon)*
Carlisle, Kenneth *(Lincoln)*
Chapman, Sydney
Clark, Sir W. *(Croydon S)*
Coombs, Anthony *(Wyre F'rest)*
Cope, Rt Hon John
Cormack, Patrick
Curry, David
Dorrell, Stephen
Douglas-Hamilton, Lord James
Durant, Tony
Evennett, David
Fallon, Michael
Fearn, Ronald
Field, Barry *(Isle of Wight)*
Fookes, Dame Janet
Forman, Nigel
Forth, Eric
Franks, Cecil
Freeman, Roger
French, Douglas
Garel-Jones, Tristan
Gill, Christopher
Gow, Ian
Grant, Sir Anthony *(CambsSW)*
Greenway, Harry *(Ealing N)*
Greenway, John *(Ryedale)*
Gregory, Conal
Griffiths, Sir Eldon *(Bury St E')*
Ground, Patrick
Gummer, Rt Hon John Selwyn
Hamilton, Hon Archie *(Epsom)*
Hamilton, Neil *(Tatton)*
Hampson, Dr Keith
Hannam, John
Hargreaves, Ken *(Hyndburn)*
Harris, David
Hawkins, Christopher
Hayward, Robert
Heathcoat-Amory, David
Heseltine, Rt Hon Michael
Hind, Kenneth
Hordern, Sir Peter
Howard, Michael
Howarth, Alan *(Strat'd-on-A)*
Howarth, G. *(Cannock & B'wd)*
Howells, Geraint

Hughes, Robert G. *(Harrow W)*
Hunt, David *(Wirral W)*
Irvine, Michael
Jack, Michael
Jackson, Robert
Janman, Tim
Jones, Gwilym *(Cardiff N)*
Jopling, Rt Hon Michael
Kennedy, Charles
Key, Robert
Kilfedder, James
Kirkhope, Timothy
Kirkwood, Archy
Knapman, Roger
Knight, Greg *(Derby North)*
Knight, Dame Jill *(Edgbaston)*
Knowles, Michael
Lang, Ian
Lawrence, Ivan
Lee, John *(Pendle)*
Lightbown, David
Lilley, Peter
Livsey, Richard
Lloyd, Sir Ian *(Havant)*
Lloyd, Peter *(Fareham)*
Macfarlane, Sir Neil
MacKay, Andrew *(E Berkshire)*
Maclean, David
McLoughlin, Patrick
McNair-Wilson, Sir Michael
Major, Rt Hon John
Marshall, John *(Hendon S)*
Maude, Hon Francis
Mills, Iain
Miscampbell, Norman
Mitchell, Andrew *(Gedling)*
Mitchell, Sir David
Moate, Roger
Montgomery, Sir Fergus
Moore, Rt Hon John
Morrison, Sir Charles
Moss, Malcolm
Moynihan, Hon Colin
Mudd, David
Nelson, Anthony
Nicholson, David *(Taunton)*
Nicholson, Emma *(Devon West)*
Paice, James
Parkinson, Rt Hon Cecil
Patnick, Irvine
Patten, Chris *(Bath)*
Pawsey, James
Peacock, Mrs Elizabeth
Portillo, Michael
Price, Sir David
Raison, Rt Hon Timothy
Redwood, John
Riddick, Graham
Roe, Mrs Marion
Rost, Peter
Rumbold, Mrs Angela
Sainsbury, Hon Tim
Shaw, David *(Dover)*
Shepherd, Colin *(Hereford)*
Skeet, Sir Trevor
Speller, Tony
Spicer, Michael *(S Worcs)*
Steel, Rt Hon David

Stradling Thomas, Sir John
Sumberg, David
Summerson, Hugo
Taylor, Matthew *(Truro)*
Thorne, Neil
Thornton, Malcolm
Thurnham, Peter
Townend, John *(Bridlington)*
Trippier, David
Trotter, Neville
Twinn, Dr Ian
Waddington, Rt Hon David
Wallace, James

Waller, Gary
Warren, Kenneth
Wheeler, John
Widdecombe, Ann
Wood, Timothy
Woodcock, Dr. Mike
Young, Sir George *(Acton)*
Younger, Rt Hon George

Tellers for the Ayes:
   Mr. James Arbuthnot and
   Mr. Tim Devlin.

NOES

Adams, Allen *(Paisley N)*
Armstrong, Hilary
Barnes, Harry *(Derbyshire NE)*
Barron, Kevin
Battle, John
Beaumont-Dark, Anthony
Bell, Stuart
Bermingham, Gerald
Bidwell, Sydney
Bonsor, Sir Nicholas
Bowden, Gerald *(Dulwich)*
Brown, Nicholas *(Newcastle E)*
Buckley, George J.
Caborn, Richard
Callaghan, Jim
Campbell-Savours, D. N.
Clark, Dr David *(S Shields)*
Clarke, Tom *(Monklands W)*
Clay, Bob
Cohen, Harry
Cook, Frank *(Stockton N)*

Cousins, Jim
Cryer, Bob
Cunliffe, Lawrence
Dalyell, Tam
Davies, Rt Hon Denzil *(Llanelli)*
Davis, Terry *(B'ham Hodge H'l)*
Dixon, Don
Duffy, A. E. P.
Eadie, Alexander
Eastham, Ken
Evans, John *(St Helens N)*
Flynn, Paul
Foot, Rt Hon Michael
Foster, Derek
Fraser, John
Garrett, John *(Norwich South)*
Godman, Dr Norman A.
Griffiths, Nigel *(Edinburgh S)*
Hanley, Jeremy
Haynes, Frank
Hinchliffe, David

Home Robertson, John
Hughes, John *(Coventry NE)*
Illsley, Eric
Jones, Barry *(Alyn & Deeside)*
Jones, Martyn *(Clwyd S W)*
Lamond, James
Lewis, Terry
Loyden, Eddie
McCartney, Ian
Macdonald, Calum A.
McFall, John
McKay, Allen *(Barnsley West)*
Mahon, Mrs Alice
Malins, Humfrey
Martin, David *(Portsmouth S)*
Meacher, Michael
Meale, Alan
Michael, Alun
Michie, Bill *(Sheffield Heeley)*
Moonie, Dr Lewis
Nellist, Dave
Neubert, Michael
Norris, Steve
Patchett, Terry
Pike, Peter L.

Powell, Ray *(Ogmore)*
Redmond, Martin
Richardson, Jo
Rowlands, Ted
Ruddock, Joan
Skinner, Dennis
Smith, Andrew *(Oxford E)*
Smith, C. *(Isl'ton & F'bury)*
Smith, J. P. *(Vale of Glam)*
Smith, Tim *(Beaconsfield)*
Steinberg, Gerry
Strang, Gavin
Taylor, Teddy *(S'end E)*
Vaz, Keith
Walley, Joan
Wardell, Gareth *(Gower)*
Wareing, Robert N.
Welsh, Michael *(Doncaster N)*
Winnick, David
Wise, Mrs Audrey
Young, David *(Bolton SE)*

Tellers for the Noes:
   Mr. Richard Shepherd and
   Mrs. Ann Winterton.

Question accordingly agreed to.

Bill read a Second time and committed.

BUSINESS OF THE HOUSE

Ordered,

That, at this day's sitting, the Employment Bill and the Pesticides (Fees and Enforcement) Bill may be proceeded with, though opposed, until any hour.—*[Mr. Heathcoat-Amory.]*

Employment Bill

Postponed proceeding on further consideration of the Bill, as amended (in the Standing Committee), resumed.

New Clause 19

INTEREST ON INDUSTRIAL TRIBUNAL AWARDS

'In Schedule 9 to the 1978 Act (procedure etc. of industrial tribunals), for paragraphs 6A there shall be substituted the following paragraph—

"6A—(1) Industrial tribunals shall have the power to award simple interest on sums payable in pursuance of their decisions (principal awards) in accordance with this paragraph.

(2) The decision as to whether to award for interest on a principal award shall be in the discretion of the tribunal, but it shall be for the party against whom the principal award is made to show cause why some interest should not be awarded.

(3) Interest shall be awarded at a rate not exceeding the rate for the time prescribed pursuant to section 17 of the Judgments Act 1838.

(4) Interest shall accrue on all sums awarded by a tribunal, without any need for a decision to that effect by the tribunal, at the rate referred to in subparagraph (3) above from the date when the tribunal's decision is sent to the parties with the date of payment.

(5) The tribunal shall have no power to exclude the application of subparagraph (4) above.

(6) Interest shall not be awarded for a period commencing before:

(a) in the case of an award under section 53(4) of section 72 of this Act, the effective date of termination as defined by section 55;

(b) in the case of a redundancy payment, the relevant date defined by section 80 of this Act;

(c) in the case of an order under section 11(8) of this Act the date when the relevant deduction or payment was made;

(d) in the case of a guarantee payment, the date in respect of which the payment is claimed;

(e) in the case of a payment to which an employee is entitled by virtue of section 19 of this Act, the date when the period of suspension began;

(f) in any other, the date when application was made to the tribunal.".'.—[*Mr. Wallace.*]

Brought up, and read the First time.

10.27 pm

Mr. Wallace: I beg to move, That the clause be read a Second time.

The purpose of the new clause is to introduce, at the discretion of the tribunal, interest on awards made by the tribunal from dates preceding the announcement of the decision to make an award and for compulsory interest from the making of the award.

I understand that last year there was a consultative paper published by the Department of Employment indicating an intention to bring in interest on tribunal awards, although draft regulations are still awaited. This would appear an appropriate opportunity to press ahead with that.

The powers under schedule 9 of the Employment Protection Act 1978 invest the Secretary of State with power to confer interest on tribunal awards, but experience has shown that that power has seldom, if ever, been used. Indeed, the power is only to award interest on sums from the date at which the judgment is made and not the date from which the wrong has been perpetrated and in respect of which an award has been made. That differs from most other cases in which there has been a delict or a tort, where the interest is usually payable on a settlement from the date at which the wrong was committed.

I believe that the reason often proffered for that difference is that it is argued that the tribunal system operates more quickly and therefore people who are in receipt of awards have not been out of pocket for as long. I believe that it would be accepted by hon. Members on both sides of the House that litigation in the courts involving a tortious action can sometimes go on for many years. Therefore, there is often a significant difference. That ignores, however, those cases where for some reason or another, and sometimes not through any fault on the part of the claimant, a case going to a tribunal can be drawn out. It may even then go on to appeal, and, therefore, it can be some considerable time before an award is made.

The purpose of the new clause is to insert a new paragraph into schedule 9 of the 1978 Act to the effect that industrial tribunals would have the power to award simple interest on sums payable in pursuance of their decisions. That would be made at the discretion of the tribunal, although there would be a presumption in favour of interest being made payable, and it would be for the party on the losing side to put forward an argument showing why that should not be the case. One can foresee circumstances in which it might be argued that there had been time wasting caused by the claimants.

The interest awarded would be at the judicial rate prescribed by law under the Judgements Act 1838. Interest rates are not prescribed in such a statutory form north of the border, and it would not be unreasonable for Acts of Parliament that straddled the border to provide for the same rates.

10.30 pm

Subsection (4) relates to those sums of interest accruing from the date of announcement of the award. The rate would be compulsory, and not at the tribunal's discretion. Subsection (5) describes the dates from which the tribunal would have discretion to award interest. Subsection (6) should refer to section 53(4) "or" and not "of" section 72 and the effective date of termination. In cases of written or unfair dismissal, that would be the date of dismissal as defined by the legislation. In the case of redundancy payments, it would be the date of leaving. The purpose of the subsection is to make clear the date from which interest may be awarded.

On at least two occasions the judiciary has expressed a view on the tribunal's lack of power in awarding interest. In 1981 in UCATT *v.* Brain in the Court of Appeal, Lord Justice Donaldson, who is now Master of the Rolls, said:

"There is no power to award interest on money awarded by a Tribunal as compensation for unfair dismissal ... Whatever the reason, I think the time has come when Parliament, if it has a convenient opportunity, ought to consider whether it is really right that employees who are unfairly dismissed should not only have to wait for their money, which may be inevitable, but when they do wait for it they should get compensation in depreciated currency as a result of the passage of time and without interest."

That is a powerful judicial dictum. Lord Justice Donaldson calls for Parliament to consider this matter at "a convenient opportunity" and I can think of no more convenient opportunity for the House to address itself to a judicial plea than 10.31 pm on Report on the Employment Bill.

In the 1987 Caledonian Mining case Mr. Justice Popplewell echoed Lord Justice Donaldson's plea and said:

"We cannot pass from this case without expressing our dismay at the present position about interest. It will be observed that these men were dismissed over three years ago and have therefore been left out of their money for some time. The time that it has taken for this matter to be resolved is due to no fault of theirs. It is difficult to understand why interest which is available to parties in the high court should not be available to litigants before an Industrial Tribunal which is intended to be less formal. It is a blot on the administration of justice."

Those are strong words from the judicial bench.

I hope that the House will take this opportunity to remove this blot on the administration of justice. The new clause does not insist on interest rates above the level that would normally be expected to be paid in judicial cases. It reflects the concern which has been expressed more than once by the judiciary. It tries to tackle an anomaly.

There has been little give in Committee and on Report by the Government on Opposition amendments. I hope that the new clause commends itself to the Government. Even if the Minister tells us that the wording is not suitable, an undertaking to introduce the measure in another place in a proper form would suit our purposes. I commend the new clause to the House. It will ensure that there is greater justice for those who take their case to an industrial tribunal and are successful.

The Parliamentary Under-Secretary of State for Employment (Mr. Patrick Nicholls): The hon. Member for Orkney and Shetland (Mr. Wallace) is entirely right to imply that throughout Committee we always responded to good points. I assure the hon. Gentleman that our attitude this evening will adhere to that tradition to the full.

The effect of the new clause is twofold. First, it would provide directly for interest to accrue from the promulgation of industrial tribunal decisions and so bypass the Secretary of State's existing order-making power under the Employment Protection (Consolidation) Act 1978, as amended, which provides for interest on tribunal awards. Secondly, it would give industrial tribunals a discretion to provide for interest on awards to accrue, even before the promulgation of their decisions.

The first of those aims is unnecessary. In the consultation paper on industrial tribunals issued last year, to which the hon. Member for Orkney and Shetland referred, we stated our intention of implementing the order-making power in the 1978 Act to enable interest to be payable on tribunal awards. The proposals in the consultation paper were generally welcomed and, on present plans, the necessary order will be laid later this year. While it may be argued that there may have been some delay on this, I hope that the hon. Gentleman will accept that his new clause is, in the event, unnecessary.

The second aim of the new clause—to provide for interest to apply even before a tribunal award—is unacceptable. In our view, the existing powers in the 1978 Act as amended are perfectly adequate and strike a fair balance between the interests of the applicant and the interests of the respondent. Therefore, the Government would say——

Mr. Wallace: The Under-Secretary talks about seeking power to award interest before a decision is made. I may have been ambiguous and I apologise to the House if I did not express myself clearly. We seek interest from a date

preceding the award, from the date of the wrong. That applies in most cases of tort. Why should it be different in cases of redundancy or dismissal?

Mr. Nicholls: I am sorry if I misrepresented the hon. Gentleman. I was perhaps paying too much attention to the wording of the new clause rather than the intent as the hon. Gentleman expressed it. There is no doubt that the wording of the new clause, particularly subsection (6), if accepted, would enable interest to run, not merely from the date of judgment, but from some previous date. According to the wording of the new clause, it need not even be the date on which the action commenced. It could be the date from which the wrong accrued. That is a novel proposition, and certainly it is not the way in which the High Court or the county court work.

The hon. Gentleman referred to the words used by Mr. Justice Popplewell in the 1987 case, when he talked of "a blot on the administration of justice."

My recollection of that case, backed up by the fact that I have the law report in front of me, was that the point made in the judgment was that the defendants had been kept out of their money for three years. The judgment was given in 1987, although the tribunal hearings had been in 1984. Therefore, the blot on the administration of justice was the fact that three years had elapsed before judgment was given. It is precisely that sort of blot on justice with which the order, which will be laid in due course under the 1978 Act, would deal.

Mr. Christopher Hawkins (High Peak): Is my hon. Friend saying that to pay interest from the date of the wrongdoing would be novel? Surely the Inland Revenue charges interest on money owed to it, not from the date of the hearing but from the date from which the money was originally owed. That is similar to what is proposed by the new clause.

Mr. Nicholls: Mercifully, my duties do not include justifying the Inland Revenue and all its works. However, I hear what my hon. Friend says and feel more than a twinge of sympathy with him. What we propose about the implementation of the power in the 1978 Act is very much in accordance with general practice at the moment in relation to both High Court and county court matters, and deals precisely with the point about the blot on the administration of justice made by the hon. Member for Orkney and Shetland.

Mr. Haynes: It is all right for the Minister to brush to one side the question of Inland Revenue and interest. It works only one way, and it works only one way here. That is why the hon. Member for Orkney and Shetland (Mr. Wallace) tabled the new clause. Let us have the facts of life, and the Minister at the Box telling us home truths about interest in relation to tribunals. He knows as well as me that many workers suffer because they cannot get to the tribunal; there are that many wanting to go.

I can remember when the Government were telling the National Coal Board to close pits willy-nilly. Some people wanted to claim their rights at the tribunal for unfair dismissal—oh yes, there were a lot of unfair dismissals during the miners' dispute. The Minister will probably remember that, although he may not have been a Minister at the time; if I remember rightly, he used to sit at the back of the Chamber. I used to enjoy some of his contributions,

[*Mr. Haynes*]

and I followed some of them because they had upset me. He has upset me this evening as well, because he has not spoken correctly and truly to the new clause.

If a person owes money to the Inland Revenue he will be charged interest on it, but if it is the other way around —if the Inland Revenue owes the person money—there is no question of interest. [HON. MEMBERS: "There is."] It is high time that it was changed. Someone says, "There is", and I hope that it is a Whip: I hope that he will stand up and say what he means. I happen to know that it does not work that way round.

It could take a person three years to get his unfair dismissal case to the tribunal, given the Government's actions in industry and what they have done to workers' rights. Never mind the employer; this lot look after him. I am talking about the worker—the person who provides the necessary. The employer could not enjoy himself without the employee's contribution.

The new clause asks for fairness to the employee. If it is to take a long time for the case to reach the tribunal, interest should be paid: there is no doubt about that. I hope that the Minister will get up and say, "I agree with the new clause." He has not said that yet. Why does he not speak one way or the other, so that we know exactly where he stands? [*Interruption.*] That is a Whip interfering with what I am saying. He should not be saying anything. He is sat there yawping at me. If he wants to say anything, Mr. Deputy Speaker, he should indicate that to you and then get up and make his contribution.

If we vote on the new clause, I want to know which Lobby the Minister will go into. Will he support it or not? Sitting here listening, I thought, "I wonder who wrote that speech for him."

Mr. Ian McCartney (Makerfield): He should be sacked.

Mr. Haynes: I had the impression that the Minister did not really believe what he was saying. I hope that he will get up again and tell us—I gather that he is not going to get up again, but if there is a vote we shall find out which Lobby he goes into. If you will allow me, Mr. Deputy Speaker, I shall come back later and tell him what I think about him. He has the opportunity to speak again: I will give him the right—and I am sure that you will, Mr. Deputy Speaker—to stand up again at that Dispatch Box and tell us what he is going to do, what he really means and whether he supports the new clause.

The Minister may talk about Mr. Justice Popplewell, but we are talking about the facts of life. There is no need to point to the hon. Member for Orkney and Shetland; he has made his case. I am talking about the Minister. He sits on the Government Front Bench, and he speaks tonight on behalf of the Secretary of State, who sits there laughing his head off as though it were all a big joke. [*Interruption.*] Does someone want me to give way? [HON. MEMBERS: "No."] Hon. Members have taken me off my train of thought now; I do not know where I am. Oh yes, I was talking about the grin on the face of the Secretary of State.

This is a serious matter, and the right hon. Gentleman ought to know better. I have served with him on the Committee stages of various employment Bills. We got on ever so well, but tonight the Minister is not saying at the Dispatch Box the things that I want to hear. I hope that we shall hear whether or not he agrees with the new clause. If

he does not inform us verbally, we shall certainly know the answer if there is a vote. Make no mistake—I am coming back to that point.

10.45 pm

Mr. McCartney: I support the clause as someone with a number of years' experience representing employees at industrial tribunals. I refer to employers who either do not want a tribunal to consider a dismissal or who, in the period leading up to the hearing, employ methods, fair or foul, to ensure that the hearing does not take place for a considerable length of time after the dismissal in question.

The proposed clause is more than a form of redress for employees whose tribunal appeals are successful after legitimate delays, because it will also spell out the situation to employers who exploit the system to delay hearings or to dissuade employees from taking their cases to the tribunal. At every stage, employers and their solicitors are able to exploit the law to delay proceedings, to the point where the employee will in many cases give up, or where important witnesses to the dismissal, having themselves found employment elsewhere, are no longer easily available.

When a submission is made to a tribunal, it immediately writes to both parties requesting additional information to be passed to ACAS. That offers the bad employer acting against the employee's interests the first opportunity to procrastinate. That is the point at which consultations should take place with ACAS in the hope that an amicable settlement can be reached. If the employee's complaint is found to be legitimate, negotiations can be held and steps taken to resolve the matter, rather than resort to a formal hearing before the tribunal. Alternatively, it may be found that the employer acted reasonably in all the circumstances.

At present, not just weeks but months can go by before an employer agrees to meet with ACAS or to provide it with information on which to decide whether the employee's original submission to the tribunal was legitimate. After the existing initial stage that provides for ACAS to meet the employer and the employee, often the employer fails to provide sufficient information as the basis on which to hold discussions with all the parties concerned.

ACAS will give the employee, or his legal or trade union representative, an opportunity to address themselves to the evidence. By then, the claim may be into its sixth or ninth month, but the tribunal has not yet been consulted. The employee may then be forced to ask the tribunal for further particulars. The hon. Member for Orkney and Shetland (Mr. Wallace) may wish to press the Minister and ask him for further and better particulars and for the reasons why he will probably oppose the new clause.

Another few weeks, even two months, may go by as the employer is forced to provide further and better particulars. Then there is a meeting with ACAS after which ACAS submits a report to the tribunal chairman who may decide to have an initial hearing to decide whether the matter should proceed to a full hearing of the tribunal. Another eight to 12 weeks may go by until the date for a further hearing is fixed. It can take more than a year to establish whether there should be an initial hearing. It is completely unreasonable that under the law as it stands a former employee with a legitimate claim may be unable to put his case to a tribunal until more than 12 months after the original complaint.

After the initial hearing, a tribunal may decide that there are legitimate reasons for the complaint to have a full hearing. At that stage, the employer, or the employer's legal representative, may step in again seeking additional information from the former employee. For example, if female employees claim that they are receiving less remuneration than their male colleagues, the employer will present a detailed submission asking them for further details about how they calculate their claim in respect of the way in which they regard the job. That may take another three or four months. An employer may give ACAS the impression that it may consider negotiating. For example, the former employee may be in a new post and it may be necessary to calculate the time from the original dismissal to the taking up of the new post so that there can be appropriate discussions about compensation. While all that takes place, time is continuing. At the end of the negotiations the employer may then tell ACAS that it is prepared to go to a full hearing. Another few months have passed without the employee receiving a settlement.

When the case proceeds to a full hearing all the relevant documents have to be prepared. In many instances the cases are very complex in terms of trying to establish a case of unfair dismissal or constructive dismissal whereby there has been a transfer of undertakings and determining whether such a transfer took place under the Employment Protection Act 1975. It takes considerable time to establish evidence, particularly when an employer is not prepared to play his or her full part in establishing the facts of the case.

Ultimately it could take between 18 months and two years and sometimes longer, and cases become unnecessarily complicated by the misuse of legislation or the administrative practices of ACAS or the tribunal system. An employer can deliberately eke out the case to put off the potential hearing of a tribunal.

In many cases there are legitimate reasons for delay. For example, it is legitimate for ACAS to establish as soon as it can practically do so whether a former employee should proceed with a legitimate claim. It is also important that ACAS has the opportunity to try to negotiate a settlement. In most cases a negotiated settlement is in the best interests of the employee or group of employees who have been dismissed. There are legitimate reasons why substantial delays can occur before a tribunal hearing. That is covered in the first part of the new clause.

The Government will not accept, mainly because of their ambivalence to employees' rights, that a substantial number of employers are not prepared to abide by the rules and play fair or adopt a reasonable attitude. Under the new clause, if an employee succeeds in action taken against such unreasonable behaviour, the employer will have to meet the financial consequences of delaying the proceedings of the tribunal.

Under the current law, rightly there is an obligation on the former employee to establish the reasonableness of his case. At an early stage of the proceedings, if it is clear to the tribunal or ACAS that the employee's submission is unreasonable, it is made clear to the employee that if he proceeds the tribunal may award costs against him. I do not object to that provision because I accept that it is a safeguard against frivolous and vexatious applications against an employer. However, if such protection is available to an employer there must be a quid pro quo for employees, and the new clause offers ample opportunity for that.

Conservative Members have mentioned decisions of the High Court and Court of Appeal. However, they are insufficient to protect many people who try to use the tribunal system but are frustrated by the ability of employers, individually or through their solicitors, to use the system to the full. On many occasions, applicants withdraw rather than go through the lengthy procedures and worries of pursuing a complicated case of unfair dismissal.

Mr. Haynes: I am listening carefully to what my hon. Friend is saying. I am convinced that the Minister is following every word and fully understands what my hon. Friend is saying. My hon. Friend probably does not realise that the Minister is a solicitor; he is legally qualified. He has probably represented employers from time to time. My hon. Friend has specifically referred to delay. I believe that the Minister was appointed to his post as he knows employment law from A to Z because he has been involved in it himself.

Mr. McCartney: I thank my hon. Friend for his perceptive comments. I apologise to the Minister; I did not realise that he was a member of the legal profession—the best paid closed shop in Britain, although that is currently under threat if one believes the squeals of some Conservative Members during Prime Minister's Question Time.

I represented some women appearing before a tribunal in Liverpool. Prior to entering the room I was reviewing the evidence that we were to put to the tribunal. In the room next to us, which had wafer-thin walls, was the barrister representing the employer. He was telling the employer that his best course of action was to apologise to the chairman of the tribunal and accept the former employee's submissions as it had already cost him £160 for an hour's consultation and would cost him a further £160 an hour if he wanted to proceed. He felt that at the end of the day the employees' submission would be successful. When I and the two women concerned and some people waiting for another case heard that, we felt rather confident on going into the tribunal some minutes later.

11 pm

There is a substantial financial kickback for those who, on occasions, wish to eke out proceedings leading up to or during the tribunal. The payments for the legal profession are substantial. The barrister to whom I referred was acting honourably in advising his client not to proceed at the cost of £160 an hour but to quit before the cost increased. But that is not always the case and some tribunals have sat for more than a day when it has been clear from the outset that, on the evidence provided, there should have been a settlement long before in favour of the former employees. Only the intransigence of the employer in trying to ensure that the tribunal did not take place or to frustrate it so that the case would not be put by the former employees has prevented such a settlement.

The hon. Member for Orkney and Shetland is right that in those circumstances a former employee should not lose out financially. There should be a penalty not only for being unable to come to an amicable arrangement but for having wasted the time of ACAS and the tribunal. There

[*Mr. McCartney*]

are occasions when people put up a vexatious defence to applications by former employees and in those instances they should be penalised financially.

In other legislation the Government have introduced financial penalties to prevent organisations or individuals from utilising tribunals. The most recent example is the Secretary of State for the Environment's instructions to impose severe financial penalties on developers and local authorities who continue with appeals against certain decisions.

The principle has already been acceded to by the Government on the misuse of tribunal and appeal procedures in other areas, so why, in the area of industrial relations, do the Government only grudgingly accept that such a problem exists but do nothing to protect employees against the misuse of the system by employers? Is it not probably because pressure from some employers' organisations is somewhat clouding the Minister's view about such matters? On the one hand, the Government give the impression of providing additional employees' rights, but the application of the legislation reduces employees' abilities and allows the employers free range to frustrate the ability of former employees to seek redress at industrial tribunals.

Mr. Leadbitter: Will my hon. Friend put the position in a nutshell? As I understand it, the new clause does not ask the Government to deviate from the general principle of simple interest at the point of award but says that the simple interest on the award shall be paid from the point of dismissal. That is not a major step for the Government. Will my hon. Friend suggest at an appropriate point that we are not moving away from the general principle that the Government have already accepted—that simple interest at the point of award is apparently acceptable? We are asking, in the name of natural justice, that simple interest shall be payable from the point of dismissal.

Mr. McCartney: My hon. Friend is right. The Government should accept that an employer who frustrates the attempts of a former employee to have a case considered by a tribunal or who extends unnecessarily the proceedings leading up to a tribunal hearing—when in the view of ACAS at the secondary stage it was a case which was worthy of consideration by a tribunal—should suffer a financial penalty. An employer in that position should face a financial penalty if, at the end of the day, the former employee succeeds with his or her case. Why do the Government consider that to be unreasonable?

Mr. Allan Rogers (Rhondda): Does my hon. Friend accept that the Government's position on this matter is not clouded or distorted by recommendations that may have been made by employers' organisations? Their position arises simply from the political prejudice of the Minister and his colleagues, who hold an "employee bad, employer good" view. No pressure is being placed on the Minister to refuse to make the change to the Bill that we recommend. His political dogma and prejudice will not allow him to accept a simple amendment such as this.

Mr. McCartney: My hon. Friend is probably right. Hon. Members who serve on a regular basis on Committees examining Bills know only too well how the Government refuse to accept amendments which would clearly improve the legislation under consideration. I see my hon. Friend the Member for Jarrow (Mr. Dixon) looking at me invitingly. I assure him that I am not making an oblique reference to another measure. Clearly, we are batting on a sticky wicket in trying to argue for common sense, for a sense of justice and for fair play. We are trying to ensure that when legislation leaves this place it will work. The Government have already secured the principle of the Bill in Committee and on the Floor of the House. Let us now try to improve it.

Mr. Leadbitter: My hon. Friend will be aware that, having accepted as a reasonable principle that simple interest shall be paid from the point of dismissal, the new clause provides that if an employer can show just cause why it should not be paid, that claim will be taken into account and, if proven, accepted. The onus is on the employer to show why it should not be paid. In other words, there is no reason why the Government should not accept the new clause.

Mr. McCartney: My hon. Friend is correct, and I can give an example of the way in which legislation works in that way now at the conclusion of a tribunal hearing. I am thinking of what happens when there is an application for costs in addition to normal costs, either because the employer's application was vexatious or because the timescale involved in bringing witnesses was extended beyond what had been anticipated, making the cost of reimbursing witnesses more expensive. At that stage a request can be, and usually is, made to the chairman of the tribunal. At that point the employer can object, on two grounds: on the ground of the principle that the payment should be made and, if that falls, on the ground of the level of the reimbursement. In either case he can request that the former employee or his representative go on the witness stand under oath and establish the facts on the basis of which the application is made. Only after that procedure does the chairman of the tribunal either give a ruling or consult with his two colleagues and come back with a decision.

In every instance the rights of the employer are protected and that is precisely what the position would be in respect of any tribunal after the acceptance of this clause. The employer's rights would be protected absolutely both by the way that the clause is worded and by the way that it would be applied in due course by the tribunal.

So the position is absolutely clear. The Minister cannot argue that the clause has a major defect in the sense that it undermines the rights of the employer at the tribunal in the calculation of interest. The employer is protected throughout. The only change that this clause makes is to make it clear to those employers who wish to undermine the tribunal system that there will be a financial penalty to be met if at the end of the day their case is not accepted by the tribunal. It is as simple and as clear as that and I cannot think of any reason why the Government cannot accept this new clause willingly. Let us make the best of this bad Bill and at least improve it in some ways.

Throughout the procedure of getting to a tribunal the onus is on the employee to show that there is good cause to submit the complaint to a tribunal. The employee submits it to a tribunal in the absolute knowledge that if the application is judged vexatious or there is anything wrong with the way in which the evidence is produced to the tribunal and if the hearing goes against him he can be liable for substantial costs. If that is the position for employees now, why should it not be the position for employers after the passing of this Bill?

Ms. Jo Richardson (Barking): We shall be voting with the hon. Member for Orkney and Shetland (Mr. Wallace) on this interesting, ingenious and useful new clause. We have heard a very powerful case put by my hon. Friend the Member for Makerfield (Mr. McCartney), who is clearly an expert on this matter. We should all be grateful to him for the way in which he described the various cases.

We have all come across cases in our own experience, either as Members of Parliament, or perhaps in a former life, or perhaps in a double life if we are continuing that former life while being a Member of Parliament, as some hon. Members seem to be doing. In my own limited experience as a constituency Member—and I mean limited by being a Member of Parliament—I have found a very large number of cases over the years of people who have had to wait months and months, not knowing what is happening, when their case will come to court or when the appeal will be heard. Why should it always be the employer who has the whip hand, as it were, and who can always in some way, often ingeniously, put things off? Cases of unfair dismissal always disadvantage the aggrieved person throughout the procedure.

I find it amazing that the Minister can toss the new clause aside in so brief and dismissive a way. At the beginning of his remarks, I thought that he was going to accept it because he seemed to be sympathetic to the first point. We are, of course, glad to hear that the Government will eventually—whenever "eventually" is—lay an order. However, why should we have to wait for that? Why should we always be pushing when there is, apparently, an open door? The Government themselves have introduced the Employment Bill. If the Government are as near as the Minister says to introducing such a provision and he has an order ready to be laid, why did he not include this provision in the Bill? Why did he leave it out and why is he still leaving it out?

11.15 pm

The Minister referred to the point about interest being payable at the point of dismissal or, as he said, when the wrong occurred. Why not? My hon. Friend the Member for Ashfield (Mr. Haynes), I believe——

Mr. Haynes: Yes, my dear.

Ms. Richardson: Do not "my dear" me. My hon. Friend, in his usual style of hitting straight between the eyes, after which they all fell down laughing, put his finger on the point. He has shown that the point about the Inland Revenue—which Conservative Members, not Opposition Members, have raised—is the most telling. In my experience as a Member of Parliament dealing with constituency cases, whenever the Revenue is owed money, it wants its interest immediately from the point at which the money was owed. Sometimes people have the temerity when they are owed money as taxpayers—which frequently happens—to say, "I want money on the interest you have been holding from me". It may have been held for some time if there has been a mistake for several years. However, I have never found a way of persuading the Inland Revenue to pay interest. That is most unfair.

Mr. Jeremy Hanley (Richmond and Barnes): That is not true.

Ms. Richardson: I should be delighted if the hon. Gentleman would tell me how to persuade the Revenue.

Mr. Hanley: It is not fair to say that the Inland Revenue does not pay interest on overdue tax because it does. As a professional chartered accountant, my experience is that it has always been most fair. I have no brief to defend the Inland Revenue on this matter. I am merely trying to explain my experience.

Ms. Richardson: The hon. Gentleman is a chartered accountant. The majority of my constituents do not have chartered accountants to do their accounts. *[Interruption.]* Hold on a moment. They simply know that they are owed money. At some stage, they are told by the Revenue that a mistake has been discovered and that they are owed some money. Perhaps I should have come to the hon. Member for Richmond and Barnes (Mr. Hanley) professionally. I have had several cases over the years in which I have written to the Revenue and have said that a woman or man has been owed money for two or three years. I have asked why the interest cannot be paid, but I have never won a case yet.

Mr. Rogers: Will my hon. Friend press the hon. Member for Richmond and Barnes (Mr. Hanley) on this issue? I have never heard of an instance in which the Inland Revenue has paid interest on moneys that have been paid by a taxpayer and which it is to refund. I hope that my hon. Friend will press the hon. Gentleman to give one instance in which the Inland Revenue has done so.

Ms. Richardson: I should be glad if the hon. Member for Richmond and Barnes would do that.

Mr. Hanley: Not only is interest payable in the circumstances that have been described; it is even tax free.

Ms. Richardson: The hon. Gentleman should conduct a seminar, in his capacity as a chartered accountant, to tell Members of Parliament how to tackle the Revenue on behalf of their constituents. I have certainly never come across such a case.

Mr. Hawkins: It is simple. One merely appeals against an assessment and if one wins the appeal, interest will be awarded against the Inland Revenue.

It is a side issue whether the Revenue pays, as well as receives, interest. The important point is that it is not normal in legislation for interest to be paid from the date of the event—from the date on which it is owing. I should love someone to comment on what Mr. Justice Popplewell said. The injustice to which I believe he was referring was not the payment of interest from the date of the court case; it was the payment of interest in the case where employers purposely delayed the case, sometimes for three years, and so deprived the person who should have received money of the interest that he could easily have earned in a building society. That is the injustice which we have been asked to put right but which, I am sad to say, we do not put right in the Bill.

Ms. Richardson: To return to the Inland Revenue point, perhaps we are talking about two different angles. The hon. Members for High Peak (Mr. Hawkins) and for Richmond and Barnes appear to be thinking of different circumstances. Suppose that a person claims that he or she

[*Ms. Richardson*]

has been overpaying tax, engages an accountant—or anyway knows how to proceed—and goes to appeal. The outcome of that appeal may be a decision that interest is payable. I can envisage that happening. But I am thinking about a different kind of case, in which the Revenue has written to someone saying, "Dear Sir"—it is never "Dear Sir or Madam"—"We have found that we have made a mistake. We owe you £200, which we took from you wrongly in 1978." In that case, it is not a question of going to appeal; the Revenue has admitted its mistake. But even if one writes to the Revenue and says, "You owe that person interest," the person never gets the interest out of the Revenue. I beg the hon. Members for High Peak and for Richmond and Barnes to think about that point. We are not talking about the professional cases in which the taxpayer goes to appeal. That is different, I agree.

Mr. Rogers: That is an award.

Ms. Richardson: Yes, it is an award.

Let me return to the main point, as I want to leave time for the Member for Orkney and Shetland to reply——

Mr. McCartney: Conservative Members may not concede the point about the Inland Revenue but we should draw the Minister's attention to the booklet issued by the Department of Employment about industrial tribunal procedures, page 11 of which deals with the award of costs or expenses. It advises employees about the awards of costs and expenses against them and says:

"an award of costs may follow a warning given at a pre-hearing assessment."

I referred to that in my remarks. It continues:

"This may apply even if the application is withdrawn and the case does not go on to a hearing."

That clearly states that an employee can have costs awarded against him backdated to the date on which the application was made. The calculation could only be made from that date. The award of costs could only be for the period from the date on which the application was made to the date on which it was withdrawn. The point is already conceded in respect of employees in the Department's own booklet, yet the Government are still not prepared to meet the request in respect of employers.

Ms. Richardson: My hon. Friend has made an excellent point, and I hope that the Minister will look again at the booklet, in which the position is simply stated. I hope that the Minister will think again. The hon. Member for Orkney and Shetland has made a good and honest attempt, and introduced a very good debate, in trying to persuade the Department of the justice of what he and we believe.

I hope that the House will support new clause 19. If it is in some way defective, the Minister can have it redrafted and then reintroduce it on another occasion. It is not good enough for him simply to say that the first part of the new clause is not necessary because, at some future date, he will lay an order and with little explanation to say that the second part is not acceptable.

Mr. Wallace: This has been a somewhat longer debate than I had anticipated, but, as the hon. Member for Barking (Ms. Richardson) said, it has been a good debate. I welcome the Opposition's support for the new clause. It is regrettable that the Minister's response was so brief and

so dismissive. I welcome his announcement that the long-awaited regulations will be tabled in the not-too-distant future. However, I am sure that he would accept that that goes only a small way towards what the new clause seeks to achieve.

A fair point was made about why the position should be any different between the Inland Revenue charging interest and an employee charging interest when the payment has been delayed for some considerable time and he has, therefore, lost the opportunity of gaining interest on that capital. Part of the purpose of the new clause is to rectify that position. If someone has pursued a claim for redundancy through an industrial tribunal and been given a lump sum award at that time, he could have invested it and gained interest. Why should he be denied interest on that money which, over some years—or even one year with the current rate of inflation under this Government—has been devalued? I disagree with the suggestion of the hon. Member for Makerfield (Mr. McCartney) that there should be some penalty. Interest is not a penalty; it is a fair sum.

Mr. Leadbitter: The hon. Gentleman is on the right track. The date of that award is neither significant nor pertinent because the award itself relates to dismissal. Interest on the award should therefore be payable from the date of dismissal.

Mr. Wallace: The hon. Gentleman is right. I am not trained in English law, but Professor David Walker, an eminent professor of Scots law, said in the second edition of his work on delict:

"Accordingly the earliest date from which interest may be ordered to run is the date when the right of action arose."

The word "may" makes it discretionary and what the new clause proposes is discretionary.

This is the United Kingdom Parliament, and if the Minister feels uneasy because the new clause does not coincide with what he knows to be English law, I ask him to think again because it may well coincide with what Professor Walker says is possible under Scots law. It is not intended in any way to be a penalty; it is intended to ensure justice and fairness. In the absence of any assurance that that point is taken on board by the Government, we will press the new clause to a Division.

Mr. Nicholls: Even in this relatively short debate a number of important points have been raised to which I wish to respond. It is obvious to me, if not to every hon. Member in the Chamber, that the Opposition have been pushing at an open door. The principle of interest being payable on awards made by industrial tribunals was conceded in the 1982 Act, which amended the 1978 Act. It has now been conceded in practice because the Government are consulting about a scheme for the payment of interest.

The hon. Member for Barking (Ms. Richardson) posed the perfectly fair question, why bother to do it that way when an appropriate Bill is going through Parliament? We believe that we have something rather better than a Bill —a statute with an order-making power. We have gone out to consultation and said that we will introduce a scheme later this year. So the principle was conceded as long ago as 1978 and the practice has now been conceded as well.

11.30 pm

The only point of difference between the hon. Gentleman and me is whether such a scheme should provide for the payment of interest as from the date of judgment or whether it should be from the date of wrongdoing. I heard what my hon. Friends said about the Inland Revenue. That is not an appropriate analogy. Insofar as it was appropriate, it was an expert opinion from chartered accountants. It was advice which on this occasion was free. Free advice from chartered accountants is a treasure much to be prized. My hon. Friend was wrong about interest being payable.

By far the better example was the reference to court cases by the hon. Member for Orkney and Shetland. The point about court cases is that the general rule is that interest runs from the time of judgment. In exceptional circumstances it can run from the time of wrongdoing, but in practice that happens only in exceptional circumstances because inevitably it can take a considerable time to get the hearing to court.

A great deal of play has been made of the Caledonian Mining case and the remarks of Mr. Justice Popplewell. One dislikes to blur an interesting debate by referring to facts, but the point about that case is that reference was made in the judgment to the plaintiffs having been kept out of their money for three years. That was the time it took from the case being heard at first instance until it was disposed of on appeal. It took only a few months to get the case to the tribunal. So the blot on justice that has been referred to time and time again relates not to the time in tribunals where cases are heard relatively quickly but to the date of judgment. That is the usual position. That is what applies in courts of law. That is why I say in this case that the Opposition are pushing at an open door.

Mr. Wallace *rose——*

Mr. Nicholls: I will give the hon. Gentleman the last chance.

Mr. Wallace: The Minister has conceded that it is more appropriate to look to courts but he said that there were exceptional circumstances where interest would be allowed from a date preceding the date of judgment. The new clause allows discretion. It is not mandatory. I accept that the presumption is in favour of it. I would see it as being very much second best, but would the Minister be more disposed towards the new clause if the presumption was reversed and the person had to argue for it? That would be better than what the Minister proposes, although it would not go as far as I would wish. Is the Minister prepared to consider that?

Mr. Nicholls: Obviously the hon. Gentleman is finally accepting that there is more force in what I said——

Mr. Haynes: On a point of order, Mr. Deputy Speaker. Is it right and proper for the Minister, during a debate of this kind, to say to an hon. Member that he will give him the last chance? I am asking for a ruling from the Chair. The way the Minister is carrying on is shocking, and I think you ought to tell him so, Mr. Deputy Speaker.

Mr. Deputy Speaker (Sir Paul Dean): I have heard nothing out of order from the Minister.

Mr. Nicholls: As the hon. Member for Orkney and Shetland well knows, we are dealing with a structure of tribunals where a case can be heard quickly, as opposed to

a court where it can take a considerable time. That is the significant difference, and that is why I cannot go all the way with the hon. Gentleman.

Mr. Rogers: I am participating in the debate at this stage because of the remark by the Minister about giving the hon. Member for Orkney and Shetland (Mr. Wallace) the last chance to speak. It is not the Minister who determines the length of debate.

The only reason the Government are not prepared to accept the new clause seems to be because of their political prejudice and deep-seated dogma on industrial relations. The whole basis of their presentation of the Bill is that they want to argue employer, good—employee, bad. If any hon. Member makes a constructive suggestion that would improve the Bill, as the hon. Member for Orkney and Shetland did, we see immediately the hackles of prejudice and dogma rise on the backs of Ministers.

It does not matter that my hon. Friend the Member for Makerfield (Mr. McCartney) or the hon. Member for Orkney and Shetland have put forward their case in a proper fashion. The Opposition's attitude to the debate is, in a sense, cynical, because we know that the Minister will not accept any proposition that is reasonably based.

When the Minister puts forward instances to justify the case, he does it without a sense of common justice and fair play. The litigants whom we are thinking about in this situation are ordinary people, who often receive wages, and who are involved in disputes, or, perhaps, are made redundant because of circumstances that are beyond their control. They are suddenly confronted with their employers being difficult and do not want—to use an expression that we use in the valleys—to give them their fair due for their legitimate rights.

Let us suppose that a person is entitled to £2,000 for a period of service of employment and, perhaps, an even longer period of future unemployment. If the employer is difficult, he can drag the matter out, as mentioned by the hon. Member for Orkney and Shetland, and by the time —at the Government's present rate of inflation—that £2,000 is paid, under the proposals in the Bill it could be worth considerably less. On the basis of common justice and fair play, it should be paid at the time that the person is due the money. It is not beyond an employer who is devious, or even just cheap—the sort of person who supports the Conservative party—to delay, knowing that at the end of the day the amount of money that he will pay out will be worth much less than at the time when it should have been paid.

The Government are wrong in not accepting this reasonable new clause. I know that if we argued right through the night we would not convince this Minister —the Minister who during the past year stood at the Dispatch Box and suggested that women should work in the coal mines, which was something that most people thought had gone out in the last century. A Minister who can justify that proposition could justify anything. One thing that I would not look for from this Minister is——

Mr. McCartney: On the question of compensation and its fairness, even when compensation must be paid, for example, when an employer refuses to make a reinstatement at the end of a tribunal—when an employee has sought reinstatement and not a financial contribution —in the calculation of the compensation for the failure to reinstate, there is a statutory requirement on the employee

[*Mr. McCartney*]

to prove that within the period leading up to the tribunal he has sought gainful employment. If that is not proven, the compensation can be reduced accordingly. Therefore, at all stages in the procedure there is an obligation on the employee that will determine the final amount of compensation. If that is the case for the employee, this minimal requirement on the employer should be accepted by the Minister.

Mr. Rogers: Yes, but my hon. Friend should not be surprised by the ethic put forward by the Government. It underlies the Government's attitude. They try to project that they are in support of individuals, that they protect individuals and that they want to look after individuals, but, of course, that is only applicable if the individual can buy into the legal system—if he can afford the legal system. For so many individuals the only way that they can get into the legal system is by forming associations or affiliations, such as trade unions. However, the Government have attacked trade unions and their ability to defend individuals. It is a concerted political attack based on their prejudices and political dogmas.

Mr. McCartney: My hon. Friend makes an interesting point about the Government's political dogma. Perhaps they do not want interest to be paid from the date of dismissal because of the Chancellor's high interest rate policy and the damage that will be done to employers who lose a case.

Mr. Rogers: I agree with my hon. Friend. The Government are concerned with, for example, the right of individuals in Poland to form themselves into a trade union. They mouth hypocritical statements about the rights of trade unions and blows for democracy. At the same time, they use the power of the state over individuals who want to exercise their trade union rights in this country.

The Government's pathological hatred of trade unions goes back to the Heath Government. We know its basis. I do not expect any common justice from the Government or the Minister. The time for reasonable arguments and debate in the Chamber has gone. On many issues, the Government say no, no, no. They decide where they want to go. The way in which the Government are trying to destroy the Health Service is just another symptom of their dogma. We are seeing in the Government's intransigence and negativeness their political prejudice and dogma. There has never been a more dogma-ridden Government in this century. I hope that we will press the motion to a vote.

Mr. Wallace: Yes.

Mr. Rogers: The hon. Member has agreed. Unless one of my colleagues speaks in the debate, the Division will come fairly soon.

Mr. Leadbitter: I notice that, in responding to the debate, the Minister appeared to have a brief before him. He appeared to present to the House something on which his mind was already made up. That is out of character for him.

Mr. Rogers: No.

Mr. Leadbitter: It is out of character because we are not asking a great deal in new clause 19. We are saying that the general principle has been accepted. We are talking only about the time scale.

The Minister referred to a state of wrongdoing. Once the tribunal makes a declaration in favour of an applicant —in this case, the employee—that state of wrongdoing is removed. The question is whether in a state of equity the person who has been given the award should have simple interest from the date of judgment or from the date of dismissal. The state of wrongdoing has been removed. Therefore, the new clause gives the Minister another point in his favour. If an employer can show just cause why interest shall not be paid from the date of dismissal, the tribunal will uphold his decision.

Why are the Government intervening in a democratic process? In effect, the tribunal says to the employer, "Your state of wrongdoing vis-a-vis the employee has been removed". It may take months for an employee to get his case before the tribunal, through no fault of his, so why cannot the award be bolstered by a state of equity, natural justice—whatever one calls it—and an innocent employee given simple interest from the date of dismissal?

Mr. McCartney: Will my hon. Friend refer to paragraph 6(b) of the new clause which says that interest shall not be awarded before

"in the case of a redundancy payment, the relevant date defined by section 90 of this Act;"?

It raises a curious anomaly in the Minister's case. If a redundancy took place, redundancy payments would be paid from the date of the redundancy, but if an appeal were made to a tribunal which decided that the redundancy was not a redundancy but an unfair dismissal, unless the new clause was accepted, the award would not start from the date of the redundancy, as a redundancy notice would require under the Employment Bill, but from the date of the tribunal. It would be completely wrong if, having proved at a tribunal that a redundancy did not exist, compensation was awarded only from the date of the tribunal, not the redundancy.

Mr. Leadbitter: My hon. Friend is correct. About a year ago an employee found himself in a difficulty, not of his own making, but due to a personality conflict between him and his chief officer. The young man went to a tribunal and was exonerated. However, when he returned to the local authority, which I shall not name because it would be imprudent to do so, it remained adamant and did not provide a response to the tribunal's decision.

Ordinary working people are not lawyers, but depend entirely upon their occupation. Therefore, they go to a tribunal in a state of complete innocence. They do not know what is going to happen. But those on the tribunal who professionally consider a person's predicament and decide to award in his or her favour are saying that he or she has been relieved of a state of wrongdoing. If the process has taken several months, it seems, in equity, that the award is intended to refer to the date of dismissal, not of the award.

I do not wish to take up too much time tonight, and the Minister may be unable to respond, but I wish to make the point that the Minister had a brief. I understand that because I have been here long enough. I am not recriminating the Minister; that is the last thing that I want to do. However, I would like to feel that the Minister will return to his Department and discuss the mood of the House with the Secretary of State for Employment.

On both sides of the House there is substance in the idea that an ordinary working person, having been exonerated by an award, could reasonably expect the award and the simple interest to come from the date of dismissal.

Mr. Rogers: I notice that when my hon. Friend appeals to the better nature of the Minister and Conservative Members, as he has in his speech, all he had by way of response was a rather cynical grin. I do not wish to make a personal statement against my hon. Friend, but I wish that he would not accord to Conservative Members virtues that do not belong to them. To suggest that they are reasonable people who will accept a reasonable case is not valid. They are motivated by political dogma and prejudice, and all the reasonable arguments that may be advanced fall on deaf ears.

Mr. Leadbitter: I understand my hon. Friend's view, but we are dealing with a limited number of cases, although it may vary according to the time of year. We are dealing with ordinary working people. I feel that I know the House of Commons. If the Minister is not in a position to give an undertaking now, I hope that he will understand the temper of the House. We are asking for something very small, although the principle is very important. If an hon. Member on either side of the House was placed in the position of an employee going before a tribunal and gained an award, would he find it difficult to understand that that award should apply from the date of dismissal and not from the date of the tribunal's judgment?

I hope that the Minister will discuss the matter with the Secretary of State. It is not important to him as a Minister, or to me, or to any hon. Member on either side of the House; we occupy favoured positions as elected Members of the House of Commons, and we are very well off. But we are talking about people who may be very poor indeed, and who need the benefit of our prudence.

Mr. Clelland: My hon. Friend the Member for Hartlepool (Mr. Leadbitter) has appealed to the Minister to look to the justice of the case being put forward. I feel, however, that here we are dealing not with justice but with attitudes. My hon. Friend the Member for Rhondda (Mr. Rogers) is quite right in that repect.

We may speak of the simple justice of giving someone interest on money that he may have been owed for a considerable time—for such cases are often delayed in the way described by my hon. Friend the Member for Makerfield (Mr. McCartney). We are discussing not only the payment of interest but the payment of the compensation itself, and often such compensation is inadequate, not only in terms of meeting the wrongdoing often involved in unfair dismissal or the denial of redundancy payments, but in terms of meeting the lost earnings that may have resulted.

In Committee, I drew the Minister's attention to a case on record in which an industrial tribunal found that an applicant had been unfairly dismissed. Winding up the case, the chairman said that had it not been for the legal maximum he would have been entitled to far more compensation, and that the tribunal would have wished to give him far more. Although such remarks were made by people who had been through the facts of the case, the

Minister was not willing to give way to that argument, and it is even less likely that he will give way to the argument being put tonight.

Mr. Rogers: I have been arguing on the basis that the Minister will not give way to any argument, because of his prejudices and dogma. One reason why he is not giving way on this issue may be what could loosely be termed political childishness. When he gave the hon. Member for Orkney and Shetland (Mr. Wallace) what he thought was his "last chance" to speak—some last chance that was— the Minister said that he had already conceded the point in principle, and that the Government were prepared to bring in the measure in an order at a later stage. Before my hon. Friend sits down, perhaps he will reflect on the motives behind the Government's attitude.

Mr. Clelland: Part of the problem is that when perfectly reasonable arguments are made by the Opposition in Committee or in the House, the Minister sees it as his job not to listen to them, and then to say, "That sounds all right to me. We may not agree with the wording, but we shall devise something that will better fit the Bill," but rather he takes a macho view and considers that his task is to defeat the Opposition rather than to produce reasonable legislation.

The attitude to which my hon. Friend the Member for Rhondda drew attention was amply displayed when we debated that part of the Bill dealing with employment rights.

Mr. McCartney: Perhaps my hon. Friend will probe the Minister as to his attitude towards the Employment Act 1982—the Tebbit Act—under which retrospective payments amounting to £2 million were made to 400 people who alleged unfair dismissal because of their refusal to join a trade union, when their cases had already been dismissed at tribunal hearings. Nevertheless, sections 1 and 2 of that Act enabled them retrospectively to enjoy huge awards.

Mr. Clelland: The Government's prejudices are well known, and my hon. Friend draws attention to a particular case that illustrates them. The Government have shown on many occasions that they can twist the law to favour their particular prejudices, while denying justice to those entitled to it.

In Committee, we suggested that from day one of their employment, people should be entitled to the full range of employment rights. The Minister's argument against that proposal was that employees would use those rights against their employers. That revealed that the view of the Minister and of the Government is that such rights serve not to protect employees against their employers but as weapons for employees to use against their employers. That reveals a great deal about the Minister's psychology when it comes to industrial relations, and says much about why he will not accept the justice for which the proposed new clause provides.

Question put, That the clause be read a Second time:—

The House divided: Ayes 60, Noes 154.

Division No. 224]   **[11.57 pm**

AYES

Alton, David	Battle, John
Armstrong, Hilary	Beith, A. J.
Barnes, Harry *(Derbyshire NE)*	Bell, Stuart
Barron, Kevin	Blunkett, David

Bruce, Malcolm *(Gordon)*
Buckley, George J.
Clay, Bob
Clelland, David
Crowther, Stan
Cryer, Bob
Cunliffe, Lawrence
Davis, Terry *(B'ham Hodge H'l)*
Dixon, Don
Evans, John *(St Helens N)*
Fearn, Ronald
Flynn, Paul
Foster, Derek
Fraser, John
George, Bruce
Godman, Dr Norman A.
Golding, Mrs Llin
Haynes, Frank
Home Robertson, John
Howells, Geraint
Hoyle, Doug
Hughes, John *(Coventry NE)*
Illsley, Eric
Kennedy, Charles
Leadbitter, Ted
Lewis, Terry
Livsey, Richard
McCartney, Ian

McKay, Allen *(Barnsley West)*
Meacher, Michael
Meale, Alan
Michael, Alun
Michie, Mrs Ray *(Arg'l & Bute)*
Mowlam, Marjorie
Nellist, Dave
Pike, Peter L.
Powell, Ray *(Ogmore)*
Prescott, John
Redmond, Martin
Richardson, Jo
Rogers, Allan
Salmond, Alex
Skinner, Dennis
Smith, Andrew *(Oxford E)*
Smith, J. P. *(Vale of Glam)*
Snape, Peter
Steel, Rt Hon David
Strang, Gavin
Wareing, Robert N.
Welsh, Andrew *(Angus E)*
Welsh, Michael *(Doncaster N)*
Wise, Mrs Audrey

Tellers for the Ayes:
    Mr. Archy Kirkwood and
    Mr. James Wallace.

NOES

Alexander, Richard
Alison, Rt Hon Michael
Amos, Alan
Arbuthnot, James
Arnold, Jacques *(Gravesham)*
Ashby, David
Aspinwall, Jack
Baldry, Tony
Batiste, Spencer
Bennett, Nicholas *(Pembroke)*
Bevan, David Gilroy
Blaker, Rt Hon Sir Peter
Boswell, Tim
Bottomley, Peter
Bottomley, Mrs Virginia
Braine, Rt Hon Sir Bernard
Brazier, Julian
Bright, Graham
Butterfill, John
Carlisle, Kenneth *(Lincoln)*
Carttiss, Michael
Chapman, Sydney
Coombs, Anthony *(Wyre F'rest)*
Cope, Rt Hon John
Davis, David *(Boothferry)*
Devlin, Tim
Dorrell, Stephen
Douglas-Hamilton, Lord James
Durant, Tony
Evennett, David
Fallon, Michael
Favell, Tony
Fishburn, John Dudley
Forman, Nigel
Forsyth, Michael *(Stirling)*
Forth, Eric
Fowler, Rt Hon Norman
Freeman, Roger
French, Douglas
Gardiner, George
Garel-Jones, Tristan
Gill, Christopher
Glyn, Dr Alan
Goodson-Wickes, Dr Charles
Gow, Ian
Greenway, John *(Ryedale)*
Griffiths, Sir Eldon *(Bury St E')*
Griffiths, Peter *(Portsmouth N)*
Gummer, Rt Hon John Selwyn
Hague, William

Hamilton, Hon Archie *(Epsom)*
Hamilton, Neil *(Tatton)*
Hampson, Dr Keith
Hanley, Jeremy
Hargreaves, A. *(B'ham H'll Gr')*
Hargreaves, Ken *(Hyndburn)*
Harris, David
Hawkins, Christopher
Heddle, John
Heseltine, Rt Hon Michael
Hind, Kenneth
Howarth, Alan *(Strat'd-on-A)*
Howarth, G. *(Cannock & B'wd)*
Hughes, Robert G. *(Harrow W)*
Hunt, David *(Wirral W)*
Irvine, Michael
Jack, Michael
Jackson, Robert
Jones, Gwilym *(Cardiff N)*
King, Roger *(B'ham N'thfield)*
Kirkhope, Timothy
Knapman, Roger
Knight, Greg *(Derby North)*
Knight, Dame Jill *(Edgbaston)*
Knowles, Michael
Knox, David
Lee, John *(Pendle)*
Lightbown, David
Lilley, Peter
Lloyd, Peter *(Fareham)*
Lyell, Sir Nicholas
Macfarlane, Sir Neil
Maclean, David
McLoughlin, Patrick
McNair-Wilson, P. *(New Forest)*
Malins, Humfrey
Martin, David *(Portsmouth S)*
Maude, Hon Francis
Maxwell-Hyslop, Robin
Mayhew, Rt Hon Sir Patrick
Meyer, Sir Anthony
Miller, Sir Hal
Mills, Iain
Mitchell, Andrew *(Gedling)*
Mitchell, Sir David
Moore, Rt Hon John
Morrison, Sir Charles
Moss, Malcolm
Moynihan, Hon Colin
Neubert, Michael

Nicholls, Patrick
Nicholson, David *(Taunton)*
Nicholson, Emma *(Devon West)*
Norris, Steve
Page, Richard
Paice, James
Patnick, Irvine
Patten, Chris *(Bath)*
Porter, David *(Waveney)*
Powell, William *(Corby)*
Raffan, Keith
Raison, Rt Hon Timothy
Redwood, John
Ridley, Rt Hon Nicholas
Rowe, Andrew
Rumbold, Mrs Angela
Ryder, Richard
Sainsbury, Hon Tim
Shaw, David *(Dover)*
Shepherd, Colin *(Hereford)*
Shersby, Michael
Smith, Tim *(Beaconsfield)*
Soames, Hon Nicholas
Speller, Tony
Spicer, Michael *(S Worcs)*
Stanbrook, Ivor
Stanley, Rt Hon Sir John
Stevens, Lewis
Stewart, Andy *(Sherwood)*
Stradling Thomas, Sir John

Sumberg, David
Summerson, Hugo
Taylor, Ian *(Esher)*
Taylor, Teddy *(S'end E)*
Thompson, Patrick *(Norwich N)*
Thorne, Neil
Thurnham, Peter
Townend, John *(Bridlington)*
Tracey, Richard
Trippier, David
Trotter, Neville
Twinn, Dr Ian
Vaughan, Sir Gerard
Waddington, Rt Hon David
Waller, Gary
Ward, John
Wardle, Charles *(Bexhill)*
Watts, John
Wells, Bowen
Widdecombe, Ann
Winterton, Mrs Ann
Winterton, Nicholas
Wood, Timothy
Woodcock, Dr. Mike

Tellers for the Noes:
    Mr. David Heathcoat-Amory
and
    Mr. Tom Sackville.

Question accordingly negatived.

Clause 7

REPEAL OR MODIFICATION OF PROVISIONS REQUIRING DIFFERENT TREATMENT OF DIFFERENT CATEGORIES OF EMPLOYEES

Mr. Lee: I beg to move amendment No. 2, in page 6, line 23, at end insert—

'(4A) In section 17 of the Offices, Shops and Railway Premises Act 1963 (fencing of exposed parts of machinery)—
    (a) subsection (3),
    (b) in subsection (4), the words from ", except when any" onwards, and
    (c) subsection (5),
shall cease to have effect.'

Mr. Deputy Speaker: With this it will be convenient to take Government amendments Nos. 8, 10 and 13.

Mr. Lee: These amendments to schedules 3 and 7 and clause 7 deal with a matter that is virtually a technicality, but they have been tabled to ensure that safety standards remain at the present high level. If the amendments are not passed, there is a theoretical possibility that young people and adults may be at risk from dangerous moving parts of certain kinds of machinery.

At the moment dangerous machinery must be fenced and people may not clean or maintain it while it is moving, with one exception, that if examination, lubrication or adjustment are "immediately necessary" while the machinery is in motion, regulations can be made to allow this. If they are made, they must specify that only persons over 18 can carry out this work—section 17(5). But such regulations have never been made. So at present the law is that no one cleans or maintains dangerous machinery while it is moving.

Since the regulations envisaged in the original Act, if they had been made, would have had to specify that the maintenance could have been done only by persons over 18, the provision allowing them was caught by our general principle that unused legislation curbing the work activities of under-18-year-olds should be repealed; and we have taken the advice of the Health and Safety Commission and repealed it.

But the result is that while regulations are no longer allowed to be made to specify that over-18-year-olds may carry out such work if it is immediately necessary, the work can, by virtue of section 17(3) and part of section 17(4), be done if, in the same way, it is immediately necessary, by anyone, without let or hindrance.

To ensure that our Bill maintains safety as well as removing this unused legislation, we also need to repeal the section of the Offices, Shops and Railway Premises Act 1963 which allows examination, lubrication or adjustment to be carried out on moving machinery if it is immediately necessary. If we did not, employers could ask persons of any age to maintain dangerous machinery while it is moving, with no precautionary regulations needing to be prescribed first.

There has never been a call for such regulations to be introduced. In other words, the kind of machinery that we are talking about does not need to be in motion for those maintenance purposes.

The effect of our amendments is that the requirement to fence these machines safely will now be an absolute requirement, thus maintaining if not improving safety standards. I hope that hon. Members will support the amendments.

12.15 am

Mr. Harry Barnes: There has been an amazing transformation in the Government, for they are now concerned with safety. They can claim, for the first time, to be showing some compassion. So far we have had to deal with a host of matters concerning young people, women in the pits and other issues on which the Government have refused to make any concessions. That is why I am suspicious about this series of Government amendments.

Why are they amending clause 7 in this way? After all, clause 8 is concerned with young people, and one would have thought that that, rather than clause 7, should be amended. Or perhaps we need an entirely new clause to deal with the safety aspects to which the amendment refers. Clause 7 is entitled:
"Repeal or modification of provisions requiring different treatment of different categories of employees."
It would be more correct to call it the clause which forces women to work underground in coal mines. That being so, we must ask whether the amendment is appropriate to that clause, subsection (1) of which amends the Mines and Quarries Act 1954 to stop winding and rope haulage and conveyors from being restricted to male usage only. Subsection (2) of the clause amends the same Act to allow women and young persons to do heavy underground work. Subsection (3) provides for women working underground to work significant numbers of hours and to work whole shifts involving overtime. Subsection (4) amends the Factories Act 1961 to allow women and young persons to clean machinery, especially underground machinery, in pits. Subsection (5) allows much of the same underground nightmare for women to be enforced in the schedules to the Bill.

Why are we now offered an amendment to such a clause by way of altering the Offices, Shops and Railway Premises Act 1963? There are not many offices, shops or railway premises down the pits, although there are man-riders, which presumably in future will be called man and

woman-riders or perhaps person-riders. There are also coal trucks which are sent along rails to enable the onsetter to send coal up to the surface. But they have more similarity with railways than with railway premises, shops and offices.

Amendment No. 2 is modest, as the Minister said, in that it excludes two and a half sections of section 17 of the Offices, Shops and Railway Premises Act 1963, presumably on the ground that they cover superfluous areas in terms of protection that at present exist for those guarding machines. Section 17(1), which will remain, says:
"Every dangerous part of any machinery used as, or forming, part of the equipment of premises to which this Act applies shall be securely fenced unless"—
and then we have the get-out bit—
"it is in such a position or of such construction as to be as safe to every person working in the premises as it would be if securely fenced."
I am sure that employers could drive a horse and cart through both provisions. Why is it necessary to remove the provisions in subsection (3), part of subsection (4) and subsection (5), because employers will be able to carry on doing what they have been doing with the legislation as it stands at the moment? The removal of those subsections makes little difference. On the surface it improves the former Act but there is really little advantage.

Section 17(5) of the 1963 Act, which is to be removed, is a key element for the Government's purpose. It refers to
"such persons who have attained the age of eighteen".
There is no mention of underground coal mines, women in the pit or the primitive working conditions in a mine, including the absence of lavatory facilities, which we discussed at great length in Committee, and the other problems that exist in connection with women working in a pit, unless there is a vast improvement in conditions for everybody working in a pit.

Government amendment No. 2 has more to do with clause 8 of the Bill because that is concerned with the removal of restrictions relating to the employment of young persons. Although young persons are normally in this legislation referred to as persons aged 16 to 18, at least those over 18 are a bit nearer to this clause than they are to the clause that deals with women in the pit. It would be more appropriate with regard to the Offices, Shops and Railway Premises Act 1963, which covers wider areas than the pit, to include it in a clause such as that.

The paradox is that any future Government scheme to protect women by removing them from the primitive conditions in a pit would have to alter all the subsections of clause 7 except the provision that is in front of us at the moment. That indicates to me that this provision is irrelevant to the clause that we are discussing. Does it not show that the amendment is out of place here? Perhaps the Government should go back to the drawing board. They will find drawing boards in offices, shops and railway premises but not in pits—unless they are used as shovels in the pit as part of the toilet facilities.

Mr. Lee: The hon. Gentleman is being uncharacteristically churlish about an amendment that initially he supported in broad terms.

To answer his technical questions, the reason we are altering clause 7 and not clause 8 is that the amendment essentially concerns treating young people and adults the same rather than simply removing a restriction on young

[*Mr. Lee*]

people. The Government amendment makes doubly sure that young people will not be at risk from maintaining moving machinery.

We are supported in our approach by the Health and Safety Commission, which the Opposition in Committee continually quoted at us. The commission agrees that section 17(5) should be repealed. Its advice is that the provision is "obsolete" and that

"if needed regulations can be made under the Health and Safety at Work Act."

The amendments that we are now debating maintain a high safety standard.

Question put, That the amendment be made:–

The House divided: Ayes 128, Noes 5.

Division No. 225]   **[12.24 am**

AYES

Alexander, Richard	Kennedy, Charles
Alison, Rt Hon Michael	King, Roger (B'ham N'thfield)
Alton, David	Kirkhope, Timothy
Amos, Alan	Kirkwood, Archy
Arbuthnot, James	Knapman, Roger
Arnold, Jacques (Gravesham)	Knight, Greg (Derby North)
Ashby, David	Knowles, Michael
Baldry, Tony	Knox, David
Batiste, Spencer	Lee, John (Pendle)
Bennett, Nicholas (Pembroke)	Lightbown, David
Bevan, David Gilroy	Lilley, Peter
Boswell, Tim	Livsey, Richard
Bottomley, Peter	Lloyd, Peter (Fareham)
Bottomley, Mrs Virginia	Lyell, Sir Nicholas
Brazier, Julian	McLoughlin, Patrick
Bright, Graham	McNair-Wilson, P. (New Forest)
Carlisle, John, (Luton N)	Malins, Humfrey
Carlisle, Kenneth (Lincoln)	Martin, David (Portsmouth S)
Chapman, Sydney	Maude, Hon Francis
Coombs, Anthony (Wyre F'rest)	Maxwell-Hyslop, Robin
Cope, Rt Hon John	Mayhew, Rt Hon Sir Patrick
Davis, David (Boothferry)	Meyer, Sir Anthony
Devlin, Tim	Miller, Sir Hal
Dorrell, Stephen	Mills, Iain
Douglas-Hamilton, Lord James	Mitchell, Andrew (Gedling)
Durant, Tony	Mitchell, Sir David
Fallon, Michael	Morrison, Sir Charles
Favell, Tony	Moss, Malcolm
Fishburn, John Dudley	Moynihan, Hon Colin
Forsyth, Michael (Stirling)	Neubert, Michael
Forth, Eric	Nicholls, Patrick
Fowler, Rt Hon Norman	Nicholson, David (Taunton)
Freeman, Roger	Nicholson, Emma (Devon West)
French, Douglas	Norris, Steve
Gill, Christopher	Paice, James
Goodson-Wickes, Dr Charles	Patnick, Irvine
Greenway, John (Ryedale)	Raffan, Keith
Griffiths, Sir Eldon (Bury St E')	Raison, Rt Hon Timothy
Griffiths, Peter (Portsmouth N)	Redwood, John
Hague, William	Ridley, Rt Hon Nicholas
Hamilton, Hon Archie (Epsom)	Ryder, Richard
Hanley, Jeremy	Sackville, Hon Tom
Hargreaves, A. (B'ham H'll Gr')	Sainsbury, Hon Tim
Hargreaves, Ken (Hyndburn)	Shaw, David (Dover)
Harris, David	Shepherd, Colin (Hereford)
Hawkins, Christopher	Shersby, Michael
Heddle, John	Smith, Tim (Beaconsfield)
Heseltine, Rt Hon Michael	Stanbrook, Ivor
Hind, Kenneth	Stanley, Rt Hon Sir John
Howarth, Alan (Strat'd-on-A)	Steel, Rt Hon David
Howarth, G. (Cannock & B'wd)	Stevens, Lewis
Howells, Geraint	Stewart, Andy (Sherwood)
Hughes, Robert G. (Harrow W)	Stradling Thomas, Sir John
Hunt, David (Wirral W)	Sumberg, David
Irvine, Michael	Summerson, Hugo
Jack, Michael	Taylor, Teddy (S'end E)
Jones, Gwilym (Cardiff N)	Thompson, Patrick (Norwich N)

Thorne, Neil	Wardle, Charles (Bexhill)
Thurnham, Peter	Watts, John
Trippier, David	Wells, Bowen
Trotter, Neville	Widdecombe, Ann
Twinn, Dr Ian	Wood, Timothy
Waddington, Rt Hon David	
Wallace, James	Tellers for the Ayes:
Waller, Gary	Mr. David Maclean and
Ward, John	Mr. David Heathcoat-Amory.

NOES

Barnes, Harry (Derbyshire NE)	
Cryer, Bob	Tellers for the Noes:
Lewis, Terry	Mr. Kevin Barron and
Skinner, Dennis	Mr. Allan Rogers.
Welsh, Michael (Doncaster N)	

Question accordingly agreed to.

Clause 10

TRADE UNION DUTIES FOR WHICH TIME OFF MUST BE ALLOWED BY EMPLOYER

Mr. Nicholls: I beg to move amendment No. 30, in page 9, line 10, after 'out', insert '(i)'.

Mr. Deputy Speaker: With this we may discuss Government amendments Nos. 31 to 34.

Mr. Nicholls: Amendments Nos. 30 to 34 are purely technical and in no way change the underlying purpose of the clause. That said, they fall into two distinct categories. Amendments Nos. 33 and 34 remedy a defect in the drafting of section 32 of the Employment Protection (Consolidation) Act 1978. The need to put forward the amendments arises out of a recent Court of Appeal decision in the case of Adlington *v.* British Bakeries (Northern) Limited. The case was decided during the Committee stage and was referred to by the hon. Member for Preston (Mrs. Wise).

The purpose of clause 10 is to remove the anomoly in section 27 of the 1978 Act, which was revealed in the 1982 Court of Appeal case of Beal and Others v Beecham. The amendments seek not to change the purpose of the clause, but to amend the law to remove that anomaly. The clause does not alter the law in any other respect.

Mr. Strang: The Minister will recall our discussions in Committee on a clause to which we take great exception. I am not wholly convinced that the amendments are entirely technical and I wish to probe the matter a little further, especially on amendment No. 31.

The issue has a long history going back to the Employment Protection (Consolidation) Act 1978, which was introduced by the Labour Government. Section 27 of that Act clearly laid down the circumstances under which an employee could have paid time off for legitimate trade union activities. There was some opposition to that legislation from the Conservative party. I say "some" because in those days the Tories' extreme attitude towards the trade union movement was not fully manifest.

During those debates a number of hon. Members sought to limit the circumstances under which people could have paid time off. The position is clear because an ACAS code of practice, which was envisaged in the Act, defines the duties for which trade union officials can have paid time off. They include:

"(a) collective bargaining with the appropriate level of management;

    (b) informing constituents about negotiations or consultations with management;

    (c) meetings with other lay officials or with full-time union officers on matters which are concerned with industrial relations between his or her employer and any associated employer and their employees;

    (d) interviews with and on behalf of constituents on grievance and discipline matters concerning them and their employer;

    (e) appearing on behalf of constituents before an outside official body, such as an industrial tribunal, which is dealing with an industrial relations matter concerning the employer; and

    (f) explanations to new employees whom he or she will represent of the role of the union in the workplace industrial relations structure."

It is our view that the ACAS code of practice, amplified by various court cases, lays down a reasonable legislative framework determining when a trade unionist should be entitled to time off paid for by his employer. We take exception to the clause because it seeks to change all that. It seeks to remove the applicability of the ACAS code of practice and to insert a new definition of the circumstances in which a trade union official would be entitled to time off, namely, the definition in the Trade Union and Labour Relations Act 1974.

It is symptomatic of the Government's whole approach to these matters that the definition which is to be operative is the definition of a trade dispute. Time and time again we have to remind Government Members that, contrary to the impression that they and the organs of the press that support them give, full-time trade union officials spend 95 to 99 per cent. of their time not in seeking to encourage people to withdraw their labour but in seeking to avoid disputes and secure agreements. Often their intervention has the effect of preventing people from coming out on strike or taking industrial action.

The vast bulk of their time is spent on helping the process of industrial relations which means helping to avoid disputes and breakdowns in relations between management and workers. Generally it is only a small fraction of their time that is involved in strikes and other forms of industrial action. It is sad that the Government should seek to revert to the definition of a trade dispute to lay down the conditions that have to be fulfilled for a worker to have paid time off for trade union activities.

It was made clear in Committee how restrictive the provision will be. For example, under present legislation, if a national trade union such as the Amalgamated Engineering Union organised a conference on the car industry, provided the conference was about industrial relations and other aspects of the industry, it could reasonably expect that all its members who were active in the car industry, where there was an agreement between the AEU and the company, would be entitled to paid time off to attend the conference. So it would not matter whether the AEU convenor was based at the Rover Cowley plant or at the Nissan Washington plant; the same criteria would apply. In the example that I have given the convenor would be entitled to paid time off.

What the legislation does is alter that position and it creates a situation where, whether the trade union convenor will have paid time off will depend on the actual collective agreement that is in force between the trade union and the employer at the particular plant or company in question. Therefore, I believe it to be the case that, if there is a rather restrictive agreement between Nissan and the AEU, one could find that a convenor at the Nissan plant would not be entitled to paid time off, but a convenor at the Rover plant, where there is a more traditional type of agreement, would be. That was one of the points that came out in Committee.

12.45 am

One of the most incredible justifications for that change in the legislation was to give employers greater certainty. The implication was that there was a certain ambiguity in the current legislation as to when a trade unionist was entitled to paid time off. However, it does the very opposite, as my example illustrates. Instead of there being a uniformity across the board, as applies at present and is basically laid down by the ACAS code of practice to which I have referred, we shall be moving into a situation where the entitlement to paid time off will vary, not according to the nature of the event—for example, a conference or training school—that the trade union official wants to attend, but according to the nature of the collective agreement between the employer and the trade unionist.

It must be pointed out that the Government completely failed to sustain their case that that would lead to a position of greater clarity and predictability for employers in relation to paid time off for trade unionists. It must further be said that the first indication that we received of the Government's intention in that area goes way back to the White Paper, "Building Businesses. . . . not Barriers". That sought to imply that that requirement, which goes back to the Employment Protection Act 1975, was something of a burden on employers. That being so, Ministers have still not made the slightest attempt to describe that burden on or cost to employers. There is no suggestion of any quantification of those.

No one has sought to indicate what the average financial cost or burden in any year is to any particular employer, whether large or small. Indeed, I do not believe that any hon. Member on either side of the House really believes that the entitlement to paid time off by trade union officials, as it operates in this country at present, is in any way a disadvantage or some sort of burden to employers, which makes our firms less competitive than those elsewhere.

Mr. Bob Cryer (Bradford, South): Does my hon. Friend agree that the exact reverse would be the truth? If the arrangement for paid time off is left to individual collective agreements between a trade union branch and an employer, it will surely lead to accusations of disparities between agreements—as to employers giving time off or not, as the case may be, to go to the sort of conference mentioned by my hon. Friend—which will in turn lead to more pressure for negotiations to allow time off to reach parity with other sections of the industry. That in itself could lead to an industrial dispute about the very legislation that the Government are proposing to introduce. A national agreement laid down and applying, through statute and national convention, across the board is obviously a way of avoiding disputes between sections of an industry, whereas the Government's proposals are a recipe for conflict.

Mr. Strang: I do not have the slightest doubt that the situation will develop in that way. Codes of practice and case law make people's position clear. It is not clear in this measure. There will be opposition by employees when they find that they are no longer entitled to paid time off.

[*Mr. Strang*]

Paid time off will be determined by collective agreement, but there are collective agreements and collective agreements. Some, such as the one between the trade unions and the Ford Motor company, are almost comparable to legislation, so well-honed are they. They are clear-cut and precise. But many other collective agreements fall a long way short of that and whether there is time off to undertake a particular activity is open to interpretation.

Disagreement and disharmony will be promoted when a trade union has one interpretation of a collective agreement and the employer has another. We can rest assured that the employer will interpret it as meaning that the official is not entitled to paid time off while the trade union will take the opposite view. The union's rational response will be to bring pressure to bear on the employer to achieve that paid time off. Notwithstanding what is included in the collective agreement, it is always possible to negotiate a supplementary agreement providing specificaly for paid time off for a particular purpose. There will be a clear incentive for workers to bring pressure to bear on employers—perhaps even embarking upon industrial action—to negotiate a supplementary agreement to give paid time off to attend the kind of conference that I have mentioned.

Surely most reasonable people recognise that it is in industry's interests that managers and trade union officials are well educated. Some trade union officials are involved in just certain matters—for example, national pay negotiations—but even people without experience in the workplace know that shop stewards play a pivotal role. Consequently, it must be in the interests of large, complex operations that those people have an opportunity to be as well-educated and well-informed as possible. Of course they should be well-informed about industrial relations and negotiating procedures, but they should also have the widest opportunity to educate themselves about their industry and to widen their horizons.

In Committee, I asked whether a trade union convenor would be entitled to paid time off to attend a conference on the implications for his industry of the single European market in 1992. We did not get an answer. It is clear that often convenors will not be entitled to paid time off. Of course, it will be possible to negotiate an agreement to achieve that, but the Government are backward in the way in which they have enacted legislation to restrict the scope for working people to attend courses and broaden their education.

No one seriously suggests that British industry gravely under-performs, that our output has been greatly reduced or that our productivity has been adversely affected because too many trade unionists have been getting paid time off to attend various courses—far from it. I suspect that not only Opposition Members but many managers and employers would argue that industry would operate more efficiently if more active trade unionists had more opportunities to participate in conferences on education and so on. That would broaden their understanding and enable them to become more knowledgeable not only about industrial relations and negotiating procedures but the nature of their industry's market.

The measure has not been justified by the Government. Certainly, as I have indicated, the two main arguments put forward by the Government, have not been substantiated. They have not produced any evidence to show that the current requirement is a burden to industry. It is nonsense to argue, as they have done, that the changes will bring greater certainty.

We are talking about a large number of people and a range of courses. In 1989, 60,000 shop stewards and trade union representatives will go on training courses arranged by their union or the Trades Union Congress. The trade unions and the TUC spend £6·5 million on training, of which 25 per cent. is grant-aided by the Government.

I am not suggesting that the new legislation will mean that participants on every course organised by the TUC or the unions will not be entitled to paid time off. That does not apply to health and safety representatives: they are governed by separate regulations and there is no restriction on their entitlement to paid time off for trade union activities.

A large number of courses are attended by thousands of trade unionists every year. In the main they are attended on the basis of paid time off. In those circumstances it is wholly reprehensible for the Government to enact a measure which will limit the opportunity for some, not all, trade unionists, to participate in the courses.

The Minister argued that the amendments were technical. I would appreciate greater clarification of that argument. Amendment No. 31 deals with a paragraph that is to be substituted in the Employment Protection (Consolidation) Act 1978. The words to be removed are:
"any matters specified in section 29(1) of the Trade Union and Labour Relations Act 1974"
and the words to be inserted are:
"negotiations with the employer that are related to or connected with any matters which fall within"
section 29(1) of the Trade Union and Labour Relations Act.
That is not technical in the way that the word is normally used in the context of amendments. It changes the Bill so that the courts will interpret it differently from the way in which they would if it remained unamended.

I seek Government guidance on this matter because when I was studying it I was not sure whether the change would marginally improve the position for the trade unions and us. I thought that the phrase
"related to or connected with"
went wider than the wording
"any matter specified in section 29(1)".
If my view was correct, it would mean that that was not a major change but would slightly improve the position. I say "slightly" because such a change would be only marginal and would in no way mitigate the enormity of the amendment, which—as we explained at some length in Committee—we consider an absolute outrage. It cannot be justified on the ground that, as the Government claim, it will help business. It is clear from the inadequacy of the Government's attempts to justify the amendment that it is born out of their continuing vendetta against the trade union movement.

1 am

The amendment is intended to undermine and weaken the trade unions. It is the product of an era when the Government believed that there were votes to be had from portraying the unions as the opponents—the enemies—of real progress. I am not sure whether they still believe that votes can be won on that ticket; I suspect that their own polls will tell them that such votes are becoming fewer and fewer, and that the unions are more popular now than they have been for decades. The idea that they are somehow responsible for the major problems facing the nation—inflation, mass unemployment and a huge balance of payments gap—is nonsense.

I would like to think that, whatever the Government's political motivation, the extent to which they can be encouraged to implement vindictive legislation on the basis that it will win votes is being reduced. This, however, is another element in the saga of legislation aimed at attacking the legitimate trade union movement. We got another whiff of the Government's attitude at the weekend, when the Secretary of State made some reference to introducing future legislation to deal with unofficial action. That was bound to receive some coverage in the light of the unofficial action on the London Underground, but the idea that action can be taken to prevent people from striking unofficially is hardly sustainable.

Do the Government intend to introduce legislation to fine or otherwise penalise the unions? That is nonsense, because unofficial action, by definition, is action taken in defiance of trade union instructions. Will they seek to imprison the organisers of such action? In the case of the London Underground action, it is extremely unlikely that they would ever find the organisers. Even against the background of, for instance, the action that the Government took over GCHQ to undermine basic human liberties relating to the right to engage in trade union activity, it is hard to believe that they would legislate for people to be locked up simply because they sought to withdraw their labour. Whether or not the Secretary of State was serious, I suspect that, when they examine the proposal, the Government will find it impracticable.

What is disturbing, however, is that the Government still seem to be considering legislation to trammel and restrict trade union activities further. All the evidence—including much of the evidence obtained by the Government on the consultative documents issued in connection with the Bill—has asked them not to take such action.

In respect of a Bill debated in the last Session, the extent to which representations were made by the Confederation of British Industry, the British Institute of Management and the Institute of Personnel Management, implying and sometimes explicitly arguing that the Government had gone more than far enough, was remarkable. That was the view even of organisations that supported the Government when they first enacted employment legislation on being returned to power.

The idea that the Government can further attack trade union rights is wholly indefensible. I do not believe that it has many supporters. It represents simply a continuation of the Government's policy of attacking and undermining trade union activity. That does not reduce union disputes. It must be clear even to the Government that the main reason for the reduction in industrial disputes is mass unemployment. Because of its scale, the average worker feels lucky to have a job and in those circumstances is not in a position to withdraw his labour. However, in some areas—and particularly London—there is not only full employment but employers are finding it hard to recruit. As a consequence, the unions' bargaining power is enhanced and there is a prospect of industrial action. The situation is exacerbated by the sharp rise in the cost of living.

We bitterly resent clause 10. I ask the Minister to answer my question relating to amendment No. 31, as I am genuinely uncertain as to its true effect. I cannot regard it as a technical amendment. The Minister referred to a recent case that was cited in the Standing Committee, and he may have been implying that the amendment would ensure the same outcome. If that is so, I regard the amendment as purely technical. Perhaps the Minister will explain precisely the implications of amendment No. 31.

Mr. Harry Barnes: We are debating important matters relating to time off for trade union duties and for involvement in training. I prefer to talk about the opportunities for education. Trade unionists do not have to be taught by rote, but need to understand difficult and complex situations in which different views, values and arguments must be taken into account.

The question must be asked whether we are here dealing with purely technical amendments or with something considerably more significant. The changes made in Committee and the defeats that Labour suffered there were certainly significant.

At least four pieces of legislation must be carefully examined. They are the Employment Protection (Consolidation) Act 1978, the amendment in Committee which referred the Trade Union and Labour Relations Act 1974 to the Employment Protection (Consolidation) Act 1978, and the amendments now before the House, which can be interpreted in many different ways and certainly need clarifying. The original Employment Protection (Consolidation) Act 1978 stated that trade unionists should be allowed time off

"(a) to carry out those duties of his as such an official which are concerned with industrial relations between his employer and any associated employer, and their employees; or

(b) to undergo training in aspects of industrial relations which is—

(i) relevant to the carrying out of those duties; and

(ii) approved by the Trades Union Congress or by the independent trade union of which he is an official."

That is being destroyed and specific measures were introduced in Committee stating that those provisions should be available only for matters involving trade disputes as defined in the Trade Union and Labour Relations Act 1974. However, it was argued that other items could be involved in recognition agreements which might still be debated.

The hon. Member for Pendle (Mr. Lee), who answered the debate in Committee, was quite insistent that recognition agreements were of vast importance and significance. In a 22-minute speech, during which there were eight interventions, he managed to mention recognition agreements 11 times and said:

"We agree that, in principle, training of trade union officials is a good thing. In our view, trained shop stewards are better than untrained shop stewards".

He continued:

"Clause 10 is not inconsistent with that view in any way. All it states is that the employers' obligation to allow paid time off for training and other trade union duties must be governed by the terms of the recognition agreement with the trade union. What is unreasonable about that?"—[*Official Report, Standing Committee A,* 28 February 1989; c. 354.]

The amendments might destroy the possibility of the recognition agreement being taken into account. Our argument in Committee was that the recognition agreement would be undermined in regard to time off for trade union duties by clause 10 which would alter the legal

[*Mr. Harry Barnes*]

framework in which trade unions could negotiate. The Government did not take that view. They believe that negotiations have nothing to do with power relationships in industry and that two good-natured people chatting together can sort things out.

What does amendment No. 32 mean? It introduces a fresh provision about other training and educational duties that could be involved. It states:

"(i) any other duties of his, as such an official, which are concerned with the performance, on behalf of employees of the employer, of any functions that are related to or connected with any matters falling within that provision and that the employer has agreed may be so performed by the trade union;"

The second part of the amendment seems to refer to recognition agreements. But to what does the first part refer? Why do we need fresh language now? Is there a legal possibility that the second part of the amendment would be tied in with the words "falling within that provision" to clause 10(a)(i), which refers to section 29 of the Trade Union and Labour Relations Act? Is it possible that, although a matter was included within a recognition agreement, the employer could disobey that recognition agreement because the agreement on time off for trade union studies exceeded the provisions of the Trade Union and Labour Relations Act? If my interpretation is correct, if flies in the face of what we were told 11 times in Committee by the hon. Member for Pendle.

1.15 am

In Committee, the Minister said that health and safety provision would not be affected, but amendment No. 32 might affect it. It says:

"any other duties of his, as such an official, which are concerned with"

negotiations with an employer

"that are related to or connected with any matters falling within"

section 29(1) of the Trade Union and Labour Relations Act 1974.

The words

"that are related to connected or with any matters"

throw the matter wide open and make an improvement. Are negotiations with an employer possible negotiations under the appropriate section of the Trade Union and Labour Relations Act or are they actual negotiations, which will depend on power relationships within an industry and may be highly restrictive, given the other trade union legislation that has been passed in recent years? Clause 10(a)(i) may be highly restrictive, and may add to the problem with clause 10(a)(ii) if it is interpreted in the way that I suggested earlier.

There is much need for time off for trade union duties and education. The Bill, which is of much interest to trade unionists, young people, women who may have to work in a pit and disabled people, may exclude from discussion matters such as time off for trade union duties, terms of employment, the allocation of work duties, matters of discipline, membership of a trade union, facilities for trade union officials and machinery for negotiation. A legal interpretation of the Bill might restrict such activity.

I should like more detail of the Bill's provisions and why the amendments are necessary. To argue that they are technical and that therefore we need not worry too much about them does not carry much weight because other measures described in Committee as technical which were opposed by Labour Members produced serious problems for working people.

Mr. McCartney: I thank you, Madam Deputy Speaker, for your kind remarks about my recent illness. I hope to prove that I am back to full fitness as I catch your eye again and again. That is not a threat.

Madam Deputy Speaker (Miss Betty Boothroyd): It is a promise.

Mr. McCartney: You said it, Madam Deputy Speaker.

The clause is important. We are trying to elicit from the Government the true intention behind their proposals. In his detailed analysis, my hon. Friend the Member for Edinburgh, East (Mr. Strang) clearly showed that in practice on the shop floor it is vitally important that trade unions are able to use legislation when their legal rights are challenged. That applies particularly in industries where trade unions are in a weak position, not necessarily because of low membership but because of the way in which that membership is situated in particular industries and the relationship between employees and the companies in those industries.

It is important that legislation does not create further imbalances which reduce the ability of working people to join a trade union and to make recognition of that union effective by the way in which an employer provides resources and facilities, such as time off, for the trade union representatives to carry out their duties.

As a former shop steward, I have always taken the view that it is paramount in good industrial relations that an employer recognises the work of trade unions in the workplace and the way in which they can make a positive contribution to the development of the company and, in the day-to-day management of a company, their contribution in terms of developing strategies and improvements in work force techniques, the development and use of new technology, and the way in which relationships and communications can be improved in an industrial setting.

All that can be done only by the active co-operation and involvement of trade unions. Where that co-operation is sought, it can be effective only when trade unions have the right to ensure that their contribution is underpinned by time off and other resources.

As my hon. Friend the Member for Derbyshire, North-East (Mr. Barnes) said, in Committee the Minister said that all those matters were covered by recognition agreements. That is significant, because recognition agreements are central to whether trade unionists have any rights under current legislation.

For example, the first part of clause 10 says:

"In section 27(1) of the 1978 Act (duty of employer to permit employee who is an official of an independent trade union recognised by employer to take time off to carry out certain trade union duties)"

That recognition is vital to whether a trade unionist can, in reality, effectively carry out his or her work on behalf of the trade union and the work force.

The reality is that under the Government ACAS, in its handbook for small firms, says that there is no statutory obligation on the employer to recognise the trade union. An employer who refuses to recognise a trade union undermines completely what the Minister said, because it, follows from that that there is no recognition of statutory rights.

Again, hedging its bets and advising on representation rights, on page 57 of the handbook, ACAS says:

"Sometimes employers do not think there is enough strength of feeling for trade unions within the workforce to justify full recognition."

We all recognise that as the first excuse by employers to prevent trade unions being recognised.

It goes on:

"Instead they may agree to representation rights which do not provide for full negotiations with the employer but entitle members to be represented by their union individually eg, in disciplinary cases or if the employee has a grievance".

Here we are talking about a situation where an employer may give certain rights, but there is no full recognition agreement. That agreement does not, therefore, meet the test set out by the Minister in Committee because it does not deal with facilities, training and time off. If the trade union does not accept that, the result is no union recognition.

In giving an example of what can happen, I will not name the company because the individual concerned is still employed, albeit tenuously, by the firm. I wrote to the Minister some time ago about this case and received an unsatisfactory reply, in which I was sent a leaflet about the employment of disabled workers, was reminded that an employer did not have to recognise a trade union and was told that the Government could not intervene.

My example involves a woman who was employed by a company which was taken over by a large retail organisation. The original employer had employed her under the provisions for employing disabled workers; the lady in question has suffered from major disabilities since birth. The original employer recognised trade unions and the value of employing disabled people. Following the takeover, the new employers informed the trade unions concerned that the company would no longer recognise unions in negotiation proceedings and would not offer the right of representation to individual employees.

The new company told the employees in the company in Wigan which had been taken over that working arrangements would be changed in a significant way. For example, the girl in the example I am giving had been employed as an assistant at a cash desk. Her job description was changed and she was to become a sales person with a weekly and monthly sales target to reach. Her disabilities were such that she was unable to reach those targets and she became liable to disciplinary proceedings by the company.

The company told her that it would not recognise her trade union and attempted through harassment to discipline her because, as I say, her disabilities prevented her from selling sufficient television sets, video recorders and other machines to the public.

When I wrote to the company pointing out the previous arrangements and claiming that the young lady should at least have the right to be represented by the trade union concerned at a disciplinary hearing, I was told that, because there was no recognition agreement, it had no requirement to allow her to be represented. However, the company said that it would allow her to have present a friend who was not employed by the company.

At that stage I wrote to the Minister claiming that that was unsatisfactory, with the harassment of a disabled person whose statutory rights were being undermined. The Minister washed his hands of the whole affair. He turned a blind eye and would not intervene, even though a major national company was harassing a disabled worker because it was claimed that she was not reaching sales targets.

It is in such cases, where partial agreements exist or where no agreement exists, that the rights of trade unions to represent individuals are undermined. In Committee, the Minister said that all would be well so long as there was an agreement. I have shown that employers who do not want to provide facilities for trade unionists just do not make agreements or they restrict such agreements as they are prepared to make. The Government amendments represent further restrictions on agreements, which will be interpreted in such a way that the rights that unions have to represent their members will be further eroded.

1.30 am

My hon. Friend the Member for Edinburgh, East (Mr. Strang) raised the issue of 1992, which is vital to all trade unionists in the United Kingdom. I will use an example here too from my own constituency.

Heinz is one of the major employers in Wigan and we have a good relationship with it as a company. This example is not an indication of what Heinz may or may not do in the sense of the many policy statements that have been issued, but it shows what could happen after 1992 unless the Government give some clear guidelines to employers such as Heinz.

Currently Heinz has two factories in the United Kingdom and has acquired over a number of years factories in Portugal, Spain, Holland and Italy. The factory in Wigan, which is the largest manufacturing base in Europe, is the area for the production of baby foods —where a controversy has recently been raging—baked beans, ravioli and the like. The factory at Harlesden in north London produces pastas, such as spaghetti, Weight Watchers and other such lines and pickles. In 1992 these units could be in competition with factories in Europe. For example, the factory in Holland has almost the same production capacity as that in Wigan and a very similar product range.

Madam Deputy Speaker: Order. I am sure that the hon. Gentleman is coming to the amendment before us, which deals with time off for trade unionists.

Mr. McCartney: That is precisely the point that I want to make about 1992, Madam Deputy Speaker.

The production capacity of the factories in Spain, Italy and Portugal is such that it could lead to significant changes by switching production from the United Kingdom to the European sector, as has happened with the Ford Motor company and other companies in the engineering industry. Come 1992, will there be obligations and rights for trade unionists in Britain to sit down with their counterparts in Europe to discuss the implications of 1992, the overall level of production in Heinz as a company, the role of each of the production bases in Europe and the benefits or otherwise of switching production between factories?

Unless there are statutory rights as between factories, the rights of workers after 1992 in this sector of the food industry will be radically undermined even if the employer is a decent employer, so it is vital that there is a clear indication from the Minister that he is not going to rely on the so-called recognition agreements, because in many instances they will not be agreed between employers and trade unionists, but will set down specifically the right of

[Mr. McCartney]

workers to have their trade union recognised and specify that minimum standards must be provided for the trade union to operate on behalf of its members.

That brings me to an issue on bargaining and training. *[Interruption.]* Does the hon. Member for Sheffield, Hallam (Mr. Patnick) want to intervene? I know he is a champagne lout——

Madam Deputy Speaker: Order.

Mr. McCartney: The hon. Gentleman needs your protection from these remarks, Madam Deputy Speaker; he is very sensitive. I do not want to take the time of hon. Gentlemen if they want to make a positive contribution to the debate, as I am genuinely attempting to do.

On the issue of training, in terms of both bargaining and health and safety, many instances of a breakdown between employers and employees are the result of inadequate consultation over the bargaining system and the rights of employees within that system in terms of their being specifically involved in bargaining and of how those systems are refined in the sense of interpreting them. It happens both in terms of those specifically involved in bargaining and how those bargaining systems are refined in the sense of interpreting them, which involves the general work force, and in interpreting bargaining representation.

Good employers—and there are many in the United Kingdom—prefer to provide the opportunity to ensure that where bargaining arrangements exist, the trade unions involved in them are training to ensure that they have an absolute knowledge and grasp of the bargaining procedures and that they also understand and are involved in how decisions are transmitted to the work force. The Minister has not responded positively to my hon. Friend the Member for Edinburgh, East (Mr. Strang). He has not said that there must be specific protection in the Bill for training on bargaining agreements. The same is true of health and safety and other matters. Unless the Minister becomes more positive, the Opposition can continue only with the clear understanding that this Government use employment legislation to weaken the rights of trade unionists and employees, and do so specifically to change the balance of power in industry and to weaken and undermine the ability of employees to negotiate. In doing that, rather than protecting and enhancing industrial relations, they are undermining industrial relations.

Mr. Michael Welsh (Doncaster, North): It is of great importance to industrial relations that workers are educated about them. The average age of people working for British Coal is about 34. The chairman of British Coal has said that he will welcome the opportunity to give courses to educate young people in trade unions in industrial relations and collective bargaining. I believe that you would welcome that, Madam Deputy Speaker, although the Government will not.

Mr. McCartney: My hon. Friend is right. I welcome the fact that British Coal has recognised the error of its ways in previous years and is now attempting to improve the ability to communicate and the involvement of trade unions.

Another area in which I would welcome a greater degree of training and involvement of trade unions and

employees is in negotiations and discussions on pension provisions. Here again, it is vital in the bargaining procedures and in the recognition agreement, by which the Minister lays great store, that there is clear recognition of the need for time off with pay for employees' representatives to be involved in the negotiations on pension provisions for employees. That is vital, given the changes in legislation in recent years about rights in connection with pensions and the ability of employers and employees to switch pensions between companies and divisions of individual companies. Unless employers recognise the need for time off for training and involvement in the negotiations and administration of pension schemes, employees will again be at a distinct disadvantage.

Mr. Harry Barnes: The Trade Union and Labour Relations Act 1974 has now been altered as a result of the changes that took place in Committee. The position now is that the definition of trade disputes will determine what it is that employees are allowed to be educated about. There are seven categories in the 1974 Act, but none of them makes any direct reference to pensions being a possible item under discussion. It would have to be argued that terms and conditions of employment, which are one category under the Act, should be considered. It is possible that, within law, the terms and conditions of employment do not include pensions because they are not directly part of working, but are a benefit that people receive when they have left work.

Mr. McCartney: My hon. Friend is right. He referred earlier to the Minister's remarks in Committee, and to the great store that the hon. Gentleman set by recognition agreements. If a recognition agreement is all that an employee can rely upon in his relations with his employer, it must include his absolute right to involvement in the determination and administration of any pension scheme that the company may operate independently of, or in conjunction with, other companies. That right must be included if the recognition agreement is to mean anything.

We must also consider what would happen under the Bill as amended if an employee who was up on a disciplinary charge were sacked by the company and went to a tribunal. Let us suppose that the shop steward wants to represent that employee against the company. Would the amendment prevent a shop steward or workplace representative from having time off with pay to act on behalf of the employee?

Mr. Cryer: The brutal new law passed by the set of savages who are in government at the moment removes benefit for 26 weeks. Because of that, employers often send representatives to tribunals dealing with cases amounting, in effect, to cases of unfair dismissal, to claim that the employee has been fairly dismissed and was in breach of some disciplinary procedure or other. That allows employers to disbar employees from 26 weeks' benefit. If the worker does not have the right to similar representation, the employer can make a one-sided case, in which the worker comes off worse. My hon. Friend the Member for Makerfield (Mr. McCartney) is making an important point.

Mr. McCartney: I thank my hon. Friend for that intervention, but my worries go even further. Even if an employer refuses to allow a shop steward to represent an employee who has been dismissed or disciplined, that employee should still have the right to call on fellow workers as witnesses in any disciplinary proceedings. Will the Minister give a commitment that employees will be given time off with pay to act as witnesses on behalf of the disciplined employee or employees? If not, it can be argued that significant changes are afoot in trade unionists' right to representation.

What happens if a trade union representative proposes to represent an employee at a Department of Social Security appeal tribunal concerning the payment of a benefit in respect of an absence resulting from an industrial accident or injury? An employee who has sustained an accident at work may have been excluded from claiming a number of benefits for which he is, in fact, eligible, and he may ask for his trade union representative to represent him at the tribunal. There is a direct correlation between the accident at work and the employee's right to claim the benefit and his workplace trade union representative therefore has a right to represent him. In such circumstances, is it not fair and right that the employer should allow that trade union representative time off with pay to represent the employee at the tribunal? It is not at all clear whether the amendment would undermine that basic principle.

I know that a number of my hon. Friends wish to participate in the debate. Let me finish, therefore, by asking the Minister a specific question about the rights of disabled workers, particularly in respect of recognition. Does he agree that it is about time that the Department of Employment made it clear that there is a duty on major employers to make provision for disabled people in the workplace? Where there is evidence that the rights of those disabled people have been undermined, should not the Department take it upon itself to ensure that that state of affairs does not continue?

1.45 am

It would be absolute nonsense and a sham if the Department were to issue leaflets telling employers of the need to recognise the rights of the disabled in the workplace while at the same time the Minister writes to Members of Parliament saying that if employers undermine existing rights it is nothing to do with the Department, but a matter between the employer and the employee. Have we really reached the stage when the disabled can be so flagrantly disregarded by the Government and their position so undermined that there is harassment to get rid of disabled employees? That is wholly unacceptable. I hope that the Minister will assure us that he will take steps to strengthen the rights of the disabled in the workplace.

Mr. Cryer: It often strikes me that Tories are much more interested in machinery than in people. If, for example, an employer wished to introduce new machinery, there would be long discussions in the board room, new training provision and assessments of the machines' output, the installation costs and the degree of protection for the machinery—most of it imported under the Tory Government. Yet the Government rarely understand that there must be the same degree of scrutiny and education on behalf of the employees.

This nation's most important asset is its people. The relationship of people to machines and to each other is a continuing process of negotiation in industrial relations. If

people are to be allowed to retain their dignity, they must operate within independent trade unions. The Government love the trade unions to operate anywhere other than in the United Kingdom. The Prime Minister dances with delight about the trade union movement in Poland—not because she is concerned with trade unions or, indeed, anyone in particular in Poland, but because she thinks that any movement among the people in Poland must inevitably lead to the breakdown of the system so that private enterprise capitalism and the enterprise culture can be instituted.

The right hon. Lady claims concern for the trade unions. We are members of a party that sprang from a trade union movement, that came into being because the factor of production called labour—a collection of people —demanded dignity and the right to participate, at the very least, in the productive processes. I work to make labour superior to capital. I hate the process in which the owners of capital dictate to labour in that list of the factors of production. However, because that process exists, I seek to give working men and women—labour—an opportunity to exercise some dignity. Time off for trade union activities is part of that pattern of preserving human dignity.

Tory Members know that the board rooms where most of them spent many years are not tatty or badly ventilated. The directors make sure that they are well furnished, well lit and well ventilated, so that discussions can be held in quiet circumstances. If they concede reasonable canteen conditions for the workers, it is sometimes done with enthusiasm but sometimes with an ill grace.

The clause and the amendments are trying to take away some established rights that have been built up over the years for trade unions to participate in a limited range of activities, with time off from work with pay. As I mentioned in an intervention to my hon. Friend the Member for Edinburgh, East (Mr. Strang), who made a good, comprehensive speech, the proposal, which will mean that the terms and conditions for time off with pay will depend on local collective agreements, is a formula for further conflict.

If a national code of conduct is produced by ACAS or another reputable organisation, it has the imprimatur of a code of guidance even though it may not be legally enforceable. There would be standard terms and conditions for time off for each factory. Therefore, if there was a meeting of trade unionists to reach a collective understanding, there would not be an argument about why Fred Smith or Charles Jones, convenors from the factory in Birmingham, Norwich or Nelson, were not there because their employer would not give them time off. Otherwise, argument might start about why A should be given time off and B should not, and why C should get only half the time necessary for the discussion on training or whatever. Inevitably there would be pressure from the workpeople and from the individuals themselves, or perhaps from the individuals to start with, spreading to the work force, who would say that their representatives should have the same rights as representatives of other firms doing the same sort of work and seeking the same sort of training.

A union might organise a conference on 1992. The Secretary of State for Trade and Industry, Lord Young of Graffham, did not start the campaign on 1992—with glossy pamphlets and massive public expenditure—in a back street. As I recall, he set it off with a series of

[*Mr. Cryer*]

breakfasts, all paid for by the taxpayer, for industrialists. He thought that he would give industrialists a chance to chat together about it. But if an employer decides that a trade unionist is not to be allowed to attend a conference on 1992, that will be the sole decision of the employer.

Amendment No. 32 refers to

"any other duties of his, as such an official, which are concerned with the performance, on behalf of employees of the employer, of any functions that are related to or connected with any matters falling within that provision and that the employer has agreed may be so performed by the trade union".

The phrase "the employer has agreed" means that it will be a unilateral decision. I do not think that that is right. The best arrangements in a workplace are made by collective discussion and agreement.

The unilateral decision of the employer will apply to an activity that might well cover the obsession of the current Government advertising campaign with the wonderful benefits of 1992. The textile unions might want to organise a conference on burden-sharing arrangements for textile imports by 1992 after the renegotiation of the existing multi-fibre arrangement. That would be a legitimate discussion because it would be a matter about which both the employers and the employees in the textile industry would be very much concerned. The discussion could be about other things, such as the high interest rates created by the Government's economic policies, short-time working, loss of jobs or lack of investment.

However, under these proposals, in the textile industry, for example, Courtaulds may have a collective agreement that allows its shop stewards time off, but another firm, such as Bulmer and Lumb or Benson and Turner in my constituency, might say, "We do not think that you should have time off." Therefore, a conflict will arise. The trade union movement will naturally attempt to obtain standard terms and conditions for every one of the organised workplaces, and it is only right that it should do so. It would be unjust if there was a disparity in attendance at such a conference as I have outlined, where the discussion would concern the future of the textile industry, which is still important to northern areas, such as Yorkshire and Lancashire. The Minister's proposal to alter the Bill, which is not a very fruitful Bill in any event, is, therefore, likely to cause conflict.

Mr. McCartney: Will my hon. Friend consider the situation whereby employees are now having to consider involvement in competitive tendering in the Health Service and in local government services? It is necessary for them to be involved for the first time in the tendering procedure and their ability to be so involved is linked to their ability to have paid time off to secure the right education and background to develop ideas for submitting tenders, for checking tenders and for validation of tenders. I know already of situations where trade unionists are being told that they will not be allowed paid time off for such activity. Will my hon. Friend indicate whether he believes that the amendment will undermine that position even further?

Mr. Cryer: Clearly, if there was a trade union conference called about those circumstances, in which the aim of the trade unions would be almost certainly to secure tenders and to obtain jobs for their members, paid time off should be allowed. We must remember that the

background to the discussions is not a deep underlying antagonism of the trade union movement to capitalism and all its works, but the aim of protecting its members, to preserve jobs and, indeed, to improve the efficiency of the enterprise in which its members work. There are many examples where trade unions have entered into agreements on productivity arrangements. For example, in the textile industry, three-shift working, changes in staffing, the flexibility of staff and the introduction of new machinery have all been accepted because the trade unions have been co-operative. As a matter of interest, many thousands of textile workers who lost their jobs did not have the co-operation of their employers, which they so richly deserved.

My point is that the trade unionists may well wish to go to a conference, because they see a conference about public procurement as an important means of securing the future viability of the factory in which they are working. However, under amendment No. 32 it would be entirely up to the employer as to whether they would be allowed to go or not, which is wrong.

There are many moves which will vitally affect jobs in our country. For example, there is the public procurement directive of the EEC, in which it states that tenders of public bodies will have to be put out to the whole of the Common Market. That could be a threatening provision for jobs in the United Kingdom, which has a massive balance of payments deficit. If the directive is introduced without safeguards, the proportion of our public procurement trade from non-member states could rocket from its present level of 2 per cent. of £4 billion. The trade union movement would hold meetings at weekends and outside working hours, but inevitably part of the working week would have to be used. I am talking about activities which fall within the amendment and which would be mounted because of concern by trade unions for their members' jobs.

2 am

It is wrong that the employer should have the sole decision-making capacity. As my hon. Friend the Member for Makerfield (Mr. McCartney) said, trade unions need to be independent so that they cannot be suborned or silenced when representing their members at disciplinary hearings. An employer may say, "I will not give you time off to represent a trade union member in a case appealing against my decision." In all fairness, that must happen. An industrial or social security tribunal hears evidence from both sides. The outcome of discussions that take place before a tribunal hearing is not a matter for the employer.

It is similar to a plaintiff in court being denied representation when a defendant has representation. Everyone would say, "That is unjust." Under this legislation, a one-sided case can be presented by an employer, who can afford to employ a solicitor. Industrial tribunals have been legalised away from the basic formality that they were established to provide—not by workers but by employers, who obtained and paid for the services of solicitors and barristers. That is one reason why the right of trade union officials to time off should be made clear. That would provide the justice that most people recognise as important in a court of law and in social and industrial tribunals.

Mr. Bob Clay (Sunderland, North): Will my hon. Friend cast his mind back to the remarks made by my hon.

Friend the Member for Makerfield (Mr. McCartney) on the role of trade unions in discussions on local authority privatisations? Apart from local authority privatisations being forced through Parliament by the Government, a growing number of management and employee buy-outs are taking place, encouraged by the Government. Has it occurred to my hon. Friend that in many ways the Government's proposal operates against their competition policies? Management could use the discretion that they will have if the amendment is passed to discriminate between one employee or management buy-out and another. Sometimes trade union officials would be allowed time off to develop business plans and prepare buy-outs and sometimes they would not. That would be not merely unfair but corrupt.

Mr. Cryer: My hon. Friend is right. In a sense, it would amount to insider dealing, with employers using their position under apparently unconnected legislation to manipulate decisions and keep trade unionists out of one set of negotiations while allowing them to participate in another. That is an important point, because yet again the decision-making apparatus is in the hands of the owners of capital, while labour is, in every sense, at their mercy. Many important moves are taking place in legislation due to the Government's decisions.

For example, it would be reasonable for employees of the National Health Service to have time off to discuss the takeover of the cleaning services. I have an exact case in point. Trade unions were, as it were, privatised by an organisation called Taylor Plan. Employees to whom a wage award had been made during their period of service found that, if they left service before the payment was handed over, Taylor Plan refused to make the payment. That happened to employees who worked when the award was negotiated and when it was operative, but had not been paid out because of delays in computer programming, the post or whatever excuse the administration produced.

If people are struggling from week to week to meet payments for rates, electricity and gas, and are driven to get electricity tokens from the Yorkshire electricity board to feed their electricity meters because they are scrimping and saving week by week, a back payment is important. It is essential that their trade union representatives should be able to participate in discussions to ensure that collective agreements on privatisation are at least equal to those agreements that they have already negotiated with the public authority.

The Government produce the change in circumstances because, by the back-door privatisation of the Health Service, they require health authorities to sell off their cleaning and other services. They did it first to cleaners and are now trying to do it to doctors, from whom, I am delighted to say, they are encountering enormous resistance, and to local authorities. Therefore, there are more reasons why trade unions need the opportunity to discuss the changes taking place in working practices, ownership and negotiations which arise solely out of the mad theological doctrines of the gangsters who currently govern our nation, but whose time, I am happy to say, is running out. It is important to clarify the trade unions' position.

My hon. Friend the Member for Edinburgh, East, and no doubt the Minister, would say that different rules affect health and safety at work. Time off is allowed for health and safety at work matters but is in the process of becoming highly qualified for other matters. I wonder why. Is it because, with health and safety at work, there is a clear link between the loss of hours of work and industrial injury, and, therefore, it is sensible, even to the class warriors of the Right wing in the Government, to give time off to discuss health and safety at work to prevent a loss of hours? However, the relationship between time off and industrial relations, and the panoply of associated ideas, is not quite so plain.

Good industrial relations spring from the confidence of two sections of industry, employers and workers, in each other. If employer and employees are bickering over who is to have time off in every circumstance, week after week, it erodes that confidence. It reduces morale on both sides, leading almost inevitably to a lowering of productivity, and is entirely counter-productive. I should have thought that the rationale for allowing time off to cover health and safety provisions should apply across the board.

As I have said before in the House, it is difficult to examine the statistics relating to industrial injury and those relating to strike action because the Government have removed from the 1984 statistics those relating to time lost through injuries requiring three or more days off work. If the Minister examines those statistics, however, he will find that in any average year more days are lost through industrial injury than through strike action. The Government should cast aside their shibboleth that trade unionists are always organising strikes, and look at the reality in industry: that trade unionists want to protect their members' jobs, want a wide range of interests to be associated with those jobs and want an educated and confident work force in a factory where some mutual trust and confidence exists. The Government's qualification for time off will not produce that.

As my hon. Friend the Member for Edinburgh, East (Mr. Strang) pointed out, the Government have provided no assessment or calculation as a basis for that qualification. Although I was not on the Committee, I understand that there, too, no information was produced to enable the Government to point to a lowering of productivity or an increase in industrial disputes as a result of the existing legislation and code of practice. If that is the case—as I firmly believe—it is another instance of the blind prejudice of a Government who provide the men and women working in the diminished number of factories still remaining with the best example of class warriors. It is the Government who want to attack organised working men and women, and to diminish their aims of dignity and parity with the owners of capital.

I have no doubt that the Government will proceed with their amendments, but we shall still have won the arguments, and the arguments here will be transferred to the factories. The Government amendments are a first-class formula for disputes between employer and employee, and for a lowering in morale, tone and output wherever the new rules apply.

Mr. Nicholls: Running through the debate has been the theme that the Government amendments are not technical, and I accept that that is a justifiable concern on which I shall try to satisfy the House.

The hon. Member for Edinburgh, East (Mr. Strang) put his finger on it when he talked about the way in which the system should operate, and when he said that the purposes for which people would be able to take paid leave

[*Mr. Nicholls*]

would be determined by the existing collective agreement. I think that the implication was that the matter should be left to the common sense of employers and employees alike, without Government interference. For all I know, that may have been the intent of those who drafted the 1978 Act, but in practice it worked out in precisely the opposite way.

2.15 am

It became clear at a relatively early stage, and certainly in the Court of Appeal case of Beale and others *v.* Beecham Group Ltd., not that unions were able to reach agreement with an employer as to the matters for which an employee would be entitled to paid leave but that the matter went further than that. The effect of the Court of Appeal's decision in the Beale case was that, once there was recognition of collective bargaining, it became virtually impossible for the employer to say, "I did not mean collective bargaining in its entirety but particular aspects of collective bargaining." Once there was recognition of agreement on collective bargaining, it meant whatever the union wanted it to mean. Clearly use was being made of the original purposes of the 1978 Act, which was far too wide, and the Government felt that that scenario should be addressed.

In the context of the Bill, the Government introduced clause 10 whose purpose—despite the inevitably complex drafting—is easy enough to understand in layman's terms, even if the lawyers are not always satisfied. Its purpose is to ensure that employers will have only to provide paid leave for matters that they recognise in respect of the unions concerned. That is why clause 10 was originally drafted in the way that it was.

However, even while the Bill was in Committee, and as clause 10 itself was being debated, the Court of Appeal made a good attempt, as it turned out, to address the problem that Beale brought to prominence. It did so in the case of Adlington *v.* British Bakeries. The rationale was that, even in respect of an item covered by a recognition agreement, and notwithstanding the dictum in the Beale case, there should still be a degree of proximity between what was being claimed in relation to paid time off and actual negotiations. The Adlington case introduced the concept not only of theoretical recognition but proximity to actual negotiations. In the context of that decision, the Court of Appeal addressed the same problem that the Government attempted to address with clause 10.

At that stage, parliamentary counsel clearly had to examine the drafting of clause 10 and decide whether it needed adjusting in the light of Adlington; or, in layman's terms, to see whether any useful ingredient in the Adlington case had not been taken into account in clause 10. Parliamentary counsel reached the conclusion that the concept of proximity was useful and one that clause 10 alone would not address. It was with a view to retaining that concept of proximity that the amendments now before the House were devised.

Amendments Nos. 30 to 34 fall into two distinct groups. Amendments Nos. 30, 31 and 32, within the intention of clause 10, preserve the proximity concept contained in Adlington, whereas amendments Nos. 33 and 34 deal with a different matter entirely.

The hon. Member for Derbyshire, North-East (Mr. Barnes) raised the issue of associated employers, and in

doing so he identified the purpose of amendments Nos. 33 and 34. Incidentally, I correctly described amendments Nos. 30 to 34 as technical because they are, in the sense that, once one accepts the purpose of clause 10—which I realise Opposition Members do not—and the fusing of the proximity concept with Adlington, the amendments become a purely technical exercise, but in the way of these things, it is not a simple one. They are technical amendments to that extent.

Amendments Nos. 33 and 34 take the opportunity to remedy a defect in the drafting of section 32 of the Employment Protection (Consolidation) Act 1978. The irony is that that defect would have been apparent on the face of the 1978 Act. Section 32 sets out the definition of the term "recognised" as it applies to independent trade unions for the purposes of sections 27 to 31(a)—the time-off provisions. Amendment No. 31 would amend section 32 of the 1978 Act because the definition of "recognised" is redundant and has been so since 1978, because "recognised" means

"recognised by an employer or two or more associated employers".

But sections 27(1) and 28(2) of the 1978 Act to which the definition applies speak of "an employer" and

"an independent trade union recognised by him".

So the reference in the statutory definition to "associated employers" is clearly otiose, and this is a good opportunity to remove it. That is the purpose of amendments Nos. 33 and 34.

Amendments Nos. 30, 31 and 32 would preserve the proximity concept in Adlington. Notwithstanding that, the hon. Member for Derbyshire, North-East asked me specifically about amendment No. 32.

I reiterate that the purpose of clause 10 is to give a right to time off for duties which are connected not with negotiations but with the performance of other functions such as representation through a grievance procedure which the employer has agreed to allow the union to perform. Amendments Nos. 31 and 32 are connected. They both seek to ensure that that proximity concept is retained.

I appreciate that the amendments are not easy amendments, but I assure the House that all they do is ensure that clause 10 stands, while at the same time clearing up an anomaly in the 1978 Act and making sure that the concept of proximity is retained.

In all fairness, the point made by the hon. Member for Bradford, South (Mr. Cryer) needs to be addressed. In effect, the hon. Gentleman was saying that he had spotted what the clause was all about. He did not refer to paid time off, although that is what we are debating, but he disapproved of the fact that the employer should decide and he suspected that that is what the clause is all about. The hon. Gentleman is absolutely right. He spotted precisely what the clause is all about. Despite the words that the lawyers choose for us, the principle is simple enough. If the employer is expected to give paid time off for matters for which he has recognised the union, it is right that it should be only for those matters for which he has recognised the union. The employer has decided to recognise the union for those purposes, so it is complete nonsense that, merely because an employer recognises a union for one purpose, he should suddenly find that in practice he is obliged to pay for some other purpose.

The underlying purpose of clause 10 and the amendments is to ensure that, if an employer recognises a union for a particular purpose, that is the purpose for which paid time off is given. Ultimately the employer pays the wages. I am not hiding it from the hon. Gentleman that the employer should be entitled to say to the trade union, "I recognise you for this purpose; therefore, you are entitled to paid time off. I do not recognise you for that purpose; therefore, you are not."

When I moved the amendments formally I said that they were technical. They are technical. At the same time I accept that they are complex, but I trust that, even at this hour, I have given the House some elucidation. We shall find out in a moment or two whether I have given any comfort.

Question put, That the amendment be made:—
The House divided: Ayes 103, Noes 30.

Division No. 226]   **[2.24 am**

AYES

Alexander, Richard	Lilley, Peter
Alison, Rt Hon Michael	Lloyd, Peter *(Fareham)*
Amos, Alan	Lyell, Sir Nicholas
Arbuthnot, James	Maclean, David
Arnold, Jacques *(Gravesham)*	McLoughlin, Patrick
Ashby, David	Martin, David *(Portsmouth S)*
Batiste, Spencer	Maude, Hon Francis
Bennett, Nicholas *(Pembroke)*	Maxwell-Hyslop, Robin
Bevan, David Gilroy	Mayhew, Rt Hon Sir Patrick
Boswell, Tim	Meyer, Sir Anthony
Bottomley, Peter	Mills, Iain
Brazier, Julian	Mitchell, Andrew *(Gedling)*
Bright, Graham	Mitchell, Sir David
Carlisle, Kenneth *(Lincoln)*	Moss, Malcolm
Chapman, Sydney	Moynihan, Hon Colin
Coombs, Anthony *(Wyre F'rest)*	Neubert, Michael
Cope, Rt Hon John	Nicholls, Patrick
Davis, David *(Boothferry)*	Nicholson, David *(Taunton)*
Devlin, Tim	Nicholson, Emma *(Devon West)*
Dorrell, Stephen	Norris, Steve
Durant, Tony	Paice, James
Favell, Tony	Patnick, Irvine
Fishburn, John Dudley	Raffan, Keith
Forth, Eric	Redwood, John
Fowler, Rt Hon Norman	Ridley, Rt Hon Nicholas
Freeman, Roger	Ryder, Richard
French, Douglas	Sackville, Hon Tom
Garel-Jones, Tristan	Sainsbury, Hon Tim
Gill, Christopher	Shaw, David *(Dover)*
Greenway, John *(Ryedale)*	Shepherd, Colin *(Hereford)*
Gregory, Conal	Shersby, Michael
Griffiths, Sir Eldon *(Bury St E')*	Smith, Tim *(Beaconsfield)*
Griffiths, Peter *(Portsmouth N)*	Stevens, Lewis
Hague, William	Stewart, Andy *(Sherwood)*
Hamilton, Hon Archie *(Epsom)*	Stradling Thomas, Sir John
Hanley, Jeremy	Summerson, Hugo
Hargreaves, Ken *(Hyndburn)*	Taylor, Teddy *(S'end E)*
Harris, David	Thompson, Patrick *(Norwich N)*
Hawkins, Christopher	Thurnham, Peter
Heddle, John	Trippier, David
Hind, Kenneth	Trotter, Neville
Howarth, Alan *(Strat'd-on-A)*	Twinn, Dr Ian
Howarth, G. *(Cannock & B'wd)*	Waddington, Rt Hon David
Hughes, Robert G. *(Harrow W)*	Waller, Gary
Hunt, David *(Wirral W)*	Wardle, Charles *(Bexhill)*
Irvine, Michael	Watts, John
Jack, Michael	Wells, Bowen
Jones, Gwilym *(Cardiff N)*	Widdecombe, Ann
King, Roger *(B'ham N'thfield)*	Wood, Timothy
Kirkhope, Timothy	
Knapman, Roger	Tellers for the Ayes:
Knowles, Michael	Mr. David Heathcoat-Amory
Lee, John *(Pendle)*	and
Lightbown, David	Mr. Michael Fallon.

NOES

Alton, David	Battle, John
Barnes, Harry *(Derbyshire NE)*	Buckley, George J.
Barron, Kevin	Clay, Bob
Clelland, David	Nellist, Dave
Cryer, Bob	Redmond, Martin
Cunliffe, Lawrence	Richardson, Jo
Dixon, Don	Skinner, Dennis
Foster, Derek	Strang, Gavin
Godman, Dr Norman A.	Wallace, James
Home Robertson, John	Wareing, Robert N.
Howells, Geraint	Welsh, Andrew *(Angus E)*
Hughes, John *(Coventry NE)*	Welsh, Michael *(Doncaster N)*
Illsley, Eric	Wise, Mrs Audrey
Kennedy, Charles	
Kirkwood, Archy	Tellers for the Noes:
McCartney, Ian	Mrs. Llin Golding and
McKay, Allen *(Barnsley West)*	Mr. Frank Haynes.
Meale, Alan	

Question accordingly agreed to.

Amendments made: No. 31, in page 9, line 11, leave out from 'with' to 'section' in line 12 and insert
'negotiations with the employer that are related to or connected with any matters which fall within'.

No. 32, in page 9, leave out lines 15 to 17 and insert—
'(ii) any other duties of his, as such an official, which are concerned with the performance, on behalf of employees of the employer, of any functions that are related to or connected with any matters falling within that provision and that the employer has agreed may be so performed by the trade union;'.
—*[Mr. Lee.]*

Clause 16

PRE-HEARING REVIEW OF PROCEEDINGS BEFORE INDUSTRIAL TRIBUNAL

Mr. Wallace: I beg to move amendment No. 35 in page 12, line 18, leave out lines 18 to 21 and insert—
'(i) by the Tribunal; or
(ii) as determined in accordance with the regulations, by any chairman being a member of the panel of chairmen.'.

Madam Deputy Speaker: It will be convenient to discuss at the same time the following amendments: No. 36, in page 12, line 31, leave out '£150' and insert '£50'.

No. 38, in page 12, line 42, after 'order', insert
'but the sum so specified shall not exceed 2% of the sum for the time being prescribed for the purposes of section 75(1) of this Act.'.

No. 37, in line 42, at end add—
'(4) Where regulations are made which authorise the making of an order of the kind referred to in subparagraph (2)(a) above, nothing in this Act or in those regulations shall authorise the making of such an order unless—
(a) the party against whom the order is made has had not less than 3 weeks' notice of the pre-hearing review, or has agreed in writing to waive such notice;
(b) that party has had an opportunity to appear in person or be represented at the pre-hearing review, or to submit written representations if he so elects;
(c) the tribunal or person which makes the order has made such enquiries as are reasonable in the circumstances, including his financial obligations, and is satisfied that—
(i) it is reasonably practical for that party to pay the deposit within the time within which it is ordered to be paid;
(ii) undue hardship will not be caused to that party if the deposit is paid by him and is not refunded to him;
(d) the tribunal or person which makes the orders considers in the light of the originating application and entry of appearance, any representations in writing which have been submitted and oral argument advanced by or on behalf of a Party, that

the contentions or any particular contentions of the party against whom the order is made appear or appears to have no reasonable prospect of success.'.

No. 39 in page 15, line 21, after 'Act', insert—

'(c) an order under section 16(3) which increases the sum specified in paragraph 1A(2)(a) of Schedule 9 to the 1978 Act.

Mr. Wallace: The amendment relates to the administrative and initial arrangements in clause 16 for pre-hearings before industrial tribunals. Its purpose is to ensure that, when determining whether a case receives a pre-hearing review, that determination shall be carried out only by the tribunal or by a chairman who is a member of the panel.

The clause as drafted makes provision for the promulgation of regulations permitting
"such persons as may be determined by or in accordance with the regulations"
to conduct a pre-hearing review. That vague phrase could cover a multitude of sinners as well as a multitude of virtuous people. It would be unsatisfactory to leave that form of words unamended. The British Institute of Management feels that it would be better if we retained the present system of informal discussions that often take place before a tribunal goes ahead, rather than the formalised structure set out in the clause.

However, if we are to have an institutionalised pre-hearing review, it should be undertaken by the appropriate body—either by the tribunal or by those who, because of their qualifications and experience, have been selected to be members of the panel of chairmen, and that would be the effect of amendment No. 35.

Amendment No. 36 would reduce the deposit which any pre-hearing review could impose from £150 to £50. The history of this provision is somewhat chequered. When the Government first proposed the idea of a threshold fee, they suggested £25 but thought that it should be paid by all comers; there was to be no element of discretion. That proposal met with little approval when it went out for consultation, and it was rejected. In the light of that, the Government thought again and proposed that it be increased from £25 to £150, but making it conditional on the outcome of a pre-hearing review, no doubt on the basis that they were trying to weed out frivolous or vexatious claims.

One might have thought that before going ahead with a proposal which, in an almost novel way, introduced a financial threshold that a person must cross before putting his or her case to a tribunal, there would have been an overwhelming body of evidence to show that under the present arrangements there was widespread abuse. But there does not appear to be much authority for that proposition.

Indeed, the bodies which have made comments on this provision—for example, the employment committee of the Law Society and the Law Society of Scotland—have commented that there is no body of evidence to suggest that there has been a great number of frivolous cases clogging up the tribunal system. Those bodies, along with others, find it a regrettable precedent that we are introducing into our system of justice this admission fee before people can take their case to a proper hearing.

In many respects it would be better if there were no deposit at all and if this review did not exist. But, if there is to be a deposit, it is our contention that £50 would be easier to find for less well-off employees, who, perhaps

because they have become unemployed, are much more likely to be involved in tribunal cases. Whether the Government may say about its being wrongly put about that in every case there will be a £150 deposit—I accept that that is not what is proposed here—one knows full well that that sort of idea gains currency. That in itself might deter people from taking the initial step in trying to achieve justice, as they see it, in the case of a claimed wrong. People with valid claims might never get to the stage of lodging them.

Therefore, we propose a sum which is much more realistic, although it would be very difficult for many people to find even £50 and possibly they would have to be given some time to pay. But it would be more within their ability to pay than the sum proposed in the Bill as it stands.

At this point I should refer to amendment No. 38, which I have no doubt the Minister will suggest contradicts what I have just said about amendment No. 36. I accept that there is a contradiction and something of a fallback position in amendment No. 38, because if the 2 per cent. figure were to apply in present circumstances the sum would be £170 rather than £150. We have sought to put this in because, as things stand, the Secretary of State could by regulation and subject to the negative procedure, amend the sum of the deposit from £150 to any figure at all by substituting
"such other sum as is specified in the order."

No limit is put on it, and it is unsatisfactory that that carte blanche should be given to the Minister subject only to the briefest scrutiny in the Committee on Statutory Instruments, which would not be allowed to amend and would have only a limited opportunity to discuss the principle behind it. That is why we have suggested that there should be an attempt to link the deposit to the award payable, so that if there is any suggestion that the deposit should go up it would be necessary to increase the maximum award. That would impose a realistic restraint on the actions of any future Secretary of State, or indeed the present one, if he sought to abuse the procedure which is set down here.

Amendment No. 39, if carried, would make it necessary for these regulations or any substitution sum to be subject to the affirmative procedure. This would indicate the importance of this as a fundamental principle of justice not just related to the question of industrial tribunals. We are dealing here with people's rights and it is an important departure in the administration of justice in this country. It is not an incidental matter and when we are dealing with such a fundamental matter the affirmative procedure is much more appropriate.

The only amendment to which I have not yet referred is No. 37. This is an important amendment because it seeks to set some parameters within which the pre-hearing review must operate. It ensures, for example, that the basic precepts of natural justice are observed and that adequate time is given by one party to the other if a pre-hearing review is sought with the likelihood of a deposit ensuing. It ensures the right to representation or, if there is no representation, the right either to be heard or to make written representation. It tries to ensure that orders are not made against people who cannot realistically comply with them, in which case a deposit really amounts to a dismissal of the claim. The amendment proposes that it would be incumbent on the tribunal or the chairman to ensure that such a sum was not imposed if the effect would be that the claimant was unable to take the claim any further. It also proposes that deposits would be imposed only in circumstances in which costs awards could be made under the present rules.

2.45 am

Much of what is proposed in clause 16 is a sorry departure from the present system. There is no evidence that the present system is being abused and Opposition Members—of whom there are still a number here even at this late hour—regret very much that a fee is to be introduced into our system. Given that that is the case, and although it is perhaps optimism triumphing over reality, given the Government's attitude to any Opposition amendments, we tried to propose a halfway house, and to put some parameters and restraints on the Government's proposals. It is in that spirit that we move the amendments.

Mr. Nicholls: The hon. Member for Orkney and Shetland (Mr. Wallace) has raised a number of points on the amendments and I will do my best to deal with them.

Clause 16 as drafted gives the Secretary of State the power to make regulations authorising pre-hearing reviews to be carried out either by the tribunal chairman or by the full tribunal, which would obviously include the lay members as well as the chairman. That is also the effect of amendment No. 35, so to that extent it is difficult to see the difference in substance between the amendment and the Government's proposal, although, if I understood the hon. Gentleman correctly, he was concerned that there was reference in clause 16 to "such person", which may have raised a doubt in his mind about what was intended. We are advised that that formula has to be used because the regional chairman might be sitting and the regional chairman is separately defined under the regulations, or the president himself could be referred to. That is why that formulation is used. Clause 16, as drafted, already does what the hon. Gentleman has in mind.

Amendment No. 36 is, as the hon. Gentleman said, a halfway house. It proposes to reduce from £150 to £50 the maximum deposit for a pre-hearing to be ordered. I dare say that the hon. Gentleman would think it rather ungenerous of me to say that if he is prepared to concede the principle of a deposit, our judgment is as good as his. He would say that he does not concede the principle, but lives in the real and practical world and hopes that Ministers do as well. If one concedes, if only for the purposes of the argument, that some deposit is appropriate, it is a question of where one draws the line. Neither £50 nor £150 is a princely sum. In each case, the sum would be only a maximum. There is no question of a tribunal being under an obligation to order a sum at all. Although it may seem to be the judgment of Solomon, we take the view that £150 is right.

Amendment No. 37 seems to us to be unnecessary because virtually all the matters that it covers would be covered by regulations which are due to be made under clause 16 in any event.

The Government take the view that amendment No. 38 unduly fetters the discretion of the Secretary of State in determining the size of the maximum deposit. It would also be unnecessarily complicated. I accept that the amendment is ingenious, but it is difficult to see the logic in trying to enshrine in law a mathematical relationship between the compensatory award maximum and the deposit maximum.

Clause 16 allows the Secretary of State from time to time to alter the limit on the amount of a deposit, and clause 21(4) makes any order altering the limit subject to the negative resolution procedure. Amendment No. 39 would provide that the draft of any such order would have to be laid before, and approved by resolution of, both Houses of Parliament. This debate echoes a number of debates that we had in Committee about whether the affirmative or the negative procedure should be used. Someone—it may even have been me—suggested that such debates entailed an element of ritual and that, in the unlikely event that our roles were ever reversed, Ministers might one day be Opposition Back Benchers and arguing the opposite view. Lively though my imagination is, I cannot encompass that prospect at this time in the morning.

The Government regard this as precisely the sort of matter that should be dealt with by the negative resolution procedure. Therefore, while I should have liked to tell the hon. Gentleman that his optimism would triumph over his experience, I cannot recommend his amendments to the House.

Ms. Richardson: It is rather unfair of the Minister to hint that the hon. Member for Orkney and Shetland (Mr. Wallace) was abandoning the principle of opposition to the £150 deposit. I do not think that he was. He was at pains to say that this was an honest attempt to arrive at a halfway house. Let me say to him and to the Government that the Opposition Members also stick by the principle that we are opposed to the £150 deposit. Like the hon. Gentleman, we should have preferred the clause to be deleted. Nevertheless, the amendments represent a good way of rehearsing our extensive arguments in Committee and of placing on record the opposition that remains to the concept of a deposit of the size envisaged in the Bill.

It is all very well for the Minister, in a fairly light-hearted way, to dismiss £150 as not much. To the majority of working people, £150 is quite a lot. To many people, £50 is quite a lot. To suggest that it does not amount to much more than a row of beans—I am not saying that the Minister used those words; he did not—is to underestimate its importance. I remind the Minister that during the consultation procedure a number of prestigious bodies expressed their opposition. The British Institute of Management was not totally opposed to a deposit but argued that it would be much more of an obstacle for an employee than for an employer. We can all echo that. The BIM also suggested that employers might automatically apply for an order.

The Engineering Employers Federation felt that, although the £150 deposit would not deter those backed by a union, it might deter—would deter—those who were not unionised but

"might have a genuine case".

Given the Government's antipathy to unions, one would have expected them to give a little thought to those who are not unionised.

The TUC, the Equal Opportunities Commission and the National Association of Citizens Advice Bureaux were wholeheartedly against the £150 and the Government would have been wiser to listen to their advice. As it is, the Government will oppose the amendments, which will be lost in the mists of time—whatever time it is now. We shall have to see what happens. If statistics are kept after the

[*Ms. Richardson*]

provision for a deposit becomes law, I am sure that they will show that many genuine cases will not be taken to a tribunal.

We must recognise that not only will many of those faced with a £150 demand not be able to pay it, but that many people will not even take their cases to a tribunal because of the possibility of that deposit being demanded. Although the Minister has said that it is a deposit and that £150 is the maximum, it will deter people.

We want a system of industrial democracy that does not result in any employee, whether or not unionised, being deterred from pursuing his or her rights as he or she perceives them. The clause is just another way of the Government putting blocks in the way of the employed and giving an advantage to the employers. We should prefer the clause to be deleted but, given that that is not a possibility because our amendment was not selected, we shall wholeheartedly support these amendments.

Mr. Haynes: I am not surprised that we are debating such important amendments, which I welcome. The Opposition are opposed to any deposit. It is immoral of the Government to impose a deposit of £150. Ministers have their heads in the clouds; they do not have their feet on the ground; they do not understand the problems of low-paid workers. The Government do not want workers to belong to a trade union and encourage them not to be.

When I was a trade union official in the mining industry in the Nottingham area, members made their contributions each week and that entitled them to certain benefits. If the deposit had been law then, one benefit would have been that the union would probably have paid the £150. That is what happens in the trade union movement. The Ministers belonged to a closed shop in their previous professions and are, perhaps, still associated with those professional organisations. I cannot understand why they argue against the closed shop in trade unions. The closed shop means protection for members. The Government are imposing a penalty of £150 on workers who have had a shoddy deal from their employers and have had to take their cases to an industrial tribunal. It is immoral, although I am no longer surprised by many of the Government's actions.

3 am

The Government encourage low pay for workers. We have plenty of low-paid workers. If a worker is not in a trade union, he will have to find £150, probably just after losing his job. Where does the Minister get his ideas from? Has he really thought this out? He is nodding his head but I do not think that he has thought it out. He has not got his feet on the ground. He has not worked in the areas in which many Opposition Members have worked. We understand fully the implication of a £150 deposit.

It annoys me when I hear the Secretary of State for Social Security shooting his mouth off about how well off people are. We have poverty in this nation. We have people on very low earnings. The hon. Member for Pendle (Mr. Lee), the Minister responsible for tourism, is encouraging more and more people into tourism to work for very low wages. If there is an unfair dismissal and the person wants to go to the tribunal, how the hell does the Minister think that that person will manage to get a fair deal? The worker will not be able to go to the tribunal because he cannot afford the £150. We must remember that there is always the danger that he will lose, even though he has a first-class case. That is why the £150 deposit is immoral.

I am surprised—no, I am not surprised that this is happening under the mob that we have in government. Mark my words; when we kick out that lot on the Government Benches——

Mr. Lee: Never.

Mr. Haynes: The Minister will eat his words one day. He might be one of those who will go and who may have to go back into practice again, with nice, big, cosy earnings in the closed shop.

Mr. McCartney: At £150 an hour.

Mr. Haynes: Yes, representing employers at tribunals, getting rich pickings. We are talking about people in the lower income group who are in serious financial difficulty. It is not funny; it is a serious matter. The Minister should be in a position to find out about poverty. I know what it is all about, as my father did before me. I have lived in poverty; I have breathed it and slept in it. I know how people are suffering when they are not getting the earnings that they should.

Mr. Teddy Taylor (Southend, East): I accept what the hon. Gentleman says—I think that he knows that I am a lifelong trade unionist—but does not he accept that there is another side to the matter? With all the new responsibilities, rules, regulations, restrictions and conditions that are being imposed on the United Kingdom Parliament and Government in consequence of EEC directives, as most of the Bill is, employers will spend all their time going to tribunals instead of getting on with the job of production. The hon. Gentleman's party has new enthusiasm for all this nonsensical bureaucracy that is making the life of industry a nightmare. Does he accept that there is another side to the story and that perhaps something should be done about it?

Mr. Haynes *rose*——

Mr. Deputy Speaker (Sir Paul Dean): Order. I am sure that the hon. Member for Ashfield (Mr. Haynes) will not be tempted to broaden the debate.

Mr. Haynes: You have jumped the gun, Mr. Deputy Speaker. I understand why. The hon. Gentleman has an argument and he is using it and he is trying to use me as well, but I am not going down the EEC road tonight. I do not think it would be fair. But I understand why the hon. Member for—[HON. MEMBERS: "Southend."] I am talking about the hon. Member for Southend, East (Mr. Taylor). I know, because he has said it so often before. We have had debates in the early morning on these directives from Europe.

The point is that I maintain my argument and I will never change. The Conservatives will never change, but we will change the system in here—that lot will be over here and we will be over there. We will put things right, and I promise the Minister that it will happen at the next election, because the people outside have had enough. They do not want any more, but they have three more years, so we will have to make the best of it. However, there is worse and worse to come. With such proposals as this, matters will get worse and worse. A lot of people in my constituency are suffering under the Government, and here they go again—a lower-paid worker must pay a deposit of £150 to fight a case which it is possible that he might lose. It really is immoral.

My hon. Friend the Member for Barking (Ms. Richardson) said at the Dispatch Box only a few minutes before I started to say my piece that what the Government were doing is wrong and that we do not accept that that payment should be made. It is not fair, it is completely immoral, and I believe that we should vote for the amendment. I hope that some of the Conservative Members will change their minds and see the unfairness involved. I am living in hope, I know. If they are honest with themselves, they will vote with us tonight on these amendments. *[Interruption.]* They will probably not have enough for a closure, because they are dipping very fast. There were 103 at the last count. The Government Chief Whip has a job to get out there and get them in, in the hope that they will win a vote tonight, because at the moment they are on a loser. Conservative Members are going down and down, but we are still here fighting on behalf of the people we represent, especially those lower-paid workers.

Mr. McCartney: They could not raise a deposit between them.

Mr. Haynes: My hon. Friend is quite correct. I think that you have had enough of me, Mr. Deputy Speaker.

Several hon. Members *rose——*

Mr. Haynes: I think that I will stay a bit longer, because they are a bit upset over yonder. The Minister always tells me that he loves Frank Haynes to be called. He knows that I will have a go at him, but I am a different man in here from what I am outside, because in here I fight like a dog for what I believe in—a mad dog too, perhaps. I will fight for what I believe in in the same way as the great grandfather of the hon. Member for Pembroke (Mr. Bennett) did. He must be turning in his grave at some of the things that the hon. Gentleman has done in this Chamber. The great grandfather of the hon. Gentleman was a fighter for the working class people, especially the lower paid workers. When I was a young lad, people worked in the pits for peanuts. Safety came last and profits were at the top of the list for the coal owners. That is what Toryism is all about. People, especially in this country, know what Socialism is about, and, by God, soon they will get some more Socialism and we will get some more fairness in the interests of the people and not just of certain individuals.

A lot of the company bosses are feeding money into the Conservative party funds, and there is a connection here. I believe that the Minister has taken that point well home. I think that he understands what I am trying to say to him. The message is coming over to the electorate loud and clear. The next election cannot come soon enough, and we will win it. The tragedy is that I will not be coming back here after it. I have enjoyed my time here and I will enjoy what is left. No doubt, in the future I will have something to say to the Minister about his policies.

I am asking the Government to back off and accept what we have said. The amendment does not go as far as I would like, but at least the Democrats are going part of the way.

Mr. Barron: They are Liberals.

Mr. Haynes: No, they tell me that they are Democrats. I am not going to argue about it. The Democrats are going part of the way. Because the Labour amendment has not been selected, we are forced to go along with the Democrats' suggestion. We support them to the hilt. We will be in the Division Lobby with them, and I hope that some Tories will be with us.

Mr. Wallace: I think that the Minister said that if Ministers lived in the real world, hope would triumph—he went on to prove that they do not—but he made that comment late at night and perhaps did not mean to phrase it in that way. It outlined what many of us have found throughout the debate—no matter how reasonable we try to make our amendments, the Government do not meet them even a third or a half of the way.

As for the real world, the hon. Member for Ashfield (Mr. Haynes) made a valid point——

Mr. Haynes: Several.

Mr. Wallace: Several valid points, but one in particular about the £150. We are talking about people not just on low pay but on no pay, which is why they go to an industrial tribunal. That sum may be the maximum amount to be paid, but it is a colossal sum for them. Its imposition may debar people from seeking justice.

I am not always satisfied by assurances from Ministers that "these matters will appear in regulations." If that is so, the Government should have nothing to fear in laying down statutory parameters. I accept the Minister's comment that the term "such person" is necessary to cover this group of chairmen of tribunals. For that reason, I will not seek a Division on amendment No. 35. Amendment No. 36 goes more to the heart of what we have been driving at. Although we would prefer to have no deposit, our proposal is more realistic than the Government's provision.

Amendment negatived.

Amendment proposed, No. 36, in page 12, line 31, leave out '£150' and insert '£50'.—*[Mr. Wallace.]*

Question put, That the amendment be made:—

The House divided: Ayes 24, Noes 106.

Division No. 227]   **[3.13 am**

AYES

Alton, David	McKay, Allen *(Barnsley West)*
Barnes, Harry *(Derbyshire NE)*	Meale, Alan
Barron, Kevin	Nellist, Dave
Cryer, Bob	Richardson, Jo
Cunliffe, Lawrence	Skinner, Dennis
Dixon, Don	Strang, Gavin
Foster, Derek	Wareing, Robert N.
Golding, Mrs Llin	Welsh, Andrew *(Angus E)*
Haynes, Frank	Welsh, Michael *(Doncaster N)*
Home Robertson, John	Wise, Mrs Audrey
Howells, Geraint	
Hughes, John *(Coventry NE)*	Tellers for the Ayes:
Kennedy, Charles	Mr. Archy Kirkwood and
McCartney, Ian	Mr. James Wallace.

NOES

Alexander, Richard	Bottomley, Peter
Alison, Rt Hon Michael	Brazier, Julian
Amos, Alan	Bright, Graham
Arbuthnot, James	Carlisle, Kenneth *(Lincoln)*
Arnold, Jacques *(Gravesham)*	Chapman, Sydney
Ashby, David	Coombs, Anthony *(Wyre F'rest)*
Batiste, Spencer	Cope, Rt Hon John
Bennett, Nicholas *(Pembroke)*	Davis, David *(Boothferry)*
Bevan, David Gilroy	Devlin, Tim
Boswell, Tim	Dorrell, Stephen

Durant, Tony
Fishburn, John Dudley
Forth, Eric
Fowler, Rt Hon Norman
Freeman, Roger
French, Douglas
Garel-Jones, Tristan
Gill, Christopher
Goodhart, Sir Philip
Greenway, John *(Ryedale)*
Gregory, Conal
Griffiths, Sir Eldon *(Bury St E')*
Griffiths, Peter *(Portsmouth N)*
Hague, William
Hamilton, Hon Archie *(Epsom)*
Hamilton, Neil *(Tatton)*
Hanley, Jeremy
Hargreaves, Ken *(Hyndburn)*
Harris, David
Heddle, John
Hind, Kenneth
Howarth, Alan *(Strat'd-on-A)*
Howarth, G. *(Cannock & B'wd)*
Hughes, Robert G. *(Harrow W)*
Hunt, David *(Wirral W)*
Irvine, Michael
Jack, Michael
Jones, Gwilym *(Cardiff N)*
King, Roger *(B'ham N'thfield)*
Knapman, Roger
Knowles, Michael
Lee, John *(Pendle)*
Lightbown, David
Lilley, Peter
Lloyd, Peter *(Fareham)*
Lyell, Sir Nicholas
Maclean, David
McLoughlin, Patrick
Martin, David *(Portsmouth S)*
Maude, Hon Francis
Maxwell-Hyslop, Robin
Mayhew, Rt Hon Sir Patrick
Meyer, Sir Anthony
Mills, Iain
Mitchell, Andrew *(Gedling)*

Mitchell, Sir David
Moss, Malcolm
Moynihan, Hon Colin
Neale, Gerrard
Neubert, Michael
Nicholls, Patrick
Nicholson, David *(Taunton)*
Nicholson, Emma *(Devon West)*
Norris, Steve
Paice, James
Patnick, Irvine
Raffan, Keith
Redwood, John
Ridley, Rt Hon Nicholas
Rowe, Andrew
Ryder, Richard
Sackville, Hon Tom
Sainsbury, Hon Tim
Shaw, David *(Dover)*
Shepherd, Colin *(Hereford)*
Shersby, Michael
Smith, Tim *(Beaconsfield)*
Speller, Tony
Stevens, Lewis
Stewart, Andy *(Sherwood)*
Stradling Thomas, Sir John
Summerson, Hugo
Taylor, Teddy *(S'end E)*
Thompson, Patrick *(Norwich N)*
Thurnham, Peter
Townend, John *(Bridlington)*
Trippier, David
Trotter, Neville
Twinn, Dr Ian
Waddington, Rt Hon David
Waller, Gary
Wardle, Charles *(Bexhill)*
Watts, John
Wells, Bowen
Widdecombe, Ann
Wood, Timothy

Tellers for the Noes:
    Mr. Michael Fallon and
    Mr. David Heathcoat-Amory.

Question accordingly negatived.

Clause 18

DISSOLUTION OF TRAINING COMMISSION

Amendment made: No. 18, in page 13, line 27, leave out ", apart from this section,".—[*Mr. Fowler.*]

Schedule 5

DISSOLUTION OF TRAINING COMMISSION:
SUPPLEMENTARY PROVISIONS

Amendments made: No. 19, in page 26, line 11, leave out ', in relation to any time falling on or after that date'.
    No. 20, in page 26, line 25, leave out
'office or place of business'
and insert "principal office".—[*Mr. Fowler.*]

Clause 19

TRANSFER OF STAFF EMPLOYED IN SKILLS TRAINING AGENCY

Mr. Strang: I beg to move amendment No. 23, in page 13, line 30, leave out clause 19.

Mr. Deputy Speaker (Sir Paul Dean): With this we may take the following amendments: No. 24, in page 14, line 7, at end insert—

'(2A) The Secretary of State shall make arrangements for the continuation of a "Skillcentre Network.".'.
    No. 26, in page 14, line 10, at end insert—
'(3B) After the transfer of an undertaking, civil service terms and conditions of employment shall continue to apply, unless altered by negotiation and agreement with the relevant trade unions.'.
    No. 27, in page 14, line 10, at end insert—
'(3C) After the transfer of an undertaking, civil service pension arrangements shall continue to apply, unless altered by negotiation and agreement with the relevant trade unions.'.
    No. 28, in page 14, line 19, at end insert—
'The Secretary of State shall make such arrangements as necessary to ensure that after a transfer of an undertaking, the same amount and quality of training is delivered.'.
    No. 29, in page 14, line 40, at end insert—
'(9) This section shall not come into force until the Secretary of State has established a body of relevant organisations to monitor the training services delivered after the transfer of an undertaking.'.

Mr. Strang: Clause 19 follows from the Government's decision to privatise skill centres, which we deeply deplore and which has important consequences for the staff employed at them, who are currently civil servants.

The proposal stems from the Government's announcement in last December's White Paper "Employment for the 1990s" indicating their intention to privatise the Skills Training Agency. However, their arguments were flawed. The White Paper stated:

"The Skills Training Agency would be in a better position to seize these opportunities if it were to move into the private sector where it could adopt the best commercial practices. The Government are therefore taking professional advice on the feasibility of such a move."

In essence, the Government are free to run the agency as they wish. It is within their power to decide that, and whether or not the agency is in the public sector does not really matter. If the Government want the agency to be run as a commercial operation, they have only to instruct the civil servants in charge to run it that way. If the Government want the agency to concentrate on certain areas where a need for greater training provision has been identified, they have only instruct the people who run it to do that instead.

I make that point because sometimes it is suggested that it is impossible to run an activity in the public sector commercially or efficiently. British Airways is currently operating very efficiently in the private sector under the chairmanship of Lord King, but before its privatisation, the Government gave British Airways a remit to slim down and become profitable. British Airways operated in the public sector, in preparation for privatisation, as a relatively efficient, profitable and slimmed-down company. It could have continued doing so in the public sector. That illustrates that there is nothing in the argument that the Skills Training Agency must be moved into the private sector before it can perform in a certain way. It will do so anyway if the people running it are asked to make it function in a specific way; and if the Government are not satisfied with their performance, they can be replaced by people having the wherewithal and ability to make it do so.

Our main reason for opposing the clause is that all the evidence, including the Government's own documents, suggests that British business has failed adequately to invest in training, and that its record is poor by comparison with its European competitors. In those circumstances, how on earth can it make sense to remove from the public sector a training provision that the

Government can influence and transfer it to the private sector—when the record of private training sector even in the Government's eyes, and certainly in ours, is poor?

With the agency taking over the responsibilities of the Training Commission, a substantial proportion of the so-called national task force now comprises large, private industrial companies. Having acknowledged that, apart from some notable exceptions, British business has failed to take training sufficiently seriously, it seems a remarkable conclusion to put the people who have apparently failed in charge, or at least to give them a major say over the Government's expenditure on training and at the same time to move out of the public sector the skill centres which are wholly owned by the Government and through which the Government can lay down what training should be provided.

3.30 am

The argument that the agency is losing money does not stand up as it is a wholly artificial exercise. The Secretary of State's announcement referred to the fact that the agency had made a profit in some years but had made a substantial loss in others. I do not have the figures to hand, but I recall that it made a profit in 1987-88 or 1988-89. That was partly accounted for by the fact that the Manpower Services Commission was committed to using the skill centres to provide some of the training that it was financing.

In the current year, the gross cost of the training centres is about £53 million, whereas the Government's planned expenditure for the Training Agency is £2,860 million. It is an artificial point to argue that the skill centres are losing money. One could stop them losing money by instructing the managers to organise the scheme or slim it down so that it would no longer lose money. Alternatively, one could acknowledge that the Government are spending a substantial sum of money on training and that it may make sense to use some of that money to provide opportunities at the skill centres that are not available elsewhere and cost money. The argument that the skill centres should necessarily be profitable is not valid.

The skill centres have existed for a long time. They first came into being in the aftermath of the first world war. They have a good record. Some excellent people work in the skill centres, which have provided tremendous opportunities and valuable training, particularly for the long-term unemployed. Many women have been able to acquire the necessary skills for jobs which are usually carried out by men, and we would all encourage that. Skill centres can be proud of the contribution which they have made to training in Britain over the years.

That is not to say that one should accept the current arrangements or concede that the training courses and facilities which they currently provide are the right ones for the 1990s. However, while they are part of the Civil Service, and part of the Government, at least the Government can decide what facilities are provided in these centres. There is no question but that in many localities skill centres have identified skills shortages and have made a significant contribution to training the most difficult people to train, such as those who have been unemployed for some time. We reject the Government's approach. It is ludicrous for them to argue that they can enhance and improve training provision in this country by privatising a fraction of the training facilities that accounts for a small proportion of Government expenditure on training.

It is clear that training provision will be privatised, and it would be helpful if, in the time available—we do not wish unduly to prolong proceedings—the Minister said a little more about the progress of the management buyout. He explained in Committee that the Government are quite happy that the deputy chief executive, Mr. Bishell, is leading a management buy-out, which would rule out the purchase of local skill centres by local consortia. Is that still the most likely option? I know that the Government are not excluding further options, even at this late stage.

Labour Members should like an assurance that assets will not be disposed of at knockdown values and that the market value of sites will be reflected in their sale price. Under the British Aerospace privatisation, assets were sold for a price below that implied in the overall package. The Minister should give an assurance that sites—the market value of some of which is quite favourable—will not be disposed of at knockdown prices. I have heard one or two suggested figures for skill centres and sites that are, to put it mildly, well below what one would expect the assets to realise if they were sold separately in the market.

We are not trying to impose an undue burden on the new outfit. We are opposed to privatisation, but once it goes ahead it is in everyone's interests that it should provide more training. We are worried that, assets having been acquired, there will be a gradual process of rationalisation and asset-stripping and that the privatised operation will make a reduced contribution, quantitatively if not qualitatively, to training.

Clause 19 is not about privatisation but about the terms and conditions of employment of civil servants employed in the centres. It ensures that when skill centres are transferred to their new owners, the Transfer of Undertakings (Protection of Employment) Regulations 1981 are employed for all staff. However, because civil servants often enjoy better conditions than they might in the private sector, and because we fear that the service offered by skill centres will suffer, we are proposing amendments to safeguard the rights of employees and the standards of service that they offer.

Amendment No. 24 would mean that the Secretary of State would have to make arrangements for the continuation of a skill centre network. We believe that privatisation will be followed by the breaking up of the national effect on retraining into a service that ranges widely in quality from area to area. The amendment should cause the Government no problems if they are committed to the continuation of national training, while allowing for separate management.

Amendment No. 28 would require the Secretary of State to ensure that privatised skill centres will provide the same amount and quality of training.

Amendment No. 29 would greatly assist the Minister in pursuit of that goal. It provides for the setting up of a watchdog body for monitoring the training services that are delivered after privatisation. We do not specify which organisations should sit on that body, but say only "relevant" organisations. We have in mind a body along the lines of that which was set up to monitor the performance of British Telecom when it was privatised, and feel that it should comprise representatives of trade unions, the unemployed and employers' representatives to

[*Mr. Strang*]

safeguard against the sort of defects that we believe are apparent in the body that is supposed to be supervising British Telecom.

We have advanced amendment No. 26, which concerns the terms and conditions of employment of civil servants who are currently employed in connection with skill centres. Amendment No. 27 relates to their pensions. Both amendments state that they will continue to apply unless they have been altered by negotiation and agreement with the relevant trade unions.

We recognise that the Government have given certain undertakings, and the purpose of the clause is to ensure that the civil servants retain their accrued rights in relation to pensions, redundancy and employment conditions. However, as the Minister said in Committee, after privatisation anything can happen. We want to tie the Minister down more clearly because we believe that there should be some commitment to the civil servants which goes beyond the point of transfer.

In Committe the Minister made a statement on pensions. He said that they

"must be covered separately by arrangements in the terms of sale. The details will be a matter for the sale negotiations, but . . . arrangements to provide for pension terms which, taken overall, are comparable with those that apply now will be part of the conditions of sale."

If we are to accept that rather bland assurance, amendment No. 27 would give it some substance while offering new employers some flexibility. Unfortunately, there is nothing in this or any other Bill that would guarantee civil servants similar pension rights, and they and their unions are right to be sceptical of the Government's real commitment and intentions.

As the proposals stand, anybody with more than two years' service can leave the pension rights that they have accrued in the Civil Service scheme. Employees with less than two years' service do not have that right. I put it to the Minister that one can leave one's rights in other pension schemes after less than two years; so why is it necessary to have a cut-off of two years?

Similarly, we ask the Government to match their words with actions and accept amendment No. 26 on the terms and conditions of employment—of which pensions do not form a part. Again, we suggest that it will be only a matter of time before those rights are eroded.

On the question whether a privatised civil servant will be required to move willy-nilly under the new management, the Minister gave a curious answer in Committee. He said:

"The position will remain broadly the same when they move to new ownership but may change slightly, particularly if the network is not the same as it is now."—[*Official Report, Standing Committee A,* 16 March 1989; c. 532.]

Given that the network is highly unlikely to remain unchanged, where does that leave the movement of employees of skill centres?

It may not be unprecedented—I hope that the Minister will say what the precedents are—but this is a remarkable and traumatic issue for the civil servants. There are many instances in the implementation of such a policy where civil servants are given some choice. They can take redundancy or obtain a transfer into another area of the Civil Service, remaining civil servants.

But these civil servants are not being given that choice. They are being compulsorily privatised. The Minister probably knows already that many of them deeply resent that. Many believe in the idea of public service. They want to be civil servants. They like being civil servants and they are deeply angry that, without any warning or mandate, they can be suddenly told that on a particular day, which is not far off now, they will cease to be civil servants, even if they would rather have continued as civil servants, perhaps in some other area of the Department of Employment's general activities or some other area of the Civil Service.

It is highly unsatisfactory that that should be the plight of people in the Civil Service, and I refer not just to those in the higher echelons of the service but to people with a commitment to working in the public service, who believe that by working as civil servants, particularly in this area, they have a valuable role to fulfil.

In the past I was in contact with instructors in the establishments, through the links I had with the old Civil Service Union. Many of those people are dedicated to their task and it is deeply regrettable that they should find themselves compulsorily transferred to a private organisation. We cannot know what the future holds for such an organisation because inherent in the exercise is the fact that once it is sold off, it must operate independently in the market place. Indeed, we have no guarantee that it will continue to provide training in 10 or 20 years hence.

This proposal was brought forward as a new clause during the final stages of the Committee stage debates. We are glad of this opportunity to raise the issue on the Floor of the House. The Minister has an obligation to the House to deal with these issues, but he has a wider obligation to the staff, the trade unions and the country to answer the questions that we have asked.

3.45 am

Mr. McCartney: It is a tragedy that at 3.45 in the morning we should be debating the issue of training in Britain and the demise of a co-ordinated national training effort which has involved the public and private sectors, local authorities and Government in the development of employment and training initiatives.

I was in local government for six years and worked closely on issues of this type, including with the MSC on general employment projects and on the technical and vocational education initiative. I found it vital to have local authorities involved with the Training Commission and private employers to develop the education system so that it became able to meet the needs of industry. I found it an uplifting experience.

It is regrettable that, because of their policies, the Government have tended to withdraw from that type of close co-operation between local authorities and the public sector in general. They are now trying to organise it solely on the basis of the market place, and that will prove to be a tragedy in the short and long-term. After all, our competitors in Europe and further afield are not leaving their training initiatives to market forces. They appreciate the need to co-ordinate and develop employment and training initiatives as an entity to enhance the development of their economies.

It is tragic that the Government should be taking these steps at a time when we have major skill shortages in various parts of the country. That is the case, for example, in the north-west, because of 10 years of decline and lack of investment, while in other areas there continues to be a lack of skilled manpower even though local economies are booming. The shortfalls in the YTS and the short-term nature of earlier training schemes have left us with a skill base lower than we had 10 years ago. That will act to the long-term detriment of the public and private sectors.

With the abolition of the metropolitan authorities, we saw, for example, in Greater Manchester, the ending overnight of joint initiatives between the MSC and the local authority. Millions of pounds each year went into joint ventures and training at skill centres and places of employment. We have not recovered from the loss of that type of resource.

We have a skill centre in my area. The local authority has developed round it, so to speak, a development company involving a major new initiative of an industrial estate. It is one of the most modern industrial estates in the north-west. Its infrastructure is superb and it is attracting new industry. The skill centre is linked with the information technology centres and a system has been developed whereby the local authority, through its employment initiatives with the private sector, is trying to develop a co-ordinated approach to training in our area. Yet at the same time there is an attempt by the Government to leave all this to market forces.

Market forces by themselves are totally inadequate to deal with the needs of private industry and to link that with the resources being spent at the public level by local authorities and in some instances by Government so as to get the best value for money and develop in such a way that we involve as many people as possible in retraining, the rehabilitation of the long-term unemployed and the disabled and the development of new skills and techniques. This is essential in terms of the development of the economy.

We have realised in the north-west, with the demise of much of our industry in textiles, heavy engineering and shipbuilding, the need to develop a different structure of employment in the region. That means the introduction of new skills and technology, but that cannot be achieved in either the short or the long term without a co-ordinated approach to training and the development of new skills and the provision of resources to identify those new skills and enable people to learn them.

Amendment No. 24, if carried, would give us an opportunity to make sure that, although skill centres are privatised, the essential nature of the network is retained and they have a chance to work with the private sector, local authority and other public sector initiatives. Even though I am totally opposed to the idea of urban development corporations, while they exist they have a role to play in the development of the economy in the urban areas of Salford, Manchester, Liverpool and other such places. Their activities need to be co-ordinated with the work of skill centres and should not be completely divorced and left to market forces.

It is also important that quality and quantity are not reduced. Over the last decade both the quality and the quantity of the training needed to develop the economic base of the regions have been reduced substantially in many parts of Britain. And we are faced with a Government privatising these organisations for ideological reasons and not looking at what is required in terms of a co-ordinated approach to training in the private and public sector.

I look to the Minister to give me some assurances, given the unique role of the skill centres as the dynamo in my local economy and the overspill effect that has occurred in terms of the other initiatives that have been taken, some in the past directly with the Government through the MSC, the Department of Education and Science and the Department of Employment. We have seen over four or five years the development of such schemes and the involvement of both the private and the public sector, but the Government's proposals are putting an end to all this. There were approaches last year to the TUC about Government proposals interfering with the then role of the MSC, then deciding to get rid of the Training Commission and to privatise what is left of the skill centres. There seems no sense in the Government doing that and then not coming forward with initiatives to protect the present network of skill centres, which, in protecting that network, will protect the work done in the regions by skill centres and other organisations to enhance and develop new skills in local economies.

My hon. Friend the Member for Edinburgh, East (Mr. Strang) has asked the Minister for commitments on staff, which are important and are similar to the plea made recently about staff in the Department of Energy under the Electricity Bill. We are seeking not only a commitment on current staff, but a general commitment on the level of employment within the new, privatised skill centres. Unless there is a commitment about the level of employment and the quality of the trainers, the role of skill centres will be seriously undermined, as will the training that they provide and the quality and quantity of that provision.

Over the past few years, there has been a tendency in some skill centres to cut short, often at short notice, some of the programmes that are being developed, as a result of cuts at some of the centres. That has led to many instances of the staff becoming demoralised and the people who are trying to take advantage of the schemes have found themselves in difficulties. They have had to come off schemes before they are completed, or are threatened with having to do so. That does not add up to a modern approach to training in new skills.

One would expect such things to happen at the turn of the century, but not with training for the new technology for the next century and not when in Europe, the far east, the middle east, America and even central America, there are initiatives by Governments and industries that will undermine our export drive. We need to develop and strengthen our economy in the regions, yet at this very point, the Government are reducing resources overall and then asking us to accept that market forces will see us through. That is unacceptable.

I want the Minister to give some commitments about the skill centres in the north-west, such as the one in my constituency, and to say what his intentions are about developing and building on initiatives taken by some local authorities—initiatives taken in good faith with his Department. Many capital resources and much ratepayers' money have been put into those initiatives, yet we are now uncertain about the Government's policy on skill centres. If the Minister gives us some undertakings on that, our worries will be eased. I view with some trepidation the decision of the Minister and the Government to opt out of developing a national policy on training, in terms of quality and quantity.

Mr. Haynes: I see the proposal as part of the Ridley blueprint under which the Government, when they came

[*Mr. Haynes*]

to office in 1979, were determined to destroy certain aspects of life before 1979. There is a very successful skill centre in the town of Kirkby-in-Ashfield in my constituency, with a first-class team providing training and giving an excellent service. I pay a tribute to the staff of that skill centre, and a tribute was paid by all the apprentices who went to the skill centre over a long period. Yet here, once again, the profit motive has now come into operation. It seems that because of the reason given by my hon. Friend the Member for Edinburgh, East (Mr. Strang), it has been done with indecent haste, without proper consultation with the people who are providing the service. The Government have gone ahead willy-nilly with the preparation for privatisation.

It may be that some of the skill centres were losing money, but the important point is that they were providing a first-class service in the locality. Nottingham county council and Ashfield district council were doing a first-class job in conjunction with the skill centre in my constituency. We had a wonderful connection with the youth organisations. Everyone used to get together to discuss what they felt should be happening in the interests of youngsters leaving school, who could not find work but who were receiving expert training in the skill centre, and in the interest of adults who could not find work and needed to be retrained.

4 am

In addition, we had school involvement in my constituency and in Nottinghamshire generally. Local business was involved. Committees were set up, on which all the organisations were represented. They would feed information in with a view to helping to provide a better service. The one thing that stuck in the Government's craw was the involvement of the trade union movement in skill centres. Lo and behold, the present Secretary of State for Northern Ireland, then Secretary of State for Employment, cut off many of the skill centres and destroyed the centre in Kirkby-in-Ashfield in my constituency. We were left without a skill centre, with nowhere for people to go. We provided a service from people outside the constituency as well; yet, here we go, into the private sector.

The Government closed down many skill centres—just as they closed the pits—with a view to keeping hold of the profitable ones. They did that so they could fatten them up and hand them over, just as they have with electricity, water, gas and British Telecom. It happened to all those industries first, and now it is happening with skill centres, which I maintain are doing a first-class job.

The thing that worries me most is that the Government will get away with it. They have the majority to do anything in this place. They do not listen to Opposition Members' sensible suggestions. I am sorry that I have sung the Parliamentary Under-Secretary to sleep. Perhaps he is simply closing his eyes and listening; I hope so, because Opposition Members have a real story to tell about skill centres.

I am worried about the watchdog body that is to be set up once skill centres go into the private sector. I should like to know who its members will be. Will it be like the other groups that have been set up by the Government? It will probably consist of members of the Conservative party being paid off with a little job as part of a watchdog body

to see that the private sector does the job properly. It will probably be jobs for the boys with blue eyes, because the Conservative party's colour is blue. That is probably what will happen. The Government will look after the laddies who have served the Conservative party over the years. They will provide them with a job keeping an eye on the skill centres.

I wonder, if that happens, whether they will do a proper job. If the Government get away with the proposal in the Bill, all manner of organisations need to be represented on the watchdog body—particularly the trade union movement. If I were a member of the Conservative party——

Mr. Andy Stewart (Sherwood): We would not have you.

Mr. Haynes: The hon. Gentleman has woken up. He has been asleep since the debate began. He normally is. *[Interruption.]* I never interrupt the hon. Gentleman when he speaks, yet he is interrupting me. The hon. Gentleman is helping to close pits in the Nottingham area by voting for the Government's economy policy—*[Interruption.]* He is still shouting and bawling.

I am concerned about the sort of people who will be appointed to serve on the watchdog body. There should be fair and proper representation across the board. If I were sitting on the Conservative Benches I should probably want management from different organisations to serve on that body. That is only fair because the Conservative party is in power. However, to make the body fair we also need those who represent trade unionists. I fear that it will not be fair if the Government do not go about this matter in the right way.

The Government are moving skill centres into the private sector, where the profit motive will prevail. Will money be properly spent in the interests of the skill centres and the trainees? I hope that the Minister will assure us that the appointments to the watchdog body will be fair and that the profit motive will not prevail over a fair and proper system.

The Minister of State, Department of Employment (Mr. John Cope): I fully appreciate that Opposition Members do not accept the underlying policy of privatising the Skills Training Agency. The present position of the STA is unsustainable, and anyone who does not think that needs only to study the Public Accounts Committee report to discover the true position. It broke approximately even in 1987, but in the remainder of the past five years it spent a great deal more than its income. As the PAC pointed out, it has been subsidised surreptitiously by the MSC and the Training Commission, and the PAC rightly said that that should not continue.

I was asked about the progress of the management buy-out. I understand that the initiative led by Mr. Bishell is proceeding. All contacts with potential purchasers— some 40 organisations have expressed interest—are being handled by Deloittes, which is advising the Government on the sale. I am not, therefore, in a position to comment on the individual prospective purchasers. Our position on the management buyout remain that which has been stated by myself and by my right hon. Friend the Secretary of State.

Our professional advisers are preparing the necessary documents for the sale of assets, which include an up-to-date assessment of the value of every property. My right hon. Friend gave a clear assurance to the House on 13 March that the Government would share in any development gains in the years immediately following the sale, and we propose to make provision for that. First we must get a valuation of all the properties. That is being done for us, following a competitive tender, by King and Company, which is advising on the property aspects of the sale.

Clause 19 and most of the amendments relate to the protection of the staff. My right hon. Friend the Secretary of State explained at the time of the announcement that he would table what has turned out to be clause 19. The purpose is to ensure that the staff of the STA are protected by the application of the Transfer to Undertakings (Protection of Employment) Regulations 1981. That is basically what the clause does.

My right hon. Friend also undertook to ensure through the contract of sale that all staff who transferred into the private sector are satisfactorily covered by pension arrangements. I am happy to repeat that undertaking in response to amendment No. 27.

The hon. Member for Ashfield (Mr. Haynes) referred to haste. We also heard references to the morale of the STA staff. I ask the hon. Gentleman to bear in mind that it is very important that we should end the uncertainty that has hung over the STA not only since the announcement by my right hon. Friend the Secretary of State or the White Paper to which the hon. Member for Edinburgh, East (Mr. Strang) drew attention, but for a number of years because of its position. In the interests of the staff, apart from anything else, we should progress matters as fast as possible. That is an important aspect for us all to bear in mind.

In his statement my right hon. Friend also made it clear that we want to preserve as many skill centres as we can to provide a national network. We agree with the Public Accounts Committee that there is no case for subsidising the skill centres. That is particularly so when about one third of them are seriously under-utilised. At the same time, we are anxious to make it clear that we are selling a training business. We are interested only in bids from people who want to run an effective training business. It is on that basis that we shall consider the bids. We want to see a continuing skill centre network in the private sector.

We believe that it would be wrong to set in aspic the present amount and quality of training, as amendment No. 28 suggests. It seeks to permit no change at all, although I gather from the speech of the hon. Member for Edinburgh, East that that is not entirely what he had in mind. I have already made it clear that removing clause 19 from the Bill, as amendment No. 23 seeks, would not prevent the sale of the skill centres. The clause safeguards the position of staff who transfer with the business. It is similar to provisions that have been included in many of the previous privatisations. It is important to make clear what it does.

The terms and conditions of employment and the collective agreements that apply at the time of transfer will be continued by regulations with the new employer. After the transfer, changes to the position that exists at that time will be a matter for agreement through the normal processes of collective bargaining, but it is not a case of anything happening then regardless, as was suggested.

There is no compulsion on either side to reach a new agreement. If both sides are happy with the arrangements as they stand at the time of transfer, the same conditions will continue. The process of reaching a fresh agreement is voluntary on both sides. Until then, the clause and the regulations will ensure that the existing arrangements will continue. Amendment No. 26 therefore becomes unnecessary.

On amendment No. 27, I have already mentioned that occupational pensions are excluded from the Transfer to Undertakings (Protection of Employment) Regulations. They are not covered by what I have just said. However, I have referred also to the undertaking which has clearly been given not only by myself, but by the Secretary of State.

4.15 am

Amendment No. 29 provides for some sort of monitoring. I cannot tell the hon. Member for Ashfield who or what sort of person would be involved in the monitoring, because it is not our proposal. It is the proposal contained in amendment No. 29, which was moved by the Opposition. Clearly, the hon. Gentleman was suspicious about who might be put on such a board and we might share that concern. However, it appears that amendment No. 29, in providing for such monitoring, displays a prejudiced view of the private sector. After all, the essential condition for success in the private sector is to provide what the customer wants to buy. The STA's potential customers will not want to purchase inadequate training that does not meet their needs. The customer is, in fact, the best monitor, and to satisfy him is what we are seeking to achieve.

The hon. Member for Makerfield (Mr. McCartney) mentioned TVEI, which does not really come into the amendment, but it is not for me to quarrel with that. However, in passing I assure him that TVEI certainly continues to develop and has a much larger budget than the STA—and a rising one. The Government are spending far more on training across the board than our predecessors did 10 years ago. We are, of course, developing the system. I do not always expect Opposition Members to like what we are doing, but to suggest that we have decreased the Government's involvement in training, including financially, when compared with 10 years ago, is entirely wrong. To speak as if the STA was the only public sector element in training and education is wrong. It is one, and, as the House knows, we are proposing to change its arrangements.

We believe that the skill centres can best serve the training needs in all parts of the country by becoming more competitive and more viable training businesses, with a clear commercial focus and the ability to compete on level terms with other providers of training. However, it is important that the staff who transfer to the private sector have proper protection, which is what clause 19 achieves. I believe that it should stand unamended.

Mr. Strang: It goes without saying that we are not persuaded by the Government's arguments, and we certainly will want to vote on the first amendment.

Question put, That the amendment be made:

The House divided: Ayes 18, Noes 113.

Division No. 228] **[4.17 am**

AYES

Barnes, Harry *(Derbyshire NE)*	Golding, Mrs Llin
Cryer, Bob	Home Robertson, John
Cunliffe, Lawrence	Hughes, John *(Coventry NE)*
Dixon, Don	McCartney, Ian
Foster, Derek	McKay, Allen *(Barnsley West)*

Meale, Alan
Nellist, Dave
Richardson, Jo
Skinner, Dennis
Strang, Gavin
Welsh, Andrew *(Angus E)*

Welsh, Michael *(Doncaster N)*
Wise, Mrs Audrey

Tellers for the Ayes:
 Mr. Robert N. Wareing and
 Mr. Frank Haynes.

NOES

Alexander, Richard
Alton, David
Amos, Alan
Arbuthnot, James
Arnold, Jacques *(Gravesham)*
Ashby, David
Baldry, Tony
Batiste, Spencer
Bennett, Nicholas *(Pembroke)*
Bevan, David Gilroy
Boswell, Tim
Bottomley, Peter
Brazier, Julian
Bright, Graham
Carlisle, Kenneth *(Lincoln)*
Chapman, Sydney
Coombs, Anthony *(Wyre F'rest)*
Cope, Rt Hon John
Davis, David *(Boothferry)*
Devlin, Tim
Dorrell, Stephen
Durant, Tony
Favell, Tony
Fishburn, John Dudley
Forsyth, Michael *(Stirling)*
Forth, Eric
Fowler, Rt Hon Norman
Freeman, Roger
French, Douglas
Garel-Jones, Tristan
Gill, Christopher
Goodhart, Sir Philip
Greenway, John *(Ryedale)*
Gregory, Conal
Griffiths, Sir Eldon *(Bury St E')*
Griffiths, Peter *(Portsmouth N)*
Hague, William
Hamilton, Hon Archie *(Epsom)*
Hamilton, Neil *(Tatton)*
Hanley, Jeremy
Hargreaves, Ken *(Hyndburn)*
Harris, David
Heathcoat-Amory, David
Heddle, John
Hind, Kenneth
Howarth, Alan *(Strat'd-on-A)*
Howarth, G. *(Cannock & B'wd)*
Howells, Geraint
Hughes, Robert G. *(Harrow W)*
Hunt, David *(Wirral W)*
Irvine, Michael
Jack, Michael
Jones, Gwilym *(Cardiff N)*
Kennedy, Charles
King, Roger *(B'ham N'thfield)*
Knapman, Roger
Knowles, Michael
Lee, John *(Pendle)*
Lightbown, David

Lilley, Peter
Lloyd, Peter *(Fareham)*
Lyell, Sir Nicholas
Maclean, David
McLoughlin, Patrick
Martin, David *(Portsmouth S)*
Maude, Hon Francis
Maxwell-Hyslop, Robin
Mayhew, Rt Hon Sir Patrick
Meyer, Sir Anthony
Miller, Sir Hal
Mills, Iain
Mitchell, Andrew *(Gedling)*
Mitchell, Sir David
Moss, Malcolm
Moynihan, Hon Colin
Neale, Gerrard
Neubert, Michael
Nicholls, Patrick
Nicholson, David *(Taunton)*
Nicholson, Emma *(Devon West)*
Norris, Steve
Oppenheim, Phillip
Paice, James
Patnick, Irvine
Raffan, Keith
Redwood, John
Ridley, Rt Hon Nicholas
Rowe, Andrew
Ryder, Richard
Sainsbury, Hon Tim
Shaw, David *(Dover)*
Shepherd, Colin *(Hereford)*
Shersby, Michael
Smith, Tim *(Beaconsfield)*
Speller, Tony
Stewart, Andy *(Sherwood)*
Stradling Thomas, Sir John
Summerson, Hugo
Taylor, Teddy *(S'end E)*
Thompson, Patrick *(Norwich N)*
Thurnham, Peter
Townend, John *(Bridlington)*
Trippier, David
Trotter, Neville
Twinn, Dr Ian
Waddington, Rt Hon David
Wallace, James
Waller, Gary
Wardle, Charles *(Bexhill)*
Watts, John
Wells, Bowen
Widdecombe, Ann
Wilshire, David
Wood, Timothy

Tellers for the Noes:
 Mr. Tom Sackville and
 Mr. Michael Fallon.

Question accordingly negatived.

Clause 21

ORDERS

Amendment made:
No. 3, in line 26 after 'applies,' insert—
'(aa) an order under section 19,'.—*[Mr. Fowler.]*

Clause 23

SHORT TITLE, COMMENCEMENT AND EXTENT

Amendment made:
No. 5, in line 14 at end insert—
'(bb) section 19,'.—*[Mr. Fowler.]*
Order for Third Reading read.

4.26 am

Mr. Cope: I beg to move, That the Bill be now read the Third time.

The Bill removes unnecessary restrictions and, in so doing, widens the employment opportunities for women and young people. It also contributes to a new national framework for training. It simplifies the regulation of business and strikes a fairer balance between employers and their employees. At the same time, it takes away no vital safeguards from anyone.

It is not a revolution in employment law, but an important and constructive measure which should enjoy the support of the House.

4.29 am

Ms. Jo Richardson: Nearly five months ago, along with many other hon. Members, I sat on these Benches for the Second Reading of the Bill and heard speech after speech from Conservative Members the like of which I had never heard in the House before. All of a sudden, the Government wanted to improve the lot of women: after years of eroding women's rights and opportunities, they had apparently seen the light. The more cynical of the commentators observed that the Secretary of State's personal road to Damascus had to do less with ending discrimination than with the realisation that the votes of women would determine the result of the next general election—and I hope they will.

I was prepared to give the right hon. Gentleman the benefit of the doubt. After all, the Bill was going to allow women to clean dangerous machinery and to go down the mines: what more could any self-respecting woman want? Then I thought, "Wait a moment. What about a universal maternity grant?" The Government abolished that. "What about maternity leave as of right?" The Government are the only Government in western Europe to refuse us such provisions, all of which are connected with employment. "What about improved child care facilities, which are crucial to women who are working?" We have the least publicly funded child care facilities in Europe. "What about parental leave?" Time after time, the Government disgracefully block the European draft directive. "What about equal pension and retirement ages?" We debated that specifically, but the Government say that the position is far too complicated at present.

I looked through the Bill in vain for a major contribution to reducing sex discrimination at work. There was a long-overdue repeal of section 51 of the Sex Discrimination Act, but only in relation to employment and training. There was nothing to counter, for example, sexual harassment at work, which is a major obstacle to women remaining in some jobs; nothing to end low pay, a phenomenon that affects women disproportionately; nothing to recognise the contribution to the economy of part-timers, most of whom are women. In the last sitting on Report we moved a new clause that would have given part-time workers full employment rights, but the

Government showed what they really thought of women workers, particularly part-time women workers, by denying them a set of basic rights that are available almost everywhere else in the European Community.

If truth be told, most of the gestures towards women in the Bill have been forced on the Government by Europe. They do not, however, begin to make a start on the fundamental discrimination, which is very deep-seated; instead they have been used callously by the Government as a mask to hide the real aims of the Bill. Having exhausted their attacks on trade unions, the Government have turned their attention back to employees and afresh to unpaid union officials. The removal of the rights to written disciplinary procedures and reasons for dismissal of many employees are unnecessary and bad enough; the removal of the status of civil servants from people working in the Skills Training Agency is a disgrace. Many such employees are following a Civil Service career.

I was impressed—I thought about it carefully only a few minutes ago—when my hon. Friend the Member for Edinburgh, East (Mr. Strang) said that many people were proud to be civil servants. That is indeed the case, but overnight, without the option of a transfer elsewhere in the Civil Service, they are no longer to be public servants.

The loss of rights in the Bill, and in much of the legislation of the past decade, is now accompanied by a reduction in the ability to seek redress when the remaining rights are infringed. Lay officials—shop stewards—are to be limited in the paid time off they are allowed for trade union activities. We had a debate about that tonight. It is clearly intended to limit the amount and quality of advice that such officials are able to offer fellow workers. As one of my hon. Friends pointed out, shop stewards often assist employees who take cases before an industrial tribunal.

The Bill will allow the chairs of tribunals to charge an applicant £150 if he wishes to proceed with a case. But the most disturbing of all the clauses is that which "allows" young people to work unrestricted hours in factories and shops. That clause is a disgrace. Young people aged between 16 and 18 will, when asked, be required to work more than nine hours per day, more than 48 hours a week —and many will have to start work before seven in the morning and finish after eight at night. They will have no right to refuse to work those hours.

Statistics show that the younger one is the more likely one is to have an accident. YTS accident rates have doubled over the past three years. Young people need special protection. The Opposition realise that, and so does Europe. However, the Government respond by introducing a Bill that contravenes the European social charter. Earlier, the Government rejected new clauses that would have helped the disabled. What a disgrace that they should have been turned down. They would at least have made the Bill worth while.

The Bill represents a missed opportunity. There can be no doubt that the number of young people coming on to the labour market will fall by almost one quarter by the early 1990s. Something must be done, but the answer is surely not deregulation—which Conservative Members cling to like a sinking ship. It will not solve anything. I wish we could persuade the Government to face up to the crying need for a proper training programme, adequately funded and supervised, and offering real jobs at the end of it.

The unemployed need training and retraining, but so do other workers and women returning to the labour market after taking care of their children or of their elderly or disabled relatives. Such are the initiatives that will provide the answers in a changing labour market and to discrimination against women, which is still rife. The so-called Employment Bill does nothing to provide any answers, and I urge my right hon. and hon. Friends to vote against its Third Reading.

4.37 am

Mr. Wallace: When the Bill received its Second Reading, my right hon. and hon. Friends tabled a reasoned amendment, which was voted on, which stated that, while we welcomed certain parts of the Bill— specifically those extending equal opportunities to women —we expressed regret that the Bill failed to provide adequate protection for young people and diminished many employees' rights.

We hoped that a number of the Bill's provisions could be amended during its Committee and Report stages, but it has been clear throughout that the Government were unwilling to accept even the most reasonable of the Opposition's amendments and insist instead on the Bill being as they want it, without making any concessions.

I commend the first part of the Bill in respect of equality for women. I do not envisage that it will mean a return to sending women down coal mines, as has sometimes been graphically suggested by those most opposed to that part of the Bill. It is more likely to permit women pursuing engineering courses and who are currently unable to take up employment in mining to do so. That will open up opportunities for women that do not currently exist.

As the hon. Member for Barking (Ms. Richardson) indicated, the Bill's most sinister provision is that relating to the employment of young people. While we accept that there is a large volume of anomalous legislation, and do not quibble about it being removed from the statute book, the risk is that doing so will put the baby out with the bath water. It appears that many forms of protection that have existed for many years, with good reason, will also be removed. Not only Opposition Members have expressed concern; throughout our debates quotations from bodies such as the CBI have suggested that the Bill could lead to the exploitation of young people by unscrupulous employers.

In passing the Bill, we have to disassociate ourselves from at least one important part of the European social charter. I find it difficult to accept that such legislation can be advanced in the name of progress when we are taking a step back from our international obligations.

The Bill restricts the rights of individual employees in a number of important ways—with regard to disciplinary procedures, time off for trade union duties and the period of employment necessary to qualify for a statement of reasons for dismissal. As we have debated at some length, there is the opportunity for employers to insist on pre-hearing reviews and the necessity for employees wanting to pursue a case to have to put down a deposit. In a number of cases the Government have argued that the Bill is taking down barriers and relieving the burden on small businesses.

However, as it did before Second Reading, the British Institute of Management has written to many Members of Parliament as it looked forward to Report and Third Reading, specifically about the extension of the qualifying period for a written statement of reasons for dismissal. It

[*Mr. Wallace*]

accepts that that brings the period into line with the qualifying period for a claim of unfair dismissal. However, it states:

"we do not see this as a comprehensive argument in its favour. 78 per cent. of BIM members, when questioned in October last year, stated that the current level of employment protection was 'about right'. Only 11 per cent. thought there was 'too much'.

That gives the lie to the Government's contention that in some way the Bill will lift the burden on small businesses. It appears that a large number of businesses think that the balance is about right.

The Bill does not stem from any real desire to lift burdens but is a manifestation of an attitude that pervades the Government, who consider industry to be a battlefield between employers and employees in a constant battle as to which side should get the upper hand. Quite clearly, they are taking the opportunity to give the upper hand to employers. The Bill is a rejection of any idea of a social dimension to 1992 and greater European unity. Many of our continental counterparts see industry as more of a partnership. The Government totally repudiate that view, and the Bill is a manifestation of their attitude.

As I said earlier in regard to equal rights for women employees, we commend some of the Bill's provisions, but its balance is such that, not least because the Government have been extremely unwilling to accept any amendments to it, have struck with what they want to put on the statute book and have been deaf to even reasoned argument, we shall oppose the Bill on Third Reading.

4.43 am

Mrs. Audrey Wise (Preston): The Bill is mean and nasty and therefore is a good reflection of the Conservative party and is very worthy of the Government. It is mean and nasty because it takes away even quite small rights from employees while making sanctimonious statements about extending freedom. A Government who bother to remove the right to written reasons for dismissal and to written descriptions of disciplinary proceedings are a mean Government. A Government that remove protection from young people, which may lead to them working nights and for unlimited hours, are a nasty Government. The Government have done that in the name of extending opportunities for young people, which is disgraceful.

The Government have said that the Bill extends employment opportunities for young people and that it will increase the number of jobs available to them. When challenged to say how that would happen, as the Bill only removes protection and makes it possible to employ young people in conditions in which they should never be employed, the Government said, "The Bill will not create jobs offering unlimited hours, constant nights or fancy shifts." If that is so, why does the Bill make provision for such conditions? The Government cannot say that opening the door to unlimited hours or shift work so as to provide more opportunities for young people to work will not have that effect and yet produce more jobs. That is a completely untenable argument.

I hope that the Bill will have no effect, but if it does it will be no thanks to the Government—it will be despite them. They sought to extend not the rights of any worker or any good employer but simply the rights and freedoms of the worst employers to compete in the worst possible way. The Bill is bad not only for working people but for good employers. I was astonished by how often in Committee I argued the case of the good employer. I felt justified in doing so because any decent employer will look with dismay at the freedom given to his competitors to compete at the lowest possible levels of personnel management.

The Government have said that the Bill extends opportunities for women. I hope that the hon. Member for Orkney and Shetland (Mr. Wallace) is right in saying that the Bill will extend opportunities for genuine careers for women, but I doubt it. I do not know whether it will result in women going down pits, but if it does not, it will simply be because employment in the mining industry is contracting. It is an expression of a peculiar sense of humour to extend to a new group of people who have not asked for such an extension the right to work down a mine when employment of people who want to work in mines is being forcibly reduced.

The Bill shows that the Government do not care about working people, or about the sensible procedures of the House. The Government have not made any concessions and they have not felt it necessary to produce reasoned arguments. Their arguments in Committee at times bordered on the bizarre. They have not been embarrassed when they have been caught out with the absence of facts.

We have been discussing young people, and I want to refer once again to the fact that the Bill changes the definition of young people. The glorious freedom to work nights will now begin when youngsters are aged 15 years eight months.

When I asked in Committee how many under-16-year-olds would be affected by the Bill, the Government did not know. They did not even care. Yet I discovered from the Department of Education and Science, the colleagues of the Ministers on the Government Front Bench now, that it will affect more than 100,000 young people under 16. A Government who are as careless of information and fact, who do so little preparation and who, at the same time, bleat on perpetually about extending freedom are a Government worthy of nothing but contempt, as is the Bill.

4.49 am

Mr. Harry Barnes: The Government were pushed into the first six clauses by the directive of the Council of the European Community. However, they were pushed into them rather slowly because the directive was dated 2 February 1976 and they produced them in a minimal fashion, as was illustrated by the Opposition's amendments on which we were defeated in Committee.

Those amendments sought to reduce the under-representation of women by arguing for positive discrimination and for consultation on and reviewing of legislation with the Equal Opportunities Commission, which was not allowed in some areas, and to improve compliance with the statutory provisions that we were at that time enacting, and extending the provisions to religious orders, among others. None of those moves were accepted. No member of the Committee broke ranks on any amendment put forward by the Opposition.

Our one success on the first six clauses seemed to be a modest amendment to have the Equal Opportunities Commission consulted when new minimal improvements to the Sex Discrimination Act 1975 could be overridden.

that appears in clause 6 which deals with the Secretary of State's power to exempt particular acts of discrimination required under statute. The argument was that certain legislation might emerge that it did not know about and it might need the action in some circumstances to evade what it was doing in a limited way within the other five areas.

I moved that amendment in Committee, and when the Minister promised to bring a reworded version forward on Report I begged leave to withdraw the amendment. That was done, but I have not seen that promise fulfilled. That promise can be found in the Committee *Hansard* for 31 January at columns 90 to 94. If we are not getting that now, will it be promised in another place?

After the first six clauses in response to the EC directive on sex discrimination, the Government thought that it would be a clever wheeze to present clause 7 which seeks to push women into working in the pits. The one great danger is that women who register as unemployed may be directed towards jobs in the pits, and, if they refuse them, will be deemed not to be actively seeking work and thus lose benefit.

That wheeze sought only to embarrass the Opposition. It was the Opposition who believed in equal opportunity. The Government were having only a mild version forced upon them and were going as reluctantly as possible towards it. They thought that it would be a good debating point—a good turning of tables—to confront the Opposition with a crude version of equality in the pits. I can see no other reason for their seeking to do that.

The Opposition took up the challenge, accepting the principle, given positive improvements for men and women in the pits, particularly ergonomic, health and safety, toilet and lavatory facilities improvements. Neither the Government nor any Conservative Members gave any support to any of those suggestions in Committee or on the Floor of the House.

We reject the idea of putting women in crude and primative conditions. Even men should not be working in such conditions, but the men who work in them in the mines do not want their daughters and wives to work in such conditions. That view should be respected by all. It is certainly respected by daughters and wives in mining communities.

With the "women in the pits" debate we confronted the whole issue of major burdens being placed on working people by the Bill. Reference has been made to the protection that used to be afforded to youngsters between 16 and 18; 75 per cent. of them have been protected in such matters as hours of work, numbers of days to be worked and meal breaks. Those protections are going. How can human beings do that to young people?

Those who are prepared to do it may be ignorant about conditions in the pits, but they must meet youngsters and talk to them about their feelings. Were they not once young themselves? Were they all workaholic whizz kids who were unconcerned about what was going on around them? They may indeed have been like that, for they have no understanding of what life is really like. Youngsters should have better things to do than be forced by legislation of this type to do nothing but work.

In Committee and on Report we attempted to protect the disabled, allowing them job opportunities and hindering dismissals. It has become clear that there is not an ounce of compassion among Conservative Members for women, for the young or for the disabled. Trade unionists are again taking a bashing over time off for union activities. The only move on that front in Committee came from Tory Members who wish to foist on trade unions still greater burdens and to bash the last remnants that remain of closed shop activities.

The Bill contains other anti-social matters, including the removal of the right of many people to dismissal notices, and there has been a lack of response to the reasonable concern voiced by many people about the functions and duties of industrial tribunals. Rather than develop those matters, I shall conclude by mentioning a matter that we have not debated, partly because until tonight we have been too polite an Opposition. We have allowed the Bill to progress under protest only, being anxious to debate the measure without the threat of the guillotine.

The subject to which I refer is Northern Ireland. Clause 20 applies the entire measure to Northern Ireland by Order in Council, mainly under the negative resolution procedure. If the writ of the Bill should not extend to an area, that area must be Northern Ireland. The House has just passed fair employment legislation applying to Northern Ireland. It received all-party support and was opposed only by diehard Ulster Unionists.

How can there be fair employment when the young are exploited, when the disabled are dismissed as of no concern and when trade unionists are hounded? The way to help Northern Ireland is the way to help the rest of the United Kingdom, and that is by rejecting disgraceful Bills such as this.

4.58 am

Mr. Nellist: If the economy was really going forward, the Bill would be unnecessary. If we were in the seventh —or is it the eighth?—successive year of economic growth, as the Chancellor keeps on assuring us, the Bill would not be required. If we were witnessing genuine falls in unemployment rather than a largely statistical manipulation of the figures, and if we were having a rise in the number of well-paid jobs, the Bill would be superfluous.

The boom that was engineered, particularly in the 18 months before the 1987 general election, is fragile and its time is almost up. Hence this legislation. Investment is low, productivity and production are virtually static and trade has nose-dived. Yet the Government continue with their 10-year strategy of preparing the legislative framework to ensure that when the fragile boom is seen not to be present they will have the necessary bits of paper in place to restrict trade unions as organisations and workers as individuals from opposing reductions in living standards and working conditions. This is the sixth major attack in 10 years continuing that pattern.

As colleagues have said, not only on Report but in the many hours in Committee, this Bill removes individual workers' rights gained primarily during the 30 years following the second world war. What was given by employers and industrialists and the Tory party of those days with the left hand is now being savagely snatched back with the right. It is the cynical disregard of workers' interests in the interests of profit that is the prime function of this Government and of the party that introduced the Bill. It is not about creating jobs or improving conditions but about increasing exploitation and removing rights from individual employees.

The first section of the Bill—about which my hon. Friend the Member for Derbyshire, North-East (Mr.

[*Mr. Nellist*]

Barnes) has just spoken—comes under the guise of a gesture towards sex equality. However, it is not equalising upwards and improving all protective legislation for men and women, but equalising downwards from the existing protective legislation on the statute book. It achieves equality, not by increasing protection for men but by reducing it for women, particularly in such things as the cleaning of machinery with dangerous moving parts. That shows the interest of this Government. They are not for equality; they are for reducing to the lowest common denominator wherever they can get away with it.

Clause 7 is about repealing the ban on women working underground. I do not intend to repeat the arguments in Committee, when I spoke for an hour and a quarter on that clause alone. I made a promise in Committee because, like most if not all the members, I spoke on the basis of second-hand knowledge, of conversations with miners and their families, without direct personal knowledge of a working pit, although I have been down a couple of redundant slate mines. I promised to spend a day in a working pit before we reached Report and I did that as a guest of the management and trade unionists of the Keresley colliery outside Coventry at the beginning of May. That reinforced in my mind the points I made in Committee about the conditions of work for miners in British pits and the inherent danger not only of dust, chemicals and heat but of the roadways. I travelled along hundreds of metres of roadways that were less than $3\frac{1}{2}$ to 4 ft high. It confirmed all the points that we had made.

What we wanted from the debate on that part of the Bill were ways of improving the existing working conditions of miners, not of introducing more workers into those inadequate conditions. But all the way through the stages of this Bill the Tory party has rejected any amendment to improve working conditions in regard to health and safety, sanitation, heat, dust, chemicals or redesigning of machinery or protective equipment.

Clause 7 was essentially a blue herring. It was designed to divert attention from the way in which the Bill was reducing working conditions for women and youth in particular.

The Liberal spokesman, the hon. Member for Orkney and Shetland (Mr. Wallace), said a few moments ago that it will open opportunities for women. From March 1984 to March 1988 the number of pits in this country was reduced from 170 to 94 and over 90,000 jobs disappeared from the pits.

We are not here as legislators to discuss abstract rights, to discuss things like academics in ivory towers; we are here to discuss practical legislation in the real world. What was needed, and what was totally absent from this Bill, was movement towards increasing genuine opportunities for the employment of women, particularly working-class women, which would have needed such things as work-place nurseries and ending the tax on them, and improved maternity leave and maternity grants. The amendments and points that we put in Committee in that direction were decisively and unanimously rejected by the Government.

The other major area of the Bill is the sweeping away of current restrictions on the employment of young people, especially in terms of the number of hours a week that they can work. Those provisions are about increasing the exploitation of young people who, as my hon. Friend the

Member for Preston (Mrs. Wise) has repeatedly said, may be as young as 15 years 8 months old. I make the same point today as I made three times during the passage of the Bill. There is not a single Tory Member who would raise his hand and tell us that he would put a daughter or a son of his at 15 years 8 months old into a bakery on nights and working more than 54 hours a week. Yet that is precisely what they are asking the working-class youth of this country to work when, or if, the Bill becomes law.

All through the discussions, we have been told that these matters could safely be left to market forces and negotiation. My hon. Friend the Member for Derbyshire, North-East (Mr. Barnes) made the point in a stage whisper in Committee. He said that the only promise we were getting from the Tory party on young people's hours of work was that no young person would be forced to work more than 24 hours in any single day.

The Government are doing nothing to improve the conditions of young people. They have swept away the wages councils for the under-21s, they have abolished benefits for 16 to 17-year-olds to conscript them on to the youth training scheme and now they are grafting on this deterioration in hours and working conditions for those youngsters who are in jobs. We spelled out the inevitable consequence during the passage of the Bill. There will be an increase in the number of accidents among young people.

As Nye Bevan used to say, one does not have to look in the crystal ball when one can read the book. Any analysis, especially since the expansion of the youth training scheme, which considers young people at work, especially in non-unionised and unsupervised areas, shows a doubling of accidents. The trend will continue at the end of long shifts for younger people of 15 years 8 months. Responsibility for the blood from the increase in accidents, the amputations and possible fatalities will rest squarely on the Treasury Bench of the House of Commons, which introduced and pushed the Bill through.

The Government see young people as cheap labour. Okay—at 5.5 am, with perhaps a couple of dozen of us voting against the Bill, it will receive a Third Reading. However, we will take the only responsibility left open to us, not only as politicians, but as active trade unionists. We will take the campaign out of this Chamber, once the Bill is passed, back into the trade union movement, and we will insist that our trade union organisations actively recruit young people, as they have done in the past, but in recent years have perhaps not done sufficiently well. To paraphrase the old black and white television advertisements of the 1950s, we will get the strength not of the insurance companies, but of the trade union movement, around those young people. The collective protection of the trade unions is the only barrier to the increase in accidents upon which we can build.

The Bill also weakens individual workers' rights on redundancy, time off for trade union duties and access to industrial tribunals unless people can afford a £150 deposit. It may not be exactly a tax on justice, but there is no other phrase for it.

The Bill also dissolves the Training Commission. That is part of the Government's strategy to weaken the ability of workers to defend themselves and to have free, democratic and effective collective representation through the trade union movement.

As my hon. Friend the Member for Preston also said, the Bill is vicious and mean. It is an anti-working class measure. If—or, more likely, when—it receives its Third Reading in a few moments, we, as Labour Members, will have to take the fight out of this Chamber into the real world and to the working-class movement of Britain. We must seek to encourage working people to reimpose on employers by negotiation, organisation, and, where necessary, industrial action the rights that have been legislated away by the Tory party.

The Bill will be passed, but if Tory Members, especially those with close connections with business, think that that is the end of the matter and that once the proposals are down on a piece of paper, workers' rights will be removed and the door will be open to the increased exploitation of young people and women workers in particular, they should not hold their breath. The time is not far away when rights will be reimposed—the right to a decent job, to decent pay and to a safe working environment, for which the Tory party and the Government care naught.

5.10 am

Mr. Cryer: Trade unionists in the textile industry have co-operated in shift working, in changes in working practices and in the introduction of new machinery. They have not received the gratitude of the Government or the employers. They have been kicked in the teeth. Since 1979, 150,000 to 200,000 jobs in the textile and clothing industries have disappeared. The notion that by introducing yet more flexible working and removing protection for women and young people the Government will somehow generate a boom in the manufacturing or service industries is, quite simply, an illusion. The Bill is intended to enable the Government to pass on to employers means of attacking ordinary working men and women yet again—and particularly women.

Under recent social security legislation, people must be able to demonstrate that they are actively seeking work. In addition, the power now exists to require women to take night work. In the same legislative process the Government are arranging for the passage of a private Bill —the British Rail (Penalty Fares) Bill. With the help of the organisation of the Chief Whip to secure the Tory vote, British Rail seeks means of destaffing stations and installing more ticket machines. The self-same women who are forced to take night work under threat of penalties against them will not find public transport staffed by people who can help them in any dilemma that they may face in this increasingly violent Tory society; they will be exposed increasingly to the violence that surrounds them. They will be placed in that position by a network of legislation that is oppressing them, of which the Bill is an example. On cold winter mornings, when they hear footfalls on the path behind them as they go to the station —Tory legislation has meant that bus services have been sadly diminished—and look for friendly help, it will not be there.

Responsibility will rest squarely with the Tory legislators as they sit there in their smug somnolence tonight, making funny little remarks about the circumstances, in their jokey, contemptuous, hard-hearted and vicious manner. I note that the hon. Member for Bromsgrove (Sir H. Miller), for example, finds the whole thing terribly amusing. No doubt the women in Bromsgrove will be pleased to hear that their Member of Parliament finds the predicament in which the legislation will place women in general overwhelmingly amusing.

Clause 10 robs trade unionists of the right to participate in conferences and to attend meetings that are relevant to their jobs and their industry. In future, such participation will depend on collective agreements argued out in each factory, rather than on a national arrangement under which every employee throughout the country knows and understands his position. That is a recipe for industrial unrest; it is being pushed through by the Government as a further attack on trade unionists and trade unions.

The Bill contains some shoddy little measures. Clause 11, for example, provides that one must work for two years continuously before an employer is required to put in writing the reasons why one is facing the trauma of dismissal. It is a shoddy bit of vindictive pettiness towards working people to remove a burden from employers by telling them that they need not write down their reasons. The Government have produced no evidence that the removal of a simple obligation to set out the reasons for the exercise of an employer's enormous power—for the person facing dismissal, almost an awe-inspiring power —would result in the diminution of employment in small businesses or in the output of manufacturing industry.

The Government intend to impose a tax on justice, despite the fact that, once again, they have produced no evidence to show that resort to an industrial tribunal is made flippantly, vexatiously or frivolously or that it is not a genuine attempt to seek justice. If that is the case—and the Government have produced no evidence to prove that it is not—it is an unfair and onerous penalty that people should be asked to pay a £150 deposit for a pre-hearing review. Millions of people struggle from week to week to find the money to pay their bills. It is outrageous to ask them to produce £150 on top of their many outgoings and, for many people, it will be an effective bar to access to justice.

I echo the words of my hon. Friend the Member for Barking (Ms. Richardson) about the provision that will allow women to work in coal mines. It is a removal of the protection for women and young people. To translate working in the most harrowing and awful conditions in pits as some sort of gain is to treat women with contempt and disdain. At the next general election we shall make much of this legislation and demonstrate to women that the Tory party has betrayed them.

Question put, That the Bill be now read the Third time:—

The House divided: Ayes 106, Noes 20.

Division No. 229]   **[5.16 am**

AYES

Alexander, Richard	Dorrell, Stephen
Amos, Alan	Durant, Tony
Arbuthnot, James	Fallon, Michael
Arnold, Jacques *(Gravesham)*	Favell, Tony
Ashby, David	Fishburn, John Dudley
Baldry, Tony	Forsyth, Michael *(Stirling)*
Batiste, Spencer	Forth, Eric
Bennett, Nicholas *(Pembroke)*	Fowler, Rt Hon Norman
Bevan, David Gilroy	Freeman, Roger
Boswell, Tim	French, Douglas
Bottomley, Peter	Garel-Jones, Tristan
Brazier, Julian	Gill, Christopher
Bright, Graham	Goodhart, Sir Philip
Carlisle, Kenneth *(Lincoln)*	Greenway, John *(Ryedale)*
Chapman, Sydney	Gregory, Conal
Coombs, Anthony *(Wyre F'rest)*	Griffiths, Sir Eldon *(Bury St E')*
Cope, Rt Hon John	Griffiths, Peter *(Portsmouth N)*
Davis, David *(Boothferry)*	Hague, William
Devlin, Tim	Hamilton, Hon Archie *(Epsom)*

Hamilton, Neil *(Tatton)*
Hanley, Jeremy
Hargreaves, Ken *(Hyndburn)*
Harris, David
Heddle, John
Hind, Kenneth
Howarth, Alan *(Strat'd-on-A)*
Howarth, G. *(Cannock & B'wd)*
Hughes, Robert *(Aberdeen N)*
Hunt, David *(Wirral W)*
Irvine, Michael
Jack, Michael
Jones, Gwilym *(Cardiff N)*
King, Roger *(B'ham N'thfield)*
Knapman, Roger
Knowles, Michael
Lee, John *(Pendle)*
Lightbown, David
Lilley, Peter
Lloyd, Peter *(Fareham)*
Lyell, Sir Nicholas
Maclean, David
McLoughlin, Patrick
Martin, David *(Portsmouth S)*
Maxwell-Hyslop, Robin
Mayhew, Rt Hon Sir Patrick
Meyer, Sir Anthony
Miller, Sir Hal
Mills, Iain
Mitchell, Andrew *(Gedling)*
Mitchell, Sir David
Moss, Malcolm
Moynihan, Hon Colin
Neubert, Michael
Nicholls, Patrick
Nicholson, David *(Taunton)*

Nicholson, Emma *(Devon West)*
Norris, Steve
Oppenheim, Phillip
Paice, James
Patnick, Irvine
Raffan, Keith
Redwood, John
Ridley, Rt Hon Nicholas
Rowe, Andrew
Ryder, Richard
Sainsbury, Hon Tim
Shaw, David *(Dover)*
Shepherd, Colin *(Hereford)*
Shersby, Michael
Smith, Tim *(Beaconsfield)*
Speller, Tony
Stewart, Andy *(Sherwood)*
Stradling Thomas, Sir John
Summerson, Hugo
Thompson, Patrick *(Norwich N)*
Thurnham, Peter
Trippier, David
Trotter, Neville
Twinn, Dr Ian
Waddington, Rt Hon David
Waller, Gary
Wardle, Charles *(Bexhill)*
Watts, John
Wells, Bowen
Widdecombe, Ann
Wilshire, David
Wood, Timothy

Tellers for the Ayes:
      Mr. Tom Sackville and
      Mr. David Heathcoat-Amory.

NOES

Alton, David
Barnes, Harry *(Derbyshire NE)*
Cryer, Bob
Cunliffe, Lawrence
Dixon, Don
Foster, Derek
Golding, Mrs Llin
Howells, Geraint
Hughes, John *(Coventry NE)*
McCartney, Ian
Meale, Alan
Nellist, Dave

Richardson, Jo
Skinner, Dennis
Strang, Gavin
Wallace, James
Wareing, Robert N.
Welsh, Andrew *(Angus E)*
Welsh, Michael *(Doncaster N)*
Wise, Mrs Audrey

Tellers for the Noes:
      Mr. Allen McKay and
      Mr. Frank Haynes.

Question accordingly agreed to.
Bill read the Third time, and passed.

Rights of the Child (UN Convention)

Motion made, and Question proposed, That this House do now adjourn.—*[Mr. Chapman.]*

5.27 am

Mr. Ken Hargreaves (Hyndburn): Even at this late hour I am grateful for the opportunity to raise my concerns about the proposed United Nations convention on the rights of the child. I apologise to the Minister for any inconvenience caused to him by being here at this late hour. I welcome to the debate my hon. Friend the Member for Maidstone (Miss Widdecombe) and the hon. Member for Liverpool, Mossley Hill (Mr. Alton).

The recent events in China have filled us all with sadness, horror and anger, because the most basic of all human rights—the right to life itself—has been taken away from more than 7,000 young people. Our sadness, our horror and our anger are justified. No one has the right to destroy innocent human life in that way.

Those of us in the pro-life movement, who believe that life begins at conception, feel the same sadness, horror and anger about the 170,000 children in this country who are killed by abortion every year. Their lives are sacred and should not be forfeited because they are inconvenient to their parents, any more than the lives of the Chinese students should have been forfeited because they were inconvenient to the state.

The right to life is paramount and must be recognised as such from the moment that new life begins, at conception. That right embraces the entire process of human growth and development. The constantly increasing numbers of abortions and the growing social and legal acceptance of terminating the lives of handicapped children show that the child needs special protection before as well as after birth. I am concerned that the proposed United Nations convention on the rights of the child will not fully recognise the right to life.

The proposed convention is meant to update and upgrade the 1959 United Nations declaration on the rights of the child, but, unlike the declaration, the convention will have the force of law. Its purpose is to enumerate the rights of children and to secure a commitment from states that they will endeavour to bring their laws and practices into conformity with those rights. The 1959 declaration made two references to the child before birth. The preamble stated:

"Whereas the child by reason of his physical and mental immaturity, needs special safeguards and care, including appropriate legal protection before as well as after birth."
Principle 4 of the declaration said:

"Special care and protection shall be provided both to him and his mother, including adequate pre-natal and post-natal care".

The proposed convention, drafted by a working group of the United Nations Human Rights Commission in Geneva, which had been working on the text for some 10 years, made no mention of the unborn child. Attempts specifically to protect the unborn child in the convention were made in 1980, but opposition from some countries with liberal abortion laws prevented the inclusion of any reference to the child before birth.

Article 1 of the draft now contains the following definition of a child:

"For the purpose of the present convention a child means every human being below the age of 18 years, unless under the law applicable to the child, majority is attained earlier".

There is no reference to the point at which childhood begins. This ambiguity on the beginning of childhood was clearly approved by the working group to allow states with differing laws governing the rights of the child before birth to interpret article 1 in different ways. The great opportunity to challenge states to improve the legal protection offered to the child before birth by using objective criteria to identify the point of commencement of childhood was not utilised.

Following international protests about the failure of the convention to protect the child before birth, last November's meeting of the working group reopened the issue. On 29 November, a reference to the child before birth was inserted in the preamble to the draft. It now reads:

"Bearing in mind that as indicated in the declaration of the rights of the child adopted by the General Assembly of the United Nations on 20th November 1959, the child, by reason of his physical and mental immaturity, needs special safeguards and care, including appropriate legal protection before as well as after birth."

That is the only reference to the child before birth in the convention and even that was inserted only in exchange for the states which wanted such protection for unborn children agreeing to a comment being added as follows:

"In adopting this preambular paragraph the working group does not intend to prejudice the interpretation of article 1 or any other provision of the convention by state parties".

It is clear that the interpretation of the word "child" leaves the way wide open for countries where abortion is legalised to interpret the convention as excluding the child before birth. Their adoption of the convention will not therefore be inhibited by the fear that by doing so they will have to amend existing abortion laws.

It is unfortunate that, solely because of their abortion laws, the majority of the delegates of the working group should have decided to omit the important words "from the moment of conception" from article 1. The great increase in medical knowledge about the nature and development of the child before birth in the 13 years since the declaration would, in the ordinary course of events, have made it natural to stress the importance of medical care for children before birth. All countries now recognise the importance of that and make provision for it in their medical services.

It is disgraceful that, in 1989, because, for the purpose of abortion laws, children are treated as chattels rather than people, an important convention on the needs and rights of children should deliberately exclude mention of their needs and rights before birth. Due to the present abortion laws, the convention was unable to deal with the specific duties and responsibilities of parents towards their children before birth.

The effect on children of the behaviour of their parents during the nine months of development in the womb is increasingly recognised in medical circles. It would have been of benefit to all human beings if that had been explicitly recognised in the convention.

The new convention should contain within its preamble a statement on the need to provide legal protection before, as well as after, birth. It should reaffirm the principles, contained in the current declaration, that the best interests of the child shall be the paramount consideration in the enactment of laws. It should reaffirm the principle that a child who is physically, mentally or socially handicapped should be given the special treatment, education and care required by his or her condition.

I welcome the Government's commitment to the family and the importance of family life. However, such commitment will not ring true with the general public unless the Government are seen to be doing everything in their power to protect the weakest and most vulnerable member of that family: the unborn child. Therefore, I hope that the Government will seek to ensure that the text eventually agreed for the proposed convention will recognise that a human child is human, both before and after birth, and that human rights—rights which attach to a being by virtue of being human—will attach to a child before and after birth.

Unless that clarification to the proposed convention is made, the impression will be given that the United Nation's commission regards some humans as not being entitled to human rights, and that the commission may decide which humans are so entitled, and which are not. Such an attitude would discredit the commission, the convention and the Government if they were seen to support it.

5.38 am

Mr. David Alton (Liverpool, Mossley Hill): That hon. Members on both sides of the House have stayed throughout the night and are here at just after half-past 5 in the morning to debate this important issue demonstrates that neither the issue nor the Members who are concerned about it will go away, and that it is a matter that the Government must face. I and I am sure many millions in this country are grateful to the hon. Member for Hyndburn (Mr. Hargreaves) for having used his Adjournment debate to raise this important matter. I am grateful to the Under-Secretary of State for Health for having persevered through the night to be here to answer the important points which have been made this morning. I wish to underline those points in my brief contribution, and I am grateful to the hon. Member for Hyndburn for allowing me to intervene.

Going back, not just to 1959 but to 1948, to the immediate aftermath of the second world war, when we had experienced such massive atrocities on a scale never before experienced by humankind, the United Nations passed a declaration which asserted unequivocally and unambiguously that everyone had the right to life. Over the intervening 40 years that commitment has been watered down, eroded and evaporated as successive Governments in different parts of Europe have become more and more edgy about providing a substantive assurance on the right to life.

During the past 20 years in this country we have allowed 3 million abortions of unborn children. I do not believe that anyone who was in this Chamber in 1967 when the original legislation was passed ever believed that the taking of life would occur on such a massive scale. There are 174,000 abortions annually and about 600 abortions every working day. That is the heedless plunder of our creation and it is not only happening here. In the United States of America, there are about 1·5 million abortions annually, and in China, to which the hon. Member for Hyndburn referred, there were 5 million abortions last year.

In my view, abortion is the ultimate form of child abuse. We should not be surprised that so many terrible things happen to the child on this side of birth when we allow the destruction of the child before it can be born.

[*Mr. David Alton*]

When we consider some of what takes place in this country's private clinics and hospitals, it seems that we have turned them into charnel houses. Abortions can take place legally as late as 28 weeks into gestation. The fact that a child that is perfectly viable, or even a child without viability that is clearly human, can be destroyed by being torn apart piece by piece demonstrates that our claims to call ourselves civilised are not justified.

This is happening on an horrific scale, but it has been politely placed out of sight and out of mind. The Minister should not underestimate the potency of the issue. Britain took a lead, some 150 years ago, in ending the international trade in slaves, and the United States quickly followed our example. If today we take the first steps back from this ugly trade in abortionism—if we turn the tide, take the fight to the United Nations and reassert the statements made in 1948 in the UN declaration of human rights that everyone has the right to life, and the 1959 declaration that life begins at conception—I believe that we will be performing a major service to mankind.

This question is far too important to be left to obscure debates held in private Members' time, and be relegated to "conscience questions", which is shorthand for preserving the status quo. The pro-life amendment to the United Nations convention would be a first step towards restoring a rational sense of balance to the debate and away from the status quo. It would recognise that no one has the right to end the life of another. To say that it is our right to choose to take another person's life is a spurious assertion: it is never our right to make that choice. It is merely the ultimate refuge of a selfish society.

The House will wish to thank the hon. Member for Hyndburn for initiating this debate, and I look forward to the Minister's reply.

5.41 am

Miss Ann Widdecombe (Maidstone): Let me also congratulate my hon. Friend the Member for Hyndburn (Mr. Hargreaves) on securing this important debate, and thank the Minister for having lasted through the night. If if falls to his lot to reply to my Adjournment debate on Thursday, I hope that it will be at a slightly more congenial hour.

The fact that two Adjournment debates this week deal with the subject of abortion demonstrates the level of parliamentary concern and, indeed, determination that the issue will not go away and must be resolved. When my hon. Friend the Member for Hyndburn made the point that there was no proper definition in the United Nations convention of where childhood began, he put his finger on the main weakness of the case for not defining the rights of the child.

If we had defined when childhood began, the case of the Carlisle baby would not have come about. It is popular among our opponents to talk merely about the woman's right to choose, and to refer to "the foetus", never the baby or the unborn child. It is difficult to see that the Carlisle baby, whose case I shall be raising on Thursday, could possibly be described as anything other than a child or a baby. That baby was no different from babies all over the world in incubators, being loved and cherished with all the resources of medical science placed at their disposal. Had there been some definition of where childhood began, it

would have been impossible for its case to occur. If we recognise the rights of children before birth, as we do to a limited extent in this country—that is, we recognise their rights at 28 weeks—there is no way that we can ignore so comprehensively their rights after birth.

There is a second parallel between the Carlisle baby case and the United Nations convention. My hon. Friend the Member for Hyndburn rightly pointed out that, by its refusal to define where childhood begins and to give rights to the unborn child, the convention allows nations to interpret it as widely as they choose. In other words, it condones the cover-up. Instead of doing what most international treaties do—set standards to which everyone must adhere—it says that everyone can do what they like.

The most massive cover-up, which I shall be speaking about on Thursday, occurred at Carlisle general hospital in the summer of 1987, when the mother concerned was not even told that her child of six months had lived; the priest who brought the matter to public attention had his contract terminated or at any rate not renewed; a request for a coroner's inquest, which is usually a formality, was turned down; and a live child was not registered at birth. That is the kind of situation that could arise from the United Nations convention—and I see you, Madam Deputy Speaker, rising to tell me that my remarks are too wide of the debate.

Once we say that there is no need to define the rights of the unborn child and that nations can do what they like, we are saying that the born child also has restricted rights and that politicians, doctors and coroners should be left to interpret the law as it stands instead of setting objective standards and punishing very severely those who transgress them.

5.45 am

The Parliamentary Under-Secretary of State for Health (Mr. Roger Freeman): My hon. Friend the Member for Hyndburn (Mr. Hargreaves) graciously apologised for any inconvenience caused to me by participating in the debate at a quarter to 6 in the morning. There is absolutely no inconvenience to myself, but it would be fair and courteous to apologise to you, Madam Deputy Speaker, and to all the servants of the House, for keeping you up so late.

The hon. Member for Liverpool, Mossley Hill (Mr. Alton) rightly said that abortion is an important national issue. I believe that it is worth debating at 5.30 in the morning just as much as at 5.30 in the afternoon. I have no doubt that we shall be returning to these important issues many times, and my hon. Friend the Member for Maidstone (Miss Widdicombe) gave me a trailer of the debate on Thursday, in which I shall certainly participate.

I congratulate my hon. Friend the Member for Hyndburn on choosing such an important topic for his Adjournment debate. He drew attention both to important United Nations negotiations now under way and, more specifically, to the sensitive issues of abortion and embryo research on which right hon. and hon. Members in all parts of the House have sincere and deeply held views. Although a Minister serves to express the Government's view in the hope of enlightening the House as to the facts of the case in question, we all of us—myself included—have deeply held views on abortion and embryo research, and we shall express them at the appropriate time.

I listened very carefully to my hon. Friend's remarks in the context of the draft United Nations convention on the rights of the child. It may be helpful if I say a few words about the convention, which was prepared by a working group established by the United Nations commission on human rights in 1979. The United Kingdom was a member of that working group and played a leading role in the drafting of the convention. As a member of the working group, the Government always sought to ensure that the draft reflected our national policies and the principles of the 1959 United Nations declaration on the rights of the child.

The working group has completed its work on the text of the convention, which is now in its final form after almost nine years of detailed discussion. The draft is due to go to the United Nations General Assembly in New York for adoption later this year. It is the Government's intention to sign and ratify the convention soon after its adoption, because, in our view, it is right for this country to be associated with that important statement of international commitment to improving the health and welfare of children throughout the world.

My hon. Friend the Member for Hyndburn rightly drew attention to one or two articles of the convention, but it is an extensive draft covering some 40 articles dealing with children's rights over a very broad range of issues. I am sure that he would wish to lend his support to the convention in that sense.

Once adopted, the convention will be the first international treaty to deal specifically and over a wide field with the human rights and fundamental freedoms of children. The convention will establish minimum standards for the survival, protection and development of children. The Government warmly support the convention's aims.

The working group has been engaged in considerable debate on many of the issues tackled in the draft convention. Among these have been questions about the extent to which it applies to the unborn child. This of course is closely related to the points my hon. Friend has most eloquently drawn attention to this morning. Participating countries have inevitably adopted widely differing positions on this issue. It was the working group's practice to proceed by consensus, and the views of all contributing countries had to be taken into account in drafting this international instrument. That may seem a trite comment, but this is the way in which international treaties and conventions are prepared, as perhaps my hon. Friend the Member for Maidstone knows.

It is, in the Government's view, esential that the convention should not affect the right of Parliament to decide on appropriate legislation in the fields of abortion and embryo research. In this we are of course at one with many other countries and the issues which are of concern to us must also be exercising their minds. The extent of legislative protection that should be given to human embryos and foetuses is a matter of great debate and difficulty in many countries, not just in the United Kingdom. We must all recognise that on these issues there are deep and sincerely held, but widely differing, views. It is for this reason that in this country Governments have traditionally taken a neutral stance on issues such as abortion and human embryo research, regarding them as matters of individual conscience.

As regards the law on abortion, the House is well aware that our present legislation dates from 1967 when Parliament decided to build on an existing framework of criminal law on this subject. Parliament decided on these arrangements on a free vote. The 1967 Act sets out the circumstances in which termination of pregnancy may legally be performed if statutory arrangements are satisfied. The Abortion Act has to be read alongside the Infant Life (Preservation) Act 1929, whose basic purpose is to protect the life of the unborn child except where termination of pregnancy is necessary to save the life of the mother. It is open to Parliament to alter some or all aspects of this legislative framework. I know that many hon. Members have strong views on the subject, and the matter has been frequently debated since 1967. It is this complex and controversial position which the Government have to take into account in considering the draft convention.

I am very well aware of the strong and conflicting views hon. Members and others have expressed on the whole issue of abortion. There was a long and valuable debate in the House on 16 December 1988 about the unborn child and my hon. Friend has made good use of the opportunity to draw attention this morning to the issues discussed on that and many other occasions.

The conflict of opinion on abortion applies equally to research involving human embryos. Advances in science and medicine over the past few years have made practicable a whole range of procedures and treatments which could not even have been contemplated previously, but as we all recognise, such scientific advance brings with it problems as well as benefits. In particular, as the Warnock report emphasises, it gives rise to many profound and difficult questions of rights and duties, both ethical and legal on which each of us will have our own view. There is, however, one thing on which I am sure we all agree—the need to provide a clear legislative framework in which future developments can take place.

In our White Paper, "Human Fertilisation and Embryology: A Framework for Legislation", we set out our proposals in this field. Two are particularly relevant to this debate; first, the establishment of a statutory licensing authority to control centres engaged in such procedures as in vitro fertilisation; secondly, to have a free vote on alternative clauses on embryo research in the Bill. One would outlaw it altogether; the other would allow it under strict controls. In that way Parliament will be able to reach a decision on this particularly sensitive issue on the basis of individual conscience.

Mr. Alton: I am grateful to the Minister for that important assurance that there will be a vote on embryo experimentation. Is he prepared to give the House an assurance that the same opportunity to vote in Government time on late abortions will also be provided?

Mr. Freeman: As the hon. Gentleman well knows, that is a matter not for me but for my right hon. Friend the Lord President and others. I can assure the hon. Gentleman that I will draw to my right hon. Friend's attention hon. Members' comments in this brief debate. He is in no doubt about the strength of feeling on the issue, and I can do no more than convey to him the feelings of hon. Members who have participated in this debate and their views on the subject. We have made a firm commitment to bring forward legislation on these matters within this Parliament, and I should like to reaffirm that commitment.

[*Mr. Freeman*]

I am aware that many hon. Members would like to see changes in the abortion law included in the forthcoming legislation. Their arguments will be carefully considered when the legislation is prepared. I am sure that in the debates on the legislation there will be much discussion on the issues ably raised by my hon. Friend the Member for Hyndburn.

The central subject of the debate is the draft convention on the rights of the child. It has been helpful to have hon.

Members' views and I hope that my reply has shown that in considering the position on the final text of the work on the draft convention the Government are fully seized not only of the importance of the subject as a whole but of the sensitivity which some aspects of it hold for hon. Members. We shall certainly bear these closely in mind in bringing into harmony the convention and the legislation in this country.

Question put and agreed to.

Adjourned accordingly at five minutes to Six o'clock.

House of Commons

Wednesday 7 June 1989

The House met at half-past Two o'clock

PRAYERS

[MR. SPEAKER *in the Chair*]

Oral Answers to Questions

SCOTLAND

Health Service (Women)

1. **Mrs. Fyfe:** To ask the Secretary of State for Scotland whether he has any plans to consult women on the Health Service.

The Parliamentary Under-Secretary of State for Scotland (Mr. Michael Forsyth): My right hon. and learned Friend has consulted a wide range of organisations and professional bodies about the Government's proposals for reform for the NHS. The views submitted will reflect the views of men and women alike.

Mrs. Fyfe: Now that the Prime Minister has set a new standard in personal health care by treating herself to electric mud baths when she is feeling under par, will the Minister explain to Scottish women why they and their families have to have the cheapest medicines and hospital care, and why they have to undertake so-called community care at great cost to their incomes, career prospects, leisure and health?

Mr. Forsyth: What the hon. Lady says is rubbish. No one in Scotland is required to take the cheapest medical care. The provisions in the White Paper and the basis on which the National Health Service is run in Scotland are that patients should have access to the best possible medical care, which does not always mean the most expensive.

Sir Hector Monro: Does my hon. Friend agree that women doctors who often work part time in general practice or elsewhere in the Health Service have an important part to play? Does he further agree that under the new contract their position is safeguarded and enhanced, and that they can look forward to a good future?

Mr. Forsyth: Yes, I very much agree with my hon. Friend. The new contract which has been accepted by the general practitioners' negotiators protects the position of part-time women doctors. My hon. Friend is right to draw attention to the importance that we attach to having more women doctors in the Health Service, both for the extension of patient choice—many people would prefer to see a woman doctor—and because many women doctors bring precisely the kind of expertise in preventive medicine that we aim to encourage in the Health Service.

Mrs. Margaret Ewing: On behalf of the women of my constituency and of the community of Moray, I welcome the Minister's announcement last week that a new obstetric and maternity unit is to be built in Elgin in less than 10 years. When does the Minister envisage the option appraisals being completed and the first stone laid?

Mr. Forsyth: I thank the hon. Lady for her general welcome to the proposals. As she knows, the independent working group that we set up to examine maternity facilities in Moray saw the establishment of a specialist unit as a legitimate goal and suggested that it would take 10 years. I have asked the Grampian health board to try to achieve a specialist unit more rapidly than that. I have met the chairman of the health board and asked him to proceed with the greatest possible speed. As the hon. Lady knows, there are particular problems connected with the site at Dr. Gray's hospital in Elgin, but I assure her that every effort will be made to overcome them and to bring the facility into being as speedily as is physically possible.

Mr. David Marshall: Despite the Minister's answer to his hon. Friend the Member for Dumfries (Sir H. Monro), is it not true that the proposals for the National Health Service will lead to a reduction in the numbers of women doctors—especially those working part-time in the service? What effect will the proposals have on the career structures of part-time women doctors in the Health Service?

Mr. Forsyth: The proposals will not reduce the number of part-time women doctors or affect them adversely. I note that the hon. Gentleman produced no justification for his statement——

Mr. Dewar: Ask the doctors.

Mr. Forsyth: The doctors argued that it was essential to alter the criteria for the basic practice allowance, to set them at levels at which the allowance was payable, to begin with, for 400 patients and would continue up to 1,200 patients. We responded to that by doing precisely what the doctors asked, and the position of part-time women doctors has been protected as a result.

Freedom of Speech

2. **Mr. Amos:** To ask the Secretary of State for Scotland whether he will consider extending section 43 (Freedom of speech in universities, polytechnics and colleges) of the Education (No. 2) Act 1986 to Scotland.

10. **Mr. Andy Stewart:** To ask the Secretary of State for Scotland what representations he has received seeking the extension of section 43 (Freedom of speech in universities, polytechnics and colleges) of the Education (No. 2) Act 1986 to Scotland.

Mr. Forsyth: It was decided in 1986 not to extend to Scotland the provisions in the 1986 Act which became section 43 as there was little evidence in Scotland of the problems that prompted the legislation south of the border. Since then there has been very little evidence of disruption of free speech in universities or colleges in Scotland.

Mr. Amos: I am grateful to my hon. Friend for that answer. As our universities are funded nationally, how can he justify the fact that the law as it relates to Scotland in this matter is different from the law relating to England?

Mr. Forsyth: My hon. Friend is right to draw attention to the importance of freedom of speech being a feature of our universities and colleges north and south of the border. I think that it is right to say that the Left have been more disruptive in universities south of the border—hence the need for the 1986 provisions. I can certainly assure my hon. Friend that when there are problems north of the border we shall address them.

Mr. Stewart: May I take this opportunity to congratulate students attending Scottish universities on accepting the principle of free speech? We take free speech for granted, but there has been a grave loss of life and sacrifice by Chinese students trying to achieve the same freedom. If the situation deteriorates will my hon. Friend consider keeping the matter under review?

Mr. Forsyth: My hon. Friend is right to draw attention to the responsibilities on students and especially on student unions to ensure freedom of speech in universities and colleges in Scotland. I understand that the Conservative candidate in Glasgow, Central was joined in support by Chinese students at his press conference today in Scotland.

Mr. McFall: When the Minister visited Glasgow college on 20 October last year there was a spontaneous demonstration against him of the type that takes place whenever he visits in Scotland. After that demonstration the Minister went out of his way to commend the students on their responsible actions. Will he take this opportunity to reinforce that comment and relate it to all Scottish students and thus emphasise that there is no need to introduce such legislation in Scotland?

Mr. Forsyth: I remember that demonstration. I also remember the demonstration which greeted me in the constituency of the hon. Member for Moray (Mrs. Ewing). At that time many of the placards being waved said, "Thanks for coming, Michael". That was entirely spontaneous. I regret to say that that was not what the placards said when I visited Glasgow college. I can certainly assure the hon. Gentleman that so long as students behave responsibly they will not need to look to the House to embark on legislation to keep freedom of speech in our universities and colleges.

Mr. McLeish: I am pleased to note that the Minister now endorses the good nature, good sense and good behaviour of Scottish students. I am also pleased to see him distance himself from the hard Right on the Conservative Back Benches who use education in Scotland as a plaything. Is he aware of the review of the 1986 Act being undertaken by his right hon. Friend the Secretary of State for Education and Science? That Act is not functioning well and I sincerely hope that we shall not have any of that nonsense in Scotland. Will the Minister addresss himself to the real issue in Scottish education, which is the under-investment in higher education and not the behaviour of students?

Mr. Forsyth: There have been a record number of students as a result of the Government's investment in higher education. I am not distancing myself from any of my hon. Friends. They have rightly underlined the importance of freedom of speech in universities and colleges and I have given a clear commitment that, should Scotland experience the kind of problem that occurs in England, we would not hesitate to go down the legislative road. While student unions carry out their proper responsibilities there is no need for the House to become involved in their affairs.

Conservation (Woodlands)

3. **Mr. Key:** To ask the Secretary of State for Scotland what encouragement is given to conservation groups in the United Kingdom, including the Wiltshire Trust for Nature Conservation, to undertake projects in Forestry Commission woodlands.

The Parliamentary Under-Secretary of State for Scotland (Lord James Douglas-Hamilton): The Forestry Commission actively encourages local conservation groups to undertake projects in its woodlands. The Wiltshire Trust for Nature Conservation is represented on Forestry Commission conservation committees and advises the commission on the management of three sites, managing part of one of them on a leasehold basis.

Mr. Key: We are fortunate that the Wiltshire trust has been blazing a trail in that respect, but does my hon. Friend agree that the Forestry Commission has been a bit slow to establish joint projects and joint funding involving local environmental groups, and that where that is achieved it gives tremendous new access and recreation not just for tourists but for local people?

Lord James Douglas-Hamilton: I agree that it is important for tourism that we should strongly support environmental measures and I am glad that Somerford common was given much prominence in the leaflet that the Forestry Commission helped to produce. We give considerable funds—£200,000—to environmental groups. Scottish Office funds do not stretch as far as Wiltshire, but I will draw my hon. Friend's point to the attention of the Forestry Commission's chairman and that of my right hon. and learned Friend the Secretary of State and my right hon. Friend the Secretary of State for the Environment. This year we are contributing £250,000 to setting up the Scottish Woodland Company and we may commit anything up to £50 million over the next 20 years in order greatly to improve environmental standards in the central lowlands of Scotland.

Mr. Kirkwood: Has the Minister seen press reports circulating in the Borders region that statements were made by Scottish Office Ministers to Conservative candidates suggesting that £500,000 might be available for the Borders road authority to engage in environmental and forestry projects in that region? Does the hon. Gentleman approve of that method of making announcements? Will he now make an official announcement and get round to making real funding available so that the roads authorities in areas such as the Borders can repair and maintain the links to trunk roads being destroyed by the forestry industry?

Lord James Douglas Hamilton: I met deputations from the Borders region and from Dumfries and Galloway region to discuss roads affected by forestry extraction. We responded after the public expenditure survey round last autumn when we were able to take their points on board. I shall look into the hon. Gentleman's point about the reports, which I have not seen, but we are very much in favour of improving environmental standards everywhere in Scotland.

Dr. Moonie: With due regard to the Minister's concern for the environmental impact on forests, what research has his Department commissioned in the past two years into the effects on Scottish woodlands of English pests?

Lord James Douglas Hamilton: I cannot give the hon. Gentleman the exact figure, but I can tell him that we are spending about £6 million on looking into the problems of acidification, which are substantial.

Mr. Adley: I hope that neither the Opposition nor my hon. Friend will regard me as an English pest. Is my hon. Friend aware that we are entirely happy that the Forestry Commission has its headquarters in Edinburgh and that his Department answers our questions on forestry matters, but that it would be helpful if we could occasionally have answers on the problems in England for which he is ministerially responsible? He has now written referring me to my right hon. Friend the Minister of Agriculture, Fisheries and Food on a matter that I raised with him at a previous Scottish Question Time. Is it still Government policy to encourage the Forestry Commission to sell off land for the highest possible price?

Lord James Douglas Hamilton: Certainly as far as disposals are concerned, 140,000 hectares have been sold and receipts exceeded £120 million. Obviously certain areas that are surplus to requirements should be sold. It is important that the Forestry Commission should continue to supply timber mills on a steady basis, as that is important for their prosperity and for those whom they employ. I gave a full answer to my hon. Friend's point, which he raised on a previous occasion, in writing last night.

Collieries

4. **Mr. Eadie:** To ask the Secretary of State for Scotland whether he has calculated the loss of revenue to Midlothian district as a consequence of the proposed closure of Bilston and Monktonhall collieries.

The Secretary of State for Scotland (Mr. Malcolm Rifkind): The closure of the collieries will, of course, mean some overall loss of income and spending power to the area. But any loss of rate income to the district council will be compensated for in subsequent years through a corresponding increase in revenue support grant.

Mr. Eadie: The right hon. and learned Gentleman should be aware that 7,000 jobs have been lost in the mining industry in Midlothian since 1978. The Secretary of State claims that the financial impact is very light, but is he aware that we have already undertaken a preliminary survey of the economic impact, which suggests that Midlothian will lose at least £20 million? A small area such as Midlothian cannot afford such a loss. Will the right hon. and learned Gentleman consider meeting Midlothian district council with me to discuss that devastating problem?

Mr. Rifkind: I have just signed a letter to the hon. Gentleman agreeing to such a meeting. Income from employment in the area will fall as a consequence of redundancies, but excluding redundancy payments, a net loss of disposable income of around £4 million per annum has been provisionally estimated as a result of recent decisions. The hon. Gentleman will be pleased to learn that unemployment in his constituency fell by more than 32 per cent. in the past two years, from 4,700 to 3,300. Although that figure is still far too high, it is encouraging that the trend is significantly in the right direction.

Health Service (Competitive Tendering)

5. **Mr. Michael Brown:** To ask the Secretary of State for Scotland if he will make a statement on progress on competitive tendering in the Health Service in Scotland; and if he will make a statement.

Mr. Michael Forsyth: Since the last general election, savings from competitive tendering have increased from £600,000 to £25 million on 74 contracts. That represents substantial additional resources for patient care in Scotland's health service over the next three to four years. Boards will continue to make progress in both the scope and range of services to put to competitive tender and are much encouraged by their success to date.

Mr. Brown: Bearing in mind the Opposition's attitude to competitive tendering, is it not the case that they would be prepared to deny £25 million of additional resources for patient care in Scotland? Is not that £25 million of extra care the direct result of my hon. Friend's decisions?

Mr. Forsyth: Yes, my hon. Friend is correct. Boards can use savings for direct patient care. The resources released so far could buy more than 2,000 kidney dialysis machines, or pay for 8,000 hip replacement operations or about 4,000 heart bypass operations.

Mr. Dewar *indicated dissent.*

Mr. Forsyth: The shadow Secretary of State for Scotland scoffs, but he was among those who indulged in disruption to prevent competitive tendering and saw 3,500 operations cancelled in Scotland.

Dr. Reid: What instructions has the Minister issued to Scottish health boards about value added tax for the purposes of competitive tendering? Is he aware of the Treasury circular of August 1988 which lays down specific guidelines on the conditions under which VAT may be refunded to health authorities when it is incurred in putting work out to private tender? Why has that circular been ignored, and why have health boards been advised instead that the matter is under review? Is it not because strict compliance with Treasury conditions would reveal that much of the savings that the Minister boasts about are bogus?

Mr. Forsyth: VAT policy is a matter for my right hon. Friend the Chancellor of the Exchequer. I am aware of the circular, with which health boards are complying. They are asked to disregard VAT when evaluating in-house contracts as compared with those of private enterprise. However, the hon. Gentleman's analysis of the situation is incorrect. Three-quarters of the contracts awarded, and the bulk of the savings, have been achieved as a result of in-house tenders being accepted on which VAT was never levied. When making a comparison between in-house and private sector tenders, VAT is disregarded because it is a receipt to the Exchequer. The key point is that savings are made to the public purse as a whole.

Mr. Galbraith: Why is the Minister conniving with the likes of the Scottish National party through competitive tendering in Tayside to sack some of the lowest-paid workers in Scotland? Is it not the case that competitive tendering in the National Health Service is subject to some extremely dubious accounting practices in which many costs to the private contractor are hidden, to the disadvantage of the in-house tender? Does the Minister agree that it is time that we had a full investigation into accounting practices and competitive tendering in the National Health Service and that until that is complete we should halt further competitive tendering within the National Health Service?

Mr. Forsyth: The hon. Gentleman's previous position was that there were no savings to be made. Now that savings of £25 million have been made, we are getting bluster. As for conniving with the SNP to make people redundant, the hon. Gentleman will be aware that three quarters of the contracts in the Health Service are the result of successful in-house bids. When people have been made redundant, they have received redundancy payments and many have been re-employed by the private sector. The public interest demands that the best possible value for money be obtained. The hon. Gentleman should look to the conduct of his colleagues in Lothian where, as a matter of political prejudice and ideology, the Labour party has put the ratepayers' interests second.

Devolution

6. **Mr. Tom Clarke:** To ask the Secretary of State for Scotland what is Her Majesty's Government's policy on devolution for Scotland.

Mr. Rifkind: We believe that the present constitutional arrangements provide for full and fair representation of Scotland's interests.

Mr. Clarke: Will the Secretary of State accept that in denying Scottish people a legitimate say in their own affairs, he is flying in the face of the views of the vast majority of Scots, who support Labour party policy, and that in so doing he has given short-term succour and comfort to a separatist minority view whose slogan is as unrealistic in Scotland as it is unworkable in Europe?

Mr. Rifkind: We believe that Scotland, England and the rest of the United Kingdom see this Parliament at Westminster as our parliament. It is the Parliament of Scotland as it is the Parliament of England, and no citizen of Scotland is denied any rights available to any citizen elsewhere in the United Kingdom. One of the problems of the hon. Gentleman's party's proposal for devolution, apart from its other defects, is that together with all the other proposed reforms it would exchange a system in which Scots pay two taxes for a system in which Scots would pay four taxes. The Labour party wishes to replace the community charge with a property tax and a local income tax, to have Scots paying income tax to the United Kingdom Government and to give a Scottish assembly power to levy a supplementary income tax. Four taxes for two does not seem likely to be in Scotland's interests.

Mr. Bill Walker: Does my right hon. and learned Friend agree that many of the proposals under the so-called banner of devolution are very difficult to distinguish from separatism, as is the question of Scotland's presence in Europe? Is it not interesting that the hon. Member for Glasgow, Govan (Mr. Sillars) has withdrawn his question about separatism from the Order Paper and is not present in the Chamber, perhaps because he knows that he has no real case to put forward?

Mr. Rifkind: My hon. Friend is quite correct. In regard to the first part of his question, I am bound to say that I think that the Labour party is running scared. The ridiculous slogan "Independence in the United Kingdom", which has neither grammatical sense nor political wisdom, will live to haunt the Labour party.

Mr. Salmond: Will the Secretary of State tell us if, in his estimate, support for the independence in Europe policy is running at 52 per cent. or at 61 per cent. as variously estimated by Systems Three? If the people of Scotland regard this Parliament as a parliament for all the United Kingdom, what does the Secretary of State think the reaction would be in Scotland to the fact that five out of the first 10 questions at Scottish Question Time are from English Tory Members?

Mr. Rifkind: English Members may have tabled some questions, but at least they had the courtesy to turn up to ask them, unlike the hon. Member for Glasgow, Govan (Mr. Sillars), who, having been elected to the House, yet again manifestly fails to appear. Even when he tables a question that would undoubtedly be reached, he withdraws it because he has not the guts to be here to carry out his parliamentary responsibilities.

Mr. Gow: Is my right hon. and learned Friend aware —[*Interruption.*]

Mr. Speaker: Order. I ask the House to settle down; it is very bumpy today.

Mr. Gow: Is my right hon. and learned Friend aware that I am a Scotsman? Is he further aware that Conservative Members share his view that a legislative assembly in Scotland would put the Union at risk? Will he remind his right hon. Friend the Secretary of State for Northern Ireland of that truth?

Mr. Rifkind: I have always thought of my hon. Friend as one of the most Scottish of my colleagues, and we are delighted that he is participating in our proceedings. I strongly believe that the Labour party's proposals for Scottish constitutional change would damage the United Kingdom. My hon. Friend will, as he has before, put questions about Northern Ireland to my right hon. Friend the Secretary of State for Northern Ireland.

Mr. Dewar: If the Secretary of State thinks that the hon. Member for Eastbourne (Mr. Gow) is the most Scottish of his colleagues——

Mr. Rifkind: One of them.

Mr. Dewar: That is an important caveat, but it suggests basic doubts about the Secretary of State's judgment. Does the right hon. and learned Gentleman agree that, in voting this week for its own identity, the Institute of Chartered Accountants of Scotland was applying to its own affairs the principles of devolution and the case for passing power to Scotland? Will he join me in welcoming that and recognise that his party will never be a credible force in Scotland if it displays a thrawn refusal to listen to public opinion, putting it on a par with the Scottish National party, which, in refusing to join the constitutional convention, is apparently working on the principle that there should be no compromise with the electorate?

Mr. Rifkind: The hon. Gentleman must appreciate that one of the stems of the unitary state and Parliament in which we participate is that, over the past 250 years, the Scottish national identity has been preserved and enhanced. It applies not only to chartered accountants but to the Scottish legal system, of which the hon. Gentleman and I are members. It illustrates that it is not inconsistent with a unitary Parliament and a United Kingdom that Scotland's national indentity, institutions, culture and heritage can be preserved and enhanced.

Mr. Tom Clarke: On a point of order, Mr. Speaker. In view of the Secretary of State's unsatisfactory answer, I shall seek to raise the matter again on the Adjournment.

Community Charge

7. **Mrs. Ray Michie:** To ask the Secretary of State for Scotland what is his Department's latest estimate of the administrative costs of collecting the community charge in *(a)* Argyll and Bute, and *(b)* Scotland.

8. **Mr. Dalyell:** To ask the Secretary of State for Scotland what is his latest estimate of the costs of collection of the poll tax in relation to the costs of collection of the rates.

The Minister of State, Scottish Office (Mr. Ian Lang): The administrative cost of community charge collection for Scotland in 1989-90, including registration work but excluding the costs of operating the rebate scheme, is estimated by local authorities at £31·8 million. The cost of rates collection in 1988-89 was £17·3 million. Estimates of district councils' costs are not available centrally.

Mrs. Michie: Is the Minister aware that the cost of implementing the poll tax is continuing to escalate? In Argyll and Bute, extra staff have had to be taken on. In Strathclyde, 720,000 changes have already had to be made to the poll tax register. Strathclyde is having to pay £8 million more than the Government's estimated cost of implementation. How can the Minister justify this escalating cost and bureaucracy to implement the poll tax?

Mr. Lang: On the contrary, the costs now coming in are lower than those originally estimated when we published the Bill. If the hon. Lady compares the cost of implementing the community charge with that of a local income tax, which is favoured by the Social and Liberal Democratic party and others, she will find that a 1981 White Paper estimated the additional cost of collecting a local income tax at £500 million, in addition to which it would have involved the employment of tens of thousands of additional civil servants.

Mr. Dalyell: What evidence is there that costs are lower? Does the Minister deny the Strathclyde figure that, whereas the cost of collecting rates was £17 million, the cost of collecting the poll tax is at least £36 million?

Mr. Lang: What I said was that the costs are lower than those originally indicated when we published the Bill. The costs overall are higher for collecting the community charge because something like double the number of people pay, but the cost is roughly the same per head of the

population. I think that that is a price worth paying for the extra fairness and accountability that derives from the community charge system.

Mr. Buchanan-Smith: Can my hon. Friend tell me how much extra the community charge payers of Grampian have to pay because of the decision of the Labour-controlled city of Aberdeen district council not to operate the administration of the charge?

Mr. Lang: Such figures are not available to me at present, but it is undoubtedly the case that as a result of the decision of 15 district councils in Scotland not to assist in the handling of the community charge, considerable numbers of people are being put at risk, including the most vulnerable in society who may be unable to get rebates punctually.

Mr. John Marshall: Can my hon. Friend tell the House how the cost of collecting the community charge compares with the suggested costs of collecting the two local government taxes proposed by the Labour party?

Mr. Lang: My hon. Friend raises a sensible point. I have already indicated that the cost of a local income tax would be massive compared with the community charge. The community charge itself has a cost of collection of less than half of 1 per cent. of the total expenditure of local authorities. I think that helps put the matter in perspective.

Mr. Douglas: Is the Minister including the cost of the humiliation of individuals who have to register their offspring, parents, husbands or wives who are severely mentally impaired? How does he estimate that cost? Will he consider the anomaly whereby the services subvent service men who find themselves having to pay high community charges? Why can the Ministry of Defence do that for service men who may be highly paid when the same cannot be done for the disabled?

Mr. Lang: The arrangements for service men reflect broadly the arrangements that existed under the domestic rating system. As to humiliation, I recognise no humiliation in a system that invites all adult members of the population, with a few exemptions, to contribute to the cost of local authority expenditure and thereby play a fuller part in local authority democracy.

Local Authority Income

9. **Mr. Harry Greenway:** To ask the Secretary of State for Scotland what proportion of Scottish local authority income comes from *(a)* central Government funds, *(b)* the non-domestic rate and *(c)* the community charge; and if he will make a statement.

Mr. Rifkind: A total of 52 per cent. of Scottish local authority income in the current year will come from central Government funds, 27 per cent. from non-domestic rates and 21 per cent. from community charges. The proportion to be raised from community charges is higher that it need have been because many authorities have budgeted to increase their spending by well over the rate of inflation.

Mr. Greenway: Community charge payers will note that answer. Does my right hon. and learned Friend agree that the recent announcement that Scottish business ratepayers will achieve level playing fields with their English counterparts is good news for Scottish industry, for Scottish jobs and for everyone who cares for Scotland?

Mr. Rifkind: Yes, indeed, it has been a feature for many years of the Scottish business and industrial community that it has had a higher non-domestic rates burden than that south of the border, primarily because of higher local authority spending. Despite the cause of the problem, this Government are the first to ensure that that will cease and that in the United Kingdom we will have a common level of non-domestic rate poundage, thereby bringing the equivalent of £250 million of reduced rates burden to business and industry throughout Scotland.

Mr. Ernie Ross: Does the Secretary of State concede that his control of non-domestic rates will mean that if local government is to respond to the needs of the local business community, the cost of the expectation of increased services by non-domestic ratepayers will fall directly on domestic poll tax payers? How does he intend to help local authorities because of that?

Mr. Rifkind: I have to remind the hon. Gentleman that, as I understand it, local authorities have welcomed our plan to reduce the burden on the industrial and business community in Scotland because they appreciate, even if the hon. Gentleman does not, that that not only will be of benefit to industry but will have consequential benefits for jobs and the overall prosperity and competitiveness of the Scottish economy.

Mr. Wallace: The Secretary of State will recall that when the Green Paper was published he said that there would be special arrangements for Orkney and Shetland because of the high proportion of non-domestic rates from the oil terminals and, in Shetland's case, because of the debt repayment policy that would mean lower non-domestic rates at a time when oil revenues were going down. In the light of his recent announcement, what steps does he propose to take to flesh out the proposals for special arrangements?

Mr. Rifkind: Yes, we said in our announcement on business rates that there would have to be special arrangements for Orkney and Shetland because of the facts to which the hon. Gentleman referred. We are currently considering what those might be and there will be discussions with officials from the two island authorities to identify the most appropriate course of action.

Mr. Favell: Is it not a fact that following revaluation, the rating system in Scotland was highly unpopular and that it was only this Government who had the guts to do anything about it, unlike the gaggle of frustrated Socialists on the Opposition Benches, who have nothing to offer but wrecking tactics?

Mr. Rifkind: My hon. Friend is right, except in one respect. Labour Members are not offering simply wrecking tactics; they are offering in exchange for the community charge a property tax and a local income tax. They seem to believe—*[Interruption.]*—that two unpopular taxes will somehow be more acceptable to the people of Scotland than one form of rates or community charge. I notice that they are now trying to deny that, but the evidence is in their own policy documents, so we are entitled to refer to it.

Mr. Maxton: Does the Secretary of State accept that there has been a massive reduction in the level of Government grant given to local authorities in percentage terms, from 68·5 per cent. in 1979 to the present 55 per cent.? That would realise £589 million at present, which would mean £151 per poll taxpayer in Scotland, if it were distributed in that way. Does he agree that it was that reduction in grant that put pressure on the rating system and which led the Government to introduce the absurd and unfair poll tax, which is now putting the burden directly on the very poorest in our community?

Mr. Rifkind: I remind the hon. Gentleman that it was the last Labour Government who were responsible for the single biggest reduction in what was then called the rate support grant. I notice also that although speaking from the Opposition Front Bench, the hon. Gentleman did not contradict my remarks about the Labour party proposing to replace the community charge with two separate taxes —a property tax and a local income tax.

Crown Estate Commissioner

11. **Mr. Macdonald:** To ask the Secretary of State for Scotland what plans he has to undertake a further review of the Crown Estate Commissioners' powers in Scotland.

Mr. Rifkind: I have no plans to do so.

Mr. Macdonald: I appreciate that the Secretary of State has just recently completed a review, but does he not think that the whole issue needs to be looked at again, following the clumsy and inadequate way in which the commissioners have handled the allocation of test drilling permission for mineral deposits off the west coast of Scotland? Those deposits could eventually be very significant, so does the Secretary of State not think that it is time that such matters were handled by local and central Government working jointly and not left to the Crown Estate Commissioners, who are undemocratic, unaccountable, not especially experienced in this regard and deeply resented in the Highlands and Islands?

Mr. Rifkind: My understanding is that with regard to the particular incident to which the hon. Gentleman refers, the Crown Estate Commissioners have complied with well-established procedures. Indeed, on this occasion, they have consulted more widely than is usual. At present, all that is being considered is permission for prospecting purposes, not for actual mining, and that involves core sampling, seismic surveys and spot dredging of samples. The consultation procedure has been substantial. If, as a result of that, any further application were to be made, a more widely based consultation process would be required, which would have to be independently and expertly assessed. There would then be a full consultation process conducted by the Scottish Office, involving relevant Departments, local authorities, statutory agencies and others with a legitimate interest in the matter. At this stage, all that is being contemplated is permission for prospecting purposes. Any further action would require the much more substantial procedure that I have just outlined.

Mr. Kennedy: Will the Secretary of State note that many in the Highlands and Islands will think, listening to that response, that the Crown Estate Commissioners have carried out a more thorough consultation procedure than normal—which would hardly be difficult? Given the growth of fish farming activity, does the Secretary of State not think that there is a strong need now for more local, democratic accountability for seabed leases and the like and that local authorities should be involved in that planning procedure, rather than it being left to an unelected and thoroughly publicly unaccountable body —the Crown Estate Commissioners?

Mr. Rifkind: The Government have just undertaken a review of the position of the Crown Estate Commissioners. As a result of that, I have just established a fish farming advisory committee and Lord Grieve has agreed to be the chairman of that committee. It will advise the Crown Estate Commissioners on how to deal with cases in which there is an objection to an application for a seabed lease from one or more of the statutory bodies represented on the committee. Cases of particular difficulty will be referred to the Secretary of State for advice and the Crown Estate Commissioners have undertaken to take into account the views of the Secretary of State on any controversial matters. There has been a substantial improvement in the appropriate procedures, which will ensure that the Crown Estate Commissioners will, in practice, take into account exactly the kind of considerations that would be relevant to other planning applications.

Sir Nicholas Fairbairn: Does my right hon. and learned Friend appreciate that, to get over the difficulties of this apparently unelected body, it would be a suitable customer to be made into a private agency? Will he quickly consider whether it can be so converted and removed from the clutches of the state?

Mr. Rifkind: It is not so much the state, as the Crown for which the Crown Estate Commissioners are responsible. My hon. and learned Friend's suggestion, ingenious as it is, may not be entirely appropriate to a body that is responsible for administering the Crown's estates.

Mr. Wilson: I am sure that they will be quaking in their boots in Buckingham palace at the suggestion by the hon. and learned Member for Perth and Kinross (Sir N. Fairbairn) that the Crown Estate Commissioners should be privatised.

The replies given by the Secretary of State are inadequate and alarming. If indeed a review of the Crown Estate Commissioners has been carried out, I am disappointed that he can still give such complacent and inadequate replies. The consultation procedures, about which my hon. Friend the Member for Western Isles (Mr. Macdonald) asked, were totally inadequate. Once again, Scottish coastal communities were left to find out at second or third hand about proposals that could have profound implications for their futures. The Secretary of State must accept that that is unacceptable and that the fate of Scottish coastal communities should not be in the hands of an organisation whose prime function is property development in London and the maintenance of Regent's park.

Mr. Rifkind: The hon. Gentleman should do his homework. The Crown Estate Commissioners carried out wide consultations, including consultation with the local planning authority.

Mr. Wilson: They did not.

Mr. Rifkind: The hon. Gentleman says that they did not. They did. He should check his facts before making such allegations. For the purpose of prospecting, the Crown Estate Commissioners carried out wide consultations, including consultation with the local planning authority. I believe that that was quite sufficient. I have already pointed out that if, as a result of prospecting, the company wished to go further, a much more exhaustive process would be undertaken, conducted by the Scottish Office, and that would provide the safeguards in which the hon. Gentleman is interested.

Community Charge (Churches)

12. **Mr. Strang:** To ask the Secretary of State for Scotland what representations he has received from the principal Churches in Scotland on the poll tax.

Mr. Lang: My right hon. and learned Friend has received a number of such representations. In particular, representations have been made on the impact of non-domestic sewerage charges on churches, church halls, charities and other organisations. I share the concern expressed and I am glad to be able to announce to the House today that we are changing the arrangements so that such bodies which already obtain some relief from non-domestic rates and from water rates will also obtain some relief from non-domestic sewerage rates. I shall be bringing forward proposals shortly. Consultations with COSLA will be put in hand at once.

Mr. Strang: Although we welcome that concession, we hope that it will amount to complete exemption for church buildings in the payment of sewerage rates. Will the hon. Gentleman take on board the need to match the 50 per cent. reduction on domestic rates payable on accommodation provided for Church of Scotland ministers and priests with a comparable concession in the poll tax? Surely the hon. Gentleman understands the dramatic effect of the changes on the finances of the Church of Scotland and the Roman Catholic Church in Scotland.

Mr. Lang: The community charge is, of course, a different system, being a charge for personal services rather than a property tax, and it would not be appropriate to have special arrangements for ministers. However, we have extended the mandatory relief on certain church property from 50 per cent. to 80 per cent., which may help to some extent.

We propose to introduce legislation to reduce to between 50 per cent. and 25 per cent. of net annual value the proportion of rateable value against which the sewerage rate is levied. That arrangement applies at the moment in the context of water rates.

Mr. Steel: Is it not a little difficult to know how warmly to welcome this concession until we know— *[Interruption.]* Will the Minister please listen to me? It is difficult to know how warmly to welcome the concession until we know its exact relation to the charges made before the poll tax was introduced. Can the Minister tell us how much the concession will be worth?

Mr. Lang: I had hoped that the right hon. Gentleman would have said "benvenuto". I hope that he will welcome the arrangement. A church in the Lothian region, for example, with a rateable value of £7,000 would currently have sewerage charges of £280, but they might be reduced to £70 under the concession.

Mr. Jack: Does my hon. Friend think that members of the principal Churches in Scotland will come to recognise the inherent fairness of the community charge, the help that it gives to the single Scot and the generosity of the rebate scheme?

Mr. Lang: My hon. Friend is right to suggest that the inherently greater fairness of the community charge compared with the domestic rating system is self-evident. I am sure that ministers of the Church will come to appreciate that and to agree that it is far more appropriate that personal services provided by local authorities should be paid for by individuals rather than simply on the basis of property.

Mr. Canavan: Will the Government consider scrapping the poll tax, which had been described by various Church representatives as an immoral tax, as well as being expensive to administer and difficult to collect? In the light of recent estimates by Scottish local authorities that more than 30 per cent. of people on the poll tax register—well over 1 million people—have failed to pay their first instalment, will the Minister tell us his views on what level of non-payment would be required to force the Government to think again about abolishing this iniquitous tax?

Mr. Lang: It is clear from figures provided by local authorities that the level of payment is such as to render the hon. Gentleman's question irrelevant. I am sure that anyone assessing the community charge and taking account of the rebate system—which takes particular account of the needs and circumstances of the low paid, for which more than 1 million applications have been received—would recognise that a broader-based tax, such as the community charge, is a fairer and more appropriate way to pay for local authority services than the rating system that fell on only four out of every 10 adults.

Mr. Buchanan-Smith: Unlike the right hon. Member for Tweeddale, Ettrick and Lauderdale (Mr. Steel), I welcome my hon. Friend's announcement. Is he aware that it will be warmly welcomed, not only by the Churches, but by the many community associations that run halls and voluntary organisations? Is he further aware that in my constituency some local halls were faced with an increase in rates of as much as 1,000 per cent., and in some cases a potential increase of 5,000 per cent.? That is the extent of the concession announced by my hon. Friend, and I congratulate him on it.

Mr. Lang: I am grateful to my right hon. Friend for his comments. I believe that my announcement will be widely welcomed throughout Scotland and will be of particular advantage to the Churches, bodies and organisations to which my right hon. Friend referred. The sum involved of £3 million is equivalent to about 2 per cent. of total sewerage charges.

Mr. Foulkes: We might as well be in Hong Kong.

Mr. Dewar: I shall refrain from commenting on my hon. Friend's remark.

Does the Minister accept, in general terms, the right of the Churches to speak out against a tax that they believe to be socially divisive and unjust? If so, will he distance himself from the petulant and rather undignified complaints of the chairman of the Scottish Conservative party and the Minister of State, Department of Education and Science about those Churchmen who expressed their concerns about the impact of the poll tax? Is it not right that anyone whose conscience is troubled should protest against a tax that was described by the right hon. Member for Henley (Mr. Heseltine) as placing on an equal footing in the eyes of the tax collector

"the rich and the poor, the slum dweller and the landed aristocrat, the elderly pensioners living on their limited savings and the most succesful of today's entrepreneurs."—[*Official Report*, 16 December 1987; Vol. 124, c. 1141.]

Mr. Lang: I certainly agree that it is appropriate for the Church and for members of Churches to express views on a wide range of issues, and no doubt the community charge comes under that category. I do not recognise the hon. Gentleman's description of the community charge, which clearly takes no account of the extensive rebate system, for which we estimate that some 30 per cent. of the adult population of Scotland may be eligible. It is the rebate system that makes the fairness and generosity of the community charge, taken overall, acceptable. It provides a better and fairer way of paying for the cost of local authorities.

NHS (Reform)

13. **Mr. Bill Walker:** To ask the Secretary of State for Scotland what representations he has received from general practitioners in Tayside about the Government White Papers on the Health Service.

Mr. Michael Forsyth: About 80 letters have been received from general practitioners in Tayside, direct or through hon. Members, referring to various matters arising from the Government's White Papers "Promoting Better Health" and "Working for Patients".

Mr. Walker: I thank my hon. Friend for that reply. Is he aware that at meetings I had with individual GPs and with representatives of GPs in Tayside it became clear that the GPs had not understood—[*Interruption.*]—properly and fully just how much control they would have over decisions affecting where they could send their patients —because the payment will follow the patient—and how important that was for the popular community cottage hospitals in the future?

Is he further aware that doctors were horrified when they were made to realise that the lies contained in the leaflet distributed by them on behalf of the BMA were making many pensioners unhappy and concerned because of the fear that in future they would not be able to get their prescriptions and receive treatment, and as a result of that they propose to do something about it?

Mr. Forsyth: There is no justification whatever for patients being frightened or misled about the White Paper proposals. We have had a positive response from GPs in Scotland—[*Interruption.*] Indeed, the new contract which has been agreed by their negotiators is based very much on the proposals which were put forward in Scotland.

In response to Opposition Members who scoff at the assertion by my hon. Friend the Member for Tayside, North (Mr. Walker) about the degree of interest in the extent of control which GPs can obtain as a result of

GP-based budgeting and self-governing hospitals, I can say "yes" to my hon. Friend and tell him that I have received from his constituency representations not only about self-governing hospitals but about GP-based budgeting, with considerable enthusiasm being shown by the persons concerned.

Mr. Foulkes: May I inform the hon. Member for Tayside, North (Mr. Walker), as a psychologist— *[Interruption.]* He is not; I am. May I inform him that there is absolutely no evidence to show that the general practitioners in Tayside are any less intelligent than the GPs in Ayrshire? All the GPs to whom I have spoken in Ayrshire understand only too well what is meant by the White Paper. They have passed a resolution unanimously condemning it and asking the Government to withdraw it.

If members of the Government, and in particular the Minister, mean anything when they use the word "consultation"—if they are not to be seen as people who are not men of their word—the only honourable action for them to take now is to withdraw the White Paper.

Mr. Forsyth: I am tempted to reply to the hon. Gentleman by saying "physician, heal thyself." I had a meeting with GPs in Ayr on Monday. After an hour's discussion with them I formed the same conclusion as my hon. Friend the Member for Tayside, North (Mr. Walker) —that many of the details concerning our proposals were not understood and had not been communicated to them.

I am happy to tell the House that the objectives of our White Paper—to increase patient choice, to increase the emphasis on preventive medicine and to make the NHS more responsive to the needs and wishes of patients—are objectives which all of those GPs were happy to endorse. The mechanisms, mechanics and best way forward are issues on which GPs should not pass resolutions of condemnation. They should roll up their shirt sleeves and help us to get this right.

Mr. Hind: When my hon. Friend replies to the representations from the GPs in Tayside, will he emphasise that indicative budgets, both practice and drug budgets, mean that no patients need fear lest the resources for their treatment will not be available? Will he ask them to withdraw the leaflet from the BMA, which unnecessarily winds up elderly and sick patients and makes them fear that the necessary resources will not be available?

Mr. Forsyth: I wrote to the British Medical Association in Scotland asking it to withdraw the leaflet from Scotland. I received a reply saying that the leaflet had been produced in London and that it did not take entire responsibility for it. I also pointed out the assertions in that leaflet about our proposals, which are frankly just untruths. The response from the BMA in Scotland did not seek to defend the assertions which are made in that leaflet. I believe that events have moved on and that there is a coming together to get the proposals right, certainly in regard to the contract.

I agree with my hon. Friend that it is completely irresponsible to say to any patient that he will be denied treatment or drugs as a result of the proposals. That is not true. No general practitioner, whether a budget-handling GP or a GP subject to indicative budgets, will find that he does not have the resources to treat the patients. Opposition Members who say such things are causing needless anxiety to patients.

Mr. Robert Hughes: The hon. Member for Tayside, North (Mr. Walker) has made astonishing charges of ignorance against doctors in Tayside. Is he saying, however, that it is because the doctors are too thick to understand the White Paper or that the Minister is too thick to explain it properly?

Mr. Forsyth: I am saying that the type of intellectual approach that the hon. Gentleman has shown in his question is not one that I would expect from doctors. I would expect doctors to study the proposals carefully, to form a considered judgment, to identify the particular aspects causing them concern and to discuss with the Government the best way forward. That has not always been the case, but I accept what I think is implicit in the hon. Gentleman's question, which is that the vast majority of doctors will rightly see the way forward as being one which looks to their patients' interests. The White Paper is based on putting the patient first and ensuring that the Health Service delivers the best possible quality of care with the substantial additional resources that are available within the NHS.

Short Brothers plc

3.31 pm

The Secretary of State for Northern Ireland (Mr. Tom King): With permission, Mr. Speaker, I wish to make a statement about the privatisation of Short Brothers plc.

Since last July the Government have been working with the management of Shorts to seek a successful transfer of the company to the private sector. On 3 March I advised the House that I had selected two out of the six preliminary proposals for the purchase of the company, and had invited those two to submit final proposals by 30 April. They were the Canadian company Bombardier, and a partnership of GEC and Fokker. Their final proposals have now been fully reviewed, and I can advise the House that I have today approved heads of agreement for the sale of Short Brothers plc to Bombardier.

Under the heads of agreement, Bombardier will pay £30 million for the share capital of Shorts. On behalf of the Government, I have offered Shorts, under its new ownership, grants of £79 million for new capital investment in the next four years and of £18 million for other costs, mainly for training. As regards the company's existing liabilities, the £390 million loan advanced by the Government earlier this year to repay commercial debts for past losses will be written off. I have also agreed to advance a further £275 million to recapitalise the company, to repay the remaining borrowings and to meet anticipated losses on existing contracts.

Of this sum at least £60 million will be in the form of an interest-free loan. That loan will be progressively cancelled as specified targets are met, but would be immediately repayable in the event of a material breach by Bombardier of the commitments it has given in relation to the future of the company. The Government will of course continue to fund the company until the completion of sale but as I announced on 10 January 1989, Government undertakings in respect of Short's liabilities will be withdrawn at privatisation as far as new obligations are concerned.

Beyond the period covered by the terms of the heads of agreement, Short's eligibility for assistance will be on the same basis as other private sector companies in Northern Ireland. In this respect, as I announced on 22 March 1989, I plan to repeal my powers in relation to Shorts in public ownership contained in the Aircraft and Shipbuilding Industries (Northern Ireland) Order 1979.

The terms of the agreement are subject to contract and also a number of conditions including the approval of the European Commission. The necessary estimates will be laid before the House at the appropriate times.

Bombardier recognises the important position occupied by Shorts in the Northern Ireland economy and intends to acquire the company as a long-term investment and to maintain it as a complete entity. Its objective is to develop the three main divisions of aircraft, aerostructures and missiles. In particular, Shorts aircraft division will become a full partner in the detailed design and development of the Canadair RJ regional jet and I have agreed to offer £18 million towards development costs on Short's part of this work.

Bombardier is a Canadian group with a range of products in the transportation industry. In 1986 it acquired Canadair, an aerospace company similar in size to Shorts, from the Canadian Government, and has since developed it successfully. It has recently launched its new regional jet for the short to medium range market. Overall, I believe that its activities provide an excellent fit with those of Shorts.

This agreement with Bombardier for the acquisition of Shorts opens the way for the transfer of the company from public ownership to the private sector. The scale of the sums involved illustrates very clearly the problems that the company has faced in public ownership and as a relatively small enterprise in the complex and competitive arena of aerospace. At the same time, it has developed products and skills which, with the right leadership and organisation, can once again make Shorts a successful and viable operation which contributes fully to the economy of Northern Ireland. The Government believe that operating under the commercial disciplines of the private sector and as part of a larger group under Bombardier's ownership, gives Shorts the best possible opportunity for a much brighter future and fully justifies this substantial investment of public funds.

Mr. Jim Marshall (Leicester, South): I thank the Secretary of State for answering the question that I put to him some days ago, asking that he should make a decision on the future ownership of Shorts prior to the opening of the Paris air show. Perhaps it is appropriate that a decision has been made on the eve of that show.

We welcome the fact that a decision has been made because it will remove the uncertainty which surrounds the future ownership of Shorts. We also welcome a bid, which, we hope, will seek to maintain the company as a single entity, and its product range.

It will come as no surprise to the Secretary of State to learn that we still continue to dislike the Government's privatisation policy, in particular as it applies to Shorts. Our view has been, and remains, that if the Government had been prepared to provide the level of financial assistance that they are now prepared to give to get rid of the company, Shorts, as a publicly owned company, would have flourished and could have been profitable. However, once the Government persisted in their privatisation policy, we made it clear some time ago that, out of the two bids that the Government were actively considering from Bombardier and GEC-Fokker, the decision should be made in Bombardier's favour. We are delighted that the Secretary of State has seen fit to accept our view.

Does the Secretary of State agree that, important though today's announcement is, of even greater importance is the future strategy for the development of the company in view of its pivotal importance to the economy of Northern Ireland? Paragraph 4 of the Secretary of State's statement refers to the commitments that Bombardier

"has given in relation to the future of the company."

It does not say that commitments will be, or may be, given but that commitments have been given. I and my party do not feel that those commitments were fully and adequately expounded in the Secretary of State's statement. It is those particulars and specifics lacking from the statement on which I wish to question the Secretary of State.

First, during his discussions with Bombardier, has the Secretary of State received any assurance about the existing product range and likely levels of employment? Secondly, I am sure that the Secretary of State agrees that Shorts is a centre of technical excellence. In view of that, has he received any assurance that the company will continue with research and development at the very frontiers of high technology?

Thirdly, the success of the bid depends greatly on the financial arrangements announced today by the Secretary of State. However, as he said, those will depend on the agreement or acquiescence of the European Commission. Have there been any preliminary discussions with the European Commission, and, if so, in which direction are they likely to go?

Fourthly, the House will know that Bombardier, although a successful company, is small in international terms. It employs 13,000 people worldwide. It is to take over a company in the north of Ireland, Shorts, which employs about 7,000 people. In those circumstances, is the Secretary of State convinced that the enlarged company has the necessary level of managerial expertise and sources of profitability to ensure its survival?

Fifthly, will the Secretary of State seek to ensure that, between today and the final takeover by Bombardier of Shorts, all members of the work force will be involved in full consultation with the Government, the present Shorts' management and the management of Bombardier?

Finally, Shorts has a distinguished past and deserves a soundly based future. We hope that that can be assured, not just for the sake of the company, but also for the economy of Northern Ireland as a whole.

Mr. King: I am grateful for the hon. Gentleman's comments about Bombardier and the decisions that we have made. Anybody who has any idea of the history and present position of Shorts and who thinks that its problems will be solved merely by pushing more money at them without changing ownership is mistaken. It is absolutely vital to give it the structure of a larger group, within the aerospace world. If we do not we shall simply be pouring more money after the substantial sums that we have already spent. I should have thought that the hon. Gentleman would have reflected on what the structure was that led to the calls for such substantial sums of money. Today, I have announced assistance of £780 million for that. Putting more money in without a substantial change in the arrangements would have been inconceivable.

I am satisfied of Bombardier's commitment to making a success of Shorts as a single company in Northern Ireland. That is one of the commitments into which Bombardier has entered. It will seek to maintain in totality the expertise, research and design development, which it sees as assets and values.

Bombardier took over Canadair which, at the time, was a loss-making, state-owned company in Canada that employed 5,000. Under Bombardier's leadership and ownership, within three years the company is now profitable and employs 6,500—1,500 more than when it was taken over. That must be real encouragement. Anybody who knows the chairman, M. Beaudoin—I have seen him in Belfast today—will know the high price that he attaches to communication with the people who work in the company.

Rev. Martin Smyth (Belfast, South): On behalf of my colleagues and the people of Northern Ireland, and of Belfast in particular, I welcome this statement. Bearing in mind the interval between the announcement of the privatisation and the buy-out of Harland and Wolff, will there be a similar prolonged period which will add to the

doubts and questions about Short's future, or does the Secretary of State foresee a speedier conclusion to these negotiations? He will know that there has been a loss of morale and that workers have left Shorts and that some have even been enticed abroad to look after their own futures because the future of the firm was in doubt.

I also welcome the fact that money has been put into training. Shorts used to have a fine training programme. Do I take it from the announcement that it will now return to on-the-job training in aircraft design and manufacture as well as other forms of training? I welcome the injection of capital, because although all have agreed that money was put into Shorts in the past, more money was needed in this area to give the company the proper tools for the job.

My colleagues and I await developments. Does the Secretary of State foresee any real difficulties with the Office of Fair Trading or the European Commission?

Mr. King: I am grateful to the hon. Gentleman, who speaks on behalf of himself and of his hon. Friends. He has a direct constituency interest, but everyone would recognise that Shorts affects the interests of all in Northern Ireland because of its important position.

I hope that there is a difference between what happened with Harland and Wolff and these negotiations. The management buy-out and the involvement of employees gave rise to a more complicated procedure, with the prospectus and the offer of shares in the new company. My best expectation is that if, as I hope, we are successful with the European Commission and the Office of Fair Trading, it will be possible for the matter to be concluded within three months.

As for training and the future of the company, this has been a difficult time because the employees, perhaps more than anyone else, knew how serious the company's position was and had been for some time. They knew about the large losses that were being made. If it had gone on as it was, the company had no future. Now it definitely has one—a future in which the Government and Bombardier are prepared to invest. Most importantly of all, provided that all who work in Shorts are committed to ensuring that they make the maximum contribution, if these are to be new investments, new facilities and new products, this will be an exciting development for Shorts and for Northern Ireland.

Mr. Kenneth Warren (Hastings and Rye): I congratulate my right hon. Friend, my hon. Friend the Member for Gosport (Mr. Viggers), and the officials who have supported them in their difficult negotiations and who are not often mentioned.

Is it not good that, on the eve of the Paris air show, the competition that my right hon. Friend has mounted and which has been decided clearly shows the value of Shorts in the international aerospace community? Bombardier is a growing force in international aerospace, as the acquisition of Shorts will show. I hope that my right hon. Friend agrees.

I hope, slightly egotistically, that my right hon. Friend will be kind enough to acknowledge that the Government have entirely agreed with the report by the Select Committee on Trade and Industry on this matter of privatisation.

What guarantee can my right hon. Friend give that the security of the missiles division will be maintained, given

[*Mr. Kenneth Warren*]

the sensitive work in which it is engaged? Lastly, is the £18 million which my right hon. Friend has committed to the Bombardier civil aircraft project the end of a commitment?

Mr. King: I have set out the main commitments but I have made it clear that in future the Government will treat Bombardier-Shorts in the same way as a normal private sector company in Northern Ireland.

I particularly appreciate my hon. Friend's comments about my hon. Friend the Under-Secretary of State for Northern Ireland, the Member for Gosport (Mr. Viggers). The difficulty about the whole situation was that this change was absolutely vital if Shorts was to survive. It was not entirely possible to let people in Northern Ireland really understand the seriousness of the situation. We tried to get an element of realism in the approach, but that was not always appreciated. My hon. Friend the Member for Gosport had to take a great deal of flak over that and he deserves great credit for the successful outcome that I have been able to announce to the House.

The agreement offers an exciting prospect for the future. I know that it is very closely in line, although not totally in line, with some of the recommendations that my hon. Friend the Member for Hastings and Rye (Mr. Warren) and his colleagues in the Select Committee pressed upon us.

Mr. Seamus Mallon (Newry and Armagh): I welcome this announcement, and especially the fact that it will end indecision for the work force in the North of Ireland. I am sure that the Secretary of State agrees that, when £800 million of public money is used, it should be used to the advantage of all sections of the community. Will he tell the House what requirements have been written into the agreement to ensure that discrimination in employment at Shorts will end once and for all? What security arrangements have been insisted upon by the Government so that no more missiles or information about them can be stolen from Shorts to the advantage of terrorists in the North of Ireland and their paymasters in the wretched South African Government?

Mr. King: No missiles have been stolen from Shorts and we are determined to make sure that none will be stolen. I make that absolutely clear. If the hon. Gentleman is referring to a demonstration cutaway model stolen from a TA centre, that is a rather different matter. None the less, I need hardly say that we take that very seriously and have been anxious to ensure that proper precautions and proper security are in place.

The hon. Gentleman spoke about public money. This is a substantial injection of public funds for the benefit of Northern Ireland. It is for the benefit of the economy of Northern Ireland and not for the benefit of one community or another. That is important and it is fully understood in the commitments and obligations that Bombardier will enter into. The company fully accepts the laws that obtain in Northern Ireland and I know that it will seek to be a good employer in the Province. It will bring great benefit because the injection of new ideas and a different approach can only be of benefit.

The company will be working together with the recognised skills and abilities that exist in Shorts and, as I said in my statement, that is a very happy fit indeed. I certainly look to this to make a major contribution to the

Northern Ireland economy. That is the justification for investment on this scale, and it will benefit all the people of Northern Ireland.

Mr. Ian Gow (Eastbourne): While unreservedly welcoming my right hon. Friend's statement, may I ask whether he agrees that the story of Shorts while it has been in the public sector has been a very unhappy and costly story indeed? Will my right hon. Friend learn the appropriate lessons from the experience of this company being in the public sector? In so far as there are any other companies which his Department still owns in Northern Ireland, will he undertake to put them into the private sector at the earliest possible moment?

Mr. King: My hon. Friend has made a shrewd and absolutely accurate observation. The figures demonstrate the scale of the problems that have arisen and which are partly connected to market conditions and partly to the size of the company. I profoundly believe that the difficulties owe a lot to the problems that public ownership can bring and the lack of motivation that can flow from it.

My hon. Friend the Member for Hastings and Rye (Mr. Warren) invited me to pay tribute to our officials. I know that my hon. Friend the Under-Secretary of State for Northern Ireland, the Member for Gosport (Mr. Viggers), would wish to be associated with that. The officials are not often mentioned and have taken much criticism during this process. Two or three years ago not many people would have held out many prospects for the survival of Harland and Wolff or Shorts. There has been a massive undertaking and all the people who work for Harland and Wolff and Shorts now have the real chance of a much brighter future. That prospect owes much to the dedicated and hard work of the team in the Department of Economic Development as well as to the companies.

Mr. Doug Hoyle (Warrington, North): I welcome the Secretary of State's announcement. He knows my view, that it would have been better to have kept Shorts in the public sector, but does he agree that it is good to bring the uncertainty to an end?

Secondly, as Bombardier makes a jet similar to Short's FJX, will the FJX project come to an end? Does being full partners in the aircraft side mean being full partners in the design, research and development of any future aircraft and those in the Short range?

Thirdly, will the redundancies that have been announced, particularly in the white collar sector, be withdrawn, or will they stand?

Fourthly, what guarantee has the Secretary of State sought from Bombardier that it will continue in Northern Ireland? Will the Government continue to have a holding to ensure that Shorts continues as an integrated entity in Northern Ireland?

Mr. King: The RJ has already been launched. The FJX is some years away from that possibility. It is still only a design concept but some work has been done on it. Bombardier is impressed with some of its concepts and looks to Shorts to be a full partner in the detailed design work on the regional jet and in the design and development of further aircraft that may flow thereafter. I can give the hon. Gentleman that assurance.

Bombardier is making a significant commitment to the future. It wishes to develop into a substantial group within the aerospace industry. It has given a commitment that

Shorts will remain as a single company and continue in Northern Ireland and our financial proposals are linked to the maintenance of those commitments.

Mr. James Kilfedder (North Down): The excellent work force and management of Shorts will be thankful that the decision has been made at long last, because the delay has meant the loss of many jobs and of young, highly skilled technical and craft workers. A substantial amount of public money is to be invested in Shorts, for which the people of Northern Ireland are deeply grateful, but I repeat that, as I said six months ago to the Secretary of State in the House, it is time for the Northern Ireland Office to send out not English Ministers but a representative delegation of politicians, Unionist and nationalist, Protestant and Roman Catholic, to the United States and elsewhere to seek the jobs and investments that are needed in Northern Ireland.

Mr. King: If I heard the hon. Gentleman correctly, he welcomed the announcement and I am grateful for that. He has previously said that it would be appalling if Shorts were split up and sold off in parts and I hope that he welcomes the fact that that will not be the case. I am glad now to have his support for this important development in privatisation.

I would welcome, and I know my right hon. Friend the Minister of State would, the assistance of politicians—elected Members—from Northern Ireland in the work that we try to do to bring jobs to Northern Ireland. That is the first offer of assistance that I have had and, if it is echoed, I shall be glad to see it happen.

Mr. John D. Taylor (Strangford): The Secretary of State will recognise my interest in Short Brothers because the company has plants in Newtownards and Castlereagh. We welcome Bombardier to Northern Ireland. The right hon. Gentleman's statement is better late than never; the delay associated with the whole matter has created great unrest within Northern Ireland and has certainly hit the morale of the company's staff. The damage done by delays and by the Ministers responsible during the past year is deplorable.

The lack of investment by present Northern Ireland Office Ministers in recent years has been one of the main reasons for the decline in the fortune of Short Brothers. It can be fairly said that when another Government were in power the losses were not as bad and there was investment. The problem at Short's in recent years has been lack of investment, yet today we learn that £700 million and more is being spent to get rid of the company. Delays have also cost the loss of another 700 jobs in the past four weeks. We must not run away from the facts of the situation created by the Minister responsible for handling the future of Short Brothers.

What are the commitments to Short Brothers and to Northern Ireland? Will the company's three main sectors remain in Northern Ireland? If so, is there any time limit? What about the plant in Newtownards? What guarantee is there that Short's will continue to maintain a separate plant in the borough of Ards? What about the successful Belfast city airport which Short Brothers developed in recent years? Is it included in the sale or is the intention to hand it over to the monopoly control of the Northern Ireland Airports Authority? Can the Secretary of State guarantee that Belfast city airport will continue to exist as a separate entity? Will the right hon. Gentleman confirm

also that Short Brothers will not only be involved in the design of the regional jet but its manufacture and that the FJX is herewith abandoned?

Mr. King: The right hon. Gentleman spoke of a "deplorable" delay. I think that that was a pretty deplorable contribution. First, I welcome the right hon. Gentleman's interest and am glad to have at last his involvement and his direct addressing of the problems affecting 7,000 people, some of whom are his constituents. That is the first time that I have heard directly from the right hon. Gentleman about their concerns and interests.

The right hon. Gentleman should inform himself better about the realities of the situation. He referred to investment during the term of an earlier Government. What happened to the money that this Government provided? It went in losses because no provision was made for new products. Because the world was becoming more competitive, products also had to be sold at increasingly lower prices. Profits went and losses were incurred. That is why—I now answer the question of the hon. Member for Warrington, North (Mr. Hoyle)—700 redundancies have already been announced and I fear that they will have to proceed. I hope that thereafter—as a result of the new management, new organisation and new opportunities—there will be more jobs and not fewer. I have already drawn attention to Bombardier's record with Canadair.

Belfast city airport is included in the arrangement, so it will remain separate. There are commitments, and there are safeguards against any deals being done to the disadvantage of Northern Ireland. As the right hon. Gentleman rightly said, the airport is an important Northern Ireland asset. I can also confirm that Bombardier will be involved, not only in the design of the regional jet but its manufacture.

Mr. Robin Maxwell-Hyslop (Tiverton): Will my right hon. Friend confirm that the technical contribution which over the years Queen's university of Belfast has made to the success of Shorts and to its potential was one of the valuable factors which Bombardier took into account? May I also put in a word of gratitude to Mr. Rodney Lund, who took over the chairmanship of what was otherwise a moribund company at an extraordinarily tense and difficult time, and express the hope that we have seen the last of restrictive practices on the part of the work force, which would have brought even a state-financed company to its knees and which have no part in the real world of which Shorts is now part, with the best opportunity it has ever had of securing its commercial future since it was expropriated by Sir Stafford Cripps with virtually no compensation to its shareholders, and therefore was not creditworthy as a free-standing and real part of the world aircraft industry?

Mr. King: I am grateful to my hon. Friend, who knows Shorts as well as, if not better than, any other Member of the House and who has taken a close interest in the company. He is well aware, and rightly so, of the real contribution that Queen's university can make in technical and research work. I have no doubt that Bombardier will wish to ensure that those close relationships continue as they benefit Shorts and so many other companies in Northern Ireland. In regard to restrictive practices, this is a very important day, which, as my hon. Friend said, could be the start of the best opportunity Shorts has ever had.

[*Mr. King*]

Bombardier is making its commitment. I am recommending to the House that public funds should be injected to make that possible. It will now depend crucially on the response of all who work in Shorts whether that opportunity is taken successfully. I am grateful to my hon. Friend for mentioning Mr. Rodney Lund. We certainly appreciate his tenure as chairman at a very difficult time.

Mr. Charles Kennedy (Ross, Cromarty and Skye): May I echo the sentiments already expressed on both sides of the House about the announcement, which is all the more welcome on the eve of the Paris air show? In rightly paying tribute to the management and work force at Shorts, and through the commitment which has been shown by Bombardier, will the Secretary of State sketch in a little more detail the heads of discussion which, in his view, remain outstanding between his Department and the European Commission over the three-month period which he envisages it should take finally to conclude a European level the details of the package that he has announced today?

Mr. King: In respect of that, obviously it is necessary to get European Community approval for very substantial injections of public funds. The European Community will wish to be satisfied that they are not subsidies and distortions of fair competition within the European market. That is the key issue that has to be resolved. Having said that, I am grateful to the hon. Gentleman for what he has said. The announcement has been widely welcomed. The House may be interested to know that I advised the unsuccessful bidders this morning. I spoke to Mr. van Duinen, the acting chairman of Fokker, and I was encouraged by his response, as Fokker will continue to be a very important partner for Shorts. At midday I was pleased to hear the very positive statement by Fokker welcoming the announcement and the end to uncertainty and stating that it believed that Shorts would be in excellent hands in future.

Sir Giles Shaw (Pudsey): May I add my congratulations to those received by my right hon. Friend and his team on his second excellent announcement after his statement on Harland recently? It is little short of miraculous that he has been able to bring those two difficulties safely home at this time. May I remind him, if he needs reminding, that the £780 million which he has now disclosed as the dowry for this enterprise is a direct reflection of the real problems of public sector competition in the aerospace industry? Is he satisfied that Bombardier has the capital resources as well as the immediate resources to find £30 million of share capital to enable development to continue? Finally, will he emphasise still further Short's relationship with the MOD in vital defence operations?

Mr. King: I am very grateful to my hon. Friend, who used the word "miraculous." If I had been asked that question two years ago, I would have used a similar word, because we faced a daunting task. The sale is important to progress and the atmosphere and attitude in Northern Ireland. It will be seen that companies can succeed by their own efforts and will do much to kill the image that exists in some parts of the United Kingdom that Northern Ireland can exist only on subsidy and assistance. My hon. Friend knows from his experience that there are a number of highly successful, profitable and hard-working firms in Northern Ireland. I look to see Harland and Wolff and Shorts join those companies.

The cost involved is not £780 million but £750 million. Bombardier is paying £30 million for the share capital, and I am satisfied that it has the resources to do so.

Mr. Tam Dalyell (Linlithgow): On this question of attitude, is the Secretary of State aware that some hon. Members would like, metaphorically, to vomit when they hear the reactions of some Northern Ireland Members? What firm this side of the water has ever received anything like £780 million of Government money? Should it not be recognised in Northern Ireland that for 20 years it has received resources that many of our constituents have not, and at least we should like them to acknowledge that?

What is likely to be the European Commission's attitude to the sale, and is it within regulations? Has there been any discussion about end user certificates, which created so much difficulty last year in relation to arms to Afghanistan? Has there been any discussion with Bombardier about end user certificates in relation to missiles in particular?

Mr. King: On the latter point, the rules will remain as they are. I say to my hon. Friend the Member for Pudsey (Sir G. Shaw), who asked about the Ministry of Defence, that the Ministry of Defence is familiar with Bombardier, from which is has purchased products.

The hon. Member for Linlithgow (Mr. Dalyell) promised to keep his vomiting metaphorical. I understand his reaction to the churlish and thoroughly unpleasant approach of the right hon. Member for Strangford (Mr. Taylor). We believe—I have fought to ensure a future for Northern Ireland—that Northern Ireland has particular problems, but all the people in Shorts whom I saw this morning appreciate that this is a remarkable and substantial investment, and a substantial gesture from which they will benefit. One or two of their representatives should show greater spirit of generosity and appreciation.

Discussions with the European Commission will be tough, but I believe that we can achieve success. Substantial public investment is being made in one company and skilful negotiations will be necessary, but I believe that we can achieve success.

Mr. Michael Brown (Brigg and Cleethorpes): does my right hon. Friend agree that one of the problems with the Northern Ireland economy over the past 20 years of political and security troubles is that it has been heavily dependent on the Government? One of the joys of his statement—although initially some hon. Members may recoil in horror at the amount of public funds being made available—is the prospect for the future of the Northern Ireland economy and Shorts in particular. We are transferring a substantial part of the economy to the private sector, thereby offering greater stability and prosperity for the future of the Northern Ireland economy.

Mr. King: I am very grateful to my hon. Friend. What he says is precisely the point. I foresaw no future for Shorts unless there was a change of motivation and unless the benefits of private sector commercial discipline could be felt. It has suffered, needs new investment and a freeing of its debt burden. We shall do that and give every possible encouragement to the people in Shorts to show what they can achieve. The Paris air show will show everybody what a competitive world aerospace is. The buoyancy of the air show will show what a good opportunity this is for the people who work for Short Brothers.

Mr. Harry Barnes (Derbyshire, North-East): In the first four years, 70 per cent. of the capital will be provided from public funds. Would it not be appropriate, therefore, at least during that period, for 70 per cent. of the equity to be controlled publicly? Have the trade unions in Shorts been consulted? What is their attitude to the proposals?

Mr. Speaker: Briefly.

Mr. Barnes: Last night we discussed the Employment Bill which will attack the position of young people and will lead to other problems. How is it likely to help the position in Shorts?

Mr. King: On the question of the funds being made available, part of them will recapitalise the company, part will repay remaining borrowings and moneys already lost and part will meet anticipated losses on existing contracts. Those are real and substantial costs that will occur in the ensuing period. As regards other funds, I made clear in my statement the way in which the performance of Bombardier and the maintenance of the assurances that it has given will be tied in against the interest-free loan to which I referred. On the question of the trade unions, many efforts have been made to keep all the work force and the trade unions informed of the objectives and of progress. Indeed, they were fully informed today.

Dr. John G. Blackburn (Dudley, West): Will my right hon. Friend accept the congratulations of the House and the warm tribute to the Minister for bringing a difficult set of negotiations to a satisfactory conclusion? I visited the company within the last six months. The fact that there is an £18 million investment for research and development is a testimony of our commitment to the company. The provision for the Government to take back £60 million if performance targets are not met is very important. That arrangement is in stark contrast to the financial structure created for the De Lorean company. Will my right hon. Friend assure the House that the financial targets will be strictly adhered to for the safety of the public purse?

Mr. King: We are anxious to ensure that the commitments and assurances that we have had are properly achieved. My hon. Friend correctly notes that that is the clear purpose of the arrangements. I am grateful for what he said about the efforts of my hon. Friend. As my right hon. Friend the Chief Secretary is here as well, we should also recognise the wider support that we have had in this important development.

Mr. Bob Cryer (Bradford, South): In view of the need to secure the future of jobs in the company, can the Secretary of State assure us that no civil servants or consultants involved in assessing the position were involved with the last project in which a representative of the enterprise culture was in receipt of such largesse from the taxpayers' pocket on a much larger scale? I refer, of course, to John Z. De Lorean. Can the Secretary of State also assure us that none of the £780 million will find its way into Conservative party funds from grateful recipients?

Just in case the Secretary of State intends to reply that I was a member of the Government who gave the money to De Lorean, it is not true, because I was not.

Mr. King: I think that the hon. Gentleman suddenly saw the terrible chasm opening before him just before he sat down. If he had not done so, I would not have dreamt of mentioning that he was associated with the Government who entered into what subsequently proved to be a most unfortunate arrangement. We in this Government approach things in a different and more cautious way. We have been criticised in a relaxed manner by the right hon. Member for Strangford (Mr. Taylor) for too much delay. We have a heavy responsibility to the House and to the taxpayer when such substantial funds are involved. We do not rush into things. We try to ensure that the taxpayer gets the best return and the best bargain for substantial expenditure.

Several Hon. Members *rose——*

Mr. Speaker: I will call the two hon. Members who have been standing in view of their long-standing interest in this matter, but I ask them to be brief, please.

Mr. James Cran (Beverley): I too would like to congratulate my right hon. Friend on achieving what I consider to be the impossible, given the hearings we had in the Select Committee on Trade and Industry and especially against the background of the many fears that were expressed, none of which has come to fruition. Does my right hon. Friend not agree that this has been far too long in the coming, given that the Government announced their intention to privatise in 1984? I welcome the amount of public funds going into this venture because of its special nature. However, will my right hon. Friend illuminate for the House what the company itself is putting into future investment, aside from the £30 million in equity participation?

Mr. King: In respect of the sums involved, the significant amount of money I announced for capital expenditure—£79 million—is, of course, our contribution towards the capital investment that the company will be making. From that, my hon. Friend can form an idea of the substantial investment on top of the £30 million for the acquisition of the present Short shares that the company will be making. Together with that, there will be an opportunity for it to be a full partner in the RJ programme being launched just now, which is an important commitment and investment.

Sir Michael McNair-Wilson (Newbury): I want to congratulate my right hon. Friend and his ministerial team on the most satisfactory conclusion with Bombardier. However, how will my right hon. Friend safeguard the classified nature of the guided weapons work being carried on by the company, especially Starstreak, which is a sought-after missile in the international market?

Mr. King: My hon. Friend is right. Starstreak is a critical and important product with a high security classification. The present arrangements will remain in force and will be an important safeguard. My hon. Friend is right to identify the importance of the issue.

Alar

4.22 pm

Mr. Malcolm Bruce (Gordon): I beg to ask leave to move the Adjournment of the House, under Standing Order No. 20, for the purpose of discussing a specific and important matter that should have urgent discussion, namely,

"The need to ban the chemical Alar, the apple spraying product."

The request is specific because the product is a chemical growth regulator which helps to make more buds set and grow into mature fruit, so it is being sprayed at this time of year. The matter is important because the chemical is especially dangerous for children, who eat far more apples and apple products for their body weight and have longer to develop the cancers associated with this product. The matter is urgent because we have learnt in the past 24 hours that the American Government have banned the use of this product. We are anxious to ensure that the British Government either do the same or explain why they are not going to do so.

I and my colleagues have expressed concern on this matter and have been in correspondence with the Minister of Agriculture, Fisheries and Food. Although the United States Government are now determined to ban the product, I received a letter from the Minister on 31 May saying that the British Government did not intend to ban the product and did not believe that the product was especially harmful. We need to know from the Government exactly how the British examination has come to an apparently opposite conclusion from that drawn by the American authorities.

The Government have also said that if they find that there is any evidence that should cause public concern, they will publish it. They stated to the Select Committee on Agriculture that they would ensure that the information made available to the Advisory Committee on Pesticides would be made available to the public. I am sure that you, Mr. Speaker, would accept in the light of this development in the past 24 hours that the Government should tell the House exactly what they intend to do about this product. If they intend to ban it, they should do so now and inform the House. If they do not, they should publish all the information available to them and explain why they do not intend to ban it.

Mr. Speaker: The hon. Gentleman asks leave to move the Adjournment of the House under Standing Order No. 20, for the purpose of discussing a specific and important matter that he believes should have urgent consideration, namely,

"The need to ban the chemical Alar, the apple spraying product."

I have listened with care to what the hon. Gentleman has said. As he knows, my sole duty in considering an application under Standing Order No. 20 is to decide whether it should be given priority over the business set down for today or tomorrow. I regret that the matter that the hon. Gentleman has raised does not meet the criteria of Standing Order No. 20 so I cannot submit his application to the House.

BALLOT FOR NOTICES OF MOTIONS FOR FRIDAY 23 JUNE

Members successful in the ballot were:

Mr. Roger Gale

Mr. Simon Burns

Mr. Irvine Patnick

EUROPEAN COMMUNITY DOCUMENTS

Ordered,

That the proposals described in the unnumbered Explanatory Memorandum submitted by the Department of Employment on 2nd June 1989 relating to safety and health of workers at work be referred to a Standing Committee on European Community Documents.—[*Mr. Chapman.*]

Political Honours (Amendment)

4.24 pm

Mr. Bruce Grocott (The Wrekin): I beg to move,

That leave be given to bring in a Bill to restrict the granting of honours for political purposes.

It is 10 years since, shortly after assuming office, the Prime Minister restored the power that previous Prime Ministers had had to grant honours for political purposes. This is a particularly urgent matter because, in 10 days' time, there will be a new Queen's birthday honours list, with some 1,000 names on it and some 250 different distinctions and decorations being awarded, ranging from peerages at the top to the British Empire medal at the bottom.

Few hon. Members would object when some recognition is given to people who otherwise receive little reward or recognition—those who are outstanding in times of national disasters and those who for long periods provide voluntary service to their communities. But that is not what is happening under the honours system as managed by the Prime Minister. Indeed, it rarely happened under the honours system in the past.

In the past 10 years, the honours system has had two main characteristics. There has been a massive exercise of patronage by the Prime Minister. It may be called the Queen's birthday honours, and it may be the Queen's birthday, but the honours are the Prime Minister's. In addition, the kind of honour that is given depends not so much on what a person has done as on who he or she is. It is closely related to rank in society. We do not yet know whether in the forthcoming Queen's birthday honours any awards will be given to the people who were involved in the rescue operations after the Lockerbie air disaster, the Clapham disaster and, more recently, the Hillsborough disaster, but we can predict with certainty that the recognition given to them will be nothing compared with the recognition given to a time-serving Conservative Member of Parliament or an industrialist who gives large sums to the Conservative party.

It is historic fact that in the same honours in which the Prime Minister's adviser on publicity and public relations received a knighthood, the fireman who was badly injured in the Bradford fire received the British Empire medal, the lowest of awards that can be given. For anyone who is in any doubt, the citation for the British Empire medal spells it out beautifully: it is to be

"awarded to those who do not qualify by rank for a higher medal".

We know that, whatever aspect of our society is being recognised, the honour depends on a person's rank. If an honour goes to the Civil Service, the permanent secretaries get the knighthoods; the clerical officers, if they get anything at all, get the lowest rank of honour. A knighthood comes as automatic rank for a permanent secretary—*[Interruption.]* Conservative Members are apparently horrified at the prospect of recognition of rank in our society differing from that.

We know that if honours are to be given to the Health Service, knighthoods go to the chairmen of district health authorities but if nurses and hospital porters were to be recognised, which they are not, the honour would be at the lowest rank. If awards are to be given to the education service, the knighthoods go to the vice-chancellors of universities while teachers in busy city-centre comprehensives get nothing or the lowest level of award.

My Bill has two objectives. I am sure that the main part of it will be non-controversial and therefore not opposed. It is taken from an editorial in *The Times* on 31 December 1987, which stated:

"Honours should be taken out of the direct gift of the Prime Minister and politicians. They should be controlled by a strong, independent body."

I agree wholeheartedly with that statement, but I would go even further. We need a commission of inquiry into the honours system to determine whether it continues to serve any useful purpose in our society.

The way in which the Prime Minister has used the honours system is quite disgraceful. For example, the main characteristic in the decision whether to reward an industrialist is not the contribution that his company has made to the economy, but the contribution that it has made to Conservative party funds. Two thirds of the 110 industrialists awarded knighthoods or peerages by the Prime Minister represent companies which contribute to Conservative party funds. Yet only one third of the top 200 companies contribute to Tory party funds. The chance of an honour is roughly doubled if an industrialist contributes to Conservative party funds. That is outrageous and should be stopped.

Another aspect is the granting of honours to Conservative Members of Parliament. When I returned to this place after an absence of eight years I recognised many familiar faces on the Conservative Benches, but I could not get used to the fact that almost all of them had knighthoods. I have done a little checking and discovered that 100 of them have knighthoods and that only four Conservative Members with continuous service since 1964 do not have one——

Hon. Members: Name them.

Mr. Julian Critchley (Aldershot) *rose*——

Mr. Grocott: The hon. Gentleman and his three Friends deserve the admiration of the whole House.

We know of the awards given to the ideological supporters of the Conservative party in the past 10 years. Massive awards have been given to Aims of Industry, the Centre for Policy Studies, and the Institute of Economic Affairs—presumably on the basis of the economic advice that it has given to the Government. Now that the Government's economic policy is falling apart, I wonder whether the awards will be handed back.

I find it a disgraceful practice to reward journalists for doing their job, and I speak as a member of the National Union of Journalists. The overwhelming majority of those given awards are known for their political neutrality, such as Lord Wyatt, but the one group that will not receive awards anything like those given to Lord Wyatt are those doing such an outstanding job reporting what is happening in China under conditions of great danger.

I doubt whether this uncontroversial Bill will be opposed. If it is, I hope that it will not be opposed by any hon. Member who has been either a beneficiary of the present system or hopes to be so in the future. It is common sense to recognise after this length of time that the honours system has been abused by the Prime Minister. We should scrap the present method of fixing political honours and set up a public inquiry. The House should support my Bill.

4.34 pm

Mr. Neil Hamilton (Tatton): As one who qualifies under the criteria laid down by the hon. Member for the Wrekin (Mr. Grocott) of neither having been a beneficiary, nor likely to be one, of the honours system—[*Interruption.*] I am encouraged by the objections of my right hon. Friend the Patronage Secretary. I do not know whether it is an indirect attempt to shut me up. In the past, that has sometimes been his objective.

It would be wrong to allow this opportunity to pass without a sensible point of view being put across. I am surprised at the sensitivity—indeed, the gall—of the hon. Member for The Wrekin (Mr. Grocott) in introducing a Bill of this kind. He was a Back-Bench supporter of a previous Administration, which we recall with some fondness, headed by Lord Wilson of Rievaulx, so I can only regard the hon. Gentleman's speech today as a kind of atonement for some of the events that occurred in 1976. We recall that Lord Wilson in the honours list of that year not only provided titles for people, but for many of them he provided official residences as well, particularly residences with a high degree of security—with bars on the windows.

I do not know whether hon. Members representing the centre parties in the House intend, if there is a Division. to support the hon. Member for The Wrekin, but we recall with fondness another man of high principle who held the highest office of state open to a mere commoner—Mr. Lloyd George, who did many great things in the course of his long Administration, the greatest of which was the sale of peerages on a very substantial scale indeed. I do not recall that in the days of the "lavender list" we had any calls for witch-hunts in No. 10 Downing street by, for example, the hon. Members for Linlithgow (Mr. Dalyell), for Walsall, North (Mr. Winnick) and all the other great men of rectitude on the Opposition Benches. Nor do I recall recently—say, just before the last election—the right hon. Member for Islwyn (Mr. Kinnock) being slow off the mark in using the honours list to reward his former right hon. Friend, now Lord Cocks, for the great services that he had rendered to the Opposition in making way—we were delighted at the occurrence—for the hon. Member for Bishop Auckland (Mr. Foster). Clearly, the honours system has its uses from time to time for Opposition Members.

Perhaps I may recall an utterance by the late Lord Keynes, who said that dangerous human proclivities could be canalised into relatively harmless courses by the making of money. We do it far mor effectively and cheaply by the maintenance of an honours system. The worst corruption that we have witnessed in this country in recent years has been the corruption that comes from Socialism, whereby the Government of the day bribe the electors with their own money—[*Interruption.*]—as in the Hull by-election of 1967, which brought the hon. Member for Great Grimsby (Mr. Mitchell) to the House, although we do not often see him these days, except on television.

The honours system provides a relatively harmless and costless way of rewarding people who perform great functions to the state. Honours are awarded in all walks of life. We have the sportsman of the year, for example. Last year we could have given the Leader of the Opposition the award of foreign traveller of the year for the great services that he performed in Zimbabwe. This year he may qualify for the title of broadcaster of the year for the signal services that he has performed for the Conservative party in recent weeks on BBC radio.

The hon. Member for The Wrekin, in his egalitarian extremism, seems sadly out of touch with the new model Labour party. I do not know whether he is forming an alliance with the right hon. Member for Chesterfield (Mr. Benn), whose desire it is to abolish the whole honours system and perhaps replace it with a kind of dishonours system with the public stripping of double-barrelled names, the expunging of entries from Who's Who, the public burning of pedigrees and the presentation of a certificate of proletarianism to prove that one can be prolier than thou.

The right hon. Member for Chesterfield (Mr. Benn) cane up with the wizard idea just before the last election of creating 1,000 peers in order to abolish the House of Lords. But then, of course, he realised that the whipping system in the House of Lords is perhaps rather less strict than it is in this House and that he would not be able to achieve his objective. It would be a shame indeed to abolish the only real opposition to the Government in this country today, which is in the House of Lords. I say that just to show that I can be fair-minded.

It would also be a shame to frustrate the legitimate expectations of my right hon. and hon. Friends. Mention has already been made in an oblique way to my hon. Friend the Member for Aldershot (Mr. Critchley), of whom it must be said that any attempt to honour him would be merely to put tinsel on the Christmas tree, as he carries such great dignity in any event that it would be impossible to expand it. It would be a shame, too, to frustrate the legitimate desires of the many Labour councillors who petition Conservative Members of Parliament from time to time for some recognition of the great work that they perform in the interest of the public. I am sure that hon. Members will readily agree that the rewards of public life are few and small when compared with the great sacrifices that we make for the benefit of the public.

I hope that all my hon. Friends and perhaps some Opposition Members who have nothing else to look forward to but the prospect of some meretricious honour of this kind, will join me in the Lobby in opposition to the Bill.

Question put, pursuant to Standing Order No. 19 (Motions for leave to bring in Bills and nomination of Select Committees at commencement of public business):—

The House divided: Ayes 134, Noes 128.

Division No. 230]   **[4.40 pm**

AYES

Adams, Allen *(Paisley N)*	Canavan, Dennis
Allen, Graham	Clarke, Tom *(Monklands W)*
Archer, Rt Hon Peter	Clelland, David
Armstrong, Hilary	Clwyd, Mrs Ann
Ashton, Joe	Cook, Frank *(Stockton N)*
Barnes, Harry *(Derbyshire NE)*	Corbett, Robin
Battle, John	Corbyn, Jeremy
Bell, Stuart	Cousins, Jim
Benn, Rt Hon Tony	Cryer, Bob
Boyes, Roland	Cunliffe, Lawrence
Bradley, Keith	Dalyell, Tam
Bray, Dr Jeremy	Darling, Alistair
Brown, Nicholas *(Newcastle E)*	Davies, Rt Hon Denzil *(Llanelli)*
Caborn, Richard	Davis, Terry *(B'ham Hodge H'l)*
Callaghan, Jim	Dixon, Don
Campbell, Ron *(Blyth Valley)*	Dobson, Frank
Campbell-Savours, D. N.	Duffy, A. E. P.

Dunnachie, Jimmy
Eastham, Ken
Evans, John *(St Helens N)*
Ewing, Mrs Margaret *(Moray)*
Fatchett, Derek
Fields, Terry *(L'pool B G'n)*
Fisher, Mark
Flannery, Martin
Flynn, Paul
Forsythe, Clifford *(Antrim S)*
Foster, Derek
Foulkes, George
Fraser, John
Fyfe, Maria
Galbraith, Sam
Garrett, John *(Norwich South)*
Godman, Dr Norman A.
Golding, Mrs Llin
Gould, Bryan
Grant, Bernie *(Tottenham)*
Griffiths, Nigel *(Edinburgh S)*
Griffiths, Win *(Bridgend)*
Grocott, Bruce
Hattersley, Rt Hon Roy
Haynes, Frank
Heffer, Eric S.
Henderson, Doug
Hinchliffe, David
Hogg, N. *(C'nauld & Kilsyth)*
Howells, Dr. Kim (Pontypridd)
Hoyle, Doug
Hughes, John *(Coventry NE)*
Hughes, Robert *(Aberdeen N)*
Hughes, Roy *(Newport E)*
Illsley, Eric
Jones, Barry *(Alyn & Deeside)*
Kennedy, Charles
Kilfedder, James
Lamond, James
Leighton, Ron
Lestor, Joan *(Eccles)*
Livingstone, Ken
Loyden, Eddie
McCartney, Ian
McFall, John
McKay, Allen *(Barnsley West)*
McLeish, Henry
Madden, Max
Mahon, Mrs Alice
Mallon, Seamus
Marek, Dr John
Marshall, Jim *(Leicester S)*

Martlew, Eric
Meale, Alan
Michael, Alun
Michie, Bill *(Sheffield Heeley)*
Mitchell, Austin *(G't Grimsby)*
Moonie, Dr Lewis
Morgan, Rhodri
Morley, Elliott
Mullin, Chris
Murphy, Paul
Nellist, Dave
O'Neill, Martin
Patchett, Terry
Pike, Peter L.
Powell, Ray *(Ogmore)*
Quin, Ms Joyce
Radice, Giles
Randall, Stuart
Redmond, Martin
Reid, Dr John
Richardson, Jo
Robinson, Geoffrey
Rogers, Allan
Ross, Ernie *(Dundee W)*
Ross, William *(Londonderry E)*
Ruddock, Joan
Sedgemore, Brian
Sheldon, Rt Hon Robert
Short, Clare
Skinner, Dennis
Smith, Andrew *(Oxford E)*
Smith, C. *(Isl'ton & F'bury)*
Smith, Rt Hon J. *(Monk'ds E)*
Soley, Clive
Steinberg, Gerry
Strang, Gavin
Straw, Jack
Turner, Dennis
Vaz, Keith
Wall, Pat
Wareing, Robert N.
Welsh, Andrew *(Angus E)*
Welsh, Michael *(Doncaster N)*
Williams, Alan W. *(Carm'then)*
Wilson, Brian
Wise, Mrs Audrey
Worthington, Tony
Young, David *(Bolton SE)*

Tellers for the Ayes:
    Mr. David Winnick and
    Mr. Kevin Barron.

NOES

Adley, Robert
Alexander, Richard
Alton, David
Arbuthnot, James
Arnold, Jacques *(Gravesham)*
Aspinwall, Jack
Baldry, Tony
Barnes, Mrs Rosie *(Greenwich)*
Beaumont-Dark, Anthony
Beith, A. J.
Bennett, Nicholas *(Pembroke)*
Bevan, David Gilroy
Blackburn, Dr John G.
Bonsor, Sir Nicholas

Boscawen, Hon Robert
Bowden, Gerald *(Dulwich)*
Boyson, Rt Hon Dr Sir Rhodes
Brazier, Julian
Bruce, Malcolm *(Gordon)*
Buck, Sir Antony
Budgen, Nicholas
Burns, Simon
Butler, Chris
Butterfill, John
Carlisle, John, *(Luton N)*
Carrington, Matthew
Clark, Dr Michael *(Rochford)*
Clark, Sir W. *(Croydon S)*

Coombs, Anthony *(Wyre F'rest)*
Coombs, Simon *(Swindon)*
Cormack, Patrick
Cran, James
Curry, David
Devlin, Tim
Dicks, Terry
Dunn, Bob
Evans, David *(Welwyn Hatf'd)*
Evennett, David
Favell, Tony
Fearn, Ronald
Forman, Nigel
Fox, Sir Marcus
Franks, Cecil
Fry, Peter
Gardiner, George
Gilmour, Rt Hon Sir Ian
Gow, Ian
Grant, Sir Anthony *(CambsSW)*
Greenway, Harry *(Ealing N)*
Hague, William
Hanley, Jeremy
Hannam, John
Harris, David
Hayward, Robert
Heddle, John
Hicks, Mrs Maureen *(Wolv' NE)*
Higgins, Rt Hon Terence L.
Hind, Kenneth
Howarth, G. *(Cannock & B'wd)*
Howell, Rt Hon David *(G'dford)*
Howell, Ralph *(North Norfolk)*
Howells, Geraint
Hughes, Robert G. *(Harrow W)*
Irvine, Michael
Janman, Tim
Johnson Smith, Sir Geoffrey
Kirkwood, Archy
Knight, Greg *(Derby North)*
Knight, Dame Jill *(Edgbaston)*
Knowles, Michael
Latham, Michael
Lawrence, Ivan
Lawson, Rt Hon Nigel
Lee, John *(Pendle)*
Lloyd, Sir Ian *(Havant)*
McCrindle, Robert
Macfarlane, Sir Neil
MacKay, Andrew *(E Berkshire)*
McLoughlin, Patrick
Malins, Humfrey

Maples, John
Marlow, Tony
Marshall, John *(Hendon S)*
Mills, Iain
Miscampbell, Norman
Mitchell, Andrew *(Gedling)*
Mitchell, Sir David
Moate, Roger
Moss, Malcolm
Nicholson, David *(Taunton)*
Onslow, Rt Hon Cranley
Oppenheim, Phillip
Patnick, Irvine
Pawsey, James
Powell, William *(Corby)*
Price, Sir David
Raffan, Keith
Redwood, John
Rhodes James, Robert
Riddick, Graham
Roe, Mrs Marion
Rost, Peter
Shaw, David *(Dover)*
Shaw, Sir Giles *(Pudsey)*
Shaw, Sir Michael *(Scarb')*
Shephard, Mrs G. *(Norfolk SW)*
Shersby, Michael
Sims, Roger
Skeet, Sir Trevor
Smith, Tim *(Beaconsfield)*
Steel, Rt Hon David
Sumberg, David
Summerson, Hugo
Tapsell, Sir Peter
Taylor, Ian *(Esher)*
Tebbit, Rt Hon Norman
Thorne, Neil
Thornton, Malcolm
Townend, John *(Bridlington)*
Vaughan, Sir Gerard
Walker, Bill *(T'side North)*
Wallace, James
Walters, Sir Dennis
Wardle, Charles *(Bexhill)*
Widdecombe, Ann
Woodcock, Dr. Mike
Yeo, Tim
Young, Sir George *(Acton)*

Tellers for the Noes:
    Mr. Michael Brown and
    Mr. Neil Hamilton.

Question accordingly agreed to.

Bill ordered to be brought in by Mr. Bruce Grocott, Mr. Don Dixon, Mrs. Maria Fyfe, Mr. John Garrett, Mr. James Lamond, Dr. Lewis Moonie, Mr. Jeff Rooker, Mr. Ernie Ross, Mr. Dennis Skinner and Mr. Dennis Turner.

POLITICAL HONOURS (AMENDMENT)

Mr. Bruce Grocott accordingly presented a Bill to restrict the granting of honours for political purposes: And the same was read the First time; and ordered to be read a Second time upon Friday 7 July and to be printed. [Bill 150.]

Opposition Day

[12TH ALLOTTED DAY]

Government Economic Policy

Mr. Speaker: Before I call the right hon. and learned Member for Monklands, East (Mr. Smith), I must announce to the House that I have selected the amendment in the name of the Prime Minister. In view of the late start to this debate I propose to limit speeches to 10 minutes between 7 and 9 o'clock, but I ask those hon. Members who may be called before then to bear that limit in mind.

Mr. Nicholas Bennett (Pembroke): On a point of order, Mr. Speaker. You have not announced whether you intend to call the amendment standing in my name, which is supported by 24 of my colleagues, or the amendment tabled by the Democrats. I recognise that there are a number of amendments to the Labour party motion and that it may not be possible to call all of them, but I seek your guidance. You will recall that in the unpublished and unbroadcast part of a radio interview some 10 days ago, the Leader of the Opposition, when asked about his economic policy, said, "I am not"——

Mr. Speaker: Order. The hon. Gentleman knows that it is only possible for me to call one amendment and I have nominated it, so I have answered his question.

Mr. Bennett *rose*——

Mr. Speaker: Order. It is not a point of order and I cannot deal with it.

Mr. Michael Brown (Brigg and Cleethorpes): On a point of order, Mr. Speaker. I recognise that you have decided to select the amendment in the name of my right hon. Friend the Prime Minister only. During the debate, however, will it be possible for the 25 hon. Members who have signed the amendment in the name of my hon. Friend the Member for Pembroke (Mr. Bennett), should they catch your eye, to refer to the speech recently given by the right hon. Member for Llanelli (Mr. Davies) regarding the views of the Leader of the Opposition and his views of that right hon. Gentleman's economic policies?

Mr. Speaker: The hon. Gentleman is an old parliamentary hand and he will know that the debate is confined to the Opposition motion and the Government amendment. He must keep his speech within those confines.

4.54 pm

Mr. John Smith (Monklands, East): I beg to move,

That this House deplores the confusion and disarray of the Government's economic policy, the record balance of payments deficit, the rising rate of inflation and the damaging level of interest rates; notes with concern the continuing neglect of the real economy and the failures to invest adequately in education and training, research and development, and the regions, which undermine Britain's prospects of success in the single market of the European Community after 1992; and calls upon the Government to give urgent priority to such supply side investment in order to reduce the balance of payments deficit and begin to create a strong, balanced and competitive economy for the 1990s.

When he presented his Budget in March 1988, the Chancellor of the Exchequer exhibited a sublime degree of self-confidence. His Budget gained fulsome praise from the Prime Minister, who said that it was "brilliant". She was not in any way inhibited by the fact that she had sabotaged his exchange rate policy a few days before. The House will recall the Chancellor's confident boast, given in his wind-up to the debate on the Budget resolutions, that Britain was

"experiencing an economic miracle, comparable in significance to that previously enjoyed by West Germany and still enjoyed by Japan."—[*Official Report,* 21 March 1988; Vol. 130, c. 109.]

In presenting his Budget, the right hon. Gentleman said:

"the present . . . upswing, unlike almost all its predecessors, has not led to any resurgence of inflation".—[*Official Report,* 15 March 1988; Vol. 129, c. 994.]

The Chancellor, warming to his task, said in the wind-up to the Budget debate:

"we are now talking about getting it down from something between 3 and 4 per cent."—[*Official Report,* 21 March 1988; Vol. 130, c. 110.]

As for the balance of payments, there would be

"no difficulty in financing a temporary current account deficit of this scale".—[*Official Report,* 15 March 1988; Vol. 129, c. 994.]

But the self-confidence and the self-congratulation proved to be short-lived, because it was based on blissful ignorance, the sort of ignorance demonstrated by a man on the top of a ladder who does not know he is about to fall off. The so-called temporary current account deficit soared to more than £14 billion and has been sliding relentlessly further into the red ever since.

Inflation, described by the Chancellor in a phrase that will haunt him as "a temporary blip", has doubled to 8 per cent. So, today, far from talking about temporary blips, the Chancellor prefers to warn us, as he said in his OECD speech of last week,

"against people who are impatient for quick results".

That was his message to the OECD Ministers in Paris.

But, as interest rates blip higher and higher for longer and longer, is it any wonder that people are losing confidence in Conservative economic policy? With interest rates moving to 14 per cent. perhaps higher, with soaring borrowing costs threatening investment in industry and risking overkill and recession, is it surprising that people are becoming impatient for some results? But whose expectations was the Chancellor really trying to calm?

On the day the right hon. Gentleman announced the latest increase in interest rates he was addressing the Tory women's conference. He was reported in *The Independent* as having opened his speech to the Tory women by saying as follows about the timing of the interest rates:

"I had two conflicting thoughts. I thought it was a rather tactless time in the middle of the women's conference. Then I thought—where else could I look for such mature, intelligent, responsible support?"

They heckled him. I think the Chancellor has a problem with Tory women—[*Interruption.*]—because there is another place, not too far from where he lives where there is not much in the way of mature, intelligent and responsible support for him. The Prime Minister, in an extremely revealing interview in the *Glasgow Herald* told us about the nature of her relationship with her Chancellor of the Exchequer. She said:

"Nigel is a very good neighbour of mine, and a very good Chancellor. Geoffrey is a very good Foreign Secretary. I am not going any further. You know I have to do reshuffles from time to time. I hate them. Why?—because I have a very good Cabinet. But I know that there are young people who have to have an opportunity, as others had it. I hate them."

I think she must mean the reshuffles.

"I have to work myself up because I know that I have to do them. I hate them."

And then, ominously:

"So will they."

Good neighbourliness is highly relevant to the confusion and disarray which lies at the heart of Government policy, and, on that subject, my sympathies are, to some extent, with the Chancellor of the Exchequer. After all, when he picks up the telephone and wants to get through to No. 10, it must be rather disconcerting to be told, "Walters here. Would you like to speak to Griffiths?" It is not clear who the real Chancellor of the Exchequer is. We have here the nominal Chancellor of the Exchequer.

Although he and the Prime Minister are neighbours, he should take account, as many of us who are aficionados do, of the theme song of the "Neighbours" programme which we hear twice a day on BBC television. The song goes:

"Neighbours—everybody needs good neighbours.
Just a friendly wave each morning helps to make a better day.
Neighbours need to get to know each other.
Next door is only a footstep away.
Neighbours—everybody needs good neighbours.
With a little understanding, you can find a perfect blend.
Neighbours should be there for one another.
That's when good neighbours become good friends."

The Chancellor of the Exchequer may be a good neighbour, but Walters and Griffiths are the good friends. Time after time, in the management of his policy, he has been up-ended by the Prime Minister's own intervention.

The Prime Minister wants some quick results, as Britain's inflation rate soars to 8 per cent. and the ludicrous target of zero inflation looks ever more absurd. To avoid the verdict of the judge and jury, the Chancellor has resorted to the lame excuse of the international trend, his flimsy international alibi. At the Organisation for Economic Co-operation and Development he talked about G7 inflation. What on earth is that?

The phrase is intended to give the impression that inflation is a national contagion that no one can avoid, the mere fact that one is alive means that one will catch it and that it does not have much to do with the Chancellor. It is instructive to look at the inflation rates of the other G7 countries. Japan has 1·2 per cent., the Federal Republic has 2·7 per cent., France has 3·4 per cent., the United States of America has 5 per cent., Canada has 4·6 per cent. and Italy has 6 per cent. The average is 4·4 per cent., while Britain has 8 per cent.

There is no such thing as G7 inflation, but there is British inflation, which is not externally caused. Neither oil nor other key commodities have risen spectacularly in this decade, as they did in the 1970s. The resurgence of inflation is domestically driven and caused by the Government's mismanagement of demand, their foolish credit boom, their own utility price increases and the Tories' inflationary "own goals," to borrow a phrase favoured by the Confederation of British Industry.

The mismanagement of demand has made worse the most serious problem of all: Britain's worsening balance of payments deficit. The 1988 Budget combined foolish and unfair tax cuts with an unsustainable credit boom and dramatically aggravated Britain's emerging external deficit. Sadly, that deficit is no mere temporary blip. Since 1982, Britain's non-oil current account has been in deficit and has grown worse every year except 1985. That long-running trend of deterioration, concealed for a while by North sea oil, is at the heart of Britain's balance of payments deficit.

However, the Chancellor refuses to acknowledge the problem. He has seriously and consistently underestimated its scale. Absurdly, Treasury Ministers claim that the deficit is a sign of success. The Chief Secretary to the Treasury does so regularly. By implication, the growing surpluses of Germany and Japan are evidence of economic failure, and their expanding role as the world's foremost creditor nations must be a lamentable national humiliation for them. Alternatively, the Treasury likes to present the deficit as yet another temporary event: a short-term result of excessive demand and a temporary misalignment of demand and supply in the economy. But the deficit is a long-term structural problem that will not be cured merely by the easing of domestic demand.

Since the Chancellor fails to understand the cause of the deficit it is not surprising that he cannot accurately forecast it. In 1988, we were told that it would be £4 billion and it was £14 billion. This year, the Chancellor says that it will be about the same, £14 billion, but so far this year we are heading for a new record deficit of more than £17 billion. When he replies, will the Chancellor explain why the European Commission, the International Monetary Fund and the OECD have all forecast a further record slide into the red this year? The OECD's latest forecast, available to the Chancellor in Paris last week, reportedly predicted that Britain would run record deficits this year and next.

What is the explanation for that discrepancy, given that the OECD forecast must be agreed with the Treasury? I trust that the Chancellor, this afternoon, will tell us the Treasury's revised forecast for the balance of payments this year. Clearly the figures that he gave the House in his Budget statement not so long ago are no longer credible in the House, at the OECD or in the financial markets.

The forecasts are important because they reveal how long high interest rates will be needed to attract the hot money flows which the Chancellor wants in order to finance the balance of payments deficit. High interest rates are not merely a device to curb inflation, but the price we must pay for living beyond our means. We are having to pay the Lawson risk premium, the speculator's ransom, required to attract capital into sterling and finance the balance of payments deficit. That price is rising, as the market's confidence in the Government's economic policy falls.

The Government have failed to tackle the weakness of Britain's economic fundamentals: the burgeoning balance of payments deficit and the resurgence of inflation. Those are facts which no amount of hype about Thatcher miracles can conceal from the currency markets or the electorate. The Government's dependence on higher and higher interest rates is more and more a sign of policy weakness and evidence of confusion and disarray, rather than a firm policy resolve.

A good example of that confusion and disarray arose at Prime Minister's Question Time on 23 May, when the Prime Minister, in answer to a question from my right hon. Friend the Leader of the Opposition, clearly implied that, at 13 per cent., interest rates were adequate to curb domestic demand. The evidence of a slowdown in the credit boom is growing, if not yet fully conclusive.

[Mr. John Smith]

However, 13 per cent. was not enough to satisfy the currency speculators and failed to buy off their anxieties about the British economy.

Here revealed is the self-inflicted contradiction of the Government's economic policy. The Chancellor has chosen to rely on high interest rates as a universal economic panacea, but interest rates are a double-edged sword. They are a weapon that cuts both ways: raising the exchange rate and curbing demand. Those two objectives can conflict, and that is precisely what is starting to happen in the British economy. As demand begins to fall away, high interest rates threaten overkill and recession. However, the Chancellor still needs to attract that hot money to finance his external deficit.

Mr. John Townend (Bridlington): If he disagrees with the present rate, would the right hon. and learned Gentleman be good enough to tell the House what the appropriate rate of interest should be at the present time?

Mr. Smith: I do not agree that the only weapon that we should use should be interest rates. As we have made clear on numerous occasions, there are other methods— *[Interruption.]* I shall give way to the Chancellor if he will tell me what he thinks the appropriate rate should be. Not only is this House interested in whether he thinks they should be higher; even more importantly, does the Prime Minister think that they should be higher? The markets never know whether the Chancellor, the Prime Minister or Sir Alan Walters speaks for the Government.

Mr. John Redwood (Wokingham): If the right hon. and learned Gentleman believes that the credit boom is slowing down, why is he recommending credit controls? Is he aware that credit controls and the exchange controls that they would require are illegal under the EEC arrangements which are being put in place for 1992?

Mr. Smith: There are some signs that the boom in demand is slowing down—and I am not surprised. If one takes £50, £60 or £70 a week out of people's incomes by means of increased mortgage payments, they cannot spend the money on goods produced at home or imported from abroad. But if there is a need to control demand, it should not be met by further increases in interest rates. It should be done by credit controls. Before the hon. Member for Wokingham (Mr. Redwood) departs too far from his former friends in the No. 10 policy unit, he had better read what they are sedulously leaking to the press day after day —that they are considering forms of credit controls as an alternative to the Chancellor's reliance on interest rates. I would not presume to give the hon. Gentleman political advice about his future career, but there is no need for him to stick his neck out too far on this subject.

The confusion between the Prime Minister and the Chancellor over interest rates and monetary policy merely exacerbates the inherent conflict within the Government's foundering economic strategy. No. 10, as the hon. Member for Wokingham reminded us by implication, is returning to monetarism and wants to avoid any further rise in interest rates. The City catches wild rumours that the Chancellor has resigned, but the Treasury line remains that interest rates will stay as high as necessary for as long as necessary. Is that still the Government's policy?

The Chancellor of the Exchequer (Mr. Nigel Lawson): Yes.

Mr. Smith: In that case, they had better get a grip on some of the advisers in No. 10 who tell the press that another Government policy is to be followed.

In all this confusion and disarray one searches in vain for the medium-term financial strategy, that wonder of modern economics in which the Chancellor would repudiate day-to-day management of the economy, disparaging it as flying by the seat of one's pants, in favour of medium-term targets. But the medium-term financial strategy has turned out to be just another temporary blip in the history of modern economics. The medium-term financial strategy has been aimlessly drifting in ever decreasing circles until it has finally disappeared up the Chancellor's own monetary targets.

Recently, the Chief Secretary to the Treasury bravely attempted to resuscitate the medium-term financial strategy when speaking to a conference of small businesses, called "Small Businesses: The Quiet Revolution". He told the conference—I quote from his Treasury handout—

"Government policy now operates in a medium-term framework which gives individuals and firms the confidence to plan ahead."

He was speaking on Wednesday 24 May, the same day on which interest rates rose to 14 per cent., the tenth such jump in borrowing costs since last summer. That is the medium-term plan to give small businesses confidence with which to plan.

I shall tell the Chancellor, who seems sceptical, what the small businesses said about his 14 per cent. interest rates. The National Federation of Self Employed and Small Businesses received the news with dismay, commenting that each percentage point increases the cost to industry by an extra £250 million. The federation complained that small businesses will be hit hardest, and went on to say that they were the pawns in the Government's move to defend the pound. So much for the medium-term financial strategy and the confidence it engenders.

I asked the National Federation of Self Employed and Small Businesses to give me an example of what it meant, which it did, calling it "Real Example No. 1". It concerns a company in Gwent, a supplier of equipment to the heating and plumbing industry. Its owner borrowed £25,000. His repayments on 19 May, when he first took out the loan, totalled £343 a month. This year, on 18 May 1989, his bank statement showed that the repayments had gone up to £552·44. He is also suffering from bad debts on the part of his creditors, because they, too, are being squeezed. If interest rates rise to 15 per cent., as the federation says seems likely, his repayments on the loan will have doubled. So much for the medium-term financial strategy and for encouraging small businesses.

The truth is that higher interest rates are a costly and ultimately futile attempt to restore confidence in the Government's failed economic policy. They will hurt British industry and British families, and especially home owners, whose mortgage misery is caused by a tax this year on home ownership—the price of the Chancellor's earlier mistakes.

Sir Peter Hordern (Horsham): Since the right hon. and learned Gentleman is so much against high interest rates, as he openly told the House, may we take it that the Opposition's policy is a return to hire purchase controls and to a reduction in the exchange rate, as is openly avowed by the hon. Member for Dagenham (Mr. Gould)? Is it Labour Government policy to devalue sterling against all other currencies and to reimpose hire purchase controls?

Mr. Smith: I have made it clear so often that I tire of repeating it that my objection to higher interest rates is that the Government use them as the only weapon of policy to restrict demand. I have argued that there should be alternative credit controls, and that they should not be dismissed dogmatically. Indeed, one of the delegates at the Tory women's conference spoke out to that effect, and the hon. Gentleman, like some of his hon. Friends, should be careful that he is not outflanked by a change of policy under which the Government introduce some form of credit control——

Mr. Robert Hayward (Kingswood): The right hon. and learned Gentleman has been on his feet for precisely 20 minutes. As this is the first economic debate since the publication of the Labour party's review, will he make clear what his party would do and what the cost of its programme would be?

Mr. Smith: I gave way in an excess of generosity, thinking that the hon. Gentleman would involve himself in the controversy in which I was engaged with the hon. Member for Horsham (Sir P. Hordern). However, if he will contain himself, I shall develop the points in our motion.

Mr. Nicholas Bennett *rose*——

Mr. Smith: The markets' judgment of the Government's economic policy and the resulting fragility of sterling cannot be reversed by high interest rates alone. Such rates are a recipe for further industrial decline, as soaring borrowing costs become an intolerable burden on British industry. Real confidence will be restored only when the Government start to tackle the fundamental problems of the British economy and stop indulging in what *The Daily Telegraph* recently called
"rhetorical self-indulgence abroad accompanied by an ever-burgeoning culture of economic self-gratification at home"—
something with which we have grown familiar over the weary 10 years of this Government.

Real confidence will return, as those on all sides of industry know, only when we in Britain invest in the supply side of the economy with the same relentless determination as West Germany does. If we are to boost our industrial capacity and trading performance we must invest, as our motion states,
"in training, research and development, and the regions",
and especially in manufacturing industry. Only investment can build the strong and competitive economy that Britain needs to meet the challenge in Europe after 1992.

Despite the Government's receipt of £78 billion in North sea oil revenues—one statistic that the Government seek to smother: we never hear the apologists in No. 10 drawing our attention to the existence of North sea oil revenues—we have massively under-invested, especially in the manufacturing tradeable sector of our economy. Investment in the manufacturing sector has only just crawled back to the level achieved by the last Labour Government, and the cumulative loss over 10 years amounts to about £18 billion of investment forgone. We

have squandered North sea oil and have failed to invest, while our major rivals without that unprecedented windfall have raced ahead.

In that excess of self-indulgence which characterised his 1988 Budget speeches, the Chancellor arrogantly compared Britain's so-called economic miracle with that of West Germany. He was so disparaging as to refer to the West German economic miracle in the past tense. We have heard that the West German economy is sclerotic, arthritic and hidebound and somehow much less efficient intrinsically than the bounding, vigorous economy that characterises the United Kingdom.

Let us look at our feeble performance compared with West Germany's investment record in manufacturing, research and development and training. The share of GDP invested in manufacturing in West Germany in the eight years from 1980 to 1987 is more than 50 per cent. higher than for the same period in the United Kingdom. Is it any wonder that West Germany's share of world trade since 1980 has gone up from 19·9 per cent. to 21·5 per cent. while that of Britain has fallen from 9·7 to 8·1 per cent.? Is it surprising that our deficit in manufactures with West Germany has grown from the £2 billion that the Government inherited to the £8·5 billion that it is now?

I looked through a list of figures comparing British investment with that in West Germany, and I shall select a few. West Germany spends £432 per employed person on research and development compared with only £265 in the United Kingdom. Over 70 per cent. of engineers in West Germany have recognised qualifications compared with 40 per cent. in the United Kingdom. The figure that I find the most shaming of all is that only 30 per cent. of our work force have recognised qualifications equivalent to at least one O-level, compared with 70 per cent. in West Germany.

Let us look at West Germany's investment in machine tools. In 1987, it spent £3 billion on machine tools, compared with £670 million in the United Kingdom. West Germany now installs as many new robots every year as the total number of robots in place in Britain. Overall, machine tool purchases have increased by 100 per cent. in West Germany against a rise of only 10 per cent. in the United Kingdom. That is what is happening in West Germany. What is happening here?

I hope that the House will not feel that it has to rely on any kind of biased statistic on a matter as serious as this. That is why I shall quote what the Engineering Employers Federation said two days ago in the *Financial Times*. It said:
"The federation predicts the negative trade balance in all engineering products will worsen by 30 per cent. from a deficit of £8·9bn in 1988 to £11·6bn this year."
It says:
"Aerospace products will be the only significant UK metal-using manufacturing sector to remain in the black in international trade this year, . . . Mechanical engineering, for the first time in recent years, will slip into the red, moving from a positive balance of £166m last year to a deficit of £1·6bn this year, the federation estimates.
The engineering industry last had a positive trade balance, of £2·8 billion, in 1982. Last year the deficit more than doubled from £4·2 billion in 1987."
That is the sad tale of what is happening in a crucial part of our manufacturing sector. No wonder our balance of trade and our consequent balance of payments deficit are frightening.

Mr. Kenneth Hind (Lancashire, West): In 1988, there was a record increase in investment in the United

[*Mr. Kenneth Hind*]

Kingdom, of 14·5 per cent. At present, investment in British industry is at a record level. The right hon. and learned Gentleman talks about increasing investment. The only way that he would bring that about is by increasing taxation and putting public money into industry.

Mr. Smith: The hon. Gentleman does what all apologists for the Government do. He seeks to confuse investment in the manufacturing sector with investment in business overall. He includes in his figures investment in casinos, leisure developments and the like. I have concentrated on investment in the manufacturing sector. The hon. Gentleman knows, and the Chancellor will not dispute, that investment in the manufacturing sector has just recently crawled above its 1976 level.

Mr. Phillip Oppenheim (Amber Valley) *rose*——

Mr. Smith: I have given way repeatedly and I must get on.

Instead of following the example of successful competitors the Government continue the decade-long neglect of our manufacturing industry, the internationally tradable sector of our economy. That is the fundamental fault in the British economy and the fundamental flaw in the Government's policy. They compound this error, which is right at the heart of the matter, with confusion and disarray in the day-to-day management of the economy, especially on the demand front.

Before March 1988 the Chancellor was shadowing the deutschmark at the level of DM 3 to the pound. That was until the Prime Minister brutally overruled him, as she pointedly reminded him recently. More recently, the Chancellor has been assuring markets of his firm intention to raise interest rates as high as is necessary for as long as is necessary. No doubt he will seek to make that clear again today and the markets will ask, as they ask every time he says it, whether the Prime Minister agrees with him. Two weeks ago in an answer at Prime Minister's Question Time the right hon. Lady cut the feet from under him and precipitated a currency fall which in turn brought another increase in interest rates. Hardly a day goes by when we do not have a further indication of dissent and confusion in that border zone between No. 11 and No. 10 Downing street.

Mr. Tim Yeo (Suffolk, South) *rose*——

Mr. Smith: No, I shall not give way.

On the No. 10 side of that zone there are some influential lodgers. There is Sir Alan Walters, the real Chancellor of the Exchequer, and the monetarist guru Professor Brian Griffiths. They are there to torment the Chancellor, and as he gets through and speaks to them, he no doubt remonstrates with them for conspiring against his policies. I do not envy the Chancellor in his difficulty in seeking to make some sense of the policy to which he is committed. He ought to get support from the Prime Minister once the Government have decided upon their economic policy. This country cannot have its economy managed by constant warfare between Nos. 10 and 11 and all the consequences that have flowed from that in recent months.

Mr. Ian Taylor (Esher) *rose*——

Mr. Smith: I will not give way to the hon. Gentleman. [*Interruption.*]

I thought that I had been making clear almost to the point of repetitive boredom the Opposition's commitment to tackling the fundamental problem of Britain's economy, which is the supply side problem. I am making clear not only our disagreement about the incompetent demand management that is practised by the Government but our disagreement about their excessive reliance on interest rates as the only weapon. Can we get that clear?

I should like all Conservative Members to deal with the policy. I should like them to start explaining why we invest less than West Germany. I should like them to tell us why they do not speak up for small businesses, which complain so vociferously about the effect of higher interest rates. [*Interruption.*] Perhaps the next time that I meet a representative of small business I will tell him that the hon. Member for Dover (Mr. Shaw) laughed when I raised this matter.

Mr. David Shaw (Dover): Will the right hon. and learned Gentleman accept from a small business man that the Labour party policy for the small business man has been a total and utter joke throughout the party's history? The Labour party has never had any policy to help small businesses and its 1979 and 1983 manifestos had nothing in them about small businesses.

Mr. Smith: I have changed my mind. I shall not report to the National Federation of Self Employed and Small Businesses; I shall send *Hansard* as a good example of the lucidity with which Conservative Members approach some of the problems of small businesses. Small business men will not find that tirade very convincing because they have to accept the reality of the 14 per cent. interest rate that the Government have inflicted upon them.

Sir William Clark (Croydon, South) *rose*——

Mr. Smith: The Chancellor's problem in seeking not only to devise a policy——

Sir William Clark *rose*——

Mr. Smith: No, I shall not give way.

The Chancellor's problem is not just in deciding what his policy should be but in making sure that it is adhered to. In that circumstance, he is not comforted by what the Prime Minister said in her interview in the *Glasgow Herald* when she held out two possibilities for people who were retiring from the Government. She said:

"They can have a great career on the Back Benches. They get respect there, you know."

I do not know whether the Chancellor will follow that happy route. The signposts along that route are Old Bexley and Sidcup, Shropshire, North, Henley and—I say this almost with some affection—Chesham and Amersham. Those are the signposts to the road to self-respect. The Chancellor may not find them all that beguiling.

Sir William Clark *rose*——

Mr. Smith: The hon. Gentleman has been a bit tiresome, so I shall give way to him.

Sir William Clark: I am grateful to the right hon. and learned Gentleman. He is criticising the Government's policy on investment in manufacturing industry. Would he be kind enought to tell the House what is the Labour party's policy to accelerate investment in manufacturing industry? Does it require an injection of taxpayers' money which will lead to increased taxation, or not?

Mr. Smith: One of the things that we should not do is to run a high interest rate policy which makes it almost impossible for people to invest in manufacturing industry. If the hon. Gentleman takes the trouble to read our policies with the care that I am sure most of his researchers are busy doing so at the moment, he will find the answers to the questions that he raises.

What we are debating here today is the confusion and disarray in the Government's economic policy. *[Interruption.]* Conservative Members find it entertaining if someone disagrees with his Front Bench. I say one thing back to them—Old Bexley and Sidcup to you.

The fact is that there is confusion and disarray in the Government's economic policy. A child could see that. Their short-term tactics are as muddled as their strategy is inadequate. That is why today, on behalf of a troubled nation, we call them to account.

5.33 pm

The Chancellor of the Exchequer (Mr. Nigel Lawson): I beg to move, to leave out from "House" to the end of the Question and add instead thereof:

"congratulates Her Majesty's Government on its economic policies which have led to output, investment, and manufacturing productivity growing faster than in any other major European Community country in the 1980s; applauds the Government's firm anti-inflationary stance, and the action it has taken to exert further downward pressure on inflation; and commends the Government's supply side policies which have brought industry's profitability to a 20 year high, led to record rates of new business growth, and seen the creation of nearly three million new jobs since 1983.".

The first thing to be said about the speech that we have just heard from the right hon. and learned Member for Monklands, East (Mr. Smith) is that it bore no relation whatever to what is happening in the real economy. The one thing that it did bear a close resemblance to was every other economic speech that he has made over the years. However, I have to say, in a spirit of great affection, that the trivia element was even higher than usual. In fact, it was pretty nearly 100 per cent.

It is remarkable how, whatever the economic circumstances, whether inflation is rising or falling, whether unemployment is rising or falling, whether sterling is rising or falling, whether he professes to be concerned about the threat of recession or the dangers of overheating, up the right hon. and learned Gentleman pops with the same solution—more public spending on training, research and development and investment.

Now let me try to find some common ground. I cannot accept the right hon. and learned Gentleman's assumption that these things have merit—*[Interruption.]* These are serious matters and Opposition Members should listen to what I have to say. I cannot accept the right hon. and learned Gentleman's assumption that these things have merit only to the extent that they are paid for by the taxpayer, but I entirely agree that we want to see more training, more research and development and more investment. That is precisely what we are seeing at the present time. Expenditure on training is rising fast and is now running at well over £20 billion a year. Spending on industrial research and development has also been growing steadily year after year. In 1987, the most recent year for which figures are available, industrial research and

development was more than 30 per cent. up in real terms over the comparable figure for Labour's last year in office —that is what has been happening—while total civil R and D, as a share of GDP, is well above the European Community average. Those are the facts.

As for investment, that too is at its highest level ever and still rising fast, with manufacturing investment particularly strong. Indeed, total business investment in the United Kingdom now represents the highest proportion of GDP ever recorded. Whereas under Labour, total investment scarcely grew at all, in the 1980s under this Government we have seen investment growing substantially faster than consumption and faster than in all the other countries of the European Community.

All that is a clear sign of a healthy and vigorous economy, one far removed from the picture painted by the right hon. and learned Gentleman, who simply demonstrates how hopelessly out of touch the Labour party is with the reality of life in Britain today.

Mr. Chris Mullin (Sunderland, South): According to figures supplied to me yesterday by the Department of Trade and Industry, manufacturing investment in the north-east—the area that I represent—in 1987, the latest year for which figures were available, was 53 per cent. of what it stood at in 1979. How does that square with the economic miracle?

Mr. Lawson: Even the right hon. and learned Member for Monklands, East admitted that manufacturing investment in Britain today is at an all-time record level.

Mr. John Smith: Will the Chancellor please tell us by how many percentage points investment in manufacturing industry today is above what it was when the Government took office?

Mr. Lawson: What I will tell him is that not only is it above and rising fast, but manufacturing output, which he considers of such importance, fell under the Labour Government and has risen substantially under this Government. That is the difference between our records on manufacturing.

What we have heard today from the Opposition is in no sense a new phenomenon. I recall, as some other hon. Members may, the censure debate on the economy that was mounted by the Opposition in January 1985—the last occasion on which interest rates were increased to 14 per cent. In that debate the Leader of the Opposition said:

"We know that the Chancellor of the Exchequer wants a high growth rate. We know that he wants a low inflation rate and we know that he wants everybody to go busily about their business. But given his record, that is not really on."— *[Official Report,* 31 January 1985; Vol. 72, c. 421.]

Mr. Neil Kinnock (Islwyn): That is right.

Mr. Lawson: The right hon. Gentleman says that that is right, but it is wrong. It is wrong in every particular. Since January 1985 British business and industry have had four of the best years that they have ever known. Since January 1985—I am taking about the particular things to which the right hon. Gentleman referred in 1985— *[Interruption.]* If the right hon. Gentleman wishes to get to his feet he can.

Since January 1985, growth has averaged 3·5 per cent. a year, inflation has averaged 5 per cent. and unemployment has fallen by more than a million—so much for the right hon. Gentleman's predictions.

Mr. Kinnock: In the course of doing all that, the Chancellor of the Exchequer—unforgiveably—has given us policies that result in a massive and possibly incurable balance of payments and balance of trade deficit. One of the reasons why he has managed for a part of that time to restrain inflation is that the balance of payments and dependence on foreign manufactured imports restrained inflation. Now that the Chancellor is having to revert to his policy of reliance on interest rates, inflation is shooting up and will go up further than even he wants.

Mr. Lawson: What is abundantly clear is that, four years after the 1979 debate, we can see that the right hon. Gentleman was wrong about growth, wrong about inflation and wrong about unemployment. In four years' time we shall see precisely that he was wrong about everything that he says today.

The plain fact is that, over the past five years, Britain has created more new jobs than any other European country, and we have more people in work today than ever before in our history. No wonder the right hon. and learned Member for Monklands, East did not say a single word about unemployment in the whole of his speech—a subject about which we always used to hear so much. The right hon. and learned Gentleman's speeches used to be about nothing else, but now we hear not a single word about unemployment.

At one point, the right hon. and learned Gentleman referred in a most emotional way to the question of small businesses. Let me mention just one more indicator of the new-found strength of the British economy—a strength that has spread from the south of England to the midlands, to Wales, to the north and to Scotland—and that is precisely the pace of new business formation, which last year achieved a record rate, net of closures, of more than 1,300 new businesses a week. That is what is happening to small businesses, and it is a far cry from the picture painted by the right hon. and learned Gentleman in his speech. That figure is net of liquidations—1,300 more businesses each week.

If the right hon. and learned Gentleman wants to make speeches about industrial decline, he should have reminded the House of the state of British industry in 1979 after five years of Labour Government. That was indeed an example of how not to run an economy. Industry was unproductive, unprofitable and strike-ridden—crippled by Government controls and interference, and often only propped up by state handouts, all financed by penal rates of taxation—*[Interruption.]*

Mr. Cranley Onslow (Woking): On a point of order, Mr. Deputy Speaker. Given the acoustics of the Chamber, I know that it is very difficult for you to hear sedentary interventions from the Opposition Front Bench, but if you watch the lips of the Leader of the Opposition you will see that he is continually trying to interrupt my right hon. Friend the Chancellor. Can you persuade him to shut up?

Mr. Deputy Speaker (Mr. Harold Walker): Order. I like to think that I have learnt a lot in the Chair, but I have yet to learn lip-reading. It seems to me that noise is coming equally from both sides of the Chamber. We could do with less sedentary noise from all parts of the House. I should like to hear the Chancellor of the Exchequer.

Mr. Lawson: I was saying, Mr. Deputy Speaker, that since 1979 the British economy has been transformed—a fact that has been acknowledged throughout the world. It is an economy immeasurably stronger and more confident than it was 10 years ago.

Mr. Geoffrey Robinson (Coventry, North-West): How can the economy be seriously presented in that way? After four years of the Chancellor's policies, which he calls good policies, we have under his Government record interest rates, record inflation and a record balance of payments deficit. What can be right about policies that have brought us to that point?

Mr. Lawson: It is certainly very far from record inflation, which the Labour party knows about.

I come now to the question of inflation. I readily concede that we have not yet exorcised the spectre of inflation.

Mr. Kinnock: What spectre? It is real.

Mr. Lawson: That is the problem we face today, and it is a problem that the right hon. and learned Member for Monklands, East conspicuously failed to address in the whole of the length of his speech in any remotely coherent way. The deficit on the current account of the balance of payments, which he dwelt on at such length, is itself a problem only to the extent that it is a symptom of excessive domestic demand. Exports continue to do well, and over the past three months exports have been up 8·5 per cent. over a year ago.

No, it is the problem of inflation that the House needs to address today. Once we master that—as we can and will —the British economy is set for an even better decade in the 1990s than we have known in the 1980s.

The rise in inflation that we are experiencing today is a worldwide phenomenon.

Mr. Stuart Bell (Middlesbrough): The Chancellor says that inflation is the major issue that faces the House, which is true, but is he saying that he has no policies at all for the next few years to reduce the balance of payments deficit?

Mr. Lawson: The reduction of excessive domestic demand will itself cause in due course an improvement in the current account of the balance of payments. I have made that clear time and time again.

The rise in inflation that we are experiencing today is a worldwide phenomenon. Taking the seven major industrial countries as a whole—that is what the G7 are, as the right hon. and learned Member for Monklands, East seemed not to know—inflation is now at its highest level for almost five years. Indeed, over the past six months the rise in recorded inflation in the United Kingdom has been only marginally greater than the rise in inflation in the G7 as a whole. That is only because, unlike most of the rest of the world, we include mortgage interest payments in our retail price index—*[Interruption.]* The Opposition do not like the facts, but they are going to get some facts. On a genuinely comparable basis, inflation in this country has increased over the past six months by less than in the G7 as a whole.

The right hon. and learned Gentleman may care to know that, while admittedly our recorded inflation rate is currently some 3·5 per cent. above the G7 average—that is true—during the whole of the period of the last Labour Government, of which he was a member, the United

Kingdom inflation rate averaged 6·5 per cent. above the G7 average. If the right hon. and learned Gentleman wants to make comparisons, let him have the facts.

Nor is what we are seeing today, either here in this country or worldwide, in any sense a return to the levels of inflation that we suffered in the 1970s. Indeed, the current underlying rate of inflation in the United Kingdom of 5·9 per cent. as measured by the RPI excluding mortgage interest payments, is well below the lowest level ever reached in any month throughout the whole of the lifetime of the last Labour Government, let alone their appalling 27 per cent. peak, so I am not going to listen to any strictures from the Labour party about inflation. I am not interested in the slightest in what the Opposition have to say about inflation.

Even so, inflation is clearly too high and must come down—and it will come down as the measures that have already been taken work their way through. Those measures are a tightening of monetary policy through higher interest rates within the context of a substantial Budget surplus.

Over the past year, interest rates have been raised very substantially and the medicine is clearly working. The housing market, which was such a powerful engine of consumer borrowing and spending, has subsided dramatically with prices levelling off in some areas and in most of the south-east actually falling. At the same time, turnover has fallen markedly, too. Retail sales have shown little or no growth since last summer and the growth in the narrow measure of the money supply—M0—has slowed down sharply since last September and is clearly headed back towards its target range. That is encouraging, though I have to say that I will not be content until it is well within that range.

Mr. D. N. Campbell-Savours (Workington): How can a small manufacturer of a particular product in Workington compete with a German manufacturer of exactly the same product when the interest rate paid by the business-man in Workington may well be far in excess of 14 per cent. and the German is able to borrow at perhaps 5 per cent.?

Mr. Lawson: I can tell the hon. Gentleman this—a small businessman in Workington or anywhere else in the United Kingdom has far more to fear from the rampant inflation that would follow from Labour policies than from any rise in interest rates.

Inevitably, there is a further time lag between the effect of tighter monetary policy on the growth of spending, which has now been evident for some time, and its effect on inflation.

In my Budget speech, I indicated that inflation was likely to rise for some months further to reach about 8 per cent. including mortgage interest payments, before falling back again in the second half of the year. Given the impact of higher oil prices, it is now clear that the peak will be slightly higher than this, and could well be reached quite soon. However, from the summer a gradual fall should take place as the policy has its full impact.

To repeat, the Government are determined to take whatever action is necessary to bring inflation down. Thus, although it is clear from the evidence of the domestic economy that spending—and, in particular, consumer spending—is slowing down at a satisfactory pace, I judged it necessary two weeks ago to raise interest rates by a further 1 per cent. in order to avoid taking risks with

inflation. I could not ignore the fall in the exchange rate which had occurred, and which threatened to undermine the firm anti-inflationary stance we have taken. That remains our position. There is, indeed, now a widespread and well-established understanding of the problems which currency depreciation brings in its wake. As the right hon. Member for Leeds East (Mr. Healey) said:

"Hard experience confirms the findings of economic research—that . . . depreciation can no longer be treated as a soft option."

But that was said as long ago as October 1978. The Labour party has had plenty of time since then to unlearn this lesson; and unlearn it it has. So we now have the spectacle of the Leader of the Opposition adopting once again Labour's instinctive devaluationist stance—arguing that sterling is overvalued and should depreciate substantially. We wholly reject this devaluationist and defeatist view, as indeed we always have done.

Mr. Kinnock: The Chancellor of the Exchequer told us that to prevent the pound from falling he had to intervene with 14 per cent. interest rates. Are we to believe that every time the Prime Minister makes an incautious remark in the House and causes a fall in sterling he will have to raise interest rates by 1 per cent.?

Mr. Lawson: If it is the case—and I do not know whether it is—that my right hon. Friend's remark in the House had an adverse effect on the markets, it is because the markets wholly misinterpreted what she was saying.

I have already referred to the censure debate of January 1985. Let me repeat what I said in my Budget speech in March of that same year, 1985. In 1985, I said this:

"There are those who argue that if we stick to sound internal policies, the exchange rate can be left to take care of itself . . . but significant movements in the exchange rate, whatever their cause, can have a short-term impact on the general price level and on inflationary expectations . . . So benign neglect is not an option . . .

There is no mechanical formula which enables us to balance the appropriate combination of the exchange rate and domestic monetary growth needed to keep financial policy on track, but a balance still has to be struck, and struck in a way that takes no chances with inflation."—[*Official Report*, 19 March 1985; Vol. 75, c. 785.]

That is what I said then, and that is what we did then, and inflation, which had risen uncomfortably, duly came down again and did so without any adverse effects on British industry.

The plain fact is that monetary policy is and always has been the only means of curing inflation. This means setting interest rates and holding them at the level needed, and for the time needed, to do their work. This is the weapon which has been tried and tested in the past. It is the weapon on which all the other major economies necessarily rely as they, too, struggle with the forces of inflation. As I have already pointed out, it is once again having the desired effect.

I accept that effect is not painless. As a result there are always those who seek to peddle some easier alternative. As we have heard from the right hon. and learned Member for Monklands, East today, the Labour party's magic cure is credit controls. I have to tell the House that this is purest fantasy. To listen to the right hon. and learned Gentleman, would imagine that the bulk of household credit comprised hire purchase or credit cards. That is another example of how totally out of touch the Opposition are.

Of total household debt, some 85 per cent. is on mortgages. The total of credit card and hire purchase

[*Mr. Lawson*]

lending—the two together—amounts to only a little over 5 per cent. of household debt, so it is nonsense to imply that introducing controls on hire purchase or credit cards would do anything significant to reduce the growth of consumer credit, or to allow interest rates to be one whit lower. In any event any such controls would be simplicity itself to get around.

As for direct controls on bank lending, these proved increasingly ineffective in this country even before exchange control was abolished. Today they would simply provide a field day for foreign lending institutions. But of course it is only natural for the Labour party to hanker after the ration book and the queue, which for the Opposition is not so much a means to an end as something to be desired for its own sake.

There are also other, more sophisticated nostrums to which the right hon. and learned Gentleman alluded—neither of them, I have to say, in any way new—and which are currently being touted in the public prints.

Monetary base control was something we looked at very carefully when we first took office. The arguments were set out fully in the 1980 Green Paper on monetary control. I remember it well because I was Financial Secretary to the Treasury at the time, and had particular responsibility under my right hon. and learned Friend the present Foreign Secretary for that Green Paper.

Despite its theoretical attractions, monetary base control has severe practical difficulties, which is perhaps why no major country has adopted it. After full consultation and public discussion we decided not to proceed with it, and that remains the position today. Moreover, in essence monetary base control is another way of generating the level of short-term interest rates needed to curb inflation. It is in no sense an alternative to high interest rates.

The other proposal much aired of late is that we should over-fund—which in present circumstances would mean refraining from using the Budget surplus to repay the national debt. Over-funding was not a device that in fact we used in our first two years, which were so critical in the battle against inflation, but for a time thereafter it did play a part in policy; but it produced increasing distortions—the so-called "bill mountain"—in return for little practical benefit, and was accordingly dropped as an instrument of policy some four years ago. It is an illusion to suppose that over-funding can, of itself, tighten monetary conditions, since money drained out of the system by selling gilt-edged securities over and above the Government's strict funding requirements has to be put back into the system elsewhere.

In short, there is no substitute, and never has been any substitute, for the use of short-term interest rates. To use a hallowed phrase, which I hear Opposition Members uttering from a sedentary position, there is no alternative. The only thing is that they would never have the guts to carry out a policy of this kind if they were ever discharged into office.

The right hon. and learned Member for Monklands, East went on at great length about his confusion over the Government's economic policies, and about alleged differences within the Government. Let me take this opportunity to make the Government's position perfectly clear. Our overriding objective is to bring inflation back down. To do that, we will keep interest rates at whatever level is necessary for as long as is necessary. We will maintain our existing funding policy and our existing monetary techniques, and we will not allow the firmness of our monetary stance to be undermined by a depreciation of the exchange rate. These are the policies that have successfully brought inflation down in the past, and will do so again.

That is where we stand, but where does the Labour party stand on these vital issues? Where does it stand? I have given a full statement of our position and our policy, and we heard nothing at all about the Labour party. [*Interruption.*]

Mr. David Shaw: Give way to them.

Mr. Lawson: I will readily give way to the kebab experts.

Mr. Alex Salmond (Banff and Buchan) *rose——*

Mr. Lawson: I am not aware that the hon. Member is a member of the Labour party, but I will let him speak for it.

Mr. Salmond: Has the Chancellor considered the impact of his high interest policy on areas of the country that are not overheating? Does he believe that at present the Scottish economy is overheating? If it is not, why should Scottish manufacturing industry, farmers and fishermen pay penal interest rates resulting from the inflationary problems being generated in the south-east?

Mr. Lawson: If the hon. Gentleman knew anything about the Scottish economy, he would know that the Scottish economy is doing extremely well at the present time. Scottish business-men are extremely satisfied with the policies of this Government, and Scottish business and industry are scared stiff of any hint of separatism, which the hon. Member supports.

After two long years of agonising reappraisal, the Labour party has at least come up with a voluminous policy review, but it has absolutely nothing to say on the key issue of inflation—nothing at all. One of Labour's economic advisers, who apparently asked not to be identified, explained to *The Independent* newspaper on the day the economic section of the policy review was published:

"they've no idea what to do on inflation."

Indeed, everything the Opposition advocate would simply ensure, just as it did when they were last in office, that inflation went through the roof—massive increases in public spending, with no idea of how to pay for them; a new tax on saving, with national insurance contributions levied on savings income; lower interest rates—we have heard this from them today—and, of course, devaluation. All these would send inflation soaring through the roof, and what defences would they erect to stem the inflationary torrent which all this would unleash? Higher taxes, perhaps? That is what the hon. Member for Newcastle upon Tyne, East (Mr. Brown), an Opposition Treasury spokesman—and I see him nodding—told us on television last week. That is very interesting, but, curiously, we heard nothing about that from the right hon. and learned Member for Monklands, East today. Perhaps we shall hear more.

According to the Leader of the Opposition, in his very interesting interview with Mr. James Naughtie, Labour would resort to price controls, credit controls and import controls. So much, incidentally, for Labour's commitment to the single European market and 1992.

As the right hon. Member for Llanelli (Mr. Davies) —and I am glad to see him in his place—a Treasury Minister in the last Labour Government, so aptly put it the other day:

> "The Labour Party idea that you should have credit controls is rubbish. There is no way you can control credit except by controlling the price of credit, and the price of credit is Bank Rate. The Opposition front bench, in short, is all over the place."

Mr. Denzil Davies (Llanelli): If the right hon. Gentleman wishes to advance an argument about credit controls versus interest rates, that is all very well, but will he now answer a question? Why, after four years with him as Chancellor of the Exchequer, does Britain have the highest rate of inflation, the worst balance of payments deficit and the highest rate of interest throughout the industrialised world? Why can other countries do so much better than him and the Prime Minister?

Mr. Lawson: I do not want to be unkind to the right hon. Gentleman, who has made a constructive comment on the Labour party's policies, but what he said is simply not true. We do not have the worst record by any means in the industrialised world. In a number of ways, we have the best record in the industrialised world.

Mr. John Smith: Will the right hon. Gentleman say which member of the OECD has a worse record in those three important respects?

Mr. Lawson: I will tell him, if he likes, of a member of G7, not merely the OECD or the EEC. On a comparable basis, the Italian rate of inflation is higher than ours. Italy's rate of inflation is 6·7 per cent. and ours is 5·9 per cent., and that is a fact.

Mr. Kinnock: The right hon. Gentleman refers to one indicator. Will he say why we had a trade surplus with Italy in 1979 but now have a £2·1 billion annual trade deficit just with Italy?

Mr. Lawson: The performance of the Labour Government was so lamentable that they were chucked out of office. If the right hon. Gentleman wants to stand on the performance of the last Labour Government, Conservative Members would be happy for him to do so.

Mr. Graham Allen (Nottingham, North) *rose——*

Mr. Lawson: No, I have given way enough.

We have learnt a little bit more, as was clearly revealed in the Naughtiegate tapes, which we now have available and from which I will read only a brief extract:

> "Kinnock: I'm not going to—"
> *[Interruption]* Labour Members should listen to the pearls of wisdom from the leader of their party. It goes like this:
> "Kinnock: I'm not going to sit here and be bloody quizzed on the alternatives. He's the Chancellor of the Exchequer . . . I'm not going to be bloody kebabed talking about what the alternatives are. We're not in control of it.
> Naughtie: Why don't you say that in as strong terms as you want to?
> Kinnock: But wait a minute. Opposition leader asked what he would do. Opposition leader says, 'to cut a long story short, we don't know.'"

Of course, there we have it. *[Interruption.]* They do not know, and they know they do not know.

Mr. Ian Gow (Eastbourne): On a point of order, Mr. Deputy Speaker. I could not quite hear the last words of my right hon. Friend the Chancellor, and I wonder——

Mr. Deputy Speaker: Order. If the hon. Gentleman and his right hon. and hon. Friends had been quieter we might all have heard.

Mr. Lawson: They are windy—they do not want to give us a hearing.

The Labour party does not know, and what is more it knows that it does not know. The Leader of the Opposition blathers about controlling this, that and the other—he cannot even control himself. So far from running the economy, he could not even run a kebab stall. Despite all the packaging and all the razzamatazz, despite the 88 pages of fine print, despite what must have been hours of careful coaching by his minders, the right hon. Member for Islwyn (Mr. Kinnock) and his party are no more fit to govern now than they were in 1979, 1983 and 1987. Labour Members know it, and so does the country.

6.9 pm

Mr. A. J. Beith (Berwick-upon-Tweed): I suppose that it is of the essence of these debates that Chancellors are not expected to add to the known facts about Government policy in the course of their remarks lest they cause further runs on the pound or further misinterpretations. But the Chancellor gave one or two things away. For example, he said that the rate of inflation will go higher even than he has most recently predicted and that by the end of the summer it should—he merely said "should" and not "would"—start to fall. With our climate, the end of the summer is a conveniently variable feast. Whether the Chancellor's forecast will be fulfilled remains a question.

The Chancellor also made great play of the fact that the markets had misinterpreted what his right hon. Friend the Prime Minister had said, which gave rise to the run on the pound and to the current interest rates. What they misinterpreted was the Prime Minister saying that she thought that the Chancellor's policies were working. I presume that she will say that again on a number of occasions. I am sure that the Chancellor hopes that expressions of confidence in his policy will be made from time to time. Will they have the same effect every time that they are uttered? If so, will we see a rise in interest rates as an automatic consequence?

The right hon. and learned Member for Monklands, East (Mr. Smith) set out accurately and amusingly the key defects of the Government's policy. Bearing in mind Mr. Speaker's injunction, I do not want to go over the ground that the right hon. and learned Gentleman covered.

We must concentrate on certain key elements. One is the Government's failure to tackle inflation. For some years the Government had a stock of excuses which they brought out to explain the inflation that was around in the system. One excuse was that it was due to previous failure to control the money supply. Now they claim that they have the money supply under control. Then it was oil prices. Despite some recent increases, oil prices present nothing like the problem that they presented in the early years of this Government, or of the previous Government.

Sometimes the Government blamed the trade unions. Now they reckon that they have the trade unions under control. Sometimes they blamed the Labour Government. When they were not doing that, they blamed the right hon.

[*Mr. A. J. Beith*]

Member for Old Bexley and Sidcup (Mr. Heath) and his Government, of which some of them were members. Incidentally, when the right hon. Gentleman was last heard of, he was supporting the Conservative Euro-candidate in Inverness. Whether it is a case of him being fed to the Free Presbyterians I do not know, but nothing seems to have been heard of him since.

The Government have produced a new set of excuses for inflation. First, it was a blip. As inflation began to rise from the slumber induced by 3 million unemployed, what was their reaction? They said that it was just another blip. It is clearly a far worse problem, and putting up interest rates has not made it go away. Then the Government said that it was a sign of success and an indication that their policies were working, but that we had slightly over-performed and gone a little too far in the right direction. No one can remember Japan or Germany suffering from over-performance that produced such inflation rates. If that was success, it almost made failure seem tempting.

The latest excuse is that inflation is increasing the world over. If our competitors were suffering from inflation rates of nearly 8 per cent., we might have reason to attach importance to that argument but with rates like 3·6 per cent., 3 per cent., 2·4 per cent. and 1 per cent., that argument can hardly be taken seriously.

Inflation must be tackled more seriously and more effectively. The Chancellor talked about exorcising the spectre of inflation. My rather low-Church views make me no expert on exorcism but I always thought that it required bell, book and candle—in other words, a whole series of measures, not just one. The Chancellor is an inefficient exorcist, insufficiently trained and equipped for the task. He must recognise that a broader strategy will be needed. The measures that he has taken, confined as they are mainly to interest rates, run the risk of inducing recession. Unless he broadens them, we will get the worst of that recession sooner or later.

It is difficult to imagine in what direction the Chancellor will move when there is fundamental disunity within the Government even about what the basic economic indicators are and mean. One understands that the Chancellor does not attach much importance any more to M0 as a monetary indicator, but the Prime Minister's principal adviser thinks that it is the only important monetary indicator. The Chancellor does not think that broad money indicators are important either. Perhaps that is because they are so far from their target rates that he does not want to refer to them.

The Prime Minister may not want to buck the market, but the Chancellor is engaged in the task of bucking the market. That is what his policy is all about. It is about trying to buck a market that does not believe that our economy and our currency are worth what we say they are worth. Therefore, we have to keep putting up interest rates to convince the market otherwise.

What has been lacking from the debate so far has been any clear indication of alternative policies that would meet the need. There are some alternative policies in the Opposition motion to which I can give strong support and which I believe are genuinely necessary, such as greater investment in training, tackling the skill shortage and greater investment in research and development and in

regional policy. All those are necessary to tackle inflation in the long term. Indeed, they are necessary if we are to have a fair and more just society, but they will not exert much influence on inflation in the short term.

The weakness of the motion is that it does not say much about what we should do now. There is confusion about whether the Labour party wants import controls or credit controls. Perhaps the reference to import controls was the result of the Leader of the Opposition being nonplussed in an interview. My picture of the interview is like the similarly blue-suited and white-collared figure in the famous painting who was being questioned by a harsh interrogator. The little boy was asked, "When did you last see your father?" I have in mind a picture of the Leader of the Opposition standing there, appalled that he should be asked such an unfair question as, "What would you do?" The little boy in the painting emerged from the exchange with more dignity than the Leader of the Opposition.

Mr. Hind rose——

Mr. Beith: Perhaps the hon. Gentleman would let me proceed a little further into what I think the Government should be doing. If he feels that there are omissions in what I say, I shall give him the opportunity to speak.

Mr. Hind: The hon. Gentleman has rightly pointed to the message that the right hon. and learned Member for Monklands, East (Mr. Smith) has given the House about what Labour would do. Does the hon. Gentleman agree that no policy has been put forward by the Labour party to deal with inflation? The Labour party has given no idea of its interest rate policy or its tax policy. All that we have had are fuzzy, supposed panaceas that amount to nothing. We want something more specific.

Mr. Beith: I agree entirely with the hon. Gentleman on that.

Mr. Norman Hogg (Cumbernauld and Kilsyth): If the hon. Gentleman agrees with that, will he tell us how the Social and Liberal Democrats would deal with inflation?

Mr. Beith: If the hon. Gentleman had not interrupted me, I would have gone on to do precisely that.

First, I want to say why I do not think credit controls are an effective mechanism. I do not think that the Labour party has come to terms with the real world if it imagines that the imposition of credit controls on a system of free capital movement would have a significant impact on the economy and on the rate of borrowing. I do not want to create a society in which credit controls are the stock in trade of Government policy. I do not want our citizens to have to encounter the Government every time that they go into a shop to buy a commodity. That is not the kind of society that I want to create. I think that it is an admission of failure if we even have to attempt to return to that kind of world.

We have to make our position clearer on other policies that are relevant to tackling inflation. One is the exchange rate mechanism of the European monetary system. It is a reputable argument that if we had been in the exchange rate mechanism for a reasonable time, say, two or three years, we would not have the rate of inflation or the interest rates that we now have. Indeed, a powerful discipline would have been exercised on monetary policy in a period when it is recognised, even by the Chancellor, that monetary policy was too lax. Yet the Government intend to join the system only when the time is right. We all know that that time will not be so long as the right hon. Lady is in charge. The Labour party still has not committed itself. It says in its policy review:

"substantial change would be required before we could take sterling into the Exchange Rate Mechanism."

The Labour party does not specify what that substantial change is and it remains a reluctant potential convert to British membership of that system. Indeed, the hon. Member for Dagenham (Mr. Gould) has long been a resolute opponent of it.

There are a number of measures that we have already argued are relevant in such a situation. One on which I know the Labour party agrees is that the public sector price increases in water and electricity, for example, which arise directly out of privatisation, should not be taking place. They are Government-induced inflation and are not a response to cost pressures. They arise directly out of the attempt to make the industries saleable, and the Government could have acted on that already.

Secondly, the Government could do more to promote savings. The measures that they have taken in the Budget are not sufficient to induce savings from new savers—from people who are currently not saving. The Chancellor has the opportunity to act on that.

Thirdly, I was interested in the Chancellor's comments on funding policy. The Chancellor delivered a criticism of the idea that we should change policies on funding, as though somebody in the course of the debate had already suggested that. I wondered to whom the Chancellor's remarks were directed. They could not have been directed towards the right hon. and learned Member for Monklands, East because he did not suggest such a change. They must have been directed——

Mr. Giles Radice (Durham, North): To Professor Alan Walters.

Mr. Beith: I certainly do not believe that the Chancellor was anticipating what I was going to say. Clearly, his remarks must have been directed at the Prime Minister's advisers. However, the mere fact that Professor Alan Walters suggests something is no reason for not taking it seriously. The fact that there is an area of policy which both monetarists and Keynesians consider to have some prospect of having a beneficial effect on anti-inflation policy is sufficiently surprising in itself to make one think that it should be taken seriously.

There is good reason to believe that if the Government —to put it in a simpler way than some of the commentators have—overfund, borrowing more than they need to do at a time of substantial public sector surplus, it could have the effect, among others, of raising the longer-term interest rate. There are fears about the consequences of that, but the Chancellor's current policy is based on the assumption that high interest rates will ensure that the rest of the economy responds to those high rates and that inflation will not take off. He should know full well that high interest rates bear most heavily on the domestic borrower and on small businesses, not on large companies.

Generally, the larger companies are able to borrow long term and have been insulated from the effect of high interest rates. That means that it is often small and innovative businesses which are struggling hard with high interest rates. The Chancellor says that they have got to suffer this to drive inflation out of the system, but he will not drive inflation out of the system if the effect is confined to that sector and does not extend to the large firm sector, which is benefiting from the much lower long-term interest rates. The gap between long-term and short-term interest rates does not seem to be a sensible part of economic policy. We all want to see the short-term interest rate brought down, but the current disparity between the two has an element of unreality about it.

The Chancellor was far too ready to dismiss one measure which, as an almost unarmed Chancellor, he could reasonably consider, which is the use of funding policy to exercise some effect on inflation. Whether he wants to believe in that policy as a monetarist, believing, as some monetarists do, that such a policy exercises restraint on the money supply, or as a Keynesian, viewing it as something that would have an effect on the yield curve and on long-term interest rates, either way it is likely to have some short-term impact on inflation. Surely we are looking for short-term measures at present which can have some beneficial effect. We have argued that the Chancellor should add some measures to his armoury and that is another that could be added to that list.

Clearly, some of the problems that the Government have faced have been problems of market perception of Government policy or market misunderstanding, as the Chancellor would say. We still have no clear explanation of the balance of power in the Government's economic policy. In a small way, it is like trying to weigh up what is happening within the power structure in Peking. We do not know who is in charge. As long as that is the case, the market will take cognisance of the fact and it will lead to short-term pressures, which will give rise to further increases in interest rates.

There are short-term disadvantages and dangers in the Government's present disunity, but there are also long-term dangers. That disunity also relates to Britain's role in Europe, Britain's place in the European monetary system and the extent to which Britain will become involved in the development of European currency and a European central bank. The danger of the Government's present attitude of hostility in varying degrees is that Britain will exclude itself from developments that it should be leading.

Our long-term economic prospects will be severely damaged both in general terms and because London will not be able to take its place as the natural financial centre of Europe. On many European issues, Britain is not merely missing the train, but throwing away the ticket at the same time. In the long term, that is as damaging for Britain as is much of the short-term damage which is being caused by the disunity between the Prime Minister and the Chancellor.

6.25 pm

Mr. Cranley Onslow (Woking): I want to make a short speech, so I shall make no reference to the opening speech of the right hon. and learned Member for Monklands, East (Mr. Smith) other than to say that, although it contained some amusing bits, that did not conceal the fact that it was fundamentally shallow and unconvincing. Most of my hon. Friends feel the same way about it.

Mr. Radice: The great economic expert.

Mr. Onslow: One does not have to be an economic expert to be able to judge a shallow and unconvincing speech.

[*Mr. Onslow*]

I want to refer briefly to one other Opposition Member. The performance of the Leader of the Opposition was just as we have learnt to expect. As my right hon. Friend the Chancellor said, he is a man who could not control inflation because he cannot control himself and we saw that demonstrated again today in the way in which he clowned it up in a sedentary position on the Front Bench. Reflecting on the reports of his interview and the episodes that did not reach the microphone, I noted that the hon. Member for Dagenham (Mr. Gould) said of his right hon. Friend the Member for Islwyn (Mr. Kinnock) that he was a man of immense self-discipline. For a man to make such a statement with a straight face, as I presume he did, tells us more about himself than about anyone else. The hon. Member for Dagenham does not make a very percipient judgment on some of his colleagues.

I want to test the credentials——

Mr. Doug Hoyle (Warrington, North): Tell us what you want to do.

Mr. Onslow: I will tell the hon. Gentleman what I want to do. I want to test the credentials of the right hon. Gentleman's leadership and his party. I hope that he will not mind my doing so and I am sure that he will not be sensitive about that. I want to ask some questions that I hope the hon. Member for Dagenham will be prepared to answer and that many of us hoped that the right hon. and learned Member for Monklands, East would have answered in his opening speech.

The first question is that if we suppose that the Opposition had the opportunity to deal with this situation, what would they do? Where would the money come from? It is fair to put that question on the basis of some points that others have already managed to squeeze out of the Labour party's reluctant spokesmen. It is fair to ask what the basic rate of income tax would be under a Labour Government. We know from a reply by the right hon. and learned Member for Monklands, East to a question from Jonathan Dimbleby on 12 February that there would be changes in the basic rate of income tax paid by 95 per cent. of the taxpaying public. The right hon. Gentleman went so far as to say:

"some will pay less, some will pay more, some will pay the same."

We and the public would like to know how many of that 95 per cent. will pay more and how much more they will have to pay. It is not unfair to put the questions in those terms.

My second detailed question is whether the right hon. Gentleman and his colleagues have made any estimate of how many pensioners would be made worse off as a result of Labour's proposals to impose an investment income surcharge. The Labour party is committed to that, so it seems fair to ask on behalf of the taxpaying public and pensioners, in particular, who have some savings, how many of them would be hit by such a proposal if, by some misfortune, it was ever possible for it to be implemented.

I have asked where the money would come from because the Labour party has a clear commitment to spend a great deal more money if it were in government. In its policy review, there are numerous spending pledges. Does any Labour Member have any idea what those pledges add up to in cost terms? If so, may we please be told? If not,

may we please be told? In an economic debate, a party that wishes to be taken seriously should be able to cost its proposals.

By how many billion pounds—not million pounds— would a Labour Government intend to increase public sector investment, and hence demand? In asking that question, I am placing the Labour party in some difficulty because it defines its terms in a way that suits it rather than in a way that adds to general understanding. I recognise that, in using the word "investment", the Labour party rules out the factor that many of us consider important —the profitability of such investment. Experience has shown that the Labour party tends to equate expenditure with investment. I imagine that it admits that an increase in expenditure, even if it is called investment, must increase demand. Will some Labour Member please tell us what effect that will have on inflation? Presumably, increasing demand is likely to increase inflationary pressure. To say that the Labour party is concerned only with manufacturing industry begs more questions, and that does not strengthen its case.

I shall ask another question, to which I suppose I will not get an answer, but I will ask it just the same. Does the Labour party want the exchange rate to remain at its current level or does it want it to be lower? Has the Labour party made an estimate of the increase in consumer credit that would result from its proposal to reduce interest rates? I understand from the speech of the right hon. and learned Member for Monklands, East that he does not wish to rely on higher interest rates alone, so presumably he intends that interest rates should be reduced—in spite of the wise advice that the right hon. Member for Llanelli (Mr. Davies) has given.

If there are to be credit controls under a Labour Government—if that ever comes about—what sort will they be? How will they be administered? To what will they apply? May we be told more about them? May we please be told more about the import controls to which the Leader of the Opposition apparently committed his colleagues in that celebrated non-interview? To what will they apply? How will they be administered? How will they be reconciled with our international obligations? How long will it be before we are back to price controls? There is already a sign in the Labour party's policy review that under a Labour Government there will be price controls on water and electricity. What else is to be subject to price control?

Finally, if I may put this indelicately, will the hon. Member for Dagenham define what he means by the "real economy"? Having heard what the Opposition have said on this and many other occasions, Conservative Members have little doubt, as I think have people outside, that the real Socialist economy is one of controls, strikes, runaway inflation and national disaster.

6.33 pm

Mr. Norman Hogg (Cumbernauld and Kilsyth): I am grateful for the opportunity to contribute to this important debate. I certainly support the official Opposition motion because it identifies the problems in the economy and sets out in general terms the steps that are required to rectify weaknesses. I want to relate my remarks particularly to the Scottish economy and I hope that hon. Members will forgive me for doing so. There are important differences between the economy in Scotland and the eonomy in the rest of the United Kingdom. I am sorry that representatives of the Scottish National party have vanished from the Chamber. One short intervention during the Chancellor's speech is not a contribution from a party that claims to speak for Scotland. The absence of SNP Members from the Chamber is deplorable.

The problems faced by the Scottish economy are the direct result of the Government's policies. The Government hope that many small businesses will be set up in Scotland and that those small businesses employing small numbers of people will take the place of the traditional industries that have vanished over the past decade. The Government seem to put their faith in electronics, in light engineering, in engineering in support of the electronics industry and in service industries. In my constituency, there has been some success in attracting such industries. OKI, a high-technology industry, recently opened, and low-technology firms such as Hinari, which manufactures televisions, have started operations. The success in bringing such firms to Scotland has been due to the work of Locate in Scotland and the development agencies which operate in the five new towns. The big push has been for small businesses, but they have been badly affected by a 14 per cent. interest rate.

I was interested to hear what the Chancellor said about the success in attracting small businesses to Scotland, but he did not say how a 14 per cent. interest rate would facilitate their development. Those small firms often operate to small margins. The margin for reinvestment is very much smaller, given their nature, than it is for larger firms. Initially, under-investment is often a feature. I worry greatly what is happening to small firms in Scotland. I do not believe that the statistics cited earlier this afternoon will hold up much longer.

Companies are disappearing because of the difficulties with which they are faced. Estimates in Scotland show that a one percentage point increase in interest rates can cost industry as much as £20 million or £25 million. Extra costs also fall on those who run small businesses. Often they are home owners in those places where industries and businesses are being set up. The average mortgage in Scotland is £45,000, which means that home owners have had to find an extra £100 per month because of increased interest rates. Often they are the young, high-flyer managers who are so necessary for the success of small businesses. The position will not improve in the short-term. If the building societies follow the bank interest rate increase with an increase in their rates, the position will become very worrying.

Sir Nicholas Fairbairn (Perth and Kinross): Before the hon. Gentleman bleeds his heart blue, will he remind us of the number of small businesses in Scotland that we lost under his Government and of the increased number under our Government? Will he remember that, thanks to our fiscal policies, the number of small businesses in Scotland has mushroomed? That is all thanks to our reversal of his Government's policies, which, whatever they are wrapped in, a future Labour Government would put back to destroy small businesses again. Will the hon. Gentleman give the Government a pat on the back because big business, namely, Ravenscraig, is safe and healthy, thanks to our economic policies?

Mr. Hogg: I cannot do that because the hon. and learned Gentleman is not correct. During the first two years of the decade of Conservative Government my constituency lost 2,000 jobs, which was precisely the number created by the Labour Government during the preceding four years.*[Interruptions.]* The hon. and learned Gentleman should pay attention to what I am saying before he interrupts me because I paid tribute to the work of Locate in Scotland and the development agencies in the five new towns, which have been responsible for 70 per cent. of all inward investment to Scotland since the second world war. The Government know that they must protect Ravenscraig because if it were lost, that would end any Conservative changes in Scotland. The Government's position in Scotland is parlous enough without threatening the future of Ravenscraig.

Before I was interrupted, I was talking about interest rates. I had hoped that the Chancellor would give some encouragement to home owners, but he said nothing on that matter. I had hoped that he would announce a freeze on mortgage interest rates, by agreement with the building societies, but he did not do so. I am afraid that that is the hallmark of the Treasury Bench and its inflexible approach to the economy.

Mr. Hind: The hon. Gentleman said that he was surprised that my right hon. Friend the Chancellor had not agreed a freeze on mortgage interest rates with the building societies. If building societies lost money as a consequence of uncompetitive rates compared with the banks, how would the loss be made up to them so that they could continue to lend, especially to first-time buyers, the money that is much needed for mortgages?

Mr. Hogg: Any such freeze would be short term. If the hon. Gentleman had any confidence in the Government's economic strategy he would accept that a short-term policy would not result in the difficulties to which he referred. If he is confident that the Government are right, I do not understand why he does not support the call for a mortgage freeze.

In addition to interest rate difficulties, inflation is now running at 8 per cent., with every possibility of rising further. That eats into our standard of living and is a disincentive to companies to invest. There is also a balance of payments deficit which, on a year-on basis, could run as high as £17 billion. The danger is that the country will be caught in a pincer movement between an industrial slump and price inflation.

The Chancellor's policy is not working in Scotland, unless its aim is to curb spending on Scottish products and investment in plant and machinery. When interest rates are used to bolster the pound, firms lose their competitive edge in export markets. Scotland is being asked to help to cool down the over-heated south-east. There is no boom in Scotland, despite what the hon. and learned Member for Perth and Kinross (Sir N. Fairbairn) said, but it is being asked——

The Economic Secretary to the Treasury (Mr. Peter Lilley): The principal Scottish forecasting body, the Fraser of Allander Institute, records that the Scottish economy grew last year more rapidly than that of the remainder of the United Kingdom and forecasts that it will do so again in the coming year.

Mr. Hogg: I shall refer to the Fraser of Allander Institute later in my speech.

[*Mr. Hogg*]

Scotland is being asked to accept the medicine being dished out to the south-east although it does not suffer from the same problems. The latest figures—not from the Fraser of Allander Institute, but from the Scottish Office —show a fall of 3 per cent. in manufacturing output for the last two quarters of 1988—the largest fall in five years and a consequence of earlier rate rises. The boom is being nipped in the bud and the threat of recession once again looms over the Scottish economy.

While output fell in Scotland by 3 per cent., it rose in the remainder of the United Kingdom by 0·7 per cent. We heard a great deal about total output in the Chancellor's speech. The Scottish construction industry's output fell by 8·7 per cent. while that of the remainder of the United Kingdom rose by 2·6 per cent. The electrical instrument engineering industry, so important to Scotland, suffered a fall of 12 per cent. against a United Kingdom rise of 2 per cent. There was a fall in investment goods of 9·6 per cent. against a United Kingdom rise of 1·7 per cent. If there is cheer for Scotland in all that, what is the Treasury's prediction for Scotland for the next 12 months? What is the future for the Scottish economy?

The Fraser of Allander Institute is certainly not a friend of the Labour party. I readily accept that and understand why the Minister is so quick to pray in aid anything that it might say. However, even that institute has identified pessimism among manufacturers as worse now than at any time since the oil price collapse in 1986. It says that the decline in manufacturing must soon filter through to the labour market. What is the Government's prediction for unemployment levels in Scotland during the next 12 to 18 months? There is a loss of confidence in Scottish industry that is directly attributable to the Government's policies.

Where does all that leave Scotland as it faces the advent of 1992? Professor Neil Hood, who has close connections with the Scottish Development Agency and with Locate in Scotland, said that Scotland is insufficiently prepared for 1992. My constituency is industrial—the sort of place about which the Government are fond of saying, "This is where success lies." However, as I go around my constituency I find confirmation of what Professor Hood said and, indeed, of what the Fraser of Allander Institute said about pessimism among manufacturers. In addition to all those problems the Channel tunnel will not help the northern or Scottish economies.

The Government's record in Scotland shows a decline in manufacturing and a fall in the number of employees in manufacturing as high as 34 per cent. Regional grants have fallen from £289 million in 1978-79 to £95 million in 1989-90. The Government can account for only 30,000 jobs created in Scotland between 1983 and 1986, yet 700,000 were created in the south-east during the same period.

Scotland has no confidence in the Government's policies and that will be reflected in the European election results a week on Thursday and in the Glasgow, Central by-election on the same day. The Government came second in that constituency at the last election and it will be interesting to note where they come this time.

Judged by any indicator, the economy is in trouble, and the position is much worse north of the border. The Government have failed to support the Scottish economy, failed in education and training and failed in investment.

They have not failed, however, in their record of low support for their policies. In all the years that I have been active in politics, I cannot recall a time when the Government had such low support among the Scottish people. They are in for a severe shock in the European elections and the Glasgow, Central by-election. I am confident that the Labour party will gain the seats because it is clear in Scotland that that is where the future lies. There will be a Labour Government; that is coming soon, and the sooner the better.

6.50 pm

Mr. Tim Smith (Beaconsfield): The hon. Member for Cumbernauld and Kilsyth (Mr. Hogg) argued that the economic situation in Scotland was somehow different from that of the rest of the United Kingdom because, he said, there was no overheating in the Scottish economy. In a telling intervention, the Economic Secretary said that in a recent period Scotland had enjoyed a higher rate of growth than had the rest of the country. Inflation is a problem wherever we find it in our economy. It is as much a problem for Scottish businesses as it is for any other British businesses, and the hon. Gentleman admitted that inflation was a disincentive to invest.

That is precisely what it is. If small businesses must choose—it is not a pleasant choice to have to make— between high interest rates and getting inflation down, they must accept that it is in their interest to reduce inflation as quickly as possible, and high interest rates will achieve that end.

The Chancellor announced that the net growth of small businesses in the United Kingdom has been higher than ever before. I have a simple message for the Chancellor. I urge him to stick to his guns, to persist with his policy and to continue to concentrate on getting inflation down. That must be our top economic priority.

There has been much talk in the debate about short-term measures. For example, the hon. Member for Berwick-upon-Tweed (Mr. Beith) said what he would do in the short term, although he rightly rejected the possibility of credit controls. He spoke of over-funding, and the Chancellor explained why that would not be effective.

We knew when the policy was introduced that it would take time to work through, and it will. He must think back a couple of years, to the events of late 1987 and black Monday; it is fair to date recent events from that time. The right hon. and learned Member for Monklands, East (Mr. Smith) wanted the Chancellor to go further at that time in reducing interest rates. The fear in late 1987 and early 1988 was of a recession because nobody knew how the real economy would respond to the sudden collapse of the financial markets.

Industrialists today wonder why politicians and ecomomists were so concerned at that time. They say, "Our businesses were going well and we were doing good business. What did a sudden collapse in the stock market matter?" They were unconcerned, and so far from having a recession in 1988, we had high growth stimulated by low interest rates, though it was higher than we could ultimately sustain. The policies of the right hon. and learned Gentleman would merely have exacerbated the problem.

The policy, if mistaken, was right at the time, but we must now put matters right. It will take time for that to happen and for the Chancellor's policies to work through. Patience is required, and I appreciate how difficult that is for an owner-occupier whose monthly mortgage payments have gone up substantially in the last 12 months. People in that position are bound to be impatient. They want the interest rate to fall so that their monthly payments can fall.

I am convinced, however, that when the situation is explained properly to people, they appreciate that the present measures are necessary if we are to avoid a repeat of the inflationary trends of the last 20 or 30 years. That is why our top priority must be to get inflation down.

I fear that there could be a danger of over-reacting. I was disappointed at the recent rise in interest rates. I felt that it had been at 13 per cent. for quite a time, and it seemed that the policy was working. I remain convinced that it is working. I hope that it will not be necessary for the Chancellor to raise interest rates again, although I support him when he says that he will maintain interest rates at their present levels until he is satisfied that inflation is on a downward path and that, if necessary, he will raise them further.

I read with interest an article in the CBI magazine by the confederation's director-general headed:

"Danger: Scribblers in the dark."

It appears that the director-general, John Banham, is as unhappy about some scribblers as is the Chancellor. Mr. Banham complained about information that sometimes appeared in press stories concerning the economy. He wrote:

"Recent headlines have blared bad news which was just plain wrong."

For example, although one headline said 'Export slump in February" Mr. Banham wrote:

"in fact, seasonally adjusted, exports . . . were 9·5 per cent. in volume up on the same period last year."

Another headline declared:

"'Import surge continues'—yet imports of consumer goods in the three months to the end of March were down, in volume terms, compared with the preceding three months."

Later in the article, Mr. Banham wrote—and he should know, representing a huge proportion of British industry —that the Government's policy was working. He said:

"Consumer spending has slowed right down. This was clear from the CBI's Distributive Trades Survey as early as last autumn . . . The slowdown will affect other sectors of the economy as we move through the year. Distributors' stocks have built up and this means less orders—for importers as well as United Kingdom producers. . .Investment is, at present, holding up well . . . Capacity utilisation is easing."

There is plenty of evidence to show that the Chancellor's policy is working, and that is why we must stick to our guns. Then we will see, as the year progresses, that the figures start to come right.

Other people have more confidence in the British economy than some of our commentators, and I have details of a number of recent examples of people putting their money where their mouths are and investing in the British economy. On successive days in April there were announcements to that effect. The first came from Toyota, with news of a large investment in Derbyshire. Then Bosch announced a large investment in south Wales.

I was particularly pleased that Robert Bosch Ltd decided to invest in Britain because the company has its United Kingdom head office in my constituency. Up to now the company has been importing everything that it sold in this country. Now it is to establish a car component factory in south Wales which will eventually employ 1,200

people and create another 1,500 jobs. The investment will total £100 million and I am told that 80 per cent. of the output will be exported.

There are many other examples of inward investment, and we have heard about the success of the Scottish development agency in attracting overseas investment to Scotland. It is clear, therefore, that this type of investment is occurring throughout the country. Many overseas investors are coming here in preference to other countries. When I discussed with Robert Bosch why it had chosen the United Kingdom—remembering that there is great competition throughout the European Community for this type of investment; Bosch already has a large investment in Spain, where it employs 6,000 people—I was told that the company had confidence in our economy, that it believed that the United Kingdom was a stable area in which to invest, that prospects here were good, that industrial and labour relations were good and that manufacturing productivity had risen substantially. Foreign companies have confidence in our economy. My hon. Friends and I have confidence in my right hon. Friend's policies. I am sure that, given time, they will succeed.

Several Hon. Members *rose——*

Mr. Deputy Speaker: Order. I remind the House that Mr. Speaker earlier announced that speeches falling between 7 o'clock and 9 o'clock would be subject to the 10-minute limit.

6.58 pm

Mr. Denzil Davies (Llanelli): The Chancellor made what one could describe as a knockabout speech. He failed to answer the central question why, after 10 years of Conservative rule, with the present Prime Minister in charge, Britain has the highest inflation rate in western Europe, has by far the worst balance of payments deficit of all the industrialised nations and has the highest interest rates among all our main industrial competitors. For that sorry state of affairs only one person can accept the blame, and that is the Prime Minister. She is very fond of blaming everyone else inside and outside of the Government. She cannot, in fact, blame the trade unions for this sorry state of affairs. The public sector, high rates of income tax, the dreaded public sector borrowing requirements—or what she used to describe as the frontiers of Socialism—have all gone. All those dragons from the past have either been slain or at least caged. The blame lies with her policies and, indeed, those of the two Chancellors who have held office in the past 10 years.

When the Government came to power in 1979, they made the control and the reduction of inflation their main target. One way they would do that—a point that was made recently in an article in *The Sunday Times*—would be by increasing the supply of British goods by improving the supply side of the economy, and by controlling and reducing by monetarist means the money supply. They would increase the supply of goods and reduce the supply of money and thereby try to get inflation down.

The Prime Minister's first Chancellor, the present Foreign Secretary, was certainly able to reduce the supply of money. However, in doing so—I accept that that was combined with a world recession—he diminished Britain's industrial capacity and its ability to increase the supply of goods.

[*Mr. Denzil Davies*]

The right hon. and learned Gentleman, the present Foreign Secretary, is a mild man, but when it came to reducing the money supply he was a veritable rottweiler. With his tight monetary targets—we all have examples in our constituencies—he managed to mangle large sections of British manufacturing industry. A number of industries disappeared, never to appear again.

There were some productivity gains, but the price that was paid in productivity gains was far too low in respect of the industries that were destroyed.

The right hon. and learned Gentleman then went to the Foreign Office and the present Chancellor took over. I would not describe the right hon. Gentleman the present Chancellor as a monetarist, but at least he is reported to understand monetarism. If he does understand monetarism, he will also understand its limitations—especially in an open financial system, such as is the British economy. The contradiction in monetarism is that, although it is thought to be, and is, a Right-wing financial ideology, one of the best countries in which it could be practised would be the German Democratic Republic, because a command economy is much more capable of controlling the money supply than an open economy.

During the Chancellor's period in office, he has kept missing his monetarism targets, changing his monetary targets and relaxing his monetary targets. In fact, over the years he has considerably increased the supply of money in the economy, so that today what is called "broad money" —he never mentioned that in his speech, because now his target is "narrow money"—which is notes, coins and bank deposits, is probably running at the rate of 20 per cent. or more. On top of all that we have had the tax-cutting Budgets—especially the one two years ago—which have flooded the system with even more money.

However, the trouble by then was that the supply of domestic goods had been so curtailed as a result of the policies of his predecessor in the first four years that the increase in the supply of money, which the Chancellor engendered, has left us with high inflation rates and an horrendous balance of payments deficit, because that was the only way in which the goods could match the money in the economy.

So a Government, who started off 10 years ago determined to increase the supply of goods and reduce the supply of money, now find themselves in the extraordinary position, through mismanagement, of having reduced the supply of goods and having increased the supply of money.

What is to be done? The Chancellor is in a corner. He is caught between the foreign exchange markets, domestic inflation and the hang-ups of his neighbour next door. I am sorry to say that the person who does not understand monetarism is the Prime Minister. The Prime Minister thinks that she understands monetarism and she wants to be a monetarist, but then she recoils from some of the harsh consequences of monetarism. She brings in professors from America or gurus. I thought that the Chancellor dealt very well with Tim Congdon, but the Prime Minister did not look very happy. The Chancellor could not see her face, but she did not like it. She was not too happy at that point in the Chancellor's speech. I do not believe that she does understand monetarism, and I have some sympathy with the Chancellor in having to deal with her in that respect.

As I think I have said before, I do not believe that old-fashioned credit controls or, indeed, new-fangled deposit controls, imported from America by Professor Walters, can solve the problems. In the end, if the policy is just about monetarism, it will be about high interest rates. Our complaint is that the policy should not just be about monetarism.

I believe that there are alternatives, although they would not have a dramatic effect. The House knows very well, sadly, through debating the British economy over the past 20 years, that there are no immediate panaceas, and certainly not in fiscal or monetary policy. We need a substantial restructuring of the British economy to solve our real problems. There are some things, however, that can be done without relying entirely on a monetarist policy and on high interest rates.

It is no secret that the Chancellor wants to join the exchange rate mechanism of the EMS, but the Prime Minister will not let him. It is difficult for me to say this, but the right hon. Lady should now stop being silly and should allow the Chancellor to go to Europe and negotiate entry into the EMS. She should let him go quietly on Sunday afternoon. He could join the other Finance Ministers in some West German spa town and he could negotiate entry into the EMS and a realignment of currencies. I believe that that is what he wants to do. The Treasury is right. However, the right hon. Gentleman's next-door neighbour prevents him from doing so.

Membership of the exchange rate mechanism would restore confidence to economic policy, provide some stability for the pound, and take some pressure off interest rates. Whether we like it or not—thanks considerably to the mismanagement of the economy over the past 10 years and the reduction in Britain's manufacturing capacity— sterling is rapidly ceasing to be a world currency. It is still trying to behave as if it were a world currency, but it is rapidly becoming a regional one.

Most of our balance of payments deficit in manufactured goods is with western Europe. In fact, most of our balance of payments deficits altogether are with western Europe. The world currencies today are the deutschmark, the yen and the dollar. I am sure that the Chancellor enjoys himself when he goes to the G7 meetings but, with all respect to him, he is really a bit player on the world stage. It is the yen, the dollar and the deutschmark that count. We should recognise the fact, at last, that sterling is a regional currency. More than half of our trade is with the EEC and that proportion will increase as 1992 approaches.

If this were not such a dogmatic Government, the Chancellor could also reverse some of the income tax cuts that he so foolishly put into effect two years ago. He should make the income tax system progressive again. He should introduce further rates and raise some money in taxation to balance his policy between monetarism and a fiscal policy. Of course, he will not do that either. If he did that, pressure would be taken off interest rates and industry.

None of that will happen. Interest rates may well have to go up again to stop a run on the pound. There will be a recession. Whether one calls it a hard or a soft landing, the only way that inflation can be brought down by monetary means and high interest rates is by creating a recession. Unemployment will rise and British industry will again pay a heavy cost. We are back where we were when the Government first came in, with policies to reduce the money supply which, in turn, reduces the supply of domestic goods.

There will not be much improvement in the balance of trade. In a very careful statement, the Chancellor appeared to indicate that it will take some time before the balance of trade improves. Ten years have gone by since the Government came to power—10 years of great opportunity, of very favourable international conditions on inflation and on commodity prices and of great opportunity at home in terms of £75 billion in oil revenue. However, those 10 years have been wasted. The Prime Minister can blame no one but herself for that.

7.9 pm

Sir Ian Gilmour (Chesham and Amersham): I agree with the right hon. Member for Llanelli (Mr. Davies) that we should join the EMS at the right exchange rate. I understood him to say—I may have misheard him—that the Government have reduced the supply of goods. I do not believe that he could possibly have meant that, because although we all have some criticisms—at least I do—of the Government's economic policy, I do not believe that anyone can seriously say that they have reduced the supply of goods.

I am sure that we would all agree, however, that the consumer boom got out of hand last year. Since mid-1985 the growth in consumption has been 6·1 per cent. a year —far greater than in any other period. Although that growth was conspicuously set off last year, it would be a grave error to say that it was merely a short-term problem or a short-term blip. It is much more deep-seated than that.

The right hon. Member for Llanelli referred to the monetarists of earlier days. There is a view going round that the monetarist experiment of the early 1980s was a great success and that all would have been well if my right hon. Friend the Chancellor had continued with such policies and maintained a firm control of the money supply. That view has been argued recently by Mr. Tim Congdon, who has been making some good forecasts. That argument does the Chancellor a serious injustice and I am happy to defend him from it. The fall in inflation in 1983 to 4·5 per cent. could hardly have been the result of controlling the money supply one or two years previously, because M3 rose 16·5 per cent. in the year to the second quarter of 1981 and 14 per cent. in the year to the second quarter of 1982. In any case, the years of alleged monetarism were far from being the halcyon days now depicted. I do not believe that anyone would reasonably want to return to them and my right hon. Friend is right not to do so.

Between the second quarter of 1979 and the second quarter of 1986, total output grew by an average of 1·25 per cent. a year and unemployment rose by 2 million. Inflation did fall, thank heavens, to 2·5 per cent. in 1986, but, obviously, that was not the result of controlling the money supply, because the money supply was not controlled. During the years it grew at an average of 14 per cent. a year. I think the right hon. Member for Llanelli possibly misunderstood that point.

Whatever mistakes the Chancellor or the Government may have made recently, my right hon. Friend was certainly not guilty of abandoning a successful monetarist policy. All that has happened has been to advance, by about two or three years, a crisis that was going to occur anyway.

As I have endlessly pointed out, economic growth can never be permanently sustained unless the growth of domestic demand is appropriately balanced by a growth of exports. Unfortunately, over the entire post-war period, long before the Government took office, there has been a persistent weakness in the ability of British industry to compete successfully. By the end of the 1970s it was already clear that if we continued to lose market share —particularly in our own markets—a critical point would soon be reached. That problem was masked for a bit by North sea oil, but certainly not now.

Our troubles spring not from the abandonment of monetarism but from the fact that the Government never addressed the problems of industry's competitiveness. Although the Government have bashed the trade unions handsomely, probably their policies have made our competitive position not better, but worse. The first three years of the Government—1979 to 1982—far from being halcyon days, look like a catastrophic mistake. Although we were continually assured that there was no alternative —I was glad to hear my right hon. Friend reintroduce that well-known phrase this afternoon—and that solid foundations were being laid for non-inflationary growth, what happened was that deflation merely dug a great crater from which our industry has been able to climb out only at a serious competitive disadvantage.

The combination of a collapse in demand and an over-valued exchange rate led to widespread scrapping of plant. For three years, investment in manufacturing was lower than capital consumption, so there was a fall in productive capacity. That must be one of the main reasons why, although the growth of output from 1979 until now has been exceptionally slow and unemployment has risen by nearly 1 million, we are now up against the limits of our capacity to produce, while inflation is climbing back uncomfortably close to the figure we inherited from the Labour party.

The main point is that the increase in import penetration is emphatically not a phenomenon that belongs to the past three years of consumer boom. It has been an almost continuous process during the past 10 years and before that. The rise in the proportion of imports of manufacturing to GDP from 14 to 18 per cent. between 1979 and 1985 was as large as it was between 1985 and 1989 when it rose from 18 to 22 per cent. One of the necessary conditions for continued growth is a cut in domestic demand. That is obviously right, because the deficit in our balance of payments is now at least 4 per cent. of GDP. At the same time, however, further growth of output is being constrained by lack of capacity.

At the moment, I cannot see from any constellation of policies now in prospect that the other necessary condition for continued growth—that net export demand will rise enough, if at all—will be fulfilled. It is not hard to see what should happen. The cut in domestic demand obviously should be confined so that the damage is limited to consumption rather than blighting the welcome recovery in investment in the past year, which at long last has got going. That cut in demand also should not frustrate the much-needed increase in net export demand.

Unfortunately, the instruments of policy which the Government have chosen—high interest rates and a high rate of exchange—do not meet those requirements.

[*Sir Ian Gilmour*]

Obviously, high and, possibly even higher, interest rates are particularly bad for investment. A high rate of exchange makes investment in exporting industries, as well as exports themselves, unprofitable. Moreover, high interest rates coming at a time when household indebtedness has been encouraged to grow to unprecedented levels causes severe, random and unmerited distress.

The best way to cut domestic demand was not advocated by the right hon. and learned Member for Monklands, East (Mr. Smith), for obvious reasons. It was, however, advocated by the right hon. Member for Llanelli. Surely the right club for the Chancellor now to take out of his bag is one to put up income tax. If income tax was increased, interest rates could be reduced without causing a loss of confidence in sterling. In due course there could be a reduction in the exchange rate with much less risk of inflation. Under those circumstances there would be a much better prospect of growth coming from exports and investment, in which case growth could be sustained.

I do not accept that the existence of a Budget surplus, as measured by the PSBR, means that one should not increase taxation. It is the state of the economy that matters and if a cut in demand is, by general assent, required—as it is—the mere fact that there is a surplus in the public sector accounts tells us nothing about whether the chosen instrument should be fiscal or monetary policy.

Mr. David Nicholson (Taunton): My right hon. Friend knows that I listen to his speeches with great interest. How would an increase in income tax contribute to pay claims and pay settlements that are currently giving cause for concern?

Sir Ian Gilmour: I recognise that difficulty, but an awful lot of people who receive wages are also buying houses so it is no good thinking that high interest rates do not affect wage claims.

The Government are looking ahead to the single market of 1992, but on present trends, it is likely to be a mixed blessing for the country. It is therefore vital that we should try to use the mechanisms of the European Community to develop a thriving and competitive industry. That would meet the needs of the hon. Member for Cumbernauld and Kilsyth (Mr. Hogg) and of those areas that currently have high levels of unemployment. It means playing an active role in the formation of Community policies and not seeking to turn it into a glorified free trade area. That is not what the Community is about and it would be directly contrary to British national interests.

The Government have, I fear, wasted a good deal of time since they cottoned on to the deterioration in our trading position. If they go on relying on their one club, they may find themselves in an electoral bunker as well as other ones. Moreover, their one club is particularly inappropriate since, for understandable reasons, the Government are extremely reluctant to use it. Therefore, the Government are in danger of going from a one-club policy to a no-club policy, as a result of which little would be done.

I hope that the exchange markets and foreign Governments have gained confidence from what my right hon. Friend the Chancellor has said this afternoon, but it is high time that a new and better policy was brought in.

7.19 pm

Mr. Giles Radice (Durham, North): I shall confine most of my remarks to the balance of payments deficit, for three main reasons: first, because the deficit is big and growing; secondly, because it takes out of the Government's hands the power to run our own economy; thirdly—here I agree with the right hon. Member for Chesham and Amersham (Sir I. Gilmour)—because it reflects our failure to pay our way in the world.

The Chancellor has consistently underestimated both the size of the deficit and the speed at which it has grown. In March 1988, he forecast a deficit for the year of £4 billion. At the time of the Budget he told the House that it would be equivalent to 1 per cent. of GDP and that he foresaw no difficulty in financing what he called a temporary current account deficit of that scale. By last November, in his autumn statement, he revised the forecast for 1988 upwards to £13 billion. The deficit for the year turned out to be £14·5 billion, £10 billion worse than the Chancellor had estimated in the 1988 Red Book.

As hon. Members well know, the forecast in this year's Red Book also gives a deficit for 1989 of £14·5 billion. As our Select Committee report stated, even to maintain a similar level of deficit in 1989 as that for 1988, the Treasury must rely on an extremely ambitious reversal in the behaviour of both exports and imports. So far, the monthly figures have been extremely discouraging.

Taking the first four months' figures together and putting them on an annual basis, the deficit now runs at more than £18 billion a year. To put that figure in perspective, as a percentage of GDP it is well over 3 per cent. I think that the right hon. Member for Chesham and Amersham was right and that it is nearly 4 per cent. It is greater than the deficit in any other major industrial country. Contrary to what the Chancellor said in March 1988, the deficit is neither small nor temporary. Furthermore, there is no evidence of any country of a comparable size sustaining a deficit of that level for any length of time.

One view which has been sedulously encouraged by the Chancellor is that somehow the balance of payments deficit no longer matters in the way in which it used to in the 1960s. His argument goes something like this: by definition, all economies cannot be in surplus. Some will be in surplus and others in deficit. His argument runs that, in a world in which there are free flows of capital, which is very much the case at the moment, some countries will export capital and others will import it. His implication is that Britain will be an importer of capital.

Last year, the Chancellor advised the Select Committee, making up economic theory as he went along, that the countries with current account deficits would tend to be those in which the investment opportunities were attractive because they attracted mobile savings. He has also argued that we are constantly using the import of capital to re-equip British industry.

According to the Chancellor, by running a larger current account deficit we are not only doing the rest of the world a favour, but helping ourselves. The Chancellor also tells us that there is no reason why we cannot continue to run a large balance of payments deficit for a considerable length of time. What a wonderful world it would be if it were really like that. We do not need to be old-fashioned mercantilists to see that there are flaws in the Chancellor's argument. Of course there is a case for financing a temporary deficit, but if it is large and continuing, it will produce considerable dangers and risks.

If we have to finance a deficit the size of ours, and continue to finance it over a number of years, we will virtually be putting the economy into the hands of the holders of sterling. A Chancellor with a deficit of that size is bound to shape his policy according to the currency markets. As my right hon. and learned Friend the Member for Monklands, East (Mr. Smith) said, it will mean that British interest rates will have to be at such a level that they continue to attract the holders of sterling. If we continue to run deficits at this level, our interest rates will have to be considerably higher than those of our main rivals. Therefore, we shall have to continue to increase the level of our interest rates. We have already seen the impact of high interest rates on mortgage holders and industry. How much worse could the position become? Our higher interest rates will undermine the investment plans of industry, particularly small businesses, and cripple the prospects of British exporters.

It is quite possible, indeed highly likely, that, despite the interest rate differential, the holders of sterling will lose patience with the British economy. If that happened, our fate would be totally in the hands of the market. A run on the pound and a precipitous fall in the value of the currency would follow, with all that that could mean for the British economy. The fact that there has been considerable official intervention in the market during the past month and that our reserves fell by more than £1 billion in May, is a sign that, despite the Chancellor's propaganda, the Government are acutely aware of the risks of their policy.

I agree with the right hon. Member for Chesham and Amersham that it is entirely obvious that our current account deficit is not some benign phenomenon but a symptom of serious structural problems which, for most of the 1980s, were masked by North sea oil.

How far are British goods over-valued? The Red Book shows that, during the past two years, there has been a significant loss of competitiveness. Sooner or later there will have to be an adjustment. Even more disturbing is evidence, during the 1980s, of a growing import penetration, particularly of manufactured goods. The figures are there for all to see. We can look at the latest OECD report and listen to what the National Economic Development Office has to say. A table in the Red Book must be extremely disturbing for the Government.

I agree with the analysis of the right hon. Member for Chesham and Amersham that the recession knocked out at least 20 per cent. of British manufacturing capacity. We failed to replace that capacity with enough of the newer industries and products which can compete successfully with our industrial rivals.

As the Director General of NEDO said in his March memorandum:

"The range of products in which the UK is internationally competitive may be limited, and when demand grows as fast as in 1988 the goods British producers no longer manufacture competitively may have to be imported."

He goes on to state, in an extremely disturbing conclusion:

"if we simply cannot produce the goods we are now importing, the relief of demand pressures will only slightly improve the balance of payments."

It is an extremely pessimistic conclusion. In short, we are in danger of becoming a nation which, year in, year out, imports more than it exports. Our present policies no longer seem to pay our way in the world.

In conclusion, the balance of payment deficits matter. Sooner or later they must be brought under control and we shall need a responsible policy on demand, which we do not have at the moment. I agree with the right hon. Member for Chesham and Amersham that we need to ensure that our goods are not over-valued. I agree with my right hon. Friend the Member for Llanelli (Mr. Davies) that we ought to join the EMS. As my right hon. and learned Friend the Member for Monklands, East said, we will need more rigorous policies on the supply side.

If the Government fail to act on the balance of payments they will hand over control of the British economy to the holders of sterling. As the Chancellor well knows, they are rapidly losing confidence in the Government's handling of the economy. As my right hon. and learned Friend the Member for Monklands, East said, they are uncertain who is running the economy. Once they lose confidence in the economy, they will force on our Government and economy an adjustment in a way and at a time that could be harmful to the long-term prospects of the British economy.

7.29 pm

Mr. William Powell (Corby): The right hon. and learned Member for Monklands, East (Mr. Smith) is a jolly fellow and he hugely enjoyed himself this afternoon. He always exhibits some of the most engaging characteristics of his profession as a barrister. He has to the fullest degree the forensic skills and the analytical abilities that we would expect in a man of his profession, but, like me, he has spent far too much of his time defending criminals, and to defend criminals one has to have destructive analytical abilities. There is no necessity to put together the patient, constructive policies that are needed when holding the office of Chancellor of the Exchequer, to which the right hon. and learned Gentleman aspires.

Of course, the right hon. and learned Gentleman is a wise man, too. He knows perfectly well that he does not want to saddle himself with any of the flotsam and jetsam of the policies that emanate from the party on whose behalf he speaks. He is determined to commit himself to nothing on the future policies of a Labour Government. It was, as always from him, a class performance. He roared with laughter through most of it, and he will be taken no more seriously in the House than outside it.

I want to return to the themes of the speech of my right hon. Friend the Member for Woking (Mr. Onslow). The questions that he posed, to which we shall not get an answer today, are those from which the Labour party will be unable to run away. If the wishes of the hon. Member for Cumbernauld and Kilsyth (Mr. Hogg), who looked forward to the prospect of the return of a Labour Government, are to be fulfilled, the questions posed by my right hon. Friend the Member for Woking will have to be answered. I hold the hon. Member for Cumbernauld and Kilsyth in considerable affection, but he was clearly wrong about one thing—the imminent return of a Labour Government. At best, that is three years away. Anyone who imagines that a general election will be held in two years' time, or in just over two years' time, with any

[*Mr. William Powell*]

prospect of the Labour party winning it, is living in cloud-cuckoo-land. At best, the Opposition can hope for one about three years from today. If we have one before then, we shall not have another Labour Government in three years' time—that will be in seven or eight years' time, a very long time for the hon. Gentleman to wait. Meanwhile, real problems will have to be confronted by the party that he represents.

It is always nice to hear the right hon. Member for Llanelli (Mr. Davies). We hold him in considerable respect and affection. This decade has been a testing time for him. He has had to come to terms with some of the unpleasant and unfortunate aspects of his party's policies. As defence spokesman, and now as a commentator on economic affairs, he is always robust and independent—and he can afford to be, because his prospects of office in any future Labour Government have long since disappeared. So, from the Back Benches, he can give us the benefit of his wisdom and his commentaries on the policies being advocated by his party's Front Bench spokesmen, and very revealing they are, too.

Fundamental policy questions will have to be answered because they will be asked again and again. The right hon. and learned Member for Monklands, East said that interest rates were too high. He seemed to support a policy of high interest rates—but not quite as high as they are now—to be combined with credit controls, the nature of which he was unprepared and unable to spell out.

Mr. Allan Rogers (Rhondda): In his lengthy six-minute preamble, the hon. Gentleman has dwelt on the trivia spoken by my right hon. and learned Friend the Member for Monklands, East (Mr. Smith) and by everyone else who has participated in the debate. He has given us a wonderful commentary, but as he is a supporter of a Government who have been in power for 10 years, will he comment on the Government's handling of the economy instead of discussing this destructive trivia?

Mr. Powell: The point made by the hon. Gentleman which will be noted most keenly was his reference to the trivia in the contribution made by the right hon. and learned Member for Monklands, East.

The Labour party will have to answer questions. What level of inflation is acceptable? What level of interest rate would the Opposition support? What level of public borrowing do they regard as sustainable and acceptable? What level of taxation? Are we to return to the days of restrictive practices, of overmanning and of secondary picketing? All these questions, asked by my right hon. Friend the Member for Woking, will not disappear.

Unfortunately, the hon. Member for Durham, North (Mr. Radice) is not a historian. He is an economist who has forgotten his history. What has happened in the 1980s has been the product of what happened in the 1970s, by the end of which this country had been brought to its knees. The nation, the House and the Labour party know that. In the 1980s we have had to begin the process of reconstruction. I, like many of my right hon. and hon. Friends, have seen it in my constituency. The Corby steelworks was closed by the Labour party, which brought my constituents to their knees. In the course of this decade we have had to rebuild and have done so extremely

successfully. Employment has never been as high as it is now; nor has investment. Factories are being built all the time, and training is taking place.

The right hon. and learned Member for Monklands, East mentioned the need to improve education. That was another of his light-hearted points, because every measure that has been brought forward to improve the quality and standards of education in this country has been opposed in the House by the party that he represents. Given this opposition, this "Mr. No" attitude on the part of the Labour party to any proposal designed to improve matters, the country is entitled to take note that these people are not serious about their ambition to govern.

I want to draw two matters to the attention of the House. I remember talking last year in Germany to senior executives of that country's biggest bank. I asked them what advice they were giving to their clients about placing investment. They said that there were three places in Europe in which to invest: the corridor between Munich and Stuttgart, the greater Paris area and the whole of Great Britain. They were telling their clients that the most promising place in which to invest was the whole of Great Britain. My hon. Friend the Member for Beaconsfield (Mr. Smith) referred to the Bosch investment in south Wales, and there are many other similar examples in the regions. The need for such investment in the regions has already been mentioned.

I close with another telling statistic. Shortly before he died, that great Conservative Franz Josef Strauss was in this country, analysing the difference between the German and British economies. He said that the average hourly wage in West Germany which an employer has to pay is DM31, half of which goes on wages and salaries and the rest on social insurance costs of one sort or another. The equivalent figure in Great Britain is DM21, an hour. Our competitive advantage over Germany is considerable and we must not lose that opportunity. Any glimmer of a policy that we hear from the Opposition is designed solely to destroy that competitive advantage, not to reinforce it. As long as that is so, they are not worthy of the confidence of our people.

7.39 pm

Mr. D. N. Campbell-Savours (Workington): Unlike the hon. Member for Corby (Mr. Powell), I do not wish to indulge in a harangue directed at hon. Members on the other side of the House. I wish to do as the Chancellor suggested and try to establish where there is common ground and whether we can proceed, perhaps not altogether with alternatives that I regard as ideologically acceptable, but on lines that the Government might be willing to accept in principle. We can agree that last year's current account deficit was £14·7 billion, which is 3·2 per cent. of GDP, and that we have a projected deficit this year of between £17 billion and £18 billion. We can also agree that we face a rapidly deteriorating balance of trade. Import penetration has doubled since 1970.

The Government publishes a booklet on United Kingdom overseas trade statistics, from the various sections of which one can glean the statistics about finished and semi-finished goods. One can select headings such as glass, footwear, domestic electrical goods, furniture, sports goods, beer and coal. I found today that there are even statistics about condoms, on which Britain has a substantial trade deficit, a major part of which is due to our European partners. Exports rose 10·1 times over the period 1970-88 and in the crucial area of consumer items exports rose 9·6 times. In the same period, imports rose 35 times. All the figures are identified in the overseas trade statistics.

The Government believe that they can offset some of the deficit by way of invisibles, although they now have to admit that there has been a substantial reduction in the invisible balance over the three years since 1986, from £8·5 billion in 1986 to £5·9 billion in 1988, so the Government can no longer depend on that area despite the substantial investment which took place overseas following the abolition of exchange controls.

How can we reduce the manufacturing deficit? I have a constructive proposition for the Government which does not necessarily require major ideological compromise. It depends on the private sector and I hope that the Government will seriously consider it. We should have a sectoral approach to the restoration of the manufacturing economy and it should be achieved by pump priming—what Walter Eltis, director-general of the National Economic Development Office recently referred to as "product loss areas". I am sure that the Minister knows what that means.

I wish to consider an area that I knew many years ago as an example of where this could work. Before I came to the House I was a clock manufacturer and one of my interests in clock manufacturing, over and above my commercial interests, was to examine what was going on in the electronic quartz clock movement market. I came to the House in 1979 and within two years the only British manufacturing plant of electronic quartz clock movements in the whole United Kingdom was in Wishaw, in the constituency of my hon. Friend the Member for Motherwell, South (Dr. Bray) and it faced closure. The factory was owned by Smith's Industries and I and my hon. Friend the Member for Motherwell, South went to the Department of Trade and Industry to argue the case for sectoral support. We did that on the basis that it was the only remaining quartz clock manufacturer in the whole of the United Kingdom, but Ministers turned us down. At the time, about eight years ago, I told the Minister that if that firm closed, within a few years the whole market would be dominated by electronic quartz clock movements made in Germany, Switzerland, Japan and France.

As a result of checks that we have made in the past few days I can now tell Ministers that every quartz clock movement in the United Kingdom, except for those fitted to Metamec clocks which are made by a firm in Norfolk which produces its own movements but only for its own finished products, is now imported from the continent. The manufacturers are Ahttori from Japan, Jungans, Hannart, Staiger and Kienzle from Germany, and those firms totally dominate the United Kingdom market. Anyone who goes through the trade statistics in the way that I have suggested will find that that has happened in many sectors of British industry.

Is it not in the national interest to restore areas that are critical to specific industries? I have mentioned only the clock industry. Is it not wise to examine what has happened in that area in the way that the National Economic Development Office used to do under the Labour Government? Working parties used to examine and define the area of loss and then set out with the National Enterprise Board and other organisations to try to promote the redevelopment of investment. Today

NEDO has 16 working groups, but they only make recommendations. They advise manufacturing industry, whereas previously they were in a stronger position in terms of investment decisions.

At very little expense, the Government could set up an industrial reorganisation corporation. Only civil servants would be involved and they could identify, in the same way as NEDO did in the 1970s, product loss areas where there should be manufacturing to substitute for imports. They could identify sponsors in the private sector. In the case of clock manufacture, they could go to a company such as Metamec which has experience of movement manufacture in the United Kingdom and say, "We want to re-establish a foothold in this market because almost 100 per cent. of the market is dominated by imports." The company could be offered substantial sectoral grant support of perhaps as much as 50 per cent.

I add no rider that it should be a regionally based industry, because I understand that the Government want to rely on more market-oriented policies to develop the regions. My proposal is simply that the Government adopt a sectoral approach with substantial grant aid to re-establish our position in markets that are subject to heavy import penetration. The sectoral sponsors would raise the other 50 per cent. of the capital necessary to set up the plants. They could put up perhaps half the 50 per cent. by borrowing, which might be a requirement of the Government. The companies could go to the markets to raise money for sectoral developments and might even float on the stock exchange in the same way as Eurotunnel, whose offer was speculative.

Market penetration targets could be set by the industrial reorganisation corporation with the private sector sponsors. Apart from the grant assistance to get the companies off the ground, there would be little further public support. The enterprise would be totally privately controlled with no state interference apart from endeavouring through the corporation to establish some sort of target arrangement for markets. The Minister may say that that will not work. I talked to Metamec today about it. The company's managing director, Mr. Herbert Hanna, told me that the company tried to do that three years ago and had to put up all the money. It spent £2 million developing a plant to produce the movement that I have mentioned, but because of the absence of a United Kingdom sectoral grant the company simply could not compete.

Sectoral grant is available in West Germany, which also has research and development grants and grants from the local authorities and the Länder Parliaments in Germany through regional industrial committees. The technology went in but Metamec was not able to effect the model changes necessary to keep pace with German advances in technology.

Mr. Hanna told me that if a private sector offer were made to him, substantial grant was available for putting down the equipment, and he had to go to the market to raise a quarter of the capital required, it would have an almost immediate effect on Britain's market for clock movements. He said that within a matter of months the company would be hiring another 250 people in the Norfolk area. He knows that all that the British market wants is a cheap movement that works, is reliable and is internationally competitive. We are talking about tight competitive conditions where Kienzle can sell a quartz

[*Mr. D. N. Campbell-Savours*]

movement into the United Kingdom market for as little as 85p per unit. Mr. Hanna said that Britain would otherwise inevitably fail to get back into that area of the market.

It is not only in the clock sector that that can take place. I have identified a series of sectors in which the market is almost entirely dominated by imports. The market for trainer shoes is almost entirely dominated by imports, except for high quality products such as New Balance, which has a factory in my constituency. Why cannot we produce such goods here in the United Kingdom when everyone knows that, as the hon. Member for Corby (Mr. Powell) accepted, labour is cheaper in the United Kingdom?

One can cite the wire and cable sector; major parts of the chemical industry; photographic materials; cameras; watch movements; hosiery; the white cloth used by most cloth manufacturers when they print their fabrics ready for the market; video equipment and personal computers, which invariably carry a British name such as Amstrad but which, when one looks at the back of the machine, have been made in Japan, Korea or some other country in the far east. In office machinery and data equipment import penetration stands at 93 per cent. In man-made fibres it is 38 per cent.; in instrument engineering, 58 per cent.; in electrical and electronic engineering 49 per cent.; and in the boot and shoe and leather goods trade it is also 49 per cent.

If Britain adopts a sectoral approach, based on private sector investment in the way that I suggest, the Government's ideological position will not be compromised. That is the only way to interfere directly in manufacturing industry to reduce substantially the trade surplus. We cannot rely on market factors any more. We need positive intervention.

7.51 pm

Mr. David Shaw (Dover): My constituents want me to thank the Government and my right hon. Friend the Chancellor for the successful way in which the economy has been managed. They remember the way in which the economy was managed by Labour. Now we have lower inflation and people such as pensioners have benefited. Now we have lower unemployment and the young and the school leavers have benefited. Now that Britain has the highest employment in its history, women have benefited, with more job opportunities than they ever had under Labour. Now we have higher wages from which nurses and other deserving people have benefited, as well as all wage earners. In other words, we have all benefited from the Government's policies.

It is true that interest rates are not at the level that we would like, but they have increased in all major industrialised countries. In those countries inflation has been increasing. For example, Dr. Richard Rahn of the United States chamber of commerce has shown that inflation in the United States of America has risen from 5·1 per cent. to 6·4 per cent. The United States Federal Reserve has tightened its monetary policy still further, even to the point of risking recession. Britain has no choice but to stay competitive and to squeeze out inflation by increasing interest rates. The Government have been right to push the regrettably necessary policy of higher interest rates in order to achieve a more successful economy during the 1990s.

The Opposition make much fuss about the current account deficit. That is strange, since foreign currency assets in Britain are at an all-time high, equivalent to some 10 years of deficits at the current level of deficit. Why do Labour make so much fuss about that deficit? It may be to hide their own mistakes. Labour killed our manufacturing industry during the 1970s, when low productivity was encouraged and when low investment was necessarily accompanied by low profits, as any Opposition Member must realise. Without high profits there cannot be high investment.

In 1976 there was a surplus in motor cars and accessories because that account and the balance of trade in it ran well. By 1979, when the Labour party left office, there was a deficit in motor cars and accessories because the amalgamation of companies such as British Leyland failed. Labour's industrial policy had failed. The Industrial Reorganisation Corporation and other Labour policies on planning the economy and industrial markets had failed.

Now, in 1989, it is likely that a major improvement in the balance of trade in manufacturing is on its way. We have new car plants. Nissan is producing record levels of cars. [*Interruption.*] If the hon. Member for Hackney, South and Shoreditch (Mr. Sedgemore) wishes to intervene, I shall be delighted to give way to him.

Mr. Brian Sedgemore (Hackney, South and Shoreditch): I was just thinking that it is possible to argue a case chronologically. The hon. Gentleman was talking about the so-called devastation of our manufacturing industry between 1975 and 1979 and then he leapt from 1979 to 1989. Would he care to work through the figures from 1979 to 1981?

Mr. Shaw: I am delighted to point out that one of the Government's great successes has been to reduce employment in manufacturing industry by some 2 million people, leaving manufacturing industry in a much more efficient state than it was under Labour. Hon. Members must accept that 5 million people in Britain are now producing more than were 7 million in manufacturing industry under Labour. That is success. British industry has higher productivity now than it did under Labour. [*Interruption.*] I am confident that I am driving my points home because of the reaction of Opposition Members.

We heard earlier about the Labour party's new policy document, but the one group of people who were not prepared to talk about it was Labour Members. It was my right hon. Friend the Chancellor who had to dissect the document. I note that the Labour party's new policies take us back not to the 1970s, but to the 1960s. I remember that in the days of Harold Wilson the Labour party was long on promises and short on answers. That certainly seems to describe today's new policy document from the Labour party.

The Labour party now promises us low interest rates. It believes that we can isolate ourselves from the rest of the world. It believes that if the rest of the world has high interest rates we can somehow have low interest rates. Many years ago King Canute tried to hold back the waters but he failed, just as those who try to hold back the waters of high interest rates in the rest of the world will fail. [*Interruption.*] I have already given way to the hon.

Member for Hackney, South and Shoreditch. I shall be delighted to do so again if he has anything useful to say, but he did not previously so it is probably not worth giving way to him again.

Increased public expenditure is still being put across by the Labour party as being the answer to our problems. We do not have the problems that the Labour Government had. We do not need cures for increased public expenditure. They did not work in the 1970s. The Labour party did not have the money to increase public expenditure in the 1970s. It is amazing that the Labour party should still believe that public expenditure can be increased and that interest rates will remain low. How can we issue more debt to finance increased public expenditure and yet reduce interest rates? If someone has to borrow money, they have to pay high interest rates. That market fact cannot be bucked. The Labour party's policy is a contradiction.

I regret that the hon. Member for Islington, South and Finsbury (Mr. Smith) is not here today. I often listen with interest to his speeches. Earlier this year he said that we must have lower interest rates and a more stable and competitive exchange rate. If interest rates are lower than market conditions require, foreigners will not hold pounds and we would have to devalue. Therefore, low interest rates, cannot, as he says, go hand in hand with stable and competitive exchange rates. Indeed, stable and competitive exchange rates cannot go together because if an exchange rate is stable it is unlikely to be competitive and if it is competitive it is not likely to be stable. The more one examines Labour's policies——

Mr. Tony Worthington (Clydebank and Milngavie): Will the hon. Gentleman repeat that?

Mr. Shaw: I am sorry if the hon. Gentleman, like many Opposition Members, cannot follow the economic facts of life. The more one examines Labour's policies the more one finds that they are based on the mathematics of wishful thinking. It is a very special version of mathematics, taught only at the Walworth road school of policy review.

The Opposition claim they have a new economic policy but the right hon. and learned Member for Monklands, East (Mr. Smith) again and again refused invitations earlier in the debate to outline Labour's proposals. Why did he decline to tell the people of this country about them? We must conclude that it was because those policies are not capable of being argued in rational debate on the Floor of this House. That point was proven when the Leader of the Opposition ran away from his BBC interview on economics. What kind of a man runs away from an interview on economics? The Opposition claim that they now understand competition and the market, but I do not believe that they have an economic policy that can compete with that of the Government. I shall support the Government amendment in the Lobby tonight.

8 pm

Mr. Doug Hoyle (Warrington, North): One of the problems we face in this debate is not knowing how long the Chancellor will be in his job. We do not know when that dreaded knock will come and he will be ushered into No. 10 and told that he is on his way. It is difficult to propose any long-term solutions to a person who may have only a short-term contract.

The Chancellor and the Prime Minister both have strong views on keeping inflation down, but we hear nothing these days of zero inflation. It is no longer bedtime reading for the young in every Conservative household. It has disappeared out of the window. When the Minister replies, I shall be pleased to hear when that target will be achieved.

We do know that inflation is higher in this country than any other in the EEC except Greece and Portugal. There seems to be some complacency about our record by comparison with the rest of the Community, with the Government saying that all is right, but this country is paying a very high price for having the Government in office. My right hon. and learned Friend the Member for Monklands, East (Mr. Smith) was right to point out that the failure to invest on the supply side is now catching us out. British industry continues to lag behind because of failure to invest. It also faces high interest charges and rising costs as a consequence of gas privatisation and the proposed privatisation of the power industry. British industry costs are far higher than those of its competitors in Germany or France, which makes domestic companies even more uncompetitive than they were.

The Department of Trade and Industry and even the noble Lord the Secretary of State himself talk only of a venture economy. We get from them tinsel rather than substance. To hear Conservative Back Benchers, one would think that Labour was in office, because Government Members spend all their time attacking Labour policies while not one of them gives an iota of information about what they would do.

We are heading for a record Community trade deficit of £18 billion, yet the Government's only response is to raise the interest rate time and time again. It now stands at 14 per cent. and all the signs are that it will rise to 15 per cent., which will make a bad situation even worse. Britain's metal industries are falling into deficit, and we shall shortly be left with only aerospace. When a Labour Government were in power, our engineering industry was in the black. Today, the trade deficit in engineering products has deteriorated by 30 per cent., rising from a deficit of £8·9 billion in 1988 to £11·6 billion in 1989.

In the years 1985 to 1988, for which the hon. Member for Dover (Mr. Shaw) claimed a special degree of Government success, the deficit increased by 600 per cent. Does he call that a success story? Our trade deficit with West Germany is a calamity. Last year it totalled £845 million, which is the biggest deficit with any of our trading partners. The deficit trebled between 1979 and 1988, yet Conservative Members have the cheek and impudence to speak of that as a success story. I should not like to experience a Conservative failure.

Another Government ploy, particularly from 1979 onwards, was to say, "It does not matter much about the metal-bashing industries because the sunrise industries such as information technology will be our saviour." Information technology was the in thing which would save us all, but our IT trade deficit is rising year by year. I sit on a Committee that has just produced a report on information technology. Its advice to the Department of Trade and Industry was ignored because it would have interfered with the market. As long as we rely on market forces alone, we shall never recover from our IT trade deficit or have any hope that information technology will be our saviour. The situation will only get worse.

[*Mr. Doug Hoyle*]

Whenever we spell out to the Government what ought to be done, they make no response and refuse to face the facts. I do not know where the hon. Member for Dover gets his figures about motor vehicles. Last year, we imported from the Common Market £6 billion more in motor vehicles that we exported.

Mr. David Shaw: I was making the point that we enjoyed a surplus in 1976 but suffered a small deficit in 1979. I do not deny that the deficit increased, but for the first time the trend is reversing. That has been shown up in the Oxford Economic Forecasting studies. By the mid-1990s, we may return to a trade surplus on motor vehicles as a consequence of the new efficiency that will come with Nissan and Toyota. That Government achievement cannot be denied.

Mr. Hoyle: I just wonder where the hon. Gentleman lives. I think his problem is that he gazes out to the Channel without looking at the mainland behind him. It is remarkable that the hon. Gentleman can make such a statement. I repeat that we suffered a record £6 billion deficit in our trade with the EEC.

Mr. Calum Macdonald (Western Isles): The hon. Member for Dover (Mr. Shaw) is really saying that after 10 years of pandering to British management, the Government have given up on it and now rely upon foreign management to get Britain out of the mess that it is in.

Mr. Hoyle: Absolutely. The Government's problem is that they have no faith in Britain. It does not matter who owns our industries. They just hope that the Japanese will capture the European market for Britain and rescue our record £6 billion trade deficit with the EEC that the Government created.

It is nonsense for the Government to continue to claim a success story. One of the consequences of the Government's present policy will be that unemployment will rise again, especially in the areas represented by Opposition Members. Barclay's Economic Review estimates that there will be a 200,000 rise in unemployment, but, I think that that estimate is probably rather low.

The Government are producing slogans instead of remedies. As has been said, the problem is that the Government are running a casino economy. They are like gamblers who are drunk on the roulette wheel. All they are doing is throwing chip after chip into the casino. We can no longer afford the luxury of this Government, nor can we afford their incompetence.

Several Hon. Members *rose——*

Mr. Deputy Speaker (Sir Paul Dean): Order. I am very grateful to those hon. Members who have co-operated so well in observing the 10-minute limit on speeches. The wind-up speeches are expected to begin at 9.20 pm and five hon. Members still wish to speak. If my mathematics is correct, that means that I can now relax the 10-minute limit on speeches, but I hope that hon. Members will bear in mind that five hon. Members hope to speak between now and 9.20 pm.

8.11 pm

Mr. Kenneth Hind (Lancashire, West): The hon. Member for Warrington, North (Mr. Hoyle) said that Conservative Members have criticised the Opposition. I join in those criticisms. The Opposition introduced the debate to criticise Government policy. National politics today is essentially a two-horse race. The Conservative and Labour parties agree that the centre parties are a broken force: therefore the public look to the two major parties for policies for the future. It does not come well from the Opposition simply to ask what the Government will do when recently they have produced a detailed document for public examination setting out what they would do if they were in power. Therefore, it is fair for us to say to the Opposition that we accept that there are problems in the economy, but we and the public are entitled to know what they would do if they were in power. We have repeatedly asked that question in today's debate.

The right hon. and learned Member for Monklands, East (Mr. Smith) opened the debate by making a number of points that revealed the weakness of the Opposition. But what are the strengths of the Government's present position? In the past four years, unemployment has fallen by 1 million. Since 1982, more jobs have been created in Britain than in the rest of Europe put together. Inflation has fallen to an average of 5 per cent. per year, there have been major reductions in taxation and an average annual growth in industry of 3·4 per cent. We have the highest productivity growth in the OECD except Japan. The growth in small businesses has mushroomed, creating 1,300 new businesses a week. Company profits are higher than they have been for 20 years. Despite the criticisms from the Opposition, manufacturing industry has grown by 7 per cent. in the past two years—twice the growth in the economy. That is a major achievement.

The right hon. and learned Member for Monklands, East leads the Opposition charge and states that what is required is new investment in training, research and development and new machinery. I agree with him. We all agree on that, but we recognise that to close the gap between our imports and exports we need to increase the capacity of British industry. Our industrial base has to grow. My right hon. Friend the Chancellor of the Exchequer has encouraged that. In 1988-89, the last year for which detailed figures are available, there was a 14·5 per cent. increase in investment in British industry and we are now witnessing record levels of investment, achieving precisely what the right hon. and learned Member for Monklands, East wants us to achieve.

A large proportion of our trade deficit is created by new machinery which is imported only to increase the British industrial base to close the gap between imports and our exports. In 1987 half our trade deficit was made up of imports of machinery into the United Kingdom. British industry has the confidence to expand and to create jobs, and that is a major achievement.

Mr. Worthington: I wish to ask the hon. Gentleman a simple question. Why is capital machinery being imported?

Mr. Hind: We have to go back a fair number of years. I regret that much of our manufacturing industry was killed off in the 1960s and 1970s and cannot easily be replaced. Anyone who knows anything about economics knows that, at the first sign of an upswing in any economy, the manufacturers of machinery benefit first. However, we do not have as big a machinery industry as we should like, so we have to import machinery, but we have the beginning of the upswing and the about-turn that will help to close our trade gap.

The major enemy that the Government face is inflation. I fully support the line taken by my right hon. Friend the Chancellor of the Exchequer when he put that at the top of the problems that we face. He is right to attack that problem as his first priority. There is pressure on the pound at the moment because of the improvement in the American economy and external pressure. There is an increase in inflation across the board in the G7 countries. It is no good Opposition Members saying that it is not happening elsewhere. Of course it is happening elsewhere and that is recognised, but unfortunately we in Britain have a greater dose of the disease than we should like, but we know that the cure lies in introducing higher interest rates to suppress demand and reduce inflation.

No one should think that the Conservative party likes high interest rates. No one who has worked in any industry wants high interest rates. We can see the damage that they do and I am sure that my right hon. and hon. Friends agree that they are a short-term measure which will improve our financial performance and help to close our trade gap, dampen down demand and reduce imports. That solution is working now. Mortgage inflation is beginning to reduce.

The Opposition suggested introducing credit controls, particularly for credit cards, but that is such a small part of the problem, representing less than 5 per cent. of debt, that it will not tackle the problem. It will take time, but the economy is stronger than it has been for many years and that has been shown by the winds that it has faced in the past few years—black Monday, the crash in the world markets, the fall in the value of sterling a few years ago and various problems created in the economy by the fall in oil prices. The British economy has been strong enough to weather those storms and will be strong enough to weather the problems that we are facing at present.

The Opposition have offered no solutions. The right hon. Member for Llanelli (Mr. Davies) is on record in *The Independent* saying that the Opposition have no idea how to deal with inflation. One of the Labour party's advisers was quoted in *The Independent* as saying that it has no idea what to do about inflation. The Leader of the Opposition admitted in an interview with James Naughtie of the BBC, which has been hidden away in the archives and which we will never hear, that he did not know what to do about it. He said, as have Opposition Members throughout the debate, that the Government are in power, so, "Let us see what they can do about it." The British public are entitled to ask the Labour party what it would do if it were in power.

In an interview this morning, the right hon. and learned Member for Monklands, East ducked a question about control of sterling. He could not speculate on the appropriate level of the pound because he does not have an idea what it should be. The Opposition have no policy to deal with the pound, which is an essential part of managing the economy.

The Labour party has produced a document outlining its policies for the future. It clearly emerges from it that the Labour party is the party of higher taxation. It proposes to return to the old remedies such as raising taxation and renationalisation. The right hon and learned Member for Monklands, East ducked my question when I challenged

him in an intervention about how new investment will be financed. It will be financed using ratepayers' money, by raising taxes and using that increased taxation to intervene in industry. Higher taxation, intervention and failure to control inflation and the pound will increase inflation and make a bigger mess of the economy than the Labour party has done previously. We all remember what a terrible mess it made of the economy in 1976.

The abolition of the upper earnings limit on national insurance contributions will make anyone earning more than £17,000 a year worse off. The married couple's allowance will gradually be withdrawn, making 12 million couples worse off as they lose indexation. Labour has taken a step backwards from the clear-cut pledge to restore cuts in the basic rate of income tax. It is trying to conceal its intention by talking about an income tax regime of many different rates. The right hon. and learned Member for Monklands, East admitted that any reform of income tax along the lines proposed will make some basic-rate taxpayers worse off.

We have asked the Labour party to cost its programme. It ducks the question because it knows that it will inevitably lead to higher rates of tax, increased inflation and lower standards of living and show that they are not in a fit state to control the economy or run the country.

I should like to mention a matter to which my hon. Friend the Member for Dover (Mr. Shaw) referred. We must consider expert forecasts of the performance of the British economy. The survey by Oxford Economic Forecasting, which was published on 31 May, predicts that manufacturing industry will boom throughout the next decade, generating thousands of new jobs. By 1995, manufacturing output is expected to be 60 per cent. higher than today. Car production is forecast to rise from 1·25 million today to 2 million by 1995, helped by the dramatically improved efficiency and profitability of United Kingdom car plants. Such profitability will run right through the British economy.

The Chancellor of the Exchequer and Conservative Members accept that mistakes have been made in the past, but the right policy to correct the economy is being pursued, despite the criticisms of the Opposition. The Government do and mean what they say. At least we are prepared to say to the public, "This is where we stand, and this is what we shall do," unlike the Opposition, making it clear that we are fit to govern this country and that they are not.

8.25 pm

Mr. Tony Worthington (Clydebank and Milngavie): I wish to return to the central problem—the fact that Britain is not paying its way.

Last year we ran a current account deficit of £14·7 billion, and it seems that this year's deficit will be £18 billion to £20 billion. I treat the problem seriously because the Chancellor has always done so with other countries. A few years ago he lectured the Americans about a deficit of 3 per cent. of gross domestic product, but our deficit is now 3·2 per cent. of GDP. The Chancellor lectured debtor nations, whether they were developing or developed countries, when they were in deficit. He never visits Japan or Germany and says, "How weak your economy is—it is in surplus." Strangely, our economy is supposed to be the only strong economy with a record deficit.

[*Mr. Tony Worthington*]

It is difficult to find a part of the world with which we are not running a deficit. We are not running a deficit with north America, but the surplus is falling. We are not in deficit on oil, but that surplus is also falling. The reason why we are in deficit is that after 10 years of Tory Government we cannot compete effectively with other countries. When Tory history books are written, the chapter on the period between 1979 and 1981 is always missing.

Absurd reliance has been placed on service industries. When Labour Members said that we needed manufacturing industry to survive, we were criticised by the Financial Secretary to the Treasury and others for concentrating only on that sector. The chickens are coming home to roost and what we have been saying for many years about the Government's neglect of manufacturing industry is being proved correct. My hon. Friend the Member for Workington (Mr. Campbell-Savours) said earlier that we must play a more interventionist role in manufacturing industry, perhaps on a sectoral basis. It is certainly difficult to see how market forces can cause manufacturing industry to re-emerge.

We run deficits on almost everything. One would have thought that we produce a lot of potatoes, yet we export £18 million-worth and import £58 million-worth. The picture is similar for sports goods.

Mr. Macdonald: And condoms.

Mr. Worthington: Condoms are mentioned yet again, which reflects some hon. Members' obsession with them, but there is only a £3 million deficit there. Last year, we exported £64 million-worth of coal but imported £427 million-worth. Twenty years ago, no one would have believed that we would be running a £24 million deficit on carbonated water.

In the 18 years from 1970 to 1988 there was a 23-fold increase in imports of capital goods and a 35-fold increase in imports of consumer items. In those 18 years there was less than a tenfold increase in exports. There was a 78-fold increase in car imports but only a sixfold increase in car exports. We assemble cars but although the wages are earned in this country the profit and the control are elsewhere.

We can no longer rely on oil as a surplus. The surplus in 1985 was £8·1 billion but by 1988 it had been reduced to £2·3 billion. We can no longer rely on invisible exports. In 1986 they amounted to £8·5 billion, but by 1988 they had fallen to £5·8 billion. Earlier we were told that we need not worry about the deficit because we were importing capital goods. We are indeed importing them—we have ceased to manufacture capital goods.

The hon. Member for Corby (Mr. Powell) pointed out that the average wage in Germany is 31 deutschmarks per hour and that the average wage in this country is 21 deutschmarks per hour. He said that we had a competitive edge. It is strange that Germany is beating us hollow on wages as well as having all the social benefits, extra training, better pensions and nurseries for children that we are denied.

We had the clearest confession from the hon. Member for Corby that the Government's strategy is to seek a low-wage economy, but the people do not want a low-wage economy. They want an economy with high wages, high education standards, better research and development. They want a Government who believe in the future of the United Kingdom as an economy which can compete with countries like Germany.

The speech of the hon. Member for Corby reminded us of the words a few months ago of the director general of the CBI, who said that a combination of British productivity and German social costs would be lethal for this country. He was right. That is the legacy that the Government have given us.

It is essential that we abandon our non-interventionist strategy in industry. There are no grounds for thinking that work will return to many areas simply by leaving things to market forces. Capital remains the most portable of the factors of production and it can go anywhere in the world. Labour has to stay here; it should stay here and should have a good life. Certainly we need far more investment in education and training. We should abandon the pretence that the employment training scheme is anything other than a means of lowering unemployment figures. It is an insult to the people to pretend that the employment training scheme will provide adequate training for people to compete in the modern world.

We have a capital-oriented economy on the Government Benches. We need an economy much more oriented to the needs of the people. There has been much reference in the House to the creation of jobs. Jobs may have been created in some parts of the country but in Strathclyde, the region that I represent, total employment had fallen in September 1988 to 767,000, a decline of 10,000 jobs since September 1987, and the number of jobs in manufacturing industry had fallen by 162,000, or 49·7 per cent. Since 1979, the last peak in the trade cycle, Strathclyde's total employment is estimated to have fallen by 220,000 or 22·3 per cent. Strathclyde's share of employment in the United Kingdom has fallen from 4·3 per cent. to 3·5 per cent. since 1979. That is the economy within which I live and work. That is the reality of life there and in Glasgow, Central, where male unemployment in Bridgeton and Dalmarnock is 38·2 per cent.

All that the Government promise us is that there will be a decline in the economy over the next few years while their high interest rates continue to take effect. The Government have to recognise that the only hope for many parts of the country is for them to abandon dependence on market forces. They must realise that in area after area we have no products to sell and that the only way to have products is by taking a much more interventionist stance.

When we lost television manufacturing to the Japanese, we then lost video, compact discs and all the developments that occurred after that. My hon. Friend the Member for Workington (Mr. Campbell-Savours) referred to the knock-on effect of the loss of production of quartz digital mechanisms for clocks, and showed how we have lost products in one area after another. We must abandon reliance upon market structure and take a much more interventionist role.

8.37 pm

Mr. Tim Janman (Thurrock): I congratulate the Chancellor, the Government and my hon. Friends on the Front Bench on the many positive aspects of the economic advance that we have made over the last decade. Deregulation, lower taxation, privatisation and the control of public spending—all the things that the Labour party never sought to do when in power—have led to increased productivity, investment and profitability in British industry, and to a longer period of sustained real growth in the economy than we have seen for many decades, whereas in the past we were continually in stop-go cycles.

All that could be undermined if inflation is not brought under control. It is vital to regain full discipline of the money supply. I want to concentrate on one concern—that broad money is no longer targeted and has not been targeted for some time; broad money is no longer under control. I acknowledge that narrow money has been brought under control, although clearly it was out of control until fairly recently. The December 1988 increase in M0 was the biggest monthly increase since 1979. Recent figures show that the interest rate increases, which the Chancellor was correct to bring in, have been working and that narrow money growth has been tumbling.

That is shown by some recent statistics. In the year to January, narrow money increased by 7·4 per cent., in the year to April, it increased only by 5·7 per cent. and in the six months to April, narrow money has been increasing at an annual rate of only 0·9 per cent. That is one of the key ingredients in bringing inflation under control and getting it out of our economic system.

My concern is that broad money is not under control. If we look at the rates of growth in M3 and M4, we see that those rates of growth are far too high. In the 12 months to April this year, M3 grew at 20·6 per cent. Over the six months to April, it grew, annualised, at 19·1 per cent., and over the three months to April, it grew, annualised, at 18·8 per cent. The equivalent figures for M4 money supply growth show 18·1 per cent., 16·7 per cent. and 20 per cent. increases.

The figures for narrow money are welcome and, if anything, narrow money growth over the past few months has been slightly too tight compared to current and expected general growth in the economy. But the M3 growth and the M4 growth are not acceptable. Those figures are the result of printing money last year to buy deutschmarks and of attempts to fix or control exchange rates by allowing the commercial banks to throw money at the problem. The strength of sterling should not be a major consideration in counter-inflation policy. It should be the result of counter-inflation policy achieved through sound money policies, which we have still not wholly achieved or certainly have not been achieving for the past few years.

There was a considerable time after 1979 when we were well on the way to achieving sound money and well on the way to achieving zero inflation. Our policies achieved an inflation rate of less than 3 per cent. in mid-1986, when inflation reached a trough of 2·4 per cent. Sceptics will say that broad money is not important. However, taking into account the longer time lags that exist, the M4/retail price index relationship is clear.

I want to go through some figures for the period from 1972 to the present, which clearly show that there is a relationship between broad money and inflation, albeit not quite as tight or with such short time lags as with narrow money. In 1972 and 1973, the average increase in broad money on the M4 measure was 22 per cent. From January 1974 to August 1975, inflation increased from 12 per cent. to 26·9 per cent. During 1974, broad money growth was reversed and it went down to a trough of 12 per cent., which resulted, in July 1976, in inflation coming back

down to 12·9 per cent. During 1975, with the election of a Socialist Government, we inevitably saw an irresponsible increase in broad money supply growth——

Mr. Bryan Gould (Dagenham): The election was in 1974.

Mr. Janman: I am quite aware that the election was in October 1974, but in 1975, the Labour Government had already escalated broad money supply growth to 16 per cent. That increase resulted in inflation peaking in June 1977 at 17·7 per cent. During 1977, as a result of the International Monetary Fund coming in, broad money supply was again reduced to a trough of 11 per cent. growth on an annualised basis and this worked through to produce a reduction in inflation to 7·4 per cent. in June 1978. During 1978, while inflation was coming down, broad money supply again reached a peak growth rate of 18 per cent., which in turn, in May 1980, produced an inflation rate of 21·9 per cent.

During 1982, after this Government's heroic Budget in 1981, broad money again reached a trough of 13 per cent. in annualised growth terms and this resulted, in May 1983, in inflation coming down to a low of 3·7 per cent. In more recent years, between 1983 and 1986, broad money, on the M4 criteria, grew between 13 per cent. and 14 per cent. and that resulted in inflation between 1984 and 1987 averaging 4·7 per cent. The disturbing news is that, between the fourth quarter of 1987 and the fourth quarter of 1988 inclusive, broad money has been allowed to creep up to a growth range of 16 per cent. to 18·5 per cent., which has unfortunately resulted in an inflation rate of about 8 per cent. in April 1989.

I am not saying that narrow money is not important, because it is probably more important than broad money, but I am trying to show that broad money is also an important consideration. If we take snapshots of two periods in the middle and late 1980s, we can see that that is the case. Between the fourth quarter of 1984 and the fourth quarter of 1985, the annualised rates of broad money varied between 12·8 per cent. and 13·8 per cent. The equivalent figures for narrow money were 5·6 per cent. and 3·3 per cent. In 1986, allowing of course, for a time lag, that resulted in inflation coming down to 3·4 per cent., with the lowest figure in the middle of 1986 being 2·4 per cent.—the lowest figure for about 20 years, which was a fantastic achievement at that time.

If we now look at the 1987-88 picture, we see that between the fourth quarter of 1987 and the fourth quarter of 1988, broad money grew at a rate of between 15·3 per cent. and 18·6 per cent. and narrow money has been allowed to increase to growth rates of between 4·2 and 8·5 per cent. over that same period of five quarters. That has resulted in the current inflation rate of 8 per cent. and rising.

From those figures it is clear that we can conclude that not only is narrow money supply important in looking at inflationary trends and seeing what is going to happen in the future, but so is broad money. Broad money targets, preferably M4 targets, should again be set and achieved, although I take the view that those broad money targets can be more liberal than they otherwise would need to be if narrow money is under control. If we go back to having targets both for broad money and narrow money, and try to achieve and be seen to achieve those targets, I am confident that that will give a signal to the financial

[*Mr. Janman*]

markets that the Government are serious about maintaining sound money and about attempting to achieve 0 per cent. inflation.

There is an article in *The Guardian* today in which several hundred words are printed to try to show that there is no connection or no particular relationship between either narrow money or broad money and inflation, but the graph printed at the end of the article shows exactly the opposite. The graph shows a clear relationship between narrow money and the retail prices index, and with a time lag, with broad money. The figures show that to achieve zero per cent. inflation, we need to bring down broad money growth to not more than 10 to 11 per cent. per annum and narrow money, on which we have already perhaps gone slightly further than we need to, should be brought down to an annualised rate of no more than 1 to 2 per cent. growth at present.

This particular aspect of economic policy, about which this evening's debate has given me an opportunity to speak, is a matter about which I have some concern and which I would ask my right hon. Friend the Chief Secretary to review. It is not a matter about which one should be dogmatic and there are no simplistic solutions. If we look at the trends and the figures, and the fact that over the past few years we have ditched broad money targets, whereas for the first four or five years in office after 1979 we had such targets, it is clear that to achieve that worthy target of zero per cent. inflation, we need to keep high interest rates for as long as we need to. We need to allow exchange rates to float freely. We should encourage the Bank of England to sell securities to the banks to mop up that 7 or 8 per cent. of broad money that needs mopping up.

When considering the tenor of our economic policy and all the measurements upon which our economic success can be judged, it is ludicrous for the Opposition to deny that the past 10 years have brought this country excellent economic success. It is even more ludicrous for them to snipe at the Government's achievements when clearly, from the leadership of the Labour party downwards, Labour Members have no realistic alternative to put in its place and no understanding of how they can even try to find an alternative. We must consider having both broad and narrow money targets. If we do that, we shall have policies that will achieve the target, which we all want, of sustained zero inflation.

8.50 pm

Mr. John Battle (Leeds, West): One line in the Chancellor's response to our motion drew my attention —his claim that so far not a word had been said about unemployment. I was surprised that he drew attention to what might be described as the forgotten factor whenever Conservative Members participate in a debate on economic policy. I should like to focus on the forgotten factor of unemployment.

As we have commented throughout the debate, when we have a Government who have given us record interest rates and a record trade deficit, we should not forget that they have also given us a record unemployment level. It is still unacceptably high. The unemployment level represents not figures, numbers and statistics but real people who do not have jobs. It is worth reminding the House

that, according to the Government's figures, nearly 2 million people are still without work. The Unemployment Unit estimates that we should add at least 500,000 to that figure to take account of changes in methods of calculation.

There is talk about handling inflation and references have been made to the Government having the single instrument of interest rates. There is another secret, unmentionable weapon—unemployment. The Prime Minister offered the following economic advice in February 1981 to readers of *Time* magazine:

"bringing down inflation does mean that you have increasing unemployment and I don't know of any other way of doing it."

Clearly, unemployment is a weapon in the Government's armoury, although they are not anxious to stress that. However, this year's economic policy statement paragraph 3.04 in the Red Book, "Financial Statement and Budget Report 1989-90", refers to the labour market, and spells it out:

"Unemployment . . . is most unlikely to continue falling". What else can that mean, except that unemployment is expected to rise? That is the basis of the Government's economic and budget strategy.

My hon. Friend the Member for Warrington, North (Mr. Hoyle) referred to *Barclays Economic Review,* which has estimated that unemployment will increase in real terms by at least 200,000. On 21 April, the Parliamentary Under-Secretary of State for Employment was asked in a written parliamentary question when he expected

"unemployment levels will fall to the 1979 level".

He replied:

"The Department does not forecast future levels of unemployment."—[*Official Report,* 21 April 1989; Vol. 151, c. 347].

We are entitled to ask why on earth not, when it seems to be part and parcel of the Government's strategy. The country knows that since 1982 the Government's unemployment figures have been subjected to 24 changes in the method of counting and there are another four to come. According to the Government's figures, unemployment has been more than 3 million for nearly six of their years in office.

I shall draw attention to one group that is often forgotten—the long-term unemployed, who, understandably, could be the most aggrieved at the talk of the economic boom in Britain and all that we hear about economic miracle of the Government's policies. The proportion of people who have been unemployed for more than a year rose from 25 per cent. in 1979 to 41 per cent. last year. It is not that those people were in and out of jobs. They and their families were paying the long-term price for the Government's faulty economic experiments.

There are regional inequalities in the distribution of employment. The 1988 "Regional Trends" shows that the Yorkshire and Humberside region, part of which I represent, had the highest proportion of people in the United Kingdom who had been unemployed for between one and two years—17·2 per cent. That region had the second highest proportion of people who had been unemployed for between two and three years—9·4 per cent. It had the fifth highest proportion of people who had been unemployed for more than three years—22·7 per cent. Unemployment is still high in the region. It has the second highest level of unemployment generally, with more than 270,000 people still unemployed. To take a smaller area, long-term unemployment in West Yorkshire is 42 per cent.

When dealing with statistics, how often do we forget the hopelessness of the long-term unemployed? On 4 May 1980, in the *News of the World,* the Prime Minister was reported as saying:

"I could not live without work. That is what makes me so sympathetic towards those people who are unemployed. I do not know how they live without working."

Under this Government many of the long-term unemployed have had to live without work, and it seems that the Prime Minister either has forgotten her sympathy for them or is pretending that they no longer exist.

We are entitled to ask what future the Government offer to people in my constituency who are living with long-term unemployment, with no hope of employment for their children. When considering the prospects, we need look no further than the CBI quarterly report. Its industrial trends survey points out that, after a period in which manufacturing employment has risen, firms now expect to cut their work forces. No region comes out of that survey worse than my region of Yorkshire and Humberside. Commenting on the report, the *Sunday Times* said:

"it suggested that firms are still tending to cut back employment rather than make a determined effort to rein back pay. Indeed, the CBI's own evidence on skill shortages, with more than a fifth of companies regarding them as a constraint on output, suggests that many firms have no option but to meet employees' demands.

The more fundamental point was that economic behaviour still conforms to the view that there is a trade-off between unemployment and inflation. In addition, if we regard the current-account deficit as in part an outlet for inflationary pressures, there is also a trade-off between the jobless total and the trade gap."

Mr. Janman: I have no quarrel with the hon. Gentleman's genuine concern about unemployment, and it is true that at the beginning of this decade there was a period of high unemployment. Given that every Labour Government have ended their term of office with higher unemployment levels that when they took office, can the hon. Gentleman tell the House how the return of a Labour Government would improve matters?

Mr. Battle: I must make it absolutely clear that the levels of unemployment under Labour Governments were a great deal less than those under this Government.

The paper presented by the Centre for Economic Policy Research, entitled "The Thatcher Miracle", points out that the unemployment-inflation trade-off has not disappeared during the past 10 years but has simply been clouded by the existence of North sea oil. That is the key point. The centre points out that the level of unemployment required to reduce inflation—the non-accelerating inflation rate of unemployment—would have to be well above the current jobless total.

To achieve a steady rate of inflation of even 4 per cent. to 5 per cent. under current Government policies would require a higher level of unemployment. Higher unemployment levels will be inevitable in regions such as mine as a consequence of the Government's efforts to reduce inflation, yet the Government's response in a written answer was that the Department did not forecast future levels of unemployment. Perhaps they dare not do so; perhaps they are deliberately suppressing economic data. We have the right to challenge the Government on why they will not forecast the levels of unemployment that would be a consequence of their policies.

What will happen when unemployment rises? It will be much easier for employers to dismiss workers or to make them redundant, because workers' rights have been undermined through legislation to eliminate trade unions, the reduction of wages councils' minimum provisions and the removal of social security entitlements. Even during the past few weeks, the Government have introduced measures to ensure that unemployment will no longer be seen to rise because those who do not accept low paid jobs will be taken out of the social security records. Perhaps, even now, officials at the Departments of Employment and of Social Security are working at their computers trying to find programmes for new ways to conceal the unemployment figures when they begin to rise again. At the very least the Government have a duty to spell out the Labour market implications of their economic policies.

In a party political broadcast on 4 May 1977, the then Leader of the Opposition—the right hon. Member for Finchley (Mrs. Thatcher)—said:

"Sometimes I have heard it said that Conservatives have been associated with unemployment. We would have been drummed out of office if we had had this level of unemployment."

At that time unemployment stood at 1·3 million. Since then, and for every year of this Tory Government's office, the level of unemployment has been higher than 1·7 million. When the Prime Minister was Leader of the Opposition she said that a Government presiding over 1·3 million unemployed should be drummed out of office, so perhaps the time has come for her Government to be drummed out of office. Who, other than the long-term unemployed—the forgotten factor of the economy—have more right to beat that drum loudly and call upon the Prime Minister and the Chancellor not to get their act together? They manifestly cannot get their act together. Together they should go.

9.3 pm

Mr. Calum Macdonald (Western Isles): The hon. Member for Thurrock (Mr Janman), who has unfortunately left the Chamber, showed why the Conservative Government have got the economy so badly wrong over the past 10 years. The hon. Gentleman was becoming further and further lost in the clouds of monetarist mysticism with his talks of M0, M4, M25, and so on. The Conservative party used to boast that it was the party of household economics. I should love to hear the hon. Gentleman giving a speech to housewives and to hear what they made of it. The hon. Gentleman's speech was difficult to follow, but I think that the gist was that the Government had it right at the time of the big recession, but that in the past few years they had made a terrible mess of things.

While I do not wish to go over ground that has already been traversed in the debate, I cannot resist referring to the latest issue of *Business* magazine, not only for the value of its leading article but because I recall Conservative Members referring to that magazine a couple of weeks ago, citing the then leading article which was headlined:

"Born again Britain. How industry is getting it right."

[*Mr. Calum Macdonald*]

I remember well how that magazine was held aloft and waved regularly at Question Time, with Conservative Members proclaiming that industry was once again confident of the British economic miracle.

The latest issue of *Business* magazine has a different tone to its leading article. It is not "Born again Britain" but
"How Britain lost its balance"
and the first sentence of the article reads:
"Britain is gripped by a trade crisis."
There is no better illustration of the collapse in business confidence than the change in tone of *Business* magazine and its attitude towards the Government's economic policy. The magazine's latest article goes on to say that its analysis suggests
"that the country might be facing a trade crisis even more deep-seated and fundamental than recent monthly figures indicate."
In this debate various figures have been given for the different industrial sectors. It is clear that one by one they have all slipped further into deficit. What I find most telling—this has not been mentioned in the debate—is the fact that we have now slipped into deficit in the umbrella trade. I should have thought that if there was one area in which Britain could stay ahead, it was in the manufacture of umbrellas, but we are now importing £28·7 million-worth of umbrellas compared with exports worth £6·4 million. That must surely be a latter-day example of carrying coals to Newcastle.

When we examine the various regional sectors with which Britain trades, we find the same dismal tale. We are in deficit with all but two of the world's regional trading blocs, the two exceptions being the Arabian countries and North America. Amazingly, we are in deficit with the Socialist bloc. Indeed, we are in deficit with Russia. Even Mr. Gorbachev's perestroika has outstripped our Prime Minister's economic miracle.

It is important to note that the item so often pointed to in the past—our export surplus on invisibles—is no longer sufficient to keep our heads above water. Even that has decayed over the years. Whereas our surplus in invisibles was running at £8·5 billion in 1986, it slipped last year to £5·9 billion. In all those sectors we see a steady decay in Britain's economic situation, such that *Business* magazine concludes that the Government have managed to
"dig the biggest hole in Britain's economic history."
If that is the view of that magazine, it is little surprise that the financial markets are showing less confidence in the Government's performance. The key to finding our way out of the present difficulty must be to tackle the long-term underlying structural problems that the country faces.

Conservative Members regularly jump to their feet to ask what we, the Opposition, would do in this situation. It is certainly a difficult task to devise the Houdini trick that will get the Government out of the present mess. I do not believe that this is the right kind of approach. Our approach should not be to find some way of slipping out of a particular conjunction of bad figures in one month. Our approach should be one that is rigorously applied over a number of years and one which will resolve the long-term problems of the British economy.

The hon. Member for Lancashire, West (Mr. Hind) said—it was about the only point on which I agreed with him—that a solution to the present crisis would take time. It definitely will take time; there are no immediate solutions. The Government, however, have had time enough and they have only got us deeper into our economic mess and have not brought us any nearer to resolving it.

It was interesting that, when during his speech the Chancellor felt himself to be in a position of weakness, he turned to what he called some area of common ground. He said that he recognised the problems to which we have pointed, such as those in education and in training, but the point is that after 10 years of this Government and four years of the right hon. Gentleman as Chancellor we are no nearer resolving any of those problems.

My right hon. and learned Friend the Member for Monklands, East (Mr. Smith) cited the very telling example of the level of training in this country as compared with West Germany. In West Germany 70 per cent. of the working population are trained to the equivalent of having at least one O-level, whereas in this country it is 30 per cent. That is after the Government have been in office for 10 years, so it is no use Conservative Members saying that solutions take time or the Chancellor saying that he recognises the problem—the Government have had 10 years to deal with the problems and nothing has been done.

Mr. Allen: I must have misunderstood the Chancellor's remarks, because I thought that the common ground that he was seeking was between No. 11 and No. 10 Downing street, as my right hon. and learned Friend the Member for Monklands, East (Mr. Smith) elucidated.

Mr. Macdonald: I think that the Chancellor has given up on that. That is why he was hoping to strike up a friendship with my right hon. and learned Friend the Member for Monklands, East.

The policies that the Government have pursued to try to fight their way out of the economic hole that this country is in boil down largely to privatisation, reform of industrial relations and taxation policy. I do not believe that anyone could sensibly argue that privatisation has made an iota of difference to this country's competitive performance. The Conservative party has made much the same mistake that we tended to make at one time, which was to think that a simple operation in nominal ownership would actually introduce some zest and vim into trading performance. It did not happen when we nationalised, and it certainly has not happened after privatisation.

This summer of strife must take its place among other famous seasons of industrial discontent. That shows how weak, one-sided and inadequate the Government's approach to industrial relations has been. Industrial relations are still characterised by a mediaeval culture of industrial lords and industrial serfs. There is still the primative indignity of separate canteens and toilets in too many factories. All that there has been in the past 10 years is an alteration in the balance of power between management and labour. There is still the old situation of conflict—the subdued warfare that is peculiar to Britain. It is one of our great social shames and a great source of industrial weakness.

Despite everything that has been said today by Conservative Members, the Government have still failed to reduce taxation. They have, indeed, increased taxation as a proportion of national wealth. Moreover, it is an entirely false goal to consider that the simple totem of reducing taxation will reinvigorate the economy. Sweden has high taxation rates, but it has one of the richest economies in Europe. One should not conclude, however, that if one increases taxation one will have a wealthier society. Nevertheless, the example of Sweden certainly makes people think twice about making a simple equation between reducing taxation and increasing wealth and industrial initiative.

The Chancellor likes to think of himself as a tax reforming Chancellor. We have also heard a great deal from the Government about how keen they are to improve efficiency in various sectors. They often talk about the National Health Service in this context. I was surprised, therefore, to discover how poorly the efficiency of the Inland Revenue compares with other countries. The collection costs of the Inland Revenue service absorb 2 per cent. of income tax receipts—twice the amount absorbed by the similar service in Sweden, a country often cited as an example of administrative efficiency. It is staggering that our collection costs are four times greater than those in the United States of America which employs the same number of people to handle twice as many taxpayers. The tax reforming revolution is a sham, the industrial miracle is a sham and, day by day, those shams are ever more exposed.

9.16 pm

Mr. David Nicholson (Taunton): This is, after all, an Opposition Supply day, but we have heard little from the right hon. and learned Member from Monklands, East (Mr. Smith) or from the hon. Member for Western Isles (Mr. Macdonald) who spoke of shams, about Opposition policy.

During the speech of the right hon. and learned Gentleman, I was struck by the appearance of the Leader of the Opposition trying to show his weight and, perhaps, to overshadow his shadow Chancellor. The bicentenary of the French revolution is coming up next month and I was struck by the contrast between the two right hon. Gentlemen—one representing the great voice of Danton and the other the trim figure of Robespierre. Every French pupil and perhaps one or two English pupils know what Robespierre did to Danton and what eventually happened to Robespierre.

To run an economy and to present an alternative economic policy a degree of comradeship, agreement and fraternity is needed. When I observe the Labour party I am reminded of a remark about the French revolution that my right hon. Friend the Member for Chesham and Amersham (Sir I. Gilmour) is often fond of quoting:

"Having seen what was done in the name of fraternity,
If I had a brother I should call him cousin."

Mr. William Powell: Will my hon. Friend give way?

Mr. Nicholson: I am sorry, but I only have two minutes to go.

Reference has been made to trade deficits and to various business forecasts. It is interesting to refer to the British Chambers of Commerce quarterly economic survey for the first quarter of the year, which was published last month. That showed that, after a slack growth in export orders towards the end of last year, in the first quarter of this year export orders were firmly up. That survey covered 3,000 businesses in 12 regions. I was particularly pleased to notice that in the south-west there was an increase in the export orders. The hon. Member for Leeds, West (Mr. Battle) spoke about regional imbalance, but I was pleased to note that that increase in export orders also occurred in the north-east.

The survey report also stated:

"There is now clear evidence that the effect of interest rate rises has now put the trend in home orders growth firmly on a downward path."

This will encourage my right hon. Friend the Chancellor, who has been looking to high interest rates to cool down home demand. Despite the difficulties which have been caused for many people and businesses, the first quarter survey also shows that business confidence in increased growth in turnover is increasing, as is confidence in profitability growth, and I am pleased to welcome that.

I receive many letters from retired people in my constituency. Often, they are from solid Conservative voters who are not entirely happy with aspects of Government policy. One thing which they absolutely emphasise, and which concerns them because they lived through the Labour Government of the 1970s, is that the Government must reduce inflation.

I hope that this debate will show the whole-hearted support for my right hon. Friend the Chancellor which comes from his colleagues in the Conservative party and in the House.

9.20 pm

Mr. Bryan Gould (Dagenham): We have had a valuable and interesting debate, of which one of the most interesting features has been the marked change of mood as we discussed today's economy. We have certainly heard some assured and skilled contributions from the Opposition. It has been noteworthy that the Government have had some difficulty in finding enough speakers to keep the debate going. Perhaps that was because those Government Back Benchers who have contributed have exhibited some anxiety about the current state of the economy. There has been some tendency towards admitting mistakes, even a little self-criticism.

The Chancellor was largely immune to that trend and was his usual boastful self. However, even the Chancellor was just a little muted. I also noted that his speeches contained no blips. A year or six months ago his speech were full of blips. There were so many blips that his speeches often sounded like the Greenwich time signal, but he now finds it a little more difficult to dismiss some of his handiwork as mere blips.

He forecast 4 per cent. inflation, then 7 per cent., then 8 per cent. and he was constrained to admit today that it may go beyond 8 per cent. That can hardly be regarded as a blip. He has raised interest rates no fewer than 10 times, to their current level of 14 per cent., and he assures us that he stands ready to raise them yet further. That is hardly a blip. A trade deficit, which he forecast as £4 billion last year, turned out to be £14 billion. He said that it would be £14·5 billion this year, it is already heading for £18 billion and he concedes that it will take some time to deal with it. That can hardly be regarded as a blip. From Conservative Members today we have heard, not a series of blips, but a long cry of pain, which has been echoed by many families in Britain and much of British industry.

That is not the only change that we have noticed in the Chancellor's presentation of his policy. Barely a year ago the Chancellor was forecasting inflation of 4 per cent. and a balance of payments deficit of £4 billion. He was saying, by implication, that the correct rate against the

[Mr. Bryan Gould]

deutschmark, which he was implicitly shadowing, was 3 deutschmark to the pound. When asked to pronounce on the subject he made it clear that 3 deutschmark 10 pfennigs was unsustainable, and he may be right.

A year or so later, our inflation rate is twice that of Germany. If a rate of 3 deutschmark 10 pfennigs was unsustainable a year ago it must be doubly unsustainable today. The Chancellor goes to the barricades in defence of an exchange rate against the deutschmark of 3 deutschmark 10 pfennigs. The Chancellor may be prepared to spill his last drop of blood in defence of that new target, but it comes a little hard when he is prepared to spill the blood of others in support of something which he so recently invented.

Not often do I feel a twinge of sympathy for the Prime Minister, but even the hardest-hearted among us can feel a little sympathy for her if she feels a little bemused by these gyrations on the part of her Chancellor. She herself has changed her stance somewhat. We do not hear too many references these days to her brilliant Chancellor. Her comments are decidedly less flattering. She vouchsafed to the World Service that mistakes had been made, and that the mistake had been to shadow the deutschmark, for which we know exactly who was responsible. It was that mistake which pushed up inflation, so the prime ministerial finger was pointed directly at her Chancellor.

On 23 May the Prime Minister said in this House that she saw no reason to put up interest rates. Less than 24 hours later she was directly contradicted by the Chancellor —one assumes that she went along with it—who promptly put up interest rates. That was more evidence of the growing divergence between the Prime Minister's view of the economy and what the Chancellor thought was required and desirable——

Mr. Tim Smith: Will the hon. Gentleman give way?

Mr. Gould: I want to conclude this little catechism.

Underlying all this is the Prime Minister's famous nostrum, "One cannot buck the market." As we see the Chancellor wrestling with the foreign exchange markets, urging them to support the pound and pushing up interest rates, we realise that he is trying to do exactly that—buck the market. He is engaged, as the central tenet of his economic policy, in trying to do something which the Prime Minister says cannot be done—and that encapsulates the nub of the problem, which is that the Chancellor and the Prime Minister were fair weather friends. They would stick together while the going seemed good, but as soon as it got tough they set off on different paths.

We know what path the Chancellor is on. He may sometimes strike a rather undignified posture as he proceeds along it, trying to stand on his head as he moves along, but at least the path is clear. He continually tells us —he said so again today—that he is determined to push up interest rates every time there is bad economic news and every time sterling comes under pressure. There is no shortage of bad economic news; the problem for the Chancellor is that he is so often called to account to make good that threat, promise or boast, whichever it is. The problem is that promising in advance to be tough and to ask others to take the necessary medicine is good tactics and policy as long as the action does not have to be taken.

When it has to be taken, and then taken again and again and again and again and again and again and again and again and again, it starts to lose some of its magic. It also starts to lose some of its credibility.

The markets have called the Chancellor's bluff, and they now demand thick and fast, almost day by day, that he should make good his threat, promise or boast. If he does not, they will conclude, as we shall, that the Chancellor's stated policy is no longer the policy being applied by the Government.

Having raised interest rates no fewer than 10 times, the Chancellor now faces the following comment from a respected City adviser—not a teenage scribbler, but Roger Bootle of Greenwell Montagu, who said on 5 June:

"To all intents and purposes the policy of relying solely on short-term interest rates to effect a major turn-round in the United Kingdom economy has failed".

That is the judgment of the City. The Chancellor persists with his one-club policy, however damaging it may be to personal and family budgets or to British industry. The CBI survey, the most pessimistic in two years, shows that business confidence and export orders are at their lowest ebb for two years.

Mr. Tim Smith: Will the hon. Gentleman give way?

Mr. Gould: I shall give way in a moment.

The Chancellor persists with interests rate hikes even though they have been shown in recent months to be almost totally ineffective in securing his own stated policy objectives. High interest rates have not reduced inflation. So far as we can measure their impact, they have pushed it up. Interest rates are a price, and like other prices will feed through into the RPI as the Chancellor well knows. Why else is he so anxious to get mortgage rates out of the RPI? He persists with interest rate rises even though they have notably failed to reduce demand. Vehicle sales are at their highest ever level and yesterday consumer credit was still soaring ahead. The Chancellor has found that increasing interest rates and pushing up the value of the pound does not reduce demand. It stimulates it because every over-valued pound will buy more cheap imports than it should. He is caught in that cleft stick.

Mr. Tim Smith: What is the hon. Gentleman's view on the value of the pound? Does he want to see it go up or down or would he prefer to see it stay the same?

Mr. Gould: I am inclined to say that it is difficult to buck the markets. The Chancellor insists on pushing up interest rates to ridiculous and dizzying levels which do great damage, and one of the consequences is that the pound is held at an over-valued level. As the CBI makes clear, that makes it difficult for British industry to compete. The paradox is that the Chancellor uses interest rates to try to dampen demand, but as fast as demand comes down, the supply side of British industry is damaged. That discourages investment, reduces our competitiveness and makes it more difficult for British industry to meet demand.

The Chancellor persists with an interest rate of 14 per cent. and threatens us with 15 per cent. I invite him to tell us why it is that, after 10 years of Tory stewardship, with inflation at the highest level in the G7 countries and a record trade deficit, we have to have an interest rate of 14 per cent.—twice as high as the German interest rate. What is the purpose of that? Why is it so essential for us to have the interest rate at such a level? We are entitled to a straightforward and simple answer, and the Chancellor has the opportunity to put the answer on the record. I invite him to do so.

The Chancellor's problem is that, every time he pushes up interest rates, he makes the basic situation inherently more unstable and makes us more and more dependent on hot money. He makes the rate for sterling more and more vulnerable and makes the prospect of a hard landing more and more likely. No wonder the Prime Minister is distancing herself from a Chancellor who seems to have lost control. No wonder her office briefs the weekend press to the effect that the Chancellor is now under threat. Is it surprising that she told the *Glasgow Herald* that, although he is a good neighbour, she will go no further? When the hard landing that the Prime Minister now expects occurs, she has decided that part of the wreckage that will have to be cleared off the runway is the Chancellor himself.

The problem is that the evidence is mounting daily that the Chancellor has lost the argument. Since rates went up on 24 May, sterling has continued to be under pressure. Every day that goes by without the Chancellor making good his boast suggests more and more strongly to the markets that the Chancellor is no longer running the show; that other counsels now weigh the Prime Minister. If we continue to see pressure on sterling for the remainder of the month and we do not see the Chancellor raising interest rates, we can all afford to draw the obvious conclusion.

The Chancellor is in trouble and that may be why today he chose—unwisely some may think—to fight back. First, he ticked off the Prime Minister for her indiscretion on 23 May. Judging by the expression on her face, he did nothing to make his position more secure.

The Chancellor then decided to conduct a little seminar on the practical deficiencies of monetarism. There was a delicious irony about his dismissal of monetary-based control and over-funding, but what was remarkable about that was that it must have been the first time that any hon. Member present could recall a lesson in economics being delivered by a Chancellor to the Prime Minister in public and on the Floor of the House.

Then, perhaps most unwisely of all, the Chancellor assented to the proposition that there is no alternative. Those of us who could see the Prime Minister's expression and who also noticed some of the occupants of the Government Front Bench will fear that, in that as well, he may prove to have been mistaken.

The problem is that all this is too late. The Chancellor has lost the argument because the Prime Minister is now listening to other advice. Sir Alan Walters is telling her that a mistake was made in shadowing the deutschmark, that the price for that mistake has to be paid, that a fall in sterling as a consequence of that mistake cannot be avoided, so it is impossible and futile to try to buck the market by pushing up market rates in order to defer the evil day. I would not embarrass right hon. and hon. Members by naming them, but I see that there are those on the Government Benches who entirely agree with that analysis.

That is bad news for the economy because it suggests that the Prime Minister, with her new advisers, is now intent on a return to the basic rigours of monetarism. That is bad news because it means that we are about to re-enter the sort of recession that was created in 1980-81, which wiped out fully one fifth of British manufacturing industry.

But that is even worse news for the Chancellor. It means that the Chancellor's strategy is in tatters and his reputation in shreds, and with very good reason. His legacy is an under-invested, ill-equipped badly trained economy, saddled with an inflation, interest rate and trading deficit burden, which means that we are in no shape to face the fierce competition of the 1990s and the single European market. The only hope for the economy is that we should make a new start, and the European elections on 15 June give us the chance to take the first step towards it.

9.37 pm

The Chancellor of the Duchy of Lancaster and Minister of Trade and Industry (Mr. Tony Newton): I had intended to start by saying that we had a wide-ranging, if in some respects rather predictable, debate. It has certainly been predictable, not least the last thirty seconds or so of the speech made by the hon. Member for Dagenham (Mr. Gould), but it has certainly not been wide-ranging enough to give us one second's insight into the policies of Her Majesty's Opposition. That has been the most striking single fact about the whole debate. [*Interruption.*]

Mr. Speaker: Order. The Opposition Front Bench spokesman was heard in silence.

Mr. Newton: In a speech that made a ritual genuflection to the terms of the Opposition motion, which at least purports to have something to do with economic policy, the hon. Member for Dagenham made reference to what I know he is prone to describe as "the real economy", which the motion also mentions—and the neglect of which is one of the themes of that motion. I leave aside the question of what that phrase is supposed to mean, although the more I listen to or re-read the speeches of the hon. Member for Dagenham, the more difficult I find it to discern the distinction that he draws between one aspect of economic activity and another.

Whatever distinction the hon. Gentleman draws, it is clear that by any measure of output, jobs or investment, the real economy—and I presume that output, jobs and investment are what he means by "the real economy"— shows no sign of neglect. On the contrary, over the past two years unemployment has fallen. My right hon. Friend the Chancellor remarked how interesting it is that we hear so little from the Opposition about unemployment.

Mr. Battle: As the Minister did not hear some of the contributions made by my hon. Friends, perhaps he will say why unemployment under the present Government has been higher every single year than it was under any Labour Government.

Mr. Newton: Over the past two years the rate of unemployment in the United Kingdom has continued to fall faster than in any other major industrialised country. On agreed international definitions the United Kingdom's unemployment rate is about $2\frac{1}{2}$ percentage points lower than the European Community average. The United Kingdom has a lower unemployment rate than Spain, Italy, France, Belgium, Ireland, Greece and the Netherlands.

What is more, we have enjoyed much greater success than other European countries in creating jobs. Since March 1983, the number of people in employment increased by nearly 3 million to more than $26\frac{1}{2}$ million,

[*Mr. Newton*]

which is the highest number of people at work ever in this country. The latest available international comparisons —I know how keen Opposition Members are on international comparisons—show that the increase in the number of people in employment in the United Kingdom between 1983 and 1987 was greater than in the rest of the European Community put together. That is one of the achievements of the real economy.

Mr. Kevin Barron (Rother Valley): Will the Minister give a British comparison and say when unemployment in this country is likely to return to the numerical level of 1979?

Mr. Newton: Given the speed at which the economy has been growing and the pace at which unemployment is falling, we can certainly look forward to a further reduction. The hon. Gentleman knows very well that it would not be right for me to make a prediction of the kind that he seeks. He knows also that under this Government unemployment has fallen faster than the rate promised by the Opposition at the time of the last general election.

All United Kingdom regions have shared in the downward trend in unemployment, with the west midlands and Wales experiencing the biggest reductions over the past year. That reflects the fact that, during the 1980s, the United Kingdom has grown faster than all other major countries of the European Community, whereas in the two previous decades it was at the bottom of the growth league. The same holds true for investment. We have heard a great deal from Opposition Members about investment. In the 1980s the growth of total investment in Britain was higher than in any major European country, after being very much lower in the 1960s and 1970s. As my right hon. Friend said, last year alone the growth in business investment was more than 14 per cent. and we expect a further substantial rise this year.

Mr. Mullin: Yesterday, the Minister's Department supplied me with figures for the level of manufacturing investment in the north-east of England, which includes my constituency. In 1987 they were 53 per cent. of what they were in 1979. Those figures were supplied by the Minister's Department. I drew them to the attention of the Chancellor of the Exchequer but he chose not to address them. Would the Minister care to do so?

Mr. Newton: Since the period to which those figures relate, there has been a substantial further increase in investment. One has only to go to Newcastle and the north-east to know how much investment is being made there and how the spirit and confidence of industry in the north-east has increased.

Mr. Pat Wall (Bradford, North) *rose——*

Mr. Newton: I shall not give way for a moment.
The hon. Member for Dagenham and the right hon. and learned Member for Monklands, East (Mr. Smith) have persistently failed to acknowledge the extent to which we have achieved a substantial increase in investment in the economy and we have changed the pattern of decades in which our consumption consistently rose faster than our investment. In the past seven years we have produced a pattern in which, for the first time in a generation,

investment has grown twice as fast as consumption. During the 1970s, consumption rose almost five times faster than investment.

Mr. Wall *rose——*

Mr. Newton: In view of the hon. Gentleman's persistence, I shall give way.

Mr. Wall: The Minister talks about patterns of investment. Investment in manufacturing industry has barely reached the level that it was in 1979. Investment in financial and service industries has doubled in that time, but investment in the infrastructure has halved. Surely anyone can understand that if we do not create wealth and support the infrastructure we shall be unable to support the banking and service side of the economy for any length of time.

Mr. Newton: I have two points in response to that. First, the shifting pattern between manufacturing industry and other aspects of the economy is part and parcel of the development of all advanced industrial economies. The strength of the financial services and other sectors so despised by Opposition Members is not the least of the achievements of the present Government in the past decade. Secondly, just a few weeks ago we had a debate on manufacturing industry and the hon. Member for Dagenham made a speech in which virtually his entire argument was that manufacturing industry was not stronger than it had been for a considerable time. He said that the level of investment in manufacturing had still not quite reached the level that it was in 1979. I said to him then that that argument was a figleaf which would last very little time. Indeed, within a week, the figures showed that manufacturing investment in Britain was at a record level.

Mr. Gould: I am glad to welcome the Government's achievement in at last bringing manufacturing investment back to the level that it was in 1979. But the Minister misrepresents my speech. My major point to show the decline in manufacturing industry was the turnround of £19 billion in our trade in manufactured goods. I wonder whether the Chancellor of the Duchy can explain that away.

Mr. Newton: I was about to deal with the balance of payments position. It is not in dispute between the hon. Member for Dagenham and me—whatever view we take about the right position of manufacturing industry in the economy and what I regard as the rather antique approach of the hon. Gentleman—that manufacturing output has risen steadily and now stands at record levels; that manufacturing productivity has increased at a pace not experienced in the economy for decades; and that manufacturing investment has risen sharply, not least over the past few years.

The hon. Member for Dagenham ignored the fact that not only the quantum but the quality of investment and what it achieves for productivity and output is important. The increase in productivity of British manufacturing industry bears witness to the greater profitability and higher quality of investment since 1979.

For British manufacturing industry, the 1970s were a period of overmanning, stagnant productivity, declining profitability and dismal industrial relations. Many companies were not gaining the full benefit from their investment. During the 1980s, the growth of productivity in manufacturing has been faster than in any major manufacturing country, and manufacturing productivity has improved 50 per cent. since the beginning of the decade.

The hon. Member for Dagenham spoke little about what he termed the "real economy". He did not refer to the substantial turnround that has occurred in some of our important industries, not least our important manufacturing industries. I shall take one example to which Labour Members frequently devote attention—the vehicle industry. The production of passenger cars in 1988 was 7 per cent. higher than 1987. More cars were produced in this country last year than since 1977, and that trend is continuing. The same pattern emerges for commercial vehicles, with 318,000 being produced in 1988, which was no fewer than 29 per cent. more than in 1987. The success stories of the individual companies can be seen.

Mr. Rhodri Morgan (Cardiff, West) *rose——*

Mr. Newton: I shall complete this point, which is of some significance, not least in relation to the questions that the hon. Member for Dagenham asked.

Just under 1·25 million motor cars were produced last year, compared with just over 1 million in 1979.

Mr. Gould: What about the trade balance?

Mr. Newton: I shall come to that in a moment.

In 1974, 1·5 million cars were produced. During the period of the last Labour Government, the production of cars fell by about 300,000 or 500,000, but it has recovered by about 200,000 since the Government took office.

I shall tell the hon. Member for Dagenham what happened to the import penetration of motor cars. In 1988, it was almost the same as in 1979, but between 1974 and 1979 it doubled from 27·9 per cent. to 56 per cent. That is when the worsening of trade in that crucial sector occurred, and it is clear from what is happening to production and investment, not least inward investment, in the British motor car industry that we are now beginning to recover from that disastrous position that the last Labour Government created.

Mr. Morgan: The Minister keeps reeling off trade deficit-defying, wondrous success stories. He leaves us with a question. If our batting averages are so good, how come we are losing all the test matches?

Mr. Newton: The point is almost exactly illustrated by what I have just shown in respect of motor cars. During the 1970s and to a substantial extent the 1960s as well, the policies, in so far as there were any, advocated by Opposition Members led to poor industrial relations, low increases in productivity and low increases in investment. Not least, credit controls such as the Labour party now advocates had a serious effect on many consumer goods industries. One industry after another began to sink in the same way as the motor car industry sank, as was shown clearly by the figures that I have given.

Of course, it has taken time to make inroads into the problems and to turn things round, but it can be seen clearly not only in the motor car industry but in other industries that productivity and output have been rising and that there is more investment. The scope for an improvement in performance that we all want to see has increased steadily.

The hon. Member for Clydebank and Milngavie (Mr. Worthington) spoke of the loss of the television industry. In the light of the point that the hon. Gentleman made, it is worth noting that in the first quarter of 1989 we had a trade surplus in colour television sets and video tape recorders. That reflects in part the contribution being made by inward investment which shows that people around the world do not accept the analyses of Her Majesty's Opposition of the British economy, and that they are voting with their feet by coming to do business with us in the construction of factories.

The fundamental strengths of the economy are clear from the record to which I have referred, with its sustained growth, its falling unemployment, its surge in investment in manufacturing and throughout the economy, and the extent to which people from other parts of the world are voting with their feet by doing business here. That strengthening results from the policies that the Government have pursued.

The debate has been remarkable for its confirmation that the Opposition have no serious policy. The right hon. and learned Member for Monklands, East told us that he would be coming to his policy and to what he would do about inflation. He never did; he could not because he does not know. In that he has at least achieved unity with his leader. We have already heard about the celebrated interview with James Naughtie. I am in the unhappy position of not being able to quote most of it because, even if it were printable in the *Evening Standard,* it would not be quotable in the House within the terms of order. I can quote the reporter's magnificent description of what happened:

"The disagreement began after Mr. Naughtie, a respected and experienced journalist, asked Mr. Kinnock what would be his plans on bringing down interest rates. A long silence followed".

The approach of the Leader of the Opposition is not just that he has not got a policy, but that it is not even fair to expect him to have one. His excuse is that he would not be starting from here. Of course he would not be. We know where he would have started. He would have started where the last Labour Government left off, with inflation higher, with investment lower, with growth slower and with the country's industrial relations in a shambles. Neither the House nor the country has any intention of going back down that road with him.

Mr. Derek Foster (Bishop Auckland) *rose in his place and claimed to move,* That the Question be now put.

Question, That the Question be now put, *put and agreed to.*

Question accordingly put, That the original words stand part of the Question:—

The House divided: Ayes 184, Noes 315

Division No. 231]   **[10 pm**

AYES

Adams, Allen *(Paisley N)*	Beckett, Margaret
Allen, Graham	Beith, A. J.
Alton, David	Bell, Stuart
Anderson, Donald	Bermingham, Gerald
Archer, Rt Hon Peter	Bidwell, Sydney
Armstrong, Hilary	Blair, Tony
Ashley, Rt Hon Jack	Blunkett, David
Ashton, Joe	Boyes, Roland
Barnes, Harry *(Derbyshire NE)*	Bradley, Keith
Barnes, Mrs Rosie *(Greenwich)*	Bray, Dr Jeremy
Barron, Kevin	Brown, Gordon *(D'mline E)*
Battle, John	Brown, Nicholas *(Newcastle E)*

Bruce, Malcolm *(Gordon)*
Buckley, George J.
Caborn, Richard
Callaghan, Jim
Campbell, Menzies *(Fife NE)*
Campbell, Ron *(Blyth Valley)*
Campbell-Savours, D. N.
Canavan, Dennis
Cartwright, John
Clark, Dr David *(S Shields)*
Clarke, Tom *(Monklands W)*
Clay, Bob
Clelland, David
Clwyd, Mrs Ann
Cohen, Harry
Cook, Frank *(Stockton N)*
Cook, Robin *(Livingston)*
Corbett, Robin
Corbyn, Jeremy
Cousins, Jim
Crowther, Stan
Cryer, Bob
Cunliffe, Lawrence
Cunningham, Dr John
Dalyell, Tam
Darling, Alistair
Davies, Rt Hon Denzil *(Llanelli)*
Davies, Ron *(Caerphilly)*
Davis, Terry *(B'ham Hodge H'l)*
Dixon, Don
Dobson, Frank
Douglas, Dick
Duffy, A. E. P.
Dunwoody, Hon Mrs Gwyneth
Eastham, Ken
Evans, John *(St Helens N)*
Ewing, Mrs Margaret *(Moray)*
Fatchett, Derek
Fearn, Ronald
Field, Frank *(Birkenhead)*
Fields, Terry *(L'pool B G'n)*
Flannery, Martin
Flynn, Paul
Foster, Derek
Foulkes, George
Fraser, John
Garrett, John *(Norwich South)*
George, Bruce
Gilbert, Rt Hon Dr John
Godman, Dr Norman A.
Gould, Bryan
Grant, Bernie *(Tottenham)*
Griffiths, Nigel *(Edinburgh S)*
Griffiths, Win *(Bridgend)*
Grocott, Bruce
Harman, Ms Harriet
Hattersley, Rt Hon Roy
Haynes, Frank
Henderson, Doug
Hinchliffe, David
Hogg, N. *(C'nauld & Kilsyth)*
Howarth, George *(Knowsley N)*
Howell, Rt Hon D. *(S'heath)*
Howells, Geraint
Howells, Dr. Kim (Pontypridd)
Hoyle, Doug
Hughes, John *(Coventry NE)*
Hughes, Robert *(Aberdeen N)*
Hughes, Roy *(Newport E)*
Illsley, Eric
Ingram, Adam
Janner, Greville
Jones, Barry *(Alyn & Deeside)*
Jones, Ieuan *(Ynys Môn)*
Jones, Martyn *(Clwyd S W)*
Kennedy, Charles
Kinnock, Rt Hon Neil
Lamond, James
Leadbitter, Ted

Leighton, Ron
Lestor, Joan *(Eccles)*
Lewis, Terry
Livingstone, Ken
Lloyd, Tony *(Stretford)*
Lofthouse, Geoffrey
Loyden, Eddie
Macdonald, Calum A.
McFall, John
McLeish, Henry
Madden, Max
Mahon, Mrs Alice
Mallon, Seamus
Marek, Dr John
Marshall, Jim *(Leicester S)*
Martlew, Eric
Meacher, Michael
Meale, Alan
Michael, Alun
Michie, Bill *(Sheffield Heeley)*
Michie, Mrs Ray *(Arg'l & Bute)*
Mitchell, Austin *(G't Grimsby)*
Moonie, Dr Lewis
Morgan, Rhodri
Morley, Elliott
Morris, Rt Hon A. *(W'shawe)*
Morris, Rt Hon J. *(Aberavon)*
Mowlam, Marjorie
Mullin, Chris
Murphy, Paul
Nellist, Dave
Oakes, Rt Hon Gordon
O'Brien, William
O'Neill, Martin
Orme, Rt Hon Stanley
Pike, Peter L.
Powell, Ray *(Ogmore)*
Prescott, John
Quin, Ms Joyce
Radice, Giles
Randall, Stuart
Redmond, Martin
Rees, Rt Hon Merlyn
Richardson, Jo
Robertson, George
Robinson, Geoffrey
Rogers, Allan
Rooker, Jeff
Ross, Ernie *(Dundee W)*
Rowlands, Ted
Salmond, Alex
Sedgemore, Brian
Sheerman, Barry
Sheldon, Rt Hon Robert
Short, Clare
Skinner, Dennis
Smith, Andrew *(Oxford E)*
Smith, C. *(Isl'ton & F'bury)*
Smith, Rt Hon J. *(Monk'ds E)*
Snape, Peter
Soley, Clive
Spearing, Nigel
Steinberg, Gerry
Strang, Gavin
Straw, Jack
Turner, Dennis
Vaz, Keith
Wall, Pat
Wallace, James
Walley, Joan
Wardell, Gareth *(Gower)*
Wareing, Robert N.
Welsh, Andrew *(Angus E)*
Welsh, Michael *(Doncaster N)*
Williams, Rt Hon Alan
Williams, Alan W. *(Carm'then)*
Wilson, Brian
Winnick, David
Wise, Mrs Audrey

Worthington, Tony
Young, David *(Bolton SE)*

Tellers for the Ayes:
   Mr. Allen McKay and
   Mrs. Llin Golding.

NOES

Adley, Robert
Alexander, Richard
Alison, Rt Hon Michael
Amery, Rt Hon Julian
Amos, Alan
Arbuthnot, James
Arnold, Jacques *(Gravesham)*
Arnold, Tom *(Hazel Grove)*
Ashby, David
Aspinwall, Jack
Atkins, Robert
Baker, Rt Hon K. *(Mole Valley)*
Baker, Nicholas *(Dorset N)*
Baldry, Tony
Banks, Robert *(Harrogate)*
Batiste, Spencer
Beaumont-Dark, Anthony
Bellingham, Henry
Bendall, Vivian
Bennett, Nicholas *(Pembroke)*
Benyon, W.
Bevan, David Gilroy
Biffen, Rt Hon John
Blackburn, Dr John G.
Blaker, Rt Hon Sir Peter
Bonsor, Sir Nicholas
Boscawen, Hon Robert
Boswell, Tim
Bottomley, Peter
Bottomley, Mrs Virginia
Bowden, Gerald *(Dulwich)*
Bowis, John
Boyson, Rt Hon Dr Sir Rhodes
Braine, Rt Hon Sir Bernard
Brandon-Bravo, Martin
Brazier, Julian
Bright, Graham
Brooke, Rt Hon Peter
Brown, Michael *(Brigg & Cl't's)*
Bruce, Ian *(Dorset South)*
Buchanan-Smith, Rt Hon Alick
Buck, Sir Antony
Budgen, Nicholas
Burns, Simon
Burt, Alistair
Butcher, John
Butler, Chris
Butterfill, John
Carlisle, John, *(Luton N)*
Carlisle, Kenneth *(Lincoln)*
Carrington, Matthew
Carttiss, Michael
Cash, William
Channon, Rt Hon Paul
Chapman, Sydney
Chope, Christopher
Churchill, Mr
Clark, Hon Alan *(Plym'th S'n)*
Clark, Dr Michael *(Rochford)*
Clark, Sir W. *(Croydon S)*
Clarke, Rt Hon K. *(Rushcliffe)*
Colvin, Michael
Conway, Derek
Coombs, Anthony *(Wyre F'rest)*
Coombs, Simon *(Swindon)*
Cope, Rt Hon John
Cormack, Patrick
Couchman, James
Cran, James
Critchley, Julian
Currie, Mrs Edwina
Curry, David
Davies, Q. *(Stamf'd & Spald'g)*
Davis, David *(Boothferry)*
Day, Stephen

Devlin, Tim
Dicks, Terry
Dorrell, Stephen
Dover, Den
Dunn, Bob
Dykes, Hugh
Eggar, Tim
Emery, Sir Peter
Evans, David *(Welwyn Hatf'd)*
Evennett, David
Fairbairn, Sir Nicholas
Fallon, Michael
Favell, Tony
Field, Barry *(Isle of Wight)*
Fishburn, John Dudley
Fookes, Dame Janet
Forman, Nigel
Forsyth, Michael *(Stirling)*
Forth, Eric
Fowler, Rt Hon Norman
Fox, Sir Marcus
Franks, Cecil
Freeman, Roger
French, Douglas
Fry, Peter
Gale, Roger
Gardiner, George
Gill, Christopher
Gilmour, Rt Hon Sir Ian
Glyn, Dr Alan
Goodhart, Sir Philip
Goodlad, Alastair
Goodson-Wickes, Dr Charles
Gorst, John
Gow, Ian
Grant, Sir Anthony *(CambsSW)*
Greenway, Harry *(Ealing N)*
Greenway, John *(Ryedale)*
Gregory, Conal
Griffiths, Sir Eldon *(Bury St E')*
Griffiths, Peter *(Portsmouth N)*
Grist, Ian
Ground, Patrick
Gummer, Rt Hon John Selwyn
Hague, William
Hamilton, Hon Archie *(Epsom)*
Hamilton, Neil *(Tatton)*
Hampson, Dr Keith
Hanley, Jeremy
Hannam, John
Hargreaves, A. *(B'ham H'll Gr')*
Hargreaves, Ken *(Hyndburn)*
Harris, David
Haselhurst, Alan
Hawkins, Christopher
Hayward, Robert
Heathcoat-Amory, David
Heddle, John
Hicks, Mrs Maureen *(Wolv' NE)*
Hicks, Robert *(Cornwall SE)*
Higgins, Rt Hon Terence L.
Hind, Kenneth
Hogg, Hon Douglas *(Gr'th'm)*
Hordern, Sir Peter
Howard, Michael
Howarth, Alan *(Strat'd-on-A)*
Howarth, G. *(Cannock & B'wd)*
Howell, Rt Hon David *(G'dford)*
Howell, Ralph *(North Norfolk)*
Hughes, Robert G. *(Harrow W)*
Hunt, David *(Wirral W)*
Irvine, Michael
Irving, Charles
Jack, Michael
Jackson, Robert

Janman, Tim
Johnson Smith, Sir Geoffrey
Jones, Gwilym *(Cardiff N)*
Jopling, Rt Hon Michael
Kellett-Bowman, Dame Elaine
Key, Robert
Kilfedder, James
King, Roger *(B'ham N'thfield)*
Kirkhope, Timothy
Knapman, Roger
Knight, Greg *(Derby North)*
Knight, Dame Jill *(Edgbaston)*
Knowles, Michael
Knox, David
Lamont, Rt Hon Norman
Lang, Ian
Latham, Michael
Lawrence, Ivan
Lawson, Rt Hon Nigel
Lee, John *(Pendle)*
Lennox-Boyd, Hon Mark
Lightbown, David
Lilley, Peter
Lloyd, Sir Ian *(Havant)*
Lloyd, Peter *(Fareham)*
Luce, Rt Hon Richard
Lyell, Sir Nicholas
McCrindle, Robert
Macfarlane, Sir Neil
MacGregor, Rt Hon John
MacKay, Andrew *(E Berkshire)*
Maclean, David
McLoughlin, Patrick
McNair-Wilson, Sir Michael
McNair-Wilson, P. *(New Forest)*
Madel, David
Major, Rt Hon John
Malins, Humfrey
Maples, John
Marlow, Tony
Marshall, John *(Hendon S)*
Marshall, Michael *(Arundel)*
Martin, David *(Portsmouth S)*
Mates, Michael
Maude, Hon Francis
Mawhinney, Dr Brian
Maxwell-Hyslop, Robin
Mayhew, Rt Hon Sir Patrick
Mellor, David
Meyer, Sir Anthony
Miller, Sir Hal
Mills, Iain

Miscampbell, Norman
Mitchell, Andrew *(Gedling)*
Mitchell, Sir David
Moate, Roger
Monro, Sir Hector
Montgomery, Sir Fergus
Moore, Rt Hon John
Morris, M *(N'hampton S)*
Morrison, Sir Charles
Moss, Malcolm
Moynihan, Hon Colin
Mudd, David
Neale, Gerrard
Newton, Rt Hon Tony
Nicholls, Patrick
Nicholson, David *(Taunton)*
Nicholson, Emma *(Devon West)*
Norris, Steve
Onslow, Rt Hon Cranley
Oppenheim, Phillip
Page, Richard
Paice, James
Parkinson, Rt Hon Cecil
Patnick, Irvine
Patten, Chris *(Bath)*
Patten, John *(Oxford W)*
Pattie, Rt Hon Sir Geoffrey
Pawsey, James
Peacock, Mrs Elizabeth
Porter, Barry *(Wirral S)*
Portillo, Michael
Powell, William *(Corby)*
Price, Sir David
Raffan, Keith
Raison, Rt Hon Timothy
Redwood, John
Renton, Tim
Rhodes James, Robert
Riddick, Graham
Ridley, Rt Hon Nicholas
Ridsdale, Sir Julian
Roberts, Wyn *(Conwy)*
Roe, Mrs Marion
Rost, Peter
Rumbold, Mrs Angela
Sackville, Hon Tom
Sainsbury, Hon Tim
Sayeed, Jonathan
Scott, Nicholas
Shaw, David *(Dover)*
Shaw, Sir Giles *(Pudsey)*
Shaw, Sir Michael *(Scarb')*

Shephard, Mrs G. *(Norfolk SW)*
Shepherd, Colin *(Hereford)*
Shepherd, Richard *(Aldridge)*
Shersby, Michael
Sims, Roger
Skeet, Sir Trevor
Smith, Tim *(Beaconsfield)*
Soames, Hon Nicholas
Speller, Tony
Spicer, Sir Jim *(Dorset W)*
Spicer, Michael *(S Worcs)*
Stanbrook, Ivor
Stanley, Rt Hon Sir John
Steen, Anthony
Stern, Michael
Stevens, Lewis
Stewart, Andy *(Sherwood)*
Stewart, Rt Hon Ian *(Herts N)*
Stradling Thomas, Sir John
Sumberg, David
Summerson, Hugo
Tapsell, Sir Peter
Taylor, Ian *(Esher)*
Tebbit, Rt Hon Norman
Temple-Morris, Peter
Thatcher, Rt Hon Margaret
Thompson, D. *(Calder Valley)*
Thompson, Patrick *(Norwich N)*
Thorne, Neil
Thornton, Malcolm
Thurnham, Peter
Townend, John *(Bridlington)*
Townsend, Cyril D. *(B'heath)*

Tracey, Richard
Tredinnick, David
Trippier, David
Trotter, Neville
Twinn, Dr Ian
Vaughan, Sir Gerard
Viggers, Peter
Waddington, Rt Hon David
Wakeham, Rt Hon John
Walker, Bill *(T'side North)*
Walker, Rt Hon P. *(W'cester)*
Waller, Gary
Walters, Sir Dennis
Ward, John
Wardle, Charles *(Bexhill)*
Watts, John
Wells, Bowen
Wheeler, John
Widdecombe, Ann
Wiggin, Jerry
Wilshire, David
Winterton, Mrs Ann
Winterton, Nicholas
Wolfson, Mark
Wood, Timothy
Woodcock, Dr. Mike
Yeo, Tim
Young, Sir George *(Acton)*

Tellers for the Noes:
  Mr. Tristan Garel-Jones and
  Mr. Tony Durant.

Question accordingly negatived.

Question, That the proposed words be there added, *put forthwith pursuant to Standing Order No. 30 (Questions on amendments), and agreed to.*

MR. SPEAKER *forthwith declared the main Question, as amended, to be agreed to.*

Resolved,

That this House congratulates Her Majesty's Government on its economic policies which have led to output, investment, and manufacturing productivity growing faster than in any other major European Community country in the 1980s; applauds the Government's firm anti-inflationary stance, and the action it has taken to exert further downward pressure on inflation; and commends the Government's supply side policies which have brought industry's profitability to a 20 year high, led to record rates of new business growth, and seen the creation of nearly three million new jobs since 1983.

Offenders

10.15 pm

The Minister of State, Northern Ireland Office (Mr. Ian Stewart): I beg to move,

That the draft Treatment of Offenders (Northern Ireland) Order 1989, which was laid before this House on 9th May, be approved.

This is the first of two orders before the House tonight. With the agreement of the House, it will be convenient to discuss also the second motion:

That the draft Community Service Orders (Northern Ireland Consequential Amendments) Order 1989, which was laid before this House on 9th May, be approved.

That order is purely consequential on the first. I appreciate that it will have to be moved separately.

The first draft order comprises a package of measures which primarily concern the powers of the courts to deal with offenders and which, I am glad to say, have been generally welcomed. While some relate chiefly to juveniles, there are others which have implications for adults. A number of the changes are designed to bring the law in Northern Ireland into line with that of England and Wales. Experience of the operation of existing law in the Province has led to other changes which I shall describe.

In the case of the measures concerning juvenile justice, I remind the House that these arise from the report of the children and young persons review group published in 1979 which came to be known as the Black report, after its chairman. These measures introduce a number of new non-custodial options which should lead to a decrease in the number of juveniles in custody.

Article 3 will extend the powers of the courts to attach what are commonly known as "fourth conditions" to probation orders so as to provide greater flexibility in their use. The changes to the Probation Act (Northern Ireland) 1950 are similar to those provided for England and Wales by the Criminal Justice Act 1982 and will enable the court to make it a condition of a probation order that the offender attends an activity centre or a day centre for a maximum of 60 days.

Article 4 provides that, where a juvenile is jointly charged with an adult, he or she may be referred to the juvenile court for both trial and sentence if the adult defendant pleads guilty and the juvenile pleads not guilty. Under existing law, a juvenile charged jointly with an adult must be tried in an adult court and may be referred to the juvenile court only for sentence. I am sure hon. Members will agree that it is more desirable that juveniles should attend a court which is constituted to meet their needs.

Article 5 provides for the extended use of attendance centre orders, which can often be a useful alternative to custody. In Northern Ireland, these orders may be imposed only on persons under 17 years of age, and indeed the latest available figures indicate that about 70 per cent. of attendance centre orders are imposed on persons aged 15 or under. In view of the young age of the majority of persons who are ordered to attend an attendance centre, it is proposed to place a responsibility on the parents to produce their children at the centre at the specified time. This is important, because failure by the child to attend the centre could lead to a more serious disposal.

Articles 6 and 7 deal with custodial sentences. In Northern Ireland, young persons under 17 may be sent to a training school where the child or young person is found guilty of an offence, which, in the case of an adult, is punishable by imprisonment. Under present law, a training school order gives authority to detain the child or young person for a period of up to three years. However, he or she may be released on licence at any time after committal, except that if this is proposed within 12 months of committal, the consent of the Secretary of State is required. Article 6 of the order will reduce the maximum period of detention from three to two years. It will also reduce the period within which the consent of the Secretary of State is required from 12 months to six months. These changes should help to reassure those who expressed concern about the length of time that young persons might have to spend in custody.

Article 7 will increase the maximum period of detention in a young offenders centre from three years to four years. This is not intended to increase the length of the term of detention in individual cases. Instead, it will mean that a number of young offenders who are given a term of detention of between three and four years will be eligible for admission to a young offenders centre rather than to prison, a facility much better suited to their needs.

Articles 8 and 9 deal with the abolition of the common law power of the courts to record sentences and its replacement by an enhanced power to suspend sentences. Recorded sentences, which are peculiar to Northern Ireland and the Republic of Ireland, are similar to suspended sentences, in that sentence can be deferred while the convicted person enters into an obligation to be of good behaviour during a specified period.

However, in the case of the recorded sentence, there is no limit on either the sentence or the period during which the person may be bound over. In addition, it lacks the flexibility of a suspended sentence as it must be reactivated in full if the person reoffends within the operational period. Because of that inflexibility, injustices can arise if, for example, there is a subsequent conviction for a trivial and quite unrelated offence which automatically reactivates the recorded sentence. We therefore consider that the power to suspend sentences is more satisfactory and that the new provisions will achieve this.

I referred earlier to the provisions of articles 3 and 5, which aim to provide alternatives to custodial sentences. The aim of article 10 is similar. That will reduce the age for community service from 17 to 16 and, again, that corresponds to a change introduced for England and Wales by the Criminal Justice Act 1982. Because the age for community service in Northern Ireland at that time was 17, the 1982 Act imposed a restriction on courts elsewhere in the United Kingdom to ensure that a community service order was not imposed on a person under 17 who intended to reside in Northern Ireland. As the effect of the treatment of offenders order will be to make 16 the age for community service throughout the United Kingdom, that restriction is no longer necessary and is removed by the Community Service Orders (Northern Ireland Consequential Amendments) Order.

I return now to the treatment of offenders order. Article 11 will amend the powers of the courts to defer sentence and provides that the period of deferment will run from the date on which it is announced rather than, as at present, from the date of conviction. That change will ensure that the defendant will obtain the benefit of a full six months period to enable him or her to demonstrate to the court, either by making reparation for the offence or by a change in circumstances—for example, by finding a job or getting married—that he or she has both the desire and the ability to stay out of trouble. Again, that mirrors present law in England and Wales.

Article 12 will increase the maximum penalty for a number of offences to bring them into line with similar penalties that are available in England and Wales. The maximum penalty for indecent assault on a female will be increased from two to 10 years, and the maximum term of imprisonment for attempted rape or assault with intent to commit rape is to be increased from seven years to life imprisonment. The maximum penalty for child cruelty, which was increased recently for England and Wales by the Criminal Justice Act 1988, is to be increased from two years to 10 years. Although I am glad to say that the evidence does not suggest that such crimes are widespread in Northern Ireland, the House rightly regards them as very serious offences for which substantial terms of imprisonment may often be appropriate.

Finally, article 13 will, for the first time, enable a number of young offenders who are remanded in custody to be held at the young offenders centre. Under present arrangements, all male persons over 17 who are remanded in custody are held in Her Majesty's prison, Belfast. As some spare capacity exists in the young offenders centre, it is sensible and much more suited to their needs to allow a number of young persons to be held there while on remand.

Taken as a whole, this package of proposals should provide the criminal courts in Northern Ireland with useful additions to their powers to determine the most satisfactory disposal for both young and adult offenders and offer greater scope for the use of alternatives to custody.

I commend the order to the House.

10.23 pm

Ms. Marjorie Mowlam (Redcar): We welcome this opportunity to consider young offenders in Northern Ireland. Sadly, such offenders are not focused upon often, as we spend so much of our time discussing the sentencing and treatment of terrorists.

There are few surprises in the orders, but we consider that they are a further example of the Government's piecemeal approach to young offenders. There is no clear overall strategy and no coherent plan to deal with young offenders in Northern Ireland. We had hoped that the Government would use the orders as a means to introduce such coherence, but, instead, we have been presented with the piecemeal approach tonight.

We would like to see provisions that were more rational and relevant and that would strike a balance between punishment, reform and rehabilitation. The Government have not offered us that recipe tonight.

The orders try to tackle the problems of young offenders in Northern Ireland. We had hoped that a clearer, twin-track approach would have been adopted by the Minister. We would have liked the provisions to deal in a sensitive and constructive manner with offenders and, at the same time, give more emphasis to preventing those crimes from taking place. If we attempt to take preventive action it is necessary to study the crimes that are common among young people, including theft, burglary, vandalism or the particular problem that has developed in Belfast, of which I am sure the Minister is aware—joy-riding. That has grown in popularity in recent months. We must understand the rationale behind such crimes if we are to prevent them and we must understand why young people commit them.

We would like to think that, among other things, the Government would address the problems of frustration, boredom, despair bred from unemployment, lack of decent housing and lack of money. The preventive framework set down by the Government is not impressive.

In Northern Ireland, unemployment among young people is above 16 per cent. The Minister should also consider the implications of the 1987 decision to take away the funding for the education service, which is targeted directly on young offenders. That service represented preventive action against crime and the Minister should have left it intact. Another important consideration is the fact that benefit has been taken away from 16 and 17-year-olds. That age group now has no link with the society. If they are not in full-time education or not in a job they have no reason to connect with society. The Minister should consider the implications of that decision carefully when studying preventive action against crimes committed by young offenders.

The preventive work that has taken place has occurred not because of the Government, but despite them. I am sure that other hon. Members would like to give credit to the voluntary sector in Northern Ireland, which has done so much work with young offenders. We are not merely thinking of the Northern Ireland Association for the Care and Resettlement of Offenders—NIACRO—and its employment initiatives, particularly the after schools.

It would be useful if the Minister clarified some of the implications of the orders as they do little to help to deal with young offenders. It is clear that a court will be able to stipulate, as part of a probation order, that an offender attend certain places or activities. It would be useful to know whether the Minister has had any planning or funding discussions with the voluntary sector about that provision. I am sure he is aware that day centres in Northern Ireland, unlike those in England and Wales, are not funded by local authorities but lie within the voluntary sector. There is a greater need for communication and planning in Northern Ireland than there is in England and Wales.

It would also be useful if the Minister were to give us more details about the community service orders. In his introduction he stated that they are an "alternative to custody," but I am sure that he is aware, as are other hon. Members, that they often become an alternative to non-custodial options.

It would be useful to know what discussions the Minister has had, particularly with probation officers, about the compulsory nature of the orders. We appreciate the rationale for the compulsion, but I am sure that if the Minister has talked to probation officers about this he will have found that problems arise when compulsion is built into a relationship between a young offender and a probation officer, because developing that relationship is largely based on trust. I have talked to many probation officers across the water and in England and Wales, and the compulsory element of the legislation, as it matches up to legislation this side of the water, worries them.

We would appreciate the Minister's comments on attendance centre orders, which the Opposition greatly welcome. The creation and use of attendance centre orders will be useful. However, we are greatly concerned that only one centre is open in Belfast. Under the Children and

[*Ms. Marjorie Mowlam*]

Young Persons (Northern Ireland) Act 1968, as I understand it, a young offender can attend one of the centres only if he or she lives within 10 miles of it. Therefore, although they will be useful, their use will be limited to certain groups within the Province. What plans, if any, has the Minister for further development of attendance centre orders?

Two parts of the provisions particularly disappoint me, and the first concerns the training school orders. The Opposition are keen for them to be done away with, because the money and staffing could be used for community projects which, in the long run, would be much more useful for young people. Much of the informed opinion in the Province acknowledges that the training schools have failed to work for many young offenders.

We would be grateful if the Minister would comment on the increase in the maximum terms that he outlined when referring to article 7. It represents a classic example of the Government's belief that, by definition, stiffer penalties result in success. There is very little evidence to prove that long sentences reduce the likelihood of sex attackers reoffending. It would be useful if the Minister could bring some to the House tonight. The assumption that a more punitive measure will produce success needs substantiation. It seems to be the ideology, or prejudice, behind much of the Government's thinking on young offenders.

The orders have offered the Government an opportunity to make a radical overhaul of the young offender system in Northern Ireland. Sadly, they have not taken that option, but have produced piecemeal provisions, lacking in coherence and clear planning. We hoped that they would take the chance to outline much more clearly the preventive action that they would like to take to reduce the number of young people sentenced to custody and, most importantly, to encourage and develop new, innovative methods for dealing with offenders. Sadly, the Government have missed the opportunity to develop such initiatives, and have merely introduced the orders which reveal the same stubborn, misguided beliefs of previous legislation and the belief that punitive sentencing deters crime.

That is the basis of the policy which we have seen fail in Northern Ireland since the Black report. Tonight, we hoped that the Government would have listened more carefully to the united advice of informed opinion in the Province that would have asked for a much more radical cutting edge to the legislation which has been introduced this evening.

10.34 pm

Mr. James Kilfedder (North Down): I welcome the opportunity to follow the hon. Member for Redcar (Ms. Mowlam), whose thoughtful and caring speech is to be commended. I hope to be able to refer to some of her points later in the short time available.

It is a sad comment on our times in Northern Ireland that Northern Ireland business comes on so late in the evening. We were fortunate that it started just before 10.30 pm today, but it has been much later on other occasions.

I want to refer to two parts of the legislation. First, I welcome the increase in the penalty for indecent assaults on females, bringing Northern Ireland into line with

England and Wales, where the maximum penalty is now 10 years. Making life imprisonment the maximum penalty for attempted rape or assault with intent to commit rape is belated recognition of the increasing number of such attacks, not only in Northern Ireland but throughout the United Kingdom. I hope that the courts will use their new sentencing powers in Northern Ireland to protect women, who often feel so vulnerable. The media recount many such assaults, often committed in frightening circumstances.

I also welcome the increase from two to 10 years in the maximum penalty for cruelty to children. Sad to say, we live in an age in which children can be treated with appalling cruelty by sadistic or uncaring parents, and every effort must be made to curb such ill treatment.

It is impossible in this limited time to debate the order in its entirety. As the hon. Member for Redcar said, this is a rare opportunity to debate the needs of children and young offenders, and it is sad that our time is so limited. I shall therefore restrict myself to some observations on the treatment of young offenders.

I must concur with NIACRO, which criticised the order. The hon. Member for Redcar followed that body in saying that this is another example of the piecemeal approach adopted by the Northern Ireland Office. There is no comprehensive policy for children and young persons in Northern Ireland, nor any overall plan or coherent strategy. NIACRO referred to the Black report and alternatives to custody. I cannot go into the recommendations of that report now. Suffice it to say that there is tremendous anxiety in Northern Ireland about the amount of juvenile crime. It is often prompted by drink or drug abuse, a disturbed family background or inadequate discipline, although I hasten to add that those are not the only reasons for delinquency.

The primary responsibility for the care and control of children and young persons must lie with the parents, but they should not stand alone. Standards must be established for the youth of today, as in years gone by, and the school and church have a central role to play in providing the child or young person with guidelines as well as discipline and support.

In this age of unemployment, to which the hon. Lady also referred, and of drink and drugs, the insidious undermining of society by television programmes, and the craving for money to feed into slot machines and to purchase items with which to keep up with someone else's lifestyle in the pop world, it is not surprising that delinquency is on the increase. That is why Northern Ireland needs good schools, with classes of reasonable size and proper discipline.

We also need an adequate police force. After all, the police are the representatives of law and order and should command respect. Police officers need to be seen walking about our housing estates and the streets of our towns.

The police must have the support of the public. It is no use if, when the police call at the home of a young person about his misconduct, the parents automatically side with their son.

More needs to be spent on facilities for young people, so that they have every chance to make good use of their leisure time. It is a shame that in parts of North Down proper facilities are not available. One such area is Holywood, but it is not unique. Many areas in the Province lack proper facilities for young people. The Government should set up an inquiry to find out which areas suffer from such deprivation and then ensure that the local authority in conjunction with Stormont makes money available. More also needs to be spent on the probation service.

All those things require expenditure, but I think I am taking up the theme put forward by the hon. Member for Redcar when I stress the prevention of delinquency as much as treating those who offend against the law. We need money if we are to deal with the problems. Who would deny that which may prevent young people from falling into delinquency or assist them back to the straight and narrow path? Needs must be balanced against cost. What is the present cost of residential care in Northern Ireland and what success has such care achieved? We need to know the cost of custodial treatment, whether the taxpayer is getting value for money and whether the treatment is helping children and young persons in Northern Ireland.

It is generally agreed by experts that the re-conviction rate for young people placed in institutions is extremely high. That may also be the experience in Great Britain. My hon. and learned Friend the Member for Blackpool, North (Mr. Miscampbell) nods in agreement. He above all hon. Members present knows about such matters. The Howard League for Penal Reform has emphasised that a spell in custodial care can easily confirm a young person in a delinquent way of life. Of course, in some cases young people must be placed in custody, in restraint in a home, because they have refused all other treatment, defied the treatment offered or have committed an offence which merits custodial treatment.

There is certainly a need for effective sanctions which reflect the condemnation of the entire community and the grief that the crime has caused to the victim. Such sanctions must also provide a reasonable prospect of correcting the offender and turning him from delinquency. Sadly, custodial sentences are sometimes given to young people who might benefit from a different type of treatment. We must consider the cost of custodial treatment. If the Minister cannot give that information now, I hope that he will write to me.

More and more crimes are being committed without anyone being found guilty and many such crimes are committed by children and young persons. That is why there is a need for more police officers, whose presence will deter potential offenders. They may also be able to catch offenders. I have complained many times that there are not enough police officers in North Down, which has a large and ever increasing population. Why has the number of community police officers been reduced in North Down? They carried out a useful job in Bangor and in other parts of my constituency.

Whether an adult or a young offender commits an offence when drunk, the public house or off licence which sold the drink to him should also have to face some financial penalty. Public houses and off licences make large profits out of drink, the pubs often staying open until late hours and then spewing their patrons on to the streets. I see people in Bangor late at night and in the early hours of the morning engaging in what I can only describe as anti-social behaviour. Before long they may commit some crime, such as smashing a window or threatening someone, in the vicinity of the public house where they have spent a great deal of time and money consuming alcohol. A disgraceful situation exists in Bangor, which I am sure is typical of many towns in Northern Ireland.

We must bear that in mind when discussing the treatment of offenders because that situation cannot be tolerated much longer. There must be some sanction on public house owners, who are only too delighted to welcome people in but do not care tuppence what those people do when they leave the premises.

Mr. Norman Miscampbell (Blackpool, North): How on earth can anyone prove who sold a person too much alcohol, whether it be in a pub or an off licence, or whether it was the responsibility of the last licensee who sold the person alcohol? How on earth can that be made an offence? There would never be a conviction.

Mr. Kilfedder: I do not share my hon. and learned Friend's pessimism. He may have sat too long on the bench. I view the matter from the point of view of the public. Something must be done. Those who sell drink make vast profits out of the people who buy it but they do not care what happens to those people when they leave the public house.

Police officers may see someone leaving a public house and they often go into public houses to watch what the patrons are up to. If such a police officer says that somebody drank alcohol in certain premises it should be possible to apply a sanction against the owner of that public house. That is the only way in which we shall ever stop the vile behaviour of people who drink in public houses in Bangor and elsewhere. I should add that many people who frequent public houses behave in a decent and sociable way, but I am talking about those who have no regard for other people or their property.

How many of the 14 to 17-year-old males who appeared before juvenile courts were sent to borstal or detention centres in the last year for which figures are available compared with 10 or 20 years ago when the Northern Ireland treatment of offenders legislation was enacted? The treatment of young people is a precise science. A study was carried out in conjunction with magistrates in Leeds where 50 per cent. of young truants were given supervision orders and 50 per cent. had their cases adjourned periodically and were given a magisterial wigging but nothing else. Those truants whose cases were adjourned and to whom the magistrates addressed a few remarks did much better than those who were given supervision orders, in terms both of school attendance and delinquency rates.

That study contains a lesson for all of us and the experts in this precise science. We need to spend more time considering why young people in particular engage in deviant behaviour and studying how to deal with that situation, for the benefit not only of the public but of those guilty of delinquency.

10.49 pm.

Mr. William Ross (Londonderry, East): As usual, we find ourselves considering late at night Northern Ireland legislation under the Order in Council procedure. I make my now traditional protest because this matter is one that should be dealt with by a Bill, not by an Order in Council late at night. Later, I shall say why I believe that a Bill is required in this particular case.

Reference has been made to the Black report published in 1979, yet the jigsaw picture is still being built up bit by bit, though perhaps not in quite so an unrelated way as the hon. Member for Redcar (Ms. Mowlam) would have us believe. We are taking far too long. The Black report was

[*Mr. William Ross*]

comprehensive and detailed, and most of its recommendations should have been dealt with in a far shorter time scale than that which we are currently observing. I remember the Black report debates, which were fairly thorough, and I see no reason for such delay before all of its recommendations are made law.

The argument as to how one reforms criminals has waged much longer than the 10 years that have elapsed since the Black report, and will probably continue for many a day yet if we are to strike the right balance between a punishment that fits the crime and reform—especially in relation to the young criminal, guilty of the loutish vandalism that so besmirches many towns and villages throughout Britain, never mind Northern Ireland. We must make such offenders face the consequences of their crimes.

It is easy to smash something or to cause difficulty, pain, terror and hardship. But many of those who commit such crimes seem to live their lives with no sense of personal conscience or discipline. Anything that we can do to instil a sense of responsibility for their own actions and towards the welfare of others and of society in general must be welcomed. However, I am not certain that we shall get all the answers from the legislation that is now before the House.

The hon. Member for North Down (Mr. Kilfedder) said that much of the responsibility for people's action lies in the home, the churches and the schools. I believe that it is in the home that an individual's sense of personal responsibility begins to develop and is nurtured to rule his life and his actions. Far too many cases of bad parenting bring out evil in young people.

The hon. Member for Redcar said that one reason for bad behaviour was lack of money. However, most young people complain that they lack enough money. We all like to have money when we are young. From what I have seen of the well-off yobboes in the south of England, I do not think that money would help to improve their behaviour at all. Bad behaviour has nothing to do with money, or the lack of it, but with the personal discipline that is instilled in young people in their own homes. Far too many parents throughout the United Kingdom do not take their responsibilities seriously enough.

The Minister remarked that parents will have to take their children to an attendance centre, which is a good thing. Perhaps it would be better if parents had to bring their children into school every day, as they would have responsibility for the children they bring into the world, and the children would not grow up to be quite so nasty.

As many of the problems that we are discussing are the consequence of loutish, yobbish behaviour by young adults, I welcome the reduction from 17 to 16 in the age at which they are forced to face the consequences of their action in court. Our object should be to prevent reoffending as far as possible. Like the hon. Lady, the Member for Redcar, I commend the efforts already made by voluntary and community groups. They do a tremendous job, but they need to be carefully monitored in case undesirable individuals take control, and that is an ever-present threat in Northern Ireland. If they are carefully monitored and properly run, those organisations have a great part to play, provided that the Government give them the funding to do their job.

A number of interesting factors emerge from a brief examination of the crime profile in Northern Ireland. An excellent publication by the probation board in Northern Ireland reveals that at approximately 3,800 offences per 100,000 population, the crime rate is less than in 40 of the 42 police force areas of England and Wales. Either Northern Ireland is still a much more law-abiding place than most of the rest of the United Kingdom, or a much higher percentage of crime is reported in England and Wales than in Northern Ireland. I do not know whether that is so, but I find it astonishing that the crime rate in Northern Ireland is lower than it is in 40 of the police force areas in England and Wales.

Clearly, the root cause of many of the problems in Northern Ireland is the terrorist campaign. It is not surprising that armed robbery is much higher on the list of crimes in Northern Ireland than it is in the rest of Britain.

The profile of the prison population starkly reveals the effect of terrorism in Northern Ireland. It reveals that 25 per cent. of the prison population in Northern Ireland are serving life sentences, compared with 6 per cent. in England and Wales. That is a direct result of the terrorist campaign. If it were not for the terrorist campaign, prisoners serving life sentences would represent a lower percentage of the prison population in Northern Ireland than they do in England and Wales as there is much less really violent crime. Without the terrorist life sentences, I suspect that there would be very few prisoners serving life sentences in Northern Ireland.

In April this year, 7 per cent. of sentenced prisoners were aged between 16 and 20, and 72 per cent. of those over 21 were convicted of scheduled offences—or terrorist crimes. In other words, seven out of 10 of the people in prison in Northern Ireland are there as a result of the activities of terrorist organisations. That is a huge proportion. If that is taken out of the equation, Northern Ireland is clearly a peaceful, law-abiding society, strange as it may seem.

The hon. Member for North Down (Mr. Kilfedder), who mentioned what happened in Bangor, was referring to quite unacceptable behaviour that should be stopped. But the police cannot stamp it out because they are so tied up in solving terrorist crime, and we all appreciate that.

Mr. John Taylor (Strangford): Because there are a lot of Conservative voters there.

Mr. Ross: The right hon. Gentleman is correct, there are a lot of Conservative electors there; perhaps the wealthy section of the community is committing all the offences along the sea front and wherever else. It is apparent from the south-east of England that it is not poor kids who are committing offences in the area.

An interesting statistic appears in the probation service's report, and it astonished me when I first learned of it 18 months ago. Fine defaulters represent more than half the sentenced receptions in prison in Northern Ireland. Does the Minister find that a disquieting as well as an amazing fact? Is the figure for this side of the Irish sea the same? If so, it is about time we stopped putting people in prison for not paying their fines. They should be made to do community service. What sort of unpaid work does an offender have to do under a community service order? An offender has to do gardening, labouring, painting and decorating, work with senior citizens and to help with youth clubs and voluntary organisations. Such tasks are tailormade for people who do not pay their fines.

If someone is sentenced to imprisonment for about a fortnight they can be released after only two days, or, if they are fortunate, only one day.

Mr. Seamus Mallon (Newry and Armagh): It sounds as though the hon. Gentleman could write a book about it.

Mr. Ross: I assure the hon. Member for Newry and Armagh (Mr. Mallon) that there is nothing like personal experience for discovering facts. He should try it some time and show whether he has the courage of his convictions, which he so often proclaims in the House.

If someone who takes home £70 or £80 a week is fined £150 or seven days' imprisonment, he will take the seven days, as he will probably serve only two and a half anyway. The cost of keeping such a person in prison must be astronomical. We should consider this issue sensibly and try to do something about it.

Community service orders should be made on folk for whom they will be effective. I am sure that many old people need their hedges or grass cut. I would sooner send out a chap who has not paid his fine to do community work than some young thug who may case the old person's house and return the following week and clean up. This is a fruitful sector for reassessment of sentencing policy.

I remember the creation of the probation service in Northern Ireland, which is different from the service throughout the rest of Britain.

Mr. James Molyneaux (Lagan Valley): It is more efficient.

Mr. Ross: Is it a more efficient service? If it is doing as well as it appears to be, why has it not been tried over here? Given the crime rate here, it appears to be more necessary. Some hon. Members are fond of saying how bad things are in Northern Ireland and what a terrible place it is, but the service is doing well and the Government are sitting on their hands and refusing to modernise it. I should have thought that this modernising, efficient, privatising Government would have wanted to introduce this successful system in the rest of Britain so that it can benefit from the experiment that has been so successful on the other side of the Irish sea.

Mr. Roy Beggs (Antrim, East): Does the hon. Gentleman agree that the excellent probation service in Northern Ireland could be improved if the case burden on each officer were further reduced?

Mr. Ross: That possibility had not occurred to me. No doubt the case work is heavy but if it is paying such rich dividends, more expenditure on the service might be a good investment. If we can reform these young people and improve their behaviour, it will be time and effort well spent.

Other factors should be taken into consideration. The courts should make full use of community service orders. I have suggested one area where their use could be extended. As well as making good use of the orders, the authorities in Northern Ireland ensure that they are carried out in full. I confess that Northern Ireland is a very different place from central London, if only because of the

size of the population. In smaller towns and villages individuals are more easily located and can be made to do the work.

If a sentence is passed and if someone is told that he must do certain things to discharge his liability, the end is much worse than the beginning if the authorities do not ensure that the liability is discharged. The service would become a laughing stock. If community service orders are used, the Government should make sure that the system is carried out properly.

It is sad that some 60 per cent. of those who are given community service have four or more previous convictions. There may be good reasons. Perhaps the Minister could tell us why there is such a high level of repeat performances.

On the structure of the probation board, we are told that it will consist of

"(a) a chairman, deputy chairman, and not less than 10 or more than 18 other members, appointed by the Secretary of State for Northern Ireland;

(b) not more than 5 members co-opted by the board with the approval of the Secretary of State. (This power has not been used)."

Why is there such a wide range of 10 to 18 members and why is the power referred to in paragraph (b) provided if it is not being used?

The subject is of great interest to everyone who is concerned about getting rid of loutish behaviour in the community. There are critical factors about the implementation of the orders. The probation board draws attention to one:

"There is some evidence in England and Wales to suggest that the growth in Probation Orders has replaced lower tariff disposals of the Court such as a fine. It is therefore vital in the operation of this new legislation in Northern Ireland that the new intensive Probation Supervision is not used as a substitute for lesser penalties but is used instead of a custodial sentence."

That is important. I should like an assurance from the Minister that that advice is being accepted.

NIACRO expressed considerable concern about the level of funding for day centres. Perhaps the Minister will tell us about that. How many day centres will there be, where will they be sited, and how widely does he intend that they should be used?

On paper, there are quite a few staff, but keeping a check on young offenders, making sure that they behave themselves and keeping a close eye on their out-of-school activities, so to speak, is difficult. I do not think that it can be done cheaply, but it pays rich dividends. Staffing should be examined again.

It seems that there was a call in the Black report for an integrated strategy. The hon. Member for Redcar made a complaint. I do not believe that a complaint is fully justified. I am complaining not about the development as such, but about the long time that it has taken for that development to happen. As I said earlier, I would like the structure to be created and put in place very soon. Adding bits and pieces is not good enough. We need a comprehensive set of proposals to be brought forward to deal with other matters concerning young people. There is much work going on in that area. Can we be given a time scale for its completion?

I have a quibble about article 12, which is the tiddly bit that was slipped in, I believe. The article deals with the increasing of maximum terms of imprisonment for offenders in cases of child cruelty and assaults on and rapes of women. We are told that the maximum penalty for

[*Mr. Ross*]

indecent assault on a female will rise from two to 10 years imprisonment. That brings the penalty for assault on a female into line with that for assault on a male. That is the only reason we are given for the increase. There is no explanation of why 10 years rather than two years is right for offences against either sex. Can we be given those reasons? Why should the penalty not be 15 years, or remain at two years?

The Government say that the increase in the penalty for child cruelty reflects the concern arising from a number of recent cases. I thought that one of the basic precepts was that hard cases make bad law. Hard cases probably make good law in this instance, but that is by the way. Is public concern the best reason the Government can give for multiplying the possible sentence by five? Why do we not have a more detailed explanation of why the Government decide on certain levels of sentencing, rather than the Government just saying what they have about these?

The reason given for increasing the penalty for attempted rape is that it is similar to the increase in England and Wales brought about by the Sexual Offences Act 1985. That brings me back to my first point. If these matters were being dealt with by Bill instead of by order, the Minister could not get away with the bland statement that the penalties were being increased to bring them into line with what happens in England and Wales. He would have to give a full and clear explanation in the House and in Committee of the Government's reasons for deciding on those periods of imprisonment.

I am not saying that those periods are wrong; I just want to be told why they are right. I want to be told in detail and through the Bill procedure. I want to be told in Committee and I want to be able to question the Minister in a way that I can never question him in this nonsense that we go through here, night after night. We are not able to question, not able to obtain answers and not able to dot an i or cross a t. That is not good enough and it has been going on for almost 20 years too long.

11.13 pm

Mr. Seamus Mallon (Newry and Armagh): I regard these orders as important pieces of legislation, not so much for what is in them—although there is much substance and much good in them—as for the implications of the elements that are not included and the limit of the scope of the orders. It is almost impossible to seek a solution to the problems about which other hon. Members have spoken, without considering the context in which the problems exist. I do not see how we can discuss these orders unless we discuss the context in which young people find themselves.

I am not talking about the people with money who behave in a loutish way in places such as Bangor on a Saturday night. Such behaviour occurs in every other village and town and probably in every country in the world. I am talking about young people from deprived backgrounds, who have never worked, whose fathers and grandfathers have never worked and who, in their own hearts, know that they will never work. They do not have a stake in society. They have been thrown into the trap of despair before they are even adults. If we are ever to get to the root of the problem, we must tackle that aspect.

During today's excellent debate on the economy, it struck me forcefully that if one of the young people to whom I spoke last night when canvassing in a deprived area had been sitting here today he would have heard about a different world. His economy is not the economy of today's debate. He will never see it, because he will not be employed. He sees around him not just financial deprivation but terrible social and environmental deprivation. From the hour he is born, he lives in that deprivation, which in the North of Ireland is exacerbated by many factors, not the least of which is violence. Many young people fall into that trap early in their lives. They are the people whom we should consider, not the people in the flashy cars who screech around the town late at night, having had a skinful of drink.

The issues are compassion and concern for people who, through no fault of their own, find themselves in a difficult position. That is why the legislation is so important. It could be improved, but only by looking at the scope of the problem. We have heard that 16 to 19-year-olds constitute a higher percentage of the prison population in Northern Ireland than in any other European country. The figures are exaggerated by the number of young people who have been convicted of scheduled offences, but that is not the whole story. Under legislation, imprisoning people has been an easier option than the constructive approach of rehabilitating them. That is one reason why the prison figures are so unbalanced. Unless we aim at rehabilitation, custodial sentences will continue to be the norm, not for the right reason but because it is an easy option which gives less trouble to the judicial bench and everyone else involved.

The hon. Member for Londonderry, East (Mr. Ross) referred to fine defaulters. We should consider that valid point because there are alternatives to imposing fines which will not be paid anyway, but the options have been reduced by this legislation. The Minister will correct me if I am wrong, but I understand that a person in England and Wales who defaults is arrested and brought before the courts, which can exercise options. That does not happen in the North of Ireland. A person who defaults is immediately sent to prison and the courts do not have the discretion to try another approach. That, too, contributes to the prison figures in the north of Ireland. It makes no sense to have such a difference between England and Wales and the north of Ireland. From one point of view, it is careless, and from another it is extremely punitive.

Our thrust must be towards rehabilitation rather than punishment and towards creating an alternative to imprisonment for fine defaulters.

Mr. William Ross: I made the point that that is an economic benefit for those, especially the unemployed, who are prepared to spend two or three nights in prison rather than pay the fine. Surely it would far better if they did something useful for the community.

Mr. Mallon: I readily take the hon. Gentleman's point. If I may be anecdotal for a moment, I started my career working in a training school for young offenders. At that time such schools were called reformatories. One person, whom I shall call Joe, went to the city centre in Belfast each time he was released and threw a brick through the biggest window that he could find so that he would be sent back to the reformatory. It was the only place of stability that he had known during his poor life. It would be no use talking to that kid about a fine because it would be irrelevant. It would be no use talking to the people mentioned by the hon. Member for Redcar (Ms. Mowlam) because they would not have the money to pay a fine. We must find a constructive way of showing such people that the sort of offences that they have committed are not just bad for society but bad for their own lives and those of their children. That might go some way towards solving the problem.

I wish now to discuss a sensitive part of the problem. I do not think that this sort of legislation, in its totality, will work without two factors. First, it must be worked properly by magistrates and judges. I have my doubts about that. I have the highest regard for those who sit as magistrates and judges, but there are some people who should not sit as magistrates and judges. Anyone dealing with young people in the North of Ireland recognises that fact.

I cite another personal experience. One of the ways in which the Black report has not been accommodated is by not removing non-attendance at school from this legislation and putting it into the education sphere. I dealt with the case of a young boy who was not attending school. His father did not attend the court hearing. It is true that that young boy should have attended school and that the father should have appeared at the court. The bench gave the order for the police to arrest the young boy on the school bus and take him to a training school. There was no reference to the family. There were no options. I do not blame the police, because they did not have any options. That was a most insensitive approach, but it has been repeated time and again by the same magistrate. That is a matter of record.

Unless the magistrates and judges operate this legislation in the spirit in which it is written, working towards the aims that it embodies, it will fall down. If they perceive the easy options to be imposing a fine or putting a young person in prison, some of them will do that, because some of them do not have the humanitarian approach that is required if we are ever to solve the problems of young offenders.

The second factor, which has already been mentioned, is a comprehensive approach to the problem. You will notice, Mr. Deputy Speaker, that we are all using the same terminology. I readily admit that the good briefings that we have received from concerned people in the north of Ireland have rightly stressed that problem. There is an a la carte approach not only to this legislation but to the whole of Northern Ireland legislation. To mix a metaphor, it is like choosing dolly mixtures—a piece of this legislation and a consequential amendment to tie it in with another piece of legislation, and so on. Anyone who has ever dealt with the Emergency Provisions Act, the Prevention of Terrorism Act, the public order legislation and this legislation knows that he needs about six Acts to cross-reference.

We do not want any sleight of hand, such as the reference in the explanatory document to the Black report and the children and young persons review group. That is sleight of hand because it implies that the measure is in accord with what was proposed. We want a complete children and young persons measure for Northern Ireland in its totality, a measure which will deal with all the problems on the basis of the Black report. The Government must not pick bits out of the report when it suits them, leaving other bits out when it does not suit,

thereby creating a bag of dolly mixtures, so to speak, with a great deal of cross-referencing having to be done. That cannot lead to efficiency, effectiveness and justice.

Mr. William Ross: Will the hon. Gentleman join the Ulster Unionist party in asking that this matter be dealt with by way of a Bill? That would enable us to show a degree of cross-community support in the interests of all the people in Northern Ireland. That is the only means by which we will achieve the kind of investigation that the hon. Gentleman is seeking.

Mr. Mallon: For a moment I thought that the hon. Gentleman was inviting me to join the Ulster Unionist party—an offer which I appreciate but must decline. However, I willingly join Ulster Unionist Members in making the demand to which he refers. Having deliberated for many long hours on the emergency provisions and the prevention of terrorism legislation, I have no hesitation in joining those Members in trying to obtain children and young offenders legislation which is comprehensive and strategic and deals with all the problems in one measure. Indeed, I would join anybody in seeking that end. Unless we can examine such a measure line by line, we shall end up with a bit of this, a bit of that, with consequential amendments here and there, and everything in the garden will be rosy except the net result.

I do not propose to discuss the detail of the orders, much of which has been covered, but will the fourth conditions be used and, if so, how? How can they most effectively contribute to the welfare of society and of the young people involved? Will there be enough funding for day centres? I gather that there will be just one day centre and that it will be in Belfast. There will not be one west of the Bann, so there will not be the reasonable accessibility that will be required if the bench is to have the option of pursuing that course rather than imposing a fine or custodial sentence.

I take it as a compliment to those of us west of the Bann when it is implied that we do not have the same degree of law-breaking by young people. It would be nice if that were the case. Even so, are we to throw on to the voluntary groups the onus, and on an ad hoc basis and almost weekly, the task of setting up a day centre situation—not a day centre—which will be able to cope adequately? I have discussed this with various people, who say that they are confident of being able to deal with the problem by means of existing funding and their own structures. I hope that they are right, but I fear that we shall have to tackle the joint problems of the number of centres and the siting of them.

I welcome in this legislation the removal of the negative conditions which have applied, and which I believe still apply, in England and Wales. They are unenforceable and in most cases they make no sense. Generally, they cost more time, money and energy than they are worth. I compliment the Minister on having had the good sense to leave that aspect out this legislation. It shows that he and his advisers listened to those with experience of this in England and Wales.

I welcome article 6, which relates to training schools. The term of the order is to be reduced from three years to two years

"or until he attains the age of nineteen".

The period during which a detained person may not be placed out under licence without reference to the Secretary

[*Mr. Mallon*]

of State is to be reduced from one year to six months. These reductions are improvements. They represent an act of faith in the legislative approach.

Article 7 deals with the extension of the maximum term of detention in young offenders centres from two years and 364 days, as I understand it, to four years. If that means that fewer young people will go to prison, that is grand. That would be a positive step forward. However, if young offenders' centres are to be turned into alternative prisons, that is bad. Such a move would confuse the issue and substantially change the complexion and context of young offenders centres. Such a change should be monitored. We must at least question the possible consequences. An increase in non-custodial sentences could ensue.

Will magistrates and benches generally take these provisions in the spirit in which they are written? If they do, we are on the way to solving the problem. If they do not, we shall be moving away from a solution.

The minimum age for a community service order causes a problem. I am confused about this, and I think that the same can be said for the proposed legislation. We are talking of young people who reoffend and increase the tariff for themselves. In effect, there is a postponement of the custodial sentence. That does not benefit the system or the circumstances of the individual. There is an inherent danger which must be reconsidered. Is there an alternative? I think that there is. There must be a clear separation between the ages of 16 years and 17 to 21 years. If the domino effect is to start at 16 years and continue through to 21 years, the result will be immensely counter-productive and unintended.

Article 13 provides for an option to remand young people to young offenders centres. Will the option be exercised by magistrates and judges? I would much prefer a mandatory provision that young people should be remanded to young offenders centres for non-scheduled offences. Better still, they should be remanded to the type of centre which could have been established under the Treatment of Offenders Act (Northern Ireland) 1968. I am talking not of Risley but of a properly staffed, run and thought out remand centre for young people. There is a danger that in the end the easy option will be taken.

Some young offenders are imprisoned for long periods at the Secretary of State's pleasure, having been convicted of scheduled offences, and in many cases having committed horrific crimes. Nethertheless, they are still young offenders. I shall not dwell on the matter, because there will be other opportunities to ask again and again that the review procedure for those young offenders be overhauled quickly, dramatically, and in a way which demonstrates, as I think everyone agrees, that the present system is unjust, unfair and, in many ways, unworkable. Surely we must include in our consideration young offenders who remain in prison at the Secretary of State's pleasure.

I pay tribute to the Probation Board, which has an onerous task. It is funded by the Secretary of State but it is then left to do its job. There is nothing between the board and its funding. It is the board to which the voluntary groups have to be responsible. The members of the board deserve tremendous credit. They have done a magnificent job in difficult circumstances. I should love to think that the Northern Ireland Office and the Secretary of

State and the Minister would do those people the greatest courtesy by listening intently when they ask for a comprehensive and strategic approach to the problem rather than the dolly mixture approach adopted so far.

11.34 pm

Mr. Ian Stewart: With the leave of the House, I shall reply to the debate.

During the past hour, we have had a wide-ranging debate. Some of it has been related specifically to the contents of the orders, but much of it, for perfectly understandable and justifiable reasons, has dealt with young offenders, their offences and general sentencing policy. I hope that the House will understand if I concentrate on those matters directly related to the orders. I shall not, however, overlook what has been said tonight about the wider matters.

The hon. Member for North Down (Mr. Kilfedder) suggested that the proprietors of public houses should carry some responsibility for drunkenness. He also spoke about sentencing policy, but that is a question for all of the United Kingdom. I shall draw the attention of my right hon. Friend the Home Secretary to the general matters discussed.

I am not an expert on the law in England and Wales, but some of the suggestions given tonight appear to involve some practical problems of implementation, as pointed out by my hon. and learned Friend the Member for Blackpool, North (Mr. Miscampbell). Some interesting comments have been made about judicial and sentencing policy that applies throughout the United Kingdom in addition to the policy directly related to Northern Ireland. I have taken note of what has been said.

The hon. Member for Londonderry, East (Mr. Ross) asked about the timing of the Treatment of Offenders (Northern Ireland) Order. He pointed out, quite fairly, that it is a number of years since the Black report was completed and originally discussed. It has taken many years to bring forward the proposals because the question of training schools proved an extremely contentious one on which a wide range of views were expressed by those reacting to the proposals. It was not until 1986 that a decision was eventually taken that training schools should continue, but that the terms should be reduced. That decision has been implemented under article 6 of the order. In a sense that decision represented a compromise, but it was also a reflection of the consensus, which contained widely different views about the possible role of the training schools.

In the context of the Treatment of Offenders (Northern Ireland) Order and the general debate on sentencing, training schools have been considered in the light of their use by and for offenders. Hon. Members will be aware, however, that such schools are also used for care cases. One cannot take a simple view of such schools based on the care of offenders; we must remember the other role of those institutions.

A number of hon. Members have spoken about the co-ordination of particular measures and our decision to put the measures dealing with the treatment of offenders in one parcel even though it does not cover the range of issues that are relevant to the behaviour of young people or the non-offence aspects of the problem. In many ways it would be convenient to draw more legislation together, but the House should recognise that a number of the matters fall under the responsibility of different Departments in Northern Ireland, just as they do in the rest of Great Britain. Whereas the general law relating to children is a matter for the DSS or the Home Office, issues relating to offenders in Northern Ireland fall under my responsibility and are solely a Home Office concern in the rest of the United Kingdom.

There are practical problems in relating those two issues in the legislation, but I assure hon. Members that great care is taken. I should like to pay tribute to my officials and others who have played a part in drawing up these measures and ensured that the wider picture is carefully assessed.

We intend to produce a children and young persons order for Northern Ireland in the next Session of Parliament. It will deal with a range of matters——

Mr. John D. Taylor: Will the Minister give way?

Mr. Stewart: I shall give way in a moment if the right hon. Gentleman will allow me to finish my comments. The order will deal with a range of matters which were also covered in Black report and are certainly in need of attention in the House. It will parallel developments which are taking place in England and Wales through the Children Bill.

Mr. Taylor: I welcome the Minister's statement that new comprehensive legislation on this subject will be introduced, but I regret the fact that he referred to an order. In light of the views expressed by the official Opposition, the hon. Member for Newry and Armagh (Mr. Mallon) and, of course, by Ulster Unionist Members, will he consider introducing a proper Bill, with rights for full parliamentary debate and amendments?

Mr. Ian Stewart: I noted the comments of the right hon. Gentleman and other hon. Members from Northern Ireland who have raised this point this evening. As they will know, my right hon. Friend the Secretary of State has said that he will be willing to consider the procedures by which we take Northern Ireland business through the House, particularly the possibility of having debate through a Northern Ireland Committee. He remains open to discuss those possibilities with representatives from Northern Ireland.

I cannot undertake, and it would be irresponsible of me to do so, that the House is likely to be able to provide——

Mr. Mallon: Will the Minister give way?

Mr. Stewart: If the hon. Gentleman will possess himself, and if other hon. Members will allow me even to complete my sentences, of course I shall give way.

I cannot foresee a time when the House will have the available capacity to deal, in full primary legislation through Bills and Acts, with all legislation for Northern

Ireland, much of which substantially replicates that which is enacted in England, Wales or the rest of the United Kingdom.

Mr. Mallon: I welcome the Minister's confirmation that there will be some form of legislation for Northern Ireland for children and young offenders. Will he go further and say that it will be fresh legislation, which will supersede existing legislation and will not be consequential either on that which we are discussing tonight or on an Act dealing with children and young offenders which might be introduced for England and Wales?

Mr. Stewart: As the hon. Gentleman will know, all Northern Ireland legislation is considered in relation to the particular circumstances of that Province. I am not the Minister responsible for this particular legislative proposal, but I shall convey the hon. Gentleman's comments to my hon. Friend the Parliamentary Under-Secretary of State.

I wish to illustrate not merely that we need to tackle the recommendations of the Black report, and other discussions on this matter, consistently over a period, but to emphasise that none of our decisions are taken in the sort of isolation which the hon. Member for Redcar (Ms. Mowlam) unfairly suggested.

It being one and a half hours after the motion was entered upon, MR. DEPUTY SPEAKER *put the Question, pursuant to Order [26 May].*

Resolved,

That the draft Treatment of Offenders (Northern Ireland) Order 1989, which was laid before this House on 9th May, be approved.

NORTHERN IRELAND (COMMUNITY SERVICE)

MR. DEPUTY SPEAKER *then proceeded, pursuant to order [26 May], to put the Question on the remaining motion relating to Northern Ireland.*

Motion made, and Question put.

That the draft Community Service Orders (Northern Ireland Consequential Amendments) Order 1989, which was laid before this House on 9th May, be approved.—*[Mr. David Hunt.]*

Question agreed to.

PRIVILEGES

Ordered,

That Mr. Attorney General, Mr. Tony Benn, Mr. John Biffen, Sir Bernard Braine, Mr. Frank Dobson, Sir Philip Goodhart, Mr. Terence L. Higgins, Sir Peter Hordern, Sir Russell Johnston, Mr. Michael Jopling, Mr. John Morris, Sir Charles Morrison, Mr. Stanley Orme, Mr. Cranley Onslow, Mr. Merlyn Rees, Mr. Peter Shore and Mr. John Wakeham be members of the Committee of Privileges.—*[Mr. David Hunt.]*

Snapethorpe Hospital, Wakefield

Motion made, and Question proposed, That this House do now adjourn.—*[Mr. Chapman.]*

11.45 pm

Mr. David Hinchliffe (Wakefield): I am grateful for this opportunity to raise the proposed closure of Snapethorpe hospital. It is of the greatest concern to my constituents.

At the outset, I express my gratitude to the Minister for agreeing to meet me in a fortnight's time to discuss this important matter. This debate is about the proposed closure of the most modern hospital in my constituency. It is about the potential for the future use of the excellent facilities and environment at Snapethorpe. It is about the questionable way in which the hospital has been run down over 10 years, and the way in which local opinion about the hospital's future has been treated with utter contempt by the Wakefield health authority and the Yorkshire regional health authority.

The debate is also about the Government's policy towards medium-sized and small hospitals such as Snapethorpe, and about the Government's policy on initiatives for community care of the sort put forward by the local authority in Wakefield in respect of Snapethorpe hospital.

The formal campaign to save Snapethorpe hospital from closure has recently celebrated 10 years of existence. It would be appropriate for me to express my sincere appreciation to the many people and organisations who have been involved in that campaign over 10 years. I should like to mention especially Alice Lannagan and Penny Roberts, two former nurses at the hospital—when it was in operation—who have worked ceaselessly as chair and vice-chair of the campaign for 10 years.

I want to mention the Wakefield trades council and the local Labour party, which have continued to fight to retain the hospital; also the Wakefield community health council which has never ceased to reflect the views of Wakefield's people on this issue; and my predecessor as the Member for Wakefield, Walter Harrison, who sought vigorously over many years to ensure that the hospital was kept open and in public use. It would be remiss of me not to mention that several stalwart campaigners for the hospital in these 10 years are unfortunately no longer alive to witness this latest chapter in the fight.

The fact that, after 10 years, the district and regional health authorities have still not disposed of Snapethorpe is evidence that the campaign has been extremely effective and fully justifies the efforts made in it. The way in which the closure of Snapethorpe has been engineered is a matter of deep concern.

I do not usually read *The Times,* but someone drew to my attention the parliamentary sketch in that paper of 26 April, which reported health questions from the previous day, when I had raised the issue of Snapethorpe hospital. The article states:

"'But Snapethorpe Hospital hasn't had a patient since 1984,' sneered Junior Minister David Mellor at a Labour back bencher, David Hinchliffe (Wakefield), who had asked about a hospital closure. Laughter followed, at Hinchliffe's expense. Only later did one reflect that Health Authorities empty hospitals before closing them. Mellor was offside."

The penultimate sentence in that quotation is unintentionally highly perceptive, because the manner in which the hospital was emptied was a scandal in itself. My predecessor Walter Harrison described the Snapethorpe

problem as "closure by stealth". That sums up what has happened to this important hospital in the past 10 years. The highly questionable way in which the rundown occurred merits more attention than I am able to give in this short debate. However, some important matters need to be brought to the attention of the Minister. First, the health authority has for 10 years sought the closure of the hospital but has never had the courage to face local people and admit its real intentions. Over many years we have been given all sorts of excuses for ward closures but all along we have been told officially that there has never been any intention to close the hospital. However, that is the proposal before the Minister.

Secondly, arbitrary decisions have been made by unaccountable hospital consultants who in some instances —I stress "some instances"—have been more concerned about the personal inconvenience of travelling to Snapethorpe hospital than about any issue of patient care. They have withdrawn from the treatment of patients at the hospital and have made it inoperative.

Thirdly, my constituents have been deprived of the infectious diseases facility that was valued and used over many years and relatives, without cars, of patients who suffer from such diseases face three bus journeys to the far side of Leeds to the Seacroft hospital. As a result of the closure of Snapethorpe hospital and in particular the Barden ward, the excellent convalescent facilities at that hospital no longer exist. Wakefield health authority has taken no action to provide convalescent facilities elsewhere in its area. That means that my constituents are now deprived of any form of convalescent facilities and I am especially concerned about that because I receive information about a significant number of people who have been prematurely discharged from hospital. Those people would have benefited from a week or a fortnight of recuperative care in the facility of the kind that Snapethorpe hospital used to offer.

As I have said, the debate is also about Government policy on medium and small hospitals. On 22 May 1980 the Government issued a consultative paper entitled "Hospital services—the future pattern of hospital provision in England". That made clear the Government's belief that medium and small hospitals should play a more important role than they were playing at that time. That was a significant policy statement by the Government and it was produced by a Minister of Health who, at the invitation of Walter Harrison, visited Snapethorpe hospital and blocked a proposed temporary closure. That was unanimously welcomed by Wakefield people.

The press release that accompanied the consultative paper said:

"The time has come for a critical look at the giant 'super' hospital with over 1,000 beds—impersonal, complex and remote . . . these hospitals are frequently remote from the people they are intended to serve, also they lead to the closure of smaller hospitals which are much loved and much needed by their local communities."

Perhaps when the Minister replies to the debate he will tell us what happened to those worthy expressions of concern for just the kind of situation that we have in Wakefield. In Wakefield a much loved, much needed and much valued hospital which was donated to the people of Wakefield in the 1930s by a benefactor, is to be closed because of a huge development on the Pinderfields hospital site. That site is inconvenient for vast numbers of people in Wakefield. As the Minister may know, Snapethorpe is at the centre of the local community and it can be argued on behalf of the majority of my constituents that Pinderfields hospital simply is not in as convenient a position as Snapethorpe.

It is important that the Minister responds to the clear policy statement of 1980. I am not aware of the Government formally changing their view on this matter, and the policy statement relates directly to hospitals of the kind that we are discussing. Snapethorpe is a small and valued local community hospital.

I said at the outset that we are also considering local initiatives in community care. The Minister may have been informed that Wakefield metropolitan district council has formulated detailed plans to use Snapethorpe as a focal point for community and support services for the elderly and disabled with a range of much-needed provisions, including shelter, extra care units, workshops for the disabled and a day centre.

Since I became a Member of Parliament I have had detailed discussions over a number of years with various members and officers of the local authority about its proposals, which would provide valuable facilities for the people of Wakefield, and for which there is considerable support among my constituents.

The local authority has had detailed discussions at officer and member level with the Wakefield health authority about its proposal. Wakefield council, in effect, sought the joint use of Snapethorpe hospital. It is that point that I hope the Minister will deal with tonight. For whatever reason, at the behest of the Wakefield health authority those discussions were discontinued after the removal of Sir Jack Smart as the authority's chairman.

There is a will within the district council to continue that dialogue and I am sure that that will be supported by the vast majority, if not all, of my constituents. The local authority pressed the health authority to support the continued use of Snapethorpe. I envisaged the provision of respite nursing care and the reinstatement of the much-needed convalescent facilities that had been withdrawn by the health authority. Those facilities would, if they were provided by the Wakefield health authority as part of a joint venture, fit in ideally with the local authority's provisions to form the basis of an excellent initiative which would enable people to remain within the community with support. Sadly, the minds of Health Service managers nowadays seem to operate like cash registers and Wakefield health authority has no vision of what could be achieved.

The Minister knows that I have tabled a number of questions about the performance-related pay and one area that concerns me is that hon. Members such as myself cannot discover under what circumstances performance-related pay is given to Health Service managers. But I am aware that one of the performance objectives is the achievement of hospital closures and it is likely that, if the closure of Snapethorpe is ratified by the Secretary of State, the general manager on a salary of £35,000 a year could receive a performance-related cash bonus.

It is nonsense that a person paid from public funds should receive a bonus from public funds for achieving such a closure completely against the wishes of those who pay him. The Government must look at the way in which performance-related pay operates, particularly in relation to hospitals such as Snapethorpe.

Snapethorpe has been empty for some considerable time and the officers of Wakefield health authority had no intention other than to see Snapethorpe sold as a valuable asset.

The permanent closure and disposal of Snapethorpe was discussed at a meeting of the Wakefield health authority on 22 December 1988. A report written by officers of the Wakefield health authority on the local authority's plans said:

"none of the proposals would have a significant direct benefit to the local health service."

That made clear the officers' belief that the proposals of Wakefield district council would not have a bearing on the Health Service within the Wakefield authority.

I find it astounding that anyone looking at the proposals for community services of the kind that I mentioned earlier could reach the conclusion that those provisions would not have a bearing on the health services. It says something about the people who are now running the National Health Service at local level that they are unable to anticipate just how much the local health service could benefit from the kind of initiatives we propose.

We hope that the Government's long overdue response to the Griffiths report will be made before long and that they will consider proposals of the kind being put forward by Wakefield. They should be supported by the Government because they are about ensuring that people remain in the community and do not enter institutional care that they do not require. The council's proposals would ensure that many people who would otherwise be hospitalised will remain in the community with day care, with day support, and with the help of the other initiatives proposed, rather than end up in long-term institutional care. If that does not have a direct bearing on the local health services, I do not know what has.

I want to give the Minister adequate time to respond to my comments. I am sure that he is well briefed. Although these are early days in the hon. Gentleman's role as Under-Secretary of State for Health, he is certain to have had already his fair share of grief from Back Benchers such as myself fighting for much loved local hospitals. I know that the hon. Gentleman will have to respond to another Adjournment debate later this week, and I sympathise with him for having to remain here until such a late hour to deal with such issues.

By comparison with the arguments advanced by other right hon. and hon. Members, not all can boast, as I can, the proud history and excellent potential of Snapethorpe hospital. Not all can boast of formal objections to the proposal to close the hospital not only from the constituency Member of Parliament but from hon. Members representing surrounding constituencies. They include my hon. Friends the Members for Dewsbury (Mrs. Taylor), for Leeds, Central (Mr. Fatchett), for Hemsworth (Mr. Buckley), for Pontefract and Castleford (Mr. Lofthouse), and for Normanton (Mr. O'Brien). They have all, without prompting, but knowing of the strength of feeling about Snapethorpe, objected formally to the health authority.

Not all right hon. and hon. Members can boast the support of all political parties at local level for the future of their hospitals. Wakefield Conservative party fully supports the future of Snapethorpe. It does not say very much about the matter except at election time, but it does support the hospital's future. Had I been defeated at the last election, I would fully have expected the elected

[*Mr. David Hinchliffe*]

Conservative Member, God forbid, to be making a plea for the hospital's future in my place, because I know that the Conservative candidate shares my concern.

Not everyone can boast that their hospital has been visited by two Health Ministers and by at least three shadow Health Ministers, all concerned about its threatened closure. And not all right hon. and hon. Members can boast petitions containing the signatures of 100,000 local people supporting their hospital's future. Surely none can boast the level of local commitment that has enabled the fight to retain Snapethorpe hospital to continue for more than a decade.

Snapethorpe has a future in the hands of local people. There are clear proposals to ensure that it will have a future of use to the community; a future of carrying on the good work that it has performed as a hospital over many, many years. I appeal to the Minister to block the proposed permanent closure so that the hospital may enjoy that future.

12.4 am

The Parliamentary Under-Secretary of State for Health (Mr. Roger Freeman): The hon. Member for Wakefield (Mr. Hinchliffe) is a doughty fighter for his constituency causes. I pay tribute to him for his energy and his relentless efforts in pursuit of his constituents' interests. That must be right and I make no complaint about it, however many parliamentary questions, Adjournment debates or letters there are. It is his duty and his responsibility and I respond with enthusiasm and a willingness to reason with him. Ultimately we have to exchange argument and discussion on the basis of reason and what is in the best interests of his constituents who are patients of the National Health Service but within limited resources. Resources were always limited. They were limited under the Labour Government and they are limited under the present Administration in any one year. We have to make the best use of the resources available.

I have nine minutes to address some of the points that the hon. Gentleman has raised. One of his key points was about community hospitals. The Government firmly believe that community hospitals have a role to play in the National Health Service. I am bound to say that the argument in support of community hospitals is stronger in rural areas than in urban areas.

I do not know the borough of Wakefield. I have passed through it but I have not visited it. I am sure that the hon. Gentleman will appreciate that in an urban area, or a comparatively densely populated area, the argument for having several separate community hospitals is very different from that in the sparsely populated areas of Norfolk where I was last week, when it was put to me that very sophisticated, high-technology medical equipment was not so important and could be provided in the provincial cities and towns, but it was important that commmunity hospitals should remain to provide non-acute services. That is an important policy and we stand by it, but, as I am sure that hon. Gentleman will agree on reflection, it is more relevant to rural areas than to urban areas.

The hon. Gentleman raised the specific issue of Snapethorpe hospital. As he said, he, I and a delegation are to meet on 20 June. It is somewhat unusual to have the Adjournment debate before the meeting. Nevertheless it will serve as a benefit in putting the hon. Gentleman's comments on record for the Department and the district health authority to study beforehand. I shall certainly study them before the meeting.

It might be helpful if I spent three minutes putting on record the sequence of events which has led up to the current proposal for the permanent closure and disposal of the hospital. I shall try to deal with the hon. Gentleman's two main points.

Snapethorpe hospital opened in 1933 and originally had a complement of 103 beds. The benefactor of the hospital, as the hon. Gentleman has pointed out in a recent series of questions in the House, was a Mr. Benjamin Sykes. The hospital site and buildings were later vested in the Secretary of State under the National Health Service Act 1946, free of any trust.

The transfer of services at the hospital to elsewhere in the Health Service occurred over a period of years, culminating in its temporary closure in April 1984. That has been the situation since then. For the past five years it has been relatively unused; only one service remains—the sterile supplies unit. This state of affairs has been the result largely of clinical and not administrative decisions.

As long ago as 1978, the consultant in charge of the infectious diseases unit based in Elgin ward decided that he could no longer provide a fully comprehensive service at the hospital. Over the three preceding years the average bed occupancy of this 12-bedded ward had never exceeded 50 per cent. At that time the seriously ill patients were always transferred to Seacroft hospital in Leeds. The service was subsequently transferred completely to Leeds together with the resources.

Further clinical decisions to return Dewsbury chest patients to their home health authority and to close a pre-convalescent ward showing a negligible bed occupancy resulted in only one ward remaining in use. Both decisions received community health council approval. The remaining ward, Barden, stayed open to provide a chest service to Wakefield.

In July 1980, the health authority commenced consultation on the closure of Barden ward, along with other proposals for the closure and change of use of facilities within the district. Closure was opposed by the CHC and the matter was referred to Ministers for a decision. In 1981, full closure was deferred pending a further review of services. In April 1984, the then Minister of State, my right hon. and learned Friend the present Secretary of State, agreed to temporary closure. The hospital has remained closed since that time.

In November 1987, the health authority resolved to consult again on permanent closure. The consultation process has now been completed and because of the continued opposition of the community health council, the matter has again been referred to Ministers. I assure the hon. Member for Wakefield that Ministers will wait until the meeting is held so that we can take full account of the representations that he and others will make.

The health authority has considered the possibility of providing acute services at Snapethorpe, but the hon. Gentleman is aware of the hospital at Pinderfields in which £25 million is to be invested to enhance the capacity of that excellent hospital to 700 beds. Acute services are more sensibly located at the district general hospital.

I am advised that the buildings at Snapethorpe are not suitable for the long-term care of elderly people and would have to be rebuilt. I am further advised that they are not suitable for refurbishment, but if they are perhaps the hon. Gentleman will so advise me at the meeting. Back-up services would be located four miles away at the district general hospital. Mentally handicapped people are provided for in Wakefield, and other plans and facilities are available for mentally ill people.

I am advised that, within limited resources, the district health authority has decided that providing further services on site, bearing in mind that the buildings could not sensibly be used in their present state and would have to be demolished, is not top of the list of its priorities.

The hon. Member for Wakefield referred to a joint venture with the local authority. We welcome joint ventures with local authorities. The Department of Health has not issued any instructions about joint ventures and encourages them. When the Government have announced their conclusions following the review of Sir Roy Griffiths' report into community care—an announcement will be made soon—doubtless district health authorities and local authorities will reconsider the provisions of facilities in the community for the different client groups that the hon. Gentleman cited.

At present the health authority believes that it would be in the best interests of the patients it serves for the site to be sold and for the proceeds to be used now to the benefit of the patients in the area. That is not to say that in the future, with more resources or different priorities, the health authority could not decide, perhaps jointly with the local authority, to provide additional services on a different site within the urban area. Surely it is better, after five years of planning blight and the facilities lying empty, for the uncertainty to come to an end, the site sold and the proceeds reinvested immediately to the benefit of patients in the area.

I look forward to meeting the hon. Member for Wakefield and his delegation shortly.

Question put and agreed to.

Adjourned accordingly at thirteen minutes past Twelve o'clock.

House of Commons

Thursday 8 June 1989

The House met at half-past Two o'clock

PRAYERS

[MR. SPEAKER *in the Chair*]

PRIVATE BUSINESS

ASSOCIATED BRITISH PORTS (No. 2) BILL

Order for Third Reading read.
To be read the Third time on Thursday 15 June.

ASSOCIATED BRITISH PORTS (HULL) BILL

ISLE OF WIGHT BILL

TEES (NEWPORT BRIDGE) BILL *[Lords]*

TYNE AND WEAR PASSENGER TRANSPORT BILL

Orders for Third Reading read.
To be read the Third time on Thursday 15 June at Seven o'clock.

BRITISH RAILWAYS (PENALTY FARES) BILL *[Lords]*

LONDON REGIONAL TRANSPORT (PENALTY FARES) BILL *[Lords]*

Orders for Consideration read.
To be considered on Thursday 15 June.

NEW SOUTHGATE CEMETERY AND CREMATORIUM LIMITED BILL

Order for Consideration read.
To be considered on Thursday 15 June at Seven o'clock.

HYTHE, KENT, MARINA BILL

LONDON UNDERGROUND (VICTORIA) BILL

BRITISH FILM INSTITUTE SOUTHBANK BILL

Orders for Second Reading read.
To be read a Second time on Thursday 15 June.

Oral Answers to Questions

NATIONAL FINANCE

Pay Rises

1. **Mr. Cohen:** To ask the Chancellor of the Exchequer what information he has on the pay rises awarded to directors in the last period for which figures are available, if he will indicate the economic effect of all workers having a similar pay rise this year; and if he will make a statement.

The Chief Secretary to the Treasury (Mr. John Major): Pay is for the parties involved to agree and it is not for the Government to intervene.

Mr. Cohen: What a cop-out answer! How does the Chancellor justify an average increase of 23 per cent. for top directors when inflation is 8 per cent. and workers are having to accept much less than that? How does the Chief Secretary justify a 20 per cent. increase for ICI bosses, 34 per cent. for Unilever's boss, 43 per cent. for Barclay's boss, 47 per cent. for Cadbury's boss, 48 per cent. for BP's bosses, 58 per cent. for Sun Alliance bosses, 100 per cent. for Legal and General's bosses and 100 per cent. for P and O's? Is not the reason that the Conservatives and those directors have the same incestuous class interest? Regardless of the economic effect, there is Government condemnation for workers' pay rises and a free-for-all for top directors.

Mr. Major: I am bound to say that I think that the hon. Gentleman has a rather limited view of directors. Contrary to his vivid expression, the vast majority are able, efficient and effective, and we need the best management. Notwithstanding that, I have never justified wage or salary increases that are unjustifiable, and I do not do so now. It is not, however, for me to determine what is or is not justifiable in that respect.

Mr. Bill Walker: Does my right hon. Friend agree that there are only two resources in any company—money and people—and that it is the way in which those resources are managed and deployed that results in profitability or loss in operation? It is only right that those who create the profits should, as a result of the shareholders' wishes, be properly remunerated.

Mr. Major: My hon. Friend makes his point extremely clearly, but I repeat that I am not directly responsible for or concerned with the matter. Pay is a matter for those who negotiate and determine it, and it is not for the Government to intervene.

Personal Disposable Income

2. **Mr. Nicholas Bennett:** To ask the Chancellor of the Exchequer what was the growth of real personal disposable income for the latest full year for which figures are available.

The Paymaster General (Mr. Peter Brooke): Real personal disposable income is estimated to have grown by 5 per cent. in 1988.

Mr. Bennett: I thank my right hon. Friend for his reply. Can he confirm that under the Government real disposable income has risen by about one third, partly as a result of the Government's tax-cutting policies, and has he any calculation of the effect on real disposable personal income if Labour's policies were put into effect?

Mr. Brooke: My hon. Friend's first point is correct, in the context of the real take-home pay of a married man with two children who is on male average earnings. As for the second point, we know so little about Labour's policies that any observation of mine would be purely speculative —which strikes me as an appropriate adjective to apply to the policies.

Ms. Short: Does the Minister agree that not everyone has received a 5 per cent. increase as there has been enormous inequality in its distribution? Is he aware that the worst-paid 20 per cent. in society are increasingly worse off and we are becoming a more unequal society? Does that not concern him? Does he not think that the Government ought to look at the provisions made right across Europe for some national minimum wage rather than allowing inequality to grow in Britain?

Mr. Brooke: The hon. Lady is not well informed in the first part of her question. Perhaps she should put in a little more research in future. As to the second part of her question, that proposal is contained in the social charter, on which the Conservative party looks forward to vigorous debate.

Mr. John Marshall: Does my right hon. Friend agree that minimum wage legislation would create unemployment in this country? Does he further agree that the percentage of gross domestic product being spent on the elderly is higher in Britain than in 10 of the other Community countries?

Mr. Brooke: My hon. Friend is perfectly correct in both his observations.

Dr. Marek: The Paymaster General will know that in calculating real personal disposable income, interest paid to savers is offset by mortgage interest paid to building societies. Does he accept that generally speaking the saver with £30,000 in a building society is not the same person who has to borrow £30,000 to finance the purchase of a house? Will he now admit how much real personal disposable income has been lost in the past year by the man or woman with an average mortgage?

Mr. Brooke: The hon. Member for Wrexham (Dr. Marek) is broadly speaking correct in his surmise about the unlikelihood of coincidence. As to the second part of his question, he knows very well that the policy pursued by my right hon. Friend the Chancellor to bring down inflation is directed specifically to that aim and my right hon. Friend has said that when inflation visibly comes down, interest rates will follow.

Personal Equity Plans

3. **Mr. Baldry:** To ask the Chancellor of the Exchequer what estimate he has of the number of personal equity plans now in existence.

The Chancellor of the Exchequer, (Mr. Nigel Lawson): About 450,000 personal equity plans have been taken out to date.

Mr. Baldry: Does my right hon. Friend agree that the welcome boost to personal equity plans in this year's Budget will increase the number of people who have a personal stake in the success of British business and encourage businesses to invest further because their ability to raise equity will thus be enhanced? Given all those advantages, does my right hon. Friend not think it somewhat sad that the Labour party should oppose this year's Budget proposals to expand personal equity plans? Does that not reflect the Labour party's inherent opposition to the spread of wider share ownership and a property-owning democracy?

Mr. Lawson: Yes, indeed. My hon. Friend is quite right. The Labour party is wholly opposed to share-owning democracy and they were opposed to property-owning democracy. Indeed, for years and years they opposed the sale of council houses to their tenants until eventually public feeling was so strong that they had to change their ways. The measure in this year's Budget will give personal equity plans a new boost. One of them—permitting new issue shares to go into personal equity plans instead of, as previously, purely cash—is an important change. I can announce today that this facility will be extended to shares issued by building societies when converting to plc status, and this includes the Abbey National.

Mr. Cryer: If the Chancellor of the Exchequer is so committed to a share-owning democracy, will he introduce legislation to allow shareholders to determine whether a small clique of Tory sycophants in the boardroom hand over shareholders' money to the Tory party, or is he stopping short of spreading democracy to shareholders so long as the Tory party coffers are substantially swollen, like himself?

Mr. Lawson: The hon. Member's paranoia becomes increasingly tedious. Company shareholders can, if they are dissatisfied with the management of any company, vote that management and vote those directors out of office —and that is democracy.

Labour Statistics

4. **Mr. Brazier:** To ask the Chancellor of the Exchequer for how many months adult unemployment has fallen continuously in the United Kingdom.

Mr. Major: Unemployment in the United Kingdom has fallen for 33 months in succession.

Mr. Brazier: Does my right hon. Friend agree that unemployment has fallen in every region, especially among the long-term unemployed? In the past 10 years, we have moved from above the EEC average to well below it. Does he agree that there can be no greater testimony to the performance of the Government on unemployment than the silence of the Opposition on the subject yesterday?

Mr. Major: There was certainly a deafening silence on the Opposition Front Bench yesterday. My hon. Friend is entirely correct. The fast falls in the west midlands, Wales and Yorkshire are especially welcome. There have been remarkable reductions in long-term unemployment in every region.

Mr. Heffer: It would have been remarkable if unemployment had not fallen, given that it had risen to such high levels under this Government since 1979. Is it not clear that despite the falls in unemployment, which I do not deny for one moment, under the capitalist system unemployment comes down just as it goes up, but the Government have not achieved the lower levels of unemployment which existed under Labour? The levels are still far higher than they were when the Government took office.

Mr. Major: The hon. Gentleman overlooks a point which is material to his concern—that there are more people in work today than there have ever been. The dramatic falls in unemployment have exceeded even the most optimistic forecasts two years ago—certainly those of the right hon. Member for Birmingham, Sparkbrook (Mr. Hattersley), who forecast at the general election that unemployment would increase, since when it has fallen by over 1 million.

Mr. Waller: My right hon. Friend said that unemployment had fallen especially fast in areas previously regarded as the more deprived parts of the country. Does he agree that this shows that those who talked in the past of the inevitability of the north-south divide were somewhat misguided and that the north has qualities and reservoirs of skill which should attract many people to the north?

Mr. Major: I agree with my hon. Friend. On the many visits that I have made to the north in recent months, I have been extremely impressed by the way in which the economy is growing and by the confidence and investment in industry. It is clear that the best regional policy is the sustained economic growth that we have experienced in the past few years.

Mr. John D. Taylor: Does the Minister expect unemployment to continue to fall for the rest of this year?

Mr. Major: We never make predictions about unemployment. We declined to do so last year, since when it has continued to fall dramatically. As I reminded the House a moment ago when quoting the right hon. Member for Sparkbrook, predictions about unemployment are unwise.

Mr. Andrew MacKay: As the spectre of unemployment fades as a result of the Government's economic policies, does my right hon. Friend agree that industry faces a new problem—skill shortages? Are Ministers addressing the problem to ensure that more skills are developed and fresh people brought into the labour force, including women?

Mr. Major: That is an important point. As my hon. Friend will know from the public expenditure round last year, substantial additional resources have been made available for skill training. I hope that as industry is increasingly profitable it will devote more of its resources to training present and future workers.

Foreign Aid

5. **Mr. Dalyell:** To ask the Chancellor of the Exchequer if he will make a statement on the most recent discussions of the IMF on help to *(a)* Brazil, *(b)* Zaire, *(c)* Indonesia and *(d)* Nepal.

Mr. Brooke: The discussions to which the hon. Member refers are, of course, confidential. Brazil, Zaire and Nepal

have drawn on IMF facilities within the past three years. Indonesia has not applied for IMF assistance in that period.

Mr. Dalyell: What measures will the Paymaster General promote in the World Bank and the IMF to ensure that the IMF's structural readjustment programmes do not accelerate the destruction of the rain forests?

Mr. Brooke: IMF programmes are macro-economic and do not relate directly to issues such as the environment. The environment is a matter for the World Bank. IMF programmes create conditions for economic growth which, by leading to the alleviation of poverty, would tend to reduce pressure on the environment.

Mr. Harry Greenway: How do the IMF programmes for underdeveloped and developing countries compare with the IMF rescue operation for this country under the last Labour Government?

Mr. Brooke: That is a slightly larger question than that asked by the hon. Member for Linlithgow (Mr. Dalyell), but there is never any harm in my hon. Friend reminding the House of conditions 12 or 13 years ago.

Mr. Chris Smith: So far, the Government have been lukewarm, at best, in their efforts to alleviate the massive debt problems of many of the developing countries, and their reluctance to associate that with environmental concern, as shown by the answer that the right hon. Gentleman has just given, makes the position even more worrying. Can the right hon. Gentleman not see the common sense in securing environmental gains for the safety of the planet as a whole while at the same time lightening some of the crippling debt burdens of countries such as Brazil?

Mr. Brooke: Taking the hon. Gentleman's question at face value, the Government fully support the World Bank. As to the enhanced structure adjustment facility, the United Kingdom has led the way in supporting the efforts of the poorest countries to adjust their economies. The IMF pays its way through ESAF, to which the United Kingdom has made one of the largest contributions, providing a subsidy on up to £1 billion special drawing rights of ESAF lending.

Interest Rates

6. **Mr. Tom Clarke:** To ask the Chancellor of the Exchequer what are the current interest rates in *(a)* the United Kingdom and *(b)* the rest of the G7.

Mr. Lawson: Three-month money market rates in the United Kingdom currently stand at 14 per cent., compared with an average of 8·6 per cent. in the rest of the G7.

Mr. Clarke: Given those appalling comparisons, is the Chancellor aware that the Small Business Research Trust recently conducted a survey which showed that a quarter of its members were deeply worried about the impact of interest rates on their businesses? What steps does the right hon. Gentleman intend taking to allay their fears, or can they expect things to become even worse?

Mr. Lawson: Let me say two things in reply to the hon. Gentleman's question. First, on the fact of short-term interest rates in the United Kingdom being above the average for the rest of the G7, there is nothing new about that—nothing new at all. They have been consistently higher over the past five years. During those five years, there has been a massive increase in investment of all kinds. There has been a record growth of new businesses —indeed, business and industry generally have done better than they have ever done before—so I think that the hon. Gentleman is wholly mistaken in drawing the conclusions that he does.

On the second point, I would say to the hon. Gentleman that of course what would be far, far worse for small businesses would be to see the sort of levels of inflation that we saw under the last Labour Government, and we are determined that we shall never go back to that.

Mr. Ian Taylor: Does my right hon. Friend agree that the speech yesterday by the right hon. and learned Member for Monklands, East (Mr. Smith) undermining the interest rate policy would have the effect of undermining the exchange rate, which would import inflation into this country? Does my right hon. Friend agree that the right hon. and learned Gentleman's policies would therefore be more inflationary?

Mr. Lawson: Yes, indeed. It was quite clear from the debate that we had yesterday that the Labour party has no policy at all to fight inflation. The only policy it has is one to put inflation up, through massive increases in public expenditure, through increased taxes on savings, through devaluation and through lower interest rates.

Mr. Robert Sheldon: As the Chancellor has ruled out credit controls, even of a limited kind, is it not clear that his only weapon has been ludicrously high interest rates? As this has been fed directly into the RPI, is it not also clear that wage claims are higher than they would otherwise have been, producing a further level of inflation for which the right hon. Gentleman is responsible?

Mr. Lawson: I entirely agree with the implication in the right hon. Gentleman's question that it is absurd that we have mortgage interest payments in the RPI, unlike most other countries. The right hon. Gentleman is perfectly right about that. But as for ludicrous interest rates, the only ludicrous interest rates were the interest rates during the last Labour Government when he was a Treasury Minister, which were negative in real terms. Negative real interest rates rob the saver and do great damage to the economy. That is what we had under Labour.

Mr. Gill: Will my right hon. Friend take this opportunity to remind the House that one cannot establish sound security on borrowed money? Will he exhort the nation to follow the Government's example in repaying debt, thereby reducing the burden of interest?

Mr. Lawson: My hon. Friend is right. It would, indeed, be very much better in many ways if the appetite for borrowing was somewhat moderated. This is a free country—a free country—and people and companies are entitled to borrow what they wish to borrow and what they feel is prudent to borrow and I do not wish any change in that. Nevertheless, I do feel that the higher interest rates we have now might be to some extent a discouragement to borrow and an encouragement to save and, indeed, that is what we see happening at the present time.

Mr. Beith: How can very high short-term interest rates drive inflation out of the system when they bear disproportionately on small businesses and not on the larger businesses, which borrow mainly in the long term? Unless the Chancellor has some change of policy, will the position not be that smaller business will take more and more of the medicine that is not working on the system as a whole?

Mr. Lawson: The main difference—the most important difference—between the effect of long-term interest rates —which, the hon Gentleman is quite right, are well below short-term interest rates tend to bear more heavily on consumer spending because consumer borrowing is linked to short-term interest rates whereas, as he pointed out, a great deal of investment is linked to longer-term interest rates and, therefore, the only sense of what he is saying is that the depression of the growth of demand which is necessary in his judgment should be more directed towards investment and less towards consumption. That is not something with which I agree.

Mr. Gordon Brown: Now that mortgage rates have been 10 per cent. or above for almost all the past 10 years, now that borrowing costs are just about the highest in Europe and now, as the Chancellor confirmed yesterday, that home owners face a summer of high mortgages and rising prices, does the right hon. Gentleman still dismiss the anxieties of home owners throughout the country? Does he still repeat the advice he gave earlier that they should cut back on something else?

Mr. Lawson: What I do say is that the 10 years to which he referred have been 10 years of unprecedented success for the British economy.

Balance of Payments

7. **Mr. Martyn Jones:** To ask the Chancellor of the Exchequer what was the balance of payments for the first quarter of 1989.

The Financial Secretary to the Treasury (Mr. Norman Lamont): The current account deficit in the first quarter of 1989 is provisionally estimated at £4·4 billion.

Mr. Jones: Is the Minister aware that only this Monday the Engineering Employers Federation predicted that in 1989 the only industry in Britain which will be in surplus with the rest of the world and which is a major metal user will be the aerospace industry?

Mr. Bill Walker: What about whisky?

Mr. Jones: That industry does not use metal, so far as I am aware. Does the Minister not consider that that is a major blip on the economic policies of the past 10 years?

Mr. Lamont: It is not necessary for the current account to be in surplus in every sector. I regard projections for individual sectors as insignificant. It does not matter if we are in deficit in one sector, such as engineering. As a result of the measures that my right hon. Friend the Chancellor has taken, demand in the economy will slow down and the position on the current account will improve.

Mr. Boswell: Has my right hon. Friend noticed that the balance of payments includes an unusually high proportion of imports of investment goods? Will they not contribute to a more efficient industrial structure in the future?

Mr. Lamont: My hon. Friend is right. About one quarter of the value of manufactured imports between 1987 and 1988 was accounted for by consumer goods, including cars, with the remainder—fully three quarters —made up of goods for production and investment. That illustrates that, as my hon. Friend says, part of the current account deficit has been accounted for by firms tooling up for investment and higher production.

Mr. Macdonald: Will the Financial Secretary explain why the Government have approved the recent OECD report, which shows the balance of payments deficit getting still worse next year?

Mr. Lamont: I think that the hon. Gentleman is mistaken. The report has not been published or released, and he has no basis of saying that the Government have approved it.

Mr. Kirkhope: Does my right hon. Friend agree that the high levels of investment in manufacturing industry and the recent high level of inward investment as a result of the attraction of the Government's economic policies will result in a much better balance of payments as we progress into the 1990s?

Mr. Lamont: It is not just the high level of investment in manufacturing that matters but investment in the whole economy, and I am sure that the record level of investment in the whole economy is a very good thing for the long-term benefit of the economy. In that respect, my hon. Friend is right.

Mr. John Smith: Do the Government still adhere to the forecast of a balance of payments deficit of £14 billion this year? If not, when will the Minister announce that it is going to get worse?

Mr. Lamont: As the right hon. and learned Gentleman knows, the Government's forecasts are updated in the Autumn Statement. We still stick to the view that the current account deficit in the second half of the year will be lower than it was in the first, as was said in the Red Book, and, indeed, the figures and trends are there to show that. Export volumes in the past three months are up $1\frac{1}{2}$ per cent. on the previous three and the trend is upwards, while imports are beginning to stabilise in response to the slowing down of consumer demand, which is exactly what the policies of my right hon. Friend the Chancellor were designed to achieve.

Income Tax

9. **Mr. Butler:** To ask the Chancellor of the Exchequer if he will make it his long-term policy to abolish income tax.

Mr. Lawson: In my Budget last year, I set the target of reducing the basic rate of income tax to 20 per cent. as soon as it was prudent and sensible to do so. That remains the target.

Mr. Butler: Does my right hon. Friend believe that there is some innate benefit in income tax? With strong economic growth, is it not conceivable that we could do away with the tax altogether?

Mr. Lawson: I think that that is unlikely to occur during my time as Chancellor of the Exchequer.

Mr. Battle: Will the Chancellor tell the House how much of the burden of taxation has shifted to indirect taxes such as VAT? How much will indirect taxation increase as he proceeds with his policy of reducing direct taxation?

Mr. Lawson: The increases in direct taxation that have occurred during the time that I have been Chancellor of the Exchequer have been negligible—in fact, very small indeed. Nor during my time as Chancellor of the Exchequer have I increased the national insurance rates, so let us get that straight. What I will say to the hon. Gentleman is that if the policies which have been proposed by the Labour party were ever put in practice, we would see a very substantial increase in income tax at almost all levels.

Sir William Clark: Does my right hon. Friend agree that Conservative Governments reduce income tax because they always control public expenditure wisely, whereas Labour Governments invariably increase income tax because they are profligate in their public spending?

Mr. Lawson: My hon. Friend is right, and that is how we have been able to get income tax down and that is how we will be able to get income tax down still further in the years that lie ahead, to the great benefit of the economy as a whole and also giving individuals a wider choice of how they spend the money that they earn. As for the Labour party and their spending plans, they have yet so far still failed to answer the question put to them by the right hon. Member who was formerly running the GLC—I cannot remember his constituency at the present time—*[Interruption.]*—Brent, East (Mr. Livingstone)—who said very pointedly that they have not said where they are going to find the money to spend on all those programmes.

Inflation

10. **Mr. Duffy:** To ask the Chancellor of the Exchequer what is his estimate of the underlying rate of inflation for the British economy; and whether he will make a statement.

Mr. Brooke: The best guide to the underlying rate of inflation is provided by the RPI excluding mortgage interest payments—*[Interruption.]*——

Mr. Speaker: Order.

Mr. Brooke —which currently stands at 5·9 per cent.

Mr. Duffy: Why did not the right hon. Gentleman's right hon. Friend receive a more encouraging response today from sterling and the market in view of his very sturdy reaffirmation in last night's debate of his well-known and well-tried counter-inflationary policy?

Mr. Brooke: That, if I may say so, seems to be a question more for the markets than for me. The markets have, in fact, been thoroughly calm.

Mr. Gow: Will my right hon. Friend reaffirm his commitment to maintaining high interest rates until we abate the rate of monetary growth? Will he reaffirm the commitment of the Government to move towards stable prices at the earliest possible moment?

Mr. Brooke: My right hon. Friend the Chancellor of the Exchequer made that wholly clear yesterday. I am delighted to echo him today.

Mr. Nicholas Brown: Is it the Government's view that shadowing the deutschmark has helped to cause inflation in the past?

Mr. Brooke: That question, again, goes somewhat wide of the original question that I was asked. As the hon. Gentleman has risen from the Opposition Front Bench, let me say that one of his Front Bench colleagues earlier this week said on television that inflation was higher now than when the Labour party went out of office. As the RPI was then 25 per cent. higher, and the RPI without mortgage interest payments was 50 per cent. higher, it seems to me that the Opposition Front Bench is seeking to rewrite history.

Manufacturing Investment

11. **Mr. Arbuthnot:** To ask the Chancellor of the Exchequer what is the latest official projection for the growth of manufacturing investment in 1989.

12. **Mr. Gerald Howarth:** To ask the Chancellor of the Exchequer what is the latest official projection for the growth of manufacturing investment in 1989.

Mr. Lawson: The latest DTI investment intentions survey, published in December, projected manufacturing investment in constant prices to rise by a further 11 per cent. in 1989 on a year earlier. The latest CBI "Quarterly Trends Survey", published in April, confirms this buoyant outlook.

Mr. Arbuthnot: Is it not clear that it is the policies of the Government that have created the climate where manufacturing investment, output, profits and productivity are all increasing satisfactorily? Can my right hon. Friend say how long and to what extent that trend is likely to continue?

Mr. Lawson: As far as I can tell my hon. Friend the prospects are very good indeed. We now have a situation in which business investment is at the highest proportion of GDP that it has ever been in our history. Company profits are high; company confidence is high. Therefore, the prospects for further investment are also excellent. As for manufacturing industry, it is interesting that during the period that I have been Chancellor of the Exchequer the average annual growth of manufacturing investment has been 9 per cent. compared with the period of the whole of the last Labour Government, which was roughly the same period of time, or a little bit less, when the growth of manufacturing investment was only 2·3 per cent.

Mr. Howarth: While welcoming the record rate of investment in manufacturing industry that has taken place under the Conservative Government, may I tell my right hon. Friend that nowhere in the United Kingdom is there more evidence of the revitalisation of British manufacturing industry than in the west midlands where the latest quarterly report of Walsall chamber of commerce shows that no fewer than 46 per cent. of companies are revising upwards their plans for manufacturing investment this year.

Mr. Lawson: I am particularly glad to hear that from my hon. Friend. Indeed, as a Member representing a midlands constituency myself, I am well aware of the successful economy of the midlands and the reinvigoration of the midlands and the high degree of investment that is going on there. Of course, as my hon. Friend will be the first to admit, it is not something confined solely to the midlands; this is now occurring nationwide.

Mr. Pike: Does the Chancellor recognise that his complacency hides the wide regional discrepancies between investment in manufacturing industries? Is it not a fact that, if there were more investment in our key manufacturing regions, the Government would do a lot more to improve the unemployment figures and our balance of payments? Does he recognise that investment in the north-west region—a key manufacturing region—according to the Government's latest available figures, is 38 per cent. below the 1979 level?

Mr. Lawson: There have always been differences between different regions, and there always will be. This is not something new. But what I find extraordinary in the question asked by the hon. Gentleman, and, indeed, by most, if not all, Labour Members, is their exclusive concern with manufacturing industry and manufacturing industry's investment. Manufacturing industry and manufacturing industry's investment are indeed very important, but the whole of the rest of British industry is important too. Some time hon. Gentlemen should recognise that the other 75 per cent. of the economy does in fact exist.

Mr. Orme: Will the Chancellor address himself to the fact that, if we are going to do anything about the balance of payments deficit, we have to manufacture to export? What has happened to our manufacturing exports over recent years? How does he explain those?

Mr. Lawson: I am glad to say that our manufacturing exports over recent years have done extremely well. Indeed, total exports, in which manufacturing accounts for a very large part, in the last three months were $8\frac{1}{2}$ per cent. in volume terms above a year ago.

Mrs. Peacock: Does my right hon. Friend agree that investment in manufacturing industry, which is important to many of us who represent such areas, has been absolutely tremendous in recent years, especially in Yorkshire? Does he agree that that is a sign of confidence in the future economic success of the country, and that, instead of decline and dereliction, we now have many new factories and many new jobs?

Mr. Lawson: My hon. Friend is quite right, and I know the very great concern and interest that she has always shown in business and industry in her own constituency. It is indeed a striking fact, as I pointed out a moment ago, that over the past five years manufacturing investment has been growing at the rate of 9 per cent. a year, and it is set to grow still further.

Mr. John Smith: Can I ask the Chancellor the same question that I asked him yesterday, but which he did not answer? By how many percentage points has investment in manufacturing industry increased since 1979?

Mr. Lawson: Investment in manufacturing industry in quantum is only slightly above what it was in 1979, but it is, of course, heading still further up. Manufacturing output has also risen very sharply indeed under this Government, unlike under the last Labour Government, when manufacturing output actually declined.

Manufacturing Output

15. **Mr. Ward:** To ask the Chancellor of the Exchequer what has been the annual rate of growth of manufacturing output over the last two years.

Mr. Major: In the two years to the first quarter of this year, manufacturing output grew at an average annual rate of 7·1 per cent.

Mr. Ward: Does my right hon. Friend agree that the news about investment in manufacturing that we have just heard is good news for tomorrow? However, the answer that he has just given indicates that the supply side boom, which the Government have been working for, is with us today.

Mr. Major: My hon. Friend is right. The strength of manufacturing output shows clearly that the supply side changes of recent years are working. My hon. Friend will be pleased to know that the levels of investment that we have seen recently will ensure that that continues.

Mr. Mullin: In view of the lavish claims being made about the level of manufacturing investment, will the Chancellor have another go at explaining the figures that I put to him yesterday—that according to the latest figures from the Department of Trade and Industry, manufacturing investment in the north-east stands now at 53 per cent. of what it did in 1979?

Mr. Major: That relates to manufacturing output. In fact, manufacturing investment has risen by 14½ per cent. in the last year to a record level.

Economic Growth

16. **Mr. Oppenheim:** To ask the Chancellor of the Exchequer what was the rate of economic growth in the latest year for which figures are available.

Mr. Major: Gross domestic product is estimated to have grown by 4½ per cent. in 1988.

Mr. Oppenheim: Is it true that, whereas a great deal of investment in manufacturing in the 1970s was directed by politicians into uneconomic enterprises or into uncommercial capacity, it is now being directed by private industry into proper jobs and proper industry? Perhaps that is why, whereas under the last Labour Government manufacturing output fell, it has risen sharply under this Government.

Mr. Major: That is right, and it is why we are now well into the eighth successful year of sustained growth of more than 3 per cent. During the past seven years there has been a combination of strong and steady growth that has not been matched since the war.

Mr. Campbell-Savours: Would there not be a substantial increase in growth if the Government adopted a positive policy of import substitution? Will the Minister reflect on my modest contribution to last night's debate, when I set out a scheme for private sectoral support for industry that would lead to a substantial number of jobs, cost the state very little and, to some extent, reduce the trade deficit? Will the Minister read what I said last night and, perhaps, drop me a line about it?

Mr. Major: I always read carefully what the hon. Gentleman has said, although some of the ideas that he advanced yesterday were tried not wholly successfully in earlier years. I welcome the efforts many industries are now making to provide goods to be sold at home at competitive rates as an alternative to imports. I hope that they will continue to do that.

PRIME MINISTER

Engagements

Q1. **Mr. Thurnham:** To ask the Prime Minister if she will list her official engagements for Thursday 8 June.

The Prime Minister (Mrs. Margaret Thatcher): This morning I presided at a meeting of the Cabinet and had meetings with ministerial colleagues and others. In addition to my duties in this House I shall be having further meetings later today.

Mr. Thurnham: During the course of my right hon. Friend's busy day, will she find time to read Paul Twyman's excellent pamphlet entitled "1992, Crossroads for Free Enterprise"? Will she use her best endeavours to ensure that Europe takes the road of free enterprise so that we can look forward to the day when the whole of Europe, from the Atlantic to the Urals, is rid of creeping Socialism and tyrannical Communism?

The Prime Minister: I have indeed read that pamphlet and I agree with its conclusion that we face a choice in Europe between corporatism, central control and regulation—as is supported by the Opposition—and the creation of a genuine single market in which enterprise can flourish and the energies and talents of people be set free to generate wealth and bring about further social improvement. That is the sort of Europe that the Conservative party wants and for which we shall be campaigning in the forthcoming election.

Q2. **Mr. Barron:** To ask the Prime Minister if she will list her official engagements for Thursday 8 June.

The Prime Minister: I refer the hon. Gentleman to the reply that I gave some moments ago.

Mr. Barron: Will the right hon. Lady confirm that on Monday evening she will be joining me and my right hon. Friend the Leader of the Opposition in voting in favour of the televising of the proceedings of this House?

The Prime Minister: I must disappoint the hon. Gentleman, in that I shall not be here on Monday evening. I wish to make it clear that if I were here, I should be supporting the Lord President.

Mrs. Currie: Has my right hon. Friend noticed that the right hon. Member for Yeovil (Mr. Ashdown) is missing from the Chamber this afternoon as he has buzzed off to Hong Kong? He is not, therefore, here to ask his usual silly questions—*[Interruption.]*

Ms. Short: The hon. Lady is not in order.

Mr. Speaker: Order. It must be a question for the Prime Minister.

Mrs. Currie: Does my right hon. Friend agree that although there is considerable sympathy with and understanding of the worries of the people of Hong Kong, it would be wrong to give anyone the idea that millions of people could come and settle in this country overnight? Does not the future of the colony lie with China?

The Prime Minister: As both my right hon. and learned Friend the Foreign Secretary and I have said, we are deeply concerned about Hong Kong and the natural feelings of its people. We have said that we are prepared to consider ways of obtaining greater flexibility under the present rules to allow an increasing number of people to come to this country under the several different limbs of the immigration rules and the British Nationality Act 1981. We shall consider that matter carefully in the coming days and, if need be, come to the House if we need additional powers.

Q3. **Mr. Nigel Griffith:** To ask the Prime Minister if she will list her official engagements for Thursday 8 June.

The Prime Minister: I refer the hon. Gentleman to the reply that I gave some moments ago.

Mr. Griffiths: How does the Prime Minister justify the shameful decision of Tayside Tories to support the Nationalists where SNP means "sacking 900 people"?

The Prime Minister: I do not think that I should get involved in that. I am sure that Tories support Tory policy.

Q4. **Miss Widdecombe:** To ask the Prime Minister if she will list her official engagements for Thursday 8 June.

The Prime Minister: I refer my hon. Friend to the reply that I gave some moments ago.

Miss Widdecombe: Will my right hon. Friend find time in her busy schedule to visit Maidstone general hospital, which was built under the aegis of this Government after years of obvious neglect and which even now is just expanding to include a mass radiography unit? Does she agree that this is tangible proof of the Conservative commitment to the National Health Service?

The Prime Minister: Yes, and I am delighted to hear of its success from my hon. Friend. It is an example of the improvements that are occurring throughout the country in the NHS because we are spending three times as much on the NHS as was spent under Labour. Whereas Labour cut the capital programme for hospital building, we have increased it by 40 per cent., and I am glad that my hon. Friend's constituency is a beneficiary.

Mr. Kinnock: Is the Prime Minister aware that the chief executive of London Regional Transport says that the only way to reduce rush hour overcrowding on the Underground is substantially to increase fares so that people cannot afford to travel at those times? Does the right hon. Lady agree with those views?

The Prime Minister: If there are requests for increased fares and they are designed to lead to increased service, of course those would be considered. I would point out that on transport matters, as on most other things, the Government have put an increasing amount to the capital spent on transport.

Mr. Kinnock: Why does not the Prime Minister stop wriggling and simply say whether she thinks—*[Interruption.]*

Mr. Speaker: Order.

Mr. Kinnock: Will the Prime Minister say whether she thinks the ability of people to get to their work in London should be rationed by fares regulated by price?

The Prime Minister: I thought that on a previous occasion the right hon. Gentleman had agreed with me that if one gets increased service, one should expect to have to pay for that improvement. He seems totally to have forgotten that.

Mr. Kinnock: Can the Prime Minister explain how, if one is charging fares that stop people travelling, one is increasing service to them?

The Prime Minister: There have been a number of proposals from London Underground for increasing the standard of service. The right hon. Gentleman, as usual, wants something pretty well free, provided that someone else pays.

Q5. **Mr. Roger King:** To ask the Prime Minister if she will list her official engagements for Thursday 8 June.

The Prime Minister: I refer my hon. Friend to the reply that I gave some moments ago.

Mr. King: I congratulate my right hon. Friend on her recent visit to the west midlands. Will she confirm that no Conservative Euro-candidate is opposed to our member-ship of the European Economic Community? What message does she have for the numerous members of the other parties in respect of their attitude to the hard Left campaign group of the Labour party?

The Prime Minister: Yes, of course I confirm that, unlike the Labour party, all our candidates in the Euro-elections believe that Britain's future lies in the European Community. A Conservative Government led by my right hon. Friend the Member for Old Bexley and Sidcup (Mr. Heath) had the vision to take Britain into the Community—*[Interruption.]*

Mr. Speaker: Order. Interruptions waste a lot of time.

The Prime Minister: A successor Conservative Government have made such a success of Britain's membership.

Mr. Maginnis: Has the Prime Minister been informed by the Secretary of State for Northern Ireland that at a dinner party in Hillsborough castle, the deputy chairman of the Police Authority for Northern Ireland described the former Chief Constable—and I apologise to the House for the language—as a "black bastard", accused him of having previously kicked the—I will not use the four letter word beginning with "f"—out of Roman Catholics, and that the deputy chairman further described the police as "black thugs"? Is that the sort of behaviour the right hon. Lady expects from the deputy chairman of the Police Authority for Northern Ireland? When the right hon. Lady has verified what I have said, will she take steps to ensure that that person is removed from the authority?

The Prime Minister: I am in no position to know whether or not the account of the hon. Gentleman is accurate. My right hon. Friend the Secretary of State for Northern Ireland says that the answer to the first part of the question is no, Sir. It is monstrous to try to repeat an alleged account of a conversation under such circumstances, and I totally condemn it. The hon. Gentleman knows that we fully stand behind the police in Northern Ireland in the excellent and wonderful work that they do.

Mr. Nicholas Winterton: Is my right hon. Friend aware that an increasing number of industries in this country are concerned about the policy of high interest and exchange rates, and that those two policies are torpedoing the very sector of the British economy which could reduce our balance of trade deficit and assist in reducing inflation? Will she look at other policies, particularly that of asking the Bank of England to request the clearing banks to place substantial deposits, which would be very beneficial for Britain's manufacturing industry?

The Prime Minister: There are two points. As my hon. Friend is aware, increases in interest rates are not readily acceptable, but are far less damaging than a perpetual increase in inflation. Secondly, as he will also be aware because he takes much interest in industrial matters, a 1 per cent. increase in wages is about four times as damaging as a 1 percentage point increase in interest rates. There has been an increase in wages of 9 per cent. in the past year.

Q7. **Mr. Knapman:** To ask the Prime Minister if she will list her official engagements for Thursday 8 June.

The Prime Minister: I refer my hon. Friend to the reply that I gave some moments ago.

Mr. Knapman: Has my right hon. Friend seen press reports stating that a mother of three, a Lambeth Labour councillor, has claimed £20,000 expenses in one year? Does my right hon. Friend agree that that is absurd, and a backdoor way of appointing full-time councillors?

The Prime Minister: I have seen such reports. In the White Paper responding to the Widdicombe report, we announced our intention to introduce a flat-rate allowance to prevent councillors exploiting an attendance-based allowance system.

Rain Forest

Q8. **Mr. Dalyell:** To ask the Prime Minister if she will seek to include on the agenda of the Madrid summit, European Economic Community policy towards debt-for-nature swaps in relation to conservation of the rain forest.

The Prime Minister: I welcome the debt-for-nature swaps agreed voluntarily between commercial banks, conservation organisations and debtors, although their role is likely to remain small in relation to both developing country debt and environmental problems. The agenda for the European Council has not yet been agreed, but environmental issues may well be raised.

Mr. Dalyell: May I ask the Prime Minister a question of which I gave her Office a little notice? Does she support the European Parliament's resolution of 26 May on tropical timber products?

The Prime Minister: I am grateful to the hon. Gentleman for giving me notice. The resolution, which is addressed to the Commission for initial consideration, deals with a number of aspects relating to trade in tropical timber. My right hon. Friends in the DTI, with their officials, are looking at its full implications.

Mr. Bell: In relation to the Prime Minister's earlier response as to our success in the European Community——

Mr. Speaker: Is this related to rain forests?

Mr. Bell: In relation to rain forests and the European Economic Community, should we not have a proper social contract throughout Europe?

The Prime Minister: It is much more practical for us to do what we do to assist the continuation of the rain forests and that is one of the reasons why we should be proud of being British.

Engagements

Q9. **Mr. Ken Hargreaves:** To ask the Prime Minister if she will list her official engagements for Thursday 8 June.

The Prime Minister: I refer my hon. Friend to the reply that I gave some moments ago.

Mr. Hargreaves: As tickets for the West German national lottery are now circulating in Britain, is it not time to consider the setting up of a national lottery here so that the proceeds of such a lottery can benefit the British people?

The Prime Minister: As my hon. Friend knows, that question comes up from time to time, but we have never set up a national lottery. People want a national lottery for many different reasons, but I would be slow to consider setting one up because enough money already goes to gambling of one sort or another and such a lottery would be damaging for a number of local fund-raising occasions which are far more profitable.

Business of the House

3.30 pm

Mr. Frank Dobson (Holborn and St. Pancras): Will the Leader of the House tell us the business for next week?

The Lord President of the Council and Leader of the House of Commons (Mr. John Wakeham): The business for next week will be as follows:

MONDAY 12 JUNE—Until 7 o'clock, private Members' motions.

Debate on a motion to approve the report of the Select Committee on Televising of Proceedings of the House (HC 141).

Motion to take note of EC documents on insider trading. Details will be given in the *Official Report*.

TUESDAY 13 JUNE—Progress on remaining stages of the Local Government and Housing Bill.

Motion to take note of EC documents on broadcasting. Details will be given in the *Official Report*.

WEDNESDAY 14 JUNE—Conclusion of remaining stages of the Local Government and Housing Bill.

Remaining stages of the Police Officers (Central Service) Bill *[Lords]*.

THURSDAY 15 JUNE—There will be a debate on the arts and heritage on a motion for the Adjournment of the House.

The Chairman of Ways and Means has named opposed private business for consideration at 7 o'clock.

FRIDAY 16 JUNE—Private Members' motions.

MONDAY 19 JUNE—Remaining stages of the Self-Governing Schools Etc. (Scotland) Bill.

[Monday 12 June 1989

Relevant European Community Documents

  (a)   7310/87   ⎫
                          ⎬ *Insider Trading*
  (b)   8810/88   ⎭

Relevant Reports of European Legislation Committee

  (a) HC 43-iii (1987-88) para 5, HC 15-xxiii (1988-89) para 1 and HC 15-xxiv (1988-89) para 1

  (b) HC 15-i (1988-89) para 8, HC 15-xxiii (1988-89) para 1 and HC 15-xxiv (1988-89) para 1.

Tuesday 13 June 1989

Relevant European Community Documents

  (a)   5574/88   ⎫
                           ⎬ *Broadcasting*
  (b)   *Unnumbered*⎭

Relevant Reports of European Legislation Committee

  (a) HC 43-xxvi (1987-88) para 5, HC 15-xvii (1988-89) para 1 and HC 15-xxi (1988-89) para 1.

  (b) HC 15-xxiv (1988-89) para 3.]

Mr. Dobson: I thank the Leader of the House for his statement.

I wish to register our strongest objection to the proposal that the Select Committee's report on the televising of the House should be debated on Monday and that only half a day should be devoted to it. It is a most important matter which affects every Member of the House and every one of them is entitled to have time to consider the report, to discuss it with colleagues and to feel assured that all points of view will be expressed in the debate.

The Select Committee held 32 meetings and considered oral evidence and 250 written submissions, including 90 written submissions from hon. Members. Therefore, it seems peculiar that the House should be expected to deliberate and decide on the matter after just three hours of debate late one evening.

The Opposition believe—most of us anyway—that the British people are entitled to see and hear what their elected representatives are doing. In view of the Prime Minister's statement at Question Time today, can the Leader of the House confirm that there will not be any late effort by the Government to sabotage the televising of the House and that the payroll vote will be expected to support the report when he recommends it to the House on Monday? [HON. MEMBERS: "It is a free vote."] We all know what free votes are like.

On Monday, the Secretary of State for Employment will attend the Labour and Social Affairs Council of the European Community and we understand that he will be trying to undermine the European directive on health and safety in the workplace. Will the Leader of the House give us an undertaking that the House will be allowed to debate the outcome of Monday's meeting at an early date?

I come back to two standard items. First, when can we expect to have the Government's response to the Griffiths report on care in the community, and when can we expect to debate it? Secondly, when will the Secretary of State for Education end his protracted and apparently hopeless discussions on the introduction of student loans instead of student grants so that we can have the promised debate?

Finally, will we have an early opportunity to debate a possible dog registration scheme or any other practical measures to restrain uncontrolled dogs from savaging innocent passers-by? Unlike some topics that we debate in the House, it might be possible for us to do something about this problem.

Mr. Wakeham: The hon. Gentleman asked me five questions about the business for next week. I am bound to say that I am rather surprised at his tone on the first question about the debate I have arranged on the report on televising the House of Commons. The House has made a decision on the principle of holding an experiment and it does not therefore seem necessary for there to be a long debate to discuss the matter again. The question is whether this is the right procedure. He played a full and active part, for which I am extremely grateful to him, in the work of the Select Committee. The report has been made available for Members to study and it is right that we should get on and deal with it. I believe that the time that I have allocated is adequate. The House has had a full day's debate on the matter and it is now being invited to approve the report of the Select Committee. I do not think that a prolonged debate is necessary, but I will table a motion to ensure that any amendments which you, Mr. Speaker, may select can be disposed of.

I will refer the European matter concerning health and safety to my right hon. Friend the Secretary of State for Employment and perhaps we can have discussions through the usual channels.

I am well aware of the continuing interest in the Griffiths report and in the Wagner report. I can assure the hon. Gentleman that we attach great importance to this issue. As I have said before, this is a complex and sensitive area where we must give thorough consideration to all the options. Our deliberations are continuing and we shall bring forward our proposals in the near future. That will be the time for consideration of any further debate.

On the question of top-up loans, I will make a slightly different statement from that which I have made before. The position on student loans is that my right hon. Friend hopes to be able to report to the House fairly soon his conclusions on the administration of this scheme. The right time for any debate will be after that, but I will certainly keep the hon. Gentleman's request in mind.

With regard to dogs, I cannot promise a debate next week, but I point out to the hon. Gentleman that one of his hon. Friends will raise an Adjournment debate on the subject next Thursday to which a Minister will be responding.

Sir Philip Goodhart (Beckenham): As a major conference on Vietnamese boat people is to be held in Geneva next week, may we have an early statement from the Foreign Secretary on Hong Kong so that some of us can protest about the shameful proposals put forward to ship the boat people back from Hong Kong to Vietnam, a country with an appalling record on human rights and economic mismanagement?

Mr. Wakeham: I know that my hon. Friend recognises the seriousness of the problem. He is correct in saying that there will be a United Nations conference in Geneva next week, and my right hon. and learned Friend the Foreign Secretary, accompanied by the Governor of Hong Kong, will attend it. Its aim is to produce a comprehensive and durable solution to the problems of the Vietnamese boat people. We shall be pursuing immediate relief for Hong Kong's current boat people crisis both at the conference and in the coming months.

Mr. A. J. Beith (Berwick-upon-Tweed): Is it not essential that we have a debate on Hong Kong soon, because in all our previous debates there was certainly no assumption that the transfer under the Sino-British agreement would be to a regime that was butchering its own citizens or to a country that might be on the verge of civil war? Surely the whole question has to be addressed afresh in the light of the circumstances.

Mr. Wakeham: I agree that a debate on Hong Kong is something to which we must address ourselves. It is a question of timing. The Foreign Affairs Committee is currently taking evidence on various matters connected with Hong Kong, and it may be that the best time for a debate is after its report is available.

Mr. Alick Buchanan-Smith (Kincardine and Deeside): In the light of press reports this morning that the Government have decided that a price auction will be the ultimate determinant of the award of independent television franchises, can my right hon. Friend say when the House will be told what those conclusions are? Is he aware that many Conservative Members feel that, rather than having a price auction, quality has to be given the highest priority?

Mr. Wakeham: My right hon. Friend the Home Secretary will make known shortly his conclusions on that and other aspects of our recent Broadcasting White Paper. I should not want to comment further now on speculative

press reports. My right hon. Friend is experienced enough to know that he must wait until my right hon. Friend the Home Secretary makes his statement.

Mr. Merlyn Rees (Morley and Leeds, South): The right hon. Gentleman reminds the House that we voted in favour of an experiment in televising the proceedings of the House and that the Select Committee's scheme for that experiment is what we shall be voting about on Monday night. Will the right hon. Gentleman confirm that, six months after the beginning of that experiment, or whatever is the period, the House will have another opportunity to return to the major issue of whether its proceedings should be permanently televised? Is not Monday's debate concerned only with the experiment?

Mr. Wakeham: Absolutely. The right hon. Gentleman is right, as he so often is in respect of these matters. The purpose of Monday's debate is to approve or not to approve the Select Committee's report. The decision of the House to allow the experiment will not be altered one way or the other by what happens on Monday. At the end of the experiment the House will be able to make a judgment as to what should happen in the future, presumably on a permanent basis.

Mr. Michael Latham (Rutland and Melton): I am sorry to go on about this matter, but is my right hon. Friend yet in a position to say when something will be done about constituents queuing in the rain to get into this place? That matter has been discussed by the relevant Committee for a very long time. I know that there are difficulties about the other place, but they are surely not insuperable and could be overcome.

Mr. Wakeham: I agree with my hon. Friend that the matter is taking rather longer than he or I would like and that the problems ought not to be insuperable. The proposals of the Accommodation and Administration Sub-Committee are being considered by the responsible authorities and the relevant Committee of the other place. It is hoped that an initial response will be received in the near future.

Mr. Jack Ashley (Stoke-on-Trent, South): Is the Leader of the House aware that 11 minutes ago, at 3.30 pm, the final report on disabled adults from the Office of Population and Censuses Surveys was published, and that it reveals shocking disparities in the services and equipment provided to the disabled, especially those who are old, deaf or blind? It is outragous that disabled people should be deprived of proper amenities. May we have a debate on that subject next week?

Mr. Wakeham: I am afraid that the answer is no, we cannot have a debate next week. The right hon. Gentleman knows where I have been for rather longer than the last 11 minutes and will appreciate that I have not had an opportunity to study the report. Of course I shall do so, and so will the Ministers responsible. The Government will make an apropriate response in due course.

Sir Michael McNair-Wilson (Newbury): If I am to show myself as being at all sensitive to my postbag, I must press my right hon. Friend to reconsider his decision concerning a debate on dog registration. He will be aware that an effective scheme operates in Northern Ireland, but it seems to be peculiar to the Province. As there is so much concern about the number of stray dogs now in society, if that is the

[*Sir Michael McNair-Wilson*]

right word, and about the number of attacks on people recently by particular breeds of dogs, he will know that there is increased public concern also at the ending of the dog licensing scheme in the United Kingdom, except in Northern Ireland.

The dog population seems to be somewhat out of control, and, although local authorities can impose their own dog registration schemes if they wish to do so, none has. If the problem is not to reach epidemic proportions, the Government must find time for a debate to consider the whole question of dog control, whether or not a registration scheme turns out to be the right solution.

Mr. Wakeham: I acknowledge the fact that my hon. Friend has received many letters on the subject. So have I, and a number of right hon. and hon. Members sent others to me to answer. I indicated earlier that the hon. Member for Dundee, East (Mr. McAllion) has secured an Adjournment debate for next Thursday, which will provide an opportunity for him to raise points for the Minister to answer. It appears to me that, subject to your view, Mr. Speaker, some of my hon. Friend's points may also be relevant to the debates on the Local Government and Housing Bill that I announced. My hon. Friend should await the comments of my right hon. Friend the Secretary of State for the Environment and of Home Office Ministers on that subject.

Mr. Max Madden (Bradford, West): Yesterday the Secretary of State for Health announced that a list of 200 hospitals, including hospitals in Bradford and other parts of Yorkshire, were allegedly claiming to be interested in being privatised and becoming self-governing. Will the Leader of the House urge the Secretary of State to make a statement to the House explaining why on earth he is opposed to ballots of people living in health authorities where hospitals are believed to be interested in becoming self-governing, to enable them to express their views, and also ballots of staff whose livelihood depends on the future of those hospitals? Why are the Government so eager to allow ballots on whether schools should opt out of state education and whether council estates should change their landlords, but so implacably opposed to ballots on health care and the future of NHS hospitals?

Mr. Wakeham: It seems to me that the hon. Gentleman must be rather frightened of the proposal, given the vehemence of his opposition to it. He is distorting the position substantially. The position is that 178 units around the country have expressed an interest in the proposals for self-government on a no-commitment basis. All those with an interest in the mater will have an opportunity to express their views on individual proposals before any formal application is made, and district health authorities will continue to be responsible for overall planning for health care and the needs of their resident populations.

We think it very encouraging that so many hospitals and units are interested in becoming self-governing. Doctors, nurses and managers want to explore the idea further, because the increased management freedoms will enable them to give patients a better service, while remaining fully part of the National Health Service. That seems a perfectly sensible way to proceed.

Mr. Nicholas Bennett (Pembroke): Will my right hon. Friend draw the attention of my right hon. Friend the Secretary of State for the Environment to the new clauses to the Local Government and Housing Bill that my hon. Friends and I have tabled which are designed to deal with councillors who owe massive amounts in rents and rates —and, in future, community charge—under which councillors who did not pay rent and community charge would in future be disqualified from membership of local authorities?

Mr. Wakeham: I shall certainly draw the new clauses to my right hon. Friend's attention, but I suspect that he already has them in mind and is considering an appropriate response at the right time.

Mr. Nigel Spearing (Newham, South): The House will be grateful to the right hon. Gentleman for making it clear that he is to put down a motion to enable any amendments selected by Mr. Speaker for Monday's debate on broadcasting of Parliament to be taken. Will he, however, extend his duties to Tuesday's debate on pan-European legislation on broadcasting? In view of the important issues raised by EEC matters, is there not a risk that an hour and a half is a little too short? Perhaps on this occasion a suspension motion would be in order.

Mr. Wakeham: The hon. Gentleman always makes his requests in a courteous and persuasive manner, and I certainly undertake to have discussions through the usual channels to establish whether such action would be in the general interests of the House.

Mr. Nicholas Winterton (Macclesfield): I fully support the request of my hon. Friend the Member for Newbury (Sir M. McNair-Wilson) for a major debate on a dog registration scheme, but may I make the further request: that the Government come up with a decision on the Griffiths report as soon as possible? It is very difficult for those of us who take an active interest in the Health Service to consider its future, and particularly the White Paper "Working for Patients", without knowing precisely where the Government stand on the report. Moreover, the longer that the Government delay, the more psychiatric hospitals are being closed. We are selling the future. I strongly believe that we need long-stay care for a large number of people suffering from mental illness.

Mr. Wakeham: My hon. Friend adds his considerable weight to the remarks about dogs and I note carefully what he has said, although I thought that I had been reasonably forthcoming in a busy week. I fully understand my hon. Friend's desire that the Government should produce their considerations of these matters and make public their position on the Griffiths report, but he will agree that we had better get it right rather than be too hastily wrong. My hon. Friend has a reputation for expressing his views fairly vocally, and if we get it wrong we might get some stick from him.

Mr. Dick Douglas (Dunfermline, West): Does the Leader of the House recall that in a previous Parliament the Select Committee on Defence twice was highly critical of the Government's decision to contract out Her Majesty's dockyards? Will he give an undertaking, either via a statement by a responsible Minister next week or on some other appropriate occasion, that we shall have some information about what exactly is happening at Rosyth?

There are signs that Thorn EMI is to pull out and that Babcock is reshaping its corporate structure. That induces severe unhappiness in the labour force, to put it mildly, and casts doubt on the long-term commitment of those contractors to remain with the project.

Mr. Wakeham: I know the long and detailed interest that the hon. Gentleman takes in these matters, and I remember the report to which he refers. At this time of year we tend to have debates on defence. We are to debate the Army today. I would not want to stretch the hon. Gentleman's ingenuity too far by suggesting that he should bring that into the debate. However, we shall be having a debate in the near future when I am sure that the hon. Gentleman will be able to make his point. In the meantime, I shall refer the matter to my hon. Friend the Minister of State for the Armed Forces, who was listening to what the hon. Gentleman said.

Mr. Henry Bellingham (Norfolk, North-West): My right hon. Friend may have covered this matter in previous business questions, but he will be aware that, until recently, when an hon. Member signed an early-day motion his name appeared on the Order Paper the next day. However, now, if one signs an early-day motion that is more than a week old, it appears only every Thursday. Why has that change taken place? Does he agree that it devalues early-day motions? Cannot we return to the original system?

Mr. Wakeham: I hope that my hon. Friend will not take it amiss when I say that his question is rather like night following day. There were complaints about the existing system and suggestions that it was being abused. The Accommodation and Administration Sub-Committee looked at the matter and some new proposals have been produced. We are now trying those new proposals, and we had better see how we get along for a little longer before we start changing them again.

Mr. Win Griffiths (Bridgend): I am grateful to the Leader of the House for giving an assurance that we will have a debate on the European Community proposal for a framework directive on health and safety at work. Can he assure us that the debate will be held in the very near future rather than at some indefinite time?

Mr. Wakeham: I am not one to be churlish to anyone who says anything kind to me on these occasions, but it is not quite what I said in answer to the hon. Member for Holborn and St. Pancras (Mr. Dobson). I said that I would refer his question to my right hon. Friend the Secretary of State for Employment, and I did not give any undertaking.

Mr. Harry Greenway (Ealing, North): Will my right hon. Friend reconsider his answer to my hon. Friend the Member for Newbury (Sir M. McNair-Wilson) and his refusal of a debate on dog registration? In my constituency, on the large High Lanes estate, the Post Office has three times suspended deliveries of mail because of attacks on postmen by stray dogs or dogs which are out of control. The need for a debate is urgent.

May we also have a debate on the environment, and particularly on the need to save playing fields from Socialist councils such as Ealing which is seeking to build on 17 acres of the beautiful Cayton road playing fields belonging to Ealing Green high school?

Mr. Wakeham: I wish that I could help my hon. Friend by finding time for a debate. The second issue that he raised is important, but I fear that he will have to use his considerable ingenuity to find a way of raising it.

As to my hon. Friend's first point, I cannot add to what I have said to hon. Members, except to say that in practice the problem is not so much the registration of dogs as owners of dogs being responsible for and taking proper care of their dogs. That is what lies at the heart of the trouble.

Mr. Dennis Skinner (Bolsover): The Leader of the House will recall that several months ago the Secretary of State for Energy declared that he would introduce amending legislation regarding the restart scheme as it applied to mineworkers. Despite several requests, the amending legislation, which will affect a considerable number of people who have been made redundant in the past 12 months, still has not been introduced. Will the right hon. Gentleman have a word with the Secretary of State for Energy to get the matter on board? If parliamentary time is not available, the Leader of the House could dump the Associated British Ports Bills and kill two birds with one stone. As that affects the Secretary of State for Employment and there is a need for co-ordination, the right hon. Member for Old Bexley and Sidcup (Mr. Heath) who has been brought back into favour by the Prime Minister, could act as an overlord to get the two Departments together to bring the legislation forward.

Mr. Wakeham: As usual, the hon. Gentleman goes in for a touch of overkill in his question. I know that, as always, he is trying to be helpful. He asked whether I would have a word with my right hon. Friend the Secretary of State for Energy, and the answer is yes.

Mr. David Winnick (Walsall, North): No doubt strong protests will be made about the way in which a BBC crew has been roughed up by security thugs in China. However, dealing with a domestic matter, will a statement be made next week explaining why the Minister of State, Foreign and Commonwealth Office waited a week before admitting that he had lunch with a BBC correspondent from whom the story originated that the expulsion of Soviet citizens had something to do with the possible blackmailing of Labour Members of Parliament? He claims that he was misunderstood, poor chap. The Government use their propaganda and news machinery to smear their political opponents but deny the story when the going gets rough.

Mr. Wakeham: The hon. Gentleman's allegations are disgraceful. My hon. Friend the Minister of State issued a comprehensive statement on 2 June about the background to those unfounded reports. I repeat that Labour Members were not associated with the matter. If the hon. Gentleman were an honourable gentleman all the time, he would accept that assurance.

Mr. Harry Cohen (Leyton): May we have a debate about the policy of higher fares on London Underground? Some hon. Members believe that it is further evidence that public transport is not safe in the Government's hands. If people are priced off the tube, the roads will be made more congested. Some hon. Members want to argue that more public investment and an integrated planned transport system is needed for London.

Mr. Wakeham: I should welcome a debate on London Transport and an opportunity for the appropriate Minister to say how much investment has been made in the Underground system—considerably more than by the Government of which he was a supporter.

Mr. D. N. Campbell-Savours (Workington): Is the Leader of the House aware that among those who are opposed to the televising of the proceedings of the House are hon. Members who would wish to compromise on the matter? Is he aware that I shall be tabling—within a matter of minutes after the right hon. Gentleman has tabled his motion—a series of amendments that deal with a compromise position, such as on the question of a dedicated channel for Select Committees and Standing Committees? Will he discuss with the parties concerned the possibility of my amendments being selected? If they are, a number of hon. Members will want to support them. I am worried that if they are not selected hon. Members will not have a chance to take a compromise view on the matter.

Mr. Wakeham: The hon. Gentleman takes himself seriously, and, even if no one else does, I try to do so. I would be unwise to comment on his amendments until I have seen them; and he would be unwise to table amendments until I have tabled the motion.

Mr. Campbell-Savours: That is what I said.

Mr. Wakeham: The hon. Gentleman is wise to take that course of action. He will recognise that the selection of amendments is a matter not for me but for Mr. Speaker.

Mr. Tam Dalyell (Linlithgow): May I quietly ask the Leader of the House how he and his colleagues would feel if they listened to the 9 o'clock news and heard that a group of them had been subject to blackmail, unspecified, and found that, at the end of the news, no qualifications were made to that statement? May we have a statement next week on exactly what happened at the Mijanou restaurant on 25 May?

Is it by chance the same thing about which Colin Wallace was complaining, which has been well detailed in Paul Foot's serious book "Who framed Colin Wallace?" which has just been published by Macmillan? It is not a matter of loony Lefties and Colin Wallace making these allegations. The loony Lefties would include His Grace the Duke of Norfolk, who believes Wallace, and the second Earl of Stockton, who is recorded as believing him. Is it a matter of the systematic rubbishing by security services of Labour MPs? The Lord President cannot say that the statement is unfounded and disgraceful. There are facts, and I ask the Minister quietly and sensibly to respond to them.

Mr. Wakeham: I shall answer the hon. Gentleman equally quietly. He would be the first to complain if he thought that the Government were responsible for the news on the BBC at 9 o'clock at night. In a free society, the BBC must report, under its own responsibility, what it believes to be happening and stand by it. My hon. Friend the Minister of State, Foreign and Commonwealth Office has made his position absolutely clear. That is the end of it as far as he is concerned.

Mr. Bob Cryer (Bradford, South): May we have a statement—it is overdue—next week on the capitulation by the Secretary of State for Transport in accepting the ending of a derogation from the weight limit of 38 tonnes for juggernauts, which was solemnly pledged to the House in 1982 in a debate on the Armitage report, and in allowing a weight limit for juggernauts which has been fixed by the Common Market at 40 tonnes as an interim move towards an overall limit of 44 tonnes, the Common Market standard? Are the Government satisfied that our roads and bridges can take 40 tonnes gross vehicle weight? Should not the Secretary of State for Transport explain to the House why the Government are spending £1 billion on improving our roads to carry more and more juggernauts, which will not be confined to any improved roads but will wander around the whole country, bringing even more disruption and oppression to traffic and to villages and towns?

Mr. Wakeham: My right hon. Friend successfully negotiated a satisfactory end date for United Kingdom derogations from the Community maximum lorry weight limits. Against a Commission proposal that our derogation should end in 1996, he insisted that we needed more time to bring sufficient of our bridges up to a suitable strength—which is part of the hon. Gentleman's point. That was a major achievement. The 40 tonnes gross limit and 11·5 tonnes drive axle limit shall not apply in the United Kingdom until 1 January 1999.

Mr. Keith Vaz (Leicester, East): May we have a short statement early next week on the position of British citizens still in China? I have a constituent, Miss Elaine Sweeney, of Humberstone in Leicester, who is in Chengdu in Situhan province. I am grateful to the Foreign Office for the steps that it has taken to ascertain her whereabouts. She telephoned her mother this morning.

I am concerned about the arrangements that are to be made by the Foreign Office for the return of British citizens. Today I spoke to five Foreign Office officials to obtain confirmation of the arrangements for her return, but they were not in a position to tell me what was to happen. On the World Service this morning, I heard that the American Government had taken some responsibility for British citizens in that province. Does the right hon. Gentleman agree that it would be more appropriate for the Foreign Secretary to write to hon. Members with an interest in this matter to tell them when another Government are involved and to ascertain, as a matter of urgency, what arrangements can be made for the return of those British citizens?

Mr. Wakeham: The whole House will want to pay a warm tribute to the work being carried out by our ambassador and the staff of the British embassy in China, who are dealing with some very difficult problems in trying conditions, as are many journalists and reporters who are seeking to do their job there as well. I do not want to say anything other than that. However, I can say to the hon. Gentleman that the young lady about whom he is concerned is well and is booked on an aeroplane to leave the country. I hope that that is satisfactory.

Points of Order

Mr. Bob Cryer (Bradford, South): On a point of order, Mr. Speaker. You have heard several requests for a debate about a dog registration scheme. May I draw your attention to the fact that an amendment has been tabled to the Local Government and Housing Bill, to require a dog registration scheme to be instituted by the Minister for

Local Government by means of a statutory instrument, with a requirement for an explanation if the Minister does not provide such a scheme? In view of the widespread concern, especially after the reports of rottweilers attacking young children and old women, it would be helpful to the House if you gave careful consideration to the request for a debate in examining the selection for amendments on either Tuesday or Wednesday, when the Bill will be considered. It would be extremely helpful if you would bear the request in mind, with a view to making a selection that includes that amendment.

Mr. Speaker: I certainly give that undertaking to the hon. Gentleman.

Mr. Harry Cohen (Leyton): On a point of order, Mr. Speaker. May I ask you to look at the two most recent answers to me from the Minister for Local Government about the poll tax? He begins by saying that the Government are not introducing a poll tax. You will recall that you recently described it as a poll tax yourself. May I therefore ask you to look at that? We need to have an assurance that the Government will not use that as an excuse to refuse to answer such questions.

Mr. Speaker: Every hon. Member may describe legislation in whatever way he likes. I never described it as a poll tax. I use the words laid down in the Local Government Finance Bill 1988.

The Army

Motion made, and Question proposed, That this House do now adjourn.—*[Mr. Chapman.]*

[Relevant documents: First Report from the Defence Committee of Session 1988-89 on the Future of the Brigade of Gurkhas (HC 68) and the Government's Reply thereto (Cm.700).]

Mr. Speaker: Before I call on the Front Bench I must point out that many right hon. and hon. Gentlemen wish to participate in this debate. I propose to put a limit on speeches of 10 minutes between 7 pm and 9 pm, but as we have had an early start, I hope that it may be possible to relax that limit. In fairness to all, I hope that those called before 7 pm will bear that limit broadly in mind.

4.7 pm

The Minister of State for the Armed Forces (Mr. Archie Hamilton): This year, we celebrated the 40th anniversary of NATO. During the past four decades, the collective strength and efforts of the Alliance have maintained peace in Europe in the face of the overwhelming military power of the Soviet Union and the Eastern bloc. This year has also seen the 10th anniversary of a Conservative Government, who have not only provided this country with secure defences, but have also played a full part in NATO's search for dialogue and co-operation in East-West relations. Thankfully, NATO's approach has now evoked a response from the Soviets.

There are welcome signs now that the Soviet leadership is moving away from its past exaggerated reliance on aggressive military power as the basis of the Soviet Union's status as a world power. We are determined to encourage and build on this new mood, but we should not be blind to the massive military strength that the Warsaw pact still retains. The recent promises of reductions in its forces are a step in the right direction, but even after the reductions announced last December are implemented, the Warsaw pact will still outnumber the West by 2·4:1 in tanks and artillery in Europe and by 1·8:1 in combat aircraft. That is a huge imbalance which is inconsistent with the requirements of any "defensive doctrine".

Mr. Martin O'Neill (Clackmannan): Before the Minister leaves that point, will he tell us the ratios that normal military strategy requires to make no offensive attack worth while? Are we not talking about ratios of about 3:1 at least before commanders would consider that they had sufficient advantage to guarantee an offensive attack any chance of success?

Mr. Hamilton: I have certainly not heard the figure. The thing that matters is the concentration of forces for an offensive attack. That is the significant matter, and that is one of the factors that will have to be considered in the CFE talks. We must ensure that the forces that we are left with are dispersed widely enough to prevent a concentrated attack—the one thing that would undermine the security of the West.

If we are to be certain of preserving our freedom and security, NATO needs collectively to remain able to show the Warsaw pact that it can gain no possible advantage by trying to pursue its objectives by the use of military force in Europe. The government are not prepared to abandon the policies that have kept the peace for so long. We will not abandon the nuclear element of Western defence,

[*Mr. Hamilton*]

which history has shown is the only way in which the aim of preventing all forms of war in Europe—conventional and nuclear—can be achieved, and which is accepted by all members of the Alliance. The Labour party wants to throw away the policy or flexible response which has ensured that Soviet leaders have never felt tempted to use their massive military strength against a NATO country.

Our deterrent policy ensures that any aggression would involve the prospect of unacceptable losses, disproportionate to any conceivable gain. That involves having available to the Alliance a range of options so that a potential enemy is faced with a series of possibilities that cannot be predicted with certainty. Creating uncertainty in the minds of our potential enemies about how, precisely, the West would respond to aggression is one thing. Creating uncertainty in the minds of our allies about our commitment to the agreed policies of the Alliance is another. With this Government, our allies can be certain that the United Kingdom will continue to provide the full range of effective forces and a full contribution to the mutual commitments of NATO membership that are necessary for our defence and that of our allies.

The Army plays a crucial part in this country's commitment to NATO's common defence, principally through its role in the defence of Europe's central region. The centrepiece of this contribution is the British Army of the Rhine, which provides armour, infantry, artillery and air defence units—as well as regiments of Lance missiles and artillery, which are capable of firing nuclear warheads —as part of NATO's Northern Army Group. In war, it would form a fully integrated part of the forces available to NATO's Supreme Allied Commander Europe to carry out NATO's agreed strategy of forward defence and flexible response.

Over the past 10 years the Government have spent about £20 billion more on our conventional forces than would have been spent if spending had continued at the 1978-79 level—its level under the last Labour Government. Because of that we have been able to provide the forces and the equipment necessary to maintain a full contribution to this strategy, and I shall today describe some of the ways in which we shall ensure that the Army can continue to play a full part.

Mr. Tam Dalyell (Linlithgow): As a tank-crew national service man in the British Army of the Rhine—possibly it is a residual interest—may I ask the Minister whether the complaints about BAOR accommodation that some of us have heard are founded? Some of the SS barracks which were very good when I was a national service man must surely be deteriorating.

Mr. Hamilton: I did not receive many complaints about Army barracks when I visited the Rhine Army recently. We are constantly spending money on updating and improving them, and there is no question of their being left in their pre-war state. Even though some of the accommodation is not up to the standard that we would like, we find money for improvements whenever we can.

Over this period the capability of BAOR has been increased considerably, and we are continuing to provide for extensive improvements in each of the key areas of firepower, mobility and protection.

During the past year, a sixth regiment of Challenger 1 tanks has been introduced. A seventh regiment is on order, and in December last year we decided that all Challenger tanks will be retrofitted with the new Charm 120 mm main armament. The first regiment will be equipped in the early 1990s. We also intend to replace the Chieftain tank as soon as possible, and as my right hon. Friend announced on 20 December, we have given Vickers Defence Systems the opportunity to show that it can deliver Challenger 2 to specification, time and cost. The demonstration phase is due to end in September 1990. Vickers must also show that it is able to develop improved ammunition for the tank's main armament so that it can match the technical developments of the future. We also placed an order in January this year for a further batch of Challenger armoured repair and recovery vehicles which will significantly enhance the combat effectiveness of our armoured forces.

The multiple-launch rocket system will start to be deployed from next year. Three regiments' worth have been ordered. This system will increase the range and potency of the Royal Artillery, initially with a rocket which will dispense bomblets designed to attack personnel and lightly armoured targets. MLRS2, which will dispense anti-tank mines, is under consideration for the mid-1990s, and MLRS3, which will be designed to dispense terminally guided anti-armour munitions, is being developed as a multnational collaborative venture for the latter part of the 1990s. Phoenix, a remotely piloted vehicle which is nearing the end of development, will provide improved targeting information.

A new 155 mm self-propelled howitzer, due to enter service from the early 1990s to replace the Abbot self-propelled howitzer and some of our older M109 systems, will not only provide a significant improvement in the artillery's firepower but should also provide excellent value for money for the taxpayer. A decision on this will be made shortly.

We have continued to improve the equipment of the infantryman. The LAW80 man-portable anti-tank weapon has been in service since January last year. Some 90,000 SA80 rifles are now in service in two versions, the individual weapon and the light support weapon. The weapon is generally well liked and has significantly increased infantry firepower. It is much more accurate than its predecessor, it allows more ammunition to be carried for the same weight, it is more compact, and it has a higher rate of fire.

A development contract was awarded in September last year for the important TRIGAT missile project. This programme, on which we are collaborating with France and West Germany, is aimed at replacing our current anti-tank missiles with more powerful third-generation systems in the mid to late 1990s.

Deliveries of the Warrior mechanised combat vehicle, armed with the 30 mm Rarden cannon, continue. Two battalions are now complete, and two are in the process of receiving their new vehicles. In all, we have ordered 13 battalions' worth of the armoured personnel carrier version. Other versions will carry out more specialised tasks. Our initial impressions of this British-designed and built vehicle are very encouraging and it will enable the infantry to support armoured units more closely. Protection for non-armoured infantry battalions with a

NATO role has also been greatly improved, now that deliveries of the Saxon wheeled armoured personnel carrier are complete.

Our development of the use of helicopters on the battlefield continues. Our studies have shown that both tanks and helicopters armed with anti-tank missiles have an essential role on the battlefield. Although both can destroy armour, the greater range and mobility of the attack helicopter makes it more suitable for reserve operations and swift counter-attacks. Helicopters are, however, relatively vulnerable to enemy fire and cannot provide the same ability as the tank to hold ground for long periods, or provide firepower support for dismounted infantry.

We are still considering the next generation of attack helicopter for the Army, and we have continued to improve the TOW missile on the Lynx anti-tank helicopter and to develop the ability of the helicopter to fight at night using thermal imaging and image intensification equipment.

The conversion of 24 Brigade to the air-mobile role began in April last year. An Army Air Corps regiment, equipped with anti-tank and utility Lynx and Gazelle helicopters, will be part of the brigade and will begin to form at Dishforth this year. Further support for the brigade in the short term will be provided by RAF Chinook and Puma helicopters.

To strengthen the army's ability to defend itself against the air threat on the future battlefield, we intend to replace the current Rapier system from the mid-1990s with the new, advanced Rapier 2000, which is now under development. We have also decided to form a third air defence regiment armed with the new high-velocity missile currently being developed by Short Brothers.

Mr. Dalyell: Has the Minister read the interesting autobiography by his right hon. Friend the Member for Chingford (Mr. Tebbit), in which he asserts that the Ministry of Defence was really completely unconcerned about the industrial future of Westland? I do not think that I distort it. Can we have the assurance that the Ministry of Defence is now extremely concerned about the industrial future of Westland and will gear its requirements to that industrial future?

Mr. Hamilton: It would be more accurate to say that the Ministry of Defence is most concerned about getting value for taxpayers' money. If, at the same time we can serve the British industry, that is a bonus. However, I do not believe that we are here exclusively to maintain any part of British industry. It would be a mistake for British defence manufacturers to work on that assumption. When it comes to helicopters, one of the problems is that we do not have a continuing demand for them and, therefore, Westland, if it is to have a good future, must look for export orders, as well as relying on the Ministry of Defence for orders.

Mr. John Wilkinson (Ruislip-Northwood): Will my hon. and gallant Friend clarify in greater detail the Government's policy on helicopter procurement? When the Government are considering the anti-armour role are they looking at aircraft other than the light attack helicopter, such as the Apache and the PAH2? On the question of the transport role for the brigade at Catterick,

is my hon. Friend considering aircraft other than the EH101 to provide troop lift in the longer term, or is the EH101 to be the aircraft to be bought?

Mr. Hamilton: When it comes to the light attack helicopter, we are indeed looking at alternatives, and the Apache is one that is under consideration. However, we must bear in mind that that is a fantastically expensive aircraft. I am sure that our consideration will be influenced by the cost of it.

As my hon. Friend knows, the difficulty with the EH101 is that although we have not reached anything like the position of having the aircraft, it is the only aircraft even in plan, of its size. Therefore, when considering carrying ability, we would have to think probably in terms of quite a different size of aircraft, if we were not to have the EH101. Certainly, our minds are open on that, too. We are hoping that the development of that aircraft will move ahead, but there are difficulties with it at present.

Sir Jim Spicer (Dorset, West): My hon. Friend made the point, with which I am sure we would all agree, that it is incumbent on any company, including obviously, Westland, to look for export orders. However, are we not truly in a chicken and egg situation, because export orders are bound to depend on the home Government being prepared to place their faith in the manufacturer and live up to the expectations that they have accorded a company in terms of placing firm orders? Until those firm orders are placed, it is almost impossible for any manufacturer, however good its product may be, to go out into the field and say, "We have a good product," because the first question that it will be asked is, "If it is so good, why have not your Government bought it?"

Mr. Hamilton: I take that point, but I believe that my hon. Friend would also accept that one of the advantages of the link that Westland has with Sikorsky is that it has a proven aircraft that it can manufacture under licence from Sikorsky. One would hope that that would improve its export opportunities. The role that the Army fulfils at home and abroad is to protect the people of this country and our allies, and to defend the way of life that we enjoy in the West. The skill and professionalism with which the Army carries out that task is worthy of the very highest praise, and is something that impresses me at each unit and exercise that I visit.

In the United Kingdom, the Army is, of course, deployed in Northern Ireland to support the RUC in combating the men of violence, whose aim is to kill and to destroy our way of life.

At present, there are 19 major Army units in Northern Ireland, of which nine are battalions of the UDR, which carry out their task with the utmost professionalism and dedication. There was one major change in 1988—the creation of Headquarters, 3 Infantry Brigade, at Armagh which now directs Army operations in the border area and allows the other two brigade headquarters to concentrate on supporting the RUC in other areas where there is a high level of terrorist activity.

Service men face risks both on and off duty in Northern Ireland. Regrettably during 1988 a naval recruiting officer and 33 regular army and UDR soldiers, most of whom were off duty, were murdered by terrorists, and 229 injured. So far this year six soldiers have been murdered and 73 wounded. The callous attitude of the IRA was typified last year by the murder of six off-duty soldiers who

[*Mr. Hamilton*]

were taking part in the Lisburn fun run in June, to raise money for charity, and an off-duty UDR soldier was shot down in front of his wife and children while they were on a family shopping trip.

Nor is this campaign of murder confined to Northern Ireland, as a number of incidents both in Europe and on the mainland of Great Britain since the last Army debate have shown. In Europe, one soldier and three RAF men were murdered last year in terrorist attacks. One soldier was killed in the bombing at Mill Hill. Thankfully, timely action by the security forces prevented the horrific carnage that the terrorists hoped to achieve at Tern Hill and in Gibraltar. I can assure the House that this Government take very seriously the need to maintain and, where possible, enhance the security of the Armed Forces and we shall continue to be vigilant.

Mr. Jonathan Sayeed (Bristol, East): Will my hon. Friend take this opportunity to congratulate the American ambassador Mr. Catto on his condemnation of the IRA and the clear message that he sent back to the United States not to support Noraid and help those murderers?

Mr. Hamilton: I shall certainly do as my hon. Friend asks. There has been encouraging support both from the Reagan Administration and, subsequently, the new Administration in condemning the activities of Noraid and in making the point to the American people that they are supporting a terrorist organisation and that nothing is served by doing that.

The resurgence of terrorist activity in 1988 has highlighted once again the outstanding dedication and courage of our service men and women in the face of dangerous and testing circumstances. There are no short-term solutions and the fight against terrorism will be a long one. However, last year the Army, with the assistance of both the Royal Navy and the RAF, achieved a number of notable successes in support of the RUC. More than 500 weapons, 100,000 rounds of ammunition and nine tonnes of explosives were seized by the security forces in 1988. Some 205 bombs were made safe through the extraordinary bravery and skill of our bomb disposal teams. There can be no doubt that those achievements have saved the lives of many civilians and service men who would otherwise have been added to the number already murdered by the terrorists.

In their futile campaign of murder, the terrorists have also brought imprisonment and death upon themselves. In Northern Ireland 127 people were convicted last year of serious terrorist offences. In addition, eight terrorists in Northern Ireland paid for their murderous activities with their lives—five when they were intercepted in the act by the security forces and three who killed themselves with their own bombs. Another terrorist was killed in February this year by a bomb that he was attempting to attach to a former workmate's car.

Those deaths, and the repeated murder of civilians by terrorists in Northern Ireland, illustrate all too clearly the bankruptcy of the terrorists who, after 20 years, have nothing constructive to offer, even to those from both communities whom they falsely claim to represent. The men of violence scar many lives with tragedy, not only those they murder and maim, but the families of their victims. They offer nothing but destruction and despair to the communities of Northern Ireland. No one has the right in a democratic society to put aside the law or to use murder when they fail with the ballot box.

It is regrettable that it is clear that the IRA still retains large quantities of sophisticated arms and ammunition, and still intends to carry out a major campaign of violence and intimidation. As long as is necessary, therefore, the Army will continue to play its part in the vital task of maintaining the rule of law. Hon. Members on both sides of the House are keen to have the soldiers off the streets again; it is only the terrorists who keep them there.

I come to other matters and to other ways in which the Army is planning to meet the changing circumstances of the future.

Mr. Eric S. Heffer (Liverpool, Walton): I am not arguing with the Minister in any way over his remarks about terrorism, but before making those remarks he said that the role of the Army was to defend our way of life. Will he define that more clearly? What does he mean by "our way of life"? If he means the right to have free elections, to have freedom of speech, the right to demonstrate, the right to have a free press, to have free trade unions which have the right to strike, to have control over the armed forces and the police by the civil authorities and so on, I would have no argument with him.

The Prime Minister, however, tends to talk about freedom as though it meant freedom for the capitalist system. For her, apparently, it means nothing else. Certain people in Europe are simply putting forward a social document which seems to be hardly Socialist in character. But the Prime Minister gets all upset and says, "We do not want that Socialism here".

Mr. Julian Brazier (Canterbury): People were being killed while a Labour Government were in power, not just while we have been in power——

Mr. Heffer: If the hon. Gentleman will keep his damn mouth shut, I will try to make my point.

Hon. Members: Order.

Mr. Speaker: Order. The hon. Member is making an intervention. It must not be a speech.

Mr. Heffer: If the hon. Member for Canterbury (Mr. Brazier) will stop making a sedentary intervention in my intervention, I will be able to make my point.

Will the Minister define precisely what "our way of life" means to the Government, especially as the Tories seem to be making it almost impossible for workers to take strike action at any time and under any circumstances?

Mr. Hamilton: I should have thought that the main freedom being defended by the armed forces of the nation was the freedom to elect the Government that the people want. If life is as abhorrent to people as the hon. Gentleman makes out, they will decide that it is time for a change of Government. I do not see that as being remotely likely. Indeed, if the Labour party continues to be seen to support continual obstructive strikes across the country, the chances of us remaining in power indefinitely are very good indeed.

As the House will be aware, the Secretary of State announced on 22 May the Government's plans for the future of the Brigade of Gurkhas. Those plans make it clear that, despite the loss of their current main role in Hong Kong in 1997, there is a worthwhile and viable future for these fine fighting men in the British Army, based on a viable brigade structure that would comprise about 4,000 personnel, serving in discrete units which will preserve their distinctive identity and traditions.

It is clear from some of the reactions to my right hon. Friend's announcement that a number of people have missed the point that we are talking about a decision which will not have full effect for another eight years. There will be no reductions in numbers overnight. Indeed, the earliest that any changes could start to be made is in 1992, and it will not be necessary to take decisions about that until well into next year.

The House will recognise that it would be neither prudent nor practicable to be categoric at this stage about the precise number of troops that will be in the brigade after 1997 or, as so much will depend on circumstances at the time, their exact roles or deployments. The Government have, however, given a clear demonstration of their commitment to the Gurkhas by giving them such an assurance about their future so far ahead.

We have also made it clear that a brigade of about 4,000 is open to review in the light of circumstances, including whether the Gurkhas could help to overcome any more general manpower shortages in the Army resulting from adverse demographic trends. When the first decisions on numbers become necessary, we should also be much clearer about the precise effects that demographic changes will have on the Army as a whole.

The Government believe it would be wrong to see the retention of the Gurkhas purely as a solution for demographic problems, with the implication that, if those problems disappear, so will the Gurkhas. The Government's plans are founded on the assumption that, regardless of demographly, we shall, on the basis of the information available at present, wish to retain a significant Gurkha force with roles within the mainstream of the Army's defence commitments. It is on that assumption that the figure of about 4,000 announced by right hon. Friend is based.

Mr. A. E. P. Duffy (Sheffield, Attercliffe): Will the Army meet its recruitment target this year?

Mr. Hamilton: It will not meet its recruitment target this year and, on the whole, the trend gets worse as we progress.

Mr. O'Neill: I am not sure whether the House should welcome what the Minister said about the Gurkhas. Is he in any way moving away from the Secretary of State's statement of 28 May, or is he merely dressing it up in a different form?

Mr. Hamilton: I am merely elaborating on my right hon. Friend's statement. He said that there would be about 4,000 in the Brigade of Gurkhas and that is what I am saying. I am also saying, as has my right hon. Friend, that we will look at whether any extra people, above the 4,000 will be needed in terms of the demographic trends. All the signs show that they will be.

Mr. Sayeed: If, as proposed, we reduce each battalion to three companies rather than four, how will the Gurkhas deal with wartime attrition?

Mr. Hamilton: At the moment there are four companies in the battalions based in Hong Kong because of the heavy task which they have to perform. Therefore, they are at a much higher level of strength than a British battalion over here. We reduced the number of companies from four to three purely because those in Hong Kong have much higher demands placed upon them.

But of course, the House would expect me to say all this. So perhaps I could quote from a letter to the *The Times* published on 31 May from Field Marshal Lord Bramall, who as well as being a distinguished former Chief of the Defence Staff is President of the Gurkha Association. In it he said:

"The Government's statement was a positive, helpful and sensible one. In the place of uncertainty the Government was planning firmly for the Brigade of Gurkhas to have a worthwhile and viable role after 1997, and to do so at a basic strength of a four-battalion group, instead of the existing five, and with all the Gurkha regiments intact."

He went on:

"I believe the Government has kept faith with the hillmen of Nepal who, for over 170 years, have rallied to the support of this country, however adverse the circumstances or gloomy the forecasts; and who, in large numbers, have laid down their lives with the utmost gallantry for our security and our future."

There is little further that I can add other than warmly to endorse that eloquent tribute to the Gurkhas. The Gurkhas are rightly renowned for their traditional infantry skills, but they are also very adaptable. They have an assured future as part of the British Army and I am sure that they will meet every new challenge that they will have to face in the future.

I have mentioned the potential effects of demographic changes, and I would like to dwell a little on this problem, which the Army, in common with all large employers will increasingly have to face. The Army is a very major employer of young people, recruiting over 20,000 each year. In future, the Army will be competing for a sizeable share of a reducing resource at a time when employment prospects for young people are forecast to expand. We expect that by 1994 the number of young men aged between 15 and 19 will reduce by some 20 per cent.

In response to this problem the Army commissioned a major study into the problems of Army manpower supply in the years ahead known as MARILYN. I have today placed an abridged version of this report in the Library of the House. The study explores a range of possibilities and will underpin much of our future work on this subject. It is not itself a statement of Government policy and not all the proposals identified will necessarily be implemented.

Mr. Menzies Campbell (Fife, North-East): Why was not the abridged version of the report placed in the Library before today to give hon. Members the opportunity to look at it, consider its terms and, I hope, make rather more constructive contributions to today's debate?

Mr. Hamilton: I apologise to the hon. and learned Gentleman if he has not had enough time to look at the report. There was some work to do on abridging the original version, and we wanted to get the report into the Library before the debate took place. I am sorry that that could not have been done earlier.

Mr. O'Neill: Who was responsible?

Mr. Hamilton: A number of people asked me for an abridged version of MARILYN and I was able to send them a copy before the debate.

Mr. O'Neill: That was selective.

Mr. Hamilton: It was selective according to the numbers asked for.

We are now aiming to tackle the problem on two broad fronts—by improving recruitment and retention. Retention is important in providing continuity of experience and expertise, and in ensuring that we get the best return possible on our recruiting and training investment. Officer premature voluntary release, although more or less stable over the last two years or so, is running at about 650 a year, and soldier PVR is now about 3 per cent. These figures certainly do not amount to a stampede but they are higher than we should like.

Towards the end of last year, therefore, we provided around £1 million extra for the Army recruitment budget, with the aim of carrying out a couple of pilot television advertising campaigns in the regions. Those have proved very successful, increasing inquiries by 150 per cent. in those areas where the commercial was run. In March this year we launched a major television campaign, the first for eight years. Extra funding of almost £5 million will be provided to the recruiters this year, which will be spent on more television and other advertising as well as an up-to-date management information system to ensure that our efforts are properly and effectively targeted.

We have also looked closely at the way in which the Army runs its recruitment effort to remove unnecessary wastage and to encourage a more flexible and imaginative approach. For example, we shall be looking to boost officer entry by encouraging late entrants and reinstating reservists in specialist areas.

With soldier recruitment, I know that there has been speculation about whether we are planning to reduce our entry standards. In previous years we have been able to be very selective and take only the best—those who considerably exceeded our minimum requirements. We shall no longer have that luxury and so we are intending to spend more time in the early stages of training. We have, for example, instituted a physical development course for those who fail the entry fitness test. Over 250 have attended the course since last August, and most have passed into basic training. It is interesting to note that their wastage rate has been no higher than other recruits.

We need to turn as many inquirers as possible into applicants and as many applicants as possible into trained recruits. Everyone in the chain of command is being made aware of the problem and the need for them to make a personal contribution to reducing wastage and improving retention.

It is clearly important that we have a remuneration package which enables us to attract and retain the officers and soldiers that we need, but people do not leave the Army solely because of pay. Job satisfaction, worries about a second career, family pressures and a number of other factors play a part. I can assure thae House tht we are looking at all those areas.

Hon. Members will be aware that we are looking at the scope for widening the opportunities open to women in the Army. Although we do not envisage changing the long-standing policy of not employing women in direct combat roles, we believe that a significant additional number—I envisage that being well into four figures rather than three—of valuable and challenging jobs can be made available to women.

The House is also aware of our position on recruitment from the ethnic minorities. We have made clear our disappointment over the rate of applications from black and Asian youngsters, who represent only 1·25 per cent. of our Army recruits. That is something that we must correct and we look forward to the results of the consultancy study that we have commissioned which will help us decide how to target our recruitment efforts to best effect.

In short, we do not underestimate the scale of the problem and the potential difficulties that we face, and those are being tackled now. There is much that we can do to help ourselves by identifying management practices appropriate to changed circumstances. The demographic trough will not go away, but I intend to ensure that the Army will be able to respond to it in a well balanced and sensible way.

Of course, we cannot consider the future of the British Army without taking into account developments in the international arena and, in particular, the conventional arms negotiations taking place in Vienna.

My right hon. and learned Friend the Foreign Secretary set out the Western aims for those talks in March when he introduced the NATO proposal—in essence, a major reduction, to equal levels, in the key armoured forces essential for large-scale aggression and surprise attack. The recent NATO summit was able to extend that and, in addition, to propose reductions in aircraft, helicopters and manpower—a direct and speedy response to expressed Eastern concerns.

The opportunity is there now for progress towards an agreement. The timetable suggested by President Bush is an ambitious one, and represents a challenge to which everyone, not least Mr. Gorbachev, can respond. The negotiations have got off to a good start, and there is a greater degree of agreement on objectives and goals than emerged over many years in the mutual and balanced force reduction talks. The agenda, I might add, is a Western one, and the Soviets, here as elsewhere, are responding to Western initiatives and ideas. Of course, when Mr. Gorbachev claims that he is tabling a "bold new initiative" our media are liable to take him at his word and forget that we are seeing Western proposals being played back to us.

I am convinced that the Soviet response emanated from a realisation in Moscow that NATO was not prepared to be cowed or browbeaten by threats and that the Western Alliance remained cohesive and strong whilst forging ahead in advanced defence technology. Our steadfast adherence to sensible policies is now bearing fruit in the radical developments in East-West relations.

That commitment to strong defences in NATO was confirmed at the recent summit in Brussels. NATO also confirmed the continuing need for land, sea and air-based nuclear systems in Europe, including ground-based missiles; the rejection of a third zero in SNF negotiations in the clear statement that any negotiation should only lead to partial reductions in short range nuclear systems, and the unanimous view that negotiations on SNF should not commence until agreement on CFE has been reached and implementation is under way; and that there should be no implementation of reductions in short-range nuclear systems until conventional force reductions agreed under CFE have been completed. It was indeed an important summit, establishing a firm basis on which the Alliance can move forward.

Contrary to gloomy prognostications from the commentators, NATO emerged with a united and forceful view of its policies and vision. I recommend to hon. Members the full and unequivocal exposition in the comprehensive concept of the realities of Alliance security which Opposition Members seem neither to understand nor to accept. That concept was fully endorsed by all our NATO allies.

Those same allies will be pretty depressed if they have bothered to read the latest policy statement on defence from the Labour party. They will learn that the Labour party rejects the NATO strategy of flexible response and wants to see the end of short-range nuclear systems altogether. The Labour party intends to stand alone in Europe and reject the cornerstone of NATO defence policy that has kept the peace in Europe for so long and has forced the Soviets to the negotiating table.

Mr. Frank Cook (Stockton, North): Is the Minister suggesting that France supports the doctrine of flexible response when he says that Britain is alone in rejecting it? Can he be serious?

Mr. Hamilton: I did not say that Britain stands alone; I said that the Labour party stands alone in rejecting flexible response as the keystone to the defence of the NATO Alliance. The French adhere to flexible response. They may not be military members of NATO, but they adhere to the concept of flexible response which is being rejected by the Labour party.

Mr. Heffer: Conservative Members complain about people standing alone in relation to Europe, but the Prime Minister constantly tells us that she is standing alone on issue after issue. I do not complain about that. If she thinks that that is the correct thing to do, she has every right to do that. If the Labour party is standing alone and standing up for something for once, I shall be delighted.

Mr. Hamilton: The hon. Gentleman may well be delighted, but my right hon. Friend the Prime Minister was delighted with the outcome of the summit talks and with the fact that we reached an agreement that was shared by all our NATO allies.

Mr. Brazier: My hon. Friend has given way many times and I thank him for doing so again. For the benefit of the hon. Member for Stockton, North (Mr. Cook) and for Liverpool, Walton (Mr. Heffer), will my hon. Friend confirm that France not only supports the doctrine of flexible response but has just modernised its own short-range land-based weapon system with Hades?

Mr. Hamilton: I was making that clear to Opposition Members. France is very much a believer in flexible response and believes that we should not rely solely on ballistic missiles but should have a number of nuclear systems with which to reverse any attacks that we might receive.

But, of course, it is not only flexible response that is rejected by Labour. So is Britain's independent nuclear deterrent which, as our allies have once again explicitly stressed at the summit, contributes to the overall deterrence strategy of the Alliance.

We have heard much recently from the right hon. Member for Islwyn (Mr. Kinnock) to the effect that he has rejected unilateral disarmament as Labour policy, but has he? The only thing that has changed in the Opposition's policy is that where before Labour would give away Britain's nuclear weapons now they will negotiate away our deterrent.

If a Labour Government were ever elected by the people of this country two things could be guaranteed.

First, the many CND members of the Labour party in this House would lobby furiously to see Britain's nuclear deterrent negotiated away. Secondly, President Gorbachev would be over here as soon as he decently could offering perhaps two or three times as many Soviet warheads in return for Trident—and the Labour party is committed to deal. As a result, Britain would lose all its nuclear weapons and the Soviets would be left with thousands. That may not be unilateral disarmament but the result is the same.

We live in an unpredictable world. Although no one can disinvent nuclear weapons, the Labour party is prepared to see Britain stripped of her independent nuclear deterrent. Labour's defence policy will be no less dangerous in the next election than it was in the last; it will undermine the NATO Alliance and threaten the security of these islands.

The British people realise this and that is why Labour has no more chance of winning the next election than it did the last.

4.50 pm

Mr. Martin O'Neill (Clackmannan): The predictable format of the Minister of State's speech was followed almost to the letter: the 40 years of peace through NATO, the quick reference to the sterling work of the armed forces, to which we all subscribe, a little bit about morale, a bit about fighting terrorism and then a bash at the Labour party at the end—very much the usual stuff.

It is regrettable that it has taken so long for this debate to be held. Normally these debates are over if not by the end of the year at least by the end of January. While we have looking over our shoulder, as it were, the White Paper on the estimates, it would be unhelpful for us today to stray too far into that. I am quite happy to discuss at the appropriate time the relevant parts of the Labour party's defence white paper, which will be a green paper, of course, until it goes to our conference. But that is certainly not our purpose today.

My one regret is that this speech is not being made by my hon. Friend the Member for Knowsley, South (Mr. Hughes), who is sadly not with us today because he has recently had an operation and is still in hospital. I am sure that friends and colleagues hope, as I do, that he will make a speedy recovery.

I associate myself with the tributes paid by the Minister to the Army for the contribution that it makes to the defence of these islands, the role that it carries out in Europe and the work that it does in places such as Belize and Hong Kong. There are many examples of the kind of work done by our troops, very often in discreet and community-spirited ways. The Minister has already referred to the callous and heartless killing of soldiers who were participating in a fun run for charity last year. It is that kind of work that many of our young men actively participate in for the benefit of the community far beyond the 9 to 5 hours that many people seem to associate with work in many areas. Our young men are a credit to their regiments and to the youth of this country as a whole.

The most important contribution that the Army makes, however, is to NATO and above all to the British Army of the Rhine, including those troops in the United Kingdom who are deployed ready to be transferred to the continent at any time of crisis. Certainly in the last 10 days of the run-up to the NATO summit and the subsequent Government retreat, these questions of the size of our

[*Mr. Martin O'Neill*]

armed forces have once again come under the scrutiny of the press, as I hope that they will today and in the weeks ahead come under that of the House. It will take some time for us all to appreciate the complexity of the comprehensive concept and the implications of the summit communiqué.

I was fortunate enough to be in Rome on Monday to hear Ambassador Lodogar and Ambassador Dobrynin talk about some of the difficulties which the summit will throw up, and the task of definition which the allies have set themselves over the summer is a very important one. We recognise that until 7 September it will not be possible to answer a number of the questions that we shall be asking today, but in this debate we shall raise some questions which the Minister should try to address in winding up. We want to know the implications for the British Army of the Rhine and for the other allied forces of the cuts which President Bush has announced with regard to United States forces. I do not think that it would be correct for us to say at this time that we should join the French in being counted in because I believe that the different arrangements which the French have with the Alliance are such that this would add an undue complication. We want to get cuts and we want to get them quickly.

Hon. Members who participate in these debates know that over the months and years I have been arguing that we should have been far more positive in response to some of the Gorbachev initiatives—so-called initiatives, because in many instances they were elaborate public relations exercises which looked very good and promised a great deal but were dependent upon a response which, sadly, was not forthcoming until President Bush's belated, I think, but highly welcome statement prior to the summit. We can see from the initial response from the Soviet Union that there are considerable grounds for optimism but at the same time certain uncertainties which we have to look at.

I hope that we can move quickly on this and that the September deadline can be met. It might be interesting if, in winding up, the Minister could share with the House some of the thinking. For example, the Prime Minister was adamant on Tuesday that no British Tornados would be involved in any of the cuts. On the other hand, if we set aside the Prime Minister's prejudices for the moment and look at the question of helicopters, will these be included? If so, will it be the Army's helicopters or the RAF's? Will the Army and the RAF still have joint control over helicopters? This is an old argument which always crops up. I notice in today's *Jane's* that the Australians have now grasped the nettle and taken away the choppers from the RAAF and that these are now solely under the control of the Army. I believe that in an Army debate of this nature this question should be addressed.

We have had a lengthy and rather depressing disquisition by the Minister on the various types of helicopters. I have listened to hon. Members on both sides of the House talking about the future of helicopter procurement and there seems to be a characteristic indifference by the Ministry of Defence to the industrial implications of a confused policy of procurement. We have to recognise that, if we are to sustain a manufacturing base in this country for any kind of helicopter, it is the

responsibility of the Government, as the main customer of those manufacturers, to create the circumstances in which exports can be obtained. As has been heard from the Government Benches, the weakest possible case that one can put to a foreign customer is to start by saying that our Government have yet to make up their mind what they want.

In one defence debate after another and in one Army debate after another a succession of Ministers—usually a different one each time, but the script is always the same —have said that they have not yet made up their minds what to do. We need far stronger assurances as to the intentions regarding this part of our manufacturing base, because we are running out of time. We must not forget that, come 1992, whoever is in the European Parliament and whoever is at the Government Dispatch Box, we need to ensure that we have a place in the manufacturing of helicopters. If we do not get it right quickly, we shall be considerably weaker when the appropriate section of the Single European Act comes into play—and defence procurement is one feature of the new arrangements.

As to the implications of the summit, traditionally we have heard that the argument for short-range nuclear forces in Europe is twofold. The first is that they bridge the conventional gap between the Warsaw Pact and NATO, and that because of the willingness of the Soviet and eastern European Governments to spend vast amounts of money on defence, those Governments were able to build up sizeable comparative advantages over the West in certain areas of conventional defence. As democratically-elected Governments in the West were not always as committed as British Labour or Conservative Governments have been to support defence expenditure, and have not supported the Alliance in the way that they should, they have hidden behind short-range nuclear forces.

If there is a positive response to President Bush's initiative, and if by 1992-93 the parity or below parity that we seek is achieved, one of the fundamental arguments for SNF forces in Europe—the gap to which I referred—will be removed.

The second argument for SNF has been inelegantly but precisely put—that the Americans are not prepared to have troops here if there is no nuclear guarantee. When we go to NATO, we hear the phrase, "No nukes, no troops." The Germans are still not satisfied, but their time may have been bought by the allies, at least in respect of the German short-range question. However, the problem will not go away. If Chancellor Kohl is returned to power, it will only be with the support of the Free Democrats, which means the presence also of Foreign Minister Genscher in the Cabinet. If he is in the Cabinet, there will be arguments in favour of the albeit step-by-step removal SNF. Genscher, ever the populist, and looking over his shoulder at the narrow margin between his political existence and non-existence under the German electoral system, will make continued calls for the removal of short-range nuclear forces. If the host country for the majority of SNF is not prepared to allow them, I cannot see the Alliance standing by last year's communiqué.

Since the Brussels summit last March, the situation has changed from one of discussing modernising Lance to debating the continued deployment of existing SNF, and to discussing those forces' possible removal in two or three years' time, subject to other developments. The confidence with which the Americans view the prospects of a positive Soviet response to the Bush initiative suggests that that item will be on the agenda fairly quickly.

Although SNF will not be removed until 1992-93, discussions could take place by the end of next year. If agreement is reached on definitions and a deal is settled within six to 12 months, implementation will proceed, according to President Bush's remarks, as speedily as possible. If implementation continues apace, there will be considerable pressure in Germany to comply not least because there will be elections to the Bundestag in December 1990. From the point of view of Genscher and Kohl, there could be no better preparation for those elections than for them to be able to tell their electorate, "We are discussing the dismantling of short-range nuclear forces."

The British Government should not kid themselves as to the length of time that SNF will remain in Europe and the Prime Minister still be walking in step. People decided to leave that unfortunate and unpleasant topic to one side for a little while so that they could get out of Brussels last week as quickly and as safely as they could, but the Minister would be wrong to imagine that a flexible response will remain in its present form.

We also have an interest in the threat posed by SNF to the 55,000 British troops in the central region. Another element is the anxiety expressed to me last year by the German Foreign Minister, and acknowledged by the German Defence Minister, that SNF is no longer regarded as a viable political weapon. Germany sees it as quite possible that the force to space ratio argument to which the Minister referred will apply and that the commanders in the field—to whom the Prime Minister referred on Tuesday as being the people who must make fast decisions —will be left to decide whether or not to use nuclear weapons when confronted by a sudden invasion. Neither the Prime Minister nor the Minister may appreciate that argument, but many right hon. and hon. Members in all parts of the House do.

Mr. Michael Mates (Hampshire, East): The hon. Gentleman is right about German anxiety, but he mentions only our short-range nuclear weapons and our modernisation plans. We have 88 systems, and I can tell the hon. Gentleman that every one of the commanders in the British and American armies of the Rhine is much more worried about the 1,200 already modified Soviet short-range nuclear weapons. Is the hon. Gentleman not worried about them too?

Mr. O'Neill: Yes, and that is exactly the point I am trying to make. If and until our modernisation programme proceeds, that disparity between our forces and the overwhelming superiority of the Soviets will continue for a considerable length of time. It is thus in our interests to start negotiating for the removal of SNF as quickly as possible. It is argued repeatedly that we should negotiate only from a position of strength, but we cannot afford to wait until we can do that.

Mr. Mates: So Labour would have us give up our short-range nuclear forces?

Mr. O'Neill: No, not give them up but talk about dismantling them—we should recognise that to do so would be to our advantage and that of the German people. There is a consensus across the political spectrum in the Federal Republic that that action should be taken. That consensus is recognised by the American President, whose support for the present coalition stems from his wish not to see it out of power, because he would then have to deal with a coalition led by Social Democrats with which the Labour party would have considerable sympathy, as would a number of other Governments in the NATO Alliance. The Minister over-eggs the pudding when he suggests that everyone who signed the Brussels communiqué did so in a spirit of complete unanimity. I know of one right hon. Lady who signed it but who does not agree with every jot, dot and comma of it—and no right hon. or hon. Member believes that she does.

I believe that the flexible response strategy of the Alliance is out of date and should be changed, but that can be done only through serious discussion within the Alliance and disarmament talks of a kind that we can throw our weight behind. What worries me at present is that, although the Americans and the Germans are committed to the comprehensive concept and the implementation of the changed arrangement proposals in the summit communiqué, I have yet to see any clear and frank support from the Prime Minister, who was most unconvincing at the Dispatch Box on Tuesday.

The Prime Minister has said that she will have nothing to do with a sizeable or meaningful contribution to the initiative which probably above all else makes the package attractive to the Soviet Union—the inclusion of aircraft in the proposals. It is a mark of the statesmanship of President Bush that he identified that initiative as a breakthrough that would win over the Soviets, who had asked for it, and he should be given credit for that. The Prime Minister's response has been characteristically grudging and curmudgeonly, and it is fortunate indeed that the other 15 members of the Alliance are bringing good sense to the issue.

The Minister has not had much time to read the fine print of the communiqué, but it would be useful for us to have some idea of the Government's thinking about dual capability and what systems might be considered suitable candidates. Perhaps, for instance, he could give us his views on the 155 mm and 203 mm systems, which I certainly consider suitable.

There are tremendous grounds for optimism on both sides of the European divide—for instance, the election results in Poland, the encouraging developments in Hungary and, indeed, the Soviet Union itself, where the degree of openness in debate has surpassed even that experienced by Conservative Members at their annual party conferences. We have observed disagreements and we have seen the Soviet President being attacked, which is no bad thing.

I realise that in a number of other countries we shall have to wait a considerable time for the progress that is due. In Romania, "Socialism in one country" has been supplanted by "Socialism in one family". Czechoslovakia is perhaps a sleeping giant that has yet to turn. We have considerable grounds for hope in East Germany, but realisation of that hope is still some way away.

Mr. Wilkinson: Does the hon. Gentleman consider the 58 deaths and 500 injured in Uzbekistan, the gassing of 20 in Tbilisi and the unrest in Armenia, which has also caused deaths, a hopeful sign? Or does it suggest to him that the Soviet Union is prepared, if necessary, to use armed force within its own republics and might even do so outside?

Mr. O'Neill: It is true that a great deal remains to be done to improve the situation in the Soviet Union. It is encouraging, however, that at least some of the excesses —I do not say all—have been followed by speedy repudiation by the authorities and the arraignment of those responsible. That has happened in Georgia, although we do not know yet what is happening in Uzbekistan. I do not deny that the state of affairs in the Soviet Union is still patchy. It is very difficult to emerge in a short time from 70 years of tyranny. It is also difficult for a centralised empire to handle the ethnic problems that have emerged in some areas.

It is certainly encouraging that the Soviet Union now recognises that it is spending too much on defence. When I was there earlier in the year, I talked to some economists who said, "We used to think that we spent about 10 or 11 per cent. of our gross domestic product on defence, but we know that the CIA believed that it was more like 15 per cent; we now think that it is about 23 per cent., but we are not sure, and we would like to see the CIA's databases, which are probably more accurate than ours." Soviet expenditure on defence presents such a confused picture that attempts to cut that expenditure, although laudable, may take much longer than we would like. Nevertheless, the Soviets are endeavouring to make changes and we must give them every possible encouragement. President Bush has taken a worthwhile step along that road.

Mr. Sayeed: I accept that the economic argument has helped the Soviet Union to change its mind about building up its weapon systems. Would the hon. Gentleman agree, however, that the reason the Soviets have come to the negotiating table is that the NATO allies have remained firm? Had this country and others followed Labour party policy on cruise missiles, the Soviet Union would never have bothered to negotiate at all.

Mr. O'Neill: That is speculative in the extreme. *[Interruption.]* I am trying to answer the hon. Gentleman's question. The remarks of the hon. Member for Canterbury (Mr. Brazier) are rarely helpful, and in this case they are simply a nuisance.

The Soviet attitude to talks on short-range and long-range nuclear weapons has been transformed by the arrival of Mikhail Gorbachev and the relationship that he established with Ronald Reagan. That is the single fact that we can identify. Whether the movements within Europe, and indeed the United States, against the deployment of cruise and Pershing missiles and the arms race as it was then developing have been an important factor must be left to historians, but I believe that they have. The hon. Member for Bristol East (Mr. Sayeed) does not, but I think that we must agree to disagree. I do not intend to enter into an elaborate point-scoring exercise.

It is not to the Soviet Union or to the Warsaw pact but to China that I now wish to look, with some trepidation. We in Britain have a unique responsibility to Hong Kong, but what the Minister said about the Gurkhas does not strike me as particularly satisfactory. He seems to have said nothing more than the Secretary of State said in his recent statement announcing a 50 per cent. cut in the brigade. That is not reassuring.

In the past decade, we have learned to our cost that when wrong signals are given out to particular countries at the wrong time we pay dearly, as we did in the Falklands. Until we can obtain far better guarantees of the intentions of the People's Republic of China for the people of Hong Kong after 1997 we should not talk about cutting the Gurkhas or withdrawing troops. I believe that hon. Members on both sides of the House will wish to argue that case today.

I thought that the Minister was going to say that in the light of changing circumstances the figure of 4,000 might be raised, but he meandered around the question and never reached a conclusion. If we are told in the Minister's winding-up speech that the Secretary of State's announcement is to be put on hold, many of us will be, if not satisfied, at least reassured of the strength of the Government's intent.

Members of the Select Committee will speak for themselves, but paragraph 305 of the Select Committee report states that there are
"no grounds for concluding that a cut in the number of Gurkha infantry battalions is justified."
They were speaking not just from their hearts—this is a matter of tremendous emotion for many people in Britain —but also from their heads, after many months of well-researched work. The Secretary of State apparently found that work immensely helpful when he spoke on 22 May, but he did not pay very much attention to it. The British Army requires the Gurkhas not only for demographic reasons but because they represent a contribution to the armed forces that still has a place in the British Army. It is worth while for us to continue to support the state of Nepal by continuing to entrust the Gurkhas with the tasks that they have carried out with such distinction and valour for such a long time. We should not consider reducing our commitment to Hong Kong in any way at this time, least of all our commitment in the form of the Gurkhas.

The Minister has spoken about the security of mainland army bases where the experiences of this summer have been particularly distressing. I recognise that the Ministry has responded in a flexible and, one hopes, effective way and that the cessation of these attacks for the moment at least—that is all that we can ever say—is a tribute to the renewed and increased vigilance of our forces, and we welcome the arrangements that have been made. Car numbering may also have made a difference. Perhaps when the Minister replies to the debate he will give us some news of what has happened in that respect.

The increased threat outside Northern Ireland does not quite shape up with the Government's plans for the MOD police force. We understand that the MOD police force may well be cut in order to save money. In the past 10 years the force has been increased, but that was almost entirely due to greater demand as a result of the increased size of anti-nuclear demonstrations. While the MOD accountants see considerable opportunities to save money by substituting private security guards, those security guards have no constabulary powers of arrest, no right to bear arms where appropriate and no training in their use.

The MOD police force has a creditable record and there is considerable concern about the proposed changes to policing arrangements at the Colchester garrison. Military commanders are concerned about security and civilian police officers are worried about their capacity to take on the responsibilities of the MOD police at Colchester given the financial restraints under which the civilian police must operate. The MOD finally dropped the proposals in the face of considerable opposition. May we be assured that this bright idea will not re-emerge in other garrison towns and that the increased activities of terrorists on the United Kingdom mainland will be countered by the increased commitment of resources, equipment and personnel to the safety of the bases? We need to ensure that financial reasons will not be advanced for any changes in security. We pay tribute to the way in which the Secretary of State and his Ministers responded to the events of last year, but we should like to think that such vigilance will be maintained, as we know that it will, and that the MOD police will not be involved in any cost-cutting exercises.

In regard to the Government raising funds, I should like briefly to mention Royal Ordnance, the supplier to the armed forces, and the sale of Royal Ordnance land. It appears that the care and attention that the MOD is giving to these matters is less than it should be. The Enfield site was valued at £3·5 million and subsequently sold for between £300 million and £400 million. That suggests that the MOD is not getting the value for money that many of us assumed the Government would have been anxious to achieve.

The Parliamentary Under-Secretary of State for Defence Procurement (Mr. Tim Sainsbury): The hon. Gentleman misled the House—inadvertently, I hope—when he said that it was subsequently sold for £300 million. The site to which he referred has not been sold, has no planning permission and has had no development carried out upon it.

Mr. O'Neill: We shall have to explore that later. I understand that British Aerospace will be selling the land very soon for something in the order of the sum that I mentioned. On a number of occasions the Minister has told us that he has experience in these matters, but his experience seems to have involved a different type of land sale as these sales appear to represent a particularly bad deal for the MOD and for the nation. Perhaps I am using the word "sale" wrongly, but the proposed sale to which I am referring at the price that I mentioned represents nothing less than a complete abdication of the Government's responsibility to the taxpayer.

The Minister referred at some length to the MARILYN report, which I have read about in the press. I believe that it has now been circulated to a select few Members of Parliament and that today, as an afterthought, a copy was placed in the Library. I understand that not even the Chairman of the Select Committee has received a copy, so its circulation must be extremely restricted. A number of right hon. and hon. Members take an interest in these matters and would have regarded it as a courtesy to be told that a copy of the report was available in the Library.

Had it been placed in the Vote Office, we would have seen quite clearly when it came out, but putting it in the Library almost as an afterthought is not the best way of securing all-party support for what may be a worthwhile and politically uncontentious issue. Such clumsiness is increasingly characteristic of the Ministry and was apparent in the announcement of a statement on the Gurkhas on a Monday on a one-line Whip when many members of the Select Committee, who had spent a great deal of time working on the issue, were not in the House and did not know about it. Normally, as a courtesy, I receive word about such statements in advance. The fact that I was not here and a colleague was able to handle it was not a problem for me, but for individual members of

a Select Committee who put in a great deal of time on a voluntary basis to be treated in such a disrespectful way by the Ministry was nothing short of shocking.

Perhaps the indifference of the Secretary of State is demonstrated by the fact that he is not here today to support his own Department. I do not blame him for not listening to me because I understand his discomfort at some of the things that I have to say, but it is a matter of courtesy to the House and to his own Department that the Secretary of State should take the trouble to be here and to speak on these matters, or at least to let right hon. and hon. Members know that there are good reasons why he is not here. Had he done so, it would not have been necessary for me to raise the matter in the way that I have.

Mr. Archie Hamilton: My right hon. Friend the Secretary of State is in Brussels having discussions with other Defence Ministers. He is sorry that he is unable to be present.

Mr. O'Neill: I accept that as an excuse, or reason. If an agriculture Minister visits Brussels, statements are always made, but if NATO holds a meeting about earth-shatteringly important matters, the chances of getting a statement from the Trappist Secretary of State for Defence are almost zero.

The Minister has usefully expressed the Government's concern about recruitment, which will be a problem in the 1990s. We recognise the demographic changes that are occurring in the country and much will have to be done to attract people from sections of the community who so far have shown little interest in joining the Army. We appreciate the Government's concern about recruiting more people from ethnic minority communities. We are along way away from ethnic minorities being represented in the Army in the numbers that the size of their communities requires. We shall have to watch this issue closely because it is as important for community relations as it is for the defence of this country.

Mr. Harry Cohen (Leyton): My hon. Friend makes a good point about ethnic minorities in the armed forces. Surely it is wrong for the Government to refuse to monitor ethnic minorities in the armed forces when those minorities are simply not getting the promotions to which they are entitled. The Government should be checking that and doing something about it.

Mr. O'Neill: We have discussed this in a number of debates, in which my hon. Friend participated on behalf of his constituents. A case can be made for more scrutiny and greater monitoring. We must be assured that ethnic minorities will be attracted to the armed forces and that they will regard it as a worthwhile commitment with which they can identify.

It would be helpful if the Under-Secretary of State for the Armed Forces said something about the success of the initiatives that his predecessor took in relation to bullying. He made great play of this issue in a debate last year, and it is important that hon. Members should be updated about the concerns that the former Under-Secretary of State expressed.

The House's treatment of the armed forces is somewhat sketchy. One-day debates are often too short and unsatisfactory. Labour Members have always complained that the time lag between debates is too long.

Mr. Archie Hamilton: A two-day debate for the Army.

Mr. O'Neill: The Minister laughs and says, "A two day debate for the Army." Hon. Members should be allowed more than five days' debate on the Army, which is one of the biggest recipients of public expenditure. The Prime Minister recognises that it is one of the most important responsibilities of the state. Given that she does not recognise much as being the responsibility of the state, hon. Members should be allowed more than 10 or 11 chances to discuss the Army at Question Time and five days of debate. Regrettably, these debates occur as and when the Government have the time or nothing better to debate.

Mr. Sainsbury: What about a debate in Opposition time?

Mr. O'Neill: The Minister is well aware that Opposition time is already restricted enough. If the Government believe that the defence of the country and the time that hon. Members spend debating it are important, many hon. Members believe that more time should be allowed.

There are a number of possible developments in the defence of our country. This is an opportunity for all hon. Members to express guarded optimism for the future, but that optimism depends to an extent on what happens abroad. Our optimism for the future is mainly due to the fact that our armed forces, especially the Army, make a sizeable contribution, which we all support and believe benefits the people who serve in it and the country. I am therefore happy to participate in the debate.

5.35 pm

Mr. Michael Mates (Hampshire, East): If the hon. Member for Clackmannan (Mr. O'Neill) thinks that these debates are too short, he could oblige us by speaking for slightly less than 45 minutes. We would also get better evidence of the keenness of the Opposition if more than five Labour Members were present.

It is impossible at times not to feel a twinge of sympathy for the hon. Member for Clackmannan as he struggles to square the circle of Labour defence policy, especially when he came to the difficult passage in his speech about nuclear forces. A skilled professional acrobat can walk a tight wire and an even more skilled one can walk a slack wire. However, he canot walk a tight wire if, half way across, it drops 3 ft, which is what happens every time the Labour party tries to put together a nuclear policy that is coherent, honest and acceptable to Labour Members. When the hon. Member for Clackmannan was saying "We shall not scrap short-range nuclear forces," Labour Members behind him were shaking their heads in disapproval. When the hon. Gentleman mentioned the German concern, he did not want to address the enormous Russian superiority. I do not want to follow the hon. Gentleman, whose speech would have been better made in a defence debate rather than one on the Army, which he mentioned only peremptorily.

When the Select Committee on Defence visited the Army over the past year it found it in good heart and professional, working well and offering a service of which we can be justifiably proud. We visited British elements of battalions and troops and staff in the far east. We visited the United Kingdom land forces headquarters in Wilton and I visited many other units. Most important of all, we visited our forces in Northern Ireland. I endorse everything that the Minister and the hon. Member for

Clackmannan said about how well they are doing. It is a paradox that the worse the conditions for soldiers, the higher their morale and the harder they work for a cause for which they have been professionally trained and which they believe is right. I am sure that they have the support of all hon. Members.

Never before have we concentrated as much on one section of the Army as we have this year on the Gurkhas. Most of the Committee's working time was devoted to them and they caused it to produce the longest and most thorough report in its history. It is an exceedingly comprehensive report and I am grateful not only to my colleagues for the work that they put into it but to the Committee staff, who worked hard on our behalf, assembling all the facts to produce it. I hope that it is as helpful to the House as the Government said that it was to them.

It was slightly disappointing that such a comprehensive report was met with such an uncomprehensive Government reply. I can understand the Government's difficulty about the time scale involved and their not wanting to commit themselves to a state of affairs that may apply in 1997. The Government made two announce-ments. The first, which was most welcome, was of a firm and definite future for the Gurkhas in the Army after 1997, and everyone welcomes that. Secondly, they produced a figure that amounted to more than a 50 per cent. cut. It would have been helpful to know the thinking behind it, rather than to have the vagueness that surrounded the response and the statement by the Secretary of State.

It was helpful that, during his statement, my right hon. Friend the Secretary of State elaborated in reply to a question by me and said that it was a minimum figure, which was negotiable upwards but was unlikely to go down. I am glad that my hon. Friend the Minister of State has confirmed that. Having considered the subject so closely, we will not leave it alone. We are pleased that my right hon. Friend the Secretary of State will come before the Committee on 26 June, when we hope that we can persuade him to flesh out the thinking behind his decision, to say how he envisages the figure being achieved and to give a more detailed response to some parts of the report.

I could talk at length about the report and elaborate on it, but I see at least five members of my Committee waiting to catch your eye, Madam Deputy Speaker. I do not want to abuse the fact that you were kind enough to allow me to catch your eye first, so I will not take the House through the whole report. I should like to refer, in the context of the Gurkhas, to one serious subject to which both Front Bench speakers have alluded—the future manpower problem. The Committee covered that aspect closely.

It is axiomatic that, if we have 8,500 well-trained, loyal, well-motivated troops, our requirements for them—albeit in 10 years' time—must take account of what our needs are likely to be. When running an Army of a size that will meet the commitments of the Ministry of Defence and the Government, without fat in the system—presumably, that has been removed during the past few years—we must look first at current manpower levels and problems and then at the projections.

My hon. Friend the Minister was honest in expressing concern about the present position and how it could develop. If he had wanted to put it in exact words, he could have done little better that to turn to our report, especially the part that deals with the establishment and strength of the Army, in paragraph 129 onwards. The Committee measured the shortfall according to the Ministry's figures, but they are now out of date. The latest recruitment figures which the Ministry produced in a press release on 2 March revealed a slightly worse position than the one on which we reported. We said:

"If this shortfall reflects a worsening trend, there is cause for concern."

Ministry officials who spoke to us acceded to that point.

The Committee went on to look at shortages of infantry. It said:

"The infantry constitutes nearly one-third of the Army's manpower. It is here that the gap between strength and establishment is most acute, and is expected to be about 5 per cent. by 1 April 1989."

The 1·5 per cent. shortage in the forces as a whole has been concentrated into a shortage of 5 per cent. in the infantry. It is from the infantry that the reserve of manpower in Hong Kong will become available when we pull out.

Although we welcome the Ministry's assurances, I hope that it will address more urgently the problem of future recruitment. The MARILYN assessment—manning and recruitment in the lean years of the nineties—is realistic. The recruiting drive that is under way may be successful, but it would be a sanguine person who, given the demographic problems and changes in attitudes to our armed forces, thought that by simply spending money on television recruiting campaigns we will make good the shortfall. I do not believe that anyone in the Ministry of Defence really thinks that. We must get the message across more clearly.

When I look around the Benches I see few Members of Parliament who have had a direct connection with the services, because we are 28 years from the ending of national service. In recruiting 16 to 18 year-olds, we are for the first time recruiting from families where the father has had no military experience—he has not been called upon to do his national service. Until four or five years ago, there was always someone in the family who had served. There was always a photograph on some sideboard of the service man, however much he hated his service while doing it. When those people finished their service, they were proud that they had contributed to our country. That element is missing from every part of family life.

The Ministry of Defence would do well to try a different recruiting approach from the one that assumes that everyone knows what military service is about, what it means and what it has meant in terms of the way that our society has been built up. There is no question but that there has been a sea of change. When one goes round one's constituency talking to people, one finds that it is now the early middle-aged people who have no concept of what service life means. That starts the prospect of a recurrence of the kind of divorce between the military and civilian communities that we had at the end of the 1930s, when there had been a similarly long period during which people had not experienced service life at first hand. I hope that the Government will consider producing a more general, less macho approach to the services. Much of a service man's life is spent on the ordinary facet of service to the community—he has to fight only if the politicians' policies fail, and under the Government that is less and less likely to happen.

I want to make a brief remark about the community charge as it affects the services. Before the Whips shiver, let me say that I am not fighting any old battle—I want to raise a different aspect.

Mr. Frank Cook: A tactical withdrawal.

Mr. Mates: The hon. Gentleman knows me better than that.

There is a real problem which I want to address and on which I hope to be given some elucidation by the Ministry of Defence. The Government have decided that service men were to be treated in the same way as their civilian counterparts. That is not the right answer, because service men are different. I hope that the Ministry fought his corner hard to get them treated differently. The sensible solution would have been to make service men pay an average community charge. That could be easily done.

I am not arguing that service men should not bear the same responsibility as their counterparts, but it is not right, and is sometimes downright unfair, that a service man should be subject to the community charge payable in the area to which the services—mainly the Army—sends him. He can be posted suddenly from a low-rated area to a high-rated area through no choice of his. He can show no democratic reaction. The argument used to support the community charge is that one can vote people out, but the service man can play no part in the way in which local democracy works. He just has to lump it.

The Ministry has an equalising mechanism whereby a service man can be relieved of part of the burden of a particularly severe charge. I hope that, on looking at the anomalies that will be thrown up, and that are starting to be thrown up in Scotland, the Ministry will return to what must be the right solution—a standard community charge for every soldier, sailor and airman, and their dependants, wherever they are.

A particular problem is already arising and I want the Ministry to consider it. More and more married soldiers and officers have bought their own houses, encouraged by us. When they end their service, they do not have to start at the bottom of the property ladder, and that is right and proper. Having encouraged them to do that, we then, for perfectly good military reasons, uproot them from Hampshire and send them to Scotland or Yorkshire. That must be. Because they want to keep the family unit together, they take quarters. They will then, in many cases, be liable to pay a double community charge by being charged at their home and then being told that because they are living in quarters in Catterick, that is their major residence. They will have to pay two charges because they will be liable for the charge in their own homes——

Mr. Frank Cook: The hon. Gentleman would be as well.

Mr. Mates: That is true, but I can go where I choose. The services are different from everyone else. Other disciplined forces, such as the police forces, the ambulance forces, nurses and doctors, can say that they will not go to Yorkshire, for example, if they think that the community charge there is too high. Service men cannot say that, so they are a different and unique case and must be treated as such. It must be unfair for a soldier to buy a house wherever he thinks he will spend his post-service life and then be penalised doubly under the community charge because of a posting. If the service demands him to move, it should compensate him for it.

I hope that that problem will be considered and that we shall receive a comprehensive answer, although I realise

[Mr. Mates]

that we shall not do so today. It is a problem that will bring the community charge into disrepute vis-a-vis the services if we are not careful.

I want to speak briefly about the Falkland Islands and our defence commitments there. I am not going to argue about why or how we are there; what is important is that we are there defending the Falklands. As a result of the considerable expense that the Government have put into the Falklands and the considerable drain on the defence budget at present as a result of the forces and assets there, the Falkland Islands have become rich, especially through the fishing licences that they are able to grant. They have become rich to the extent that income from fishing licences has risen from £650,000 in 1986 to £16 million in 1988. Would it not be right to ask the Falkland Islands Government to make some contribution to our defence costs out of that great wealth?

There is a precedent for that in Hong Kong. We have a defence agreement with the Hong Kong Government because our forces are committed there very much in the interest of Hong Kong's success as a free enterprise society. The same can be said about the Falkland Islands. They are able to receive that great income only because of the great time, effort and expense put, rightly, into defending them. Given how hard-pressed our defence budget is at present and how hard-pressed it will continue to be, it would not be unfair to ask the Falkland Islands Government to make a contribution to our defence costs. I hope that the Government will do that.

5.52 pm

Mr. A. E. P. Duffy (Sheffield, Attercliffe): I hope that the House will bear with me if I speak both in the light of the Statement on Defence Estimates for 1989 and in the context of recent momentous events. The defence White Paper addresses the role and equipment of the armed forces including the Army, in chapter three. It deals in its opening chapters with the recent and significant developments that must be in all our minds, such as the challenge of arms control. However, I hope that none of us will overlook NATO's 40th anniversary. In the treatment of arms control in chapter two, I can detect the welcome hand of Sir Michael Quinlan, permanent Under-Secretary at the Ministry of Defence. No one more experienced, more authoritative or more eloquent could have been called upon to perform this exacting and sensitive task.

It is hard for many of us to remember what Europe was like in 1949—exhausted and discouraged, with its economies in ruins. That was 40 years ago. Everyone born in north America and western Europe since then has been brought up under the strength of NATO's sheltering wings. Our vitality has revived and our common defence has been assured. That is no coincidence.

From the beginning, NATO was more than a security system. It provided the means of expression of a common purpose and a common vision. It established a community of values which bound together a growing number of nations in north America and western Europe. I am proud to say that I attended its anniversary ceremony in Brussels in April. Let us wish NATO in its 40th year many peaceful and happy returns of the day. In the immortal words of the great Sophie Tucker, might we not also say of NATO,

"Life begins at forty"? All of us wonder about the next role for NATO. I believe that it will have, not simply another lease of life, but a more meaningful one.

We are debating the Army at a time of growing optimism throughout the world, with the intermediate nuclear forces treaty and the opening of the Vienna negotiations. I am proud to say that I visited Vienna last month. I visited at least half of the arms control national delegations and I can testify to the new climate there. Unlike the mood at the time of the mutual balanced force reductions there is a sense of optimism, purpose and a determination not to get bogged down. We are going places in Vienna. I am confident that we shall get results and some people are now talking about results as early as a year hence—that is, the preliminary results, not the implementation. Is this not exciting, because clearly we are on the verge of a new chapter in the difficult history of East-West relations?

I found the Soviet arms control delegation just as anxious to get results as the United States delegation and our own. I went from one to the other and back again. However, it would be wrong to think that all has changed for the good in eastern Europe as a result of Mr. Gorbachev's policies. Many human rights problems remain, so as we go forward Alliance cohesion will prove critical if we are to shape a more promising world. We cannot possibly imagine that recent developments have changed everything. The Soviet Union will remain a heavily over-armed society. Without a secure Alliance defence, it could be increasingly tempted to believe that it has the risk-free option of using force or threatening to use force against us.

Intentions are not the same as capabilities and intentions can change overnight, at little cost. They have done so frequently in modern Soviet history. Furthermore, not all capability categories were covered by Mr. Gorbachev in his United Nations speech last December. He covered battlefield firepower, but not manoeuvrability —that is availability, readiness and deployment—air defence, air attack, combined forces, mobilisation and reinforcement.

Let us consider military industrial capacity, whatever the consumer constraints in the Soviet Union. Can the Minister confirm reports that Soviet tank production levels are actually rising? I am thinking of the FST1 and the T80. Yet at the same time Mr. Gorbachev calls for a reduction in tank deployment. Whatever may be true of justice, it is not true of peace that

"It droppeth as the gentle rain from heaven".

We must work for it, with a stout heart and a cool nerve. Within the Alliance, we must work for peace together. Unity and determination must be our watchwords.

Last week the NATO summit demonstrated that there is much on which the Alliance agrees. It agrees that the Alliance continues to provide a framework of stability and that within that framework the 16 free European and north American nations should work together to pursue the Harmel guidelines. It also agrees that true security in Europe continues to require the presence of United States forces, both nuclear and conventional. However, beyond that we run into real difficulties—not new, but real, difficulties.

What level of forces do we require for deterrence? What type of nuclear forces do we need and where should they be deployed so that the risks, as well as the proven benefits, are fairly distributed? To what levels can we safely reduce, and what would such adjustments imply for forward defence and flexible response? That is one kind of difficulty, which does not concern Opposition Members or the House exclusively; it is broadly based throughout the Alliance.

Another difficulty has to do with how we can make sense of the changes taking place in the Soviet Union and eastern Europe. The North Atlantic Assembly believes—I know that my colleagues on both sides of the House will know that what I am saying is well founded—that parliamentarians, unconstrained by necessary adherence to formal Government positions, can bring a fresh perspective to NATO's deliberations, blending an understanding of, and concern for, military aspects of NATO's plans with a knowledge of the underlying reality of public opinion.

That is where we come in. No one is better placed to speak about public opinion than we are, and it is on the change. All parties represented in the North Atlantic Assembly are determined to question and confront even the most sacrosanct and sensitive elements of current NATO policy.

On the other hand, we also believe that the Western Alliance must test to the full the promises of current Soviet rhetoric. If the Soviets continue to invest heavily in military capability, that must say something about their long-term intentions towards us. As long as the Soviet Union's security and foreign policies are not subject to democratic control, NATO must keep up its guard. No defence means no détente, which, in turn, means no lasting change for the better.

The estimates show that spending is set to rise marginally. The increase is less than the rate of inflation and hence amounts to a real cut. Most concern today, therefore, will focus on the details of how the money is to be spent and how it will affect the Army. Real spending on equipment will be cut by perhaps 10 per cent., and this is the year when the uncuttable spending on Trident is near its all-time high, so conventional equipment will suffer badly.

No service will avoid going without some things that are needed. Some procurement programmes will be extended, which costs money in the long term. The White Paper does not tell Members of Parliament—never mind the voters—what they need to know. How will the equipment cuts be managed and how much will individual items of equipment cost? The White Paper does not say much about what is being done to deal with the manpower crisis to which the Minister admitted in his opening speech. That is crucial in present conditions. Are some combat units operating under strength for example?

The White Paper confirms that the Army will get its seventh regiment of Challenger tanks. But the Army also has a vital need for modern artillery and anti-tank weaponry. It is good news that the Army is to start to deploy MLRS—the multi-launch rocket system—next year, but when will the collaborative family of third generation anti-tank missile systems—TRIGAT—come into service? The Minister also confirmed that the improved Westland Lynx Mark 7 anti-tank helicopter is now being deployed in support of 1(BR) Corps in West Germany. But when will it receive infra-red TOW roof sight modules, secure radios and Ferranti AWARE radar warning receivers?

Evidence of overstretch can also be found elsewhere in the Alliance. Increases in defence spending by all our allies are unlikely because of budgetary pressures. The need will grow for more cost-effective equipment procurement, more support for the European procurement group, IEPG, more efficient deployment of resources to improve the teeth-to-tail ratio, better use of reserves and more practical co-operation between allies—that is, an examination of appropriate roles, risks and responsibilities in the Alliance, not only in the NATO area but in other vital theatres such as the Gulf. Henceforth, all of us in the Alliance will have to think smarter, not richer.

There are other lessons of the past to be remembered and stringent conditions for our success that cannot conveniently be wished away. I refer again to strong defence. A strong defence is as necessary—perhaps more so—in times of movement such as we have witnessed, sadly, on the other side of the world in recent days as in times when the status quo prevails.

United, the Western Alliance will determine events. Having rebuilt western Europe and assured the strength and cohesion of the West, NATO can fulfil its second great historic task—to facilitate peaceful change in the East. I envisage a second and more meaningful lease of life for NATO. It is the best institutional device that could be created to fulfil a number of necessary functions: first, to co-ordinate joint verification; secondly, to monitor East and West compliance; and, thirdly, to provide sanctions for violations. If NATO did not exist, we would need to invent it. There is nothing available to us that can work so effectively for East-West reconciliation and ultimately the ending of the painful and grotesque division of Europe.

6.8 pm

Dame Janet Fookes (Plymouth, Drake): I wish to deal with only one theme tonight because I am aware of your injunction, Mr. Speaker, at the outset of the debate, that we should bear in mind the fact that others wish to speak. You, Sir, addressed your remarks to hon. Gentlemen; I like to feel that that was because you felt that a lady would not need such an injunction.

Both the Minister and the Opposition Front Bench spokesman touched on my theme, which relates to the future manpower requirements of the Army, bearing in mind the alarming trend in the number of young people which will become evident by the mid-1990s. The Minister said that by 1994 there would be 20 per cent. fewer 15 to 19-year-olds coming forward. Already concern is being expressed about recruitment in the Army and the problem is likely to get worse unless urgent steps are taken. After all, it is not only the Army that is looking for bright young people—it is the Royal Navy, the Royal Air Force, the police and, of course, industry and the professions. I suspect that there will be something of a rat race and that we shall need more than attractive television advertisements to recruit.

I noted with pleasure the Minister's reference to making greater use of women in the armed services, particularly in the Army. I was not altogether surprised to hear him say that it was still not the intention to change the long-standing convention and rule that women should not be used in direct combat. I hope that my hon. Friend may consider the matter and perhaps come to modify his views in later years. It seems to me that in every sphere women are now treated on equal terms with men and it is a pity that they should not be given more encouragement in the Army. It will be an interesting race between the Army and

[Dame Janet Fookes]

the Church of England. We shall have to wait and see which can hold out longest against admitting women to its innermost portals. More seriously, I think that we shall need to look closely at the role of women and make a greater role for them in the coming years.

If recruitment techniques are important, so also is retention. That brings me to the main burden of my remarks—the question of retaining those who have already been persuaded to enter the Army. The statistics are not favourable. My understanding is that over the past five years the early loss of trained personnel has increased by some 70 per cent. When one thinks of the wastage that that represents in public funds and of the wastage to the Army in losing those who have most to offer, it is most worrying.

What are the reasons? In my view, one of the outstanding reasons as it affects the Army is the concern and discontent felt about housing arrangements. It affects all the armed services, but the Army bears a disproportionate amount of the burden—far more than the Royal Navy and more than the RAF. It springs from the nature of Army service. At any one time, more than half our Army personnel are away from mainland Britain, and even when they are in Britain they may be widely dispersed, far away from their natural homes.

Reference has already been made to the encouragement by the Ministry of Defence for people in the services to own their own homes. That is put forward as an admirable aim, as no doubt in many ways it is, but I do not believe that sufficient thought has been given to the peculiar difficulties which arise for Army personnel. Because they are so often away from home, they are obliged to be in quarters for which they have to pay. If they cannot live in their own homes, they have to let them—assuming that they can find suitable tenants who will pay up and look after the property.

I know from my membership of the council of the Soldiers' Sailors' and Airmen's Families Association that innumerable horror stories are circulating about difficult tenants. What is more, the tenancies have to be managed, and often the agents take 15 to 20 per cent. of the rent. So the unfortunate soldier is squeezed between paying for his quarters on the one hand and all the difficulties of letting a property on the other.

The alternative—not buying at all—means that on leaving the service, whether prematurely or at the end of a full term of service, the soldier has the major problem of seeking to buy a home. When one thinks of the increase in property prices over the years, one realises that there is no way in which a service man can get easily into the market. It is not surprising, therefore, that under persuasion from wives and families generally a great many promising young men are leaving the service early.

I have here a letter from the controller of SSAFA, Major-General Charles Grey, who wrote to me as an MP and as a member of the governing council of SSAFA because SSAFA sees at first hand the difficulties which arise. I quote briefly from his letter:

"As you may know, SSAFA has about 6,000 volunteers in its UK network. They cover every town and village in the country and provide trained caseworker support for Service and ex-Service families in need, or difficulty of any description. These local workers have been representing increasingly strongly about the number of homeless ex-Service families in their areas, particularly from the Army."

He also refers to the network of services, professional and voluntary, retained by SSAFA overseas and adds:

"We are now regularly faced with evidence of a widespread sense of apprehension and insecurity—particularly among Army families. This is directly attributable to their perceived housing difficulties."

Later he says:

"Service manning is not our problem; but no one in close touch with every variety of Service family, as we are, can doubt that vast sums spent on training are being wasted for want of the comparatively small investment necessary to allow families a sense of future housing security."

That is the problem. What of the solution? I have worked closely with my hon. Friend the Member for Canterbury (Mr. Brazier)—I hope, Mr. Speaker, that he will catch your eye later in the debate—who has been instrumental in bringing forward an excellent scheme. He has even proposed a new clause for the Finance Bill as the proposed scheme has tax implications. Briefly, it is an armed forces house purchase savings scheme. It seeks to allow various savings institutions, such as building societies, banks and insurance companies, to take part in a savings scheme through which a service man could save money with the same tax incentives as people in civilian life, so that at the end of the day he will have sufficient money to enable him to buy a house. The rental portion of his accommodation charges would be treated as an interest payment and the relief that he would get on that would be paid to the institution, presumably on a monthly basis. He could also add voluntary savings which would attract the same tax relief as is given to a civilian buying a house.

That proposal seems eminently sensible, and far better than trying to devise elaborate schemes to support service men buying their own houses too early when it does not make sense for them to do so. I hope that I am pushing at an open door in relation to my right hon. and hon. Friends in the Ministry of Defence, but I am concerned about my right hon. and hon. Friends at the Treasury, who are not noted for their immediate espousal of imaginative schemes which in some way affect taxation—they have to be made to see that there is a real problem in retaining manpower in the services and that while they may be saving a small amount in immediate taxation, the millions that are being wasted on people who leave the services too early have to be set against that. So far as I can see, the Treasury is not fond of sums of that kind because they do not fit into its rigid thinking. I urge my right hon. and hon. Friends in the Ministry of Defence to make the strongest possible representations to Treasury Ministers to ensure that they understand the wider implications and not just the narrow concepts so beloved of that Department of State.

I hope that my hon. Friend the Parliamentary Under-Secretary of State for the Armed Forces will deal with that subject in his reply to the debate and that he will give us a word of encouragement. If there is one thing that could be done to retain much-needed Army personnel at a time of increasingly shrinking numbers of young people, that proposal would do a great deal to solve the problem. I commend it to the House and to the Government.

6.18 pm

Mr. Menzies Campbell (Fife, North-East): I am sure that I speak for many hon. Members when I say that we find ourselves totally in accord with the thoughtful and perceptive observations of the hon. Member for Plymouth, Drake (Dame J. Fookes).

In support of what was said by the hon. Member for Hampshire, East (Mr. Mates), may I draw to the attention of Ministers the difficulties that the community charge is creating for serving men and women in the three armed services? I have a constituent who is a private in a Scottish regiment. He has chosen to buy his own house in my constituency, but he has recently been posted to a Scottish barracks. He pays a personal community charge in the district to which he has been posted but, because he has his own house which is unoccupied, he has to pay a standard community charge, that having been expressed in Scotland as a multiplier of two. That means that from the income of a private he pays three community charges.

That appears to be an extraordinary burden to put on someone who has to go where he is sent and who has taken the entirely responsible and, as I am sure the House would agree, reasonable step of buying his own home. I hope that that is a matter that the Treasury and the Ministry of Defence will look at with far greater sympathy and understanding than has necessarily been displayed in such matters up to now.

I shall say a word or two about the events of the past week, which have bulked to a certain extent in the speeches we have already heard. I am well aware that loyalty is at a premium on the Government Benches, but I am sure that even the Prime Minister's most exuberant supporters would find it difficult to consider that her conduct of events in the immediate period up to the 40th anniversary celebrations of NATO should be regarded as a model for others to follow or, indeed, for her to follow on some future occasion.

The strength of any alliance depends on the unity of its members and on the unity of its purpose. In the case of an alliance of democratic countries, having as its central purpose the preservation of democratic values, it appears all the more necessary that there should be tolerance and understanding amongst its members. Negotiating with one's allies as if they were one's enemies is hardly likely to cement an alliance. It may be emotionally satisfying, and even politically self-justifying, but it is much more likely to lead to decisions which represent the least common denominator rather than the highest common factor.

Nor in an alliance as diverse as NATO is such an alliance to be easily preserved if there is no sensitivity amongst its members about the domestic political circumstances of each other. Just as the British Army makes a substantial contribution of the highest quality to the military effort of NATO, so too should the British Government be willing to make a similar contribution to the joint political effort of the Alliance. I doubt very much that Chancellor Kohl, never mind Mr. Genscher, felt that our Prime Minister's attitude in the period immediately prior to Brussels was one that took account of the interests of Federal Germany or, indeed, the interests of NATO. We maintain such units of the British Army as we do in Federal Germany for the purposes of the Alliance. Anything that diminishes the strength of the Alliance, potentially or actually, diminishes the effectiveness of our military contribution.

Nor are we able now to ignore the geography of Europe and its history. Germany sits at its centre able to look east or west for expansion. In the past, such expansion took a physical form and a military one, but the strength of Federal Germany, at least today, lies in its economic capacity. It is little wonder then that President Bush pays attention to Chancellor Kohl's concerns. With the United States of America's balance of payments and budget deficits, he has little alternative. Defending a weakening dollar against a strengthening deutschmark requires a sensitivity to the political circumstances of federal Germany.

In the vacuum caused by the abnormally long running-in period of the Bush Administration, the United Kingdom had a remarkable opportunity to be a bridge between Europe and the United States. We did not take that chance; rather we used the time to take up positions from which ultimately we had to depart, even on the most optimistic Government interpretation of the comprehensive concept.

I believe that the whole House would join in applauding the initiative taken by Mr. Bush. It is an initiative that can justifiably be described as bold and imaginative, because, quite apart from its own intrinsic merit, it had the effect of putting to the test the statements and the offers previously made by Mr. Gorbachev. The initiative underlined that the key to arms reductions at any level in Europe is parity in conventional forces. That is self-evident from the terms of paragraph 48 of the comprehensive concept. However, there is an old rule of interpretation of documents, which is that one should always read them as a whole and not paragraph by paragraph or sentence by sentence. When one looks at the relationship between paragraph 48 and paragraph 49—the paragraph that provides that no decision about the follow-on to Lance will be taken until 1992—it is not difficult to comprehend that, if what is proposed in paragraph 48 has come to pass, or is even reasonably within grasp, there must be great doubt that there will be a political will in the United States to proceed with a follow-on to Lance. Paragraph 48, therefore, is not the end of the story. Indeed, it contains within it, when read with paragraph 49, the mechanism for its own obsolescence.

If the Bush initiative leads to a reduction in the number of United States troops stationed in western Europe, that inevitably will mean that in Europe we may have to assume, relatively, a larger responsibility for our own defence in the provision of conventional forces. That must have implications for all the armed services, but particularly the Army, and especially in the light of the demographic trends which have already been mentioned. Those trends work against the Army as much as they work against any other form of employment.

When the debate began, I like others, was minded to say that I was awaiting with interest the publication of the Government study on manpower, the MARILYN exercise, but we learned, almost as soon as the debate began, that an abridged version had been placed in the Library. I understand from members of the Select Committee that the abridged version has been available to some of them for several weeks. I believe, putting the matter no higher than this, that it is unfortunate that those of us who have an interest in these matters were not given an opportunity to make some study of that document in

[*Mr. Menzies Campbell*]

advance of the debate. Apart from anything else, it would have helped us to make comments or observations which, if not any wiser, should at least have been better informed.

Mr. Archie Hamilton: I should put the hon. and learned Gentleman right on that matter. The Select Committee was given an abridged version of the MARILYN report, but that was a classified version. It is the unclassified version that is now in the Library.

Mr. Campbell: I accept the Minister's explanation, although I note that it did not come with an apology. I still think that it is unfortunate that those of us who have an interest in these matters were not able to be better informed before the debate began.

Those manpower difficulties make it all the more difficult to understand the Government's failure to accept in their entirety the conclusions of the Defence Committee on the future of the Gurkhas. The Minister said something about the Gurkhas when he opened the debate. However, although what he said may have been slightly different in tone, it was no different in substance from what was said when the announcement was made some weeks ago. It is notable to remind ourselves that the Defence Committee argued for the same number of men and for no reduction in the number of Gurkha battalions. The Government's proposal is to reduce the number of troops by half and to reduce the number of battalions from five to four.

Apart from any moral obligation, which quite a number of hon. Members feel we have towards the Gurkhas, the manpower demands of the Army—as the Chairman of the Defence Committee trenchantly pointed out—should surely dictate acceptance of the Defence Committee's entire recommendations. I add the rider, which to some extent has already been anticipated by the hon. Member for Clackmannan (Mr. O'Neill), that recent events in Hong Kong, where the Gurkhas are stationed for certain specific tasks, should be the subject of careful analysis to establish clearly whether the decision—which, if not taken, has at least been proposed—is one to which the Government should adhere in the light of circumstances which may clearly be subject to radical change.

There appears to be some evidence that recruitment may be easier in areas of the United Kingdom where there is a traditional geographical link with particular regiments. I am sorry that the Secretary of State is not here today because I wanted to remind him of his notable participation in the campaign to save the Argyll and Sutherland Highlanders, a regiment based at Stirling castle, of which he was a distinguished officer who saw active service. The regiment had a particular link with Stirling and the surrounding countryside. I hope that the Government will take account, in what I hope will be a sophisticated approach to the recruitment problem, of the fact that such local loyalty frequently can be a much more effective recruiting sergeant than simply giving opportunities to those interested in the Army to be assigned to a regiment with which they have neither family nor geographical ties.

I wish briefly to deal with two matters to which some reference has already been made. The first is the position of ethnic minorities within the armed forces. It would be folly to pretend that that issue could be easily resolved, but it must be the case that admission to a particular regiment, however distinguished, and promotion within the Army should depend on ability and nothing else. Not only must that be the policy of the Ministry of Defence; it must be the reality. The House looks to the Minister to give us some reassurance on that matter.

With regard to the Territorial Army, if the demographic trends persist, that branch of the services will have to assume greater burdens. I hope that the Government will act to make membership of the TA as attractice as possible, not least to those who opt for early retirement from the armed services. I do not believe that the issue is necessarily simply one of money; it probably lies in a proper recognition of the role of the TA and the provision of up-to-date equipment and proper opportunities for training.

I do not expect the Minister to tell us this evening of the progress of the demonstration phase of the Challenger 2 project, but he knows that a number of hon. Members believe that the effect of the decision of 20 December 1988 was to put Vickers on probation. We await the results of the demonstration phase with great interest. It might be of some help if the Minister could say when he expects to be in a position to give the House some information; or are we to wait until the whole of the demonstration phase has been completed?

Like other hon. Members, I have been extensively lobbied by the companies bidding for the contract to supply 5,000 four-tonne trucks to the Army over the next few years. They have been generous with their briefings and modest with their hospitality. It is as well that they have not sought to transpose those adjectives. All the companies make persuasive cases. Those of us who do not have access to the results of the assessment tests, or who have no particular expertise, are undoubtedly at a great disadvantage.

I accept that a whole range of factors must be taken into account—the buy-back scheme, for example, that has been proposed by one of those competing for the contract; the proposal of another to make a large investment at Irvine, which lies close to the boundary of the Secretary of State's constituency—who would no doubt deal with that matter with his usual objectivity; others who make high claims for the United Kingdom content of the vehicles to be produced; others who emphasise the costs and others the ability of their company to fulfil the contract if awarded, thereby seeking to draw unfair comparisons with other companies. I suggest that the criteria to be adopted should be that the product chosen must be the best for the job. Financial considerations are important, but the Government should not be seduced by them into accepting a tender for a vehicle which, on capability grounds alone, they would not accept.

The men and women of the British Army are heirs to a long and valuable tradition. Their professionalism is recognised wherever they go. They can be called upon at any time to fight in dangerous conditions and they keep the peace in difficult and dangerous circumstances in Northern Ireland. They are often called upon when public services either decline or are unable to discharge their responsibilities. Those men and women deserve our commendation; they also deserve our practical support.

6.35 pm

Mr. John Wilkinson (Ruislip-Northwood): Exactly three weeks ago, almost to the hour, I was struggling to get on an aeroplane to take me out of Shanghai to Hong Kong in what was clearly a rapidly deteriorating situation. I was told that flights were fully booked until the middle of this month. I did manage to get out of Shanghai, and I am conscious of the extreme stress of those who, in the worsening crisis of the past few days, must have faced a real emergency in trying to get out with their families and whatever belongings they could take.

On 22 May I was with the Gurkhas on the borders of Hong Kong. It was the day my right hon. Friend the Secretary of State made his statement about the future of the brigade. My tour of China had been with the defence committee of the Western European Union, and had begun with a unit of the People's Liberation Army just outside Peking, although soldiers were not yet very much in evidence in the city. The students were much in evidence, as they were in Xi'an and Shanghai.

I do not wish to be too anecdotal, but when I reached Hong Kong I was struck by the optimism of the Brigade of Gurkhas and the strong feeling among its officers that the bottom figure of 4,000 quoted by my right hon. Friend would never be reached and that the Crown would have at least as much need of the brigade, probably in numbers almost up to its present strength, as far ahead as could be foreseen. Of course, the unit most under threat is the 2nd Battalion of the 2nd Gurkhas, but I was told that it had been under similar threat before and had twice escaped disbandment in recent years.

If we study what has happened in China in recent days, and if we coolly and rationally re-examine our policy towards Hong Kong, I am sure that we would all accept that it would be wise to heed the warning of the hon. Member for Clackmannan (Mr. O'Neill) and not pursue the policy announced just as though nothing had happened.

The roles of the Gurkhas in Hong Kong—the 48th Brigade—include the maintenance of British sovereignty to 30 June 1997; support of the civil authorities and the Royal Hong Kong Police in the maintenance and stability of security; training for limited war operations; assistance to the civil community in the event of natural or other disaster; and the prevention of illegal immigration to Hong Kong. In 1987, no fewer than 22,000 illegal immigrants were arrested at the borders of Hong Kong.

The scale and dimension of the problem of the Vietnamese boat people has afflicted Hong Kong to a growing extent in recent weeks. Her Majesty's Government claim that this immigration problem is merely the result of economic pressures. Nearly all refugees in history have come, at least in part, to take the terrible decision to leave their homes as a result of economic pressures. We must also bear in mind the fact that the Government of the People's Republic of Vietnam have not condemned the action of the People's Liberation Army in brutally crushing the students and other freedom-loving people. Therefore, I should have thought that, at least in part, the motivation of the boat people was to escape a politically unacceptable regime.

We hope that sense will prevail and that peace will be re-established in the People's Republic of China. If it is not, there is the threat of a major immigration problem on the frontiers of Hong Kong. Undoubtedly, if that movement of people were to persist into the future the Gurkhas would be very much needed. All the security forces involved in the apprehension of illegal immigrants would be required. The plans of Her Majesty's Government call from 1991 for the disbandment of the Royal Hong Kong Regiment, the Volunteers, who play an important part in the policing of the border. I hope that the timescale within which their disbandment is envisaged will also be re-examined.

I trust also that the Government—in view of the circumstances that have manifested themselves so horrifically in the People's Republic—will review their policy on the issue of British passports with the right of abode in the United Kingdom for ex-members of the Royal Hong Kong Regiment who, as former servants of the Crown, must prima facie view with considerable apprehension their future in Hong Kong under the sovereignty of the People's Republic after July 1997.

Another aspect of the plans of Her Majesty's Government is the withdrawal of the first of the Gurkha battalion of 48 Brigade from Hong Kong in 1992. You, Mr. Speaker, will have recollections of partition in India in 1947. You may still have been serving in the Indian Army in those dark days of mid-August 1947. The lesson of the past few days must be that it would be extremely unwise of the British authorities in Hong Kong to diminish the forces of the Crown available to support the civil power and police the frontier before the handover of power. Nature abhors a vacuum, and at a time of political uncertainty the vacuum created by the diminution of physical power could have alarming consequences.

On Sunday 21 May, my wife and I marched in Hong Kong with a huge and, at that time, apprehensive but not yet angry crowd of 500,000 people demonstrating peacefully in favour of the demands of the students and other freedom-loving people in the People's Republic. I felt then that the demonstrations in China could only end in tears. My other strong feeling at the conclusion of that march—it was the biggest demonstration ever in the colony's history—was that the peaceful manifestation of deep feeling on behalf of Chinese people in Hong Kong in favour of the aspirations of fellow Chinamen in the People's Republic could quickly turn to deep bitterness and to nasty anti-British kinds of riot.

Since then, sad to say, there have been some riots in Hong Kong but—thank goodness—they have not got out of control. Any diminution in the British military presence in Hong Kong too soon, however, could be extremely dangerous because in the last resort that presence is needed as an aid to the civil power.

Something else leads me to question the Government's decision, so far in advance of the handover of power in Hong Kong in 1997, to make at least outline decisions about the future of the Brigade of Gurkhas. The point was well outlined by the Chairman of our Select Committee, my hon. Friend the Member for Hampshire, East (Mr. Mates). The so-called demographic trough is now extremely alarming. We have a shortfall of about 5 per cent. in the infantry and the very nadir of the demographic trough will occur when the rundown of the Brigade of Gurkhas is due to start.

Traditionally, 80 per cent. of Army recruits are taken from the 16-to-19 age range. That has been the consistent pattern. Of that age range within the population as a whole, in the last decade the Army has on average recruited 0·8 per cent. By 1993, the number of 16-year-olds in the population will have dropped from the present 400,000 to 332,000, and in 1995 the low point for that age bracket will be reached. If the Army in the mid-1990s is still to obtain 80 per cent. of its recruits from that age bracket and maintain the target of recruiting it has set of 20,000 per year, the proportion of males recruited will have to go up from 0·8 to 1·2 per cent. per annum. Throughout the last decade, except in 1980, the figure has hardly ever exceeded 0·8 per cent. That is why it is rash for the Government even to suggest such a large reduction in the Brigade of Gurkhas.

Events in China have brought home to us the age-old lesson that the unexpected always happens. Not long ago we were looking to China and thinking that a magnificent reformist programme would transform the economy, that we could enjoy arms sales, have military exchanges perhaps and have a healthier relationship to our mutual good. Those hopes have been dashed and, undoubtedly, there are security policy remifications for the region—not least for Hong Kong.

There are also lessons for areas of potential instability nearer home. In an earlier intervention, I cited the ethnic unrest in Armenia, Uzbekistan and Georgia. We do not know how that pattern of ethnic unrest will develop. It could certainly lead to desperate Communist leaderships using force to suppress the national aspirations and, possible the aspirations for liberty and democracy within the countries of eastern Europe and the Soviet empire in Europe. If that were to occur, the instability could overspill and pose a threat to our security. Therefore, we should have at least the flexibility which a sensible manpower policy in our Army would allow.

In the past, we have been able substantially to increase the numbers in the Brigade of Gurkhas. In future, by closing the depot at Dharan in eastern Nepal, it will be made much harder. That is the kind of pettifogging, mean economy which absolutely baffles me. The Ministry of Defence wastes hundreds of millions of pounds of taxpayers' money without seeming to bat an eyelid, appearing to suggest that it is merely £1 billion down the drain on the Nimrod airborne early warning system. The Foxhunter radar, the alarm and anti-radiation missile, EH101, the command and control system for the type 23 have all overrun on cost. The number of examples is stupendous and horrifying. However, for an institution such as the depot of the Brigade of Gurkhas in Nepal, which costs £4 million per year to run and where the British military hospital carries out invaluable work for the local community at costs of only £2·5 million a year to run, the Government cannot find the money.

The Government have a disregard for the effect on the local community and the loyalty of the people of Nepal, particularly eastern Nepal, who have given sterling service to the Crown, which I find staggering. It could just be that the optimism of those officers in Hong Kong on Monday 22 May will prove justified. Events may turn out so that we need more Gurkhas than we think, and we may even conceivably need more than the 8,000 which are in the Brigade of Gurkhas now. If that is so, it will be difficult to achieve the necessary expansion without the depot at Dahran.

In case there are any fallacious ideas floating around that Gurkhas cannot cope with the sophisticated equipment on the central front in Europe, if the average squaddie in Glasgow, Liverpool, Newcastle or London manages to cope with basic infantry skills and jump out of the back of an armoured personnel carrier I do not think that Gurkhas will find it any more difficult. As my right hon. Friend said,

"The Gurkhas are not only extremely good soldiers who fought extremely well in many different conditions and theatres, but are clearly very adaptable. I have no doubt that they can cope with any task that they are given."—[*Official Report,* 22 May 1989; Vol. 153, c. 1092.]

I hope that Her Majesty's Government will respond accordingly.

6.54 pm

Mr. Frank Cook (Stockton, North): I could not rise and catch your eye, Mr. Speaker, at a more appropriate moment, because I want to crave the indulgence of the Chamber and start where the hon. Member for Ruislip-Northwood (Mr. Wilkinson) left off. I wish to refer to the record of that statement and the questions of that day. You and hon. Members who were present will recall that I said:

"The Secretary of State will recall that at the time of press speculation and comment when the Select Committee was considering the Gurkha's future, one school of thought of questionable origin was that the Gurkhas may be suitable for one type of warfare but not for another. I refer not to Northern Ireland but to their role in high tech, modern rapid response situations. The suggestion made in the media was that perhaps the Gurkhas do not think quickly enough. Will the right hon. Gentleman put that argument to bed once and for all and counter it, here and now?"—[*Official Report,* 22 May 1989; Vol. 153, c. 691.]

Thank heavens, the Secretary of State did so and graciously thanked me for the opportunity. Furthermore, outside the Chamber in the corridor by the Tea Room, he expressed particular thanks for my having given him the opportunity.

However, the very next day in a newspaper, the despicable opinions to which I referred were attributed to me personally without any reference to the fact that I pleaded with the Secretary of State to counter and dispel them. In addition, the said edition of *The Times* of 23 May edited in similar fashion the response of the Secretary of State. I do not mind an element of spite creeping into reports from time to time, but when it is quite so selective, judicious and partisan, I object to it. I hope that hon. Members will not mind if I correct the record today. Perhaps that newspaper will have the decency to tell its readership tomorrow, if only because it might correct the opinions expressed in some of the mail which I have received, which has been particularly critical of the wrongly attributed opinion.

To remove any doubt, not only myself, but colleagues within the parliamentary Labour party and those whom I have met on my military visits, have the highest regard for the ability, loyalty, allegiance, fighting and peace-serving qualities of the Gurkhas. It is despicable for newspapermen to allow their spite to boil over in such an uncontrollable way.

Much has been made tonight of the Select Committee report on the Gurkhas. The Gurkha units have always proved to be effective in a military sense and efficacious in a cost-saving sense. There is no doubt about that. At this time, when brigade commanders are being encouraged to count their pennies carefully and control their own budgets, I should remind the House that the Gurkha units are competitive in that way.

Before we come to a definite decision on the future of the Gurkhas, leaving aside for the moment the proposals on paper, we should remember that we are talking about, not necessarily a "cheap" form of providing for defence, because that is the wrong word, but a cost-effective form. The Gurkhas can be used in most effective roles, not only in Hong Kong but throughout the spheres of influence in which we play a defensive role.

Mr. Mates: I could not agree more with the hon. Gentleman. The Gurkhas are cost-effective not merely in the way that he described, but because they join the service for a full 15-year term. Therefore, the return on investment and the level of experience grows in each Gurkha battalion. That is in sharp distinction to the recruitment of the British Army, where the average length of service is only five years.

Mr. Cook: The hon. and gallant Member for Hampshire, East (Mr. Mates) terrifies the life out of me. I cannot allow this agreement to go too far. He steals the words from my mouth, but he says them with a great deal more elegance than I could. I thank him for his intervention. He is absolutely right.

I exhort the Minister to be careful before making any decision on the future of those Gurkha units because nothing could be worse than removing such effective combat units from our store.

Reference has also been made to NATO and its changing ideas and outlook. My hon. Friend the Member for Sheffield, Attercliffe (Mr. Duffy), the President of the North Atlantic Assembly, dealt with that in detail. I want to draw hon. Members' attention to some of the views expressed a fortnight ago at the spring session by the spokesperson for NIAG. For those who do not know what that stands for I shall quote its spokesperson. He said:

"The acronym stands for NATO Industrial Advisory Group, and the NIAG is one of the six main groups reporting directly to the Conference of National Armaments Directors . . . It is composed of delegations of industrialists from each of the NATO nations except Luxembourg and Iceland". Therefore, it is truly representative.

The spokesperson for NIAG said:

"all of NIAG's efforts are multi-national and collaborative . . . we would find ourselves being forced into collaborative programmes by the irresistible force of economics . . . no nation . . . can any longer afford to produce, by itself, all of the defence equipment that it needs . . . Just think of the number of programmes . . . which are being kept alive for political reasons only . . . The political life machine is going to have to be turned off, and 'political' programmes allowed to die . . . We must face the fact that, for the foreseeable future, the military budgets of NATO nations, at the very best, will be maintained at the zero growth level and, more realistically they are headed down . . . the trend is very definitely toward fewer programmes . . . not even the US can afford by itself to produce everything it needs . . . The military of the various countries are going to be forced to rationalise their requirements so that, hopefully, those weapons that are produced will be produced in larger quantities and unit costs can be reduced . . . the days have gone when the answer could be found within Europe alone. In the interest not only of affordability but of ensuring that the products that are built are the very best that technology can provide, the industrial collaboration has got to be transatlantic".

The unasked question is not merely where do we get our arms, but how do we get them. The Government tell us that we must have competition in order to obtain weaponry at the cheapest unit cost. Yet now, NIAG's logic tells us that we must reduce competition in order to reduce unit costs.

Questioned on those matters at the Dispatch Box earlier, the Minister said that he would ensure that the British taxpayer received value for money. How far will that value for money go if we are to have collaborative projects which span the Atlantic? If we engage in collaborative programmes with the American arms producers, to what extent will we be required to fund research and development? I am sure that the Minister will refer to this later if he takes up this line of challenge that I am throwing out.

Will that collaboration be of the kind that we were offered with Trident when the agreement was broken? The House will recall that we were promised that Trident would be maintained in this country, but now it will not. We were told that Trident would be our property, but now we find that we have joined a Trident library from which we can make withdrawals for refurbishments when necessary. I offer those thoughts to the Minister and I am sure that he will refer to them later.

Let me deal briefly with other changes that have taken place in NATO to which the President of the North Atlantic Assembly referred. There have been changes in outlook on the representation of the Armed Forces. Britain relies on the pay review board but other countries have other systems. Germany, the Benelux countries, Holland and Denmark, allow forms of trade unions. I use that term because I cannot think of a different word in the English language which will clearly describe what I am referring to. Those unions have come together to form Euro-Mil—the European military. They are staffed by responsible people.

The sergeant-major representing Euro-Mil at Antalya in Turkey this year was a Christain Democrat of fairly Right-wing political persuasion. He spoke persuasively of the need to establish a dialogue between serving men and women and the Ministries of Defence in their respective countries, and, indeed, across the NATO Alliance.

The hon. Member for Wealden (Sir G. Johnson Smith) will confirm that representatives of Euro-Mil will be meeting officers of the military committee before the next plenary session in Rome in October. That shows a fair degree of responsibility and maturity. Those people are responsible, experienced and a source of pride for us. They are worthy allies. Why do not we accord our serving men and women the same kind of respect and the same opportunity to present their anxieties and needs in terms of pay and conditions instead of their having to go through the pay review board procedure or expecting us to speak on their behalf on the five meagre occasions that we get each calendar year?

Mr. Mates: Only one Opposition Member is present on each occasion.

Mr. Cook: That may be a further reason for allowing our serving men and women a more formal and structured way in which to represent their needs. I offer that to the House for serious consideration, not for frivolous comment.

Changes are not only taking place in the North Atlantic Alliance but in the Warsaw pact, as has been referred to tonight. The North Atlantic Assembly has acknowledged

[*Mr. Cook*]

that by meeting representatives of the Hungarian and Polish Governments for discussions and they will be invited to the Rome plenary session.

I can do no better than to finish with my concluding remarks to this year's plenary session. I drew attention to the fact that in 40 years much has changed within the Alliance and the Warsaw pact. If we are serious we must assess those changes clinically. We must declare our assessment honestly and adjust our policies cautiously and collectively. Above all, we must conduct our consideration courageously and with candour. We must make the most clinical threat assessment. Does the threat still exist, if it ever did? If it does, from which direction does it come, what form does it take, can it be countered and at what cost? Only when we have done this can we perhaps discuss sensibly the issues of burden sharing.

Mikhail Gorbachev extends to us the hand of warmer friendship. If we grasp that hand we grasp the hand of the Soviet people. If we reject or inhibit his gestures we fuel those elements in the Soviet Union which seek already to obstruct or reverse the moves towards glasnost and perestroika. We must encourage change carefully and with patience. We must welcome change magnanimously and without vindictiveness. Most of all, where necessary, we must be prepared to make changes ourselves.

Several Hon. Members *rose——*

Mr. Speaker: Order. At the start of this debate I said that I would impose a 10-minute limit on speeches between 7 and 9 o'clock, but I think I would now be justified in relaxing that limit. If hon. Members will not speak for more than 12 minutes each, all those who wish to participate in this debate will be called.

7.10 pm

Sir Jim Spicer (Dorset, West): I am delighted to hear your latest words, Mr. Speaker, but I promise you that I will keep to within my 10 minutes.

First, I pay a very warm tribute to my hon. Friend the Member for Ruislip-Northwood (Mr. Wilkinson), who put very cogently indeed and in words that I am sure we would all endorse the reasons why the Brigade of Gurkhas should remain at the higher figure. In saying that, he stressed—and it needs to be stressed—that he was talking in terms of possible aid to the civil power in Hong Kong and he was not, as the Opposition Front-Bench spokesman, the hon. Member for Clackmannan (Mr. O'Neill), and also the spokesman for the Social and Liberal Democrats, the hon. and learned Member for Fife, North-East (Mr. Campbell), tried to highlight, suggesting that there might be some relationship between events in China and the retention of the Gurkhas at full strength. I know that that was not the intention, but he spelt it out in total detail. We are on dangerous ground if we start talking about the Brigade of Gurkhas being retained at 8,000 against a possible confrontation with the People's Republic of China.

Demography is a word that is very much in vogue and as we move towards the 1990s it will behove every person in this country to pay much more attention to it. Recruitment to the Civil Service and the Health Service,

but, above all, as has been made quite clear by every speaker so far, the armed forces will become very difficult indeed.

In every board room, and I hope in the Ministry of Defence as well, two items must be at the top of the agenda at all times. The first is: how can we attract new recruits and hold them? In that context I pay tribute to my hon. Friend the Member for Plymouth, Drake (Dame J. Fookes) for her speech tonight, because she highlighted one way in which we can stem the haemorrage of soldiers from our armed services. I also pay tribute to my hon. Friend the Member for Canterbury (Mr. Brazier) because it is at his instigation that we have a proposed new clause in the Financee Bill on an armed forces home purchase savings scheme. That could do a tremendous amount, and no one in the Ministry of Defence should walk away from the battle that must take place with the Treasury if we are to get a scheme such as that passed by the whole House. I would add that it has the support already of 119 Members.

That is the first question: how do we find recruits and hold them? The second is: what more can we do to make the most efficient use of our human resources when they are bound to be at a premium?

It will come as no surprise to my hon. Friend the Minister that I propose to move on and talk about the role of the helicopter on the battlefield. No one can doubt the totally defensive nature of our forces in Germany, but it must be right to question whether the present balance of equipment of those forces is the most cost-effective in terms both of the use of available manpower and of defence capability. In my view, the time is long past for making a decision. We have to go down the road of making available to our armed forces, particularly the Army, a much larger number of helicopters.

In that context, I was delighted to hear the intervention this afternoon which made it clear that the time is equally long past for us to see the end of divided control of battlefield helicopters. They should all be in the hands of the Army, not shared with the RAF.

Why do all our Western allies place so much more faith in the role of helicopters within their armed forces than we do? The figures speak for themselves. The French have about 600 battlefield helicopters, the Germans have about 800 and the United States have 8,600. I fully accept that the latter is a false figure because of the size of our armed forces when compared with those of the United States, but even if they are brought down to the same level the United States figure is 1,700 helicopters against a total figure for the United Kingdom of 380. That is quite shameful.

All the other armed forces within the Alliance have accepted the helicopter as a battle-winning factor because it is the one piece of equipment which provides real mobility, particularly on a battlefield which has become increasingly hostile and confused.

Also, anyone who has served in the armed forces must know that the helicopter is a force multiplier. The smaller the force deployed, the greater the importance of the helicopter because it can move the resources and fire power about the battlefield to meet the threat. Having a small but highly efficient and mobile Army, we need a strong helicopter force, and far more than many of the other armies in the NATO Alliance.

Sir Geoffrey Johnson Smith (Wealden): I have been following my hon. Friend's argument most carefully and I warmly support it. Does he agree that it is not only in respect of the central front of the threat that we have traditionally supposed has come from the Soviet Union —and there is still a long way to go yet—but that one of the advantages of the helicopter for a country with forces of the size that we have is that it enables us to have greater mobility and adaptability for any out-of-area responsibilities that we might be called upon to fulfil?

Sir Jim Spicer: I am grateful to my hon. Friend, who has great experience in these matters, and I very much agree with him. I am going on to develop my argument and to say exactly how the other NATO allies deal with this problem and how they have built up forces which can be used on the main front but also in connection with the out-of-area concept.

It is this concept and need which have led the United States, France, Germany and the Warsaw pact countries to equip whole divisions and brigades with helicopters as their prime movers. In general terms, the French have an air mobile division, the Germans have three Luftlande brigades, and the United States has fully equipped combat aviation brigades. In stark contrast to this picture, we have just one air mobile brigade which we all know is in the process of being formed but is woefully short of helicopters and will remain so into the foreseeable future.

I am critical of this because there is not much point in having a air mobile brigade if it does not have the true air mobility to allow it to operate effectively.

In this overall scene, inevitably within the armed services battles and frictions develop and inevitably there is a battle about the tank versus the helicopter. It is a totally unnecessary battle because it should have been fought and done with already.

Some people within the Ministry of Defence and the Army should change their thinking. They should think of the helicopter no longer as a helicopter but as a low-flying tank. If they think of it as a low-flying tank, we shall ultimately reach the stage when the gallant soldiers in our armoured regiments will willingly move on a step and use the helicopter in the way that the tank was used in the past, with all the same logistical back-up but helicopter-borne as well. Although one or two right hon. and hon. Members dissent, the tank soldier is adaptable and could move to such a role.

Mr. Mates: Certainly tanks are as adaptable as the cavalry has always been, but to equate a helicopter with a low-flying tank is perhaps as odd as equating a tank with a grounded helicopter. They are totally different vehicles needing totally different tactical deployment, and they do totally different jobs.

Sir Jim Spicer: My hon. Friend and I are both aware of that. I have usually operated from an aircraft wearing a parachute, but I understand the difference between a tank and a helicopter. It is possible for the helicopter to replace a tank on the ground in an anti-tank role and with increase in mobility on the battlefield.

Do my hon. Friend the Minister and his military advisers accept the general view that we are lagging behind all our NATO allies and the Warsaw pact in the use of helicopters? Will he give an undertaking to re-examine, now or in the near future the role of the helicopter in our defence forces and, following such a review, bring our helicopter strength more closely into line with that of our NATO allies and the Warsaw pact forces?

7.21pm

Mr. John Cartwright (Woolwich): Like other right hon. and hon. Members who have participated in the debate, I shall concentrate my remarks on the problems of demography and on the issue of the Brigade of Gurkhas. Before doing so, I wish to mention an issue that has caused considerable sadness to many of my constituents in Woolwich. I refer to the decision to transfer the headquarters of the directorate-general of defence quality assurance to Teesside.

My first point is that it has taken an incredible amount of time to reach that decision. In the early 1980s, a great deal of money and effort was invested in planning the reorganisation of the Woolwich arsenal site, including more than £300,000 on the design of a new headquarters building for the directorate-general. Early in 1984, rationalisation was proposed and detailed studies undertaken.

On 19 November 1986, the hon. Member for Epsom and Ewell (Mr. Hamilton) was kind enough to write to tell me that the Secretary of State did not want to make a decision until sites outside south-east England had been considered, and that yet another detailed study was to be undertaken. The hon. Member for Epsom and Ewell commented, perhaps optimistically, that that study would defer a decision about the arsenal for another six months, but the decision was not announced until March 1989— almost two and a half years later.

The only argument made for transferring the directorate-general to Teesside was that that offered the best prospect of overcoming shortages of specialist staff, but at the end of February 1989 staffing levels did not show any dramatic shortage. There were 1,135 in post against a ceiling of 1,250. While it is true that there was a shortage of 52 staff in professional and technical grades, that situation is no worse than in many other Ministry of Defence establishments.

The Government have not produced any evidence to show that professional and technical staff will be easier to find in Teesside than in south-east London. They only point to higher levels of unemployment in Teesside, in the hope that vacancies will be filled.

The financial savings from the transfer will be minimal. On the basis of MOD assessments, the Teesside option will bring an overall saving of £10 million over 25 years by comparison with the concentration on the Woolwich arsenal west site. However, that calculation ignores the substantial sums spent at Woolwich arsenal over the past 10 years—£22 million on maintenance, repairs and improvements, and all of which will now go down the drain. Several million pounds were spent since 1985-86 on housing directorate-general units moved to Woolwich from other locations. That is another example of the way in which the Ministry wastes money, when forward thinking would have prevented it being spent in such a profligate way.

I cannot help but think that the Ministry of Defence's major concern is the value of the 94 acres of riverside land in Woolwich that will be released by the move. I am sure that that factor in the equation weighs more heavily than any other. The move will deal a considerable blow to an area that has now lost virtually all its industrial jobs and has a long history of service to the country's armed forces. The arsenal, which will close permanently in 1993, dates back to 1671, and was predated by Henry VIII's dockyard,

[*Mr. John Cartwright*]

which was established in Woolwich in 1515. When the arsenal is moved in 1993, that link will be broken—but I hope that thought will be given to ensuring that the historic buildings remaining will feature in a lasting tribute to the contribution that the people of Woolwich made to the armed services over hundreds of years.

I turn to the demographic trough, and I am surprised that the Government have been caught unawares by it. It cannot be regarded as a sudden or unexpected problem. The downward trend in the birth rate has been in evidence since the early 1970s. The low point of the trough has been known since 1978. It was known that it would create problems for the armed forces, and that matter was referred to in the Defence Estimates statement in 1980 and in 1981. However, that was followed by total silence, until this year.

I can at least claim that I referred to that issue in a number of previous Army debates, in 1983, 1984, and 1987. But on none of those occasions did the Minister replying consider that the demographic trough was a serious enough matter even to be mentioned in his winding-up speech. I did rather better in 1988 when in a debate on the Army I again referred to the demographic trough and scored a bullseye. On that occasion, the Under-Secretary of State for the Armed Forces acknowledged the problem and that I was right to draw attention to it, but added that

"we are convinced that our policy of fair pay, and of fair conditions and allowances . . . should ensure that we keep ahead of the game and cope with the demographic trend and the small number of youngsters available to join the armed forces."—[*Official Report*, 26 January 1988; Vol. 126, c. 254.]

Given that shattering degree of complacency even as recently as January 1988, it is hardly surprising that measures to improve both recruitment and retention were not set in train much earlier. It is still strange that we have not seen the results of the MARILYN study until now, 10 years after the problem first became evident and nine years after the first reference to it in a defence White Paper. I appreciate the complexity of the problems and understand that they need studying carefully, but no one can accuse the Ministry of Defence of intemperate haste.

Other right hon. and hon. Members have mentioned the problems arising from the demographic trough and I shall not cover the same ground, but I emphasise that the 16 to 19-year-old group is declining, and that the reducing numbers available to the Army will reduce further if the Government are successful in encouraging more 16 to 19-year-olds to enter further and higher education.

For the forces, the problem is here now. The MOD set out to recruit 22,000 service men in 1988-89 and anticipated a shortfall of 2,000. The outcome was a good deal worse. The strength of the Army was expected to decline to 1·5 per cent., or by 2,000 people below establishment by 1 April 1989, but the number appears to be nearer 3,000. The Chairman of the Defence Committee reminded the House that the situation is much worse in the infantry, where the shortfall is around 5 per cent. and worsening.

The Government's proposal to improve retention is entirely sensible: clearly pay and allowances must keep pace with those in outside employment. I would argue, however, that it is equally important to ensure that the quality of life for service personnel keeps pace with that of

civilians, and that will be an expensive operation at a time when manpower, as opposed to the cost of equipment, is taking a growing share of the defence budget.

The recruitment of ethnic minorities is also absolutely right in principle, and I am glad that there is now a degree of monitoring, but it is not likely to produce dramatic results. To establish the same proportion of ethnic minorities in the armed forces as exists in the population as a whole would mean only 800 or so more recruits. Similarly, it is right that we should give women more interesting, exciting and perhaps demanding opportunities, but we should not ignore the fact that the fall in the number of young women in the population mirrors the fall in the number of young men, and the Army will face severe competition from civilian employers in attempting to attract the required quality of recruit.

Like other speakers, I hope that the MARILYN exercise and the Government steps resulting from it will bear fruit. Against the background of increasing competition for scarce manpower, however, I believe that the Army must run very fast to stand still. That is why I find it so hard to understand the Government's decision on the future of the Gurkhas.

I felt that the Government's response to the Select Committee report was extraordinarily sketchy. It contains some vague references to squadrons of engineers, signals and transport, without explaining what "squadrons" means in terms of numbers. That seems to imply a substantial cut in the number of Gurkhas employed in those specialist fields. The Committee went to some trouble to point out the folly of losing high-quality, experienced and motivated engineers and technicians whose skills are in such short supply.

The Government recognised that recruitment would inevitably become more difficult as a result of demographic changes, but did not say whether they accepted the Committee's interpretation of the forecast figures. If they accept that interpretation, it is hard to see how they can justify proposing a cut of more than 50 per cent. in the Brigade of Gurkhas. If they do not accept it, it would be interesting to know on what basis the cut was suggested.

Paragraph 17 of the Government's response leaves open a loophole in saying:
"demographic difficulties could lead to increased numbers of Gurkhas being retained."
Surely, however, we are entitled to ask when the decision is likely to be made. The Minister accepted today that recruitment targets were not being met and that the position was worsening. How much will it worsen before a decision is made? Is the number to be 4,000, 4,500, 5,000 or what?

The response talks of progressive restructuring of the brigade over several years. Again, we are surely entitled to ask what that means. Does it mean natural wastage or redundancy, and what will the costs be? Far from removing uncertainty, the response creates more uncertainty. It gives the impression that we regard the Gurkhas as a reservoir and feel that we can turn the tap on or off to suit our convenience. If we can manage with 4,000 we will; if we need more, we will simply take more. That is not the right way to approach people who have provided us with such dedicated service.

Every speaker who has mentioned the Gurkhas has commented on the extraordinary value for money that they give to the British Army. The Chairman of the Select

Committee underlined the point about retention when he reminded us that 95 per cent. of Gurkha soldiers serve at least 15 years, whereas the average length of service for a British soldier is about five years. We make a tremendous effort to keep people in the British Army, while we find it extremely difficult to persuade Gurkhas to leave. Surely that makes the point about their effectiveness.

All of us who had the honour, privilege and pleasure of taking part in the Select Committee inquiry and who came to the problem for the first time were struck by the adaptability, dedication and enthusiasm of the young men who have come forward in such large numbers from the hills of Nepal to serve with the Brigade of Gurkhas. They represent a priceless asset to the British Army. The Government seem incredibly short-sighted in seeking, in the face of all the evidence, to reduce Gurkha numbers so sharply. I hope very much that they will think again, and will do so very quickly.

7.34 pm

Mr. Robert Boscawen (Somerton and Frome): My hon. Friend the Member for Dorset, West (Sir. J. Spicer) spoke with considerable knowledge and practical experience about the helicopter needs of the forces in Europe. I wish to mention only one feature of the speech by my hon. Friend the Minister of State which rather disturbed me, on the question of Westland. In answer to an intervention, he said—rightly, in my view—that the best approach to the aerospace industry was the commercial, competitive approach. What worried me was that he did not share the enthusiasm shown by his right hon. Friend the Secretary of State when he spoke in my constituency about the development of the vital EH101 collaborative project. The Government have expressed enthusiasm about proceeding with the project, and I trust that they will give the orders in future. I hope that in his winding-up speech my hon. Friend will convince us that the Government are still enthusiastic about a project that is so vital to the future of Westland and to a great many constituents.

I did not wish to talk about the general NATO position. I was, however, struck strongly by the wise comments that we have come to expect from the robust speeches of the hon. Member for Sheffield, Attercliffe (Mr. Duffy). He said what all Conservative Members believe—that intentions are very different from capability. We would be very unwise to trust entirely to intentions before we see the capabilities of the Soviet bloc actually change, and to change our doctrine of flexible response in advance.

The reason for the existence of that doctrine, and the reason it is such an enormous advance, is that we would have no such doctrine and no means of applying it if we were left with the massive response of the strategic deterrent only in the last resort. I hope that the Opposition realise that, and will think long and hard before returning us to the previous position.

Lastly, I wish to raise two or three points that have been mentioned by hon. Members on both sides of the House and are worrying many of our constituents and have been drawn to my attention on numerous occasions about the problem of recruiting and retaining trained men in our services. They are twin problems, but they run absolutely together. However much we improve and spend on recruiting programmes, we shall not be able to recruit people when they see the people who are there already leaving in large numbers because they do not like the conditions.

Unlike some Opposition Members, I think that my right hon. and hon. Friends in the Ministry of Defence are well aware of the demographic complications and have been aware of them for some time. They are acting on ways to retain service men. So far so good, but what about the rest of the Government machine? That is what worries me. Have other Departments really got the message that they have to make changes in service men's housing, particularly in the means by which service men, especially those who have been in the forces for some time, are able to purchase their own homes?

It is 40 years or more since I was involved in various forms of soldiering but one thing has never changed and is as true today as it was then. I refer to the acuity and speed with which service men learn and understand what conditions are like for their contemporaries and friends in civilian occupations and homes. They are quick to compare, and when the gap gets too wide they seriously consider leaving. My right hon. and hon. Friends in all Government Departments have to take that into account. If they are to retain fully and expensively trained manpower in our services, they must ensure that the gap between conditions in the services and outside is not so wide as to push those already in the services out into civilian life.

My colleagues have mentioned the problem of the community charge. It is time that the Government gave us a full explanation of exactly how the community charge will affect service men in England and Wales. There are ugly rumours about what is happening in Scotland. Already service men in England foresee that they will have to pay a good deal more than they now pay in rates and they feel that is not fair. One of the main purposes of the community charge is to make local authorities more accountable. But if a service man does not stay in his barracks for more than a year or two, how can he use that accountability and vote against the local authority that has increased his community charge? Will service men have to pay a flat rate community charge? If it has been announced I am not aware of it, but I believe that the sooner my right hon. and hon. Friends announce the way that the community charge will work for service men the better.

It was fortunate and bad luck that, as so often happens the announcement on the future of the Gurkha regiment had to be made only a few weeks before the terrible atrocities were committed in Peking. However, one has to recognise that the good thing about the Government announcement in my view—I have many connections with the Gurkhas, going back a long time—was that they are to be a part of the British Army in future. That secures the future of the Brigade of Gurkhas for a very long time ahead, although their numbers may be fewer. That was a major plus and should be welcomed and the Government should be given credit for that.

The lesson that we have always had to learn is that, if we cut our commitments, we shall have to look at the size of the forces needed for those reduced commitments. That is what I believe the Government were trying to do, having stated that inevitably our commitments to Hong Kong will reduce and there will have to be some cut in the number of in our forces. Nevertheless, the situation has changed and undoubtedly the Government are now in an exceedingly difficult position as a result of the atrocities last weekend

[*Mr. Robert Boscawen*]

in China in determining the exact requirements in future. I notice that my hon. Friend made it quite clear that we are talking about what will happen at least 10 years hence, and has allowed for a great deal of flexibility. Therefore, I am not quite as concerned as other hon. Members.

We must not forget the lessons brought home to us so vividly in the Falklands campaign a few years ago when the wrong signal was given by the Government of which I was then a junior member, in announcing the withdrawal of the Endurance from the Falkland Islands. With the best will in the world the announcement at the time had not taken into account what might happen in Argentina. We should be aware of that lesson about sending a false signal in the proposals that have been made for the Gurkha regiment.

7.47 pm

Mr. Tam Dalyell (Linlithgow): I wish to raise two related issues—first, justice for an ex-soldier and, secondly, the operation of military intelligence.

A month ago *The Scotsman* newspaper reviews editor asked me to review a book called, "Who Framed Colin Wallace?" by Paul Foot, published by Macmillan. I therefore read the book extremely carefully. It reinforced the impression that I had formed some two years ago when Colin Wallace and his friend Major Fred Holroyd spoke to me for three hours in the House. I started sceptically but came to believe that they were telling the truth.

Before any Minister observes that Paul Foot is a loony lefty or makes some unfortunate comment on my own judgment in these matters, let me say that among those who have gone on record as believing Colin Wallace are His Grace the Duke of Norfolk, the Second Earl of Stockton, the publisher and Macmillan's grandson, Herbert Asquith's grand-daughter Laura Grimond, Anthony Cavendish, a friend of Sir Maurice Oldfield, the hon. and learned Member for Montgomery (Mr. Carlile), and my hon. Friend the Member for Brent, East (Mr. Livingstone) who has done a great deal of work on the subject.

Basically, Wallace's troubles began in Northern Ireland when he began asking two awkward questions of the Army authorities. The first was, why, when we know it is happening, do we let young boys be sexually abused at the Kincora boys home?

The second question was, why do we allow Army-related intelligence services to harrass politicians? This was long before the world had heard of Peter Wright; it is the reason why Wallace was thrown out of Northern Ireland, and then harassed.

I want to ask some specific questions of the Ministry of Defence. Page 9 of Foot's book says:

"Looking back on his three years at Lisburn, Tony Yarnold"—

who was a lieutenant-colonel—

"has nothing but praise and admiration for Colin Wallace. 'Let's face it, Colin was the linchpin of the whole operation. He was terrific—way ahead of us all in his knowledge, his skill with the press and his readiness for work. Everyone wanted him all the time, and somehow he was always available.'".

That is what Lieutenant-Colonel Yarnold is alleged to have said. Does the Ministry of Defence accept that view and is it on their records?

I asked the Minister whether Paul Foot on page 14 of his book accurately quotes the head of public relations on information policy, Peter Broderick, who took over as head of Northern Ireland Army Information in 1973. As I am constrained by time, the Ministry of Defence can read from the paragraph beginning

"The Army by this time (1970)"

and the next paragraph starting "Consequently". The third paragraph says:

"Colin Wallace at first became a pawn in this game. Though on the staff of public relations, he was used by Information Policy as their outlet to the press. He also had a knowledge of the Irish situation which was totally unique in the headquarters and surpassed even that of most of the Intelligence Branch. As time progressed, he was not only the main briefer for the press, but also the adviser on Irish matters to the whole Headquarters and—because of his personal talents—contributed much creative thought to the Information Policy Unit. In order to do his job, he had constant and free access to information of the highest classification and extreme sensitivity."

That was, allegedly, Peter Broderick's statement to the Civil Service appeals board in October 1975. I ask the Ministry of Defence to let me know by letter whether that coincides with its records.

Page 18 says:

"Peter Broderick's official report has a revealing sentence: 'He [Colin] acted resolutely and to effect against anyone— Republican or Loyalist—who was destroying his country.' "

That was Broderick's statement to the Civil Service appeal board in October 1975. Does the Ministry of Defence accept that?

Page 259 states:

"The third allegation in the paragraph pooh-poohed Colin's claims that he had three times been recommended for decorations, with the single sentence: 'there is no record of this'.

There was, however, a record of it. Tony Staughton"—

who was a well-respected major in the army—

"head of the MOD Information Office in 1982, told me"—

that is, Foot—

"on the telephone and in interview that he had twice recommended Colin for the MBE and was so certain he would get it that he went out and bought champagne to celebrate it. He wrote this down in a letter of recommendation of Colin to Arun District Council: 'I twice recommended him for an award for his exceptional services, and felt it was most unfair that he was not so recognised.' Colin was recommended a third time for the honour by Peter Broderick, Staughton's successor."

Are those comments and those made on page 260 by Tony Yarnold true?

Is the long "TARA" memorandum beginning on page 96 at "Reference A" and finishing

"I would recommend therefore:—

(a) We make one final attempt to get the RUC to investigate the matter or at least discuss the matter with the RUC.

(b) We obtain very clear and unambiguous authority from London to proceed with a press disclosure"

in Ministry of Defence records?

I am not in a hurry, but I ask for a letter within a reasonable time about this matter.

Is the episode of the lost pistol, outlined on page 125, accepted by the Ministry of Defence?

What was Colin Wallace's crime? I believe that it was breaking ranks about revealing wrongdoing.

That is related to what happened this week in relation to what I can only describe as the rubbishing of Labour Members of Parliament. Today's *Daily Mirror* says,

"What a source!
Waldegrave makes a meal of smear story.
FACT: The lunch—at London's exclusive Mijanou restaurant, near Victoria—was brought forward by Mr. Waldegrave's office for that day."

Was it brought forward? And why? I believe, and I say this with care and the full knowledge of the House, that someone within Government must answer whether the Minister of State, Foreign and Commonwealth Office was briefed on blackmail and Labour Members by the security forces.

On 1 June 1989, the *Daily Mirror* printed the following article for 4 million people to read:

" Control over MPs—homosexual and other blackmail.'"
This is followed by the names of four "Heathite" Tories, and four Labour politicians.

Another note says:

"'Former KGB agent—prostitute's links with Labour MPs in London. Cover up by the Home Secretary.'
Colin Wallace tells me this week: 'We would pass these lies on to journalists with the authority of the intelligence services. The aim was to damage the Labour Party, and the Heath wing of the Tory party.
The very right-wing people who ran intelligence thought that all these politicians were a menace.'"
I should like a comment on that from the Government.

It is no good hon. Members looking sceptical because Labour Members had to put up with this opening of the nine o'clock news on 25 May:

"Mike in vision. The British case against the Soviet spies —Russian diplomats were involved with Middle East terrorists, and trying to blackmail Labour MPs."
I do not like this juxtaposing of Middle East terrorists and blackmailing of Labour Members. The nine o'clock news continued:

"Good evening. Senior British sources have been explaining WHY eleven Soviet diplomats and journalists are being expelled: HOW the tit-for-tat spy row with Moscow started. They accused the Russians of involvement with Libyan and Iranian terrorists, and trying to blackmail MPs."
Again, some explanation must be given of this juxtaposing of Labour Members with a situation that never developed and which never stood up. John Sergeant's report says:

"The BBC have now learnt more details of the allegations made by British counter intelligence".
Details from whom?

"It's alleged that Labour MPs were targets for possible blackmail threats. It's also alleged that the agents were involved with Iran and Libya."
Before taking such a report from a lunchtime conversation with a Minister of State, Foreign and Commonwealth Office, who is not in the Cabinet, the BBC should have checked. And the BBC did. Yes, I understand that Mr. Checkland and Margaret Douglas have said that the BBC did indeed check. Did they check with the intelligence agencies? One of them at least we know is permanently represented, possibly, even still after Brigadier Stonham, in the BBC building. Some explanation must be offered in relation to that detail and checking.

They certainly ought to take account of how the programme finished. It said:

"Senior British sources have been giving reasons for the expulsion of Russian spies: they were believed to be involved with Middle-Eastern terrorists and blackmailing Labour MPs."
No qualification was given, and my wife and I and others who saw it that night were very shaken and hurt by it.

Some explanation is due because it seems that we have returned to all that Wallace and Foot were writing about or have written about in relation to the 1970s. Foot's book deserves an extremely detailed response. Many of my colleagues in the parliamentary Labour party are extremely angry, continually, about the blackmail story. I

believe—I take this responsibility upon myself and do not put it on my colleagues—that it originated with elements of the security services.

Just who did frame Colin Wallace? If Foot's book is wrong, there must be some riposte and explanation. Detail must be given because I have named some of those who believe that Colin Wallace is telling the truth.

Just who originated the notion of Labour MPs being blackmailed? It did not come out of thin air.

I hope that the Minister at least can give some assurances in relation to his Department, the Army.

I realise that junior Ministers cannot speak for wider intelligence services, which nevertheless come under this vote.

8 pm

Mr. Churchill (Davyhulme): The hon. Member for Linlithgow (Mr. Dalyell) will not be surprised if I do not follow him into the somewhat abstruse byways along which he has been perambulating.

I pay tribute to the forces of the Crown for the admirable way in which they fulfil the vital and necessary tasks assigned to them in the defence of Britain's and NATO's interests around the world—nowhere more than in Northern Ireland. I especially commend the men and women of the Ulster Defence Regiment, who have been subjected to relentless and cowardly attack in their homes while going about their civilian occupations and even many years after they have left the service and are in their retirement. The House owes all of them its gratitude.

I am very concerned about the desperate situation faced by service men, especially those in the Army, when trying to buy a home, particularly in the south or south-east of England, and the lack which has become apparent in recent years of any satisfactory scheme to enable them to do so. I warmly endorse the proposals of my hon. Friend the Member for Canterbury (Mr. Brazier) to provide an armed forces house purchase savings scheme. I strongly urge my right hon. Friend the Chancellor of the Exchequer to back this overdue scheme, which is provided for in amendments to the Finance Bill, which is now being considered.

I draw the attention of the House to the letter which my hon. Friend the Member for Plymouth, Drake (Dame J. Fookes) quoted and which, no doubt, other hon. Members have received. Major-General Charles Grey, the controller of SSAFA, said:

"It is becoming an increasingly common habit amongst soldiers to leave the Service just as they are entering their most valuable period, at about the age of 25, so that they can emulate their civilian contemporaries, who are at that stage entering the housing market."
The present situation is unfair not just to those serving in the Army. It is clear that it is un-cost-effective, too. This problem must be addressed.

Having had the privilege with the Defence Select Committee of seeing at first hand the Gurkhas in their various postings—in Hong Kong, Brunei, Nepal and here at home, at Church Crookham—I wish to devote my remarks to their future. Those remarkable fighting men from the hill tribes of Nepal have served the British Crown and nation for 174 years, since 1815, with the utmost distinction. In the first world war, 200,000 volunteered; 20,000 died. In the second world war, a quarter of a million volunteered; 9,000 died and a further 23,000 were wounded. Since the first world war, Gurkhas have won 13

[*Mr. Churchill*]

Victoria Crosses, the most recent in 1965, and a further 13 have been won by British officers of the brigade. After that exemplary record of service, a question mark now hangs over their future following the United Kingdom's decision to hand over Hong Kong to the People's Republic of China in 1997.

In recent years, the principal employment and role of the Gurkhas have been the defence and border security of Hong Kong, and it is clear that that role is coming to an end. The Gurkhas' skills as riflemen and jungle fighters are legendary, but for me it was an eye-opener to see the incredible flexibility of the Gurkha soldier. I shall illustrate this by drawing attention to the first report of the House of Commons Defence Select Committee, "The Future of the Brigade of Gurkhas". In part VIII, paragraph 171, the Committee says:

"A number of Gurkhas are parachute trained, and the battalion stationed in the UK is part of 5 Airborne Brigade. Judging by the way Gurkhas take to parachuting—in a typical recent P Company course 2 out of 27 Gurkhas failed, whereas the British failure rate is normally about 50 per cent."

Paragraph 175 states:

"The Queen's Gurkha Signals already carry out many tasks similar to those of British Signals regiments, and could adapt to new ones as required. In this respect, it is worth noting the gradings achieved by Gurkha signallers on Royal Signals Training Brigade courses from 1982 to 1987."

I shall not spell out the details, but the evidence showed that 67 per cent. of the Gurkhas scored grade A or B whereas only 23 per cent. of the rest of the British Army managed those scores. Let no one say that the Gurkhas are incapable of matching themselves to the exacting role required in the European theatre on the central front.

We have watched with horror the unfolding events in the People's Republic of China. Our hearts go out to the students of Peking and the civilians of China who, unarmed and peacefully, were asking no more than to build freedom and democracy in their land. Their courage in the face of ruthless and indiscriminate use of military power has commanded our admiration. As one who has had the unpleasant task of reporting wars of three continents, I pay tribute to the courage of Miss Kate Adie of the BBC and other war correspondents reporting from the front line in China.

Faced as we are with the chronic actual or potential instability of the Communist tyrannies as they stagger haltingly towards a measure of liberalisation, we are entitled to ask: is this the moment to talk of halving the strength of the Brigade of Gurkhas from over 8,000 to 4,000?

Not just China is susceptible to such instability as it tries to move towards a more liberal regime. It is not impossible by any means in the coming months that one could see similar horrors repeated within the Soviet Union, possibly in the Baltic republics of Latvia, Lithuania or Estonia, and possibly they could happen in the Soviet republics themselves, such as Georgia or the Ukraine.

There is no question but that we are now in a period which, on the one hand, has never been more hopeful in my entire lifetime and the lifetime of my generation brought up in the post-war years, because for the first time we have a constructive dialogue between East and West, with genuine warmth. One sees the determination of Mr. Gorbachev to progress to constructive disarmament and to achieve a balance of power; we must all most warmly welcome that.

On the other hand, it would be a grave mistake if we did not see the enormous stresses and strains taking place within the Soviet and Chinese societies as they try to take off the cooking pot a lid that has been kept so firmly in place for 40 years or more. There is a great danger that one could see the upsurge of nationalism in one of the many parts of the Soviet empire and that could lead to ruthless repression, not necessarily by Mr. Gorbachev, but if he did not have the courage of those who have previously held power and who have been pushed to one side for the moment during this period of detente, he and the present regime might be pushed aside, so the tanks might be sent in to repress disorder.

I find it very unfortunate that we should be considering halving the strength of the Brigade of Ghurkas at this time, not only from the point of view of the world situation, but from the point of view of our worries about the demographic trough. Already the Army is 7,000 under strength and plunging ever deeper into deficit.

If my right hon. Friend the Secretary of State does not intend to impose redundancies on the Gurkhas in 1997, one can presume only that it is intended to begin a rundown in recruitment for the brigade in the near future. I must ask my hon. Friend the Under-Secretary of State for the Armed Forces to be frank with the House about the intentions of the Ministry of Defence in that regard. When is it intended to start the rundown to achieve the figure of 4,000 by 1997? Is it really wise to run down the Gurkhas at all through the early and mid-1990s when they may be required more than ever to provide stability in Hong Kong and to cope with the disorders that may arise, possibly on a massive scale, as the hand-over approaches?

I have no doubt that the Government are in danger of making a great mistake in their decision to halve the strength of the Gurkhas. That decision has been made without adequate reference to the impact on a loyal ally of halving the resources flowing to the hill tribes of Nepal, without adequate regard to the manpower crisis faced by the British Army as we plunge into the democratic trough and without proper consideration of the new instability in China and elsewhere in the world. The decision has certainly been taken without adequate consideration of the superb cost-effectiveness of the Gurkhas who, as has been pointed out, serve a minimum of 15 years, compared to an average of five years for the rest of the Army.

I seriously urge my right hon. Friend the Secretary of State for Defence and the Government to reconsider this seriously mistaken decision and to reprieve the Brigade of Gurkhas at its present level of strength.

8.14 pm

Mr. Bruce George (Walsall, South): I hope that what I say will not be used against me in my party, but I must confess to having agreed with virtually everything said by the hon. Member for Davyhulme (Mr. Churchill). I agreed with him especially on what he said about the Gurkhas and I hope that the Government, if they are sensitive, will appreciate that virtually every speaker from all parties has condemned their decision on the Gurkhas. If this House means anything, and if the Select Committee system means anything, I hope that the Government and the Ministry of Defence will not ride roughshod over the views of so many hon. Members, who have been urging them to reconsider their decision to halve the size of the Brigade of Gurkhas.

The hon. Member for Davyhulme also spoke about the enormous changes taking place in the Soviet Union. Once one opens a Pandora's box, it is difficult to close it, although the Chinese appear to have done so successfully —in their terms. If I may digress slightly, I want to follow the hon. Member for Somerton and Frome (Mr. Boscawen) who pointed out the Government's poor timing over Endurance and the announcement on the Gurkhas. I would add another example of bad timing. I saw a wonderful picture in the latest self-congratulatory document produced by Tory central office showing a smiling Prime Minister talking to a certain leader from the People's Republic of China, Mr. Deng. Perhaps the person who included that picture wants to be disciplined by Tory central office.

It is important when one views the momentous changes in the Soviet Union and eastern Europe not to say, as some in my party have said, that the cold war is over, that disarmament has broken out and that we must now throw caution to the winds and join in the spirit begun by President Gorbachev. I am sceptical of that view, as I am of the view that, because President Gorbachev is not completely in control of things, we should do little because his good work will be overthrown and we could be left in an equally bad situation. As a good moderate, I believe that there is a point equidistant from those two extremes. One must take advantage of the initiatives emanating from the Soviet Union, one must loudly proclaim the initiatives being made by our side of the negotiating fence and one should proceed with a degree of caution recognising that, should circumstances change, one would need to have the flexibility to reverse any changes we might have made. We should be neither over-pessimistic nor over-euphoric.

In the old days—that is, two or three years ago— national security decision making in Government was fairly simple. There were problems in getting defence budgets through and problems within NATO, but as there was a definable adversary, resources and unity largely secured eventually. Now the rules of the game have changed. Relations between countries in NATO are changing. Relationships between countries in the Warsaw pact are changing, as are relationships between the respective alliances. That requires a great deal of intelligence and rationality within the Alliance of 16 nations which, by definition, permits decisions to be made slowly and as a result of a great deal of compromise. I hope that we are on the right track and I personally welcome considerably the leadership shown, eventually, by the United States and the successful visit of President Bush to Brussels.

The question we have to ask is whether the Soviet Union has changed. Does it threaten us, or has that threat diminished? How serious is President Gorbachev, and how serious are his numerous initiatives? It is difficult to make a final judgment, but his unilateral cuts announced initially in December at the United Nations and the consequent cuts by his allies in the non-Soviet Warsaw pact countries are militarily quite significant. It is true that there was a public relations element and that to some extent the Soviet Union and its allies were scrapping aircraft and tanks that should anyway have been scrapped. Nevertheless, we should not be too dismissive of Mr. Gorbachev's gesture because it has some military significance. Many have said that it has given NATO an extra week or 10 days' warning time. I think that we should say, "Fine, we agree with what

you have done, as far as it goes. We shall wish to verify it but we congratulate you, nevertheless, on what you have done so far."

I wonder whether we should have been a little more smart in our own attitude to public relations. Let us be honest about it: in the past three or four years virtually all NATO Governments have unilaterally announced cuts that make the cuts announced by the Soviet Union and its allies seem almost marginal. Look at the cuts announced here. In the next few years our defence expenditure is to fall to 3·9 per cent. of gross domestic product. That is quite incredible. I urge Conservative Members, when addressing CND meetings, to tell them enthusiastically how structural disarmament has proceeded under them at a great pace in the past two or three years.

A recent authoritative American document, "Report on Allied Contributions to the Common Defence", shows the growth in defence spending in each NATO country. Britain emerges well—or badly, depending on one's perspective. Those who favour high defence expenditure will feel that the Government emerge badly as there are only four countries in NATO whose annual spending on defence has increased less over a 10-year period than that of the British Government. We are making what are virtually unilateral cuts and all our allies are doing the same. Perhaps in the propaganda game and to persuade public opinion we should have been more prepared to say that unilateral cuts are not the sole prerogative of the Soviet Union—that we have done our bit and made our contribution and that we should not feel embarrassed or left behind by the initiatives taken by Mr. Gorbachev.

I return to my main theme: is Mr. Gorbachev serious? He has made some dramatic changes in defence spending. He recently announced that 15 per cent. of GDP was devoted to defence in the Soviet Union. That is four times the amount to which the Soviet Union has previously admitted. Furthermore, he virtually admitted that that was not all—that it was merely the budget of the Ministry of Defence and did not include research and development and all sorts of other items.

When I was in eastern Europe recently I met a chief of general staff. I said to him, "You have recently announced cuts in defence expenditure, but from what base line?" He said, "We do not know." How can we take seriously all the claims that defence expenditure is being cut? Nevertheless, I think that the Soviet Union has made a good start on defence expenditure.

Has doctrine changed? I believe that it has been changing, and was probably changing even before Gorbachev came to power. I feel strongly that the initiatives originally derived from Andropov and that when he died Gorbachev was chosen to implement the reforms. Military doctrine had begun changing a few years before. But before we accept that its military doctrine has become completely defensive and that it aims for a "reasonable sufficiency", we must ask the Soviet Union about it and exchange views on it. That process has begun. We must improve confidence-building measures and observing exercises. We must look, too, at Soviet training patterns. One good way of finding out whether the Soviet Union's doctrine has changed is to watch how it trains and exercises its armed forces. However, it is difficult to change training and exercising practice suddenly. A change in doctrine involves a change in training, equipment and strategy, and that is difficult to effect swiftly.

[*Mr. Bruce George*]

Dramatic changes are emerging—not just in the Soviet Union but in eastern Europe. A few weeks ago I travelled to Budapest from Vienna—by train as it happens, because I was paying my own fare. I said to someone in my compartment, "Now that we are passing the border between Austria and Hungary, have a look at the iron curtain." The train slowed down, and I looked, but I could not see it. It had gone. A few days before I had visited the national headquarters of Solidarity in Warsaw. Two months earlier, the organisation was still banned, yet here it was fighting parliamentary elections. That is a staggering example of how things have changed in eastern Europe —at least in some countries in eastern Europe. We must take advantage of circumstances. We must be neither over-optimistic nor over-cautious.

This is an important debate for me. It is the first for nine or 10 years in which the views that I have expressed have not been too far removed from those of my party. I am delighted to be able to speak in those circumstances. I recall reading about those who supported President Roosevelt. After he was chosen at a convention, everybody was for him. His organisers therefore distinguished between his supporters by adding an asterisk after the names of those who had supported him before the convention.

I have been a multilaterist for many years. I would say to my hon. Friends, "Welcome back." It has been a lonely nine years. The Minister expressed clear irritation at the fact that the Labour party will not be quite such a push over as it has been in the past two elections. If we can succeed in getting our policies through the party conference, it will be much more difficult to castigate the Labour party as an aberration.

A few weeks ago I was criticised in the House for expressing my disappointment that consensus had disappeared. I have no sense of shame in saying that I believe, as many do, that politics should cease at the water's edge. We should devise security policies with which all political parties and most of the population sympathise. I hope that we are going some way towards re-establishing a sort of consensus, if not an absolute consensus, on security so that the issue of defence can be removed in part from the cut and thrust of the political arena.

Mr. Churchill: Can the hon. Gentleman explain to the public at large how someone—not the hon. Member—can proclaim himself to be a multilaterist and yet retain membership of CND?

Mr. George: My time is almost up and I shall not follow the hon. Gentleman down that road.

I was serving on the Select Committee on Defence when it investigated security in military installations, and I have an obsession with the reform of the private security industry.

Royal Ordnance, which is owned by British Aerospace, has decided to throw out the Ministry of Defence police at its plant in Westcott near Aylesbury and replace them with its own private guarding force. I can think of nothing more stupid. The brochures produced by the Westcott plant— on which I shall not elaborate—show what is produced there. What is produced would be of enormous benefit to a potential terrorist. I fear what may happen once the Ministry of Defence police are removed. They are well trained and well led. They have access to arms and they have back-up from Bicester nearby. They have a tradition of service in defending our military installations. They are to be replaced by largely untrained people with not so much as a truncheon between them. Bearing in mind the sensitive nature of what is produced at Westcott, this is a stupid, stupid decision.

The company has been less than honest with the Thames Valley police and with the Ministry of Defence. I hope that, bearing in mind my remarks and the information that I propose to convey to them, the Government will call in British Aerospace and the management at Westcott and review and change the decision. If the decision is not changed, the guarding force that will be employed will not be up the task. No one has been recruited yet. Will people be recruited from an area of low unemployment? It is a stupid decision. We cannot play games with the security of national assets. I hope that even at this late juncture the Ministry of Defence will seek to retain the MOD police. The Ministry will be applauded if it intervenes and achieves that objective.

8.29 pm

Mr. Neil Thorne (Ilford, South): It is a great pleasure to take part in the Army debate, particularly as I have been associated with the Anglo-Nepalese all-party parliamentary group for the last 10 years, first as secretary and now as chairman. I was delighted when my colleagues on the Select Committee on Defence agreed that we should consider the future of the Gurkhas. That was an innovation because the majority of Select Committee reports are about actions that have been taken by Government rather than recommendations to Government as to what action should be taken.

I regret, therefore, that the Secretary of State, for whom I have the highest regard, could not be more positive when he made his recent statement on the future of the Gurkhas to the House. I appreciate that he was talking about the position post-1997. Of course, it is difficult for any politician to bind himself or a successor that far ahead. Nevertheless, I took some comfort from his remarks because I interpreted them to indicate that the 4,000 that he mentioned was the basic minimum, below which the Government would not go.

I should like to think that, because of the demographic trough about which we have heard so much in this debate, and for other reasons, we may find that post-1997 we shall require more Gurkhas rather than fewer. I hope that by that time we shall be thinking in terms of 10,000 Gurkhas. We know that there are 30 competitors for every Gurkha place. That means that the quality of the troops that we obtain from Nepal is extremely high.

It has already been mentioned that we have had a relationship with the Gurkhas since 1815. Next year is the 175th anniversary. The service that we have been given has been unstinting, and we should be profoundly grateful for it. Therefore, the aid that we give to Nepal is really paying back in a small way what we have taken from the country in its manhood over those many years. I look upon aid to Nepal in a different light from aid to any other country for the very good reason that we are paying for services rendered. It would be a tragedy if we were to give the impression that we did not intend to carry on doing that.

We must ask a number of questions of the Secretary of State about the future of the Gurkhas. In the past the

Gurkhas have been considered to carry their own reserves because they have had four companies. Is it intended that British reservists will in future provide that element? Will we be looking perhaps to the Territorial Army to give that support? That would certainly be an innovation. If the Government propose to cut numbers, they must state fairly soon whether they intend to do that entirely by natural wastage or whether they propose redundancies. If there are to be redundancies, on what basis would they be made and how would redundancy affect pensions?

At the moment there is a permanent cadre of British officers. Four infantry battalions of a smaller size would have a significant effect upon that. Can we be assured that there will be sufficient left to sustain an appealing career structure for the remaining officers? I remind my hon. Friend that Gurkha officers have been a source of the leadership of the British Army for many years and that they have been able to maintain a very high profile.

One of the bases of Gurkha service is the family permission whereby the Gurkha soldier above a rank of staff sergeant can have his family with him at all times. Below that rank the soldier is accompanied by his family for a certain proportion of his service. That is important to the Gurkha soldier because he tries to manage his affairs in such a way that the birth of his children takes place during the period when he has family permission and has the benefit of using hospitals run by the British forces. The future of family permission must be made clear.

We would also like to know where in the United Kingdom the brigade is to be based. I hope that we shall soon have information about that. Will the training depot be situated in the United Kingdom when there is a move from Hong Kong? That is another important question to which we need an answer.

Dharan has been referred to already. It is a source of great sadness to me that, a year before the Select Committee went to Nepal to make its report, a decision had been taken and announced that Dharan was virtually to be abandoned. Some backtracking has taken place since, but in my view the decision was wrong because we make a valuable contribution to the infrastructure of that region of Nepal. Anyone who has been to that part of the world will be aware of the position. I cannot imagine that any politician who had been there could have made such a decision. I feel certain that the decision was taken blind because I do not think that there would have been such a decision otherwise.

I hope that my hon. Friend can assure me that the welfare facilities, and the personnel and stores transiting facility will continue there, as well as the agricultural resettlement training, which is very important to the economy of Nepal. There is a very good agricultural school and a building trades school there for retired soldiers whose future is in question. We must have answers about their future and about the financing of the hospital once the British military hospital closes. We need an assurance about long-term funding.

Hon. Members on both sides of the House have been concerned about the future of Hong Kong after the British leave in 1997. My hon. Friend should consider whether it would be possible to reassure the people of Hong Kong by coming to an arrangement whereby the Chinese Government fund a residual presence of Gurkha soldiers in Hong Kong, over at least part of the 50-year guaranteed period post-1997. We have such an arrangement in Brunei whereby the troops still serve under the British Crown. If the Chinese are serious about their guarantees to the people of Hong Kong, I cannot see why a similar arrangement could not be entered into with China. I am sure that that would give a great deal of reassurance to the people of Hong Kong that their future was not likely to be turned upside down by the presence of Chinese forces behaving as they have so recently in Peking.

A completely different point of great concern to me is the future of battlefield communications. In the past we have been extremely well served by battlefield communications in the British Army, which has a reputation second to none in the world. One reason is that we can communicate on the battlefield so expertly at all levels. In order to do that, we have relied upon a number of companies in this country bringing forward their expertise.

One of those companies was founded in my constituency—the Plessey company. At present, the Plessey company is under the considerable cloud of a possible takeover from a predator, which is partly foreign, Siemens, and partly from home, GEC. There is no way under these conditions that the Plessey company can continue to carry out its extensive research and development programme efficiently, on which it spends some 22 per cent. of its turnover, this being about twice as high as any competing company. I fear that, if this state of affairs is allowed to continue and that company is subjected to that kind of pressure much longer, we shall not retain our edge over other troops in the battlefield.

I believe that it is in the national interest, and national security in particular, for the Ministry of Defence to say that, if the conditions that were laid down by the Monopolies and Mergers Commission cannot be carried out to the letter, it has a duty to the country to announce that quickly and remove the cloud as soon as possible. The staff of the MMC are not security cleared so they cannot be told exactly what is going on in research and development.

I congratulate my hon. Friend the Member for Canterbury (Mr. Brazier) on so steadfastly pursuing his home ownership scheme. Undoubtedly that is one of the keys to recruiting and retaining Army personnel. I hope that the Ministry of Defence can get the message over to the Treasury that we must be more flexible and we must take bold decisions before it is too late.

I remind my hon. Friend the Minister that the Territorial Army is a key issue in the defence scenario. I spoke in a debate a few days ago concerning the TA, and I referred specifically to the need for the TA messes to be the best possible clubs in every area in which they are present. If that is not done, we cannot expect to train and retain the personnel that we need. Will the Minister assure me that that matter is receiving his attention? We should ensure that this is the case not only for 36 Signal Regiment which is to have a new headquarters built in my constituency during the next few months, but for all others throughout the country. They must all have excellent recreational facilities for Territorial soldier at all levels.

I hope that my hon. Friend can answer at least some of those questions tonight.

8.42 pm

Mr. Harry Cohen (Leyton): I am pleased to speak after the hon. Member for Ilford, South (Mr. Thorne), as I did on Tuesday night on his Redbridge market Bill. After that debate, our former colleague Matthew Parris in his

[*Mr. Harry Cohen*]

excellent article in *The Times* described the hon. Gentleman as the "monocled Colonel Thorne, OBE, TD". It is thus absolutely fitting that he should be speaking in this Army debate.

This could be a very wide-ranging debate. A number of issues have not so far been touched upon, for example, forces' widows who are treated abominably by the Government. Indeed, women in other countries have to go round with begging bowls collecting money to support their sisters in this country. That is a scandal. Another example is the ex-service men who have been exposed to radiation. The Government are dragging their feet and refusing to give proper compensation to the victims or their families. Indeed, we have hardly touched upon the Government sell-off of the Royal Ordnance factories, which was a planned £100-million-plus rip-off of public assets for which the Government were responsible and which they are now trying to cover up. Those are other important issues, to which we shall return.

This is a debate on the Army, and I pay tribute to all those individuals who perform their tasks effectively and efficiently. It is the policies that are imposed upon them and which they are forced to implement that are too often wrong. It is the Government's fault, especially in the field of nuclear and conventional weapons.

There was an excellent cartoon in *Tribune* showing a couple of men walking past two billboards. The first billboard said, "Gorbachev's new arms cuts" and the second said, "Mrs. Thatcher's new nuclear weapon". One guy turned to the other and said, "She will be telling us next that we need these nuclear weapons to defend ourselves against disarmament." That is the situation we are in.

There has been a whole list of defence initiatives from President Gorbachev. The INF agreement is a great tribute to his will in getting a reduction in a range of nuclear weapons—some 4 per cent. of the world's nuclear weapons. Other initiatives are his unilateral cut in conventional weapons, and his action to try to cut back and remove chemical weapons. Russia has announced the first factory to crunch and destroy chemical weapons, which is an important new factor.

President Gorbachev has put into practice the concept of asymmetries. It is time that the West joined in that concept and made some asymmetrical cuts, too. As a result of those initiatives, the Soviet threat, which so many of us thought was a myth in any event, has diminished, certainly in the public mind. It is now down to single percentages. It is only the Conservatives who live in a bygone age, who still cling to that cold war notion of the Soviet threat. The reason for President Gorbachev's initiatives is, of course, economic—perestroika. He wants to bring money to his own people instead of wasting it on military and nuclear costs.

Another reason is the risk of accident. President Gorbachev has the experience of Chernobyl and he knows that there will be more nuclear accidents in the nuclear arms race to create weapons. He knows, too, the danger that lies in their use. Indeed, the Pentagon produced a report——

Mr. Mates: Will the hon. Gentleman give way?

Mr. Cohen: No, I shall not give way.

The Pentagon produced a report, "Discriminate Deterrence", which talks about using nuclear weapons in a limited way against some Third-world countries.

Then there is the danger of proliferation. In the past few weeks we have seen, for example, that India has its new intermediate range weapons, AGNI, which could have a nuclear capability. Indeed, the Prime Minister, in her discussions with President Bush, talked to him about the United States providing nuclear weapons in Argentina. Such a proliferation poses a great threat. President Gorbachev has recognised that threat and that has prompted the promotion of his initiatives. Those are reasons for us, too, to run down our nuclear weapons in the context of the arms race.

President Gorbachev's latest proposals should be considered by the House. His proposal of 1·35 million troops on each side within six years should receive a positive response from the Government. So, too, should the common ceiling in tanks, artillery and armed troop carriers, combat aircraft and helicopters. President Gorbachev has suggested a three-stage proposal with elimination in two to three years of asymmetries and reductions to equal collective ceilings—10 to 15 per cent. lower than the lowest level possessed by either alliance. The Government should also consider President Gorbachev's proposals for cuts of 25 per cent. on each side and the establishment of a purely defensive conventional arms posture.

Then, of course, there is the proposal for the thinning out of the front line in Europe. That, of course is directly counter and opposite to NATO's backward strategy of so-called forward defence, which is a much better strategy.

Another proposal which has not been touched on by any Minister or anyone in the West is that the Soviets have offered to remove their entire nuclear ammunition from their allies if the United States does the same. Yet that has not even been referred to by NATO. There are opportunities to pick up those initiatives and to obtain parallel reductions in both nuclear and conventional forces.

The proposals made by President Bush must be viewed against those initiatives. His offer to cut United States troops in Europe by 30,000 to 275,000 is very welcome, but it ignores a couple of factors. It ignores all European armies, which I believe should also be substantially reduced. It also does not take account of America's increasing number of nuclear weapons in Europe, such as those at Upper Heyford, where a direct increase in the number of F111s is planned.

NATO adopted the comprehensive concept, and the Prime Minister quoted from it on Tuesday. Paragraph 27 states:

"The Allies' sub-strategic nuclear forces are not designed to compensate for conventional imbalances."

Paragraph 44 states:

"But the sub-strategic nuclear forces deployed by member countries of the Alliance are not principally a counter to similar systems operated by members of the WTO."

What are they for, if they are not to counter conventional imbalances or nuclear forces? What are they for, other than to be kept, come what may, despite there being no cause to keep them? It would be difficult to be more provocative towards other countries.

The NATO communiqué states about dual-capability aircraft that it will "include reductions by each side to equal ceilings at the level of 15 per cent. below current Alliance holdings of helicopters and of all land-based combat aircraft in the Atlantic-to-the-Urals zone."

That is very welcome, but the Prime Minister has now said that Britain's dual-capability aircraft will not be included in the discussions. That makes NATO's commitment rather hollow.

The comprehensive concept ignores France. Tucked away in an footnote on page 4, the NATO communiqué states:

"France takes this opportunity to recall that, since the mandate for the Vienna negotiations excludes nuclear weapons, it retains complete freedom of judgment and decision regarding the resources contributing to the implementation of its independent nuclear deterrent strategy."

France is saying that it is out of the discussions. NATO certainly is not coming to terms with Gorbachev's initiatives, let alone matching them.

The summit was an enormous defeat for the Prime Minister. It was a blow to her modernisation, block negotiation stance. The replacement for Lance has probably been delayed indefinitely and negotiations will commence on strategic nuclear forces. The Prime Minister is not a multilateralist. When a Conservative Member said during Question Time that the Government were the true multilateralists, the right hon. Lady was embarrassed. She does not want to get rid of nuclear weapons—she favours using the INF agreement to re-arm. She wants modernisation and a new arms race. She is out of date, irrelevant and dangerous. She is also two-faced—she smiles with President Gorbachev, but there is great hostility and opposition beneath the smiles.

The Gorbachev initiative provides a great opportunity to rid Europe of nuclear weapons and to reduce conventional forces. There could be stability at a much lower level of arms. Britain could play its role by getting out of the nuclear arms race, which would release resources from warfare to welfare and for the needs of mankind throughout the world. We need to get rid of the Tory nuclear-wild Government before Britain can play its proper role.

Several Hon. Members *rose——*

Mr. Deputy Speaker (Mr. Harold Walker): Order. Three hon. Members are still seeking to catch my eye. I understand that Front Bench spokesmen hope to begin their replies at 9.25 pm. I hope that hon. Members will pay regard to the arithmetic.

8.54 pm

Mr. Norman Miscampbell (Blackpool, North): I am sure that there will be no difficulty in all three hon. Members contributing to the debate in the time available.

I wish to follow the splendid speech of my hon. Friend the Member for Plymouth, Drake (Dame J. Fookes) and discuss not overall Army responsibilities or materials supply, but the most pressing matter of how we are to man the equipment in future years. There is a vital need for the Army to retain its personnel and to recruit those needed to man our defence forces. The Minister's speech clearly recognised the problem. It has certainly been recognised by every unit that I have visited during the past year and a half, and there were quite a number of them. We recognise not only the demographic decline but the inevitable civilian competition from those who want to employ the very people that the Army needs, such as specialists and personnel of intelligence and initiative.

The manning of missiles and tanks depends on retaining the personnel. To achieve that, we must provide the soldier with a good career—and that means not just satisfying the soldier, but satisfying his wife and children so that they will want him to stay in the Army. The foundation of that satisfaction must be the knowledge that, after whatever length of service, the soldier will have a happy resettlement—to use current economic jargon, a soft landing. To achieve that a number of issues must be tackled. A better degree of training both for the soldier and his wife is required. Of course, SSAFA helps with training and others also lend a hand. The soldier and his wife need to learn the skills to allow them to set up home in civilian life with a great more ease than is currently the case.

In home postings, especially in the south of England, it is relatively easy for wives to get jobs, but a great deal of hardship occurs in away-from-home postings. I saw this clearly when I visited Holywood in Northern Ireland, where a regiment had gone for two years. The wives had followed their husbands and found that there was no work there for them. Wives with skills who had had good jobs in Aldershot found themselves offered the most menial tasks on the Down coast, and of course they found that disconcerting.

Something must be done to help the wife who must give up her job to follow her husband, and we want wives to accompany their husbands. I cannot see why, for those who have been in employment, some unemployment benefit could not be payable when they move overseas or to Ireland. Nor do I understand why, alone among those who serve the state, we ask them to pay for accommodation overseas. Perhaps we should consider—the Navy appears to be doing this with great success—initiating the custom of periodic bonuses for those who stay on as their service progresses.

I am anxious to keep my remarks short and will leave out much of what I would otherwise have said. I must, however, refer to the problem of housing and the growing feeling of discontent among people as they progress through their service lives and feel that they will not be able to get a home when they come out. My hon. Friend the Member for Canterbury (Mr. Brazier) made a number of suggestions. Those and similar proposals have been made time and again, but tonight I have time only to commend them.

As one who has not given a vestige of support to the community charge from beginning to end, for Scotland or anywhere else, I feel that what we propose for the Army by way of the community charge needs thinking through. When a regiment is told that at the appropriate time it will move to inner London on guard duty, its reception to that news must be like the sepoys' reception in the middle of the last century to being given greasy cartridges, which they did not like. I do not know what a soldier will do when told that he is to go into Westminster where, whatever is said, the community charge will be £500 to £600 a head. How will soldiers pay that, and why should they pay it? I need say no more about homelessness or the community charge.

We spend enormous sums retraining people, and we lose those who are trained at enormous cost. Any rational application of economics and cost-effectiveness must show

[*Mr. Norman Miscampbell*]

that a tiny proportion of money spent on making life better for those who are already in the services would pay handsomely.

It is a question of making the wives feel not just that their men are contented husbands. We want them to continue to want to help them remain contented. In that way they will be content to be the wives, and families, of soldiers. Unless we tackle the matter in that spirit we shall have losses, and they will be inexcusable.

9.2 pm

Dr. Alan Glyn (Windsor and Maidenhead): I wish at the outset to thank the Minister for at last allowing the rebuilding of Victoria barracks, Windsor, for which I have been pressing for eight years. My hon. Friend the Member for Kettering (Mr. Freeman) was good enough to come with me to see the site and, following that, the Under-Secretary of State for the Armed Forces announced in a written reply that he had given

"Approval to proceed with the rebuilding of Victoria barracks on the site of the old barracks at Windsor",— [*Official Report,* 18 May 1989; Vol. 153, c. *274.*] That has given great satisfaction not only to the Household Division but to the colonel of the regiment, Her Majesty.

Paragraph 46 of the Defence estimates gives an excellent analysis of the disparity that exists between ourselves and the Warsaw pact. Even if satellites such as Hungary and Poland split off, the Warsaw pact will have enormous superiority. So we must continue with our policy of having a flexible response and we must retain the nuclear capacity. Who knows what may happen? What happened in Peking could happen in Red square.

We must face the problems of the demographic trough, combined with the possible loss of 35,000 United States troops. Somehow we must fill that gap. Our special relationship with America still exists. Even so, the removal of 35,000 troops presents a problem with which we must deal.

That will be done by ensuring that we recruit enough people, and to do that we must offer them the right terms of service, always remembering that we are competing with industry, espcially in technology. Unlike other countries, we do not have a system of national service. I suggest that we must find an alternative, and perhaps we should press employers to make it compulsory—with, of course, sufficient allowances being provided—for people to do service. They could become Territorials or former Regulars could retrain at frequent intervals, so enabling us to have a strong reserve.

I was impressed by the suggestion of my hon. Friend the Member for Plymouth, Drake (Dame J. Fookes) for the further use of women in the services, which would give even more flexibility. We shall still need the Gurkhas.

The Defence Estimates show that the volunteer services have risen from 73,000 to 90,000 but that is still not enough. I must also refer to the important issue of the SSAFA letter, which was mentioned by my hon. and learned Friend the Member for Blackpool, North (Mr. Miscampbell). It was written by General Grey, whom I telephoned to discuss the matter. The issue was also raised by my hon. Friend the Member for Canterbury (Mr. Brazier). We must recognise what the SSAFA letter says. I am sure that all hon. Members would agree with that.

Chemical weapons are the most dangerous of all because they are so difficult verify, even by satellite. The comparison between our openness and that of the Russians is well illustrated in paragraph 226 of the Defence Estimates. The imbalance which would result from the proposals of the Soviet Union is insufficient. As the Prime Minister said when she reported on the NATO summit, short-range missiles must remain until the Soviet Union has carried out its arms reduction policies. West Germany objects to short-range missiles but they would land in East Germany, the home of the Soviet allies. We should not relax our grip or drop our guard.

I am convinced that if we continue to negotiate in a strong and tough way we shall be able to achieve a settlement with the Soviet Union. We should always remember that policies could change if Gorbachev were beaten and the same were to happen in Russia as has occurred in China. We must always watch these points, be on our defence and ensure that we are never below the strength of Russia, which can pull hidden troops from the Urals. Let us always remember to negotiate from strength to obtain the security we need.

9.7 pm

Mr. Julian Brazier (Canterbury): I am most grateful to hon. Members for speeding up their speeches to fit me in, and to Ministers for compressing their speeches. I thank my hon. Friend the Member for Plymouth, Drake (Dame J. Fookes) and my seven other colleagues who spoke in support of my armed forces house purchase savings scheme.

I have been encouraged by the constructive discussions that I have had with the Secretary of State and my hon. Friend the Member for Romford (Mr. Neubert) on the subject. Both have shown considerable flexibility of mind in the solutions which they are willing to look at.

Of the householders in this country, 63 per cent. are home owners. All householders with mortgages are entitled to tax subsidies in the form of mortgage interest relief. A further 28 per cent. of households are either council or housing association tenants and, through their rent payments, they can, if they choose, attract a different form of subsidy: an accumulating discount on the purchase of that property. Sadly, the Army and parts of the Royal Air Force are shut out of that system and are firmly in the other 9 per cent. Comparatively few soldiers —the last figure I saw was 26 per cent.—own houses. Those who do have serious difficulties of the sort already covered by my colleagues.

I wish to stress one simple point, and read out some of the letters which I have received to illustrate it. The solution to the Army's house purchase problems does not lie with encouraging soldiers to buy houses while serving. Unlike the Navy, and part of the Royal Air Force, whose families are comparatively static, about half the Army's families are outside mainland Britain and the rest are extremely mobile. House ownership for a serving soldier does not mean home ownership or owner-occupation, but rather the absolute nonsense of trying to run two households with all the problems that being an absentee landlord entails.

Mr. O'Neill: Does the hon. Gentleman know whether service men living in service accommodation can acquire credits which could be used if, for example, they bought a council house allocated to them after they left the service?

Mr. Brazier: I am delighted to confirm that the hon. Gentleman is right. Should a service man subsequently obtain a council house, thanks to my hon. Friend the Member for Elmet (Mr. Batiste) those credits can be taken into account. However, the difficulty is that that very measure has resulted in councils being even more reluctant to allocate council houses. In many cases service men simply cannot get them at all, especially if they do not have children.

The message is simply that the solution to the Army's housing problem does not lie in encouraging people to become involved in buying houses during their service. The purchase of a house should be at or near the end of their service.

At the moment a soldier has no alternative, and I wish to read out a number of letters to illustrate the problem. The first comes from a flight lieutenant from one of the branches of the Royal Air Force, which has a similar problem. He said:

"While stationed in England I bought my own house. It is the only property I own. On being posted to Germany I rented my house and moved into married quarters at a cost of £180 a month. Almost half of the monthly rent I am receiving for the house goes in expenses—rates, agent's fees, insurance etc. This means that I am £75 a month short after paying my married quarters rent. Yet the law does not allow the married quarters rent to be offset against the let house so that the whole of the net income on that house is treated as though it is profit, meaning a still further loss of £26 a month."

Of all those who have written to me, that man is the best off because he has a letting arrangement which works.

The Federation of Army Wives has sent me a long brief with case after case of lettings that have turned into disaster. I quote just one. A major with three children was posted to BAOR. His tenant cleared out owing rent, electricity bills, telephone bills. He left the house in a dreadful state. The major travelled back to the United Kingdom at his own expense, decided to cut his losses and sell. He is now not able to enter the housing market again.

The next letter comes from a serving officer, who wrote:

"I have shown this paper to the six military serving members of my staff and to some of the retired ones. All with one voice have said 'If only a scheme like this had been in operation when I got married.'"

The crucial sentence comes at the end of his letter.

"Anything would be better than the present moral blackmail to follow the drum and accept the very real problems of letting one's own property."

That is the nub of the problem. Officer and soldier are faced with moral blackmail of either having to buy a house and go down the hideous route of trying to run two households with all the hassles and problems that tenants bring, which in most cases they resolve by leaving the Army, or to do nothing at all and end up homeless.

All those cases concern officers. Comparatively few NCOs even try to buy at the moment. Let me quote a letter from the wife of one:

"My husband is an NCO in the Army and I am stationed in London. As we have no children at the moment and I am earning a good salary in London, we decided the time is right for us to purchase a flat."

Then news of the posting came, along with all the problems that have been referred to—the loss of the wife's job, and so on. She ends the rather sad story by saying:

"It is because of my feeling of being penalised because of my husband being in the Army and our subsequent loss of our flat that I felt that I had to write to you and applaud your fight on our behalf. I only hope that we, along with many other families in the armed forces, will benefit from your campaign."

The last letter that I wish to quote is particularly sad. It comes from a lady I know whose husband is a major and would have been classified as a high flier. He has all the right credits to go up to very senior service in the Army. The extract is this:

"Some years ago we managed to get a foothold on the property market and now struggle to maintain a mortgage while paying for a married quarter. We have a mortgage of £40,000"—

comparatively small; they got in before the latest rise in prices—

"but unlike many other service families we suffered the inevitable problems of letting. For a period of six months we received no rent and for a further six months we had a tenant who did not pay and who stole or damaged so much that we incurred yet more expense. We then had one year of trouble-free letting but of course we had to pay agent's fees and tax on the rent received then."

She goes on to make the same point as has just been made about wives. She ends by saying:

"If a scheme like yours were to be introduced this year we would be able to sell our home, put the money into it and we could then stay on in the Army."

Then comes the saddest sentence of all:

"Sadly, the Army is an anachronism; it looks as if we will no longer be able to afford to subsidise it."

My hon. Friend the Member for Drake quoted a statistic from a brief that went round earlier which showed that premature voluntary release had risen by 70 per cent. in the Army in five years. In reply to a parliamentary question a few days ago, I discovered that in the latest quarter of this year, taking it back six years now, the figures having just become available, it has risen by 140 per cent. between the first quarter of 1983 and the first quarter of 1989.

We cannot go on saying to our soldiers that their alternatives are to do nothing and be homeless or get involved in this hopeless arrangement. We cannot keep people much past the age of 25 in the Regular Army and the age profile of the Army reflects that.

My hon. Friend has been most flexible and willing to listen to my suggestions and I know that he and his officials have worked extremely hard in this matter. I will end by giving him a shopping list of items which it seems to me are essential to make any scheme work—there is no reason why he should take my proposal off the shelf. There are four. The first is the easiest of them because since the Budget it is available already. It must be a fully tax-exempted scheme as a house is fully tax-exempted. The new PEP scheme in the Budget is fully tax-exempt; no tax of any sort is paid on money generated within the scheme.

The other three items are new. The second is that it is very important that a soldier going into this scheme, which is in lieu of a house—and he is only shut out from buying a house because he is in the Army—should be able to get the equivalent of mortgage interest tax relief, a benefit for which the 63 per cent. who are home owners are eligible if they have mortgages. It is in lieu also of accumulated discount on a council house.

The third is that he must get some return out of his existing housing payment. Most of these are single-income families and the difficulties in getting work for wives in some parts of England have been referred to. There are hardly any jobs for wives abroad. They are the only category of public servant, indeed almost the only category of people of any sort, who are made to pay accommodation charges when they are abroad.

[Mr. Brazier]

The fourth is a detailed but important item. It is very important that there is no upper limit on contributions to the scheme. Obviously there is an upper limit on tax relief but, just as civilians when they buy a house group together what bits of capital and income they can raise, so people should be able to put whatever capital they want to into this nest egg to accumulate in this tax-free environment, subject to the same tax exemption limits as their civilian counterparts have on mortgage interest relief.

We owe it to all the members of our armed forces to enable them to have a secure housing future. The MOD has shown imagination in the schemes that it has brought forward in encouraging those members of the armed forces who can be owner-occupiers, the Navy and part of the Royal Air Force by making it possible for them to do so, but I must leave my hon. Friend with the thought that such measures are a complete and utter mistake for the Army. They are not only a waste of money but a delusion leading people down the wrong route. We must instead provide our soldiers with an alternative so that those with 22 years' service do not need to write to me again saying that they are on a five or 10-year waiting list for a council house when they would almost certainly be owner-occupiers otherwise.

I commend those thoughts to my hon. Friend the Minister.

9.19 pm

Sir Geoffrey Johnson Smith (Wealden): I will utter just one or two sentences. I wish to place on record that my hon. Friend the Member for Canterbury (Mr. Brazier) has widespread support on the Conservative Benches for his remarks, and I know from the nodding heads of Opposition Members that they support him too. I am sure that my hon. Friend's comments were listened to with great respect by my hon. Friend the Minister.

9.20 pm

Mr. O'Neill: With the leave of the House, I may say that tonight's debate has been wide-ranging in some respects but has featured several recurring themes. The subject of the Brigade of Gurkhas was raised in almost every contribution except the last two. It is rare in defence debates for there to be a consensus, but it is the unanimous wish of right hon. and hon. Members in all parts of the House to retain the Gurkhas at their present level of strength.

Tonight's debate would have occurred regardless of what happened in Peking, but recent events in the People's Republic of China have given it an extra edge. It is significant that senior Members such as the hon. Member for Somerton and Frome (Mr. Boscawen)—who does not make regular speeches in Army debates, partly because of his many years of service in the Whips' Office—forcefully made the point that we all remember what happened when the signal went to withdraw the Endurance. The hon. Member for Somerton and Frome made that point in a straightforward way but most graphically.

I do not envisage Hong Kong being another Falklands but I do not want to take any risks. The presence of the Gurkhas in Hong Kong sends signals not only to those outside the colony but to those living there, which is of equal importance. We owe them a substantial responsibility. Just because Hong Kong is far away and its culture is different from ours does not mean that our responsibilities there will begin to end some time around 1997 if circumstances are not as we should like them to be.

I ask the Government to take on board the fact that every right hon. and hon. Member who has spoken on that subject is of one mind. The Minister of State for the Armed Forces somewhat disingenuously commented at the beginning of the debate that he is trying to shift with the situation, to try to point up the possibility that his right hon. Friend the Secretary of State for Defence will think again. The House is asking the Secretary of State to think again, and when he reads *Hansard* he will discover time and again that right hon. and hon. Members are not happy with what has been said. I am sure that that view is held in all parts of the House.

It is significant that the only person who could be prayed in aid of the Government's view is Field Marshal Lord Bramall, in his letter to *The Times*. However, during the course of the evening I have been able to find something else said by Lord Bramall which may be of interest to the House. It appears that Lord Bramall can be prayed in aid by a number of people, and certainly I have tremendous respect for his judgment and views.

In last year's debate on the Defence Estimates in another place, Lord Bramall referred to the £20 billion that the Government spent on conventional defence since 1979, which was also mentioned in the Minister's speech today. Lord Bramall commented:

"The Government can be proud that as a result of seven years of sustained growth between 1979 and 1986, induced both by the Falklands campaign and by the Government's adherence to the NATO 3 per cent. growth target (an intention, I have to say, which was first announced, as the noble Lord, Lord Mulley, will know, by the last Labour Government)".

He continued:

"The Government would always want to see themselves as strong on defence. Indeed, they have done much, first to get forces' pay on a proper basis—and here I give credit to the noble Lord, Lord Mulley, who started the process when he was Secretary of State."—[*Official Report, House of Lords,* 12 July 1988; Vol. 499, c. *727-8.*]

I do not want to start an exchange of "Oh no you didn't—Oh yes we did." I am merely trying to put the record straight. The Minister of State has been in the House for long enough, and has been connected with the Ministry of Defence for long enough as a Whip, a junior Minister and a Minister of State, not to insult the intelligence of the House with obviously misleading items of information to the effect that the increase in the Government's conventional spending is wholly attributable to decisions made by them. Many were set in train long before the present Government came to office. *[Interruption.]* The Minister is careful enough to say from a sedentary position that he did not say that, but that is what he meant to convey, as anyone with half a brain would have worked out when he said it. I wanted to use the right quotation, and I consider evidence from someone of Lord Bramall's seniority more than worth praying in aid.

In his speech on the Estimates last year, Lord Bramall drew attention to the deep-seated anxieties shared by many people about aspects of procurement. I will confine my remarks on that subject to one or two points that have arisen in today's debate. Everyone was relieved, I think, at the decision to go for a British tank, and no one disputes that the arrangement with Vickers is probably the most sensible option. We shall be buying a tank that is not yet in operation in our own or any other army—it is often forgotten that the Americans and Germans do not have such tanks in service yet and that we are going through the process of testing and trying them.

This summer once again sees the Canadian army competition, and I am not sure that it was sensible to arrange for the British not to be present. I may be wrong, but I was under the impression that British Army teams would not be competing this year. The Minister nods to confirm that. I think that that is regrettable. In my view, our armed forces can only benefit from such participation. That they will not do so well because their kit is not what it might be is a matter for speculation. As they lost a place a couple of years ago, I would expect them to try their damnedest to make the impact that their professionalism requires. I ask the Minister to think again, and to let us know the Ministry's current view.

Will the Minister also tell us why we are not replacing the Milan anti-tank missile, as the French and Germans are replacing its counterparts in the 1990s? We also seem to be slipping behind the French and Germans in battlefield air defence. For every two main battle tanks that we have, there is one air defence system, but for every two that the Germans have there are 1·5 air defence systems—that is to say, 50 per cent. more—while the French have almost one air defence system for every tank. I realise that what I have said is open to criticism on the grounds of over-simplification; nevertheless, the authors of Jane's "Battlefield Air Defence" were concerned about the matter, and I feel that it is legitimate to raise it in a debate of this nature.

Another aspect of procurement has not been mentioned today, perhaps because one or two hon. Members who have made it their hobby horse are not present. There is still a good deal of anxiety in the House about the demountable rack offloading and pickup system, known as DROPS. BAOR requires trucks capable of loading and off-loading supplies in the field. We know of the complaints about the equipment which was lent to the MOD and the problems in getting them investigated. The Comptroller and Auditor General has looked into the matter, but he has been hampered by the fact that it appears that the National Audit Office does not have the right technical advice to reach a judgment, so the matter has still not been settled. There is a strong case for looking very closely at DROPS and for there to be a proper statement in the House at some stage.

We have discussed Ptarmigan and raised the need for effective communications for BAOR, particularly as the amount of information that needs to be distributed on the modern battlfield is increasing rapidly. The Ptarmigan tactical communications network is supposed to fulfil those requirements, but there have been reports that the system does not have the capacity to meet the Army's future needs. The introduction of BATES, the battlefield artillery target engagement system, and ADCIS, the air defence command information system, will substantially increase the demands that will be made on Ptarmigan.

It was originally planned to purchase 32 mobile trunk nodes, but in the end only 26 were acquired and there is substantial doubt as to whether that will be sufficient. Just a few weeks ago in *Jane's Defence Weekly* a communications commander called for the number to be restored to 32. Certainly the Ministry should look at a number of matters relating to Ptarmigan.

It may be that all the answers on procurement are not available tonight, but I understand that before the summer we shall be debating the Estimates. I should like to think that when we debate more detailed matters of procurement, the Minister will be able to give the House more information. If he can give us some information tonight, so much the better, and if he cares to write to me I shall be happy to receive his letters. I give notice that we shall be returning to these detailed matters in the Estimates debate relating to procurement for the Army and particularly BAOR. It is legitimate that we raise the matter tonight and receive some information.

A number of interesting points have been raised. My hon. Friend the Member for Walsall, South (Mr. George) expressed concern about the security arrangements for Westcott and his longstanding concern about MOD security. He deserves an answer. The speech by my hon. Friend the Member for Linlithgow (Mr. Dalyell) requires a substantial reply. The House will benefit, perhaps not this evening but certainly in future, from a substantial answer to those serious questions. If the Minister chooses not to put them on record but to write, I know that my hon. Friend would like to hear from him as quickly as possible and I should like to see the replies.

My hon. Friend the Member for Sheffield, Attercliffe (Mr. Duffy) made an extremely thoughtful speech. I know that he could not be here for the wind-up and he has apologised. My hon. Friend takes his duties as President of the NATO Assembly very seriously. He raised a number of serious questions and made a useful contribution to the debate. He raised serious issues about the problems of joint procurement and collaboration and co-operation within NATO. We are all grateful to him for his remarks and I hope that the Minister will be able to meet many of his requests.

He raised one point of response to the speech by the Minister of State. Perhaps the Minister could tell us whether the new MLRS sytems will be purely conventional or whether they will be dual-capable and whether they will use nuclear shells or merely conventional shells. That information will be of some assistance when we come to assimilate the significance of the communiqué produced last week in Brussels.

The hon. Member for Ilford, South (Mr. Thorne) made passing reference to the bid for Plessey. The silence of the Ministry of Defence about the bid has been almost deafening, although its previous position about the takeover of Plessey was well known and its representations were a matter of public debate. A clear statement will have to be made soon giving the Ministry of Defence's view, as it is critical to consideration of the bid.

A number of issues have been raised, and I have touched on only some of them. I and other hon. Members believe that President Bush's offer and NATO's response to it merit consideration. We shall doubtless return to the subject in the summer and autumn. Understandably, we have been discussing more basic and fundamental issues, but consideration of the Gurkhas enabled us to debate demographic trends and future recruitment.

Many useful contributions have been made about pay and rations and Army life. At times, we tend to leave these matters to bodies such as the pay review board. It is desirable that such issues are removed from the political arena and left to a group of experts, so that neither one side nor the other deals with the cash element. It has emerged from the debate that there are serious potential

[*Mr. O'Neill*]

social problems under the surface among the armed forces. They are emerging because of the dramatic changes that have recently occurred in the property market.

From my own constituency experience, I am aware that non-commissioned officers and men in the ranks do not experience some of the difficulties that have been alluded to in obtaining council accommodation. It may be that I deal with a Labour authority which has bigger housing stocks and that in other parts of the country, where housing stocks are smaller, the problem assumes different significance. There is worry among all ranks about accommodation.

The hon. Member for Canterbury (Mr. Brazier), whom I am wont to criticise and bash whenever I can, for once is right. I have not looked at the fine print of the amendments to the Finance Bill that he has tabled. I am not trying to damn him with faint praise, but I appreciate the vigour with which he is pursuing the matter. Like the Gurkhas issue, there is no division across the Floor of the House about the principle of this. We may disagree about the fine details, but they can be ironed out, which is what the House, at its best, is supposed to do.

We have had a useful debate. Some issues have not been considered as closely as they might have been. My hon. Friend the Member for Walsall, South is coming out of the cold, or other people in our party are coming out of the cold—I am not sure which, and I will not say one way or the other. There has been an uncharacteristic degree of unanimity among Labour Members and broad agreement across the Floor of the House on a number of issues. The Government would be well advised to pay close attention to what has been said because it is not party advantage that is at stake but the good name of the Army, the morale of the men and women who serve in it and, ultimately, the defence of this country. I urge the Government to think seriously about what hon. Members have said today.

9.39 pm

The Parliamentary Under-Secretary of State for the Armed Forces (Mr. Michael Neubert): As a veteran of no fewer than two single service debates since taking up my post, I have been struck again by the diversity and authority of the contributions by hon. Members on both sides of the House. I shall try to respond to as many points as I can in the time left available to me, but the House will understand that I shall also want to make some comments of my own.

My hon. Friend the Minister of State for the Armed Forces spoke of the encouraging signs of change in the Soviet Union, but not all news that comes from the East is encouraging. While a massive military capability exists in the Soviet Union, the West must retain the wherewithal to deter aggression. The Government will continue to ensure that this remains so. To succeed, we must maintain the support of the British public and recognise the debt owed to those men and women in our armed forces. For that reason, I am particularly pleased that tribute has been paid on both sides of the House to their sterling work.

We welcome the Bush proposals at the recent NATO Alliance summit and we now await the response of the East. As always, there is much detailed work to be done within NATO and it is too early to assess the implications for the United Kingdom in general and for BAOR in particular. It is worth pointing out that reductions envisaged for NATO are small compared with those being sought from the Warsaw pact to remove the existing large conventional superiority. I am afraid that I must disappoint the hon. Member for Clackmannan (Mr. O'Neill) in giving that response at this early stage in the development of arms control.

We do, however, share in the triumph that we believe the NATO summit represented. I regretted, but was not surprised by, the rather sour comments made by the hon. and learned Member for Fife, North-East (Mr. Campbell) on the part played by our Prime Minister in those negotiations. It may be that by his choice of party and policy he has condemned himself to a role of spokesman that is about as effective as trying to light a match in a force 10 gale. He naturally resents the dominant role that my right hon. Friend the Prime Minister plays in world councils. We are prepared to pay tribute to the part that Britain has played in reaching this advantageous arrangement, which has taken the initiative in arms control for the first time for some months.

The Army continues to play key roles in the defence of the United Kingdom and in the forward defence of the European mainland. In addition, it continues to provide vital assistance to the forces of law and order—against the men and women of violence in Northern Ireland—as well as assistance to communities and Governments all over the world. This year has seen the Army in action in all these guises and the House is right to applaud them. From the jungles of Belize to the streets of Northern Ireland, our service men and women serve with great distinction and professionalism.

In this latter context, the hon. Member for Clackmannan asked about measures taken to counter the terrorist threat. He was good enough to acknowledge that the Government have in hand extensive new work to improve the security of service establishments. In this, the Ministry of Defence police will continue to play their part. This does not mean that every civilian-guarding task requires its specialist skills, but I can assure the House, especially the hon. Member for Walsall, South (Mr. George), that any adjustments to the size of the force will have full regard for its value in the security context. In addition, the Army is continually refining and improving the organisational and operational arrangements to support the RUC in Northern Ireland. These have been successful and, together with measures taken by my right hon. Friend the Secretary of State for Northern Ireland, have frustrated the IRA in any attempts to make greater use of the large quantities of arms and ammunition that it possesses.

I should like to dwell on some of the more newsworthy activities in which the Army has taken part over the past 12 months which illustrate the variety of tasks that the service may be called upon to perform. I shall give examples of the Army in action which may be unexpected to the public at least, if not to Parliament. In Nepal, British military staff treated almost 900 casualties and carried out more than 300 operations in the wake of the earthquake there last August. Following hurricane Gilbert in Jamaica in September, Royal Engineers from the Belize garrison carried out much-needed repair on hospitals and children's homes. In Vanuatu, another team of sappers is working to repair cyclone damage under the auspices of the Overseas Development Administration.

Closer to home, and perhaps the most difficult and distressing work carried out this year, was at the sites of the tragedies at Lockerbie and Kegworth. Up to 500 service men were present at Lockerbie on any one day, and some 8,000 man days of service assistance were provided. Some of the work was especially harrowing and those involved deserve the highest praise.

The army responded to many other calls for assistance, such as in the clearance of unexploded ordnance. Some 200 calls were answered in Great Britain, involving, for example, several world war 2 German 500 lb bombs. Those at Stanford-le-Hope and near Billingsgate fish market in London required the evacuation of large numbers of local residents.

Assistance was also given to the Home Office in the past year in manning temporary prisons at Alma Dettingen barracks and Rollestone camp. The soldiers involved demonstrated very well the sheer adaptability of the modern service man.

Perhaps the most under-rated of all the Army's commitments is the contribution it makes to the various international peace-keeping forces. For many years, we have provided contingents for the United Nations force in Cyprus and the multinational force of observers in the Sinai. Our garrison in Cyprus has provided support for the United Nations there and for United Nations forces in Lebanon, that terribly troubled country. Most recently, we have provided the signals staff for the United Nations transition assistance group in Namibia. Despite serving in conditions of virtual turmoil in this case, British personnel are highly regarded for the work they have done.

It has become clear that one of the main issues exercising the House—and that can be judged by the contributions of many of my hon. Friends and other hon. Members—is the question of the Gurkhas. My hon. Friend the Member for Davyhulme (Mr. Churchill), in particular, spoke feelingly and forcefully about that. I hope that tomorrow, hon. Members will reread what my hon. Friend the Minister of State for the Armed Forces had to say at the beginning of the debate about the Gurkhas. The hon. Member for Clackmannan raised the question of the future of the Brigade of Gurkhas and the current position in China. The Government are well aware of our security obligations to Hong Kong.

My hon. Friend the Minister of State for the Armed Forces made it clear that no reductions in Gurkhas would be made before 1992 and that no decision on the matter need be taken until well into next year. Surely that is the way to look at the statements made by my right hon. Friend the Secretary of State in the House about the future of the Gurkhas. As he himself said, the figure of 4,000 is a minimum. Surely what is significant—this is a point to which insufficient importance has been given tonight—is that the brigade structure will remain and all the Gurkha regiments will be intact. If that is encouraging to the President of the Gurkha Association, my hon. Friends and other hon. Members might also take encouragement from it. We are talking of some years ahead, not next month or next year. A commitment has been given not only to 4,000 men, but to the brigade structure of the Gurkhas. Surely that should be some reassurance to my hon. Friends and others tonight.

My hon. Friend the Member for Ruislip-Northwood (Mr. Wilkinson) spoke about the Vietnamese boat people —another tragic problem which has intensified in recent weeks. We are seeking to assist in a number of ways in Hong Kong. Troops of the Hong Kong garrison have already erected several temporary tented holding camps for the boat people. We are providing stocks of tents, water and water purification equipment, which are being used to help to set up these facilities. Troops are currently building a large tented camp to house Vietnamese boat people at Sek Kong military airfield.

Another issue mentioned in a number of speeches, notably that of my hon. Friend the Member for Dorset, West (Sir J. Spicer) was the question of helicopters. I repeat that the Government fully recognise the importance of helicopters on the battlefield. As my hon. Friend the Minister of State for the Armed Forces said in his opening speech, our development of this capability continues. I shall not repeat my hon. Friend's remarks about our existing plans for improvement. The key point is that we should ensure that the balance of systems is for the destruction of armour is maintained. Helicopters and tanks both have a role to play, as we and our allies recognise.

I agree that helicopters are of considerable use out of area but, as with other equipment, our priority must be to meet NATO requirements while building in the flexibility necessary for out-of-area operations where appropriate.

The command and control of helicopters has recently been studied by the Ministry of Defence and it has been concluded that no significant changes should be made to the current arrangements.

My hon. Friend the Member for Dorset, West described helicopters as "low-flying tanks". As the House knows, one of my responsibilities is for low-flying training, so the concept of low-flying tanks did not immediately fill me with enthusiasm, in that context at least.

Mr. Cohen: The Minister referred to command and control and said that he did not think that there was any need to change the arrangements for the communications system. One problem is that the system cannot distinguish between friend and foe. Does not the Minister think that that makes it worth altering?

Mr. Neubert: I think that the hon. Gentleman is on another point. It might be better for him and the House if I moved on to my next subject, which is training.

To maintain the level of professionalism that we have all come to expect from the British Army it is necessary that training is as effective and realistic as possible; exercises are vital in that respect. In 1988 Exercise Iron Hammer, which took place in Lower Saxony, involved 3 Armoured Division together with some 3,300 regular and Territorial Army personnel from the United Kingdom.

In the United Kingdom there was a series of military home defence exercises in the autumn. These tested our preparation to defend ports, airfields and other facilities, essential to our ability to sustaining war on the continental mainland, and the exercises involved not only Regulars from all three services, but Regular reserves, the TA and the Home Service Force.

In the United Kingdom, the Army needs large areas of land for training. We are determined to ensure that the size of the defence estate is kept to the minimum necessary to support the armed forces and, where possible, we take steps to rationalise our holdings and to dispose of land that is no longer essential to our purposes. Nevertheless, our current holdings cannot satisfy fully the training needs

[*Mr. Neubert*]

of the Army and we must continue to acquire additional land for training, usually by extending existing training areas.

Why do we need the land? All soldiers require the use of small arms ranges and local training areas within easy reach of their barracks, and large areas of land are needed for exercising whole units or groups of units. Modern weapons require larger danger areas than before to accommodate their greater range and power and new tactics for increasingly mobile units demand wider areas of land over which to conduct realistic manoeuvres.

We are assessing carefully the scope for using computer weapon simulation techniques but, although the introduction of weapon simulators can help to develop individual military skills and reduce some of the pressures on training land, they can never replace the need for training in the field in conditions resembling those that might be encountered in war. Moreover, simulators do not remove the need for soldiers to handle and fire the real weapons that they would use in battle.

In his opening speech, my hon. Friend described the positive response that the Army was making to the challenge posed by the demographic trough—a recurring theme of today's debate. I make no apology, therefore, for returning to the subject. The Army is by far the most manpower-intensive of the three services, employing roughly as many as the other two put together. The message that I should like to leave with the House— especially my hon. Friend the Member for Hampshire, East (Mr. Mates)—is that we are not planning to fail. We need to ensure that resources are deployed to maximum efficiency in order to meet the manpower challenges of the next decade and beyond.

In deference to my hon. Friend the Member for Plymouth Drake (Dame J. Fookes) perhaps I should add the word "womanpower". We take seriously the wider role of women in the armed forces. We noted my hon. Friend's reference to women being assigned to combat roles in the Church of England. Being Conservatives on this as on other matters, we hope that that was not her bid for a bishopric—although, if it came to it, I think that she would make a very good bishop.

Pay and conditions of service play a vital part in ensuring that sufficient manpower of the right quality can be recruited and retained. The Government accepted in full the recommendations of the Armed Forces Pay Review Body both in 1988 and 1989. We also announced during last year major changes to the allowances paid to members of the armed forces, designed to ensure that they are up to date, cost effective and appropriate to the needs of service life. The policy is to encourage accompanied service, and the package of allowances, of which I will say more in a moment, reflects that policy.

Turbulence is an inescapable feature of army life. But this can on occasion conflict with family responsibilities. In an era when so many women, including Army wives, quite rightly expect to pursue careers of their own, there can be difficulties. We have devoted quite a lot of time recently to thinking how we can accommodate this change in expectations.

That brings me to the major topic of housing that was mentioned by so many of my hon. Friends, and in particular by my hon. Friend the Member for Canterbury (Mr. Brazier) who has made it very much his personal campaign.

Difficult choices can arise for the individual who will naturally want his family with him but who will also, like his civilian counterpart, want to become a home owner. We recognised these difficulties in last year's review of armed forces allowances when we introduced the home owner's relocation package.

Under these arrangements, a service man living in his own house who decides to move home when posted to a new station some distance away is reimbursed the cost of estate agent's and legal fees up to a maximum, at present, of £2,500. In addition, he will be entitled to removal at public expense and to receive disturbance allowance. Equally, those who prefer not to relocate their home but elect to let their houses and move into married quarters are entitled to financial help with the costs of tenancy arrangements. These changes represent significant improvements to the conditions of service of the service man and woman.

We also offer surplus married quarters for sale to service men at a 30 per cent. discount. This has proved popular and since the scheme's inception in 1983, nearly 2,000 married quarters have been sold under these arrangements and a further 440 sales are in the pipeline. Clearly there is a finite number of surplus married quarters that can become available but we shall continue as long as possible to identify and release surplus quarters for disposal in this way.

The Army has also been considering other ways in which it can assist its personnel to enter the housing market. At the beginning of the year, we launched the buy, let and settle options which have been developed by private companies in conjunction with the Army and are designed to meet the specific needs of Army personnel. Under these schemes, service men will be offered a comprehensive package which will include help with finding a suitable property arranging mortgages and, when appropriate, making arrangements for property management and tenancy agreements. While these schemes do not necessarily meet everyone's requirements, they do, nevertheless, offer a useful and welcome service, particularly to the service man stationed abroad.

We have also been giving serious consideration to the establishment of a scheme to house ex-service men through the medium of housing associations in order to address the difficulties arising from the contraction of council housing stock to which reference has been made. We are currently looking at two sites in the south of England which might be suitable for a trial scheme, and are obtaining external advice on how such a trial might be taken forward.

My hon. Friend the Member for Canterbury and others have made suggestions as to how the current position might be improved. As my hon. Friend said, we have had discussions with him. My right hon. Friend the Secretary of State has played an enthusiastic part in those discussions and we have been considering a number of different measures. We are attracted to a scheme in which service men, who are not home owners because of the mobility required of them by their service career, might benefit from a saving scheme linked to the eventual purchase of a property. But there are a number of detailed considerations and a great deal of work to be undertaken before a scheme of this kind can be established.

From what I have said, I hope the House will agree that there is a considerable degree of assistance already provided to assist Army personnel with their housing requirements. We shall continue to examine ways in which we can provide further assistance in this area.

Mr. Dalyell: Will the Minister write to those hon. Members whose comments he has not answered?

Mr. Neubert: Of course, I shall hope to write to all hon. Members whose points have not been answered in my closing speech.

I shall return to the theme of recruitment and retention, which has played such an important part in the debate, and talk about the Army career. With the clock ticking against me, I can only allow myself the very shortest time in which to do this. I would say, however, and I am sure that I would be joined in this by all hon. Members, that life in the Army remains a fine career. We commend it to young men and women now and through the 1990s.

It being Ten o'clock, the motion for the Adjournment of the House lapsed, without Question put.

Abortion (Carlisle Baby Case)

Motion made and Question proposed, That this House do now adjourn.—[*Mr. Heathcoat-Amory.*]

10.6 pm

Miss Ann Widdecombe (Maidstone): I am most grateful for the opportunity to raise this issue tonight. I thank you, Mr. Speaker, for selecting this debate on the topic of the Carlisle baby. The case has been raised in questions to various Ministers and also as part of the general abortion debate, but it raises so many issues of national importance, affecting all regional and district health authorities and hospitals where abortions are carried out, that it really deserves a debate of its own.

I have given my hon. Friend the Minister notice of the principal questions that I intend to raise in the hope that many of those hitherto unanswered questions will be answered, and that certain things that went on in Carlisle will finally come out into the light of day.

In raising the issue, I have confined myself to the material contained in affidavits, sworn properly before a solicitor, information given to the priest, the chaplain of Carlisle city general hospital, and certain press coverage that has gone unchallenged.

Nevertheless, I recognise that not all hon. Members share my concern about the events in Carlisle in July 1987. I offered my hon. Friend the Member for Berkshire, East (Mr. MacKay), who I know to be entirely honourable and who would therefore have confined his time appropriately, the opportunity, if he wished, to intervene in the debate, but, alack, this place is as empty of himself as the arguments of the pro-abortionists on the subject are of reason and merit.

In summary, on 21 July 1987, a woman was admitted to Carlisle city general hospital, 21 weeks pregnant, for an abortion. No injection was used to ensure that the child would be born dead, and the method used was the prostaglandin method. In the event, the child was born alive. She lived for three hours, during the course of which she was baptised by one of the nurses. She was left gasping on a kidney dish. No ventilation or incubation equipment was available. Two nurses were left to cope with the situation alone without proper supervision. When the child died, no death certificate was issued, and no birth certificate has ever been issued.

The mother did not find out for six months that the child had lived. When eventually the facts came to light, through the good offices of a Catholic priest, a police file was prepared on the case that led the coroner in Carlisle to recommend that it was in the public interest that an inquest should be held. Normally it is routine that an inquest would follow, but on this occasion it did not.

The case raises a large number of questions, both about the compliance of our hospitals—in the NHS and the private licensed clinics—with the Infant Life (Preservation) Act 1929 and about the conduct of late abortions in general.

The 1929 Act states:

"any person who, with intent to destroy the life of a child capable of being born alive, by any wilful act causes a child to die before it has an existence independent of the mother, shall be guilty of . . . child destruction".

That is any child capable of being born alive—and the Carlisle baby was born alive.

That same Act states that at 28 weeks there

"shall be prima facie proof"

[*Miss Ann Widdecombe*]

that the child will be capable of being born alive. It does not say "before 28 weeks there is no proof". It simply gives absolute protection after 28 weeks. If anyone has reason to assume that a child before that time is capable of being born alive, to procure its death is an act of child destruction. That is made very clear under the 1929 Act, and it is clear in the Abortion Act 1967 that nothing in it negates the provisions of the 1929 Act.

We are faced with a very strange situation. A piece of law states that it is child destruction to kill a child before it has an independent existence from its mother if it is capable of being born alive. Yet widely practised in the private clinics is the diabolical method of D and E in which the child is dismembered alive, without anaesthetic, in the womb. Is my hon. Friend the Minister really satisfied that our NHS hospitals and the private clinics that he must license are complying with the law? In the NHS hospitals, where that diabolical method is not practised, an injection of urea or saline is given to a child before abortion by the prostaglandin method. How does ensuring that the child is born dead possibly comply with the 1929 Act? As we now know that children can survive independently of the mother as early as 24 and possibly 23 weeks, what possible reason can there be for allowing any abortions after those weeks if the 1929 Act is to be complied with? That has been generally recognised.

We have another complaint, because not only is it permissible to kill those children in hospitals, despite the 1929 Act, but, just to make a sop in the direction of complying with the Act, there is a set of regulations. They were enunciated by the then Secretary of State, Mrs Barbara Castle, on 21 October 1975, when she said:

"In the National Health Service the Select Committee's recommendation that terminations after the twentieth week of pregnancy"—

the Carlisle baby was 21 weeks—

"should be carried out only in hospitals possessing appropriate facilities, including resuscitation equipment, have been accepted, and discussions have been held with regional medical officers who will be responsible for the implementation of the recommendations."—[*Official Report*, 21 October 1975; Vol. 898, c. 245.]

Furthermore, in approving private clinics the Secretary of State demands that they have ventilation and incubation if they are to carry out terminations after the 20th week; demands that there should be staff instructed in their use and available to use them; demands that arrangements be made for the child to be taken to the nearest special baby care unit. I am sure that we do not expect less from the NHS than we expect from the private sector. I ask my hon. Friend the Minister whether at any time the East Cumbria health authority gave notice to him, or to any of his predecessors, that it could not comply with the conditions set out in 1975 and re-enacted ever since.

Was my hon. Friend under the impression that Carlisle city general hospital could comply with those regulations? If he was not, what steps has he taken to ensure that other hospitals, in other areas, that have not had the horror of this case and therefore have not come to public notice, can comply with those simple provisions about ventilation, incubation and trained staff?

Why were two nurses left unsupervised? Why were no instructions given by the consultant who had authorised and, indeed, started the abortion? Why was their only telephone contact with a junior doctor who was on duty that night? What was done by senior medical staff in Carlisle city general hospital that night? Is all that normal procedure at Carlisle? Is it normal for nurses to be left unsupervised to cope with very complicated and unexpected cases? If so, is that also done elsewhere? Is my hon. Friend aware that the junior doctor on duty that night did not wish to participate in abortions? Wherefore the workings of the conscience clause?

I come now to the cruellest point of all. It appears that the diagnosis was possibly wrong. The abortion was carried out under section 1(1)*(b)* of the 1967 Act, which states that abortion is permissible where

"there is a substantial risk that if the child were born it would suffer from such physical or mental abnormalities as to be seriously handicapped."

In this case the diagnosis was that the father had a mild form—and it was mild—of Ehlers Danlos syndrome, which the child in turn had only a 50 per cent. chance of inheriting and which ranges from a very minor disability to being quite serious in some forms. Can that be described as a substantial risk? If the Minister had to take a bet on such odds, would he think it likely that the odds were in favour of the child coming out handicapped? No proper analysis was made of whether that diagnosis was right or wrong.

We come to the aftermath of the Carlisle case and to what I can only describe as a massive cover-up. There was a police investigation and a recommendation for an inquest. It is not my hon. Friend's responsibility to approve inquests, but may I ask him to say in how many other instances of death in an NHS hospital where a coroner has recommended an inquest has that recommendation been turned down? How often does that happen?

Is there or is there not a law which says that live births shall be registered? Why was the Carlisle baby not registered? Why, when it had lived for three hours— wanted, normal and baptised—was there no death certificate? Why was the mother not offered the option of a funeral, which is offered even in the case of stillborn babies, let alone those who have lived? Why was not the mother told of the true situation for six months? Why was it left to a priest to bring the matter into the light of day, and why was the priest's contract not renewed? Is it true, as the nurses have stated, that their union advised them to keep quiet and not to take any legal action?

Will the Minister admit that a thorough overhaul of procedures is needed and that what happened in Carlisle that night brings credit to nobody and that the regional health authority must answer properly for its implementation of the ventilation and incubation requirements? Will he also agree, chillingly, that there was a similar case in 1983, alas not the subject of so much publicity?

When that little light was extinguished in Carlisle, a great darkness fell on the NHS, on its civilisation and on its compliance with basic law. Does the Minister agree that for a live, wanted, normal, baptised child to live for three hours on a kidney dish—not even in a warm cot and not in its mother's arms—not in an incubator but on a kidney dish, is a disgrace? Will he join me in regretting that the case was not resolved in the light of day?

I now make a statement of fact and I do not make it threateningly. I have not tonight named any of the staff involved, the chairman of the regional health authority, the hospital administrator or anybody else, not even under privilege, but if a similar case occurs again in any part of the country a considerable body of parliamentary opinion will insist that that case is solved in the light of day, even if it means coming up with names and personal identities in the House.

I summarise my questions to the Minister and I would like him to answer all of them. I hope that I have left him sufficient time in which to do that. How does killing a child before birth tie in with the Infant Life (Preservation) Act 1929? What is the point of insisting that ventilation equipment shall be available if the child is allowed to be killed? Will the Minister consider outlawing completely the barbaric D and E method? Does he expect the NHS to match the standards that he lays down for private hospitals? Did East Cumbria ever indicate that it could not comply with the regulations and, if not, why was ventilation not available that night? Why were two nurses left alone unsupervised? In how many other instances of death on NHS premises has a recommended inquest been refused? Why was there no birth certificate? Why was there no death certificate?

Does the Minister agree that there was a cover-up and, if he does, what disciplinary action was taken, and if none was taken, what steps will be taken to ensure that this never occurs again? Why was the mother not told for six months that the child had lived? Why was the priest's contract not renewed? Is the Minister satisfied that the abortion complied with section 4 of the 1967 Act, and does he agree that that section is widely abused and that this is only one instance of it? What steps has he taken to revise the regulations or to re-emphasise them, in the light of the Carlisle case, to all regional health authorities? Why was there no option of a funeral?

I hope that the Minister will answer those questions. They all need answering. If they are not answered, this issue will be properly raised again in the House.

10.10 pm

Mr. Ken Hargreaves (Hyndburn): I am grateful to my hon. Friend the Member for Maidstone (Miss Widdecombe) for allowing me to make a brief contribution to the debate. We should be grateful to her for raising this important case and to the Minister for being here for the Adjournment debate this evening. I believe he has replied to every Adjournment debate this week, and I am grateful to him.

The Carlisle baby case is disturbing, as the facts outlined by my hon. Friend the Member for Maidstone have brought home to us. On Tuesday, the Under-Secretary of State for Health said:

"The Abortion Act has to be read alongside the Infant Life (Preservation) Act 1929, whose basic purpose is to protect the life of the unborn child, except where termination of pregnancy is necessary to save the life of the mother."—[*Official Report,* 6 June 1989; Vol. 154, c. 206.]

That did not happen in this case. There was no protection for the child under the Infant Life (Preservation) Act. It was not only capable of being born alive, but was actually born alive. There is no doubt about that. However, there was no prosecution, and not even an inquest.

Nobody comes out of the case well. The hospital authorities, the Home Office, and the health authority do not. The Church does not because it could have done more to ensure that the chaplain was reinstated. Many people have a lot to answer for. We intend to continue to press this case until we have satisfactory answers.

10.12 pm

Mr. David Amess (Basildon): I entirely endorse the comments of my hon. Friend the Member for Maidstone (Miss Widdecombe) and I admire her tenacity on this issue and all her supportive remarks about abortion.

In December, I and a number of colleagues raised, at Home Office questions, the Carlisle baby case and my hon. Friend the Under-Secretary for the Home Department was frank in his replies. He said:

"There has been only one conviction for child destruction in the past ten years."

He continued:

"There is quite clear and compelling evidence that the rebuttable presumption should arise not at 28 weeks but at 24 weeks,"—[*Official Report,* 15 December 1988, Vol. 143; c. 1074.]

I recently asked my hon. Friend the Minister a number of questions about abortion and I shall not detain the House with his answers today. He was frank and the number of late abortions carried out make one sad, particularly the fact that an abortion was carried out on a 10-year-old.

In an Adjournment debate in 1986, I raised the issue of abortions in private clinics. I am not happy with the procedures carried out. I do not expect my hon. Friend to respond tonight, but I hope that in due course he will write to tell me what advice his officials give to private clinics.

Is it a wonder that we face social problems and that life has become cheap when the number of abortions carried out in the United Kingdom is so high? I certainly hope, as would the majority of hon. Members, that well within the lifetime of this Parliament we shall have a clear opportunity to vote on the stage at which abortions can be carried out in this country. I very much hope that we shall vote to reduce the legal limit and that the Infant Life (Preservation) Act will no longer be the nonsense which it so clearly is today.

10.19 pm

The Parliamentary Under-Secretary of State for Health (Mr. Roger Freeman): My hon. Friend the Member for Maidstone (Miss Widdecombe) was fortunate to secure this Adjournment debate tonight. I think that she described the case as distressing and sad, and I agree with her. Her contribution to the debate and those of my hon. Friends the Members for Hyndburn (Mr. Hargreaves) and for Basildon (Mr. Amess) were illuminating and important.

In the 11 minutes left I can answer but a few of the points raised, but I shall study the reports of this debate. My hon. Friend raised a number of issues and was kind enough to give me an outline of the points that she intended to raise. I hope that she will bear with me and accept an answer in correspondence to many of the points that she raised. Likewise, I shall write to my other hon. Friends.

The debate has centred on the Carlisle baby case—a termination of pregnancy on grounds of likely serious physical handicap which took place in Carlisle hospital in July 1987. I am anxious to demonstrate to the House that this case has been closely examined by the health authority and by the Department of Health, and also, as regards the matter of an inquest, by the Home Office. But in doing this I have to bear in mind two different matters. The first is that of patient confidentiality. Termination of pregnancy is for the women concerned inevitably stressful and it is

[*Mr. Roger Freeman*]

therefore clearly important that the usual standards of confidentiality should be adhered to with particular rigour. The second is the question of possible legal proceedings on behalf of the women. I am advised that this question is still outstanding and I have therefore to bear this closely in mind in what I say briefly tonight.

When the various concerns about the case became apparent the East Cumbria health authority set up an internal committee of inquiry which included an independent gynaecologist, and produced conclusions and recommendations. The committee concluded that the termination of pregnancy was properly performed within the requirements of the Abortion Act but that there was some disregard of the patient's right to confidentiality and lapses in communication at and after the event. Its report, which identifies the staff involved and gives details about the patient's circumstances, is confidential. In the light of the committee's findings and recommendations the authority has tightened its procedures in various ways to ensure that they are in line with best practices. Written guidance to both medical and nursing staff has been strengthened and staff have been reminded that all information relating to patients must be kept confidential.

My hon. Friend asked first about resuscitation equipment and the 1975 Select Committee report. The Committee's recommendation that termination after the twentieth week of pregnancy should be carried out only in hospitals possessing appropriate facilities was accepted and in the NHS responsibility for its implementation has been the responsibility of regional medical officers. The Committee's recommendation was discussed with RMOs in September 1975. They said that there would be no difficulty in implementing the recommendation.

In March 1983 RMOs were reminded that the Department wanted to ensure that all NHS gynaecological staff who undertook late abortions were aware of the requirement that resuscitation equipment should be available. The RMOs felt that this requirement was sufficiently well known and observed by NHS consultant gynaecologists, and saw no need for the Department to issue particular guidance on the subject. In the Carlisle baby case the position is that if a decision had been made by the doctor concerned to resuscitate the foetus the necessary equipment was available on site and would have been on the scene within a matter of a very few minutes.

My hon. Friend asked about the Infant Life (Preservation) Act 1929 which makes it an offence to destroy the life of a child which is capable of being born alive. In any particular case it is a matter for the clinical judgment of the individual doctor whether a foetus, at any age, is capable of being born alive. Doctors are properly mindful of the requirements of the Act and do not carry out an abortion, by any method, when they consider that a child is capable of being born alive. As for the method used to perform an abortion, that too is a matter for the clinical judgment of the doctor involved having regard to all the circumstances of the particular case.

I am sure that my hon. Friend will agree that we should not put ourselves in the position of clinicians, making a judgment about whether a child is capable of being born alive. It is for the courts to make a determination given the circumstances of a particular case and I would not wish to go further than that.

My hon. Friend asked about the supervision by the nursing staff and specifically about the nursing staff present at the termination. They were not alone and they were not unsupervised. Two nurses were caring for the woman under the supervision of a sister. The doctor was called on delivery and attended quickly. He decided not to attempt to resuscitate the foetus and informed nursing staff to that effect. That was entirely a matter for his clinical judgment.

The question of deaths on National Health Service premises where a recommendation for an inquest is turned down, is a matter for my right hon. Friend the Home Secretary and I will see that my hon. Friend's comments are brought to his attention.

My hon. Friend asked me why the baby's birth was not registered. The Births and Deaths Registration Act 1953 requires that any child born alive shall be registered and if the child subsequently dies the death also falls to be registered. Where more than 12 months have transpired since a birth or a death the registrar general's authority is required for the registration. In considering any such application for registration after 12 months the registrar general needs to be satisfied that a registerable live birth or death has occurred. I understand that no such application has been made in this case.

My hon. Friend asked why the mother was not told for six months that the baby had lived. The doctor made a clinical judgment that this was not a live birth. In the circumstances staff decided to say nothing to the mother after the doctor made his decision.

My hon. Friend asked about policy on burial arrangements. At the time to which these events refer it was the health authority's general policy to offer ordinary burial for stillbirths but not for terminations of pregnancy. This policy has now been extended to cover situations in which the foetus is over 20 weeks' gestation and guidelines have been issued to staff that burial of the foetus should be offered to the mother in these circumstances.

As regards the incineration of the foetus, this was the health authority's normal practice at the time, but, as I have already said, the procedure has now been changed. In cases over 20 weeks' gestation the foetus is now retained for 48 hours to allow for a request for burial.

My hon. Friend asked about the priest's contract. As she knows, the Department of Health does not intervene in the decisions of statutorily independent health authorities as they relate to questions of employment of individuals, and it would not therefore be appropriate for me to comment.

My hon. Friend asks for an assurance that the lessons from the Carlisle baby case will be learned. It is clear that this was in many ways an exceptional case. It attracted considerable publicity and has been closely studied in the Department, culminating in correspondence between the Minister for Health and the chairman of the authority, who assured us that the lessons of this very sad episode have been fully learned. The Department will also take close account of this case in its future administration of the Abortion Act 1967.

My hon. Friend implied that the diagnosis of handicap in this case was wrong. This is a misunderstanding of the position under the Abortion Act 1967. The Act requires that in cases such as this doctors should give an opinion, in good faith, that there is a substantial risk that if the child were born it would suffer from such physical or mental abnormalities as to be seriously handicapped. This is a matter of clinical judgment and I have no reason to believe that the Abortion Act is not being properly observed on that point.

I have gone into some detail, as far as the requirements of confidentiality and possible legal action allow, about the facts of the particular case which has given rise to concern. I hope that hon. Members will accept my assurances and those of the Minister for Health, who has also looked into this matter, and of the Home Office that this case has in its various aspects been closely studied. On the general question of late abortions, my Department will continue to ensure that the law and practice on this extremely difficult subject are administered as closely as possible. This is of course entirely without prejudice to any changes in the law on abortion which Parliament may see fit to adopt in the future and which it would not be right for me to discuss in any detail in this Adjournment Debate. I am, however, grateful to my hon. Friend for giving me the opportunity to set out the position.

On the general question of abortions, let alone late abortions, it has of course been long-standing practice in the House for Members to be able to express their own personal views on this issue. As regards that general policy, the Government have been consistent and, like my hon. Friend, I find this case extremely distressing and sad. Whatever my own personal feelings, I see it as my duty tonight and in future correspondence with my hon. Friend to answer the facts of the case so as better to inform not only my hon. Friend but all hon. Members. In answering those questions of fact, one's own personal views or opinions concerning the issues that have been raised are in no way implied.

I undertake to write at length and to answer as comprehensively as possible the points raised by my hon. Friend.

Miss Widdecombe: With the leave of the House, Mr. Speaker, may I thank my hon. Friend for his very comprehensive reply to a long series of questions? I am grateful to him. Throughout his reply ran the theme that a live child does not have rights so long as it is the product of an abortion. To take the burial question, it was a live child; it should have been registered; it should have had a death certificate. Merely because it was the product of an abortion does not mean that it had fewer rights than a child born prematurely.

Question put and agreed to.

Adjourned accordingly at half-past Ten o'clock.

House of Commons

The House met at half-past Nine o'clock

PRAYERS

[MR. SPEAKER *in the Chair*]

BILL PRESENTED

ITINERANTS (CONTROL)

Miss Ann Widdecombe presented a Bill to make stop notices applicable to caravans: And the same was read the First time; and ordered to be read a Second time upon Friday 23 June and to be printed. [Bill 152.]

Drug Abuse

9.34 am

Mr. Chris Butler (Warrington, South): I beg to move,

That this House commends the Government for the high priority it gives to the problem of the misuse of drugs; calls for sustained and properly co-ordinated attempts to reduce supplies of such drugs from abroad, for the maintenance of effective deterrents to drug abuse and of effective controls on availability, and for a developing and monitored programme of prevention and education to minimise potential demand; and calls urgent attention to the problem of intravenous drug abuse aggravating the risk that AIDS presents to the population of the United Kingdom.

The founder of the Royal College of Physicians, Thomas Sydenham, said:

"Bless the Lord for giving opium to the human race."

Three hundred years on, a recent opinion poll shows that the British public believe that narcotic drugs are the greatest threat facing the United Kingdom. It is often said that where the United States leads, we follow some years later. The scale of the problem in the United States is truly immense.

There are reckoned to be 38 million illicit drug users in the United States. There are 12 million regular users of cocaine, to the extent that it is now believed that the cocaine market in North America is saturated. Prices are falling there and there is wide availability, despite the fact that 127 tonnes of cocaine were seized by the United States authorities. There are 18 million regular users of marijuana in the United States and 500,000 heroin addicts. This causes immense cost to United States society in terms in crime, policing, the judicial system and medical treatment amounting, it is estimated, to $54 billion a year.

The drug policy review group in this country believes that the equivalent United Kingdom costs annually are £3·8 billion. If we were even to begin to reach United States levels, that figure could easily be doubled. We have not yet begun even to register the costs of crack, which are already inflicting tremendous wounds on United States society, although it has already arrived here, as the recent riots in Wolverhampton showed. The word on the streets in Warrington, my constituency, is that crack is available in the night clubs there, as are many other drugs. Many people travel quite a long way to get their drugs from the Warrington night club scene.

In the first half of the 1980s, new addicts increased at the rate of 25 per cent. a year, so that by 1988 the total number of known addicts was five times that in 1978. In 1986, notifications of new addicts fell, but they rose again in 1988. It is estimated that notification underestimates the total number of addicts by between 5 and 20 times. In 1988, 270 kg of heroin were seized, but it is estimated that only 10 to 15 per cent. of all drugs reaching the population are stopped by such seizures. In 1988, too, 300 kg of cocaine were seized, but the police say that very large quantities of cocaine are reaching our shores.

There were no increases in notifications of cocaine addicts in 1988, but the police and other agencies report widespread availability. That will reflect itself in future notifications of addicts. The police believe that cocaine is the major threat facing this country in the coming years. In some areas, it is already cheaper than heroin.

The Advisory Council on the Misuse of Drugs estimates that there are between 75,000 and 150,000 opiate users in the United Kingdom. There is a similar number —between 75,000 and 150,000—of non-opiate users. That

[*Mr. Chris Butler*]

excludes cannabis. If we were to take the worst scenario —a total of 300,000 regular uses—that would fill our gaols six times over.

The problem is clearly out of hand. It is true to say that we are now staring down the barrel of the gun. Some people write off the drug problem as the problem of "Sin City"—London—or they write it off merely as a problem that affects a section of our society: hippie dinosaurs, perhaps, or the champagne set, or ethnic minorities. It is true that London accounts for some two thirds of the problem, but it is truly now a national problem. There is hardly a city, town or hamlet that is not affected in some way.

The problem is certainly not confined to one section of the community; it affects all social classes. Drug abuse has exploded, and with it crime, as many must finance their habit by dealing in drugs and prostitution. The contribution that that makes to the crime wave is commonly underestimated: Home Office research in 1983 suggested that in the Wirral 15 per cent. of burglars were notified addicts, and further research in 1985 suggested that about 50 per cent. of all burglars in the area were drug misusers. If that is multiplied to give a nationwide figure, the result is truly staggering. I wonder whether the crime wave of recent years could be correlated with the increase in drug abuse. Dr. Tim Harding of the university of Geneva reckons that between 25 and 30 per cent. of all prisoners have been opiate users.

It seems at times a hopeless battle, and there are those who wish to void the field. Some extreme libertarians believe in decriminalisation, feeling that people should be allowed to go to hell in their own way. That, however, ignores the extreme social cost that would accompany even decriminalisation. Families are certainly affected by addicts who are hooked into their habit.

Highly intelligent and respected drug experts also believe in decriminalisation, feeling that the costs of the present regime are so high that it is the only answer. In their view prohibition has failed, as it was doomed to fail, and indeed has aggravated the problem by opening the doors to gangsterism. They cite Amsterdam as an example of a good liberal approach. In that city, possession of cannabis is no longer an offence: it can be freely bought in cafes with a cannabis leaf in the window.

Decriminalisation is not the answer; Amsterdam is not paradise. In fact, drugs have made it a rather seedy and sleazy city. At best, decriminalisation would lead to greater availability of drugs, and—as the Advisory Council on the Misuse of Drugs has pointed out— increased availability would tend to lead to increased chances for others to be dragged into the habit. At worst decriminalisation would lead to large conglomerates getting in on the scene—as has happened with tobacco and alcohol—and promoting it, subtly and not so subtly. I believe that decriminalisation is a policy of despair.

Mr. Stuart Randall (Kingston upon Hull, West): I have been listening carefully to the hon. Gentleman and I agree that the dangers to which he referred exist. Does he not recognise, however, that in this country only about 10 per cent. of addicts are known by the helping agencies, whereas in Holland the figure is about 75 per cent? Does he not agree that, although decriminalisation has many negative aspects, the other side of the coin would be that massive benefit, which would be a major factor is stamping out drug-taking?

Mr. Butler: If the hon. Gentleman will bear with me as I develop my argument, I think that he will see the same way out of the maze as I do.

Until 1960 the policy of controlled availability left us free of the problems faced by the United States. Since the 1920s alcohol and drugs had been strictly prohibited there, and although the prohibition of alcohol collapsed amidst a sea of gangsterism, drug prohibition continues with the result that gangsterism flourishes and 5,000 new heroin users are accumulated every day.

In 1960, the Brain committee said that in the United Kingdom everything was all right—certainly in comparison with the horrors of the position in the United States. The market was effectively undercut by the official supply, and in the 1950s and 1960s, certainly, there were some 500 addicts among a population of about 50 million. The small number of addicts were maintained on unadulterated drugs, and there were few crimes associated with them.

What went wrong? In the early 1960s a large number of north Americans came to this country and exploited some unscrupulous GPs, who prescribed drugs in considerable amounts. Sizeable profits were made by both the doctors and the north Americans engaging in their transatlantic trade. The result was the Dangerous Drugs Act 1967, and the setting up of a number of licensed clinics around the country to replace the GPs. There were too few, however, and it was difficult to recruit psychiatrists prepared to staff the centres and run the risk of encountering the problems of agression associated with drug addicts.

In effect, the clinics retreated from their target market. They became associated with bureaucracy, and with unreasonable attempts to wean addicts off their habit. We had begun to retrace our steps down the American path. The number of addicts rocketed, and in the United Kingdom it was open season for internationally organised crime.

The question I wish to raise, which is connected with the intervention by the hon. Member for Kingston upon Hull, West (Mr. Randall) is whether we can now return to the benefits of registration. We have accumulated some 20 years of damage, and we have a vastly greater problem on our hands. I believe that we can return to registration, and that in any event, the pressure of events is taking us there.

Merseyside has a high prevalence of drug abuse: a conservative estimate is that it contains about 15,000 regular heroin users, 40 per cent. of whom inject. A quarter of all 15 to 20-year-olds have tried illicit drugs, and one tenth of them are regular users. Merseyside strikes me as an excellent illustration of how to find the path back to the benefits of registration. Since the mid-1980s it has followed a policy of harm reduction, endorsed by the advisory council. That policy accepts that abstinence is not the only objective of treatment: to concentrate on abstinence is to exclude the large proportion of drug users who are committed to long-term abuse and who will not listen.

If drug abusers will not abstain, the next best step does not involve banishing them to the black market; it involves minimising the consequences to themselves, the community and society. For such a policy to be effective such services need to be accessible, confidential and—that awful term—"user friendly". AIDS prevention must take priority over drug prevention: those who will not abstain must be encouraged not to inject. If they refuse to do that, they must be encouraged not to share needles, and if they will not do that, they must be encouraged at least to use clean equipment.

The methods of the Merseyside policy include long-term maintenance on drugs, the provision of syringe exchanges, information about cleaning syringes, and even free supplies of condoms and associated material. It also involves a large team of outreach workers in the homosexual community, working among rent boys and prostitutes. Generally, the policy has begun to reach the addict population which until now has remained largely submerged.

Does the Merseyside policy work? There is evidence that it does. There has been a reduction in local crime around the centres that provide such services, and there is insignificant leakage of drugs from the clinics into the addict population at large. For six months the local police examined all arrested drug addicts and did not find one with clinic drugs to which he was not authorised. The Merseyside policy attracted an unreached population. At least 1,000 people became involved with the Liverpool exchange scheme and only one third of those people had previously been in contact with any drug service.

If drug equipment is not returned there are grave dangers of re-use and unauthorised disposal, but the Merseyside exchange scheme achieves a fair balance of exchange. There has been a general reduction in needle sharing, but I suppose the ultimate criterion is how far the HIV virus has spread in Merseyside. It is remarkable that the figures are extremely low there. In the Merseyside area only 14 drug addicts are HIV positive and they all acquired their infection from outside the area before 1985. Tests on 105 addicts and prostitutes known to have engaged in risky behaviour showed a 0 per cent. rate of HIV infection. There are no known cases of local infection with HIV from drug abuse.

The policy of outreach, maintenance and user friendliness begins to show us how we can return to the path of making registration work again. Under the threat of AIDS that will increasingly be the pattern. AIDS is a bigger threat to individual health and to the health of our society than drug abuse, but drug abuse involving the sharing of needles can spread the virus at a devastating speed. It spreads it first into the drug population at large and secondly into the heterosexual population.

In Thailand where there are very many herion addicts, three years ago HIV infection rates were 0 per cent. among drug addicts. Two years ago the rate was 1 per cent. and last year it was 50 per cent. That demonstrates the truly explosive spread that can result from needle sharing in a herion-taking community. Tourists contemplating going to Thailand for rest and recreation should think again.

In some parts of the United States up to 70 per cent. of addicts are now HIV positive. Fifty-three per cent. of all AIDS deaths in New York are of drug addicts and 50 per cent., that is 100,000 of New York's 200,000 drug abusers, are already HIV positive. The majority will go on to develop the disease and will die shortly afterwards. Nationally in the United States 30 per cent. of all drug users are estimated to be HIV positive. In the United Kingdom the 1986 equivalent figure was 10 per cent., but it will have increased since then. However, in Scotland the figure reaches up to 60 per cent. especially in the Lothian region. That has caused a heterosexual epidemic in

Scotland to the extent that in the Edinburgh region 1 per cent. of the heterosexual male population between the ages of 15 and 45 are now HIV positive.

What is worse is that many drug addicts turn to prostitution to finance their habit. In April 1988 of 35 women in Glasgow known to be HIV positive 26 were working as prostitutes. That is a violent focus of infection. Last year during the debate on the Criminal Justice Bill I argued that deliberate or knowing infection of another person with AIDS should be made a criminal offence. I believe that more strongly than ever. I realise that there is a problem in proving the case, but at least the law would be there as a deterrent as well as to be used. It is not only intravenous drug users who are at risk of AIDS. In 1987 a study of prostitution in New York showed seropositivity rates among crack users as great as the rate among heroin users and seropositivity rates among crack users in the Bahamas are similarly high.

Mr. Tony Baldry (Banbury): All the problems that my hon. Friend describes come together in a horrendous nightmare in the sort of hospital that I saw in Newark, New Jersey. That hospital contained complete wards of babies who were born with AIDS because their mothers were drug addicts who resorted to prostitution to pay for their drug addiction and became AIDS victims. That meant that children born of prostitute mothers were already suffering from AIDS. That is the spectre which awaits this country if we do not tackle the crack problem effectively and now.

Mr. Butler: I am grateful to my hon. Friend for filling out the generally bleak picture that I am painting. Fifty per cent. of all HIV positive mothers can expect to give birth to HIV positive children, and that is sad. In Africa about 50 per cent. of all people infected with HIV are young children.

Mr. Randall: The picture that the hon. Gentleman has just painted is very bleak, but does he not agree that a major problem in this country is getting people to come forward? Misusers do not come forward and until we get to grips with that we will fail to provide the crucial helping services.

Mr. Butler: I thought that to some extent I had dealt with that in terms of the outreach programmes in Merseyside where people do not just wait for addicts to come in but send workers out into the various risk communities to find the addicts and offer them services in a user friendly way. It is not only a matter of a carrot but of a stick and I shall shortly deal with that.

Mr. Randall: I think that the hon. Gentleman will agree that while the Merseyside approach is quite radical, it is not the approach across the country as a whole. The situation is patchy from area to area, and until we spread the notion that people must come forward and provide a safe environment in which people can do that we shall have problems. The prison population is a good example.

Mr. Butler: Once again the hon. Gentleman makes my point for me. I am not defending the Government, because I think that Britain has been going wrong in this field for more than 20 years. In many ways prisons are the key to the spread of HIV infection. Dr. Tim Harding who is the prison medical officer in Geneva prison and reader in legal medicine in Geneva has carried out a well-conducted study

[*Mr. Butler*]

of five European gaols. He estimates that one tenth of all prisoners in those gaols carry HIV. He carried out a study in France among 500 consecutive newcomers to Fresnes prison and found a 12·6 per cent. rate of HIV positivity. He says:

"In prisons considerable numbers of intravenous drug addicts, a high proportion of whom are probably AIDS carriers, can be expected to have occasional homosexual contacts . . . induced homosexual behavour provides a 'bridge' between a known high risk group of (intravenous drug abusers) and individuals who may later become a source of infection through heterosexual contacts"

Graham Medley from Imperial college London says that needle-sharing in British prisons produces between 33 and 344 AIDS infections in prison every year. Staff at Risley remand centre tell me of the extreme difficulty that they have in screening visitors and stopping them from bringing in drugs. They also have to engage in the very unpleasant business of cell searches looking for drugs and syringes. Sweden, which is a paragon of human rights, has solved the problem by daily screening of prisoners' urine. Will my hon. Friend the Minister consider such an experiment here? The current methods of control are certainly inadequate. I do not believe that the provision of condoms to prisoners is the answer. They have a high failure rate for such high-risk activities and may cause more damage than they are worth. Information is the only vaccine that we have, and it is especially important to the prison scene. Part of the vital information that is needed by the authorities and prisoners is prisoners' HIV status, by which they can base their behaviour in prison and outside afterwards.

I am talking about regular testing of the prison population. I know that the medical authorities are devising tests using saliva rather than blood, which might make testing easier. Some people would say that testing offends civil rights, but prisoners have already lost most of their civil rights by being in prison, and survival of society must begin to take precedence over individual rights, as it always has in the past when we have faced pandemics of this kind.

The nettle has been grasped elsewhere. Spain screened its prisoners and found an 18·7 per cent. HIV positivity rate. Parts of the Basque country and Catalonia found a 50 to 55 per cent. positivity rate. Bavaria began testing its prison population in 1985. By 1987, it had tested 97·3 per cent. of its prison population voluntarily, and found a 1·48 per cent. positivity rate. Sweden positively encourages testing of new prisoners. Italy positively encouraged testing of new prisoners and found a 16·8 per cent. positivity rate. Testing can be done without a cataclysm for human rights.

I should like my hon. Friend the Minister to say what progress has been made with anonymous testing in prisons, which was promised by the director of the prison medical services in November 1988. The danger is that if we do not grasp the nettle, prisons in the United Kingdom will become a major crossover point to the heterosexual population outside.

Enforcement is the stick that I mentioned to match the carrot. If we are to renew a drive back to making registration work, we shall have to be even tougher on many of the criminals who populate the drug world. We need the stick and the carrot to identify, isolate and control the problem. Merseyside's prescribing and general policy

is correct, but I am not so happy about its penal policy. Cheshire police are happy with the support that it receives from the courts, but when it engages in joint operations with Merseyside police both forces hope that the trial will be held in Cheshire because they believe that the Merseyside courts will be soft on pushers. A quarter of marijuana users in the Merseyside area are cautioned, whereas in Greater Manchester the rate is only 5 per cent. The possession of class A drugs can result in a seven-year prison sentence and an unlimited fine, but in May 1988 Merseyside police extended the possibility of a caution to those found in possession of heroin. It is no good taking a harsh public stance on drugs if the actuality is soft beneath. It sends out the wrong message to drug addicts and the population at large. It is not right that there should be differing standards of justice throughout the country. There should be uniform severity for pushers and uniform strictness for those who are found in possession and have not acquired drugs in the proper registered manner.

The Drug Trafficking Offences Act 1986 is a most valuable piece of legislation. It has enabled the police to track the devious spread of assets which drug traffickers insert into complex banking systems, but it takes up much police time. The police have managed to confiscate £8 million worth of assets, but that has cost them much money and I wonder whether there is a case for the police being able to reclaim the costs that they incur in confiscation. I am aware of the problem with hypothecation of revenue, but I suggest that there is a precedent because in the past the secret services have often flourished with the aid of confiscated assets that the Treasury has not nosed in on.

Another problem with that otherwise exellent Act is that the prosecution does not follow its spirit sufficiently. Prosecuting authorities demand that the police prove that assets of drug traffickers were acquired illegally. The Act placed a welcome burden on the defendant to prove that he had acquired his assets legally. I hope that my hon. Friend the Minister will lean on prosecuting authorities to make them observe the spirit of the Act.

The importation and distribution of drugs are not two separate issues. The relationship between the police and Customs is better, but it could be improved. Customs is a national organisation and the police are not, which in joint operations causes logistical difficulties. It is time that we had a national agency similar to the Federal Bureau of Investigation or the Drugs Enforcement Agency. I have always been an admirer of Elliot Ness and the "Untouchables". As we already have a national intelligence unit, it is time that we had a national operational unit, pooling the skills of police, Customs and the Home Office's drug branch. Such a group of "Untouchables" would form a national drugs directorate that would co-operate internationally with, perhaps, a European task force that relies on a European intelligence base. There has been much talk recently about integration with Europe. I do not agree with full integration yet, but such integration and co-operation would be sensible and not a symptom of "Bexleyism." International crime must be combated by an international effort.

I applaud the decision that the Government took in October 1983 to restrict parole for drug traffickers sentenced to more than five years' imprisonment because it gives the right message to pushers. Will my hon. Friend the Minister assure me that that restrictive policy will continue? We should not pursue the objective of a lower prison population and be lax with dealers in death and misery. Unfortunately, I disagree with my predecessor, Lord Carlisle. His Committee's report states that we should abandon this restrictive policy. The Committee believes that everyone should be entitled to parole after serving half of a four-year sentence or more. Now is not the time to be soft on drug dealers.

Many drug couriers and dealers imprisoned in Britain are foreign. Local review committees are tempted to deport them before they complete their sentence. The motivation is clear—to get rid of the scum and lessen the burden on the British taxpayer. Many couriers are sad cases who have been manipulated by more malign minds, but sympathy is the wrong attitude because they have often been picked to give that kind of aura. A premature return to their countries of origin would give the message that Britain is a soft touch. Certainly, the possible gains to people coming from Third world countries are immense if we do not make them aware of the potential risks.

I am glad that I concur with my predecessor on this point. He said:

"for the professional drug trafficker who has a large nest-egg hidden way in some foreign bank, a free ticket back home will not amount to much of a punishment compared with a few years in prison here."

I hope that my hon. Friend the Minister can ensure that the parole board will treat potential deportees in the same way as it treats other inmates of British gaols.

There is also the international aspect of enforcement. The United Kingdom co-operates in the United Nations commission on narcotic drugs and in the Pompidou group, and in that way there is international co-operation in reducing the availability of drugs. The Overseas Development Administration, the Foreign and Commonwealth Office and the Home Office spend millions of pounds a year on drug projects abroad, including crop eradication and crop substitution. No doubt, other hon. Members will wish to explore those international aspects more.

I am particularly concerned about the Caribbean basin. The Caribbean has become much afflicted with the problem, with money laundering and high increases in domestic addiction occurring. It has become a trafficking centre for north America and the consuming countries of Europe. We have a relationship with the dependent territories and Commonwealth countries there. We have a particular responsibility and influence there, too. We have given some assistance, through launches to the Turks and Caicos islands and the British Virgin Islands, and in 1988 we sponsored a Commonwealth drug law enforcement conference in Barbados, but we could do more. I know from personal experience that one can walk down the streets in the Bahamas and be regularly accosted and offered coke. That is a blot on the Caribbean basin. In some areas there is strong evidence of official complicity in the drug trade, to the extent that it raises questions about the governance of those islands. I know that some of these islands are our friends, but friendship implies frankness, and if they are unable to put their houses in order there may be temptation for some international action to be taken to do it for them.

Drug prevention through the medium of education is important. In America, drug-crazed schoolchildren in sink schools in inner cities often make shootings and rapes on stairwells almost unremarkable. There is a great problem of a drug-ridden, ruthless, amoral, often unparented

underclass, and it is making the Americans think hard about their social policy. In the United Kingdom, the number of heroin addicts under 21 is rising, but the school population of 6 million is, as yet, almost untainted by narcotics. I hope that cultural pressures and education will keep it that way.

The most important socialising force and force for good in this respect is the family. Families do get it wrong. Prison officers at Risley have told me of parents who bring in drugs for their children on remand. If the family breaks down, we will certainly lose a potential force for much good, because the family is the unit in which children realise that they have responsibilities to people other than themselves. The Conservative party is often said to be the party of the family, but, sadly, since 1979 the illegitimacy rate and the rate of cohabitation without marriage have doubled, which does not say much for the party of the family. Much can be done to reinforce the family as an economic unit and bring home to fathers the responsibilities of parenthood. That should be a major priority for political parties, and I believe that a prize will await those who realise it at the next general election.

Much good work is done in schools by bodies such as TAGADE. The life education centres of the Rev. Ted Noffs offer a promising line of bringing home to children the wonders of the workings of their bodies and giving them a positive feeling of self-respect for their health. The image of sparkling life is presented to them, compared with the automatic turn-off of grisly death and, perhaps, the turn-on of the forbidden. The media often fall into this trap. They often portray drugs as a symptom of the naughtiness of the champagne set, as adventures into the forbidden, or they portray crack as the coming thing for the "in" set. The reality is that drugs are used to bolster the self-esteem of those who take them. They are a grubby, dirty business and are taken by people who are inadequate. Drug taking should be presented as that. The media have a responsibility to evaluate their presentation just as much as the Government do, but I suppose that asking for self-regulation in the media these days is like crying in the wind.

The Government are feeling their way in their anti-drugs propaganda. They spent about £2 million on it last year. In 1987, they engaged in a campaign to persuade misusers not to inject and never to share. The preliminary results of research show that that campaign was ineffective and may even have been counter-productive. We now know that simplistic slogans for mass consumption, such as, "Just say no" or authoritarian approaches to schoolchildren are not the ways to do it. Many preconceived notions about campaigns of such promotions have had to be jettisoned in the light of research. It is vital that, if the Government engage in these promotional campaigns, they do the research to evaluate the effect. There is no point in spending millions of pounds if the result is fruitless or possibly harmful.

Clearly, prevention of drugs is better than cure, especially because a cure of drug addicts is rarely achieved. As with enforcement against crime in general, enforcement in this respect is late in the day. It is far better that children and young people learn from their families, schools and general culture that it is wise never to begin. The challenge is enormous, with some 300,000 regular users of drugs. I hope that we can rise to take the difficult decisions to meet it.

10.17 am

Mr. Tim Rathbone (Lewes): I am proud to be the first to congratulate my hon. Friend the Member for Warrington, South (Mr. Butler) on initiating this debate on what must be one of the most important problems—if not the most important—facing society, not just in this country but in the Western world. It is sad that the peculiarities of parliamentary procedure mean that these debates are likely to take place only on Friday mornings, when many hon. Members have constituency engagements or, at this time of year, compaigning engagements. Those who have gathered here are interested in this subject. I should like to embrace the views of my hon. Friend the Under-Secretary of State for the Home Department who leads the Government in chairing the inter-ministerial group on this subject.

I fear that I must make one political comment—the only one—and note the paucity of the Opposition's attendance. Apart from the necessary Front-Bench spokesman—the hon. Member for Kingston upon Hull, West (Mr. Randall), whom we are glad to see—there are no other members of the Labour party and no members of the Social Democrats, the Social and Liberal Democrats or the Ulster parties. Perhaps most noteworthy of all, there are no hon. Members from Scotland present. Part of the greatest problem we face in this country is, tragically, north of the border.

Mr. Randall: I want to place on record that apart from Front Bench Members, there are only six Conservative Members in the Chamber.

The Parliamentary Under-Secretary of State for the Home Department (Mr. Douglas Hogg): There are no Labour Members present on the Back Benches.

Mr. Rathbone: Statistics can be used to prove anything.

Mr. Hogg: There are seven Back-Bench Conservative Members present.

Mr. Rathbone: I believe that there is a miscount from my Front Bench.

The truth is that drug misuse is the most horrifying problem. I agree with everything that my hon. Friend the Member for Warrington, South said, with one proviso. He mentioned that AIDS was an even more pressing problem than drug abuse. I have to take the opposite point of view on that. Whatever the horrors of AIDS and whatever the greater likelihood of those who suffer from AIDS dying before their time compared to the likelihood of those who take drugs dying before their time—and statistics are not available to prove the matter one way or another—until we get to grips with the problem of drug misuse, we shall be incapable of getting to grips with at least the behavioural activities that lead to the spread of AIDS. AIDS is both a behavioural and a medical problem. With the marvellous innovative spirit that exists in the human race and the scientific knowledge which is discovered so swiftly nowadays, I hope sincerely that we shall see further developments in the study of AIDS which will lead to treatment for it. It is welcome news, which came out only in the past week, that at last the virus has been traced back to its source and that is, perhaps, the start for finding a treatment for it. I hope that my hon. Friend the Member for Warrington, South will take my criticism in good spirit, because it in no way negates the importance of this debate.

My hon. Friend the Member for Warrington, South raised two broad aspects of the problem—trafficking and demand reduction. I was privileged to attend a United Nations-sponsored parliamentary meeting in Vienna just two weeks ago. It was sponsored by the United Nations fund for drug abuse control—UNFDAC—and it was attended by representatives from Italy, including those representing the anti-Mafia commission of the Italian Parliament. It was also attended by representatives from the Federal Republic of Germany and by my hon. Friend the Member for Westminster, North (Mr. Wheeler) in his capacity as Chairman of the Select Committee on Home Affairs. I attended in my capacity as chairman of the all-party drug misuse group. The meeting concentrated on the aspect of trafficking. That is, of course, an aspect of drug misuse that falls very much in the international sphere. One of the points made, particularly by the Italian parliamentarians, was the way in which the crime syndicates have assumed such an immensely worrying international dimension because of their ability to penetrate all the most sensitive sectors of the political, economic and social structures of an ever greater number of countries.

That penetration is especially noticeable in south America. However frustrated we may be when looking at the problem from our side of the Atlantic and north of the equator, we should realise how much the problem still exists in the countries of south America. We should commend the immense job the people there do in trying to come to grips with that horrible domestic problem— horrible in every aspect. One cannot look lightly on the problem faced in Colombia, where 18 judges were killed last year, which at one terrorist stroke undercut society's ability to rule itself, and the inclination of judges, who are human beings like ourselves, to implement proper justice in the future. We should seek ways in which we can buoy up their ability to administer justice, as well as their ability to keep law and order.

I want to remind my hon. Friend the Parliamentary Under-Secretary of State for the Home Department that I was a little depressed on that score. When I questioned our right hon. Friend the Secretary of State for Defence about whether he had any plans for a meeting with his Colombian counterpart, he said that he had no plans to do so. That may be as a result of the exigencies of his diary and I hope it is no more than that. However we must not overlook ways in which we can help the enforcement of law and order by giving military advice and assistance, which is what is so often required, as well as political advice and aid in the work of drug misuse officers on the ground.

Mr. Randall: I would be grateful if the hon. Gentleman would give me some clarification. I was interested to hear what he said about buoying up the criminal justice system after the death of the 18 judges. Can he tell the House a little more about how he feels Britain, as an external country, can help to buoy up the criminal justice system in Colombia?

Mr. Rathbone: The hon. Gentleman anticipates what I was about to say. There are three areas in which we could buoy up the criminal justice system in Colombia. One way falls into the ambit of the United Nations. The completion of the United Nations convention on drug misuse and its adoption and ratification can be encouraged by this country. It will provide a yardstick or backdrop against which all other international and domestic activities can be measured and encouraged.

The second area is that of military assistance. The illegal growing, distillation and warehousing of those illegal products is carried out deep in the forests of huge countries in that under-populated continent. It is logistically and militarily an enormous effort to track down wrongdoers and to take action against them. What we would consider to be a police or Customs exercise in this country is a military exercise in Colombia. Military communications are important there. The drug barons who are earning, by the lowest estimates, about £50 billion a year from drugs trafficking—more than the gross national product of some south American countries—have the wherewithal to buy the best communications equipment as well as the best armaments. To get hold of the best communications equipment, they go to the best sources. We must match them with the equipment used by the authorities in those countries.

The traffickers have armaments with which to defend themselves, as they put it, or to push their illegal traffic in a terrorist way, as I would describe it. We must ensure that the powers of law and order in those countries have the necessary armaments. It comes down, in the end, to giving those countries sufficient hard currency, through trade, to buy those armaments, or at least to encouraging them to use loans and grants from international and national sources for the recruitment and training of internal forces of law and order.

Thirdly—and this was perhaps what prompted the question of the hon. Member for Kingston upon Hull, West as it is the most difficult aspect—we have a role to play in encouraging, and making it easier for, those countries to pass laws that can be properly applied. They need both adequate internal laws to help them to grapple with the problem and an international framework of laws in which the drug barons can be trapped. The British Government have taken the initiative and have struck bilateral agreements with several countries under which drug trafficking assets can be traced and confiscated and information exchanged. That is a marvellous illustration of the sort of bilateral action that can be taken.

We have enormous experience of constitutional affairs and we could help the countries to draft laws or amend their present laws so that they can be applied more easily. That was one of the matters that arose in our meetings with the German and Italian parliamentarians. The communiqué that all three participating countries agreed said that

"given the increasingly serious problems of a number of countries and the noted inadequacy of national and international measures adopted so far, is was essential to consider as a matter of urgency new initiatives, giving priority to the delicate areas of criminal investigation, the identifying of international drug traffickers and the bringing of such criminals to justice."

I pay tribute to British drug liaison officers. I know from my limited personal experience and from what I have heard that they do a terrific job. I shall not go into great detail: I shall certainly not identify the individual or countries concerned as many of those gentlemen live in fear of their lives. Both those from the police and from Customs and Excise do the most marvellous job, and they have perhaps done more to increase the entrapment of

drug traffickers and the capture of drugs being trafficked than any other single well-directed activity could have done.

Mr. Randall: I listened carefully to the hon. Gentleman's three points. Does he agree that because the revenues that can accrue from the production of drugs are so massive, there is a great incentive for certain Governments to do no more than pay lip service to their desire to rid their country of drugs? How can one square the wish to participate in efforts to get rid of drugs with the reduction of revenues which, to some of the poorer countries, are massive?

Mr. Rathbone: That is a tricky question, which was alluded to by my hon. Friend the Member for Warrington, South. My hon. Friend referred to the Caribbean basin, where evidence emerges all too often of direct links—not only national links, for the benefit of the national treasury but personal links for the benefit of personal treasuries —between drug traffickers and those who stand to gain from their activities.

Let me correct an insinuation that the hon. Member for Kingston upon Hull, West made. The moneys that the drug barons earn form at most a very small part of the gross national product of the countries concerned. It is true that traffickers may live in those countries and use some of the money that they gain, but in the main, the moneys are part of international funds that swill around the world—from one interest-bearing instrument in one country to another interest-bearing instrument in another. Most of the funds are not used in the homeland, as the traffickers do not have to use much of the money—the huge amounts—that they gain to maintain their factories and armies. A stage further down the line, the growing of drugs is of only marginal benefit to the national economy, although, compared with traditional vegetable crops, it can be of immense benefit to individual incomes. It is tragic that it is not the producers but the barons who benefit.

May I ask my hon. Friend the Parliamentary Under-Secretary of State for the Home Department whether the Government will continue their efforts to devise ways of improving international liaison by drug liaison officers and providing an international base for their work? A British drug liaison officer in a particular country or city should be in a good position to do work for the German or French police as well as the British police. Conversely, a German, Dutch or French drug liaison officer should be able to work for the benefit of the British police.

My hon. Friend the Member for Warrington, South referred to the international position and to the United Nations. I would also draw attention to the activities in Europe, which are equally important to us and to the other countries of western Europe. It was in that context that two weeks ago the Pompidou group of Ministers met in London under the chairmanship of the Home Secretary and under the wing of my hon. Friend the Under-Secretary. The Pompidou group was set up by the Council of Europe, which has taken a considerable interest in the problems of drug misuse through its Legal Committee and through its Social, Health and Family Affairs Committee, of which I am pleased to be a member. It was in the spirit of Council of Europe Assembly recommendation 10.85,

[*Mr. Rathbone*]

calling for genuine political co-ordination and action at European level that the Pompidou Ministers were called together two weeks ago.

My hon. Friend made an important reference to the sense of urgency that we must now feel about the danger to Europe from cocaine and, increasingly, from crack. We must not wait for the effects of that new drug to turn up in the health records before planning preventive action. So often it is not until the medical world feeds back reports of a problem to the social or political worlds that action is taken. I plead with my hon. Friend the Minister—most especially wearing his hat as chairman of the interdepartmental Minister's group—to impress on his colleagues that they should not wait for dramatic and horrifying statistics to be fed in from representatives of the Department of Health before taking action.

The problem is put into more dramatic perspective because of the growth of crack. There is nothing peculiar about that derivative of cocaine. It is easy to make, cheap to buy and therefore cheap to sell. It has two quite horrific properties, the first being its immediate and shortlived effect leading to the propensity to buy again being all that much stronger. Because it is cheap to buy, there is a vicious downward spiral.

Mr. Tristan Garel-Jones (Comptroller of Her Majesty's Household): Like alcohol.

Mr. Rathbone: It can be like alcohol, as my hon. Friend has suggested from his special knowledge of these matters, but with alcohol one has to consume a considerable amount and get into an alcoholic curve before becoming a truly licensed alcoholic.

The second horrifying property of crack is that, unlike cocaine or herion, which have to be taken for·12 or 18 months before addiction, if crack is taken only three times it is highly liked to lead to complete addiction. Its availability because it is cheap and the characteristic that makes people want ever more of it are enormously worrying aspects. Unless we get it right, another potentially worrying aspect will be the easing of frontier controls in 1992. We must be sure that as we lower the Customs and immigration barriers in Europe—for the very good reason of making Europe a more coherent and cohesive entity—we do not make it easier for drug traffickers to move drugs around the European Community.

As I have already said, the Government have shown great initiative in dealing with the proceeds from crime. They have, first, introduced legislation into this country; secondly, tracked down the sources of illicitly earned funds; thirdly, struck bilateral agreements with other countries; and, fourthly, encouraged multilateral agreements wherever they can be made. As my hon. Friend the Member for Warrington, South said, huge amounts of money are involved. I plead with my hon. Friend the Minister, as many of us have pleaded with his colleagues, to use the money seized from tracking down drug traffickers for the encouragement and improvement of the forces of law and order in their good work.

The Treasury is opposed to that suggestion because it wants to avoid hypothecation. One argument is that it would be unfair for the police force that happened to be active—or luckily active, as some would say—and had

struck gold then to be given the benefit of that money. Some might say that it is impossible actually to plan those activities on a basis of occasional bunce funds. Those are not worthwhile arguments. We are not suggesting that such money should be built in as part of the regular budget of police forces or drugs intelligence units. However, where certain actions should be taken—for example, the establishment of better computer intelligence networks and better training—it would be criminal of the Government not to make those criminally gained funds available to aid the fight against the drug criminals.

Mr. Anthony Nelson (Chichester): I am aware of my hon. Friend's close interest in this matter, and also in the police manning of our county of Sussex. Does he agree that the problem of drug abuse and addiction, while especially evident in Metropolitan areas, also extends very much to the provinces? Is it not the case that in areas such as ours there is little prospect of improved manning on the ground, so that the policeman on the beat can deter trafficking, unless there is additional financial provision? Our pleas year after year for a more adequate police complement have not been met. The Government should carefully consider my hon. Friend's proposal as a possible means of tackling this specialist problem, which is one not just of the cities, but of country areas.

Mr. Rathbone: I am enormously grateful to my hon. Friend and political neighbour for drawing attention to that point and for reminding the House and the Minister of the needs of East and West Sussex. It is regrettable that requests for a greater police complement from the police authority and the chief constable—to whom I pay tribute for his work for the communities in East and West Sussex —have not been met.

I am not actually talking about funds from drug trafficking going into the budget for officers on the beat. That is another pressing question that I look forward to pursuing with my hon. Friend both in the House and elsewhere. My suggestion is that those funds should be used, not just for a police force, but for a national force to help the national effort. They could be a cornerstone for the intriguing idea put forward by my hon. Friend the Member for Warrington, South for a national drugs misuse fighting body. What better way to use those funds than to get such a scheme off the ground?

As I mentioned earlier, there appeared to be an immensely satisfactory outcome from the recent Pompidou group discussions. I commend the Government on their proposal for an international demand reduction conference next year, which will be especially welcome in the specific context of the threat, from cocaine. It is an admirable idea that is being substantiated by the Government's willingness to fund it. In that area, as in many areas of the fight against drugs misuse, the Government are offering support not only in words but in the necessary funding.

That leads me into the second area. I apologise to the House for taking so much time, but I believe that it is an enormously important subject. I hope that I am not repeating what my hon. Friend the Member for Warrington, South has said, nor, indeed, unwinding any of the wise words that my hon. Friends will be adding later on.

In his summing up, my hon. Friend the Member for Warrington, South said that we must make more people aware of how wise it is never to begin. I believe that, whatever we do towards reducing production—there is much more that we can do—however we can better inhibit and overcome, reduce and, perhaps, in some areas even eliminate trafficking, and whatever we do to improve treatment, we will not get to the crux of the drugs misuse problem until we reduce demand.

It is a problem that is no longer confined to big cities, to a social élite or to any particular sub-section of deprived or well-off people in the developed world. In those countries, where hitherto the major problem of drug misuse has been the problem of containing production, we have seen—as everybody forecasted would be the case—a quite horrible increase in drug misuse.

It is worth mentioning in that context that not only are people in the production countries becoming drug-addicted, but the consumption countries are becoming production-orientated. I believe that it is still right to say that the largest cash crop in the ninth largest economy in the world happens to be marijuana; and the ninth largest economy in the world happens to be the state of California in the United States of America. I cite that as an instance of how we can no longer talk about production and consumption countries we are all in this horribly together.

To come to grips with the problem of demand, it is crucial to build a better understanding of what prompts it. I would ask my hon. Friend the Minister to touch on what the Government are doing within our marvellous National Health Service to encourage medical and genetic research into what may underlie drug misuse.

I know that in the United States there are studies into the genetics of those who have become misusers of alcohol as well as of drugs. There are indications, to put it no higher, that whatever a person's social or family background, the most likely cause underlying a person becoming entrapped into drug or any other misuse is a genetic propensity to such misuse. If that is the case and we are finding a new channel of approach—a genetic approach—to the problem, we should carry out more research in that area in this country, so that we will be better able to come to grips with the problem. However, it is not only medical research that is necessary, but social studies and research into the number of addicts and where they are.

In Brighton we have an extraordinarily well set-up drug unit, which is under the wing of the East Sussex county council. That unit draws together social, medical and police services. It has a well-conceived well-planned and well-costed research project, so that it can understand the problem of drug misusers on a numerate basis in Brighton, which has a great problem. I was disappointed, however, to discover that it was impossible for that unit to get funding from the district or regional health authorities and that it had to tap other sources for funds. Thank goodness it has been successful in doing so, because that research will make an enormous contribution to all of the other efforts that it applies so manfully—I suppose that I should say "womanfully"—in the battle against drug misuse in that town. It is only after we have a better understanding of the problem that we can ensure that all our activities impinge properly and most effectively in the fight against drug misuse.

My hon. Friend the Member for Warrington, South raised queries about the advertising campaigns that have been run so far, and I would add my own question mark to those. We must be certain that in this complex area of human behaviour advertising campaigns, first, communicate and have an immediate effect along the lines for which they were designed, and, secondly, that their effect has some form of longevity which makes them worth while. I feel that, while those advertisements are visible and dramatic because of their visibility, the rather longer-term and more mundane methods of health education and drug advice for the medical profession, for parents, for teachers and for high-risk groups are really the way in which to tackle the problem.

In my area—and my hon. Friend the Member for Warrington, South drew attention to one in Merseyside—we have a first-class drug advice and information service. It is well publicised, it has become very well used and it is a point of reference for those people who are worried about getting tempted into drugs or, having been tempted, are worried about the effect that it is having. Perhaps most importantly, it is a source of information for parents who are concerned that their children may be in the process of being tempted and want to know what they can do to intervene in that process and cut it off.

I commend the Government on their funding for the next three years of drug advisers in schools. They anticipated the motion of my hon. Friend the Member for Warrington, South, because they have taken on the additional task of advising on AIDS, and I believe that they might also take on the task of advising on alcohol. It is absolutely essential to have within each school a teacher identified as a source of knowledge about addiction of all sorts and who can recognise those addictions in children.

As my hon. Friend the Member for Warrington, South did, I draw attention to the life education centre programmes, which were started in Australia by the Rev. Tom Noffs, and which have been started to such good effect in parts of this country. It is a sophisticated but simple device for injecting into young people's minds a greater awareness of the value of a healthy lifestyle and a healthy body. It is a simple caravan with a trained teacher inside using displays as extraordinarily dramatic and innovative methods of communication. It visits a school and in two hours can take an entire age group through one of its classes. There are different classes for each age group from five to 15. Therefore, it can cover a normal school in less than a week. The caravans have proved effective in parts of Essex and they are now part of life in the Isle of Man. They have been visited by Ministers from all the Departments within my hon. Friend the Minister's ministerial group. I am pleased that my right hon. Friend the Prime Minister participated in one such session in a caravan brought into No. 10 Downing street a few months ago. She was enormously impressed.

Mr. Alan Williams (Swansea, West): On a point of order, Madam Deputy Speaker. I apologise to the hon. Member for Lewes (Mr. Rathbone) but I shall interrupt his speech for only a moment. We wonder whether there has been a request for a statement to be made this morning. We had expected one on the new and somewhat novel proposal for a carbon tax which emerged yesterday. You will understand, Madam Deputy Speaker, that we want to know the status of that announcement from the Secretary of State for the Environment and the amount of the tax.

I intervene at this point because the announcement seems to be based on a completely new principle that goes way beyond the principle accepted by both sides of the

[*Mr. Alan Williams*]

House that the polluter pays. It seems to be based on the idea that a tax should deter the use of coal. It is a hidden boost to the preference for nuclear power held by the Secretary of State for the Environment and the Prime Minister. If there has been no request for a statement today—since no Minister is present I assume that that is the case—I should like to take this opportunity, through you, Madam Deputy Speaker, to say that we expect a statement on Monday.

Madam Deputy Speaker (Miss Betty Boothroyd): I can tell the House and the right hon. Gentleman that Mr. Speaker has received no such request this morning.

Mr. Edward Leigh (Gainsborough and Horncastle): Further to that point of order, Madam Deputy Speaker.

Madam Deputy Speaker: Order. Is it a new point of order?

Mr. Leigh: It is further to the previous point of order.

Madam Deputy Speaker: I will hear it.

Mr. Leigh: This is a major debate on a serious international and national problem. The right hon. Member for Swansea, West (Mr. Williams) has brought in his friends from the press to listen to a totally bogus and dubious point of order which has nothing to do with the——

Madam Deputy Speaker: Order. I have answered the point of order. The hon. Member for Gainsborough and Horncastle (Mr. Leigh) has endorsed my feelings. This is an important debate and we must proceed with it.

Mr. Harry Greenway (Ealing, North): Further to that point of order, Madam Deputy Speaker.

Madam Deputy Speaker: I doubt whether there can be anything to add to that point of order or to my reply.

Mr. Harry Greenway: I wonder whether it was made clear to you, Madam Deputy Speaker, in the question whether there had been a request for a statement that the Secretary of State had made it clear——

Madam Deputy Speaker: Order. There can be no debate on this matter.

Mr. Rathbone: There are various types of misuse and we happen to be debating——

Mr. Butler: In my speech I mentioned the media's responsibility in reporting about drugs. It was fascinating to watch the Press Gallery fill up on that spurious point of order and then to empty as soon as the point of order was finished. Does that not underline my point about the media's responsibility in this matter?

Mr. Rathbone: I endorse my hon. Friend's comments. Giving the gentlemen of the third estate the benefit of the doubt, I hope that they came in to find out how well the debate was going, to hear the points being made and to see the extremely poor turn-out on the Opposition Benches, except during that spurious point of order. Of course, the point of order did not deal with an unimportant subject but it may be straying far from the subject of the motion

to attempt to include the misuse of the environment in a debate on drug misuse rather than to treat it as a separate subject.

Mr. Randall: The hon. Gentleman has raised yet again the question of attendance. I deplore low attendance. Is the reason why there is such poor attendance on the Conservative Benches the fact that the party is now seven points behind in the poll or is it because Conservative Members are not interested in drugs?

Mr. Rathbone: We do the important subject of drugs no service by trying to inject into the debate the scoring of cheap political points. The hon. Member for Kingston upon Hull, West understands this matter and has expressed concern. It is not in his nature to be prompted into such behaviour by the presence of a Whip on the Opposition Front Bench.

I was describing the operation of the life education centre schemes in this country. That scheme is one, probably the best, of the specific schemes designed to get to the base of the problem of drug misuse by dissuading people from becoming involved in drugs in the first place. If there is a chance that I am right—I believe that I am —the scheme deserves Government support in order to enable it to administer a national expansion of its activities and to help it train teachers as well as to provide the capital cost of equipment so that in the not too distant future we can hope to see 'such centres operating in every local education authority. Some will require more units than others; that will depend on the size of the education authority. Such schemes should provide for every school in the country an opportunity for the young to participate in the education programme for two hours of each of the 10 formative years of their life. If that is done, in 10 years we will be able to say that my hon. Friend the Member for Warrington, South, in initiating the debate, turned a corner in coming to grips with the horrible problem of drug misuse, and the House and the nation would be indebted to him for that.

11.7 am

Mr. Charles Irving (Cheltenham): I congratulate and thank my hon. Friend the Member for Warrington, South (Mr. Butler) for what we must all agree was a compelling and telling speech. I hope that my hon. Friend the Minister, who has already done a great deal, will take on board some of the points that he raised.

Awareness is growing rapidly in the community about the horrific dangers of drug misuse. Crack is now easily available on street corners at £5 or £10 a go. It is time we exploded the cornershop cocaine, which is what it is. That cheap and highly addictive cocaine-based drug has brought nightly carnage to the streets of many American states. Profits from the trade in it have drawn youngsters, some scarcely in their teens, into a net of crime, often ending in death, as crazed addicts and dealers settle their grievances with guns.

Crack is smoked, not snorted and goes quickly to the brain. It can be bought for a few pounds and it is cheaper than a gun. It is now starting to show its ugly face in Britain as the drug bosses who set up the deadly trade scent the possibility of big profits. Britain, with a population about a quarter of the size of the United States conveniently concentrated into big cities, has many areas where disaffected and unemployed people become easy prey. The *Western Daily Press* recently produced a compelling article by Simon Pipe with evidence of the drug abuse problems in the Bristol area. That was an humane expose which is well worth reading.

Already, Wolverhampton and the south west have experienced the disorder that crack brings. It is a drug which brings destruction, despair and death to the addicts and those around them. The spread of crack must be stopped before it brings us the hell on earth which it has visited on America.

Crack is one cigarette puff away from the dirty needle syndrome and the AIDS virus which will cost the economy billions of pounds in medical care and loss of earnings in the next 10 years. Drug abuse runs the parallel risk of sending the AIDS epidemic into a freefall. The HIV virus marches on relentlessly with no vaccine in sight to end sufferers' misery. Prisons are a known breeding ground for it and regional secure units are a myth. The next century approaches with the ominous legacy from the 1900s and the fear that drugs and AIDS, especially in prisons, will become hideously out of control.

Crack is terrible. It is deadly and has a street value running into tens of millions of pounds. It is the purest, most lethal form of cocaine and its users become addicted and dependent. Surely it is essential that even greater efforts should be made to harness the skills and the brilliance of health and education officials, both regional and national. They must wake up to the growing threat before it becomes a horrible reality and turns all of us into victims.

The evil purveyors have targeted Britain and the invasion is already here. Parents in virtually every constituency are crying out for help. All we can suggest is working parties and conferences, the involvement of European sources and even the Home Secretary. As far back as 1983, he warned of the tragedies that lay ahead; six years later we have little to show, and working parties are still talking.

It is simply not enough to punish offenders. The probation service, housing associations such as Stonham, of which I have the privilege of being chairman, and NACRO have much to offer in the way of providing a secure haven for addicts and using the techniques available to wean them off drugs. However, when we want to offer the services of these nationally sponsored bodies we are met with a brick wall: there are no resources.

For many potential victims, the threat of greater punishment will only increase the lure and it will certainly increase tension between the police and those involved. The pushers need heavy punishment, and the addicts and their families need the nation's help.

Crack respects no boundaries and no classes. It traps the vulnerable, desolate and hopeless with the chance of a quick, cheap thrill which rapidly becomes a destructive addiction, leaving users physically damaged and mentally dependent. Cardboard box city will not be confined to the Thames but will spread throughout the country bringing the tragedies that we already see in some of our bigger cities. To combat that, a massive programme of education is needed to alert youngsters and parents to the great social and personal dangers of this drug. The police, social services, local authorities and health services must link together to stop this drug plague. There should be no holds barred or money spared in our efforts to relay the message through schools, clubs, television and doctors' surgeries. There is nothing to be said in favour of crack. It has no

mindbender defenders, as had LSD, and there are no arguments in favour of it such as those put forward by people who want legislaton to liberalise the use of marijuana.

I do not underestimate the difficulties that the Home Office faces in trying to resolve the problem. I do not underestimate the sterling efforts of my hon. Friend the Minister. However, we have a unique opportunity which comes rarely in this House, to urge, plead and beg that something be done quickly.

I have stuck to my usual 10-minute speech, Madam Deputy Speaker.

11.16 am

Mr. Edward Leigh (Gainsborough and Horncastle): I am grateful to my hon. Friend the Member for Warrington, South (Mr. Butler) for giving the House the opportunity to debate what has become a devastating international problem. I hope, like my hon. Friend the Member for Cheltenham (Mr. Irving), not to detain the House more than a few minutes. In my few remarks I intend to survey the world situation, which has not so far been done in detail, to consider what the Government are trying to do to meet the problem and, in the last few moments of my speech, to offer a few thoughts of my own.

We have heard much about the problem in the United Kingdom. According to the Home Office statistical bulletin of 11 April 1989:

"The number of new and former drug addicts notified to the Home Office increased by 1,100 between 1987 and 1988, almost reaching the peak number recorded in 1985."

Although there had been an apparent levelling off in heroin addiction, that has now proved not to be the case, and there has been an upturn.

As hon. Members have already made clear this morning, cocaine is a much more worrying problem. In London a kilo of cocaine is worth four to five times the price in Miami. This financial incentive, coupled with the apparent saturation of the American market, makes Europe an attractive proposition. The experience of the Bahamas and the United States is that crack will not become readily available until there is a large stockpile of cocaine. Recent events in Wolverhampton may point to the fact that a stockpile has been built up. I can put it no better than my right hon. Friend the Home Secretary, who said in a press release on 18 May:

"Crack is the spectre I see hanging over Europe. Prior to 1985 crack was an almost unheard of term in the United States. It is now a major drug in 49 out of the 50 States."

As my hon. Friend the Member for Cheltenham made clear in his pertinent remarks, crack is a devastating phenomenon of which this House should be aware, and it is the more worrying in that dependence on it is far more devastating than dependence on heroin. It seems that Latin American groups are setting up distribution chains in Europe. Put at its simplest, cocaine supply is moving from an individual, entrepreneurial business to a multinational one.

It is important that the House should be aware of what is happening overseas. There is a continuing and worrying growth of addiction. It was recently estimated that in Karachi one in nine young men were heroin addicts. Bolivia, with a population of six million, estimates that it has 250,000 addicts. According to the World Health Organisation—a point made by my hon. Friend the Member for Warrington, South—HIV infection among

[*Mr. Edward Leigh*]

heroin injectors in Thailand has risen from 0 per cent. three years ago, to 1 per cent. two years ago, to a staggering 50 per cent. last year.

It is unlikely that there will be any significant reduction of production. The golden triangle is even more lawless, and the golden crescent is unlikely to be contained until the situation in Afghanistan is resolved. There has been some success in dealing with cocaine in Bolivia, but there was an upward trend in Brazil, although cocaine production there is relatively low grade. The United States Drugs Enforcement Agency estimates that there has been a 25 per cent. increase in production in Peru. All this shows the problems that we face.

I am indebted to my hon. Friend the Parliamentary Under-Secretary of State for Foreign and Commonwealth Affairs, who recently addressed the parliamentary all-party drug misuse group to which he gave an interesting analysis of what is happening in Peru, which he recently visited. His experiences there make grim reading:

"To get to a first stage laboratory took one hour by helicopter and required the protection of two other, heavily armed helicopters. It took considerable time to find the laboratory, which was under the canopy of the jungle. The site had three to four huts for production, a power house, dormitory and cooking facilities. In the course of that journey, four more factories were spotted, three of which were still in production. In a small area there were estimated to be 100 factories. The scale of production was massive and the whole of the Peruvian army could not seriously impede the scale of cultivation and production. The physical act of manually eradicating the crops was extremely difficult and yet if substitute crops were to be produced, chemical eradication was not possible. Colombia was doing a tremendous job, but the problems were immense. The Head of the Drug Squad had a $2 million price tag on his head. There was considerable corruption. The judiciary was increasingly unlikely to convict for drug offences. Despite these impediments, Colombia was becoming more sophisticated and successful in tracking planes."

It seems from this report that the authorities are only scratching the surface of the problem.

That is the international epidemic that we face and the source of the spectre that my right hon. Friend described as hanging over Europe, and it is why this debate is timely. What are we doing in this country? The new convention against illicit traffic in narcotic drugs and substances which was signed in Vienna in December 1988 provides an international framework for co-operation against trafficking. More training continues to be provided, with the exchange of enforcement officers and an increase in the number of United Kingdom Customs and police officers.

A number of problems remain to be dealt with, not least the under-resourcing of the United Nations drugs bodies. Despite the best efforts of the Government to promote international co-operation, at best we are only holding our own.

Hon. Members have mentioned what the Government are doing domestically in terms of detection and enforcement. In an interesting Adjournment debate on 2 May, my hon. Friend the Minister of State, Home Office said:

"The strength of the police force drug squads in England is more than 40 per cent. greater than it was at the end of 1983".—[*Official Report,* 2 May 1989; Vol. 152, c. 156.]

It is easy for us armchair analysts to claim that the Government are not doing enough, but that quotation shows that there has been a big increase in police drug squads.

The interesting Home Office document, "Tackling Drug Misuse: A Summary of the Government's Strategy", makes it clear that the Government take this problem seriously and have increased the penalties. I refer the House to paragraph 5.7. No doubt my hon. Friend the Minister will tell us in detail what the Government have been doing and intend to do.

I end with my personal thoughts on this problem. The Government are doing a great deal, but is it enough? I am reminded of a block of flats. On the ground floor live people who are producing substances with the potential to kill our children. What do we do? First, we politely complain. Secondly, we ask them to set their house in order. Thirdly, we might give them the resources with which to do that. All that is good and it has been happening. Ministers have visited South America and have attempted to increase international co-operation. They have talked of giving more resources. That is all very well, but is it enough?

As I have said, the situation in South America is getting out of control. Can the Western world go on accepting what may be an attack on the very nature of our society? I do not think so. Unless certain countries, such as Bolivia, can get to grips with this problem it may become necessary for the international community to take action.

Mr. Randall: Such as?

Mr. Leigh: I do not want to speculate at this stage; neither do I want to underestimate the appalling spectre that hangs over us. Those countries do not have the resources to tackle the problem and it may be necessary to adopt other methods.

We have talked about deterrence. The document to which I referred shows that the Government have increased penalties.

Mr. Randall: I should like to press the hon. Gentleman on this. I know that he is sincere about this, as are we all. Earlier, I pressed the hon. Member for Lewes (Mr. Rathbone) on the same point. The problem is immense. We are talking of independent sovereign countries, and I am at a loss to know exactly what we can do to overcome the massive forces at work in them. An enormous amount of money is being made. What action is the hon. Gentleman specifically recommending?

Mr. Leigh: The hon. Gentleman must draw his own conclusions. I speak as a Back Bencher. Even so, this is a sensitive area and I would prefer to hint rather than to make concrete statements. I drew the analogy with the block of flats for a good reason, and I stick to it. We ask for the police to be brought in if what is happening on the ground floor endangers our children. These are sensitive matters and our debate may well be heard in other places.

We have spoken of deterrence. The problem is enormous and the potential gains are vast. The international trade is worth £50 billion. Deterrence may not be enough. No hon. Member is asking for the death penalty to be imposed for international drug traffickers or smugglers, but this is not just a moral issue. There have been many debates on the rightness or wrongness of imposing the death penalty. The House has taken a decision. Some hon. Members take the view that to impose the death penalty would always be wrong in any circumstances. Others believe that because most murders are committed within the family, the death penalty should not be imposed. What will happen, though, if the international control of drugs breaks down, resulting in a breakdown of law and order on our streets to the extent that has occurred in Washington? I have lived for most of my life in this capital city and have never been afraid to go out at any time of night. I am a big chap, but I would not walk at night on the streets of Philadelphia or New York.

The response of the United States Government to the problem has been grotesquely insufficient. There has been a major breakdown of society in many inner city areas in the United States. The problem is not wholly drug related. Some of it relates to the breakdown of the family unit. Some of it relates to certain welfare concepts, but that is another issue. If, however, there were a breakdown of law and order in inner city areas in this country and the police started to lose control, it would no longer be a moral issue. Society—not individuals—would be under attack. In the past, society has taken the decision that it has the right to defend itself from foreign aggression by the use of force or violence. If society is placed under that kind of pressure, hon. Members might say that we ought to follow the example of other countries and impose the ultimate deterrent to deal with the problem. I know that the problem cannot be solved by deterrence alone and that the Minister will tell us that prevention is very important and that international co-operation is vital.

I have tried to explain the seriousness of the problem. Unless other measures are successful, we may have to consider using more extreme measures. I would not want to use them, but eventually they may prove to be necessary.

11.32 am

Mr. Peter L. Pike (Burnley): I shall follow the example of the hon. Members for Cheltenham (Mr. Irving) and for Gainsborough and Horncastle (Mr. Leigh) and will make a short contribution to the debate. I welcome the opportunity that the hon. Member for Warrington, South (Mr Butler) has given us to debate this important issue, on which there is a great deal of unanimity on both sides of the House. We all recognise the need to combat the evil of bringing drugs into this country and the consequent evil of pushing drugs, with all its implications. To push drugs is one of the most evil crimes, and we must take the strongest possible action to combat it. The taking of drugs can ultimately lead to death. Drug pushers commit an act that is tantamount to murder by making drugs available to people, some of whom become hooked on them and ultimately die.

The families of those who take drugs are also affected. Drug-taking can destroy family life. A person can become so obsessed with taking drugs that he resorts to crime to get money to pay for them. I have met many constituents who need a great deal of support during extremely difficult periods in their family life. When people get into debt and resort to crime, one often finds that drugs are involved, but that is not so in all cases.

The problem is not confined to big cities or to certain classes of people. It affects small towns throughout the country, including Burnley. There is a tendency to ignore the drugs problem. We shall be unable to tackle it unless we recognise that it is a problem. A press campaign in my constituency is being led by a local reporter, Ian Pilkington, of the *Burnley Express and News*. The campaign is called "Drug Alert". Every week the *Burnley*

Express and News draws attention to the problem and tries to ensure that at local level it is being tackled. A local solicitor, Mr. Dearing, is also trying to make people aware of the fact that there is a drugs problem in Burnley and that it is not confined to Liverpool and Manchester.

We must provide additional resources for hospital units that are trying to get people off drugs. There is a unit in Prestwich that serves a large area, but only a very small number of beds are reserved for drug addicts. Additional facilities are needed in Lancashire and elsewhere in the north-west. The Burnley, Pendle and Rossendale district health authority has authorised an increase in the number of people who are helping drug addicts, but we are only tinkering with the problem. Far more people are needed to tackle it. The National Health Service is under pressure, but provision for dealing with the drugs problem should be treated as a priority. It should not have to compete with other hospital services. If adequate provision is made to tackle the drugs problem, it must not lead to money being taken away from other services. That would be wrong.

Far more must be done to educate young people. Somebody in every school should be responsible for doing that job. Young people should also be educated about the dangers of AIDS. The sharing of needles is one of the major causes of the spread of AIDS. We have underestimated how much money will be needed by the National Health Service, the social services and the education authorities to tackle the AIDS and the drugs problem. The sooner we wake up to that fact, the sooner we shall be able to overcome these issues. The cheapest and most effective way to tackle the drugs and the AIDS problems is to spend money on the education service so that young people are made fully aware of what might happen.

We must make every effort to stop drugs from being brought into the country. Hon. Members on both sides of the House recognise the difficulty of doing that, but we must ensure that the resources are there. Many of the Government's actions over the past few years have received the support of hon. Members—for instance, the confiscation of money made from the sale of drugs. A prison term will not be a sufficient penalty if the offender can later benefit from the profits that he made before his imprisonment.

Resources are needed for education, the Health Service and the social services: full support is needed for the family which might otherwise be destroyed by the drug problem of one of its members. Many such families do not know where to turn.

There is considerable unanimity on this problem. We must devote resources to ensuring that it does not increase, in the hope that we may ultimately see a reduction.

11.41 am

Mr. Harry Greenway (Ealing, North): I join those who have congratulated my hon. Friend the Member for Warrington, South (Mr. Butler) on initiating one of the most important debates that I have heard in the House. The drug problem affects the survival of our land and our society, and is a no less important subject for debate than war. This is, indeed, a war of a fundamental nature.

First, let me ask my hon. Friend the Minister to address his mind to the growing number of individuals and small groups now pressing for the legalisation of soft drugs such as marijuana. I should like his assurance that, as long as

[*Mr. Harry Greenway*]

the present Government remain in power, such drugs will not be legalised. Professor Francis Camps, Home Office pathologist for some 20 years and an outstanding man, said that soft drugs always led to hard drugs and hard drugs to death. To legalise marijuana, therefore, is to put people on the road to hard drugs and thence to death. Francis Camps, than whom few people can have had more experience of drugs—he observed their effects when performing autopsies on those who had died of their addiction—observed that the average length of the cycle from the first soft drug to death was seven years, although people often lasted for a shorter time than that.

Mr. Rathbone: I may be anticipating what my hon. Friend is about to say. I hope, however, that he is not implying that the only threat of soft drugs is the fact that they lead to hard drugs. Although some years ago there was a school of thought that held that marijuana, for instance, did not do any great harm, there is now almost incontrovertible evidence that it is physically debilitating for the taker. Soft drugs of themselves are bad for people.

Mr. Greenway: I am grateful to my hon. Friend, who has made my next point for me. Soft drugs are indeed highly damaging, and can lead to prolonged illness and death. My initial point was merely that if soft drugs lead to hard drugs the progress towards death is accelerated. I hope that my hon. Friend the Minister will give me the assurance for which I have asked—and also that he will forgive me for leaving the Chamber for some time after my speech to undertake a school engagement.

In his admirable speech, my hon. Friend the Member for Warrington, South referred to the spread of AIDS through the multiple use of needles by drug addicts and others. We all know of the tragic consequences of that practice, which continues despite the Government's excellent record in making more needles available to those who require them for medical purposes. There is now no need for any needle to be used twice.

A friend of mine, a Church of England clergyman, in addition to his parish work, has dedicated his life to taking into his home AIDS sufferers of all ages, particularly younger people. He told me the other day that there were always about four in his home, and that about two died each year: if I may use a crude term, he has a "throughput". He spoke movingly and disturbingly of a 17-year-old suffering not only from AIDS but from senile dementia induced by his condition. Think of the devastating effect on that young life.

I want to trumpet my friend's achievement. The world needs to know what he is doing, to gain an even greater appreciation of the horrors of AIDS and the suffering of patients and those who care for them. Those who devote their lives to nursing AIDS sufferers are doing a wonderful thing, but what they must watch imposes on them extreme emotional distress.

My hon. Friend did not mention a drug problem of considerable and, I fear, growing proportions: glue-sniffing. It is as much a drug problem as any other, and is increasing particularly in schools, in some of which one in 10 children is said to be sniffing glue. The number of deaths is rising steadily each year, as is the suffering involved, despite an Act passed about two years ago under which those selling glue kits to known would-be sniffers can receive severe punishments, including imprisonment.

The problem is most common in deprived areas. It occurs among children of all ages, including tiny tots who find it interesting and fun and who stagger about after sniffing. A few months ago I heard of a teenager who, having sniffed glue, believed himself to have superhuman strength and kicked down a hard wooden fence when wearing pumps, knocking it to the ground and causing great damage. Violence is induced by glue sniffing.

We are not solving the problem, and, although it has not been mentioned much lately, it is still there and growing. While everyone is anxious to see substances that glue sniffers are keen to use removed, it is not always possible to remove such substances, or other things such as boot polish from the shops, glue sniffers like to abuse boot polish. I ask the Minister to step up prevention through education and to combine that with stiffer penalties for pushers of glue kits, wherever they are found. In particular we must concentrate on the education of children and families to prevent glue sniffing.

When it is not curbed, glue sniffing leads to soft and hard drugs and can take away a person's mind. A few weeks ago I heard about a prisoner of 24 whose mind had completely gone as a result of glue sniffing over several years. He was not able to respond even to simple instructions and simply sits and stares into space. His life is effectively ended even though he is only 24. That is not an imported problem because it is within our own society and continues to grow.

Mr. Pike: Glue sniffing can be started when people are very young. Does the hon. Gentleman think that there has been sufficient research about the progress from glue sniffing to soft and hard drugs? Perhaps there should be more research to see how that type of problem emerges.

Mr. Greenway: The hon. Gentleman makes a fair point. Much more research into how it starts should be undertaken and we should find out more about how it may be cured. It starts most simply by one child influencing another. As I know from my long experience of teaching, little children get a great kick out of being with older children. If the older children smoke, the younger ones soon want to do the same, even if they are only about the age of three. The same is true of glue sniffing. When older children glamorise it, as they regrettably do, younger children become interested in it, partake of it and become addicted. Much more research would be valuable and is urgently required.

The broad question of drugs coming into Britain was raised by my hon. Friend the Member for Warrington, South and developed by my hon. Friend the Member for Lewes (Mr. Rathbone) who said that the international trade in drugs is about £50 billion. We need to think again about our Customs procedures. We are now employing fewer Customs officers than ever before in relation to the number of people travelling. Examining the baggage of the millions of people who travel each year is an enormous problem. We now have a system which is common in the European Community and in many parts of the world. The system has been a failure.

When people declare what they have bought, as I did a few months ago, they have to join a queue of 20 or 30 people. The people in that queue will be handled by two or three Customs officers, one of whom seems to leave the moment that the queue appears while another goes off for a cup of tea. That leaves one Customs officer to deal with a queue that grows quite quickly. By definition, each person in the queue has much to discuss and almost certainly will have to open bags to show what is in them. That is a lengthy process and people may have to wait for several hours, having gone to the trouble of being honest and declaring what they have bought. They then discover that they are free to go through, as I discovered on the occasion that I mentioned.

Because of that cumbersome system many people go for the "nothing-to-declare" booth even though they have items that should be declared. They do that not because they are dishonest, but for personal convenience and to save time. There is no guantlet to be run in the "nothing-to-declare" section and large numbers of people go through it. Many of them know that they have much to declare and many must have hard and soft drugs because a large quantity of such drugs is still known to be coming into the country. That is serious and unsatisfactory.

I appreciate the worry that the Customs process imposes upon the Home Office, but I ask my hon. Friend the Minister to consider whether the time has come to revert to the former process in which everyone was automatically expected to declare rather than having the choice of opting for the green or red channel. That would lead to a greater chance of people being apprehended, and people who need to be seen could do so through a process that is not as lengthy as the present red channel process.

I commend the Home Office on the policy enacted in legislation of confiscating the profits of those who gain from the sale of drugs. I know that that legislation has been highly effective and is one of the great improvements in the law of the 1980s. As the hon. Member for Burnley (Mr. Pike) said, we need more education on the subject in schools. Those who say that there is no drug problem in schools cannot substantiate the assertion. I have shown that glue sniffing is certainly a problem in schools and the same may be true of other drugs. However, the problem is still much smaller than it might be. The system of an efficient education officer per local authority which was initiated by the Government is vital, and will help to keep the problem at bay. I hope that it will eliminate the problem altogether.

11.48 am

Mr. Robert Hayward (Kingswood): I join my hon. Friends in welcoming the opportunity to debate the subject of drugs. I should like to address one specific aspect of drug abuse, and that is the use of drugs in sport. Sportsmen and sportswomen in all sports, especially those who reach high levels, are role models and peer groups who set examples to youngsters. Youngsters feel that if senior sportsmen can take drugs they might as well do the same. I commend sportsmen from around the world, such as Carl Lewis, who have gone out of their way to make it clear that they do not take drugs and to discourage others from doing so.

It is relevant to talk about drug abuse in sport about nine months after the events at the last Olympics, which received enormous worldwide publicity, because it allows us to consider the progress that is—or in some cases, tragically is not—being made. In Reykjavik last week, my hon. Friend the Minister for Sport presented, on behalf of European Ministers, a draft anti-doping convention, which is to be commended. Page 5 of the convention mentions the association between general drug abuse in society and drug abuse in sport. It says that the object of the convention is to emphasise

"the dangers to health and the harm to ethical values inherent in doping in sport."

That succinctly shows the influence that sportsmen can have on our values.

Discussion in Reykjavik was useful. Unfortunately, it occurred many months after the events in Seoul, and it may be several months before the convention is ratified by one country. Even countries regarded as being in the lead in tackling drug abuse, such as Norway, Australia and Britain—who we hope will be joined by Canada when the Dublin commission has completed its report—are moving slowly.

I welcome the recommendations of the convention, but, unfortunately, it makes no suggestions about the length of bans for those found to have taken drugs. It makes no recommendations about sponsorship, which one might reasonably have expected. I hope that, the convention having been ratified, anyone who is found guilty of taking any of the major banned drugs—I accept that some drugs are taken in error or in association with medicine—will be banned for at least three years, and possibly four, for a first offence and for life for a second. International sport cannot accept what occurred with Slopaniek and others who, having been banned for two years, were allowed to return to the world athletics championships and Olympics to win a gold medal and set what are classified as world records. It is laughing in the faces of any efforts to ban drugs if such people are allowed to return so soon. We need—and this is suggested in the convention—random and unannounced testing in all sports, with independent collection. Without such policies there will be no major drive against drug abuse in sport.

I am pleased to say that 19 governing bodies of sport in the United Kingdom have either adopted policies that meet the convention's requirements or are in the process of doing so. Beyond the 19 listed, amateur tennis is making substantial efforts to catch up, and I hope that it will be able to join the list soon.

In addition to signing the draft convention, each country should adopt a policy for individual competitions, whereby anyone who is in the list of top 10 competitors according to the previous season's performances is a prime target for random and unannounced testing. I welcome the willingness of the Sports Council and other sports councils in Europe to fund tests, not only in the United Kingdom but other parts of the world, of individuals who are recognised as leading competitors. The Sports Council regularly visits the Canary Islands to test competitors who are training out of season, which is a welcome development.

It is interesting to consider the scale of drug abuse in sport, given that we are talking about role models. Daley Thompson, who should know about world competition, not only because of his phenomenal achievements but because he trains in the Canaries and Los Angeles and therefore mixes with leading world athletes in Europe and the United States, estimated that while

"30 per cent. of Britons had used drugs to improve their performance"

[*Mr. Robert Hayward*]

80 per cent. of American athletes had used drugs to improve their performance. Those are quite staggering statistics.

I said that we are making progress, and last year the Sports Council funded 3,400 tests, of which 14 were found to be positive. The cost of carrying out those tests in the United Kingdom and abroad was £478,000, showing that testing can have an enormous effect for a relatively small outlay. Britain is fortunate in being able to bring pressure on some sports because they receive funds from the Sports Council. If those sports do not adhere to a policy similar to that which the Government are advocating, they will lose their grants.

Major sponsors, as I suggested in relation to the anti-doping convention, should look carefully at the sports that they support. They participate in not only amateur but professional sports. Regrettably, there will be no testing at Henley, Wimbledon or the British Open golf championship this year. While we are making progress, some of which is very slow, some of the major British sporting events, only nine or 10 months after the events in Seoul, do not recognise the importance of dope testing. It costs little to prove to sponsors that sports are clean. if they can show that they are clean, it will give a clear message to our youth.

I referred to the difference that Daley Thompson identified between the number of British atheletes who had used drugs, as he estimated it, and the number of American athletes who had done so, as he estimated it. He is in a good position to know what is going on in sport. I should like to dwell on American sport, because it is generally believed in America that it is making progress in tackling drugs in society and sport. My hon. Friend the Member for Gainsborough and Horncastle (Mr. Leigh) referred to that belief. Unfortunately, it is not so. I raised the subject with my hon. Friend the Minister for Sport on an Adjournment debate about five and a half years ago. I said that in 1982 there had been no drug tests at 51 major European sporting events or at any of the major sporting events in the United States. What progress has been made? The track athletes club in the United States said that it was willing to accept short notice testing, but it has not done so yet. Weightlifting authorities in the United States announced two years ago that they were prepared to accept testing, but not one test has been carried out in a weightlifting contest in the United States. The United States reached agreement with Russia to have an exchange on testing, but no document has been produced that could be signed, let alone any test being carried out in the United States.

It is a sad comment on American sport that, only this week, the chief medical adviser to the United States Olympic Committee, Dr. Robert Voy, resigned because of the total lack of progress in the United States on dope testing. Yesterday, I took the opportunity to speak to him. I asked him to clarify why he had resigned. He made it clear that one of the prime reasons was the total lack of commitment—to use his phrase, "The USOC has put dope testing on the back burner." There is no evidence that the USOC will act on the report of the Dubin commission. It is clear that Canadian sports of all forms will take urgent, clear and positive action.

No American sport, with one exception, is willing to take the same steps. The one exception in the United States is cycling which, having been confronted by the embarrassment of having competitors return home from competitions for fear of being dope tested, has decided to throw everything open and is willing to have dope testing in any circumstances. Despite the embarrassment of having had American competitors leave in droves from the Pan-American games a year before the Olympics, not one other American sport has made any progress. In competitions last year in Europe, track athletes from America, including discus throwers and pole vaulters, withdrew because they suddenly discovered that there would be dope testing, carried out with the assidulty pursued in Europe but not in the United States.

It is interesting to note why so many sports in the United States are not willing to take action. Echoing Dr. Robert Voy's words, they are hiding behind the veil of the legal system. Before the last Olympics, the director of sport sciences for the National Collegiate Athletic Association, Mr. Frank Uryasv, said:
"the legal system makes it almost impossible"
to drug test.

It is interesting that cycling in the United States does not face that problem although it has opened up its doors, but other sports are willing to continue along those lines.

Mr. Rathbone: I draw the attention of the House to the extraordinary comparison between those statements and the readiness in the horseracing world to spot-test horses. Is it not peculiar that we can do this for animals but not for human beings?

Mr. Haywood: As my hon. Friend says, there are many anomalies. We are making progress in horse racing, although I admit that it is not a matter about which I know much. There have been disqualifications this season in this country. It is important that all sports adopt policies similar to that outlined in the doping convention.

Mr. Harry Greenway: My hon. Friend the Member for Lewes (Mr. Rathbone) rightly said that there is regular dope testing of all horses at all race meetings. The same is true of all other aspects of equestrian sports. For example, in event riding the horses are severely tested because their performance can be enhanced by drugs. The same is true of greyhound racing in this country.

Mr. Haywood: I thank my hon. Friend for his comment. As my hon. Friend the Member for Lewes (Mr. Rathbone) pointed out, not just the human sports need to be tested to ensure that victory is clean and honest.

Five sports in the United States, along with cycling, were willing to open their doors, but they gave up because of the lack of positive action by the USOC. Yesterday, the Sports Council told me that, as far as it was aware, United States professional golf just did not want to know about testing. We are talking not purely about Olympic sports or sports involving humans; a range of professional sports is involved. It cannot be presumed that performance in any sport does not improve with the use of drugs. It should be assumed that every sporting performance improves with the taking of some form of drugs.

I recognise that in the United States sport is in a different form. There is no equivalent to the Sports Council, so one must consider alternative means of making progress. I have referred to golf. More than any other sport, American football and American basketball are probably riddled with drug-taking. In 1986 the collegiate football teams had 40 teams Bowl-bound, to use their expression—they were about to play in one college bowl or another—and they announced that there was to be random testing. We are talking about 40 teams and between 2,000 and 2,500 footballers. Random testing was carried out on about 10 per cent., so let us assume that between 200 and 250 people were tested. Despite the fact that the tests were announced in advance and people could take masking agents, there were 21 positive tests. The NCAA announced that, because it had found that only 10 per cent. of all those tested were positive, there was no evidence of drug-taking so it would discontinue such a policy. That is a tragedy and it fills me with disbelief.

Collegiate football argues that it cannot afford testing. I have already said that the total cost for testing in all the sports in Britain that are involved so far was only £487,000. I have suggested that British sports should test individuals who appear in the top 10 rankings of their competitions. In American collegiate football it would be easy to say that the top 10 colleges involved—Notre Dame, the universities of Miami, Florida State, Oklahoma, Nebraska and Michigan, the university of South Carolina and the like—would be the prime targets for random tests. What a message would be sent out to American youth if it were announced that the prime athletic achievers in collegiate football were to be tested.

The criticism of costs beggars belief. Most of those universities that I identified have major medical schools attached to them. They could ask their students, as part of their research, to carry out dope testing of their sportsmen. That would be the best way of making progress in collegiate football and then making progress in professional sport.

I suggest, as I did in relation to European sports, that the major sponsors in American, British, European and worldwide sport give serious consideration to withdrawing sponsorship unless they are certain that the sporting event is clean. I am not suggesting that the sports are not clean. I said that golf in the United States did not want to know. Perhaps drugs are not used, but we do not know because there have not been any tests.

I am not suggesting that any of the sponsors that I have mentioned sponsor drug-ridden events, but they do not know whether they do. They should be able to say, "We know that these events are clean." The major banking institutions, such as Citicorp and Chase Manhattan, companies such as Pepsi-Cola and Coca-Cola, the NBC and ABC, which buy the sporting rights, and Texaco and other big oil companies should ask the sports events that they sponsor, "Can you make a categoric assertion that this event is clean?" Without such a policy on sport, everything that the American Government say that they are attempting to do can be laughed at.

How can William Bennett, the head of the American drug task force, say, "We are taking this issue seriously" when the President of the United States welcomes and congratulates teams that have won major bowls, major sporting events, but which cannot stand up and say that they are clean? It should be an embarrassment not only to Mr. Bennett but to President Bush and other members of the American Administration that the most public aspects of American society are not clean of drugs, and that apparently little effort is made to make them clean. I should like to see in the United States major progress not in words but in action.

Although I have criticised America for its marked failure to make progress, I hope that, worldwide, we shall not sit back and say that it is only like that in the United States. It is not. We have a long way to go in Britain and in Europe. It was only last year that Birgit Dressel, a German heptathlete, died as a result of drug overdoses in an attempt to lift herself from being between 30th and 40th in the world's heptathletes into the top 10. That is a sad commentary on drug abuse in sport. We must make massive progress in this country because, as I said earlier, only by making progress in sport shall we be able to set an example to the youngsters in society as a whole. By setting that example, we shall have taken one step—and only one step—in making progress towards eradicating the drug problem within society today.

12.20 pm

Mr. Tony Baldry (Banbury): The whole House owes a debt of gratitude to my hon. Friend the Member for Warrington, South (Mr. Butler) for having introduced this important debate. It has enabled hon. Members to speak with some insight on a subject that concerns us all. The speech of my hon. Friend the Member for Kingswood (Mr. Hayward) was a classic example of an ideal speech in this House. My hon. Friend has deep knowledge of a particular aspect of this subject. He has carried out research and looked into the matter, and has shared his findings with the rest of the House to the enhanced benefit of us all.

The Guardian on 19 May, in its first editorial, said:

"Drug addiction is already perceived as the single biggest threat facing Britain. A survey of parents published yesterday, puts drug abuse far ahead of all other risks threatening the future of their children: well ahead of Aids, pollution, mugging, drink, tobacco, unhealthy foods and accidents. But serious though the present drug problem has become, an even more serious threat looms on the horizon: crack."

Speaking as the parent of two young children—I know that many other hon. Members are also parents—I suspect that one of the spectres that haunts us all is drugs.

All of us, from time to time, have had a glimpse of hell. For our grandfathers, it was probably the trenches of the first world war and the carnage there. For our fathers, it was the hell of Auschwitz and Belsen and the destruction of that time. By comparison, my glimpses of hell have been less horrific, though none the less frightening. I am thinking of the feeding camps of Ethiopia and the mass starvation there. I also think of a day that will stick in my mind for a long time and to which I alluded earlier. I visited a children's hospital in Newark, New Jersey, which was largely full of young babies who had contracted AIDS in the womb. Their mothers, by and large, were women who had become drug addicts for a variety of reasons. They had taken to a life of prostitution to pay for their drug addiction and a vicious circle of prostitution, drug addiction and prostitution had led them in an ever downward spiral. When they became pregnant, their babies become infected with AIDS.

It is difficult to look at such a large number of children who, through no fault of their own, have been born with the most terrible illness and for whom life will be short and fraught. Fortunately, as yet, there are no hospital wards in this country where one can see similar scenes, but, unless we get to grips with the drug problem in this country, such a spectre awaits us.

Crack is a cocaine-based narcotic and will make the drugs problem worse, as the United States experience

[*Mr. Tony Baldry*]

clearly demonstrates. As the House will probably know, it is produced by cooking cocaine hydrochloride with baking soda and water. When the mixture cools, it crystallises and can be cut into squares, commonly known as rocks. It is consumed by heating the rocks and inhaling the vapour. The rush reaches the brain within seconds and addiction is acquired far more quickly than with other drugs. Worse still, there is no substitute drug which can be offered to addicts in rehabilitation. That has made them more reluctant to seek help than opiate users, such as heroin addicts. I speak as a member of the Bar who, from time to time, has had to defend addicts to heroin and other drugs. Heaven knows, it is hard enough to persuade heroin addicts to seek proper help and support. There are 100,000 heroin addicts in this country.

More alarming still is the increasing level of violence associated with the dealing in and use of crack. Those who smoke it are said to experience a feeling of omnipotence and paranoia which, in the United States, has led to an increasing number of shootings of police officers as well as other crimes of violence.

In the past four years, there has been a six-fold increase in the seizure of cocaine in Europe. In Britain, Customs and Excise seized about 220 kg in the first three months of this year alone, compared with 35 kg in the whole of 1984. It is worth dwelling on those figures. Of course, 35 kg of a drug such as cocaine is, in itself, a pretty substantial problem. My right hon. and hon. Friends at the Home Office by their actions have already acknowledged that the seizures represent only a fraction of the illegal drugs being smuggled into this country.

Three or four years ago, even in the United States, crack would not have been seen as a problem. Yet in three years it has gone from being a minor problem in the United States to one that is reaching epidemic proportion. We, at least, have the advantage of being forewarned. We know the spectre that could face us. Clearly, Europe is increasingly in the sights of the drug barons in south American countries such as Colombia and Bolivia. It seems that production in south America has increased to the point where the north American market is saturated, so the south American traffickers are now targeting the United Kingdom and the rest of Europe as additional outlets. It is horrific to think of drug trafficking as akin to the export trade, but that is certainly how the drug traffickers of south America look at it. One has only to recall the activities of ex-President Noriega of Panama, who made drugs one of that country's major exports to realise the problems that we face in Europe.

Crack is extremely addictive. Smokers seem to become hooked after smoking it as few as three or four times. By contrast, even cocaine can be smoked for 13 to 14 months without addiction. Already, the introduction of crack into this country is having an impact on the behaviour of pushers, who appear to have slashed the price of cocaine so as to widen the market. The street price has fallen from about £100 per gramme 18 months ago to as little as £40 in the east midlands and even £30 in parts of London. It seems almost obscene to allude to drug dealing as akin to business but clearly the drug pushers want to persuade people to switch brands—to go up market and change to crack. The reason is that it doubly benefits the pushers, who boost their income with each gramme of powder that

is turned into crack and increase their revenue because crack produces such as intense and short-lived high that the user's craving and consumption far outstrips the craving and consumption of the cocaine snorter.

There is a strategy operating in some parts of Britain whereby cannabis is deliberately withheld from the streets and cocaine offered in its place. In some parts in Britain crack is on sale for as little as £20 a hit. That is terrifying because many youngsters can lay their hands on £20 with a bit of petty thieving, whereas in the past drugs such as heroin may have been more expensive.

Mr. Rathbone: My hon. Friend may not be painting a gloomy enough picture. One can get a hit or fix of crack for as little as £2 or £3.

Mr. Baldry: I am sure that my hon. Friend is right. That is even more horrifying because many youngsters can acquire £2 or £3 by way of pocket money these days.

Last September police raided a flat on an estate in south London and discovered large quantities of drugs in a crack factory fortified with steel doors. Armed police had to use oxyacetylene torches and a hydraulic ram to force their way in. That estate, which houses about 3,000 people is, alas, already known by locals as "crack city". Customers come from all over the country to buy crack in the centre of that estate. One local resident said:

"There are times when it's like Waterloo station in the rush hour . . . Sometimes you can get 15 street dealers outside the pub. We get really big teams, from all over the place. Sometimes a dealer will arrive with four or five blokes minding him."

The police have taken to wearing bullet-proof vests when raiding the estate. That is horrific. We are talking about a housing estate not more than 15 minutes away from the Palace of Westminster, and it is only a matter of months since armed police wearing bullet-proof vests had to raid it. Hon. Members have referred to Elliot Ness and "The Untouchables", but we are already seeing horrific signs of things happening here that hitherto have been associated with the United States.

Mr. Randall: I welcome the hon. Gentleman's vivid description of the possible consequences of the arrival of crack. A number of hon. Members have suggested that we are just about holding our own in the containment of drug misuse, but does the hon. Gentleman not agree that some radical changes in our drugs policy may be needed if we are to contain this new drug which he has described in such strong terms?

Mr. Baldry: Yes, and I have no doubt that my hon. Friend the Minister will outline some of the initiatives that the Government have been taking. All the evidence suggests that my right hon. Friend the Home Secretary has clearly understood the spectre of crack. After all, it was he who made it clear to the Pompidou group of the Council of Ministers exactly the spectre that Europe faces from the introduction of crack.

Many hon. Members may recall that a few weeks ago there was a debate on the inner cities on an Opposition Supply day. It was, perhaps ominous that on that very night there was a riot in Wolverhampton. It did not involve lager louts. it was not an alcohol-related riot—it was a riot following the discovery of a quantity of crack. The incident began with a drugs raid on a public house suspected of being the focus of drug dealing. It degenerated into a fight between local youths and the police officers, who were quickly backed up by properly equipped riot squads. There was looting, vandalism and arson, but it was clear that much of that was inspired by the drug pushers trying to protect their interests.

I have no hesitation in saying that the police, both in Wolverhampton and in south London, were right to go in hard and pursue the matter to the end. It must be fully understood that those who deal in crack will be dealt with heavily. I am sure that the courts will also make that quite clear. It is a telling point that on this very day *The Times* reports that a young person aged 22 was yesterday remanded in custody charged with possessing crack. It is the first case of its kind in Britain, so it is appropriate that we should have this debate today.

During recent years police throughout Britain have become professional and sophisticated in their war against drugs and they have responded positively to the new threat of crack. Scotland Yard has set up a 17-man intelligence unit to study links between the crack market and certain sections of the population. There is a difficult problem, which the House and the country must face honestly but with a degree of sensitivity. One of the areas where crack appears to have become prevalent most quickly is the inner city, which houses large numbers of black and West Indian youths. A senior police officer is reported as saying that a great deal of the crack trade is imitative of what is happening in certain sections of Washington and new York and that much of it is Jamaican inspired. The incidence of crack among a minority in the Afro-Caribbean community in inner London creates a difficult problem which, although it must be handled positively, must also be handled with sensitivity if it is not to look as though we are somehow asserting that crack is a black problem. Crack poses a problem that affects us all, but it appears to be easier for crack pushers to penetrate the Afro-Caribbean communities rather faster than other communities.

I have no doubt that many black community leaders will be highly apprehensive that if we as a community do not act together, crack here will become a focus in the same way as it has devastated numbers of black communities in American cities. It is a tragic comment that in some precincts in the United States half the young people are crack addicts and there are daily street battles between drug groups.

My right hon. Friend the Home Secretary has referred to crack as a plague. It is perhaps worth reminding ourselves of the lines written at the time of the black death:

"We see death coming into our midst like black smoke, a plague which cuts off the young and has no mercy".

That is certainly the effect of crack. It is a plague which cuts off the young and has no mercy. The drug has spread like a plague across the United States, especially the poorer inner cities. My right hon. Friend the Home Secretary was right to say:

"If crack ever becomes deeply rooted in Europe the outlook will indeed be bleak. Our job must be to work together urgently to ensure that the United States experience is not repeated here."

As many of my hon. Friends have said today, crack and similar drugs must be tackled on two fronts—supply and demand. I know that Home Office Ministers have been active in both areas, with initiatives such as more money for the United Nations anti-drugs programmes and, beginning next April, programmes to train Customs officers from the producer and transit countries. It is, of course, an international problem. We might be the

recipient, but drugs go through a number of other countries. It is therefore important to work together. The British Government have given £2 million to help to improve the equipment of the law enforcement agencies in countries along the supply route. I am sure that Ministers will be working towards persuading our partners in the European Community that there should be an effective European convention which makes it possible to confiscate traffickers' profits and to tackle the problem as a community.

There may be limits to the success of controls over supply, because the rewards are so high and the potential loopholes so large. After all, the product is not difficult to transport. I have been involved in cases, as I am sure have other hon. Members who are also members of the Bar, where drugs have simply been sent through the post. Try as it may, the international sorting office of the post office cannot examine every parcel that comes into the United Kingdom. We must, therefore, not only tackle supply, but also seek ways of controlling demand.

In recent years, we have seen that controlling demand can be effective by means of, for example, media campaigns, school education programmes on such things as drug abuse, and an increase in funds for treatment and drug rehabilitation projects. My hon. Friend the Under-Secretary of State, who is to respond to the debate, is chairing a ministerial group on the misuse of drugs. I believe that such groups are beginning to become effective —not only the one dealing with the misuse of drugs but also the one dealing with alcohol abuse, which my right hon. Friend the Leader of the House is chairing.

My right hon. Friend the Home Secretary has already called for initiatives to tackle crack and to step up education programmes to warn young people of the highly addictive effects of the drug and to stress the concern among doctors that, sadly, there is no way to wean addicts off the drug. I hope that at some time it might be possible to send a straightforward leaflet on crack and its dangers to every parent in the country. After all, we are becoming increasingly used to schools sending out information to parents. This is a challenge to every parent and something about which everybody should be concerned.

There are one or two important ramifications of the crack problem which it is important to take on board, particularly with the European elections taking place next Thursday. Many of my right hon. and hon. Friends wish to see a Europe sans frontiers. Metaphorically, we all understand what that means—a Europe with no trade barriers. That has been translated into a belief that we should also have a European Community in which there are no frontier posts or border controls. Therefore, if an illegal substance entered the European Community in southern Greece, it could reach northern Scotland without having to pass another border control or frontier check. That would be lunacy because it would be much easier for drug traffickers to move drugs around the Community. I hope that Home Office Ministers will resist attempts to dismantle border controls. Some checks should be retained and there should continue to be increasing co-operation between the police and drug enforcement authorities throughout Europe in exchanging intelligence with Customs officers, police officers, drug officers and others, so that there is a Community effort, in which border controls form a useful part.

In the next few months the fight against crack will be crucial. The actions within the next few months of

[*Mr. Baldry*]

Parliament, my right hon. and hon. Friends in the Home Office and those in the European Community will determine whether we succeed in that fight. From the actions that Home Office Ministers have already taken, there is every indication that they are determined that we should succeed. The rest of us in the House must play our part in awakening public opinion with sense of alarm about what may take place. We must persuade vulnerable communities that crack represents the most serious threat that they face. By the time they find out for themselves, it may be too late.

The House owes a debt of gratitude to my hon. Friend the Member for Warrington, South for having introduced the debate. This is one of the most horrific threats to face the country for a long time. No words that we can utter in the Chamber are sufficient to stress to every parent and every community leader in the country that crack has to be defeated quickly.

12.48 pm

Mr. Stuart Randall (Kingston upon Hull, West): I congratulate the hon. Member for Warrington, South (Mr. Butler) on his motion. We have had a valuable debate. It has been comprehensive and it is good to see the House united on matters such as this. Apart from a slight flurry on the Conservative Back Benches, no party points have been made today. The House appreciates the seriousness of the problem and the way in which crack, in particular, could affect our society.

I am glad that the hon. Member for Banbury (Mr. Baldry) made such an emphatic speech about crack because I was going to take a similar attitude towards it. I raised the matter with the Home Secretary during the last Home Office questions and asked what initiatives the Government would take to combat the threat to our society. Even if the Parliamentary Under-Secretary does not answer any of my questions I hope that he will today take the opportunity to tell us precisely what initiatives the Government plan to take to combat crack.

We have had a constructive debate today and I intend to continue it. Conservative Members have said that we are just about holding our own in the drugs battle and have referred to the activities of yet another working party. That demonstrates that there is concern that the Government's policy is not getting to grips with the problem. Crack threatens our society and our democracy. If we are only holding our own in the battle with other drugs, what on earth can we do to contain this new drug which is so addictive, has spread throughout the United States over a three year period and is now used in massive proportions. A person can be addicted to crack after using it only three times.

I hope that the parliamentary Under-Secretary will say a little more and be a little more constructive than the Home Secretary was during the last Home Office questions when he merely highlighted the problem. The speech of the hon. Member for Banbury was admirably constructive. Experience in the United States has shown many of us that this is a huge problem and we urgently need some solutions from the Government. That will involve a review of resources including money, manpower, technology, and

medical research. It is not enough merely to have another meeting of the Pompidou group but there must be action to prevent the spread of this horrifying drug.

As the hon. Member for Banbury said, the use of the drug throughout the United States has devastated communities and has resulted in violence which we have also seen in Wolverhampton. The drug has a great effect on those who take it, become high and behave in an extraordinary fashion. As the hon. Gentleman also said, Ministers have been active. They have put forward money to try to solve the problem. It would be unfair to dispute that. But is the policy working? I can put my hand on my heart and say that I am not confident that the Government's existing drugs policy is working. I say that in the most constructive way because the subject is too serious for one to be flippant.

I congratulate the hon. Member for Warrington, South. He made a progressive speech and injected into the debate a number of new ideas which must be given serious consideration when tackling the problem of drugs.

Three tests should be applied when assessing the Government's success in tackling drug abuse. First, how successful has Government policy been in discouraging people from taking drugs? Secondly, how successful have the Government been in discovering the sources of drugs and reducing their supply? That is an international as well as a national problem. Thirdly, how successful are the help and services provided to encourage drug addicts to give up drugs and to stay off them indefinitely?

We have heard in the debate that many factors are involved in assessing the success of Government policy. The third edition of the Home Office document entitled "Tackling Drug Misuse"—I compliment the Minister on the quality of the document: it is very readable—shows in figure 1 that, after a period of relative stability in the 1970s, the misuse of drugs greatly increased in the first half of the 1980s. The number of drug addicts notified to the Home Office increased in that time from about 2,500 to about 9,000. However, addicts notified to the Home Office constitute only a small proportion of the total number of chronic misusers of drugs.

The upshot is that since 1980 we have experienced a worrying increase in the numbers of chronic misusers. The Government will argue that what has happened here is but part of an international phenomenon which has affected many western countries. There may well be an element of truth in that. Nevertheless, the Government are responsible for limiting the demand for drugs and restricting their supply to this country, and Government policy is at least partly responsible for the alarming increase in drug misuse.

It is clear from today's debate that the House shares my reservations about Government policy and believes that we are only just holding our own. We are creating too many committees, as hon. Members have pointed out in their constructive speeches.

I do not believe that the Government have done all that they could to reduce the supply of drugs to the United Kingdom. There is a vast number of different ways in which drugs can be brought into this country, and it is clear that it is impossible to prevent all drugs from entering. However, if we are really determined to restrict the supply, more manpower, money and technology are needed. Is the Minister satisfied that enough staff have been employed to reduce the supply of drugs to the United

Kingdom? Do we still have enough Customs and Excise officers to tackle this massive job? In the end, it comes down to Government priorities.

In an intervention during the speech of the hon. Member for Lewes (Mr. Rathbone), the hon. Member for Chichester (Mr. Nelson) said that in his county the resources that have been made available for drugs research are limited and that it was sad that requests are not being met for additional police officers to carry out drugs-related work.

The third test of Government policy is how successful they are in encouraging drug addicts to give up using drugs and stay off them. The Hull and East Yorkshire council for drug problems, which has a very successful track record, believes that the Government's attitude, and that of the medical profession, has had a deleterious effect on the treatment of chronic drug misusers. The Government's Advisory Council on Misuse of Drugs recommended in its two-part report on AIDS and drugs misuse that specific action should be taken to stop the spread of the HIV virus in prisons through the use of condoms. That recommendation was rejected by the Government. The matter was raised by the hon. Member for Warrington, South. I hope that the Minister will explain why the Government decided not to accept that recommendation.

The report also proposed that there should be comfortable withdrawal from drugs for prisoners. It would involve the use of methadone as an alternative drug. The Hull and East Yorkshire council for drug problems has advised me that the Government have rejected that approach. Their general view is that prisoners should not be provided with the alternative approach to drug withdrawal that was recommended by the Advisory Council on Misuse of Drugs. In other words, prisoners should experience cold turkey. The Hull and East Yorkshire council for drug problems believes that a safe environment is needed so that prisoners with a drugs problem feel confident enough to go to the prison authorities and admit it. Then they could be properly treated.

It is estimated that the helping agencies in the United Kingdom know about 10 per cent. of the drug users in their communities. That has to be contrasted with about 75 per cent. in Holland. I have already raised the matter with the hon. Member for Warrington, South. It demonstrates the different approach and attitude to drugs between the two countries. I should be grateful if the Minister would comment on that.

I have been advised that drug addicts in the United Kingdom come forward only when they have no money and cannot therefore buy drugs. We must encourage more people who use drugs to make themselves known to the helping agencies so that help can be given to them.

The helping agencies have also advised me that the attitude of the medical profession does not always help drug addicts. The general feeling is that people should stop using drugs. In practice, doctors prescribe methadone only if they believe that people will come off drugs quickly. The Hull and East Yorkshire council for drug problems also believes that régimes are usually set up for doctors rather than for drug users. Consequently, most drug users start to take drugs again. The helping agencies believe that the medical profession needs to listen more than it does to what drug users say so that they can be helped to reduce their dependency on drugs. At the moment, almost all drug addicts fail to do so.

The inconsistency of the medical profession seems to be a matter of concern to the helping agencies. Some parts of the country have a good range of services designed to help addicts—the hon. Member for Warrington, South described the services in Merseyside—but in other parts such services can be described only as poor or non-existent. I should welcome the Minister's comments on that fourth point.

In Holland "methadone buses" are used to encourage drug addicts to break the habit, and I understand that such services also exist in Merseyside. Those at the grass roots in the helping agencies believe that they should be more comprehensively available. Needle exchanges, which are vital to a reduction in the transmission of HIV through the use of dirty and shared needles, are only now being organised in some cities.

The helping agencies have also expressed concern about the Government's attitude to women drug users. I am told that few rehabilitation units take in children along with their mothers. As a result fewer women come forward, fearing that their children may be taken away if they admit to their drug problem. This is my fifth point: it is important to recognise that women addicts can care just as much for their children as those with no addictions.

The helping agencies feel that the Government are concentrating too much on the injection of heroin and other opiates: clearly the risk of contracting AIDS arises from infected needles irrespective of the drugs that are used. They believe that the Government should also emphasise that users of amphetamines—including "recreational" users who may inject themselves on Saturday evenings—are just as vulnerable to AIDS, if they are using contaminated needles. I should like the Minister to comment on that as well.

The hon. Member for Warrington, South began his excellent speech by talking about the lack of a registration scheme for crack. I agree that such a scheme is needed, especially as the availability of crack seems far greater than I had thought. Press statistics suggest that it is not widely available, but hon. Members on both sides of the House have said today that it can be obtained for as little as £2 —or, according to one hon. Member, for between £5 and £10.

The hon. Member for Warrington, South said that the probable number of addicts in this country is between five and 20 times the number of registered addicts. Home Office statistics in the report to which I referred earlier show that drug seizures have generally increased, with a slight turndown in recent years. However, the amount of drugs seized is a small proportion of the total amount brought into the country. That is worrying and if the same thing applies to crack we are in danger. Crack is a manufactured drug and I understand that it is made from cocaine. Movements of such drugs will take place throughout the European continent from various parts of the world.

The statistics produced by the Home Office suggest that our fears about the extension of the use of crack are well-founded. If one assumes that the amount of crack that will not be seized is in the same proportion as the amount of other drugs that are not seized one realises that we have a big problem. We have a drugs crisis on the horizon—I hope that I am not overstating the case—that will affect many parts of the country, especially the inner cities, the

[Mr. Stuart Randall]

areas of deprivation and the ethnic communities. I cannot stress enough that we are on the verge of a serious problem.

The police think that cocaine will pose a major problem in future and, as we know, crack is a derivative. In some parts of the country there is an extraordinary correlation between drug taking and crime. Not unreasonably we can expect far more crime if the use of crack increases. The Government parade statistics, as one would expect them to do, that crime is decreasing. However, violent crime is increasing at an alarming rate. The Government's policies could lead to a greater circulation of crack and that could lead to an increase in violent crime. I do not say that in a negative way but simply because I am extremely worried.

The hon. Member for Warrington, South spoke about Amsterdam and the Dutch situation. He did not fully develop that argument nor shall I because I do not know all the details. One of the arguments—which I do not advocate—for legalising drugs is that one can prevent or to some extent control, overdosing. Overdosing usually occurs when somebody who is taking an impure drug comes across a pure drug and does not know the difference and overdoses himself. There are many threats to the argument about legalising drugs but my intuitive reaction is to say, "No way." However, we must take into account the failure of our policy on primary care.

Mr. Butler: I think that the terms that we use in the debate must be more precise. Is there a difference between decriminalisation, which makes it totally legal for anybody to possess drugs in any circumstances, and a system of registration? One needs to distinguish between decriminalisation and the legal availability of drugs within a registered framework surrounded by a tight criminal framework of the type that I developed in my speech.

Mr. Randall: The hon. Gentleman makes an excellent point. We must have a registration scheme to ensure that we know who is who, which is important in the fight against drugs. We must ensure that the problem of over dosing is controlled as much as possible. Britain's helping agencies are aware of only 10 per cent. of addicts whereas in Holland the figure is 75 per cent.

The hon. Member for Warrington, South described the Merseyside case in some detail. It is important that the argument, which has been described by some people as, "just say no", is considered. It is a specialised subject, but I fear that, as politicians, our first reaction is to say no to any form of drug taking. As policy on primary prevention so far has been fairly ineffectual, alternatives must be considered.

I am glad to hear that the Merseyside policy is working and reaching the addict population. I am especially glad —I cannot emphasise this enough—that the AIDS virus seems to be under some sort of control. We must consider the Merseyside experience carefully and gain knowledge from it. The threat of AIDS is greater among drug users. The sharing of needles can spread the HIV virus, with staggering results. The use of heroin has had a massive effect.

The hon. Member for Warrington, South referred to prostitutes. I share his view that it verges on evil for a prostitute who is HIV positive to carry out her trade, thereby placing anyone who goes with her at risk of catching the virus.

I am worried that within the closed community of prisons—Hull prison is experiencing the problem—needle sharing is occurring, resulting in many reported infections. I was interested by the comments of the hon. Member for Warrington, South about prisons in Sweden, where prisoners are screened daily so that the authorities know who is vulnerable. I think that lessons could be learned from that experience.

Mr. Douglas Hogg: The hon. Gentleman referred to increasing evidence of infections within the prison system. There is no evidence of a person becoming HIV positive as a result of any act in a prison.

Mr. Randall: Did the Minister say "as a result of any action in a prison?"

Mr. Douglas Hogg: There is no evidence that anyone has become HIV positive as a result of any action in a prison by way of homosexual activity or drug taking.

Mr. Randall: I am grateful to the Minister for correcting me on that.

Mr. Butler: The reason why evidence is not available is that it has not been looked for.

Mr. Randall: The hon. Gentleman believes that there is a problem, but I accept what the Minister says. Even if no one in prison has contracted the AIDS virus, we should consider carrying out the kind of tests that are undertaken elsewhere. To tackle the AIDS problem, we must be persistent in ensuring that tests are carried out. It is interesting that the Swedish authorities feel that it is necessary to have these tests in prisons. It is interesting also that we feel that there is no need for such tests because we believe that no one has picked up AIDS in our prisons. I accept what the Minister says—he is responsible for prisons.

It is crucial that we do all that we can to prevent pushers from earning profits from drugs. We must persist with the confiscation of assets. I hope that, through the European ministerial groups and working parties, we will pursue this matter as strongly as possible. The Pompidou group of the Council of Europe and the Government have spent money in certain countries where it has been deemed desirable to grow alternative crops to drug-based crops. We seem to be making little headway in the Caribbean islands. I do not know whether other hon. Members share my view, but I cannot grasp whether we are winning, losing or standing still. Perhaps it is an impossible question to answer. I feel from reading reports on what is happening in the Caribbean that there are immense problems.

I hope that the Minister will let us know the Government's policy on harm reduction and primary prevention. I shall quote an article in the May/June edition of *Drug link* which impinges directly on the Government's policy. Under the heading "Beyond 'Just Say No'" it contends:

"drug education should go beyond primary prevention".

The article refers to the attempt to stop people taking drugs and says:

"Most of the kinds who don't use drugs are not influenced by drugs education. It has, at best, a neutral effect. Drug education should encompass the best aspects of primary prevention programmes. It should give information, it should get kids to examine their attitudes, to examine social, legal, political, historical, cultural and health issues. Most importantly, it should look at secondary prevention strategies, ie how to prevent kids harming themselves from drug use."

To paraphrase, the article also says that, in general, primary prevention of whatever kind, seems to be ineffective. It seems to lack a social, cultural and political dimension and to focus instead on the individuals, adopting a victim-blaming approach. It deals with stereotypes and isolates and castigates drug users as deviants. It is negative and does not address the problems of young people who reject the message. Any outcome other than not taking drugs must be seen as a failure. Primary prevention is based on flawed assumptions about behaviour change. It focuses on the expertise of the educator, as opposed to the young people's experience and it does not take into account a period in everyone's life called adolescence, during which people like to take risks. That is strong criticism. The article suggests that primary prevention, which is at the core of the Government's policy, does not work. The people who wrote that article are at the grass roots, dealing with the helping services for drug addicts.

Mr. Rathbone: The hon. Gentleman has not identified the author of that article and my memory does not serve me well enough to identify him. I believe that the article is referring to propaganda and advertising, but not to the activities of teachers responsible for drugs problems in schools. Whatever the article is referring to, the problems could be overcome at a stroke if the Government gave support to the life education centres to which I referred in my own speech.

Mr. Randall: The hon. Gentleman makes a good point. The authors of the article are Ian Clements, Julian Cohen and Pat O'Hare. The article begins by saying:

"Drug education in schools seems to be up a blind alley —approaches aimed at preventing drug use are ineffective and those aimed at reducing harm are unacceptable."

The article reflects an alternative approach to the issue and goes on to say:

"Our underlying assumptions are that drug use is part of normal behaviour and will take place. The moral high ground has in the past been claimed by the 'just say no' lobby who, while accepting that some young people will ignore their advice, see these as inevitable casualties in their attemps to prevent drug use to the exclusion of other aims. Our view is that the moral high ground lies with developing strategies aimed at minimising harm to individuals and communities."

I felt that it was worth putting that alternative on the record, so we can consider it later on.

The hon. Member for Lewes (Mr. Rathbone) made an interesting speech. I know that he has been active in the all-party drug misuse group, together with my hon. Friend the Member for Islington, South and Finsbury (Mr. Smith).

Mr. Rathbone: And my hon. Friend the Member for Warrington, South (Mr. Butler).

Mr. Randall: Yes, the hon. Member for Warrington, South is also a member of that group. I welcomed what the hon. Member for Lewes said. However, the way in which he referred to his three measures for restoring some sort of criminal justice system in Colombia made me slightly bemused, although I acknowledge the hon. Gentleman's expert knowledge on these matters. Indeed, I tackled him on those measures in one of my interventions. I am not sure that Governments can be bought off. The hon. Gentleman suggested that there should be help in buying communications equipment and in providing intelligence information and, possibly, weapons. I believe that although the exchequers of those countries may not, on paper, be receiving anything from the drugs crops, the opportunities for them to be bought off with very large sums of money must make it possible that they are benefiting from the drugs. The hon. Gentleman advances a high risk strategy, which raises doubts and questions in my mind, although I am not sure that I have an alternative.

The hon. Member for Lewes also talked about drug liaison officers. I agree that drug liaison officers in different countries should co-operate and use common information systems—especially in the EEC countries because of the special relationship that we share.

The hon. Member for Chichester (Mr. Nelson) referred to the provision of police for drugs work in rural areas. He was absolutely right that our rural areas encounter problems; it is not just London or the inner cities. The hon. Gentleman said that it was sad that requests to the Government for additional police officers for drugs work had not been met. I cannot understand why the Government are not making resources available.

The hon. Member for Lewes said that California was the ninth largest economy in the world and that the largest part of its economy derived from drugs.

Mr. Rathbone: The largest cash crop.

Mr. Randall: Yes, the largest cash crop. The matter arose in the American presidential elections and President Bush made great play of it. I hope that the American Government will take a much tougher line than they have taken in the past. The problem lies not only outside but within the boundaries of the United States. The Americans say that they are going to tackle the problem in Colombia or in other south American countries yet at the same time drugs are a massive cash crop in their own country.

Medical research in also important, in addition to social research, and we must spend more on it. Hon. Members have referred to advertising campaigns. The people to whom I have spoken at grass roots level—in the helping agencies—believe that a number of campaigns, including those encouraging the use of clean needles and discouraging the sharing of needles, have been ineffective. Our schools display an element of rigidity on the question of drugs. Especially now that crack is firmly on the scene, we need to review our methods of promulgating our message about drugs. If we are not succeeding, the money is not being well spent and the Government should reconsider. Perhaps the Minister will tell us whether the money that is being spent is being spent effectively and whether he feels that the reports that I have received are not as accurate as I have been led to believe.

The hon. Member for Cheltenham (Mr. Irving) made an excellent point about crack. he said that one could buy it for £5 to £10 a go. He told us of parents crying out for help, while we hold conferences on European co-operation. That as a telling point. The working parties are still talking three years later, but the parents still have problems.

Today's debate has been excellent and has shown the great concern of hon. Members on both sides of the House. We have widely discussed the problem of crack and the crisis that we now face. We know that that and other

[*Mr. Randall*]

drugs debilitate our society. I hope that the Minister will answer the very many questions that have been raised today.

1.35 am

Mr. Hugo Summerson (Walthamstow): Drug use and abuse has a long history. It goes back hundreds of years, to the time of the Crusades, when the Assassins of Palestine were one of the great powers in that area. They were all doped up to the eyeballs by the Old Man of the Mountains and they did terrible things to our men in Palestine. That was some time ago, but over the centuries there have been many other incidences of drug abuse. In London, during the time of Sherlock Holmes, there were the famous opium dens on the river. I am sure that the House will recall one famous scene where Holmes was found by Dr. Watson lying on a bunk puffing away at an opium pipe.

Drugs have been used for various reasons, such as to ensnare people's minds, and for pleasure. I suspect that today many drugs are abused simply because people are bored. The reason is clear to those who visit many council estates, with their high-rise blocks and terrible staircases that people always have to use because the lifts are broken down for the umpteenth time. No one ever parks his car in the underground spaces because the cars are vandalised or burnt and the car parks are used by the criminal fraternity for stripping stolen cars. There is evidence of drug abuse in such areas because the young people living there say, "What else can we do? We are fed up with watching television. We do not want to watch Sky, with its promise of 100 new channels because they will be even more boring." Those youngsters feel that in drugs they have something new, something exciting and something dangerous because it is against the law.

My first plea is for a little more life to be injected into such areas. A good start would be pulling down some of the tower blocks and sending those living in them to more civilised and sensible surroundings. They want little houses with gardens. That would strike at the heart of those who use the soullessness of the decay of council estates to push their lethal products on those who have the misfortune to live there.

I went to Washington D.C. last year for a conference and found the rate of killings among drug dealers quite terrifying. More than 300 people died violently last year in Washington, mainly because of shoot-outs between rival drug gangs. One of the worst aspects was that Capitol Hill itself was one of the most dangerous places in the capital of the United States of America. Everyone on our trip was warned not to go anywhere near Capitol Hill after dark because of the serious dangers there. I ask the House to imagine what it would be like if drugs got such a grip on this country that Parliament square itself became dangerous for our people and for the tourists. That is what has happened in the United States, and I only hope and pray that it does not happen here.

Another worrying aspect is the copycat tendency. Many people look up to those in the pop scene or who are media figures; they look on them as gods. They do not realise that those gods are made of base material and have feet of clay.

All too often, people on the pop scene use drugs. They have an enormous influence on society. The young will look to them and say, "So and so uses drugs. It is obviously the in thing to do, so I shall do the same." There have been instances, too, of well-known media figures using drugs.

We can sit in the House and talk about the matter but all that the young people will think is, "Oh well, they are only blimpsih, old fuddy-duddies". They will not pay any attention to us, but they will pay attention to those to whom they look up—people in the media, on the pop scene and, perhaps, even footballers. Let us see if we can get some of those people on our side to put the message across —those to whom potential drug abusers will look and to whom they will listen.

I listened to the hon. Member for Kingston Upon Hull, West (Mr. Randall) with great interest. He certainly described in immense detail exactly what he thought about the problem. I defer to him, a man of his years and experience, and I have therefore, cut my speech. I would have said more, but the hon. Gentleman's words of wisdom have made up for my shortened speech.

I fully applaud the Government's efforts to date. I am sure that we shall hear from my hon. Friend the Under-Secretary that the Government intend to do even more not only to root out this vile trade and the vile use of drugs in our country, but to prevent it spreading any further.

1.41 pm

Mr. John Marshall (Hendon, South): Listening to the hon. Member for Kingston Upon Hull, West (Mr. Randall) who spoke at great length, one could not help thinking that they also serve who only sit and wait. Unlike him I shall show that brevity is the spice of wit.

How often have we heard during the debate the question, "what are the Government doing about drugs?". While the Government have a responsibility to stem and staunch the supply of drugs, the responsibility for effecting the demand for drugs goes much wider than the Government. It is one shared by us all as parents, teachers, religious leaders, doctors and social workers. We must ask ourselves the basic question: why is it that at a time of unprecedented prosperity, so many feel the need for the artificial stimulus provided by drugs?

I believe that we are reaping the whirlwind from the permissiveness of the 1960s. At that time, leaders in our society were willing to sign letters to *The Times* suggesting that soft drugs should be legalised and people were willing to suggest that soft drugs were chic. Those who created a climate of opinion then are responsible for what is happening today. Those, such as the authors of TW3— "That Was the Week that Was"—who were willing to destroy traditional values and who were able to sneer and to destroy, but were able to produce nothing positive to put to society, are responsible for what is happening today.

We have a society that is better educated and more prosperous, but still more anxious to indulge in drugs. That is because, as a society, too many lack a faith and a vision for the future. I believe that, if we are to cure that problem, the churches should be taking more of a role. We all know the views of the churches on the community charge. We all know the views of the Bishop of Durham on the resurrection, but I would like to hear his views on drugs, and some of the major problems facing us as a country.

I cannot conceal the contempt, the anger and, indeed, the hatred that I feel for drug traffickers, because they are willing to sell drugs to others, oblivious of the consequences that those individuals will suffer. They are willing to trade in misery and in degradation. I believe that no penalty can be too great for any drug trafficker. I welcome the fact that the Government have been responsible for substantially increasing the penalties for drug trafficking.

The drug barons of the world know no boundaries. The chains of command spread over many countries and pass through many frontiers. The Government are right to ensure that the corrective action and the campaign against drug barons are also international. However, does my hon. Friend the Minister believe that stationing merely 12 drug liaison officers in the principal producing and transit areas is enough?

Mr. Douglas Hogg: There are 15.

Mr. Marshall: Is that enough? I have my doubts. On that note, I give way to my hon. Friend the Member for Maidstone (Miss Widdecombe) who has been patient this morning.

1.46 pm

Miss Ann Widdecombe (Maidstone): I congratulate my hon. Friend the Member for Warrington, South (Mr. Butler) on securing the debate. I do so in that brief sentence because I have been driven to undue truncation of my speech due to the verbosity—or rather, the eloquence —of the hon. Member for Kingston upon Hull, West (Mr. Randall). I congratulate the Government on the considerable initiatives and spending that they have undertaken in connection with drug misuse and on the wholly correct priority that they have given to it.

The establishment in 1984 of the interdepartmental ministerial committee on the misuse of drugs has been extremely productive, as have the mass media publicity campaign undertaken, promoted and funded by the Government, and the Government's participation in international initiatives such as the 1988 United Nations convention. All of that proves that the Government are committed to tackling the problem. We welcome the support of the hon. Member for Kingston upon Hull, West for those initiatives.

The secret of reducing the demand for drugs is the education of the young. It is crucial that we produce a generation of young people who will despise the use of drugs as stupid and ridiculous, even if they are not prepared to regard them as immoral. That is the argument that we have to win. We should be asking why young people experiment with drugs. Well, why do they smoke and drink? Even though smoking is declining within the population as a whole, there is a rise in teenage smoking, particularly among young girls, and the increase in drink-related offences among teenagers is ample testimony to our failure to convince them of the dangers of alcohol. For the young, prohibition is often the equivalent of a dare and death is remote and unreal—unless, tragically, it happens to one of their peers when the shock can be salutary and thought-provoking.

It is not only the young who suffer from the malaise of "It can't happen to me." Many people of mature years do not moderate their sexual behaviour despite the chilling message of the campaign against AIDS. It is a piece of conventional wisdom that most people will believe in the reality of AIDS only when someone they know dies from it, but I suspect that even then some will hear the splash of the ferryman's oars for only a short time before convincing themselves that everything is all right and that that person was simply unlucky.

Our social climate is a product of the decade of delusion —the 1960s—and people are not expected to bear the consequences of or take responsibility for their actions. If someone commits a premeditated crime, their background was deprived; if they cheat to obtain credit, it is the fault of the finance company for making credit available; if there are difficulties in marriage, people get a divorce, even if the marriage has lasted only a year; if someone is inconveniently pregnant, they have an abortion; if people do not want to work even if work is available, they claim social security; and if they smoke, or drink to danger point, they believe that the NHS will make them better.

A natural conclusion of all that is that people will think that there is no real danger and that they have no responsibility to consider the question of drugs. That is the result of the mentality of those brought up by 1960s parents. We have to eradicate that mentality, which will take as long as it did to inculcate it. We have to look for some short-term measures and ask ourselves what will convince the young.

My hon. Friend the Member for Walthamstow (Mr. Summerson) suggested that youngsters are convinced by words of wisdom from those whom they respect. Peer group pressure, the hatred of being the odd one out and the views of their own age group also convince the young, and that is important. It is time we made much more use of young people in helping and educating young people with the drugs problem. Where the didactic approach does not work, the shared experience approach may. We could successfully use the young who have had, and overcome, drug problems to teach other young people of the dangers involved. They will listen more carefully to those of their own age.

We must strip the glamour image of drugs, touched on by my hon. Friend the Member for Walthamstow. Earlier, I asked why young people drink and smoke. It is because grown-ups do so and because they see their heroes and favourite characters in glamorous TV series doing so. Every time a well-known personality is convicted of a drug offence, that is seen by the young as an endorsement of drug use, which we call abuse. We must come down with extremely tough penalties on those in positions of influence and in the public eye who use drugs and set a deplorable example.

I shall particularly welcome an answer from my hon. Friend the Minister on the use of young people in the education campaign.

1.51 pm

The Parliamentary Under-Secretary of State for the Home Department (Mr. Douglas Hogg): It is extraordinary that we should have had so few debates in recent years on an issue which is so important to the nation and involves a substance so destructive to individuals. That is true of drug misuse and individual drugs, which have rarely been

[*Mr. Douglas Hogg*]

the subject of debate in this House. Therefore, the House is indebted to my hon. Friend the Member for Warrington, South (Mr. Butler) for giving us the opportunity to discuss and consider such an important issue. I say that not least because it gives me the opportunity to emphasise the high priority that the Government give to problems associated with drug misuse, and to outline in broad terms, the nature of our present policies and those that we are likely to pursue.

Before I set about that, may I say how much I agree with the remarks of my hon. Friend the Member for Maidstone (Miss Widdecombe) when she reminded the House that this is not exclusively a Government matter. Of course, they have an important role to play, but so do individuals. It is jolly good to remind individuals that they, and society as a collection of individuals, have a moral responsibility for their actions, those of their neighbours and the consequences which so often ensue.

I shall begin by giving a snap-shot picture of the drug scene as I see it both in general and in particular. I shall then outline in broad terms the nature of our present policies and answer more extensively the points made by hon. Members during this important debate.

The nature and extent of drug use varies from year to year, drug to drug and area to area. Those variations are caused by a variety of factors including availability, fashion, tradition, price, and quality. It is a mistake to suppose that a particular sort of drug misuse which might be prevalent in central London is also prevalent in Lincolnshire. They may well be different, and, therefore, we should be careful when analysing a drug problem to keep in mind the fact that, though present throughout the country, it is not the same throughout the country.

Trends are worrying, whether measured in terms of seizures or in terms of the rising number of addicts. Both records show that the trend is increasing, which is worrying. In part, one could say that increasing numbers of seizures are signs of greater efficiency on the part of Customs and the police. The increase in the number of registered addicts points at least in part to a closer compliance with the law on registration, but I do not take undue consolation from these facts because the underlying trend, which is reflected at least in part in those increases, is worrying.

In this context, I shall mention cocaine, of which crack is a derivative. For the second year running, seizures of cocaine have exceeded those of heroin in volume terms. I acknowledge that that is partly the result of increased police and customs efficiency, but it also tells us that Europe in general and the United Kingdom in particular are being made the subject of the importation of cocaine by Latin American traffickers.

For this, there are a number of reasons, of which three are worth mentioning, First, hon. Members have mentioned the difference in price in the United States and the United Kingdom where a much higher return is to be secured. Secondly, the United States market is not capable of indefinite expansion. I do not want to use the word "saturation" which has been used by a number of hon. Members, but I accept that there is a limit to the United States market's potential for expansion, so it is inevitable that traffickers will look to Europe.

Thirdly, the interdiction policies being pursued by the United States Government, although in no sense successfull overall—they interdict only 20 per cent. of the whole—serve as a deterrent. Many traffickers will be looking to Europe as an easier place in which to expand the market. The trends, especially in cocaine, are extremely worrying.

I shall quickly say something about particular classes of drug. There were encouraging signs of decline in the reported misuse of heroin in 1986-87. That was probably more due to supply than to anything else. However, since then there has been a 20 per cent. increase in seizures. That trend is likely to continue.

We do not know the total numbers of misusers—nor can we, because it is an unlawful activity; but it is estimated that there are 100,000 regular heroin misusers, of whom probably half are regular injectors. Certainly, more than half of the notified addicts are.

For the second year running, volumes of cocaine seized have exceeded those of heroin seized. As I said, crack is a derivative of cocaine, and I have no doubt that when substantial quantities of cocaine are present in a community, there is a high risk that it will be transformed into crack. At the moment the figures are not, in themselves, terribly alarming. There were 27 seizures of crack in the first three months of this year, 13 seizures in 1988 and six in 1987. but if I have to state an opinion, it is that those figures are but the tip of an iceberg. I believe that there is a high risk that a serious problem of crack misuse will develop in this country. I cannot express the level of that risk; it is not sensible to try. I merely tell the House that there is a high risk which we are duty bound to tackle.

The illicit production of amphetamines in the United Kingdom is now probably the major source of amphetamines available to misusers. As has been rightly said, in particular by the hon. Member for Kingston upon Hull, West (Mr. Randall), amphetamines are injected quite as much as heroin is injected. The risks associated with amphetamine injection are just the same.

Cannabis remains the most widely misused drug. It is important to maintain pressure on cannabis misuse, if only because, to do otherwise, would send wholly the wrong signals to misusers and drug traffickers.

My hon. Friend the Member for Ealing, North (Mr. Greenway) asked me about decriminalisation in general, but particularly about the decriminalisation of marijuana. There is no prospect whatsoever of this Government at any time decriminalising the use of any of the drugs with which we are now concerned. In particular, there is no prospect of the use of marijuana being decriminalised. It will remain subject to the existing criminal law.

That concludes the snapshot that I wanted to take. It is a serious problem which, in many respects, is getting worse, so I shall now try to deal with what we need to do about it. As I do so, I shall attempt to answer points that have been made by Opposition Members and by my hon. Friends. I hope that I shall also have sufficient time in which to answer specific questions that have been raised.

We all agree that there can be no single solution to the problem of drug misuse. If any Government are to stand any hope of success, they must have a broadly-based policy that addresses the various elements of the problem. From time to time the emphasis of that strategy will shift in order to meet particular anxieties or developments. I shall summarise briefly the five elements of the policy and then develop them—again briefly. First, we must reduce supplies from abroad. Secondly, we must improve the effectiveness of enforcement. Thirdly, we must tighten up on deterrence and domestic control. Fourthly, we must reduce demand through prevention and education. Fifthly, there must be improvements in treatment and rehabilitation.

That process is supervised and co-ordinated by a ministerial group on the misuse of drugs, which I have the privilege to chair. Ministers and officials from a variety of Departments with an interest in the problem have been brought together in the group. The group's function is to act as a catalyst and as a means of co-ordinating policies across Government because, by the nature of things, the policies span Departments. It has proved to be an extremely useful vehicle for changes in policy.

A number of hon. Members have referred to supply, an issue of very great importance. We have been extremely active in our attempts to reduce the supply of imported drugs. We give supply a high priority in our bilateral and multilateral relations with other countries. We play an important part in the United Nations commission on narcotic drugs. We are active in the Council of Europe's Pompidou group. We chaired the group meeting last month that considered in particular cocaine and other drugs. We have also played a prominent part in the United Nations convention on illicit drug trafficking.

We are also important international donors: we are the fourth largest donor to the United Nations fund for drug abuse control. We have contributed to specific projects maintained by the fund; for instance, £3·4 million is committed to an opium eradication and substitution project in Pakistan, and £2·2 million to drug-related development projects in Bolivia. In 1987 my right hon. Friend the Home Secretary secured agreement to an increase from £500,000 a year to some £2 million in the Home Office budget for law enforcement and drug-related assistance in key producing countries from which drugs are reaching the United Kingdom.

My hon. Friend the Member for Lewes (Mr. Rathbone) raised a helpful point. He is right in saying that a number of countries, particularly in Latin America, look to us for specific enforcement aid. We are willing—within the budgets that we have set ourselves—to assist producer countries, especially those in Latin America. The justification for that is that those countries are assisted to carry out enforcement measures for themselves, and also that it demonstrates our commitment to the policy of co-operation. We look much more favourably on enforcement-related bilateral aid than on eradication measures. Unless supported by huge sums, capable of providing enforcement and income replacement, eradication measures are probably not the most effective policy, and we cannot provide such sums. Moreover, by providing specific enforcement-related assistance we can achieve a perceptible result.

Let me give some examples of the assistance provided for Latin American countries, or those involved with cocaine, in the 1988-89 budget. In Bolivia we have provided equipment for radios. In Peru we have provided a radio support car and aircraft spares. In Colombia we have provided radio and computer equipment. In Jamaica we have provided a United Kingdom-based Customs training course, together with training in computers. In Brazil we have provided radio equipment. In the British Virgin Islands we have provided a drugs squad officer and

drug surveys. In Venezuela we have provided United Kingdom Customs training courses. I feel that such specific aid, directed at particular needs, is of especial value.

We have also been extending the provision of drug liaison officers. I entirely agree with those of my hon. Friends who have spoken warmly of them. We now have some 15 DLOs throughout the world, posted in the areas that we expect to be most relevant to our internal problems, and we intend to increase their number. I entirely agree with what my hon. Friend the Member for Hendon, South (Mr. Marshall) said on that subject.

Let me return to a point made by my hon. Friend the Member for Lewes. I certainly think that there is scope for co-operation between DLOs from this country and those from other friendly countries such as Germany, which I think he mentioned. The work is carried out on a more ad hoc, person-by-person basis at present, if only because we probably have the most sophisticated method of distributing intelligence through the National Drugs Intelligence Unit, which is not matched by the majority of other European countries. I agree with my hon. Friend about emphasising the importance of co-operation. Where DLOs get information that is relevant to a friendly country, I hope that they will take steps to inform their counterparts either through the NDIU or directly through their counterpart DLOs in post.

The Council of Europe has been mentioned. We had a meeting in May and focused on several issues, most notably on cocaine and the confiscation of drug traffickers' assets. It was an important conference, not least because it demonstrated to my satisfaction that the United Kingdom policy on combating drug misuse is the most developed of any country in central Europe. I found that rather reassuring.

We have taken several steps but I shall mention just two of them. In reply to a point made by my hon. Friend the Member for Lewes I can say that we have set up a working party, the object of which, in part, is to analyse the kind of causes that lead people to drug misuse. It will also try to establish a clearer profile of a typical drug misuser, most notably a user of cocaine. In reply to my hon. Friend the Member for Walthamstow (Mr. Summerson) I can say that many of the problems are associated with boredom —perhaps that is one way to express it—and certainly with the quality of life and prospects for prosperity that people perceive. There is no doubt that a person living in a deprived area is more at risk than one who does not live in such an area.

The other feature of the conference was our announcement of our intention to host an international conference on demand reduction. I am grateful to my hon. Friends for welcoming that. I regard it as important and we are anxious to see producer nations becoming involved in the process.

Some hon. Members rightly raised the question of 1992 and the single European market. They asked if the single market would result in the dismantling of our controls at ports of entry. The answer is no. My right hon. Friend the Home Secretary has made it quite plain by treaty and by statute that we have retained the right to maintain at the ports of entry such controls as we deem necessary to prevent the importation of drugs and other criminal articles such as weapons, and to prevent the passage of terrorists. I hope that that will be of some reassurance to hon. Members.

[*Mr. Douglas Hogg*]

I shall now turn to the policies that we are pursuing on the domestic front. The hon. Member for Kingston upon Hull, West and my hon. Friends the Members for Lewes and for Chichester (Mr. Nelson) questioned whether we were dedicating sufficient resources to enforcement. We have dedicated substantial resources to it and I hope that I will be able to satisfy hon. Members about that. In recent years Customs resources have been substantially increased. Since 1979 we have trebled the number of Customs and special investigators. In the four years between 1984 and 1988 we increased preventive posts by 854. In 1988-89, 450 additional staff were assigned to Customs work, mainly in the field of work connected with preventive measures on drugs. I shall not go into the details because of time, but I can say that we are spending substantial amounts on equipment.

As the House will know, we have set up 17 drug wings, consisting of 221 police officers. We have doubled the capacity of the national drugs intelligence unit, which we established in 1985, and 50 additional officers have been engaged on drugs work in the metropolitan area. We have increased the number of drug squads by 40 per cent. since 1983.

I know and recognise the interest in using the proceeds of confiscated assets for police work. My hon. Friend the Member for Warrington, South and my hon. Friend the Member for Lewes are specifically interested in the subject. There are more powerful arguments against that concept than has been appreciated. I recognise that some people hold different views on hypothecation, but it is difficult in principle to have a policy of hypothecation—of dedicating a particular stream of income to a particular head of expenditure. It is undesirable to give a police force or any enforcement agency a pecuniary interest in an inquiry, and I fear that it would distort policing policies. It is jolly difficult to determine, where a number of police authorities and Customs are working on a case, how to apportion moneys between forces. I attach more importance to the windfall argument than does my hon. Friend the Member for Lewes.

The Home Office is considering the possibility of a central pot, to use jargon, to assist with exceptional expenditure. General drug policing needs should be reflected in bids made by police authorities to my right hon. Friend the Home Secretary, which will be considered by the inspectorate in the normal way. I do not believe that there is a substantial shortfall in our enforcement effort.

There has been wide agreement on deterrence. I am glad to be able to say to my hon. Friend the Member for Warrington, South that we have substantially increased penalties for trafficking in class A drugs; the maximum sentence is now life imprisonment. Further, the courts have been imposing ever increasing sentences.

We have been refusing parole to those sentenced to imprisonment for five years or more for class A drug offences. To put the policy more exactly, parole has been extremely restricted. It would be wrong for me to foreshadow, in an ad hoc way, what our response to the recommendations made by Lord Carlisle's committee will be. My hon. Friend the Member for Warrington, South should not draw any adverse inference from that, I am merely saying that I do not think that it would be right to respond in an ad hoc way to an extremely important report.

Mr. Randall: Does the central pot to which the Minister referred apply only to England and Wales or to Scotland and Northern Ireland as well?

Mr. Hogg: It is a possible Home Office measure, so it will apply to the police forces of England and Wales. As the hon. Gentleman knows, policing in Scotland is a matter for my right hon. and learned Friend the Secretary of State for Scotland.

The policy of confiscating drug assets has proved extremely important. We have made confiscation orders to the value of £11 million. I regard that as an extremely important sanction, and it prevents the reinvestment of moneys gained from such activity in future crime. I regard this as a penalty of considerable importance in our strategy. I shall not develop at length how we intend to carry it further, save to say that I attach high importance to the making of reciprocal bilateral agreements. We have made six already and we intend to push forward at all possible speed with further bilateral agreements and to proceed as quickly as we can within the Council of Europe on a multilateral agreement.

I apologise for going faster than I would wish, but I know that my hon. Friend the Member for Warrington, South wishes to speak at the end of the debate and I should like to make time for him. The demand side is an extremely important side of our policy. One of the most interesting and disturbing features of my recent visit to the United States was that, although the Coastguard has an effective operation to intercept cocaine run from Latin America to Florida—it surpasses anything that I have seen before, with ships, men, radar and aircraft; it has an air wing and is like a military operation—it estimates that it interdicts only 20 per cent. at most of the traffic coming into the United States. We must consider questions of demand reduction at the forefront of our policy.

Demand reduction can take various forms. National advertising can be important. I have in mind our heroin and AIDS campaigns. I do not agree with the criticism by my hon. Friend the Member for Warrington, South, who suggested that national advertising was not effective. There have been various assessments of the efficacy of our national programmes. There has been a much greater willingness among young people to say no to heroin and we have been successful in portraying heroin as a dirty drug. I agree that there are many limitations with a national scheme. One must somehow get the message across in a credible manner. One must not put across a message that is irrelevant to the experience on the streets. There is a hazard in talking about cocaine when cocaine is not universally available. Partly for that reason, during our last campaign we also had three underpinning local regional campaigns that were addressed to more specific needs in particular areas. I suspect that in future we may look as much to those local regional campaigns as we do to a national one.

My hon. Friend the Member for Maidstone made a good point about demand reduction in schools. We need to involve young people in the communication of the message in schools. I recognise that folk such as I are not very credible in a range of schools which one could mention. I am afraid that we must recognise that sad fact.

We need to tailor the message to the community in which it is delivered. We have been acting through education co-ordinators. We have created in every education area education co-ordinators whom we have funded through central resources. That is extremely important. We have assisted also with in-school training and the preparation of training packages. Against a background of crack, we will have to ask ourselves whether we need to do more to deliver locally messages of demand reduction. That must go wider than the schools. It is one matter that I want to consider closely following my return from the United States.

I should like to answer a number of points that I have not so far covered. My hon. Friend the Member for Warrington, South requires the thanks of the House for having raised this matter. He has introduced a variety of important issues. I am glad that he supported us on the issue of condoms. I have been asked by the hon. Member for Kingston upon Hull, West to say why we are opposed to the issue of condoms in prisons. The main reason is that we believe that the issue of condoms would be likely to result in a greater prevalence of homosexual activity. Because of the failure rates associated with condoms, we fear that the result would be to increase and not to diminish the risk of HIV being present in prisons.

My hon. Friend the Member for Warrington, South was right about training. As he knows, we have created a video training package for prisoners and staff and we are anxious that those video packages and training materials should be available throughout our prisons.

The question of the treatment of prisoners who are suffering from drugs was raised. It is not right to say that periods of cold turkey are a part of prison service department policy. It is right to say that it is a clinical matter for medical officers. To express a non-clinical opinion—my own—it seems right that where a person's treatment requires maintenance, if necessary by methadone, that, subject to the medical officer's clinical view, would be appropriate. If somebody is already on a treatment programme when he comes into the prison system, I would hope that medical staff would identify that fact and continue with the maintenance programme.

My hon. Friend the Member for Warrington, South also touched on the question of compulsory testing. As he knows, it is not our policy because there is no cure. It also would impose grave social and economic sanctions, and we do not have such testing outside the prison system. It would, in any case, require legislation. Our policy, therefore, on testing in the prison system is to make it voluntary. Broadly speaking, prisoners should be treated in the same way as persons outside prisons.

We were also asked about what we were doing to eliminate drugs in the prison system. As the House knows, we have abolished the right of remand prisoners to receive food from outside during the remand period. That was done simply to prevent remand prisoners having drugs brought in. We have also increased searches and the use of sniffer dogs.

Ninety per cent. of the finds of drugs in prisons are cannabis. I cannot remember the exact figure for the finds of syringes and needles, but I know that the figure is less than 100. Although one can become disturbed about it and although it is right to watch the situation, the suggestion that the injecting of drugs is commonplace in prisons is wrong. There is no evidence to support that.

My hon. Friend the Member for Warrington, South also raised the matter of anonymous screening. The prison service department will hope to take part in the scheme and the policies that are being put in place by the Department of Health and which will rely on the project put forward by the Medical Research Council for a programme of anonymous testing.

The House will want to allow my hon. Friend the Member for Warrington, South to have a brief word at the conclusion of our debate, so I will summarise my remarks by saying that I have tried to give some idea of Government strategy in this matter. I have tried to respond to particular points and I apologise for not dealing with them all. We have committed substantial resources to this matter to the extent that if we see that there is a further requirement or an additional risk, we shall act as positively as we have done in the past.

2.28 pm

Mr. Butler: I am grateful to you, Mr. Deputy Speaker, for allowing me an opportunity to speak again. It is important for me to emphasise that we have had a constructive debate today about a subject that is important to the future of our nation. We have heard contributions from various parties, and the debate has shown the House in a good light as it has shown all of us contributing constructively and with a degree of unity that I find rare. That makes me a little prouder to be a Member of this institution at the moment.

My hon. Friends the Members for Lewes (Mr. Rathbone) and for Gainsborough and Horncastle (Mr. Leigh) referred to the international aspects of drug abuse. It is a global problem which needs to be tackled by global co-operation, but unfortunately we do not even achieve adequate co-ordination between our national agencies to tackle the problem. My hon. Friends the Members for Lewes, for Banbury (Mr. Baldry) and for Cheltenham (Mr. Irving)——

It being half-past Two o'clock, the debate stood adjourned.

Orders of the Day

Private Members' Bills

LICENSING AMENDMENT (SCOTLAND) BILL

As amended (in the Standing Committee), considered.
Motion made, and Question, that the Bill be now read the Third time, *put and agreed to.*
Bill accordingly read the Third time and passed.

WEIGHTS AND MEASURES (AMENDMENT) BILL

Order for consideration in Committee read.

Hon. Members: Object.

Mr. Deputy Speaker (Mr. Harold Walker): Consideration what day?
No day named.

COAL MINING SUBSIDENCE (DAMAGE, ARBITRATION, PREVENTION AND PUBLIC AWARENESS) BILL

Order for Second Reading read.

Hon. Members: Object.
Second Reading deferred till Friday 16 June.

BRITISH RACING COMMISSION BILL

Order for Second Reading read.

Hon. Members: Object.
Second Reading deferred till Friday 16 June.

FOOTBALL SPECTATORS (No. 2) BILL

Order for Second Reading read.

Hon. Members: Object.
Second Reading deferred till Friday 16 June.

FIRE SAFETY INFORMATION BILL

Order for Second Reading read.

Hon. Members: Object.
Second Reading deferred till Friday 23 June.

PUBLIC SAFETY INFORMATION BILL

Order for Second Reading read.

Hon. Members: Object.
Second Reading deferred till Friday 23 June.

PROTECTION OF RESIDENTS IN RETIREMENT HOMES BILL

Order for Second Reading read.

Hon. Members: Object.
Second Reading deferred till Friday 23 June.

GAMING MACHINES (PROHIBITION ON USE BY PERSONS UNDER EIGHTEEN) BILL

Order for Second Reading read.

Hon. Members: Object.
Second Reading deferred till Friday 23 June.

BRITISH NATIONALITY (HONORARY CITIZENSHIP) BILL

Order for Second Reading read.

Hon. Members: Object.
Second Reading deferred till Friday 7 July.

RIDERS OF EQUINE ANIMALS BILL

Order for Second Reading read.

Hon. Members: Object.
Second Reading deferred till Friday 16 June.

CONTROL OF LITTER (FINES) BILL

Order for Second Reading read.

Hon. Members: Object.
Second Reading deferred till Friday 7 July.

AGRICULTURE (CONTROL OF NITRATES) BILL

Order for Second Reading read.

Mr. Deputy Speaker: Second Reading, what day? No day named.

BUSINESS OF THE HOUSE

Ordered,
That, at the sitting on Monday 12th June, if proceedings on the Motion in the name of Mr. John Wakeham relating to Televising of Proceedings of the House have not been previously disposed of, Mr. Speaker shall at Ten o'clock put any Questions necessary to dispose of them and of any Amendments to that Motion which may have been selected by him and which may then be moved; and proceedings in pursuance of this Order, though opposed, may be decided after the expiration of the time for opposed business.
Ordered,
That, at the sitting on Thursday 15th June, the Motion in the name of the Prime Minister for the Adjournment of the House shall lapse at Seven o'clock, if not previously disposed of.—[*Mr. Sackville.*]

Bank Hall Hospital, Burnley

Motion made, and Question proposed, That this House do now adjourn.—*[Mr. Sackville.]*

2.33 pm

Mr. Peter L. Pike (Burnley): I wish to raise the proposed closure of Bank Hall hospital in Burnley. Let me make it clear at the outset that I shall argue about the reduction in the level of service provided to the people of Burnley rather than about the building itself, which dates back to the 18th century and needs a considerable amount spent on it. It was the former home of General Scarlett, who fought his first parliamentary election in Burnley as a Conservative candidate, fortunately unsuccessfully. He was the victor in the charge of the heavy brigade which took place on the same day as the charge of the light brigade.

The closure highlights yet again the financial restraints that the Government are imposing on the Health Service and the reduction in the provision of services. It will cut still further the facilities available to the people of Burnley, Pendle and Rossendale. This will be the third hospital closure in two years. The Hartley hospital in Pendle and the Victoria hospital in Burnley have both been closed and we have now to consider the closure of Bank Hall hospital.

It is somewhat surprising that at exactly the same time as the announcement of the consultation was made in the local press, a Dr. Gupta of Blackburn and a consortium of eight other people announced the purchase of the former Victoria hospital for £550,000—£350,000 to go to the region and £200,000 to the district health authority—to open a private residential and nursing home for the elderly. Once again, that highlights the way that the Government are shifting their responsibility and the public responsibility to provide care for the elderly. It is time that they put forward clear proposals about the care that should be provided.

I am not opposed to those who have sufficient resources choosing to go into private residential or nursing accommodation, but increasingly to force people to do so is quite wrong. The key element in supporting the private sector, as the Government do, is that a profit element comes into the provision of care. I am not suggesting that some of the nursing and residential homes do not provide a high standard of care, but it is obscene to make profit out of old age. Society and the Government have a responsibility for the care of the elderly.

The consultation exercise has a closing date of 5 July for submissions. That is a reduction of the period laid down from three months to two months, the main objective being to save money—exactly the reason why we are considering the proposed closure. Once again the National Health Service is being tailored to meet financial restraints rather than what should be the priority objective of meeting the needs of those whom it serves. The *Lancashire Evening Telegraph* of 8 June carried the editorial headline:

"'Shoestring' an unwelcome NHS buzz-word."
The final paragraph of the editorial stated:

"Like the British Medical Association's current telling campaign about the present drive for an even more businesslike approach to the running of the health service, we believe it won't do much for patients if the shoestring outlook to funding still stays in place."

The problems that we face with the proposed closure of Bank Hall and the general problems of the NHS are caused by the Government's shoestring approach and the

necessity for health authorities to cut, cut and cut again to meet budget objectives laid down by the Government. The simple truth is that whenever a health authority makes a cut or a closure to meet the criteria laid down by the financial restraints imposed by the Government, in another 12 months it will have to make yet another cut or closure. If the Bank Hall closure goes ahead, some of the elderly will be moved to Marsden hospital but within two or three years that hospital, too, will be considered for closure. Consultation about closing it a few years ago was deferred, but we know that closure will be proposed again in the foreseeable future.

The interim short-term programme of the health authority for 1989-90 and 1990-91 has been on the basis of achieving savings of £934,000 minimum to £2·5 million. That again highlights the fact that the health authority constantly has to spend its time concentrating on meeting the Government's financial restraints. Those savings mean cuts in what is already an insufficient level of service provision to the people of Burnley. The short-term programme assumed the Bank Hall closure and anticipated that the consultation exercise would receive a favourable response.

I have referred to the *Lancashire Evening Telegraph* editorial of 8 June, and on the same day there was a news item covering the same issue. In that article, councillor McGeorge said:

"I cannot see any advantage to patients in this closure and they are what count."
Councillor McGeorge is the Labour leader of Burnley council. However, in case the Minister thinks that it is just one party that is protesting, I shall quote the words of a Conservative member of the council who spoke at the same meeting. He said:

"On this side of the council we don't want to see Bank Hall close either.

We don't think anyone can say that private nursing homes can replace the service offered at Bank Hall. I only hope that people who have decided to shut Bank Hall are prepared to accept responsibility of what might happen."
At the end of the day, it is the health authority that is making the decision, but it is making it because of the constraints put on it by the Government.

Councillor Kevin Kirkham of the SLD also spoke. He said that he agreed wholeheartedly with what councillor McGeorge, the leader of the Labour group, had said. An article in *The Burnley Citizen,* which also came out on 8 June stated:

"Councillor Butterworth, who is chairman of the League of Voluntary Workers for Burnley's remaining hospitals added: 'Bank Hall should be kept open and all hospital closures should be opposed'."
The *Burnley Express and News,* which came out today, described the proposed closure as

"Criminal and horrifying for the elderly and long-stay patients accommodated there."
Councillor McGeorge is quoted as saying that

"the gloves have now come off. We are going to fight this all the way."
He went on to call on the community health council to join the fight and not, as in the past, cop out and agree with the proposals being made by the health authority. I shall be fully involved in that fight, and I shall fight every inch of the way to ensure that we do not see a further reduction in service level provision for the people of my area.

Mr. Wolstenholme, of the Burnley, Pendle and Rossendale health authority, sent a document to the unions saying that, in addition to the problems for the

[*Mr. Peter L. Pike*]

patients involved, there would be reductions in staff. In a letter sent to the National Union of Public Employees, he said:

"Whilst some staff will be needed to transfer to Marsden Hospital with the patients such an arrangement will not be extended to cover all the staff presently at Bank Hall Hospital."

That, too, shows further job reductions.

The health authority's policy and resources committee, in its integrated planning statement for 1989—it has not yet been approved by the full district health authority—indicated other problems as well as that of finance. I have already briefly referred to the growth of private residential and nursing homes. That document says:

"The rapidly expanding number of private residential and nursing homes has also had an effect upon the service demands for this client group. Over the past five years, the number of private nursing home places has increased by approximately 23 per cent. and the number of residential home places by 25 per cent."

It goes on:

"Work had been due to proceed on the new Geriatric Unit at Rossendale General Hospital in 1989-90, but this scheme has now been omitted from the Regional Capital Programme. The District is now seriously concerned over the standard of care that can be provided to the elderly at Rossendale when the service is severely limited by grossly inadequate accommodation which was condemned over 10 years ago."

That shows not only the Bank Hall closure threatening the service level provision, but provision that would have been made at Rossendale general hospital being dropped from the programme. Of course, many of the people who cannot go into Rossendale would have been accommodated in Bank Hall hospital in Burnley.

The consultation document says:

"Major changes in the pattern of care of elderly people have occurred in recent years which to a large extent is due to the development of the private sector nursing home and rest home provision, and in part of technological changes in medicine. In 1983-84 the District Strategic Plan recorded that there were 385 places available in private homes for the elderly and 87 places in private nursing homes. By the beginning of 1989 this figure had risen to 1,500 places and 400 places respectively and is set to rise even further by 1990-91."

There is a public responsibility to care for the elderly, whether through the health authority or the social services. The House still awaits the Government's response and a debate on the Griffiths report, community care and the many other issues linked with problems such as the closure of Bank Hall hospital.

There will be a reduction in beds for the elderly from 43 to 26, and, because of the way the beds will be relocated, the provision of beds for children will be reduced from 65 to 54—yet another cut in services. A considerable amount of money is being spent to move the children's ward from Marsden hospital and to move the elderly from Bank Hall hospital to Marsden hospital. About £90,000 will be spent on adapting accommodation at Marsden hospital and £200,000 will be spent on transferring the children's ward from Marsden to Burnley General hospital.

Our main argument is that there will be a reduction in service provision. Areas such as Burnley, Rossendale and Darwen, and Pendle have particular problems because many people have worked in industries which cause chest problems and so on in old age. Also, many young people are leaving the towns because the Government's policies

have reduced the amount of work available. We therefore need a higher than normal level of Health Service provision, particularly for the elderly.

I know that the Minister will refer to the developments at the Wilsonhey unit and Pendle community hospital. I welcome the developments and I do not say that we cannot change the use of a building, but I and the people whom I represent believe that there is insufficient provision now. Cuts will not be accepted by the people of Burnley, Rossendale and Darwen or Pendle. If the Government do not recognise that and make the necessary resources available, they will lose two seats at the next general election.

Care of the elderly is a public responsibility. The Government should wake up to that responsibility and make resources available to health authorities and county council social services so as to meet the needs of the community that those bodies serve.

2.47 pm

The Parliamentary Under-Secretary of State for Health (Mr. Roger Freeman): I congratulate the hon. Member for Burnley (Mr. Pike) on his success in the ballot. I should like to give the House the background to the proposed closure of geriatric facilities at the Bank Hall hospital. As the hon. Member for Burnley pointed out fairly, the proposal is only at the consultation stage and has not yet been considered by the North Western regional health authority. If there is an objection by the community health council, it will be considered carefully by the health authority. If there is a sustained objection, it will come to Ministers for further consideration. The hon. Gentleman knows that and pointed it out.

I hope that the House will permit me to comment briefly on the provision of patient services generally in the Burnley, Pendle and Rossendale districts. The Burnley, Pendle and Rossendale district health authority provides a full range of health care services for a local population of about 227,000.

The hon. Member for Burnley referred to cutbacks. For the period from 1982 to 1987-88, the latest full year for which we have figures, in-patient treatments were up by 15 per cent. to 32,000 patients per annum and out-patient treatments were up by 7 per cent. to 165,000 patients per annum. I fail to see how the hon. Gentleman can sustain his argument that there have been health cutbacks. The level of resource funding, to which I shall turn in a minute, is a different issue. The record shows that the hon. Gentleman cannot sustain his argument, because patient care measured in terms of in and out-patient treatment, has risen. The number of people treated by community nurses in the district has also risen by 29 per cent. to 35,000 per annum.

Those figures do not show the increase in the quality of care that has also taken place and which reflects the staff's dedication and commitment. I know that the hon. Gentleman will join me in thanking and congratulating the health authority staff. As politicians, we do not thank Health Service staff enough. We take them for granted, and, as a Health Minister, I join the hon. Gentleman in congratulating the staff who work in his constituency.

The right hon. Gentleman asked me about the Griffiths report and I can only repeat the commitment given to me by my right hon. and learned Friend the Secretary of State for Health and the Prime Minister that we shall shortly bring to the House our conclusions on the second Griffiths report on care in the community. They were extremely important, and were deliberately omitted from the White Paper "Working for Patients" because our thoughts and deliberations had not been concluded. However, they will shortly be complete and we shall bring them to the House.

A more tangible sign to the local community of the Government's commitment to improve services is the local building programme, in particular, the completion of the Burnley general hospital phase 3 development, the Wilson Hey unit. That has provided 49 paediatric and surgical specialty beds, with a playroom and outside play area for the children, 105 surgical beds, four high-dependancy beds, three operating theatres and one minor operating theatre, at a total cost of about £6·1 million. A further £5·9 million project to expand Pendle community hospital is also well under way to providing an additional 72 geriatric beds by May 1991. Those new buildings and the facilities which they contain will ensure that the improvements in patient care achieved in recent years will continue well into the future.

I take further issue with the hon. Gentleman. I do not think that he would dispute the figures that I have given because they are facts. It is not sensible to equate hospital closures with cuts. They are sometimes necessary because buildings are worn out and beds, wards and hospitals need new buildings.

The hon. Gentleman implied that any closure was wrong, although, to be fair, he qualified that. He referred to Hartley and Victoria hospitals. Closures are merely signs of the re-provision of health care services. As I have already said, the Health Service is spending £12 million on new capital projects in the health authority area. That is an example of our commitment constantly to improve the care and provide it in a more modern and acceptable way, which is in the patients' interests.

Mr. Pike: Will the Minister accept the important point that, within this consultation paper, a reduction of beds, both for the elderly and children is clearly shown?

Mr. Freeman: That is not right. I am informed that the elderly use 80 per cent. of the 43 beds currently available at the hospital, which gives a figure of 34. I am informed that the replacement Deerplay ward at Marsden hospital will provide 26 beds and that a further 10 beds will be available at the district general hospital for family respite. They will not be beds for members of the family to use as patients, but so that they can enjoy some respite. That makes a total of 36 beds. Therefore, I do not agree with the hon. Gentleman that, in the short term, facilities will be reduced.

I also take issue with the hon. Gentleman's argument that private nursing health care and residential homes are wrong in principle. He implied that they were immoral because a profit is made from them. I disagree. Private nursing homes and residential homes, when properly organised and providing a good quality of care, are perfectly acceptable. As the hon. Gentleman well knows, patients are supported, when appropriate, by the Department of Social Security through income support.

Mr. Pike: The Minister will realise that, given the limitations on the money provided, families have to supplement the cost, sometimes with great difficulty.

Mr. Freeman: I am aware of that. For nursing homes, the state provides about £200 per patient per week. I know that fees often run in the range of £230 to £240 a week, implying some contribution from the savings of the elderly persons or their families. That is a significant degree of support. Private health care can march in step with the NHS in terms of the quality of care delivered.

The hon. Member for Burnley asked me about staff protection. I am informed that the Burnley, Pendle and Rossendale health authority, after consulting the district joint negotiating consultative committee, has already adopted a policy for staff protection in the event of any change or use of premises, and that policy will be fully implemented.

Turning to the Bank Hall hospital, the opening of new and better NHS facilities must rightly be accompanied by a rigorous examination of the continuing use of older existing beds. The Burnley health authority has considered how the hospitals in the district are being used, the services they provide and the level of patient activity involved. It has also considered the capacity of the private sector to meet the needs of elderly patients for nursing care.

Major changes in the pattern of care of the elderly have occurred in recent years and are due to a large extent to the development of private sector nursing homes and, in part, to technological changes in medicine. We all welcome the fact that people are living longer. Although there are many more elderly patients and many more are being treated, it is a fact that the pattern of treatment has changed. The average stay in hospital for geriatric patients is much shorter, and because the number of beds has been maintained in the health authority concerned, and the average use of beds is decreasing, even after the demographic pressures, the occupancy of beds is falling.

In Bank Hall, the decrease has been from 90 per cent. to 82 per cent. occupancy, as the average length of stay has fallen from 227 to 108 days. This is partly the result of the greater availability of residential places in the private sector. Elderly patients can readily find a place which provides nursing care, following a period in hospital for active medical treatment. In the past, many such patients would have been kept in hospital for want of suitable alternative accommodation. I am sure the hon. Gentleman joins me in welcoming this move, whether it takes place within the Health Service or without it. Patients who are medically cured should not be in wards in hospital. They prevent others from being treated there and it is not good for their morale or general wellbeing.

Taking account of these developments, the district health authority has concluded that there is a need to rationalise hospital services in the district. That is the reason for the proposal to close Bank Hall hospital. As a result, financial, medical and nursing resources can be used to greater effect within the NHS.

The option favoured by the district health authority and set out in its consultation document is for the closure and disposal of Bank Hall while expanding services for elderly people at Deerplay ward at Marsden hospital in Burnley. The proposals are set out for consultation under arrangements that apply to all proposals for a significant change in patient services. This is covered in departmental guidance issued in October 1975.

The hon. Gentleman mentioned the time scale for consultations. The normal provisions will apply in this case—a three-month period for consultation at district health authority level, taking us to the end of July. I hope

[Mr. Freeman]

that all the parties involved will play their full part, as, I am sure, will the hon. Gentleman. I hope that the community health council and all involved will make constructive comments on the proposed closure and on alternative ways in which patients should be cared for.

Finally, I turn to the main theme of the hon. Gentleman's speech, the level of funding. He said, fairly, that he is specifically concerned not about this particular site or about its future but about the level of funding. The White Paper proposes that the basis of funding should be changed—first, through the regions and, secondly, through the regions to the districts. We wish to fund district health authorities on the basis of weighted capitation—on the number of residents in a particular district health authority area, weighted by their relative age and morbidity, which in turn will reflect various social and industrial health factors—and the relative cost of providing health care. A more automatic system of allocating taxpayers' resources will, we believe, be fairer and more certain and will enable Health Service managers to plan with greater confidence for the future.

I do not know about the particular demographic and population pressures in the hon. Gentleman's health authority area. However, when the new system is in place —the successor to the old resource allocation working party targets for regions, and, through them, for districts, and the targets that Ministers, of whatever Government, chose to aim for in terms of resource allocation, a system that served us well for many years—it will reflect fairly population movements, population growth and the other factors that I have mentioned. There will then be less criticism of whether one area has been more or less fairly treated than another.

When the new system of allocating funds is in place, I hope that the hon. Gentleman will agree that it will be for the health authority to decide local priorities. I hope that greater attention will be paid to using finite resources effectively in any year. The resources of any Government, of whatever political complexion, are finite. After a health authority has received finite resources in any particular year, it must use them effectively and efficiently. Both the hon. Gentleman and I agree that we want to improve both the quality and the quantity of health care.

Question put and agreed to.

Adjourned accordingly at two minutes past Three o'clock.

House of Commons

Monday 12 June 1989

The House met at half-past Two o'clock

PRAYERS

[MR. SPEAKER *in the Chair*]

Oral Answers to Questions

TRANSPORT

Rail Services (Report)

1. **Mr. Matthew Taylor:** To ask the Secretary of State for Transport if he will obtain a copy of the National Economic Research Association's report on the quality of rail services for his departmental library.

The Secretary of State for Transport (Mr. Paul Channon): It already has one.

Mr. Taylor: I hope that the Secretary of State has a copy of the report sitting on a shelf at home and that he has had an opportunity to read it. If he has, he will be aware that it highlights fewer seats on trains, despite more traffic on the railways and the sort of overcrowding that I experienced travelling from Cornwall to London last night. Many people had to stand from well before Plymouth until they reached London. I experienced, together with many other people, the difficulties of travelling on British Rail at a time when it is underfunded. The report highlights all those problems and calls on the Government to invest in rail, get traffic off the roads, reduce lorry traffic through towns and villages and do something about congestion. Will the Minister act on the report and proceed quickly to ensure safe public transport in this country?

Mr. Channon: I am sorry that the hon. Gentleman had a difficult journey, and I understand the problems that he raised. Not only do I have a copy of the report at home but I have read it with care and have had a meeting with the trade unions about it. It contains much good stuff; I do not agree with all of it, but I agree with much of it. We are acting on many of the report's recommendations. The hon. Gentleman mentioned overcrowding, which I accept sometimes is a problem on some InterCity lines. He will be pleased to learn that I have today approved investment by InterCity in 31 extra mark IV coaches, at a cost of £8·5 million, which will allow electrified trains to run on the east coast main line with more coaches, which will relieve congestion and cascade on to other lines.

Mr. Adley: As the report to which the question refers relates investment to service, and as we have just finished praying, may I ask my right hon. Friend to consider the following matters? The statement that he made a few days ago in the House has given road builders a bonanza, with the minimum of research, while British Rail must climb a high hurdle every time it wants to present proposals to my right hon. Friend. Will he consider the fact that France builds railways in the prospect of doing business, whereas British Rail must prove in advance—sometimes against all the odds—that it can do the business before it is given investment approval?

Mr. Channon: Although I have had many talks with my hon. Friend, I have yet to convince him that, whatever the height of the hurdle, British Rail always manages to climb it. *[Interruption.]* I am looking forward to debating the amount of investment made in British Rail, which we shall deal with in a later question, when I shall show that in real terms investment is considerably larger than at any time under a Labour Government.

Mr. Anderson: If progress is to be made, is it not important that those who take the key decisions have personal experience of the quality of British Rail? It is said that over the past decade the Prime Minister has travelled on it only once—and only for a short distance. Will the Secretary of State therefore try to persuade her to use British Rail from time to time?

Mr. Channon: That is all very well. The Prime Minister is keen to support British Rail and has supported its investment programmes, as have the Government collectively. In contrast to the hon. Member for Truro (Mr. Taylor), I had an excellent journey on British Rail this morning.

London Transport

2. **Mr. John Marshall:** To ask the Secretary of State for Transport when he last met the chairman of London Transport; and what was discussed.

Mr. Channon: On Thursday 8 June, at a meeting of my London passenger transport group, which discussed the central and east London rail studies.

Mr. Marshall: Does my right hon. Friend agree that the long-suffering commuters of London will have no sympathy for a strike over the retention of a promotion system based on Buggins' turn rather than ability? Does he agree that a wage claim of £3,000 a year is quite extraordinary and unjustified? Does he agree that common sense rather than greed and avarice should be the guiding light of London Transport?

Mr. Channon: I agree that prolonged industrial troubles on the London Underground are extremely damaging to travellers. They will not help to resolve the problems, and the House should urge that there should not be such industrial action.

Mrs. Dunwoody: Is the Secretary of State aware that a sad lack of common sense is being displayed by the management of London Underground, who seem to believe that the way to improve the service is to price as many passengers off it as possible? Is that sensible or far-seeing management? What plans does the Secretary of State have to encourage management to improve the service?

Mr. Channon: The hon. Lady knows that a question on the central London rail study has been tabled, and we shall deal with it soon.

Mr. Prescott: That is nothing to do with it.

Mr. Channon: The hon. Gentleman says that it has nothing to do with it. I am about to answer the hon. Lady's question.

Mr. Snape: Get on with it, then.

Mr. Channon: It is not easy with the hon. Member for Kingston upon Hull, East (Mr. Prescott) sitting there. I have received no proposals on fares from LRT. I understand that it is concerned, rightly, about safety and congestion. I have already approved more than £200 million investment in safety measures and £700 million investment to improve the Central and Northern lines. I would have to hear convincing arguments from LUL before I agreed to pricing people off the Underground.

Mr. Higgins: Will my right hon. Friend have discussions with the chairman of London Regional Transport about the way in which traffic cones seem to be breeding in central London as well as on motorways? Yesterday, they were fouling up the approaches to the A40. Will my right hon. Friend open a hotline so that members of the public can point out where traffic cones have been left in places unnecessarily, simply because someone has been too lazy to move them out of the way?

Mr. Channon: I shall certainly consider my right hon. Friend's comment. I am not sure that it is a matter for the chairman of London Regional Transport, but I shall certainly get in touch with my right hon. Friend about those cones.

Mr. Prescott: Does the Secretary of State accept, as no doubt the chief secretary will do in the future, that the fare increases on the Underground system, which, since 1980, have been three times higher than inflation, result directly from his policy that all costs should be covered by fares? That is the opposite of the position in Europe which, with a public subsidy system, has produced the better quality service and cheaper fares that are so different from the London system, which is a shame to us.

Mr. Channon: I do not agree with anything that the hon. Gentleman said. Investment in London Underground is increasing continually and is running at historically high levels—[HON. MEMBERS: "Answer the question."]. I am entitled to answer in the way that I want. I do not agree that the fares are higher in real terms than they were some years ago. The hon. Gentleman's question is based upon a misapprehension.

Mr. Hanley: The majority of people in London believe that the answer to London's traffic problems lies mainly in improved services, and the Underground plays a large part in that. In his discussions with the chairman of London Regional Transport, will my right hon. Friend ensure that, because of the great demand on services, London Underground will provide more and longer trains as soon as possible?

Mr. Channon: I agree with all that my hon. Friend has said. He will be extremely pleased to know of the enormous increase in investment in London Underground, which is running, in 1988-89 prices, at £284 million a year. When the Labour party and the GLC had control of it, investment was less than half that level.

London Underground (Automatic Barriers)

3. **Mr. Tony Banks:** To ask the Secretary of State for Transport if he will make a further statement about ticket barriers on the London Underground system.

The Minister for Public Transport (Mr. Michael Portillo): I understand that a report from the independent consultants on the working of the Underground ticketing system is expected shortly.

Mr. Banks: Will the young and up-and-coming Minister please explain to me how London Underground Limited can carry on installing ticket gates when virtually no one in London approves of them? Has the hon. Gentleman seen the chaos at, for example, Westminster Underground station, where the authorities have to lock the gates open because of the pressure of people? Will he please call in London Underground to tell it to stop this ridiculous scheme which, I remind him, would never have been allowed under the good old GLC?

Mr. Portillo: I have considered the problems of congestion in a number of our stations. I do not think that the ticketing system is the main contributor. There are other reasons for the congestion. The railway inspectorate and the fire brigade have looked at the gates. We have asked consultants to look at them, and their report will be available shortly. The hon. Gentleman often urges us to adopt the systems that operate abroad. I point out that gates at exits are to be found in Hong Kong, Singapore, Washington, San Francisco, Seoul, Philadelphia, Illinois, Tokyo, Osaka and on the Paris RER.

Mr. Harry Greenway: Will my hon. Friend undertake not to return to the old days of the GLC, which doubled the fares and doubled the rates in 1981? Will he give Londoners an assurance on the effect of these gates in a fire?

Mr. Portillo: That has been the subject of the study by the railway inspectorate and the London fire brigade. Emergency buttons are positioned in various places where the staff can operate them, so that all the gates fly open. Recently, the Underground has checked that in the event of a power failure—even a single-phase power failure—the gates would open automatically. That is the basis on which the railway inspectorate and the London fire brigade have felt confident in approving those systems.

Mrs. Clwyd: Will the Minister look a the chaos that all too frequently occurs at Gatwick airport, where passengers from airlines find it almost impossible to purchase a ticket? Is the Minister aware that late at night, only one window out of eight——

Mr. Speaker: Does the hon. Lady mean Gatwick underground?

Mrs. Clwyd: I am talking about passengers attempting to get on to the Underground from the airlines.

Mr. Speaker: Order. This is very wide of the question.

Central London Rail Study

4. **Mr. Livingstone:** To ask the Secretary of State for Transport if he has made a decision about the options contained in the central London rail study; and if he will make a statement.

Mr. Channon: Not yet, but I hope to do so later in the year.

Mr. Livingstone: The Secretary of State expressed regret that the rail study did not make reference to the north London line, a vital part of the London transport network. Will he exert whatever pressure he can on British Rail to prevent the closure of Primrose Hill station, which will throw further pressure on to London Transport because it is British Rail's clear intention now to reduce the number of trains running on the Watford line to Liverpool Street, from five an hour to one an hour? How can the Secretary of State justify that, given the present congestion on the Tube?

Mr. Channon: I am sure that the hon. Gentleman will welcome the fact that we are considering carefully all the options contained in the central London rail study, which presents some imaginative and important proposals for improving London's transport in the future. The question of the north London line is being considered carefully, as it relates also to the east London rail study. I will consider the hon. Gentleman's later points. In general, we are now engaged in some of the most important and radical suggestions to try to solve London's traffic and Underground problems over the next couple of decades.

Mr. Dykes: Does my right hon. Friend agree that these massive plans will be vulnerable to excessive delays because of their complexity? Will he reassure the House that we shall proceed rapidly with the proposals, because we could have endless arguments about all the different options? Can we get digging as soon as possible?

Mr. Channon: I note my hon. Friend's support for the proposals. My aim is to come to conclusions in the very near future—or nearish future—and to come to the House, as I said in answer to the hon. Member for Brent, East (Mr. Livingstone), with definite proposals later this year.

Ms. Ruddock: May we assume from the right hon. Gentleman's reply, therefore, that he is denying the reports which have already appeared in the press that he has made decisions? Will he tell the House about the shape and finance of London's new rail links? Will he tell us whether he has authorised British Rail and LRT to prepare a private Bill? Most important of all, will he give us some idea of the cost of the Paddington to Liverpool Street line and the level of fares increases that will be necessary if he continues to insist that the passengers must pay?

Mr. Channon: As I have told the House on a number of occasions, no decisions have been taken. It will be very nice if it is possible—and I hope that it will be—to have a Bill in November dealing with one of the solutions to the problem, although it is impossible to be certain at this stage. No decisions have been taken, so I cannot instruct people on these matters. The hon. Lady mentioned fares. The question of financing whatever proposals come forward has to be studied. Fares will have to play their part. There is also the option of Government grants and of contributions from developers.

Drink-Driving

5. **Mr. Arbuthnot:** To ask the Secretary of State for Transport what further plans he has for tackling the problem of drinking and driving.

The Minister for Roads and Traffic (Mr. Peter Bottomley): We have today launched a new campaign, with the help and co-operation of the medical services, the police, the insurance industry and the brewers and retailers. Two new television commercials will be shown. New posters and publicity material are available for use by road safety officers throughout the country. The basic message continues to be that drinking and driving wrecks lives and that it is unnecessary and unacceptable.

Mr. Arbuthnot: Will my hon. Friend confirm that if other insurance companies follow the line recently taken by Pearl Assurance, motorists who insist on continuing to drink before they drive will find that they are likely to face a nasty financial shock, even if they do not kill or disable somebody?

Mr. Bottomley: My hon. Friend has a good point. At the moment an insurance company does not need to pay out for those who drive unroadworthy vehicles. Pearl Assurance has simply applied the same principle to those who are not roadworthy drivers. The company will not necessarily pay out to mend such a driver's car and may claim back any third party payments that it has to make. I do not see any reason why the 19 out of 20 of us who do not drink and drive should have to continue to subsidise those who do. We are sufficiently at risk of our lives as innocent victims and I do not see why we should pay out money as well.

Sir Dudley Smith: While every sensible person must be against drinking and driving, is it not correct that we have a good record compared with other European countries, thanks largely to the efforts of my hon. Friend's Department?

Mr. Bottomley: It is certainly true that the campaigns initiated over the years by my right hon. Friend the Secretary of State have paid off tremendously in saving lives. The death trend in Britain is very much better than, for example, in Finland or even New South Wales, which go in for other strategies.

We must change people's understanding and their behaviour, using allies in the drinks trade, so that wherever people go to drink, they can have alcohol-free drinks if they are driving. That is the host's responsibility. It is the passenger's responsibility to pick an alcohol-free driver and it is primarily the driver's responsibility to decide between the throttle and the bottle. The trouble is that even at the present reduced levels, the killing season is now with us.

Public Inquiries

6. **Mr. Baldry:** To ask the Secretary of State for Transport if he has any proposals to improve the system of transport public inquiries.

Mr. Peter Bottomley: The public inquiry system is kept under review. All suggestions for change are given careful consideration. We are satisfied that for the great majority of road proposals the present inquiry system works well. We need to safeguard the rights of those affected by our proposals.

Mr. Baldry: Is my hon. Friend aware that I am somewhat disappointed by that reply because, as my hon. Friend must be aware, it took some 30 years from Ernest

Marples promising that the Banbury bypass would be built as a matter of priority for substantial construction on the M40 to begin? Will my hon. Friend take a Genghis Khan approach to the public inquiry system to simplify it substantially, to shorten it and to shut up those professional objectors who are in the vanguard in calling for infrastructure investment in general but who seem to oppose every infrastructure investment in particular?

Mr. Bottomley: The answer is that I am not sure. As my right hon. Friend the Secretary of State said, we need to save time before we get to the inquiry stage. Three quarters of inquiries take two weeks or less and consider people's legitimate interests. However, time is wasted by the Department in trying to find an acceptable route. Where there is controversy—with the exception of Worthing—perhaps one way would be for people to decide whether they want the bypass—if there is to be one—to run east, west, north or south before the Department commits too much time to fighting fruitless battles. We need to fight for people's interests in a safer environment, with safer roads, and better industrial access. Perhaps then, as my hon. Friend wants, we could save a great deal of time.

Mr. Allen: What is the Minister's view on the circumventing of public inquiries into major transport matters by the use of the private Bill procedure in this House? Will he make representations to his right hon. Friends to ensure that in future all major transport issues are examined publicly so that all witnesses can give the evidence that they feel is appropriate?

Mr. Bottomley: It is odd that the hon. Gentleman has suggested that having a matter considered by the House of Commons is in some way to get away from a public inquiry. That is the way in which most of the railways have been built in this country and it is the way in which most people would like them to continue to be built.

Mr. Madel: Does the White Paper on roads take account of the expenditure implications of any delays in the construction of bypasses caused by lengthy controversial public inquiries, because every month of delay has an inflationary effect on the final bill?

Mr. Bottomley: It should not, as inflation comes down again. The important point is that we do not want to lose any time unnecessarily. Each pound spent on the roads brings a £2 return and we are getting a return of about £160 million per year from the present road programme in road casualty reductions alone. Therefore, as my hon. Friend has said, it is important that we get on with the programme.

Mr. Prescott: Will the Minister confirm that the Government are seriously considering replacing roads public inquiries by the private Bill procedure of this House to avoid giving people the opportunity of having their views heard? As the Minister is concerned about delays, will he confirm that the Birmingham northern relief road has now been delayed directly because of the Green Paper on private financing and that, instead of getting their road, the people of that area now face the possibility of a toll road?

Mr. Bottomley: The answers to the two specific questions on the inquiry are no, and not necessarily. The only person who has suggested the use of Bills for a large number of road schemes is the director of Friends of the Earth. I was not persuaded by him and I am not persuaded by the hon. Member for Kingston upon Hull, East (Mr. Prescott).

Mr. Charles Wardle: My hon. Friend's announcement later this week of alternative proposals for the Hastings, western and Bexhill bypass will be a welcome sign of further progress on the Dover to Honiton trunk road link. However, if a public inquiry follows the eventual publication of draft orders, when does my hon. Friend imagine the road will be complete?

Mr. Bottomley: The answer to that is NIMTOO—not in my term of office—although we want to make as much progress as we can.

Manchester Airport (Rail Link)

7. **Mr. Andrew F. Bennett:** To ask the Secretary of State for Transport if he will make a statement on the progress of a rail link to Manchester airport.

Mr. Portillo: We expect to receive a formal investment proposal from British Rail shortly.

Mr. Bennett: Will the Minister confirm that there appears to have been a last-minute financial hiccup in the negotiations between the Department and the Greater Manchester transport authority in the past couple of weeks? Can he confirm that the problems have now been smoothed out and that there is nothing to stop the construction of the rail link going ahead later this year?

Mr. Portillo: I must wait and see what British Rail's investment case is. The hon. Gentleman may have been referring to the question of resource allocation for the PTA share of the cost in the next financial year. I am happy to agree in principle that the allocation should be covered. The hon. Gentleman asked about timing. I am well aware that if the rail link is to be built, it should be phased in carefully with the new terminal, which is due to open in April 1993.

Mr. Eastham: May I impress on the Minister the fact that Manchester airport has been applying for the rail link for the past 10 years? I hope that the Minister will make it clear to British Rail that we want no more unnecessary delays. Given the money that has been spent on Gatwick, Stansted and Heathrow, is it not about time that the north-west had its share of expenditure?

Mr. Portillo: I do not think that the time spent in establishing the case has been wasted in any way. Perhaps the hon. Gentleman can take comfort from what I have said—that it is well understood that the important factor in the timing of the rail link is that it should fit in with the new terminal planned for April 1993. If Ministers receive the investment proposal shortly, we shall be in good time to phase the link in with that.

Mr. Favell: Is the Minister aware that the car park at Manchester airport is now immensely expensive, especially for the holiday traveller? Does he agree that a rail link would be a great boon to those who save up to go on holiday once a year?

Mr. Portillo: My hon. Friend makes an interesting additional point. I think that the investment case made to me by British Rail will be made in the light of all the circumstances, and of all the extra traffic that can be attracted. I look forward to seeing that proposal shortly.

Midland Rail Electrification

8. **Mr. Allen:** To ask the Secretary of State for Transport if he will meet the chairman of British Rail to discuss an investment plan for the electrification of the midland main line.

Mr. Portillo: It is for British Rail to propose those electrification schemes which it believes to be worth while.

Mr. Allen: Is the Minister aware that people who travel on the line through the east midlands to Nottingham are heartily cheesed off at the Government's attitude to the electrification of the east midlands line? It is a scandal that the Government are prepared to find perhaps £$\frac{1}{2}$ billion for environmental improvements where they see electoral advantage and yet cannot allow or encourage British Rail to spend a mere £100 million to electrify the line through the east midlands. Will the Minister look again at the rate of return that he has demanded that British Rail should make on its capital and make it more feasible for British Rail to electrify the line? The east midlands needs the line. It needs electrification. Without that, we shall become an economic backwater. It is not good enough for the Government to keep washing their hands of the issue.

Mr. Portillo: I take it that what the hon. Gentleman really wants is an improved service to Nottingham and Sheffield. We have just had announced an improvement of 10 minutes in the journey time to Nottingham and an increased frequency of service. There is a new 7.30 am train which will doubtless be useful to the hon. Gentleman personally. Following the announcement by my hon. Friend the Secretary of State about the east coast main line, it may now be possible to transfer trains from that line to the east midlands line to give Nottingham and Sheffield an hourly service.

Electrification is a separate matter, and it is not likely to bring much of an improvement in journey time. I believe that the question of electrification will arise at a later date, when the line is due for reinvestment. The rolling stock on the present line is well within its working life at the moment.

Mr. Ashby: My hon. Friend will recall that a long debate on this matter was initiated last year by my hon. Friends the Member for Harborough (Sir J. Farr) and for Bosworth (Mr. Tredinnick) and myself and that the hon. Member for Nottingham, North (Mr. Allen) was notably absent from it. We spoke then of the need for electrification in view of the great changes that had taken place, particularly the Toyota plant. Will my hon. Friend undertake to ask the chairman of British Rail to look again at this matter, in the light of the facts that more investment is being made in the east midlands and there is a crying need for investment to provide a direct link via the Channel to France to bring prosperity to the midlands?

Mr. Portillo: The chairman of British Rail is well aware of my hon. Friend's opinion and those of many of my hon. Friends who have spoken so strongly in favour of electrification. The quality of service is important, not electrification per se. I hope that my hon. Friend is pleased

both with the current improvements and with those that I announced today, which are the result of my right hon. Friend's statement about additional rolling stock.

British Rail (Privatisation)

9. **Mr. Snape:** To ask the Secretary of State for Transport what recent discussions he has had with the chairman of British Rail about privatisation proposals for British Rail.

Mr. Channon: Privatisation is one of the topics that I discuss from time to time with Sir Robert Reid.

Mr. Snape: That was a terrific answer. Is the right hon. Gentleman aware that after years of running the railways on a Government-sponsored shoestring, to tell British Rail management that privatisation is the only answer to its problems is creating massive uncertainty within the industry? Is not talk of a return to the large regional railway companies simply nostalgic nonsense? Does not the United Kingdom, like other advanced industrialised nations, need a publicly owned, properly funded national railway system?

Mr. Channon: As I have told the House on many occasions, we have not decided about privatisation. I welcome British Rail's recent impressive performance, as do many hon. Members, and privatisation could reinforce that. However, I shall pursue that only if I am convinced that it will lead to an improved service to the customer. That is why I have given the hon. Gentleman this answer, I note his views about large regional companies.

Mr. Gregory: Does my right hon. Friend agree that there is a pent-up feeling that British Rail should be privatised for the benefit of both rail users and British Rail employees? Would not the employees welcome the opportunity of a share option scheme, something that has been consistently denied to them by the Opposition, and especially those working on the east coast main line? They will be delighted with today's announcement of 31 new coaches, which will mean even greater improvements. The sooner they have them, the better.

Should not the chairman of British Rail urgently consider the privatisation of certain sectors, including catering and the property board, both of which have been lacklustre?

Mr. Channon: My hon. Friend is right to say that there is a great deal of interest in and support for privatisation. There is no evidence from British Rail's performance to support the view that any uncertainty over that issue is causing any damage——

Mr. Snape: That is why I asked the question.

Mr. Channon: The hon. Gentleman did make that point.

We must decide on the long-term future of the railways without unnecessary delay. I note the views expressed by my hon. Friend the Member for York (Mr. Gregory) and will bear them in mind.

Mr. Dalyell: What does Sir Robert Reid say from time to time about the technical feasibility of privatisation?

Mr. Channon: Sir Robert Reid, not I, should speak for himself on these matters. British Rail is co-operating fully with the work in hand and the board has taken no formal position on privatisation.

Mr. Redwood: When considering privatisation, will my right hon. Friend take into account the need to make the railways more enterprising and more responsive to growth opportunities? I am thinking especially of the Earley power station site development in my constituency, where a nationalised industry appears to be reluctant to install a station that is much needed. Will my right hon. Friend ensure that the ability to go for growth and for new passengers is written into the privatisation proposals?

Mr. Channon: I shall study what my hon. Friend has said. Most hon. Members, certainly Conservative Members, know that privatisation in a large number of areas has released the initiative and enterprise of many state industries, has provided growth opportunities and is heartily to be desired.

Road Casualties

11. **Mr. Colin Shepherd:** To ask the Secretary of State for Transport if he will indicate the general trend in road casualty figures.

Mr. Channon: Casualties in road accidents reached a post-war peak of over 397,000 in 1965. Since then, the trend has generally been downwards. In 1987, the latest year for which full details are available, there were 311,500 casualties. During the same period, the trend for deaths in road accidents has also been downwards, falling from 7,950 in 1965 to 5,125 in 1987.

Provisional figures for 1988 show a slight upturn in total casualties to 321,700, but road deaths show a continued fall, to an estimated 5,041 in 1988.

Mr. Shepherd: Does my right hon. Friend agree that many families will be eternally grateful to him for his success in bringing down the number of road deaths, although, naturally, there is still some concern about road casualties? What action is my right hon. Friend taking in respect of the various organisations that have an interest in making representations on his response to the North report?

Mr. Channon: I am extremely grateful to my hon. Friend. My predecessors, my colleagues in the Department and the Department itself have done an immense amount of work on this important topic. In July 1987, I set the target of reducing road casualties by one third by the year 2000. Traffic is increasing considerably. My hon. Friend rightly referred to the North report. Naturally, we shall carefully consider any representation that has been made to us. We have already received a large number, and we are considering them carefully. We have already been able to take some action about high risk offenders.

Mr. Roger King: My right hon. Friend will be aware that one way of combating the road casualty figures is to make sure that motor vehicles are roadworthy. Would he care to comment on the European meeting of Ministers, at which a new tyre directive was devised, and tell us when it is proposed to be introduced?

Mr. Channon: I thought that my hon. Friend would be pleased about the new tyre directive. I read his powerful speech a few days before the European Council meeting. I am not sure whether I am in total agreement with him about the matter, but I think that he will be pleased about the new 1·6 mm tyre tread directive which will come into force in the middle of 1990. If I have that detail wrong, I will write to my hon. Friend.

Channel Tunnel

14. **Mr. Gerald Bowden:** To ask the Secretary of State for Transport what representations he has received from British Rail about the need for a second Channel tunnel rail terminal at Waterloo in addition to that at King's Cross; and if he will make a statement.

Mr. Portillo: British Rail has been planning for some years to locate its London terminal for Channel tunnel passenger trains at Waterloo and for it to be in operation by 1993. Powers for that were granted in the Channel Tunnel Act 1987. It is now proposing to locate a second London international passenger station at King's Cross.

Mr. Bowden: Will my hon. Friend confirm that the only reason for such a grandiose arrangement at Waterloo is to accommodate the passport and immigration controls and for the convenience of Customs clearance? Is it not time that the authorities brought their procedures into line with those on the continent, where Customs, passport and immigration controls are done on the train? There would then be no need to have such a grand, expensive development at Waterloo.

Mr. Portillo: I do not think that my hon. Friend is entirely right in saying that that is the only reason. A large number of passengers will use the services, and that is why British Rail is having to think about two termini to cope with more than 15 million passengers a year. The Customs clearance matters are not settled. They are still being discussed within the Government. I recognise the force of the argument that, for the convenience of customers, it is much the easiest thing to have the same sort of arrangement as we have at airports, whereby people would carry their suitcases through Customs and clear quickly after they have left their trains.

Mr. Spearing: Have the Government not made a complete mess of the matter? Is it a fact that British Rail representatives told the Select Commitee that they did not need another terminal other than at Waterloo? We now need one at King's Cross and, apparently, a third one at Waterloo. Is it not time that the Government had a complete strategic survey of the matter to include other sites such as Stratford and show the country that they mean what they say about the planning and transport inquiries on which a question was answered earlier this afternoon?

Mr. Portillo: I am rather confused by the hon. Gentleman's reference to a third terminal at Waterloo. My understanding is that there is to be a terminal at Waterloo. That is covered in the Channel Tunnel Act 1987. The proposal is now for a second terminal at King's Cross. There is no proposal for a third terminal. It is for British Rail to demonstrate whether it should be at King's Cross or at Stratford. During the debates on the King's Cross Bill there will be an opportunity for the hon. Gentleman and others to consider the important arguments that have been made in favour of King's Cross as against Stratford.

Drink-Driving

18. **Mr. Michael Brown:** To ask the Secretary of State for Transport how much his Department is spending on drink-drive advertising in the current year.

Mr. Peter Bottomley: About £2 million is being spent on new television commercials, air time, new publicity materials, and support for local road safety officer campaigns. That relatively small sum is multiplied many times by the coverage of the subject in the media, including thoughful television coverage, such as the recent BBC "Horizon" programme, and by reporting of drink-drive cases. The campaign is being heavily supported by material produced by the Brewers Society, by individual brewers and by the club movement.

Mr. Brown: Does my hon. Friend agree that that is a vast amount of public money? While I am sure that we would all agree that that is absolutely necessary, does he agree that it is hardly logical? Surely the media in their news bulletins should give as much attention to lives lost through drink-driving as they do to any rail or aeroplane disaster.

Mr. Bottomley: It is true that, if between 800 and 900 people lost their lives in the air, at sea or on the railways, the media would be concentrating all the time on why and how that happened. If I had had the courage I would have announced this morning that no public money was to be spent on advertising, because then every television programme and newspaper would have to be explaining why drink-driving is so dangerous. I have not such courage.

ATTORNEY-GENERAL

Advice to Ministers

Mr. Dalyell: To ask the Attorney-General, pursuant to his oral reply to the hon. Member for Walsall, North on 8 May, *Official Report,* column 553, what assessment he had made of the implications for the treatment of documents containing his advice to Ministers and others of the recently revised Cabinet Office guidance on Government information.

The Attorney-General (Sir Patrick Mayhew): None.

Mr. Dalyell: As one who sat on this Bench and heard Jack Profumo make statements to the House, does the Attorney agree with Harold Macmillan that it is rather important to our system of government that Ministers do not tell lies to the House? In those circumstances, as a major Law Officer of the Crown, what did he think when he heard that Sir Leon Brittan had said that the most intimate advisers to the Prime Minister, Mr. Powell and Mr. Ingham, had absolutely abused his letter raising question on the Prime Minister's behaviour? Is the senior Law Officer entirely happy in that rather bad company?

The Attorney-General: As the question began with a premise that I most certainly do not accept, I have nothing that I can usefully add in response to it.

Director of Public Prosecutions

40. **Mr. Janner:** To ask the Attorney-General when he last met the Director of Public Prosecutions; and what matters were discussed.

The Solicitor-General (Sir Nicholas Lyell): On 7 June. We discussed a variety of matters of Departmental interest.

Mr. Janner: Did the Minister discuss with the Director of Public Prosecutions the inability of the law to deal with cases of incitement to racial violence and the likelihood of greater danger as a result of the Rushdie affair? Does he agree that the law is not capable of dealing adequately with such public order offences and that it should be strengthened? Are the Government considering such strengthening?

The Solicitor-General: Policy is, of course, a matter for my right hon. Friend the Home Secretary, but basically, no, I do not agree with the premise of the hon. and learned Gentleman's question. I do not believe that anything that he has put in his question has made it out.

Mr. Stanbrook: Will my hon. and learned Friend please discuss with the DPP the implications of the case of Gooch, who was convicted at the Old Bailey of the manslaughter of his wife, my constituent, where the judge said that there was no justification for accepting the plea to manslaughter rather than the charge for which he was brought before the court, namely murder? In cases of that kind, would it not be better for the CPS to clear a reduction from the charge of murder with the trial judge privately beforehand and thus avoid giving the impression in court that the reduction in the charge had been done at the convenience of the CPS?

The Solicitor-General: I shall certainly look into the matter and write to my hon. Friend. It may be useful to say that, against an open question, it would be helpful if my hon. Friend could either write a letter or put down a specific question.

Mr. Fraser: Can the Solicitor-General help us on the question of prior publicity and prosecutions? Does he recall that in December the Attorney-General told the House, in the Father Ryan case, that juries have a "scrupulous disregard" of what they see and hear elsewhere and that the risk of publicity affecting their ability to try a case fairly does not exist? Can he say, first, whether those remarks and those of the Prime Minister applied only to the Ryan case or are they general? Secondly, can he say that there is no doctrine applied by the Director of Public Prosecutions to the effect that the prior publication of reports, such as the King's Cross report or a Department of Trade and Industry inspector's report, acts as a debarment to a subsequent prosecution? Thirdly, can he tell us why the consideration by the Director of DTI reports is taking so long?

The Solicitor-General: It would be in rare cases that prior publication became a debarment to prosecution, but one must look at each case on its merits. The House will have in mind particular cases in recent weeks, which would obviously have a very different effect from other cases that we have discussed.

City Fraud

41. **Mr. Skinner:** To ask the Attorney-General whether he has any plans to meet the Director of Public Prosecutions regarding City fraud; and if he will make a statement.

The Attorney-General: I meet the Director of Public Prosecutions for discussions frequently, and plan to continue to do so. Subjects include the handling of fraud cases, whether arising in the City or elewhere. Some cases of serious and complex fraud, however, are now handled by the serious fraud office.

Mr. Skinner: I wonder whether the Attorney-General or the DPP have a quiet little chuckle to themselves when they meet and discuss things such as City fraud as opposed to laws affecting trade unions? Is it not rather odd that in our society people such as Peter Cameron-Webb and Peter Dixon—city fraudsters who got away with £40 million—are not extradited now that five years has elapsed and yet when workers go before the courts, the judges find the appropriate sentences in some old or new law book in order to hammer the railwaymen, the miners, the seafarers and now the dockers? Surely the truth of the matter is that in our society, run by the Tory Government, there is one law for the bosses and City crooks and one for the workers.

The Attorney-General: I am afraid that, yet again, the wish has been the father to the thought. The confusion in the question lies between the ability to extradite from the United States in which we are bound by——

Mr. Skinner: You let them go.

The Attorney-General: The hon. Gentleman asked a question as well as making a long speech and I am giving him the credit of expecting an answer to it, which I am trying to give.

In the case of extradition from the United States, we are bound by the provision of the United States extradition law. In the case of prosecution for fraudulent and criminal conduct we are bound by our own provisions. The hon. Gentleman refers to the Lloyd's scandals. He may know, but he did not mention it because it did not suit him, that there is a prosecution now in train against a number of those who have been charged with offences in the course of the Lloyd's scandals. Under the administration of the serious fraud office and the Office of the DPP I can tell the hon. Gentleman that the criminal law is administered without fear or favour, affection of ill will.

Mr. Latham: Will my right hon. and learned Friend confirm that he and his fellow Law Officers take such offences extremely seriously? Will he also confirm that they are being dealt with as quickly as they can by the police, because that does not always appear to be the case?

The Attorney-General: I confirm each of those questions, but the police, of course, are outside my ministerial responsibility. I suggest that the attitude of this Government to serious fraud may be judged by the fact that we have invited Parliament to legislate to introduce the serious fraud office, with unique powers, which have led to cases bring brought to court months and sometimes years earlier than would otherwise have been possible. The House need not accept my word on that, but take the word of the Commissioner of Police for the City of London in his most recently published report, in which he paid great tribute to the serious fraud office at the end of its first year of operations.

Diplomats

42. **Mr. Tony Banks:** To ask the Attorney-General what is his policy in respect of the prosecution of diplomats.

The Attorney-General: Individuals enjoying diplomatic immunity may not by law be prosecuted unless there is a waiver of that immunity on behalf of the diplomat's own state. Whether it is appropriate to seek such a waiver is a matter for my right hon. and learned Friend the Foreign Secretary.

The question whether a diplomat should be prosecuted will, subject to waiver, be determined by reference to the code for Crown prosecutors.

Mr. Banks: Is the Attorney-General aware of the scandal of unpaid parking fines that a number of embassies have been running up? Is it not about time that he asked his right hon. and learned Friend the Foreign Secretary to go for a waiver of diplomatic immunity against those individuals who are persistent offenders? If he cannot obtain a waiver, he should declare them persona non grata, because it is about time that some stern action was taken against those people.

The Attorney-General: I agree with the hon. Gentleman that there is great public resentment about those who abuse diplomatic status in the way that he has described. Whether a waiver should be applied for has to be a matter for my right hon. and learned Friend the Foreign Secretary who, I can assure the hon. Gentleman, will be made aware of the hon. Gentleman's feelings.

EC (Fines)

43. **Mr. Teddy Taylor:** To ask the Attorney-General if he will publish a paper outlining the rights of access to United Kingdom courts for individuals and companies which have fines imposed on them by the European Community; and if he will make a statement.

The Solicitor-General: No, Sir. National courts have no power to review the legality of fines imposed by the European Commission. Individuals and companies who wish to test the legality of such fines, may institute proceedings against the Commission in the European Court of Justice in Luxembourg.

Mr. Taylor: Could my hon. and learned Friend say whether, as one who believes in justice, he is worried that, under the mergers directive, the European Community can appoint inspectors who can walk into any British company that they think might be affected, obtain access to its premises, demand to see its papers, ask for information on the spot, and if they are not satisfied with the information, impose immediate fines of many tens of thousands of pounds, even per day? Is it not an outrage that, in a country which believes in democracy and the rule of law, individuals can be fined massive sums, and their only recourse is to go to the European Court, which might actually increase the fines? Are not the Government willing to take seriously the fact that the basis of British law, that one should have access to the courts before fines are imposed, is totally undermined both by this directive and one other that preceded it?

The Solicitor-General: I read my hon. Friend's speech in the recent debate and the answer given on behalf of the Department of Trade and Industry. From a legal aspect, any such company has a right of recourse to the European Court of Justice at Luxembourg.——

Mr. Taylor: Three years later.

The Solicitor-General: Whether or not the fine is valid must be decided by the European Court of Justice, to which companies have access. However, the policy matters, as my hon. Friend will appreciate, were those raised in the debate and answered on behalf of the Department of Trade and Industry.

OVERSEAS DEVELOPMENT

Nigeria

45. **Mr. Watts:** To ask the Secretary of State for Foreign and Commonwealth Affairs if he has any plans to visit Nigeria.

The Minister for Overseas Development (Mr. Chris Patten): My right hon. and learned Friend hopes to visit Nigeria for the next round of United Kingdom-Nigeria bilateral talks. The Minister of State, Foreign and Commonwealth Affairs my right hon. Friend for Wallasey (Mr. Chalker) will be visiting Nigeria from 25 to 27 June to open an oil and gas seminar.

I visited Nigeria from 25 to 31 May, to attend the 25th anniversary meetings of the African development bank and fund, to discuss our biliateral aid programme with Nigerian Ministers and to visit technical co-operation projects.

Mr. Watts: In considering further our bilateral aid programme will my right hon. Friend consider giving priority to increasing the number of training places for Nigerians at United Kingdom educational institutions, including the Thames Valley college in my constituency , which has longstanding connections with Nigeria?

Mr. Patten: I know how distinguished a record the institution has in providing training for people from other countries. This year, in the United Kingdom, we shall be training about 480 students from Nigeria in one discipline or another, with the help of taxpayers' funds. We hope to increase that figure to 600, or more.

Mr. Winnick: When the visit to Nigeria takes place, will the British position on current events in China be explained? Will the Minister explain to the Nigerian Government our deep concern over the way in which British citizens involved in the media are being roughed up and subjected to brutal treatment by security thugs in China?

Mr. Patten: I congratulate the hon. Gentleman on the way in which he introduced that extremely important question on to the Floor of the House. Of course, we make clear our concern about those issues to everyone, and I am sure that the Nigerians are as concerned about them as others. Since I was in China last month, in Tiananmen square at the beginning of the demonstrations and hoped, like the rest of the House, for a different outcome, I very much share the concern of the hon. Gentleman.

Mr. Soames: Is my hon. Friend aware that there are no elephants in Nigeria but that, if there were, he should tell the Nigerian Government that although this Government have taken dramatic and important steps to ban the import of ivory, they have left out one important thing: ivory can be stained by smoking, so the clause that forbids the import of all new ivory should be extended to cover the import of all ivory.

Mr. Patten: There are many places in which one would not find the elephant, including my hon. Friend's constituency. However, he raises a point of considerable importance. He was right to draw attention to the intitiative taken by my noble Friend the Minister of State, Department of the Environment. I shall certainly draw my hon. Friend's comments to the attention of my noble Friend.

My hon. Friend will also be aware that we are doing a good deal in Zimbabwe, Kenya and elsewhere to support the strengthening of the institutions in those countries which help to conserve wildlife.

Mr. Speaker: I hope that the House will agree that we should not go wide of the question. To do so is to the detriment of those who have questions lower down the Order Paper.

African Development Bank

48. **Miss Widdecombe:** To ask the Secretary of State for Foreign and Commonwealth Affairs if he will make a statement on the annual meeting of the African development bank in Abuja.

Mr. Chris Patten: I attended, as governor for the United Kingdom, the recent annual meetings of the African development bank and fund in Abuja, Nigeria. The meeting also marked the 25th anniversary of the bank's establishment. We reviewed the bank's policies and programmes and we affirmed the importance of using its resources effectively particularly in view of the difficult challenges facing many African countries. I was asked to give a keynote speech on behalf of the non-regional member countries.

Miss Widdecombe: Will my hon. Friend also confirm that, in addition to helping the bank to support structural development, he will try to persuade it to do more to protect the African environment?

Mr. Patten: I very much share my hon. Friend's point of view. In one of the two speeches I made at the bank's meeting I set out our concern about environmental issues. The threat posed to marginal land by population pressure and by environmental degradation is well understood. We know the impact of tropical deforestation. We have therefore launched a significant forestry initiative under the aegis of the tropical forestry action plan, and eight countries in Africa are participating in it.

Mr. Tony Banks: Since there are some elephants left in east and central Africa, will the Minister, when he goes to the meeting, encourage the making of loans to the African countries which are doing their best to try to protect their remaining herds of elephants? What can the hon.

Gentleman's Department do to support African countries which are taking a highly responsible attitude to the conservation of elephants?

Mr. Patten: As I said in reply to an earlier question on this subject, we are already providing funds in grant form to help other countries in sub-Saharan Africa, such as Kenya and Zimbabwe, to strengthen their conservation departments, so that not only elephant but other wildlife can be preserved. In Kenya, we have a large programme which we are considering increasing, not least by the provision of capital equipment such as radios and trucks.

Aid

49. **Mr. Skinner:** To ask the Secretary of State for Foreign and Commonwealth Affairs what was the proportion of gross national product given in overseas aid in 1979 and in 1988 or the latest available year; and if he will make a statement.

51. **Mr. Corbyn:** To ask the Secretary of State for Foreign and Commonwealth Affairs what was the proportion of gross national product given in overseas aid in 1979 and in 1988 or the latest available year.

Mr. Chris Patten: The proportion of GNP given in net official development assistance in 1979 was 0·51 per cent. In 1988 it is provisionally estimated at 0·32 per cent.

Mr. Skinner: Those are abysmal figures. At a time when the Government have been able to pay back more than £14 billion of Britain's national debt in the past financial year it would have made much more sense if the figures the Minister gave had been at last comparable to the United Nations 0·7 per cent of GNP. That, on top of giving aid to some of these countries to pay off their debts, would have been a much more worthwhile gesture from one of the most developed countries—ours—even though it is run by a Tory Government. Why does not the Minister make amends this time? The Chancellor will tell him that there will be another massive pay-off of the national debt this year. Why does not the Minister ask him for a large proportion of that—say £1 billion—to help Third world countries?

Mr. Patten: Last year the hon. Gentleman and others criticised me when I announced that our aid/GNP figure had fallen. I am surprised that the hon. Gentleman is so reticent with his congratulations now that I have announced that it increased by 14 per cent. in 1988 over 1987. The House will know that, for me, the vital figure is the one for the total volume of our aid programme. I am pleased to say that that is increasing this year over the planned figure for last year by 12 per cent. in cash terms or 7 per cent. in real terms.

Mr. Jacques Arnold: Does my hon. Friend agree that one of the principal problems for the ratio is the rapid growth in our GNP, and that the figure that developing countries are looking for is the absolute amount that has been put into their countries and on what it is being spent?

Mr. Patten: Of course my hon. Friend is right. This year we shall spend about £165 million more on our aid programme than was planned to be spent last year. If there were to be a Labour Government—perish the thought—I am sure that they would be able rapidly to increase the aid/GNP proportion because the growth rate would fall like a stone.

Miss Lestor: If the Minister is looking for some sort of praise, I shall say to him that I am glad that pressure from the Opposition and from the aid lobby in particular has enabled him to make the announcement of the small increase in the amount of GNP devoted to aid. However, it is extremely small and he is well aware that the figure is well below the average for members of the European Community, for which the last figure given was ·50 per cent. of GNP. Does he not agree that it is deplorable that not only are we well below standards in the EEC on the provision of clean water, and on consumer protection and employment protection rights, but we are below standard on the provision of aid to the Third world? When will he come to the House and announce a timetable for reaching the UN target of 0·7 per cent.?

Mr. Patten: I thank the hon. Lady for what I take to have been a bouquet in the earlier part of the question. I am not sure whether the latter part of her question will have ignited the European election campaign to the fever pitch that we all expect by Thursday. Once again I say to the hon. Lady that the figure that I announced for our aid/GNP proportion represents a 14 per cent. increase in 1988 over 1987. It is not without significance that our aid programme this year is 7 per cent. higher in real terms and 12 per cent. higher in cash terms than last year.

Statements

3.31 pm

Mr. Dennis Skinner (Bolsover): On a point of order, Mr. Speaker. I know that you spend time over the weekend trying to get away from the politics of this place and I know that that is difficult for you because you have to get your tackle ready for Monday morning. In view of the efforts that you have been making to keep abreast of events, I have no doubt that you have noticed that there is an almighty row going on between the Prime Minister and the Chancellor of the Exchequer. Hon. Members ask on points of order, "Mr. Speaker, have you had any request for the Minister for so-and-so to make a statement?" I shall not ask that, but instead ask whether you have had a request from the Prime Minister and from the Chancellor of the Exchequer to make a statement so that we can hear about the conflicting reports? It is high time that we had it all out in the House from the Prime Minister and the Chancellor of the Exchequer, and then you would not have to keep sticking your nose in and watching the goggle box to find out what is going on.

Mr. Speaker: I have had requests neither from the Chancellor nor from the Prime Minister.

Consumer Protection

3.33 pm

Ms. Joyce Quin (Gateshead, East): I beg to move,

That this House is of the opinion that government policies have failed to benefit the consumer and have not ensured that the consumer interest is properly taken into account in the run-up to 1992 and the single European market; and calls on the Government to reform and up-date the 1987 Consumer Protection Act, to introduce a new system of labelling of goods in order to provide accurate information on their health, safety and environmental implications, to implement fully the European Economic Community product liability directive and facilitate a speedy adoption of the product safety directive, and to make provision for regular and systematic consultation with consumer organisations on all aspects of 1992 legislation.

I am pleased to have the opportunity to introduce for debate a subject of my choice. I feel slightly schizophrenic in that I am raising for debate a subject for which I have Front Bench responsibility, although it is through the private Members' ballot that I have been able to bring forward this subject. Perhaps it would be more accurate to say that this is a subject for which I have partial Front Bench responsibility, because it is my contention that the Government have failed the consumer, and neglected consumer interests, across the whole range of their Departments and policies. I shall refer to the work of Ministers of several Departments and to how their policies have impinged on the consumer and given the consumer a raw deal.

Not least of the problems, as the motion says, is that the Government have failed to safeguard the consumer from the effects of the opening up of the single Europe market in 1992 and all the legislation that is involved. I make no apology for the fact that this afternoon I shall refer to many of the European issues facing consumers. This is a particularly appropriate time to do so, as we are in the last few days before the European elections. The debate on whether Europe will benefit the consumer and the average citizen of the EEC, as well as what its effects on business will be, are subjects about which we are all rightly concerned.

On many occasions, the Government have claimed that their free market approach to economic policy automatically favours the consumer, offering greater choice and reasonable prices through unfettered competition. This attitude, which can most kindly be described as naive, has come to look more and more untenable during the Government's term of office. I shall aim to show that what is now needed is a considerable improvement in consumer protection and consumer rights, both domestically and via the European Community, including the right of the consumer to be fully informed, the right to be consulted, the right to easy and inexpensive channels of legal redress, improved rights of compensation, and so on.

Mr. Teddy Taylor (Southend, East): What makes the hon. Lady say that the European Community is in favour of informing the consumer and giving out information? Is she aware that the Consumer Protection Act 1987 removed origin marking, which was one of the best consumer information services, solely because of an instruction from the EEC? How can she say that that body helps the consumer when the average family in Britain pays an extra £13 a week for its food directly as a result of the EEC?

Ms. Quin: The EEC has had mixed effects on consumers. I shall not be wholly praising the EEC, but nor shall I be wholly condemning it. I shall be picking out the various elements of EEC consumer protection and looking at those examples that need reinforcing. I shall not hesitate to criticise certain aspects of EEC legislation that harm the consumer. It would not be wise to take an oversimplified view of the EEC. I hope that the point that I was making will become clearer to the hon. Member for Southend, East (Mr. Taylor) in the debate.

Let us examine some of the recent actions of Government Departments and see what effects they have had on the consumer. One of the main issues, about which we have had several debates and questions, is the failure of the Ministry of Agriculture, Fisheries and Food to protect the consumer. That is particularly true of consumers' worries and fears about food quality and safety. While modern farming practice is good at producing the quantity that is needed—in many cases, it goes way beyond that, with the production of large-scale surpluses—there is nevertheless more and more consumer concern about the quality of food and, in particular, about the amount of information the consumer is given about the treatment of food.

Recently, I asked the Minister of Agriculture, Fisheries and Food a question about the use of tecnazene—a chemical that inhibits the sprouting of potatoes, thereby improving their shelf life. Potatoes treated with it are not safe for human consumption for six weeks following the administration of the treatment. The Minister informed me that last year about 20 per cent. of potatoes in Scotland were treated with tecnazene, and that a similar percentage were treated in England and Wales, although figures were not available. Apart from expressing my concern that the Minister did not have the figures available immediately, my principal reaction was that consumers are unaware whether the potatoes that they buy have been so treated. If they were treated, they do not know when that happened or whether the potatoes that they are buying fall within the safety limit.

Much concern has recently been expressed about the use of Alar on apples. Again, consumers have no way of knowing whether the apples that they are buying have been treated.

We are now being told that the Government are likely to permit the irradiation of foodstuffs. I oppose that strongly and believe that we should oppose it within the EEC rather than giving way in advance, which is what we appear to be doing. At the very least, food that has been irradiated should be clearly labelled. That will cause the Ministry of Agriculture, Fisheries and Food problems because there is no foolproof test to show whether foodstuffs have been irradiated, which is a further reason why the process should be banned until a system of proper testing and labelling is devised.

The Consumers Association is calling for the mandatory labelling of all foodstuffs, and perhaps the Minister will comment on that. One of the failings of the Consumer Protection Act 1987 is that agricultural produce is excluded. When the Act was being considered, Labour Members pointed out that defect in the legislation. I am delighted that my right hon. Friend the Member for Swansea, West (Mr. Williams) is present because he led for the Labour party on that issue.

To many hon. Members, it seems that the producer rather than the consumer has the upper hand under the Government's agriculture and food policies. Only through the introduction of an organisation such as the food standards agency, which the Labour party has recently called for, will the balance begin to be redressed.

The activities of other Departments work against the consumers' interests. The most flagrant example is the Government's privatisation programme, especially that of the natural monopolies of water, gas and electricity. From contacts with my constituents and my recent experience gained in canvassing at by-elections, I am aware that, while all those measures are unpopular with the voter, the privatisation of water most enrages consumers. People were especially enraged by the advertising campaign, which told them what they already knew—that they are served by a network of water authorities and that water is delivered to their houses—and the pre-privatisation price rises, which they regard as a massive consumer con.

Most British people are drinking water that falls below EEC standards. Most consumers know that the pressing priority is not selling off water to private interests but investing in the necessary infrastructure and remedial works to ensure that water quality, whether it be drinking or bathing water, is fit to use. I strongly believe that safety and health factors are much more in the consumers' interest than the Government's obsession with privatisation.

The National Consumer Council has pointed to many of the problems facing consumers when having to deal with private monopolies. Page 5 of its publication "In the Absence of Competition" states:

"The monopolist can charge prices higher than the consumer would pay in a competitive market and can therefore make excessive profits."

The publication goes on to argue, rightly, for regulation on prices and quality and for proper penalties whenever there is a failure to abide by whatever system of regulation is agreed. The NCC wishes also to ensure that consumers are compensated for any reduction in quality. Consumers are worried that the Government's determination to please their corporate supporters means that consumers will end up with woefully inadequate safeguards. The pre and sometimes post-privatisation price rises have given us prices for certain utilities that are higher than those of our competitors, so not only consumers but industry is set to lose out in the run-up to 1992. Consumers and users are suffering because of Government actions and failings in other Departments. One example is Britain's transport network, which is crumbling because of lack of investment and a short-termist approach brought about by Government cuts and economies which turn out to be false economies when we consider the nation's long-term needs. Whether it is the decaying London suburban rail network, the lack of infrastructure linking the regions to the Channel tunnel or the chaos through bus deregulation in certain areas such as mine in Tyneside, the consumers as users of the services have to bear the consequences of lack of Government support. There is a lack of Government support not because there is no money available for such badly needed investment but because, through dogma, the Government refuse to spend it.

Mr. Tony Favell (Stockport): Has the hon. Lady overlooked the massive injection of cash for our road system which was announced only two weeks ago by the Department of Transport?

Ms. Quin: I have not overlooked that. It is a bone of contention in my region in the north-east. We feel that some of the roads in our area that have been in desperate need of upgrading for many years—the A1, particularly north of Newcastle, and the A69, from Newcastle to Hexham—are not getting the cash injection that is needed. People in my region are worried because, although the announcement is welcome in certain areas, we still will not be adequately linked to the Channel tunnel. That injection of cash is nowhere near the amount that is needed if we are to compete properly in 1992.

Under the last Labour Government, there was a Department of Prices and Consumer Protection, headed by a Minister with Cabinet rank. Under the Conservative Administration, consumer affairs have been progressively downgraded, so that it is now the responsibility of a junior Minister in the Department of Trade and Industry. That is an obvious illustration of the lack of importance that the Government attach to consumer affairs. Labour's current policy review again talks about a Cabinet Minister for consumers to protect them and give them rights under Government policies.

The record of the Department of Trade and Industry does not give consumers grounds for confidence that their future is safe in its hands. The Department deals with many matters that are vital to the standards, quality and reliability of the goods we buy. Pricing policy, price indications, weights and measures and labelling are all within the Department's remit. Yet it is clear that when dealing with that variety of issues the Department's instinct is always to come down in favour of voluntary action and self-regulation. Indeed, the Minister is nodding enthusiastically as I say those words.

Self-regulation seems to be the Department's watchword. Yet consumer organisations and consumers want statutory requirements on standards and labelling that are arrived at independently of any firm or industry which in the normal commercial way has a vested interest in persuading consumers to buy its goods. The consumer wants independent and impartial information, but the Government are consistently failing to provide it.

There was great disappointment, for example, about the Goverment's action on misleading price indications, because the code was not given the full statutory backing which many would have liked. Another issue that has come to the House's attention recently is the system of determining the accuracy of weights and measures. Here, too, the Government seem intent on ignoring consumer protestations. As hon. Members will know, a private Member's Bill—the Weights and Measures (Amendment) Bill—is currently before the House. The Under-Secretary of State for Industry and Consumer Affairs has declared his support for the Bill, although it represents the abandonment of a previous all-party agreement on how to change the weights and measures system. The all-party agreement was embodied in the recommendations of the Eden committee, which met three or four years ago. The committee recommended self-verification of weighing machines in certain circumstances only because the safeguards included were acceptable to industry, consumers and local authority trading standards officers.

The Bill was drafted only after consultation with industry. The Bill's promoter has, rightly, declared an interest, in that he is consultant to the National Federation of Scale and Weighing Machine Manufacturers. Although he has subsequently tabled some amendments, the Bill is still unsatisfactory to consumer organisations, which rightly feel that it was the Government's job—which they were committed to do—to bring forward the recommendations of the Eden committee, which were agreed by all parties, in the appropriate legislative form.

Just today I have seen a report that self-regulation and the voluntary approach are to be extended to estate agents and that a voluntary code of practice is being suggested. One newspaper reports that the hon. Member for Walthamstow (Mr. Summerson) has said that he will be calling for a statutory code. If he does so, he will have the Opposition's support. We believe that this is an important matter and that neither a voluntary approach nor self-regulation is appropriate. Estate agents should be obliged through legislation to act responsibly towards consumers.

Another example of the Government's obsession with the self-regulatory approach was provided by the Chancellor of the Duchy of Lancaster when he spoke at a recent conference about the increasingly important phenomenon of what has come to be called "green" or "environmentally conscious" consumerism. In responding to the desire of consumer organisations for a proper system of labelling which would give consumers accurate information about the environmental impact of the goods they are buying, he said that, while he understood the desire to introduce environmental labelling, he favoured a voluntary approach.

I should like an environmental labelling system to be introduced as a matter of urgency. The voluntary approach is not the answer. We need a developed form of the West German Blue Angel eco-label, which is independently assessed and in the administration of which consumer organisations and environmental groups, as well as industry, are represented. I believe that that system is funded by industry but that industry is happy to accept the independent recommendations of the body that administers the scheme.

Mr. Favell: Has the hon. Lady observed that environmental labelling is now proving good business to many retailers and manufacturers and that market forces are bringing about what the hon. Lady is requesting at no extra cost to the consumer, whereas if the House were to enact the legislation for which she is calling a vast army would be needed to ensure that each label contained the correct information?

Ms. Quin: The Blue Angel system in West Germany is funded by industry, and does not, therefore, involve Government money. In any case, such a system need not be expensive. I shall be dealing in a few minutes with the hon. Gentleman's point about industry itself becoming more environmentally conscious.

Incidentally, the Under-Secretary of State for Industry and Consumer Affairs did not respond to a question that I put to him during Trade and Industry Question Time not so long ago when I asked him his views on environmental labelling. I hope that he will take the opportunity of giving the House his views on that issue today.

It seems that at last the Government are beginning to realise some of the commercial implications in the important trend towards green consumerism. However, a great deal more needs to be done to encourage industry to respond to the boom in demand for environmentally friendly products. That will be especially important if our

[*Ms. Quin*]

"green" consumers are to be able to buy British goods instead of imports from, say, West Germany where green consumerism and industry are more advanced. I need hardly remind the House that we are already running a massive trade deficit with West Germany. Although the Government are beginning such a campaign and industry is starting to respond, I should like more progress. The Government have been prepared to spend many millions of pounds on glossy advertising campaigns in recent years and this is one area in which Government advertising might be welcome.

Consumer organisations are already doing a good job in making consumers aware of the environmental implications of much of what they buy as well as in pointing out the dangers of the pseudo-green claims that manufacturers sometimes make. While I accept the point made by the hon. Member for Stockport (Mr. Favell) that industry is becoming more environmentally minded, I am afraid that there is also some phoney greenery in industry. One can sometimes be tempted to buy a product which claims to be environmentally friendly but which turns out to be wrapped in unfriendly, non-biodegradable packaging. We must take a good, cool and hard look at the claims of many manufacturers to be environmentally sensitive, because they are not always what they seem.

I am glad that there is also growth in the setting up of consumer organisations specifically to highlight environmental concerns and the need to promote green and socially responsible consumerism. I refer to the valuable work of the Women's Environmental Network, which recently produced a good report on dioxins, and to its campaign to encourage the production of chlorine-free paper products.

Mr. Malcolm Bruce (Gordon): On that important point, and taking up the earlier intervention of the hon. Member for Stockport (Mr. Favell), does the hon. Lady agree that one of the problems is that the Government's reaction tends to be that if the market will bear the offer of a choice of dioxin-free produce, so be it, but that they are not prepared to intervene to ensure that that choice is made available? Is not that the fundamental difference between the Government's philosophy and what consumers really want?

Ms. Quin: I agree that that is exactly what is happening, although it is not just to help consumers and consumer organisations but because there is a vital need to protect the environment that we should be taking more interventionist action than most of us would otherwise like.

New Consumer, an organisation whose headquarters are in Newcastle, is doing research into the environmental and social implications of many of the goods and services that are currently being provided. I think that I am right in saying that the Consumer Protection Act 1987 had to be put on to the statute book rather hastily in time for the general election, and Labour Members criticised it at the time as far too weak. It already needs strengthening and updating, in line with some of the difficulties experienced by consumers since it was passed and some of the new developments, particularly the environmental developments that I have described. Better labelling is a key factor,

but it is also clear that EEC legislation will be increasingly relevant, and I shall refer in more detail to EEC matters later in my speech.

The consumer also needs much easier and cheaper access to legal redress. Hon. Members may remember the recent case of two sisters who were accused of shoplifting by Tesco. Although in the end they were pronounced completely innocent, they faced ruinous costs. An improvement in the legal aid arrangements is vital for consumers.

We also need a proper statutory code of advertising practice and proper powers to order the correction of misleading advertisements. That would certainly help to counter the many misleading advertisements that appear in newspapers in which loan sharks offer people easy credit without explaining to them that there is a catch, or displaying the rates of interest that they will have to pay.

As I said, agricultural produce and unprocessed foods will also need to be brought within the Act.

There are other anomalies. The Food and Drugs Act 1955 does not cover microwaved or cook-chill food. That is not surprising, but both have recently caused outbreaks of food poisoning and they should be covered.

It would be nice if the Government would announce today their help and support for the establishment of a proper, comprehensive, nationwide network of consumer advice centres. The citizens advice bureaux and many specialised advice agencies do a terrific job, as I know from my contact with them, but I am perturbed by the fact that the network of local authority consumer advice centres has been cut, largely because of the Government-imposed economies that local authorities have had to make. I am even more perturbed to learn that the Government do not even seem to keep centrally the figures relating to the number of local authority consumer advice centres or information about where they are to be found. That lack of figures was made clear in an answer given by the Under-Secretary of State for Industry and Consumer Affairs to my hon. Friend the Member for Dunfermline, East (Mr. Brown).

Some excellent consumer advice centres disappeared when the Government abolished the metropolitan county councils. That was certainly the case in Tyne and Wear, where the Tyne and Wear consumer advice centre did a very good job. The result of all these cuts is that there is now patchy provision of consumer advice, with certain regions clearly under-served. I am glad that the Labour party's proposals in recent policy documents would rectify that deficiency.

The Government should closely examine the so-called lemon laws in the United States because its consumer protection legislation could teach us a great deal. It is difficult for people in Britain to get defective goods replaced or to obtain adequate compensation. Years after the problems were first highlighted, there are still far too many cases of, for example, substandard cars being sold and then purchasers having tremendous difficulty in obtaining compensation or a replacement vehicles. There are also far too many examples of poor garage servicing, with cars sometimes being delivered back to their owners in conditions that might endanger them and even other road users.

Mr. Conal Gregory (York): The hon. Lady made a valid point about the difficulty of maintaining good consumer standards because of scarce resources in many local authorities. Will she pay tribute to the local authorities' co-ordinating body on trading standards? I believe that my hon. Friend the Minister takes his responsibilities seriously —for example, he has made resources available to tackle the problem of flammability of upholstery. However, it would be ridiculous for every local authority to carry out that exercise when it could be co-ordinated by one or two local authorities. It is therefore right that proper co-ordination is acknowledged.

Ms. Quin: I am happy to acknowledge the importance of proper co-ordination and also the good work of the Association of Trading Standards Officers. However, the hon. Gentleman will not be surprised if I do not agree with all of his remarks. It is astonishing that the Government are no longer even informed about the remaining number of local authority advice centres. They have not carried out a study to determine the areas where consumers need a resumption of that service.

I wish to refer to other issues which consumer organisations have raised directly with me and which I hope the Minister will consider. The Consumers Association is concerned about the lack of an adequate certification scheme for gas equipment. Before British Gas was privatised, it had to approve all domestic gas appliances to ensure that they met the appropriate British standard. As, in theory, British Gas is no longer a monopoly, there is no longer any requirement for such items as gas-fired boilers and heaters to meet any particular standard, although I understand that gas cookers are covered by some regulations. The Commission in Brussels has issued a directive that all British gas appliances must meet safety requirements, but the responsibility for that rests solely with the manufacturer as there is no requirement for independent verification. That is another example why we believe that the self-regulatory and voluntary approach is not appropriate.

The Consumers Association is also concerned about the wiring of electric plugs on home appliances. Like most consumers, I am annoyed that I have to buy a plug separately from an electric appliance. Legislation is necessary to ensure that consumers can buy appliances that are already fitted with plugs. Because of the great variety of prices for goods, without legislation consumers may still buy the appliances and plugs separately if that makes the total purchase less expensive. A survey by *Which?* highlighted th problem of consumers not knowing how to wire plugs correctly, which could lead to accidents.

In the latter part of my speech I will deal with consumer affairs within the EEC and, in particular, the consequence for British consumers arising from the opening of the single European market in 1992. Recently the Consumers Association and the London-based Consumers in the European Community Group produced interesting research and literature on the consumer in 1992. The publications of those bodies made important recommendations to the Government and to European institutions. I hope that, by now, the Minister has read them. When I referred to them at the last Department of Trade and Industry Question Time, he said that he had not read them. They are essential reading for many people, even before European election day on Thursday.

A Department of Trade and Industry press release refers to a speech that the Minister made before the Scottish Consumer Council. It states that the Minister

"dismissed criticisms that the Government neglected consumers in planning for the Single Market in 1992.

'Nothing could be further from the truth. We recognise the Single Market is everything to do with consumers.'

Mr. Forth explained that the Government's awareness campaign was deliberately targeted at businesses because it was they who needed to gear themselves up for change, whereas consumers do not have to make special plans."

However, consumers certainly need to be aware of all the decisions being made in the run-up to 1992. I am sure that they wish to know whether their interests will be safeguarded. Consumer organisations certainly need to be geared up just as much as industry does, because they have the job of advising their members and the general public about legislative changes and changes that must be introduced if the consumer is to have adequate protection.

In his press release, the Minister went on to say that he wanted to explode three myths. The first concerned the statement:

"the Single Market will not result in lower safety standards." The second related to the statement:

"Furthermore, the UK will continue to negotiate to ensure that the harmonised European standards take place at the higher end of the spectrum—levelling up and not down."

There is a certain inconsistency in those two myths. If it is true that standards are not to be endangered, why is it so important to negotiate to ensure that they are not so endangered? The negotiations are important, and the results will determine whether standards are to be reduced or raised as we hope.

On 1 June, the Minister attended a meeting of the EEC Consumers Affairs Council. Given all the EEC directives that have already been agreed and those that are currently under negotiation and affect the consumer, the agenda for that meeting could have been endless. However, in answer to one of his hon. Friends at Question Time, the Minister seemed to say that such meetings were rather pointless and infrequent. None the less, some positive gains seem to have been made by the meeting.

The Parliamentary Under-Secretary of State for Industry and Consumer Affairs (Mr. Eric Forth): It is important that the House understands that the setting of agendas and the frequency of the meetings, as the hon. Lady probably knows better than any other hon. Member, are entirely for the presidency. The Spanish presidency chose to wait this length of time before having a meeting. The Greek presidency immediately beforehand did not choose to have a meeting with the Council of Ministers. I am sure that the hon. Lady understands that.

Ms. Quin: I accept partly what the Minister has said, but, given the number of directives that directly affect the consumer, I wonder whether he will now be arguing for more frequent meetings of the EEC Consumer Affairs Council than has been the case.

Some gains appear to have been made at the meeting, notably the joint position agreed by the Council of Ministers on a common system for calculating the annual percentage rate of interest under the consumer credits directive, which I welcome. However, other developments at the meeting give rise for concern. I understand that the draft directive on package travel was raised by the European Commission, but that the United Kingdom Minister was strongly opposed to the directive, even though all consumer organisations to which I have spoken are very much in favour of it, as it offers better protection for the consumer than anything at present.

[*Ms. Quin*]

I remind the Minister that it was not only Labour but Conservative Members of the European Parliament who, in the European Parliament supported amendments which in certain cases strengthened the directive for the benefit of the consumer. However, perhaps that is just another area where there are disagreements within the Conservative party over European issues. There certainly appears to have been a difference of view on that issue between Conservative Members of the European Parliament and the attitude adopted by the Minister with responsibility for consumer affairs.

Mr. Robert G. Hughes (Harrow, West): The hon. Lady is talking about differences of view apparently within the Conservative party on the future of the European Community. Will she confirm that the former leader of the European Parliament Labour group said:

"It is obvious the Common Market is utterly incapable of reforming itself. The sooner Britain gets out the better"?

He said that in 1987, and that is perhaps why he was sacked from that job. However, the new leader said:

"The Common Market . . . has been a disaster for British people."

Does that go along with the pro-European flavour that the Labour party is pretending to give to the British people?

Ms. Quin: The hon. Gentleman, of course, has used the labels loosely. I do not know whether he was here when I responded to an earlier intervention, when I said that in my speech I would be criticising certain aspects of the EEC and praising others. I believe that there is a mixture of good and bad, certainly in consumer protection. If we want to widen the debate to talk about the state of the major parties as we approach the Euopean election, I would say that the Labour party is in much better shape to fight that election, and has been much more united that the Conservative party has been during recent weeks.

Will the Minister continue to oppose the draft directive on package travel? If so, will he take national action to prevent tour operators from continuing to breach the code of the Association of British Travel Agents? The breaches of that code were highlighted recently in a report from the Office of Fair Trading. I note that the Minister said something recently about the creation of a holiday ombudsman. While I see the need for someone in authority to follow up the many complaints about package travel, I do not believe that that will in any way contradict the need for an EEC directive in the form that will most benefit consumers.

At the EEC Consumer Affairs Council on 1 June there was a worrying lack of agreement on the general resolution covering consumer protection and 1992. I have been told that our Minister was in a minority of one in disagreement on an issue which centred on EEC rules on the safety and quality of consumer products. The British view was said to mystify the other member states, in that the Minister made no attempt to find a solution that would have allowed an overall agreement. As usual, we have managed to antagonise the other member states without having achieved anything in return. Perhaps the Minister will tell us by what steps he proposes to reach agreement at the next meeting of the Council on that issue.

At the meeting the priority to be given to consumer education was also discussed. Apparently, Ministers do not disagree about the necessity for some system of consumer education within the member countries, but I wonder whether the Government's recent refusal to countenance the use of the Lingua programme in schools will signify a similarly negative approach to consumer education. I believe that the better informed and educated consumers are, the better that is for our society.

There are other EEC-related issues to which I shall refer briefly. The product liability directive was agreed and is already in force, but it has not been satisfactorily implemented in the United Kingdom to the full advantage of the consumer. The development risks defence, which was a contentious issue at the time of the Consumer Protection Act 1987, has proved to be a problem in relation to the United Kingdom's implementation of that directive.

The United Kingdom should work determinedly for the adoption of a product safety directive which would underpin many of the agreements on standards and so on set within the EEC as part of the 1992 programme. Without a directive such agreements on standards will be unsatisfactory.

The current EEC standards and those to be adopted on a range of consumer products also raise different issues. I shall not go into details, but there is concern among consumers in this country about the standards relating to refrigerators—that is particularly important because of recent worries about food—cooker surface temperatures, electric room heaters, spin extractors, ultra-violet skin treatment appliances, hedge trimmers, chain saws and so on. A tremendous variety of goods and products are part of the discussions on the harmonisation of standards in 1992. The list of issues related to consumer protection is long, but the conclusion is obvious. In all the regulations and the negotiations on safety standards, those standards should be set at the highest level.

Mr. Favell: We are living in a fast changing world. Is the hon. Lady suggesting that the EEC should set standards for every product on the market now or in the future? If so, she is living in cloud-cuckoo-land. It is impossible for every product to be examined and a standard set before its manufacture and retail.

Ms. Quin: I am sure that the hon. Gentleman is aware that a more general system for standardisation has already been agreed in Europe. Within that general system one must try to ensure that the standards are as high as possible. That need also reinforces my earlier point about the need for a product safety directive to underpin many of the broader agreements on standards that have been reached.

The EEC cannot simply be about a Europe open for business; it must be about consumers and society. The Community must benefit all citizens within Britain and Europe. The Government may protest that they are concerned to see standards for consumers set as high as possible, but the Government's opposition to recent EEC initiatives to improve the health and safety of workers is well known. I believe that the health and safety of consumers cannot be anything but a related issue.

The organisations concerned with the well-being of the consumer need to be consulted more about all aspects of 1992 legislation. The Consumers Association and the consumers of the European Community group made that point strongly recently. Consumers must be formally involved in the European standard-making process. From contact with the European institutions, many of us know that many of the EEC decisions are taken by officials behind closed doors. Therefore, it can be extremely difficult for consumer organisations and others to have an adequate input in such decisions.

We are all consumers, and when talking about consumer protection and rights we are talking about something which is vital to a civilised society in which commercial forces operate for the general good, not to the public detriment. Therefore, concern for the consumer is an essential part of concern for society as a whole. Given this Government's record, I do not think it will surprise anyone that it will become increasingly clear that the Labour party is the natural ally of the consumer, to which the consumer will increasingly look in the future.

4.25 pm

Mr. Michael Jack (Fylde): I shall comment on one or two of the points made by the hon. Member for Gateshead, East (Ms. Quin), and address one or two agricultural issues. In doing so, I declare an interest to the House because I am the parliamentary adviser to the Produce Packaging and Marketing Association.

In Committee, we had an interesting debate on a European directive on product labelling in the produce industry. We raised issues such as Alar and the other chemicals which the hon. Lady mentioned. The controversy surrounding Alar is a classic example of how information emanating from the consumer industry in the United States, where there were clearly differences of opinion about whether Alar was as bad as one group said, was suddenly picked up by the consumer body here and led to a major scare. When it examined the scientific evidence which lay behind the scare, our own committee on pesticides, which is an independent body with no commercial or Government connections other than the fact that it reports to a Government Department, found no scientific evidence for banning Alar for the treatment of fruit.

The debate did not go on to expose the wider issue of the benefit to the consumer of using Alar. It ensures that apples stay on trees and do not fall off too early and means that the consumer is not presented with a poor quality, bruised fruit which may have other disadvantageous aspects. A hint of a problem is seized on without scientific evidence and promulgated as a new gospel. The scientific evidence surrounding Alar suggested that, for an individual to obtain the same level of input of Alar as did the mouse with the tumours, he or she would have to eat 25,000 times the normal human consumption of apples. I cite that as an example to show that realistic and scientific evidence must lie behind our discussion of many of these consumer issues.

Consumerism touches on the important issue of information. Often, when a consumer has to make a choice about goods, he or she has to fight a battle against ignorance. The hon. Member for Gateshead, East was strong on solutions, but weak on how we could improve the information flow to the consumer. She also gave the impression that we have little consumer protection and that what there is is utterly ineffective. She made it sound as if we were standing at the abyss of consumer abuse, and that she, on behalf of the Opposition, had all the solutions. That is palpably not true.

I have looked for facts and figures to aid me on the subject of information. An article in *The Sunday Times* of 6 November 1988 showed that:

"According to the Office of Fair Trading (OFT) 40 per cent. of people in the sample of 2,000 did not know the seller is responsible for correcting matters if, say, an electric kettle does not work."

If we are still at the basic stage of educating the consumer about his or her rights under existing law, I see little hope for the panopoly of legislation suggested by the Opposition in this debate as a solution to the mind-boggling range of problems before us.

Mr. Frank Cook (Stockton, North): The consumer's fault.

Mr. Jack: I am not blaming the consumer for this. I am pointing out that one of the key aspects in any consumer transaction is information. Even if European directives or regulations covered every item mentioned by the hon. Lady, could we say with confidence that the consumer would quickly become aware of them and act on them? A short time ago, in November 1988, 40 per cent. of a large sample did not know their basic consumer rights, so I doubt whether a lot of new legislation would take us any further forward.

I note also that the present consumer legislation ventures into the realms of second-hand goods. The Sale of Goods Act 1979 deals with that point. Many of us have received letters from our constituents complaining about defects in products that they have bought, especially second-hand products, yet the Sale of Goods Act already protects people in this respect.

Mr. Ian McCartney (Makerfield): Would it not have been better if the Government had spent millions of pounds on advertising on television and explaining consumers' rights instead of publicising the privatisations of the water and electricity industries in the past few weeks?

Mr. Jack: The hon. Gentleman might have made a more telling point if he had paid tribute to the £50 million that the Government put into trading standards and the £8 million grant-in-aid that the Department of Trade and Industry gives to the citizens advice bureaux. So it is not true to say that we are not meeting our financial responsibilities to look after the consumer. The Securities and Investments Board has produced a video and booklet discussing its own affairs.

It can be seen from these examples that consumerism is a complicated business. It covers every sort of purchase of goods or services, and it takes a lot of effort to get through the basics that we already have. I fear for what may happen if the line adopted by the hon. Member for Gateshead, East is pursued; we shall have yet another Euro mountain—this time, a paper mountain of ideas that may be well intentioned but are weak when they come to be applied.

I have some limited experience of consumer affairs—at one time I was employed by Marks and Spencer and had to deal with consumers' inquiries. It was interesting to see how even that reputable business encountered the problem, when dealing with consumers, of working out whose the responsibility is when something goes wrong. We had to point out, for example, that inadequate attention to washing instructions on shirts might result in holes appearing in them, and that was not the company's

[*Mr. Jack*]

fault. If we take some of the hon. Lady's arguments to their logical conclusion, industry will be made responsible for every fault, which would be wrong.

From the front line of a retail establishment we observe a strong relationship between the price of goods and services and their quality. The Conservative Government can take credit for having increased earnings by record amounts. We have reduced taxation and put more money back in the pocket of the consumer, so that, generally speaking, he can afford a higher standard of goods.

Mr. Allen McKay (Barnsley, West and Penistone): Rubbish.

Mr. Jack: If the hon. Gentleman had worked in a retail environment as I have, in Marks and Spencer and latterly in the produce industry, he would have clearly understood that we are upgrading. When did he last visit his local Tesco? The range of goods on display there and in Sainsburys has vastly improved in quality compared with a few years ago because people can now aford to pay for quality.

Inherent in the Opposition's argument is the seductive idea that consumers can be safeguarded. People do not like buying goods that fall apart and are inherently poor in quality and safety. They quickly say, "No, that is not for me." They prefer to buy a good branded item that has been proven in service and they buy it from a reputable retailer. In that way, the market place can best serve the consumer in giving adequate consumer protection.

The laws on goods of a merchantable quality start to open the door to ways in which people can obtain redress if poor quality goods are offered. I had an example of this when I bought my wife a handbag which fell to pieces. After much remonstrating with the shopkeeper, I took him to the small claims court and won the action on the ground that the goods were of unmerchantable quality. I know that the existing legislation works and provides good and cheap redress for the consumer who runs into a problem. That answers the point made by the hon. Member for Gateshead, East about the expense of the law. The area of the small claim is the one that most often hits the consumer, and it is the area in which the consumer most often seeks protection through the law.

I have been involved in an interesting area of consumer protection. For the past 18 months I have been working with members of the House Builders Federation to produce a code of practice to regulate the area of private sheltered accommodation for the elderly. It deals with a classic consumer problem that started in an industry that was growing rapidly and had growing pains. Its management and sales style led to problems in that people were getting a deal that was not quite the one that they thought they should be getting. Service charges were going up more rapidly than people had anticipated and the quality of the service in the industry was not as good as they had expected.

We worked first with Age Concern to identify the problem more clearly and with the House Builders Federation to produce a code of practice. On 27 June, before the whole of the industry and with the help of the National House-Building Council, we shall launch a voluntary code of practice to regulate some of the excesses in sheltered accommodation. The code will give excellent protection to buyers. We have interlocked that code of practice with the rules and regulations of the National House-Building Council on housing quality. If a house builder does not acknowledge the National House-Building Council rules, he cannot get the "build" mark and without that he cannot sell his house of flat. That cunning interlocking of an existing regulatory mechanism in house building with our code of practice on sheltered accommodation will provide for the first time truly meaningful protection against abuse in that area.

There will be an element of discipline because somebody who buys sheltered accommodation in a development and finds that it is not being run in accordance with the good practice in our code will be able to go to the National House-Building Council which will be able to discipline its members. That discipline puts the house builder in a difficult position, because he may not be able to sell the property that he has built. I put that example before the House because the hon. Member for Gateshead, East condemned any kind of voluntary code of practice. The work that we have carried out in this area and on the many other voluntary codes which are registered by the Office of Fair Trading under the 1987 Act is a useful and effective way to go forward in consumer protection.

In relation to the 1987 Act, I have mentioned our code of practice. One of the key features in the Act is the question of misleading price indicators. That is a valuable addition to our consumer protection law. It means that for the first time in sheltered accommodation people will not be able to make false claims about the way that service charges are likely to go. That is a good example of a piece of general—not specific—legislation that helps a group of consumers. Would those consumers be aware of that protection if it were not for the information emanating from my code of practice? It has generated much newspaper comment, and I pay tribute in particular to *The Daily Telegraph* which has assiduously followed through on the code. Newspapers have a vital role to play in putting forward such consumer information, because they reach a large number of people and can get the message across quickly and effectively so that people can react accordingly.

It never fails to amaze me that we still have the confidence trickster, or the pressurising salesman. Many consumer problems that we are seeking to address result from such people. We have all heard stories of double-glazing salesmen saying, "If you don't buy today, you will lose your 25 per cent. discount." Those are the main bones of contention, rather than some of the more sophisticated consumer arguments put forward by the hon. Member for Gateshead, East.

The hon. Lady mentioned the interesting case of the produce industry and Europe. There is already European legislation on common grading standards. All produce sold as class 1 in Europe has to follow these rules and regulations. They are down there, they are agreed to, they are in statute. Has the hon. Lady ever bought a bruised apple, a soft tomato or a flabby lettuce? I imagine that she is honest enough to admit that she may have found such defective produce. However, the EEC grading standards say that such produce should not be sold. The point is that we need good, human input to make the standards work. That is why people such as trading standards officers and Ministry inspectors have an important role to play.

Above all, the trust that the buyer and the seller have in one another is what will determine whether rules and regulations are followed through, and followed assiduously. That is the best form of protection for the consumer. It will mean that if leading retailers find that products are not in line with their specifications they will take action straight away. They will not need an inspector. However, the human input is required to make the rules and regulations work. The hon. Lady put forward many specific ideas, but I wonder whether we shall have the resources to make them work. I know that what made our rules and regulations work in the produce industry was our agreement that we wanted to make a high quality product, because if we did not, our customers would not buy it. That is straightforward and simple.

Other common European regulations work to our mutual benefit. The hon. Lady's suggestion that there should be a European statement on safety can be compared with the reality of what happens in the motor industry. Cars have been produced for a long time, so we have construction and use regulations that lay down the technical specifications against which cars can be built. They are highly geared towards producing safe motor cars.

What will happen in 1992 will lead us further down that road, because we shall then have common standards. That is the right way to go, rather than the way in which the hon. Lady is pointing us. Making general statements about safety in a technical sector such as that of motor cars is no substitute for the detailed objectives of our construction and use regulations and the pan-European requirements for cars on, for example, exhaust emissions. Specific and detailed regulations are worthwhile, but general statements tend to be meaningless.

The hon. Lady's speech gave the impression that there is no legislation on safety. I am glad to see that she now shakes her head, because that underpins the point that I am making. In many sectors—for example, motor car manufacture—excellent legislation deals with the consumer protection and safety issues to which she drew the attention of the House.

I should like my hon. Friend the Minister to look at a few specific points because no one can claim that consumer protection is perfect. The Consumers Association magazine *Which?* does an excellent job in highlighting the continuing need for activity, and local citizens advice bureaux are a useful source of information. I work closely with my local office in Lytham St. Annes. It keeps me fully appraised of important factors.

I am concerned about one or two points in particular. One is consumer credit. Many people, perhaps through lack of education and information, take on consumer credit obligations that they later cannot meet. I was disappointed when the previous Minister would not take up an idea that I put to him. It was that everybody, on taking out a consumer credit agreement, would be given a booklet laying down precisely the nature of the agreement that he was taking on and the obligations that it gave him. It is all too easy to get credit from a shop. Those who may not be as financially aware as others suffer when they take on such obligations without due notice of what they have let themselves into. The credit industry could do something like this itself, but to make certain that it does it should be required to give the information to the consumer. Caveat emptor—let the buyer beware—but the buyer must be aware to beware.

Mr. Favell: Consumer credit is an issue that exercises all our minds and I regularly come across not only young people but parents who are worried about their children who get into debt. As my hon. Friend will be aware, as an infant, which one is until one is 18, one is not responsible for repaying debts. However, once one has reached the age of 18 and is free to vote and fight for one's country, one is responsible for getting out of debt, if one is in debt. That should be spelt out loud and clear.

Mr. Jack: I thank my hon. Friend. I do not disagree with his solution. However, I am concerned about the question of information, and I should like to see more information made available when people take out credit. There are financial implications and obligations in taking out a life assurance policy, and there is a cooling off period during which one can decide whether the policy is exactly what one wants and one can study the implications of one's signature on the bottom line.

Some interesting things have been said by Opposition Members about guarantees. I notice that in 1986 the Office of Fair Trading estimated that the amount spent by consumers on unsatisfactory goods was £3·5 billion on cars and accessories and £346 million on household appliances. I do not want to detain the House unnecessarily by reviewing the question of guarantees, but the Department could do much good for consumers by looking at the terms of guarantees, particularly those that say, "Woodworm treatment: guaranteed for 20 or 25 years." How many companies will be around for such a time to honour long-term guarantees? We all look to guarantees as a reassurance that the product will do the job that it says it will. We should look at the bonding of guarantees, and I know that such a move is supported by the National Consumer Council.

Let me pray in aid of my argument on the general subject of the direction of Community law on consumer protection a speech made by Sir Gordon Borrie which was published in the *Journal of Business Law* in March 1988. I hope that the hon. Member for Gateshead, East will have a chance to look at it. Sir Gordon says that, originally, the Commission tried to introduce many directives on specific functions, but that they were not taken up very much. He went on to say that the Community developed, in a way that he approved, its approach to more general statements on the subject of consumer law. That is an important observation, by one who sees that as a welcome direction in which the Community should go. It also underlines why the Government are sometimes the odd man out. They see Europe trying to be prescriptive and detailed when what it needs to do is to set the scene, point out the problem and then allow the individual Government, and then the individual state, to solve the problems. The most appropriate and Conservative way of proceeding is to trust the individual, to give him information and to provide him with a framework of protection, which is what the Government have done. I am certain that on Thursday people will take that view rather than agree with the hon. Member for Gateshead, East.

4.49 pm

Mr. Alan Williams (Swansea, West): May I argue one specific case and cause—the need for a complete and separate department of consumer affairs? About 15 years ago, I was Minister of State for the Department of Prices and Consumer Protection. I shall argue for a return to the

[*Mr. Alan Williams*]

basic concept but not the form. I shall be relatively non-political, and while I shall criticise the Government I shall also be critical of the period for which I and my colleagues were responsible for consumer protection.

It is important to emphasise a point that tends to be forgotten. Implicit in talk of the consumer society is that the consumer is king. The history of the consumer society has been one of erosion of the consumers' power in the market place and of an increasing need for the Government or, now, the EEC as a sort of continental authority to back up the consumer's diminishing power. Long gone is the day of the local market, when local producers and local sellers knew local buyers and were dependent on their reputations in the local market. At that time, there was parity of status between individuals. By the nature of the highly desirable changes that had to occur if we were to move to the levels of affluence that the western world now enjoys, a market has inevitably evolved in which that relationship altered massively against the power of the consumer. Mass marketing and mass production removed the decision-maker from the purchaser, making it more difficult for consumers to make representations that matter and count.

Some of the new techniques that are used, such as the use of quality control, have led to the market place discovering errors and, if enough pressure is applied, suppliers putting them right. A quality control system that checks one in every 10 products detects a mechanical error in the system, but the converse is that there is a one in 10 chance of discovering an inadvertent human error. Statistically, such human errors pass through the system more than is identified. If a remote marketing company or remote international manufacturer is involved, it is difficult for the consumer to obtain redress.

Mr. Alistair Burt (Bury, North): Is not the remoteness that the right hon. Gentleman is describing covered by the most basic of our Sale of Goods Acts, which allows a consumer who has bought a defective product to return to the local shop where he bought it and demand redress rather than have to try to seek redress from a remote manufacturing company? The process is rather closer to home and easier for the consumer than the right hon. Gentleman is suggesting.

Mr. Williams: It can be as difficult to obtain redress from a mass marketer as it is from a mass producer. I have written many letters to firms that have branches nationally on behalf of my constituents, because sometimes it is very difficult for them to obtain their legal rights. That is not a political point but a reality of the market place.

That problem is exacerbated by the fact that it is difficult for the consumer to know whether he is making a good or bad purchase decision at the time of purchase because of the increasing complexity of products. Domestic appliances are becoming increasingly complex, products such as foodstuffs have increasingly complex additives and there are technical problems with the irradiation of food. The complexity of products makes it more difficult for the consumer to make a considered judgment about the version of a product that he should buy. It is important, therefore, that there is back-up to

ensure that if something subsequently goes wrong with a product the consumer can be adequately assured that it will be put right.

The House has had to take action against even reputable international producers, who have not hesitated to use the complexities of the law to shelter from what consumers consider to be their rights. One or two hon. Members who are present today were present when we discussed exclusion clauses. The hon. Member for Fylde (Mr. Jack) referred to guarantees. I well remember the exclusion clauses that we had to make illegal whereby major companies were offering people guarantees that, if they were silly enough to sign and return, removed the rights that they already had at law and conferred on them a lesser set of rights.

The use and type of the market, the nature of products and the increasing sophistication of those who want to protect their selfish interests against those of the consumer have diminished consumers' rights. Further, we are moving increasingly into a credit economy—I shall not make any political points about that, tempting though it is —one of the inevitable effects of which is that if someone makes a mistake they may pay for it long after they are able to get any use from a faulty product.

It is clear that a countervailing force is needed in favour of the consumer. The hon. Member for Fylde referred to Sir Gordon Borrie. I was in the middle of an interview with Shirley Williams to appoint him when I was called out by Jim Callaghan and switched from the Department of Prices and Consumer Protection to the Department of Industry. Despite the shortcomings of the Department of Prices and Consumer Protection, for a while it reversed the power balance within Whitehall between the consumer and producer to such an extent that the Confederation of British Industry began to squeal that protection had moved too much in favour of the consumer.

I hope that the Under-Secretary of State for Industry and Consumer affairs has found his work fascinating. What I am about to say is not a personal attack on his role, because one must first be an Under-Secretary and then a Minister of State before becoming a Secretary of State. Since the Conservative party came to office, there has been a progressive erosion of the protection for the consumer that was provided in the 1970s. We saw first the abolition of the separate Department of Prices and Consumer Protection and then the subsuming of consumer responsibility within one of the major industrial sponsoring Departments. Within that Department we saw the downgrading of ministerial status so that, instead of the job going to a separate Cabinet Minister, it was given to a Parliamentary Under-Secretary of State. Under-Secretaries of State can argue their corners belligerently —I am sure that that is true of the Under-Secretary of State for Industry and Consumer Affairs—but the final say rests with senior Ministers. Those who have been members of the Government know the close relationship that exists in a sponsoring Department between the sponsored industries, their officials and their Ministers. It is difficult for a Parliamentary Under-Secretary of State to win the argument in an enormous Government Department, with a hierarchy of Ministers of State who are responsible for different sectors of the economy and a Secretary of State who believes that 95 per cent. of his responsibility is directed towards industry and commerce.

Mr. Forth: Does the right hon. Gentleman accept that important changes have taken place in the Department since he was such a distinguished member of the ministerial team? The sponsoring relationship has been radically changed as well so that there is now, deliberately, no direct involvement by the Department with industries in the way that he may recall from his days in the Department. That may well have changed things greatly in the context of the right hon. Gentleman's argument.

Mr. Williams: I well understand that point. I understand that the sponsoring divisions no longer exist, but an analysis of the work of civil servants within the Department would show that their work time is devoted more to industry and commerce than to consumer interests.

The sponsoring Department even appoints the consumer watchdogs. The Department of Energy, which has a close relationship with the gas, electricity and coal industries, appoints the members of Ofgas. Because of technology investment, the Department of Trade and Industry has a close relationship with British Telecom. It appoints the members of Oftel. That is not to say that Professor Carsberg is not a formidable man and that he will not do a good job, but the person who is responsible for consumer interests is aware that the Minister who decides whether to reappoint him must consider the demand by the industry that his office is intended to monitor.

The hon. Member for Fylde argued a case for self-regulation and I was interested in the instance that he put forward. The reality is, however, that a voluntary code is only as strong as the coverage of the trade association that has underwritten it and that association's will to enforce it. If a trade association covers only 60 per cent. of the suppliers of a particular good or service, another 40 per cent. are outside its scope. That makes it difficult for the trade association to take a tough line with its members, because they are likely to say, "We will do exactly the same. We will go outside."

It is not just that responsibility for consumer protection has been relegated—it is highly fragmented between Departments. The Ministry of Agriculture, Fisheries and Food is responsible for food standards. Even if we accept that Ministers want to ensure that food is safe and standards are high, the Department is automatically laid open to allegations of whitewash the moment a major case arises and it appears to be dilatory. In terms of self-interest, it makes sense to take those responsibilities from that Department and give them to a separate Minister for Consumer Affairs.

The Treasury is responsible for credit policy. Incongruously, the Department of Employment—a matter of great interest to the hon. Member for York (Mr. Gregory)—is responsible for tourism. That is an anomalous allocation of responsibilities. The Department of Energy has responsibility for gas and electricity. The Department of the Environment has water responsibilities. The Department of Trade and Industry is responsible for safety standards in respect of weights and measures and such large sectors of industry as British Telecom. The Home Office has responsibility for standards in television, radio and the media generally. The Department of Transport has responsibility for consumer interests in relation to those companies that supply ferry, air and rail services. Legal services come within the Lord Chancellor's

domain. Taking a wider view of the consumer, all those instances ignore the consumer element in education, health and so on. There has been fragmentation of responsibility for consumer interests in so many Departments that it is difficult to get a cohesive and coherent consumer strategy.

In 1974, we had the Department of Prices and Consumer Protection. It did a worthwhile job within a limited context. By creating a Department, the Government pulled together people with a single objective, but the Department failed because its scope was too narrow. Without the price element, it did not merit the status of a Department. Originally, the prices side took half the Department's work but, as that became less important, it was clear that the Department was not viable as an administrative entity. That happened not because the concept of an independent Department was wrong but because the Department was too narrowly based.

One of my first battles in the Department took place when I wanted to take responsibility for safety from the Home Office, which, in fairness, the Home Office was only too happy to relinquish. I lost the battle to get tourism from the Department of Trade. The Department flatly refused to surrender to the Department of Prices and Consumer Protection responsibility for package tours, hotel standards and so on. Clearly, those aspects should have been covered by a separate Department.

It is time that we stepped back, looked again at the consumer functions that are submerged throughout Whitehall and considered which could and should be extracted—not which ones the Departments are willing to give up—and given separate Cabinet status through a Department of Consumer Affairs. Such a Department would have the muscle to match the powers of the sponsoring Departments. It will be even more important after 1992 when we have to struggle with Brussels as well as Whitehall.

5.9 pm

Mr. Conal Gregory (York): I welcome the opportunity to debate this key subject and I congratulate the hon. Member for Gateshead, East (Ms. Quin) on her perspicacity in pursuing it. For a long time, I have had an interest in consumer matters. In the 1983-87 Parliament, I took the initiative through a private Member's Bill to pioneer the Consumer Safety (Amendment) Act 1986, which became law.

Although Conservative Members may be full of moans and groans—and I shall add to those shortly—I must say at the outset how delighted I am that the Under-Secretary of State for Industry and Consumer Affairs and his colleagues take the matter so seriously. I want to draw the House's attention particularly to the fact that the Government acted with great speed a short time ago in introducing regulations to ensure that much safer upholstery was used for furniture. With the hon. Member for Makerfield (Mr. McCartney), I expected to have to carry out an all-party campaign, which might have taken years to achieve such a regulation. However, the carpet was removed from under us and he and I were delighted by the speed with which the Department of Trade and Industry acted.

The Government have protected the consumer and the Consumer Protection Act 1987 is but one of the initiatives taken by the Department of Trade and Industry. Although I welcome the debate, I deplore the tone of the motion. I

[*Mr. Conal Gregory*]

recall the Labour party's lack of interest for a long time in consumer matters when it was in office and I urge my right hon. and hon. Friends to reject the motion.

The Consumer Protection Act 1987 exempts second-hand goods from the general safety requirements. Although some second-hand goods such as electrical goods are covered by specific safety legislation, others are not. The safety of second-hand and repaired tyres is wholly uncontrolled and there is considerable evidence that potentially dangerous tyres are being sold to the public without any warning or advice about previous use or, more important, major repairs.

The hon. Member for Gateshead, East will recall that section 14 of the Trade Descriptions Act 1968 deals with:

"False or misleading statements as to services".

Section 14 has proved virtually unworkable because it requires a level of proof far in excess of that required by other trading standards legislation. It was a Labour party initiative, but it has not worked in practice although trading standards officers have tried to make it work. The Labour party also scratched at the surface of major issues, such as misdescribed holidays, which I shall speak about in detail in a moment. Do the Government intend to review the provisions and to bring them into line with section 1 of the Trade Descriptions Act 1968, which applies to all goods?

The hon. Member for Gateshead, East referred briefly to loan sharks and I wholly concur with her remarks. Too many people are getting into debt with second or third mortgages. I am concerned, as I am sure you are, Mr. Deputy Speaker, if you have read the national press today, to see that some hon. Members are trying to persuade the Minister to remove warning statements such as "Failure to maintain payments may mean you forfeit your house." That warning should be displayed by all reputable bodies to those seeking a loan. I am surprised that certain finance houses have been trying to persuade hon. Members to have such warnings removed.

Another important matter is shop notices. I was appalled to hear about certain notices in Winchester, to see them in Coney street in York, and in other places, advertising closing-down sales, but without any apparent intention to close down. I remember that a jeweller's shop in Regent street claimed that for some 10 or 12 years. However, in Winchester, the notice said that it was only four days until the closing down sale and another was written in similar terms. When are those shops intending to close down? Will it be next week, next month or the year 2000? Shops can continue with such notices and keep refreshing them. As long as no malice is intended, members of the public can be hoodwinked. If they are not familiar with a town or city, they may believe that they are entering a shop where prices have been reduced artificially because it is closing down.

I want now to turn the spotlight on the travel trade, in view of its importance, and its lack of response to complaints. The trade's constant inability to take action has seriously undermined consumer confidence. After the purchase of a car, a holiday is probably the most expensive regular item bought out of a family budget. Travel agents and operators alike market dreams that rarely reach expectations. In 1977, fewer than 4 million package holidays were sold. The growth in package holidays has

been so dramatic that Britain's tour operators expect to offer just under 14 million charter holidays with a value of £3·7 billion in the year to the end of March 1990.

However, consumer satisfaction has hit rock bottom. The Office of Fair Trading reports that as many as one in five people make a formal complaint about their package holiday and that 40 per cent. of foreign trips are plagued by difficulties. Part III of the Consumer Protection Act 1987, which came into force on 1 March this year, presumably gives consumers more protection over pricing. The guidelines state:

"Travel agents should make sure that correct price indication for holidays is made clear to consumers before booking."

Our travel agents would do well to have those guidelines placed before every clerk ,in every booking office, whether Lunn Poly, Thomas Cook, the Co-operative, Hogg Robinson or whichever, and to be reminded of them every 10 minutes of the day for a good month. Do the guidelines mean that consumers should be given accurate prices with no hidden extras?

Ms. Quin: I agree with much of what the hon. Gentleman has said. Will he inform us whether he supports the European Community directive on package travel? The Parliamentary Under-Secretary of State for Industry and Consumer Affairs does not.

Mr. Gregory: The hon. Lady has pre-empted my remarks. I give hearty support to that directive, which does not go far enough.

I want to deal now with the problem of inaccurate fares. Travel agents frequently fail to find the lowest fare. In a survey carried out by *Which?* published in May, 83 per cent. of travel agents quoted the wrong fare. I want to stress for the record that the figure was not 8·3 per cent. but 83 per cent. The agents were not asked a difficult question. They were asked to quote the cheapest scheduled air fare to Geneva, Paris or Brussels. Only 17 per cent. of agents found the cheapest fare. Some quoted more than £82 too much, either through incompetence or through instructions to quote only the fares of certain airlines.

Most operators' forms insist that insurance is taken out at the time of booking and not a minute later, and suggest that otherwise the form in invalid. They require the consumer to accept that, unless they tick a box to the contrary——

Mr. Favell: I bow to my hon. Friend's superior knowledge on consumer affairs and, in particular, congratulate him on being a pioneer in consumer legislation in recent years. However, does he agree that it is fair to point out that Britain is a European leader in the provision of cheap package tour holidays? One hears regularly of people from abroad flying with scheduled air fares to this country to take advantages of the many offers here. Are not the reasons why the industry is so successful the fact that tour operators have entered into voluntary agreements and the activities of a private organisation, the Consumers Association, and *Which?,* its journal?

Mr. Gregory: My hon. Friend may be correct to say that the industry has the greatest proportion of sales, but it also has the greatest number of complaints. Rarely do people go back to the agent who has booked their passage. I recall seeing a cartoon recently of an individual in a travel agents who was asked by the clerk where he wanted to go.

He said that he would like to go on holiday somewhere close to his baggage. That does not strike me as wholly inappropriate.

I have already referred to the difficulties with travel insurance forms. In addition, the cover is inadequate and the premiums are unacceptable. Holiday insurance premiums are usually higher than any broker would obtain and the cover is not as extensive. Exclusion clauses apply if someone becomes redundant or pregnant after booking a holiday, but that booking could have been made many months before the intended holiday. Therefore, the question of liability must be considered.

I also draw my hon. Friend's attention to the fact that many agents are either misinformed or unimaginative. If a consumer purchases a product, it should serve the purpose intended. There is little point in recommending a hotel or venue with no lift or in an area with steep hills for someone who is physically disabled, because such a recommendation could mean that that person is confined to just a few rooms of the hotel.

I do not wish to restrict my remarks entirely to the retail sector and to the travel agents because they often say, "That is not our problem—not in our back yard. The difficulty is with the tour operator." Tour operators have a cavalier approach, often cancelling holidays outright or changing dates. I shall give an example. A couple from Tamworth booked a holiday in Turkey with Intasun. It was cancelled. They were offered an earlier date but could not take it. The holiday was supposed to be a celebration. They chose to take a holiday in Scotland instead and I am jolly pleased that they did so.

Tour operators also change the timing of journeys. I know of pensioners who booked a holiday in Corfu with Horizon specifically because the tour was to depart at 1·40 in the afternoon and return at 8 o'clock at night. However, within days of the intended departure, those people learnt that they were to leave at 11·25 in the evening and return home at 5·40 in the morning. Understandably, they cancelled because the new arrangements represented a quite separate contract from the one that they had entered into.

Many people would like to use their local airport, which makes more sense than bussing people halfway across England. It was for that reason that a family with young children and an elderly aunt chose a holiday that started from Luton, their local airport. However, the operator switched it to Gatwick, a one and a half hour train journey away.

There is also the vexed matter of surcharges, which are not explained and which are operated on a maverick system from one operator to another. Indeed, some firms quote different surcharges for the same holiday. Kuoni Travel Ltd., which normally has a very good reputation, produced separate brochures that quoted different sterling rates for the same holiday. Therefore, people on the same package could face different surcharges—could anything be more ludicrous than that? Yet one faces an uphill struggle if one wants the trade body, the Association of British Travel Agents, to take effective action.

There is also the problem of hotel changes. One can find the chosen destination to be fully booked once one is abroad. I know that ground handlers try to help by putting people in cheaper accommodation for say three nights and then switching their hotel or making the facilities of the intended hotel available later, although they may be four streets away.

Holidaymakers travelling abroad expect a high standard of safety in the hotels and apartments in which they spend their holidays. However, the safety levels all too often fall well short of those required in the United Kingdom. I am sure that many hon. Members regularly watch the Esther Rantzen programme on Sundays and will have been appalled to learn of potential hazards such as lifts without internal doors, inadequate railings on stair and balconies, the lack of life-saving equipment at swimming pools and dangerous cots. A list of consumer dissatisfactions would be longer than a month's supply of *Hansard,* yet operators continually seek to get out of the problems by saying, "Take your claim to the ground handler in the country in which you suffered on that holiday." Clearly, United Kingdom operators and United Kingdom agents should accept their responsibilities.

Mr. Robert G. Hughes: My hon. Friend has made some valuable and important points, especially about safety. Has he received many complaints, and has he any reflections, about the other side of the coin—the medical care that people seem to be denied by so many companies? Many of the company representatives seem to deny the people in their charge access to the medical care that is available or that should be available from the expensive insurance that those people have taken out. Such representatives are risking the lives of the people who put their trust in them.

Mr. Gregory: I echo my hon. Friend's remarks. Ground handlers seem to be ignorant of the E111 form and its uses. They seem constantly to depend on the travel insurance that has been taken out and do not provide the adequate safeguards to which most consumers are entitled unless the holidaymakers have taken out a more expensive policy with an organisation such as Europ Assistance, which is again to the benefit of the travel agent, when such safeguards could and should have been organised more properly at the beginning of the process.

When my hon. Friend the Under-Secretary replies to the debate, I hope that he will at least confirm that he is unhappy about safety levels and that he would like to see greater responsibility from the tour operators and agents. I hope that he will call on them to ensure that they accept liability, because operators cannot continue to shirk that important point. The regular horror stories in all our postbags would not be so intense if the travel trade took its responsibilities seriously and did not make so many errors in the first place. It should be prompt in offering proper compensation.

Far too many operators try the hard-sell through glossy brochures and have no compunction about cancelling holidays outright or offering different destinations, departure times, airports and flight times.

The message that appears to be coming through is that, although one may have thought that one had entered into a contract, one cannot be sure if, when and where one is going on holiday.

Much of the anger and frustration could be deflected if the travel trade offered adequate compensation. Two tour giants, Thomson Holidays and Horizon, last year launched "no cancellation" offers. I am sure that with his laissez-faire approach my hon. Friend would say that they are splendid companies to do so. That offer seemed to be a guarantee that arrangements would be honoured and that the small print would not be invoked. However,

[*Mr. Gregory*]

consumers booking with those companies already know that that offer is not worth the paper that it is printed on because the companies have been sliding out of their responsibilities, offering as little as £15 compensation. That is derisory and it ill becomes their press officers to have made so much of their approach last year.

Tour operators have had their chance in voluntary codes of conduct and have been found lacking all the way along. The time has come for some Government intervention. It is because Government action is called for that I turn now to the EEC draft directive on package travel. It contains a great deal of commonsense and even the Association of British Travel Agents, which is the main body for both agents and operators in the travel trade, has stated that it

"accepts that there is a need for additional protection for EC travellers."

That is quite a statement from ABTA, which rarely admits anything. I am delighted that it has accepted that point even though, in its consultation documents to the Minister, it has tried to erode each point of the draft directive. I am glad of that admission from ABTA because we need some redress and the consumer, whom we are trying to support in this debate, needs help.

Press comments have suggested that my hon. Friend the Minister would like a package holiday ombudsman. Indeed, the consumer must have statutory rights which could, by all means, be backed up by a trade body. An ombudsman would be welcome, but we need a trade that is willing and anxious to participate and the holiday trade seems reluctant to do so.

The draft directive calls for compensation to holiday makers who have reasonable complaints. ABTA's submission states:

"Many of the risks resulting from the Directive would be uninsurable."

I wonder whether ABTA has heard of Lloyd's of London. Perhaps we could introduce the two parties to each other because there is no such word as "uninsurable".

I remember debating insurance with the right hon. Member for Swansea, West (Mr. Williams) when discussing the major consumer legislation of the previous Parliament. We discussed covering the liability for pharmaceutical risks, the extent to which consumers were exposed to risks with new pharmaceutical products and the extent to which the risk was insurable. The answer is that it was insurable; Lloyd's is prepared to underwrite the risk. It is unrealistic, and unbecoming, for a great tour industry not to fulfil its responsibilities properly.

ABTA says that consumers can only realistically expect an organiser to use his best endeavours and have third party liability, which would be limited. In other words, ABTA seeks to transfer liability to anyone other than itself —to the ground handler or to the consumer, perhaps, for having been unfortunate enough to book a package holiday in that particular place. ABTA is shirking its responsibility.

Let us consider the objections. The travel trade says that it is reluctant to offer compensation or take responsibility for the difference in price of the holiday if the price has increased by more than 2 per cent. Other industries quote forward, and stick to their quotes. Take the example of the motor car industry. One may book a new motor car three or four months in advance. The price

may change, but a contract has been entered into and the motor trade honourably allows the purchase to take place at the earlier price.

ABTA says that bland and unhelpful expressions would enter the brochures—for example,

"There are sporting facilities usually available."

But that is all that the consumer gets now. Virtually no operator and few agents reveal information about noise. One rarely knows, for example, whether a hotel is close to a busy road. Then there is proximity to the beach. I have yet to see a brochure that properly informs its readers whether it is a sand or a shingle beach. Few say whether there are lifts in the property or set out costs of using a swimming pool, towels or a sunbed. Anyone who has been to the Mediterranean will be aware that war almost breaks out on the beaches between the British and the Germans over the availability of sunbeds. One may discover unexpectedly that there are no shops at the airport. That is one problem that Intourist faces, as I discovered when I had the pleasure of visiting Moscow and Leningrad over Easter. For someone with a young family, it is vital to be able to find soft drinks at the airport, especially if one is to be held there for three or four hours or, as in my case, five hours. We went without refreshment.

What compensation do operators offer for such delays? I cannot find a brochure that offers a penny until 12 or more hours have elapsed. Imagine that. A holidaymaker may go to the airport an hour or two before the required time for the flight and may have to wait 11 of the 12 hours without compensation. The start or end of a holiday should not be ruined by excessive delays such as that, and we need compensation for shorter delays. In the case of someone who has gone on a weekend break, half a day —a large proportion of the time available—will already have been used, yet he will be offered little or no compensation.

In view of that catalogue of complaints, it is not surprising that Blackpool attracts more British visitors that Italy, Greece, Yugoslavia and Turkey put together, and long may that last. Operators offering the splendid United Kingdom destinations operate with one hand tied behind their backs. Holiday packages in Great Britain and Ulster are first class, and all concerned take their responsibilities seriously, but those selling primarily overseas lack consumer commitment.

We have waited too long for the overseas package holiday trade to put its house in order. Now is the time to act, and every traveller will journey with confidence this summer if he knows that the British Government have insisted on a fair deal.

Several Hon. Members *rose——*

Mr. Deputy Speaker (Mr. Harold Walker): Order. Unless speeches are shorter, some hon. Members will be disappointed at 7 o'clock.

5.34 pm

Mr. Tam Dalyell (Linlithgow): We are indebted to my hon. Friend the Member for Gateshead, East (Ms. Quin) for raising many important issues. I declare an interest, as the speech that I shall make had its genesis a fortnight ago when I looked at some of my flowers and vetegables and found that they were covered with greenfly when they ought not to have been covered with greenfly. I am indebted, too, to Nicholas Carter, a senior scientist at Rothamsted, who provided me with a great deal of information.

The subject of my speech is the future of the national insect survey at a time when aphids are filling fields and gardens throughout the summer. If this were a personal complaint, I should not raise it in the House, but as it is a widespread complaint, about which something could be done, and as the Government are taking unjustifiable action in cutting agricultural research, I feel fully entitled to do so.

We have had a mild dry May, and the biggest explosion in the aphid population for 15 years. Greenfly, blackfly and other pests are threatening crops but apparently it is intended that the Rothamsted insect survey should close many of its insect traps, provide less information about the spread of aphids and cut its forecasting activities, which are vital to farmers.

One consequence will be that more insecticide will be sprayed as an insurance, in the absence of information about pests. I am especially grateful to my hon. Friend the Member for Gateshead, East, therefore, for bringing me into order by making environmental consequences part of the subject of her motion.

The Rothamsted survey monitors insects using traps sucking insects out of the air and collecting them for future counting and analysis. The first British suction trap was set at Rothamsted experimental station in 1964. By 1970, 10 more traps had joined the survey. By last year, 23 traps, each 12·2 m tall, were in operation—including six in Scotland. As a Scottish Member, I emphasise that we are greatly concerned about the problem that is now upon us in Scotland.

Rothamsted has the most extensive network of suction traps in the world. During 446 site-years its researchers have counted almost 10 million aphids from 300 species. This invaluable database, which allows scientists to make accurate predictions about times of infestation by many aphids, is threatened by the Government's policy on agricultural research, which they regard as a commercial spin-off. An unpublished Government review of agriculture research and development, known as the Barnes report, has identified aspects of Rothamsted's work, such as its forecasting activities, as near market as it can save farmers money by pinpointing times at which they need to apply insecticides to their fields. The Government believe that that work should be paid for by the farmers.

Funds for the insect research survey which come through the Agriculture and Food Research Council's institute of arable crops research are being reduced. As a result, the survey will have to close some traps completely and monitor others for only part of the year. The IRS weekly publication *The Aphid Bulletin and Aphid Commentary,* distributed by post, free of charge, to more than 300 interested people will not appear this year.

The Government's shortsighted approach threatens an unrivalled database for entymological and ecological research, as well as for farmers. It is likely to lead to the more profligate spraying of chemicals by farmers, who will be unaware of the true extent of any likely aphid attack. The loss of data also threatens efforts to assess whether environmental changes, including climatic changes, are having long-term effects on the insect population.

Workers who empty suction traps look not only for aphids but for aphids' many predators such as ladybirds, hover flies, lacewings, spiders and beetles. All those captured are kept and catalogued. The damson hop aphid attacks hops. Insecticides can prevent it from causing larger reductions in the yields of hop gardens in Herefordshire and Kent every year. The spraying of insecticides has been so intensive that the damson hop aphid has developed a resistance to many of the chemicals used. The time to spray for maximum effect is when the aphid migrates from its winter hosts—damsons and sloes—to hops. Samples taken in Kent and Hereford over the past 15 years combine with weather details to provide a good database from which to project the start and finish of the migration. The samples revealed that it is possible to use data on temperatures in early spring, rainfall figures for winter and spring and the amount of sunshine in summer to predict the migrations.

All that work is threatened, yet with greenhouse effect conditions, it is even more important. For example, the black bean aphid spends the winter on spindle trees and migrates to crops such as spring beans in May or June. Suction traps provide more data, from an elaborate system of constantly updated forecasts, of the size and timing of the migrations. The system was developed by IRS together with the Government's agricultural development and advisory service and Imperial college, London. Forecasts are based on the size of the previous autumn's migration as measured in suction traps, egg sampling and sampling of aphids on spindle trees in the spring and, finally, the early stages of spring migration. In 1989 researchers expect damage to bean crops in much of eastern England and the west midlands. Crop infestation by aphids has already occurred some two weeks earlier than usual.

You asked us to be brief, Mr. Deputy Speaker. I think that I have made my point in general and, as the Minister is nodding, I assume that he believes it to be a serious point. Nicholas Carter and others—I consulted widely before the debate—have produced a great deal of information, of which much is available to gardeners. Long-term data such as those provided by the IRS will prove valuable in determining trends in aphid population biology, and such trends may be linked to changes in land use or climate. That role for the survey has not yet attracted a great deal of attention, but it may turn out to be its most important as concern about the changing climate gathers ground. Unfortunately, the long-term monitoring that is essential to such work is often the poor relation of science because it is non-experimental and needs no sophisticated equipment. Thus the Natural Environment Research Council gives a low priority to its biological records centre. The problem is that long-term monitoring is often incompatible with short-term decisions about funding. Once a continuous sequence of data is broken, it can never be recovered.

If such work is interrrupted, let alone brought to an end for some short-term financial gain—quite frankly, an accounting gain—to make the books of a Department look good, great damage will be done. There must be some sort of sequence in that work. There are several million gardeners in this country. Indeed, the Minister represents a Worcestershire constituency. Worcestershire is famous for its gardens and many of the Minister's constituents will think it a heck of a pity if any of the work relevant to the national insect survey is interrupted.

I note that the Under-Secretary of State for Scotland has done me the courtesy of coming into the Chamber. He represents a beautiful part of a beautiful city and I can assure him that his constituents are most concerned about

[*Mr. Tam Dalyell*]

the problems of aphids such as greenfly and blackfly. If the Under-Secretary does not believe that, he should ask his constituents in Davidson's Mains. I hope that the Scottish Office will take an interest in this matter. I shall tell him exactly what I have said and where I obtained my information when we are behind the Chair. I am hoping for two detailed answers—one from the consumer Minister, once he has contacted his MAFF colleagues, and the other from the Scottish Office.

5.44 pm

Mr. Robert G. Hughes (Harrow, West): I apologise to the hon. Member for Linlithgow (Mr. Dalyell) for not wishing to follow his speech because, quite frankly, I did not understand it—[*Interruption.*] Some of us admit that we do not understand matters, unlike certain Labour Members who interrupt from sedentary positions.

I congratulate the hon. Member for Gateshead, East (Ms. Quin) on raising this important subject for debate. I apologise for having missed the beginning of her speech, but I was doing some work on something to do with Europe that will occur later in the week, although what it is escapes me for the moment. I was disappointed with much of what she said. She gave a long shopping list of aspirations and ideas about what could be controlled and what sort of standards should be introduced, but I heard no strategy for how to do that. I assume that her remarks came from the same stable as those of the right hon. Member for Swansea, West (Mr. Williams), although he put forward a strategy largely based on his experiences as a Consumer Minister. I had a great deal of sympathy with what he said, although I did not necessarily agree with his strategy.

Two separate roads could be taken in approaching this problem. I am not entirely sure that the Labour party and I want to take the same road. It is right that people should be protected from buying dangerous goods or a service that does not live up to its description. A number of ideas have been put forward by hon. Members on both sides of the House suggesting changes in the law, new regulations and new codes of conduct.

I do not want to go down the road of seeking to tell people what are the best options in what is available, but from much of what the hon. Lady said I detected her wish to go down that road. She concentrated many of her remarks on information. My experience of some of the consumer information services provided by local authorities is that they tell people, "This is the range of goods available and this is what we think you should buy." Local authorities are not equipped to give such advice. It is certainly not the purpose of Government, whether central or local, to spoonfeed people as though they always know what is best, what consumers should be buying and how they should spend their money. Spoonfeeding is very much a Labour party approach—indeed, it is exactly the approach set out in its 1983 election manifesto. No doubt that is why it did so disastrously. The manifesto contained 100 pages telling people how the Labour party would run their lives for them. From the hon. Lady's remarks, that still appears to be very much the Labour party's approach.

Mr. Frank Cook: The hon. Gentleman would do well to concentrate on what my hon. Friend the Member for

Gateshead, East (Ms. Quin) said rather than on what he wishes she had said. I hope that he will now get on with the reality rather than the fantasy.

Mr. Hughes: The hon. Gentleman was rather peripatetic during the hon. Lady's speech. I thought that he entered the Chamber after me and so could not have heard all that she said. I can understand his wish that the Labour party's 1983 election manifesto did not exist. Perhaps he wishes that he had not stood on that manifesto.

Ms. Quin: At what point during my speech did the hon. Gentleman enter the Chamber? He complained about the absence of a strategy, yet I began my speech by saying that consumer interests needed to be taken into account across Government Departments. I referred to certain matters that were later taken up and enlarged upon by my right hon. Friend the Member for Swansea, West (Mr. Williams).

Mr. Hughes: I am grateful to the hon. Lady for clarifying that point and I shall certainly read the early part of her speech. I remember looking at the clock when I entered the Chamber at 3.42 pm. I am, of course, delighted to hear that the hon. Lady covered those points.

I wish to take a different approach from other hon. Members to the food issue, and pick up a phrase used by the right hon. Member for Swansea, West. He said, in many ways quite rightly, that gone are the days of the local buyer knowing the local producer. Of course those days have gone. We do not necessarily know who produces the goods. It is important that people should have trust in stores such as Marks and Spencer and Sainsburys and the manufacturers.

That point has been brought home to parents who are concerned about the problems that have been faced by some baby food manufacturers. It is interesting to look at the manufacturers' different responses. Farleys had a milk problem. It is instructive for all food manufacturers to think carefully about what caused the problem in the Farleys factory. In the end, the company went out of business or had to be bought out by, I think, Boots. The company went out of business because people lost trust in it. Did they lose trust in that company because of the problem in the factory? They did not. They lost trust in the company because of the way in which it reacted to the problem in its factory.

The managing director of the company appeared on BBC television and said that there was a problem. That was several days after the problem appeared in the factory, and, until then, the company had failed to tell the public about it. When he finally admitted that there was a problem, in that live BBC interview, the managing director advised people not to buy that company's products any more and to throw away the products that they had at home. The advice to throw those products away was rather ungenerous. As subsequent manufacturers who have had similar problems have said, the managing director should have said, "Return the products to us and we will refund your money." That would demonstrate a more generous attitude.

What finally killed the Farleys company was reluctance on the part of the senior executive to admit that there was a problem in the factory and the company's failure to close the production line when the problem was discovered. As a parent, when I heard that the company had not closed its production line, I lost confidence in the company. I was clearly not alone, as the company went bankrupt.

Mr. Frank Cook: Quite right, too.

Mr. Hughes: I hope that I heard the hon. Gentleman say from a sedentary postion, "Quite right, too." I agree. *[Interruption.]* One day the hon. Gentleman will treat hon. Members to a speech. It will be a rare thing. He makes only sedentary contributions when I am in the Chamber.

There has been a marked difference in the problems that are faced by other baby food manufacturers such as Cow and Gate. As the parent of two small boys, I still have every confidence in Cow and Gate and other companies.

Mr. McCartney: And Heinz.

Mr. Hughes: I am grateful to the hon. Member for Makerfield (Mr. McCartney) for mentioning Heinz. I am sure that he will agree that those companies were totally honest and, therefore, deserve the support and trust of all parents. From what they say about their sales figures, it is obvious that they are getting that trust. We place enormous trust in the retailer and the producer. Whatever the Government might do and whatever regulations might be in force, that trust is foremost in buyers' minds.

I may have missed what the hon. Member for Gateshead, East said, but I was surprised that she did not pay tribute to the consumer safety statistics that have been collected by the DTI. Important changes have been made in the updating of consumer safety statistics and the basis on which they have been collected, including the extension of the system to cover leisure accidents. I am the sponsor of the Safety in Children's Playgrounds Bill. Many groups are seeking to improve safety standards in children's playgrounds. It is important for them to get from the DTI relevant statistics about the number of children who need to be hospitalised, and why. It is easy to have a preconceived idea of why accidents happen in play-grounds. For instance, most people believe that the hard surfaces in two thirds of our playgrounds cause most accidents in playgrounds. However, the DTI has revealed that most accidents happen because children collide while running from one piece of play equipment to another. Without further statistics, how can we introduce further legislation, standards or codes of practice, as I hope that the Department of the Environment will do?

It is important to pay tribute to the work of the DTI——

Mr. Harry Barnes (Derbyshire, North-East): On a point of order, Mr. Deputy Speaker. What is the relevance of the contribution by the hon. Member for Harrow, West (Mr. Hughes)? His remarks about play schools and playgrounds are interesting, but how are they related to the EEC? He is talking about the presentation of British standards rather than EEC standards. Some hon. Members have been waiting a considerable time to debate the poll tax.

Mr. Hughes: People will read that intervention with great interest and note that the hon. Member for Derbyshire, North-East (Mr. Barnes) is clearly not interested in safety in children's playgrounds, and the parents in his constituency——

Mr. Barnes *rose——*

Mr. Deputy Speaker: Order. I draw the attention of the hon. Member for Harrow, West (Mr. Hughes) to the terms of the motion. I am bound to say that he seems to be ignoring the motion, whatever the merits or demerits of any later debate may be. I ask him to have regard to the number of hon. Members who are waiting to speak in a short debate.

Mr. Hughes: I acknowledge that point, Mr. Deputy Speaker, but the hon. Gentleman's point of order is rather amiss. As you will have read, Mr. Deputy Speaker, the first line of the motion states

"To call attention to the failure of the Government to protect the consumer".

It goes on:

"that government policies have failed to benefit the consumer".

I was making consumer points. They belie the motion. I should have thought that it was not only reasonable but important for those points to be made.

It is essential to have not only consumer safety statistics but consumer safety campaigns. I congratulate my hon. Friend the Minister on conducting the campaigns. The first was on toy safety. Most of us in the peak shopping time before Christmas saw giant teddy bears in the shops, with retailers helping to promote the safety message. There has been an improvement in consumer awareness of fireworks safety. Fireworks are dangerous things. Anything that can be done to limit their use or to persuade people not to use them is good.

There have been electric blanket campaigns designed to encourage the elderly in particular to get their old electric blankets serviced. There is nothing that the Government can do to make that happen. How can we get someone to take an old electric blanket to be serviced merely because the Government say so? However, people can be persuaded, and persuasion is important. In conjunction with the Child Accident Prevention Trust, two booklets on child safety equipment and on the safety of nursery equipment have been made available through the clinics to all new parents. I was impressed, when our last baby was born five months ago, when I received copies of those booklets. I pay tribute to the Minister for making those booklets available.

The hon. Member for Gateshead, East said that part of the Government's response to the issue—as she put it, the Government's inadequate response—was privatisation. I do not understand how she can make that point. She said that privatisation had failed to protect the consumer, especially in terms of price. If one considers the prices charged for electricity and gas, they are lower in real terms than those charged previously—certainly those charged under the Labour Government. Those who pay electricity and gas bills know that prices are lower than they were, and that they have not gone up in line with inflation. *[Interruption.]* It is interesting that Opposition Members either laugh or shout ridiculous comments from a sedentary position, when both the Labour party and its friends in office, the Liberals, did so much to hike up the prices of those two basic commodities. They know that they are responsible for the twin evils of high prices and under-investment in those two industries.

Privatisation of those industries has, first, protected the consumer by keeping the prices down, and, secondly, has caused a substantial rise in investment in those industries, which is another important protection for the consumer.

Mr. McCartney: What about water charges?

Mr. Hughes: I shall be coming to those.

Ms. Quin: Will the hon. Gentleman tell us which would be his priority—privatisation of the water industry or bringing our water quality up to EC standards?

Mr. Hughes: As the hon. Lady has mentioned the water industry, I will comment on it now. We must compare the record of this Government with that of the Labour Government. As we know—after all, the chairman of the Water Authorities Association has told us this—we are still suffering from the massive under-investment of the Labour Government, which is causing problems on our beaches and with our water supply.

Mr. Frank Cook: Will the hon. Gentleman give way?

Mr. Hughes: I shall give way when I have answered this point.

That under-investment is still causing problems. *[Interruption.]* It is all very well saying that was 10 years ago, but it is the experts who are trying to run those businesses who tell us the answers, not hon. Members speaking from a sedentary position.

Water privatisation will give us a guarantee that we can have decent standards for our water supply, because the supply will have to be to the standards laid down by the National Rivers Authority. The Labour party, having voted against all those provisions in the Water Bill, has put itself on to the side of those people who are the polluters of the water supply and who do not care about higher standards for water. Of course, we shall have higher water standards. We do not need the Labour party, with its dreadful record in government, to give us any lectures on that point.

Those are important areas for consumer protection. I believe that the Government have a good record on consumer protection, and that they have given it a higher priority by ensuring that there is real work carried out, rather than the pretence of a Ministry. We have heard from the Labour party today that it wants to return to the pretence of wrapping these things up in words. It wants to over-regulate and to tell people that politicians can make decisions better than ordinary people making their purchases. I do not believe that that policy will wash with the public. They want the freedom to make their own decisions, providing that they know that they can have protection from shoddy goods and from false promises. Once we have made more strides in that direction, as we shall in the next few years, people will understand, as in so many other areas, that the Labour party's approach to this matter is entirely fraudulent.

6.4 pm

Mr. Malcolm Bruce (Gordon): I fear that the hon. Member for Harrow, West (Mr. Hughes) missed almost every relevant point at the core of the debate. If one wants to take the two extremes of the argument, there is the extreme view that says that the free market will solve all our problems and the one that says everything will have to be regulated down to the last detail. Having said that, the main contributors to the debate are saying neither of those things. I believe that the constructive debate is to recognise the limitations of the market place and those of the regulatory authority, and determine how one can secure a sensible balance. That is how we might achieve a constructive debate.

Given that the context in which the motion is set is the move towards the single market in 1992, the point to stress at the outset is that there is obviously an argument as to what the single market will mean for the consumer. I want to make it clear that I believe that the single market offers great opportunities for the consumer. The creation of a unified economy of more than 320 million people offers a very wide range of choice and opportunity for the consumer, economies of scale for the producer, which will help to bring down costs by securing access to a bigger market, and a higher rate of innovation, both of the product and of technology. Those are the kind of benefits that I believe can and should accrue. Indeed, I am advised that a report by Alber and Ball to the European Parliament in 1983 estimated that the existing regulations across the Common Market amounted to the loss of a week's wages for every worker within the Community. One must assume, therefore, that removing many of those restrictions will be of positive benefit.

I want to make it clear that I believe that the single market is something to be welcomed and to be encouraged. I understand the arguments from Conservative Members that we do not want to go into that situation only to impose a whole range of alternative regulations. I believe, however, that we need to approach the matter in an objective and sensible manner. One argument is to say that a free market is the best possible protection for the consumer. My comment on that is, perhaps, but "it ain't necessarily so," and that there are tendencies within a free market to create monopolies and a situation where consumers are disadvantaged and where they need active intervention to secure redress.

The hon. Member for Gateshead, East (Ms. Quin) and other hon. Members have mentioned the Government's programme of privatisation. I do not want to dwell on that matter for very long, but it is worth saying that in the run-up to the privatisation of British Gas and to the current privatisation of electricity, the Government have pursued a policy of deliberately raising the prices of those commodities to the consumer by a rate far higher than the rate of inflation. I do not have to defend the last Labour Government—indeed it is not my intention to do so—but to refer to something that happened 10 years ago and to ignore the fact that the price of oil went over $40 at that time——

Mr. Robert G. Hughes: Here are the excuses.

Mr. Bruce: The hon. Gentleman says than any excuse will do, but $40 of 10 years ago has to be compared with a price that actually dipped two years ago to $9 and is now under $20. That is a substantial difference. That rather goes with the Government's claim that they have presided over record investment and earnings. Almost every year of this century, barring wartime and the first two years of the present Government, Governments have been able to say that. If they were not able to say that, they would not have been re-elected, so it does not amount to a very substantial or radical claim.

One takeover that I feel has not necessarily added to the benefit of the consumer has been the takeover of British Caledonian Airways by British Airways, which I believe should not have happened. It was brought about as a direct consequence of the Government's refusal to recognise, when British Airways was privatised as a monopoly, that it was such a dominant player in the domestic scene that it effectively destroyed the possibility of British Caledonian Airways remaining as an independent airline. As somebody who has to make frequent use of British Airways, I do not believe that, as a consumer, I receive adequate treatment in choice or service. Too often British Airways cancels planes at short notice—it is very often the last plane of the day—very often because it has to divert that aircraft to a route on which it faces competition. Therefore, the exact opposite to what is intended follows. Because it has a monopoly on certain routes, the consumer who is completely dependent on British Airways suffers the greatest. Those who would have the opportunity to divert to another airline find that they have a choice, because British Airways cannot afford to leave them without the choice and lose the business to its competitor. The Government should address such problems and should ensure that British Airways operates as a competitor on routes, but, if it is accepted that a certain route cannot sustain two operators, the Government should ensure that the consumer is given the same treatment as would be given on a route where competition exists.

When companies have been privatised as monopolies it has been argued that regulation is necessary. That argument does not divide the House—why else did the Government introduce Ofgas and Oftel if they did not recognise that such regulations was necessary? The argument that divides the House is the extent to which that regulation should be effective. I have no doubt that when the Electricity Bill comes back to the House two important amendments accepted in the other place will be reversed. That is regrettable because those amendments were in the interests of the consumer. When the Gas Bill went through the House, I and other hon. Members pointed out that the provision of choice in the industrial sector was totally inadequate and that British Gas would be taken to the Monopolies and Mergers Commission. That proved to be correct.

One of the concerns about the single market and its implications for consumers is its effect on and drive towards mergers and takeovers. In recent years we have seen evidence of that. The takeover philosophy is different in different member states. My party believes that the obligation to prove that a takeover is in the consumer's interest should be put on the hostile predator and not on the recipient of the bid. Evidence collected by the Minister's Department suggests that the vast majority of takeovers are, almost by definition, designed not to increase competition or consumer choice, but to consolidate the larger, hostile bidder's position within the market. By definition, that is contrary to consumer interest. General statements of good will are made and we are told that economies of scale will be made and rationalisation procedures will be followed that will benefit the consumer. Analysis, however, suggests that once the bid has been accepted the consumer is worse off. Our proposals would lead to a dramatic improvement in the protection of consumer interests. It is to my continual regret that the Government have said that such takeovers are a matter for the shareholders and that consumer interests do not count. They believe that if the shareholders are willing to sell, that is the only basis on which most takeovers should be decided.

Shareholders are always delighted to sell because increasing their standing in the market place enables them to exploit the consumer for an even greater profit. Why on earth should shareholders resist such an obvious temptation? The Government and the wider community have an obligation to ensure that takeovers are examined for their possible benefit to the consumer.

It is worth making a comparison between the United Kingdom and the Federal Republic of Germany. In that country hostile takeovers are almost unknown, essentially because the structure of ownership within German industry means that it is almost impossible to secure such a takeover without the consent of the main banker of any corporation, who also tends to be the major shareholder.

As 1992 approaches Britain is increasingly vulnerable to takeovers from countries inside and outside the Community and, at the same time, we are unable to secure similar access to the ownership of those countries' markets.

It is interesting to consider the financial characteristics of the European markets in comparison to our own. Mention has already been made of consumer credit. I shall not be mealy-mouthed about it. I believe that the ethic the Government have advanced has fuelled a consumer credit boom that has fundamentally weakened our economy and has meant that many people face genuine financial hardship. I do not believe it is just a case of loan sharks, but the way in which our retailing operators conduct their business. When people go to a shopping centre they are actively encouraged to take out lines of credit for goods and services which they do not actually need, but which they are tempted to buy. They are not aware of how they will pay for such goods and services. I do not believe that consumers are adequately protected against being tempted to take on levels of credit that they cannot afford to sustain. Such credit is even more damaging since the Government have lost control of the economy and have been forced to jack up rates of interest dramatically over a short time. People now find that their level of repayments is far greater than they had anticipated or budgeted for. The code of practice that has operated in some of our retail stores must be altered radically.

It is interesting to consider the two most successful economies of the developed world—Japan and West Germany. They operate on highly conservative financial principles and the level of savings is far, far higher than our own. It is between 15 and 20 per cent. Long-term strategies are carefully considered by those countries. We operate on a short-term basis and our propensity to save could well move into a negative index soon as a direct result of the climate created by the Government.

The Government's policy is extraordinary, as they seem to encourage people to buy goods and services that are not produced in this country with money that most people do not have. On that basis it is not surprising that our economy is getting into trouble. The Government continue to claim that the thrust of their policy is the need to keep inflation under control and yet they refuse to join the exchange rate mechanism of the European monetary system. All the evidence suggests, however, that our membership of that mechanism would not only help to bring inflation under control, particularly in the long term, but that such inflationary control could be achieved with lower rates of interest. It is interesting to note that the French found a direct correlation between that and——

Mr. Favell: On a point of order, Madam Deputy Speaker. The European monetary system has nothing to do with the motion on the Order Paper and you should bear in mind that a number of hon. Members still want to speak.

Madam Deputy Speaker (Miss Betty Boothroyd): The hon. Member for Gordon (Mr. Bruce) is straying considerably from the motion on the Order Paper, but I am sure that he will bring his remarks back to the motion.

Mr. Bruce: Yes. My simple point is that every consumer I meet would like us to have a level of inflation comparable to that in France and interest rate levels comparable to those of other countries. Consumers would benefit from our membership of the European monetary system. It appears that the Prime Minister and her adviser, Professor Alan Walters, are alone in the conviction that their argument is right.

It has been argued that consumers, in order to make a rational choice in the market place, must have access to information, particularly in the case of environmental protection. Earlier it was suggested that the market was already responding to consumer concern and that retailers had managed to give people information by better labelling and that that had meant that, at no cost and without Government action, environmentally offensive products had been and were being phased out. That argument has been advanced in relation to aerosol cans and CFCs, but they represent a relatively small part of the problem in comparison to the range of environmental concerns. Many of the companies that had introduced ozone-friendly aerosols still operate large amounts of refrigeration and air-conditioning machinery and they do not make adequate provision for that machinery's disposal through recycling. Therefore, they are in danger of destroying all the marketing benefits which they have given to the consumer, because of their own industrial effluent. The consumer should know about that.

The importance of information has recently been highlighted by a couple of specific issues. In an intervention during the speech of the hon. Member for Gateshead, East I drew attention to the issue of dioxins, which she had mentioned. I represent paper manufacturers and fully understand the balance of the arguments. The American markets have proved that consumers demand information and a right to choose. They want to know whether the products that can produce dioxins are being used in the bleaching of particular paper products. They also want the right to buy dioxin-free products.

At the moment, the Government's reaction, which I have raised with Ministers, is that that is entirely a matter to which the markets should respond. That is not good enough. First, there should be regulations to ensure that the information is provided and, secondly, there should be, at the very least, a Government push to ensure that choice is provided. That has happened in the United States. One benefit of the larger single market may be that it will make that easier to happen within the European Community: I hope so.

Last week, I also raised the issue of Alar, which has been banned in the United States, but which is still used in the United Kingdom. Consumers need to know whether an apple product has been treated with Alar. If they have that information, they may well ensure that the market determines that Alar is phased out, but without it they are unable to do anything other than refuse to have anything to do with apples, which seems to be a draconian response to force on consumers.

I appreciate that other hon. Members wish to speak so I shall draw my remarks to a close. The Government should acknowledge that there is a role for them, as for local authorities, in the process of securing information, alerting the public and providing the necessary facilities. In a number of ways, the Government are being asked to promote good environmental practices and, so far, they are not providing the support needed. I commend local authorities which, for example, have established a code of practice in their contracts on the protection of tropical hardwoods and the recycling and use of CFCs. It is regrettable that, so far, the Government have not been prepared to promote an initiative to enable the recycling of CFCs or labelling—never mind a code of practice—for tropical hardwoods, ensuring that they come only from sustainable sources. If they do not come from sustainable sources, the community should be entitled to set up a collective ban against them. That is the one way in which the promotion of sustainable tropical hardwoods could be ensured. On both these issues, local authorities such as Sutton and my own council of Gordon have taken initiatives and asked the Government to support them to enable them to increase their services to the consumer. However, so far, their requests have fallen on deaf ears.

When fully developed, the single market offers a wide variety of opportunities for consumers. However, because of the wide differences within the Community, there must be a recognition of common consumer standards and the Government must recognise their responsibility to set that balance. I fear that, to date, they have not done so. I have received all sorts of concerned representations on many matters of developments in a rapidly changing market.

Those people feel that, at the very least, more information should be made available and that, if the Government are not prepared to be the agents to secure the information, the market response is often too slow.

Sheltered housing and the voluntary code of practice have been mentioned in the debate. Only last week, I was approached by a councillor, who was of a more Conservative than SLD persuasion and was concerned at the way in which nursing homes and sheltered housing operations for the elderly in the private sector seemed to be able to pitch their price according to a person's ability to pay. The industry effectively built its profit on running down people's money and was happy to allow them to continue on social security when their money had run out. That suggests simple profiteering: if it is not, I assure the Minister that there is great worry among Conservatives who feel that it looks awfully like it. Those are the sort of matters for which the Government have responsibility.

I hope that the Minister will accept that this debate is about securing a sensible balance between a totally unbridled free market and excessive regulation. The Government are in danger of leaving the balance too much on the side of the free market, which does not work exclusively in consumers' interests.

6.26 pm

Mr. Tony Favell (Stockport): This has been an interesting debate for me, and I think that I speak for other hon. Members. I am grateful to the hon. Member for Gateshead, East (Ms. Quin) for introducing this interesting subject, which has exercised the minds of the Government throughout the 10 years in which they have been in power.

The hon. Member for Gateshead, East, is wrong to suggest that the Government are not interested in consumers' interests. The Consumer Protection Act 1987 was wide reaching, far ranging and far from popular with many of the organisations and concerns which the hon. Lady would consider to be natural supporters of the Government. There was much opposition from manufacturers to the first part of the Act which, for the first time, gave the man in the street the opportunity to sue manufacturers for damage without having to prove negligence. That was completely new to British law and has been, and will be, vastly popular with the consumer. It was, of course, unpopular with the manufacturers.

Under the Act it became an offence, with certain exceptions, to provide unsafe consumer goods. For the first time, it imposed a general duty on suppliers to ensure, with some exceptions—one or two of which, particularly food, I agree with the hon. Lady ought to be reconsidered —that goods supplied were safe.

The Act also made the provision of misleading price indications an offence.

The Act said what suppliers of goods and services should not do. It is far easier for the Executive and those who have to enforce the Act to do that. It is far more difficult to do what the hon. Lady suggests: to say what the suppliers of goods should do. She suggested, and I intervened at the time, that there should be far greater regulation on the make-up of manufactured goods. In a changing world it is impossible to lay down standards for goods that people do not even think will emerge on to the market, to say what they should and should not contain.

The hon. Lady also suggested that there should be far greater labelling. Before I entered the Chamber, I bought a Marathon bar from the Tea Room.

Mr. Frank Cook: This is the first commercial.

Mr. Favell: I am not going to admit to my wife that I bought it or, at least, that I am going to consume it. It is absolutely smothered in information, most of which I do not understand. I understand that it contains fresh milk chocolate with fresh roasted peanuts and a peanut butter nougat and caramel centre. However, I do not understand 62 g E. It gives me the following nutritional information:

"Energy 1248 kJ/298 kcal
Carborhydrate 33·5 g
Protein 6·3 g
Fat 16·4 g
(of which saturates 7·4 g)"

It goes on to tell me how I can win a trip to the Super Bowl, and gives me various other guarantees, which I cannot read because the print is far too small. There are various competition rules for yet another competition. Finally, it says that it is best before 2 September 1989, which I understand, with another hieroglyphic on the side. It is the first time that I have read the cover on this product and it will be the last. I do not think that any other hon. Member has ever read one of these before.

I suggest that we keep these messages simple. Already, my hon. Friend the Minister will tell us, products' labels must show safety warnings and, on food, they must tell us the "best before" date and give details of the product. That

is fair enough, and it is quite enough to go on any label. It is simple and intelligible to someone like me and to 99 per cent. of the population.

It is unreasonable to attack the Government for failing to protect the consumer; we have a long record of protecting him or her. The first great act—some might say it was also the last—of my right hon. Friend the Member for Old Bexley and Sidcup (Mr. Heath) was to introduce his retail price maintenance legislation. That was a great act on behalf of the consumer and it was certainly not popular with those who would be regarded as the Government's natural supporters. We have not stopped there. I have no doubt that my hon. Friend the Under-Secretary will remind us of the Financial Services Act 1986, which was highly unpopular with many of the Government's natural supporters.

We are now introducing legislation to protect the consumer against the lawyers, of whom, alas, I am one. With my lawyer's hat on, I must say that that legislation is not popular with me, but I can understand it from the consumer's point of view. We are also questioning the activities of the brewers—organisations regarded by the Opposition parties as natural supporters of the Conservative party. We fear no man, however, and we are seriously looking into what we regard as the brewers' abuses of their monopoly power.

Finally, we are tackling the doctors. The doctors themselves tell us that, almost to a man, they voted for us in the last general election, but we are not in the business for votes: we are in business for the consumer. We genuinely believe that our reforms are for the benefit of the patients. They are certainly not intended merely to garner votes.

Madam Deputy Speaker: Mr. Eric Forth.

Mr. McCartney: On a point of order, Madam Deputy Speaker. I have been here since the beginning of the debate, during which hon. Members who have gone in and out have spoken for considerable lengths of time and were called out of order on numerous occasions by another Deputy Speaker. It is unfair that I should not be allowed at least two minutes in which to place on record a point to which the Minister may want to respond in writing——

Madam Deputy Speaker: Order. The Minister has said that he now wishes to respond to the debate.

6.33 pm

The Parliamentary Under-Secretary of State for Industry and Consumer Affairs (Mr. Eric Forth): I regret the position in which the hon. Gentleman finds himself, but it is not for me to get involved in the way in which the debate has proceeded—until now, it has been most orderly——

Mr. McCartney: I want to raise the issue of hazardous chemicals and of possible changes in EEC legislation which will undermine the position in Britain. If I am prepared to write to the Minister, will he make arrangements for him or a colleague in the Department of Transport to meet me to discuss this matter?

Mr. Forth: I hope that the hon. Gentleman will find that whenever he contacts Ministers of any Department he will receive a courteous, full and—I hope—speedy reply. I hope that he will in this case. I certainly undertake to reply to him if he writes to me.

[*Mr. Forth*]

I am grateful to the hon. Member for Gateshead, East (Ms. Quin) for raising this matter in the way in which she has and for using what is always a precious occasion—coming high in the ballot for motions—to do so. That has enabled her and other hon. Members to set out their anxieties and some important points about the vital matter of consumer protection. It also gives me the opportunity, for which I am grateful, to set out some of my and the Government's thoughts on the subject.

I start, unashamedly and with some pride, by quoting from the White Paper put out by the Department of Trade and Industry in January 1989:

"In consumer protection, the policy emphasis will reflect the Government's belief that the best form of protection comes from consumers making well-informed choices and acting in their own interests. To achieve this, information can be more effective than regulation. However, where the case is made out for regulation on safety or other grounds, the Government will not hesitate to act."

That not only encapsulates the Government's view but it reflects the tone of many of today's contributions—and not only from the Conservative side. The hon. Member for Gordon (Mr. Bruce) made remarks along these lines. We are not necessarily separated by much on this matter. I want to deal with as many of the detailed points that have been made as possible.

To illustrate the Government's attitude, I want to give an example of the sort of approach that we tend to adopt, based on a combination of information when appropriate, and regulation when appropriate. In this context, I want to mention the promotion of timeshare developments, which has worried many hon. Members and their constituents. I have received a number of complaints about timeshare, most relating to the award schemes used to entice people to presentations at which they are often subjected to high-pressure sales techniques. Some end up signing contracts which they subsequently regret. I hasten to add that these practices are by no means universal and I have publicly acknowledged before, and do so again, the efforts of the industry, through the Timeshare Developers Association, working through its code of practice, to improve and maintain standards in the industry. The association's membership now represents about 60 per cent. of timeshares sold to United Kingdom consumers.

The Department of Trade and Industry has actively tried to promote the development of these standards. For example, in 1987, we produced a leaflet for consumers entitled, "Your place in the sun—or is it?" It warned people interested in timeshare developments to be wary of prizes, discounts and half-price offers——

Mr. Frank Cook: On a point of order, Madam Deputy Speaker. I understood that the Minister, quite properly, wanted time in the debate to reply to it. I have sat here for the best part of the debate and can remember no hon. Member mentioning timeshare. If the Minister wants to make a statement on that subject, he should take time out of the proper schedule of the House, not out of a private Member's debate.

Mr. Forth: I am trying to develop an argument that combines the provision of information, on which I have just touched, with a reference I am about to make to the role of the Office of Fair Trading, which is directly relevant to consumer protection. If the hon. Gentleman will contain himself, we shall get there fairly quickly.

I was talking about the information provided by my Department's leaflet, of which we have now distributed about 650,000 copies. Thus far have we gone with information, but from time to time that can be deemed not enough, and this is a case to which that applies.

I have therefore asked the Director General of Fair Trading to conduct a review of the whole range of timeshare problems which will cover marketing and other issues to do with United Kingdom properties advertised here, and overseas properties wherever they are promoted, and which may involve a review of legislative and self-regulatory controls. The Office of Fair Trading would then come up with such recommendations as it saw fit. The director general agrees that this is an appropriate time to examine this problem, which has recently caused some anxiety to consumers.

This is a good example of the recognition of a need for such action, and I am delighted to say that the director general has agreed to involve his staff and expertise in it. I look forward to receiving his conclusions early in the new year.

Another matter that is repeatedly mentioned is safety. I think my hon. Friend the Member for Harrow, West (Mr. Hughes) mentioned the home accident surveillance system, the provision of statistics by our hospitals which give a firm, factual basis from which to launch policy developments. It is not often appreciated that accidents in and around the home result in about 5,000 deaths a year —as many as, or more than, occur on the roads. About 3 million people receive injuries serious enough to receive medical treatment.

We must not only recognise the problem but develop policies and approaches to deal with it. This is being done. The United Kingdom legal system governing consumer safety provides a level of protection equal to, and probably better than, that in most other countries. Many speakers today have referred to the Consumer Protection Act 1987 which introduced significant changes in the law and resulted in major improvements for the consumer. The introduction of the general safety requirement in that law means that it is now a criminal offence to supply a consumer product that is not reasonably safe. This general duty has many advantages over an approach that relies on detailed and restrictive regulations covering individual products. For example, it means that the enforcement officers can take action when a dangerous consumer product appears on the market.

Mr. Michael Brown (Brigg and Cleethorpes): There is a problem with that legislation because it is not always applied in a logical fashion. My hon. Friend will be aware that the Minister of Health is considering using the powers in that Act to ban a certain brand of smokeless tobacco. When my hon. Friend the Member for Derbyshire, South (Mrs. Currie) was Under-Secretary of State, she acknowledged that cigarettes were more dangerous than the product that my hon. Friend the Minister proposes to ban under the legislation. Will my hon. Friend urge some caution about the way in which that legislation is sometimes used, because there is not always logic about the way in which it is employed?

Mr. Forth: If I did not know my hon. Friend the Member for Brigg and Cleethorpes (Mr. Brown) a bit better, I would suspect that he was being mischievous because he is trying to draw me into commenting on something that another Department may be doing. If it is using the excellent legislation that I am describing to the House, so much the better, but my hon. Friend must not try to draw me into the substance of a decision that may well be made by another Department. That Department is quite capable of coming to the right conclusion on the matter and I am sure that my hon. Friend is giving it as much advice as he can.

Several hon. Members have mentioned labelling. The Consumer Protection Act 1987 fully recognises the importance of adequate warnings and instructions in relation to the safety of products. The guidance given to the courts on the factors that they should take into account in deciding whether a product is unsafe specifically includes both the manner in which goods are marketed and the instructions or warnings that are given with the products. To support this feature of the law, my Department published an authoritative guide to producing better instructions and warnings for consumer products. That is an important area but it is not often highlighted and has not been referred to during the debate.

Giving people adequate and workable instructions on the use of products can make a considerable contribution to their safe use. We continue widely to promote that practice among manufacturers and designers, and I hope that even in the courts we will see the kind of best practice set out in the guide regarded as a benchmark for considering cases.

The Consumer Protection Act also introduced changes to the law on product liability. The system of strict liability means that it will be much easier for people injured by defective products to obtain redress through the courts. As my hon. Friend the Member for Fylde (Mr. Jack) rightly said, there is now increasing redress available other than through the full court procedure. For example, there is arbitration and the small claims procedures, and in many ways we are rapidly improving the way in which consumers, as individuals or through the many consumer organisations, can seek and obtain redress. Experience of these features of United Kingdom criminal and civil law will do much to deter those who may be tempted to supply goods that do not come up to adequate safety levels.

The motion calls on the Government fully to implement the EC product liability directive. Hon. Members may have seen reports that the EC Commission had expressed some dissatisfaction with the way in which our Consumer Protection Act implements the directive, particularly over the so-called "Development risks defence." The Government have made it clear that the Commission's objections will be considered carefully but that we believe that the Act properly implements the directive. I can confirm that the Commission has now written formally to the United Kingdon setting out its concerns, but it is usual practice, and I propose to stick to it, to preserve the confidentiality of these exchanges. However, it will be obvious from what I have said that dialogue is continuing.

Mr. Favell: Is it not true to say that we are one of only three of the 12 EC countries that have implemented the directive?

Mr. Forth: I am glad that my hon. Friend has made that point because it gives me the chance to say that we are way ahead of most of the other member states on most of the directives, not just in that regard but also in effective implementation. We tend to differ greatly from most of the other member states in the extent to which we comply with and implement directives effectively and in detail. We do that through our excellent system of trading standard officers who are independent of Government and report to local government. It is not always easy for central Government to deal with that system. Given his background, my hon. Friend well understands that our compliance with EC directives is certainly as good as that of any member state and better than that of most member states. In that respect, we are among the best Europeans, and we can be proud and happy about that.

The hon. Lady asked for the speedy implementation of the product safety directive. She knows that a proposal for an EC general product safety directive was tabled by the Commission at the recent consumer council meeting in Luxembourg. The hon. Lady spoke about that. That was the first time that Ministers had been given an opportunity to discuss this very wide-ranging proposal, and it was clear at the meeting that much more work will need to be done before the draft is anywhere near ready for detailed consideration, never mind implementation. We and other member states expressed varying degrees of reservation about the scope of that draft and about the powers proposed in it. It is in the very early stages and it would be quite unreasonable at this time to expect us to approve it or seek to amend it in any detail. It has started its procedure, and we shall work with other member states to see that it develops in a workable and effective way.

I should like to make another point about general safety matters and about the sort of action that we can take when we think that it is necessary. I have mentioned the provision of information and the general legal framework. We take action against individual products or producers when a serious safety hazard comes to our attention and we are persuaded about the nature of the hazard. I shall give two examples. In recent months, we have banned, as we are able to do under the legislation, two products. One was called "Crazy Hands", a novelty toy. We thought that there was a danger that young children might swallow it and choke. We also banned three-wheel all-terrain vehicles which were imported from the United States where they had a track record of being extremely dangerous. We thought that we were justified in banning them, and we did.

Evidence shows that most accidents are caused not necessarily by faulty products but by people's behaviour. They sometimes use them in a wrong, ill-informed or occasionally irresponsible way. Therefore, we are keen to inform people of the hazards that they may face. As one of my hon. Friends has said, we have conducted and will continue to conduct campaigns covering toy safety, the safety of electric blankets and child safety. We also run an annual fireworks campaign and a Christmas campaign.

I was recently involved in launching a campaign housed in a hazard dome. It is an imaginative and sophisticated exhibition and it will tour the United Kingdom. We hope that eventually it will be brought to millions of people. The exhibition clearly illustrates in an imaginative and exciting way the sort of hazards that can exist even in the home and the measures that people can take to avoid them. That is the sort of positive and helpful contribution that we can make to provide information about hazards and the way in which we want to tackle them.

Mr. Michael Brown: I presume that the hazards to which my hon. Friend refers are health hazards. Why is his

[*Mr. Michael Brown*]

Department responsible for those while the Minister of Health is responsible for the hazard that I mentioned earlier?

Mr. Forth: I see that I have not deterred my hon. Friend. He well knows that the hazards I am describing can result in accidents in and around the home. Details of those accidents are provided by our excellent information system which is based on hospital figures. We take steps to inform people about them so that they may be able to avoid accidents.

Many hon. Members, including the hon. Members for Gateshead, East and for Gordon (Mr. Bruce) and some of my hon. Friends, spoke about environmental implications. Of course we recognise the importance of consumers being fully informed about the environmental effects of products and services in order, if nothing else, for the market to operate effectively. We are aware of the growing interest in labelling as a constructive way in which one can tackle the problem. We welcome the moves that industry is already making to provide and improve information about the environmental impact of its products. In the Government's view, the voluntary approach is the right one, but we are keeping the situation closely under review and looking carefully at the problems that labelling poses and at the experience of other countries which have set up national schemes.

We are discussing the level of interest in such schemes with representatives of consumers, producers and retailers, not least because of the need to respond to likely moves within the European Community. However, I stress that the issues involved are not simple. It is not easy to identify what is or what is not environmentally beneficial, not to identify straightforward ways to describe these problems to the user. It is not always clear how best to illustrate or describe these factors on packaging, sometimes of small articles. We are still at the early stages, and there are many ways to identify the best ways of communicating to the consumer the environmental impact or implication of the products that the consumer is being offered in the market place.

Reference has been made to the importance of informative food labelling to help consumers to choose a healthy diet. Food labels are already required to show the name or description of the food, an ingredients list, the date of minimum durability and the name and address of the responsible packer or seller. In addition, where appropriate, details of storage instructions for use and place of origin must be given.

Food labelling is kept under regular review and the Ministry of Agriculture, Fisheries and Food responds to the need for changes as they arise. For example, it has drawn up and circulated guidelines on nutrition labelling that aim to standardise the presentation of nutrition information on food labels so that consumers can compare products more easily and to help them to choose a balanced diet. The guidelines have been widely adopted and the Ministry will continue to encourage their use until EC-wide proposals are agreed. In many ways, these proposals follow closely the United Kingdom lead and the Ministry will be able to draw on the United Kingdom experience during negotiations in Brussels.

The Ministry of Agriculture, Fisheries and Food also recognises the need to provide consumer informative material about food and to help them make best use of information on food labels. In particular, it has recently issued a revised version of its free booklet called "Look at the Label", which explains the meaning of the terms used in labelling.

In all these ways we have provided a framework for the general approach that we are taking on consumer protection and, in detail, shown how some have been able to work, either in terms of provision of information or in terms of specific cases such as the banning of the products that are mentioned.

Mr. Dalyell: As five different Government Departments are probably involved in the questions that I asked about greenfly, could we not have some response by letter from the Departments involved?

Mr. Forth: I was going to deal with the hon. Gentleman's point later, but I shall do so now. I listened carefully to his, as usual, impeccably researched and briefly presented case. I undertake to ensure that not only my Department but all other Departments involved look carefully at what he said and give a considered answer. I am sure that he would not want me to give an off-the-cuff answer. We have made careful note of what he said, and *Hansard* will be scrutinised carefully, so he will get a full and proper response.

Mr. Favell: Will my hon. Friend deal with the point about keeping information on food labelling to basics? I have already spoken about the Marathon bar label, which contains so much information that a safety warning would not be read by anybody. Most of that information is unintelligible, except to the most dedicated "muesli".

Mr. Forth My hon. Friend has made an important point of which we must not lose sight, which is that a balance has to be achieved—the hon. Member for Gordon used the word "balance" and I agree with him—between providing to the consumers usable and practical information that most would be able to understand and use, and overloading a product with unintelligible information. My hon. Friend gave a good example of something that came close to the latter description. We must be careful on what we mandate or regulate for. It is much better to leave the producers to make their own decisions about what consumers can use and make the product more attractive as a result.

The hon. Member for Gateshead, East asked about the Council of Ministers' meeting. She knows that the meeting of the Consumers Ministers covered a number of different issues, to one of which I was delighted to give my full support, that is, the effort to give consumers and their organisations a better voice in the European Community. I have met and continue to meet most of the main consumer organisations here in the United Kingdom, and we are better served than almost any other country by such organisations—a factor of which we can be proud, although we often take it for granted. It meant that when I went to the Council of Ministers' meeting I was able to support any moves—Commissioner Van Miert is interested in this—to promote the representation of consumer bodies in the European Community in the most effective way.

I was also able to reach agreement with the other member states on the directive covering consumer credit, which will be an important step forward in making the information available right across the Community, to all of our consumers. We agreed on continued support into 1990 for the European level of the hospital information system referred to by my hon. Friend the Member for Harrow, West (Mr. Hughes) in order to provide, Europe-wide, a firm statistical basis for carrying forward the detailed consumer protection policy in which we are all interested. We are interested in a policy which is on a firm statistical basis, which is why we are happy to carry along with us the other member states of the Community in continuing to fund that policy.

The hon. Member for Gateshead, East asked about something that I was unable to support, and I want to tell her why, because this is an important point. It concerned the draft resolution for the relaunch of consumer policy in the Community. There was much in the proposal that I was able to support, in particular the principle that I have just outlined—that consumers' views should be taken into account in policy development. I was also committed to the need for effective representation in all Community institutions. However, I was unable to support the resolution because of the one important point that the presidency insisted on including references to quality. The United Kingdom is fully committed to the principle that consumers have the right to effective and accurate information to ensure that they are able to make fully informed choices about the products and services available to them, but we cannot agree that it is necessary, practical or desirable for the Community to relaunch a Community consumer policy programme——

Mr. Frank Cook: On a point of order, Mr. Speaker. I understand that my hon. Friend the Member for Gateshead, East (Ms. Quin), having given the Chamber the opportunity to discuss the subject, has the right to reply. As the debate has to finish at 7 o'clock, may I ask you to protect that right and ensure that she has sufficient time?

Mr. Speaker: That right depends on the availability of time. I understood that the hon. Lady wanted only two minutes to answer.

Mr. Forth: I will be guided by what you have said, Mr. Speaker. I wanted to reply to as many as possible of the points that have been made. It would not be ungallant of me to point out that the hon. Member for Gateshead, East spent 50 minutes introducing her motion, and I hoped to take full advantage of the time to reply.

The Government's policy is based on a firm, practical and pragmatic approach which strikes a balance between a legal framework, effective action within that framework and dealing with these important matters on a case-by-case basis. I shall look carefully at what has been said during the debate, but I hope that the House will agree that the motion is an unjustified criticism of Government policy. Therefore, if there is a vote, I ask the House to reject the motion.

6.57 pm

Ms. Quin: With the leave of the House, I shall reply briefly to the debate.

I have listened carefully to the various contributions and in particular welcome those of my hon. Friends who spoke in support of my motion. My right hon. Friend the Member for Swansea, West (Mr. Williams) gave the House the benefit of his experience of dealing with consumer affairs in government. I am glad that he reinforced the point that, under this Government, consumer affairs have been downgraded, a trend which Labour is pledged to reverse. I understand that the hospital safety certificates, to which hon. Members referred, were introduced by my right hon. Friend in 1975, not by the Government.

The Minister, not surprisingly, strongly defended his position, but I hope that he has listened to some of the comments made by his hon. Friends, in particular the hon. Member for York (Mr. Gregory) who spoke strongly in favour of the EEC package holiday directive, which the Government are blocking.

Consumers have a choice in what they buy, but they cannot exercise it properly in the absence of clear and helpful labelling. Such labelling should be independently monitored because voluntary self-regulation will not be good enough.

The hon. Member for Stockport (Mr. Favell) defended the Government's position on certain vested-interest groups and said that the Government were not in the business of votes. The Government will not get many votes unless consumers believe that the Government are taking their interests far more seriously than their record over the past 10 years suggests.

I have listened carefully to all the interesting contributions that have been made, but I still believe that my motion is valid.

It being Seven o'clock, proceedings on the motion lapsed, pursuant to Standing Order No. 13 (Arrangement of public business).

Mr. John McFall (Dumbarton): On a point of order, Mr. Speaker. May I seek your protection. I came third in the ballot for private Members' motions, but today Conservative Members have wasted time. Government Whips have been drumming up support. When I look about the Chamber, I see that there is a sole Scottish Minister and no pit bull terrier from the Scottish National party. Is this another example of the alliance between the blue Tories and the tartan Tories to keep issues affecting Scotland off the political agenda——

Mr. Speaker: Order. The hon. Member came third in the ballot; the hon. Member for Derbyshire, North-East (Mr. Barnes) might feel slightly more aggrieved because he came second.

Televising of Proceedings of the House

Mr. Speaker: Before I call the Leader of the House to move his motion, I should like to say a word about the procedure to be followed. Until 10 o'clock there will be a general debate, during which all amendments may be referred to. At 10 o'clock I shall call, first, the hon. Member for Workington (Mr. Campbell-Savours) formally to move amendment (c) relating to a dedicated unedited channel, and, secondly, the hon. Member for Chislehurst (Mr. Sims) formally to move amendment (n) relating to proposed restrictions on the type of picture that may be shown. I shall then put the Question on the main Question.

Many hon. Members wish to participate in the debate. I appeal for short speeches so that as many hon. Members as possible may be called.

7.1 pm

The Lord President of the Council and Leader of the House of Commons (Mr. John Wakeham): I beg to move,

That this House agrees with the Select Committee on Televising of Proceedings of the House in its First Report (House of Commons Paper No. 141).

In February 1988, the House voted in favour of the principle of an experiment in the televising of its proceedings. It set up a Select Committee, which I had the honour to chair, to consider the way in which the experiment should be conducted. The Committee's report, which is before the House today, is the product of a substantial measure of agreement within the Committee.

Mr. Robin Maxwell-Hyslop (Tiverton): On a point of order, Mr. Speaker. I think it would be a great help for the House if we could know whether the Leader of the House, by leave of the House, will be speaking again at the end, because it could reduce the number of interruptions in his speech if it is known that he will be replying to the debate at the end.

Mr. Wakeham: If any hon. Member wishes me to answer any query, I shall be present and shall seek to intervene at the end of the debate, if that is for the convenience of the House.

There was a substantial measure of agreement within the Committee. That seemed so unlikely when we started work that the fact is well worth recording. It was an unusually large Committee—of 20 Members—combining not only different political views but very different views on televising the House, yet we were able to agree our report with only one dissenting voice—that of my hon. Friend the Member for Thanet North (Mr. Gale), who wanted to approach the problem in a completely different way, which he will set out later if he catches your eye, Mr. Speaker. A wide range of views was expressed in the Committee about the rules of coverage, and I shall say something about that later.

The essence of our proposals is that the House should retain overall control, including control of the rules of coverage. The broadcasters will gain access to the signal at a fair price, and an independent company will be given a prestige contract to produce the pictures. The viewing public will be able to see the House at work, and the taxpayer will not have to pay for it.

The administrative arrangements may seem complex, but I will explain them as concisely as I can. The basic idea is a partnership between the House of Commons, the BBC and the IBA through a joint company, which we have called the House of Commons Broadcasting Unit. The unit will provide the equipment for the experiment and employ an independent operator to produce the signal. It will recover its running costs by selling the signal to the broadcasters at a fair price. The Select Committee will monitor the experiment, and it will be assisted by an Officer of the House, whom we have called the Supervisor of Broadcasting, part of whose job it will be to ensure that these arrangements work smoothly. There will also be a "customers' committee", representing all the consumers of the signal, which will act as an informal channel of communication.

Eight remote-controlled cameras will be mounted just under the Galleries and will be as unobtrusive as we can make them. We went into lighting with some care, as many hon. Members feel passionately about the subject. Clearly, we shall need extra lighting or our constituents will see very unflattering pictures of us, with heavy shadows and bags under our eyes, but we must avoid intolerable heat and glare. We concluded that the best solution for the experiment would be to install eight space lights, which simulate the effect of chandeliers, and which would be suspended from the ceiling of the Chamber. A number of members of the Committee have seen the proposed lights in operation and have found them acceptable. We also recommend that the strip lighting under the Galleries should be upgraded to provide some additional light on the Back Benches.

The House will expect me to speak in some detail about the rules of coverage since our proposals have been given a hostile reception. Those who have expressed their views most vociferously are the representatives of the media, who can hardly be said to be disinterested observers. I say that not in any pejorative sense but am merely underlining the fact that the interests and perspectives of the House and the media are different.

Let me outline briefly the rules of coverage which we propose, the considerations which led us to our conclusions and why I believe that most of the criticism of them is misguided. We thought it right to lay down at the outset a statement of objectives to guide the director on duty. This, in many ways, is the key to an understanding of the rules of coverage, so I will quote it in full:

"The director should seek, in close collaboration with the Supervisor of Broadcasting, to give a full, balanced, fair and accurate account of proceedings, with the aim of informing viewers about the work of the House."

The words

"a full, balanced, fair and accurate account"

were carefully chosen to describe the type of coverage which the Select Committee believed to be desirable. It is, of course, precisely in the interpretation of this phrase that the differences of perspective have emerged between the broadcasters and the Committee. The broadcasters—for perfectly legitimate and understandable reasons—see it as their right and duty to film what happens in the Chamber in exactly the same way as they would an election meeting or party conference, with full journalistic licence to cut away from the speaker who has the floor and to paint an impressionistic picture by the use of a range of different camera shots and editorial techniques.

By contrast, the Select Committee felt—some Members perhaps more strongly than others—that the purpose of television coverage should be to provide something like an "electronic *Hansard*", designed to provide viewers with a factual and objective visual record of our proceedings—of speeches and statements made, of questions asked and answered and of decisions taken.

I turn now to the detailed rules of coverage which we recommend to support and implement the broad statement of objectives. I think that even the broadcasters accept, albeit reluctantly, some of the restrictions we recommend, such as the ban on the filming of the public Galleries. We also propose a number of specific guidelines for the director to observe, chief among which are the designation of a standard head and shoulders shot, limited use of wide-angle shots, a strict limitation on the use of reaction shots and a prohibition on the use of split-screen and panning shots.

Mr. Dennis Skinner (Bolsover): That sounds a bit like state censorship to me. Is the Leader of the House telling us that we shall not be able to have a three-shot of the Social Democratic party? Is he saying that if the Leader of the SDP decides to cross the Floor and join the Tory party the camera will not be allowed to pan across and show him disappearing into the arms of the Prime Minister? Is the right hon. Gentleman aware that if these restrictions had been applied to the Spanish Parliament some time ago we would have finished up with a shot not of the fellow with the gun in his hand but of the Speaker with his hands up?

Mr. Wakeham: That is a pretty old joke. The hon. Gentleman will make his speech in his own way, but the activities to which he refers do not seem to me to be the proceedings of the House of Commons; at least I hope that they are not. This experiment is to televise the proceedings of the House of Commons.

I believe that these guidelines, taken together, flow logically from our broad approach to television coverage encapsulated in the statement of objectives to which I have already referred. It is only fair at this point to mention that some members of the Committee would have preferred tighter guidelines whereas the hon. Member for Holborn and St. Pancras (Mr. Dobson) and his hon. Friends argued for a more liberal regime. Nevertheless, I believe that what we have recommended in the report represents the closest thing to a consensus about the rules of coverage that it was possible to achieve among a group of 20 Members representing such a wide spectrum of views on the principle of televising.

I now turn to our recommendations for the treatment of incidents of disorder, which have been the subject of particular controversy. As we say in the report:

"Our overall approach to this matter is governed by our absolute conviction that deliberate misconduct designed to secure televised publicity ought not to achieve its aim".

I do not think that I need to dwell on disorder in the Galleries, as it is generally agreed that the Galleries should not be televised at all. Disorder on the Floor of the House is an altogether more delicate question. None the less, starting from the proposition which I have just quoted, I believe that it was right to recommend that, in cases of disorder, the director should not focus on the Member or Members involved.

Of course, as we recognise in the report, there will inevitably be cases where the director will be unsure as to what response is required of him in a given situation. That is precisely why we urge Members to

"exercise some tolerance whilst any initial uncertainties over the interpretation of the guidelines are resolved".

I am quite sure that, provided the director has attempted in good faith to apply the guidelines in conformity with the spirit of the statement of objectives, any misjudgments by him will be treated sympathetically by the Supervisor of Broadcasting and the Select Committee.

Mr. Tony Banks (Newham, North-West): The right hon. Gentleman should not make too much of this issue, because that is not really what it is all about. If an incident were taking place on the Floor of the House, for example, if the right hon. Member for Henley (Mr. Heseltine) had seized the Mace and was swinging it about his head, would the person doing the commentary say, "Although we cannot show you this, the right hon. Member for Henley is now swinging the Mace about and he has hit three Members"?

Mr. Wakeham: Overfamiliarity with the Mace by hon. Members on either side of the House would not be shown on television in the normal course of events. As for what the commentator says, I have no plans for any restrictions. The main point is that we do not believe that those who seek to engage in such activities should be seen on television if that is their objective.

The main aim of the relationship between the Supervisor of Broadcasting and the director is to ensure that any mistakes are not repeated. I should stress at this point that, as the report makes clear, we are dealing with an experiment, and the guidelines we have recommended are for the start of the experiment. They could be modified, subject to the Select Committee's approval, as the experiment evolves. If the broadcasters wish to make representations to the Committee, they are, of course, perfectly free to do so. Any such representations will be carefully considered.

Finally, on the rules of coverage, I should like to deal with one argument which sums up the opposition to our proposals—why will the television viewer not be able to see what a person sitting in the Gallery can see? My answer is that the television viewer is going to see only what the broadcasters choose to broadcast; and, even if we had a dedicated channel, the viewer would see only the shot that the director selects. A visitor in the Gallery can allow his gaze to wander over any part of the Chamber, however irrelevant to the proceedings, or even out of the window. The basic premise on which this argument is based is, therefore, clearly spurious.

Mr. Jeff Rooker (Birmingham, Perry Barr): My point is referred to in the report. Assuming that all eight cameras will be under the Galleries, does this mean that any hon. Member who, for whatever reason—this has happened during my time in the House—chooses to speak, within order, from the Upper Galleries will never stand a chance of being shown on television to his or her constituents?

Mr. Wakeham: I remember Mr. Speaker making a statement some time ago when he said that he would not normally call someone from an Upper Gallery. If there is a problem, we can consider it during the experiment. As it is envisaged, it would not be possible for such a person to be shown on television.

I believe that the rules that we have proposed offer a sensible middle path between the position in the other place, where the less-heated debate makes it possible not to have any specific rules of coverage, and the very much

[*Mr. Wakeham*]

more restrictive rules imposed in Canada, which we considered unnecessary. As such, they provide a scheme that reflects most Members' views of the purpose of television coverage.

Mr. D. N. Campbell-Savours (Workington): I am sorry to take up the right hon. Gentleman's time. Has he any idea of the costs of running the House of Commons Broadcasting Unit and the costs for the operators?

Mr. Wakeham: The cost to the Commons will be about £500,000, of which some £300,000 will be for the archives. The cost to the Commons of the broadcasting part will be relatively small. The other costs will be borne by the broadcasters. The figure is in the report, which I think shows that the cost of the experiment will be about £500,000 for each of them. That is the sort of amount that the broadcasters will contribute. It will depend on how they run and staff the operation.

Mr. Robin Corbett (Birmingham, Erdington): The Leader of the House will remember that paragraph 59 of the report refers to assistance for the deaf. Does he agree with me that every possible pressure should be put on those responsible during this experiment to have at least subtitling so that those who are denied access to so much of our television can share in this experiment?

Mr. Wakeham: There have been a number of representations on that subject by hon. Members, including my hon. Friend the Member for Torridge and Devon, West (Miss Nicholson). We are certainly doing what we can to provide that assistance. I entirely agree with that objective.

As I said, the rules provide a scheme that reflects most Members' views of the purpose of television coverage. In doing so, they cut across the desire of the broadcasters for a more liberal regime conducive to what they regard as good television, but the very phrase "good television" gives the game away as it accords a higher priority to entertainment than information. I cannot therefore recommend acceptance of the selected amendment relating to the rules of coverage. If it were agreed to, there would be no restrictions on the size of the shot that the director could use; he would have complete freedom to take the camera off the Member speaking to show anything else that was happening in the Chamber, whether it was relevant to the proceedings of the House or not; and he could pan along the Benches at any time to show which Members were present and which were not. These do not seem to me to be suitable guidelines to start the experiment with, and I ask the House to reject the amendment.

While the rules of coverage are a matter for us, the use of the signal in programmes is quite properly a matter for the broadcasters, provided they do not use it in light entertainment programmes, political satire or party political broadcasts.

Mr. Nigel Spearing (Newham, South): I do not want to delay the Leader of the House in respect of amendment (b), but does he agree that some hon. Members think that the availability of the signal is a matter not just for the broadcasters, but for this nation and this House, although the Select Committee may not have thought so? Will the Leader of the House at least concede that there is that point of view?

Mr. Wakeham: I concede, of course, that the coverage and the way in which it is shown are matters for the House at the right and proper time, but the task with which the Select Committee was charged was to draw up the rules for an experiment in the televising of the proceedings of the House. It was not charged with considering the whole question of the way in which the proceedings should be dealt with. When I say that the rules of coverage are a matter for us, I am referring to the Select Committee and to our debate this evening, which is dealing with the report of the Select Committee. The other matters are important, but we shall come to them at another time.

Mr. Merlyn Rees (Morley and Leeds, South): In reference to the last point, I agree that the House could not possibly dictate to the broadcasters on the precise use they make of the signal coming from the electronic *Hansard* during the experiment. But how this House votes after the experiment will be determined, to a large extent, by the use the television companies make of the programmes and the use they make of the signals, especially regionally. Although we cannot control the signal, the television companies cannot ignore the feelings in this House.

Mr. Wakeham: That is absolutely true of various aspects of the experiment, especially the area with which I am about to deal—the use the companies make of the proceedings of Committees. Although we cannot dictate which parts of Committee proceedings they broadcast, the Select Committee very much hopes that the broadcasters will make good and adequate use of the Committee proceedings, as well as of the House generally, so that the experiment can be evaluated properly by all of us. Our role is to provide a signal and some guidelines, not to interfere or to attempt to dictate the way in which the signal is used.

The coverage of Committees is an important matter and I underline the importance our report attached to the work of both the Select and Standing Committees. We reached the conclusion——

Mr. Sydney Bidwell (Ealing, Southall) *rose*——

Mr. Wakeham: No, I will not give way because I want to talk about Committees.

We reached the conclusion that Committee coverage could not be approached in the same way as coverage of the Chamber. The broadcasters are willing to finance complete coverage of proceedings in the Chamber from the end of Prayers to the Adjournment on every sitting day during the experiment, but they are not prepared to finance complete coverage of every meeting of every Committee during that period. As there is no public money available to subsidise Committee coverage, the only resources available are those that individual broadcasting organisations are willing to find to pay for coverage which they wish to use. The televising of Committees can, therefore, be organised only in response to demand from the broadcasters. That may be disagreeable—and I know that some members of the Select Committee would wish it otherwise—but it is a sad fact which we cannot ignore.

The report makes clear our hope that the importance that we attach to the coverage of Committees will be fully reflected in the broadcasters' programme plans, although realism lends us to warn the House not to raise its expectations too high, particularly as regards live coverage. What matters above all is that there should be enough coverage, of a representative nature, during the experiment to enable the House to decide eventually whether televising of Committees should become permanent. On that, the broadcasters have at least said that they will try their best.

If the House agrees to the motion we are debating, broadcasting will begin with the State Opening of the new Session. We recommend that the experiment should continue until the end of July next year, which is long enough to give television a fair trial. Shortly before the end of the experiment, the House will be invited to decide whether televising the proceedings should continue on a permanent basis.

Mr. Maxwell-Hyslop: Will the televising equipment be subject to the direction of the Chairman of the Select Committee, bearing in mind that it is essential that the Chairman can see all the members of the Committee and that the members of the Committee can see all the witnesses to whom questions are being put? If the cameras prevent that from happening, is it not essential that the Chairman of the Committee should have the power to give directions to remove cameras and lighting from their position, if they are preventing the Committee, in his judgment, from doing its job?

Mr. Wakeham: I cannot agree with my hon. Friend on that subject. As the House has approved this report and, therefore, the experiment in the televising of the proceedings of the House, it must be only in the most exceptional circumstances that the Chairman of a Select Committee would seek to put the cameras out. If the Committee went into secret session, the cameras would, of course, be put out. If there are any difficulties, we should remember that this is an experiment. The Select Committee would certainly look into any problem that arose to see whether we could find a satisfactory solution.

Dr. Norman A. Godman (Greenock and Port Glasgow): I have a question about paragraph 87, which deals with the live coverage of Committees away from Westminster. Can we expect to see the televising of the Scottish Grand Committee sessions which are held in Edinburgh?

Mr. Wakeham: As I have said, the televising of Select Committees, Grand Committees and anything other than the proceedings of the House will be done on demand by the broadcasters who wish to do it. I understand that the broadcasters have said that the Scottish Grand Committee when it meets in Edinburgh is one of the Committees that they would very much like to broadcast. I anticipate, therefore, that that will happen and I hope very much that it will happen during the experiment. It is important that the House has the opportunity to see on television all the different aspects of our work, so that we have a better basis on which to make the final judgment, which is the most important judgment in a way, some time next year.

Dr. Godman: We might even see the Nationalists.

Mr. Wakeham: I do not want the hon. Gentleman to raise too many hopes in these matters.

Amendment (c) tabled by the hon. Member for Workington (Mr. Campbell-Savours) would prevent the experiment from going ahead unless a dedicated television channel were made available. I think that every hon. Member would agree that if the House is to be televised, the availability of a dedicated channel would be the best way of solving the difficult questions of editing, selection

and balance which trouble many of us. But the House must recognise that providing a dedicated channel on a high-powered satellite which could transmit a signal into people's homes would significantly increase the cost of the experiment to the broadcasters. To impose that requirement on them might well result in the experiment not taking place at all. So while I have every sympathy with the hon. Gentleman's objective, I do not think that we should allow the best to be the enemy of the good.

Mr. Joseph Ashton (Bassetlaw): In that case, why did the Committee not recommend that the proceedings of the House should be shown on the internal monitors we have in our Committee Rooms? It recommended only that the proceedings should be shown in the Division lobbies. Surely it would be simple to broadcast the proceedings in every office of the building.

Mr. Wakeham: It is not technically possible to do that and it is certainly impossible to do it in time to conduct an experiment that will begin in the autumn. It is, of course, possible to do so in the long term, if that is what the House wants, but it raises big issues. Some hon. Members, who may be very much in favour of televising the House, would be passionately against closed circuit television in offices and around the House. It is a matter to which we shall, no doubt, return another day.

The House has decided, after prolonged consideration, that there should be an experiment in the broadcasting of its proceedings by television. The motion before the House will enable the experiment to take place. I invite the House to support the motion.

7.29 pm

Mr. Frank Dobson (Holborn and St. Pancras): I strongly support the motion that we agree with the report of the Select Committee on Televising the Proceedings of the House. The arrangements suggested for the experimental televising of our proceedings are not exactly the ideal that I or my Labour colleagues on the Committee would have preferred, but I believe that the proposals are workable and that they meet the legitimate doubts and reservations that were expressed in the debate in February 1988 when the principle of televising was accepted by a majority of 54 votes.

It is only right that before dealing with the proposals in the report I should pay tribute to the work that has gone into its preparation. In particular, I congratulate our Clerks who have managed to boil down 15 months of Committee proceedings, hearings, technical demonstrations, an overseas visit and more than 250 written submissions into a 33-page report which is easy to read and understand. I am also grateful to our technical advisers and Officers of the House who contributed to assessing and demonstrating the practicalities of what was being proposed.

Curiously enough, I should also like to thank my fellow members of the Select Committee who put in so much effort and even made the sacrifice of a visit to Canada, during the recess. I pay tribute to the eight Conservative Members on the Committee who originally voted against televising the House but who accepted the February 1988 decision of the House and now support the recommendations for the experiment. I personally thank my hon. Friend the Member for The Wrekin (Mr. Grocott) whose

[Mr. Frank Dobson]

practical experience as a producer of television current affairs programmes was of great help to me and to other Members.

Finally, and even more novel, I pay tribute to the Leader of the House, who, having voted against televising, nevertheless worked extremely hard, both in chairing our proceedings and in private, to put together practical proposals that would be acceptable to the House. The extent of his success was amply demonstrated last Thursday when the remarkable edifice that he had constructed was topped out by the Prime Minister's announcement of her support. Some of his Cabinet colleagues are green with envy and want to know how he got such a public statement of support, but, whatever the explanation, all this means that whatever fate may befall him in the threatened Government reshuffle, the Lord President will go into the history books as the Leader of the House who brought television cameras into the Chamber. I think that he will pleased with that.

This is an historic development because it will permit the people of this country to see as well as to hear their elected representatives at work. With the exception of a number of what might be described as wholly unreconstructed exclusionists, no one can object in principle to being shown on television if we concede the principle of being reported in *Hansard,* misreported in newspapers and heard on the radio.

However, a substantial number of hon. Members have legitimate practical doubts and reservations about the impact of the cameras on the workings of this place and about the trivialising capacity of television. Much of that doubt and uncertainty springs from a politician's distrust of the news media—distrust between the reporter and the would-be reported. There will always be tension between politicians and journalists and I believe that there should always be that tension between us. It is not the job of journalists to give us an easy time but we can and do expect them to be reasonably fair. In relation to what happens in the House and its Committees, we also expect them to be reasonably representative and not unfairly selective. They must try to maintain a reasonable balance between the parties, between the Front and Back Benches and between Members from different parts of the country. As the report makes clear, to assist them in that task it is intended that the House will monitor their output.

The Select Committee's report is designed to secure our legitimate concerns without trying in turn to deprive the television broadcasters of the rights that they must have in a democracy, because a Parliament has no more right than a Government to tell broadcasters what to do.

The first proposition in the report is to protect the interests and integrity of the House by putting the whole operation of the cameras under the control of a House of Commons Broadcasting Unit, a Supervisor of Broadcasting employed by the House, and a Select Committee. That means that the broadcasters will not control the signal that is made available to them, but for the period of the experiment the broadcasters will foot most of the bill and provide the equipment. For any permament televising arrangement, the Select Committee believes that the House should establish a broadcasting unit as a Department of the House—as an electronic

Hansard—making the signal available to those who want to use it and maintaining an archive to which anyone should have access.

We have looked into the technical requirements for the introduction of remote control cameras in the House and are satisfied that the necessary improvements in lighting can be achieved without unacceptable levels of glare or heat.

Although other members of the Select Committee are satisfied that the arrangements for the remote control of the cameras will work, I still have some residual doubts about the speed of response of the cameras, especially at Question Time, and about whether they will pick up Members quickly enough. However, that is something that will become clear during the experiment.

Many hon. Members have been rightly concerned to ensure that there is television coverage of Select Committees and Standing Committees, including the Scottish Grand Committee. We have looked carefully into that and propose various experimental arrangements that we believe will prove acceptable and from which a great deal should be learnt before the experiment comes to an end. Of course, we cannot force the broadcasters to show the proceedings of Select or Standing Committees, but in our meetings with them we have emphasised our wish for such coverage. In any case, evidence from the United States suggests that Select Committee proceedings at least are likely to prove attractive to the broadcasters. They have done so there and there is no reason why they should not here.

We have also placed great emphasis on the need for coverage by the broadcasters of matters raised, whether in the Chamber, Select Committees or Standing Committees, which are of particular interest to viewers in Scotland, Wales, Northern Ireland and the English regions. That is likely to be of particular importance to Back Benchers. The Select Committee pressed the broadcasters hard to ensure that they would be able to cope technically with the additional traffic that would result from more regional coverage. Assurances were given by the broadcasters and we look to them to honour those assurances. We have emphasised to the broadcasters that their regional coverage during the experimental period will be a major determining factor for many hon. Members when the House considers whether to have the cameras in permanently.

Although the House will have direct control over the signal that is made available for both broadcasting and recording, we will not have similar control over what use the broadcasters will make of that signal. We can restrict the use of that signal——

Mr. Bidwell: I intervene now for the reason that I sought to intervene during the speech of the Leader of the House. Many of us who have been doubtful about televising over the years and who are shifting our view about it and will be greatly governed by this debate when deciding which way to vote are concerned not so much about the cameras being switched on but the conditions under which the cameras will be switched off. As I understand it, what is strange about the report is the role of the Chair—of you, Mr. Speaker—and the traditions that we have given you and that you have exercised fairly —mostly—over the years and the extent to which, if the House were——

Mr. Tony Banks (Newham, North-West): Switch him off, Mr. Speaker.

Mr. Bidwell: I am concerned about what you, Mr. Speaker, would do, but you are much too friendly for me to admonish you in any way. I am concerned about control of the cameras when the House is suspended, as it has been, mostly as a result of exercises that have already been referred to, such as the throwing of tear gas bombs that burnt a hole in the carpet. I am concerned that there seems to be no reference in the report to the role of the Chair in decision-making about when the cameras should be switched on and switched off. That point completely puzzles me.

Mr. Dobson: The report deals with that point, stating that it would be best if you, Mr. Speaker, did not have the facility to turn off the cameras because there would be great shouts, cries and rows about those occasions on which you chose to do so and, probably even more importantly, about those occasions when you did not. We should not like that responsibility to fall upon the Chair in such circumstances.

The one thing that we can do with the signal is to restrict its use, and we should restrict it in some ways. For example, as the Leader of the House has already said, the Select Committee proposed that the signal should not be used in advertisements, party political broadcasts or comedy programmes or any combination of the three, but we cannot insist that broadcasters use material which they, in their editorial judgment, do not want to use. The House can reasonably expect that broadcasters will make more use of actuality from these proceedings than they do of the still photograph with voice-over, which is what they are reduced to at present.

A number of hon. Members on both sides of the House are concerned that broadcasters may be happy, or at least willing, to obey the new rules during the experimental period and then, should the House decide to have cameras permanently, they would go wild and ignore the rules. We ought to have a standing Select Committee to ensure that the rules are kept both during the experimental period and afterwards, should the House decide to keep the cameras in permanently.

Mr. Spearing: The House may know that I was a member of the first Select Committee which dealt with sound broadcasting. We developed a very satisfactory code of practice. Does my hon. Friend agree that, at least to start with, it might be a good thing for decisions to be on a sessional basis if the television cameras became a permanent feature—for very good procedural reasons?

Mr. Dobson: I am not sure whether a sessional basis would be the right one, but we would need to make the continuing broadcasting of the House conditional upon the rules being kept.

That brings me to the present rules on broadcasting. I am a fan of the "Today in Parliament" programme and an avowed enemy of "Yesterday in Parliament". Therefore, I welcome the undertakings given by the BBC as outlined in paragraph 56 of our report, and the hope expressed there that these will be adopted by the other broadcasters. I hope that the BBC will apply them throughout its organisation.

Hon. Members will note, however, that while ITV through Channel 4 is proposing a daily afternoon programme including live coverage, the BBC is proposing such coverage only on Tuesdays and Thursdays at present. I hope that before the experiment begins the BBC will discover that we also meet on other days of the week. It seems to have enough people here on other days of the week.

Many hon. Members would like a dedicated channel which would provide live continuous coverage of all the proceedings of the House, and I am one such Member. The Select Committee looked into this, but our investigations have shown that there is no prospect of achieving such a dedicated channel by the beginning of the experiment. Our report suggests that the rapid developments in this field should be monitored and that the idea of a dedicated channel should be pursued and promoted.

Mr. Campbell-Savours: I shall read to the House letters from British Aerospace which make it clear that that company is in a position to offer two options for transmission on a dedicated channel from October this year. If the Committee did not receive similar correspondence, it can only be said that it did not ask for it. If it had, it would have received the answers that I received in correspondence and telephone conversations.

Mr. Dobson: If my hon. Friend the Member for Workington (Mr. Campbell-Savours) had read the report of the evidence, he would know that we attempted to have dealings with British Aerospace, in seeking some immediate solution to the problem of a satellite channel, but it could not deliver in time.

Mr. Bob Cryer (Bradford, South): Ex-Nimrod equipment.

Mr. Dobson: I dispute any suggestion that British Aerospace proposed to use abandoned ex-Nimrod equipment.

There is no real prospect of one of the limited number of terrestrial channels being dedicated to the continuous coverage of the House. The only practical solution is a satellite channel. If the House decides to allow the cameras in permanently, we should be prepared to finance a dedicated satellite channel as part of our commitment to parliamentary democracy.

Mr. Edward Leigh (Gainsborough and Horncastle): Those of us who did not serve on the Select Committee are grateful to the hon. Member for Holborn and St. Pancras (Mr. Dobson) and my right hon. Friend the Leader of the House for the efforts that they made in this difficult matter. Will the hon. Gentleman confirm that if, in spite of his good efforts, the House rejected the Committee's proposals, it would not necessarily result in a more liberal regime? The Select Committee would have to go back and report again, which might allow a dedicated channel to emerge. Is that a possibility?

Mr. Dobson: That is certainly possible, although I am embarrassed by the fact that, having fallen behind most other Western democracies by not allowing the electors to see the elected at work, we have now also fallen behind the Soviet Union. I think that it might be best if we got on with it.

Mr. Roger Gale (Thanet, North): Will the hon. Gentleman concede that the Western democracies to which he referred all have dedicated channels?

Mr. Dobson: They have all sorts of different methods of reception and, to my knowledge, not all of them have dedicated channels. The other major significant feature is that the market for satellite and cable television is very different in Canada and the United States, and at a very different stage in its development.

If we consider arrangements for the permanent televising of the House, we should accept that, if necessary, it should be paid for entirely from public funds if that would produce the best arrangements. It would surely be better to have public investment in promoting parliamentary democracy than to accept a second best that someone else was willing to finance.

One aspect of the report has already attracted considerable criticism, partly from the broadcasters but also from others. I refer to the proposed guidelines governing what may or may not be shown by the cameras. My hon. Friends and I argued that the guidelines were too restrictive and, despite the best efforts of the leader writer for *The Guardian,* Labour Members voted for a more relaxed approach. We accept that what happens in the Galleries should not be shown because that would lay the House open to a demo a day. It is surely right, however, that we should permit any deliberate action by an hon. Member or hon. Members on the Floor of the House that can be reported in newspapers to be shown on television. If someone behaves in a disorderly, silly or boorish manner, why should that fact be kept from the people who elected him? Evidence from abroad suggests that the voters do not like to see such behaviour and may take their vengeance at a later stage.

We should also prefer broadcasters to be permitted to show the reaction of other hon. Members to what an hon. Member is saying. That is preferable to the proposed rules in the report.

Mr. Cryer: I am interested to know why in the list of highly restrictive rules there is a rule to say that an hon. Member's papers must not be shown. Surely it would benefit the public to know if an hon. Member was reading a brief provided by a lobby organisation. That would allow the public to see not just the remote control of the cameras of the television closed shop but the remote control of hon. Members.

Mr. Dobson: There is some merit in that suggestion, but I can envisage circumstances in which an hon. Member from whatever political party might be referring to papers with a note saying, "Don't raise this unless the other lot raise it first", or words to that effect. It might be better if the information were not available.

Mr. John Redwood (Wokingham): Has the hon. Gentleman cleared this part of his speech with the Leader of the Opposition who was not keen for the public to hear the whole of his interview the other day?

Mr. Dobson: If hon. Members had not been attending this debate, they could have listened to the Leader of the Opposition on "Wogan" this evening—fully, extensively, truly and accurately reported. There is a slight difference. In future, hon. Members will know that everything they say here may be carried unless they behave in a disorderly manner, in which case it will not be carried.

Despite my reservations, I commend the whole report to the House. I shall be voting for it. I believe strongly that it deals satisfactorily with the practical objections to televising the House. What we say in the House is already reported through other news media and we should now permit its direct coverage on television. We must remember that most of what we do in this place needs to be reported if it is to have much impact. Those who report us are as much a part and parcel of the democratic process as those of us who serve in the House. We must ensure that they play their part in our democracy in a responsible way.

It could be argued that those who insisted, despite all sorts of pains and penalties, on reporting the old, undemocratic House of Commons made a greater contribution to the development of democracy than did those on whom they reported. Until then, those in power had claimed not only that ruling the country was a matter for the privileged few, but that it was only of interest to the privileged few. The journalists and the pamphleteers breached that wall of privilege.

Until the advent of modern technology we, the elected representatives, could not address directly from this House those whom we represent. Instead, we have had to rely on journalists to act as go-betweens, and on many an occasion they have been rather inadequate go-betweens. As that great democratic Socialist Aneurin Bevan pointed out when he called for the televising of the House so long ago that I was still at school, through the medium of television hon. Members can have a direct relationship with those who elect them. Neither they nor we would have to rely on the fallible intermediaries of the press. That argument still holds good.

Broadcasters must understand that the argument that television permits a direct relationship between the elected and those who elected them requires that they keep their editorialising to a minimum. That is why the continuous coverage of a dedicated channel has such appeal. Most of us accept that the news and current affairs programmes must edit what we say, but the broadcasters must behave responsibly and, in particular, keep their commentary to a minimum.

Mr. Rooker: My hon. Friend makes an important point about broadcasters on current affairs programmes keeping their comments to a minimum. The premier political programme put out by Central Television—the former employers of our hon. Friend the Member for The Wrekin (Mr. Grocott)—previewed this debate last Thursday. Jon Lander introduced this place not only as "the palace of varieties" but described the

"twice weekly shoot-out at the OK corral with Ma Thatcher and the boys."

That is a description of this place from a premier television station in its main political programme of the week. If that is the style and content of what Central Television is planning, all the forebodings of my hon. Friends, including those of my hon. Friend the Member for Holborn and St. Pancras (Mr. Dobson), will come to fruition. I hope that that does not come to pass.

Mr. Dobson: I certainly understand my hon. Friend's reaction to such a description. Hon. Members will no doubt keep a note of that sort of occurrence, to say the least, during the experiment. It may be that the actual portrayal of what happens in this place will slightly undermine the cowboy description.

Dr. Godman: From the answer given to my earlier question to the Leader of the House, can I assume that all hon. Members who served on the Committee are in favour of televising the whole of the proceedings of, for example, the Scottish Grand Committee when it meets in Edinburgh? Those meetings last for two and a half hours.

Mr. Dobson: If the Scottish television companies want to show the whole of a Scottish Grand Committee sitting in Edinburgh, they can do so. It would be fatuous to suggest that we could force upon them an obligation to do so especially if, for example, the British Open were being held at St. Andrew's. I cannot imagine that it would add to the popularity of Scottish Members if their contributions were shown rather than the last few holes of the Open.

Mr. Nicholas Bennett (Pembroke): Does the hon. Gentleman agree that we will have to consider the way in which the television companies portray the whole of the work of Parliament, not just the exciting bits? It is interesting that the only two occasions on which the proceedings of the House have been broadcast live since I entered Parliament in 1987 have been when the House has been discussing issues in which the press are interested—the televising of Parliament and the Official Secrets Act. From the number of press in the Gallery tonight, it is clear that they have turned up because we are discussing a matter of interest to them. Many hon. Members want television to give an accurate portrayal of all the work of the House, not just the matters in which the press are interested.

Mr. Dobson: Quite unusually, I have considerable sympathy with the hon. Gentleman's desires. However, in a democracy we cannot insist that the broadcasters, the journalists or anyone else show what they do not think should be shown other than if it were on a dedicated channel, which most people favour as soon as it is technically possible. We must continue to bring pressure upon the broadcasters to ensure that they provide something approaching what might be described as a representative sample of what is happening in this place.

Mr. Tony Banks: My hon. Friend is making a point that has support on both sides of the House. A dedicated channel would avoid all those problems and must be the most desired option. The report says that while the experiment is being monitored consideration will be given to the introduction of a dedicated channel. Will my hon. Friend give a firm commitment that the next Labour Government will provide for such a channel out of funds voted by Parliament and not look around for a commercial deal with some broadcasting undertaking?

Mr. Dobson: Having taken part in the Committee's deliberations, I am reasonably convinced that hon. Members on both sides of the Committee want a dedicated channel as soon as that is technically possible. Even so, it must be remembered that even if we had the power to force the provision of a dedicated channel, we would never have the power to force people to watch it. They would have the choice, and that is what we want to provide. They would probably still get the bulk of the coverage of what happens here from the news and news magazine programmes on other television channels. Nevertheless, a dedicated channel would provide the protection of ensuring that everything was shown.

Mrs. Ann Clwyd (Cynon Valley): I apologise to my hon. Friend for interrupting his peroration. Is he aware that researchers at Aston university have set up a £60,000 study into the experiment of televising Parliament, during which they will assess the behaviour, the language, the appearance and the intelligence in debate of hon. Members? Of course, Labour Members have nothing to fear from such an assessment, but has my hon. Friend considered that as the study will be carried out by a professor who specialises in television violence it may be incomplete unless a continuous feed of Parliament's activities is seen on television?

Mr. Dobson: As I have made clear, I am in favour of a dedicated channel providing full coverage as soon as that is possible. Some hon. Members would do well to fear their electors rather than a few professors from Aston university assessing their performance.

The many interventions during my speech have made it clear that there is considerable concern about the editorialising and the smart-Alicking of commentators—especially, if I may say this, of the BBC. I for one do not mind being portrayed, in Cromwell's phrase, "warts and all", but I do object to some clever dick from the BBC adding jokeshop warts to the ones that I already possess. Hon. Members will be looking carefully to ensure that what the broadcasters do during the experiment sticks very closely to the undertakings that they have given in their evidence and to the rules that we have laid down. If they do that and enter into the spirit of the experiment, as hon. Members are doing, it should work.

If what I have said by quoting various people, including Aneurin Bevan, has not entirely converted some of the doubtful Conservative Members, I put to them two soundly Tory mottos—the Churchill family motto of "Trust the People", and, if that is not good enough, they can stick with the Duke of Wellington and "Publish and be damned".

8 pm

Mr. John Biffen (Shropshire, North): The Register of Members' Interests does not disclose that I have written a book. As the book is about the House of Commons, and as its prospective sales must relate, I hope, to the growing public interest that will be engendered by television, and as this evening holds out the daunting prospect that it could be remaindered even before it is published, I thought that I should place that fact on record—at least my publisher would wish me to place that fact on record.

I congratulate my right hon. Friend the Leader of the House on giving us the chance to take a decision that will nudge further forward our experience of televising the House. It is a modest decision and it clearly has all the hallmarks of compromise. It is the classic in that sense. Also, the arch compromiser, the spectre and the moral inspirer must have been Lord Reith.

I can think of nothing more designed to dehydrate this place than the proposals in the report. I say that with no spirit of hostility but with a great sense of gratification. It is important for the House to come to a decision which clearly embraces a wide range of opinion of those who support and oppose the experiment. My right hon. Friend deserves our thanks for the skill with which he has put together a point of view that I hope will command majority support.

I am quite certain that, in the long run, the central decision cannot hold. Paragraph 26 of the report refers to a head-and-shoulders shot. That is a shampoo approach to

[*Mr. John Biffen*]

public affairs. It destroys the true character of the House of Commons. It is and always has been theatre. As long as it tries to represent the wide range of opinions that are argued outside in the saloon bar and are put in a rather different form in this place, it will retain its vitality. It must accept that the challenge of television is that it will do that with cameras. For televising to be made acceptable, we require a degree of self-restraint on the part of hon. Members and the televisers. Such self-restraint would be more difficult to secure on the part of hon. Members than of televisers. I have no doubt that it could be secured.

If Parliament wishes to retain its vitality and to secure a link and an affection with the British public, when there are plenty of other institutions seeking to rival it, it knows that it must come to terms with the most powerful element of the media. This evening we take one small step forward, but forward it is, and I hope that my right hon. Friend gets a resounding majority.

8.3 pm

Mr. Archy Kirkwood (Roxburgh and Berwickshire): I am happy to take part in this debate, and I join with the hon. Member for Holborn and St. Pancras (Mr. Dobson) in commending the Select Committee for the way in which it carried out its work and for its workmanlike and positive report. The experimentation arrangements have been clearly and succinctly set out. On behalf of my right hon. and hon. Friends, I support the conclusions set out in the report.

My right hon. and hon. Friends and I are certainly prepared positively to consider the amendments. The amendment in the name of the hon. Member for Workington (Mr. Campbell-Savours) provides that the service should be set up in a certain way. It is of prime importance to minority parties that full on-line broadcasting should take place from day one. But I would not wish to delay the holding of an experiment on that basis. In an intervention, the hon. Gentleman said that he has an explanation for getting round the problem. I look forward with interest to hearing it.

The objectives are fairly set out in the report. They are to achieve a full, balanced, fair and accurate report of the proceedings of the House of Commons—an unvarnished, warts-and-all account. My right hon. and hon. Friends and I will test the experiment on that basis, but we have our own perspective. We were elected under an electoral system that does not leave the composition of the House of Commons in proportion to the balance of votes cast in the election. No hon. Member needs any reminding that, in the last general election, our alliance parties, as they then were, secured about 22 per cent. of the vote and we ended up with just over 20 Members.

That puts us in a difficult and peculiar position. We are trying to reflect the views of about 7 million people who voted for us. The opportunities that are given to us in Parliament do not enable us to do that. That is no reflection on the way in which the Chair conducts the business of the House; I do not make that point at all. We are in a difficult position because we must try to give a decent account of ourselves to the people who voted for us. If there are only two dozen or so of us in terms of

parliamentary strength, it makes our position peculiarly difficult in terms of what we must do in facing up to broadcasting requirements.

I do not think that it is possible to discharge a responsibility to the people who voted for us in a full balanced, fair and accurate way if we are not properly treated in the allocation of broadcasting time. We do not get anything like 20 per cent. of the parliamentary opportunities under the existing conventions of the House, and that is a problem for us. We are prejudiced in the share that we get as of right in participating in the proceedings of the House.

The Procedure Committee says that it is not right to make any changes in procedure in advance of the experiment being tested. There is a certain logic in that argument but if the Procedure Committee is not prepared to admit any changes to try to make sure that the balance of minority parties, and my party in particular, are not addressed, it leaves us in a difficult position. The Procedure Committee said that it will closely monitor the experiment to see whether modifications are desirable. I lay down that marker for the future consideration of the results of the experiment.

From their evidence to the Select Committee, and from correspondence that we have had with them, we know that the broadcasters are saying that, that their coverage will be based on the number of parliamentary seats and nothing more. They regard it as no more than their duty to do that. If that is true, again, we as a substantial national but minority parliamentary party will have difficulty in trying to accommodate that approach. If we simply accept indefinitely the situation as set out by the Select Committee, the Procedure Committee and in the evidence given by the broadcasters, we cannot possibly give full value to the 7 million people who voted for us at the last election. I do not believe that, with edited highlights, there is any reason why balanced programmes cannot be produced. That is the message that I want to send out from my party to the broadcasting authorities this evening.

The principle of votes cast as a basis for allocating broadcasting time has been used in similar political contexts—certainly it has been considered in the rules for party political broadcasts. Votes have an influence and should be brought to bear when considering the allocating of broadcasting opportunities in the House. If during live coverage it is not possible to put the view of the Social and Liberal Democrats because the procedures of the House discriminate against the calling of hon. Members from that party, we believe that broadcasters should have a duty to explain why that is so. I do not believe that the Select Committee report goes far enough in making that point clear.

One of the clearest results of the experiment will be an overwhelming cry from the public for a need to change the proceedings in the Chamber. Once they have seen an unvarnished, warts-and-all account of what goes on, how matters are conducted, how time is used and what procedures and Standing Orders are employed, there will, rightly, be an outcry for a massive programme of reform of the procedures, which I would support.

In the experiment, the broadcasters must take account of the fact that they have a duty to make the proceedings intelligible in terms of such matters as hours and Standing Orders. If the Leader of the House is to reply to the debate, will he clarify the simple and interesting question that has been put to me? Supposing attempts are made to produce television programmes to demonstrate the outmoded and archaic methods that we use in the House, will there be any inhibition on the television company using edited film extracts from the proceedings to make that point? I hope that there will not be. However, some of the restrictions contained in the conclusions and recommendations of the Select Committee report put that matter in doubt. I hope that the Leader of the House will make it clear that there will be no such restriction on the way in which the rules and procedures are looked at by television companies.

Althought I have not time to develop the point here, I believe that the introducton of television cameras will precipitate the argument that the procedures of the House are ripe for change and that the way in which we conduct business here is simply not suitable to sustain the best system of government and the most efficient process of democratic participation for a modern democracy in a country such as ours. A clear need for change in that direction has been shown.

The hon. Member for Greenock and Port Glasgow (Dr. Godman) has on a couple of occasions made the point that the Scottish Grand Committee in Edinburgh should be televised. I understand, because the report makes it clear, broadcasting of Committees will have to be demand-led. In terms of the Scottish dimension, I believe that it is essential that the Scottish Grand Committee should be televised. I fear that, looked at from a Scottish perspective, many people in Scotland, if they study the television reports of the proceedings in Parliament, will think that Scotland does not receive its fair share of debating time in the House, which some of us have been saying for a long time. I need only to cite the example of the inability of Scottish hon. Members to get at the heart of what is going on in the Scottish Office, because they are restricted to only one Scottish Question Time every four to six weeks.

It is not just a Scottish problem; it is a wider regional difficulty. I note that the Select Committee report indicates that the members of the Select Committee were aware of some of the problems of getting the live broadcasts transmitted in time for programmes produced in the regions not to be prejudiced by the demands being made simultaneously over two to three busy hours of the day by the national, London and south-east broadcasting organisations.

I hope that urgent consideration will be given to the ability of smaller and regional companies to make a proper contribution and play a proper part in the televising of the proceedings of the House. To that end, is it possible for the Select Committee which is monitoring the results of the experiment—I do not know whether that is the most appropriate body to do it—to keep and publish a log over a 12-month period of what excerpts are used, in what direction and by which company in which programmes? We could then have a complete picture of what use has been made of the film that is presented by the broadcasting units. It is important that we satisfy ourselves that regional broadcasting authorities get a fair crack of the whip.

I have always supported cameras coming into the House, as most of those on the Opposition Benches have done. I believe, however, that the danger is that the broadcasters will glamorise the House as consisting of two rival teams locked in mindless opposition, as we see so often in this place, and the reasoned, middle way will always be edited out. When people watch coverage of the

Commons, they expect to see a balanced debate reflecting the views of the parties for which they voted and not just a two-party Punch and Judy show.

8.16 pm

Mr. Roger Gale (Thanet, North): I address the House as the only member of the Select Committee who voted against my right hon. Friend's report. It will be widely assumed that I did so because I am opposed to televising the proceedings of the House. Following the vote in February 1988, I accepted entirely the will of the House and I, and those who thought as I do, did our best to ensure that, if the House were to be televised, it would be done in the most effective and efficient manner possible.

I commend the report of my right hon. Friend and I congratulate him on the compromise that he has achieved. In the month that it took the Committee to debate and to prepare the report, largely stimulated by our interest, there have been considerable technological advances. The cameras have been improved and miniaturised, much greater effort than was given before has now been given to the change in lighting in the Chamber, and, as a television producer and director, I am satisfied that very many of the technical arguments that I raised when we first debated the issue have, as a result of our interest, been solved.

So why did I vote against my right hon. Friend's report? I believe that the House is about to miss a great opportunity. I moved amendments in Committee to suggest to the House that, if we are to go down this road, we should go entirely down it. I said that it is possible, as is done in the Canadian Parliament, which has been cited long and often in these debates, to provide every hon. Member with the "Oasis" information system. That is a desk-top monitor that could give every hon. Member not only television broadcasts from the House, but all other news services, the data services from the Library, the information services that would allow us to print out the pages from the Vote Office that we need on a day-to-day basis, which in itself would save I suspect several rain forests a year, and it would enable us to have a Division bell override. In Committee, Members on both sides of the House chose to reject the public expenditure that would be necessary to provide that system.

However, there is a further stage, and it is that concern to which I believe the House should only address itself tonight. If we are to carry out the televising of the House and the broadcasting by television of the House, it should be available in its entirety to the electorate.

In the 1988 debate virtually every speaker in favour of televising the House addressed himself to the enhancement of democracy. My right hon. Friend the Leader of the House and the shadow Leader of the House said that the proposal will bring the House of Commons to the people. What the House of Commons is being offered tonight and what the public are being offered is quite simply a confidence trick. It is a conspiracy designed to prevent the public from seeing the House of Commons at work. I suppose that I should take some satisfaction from the knowledge that those of us who were originally opposed to televising the House have won the argument if the motion goes through unamended tonight.

It is possible to convey the proceedings of the House unedited to the public and it is possible to do so immediately. Earlier my right hon. Friend suggested that the costs would be such as to dissuade broadcasters from

[*Mr. Roger Gale*]

embarking upon the exercise. The Opposition spokesman suggested to the House that he would really like to have a dedicated channel, but that that might delay the experiment and that it was not technically possible. Tonight the hon. Member for Workington (Mr. Campbell Savours) will seek to move an amendment to introduce a dedicated channel to the experiment. It is technically possible to do so, never mind in October, but now, and it is affordable.

Mr. Brian Wilson (Cunninghame, North) *rose——*

Mr. Gale: I would prefer not to give way to the hon. Gentleman, because, since he is a member of the Select Committee, I am sure that he will seek to catch Mr. Speaker's eye.

The cost of a satellite transponder would be somewhere between £2·5 million and £3·5 million for a year.

Mr. David Shaw (Dover): That is peanuts.

Mr. Gale: My hon. Friend says that that is peanuts and in news media terms it is. On an agency basis—the sort of system by which the newspapers, radio and television buy the Reuters service or the Press Association service—it is peanuts. The maximum cost of £3·5 million a year would be shared not only by the BBC, but every independent company in this country and among cable news network, C-Span, CBS, CBC, Australian Broadcasting and other organisations around the world whom we are told would want that service. Shared among all those organisations the cost, as my hon. Friend suggests, would be peanuts.

Mr. Tony Banks: How do we get it in Newham?

Mr. Gale: I believe that cable news network would want to carry the service on a pan-European basis——

Mr. Banks: I said Newham, not Europe.

Mr. Gale: The hon. Gentleman will forgive me as, for one fleeting moment, I thought that Newham was part of Europe.

The money could be spent on astra transponders that are available now. We would then have not only the unedited televised proceedings of the Chamber but, for the same money, we could have up to 10 sound channels with still pictures with wiped-in inserts of the person speaking. That would enable us to carry, albeit in limited form, not only the live proceedings of the Chamber from, as the Americans say, "gavel to gavel" but the entire live proceedings of up to 10 Committees simultaneously.

The satellite service would satisfy the fears of those, such as our Scottish friends, who are genuinely concerned that their service will be elbowed out of the way. They are worried that when it comes to the crunch, when the deadline comes and it is five minutes to six and there is a major story breaking in the House of Commons, they will not get the line coverage. The satellite feed, however, would provide every regional station with the sort of service that they need. It would provide those that have the Amstrad dish for £150—those who want the full satellite service from the House of Commons—with that coverage.

It is technically possible now and it is affordable. British Aerospace told the Committee—the hon. Member for Holborn and St. Pancras (Mr. Dobson) got this completely round the wrong way and he should

acknowledge that—that it could do the job in a specified time, that it had the technology for the uplink and that it could do so to an astra transponder immediately and probably to its own transponder in three years' time.

There is one additional asset that I believe some hon. Members will find interesting. With the satellite system it is possible to carry instant subtitles for the deaf. That can be done by the kind of machine that the right hon. Member for Stoke-on-Trent, South (Mr. Ashley) uses day to day in the House. The satellite system would use a slightly upgraded version of that machine. Therefore, every deaf person in this country could have an instant transcription of our proceedings and that transcription could be instantly printed on a data basis as an immediate electronic *Hansard* that any person in the country with the dish could call up.

Tonight we have an opportunity to do one of two things: we can genuinely enhance democracy in a way that all those who sought to persuade the House back in February 1988 claim that they want to do or we can offer the country and the media a con trick—the edited highlights and lowlights designed, as I have said publicly, to tart up the "Nine o'clock News" and the "News at Ten", but not much else. I hope that hon. Members on both sides of the House will support the amendment that will be moved by the hon. Member for Workington and I hope that it will be carried. If it is not, I hope that the House will reject the report and that it will tell the Committee to take it back and get it right.

8.27 pm

Mr. Brian Wilson (Cunninghame, North): I regret the tone of the speech of the hon. Member for Thanet, North (Mr. Gale) and particularly his reference to con tricks, as I believe that the proceedings of the Committee during the past year or so have been in a different spirit.

I pay tribute to the Leader of the House for the fair and open manner in which he presided over the workings of the Committee from start to finish. I approached the Committee as a novice in such matters as I had never sat on a Committee where the effort was on attaining consensus rather than emphasising division. I did not know how that could be achieved and I was interested to see how the Committee would work. Every Committee member, with the exception of the hon. Member for Thanet, North, would agree that the Committee worked well and constructively and that the report that was published, while not suiting anyone absolutely, was certainly the honest product of honest endeavour. For that we owe much to the Leader of the House. We also owe him much for the way in which he presented that report tonight.

The central aim of those of us on the Committee who supported the experiment was to attain a consensus that would be acceptable to the House. We were not particularly interested in making gestures or in standing out for points of view that would be patently unacceptable to all the House. We believed that the exercise was far too important for such an approach. For that reason my hon. Friend the Member for Holborn and St. Pancras (Mr. Dobson) and myself were a little disappointed to find ourselves vilified in, of all places, an editorial of *The Guardian*. That editorial told us that we should hang our heads in shame for putting our names to the report. I do not know whether I greatly care for the reputation of my hon. Friend, but I thought that that was a dreadful way for _The Guardian_ to treat its former Scottish football correspondent.

Those of us who worked in that spirit were prepared to accept a compromise. Of course, we knew that it would be easy for us to posture and come back to the House with a terribly liberal and radical report on how the experiment should be conducted. It would have been easy to divide the Committee. Frankly, I would have hung my head in shame if we had tried to play party politics with this and, in the process, lost the experiment. I hope that the fact that we were prepared to accept a consensus and bury our differences means that we have produced a report that will be acceptable to the House.

All the Opposition Members and the great majority of Conservatives on the Committee approached the report with an open mind. There was a school of thought that the proceedings should have been cut short and that the BBC and ITN should have walked in, said what they were going to do and we would get on with it. However, after hearing the evidence of the BBC and ITN, it was not a point of view which I could share. Those of us who instinctively favour service broadcasting were persuaded that their evidence was not good enough and that we should explore other avenues; we began to do that.

I think that everyone on the Committee would agree that technically, editorially and in every other way the Committee's work developed and improved, and new ideas were opened up as a result of what we heard from some of the independent companies which came to speak to us. On the other hand, some of them were total chancers and we were able to separate the sheep from the goats without too much difficulty.

On the Conservative side of the Committee there was, for some time, a heavy lobby on behalf of a large, independent private company. It was to the credit of Conservative Members that they did not simply lie down in front of the blandishments of the heavy lobby from that source. There was a spirit of compromise and consensus on both sides of the Committee—_[Interruption.]_ I shall not name it until after the vote. Both sides of the Committee were prepared to give ground which they could have been expected to hold.

We visited Canada, and I think that everyone who went would agree that it probably would have been better if we had done that at the start, rather than halfway through our deliberations. As a result of that visit virtually everyone agreed that we should aim for a unit of the House as it exists in both the federal Parliament and also the provincial Parliament which we visited in Toronto.

Most of us who visited Canada also preferred the more liberal regime applied in Toronto as opposed to the rigid one in Ottawa. The suggestions in our report lie somewhere between the two points. I agree with my hon. Friend the shadow Leader of the House that we would have preferred a more liberal regime in terms of rules of coverage, but we realised, once again, that if we were going to get the proposals through we would have to give some ground.

I say to those such as the right hon. Member for Shropshire, North (Mr. Biffen), the former Leader of the House, and others who criticised the report because it suggested showing merely head and shoulders that it is not that rigid. It contains the potential for a little experimentation. I believe that as the experiment continues common sense will prevail because the report does not contain the total rigidity which some of the more hysterical leader writers have suggested. Apart from anything else, it is impossible to film nothing more than someone's head and shoulders because there is always something to the left, right, behind or below which will also come out.

Therefore, although we would prefer a more liberal regime, the one proposed is certainly acceptable to me for the purposes of the experiment and, I believe, it will develop according to simple common sense.

I was particularly interested to represent the Scottish dimension and that of the English regions and Wales, to ensure a balance of coverage. The Leader of the House will remember, I certainly well remember, the noise and clamour made from hon. Members on the Nationalist Bench because they were not given membership of the Select Committee. In future, the Nationalist Bench could perhaps be leased out to the public because it is certainly not used by the people who should be sitting on it. I can only assume that the reason for the total absence of the Scottish National party Members tonight is that they are rehearsing for after November, because they will also then be totally absent. I assume that there are no Scottish Tories present because they are rehearsing for after the next general election.

We were concerned to look after the Scottish dimension technically and editorially. For the purposes of the experiment, I would much prefer that the signal was transmitted by satellite so that regional stations around the country could pick up the clean feed and use it for regional and national purposes in Scotland and Wales, where programmes will clearly have a different emphasis from those of the south of England. In the report, we urge the broadcasting companies to do that. We urge them to send the signal around the country by satellite and I hope that our suggestion will be acted upon within the duration of the experiment. We did not, however, feel that we could instruct them to do that or that it should be written into the report, but the message is very clear.

I shall take up the point made by the hon. Member for Thanet, North—and doubtless it will be taken up by my hon. Friend the Member for Workington (Mr. Campbell-Savours)—about the absolute necessity for a dedicated channel. There is nothing in the report to prevent the existence of a dedicated channel if a company wants to take the signal and show it around the country. The amendment before us is a wrecking amendment because the idea that the experiment should collapse because a few thousand people scattered around the country cannot receive the signal on their little dishes is farcical. The idea that it would be a con trick if 100 per cent. of the people watched the House of Commons under the terms of this report but a great advance for democracy if 99 per cent. watched under the terms of the report and 1 per cent. under the terms outlined by the hon. Member for Thanet, North is ludicrous.

This is a wrecking amendment. I am in favour of a dedicated channel, which will come, but it is totally irrelevent to this report and its spirit to insist that a dedicated channel should be included in it. Let us put it to the test: if any station or satellite company wants to include a dedicated channel, it can do so. Quite frankly, if the suggestion of the hon. Member for Thanet, North that there should be 10 dedicated channels, one of the Chamber and nine of Committees, on offer, even _The Sun_ would have difficulty giving away 100,000 dishes so that people could watch them.

Mr. Gale: The hon. Gentleman clearly misunderstood what I said. One satellite transponder will provide enough capacity to cover this Chamber and up to 10 Committees.

Mr. Wilson: I take the hon. Gentleman's point and doubtless my hon. Friend the Member for Workington will elaborate on it.

I support the report in its entirety and will do so in the vote tonight. This is not the end, but the beginning, of a major democratic advance in this country—there is no doubt about that. I can understand why Conservative Members might vote against it, but I cannot for the life of me understand why any Opposition Members would vote against a report which allows the electors to see what is said and done in their name. I cannot understand how anyone who pays lip service to democracy can, in the last stages of the 20th century, deny the electorate the right to see what is said and done in their name. That is the bottom line of the report.

I am not interested in the party advantages that will come out of the experiment because no one can forecast them, and that is not the way in which this matter should be measured. It should be measured as a democratic advance and anyone who fears that is in trouble with his own beliefs and principles.

The proposals in the report, when acted upon, will expose fools, reward wisdom and rubbish morons. They might change the behaviour of the House, but nothing I have seen since I came here suggests that behaviour in the House of Commons is so perfect that it does not need a little bit of change. Let us have in all that is suggested in the report by the time of the Queen's Speech. I am sure that once the cameras are in, they will stay in. Tonight, we are witnessing an important democratic advance with which I am proud to be associated and I congratulate the Leader of the House on the way in which he has led it.

Several Hon. Members rose——

Mr. Speaker: Order. May I again appeal for short contributions of five or six minutes from each hon. Member? That would enable me to call everyone who wants to speak.

8.39 pm

Mr. Roger Sims (Chislehurst): I wholeheartedly support televising the proceedings of the House for the reason given by the hon. Member for Cunninghame, North (Mr. Wilson). The House of Commons is the heart of our parliamentary democracy. It may be a system that we sometimes take for granted, but perhaps events elsewhere in the world in the past two or three weeks will make us value it more.

If the Chamber is the heart of our parliamentary democracy, it is surely important that people should see what goes on in it. There is clearly a demand that they should. We all know how many requests we receive for people to get tickets to sit in the Strangers' Gallery. Every day a queue of people waits outside to come in. With television, all our constituents will have a chance to follow our proceedings.

I favour televising our proceedings, but they should stay as they are now. We should not change our procedures to accommodate television cameras. In that respect, I agree with the report of the Procedure Committee, on which I served. The House will recall that we agreed in principle to an experiment in February 1988

and the Select Committee was set up the following month. It has not produced its recommendations precipitately and there has been some criticism of the time it has taken. The Select Committee has gone into it in great detail and is to be congratulated on its thoroughness.

I have noted with interest the arguments in favour of a dedicated channel, which would be unedited, but I have no great enthusiasm for it—although I am not against the idea. Surely only a very small audience will want to watch continuous televising of the House. Most people will see what goes on here on news programmes and in programmes about Parliament. There is also the danger, with a dedicated channel, that word will get around that there is a sort of peak viewing time during which Members will jostle for position to make speeches, and that would certainly alter the character of our debates.

Of course, editing always takes place. We are bound to be worried about it, but the press and radio have always done it. We have often read reports in the newspapers which refer to every speech in a debate except the one that we made ourselves. We have often listened to "Today in Parliament" and heard about many speeches, after which the announcer informs us that three other Members also spoke, one of whom happens to be yours truly. Nevertheless, we have to live with editing.

I want to emphasise a point that others have already made about paragraph 59 and to express the hope that help will be given with televising for the deaf, who constitute a large minority of the population. There are in this country almost 4 million people who are hard of hearing and 50,000 who are born profoundly deaf. In recent years great advances have been made in the use of subtitles and sign language on television. Of course there will be difficulties about incorporating them into a television service, but they are not insuperable. I regret that the report merely expresses the hope that every effort will be made to meet the needs of the deaf. I want a stronger commitment. This is a wonderful opportunity to widen the world for deaf people and it should not be missed.

I also support the references to the televising of Standing and Select Committees. No doubt the two 15-minute Prime Minister's questions sessions will be fully televised each week, but they are not representative of Parliament. I should have liked some of my constituents to see the work of the Standing Committee on the Children Bill in recent weeks. In that Committee, on which I served, they would have seen Members of all parties working hard and well together to produce legislation on an important and sensitive area. It was Parliament at its best, and it is to be hoped that that is the sort of proceeding that the television cameras will cover—although I regret that, for most of the Committee's proceedings, not a soul was to be seen in the press seats.

As for the rules of coverage, paragraph 5 states:
"We would welcome a degree of flexibility"
in the experiment. In paragraph 37 a statement of objectives is given, to which my right hon. Friend the Leader of the House has referred:
"The director should seek . . . to give a full, balanced, fair and accurate account of proceedings".
Has the Committee got it right to ensure that that will be done? Do its proposals incorporate the degree of flexibility to which it refers? We do not formally recognise that we have a public Gallery or that there is anyone in it; but we know that, except in the small hours, we are not alone. Surely the aim should be to allow the television viewer to

see what a person who is physically present would usually see. As my right hon. Friend said, that would not be exactly possible because the person in the Gallery can look around the Chamber, whereas the viewer will see only what the camera shows—but that is the whole point: we are discussing where the camera should be looking.

Because this is a public forum, we must recognise that there will be a temptation for people to demonstrate occasionally because they will get publicity by so doing. Television cameras will create an even greater temptation. The Committee rightly proposes restrictions, but it is also important that our constituents should be able to see what is going on here and, as far as possible, get the feel of the place and absorb the atmosphere in which debates take place.

In addition to what are described as restrictions in paragraph 38 there are specific guidelines in paragraph 39. Perhaps there is a subtle difference between them, but the directors would clearly be well advised to comply with the so-called guidelines.

Let us consider for a moment what the effect on this debate would be if it were being televised. According to the standard format, my head and shoulders would be shown as I was speaking—and nothing else. I do not profess to be the most photogenic Member of the House——

Mrs. Edwina Currie (Derbyshire, South): Oh yes you are.

Mr. Sims: It is kind of my hon. Friend, of all people, to say so. However, even if I were, 10 minutes of head and shoulders of any one person would not provide the most riveting viewing and would not be the best way of assessing that person's contribution.

What about body language? In the course of making a speech most of us use our hands, as I am unself-consciously doing from time to time. I sometimes wonder whether some of our colleagues, such as my hon. Friend the Member for Harlow (Mr. Hayes), could be rendered mute by having their hands tied behind their backs. It is important that viewers should see whether Members are using notes and to what extent they are receiving the attention of the House. Are they addressing a packed House, hanging on their every word, or are just the Member and Mr. Speaker present? Anyone in the Gallery can see that, but the television viewer, under these restrictions, will not.

What about the effect of a Member's remarks? Even as I have been speaking some of my hon. Friends have been indicating assent, or otherwise, to my remarks, and that is all part of the debate. But under these restrictions the viewer will not be able to see that. I suggest that just as it is possible to allow a director complete freedom and the television cameras enough rope with which to hang themselves—so the experiment would fail—it is also possible to be so restrictive that the experiment will be judged to have failed. I am not sure that the Committee has got the balance entirely right between complete freedom and undue restriction. My right hon. Friend the Leader of the House has said that in Committee there were differences of view on that point. Therefore, it is right that the House should be given the opportunity to decide for itself on this point.

I hope that the House will support the report, but I invite it to omit the guidelines which confine shots to the head and shoulders of the Member who is speaking and preclude panning shots along the Benches.

8.51 pm

Mr. D. N. Campbell-Savours (Workington): Over 12 months ago, I and other hon. Members were invited by Granada Television to the mock Commons studio in Manchester to debate the televising of Parliament. During those proceedings, I spoke against edited excerpts and in favour of a dedicated channel. I returned to my constituency after the programme had been transmitted and was confronted by people who said that I was opposed to the televising of Parliament. In so far as my comments had been edited, that served to confirm my reservation about the whole question of the editing of parliamentary proceedings. That is why I support a dedicated channel.

I want what Nye Bevan described in his last great speech in 1959, the re-establishment of intelligent communication between the House of Commons and the electorate as a whole. I might add that I do not want to see trivia. I have tabled three amendments, the first of which would block all transmissions from the Chamber apart from those on a dedicated channel. That amendment was not selected. My second amendment would permit edited excerpts to run concurrently with a dedicated channel over an experimental period. The dedicated channel was considered by the Committee and supported. The Committee report says:

"We believe that continuous coverage of the House's proceedings on a dedicated channel is a highly desirable objective in the public interest. The fact that we have not felt able to make any specific recommendations on the subject in this Report has nothing to do with the merits of the idea itself, which we strongly support; it stems from practical considerations related to the timing and nature of the experiment."

British Aerospace and British Satellite Broadcasting gave evidence to the Committee. However, the Committee rejected their case and the proposals that they put forward for a dedicated channel. The problem, especially in the case of the submission by British Aerospace, was that it was based on funding the scheme from terrestrial broadcasting income and the use by the consumer of a dish costing more than £500 and a dish for professional purposes that costs £5,000.

British Aerospace was never asked a most important question. It was never asked whether it could transmit on a dedicated channel proceedings of the House to be received on a £150 to £200 Amstrad dish which is currently sold by Comet and Dixon's and a host of other retailers across the United Kingdom for receiving Sky television. The price of that dish is likely to fall and its use could bypass completely the terrestrial broadcasters because programmes could be transmitted straight from Westminster and received in people's homes on a cheap dish.

Mr. Dobson: Does my hon. Friend accept that even if his proposition went through the current viewing figures for Sky television are such that there are probably more people in the Strangers' Gallery watching this debate than would see it if his proposition were accepted?

Mr. Campbell-Savours: I can assure my hon. Friend that more people watch Sky television than are in the

[*Mr. Campbell-Savours*]

Gallery for the debate, and that dishes are being sold. My amendment would provide the kind of support that is needed.

As I say, the question that I have mentioned was never put to British Aerospace. I contacted the company today and it said:

"British Aerospace Telecommunications confirms that it could provide satellite and uplink facilities for the televising of Parliament using the ECS . . . low power satellite (needing a 1·2-1·5 m receiving dish) for about £1 million pa. Based on a usage of 32 week year, 37·5 hour week"—

that is equivalent to our proceedings in their entirety apart from debates that take place after 10 pm—

"which is equivalent to £833 per hour. Signals could be received on dishes costing about £500 for this service."

I am not putting forward that proposition. The letter continues:

"If smaller receiving dishes like those used for ASTRA are the requirement then we could, in principle and subject to availability, equally well operate to that satellite from our earthstation here at Stevenage. However, the satellite transponder charges for that space segment"—

which is four times the power of the transponder that I referred to—

"are much greater and the BAe Telecommunications inclusive price for the same number of hours would be about £4m pa. This is equivalent to £3,330 per hour. It is understood that receivers from ASTRA are expected to cost less than £200 and many predict that within 12 months the price could fall to about £100."

Some people would argue that my proposition would delay implementation of the report. I went back to British Aerospace for another letter which I received today. It says:

"BAe Telecommunications confirms that it has reserved capacity on the European Communications Satellite for at least the following three years and therefore could guarantee coverage of Parliamentary proceedings from the October date which you identified in our telephone conversation.

I would also comment that the figures contained in our earlier letter from David Gregory"—

I understand that Mr. Gregory is here for the debate—

"referring to prices and availability for the use of the Astra Satellite"—

that is the Sky television £150 dish—

"were based on telephone conversations of today's date."

I then asked for a further qualification and this also arrived today. It says:

"Further to Mr. Gregory's letter to you, I can confirm that BAeTel has both the necessary ground transmission equipment and the capacity reserved on Eutelsat satellites for the next three years and as such can certainly transmit parliamentary proceedings from October this year. We can also confirm from a telephone conversation today that adequate capacity is also available on the Astra satellite for a similar period."

I read that into the record to show that British Aerospace can provide the facility from October this year if Parliament seeks to resolve the matter in that way.

Mr. Dobson: Will my hon. Friend give way?

Mr. Campbell-Savours: I am sorry, but I will not. I have already given way to my hon. Friend once, and it is now nearly 9 o'clock. I have an obligation to others who want to speak after me.

The examination of British Aerospace's option was based on the reaction of the broadcasters, who were fearful of the expenditure implications. They never considered direct broadcasting on cheap dishes running concurrently with the Committee's principal proposals. In other words,

they did not consider direct broadcasting dishes. They relied on discussion about terrestrial broadcasting being part of the process.

I shall deal now with the cost. We have two options —£1 million for a £500 dish or £4 million for £150 reduced-in-price Amstrad dishes, plus £200,000 for a sending earthstation near Westminster. There are four options for funding that. First, there is public subscription, which some hon. Members will reject. Secondly, there is the possibility of advertising, which other hon. Members will reject. Thirdly, we have specialist consumers, a number of whom were identified by British Aerospace in a memorandum to the Committee, which said:

"there is a market throughout the UK for information on the deliberations of Government in the form of continuous sound, television and text by businesses, local press, educational establishments and private citizens. The second group of users is important as a way of monitoring publicly the editorial decisions of the first."

We can also offer a service of electronic *Hansard,* and most town halls would want transmission and would pay for it. The public library system could equally subscribe, and I am also told that it is possible that the satellite companies, during this experimental period, might offer a concessionary tariff, if only with a view to getting the business long term.

Mr. Cryer: Will my hon. Friend give way?

Mr. Campbell-Savours: I am sorry, but it is 9 o'clock and I have given way once. Other people wish to speak in the debate.

At the end of the experimental period, we could either throw out the lot—something that some want to do—or we could thrown out either the dedicated channel or what I call edited excerpt television. If we were to throw out the second, should we proceed in the way that I suggest, the effect would be to increase the number of satellite dish sales. I am not saying that that is necessarily a matter that Parliament should take into account, but it would be a factor.

The fourth and final route that we may go down into the future is that of fibre optics. Along with others, British Telecom is advocating the principle of a fibre-optic network throughout the United Kingdom, on telephone lines. The cables will be capable of transmitting a television picture. In the longer term, those who do not take this service on a dish could take it on a fibre-optic cable.

9.2 pm

Sir Anthony Grant (Cambridgeshire, South-West): I entirely agree with what the hon. Member for Workington (Mr. Campbell-Savours) said, and I shall refer to that later. However, first I endorse what the hon. Member for Cunninghame, North (Mr. Wilson) said about the work of the Committee, which was one of the most pleasant and happy Select Committees on which I have served. The work was rather harder and took rather longer than I had anticipated. I pay tribute, as he did, to the remarkable leadership of my right hon. Friend the Leader of the House and to the amiability and good humour of the hon. Member for Holborn and St. Pancras (Mr. Dobson), the shadow Leader of the House, who also contributed to the work of the Committee. We were a diverse group, politically and in our views, and our discussions were vigorous but never rancorous.

Nothing that I have heard or seen since then has relieved the anxieties that I had when I voted in February 1988 against televising the House. I still retain anxieties about several points. The prime one, and the reason why I served on the Committee, concerns the rights of Back Benchers, which I wish to ensure are not further eroded. Every time we have had a so-called improvement in communications, or even in procedure, in Parliament, it has served to enhance the status and power of the Front Bench, no matter which party is in power. By definition, it has tended to diminish the influence of Back-Bench Members. There is a danger that television will accentuate this.

I put that point to a former Speaker and the present Speaker of the Canadian Parliament and they confirmed that such an outcome was a danger and had, to some extent, happened in the Canadian Parliament. Although the procedure there is different, Governments of all parties should be restrained, so far as possible, from hogging the Floor. The Select Committee on Procedure, which is well chaired by my hon. Friend the Member for Honiton (Sir P. Emery), should apply its mind to the problem, as no doubt it will in the near future.

I stress the importance of media people attending to regional coverage, which will be the only way that Back Benchers will be able to circumvent the domination of Front-Bench spokesmen. That is tremendously important if Back Benchers are not to disappear into the background in the presence of the grandees of the Front Benches.

My second concern is the quality of debate. We all know that apart from cross-party debates such as this or debates about sex, which are always very exciting, debate has been moving inexorably away from the Chamber. I fear that television will accelerate that movement. We shall, as I saw in the Canadian Parliament, cease to address each other and, increasingly, speak to the public outside, rather like party political broadcasts or horrible things like that. That was the experience in Canada, and unless we are careful the Chamber could ultimately become little more than show business, in which case we may as well hand over the presentation of Parliament straight away to actors and comedians and get on with the real discussion elsewhere. However, that is not why Parliament was formed and developed for many centuries.

Some hon. Members have expressed their concern about misbehaviour, but I feel that that worry has been exaggerated. Parliaments come and go, but exhibitionists will always be with us. Nevertheless, we shall have to watch that carefully. I do not believe that hon. Members will become much worse, but it is an illusion to suppose that suddenly their behaviour will be much better. In the sporting world, it was always said, "When the television cameras are looking on no one will be able to misbehave." The same argument has been advanced for Parliament. In truth, far from having curbed misconduct in sport, television has accentuated it. All the tomfoolery of running on to the pitch seems to be a feature of our modern sporting fields now that the cameras are on them.

I entirely understand the point made by my hon. Friend the Member for Chislehurst (Mr. Sims), whom I greatly respect. If everyone were as gentlemanly as my hon. Friend, there would be no need for any rules or laws, but they are not, either in this place or in the reporting and journalism world. My answer to my hon. Friend is that, yes, we hope to be able to liberalise and have wider coverage than we have suggested in the report, but I

always believe that it is far better to start tough and then see whether one can relax. It usually proves impossible to do it the other way round. It does not matter whether one is captaining a team or commanding a regiment, one should start tough and relax later.

Mr. Bruce Grocott (The Wrekin): Will the hon. Gentleman confirm that in Canada the rules that started tough have remained so for more than a decade?

Sir Anthony Grant: The hon. Gentleman is right about the federal Parliament, but that does not apply in the provincial Parliaments. I was not particularly impressed by that, but I hope that we can learn from Canada's experience and that in due course we will move more in the direction of the Toronto legislature than the federal Parliament in Ottawa.

I support the Committee's report in broad principle. As my right hon. Friend the Leader of the House said, it is a package. Predictably, it has been criticised by television people, who have a vested interest, and we must sustain their displeasure with fortitude. They are mostly intelligent and responsible people, and I pay tribute to them for the dedicated and interesting way in which they gave evidence to the Committee.

There was a time when it was said that Parliament was dominated by lawyers, but that no longer applies. Nowadays it tends to be dominated by journalists and media folk, and it is equally undesirable. It is essential, and the wish of an overwhelming number of Members, to keep control of the experiment ourselves and to ensure that the cameras show a broader view of Parliament than just the Chamber and the pantomime of Prime Minister's questions twice a week, which is so beloved of the BBC.

I agree with the hon. Member for Workington in his proposals for a dedicated channel, a gavel-to-gavel electronic *Hansard* or whatever it is. I should have liked such a system for radio. Many hon. Members who fear, as I do, the dangers of misleading or mischievous editing or selection in the hands of unaccountable people should support the amendment if, as the hon. Gentleman persuades me, it is a practical proposition.

The hon. Member for Workington need not worry about being ragged by his hon. Friends about fewer people in the Strangers' Gallery watching the proceedings. Not many people read *Hansard*, but it is available to them. That is the key point. I shall support the amendment. If it is lost, I shall support the report as a workmanlike and reasonable compromise in all the circumstances. I hope that we will not lose sight of the idea of a dedicated channel, which is the way forward.

Several Hon. Members *rose*——

Mr. Speaker: Order. I again appeal for five-minute speeches, which will enable me to call every hon. Member who wishes to speak.

9.10 pm

Mr. Austin Mitchell (Great Grimsby): The hon. Member for Cambridgeshire, South-West (Sir A. Grant) may like to categorise me as a journalist and media person, but in this matter I speak as a Member of the House of Commons who is concerned about the importance of this institution and this Chamber. It seems to me, as a Member of the House who is concerned with its interests, that the House is in danger of becoming an irrelevant, unimportant

[*Mr. Austin Mitchell*]

backwater unless we communicate on television with the people who now rely on television for news and information on current affairs.

Our role is not to control the Executive—we can do that only if it is afraid that we can throw it out. That function has passed from here to the people. Our role is not even to influence each other. In this Chamber we are developing and testing the arguments and putting to the people the cases for and against what the Government are doing as the raw materials on which, at the end of four or five years, they will decide whether to keep or throw the Government out. Our essential job is public education—putting the arguments before the people. We are, therefore, irrelevant and the job is incompetently done unless we reach the people through that medium. That is the essential argument for televising Parliament.

That has always been the case, and it is the case now. It is not so much that the people want Parliament televised, although 60 per cent. do, and it is not so much that they have a right to it, although they do. It is that we cannot do our job without televising Parliament.

In that light, I am not entirely happy with the Committee's report. It took far too long for the report to be produced—18 months was far too long. The report is too cautious because it is too deferential to our egos, susceptibilities and tendernesses and it attaches too little importance to the public's wishes. It is irrelevant, however, to go into that now, because the report has been agreed. Its recommendations will be developed in the light of experience. Indeed, because of the technical problems of covering the most difficult studio in the world and because of the quick interchange of debate, the recommendations will probably have to change anyway.

In any case, if the report had recommended that the speech of every Member should be prefaced by a herald from the royal chorus of trumpeters in the Gallery, that little cherubim and seraphim should be superimposed on the picture round every Member's head and that sound and applause should be dubbed in, I would have accepted that, too, because it is so important to get across the principle that the proceedings of this institution should be covered by the television cameras. If it gets the cameras in, I would accept it. That is the basis on which I accept the report.

The opposition to the report and to televising is based only on fear—fear of ourselves, of the medium and of the public outside. It is interesting that opponents of televising have moved their ground. They no longer oppose it in principle but are now trying to use other arguments, saying that we should have televising only if there is a dedicated channel and that it should be done liberally. Opposition to the principle is now concealed by other motives.

On amendment (c), I must say that I am an enthusiatic and strong supporter of a dedicated television channel, covering Parliament full time. That is essential. Indeed, I would go further and say that it is essential in this country to have a channel such as C-SPAN in the United States, which carries public affairs generally, so that the political nation can talk to the political nation. Such a channel would cover not only Parliament—because we are no longer the only forum for discussion—but the parties, the speeches, the press conferences, the pressure groups and the university seminars. I should like to see all that on television and it could be covered via satellite and via cable.

However, it is wrong to make a dedicated channel a sine qua non, which my hon. Friend the Member for Workington (Mr. Campbell-Savours) has done, in effect. It is wrong to say that we will not have the report unless we have full-time, dedicated coverage. Such coverage will come. Getting Parliament on television will strengthen the case for it. People will want to put political issues in context and there is a demand for full-time coverage, which will be voiced only when Parliament is shown on the other terrestrial channels. Yet it is wrong to make a dedicated channel a condition of the coverage.

The report is too cautious and too late. We are 10 years behind most advanced countries, five years behind the other place, which has benefited enormously from coverage on television, and one year behind any reasonable timetable in this place. However, with all its problems, with all its reservations and with all its cautiousness, the report enshrines the vital principle of bringing to the people, through the medium on which they rely for their news and information about current affairs, what is being done by their representatives in their name and on the issues that affect their lives. That is the principle which we must espouse.

As hon. Member for Great Grimsby, where people cannot drop in and out of the Chamber, even with the difficulties that obtain for people here, I believe that we need to bring Parliament to everyone throughout the country. This is an historic opportunity and an historic moment for the House. Let us seize that opportunity.

9.16 pm

Sir John Stokes (Halesowen and Stourbridge): I have spoken more on this subject than on any other subject I can remember. I am not a member of the communications industry, but just an ordinary Englishman. We must be careful not to think that we all spend all day every day looking at that awful box. It is very harmful to the nation, its manners and its morals. The hon. Member for Roxburgh and Berwickshire (Mr. Kirkwood) said that the televising of our proceedings would change our procedures. That means, I suppose, that Question Time would become everyone else's high tea time. I do not want that to happen. I want our procedures to remain as they are. I want the House to remain what it is because I love this place. It has a special character which is quite unlike that of all the other places that have been televised, which are so terribly boring that nobody watches them. This place is special and precious and we must safeguard it.

I have always felt that, in general, the coming of the television industry has been thoroughly harmful rather than beneficial to the nation. When television covers current affairs, it tends to distort, to trivialise and to sensationalise. That is why I oppose the coming of television to this House and why I find it hard to accept the report, good as it no doubt is and hard as the Committee worked. The main danger is that television is a branch of the showbiz industry and it is not suited to the quite different business that we conduct here. That is why we must have every possible safeguard built into the experiment.

I noted that the clever Mr. Bernard Levin wrote a particularly stupid article in *The Times* in which he implied that by controlling the broadcasting we were trying to make ourselves look like plaster saints. We are not. We are trying to stop the television editors and producers making us look like a non-stop variety show.

We must never forget that the public have no interest in whether the House is televised. In my 19 years here, representing about 80,000 of the best people in England, not one has ever written to me saying, "You must televise your proceedings." All the demand for televising that has been talked about is absolute rubbish. Our constituents want to be able to send good men here, men whom they can trust. They will be all right then. Let us remember that in the greatest days of this country, not only was there no television but there was no reporting, and never has this country been better governed.

However, now we are told that we can learn some lessons from the televising of the proceedings in the other place, which I still so greatly admire, despite the new life peers. Television in the other place, originally much heralded, was initially broadcast daily, first at a reasonable hour, then at a late hour. Now the proceedings are broadcast only weekly. Then it will be monthly and eventually it will vanish altogether. Let us remember also that their Lordships have no constituents and that they are not subjected to the lobbying to which we are subjected.

We are in danger of making ourselves self-important and ridiculous. Hon. Members may think that the debate will be the talk of the pubs. Well, go to the pub tomorrow —not you, Mr. Speaker—and you will not hear the subject mentioned. It is of interest only to people in the media, not to most ordinary people, who are much more interested in cricket scores and good things like that. We must have a sense of proportion. Surely the Labour party, which purports to represent the ordinary man, should hold such views just as much as the Tory party. I am surprised that it does not.

I fear that the televising of our proceedings would utterly ruin the character of this great and famous Chamber, the most famous debating chamber in the world. I very much hope that this nonsense is thrown out.

9.21 pm

Mr. Nigel Spearing (Newham, South): I have some sympathy with some of the fears expressed by the hon. Member for Halesowen and Stourbridge (Sir J. Stokes), but the House has taken a decision and unless people disagree with that decision—their moral right to do so is questionable—we shall have an experiment. Therefore, it should be as good as we can make it.

I agree with the hon. Member for Halesowen and Stourbridge, and the many other hon. Members who feel concern about this, that the perception of our constituents about the job of a Member of Parliament is that we come into the Chamber, sit in serried ranks and speak or not speak as the case may be. We all know that the job of Parliament and of parliamentarians is about much more than either being in here or in Committee, but we cannot get that across to our constituents. Sound radio tended to reinforce that wrong perception. Many people are concerned that that perception will be still more heightened by the way in which edited excerpts and highlights, emphasising the Front Benches, will be used during television news programmes and I believe that that is probably what will happen. The danger of that is

comparable to hearing a Beethoven symphony played on the timpani and the trumpet. We must do something in the experiment to counteract that.

Some people have said that "Today in Parliament" is a good programme and it is perhaps the best of the BBC's efforts. However, I wrote to the editors of the programme many years ago when I first became a Member of the House and asked why they did not mention the Adjournment debates, saying, "Surely people are interested in knowing that this cottage hospital or that bypass has been discussed." I said that the debate need not be mentioned in detail but that the fact that an hon. Member had raised a matter should be referred to. The editors said, "No, it will be of concern to only a small number of people. That is not news."

What we do here may not be newsworthy but it is important. If, as my hon. Friend the Member for Great Grimsby (Mr. Mitchell) has said, this is the biggest television studio in the world, it will be used by the media as a new source of raw material. This place is much more important than that. It should not be seen simply as a new source of visual news material. This place is the centre of the democratic operations of our nation and democracy today is on the march. We know that a great deal of what we do here today was developed in the 1680s and 1690s and that many things happened across the Channel and in North America in the 1780s and the 1790s.

We see events from all around the world on television. We see and hear about what is happening to the democratic process in Poland, Moscow and in Tiananmen square. Poland and perhaps even South Africa may be branching out towards democracy. We are not talking about just another show or more raw material for the broadcasters. We are talking about something that should be put in its worldwide context. We are the guardians of a procedure that I believe to be unique.

On Friday 9 June *The Independent* carried a translation of what one young man had written on the hoardings in Tiananmen square:

"So we appeal to the Chinese: Get rid of the tradition of pure ideology-making, of sloganising, of objectifying. These are empty democracy. They must start the process of actual operation, of practical procedures, of turning a democracy movement centred on the enlightenment of thought into that of an actual operation. They must start with the details."

The procedures of the House are practical examples of democracy in action. Our democracy may not be perfect, but at least it is in operation and, to some extent, we are pioneers. Anything that could possibly damage our proceedings must be viewed with concern.

My hon. Friend the Member for Great Grimsby is right that, unless the amendment tabled by my hon. Friend the Member for Workington (Mr. Campbell-Savours) is accepted, it will be the producers and editors who press the button and choose what the public see. It will be the executives who choose the producers, the directors of television firms who choose the executives and those who own the firms who choose the directors.

I believe that the condition of having a dedicated channel, if that is possible, as I understand it, is an important one. It would allow people who wanted to see part of an Adjournment debate to do so. A debate could be relayed to a town hall, for example. It would allow people to see their Parliament. Tonight, we are in a position to decide that all the people should be able to see

[*Mr. Nigel Spearing*]

all the time all that is said and done in their name in their Parliament. That would be a very important democratic safeguard.

I hope that my hon. Friend's amendment will be accepted, because there can hardly be a case against it. But even if it is not, I hope that the Committee will proceed along similar lines. Unless it does, the perception of this place and the way in which it works—the democratic methods that we have developed—may be placed in jeopardy. I urge the House to support my hon. Friend's amendment and the proceedings of the House as we know them and to make them open to the whole public all the time.

9.28 pm

Mrs. Edwina Currie (Derbyshire, South): I support the report and I shall vote for the motion in the name of my right hon. Friend the Leader of the House. I am delighted to note that, although so many hon. Members are busy with European elections and by-elections and even though it is Monday, we have quite a good turnout. I hope that we shall make progress tonight. I think that we shall be making history tonight and we shall remember that with pleasure in the years to come.

Let me offer a word of praise for the Committee's efforts. The press coverage of the Committee's report was not good preparation for this debate. Many of the leader writers in national newspapers hooted with laughter and cast derision on what it said. As the Opposition Front Bench spokesman ruefully admitted, the press mainly poked fun at the Opposition, and called them

"denizens of London's clubland queruling lest some unauthorised person should blow his nose in the billiards room."

That strikes me as a pretty fair description of one or two Opposition Members.

The Committee's report, however, was not like the representations of it in the press. Some of it could only have been written by a Committee. I read with amusement paragraph 21 which says:

"In addition to our proposals for House representation on the board of House of Commons Broadcasting Unit Ltd., we recommend the appointment of an Officer of the House to act as the Supervisor of Broadcasting. The Supervisor should report to a monitoring Select Committee."

That could only have been written by a Committee; what busy bees they are going to be. That sort of tone is a bit of a pity and it demonstrates some of the compromises that the Committee had to reach.

I take the point made by my right hon. Friend the Leader of the House that this is an experiment. We should go along with it and make our decision when it is over. I do not accept the proposals put forward by my hon. Friend the Member for Thanet, North (Mr. Gale). I listened carefully to his description of the technical possibilities, but he was beginning to put me off. He suggested that we might have access to 10 Select Committees simultaneously. That does not attract me, as I have had considerable difficulties with one Select Committee. I hope that my hon. Friend will understand if I demur a little at the way that he put his point.

In general, I am impressed. It is clear that a great deal of work has gone into the report. I listened to what my right hon. Friend the Member for Shropshire, North (Mr. Biffen) said about the proposal to restrict the view to head

and shoulders, which was also mentioned by my hon. Friend the Member for Chislehurst (Mr. Sims). I think it a little unfortunate to dub that as merely shampoo politics. It is a pity that the hon. Member for Great Grimsby (Mr. Mitchell) has left the Chamber—probably for a television interview—because if such shampoo politics were to encourage him to have a haircut, that might be an advantage. What is the problem? Why do right hon. and hon. Members on both sides of the House feel so concerned? I look at the hon. Member for Holborn and St. Pancras (Mr. Dobson) and bear in mind that on television we all look about a stone heavier, as he well knows. I wonder whether he is worried that constituents might be a little concerned about ample girths or that on some occasions hon. Members are not dressed as sartorially as they might want. My right hon. Friend the Leader of the House, my hon. Friend the Member for Wirral, West (Mr. Hunt)—who served on the Committee—and other right hon. and hon. Members, especially on the Conservative Benches, should be perfectly satisfied with the notion that they might be photographed from the neck down as well as from the neck up. I note that the real concern of the Committee is that it does not want close-ups, which I do not understand, but it is an experiment and we should proceed with it.

I have listened carefully to the debate and I am glad to have this opportunity to participate in it. I gained a slight impression from the Committee's report and from many Opposition Members that the House produces something —a debate, procedure or an activity—and that someone wants to interfere with it and take it from us. Paragraph 11(i) refers to consumers being the broadcasting companies whereas paragraph 37 refers to viewers. On the other hand, my right hon. Friend the Leader of the House implied that the broadcasters are the producers and that the House, in purchasing a sort of electronic *Hansard,* will be the customer. Both those approaches are fundamentally flawed because they show no awareness of the fact that the consumers are the viewers, and that the viewers are the voters. They put us here and they are puzzled why we keep them out. They do not understand what we are debating tonight—53 years after the first television broadcast in Britain; they cannot understand why we are so afeared of it.

That point was put extremely well by Robert Harris in a recent article in *The Sunday Times.* He said:

"What kind of timid and enfeebled nation have we become that we cannot be allowed to see our own legislature at work in all its noise and colour, its inefficiencies and longueurs?. . . who exactly is protecting whom. Nobody seriously believes that it is the electorate which has to be shielded from the unsavoury sight of the Commons"—

even the hon. Member for Holborn and St. Pancras in full spate.

"Quite the reverse. It is the Commons which has decided that it wants protection from the prying eyes of the public. Thus is democracy . . . stood on its head."

All it leads to is the impression outside this place that we have something to hide—not that broadcasters or viewers cannot be trusted, but that we flinch at public reaction. That is nonsense.

Mr. Richard Tracey (Surbiton) *rose*—

Mrs. Currie: I have been asked to be brief, and I shall honour that.

I shall vote for my right hon. Friend's motion because I recognise the work that has been done and because the report makes sensible suggestions. Most of all, I will vote for the report because it will get the cameras in here, and it is about time. The people will then judge, and whichever way they judge, I will be content.

9.34 pm

Mr. Tony Banks (Newham, North-West): If for no other reason, I compliment the hon. Member for Derbyshire, South (Mrs. Currie) on her choice of colours this evening; they will look very good on television. The thought of her coming at the public on 10 different channels makes even the strongest hon. Member baulk.

I owe the Leader of the House an apology. I am prepared to give him that apology this evening. The advent of the report has taken away my favourite business question. I thought that the right hon. Gentleman was dragging his feet. I thought that the report was rather like the holy grail—everyone had heard of it, but no one knew where it was. At least the report is here, but I am disappointed that it is timid. There is not the scope that I would have expected the Select Committee to come up with. I do not like the commercialism in it—the idea of setting up a limited company. I know that that might be paying lip service to the economic philosophy of the present Government, and of the Prime Minister in particular, but I do not think that it suits the House of Commons. It could even be the thin end of the sponsorship wedge. Before long, we will end up as the John Player Parliament, with Mr. Speaker's wig being sponsored by Vidal Sassoon and the hon. Member for Littleborough and Saddleworth (Mr. Dickens) being sponsored by Harrods' food hall. I do not think that we want that.

I will support the amendment in the name of my hon. Friend the Member for Workington (Mr. Campbell-Savours), although I suspect his motives. I know how he feels about broadcasting and the televising of Parliament. A dedicated channel is wanted. It will answer all our doubts and fears. It would mean that there would be no intermediary and no filter. I do not consider that we have been well served by the Press Gallery. I would like to see the director being able to aim the cameras towards the Press Gallery so that members of the public could see just how few members of the press are here, yet they manage to write so much, and so much that is incorrect, about what we say.

I do not know why *The Sun* bothers to have someone in the Parliamentary Lobby. For the life of me, if *The Sun* can have someone in the Parliamentary Lobby, so should the *Exchange and Mart, Penthouse* and, quite frankly, *Beano* and *Dandy* as well. I do not want people of that sort interposing between what goes on here and the public. That is why a dedicated channel is absolutely crucial. We should not be looking around for someone to pay for it. We should do it in the interests of democracy. We should say that democracy is beyond price in the market place and that, therefore, Parliament is prepared to put up the necessary funds.

In conclusion, I ask the Leader of the House one question. If the amendment in the name of my hon. Friend the Member for Workington is passed, will the right hon. Gentleman advise the House to support the amended substantive motion? Quite frankly, if I thought that, by supporting my hon. Friend's amendment, we were likely to lose even that which we have, clearly I will opt for the

smaller and look later for the larger, extended, dedicated channel which I know would find support on both sides of the House.

9.38 pm

Mr. Robin Maxwell-Hyslop (Tiverton): When my right hon. Friend used the phrase "the important thing is", referring to Committees, I hoped that he was going to say, "The important thing is that the experiment being conducted should not interfere with the work of the Select Committee." I have forgotten what it was that he said was important, but it was not the most important thing of the lot. Quite a number of hon. Members have said that the epicentre of effective action has moved out of the Chamber. That is certainly so. It is the Select Committees which, by being able to focus sustained questioning on witnesses, are able to get information in a way that the one question only on the Floor of the House at Question Time never can.

If questioning is to be focused and sustained in Select Committee, it is absolutely essential that every member of the Committee has a full view of the witnesses who are being examined and that the lighting is not such as to impede the Committee in its work. We could very easily achieve a situation where we look like the Toton Macoute in Haiti, where more and more Members are wearing dark glasses. Although those who recommended televising Parliament before the crucial vote never stopped assuring us that the cameras today needed no additional lighting to what we already have, having got the vote, they then assure us that there is no truth in that whatever and that greatly increased levels of lighting are needed. That, I think, was a bit of sleight of hand that the House did not deserve.

I am particularly concerned about the effect of these proposals on Select Committees, even more than the effect on the Chamber. The important thing is that the advent of television will put the public in the position that they would have been if they could have been in the Gallery or in a Select Committee meeting—it should not alter what they are seeing. That is the criterion by which we should judge the success or failure of this experiment.

The lighting must be controlled. The cameras in Select Committee must not interfere with the process of examining witnesses. If they do, the Chairman of the Select Committee must have power to order them to cease doing whatever they are doing that is breaking the focus and the sustained effect of the questioning.

I shall support the amendment of the hon. Member for Workington (Mr. Campbell-Savours), because I think it is a very valuable thing indeed that, just as nobody censors what those in the Gallery see and nobody censors what is seen in public sittings of Select Committees, the programme going out continuously will not be chopped about to the convenience of somebody other than the viewers.

9.41 pm

Mr. Bob Cryer (Bradford, South): I shall be brief because I know that a couple of other hon. Members want to speak. Although I welcome the report and I voted for the advent of televising the House, I must say that the experiment is far too closely controlled. It is as though the

[*Mr. Bob Cryer*]

Committee was very much afraid of the media rather than it being composed of people who have grown increasingly used to working with them.

The reality is that the Chamber has been withering. The attendance tonight is not too bad, but for the majority of the time a dozen hon. Members is about the maximum present. Indeed, in spite of big occasions such as the Budget, the biggest attendance that I can recall since 1987 has not been for a debate on an external crisis, on events in other countries, or on the economic crisis, but it was when the House was discussing the discipline to be handed out to my hon. Friend the Member for Edinburgh, Leith (Mr. Brown). Television cameras would help to replace such a discussion with more important issues, would gain maximum attendance in the Chamber and would encourage a reversal in the decline of attendance in what should be the centre piece of Parliament.

One does not deny the importance of Select Committees and the cross-examination of witnesses. My hon. Friend the Member for Bassetlaw (Mr. Ashton) said that the freemasons have been giving evidence this afternoon, which is a matter of great import, and that that would, no doubt, have been covered by television. The fact is, however, that the Chamber is one of the most important places in the building, where Ministers are called to account. If this place is packed, it is more forbidding for Ministers. They have to get the nuts and bolts of their cases much more ordered in their minds before they come here. As many hon. Members have said, the advent of television will, of course, increase the democratic relationship with people outside. It will also make Ministers that bit more fearful of this place, which will be all to the good.

I have strong reservations about the idea of a dedicated channel. It seems to be a recipe for undermining the proposals and not for adding to them. I do not want Parliament to be put into an electronic ghetto to be seen by everyone for about five minutes in their lives, then switched off to become a memory. If we have confidence in ourselves and confidence in this place as the forum for the exchange of views and ideas we should have the confidence to put ourselves on a par with the rest of the other events reported by the media electronically on television.

We grumble about the press and about the way in which it reports us because it does not report the words of the particular individual. None the less, the press has access to the House. There was opposition to the access of *Hansard* and opposition to the access of radio—I can recall the debates and anxieties then and I can recall the packed House for Welsh Question Time on the first day that radio was introduced to the House. Radio has taken its place in our proceedings and television will play its part.

I shall vote for the report because I see it as the beginning of television making a proper, adequate report of this debating Chamber, which should be the important focus of attention in the nation's affairs.

9.45 pm

Mr. Anthony Nelson (Chichester): I concur with some of the sentiments expressed by the hon. Member for Bradford, South (Mr. Cryer). This issue is one of commonality across the party lines and I welcome that as this is a matter peculiar to the House itself.

Although the Committee has come in for some fair criticism and comment this evening, I believe that it has had a difficult but important task in trying to read the will of the House as expressed in February 1988. It has tried to draw a line between those who wanted no television and those who wanted the most liberal coverage of the House and in doing so it has struck the right balance. Although the report may not have pleased everyone, the experiment is worth a try and it should be seen as an experiment.

Before we vote tonight we should recall the principles which have been enunciated by a number of hon. Members tonight and which led the House to support the motion in February 1988. Those principles were repeated by the hon. Member for Bradford, South. Televising the Chamber will have a demonstrable impact on the influence of Parliament over the Executive. To some extent that influence has slipped since the introduction of Select Committees, welcome as they are, in 1979. The power and influence of Government have grown. Why should we exercise a self-denying ordinance? Is it not somewhat patronising for us to say that politics should be left to us alone and that people outside are not interested? We seek their mandate and their support. We say that we should be accountable to the people, but we say that they should not be allowed to see what we do in this place.

There is a latent, pent-up demand—more so than some hon. Members have assessed—for televising the proceedings of the House. As has already been said, this matter should not be seen from the point of view of what the broadcasters wants to deliver as they may look at things in terms of the national numbers who watch their programmes. For the people of each region there are issues of great importance and those people should be entitled, not only to read and listen to the proceedings of the House, but to see and assess for themselves the mood of this place about decisions that affect their regions.

The guidelines that have been established and the rules of coverage proposed will enable a fair, true and balanced representation of this House to be shown. In Committee we sought to take account of the misgivings expressed in the numerous representations from hon. Members to my right hon. Friend the Leader of the House as Chairman of the Committee. We have set up the structure for the House of Commons Broadcasting Unit and have proposed a director of broadcasting in this House to allay some of the worst fears expressed.

If the rules prove to be too restrictive, the monitoring facility will allow those rules to be changed. It is interesting that, from this debate, it is clear that it is thought that the rules might be too restrictive and that the Committee should have been inclined to be more liberal, but those rules can be suitably amended.

The Committee gave proper emphasis to the importance of Select Committee work. Those Committees and the Standing Committees occupy much of the time of hon. Members, they are part of the proceedings of the House and they undertake important work. It is right and proper that coverage by the media and television should cover them as well.

The amendments which have been chosen by you, Mr. Speaker, the amendment of the hon. Member for Workington (Mr. Campbell-Savours) and that of my hon. Friend the Member for Chislehurst (Mr. Sims), should not commend themselves to the House. The first is essentially a wrecking amendment and the latter—*[Interruption.]* The latter amendment leaves the rules of coverage too wide to satisfy the House at this time.

Mr. Patrick Thompson (Norwich, North) *rose——*

Mr. Nelson: I shall not give way at this time, but I will explain why the first is a wrecking amendment. We are concerned with an experiment and the House was concerned that the Select Committee should bring forward recommendations for its implementation. Not unreasonably, it has tried to impose it by the autumn of this year.

Whatever British Aerospace or the hon. Member for Workington may say about the provision of a dedicated channel, which I would support in the longer term were we to have permanent arrangements, it is not a practical arrangement for the short term. If it were made a condition of the package of the main motion it might result in the whole experiment being dropped. It should be seen for what it is: a wrecking amendment, which should be dismissed by the House.

For those reasons, I hope that the House will take further the step which it embarked on in February 1988. A historic step can be taken tonight and I hope that the House will not turn back from it.

9.51 pm

Mr. Wakeham: This has been an interesting and well-informed debate, with contributions from members of the Select Committee and other hon. Members, representing a wide range of views. If I have taken one message from the debate, it is that hon. Members from both sides of the argument feel that the time has come for decisions.

The House is not being invited tonight to reopen the principle of televising the House. That argument was settled, for the time being, last February. We are concerned with the machinery for implementing the experiment. The report ensures that the House will have the chance to vote for or against the permanent televising at about this time next year. That is a point which I make to my hon. Friend the Member for Halesowen and Stourbridge (Sir J. Stokes)—and I have a shrewd suspicion about the way in which he will vote.

I am sure that the House will forgive me if I do not attempt to respond to all the points made by hon. Members. There are a number of specific points and questions with which I shall seek to deal. I am grateful for the kind things said about me in various parts of the Chamber, particularly the comments of the hon. Member for Holborn and St. Pancras (Mr. Dobson). I spend most of my time trying to put him right on one thing or another, but it was a great pleasure to work with him in Committee, as it was with the other Committee members, and the advisers and Clerks who served us extremely well. I agree with the hon. Member for Cunninghame, North (Mr. Wilson) that we learnt a lot from the witnesses who substantially improved our knowledge of the subject.

My right hon. Friend the Member for Shropshire, North (Mr. Biffen) admonished us for attaching too much weight and seriousness to the proceedings of the House. He told us that we were theatre. I thank him for his entertaining contribution.

I feel like saying to my hon. Friend the Member for Tiverton (Mr. Maxwell-Hyslop) that I feel a bit like the Irishman and would not necessarily have started from

here. I was against the experiment in the first place, and voted and spoke against it. I certainly did not persuade anybody to vote for it on the basis that the lighting would be one thing or another. The concerns which he expressed were directly expressed in paragraph 85 of our report, which stated that if any difficulties became evident during the experiment they could be looked at. We had a test of the lighting and were reasonably satisfied with the results, although, again, the experiment may offer us scope for changes.

The hon. Member for Roxburgh and Berwickshire (Mr. Kirkwood) focused primarily on the iniquities, as he and his hon. Friends see it, of our electoral system, and made two points. He drew attention to what he called the Scottish dimension of the experiment. The Committee felt strongly that the Scottish affairs and concerns of other parts of the United Kingdom should be properly reflected, and we obtained assurances from the broadcasters on that point. The broadcasters specifically expressed interest in televising the meetings of the Scottish Grand Committee in Edinburgh.

The hon. Gentleman also spoke about monitoring the broadcast output. We are considering proposals for a comprehensive monitoring exercise during the experiment, which would include political balance and regional coverage among the items to be analysed.

My hon. Friend the Member for Derbyshire, South-East (Mrs. Currie) and the hon. Members for Newham, North-West (Mr. Banks) and for Great Grimsby (Mr. Mitchell) all accused the Committee of being too timid, but for different reasons. Being accused of being reluctant and slow by those hon. Members and by my hon. Friend from different viewpoints convinces me that we have probably not got it too far wrong.

Before I finish, I want to say a word about the two amendments that have been selected. The amendment tabled by the hon. Member for Workington (Mr. Campbell-Savours) holds out the enticing prospect of a dedicated channel providing continuous coverage of our proceedings. I know that that proposition will hold appeal for many Members. I for one would very much like to have a dedicated channel, but I ask the House carefully to examine what the amendment means. If it were passed, the experiment could not take place unless a dedicated channel was established. The report makes it quite clear that, as no public money is available for this purpose, the idea of a dedicated channel can be realised only as a result of commercial decisions by the broadcasters. That is the present position; I am not talking about a dedicated channel at some time in the future.

My hon. Friend the Member for Thanet, North (Mr. Gale) argued his case skilfully, as did the hon. Member for Workington, and gave the House figures which purported to show that a dedicated channel was financially viable. My hon. Friend's and the hon. Gentlemen's enthusiasm is not matched at present by the broadcasters. Even they would agree that it would be quite wrong for the House to seek to second guess their judgement——

Mr. Campbell-Savours: If the right hon. Gentleman had heard me move my amendment, he would realise that it did not relate to terrestrial broadcasters: it is to do with a direct transmission system.

Mr. Wakeham: I appreciate that, but if the experiment cannot take place unless we have a dedicated channel some

[*Mr. Wakeham*]

broadcasters—commercial broadcasters, not necessarily existing ones—must finance it. If any broadcaster says that he wants to broadcast a satellite programme starting in October, I for one would be perfectly happy for him to do so. I am not stopping anyone doing so; anyone who wishes to apply can do so. I am suggesting that, if no one applies, that is not a case for not going ahead with the experiment.

Despite every opportunity, neither British Aerospace nor British Satellite Broadcasting came forward to us, or more importantly to the broadcasters, with a fully costed and worked-out formal position. To go broke on the basis of three letters to the hon. Member for Workington seems to me highly risky, to say the least. If the House passes the hon. Gentleman's amendment, it will in effect throw the whole experiment back into the melting pot of uncertainty and, possibly, of protracted delay. I therefore recommend that the House votes against amendment (c), although it is for individual right hon. and hon. Members to make up their own minds. *[Interruption.]* To answer the hon. Member for Newham, North-West, who asked me whether I would vote for the main Question if the amendment were passed, I still would. That does not mean that it would not involve risks.

The other amendment that the House must decide upon is that moved in a characteristically thoughtful way by my hon. Friend the Member for Chislehurst (Mr. Sims), relating to the rules of coverage. Here the argument is simple. The Committee has recommended a framework of rules which strikes a balance between the strict Canadian model and the somewhat relaxed regime which applies in the other place. My hon. Friend is proposing significantly to relax the rules proposed by the Committee in a way that I do not think would lead to the sort of coverage of our proceedings that most hon. Members would want.

There is a further practical point. It is very much wiser to start as the Committee proposes with a fairly strict set of rules and the prospect of some relaxation as the experiment develops. If a convincing case can be made in the light of experience, that is well and good. I do not think that it would be quite so easy in practice to tighten up the rules once the experiment has begun. Therefore, I advise the House not to accept amendment (n).

It is now 16 months since the House voted in favour of an experiment in televising our proceedings. The report offers a sensible, balanced and practical way to implement the will of the House, and I recommend it to the House as it stands.

It being Ten o'clock, MR. SPEAKER *proceeded, pursuant to order [9 June], to put the Questions necessary to dispose of the motion and of the amendments thereto which had been selected by him.*

Amendment proposed: (c), at end add
'provided that televised proceedings of the House are broadcast on a dedicated channel, unedited, from the start of the sitting to the rising of the House.'.—[*Mr. Campbell-Savours.*]

Question put, That the amendment be made:—
The House divided: Ayes 98, Noes 274.

Division No. 232]   **[10 pm**

AYES

Alexander, Richard	Baker, Nicholas (*Dorset N*)
Arnold, Jacques (*Gravesham*)	Beaumont-Dark, Anthony
Ashby, David	Bennett, Nicholas (*Pembroke*)
Atkinson, David	Bidwell, Sydney

Blackburn, Dr John G.	Kirkhope, Timothy
Boyson, Rt Hon Dr Sir Rhodes	Knapman, Roger
Brazier, Julian	Knight, Dame Jill (*Edgbaston*)
Browne, John (*Winchester*)	Lawrence, Ivan
Burns, Simon	Leigh, Edward (*Gainsbor'gh*)
Butler, Chris	Lord, Michael
Campbell, Ron (*Blyth Valley*)	McNair-Wilson, Sir Michael
Campbell-Savours, D. N.	Mans, Keith
Carrington, Matthew	Marlow, Tony
Carttiss, Michael	Marshall, John (*Hendon S*)
Clark, Dr David (*S Shields*)	Martin, David (*Portsmouth S*)
Clark, Dr Michael (*Rochford*)	Maxwell-Hyslop, Robin
Clark, Sir W. (*Croydon S*)	Moate, Roger
Clelland, David	Moss, Malcolm
Cohen, Harry	Mudd, David
Coombs, Anthony (*Wyre F'rest*)	Mullin, Chris
Cox, Tom	Oakes, Rt Hon Gordon
Cran, James	Page, Richard
Cummings, John	Pawsey, James
Dunn, Bob	Pendry, Tom
Emery, Sir Peter	Porter, David (*Waveney*)
Field, Frank (*Birkenhead*)	Quin, Ms Joyce
Finsberg, Sir Geoffrey	Rhodes James, Robert
Franks, Cecil	Riddick, Graham
Fry, Peter	Rooker, Jeff
Gale, Roger	Sayeed, Jonathan
Gill, Christopher	Shaw, David (*Dover*)
Glyn, Dr Alan	Skinner, Dennis
Godman, Dr Norman A.	Smith, Sir Dudley (*Warwick*)
Gordon, Mildred	Smyth, Rev Martin (*Belfast S*)
Grant, Sir Anthony (*CambsSW*)	Stradling Thomas, Sir John
Greenway, Harry (*Ealing N*)	Summerson, Hugo
Gregory, Conal	Tebbit, Rt Hon Norman
Griffiths, Sir Eldon (*Bury St E'*)	Thompson, Jack (*Wansbeck*)
Griffiths, Peter (*Portsmouth N*)	Tracey, Richard
Griffiths, Win (*Bridgend*)	Walden, George
Hamilton, Neil (*Tatton*)	Walker, Bill (*T'side North*)
Hannam, John	Wall, Pat
Hargreaves, A. (*B'ham H'll Gr'*)	Watts, John
Hawkins, Christopher	Wells, Bowen
Healey, Rt Hon Denis	Wiggin, Jerry
Holt, Richard	Wise, Mrs Audrey
Hughes, Roy (*Newport E*)	Wolfson, Mark
Irving, Charles	
Janman, Tim	Tellers for the Ayes:
Jessel, Toby	Mr. Nigel Spearing and
Kilfedder, James	Mrs Ann Clwyd.

NOES

Abbott, Ms Diane	Boateng, Paul
Alison, Rt Hon Michael	Boscawen, Hon Robert
Allen, Graham	Boswell, Tim
Alton, David	Bottomley, Peter
Amery, Rt Hon Julian	Bottomley, Mrs Virginia
Amess, David	Bowis, John
Anderson, Donald	Braine, Rt Hon Sir Bernard
Arbuthnot, James	Bright, Graham
Archer, Rt Hon Peter	Brown, Michael (*Brigg & Cl't's*)
Armstrong, Hilary	Brown, Nicholas (*Newcastle E*)
Arnold, Tom (*Hazel Grove*)	Buckley, George J.
Ashdown, Rt Hon Paddy	Budgen, Nicholas
Ashley, Rt Hon Jack	Burt, Alistair
Ashton, Joe	Butterfill, John
Baldry, Tony	Caborn, Richard
Banks, Tony (*Newham NW*)	Canavan, Dennis
Barnes, Harry (*Derbyshire NE*)	Carlile, Alex (*Mont'g*)
Barron, Kevin	Carlisle, Kenneth (*Lincoln*)
Batiste, Spencer	Cash, William
Battle, John	Channon, Rt Hon Paul
Beckett, Margaret	Chapman, Sydney
Beith, A. J.	Chope, Christopher
Bell, Stuart	Clarke, Tom (*Monklands W*)
Bellingham, Henry	Conway, Derek
Benn, Rt Hon Tony	Cook, Frank (*Stockton N*)
Bennett, A. F. (*D'nt'n & R'dish*)	Coombs, Simon (*Swindon*)
Bermingham, Gerald	Corbett, Robin
Bevan, David Gilroy	Cormack, Patrick
Biffen, Rt Hon John	Couchman, James
Blair, Tony	Cousins, Jim
Blunkett, David	Critchley, Julian

Crowther, Stan
Cryer, Bob
Cunningham, Dr John
Curry, David
Dalyell, Tam
Darling, Alistair
Davies, Rt Hon Denzil *(Llanelli)*
Davies, Q. *(Stamf'd & Spald'g)*
Davies, Ron *(Caerphilly)*
Davis, David *(Boothferry)*
Day, Stephen
Dixon, Don
Dobson, Frank
Doran, Frank
Dorrell, Stephen
Douglas-Hamilton, Lord James
Dunwoody, Hon Mrs Gwyneth
Durant, Tony
Dykes, Hugh
Eadie, Alexander
Eastham, Ken
Eggar, Tim
Fallon, Michael
Fatchett, Derek
Favell, Tony
Fearn, Ronald
Field, Barry *(Isle of Wight)*
Flannery, Martin
Flynn, Paul
Fookes, Dame Janet
Forman, Nigel
Forth, Eric
Foster, Derek
Fraser, John
Freeman, Roger
French, Douglas
Garel-Jones, Tristan
George, Bruce
Golding, Mrs Llin
Goodhart, Sir Philip
Gould, Bryan
Greenway, John *(Ryedale)*
Griffiths, Nigel *(Edinburgh S)*
Grist, Ian
Grocott, Bruce
Ground, Patrick
Gummer, Rt Hon John Selwyn
Hague, William
Hamilton, Hon Archie *(Epsom)*
Hampson, Dr Keith
Hanley, Jeremy
Hardy, Peter
Harman, Ms Harriet
Harris, David
Haselhurst, Alan
Hayes, Jerry
Hayhoe, Rt Hon Sir Barney
Haynes, Frank
Hayward, Robert
Heathcoat-Amory, David
Higgins, Rt Hon Terence L.
Hinchliffe, David
Hind, Kenneth
Howard, Michael
Howarth, Alan *(Strat'd-on-A)*
Howarth, George *(Knowsley N)*
Howarth, G. *(Cannock & B'wd)*
Howells, Geraint
Howells, Dr. Kim *(Pontypridd)*
Hughes, John *(Coventry NE)*
Hughes, Robert *(Aberdeen N)*
Hughes, Robert G. *(Harrow W)*
Hunt, David *(Wirral W)*
Hunt, John *(Ravensbourne)*
Hurd, Rt Hon Douglas
Ingram, Adam
Irvine, Michael
Jack, Michael
Johnson Smith, Sir Geoffrey
Jones, Ieuan *(Ynys Môn)*

Jones, Martyn *(Clwyd S W)*
Jopling, Rt Hon Michael
Kaufman, Rt Hon Gerald
Kennedy, Charles
Key, Robert
King, Roger *(B'ham N'thfield)*
Kinnock, Rt Hon Neil
Kirkwood, Archy
Knox, David
Latham, Michael
Leadbitter, Ted
Lennox-Boyd, Hon Mark
Lestor, Joan *(Eccles)*
Lightbown, David
Lilley, Peter
Litherland, Robert
Lloyd, Tony *(Stretford)*
Luce, Rt Hon Richard
Lyell, Sir Nicholas
McCartney, Ian
Macdonald, Calum A.
MacGregor, Rt Hon John
McKay, Allen *(Barnsley West)*
MacKay, Andrew *(E Berkshire)*
Maclean, David
McLeish, Henry
McLoughlin, Patrick
McWilliam, John
Madden, Max
Mahon, Mrs Alice
Major, Rt Hon John
Malins, Humfrey
Maples, John
Marland, Paul
Maude, Hon Francis
Mayhew, Rt Hon Sir Patrick
Meale, Alan
Mellor, David
Michael, Alun
Mills, Iain
Mitchell, Andrew *(Gedling)*
Mitchell, Sir David
Montgomery, Sir Fergus
Moonie, Dr Lewis
Morgan, Rhodri
Morley, Elliott
Morris, Rt Hon A. *(W'shawe)*
Morris, Rt Hon J. *(Aberavon)*
Morrison, Sir Charles
Mowlam, Marjorie
Murphy, Paul
Neale, Gerrard
Newton, Rt Hon Tony
Nicholls, Patrick
Nicholson, David *(Taunton)*
Nicholson, Emma *(Devon West)*
O'Neill, Martin
Oppenheim, Phillip
Paice, James
Parkinson, Rt Hon Cecil
Patnick, Irvine
Patten, Chris *(Bath)*
Patten, John *(Oxford W)*
Portillo, Michael
Powell, Ray *(Ogmore)*
Prescott, John
Price, Sir David
Radice, Giles
Rathbone, Tim
Redmond, Martin
Redwood, John
Rees, Rt Hon Merlyn
Renton, Tim
Richardson, Jo
Ridley, Rt Hon Nicholas
Roberts, Wyn *(Conwy)*
Robertson, George
Rogers, Allan
Rowe, Andrew
Rowlands, Ted

Ruddock, Joan
Sackville, Hon Tom
Sainsbury, Hon Tim
Scott, Nicholas
Sheldon, Rt Hon Robert
Shephard, Mrs G. *(Norfolk SW)*
Shepherd, Colin *(Hereford)*
Shore, Rt Hon Peter
Short, Clare
Sims, Roger
Skeet, Sir Trevor
Smith, C. *(Isl'ton & F'bury)*
Smith, Rt Hon J. *(Monk'ds E)*
Smith, J. P. *(Vale of Glam)*
Smith, Tim *(Beaconsfield)*
Soames, Hon Nicholas
Soley, Clive
Speller, Tony
Squire, Robin
Stanley, Rt Hon Sir John
Steel, Rt Hon David
Stern, Michael
Stevens, Lewis
Stewart, Andy *(Sherwood)*
Stott, Roger
Straw, Jack
Sumberg, David
Taylor, Matthew *(Truro)*

Thompson, D. *(Calder Valley)*
Thompson, Patrick *(Norwich N)*
Thorne, Neil
Townsend, Cyril D. *(B'heath)*
Turner, Dennis
Twinn, Dr Ian
Waddington, Rt Hon David
Wakeham, Rt Hon John
Waldegrave, Hon William
Wallace, James
Walley, Joan
Ward, John
Wareing, Robert N.
Warren, Kenneth
Welsh, Andrew *(Angus E)*
Wheeler, John
Widdecombe, Ann
Wilkinson, John
Williams, Rt Hon Alan
Wilson, Brian
Winterton, Mrs Ann
Winterton, Nicholas
Worthington, Tony
Yeo, Tim

Tellers for the Noes:
  Mr. Anthony Nelson and
  Mr. Austin Mitchell.

Question accordingly negatived.

Amendment proposed: (n), at end add
'except for recommendations (i), (iv) and (vi) in paragraph 39.'.—[*Mr. Sims.*]

Question put, That the amendment be made:—
The House divided: Ayes 109, Noes 243.

Division No. 233]   **[10.14 pm**

AYES

Abbott, Ms Diane
Alton, David
Armstrong, Hilary
Ashby, David
Ashdown, Rt Hon Paddy
Ashley, Rt Hon Jack
Barnes, Harry *(Derbyshire NE)*
Barron, Kevin
Battle, John
Benn, Rt Hon Tony
Bennett, A. F. *(D'nt'n & R'dish)*
Bermingham, Gerald
Blackburn, Dr John G.
Blair, Tony
Blunkett, David
Bray, Dr Jeremy
Brown, Nicholas *(Newcastle E)*
Caborn, Richard
Canavan, Dennis
Carlile, Alex *(Mont'g)*
Clarke, Tom *(Monklands W)*
Cook, Frank *(Stockton N)*
Corbett, Robin
Cormack, Patrick
Cox, Tom
Cryer, Bob
Dalyell, Tam
Darling, Alistair
Davies, Ron *(Caerphilly)*
Doran, Frank
Dunwoody, Hon Mrs Gwyneth
Eadie, Alexander
Fatchett, Derek
Fearn, Ronald
Flannery, Martin
Flynn, Paul
Gale, Roger
Gordon, Mildred
Gregory, Conal
Griffiths, Sir Eldon *(Bury St E')*
Griffiths, Nigel *(Edinburgh S)*

Griffiths, Win *(Bridgend)*
Grocott, Bruce
Hamilton, Neil *(Tatton)*
Hampson, Dr Keith
Hargreaves, A. *(B'ham H'll Gr')*
Harman, Ms Harriet
Hawkins, Christopher
Hayes, Jerry
Haynes, Frank
Healey, Rt Hon Denis
Holt, Richard
Howarth, George *(Knowsley N)*
Howells, Dr. Kim *(Pontypridd)*
Hunt, John *(Ravensbourne)*
Irvine, Michael
Irving, Charles
Janman, Tim
Jones, Ieuan *(Ynys Môn)*
Kaufman, Rt Hon Gerald
Kennedy, Charles
Kilfedder, James
Kirkwood, Archy
Latham, Michael
Lestor, Joan *(Eccles)*
Lloyd, Tony *(Stretford)*
McCartney, Ian
McKay, Allen *(Barnsley West)*
Marshall, John *(Hendon S)*
Moonie, Dr Lewis
Morgan, Rhodri
Morley, Elliott
Morris, Rt Hon A. *(W'shawe)*
Morrison, Sir Charles
Mowlam, Marjorie
Mudd, David
Mullin, Chris
O'Neill, Martin
Page, Richard
Prescott, John
Price, Sir David
Quin, Ms Joyce

Rathbone, Tim
Redmond, Martin
Redwood, John
Rhodes James, Robert
Riddick, Graham
Robertson, George
Rooker, Jeff
Sims, Roger
Skeet, Sir Trevor
Skinner, Dennis
Smith, C. *(Isl'ton & F'bury)*
Soley, Clive
Steel, Rt Hon David
Stradling Thomas, Sir John
Summerson, Hugo
Taylor, Matthew *(Truro)*

Tebbit, Rt Hon Norman
Walker, Bill *(T'side North)*
Wall, Pat
Wallace, James
Wareing, Robert N.
Warren, Kenneth
Welsh, Andrew *(Angus E)*
Wiggin, Jerry
Winnick, David
Wise, Mrs Audrey
Worthington, Tony

Tellers for the Ayes:
    Miss Ann Widdecombe and
    Mr. John Bowis.

NOES

Alexander, Richard
Alison, Rt Hon Michael
Allen, Graham
Amery, Rt Hon Julian
Amess, David
Anderson, Donald
Arbuthnot, James
Archer, Rt Hon Peter
Arnold, Jacques *(Gravesham)*
Arnold, Tom *(Hazel Grove)*
Ashton, Joe
Baker, Nicholas *(Dorset N)*
Baldry, Tony
Banks, Tony *(Newham NW)*
Batiste, Spencer
Beaumont-Dark, Anthony
Beckett, Margaret
Beith, A. J.
Bell, Stuart
Bellingham, Henry
Bennett, Nicholas *(Pembroke)*
Bevan, David Gilroy
Bidwell, Sydney
Biffen, Rt Hon John
Boateng, Paul
Boscawen, Hon Robert
Boswell, Tim
Bottomley, Peter
Bottomley, Mrs Virginia
Boyson, Rt Hon Dr Sir Rhodes
Brazier, Julian
Bright, Graham
Brown, Michael *(Brigg & Cl't's)*
Browne, John *(Winchester)*
Buckley, George J.
Burns, Simon
Burt, Alistair
Butler, Chris
Butterfill, John
Campbell, Ron *(Blyth Valley)*
Campbell-Savours, D. N.
Carlisle, Kenneth *(Lincoln)*
Carrington, Matthew
Cash, William
Channon, Rt Hon Paul
Chapman, Sydney
Chope, Christopher
Clark, Dr David *(S Shields)*
Clark, Dr Michael *(Rochford)*
Clelland, David
Clwyd, Mrs Ann
Cohen, Harry
Conway, Derek
Coombs, Anthony *(Wyre F'rest)*
Coombs, Simon *(Swindon)*
Couchman, James
Cousins, Jim
Cran, James
Crowther, Stan
Cummings, John
Cunningham, Dr John
Curry, David

Davies, Rt Hon Denzil *(Llanelli)*
Davies, Q. *(Stamf'd & Spald'g)*
Davis, David *(Boothferry)*
Day, Stephen
Dixon, Don
Dobson, Frank
Dorrell, Stephen
Douglas-Hamilton, Lord James
Dunn, Bob
Durant, Tony
Dykes, Hugh
Eastham, Ken
Eggar, Tim
Favell, Tony
Field, Barry *(Isle of Wight)*
Field, Frank *(Birkenhead)*
Finsberg, Sir Geoffrey
Fookes, Dame Janet
Forman, Nigel
Forth, Eric
Foster, Derek
Fox, Sir Marcus
Franks, Cecil
Fraser, John
Freeman, Roger
French, Douglas
Fry, Peter
Garel-Jones, Tristan
George, Bruce
Gill, Christopher
Glyn, Dr Alan
Godman, Dr Norman A.
Golding, Mrs Llin
Goodhart, Sir Philip
Gould, Bryan
Grant, Sir Anthony *(CambsSW)*
Greenway, Harry *(Ealing N)*
Greenway, John *(Ryedale)*
Grist, Ian
Ground, Patrick
Gummer, Rt Hon John Selwyn
Hague, William
Hamilton, Hon Archie *(Epsom)*
Hanley, Jeremy
Hannam, John
Hardy, Peter
Harris, David
Haselhurst, Alan
Hayhoe, Rt Hon Sir Barney
Hayward, Robert
Heathcoat-Amory, David
Higgins, Rt Hon Terence L.
Hinchliffe, David
Hind, Kenneth
Howard, Michael
Howarth, Alan *(Strat'd-on-A)*
Howarth, G. *(Cannock & B'wd)*
Howells, Geraint
Hughes, John *(Coventry NE)*
Hughes, Robert *(Aberdeen N)*
Hughes, Robert G. *(Harrow W)*
Hughes, Roy *(Newport E)*

Hunt, David *(Wirral W)*
Hurd, Rt Hon Douglas
Jack, Michael
Jessel, Toby
Johnson Smith, Sir Geoffrey
Jones, Martyn *(Clwyd S W)*
Jopling, Rt Hon Michael
Key, Robert
King, Roger *(B'ham N'thfield)*
Kirkhope, Timothy
Knapman, Roger
Knight, Dame Jill *(Edgbaston)*
Knox, David
Leadbitter, Ted
Leigh, Edward *(Gainsbor'gh)*
Lennox-Boyd, Hon Mark
Lightbown, David
Lilley, Peter
Litherland, Robert
Lord, Michael
Luce, Rt Hon Richard
Lyell, Sir Nicholas
Macdonald, Calum A.
MacGregor, Rt Hon John
MacKay, Andrew *(E Berkshire)*
Maclean, David
McLoughlin, Patrick
McWilliam, John
Madden, Max
Mahon, Mrs Alice
Major, Rt Hon John
Malins, Humfrey
Mans, Keith
Maples, John
Marland, Paul
Maude, Hon Francis
Maxwell-Hyslop, Robin
Mayhew, Rt Hon Sir Patrick
Meale, Alan
Mellor, David
Michael, Alun
Mills, Iain
Mitchell, Andrew *(Gedling)*
Mitchell, Sir David
Montgomery, Sir Fergus
Morris, Rt Hon J. *(Aberavon)*
Moss, Malcolm
Murphy, Paul
Neale, Gerrard
Newton, Rt Hon Tony
Nicholls, Patrick
Nicholson, David *(Taunton)*
Nicholson, Emma *(Devon West)*
Oakes, Rt Hon Gordon
Oppenheim, Phillip
Paice, James
Parkinson, Rt Hon Cecil
Patnick, Irvine
Patten, Chris *(Bath)*
Patten, John *(Oxford W)*
Pawsey, James
Pendry, Tom

Porter, David *(Waveney)*
Portillo, Michael
Powell, Ray *(Ogmore)*
Radice, Giles
Rees, Rt Hon Merlyn
Renton, Tim
Richardson, Jo
Ridley, Rt Hon Nicholas
Roberts, Wyn *(Conwy)*
Rowe, Andrew
Rowlands, Ted
Ruddock, Joan
Sackville, Hon Tom
Sainsbury, Hon Tim
Sayeed, Jonathan
Scott, Nicholas
Shaw, David *(Dover)*
Sheldon, Rt Hon Robert
Shephard, Mrs G. *(Norfolk SW)*
Shepherd, Colin *(Hereford)*
Shore, Rt Hon Peter
Smith, Sir Dudley *(Warwick)*
Smith, J. P. *(Vale of Glam)*
Smith, Tim *(Beaconsfield)*
Smyth, Rev Martin *(Belfast S)*
Soames, Hon Nicholas
Spearing, Nigel
Squire, Robin
Stanley, Rt Hon Sir John
Stern, Michael
Stevens, Lewis
Stewart, Andy *(Sherwood)*
Straw, Jack
Sumberg, David
Thompson, D. *(Calder Valley)*
Thompson, Jack *(Wansbeck)*
Thompson, Patrick *(Norwich N)*
Thorne, Neil
Townsend, Cyril D. *(B'heath)*
Tracey, Richard
Turner, Dennis
Twinn, Dr Ian
Waddington, Rt Hon David
Wakeham, Rt Hon John
Waldegrave, Hon William
Walden, George
Walley, Joan
Ward, John
Wells, Bowen
Wheeler, John
Wilkinson, John
Williams, Rt Hon Alan
Wilson, Brian
Winterton, Mrs Ann
Winterton, Nicholas
Wolfson, Mark
Yeo, Tim

Tellers for the Noes:
    Mr. Austin Mitchell and
    Mr. Anthony Nelson.

Question accordingly negatived.

Main Question put:—

The House divided: Ayes 293, Noes 69.

Division No. 234]   **[10.25 pm**

AYES

Abbott, Ms Diane
Alexander, Richard
Alison, Rt Hon Michael
Allen, Graham
Alton, David
Amery, Rt Hon Julian
Amess, David
Anderson, Donald
Arbuthnot, James
Archer, Rt Hon Peter

Armstrong, Hilary
Arnold, Tom *(Hazel Grove)*
Ashdown, Rt Hon Paddy
Ashley, Rt Hon Jack
Ashton, Joe
Atkinson, David
Baker, Rt Hon K. *(Mole Valley)*
Baldry, Tony
Banks, Tony *(Newham NW)*
Barnes, Harry *(Derbyshire NE)*

Barron, Kevin
Batiste, Spencer
Battle, John
Beckett, Margaret
Beith, A. J.
Bell, Stuart
Bellingham, Henry
Benn, Rt Hon Tony
Bennett, A. F. *(D'nt'n & R'dish)*
Bermingham, Gerald
Bevan, David Gilroy
Bidwell, Sydney
Biffen, Rt Hon John
Blair, Tony
Blunkett, David
Boateng, Paul
Boscawen, Hon Robert
Boswell, Tim
Bottomley, Peter
Bottomley, Mrs Virginia
Bowis, John
Braine, Rt Hon Sir Bernard
Bray, Dr Jeremy
Brazier, Julian
Bright, Graham
Brown, Nicholas *(Newcastle E)*
Browne, John *(Winchester)*
Buckley, George J.
Burt, Alistair
Butterfill, John
Caborn, Richard
Campbell, Ron *(Blyth Valley)*
Canavan, Dennis
Carlile, Alex *(Mont'g)*
Carlisle, Kenneth *(Lincoln)*
Carrington, Matthew
Cash, William
Channon, Rt Hon Paul
Chapman, Sydney
Chope, Christopher
Clarke, Tom *(Monklands W)*
Clwyd, Mrs Ann
Cohen, Harry
Conway, Derek
Cook, Frank *(Stockton N)*
Coombs, Anthony *(Wyre F'rest)*
Coombs, Simon *(Swindon)*
Corbett, Robin
Cormack, Patrick
Couchman, James
Cousins, Jim
Cox, Tom
Crowther, Stan
Cryer, Bob
Cummings, John
Cunningham, Dr John
Currie, Mrs Edwina
Curry, David
Dalyell, Tam
Darling, Alistair
Davies, Rt Hon Denzil *(Llanelli)*
Davies, Q. *(Stamf'd & Spald'g)*
Davies, Ron *(Caerphilly)*
Davis, David *(Boothferry)*
Day, Stephen
Dixon, Don
Dobson, Frank
Doran, Frank
Dorrell, Stephen
Douglas-Hamilton, Lord James
Dunwoody, Hon Mrs Gwyneth
Durant, Tony
Dykes, Hugh
Eadie, Alexander
Eastham, Ken
Eggar, Tim
Fatchett, Derek
Favell, Tony
Fearn, Ronald
Field, Barry *(Isle of Wight)*

Finsberg, Sir Geoffrey
Flannery, Martin
Flynn, Paul
Fookes, Dame Janet
Forman, Nigel
Forth, Eric
Foster, Derek
Fraser, John
Freeman, Roger
French, Douglas
Fry, Peter
Garel-Jones, Tristan
George, Bruce
Godman, Dr Norman A.
Golding, Mrs Llin
Gordon, Mildred
Grant, Sir Anthony *(CambsSW)*
Greenway, John *(Ryedale)*
Gregory, Conal
Griffiths, Nigel *(Edinburgh S)*
Griffiths, Win *(Bridgend)*
Grist, Ian
Grocott, Bruce
Ground, Patrick
Gummer, Rt Hon John Selwyn
Hague, William
Hamilton, Hon Archie *(Epsom)*
Hampson, Dr Keith
Hanley, Jeremy
Hardy, Peter
Harman, Ms Harriet
Harris, David
Haselhurst, Alan
Hayes, Jerry
Hayhoe, Rt Hon Sir Barney
Haynes, Frank
Hayward, Robert
Healey, Rt Hon Denis
Heathcoat-Amory, David
Higgins, Rt Hon Terence L.
Hinchliffe, David
Hind, Kenneth
Holt, Richard
Howard, Michael
Howarth, Alan *(Strat'd-on-A)*
Howarth, George *(Knowsley N)*
Howarth, G. *(Cannock & B'wd)*
Howells, Geraint
Howells, Dr. Kim (Pontypridd)
Hughes, John *(Coventry NE)*
Hughes, Robert *(Aberdeen N)*
Hughes, Robert G. *(Harrow W)*
Hughes, Simon *(Southwark)*
Hunt, David *(Wirral W)*
Hurd, Rt Hon Douglas
Ingram, Adam
Irvine, Michael
Jack, Michael
Johnson Smith, Sir Geoffrey
Jones, Ieuan *(Ynys Môn)*
Jones, Martyn *(Clwyd S W)*
Kaufman, Rt Hon Gerald
Kennedy, Charles
Key, Robert
Kilfedder, James
King, Roger *(B'ham N'thfield)*
Kinnock, Rt Hon Neil
Kirkwood, Archy
Knox, David
Latham, Michael
Lawson, Rt Hon Nigel
Lennox-Boyd, Hon Mark
Lestor, Joan *(Eccles)*
Lightbown, David
Lilley, Peter
Litherland, Robert
Lloyd, Tony *(Stretford)*
Luce, Rt Hon Richard
Lyell, Sir Nicholas
McCartney, Ian

MacGregor, Rt Hon John
McKay, Allen *(Barnsley West)*
MacKay, Andrew *(E Berkshire)*
Maclean, David
McLeish, Henry
McLoughlin, Patrick
McWilliam, John
Madden, Max
Mahon, Mrs Alice
Major, Rt Hon John
Malins, Humfrey
Mans, Keith
Maples, John
Marshall, John *(Hendon S)*
Maude, Hon Francis
Mayhew, Rt Hon Sir Patrick
Meale, Alan
Mellor, David
Michael, Alun
Mitchell, Andrew *(Gedling)*
Mitchell, Sir David
Montgomery, Sir Fergus
Moonie, Dr Lewis
Morgan, Rhodri
Morley, Elliott
Morris, Rt Hon A. *(W'shawe)*
Morris, Rt Hon J. *(Aberavon)*
Morrison, Sir Charles
Mowlam, Marjorie
Mudd, David
Mullin, Chris
Murphy, Paul
Neale, Gerrard
Newton, Rt Hon Tony
Nicholls, Patrick
Nicholson, David *(Taunton)*
Nicholson, Emma *(Devon West)*
O'Neill, Martin
Oppenheim, Phillip
Paice, James
Parkinson, Rt Hon Cecil
Patten, Chris *(Bath)*
Patten, John *(Oxford W)*
Portillo, Michael
Powell, Ray *(Ogmore)*
Prescott, John
Price, Sir David
Quin, Ms Joyce
Radice, Giles
Rathbone, Tim
Redwood, John
Rees, Rt Hon Merlyn
Renton, Tim
Richardson, Jo
Ridley, Rt Hon Nicholas
Roberts, Wyn *(Conwy)*
Robertson, George
Rogers, Allan
Rowe, Andrew

Rowlands, Ted
Ruddock, Joan
Sackville, Hon Tom
Sainsbury, Hon Tim
Scott, Nicholas
Shaw, David *(Dover)*
Sheldon, Rt Hon Robert
Shephard, Mrs G. *(Norfolk SW)*
Shepherd, Colin *(Hereford)*
Shore, Rt Hon Peter
Short, Clare
Sims, Roger
Smith, C. *(Isl'ton & F'bury)*
Smith, J. P. *(Vale of Glam)*
Smith, Tim *(Beaconsfield)*
Smyth, Rev Martin *(Belfast S)*
Soames, Hon Nicholas
Soley, Clive
Speller, Tony
Squire, Robin
Stanley, Rt Hon Sir John
Steel, Rt Hon David
Stern, Michael
Stevens, Lewis
Stewart, Andy *(Sherwood)*
Stott, Roger
Straw, Jack
Sumberg, David
Taylor, Matthew *(Truro)*
Thompson, D. *(Calder Valley)*
Thompson, Patrick *(Norwich N)*
Thorne, Neil
Townsend, Cyril D. *(B'heath)*
Tracey, Richard
Turner, Dennis
Twinn, Dr Ian
Waddington, Rt Hon David
Wakeham, Rt Hon John
Waldegrave, Hon William
Wall, Pat
Wallace, James
Walley, Joan
Ward, John
Wareing, Robert N.
Welsh, Andrew *(Angus E)*
Wheeler, John
Widdecombe, Ann
Williams, Rt Hon Alan
Wilson, Brian
Winnick, David
Winterton, Nicholas
Wise, Mrs Audrey
Worthington, Tony
Yeo, Tim

Tellers for the Ayes:
   Mr. Austin Mitchell and
   Mr. Anthony Nelson.

NOES

Arnold, Jacques *(Gravesham)*
Ashby, David
Baker, Nicholas *(Dorset N)*
Beaumont-Dark, Anthony
Bennett, Nicholas *(Pembroke)*
Blackburn, Dr John G.
Boyson, Rt Hon Dr Sir Rhodes
Brown, Michael *(Brigg & Cl't's)*
Budgen, Nicholas
Burns, Simon
Butler, Chris
Carttiss, Michael
Clark, Dr Michael *(Rochford)*
Clark, Sir W. *(Croydon S)*
Clelland, David
Dunn, Bob
Field, Frank *(Birkenhead)*
Fox, Sir Marcus
Franks, Cecil

Gill, Christopher
Glyn, Dr Alan
Greenway, Harry *(Ealing N)*
Griffiths, Sir Eldon *(Bury St E')*
Griffiths, Peter *(Portsmouth N)*
Hamilton, Neil *(Tatton)*
Hannam, John
Hargreaves, A. *(B'ham H'll Gr')*
Hawkins, Christopher
Hughes, Roy *(Newport E)*
Hunt, John *(Ravensbourne)*
Irving, Charles
Janman, Tim
Jessel, Toby
Jopling, Rt Hon Michael
Kirkhope, Timothy
Knapman, Roger
Lawrence, Ivan
Leadbitter, Ted

Leigh, Edward *(Gainsbor'gh)*
Lord, Michael
Marland, Paul
Marlow, Tony
Mills, Iain
Moate, Roger
Oakes, Rt Hon Gordon
Page, Richard
Patnick, Irvine
Pawsey, James
Pendry, Tom
Porter, David *(Waveney)*

Redmond, Martin
Rhodes James, Robert
Riddick, Graham
Sayeed, Jonathan
Skeet, Sir Trevor
Skinner, Dennis
Smith, Sir Dudley *(Warwick)*
Stradling Thomas, Sir John
Summerson, Hugo
Tebbit, Rt Hon Norman
Thompson, Jack *(Wansbeck)*
Walden, George

Walker, Bill *(T'side North)*
Warren, Kenneth
Watts, John
Wells, Bowen
Wiggin, Jerry
Wilkinson, John

Winterton, Mrs Ann

Tellers for the Noes
    Mr. Roger Sale and
    Mr. James Cram.

Question accordingly agreed to.

Resolved,

That this House agrees with the Select Committee on Televising of Proceedings of the House in its First Report (House of Commons Paper No. 141).

Insider Trading

10.38 pm

The Parliamentary Under-Secretary of State for Corporate Affairs (Mr. Francis Maude): I beg to move,

That this House takes note of European Community Documents Nos. 7310/87 and 8810/88 and the Supplementary Explanatory Memorandum submitted by the Department of Trade and Industry on 22nd May 1989 relating to insider trading; and supports the Government's view that a practical and workable Directive would demonstrate Member States' common desire to take vigorous action against insider trading.

The draft insider dealing directive has two principal purposes. First, it will require member states to make insider dealing unlawful. Secondly, it will require them to co-operate in obtaining and exchanging information for enforcement purposes.

The House will recollect that it was a Conservative Government who, in 1973, first brought forward legislation to make insider dealing illegal in the United Kingdom. It was this Government who, in 1980, saw the measure on to the statute book. Britain was among the leaders in Europe in legislating in this area. Since 1980 we have made further changes, in the Financial Services Act 1986, with the aim of intensifying the drive against insider dealing.

Both in the drafting of legislation and in its operation, insider dealing law is intensely difficult, as every country in the world which has enacted it has discovered. In the discussions on the directive, I have been keen to ensure that the directive reflects our considerable success in enforcing the law. Like other member states, we sought a measure that was precise, that was practical and that was enforceable. That was not the case with the original draft. But I believe that, as a result of detailed discussions in Brussels, we are very close to a text that achieves those aims.

I turn now to the text of the directive itself. At its centre are the definitions of primary and secondary insider, and the prohibition on trading on inside information. The proposals put forward last year were very broad and vague. They did not require, for example, a primary insider to know that the information that he had was inside information, but they would have caught as primary insiders people whom we regard as secondary insiders—or even not as insiders at all. The text simply prohibited the taking advantage of insider information in buying or selling any transferable securities.

That all added up to a text that went very substantially beyond our law. The text was very wide ranging and in our judgment impossible to operate successfully. It would have greatly increased the area of uncertainty for honest people without making it any easier, and possibly much more difficult, to bring wrongdoers to book. As a result of lengthy and robust discussions in Brussels, we have now arrived at a text which reflects our own experience in this area of legislation.

Mr. William Cash (Stafford): Will my hon. Friend say whether the Government intend to bring in criminal or civil sanctions with respect to the prohibitions included in the directive?

Mr. Maude: As my hon. Friend will know, our present law operates by way of criminal sanctions and, as I hope I am outlining, the directive, as it is emerging, will not go significantly beyond what our present law requires, save in one area to which I shall refer. In those circumstances, there will certainly be no need for us to contemplate legislating or enacting this by way of civil rather than criminal sanctions. However, there may quite independently of that be a case for considering whether some sort of civil sanctions provide a better and more flexible means of enforcing the law in that area.

At the same time as arriving at a text that reflects broadly our experience, it will involve a modest strengthening of our law to prohibit certain insider transactions that are not properly caught at present. The definition of primary insider reflecting our own experience is much more precise, practicable and enforceable. The primary insider is prohibited from taking advantage in full knowledge of the facts. It has a new definition of primary insider that is clear and more restrictive than the original draft, thus helping to restore the balance between primary and secondary insiders. The text now prohibits taking advantage of inside information in buying or selling transferable securities to which the information relates, and that rider was missing in the earlier text. Each of the three key problems here has been resolved.

Our present law has been much criticised from time to time for its complexity—for example, the prohibition on a primary insider dealing is more than 100 words long—and on some occasions that complexity has not been helpful in the pursuit of offenders.

I have welcomed the opportunity presented by the Brussels discussions of going for rather more clarity and simplicity and at the same time a modest strengthening of our law to prohibit certain insider transactions that are not properly caught at present.

I cannot stress too much that it is extremely important that the prohibition on insider trading does not unintentionally and accidentally forbid such ordinary and proper business practices as a takeover, or any large purchase or sale of securities, but, at one stage, the draft text did this. I can tell the House that those practical problems, together with others relating to analysts, to market markers, and to permitted stabilisation activities, have all been resolved.

The second of the directive's strands is increased international co-operation. Insider dealing, like other financial frauds, is no respecter of frontiers. It is about as easy to insider deal on the London stock exchange from Paris as it is, for instance, from Norwich. International co-operation between regulators is already, in general, good. Again, Britain is among the leaders in Europe in that respect. The Companies Bill currently being considered in Committee contains special provisions for my Department to assist overseas regulators.

I should also mention one thing that is not in the directive. At one stage considerable, and justified, anxiety was created among companies at the suggestion that the directive would require them to release much more information. They might, absurdly enough, have had to announce that they had begun to think about making a decision before being in a position to take that decision or to act upon it. That would simply have flooded the market with useless information, while harming the ability of companies to conduct their own business in a sensible and practical manner. A proper flow of information to the market is, of course, vital, but it should be meaningful information.

[*Mr. Maude*]

I am glad to tell the House that the directive now contains a provision that, while it may modestly increase the flow of information to the market, does so in a sensible and contained way.

I should also tell the House that I propose, in implementing the directive, to redeem a pledge made by this Government in 1985: that insider dealing will be made an offence in all securities, not just corporate securities and options and futures based on them. That will bring within the scope of the legislation gilts and other securities.

The motion invites the House to support the Government's view that a practical and workable directive would demonstrate member states' common desire to take vigorous action against insider trading. I believe that this is such a directive. We are and remain determined to take vigorous action against insider dealing. I commend the motion to the House.

10.45 pm

Ms. Joyce Quin (Gateshead, East): There should be no doubt that insider dealing is a major crime. Many have claimed that there are no real victims and that prices are merely driven up—that is a natural operation of capital involving the necessary winners and losers. They suggest that the principles of the free market allow for people to take advantage of such a situation to gain profit. Fortunately, however, increasingly that view is held by the minority. The majority has concluded—I believe that it is the opinion of the House—that insider dealing is a form of theft. The victims sell shares, for example, on a false basis to people in possession of privileged information that will clearly affect the price of the share.

The crime also involves a betrayal of trust, in that people use secret information to deceive and to enrich themselves. On many occasions the loser, as we know, is the investor representing the interests of ordinary people —perhaps he looks after the savings, assurances or small shareholdings of such people. Those buying and selling shares without access to such secret information are often at the mercy of their opponents. Over a short time chain reactions can occur, often across national frontiers, as a result of the electronic, internationalised market, which causes great damage to unsuspecting individuals and firms.

Given the scale of insider trading scandals in the United Kingdom in recent years, it was right to take action. The Government introduced legislation in 1980 and that was consolidated in the Company Securities (Insider Dealing) Act 1985 when criminal sanctions were introduced. Since then the maximum prison sentence for insider trading has increased from two to seven years, although the number of prosecutions for insider trading has been small despite the existence, in theory, of those penalties. I shall return to that issue later. We believe that the practical control and punishment of insider dealing is far from satisfactory currently.

We welcome the EEC directive and we shall not divide the House on it. It would be rather hard to take exception to the carefully worded motion on the Order Paper. It is important that in the large European market that is supposed to become a reality in 1992 there should be systems to control and to punish insider trading.

We welcome both the co-ordination of rules and the obligation to exchange information. It would also be highly unsatisfactory if we were trying to bring successful prosecutions for insider dealing in the large European market when much securities trading was being done across the national boundaries of national authorities which had weaker rules or did not regard insider trading as a serious offence. It is clear that if standards are more lax elsewhere there may be a temptation for people to do business in other financial centres, which could mean a move towards a general reduction in standards rather than the improvement which we wish to see.

It is also worrying that some other EC countries do not have adequate rules on insider trading at present. As I understand it, in addition to the United Kingdom, only Denmark and France penalise insider trading. Will the Minister tell us a little more about the attitude of other countries towards the directive? He seemed to indicate that agreement was likely and that many of the difficulties had been sorted out. Have any of the member countries any serious objections and are those which, to date, have not had rules on insider trading happy at the prospect of an EC directive on the issue?

The issue matters to us more than to many other countries because our securities market is by far the most important and is for us a much more important means of raising equity finance than it is in other EC countries. Therefore, although the treaty base being used for this is article 100A and although I fully understand that that article is used to govern internal market decisions, it would not be a good idea if we were outvoted on the directive because our interest is so great. Fortunately, that does not seem likely.

I note that there was a change of treaty base governing the directive. It has not been fully explained why it was necessary to change the base. Will the Minister tell us whether doing so has had any practical effect? As I understand it, both article 54 and article 100A rely on the majority voting system.

Will the Minister also give a few more details about the timetable, and how certain, if anything can be said to be certain, agreement is likely to be? I believe that there is to be a meeting of the Economic and Finance Ministers on 19 June at which this may be considered and that there is likely to be a meeting of officials before that. Will the Minister say whether that is so? Has there been ministerial representation at the various meetings to discuss the directive? How recent was that? Will there be ministerial, rather than merely official, representation when the subject is next discussed?

The fact that we have the most experience of trying to tackle the problems of insider trading within the EC does not mean that we have been particularly successful. On recent evidence, we have been far from successful. I hope that the directive will be more effective than our existing provisions. The major weakness of our regime is its failure to bring prosecutions. We have the rules, authorities have powers, evidence often seems to be available, but people are not charged and convicted.

As has been mentioned by Opposition Members in previous debates on this subject, we have reason to believe that the practice is more widespread than is usually thought. To back that up, Opposition Front Bench spokesmen and women have pointed to the high proportion of takeover bids that are preceded by erratic movements in the share prices of the companies involved.

Mr. Tim Smith (Beaconsfield): I understand the hon. Lady's frustration at the lack of prosecutions in this area, but does she think it enough to say that there seems to be sufficient evidence? Is not the problem that often there is not sufficient evidence and that it is difficult to obtain hard evidence in support of a prosecution?

Ms. Quin: There is evidence, but it is often not hard enough to make a prosecution stick. A great deal of worry is expressed in the press and elsewhere about the small number of prosecutions, and there is a feeling that the problem is not really being t ackled. I refer the House to an article in *The Independent* of 16 November of last year:

"Despite the major play the DTI has made out of its campaign against insider dealing, the crackdown has in reality been unimpressive"—

Mr. Cash: The hon. Lady will also note that in that same article it was stated of the Opposition spokesman that he drew

"attention . . . to what he believed to be 17 prima facie cases of insider dealing. His analysis of the problem, however, would certainly have caused some hilarity among professional insider dealers. He had taken 17 cases where a company's share price rose sharply ahead of a bid announcement. This, he said, was evidence of a leak and massive insider dealing."

In the part of the article to which the hon. Lady was not going to refer, the attitude of the Opposition spokesman was seriously criticised.

Ms. Quin: The hon. Gentleman must claim to be a mind reader. Since I had just begun to quote from the article, I do not know how he can say with such authority that I was not going to refer to a section that appeared later. I draw the hon. Gentleman's attention to the fact that *The Independent* article takes a line similar to one in the *Evening Standard* and to yet another in *The Economist*. The hon. Gentleman may be about to wave another sheaf of articles at me, but I assure him that I am not quoting an isolated instance. I am quoting several newspapers and journals——

Mr. Maude: Earlier, the hon. Lady referred to evidence of widespread unprosecuted insider dealing. Does she accept that the mere existence of a movement in shares shortly before a takeover bid is announced is by no means conclusive evidence of insider dealing? It may simply be evidence of the bidding company building up a platform for its bid in advance of announcing its offer. There is nothing improper in that.

Ms. Quin: I did not claim that there was. I claimed that there had been such a large number of such movements that it raised questions, which I am sure the Minister would concede.

Mr. Maude: I must press this. The hon. Lady said that there was evidence of widespread unprosecuted insider dealing. The only evidence she has referred to, apart from quoting a comment in a newspaper which persuaded none of us, was the movement of some shares before a bid. I have pointed out, and she seems tacitly to accept, that there is a perfectly plausible and proper explanation for that. I ask again: where is the evidence of this widespread unprosecuted insider dealing?

Ms. Quin: Has the Minister examined all such cases of movements and is he entirely satisfied that there have been no irregularities? Unless he has, I cannot be absolutely reassured by what he says.

Mr. Maude: Of course I have. The hon. Lady should inform herself a little better about these matters. If there is untoward movement in share prices or any evidence of dealing in advance of a bid, the stock exchange's insider dealing group conducts an investigation. If there is prima facie evidence of insider dealing, it is referred to my Department. There have been a great many such cases since the powers to appoint investigators under the Financial Services Act 1986 came into force. These inspectors have draconian powers—to quote the Opposition spokesman in the House of Lords—to gain evidence. I can assure the hon. Lady that all cases are properly investigated. If there is any evidence of impropriety it is pursued relentlessly.

Ms. Quin: I am certainly prepared to consider what the Minister has said. In preparing for this debate, I had to look back at the various debates that have taken place. I found that the Opposition did not seem to be satisfied with what seemed to be rather complacent comments by the Minister.

Perhaps I may continue to deal with the article in *The Independent,* even though that is proving difficult in view of the many interventions. The article claims:

"There are now 18 investigations under way and a further seven cases of suspected insider dealing under consideration. Some prominent City names are said to be involved. It is a fair bet, though, that few if any of these investigations will be addressing the real, endemic problem of insider dealing—that of the large-scale professional insider dealing rings. It is well known in the City that such rings, which often operate on an international scale covering a number of different markets, exist and they are big business: finding them and successfully prosecuting their members is another matter."

That seems to call for a clear system on an international level as well as on a national level. Presumably that is why most of us are in favour of the European directive.

Mr. Cash: Earlier the hon. Lady and the Minister said that the directive contains provisions to deal with matters relating to co-operation between member states and third party states as well. I do not understand the hon. Lady's point. Surely she understands that if the directive contains provisions dealing with the points raised in *The Independent* that ought to deal with the matter.

Ms. Quin: That assumes that the directive has been satisfactorily completed. I am raising matters that I hope will be taken into account in the final form of the directive. The directive has still not been completely agreed by the Council of Ministers and the debate is about putting forward ideas which we hope will be given due weight, whether or not they are actually printed in the directive at present. I hope that the directive will make the system simpler and clearer, that its provisions will be easy to enforce and that prosecutions will be easier.

There has been a mixed reaction to the directive. In the debate in the European Parliament, MEPs from Government and Opposition parties in the United Kingdom supported the directive. I pay tribute to my colleague, the MEP for Derbyshire, who presented the report on the subject and received widespread support from the other MEPs. There has been City anger at the European Community proposals which have been described as too wide and too far reaching.

I have received a brief from the Confederation of British Industry, as I am sure have other hon. Members. It

[Ms. Quin]

deals with the proposed directive, and shows that the CBI feels that there are still considerable problems of definition. The CBI brief says:

"The CBI, therefore, asks Members to ensure that:
    When the Directive is adopted—and it has to be written into UK law—there will not be any material alteration to the present UK law."

That does not seem to be a suggestion that I can support. If an alteration would mean an improvement, I do not see why there should not be a "material alteration" to the United Kingdom law.

Mr. Maude: Would the hon. Lady like to suggest the specific improvements that she would like to see us have embodied in the directive or passed into our own law?

Ms. Quin: There may be improved ways to get information and bring about prosecutions. The Government seem to be satisfied with the way things have worked out. Despite the barracking that I received when I referred to press accounts of this subject, I do not believe that all the articles in the press are unjustified or that the Government's complacency is justified.

Some final comments on the directive have been made by the Law Society, in particular in an article in the *Law Society's Gazette* of 2 June, which I wonder whether the Minister has seen. He is not responding, so I do not know whether he has. If he has not, I recommend that he does, because the submission from the Law Society makes valid points about the problems of definition and about the scope of the directive. It also makes points about the extra-territorial implications of the directive, and the Law Society is concerned that the directive appears to contemplate only transactions in which the EEC territories are involved. It asks about what happens when the insider is within a member state, but the transaction is carried out in a non-member state. Has that aspect been considered in the EEC negotiations?

The Government's explanatory memorandum, submitted by the Department of Trade and Industry on 9 September 1987, says in point 20:

"The provisions in the proposal which relate to co-operation between Member States will need to be considered in the light of other initiatives in this field—in particular, the possible convention of the Council of Europe."

What progress has there been in the Council of Europe? What implications will negotiations within the Council of Europe have for the passing of this directive?

The Government's explanatory memorandum also says that the United Kingdom has signed memoranda of understanding on the exchange of regulatory information in the financial services sector with the United States. Will that agreement extend to other EEC countries if the directive is agreed?

There remain problems about the directive that need to be sorted out. Of themselves, they do not negate the need for such a directive. The European national moves to stamp out insider trading are vital, but they also have to mean that our system becomes more rather than less effective. If this is the outcome of the negotiations in Brussels, we shall welcome the directive.

11.7 pm

Mr. William Cash (Stafford): The motion invites us to support

"the Government's view that a practical and workable Directive would demonstrate Member States' common desire to take vigorous action against insider trading."

I shall not go into all the details, because most of them are in the explanatory memorandum, but a considerable number of ambiguities need to be resolved before 19 June. This excellent document is quite remarkable in its way. It is the first time that I can remember an explanatory memorandum that has gone into such detail. It gives advice to the House, or those who wish to read these things, as to the manner in which the original proposals have been amended as they have gone through the various stages.

The hon. Member for Gateshead, East (Ms. Quin) berated my hon. Friend the Minister for perhaps not reading an article by the Law Society, published on 2 June. Judging by her concluding remarks, I have grave doubts as to whether she has read the explanatory memorandum of 22 May 1989. She referred to one in September 1987, but the important bit is the memorandum of May 1989, which came to the Select Committee on European Legislation, contained those remarks to which I have referred, and made it clear that considerable progress had been made. However, there are still a number of problems with the directive, some of which are inherent in it and some of which, no doubt, can be resolved within the framework when it is implemented under the European Communities Act 1972.

Will the new formulation about knowledge, which is the context in which insider dealing arises, impute knowledge only where Chinese walls have been breached? I appreciate that that is a fairly technical question, but it is important that hon. Members clearly understand it. I welcome my hon. Friend the Minister saying that the directive will enable us to continue to permit takeovers. He also answered my earlier question about whether it would be dealt with under criminal or civil law.

An interesting article appeared in *The Economist* today criticising the federal court of New York for the manner in which it is trying to impose its sanctions extra-territorially outside the United States under rules devised there. It raises an important question about legal reciprocity. As I said in the Committee considering the Financial Services Bill, on which my hon. Friend the Member for Beaconsfield (Mr. Smith) and I sat some years ago, when dealing with international law—and I made this point in an article that I wrote in "Lloyd's log" as well—if one is dealing with a small global village, there must be some parity between different legislative systems, because at the press of a button one can effect transactions of immense complexity. Insider dealing depends on when and how knowledge was acquired. Courts have experienced difficulty about the meaning of the words "knowledge obtained". I am glad to see the Attorney-General nodding, because an important case was considered quite recently. To fix the liability in a manner that will give rise to a prosecution that will stand muster it is essential, first, that one is sufficiently certain about the law; secondly, that the prosecuting authority is prepared to act effectively; and, thirdly, because of the nature of international transactions in a small global village, that there is some relationship between legal systems.

Serious doubt has been expressed about the vires of the treaty. We are aware of something called the vires committee, which is a forum not of medical but legal diagnosis. I believe that it has been considering carefully the way in which article 100A is being put forward as the treaty base for the directive. If we do not try to restrain the competence of the Commission—the Prime Minister made this point recently about the tobacco industry—when it tries to go beyond the lines of the treaty, we shall be in serious trouble. The European Court of Justice has a tendency towards political integration, as I have said on many occasions. It is essential that we ensure that the treaty base is the proper one.

The legal adviser to the Select Committee on European Legislation criticised the use of article 100A. I understand that the Government gave an assurance to the Committee that they would provide a statement on the manner in which the treaty base was being dealt with. I am not aware that such a statement has been produced, but I hope that it will be before our meeting on Wednesday. If we are to do our job properly, it is important that we are fully aware of the basis on which the treaty will be used, and this includes the Single European Act.

The question is: who does one prosecute? There still appears to be confusion on this important question. Is it the individual or is it the company? It appears from the explanatory memorandum that it is the individual. The British Bankers Association sent me a letter today showing that it thought that it could apply to companies as well. This matter should be resolved. Perhaps there is a simple answer, but there still appears to be some uncertainty.

It is essential that we remove ambiguities and confusion. This measure will be an important ingredient in the fight against criminal insider dealing in the Community. Other countries do not have these laws. We have had them since 1980 and we must ensure that they are used effectively. I congratulate the Government and my hon. Friend the Minister on the manner in which the matter has been dealt with so far, but there is considerable scope for removing much of the remaining uncertainty.

11.16 pm

Mr. Win Griffiths (Bridgend): I support this fairly general, straightforward and simple Government motion on insider trading. As my hon. Friend the Member for Gateshead, East (Ms. Quin) said, I do not think that any of us would deny the need for legislation. As steps are taken towards an internal market, it is obvious that legislation is needed across the Community.

I have never traded on the stock exchange. I have to rely on what others, including Conservative Members, tell me happens there. That is not to say that I believe everything that I am told. It is a fiendish and difficult area in which to legislate. The Government's legislation and the development of explanatory memorandums over the past few years as this proposed directive has been discussed at European level can only reinforce our feelings about the difficulties.

Questions have been raised about the legal base. An extract dated 7 June from the 24th report of the Select Committee on European Legislation for the 1988-89 Session was placed in the Vote Office today. It said that in its 23rd report the Committee recommended "further

consideration" of two documents—one relating to insider trading, and the other containing amendments to the original draft directive. It asked the Government

"to submit to the Committee, ahead of the debate, a statement of its position on the proposed choice of treaty base and the reasons why it no longer considers Article 54(3)(g) to be appropriate, as its earlier Explanatory Memoranda had not covered this point.

This statement has now been received from the Department of Trade and Industry and is reproduced as an Appendix to this paragraph."

I will not read out the Department's three-point explanation, but I will say that it seems to be an extremely sensible interpretation of article 54(3)(g) and its shortcomings in covering the draft directive. Article 100A, which deals with moves towards the internal market, seems the most sensible step to take.

In considering the difficulties that still exist, paragraph 35iii on page 9 of the explanatory memorandum mentions

"the uncertainty about the position of authorised stabilisation operations."

As I understand it, they have been custom and practice on the British stock exchange. From what I have read, they seem to be a reasonably harmless way of trying to establish markets for trading in companies that are new to the stock exchange. I would be interested, purely for information, to know what the Minister feels is the likelihood of proposals in the draft directive which would take account of that point, or whether there are any countries that feel so strongly about the matter that they would not consider such proposals. However, as decisions are being made by qualified majority, there will be an opportunity to carry the proposals forward.

On the issue of just when insider information is misused, there seem still to be areas that require clarification. I found the explanatory memorandum tremendously helpful in setting out the way in which the proposal and the nuances of earlier references in the directive have been changed. Nevertheless, it is still difficult for a lay person such as myself to follow the memorandum because it is nine pages long. It would be beneficial to hon. Members if the explanatory memorandum took the form of a comparison of the earlier version of the draft directive with the latest version.

Mr. Cash: I share that thought with the hon. Gentleman because I believe that it is important that people should be able to make a reasonable assessment. There is a way of dealing with the problem which is known as a Keeling schedule. It shows, in heavy black type, the amendments made by reference to the original, so one can then see the document as a whole and also the differences that have been introduced. That would be useful for legislation taken on the Floor of the House and for legislation that is taken in the Standing Committees on European Community documents.

Mr. Griffiths: The amended form of the draft directive is presented in the European Parliament papers in the form of two columns. One can read the original directive and any changes are set out opposite. The word "unchanged" is printed where the draft has remained the same. If the Government gave us a copy of the amended directive as a single document, together with all the valuable points that are made in the explanatory memorandum of the way in which further changes have been incorporated following discussions in Brussels, it would be useful in dealing with

[*Mr. Griffiths*]

legislation. I found it difficult earlier today and over the weekend to sort out exactly what the proposal was and what changes had been made.

I refer also to the article on insider trading in the *Law Society's Gazette,* No. 22, which was provided by the helpful research department in the Library and which was posted on the board this afternoon.

I should like to take up a point made by my hon. Friend the Member for Gateshead, East (Ms. Quin) about the extra-terrestrial implications of the way in which the directive is intended to work. The writer of the Law Society article, Dr. Janet Dine, of the Institute of Advanced Legal Studies and a member of the company law committee, is of the opinion that under the terms of the directive as drafted someone who has committed an offence in Britain on the Paris stock exchange may have to be extradited to Paris for the case to be heard.

If that is the case, it is a drawback in the directive. There should be some way of framing the provisions to allow the case to be heard either in the state where the person concerned lives or where he or she has initiated the offence of insider trading. As I am neither a stockbroker nor a lawyer, I do not know whether the concept of the European legal space, which is referred to so often in the context of the development of the single market and other ideas on closer co-operation, could be useful in a directive of this nature.

The Minister said that satisfactory agreement had been reached over exactly what information needs to be published and at what stage when a company is thinking about a takeover bid, but I wonder whether that agreement also covers issues relating to the disclosure of an offence. Article 2(b) of the amended directive prevents a director recommending that his company should bid for another company when he has insider information concerning that target as it would prevent the director of a target company from selling issues when he has similar information. Can the Minister tell us anything about that?

I turn to the vexed question of the effectiveness of our legislation. Several articles have been referred to, all of which I have read, if not digested entirely. One in particular struck me as saying something that deserves at least a response from the Minister. It was an article in *The Economist* on 15 October 1988 relating to the activities in buying options in Consolidated Gold Fields before Minorco's £3 million bid for that company. *The Economist* was of the opinion that if the DTI had used sections 442, 444 and 445 of the Companies Act 1985, it could have taken action against the insider trading that *The Economist* claims was happening at that time. Unlike the other reference in *The Economist* this week, glowing reference is made to the activities of the Securities and Exchange Commission in the United States where nominee accounts can be blocked when there is some difficulty in establishing exactly who is operating on the market. ConsGold tried to get information from Liechtenstein and Liberian banks that were involved in the process but it was unable to do so, naturally enough.

Mr. Tim Smith: Instead of reading articles in newspapers, why does not the hon. Gentleman try reading the Companies Act 1985 and the Financial Services Act 1986? If he did so, he would discover that the Companies Act provides precisely the sort of power that he has been describing to disfranchise shares. I understand that that power was used only the other day when the identity of the beneficial owners could not be established. The Financial Services Act contains extremely draconian powers to deal with insider trading.

Mr. Griffiths: I was saying that, on the basis of the powers that are available in the Companies Act 1985, a claim was being made that the Department of Trade and Industry had failed to act appropriately in respect of ConsGold. I am asking the Minister to comment on the accusations that have been directed against the DTI.

Mr. Richard Holt (Langbaurgh): Has the hon. Gentleman checked them out?

Mr. Griffiths: I am checking them out by asking the Minister to tell us exactly what the Department did at the time of the ConsGold affair. Did it think about implementing sections 442, 444, and 445 of the Companies Act? *The Economist* cannot be described as a mischief maker for the fair operation of free markets. It seemed that there was some weight in what it was reporting or that the Minister would be able to quell the fears to which it was drawing attention.

Mr. Holt: Has the hon. Gentleman checked this out?

Mr. Griffiths: I wish that the hon. Gentleman would rise and say something directly to me through you, Mr. Deputy Speaker, instead of muttering.

Mr. Holt: Did the hon. Gentleman carry out any research? Did he contact *The Economist* and make any attempt to understand that which he is talking about?

Mr. Griffiths: I know exactly what I am talking about. I am referring to the claims made in *The Economist* and I am asking the Minister to comment upon them. A substantial accusation has been made, for we know that the buying options amounted to about £15 million. Against that background, it seems appropriate to ask the Minister whether he thinks that something along the lines of the SEC of the United States would be a viable option on the European scene.

11.33 pm

Mr. Maude: This has been a short but enjoyable debate. I am grateful to hon. Members for the serious nature of their contributions to it.

My hon. Friend the Member for Stafford (Mr. Cash) spoke of the serious defects of the text at earlier stages. I am happy to be able to reassure him that by dint of careful negotiation those defects have been removed. As for Chinese walls, I can give him the assurance that knowledge under the directive is imputed only where it exists. The anxiety which was widespread and justifiable at an earlier stage has, I believe, been removed. My hon. Friend raised another anxiety about whether a company might be found to be guilty of insider dealing under the directive. The answer to that is no. That is another matter which has been resolved satisfactorily.

The hon. Member for Bridgend (Mr. Griffiths) asked about stabilisation. He properly referred to it as a legitimate practice in the market that exists by custom and practice. It is formally legitimised and closely regulated under the Financial Services Act 1986 or by regulations made under that Act. He will be relieved to know that further amendments to the text made during discussions remove the anxiety properly felt on that score. The hon. Gentleman made a few remarks about the explanatory memorandum that I submitted. He seemed to criticise it for being excessively lengthy, whereas my hon. Friend the Member for Stafford complimented me on the way——

Mr. Win Griffiths: What I said was that I found the memorandum extremely helpful but that it would have been more helpful if the changes described in the memorandum had been set alongside the appropriate parts of the amended directive so we could see clearly what changes had been made.

Mr. Maude: I am grateful to the hon. Gentleman for clarifying that.

My hon. Friend the Member for Stafford was complimentary about the way in which the explanatory memorandum was framed. The difficulty about the suggestion that was made is that the working papers on which discussions are held are confidential, and properly regarded as such by all the member states and by the Commission. That helps to ensure that member states are free to express their views in a sensible environment but means that it is often not possible to make draft texts available.

The hon. Member for Bridgend and my hon. Friend the Member for Stafford made a number of useful and interesting suggestions about the way in which the scrutiny programme might be improved, and I should like, if I may, to consider carefully whether we can give effect to them, because we aim to be as helpful as we can in making the process of scrutiny work.

Mr. Cash: My hon. Friend said that it was essential that we should maintain confidentiality, and gave reasons that we have heard so often before. Does he not agree that this matter is greatly overplayed and that it would be infinitely better if the texts were made available at an earlier stage? I am sure that he will be aware that the Leader of the House is considering whether that could be done. That would allow us—as happens in the Danish Parliament— the opportunity to examine the texts as they emerge so that we did not constantly have to deal with matters that were shrouded in secrecy.

Mr. Maude: I take my hon. Friend's point, and I undertake to consider it seriously, along with the other points that he made.

Let me deal with some of the issues raised by the hon. Member for Gateshead, East (Ms. Quin). She asked about the timetable for further progress. I believe that it is intended that the matter should be discussed by ECOFIN next Monday, when the United Kingdom will be represented by my right hon. Friend the Chancellor of the Exchequer. She asked about other countries' views. They must answer for themselves, although I can tell her that a number of countries have had difficulties along the way —many of them similar to the difficulties that I have outlined. Broadly speaking, those difficulties have been resolved, although some important issues remain unresolved. It may well be possible to resolve all those matters so that the measure can be agreed before very long.

The hon. Member for Gateshead, East asked who had represented the United Kingdom in the discussions. There have been discussions both in the working group and to some extent in COREPER. Ministers do not attend those meetings and it would be impossible for them to do so. Nevertheless, I have kept in close touch with the progress of those discussions. I have made sure that Ministers are informed fully and have directed the process of negotiation. It is by no means uncommon—as the hon. Lady, with her experience of these matters, will know—for something to be agreed without Ministers' attending meetings or discussing the measure formally at any stage. That does not mean to say that it happens without Ministers' informing the process of discussion, as I assure her they have in this case.

The hon. Lady referred to the role of the European Parliament and expressed pride that her colleague the MEP for Derbyshire had produced a report on insider trading. I have to tell her that the European Parliament considered the initial draft, which was, frankly, a mess: it was unworkable, it was too broad, it would not have been effective and it would have jeopardised the position of many perfectly respectable, legitimate and honest people. Yet the European Parliament warmly endorsed the proposal. She might consider whether it would be proper to temper her praise for the work of her colleague in that respect.

Ms. Quin: Has there not also been adverse reaction to the second draft because it goes wider than the first?

Mr. Maude: There have been many drafts. It has been a fact-moving negotiation. The proposal has been subject to constant amendment, broadly in the direction that we have sought, to narrow its scope so that it is both effective and enforceable.

The draft considered by the European Parliament was, by fairly common consent, thought to be hopeless. As I said, the European Parliament warmly endorsed it.

The hon. Lady marred her performance by mounting what she might claim to be an attack on the Government's performance in pursuing insider dealing. She badly misjudged it. She relied only on evidence of remarks by some commentators and she did her reputation no good. I have a very high regard for her abilities, but I feel bound to say that she did not inform herself properly.

Ms. Quin: There were a large number of articles. Can the Minister tell me that all those were wrong, that none of the cases mentioned involved insider dealing, that all prosecutions that should have been made have been made, and that no one has escaped the net of the Government's system? If so, I shall be delighted.

Mr. Maude: The hon. Lady has not referred to any case about which she can assert that insider dealing has occurred and not been pursued, and nor did any of the articles to which she referred. She relied on assertions that there was a certain amount of insider dealing that had not been subject to prosecution. It will not do to make such assertions without the slightest evidence to sustain them. The evidence relied on was the assertion that before some takeovers there were movements in share prices. I have shown conclusively that there is frequently a proper explanation for that—a company may properly be building a platform before announcing its bid. There is nothing improper in that. There is no evidence in anything to which the hon. Lady referred to show that a large amount of insider dealing is not being pursued. She should not make irresponsible assertions.

[*Mr. Maude*]

The directive, which I believe will be agreed before long, provides for a useful addition to our domestic law. It means that we can rely on sensible law being implemented and operated in other member states. It will be supplemented by the Council of Europe convention on insider dealing, which we hope to sign and ratify later this year. All in all, it is a good move forward in the fight against insider dealing. I ask the House to accept the motion.

Question put and agreed to.

Resolved,

That this House takes note of European Community Documents Nos. 7310/87 and 8810/88 and the Supplementary Explanatory Memorandum submitted by the Department of Trade and Industry on 22nd May 1989 relating to insider trading; and supports the Government's view that a practical and workable Directive would demonstrate Member States' common desire to take vigorous action against insider trading.

EUROPEAN COMMUNITY DOCUMENTS

Motion made, and Question put forthwith pursuant to Standing Order No. 102 (Standing Committees on European Community documents).

GATT NEGOTIATIONS

That this House takes note of the proposals described in the un-numbered Explanatory Memoranda submitted by the Department of Trade and Industry on 15th October 1987 and the Supplementary Explanatory Memoranda submitted by the Department on 27th October and 25th November 1987 relating to negotiations between the European Community and Japan under GATT Article XXIV.6, on 15th October 1987 relating to negotiations between the Community and Argentina under GATT Article XXIV.6 and on 21st March 1989 relating to negotiations between the Community and Canada under GATT Article XXIV.6; and endorses the Government's view that the agreements with these countries are satisfactory given the Community's obligations under GATT.—[*Mr. Garel-Jones.*]

Question agreed to.

Motion made, and Question put forthwith pursuant to Standing Order No. 102 (Standing Committees on European Community documents).

HEALTH AND SAFETY

That this House takes note of European Community Documents Nos. 5211/88, Part 1 and the Supplementary Explanatory Memorandum submitted by the Department of Employment on 20th March 1989, 10166/88 and the proposals described in the un-numbered Explanatory Memorandum submitted by the Department of Employment on 2nd June 1989, relating to safety and health of workers at the workplace; supports the broad thrust of the common position adopted on these proposals by the Council of Ministers as a step towards the establishment of high standards of safety in workplaces throughout the Community; and endorses the Government's view that United Kingdom law generally achieves the objectives of the proposal.—[*Mr. Garel-Jones.*]

Question agreed to.

PETITION

Heath Comprehensive School

11.43 pm

Mr. Harry Barnes (Derbyshire, North-East): I wish to present a petition from my constituents in the Heath and Holmewood area of north-east Derbyshire.

Derbyshire county council has proposed to the Department of Education and Science that the Heath school for 11 to 16-year-olds should be closed. Although the council has a good record as a local education authority, this part of its plan for the area is seriously flawed.

I am pleased to present and support the petition, as I was pleased to support my constituents when a deputation met the Minister on Thursday. The petition reads:

To the Honourable Commons of the United Kingdom of Great Britain and Northern Ireland in Parliament assembled. The Humble Petition of the residents of Heath and Holmewood, Derbyshire sheweth that proposals to close Heath Comprehensive school would deprive parents of the right to choose that their children be educated in a modern, well-maintained, purpose-built school of proven worth;

Cause present and future pupils increased travel problems, particularly in winter; increase stress and provide no educational benefit;

Deprive the community of an important local asset of which it is justifiably proud;

Cause increased social deprivation in an already deprived area;

Divide a community linked by the school.

Wherefore your Petitioners pray that your Honourable House will take measures to prevent the closure of Heath Comprehensive school.

And your Petitioners, as in duty bound, will pray that your Honourable House will take measures to prevent the closure of Heath Comprehensive school.

That is signed by Mrs. Sally Holland of, 5 Gorse bank, Heath, Chesterfield and another 1,018 constituents.

To lie upon the Table.

Greyhound Racing

Motion made and Question proposed, That this House do now adjourn.—[*Mr. Garel-Jones.*]

11.46 pm

Mr. Tim Smith (Beaconsfield): I am grateful for the opportunity to raise this evening the subject of greyhound racing. I am especially grateful to my hon. Friend the Minister of State, Home Office for coming to the House to reply to the debate. I am glad, too, to see a number of hon. Members present who I know have an interest in the matter, including my hon. Friend the Member for Langbaurgh (Mr. Holt).

I have raised the subject because I am a great enthusiast of greyhound racing. I have attended several meetings recently and they have been most enjoyable occasions. It may be that my hon. Friend has not been to a greyhound meeting in the recent past and I urge and thoroughly recommend him to take the opportunity to attend one.

Next week's derby, worth £30,000 to the winner, will be watched by more than 10,000 racegoers and will be followed avidly by millions of people via the media. No, it did not take place at Epsom a week ago—this is the classic of the classics, the Greyhound Derby. It is the culmination of six rounds of competition among 200 runners, and it will be run at Plough lane, Wimbledon.

This is the start of the greyhound festival week and it is an appropriate time to look at the sport of greyhound racing and how it has fared over the past 10 years.

Greyhound racing is popular, but under-financed. Attendances are going up on the more popular courses, but smaller ones are still under threat from property developers. Ten years ago there were 48 courses, but today there are only 35, which race under the National Greyhound Racing Club rules.

Crowd violence and drunkenness have never been a problem and most tracks in recent years have become much more upmarket and can offer a sophisticated dinner and evening out. Nonetheless, the underlying tendency is that the sport is getting poorer while the off-course bookmakers, through their betting office chains, are getting richer. Standards countrywide for racegoers and the greyhounds are not improving as fast as they should.

The heart of the problem is that greyhound racing, as with horseracing, is unable to extract a fair price from the off-course betting shops for the use of its product. The situation is exacerbated for dog racing, which gets no levy and only totally insignificant sums from the off-course betting industry, despite the fact that the sport now provides nearly one third of off-course betting revenue for the bookmakers. As horseracing receives an off-course betting levy administered by the Horserace Betting Levy Board, so should greyhound racing receive an off-course betting levy.

The bookmakers argue that most greyhound race meetings take place in the evenings, when betting offices are closed. However, that does not prevent punters from placing their bets on evening dogs during the daytime when the shops are open—and thousands do.

The bookmakers say that almost all their greyhound business is conducted on the afternoon meetings. That may be true, but those afternoon meetings—although the bookmakers own some of the tracks—are all part of NGRC greyhound racing and subject to NGRC rules, stewardship, licensing and discipline. All the greyhounds,

their owners and trainers are NGRC-registered. The meetings could not be run in the absence of a supervisory authority for greyhound racing whose integrity is assured by independent stewards to the satisfaction of the licensing authority and the Home Office, which has overall responsibility for the conduct of betting sports.

All off-course greyhound betting takes place on the results of racing at NGRC-licensed tracks. It amounts to more than a £1 billion turnover for the off-course bookmakers. In betting offices the same 10 per cent. deduction is made for a bet on a greyhound as for a bet on a horse. That permits the bookmaker to recover betting duty and levy. Since greyhound racing has no levy, however, that part of the money taken from greyhound punters, supposedly to cover the levy, is not passed on to greyhound racing. The bookmakers keep it and the punters do not know that. In effect, the bookmakers make a levy charge on greyhound punters and keep the proceeds to boost their own profits. Because the bookmakers are able to exploit greyhound punters in that way, it makes sense for them to maximise their greyhound racing betting, which is what they have been doing. Between the years 1977 and 1988 the amount of off-course betting turnover on greyhounds increased from 18 to 27 per cent. of the total. Betting on horses went down from 82 to 72 per cent.

As long as bookmakers are able to charge greyhound punters for a levy that does not exist, the composition of off-course betting will continue to change to the detriment of horseracing and therefore to the detriment of the horseracing levy.

The statutory 8 per cent. betting duty applies just as much to off-course greyhound betting as to off-course horse betting, so the Government have an equal interest in both. But the greyhound betting public is not being protected in the same way as the horserace betting public because greyhound racing has no levy income to help fund veterinary work, or to improve security and dope testing, particularly in the increasing use of steroids. It has no equivalent to the equine research centre or the Racecourse Security Services companies, both of which are funded by virtue of the horserace betting levy. Why should the punter who bets on a dog and pays 8 per cent. to the Government not be protected in the same way as the punter who bets on a horse and pays 8 per cent?

A levy for greyhound racing would provide the necessary financing to improve protection for the public. Annual betting turnover on greyhounds now exceeds £1·3 billion and a levy for the sport similar to the horseracing levy would yield between £10 million and £11 million. It would also remove the bookmakers' incentive to exploit betting on greyhounds at the expense of the horseracing levy.

Many people are now beginning to question the fairness of the present situation, which leaves greyhound racing out in the cold. In the absence of a levy, much thought has been given to some alternative funding mechanism to provide a proper balance between the supplier and the retailer of the betting product. The ideal alternative would have been the control by the greyhound racing and horseracing authorities of the satellite communications company which distributes betting information and live television picture commentaries from the greyhound stadium to the off-course betting shops. But here again there is a marked imbalance. Control of Satellite Information Services Ltd., known as SIS, rests with the

[*Mr. Tim Smith*]

bookmakers, who appear to have no intention of relinquishing that control, or of allowing greyhound interests to have any stake in the company.

In the first placement of SIS shares the big four bookmakers took 45 per cent. of the 60 per cent. which were allocated, the Horserace Tote took 5 per cent. and the Racecourse Association 10 per cent. This put the bookmaker in the driving seat during the vital period when the company was being established. The result has been, as we see in the latest announcement relating to the imminent placing of the remaining 40 per cent. of SIS shares, that the big bookmakers are calling the shots once again. They are saying that none of the unplaced shares will be allowed to go to horseracing or greyhound racing, at least until 1992, when there is the vague promise that the company will go public. That means that if bookmakers have their way, racing will have to join the queue for shares with everybody else.

Since Sears Securities has sold its William Hill betting shops chain to Mecca Bookmakers, a new allocation of shares has been announced. Ladbrokes, the combination of William Hill and Mecca, and Corals, the big three, are to share between them 45 per cent. of SIS, and the Tote's holding will be increased by 1 per cent. to 6 per cent., giving bookmaking interests 51 per cent. Sears Securities is to keep just under 13 per cent., leaving only 26 per cent. for the outside world. The Racecourse Association, representing horseracing, remains with its handout of 10 per cent.

Clearly the bookmakers have no intention of letting other partners into SIS and horseracing may find its negotiating hand rather short of trumps in years to come. Greyhound racing, meanwhile, holds no cards at all despite the fact that two greyhound race meetings are beamed live every afternoon into off-course betting offices.

The merger of Mecca Bookmakers, owned by Grand Metropolitian plc, and the William Hill Organisation is presently the subject of a Monopolies and Mergers Commission inquiry. The merger serves only to aggravate the situation and give the big three bookmakers and their associates a bigger stake in the control of the only means of distributing betting information to betting shops.

The merger will also further restrict competition in the betting market and strengthen the influence of the major bookmaking companies over the Bookmakers Afternoon Greyhound Services company which was established to obtain from NGRC licensed greyhound racecourses a racing service for off-course outlets during betting office opening hours. That might have developed into the ideal mechanism for paying to greyhound racing a proper price for its product. Unfortunately it has not, because the big bookmakers have also managed to usurp the sport's position there.

Two of the big three bookmakers, Coral and Ladbrokes, now own and operate four of the eight greyhound tracks which, in 1988-89, supplied the greyhound service to betting offices. A fifth track supplying the bookmaker service is Newcastle, which is owned by Ladbrokes and leased to a private company to operate. A sixth is Hackney, whose owners, Brent Walker Ltd., purchased 119 betting shops from William Hill at the time of the merger with Mecca. Bookmaking interests control six out of the eight tracks which supply greyhound racing to bookmakers.

When the law governing the control of betting at greyhound tracks was enacted it became an offence for the proprietor of any greyhound stadium to run a book or have any interest in bookmaking at that stadium. The public interest objective was to prevent organisers of races from offering betting odds against runners. The offence is now to be found in section 19 of the Betting, Gaming and Lotteries Act 1963, which remains in force today. The law applies only to on-course betting. Thus, bookmakers who are also track proprietors can run a book in their betting shops on the racing taking place at their tracks. In other words, the law does not extend to the bookmaking companies which now organise off-course betting on greyhound racing, taking enormous numbers of bets on races that they and their employees arrange at the tracks which they own.

Perhaps my hon. Friend the Minister will agree that the law appears anomalous and should be brought up to date. I am suggesting that the spirit of section 19, if not the letter of the law, is being contravened because no safeguard exists for the off-course betting public such as that which exists for racegoers. The spirit of section 19 is being abused by all the major bookmakers. Would it not make sense, in the greyhound punters' interests, to take a leaf out of horseracing's book and prohibit bookmakers from using their own greyhound tracks to supply any form of greyhound racing and betting service to their own betting shops? If the law was changed in this way, and the sport of greyhound racing was given some form of enforceable copyright in its race results, market forces might prevail.

The Government-appointed members of the Horserace Betting Levy Board have made it clear that they believe that there should be a direct market mechanism between racing and the betting industry. In the absence of this mechanism, horseracing and greyhound racing should be treated equally.

I conclude that the existing horserace betting levy should be extended to include greyhound racing and, indeed, other sports on which off-course betting takes place, although I understand that, pro rata to the two racing sports, the other sports account for only about 1 per cent. of the total. I also conclude that there should be an inquiry into off-course betting's unhealthy influence over afternoon greyhound racing.

11.59 pm

The Minister of State, Home Office (Mr. John Patten): I welcome the opportunity which my hon. Friend the Member for Beaconsfield (Mr. Smith) has given us to respond to some of the anxieties of the greyhound racing industry and of those who enjoy the sport.

I sometimes think that issues of dispute between the racing and bookmaking industries may appear to the outside world a little arcane, but the way in which my hon. Friend addressed the House this evening was a model of clarity—much more so perhaps than some of the technical and often heated exchanges that we see in the racing press, which are hard for the average person to understand. Now the greyhound industry has taken its campaign to the pages of *The Times,* in which it is advertising. That newspaper may or may not be read more widely by hon. Members than, say, *The Sporting Life.*

Racing and betting are major industries in this country. They are the major passions of some people and they are among the diversions, if not passions, of a good many more. Incidentally, I welcome the presence in the Chamber of my hon. Friend the Member for Langbaurgh (Mr. Holt) who takes an interest in these matters.

My hon. Friend the Member for Beaconsfield ended by speaking of the need for an inquiry into the problems of greyhound racing and of betting on it. I shall begin by responding to that point, and then try to deal with as many of his detailed points as I can in the time available. Those that I do not answer now I shall try to deal with immediately in writing.

I can confirm that my right hon. Friend the Secretary of State and I are carefully considering whether to hold an inquiry, and, if we hold one, whether it should include horse and greyhound racing. The need for an inquiry has been urged on us not least by the British Greyhound Racing Board, to which my hon. Friend referred. The House will know that last year, alas, the Horserace Betting Levy Board and the Bookmakers Committee failed to agree the terms of the horserace betting levy scheme for the current financial year—the 28th scheme. My right hon. Friend the Home Secretary was therefore called upon to determine the scheme.

In their submissions about the levy dispute, the three Government-appointed members of the levy board recommended the establishment of an inquiry into the long-term funding of racing. My hon. Friend referred to these three people, who served the board with such distinction. When my right hon. Friend announced his determination of the scheme on 22 March this year, he said that he understood the arguments for this recommendation—meaning the need for an inquiry. He also explained that the possible privatisation of the Horserace Totalisator Board is a factor relevant to reaching a conclusion on the need for and the scope of an independent and objective assessment of the issues within the recommendation.

My right hon. Friend added that he would announce his conclusion on an inquiry when we had received and considered the advice of Lloyds merchant bank on the feasibility of privatising the Tote. I am not in a position to announce our conclusions on that issue, but we are making progress in considering the complex issues involved and at the end of April we received Lloyd's advice on the Tote. In addition, we have assured the chairman of the Betting and Greyhound Racing Board that whether or not the funding of greyhound racing should be included in such an inquiry is most certainly among the considerations that we are taking into account. I am happy to repeat that. In our view, that is certainly the right approach. It does not seem sensible to pursue an inquiry into greyhound racing alone.

Mr. Richard Holt (Langbaurgh) *rose——*

Mr. Patten: I see that my hon. Friend the Member for Langbaurgh (Mr. Holt) is rising menacingly.

Mr. Holt: Has the Minister and our right hon. Friend the Home Secretary taken into account the latest deliberations of the Horseracing Advisory Board, which has said that it is firmly against any form of inquiry?

Mr. Patten: We take careful account of the views of the horseracing world. I am aware of the matter to which my hon. Friend refers. In recent months there have been some substantial shifts of opinion in the horseracing world about the desirability of an inquiry. Sometimes it is rather hard for the innocent Minister to keep up with the shifts in fashion about whether to have an inquiry.

Mr. Holt: I shall keep you posted.

Mr. Patten: I welcome my hon. Friend's promise to keep me posted. No doubt the two Opposition Members who are present will do the same.

We have not reached a decision about an inquiry, but if one is held it will certainly encompass the relationship between greyhound racing and off-course bookmaking. That is a pledge if we go ahead with the inquiry. It would be extremely odd to consider bookmaking separate from its relationship to horse racing which accounts for the majority of off-course betting turnover.

Greyhound racing and horseracing are also alike in being subject to constraints and in enjoying privileges under legislation for which my right hon. Friend the Home Secretary is responsible. That is not to say that an inquiry is inevitable, because many of the issues that might be covered were explored in depth and with considerable authority by the Rothschild Royal Commission on gambling which reported 11 years ago, in 1978. It is not right to say that racing's interests have been neglected in the intervening years. For example, greyhound racing and horseracing were certainly helped by the abolition of the on-course betting duty in 1987. That help by my right hon. Friend the Chancellor of the Exchequer was widely welcomed.

Mr. Alan Meale (Mansfield): I accept much of what the Minister has said about how the industry has progressed. However, as the hon. Member for Beaconsfield (Mr. Smith) said, in the last 12 months a substantial amount of money—approximately £11 million—has gone astray. It has been taken from punters in off-course betting shops and continues to be deducted from punters who presume it is being paid in tax. To me, and probably to the majority of hon. Members, that is deception by off-course bookmakers of the punters. Will the Minister see if he can find a way to direct some of that money into the greyhound industry?

Mr. Patten: I shall do my best to respond later to the general tenor of the intervention by the hon. Member for Mansfield (Mr. Meale). I hope that hon. Members will forgive me if I do not give way again because I wish to give as full a reply as possible before the debate finishes at 12.16.

I welcome the view of the hon. Member for Mansfield that he has seen some improvements. Like my hon. Friends the Members for Beaconsfield and for Langbaurgh, he will have noticed that the Government supported private Members' legislation in 1985, the Betting, Gaming and Lotteries (Amendment) Act, which abolished the limit on the number of days on which betting, and hence racing, was allowed on each greyhound track. That was a substantial advance.

In addition, means exist for exploring concerns about bookmaking, ill founded or not. It is interesting to re-read the Royal Commission's report of 1978. One passage caught my eye and I shall read it to the House and thereby run the risk of bringing to his feet again my hon. Friend the Member for Langbaurgh. It says:

"As Jane Austen might have said, it is a truth universally acknowledged that bookmakers make too much money . . . in fact, one might say that this opinion is held by everyone except bookmakers."

I do not hold those views myself.

Claims such as the manipulation of odds or betting information and alleged domination of others within or by

[*Mr. Patten*]

the bookmaking industry will, I suspect, continue just as long as bookmakers and punters do business. It shows something of the vitality of the racing industry, both horse and greyhound, that these feelings run so strongly. Such claims were considered exhaustively by the Director General of Fair Trading in 1986 and 1987. As a result, early last year, he decided not to refer the off-course bookmaking industry to the Monopolies and Mergers Commission as a potential complex monopoly.

Continuing and suitable action under current arrangements—for example, by the Home Office, the Office of Fair Trading or Customs and Excise—might, therefore, remain the best means to address the concerns and claims of the racing industry. The arguments for a comprehensive review are also strong. My right hon. Friend the Home Secretary hopes to announce his conclusion on an inquiry before the House rises for the summer recess, or, if not, in the spill-over session.

My hon. Friend the Member for Beaconsfield made a cluster of arguments for a levy on off-course bets for greyhound races, and asks two specific questions. He referred to Satellite Information Services. The greyhound industry has variously alleged that SIS is dominated by the big bookmakers, and argued either that it should be entitled to a holding in SIS, or that the placing of unissued shares in SIS should be deferred until there has been an inquiry into racing and betting. I understand the strength of feeling on this, but the Government are not answerable for SIS's conduct as a commercial company. I understand that, at present, the big bookmakers do not control the SIS board. Under the terms of the proposed sharing placing —I have gone into this with some care—the bookmakers' shareholding will reduce to less than 50 per cent. I also understand that the Racecourse Association, which also is independent of Government, is not sympathetic to the call for it to block the share placing unless or until there has been an inquiry. The current investigation by the Office of Fair Trading into the relationship between SIS and the Racecourse Association is a matter for the Director General of Fair Trading, not my right hon. Friend the Home Secretary, but I understand that the outcome of the investigation will be made public.

My hon. Friend then referred to section 19 of the Betting, Gaming and Lotteries Act 1963, and suggested that the spirit of this section might be being abused by the ownership of some greyhound tracks by off-course bookmaking companies. That section prohibits the proprietor of any greyhound track from having an interest in bookmaking on that track. That is because the proprietor can also operate his own totalisator. If he could also conduct the on-course bookmaking, he would have a monopoly of on-course betting. This does not apply to the ownership of tracks by off-course bookmakers. This was looked at in some depth by the Rothschild commission. In the absence of any evidence of abuse, it did not support the case for prohibiting off-course bookmakers from owning tracks, and nor has the Office of Fair Trading made any recommendations about it. If anyone has any evidence of malpractice, such as the fixing of races, by virtue of ownership, it is extremely important that it is brought to the attention of the Office of Fair Trading or the Home Office, and we shall deal with it urgently.

There are six principal reasons why the Government believe that the law relating to the levy on off-course betting on greyhound races should not be changed. First, it is argued that greyhound racing is entitled to a levy because horseracing has one. The arrangements for the horseracing levy are in question at present, following the dispute about the 28th levy scheme and the resulting call from members of the levy board for an inquiry. Looking back at the origins of the levy, the extent to which it was the product of several special factors that applied back in 1960 is striking. The viability of English racing——

The motion having been made after Ten o'clock on Monday evening, and the debate having continued for half an hour, MR. DEPUTY SPEAKER *adjourned the House without Question put, pursuant to the Standing Order.*

Adjourned at sixteen minutes past Twelve o'clock.

House of Commons

Tuesday 13 June 1989

The House met at half-past Two o'clock

PRAYERS

[MR. SPEAKER *in the Chair*]

BUCKINGHAMSHIRE COUNTY COUNCIL BILL *[Lords]*
Order for consideration, as amended, read.
To be considered tomorrow.

KINGSTON UPON HULL CITY COUNCIL BILL *[Lords]*
As amended, considered.
To be read the Third time.

Oral Answers to Questions

DEFENCE

Soviet Union (Arms Reductions)

1. **Mr. Bill Michie:** To ask the Secretary of State for Defence what assessment he has made of the Soviet Union's latest planned cutbacks in its European conventional forces as announced during the recent visit of United States Secretary of State, James Baker.

The Secretary of State for Defence (Mr. George Younger): We welcome the announcement of specific proposals on conventional armaments by the Soviet Union, and particularly its inclusion figures on tanks and armoured troop carriers.

Mr. Michie: Does the Secretary of State agree that President Gorbachev's latest proposals are of major importance and that reductions of 10 to 15 per cent. at the lower levels possessed by both sides, and a further 25 per cent. reduction are very much in line with NATO's proposals on tanks, troop carriers and artillery? Surely the Government must now consider further reductions in helicopter and combat aircraft and nuclear weapons in Europe.

Mr. Younger: Yes, it is encouraging that the Warsaw pact's latest proposals fit in well with proposals made earlier by NATO, and that it is now prepared to consider all combat aircraft—at least we hope that it is—in a further round of discussions. That is encouraging and justifies all the leadership that has been given by NATO in these matters.

Mr. Beaumont-Dark: Does my right hon. Friend agree that at the present time we are having many fine words, as we had from the Chinese only a few weeks ago, and that all may be well if Mr. Gorbachev survives, but his problems are where hundreds of people are being killed in Uzbekistan? This may not happen, but we should not be taken in too easily. Does he further agree that Britain's

defence is more important than just giving in when we do not know whether, in the end, Mr. Gorbachev will be the saviour or the victim?

Mr. Younger: My hon. Friend is correct. We hope that Mr. Gorbachev will continue to be successful in pursuing his reforms in the Soviet Union, but until he has delivered reductions in the Warsaw pact's enormous level of armaments, we must keep our defences strong in order to be sure that we can defend ourselves against any attack.

Mr. O'Neill: What is the importance of force-to-space ratio arguments now that we are seeing the prospect of considerable reductions in conventional defence, and what is the importance of forward defence now that we are talking about drastically reducing both sides' conventional arsenals?

Mr. Younger: The importance of both those points cannot be under-estimated. In the first case, the force-to-space ratios, which could be dramatically altered if there are reductions of the kind that we hope to see, will entail a great deal of careful military advice being made available to the negotiators, and that we have set in hand. Forward defence is a particularly important matter for NATO because, being an alliance of free democratic peoples, we are obliged to do our best to defend every inch of NATO's territory, and we must be able to do that in the future as we have in the past.

Mr. Wilkinson: In making his assessment, will my right hon. Friend bear in mind that the United Kingdom's air assets could be as well deployed to the flanks—to the reinforcement of Norway and the southern flanks of the alliance—as to the central front so that the overall arms control equation on the central front is not the only matter to be taken into account?

Mr. Younger: I agree with my hon. Friend. Britain's contribution to the defence of NATO's territory goes much wider than the central front. We shall have to give the maximum support to the negotiations in the CFE talks at Vienna and, when the outcome of those is known, we shall have to consider the best way in which to implement what we hope will be large reductions.

Trident

2. **Mr. Andrew F. Bennett:** To ask the Secretary of State for Defence if he will make a statement on the progress of the Trident programme.

The Parliamentary Under-Secretary of State for Defence Procurement (Mr. Tim Sainsbury): The Trident programme continues to make good progress within budget. We are confident that completion of the programme's various elements will be achieved on time to meet the in-service date of the mid-1990s.

Mr. Bennett: Does the Minister agree, given that the cost of Trident is escalating, that its warheads are years behind the times, that there are problemss in making the missiles work, that there seem to be problems with the Faslane development, and that the Government have not even thought about the command and control system for the whole set-up, it is ridiculously naive of the Government to assume that it will work—even if the Russians were to wait until we have a system? Is it not also naive of my right hon. and hon. Friends on the Labour Front Bench to assume that we can negotiate away such an inadequate system? Would it not be better to scrap it now and save the £10 billion plus?

Mr. Sainsbury: The hon. Gentleman is entitled to his fantasies. I thought that normally fantasies are dreamt up but the hon. Gentleman appears to read his. Nevertheless, they bear no relation to reality.

Mr. Hind: Will my hon. Friend confirm that he has no intention of scrapping the fourth Trident submarine? Will he tell the House what long-term effectiveness the Trident submarine force would have minus one quarter of its deployment?

Mr. Sainsbury: I am glad to tell my hon. Friend that we are not at the stage of scrapping it, but certainly we are contemplating ordering it in due course. If there were not four Trident submarines, we would not be able to guarantee always to have one on patrol, as is necessary and as we have done with Polaris submarines ever since they were first commissioned.

Mr. Douglas: Can the Minister give an indication of when he is likely to order of the Trident force? Will he further confirm that an in-service date of the mid-1990s means that a Trident force would be unlikely to be in possession of missiles much before mid-1993?

Mr. Sainsbury: As to the hon. Gentleman's latter point, it would be better if I were not drawn on the precise date. Normally, we do not give such dates. One does not have to be very up in military matters to deduce the in-service date expected, and the date that the hon. Gentleman mentioned is certainly the sort of time scale that we have in mind. The tender for 07 is currently under consideration and the order should be placed before the end of the year.

Mr. Speaker: Mr. David Shaw.

Mr. Shaw: Question No. 4, Mr. Speaker.

Soviet Union (Nuclear Weapons)

4. **Mr. David Shaw:** To ask the Secretary of State for Defence what evidence his Department has that the Soviets are dismantling their nuclear artillery weapons systems.

The Minister of State for the Armed Forces (Mr. Archie Hamilton): NATO allies are still considering a number of options for adjusting remaining nuclear forces following the INF agreement. Among those options is the possible deployment to Europe, including the United Kingdom, of additional longer-range dual-capable aircraft from the United States. However, no decisions have yet been taken —[*Interruption.*] I have answered the wrong question. I apologise. I shall now answer Question No. 4. I did not realise that the hon. Gentleman—[*Interruption.*]

Mr. Speaker: Order. I have heard that done before.

Mr. Archie Hamilton: There is no evidence to suggest that the Soviets are dismantling any of their nuclear-capable gun artillery systems.

Mr. Shaw: Is not my hon. Friend concerned that there is still a massive superiority of Soviet forces in relation to conventional and chemical weapons and to short-range nuclear forces? Is he not concerned that some of the so-called removal of front-line nuclear weapons by the

Soviets may turn out to be removal just for the purpose of maintenance and that they will be returned to the front line? Does he not feel that we should still be on our guard?

Mr. Hamilton: Yes, I totally agree with my hon. Friend. I remain as concerned as he that there is certainly no reluctance on the part of the Soviet Union to update all their systems, whether conventional or nuclear, and to ensure that they are fully modernised. He is right that there are plans to withdraw a very small number of the Soviet's nuclear-capable artillery but that it may be redeployed in some other form.

Mr. Flannery: Does not the Minister get the message, especially after seeing the 1 o'clock news, that Germany, which is much nearer the front line than we are, greets Mr. Gorbachev as someone who is more popular than any other international statesman? When will the Government stop basing their foreign policy on the assumption that the Russians are about to attack us at 2 o'clock next Wednesday afternoon? Do not the Government realise that the world is a changed place? It is about time that the leading figures on the Government Front Bench, and even the Chancellor of the Exchequer and the Prime Minister, get their act together and did something decent internationally.

Mr. Hamilton: The Government's defence policy is not based on the assumption that the Soviets are about to attack us any minute, but on the capability of the Soviet forces and those in the Warsaw pact. We have seen dramatic changes in the foreign policy of the Soviet Union in the past few years and we could see other dramatic changes in quite a different direction. If we did, where would we be if such a massive capability existed in the Soviet Union?

Mr. David Martin: Can my hon. Friend confirm that in the past five years alone, 95 per cent. of Soviet short-range nuclear missiles have been updated?

Mr. Hamilton: It is quite true that there has been an extensive modernisation programme of short-range Soviet systems.

F111

6. **Mr. Fatchett:** To ask the Secretary of State for Defence if he will make a statement on future deployment plans for the F111 in the United Kingdom.

Mr. Archie Hamilton: United States air force F111 aircraft are currently stationed at two airfields in the United Kingdom: the 20th tactical fighter wing at RAF Upper Heyford and the 48th tactical fighter wing at RAF Lakenheath. These aircraft represent an important part of NATO's deterrent capability. No decisions have yet been taken to change the number of F111 aircraft stationed in the United Kingdom.

Mr. Fatchett: Is the Minister aware that the Dutch Minister has announced to the Dutch Parliament that there is to be an increase in the number of F111s sited in the United Kingdom and that there has already been an agreement between the United Kingdom authorities and the United States Government? Is the Minister calling the Dutch Minister a liar or is he not giving this Parliament the information that it deserves?

Mr. Hamilton: I am not aware of what the Dutch Minister said. However, I can reassure the hon. Gentleman that no agreement has been reached on the issue of stationing more F111s in this country

Mr. Baldry: Is my hon. Friend aware that I have a letter from a senior member of the United States Congress armed forces committee which states in clear terms that that committee has not yet even begun to consider the Department of Defence's requests for new facilities at RAF Upper Heyford? Against that background, are not some of the assertions given by groups such as the Campaign for Nuclear Disarmament, about more F111s coming into the United Kingdom at the moment, a distortion of the truth?

Mr. Hamilton: Yes, my hon. Friend is quite right: they certainly are a distortion of the truth. The only work that has been carried out at Upper Heyford has been design work, which was merely to assess what sort of costs we were talking about. In practice, there has been no approval, either by the British Government or Congress for the work to go ahead.

Mr. Rogers: The Opposition are confused by the Minister's answer—*[Interruption.]*

Mr. Speaker: Order.

Mr. Rogers: According to the *Hansard* of the Dutch Parliament, the Defence Minister said that there had been an argument between this Government and the Americans. As my hon. Friend the Member for Leeds, Central (Mr. Fatchett) asked: who is telling lies? After the Wintex operation, the West Germans also have grave doubts about the efficacy of the F111s stationed in this country, particularly because their limited range means that most of them would land on West Germany. Did the Minister discuss the enhanced employment of the F111s with the West Germans before coming to an agreement with the United States?

Mr. Hamilton: The hon. Gentleman's question is based on the wrong premise. We have not reached any agreement with the United States on this and the United States has not put forward any proposal to us. It may have ideas of its own on the matter, but it has not yet come to Ministers for approval and there is no question of us having given approval.

Soviet Union (Nuclear Weapons)

7. **Mr. Thurnham:** To ask the Secretary of State for Defence whether his Department will be responding to the Soviet proposal to withdraw 500 nuclear warheads from eastern Europe.

Mr. Archie Hamilton: We welcome the Soviets' announcement that they will withdraw 500 nuclear warheads from eastern Europe, but believe that this probably represents as little as 5 per cent. of the total number of Soviet nuclear warheads deployed within the European theatre. In contrast, since 1979 NATO has withdrawn 2,400 nuclear weapons from Europe, leaving only approximately 4,600 within the theatre. The Soviet Union will therefore have to make further very substantial reductions if they are to come down to the size of NATO's nuclear stockpile in Europe.

Mr. Thurnham: I welcome the Russian proposals, but is it not vital for us to keep up our nuclear guard in the face of the continuing massive superiority of Communist forces, both conventional and nuclear? In view of the ruthlessness of the Communist leaders in Peking, does my hon. Friend think that it is time that the Labour party got into step with NATO policy?

Mr. Hamilton: Yes. My hon. Friend is absolutely right. The recent summit confirmed NATO's support for flexible response, which is an incredibly important part of our deterrent effort in NATO. In opposing that concept, Labour is out of step with all the other nations in Europe at present. It rings rather hollow when we are told in the current election campaign that Labour party members are such good Europeans when they are the only people out of step on defence.

Mr. Heffer: Does the Minister think that—just for once —the Government might deliver a positive response to the Soviet Union? Is it not clear that Gorbachev has his own problems in the Soviet Union, and that the response from the West should be positive to help him out against those generals and others who—like generals in this country— are clearly wedded to concepts of war rather than of peace?

Mr. Hamilton: Great responses have been made: that is why we have entered into serious negotiations in Vienna. We cannot be said not to be responding. It is clearly much simpler for the Soviets to make unilateral gestures because of their present enormous superiority in armaments, which enables them to make great demonstrations of slashing numbers.

Warsaw Pact Forces

8. **Mr. Jack:** To ask the Secretary of State for Defence how many bombers, fighter bombers and fighters he estimates that the Warsaw pact could currently deploy; and what resources the North Atlantic Treaty Organisation has at its disposal to counter this threat.

Mr. Younger: We estimate Warsaw pact holdings of light and medium bombers, fighter bombers, fighters and reconnaissance and electronic warfare aircraft stationed in Europe from the Atlantic to the Urals as 8,250 aircraft, compared with 3,977 such aircraft for NATO.

Mr. Jack: Can my right hon. Friend reassure aerospace workers in my constituency that, in the light of recent discussions at the NATO summit, high-quality aircraft such as the Tornado and European fighter aircraft will still be needed to meet the threat that he has identified? Can he also reassure me that he does not expect there to be a barrier to the completion of the EFA project from the still outstanding decision on its radar?

Mr. Younger: Certainly I can. First, the aircraft will be needed to replace the aircraft at present covering us in that role. Secondly, it seems likely that if, as we hope, we achieve great reductions in the amount of armaments, there will be an overwhelming need for the highest possible quality.

Mr. Cohen: Are not the majority of NATO aircraft dual-capable, that is nuclear as well as conventional? Does that not apply to a far lower proportion of Warsaw pact aircraft? If the Warsaw pact has more aircraft overall, why does not the Minister hurry to secure an agreement on a much lower level of aircraft on both sides?

Mr. Younger: That is precisely what we are trying—very successfully—to do. We have been proposing enormous reductions in common ceilings for all those weapon systems for a long time, and at long last the Warsaw pact is beginning to catch up with the West's initiatives.

Sir Geoffrey Johnson Smith: In view of my right hon. Friend's answer to the original question, does not the disparity in the strengths of the respective air forces of the Warsaw pact and NATO merely underline the necessity for us not only to retain our strength in dual-capable aircraft but for us positively to welcome the presence of the American air force in the United Kingdom?

Mr. Younger: My hon. Friend is absolutely right. There is no doubt that the existence of an alliance of free democratic nations—which is what NATO is—requires a balanced system of defence to ensure that no attack against any member of that alliance could succeed. All that is in place now. If, as we hope, that can be achieved in future with much lower levels of armaments, sound defences will still be necessary to back up our freedoms and democracy.

United States Secretary of State for Defence

9. **Mr. Roy Hughes:** To ask the Secretary of State for Defence when he next intends to meet his United States counterpart and what issues he plans to discuss.

Mr. Younger: I met Mr. Cheney at the meeting of NATO's defence planning committee last week and I hope to meet him again in the near future to discuss a wide range of matters of mutual interest.

Mr. Hughes: Will the Secretary of State consider telling Mr. Cheney that we welcome the force reduction proposals recently made by President Bush and now call for urgent talks with the Soviet Union about nuclear reductions in Europe? Meanwhile, will Her Majesty's Government consider abandoning their nuclear modernisation proposals and get down to serious and meaningful negotiations?

Mr. Younger: It would be extremely foolish to do that, although I realise that that is the established policy of the Labour party. I welcome warmly President Bush's initiative, which has made it clear that we in the West wish to see a reduction in the level of armaments. We have made it quite clear—with the support of every single one of our NATO allies, including all those that have Socialist Governments—that we believe that, for the foreseeable future, nuclear deterrence will remain our defence. For that reason, we do not think that it would be sensible to start negotiations for the reduction of nuclear weapon systems until the complete implementation of any reductions under the CFE.

Mr. Dickens: Does my right hon. Friend agree with me that the arms control talks that are now taking place are possible only because the West is able to speak from a position of military strength and that it is most important,

in this violent and troublesome world, to keep our defences intact, to maintain them, to update them and to keep close to our NATO allies?

Mr. Younger: I totally agree with my hon. Friend. If anyone does not agree, I should have thought that it would have been completely clear to him that this policy has stood us in good stead in recent years and has also been instrumental in bringing the Warsaw pact to the negotiating table. As a result, we see the prospect of a substantial reduction in the level of armaments. That is proof to me that NATO policy has worked dramatically well.

Mr. Wallace: Can the Secretary of State confirm that at the meeting last week to which he referred a decision was taken to reaffirm the 3 per cent. per annum real increase in NATO defence spending? Did the Secretary of State and Mr. Cheney suggest the extent to which they expect the respective countries to reach that target, and was any consideraton given to how that would be consistent with NATO's arms control objectives?

Mr. Younger: There was a short debate on the subject at last week's meeting. As the hon. Gentleman has correctly said, there was unanimous agreement that the 3 per cent. should be kept as a target. It has never been a target that every nation has reached, but most nations have reached it at one time or another. For that reason, it has been a vey good yardstick with which to judge various members' performances within the Alliance. We think that it is valuable to keep it for the future.

Departmental Cost-effectiveness

10. **Mr. Stevens:** To ask the Secretary of State for Defence what his Department has achieved since 1979 in cost-effectiveness.

Mr. Sainsbury: Since 1979, my Department has significantly reduced manpower numbers and the size of the defence estate and has launched a range of other initiatives aimed at improving cost-effectiveness. These have included a greater use of competition in the procurement of defence equipment, an extensive programme of contracting out support services, and a wide range of efficiency studies, including some 20 efficiency unit scrutinies. The Department is currently engaged in an exercise to achieve a cumulative improvement in efficiency of 2·5 per cent. per annum during the three years ending in March 1991.

Mr. Stevens: I am grateful to my hon. Friend for his reply. One of the impacts of the Ministry of Defence's procedure has been to bring a great many more companies on to the defence list of contractors. That has been particularly helpful in areas such as the west midlands, especially to smaller companies to which special priority has been given by the Ministry of Defence. Can my hon. Friend say a little more about the impact of these value-for-money programmes on the effectiveness of his Department?

Mr. Sainsbury: I am happy to confirm what my hon. Friend says about the value that we attach to ensuring that we have as many contractors as possible on our suppliers' list, particularly small contractors. We are continuing with the programme of presentations and publicity to suppliers to encourage them to come forward and tender for Ministry of Defence business.

Mr. Tony Banks: The Minister's first reply was a lot of old bull—*[Interruption.]* It is absolute bull.

Mr. Speaker Order. That is not a very elegant word.

Mr. Banks: I am not a very elegant person—*[Interruption.]* Tory Members should sit down and take it. When will the Minister do something about the hoarding of land by the Ministry of Defence and all those empty properties? By what right can the Government possibly attack local authorities for having empty properties when his Department has more empty properties than any other Department? When will the Minister do something about that?

Mr. Sainsbury: I am sorry that the hon. Gentleman, who is known for his interest in the arts, clearly does not have much interest in mathematics as an efficiency saving of 2·5 per cent. per annum is clearly too much for him to comprehend. There has been reference to the Department's slowness in disposing of surplus land and I cannot pretend that it has been a perfect performance in the past. The report to which he refers recognises that measures are beng taken to improve performance in future.

Mr. Conway: Is not my hon. Friend's attitude towards cost-effectiveness in procurement ably demonstrated by the Government's support for the Vickers option for the next generation of main battle tanks, which includes the engine manufactured in Shrewsbury by Perkins, which uses 50 per cent. of the fuel of any of its main competitors? Does not that determination to support British engineering at its most able demonstrate the Government's loyalty to British engineering and to cost-effectiveness?

Mr. Sainsbury: I am happy to confirm to my hon. Friend that cost in use through life cost is a very important part of the assessments we make in taking procurement decisions. Fuel efficiency is one of the factors to which we give high priority in taking those decisions.

Mr. Rogers: Part of the Government's justification for the cancellation of Nimrod was the promise of a 100 per cent. offset deal. It is now 130 per cent., but it was 100 per cent. at the time. Perhaps the Secretary of State could check that. In view of the very limited amount of offset work that that been received and is outlined in the third report of the Defence Committee, does the Minister now think that the cancellation of Nimrod was cost-effective?

Mr. Sainsbury: I am sorry that the Opposition are having such difficulty with their mathematics. The figure is 130 per cent., not 100 per cent. I refer the hon. Gentleman to the third report which is rather complimentary to the programme, including the statement in paragraph 67:

"Boeing have expressed full commitment to the offset programme; and, extrapolating figures so far available, they may well meet their offset obligation by 1995."

Warsaw Pact (Nerve Gas)

12. **Mr. Harry Greenway:** To ask the Secretary of State for Defence what information he has on the Warsaw pact nerve gas capability; and if he will make a statement.

Mr. Archie Hamilton: The Soviet Union is the only member of the Warsaw pact to have acknowledged that it has an offensive chemical warfare capability, although we believe that such weapons have been produced by other Warsaw pact countries. On its own, it possesses the largest and most sophisticated chemical warfare capability in the world and nerve agents are just one of the types of agent declared to be in its stockpile.

Nevertheless, we find it difficult to accept a number of the Soviet Union's statements about its own and its allies' chemical warfare activities. We estimate that the Soviet stockpile of chemical warfare agents is several times larger than its claim of only 50,000 tonnes.

There is an obvious need for the Soviet Union to make available much more information about its chemical warfare capabilities if the confidence necessary for a global chemical warfare ban is to be established.

Mr. Greenway: Does my hon. Friend accept that the West disarmed totally of chemical and nerve gas weapons in the 1950s, but received not a single reciprocal response from the Soviet Union, which is believed to have nearly half a million tonnes of chemical weapons? Does he agree that a similar disarmament of nuclear weapons would be a disaster and would encourage the Soviet Union and its allies to stockpile all the more, to our detriment?

Mr. Hamilton: Yes. That is absolutely right. It is an example of unilateral disarmament clearly not having worked. We did that some 30 years ago and there has been no reciprocal action on behalf of the Soviet Union. My hon. Friend is quite right to say that we would be in great danger if we got rid of our own nuclear weapons, as we are living in a world where more nations are acquiring nuclear capability.

Mr. Brazier: Can my hon. Friend confirm that those weapons give the Warsaw pact forces an overwhelming advantage, not only because they are extremely effective, but because the fact that Warsaw pact forces have them and NATO has hardly any means that the defensive counter-measures we have to take put our own troops at an enormous operating disadvantage?

Mr. Hamilton: Yes. My hon. Friend is right. Wearing the suits that are necessary to be immune from those weapons inhibits much of what our troops can do as fighting men.

Multiple Launch Rocket System

13. **Mr. Pike:** To ask the Secretary of State for Defence what proposals exist for the multiple launch rocket system to be capable of firing short-range nuclear weapons.

Mr. Archie Hamilton: The United States announced its choice of the M270 multiple launch rocket system as a launcher for a successor missile to Lance to NATO's high level group on 5 December, publicly confirming this decision the following day. The nuclear missile for the launcher has not yet been selected. The choice of launcher and missile are national United States decisions. At the recent NATO summit, the Allies recognised the value of the United States development programme and agreed to deal with the question of the introduction and deployment of a follow-on to Lance in 1992. The Alliance also recognised that ground-based missiles would be needed in Europe for as long as could be foreseen.

Mr. Pike: Will not proposals to arm the MLRS with nuclear warheads as well as conventional warheads make any future verification arrangements arising from any future treaties extremely difficult? Should not those proposals, therefore, be condemned? Will the Minister give the assurance today that MLRS to be deployed by Britain will not have nuclear warheads?

Mr. Hamilton: No. I certainly do not think that the proposal should be condemned. It is an important part of our flexible response and, as I said earlier, NATO is aligned with that concept. It has also been agreed at the recent summit that there will be no third zero on short-range nuclear forces. That was why the word "partial" was so important in terms of the reductions with which NATO was prepared to go ahead at the recent summit.

Mr. O'Neill: Does the Minister recall that the Secretary of State said on 30 January in answer to a question on BBC news that there would be a decision on the modernisation of Lance by the summer time? Now that that has been delayed until 1992, does the Minister take that as a success for British negotiation at the summit or as a failure?

Mr. Hamilton: It is extremely important to take the summit as a whole. We are very pleased with the fact that there will be no reductions in SNF forces until after the CFE conventional forces reductions have taken place. Altogether, the summit came out very satisfactorily.

Front-Line Forces (Europe)

15. **Mrs. Mahon:** To ask the Secretary of State for Defence what consideration he has given to the defence implications of the Soviet proposal to thin out front-line forces in Europe.

17. **Mr. Patchett:** To ask the Secretary of State for Defence what consideration he has given to the defence implications of the Soviety proposal to thin out front-line forces in Europe.

Mr. Archie Hamilton: Reductions in the Warsaw pact's massive concentrations of forces in Europe would be very welcome. However, its current zonal proposals would make it very difficult to sustain NATO's strategy of forward defence. Nevertheless, we are studying them with care.

Mrs. Mahon: I find that a disappointing answer. Is it not time that the Minister took President Gorbachev's offer to thin out front-line defences seriously? [HON. MEMBERS: "Reading."] With safeguards and verification, could it not mean a much lower level of forces all round? Should not NATO be thinking anyway of replacing its forward—[HON. MEMBERS: "Reading."]—defence with one of defensive defence?

Mr. Hamilton: As my right hon. Friend the Secretary of State explained earlier, a forward defence is an essential part of NATO strategy and has been agreed by NATO for some time. It is also a policy of great importance to the Germans.

Mr. Patchett: Should not NATO agree with President Gorbachev to thin out front-line troops in Europe, as we are reaching a situation in which we do not have the troops to fulfil the commitment to a forward defence policy? [HON. MEMBERS: "Reading."] Could not vast sums of military expenditure be saved without sacrificing security if NATO were to drop what, in reality, is an outdated and offensive posture?

Mr. Hamilton: We are rather moving ahead of the game. It is important that we wait for the outcome of the CFE negotiations that are going on now and have a co-ordinated response to the Soviet proposals, as well as seeing what the Soviet response is to NATO's well-tried proposals, before we start trying to replan our strategy.

Mr. Dunn: Does my hon. Friend agree that we must be careful and cautious in giving any response to any proposal emanating from the Soviet Union, especially as the Soviet Union is likely to be successful in neutralising public opinion in West Germany?

Mr. Hamilton: Yes. One certainly has to acknowledge that the ability of the Soviet Union to mobilise public opinion in the West has been impressive. We must bear in mind that the Soviet Union is going through a period of dramatic change and it does not necessarily follow that that change will always take the same direction. We may see marked reversals as well as changes in the right direction.

Mr. Ian Taylor: Will my hon. Friend put any proposals by the Soviets for marginal reductions in their forces into the context of their budgetary situation, as outlined by their Prime Minister last week, which suggested that they will have considerable difficulty in reducing their defence expenditure to below 15 to 18 per cent. of GDP? Some sources suggest that Soviet expenditure on defence and security could be as high as 25 to 33 per cent. of their total national income.

Mr. Hamilton: I totally accept that my hon. Friend is right. We are grateful for the first, or the second, shot that the Soviet Union has made at assessing its defence expenditure, but we need to see a much greater breakdown of those figures to know exactly what they mean. In the meantime, we must be careful to keep up our own defences until we have seen positive reductions on the Soviet side.

Nuclear Deterrent

16. **Mr. Riddick:** To ask the Secretary of State for Defence what steps he has taken to ensure that the United Kingdom nuclear deterrent is credible.

Mr. Younger: For our nuclear deterrent to remain credible it must be kept effective and up-to-date. To this end we are looking at options to replace the free-fall bomb which currently provides this country's independent sub-strategic nuclear capability, and are in the process of modernising the strategic nuclear deterrent through Trident.

Mr. Riddick: Does my right hon. Friend think that the deterrent value of our nuclear weapons would be enhanced or reduced by pledging to scrap one of our Trident missiles, by pledging to reduce the number of warheads and by refusing to voice a clear and coherent policy? Is he aware of any party or of the leader of any party who voices such a ridiculous policy?

Mr. Younger: My hon. Friend is absolutely correct that no deterrent would work unless a potential attacker was convinced that there was a credible weapons system that could be effective in the circumstances of an attack. It is that which makes our deterrent credible and the Labour party is foolish to put itself in the position of having an incredible deterrent that it intends to abandon.

Mr. Madden: Does not the Secretary of State realise that an increasing number of British people recognise that the nuclear weapons here are not British and not independent and that they make Britain a nuclear target? Does he not also recognise that the vast majority of people around the world want to see the abolition of all nuclear weapons so that the people of this globe can live in peace without the threat of nuclear weapons?

Mr. Younger: The hon. Gentleman is wrong on every count. What people all round the world wish to see is the abolition of all war and the abolition of war is achieved by a credible deterrent that nobody would dare to attack.

Mr. Jacques Arnold: How effective would our nuclear deterrent be in the future if we were to cancel the fourth Trident submarine?

Mr. Younger: The Trident submarine force will succeed the Polaris force, which was originally to comprise five submarines but a previous Labour Government reduced it to four. If any idea of reducing the four submarines to three in the future would mean that we could not be sure at all times that there was at least one boat on station, and that therefore the deterrent would not be credible, any party advocating that is not fit to hold office.

Royal Naval Personnel (Radiation Checks)

18. **Mr. Loyden:** To ask the Secretary of State for Defence what further radiation checks have been carried out on Royal Naval sailors and personnel exposed to nuclear weapons and reactors; and what were the findings.

Mr. Archie Hamilton: Medical records of all naval personnel are analysed annually, and any health trends are identified. There have been no special surveys to determine whether there is any evidence of medical disorders arising from exposure of Royal Navy nuclear submarine personnel to radiation. However, routine medical surveillance is carried out for those Royal Naval personnel designated as radiation workers in accordance with the Ionising Radiations Regulations 1985.

Mr. Loyden: The Minister is ducking the question. Is it not a fact that, having resisted the proper claims for compensation for ex-service men affected by atom bomb tests, the Government are now ducking their responsibilities towards naval ratings serving in nuclear vessels?

Mr. Hamilton: It is very important indeed for the hon. Gentleman to appreciate that there has been no evidence whatever of Royal Naval personnel suffering from the dangerous effects of radiation. Indeed, there is a certain amount of evidence to show that the fact that they are in submarines means that they are protected from much of the radiation to which the rest of us are exposed.

Soviet Union (Fighting Vehicles)

20. **Mr. Brandon-Bravo:** To ask the Secretary of State for Defence what evidence his Department has as to whether the Soviets are dismantling their most modern armoured fighting vehicles.

Mr. Archie Hamilton: There is as yet no evidence that the Soviets are dismantling their most modern armoured fighting vehicles.

Mr. Brandon-Bravo: Does my hon. Friend agree that we should be more concerned with practice than with promise? We have had many promises in the last few years. What steps can we take to ensure that they are put into practice? On what forms of inspection will we insist?

Mr. Hamilton: My hon. Friend is absolutely right. The whole issue of verification will be an extremely important component of any agreement that is reached on conventional or nuclear reductions. That is an important element of the talks that are now going on.

PRIME MINISTER

Engagements

Q1. **Mr. Barry Porter:** To ask the Prime Minister if she will list her official engagements for Tuesday 13 June.

The Prime Minister (Mrs. Margaret Thatcher): This morning I had meetings with ministerial colleagues and others. In addition to my duties in the House, I shall be having further meetings later today, including one with former President Reagan.

Mr. Porter: Will my right hon. Friend confirm, if confirmation be needed, her commitment to the European Community and her determination to fight for Britain and British interests within the Community? Will she accept from me that anybody who doubts that she will fight for Britain within the Community needs to have his head and his conscience examined?

The Prime Minister: Yes, we shall continue to fight for Britain's interests in a strong Community, which we believe is both in Britain's and in Europe's interest. We have fought successfully in the past and we shall continue to do so in the future.

Mr. Kinnock: Will the Prime Minister say what she intends to do to stop the crisis of confidence about the relationship between herself and her Chancellor of the Exchequer?

The Prime Minister: The right hon. Gentleman is talking nonsense—*[Interruption.]*—absolute nonsense. On Wednesday of last week, in the economic debate, out of which the Opposition came so poorly, the Chancellor set out the Government's position clearly and in some detail. He said:
"Our overriding"—
I repeat, overriding—
"objective is to bring inflation back down."
We will not be diverted from that course. As the Chancellor went on to say:
"These are the policies that have successfully brought inflation down in the past, and will do so again."

Mr. Kinnock: If there is no difficulty about the relationship, why is the pound falling?

The Prime Minister: The right hon. Gentleman reveals the depth of his ignorance.

Mr. Kinnock: Perhaps the Prime Minister will help everybody by saying what she thinks should be done now to stop the pound sliding against the deutschmark.

The Prime Minister: Had the right hon. Gentleman listened, he would have heard the answer—[*Interruption.*] —when I answered his first question. I would add that towards the end of his speech, the Chancellor, when tackling the right hon. Gentleman, repeated:

"Opposition leader asked what he would do. Opposition leader says, 'to cut a long story short, we don't know'."— [*Official Report,* 7 June 1989; Vol. 154, c. 264-65.]

Q2. Mr. Franks: To ask the Prime Minister if she will list her official engagements for Tuesday 13 June.

The Prime Minister: I refer my hon. Friend to the reply that I gave some moments ago.

Mr. Franks: Having regard to Britain's success in creating more jobs than the rest of the Common Market combined, may I ask my right hon. Friend to agree that it might be more appropriate for the European Commission to be studying British policies rather than lecturing us on its proposals for a so-called social charter?

The Prime Minister: Yes, I agree with my hon. Friend. The social charter would mean more regulation and put heavy additional burdens on industry. It would make our industry less competitive and mean that we would be less able to create the many jobs that we have created, far exceeding the record of any other country in Europe over the same period, and would result in moving jobs from Europe to Asia. We have attracted a great deal of inward investment into this country by a policy of enterprise and deregulation, and they trust us to pursue a sound economic course.

Q3. Mr. Sillars: To ask the Prime Minister if she will list her official engagements for Tuesday 13 June 1989.

The Prime Minister: I refer the hon. Gentleman to the reply that I gave some moments ago.

Mr. Sillars: Is the Prime Minister aware that in Scotland no single thing is more detested than she is, other than the poll tax, which is known in Scotland as Thatcher's poll tax? Is she further aware that 1 million Scots have not paid a penny and that that act of repudiation will be manifest on Thursday when her party is annihilated at the polls? Will she take a piece of advice and bring forward a Bill to repeal the poll tax, because her current legislation has no chance of working in Scotland?

The Prime Minister: Whatever the people of Scotland think, they have taken advantage of the policies that this Government have pursued and they have the second highest standard of living in the United Kingdom. The hon. Gentleman asked me to take advice from him. The answer is no, because he supported the Socialist policies that brought this country, including Scotland, to its knees. As he still supports those same policies I will never take advice from him. I believe that the people of Scotland are honourable enough to wish to pay a fair and reasonable amount towards the costs of local government through a community charge.

Q4. Mr. Marlow: To ask the Prime Minister if she will list her official engagements for Tuesday 13 June.

The Prime Minister: I refer my hon. Friend to the reply that I gave some moments ago.

Mr. Marlow: As it would be better—[*Interruption.*] —for all of us if the balance of payments deficit were slightly lower, and as the largest factor in the deficit— [HON. MEMBERS: "Reading."]—is the aggregate of the individual decisions to buy foreign cars—[HON. MEMBERS: "Reading."]—does my right hon. Friend agree that it is anti-social, selfish and unneighbourly to buy foreign cars when equally good British cars are available? What would she say to those self-centred economic vandals who in future persist, for reasons of bogus status or inverted patriotism, in buying foreign cars?

The Prime Minister: I agree that quite a bit of the adverse balance of payments deficit is due to the import of foreign cars. Britain's rate of growth has exceeded that on the Continent, which means that there is a good market for foreign cars in Britain. The current production of cars is above its 1979 level and is rising because we have attracted large overseas investment. It will continue to rise, not only for the companies already in this country but because of increased production at Nissan and Toyota. That will do the balance of payments a great deal of good because there will be more British-produced cars for people to buy.

Mr. Robert Sheldon: As the presence of the Chancellor of the Exchequer next to the Prime Minister is a sign of how seriously she is taking the foreign exchange movements in today's markets, is she aware that, for any given exchange rate, the level of interest rates must be set higher if there is uncertainty in the markets? Given the unprecedented relationship between the right hon. Lady and her Chancellor, is it not clear that she should end that uncertainty now by stating publicly whether she intends to back him or to sack him?

The Prime Minister: I have firmly indicated that my right hon. Friend the Chancellor's policies are the policies of the Government. Had the right hon. Gentleman listened to my previous reply he would have heard me precisely when I said that on Wednesday last week, in the economic debate—[*Interruption.*] If hon. Members do not listen they must hear it again, so that there is no room for doubt. The Chancellor set out the Government's position clearly and in some detail. He said:

"Our overriding objective is to bring inflation back down. We will not be diverted from that course."

As the Chancellor went on to say:

"Those are the policies that have successfully brought inflation down in the past, and will do so again."—[*Official Report,* 7 June 1989; Vol. 154, c. 264.]

I could read out my right hon. Friend's whole speech—it was extremely good—but it might take rather a long time.

Q5. Mr. Colvin: To ask the Prime Minister if she will list her official engagements for Tuesday 13 June.

The Prime Minister: I refer my hon. Friend to the reply that I gave some moments ago.

Mr. Colvin: Will my right hon. Friend find time today to consider the 3¼ million Hong Kong Chinese who might wish to come to the United Kingdom if the Armageddon referred to by their Governor takes place? If those people are given the right of abode in the United Kingdom, will that also give them the right ultimately to settle anywhere within the European Community? If so, does not that make the issue of Hong Kong and the Chinese as much a matter for our European partners as for this Government, and another very good reason for ensuring that there is the maximum Conservative representation in the European Parliament following the polls on Thursday?

The Prime Minister: On the particulars that my hon. Friend raises, right of abode in the United Kingdom would not in itself allow people to settle elsewhere in the European Community, whether before or after 1992. I very much agree with him that, as a matter of political co-operation, we should look to our European partners for the strongest possible support for Hong Kong and its democratic way of life and prosperity, and look to other democratic countries for support.

I agree wholly with my hon. Friend's last point. We want the strongest possible representations and turnout on Thursday for the European Parliament elections.

Mr. Ashdown: Will the Prime Minister give a few moments today to consider the plight of young Chinese students who, because of their faith in democracy, are hiding for their lives in Peking and are waiting for the knock on the door that will take them to gaol or before the firing squad? Will she now tell the House what she will say if, in eight years' time those scenes are re-enacted in Hong Kong and involve British passport holders to whom she and the Labour party have refused to give refuge?

The Prime Minister: The right hon. Gentleman does not have a monopoly of strong feeling on this matter. I think that throughout the House we feel equally as shocked and appalled as he does. That applies to both sides of the House. Just because he has been to Hong Kong and finds it easy to say things, because he has no responsibility——

Mr. Ashdown: Dishonourable.

The Prime Minister: ——no responsibility whatsoever, does not mean that he feels any more strongly than we do. While he was away, we indicated that we would be very happy to seek more flexibility in the arrangements that we already have, particularly for those who have worked for the British Government, that we would look at the other immigration rules, and that we shall be bringing forward proposals in due course. I hope that the right hon. Gentleman will appreciate that it is really in our interests to keep Hong Kong prosperous, capitalist and a free society, which is the way in which it will be most valuable in 1997 and the way in which the Chinese will need to keep it going.

Mr. Speaker: Did I hear the right hon. Member use the word "dishonourable"?

Mr. Ashdown: I used the word "dishonourable" as I did——

Mr. Speaker: I ask the right hon. Member to withdraw that.

Mr. Ashdown: I make it clear that that word was not —[*Interruption.*]

Mr. Speaker: Order. The hon. Member is a right hon. Member and the leader of his party, and I ask him to withdraw that remark.

Mr. Ashdown: The word was intended to refer to the Government's policy—[*Interruption.*]

Mr. Speaker: Whatever the right hon. Member meant, would he please withdraw that remark?

Mr. Ashdown: So far as it may have been misconstrued——

Mr. Speaker: There are other hon. Members who wish to participate in Prime Minister's Questions. Will the right hon. Member withdraw the remark in relation to the Prime Minister?

Mr. Ashdown: Naturally, Mr. Speaker, I withdraw any connotation of that word in relation to the Prime Minister. It was referring to her policy and not to the right hon. Lady.

Sir Hal Miller: Does my right hon. Friend accept that among people in Hong Kong there is a real sense of grief and shock at the loss of so many young lives, as well as a growing sense of insecurity about their personal future? Will she take an early opportunity to show that we share that sense of loss and grief as well as being determined and capable of remaining responsible for the administration of Hong Kong until 1997?

The Prime Minister: Yes, we gladly do so. In all parts of the House we feel exactly the same way about the people of Hong Kong, for whom we are fully responsible. We shall keep the administration going in the very best way possible until 1997. Then, as my hon. Friend knows, under the agreement we have reached, there will be a liaison committee that will continue for a further three years. In the meantime, we shall do all that we can to reassure the people of Hong Kong and to reaffirm our commitment to them and to their future.

Q6. **Mr. Grocott:** To ask the Prime Minister if she will list her official engagements for Tuesday 13 June.

The Prime Minister: I refer the hon. Gentleman to the reply that I gave some moments ago.

Mr. Grocott: Is the Prime Minister aware that the whole House will have noticed her failure today to give unequivocal backing to her Chancellor? Is she further aware that in last week's vote on the honours system, the only Cabinet Minister to vote in favour of honours for political services was the Chancellor? Does she know something that we do not?

The Prime Minister: I shall answer the important part of the hon. Gentleman's question. I give full, unequivocal and generous backing to my Chancellor, of whom I am very proud.

Botulism Outbreak

3.31 pm

Mr. Ronnie Fearn (Southport) *(by private notice)* asked the Secretary of State for Health if he will make a statement on the recent outbreak of botulism in Lancashire.

The Secretary of State for Health (Mr. Kenneth Clarke): I regret to report to the House that there has been a serious outbreak of an extremely rare form of food poisoning in the area of Manchester, Blackpool and Preston and also in Clwyd in Wales. I am sure that the whole House will wish to join me in extending my sympathy to those suffering from this particularly unpleasant form of food poisoning. Currently, we are aware of 14 cases clinically diagnosed as botulism, 12 in Lancashire and two in Wales.

Inquiries at Youngs Fruits Ltd. of Folkestone, Kent, where the implicated hazelnut puree was manufactured, have shown that the company supplied eight other small dairies, in addition to Acorn Foods, and Forshaw, Littletown Farm Dairy named yesterday, with puree for use in the production of hazelnut yoghurt. The local public health authorities for the areas where these additional dairies are located have all been contacted. Environmental health officers are visiting these dairies and arranging for immediate withdrawal of hazelnut yoghurts manufactured by them. I should stress that no cases have been associated definitely with hazelnut yoghurt from those eight dairies. In addition, the possible association between one case and the consumption of hazelnut yoghurt produced by Forshaw, Littletown Farm Dairy which was referred to in statements yesterday is unclear at present.

The eight other dairies which received hazelnut products from the Folkstone farm are:
Lord Crathorne's Dairy, Cleveland;
Stockmeadow Farm Dairy, Staffordshire;
Ann Forshaws Farmhouse Yoghurt, Preston;
Madresfield Dairy, Worcestershire;
Bodfari Foods Ltd, Chester;
Yieldingtree Packers, west midlands;
Grange Farm, Buckinghamshire; and
Battledean Farm, Gloucestershire.

Inquiries are still not complete, however, and my Department maintains its advice that, for the time being, the public should not eat any brand of hazelnut yoghurt.

Mr. Fearn: Can the Minister state exactly when the chief medical officer was informed of the outbreak? Can he also inform us when he first let the public know? He mentioned that the outbreak is confined to Lancashire and Wales, whereas information seems to be coming through now that one of the yoghurts was purchased in Gosport. Can he also state why the Bristol research centre on food safety is due to be closed and why five out of the seven horticultural stations are due for closure? Does he agree that the figure of food poisoning cases for this year is 60 per cent. up on last year and that his Department and the Ministry of Agriculture, Fisheries and Food are possibly to blame for this? Surely they are putting the botch in botulism.

Mr. Clarke: On wider issues than this, it is a pity that every time we have a disastrous and possibly tragic announcement people instantly leap to attribute blame, although if blame is established it must be faced by those responsible. No blame has yet been attached to anybody and I believe that that is a sensible position to maintain.

The hon. Gentleman asked when action was first taken. We were first informed of the diagnosis on Friday evening of last week. My congratulations go to the neurologists in Manchester and to the communicable diseases surveillance centre for their prompt action in identifying and diagnosing this very rare condition. It takes some time to discover exactly what the cause of this most unusual neurological condition is and they were particularly good in spotting the correct diagnosis as quickly as they did.

Once we knew, of course, we began to take very prompt action over the weekend. A local warning was issued to the public by the authorities in Lancashire on Sunday 11 June on the advice of my Department. On Monday 12 June my Department issued further statements warning the public not to eat hazelnut yoghurt. Meanwhile, over the weekend, the two dairies mentioned specifically in the statement were contacted by the local public health authorities and all hazelnut yoghurt produced by those companies was withdrawn from sale. Since then the other eight dairies supplied with hazelnut products by Youngs Fruits Ltd. have been contacted and all their hazelnut yoghurts are being withdrawn from sale.

My Department has been communicating rapidly and instantly first with the environmental health officers in the case of the farms affected and then with those who serve the areas where people are distributing the products of those farms. We are today issuing general information to environmental health officers because they will require specific scientific advice to add to what we have already said.

As all hon. Members will know, very quickly over the weekend we began to issue the most prudent warning possible to the general public, who needed to be alerted first. That advice was that nobody should purchase any brand of hazelnut yoghurt until the position had become more clear.

The point about the Bristol research centre to which the hon. Gentleman referred can be answered in more detail by my right hon. Friends with responsibility for that, but I am informed that that research centre is not concerned with any work on food safety relevant to this outbreak. I see no connection between the horticultural centres and botulism in hazelnut yoghurt.

My right hon. Friend the Minister of Agriculture, Fisheries and Food and I have made it clear that we are concerned about the increase in food poisoning generally and we have made repeated statements about the action that we are taking. I am glad to say, however, that our figures on this very rare type of food poisoning are exceptionally good. There were only nine outbreaks in this country in the period from 1922 to 1988. I compare that with 210 outbreaks in the United States of America between 1971 and 1985 and 115 outbreaks in France between 1978 and 1984. So, fortunately, we do not have a particularly serious history of botulism. Indeed, the last case in Britain was in 1987; and I am glad to say that we have not had a death from botulism since 1978, when there were four cases from which two deaths resulted.

This case is obviously serious. We are now establishing as rapidly as possible all the facts that can be established about the origin of botulism and we shall act in every possible way if any reason for further action is indicated as a result of our inquiries.

Dame Jill Knight (Birmingham, Edgbaston): Are the experts yet able to say whether the trouble comes from a process in firms dealing with hazelnuts in this way, or whether there is a danger from the processing of hazelnuts generally?

Mr. Clarke: So far, we have good reason to believe that only the hazelnut products from the one firm at Folkestone are implicated in the outbreak. Obviously, botulism is widely prevalent in the environment and precautions have to be taken against it in the case of all sorts of food, although outbreaks are more often associated with meat and fish products. As far as I am aware, there is no evidence to suggest any trouble with hazelnut products in general and at this stage we do not know precisely what has caused the outbreak associated with hazelnut products from one firm in Folkestone.

Mrs. Audrey Wise (Preston): The Secretary of State has been congratulating himself on speedy communication, but is he aware that the director of environmental health in Preston has, at each stage in the matter, received his information first from the press, not from the Department of Health? Would the right hon. and learned Gentleman like to comment on that? Would he also care to ensure that the environmental health officers are the first to receive full information, and that, at all times, they have the resources necessary to do their work, as they are the first line of defence and the public depends on them?

Mr. Clarke: I do not know whether some people communicate with the press before they communicate with my Department, but all I will say is that as soon as my Department has received evidence it has communicated directly with the environmental health officers in the areas concerned. The hon. Lady will appreciate that we are talking about the weekend, and, for understandable reasons, it was not possible to raise all the directors of environmental health instantly. First, we went directly to those directors of environmental health in the areas where the farms concerned distributed the product, and, when we found where the product was being distributed to, we contacted the directors of environmental health there. Meanwhile, we have been giving public warnings to those who might purchase hazelnut yoghurt that they should not purchase or consume it.

Mr. Michael Jack (Fylde): May I congratulate, through my right hon. and learned Friend the Secretary of State, those in Blackpool, Wyre and Fylde district health authority on the way in which they have handled the matter and the nursing care that the victims have received at the Victoria hospital in Blackpool? When does my right hon. and learned Friend expect that further public statements on the matter will be possible, and what advice will he give on post-production quality control for future monitoring of this type of problem.

Mr. Clarke: It is too soon to have a full picture of the outbreak, but, as far as I can see at the moment, everybody acted extremely promptly once the diagnosis was confirmed. I stress that this is a difficult diagnosis to make because the average doctor, including the average consultant, has never encountered a case in his career. We acted promptly once the situation became clear, as did those responsible in the Health Service, and they are caring for the unfortunate victims in every possible way. At the moment, most of them are stable and the prognosis seems reasonably good.

On monitoring, the first step is to have a proper scientific investigation of exactly what went wrong so that we can discover what caused the growth of the organism in this particular product, and, in the light of that, to see what further steps have to be taken—for example, whether it will be necessary to strengthen the law.

Mr. Jack Ashley (Stoke-on-Trent, South): Is the Secretary of State aware that the increase in convenience foods means an increase in the risks involved, which requires an increase in monitoring by more environmental health officers? What is the right hon. and learned Gentleman doing to increase the number of environmental health officers?

Mr. Clarke: The Government readily acknowledge that there is an increase in the incidence of food poisoning in this country, which is a matter of serious concern. It is quite possible that it is connected with the growth of convenience foods. For that reason, we set up the expert committee under the chairmanship of Sir Mark Richmond, vice-chancellor of Manchester university, to advise us generally on the microbiological safety of food, and we are taking every other step as well. However, the latest incident appears to involve a canned food, and canning is traditionally a pretty safe process that is not normally expected to give rise to the risk of botulism—certainly not in the case of a non-acidic food such as hazelnut puree. Nevertheless, every outbreak increases the sum of human knowledge, and we shall find out exactly what happened to allow that particular consignment of hazelnut puree to become infected.

Mrs. Maureen Hicks (Wolverhampton, North-East): The general public will be reassured by my right hon. and learned Friend's comments today, by his prompt action, and by his recognition of the seriousness of the matter. Does he agree that the sooner there is informed research into why food poisoning is increasing and how risks may be reduced, the better for all of us?

Mr. Clarke: The overall expenditure on research connected with food poisoning is being maintained. If anything, it is increasing. It is always necessary to find useful avenues of research and I am sure that whenever we find them they will be given proper priority by those of my right hon. Friends responsible for the relevant research budgets. Beyond that, all I can say is that our record on botulism is very much better than that of most other countries, but obviously we shall make every effort to ensure that we sustain that good record.

Mr. Martyn Jones (Clwyd, South-West): The Secretary of State's advisers no doubt told him that clostridium botulinum is a spore-bearing organism and therefore is very likely to be found in canned food and is a danger when canning, especially meats. That is why the record in France is worse than in this country, because of the large amount of sausages and preserved meats, rather than heat-treated meats, that the French consume. The case in Wales that the Secretary of State described probably occurred in my constituency or in its vicinity, and I should like his assurance that he has liaised with the Secretary of State for Wales.

[*Mr. Martyn Jones*]

I should like an assurance also that environmental health officers, who are struggling to keep at bay a tide of food poisoning outbreaks in this country, will have the resources and the ability to stem that tide in future. The current case is relevant because it involves small outlets that were supplied with a large amount of infected food product. Only environmental health officers can possibly help to prevent a recurrence in future.

Mr. Clarke: I hear what the hon. Gentleman, who I believe has professional expertise in the field, says. I am advised that the very much higher incidence of botulism in other countries is associated particularly with the home preservation of meat, poultry, game, fish, vegetables, and some kinds of raw fish. I do not believe that canning usually gives rise to that particular danger to any marked degree. We will find out what went wrong with the canning process at Youngs Fruits Ltd.—if anything did go wrong —and then we shall all be better informed.

Environmental health officers have a vital task, and my Department communicates with them promptly and effectively as soon as it has the scientific basis for giving the advice that EHOs require. The question of resources devoted to environmental health officers is primarily a matter for local government, but obviously resources need to be applied consistent with the risk that the public appears to face.

Mr. Geoffrey Dickens (Littleborough and Saddleworth): My right hon. and learned Friend knows that there are two cases in my constituency, and, on its behalf and on behalf of the north-west, I thank him and his Department for the speed with which they acted over the weekend, which is always a difficult time. Radio and television bombarded us with many warnings, which were most helpful and surely saved many people from being poisoned.

Does my right hon. and learned Friend agree that people have been poisoned since time immemorial and that poisoning will continue for as long as diseases find clever ways of beating us and our cures? Nevertheless, we thank the doctors and other medics for acting so quickly. Can my right hon. and learned Friend assure the parents of children and the adults who have been affected that they have a very reasonable chance of a full recovery, and that there is every reason to believe that the disease—which is a killer disease—will be contained?

Mr. Clarke: I was in the constituency of my hon. Friend the Member for Littleborough and Saddleworth (Mr. Dickens) yesterday. I was meant to be campaigning in connection with the European elections, but I found myself addressing television and radio reporters and reinforcing our warnings to the public about the consumption of hazelnut yoghurt. The media in the north-west gave wide coverage to my warnings and those of the Government's chief medical officer. Everyone acted promptly, and I again congratulate the medical staff who diagnosed the problem and those who gave the treatment. Fortunately, although it is a dangerous disease, its treatment has advanced considerably in recent years. The news on the present patients is as reassuring as can be hoped for.

Mr. John D. Taylor (Strangford): To reassure the public, can the Minister say for certain that the source of the problem is hazelnut puree and not any of the milk products involved? Do any of the firms which he has named manufacture any other flavours of yoghurt, and, if so, are they still available on the market?

Mr. Clarke: We have strong reason to believe that the hazelnut puree is responsible for the outbreak. That particular canned hazelnut puree is used only in yoghurts. In fact, yoghurt is mentioned in the title under which it is sold. Therefore, at the moment there is no reason to believe that any other type of yoghurt or dairy product is implicated in the outbreak. Obviously, in all cases of food poisoning we encounter great difficulties when trying to trace the exact source and cause. All we can do is to carry on giving the public the full extent of our knowledge as it unfolds.

Mr. Robin Cook (Livingston): May I press the Secretary of State to answer the question put by my hon. Friend the Member for Clwyd, South-West (Mr. Jones): what action has been taken by the Welsh Office in response to the cases in Clwyd? Has it provided advice to the public?

The Secretary of State will acknowledge that the figures which he quoted to the House confirm that this is the most serious outbreak of botulism for decades. Given the alarming increase in food poisoning, when will the House see the regulations on food hygiene, which have been lying in the Department in draft form for two years this month?

I wish to take up the Secretary of State's reference to the Bristol food research laboratory which he maintained was not carrying out research into food poisoning. Will he acknowledge that that was partly because last year the Government cut the grant for research into salmonella food poisoning? When will the Government start to reverse their irresponsible cuts on research into food safety?

In response to the concerns expressed about environmental health officers, will the Secretary of State acknowledge that there are currently 430 unfilled vacancies for environmental health officers? Will the Government reverse the cuts in training places which have partly contributed to the national shortage?

The Secretary of State said that it was far too early to attribute blame. Will he at least acknowledge that this is one time when he cannot blame the consumer? Shoppers need not another leaflet from his Department giving them advice, but action to ensure food safety. When will they receive it?

Mr. Clarke: I realise that the hon. Gentleman has a duty to oppose. However, when discussing serious issues of this kind, he should not scratch about to find faintly associated causes of complaint, which is what he is doing. The new responsible official Opposition might join in the public warning. I would hope that any Labour Government would, like this Government, speed up efforts to find out what has caused the outbreak.

We are in close touch with the Welsh Office. The Government's chief medical officer is responsible to the Government, and our advice was addressed to the entire population of the United Kingdom. The advice is that, until further notice, people should not eat any brand of hazelnut yoghurt, and that advice is sustained.

The hon. Gentleman knows perfectly well that the food hygiene regulations which he mentioned have nothing to do with this outbreak of botulism. He also knows that, as a result of the consultation, we are seeking to resolve the conflicting scientific and other advice which we have received and will produce the regulations as soon as possible. I have already talked about Bristol, where the research station is not engaged in food safety research——

Dr. David Clark (South Shields): That simply is not true.

Mr. Clarke: That must be taken up with the responsible Ministers. My right hon. Friend the Minister of Agriculture, Fisheries and Food will have to deal with that —[*Interruption.*]

I remain reasonably confident—I look to my right hon. Friend for advice—that it is doing no research of any kind relevant to botulism.

I have already dealt with the question of the number of environmental health officers. The resources devoted to them are a matter for local government. We all appreciate that there is an increasing problem of food poisoning in this country, and local authorities, like everyone else, must address their priorities in that connection.

The hon. Gentleman began by saying that this was the worst outbreak of the decade. That sounds sensational until we recognise that there have been no deaths from botulism in that time, and that the country has a singularly good record on botulism in general. The hon. Gentleman should make sure that the points that he makes on this particularly difficult issue are well founded.

Several Hon. Members *rose*——

Mr. Speaker: Order. I shall take points of order after the statement by the Home Secretary.

Commercial Television

3.55 pm

The Secretary of State for the Home Department (Mr. Douglas Hurd): With permission, Mr. Speaker, I should like to make a statement on the future of commercial television. I apologise for its length; a good many complicated matters need to be taken together.

The White Paper proposed a two-stage procedure for awarding licences for Channels 3 and 5 under which applicants would first have to pass a quality threshold—consisting of positive programme and consumer protection requirements—and would then go on to offer financial tenders. The Independent Television Commission would be required to select the highest bidder.

Many of those who commented on the White Paper expressed concern that those proposals might lead to a loss of quality in programming. We recognise that concern, and propose to strengthen the quality threshold. We do not consider that it would be right to do so by adding more detailed requirements in the legislation to supply specific types of programme. We therefore propose to strengthen the quality threshold by broadening the third positive requirement in paragraph 6.11 of the White Paper to read:

"to provide a reasonable proportion of programmes (in addition to news and current affairs) of high quality, and to provide a diverse programme service calculated to appeal to a wide variety of tastes and interests."

It will be for applicants to interpret that combined quality and diversity test in drawing up their programme proposals. Those who fail to satisfy the ITC that they can meet the requirement will not have their financial bids considered.

A number of suggestions have been made about the form that the financial bid should take. The chairman of the IBA proposed that it should comprise a sum fixed by the ITC and a bid by the applicant of a percentage of advertising revenue. I support that combination of elements but, to make the bidding process clearer, propose that they should be reversed. Accordingly, the ITC will fix a percentage of net advertising or subscription revenue for each licence to form the minimum sale price. Applicants will then be required to bid a lump sum, which they will pay in addition if successful. For successful applicants, both sums will be paid annually over the period of the licence to avoid the imposition of debt burdens on licensees.

Applicants will also be required to post a bond with their tender applications. Successful bidders will be required to add to that an amount which, together with the first, will add up to a substantial performance bond. This requirement will strengthen the enforcement powers of the ITC, making them stronger and more flexible than those of the IBA now. Those who fail to meet their programme promises given at the quality threshold stage will stand to lose a proportion of the bond.

We have considered carefully the arguments about the criteria for deciding tenders. I do not believe that at the tender stage, before it is clear to whom the licences will be awarded and before the nature of any network arrangement is known, it will be possible for the ITC to make fine distinctions between the quality of programme service offered by different applicants, all of whom will have passed the strengthened quality hurdle that I have

[*Mr. Douglas Hurd*]

announced today. We must avoid a return to the opaque and sometimes arbitrary selection procedures of the past, but some flexibility needs to be written into the procedure.

We propose, therefore, that the ITC should be required in the normal course to accept the highest bid, but that it should have a power, in exceptional circumstances, to select a lower bid. This power would operate only in exceptional circumstances, the ITC would be required to give its full reasons, and exercise of the power would be subject to judicial review. In addition, there would be an exceptional power for the Home Secretary, acting on the recommendation of the ITC, to veto the selection of the highest bid if its funding came from a source that was undesirable in the public interest.

The White paper proposed that in addition to the sum bid at tender applicants would have to make a levy payment to the Exchequer. The proposals I have just announced for the fixing of a proportion of advertising or subscription revenue as a part of the tender price overtake our original proposals for a levy. Successful candidates will have only to pay the two-part tender price I have outlined. There will be no levy in addition.

Some people have wondered whether the Government would impose a moratorium on takeovers at the beginning of 1993 and whether they would insist on compulsory networking for Channel 3. The Government's view on both issues has not changed since the publication of the White Paper. I understand that the chairman of the IBA is considering permitting takeovers in the period from 1990 to 1993, subject to the normal anti-monopoly rules and bearing in mind our proposals for the régime after 1992. It would not in these circumstances be either sensible or necessary to impose a moratorium on takeovers thereafter. Networking will be a matter for the Channel 3 companies themselves to decide without Government compulsion. Basic fair trading laws should ensure that no companies are excluded unfairly from any networking arrangements. We shall consider whether any further provisions are needed in the legislation to regulate the operation of any new network system in the interests of free access and fair competition.

We have received a number of representations on behalf of the 4 million viewers who are deaf or hard of hearing. We agree that particular provision should be made for them. We have therefore decided that Channel 3 and Channel 5 licensees should be required to provide teletext sub-titling for some of the programmes in their schedules. They should provide more than is provided at present.

The White Paper proposed that Channel 5 should be shared between at least two licensees. In the light of the start-up costs of the new channel and the competition it will face from the established terrestrial channels, we have now decided that Channel 5 should form a single licence. It will thus be better equipped to compete with the existing terrestrial channels.

Similarly, the White Paper proposed that there should be a separate night hours licence for Channel 3. Many of those who responded to the White Paper doubted whether a separate night hours licence would be viable, so we have looked at this again. We want to ensure, so far as possible, that the night hours are fully used. I accept the argument that they may be better exploited commercially if they are linked with services provided at a more commercially attractive part of the broadcasting day. We have therefore decided not to disturb the present situation under which the night hours may remain connected with the peak viewing period. However, we will review the position if we find that the night hours are not being fully used. Under our proposals, the ITC will be free to allocate licences for other times of the day, such as a breakfast time service.

The White Paper proposed that the ITC would be responsible for the map—for the geographical division of Channel 3 into regions. This has been generally welcomed. The Government have noted with understanding the statement of the chairman-designate of the ITC, Mr. George Russell, that he would see advantage, if possible, in retaining the existing regions.

I turn finally to Channel 4 and S4C, the Welsh channel. The White Paper made clear the Government's intention to maintain the remit of Channel 4 while at the same time providing for the selling of its advertising separately from that on Channel 3. We have considered the comments we have received on the three options in the White Paper, and in particular the helpful report by the Home Affairs Select Committee. I have written today to the Chairman of the Committee expressing the Government's gratitude for its work on Channel 4 and setting out the Government's decisions. A copy of that letter has been placed in the Library.

The Government have decided that it would not be feasible at the present time for Channel 4 to become an independent commercial company competing with the other broadcasters if, as we think essential, it is to retain its remit. The financial outlook for Channel 4 remains uncertain with the prospect of new competition. We believe that the requirement in addition to provide a return for shareholders in a private company could put too much pressure upon Channel 4 finances and place its remit in jeopardy. But we see some difficulty in Channel 4 continuing to be owned by the authority which would be responsible for regulating its output—the ITC—and we believe that any financial underpinning given to the channel should be carefully circumscribed to provide clear incentives for cost-efficiency.

We have therefore decided that after 1993, if Parliament agrees, Channel 4 should become a public trust which will be licensed by the ITC and will continue to provide the service set out in the special remit. Channel 4 would sell its own advertising, and would be subject to a baseline budget of 14 per cent. per annum of terrestrial net advertising revenue. The baseline could be amended in secondary legislation. If the channel's revenue fell below the baseline, the difference would be funded by the ITC to a maximum of 2 per cent. of terrestrial net advertising revenue levied on the Channel 3 companies, but any surplus revenues above the baseline would be shared equally between Channel 3 and Channel 4. The trust would be required to hold its share of any surplus revenues to be used as a first call if there were deficits in later years. To reduce the need for a call on the guarantee, the ITC would be empowered to require cross announcement of programmes between Channel 3 and Channel 4. Complementary scheduling would be possible, but would not be a requirement. The Channel 4 licence would run for 10 years, but the arrangements would be reviewed after seven. I believe that is a satisfactory way of securing the future of Channel 4 with its present remit.

The White Paper concluded that the arrangements for the Welsh fourth channel should remain unchanged. Some have argued that it would not be consistent with the new and more free approach to regulation for the channel to be funded by a direct subscription on the commercial companies. The position is particularly anomalous in Scotland where the ITV companies are required to finance Welsh programmes as a first call on their resources even before they make provision for their own Gaelic speakers. The Government are sympathetic to these concerns, and have decided to make a small technical change to the funding arrangements for S4C. In future, S4C revenues will not be charged as a first call on the commercial companies but will be funded out of the proceeds of the tender through the ITC.

My statement covers most of the major decisions on the future commercial television system following the publication of the White Paper. We shall need to make announcements on the remaining issues, including the key question of transmission and the future of broadcasting in Gaelic, before long. Then we shall draft the Bill.

Mr. Robin Corbett (Birmingham, Erdington): The Home Secretary and the House will understand if I do not respond in detail to the mini White Paper today. Clearly we shall return to the issue in the autumn when we consider the Bill.

The revised proposal for awarding the licences for Channel 3 and Channel 5 are no more than a figleaf behind which the Home Secretary seeks to cover his humiliation at the hands of the Prime Minister, aided by the Secretary of State for Trade and Industry. In most important respects, the bidding for the licences has barely changed from that set out in paragraph 6·9 of the White Paper which stated:

"there is no longer the same need for quality of service to be prescribed by legislation or regulatory fiat."

All that the Home Secretary has said today is that the ITC can have reserve powers to reject the highest bid, while explaining why. In my view that amounts to no more than a tiny teaspoon to bale out a well-holed ship. Is it not the very least that could be done to meet the statement made by Mr. George Russell that unless the ITC had these powers, he would find his position untenable? I commend Mr. Russell on his stand on behalf of the viewers' best interests.

The rewording of the so-called positive requirement in paragraph 6.11 does no more than express in 35 words what took just 16 words in the White Paper. Simply adding the phrase "high quality" does nothing to guarantee that it will be delivered, nor does anything else that the Home Secretary said today. In any event, what is a reasonable proportion and who will decide it?

The statement is light on what exact amounts of money are to be provided by bidders who deliver the range and types of programme which the bid promises. The Home Secretary went out of his way to make it clear that he did not regard that to be necessary. The changes in the financial arrangements at least acknowledge that Channel 3 will face increasing competition from satellite services and are simpler and clearer than the original proposals.

I am still uncertain about what the term "financially sound" means. It seems that it will mean no more than checking on whether the cash behind the bid comes from drugs or vice. That is the problem. The Home Secretary's statement, like the White Paper, is too much about cash and not sufficiently concerned with ensuring that the cash on the table will deliver real choice and quality in terms of range and standards. Will the Home Secretary confirm that bidders will not have to guarantee to programme current affairs in main viewing programmes? Is it not the case that the same remains true of children's and religious programmes?

It is unacceptable to Opposition Members—and to some Conservative Members—that an individual should be able to own two Channel 3 licences. The Opposition believe that one person should be able to own only one franchise if there is to be real diversity in the new system.

I welcome the requirement for Channel 3 and Channel 5 licences to provide teletext subtitling for some programmes for the 4 million people who are deaf or hard of hearing. I hope that that will become mandatory for all news and current affairs programmes, and for most, rather than some, programmes eventually.

I also welcome the decision not to separate off the night hours. It was patently not sensible for the Home Secretary to propose in the White Paper to take the night hours away from the BBC while requiring it to maximise its subscription services.

Becoming a trust is the least worst option for Channel 4, although we would have preferred the status quo. What is disappointing is that despite the Government's tribute to Channel 4's "striking success" their proposals are unlikely to provide enough stability for it to meet its needs in the face of stiffening competition in terrestrial and satellite services.

Even after the statement, the Government's proposals will do no more than achieve lower quality, lower standards, less public responsibility and fewer regions within Channel 3. The proposals will not use technological change to bring about more real choice. The proposals are simply a route to undermining what the White Paper called—I hope not sarcastically—the "rich heritage" of British broadcasing. The statement reveals that the vandals have won—at least under this Government.

Mr. Hurd: The hon. Gentleman has fallen into the trap into which his right hon. Friend the Member for Birmingham, Sparkbrook (Mr. Hattersley) always falls. He has chosen to comment on inaccurate press reports about our proposals even though, by the conventions of the House, he has had a bit of time—not long, I admit—to study the proposals themselves. The hon. Gentleman has talked as though all the press reports were true. The next step, if precedent is to be followed, is that Mr. Des Wilson will write a learned article suggesting that I stimulated all the inaccurate press reports to lure the hon. Gentleman into the trap into which he has fallen.

The hon. Gentleman has ignored the three changes made on the quality threshold in response to comments on the White Paper. First, the quality threshold has been stiffened so that it is similar to the proposal in the Broadcasting Act 1981. Secondly, there will be the exceptional power of the ITC. It is exceptional—I have explained the circumstances—to award a franchise to other than the highest bidder. Thirdly, and most importantly, there will be the performance bond, which the hon. Gentleman did not mention. It will give the ITC a power that the present Independent Broadcasting Authority does not have, which is a flexible and powerful way to enforce the promises that have been made. The ITC will no longer face the criticism that all it can do is to

[Mr. Hurd]

remove the franchise, which is a power, like nuclear weapons, that is difficult to use. It will have conventional weapons with which to enforce promises.

The hon. Gentleman made two points about the news. It is clear in the White Paper that news will be a requirement and will have to be included in main time. Current affairs will also be a requirement, but there is no specific requirement about when current affairs programmes should be shown. It would not be reasonable to stipulate that in legislation.

I am glad that the hon. Gentleman welcomed our announcement about subtitling for the deaf. It is proposed that Channel 3 and Channel 5 licensees should, in the first year of the licence, provide 10 per cent. more hours of subtitling than was achieved on average by the ITV companies in the previous year. The ITC will thereafter set a reasonable target each year for an increase in subtitling.

Several Hon. Members *rose——*

Mr. Speaker: Order. I remind the House that we have a busy day ahead of us with no fewer than 120 groupings of amendments and a ten-minute Bill. I shall allow questions on this important matter to continue until quarter to five, but then we must move on.

Mr. John Gorst (Hendon, North): Will my right hon. Friend accept my welcome for his proposals, especially for the flexibility that he has shown? As many of the things that he has announced today are new, will he be open to further consultation on them with interested parties or are they now final until they are encapsulated in a Bill in the autumn?

Mr. Hurd: We have tried to listen, as was our duty, to the reactions to the White Paper and to reach a balanced reaction to them. Of course, people will continue to express views in the months ahead and it will ultimately be for both Houses of Parliament to reach conclusions. To that extent, our ears can never be shut. We have reached the conclusions that we think are sensible.

Mr. Merlyn Rees (Morley and Leeds, South): The Home Secretary has made a most important statement to which he said that there were three main aspects, but I have a long list. Is there some way in which we can have a debate on this matter, Mr. Speaker, because we cannot go through it in the next half hour and believe that we shall then have dealt with it?

Professor Peacock, who produced the Peacock report was concerned about the issue of competitive tendering in the original proposals. Has he been consulted? Does the Home Secretary think that Professor Peacock would be content with the changes that the Home Secretary has made?

Mr. Hurd: On the first point, we have had a debate on the White Paper, and there will of course, be long debates on the Bill when it comes before the House. I considered whether to do this in a written statement but the Opposition would have protested if I had. I apologise again for the length of what I had to say.

Professor Peacock commented last week on the basis of press reports. We were in touch with him later in the week

to explain that those reports were so incomplete as to be misleading. It is now for him to say what he thinks about the proposals.

Mr. Alick Buchanan-Smith (Kincardine and Deeside): May I welcome what my hon. Friend the Member for Hendon, North (Mr. Gorst) said about Conservative Members welcoming the flexibility that our right hon. Friend has shown and the modifications that he has made? While obviously we want to follow through and work out the implications, especially of competitive tendering, does my right hon. Friend appreciate that those of us who come from areas with small, independent companies are still concerned because the present system has not worked badly in reflecting the quality and the character of those areas and we are left feeling nervous that price may still be the ultimate determinant of who gets the tender? Will my right hon. Friend bear in mind the financial position of those companies when compared with some of the large companies that serve the much more populated areas of this country? The possibility of a dual franchise, which would make competition more difficult, given the resources of those companies, means that we remain concerned. I hope that my right hon. Friend will consider that point a little further in relation to competitive tendering and price being the ultimate determinant.

Finally, we in Scotland very much welcome the fact that my right hon. Friend is removing the burden on companies in Scotland that have to pay for subsidising Welsh programmes when they already finance Gaelic programmes in Scotland. I thank my right hon. Friend very much for that.

Mr. Hurd: I am grateful to my right hon. Friend. I know of his anxieties because he has expressed them to me. We have had very much in our minds the anxieties of some of the smaller companies. That is very important. The decision has not yet been taken about transmission costs, which weigh heavily on a company such as Grampian. When we move forward to that consideration, we shall bear in mind what my right hon. Friend has said.

Mr. Robert Hughes (Aberdeen, North): Will the Home Secretary accept that he has no need to apologise for the length of his statement, but much more need to apologise for the fact that it was nothing more than a vacuous homily? There was no substance in it. Why did he speak about "substantial, reasonable proportions"? Why did he not tell us what the performance bond will be? Why did he not say specifically that there will be no dual ownership? Why does he not say specifically that quality will be the real test when awarding the franchises, not cash?

Mr. Hurd: I thought that my statement was so precise and detailed as to verge on the tedious, but not on the empty. There is of course a limit to the extent to which Parliament or a Bill should decide all these matters in detail. Parliament is not the regulatory authority. We must leave a certain amount to the ITC, and I have explained exactly what that is.

The statement that I made some weeks ago about ownership was of a tight regime corresponding to the views expressed by many people, including the Opposition. We do not believe that it is right for the same franchisee, the same holder, to own two large companies or to own two companies that are next door to each other. But we do not exclude—I do not think it would be reasonable to do so, if we want the small companies to survive—the possibility of someone holding one large and one small franchise.

Mr. John Wheeler (Westminster, North): My right hon. Friend has received much advice about the future of broadcasting, not least from the Select Committee on Home Affairs and its report on the future of broadcasting and the funding of Channel 4. I thank him for his generous remarks about my Committee's report and for the pleasure it gives members of the Committee to know that the financial guarantee is to be there to enable Channel 4 to continue with its diverse programming and important remit. May I ask my right hon. Friend to comment on why he has chosen a trust as opposed to option two?

In respect of Channel 3 licences, I appreciate his comments about preserving diversity and the tests that he now proposes. Will he agree that the reserve power given to the ITC must be firmly defined it it is to be effective?

Mr. Hurd: To answer my hon. Friend's final point, the House will wish to look at the wording carefully. We have not yet put it in statutory language. I have made it clear that it should be exceptional and that it should be public. One of the problems with the present system is that the decisions are like those of the oubliette—at one moment everybody is there, with the franchise holders all together, and at the next moment somebody has disappeared with no reason or explanation given and no redress. That is not, in our view, a satisfactory system.

To answer my hon. Friend's question about Channel 4, it was felt that there was a difficulty, familiar in other contexts, between having the same agency—in this case the ITC—owning and regulating Channel 4. So there should be a separation between ownership and regulation. But, equally, we decided, partly in the light of the report of my hon. Friend's Committee, that it would not be sensible to go for total privatisation—that is, option one—so we happened on the concept of a trust, which I think fits the need.

Mr. Charles Kennedy (Ross, Cromarty and Skye): Is it not a fact that in the spheres of programme quality, diversity of choice and regional sensitivity the fatal flaw in what the Home Secretary has announced today, and to which others have referred, is the lack of definition in his statement? Phrases such as "public interest," "exceptional circumstances" and "quality thresholds" are not clearly defined. Indeed, in one case he tells us that they are to be the subject of judicial review. There is not much safeguard in that in terms of the awarding of franchises and the upholding of commitments given.

I particularly underscore the anxiety expressed by the right hon. Member for Kincardine and Deeside (Mr. Buchanan-Smith) about the future of the Scottish regional companies, for which there will be little reassurance because the Home Secretary merely expresses some sympathy for the sentiment that we should retain existing regions, if possible.

The bottom line of the right hon. Gentleman's statement is that the only cast-iron guarantees he has given are in terms of cash for the Treasury and business for the lawyers, with the interests of the broadcasters and viewers being out of sight, if not out of mind.

Mr. Hurd: The hon. Gentleman knows better than that. He knows that the phrases which he criticises are used

constantly in the House and in Acts of Parliament. They are familiar to regulatory authorities and to the courts. The House will of course want to look at the phrases, and that is natural, but there is nothing particularly obscure or opaque about them.

As for the map, we propose—I hope that, on reflection, the hon. Gentleman will agree with this—that it is not sensible for the House or for the law of the land to set in concrete for ever the map of broadcasting companies. It is not there now in the law and it would be absurd to suppose that it would be sensible to put it in primary legislation. It should be left, as we propose, to the ITC, and therefore I chose my words carefully. We noticed with understanding that the chairman-elect of the ITC said—I think the hon. Gentleman would agree—that, as far as possible, he sees advantage in retaining the present map.

Sir Giles Shaw (Pudsey): I warmly welcome the majority of the statement. I congratulate my right hon. Friend on listening so fully to all the representations. That is most welcome, especially in the context of matters such as broadcasting.

I wish to ask my right hon. Friend three brief questions. The first relates to the quality of assessment, which is now so crucial in the awarding of contracts. As he did not mention regional commitment, regional programming or regional viewers, will he comment on them? Secondly, with regard to the ITC's reserve power under a performance bond, will the bond be of a significant size relative to the areas in which it is located—for example, a smaller bond for the smaller companies in the smaller areas? Thirdly, has my right hon. Friend given any further thought to the ownership of transmitters and transmission? He will recall that that is a matter of considerable concern. While I accept the present point of view, there are considerable overlaps in the existing map to which, quite frankly, the transmission issue is linked.

Mr. Hurd: I am grateful to my hon. Friend, whose three questions are much to the point. The White Paper already gives a clear commitment to the regional content of Channel 3 programmes. What I announced today was in addition to that commitment and, for the first time, it includes a proportion of regional production. My hon. Friend is right to suggest that the size of the bond will be fixed by the ITC, but it will vary according to the franchise under discussion. We are considering transmission costs and the system of transmission. When we have decided what should be included in the Bill, I shall inform the House.

Mr. Bruce Grocott (The Wrekin): Is the Home Secretary aware that he has said nothing to allay the genuine fear of virtually all those involved in broadcasting that he is presiding over a virtual collapse of programme standards? How will what he has proposed improve programme standards in any way? Will the competing companies have to publish their programme proposals in detail? How will the controlling mechanism work? How can it be that he rejects outright commercialism for Channel 4 as being in conflict with programme standards, but appears to think that outright and unbridled commercialism for Channel 3 will guarantee programme standards?

Mr. Hurd: I shall not repeat my answers to previous questions because the hon. Gentleman is simply repeating

[*Mr. Hurd*]

what his hon. Friend the Member for Birmingham, Erdington (Mr. Corbett) said and to which I have responded.

On the question of quality threshold, an applicant will come forward and after the ITC has given an illustration of what variety and diversity should mean for that particular franchise the applicant can put forward his proposals. The ITC will then judge whether the quality threshold has been passed, and, if so, the undertakings that have been given will be incorporated in the licence.

The question of commercialism and programme standards is a matter of balance. We are not suggesting that every channel should be like the BBC or Channel 4. We aim to strike a balance, with the BBC—which has not been dealt with today—remaining as the cornerstone, and with Channel 4 preserving its remit—under the arrangements that I announced today it can clearly preserve its remit, and that has been the issue—although with a lighter touch and an increased choice with respect to Channels 3 and 5. That is the balance that we seek to strike.

Mr. John Maples (Lewisham, West): Is my right hon. Friend aware that he has gone a long way towards meeting objections both about the auction process for Channel 3 and the future of Channel 4? I hope that he will not pay too much attention to the Opposition's churlish and grudging response; they seem to be incapable of taking "yes" for an answer.

Will my right hon. Friend deal with one point that was not dealt with in his statement? Has he given any further thought to cross-media ownership and the restrictions on that with respect to Channels 3 and 5?

Mr. Hurd: I am grateful to my hon. Friend and to my right hon. and hon. Friends in general for their reception to matters to which many of them have devoted a great deal of thought. In a written answer last month I set out a rather complicated set of proposals on cross-media ownership, to which I refer my hon. Friend. If I were to attempt to repeat them out of my head, I might get some of them wrong. We accept the need for tight controls and restrictions on cross-ownership not only between holders of terrestrial franchises, but between holders of terrestrial franchises and the press.

Mr. Joseph Ashton (Bassetlaw): Is the Home Secretary aware that the international hucksters will laugh at the idea of forfeiting a substantial bond? Is he aware that what he has announced is exactly what happened with TV-am —the ITV breakfast-time programme—which was launched with a fanfare of big names and all sorts of promises but rapidly deteriorated into trivia and trash once the Australians took it over? That is what will happen again. Faced with the prospect of putting on quality programmes that will not sell much advertising or trash that will, the hucksters will immediately forfeit the substantial bond to keep the franchises.

Mr. Hurd: Then they will not keep the franchises.

Mr. Roger Gale (Thanet, North): Will my right hon. Friend accept that the discarding of the proposals to impose a levy will be most welcome and that the proposed alternative financial arrangements will be much more acceptable to the ITV companies? Will he accept, too, that

the exceptional circumstances provision, under which, and only under which, any bid would be rejected by the ITC, will go a long way to meet many of the fears that have been expressed?

I shall ask my right hon. Friend three quick questions. Further to the question posed by my hon. Friend the Member for Pudsey (Sir G. Shaw), when my right hon. Friend defines the legislation for the quality threshold will he include specific reference to certain kinds of programming, particularly children's programmes?

Secondly, I am pleased that my right hon. Friend has announced the establishment of a public trust rather than any of the previous suggested options for Channel 4. However, does he really think that it is right for the independent companies, which will no longer have any vested interest in Channel 4, to have to underwrite Channel 4?

Thirdly, the announcement concerning ITV night hours is most welcome. May we hope that that line of thought will be extended to BBC night hours?

Mr. Hurd: I have a lot of sympathy with what my hon. Friend says about children's programmes. I believe that it will be difficult to specify in legislation all the different kinds of programmes which could make up variety, quality and diversity and, therefore, a good deal will have to be left to the ITC. However, that is a matter to which we shall certainly return.

I understand my hon. Friend's point about Channels 3 and 4. It is right that there should be some underwriting —limited, as we propose—of Channel 4 to ensure that the remit can be maintained. It is reasonable that the ITC should, as I suggested, draw to that limited extent on Channel 3. My hon. Friend will have noticed, however, that the safeguards are there.

I know my hon. Friend's view on the night hours, which is a matter that needs now to be considered. We have had many reactions to the original proposal, to which we must now turn our attention, and give the House our views when we can.

Mr. John D. Taylor (Strangford): I welcome generally the Home Secretary's statement. It emphasises that, first, there will be greater transparency in the way in which licences are allocated to firms, and, secondly, that there will be greater competition. Will the Secretary of State consider the system that applies in the Republic of Ireland whereby those who—[*Interruption*]—yes, I am recommending something from the Republic of Ireland— whereby those who apply for licences must present their case and answer questions in public before the licensing authority so that the public at large have a greater idea as to the basis on which a licence is allocated?

On the question of competition, will the Secretary of State bear in mind that what has been said by colleagues from Scotland on both sides of the House about regional problems apply in Northern Ireland? We would not like to see dual ownership. We would like to see emerge a company that is truly representative of the traditions of Northern Ireland—Protestant and Catholic, Unionist and Nationalist.

Mr. Hurd: I have much sympathy with what the right hon. Gentleman said about Ulster television, which is important to the life of the Province. I note what he says about public hearings, but I am not sure whether it would be sensible to embody that as a requirement in legislation.

Mr. John Greenway (Ryedale): Is it not clear from my right hon. Friend's statement that this is a Government who bring forward radical proposals for the benefit of consumers, take stock of comment from interested parties, listen and bring forward a reformed package in light of the representations made? I am sure that what my right hon. Friend has said will end a great deal of uncertainty within ITV currently.

Is my right hom. Friend aware that last week, at a symposium hosted by the Independent Television Association and chaired by Sir Alan Peacock, the concept of having a franchise awarded by competitive auction was considered feasible, provided there were adequate safeguards to prevent over-bidding? Is my right hon. Friend satisfied that the arrangements that he has introduced will achieve that objective? Does he further agree that, with the Channel 3 franchises, it will be much better to leave maximum flexibility in the hands of the ITC when drafting the legislation rather than specifying far too much and thus creating a straitjacket?

With regard to Channel 4, has my right hon. Friend given further consideration to the question of cross-promotion of Channels 3, 4 and 5?

Mr. Hurd: I am grateful to my hon. Friend for his initial remarks, with which I agree.

We need to consider the cross-promotion point, but it is difficult to lay it down in legislation. I have said something about the cross announcements that will be necessary between Channels 3 and 4.

Several Hon. Members *rose——*

Mr. Speaker: Order. I shall allow 10 minutes more on this statement. I shall do my best to call those hon. Members who are rising, providing they ask brief questions.

Mr. Mark Fisher (Stoke-on-Trent, Central): I recognise that the Home Secretary has listened to and even accepted much of the critical evidence he received on the White Paper. He has failed to act, however, on some of the crucial points precisely because he still seems reluctant to define his terms. Will he tell the House what the exceptional circumstances are under which the chairman of the ITC can refuse the highest bid?

On specific programme requirements, does my right hon. Friend accept that the only way to ensure quality and diversity of programmes, covering children's programmes, documentaries, religious and educational programmes, is the current written detailed requirements? The general terms that he is continuing to propose are wholly inadequate and will not ensure such quality and diversity.

Mr. Hurd: I do not think that I can define exceptional circumstances, and it would be absurd to do so in advance. The House will note that there is a double instrument of control; an instrument in the hands of the ITC, and an instrument in the hands of the Secretary of State acting on the recommendations of the ITC. The Secretary of State could act if, for example, money went into a bid which did not amount to foreign control—we could deal with that otherwise—but which might generate interests that were clearly hostile to this country or might mean that, in a particular part of our country, arrangements would be set up that would be clearly contrary to the public interest. It is reasonable to have both instruments.

There will be nothing vague in the franchise terms. They will be worked out in some detail and written down. The ITC will have substantially greater powers than the existing IBA to ensure that those terms are effectively enforced.

Mr. John Redwood (Wokingham): Does the Home Secretary agree that during the winter ITV1 took a lot of the market share away from BBC1 through investment in good quality drama and that that was a good commercial decision as it enabled ITV to sell its programmes abroad? Does he agree that the conclusion to be drawn is that there is no necessary conflict between quality of programming and the pursuit of commercial opportunity? With the growing sophistication of the audience, the two often go together.

Mr. Hurd: I am glad that my hon. Friend made that point. I am familiar with the argument that some of the ITV companies, if driven too hard, will spend much less money and produce cheap programmes only. I noticed from press reports that when those companies began to feel the wind a bit their reaction was to spend more on higher quality programmes.

Mr. Rhodri Morgan (Cardiff, West): Does the Home Secretary accept that our criticisms are not churlish but are based on the fact that some of us have television organisations within our constituencies? We are well aware that when the right hon. Gentleman lined up with George Russell and the ITV companies in their criticisms of the auction system, he was attacked by Right-wing ideologues, clustered around 10 Downing street. Despite his agonised squeal, "Get your tanks off my lawn", he has lost the battle, even though he has won some small victories which he has announced with great pride this afternoon.

In the main, the questions that he has said will be asked are these: "Have you got the capital?", Not "Have you got the talent?, and "What are you going to make?" which is 28·5 per cent. not good programmes.

Mr. Hurd: I do not recognise the hon. Gentleman's description of the very workmanlike discussions which we have had inside Government on this matter, nor, I think, will the House when hon. Members have studied what I have said. The hon. Gentleman misses the essential point. It is a double process. An application will come forward with programme plans and ideas to pass the quality and variety threshold. It is only after an applicant has done that—and it will be more difficult, it will be a higher test, as a result of today's announcement—that the length of his purse will become relevant.

Mr. Tony Baldry (Banbury): Does my right hon. Friend agree that, with the franchise going to the highest bidder subject to a much strengthened overriding quality test and the ability of the Independent Television Commission not to award the contract to the highest bidder if it feels that that bidder is incapable of delivering the quality, we shall have a much simpler, clearer, fairer and more straightforward system of awarding franchises than the present somewhat opaque and oblique system? Do not the changes that my right hon. Friend has announced this afternoon demonstrate that he has clearly listened to what people have been saying over the past few weeks?

Mr. Hurd: I have tried to listen; I have not had very much option but to listen. We certainly have listened hard

[*Mr. Hurd*]

and tried to respond generally. I agree with what my hon. Friend said and would simply add something about the performance bond, which has not appeared in any of the press leaks. It will be a very important technique in helping the ITC to enforce quality.

Mr. Tony Worthington (Clydebank and Milngavie): The announcements which the Home Secretary has made today are all very welcome and in the right direction, but the right hon. Gentleman will never get to the correct destination unless he abandons the original assumptions of the broadcasting White Paper. Praise has been lavished upon the Home Affairs Select Committee's report, which says that both ITV and BBC should have public service broadcasting traditions at their heart and that that would safeguard the system. Will the Home Secretary now accept that that was the correct recommendation and should be accepted?

Furthermore, will the Home Secretary think again about the situation in Scotland? It would be simply intolerable if the House did not have a say on the number of stations within Scotland and a Government-appointed quango was able to recommend that there be only one station within Scotland. Will the Home Secretary guarantee that the present three stations, or something very similar, will be maintained?

Mr. Hurd: The hon. Member talked about the original assumptions. The original assumption in the White Paper is that there is now an opportunity for a very big choice for the viewer. Instead of sitting on that and saying that they cannot have it because we are not sure that they would make the best use of it, we are trying to provide a framework within which the viewer can have increasing choice. We believe that, particularly as a result of the conclusions we have just come to, we can reconcile that with high quality. The hon. Gentleman is asking for something which has never existed before and which probably, on reflection, the House would not want—that the map should be settled by the House. It never has been before. There have been major changes in the past conducted and put through by the IBA. I do not think that it is a matter for primary legislation, and I have set out the present position.

Mr. Robert G. Hughes (Harrow, West): Does my right hon. Friend accept that his announcement today that subtitling for the deaf and hard of hearing on Channels 3 and 5 will be mandatory and will be increased in the first year by 10 per cent. will be greeted as an enormous milestone and that there will be great thanks to him from that community for what he has done? Is he able to tell the House today what he regards as the next milestone in this and what pressure there will be on the ITC to ensure that the 10 per cent. increase does not become the entire increase?

Secondly, will my right hon. Friend accept that it would be thought wrong if the logic that has led him to announce today that the night time hours of Channel 3 will stay with the franchise holder for the day time did not lead him to leave the night time hours of the BBC with the BBC?

Mr. Hurd: My hon. Friend is right on his first point; we foresee a steady build-up of subtitling year by year. I note what my hon. Friend said on his second point. We have set out in the White Paper our notions about the BBC night hours and have noted the reaction. We have not yet turned to that matter, but we will have to do so.

Mr. John McAllion (Dundee, East): The Home Secretary has said that he is in favour of increasing choice. Does he not accept that real choice for viewers will be diminished if small, locally based high quality companies such as Grampian Television do not survive? Why can he not assure the House that the exceptional power of the ITC to award a franchise to other than the highest bidder will be used to ensure the survival of companies such as Grampian?

Mr. Hurd: I do not think that it would be sensible or right to give any such assurance. I know the loyalty which the small companies attract from their viewers, and indeed from their Members of Parliament who live within their areas. That has been clear throughout these debates. However, I question whether the hon. Gentleman would be wise to suggest that the decisions about the map of television franchises should be enshrined in statute.

Mr. Speaker: I am sorry that I have not been able to call the remaining two hon. Members, but we have a very busy day ahead of us.

STATUTORY INSTRUMENTS, &C.

Ordered,

That the draft Design Right (Semiconductor Topographies) Regulations 1989 be referred to a Standing Committee on Statutory Instruments, &c.—[*Mr. Maclean.*]

Employers' Liability Bill

4.45 pm

Mr. Frank Doran (Aberdeen, South): I beg to move,
That leave be given to bring in a Bill to require employers to provide death-in-service insurance benefits for their employees; and for connected purposes.

The main purpose of the Bill is to extend the obligation on employers to insure their employees against death or injury at work. The existing scheme was introduced in 1969 and now covers the great majority of Britain's 22·5 million workers. The main difficulty with the present scheme, however, is that it still requires proof of negligence or fault on the part of an employer before a claim for compensation will be successful.

In most cases an injured employee, or his representative if the accident was fatal, will instruct a solicitor. The case will be intimated to the employers, who will pass the case to their insurers. There will be a period of haggling between solicitors and insurance companies. Many cases are settled at this stage. A great many are not and require legal proceedings.

Cases which do not go to court can take a great many months, sometimes even years, to settle. When they go to court cases certainly take years; delays of seven or eight years are quite common. Even then there is still the problem of proving fault or negligence on the part of the employers. Many employers and their insurers escape liability on technical legal grounds. The whole system is a lottery.

One particularly graphic example of the difficulties which are experienced is the case of the mv Derbyshire, which sank in 1980 with the loss of the whole crew of 44. The representatives of those 44 crew members have been involved in litigation ever since. They have been unable to prove negligence and it is unlikely that they will ever receive proper compensation for their loss. Yet they have all lost a loved one—a loved one who, regardless of the question of fault or negligence, died in the service of his employer. No disaster fund was set up and there were no visits from dignitaries such as the Prime Minister. The dependants of those 44 crew members have had to cope with the trauma of the loss of a loved one without adequate compensation to help them adjust to their new circumstances. That is a scandal in anyone's terms.

I am a firm believer in a "no fault" liability scheme. However, time and again this Government have made it clear that they are not prepared to consider such a scheme, which operates extremely well in Canada, Australia and New Zealand.

My Bill is a modest attempt to introduce some equity and justice into the very haphazard system of compensation for injury and death which our legal system has created. For the present I am restricting its operation to cases in which there is a death resulting from an accident or illness at work. The motivation for the Bill arises out of my involvement in pursuing compensation claims as a solicitor in Scotland and also out of my involvement in the aftermath of the Piper Alpha disaster, which affected so many of my constituents.

On the Piper Alpha I discovered that of the 167 men who died 31 were employed by the operators, Occidental. Those men were covered by an insurance scheme that provided their relatives with an immediate payment of £100,000 in the event of the men's death in employment.

The relatives of the other 136 victims have had to go through the normal channels of instructing solicitors to pursue their claims, with all the uncertainty that that involves. To their credit, Occidental and their lawyers have done what they could to speed up the process of agreeing compensation claims and in most cases agreement has been reached, although payment has not yet been made.

However, even this does not overcome the major problems for those who have lost a loved one. The time of most stress is immediately after the death. The survivors have to cope not only with the emotional stress of the loss, but, in most cases, with the financial loss. In the case of a young family, for example, where the loss of the main breadwinner can cause particularly serious financial problems, the difficulties are most acute.

We had a useful opportunity to discuss compensation and the anomalies involved earlier in the year when my hon. Friend the Member for Leigh (Mr. Cunliffe) introduced his Citizens' Compensation Bill. That Bill met with considerable hostility from the Government and I regret that the opportunity to deal with the real problems caused by the present system was missed.

It is not good enough to say to those families that they may have a legal right of action against an employer when that involves months, possibly years, of legal argument, financial outlay, considerably increased stress and no guarantee of success at the end of the day.

My Bill attempts to deal with those problems in a novel way. In the first place, it would oblige employers to carry compulsory insurance to provide an immediate payment to the representatives of an employee who died as a result of an accident or illness at work. There would be no requirement for proof of negligence and the payments would be ignored when the court was considering any subsequent compensation claim. There would be criminal penalties for any employer who failed to carry full insurance cover, and the court would be empowered to make an order for the full amount required to be paid under the insurance.

The Bill provides that the amount of cover per employee should be determined by regulation. That is to allow for upgrading in future. At the moment, my view is that £25,000 of cover per employee would be appropriate. That figure is reasonable, it is not excessive compared with current awards by the courts and it would be relatively cheap from the employer's point of view.

It would be open to employers to choose to provide a higher level of benefit. Many choose to do so already. One set of figures that I have seen suggests that over 20 per cent. of the work force is covered by such a scheme on a voluntary basis.

More than 22·5 million people in employment in the United Kingdom would be covered by the scheme proposed in the Bill. According to the latest annual report of the Health and Safety Commission, there were, on provisional figures, 340 fatal injuries at work in the United Kingdom last year. Since 1981 there have been 2,895 cases. In our legal system, it is likely that the majority of those 2,895 cases, where there are grounds for compensation claims, will still be unresolved.

In the absence of a no-fault scheme, the problems of delay in the legal system will continue. My Bill will provide some immediate financial assistance for those in greatest need at a time when it is most needed.

I have described the Bill as a modest measure, and indeed it is. There will be no cost to the Government or the

[*Mr. Frank Doran*]

public purse. The cost to the employers will be extremely small and, in most cases, negligible in their total employment costs. However, to those families who lose a loved one through a work-related cause it will be of the most enormous significance at a time of great stress and most need. I commend the Bill to the House.

Question put and agreed to.

Bill ordered to be brought in by Mr. Frank Doran, Mr. Henry McLeish, Mr. Ian McCartney, Mr. Jimmy Hood, Dr. Lewis Moonie, Mrs. Maria Fyfe, Mr. Tony Worthington, Ms. Clare Short, Ms. Hilary Armstrong, Ms. Dawn Primarolo and Mr. Rhodri Morgan.

EMPLOYERS' LIABILITY

Mr. Doran accordingly presented a Bill to require employers to provide death-in-service insurance benefits for their employees; and for connected purposes: And the same was read the First time; and ordered to be read a Second time upon Friday 7 July and to be printed. [Bill 157.]

Orders of the Day

Local Government and Housing Bill

As amended (in the Standing Committee), considered.

4.52 pm

Mr. Clive Soley (Hammersmith): On a point of order, Mr. Deputy Speaker. I want to express again our real anger about the way in which the Bill has been dealt with. Notwithstanding the appalling mess that the Government made of the Housing Bill 1988, which is now the Housing Act, when they brought forward about 170 amendments, they have now increased that number to at least 197 amendments and new clauses. Many other amendments have been tabled by the Opposition and by Back Benchers from various parties in the House, bringing the number of amendments up to well over 300. Yet we are expected to deal with them on the Floor of the House.

I put it to you, Mr. Deputy Speaker, that the people outside the House expect Parliament to inspect legislation carefully. We usually do that in Committee. We did that in Committee, but we still have a Bill for which the selection list was not available until 7 pm yesterday. That is no criticism of the Clerks, who have worked incredibly hard, but not to have the selection list makes life difficult for all hon. Members.

In addition, we are anxious in that four new clauses and one amendment that I had hoped would be debated tomorrow have not been selected. I have tried to speak to the Clerks today, but they are not immediately available. In view of the pressure of work on the officials of the House, I understand why.

The Opposition's new clause 18 on ring fencing in part VI and new clause 17 in part VIII on the means-testing of grant are particularly important to us. I want to place on the record that, after the initial debates in which I shall be involved, I intend to discuss with the Clerks whether those can be selected for tomorrow.

Similarly, new clauses 21 and 28, dealing with first-time house buyers, houses in multiple occupation and fire risk, about which I am also concerned, and amendment No. 199 in part VIII on the right of appeal when a person does not receive a grant are also important matters.

I recognise that your powers in this, Mr. Deputy Speaker, are limited, but I stress to you, the Government, Parliament and the country that Parliament makes a mockery of its procedures if it spends months debating a Bill in Committee and then has only two days, starting at 5 o'clock this evening, to debate masses of amendments and new clauses, the vast majority of which have come from a Government who claim to know what they are doing. They clearly do not know what they are doing. The Bill is a mess, just as the Housing Bill was a mess. We are asked to put it right in just two short days on the Floor of the House and that is an insult to our parliamentary procedures.

The Minister for Local Government (Mr. John Gummer): Further to that point of order, Mr. Deputy Speaker. I am afraid that the hon. Member for Hammersmith (Mr. Soley) protests too much. Of the amendments before the House, 162 are minor, technical or consequential drafting amendments, many of which arise from the discussions in Committee in which the hon.

Gentleman took part, and 23 amendments are the result of commitments made in Committee. No amendments represent a significant new policy.

The hon. Gentleman should not pretend that there is anything before the House that cannot reasonably be dealt with in the circumstances and which cannot reasonably arise in what is an important Bill which the Government naturally wish to get right and concerning which we have listened carefully to the Committee.

I am sad that after a Committee which proceeded with good humour and where the Government on a range of occasions sought to meet the requests of the hon. Gentleman and his hon. Friends—many of whom were not always present, but who, when they were present, put forward their requests—the Opposition should consider our efforts to meet those requests to be to our detriment rather than a matter for congratulation. Instead, the Opposition should say that it is remarkable that the Bill has no amendments of substance except those which, in large measure, the Government have agreed with the Opposition to bring forward, or merely minor, technical amendments. That should be a matter for congratulation.

Several Hon. Members *rose——*

Mr. Deputy Speaker (Sir Paul Dean): Order. We had better not continue with points of order. I can assure the hon. Member for Hammersmith (Mr. Soley) that, although I can in no way commit Mr. Speaker, I shall draw to his attention the matters that the hon. Gentleman raised about tomorrow's selection list so that he can reconsider the matter if he thinks that desirable.

Mr. Soley: I am grateful, Mr. Deputy Speaker. We regard many of the amendments from the Opposition and from other Back Benchers to be amendments of substance. One person's technical amendment, which is usually based on the Government's definition of technical, is not everybody else's idea of a technical amendment.

Mr. Frank Haynes (Ashfield): Further to that point of order, Mr. Deputy Speaker. I want to say through you that we are not a load of schoolchildren. The Opposition know what is going on. We continually have Bills that take us into the early hours of the morning because we feel that the new clauses and amendments should be debated properly. Yet the Government try to rush them through. The Government are not giving us the proper opportunity to discuss them. When a Minister stands at the Dispatch Box, especially the Minister for Local Government, and talks to us as though he is a teacher and we are the pupils in school, I say, "Come off it". The Minister has a big grin on his face now. He thinks that this is funny, but it is serious and that is why we are raising these points of order.

Mr. Deputy Speaker: We had better get started.

Mr. Gummer: I beg to move,

That the Local Government and Housing Bill, as amended, be considered in the following order, namely, new Clauses relating to Part I, Amendments relating to Clauses 1 to 14, Schedule 1, Clauses 15 to 18, new Clauses relating to Part II, Amendments relating to Clauses 19 to 25, new Clauses relating to Part III, Amendments relating to Clauses, 26 to 29, Schedule 2, Clause 30, new Clauses relating to Part IV, Amendments relating to Clauses 31 to 54, Schedule 3, Clauses 55 to 57, new Clauses relating to Part V, Amendments relating to Clauses 58 to 64, new Clauses relating to Part VI, Amendments relating to Clauses 65 and 66, Schedule 4, Clauses 67 to 79, new Clauses relating to Part VII, Amendments relating to Clauses 80 to 91, new Clauses relating to Part VIII, Amendments relating to Clauses 92 to 124, remaining new Clauses, Amendments relating to Clause 125, Schedule 5, Clause 126, Schedule 6, Clauses 127 to 135, Schedule 7, Clauses 136 to 138, Schedle 8, Clauses 139 to 147, Schedule 9, Clauses 148 to 152; new Schedules; Amendments relating to Clause 153, Schedules 10 and 11, Clause 154.

This motion has been tabled at the request of Opposition Members.

Question put and agreed to.

New Clause 30

MEMBERS' INTERESTS

' .—(1) The Secretary of State may by regulations require each member of a local authority—

(a) to give a general notice to the proper officer of the authority setting out such information about the member's direct and indirect pecuniary interests as may be prescribed by the regulations, or stating that he has no such interests; and

(b) from time to time to give to that officer such further notices as may be so prescribed for the purpose of enabling that officer to keep the information provided under the regulations up to date.

(2) Any member of a local authority who—

(a) without reasonable excuse fails to comply with the requirements of any regulations under this section; or

(b) in giving a notice in compliance with any such requirement, provides information which he knows to be false or misleading in a material particular or recklessly provides information which is false or misleading in a material particular,

shall be guilty of an offence and liable, on summary conviction, to a fine not exceeding level 4 on the standard scale.

(3) Proceedings for an offence under subsection (2) above shall not be instituted in England and Wales except by or with the consent of the Director of Public Prosecutions.

(4) Neither section 96 of the Local Government Act 1972 (general notice of pecuniary interests) nor section 40 of the Local Government (Scotland) Act 1973 (corresponding provision for Scotland) shall apply in relation to any notice given in pursuance of any regulations under this section; but such regulations may provide—

(a) that the giving of a notice in pursuance of any such regulations shall be deemed to be sufficient disclosure for the purpose of section 94 of the said Act of 1972 (disability of members of authorities for voting on account of interest in contracts etc.) or for the purposes of section 38 of the said Act of 1973; and

(b) that the proper officer of a local authority is to maintain such records of the information contained in notices given to him as may be prescribed by the regulations and is to keep those records open to inspection by members of the public

(5) A local authority shall not be entitled (whether by means of making it a condition of any appointment or by any other means whatever) to impose any obligations on their members to disclose any interests other than those that they are required to disclose by virtue of section 94 of the Local Government Act 1972, section 38 for the Local Government (Scotland) Act 1973 or any regulations under this section.

(6) Regulations under this section may contain such incidental provisions and such supplemental, consequential and transitional provision in connection with their other provisions as the Secretary of State considers appropriate.

(7) References in this section to the indirect pecuniary interests of a member of a local authority shall include references to any such interests as, by virtue of any connection between that member or his spouse and any other person, would fall to be disclosed—

(a) in the case of a local authority in England and Wales, under section 94 of the Local Government Act 1972; or

(b) in the case of a local authority in Scotland, under section 38 of the Local Government (Scotland) Act 1973, if the authority were proposing to enter into a contract with that other person.':—[*Mr. Gummer.*]

Brought up, and read the First time.

Mr. Deputy Speaker: With this it will be convenient to debate amendment (a), in line 1, after 'member', insert 'and officer of principal officer grade or above'.

Amendment (b), in line 4, after 'pecuniary', insert 'and non pecuniary, including membership of organisations such as the freemasons'.

New clause 35—*Declaration of Freemasonry*—

' .—(1) A member of a relevant council shall make a declaration, in a register maintained for the purpose by the council, of membership of any lodge or other organisation of Freemasons.

(2) Any person offering themselves for election to a relevant council who is a member of such an organisation shall make a declaration to the returning officer at the time of nomination, and any such declaration shall be published by the returning officer together with details of the nomination.

(3) For the purposes of this section, "relevant council" has the same meaning as in section 10(2) above.'.

Government amendments Nos. 126 and 127.

5 pm

Mr. Gummer: New clause 30 and amendments Nos. 126 and 127 fulfil another of the commitments contained in our White Paper responding to the Widdicombe report—the provision of a statutory register of members' major pecuniary interests. There are four main elements to the clause. First, it gives the Secretary of State power to make regulations requiring each member of a local authority to give notice of any prescribed pecuniary interests—including indirect interests, and those of the member's spouse—to the proper officer appointed for that purpose, or to state that they have no such interests. The regulations will prescribe what interests are to be declared and will also specify how the information is to be updated.

Secondly, the clause makes failure to comply with the regulations, or the provision of false or misleading information, a criminal offence carrying a maximum fine at level 4 on the standard scale—currently £1,000. Third, the regulations may prescribe the form in which the proper officer is to keep a record of such declarations, and require it to be open to public inspection.

Finally, the clause prohibits authorities from imposing any obligations on members to declare any interests other than those which they are statutorily required to do by virtue of regulations under this clause, or that they are required to disclose at a meeting under section 94 of the Local Government Act 1972, or section 38 of the Local Government (Scotland) Act 1973. I commend it to the House.

Mr. Soley: Straight away, we are into the importance of the amendments, which demonstrates that they do not concern minor issues. The Minister is right to say that the Government trailed the proposals in their White Paper concerning the conduct of local authority business, when they also undertook to involve themselves in consultations with local authorities and others. In Committee concern was expressed as to why a timetable for meetings between the Department of the Environment and the local authorities' working party was not agreed. The Committee was assured that there were no problems and that those consultations would take place. However, the working party met only once, and its second meeting scheduled for 14 June has been cancelled—which is not surprising in the circumstances.

It all makes a mockery of the Government's attempt to kid everyone that they are interested in consultations. What on earth is the use of establishing the need for consultations and then holding just one meeting when the next thing that happens is that an amendment of this kind is brought before the House? If the Government were serious about consultations they could have introduced the amendment in another place.

Why is there such haste to introduce this measure without adjudication, and why is there no amendment of the kind that was promised to define the adjudicator's role—which is one aspect about which local authorities are unsure? Whose consent will be required for proceedings to be instituted in Scotland? Will it be that of the Secretary of State for Scotland? I suspect that the Minister does not know the answer, yet we are told that the amendment is of a technical nature and of no great importance. If it is a technical amendment, it is a bit bizarre that the Government cannot answer my questions. If, as I suspect, the Minister agrees that it is a substantive amendment, why have the Government introduced it without proper consultation and without giving answers to questions that were to some extent raised in Committee?

Why are the Government imposing on local authority councillors obligations and penalties that they are not prepared to impose on themselves as Members of Parliament? It is a matter for concern for local authorities, and for my right hon. and hon. Friends and myself, that a double standard is operating. The introduction to the 1989 Register of Members' Interests sets out nine specific classifications under which Members of Parliament are required to register their interests. They are not required to disclose the amount of remuneration or the benefit that they may enjoy, or the interests of spouses or children—except in certain circumstances relating to shareholdings. Right hon. and hon. Members are not subject to a maximum fine of £1,000 for failing to disclose their interests, although such failure is considered bad form. Again, the Government are creating one set of rules for local authorities and another for themselves.

Mr. Jeff Rooker (Birmingham, Perry Barr): Apart from those exemptions, 13 years after publication of the Royal Commission report on standards of conduct in public life by Lord Salmon, it is still the case that right hon. and hon. Members cannot be charged with corruption pursuant to their parliamentary duties. It is a scandal that that exemption remains, especially when the Government introduce such legislation in respect of local councillors.

Mr. Soley: My hon. Friend reminds me of an important additional argument. In local authorities, councillors very often declare any interest and then take no further part in the proceedings.

Mr. John Battle (Leeds, West): They are not allowed to do so.

Mr. Soley: However, in this House, after declaring an interest the right hon. or hon. Member is allowed both to participate and to vote. Why should councillors be treated as second-class citizens? Do we regard local democracy as being in some way less important than national democracy? I acknowledge the relative power of the two, but local democracy is still important.

I put it to the Minister, as I have many time previously, that Conservative councillors are worried about the way in which the Government constantly denigrate, undermine and demoralise both local authority officers and councillors. What do the Government mean when they say that they want local citizens to participate in the democratic life of the country, and then surround councillors with restrictions and refuse to accept the same restrictions themselves? It is well known that some right hon. and hon. Members participate in debates and in votes in which they have a deep financial interest, or in which their friends, relatives and spouses do. If it is wrong for local councillors to debate and vote on matters in which they have an interest, surely it is also wrong for Members of Parliament to do so.

Local councillors will risk not just a ticking off. As the Minister said, the penalty will be a fine at level 4 of the Home Office scale. Is the Minister prepared to recommend a similar penalty being imposed on right hon. and hon. Members? If not, why not? We want answers to those questions before we allow the Minister to slide his amendment through.

Mr. Haynes: When the Channel tunnel was debated, one hon. Member representing an outside organisation, and receiving £8,000 for doing so, did not declare his interest in the register. My right hon. and hon. Friends played merry hell about that, but the Government did nothing.

Mr. Soley: My hon. Friend is exactly right. If the Amendment Paper were not flooded with amendments, that matter is one that we could debate in detail. We could name one hon. Member after another who has participated in debates and in votes relating to matters in which he had a financial interest. I refer to everything from visits to overseas countries and companies affected by legislation, to the Channel tunnel and to changes that the Government are making to the ownership of certain nationalised industries. Apparently, there is nothing wrong with that—but do the same as a councillor and one could end up in court and, on summary conviction, be fined. What kind of justice is that?

Mr. Irvine Patnick (Sheffield, Hallam) *rose——*

Mr. Soley: Perhaps the hon. Gentleman who is trying to intervene can tell the House how he justifies different standards applying to Members of Parliament from those that apply to local councillors.

Mr. Patnick: In cowboy films it is said "White man speak with forked tongue." I will not say that of the hon. Member for Hammersmith, North (Mr. Soley) but he must surely accept that a councillor has far more power and could be a party to influencing decisions. There is no comparison between the interests—*[Interruption.]* The hon. Member for Ashfield (Mr. Haynes) seems to be something of a comedian, but he laughs at his own jokes. I cannot see that there is a direct comparison between the powers of an hon. Member who speaks in a debate and those of a councillor who can vote something through.

Mr. Soley: I have seen the hon. Member for Sheffield, Hallam (Mr. Patnick) try to dance on the head of a pin before, but I did not think that he would get himself into such difficulties. The message is simple: in both the local authority chamber and this Chamber decisions are made which directly affect people's interests. A number of examples have already been given, such as the Channel

tunnel and other issues of that type. There is no difference between gaining from legislation and changes that go through the House, and gaining from changes that are passed through local authority council chambers. The two are synonymous in terms of the behaviour within them.

The degree of power is greater here, particularly if one takes into account what happens when Members are taken overseas to influence policy that is decided here. We are talking about influencing people with money or attractive offers of one type or another. We must be fairly flexible about that, otherwise we may shut out many activities which are necessary if we want to be well informed. Local authorities and hon. Members should abide by rules which are essentially the same, although they need not be exactly the same in every dot and comma. If we do not, we merely demonstrate to the public that we are concerned about other people's standards, but perfectly prepared to allow ourselves totally different criteria by which to be judged.

Mr. Gummer: I am not unhappy about the kind of comments being made by the hon. Gentleman. However, I wonder if he will help me: after all, statutorily, the House of Commons can make its own decisions about how to discipline its Members. It is perfectly open to him to make his point about the way in which we all have to operate within the rules of this House. The difficulty is that local authorities do not have the power to discipline their members: it is not within their competence.

If we are to set standards in local authorities we must do it in this way. That does not preclude the hon. Member for Hammersmith (Mr. Soley) or other hon. Members from ensuring that the House should insist on different rules. However, the hon. Gentleman must not mislead the House by suggesting that councils and Parliament are parallel. I am sure that he does not mean to do so but he appears to do so. It is not that the responsibilities are that different, or that his views are not perfectly reasonable, but local authorities cannot discipline themselves, whereas this House can. If it does not take the measures which he would like it to take, it is open to him to suggest them. Has the hon. Gentleman put his points to the Select Committee on Procedure which is able to carry out his suggested measures? If not, he is not in a position to make such comments.

Mr. Soley: I can deal easily with the Minister's last point. The Labour party made recommendations and, when it was in government, carried them through into law, which this Government changed. The Labour Government tightened up the regulations on Members' interests, but this Government watered them down. We set our own standards.

I have two other answers for the Minister. First, if he believes that a disciplinary procedure is the best one, he could give local authorities the power to discipline themselves.

Mr. Patnick *rose——*

Mr. Soley: I shall not give way at this stage.

The Minister did not say that he would give them those powers. It was interesting that the Minister said that he had some sympathy with what I have said. Presumably, if he does, he must recognise that we are giving ourselves a more flexible approach to this matter than we are giving to local authorities. As the Minister knows, we do not discipline hon. Members on the same basis which we are

[*Mr. Soley*]

laying down for councillors, which is that they will be fined. We do not discipline hon. Members for the same issues as those for which we intend to discipline councillors. Indeed, we intend to do more than discipline them; we propose to haul them up before the courts, convict them and fine them. That is what we are doing and that is why the Minister is wrong.

Mr. David Clelland (Tyne Bridge): I have another parallel for the Minister to comment on. As the Minister is aware, the Government are giving power and substantial sums of taxpayers' money to sponsors of city technology colleges. One of the sponsors of the city technology college in Gateshead, Laine Northern, which is part of the John Laine group, sponsors the CTC to the tune of about £200,000. It has also been awarded the contract to develop the college to the tune of more than £8 million. When was the pecuniary interest announced in that case?

Mr. Soley: I was not aware of that particular example. My hon. Friend the Member for Tyne Bridge (Mr. Clelland) has put his finger on an interesting point. As I said earlier, we could spend hours picking up examples in which hon. Members, particularly Conservatives, have been acting in a way which they regard as perfectly normal, but in which they will not allow local authorities to act.

New clause 35 to some extent spells out our philosophy. It requires a councillor to state whether he is a member of the freemasons, which we regard as an interest. The Minister will notice that we do not say that someone cannot stand if he is a member of the freemasons or that he will be hauled before the courts and fined, but simply that it is perfectly legitimate and proper for the electorate to be informed that a councillor is a member of the freemasons. That is because that group is known to have widespread interests. It is also perfectly proper if someone declares an interest and people elect him to be councillor and he carries out his role, no doubt in many cases, very well.

If the Minister is serious about interests he can, by all means, make it clear that local authority councillors must declare their interests. However, following discussions with local authorities about how far it should go, he should also work out a proper code. I recommend that there should not be an essential difference between that code and the rules which we impose on ourselves. Otherwise, we shall undermine people's confidence in our ability to make fair and reasoned judgments between the expectations which we place on others outside the House and those which we place on ourselves. If we are seen to favour ourselves we shall do ourselves and this House no service.

5.15 pm

Mr. Matthew Taylor (Truro): Although I support the Labour party when it says that hon. Members should declare their interests, I also welcome the steps by the Government, limited though they are, towards greater declaration of interests within local government.

The purpose of our amendments is to strengthen the principles which lie behind the Secretary of State's new clause in order that they might have some chance of producing the effect which he and his Ministers desire. Amendment (a) makes an
"officer of principal officer grade or above"
subject to the same requirements as councillors to declare interests of any kind to their local authority. That is a valuable requirement at any time.

I suspect that hon. Members have experienced the sort of accusations about local authority officers acting wrongly pursuant to their own interests which circulate in local areas. The amendment would not only stop any abuses that may occur, but clarify the majority of cases in which officers are probably acting quite properly, but are the subject of innuendo and rumour at local level.

At present, our case is made all the stronger by the new era of large scale tendering for a wide variety of local government contracts. In that circumstance it is surely vital that the interests of any officers with significant involvement in the process should be open to scrutiny by members of both the council and the public. When we debated the matter in Committee I drew Ministers' attention to the fact that local government officers had been directly involved, for example, in some of the opting-out and takeover of housing estates.

Allegations of extremely dubious behaviour involving Westminster city council, among others, have already been made. Some council officers have set up businesses purely to profit from the tendering process. The public must have a right to know whether such people are involved in the administration of tendering, and I do not see why a council officer should be entitled to conceal a pecuniary interest from public view when a councillor cannot.

Amendment (b) proposes the inclusion of non-pecuniary interests in the declaration to be made by local authority members and senior officers. It refers to
"organisations such as the freemasons"
so that no one should be in any doubt about the influence that can be exerted by loyalty to such organisations, and so that the public may be free to decide whether personal interests are being put before theirs.

In 1986, it took a reporter from the *Worthing Gazette and Herald* to investigate why an obvious candidate for the position of mayor had been passed over. He revealed that the new mayor was the sixth of the past seven male Tory mayors who had been a mason. I think that the people of Worthing should have had the right to know that they were giving great authority to a series of people who all just happened to be members of the same secret society. Like the Labour party, I do not seek to ban such people from local government, but I do seek to ensure that such interests are made known to the public.

In May 1974 the Redcliffe-Maud report included a national code of local government conduct, which contains much that is pertinent to the amendments. The section on public duty and private interests states that, when councillors have a private or personal interest in any question that they must decide, they must not do anything to let that interest influence their decision. But how is anyone supposed to know whether a councillor or officer has been influenced by personal interests if those interests remain secret?

The section on disclosure of pecuniary and other interests makes precisely the point that we make in amendment (b). It states:
"The law makes specific provision requiring you to disclose pecuniary interests, direct and indirect. But which are

not pecuniary can be just as important. Kinship, friendship, membership of an association, society, or trade union, trusteeship and many other kinds of relationship can sometimes influence your judgment and give the impression that you might be acting for personal motives. A good test is to ask yourself whether others would think that the interest is of a kind to make this possible. If you think they would, or if you are in doubt, disclose the interest."

Honest councillors or officers will clearly act honourably, but it is in their interest that we have tabled the amendments. If they are not merely acting honourably, but are seen to be doing so, they will be free from innuendo and rumour. Still more important, it is in their interests and those of the public and the House that people who might act dishonourably—or who might find that, unintentionally, they have allowed their interests to be swayed—make clear their interests or potential interests.

There are those who seek to abuse their position, and it is towards them that the Government aim their new clause. If they believe that it is important to make the changes that they propose, they should also accept our amendments to the new clause, which enhance it, ensure its effectiveness and extend it to many people in local government—that is, officers—and many interests—that is, non-pecuniary interests—which at present are not covered. I hope that the Minister will accept the importance of our proposals to the public interest.

Mr. Gummer: I would be the first to say that it is the proper activity of anyone who is elected to a position of responsibility, or who holds such a position, to make clear the context in which he is likely to be thought to have been swayed. I think that that may be one way of summing up what has been said by the hon. Member for Truro (Mr. Taylor)

Whether that principle is best presented by means of statutory requirements or by means of a code of conduct —and we have agreed on a code of conduct as well—is a matter for decision. I am sure that the hon. Gentleman would agree that there is a difficulty here, which I do not underestimate. I have before me a document that Haringey council asked every councillor to fill in—indeed, at one stage it insisted. Councillors had to say whether they were members of the women's institute, but not, curiously enough, whether they were members of Probus, although the Lions and the Rotary were covered. Although the most extensive of its kind that I have encountered, the document is selective: it is bound to be.

Most people would probably consider such a proposal to be an intrusion on normal behaviour. It also suggests that people will inevitably be biased in accordance with the organisations to which they belong, whereas, if we view ourselves honestly, we must admit to other biases related to what appeals and what does not, sometimes as a result of upbringing. Whatever we do, we must constantly ask, "Am I biased, for this or that reason?". Much of what the hon. Member for Truro has said is covered by the way in which councillors properly approach their jobs, and the way in which a proper code of conduct would operate.

Like the hon. Member for Hammersmith (Mr. Soley), the hon. Gentleman referred to the freemasons. I am not a member of that organisation; I hold religious opinions that make such membership impossible. I hope, therefore, that I am reasonably unbiased. I think that there is some paranoia on the subject of freemasonry, which I do not consider the most likely area of bias. People are biased in

all sorts of ways, and the idea of selecting that organisation as opposed to all the others is very peculiar: it stands out like a sore thumb in the amendments.

The electorate should be allowed to know about any organisation to which someone belongs and about which he feels strongly. I feel, for example, that abortion is wrong and is on no occasion justifiable, and I will fight against it in all circumstances. My electorate must know that that is an opinion that I hold with deep conviction. It is more important than membership of any secular organisation. It would be very odd for a declaration of that view not to be required of me, although it is clearly of great importance to the way in which council money is spent, while I would be required to say whether I was a member of the freemasons.

Perhaps the best way to decide on the difference between statutory requirements and what might reasonably be expected from a sensible interpretation of a code of conduct would be to say that the one specific, measurable and factual question is that of pecuniary interest.

Mr. Soley: I think that the Minister should take into account two aspects of the freemasonry issue. First, the freemasons are a secret society known to have extensive interests in a wide range of activities. Secondly, a member of the Cabinet—the Home Secretary—has advised police officers and others, rightly in my judgment, not to become freemasons, so that factor has been taken into account. The Government already make special arrangements relating to senior officers in certain jobs, and I think that that is very wise of them. Why does the Home Secretary not adopt the practice in this context?

Mr. Gummer: The hon. Gentleman is referring to advice given by the Home Secretary; what is proposed here is a statutory statement. I am merely saying that it is difficult to know where to draw the line.

I suggest that it would be best to make statutory the requirement to reveal pecuniary interests. They can be much more clearly measured and their influence can be much more clearly pinpointed. In the code of practice that we hope to produce we shall point to the way in which most people ought to comport themselves. To select one kind of membership and not to mention all the others would be to suggest that there is something in the nature of the membership of freemasonry which even I—I am not a member and could not be a member—would find it impossible to accept.

5.30 pm

I do not intend to spend a lot of time discussing how secret is secret, but I can think of a lot of organisations whose operations are pretty secret and they would not be covered by the amendment. There are various party political organisations that are pretty secretive about the way in which they operate and they are pretty private about the nature of their links. I do not intend to discuss them because many of them have been the bane of the Labour party for many years. However, if they are not to be included, it means that something is being suggested about freemasons which I find very difficult to accept.

Mr. George Howarth (Knowsley, North): I do not want to labour the point about freemasons, but a considerable body of information is available to us which suggests that influence is used by freemasons over the awarding of

[Mr. George Howarth]

contracts and in many other areas of public life. That distinguishes freemasons from almost any other organisation that I can think of. The Minister should not confuse what freemasons do with the completely different activities of other organisations.

Mr. Gummer: I am not sure that I take the view that economic influence is the most important influence. I am not one of those who put economics above everything else. Therefore, I suggest that other influences can be just as insiduous, hidden and dangerous. To single out one of them in this way seems to me to be a little lopsided. I am not being extreme about it. It is very much better for everyone to know about the organisations to which one belongs. A number of hon. Members on both sides of the House who have been debating these matters have set a reasonable example; everybody knows where they stand. Sometimes, therefore, we are the object of attack, but that is a much better way to go about it.

I was sorry when it was suggested that I do not know how things are done in Scotland. Things are done exactly in the same way in Scotland as elsewhere. Therefore, it would have been inexcusable if I had not known that the Lord Advocate would prosecute.

I am slightly puzzled about the demands that are being made. On the one hand it is suggested that the House of Commons should be much tougher on hon. Members. On the other hand it is suggested that it is wrong to be tough on members of local councils. That is not a very sensible argument. It is reasonable to ask for a proper declaration of pecuniary interests. If that leads the hon. Member for Truro to say that we are not being tough enough on hon. Members, the right step is not to object to the new clause but to seek to persuade the House to change its rules.

Mr. Andrew Welsh (Angus, East): Will the Minister give way?

Mr. David Winnick (Walsall, North): Will the Minister give way?

Mr. Gummer: No. I promised that I would not take too long, and I want to answer the question that the hon. Member for Truro put to me.

The hon. Gentleman asked how officers will be dealt with. There is a difference. Officers are employed by the local authority, which can impose whatever requirements it likes on its officers. It cannot impose legally the same requirements on local authority members. It does not have that kind of power. The local authority should decide what it wants its officers to state about themselves. Some officers must declare rather more about themselves than others. That is a much better way to deal with it. I hope that both in those authorities in which the hon. Gentleman has some influence and in those in which I have some influence we shall seek to ensure that officers who have any of the connections about which he spoke make clear, because the local authority insists upon it, where they stand. It is not for Parliament to impose such a requirement on local authorities. It is for local authority members to make those requirements quite clear to the officers concerned.

Mr. Matthew Taylor: I understand what the Minister says, but he lives in an idealistic world. That does not happen in practice. It is not a party-political issue because it does not arise between the different parties, whoever

may be running the local authority. However, enormous discontent has been expressed by local communities. On some occasions, local officers find themselves hauled across the coals. I can think of one recent example in my local authority. Innuendo and rumour destroyed the life of a local authority officer. There was very little that he could do about it. There was no statutory requirement that he should declare his interest. Frankly, no one would have believed him, whether he did or not, after a while. If there were a statutory requirement, people would have more confidence in the system. It would benefit the vast majority of officers who are upright and honourable. It would also protect the public in the few instances where that is not the case.

I understand what the Minister says about local authorities being able to set their own rules, but in this instance I do not believe that that is adequate. We are dealing with the conduct of public life at all levels. There should be basic rules according to which people in local government, whether they are elected or whether they are paid employees, have to work. It is for Parliament to set the basic rules according to which they work.

Mr. Gummer: I do not think that that is the best way. It should be left to local authorities. I believe in as much power as possible being given to local authorities. I have sought to provide that power. I very much hope that local authorities will shoulder that responsibility. It is not for the House to lay down rules.

Mr. Rooker: The new clause does not make clear whether the register will be available for public inspection. Can the Minister elucidate that point? It ought to be made clear because it is not clear to me. It is an important point.

Mr. Gummer: It will be available for public inspection.

Mr. Andrew Welsh: How does the Minister intend to use these powers? I notice that the new clause uses the word "may":

"The Secretary of State may by regulations require each member of a local authority".

It does not use the word "shall." How will the Secretary of State use his powers? Will he be sparked into action by a single incident, or will he target authorities? Will the regulations apply to every local authority?

Mr. Gummer: The intention is merely to give the power to do these things. I give an undertaking that the Secretary of State for the Environment, the Secretary of State for Scotland and the Secretary of State for Wales intend to use the power in the way that we have described.

Mr. Soley: With the permission of the House, Mr. Deputy Speaker. We intend to divide the House because there has been total lack of proper consultation by the Government, as they promised. Moreover, a terrible double standard is involved here, which we do not accept. The principle that people should have to declare an interest is right, but we cannot impose on others what we are not prepared to accept ourselves. Above all, we must not do it by means of this shoddy form of consultation which has resulted in just one meeting with local authorities. Consequently, the Minister has been able to answer only some of the questions—for example, about publicity. That is unsatisfactory. For that reason, we shall seek to divide the House.

Question put, That the clause be read a Second time:—
The House divided: Ayes 246, Noes 135.

Division No. 235] [5.38 pm

AYES

Adley, Robert
Aitken, Jonathan
Alison, Rt Hon Michael
Allason, Rupert
Alton, David
Amos, Alan
Arbuthnot, James
Arnold, Jacques *(Gravesham)*
Arnold, Tom *(Hazel Grove)*
Ashby, David
Ashdown, Rt Hon Paddy
Aspinwall, Jack
Atkinson, David
Baker, Nicholas *(Dorset N)*
Baldry, Tony
Barnes, Mrs Rosie *(Greenwich)*
Batiste, Spencer
Beaumont-Dark, Anthony
Beith, A. J.
Bennett, Nicholas *(Pembroke)*
Benyon, W.
Bevan, David Gilroy
Blackburn, Dr John G.
Body, Sir Richard
Bonsor, Sir Nicholas
Boscawen, Hon Robert
Boswell, Tim
Bottomley, Peter
Bottomley, Mrs Virginia
Bowden, A *(Brighton K'pto'n)*
Bowden, Gerald *(Dulwich)*
Bowis, John
Boyson, Rt Hon Dr Sir Rhodes
Braine, Rt Hon Sir Bernard
Brandon-Bravo, Martin
Brown, Michael *(Brigg & Cl't's)*
Browne, John *(Winchester)*
Buchanan-Smith, Rt Hon Alick
Buck, Sir Antony
Budgen, Nicholas
Burt, Alistair
Carlisle, John, *(Luton N)*
Carrington, Matthew
Carttiss, Michael
Cartwright, John
Channon, Rt Hon Paul
Chapman, Sydney
Chope, Christopher
Clark, Dr Michael *(Rochford)*
Clark, Sir W. *(Croydon S)*
Clarke, Rt Hon K. *(Rushcliffe)*
Colvin, Michael
Conway, Derek
Coombs, Anthony *(Wyre F'rest)*
Coombs, Simon *(Swindon)*
Cope, Rt Hon John
Couchman, James
Critchley, Julian
Currie, Mrs Edwina
Davies, Q. *(Stamf'd & Spald'g)*
Davis, David *(Boothferry)*
Day, Stephen
Devlin, Tim
Dorrell, Stephen
Douglas-Hamilton, Lord James
Dunn, Bob
Durant, Tony
Dykes, Hugh
Emery, Sir Peter
Evennett, David
Fairbairn, Sir Nicholas
Fallon, Michael
Favell, Tony
Fearn, Ronald
Field, Barry *(Isle of Wight)*
Finsberg, Sir Geoffrey
Fookes, Dame Janet

Forman, Nigel
Forsyth, Michael *(Stirling)*
Forth, Eric
Fowler, Rt Hon Norman
Fox, Sir Marcus
Franks, Cecil
Freeman, Roger
French, Douglas
Fry, Peter
Gale, Roger
Gardiner, George
Garel-Jones, Tristan
Gill, Christopher
Gilmour, Rt Hon Sir Ian
Glyn, Dr Alan
Goodlad, Alastair
Gorman, Mrs Teresa
Grant, Sir Anthony *(CambsSW)*
Greenway, John *(Ryedale)*
Gregory, Conal
Griffiths, Peter *(Portsmouth N)*
Grist, Ian
Gummer, Rt Hon John Selwyn
Hague, William
Hamilton, Neil *(Tatton)*
Hanley, Jeremy
Hannam, John
Hargreaves, A. *(B'ham H'll Gr')*
Hargreaves, Ken *(Hyndburn)*
Harris, David
Haselhurst, Alan
Hayhoe, Rt Hon Sir Barney
Hayward, Robert
Heathcoat-Amory, David
Heddle, John
Hicks, Mrs Maureen *(Wolv' NE)*
Hicks, Robert *(Cornwall SE)*
Higgins, Rt Hon Terence L.
Hill, James
Hind, Kenneth
Hogg, Hon Douglas *(Gr'th'm)*
Hordern, Sir Peter
Howard, Michael
Howarth, Alan *(Strat'd-on-A)*
Howells, Geraint
Hughes, Robert G. *(Harrow W)*
Hughes, Simon *(Southwark)*
Hunter, Andrew
Irving, Charles
Jack, Michael
Jessel, Toby
Johnson Smith, Sir Geoffrey
Jones, Gwilym *(Cardiff N)*
Jones, Robert B *(Herts W)*
Jopling, Rt Hon Michael
Kennedy, Charles
Key, Robert
Kirkwood, Archy
Knapman, Roger
Knight, Greg *(Derby North)*
Knox, David
Lang, Ian
Lawrence, Ivan
Lennox-Boyd, Hon Mark
Lester, Jim *(Broxtowe)*
Lightbown, David
Lilley, Peter
Livsey, Richard
Lloyd, Peter *(Fareham)*
Lord, Michael
MacKay, Andrew *(E Berkshire)*
McLoughlin, Patrick
McNair-Wilson, Sir Michael
Mans, Keith
Maples, John
Martin, David *(Portsmouth S)*
Maude, Hon Francis

Mellor, David
Miller, Sir Hal
Miscampbell, Norman
Mitchell, Andrew *(Gedling)*
Mitchell, Sir David
Moate, Roger
Montgomery, Sir Fergus
Morris, M *(N'hampton S)*
Morrison, Rt Hon P *(Chester)*
Moss, Malcolm
Mudd, David
Neale, Gerrard
Newton, Rt Hon Tony
Nicholls, Patrick
Nicholson, David *(Taunton)*
Nicholson, Emma *(Devon West)*
Norris, Steve
Onslow, Rt Hon Cranley
Oppenheim, Phillip
Page, Richard
Paice, James
Patnick, Irvine
Patten, Chris *(Bath)*
Pawsey, James
Peacock, Mrs Elizabeth
Porter, Barry *(Wirral S)*
Porter, David *(Waveney)*
Portillo, Michael
Powell, William *(Corby)*
Price, Sir David
Raffan, Keith
Raison, Rt Hon Timothy
Redwood, John
Renton, Tim
Rhodes James, Robert
Riddick, Graham
Ridley, Rt Hon Nicholas
Rifkind, Rt Hon Malcolm
Roberts, Wyn *(Conwy)*
Rowe, Andrew
Ryder, Richard
Sainsbury, Hon Tim
Scott, Nicholas
Shaw, David *(Dover)*
Shaw, Sir Giles *(Pudsey)*
Shaw, Sir Michael *(Scarb')*
Shelton, Sir William
Shephard, Mrs G. *(Norfolk SW)*

Shepherd, Richard *(Aldridge)*
Sims, Roger
Skeet, Sir Trevor
Smith, Sir Dudley *(Warwick)*
Smith, Tim *(Beaconsfield)*
Soames, Hon Nicholas
Spicer, Sir Jim *(Dorset W)*
Stanbrook, Ivor
Steen, Anthony
Stern, Michael
Stevens, Lewis
Stewart, Andy *(Sherwood)*
Stradling Thomas, Sir John
Sumberg, David
Tapsell, Sir Peter
Taylor, Ian *(Esher)*
Taylor, Matthew *(Truro)*
Taylor, Teddy *(S'end E)*
Tebbit, Rt Hon Norman
Thompson, D. *(Calder Valley)*
Thornton, Malcolm
Thurnham, Peter
Townend, John *(Bridlington)*
Townsend, Cyril D. *(B'heath)*
Tracey, Richard
Tredinnick, David
Trippier, David
Twinn, Dr Ian
Vaughan, Sir Gerard
Waddington, Rt Hon David
Wakeham, Rt Hon John
Wallace, James
Waller, Gary
Wardle, Charles *(Bexhill)*
Warren, Kenneth
Watts, John
Wells, Bowen
Wheeler, John
Whitney, Ray
Widdecombe, Ann
Wilkinson, John
Wood, Timothy
Woodcock, Dr. Mike
Young, Sir George *(Acton)*

Tellers for the Ayes:
Mr. David Maclean and
Mr. Tom Sackville.

NOES

Abbott, Ms Diane
Anderson, Donald
Archer, Rt Hon Peter
Armstrong, Hilary
Ashley, Rt Hon Jack
Ashton, Joe
Banks, Tony *(Newham NW)*
Barnes, Harry *(Derbyshire NE)*
Battle, John
Beckett, Margaret
Bell, Stuart
Benn, Rt Hon Tony
Bennett, A. F. *(D'nt'n & R'dish)*
Bidwell, Sydney
Blair, Tony
Blunkett, David
Bray, Dr Jeremy
Brown, Nicholas *(Newcastle E)*
Buckley, George J.
Callaghan, Jim
Campbell-Savours, D. N.
Canavan, Dennis
Clark, Dr David *(S Shields)*
Clarke, Tom *(Monklands W)*
Clelland, David
Cohen, Harry
Coleman, Donald
Cook, Frank *(Stockton N)*
Cook, Robin *(Livingston)*
Corbett, Robin

Cousins, Jim
Cox, Tom
Crowther, Stan
Cryer, Bob
Cunliffe, Lawrence
Cunningham, Dr John
Darling, Alistair
Davies, Ron *(Caerphilly)*
Davis, Terry *(B'ham Hodge H'l)*
Dixon, Don
Doran, Frank
Dunwoody, Hon Mrs Gwyneth
Evans, John *(St Helens N)*
Field, Frank *(Birkenhead)*
Fields, Terry *(L'pool B G'n)*
Fisher, Mark
Flannery, Martin
Flynn, Paul
Foot, Rt Hon Michael
Foster, Derek
Fraser, John
Garrett, John *(Norwich South)*
George, Bruce
Godman, Dr Norman A.
Golding, Mrs Llin
Griffiths, Nigel *(Edinburgh S)*
Griffiths, Win *(Bridgend)*
Grocott, Bruce
Hardy, Peter
Haynes, Frank

Heffer, Eric S.
Hinchliffe, David
Howarth, George *(Knowsley N)*
Howell, Rt Hon D. *(S'heath)*
Howells, Dr. Kim *(Pontypridd)*
Hughes, John *(Coventry NE)*
Hughes, Robert *(Aberdeen N)*
Hughes, Roy *(Newport E)*
Illsley, Eric
Ingram, Adam
Jones, Martyn *(Clwyd S W)*
Kinnock, Rt Hon Neil
Leadbitter, Ted
Leighton, Ron
Lestor, Joan *(Eccles)*
Lewis, Terry
Litherland, Robert
Lloyd, Tony *(Stretford)*
Lofthouse, Geoffrey
Loyden, Eddie
McAllion, John
McCartney, Ian
McWilliam, John
Madden, Max
Marek, Dr John
Marshall, Jim *(Leicester S)*
Maxton, John
Meacher, Michael
Meale, Alan
Michael, Alun
Michie, Bill *(Sheffield Heeley)*
Mitchell, Austin *(G't Grimsby)*
Moonie, Dr Lewis
Morris, Rt Hon A. *(W'shawe)*
Morris, Rt Hon J. *(Aberavon)*
Mowlam, Marjorie
Mullin, Chris
Murphy, Paul
Oakes, Rt Hon Gordon

O'Brien, William
Orme, Rt Hon Stanley
Patchett, Terry
Pendry, Tom
Pike, Peter L.
Powell, Ray *(Ogmore)*
Quin, Ms Joyce
Redmond, Martin
Rees, Rt Hon Merlyn
Richardson, Jo
Robertson, George
Rooker, Jeff
Sedgemore, Brian
Sheerman, Barry
Sheldon, Rt Hon Robert
Shore, Rt Hon Peter
Skinner, Dennis
Smith, C. *(Isl'ton & F'bury)*
Smith, Rt Hon J. *(Monk'ds E)*
Smith, J. P. *(Vale of Glam)*
Snape, Peter
Soley, Clive
Spearing, Nigel
Stott, Roger
Taylor, Mrs Ann *(Dewsbury)*
Thompson, Jack *(Wansbeck)*
Turner, Dennis
Wall, Pat
Walley, Joan
Welsh, Andrew *(Angus E)*
Welsh, Michael *(Doncaster N)*
Williams, Rt Hon Alan
Winnick, David
Wise, Mrs Audrey
Worthington, Tony

Tellers for the Noes:
    Mr. Allen McKay and
    Mr. Ken Eastham.

Question accordingly agreed to.

Clause read a Second time.

Amendment (a) proposed to the clause, in line 1, after 'member', insert

'and officer of principal officer grade or above'.—*[Mr. Matthew Taylor.]*

Question put, That the amendment be made:—
The House divided: Ayes 13, Noes 229.

Division No. 236]   **[5.51 pm**

AYES

Alton, David
Ashdown, Rt Hon Paddy
Barnes, Mrs Rosie *(Greenwich)*
Beith, A. J.
Cartwright, John
Fearn, Ronald
Howells, Geraint
Hughes, Simon *(Southwark)*

Kennedy, Charles
Kirkwood, Archy
Skinner, Dennis
Welsh, Andrew *(Angus E)*

Tellers for the Ayes:
    Mr. Matthew Taylor and
    Mr. James Wallace.

NOES

Adley, Robert
Aitken, Jonathan
Alison, Rt Hon Michael
Allason, Rupert
Amos, Alan
Arbuthnot, James
Arnold, Jacques *(Gravesham)*
Arnold, Tom *(Hazel Grove)*
Ashby, David
Aspinwall, Jack
Atkinson, David
Baker, Rt Hon K. *(Mole Valley)*
Baker, Nicholas *(Dorset N)*
Baldry, Tony
Batiste, Spencer
Beaumont-Dark, Anthony
Bennett, Nicholas *(Pembroke)*
Benyon, W.

Bevan, David Gilroy
Blackburn, Dr John G.
Body, Sir Richard
Bonsor, Sir Nicholas
Boscawen, Hon Robert
Boswell, Tim
Bottomley, Peter
Bottomley, Mrs Virginia
Bowden, A *(Brighton K'pto'n)*
Bowden, Gerald *(Dulwich)*
Bowis, John
Boyson, Rt Hon Dr Sir Rhodes
Brandon-Bravo, Martin
Brown, Michael *(Brigg & Cl't's)*
Browne, John *(Winchester)*
Buchanan-Smith, Rt Hon Alick
Buck, Sir Antony
Budgen, Nicholas

Burt, Alistair
Carlisle, John, *(Luton N)*
Carrington, Matthew
Carttiss, Michael
Channon, Rt Hon Paul
Chapman, Sydney
Chope, Christopher
Clark, Dr Michael *(Rochford)*
Clark, Sir W. *(Croydon S)*
Clarke, Rt Hon K. *(Rushcliffe)*
Colvin, Michael
Conway, Derek
Coombs, Anthony *(Wyre F'rest)*
Coombs, Simon *(Swindon)*
Cope, Rt Hon John
Couchman, James
Critchley, Julian
Currie, Mrs Edwina
Davies, Q. *(Stamf'd & Spald'g)*
Davis, David *(Boothferry)*
Day, Stephen
Devlin, Tim
Dorrell, Stephen
Douglas-Hamilton, Lord James
Dunn, Bob
Durant, Tony
Dykes, Hugh
Emery, Sir Peter
Evennett, David
Fairbairn, Sir Nicholas
Fallon, Michael
Favell, Tony
Field, Barry *(Isle of Wight)*
Finsberg, Sir Geoffrey
Fookes, Dame Janet
Forman, Nigel
Forsyth, Michael *(Stirling)*
Forth, Eric
Fowler, Rt Hon Norman
Fox, Sir Marcus
Franks, Cecil
Freeman, Roger
French, Douglas
Fry, Peter
Gale, Roger
Gardiner, George
Garel-Jones, Tristan
Gill, Christopher
Gilmour, Rt Hon Sir Ian
Glyn, Dr Alan
Goodlad, Alastair
Gorman, Mrs Teresa
Grant, Sir Anthony *(CambsSW)*
Greenway, John *(Ryedale)*
Gregory, Conal
Griffiths, Peter *(Portsmouth N)*
Grist, Ian
Gummer, Rt Hon John Selwyn
Hague, William
Hamilton, Neil *(Tatton)*
Hanley, Jeremy
Hargreaves, A. *(B'ham H'll Gr')*
Hargreaves, Ken *(Hyndburn)*
Harris, David
Haselhurst, Alan
Hayhoe, Rt Hon Sir Barney
Hayward, Robert
Heathcoat-Amory, David
Heddle, John
Hicks, Mrs Maureen *(Wolv' NE)*
Hicks, Robert *(Cornwall SE)*
Higgins, Rt Hon Terence L.
Hill, James
Hind, Kenneth
Hogg, Hon Douglas *(Gr'th'm)*
Hordern, Sir Peter
Howard, Michael
Howarth, Alan *(Strat'd-on-A)*
Hughes, Robert G. *(Harrow W)*
Hunter, Andrew

Irving, Charles
Jack, Michael
Jessel, Toby
Johnson Smith, Sir Geoffrey
Jones, Gwilym *(Cardiff N)*
Jones, Robert B *(Herts W)*
Jopling, Rt Hon Michael
Key, Robert
Kilfedder, James
Knapman, Roger
Knight, Greg *(Derby North)*
Knox, David
Lang, Ian
Lawrence, Ivan
Lennox-Boyd, Hon Mark
Lester, Jim *(Broxtowe)*
Lightbown, David
Lilley, Peter
Lloyd, Peter *(Fareham)*
Lord, Michael
MacKay, Andrew *(E Berkshire)*
McLoughlin, Patrick
Mans, Keith
Maples, John
Martin, David *(Portsmouth S)*
Maude, Hon Francis
Miller, Sir Hal
Mitchell, Andrew *(Gedling)*
Mitchell, Sir David
Moate, Roger
Montgomery, Sir Fergus
Morris, M *(N'hampton S)*
Morrison, Rt Hon P *(Chester)*
Moss, Malcolm
Mudd, David
Neale, Gerrard
Nelson, Anthony
Newton, Rt Hon Tony
Nicholson, David *(Taunton)*
Nicholson, Emma *(Devon West)*
Norris, Steve
Onslow, Rt Hon Cranley
Oppenheim, Phillip
Page, Richard
Paice, James
Patnick, Irvine
Patten, Chris *(Bath)*
Pawsey, James
Peacock, Mrs Elizabeth
Porter, Barry *(Wirral S)*
Porter, David *(Waveney)*
Portillo, Michael
Powell, William *(Corby)*
Price, Sir David
Raffan, Keith
Raison, Rt Hon Timothy
Redwood, John
Renton, Tim
Rhodes James, Robert
Riddick, Graham
Ridley, Rt Hon Nicholas
Roberts, Wyn *(Conwy)*
Rowe, Andrew
Ryder, Richard
Sainsbury, Hon Tim
Scott, Nicholas
Shaw, David *(Dover)*
Shaw, Sir Giles *(Pudsey)*
Shaw, Sir Michael *(Scarb')*
Shelton, Sir William
Shephard, Mrs G. *(Norfolk SW)*
Shepherd, Richard *(Aldridge)*
Sims, Roger
Skeet, Sir Trevor
Smith, Sir Dudley *(Warwick)*
Smith, Tim *(Beaconsfield)*
Soames, Hon Nicholas
Spicer, Sir Jim *(Dorset W)*
Stanbrook, Ivor
Stanley, Rt Hon Sir John

Steen, Anthony
Stern, Michael
Stevens, Lewis
Stewart, Andy *(Sherwood)*
Stradling Thomas, Sir John
Sumberg, David
Tapsell, Sir Peter
Taylor, Ian *(Esher)*
Taylor, Teddy *(S'end E)*
Tebbit, Rt Hon Norman
Thompson, Patrick *(Norwich N)*
Thornton, Malcolm
Thurnham, Peter
Townend, John *(Bridlington)*
Townsend, Cyril D. *(B'heath)*
Tracey, Richard
Tredinnick, David
Trippier, David
Twinn, Dr Ian

Vaughan, Sir Gerard
Waddington, Rt Hon David
Wakeham, Rt Hon John
Waller, Gary
Wardle, Charles *(Bexhill)*
Warren, Kenneth
Watts, John
Wells, Bowen
Wheeler, John
Whitney, Ray
Widdecombe, Ann
Wood, Timothy
Woodcock, Dr. Mike
Young, Sir George *(Acton)*

Tellers for the Noes:
  Mr. David Maclean and
  Mr. Tom Sackville.

Question accordingly negatived.
Clause added to the Bill.

New Clause 32

CONFLICT OF INTEREST IN STAFF NEGOTIATIONS

' .—(1) It shall be the duty of a local authority to secure that, so far as practicable, the interests of that authority in any negotiations with respect to the terms and conditions on which persons in local authority employment hold office or are employed are never represented, whether directly or indirectly by, or by persons who include—
  (a) a person who is both a member of the authority and in such employment; or
  (b) a person who is both a member of the authority and an official or employee of a trade union whose members include persons in local authority employment.
(2) In this section—
  "member", in relation to a trade union, includes any person who is a member of that union within the meaning of the Employment Act 1988; and
  "official" and "trade union" have the same meanings as in the Trade Union and Labour Relations Act 1988; and
  "official" and "trade union" have the same meanings as in the Trade Union and Labour relations Act 1974; and
and a person shall be treated for the purposes of this section as in local authority employment if he holds any paid office or employment under a local authority or any such paid office or employment under any other person as, by virtue of section 80(1)(a) of the Local Government Act 1972 or section 31(1)(a) of the Local Government (Scotland) Act 1973, disqualifies him for membership of any authority.
(3) This section shall come into force at the expiry of the period of two months beginning on the day this Act is passed.'.—*[Mr. Gummer.]*
Brought up, and read the First time.

6 pm

Mr. Gummer: I beg to move, That the clause be read a Second time.

The effect of the provision would be to prohibit a local authority appointing a person who is both a member of the authority and an employee of local government from representing its interests in any negotiations concerning the terms and conditions of local government staff. The prohibition would also cover any member of local government who is also an official or employee of a trade union, the members of which include persons in local authority employment. This is an attempt to ensure that conflicts of interest do not arise in staff negotiations.

Mr. Soley: The new clause is what is known as the painful elaboration of the obvious because most local

authorities—indeed, all, because I do not know of any exceptions—practise this. Why on earth the Government, who boast about not producing unnecessary legislation, choose to do this is beyond me, but if they want to go through this strange rigmarole, so be it.

Question put and agreed to.
Clause read a Second time, and added to the Bill.

New Clause 2

SCOPE OF PART I

'(1) This part shall have effect for the purpose of disqualifying a person from becoming or remaining a member of a local authority, in accordance with section 1(8), where that person holds a politically restricted post in a local authority in Great Britain.
(2) For the purposes of this part, a person shall be regarded as holding a politically restricted post under a local authority where that person is—
  (a) the person designated under section 4 below as the head of the authority's paid service;
  (b) a statutory or non-statutory chief officer; or
  (c) a deputy chief officer.'.—*[Mr. Blunkett.]*
Brought up, and read the First time.

Mr. David Blunkett (Sheffield, Brightside): I beg to move, That the clause be read a Second time.

Mr. Deputy Speaker: With this it will be convenient to consider the following:

New Clause 3

INQUIRY BEFORE INTRODUCTION OF REGULATIONS
ABOUT POLITICALLY RESTRICTED POSTS

'(1) No regulations about politically restricted posts shall be introduced under Part I before the completion of any inquiry established under subsection (2) below, and the publication of its report.
(2) The Secretary of State shall establish an independent inquiry to assess the impact on local authority employees of the numbers likely to be affected by, and of the consequences for staff morale and the quality of service of—
  (a) the operation of a £13,500 salary qualification, or such higher amount as the Secretary of State may by order made by statutory instrument specify;
  (b) the introduction of a political restriction in respect of giving advice on a regular basis to the authority, to any committee or sub-committee of the authority or to any joint committee on which the authority are represented; and
  (c) the introduction of a political restriction in respect of acting on behalf of the authority on a regular basis for communicating with journalists or broadcasters; and
  (d) the introduction of a political restriction in respect of dealing on a regular basis with members of the public in circumstances from which they might reasonably infer that the holder of the post is in a position to influence the decisions of the authority, any committee or sub-committee of the authority or any joint committee on which the authority are represented.'.

New Clause 4

VOLUNTARY CODE OF PRACTICE (PART I)

'(1) This Part shall have effect subject to the provisions of this section, and after the making of an Order by the Secretary of State.
(2) No Order shall be made under subsection (1) above unless a draft has been laid before and approved by resolution of each House of Parliament.

(3) No Order shall be made under subsection (1) above before a period of twelve months from the introduction of a Code of Practice under subsection (4) below.

(4) The local authority associations shall, as soon as practicable after the passing of this Act, prepare and publish a voluntary Code of Practice for local authorities covering the matters referred to in this Part.

(5) No Order shall be made under subsection (1) above unless the Secretary of State has reasonable cause to believe that a serious infringement of the Code of Practice has taken place, and that the making of the Order will prevent a recurrence of such an infringement.

(6) Before making an Order under subsection (1) above, the Secretary of State shall lay before Parliament a report setting out his reasons for making such an Order, with reference to any alleged infringement of the Code as specified in subsection (5) above.'.

Mr. Blunkett: In moving new clause 2, with which new clauses 3 and 4 are being considered, I want to try to disentangle the way in which certain aspects of local government practice have been distorted and promoted through the media as inferring that all those who are openly politically active in whatever capacity and who work for local government at above a salary of £13,500 are, in the words of the Minister in Standing Committee G, "acting despicably".

The Opposition need to disentangle clearly what we are and what we are not in favour of and to ask the House to vote on those matters. First, we are not in favour of people having jobs created for them so that they may continue their political activities in working time, irrespective of their contribution to the local community in the job in which they have been employed. We want to make that absolutely and unequivocally clear. As our new clause 4 suggests in relation to other matters, we seek ways of ensuring that codes of practice and reasonable standards and rules of behaviour are applied. That is quite possible and, indeed, appointments procedures for local authorities, involving members of all political parties, can be and have been devised to ensure that that objective is met.

The second and associated smear that has been deliberately followed through understandable public worries on the first point has been the interesting notion that if one works for a local authority, one should not, perhaps, be involved in any political activity of any kind; that one should be restricted from standing for office either in local authorities, for Parliament here in Westminster or for the European assembly; and that one should be restricted from being able to speak, write or canvass on behalf of a political party or a cause associated directly with a political party. We reject that inference and smear on literally tens of thousands of people who have been giving decent service not only to local government but to their communities and to the cause of democracy.

Openly speaking and the ability to write and to declare oneself in favour of a political cause is not something of which to be ashamed; it is something of which to be proud. It is something that we should welcome in a democracy. Indeed, it is something that is suppressed and oppressed in regimes which all hon. Members would be eager to condemn and which the media outside the House spend a great deal of time rightly vilifying. However, when it is near to home there is the silence of indifference. There are people who are keen to preach to others and yet reluctant to practise the same rules for themselves.

Therefore, this evening, we are proposing measures to separate those things that we think have some validity in terms of needing guidance and restriction from those things that should be accepted as a normal and reasonable part of our political life.

First, we suggest that there should be some restriction on chief officers and their deputies and on the heads of the paid service and their deputies in terms of standing for other local authorities. That is reasonable and prudent. We do not think that many people would object to that. However, we do not see why that restriction and the political restrictions to which I have referred on people's ability to take part in politics should be extended to the vast number of people to whom the Bill would apply. Following the offer that has been made to administrative, professional, technical and clerical staff in local government, after July as many as 130,000 people will be caught in the restriction that forbids those on a gross annual salary of more than £13,500 to take part in political activity. That number comprises those who work directly in the paid service and does not include those caught in other aspects of the clauses that we are debating in terms of direct restrictions, irrespective of salary level.

That number of people, who can practise their democratic rights quite openly this week in the European elections and who have the civil right to display posters and to persuade other people to vote for any political party in that election will, if the Bill is passed, find that what is legal and acceptable this week will no longer be acceptable from the time that the Bill receives Royal Assent. We shall be placed in the farcical position that at the next European Assembly elections people who work in local government and who wish to be politically active will have to join the former leader of the Liberal party in campaigning in Italy, France or West Germany where they will presumably be free to engage in political activity. But they will not be able to promote their views and campaign on behalf of members of the same party in the United Kingdom—[*Interruption.*] Does the hon. Member for Crawley (Mr. Soames) wish to intervene?

Mr. Nicholas Soames (Crawley) *indicated dissent.*

Mr. Blunkett: I am not surprised that the hon. Gentleman has nothing to say. The Government's proposals are disgraceful. They are an infringement of basic civil and human rights and they will be challenged in the European Court of Human Rights. The legal view already is that they infringe article 10 and the first protocol, article 3 of the European convention on human rights.

Mr. Patnick: Is the hon. Gentleman aware that civil servants are already bound by certain rules? Are Opposition Members changing their view on this issue, bearing in mind what they have said in advocating that the rules for hon. Members should be the same as those applying to councillors?

Mr. Blunkett: On present salary levels, industrial and non-officer grades in the Civil Service earning up to a maximum of £24,000 are not restricted. Those working in grades in a "politically restricted capacity" on salaries ranging between £17,500 and £24,000, including London weighting, would have to ask their immediate superiors for permission to engage not only in those activities which are now banned but in standing for public office. There is no comparison between the restrictions on civil servants and the £13,500 arbitrary ban, as it were, in the Bill.

Is impartiality in the public service to be judged purely in terms of whether people pretend not to hold political views? After all, one could be a sleeper—a quiet and surreptitious revolutionary—or hold all manner of views so long as one did not express them. Are we to sweep such views under the carpet, pushing them into shady corners of unacceptability? Are we to push democracy so that people are obliged to hold their views in quiet silence?

Not only is that unacceptable to us, but it demonstrates an important contradiction that emerged in Committee. If public confidence is endangered because people hold views and, as it were, practise democracy in their spare time, seeking exemption must cast doubt on their impartiality as well as questioning the advice that is given, even though, as the Minister said in Committee, the political views of the individual are not of concern. I question the fact that the individual is politically active.

The act of seeking exemption, of going to the arbitrator and asking to be permitted, because of one's job—perhaps because one is a mortuary attendant on overtime or a psychiatric social worker in the children's service—to go forward for selection for, say, the Conservative party, as the Parliamentary Under-Secretary of State for the Environment found herself doing in the 1970s and 1980s, will be tantamount to declaring oneself to be politically active.

The moment one declares oneself to be political, in accordance with the Bill, one will be labelled and blacklisted. One will have indicated that one holds views strongly enough to want to be, say, the treasurer of the local Conservative association, and in Committee we showed that that would come under the "unacceptable" category.

At general election time we may describe such a request as unacceptable, but to find Ministers now talking about an activity in their party as being in some way dangerous to the nation's democracy is beyond belief. That is why we wish to differentiate between political knock-about and propaganda that seeks to discredit individuals and the dangerous road down which we are now being led in terms of disqualifying tens of thousands of people from practising their normal political rights.

6.15 pm

If it is reasonable to believe that impartiality flows from the advice given by solicitors, accountants, surveyors or estate agents, even though they are politically active, the same must apply to local authority employees undertaking normal and reasonable tasks. That has been the case in Tory authorities with Labour activists and in Labour authorities with Tory activists, and with few exceptions there has been no malpractice. Dedication and decency have been the general rule.

In seeking to restrict the Bill to a few, clearly-designated and highly-paid senior officials, and in promoting a code of practice which would enable us to see what was and was not acceptable, local government would regulate itself, and Parliament would decide whether the code of practice had worked. We aim by that means to protect basic rights that have been acceptable in the past but which, with the passage of the Bill, will be described as "despicable".

I hope that, even at this late stage, common sense will prevail in the Government and that it will not be necessary for people to go to the European Court of Human Rights, claiming that the British Government had acted in an unacceptable and arbitrary manner. We do not have a good record in that court. We have lost on vastly more occasions than other countries. Indeed, whenever people turn to European institutions to obtain redress and have their civil rights upheld, those institutions are strengthened to the detriment of the authority of the British Parliament.

That leads people to have less confidence in securing their democratic rights at the national level. That is bad for Parliament and for Britain. It reveals us in a poor light. What the Government propose may be good knock-about politics and they may think they are getting political capital out of it, but it is a basic infringement of all that we in Britain stand for.

Mr. Matthew Taylor: We debated this issue on Second Reading and at some length in Committee, and throughout those debates Conservative Members showed no sign of understanding the gravity of what is involved in removing people's basic democractic rights in a country the political system of which is based fundamentally on people holding those rights.

The Government's proposals mean that the right of freedom of speech will be curtailed for thousands of people. The right of free association, to campaign and to do something about those things in which people believe will be removed at a stroke, yet Ministers have been unable to give satisfactory reasons for what they are doing. They have not said, for example, that what they propose is vital or that they have tried to frame other options that would not remove those fundamental liberties. They have said that it must be plain common sense and that we must simply take away those liberties. It is that more than anything that appals me about our debates.

Mr. Gummer: Is it the policy of the hon. Gentleman's party to give civil servants the right to do all those things —a right that they have never had, even as far back as the period during which the hon. Gentleman's party was last in power?

Mr. Taylor: The Minister diverts me down the lengthy route that we followed in Committee. He will recall our long and detailed arguments about procedures within the Civil Service, the greater rights of individuals to appeal and the clearer levels at which differences occur. We reluctantly accept that there is a level within local government at which there should be certain restrictions, although I should much prefer that not to be the case.

The powers being taken by the Secretary of State and the arbitrary nature of the £13,500 figure suggest that the Minister, both for political ease and to win political support from some members of the general public, has found it simpler to wipe out a whole set of liberties at a stroke. We do not even know precisely what liberties will be removed and no details will be available before we vote. We know that the provision will be imposed retrospectively and will include, at least, prohibition on holding office in a political party, speaking or writing publicly on matters of political controversy—however that may be defined— and canvassing at elections. Ministers defend the provision by saying that it will affect only a tiny number of people, but we must remember that even on their figures, on a salary bar of £13,500 it will affect 70,000 or 80,000 people —enough to elect one Member of Parliament or to provide a majority for two Members of Parliament. That is only an initial figure. There have been no commitments from Ministers—and they certainly have not been included in the Bill—that there will be suitable changes year by year to

[Mr. Taylor]

ensure that the numbers affected do not rapidly expand. There are many ways in which more people can be brought within the net, but the most obvious is through the annual pay awards. The local authorities' conditions of service advisory board estimates that a further minimum of 20,000 staff each year will fall into the restricted category simply through the normal run of pay settlements.

In addition to the Government's reference to principal officers and above, 4,000 staff will be brought in through London weighting, another 4,000 on local scales and 8,500 fire service employees. Ministers have not told us the reality of what is being done. They have given no commitment that more and more people will not be brought into the net. That is fundamental to the liberties of every citizen, not just those directly affected, because it distorts the very democracy within which we work. Certainly all hon. Members should have a special regard for that.

Ministers say that the provision will be subject to an appeal system, yet many of those affected will have no recourse to appeal. The Government intend to scrub out the liberties of many thousands of local government employees simply by putting them under other categories. Even with the £13,500 rule, which will be subject to appeal, we are asked to believe that one adjudicator can deal with the whole of the appeal system. How can that be so? Can an appeal be held in advance? Can someone say that as he is expecting a pay rise the next year and might be banned from local government he wants to appeal in advance, not be kept hanging on a fine thread, so that he knows what he can or cannot do?

We have discussed at length the difficulties of deciding how the appeal process will operate and whether it can cope, especially when the provision is initially enacted and will affect so many people almost overnight. How does the Minister envisage it working when it is thought that people have broken the rules? It will be difficult for the individual to be sure whether his actions will be assessed as taking part in matters of public controversy. Will he be thrown out of office simply because he has miscalculated what he can or cannot do? Will the public have glossy literature pushed through their doors asking them to keep an eye on local government employees who might be breaking the rules? Are people expected to report on neighbours who have political posters in their windows or have been at a vaguely political demonstration? Or will the system operate through confessions—an individual going to the adjudicator and confessing his sins? Will the adjudicator say, "Own up, you have been a bad boy and we must do something about it."

It will be impossible for the system to work in the way intended. Either there will be some sort of police state, under which everyone will be worried about who might be reporting him to the authorities, on Left or Right, as he goes about his daily life and becomes involved—or even only said to be involved—in issues of importance to his local community, or there will be a special group of people employed to monitor the system in the way that snoopers police the poll tax by going around homes to see how many tooth brushes are in the bathroom.

The Government are launching a broadside at the basis on which our democracy works without apparent awareness of the implications and without placing restrictions on the number of people who can be brought into the net. Many people will be brought into it at a later date. Will they be only local government employees or will the employees of the few remaining public utilities be included? How far will the net extend? That is a fundamental issue that should not be pushed through the House.

I support the new clauses because their aim is to ensure proper democratic debate and decision-making, to restrict the numbers involved and to delay implementation of the provision. The Minister will no doubt argue that the new clauses aim to prevent the provision ever being implemented. That is true, and I welcome it. Those hon. Members who believe in the fundamental democratic rights and liberties of the people should do everything possible to oppose such a broad brush, sweeping attack on many thousands of individuals and the many tens of thousands who the Government may say are not included, but who we know potentially will be included in future.

Mr. Kenneth Hind (Lancashire, West): What is at the root of the Government's proposal, and why I urge the House to reject the new clause, is the importance of the neutrality of the local government official and the impartiality with which he gives his advice as a servant of the community. I have some knowledge of these matters. My father was chief accountant for Salford corporation for 30 years before he joined the National Health Service in 1948. He always regarded as a prime factor in his service to the local authority the fact that he was essentially politically neutral, taking no part in any political activity, so that the advice that he gave to all parties was equal and fair and seen to be unbiased. That is the role of the local government employee—who, after all, chooses to work in local government—especially those with salaries of more than £13,500 and the designated officers whom my right hon. Friend the Minister has included within the scope of the provision——

Mr. Tony Banks (Newham, North-West) *rose——*

Mr. Hind: I am sure that the hon. Gentleman will catch Mr. Deputy Speaker's eye.

The hon. Member for Sheffield, Brightside (Mr. Blunkett) talked about the rights of the individual and of appealing to the European Court of Human Rights. That is very much going over the top in relation to my hon. Friend's modest recommendation contained in the clause.

If we look at the Civil Service and at local government officials throughout the European Community, we will find that it is expected that they will be neutral, servants of the community providing unbiased political advice to the elected representatives. That, after all, is the role of a local government officer. Considered from that point of view I am sure that we can see the sense and the purpose of the clause.

6.30 pm

Mr. Matthew Taylor: Will the hon. Gentleman give way?

Mr. Hind: The hon. Gentleman has already spoken. We wish to make progress.

The proposals contained in these clauses have been introduced because the non-existence of regulations in the immediate past was abused. The fact that we did not have much regulation in this area, so that it was possible to be a councillor on one authority and work for another, has been abused in recent years. We have seen it occurring constantly, especially in the south-east. I make it clear that it is not a problem in Lancashire and the north-west, apart from Merseyside. We have seen, however, over and over again in the south-east examples of councillors working for one local authority being given a job in another.

Mr. Bob Cryer (Bradford, South): Will the hon. Gentleman give way?

Mr. Hind: I shall not give way. I am sure that the hon. Gentleman will have an opportunity to make his point.

That sort of job-for-the-boys situation must be stopped.

New clause 4 is asking for a voluntary code of practice —in effect a series of regulations with no teeth. It is clearly a wrecking amendment that the hon. Member for Brightside has tabled to destroy the intention that is behind my hon. Friend's clause. Secondly, it asks the House to deal with each individual case that is reported to it, through the Secretary of State, so that, effectively, each individual case is resolved by the House. That is a huge waste of the legislative time of the House. It is something that should be dealt with elsewhere.

I respect the tactics of the hon. Member for Brightside, because he is in opposition, but this is a wrecking amendment that will achieve nothing. I say to my hon. Friends that it is just undermining the Bill. I advise them completely to reject the three new clauses. I commend that view to the House.

Mr. Peter L. Pike (Burnley): I believe that we are debating an important issue. This group of new clauses is relatively modest in its approach. The new clauses recognise that the Government are not likely to recognise the folly of their policy. However, at least they give them the opportunity, if they accept the new clauses, to analyse the implications of their policy. While it would delay the implementation of the relevant parts of the Bill, it would allow them to reconsider. If the Government considered the matter positively, I believe that they would recognise that it is unnecessary to move in that direction.

The hon. Member for Lancashire, West (Mr. Hind) appears to believe that a person earning £13,500 could not serve on one local authority and perform his duties in his employing authority in a way that was not reflecting his political view. I am sure that the majority of employees who earn such a salary could not in any way influence the political viewpoint or the direction in which a local authority moves. The arbitrary figure chosen is nonsensical. It penalises those, especially in London and the south-east, who, because of the higher cost of living and property values resulting from the Government's policies, must be paid a salary for a job that would attract a much lower level of salary elsewhere.

I accept that, if a council is being advised by officers on a committee, it wants those officers to give impartial advice and to carry out the decisions of the local authority. That would be expected by any local authority, whether Labour, Conservative or SLD. When we take over government, we shall certainly expect the civil servants to act in the same way and to carry out the wishes of a Labour Government. There are genuine fears that the Government are stacking the Civil Service with senior civil servants who are of their viewpoint. If the Government are concerned about political interference, they should look

into that matter. I know that a series of questions has been asked about the number of political advisers who have been appointed in many Government Departments. In fact, the Government have more political advisers in the different Departments than any previous Government.

I feel strongly that it is wrong to erode people's rights to stand for local authorities and to remove their political freedom. We see the Government continuously eroding civil liberties, freedom and rights.—*[Interruption.]* The hon. Member for Crawley (Mr. Soames) of course rejects that charge. He never speaks in these debates. He fails to recognise that consistently this Government, who talk about freedom, erode freedom by their legislation. Obviously, the constraints of the debate will not allow me to cite examples, but that is very much in accord with their policy of removing rights.

We do not know what the regulations will contain and whether they will say that local authority employees cannot display a poster or cannot go canvassing. We have seen examples of the powers given to the Secretary of State. He can make regulations under legislation, and we saw how a few weeks ago seven orders, involving 94 pages of poll tax regulations, were dealt with in an hour and a half. That shows why we are rightly concerned about what the Government are doing. That was a sham of a debate. As I said that night, we are increasingly becoming a sham of a democracy.

If the Government are not prepared to accept the new clause moved by my hon. Friend the Member for Sheffield, Brightside (Mr. Blunkett), they will make a great mistake. While it may be right that the very senior officers should not be in a position to stand for local authorities, it is nonsense to bring in this arbitrary figure and thereby remove so many people from service on local authorities and participation in political activities. The Government would really like to move a motion that no one takes part in political activities in this country unless they happen to be Conservative activities. They do not like anyone with a different point of view from the one expressed from the Conservative Benches. The Government do not believe in democracy. It is consistent with their policy to erode democracy. If they are not prepared to accept the new clauses, I fear that it will be a further serious erosion of and a restriction on the rights of local government employees, of whatever party, to express their political views and, if they so wish, to serve on local authorities.

I hope that the Minister recognises the importance of what we are debating. I stress that it is a dangerous direction in which the Government are moving. If they want to preserve democracy, freedom and people's rights, they will be prepared to accept the new clauses.

Mr. Rooker: I support the three new clauses. In all honesty, I do not believe that the modern Conservative party believes in local government. The evidence of the past few years is there for all to see, and this is just one further example. They are driving people out of local government. That is their intention, because they do not want any strain of independence or any other form of power in the land other than central Government under Conservative party control.

If the Government get their way, by and large the people who really want to contribute to society will not go into local government. They will want nothing to do with

[*Mr. Rooker*]

it. Following the financial changes, local government officers will be bereft of any decision-making powers and their other powers will be greatly restricted.

Over the past decade it has become clear—I shall not cite individuals as that is unfair—that the whole thrust of the Conservative parliamentary party has been against good independent local government. That government is not partisan and it is not political, but independent and good and the Government do not like it.

My hon. Friend the Member for Sheffield, Brightside (Mr. Blunkett) made it clear that many people in local government believe that their fundamental democratic and human rights are being severely curtailed by the Bill. He said that those people will seek to use their democratic rights to take their case to the European Court of Human Rights. I was amazed when the hon. Member for Lancashire, West (Mr. Hind)—I believe that he is in the legal profession—said that to take such a complaint to the European Court was "going over the top".

Mr. Hind: Quite right.

Mr. Rooker: Are we to assume that an amendment will be tabled to stop people exercising their right to make such a complaint? Because of our unwritten constitution the Government are able to trammel people's rights. More and more people are forced to go to courts outside the United Kingdom to seek redress. It is expensive and all possible pressure is exerted on people not to do so. To argue that it is over the top to make such a complaint to the European Court—the function of that court is to stop member states trammelling the civil liberties of their citizens—is a disgraceful remark from a parliamentarian.

Mr. Hind *rose——*

Mr. Rooker: The hon. Gentleman did not give way to any hon. Members and I shall not give way to him.

Mr. Robert G. Hughes (Harrow, West): The hon. Gentleman should give way as he attacked my hon. Friend.

Mr. Rooker: Of course I attacked him and I shall continue to do so. I will not give way to him.

The issue goes much wider because the Government's legislation does not just cover those who give advice——

Mr. Hind *rose——*

Hon. Members: Sit down.

Mr. Hind: On a point of order, Madam Deputy Speaker. Surely it is a matter of courtesy in this House for an hon. Member who criticises another, whether it is justified or not, to give way to the hon. Gentleman criticised so that he may respond.

Madam Deputy Speaker (Miss Betty Boothroyd): It is for the hon. Gentleman who has the Floor to decide whether to give way.

Mr. Rooker: If the Government's legislation just covered those who gave advice and its scope was that narrow, there would be some merit in the argument that we could debate. The Bill, however, will not just cover

those who give advice, but manual workers and people who, by and large, have no contact with the public or with councillors. That is the incredible thing about the Bill.

Frankly, we would not be having this debate today if it were not—I say this as a Member representing Birmingham—for a mere handful of isolated cases of gross abuse in London. That is the truth of the matter. Those hon. Members who represent parts of the country outside London deeply resent what has happened. What is more, that abuse could have been put right much more easily than by the introduction of the draconian measure before us today. The Bill will affect thousands of councillors and it is a smear on good local government on both sides of the political divide. All that, just because of a handful of people in certain London boroughs. No one denies that certain chief officers were twin-tracking, but it is disgraceful that this Bill has been introduced because of their actions.

I am also concerned about the definition of political activities. The Government have attacked a range of activities and people's rights and freedoms. People join political parties, but they also join political movements. Not all political movements are political parties and a fine distinction must be drawn. At one time one could have argued that the environmental movement was not a political party, although one party may have claimed to have been more concerned about the environment than others. All parties claim that today.

6.45 pm

Our constitution is unwritten and it allows the Government to do what they want. It allows them to take people's rights away, but it also allows people to complain to the European Court of Human Rights. Charter 88 is a people's movement for constitutional reform and I understand that it is supported by members of all political parties and people of no political party. That group holds meetings around the country—some of which are said to be ordinary public meetings and some of which are fringe meetings held at conferences run by political parties and other organisations. That group is seeking to campaign for wide constitutional reform on a non-party and all-party basis. Under the Bill, will membership of that group constitute political activity? Some signatories to the charter are Conservative—they are few and far between, but honourable nevertheless. It is their constitutional right to campaign, outside of political parties, for constitutional reform. We must not forget that. I plead guilty to not following the Committe proceedings as well as I should have done and I do not know whether what is meant by political activity was discussed.

The Bill is extremely dangerous. New clauses 2, 3 and 4 go some way to mitigate that danger and to meet the main thrust of the abuse that undoubtedly took place. We did not support that abuse and we would have sought to put that matter right.

Mr. Patnick: I missed the speech of the hon. Member for Sheffield, Brightside (Mr. Blunkett). It is a pleasure to listen to the logic of his argument, but it is difficult to follow.

I accept that the Local Government Act 1972, introduced by a Conservative Government, sought to distinguish between an officer who worked for the council and those people who were officers initially, but then became known as party activists. Pre-1972 it was possible to go to local government officers to seek impartial advice. I do not mean to be disparaging about the present officers in local government, but if they are responsible to political masters it is hard for them to give impartial advice.

The hon. Member for Birmingham, Perry Barr (Mr. Rooker) referred to the fact that only London councillors were twin-trackers. The *Daily Mail* of 20 November 1985——

Mr. Tony Banks: Oh no!

Mr. Patnick: The hon. Member for Newham, North-West (Mr. Banks) has made more speeches from a sedentary position today than anyone else. I have not yet seen him get up to say anything positive; he merely continues his abuse from a sedentary position— *[Interruption.]*

Madam Deputy Speaker: Order. We should have one debate at a time.

Mr. Patnick: Thank you for your protection— *[Interruption.]* Now our Member of the European Parliament, the hon. Member for Bradford, South (Mr. Cryer), is joining in.

The *Daily Mail* article stated that a quarter of Glasgow's city councillors were employed by their regional council, Strathclyde. The hon. Member for Brightside and myself had the honour to be members of South Yorkshire county council— *[Interruption.]* If the hon. Member for Bradford, South wants to intervene, I shall give way.

Mr. Cryer: All I want to say is that I am being constantly pestered by the junior Minister from the Home Office, the hon. Member for Grantham (Mr. Hogg), who keeps shouting questions at me which are entirely irrelevant, and I am merely being courteous.

Madam Deputy Speaker: I think that we ought to show a little common courtesy in this Chamber and hear only one speaker at a time.

Mr. Patnick: I apologise to the hon. Member for Bradford, South; I thought he wished to intervene.

Both the hon. Member for Brightside and I were members of South Yorkshire county council and Sheffield city council and had a chance to see if friendship across the political divide could blossom because I had the pleasure of transporting him from Barnsley to Sheffield, where we used to slither in to the next meeting.

From the four districts—Barnsley, Rotherham, Doncaster and Sheffield—many officers employed by the local authority were also county councillors. I do not say that there was anything wrong in that. I am making the point because the hon. Member for Perry Barr said it was only London people who did this and I have endeavoured to prove that it was not.

The fact is that 16 per cent. of local authority councillors of all parties in Britain are also local authority employees—that is, about 4,000 people.

Mr. Matthew Taylor: The hon. Gentleman makes a point that we have heard before and that features in the Conservative party's brief on the Bill. Can he tell us how many of those to whom he refers as being also local authority employees would come under these restrictions, because clearly many of them would be on much lower salaries and not in positions that would be included in this Bill?

Mr. Patnick: I thank the hon. Member for that wonderful intervention. If he had allowed me to finish the point that I had started to make, I would have answered that. His crystal ball is not as good as it appears to be.

Of those 4,000 people, about 58 per cent. are teachers or lecturers, to whom the twin-tracking provision does not apply—*[Interruption.]* I am sure that the hon. Gentleman has read the Bill and it does not apply to teachers or lecturers—wrongly, some may think. This was discussed in Committee and the Minister stated that it did not apply. That leaves about 1,700 people to whom the twin-tracking provision might apply, although not all will be politically restricted. So we are left with the basic number, which could be 400 to 500 councillors, who may be caught by the twin-tracking prohibition. Does any hon. Member say that that is unreasonable? There are only a few people to whom this applies and I cannot see that it is so onerous that it is taking away privilege and making people go to the European Court, although no doubt some Opposition Members will make that case.

Mr. Tony Banks: As ever, the hon. Member for Sheffield, Hallam (Mr. Patnick) missed the point. I should like to say that I compliment him on a good speech, but I would not wish to mislead the House.

The twin-tracking argument has been used to distract attention from the more insidious aspect of this Bill, which is the political restriction on officers earning £13,500. I am not particularly in favour of twin-tracking. When I was a member of the Greater London council—and the sun always shone in those days, as we all know——

Mr. Patnick: It was shining today.

Mr. Banks: No, the sun was not shining today; it was the greenhouse effect today. It was a microwave oven out there. It is all part of the ozone layer breaking down because of Government policies. The sun genuinely shone in GLC days. I was not particularly happy about officers who had heavy council responsibilities being elected members of other local authorities. I accepted the fact, but I was not happy about it.

The point—and we said this to the Minister in Committee—is that we should look at the whole matter of compensation and the way that we remunerate our councillors. We have a crazy system. We still rely very much on people giving up their careers in order to be local councillors. It seems to me that, if we are really worried about the question of twin tracking, rather than just moving in to obliterate the idea we should start talking in terms of fewer councillors perhaps, of looking at the whole structure of local government and of paying local councillors a decent salary for doing a good job.

Mr. Robert G. Hughes: I am sure that the hon. Member will wish history to record that he was an influential and important member of the Greater London council. If he felt as he has just said and was unhappy with councillors twin tracking, being local councillors and members of the GLC staff in high positions, why were there so many of them? Why did it seem to be the policy of the Labour party to promote so many people who were in Labour party positions or were Labour councillors elsewhere to high positions in the GLC? He really cannot have it both ways.

Mr. Banks: I did not say that I was unhappy; I said that I was not happy, which is not quite the same thing. Words are supposed to mean something in this place, and there is

[*Mr. Banks*]

a difference there. I was not happy, but that unhappiness arose not because people were twin tracking but because the system of local government and remuneration of councillors is all wrong.

I would be much more in favour of seeing whether there was a problem if the Government were prepared to make some serious proposals for looking at the way in which we remunerate local councillors who do a good job. We are not looking at it in that root and branch fashion. We are looking at it at a superficial level, and this symbolises the Government's approach. It is superficial and layered with malice, venom and bigotry. That is the way in which the Government approach local government.

Coming now to the £13,500 cut-off, it is typical of this Government that they attach a price to everything; they set an economic point at which there will be a cut-off. That is not a qualitative argument; it is a quantitative argument based on money. The only thing that the Arthur Daleys on the Government Benches who now run this country understand a little bit about is money. That is their level. They know nothing about the qualitative arguments that the Opposition are addressing.

The figure of £13,500 relates back, I suppose, to Widdicombe's point about principal officers. But things have moved on since then. If the figure stays at £13,500, and assuming that the Government are around for a few years yet, in the end, logically, virtually every local government officer will come within the category. Clearly the Minister, when he replies, must tell us what he intends to do about uprating the £13,500 figure because things have moved on even while the Bill has been in Committee. It is difficult now to be precise about the number of officers in local government who will be caught, but it may be as many as 130,000. I urge the Minister to tell us because, although the Government said originally that the ban would affect a mere 3 per cent. of local government employees, that figure has gone up and I want the Minister to give precisely his estimate of the number of local government officers affected.

We also need to know from the Minister what he means by political activity. Will it be so ridiculous as to include canvassing or putting up a poster? That has nothing to do with the impartial advice that local officers are giving; it has to do with their own civil rights, I would have thought, and therefore cannot be seen as affecting them in terms of the advice they give.

The hon. Member for Lancashire, West (Mr. Hind) mentioned his dear old dad, who was a local government officer. I am sure that he gave very good and impartial advice. It is a pity that some of it did not rub off on his son. I understand that the hon. Member used to be a member of the Labour party, so clearly his dad told him some good things. I only wish that his dad would carry on telling him those things because he has clearly gone all wrong since. His dad, being a sufficiently senior officer, would clearly have come within the terms of our clause. That shows that, as ever, we are being wholly reasonable.

We say that there are two good reasons why it is right that senior officers whose purpose is to give advice should not be involved in political activity, certainly of the twin-tracking sort. First, they do not have the time and, secondly, their advice is crucial. But it is nonsense to talk about £13,500 at those sorts of levels. That is the point at

which it matters. The Government are not concerned with the sort of advice that they are giving; they are saying that because that is how much they earn they should not be in a position to give advice to elected members because that advice could be called into question. That is nonsense. First, the Minister must tell us how many local government officers will be included in his net and, secondly, what is the scope of political activity. How will he revise those salary levels or levels of political activity?

This is a crude attempt by the Government to smash local authorities into a shape that appeals to Conservative Members. That approach can be seen running through the Bill. There is no finesse about it; they are simply trying to smash local authorities. That is their philosophy and their approach and that is why we ask all reasonable Members —there are one or two, although I cannot see them at the moment, but no doubt they will be coming in soon—to support us in the Lobby when they realise the appalling nature of the Bill.

7 pm

Mr. John McAllion (Dundee, East): The hon. Member for Sheffield, Hallam (Mr. Patnick) seemed to be worried by the fact that some Glasgow district councillors also work for Strathclyde regional council. That does not seem to worry the voters in Glasgow who continue to vote in overwhelming numbers for representatives of the parties who oppose this legislation. So dominant is the Labour party in Strathclyde region that the main opposition party on Glasgow district council after Labour is composed of six Labour councillors who have temporarily had the whip withdrawn as a matter of internal discipline. They outnumber the Tory group in the council by almost two to one. Conservative Members should listen to the people of Scotland rather than use them as an example to substantiate their arguments.

While I am on that subject, let me tell the Minister that the only people who are not displaying political posters in Glasgow, Central this week are members of the Conservative party who are so ashamed of being associated with legislation of this kind that they will not display their own party's posters in the by-election.

I support the new clauses, particularly new clause 4 which has a specifically Scottish angle. It proposes that no regulations can be laid until a code of practice has been agreed with the local authority associations. In Scotland, that means with the Convention of Scottish Local Authorities. It also means the politicians who have been elected by the Scottish people. At the moment, restrictions have been imposed by a Government who in no way represent the views of the Scottish people. I know that the Under-Secretary of State for Scotland, the hon. Member for Edinburgh, West (Lord James Douglas-Hamilton), is present and that he represents a Scottish constituency, but the most recent opinion poll in Scotland which was published this morning shows support for the Conservative party standing at 7 per cent. That shows that the Government do not have a democratic mandate for imposing a new system of local government to serve people who in no way support the views of the Conservative party.

It is particularly important that the Minister should give a definition of what will constitute the kind of political activity that will be restricted. It has been said that there is a difference between political actions and actions which become a movement. Scotland has many unique movements. The hon. Member for Glasgow, Govan (Mr. Sillars) is almost completely unique in that respect. Only this week in Glasgow, Central he claimed to be the true inheritor of the Red Clydesider, Jimmy Maxton, who once served well in the House. Yet at the same time he was picking up a fat salary from Rupert Murdoch's son—the same Rupert Murdoch who sacked 6,000 print workers. I would venture to suggest that had Jimmy Maxton been alive today he certainly would not have been a member of the Scottish National party working for the son of Rupert Murdoch and taking the side of the capitalists against the print workers, as the hon. Gentleman has done so unimpressively in Scotland recently.

Let us take a campaign such as that for a Scottish assembly. I hope that the Minister is listening because this is an important point which the Scottish people want clarified. Will belonging to such a campaign be a politically restricted activity? Will local government officers who earn more than £13,500 a year be denied the right to go along to the local branch meeting of their campaign for a Scottish Assembly, to go on demonstrations and to put posters in their windows in support of such a campaign?

Will the same thing apply to the new phenomenon in Scotland—the Scottish constitutional convention? Will a local government officer be restricted from expressing support for that convention? Those are important matters that must be clarified by the Minister which to date have not been clarified.

I remember a song when I was at school about a cruel law against the wearing of the green, which was a way of trying to restrict support for Irish home rule. If the Minister does not clarify the position, we shall know that this is a direct attempt to restrict support for Scottish home rule by making it illegal for many thousands of local government officers to express their support for that concept. It is important to have that matter cleared up.

Many Scottish people are taking part in non-payment campaigns against the poll tax. Will that become a politically restricted activity under the Act? I am a member of a Scottish committee of 100 who refuse to pay the poll tax and there are also many local government officers who earn more than £13,500 a year. If the Bill is enacted, will they be forbidden from taking such action next year when the poll tax is implemented in Scotland, or will they be allowed to take part in such non-party political activities?

In Committee I asked about local government officers being elected to schools boards in Scotland. Since then, teachers' unions in Scotland have made it clear that they will work with school boards and use them as one of the main engines by which to oppose the Government's privatisation policies in Scottish education. Will local government officers be able to take part in school boards and join in campaigns run by school boards against the Government education policy in Scotland without being restricted from doing so under the Bill? Teaching members of the board will be able to do that, but if they happen to be a parent member who is also a local government officer earning more than £13,500 a year, will they be restricted from openly and publicly attacking Government policy in respect of opting out and privatising Scottish education? That must be sorted out, and I hope that the Minister will make it clear when he replies.

I want to clarify how far the clause will apply to local government officers. In Committee on 7 March I asked the Under-Secretary of State for Wales, the hon. Member for Cardiff, Central (Mr. Grist), to consider the problem of a technical officer who was a councillor in Strathkelvin and Bearsden district council and who worked for Glasgow city council as a structural engineer. I asked whether technical officers would be exempt from restrictions placed upon politically restricted posts if they earned more than £13,500 a year. The Minister said:

"It depends on what they are paid, whether they regularly advise the council, have contact with the media, and whether it can be believed that because of their position on the council they have some influence on the public. There are provisions in the Bill for such cases to be considered on their merits" —[*Official Report, Standing Committee G,* 7 March 1989; c. 156-7.]

Recently in Dundee there was much political controversy about the safety of Tayside house, the headquarters of Tayside regional council. If that man had been a structural engineer working for Tayside regional council, he could have been earning more than £13,500 a year and advising the council on matters which affected that building. He certainly could have had contact with the media over that matter and he could have influenced public opinion by what he said in respect of that building. Would such an officer be in a politically restricted post in those circumstances?

It is important that the Minister should clarify such details, because the Government are interfering in matters that they know nothing about. They know nothing about Scottish local government, yet they are imposing this new system on Scotland against the will of the Scottish people, and the Opposition will continue to resist them.

Mr. Pike: Is it not the case that under the Government's competition policy a person may be employed in an identical post in a private company as that of someone working in local government and yet not be subject to restrictions?

Mr. McAllion: My hon. Friend makes a valid point. Recently in Dundee the cleaning contract for Dundee schools was lost to a private contractor because the SNP and the Tories voted for that to happen. As a consequence, Tayside regional council employees are cleaning schools in Angus, Perth and Kinross, whereas private sector employees are cleaning schools in Dundee. The same situation could arise in other sectors of local government service, with people providing the same service in various parts of the region being treated completely differently.

Private sector employees will not be subject to the Bill's provisions but anyone working for the regional council will be. That is a mighty big flaw. The House does not understand or know Scottish local government and has no right to interfere in it. It should be left to the next Labour Government to create a Scottish Parliament to deal with Scottish local government in the way that it should be dealt with.

Mr. Cryer: New clause 2 is a particularly strong indicator of the vindictive nature of the whole Bill. The matter under consideration goes back to the Local Government Act 1972, when there was another act of aggression by a Tory Government against local authorities. It proposed the abolition of a large number of smaller local authorities, all the municipal boroughs, and rural and urban district councils. They were all wiped out by the 1972 Act, and one of the Government's arguments

[*Mr. Cryer*]

for taking that course was that as larger local authorities would involve important decision taking they would attract the right calibre of officers.

Prior to 1974 and the operation of the 1972 Act, the majority of local government work was undertaken entirely by amateurs in their spare time, outside working hours. However, the very large local authorities created by the then Tory Government placed enormous burdens on people and, as a consequence, a small number of them became involved in the business of electing councillors who then had to look round for some way of supplementing their income, and they obtained local authority jobs.

Restrictions are already placed on a local authority employee who is also an elected member, so many councillors have been compelled to look outside their own areas for employment. It sometimes happens that they work for one local authority and live in the area of another, where they represent local people in a perfectly normal and proper way. However, as my hon. Friend the Member for Newham, North-West (Mr. Banks) mentioned, the burdens placed on local authority representatives are now so great that councillors in key positions find it almost impossible to sustain a full-time job.

There is a marked difference between employees in the public sector and those in the private sector. Company directors are given as much time off as they want by the board. Tory party representation in a local authority often comprises people who have a place in the board room or who are solicitors, who find it easy to get time off. That is not always the case, but it often is. However, wage earners must always obtain permission to get time off, and it is not always given. Employees of large privatised organisations such as British Telecom are given only a certain number of days off each year, which they must allocate very carefully. Such are the difficulties that have precipitated the decision by many councillors to find local authority employment.

7.15 pm

How many people find themselves both representing a local authority and working for one? Is the figure 20, 30 or 40? What percentage of the total number of councillors does the Minister seek to embrace in his legislation? He has not mentioned any number. The fact is that the vast majority of local authority committees and full councils are served by councillors who have other jobs, and who believe that they can best do so by advocating certain political views.

It is incumbent on the Minister to provide evidence of the need for the measure he proposes. What evidence is there that there has been damage done by the advocacy of so-called prejudicial information because officers of a certain local authority are Labour or Conservative members of another council? It is an implied term in an employee's contract of employment that he will use his skills and abilities to the full. Is there any recorded case of a member of the public, body or institution suing a local government officer for breach of his contract of employment, in failing to display the required standard of quality advice?

Mr. Geoffrey Lofthouse (Pontefract and Castleford): My hon. Friend will acknowledge that throughout the country many independents win local authority seats. Are the Government suggesting that independent councillors have no part to play? Will the Bill prohibit a local government officer earning more than £13,500 a year from standing as an independent for another local authority?

Mr. Cryer: That may be another implication of the clause, and no doubt the Minister will guide us through the minefield as to what is and what is not deemed to be political activity.

New clause 4 concerns the publication of a new voluntary code of practice. It has been suggested that such a code will have no effect and be of little use. However, the Government are producing codes of practice every week. They apply them to health and safety at work, for example. If Conservative Members are so critical of such an arrangement, why have they not made their views known? If a code of practice is good enough for health and safety at work, the Minister should at least consider one to serve as guidance in the way that new clause 4 proposes. It is an area where a code of practice would be useful. I have reservations about a code's value in areas such as health and safety, but in the context proposed, one would be admirable in its application. The Government will not accept new clause 4 because they are motivated by vindictiveness, not by logic or reason.

Will membership of the Campaign for Nuclear Disarmament be deemed political activity? The Minister may say, "Of course, because I want to do whatever damage I can to CND." What about the Campaign for Peace and Security through NATO, which one might argue is equivalent to CND and is run by Lady Olga Maitland—who presumably has the Minister's support? Will membership of that count as political activity?

Let us suppose that local government officers go to a meeting of their trade union, the National and Local Government Officers Association, and NALGO discusses its affiliation to the Labour party, which it does from time to time, although it is not yet affiliated. Will those local authority members who are covered by this sweeping legislation have to leave the meeting because they might be reported by other NALGO members and be barred from political activity or discussion? Will they be excluded from the political arguments about whether NALGO should be affiliated to the Labour party? It is an absurd minefield.

My hon. Friends raised the issue of putting political party bills in windows. Will the various snoopers appointed under other sections of the Act go round checking local government officers' windows to ensure that they are free from posters carrying any suggestion other than that people should vote, and do not suggest for whom they should vote?

If the Minister cannot produce, as I suspect that he cannot, any evidence of damage to the impartiality of advice and the numbers of people which these draconian measures will involve, why does he not bear in mind the fact that, when all is said and done, even if we accept some of the criticisms about there being two jobs for the boys and girls, the publicity of such arrangements is always at its most intense locally. The local papers often have a field day with such arguments and the local voters make their judgment on it. If they do not like it, they are entitled to say to the candidate that they do not like the fact that he or she has a job in another local authority and is a councillor in theirs and so will not vote for him or her. The Minister's case is untenable on every count.

The new clauses accept the desirability of senior local government officers being excluded and, by and large, the vast majority are. The Minister can tell us the percentage of those who do not take part in political activity and the tiny percentage to whom this will apply.

The proposals are modest in scope and reasonable in the way in which they lay down safeguards before the Minister makes regulations. What sort of regulations will the Minister produce? We want to know because the erosion of political rights varies from legislation passed by Ministers who are largely vindictive to the use of tanks in Tiananmen square in China. It is because of the erosion of the right to argue for a set of values that conflict begins and develops. The Bill is an exact formula for the development of doubt, misunderstanding and, above all, conflict.

Mr. Winnick: Like my hon. Friends, I work on the assumption, however old fashioned or outdated it may be to Conservative Members, that one of the main functions of the House is to defend people's rights. The most crucial function of a democracy is that Parliament should defend people's rights to go about their lawful business and exercise their rights. If those rights are to be undermined and completely taken away, it is a serious matter for the House. If we do not give it proper consideration, we shall certainly be failing in our duty.

I am suspicious of the Government's motives. Like my hon. Friends, I think that they are motivated by sheer intolerance. Even if I was not of that view, I would bear in mind their conduct over the past 10 years and be highly suspicious of any move which they made to restrict or undermine civil liberty, on which they have an appalling record. They have banned union membership at GCHQ and taken measures against the broadcasting authorities. Fortunately, a healthy suspicion always exists, not only amongst Labour Members but in the country at large.

There is no reason why anyone earning the magical sum of £13,500 should be banned from being elected to a local authority. My hon. Friends the Members for Birmingham, Perry Barr (Mr. Rooker) and for Newham, North-West (Mr. Banks) conceded that at times they were not always happy with twin tracking. I join them because there have been cases with which I have not always been happy. If abuse occurs, those cases should come before the Government so that if they believe action should be taken they can produce evidence.

However, I am not in favour of a blanket ban. If abuse has occurred which, for the sake of argument, I concede it may have done, why should there be a blanket ban covering everyone? Some Tory councillors will be adversely affected, but in the main the Government work on the assumption that the majority of councillors or prospective councillors covered by the ban will be Labour ones. If it were the other way round and the majority of people caught in the ban were Tories, I believe that no such measure would have come before us.

Mrs. Audrey Wise (Preston): Will my hon. Friend comment on another kind of twin-tracking which goes on in the House and involves those who have highly placed and powerful directorships in private industry? Is not that twin tracking infinitely more harmful?

Mr. Winnick: I do not want to be led astray, but I must say that great minds think alike. I have a note here to say that the worst form of twin-tracking and the worst kind of abuse is that of Tory Members with countless consultancies so that at times we do not know whether their loyalty and devotion is to their own constituents or to the companies which employ them. As my hon. Friend said, that is a far greater subject of concern than anything involving councillors.

As my hon. Friend the Member for Bradford, South (Mr. Cryer) said, new clause 2 puts forward a compromise. If we work on the assumption that the most senior positions in local government should not be occupied by those who are councillors or who intend to be councillors in another local authority, it would be far enough. If that were accepted by the Government, it would be an honourable way out for them, without introducing a ban that affects the most junior officers. As has been pointed out, the limit is now £13,500, but what will happen after the next pay rise, next year or the year after? Are we really to work on the assumption that even the most junior people in local government should have their political rights taken away, and that the right to stand for public office at local level, which has always been respected, should simply be taken away and abolished because the Conservative Government consider that they should be motivated by malice and intolerance?

The Minister has not made the case and it is interesting that Conservative Members have not done so either. They have not produced evidence of abuse or of any local authorities having acted in a way to show that such a measure should come into operation.

I began by saying that we should be extremely wary of any measure which undermines people's rights, and I stand by that. Unfortunatly, not a single Tory Member has seen fit even to express some reservations. What has the House of Commons come to when not one Government Member says, "All right, perhaps the Government have a case, but I have certain reservations on the basis of civil rights. I believe in people's rights and democratic rights?" Not one Conservative Member has seen fit to do that, which is a sorry commentary on the Tory party of today.

Mr. Gummer: This has been an interesting debate, not least for those of us who have sat through similar debates in Committee, because it has shown a major shift in the position of the Opposition parties.

In Committee, there was no kind of twin-tracking that did not find its advocates on the Opposition Benches. There was no question of Opposition Members saying, "Of course we do not mean that senior officers should be allowed to engage in twin-tracking." Today we have heard what we expected to hear: that the Labour party and, to some extent, the Liberals have learnt that their espousal of this kind of policy——

Mr. Matthew Taylor *rose*——

7.30 pm

Mr. Gummer: I have had some chance to listen to the debate, and now I should like to reply. If the hon. Gentleman will listen to what I have to say, he can decide whether it is true when I have finished. There is no doubt that until now Opposition Members have been prepared to defend almost any kind of twin-tracking, but now it is extremely unpopular with them.

The hon. Member for Birmingham, Perry Barr (Mr. Rooker) made the reasonable comment that people from his part of the world were very angry because our proposals were based on what he described as isolated

[*Mr. Gummer*]

gross abuses in London. There are indeed a number of gross abuses in London, but many take place elsewhere. Can it be reasonable, for example, for the chief executive of Clydebank council to be seen as an independent adviser to that council when he was an elected Labour member of Glasgow city council?

Mr. Matthew Taylor *rose*——

Mr. Gummer: No, I will not give way; I will complete what I have to say. I listened with great care to what the hon. Gentleman said.

Can it be reasonable for the chief executive of Llin valley district council in south Wales to have been at the same time chairman of the local Labour party? How can someone claim to be an independent adviser to a council and all its members if at exactly the same time he takes a clear and senior party-political role elsewhere? I do not believe that Derbyshire is in London, but Mr. Reg Race was appointed chief executive of Derbyshire county council. Even Mr. Race found the leader of Derbyshire county council impossible to work with, although he took longer to do so than many others.

The Labour leader of Bradford council was—and is now, although he is no longer leader of the council—anti-privatisation officer of Wakefield council. That does not make it easy to believe that his advice on privatisation could be seen as suitable for the whole council; after all, he clearly took a party-political view as Labour leader in Bradford. The hon. Member for Bradford, South (Mr. Cryer) may say that the electorate has a chance to decide. Bradford did decide: it decided that it did not want its affairs run in that way.

Let me tell the hon. Member for Perry Barr that abuses are widespread, and that they take place outside London. In London they are not isolated: 24 of the 40 members of Greenwich borough council——

Mr. Cryer: Fewer than half.

Mr. Gummer: Twenty-four is not less than half of 40. The hon. Gentleman ought to listen; I have listened very carefully to him.

It is said in the local paper, and not denied by the local Labour party, that 24 members of Greenwich council would be affected by these proposals. All that the Government are saying is that in the past local government has recognised that, if an officer is to be effective and to take any real part in advising those of all parties in the local authority, he must be able to show that his advice is wholly above question and is entirely impartial. For a long time individuals have made the choice that that is the role in which they wish to serve the public.

Let me say, as one who both enjoys and respects what the hon. Member for Perry Barr has to say to the House, that I believe in good, independent local government—to use his words. Evidence of that is contained in this very part of the Bill. I do not believe that good, independent local government is possible if officers in one local authority purport to be giving independent advice when they are active members of the next-door local council, figuring in a political role. That is why the Government have made their suggestions, not out of their own head but on the recommendation of the Widdicombe committee.

Perhaps the hon. Member for Walsall, North (Mr. Winnick) should spend less time being affected by the generality of his speech, which we hear time after time with the various names and places altered, but which always expresses the same desperate desire to see the same terrible, nasty reasons for everything. The hon. Gentleman must be so miserable: everybody and every circumstance is nasty, suspicious and unpleasant to him. I am so pleased that I am not his psychoanalyst. Something very nasty must have happened in the woodshed at some stage to cause this embarrassing state of affairs.

However, the hon. Gentleman need not be suspicious about the £13,500. It was not an arbitrary figure, as the hon. Member for Bradford, South suggested; he would know that if he had read the Committee proceedings in detail. It represents an attempt to provide a clear and simple figure to meet what the Widdicombe committee has proposed for principal officers. As it was obvious that the term "principle officer" meant different things in different areas and authorities, we tried to fix the level in the easiest possible way. If there is a better way, I shall be happy to employ it. I have already given an undertaking to take powers to increase the level, so that the problems that the hon. Member for Walsall, North—with his suspicious mind—might expect will not arise.

The suggestion that we are removing democratic rights, made by the hon. Member for Truro (Mr. Taylor) and others, is entirely untrue. First, it suggests that the proposal applies to far more people who are called civil servants. We consider it important to ask civil servants to take an independent position to protect other people's democratic rights, and the same is true of local government officers. We have not gone as far as the independent Widdicombe committee would wish. We arranged for people to be able to appeal to an adjudicator, with no absolute ban. Many of the examples that hon. Members have given clearly show that—as they know—the people involved would be excluded under the rules implemented by the adjudicator.

Let me make it clear that I am not misleading the House about what the hon. Member for Truro said in Committee. Both in Committee and here, however, he has seemed to suggest that some people could be excluded, but that he did not approve of the exclusions in the Bill. If it is possible to exclude some people, it is difficult to say how impossible it will be to exclude others. The hon. Gentleman cannot have it both ways: he cannot tell the House at length how difficult the arrangements would be when he starts from the position that some people ought to be excluded—

Mr. Matthew Taylor *rose*——

Mr. Gummer: Will the hon. Gentleman just let me finish this point?

In the country as a whole it is generally accepted that the best way in which local government, and indeed national government, can work is for everyone to have a clear view of the distinction between those who are party-politically elected and motivated and have obvious party-political concerns, and those whose job is to serve equally parties of any kind that are elected by the public. That distinction has always been maintained by the good practice of officers, and has never before needed definition. It is sad that the Government have had to present these proposals, which are based on the Widdicombe report, because the public as a whole welcome the proposals, having seen the decline in public decision making by those who thought that the two could be mixed. If only we lived in a world where we did not have to legislate upon such matters, it would be a better world. It should be a matter of shame to the hon. Member for Walsall, North that those who are most likely to be caught are members of his own party.

Mr. Blunkett: It was not the driving of the hon. Member for Sheffield, Hallam (Mr. Patnick) that I questioned; it was his judgment. I question, too, the judgment of Conservative Members who have argued that independence and impartiality depend on people hiding their true democratic views in an open society. That is not accepted in West Germany, under the system that we imposed upon it, or in any other part of the world.

7.45 pm

New clause 4 deals with the majority of the points that the Minister has made. We could all dream up individual items. We could name the leader of Bournemouth council, Councillor Trenchard, the head of a housing association which has been asked to take over Bournemouth's council housing. The local council is willing to give him £20,000 to put forward the case on behalf of his own housing association, in an effort to persuade council house tenants to change landlords. We could all dream up examples of that kind if it is a slanging match that the Minister wants. But it is not. It is about whether we believe that to take away people's democratc rights safeguards democracy.

If it is good enough for local authority officers on £13,500 and above, why is it not good enough for teachers? As an elected member of Sheffield city council, why should I not have been disqualified when other people on the same salary would have been disqualified? It is nonsense. The only reason can be that the Conservative party has added up the figures and believes that it has more headmasters and teachers serving local government than we do. There is no logic to it.

Opposition Members have put forward clearly who should and who should not be restricted because of their political activities. My hon. Friend the Member for Hammersmith (Mr. Soley) did so. My hon. Friend the Member for Newham, North-West (Mr. Banks) made exactly the same speech tonight as he did in Committee, except that he used different jokes on this occasion. Some Opposition Members wanted a code of practice to be established, but we were not allowed to make that point in Committee. We have been allowed to do so tonight. I am very glad. If implemented, the code of practice would provide a year in which we could test whether it would work. The Bill would not be implemented in its present form unless the code was proved not to work. That is a perfectly reasonable compromise on which the whole House should unite.

Let us lift the uncertainty from the tens of thousands of people who might want to stand in next year's elections and who might also wish to seek selection as candidates in the general election. We should lift the uncertainty from those who are worried about taking minor office in a political party, or who want to be able to canvass, to speak or to write for political parties in our democracy. Let us lift that uncertainty. Let us make sure that we are able to hold our heads high by defending democracy rather than removing it.

Question put, That the clause be read a Second time:-
The House divided: Ayes 156, Noes 227.

Division No.237]   **[7.43 pm**

AYES

Alton, David	Howells, Dr. Kim *(Pontypridd)*
Archer, Rt Hon Peter	Hughes, John *(Coventry NE)*
Armstrong, Hilary	Hughes, Robert *(Aberdeen N)*
Ashley, Rt Hon Jack	Hughes, Roy *(Newport E)*
Ashton, Joe	Illsley, Eric
Banks, Tony *(Newham NW)*	Ingram, Adam
Barnes, Harry *(Derbyshire NE)*	Jones, Martyn *(Clwyd S W)*
Barnes, Mrs Rosie *(Greenwich)*	Kennedy, Charles
Barron, Kevin	Kinnock, Rt Hon Neil
Battle, John	Kirkwood, Archy
Beckett, Margaret	Leadbitter, Ted
Bell, Stuart	Leighton, Ron
Benn, Rt Hon Tony	Lestor, Joan *(Eccles)*
Bennett, A. F. *(D'nt'n & R'dish)*	Lewis, Terry
Bermingham, Gerald	Litherland, Robert
Bidwell, Sydney	Lofthouse, Geoffrey
Blair, Tony	Loyden, Eddie
Blunkett, David	McAllion, John
Bradley, Keith	McCartney, Ian
Bray, Dr Jeremy	McKay, Allen *(Barnsley West)*
Brown, Nicholas *(Newcastle E)*	McWilliam, John
Buckley, George J.	Madden, Max
Callaghan, Jim	Mahon, Mrs Alice
Campbell, Ron *(Blyth Valley)*	Marek, Dr John
Campbell-Savours, D. N.	Marshall, Jim *(Leicester S)*
Canavan, Dennis	Maxton, John
Clark, Dr David *(S Shields)*	Meacher, Michael
Clarke, Tom *(Monklands W)*	Meale, Alan
Clelland, David	Michael, Alun
Clwyd, Mrs Ann	Michie, Bill *(Sheffield Heeley)*
Cohen, Harry	Mitchell, Austin *(G't Grimsby)*
Coleman, Donald	Moonie, Dr Lewis
Corbett, Robin	Morgan, Rhodri
Cousins, Jim	Morris, Rt Hon A. *(W'shawe)*
Crowther, Stan	Morris, Rt Hon J. *(Aberavon)*
Cryer, Bob	Mowlam, Marjorie
Cummings, John	Mullin, Chris
Cunliffe, Lawrence	Murphy, Paul
Cunningham, Dr John	Nellist, Dave
Darling, Alistair	Oakes, Rt Hon Gordon
Davies, Rt Hon Denzil *(Llanelli)*	O'Brien, William
Davies, Ron *(Caerphilly)*	O'Neill, Martin
Davis, Terry *(B'ham Hodge H'l)*	Patchett, Terry
Dixon, Don	Pendry, Tom
Doran, Frank	Pike, Peter L.
Douglas, Dick	Powell, William *(Corby)*
Dunwoody, Hon Mrs Gwyneth	Prescott, John
Eastham, Ken	Primarolo, Dawn
Evans, John *(St Helens N)*	Quin, Ms Joyce
Fearn, Ronald	Radice, Giles
Field, Frank *(Birkenhead)*	Redmond, Martin
Fields, Terry *(L'pool B G'n)*	Rees, Rt Hon Merlyn
Fisher, Mark	Richardson, Jo
Flannery, Martin	Robertson, George
Flynn, Paul	Robinson, Geoffrey
Foot, Rt Hon Michael	Rogers, Allan
Foster, Derek	Rooker, Jeff
Fraser, John	Rowlands, Ted
Garrett, John *(Norwich South)*	Sedgemore, Brian
George, Bruce	Shore, Rt Hon Peter
Godman, Dr Norman A.	Skinner, Dennis
Golding, Mrs Llin	Smith, Andrew *(Oxford E)*
Gordon, Mildred	Smith, C. *(Isl'ton & F'bury)*
Gould, Bryan	Smith, Rt Hon J. *(Monk'ds E)*
Griffiths, Nigel *(Edinburgh S)*	Smith, J. P. *(Vale of Glam)*
Griffiths, Win *(Bridgend)*	Snape, Peter
Grocott, Bruce	Soley, Clive
Hardy, Peter	Spearing, Nigel
Hattersley, Rt Hon Roy	Stott, Roger
Hinchliffe, David	Taylor, Mrs Ann *(Dewsbury)*
Howarth, George *(Knowsley N)*	Taylor, Matthew *(Truro)*
Howell, Rt Hon D. *(S'heath)*	Thompson, Jack *(Wansbeck)*
Howells, Geraint	Turner, Dennis

Wall, Pat	Winnick, David
Wallace, James	Wise, Mrs Audrey
Walley, Joan	Worthington, Tony
Wardell, Gareth *(Gower)*	
Welsh, Andrew *(Angus E)*	Tellers for the Ayes:
Welsh, Michael *(Doncaster N)*	Mr. Frank Cook and
Williams, Rt Hon Alan	Mr. Frank Haynes.

NOES

Adley, Robert	Forsyth, Michael *(Stirling)*
Alison, Rt Hon Michael	Forth, Eric
Allason, Rupert	Fox, Sir Marcus
Amess, David	Franks, Cecil
Amos, Alan	Freeman, Roger
Arbuthnot, James	French, Douglas
Arnold, Jacques *(Gravesham)*	Fry, Peter
Arnold, Tom *(Hazel Grove)*	Gale, Roger
Ashby, David	Gardiner, George
Aspinwall, Jack	Garel-Jones, Tristan
Atkinson, David	Gill, Christopher
Baker, Nicholas *(Dorset N)*	Gilmour, Rt Hon Sir Ian
Baldry, Tony	Glyn, Dr Alan
Batiste, Spencer	Goodhart, Sir Philip
Beaumont-Dark, Anthony	Goodlad, Alastair
Bendall, Vivian	Gorman, Mrs Teresa
Bennett, Nicholas *(Pembroke)*	Grant, Sir Anthony *(CambsSW)*
Benyon, W.	Greenway, Harry *(Ealing N)*
Bevan, David Gilroy	Greenway, John *(Ryedale)*
Blackburn, Dr John G.	Gregory, Conal
Body, Sir Richard	Griffiths, Sir Eldon *(Bury St E')*
Bonsor, Sir Nicholas	Griffiths, Peter *(Portsmouth N)*
Boscawen, Hon Robert	Grist, Ian
Boswell, Tim	Ground, Patrick
Bottomley, Peter	Gummer, Rt Hon John Selwyn
Bottomley, Mrs Virginia	Hague, William
Bowden, A *(Brighton K'pto'n)*	Hamilton, Neil *(Tatton)*
Bowden, Gerald *(Dulwich)*	Hampson, Dr Keith
Boyson, Rt Hon Dr Sir Rhodes	Hanley, Jeremy
Braine, Rt Hon Sir Bernard	Hannam, John
Brandon-Bravo, Martin	Hargreaves, A. *(B'ham H'll Gr')*
Brown, Michael *(Brigg & Cl't's)*	Hargreaves, Ken *(Hyndburn)*
Buchanan-Smith, Rt Hon Alick	Haselhurst, Alan
Buck, Sir Antony	Hayes, Jerry
Budgen, Nicholas	Hayward, Robert
Burns, Simon	Heddle, John
Burt, Alistair	Hicks, Mrs Maureen *(Wolv' NE)*
Butterfill, John	Hicks, Robert *(Cornwall SE)*
Carlisle, John, *(Luton N)*	Higgins, Rt Hon Terence L.
Carlisle, Kenneth *(Lincoln)*	Hill, James
Carrington, Matthew	Hind, Kenneth
Carttiss, Michael	Hogg, Hon Douglas *(Gr'th'm)*
Channon, Rt Hon Paul	Howard, Michael
Chapman, Sydney	Hughes, Robert G. *(Harrow W)*
Chope, Christopher	Hunt, David *(Wirral W)*
Clark, Dr Michael *(Rochford)*	Hunter, Andrew
Clark, Sir W. *(Croydon S)*	Irvine, Michael
Conway, Derek	Irving, Charles
Coombs, Anthony *(Wyre F'rest)*	Jack, Michael
Coombs, Simon *(Swindon)*	Jackson, Robert
Cope, Rt Hon John	Janman, Tim
Couchman, James	Jessel, Toby
Currie, Mrs Edwina	Johnson Smith, Sir Geoffrey
Davies, Q. *(Stamf'd & Spald'g)*	Jones, Gwilym *(Cardiff N)*
Davis, David *(Boothferry)*	Jones, Robert B *(Herts W)*
Day, Stephen	Jopling, Rt Hon Michael
Devlin, Tim	Key, Robert
Dorrell, Stephen	Kilfedder, James
Douglas-Hamilton, Lord James	Knapman, Roger
Dunn, Bob	Knight, Greg *(Derby North)*
Durant, Tony	Knox, David
Dykes, Hugh	Lightbown, David
Eggar, Tim	Lilley, Peter
Emery, Sir Peter	Lord, Michael
Evennett, David	MacGregor, Rt Hon John
Fallon, Michael	Maclean, David
Favell, Tony	McLoughlin, Patrick
Field, Barry *(Isle of Wight)*	Maples, John
Finsberg, Sir Geoffrey	Maude, Hon Francis
Fookes, Dame Janet	Miller, Sir Hal
Forman, Nigel	Miscampbell, Norman

Mitchell, Andrew *(Gedling)*	Smith, Sir Dudley *(Warwick)*
Mitchell, Sir David	Smith, Tim *(Beaconsfield)*
Moate, Roger	Spicer, Sir Jim *(Dorset W)*
Montgomery, Sir Fergus	Squire, Robin
Morris, M *(N'hampton S)*	Stanbrook, Ivor
Moss, Malcolm	Stanley, Rt Hon Sir John
Mudd, David	Steen, Anthony
Neale, Gerrard	Stern, Michael
Needham, Richard	Stevens, Lewis
Nelson, Anthony	Stewart, Andy *(Sherwood)*
Nicholls, Patrick	Stradling Thomas, Sir John
Nicholson, David *(Taunton)*	Sumberg, David
Nicholson, Emma *(Devon West)*	Summerson, Hugo
Onslow, Rt Hon Cranley	Taylor, Ian *(Esher)*
Oppenheim, Phillip	Taylor, Teddy *(S'end E)*
Paice, James	Temple-Morris, Peter
Patnick, Irvine	Thompson, D. *(Calder Valley)*
Patten, Chris *(Bath)*	Thompson, Patrick *(Norwich N)*
Pawsey, James	Thornton, Malcolm
Peacock, Mrs Elizabeth	Thurnham, Peter
Porter, Barry *(Wirral S)*	Townend, John *(Bridlington)*
Porter, David *(Waveney)*	Tracey, Richard
Portillo, Michael	Tredinnick, David
Powell, William *(Corby)*	Trippier, David
Price, Sir David	Vaughan, Sir Gerard
Raffan, Keith	Viggers, Peter
Redwood, John	Waddington, Rt Hon David
Renton, Tim	Waller, Gary
Rhodes James, Robert	Wardle, Charles *(Bexhill)*
Riddick, Graham	Warren, Kenneth
Ridley, Rt Hon Nicholas	Watts, John
Ridsdale, Sir Julian	Wells, Bowen
Roberts, Wyn *(Conwy)*	Wheeler, John
Rowe, Andrew	Whitney, Ray
Sackville, Hon Tom	Widdecombe, Ann
Sainsbury, Hon Tim	Winterton, Nicholas
Scott, Nicholas	Wolfson, Mark
Shaw, David *(Dover)*	Wood, Timothy
Shaw, Sir Giles *(Pudsey)*	Woodcock, Dr. Mike
Shaw, Sir Michael *(Scarb')*	Young, Sir George *(Acton)*
Shelton, Sir William	
Shephard, Mrs G. *(Norfolk SW)*	Tellers for the Noes:
Shepherd, Colin *(Hereford)*	Mr. Alan Howarth and
Shepherd, Richard *(Aldridge)*	Mr. David Heathcoat-Amory.
Skeet, Sir Trevor	

Question accordingly negatived.

Clause 2

POLITICALLY RESTRICTED POSTS

Mr. Gummer: I beg to move amendment No. 216, in page 3, line 23, at end insert 'and'.

Mr. Deputy Speaker (Mr. Harold Walker): With this it will be convenient to take the following amendments:

No. 130, in page 3, line 24, at beginning insert 'Subject to paragraph (h) below'.

Government amendment No. 217.

No. 200, in page 3, line 34, leave out '13,500' and insert '25,000'.

No. 201, in page 3, line 34, leave out '13,500' and insert '18,000'.

No. 202, in page 3, line 34, leave out '13,500' and insert '16,000'.

No. 129, in page 3, line 39, at end insert—

'(1A) The annual rate of remuneration applicable under subsection (1)(h) above, shall not include any payment specified in Schedule *(Exclusions from salary limit)* below (except, in the case of a bonus payment, where the payment is made on a regular basis such that it is regarded by both the employer and the employee as part of the basic remuneration of the post) and the Secretary of State shall by Order maintain the value of the amount in real terms in each year following the passing of this Act at a level at least equivalent to the value in the first year of operation of this Part.'.

No. 133, in page 3, line 39, at end insert—

'(1A) Subsections 1(g) and 1(h) above shall not apply to any person who is employed on a manual grade by a local authority, or to a post occupied by such an employee.'.

Government amendments Nos. 218 and 219.

No. 134, in page 3, line 49, at end insert—

'(2A) Before the making of any regulations by the Secretary of State under subsection (2)(b) above, or the issuing of any guidance to local authorities in respect of their duties under subsection (2), the Secretary of State shall consult the local authority associations and such other organisations or individuals appear to him to be concerned.'.

In clause 3, Government amendments Nos. 220 and 221.

No. 136, in page 5, line 23, leave out 'paragraph' and insert 'paragraphs (f) to'.

No. 138, in page 5, line 23, leave out 'and' and insert 'or—

(aa) that, apart from this subsection, an activity in respect of which an appeal has been made by that individual would be regarded as falling within the terms of any restriction incorporated into his contract of employment by regulations made under section 1(5) above; and, in either case.'.

Amendment No. 157:

New Schedule

'EXCLUSIONS FROM SALARY LIMIT

1. No payment specified in paragraph 2 below shall be included within any limit prescribed for the purposes of Section 2(1)(h).

2. The payments to be excluded shall be any of the following—

(a) any bonus payment for employees in manual grades, except a bonus payment made on a regular basis such that it is regarded by both the employer and the employee as part of the basic remuneration of the post;

(b) any acting-up allowance;

(c) any chargehand responsibility payment for employees in manual grades;

(d) any overtime payment;

(e) any Distant Island Allowance;

(f) any allowance in respect of work connected with the evening letting of local authority premises;

(g) any first aid payment;

(h) any travel or subsistence allowance;

(i) any disturbance allowance;

(j) any car mileage payment;

(k) any accelerated increment;

(l) any lump sum retrospective payment in respect of a grading appeal;

(m) any London or other regional or local weighting allowance;

(n) any other payment specified in regulations made by the Secretary of State.'.

Mr. Gummer: Amendments Nos. 216 and 217 are presented to the House as a result of an undertaking given in Committee that we would place on the face of the Bill the arrangements relating to posts where the annual rate of remuneration exceeds £13,500. It was suggested that they should be placed on the face of the Bill and that is what we have done. I hope that even those who would prefer that we were not doing it in this way will agree to accept the amendments as they meet the desire of Members on both sides in Committee.

Mr. William O'Brien (Normanton): There was a great deal of discussion in Committee on the matter, but the Minister has not addressed the serious situation that we consider will be created by this part of the Bill. Politically restricted posts are significant and important and the amendments standing in my name and the names of my right hon. and hon. Friends address the issues that the Minister and Conservative Members should consider seriously.

Amendments Nos. 130, 131, 133, 136, 138 and 157 are particularly important in the extensive group of amendments referring to politically restricted posts. Amendment No. 130 seeks to add at the beginning of line 24 on page 3 in clause 2:

"Subject to paragraph (h) below".

Amendment No. 131 seeks to leave out the word "not" from line 31.

We tabled those amendments because, as the Bill is drafted, many low-paid local authority staff may be designated as holding politically-sensitive posts under clause 2(3) and retrospectively banned from political activity. For example, there are six employees in the Strathclyde regional press and public relations office who are paid far less than £13,500, but who still deal with the public. One can see readily that they have no influence on council policy, but they stand to be caught by the Bill. Those staff, and others like them, will have no right of appeal to an adjudicator, which is the basis of an appeal under this system. Under the Bill, those staff will have no right of appeal to an adjudicator, although their terms and conditions of service will be changed at one fell swoop by the Bill.

8 pm

The Secretary of State will probably say that those staff can use the appeals mechanism in their own authorities, but the employers' side of the local authorities is proposing to withdraw the right of appeal to the National Joint Council as a last resort. That will weaken the appeals mechanism available to low-paid staff. Those people will not even be in a Catch 22 situation. They will be left with no democratic right of appeal as a result of the Bill. They will be politically restricted and there will be no facilities for appeal. Judicial review is not an easy option for those people.

Amendments Nos. 130, 131 and 132 seek to raise the ceiling at which political assistants become politically restricted. In Committee, the Minister persisted in describing those posts as "special advisers". I am sure that the Minister will recall my exchange with him in Committee on that very issue. I pointed out in Committee that special advisers are employed by the Department of the Environment and that the Minister has special advisers. In Committee, the Minister referred to them as "special advisers." Despite the fact that most special advisers to Ministers earn considerably more than £13,500, the Bill imposes a salary ceiling for those clause 9 appointments, but does not prevent them from being paid less. Amendments Nos. 130 and 131 seek to exempt lower-paid special advisers from the restriction on political activities. I ask the Minister to consider seriously that junior posts will be caught by the pernicious proposal in the Bill.

Amendment No. 133 is also important. I draw the House's attention to the fact that the Widdicombe report, when evaluating whether being a councillor or otherwise engaged in political activity conflicted with an officer's duty, stated:

"there can be no conflict in the case of manual workers."

No distinction was drawn between senior and other manual workers on page 161 of the report.

[*Mr. William O'Brien*]

The Minister asked where the Widdicombe report said that it was not intended to include senior manual workers. On 7 March 1989, the answer was clear. The Government's justification for abandoning the term "principal officer" was that grades could disappear. In other words, the Government are saying that grades as they now apply can disappear. That was one of the reasons given for abandoning the term "principal officer" used in the Widdicombe report.

In accepting part of the Widdicombe committee's recommendation that a general bar should apply at a particular level, the Minister should also look at the Widdicombe committee's arguments. The committee addressed areas of possible conflict of interest and decided that they were unlikely to arise for manual workers. Specific exemption would go some way to re-establishing Widdicombe's link between restriction and responsibility. The Minister has said on more than one occasion that the Government intend to be fair when applying this legislation. The position of manual workers should, therefore, be taken seriously by the Government and manual workers should be exempted from this legislation.

We made this issue abundantly clear in Committee. The £13,500 limit should relate to basic pay, excluding weighting allowances, overtime and index linking. My hon. Friend the Member for Sheffield, Brightside (Mr. Blunkett) pointed out that even the salary award that has been made to certain officers this year brings a further batch of officers into the position where they will be disqualified from taking part in political activities because they will have reached a salary of £13,500. We made it clear in Committee that in considering the salary level as the cut-off point it would be cruel for the Minister not to take into consideration the fact that overtime payments are not consistent. Bonus payments, unless they are agreed bonus payments which are paid regularly, should be taken out of the formula when considering the £13,500 figure. Weighting allowances are a further issue that should be given serious consideration and index linking should also be a part of the formula, if there has to be a ceiling of £13,500. If there has to be a figure, it is only just that index linking should be taken into consideration.

"The Bill refers to an annual rate of remuneration, and that will not include one-off payments such as bonuses unless they are so regular that they become part of the rate for the job."

We were told that by the hon. Member for Rossendale and Darwen (Mr. Trippier), the Parliamentary Under-Secrtary of State for the Environment in our deliberations in Committee. The Under-Secretary said that unless bonuses are a regular payment, they should not be taken into consideration. If that principle stands firm, it should be included in the Bill. This is an opportunity for that error to be put right.

The Parliamentary Under-Secretary of State also said:

"I shall examine carefully and tell the Committee the precise definition of the annual rate of remuneration."— [*Official Report, Standing Committee G*, 7 March 1989; c. 167-68.]

We are still waiting for that definition and I hope that the Minister can give us some clarification on those issues tonight. The best way of doing that would be to accept the amendments because they address the existing anomalies.

Further, the Minister should consider excluding from the provisions any bonus payments made to employees in manual grades, except bonus payments which are made regularly so that they are regarded by both employer and employee as part of the basic remunerative of the post. I readily accept that regular bonuses could be interpreted as part of the worker's annual wage. However, bonus payments that are not regular should not be included in any ceiling on an employee's salary.

The acting up allowance, where an employee is doing the work of a person of a senior grade for whom he or she is filling in for holidays, sickness or accident, should not be taken into consideration when determining a person's salary under the politically restrictive provisions. In addition, the chargehand responsibility payment for employees in manual grades should also be disregarded. The distant island allowances that apply in some areas of local government as a payment for the inconvenience of where a person works should be disregarded. Allowances in respect of work connected with the evening letting of local authority premises should also be disregarded because there is so much uncertainty about when a person qualifies for that payment.

Some people qualify for extra payments for their first-aid qualifications. It is only fair that such a person should not be disqualified from political activity simply because he or she offers a service to fellow workers which also benefits the employer. Because of the small remuneration paid to that person the disqualification provisions of the Bill should not be applied.

There are a number of issues in these provisions on which I should be tempted to seek to divide the House because I feel so strongly about this. I appeal to the Minister to consider the issues that we have raised and to try to assess the position as it will affect many local government employees.

Widdicombe tried to link political restrictions to levels of responsibility, recognising the need for officers in certain posts to be able to command the respect and trust of all political parties in their capacity to advise councillors and to adjudicate on certain matters. However, manual workers do not fall within the scope of that and accepting the amendments should therefore be considered.

Amendment No. 136 makes the point that the appeals system will not work in its present form. We need to extend the range of the appeals mechanism to posts held by political assistants and to designated posts as well as to those that fall within the salary restriction. That would leave heads of paid service, chief and deputy chief officers and the monitoring officers outside the appeals mechanism. In Committee the Minister stated:

"Making an appeal . . . is open to each individual".— [*Official Report, Standing Committee G*, 28 February 1989; c. 94.]

That is a misleading statement because the appeals procedure applies only to people holding a politically restricted post by virtue of clause 2(1)(h). That anomaly should be examined in detail and, indeed, our amendment would rectify it. Clause 2(1)(h) refers to people who hold politically restricted posts because they earn £13,500 or more. As drafted, no one else can appeal against all or part of the restriction imposed on them.

While we have the Minister's assurance about the type of restrictions that he envisages, such assurances are not binding on the Secretary of State. To be fair and to offer justice to those employed in local government, the Government should accept this amendment as it would rectify that anomaly. The Secretary of State is being given sweeping powers and is not bound by the assurance given by the Minister but he would be bound if he were to accept the amendment and if it were enacted.

8.15 pm

Amendment No. 138 would extend the scope of the appeals mechanism to cover political activities as well as the restrictions, or otherwise, of these "political" posts. I have received a letter from a person who has worked as an accountant in local government for over 19 years, which states:

"Most important of all, however, the Bill raises a serious question of civil liberties. What I do in my spare time is my business, and I see no reason why that should change simply because I am paid a salary of over £13,500 per annum by the local council. I would like to think that if I wished to join a political party I could do so as a matter of right, and not under special licence from the Secretary of State."

That sums up the general feelings of many people who work in local government. They see the provisions on politically restricted posts as restricting their freedoms outside working hours. That will cause conflict in many ways.

Therefore, I ask the Minister in particular and Conservative Members in general to accept our amendments. They are constructive amendments. They do not try to be difficult or to destroy the Bill. They are simply trying to ensure that justice and fairness are applied to people who work in local government.

Mr. James Wallace (Orkney and Shetland): I support this group of amendments, though we face a dilemma in dealing with them. On the one hand there is a degree of opposition generally to what is being done. On the other, we are anxious to ensure that if what is proposed happens, it happens in the fairest way possible.

I support in particular amendments Nos. 129 and 157, which aim to specify with greater certainty what precisely will be taken into account in determining the remuneration, which in turn will determine whether someone is affected by these provisions. Amendment No. 129 would exclude weighting allowances and overtime and would ensure that the figure was index-linked. It would be far from reasonable to have a sum this year which, with the inflation rates that the Government have engineered and which the Chancellor predicts will be even higher, would be worth less in real terms.

I do not know whether the Committee discussed what would happen if someone who was already an elected member of an authority suddenly found that, because of a pay increase, he had reached the disqualification figure. Would that mean a series of by-elections throughout the country?

When this matter was discussed in Committee, the Minister promised to examine it carefully and explain the precise definition of the annual rate of remuneration. Not having been a member of the Committee, I do not know what transpired. But the fact that we are now debating the matter on the Floor of the House is indicative of the fact that the Minister did not explain precisely what definition was being used.

Amendment No. 157 details a number of items which could be included in a person's remuneration, and it seeks to exclude them when determining the figure. I was particularly attracted by the item "any distant island allowance" because many people employed in local government in my constituency are in receipt of a distant island allowance. In my constituency, people are employed by single-tier authorities and there is no question of them, even at present, being allowed to stand for their local authorities—unless one was in the unlikely situation of living in Orkney and working in Shetland, though, of course, the plane timetables would not permit that to happen.

The Montgomery committee, which was charged by the Government with the task of examining the powers and functions of the islands authorities, received strong representations to the effect that there should be an allowance for people in local government islands council areas to stand for their authorities.

Consider the case, for example, of Shetland, where more than 10 per cent. of the electorate is employed by the local authority, if teaching staff are included. That is a sizeable proportion of the electorate in the population of the islands area to exclude from the right to participate in local government. It will be thought that the end of the world has arrived when it is realised that when people have been pressing for the opposite view to be taken and are saying that some relaxation should be allowed to occur, far from that happening, the Government are tightening things up, and that there can be no hope of some relaxation for the islands areas.

The three SLD amendments are designed, first, to insert a limit of £25,000 to underscore the policy that my hon. Friends and I have reiterated. My hon. Friend the Member for Truro (Mr. Taylor)—who has departed temporarily for a much-earned respite and meal—has said, in Committee and on the Floor of the House, that when replying to the debate on this matter, the Minister misrepresented him.

It has been our policy that the limits should apply to chief officers and deputy chief officers. We accept that in some parts of the country the position has been open to abuse. It remains our view that, outwith chief and deputy chief officers, what is proposed is draconian and will curtail the fundamental rights of people to participate in local democracy. Hence our amendment to insert £25,000 instead of £13,500. We believe that by fixing it at that level our policy of limiting the exclusion to chief and deputy chief officers would be achieved.

Amendment No. 201, which would insert £18,000, is a less acceptable alternative. It would achieve the stated aim of excluding all those officers who come into regular contact with councillors, who attend committees or who give political advice in all but the smallest authorities. Going further down the scale, amendment No. 202 would achieve the same aims but include the smallest authorities.

The Government must explain why they would allow civil servants earning considerably more than £13,500 to play prominent roles in local government, while not allowing local authority manual workers even to be allowed to be considered to stand for election. I raise that matter with a degree of apprehension because it might give the Government ideas about becoming even tighter towards civil servants. I hope that they will not do that. The Bill goes much too far already in limiting the ability of people to play a constructive part in the local democratic process.

In many parts of my constituency, people stand as independents for local government. We are here telling people, "You will not play a part in local government. Your contribution is not welcome and is not required." That diminishes our democracy and therefore I hope—

[*Mr. James Wallace*]

though I suspect it is a triumph of optimism over experience—that the Minister will respond positively to the amendments.

Mr. McAllion: I support amendment No. 157. The Minister said that he had agreed to include the figure of £13,500 on the face of the Bill. Having agreed to that, it is incumbent on him to state clearly what payments will be taken into consideration when calculating that £13,500.

In Scotland, the local authority areas cover large swathes of countryside. For example, Strathclyde region covers almost half of Scotland. Other regions are also large. The Highland and Tayside regions and my region cover large swathes of the Highlands, including Perthshire and all the Angus glens. Yet the administrative centre of the region is in the southern extremity, at Dundee.

Many local government officers either live in Dundee and have to travel out to the various parts of the region or live on the outskirts of the region and come into the centre, to Dundee, to work. As a result, payments such as travel and subsistence allowances and disturbance and car mileage payments do not reflect any sort of seniority in the local government structure. They simply reflect the fact that the officers must travel large distances.

It is important, therefore, that those payments are excluded from the calculation of the £13,500. If not, the provision will go against the spirit of the Widdicombe report, and I am sure that the Minister does not intend that those payments should be taken into consideration.

Mr. Gummer: The hon. Member for Orkney and Shetland (Mr. Wallace) will appreciate that there are different ways of achieving the end, and we have tried to take the figure which approximates to what the Widdicombe committee saw as representing those who should have an absolute ban on taking part in political activities. We then made it much less onerous by ensuring that, either individually or by groups, people could be excluded from that. So most of the people of whom he speaks—manual workers and the like—are likely, certainly by category, to be excluded. That will not be unreasonable, and the way in which we have laid it down seems to be the best way of proceeding.

When it comes to the question of what the £13,500 means, we have said that it means "at the annual rate" of £13,500. That would exclude any travelling or subsistence allowances of the kind to which the hon. Member for Dundee, East (Mr. McAllion) referred. That is the case absolutely categorically and without question.

It would also exclude any kind of irregular payments. It would be only what is regularly the salary or wages. Sometimes part of that is called a bonus, but if it is on a regular basis—a distinction which the hon. Member for Normanton (Mr. O'Brien) made—it is not unreasonable to make a distinction between that and what is irregular, comes occasionally and is not part of the general. There should be no difficulty in that respect.

I have also given an undertaking to uprate the figure to keep it at the level we mean it to be, which is the equivalent of principal officer, as the Widdicombe committee requested. I do not want to tie it to a specific uprating or a specific increase in the cost of living because its purpose is not to be an index of remuneration, but to try to obtain a figure that approximates to that of the principal officer

and then to maintain that. There is no intention to extend the provision to all sorts of people, and I am sure that the hon. Member for Normanton did not mean that. However, one Opposition Member suggested that we should spread the provision downwards until the office boy would be caught. I gave an undertaking in Committee, and I am happy to repeat it tonight——

8.30 pm

Mr. O'Brien: The proposed £13,500 figure relates to the bottom of the principal officer scale. Would it not be fairer to set it at the half-way mark because otherwise it will restrict minor principal officers? Will the Minister reconsider the cut-off figure?

Mr. Gummer: The House would not think that to be a reasonable argument, would it? An independent committee recommended that the level should be set at principal officer. Because of the different ways that gradings are considered in different parts of the country, it was difficult to achieve uniformity. We felt that the figure of £13,500 met, as well as was possible, the committee's recommendation. I accept that it is at the bottom end of the principal officer scale, but it is intended to catch a bag of all those above that level.

The hon. Gentleman should acknowledge that we have introduced into the system the opportunity for anyone outside the politically restricted categories to appeal to the adjudicator. He could say, "I am earning more than that, but what I do is clearly not relevant to what is envisaged in the Bill." We have written into the Bill, through an amendment—because the Opposition wanted us to do so—that the adjudication officer should take into account the elements that relate to how one defines what is a politically restricted grade. We have been careful about that. It is not an unreasonable measure because it will affect only a limited number of local government workers. To ensure that the line drawn is not so firm that it causes the difficulties referred to by the hon. Gentleman, we have included the adjudication procedure and tried to make it as clear as possible. I think that, in general, people outside the House will think it to be a reasonable mechanism.

I accept that large numbers of civil servants will be involved and there are different arrangements to deal with how they react in different circumstances. At present, a general adjudication system is not available to civil servants, and I am glad that it has been included in this provision because it fits particular needs. I suspect that large groups of people will be excluded because of the nature of their activities. Many individuals will also be excluded. However, it is important to recognise that the public will know that those who have decided that their way of helping the general community should be through the business of advising elected members must restrict themselves to that activity when they reach a level at which that is especially appropriate.

The hon. Gentleman quoted a letter from someone who said that what he did in his spare time was his own business. There are few, if any, officers in local government who subscribe to that. Most people who make a career in local government would say, "What I do in the whole of my life should be consistent with my role of advising the whole of a committee and the whole of the council." I cannot understand how an adviser to a council could possibly, at the same time, be chairman of the local Labour party or a leading figure in the local Conservative party. However eminent the hon. Gentleman's correspondent may be, I do not think that what he quoted is correct.

Mr. O'Brien: The Minister made his last point out of context, which may be indicative of the whole Bill. We said in Committee, on more than one occasion, that chief executives, chief education officers, those in charge of departments and those advising the council should be included in the scope of the provision. I have been talking about such people as caretakers, inspectors at public works departments or plumbers who, because of the structure of their local authorities, could be earning above the ceiling. The provision could catch a junior who works in the information office of his local authority but is paid less than £13,500. Surely it is right to say that such people are entitled to do what they wish with their spare time.

Mr. Gummer: There is a distinction between those two elements. Most of those who the hon. Gentleman first quoted will inevitably be excluded by the operations of the adjudicator——

Mr. O'Brien: The Minister does not know that.

Mr. Gummer: I do not know that because the directions under which the adjudicator will operate—which we said we would include in the Bill—mean that he will understand exactly the sorts of people involved.

The Opposition are taking a new stance. In Committee I referred to a Conservative councillor on one council who was also the assistant housing director of another council, dealing with the allocation of housing for individual families in a neighbouring council area. I said that I did not think that to be a proper relationship. I was perfectly prepared to say that even though he is a Conservative councillor.

I ask the hon. Gentleman once more whether it is proper for the chief executive of a district council also to be chairman of the local Labour party. Is it proper to be the chief executive of a Scottish local authority and also a Labour councillor in another local authority? The hon. Gentleman has not yet been prepared, as in honour he should be, to say that that is improper. Until he is prepared to say so, I find the Labour party's sudden conversion rather odd. It knows that the public are in favour of the provision, so it is now trying to bow to public opinion.

Amendment agreed to.

Amendments made: No. 217, in page 3, line 29, leave out from 'delegated)' to end of line 39.

No. 218, in page 3, line 41, leave out from 'of' to 'posts' in line 45 and insert

'such of the following posts under the authority, namely—
(a) the full time posts the annual rate of remuneration in respect of which is or exceeds £13,500 or such higher amount as the Secretary of State may by order made by statutory instrument specify;
(b) the part time posts the annual rate of remuneration in respect of which would be or exceed that amount if they were full time posts in respect of which remuneration were paid at the same rate as for the part time post; and
(c) posts not falling within paragraph (a) or (b) above the duties of which appear to the authority to fall within subsection (3) below,
as are not posts for the time being exempted under section 3 below,'.

No. 219, in page 3, line 49, leave out "paragraph" and insert "subsection".—*[Mr. Gummer.]*

Mr. Gummer: I beg to move amendment No. 110, in page 4, line 35, leave out 'reports' and insert
', as respects all or most of the duties of his post, is required to report'.

Mr. Deputy Speaker: With this it will be convenient to take Government amendments Nos. 111 and 112.

Mr. Gummer: The purpose of the amendment is to clarify the definition of "non-statutory chief officer" and "deputy chief officer" in clause 2. We undertook in Committee to do that.

Amendment agreed to.

Amendments made: No. 111, in page 4, line 37, leave out 'reports' and insert
', as respects all or most of the duties of his post, is required to report'.

No. 112, in page 4, line 41, leave out 'reports' and insert
', as respects all or most of the duties of his post, is required to report'.

No. 220, in page 5, line 16, leave out from 'may' and insert 'shall'.

No. 221, in page 5, line 19, leave out subsection (2) and insert—
'(2) Where—
(a) a local authority have specified or are proposing to specify any post under the authority in a list maintained under subsection (2) of section 2 above;
(b) the holder for the time being of the post applies to the person appointed under subsection (1) above for exemptions from political restriction;
(c) the post is a post falling within paragraph (a) or (b) of that subsection which has been certified by the authority to be a post the duties of which, in their opinion, do not fall within subsection (3) of that section; and
(d) the person to whom the application is made is satisfied that the duties of that post do not so fall,
that person shall direct that, for so long as the direction has effect in accordance with its terms, the post is not to be regarded as a politically restricted post and, accordingly, is not to be specified in or, as the case may be, is to be removed from that list.'.—*[Mr. Gummer.]*

Clause 3

EXEMPTIONS FROM POLITICAL RESTRICTION

Mr. O'Brien: I beg to move amendment No. 137, in page 5, line 27, at end insert—
'(2A) References in this section to a "person" shall be taken to include references to a tribunal of such persons, appointed by the Secretary of State in accordance with subsection (2B) below for the purposes of carrying out functions under this section.
(2B) Any tribunal appointed under subsection (2A) above shall comprise a Chairperson, who shall be a person with experience of local government appointed after consultation with the local authority associations, and one representative each of local authorities as employers and of trades unions with members employed in local government grades to which political restriction may apply, or such other representation as the appellant may choose.
(2C) Any decision by a tribunal appointed under this section shall be by majority vote.'.

Mr. Deputy Speaker: With this it will be convenient to take amendment No. 152, in page 5, line 42, at end insert—
'(3A) Irrespective of any appointment or appointments made in accordance with subsection (3)(a) above, the Secretary of State shall appoint a different person for Scotland than any person appointed for England and for Wales.'.

Mr. O'Brien: What we are suggesting is that, instead of reference to an arbitrator, there should be a tribunal. That

[*Mr. O'Brien*]

would be much fairer. It would be in keeping with what is happening in and around local government. It would be a mirror of what is happening in industry, where, instead of having the one person to act as an arbitrator, there is a tribunal. Therefore, we consider that amendments Nos. 137 and 152 are important.

Mr. Andrew Welsh: This debate is about the system whereby individuals can appeal for exemption from political restrictions. The Government believe that one person only should be appointed to consider applications for exemption. The amendments, by contrast, allow for a proper system of appeal regarding exemption or political restrictions. If it is right that individuals should be able fully and fairly to participate in the democratic political process, it is surely just, correct and essential that a proper system of appeal be instituted. Individuals affected by the legislation must be protected by an appeal system that is, and is seen to be, fair. Unamended, the Government proposal does not ensure that. I therefore support the amendment.

Amendment No. 137 advocates a tribunal system. It also ensures that local government expertise will be available to the tribunal, which is important. There is a mass of expertise available within the Government and it should be used to protect the rights of individuals when those individuals feel that their rights as citizens are under threat.

In the Bill, there are none of those checks and balances which are normally associated with a democracy or any proper appeal system involving any public body. The amendment seeks to give confidence to anyone involved in appealing against a decision and will be seen as such. It will give greater confidence in a system which everyone in local government will rightly treat with caution. The Government's attitude to and record in local government forces caution on every person involved with the local government system. They have good reason to be wary about what the Government are doing by attempting to shackle and hamper the work of democratically elected individuals. People would approach the new system with caution and the new system would allow them at least to have some confidence when they appeal against decisions.

Similarly, amendment No. 152 is essential properly to take into account the fundamental uniqueness of the Scottish local government system. I am glad that the Under-Secretary of State for Scotland is present. I believe that the Scottish local government system has not been adequately catered for throughout the passage of the Bill. Certainly amendment No. 152 would begin the process of taking into account the uniqueness and the differences built into our national system of local government and law. It is not good enough for the Government to take a uniform system suited to Wales and England and apply it without thought or alteration to the very different circumstances of Scottish local government.

8.45 pm

I point out to the Minister the comments of COSLA. It rightly points out that structurally the Scottish system of local government varies widely from the system in England and Wales. Not only is the functional allocation different, but Scottish local government is unique in terms of its system—for example, for islands government. I know of

no equivalent in England. There is also a diversity of large and small units of government. There is a massive diversity between one local authority containing half the Scottish population and other small local authorities. A vast range of local authorities with different needs must be taken into account by the Bill. The imbalances far exceed anything to be found in England as, in fact, do the geographical differences between the two nations of Scotland and England.

Local government in Scotland is rightly the responsibility not of the Department of the Environment, but of the Scottish Office and the Secretary of State for Scotland. Hence, regulations, orders and circulars relating to the Scottish aspect and considerations emanating from United Kingdom-wide legislation are produced by the Scottish Office in recognition of that line of responsibility. The amendment seeks to extend that reality in a way that is useful in protecting Scottish local government.

I therefore support the amendments that emanate from the vast and practical experience of COSLA and take proper account of Scotland's individual and unique local government system. I believe that the Government are being short-sighted in their approach and that they will be making an unnecessary and fundamental mistake if they do not accept the amendment. As the Scottish Minister is here to speak for himself, I hope that he will take on board the need to take into account the distinctiveness of the Scottish system and will produce amendments that will allow people to have confidence in the new system as and when it is put into operation should the Bill go through unamended.

Mr. McAllion: I support amendments Nos. 137 and 152. Amendment No. 137 has a much better formulation for adjudication than the Bill. As it stands clause 3 would provide for a single adjudicator to be imposed upon the local authority from the outside by the Secretary of State. I assume that to be the Secretary of State for Scotland, although I am not clear and it might be that the Secretary of State for the Environment would impose that adjudicator on Scottish local authorities.

I believe that the idea of an adjudicating panel which has the confidence of the local authorities and, presumably, the confidence of the Secretary of State, as he would appoint the chairperson, is much better than imposing someone from outside on local authorities. It has the advantage of being much more democratic and of being based on the co-operation of both the local authorities and the employees who work inside the local authorities.

If General Jaruzelski was imposing his will on Solidarity—controlling local authorities—in the same way that the Minister for Local Government is imposing his will on our Labour-controlled local authorities, which side would the Minister be on? If General Jaruzelski had said to Solidarity that he intended his own appointee to impose his will upon Solidarity, with no consultation with Solidarity and with no consultation with the workers, I am sure that the Minister would be singing a different tune. If the Minister chose to stand up and say that, unlike General Jaruzelski, he is elected, that is not correct. In terms of Scottish local government, the Government have no democratic mandate to impose such measures on Scottish local authorities.

Amendment No. 152 tries to provide for a separate Scottish adjudicator and tries to establish that principle in the Bill. I know that its terms are not exactly the same as those set out in amendment No. 137 as amendment No. 152 says:

"the Secretary of State shall appoint a different person for Scotland than any person appointed for England and Wales.'"

Amendment No. 137 says that the adjudication would be undertaken by a panel of three. That is just a technical point—all we want is the Minister to agree to the principle. I would be happy if the Minister accepted the principle that the Scottish chair should be appointed by the Secretary of State for Scotland, that the representative of the local authorities would be picked by COSLA and the representatives of the workers picked by the appropriate trade unions.

In Committee, I tried to raise this matter when the Minister said:

"It will be possible for one adjudicator to adjudicate in England and Wales, and another to adjudicate in Scotland, for one to do the whole lot, or perhaps for there to be three."

The Minister therefore said that almost anything was possible. I pressed the Minister about that and asked whether clause 3(3)(a) which says that the Secretary of State may:

"appoint different persons under subsection (1) above for England and for Wales"

in any way diminished

"the right of the Secretary of State for Scotland to appoint people for Scotland?"

The Minister replied:

"The hon. Gentleman is perfectly right. It is possible for the same person to be selected by the Secretary of State for Wales and, for instance, the Secretary of State for the Environment. However, we are not discussing that point."

That was a complete non-answer and irrelevant to my question. The Minister went on:

"A reasonable way in which to proceed is for me to give the Committee an undertaking to bring forward an amendment on Report that will clarify more exactly the way in which the adjudication system will work".—[*Official Report, Standing Committee G,* 7 March 1989; c. 200.]

Having studied the amendments that have been tabled tonight, I do not see any Government amendment that clarifies the way in which the adjudication system will work.

It is important for the Government to recognise that there is a separate Scottish dimension to this question which means that we must make separate provision for Scotland. It must be appropriate to Scotland and must not impose on Scotland, through the Secretary of State for the Environment or the Secretary of State for Wales, some kind of adjudicating system.

The case is overwhelmingly in favour of a distinct approach for Scotland. The local government structure in Scotland, with its regional, district and island councils, is different from that of England and Wales. It would make little sense to someone who did not have experience of Scottish local government. When the Labour party wins the next general election, the Scottish Parliament, once established, will immediately institute a further reform of local government that will make local government in Scotland even more obscure for anyone who comes from outwith Scotland and does not understand the Scottish system.

The allocation of functions between district, regional and island councils is different from the allocation of functions in England and Wales. In Scotland we have unique circumstances. Strathclyde council employs a number of staff who deal with the press and handle the public relations of that council. Many of those employees have regular contacts with journalists and several of those who deal with the media earn more than £13,500. I assume that there would be no controversy about whether those people would be placed in the "politically restrictive posts" category. Perhaps the Minister will be able to tell us if that is so. Six other members of the same council department do not have regular contact with the media, but with the public. Two of those people earn more than £13,500 and four do not. How will those four be affected by the Bill? If we do not have a Scottish adjudicator, how will he make sense of the practice of Strathclyde regional council and how will he be able to distinguish between the different categories of officials and decide whether the restrictions should be applied to them?

It does not make sense for the adjudicator not to understand the Scottish system as he runs the risk of making catastrophic errors when deciding to restrict any of the posts. Two of the officers of Strathclyde who do not deal with journalists, but who deal with the public, would have a right of appeal because they earn more than £13,500, but the other four earn less, even though they are doing the same job. The whole thing is a mess, but things would improve if there were a provision for a separate panel of Scottish adjudicators in line with amendment No. 137.

The House already recognises that local government in Scotland is accountable not to the Department of the Environment but to the Scottish Office. That is why the Parliamentary Under-Secretary of State for Scotland is present tonight. If the Government recognise the separateness of Scotland to that extent, they should go further and recognise that Scotland should have a separate adjudication system.

We are not talking about something that will have a marginal effect. Edinburgh district council has calculated that more than 500 officers are likely to be affected by the Bill. Those officers range from administrators to solicitors, the secretariat, the technical service officers, the service engineers, maintenance and repair personnel and even its theatre manager. What happens when that manager decides to stage "Harmony Row", a production by the Scottish Wildcat Theatre company, which is a play against the poll tax? Would the theatre manager be allowed to put on that play which attacks the poll tax, or would he be accused of indulging in political activity under the Bill? Such are the anomalies thrown up by this ridiculous Bill.

The only way in which to make the Bill better is to ensure that at least some kind of Scottish sanity is written into it by ensuring that there is a separate system of Scottish adjudication. I look forward to the Minister's reply.

Mr. Wallace: I support amendments Nos. 137 and 152. Amendment No. 137 calls for a panel of adjudicators and that is justified, otherwise an enormous burden would be placed on one individual. The hon. Member for Dundee, East (Mr. McAllion) has already said that more than 500 employees of Edinburgh district council are likely to be affected by the Bill. For a start, therefore, that means that potentially 500 appeals could be lodged.

In our previous debate, the Minister for Local Government was most reasonable and said that the adjudicator had already predetermined a vast number of cases, not least those affecting manual workers. Many of us would have liked to have seen that predetermination

[Mr. Wallace]

embodied in the Bill. Even if we accept the Minister's word, many people will still wish to take their appeal to the adjudicator. Perhaps the Parliamentary Under-Secretary of State for Scotland can tell us what the adjudicator's view will be of the teaching profession. A number of teachers are councillors in an authority by which they are not employed. I would welcome some reassurance about that.

The Parliamentary Under-Secretary of State for Scotland (Lord James Douglas-Hamilton): I hope that the hon. Gentleman will accept that they are specifically not included.

9 pm

Mr. Wallace: I am very grateful for that reassurance and much relieved by it—*[Interruption.]* I do not accept that they are all Tories; a good number of our councillors are teachers.

Nevertheless, this would be a tremendous burden to put upon one person. I was going to say that the Government were here creating another quango but that implies an organisation and with one person it would probably be a quan-guy. One wonders how much this person will be paid for carrying out this function, which I foresee as being, in the initial stages at least, a full-time job.

Let us think in simple terms for one moment of what this person is being invited to do. The appointee of the Government is being asked to determine whether individuals may indulge in political activity, some of which, and probably much of which, is in an interest which could well be opposed to the interest of the Government. The appointee of the Secretary of State will be asked to make that fundamental decision, which affects the rights of an individual citizen to participate in the political process. It would have been unthinkable a few years ago to put that into the hands of a Government appointee, but that is what the Government are asking us to do in this Bill.

I therefore support the idea that if this is to be done at all it should be done by an appeals body and not left in the hands of one person. It should be done by a tribunal which reflects the interests of employers, employees and the Secretary of State. Apart from anything else, that would help to share the load. When one is debating fundamental political liberties, there is no reason why a person should be expected to wait a considerable length of time for an appeal to be heard, as would be almost inevitable if the duty were imposed on one individual.

I shall be very brief with regard to amendment No. 152 which asks for a specific person to be appointed for Scotland. It has already been said that Scottish local government is an entirely separate structure. I can see no good reason why we should tag along with what the English and the Welsh are doing. We need someone who understands fully the ins and outs of Scottish local government. For the Government to refuse a quite reasonable amendment such as this would be obduracy at its worst.

I therefore hope that the Under-Secretary of State, who always aims to please, will succeed in doing so in this case.

Lord James Douglas-Hamilton: A number of interesting points have been raised and I will start with the hon. Member for Normanton (Mr. O'Brien), who spoke with

enthusiasm about appointing a tribunal. It has always been the Secretary of State's intention that the adjudicator should be a person with suitable experience. We shall most certainly keep an open mind on that matter.

As my right hon. Friend the Member for Suffolk, Coastal (Mr. Gummer) explained in Committee, we believe that the issues are fairly clear cut. We believe that it is unnecessary to establish a tribunal. I do not see why Opposition Members feel that a tribunal comprising representatives of interested groups and trade unions would serve the necessary purpose. It should be the role of an independent adjudicator alone to consider an application for exemption against a clear statutory framework, but he would be in a quasi-judicial role.

Mr. O'Brien: If the Minister accepts that it is right for the Civil Service to have an appeals tribunal—a tripartite system—why does he insist that local government should not have the same facilities? That is simply the hypocrisy that exists on the Government Benches.

Lord James Douglas-Hamilton: Widdicombe did not make the recommendation which the hon. Member is suggesting and I believe that the circumstances are different. For example, it is not possible for civil servants to stand for Parliament, but it is certainly possible for local authority officials below a certain level to do precisely that.

One of the advantages of having an independent person as compared to a panel is that he would be truly independent and not a representative of interest groups. I do not think it appropriate that trade union representatives should sit in judgment on this question. We do not see this in any sense as a bargaining matter; it is the application of a clear-cut set of criteria determined by Parliament as set out in clause 2(3) of the Bill. The adjudicator will, of course, be expected to act independently and impartially.

The hon. Member for Dundee, East (Mr. McAllion) spoke at considerable length making the case for an adjudicator for Scotland. Indeed, the hon. Member spoke about this in Committee. I accept his argument. I believe that it is right, proper and appropriate that there should be a separate adjudicator for Scotland. He or she will be appointed by the Secretary of State for Scotland under the provisions of clause 3 to serve as the independent exemptions adjudicator for Scotland. So I hope that that amendment will be withdrawn.

I want to deal particularly with the point raised by the hon. Member for Angus, East (Mr. Welsh), who asked a question which he raised a year ago in the Committee which considered the Local Government Bill, about the words "Secretary of State for Scotland". He asked whether, when the Secretary of State is referred to, these words are interchangeable. I quite understand why the provisions in subsection (3)*(a)* of clause 3 may have led to the supposition that a similar provision may be necessary for Scotland, but an express provision for Scotland not only is unnecessary but would be positively undesirable.

Subsection (3)*(a)* is intended to avoid any doubt about the power of the Secretary of State for Wales to make a separate appointment in Wales under subsection (1). No such doubt arises in relation to the powers of the Secretary of State for Scotland in this matter, but it might well arise in relation to existing legislation if the amendment were to be made.

It is a well understood convention that in a Great Britain Act dealing with matters such as local government where the Secretary of State has full territorial responsibility, powers conferred on the Secretary of State for Scotland may be exercised separately and, if necessary, differently by him within Scotland. Therefore, it is unnecessary to add an express reference to Scotland and to do so might cast doubt on the many other legislative provisions that are now read in accordance with the convention.

Mr. Wallace: Will the Minister answer my question about how much such a person will be paid? Secondly, does he accept that it is difficult for a person to be seen to be independent if he is appointed by the Secretary of State? Can he give a guarantee that the person will be barred from the same political activities from which the legislation aims to disbar council employees?

Lord James Douglas-Hamilton: I shall certainly give the guarantee for which the hon. Gentleman asks in his last question. The remuneration still has to be worked out.

Mr. McAllion: Will the Minister also give us the assurance that whoever is appointed to the position will not be a defeated Conservative candidate at a previous general election?

Lord James Douglas-Hamilton: The hon. Gentleman can, without any question, expect him to be the best person for the job.

Amendment negatived.

Clause 5

DESIGNATION AND REPORTS OF MONITORING OFFICER

Sir George Young (Ealing, Acton): I beg to move amendment No. 2, in page 6, line 40, at end, insert—
> '(c) to secure that the officer is a person who appears to have the requisite knowledge and experience to discharge the functions of the monitoring officer. Either the monitoring officer or deputy monitoring officer should be a barrister, advocate or solicitor called or admitted in any part of the United Kingdom or a member of the Institute of Chartered Secretaries and Administrators.'.

The amendment is inspired by the Institute of Chartered Secretaries and Administrators and it seeks to define the qualifications required by the monitoring officer.

The monitoring officer will be responsible for drawing the attention of the authority to any decision or omission which contravenes any rules of law or conventions binding the authority which would result in maladministration. Therefore, the monitoring officer will need a working knowledge of local government legislation and any local conventions that are binding. He will also need to know of any actions which result in maladministration or injustice by the authority.

The monitoring officer will also be required to monitor "any proposal, decision or omission by the authority, by any committee, sub-committee or officers". Therefore, a knowledge of local authority committee structures and procedures would be a distinct advantage.

The amendment ensures that the monitoring officer or his deputy is either a lawyer or a member of the institute to which I have referred, and it would require the authority to appoint an officer who would have the knowledge and experience to do the duties in a professional and thorough

manner. It would also ensure that the public would be assured that councillors receive and act upon sound professional advice.

Mr. Gummer: I have sympathy with my hon. Friend but I hope that he will accept that, on balance, it is better not to increase the number of requirements wherever that is not utterly necessary. It is up to the local authority to decide who should be the monitoring officer. I am not entirely convinced that it is right to make it a kind of closed shop of particular people with particular qualifications. In general, it is likely that monitoring officers will be in possession of one or other of those qualifications, but that will not always be so and in some local authorities the person who is the obvious choice will not fall into those categories. It is much better that the local authority should have that decision in its own hands.

I hope that my hon. Friend will agree that the care with which I have sought to listen to and discuss with the bodies representing those various groups shows that I have a high view of the responsibilities and personal needs of those senior officers. However, in the end, it is better to leave this to the decision of the local authority. I assure my hon. Friend that I shall keep a close eye on what happens, and if there is a future need to do something of the kind that he suggests, no doubt we can return to the matter.

Sir George Young: I am overwhelmed by the clarity and logic of my hon. Friend's reply, and I do not wish to press the matter further. I beg to ask leave to withdraw the amendment.

Amendment, by leave, withdrawn.

Amendments made: No. 275, in page 7, line 42, leave out from 'obligations)' to end of line 44, and insert
'or otherwise, to ensure that no step is taken for giving effect to any proposal or decision to which such a report relates at any time while the implementation of the proposal or decision is suspended in consequence of the report'.

No. 276, in page 7, line 48, at end insert—
'(5A) For the purposes of paragraph (b) of subsection (5) above the implementation of a proposal or decision to which a report under this section relates shall be suspended in consequence of the report until the end of the first business day after the day in which consideration of that report under paragraph (a) of that subsection is concluded.'.

No. 277, in page 8, line 6, at end insert—
'"business day", in relation to a relevant authority, means any day which is not a Saturday or Sunday, Christmas Day, Good Friday or any day which is a bank holiday under the Banking and Financial Dealings Act 1971 in the part of Great Britain where the area of the authority is situated;'.

Lord James Douglas-Hamilton: I beg to move amendment No. 232, in page 8, line 18, leave out 'regional, islands or district council' and insert 'local authority'.

Mr. Deputy Speaker: With this we may take Government amendments Nos. 233, 234, 237, 238, 235 and 236.

Lord James Douglas-Hamilton: The amendments all serve to correct drafting errors or inconsistencies.

Mr. John Maxton (Glasgow, Cathcart): In nearly all Scottish local government legislation of which I am aware, the terminology region, island and district authority is fairly standard, and yet the Minister appears to be changing his mind and introducing in the Bill something rather different. Is the Minister engaged in some wily plot to introduce local government reform at a later stage?

Lord James Douglas-Hamilton: I reassure the hon. Gentleman that I have no hidden agendas in that respect. The expression "local authorities" is defined for Scotland in clause 18(2) as meaning

"a regional, islands or district council or a joint board or joint committee within the meaning of section 235(1) of the Local Government (Scotland) Act 1973."

Any joint committee that is a corporate body falls within the meaning of "joint board". As we do not want the definition to embrace unincorporated joint committees, we require to delete the words "or joint committee". I will ensure that the relevant provisions will apply as intended to regional, islands or district councils and to corporate joint bodies, but not to unincorporated joint committees. The reasoning for that is that an unincorporated joint committee is not primarily responsible for the discharge of functions. Amendment No. 237 also concerns a drafting error, but I am sure that the hon. Gentleman does not wish me to pursue that.

Amendment agreed to.

Clause 6

OFFICER RESPONSIBLE FOR FINANCIAL ADMINISTRATION OF CERTAIN AUTHORITIES

Mr. Gummer: I beg to move amendment No. 167, in page 8, leave out line 39 and insert—

'(c) be a person who qualifies by virtue of section 113(2)(b) of the Local Government Finance Act 1988 (existing office holders) as a person who may be given responsibility for the financial affairs of an authority mentioned in section 111(2)(a) to (k) of that Act; or

(d) fulfil two or more of those conditions.'.

Mr. Deputy Speaker: With this, it will be convenient to debate Government amendment No. 168.

Mr. Gummer: These minor amendments ensure that local authority chief finance officers without formal qualifications are not barred from becoming chief finance officers of the City of London or from a section 73 successor body.

Mr. Tony Banks: The Minister will correct me if I misunderstood him, but he appeared to be saying that the City of London can take people on who clearly do not have the qualifications for the job. Is that what he was saying? The Minister implied that the City of London could take on unqualified people who would have been required to have certain qualifications were they employed elsewhere.

Mr. Gummer: It is simply that certain chief finance officers are permitted under section 113 of the Local Government Finance Act 1988 to hold the post of local authority chief finance officer because at the time that section 113 came into force they were already holding such a post. The amendment ensures that such chief finance officers are not barred in the future from holding the post of chief finance officer of the Common Council of the City of London or any new successor body under section 73 of the Local Government Act 1985. The amendment ensures that certain rights accorded under a previous Act will not be excluded.

Mr. Banks *rose*——

Mr. Deputy Speaker: Order. The hon. Gentleman cannot address the House again.

Amendment agreed to.

Amendment made: No. 168, in page 9 leave out line 4 and insert—

'(c) be a person who qualifies by virtue of section 113(2)(b) of the local Government Finance Act 1988 (existing office holders) as a person who may be given responsibility for the financial affairs of an authority mentioned in section 111(2)(a) to (k) of that Act; or

(d) fulfil two or more of those conditions.'.—*[Mr. Gummer].*

Clause 7

ALL STAFF TO BE APPOINTED ON MERIT

Amendments made: No. 233, in page 9, line 43 leave out from 'Scotland' to end of line 45.

No. 234, in page 10, line 2 leave out from 'authority' to 'whether' in line 3 and insert 'or parish or community council'.—*[Mr. Gummer.]*

Mr. Paul Murphy (Torfaen): I beg to move amendment No. 140, in page 10, line 7 at end insert—

'(aa) section 15 of the Disabled Persons (Employment) Act 1944 and Section 3 of the Disabled Persons (Employment) Act 1958 (Provision of Sheltered Employment by Local Authorities)'.

Mr. Deputy Speaker: With this it will be convenient to take the following amendments: No. 141, in page 10, line 18 after 'qualification'. insert—

'(ee) section 11 of the Mental Health (Scotland) Act 1984 (Training and Occupation of the Mentally Handicapped)'.

No. 142, in line 21 at end insert——

'(2A) Nothing in this section shall affect the selection of any person for a place on a sheltered placement scheme, nor the appointment of any person made in accordance with a scheme maintained by an authority for the purpose of promoting the employment of persons with a mental or physical disability.'

9.15 pm

Mr. Murphy: This group of amendments deal with the employment of people with a mental handicap. Their purpose is to clarify the fact that nothing in clause 7, which deals with appointments on merit, will cut across sheltered placement schemes or positive employment policies which are geared to the disabled and to those with a mental handicap or an impairment.

The requirement in the clause to appoint staff purely on merit threatens to make it unlawful for local authorities to adopt any policy of positive discrimination towards people who are disabled or mentally impaired. Such policies recognise that disabled people face difficulties in gaining employment, even when there are jobs available which they could do. Apart from conscious and unconscious prejudice, difficulties arise because the disabled person may not, in the past, have had access to the same educational and employment opportunities as a person without a disability, or because the disabled person may require some additional training to perform the job successfully.

A number of local authorities have adopted policies to help disabled people to overcome these sometimes serious problems and disadvantages. Legislation such as the Disabled Persons (Employment) Act 1944 and the Disabled Persons (Employment) Act 1958 recognises that local authorities have a role to play in increasing employment opportunities for disabled people. Some authorities have a responsibility as social work or social service authorities. Finding employment often reduces the reliance on statutory welfare services and can be seen as a cost-effective way of assisting disabled people.

Section 15 of the Disabled Persons (Employment) Act 1944, which is referred to in the amendment, states that facilities may be provided to enable handicapped or disabled people to gain employment. The 1958 Act allows local authorities to make arrangements for the provision of facilities for the same purpose.

Facilities provided under those powers involve the local authority in employing disabled people. For example, under the sheltered placement schemes, to which I have referred, a business agrees to provide work for a disabled person. It receives a proportion of the standard rate for the job, based on the output of the disabled person compared with the, so to speak, ordinary employee. The balance is met by the sponsor, which is often a local authority.

The crucial point is that the sponsor is the legal employer of the disabled person. If clause 7 is to have the effect intended by the Government, it must be taken to mean that jobs are to be given to those best able to do them. Clearly, that is inconsistent with such schemes whose purpose is to provide employment for people who cannot perform jobs as well as others. Since the Government support sheltered employment and, I am sure, positive discrimination towards disabled people employed by local authorities, it would seem that such a failure is an oversight. I hope that when he replies the Minister will recognise it as such.

Mr. Matthew Taylor: This is an important point which has caused concern for those involved. I cannot believe that the Minister intended the clause to have the effect described by the hon. Member for Torfaen (Mr. Murphy). Therefore, I hope that he will either accept the amendments or clarify in specific terms why people with disabilities will not be affected in the way suggested. To a layman at least, it appears that the clause would have that effect. I do not know what a lawyer would make of it. I do not think that there will be any party political controversy on this point, but it is causing concern and I hope that the Minister will make it clear to the House that the clause will not affect disabled people in the way that has just been outlined.

Mr. McAllion: Amendment No. 141 deals with section 11 of the Mental Health (Scotland) Act 1984, which involves the training and occupation of the mentally handicapped. It places a duty on local authorities to provide or secure the provision of suitable training in an occupation for the mentally handicapped.

In the past, we have tended to concentrate on training for disabled people, but there is a growing recognition that genuine employment is the key to great advances for those suffering from mental handicap. A number of innovative schemes, all of which will be prejudiced unless the amendment is accepted, are being implemented by local authorities. It would then be legally impossible to employ the mentally handicapped if employment by merit had to be applied strictly and legally. I hope that the Minister will look at the amendment sympathetically.

Mr. Gummer: First, let me assure the House that it is not the Government's understanding that the provisions will have the effect that certain people fear. Clause 7(2) makes it clear that the general provision will have effect subject to certain existing statutory provisions designed to protect particular groups, many of which have been mentioned. The hon. Gentleman has just referred to the Scottish provisions.

I have no doubt that people need have no worries. If anyone has any further anxieties, however, I shall be happy to consider them, and if there is any question that the clause will do other than what we expect it to do I shall be glad to see whether an amendment is necessary. If hon. Members wish to withdraw their amendments, certain aspects of which will cause difficulties, I shall be happy to produce an amendment to deal with any problems, although I do not expect any.

Mr. Murphy: I am grateful for those assurances, on the basis of which I beg to ask leave to withdraw the amendment.

Amendment, by leave, withdrawn.

Amendment made: No. 113, in page 10, line 10, leave out paragraph (c).—*[Mr. Gummer.]*

Clause 9

ASSISTANTS FOR POLITICAL GROUPS

Mr. Blunkett: I beg to move amendment No. 149, in page 12, line 16, leave out 'three' and insert 'four'.

Mr. Deputy Speaker: With this we may take the following amendments: No. 314, in page 12, line 16, leave out 'three' and insert 'six'.

No. 203, in page 13, leave out lines 14 to 21 and insert 'the membership of that group numbers at least five'.

No. 315, in page 13, leave out lines 14 to 40 and insert 'the number of other groups (if any) which are larger than the group does not exceed five.'

No. 150, in page 13, line 17, leave out 'two' and insert 'three'.

No. 151, in page 13, line 19, leave out 'two' and insert 'three'.

Mr. Blunkett: I shall not detain the House for long, because we debated these issues in Committee.

The Bill designates three political assistants, but it was felt that in a number of circumstances, particularly appertaining to Scotland but also in other parts of the United Kingdom, genuine flexibility would be needed to take account of the greater plurality of representation on the local authority.

I do not think that this is a matter of tremendous ideological difference. We can box with each other about whether it would be entertaining to leave particular political parties without the facility of political assistance —if they choose to take it—but that does not seem awfully clever to us. If we can provide a facility which, within reason, meets the needs of different political parties with reasonable representation on local authorities, we should provide it.

Political support in terms of secretarial, administrative and research facilities obviously takes different forms in different local authorities, and if we are too restrictive we shall be in danger of finding that people consider different ways of presenting and obtaining support for groups.

In the spirit in which we are debating tonight, I am sure that the Minister will say, as he would have in Committee, that the amendment is very reasonable.

Mr. Andrew Welsh: I wish to speak to amendments Nos. 314 and 315.

The so-called "abuse" of the appointment of paid assistants for political groups has never to my knowledge been a particular problem in Scottish local government. The Bill, however, seeks to impose rules and limitations on Scottish local councillors, and their ability to appoint assistants as and when they wish and to meet their specific needs.

My concern is that the assumptions behind clause 9 are based purely on the English model of local government and local politics, and do not fit easily or usefully with the reality of Scottish local government. There are obvious differences of size and scale between Scotland and England, as well as differences in traditions and customs. There are also differences in local government units and political affiliations, which should be taken into account in the legislation if it is to do more good than harm.

Not only are full-time paid political advisers unheard of, but they would be an absurdity in many of the smaller and more rural Scottish authorities. The Bill sets out to provide Scotland with a supposed solution to problems which it does not have, but which exist in specific parts of England.

The wording of the Bill relates only to the English three-party system. The Scottish reality can be very different. Scottish local government has consisted of at least a four-party system for some time. In certain areas, it is even more diverse than that. Therefore, my amendment seeks to provide a more realistic framework for Scottish local government and to avoid the future unnecessary problems that, if unchanged, the Bill would pose for Scotland. I am attempting not to destroy this part of the Bill but to make it more closely fit the pattern of Scottish local government.

Amendment No. 315 is a simplification. That, for starters, can never be a bad thing for a Government who are introducing an ever-growing flood of legislation. Therefore, I commend my amendment, which simplifies one portion of an extremely long Bill. It takes into account the diversity of Scotland's political life. The Bill is designed to cater exclusively for political life in Wales and England. The Government's underlying assumption is that there is a two-party system in every local authority, with perhaps an occasional nod in the direction of a possible third party. The assumption should be different in Scotland because the political reality there is different. Scotland has a three-party or a four-party system and it has had it for some time.

I am also left with the feeling that no account whatsoever has been taken of independent councillors or independent-controlled councils. Although the inexorable trend of party politics has squeezed independent councillors out of the major urban and more populous areas, independent councillors and independent-controlled councils still exist in Scotland. Obviously it is up to the electorate to decide how long that should continue, but the reality is that in addition to a three-party or a four-party system in Scottish local government, there is still a significant number of independent councillors whose needs ought to be taken into account in the interests of fairness, if nothing else.

My concern is that the assumptions about local government in England and Wales are being applied without thought or alteration to the markedly different Scottish local government scene. Hence, the amendment calls for the application of different arithmetic when considering Scotland.

The amendments provide for flexibility compared with the rigidity of the provisions in the Bill. They allow for future political changes as well as for the present reality. I am sure that the Minister has noted that all the Opposition parties agree that the Government's proposal is inadequate and that they have tabled amendments which seek to increase the numbers involved. The details may vary sightly, but the need for alteration is accepted as a common philosophy. That leaves the Government in a very isolated position.

I should like the Minister to think again. The amendments provide one method by which he can do so. They would allow for the diversity of the political scene in Scottish local government to be recognised.

Mr. Matthew Taylor: As the hon. Member for Angus, East (Mr. Welsh) has pointed out, the Opposition parties have all tabled amendments along the same lines.

The purpose of amendment No. 203 is twofold—equity and simplicity. The hon. Member for Angus, East also pointed out that the Government's rules and criteria lead to unnecessary complication. The length and the confused nature of the debate on this part of the Bill in Committee demonstrated that the Government's proposals are tortuous in the extreme and will cause havoc in council chambers up and down the land as arguments rage between third parties of equal size, large fourth parties and allegedly independent groups that may have difficulty in obtaining assistance and that may also divide into groups with very different views on the council.

In Committee the Minister did not appear to understand the problems that he and his colleagues seemed to be intent on causing for no particular good reason. I foresee real difficulties in some local authorities, particularly in Scotland, Wales and in mainly rural parts of England, as well as in Cornwall, where sizeable numbers of independents continue to get elected and play a prominent role on councils. Most importantly, our amendment brings equity between groups of different size throughout the country. Why should members of a council in a group of five on one authority have fewer rights of access to facilities to serve their constituents than a person in a similar position in a similarly sized neighbouring authority simply because the numbers of their opponents happen to divide differently or because the council has different numbers of representatives and therefore the entitlements differ according to the particular circumstances?

Under the Government's plans, a council divided equally between four political parties would be entitled to three assistants. That is the absurdity of the Government's proposals. I understand that they are trying to limit the potential costs involved, but most local authorities do not provide such assistance because local people probably would not support it, no matter which party proposed it. That is because the local electorate has a considerable say over whether such a system would go ahead and could decide whether that cost should be involved.

9.30 pm

The problem is that under the Government's scheme the freedom to make a decision locally, according to local circumstances, is not allowed. The matter may be raised again in the other place if the Government do not accept at least one of the amendments. I rather suspect that, given the nature of the party divisions in the other place, and the fact that there are Cross Benchers, they may have a greater understanding than the Government have of the nature of a debating chamber in which many groups of differing but significant size are represented, have a real involvement, and in many cases have a determining vote on the decisions that are taken. That may not happen in this House, but it happens in the other place and in council chambers across the country.

Our amendment offers the Government a simple, sensible way out which might not provide civil servants with so much fun and games when complications arise but would certainly lead to a simple, efficient and fair system within local authorities across the country.

Mr. McAllion: I shall be brief in speaking in support of amendments Nos. 149, 150 and 151.

I do not know the basis on which the Government decided to allow three political assistants for each of the three main parties in every council, but I assume that it had something to do with the result of the last general election when the votes split largely between the Tories, the Labour party and the alliance. The situation has changed since the last general election with the division of the alliance, the SDP splitting away and the rest of the alliance forming the Social and Liberal Democrats. Since then, there has also been the emergence of the Green party as a possible alternative to the Democrats and the SDP as the third main party. The situation is changing, and I know it is difficult for the Government to legislate on something which is constantly on the move.

The amendments emphasise that clause 9 simply does not relate to Scottish local government, and that should be recognised. A large number of district authorities and regional authorities are comprised of four or more representative groups. If the number of political assistants is restricted to three, the ability of almost half Scotland's local authorities to allocate political assistance to all representative groups when those groups fulfil the criteria set out in clause 9(6) will be severely restricted.

COSLA has made available to me a breakdown of more than 63 councils in Scotland. It shows that three of those councils are single party councils, 11 are two-party councils, 19 are three-party councils, 23 are four-party councils and seven are five-party councils. Therefore, in Scotland it is not fair to restrict the number of assistants to only three parties. The Government must recognise that there are four major parties competing for the support of the people in Scotland and that councils should be allowed to allocate political assistants to all main representative groups.

The independent councillors have been mentioned. I do not support the idea that they should be allowed political assistance as independent groups on councils do not necessarily share the same political perspective, and it would be very difficult for them to agree on a political assistant to represent them all as representatives from the Left and the Right stand under the same title of independent.

The situation is becoming ever more complex. In the Glasgow, Central by-election, there are no fewer than nine different political parties competing for the vote. In a recent opinion poll, the Communist party, which is not standing, did much better than some of the parties that are standing in Glasgow, Central. We cannot allow for every party that suddenly emerges on the political scene, but we must take on board the fact that there are major parties which command a large number of votes and which deserve to be eligible for being given political assistance under the Bill.

If the Conservative party is not careful, the Green party could overtake it as the fourth party, as the latest opinion polls show. If the Government do not accept the amendment, they may find that they are denying to Conservative groups in Scotland the right to appoint political assistants. I hope that the Government will realise that Scotland is different and will legislate for political assistants for the four major parties in that country.

Mr. Gummer: Some of the discussion has gone along lines that show a division between the Government and the Opposition in the sense that it has been suggested that the idea of having a maximum of three special assistants is to mirror the party structure on particular councils. That is not so. The House will be aware that originally the Widdicombe committee supported the scheme that we should have a number of such posts up to five. When the Government produced their White Paper, they proposed that we should have none at all. I listened with care to the advice given to me from hon. Members of various parties. My hon. Friend the Member for Wolverhampton, South-West (Mr. Budgen), for example, raised the question and put some pertinent points on it. I had representations from the Labour party as well.

As a result of listening to a range of views, I became convinced marginally—not with enormous enthusiasm—that it was reasonable to allow some special assistants rather along the lines of those provided for Ministers under the present system and under the previous Government. We moved away from the proposal in the White Paper.

The idea of three was a compromise in a real sense. It seemed to us that if we were going to introduce such a system, to have one for the party in power, so to speak, in a local authority and one for the opposition party was, perhaps, a little niggardly, especially where one had a mix that would make it more sensible to have three. We therefore proposed three.

Mr. Andrew Welsh: Will the right hon. Gentleman give way?

Mr. Gummer: I shall give way when I have finished the point.

I see no reason why we cannot argue for a long time about how many there should be. The hon. Member for Dundee, East (Mr. McAllion) made the point that there were many parties and many people standing under various groups. He would have denied independents the right to decide that they might like to be an independent group. Under the regulations, the system will be different from the one the hon. Gentleman suggested. If the independents, grouped together, formed the third largest party in the sense that I have described, with a significant number of members, they would be able, if they wanted and irrespective of whether I thought it was a good idea, to form such a group, and in a council that gave up to three special advisers they would be able to gain one adviser. It would be up to them.

The hon. Member for Angus, East (Mr. Welsh) felt strongly about the situation in Scotland. He might take

[*Mr. Gummer*]

into account the point made by the hon. Member for Truro (Mr. Taylor), who made the same application to the situation in England and Wales. This is not a division between the various parts of the United Kingdom. Our proposal is based on the principle that the Government have been persuaded by the arguments of hon. Members of various parties to change their original position. Generally, it has been accepted as a welcome compromise, except by one or two hon. Members, who have revealed rather different views.

Mr. Andrew Welsh *rose——*

Mr. Gummer: I shall give way to the hon. Gentleman in a moment about Scotland but should first like to say something which is not as helpful to the hon. Member for Truro. I was fascinated—I shall check it in *Hansard*—by his revelations about the unhappy relationships among the small parties of his tendency on various local councils. It was a revelation to those hon. Members who were present to hear that the hon. Gentleman does not feel that these provisions will do anything other than lead, in what I believe were his words, to "very unhappy, very difficult circumstances". I am sorry that that is his relationship with his colleagues. It is a pity——

Mr. Matthew Taylor *rose——*

Mr. Gummer: Before I give way to the hon. Gentleman, I have promised to give way to the hon. Member for Angus, East.

There is a balance to be drawn about how much of the cost of political organisations it is reasonable to ask the public to bear. Originally the Government felt that they should bear no cost, but I have been convinced that some of the cost should, indeed, be borne. We should retain what seems the reasonable figure of three special advisers. I cannot believe that it is impossible to run a small party group without such a special adviser. It seems an odd version of the current situation to suggest that that cannot be done without some support when in most councils in most parts of the country no support is given and, historically, no support has ever been given.

Mr. Andrew Welsh: The Minister has called his measure a "reasonable compromise" but I put it to him again that it is not reasonable in Scotland. I should like him to address the straightforward point that limiting the number of political assistants to three severely restricts the ability of almost half Scotland's local authorities to allocate political assistance to all representative groups when those groups fulfil the other criteria as defined in clause 9(6). It is entirely wrong for the Minister to say that he has found a reasonable compromise because his provisions will affect almost half Scotland's local authorities. That cannot be right.

Mr. Gummer: I do not think that the matter is of that order. It is perfectly reasonable to say that on any local authority the number of people involved in that activity should be restricted to three. Most local authorities have none—that is the nature of the present position—and very many hon. Members think that it is giving far too much to have any at all. I have sought a compromise and this is the compromise that I propose. Any alternative would lead many people who have been prepared to go along with this

compromise to say, "If you are going to provide all sorts of extra people for all sorts of groups, frankly we prefer to have none at all". It is a reasonable compromise and one to which I intend to stick.

Amendment negatived.

Mr. Blunkett: I beg to move amendment No. 132, in page 12, line 37 leave out subsection (4).

I might be even briefer now than on the last occasion on the ground that this is such a reasonable amendment that it would take a dedicated and extremely unreasonable man or woman to turn it down. The reasonableness of it is that, even allowing for the £13,500 level for debarring people from political activity, if someone is not likely to be felt by those with whom and on behalf of whom they are working to be unduly influenced by their political activities outside, in other words, if they are not likely to be considered to be impartial or lacking independence, the argument about forbidding them from undertaking outside political work and debarring them from outside political activities reaches the depth of absurdity.

I should like the Minister to reconsider this issue, because, while it cannot be considered earth-shattering by anybody's standards, the Government's provisions really do take the biscuit.

Mr. Gummer: Obviously, this matter could reasonably be argued by rational people. I do not believe that those who take a different view from myself are in some way peculiar or extreme. I wholly agree with the hon. Gentleman that it is possible to have a different view.

We have taken this view because Widdicombe suggested that such posts should be graded as senior officers. We think that a point within the senior officer range, which is also the bottom of the principal officer range—that is, £13,500—is about right as the maximum.

9.45 pm

We see these posts in a different light from that which the hon. Member for Sheffield, Brightside (Mr. Blunkett) put forward, and that is why we refer to a "special assistant" rather than a "political assistant." We see this as the kind of person who might, as part of a career pattern, seek at some later date to take a more active part in politics and wish to use this provision in those circumstances. We say that this would be a reasonable role for such a person to play and that this would be a reasonable sum for him or her to have.

I agree, however, that it can be a matter of disagreement between rational people. It is part of a compromise which I propose to the House. It is a compromise which arose because originally the Government intended to suggest that nobody should be available for these posts and that no such post should be designated. But I felt that it was better to propose what we have now proposed.

I accept that it would be just as rational and reasonable to propose a different mix. I am merely saying that this will commend itself even to those people, of whom there are many, who do not think we should have any of these people. I believe this to be about the right level. We shall keep it under scrutiny because it is meant to meet a particular level, and that is the level of principal officer.

Amendment negatived.

Clause 10

LIMIT ON PAID LEAVE FOR LOCAL AUTHORITY DUTIES

Mr. Blunkett: I beg to move amendment No. 144, in page 15, line 8, leave out
'it shall be unlawful for the authority to'
and insert 'the authority may'.

Mr. Speaker: It will be convenient to discuss at the same time the following amendments:

No. 145 in line 10, after 'is' insert 'up to or'.

No. 146 in line 12, at end insert
'where any time off is taken in accordance with a scheme made by the authority, and having regard to any guidance which may be issued by the Secretary of State.'.

Mr. Blunkett: There was unanimity in Committee across a wide spectrum of political opinion that the Government needed to think again about what at first appeared to be their vindictive attitude towards the level of remuneration and availability of time off to enable people to undertake council duties.

We are here dealing with the question of time off. We suggest that 26 days should be a minimum—being only half a day a week—rather than being the maximum, which would exclude people from being able to negotiate and agree time off with their employers. This change would allow people to have greater flexibility.

This issue would not have arisen to the extent that it has if we had in prospect a reasonable system of remuneration for council duties. I am aware that discussions are going on to try to find a more satisfactory formula on that front. But we do not have that yet, and we face a situation, which was revealed in Committee, which could lead to senior elected members not being able to undertake basic duties unless they were designated the mayor, the lord mayor or chairman of council, in which case they could have the requisite time off if employed by a local authority. It was mentioned in Committee that we might reach the silly situation where leaders of councils might have to double up in one of those roles to enable them to do their job. None of us wants that to happen. I certainly would not have wanted that to occur when I led a council. Indeed, if it were to happen it would lead us into a model of north American or partly European politics which would be detrimental.

We must accept that the demand here for adequate time in which to do the job is not a threat. It is not a question of elected members beginning to manage authorities or interfering with the role of those whom they employ. It is simply giving them sufficient time in which to formulate and monitor the implementation of policy and to undertake the liaison that is now necessary, even within the restricted bounds of local government. They must be able to do that work in consultation with other agencies and with central Government.

I recall telling the Minister that he and his colleagues would be in an unhappy situation if they had to travel the country meeting elected members who could not get, and certainly could not afford to take, time off to come from the north, Scotland, Wales, the south-west and the midlands to London. The whole attitude appears to be predicated on the experience of people who can pop around the corner to see Ministers, to liaise with civil servants or to take part in local authority association work—which, as everyone agrees, is important. We want people to have time off for such work and also to be remunerated.

Although it is late and there is still a great deal of business to be discussed, I should be interested to hear the Minister's view of whether someone who is prepared to hand his allowances to his employer could be permitted additional time off. In other words, if someone gave up the notion of remuneration and instead passes it to his employer, would he be allowed additional time off to carry out his duties? As the Widdicombe report suggested—and, indeed, as was suggested as long ago as 1964 in the first Maude recommendations—certain senior councillors inevitably must have time off to carry out their functions. Officials in councils are also clear about that need because without political guidance and the ability to liaise with politicians they would be in some difficulty. Of course, it would be nice from one political point of view if active politicians were kept out of the arena of spending time on policy formulation and monitoring, but wearing another hat we would all accept that that would not be right.

It is worth reminding the House that the secretary and solicitor of the county of Kent, one of the largest authorities in Britain, said on leaving that authority that he felt that the politicisation of local government came from attitudes imposed by the centre, not from the activities of elected members seeking to do their duties more effectively.

Mr. McAllion: Will the Minister take into consideration the different circumstances in Scotland? I know that he believes that there is a whole series of gross abuses, with people being paid by one authority to act as full-time councillors in another. I ask him to consider, for example, the Highland region, which covers an area of just under 10,000 square miles. It is the largest region in Scotland with about 40 per cent. of Scotland's land mass.

Someone travelling from Durness, in the north-west of Sutherland, to Inverness, which is the centre of the Highland region, would have a four-hour journey each way. The Bill allows only four hours paid time off per week, so that person could not even attend one meeting at Inverness. The journey from Ardnamurchan peninsula in the Lochaber district to Inverness, which involves the use of ferries, takes about four and a half hours each way, so someone could not even get to the council meeting at Inverness in the time allowed. The journey from Skye to Inverness, which also involves a ferry, takes about three and a half hours each way.

People living in the rural areas of Scotland will be severely affected by the imposition of a maximum of 208 hours paid leave. I hope that the Minister will take that into account and try to be fair to councillors living in remote parts of Scotland. Unless he accepts the amendments he will be discriminating against them. I note that the Scottish Office Minister is on the Front Bench and I hope that he will support the amendments, which have been proposed by COSLA.

Mr. Gummer: The issue to decide is what is a reasonable amount of time off to allow an employee in local government to take part in council activities elsewhere. We have accepted the figure proposed by the Widdicombe committee. The 208 hours referred to in clause 10 equates with the 26-day limit that it proposed. It is about half a day a week. Of course, I know that there is a division in the House, not necessarily between the two sides, but between those of us who believe that local council activity is a part-time, unpaid activity for which certain allowances

[*Mr. Gummer*]

and restricted expenses should be paid, and those who want it to become something quite different. We heard the frank words of the hon. Member for Newham, North-West (Mr. Banks) telling us what he sees local government work to be.

That is a distinction between us and would lead me to take a different view when it comes to what appears a reasonable amount of time off to work on the local council to which one is elected. I believe that this is about the right level. It is difficult for us to fix it, because, obviously, we all have different ways of looking at it and different approaches. However, we can be guided by the committee that was set up to look into the matter and the committee made that recommendation. On that committee was a very distinguished Scottish representative of local government, a man of very considerable worth. That is the figure upon which the committee decided. I believe that that is a reasonable one on which to agree.

I know that the hon. Member for Sheffield, Brightside (Mr. Blunkett) would agree that it is one of those issues that we will differ on because we start from a different view of what local authorities should do. I have a view of the great importance of local authorities, but I see their elected members as playing a rather different role from the hands-on role that the hon. Gentleman believes they should have. We have different views of the role and, perhaps because of that, we have different views on the nature of the remuneration and the like. Therefore, it is not surprising that we disagree about how many days off a year it is reasonable for a public authority to give specifically for that purpose.

I believe that we are best to keep to the individual figure of the Widdicombe committee rather than any figure that we might dream up for ourselves. I know that some people feel that this is a lot to be given in the circumstances of someone who is paid for out of the public purse, but I believe that more or less a reasonable line has been presented by the committee. I suggest to the House that it would be best to keep with this rather than any alternative.

The committee took into account—and the very nature of its composition would make it necessary for it to take into account—all the varied differences throughout the United Kingdom. I recognise that in some parts of the United Kingdom the distances travelled and the time taken are considerable. It is difficult in those circumstances to make a special arrangement, because it is also true in some individual parts of England and Wales as well as in Scotland. It is obviously much more difficult in my constituency for district councillors to travel than it would be if they sat, for example, on some authority in London. With 54 miles of coastline, people obviously have to travel great distances. However, I think, in general, that this is not an unreasonable figure, and we are here supporting the independent recommendation of Widdicombe.

Mr. Blunkett: Clearly, I shall not persuade the Minister tonight. I hope that in the discussions on remuneration he will be willing to be more flexible and reasonable, because otherwise we will end up with a local government service that rests entirely on the rich and the retired, which would not be satisfactory for anyone.

Amendment negatived.

Amendment made: No. 222, in page 15, line 29, leave out subsection (3).—[*Mr Gummer.*]

Clause 11

CONFIDENTIALITY OF STAFF RECORDS

Mr. Blunkett: I beg to move amendment No. 155, in page 15, line 43, leave out 'Subject to subsection (3) below'.

Mr. Speaker: With this it will be convenient to take amendment No. 156, in page 16, line 4, leave out subsection (3) and insert—

'(3) The following information shall be given with respect to the employees of the relevant body:—
    (a) where a relevant body employs staff at a salary of £30,000 or more, that body shall be required to disclose the number of staff paid within each salary band as calculated in accordance with the provisions of paragraph 35(1) of Schedule 6 of the Companies Act 1985.
    (b) the relevant body shall also be required to give information regarding the average number of persons employed by it in the financial year and the average number of persons employed within specified categories as determined by the Head of the Paid Service, in accordance with the provisions of paragraph 56 of Schedule 4 of the Companies Act 1985.'.

Mr. Blunkett: In Committee we were presented with an amendment that was supposed just to tidy up the situation in terms of securing rights for people's privacy. When we examined it, it turned out to be a permissive power for individuals to find out the salary levels of those whom they may suspect of undertaking political activity on salaries above £13,500. We were very concerned about that. We suggested that, while the pay of those categories of employees should always be available to public scrutiny, it was wrong that individual members of a local authority staff should be subjected to his salary level being available to someone who wished to investigate him.

The Companies Bill now before the House offers us a different situation because the Government are determined that those employees earning more than £30,000 should be excluded from the provisions of that measure. Previously that information had to be available so that the public could see the gross number of people who were earning substantial salaries. Those salaries had to be declared. My colleagues who are considering that Bill are arguing not about the individuals, but that the existing powers should be kept.

It being Ten o'clock, further consideration of the Bill stood adjourned.

Ordered,

That, at this day's sitting, the Local Government and Housing Bill may be proceeded with, though opposed, until any hour.—[*Mr. Kenneth Carlisle.*]

As amended (in the Standing Committee), again considered.

Mr. Blunkett: Just for one awful second I thought that something had happened, but then I realised that we were not to be visited.

On 6 June, in the Committee considering the Companies Bill, the Parliamentary Under-Secretary of State for Industry and Consumer Affairs argued that it was wrong for people to be as intrusive as to publish the numbers of those earning more than £30,000. The Minister for Local Government should consider the contradiction that now exists in terms of what is permissible and enforceable for local authorities for public employees, as opposed to those employed in the private sector.

We are not asking for an exact mirror image, but we are asking that the principles should be the same. Although the categories and numbers of employees should be available, the individuals should be protected from the danger of snoopers who, with the most well-meaning intentions, investigate the salaries of their neighbours or those who have irritated them in their locality. We do not believe that when the Government moved the original amendment it was their intention to create such a situation and we would like them to reconsider this matter.

Mr. Gummer: I have a good deal of sympathy with what the hon. Member for Sheffield, Brightside (Mr. Blunkett) said. It was our attempts to restrict a little the material details that are brought forward that led to this discussion in the first place.

The fact that such salary information has been available in the past has meant that the public has been able to see that the activities of the local councils have been proper. As a result of such information being available for study, local councils have uncovered obviously unsuitable arrangements as the figures did not add up when seen by the public.

The problem is that, under clause 11, information about payments gross of any deductions made by an authority to each of its employees remains open to inspection. We have moved in the hon. Gentleman's direction as we did not believe it was right that an individual employee's deductions of one sort or another, which were taken away before the payment was made, should be seen by the public. There is no reason why that should be so.

We believe that it is necessary to keep the gross payments available for inspection. The clause fulfils an undertaking that we gave in April 1988, after consulting the local authority associations and other interested parties, to restore the legal position on public inspection rights to that which everyone had thought it was before a High Court ruling in April 1986. We tried to do what everyone had thought was true until then and which had all-party support. Everyone had accepted that such information was a necessary part of the protection of the public.

I do not think that there is an analogy with companies' accounts because provisions in the Companies Act 1988 relate to information to be shown in their published annual accounts, which authorities already show in a similar form in their published annual accounts. Clause 11 is about what should be made available in the far more detailed accounting records for the purposes of public inspection, for which in companies' audit regimes there is simply no provision. Clearly, no sensible analogy can be drawn in this way.

We believe that clause 11 offers a reasonable balance between safeguarding personal privacy and providing the level of information necessary for proper accountability. However, I have real sympathy with the way in which the hon. Gentleman has presented his points. At the moment I am not convinced that we can change this arrangement without significant difficulty as regards protecting the public purse in local government spending. There are some examples, which it would perhaps be better not to go through in detail, of its having been of use in detecting fraud.

I will give an undertaking to look again to see whether there is any way in which we can achieve that public accountability without having to ask for so much information on individuals to be on public show. I have

great sympathy with the hon. Gentleman on this point. I do not like the circumstances which have made this necessary. At the moment I do not think that we can change it but if I can find a way I shall be happy to do so.

Mr. Blunkett: With that helpful and constructive assurance and referring the Minister to what his colleague said in the Committee on the Companies Bill on 6 June, in column 177, so that there can be discussions behind the scenes, I beg to ask leave to withdraw the amendment.

Amendment, by leave, withdrawn.

Clause 12

VOTING RIGHTS OF MEMBERS OF CERTAIN COMMITTEES: ENGLAND AND WALES

Mr. Michael Jopling (Westmorland and Lonsdale): I beg to move amendment No. 19, in page 17, line 15, at end insert—

'(2A) Nothing in subsection (1) above shall require a person to be treated as a non-voting member of a sub-committee of a relevant authority if—

    (a) the constitution of the sub-committee is governed by an agreement made before the passing of this Act between that authority and one or more other relevant authorities; and

    (b) the person concerned is a member of one of those other relevant authorities.'.

I tabled the amendment because I have been most anxious about the potential effect of clause 12. I believe that taking away voting rights in certain circumstances could amount to a gross unfairness that should be put right. I believe that agreements drawn up by relevant authorities setting up committees or sub-committees involving elected members of other relevant authorities being co-opted on to committees should be upheld under the terms of this Bill.

These agreements—and there are quite a lot of them, I believe—normally exist so that the present authority has available to it local knowledge of a specialised nature or because they refer to property administration following the transfer in the past of real estate between authorities for the convenience of everybody. I believe that the Bill should not encourage or permit such agreements, made in the past in all honour, to be broken and that this House should not, through this Bill, be a party to such possibilities.

I will give the House an example of what I mean. In 1938 a private owner of the bed of Lake Windermere, in my constituency—I think I am right in saying that that private owner was the uncle of our old friend Shirley Williams, who was a Member of the House for a long time —gave the bed of the lake to "the people of Windermere". After this generous gift it was administered by the new owners through the then Windermere urban district council. Then, of course, we came to local government reorganisation in the early 1970s, Windermere urban district council went out of being and the bed of the lake was given to the new authority, South Lakeland district council. That was a satisfactory arrangement.

The gift was conditional upon the lake bed being administered by a sub-committee of South Lakeland district council—the authority's leisure and tourism committee—set up with 24 members, 16 from South Lakeland district council, five from Windermere parish council and three from the Lakes parish council, with the chairman coming from the 16 district council delegates.

[*Mr. Michael Jopling*]

At that point of local government reorganisation, a formal, legalised and witnessed agreement was entered into by the three relevant authorities on 21 April 1975. Since then, all has worked satisfactorily. The agreement approved the transfer of ownership of the bed of Lake Windermere and there was a detailed constitution for the administering sub-committee. All the members of the committee have voting powers.

The trouble is that clause 12 could, in this case, enable the senior authority, South Lakeland district council, to remove the voting rights from those co-opted members of the parish council. Do not forget that we are talking about a gift to the people of Windermere, not to the much wider South Lakeland district council. There are many similar agreements and it would be wrong for such voting rights to be removed by the Bill.

I was most concerned about the situation until today. This morning I received a letter from South Lakeland district council enclosing a copy which was sent to my noble Friend the Minister for Housing, Environment and Countryside, in which Mr. Parkinson, the deputy clerk of the council, informed the Department of the Environment that at a recent meeting the council resolved to make application for exemption under clause 12(4)(g) with regard to the sub-committee.

That means that the council has decided, at a late stage —I do not know whether that had anything to do with my amendment—to seek to allow the co-opted members from the parish council to maintain their voting rights, which is a statesmanlike and welcome move and I congratulate and applaud the council on that.

The problem that caused me to table the amendment has now been resolved, but there are wider problems. That is why I suggest in the amendment that in such circumstances a sub-committee, such as the one that I have described governed by an agreement made before the passing of the Act, should not involve the taking away of voting powers. I believe that that is fair.

I am bound to admit to the House that my main motivation has been settled due to the statesmanlike behaviour and attitude of my council at a late stage. But there could well be a number of similar agreements throughout Britain where, unreasonably and in violation of previous agreements which have been solemnly undertaken, voting rights could be removed which would be a gross unfairness. I hope that when my right hon. Friend the Secretary of State replies he will be able to tell us that my amendment is acceptable to the Government.

The Secretary of State for the Environment (Mr. Nicholas Ridley): Amendment No. 19 would enable councillors of one authority to continue to be co-opted as voting members of a sub-committee of another authority if that sub-committee was established under an agreement made before the passing of the Act.

The practice of one authority being represented on a committee or sub-committee of another is not a new one. One example of such an arrangement that is enshrined in statute is the national parks committees, for which we provided a specific exemption in the Bill. Where local authorities make such arrangements on a non-statutory basis, as in the case cited by my right hon. Friend, it is usually by establishing a joint committee. Elected members from the constituent authorities of such committees would not be affected by the voting restrictions in the Bill.

10.15 pm

Where current arrangements provide for the co-option of members of one authority to a committee or sub-committee of another, normally it should not be difficult for the authorities concerned to alter those arrangements to provide for the relevant functions to be undertaken by a joint committee. Where for some special reason that course does not prove possible I will be prepared to consider granting a special exemption by way of regulations under clause 12(4)(h).

I do not think that there are a large number of cases similar to the special one my right hon. Friend cites, where the bed of Lake Windermere was granted to the citizens by a kind benefactor. As I said in my letter to my right hon. Friend, it is still open to South Lakeland district council to form a joint committee with the two parish councils. However, I accept that there may be special circumstances making that difficult, because of the unusual nature of the agreement under which the existing sub-committee was established and if no other acceptable solution can be found we shall be prepared to provide that special exemption in the regulations under clause 12(4)(g). It is under that provision that I heard tonight for the first time that the council proposes to make an arrangement to let itself through the net, as it were—and I confirm that I shall be happy to sanction that in the regulations when they are drafted, which effectively meets my right hon. Friend's point.

Clause 12 is drafted wide enough to meet any similar, rather unusual situations of the kind that my right hon. Friend described. I shall be very surprised if any genuine committees of that kind could not use one of the ways through to preserve its voting rights, which are in no way designed to disturb a situation such as that mentioned by my right hon. Friend. In the light of that solution to my right hon. Friend's particular problem and of my general assurance that the Bill is wide enough to deal with unspecified but similar cases, I hope that my right hon. Friend will withdraw his amendment.

Mr. Jopling: I am most grateful to my right hon. Friend for that full explanation of the Government's attitude. My only concern is that other authorities may not take the statesmanlike attitude adopted by the South Lakeland district council and will say, "This seems a good opportunity to disfranchise those people to whom we previously, under a solemn agreement, gave voting rights." I hope that such cases do not arise. I know of no others, and as that is so it would be churlish of me to persist with my amendment. As my particular problem is solved, and as my right hon. Friend has added to the letter I received by saying that he is prepared to allow South Lakeland district council to do what it has asked, which is very welcome news, I beg to ask leave to withdraw the amendment.

Amendment, by leave, withdrawn.

Clause 13

VOTING RIGHTS OF MEMBERS OF CERTAIN COMMITTEES:
SCOTLAND

Mr. Charles Kennedy (Ross, Cromarty and Skye): I beg
to move amendment No. 20, in page 20, line 5, at end
insert—

'(aa) a committee appointed under section 57(1) of the
Local Government (Scotland) Act 1973 at least
two-thirds of the members of which are members of the
appointing authority and the other members of which
are members of another relevant authority;'.

Mr. Speaker: With this it will be convenient to take
amendment No. 21, in page 20, line 14, at end insert—

'(dd) a committee appointed under section 57(1) of the
Local Government (Scotland) Act 1973 by the
Highland Regional Council to discharge functions of a
general planning authority, at least two-thirds of the
members of which are members of the Highland
Regional Council and the other members of which are
members of a district council within Highland Region;'.

Mr. Kennedy: The amendments propose the insertion
of two new subsections in clause 13.

The background to this specific aspect of the legislation
is that the Government's proposals are being applied to a
situation which is unique to the Highland region. Clause
13 will, with some exceptions, deny a vote to members of
sub-committees, other than the elected members of the
parent council involved.

I see that the Parliamentary Under-Secretary of State
for Scotland is present. I shall take a moment to put on
record the anxiety which this has provoked within the
Highlands of Scotland in local government circles, both at
regional and, particu-larly, district level. If the proposal
remains unamended when the legislation passes on to the
statute book, it will strike directly at the continued
operation of a divisional planning committee system
within the Highland region.

Following local government reorganisation after the
Local Government (Scotland) Act 1973, the district
councils in the Highland region, Dumfries and Galloway
and the Borders, were denied the local planning functions
of that Act. The district councils involved have always
found that unsatisfactory and, in an ideal world, would
like those functions to be devolved to them on a wholescale
basis. However, we are not dealing with that this evening.

The Highland region district councils are, in effect,
sub-committees of the regional council's planning
committee and are comprised of regional and district
councillors, all of whom are entitled to vote on the various
planning matters which come before the divisional
committees. Not all the district councils are satisfied with
that status quo. However, within the geography of the
Highland region that is better than the obvious alternative,
which would be for all planning matters, from the most
insignificant to the major, to be handled at regional level.
Therefore, in many cases, regional councillors would have
to make decisions about comparatively small, local
planning matters from which they may be extremely far
removed.

As we heard in an earlier debate on a different subject,
the land mass of the Highland regional council is colossal
and it would not make local planning sense for regional
councillors alone to adjudicate on extremely local
planning issues. It would not be sensible to expect regional
councillors, either in isolation or with a number of

colleagues from perhaps south-west Lochaber, to know
whether to grant permission to erect a bed-and-breakfast
sign in north-east Caithness. That was why there was a
hybrid divisional planning function, which has managed
to marry together the two remits involved. One of those is
that the regional tier has the ultimate planning authority
and legitimacy, but the district tier is wholly involved and
therefore councillors on district councils are able to exert
influence and have a direct vote on issues in their own
locality.

What will the position be as a result of clause 13? The
local authorities in the Highlands would wish for a
complete exemption of their divisional planning committee system from the operations of clause 13. As the Scottish
Office Minister will be aware, there have been discussions
between the Convention of Scottish Local Authorities, the
Highland region, Inverness district, representing the
various districts in the Highlands, and his own
Department.

I understand that the matter was considered too
complex to be dealt with by amendment at this stage. In
saying that, I may be anticipating part of the Minister's
response to my remarks. I gather, however, that Scottish
Office Ministers are not themselves opposed to such an
arrangement, at least in principle. There may be more
serious resistance from within the Department of the
Environment, but I hope that both the present Secretary of
State for Scotland and his immediate predecessor—and I
see that a former Secretary of State is present—will be able
to reassure the Department of the Environment that an
exemption of this type within the specific geographical
context—the contours perhaps—of Highland regional
councils would not strike at any serious principle
underlying the legislation.

I understand that Scottish Office officials have
suggested that the problem for district councils might be
overcome through the use of powers under section 56(1) of
the Local Government (Scotland) Act 1973. The districts,
however, do not accept that that would be a reasonable
course, and have therefore come up with what they
consider appropriate alternatives, the spirit of which—
along with some of the substance—is contained in these
amendments.

If district councillors are disfranchised in their planning
function in the area covered by Highland region, serious
difficulties will be created. That would be a retrograde and
impractical step, causing problems in the administration of
the bulk of planning detail within the various district
councils which together make up Highland region. To
deny district council representatives a vote in that way
would be to deny the areas that they represent and the
communities from which they come a sense of belonging
and of being slotted into what is frequently, on a
day-to-day basis, one of the most lively, controversial and
—in terms of public interest—engaging aspects of the local
government function: the debate that arises as a result of
planning applications and opposition to them.

On a number of occasions—in particular following the
publication of the Stoddart report—Inverness and Ross
and Cromarty districts sought a review of the allocation of
planning powers within Highland region. At that time the
present Secretary of State for Scotland, then Minister of
State, felt unable to support their request. Nevertheless, I
hope that, if he is unable to achieve that kind of recasting,
the Minister will concede that to pass the clause
unamended would be a backward step. Far from being a

[*Mr. Kennedy*]

further enhancement of district input to the divisional planning function, it would retreat significantly and leave us all with poorer planning procedures and control and with a much poorer democratic say.

I hope that, if he cannot accept the substance of the amendments, the Minister will tell us that the Government will act in accordance with their spirit, perhaps in another place.

10.30 pm

Lord James Douglas-Hamilton: The hon. Member for Ross, Cromarty and Skye (Mr. Kennedy) has described expertly the present position. I do not believe that there is any difference of principle or of purpose between us. The system of regional planning committees, established by the Highland regional council, is very sensible and it has worked extremely well. We see no reason why it should be disrupted. The Stoddart committee, as the hon. Gentleman said, came to the same conclusion, and the Government supported that conclusion.

The amendments are not needed to achieve that aim. Paragraph (e) of subsection (5) of clause 13 provides, in effect, for the exemption of a committee which is established exclusively for the discharge of such functions of a relevant authority as may be prescribed by regulations. The whole purpose of the provision is to make it possible for particular local committees to be exempted from the effect of clause 13(1). I am confident that my right hon. and learned Friend the Secretary of State will be able to make the requisite regulations. I assure the hon. Gentleman that my right hon. and learned Friend has every intention of doing precisely that.

To make quite sure, I give the hon. Gentleman the undertaking that I shall look carefully at the drafting that will be required. I anticipate no difficulty in that connection, but if any technical problem should emerge I am sure that the correct solution will be to amend the regulation-making power so as to remove it. If such an amendment should prove to be necessary, we shall table it at a later stage. With that assurance, I hope that the hon. Gentleman will concede that the amendments would serve no purpose that we do not already intend to achieve.

Mr. Kennedy: It is not often, particularly in Scottish politics, that an Opposition Member can wholeheartedly thank a Scottish Office Minister for a speech. However, I do so on this occasion. I found the Minister's speech constructive and reasonable. It offers the type of commitments with a view to the future stages of the Bill that we seek.

On behalf of the local authorities and my parliamentary colleagues who have brought the matter to the attention of the Minister and his Department's officials, may I take this opportunity to thank him for his extremely welcome speech and for the positive way in which the Government have responded to our request. [*Interruption.*] I hear some hon. Members saying, "Check it tomorrow." With that final proviso, I beg to ask leave to withdraw the amendment.

Amendment, by leave, withdrawn.

Schedule 1

POLITICAL BALANCE ON LOCAL AUTHORITY COMMITTEES ETC.

Amendments made: No. 237, in page 134, line 39, leave out from 'is' to end of line 41 and insert '—

(a) a joint board within the meaning of section 235(1) of the Local Government (Scotland) Act 1973;

(b) a board or committee appointed by one or more relevant authorities in exercise of a power conferred by a local enactment, being a board or committee seats on which are required to be filled by the appointment of members of the authority or of those authorities;

(c) a joint committee appointed by two or more relevant authorities under section 57(1)(b) of the Local Government (Scotland) Act 1973.'.

No. 238, in page 135, line 40, leave out 'regional, islands or district council' and insert 'local authority'.—[*Lord James Douglas-Hamilton.*]

Clause 16

EXCEPTIONS TO AND EXTENSIONS OF POLITICAL BALANCE REQUIREMENTS

Mr. Matthew Taylor: I beg to move amendment No. 204, in page 23, line 35, at end insert—

'( ) No party or group representing 10% or more of a nominating body shall be totally excluded from the committee or sub-committee to which nominations are being made.'.

We strongly support the principle that underlies proportionality on committees. That point is dealt with in this clause. To that end we have tabled amendment No. 204. Despite Ministers having made their intentions clear, the Bill does not specifically provide for the protection of minorities. There are some local government politicians who are determined to frustrate the Government by ignoring the spirit of the clause.

The Secretary of State will be aware of the example that I shall use to illustrate my point. It concerns Cambridge city council and Cambridgeshire county council, though it is by no means the only example. In Cambridge there is a joint traffic management sub-committee, consisting of councillors from both councils. This year an arrangement has been reached between the majority city Labour group and the majority county Conservative group to exclude Democrats and to share the 10 seats equally between themselves, despite the fact that we hold seven of the 42 city seats and 10 of the 77 county seats.

A motion was put to the city council supporting the principles that are included in this clause, but Labour and Conservative members united to defeat it. Socialist members claimed that the Bill would not apply to that committee and therefore we seek to amend the Bill.

I hope that the Minister will accept that the amendment would strengthen the Bill because clearly there are those who intend that these provisions should be held in contempt. It is not always the Democrats who are in danger of being squeezed in that way. Other parties in other local authorities are in similar circumstances. It is not a partisan point. Presumably the Minister accepts that, otherwise he would not have produced the provisions in this part of the Bill. Amendment No. 204 seeks to ensure only that the Government's intentions are adhered to. In that spirit, I hope that the Minister will accept the intention of the amendment.

The Parliamentary Under-Secretary of State for the Environment (Mr. David Trippier): I am anxious to respond in the same spirit which has been evinced by the hon. Member for Truro (Mr. Taylor). I am very happy to look at the specific example which he has given the House.

My purpose is to convince the hon. Gentleman that his amendment is unnecessary. The Bill is being considered on Report and the legislation has not been enacted, so it will be interesting to discover whether the example which he cites will be caught by the legislation.

On the amendment which he tabled, simple arithmetic shows that any committee consisting of more than 10 members would be expected to include at least one representative of a party which comprises 10 per cent. or more of council members. Such an individual would be excluded from smaller committees of fewer than 10 members—and the amendment refers to sub-committees.

Mr. Matthew Taylor: The Minister is wrong about that. If there were fewer than 10 committee members, there would still have to be at least one representative of a group that represented 10 per cent. of the council. That group would then be disproportionately represented. Under the amendment at least it would be represented.

Mr. Trippier: I understand the purpose of the hon. Gentleman's amendment. He kindly paid tribute to the fact that the Bill was seeking fairer proportional representation—if I dare use that expression—in terms of membership of committees.

Mr. Tony Banks: I have never fully understood the concern about representation of minority parties on committees such as local authority policy committees. Why are the Opposition not invited to have representation in Cabinet, for example? Why is it that Opposition parties are not represented in Cabinet? Why is it that we have a system in Westminster that totally excludes any Opposition Members on the policy-framing body of Government—the Cabinet—yet we impose it in local government? I do not understand that.

Mr. Trippier: I caution the hon. Gentleman not to press his point too far. If he is suggesting that he or right hon. Members on the Opposition Front Bench would like to be members of the Cabinet or its Committee, given that there is collective responsibility among Ministers, he would have to be prepared to share responsibility for decisions which the Government take. I wonder whether that would be stretching credulity to breaking point. If that is official Labour party policy, let us hear about it, preferably from the Leader of the Opposition. I doubt whether we shall hear much more about it.

Mr. Nicholas Bennett (Pembroke): When I was Conservative leader on a London borough, one of the things which most annoyed me was the fact that we, as the major opposition party, were excluded from the policy committee of the council which actually fixed the rate. The difference between a local authority committee and the Cabinet is that a local authority committee is an executive

committee which can put council policy into practice, without any further discussion. All Cabinet decisions have to be ratified by law through this House. That is a major difference. It is right that all elected councillors should have a say in the policy of the authority before it becomes law in the council.

Mr. Trippier: I do not know how far we are able to stray on this particular point, Mr. Deputy Speaker, before you rule us out of order. The most specific point that I can make to the hon. Member for Newham, North-West (Mr. Banks) is that in local government the whole council is responsible for the executive decisions. In national Government, the Government are a separate executive.

Mr. Soley: I offer the helpful advice to the Minister that the Chancellor of the Exchequer is doing a good job for the Opposition in the Cabinet. I think that he should be encouraged.

Mr. Deputy Speaker (Sir Paul Dean): Order. I hope that we are not going to stray into higher constitutional principles.

Mr. Trippier: I was only going to reply briefly, before you ruled me out of order, Mr. Deputy Speaker, that the greatest advantage we have at the moment is the right hon. Gentleman the Leader of the Opposition, especially in view of the remarks that he made over the weekend.

However, I will now reply to the point raised by the hon. Member for Truro. Main council committees, as the hon. Member for Newham, North-West will agree, normally consist of more than 10 members. The rules at least provide for members from an opposition group to be represented even on very small committees. The amendment would make it difficult or impossible for some councils to set up small committees to deal, for example, with urgent matters. Those of us who have served in local government know that there have to be committees or sub-committees set up for that precise purpose. If, for example, there were two minority groups with more than 10 per cent. of members, such small committees, under the terms of the amendment, would have to consist of at least five councillors from the majority party for them to retain a majority. I suggest to the House that that would be excessively bureaucratic.

I remain unconvinced by the thrust of the amendment. However, having given the undertaking to the hon. Member for Truro that I will look with great interest at the example he gave to see whether it will be caught by the Bill, I hope that he will withdraw the amendment.

Mr. Matthew Taylor: I have listened with care to what the Minister said. Given that he has undertaken to look at the specific example I gave and see whether the difficulties I illustrated are likely to arise, I do not wish to press the amendment. I understand the Minister's concern about the terms of the amendment. I beg to ask leave to withdraw the amendment.

Amendment, by leave, withdrawn.

Clause 17

DUTY TO ADOPT CERTAIN PROCEDURAL STANDING ORDERS

Mr. George Howarth: I beg to move amendment No. 147, in page 24, line 6, after 'State', insert
'subject to subsection (1A) below'.

Mr. Deputy Speaker: With this, it will be convenient to consider amendment No. 148, in page 24, line 13, at end insert—

'(1A) no regulations may be made under this subsection except in circumstances where, in relation to an individual authority, that authority has not, within twelve months of the passing of this Act—

(a) considered proposed revisions to its Standing Orders, having regard to the content of guidance issued by the Secretary of State;

(b) made such revisions to its Standing Orders as it considers reasonable as a result of such consideration.'.

Mr. Howarth: Amendment No. 148 is consequential upon amendment No. 147. We are seeking to amend clause 17, which gives the Secretary of State power to regulate and, subject to such variations as may be authorised by regulation, to impose on local authorities the duty to adopt certain procedural standing orders. The amendment seeks to delay that process, so that if the Secretary of State has issued some suggestion or guidelines about what should be contained within the standing orders of any given local authority or group of local authorities and they do not comply within 12 months, the Secretary of State can make a regulation for them to do so.

The amendment arises because we have argued consistently that too much compulsion is placed on local authorities to do things that, in most cases, are not necessary. Earlier this evening, in a debate on another group of amendments, my hon. Friend the Member for Birmingham, Perry Barr (Mr. Rooker) made the point that local authorities generally were being expected to do many things and to comply with many changes as a result of some Government-perceived abuses by a handful of local authorities, mostly in the London area. To some extent, I agree with my hon. Friend.

As the Minister knows, I served on a local authority for about 14 years and we never moved outside our own standing orders. We had perfectly adequate standing orders with which we complied for the most part. If anybody breached those standing orders, it was pointed out to him and dealt with effectively. From time to time we amended them, as circumstances changed.

There is nothing unique about that. The majority of local authorities have adequate standing orders that enable them properly to carry out the duties and responsibilities of a council. We do not see why the vast bulk of those local authorities should be compelled by the Minister to carry out various changes to their standing orders, as determined by the Minister.

It is particularly rich that this Secretary of State, who spends more time in the courts than almost any Secretary of State in history answering for the irregularities of his Department, should be forcing local authorities to change their standing orders to meet some as yet unspecified regulation that the Government may wish to apply.

10.45 pm

The clause is not necessary but, given that it exists, if the Secretary of State wants to take those powers, why does he not say to the local authorities, "Here are some suggestions. You have 12 months to consider them. If you have not considered them after 12 months, I have reserve powers to do something about it"?

We do not like this compulsion, which is neither necessary for most local authorities, nor useful. It is deeply offensive to the vast bulk of local authorities and I urge the Minister at this stage, if he is serious about wanting to do something, to accept our amendment as it will give him those reserve powers without having to take draconian steps at the beginning of the process rather than waiting 12 months to see what happens.

Mr. Trippier: I should have guessed that the hon. Member for Knowsley, North (Mr. Howarth) would be selected to move the amendment because he is always so nice and reasonable about everything. I am delighted that he referred to his local authority of Knowsley so many times in Committee. It is not very surprising to many Conservative Members that Knowsley has not had much trouble with its model rules as it has only one Conservative member on its council. I do not suppose that he could have done much about the opposition——

Mr. George Howarth: There are four now.

Mr. Trippier: I apologise. It seems that there are now four. We must have won one or two council by-elections since I paid my last official visit there. It is certainly a high percentage increase.

It may well not be necessary to implement and to make statutory the model rules and I shall not be too hard about that point. However, I draw the House's attention to the fact that the Widdicombe committee recommended that the clarification and strengthening of standing orders might take the form of statutory provision. As we explained in the White Paper, "Conduct of Local Authority Business"—it is there for all to see—the Government would prefer voluntary guidance to be prepared by the local authority associations and the relevant Government Departments. That is already in hand. A working party of representatives of Government Departments and the local authority associations is at present preparing revised draft model standing orders. As we explained in the White Paper, we believe it is right to take powers to enable a statutory core of standing orders to be prescribed should that be judged desirable. The Government consider that core standing orders should cover various topics such as—these were discussed at the meetings to which I referred—the right of the minority party to put a matter on the agenda of the council or one of its committees or sub-committees; and provision to give chief officers the right to advise orally or in writing on any matter coming before a council or its committees for decision provisions to limit the powers of councils to suspend their standing orders.

Clause 17 would provide a power to require these on a uniform, national basis. I have looked carefully at the amendment proposed to clause 17 and it seems to me that its general objective is to leave the question of the adoption of standing orders entirely on a voluntary basis. Seemingly that is what the hon. Member for Knowsley, North is suggesting. I hope to convince the hon. Gentleman that we are approaching the matter on that basis but feel it right that there should be a power to enable a statutory core to be prescribed if necessary.

I hope that the amendment will be either withdrawn or rejected.

Amendment negatived.

Clause 17

DUTY TO ADOPT CERTAIN PROCEDURAL STANDING ORDERS

Amendments made: No 114, in page 24, line 13, at end insert—

'(1A) Without prejudice to the generality of subsection (1) above, regulations under this section may require such standing orders as are mentioned in that subsection to contain provision which, notwithstanding any enactment or the decision of any relevant authority or committee or sub-committee of a relevant authority, authorises persons who are members of such an authority, committee or sub-committee—

    (a) to requisition meetings of the authority or of any of their committees or sub-committees;

    (b) to require a decision of a committee or sub-committee of the authority to be referred to and reviewed by the authority themselves or by a committee of the authority;

    (c) to require that a vote with respect to a matter falling to be decided by the authority or by any of their committees or sub-committees is to be taken in a particular manner.'.

No. 115, in line 17, leave out from 'appropriate' to end of line 20.

No. 235, in line 25, leave out 'regional, islands or district council' and insert 'local authority'.—[*Mr. Gummer.*]

Clause 18

INTERPRETATION OF PART I

Amendments made: No. 236, in page 25, line 9, leave out 'or joint committee'.

No. 126, in line 13, after 'omissions;', insert—
'"proper officer"—

    (a) in relation to a local authority in England and Wales, has the same meaning as in the Local Government Act 1972; and

    (b) in relation to a local authority in Scotland, has the same meaning as in the Local Government (Scotland) Act 1973;'.—[*Mr. Gummer.*]

New Clause 23A

EXPENSES OF COMMISSIONS FOR LOCAL ADMINISTRATION

' .—(1) The following provisions shall be substituted for paragraphs 6 to 11 of Schedule 4 to the Local Government Act 1974—

"*Expenses of the Commissions*

6.—(1) Each of the Commissions shall be treated as if they were a specified body for the purposes of sections 78 and 79 (revenue support grant) of the Local Government Finance Act 1988 ("the 1988 Act"), and those sections shall accordingly have effect with the following modifications.

(2) Before making a determination under section 78 of the 1988 Act, the Secretary of State shall, except in the case mentioned in paragraph 8 below, take into account estimates of the expenses of each Commission together with any observations thereon made and submitted to him in accordance with paragraph 7 below.

(3) The Secretary of State may also take into account any other information available to him as to the expenses of the Commissions, whatever its source.

(4) A determination under section 78 of the 1988 Act shall not be invalid merely because the requirements of paragraph 7 below were not complied with.

(5) For the purposes of section 78(7) of the 1988 Act, each Commission shall be treated as if they were also a notifiable authority.

7.—(1) Each Commission shall prepare an estimate of the expenses which they will incur in the forthcoming financial year with a view to submitting it to the Secretary of State.

(2) Each Commission shall send copies of the estimate to such representatives of local government as the Secretary of State directs for consideration by those representatives.

(3) Any observations by those representatives shall be submitted to the Commission within one month of the receipt of the Commission's estimate, and it shall be the duty of the Commission to take any such observations into consideration before submitting their estimate of their expenses to the Secretary of State.

(4) Each Commission shall, not later than such date in any year as the Secretary of State specifies in writing to the Commission, submit their estimate of their expenses for the forthcoming financial year to the Secretary of State together with copies of all observations made under this paragraph by the representatives of local government or, if none were made, together with a statement of that fact.

8. Where a Commission fail to submit an estimate of their expenses for the forthcoming financial year under paragraph 7 above, the Secretary of State may, for the purposes of a determination under section 78 of the 1988 Act, assume those expenses to be such as he sees fit."

(2) Any thing done before the passing of this Act which corresponds to a thing authorised or required to be done by any provision of the paragraphs 6(2) and (3), 7 and 8 substituted by subsection (1) above and done for the purposes of sections 78 and 79 of the Local Government Finance Act 1988 shall be treated as validly done under that provision and those sections shall have effect accordingly.

(3) The foregoing provisions shall have effect for the financial years beginning on or after 1st April 1990.'.—[*Mrs. Virginia Bottomley.*]

Brought up, and read the First time.

The Parliamentary Under-Secretary of State for the Environment (Mrs. Virginia Bottomley): I beg to move, That the clause be read a Second time.

Mr. Deputy Speaker (Sir Paul Dean): It will be convenient to consider at the same time Government amendment No. 119.

Mrs. Bottomley: The Government have tabled four new clauses to part II which completes the package of reforms to the local ombudsman service outlined in the White Paper in response to the Widdicombe report. All these have the aim of making the local ombudsman more effective and efficient.

In Committee, measures were debated to improve compliance with the recommendations of the report. We now seek to introduce further provisions by means of new clauses 23A, 24 and 26 together with the consequential amendments Nos. 119 to 122 to give effect to the White Paper's outstanding proposals. These concentrate on the administrative details of the service and provide new arrangements for funding the English and Welsh commissions, new consultation arrangements with local authorities and other bodies within jurisdiction, to replace the representative body, an additional power for the commissioners to give advice and guidance on good administrative practice and a power for the Secretary of State to appoint advisory commissioners.

Mr. Soley: We covered this matter in some detail in Committee, so I will not traverse the ground again. At some stage we shall have to examine the functioning of the local authority commissioner because, useful and good though the work is, it is important, as we pointed out in Committee, given that it deals with local government affairs, for saying that local government should have some say in the financing and organising. Nor must we undermine the role of councillors, which was one of the strongest points we made in Committee. I also pointed out then that if the same standards that applied to local authorities were applied to private business we might have better services from private business for customers, and towards the people who work for those businesses. For the moment I will not debate the matter further.

Question put and agreed to.

Clause read a Second time, and added to the Bill.

New Clause 24

ANNUAL REPORTS OF COMMISSIONS: NEW PROVISIONS

' .—(1) The representative body for England and the representative body for Wales designated under section 24 of the Local Government Act 1974 are hereby dissolved and accordingly that section shall cease to have effect.

(2) After section 23 of that Act there shall be inserted the following section—

"*Annual reports for representatives etc.*

23A.—(1) For the financial year ending in 1990 and for each subsequent financial year, each of the Commissions shall prepare a general report on the discharge of their functions and shall submit it—

(a) to such persons as appear to the Commission to represent authorities in England or, as the case may be, authorities in Wales to which this Part of this Act applies, and

(b) in the case of such authorities as are not so represented, to those authorities.

(2) The report shall be submitted as soon as may be after the Commission has received the reports for the year from Local Commissioners under section 23(11) above, and each Commission shall submit copies of those reports, together with their own report.

(3) Each Commission shall arrange for the publication of the report submitted by them under subsection (1) above and of the reports of which copies are submitted by them under subsection (2) above.

(4) Before arranging for the publication of a report under subsection (3) above the Commission concerned shall give a reasonable opportunity for the representative persons and authorities to whom the report was submitted to comment on it.

(5) Without prejudice to the generality of subsection (4) above, comments made by the representative persons and authorities by virtue of that subsection may relate to particular classes of authorities to which this Part of this Act applies.

(6) Where the Commission for Local Administration in Wales consist of only one Local Commissioner, section 23(11) above and subsection (2) above shall have effect with the necessary modifications.".'—*[Mrs. Virginia Bottomley.]*

Brought up, read the First and Second time, and added to the Bill.

ADVICE AND GUIDANCE BY COMMISSIONS FOR LOCAL ADMINISTRATION AND SCOTTISH COMMISSIONER

' .—(1) In section 23 of the Local Government Act 1974 (appointment and functions of Commissions for Local Administration) there shall be inserted, after subsection (12), the following subsections—

"(12A) Each of the Commissions may, after consultation with the representative persons and authorities concerned, provide to the authorities or any of the authorities to which this Part of this Act applies such advice and guidance about good administrative practice as appears to the Commission to be appropriate and may arrange for it to be published for the information of the public.

(12B) The representative persons and authorities concerned are—

(a) for the purposes of subsection (12) above, such persons appearing to the Commission to represent authorities in England or, as the case may be, authorities in Wales to which this Part of this Act applies, and in the case of such authorities as are not so represented, those authorities; and

(b) for the purposes of subsection (12A) above, such of those persons and authorities as the Commission think appropriate."

(2) In section 21 of the Local Government (Scotland) Act 1975 (appointment and functions of Commissioner for Local Administration in Scotland) there shall be inserted, after subsection (4), the following subsection—

"(4A) The Commissioner may, after consultation with such associations of local authorities as appear to him to be appropriate, provide to the authorities to which this Part of this Act applies such advice and guidance about good administrative practice as appears to him to be appropriate and may arrange for it to be published for the information of the public.".'.—*[Mrs. Virginia Bottomley.]*

Brought up, read the First and Second time, and added to the Bill.

New Clause 26

ADVISORY COMMISSIONERS

' .—(1) Section 23 of the Local Government Act 1974 (constitution and functions of Commissions for Local Administration) shall have effect with the amendments specified in subsections (2) to (4) below.

(2) In subsection (1), at the end, there shall be added the words "but each of the Commissions may include persons appointed to act as advisers, not exceeding the number appointed to conduct investigations."

(3) In subsection (3), after the words "Parliamentary Commissioner" there shall be inserted the words "or an advisory member".

(4) In subsections (4), (5) and (6) the word "Local" shall be omitted.

(5) In Schedule 4 to the said Act, in paragraph 3 (remuneration), at the end there shall be inserted the following sub-paragraph—*[Mrs. Virginia Bottomley.]*

Brought up, read the First and Second time, and added to the Bill.

New Clause 15

POWER OF LOCAL COMMISSIONER TO SEEK COSTS AND DAMAGES

'Where a local authority fails to take action to remedy the injustice to the person aggrieved and to prevent similar injustice being caused in the future the local commissioner shall have the power to institute legal proceedings against the local authority on behalf of the complainant who has suffered injustice and to seek from the court damages and the recovery of any costs involved in both the initial investigation and any subsequent proceedings.'—*[Mr. Nicholas Bennett.]*

Brought up, and read the First time.

Mr. Nicholas Bennett: I beg to move, That the Clause be read a Second time.

The purpose of this new clause is to ensure that if a local authority ignores the findings of the ombudsman where a case of injustice has taken place, the local ombudsman should have the power to institute legal proceedings against the local authority on behalf of the complainant who has suffered injustice, and seek from the court damages and the recovery of any costs involved in both the initial investigation and any subsequent proceedings.

The new clause arises out of an intervention that I made on Second Reading and from subsequent correspondence with the Minister of State concerning the case of Mr. and Mrs. Quinn, constituents of mine who used to own a property in Coventry. When they wanted to sell the lease of a fashion store which they owned there for £37,300, the Coventry city council insisted on buying it for £20,000, although my constituent had a buyer at £17,300 more. Later the council sold the same property for £51,000 and the ombudsman ruled that the city council had been guilty of maladministration and had lost my constituents £17,300. Two ombudsman reports found the city council guilty, yet it refused to act. Its leader, Mr. Jim Cunningham, said that although the Minister had said that he might have to change the law to force recalcitrant councils to abide by the rulings of ombudsmen, it would not alter its decision. I understand that the Government have taken no subsequent action.

I draw my right hon. Friend's attention to a leading article in the *Coventry Evening Press*, which said that the council had been found guilty for a second time of

"a spivish piece of sharp practice . . . By cocking another snook at the Ombudsman's findings the council has shown itself markedly unfit to criticise the worst excesses of private enterprise sanctioned under the Thatcherism it claims to despise."

I do not agree with that last comment, but if local authorities continue to ignore the findings of the ombudsman he should be given teeth. My new clause would give him the right to bite councils if they cocked a snook.

Mr. Wallace: In general I endorse the aims of the new clause. For local councils wilfully to ignore the recommendations of the ombudsman is a denial of justice, especially for the individual. There should be some authority to enforce a judgment for damages.

I part company with the new clause in that it seeks an award of costs against the local authority for the initial investigation and subsequent proceedings. I would not object to an award of costs incurred by the complainant, but if I were a poll tax payer in a local authority that had been found guilty of maladministration I would think it very rich indeed if I had to cough up for what was essentially a transfer between two public bodies. To seek the award of such costs would be unfair to the poll taxpayers, but for individual rights——

Mr. Nicholas Bennett: Does the hon. Gentleman agree that the generality of taxpayers should not have to pay for the refusal of a particular local authority? If anyone has to pay, it should be the poll tax payers in that local authority, who could then make judgment on that local authority at the next election.

Mr. Wallace: It is a transfer from one public body to another. It would bear much more heavily on individual poll tax payers in a local authority than it would if it were paid for through the generality of taxation. Nevertheless, the extent to which the new clause asserts the importance of individual rights encourages me to vote in favour of it.

Mr. Soley: I do not think that the hon. Member for Pembroke (Mr. Bennett) has any intention of pressing his new clause to a Division, and so he has again misled his

constituent. If he did press it to a Division, he would not only have to vote against his own Government but he would have to consider the possibility of imposing exactly the same conditions for the Government ombudsman. If he did that to his party he would be pulled down to see the Whips, who would box his ears and tell him not to be so silly in future. That is what the Conservative party does to hon. Members who stray from the party line.

There is a case for saying that the views of the ombudsman must seriously be taken into account, and in almost all cases they are. The important point is that the courts exist to be used properly and the electorate is the final judge. If the Government or any Conservative Member were serious about the new clause, they would insist on it applying to the Government ombudsman. There would then be arguments about whether the taxpayers should pay for that.

There is another problem for Conservative Members who support the new clause. One day there might need to be an ombudsman to redress some of the grievances in the private sector, and perhaps—just perhaps—some of those Members would have to pay for that.

Mr. Gummer: I am not sure that the House will feel that that last intervention served much purpose except to divert attention from the seriousness of the case which my hon. Friend the Member for Pembroke (Mr. Bennett) has raised. I am unhappy when a local authority refuses to accept the impartial decision of the ombudsman. It is just as wrong if it is a Conservative authority as it is if it is a Labour authority. That is why in the next few days I am taking action to bring home to a Conservative council near Coventry a similar circumstance. It was not as serious in terms of money and perhaps more excusable in terms of the decision, but it was still a refusal to accept the independent adjudication of the ombudsman.

11 pm

The case that my hon. Friend the Member for Pembroke raises is one which I think nobody but the purblind supporters of a particular circumstance could possibly defend. There is no doubt that Coventry owes this couple £17,500. On two occasions that has been the adjudication. I do not believe that my hon. Friend expressed the case with his usual sharpness because he missed out the important aspect. The local authority sold the property, which it had insisted upon buying, at a price £17,500 less than had been negotiated, to the very people with whom the sale had been negotiated. Therefore, what happened was that my hon. Friend's constituent arranged a sale for his wool shop at £17,500 more than the local authority paid him, only to find that the local authority sold that shop on to the very people to whom it had agreed to sell in the first place. In other words, the matter was clear and significant. It is not surprising, therefore, that the Coventry city council stands condemned by the ombudsman, condemned by its own local paper and I think condemned by any right-thinking person. I am sorry that it has taken that step, because Coventry is a great city which does not deserve such a decision.

I must ask what would happen if I either supported the proposal of my hon. Friend the Member for Pembroke or if I were to find another way of making the decisions of the ombudsman enforceable by law. A large number of authorities are accustomed to solving such problems during the discussions. Labour, Liberal and Conservative

[*Mr. Gummer*]

authorities often realise, part the way through discussions, that on balance they should have made a different decision or dealt with the problem in a different way. Perhaps they still maintain that they were right, but to gain the support of the community they feel that they should handle the matter differently. That happens so often and to such great effect in hon. Members' constituencies, and is for the benefit of their constituencies, that I am loath to move towards the proposals in the new clause. Every time that the local government ombudsman started his discussions he was met with a very legalistic response because the local authority would know that it might end up being forced by law to do something. That is the real issue.

Mr. Soley: The Minister has come round to the point that I suggested he would—it is a nonsense suggestion. His earlier comments, incidentally, were largely creative literature about Coventry, as any reading of the debate in Committee will tell him, but will he bear in mind that his party's councillors supported the Coventry council in Committee?

Mr. Gummer: The hon. Gentleman has already perpetrated that inaccurate statement and he must withdraw it. It was Conservative councillors who brought the issue before the general council, otherwise the council would not have discussed it. The council divided and the Conservatives voted against the decision of the council. The hon. Gentleman is not right and he must not repeat statements that are wrong. He has done it before and he has been shown to be wrong.

Mr. Soley: Is the Minister denying that the Conservative councillors on the committee that dealt with the issue—remember they were the ones who went into detail—approved?

Mr. Gummer: The Conservative party on the council insisted that the matter be brought before the general council when they voted against the council. It is no good trying to ignore what happened. Even if the Conservatives had supported it lock, stock and barrel it was wrong and it should not have happened. Similarly an action by Hinckley and Bosworth, next door to that council, is wrong and should not have happened. That council should also accept what the ombudsman has said.

I hope that the House will note that, throughout this discussion, I have been willing to criticise Conservative as well as Labour councils, but that Opposition Members, as usual, have a partial view of the truth. The Coventry council, whatever party may run it, should not have disobeyed the proposition of the ombudsman. It cheated a small business man of £17,500. It has been found to have cheated on two separate occasions and I am sorry that the citizens of that city have been presented to the outside world in such a manner.

Mr. Nicholas Bennett: Leaving aside the smart Alick remarks of the hon. Member for Hammersmith (Mr. Soley), who is not interested in the case of individual people who have received such treatment, in future will the Department of the Environment——

Mr. O'Brien: This is a charade.

Mr. Bennett: Will the Department consider the progress of ombudsman cases? If the ombudsman's findings are ignored in a succession of cases, will the Department come back to this matter?

Mr. Gummer: First, I want to answer the hon. Member for Normanton (Mr. O'Brien) who spoke about a charade. Before the hon. Gentleman shouts out what he does not understand, he should know that I have spent a great deal of time trying to find a way to make Coventry and other councils accept the law. I have found that there is an easy way to do that, but that that carries a disadvantage that is greater than the advantage. If Opposition Members think that this is a charade, they do not appreciate how seriously we judge when someone is cheated out of money by a public authority. What is even more serious is that an hon. Member of this House should say that such action was wrong. Does the hon. Member for Normanton think that it was wrong for the council to deny the ombudsman's report?

Mr. O'Brien: The charade refers to the hon. Member for Pembroke (Mr. Bennett) who has no intention of pressing the new clause—we knew that from the start. He is being unfair to his constituents and his actions constitute a charade.

Mr. Gummer: I repeat the question—was it wrong to cheat that family of £17,500?

Mr. Soley *rose——*

Mr. Gummer: I want the hon. Member for Normanton to tell me whether the council was wrong.

Mr. O'Brien: This is a night of charades.

Mr. Gummer: Once again the hon. Gentleman refuses to say that he believes that the council was wrong.

Mr. Soley *rose——*

Mr. Gummer: No, I shall not give way as the hon. Gentleman has had every opportunity to make his case.

The House can make a distinction between those on the Conservative Benches who have publicly admitted that the actions of a Conservative council were wrong—as well as those of a Labour council—and the actions of Opposition Members who, when challenged to say whether it was right to cheat someone of £17,500, were not prepared to admit it.

I am sorry that I cannot support my hon. Friend the Member for Pembroke, but I believe that there are good reasons for not doing so.

Mr. Nicholas Bennett: I have listened with care to the arguments put forward by my right hon. Friend. I am satisfied that he has put forward strong objections to this new clause and I beg to ask leave to withdraw it. However, I will keep an eye on the situation and if this matter and other matters like it are not resolved I will bring the issue back on a future occasion.

Motion and clause, by leave, withdrawn.

Clause 22

CONSIDERATION OF ADVERSE REPORTS: SCOTLAND

Lord James Douglas-Hamilton: I beg to move amendment No. 230, in page 30, line 32, leave out from 'committee' to end of line 36 and insert

'as is mentioned in section 23(2) of this Act; or
(b) an education committee appointed under section 124 of the Act of 1973;'.

Mr. Deputy Speaker: With this we shall take Government amendments Nos. 231, 239 and 240,

Lord James Douglas-Hamilton: Amendments Nos. 230 and 231 are drafting amendments.

I draw your attention, Mr. Deputy Speaker, to the fact that amendments Nos. 241 and 242, which are not linked with amendments 239 and 240 are identical, and with your leave I will speak to them too.

These amendments are designed to address the rather different Scottish circumstances in terms of arrangements for consultation between central Government and local government. I do not think that I need to go into them in greater detail.

Amendment agreed to.

Amendment made:— No. 231, in page 30, leave out lines 41 to 47 and insert

'a joint committee—
(a) established under section 56 of the Act of 1973 or under paragraph 7 of Schedule 10 or paragraph 6 of Schedule 20 to that Act (local authority, education and social work joint committees); or
(b) referred to in paragraphs (a), (b), or (e) of section 23(2) of this Act (fire, police and local government and teachers' superannuation joint committees).'.
—*[Lord James Douglas-Hamilton.]*

Clause 24

National Code of Local Government Conduct

Mr. Matthew Taylor: I beg to move amendment No. 205, in page 25, line 1, leave out

'for the guidance of members of local authorities'.

Mr. Deputy Speaker: With this we will take amendments Nos. 206, in page 32, line 2, leave out 'recommended'.
and 207, in page 32, line 29, leave out 'guided' and insert 'bound'.

Mr. Taylor: I and my hon. Friends have tabled these amendments because without them, in our view, clause 24 is a worthless piece of bureaucracy designed to do nothing but facilitate the contempt in which many members of both Labour and, particularly, Conservative councils continue to hold the current national code of local government conduct.

As I have said, those councillors—and they are the overwhelming majority from all parties—who are honourable people will naturally accept whatever guidance is given them by the Secretary of State so long as it continues to be in the spirit of the current code. However, if the need is to improve the quality of local government it is not to those people that the Secretary of State needs to be addressing himself. It is to others who do not follow that code in a way that I believe is fitting within local government and who do not accept the guidance contained in the code.

Clearly, Ministers believe that they should follow the code, but when it comes to people such as, for example, the Conservative leader of Kingston council, who, despite having been given several specific opportunities, refuses to endorse the code, we cannot have confidence that they will follow it. Asking such people to be guided by such a code is like asking a kleptomaniac to be guided by the Ten

Commandments. It just will not happen. They clearly do not believe that they should be so guided. They will not be so guided and the Ministers should be doing something about it. Any councillor who is not prepared to be bound by the national code of local government conduct should clearly not be a councillor in the first place.

The amendment is designed to ensure that councillors, when elected and working on local authorities, are so bound. If Ministers genuinely believe that they should follow the code there is no reason for them not to accept these amendments. I hope that the hon. Lady who is to reply will accept that this is about controlling those who are determined, despite holding positions of responsibility, not to be bound by the code unless they have to be. Nothing in the Bill will do anything to affect the conduct of those who are determined not to follow the Minister's wishes and what are my wishes and, I suspect, the wishes of the overwhelming majority of the population.

11.15 pm

Mrs. Virginia Bottomley: I will not disagree with the hon. Gentleman about the importance, the value and indeed the necessity of increasing the code's prominence. That is why we have been busy updating the national code of local government conduct, which will be prescribed by the Secretary of State and approved by Parliament. Councillors will be required, on taking office, to declare that they will abide by the code.

I am not able to accept the hon. Gentleman's amendment because it reflects a misunderstanding of the nature of the code. It is a frame of reference providing broad principles and general guidance to members, but it is not a definitive rule book. It lays down important standards of behaviour, but it deals with matters which, by their nature, are not sufficiently clear-cut to be given statutory force.

The imposition of a requirement of the kind suggested by the hon. Gentleman would require a different approach to the format, style and content of the code and that would risk damaging its value altogether by trying to make it something that it clearly cannot be. To impose the code on members and to alter its advisory status would endanger the acceptability of the code among members and complicate the code.

However, we are strengthening the code, updating it and my right hon. Friend the Secretary of State will prescribe it. In addition, there is the material difference that the local ombudsman, on investigation of a case, will, if he believes that maladministration has resulted from a breach of the national code, be required to name the individual involved unless he believes that it would be unjust to do so.

I hope that the hon. Gentleman agrees that that represents a significant enhancement of the status of the code and will make all involved realise the weight that the Government attach to it.

Mr. Matthew Taylor: I am not satisfied that anything will be done to tackle the abuse of current councillors who say that they do not accept the nature of the code. Simply asking them to agree to be guided by it means little if they do not believe in the principles that it embodies in the first place. Nothing that the Minister has said will do anything to make them follow it.

However, I shall not press the amendment since we are about to debate two amendments which may allow the

[*Mr. Matthew Taylor*]

Minister to modify her position. If she accepts amendment No. 208 it will give the ombudsman the power to take some action against individuals who act in the way that I have suggested. However, I shall come to that matter in a moment. In that respect only, I beg to ask leave to withdraw the amendment.

Amendment, by leave, withdrawn.

Amendments made: No. 239, in page 32, line 8, after 'consult', insert—

'(a) as respects England and Wales'.

No. 240, in page 32, line 8, after 'government', insert 'and

(b) as respects Scotland, such associations of local authorities'.—[*Lord James Douglas-Hamilton.*]

Clause 25

ANONYMITY IN REPORTS ON INVESTIGATIONS

Mr. Matthew Taylor: I beg to move amendment No. 208, in page 33, line 15, at end insert
'where the local commissioner is of the opinion that the maladministration or breach of the National Code of Local Government Conduct is of a serious nature he may recommend to the Secretary of State that the member be barred from office for an appropriate period'.

Mr. Deputy Speaker: With this it will be convenient to take amendment No. 209, in page 33, line 30, at end insert
'where the local commissioner is of the opinion that the maladministration or breach of the National Code of Local Government Conduct is of a serious nature he may recommend to the Secretary of State that the member be barred from office for an appropriate period'.

Mr. Taylor: I mentioned these amendments a second ago when I noticed that the Minister had a quick look at what was coming. Perhaps she forgot to mention earlier that she had decided to accept these amendments, so that we need not be concerned about the previous group—at least, I hope so.

These amendments follow logically from the argument that I have just presented. It is clear that if the national code of local government is to be effective, there must be some sanction on local councillors.

The Minister has already said that she does not believe that people should be bound by law to follow the code of conduct. However, the amendments would give the local commisioner the power to take action where there were serious breaches of the code by offences which in his view made the perpetrators unfit to hold office. In that way we would give the local commissioner some teeth so that the public and other councillors could see that justice was being done.

I hope that it would never be necessary for such powers to be exercised because councillors seeing that such powers existed would follow the code rather than simply pledging themselves without feeling constrained to follow it in practice.

The amendment specifically says:
"where the local commissioner is of the opinion that the maladministration or breach of the National Code of Local Government Conduct is of a serious nature he may recommend to the Secretary of State that the member be barred from office for an appropriate period."
Clearly, ultimately, the decision would lie with the Secretary of State, but it would be only after a thorough investigation and only in the most extreme circumstances.

If the Minister believes that councillors should follow the code of conduct, she must believe that ultimately there ought to be some form of sanction against councillors who do not observe it properly. In too many cases the reality is that councillors display a cynicism both to their directorate and to their council. Unless changes are made, not only will the code be ineffective, but the Government will make a mockery of their own attempt to argue that codes of conduct should be observed.

Mr. Soley: I understand the hon. Gentleman's intentions, but they are ill-advised. As I said in Committee, it is always a mistake to attempt to establish structures that override democracy. The hon. Gentleman said that the local electorate are often cynical about councillors. I can tell thim that they are often cynical about Members of Parliament, too. If the hon. Gentleman is prepared to see councillors overridden, he must be prepared to see right hon. and hon. Members overridden by the commissioner for parliamentary business, with the power to say, "This Member has behaved improperly and therefore should be debarred." Ultimately, it is far more critical in defending democracy to ensure that the final say remains with the electorate.

Mr. Wallace: The hon. Gentleman touches on a delicate area. A comparable situation for Members of Parliament is the declaration of a Member's interests. Does he believe that any sanction should attach to a right hon. or hon. Member who fails to comply with that requirement?

Mr. Soley: The House debated that issue earlier, when I remarked that it was wrong to treat councillors differently from Members of Parliament and that there should be broad but similar guidelines covering all elected representatives. There is a proper debate to be had about the extent to which such a person should be allowed to participate and vote in a debate in which he has a personal interest. The point was made in an earlier debate—and I am not being critical of the hon. Member for Orkney and Shetland (Mr. Wallace) for not being present in the Chamber at the time—that there should be similar rules for right hon. and hon. Members as there are for councillors.

I am making the more fundamental point that if one believes in the primacy of the electorate, one must let them decide for themselves—even though I am the first to agree that, at times, they are cynical about councillors and Members of Parliament.

The danger in the last group of amendments from the hon. Member for Pembroke (Mr. Bennett) was that, under them, the local authority ombudsman could have debarred many of the Coventry city councillors, both Labour and Conservative. Despite what was said by the Minister—and the word "cheats" was used—anyone who reads the details of the Coventry case, which was incredibly complex and endured for many months, and in which there were two sides to the argument, will be aware that if the local authority had followed the ombudsman's recommendations the councillors might have been surcharged. One can imagine the problem that would have arisen if the ombudsman had had the right to disbar them from office. We cannot go down that road, which poses a danger to parliamentary and local democracy. Although the amendments are well intentioned, the end result would be a form of executive decision-making that overrode elected members—and that would be undesirable.

Mrs. Virginia Bottomley: I agree with the hon. Member for Hammersmith (Mr. Soley) that the amendments are well intentioned. We are united in wanting to ensure that the national code is widely regarded and highly respected, and is observed. The hon. Member for Truro (Mr. Taylor) hopes that it will never be necessary for my right hon. Friend the Secretary of State for the Environment to take certain steps. As matters stand it would be impossible for him to do so, because he does not have the power to bar a local authority member from office.

The Register of Members' Interests has already been debated, but the national code is a different issue concerning more general conduct and the way in which local government members should behave and discharge their responsibilities—which is much harder to enforce strictly, by statute. However, the measures already outlined for identifying a particular member who was in breach of the code which had led to maladministration will have a dramatic effect.

The hon. Member for Truro questioned whether we had a cynicism towards local councils and the electorate. We have a great deal of confidence in local councils and the electorate. Once a member has been identified as having breached the code, giving rise to maladministration, I have confidence that councils and the electorate will take the necessary steps.

Mr. Matthew Taylor: When I am told that my amendments are well intentioned I know that the Liberal party still survives within the Social and Liberal Democrats. I listened to what the Minister said and hope that she will be proved right in practice.

I beg to ask leave to withdraw the amendment.

Amendment, by leave, withdrawn.

Clause 27

RESTRICTIONS ON PROMOTION OF ECONOMIC DEVELOPMENT

Mr. Battle: I beg to move amendment No. 248, in page 34, line 41, at beginning insert
'Subject to subsection (2A) below'.

Mr. Deputy Speaker: With this it will be convenient to take the following amendments:

No. 249, in page 34, line 41, at beginning insert
'Subject to subsection (3A) below'.

No. 250, in page 35, line 1, after 'above', insert
'but subject to subsection (2A) below'.

No. 251, in page 35, line 1, after 'above', insert
'but subject to subsection (3A) below'.

No. 252, in page 35, line 7, at end insert—

'(2A) No Regulations made under subsections (1) or (2) above shall operate to prevent a relevant authority which does not have assisted area or aid status for exercising its power to provide financial assistance by way of grants, loans or guarantees under section 26(2) above, or otherwise to create any restriction which would have a differential effect on the exercise of such powers for those purposes as between authorities in different areas.'.

No. 253, in page 35, line 16, at end insert—

'(3A) No Regulations made under subsections (1) or (2) above shall prohibit the exercise by a relevant authority of its powers under section 26(2) in relation to activities

   (a) which fall within the scope of any scheme for the promotion of employment, training or enterprise sponsored by any Department of State; or

   (b) in respect of which the authority receives financial assistance from the European Community.'.

No. 254, in page 35, line 19, at end insert—

'(4A) The Secretary of State shall, within two years of the first date on which any regulations under this section come into effect, undertake a review of the operation of such regulations, and publish the results.

(4B) The Secretary of State shall, as part of the conduct of any review established under subsection (4A) above, consult the local authority associations and such other organisation or individuals concerned with the promotion of local employment and enterprise as appear to him to be concerned.'.

Mr. Battle: We now move on to part III of the Bill which deals with economic development. We welcome the introduction of clause 26 and the introduction of the new economic development powers. We found it surprising that, although one clause introduces the new power, it is followed by another three pages in part III which take away the provisions of the power. The margin note to clause 27 defines them as:

"Restrictions on promotion of economic development."

The restrictions will be left to regulation, and we do not yet know what that will be. To that extent it will be in the hands of the Secretary of State. We should sort it out here and now, on the face of the Bill, and ask whether it is necessary to restrict this power once it has been given. The power seems to be given with one hand and swiftly taken away with the other.

Economic development is not new in local authorities. Certainly, some of them have played a vital role in the analysis of the development of the local economy, and have contributed to it. Before I came to the House I served as a member of Leeds city council which was active in the early 1980s in precisely this way, and we used what provisions we could from the urban programme and other sources.

It is fair to say that Government priority in economic development tends to be focused particularly on travel-to-work areas and areas with assisted status. Under the new regulations, will the power be restricted to those areas? If so, many local authorities will miss out because the designations of those areas and often the industries that cover them cover wide areas that mask real areas of deprivation and areas in need of economic development.

I shall give an example from Yorkshire and Humberside to illustrate my point. Unemployment at the coast in the town of Bridlington stands at 19 per cent. but that is covered by the Bridlington and Driffield travel-to-work area in which the unemployment rate is only 4 per cent. The local problem in Bridlington is disguised because the case is judged simply by the travel-to-work area.

In my own city, Lord Joseph, who represented a part of Leeds, redefined the boundaries of the travel-to-work area. In defining the relationship between Leeds and Bradford, a part of south Leeds, which was one of the poorest parts of the city, was left out of the travel-to-work area for assisted area status purposes. The Pudsey area which was one of the wealthiest parts of Leeds was drawn in under the Bradford assisted area status. Substantial pockets of inner-city deprivation can be masked in that way. In my constituency, Armley is practically an urban village of the kind that grow up around key local industries such as textiles and engineering. Where those industries have been hit hard there are pockets of unemployment.

[Mr. Battle]

The local authorities that engage in economic development are not only in the large cities, but in rural areas where the population may be much smaller. Many rural authorities are involved in such development, through grants and loans to small businesses and the like. Their official statistics, when compared with the figures for densely populated areas such as the large cities, will not show up the local need.

11.30 pm

But value of assistance to local areas ought to be widely recognised. For example, Ashford, Kent—in the over-heated south-east—uses financial powers to relocate badly-sited small businesses. It may need to exercise those powers even more if British Rail's proposals go ahead. Why not? There is no reason for Ashford to be penalised, and no reason for it not have discretion to exercise the new power.

I shall not rehearse our Committee debate; the Minister's response then, however, gave us the impression that we were talking about financial assistance itself rather than the primary power. Our concern is with the power itself; why not leave it with local authorities, and let them choose whether to provide financial assistance?

The Institute of Local Government Studies at Birmingham university recently carried out a survey on the impact of possible geographic restrictions if the new power is applied. Of the 330 authorities that responded, 148—about 40 per cent.—were identified as having no special-area status, and of the authorities providing direct financial assistance nearly half were located in the south-east. Most were in the shire districts, with a moderately sized population; about half were Conservative-controlled and one third Labour-controlled. One conclusion in the report states:

"the findings suggest that the restriction of powers to give financial assistance to businesses to places with special area designation would curtail these activities in a number of highly active authorities, some of which are operating in areas of high unemployment. In addition, a number of authorities which do not offer financial assistance at present are active in other fields of economic development. They may also be prevented from expanding their activities, for example to respond to change in local unemployment rates, if the proposed restrictions are enacted".

It is clear that the regulations could well have that effect, inadvertently or otherwise. We are not in a position to say, because we do not know what will be in them. We do not think that some authorities should be penalised as against others. I repeat that we are not talking about the amount of financial assistance; indeed, the Government have the power to cap such assistance. What we are talking about is the power itself. The power presented in clause 26 is welcome; why can it not be for all?

Mrs. Virginia Bottomley: I welcome the hon. Gentleman's support for the rationalisation of the economic development power in the Bill. As he said, local government has been involved in economic development over the years but has had to use a wide range of measures to justify it. Even section 75 of the Weights and Measures Act 1986, I understand, can be used as a basis for setting up an advice system for consumers, and it is important to give the powers some coherence.

The hon. Gentleman said that much of the Bill is concerned with restrictions and limitations. We believe that that is appropriate. Because of these measures, the hon. Gentleman's constituency and those of many Opposition Front Benchers are likely to benefit more than my constituency or that of my right hon. Friend the Member for Suffolk, Coastal (Mr. Gummer). Consultations are taking place with local authorities on the precise form of the regulations. The hon. Gentleman believes that they should not prevent local authorities giving assistance in grants, loans and guarantees where those authorities do not have assisted area status or otherwise discriminate between authorities. We want to find a way of having regard to the criteria that face different local authority areas and ensuring that they can use the economic development power, especially through loans, grants and guarantees. This would be inappropriate in some of the more privileged areas.

The amendments taken with amendment No. 248 relate to concern about the unnecessary and unhelpful restrictions on the scope of the regulations as they apply to other Government Departments and the European Community. I assure hon. Members that my Department keeps in close touch with all other Government Departments that have an interest in the use of the new power. In that way, we can ensure that the power that we are giving local authorities does not have an adverse effect on those activities in which they are involved at the request or on behalf of other Government Departments.

The amendments mention training. It is important to emphasise that the Government have a strong view about the crucial importance of training in establishing businesses. It is certainly not our intention that the regulations should inhibit that in any way.

Amendment No. 254 provides that, if the regulations cause any difficulty, there will be a requirement to review them within two years. That is unnecessary. We shall continue to examine the effect of the regulations.

I hope that the hon. Member for Leeds, West (Mr. Battle) accepts that there are certain economic development measures that it is appropriate and right to target towards areas of greatest need. We wish to finalise those matters in collaboration and on the basis of discussion with local authority associations. It is important to ensure that those powers operate in conjunction with the provisions of other Government Departments and assistance from the European Community. We shall, of course, continue to examine the operation of these measures and review them accordingly. I hope, therefore, that the hon. Gentleman will not feel it necessary to press his amendment.

Mr. Battle: The Minister referred to other Government Departments—that was an interesting analogy. In providing nationwide support under the enterprise initiative or the enterprise allowance scheme, the Government recognise that if they give an enabling power, they need not impose restrictions. Can I instead suggest that local authorities should determine whether to exercise that power? When talking about the economy, Ministers have referred to level playing fields. I see no reason why we cannot have a level playing field in determining the use of a local authority's economic power.

We are still left with unspecified restrictions. The Government seem to be uncertain about clause 26. They are prepared to introduce it, but it is as though they are feeling their way with a piecemeal introduction because they are not willing to go the whole way in letting local authorities use the power.

This is not a special pleading for my own constituency. Leeds has lost its assisted area status; it has gone to Bradford. The irony is that I am pleading on behalf of many unemployment black spots in the south, such as Thanet and Clacton, and areas such as Selby. These areas could well use the new start up and small business provision. It should be a nationwide power. It ought not to be restricted.

We ought to divide the House and press the Government not to restrict the power. We should prefer it to be available to all local authorities. We cannot live in the hope that unspecified restrictions will be provided in the future, according to circumstances. Every local authority would then have to appeal directly to the Department, according to its own particular circumstances. Either it is a general power or it is not.

Mrs. Virginia Bottomley: The economic development power is an important power. Any question of restriction applies only to grants, loans and guarantees of borrowing to businesses run for profit. All other forms of assistance will be permissible everywhere. All inner urban areas, rural development areas and derelict land clearance areas will be included.

The Government are happy to consider other areas, but it is important to stress that consultations are still taking place to ensure that there are no arbitrary cut-offs. I repeat that it is the provision of financial assistance that will be restricted. Other forms of assistance—training, advice and guidance—will be available throughout the country.

Mr. Battle: Again the Minister has missed the point. I am not talking simply about ITEC training. The key point relates to loans and grants to small businesses. Of course the question is whether a business is being run at a profit. I hope that the Government are concerned that businesses should be run at a profit. It is not a charitable operation; it has to do with economic development.

I should have thought that the Government would be surprised that we are pressing the issue, because we agree with them on that point. However, the Government say that they intend to restrict the power in the case of of some authorities but not in the case of others. The question has nothing to do with the amount of money. It is simply whether any local authority in Britain can exercise that power. I am still not happy with the Minister's reply. Therefore, I shall press the amendment to a Division.

Question put, That the amendment be made:—
The House divided: Ayes 49, Noes 154.

Division No. 238]   **[11.42 pm**

AYES

Abbott, Ms Diane
Banks, Tony *(Newham NW)*
Barnes, Harry *(Derbyshire NE)*
Battle, John
Beith, A. J.
Bermingham, Gerald
Blunkett, David
Brown, Nicholas *(Newcastle E)*
Clay, Bob
Cohen, Harry
Corbett, Robin
Crowther, Stan
Cryer, Bob
Cunliffe, Lawrence
Davis, Terry *(B'ham Hodge H'l)*
Dixon, Don
Foster, Derek
Golding, Mrs Llin
Howarth, George *(Knowsley N)*
Howells, Dr. Kim (Pontypridd)
Illsley, Eric
Ingram, Adam
Kennedy, Charles
Lewis, Terry
Livsey, Richard
Lofthouse, Geoffrey
Loyden, Eddie
McAllion, John
Maxton, John
Meale, Alan
Michael, Alun
Morgan, Rhodri
Murphy, Paul
Nellist, Dave
O'Brien, William
Patchett, Terry
Pike, Peter L.
Prescott, John
Robertson, George
Skinner, Dennis
Smith, C. *(Isl'ton & F'bury)*
Smith, J. P. *(Vale of Glam)*
Soley, Clive
Spearing, Nigel
Taylor, Matthew *(Truro)*
Wallace, James
Welsh, Andrew *(Angus E)*
Welsh, Michael *(Doncaster N)*
Wise, Mrs Audrey

Tellers for the Ayes:
Mr. Frank Haynes and
Mr. Allen McKay

NOES

Aitken, Jonathan
Alison, Rt Hon Michael
Amess, David
Amos, Alan
Arbuthnot, James
Arnold, Jacques *(Gravesham)*
Ashby, David
Atkinson, David
Baker, Nicholas *(Dorset N)*
Baldry, Tony
Bendall, Vivian
Bennett, Nicholas *(Pembroke)*
Bevan, David Gilroy
Boscawen, Hon Robert
Boswell, Tim
Bottomley, Peter
Bottomley, Mrs Virginia
Bowden, Gerald *(Dulwich)*
Brown, Michael *(Brigg & Cl't's)*
Burns, Simon
Carlisle, John, *(Luton N)*
Carrington, Matthew
Carttiss, Michael
Chapman, Sydney
Chope, Christopher
Clark, Dr Michael *(Rochford)*
Clarke, Rt Hon K. *(Rushcliffe)*
Conway, Derek
Coombs, Anthony *(Wyre F'rest)*
Coombs, Simon *(Swindon)*
Cope, Rt Hon John
Couchman, James
Currie, Mrs Edwina
Davies, Q. *(Stamf'd & Spald'g)*
Davis, David *(Boothferry)*
Day, Stephen
Douglas-Hamilton, Lord James
Durant, Tony
Emery, Sir Peter
Fallon, Michael
Favell, Tony
Fishburn, John Dudley
Forman, Nigel
Forsyth, Michael *(Stirling)*
Forth, Eric
Franks, Cecil
Freeman, Roger
French, Douglas
Gale, Roger
Garel-Jones, Tristan
Gill, Christopher
Goodhart, Sir Philip
Greenway, John *(Ryedale)*
Gregory, Conal
Griffiths, Sir Eldon *(Bury St E')*
Griffiths, Peter *(Portsmouth N)*
Grist, Ian
Gummer, Rt Hon John Selwyn
Hague, William
Hamilton, Neil *(Tatton)*
Hargreaves, A. *(B'ham H'll Gr')*
Harris, David
Hayes, Jerry
Heathcoat-Amory, David
Heddle, John
Hicks, Mrs Maureen *(Wolv' NE)*
Hind, Kenneth
Hogg, Hon Douglas *(Gr'th'm)*
Howarth, Alan *(Strat'd-on-A)*
Hughes, Robert G. *(Harrow W)*
Hunt, David *(Wirral W)*
Irvine, Michael
Jack, Michael
Jackson, Robert
Janman, Tim
Jessel, Toby
Jones, Gwilym *(Cardiff N)*
Jones, Robert B *(Herts W)*
Knight, Greg *(Derby North)*
Lightbown, David
Lilley, Peter
Lord, Michael
MacGregor, Rt Hon John
Maclean, David
McLoughlin, Patrick
Maples, John
Miller, Sir Hal
Mitchell, Andrew *(Gedling)*
Mitchell, Sir David
Moss, Malcolm
Moynihan, Hon Colin
Needham, Richard
Nicholls, Patrick
Nicholson, David *(Taunton)*
Nicholson, Emma *(Devon West)*
Norris, Steve
Paice, James
Patnick, Irvine
Patten, Chris *(Bath)*
Pawsey, James
Peacock, Mrs Elizabeth
Porter, Barry *(Wirral S)*
Porter, David *(Waveney)*
Powell, William *(Corby)*
Raffan, Keith
Redwood, John
Renton, Tim
Rhodes James, Robert
Riddick, Graham
Ridley, Rt Hon Nicholas
Ridsdale, Sir Julian
Roberts, Wyn *(Conwy)*
Rowe, Andrew
Sackville, Hon Tom
Shaw, David *(Dover)*
Shaw, Sir Giles *(Pudsey)*
Shephard, Mrs G. *(Norfolk SW)*
Shepherd, Colin *(Hereford)*
Shepherd, Richard *(Aldridge)*
Skeet, Sir Trevor
Smith, Sir Dudley *(Warwick)*
Smith, Tim *(Beaconsfield)*
Soames, Hon Nicholas
Stanbrook, Ivor
Stanley, Rt Hon Sir John
Stern, Michael
Stevens, Lewis
Stewart, Andy *(Sherwood)*
Stradling Thomas, Sir John
Summerson, Hugo

Taylor, Ian *(Esher)*
Taylor, Teddy *(S'end E)*
Temple-Morris, Peter
Thompson, D. *(Calder Valley)*
Thompson, Patrick *(Norwich N)*
Thurnham, Peter
Townend, John *(Bridlington)*
Tracey, Richard
Trippier, David
Twinn, Dr Ian
Viggers, Peter
Waddington, Rt Hon David
Wakeham, Rt Hon John
Waller, Gary

Wardle, Charles *(Bexhill)*
Warren, Kenneth
Watts, John
Wells, Bowen
Wheeler, John
Widdecombe, Ann
Wilkinson, John
Winterton, Nicholas
Wood, Timothy
Young, Sir George *(Acton)*

Tellers for the Noes:
    Mr. Kenneth Carlisle and
    Mr. Stephen Dorrell.

Question accordingly negatived.

Clause 28

GUIDANCE AND CONSULTATION ABOUT PROMOTION OF
ECONOMIC DEVELOPMENT

Mr. Andrew Welsh: I beg to move amendment No. 316, in page 35, line 24, leave out subsection (1).

At 11.53 pm, I will be as brief as possible. The amendment——

Mr. Tony Banks: Take your time, kid.

Mr. Welsh: The amendment seeks to delete subsection 28(1), which will impose a duty on local authorities to seek guidance from the Secretary of State about any expenditure on the promotion of local economic development. The Bill places yet another statutory obligation on local authorities to put themselves into the clutches of the Secretary of State when they simply set about exercising the powers of economic promotion allocated to them.

Local government can, and should be, a significant and knowledgable contributor to local economic regeneration and a prime motivator in encouraging local economic activity.

My fundamental objection is to yet another example of unnecessary central Government interference with duly given local government powers. Clause 28(1) sets out to shackle local government in its attempts to determine the exact nature and requirements of local industrial promotion. As ever, with the anti-local government mob which now runs the United Kingdom's central Government, central Government will determine what will and what can be done by local authorities in such matters. That is yet another clawing back of power from local government to central Government, and is another unnecessary demand on local authorities.

My objection is that I do not believe that central Government is always right in such matters. Local authorities have few enough industrial powers devolved to them and little enough cash to meet their industrial problems. Therefore, it is somewhat unnecessarily heavy-handed of central Government to take these further restrictive powers over duly elected local councils.

Local authorities know the local situation and the industrial development and promotional needs of their local areas in a way that is quite impossible for central Government. That is why they should be allowed full control in getting on with such matters to ensure that there is industrial regeneration and innovation in their areas.

However, the Bill seeks further to stop the scope for such initiatives in the industrial promotion that is at the heart of any new initiatives and developments locally. I

know from first hand the expertise and ability of local authority staff—men and women who understand and who know personally the economic profile of their areas——

Mrs. Virginia Bottomley: I am not entirely clear whether the hon. Gentleman is aware that these measures do not apply to Scotland.

Mr. Welsh: The hon. Lady will have noticed that I have not specifically mentioned Scotland, which I normally do. I am sure that the expertise that I have found at first hand exists also in English local authorities.

Local government should be given the powers and the authority to get on with those activities because local authorities know the local situation.

Mr. Nicholas Bennett: Will the hon. Gentleman give way?

Mr. Welsh: Oh dear.

Mr. Bennett: I am most grateful to the hon. Gentleman for giving way. I simply want to place on the record the fact that we welcome his part in English legislation and hope that we can take part in Scottish legislation.

Mr. Welsh: Well, it is a return match for the interference that the hon. Gentleman has made in my country's legislation. Perhaps I am getting one back, but I hope that I am doing so in a positive and useful way.

Local authorities know best how to promote local industry in their areas because they know the economic needs in a way that central Government cannot. Why should local government officials, under policy guidance from democratically elected local councillors, not be allowed to get on with their work of dealing with the local economic problems without always being hedged in by legislation and by Big Brother in central Government? Legislation has already severely limited the powers and initiative allowed to local people. My fundamental objection is that the Bill worsens rather than improves the situation. Economic development, promoted and encouraged with sensitivity by people with local knowledge and, more importantly, the power to get on with the job, would be a far better objective than that of this part of the Bill.

I do not in any way object to local authorities having a duty to report on their plans in each financial year to ensure that local plans fitted in with the Government's broader strategic economic planning function. That is why my amendment seeks to remove the first subsection only of clause 28. Local authorities have been given little enough freedom of action and few enough resources to create employment and to encourage local enterprise. My amendment would at least free them from one more unnecessary restriction on their powers of action.

Mrs. Virginia Bottomley: Apart from the explanation to the hon. Member for Angus, East (Mr. Welsh) that this provision is not available in Scotland at the moment, I should like to inform him that the Convention of Scottish Local Authorities has welcomed the fact that more time will be allowed for the development of the separate proposals for Scotland. However, judging from the hon. Gentleman's remarks, perhaps he would not like the power to be extended there.

Mr. Maxton: I am also sure that the party of the hon. Member for Angus, East (Mr. Welsh) has little or no influence in COSLA, which is almost entirely dominated by the Labour party.

12 midnight

Mrs. Bottomley: The amendment is unnecessary. The Secretary of State may give guidance under subsection (1). While obviously it will probably be necessary for guidance to be given in the form of circulars at the time of the regulations being enacted, it is not necessarily our intention to issue further specific guidance to local authorities.

If specific guidance were to be made available, it is most likely that it would be aimed at promoting value for money or consistency between central Government and local authority initiatives. In short, it would be only practical assistance which would be helpful and sensible for local authorities to see. They would be required only to take it into account, and, having taken it into account, it would be for them to make up their minds on the matter.

These economic development powers will be helpful and of great benefit to local government, and I therefore hope that the hon. Gentleman will withdraw his amendment.

Mr. Andrew Welsh: As my attempt to be helpful seems to have been somewhat rebuffed by English hon. Members, I beg to ask leave to withdraw the amendment.

Amendment, by leave, withdrawn.

Clause 29

Amendments of existing power to incur discretionary expenditure

Lord James Douglas-Hamilton: I beg to move amendment No. 244, in page 36, line 11, leave out 'this section' and insert
'subsections (2) to (9) below'.

Mr. Deputy Speaker: It will be convenient to discuss at the same time Government amendments Nos. 123, 245, 124 and 246.

Lord James Douglas-Hamilton: The purpose of this series of amendments will be welcome. It is designed to remove an anomaly which came to light as a result of the tragic events at Lockerbie last December. Obviously, tribute has been paid to the magnificent efforts of local authorities, especially but not exclusively the authorities most directly involved.

As part of the wider response, local authorities in England and Wales wish to contribute to the disaster fund that was set up by Dumfries and Galloway regional council, but it was found that the power which local authorities in England and Wales would normally use to make such a contribution—section 137(3) of the Local Government Act 1972—did not extend to cover appeals set up by Scottish local authorities unless the civic head of an English or Welsh authority was associated with the appeal.

The series of amendments rectifies that situation on both sides of the border reciprocally. The effect is that where the civic head of a local authority launches an appeal, any local authority will be able to contribute.

Mr. Maxton: My hon. Friends and I welcome this series of amendments, which will prove extremely useful. I am sure that Scottish local authorities will now wish to contribute towards the Hillsborough fund in the same way that English local authorities wish to contribute to the Lockerbie appeal.

Amendment agreed to.

Amendment made: No. 123, in line 44, at end insert
'and

    (c) at the end of paragraph (c) there shall be added "or by such a person or body as is referred to in section 83(3)(c) of the Local Government (Scotland) Act 1973".'.—[*Lord James Douglas-Hamilton.*]

Sir George Young (Ealing, Acton): I beg to move amendment No. 9 in page 37, leave out lines 28 to 43.

Mr. Deputy Speaker: It will be convenient to discuss at the same time the following amendments: No. 8 in page 37, leave out lines 44 to 48.

No. 282, in Schedule 2, page 139, leave out lines 1 to 21.

Sir George Young: These three amendments which stand in my name enable the House to consider a matter on which the Committee was unable to reach a decision without the casting vote of the Chairman. They deal with the important matter of how voluntary organisations of the metropolitan counties are funded. In a nutshell, the Government wish to remove the section 48 funding power introduced in the Local Government Act 1985.

There are two arguments against what the Government plan to do, one of principle and one of practice. The argument of principle is that it is seen to be in conflict with undertakings given in good faith at the time of abolition which set up a secure funding framework for voluntary organisations in metropolitan counties which covered more than one local authority area.

The argument of practice against what the Government plan to do is that at a time when we are trying to reduce manning in local authorities, the arrangements proposed by the Government would increase manpower in those local authorities that have to scrutinise the voluntary sector and would involve the complex relationships that exist between local authorities as they try to justify their spending under section 137.

The Government argued that abolition of domestic rates gave an opportunity to abolish section 48 and bring the mets into line. They undertook to discuss with the local authorities the practical difficulties that we came across in Committee. In fairness to the Government, they have held discussions with representatives of the voluntary sector to try to find a way through the problem.

Having seen the minutes of those meetings, I remain convinced that it would be right for the Government to abandon the strategy on which they are embarked and to leave section 48 alone as a separate funding power in its own right for the voluntary sector and the metropolitan counties. It would reassure the voluntary sector, which has now established a funding arrangement under the new regime, if the Government said that, on reflection, their strategy is not, perhaps, the best one and that it would be better to leave section 48 as it stands.

Mrs. Virginia Bottomley: The Government have given careful consideration to the points raised in Committee, especially those made by my hon. Friend the Member for Ealing, Acton (Sir G. Young). As he said, section 48 was introduced to help voluntary organisations after the

[*Mrs. Virginia Bottomley*]

abolition of the GLC. Many voluntary organisations were performing an excellent function and it was thought right that they should receive assistance, especially as they were losing the product of the 2p rate from one tier of local authority.

We have now carried out a complete review of the limit on expenditure under section 137. We intend to ensure that spending for which there is no other statutory basis should be achieved on a different assumption—that it should be £5 per head of the adult population. There was great debate in Committee about how the section 137 proposals would work in with the section 48 scheme. There was an anomaly at the time of the abolition of the GLC and in the context of the new regime it was difficult to justify extending the arrangement.

We shall accept my hon. Friend's amendments. We have reconsidered our proposals and agreed upon a better basis. Clause 29(9) is directed at redressing the anomaly. It is a precise provision that states clearly that any expenditure under a section 48 scheme that cannot be attributed to a specific power is to be counted against the section 137 limits of the constituent councils.

As my hon. Friend said, it would impose an unnecessary burden on the schemes if it had to be assessed whether each grant could be justified under powers other than under section 137. It was argued that it would make the construction of the budget—especially in London, with 33 authorities involved—extremely difficult if each had to consider not only the cash required but the impact of individual grants on their own programmes.

As a result of meetings with the staff of the London section 48 scheme and the lead authorities of other schemes, we decided to reconsider the matter. We propose to build on the fact that the section 48 schemes have now settled into fairly regular patterns of spending. My hon. Friend's amendment will remove the special treatment of section 48 expenditure that cannot be referred to any specific power of the authorities. Instead, we shall reduce the limit on expenditure under section 137 for the constituent authorities of the section 48 schemes by an amount approximately equal to their expenditure under section 48, and which, elsewhere in the country, would have to score against the section 137 limit.

We want to discuss further with the authorities concerned the precise amounts involved. We believe that section 48 expenditure—which has made an important contribution to voluntary organisations in the London and other metropolitan areas—as well as the possibility of section 137 expenditure will be safeguarded.

Mr. Soley: We are always grateful for small mercies. It took a near defeat for the Government in Committee to make them reconsider the matter. Indeed, it was only the Chair's casting vote that saved them.

It should be put on the record that not only the former GLC area is affected, but metropolitan areas generally. Indeed, in Committee on the abolition Bill we warned the Government that the voluntary sector would be in some difficulty. The voluntary bodies have been worried and the hon. Member for Ealing, Acton (Sir G. Young) has done them a service. However, I do not think that the amendment goes far enough and if the Government are serious about helping the voluntary sector they will have to go further.

Sir George Young: I was delighted to hear what my hon. Friend said. I know that her words will be welcomed by the voluntary organisations in London and in the other metropolitan counties. Nine minutes past 12 is not the time to engage in a detailed discussion about how the reduction in section 137 will take place. However, I note that she has undertaken to negotiate with the people concerned.

It is right to pay tribute to the work of Ministers, whose commitment to the voluntary sector has never been in doubt. I welcome the fact that they have shown flexibility —which I always knew was there—in coming to the decision to leave section 48 as a funding power in its own right.

Amendment agreed to.

Amendments made: No. 8, in page 37, leave out lines 44 to 48.

No. 245, in page 37, line 48, at end insert—

'(10) In section 83(3) of the Local Government (Scotland) Act 1973 (contributions permitted to charitable and public service funds etc.), at the end of paragraph (c) there shall be added "or by such person or body as is referred to in section 137(3)(c) of the Local Government Act 1972".'.—[*Mr. Gummer.*]

Schedule 2

LOCAL GOVERNMENT ACT 1972, SECTION 137, AS AMENDED

Amendments made: No. 124, in page 137, line 45, at end insert

'or by such a person or body as is referred to in section 83(3)(c) of the Local Government (Scotland) Act 1973'.

No. 282, in page 139, leave out lines 1 to 21.—[*Mr. Gummer.*]

Clause 31

APPLICATION OF PART IV

Amendment made: No. 87, in page 40, leave out line 21.

Clause 33

EXPENDITURE TO BE CHARGED TO REVENUE ACCOUNT

Amendments made: No. 88, in page 42, line 5, at end insert

'and the reference in subsection (5) below to expenditure incurred by a local authority shall be construed in accordance with this subsection'.

No. 89, in page 42, line 11, at end insert—

'(5) Nothing in this section or the following provisions of this Part shall permit an authority to charge to a revenue account which they are required to keep by virtue of Part VI or any other enactment any expenditure incurred by a local authority which could not otherwise be so charged.'.[*Mr. Gummer.*]

Clause 34

EXPENDITURE EXCLUDED FROM SECTION 33(1)

Amendment made: No. 38, in page 43, line 8, at end add—

'(5) Where, by virtue of subsection (1) above, expenditure of any description is excluded from the obligation in section 33(1) above, it shall also be excluded from any requirement arising under any enactment (including an enactment in Part VI of this Act) under which the expenditure is required to be charged to a revenue account or any particular revenue account; but if—

(a) an authority decide that expenditure of that description should be charged to a revenue account as mentioned in subsection (1) above, and

(b) under any such requirement that expenditure (apart from this subsection) would have to be charged to a particular revenue account,

that expenditure may be charged only to that revenue account.'.—*[Mr. Gummer.]*

Clause 40

CREDIT ARRANGEMENTS

Amendment made: No. 90, in page 48, line 20, leave out from 'made' to 'the' in line 22 and insert—

'(a) on the assumption that the option will be exercised or, if the option could be exercised in different ways, on the assumption that it will be exercised in each of those ways, and

(b) on the assumption that the option will not be exercised, and if, on any of those assumptions'. —*[Mr. Gummer.]*

Clause 41

INITIAL AND SUBSEQUENT COST OF CREDIT ARRANGEMENTS

Amendment made: No. 91, in page 49, line 22, at end add—

'(5) In the application of this section to a credit arrangement which consists, in whole or in part, of a contract, the consideration under which falls within subsection (7) of section 40 above,—

(a) if the credit arrangement exists only on the basis of one of the assumptions in that subsection, the local authority shall make that assumption for the purposes of this section; and

(b) if the credit arrangement would exist on the basis of any two or more of those assumptions, the authority shall for the purposes of this section make whichever of those assumptions seems to them most likely.'. —*[Mr. Gummer.]*

Clause 42

LIMITS ON POWERS TO ENTER INTO CREDIT ARRANGEMENTS

Amendments made: No. 92, in page 49, line 42, leave out 'charged to' and insert 'set aside from'.

No. 93, in page 49, line 45, leave out 'charge' and insert 'set aside'—*[Mr. Gummer.]*

Clause 43

VARIATION OF CREDIT ARRANGEMENTS

Amendment made: No. 94, in page 50, line 13, at end insert—

'(1A) If, in the case of a credit arrangement falling within subsection (5) of section 41 above,—

(a) the option in question is exercised in a way different from that which was assumed for the purposes of that section, or

(b) it was assumed for the purposes of that section that the option in question would not be exercised but it is in fact exercised,

the exercise of the option shall be regarded for the purposes of this section as a variation of the terms of the credit arrangement; and if, in such a case, it was assumed for the purposes of section 41 above that the option would be exercised (or would be exercised in a particular way) and it subsequently appears to the local authority that it will not in fact be exercised, the option shall be assumed to have been abandoned and that abandonment shall be regarded for the purposes of this section as a variation of the terms of the credit arrangement.'.—*[Mr. Gummer.]*

Clause 45

BASIC CREDIT APPROVALS

Mr. Tony Banks: I beg to move amendment No. 169, in page 52, line 27, after 'shall', insert
'after consultation with the local authority associations'.

Mr. Deputy Speaker: With this it will be convenient to take amendment No. 170, in clause 47, page 53, line 25, leave out from 'Minister' to end of line 27 and insert
'shall consult the local authority associations on factors to be taken into account'.

Mr. Banks: Amendments Nos. 169 and 170 relate to clauses 45 and 47, which set out the method of controlling local government capital expenditure. Clause 45 states that the Secretary of State shall, before the beginning of each financial year, issue each local authority with a notice setting out a credit approval; that is how much it can borrow by various methods. It states that not only the total amount should be specified, but subsection (4) describes the period over which the various loans must be made.

I am seeking try to infuse into the proposals a little consultation, which the Secretary of State should have with the local authorities, which are so dramatically affected by the proposals. We find it extraordinary that the Secretary of State should consider setting out all the financial expenditure of a local authority without consulting the local authority associations.

Those matters were raised in Committee and we were hoping—indeed, we were expecting—an amendment very much like our own from the Government. In Committee we were led to believe that the Secretary of State would welcome an amendment along those lines, and the Minister for Local Government said so in the course of debate on 6 April 1989 which is reported in columns 696 to 698 of the *Official Report.* If the Minister is not prepared to accept the form of words enshrined in the amendments, will he tell us what form of consultation his proposals will take?

12.15 am

Mr. Gummer: The hon. Member for Newham, North-West (Mr. Banks) has put forward a reasonable case for the circumstances outlined. The problem is that we are discussing a range of matters and it would be difficult to consider that it would be sensible to discuss such matters in general as they must be discussed individually.

My officials often discuss with the local authority associations the methodology of distributing housing investment programme and other services block capital allocations. Indeed, the latter are usually distributed on the basis of recommendations made by the local authority associations. There has also been extensive consultation with the local authority associations on the new system of capital finance. We shall, of course, be continuing this detailed consultation, although I hope that, in future, the working papers will not be referred to as "leaks". In particular, we shall be inviting comments on the regulations to be made under this part of the Bill. But on our past performance no one could doubt our willingness to listen to the views of the local authority associations as that is crucial to what we are doing.

Although a local authority will receive one basic credit approval, that approval will cover several services. It will

[Mr. Gummer]

be compiled from annual capital guidelines for each of those services. So it would not be very productive to hold formal discussions on the total level of basic credit approvals. Discussions should focus on the service by service annual capital guidelines which will be the building blocks of the structure. The best course for representations about credit approvals ought to be to Ministers and officials of the relevant service Department. That is what we seek to do.

There are, and will be, many opportunities open to local authority associations wishing to discuss the size of credit approvals with the appropriate service Departments. Obviously procedures vary from Department to Department, but representations can be made at both ministerial and official level. My colleagues and I will be willing to discuss the volume and methodology for distributing credit approvals with representatives of the associations either in a body such as the Housing Consultative Council or in a meeting specially convened for the purpose.

I am happy to give all those undertakings to the House. It is better to do that than to do so within the terms of a narrow amendment. I am not seeking for the hon. Gentleman to withdraw or not to press his amendments in order to avoid the type of consultations that I have mentioned. The opposite is true: I want them to continue on the broadest possible front. I do not believe that there is any doubt that the local authority associations would believe that we have not sought, and will not continue to seek, discussions and consultations on such matters. Those associations do not always agree with what we have decided, or agree among themselves about what we should have decided. Such is the nature of those discussions.

I hope that, given my undertakings, the hon. Gentleman will find it possible to withdraw his amendment.

Mr. Tony Banks: I accept what the right hon. Gentleman says about being prepared to listen, but the point is whether any action follows, otherwise one is asking local authorities to participate in a facade of consultations. Consultations must mean that there is the real possibility that Ministers and the officials on the other side of the table are open to persuasion.

What bothers me is that we are talking about a multitude of Departments and I am rather concerned about co-ordination between those Departments if the expenditure cannot be discussed and decided upon in one go. However, having entered those caveats and in view of what the Minister has said, I beg to ask leave to withdraw the amendment.

Amendment, by leave, withdrawn.

Clause 47

CRITERIA FOR ISSUING CREDIT APPROVALS

Mr. Tony Banks: I beg to move amendment No. 171, in page 53, line 36, leave out from 'received' to end of line 38.

Mr. Deputy Speaker: With this it will be convenient to discuss amendment No. 172, in page 53, line 40, leave out 'or likely to be received'.

Mr. Banks: Clause 47 sets out the criteria that the Secretary of State shall use when fixing total credit approvals for local authorities. The clause sets out two things to which the Secretary of State should have regard and among other factors they are

"any grants or contributions which it appears to him that the authority concerned have received and are likely to receive" within the year and any capital receipts that the local authority has received or is likely to receive within the year.

The amendments seek to remove from those factors capital receipts as one of the things that the Secretary of State shall take into account when fixing total credit approvals.

I move the amendments more in hope than in expectation.

Mr. Gummer: The hon. Gentleman is on to a good point when he rightly suggests that it is not easy to take into account future receipts and that that is what he wants to restrict.

It is important to reconsider the example I gave in Committee. When an authority has completed the sale of its housing stock and is about to receive the proceeds of the sale and those proceeds greatly exceed the authority's capital programme for several years to come, it would be ridiculous for us to have to ignore that information simply because the totality of the proceeds had not yet reached that authority, but was about to reach it.

One of the purposes is to ensure that we are able to give more capital allocations in accordance with need. Under the present system we are tied to giving capital allocations where there are considerable receipts in any case and people have considerable opportunities to spend. Then, in addition, they get capital allocations, which reduces those available for local authorities in much greater need.

I do not think there is any difference between the two sides of the House on what we are trying to do here. It would be wrong to restrict the Secretary of State's ability to take into account such future receipts as I have indicated. I accept that it is not an easy matter. We shall handle it with very considerable care. We have not yet decided exactly how best to do it, but the case I have quoted is very much the kind of case that we have in mind. There is nothing secret or special behind this proposal. It is merely that we shall be able to have more capital allocations available for those whose needs are not met by their ability to spend from their own capital receipts.

Mr. Banks: A number of problems still arise even given what the Minister has said. Although one can misunderstand what can be read between the lines, perhaps the Minister shares some of my unease about this aspect of the Bill, in particular with regard to how he proposes to find out what future capital receipts a local authority may have and how he proposes to estimate what they might be. There is the matter of the prospects for interest rates. It will be extraordinarily difficult for anyone to say for sure how interest rates will move.

I know that there will be continuing discussions with local authorities and, that being so, I beg to ask leave to withdraw the amendment.

Amendment, by leave, withdrawn.

Clause 49

Capital receipts

Amendments made: No. 95, in page 55, line 5, after 'if', insert
'at the time of disposal'.

No. 224, in page 55, line 25, at end insert
'but, in the case of a disposal made before that date, the reference in paragraph (a) or, as the case may be, paragraph (b) of subsection (1) above to the time of the disposal shall be construed as a reference to 1st April 1990'.

No. 96, in page 55, line 26, at beginning insert
'Subject to subsection (3B) below'.

No. 97, in page 55, line 30, leave out from beginning to 'sums' in line 32 and insert
'are represented in the authority's accounts for the financial year ending immediately before that date either by amounts shown as capital receipts which are unapplied as at the end of that year or by amounts included in the balance as at the end of that year of any fund established by the authority under paragraph 16 of Schedule 13 to the Local Government Act 1972, those'.

No. 98, in page 55, line 35, at end insert—
'(3A) So far as may be necessary for the purposes of this Part, a local authority shall identify which (if any) sums falling within paragraphs (a) and (b) of subsection (3) above are represented by amounts included as mentioned in that subsection in the balance of a fund established as so mentioned.

(3B) Subsection (3) above does not apply to a sum in respect of which an amount shown as an unapplied capital receipt or included in a balance as mentioned in that subsection is, on 1st April 1990, held in an investment which is not on that date an approved investment; and, so far as may be necessary for the purposes of this Part, where on that date a local authority hold investments which are not then approved investments, the authority shall identify which (if any) of the amounts so shown or included are to be treated as held in such investments.'.

No. 117, in page 55, line 48, leave out 'seven days' and insert 'three months'.—*[Mr. Gummer.]*

Clause 50

The reserved part of capital receipts

Mr. Tony Banks: I beg to move amendment No. 178, in page 56, line 24, leave out '75' and insert '20'.

Mr. Deputy Speaker: With this we shall take the following amendments: No. 210, in page 56, line 24, leave out '75' and insert '10'.

No. 179, in page 56, line 25, leave out '50' and insert '20'.

No. 211, in page 56, line 25, leave out '50' and insert '5'.

No. 180, in page 56, line 32, leave out '100' and insert '20'.

Mr. Banks: These amendments relate to one of the most controversial aspects of the Bill, which sets out how the local authority must use its capital receipts, from both the disposal of housing stock and the sale of land.

In the past, as we know, local authorities have been able to use 20 per cent. of the capital receipts for capital works and the remainder for non-prescribed expenditure, or alternatively to use a further 20 per cent. of the remainder in subsequent years towards further prescribed expenditure. It is now proposed that only 25 per cent. of capital receipts from the sale of housing can be used and only 50 per cent. of capital receipts from the sale of land, while the remainder, now called the reserved part, must be applied against debt.

These amendments, which are a mixture of SLD and Labour amendments, seek to look once again at how much should constitute the reserved part and how much freedom the local authority should have in disposing of capital receipts that have come from the sale of what are, after all, assets accumulated by the historic effort of local authorities over many years.

It is the local authority with a mandate from the local people that decides to build houses or acquire land and it is quite absurd that the disposal of those same assets, whether voluntary or forced, should not leave the local authority the freedom to decide what next to do with its own assets.

The Government argue that local authority debt is massive and needs to be controlled, but I remind the Minister that as a proportion of the gross domestic product local authority borrowing fell from 1·4 per cent. in 1980-81 to 1 per cent. in 1985-86 and over the same period long-term local authority debt as a proportion of GDP fell from 15 per cent. to 13 per cent. Loans outstanding as a proportion of gross annual revenue expenditure fell from 135 per cent. in 1980-81 to 117 per cent. in 1986-87. The Government need to bear in mind that in reducing the part of the capital receipts available for use they are reducing the incentive to local authorities to dispose of their assets, and that is obviously contrary to the Government's intentions.

The Under-Secretary of State for the Government, the hon. Member for Rossendale and Darwen (Mr. Trippier), made a number of statements in Committee. In particular, he said:

"We have made it clear that we wish to provide exemptions from in-and-out transactions, which exist in the present system, and we need the regulation-making power to do so."

I hope that the Minister will be a little more clear about that. He undertook to consider whether an amendment would be an appropriate way of achieving that rather than the sweeping powers that he confers upon himself in clause 50(3), (4) and (5). Has he further considered that point? If so, what are his conclusions?

Secondly, the position of a local authority that has no debt is still open to speculation. In Committee the Minister said:

"I accept that we have to consider what might happen when an authority has no debt . . . We are considering that matter carefully . . . We have not ruled out further amendments which would provide alternative solutions."—*[Official Report, Standing Committee G,* 6 April 1989, c. 737-8.]

It is absurd to suggest that a local authority that has no debt must still be forced to set aside 75 per cent. of its capital receipts for future debt which becomes less and less likely to be incurred as its capital receipts accumulate because it is not allowed to use them. What does the Minister for Local Government intend to do about that?

I understand that the Under-Secretary of State for the Environment also gave an undertaking in the same debate in Committee that he would shortly list the capital receipts that would be exempt from the new rules. Can he now honour that undertaking, and, if not now, when will he be in a position to do so?

Opposition to clause 50 is strong. If a local authority is elected with a mandate to build houses, to modernise its school and to build homes for the elderly, and has the means to do so from its own resources, it is abhorrent that the Government should take it upon themselves to override that mandate and say that the local authority cannot use the resources that it has conscientiously built

[*Mr. Banks*]

up over the years to meet those promises. Clearly, the abolition of local government is not far off and one of the accusations that we have levelled against the Government is that they are completely undermining the process of local accountability.

When the European Parliament threatens to overrule the Government, even on such a minor matter as to whether there should be a health warning on the front rather than the side of a cigarette packet, the Government's reaction is one of outrage. They are up in arms threatening a constitutional crisis. But on this important matter—the use of capital receipts for essential projects—the Government seem willing to ride roughshod over the wishes of local people. I hope that the Minister for Local Government will address himself to those points.

Mr. Matthew Taylor: The Minister is eager to respond and I shall not delay him long. I support the hon. Member for Newham, North-West (Mr. Banks). The main difference between the amendments is that ours are more radical in giving local authorities greater freedom to respond to the needs of local people.

The point that I want to reinforce is that there is surely an economic absurdity in the Government's eyes in enforcing the repayment of debt. In many cases local authorities are paying fixed rates of interest as low as 6 per cent. Surely Ministers can see that it is madness to replace low interest bearing debts with higher interest rates which have resulted from the Chancellor, with the Prime Minister's help, messing up the national economy. They now seem to want to transfer those high interest rates, which we have as a result of the difficulties that the Government have got into nationally, to local authorities, quite needlessly, to the detriment of local people and local authorities.

Our amendments, the most radical put forward here tonight, are a way of meeting the requirements of local authorities. I do not accept the Minister's view that they undermine the national economy. It is crucial that such amendments are passed if local authorities are to start to tackle the real problems on a range of issues that they face within their local communities. I could outline them, but I suspect that at this time of night right hon. and hon, Members will be relieved to hear that I do not intend to do so. Nevertheless, the amendments are important.

12.30 am

Mr. Gummer: There has been, under both Labour and Conservative Governments, a clear need to control the total amount of public sector capital expenditure. There is certainly a difference of opinion between the hon. Members for Truro (Mr. Taylor) and for Newham, North-West (Mr. Banks). Neither is very near to power, but the hon. Member for Truro is much further away from it, and therefore is at liberty to make proposals that no Government could possibly adopt.

To do as the hon. Member for Truro suggests is to say that those authorities that happen to have considerable capital receipts for all kinds of historical reasons will do all the capital spending—because as they undertake that expenditure, the only way to keep the generality of public sector spending under control is to reduce the allocations that the Government make to those authorities without any capital receipts. The hon. Gentleman's recipe is just a

more extreme version of that presented by the Labour party. Both would mean that the very authorities having the greatest needs and the smallest chance of capital receipts would pay the cost. They are the authorities— often elected on precisely the mandate described by the hon. Member for Newham, North-West—that often depend more on central Government allocations for capital spending because, while they have no resources themselves, their needs are considerable.

The purpose of the changes we are making is to ensure that it will be easier to give to local authorities in greatest need allocations to spend on the capital projects that they must undertake. Until now, allocations have been continuously eroded because of the considerable latitude available to local authorities able to realise assets and having a considerable amount in the bank—either as a consequence of cascading or because of the value of assets they sold in any one year. They were able to spend so much that every year the Government were compelled to reduce the allocations available to others.

The odd point about the proposals of the hon. Member for Newham, North-West is that they would hit local authorities exactly like his own. The authorities that ought to be most concerned are those having large historical assets and whose allocations are restricted so that authorities in greater need may be helped. That is a much fairer system.

As to paying off debt, the hon. Member for Truro could not have studied my detailed comments. I made it clear again and again that no one is being forced to pay off advantageous loans of the 6 per cent. variety. But where local authorities realise capital, they must apply a substantial part of the resources thus realised to debt repayment—either by discharging such debts or by establishing a fund as a contra to them. Provided that local authorities build up such a fund and use the interest from it for other purposes, they do not have to pay off advantageous debts. However, they must not spend that money a second time without making provision to repay any debts already incurred.

When the hon. Member for Newham, North-West says that local government debt is not very great as a proportion of the gross national product, of course it is convenient to use those figures today because the GNP has grown so fast under this Government. It is an interesting way of using the success of the Government's economic policy as part of the judgment.

If the hon. Member for Newham, North-West had his way, the allocations to other authorities would be reduced. Many of the resources released in the way which he describes are not 100 per cent. local authority resources. Many of them have, in the past, been provided by the general taxpayer, by Government grants and the like. I have no intention of taking away those resources. I am merely saying that it is unacceptable to distort the system of the provision of capital allocations and the Government's responsibility to help local authorities with real needs by giving capital allocations. The balance that we are trying to present should help the very authorities that Opposition Members are supposed to support. Therefore, I find their amendments surprising. If the House were to pass them, it would do great harm to the very authorities which they are often most concerned to defend.

Mr. Allan McKay (Barnsley, West and Penistone): I have given due consideration to the Minister's argument, but what then of the Government's promise, when they decided to sell council houses, that local authorities would be able to use their old receipts to replace the council houses which had been sold? What about the Government's promises in relation to the homeless and those who are now on extended waiting lists? What about the local authorities which always charged an economic rent and did not take anything from the rate fund? Will not the Government's proposed system take from the pockets of those local authorities the assets for which they paid over many years?

Mr. Gummer: None of the hon. Gentleman's comments accords with the facts. It is already true that, over the years, local authorities have been able to spend a high proportion of those assets and have spent many more millions of pounds than the assets referred to when the original statement was made by Lord Joseph. Much more than was promised has already been spent. There is no argument and the hon. Gentleman knows that.

In addition, there is no argument to suggest that those assets are being taken away from anyone. What is being said is that where debts have been incurred, and the assets on which they were incurred have been sold, at least part of the assets released should go towards the redemption of the debt. Otherwise, it would be as though someone who borrowed £8,000 for a car and then sold it said that he had £7,000 to spend. He would not because first he would have to repay the debt. We must acknowledge that it is the double spending of many of these assets which has harmed us so much.

Under the present system, the very local authorities with the needs of which Opposition Members speak are often not the ones with the assets to meet those needs. If we are to provide that money, the best way to do so is to ensure that we have greater freedom to allocate capital expenditure, which is what we are trying to do.

What the Opposition propose would do great harm to those very authorities which are most in need, which is why we are trying to change the system. Most people, other than those who are purblind, agree with what we are trying to do and believe it to be fair. That explains why the Association of Municipal Authorities has been so quiet and has not supported some of the proposals put forward by the Opposition today.

Mr. Tony Banks: I find it difficult to accept what the Minister says. He comes here in his saintly role and tries to suggest that he is doing the local authorities a great favour. It is difficult to find any local authorities which agree with him. I do not know to which local authorities he is dispensing his favours. I cannot find any: there are certainly none in the London Boroughs Association or the Association of London Authorities, and I am talking about Conservative, Liberal and Labour authorities in London. I am sure that the same is true of other authorities. No one seems to want his help and, therefore, I can only assume that he does not realise that his suggestion is totally unacceptable to local authorities of all political complexions.

As far as I can see, this is a final perpetration of the fraud carried out against local authorities. My hon. Friend the Member for Barnsley and Penistone (Mr. McKay) mentioned the understanding on which local authorities

were made to sell council houses: that all the capital receipts would be used to build new homes. That gave the idea considerable appeal for a number of authorities, but it has been gradually whittled away. Authorities are now being told that, notwithstanding any needs that they may have, they will have to use 75 per cent. of receipts for the realising of debt, without regard to their assets.

I should like the Minister to give an undertaking that he will consider the assets of each local authority against its debts. I am convinced that most if not all authorities could cover their existing debts through the value of the assets that they still hold. That seems a fairly straightforward economic proposal, which even the Minister and his hon. Friends should be able to grasp—even at this late hour.

The Minister talks about a local authority being forced to sell its own property, and then—in his words—being allowed to spend the money a second time. A council building new structures is not spending in the crude sense, but reinvesting. Against that spend comes a realisable asset.

I am not at all happy with what the Minister has said. No local authority of which I know offhand will be prepared to take the poisoned chalice that he is offering in his saintly role this evening. However, I shall not press the amendment.

Mr. Soames: Why not?

Mr. Banks: Do not push me.

I am sure that we shall find other occasions on which to return to this matter. I beg to ask leave to withdraw the amendment.

Amendment, by leave, withdrawn.

Clause 52

CAPITAL RECEIPTS NOT WHOLLY IN MONEY PAID TO THE AUTHORITY

Amendments made: No. 67, in page 59, line 14, leave out 'a sum' and insert 'an amount'.

No. 68, in page 59, line 17, leave out 'sum' and insert 'amount'.—[*Mr. Gummer.*]

Clause 53

AGGREGATE CREDIT LIMIT

Amendment proposed: No. 174, in page 60, line 5, leave out

'the first six months of'.—[*Mr. Tony Banks.*]

Question, That the amendment be made, *put and negatived.*

Clause 54

DUTY TO SET CERTAIN SUMS ASIDE AS PROVISION TO MEET CREDIT LIABILITIES

Amendments made: No. 69, in page 60, line 39, leave out 'sum' and insert 'amount'.

No. 70, in line 43, leave out 'a sum' and insert 'an amount'.

No. 71, in line 48, leave out 'set that payment aside' and insert

'at the time the payment is received, set aside an amount equal to that payment'.

No. 72, in page 61, line 5, leave out 'set aside' and insert 'at the time'.

No. 73, in line 7, after 'payments', insert

'is received, set aside an amount equal to the payment'.

No. 74, in line 10, leave out 'that sum shall be set aside' and insert

'they shall, at the time the sum is received, set aside an amount equal to that sum'.—[*Mr. Gummer.*]

Mr. Murphy: I beg to move amendment No. 181, in page 61, line 13, at end insert—

'(6) The calculation of the minimum revenue provision referred to in Part IV of Schedule 3 to this Act shall permit other proper practices to be used for the redemption of debt.

(7) A local authority shall determine its minimum revenue provision in accordance with proper practices and the duty to determine such provision shall be performed before the beginning of the financial year to which the provision is to relate.'.

The purpose of the amendment is to permit local authorities to determine the provision to be set aside from revenue accounts to meet credit liabilities, in accordance with proper practices, as alternatives to the "reducing balance" method specified in schedule 3. In Committee the Minister implied that the reducing balance method now proposed in place of the original proposal for equal instalments of principal was generally welcomed by local authorities. That is true, but only in the sense that it was marginally less bad than the original proposal.

The clause, as drafted, means that conflict is possible. The amendment is designed to resolve that conflict by allowing codes of practice to be on an equal footing with statute. In other words, it allows local authorities to calculate the minimum sum that they have to set aside to meet credit liabilities by reference to the rules set out in the schedule or any other set of proper practices at the discretion of the individual local authority.

Local authorities have traditionally been free to manage their debt in the way they felt best and to take advantage of opportunities that arise to minimise their overall payments. A code of guidance on the average maturity of debt has been agreed between local authorities and the Treasury and has proved useful in giving local authorities flexibility and in meeting the concerns of the Treasury. The Government's proposal to force councils to repay a specified percentage of their outstanding debt each year has no standing within the accountancy profession, and the Chartered Institute of Public Finance and Accountancy has already expressed its doubts about the new scheme.

12.45 am

There are well-established alternative methods of repaying debt which are preferable to the Government's proposals on economic, efficiency and practical grounds. The sinking fund method is one example and annuity payments is another. No one with any real appreciation of the problems of debt management would have dreamt of imposing this system upon local authorities. It will start a random set of changes in local authority debt repayments which have no merit in themselves and cannot be justified on proper accounting grounds.

Mr. Gummer: There is obviously a fundamental difference between us on this matter. There are problems with some of the mechanisms of accounting for debt. If a local authority decides on some methods, there is little immediate impact on major borrowing decisions, whereas most of us agree that it is important to have at least an initial clear impact so that people can make a realistic decision as to whether they want to spend so much money through borrowing.

The advantage of the reducing balance method is that, first, it looks at the totality of an authority's debt and not bits of it—that is what the Government have to do when considering any of their major economic indicators in this way.

Secondly, under the reducing balance method, the marginal effect of new borrowing is felt more sharply at the time the decision is taken to borrow. That is surely sensible and prudent, not least because local authority debt is not like personal debt. When one borrows money, one knows that it must be paid back within one's lifetime and that one is going to pay it back. A local authority is not in that position. Those who make the decision know that when the burden of paying back is faced, they will not be around to carry the cost. The danger is that the council will pass on the burden of the decision to future generations, to a new set of electors and totally different people.

Thirdly, the needs assessments on which we base our grant to local authorities have always been based on the reducing balance method. That may well continue in the new system, both on housing subsidy and for needs assessments. It seems to me that if we are paying grant on the assumption that a minimum amount of provision for debt redemption is being made, that minimum provision should be made.

It seems reasonable to say that the only way to have a sensible policy of debt redemption is to have one that, first, looks at the whole of the authority's debt; secondly, bears in some way on those who immediately initiate the debt; and, thirdly, has some reference to the way in which the needs assessment for debt and for debt redemption are made. Those three factors lead me to believe that the reducing balance method is the best one.

This method has been widely welcomed. It has not been accepted in the curmudgeonly way that the hon. Member for Torfaen (Mr. Murphy) suggested. We have moved a long way to try to meet the requirements of local authorities, and many of them have recognised that. We do not want to return to a situation in which a local authority can choose a system which means that those who make the decision and benefit from the initial spending are not the people who feel the weight of the cost of the debt or make a substantial contribution towards completion of its redemption.

Mr. Murphy: The Minister is right when he says that there is a major difference between himself and us which is irreconcilable. I should like to ask him a question about the proposed method of providing for the cost of capital expenditure and whether it will increase the expenditure of some local authorities. Will he give the House an assurance that grant will be adjusted to avoid any of those additional costs falling on poll tax payers next year?

Mr. Gummer: Community charge payers next year will pay the costs that will arise from the arrangements that we come to with local authorities. We are discussing a number of matters, including the way in which we shall account for capital expenditure and its cost, but we have not yet reached a final decision.

Amendment negatived.

Schedule 3

Provisions Supplementing Part IV

Amendments made: No. 159, in page 139, line 49, leave out '(d)' and insert '(e)'.

No. 78, in page 140, line 43, leave out first 'sum' and insert 'amount'.

No. 79, in line 43, leave out second 'sum' and insert 'amount'.

No. 80, in line 46, leave out 'sum' and insert 'amount'.

No. 160, in page 141, line 3, at beginning insert—
'(1) Subject to any prescribed modifications'.

No. 161, in line 14, at end insert—
'(2) In sub-paragraph (1) above "prescribed" means prescribed by regulations made by the Secretary of State.'.

No. 162, in line 27, at end insert—
'9A.—(1) At any time on or after 1st April 1990, a local authority's credit ceiling shall be determined, subject to any prescribed modifications, in accordance with the following provisions of this Part of this Schedule.

(2) In sub-paragraph (1) above "prescribed" means prescribed by regulations made by the Secretary of State.'.

No. 81, in line 37, leave out 'any sum' and insert 'an amount'.

No. 82, in line 39, leave out 'sum' and insert 'amount'.

No. 83, in line 40, after 'paragraph', insert 'that ceiling'.

No. 84, in line 49, leave out 'a sum' and insert 'an amount'.

No. 85, in page 142, line 2, leave out 'a sum' and insert 'an amount'.

No. 86, in line 4, leave out from 'year' to end of line 9.

No. 118, in line 9, at end add—
'11A.—(1) If, at any time on or after 1st April 1990, any debt of a local authority is reduced or extinguished by virtue of such a payment as is referred to in section 134(1)(b) of this Act, the authority's credit ceiling shall at that time be reduced by an amount equal to the reduction in the debt or, as the case may be, to the amount of the extinguished debt (and, by virtue of this paragraph, the credit ceiling may, accordingly, be a negative amount).

(2) If, at any time on or after 1st April 1990, a local authority are required under section 134(7)(b) of this Act to repay or pay any sum to the Secretary of State, the authority's credit ceiling shall at the time that sum is repaid or paid be increased by an amount equal to that sum.'.—[*Mr. Gummer.*]

Clause 55

Use of sums set aside to meet credit liabilities

Amendments made: No. 75, in page 61, line 14, leave out
'Where a local authority set aside any sums'
and insert
'Amounts for the time being set aside by a local authority'.
No. 76, in page 61, line 16, leave out 'those sums'.

No. 77, in page 61, leave out lines 26 to 28.—[*Mr. Gummer.*]

Clause 58

Application of, and orders under, Part V

Mr. O'Brien: I beg to move amendment No. 288, in page 64, line 20, at end insert—
'(3A) Nothing in this Part shall apply to a company in receipt of funds from the European Regional Development Fund on behalf of the relevant local authority'.

This is a very important amendment for many local authorities. Part V deals with companies in which local authorities have an interest. Many local authorities have been working hard to attract European regional development fund assistance. The Government should place on record the practical implications of this part of the Bill in terms of European grant aid to Britain.

There is concern that ERDF moneys could be lost if the Government do not accept the need for joint ventures. ERDF requirements stipulate that in order to gain assistance the body should be a public authority, or should act as though it were a public authority. It excludes applications from individuals and private sector organisations. A minority interest is unlikely to be sufficient to satisfy European conditions of assistance because public money is not regarded as secure.

My authority, Wakefield, is involved in this exercise. If ERDF money is not made available to it, it could have traumatic consequences. The implications of the legislation affecting companies will force local authorities to relinquish control of or influence over a company when existing or future capital requirements take the authority beyond its stated control total. That will lead to a dilution of the public interest to 20 per cent. or less and therefore to a substantial reduction in local authority activity if provision is not made for ERDF money to be paid to companies over which local authorities exercise influence.

An example is the National Exhibition Centre in Birmingham. An example from the NEC agreement illustrates the point that I am making. Article 5 of that agreement states in paragraph (a) that until 1 July 2019 "the Commission's approval shall be obtained before any application is made to the Treasury for consent to any new issue of shares in the NEC Ltd., or to any disposal of existing shares in NEC Ltd., to any person or body other than the Secretary of State or a local authority for the purpose of the Local Government Act 1972;"

Paragraph *(b)* is extremely important. It states:
"Birmingham City Council shall not, without the prior approval of the Commission, transfer any part of its share holding to the Birmingham Chamber of Commerce;"

Paragraph *(c)* states:
"NEC Ltd., shall not, without prior approval of the Commission, dispose or offer to dispose of all or any of its interests in the Birmingham Convention Centre."

It is clear that if the Bill does not make provision to protect the payment of European regional development fund moneys to local authorities, local authorities could lose a great deal of support. I ask the Minister to consider the amendment extremely carefully.

Mr. Pike: If the Government do not accept the amendment, will the project being undertaken by Lancashire Enterprises in conjunction with Lancashire county council and the borough councils to revitalise the Leeds-Liverpool canal corridor be put in jeopardy? The project is bringing in considerable European funding and is vital to Lancashire.

Mr. O'Brien: My hon. Friend gives a further example of the importance of the amendment. I quoted the National Exhibition Centre in Birmingham. My hon. Friend has said what could happen in Lancashire and other colleagues could give further examples as to what could happen in their regions. The evidence before the House tonight makes it clear that the Government ought to give the amendment careful consideration. I urge the Government to accept the amendment in the best interests of local authorities throughout the regions as it will affect the economic wellbeing of local authorities.

Mrs. Virginia Bottomley: In general terms, ERDF grants for infrastructure investments are intended to

[*Mrs. Virginia Bottomley*]

support public-sector investments. In May 1987 the European Commission confirmed that local authority controlled companies were eligible for ERDF grants. In addition, the Commission confirmed that other companies would also be eligible if they had sufficiently close links with the public sector. The proposals in part V are precisely to provide a statutory framework for local authorities' interests in companies.

At present, when local authorities become involved in companies, all too often they are absolutely free of the statutory regulations governing financing propriety and accountability. When it comes to ERDF moneys in particular, it is difficult to argue that the relationship with the local authority should be anything other than extremely close.

The eligibility for ERDF grants of companies in which local authorities have interests stems from their links with the local authorities concerned.

The amendment seeks to ignore that and proposes that any company in receipt of an ERDF grant should be exempt from the provisions contained in part V of the Bill. That is quite unacceptable as a company could enjoy the benefit of grants payable to public sector bodies by virtue of its connections with local authorities but would not be subject to public sector disciplines. For example, a local authority could set up a company which it wholly owns to carry out an infrastructure project. The company could then claim ERDF grants for the project. Under the terms of amendment No. 288 that company would then be free to borrow unlimited amounts, possibly guaranteed by the local authority concerned and generally conduct its business in any manner it or, more appropriately, the local authority wished. I am afraid that the amendment would create a simple and obvious method for avoiding the controls that should properly be applied to local authority business. I hope that I have won the argument.

The hon. Member for Normanton (Mr. O'Brien) referred to two particular areas of concern. The position of the National Exhibition Centre is being considered carefully at the moment. The Lancashire Enterprise project, which I have had the pleasure of visiting, is not in any jeopardy. The amendment would seriously undermine what we are trying to achieve, and I strongly urge the House to reject it.

1 am

Mr. O'Brien: The Minister is trying to face both ways. She is saying—[*Interruption.*] I can understand that hon. Members do not believe that, but it is true. She is saying that local authorities that receive EC money and form companies should conform to Government disciplines. That can be achieved without the legislation we are considering. She referred also to the two examples that I gave and has admitted that they must be looked at in detail, because there are certain provisions that are relevant. Those examples are mirrored in local authorities throughout Britain.

The Minister should examine carefully the points she has made. What she has said does not ring true when one considers what is happening in local authorities. The Government should reconsider their proposal.

Amendment negatived.

Clause 59

COMPANIES CONTROLLED BY LOCAL AUTHORITIES AND ARM'S LENGTH COMPANIES

Amendments made: No. 22, in page 65, line 8, leave out 'by nominees of the local authority or'
and insert
'in any one or more of the following ways, namely, by the local authority, by nominees of the local authority and'.

No. 23, in page 65, line 12, leave out 'either' and insert 'in any one or more of the following ways, namely, by the local authority'.

No. 24, in page 65, line 14, leave out 'or' and insert 'and'.

No. 25, in page 65, line 19, leave out 'applies' and insert 'and subsections (4) and (5) of that section as they have effect in relation to subsection (3) apply'.

No. 26, in page 65, line 34, leave out from 'to' to 'applied' in line 36 and insert
'any financial year if, at a time before the beginning of that year, the authority resolved that the company should be an arm's length company and, at all times from the passing of that resolution up to the end of the financial year in question, the following conditions have'.

No. 27, in page 65, line 38, leave out 'is' and insert 'was'.

No. 28, in page 65, line 43, leave out 'are' and insert 'have been'.

No. 29, in page 66, line 16, at end insert 'for other than commercial reasons'.—[*Mr. Gummer.*]

Clause 60

COMPANIES SUBJECT TO LOCAL AUTHORITY INFLUENCE

Mr. O'Brien: I beg to move amendment No. 289, in page 66, line 50, after 'aggregate', insert 'within any period of twelve months'.

Mr. Deputy Speaker (Mr. Harold Walker): With this it will be convenient to consider the following amendments:
No. 290, in page 67, line 1, after 'made' insert 'that period of twelve months'.

No. 291, in page 67, line 4, after 'guaranteed', insert 'in that period of twelve months'.

No. 292, in page 67, line 8, after 'owned', insert 'at any time within that period of twelve months'.

Mr. O'Brien: The four amendments all refer to the same principle. We request that after the word "aggregate", the words
"within any period of twelve months"
should be inserted. The purpose of the amendments is to fix a time limit for calculating business association when the local authority has made a grant or loan, or holds stocks or shares in a company. Amendment No. 289 is in line with the 12-month period specified in clause 60(3)(a), where the relationship of payment to turnover is defined.

Clause 26(3) specifically permits local authorities to invest in commercial, industrial or public undertakings and to acquire shares or loan capital in such companies. We consider that the private sector often wishes to see and values a degree of local authority involvement, especially because of the expertise that the local authority can offer.

I want to refer to the question of a company whose principal business is the disposal of waste. Obviously, local authorities, especially the metropolitan authorities, are involved in the question of waste disposal and the production of heat or electricity from waste.

We suggest that, where there is a particular involvement, the time limit for calculating business association should be 12 months, as referred to in other parts of the Bill. Indeed, as was made clear in Committee, a significant amount of concern about that could be found among Conservative Back-Benchers. The hon. Member for Ealing, Acton (Sir G. Young) referred to personal associations in local authorities and to local government influence.

There is a substantial need for the Government to consider the amendment and our suggestion that references to a six-month period should be amended to read "12-month period" in order to give local authorities better opportunities for accountancy in that area of business association.

Mrs. Virginia Bottomley: It is important to make a distinction between everyday transactions between local authorities and influence companies and capital grants. For everyday transactions, the test in clause 60(3)(a) is only satisfied within a perod of 12 months if such payments account for at least half the company's turnover. However, the test in clause 60(3)(c) relates specifically to a company's capital base and the proportion of that which has been supported by grants, loans or other forms of support from a local authority.

It would not be appropriate to qualify that to apply only to grants, etcetera, provided within a specific period as proposed in the amendments. The test must be an absolute one because a company that has relied on a local authority's support for at least half its capital base would almost certainly be subject to that authority's influence, irrespective of when the support was provided. When that is coupled with a 20 per cent. or higher personnel link, the company would undoubtedly be subject to the dominant influence of the authority.

I strongly urge the House to reject the amendment.

Amendment negatived.

Amendments made: No. 30, in page 67, line 17, leave out 'or subject to the influence'.

No. 32, in page 67, line 34, leave out 'or subject to the influence'.—*[Mrs. Virginia Bottomley.]*

Further consideration of the Bill adjourned.—*[Mr. Kenneth Carlisle.]*

Bill, as amended, (in the Standing Committee), to be further considered this day.

Broadcasting

Mr. Teddy Taylor (Southend, East): On a point of order, Mr. Deputy Speaker.

Mr. Deputy Speaker (Mr. Harold Walker): Perhaps I may anticipate the hon. Gentleman's point of order. I should have announced to the House that Mr. Speaker has selected the amendment in the name of the hon. Member for Thanet, South (Mr. Aitken). Was that the point of order?

Mr. Taylor: No, it is a different point of order. I think that you, Mr. Deputy Speaker, will be aware that this is a desperately important proposal. May I appeal to the Government and ask them to consider whether it makes sense to debate at 1 o'clock in the morning the first-ever measure to give the non-elected Commission controls over British broadcasting? As it is such a desperately important issue, I appeal to the Government not to move the motion at this crazy hour.

Mr. Deputy Speaker: Order. That is not a matter for the Chair.

1.8 am

The Minister of State, Home Office (Mr. Tim Renton): I beg to move,

That this House takes note of European Community Document No. 5574/88 and the Supplemenary Explanatory Memorandum submitted by the Home Office on 30th March 1989 and the proposals described in the unnumbered Explanatory Memorandum submitted by the Home Office on 7th June 1989 relating to broadcasting activities; and endorses the Government's view that since these provisions now follow closely those of the Council of Europe's Convention on Transfrontier Television, they should be welcomed as contributing to the reduction of barriers to trade and the maintenance of the internationally-held principles of free-flow of information.

Before going any further, I advise my hon. Friend the Member for Southend, East (Mr. Taylor), who I know will be speaking to the amendment, that one reason why we are debating the motion tonight is that the matter will be discussed at the Internal Market Council later today and it was thought appropriate that the House should have the opportunity to air its views on the draft directive before the Internal Market Council meets. I shall deal with that point at greater length in a moment.

Even at this late hour, it is a fortunate coincidence that we are debating the draft directive on what, for *Hansard* purposes at least, is the same day as that on which my right hon. Friend the Home Secretary announced a range of exciting and far-reaching decisions that will affect British commercial television in the 1990s.

The same spirit of preparing in some measure for a new broadcasting world permeates the draft European Community directive that we are discussing. More and more television broadcasts in Europe will become transnational, on satellite or cable. They will stretch across borders and they will ignore frontiers. So there are needs for a minimal set of international rules in Europe on such matters as advertising and sponsorship to make certain that what one country is broadcasting does not cause offence or break all the traditions or standards of another country in Europe that is receiving that broadcast. It is against that background that I ask the House to examine the directive.

[*Mr. Tim Renton*]

I am aware of the desire of the Select Committee on European Legislation to debate the matter and I am sorry if some hon. Members feel that the debate should have taken place earlier, although my hon. Friend the Member for Southend, East suggested that it should have taken place at a later stage. The Government felt that it would be appropriate to await any possible changes to the Community's proposals which might be suggested by the European Parliament before arranging a debate so that such changes could be taken into account.

In the event, changes were suggested by the European Parliament following its second reading of the Community's proposals on 24 May, and this is the first opportunity that we have been able to find since then to hold the debate.

Mr. William Cash (Stafford): Will my hon. Friend explain to me, a member of the Select Committee on European Legislation, why we could not debate this issue before a common position was adopted, despite the fact that a recommendation to that effect was put forward by the Select Committee in its report some time before a common position was arrived at?

Mr. Renton: I cannot add to what I said. We took the view that it was sensible, as the draft directive had been changed many times—there have been four explanatory memoranda from the Home Office to the Select Committee on European Legislation detailing the various changes that have been arrived at—that the debate should not take place until the European Parliament had had an opportunity to suggest any changes. Those were not made until 24 May, and this is the first opportunity since then, given the Whitsun break, to debate the matter.

I am pleased to tell the House that we have made substantial progress on this subject——

Mr. Jonathan Aitken (Thanet, South): Come off it.

Mr. Renton: There is no question of coming off it. I shall go in considerable detail into the matter and I suggest that my hon. Friend listens carefully to the details of the progress that we have made, on the basis of which we are now able to recommend the House to endorse the attitude to the directive as set forth in the motion.

We have made such progress that the Community proposals are now fundamentally different and much more acceptable than those which the House debated on 20 January 1987. At that time the Government and the House were concerned, and rightly so, over a draft directive which appeared to introduce more restrictions on free trade than it would have removed. It had been drafted in such a way that it would have created more obstacles to the free flow of television programmes than it would have eliminated.

We had, for example, serious reservations about the Commission's approach on copyright, which depended ultimately on the imposition of a statutory licence. Nor did we believe that there was a case for fixed numerical quotas imposed on everyone from Brussels. Rather than the establishment of general principles to provide flexible regulation to meet the domestic needs of individual countries, the draft directive then contained such a fine level of detail that it was likely to lead to more rather than less restriction.

On that basis we were attracted to the idea of regulating European broadcasting by a Council of Europe instrument. At the Vienna conference of broadcasting Ministers in 1986, we were instrumental in securing agreement for the preparation of a Council of Europe convention on transfrontier broadcasting. We regarded the Council of Europe as a more appropriate forum for regulating these matters because its approach is more flexible and because it provides a much larger grouping of European states, 22 countries rather than the 12 represented by the Community. As the House knows, our emphasis was on the Council of Europe convention. Thereafter, in late 1987 and throughout 1988 and 1989 it has made significantly speedier progress than the directive.

At the Council of Europe conference of broadcasting Ministers in Stockholm last November, which I had the great pleasure to attend, it was clear that there was a collective political will to reach agreement on the outstanding points in the convention as quickly as possible. It also marked, and I emphasise this, a major turning point on the draft directive. Once the final shape of the convention became clear, we devoted much effort to securing amendments to the draft directive to bring it into line with the convention. Our approach was supported by the conclusion of the European Council in Rhodes last December that the future work of the Community in relation to broadcasting should be based on that of the Council of Europe and that the directive should be adopted in the light of that convention.

The agreement reached by the European Council was very satisfactory because it meant that, in general, the directive would follow closely the provisions of the convention. We had worked hard in negotiations on the convention to arrive at provisions that would not adversely affect United Kingdom broadcasting and advertising interests.

Those provisions substantially met all the points about which we had reservations in the draft directive—I shall list them later—and they were, therefore, in our judgment an acceptable basis for European legislation.

Mr. Teddy Taylor: I have with me the *Hansard* for the debate on 20 January 1987, during which this very issue was discussed. The point made by the then Minister was that while the negotiations were taking place the Commission was bent on establishing competence in that area. He said that, despite the Commission's endeavour to take over the Council of Europe's proposals, it was a part of the argument that the Government would not fall for. Can my hon. Friend the Minister tell us why the Government fell for it?

Mr. Renton: With the greatest respect to my hon. Friend, he is trying to see booby traps and plots where none exist. He should be fair in his quotations. I shall quote remarks made by my predecessor in that debate. He said:

"The fact of the matter is that Community competence exists."—[*Official Report*, 20 January 1987; Vol. 108, c. 843.] The fact that the Community has competence in broadcasting has been argued not only by the Commission a great many times, but it has been upheld in the European Court on a number of occasions.

Mr. Taylor *rose*——

Mr. Renton: I shall give way to my hon. Friend for the last time. He will have his opportunity to make his points.

Mr. Taylor: During the debate on 20 January 1987, the then Minister was asked whether the Government's view was that the Community should have competence in this issue, to which he replied "No".

Mr. Renton: I have just quoted what my predecessor said. The Government accept the fact that the Community has competence in the issue of broadcasting——

Mr. Taylor: No.

Mr. Renton: I must explain the present position to my hon. Friend. The court has decided on many occasions that broadcasting is to be regarded as an economic service under the terms of the treaty. That is the final state of play. We have consulted legal opinion, which has confirmed that view.

I assure my hon. Friend that, despite his concerns and echoing back to the debate of 1987, I can now recommend the draft text to the House because all the amendments to it that we have achieved mean that it sits closely alongside the Council of Europe's convention on transfrontier broadcasting—a convention that we have already signed.

Mr. Nigel Spearing (Newham, South): I thought that it might be convenient to clear the legal matters before we go any further. Leaving aside the question of the scope of the Single European Act, and in this case article 57, the hon. Gentleman's memorandum dated 7 June, which he deposited in the Vote Office, tells us that the proposal is presently conceived under articles 57(2) and 66 of the treaty. Is there any likelihood of any change in that? The phraseology suggests that there could be, although I rather doubt it. Before the hon. Gentleman concludes, will he tell us whether there is likely to be a vote on this? It is awaiting qualified majority and he may know the likelihood of its passage?

Mr. Renton: I am not aware of any likelihood that the proposal will cease to rely on articles 57(2) and 66 of the treaty. The Commission's regular view has been that those were the articles on which they relied, and I am not aware of any view that that should be changed. I cannot advise him of whether there is likely to be a vote on this. I believe, however, that it will be discussed at the Internal Market Council today. Obviously, that is something that we shall watch with considerable interest.

We came to the conclusion that the decision made by the European Council in Rhodes was satisfactory because it meant that the directive would follow closely the provisions of the convention. We felt that those provisions substantially met all the points in the draft directive about which we had had reservations in the past.

It followed from that that this signalled the need for a different approach to the directive on our part. Given our acceptance of the provisions in the convention, it would have been unreasonable to argue that we could not support the same or similar provisions in the draft directive. That position has since been reinforced by our decision to sign the convention when it opened for signature on 5 May. Nine other member states of the Council of Europe joined us at that time in signing the convention, and I have no doubt that others will do so.

Before going on to comment specifically on the changes within the draft directive, I shall explain to the House why we considered it necessary to have some form of international regulation of broadcasting. That, of course, lies within the fact that until recently broadcasting has been primarily a national industry, aimed predominantly at domestic audiences. However, it is clear that television will become an increasingly international medium as satellite broadcasting leaves its footprint throughout Europe. I have heard it forecast, for example, that within a few years about 200 international satellite television channels might be beamed down to the countries of Europe.

All countries have developed means of regulating their domestic broadcasting services over the past 50 years, and those new technological developments will make desirable a measure of international regulation—minimal, I accept. There is a need both to avoid any regulatory loophole that might otherwise develop and, more positively—for the sake of British industry interested in this market—to promote a pan-European market in broadcasting.

It was not in our view sensible or desirable for satellite or cable broadcasting to develop completely outside national or international regulatory controls. As a result of the fundamental changes made to the draft directive, we believe that we can withdraw our earlier objections to the substance of the directive.

I shall list those main changes. The proposal for a 60 per cent. quota of broadcasting time to be devoted to European Community work has been amended in two ways. First, the provision is now couched in terms that require broadcasters to devote "a majority proportion" of their transmission time to European works where it is practicable to do so. There is no longer, therefore, any fixed or legally binding numerical quota. Secondly, the definition of European works has been widened to embrace works coming from Community states, non-Community states that are party to the Council of Europe convention and from other European states that have concluded reciprocal agreements with the Community. That provision is now sufficiently flexible to be compatible with the existing requirement in the United Kingdom law that broadcasters should show a "proper proportion" of European Community material. Our broadcasters regularly show about 65 per cent. of EC material within the definition that will apply to EC programmes in the directive.

Mr. Roger Gale (Thanet, North): Does that mean that if the United States signs the European convention, as it well may, its work will be classed as a European production?

Mr. Renton: There is a difference between the United States and non-Community states that are party to the Council of Europe convention. I have not heard any suggestion that the United States might sign the Council of Europe convention. It is an interesting thought, but it has not crossed my desk. Perhaps my hon. Friend will develop that idea in his speech.

The broadcasting services, such as satellite channels that depend on a substantial amount of programmes imported from the United States and elsewhere that would not find it practicable to devote the majority of their transmission time to European works, will not be impeded by the provisions. The House will be reassured, therefore, that the flexible nature of the provision will not threaten or prejudice the constitutional independence of British broadcasters. Freedom of choice will continue and there will be room for programmes from non-EC countries.

Mr. Teddy Taylor: Will my hon. Friend give way?

Mr. Renton: With respect, I have given way to my hon. Friend three times. Time is short and, given that his amendment has been selected, it would be better if he made his own speech.

The proposed 10 per cent. quota of works from independent producers can now be achieved either as 10 per cent. of programme budgets or as 10 per cent. of transmission time, on which member states can choose. This is less stringent than the 25 per cent. targets which the Government have already set the BBC and IBA in relation to independent productions.

The provisions on the duration and insertion of television advertising have been changed to reflect the corresponding provisions of the Council of Europe convention. Advertising is now limited to 15 per cent. of the daily transmission time, or 20 per cent. if it includes tele-shopping services. The amount of spot advertising within any given hour shall not exceed 20 per cent. Television advertising within the United Kingdom already falls comfortably within those limits.

Detailed rules are laid down for the time and frequency of advertising breaks. Some member states favoured grouping advertisements between programmes rather than inserting them in natural breaks. But thanks very largely to proposals we formulated and tabled, in particular on the need to retain natural-break advertising, we believe that we have secured provisions which will not adversely affect British broadcasting and advertising interests.

Although the draft directive continues to contain a ban on the advertising of all forms of tobacco products, this is in line with the corresponding provision in the Council of Europe convention which the Government accepted in order to secure agreement to the convention as a whole.

The requirement for a right of reply has been widened to refer to a right of reply "or equivalent remedies". That will enable us to continue to rely on the existing procedures operated in the United Kingdom through the Broadcasting Complaints Commission, and we will not be required to introduce any further measures. The provisions on copyright have been withdrawn.

We are also satisfid that the provisions on the protection of minors, which are in themselves unexceptionable and indeed desirable, should not have undesirable consequences for Community competence in other sectors.

It is our view that the Commission's proposals now represent a satisfactory outcome. We have successfully resisted the arguments of some member states for protectionist measures which would have imposed greater restrictions on European broadcasters and, instead, we have achieved a substantial deregulatory text fully in line with that of the Council of Europe convention.

I stress, finally, that a prime objective in supporting the directive is to foster the free flow of television programmes throughout Europe. In that context, article 2 of the draft directive is in my opinion much the most important. I firmly believe that this will promote and encourage the growth of the broadcasting industry in the United Kingdom.

I do not need to remind the House about the approach of 1992. This will be an opportunity for all British interests —and broadcasting is no exception—to expand into the European market. The potential is enormous. The development of cable and satellite technologies that ignore frontiers has created opportunities for a new and expanding market.

There is already a large gap between the European demand for television programmes and their supply. In 1987 western Europe needed 125,000 hours of programming but produced only about a quarter of this itself. By 1990 western Europe will need at least 300,000 hours of programming. The balance of trade in this field is currently very much in the United States' favour. Europe is an importer of programmes and clearly more European co-operation and co-production in making programmes that are attractive to all the European market is necessary and will be helped by the abolition of trade barriers against the sales of such programmes that is implicit and explicit in the directive.

This is a formidable challenge for the British broadcasting industry but I believe that it is one that we are very well placed to meet, for British broadcasting already has a high reputation abroad. We have, as the House knows, the creative talent, the commercial enterprise and the production and distribution infrastructure to make the most of the expanding markets elsewhere, and the development of the independent production initiative in this country in recent years is an example of how we can take advantage of an opening in the market.

We should be in the vanguard to take advantage of these new opportunities throughout Europe in the broadcasting world to the benefit of broadcasters and viewers alike. It is on that basis and in expectation of our obtaining a wider share of this European market that I ask the House to endorse our view that the draft directive should now be welcomed.

1.32 am

Mr. Robin Corbett (Birmingham, Erdington): I must confess to being a little puzzled by what I will describe as the Minister's muted euphoria over these proposals. As the hon. Member for Southend, East (Mr. Taylor) reminded the House, in January 1987 the Minister's predecessor stood at the Dispatch Box questioning the need for a directive and indeed the competence of the Commission in this matter.

I have no doubt that some of his hon. Friends will quote from the advertisement in the Sunday papers which warns voters that if they do not do a certain thing on Thursday 15 June they will be living on a diet of Brussels. I do not want to make too much of this because the mere mention of the Euro elections pours salt into the grievous wounds of the differences between the Prime Minister, the former Prime Minister and others over this Government's real attitude to the Community.

At the last debate—and the Minister knows this— virtually the whole House, not to mention the programme makers and the advertising industry, shared the view that a better way ahead lay with the Council of Europe, and that was indeed the view of the Opposition. As the Minister has confirmed, in essence what has happened is that the Commission has now decided to follow the Council of Europe, and generally, although with some reservations, that is welcomed, I believe.

I must state my reservations about the watering down of the original proposal arguing that 60 per cent. of broadcasting time should be devoted to works originating in the Community. That has changed in two ways, as the Select Committee on European Legislation helpfully noted. The 60 per cent. has not merely become a majority proportion—which in plain English I take to mean at least 51 per cent.—but is hedged with a qualifying phrase—"where it is practicable to do so".

It is not within any time limit; it implies that this will go on for ever unless we are invited to consider another directive. I hope that the Minister will tell me what that means. I accept that some countries would find even that provision for a majority proportion difficult to move towards immediately. For example, I understand that in Greece and Portugal virtually all programmes during peak-time viewing are of American origin.

Would it not have been better to make exemptions for some stated period for such countries rather than to weaken the provision for those well able to cope? Do I take it from the Minister's remark that the current United Kingdom position of the use of about 65 per cent. of EEC originated material remains, in the Government's view, the one to which we should hold rather than the looser, weaker formula of a majority proportion?

My fears are these. Because of cross-considerations, the demands of advertisers and the need here to recoup as quickly as possible the cash laid out for a franchise, the pressure will be on the programme makers and programmers to cut costs. Unless we are careful, that can only mean more American-made programmes. Or, to put it another way in the words of the Home Secretary in an interview with Independent Radio News today, "more rubbish programmes". Those were the words that he used when discussing the announcement that he had made earlier in the day to the House. The absence of a binding numerical quota means that competition will not be so much on programme quality as on programme cost.

There are some other objections as well. There is no reference to the times at which the programmes are shown. I understand, but do not accept, that the Government want as light a regime as possible, nationally and within the EC. In the context of a majority proportion of European originated works, that could mean that some programmes are pushed, either mainly or wholly, into the off-peak, late-night hours.

In that context—it is interesting that the Minister made no reference to this—we should all be properly conscious that transfrontier broadcating should not squeeze out or threaten the rich and varied cultural backgrounds of the countries joined together in the Community. It is perfectly possible—I call the Prime Minister as witness—for individual nations to preserve their essential identity while willingly co-operating. National identity need not be sacrificed upon the altar of European co-operation.

Mr. Teddy Taylor: How can the hon. Gentleman talk of co-operation when the directive makes provision for the Commission to implement the majority, and when, in paragraph 3, there is legal provision in five years' time for any new percentage to be laid down by majority voting? There was certainly co-operation in the old Council of Europe directive, but this proposal is something quite different. It gives the Commission the power to implement whatever percentage is arrived at, and paragraph 3 makes it abundantly clear that whatever percentage is not appropriate can be changed.

Mr. Corbett: I understand exactly the hon. Gentleman's point. He will not thank me if I say that when we come nearer to the position that he mentioned in five years' time, the Minister may be on the Opposition Benches and somebody else on the Government Front Bench.

I welcome the widening of the provision to embrace nations which have relationships with the Community. That is an important contribution to the growing interest in all European co-operation beyond the boundaries of the present Community and in the interests of what President Gorbachev has called "our common European home".

I have doubts about the 10 per cent. quota for works from independent producers being tied to either a choice of transmission time or programming budgets. There is the risk that all the independents will be allowed to do is the cheap game show, late-night, nodding heads type of programme with whatever high-cost, often high-quality, drama or current affairs is done, left exclusively in house. I welcome the higher targets for independent productions, and I assume that the Government have no intention of seeking to reduce them.

We are used to joint funding of programmes by British and American interests. I welcome the growing co-operation with German and French co-sponsors in particular and hope that we shall see more. That can only help to protect and promote national and Community programme co-sponsorship—the better to resist the American invasion. Perhaps the Minister can say whether American companies will be tempted to establish production facilities in Britain or elsewhere in the Community to get around the majority proportion rule. If the Americans make such an attempt, will they be permitted to succeed?

Some may view the provisions as restricting the free flow of broadcasting across frontiers, but that need not happen. But in the wake of developing technology we must ensure that nothing destroys the best that British broadcasting and that of other countries has achieved. We must never risk the single European market offering only a choice of soaps or game shows made in Britain, France, Germany or Italy. That does not represent real programme diversity, quality or variety. We want proper choice, not just more of the same.

I regret that provisions for a right of reply were dropped, and the Minister knows that I do not accept that the Broadcasting Complaints Commission represents a serious alternative. But that matter will have to wait.

Article 8 deals with television advertising and rightly proscribes any that discriminates on the grounds of race, sex or nationality. That is important, and should give another push to progress made in this country and elsewhere in ending sexual and racial stereotyping. It may be a laughing matter to some people, but it is hurtful and offensive to those who are its targets.

I particularly welcome the provisions in article 8 for ensuring that television advertising will not encourage behaviour prejudicial to health and safety or to the protection of the environment. The latter is a welcome addition and properly recognises growing concern in this country and in others about the need to stop and to reverse pollution and destruction. There is every reason why responsible advertisers, using the most powerful medium, should be part of that process.

The Minister and other right hon. and hon. Members may have noted the recent Mintel survey reported in the *Daily Mail* today. The report stated:

"The vast majority of shoppers are willing to pay up to 10p in the pound extra for products which do no harm to the

[*Mr. Corbett*]

environment . . . Seventy-seven per cent. of shoppers will pay 5p to 10p in the pound extra for 'environmentally friendly' washing powder, falling only slightly to 72 per cent. for organic food and 66 per cent. for toiletries not tested on animals."

There is a powerful message in those results both for manufacturers and for advertisers.

I hope that the House will welcome the tight restrictions on alcohol advertising, which must not be aimed at minors, claim that it enhances physical performance, or give the impression that it aids social or sexual success. I say in all seriousness that the alcohol problem in Britain and in the rest of the Community affects far more people, across a much wider age range, than does the real menace of drugs—and it causes more social and economic damage. Alcohol abuse must be taken seriously, and the proposals help in that.

I hope that the Government will learn the lessons from sporting and other events in this country that attract young people. The Minister's predecessor was critical of the earlier draft's provisions for the protection of children. They are now covered by articles 12 and 14, and, although they represent the minimum, they are none the less welcome. Responsible advertisers—and it is manufacturers or service providers who must take proper responsibility—have nothing to fear from the provisions. In any event, it would be entirely wrong to allow them to stand aside. As we have seen with British newspapers, all too often it is one product—the example I have in mind is the sewer *Sun*—that inevitably drags down standards among its competitors.

The original copyright proposals were almost universally unacceptable. I regret the absence of new proposals, but we are better without what was originally on offer. This problem must be tackled. I hope that voluntary contractual agreements work, but I wonder whether the provision for arbitration will, perversely, discourage rather than encourage agreement, since it happens after retransmission. As the Minister has explained, the copyright proposals weaken the position of owners of rights, although the proposal seeks to preserve the present position for cable.

These proposals fit fairly comfortably alongside the Council of Europe's directive, but they are not the end of the matter. Experience will doubtless show that other provisions will have to be made. As I have said, we need proposals which will not impede the free flow of television across national boundaries but which, at the same time, do not impose what Jeremy Isaacs, when he headed Channel 4, called "Euro-puddings".

Individual, national, cultural and other traditions must be guarded as an essential ingredient of transnational television. If the proposals strike that balance and protect us from any form of loss of national and cultural identity, they will have been shown to be worthwhile.

1.46 am

Mr. Jonathan Aitken (Thanet, South): I beg to move, to leave out from "activities" to the end of the Question and add instead thereof:

'but can see no merit and no benefit whatsoever in having the content of broadcasting in the United Kingdom or any other member state being subject to a European Economic Community directive; expresses concern about the extent to which the non-elected Commission is being given powers to implement the directive; believes that broadcasting and artistic merit should be the basis of broadcasting selection rather than Euro protectionism; and trusts that Her Majesty's Government will vote against this absurd proposal which is an insult to the high standards and objectivity traditionally displayed by the United Kingdom broadcasting media.'.

If a Home Office Minister was, in normal conditions and daylight hours, to come to the Dispatch Box and introduce legislation which dictated restrictive new Government terms and conditions with which television and broadcasting companies had to comply in order to put out more than half their own air time, the outcry and vehement denunciation of censorship and state control would soon ring up and down the length and breadth of this country. It says much for the nocturnal, almost clandestine, way in which we continue unsatisfactorily to monitor EC legislation that this very same offensive principle of placing state or, in this case, EC controls on half the transmission time of broadcasting companies should be greeted almost soporifically by the House at 1.47 am as a virtual non-event.

My hon. Friends and I do not think that it is a non-event. We believe that the directive is an extremely important and seminal event. My hon. Friend the Minister should feel deeply unhappy and ashamed at having to support the directive in the way in which he has been forced to do so tonight. The oddest part of his speech was his brave, or perhaps brazen, attempt to make it sound as though his speech this evening flowed naturally with and matched up to that made by the hon. and learned Member for Putney (Mr. Mellor) when he was the Minister at the Dispatch Box, debating much the same directive on 20 January 1987.

Leaving aside the two personalities, if one read the two speeches with any objectivity one would feel that it was not a harmonious flow, but Tweedledum and Tweedledee having a battle. Time and again the statements made in either one or the other cannot conceivably be matched up. If I had to pick out one clear and demonstrable clash between the two diametrically opposed speeches, I would refer to the statement made by my hon Friend the Minister tonight about how the Government had always believed that majority voting would apply to this directive.

The hon. and learned Member for Putney said:

"The point I am putting to my right hon. Friend is that we shall argue with might and main that this is such a contentious matter that it should be dealt with only by way of unanimity."—[*Official Report*, 20 January 1987; Vol. 108, c. 855.]

I could find half a dozen other examples in the two speeches. In the previous speech, they are usually accompanied by rhetorical flourishes such as "tooth and nail" or "might and main". However, at the end of all that, we received not a bang, but a whimper of a defence of what is being brought in tonight.

Mr. Renton: I know how strongly my hon. Friend feels on the subject, but I think that he is misquoting me. I did not say that we had always believed that majority voting should apply; I quoted my predecessor, saying that he had accepted in the opening of his speech that the Community had competence in respect of broadcasting, in particular because of the economic base.

I said earlier that the court had confirmed European Community competence in important aspects of broadcasting, which is a service within the meaning of the treaty. I would indeed argue that my speech flowed on from that made by my predecessor in January 1987. Not only, however, have we managed in the intervening two years to amend all the points in the draft directive that we previously found objectionable but the key case on European competence—the Dutch cable case—arose and was decided only after the Commons debate.

Mr. Aitken: I suggest that, instead of engaging in textual arguments on the Floor of the House, hon. Members read the two speeches. Let us look at the two examples defended by my hon. Friend. My hon. Friend the Member for Northampton, North (Mr. Marlow) asked:

"Is it my hon. Friend's view, and the view of the Government, that the Community should have competence in this issue?".

My hon. Friend the then Minister replied:

"No. I think it is our view that the Community's competence in this issue is extremely limited and should remain so."—[*Official Report*, 20 January 1987; Vol. 108, c. 843.]

The clear implication is that at that time the Government did not believe that the Community necessarily had full competence. Here we are talking about whether unanimity applies. It is obvious from what my hon. Friend said then that he considered that it would be essential, but tonight we are saying that it is not.

Instead of engaging in arcane textual argument—important though it may be to resolve the battle between Tweedledum and Tweedledee—let us get on to the gut issues. My hon. Friends and I feel that we should oppose the directive vigorously, on several different grounds. First, it has nothing to do with the single market or with free market forces. Those of my hon. Friends who voted for the Single European Act must be amazed to find that the Act that they thought was all to do with free trade and the toppling of barriers is now forcing television companies to accept a whole set of restrictions. I think that television companies should be free to put on any or all of the best and most popular programmes: that is true broadcasting freedom. But the freedom of the air waves will now be restricted in an astonishing seizure of new powers by what I believe to be the ideological Euro-nannies and Euro-meddlers of Brussels.

What really sticks in our gullets is the statement—which has changed only marginally—that the majority of airtime from now on will have to be given to Euro-programmes from European sources. I think that such a restriction is anti-viewer, anti-populist and, indeed, anti-American. Anti-Americanism provides much of the rocket fuel inside the EEC in favour of the directive.

I am disturbed at the hostility towards the culture and history of the English-speaking peoples that is now emanating from Brussels. Anti-Americanism is a disease that is spreading through the Commission. The fact is that, for better or worse, the taste of the British viewer—and now, we hear, even the Portuguese viewer—is strongly in favour of the United States popular culture, from Alistair Cooke's "Letter from America" to great epics such as "The Winds of War" and popular programmes such as "Cagney and Lacey", "Hill Street Blues", "Dallas" and "Dynasty". Those are the shows that viewers apparently like to watch and listen to—and do not let us forget the growing input from other parts of the English-speaking world, such as the Australian popular programme "Neighbours".

Those programmes and their successors will be placed in jeopardy. Big brother in Brussels knows what the average British family enjoys watching and he wants to stop it. Not having been able to beat the popular television

culture of the English-speaking peoples on the ratings, the Euro meddlers now want to drive these programmes off the screens by restrictive legislation. The Government should be pretty miserable at the idea of blessing a proposal that encourages that.

The Government have had to stand on their head. In January 1987, my hon. and learned Friend the Member for Putney said that he would not shrink from voting against a broadcasting Euro directive of the type that was then contemplated. For all the fine words of the Minister of State, attempting to show us that things have changed in the intervening period and that great concessions have been won, the reality is that in June 1989 we are debating only a mildly diluted version of the same unpalatable legislative brew. Far from shrinking away from it, we are asked to swallow it almost whole.

I have said that the Government are standing on their head and I must say how strange the posture of my hon. Friend the Minister looks on the issue of the right of reply. He is the Minister who has done his best to thwart the admirable private Member's Bill, the Right of Reply Bill, which has been promoted by an Opposition Member and which many Conservative Members support. My hon. Friend used strange methods. His oratorical technique in killing off that Bill could be broadly described as "praising with faint damn". He blocked the Right of Reply Bill when it came forward in the House as British legislation, but, lo and behold, this European directive contains a firm commitment to introduce the right of reply on the air waves. It is odd that my hon. Friend can be "Mr. Facing-Both-Ways" on the right of reply issue within such a short time.

The hon. Member for Birmingham, Erdington (Mr. Corbett) touched on the issue of advertising. Some of his points are to be commended, but I see others in a different light. I should like to raise a technical point that could have great implications for British television companies. Does the phrase in the directive, the duration of the programme—referring to the amount of advertising time—apply to scheduled time or running time? We appear to be confident that the British interpretation will be accepted, but there may be a triumph of hope over experience.

Mr. Renton: I should like to reassure my hon. Friend immediately. It is agreed that scheduled time is acceptable within the draft directive.

Mr. Aitken: I am glad to hear that, as no doubt will some television companies.

Article 8, which the hon. Member for Erdington praised highly, contains many noble sentiments. We are all in favour of such ideas as preserving decency, the environment and the dignity of women, but we should look at the small print. We are told that advertising must not

"offend against prevailing standards of decency",

or

"encourage behaviour prejudicial to . . . the protection of the environment"

or

"employ forms of expression which contravene respect for the dignity of women."

All those high-sounding ideals are sloppy bits of legislation when it comes down to the possibility of television companies being prosecuted for showing advertisements

[*Mr. Aitken*]

that, in someone's opinion, offend against any of those vague and ill-drafted sentiments. They sound fine but are very unsuitable when it comes to practicalities.

I return to the issue of principle and clothe it in the language of practicality. I think that I am the only Member who has had the experience of running a major television company. I suppose that there are those who would say that, in view of that company's history, it could not have been much worse if the entire EEC Commission had had its hands on the controls at the same time. Be that as it may, at least that experience gave me an understanding of what it might be like to operate a television company against the judgments of the directive.

A busy television station has feeds coming into it from all over the world. News stories are breaking all the time. The format of programmes is always changing. With all the hustle and bustle of major programme-making rolling on through the hours, it would be impracticable then to have to get out a stop watch and start to measure how many seconds of time are coming from which sources, which cartoons originate in the United States, which originate in France and to be faced—as one would be under the directive—with very tight bureaucratic restrictions because of the need for the Commission to report regularly on the minutage of the contents of programmes and ensure the application of the provisions in article 2.

Broadcasters need to be given freedom to develop ideas. They do not need the very bad new principle that the directive would introduce.

2 am

Sir Dudley Smith (Warwick and Leamington): I join other hon. Members who have criticised the ludicrous hour at which we are debating this important subject. I hope that the lesson will be learnt by those who are responsible, because it happens all too often.

I have a good deal of sympathy for the two-man band onslaught on European legislation that is waged so assiduously in the early hours of the morning. However, on this occasion I have to part company with it. As a member of the Council of Europe Assembly I have been involved in various ways with transfrontier television. I was in Stockholm when the original proposals that were much criticised—I think fairly—by my hon. Friend the Member for Thanet, South (Mr. Aitken) were thrashed out by the then 21 nations of the Council of Europe. I pay tribute to the excellent work that was done by my hon. Friend the Minister of State. But for his leadership I do not believe that we should have made the progress that we in fact made. It was a very good convention. As my hon. Friend explained, the directive follows closely the Stockholm proposals.

In this modern age, when television is bursting out in all directions, there must be regulations to govern transfrontier television. Unless a minimum set of rules can be devised, there will eventually be chaos and a great deal of undesirable material will appear on our television screens. I am one of the last to advocate the establishment of a nanny society. I echo some of my hon. Friend's criticisms of action being taken over advertisements. That could be difficult.

When the Council of Europe first considered the subject, it drew up three basic rules to govern what it was trying to achieve on behalf of the countries of Europe. I remind the House that they cover all the countries of Europe, not just those in the EEC. They were the integrity of the television company and the programme, honesty and decency.

The future will bring satellite television and the opportunity before too long to see other countries' programmes without too much difficulty. Sensible though not onerous regulation is needed. I am particularly pleased that my hon. Friend was so successful over natural breaks for advertising. I am sure that I am right in saying that this now follows closely the pattern of television advertising in this country. I think that it is appreciated by the public. If changes were made, they would be resented. The public are used to our comfortable arrangements. Advertising is not too intrusive, and it is often enjoyed and appreciated.

I sought to speak in the debate tonight to draw attention to one particular aspect which my hon. Friend the Minister should consider. Quite recently, one main French television channel has started showing hard pornography late at night. It makes the sleazy Soho cinema clubs of 10 or 15 years ago look like a vicarage tea party. It is shown on an open channel. We have four main channels in Britain and that material is shown on a main French channel. It does not take much imagination to realise that young people can stay up after 11 o'clock at night, and if they do not want to stay up they can video the programme to watch at some other time. I should like a categorical assurance from my hon. Friend when he replies to the debate that under the rules of transfrontier television in no way will it be possible for people in Britain to receive that French television channel, or any other such programmes as there is also a pornographic programme in Italy.

I am reasonably broad minded, but I was very shocked by that programme and I believe that most right hon. and hon. Members would also be shocked. The public is entitled to the protection offered by the convention and the directive to make absolutely sure that young people and others in society are not brought down to the standards to which I have referred. I hope that my hon. Friend will address that point when he replies to the debate.

2.5 am

Sir Giles Shaw (Pudsey): I shall speak briefly in general support of what my hon. Friend the Minister has said this evening. A considerable time ago the European Commission tried to get involved in the broadcasting scene. At that time we rightly refused to encourage it unless it was able to become involved on a pan-European basis. That is why the fundamental shift that my hon. Friend has put before the House tonight is so significant, not just because the Commission has accepted the Council of Europe's suggested lines of approach, which are wholly preferable to those suggested by the Commission, but because it sets a very important precedent. It suggests that when transfrontier broadcasting can extend far beyond the boundaries of the Commission's competence there might be within the Commission an awareness that it might have to introduce some system which conforms to a far wider grouping of nation states. That is an extremely important precedent.

I fully understand why my hon. Friend the Member for Thanet, South (Mr. Aitken) and others find it pretty nasty that there are possible threats to the integrity of television producers in using material which they consider the British public might wish to see. Since the advent of independent television, there have always been pretty significant restraints on the use of imported material. I think that I am right—my hon. Friend will correct me if I am wrong—in saying that the percentage of imported American material is still a factor which, under IBA regulation, has to be observed within reasonably acceptable limits.

The way in which the directive works out, if and when it is finally ratified, will depend very much on the climate of producers and the public at the time. I am charitable enough to believe—and my hon. Friend the Member for Thanet, South should take heart from this—that many issues that have come before the Commission and have resulted in directives have been applied theoretically as part of Community statute law and have not had a huge impact in various parts of the Community. The French seem to be able to devise a Poitier connection for getting round most obstructive measures, and I have little doubt that broadcasters, whose ingenuity is prodigious, will find ways and means of finding new material from other sources which might have some Community tag attached to it even if it is routed to our screens in some funny or strange way.

What concerns me most was my hon. Friend the Minister of State's passing reference to satellites over Europe, the footprint, and what will go on inside the footprint. It appears that there is great uncertainty as to how far domestic regulation or Commission regulation will have any effect upon the satellite exposure we are about to experience. To what extent does my hon. Friend the Minister feel that the steps announced tonight will be able to embrace that in a sensible yet sensitive way? We all wish to see the development and effective use of broadcasting waves as they become available for use for this purpose and we all wish to see no restraint, in a fairly general sense, of the access of the public to the media.

However, there is a real problem in the origination of satellite material and in the competence that the owners of satellites might easily find in relation to the European Community or the Council of Europe itself. The satellites operate from very distant places. My hon. Friend the Minister must be a little more sanguine if he is to believe that the step he has talked about tonight will have a measurable effect on that development in non-terrestrial broadcasting.

In general, we have come a longish way since the proposals of 1984. I welcome the proposal that my hon. Friend has laid before the House. I am certain that it is not the end of the issue and I am certain that, as time moves on and pressures move on, there will be changes and additions made to the proposal. The right to offer some competence to the Commission in this area is sensible. The first steps it is now taking are infinitely more sensible than its original ones.

2.11 am

Mr. Roger Gale (Thanet, North): I had some sympathy with the sentiments of my parliamentary neighbour and hon. Friend the Member for Thanet, South (Mr. Aitken) in his amendment, but it is a shame that he did not find it in his heart to pay tribute to the work done by my hon. Friend the Minister in securing the convention on transfrontier television.

About a year ago, the Select Committee on Home Affairs, of which I am member, visited Brussels and Strasbourg. In Brussels, we spoke to Lord Cockfield, who was then a European Commissioner. Perhaps I should not speak for my colleagues on the Committee, although I am sure that they would share my view, but I was most concerned by the languid, arrogant and almost laissez-faire attitude that the Commission appeared to be taking to what we regarded as a pressing problem, which was the imminence of the arrival in this country of satellite broadcasting and the total lack at that time of any control over the content of the programming that would and could be received in the United Kingdom.

It is fair to say—and I made some passing reference to this only 24 hours ago in this Chamber—that I am a proponent of satellite broadcasting. I see in it tremendous opportunities for education, for the exchange of culture and language, multi-channel broadcasting and choice. I do not share the view of the hon. Member for Birmingham, Erdington (Mr. Corbett) that we should fear it. I do not believe that it is a threat. I see it as an opportunity, although it is only an opportunity if it is properly used and controlled.

For that reason, having visited Strasbourg, the Select Committee on Home Affairs in its report on the future of broadcasting recommended that the Council of Europe convention proposals should be pursued with all possible speed. I must say to my hon. Friend the Member for Thanet, South that it is, if not entirely, then very largely, due to the efforts of my hon. Friend the Minister in Stockholm and elsewhere that the convention was agreed and was open for signature in Strasbourg at the 40th anniversary plenary session of the Council of Europe last month.

It is a matter of sadness to me and perhaps of some interest to hon. Members of all parties that since the convention was opened a number of countries that are members of the Council of Europe, of which the United Kingdom is proud to be one, have signed the convention. However, perhaps significantly, among the major European Community countries, France, Germany and Italy, which kicked up much of the fuss, had, at the last count, not signed the convention.

The directive reflects much of the provisions of the transfrontier broadcasting convention. My hon. Friend the Member for Thanet, South said that he felt that it was right that United Kingdom television companies should be allowed to broadcast "all and any of the best of television". With respect, I find nothing in the transfrontier convention or, by implication, in the directive that would prevent his television company, or any other, from doing precisely that.

My hon. Friend the Minister of State picked me up when I said that the United States might become a signatory to the Council of Europe convention. There is not yet—but there will be—provision for non-member states to add their names to the convention. It is likely that in due course the north American states, both the United States and Canada, and possibly Australia, may find commercial advantage in adding their names to the convention with a view to not only pan-European but possibly pan-world broadcasting. Companies such as

[*Mr. Roger Gale*]

Cable News Network may well wish to take advantages of the opportunities for transfrontier broadcasting in Europe.

We should remember that when we in the United Kingdom talk about transfrontier broadcasting, we tend to talk in satellite terms because our terrestrial broadcasting is not by satellite. However, on the continent, and within the now 23 countries of the Council of Europe, transfrontier broadcasting can mean terrestrial broadcasting. Transfrontier is a much simpler concept. Indeed, some United Kingdom programmes are watched with great interest and enjoyment on the north coast of the continent.

That experience is much more common in othe European countries. The tiny Principality of Liechtenstein, for example, has no television station of its own and relies entirely on transfrontier broadcasting—on German, Austrian and Swiss programming—for its television reception. It has expressed real and genuine concerns about intrusions on its culture. Some of us in the Council of Europe have sought to encourage that state to establish its own broadcasting systems for precisely those reasons.

Although I shall not vote for the amendment tabled by my hon. Friend the Member for Thanet, South because I agree only with its first part and not with its second part, in support of it I should say that I believe that it is wrong that this House should address this issue at this hour in the morning of the day on which the Council of Ministers will discuss the directive.

The Select Committee on European Legislation reported that

"the Commission has made it clear that it is not prepared to accept a number of major amendments requested by the Parliament, because these would have jeopardised the rapid adoption of the draft Directive."

It is referring to the European Parliament.

With great respect, there has been nothing rapid about the European Commission's progress in this matter. Indeed, it would still be discussing it cheerfully had it not been goaded into action by the Council of Europe convention, and largely by the actions of my hon. Friend the Minister of State. Having taken so long to achieve so little and to base its conclusions finally on the Council of Europe convention, perhaps it could be asked by the Minister attending the Council of Ministers later today to take just a little longer and to pay greater heed to the Members of the European Parliament.

While the transfrontier broadcasting convention, which I have welcomed as has the House publicly, is a voluntary convention, voluntarily entered into, tonight we are dealing with something very different. Indeed, as my hon. Friend the Member for Thanet, South makes clear in his amendment, the directive represents an imposition by an unelected Commission and I do not think that we can welcome that.

2.20 am

Mr. Nigel Spearing (Newham, South): I must at the outset object to the hour at which we are asked to debate this issue and to the limit of an hour and a half for the debate. I believe that we shall hear a great deal more about the content of the directive, remembering that we must in any event translate it into our own legislation. When that has happened somebody might wake up to precisely what

is involved. I wonder whether they are awake at Broadcasting house and whether these deliberations will be featured in "Yesterday in Parliament" later today. This matter is of fundamental importance to all broadcasters, present and future, in this country.

Speaking from experience, the hon. Member for Thanet, South (Mr. Aitken) made what I would call a reasonable contribution. I sympathised to a great extent with what he said. I understand that one reason for including what he called an anti-American element is an effort by the French-speaking people in the European Community, and possibly some Germans, to withstand, as it were, what they see as the tide of English language.

In that, of course, we have a natural interest. Indeed, there are feelings in this country too, about certain aspects of north America culture which can penetrate our culture and air waves more easily than they can penetrate those of France and Germany. Certainly an effort is being made by those countries, and particularly France, to retain their cultural identity, and with that the hon. Member for Thanet, South will have some sympathy, as I have.

The points that I wish to raise are treaty-based. I said some time ago that many surprises would spring from the Single European Act, and tonight we have one of them. There was not a scintilla of a suggestion when we ratified that legislation that we would be faced with this type of directive.

I accept what the hon. Member for Warwick and Leamington (Sir D. Smith) said about the need for some international arrangement on satellites. Whether that should be done through a Council of Europe convention, which this directive parallels, or through the competence of the treaty of Rome, is the point at issue. The hon. Member for Thanet, North (Mr. Gale) spoke of the need for an international arrangement covering satellites and their standards.

The Council of Europe is a good forum in which to achieve that. But what if the European Community says, "We shall not keep within the Council of Europe on this. We claim competence by majority vote to make an alternative set of proposals which are not parallel to those of the Council of Europe"—or, for that matter, even with those which the Government could not accept? We would then be in dead trouble because, as the Minister conceded, the matter would be decided by weighted majority vote.

The articles under which the directive is promulgated are strange. Article 57(2) speaks of

"the co-ordination of the provisions laid down by law, regulation or administrative action in Member States concerning the taking up and pursuit of activities as self-employed persons."

It is significant that the heading of the memorandum which the Minister produced on 7 June also used those words. It read:

"Amended proposal for a Council Directive on the co-ordination of certain provisions laid down by law, regulation or administrative action in Member States concerning the pursuit of television broadcasting activities."

The opening words of that heading follow the wording of article 57(2). The clue to it all lies in the final words:

"the pursuit of television broadcasting activities."

That is not mentioned in article 57.

It is based on another article which comes at the end of a chapter about what are called "Services"—broadcasting is a service—and that is article 66, which is so short that I can read it all;

"The provisions of Articles 55 to 58 shall apply to the matters covered by this Chapter."

It is rather like having a provision at the end of an Act of Parliament saying, "This part of the Bill applies to everything contained in an earlier part of the Bill."

As I understand it, that particular mechanism gives competence to the Community. Who, on initial reading of the Single European Act, would envisage such a backtrack mechanism? If I have that wrong, and if the Minister has the time to reply to the debate, I am sure that he will correct me. It is an example of the surprise package. All matters of regulation relating to all services of all sorts come within the ambit of article 57 which, in certain aspects, carries majority voting. In fact, the issue is even more complicated than I have suggested, but I have tried to give the bones of it.

In view of the time I shall conclude, as other hon. Members wish to speak. I feel bound to point out, Mr. Deputy Speaker, that you have powers under Standing Orders to postpone the conclusion of the debate if you feel that the matter is of such importance as to warrant that. I am not necessarily suggesting that you do so, especially as the matter has to be decided in the Council today. This is an example of the very narrow window of time in which we have to deal with these matters.

Mr. Renton: The matter does not have to be decided in the Council today. I said earlier that it would be discussed in the Interior Market Council.

Mr. Spearing: It may not be decided, but it will be discussed. Perhaps the Minister could confirm that, constitutionally, if so agreed a decision could be taken.

Mr. Renton: Yes.

Mr. Spearing: Under the complex rules of the Council of Ministers, if the Presidency so decided the matter could be put to the vote. Again, it is a matter of procedure of when the question should be put. The Presidency could put the question and wrap up the matter. The Minister is nodding. I do not suppose that the Presidency will think fit to do that because there is a consensus that it is not yet time to take that decision. It is another example of the way that this House and this country are being constrained not only by the terms of the treaty, unexpected though they are, but because of the procedures adopted by the Council of Ministers.

My final point about broadcasters is that a few weeks ago there were four important debates on the European Community. The first related to a new withholding tax, the second to merger control—which is departing these shores for Brussels—the third to public procurement and the fourth to the six-monthly White Paper. The first three matters were legislative. They were not reported on an otherwise well-regarded programme called "Today in Parliament". Its half-hour report at the end of the day did not cover any of those three debates. The programme, which is broadcast from 11.30 pm to midnight, went out two and a half hours ago and, therefore, cannot have reported this debate which, ironically, is about broadcasting. I have mentioned that as an important footnote to yesterday's debate on television and a dedicated channel. I hope that among the 200 channels there will be a dedicated channel covering all debates in the House.

2.28 am

Mr. Teddy Taylor (Southend, East): I wish to say a few words, which I hope the Minister will consider. We are discussing the vital issue of transfer of sovereignty. If anyone thinks that that is not important, he should read the *Hansard* of the debate in January 1987. The then Minister made it abundantly clear that he would fight for the Council of Europe proposal because it was abundantly different from an EEC directive. The Government said that they would fight all the way and would do everything possible to ensure that there was unanimity. They made it clear that in their view the EEC did not have any control and that the Council of Europe proposal was right.

The Minister is well aware that night after night, when no one in Britain is aware of what is happening, we are transferring responsibility from democratic bodies, Government bodies and bodies over which we and the people have some kind of control, to the non-elected EEC Commission.

The hon. Member for Newham, South (Mr. Spearing) mentioned the recent debate on merger control. We gave the Commission the power to send inspectors into British firms to ask for information and to impose fines for which they need not go to a court. This directive—which, of course, will be accepted—gives the Commission powers over British broadcasting and British broadcasting companies. What do we do about it?

If there is any doubt in the minds of hon. Members, they should look at paragraph 2 of the proposals, because there it clearly and precisely states that

"The Commission shall ensure the application of the provisions in Article 2(1)"—

which are concerned with the majority European broadcasts—

"and Article 3 in accordance with the provisions of the Treaty."

The Minister is, of course, saying what Ministers consistently say late at night—"We are glad to say that the directive is not so bad as it once was". We heard the same comment the other night about heavy lorries. We shall have heavy lorries, but they will come two years later. We had, too, the debate on mergers. Tonight the Minister is really saying, "Do not worry about this directive, because it will not do anything that will upset British broadcasters."

I hope that hon. Members will look at clause 2, because that says that we shall have to give reports about what every British broadcasting company is doing to the non-elected Commission. It will consider those reports, give opinions on them and give advice as to how the proposal should be changed. The Minister says that it is only the majority of broadcasts that must be Euro-broadcasts. Even that is not terribly clear—and that includes some Council of Europe Members. Sadly, what the Minister did not say was that, under article 3, there is a specific proposal for the Council of Ministers by a majority to change that to whatever figure, conditions or considerations that it might want. The Minister must be aware of that. It is because the Government fought this so severely and so well in 1987 that we now have something completely different. When we have something in the Council of Europe, we know that there the basic control and responsibility is left to a democratically elected parliament and bodies appointed by that parliament.

I wish that our party Whips would appreciate how serious it is when we transfer control to a non-elected

[*Mr. Teddy Taylor*]

committee. We are doing that night after night in the House, and no one is hearing about it. There was a time when I heard the Prime Minister's splendid words about how we would fight this unnecessary transfer of sovereignty. We were going to stop the Single European Act being used for what it was not intended. We were to promote free trade. What we have, however, is not the free trade that we want, but the transfer of more and more responsibility to the non-elected Commission.

For those who say that they are not terribly worried about the content of the directive, let them think about what happened recently about the sixth directive. When we debated that directive in the House we were told that there was nothing in that that could be used to affect Britain's zero VAT rating. Yet, as the Minister is well aware, we have had two recent court cases in which the Commission interfered with our zero rates.

We are doing something terribly serious tonight. If hon. Members read the directive or read the debate of 1987, or if the Minister studies the files in his Department, they will appreciate the seriousness of the matter. The Government fought a very hard battle to stop this becoming a Euro-directive. The Government said that they would fight it by "might and main". They knew that the issue here was not the question of how much sovereignty, but the question of the transfer of that sovereignty. What we are doing is starting a process whereby the control of broadcasting is switched to a non-elected body of the European Commission. That is a most dangerous thing for our democracy and, in the long term, Parliament will regret it.

I know that my hon. Friend the Member for Thanet, South (Mr. Aitken), some other hon. Members and I are a thorough nuisance keeping people up when they could be asleep. Probably our action is pointless, as our views will have no effect because of the decisions that will be taken tomorrow. Our action is utterly pointless, as this House has no power. At the end of the day, however, I do not believe that we should be fulfilling our obligations to our constituents and doing the job for which we are paid if we did not say that this decision was shocking, shameful and undemocratic. I believe that Parliament will live to regret it.

2.37 am

Mr. William Cash (Stafford): I have a paper with me that was issued from Brussels entitled "Common position adopted by the Council on 13 April 1989". To my surprise, I found that it was published on 10 April, apparently three days before the document was adopted. That is extraordinary.

Some of my hon. Friends have already have said that the legislation will be implemented by way of a United Kingdom statute. That statute must be construed in a manner that is consistent with the directive. If there are any inconsistencies, the European Court of Justice will determine the matter against the statute in favour of the directive. Parallel to the directive are the provisions of the Council of Europe convention.

My hon. Friend the Member for Thanet, North (Mr. Gale) has already said that other third-party states outside the EC may become subscribing members to the Council of Europe convention. Effectively we could be faced with

a tripartite problem—a United Kingdom statute that is interpretable through our courts to the European Court of Justice; the provisions of the directive which are within the framework of that European Court and the Council of Europe convention that could be interpreted in a different way. The directive's provisions cover——

It being one and a half hours after the commencement of proceedings on the motion, MR. DEPUTY SPEAKER *put the Question necessary for the disposal of the proceedings, pursuant to Standing Order No. 14 (Exempted business).*

Question put, That the amendment be made:—
The House divided: Ayes 11, Noes 68.

Division No. 239] [**2.37 am**]

AYES

Barnes, Harry *(Derbyshire NE)*
Clay, Bob
Cryer, Bob
Golding, Mrs Llin
Lewis, Terry
Loyden, Eddie
Meale, Alan
Michael, Alun
Skinner, Dennis
Spearing, Nigel
Taylor, Teddy *(S'end E)*

Tellers for the Ayes:
Mr. Roger Gale and
Mr. Jonathan Aitken.

NOES

Amess, David
Amos, Alan
Arbuthnot, James
Arnold, Jacques *(Gravesham)*
Arnold, Tom *(Hazel Grove)*
Atkinson, David
Bennett, Nicholas *(Pembroke)*
Bevan, David Gilroy
Boswell, Tim
Brown, Michael *(Brigg & Cl't's)*
Burns, Simon
Carrington, Matthew
Chapman, Sydney
Coombs, Anthony *(Wyre F'rest)*
Coombs, Simon *(Swindon)*
Currie, Mrs Edwina
Davies, Q. *(Stamf'd & Spald'g)*
Davis, David *(Boothferry)*
Day, Stephen
Dorrell, Stephen
Durant, Tony
Fallon, Michael
Forth, Eric
Garel-Jones, Tristan
Gregory, Conal
Griffiths, Peter *(Portsmouth N)*
Hague, William
Hamilton, Neil *(Tatton)*
Harris, David
Heathcoat-Amory, David
Hind, Kenneth
Howarth, Alan *(Strat'd-on-A)*
Howarth, G. *(Cannock & B'wd)*
Hughes, Robert G. *(Harrow W)*
Hunt, David *(Wirral W)*
Irvine, Michael
Jack, Michael
Lightbown, David
Lord, Michael
McLoughlin, Patrick
Miller, Sir Hal
Mitchell, Andrew *(Gedling)*
Moynihan, Hon Colin
Nelson, Anthony
Norris, Steve
Paice, James
Porter, David *(Waveney)*
Renton, Tim
Roberts, Wyn *(Conwy)*
Sackville, Hon Tom
Shaw, David *(Dover)*
Shaw, Sir Giles *(Pudsey)*
Shepherd, Colin *(Hereford)*
Smith, Sir Dudley *(Warwick)*
Stern, Michael
Stevens, Lewis
Stradling Thomas, Sir John
Summerson, Hugo
Taylor, Ian *(Esher)*
Thurnham, Peter
Tracey, Richard
Twinn, Dr Ian
Waddington, Rt Hon David
Waller, Gary
Wardle, Charles *(Bexhill)*
Watts, John
Widdecombe, Ann
Wood, Timothy

Tellers for the Noes:
Mr. Kenneth Carlisle and
Mr. David Maclean.

Question accordingly negatived.
Main Question put:—
The House divided: Ayes 58, Noes 7.

Division No. 240] [**2.48 am**]

AYES

Amess, David
Arbuthnot, James
Arnold, Jacques *(Gravesham)*
Arnold, Tom *(Hazel Grove)*
Atkinson, David
Bennett, Nicholas *(Pembroke)*
Bevan, David Gilroy
Boswell, Tim
Burns, Simon
Carrington, Matthew
Chapman, Sydney
Coombs, Anthony *(Wyre F'rest)*
Coombs, Simon *(Swindon)*
Currie, Mrs Edwina
Davies, Q. *(Stamf'd & Spald'g)*
Day, Stephen
Dorrell, Stephen
Durant, Tony

Fallon, Michael
Garel-Jones, Tristan
Gregory, Conal
Griffiths, Peter *(Portsmouth N)*
Hague, William
Hamilton, Neil *(Tatton)*
Harris, David
Heathcoat-Amory, David
Hind, Kenneth
Howarth, Alan *(Strat'd-on-A)*
Howarth, G. *(Cannock & B'wd)*
Hughes, Robert G. *(Harrow W)*
Hunt, David *(Wirral W)*
Irvine, Michael
Jack, Michael
Lightbown, David
Lord, Michael
McLoughlin, Patrick
Miller, Sir Hal
Mitchell, Andrew *(Gedling)*
Moynihan, Hon Colin
Norris, Steve

Paice, James
Renton, Tim
Roberts, Wyn *(Conwy)*
Sackville, Hon Tom
Shaw, David *(Dover)*
Shepherd, Colin *(Hereford)*
Smith, Sir Dudley *(Warwick)*
Stern, Michael
Summerson, Hugo
Taylor, Ian *(Esher)*
Thurnham, Peter
Twinn, Dr Ian
Waddington, Rt Hon David
Waller, Gary
Wardle, Charles *(Bexhill)*
Watts, John
Widdecombe, Ann
Wood, Timothy

Tellers for the Ayes:
 Mr. Kenneth Carlisle and
 Mr. David Maclean.

NOES

Clay, Bob
Golding, Mrs Llin
Lewis, Terry
Meale, Alan
Michael, Alun
Skinner, Dennis

Spearing, Nigel

Tellers for the Noes:
 Mr. Bob Cryer and
 Mr. Harry Barnes.

Question accordingly agreed to.

Resolved,

That this House takes note of European Community Document No. 5574/88 and the Supplementary Explanatory Memorandum submitted by the Home Office on 30th March 1989 and the proposals described in the unnumbered Explanatory Memorandum submitted by the Home Office on 7th June 1989 relating to broadcasting activities; and endorses the Government's view that since these provisions now follow closely those of the Council of Europe's Convention on Transfrontier Television, they should be welcomed as contributing to the reduction of barriers to trade and the maintenance of the internationally-held principles of free-flow of information.

Cardiff Wales Airport (Rail Link)

Motion made, and Question proposed, That this House do now adjourn.—*[Mr. Dorrell.]*

2.58 am

Mr. John P. Smith (Vale of Glamorgan): At this very late hour I should like to bring to the attention of the House a matter which my constituents, a broad spectrum of people in Wales and I believe to be of great concern —the pressing need for a surface rail link to Cardiff Wales airport.

I wish to argue the need for this on three grounds. First, I believe that there are inadequate surface transportation links with Cardiff Wales airport, road or rail. More important, unless we provide a surface rail link to serve the airport the implications for its future look very bad. The final reason is that there is already a proven case for the reopening of a passenger rail link from Barry in south Glamorgan to Bridgend in Mid Glamorgan, passing through the western Vale of Glamorgan and the town of Llantwit Major. It would skirt the airport, and it would not be a very difficult job to provide a link for both passengers and freight.

I argue my first point on the following grounds. The existing surface link with Cardiff Wales airport is the road from Culverhouse Cross in north-west Cardiff—which has a good link along the link road to the M4—through Weycock Cross. However, on that link a single-lane carriageway must cater for the considerable volume of traffic that has recently built up following developments in north-west Barry. On bank holidays, and during the nice weather that we have experienced recently, the road is even more congested. On the recent spring bank holiday I understand that it was jammed solid from Culverhouse Cross right through to the holiday resort of Barry Island, in my constituency. Any passengers attempting to reach Cardiff Wales airport to embark on either internal flights or flights abroad could well have been unable to get there.

I have it on good authority that the present position is unacceptable, and that it may well be costing the airport much-needed trade and custom. It could be argued that we are losing business unnecessarily to adjacent airports such as Birmingham and possibly even Bristol. I recognise, however, that at present the airport is doing very well in difficult circumstances. Trade has increased, and the volume of passengers and freight out of the airport has risen slightly. I understand that the number of flights and aircraft has fallen, but the aircraft that are coming in are of a larger scale and able to carry much more, which is very encouraging.

That brings me to my second point. It will not bode well for the airport's future if we fail to grasp the nettle now, and to understand the need for investment in a rail link. The accepted view is that the increase in air traffic will continue in the foreseeable future, because of reduced flight costs, more efficient aircraft and people who now have higher disposable incomes and can afford air travel. If Cardiff Wales airport is to meet the needs of increased passenger numbers and freight, it needs an adequate surface link. If we want it to be a gateway to European markets in 1992—I am sure that the Minister agrees—we must provide that link or we will live to regret it. Once again, we may find ourselves trailing behind other regions.

The need for a link has been recognised in other regions. It is of such importance that I decided to take this

[*Mr. John P. Smith*]

opportunity to bring it to the attention of the House. Other premier regional airports have introduced rail links. Birmingham has a direct rail link to its recently constructed terminal. Manchester has agreed with British Rail to provide a rail link to serve the important regional airport there. There is an agreement in Newcastle to extend the Metro system to provide a station to serve Newcastle airport. A rail link has been built into Stansted airport. Those links recognise the demand for access.

Local authorities, my colleagues, many industrialists in Wales, individuals representing the tourist industry and, understandably, the airport authority share my concern about prospects for the airport if this facility is not provided. There is a danger that the airport will start to lose custom and, in the process, its regional status. I hope that I am not exaggerating, but I am sure that the Minister and all Welsh Members share my worry. We should direct attention towards this issue.

My third argument for the surface rail link is based on the undoubted need to reopen the passenger line through the Vale of Glamorgan, which was shut under Beeching some time ago. I note with interest that at the annual general meeting of South Glamorgan county council the incoming chairwoman, Councillor Lorna Hughes, referred in her inaugural address to the long-standing need to provide a passenger rail link through the vale. There are numerous reasons for that. The most important demographic factor is the considerable expansion of local communities since Beeching.

Account must be taken of the increasing reliance on car transportation. A large number of people commute from the Vale of Glamorgan to Cardiff. It is a significant travel-to-work area. Much of the traffic congestion on the roads could be alleviated if commuters switched to other forms of transport, including public transport. The most obvious alternative form of transport, and the one that makes the most sense, is a rail line through the Vale of Glamorgan.

A line already exists. Unlike what happened in other areas, it was not removed. The line is used regularly to transport freight through the vale, to Bridgend in particular. Steam coal is transported regularly to Aberthaw power station. I understand that 11 trains a day use that line. Passengers also use the line on Sundays when repairs are being carried out to the main line from Barry, or from London to Swansea. That line skirts the airport. It would be a relatively easy task—I stress that point, bearing in mind some of British Rail's comments during the last few years—to reopen the line. When it had been reopened to passenger traffic, it would be relatively easy to provide a link to Cardiff Wales airport.

British Rail does not share that view. It has argued that the line would not be economically viable. If one examines British Rail's ability to provide new services in south Wales, one finds that its track record is neither very encouraging nor very good. New stations that have been opened in south Glamorgan, largely as a result of local government initiatives, have proved to be highly successful. I refer to the opening of Cathays station in Cardiff. That was wholly a local authority-South Glamorgan county council initiative. British Rail was obviously reluctant to open it, but it has proved to be a huge success. It was followed by a joint venture, with

Welsh Office assistance, to provide other stations, including Eastbrook Halt. Passenger transport from the Dinas Powys community increased by 60 per cent. after that station was opened. I am absolutely convinced that a similar increase in traffic would result from an extension of the line through the Vale of Glamorgan and from the provision of additional stations.

This important matter is not being given the attention that it deserves. I hope that the Minister has been listening carefully. Local people believe that the need for a rail link to Cardiff Wales airport should be recognised. A decision must be taken now because of the planning and land acquisition considerations, and even the engineering and design considerations, that will have to be dealt with during the next couple of years.

If a decision is not taken now, I fear that we shall fall behind what has been achieved by airports in other regions that have recognised the need to tackle the problem. The Secretary of State for Wales sets great store by his ability to serve the region and the community. It could well be a test for the Secretary of State for Wales to realise that we can continue to develop the Welsh economy only if we provide a rail link to Cardiff Wales airport. I apologise if I have slightly exceeded my time.

3.15 am

The Minister of State, Welsh Office (Mr. Wyn Roberts): I congratulate the hon. Member for Vale of Glamorgan (Mr. Smith) on securing his first Adjournment debate and I thank him for giving me the opportunity to say how much I support Cardiff Wales airport.

The airport provides valuable scheduled services to Amsterdam, Dublin and various destinations in the United Kingdom. Amsterdam provides a gateway to many destinations in Europe and across the world. Cardiff is served by charter flights to many places, notably the tourist areas of Europe. It is also served by regular transatlantic charter flights to such places as Orlando, Florida, New York and Toronto.

I am sure that as the skies over London become more congested, the Cardiff airport management will seize every opportunity to attract further traffic to Cardiff Wales airport. I wish them well in such ventures, which will no doubt be aided by the increasing liberalisation of the airways being brought about by the European Community

I am aware that the airport management, in conjunction with the Welsh Development Agency, has been conducting and continues to conduct surveys to determine the customer potential of new routes. These are providing much useful information as a basis on which to attract new services to the airport. I understand that with the help of those surveys, some new scheduled services to the continent are already in the pipeline and the airport is also looking to enhance its services to north America.

Cardiff Wales airport currently handles about 750,000 passengers per year. Most of those come from south Wales, the majority travelling in the peak holiday period. Some others come from the west country, particularly for the transatlantic charter services. The majority travel to the airport by car, but there is a good bus service from central Cardiff and from Barry.

I am aware that the airport management wish to see improvements to the access from Cardiff to the airport. The late hon. Member for the Vale of Glamorgan, Sir Raymond Gower, also wrote to me on this topic. Interest has been expressed both in the improvement of road access and in the provision of a rail service. The former is of course a matter for South Glamorgan county council which is the highway authority for the area. I am sure that the hon. Gentleman will agree that the Culverhouse Cross-Capel Llanilltern link is a great improvement to communications in the area.

As well as securing this debate, the hon. Member for Vale of Glamorgan has written to my right hon. Friend arguing the case for the reopening to passengers of the Vale of Glamorgan freight line, which passes near the perimeter of Cardiff Wales airport. To provide a rail link to the airport would require the reopening of a section of this line to passenger traffic. I must, therefore, first of all explain the Government's views on the reopening of new railway lines by British Rail.

The opening or reopening of any railway line is initially a decision for the British Railways Board to make in the light of the general objectives set for it by the Government. The railways board is expected to take a proper commercial approach to such proposals. It must also take into account any funds available from other sources, such as local authorities or the private sector. Any central Government funding would be dependent upon the ability of British Rail to demonstrate that the proposal will bring quantifiable economic external benefits to the community as a whole, such as relief from severe traffic congestion. Normally the Government would expect the costs of a new railway to be met by those who directly benefit.

Cardiff Wales airport is a limited company jointly owned by Mid, West and South Glamorgan county councils. Those authorities stand to benefit from any increased patronage at the airport and I am sure that it must be reasonable, in that circumstance, for the authorities to bear at least a share of any costs involved in providing improved access. Indeed, county councils have a duty to decide how best to meet the transport requirements of their areas. This would be South Glamorgan for the area including Cardiff Wales airport.

The Government's policy is that if a council adopts the reopening of a particular line, it would have to bear any capital costs of the project which cannot be supported commercially by British Rail.

The hon. Gentleman may be aware that Mid Glamorgan and South Glamorgan county councils have already collaborated on a joint rail strategy, to which he referred. The first phase of this strategy, which was funded as a project of regional or national importance, has brought considerable improvements to rail services in those counties. I understand that the counties are likely to put in a bid for a PRNI allocation for a second phase of this strategy, but it may not include a spur to serve the airport, as their last recorded view was that the current passenger levels using the airport could not justify such a link in the near future.

It seems that there are two ways in which Cardiff Wales airport might be connected to the railway. A link to the airport terminal would require a stretch of new railway line from the existing Vale of Glamorgan freight line, upgraded to passenger standards as necessary. Choice of route would be constrained by the Porthkerry viaduct and the adjacent deep cutting. Such a scheme would take some high quality agricultural land and would have serious consequences for Porthkerry village. It would be an expensive business.

An alternative would be a scheme including the reintroduction of passenger services along the Vale of Glamorgan line to a station at or near Rhoose. A station on that line would be some distance from the airport terminal and might not be very attractive, given the available bus services. The line itself would need to be upgraded and provided with new signalling to take passenger traffic. I am told that rolling stock alone would cost in the region of £1·6 million.

British Rail is aware of the interest shown generally in the reintroduction of passenger services to the Vale of Glamorgan line. It has not made any detailed assessments of the potential viability of such a service because it does not consider it necessary. In its judgment, based on experience in other parts of the country, the population of the Vale of Glamorgan is insufficient to sustain such a service. Mid and South Glamorgan county councils did look into the possibility of the inclusion of the Vale of Glamorgan line within their joint rail strategy, but they have decided that the case for this line is insufficiently strong, at least in the short term.

In his letter to my right hon. Friend, the hon. Gentleman pointed out that several airports enjoy, or will enjoy, the rail links. The hon. Gentleman has made very much the same point tonight and I accept the point. Most of those airports serve a far higher population than Cardiff Wales airport. Two of them, Birmingham and Stansted, were already close to existing passenger lines and at least one other will be served by an already expanding local suburban railway network. Even Heathrow has only relatively recently been linked to the Underground system, which affords comparatively slow access to central London. The proposed new rail link between Heathrow and Paddington will be heavily dependent on the availability of external finance before it can be built. There are many other airports, which I could list for the hon. Gentleman, with no rail links, such as Bristol and Edinburgh.

I realise that what I have just said is not very encouraging. I realise the importance to Wales of a thriving international airport and the advantages which a rail link would bring but British Rail cannot provide and service such a link unless it is commercially viable. On present indications, there does not appear to be a satisfactory economic case.

The lack of a link is not stifling growth at the airport. New charter services have been introduced this year and prospects seem promising for the introduction of further services, both charter and scheduled. I am pleased to see that the airport management has plans for further development and that it is striving to increase its business.

The airport already has runway facilities to handle the largest jets and is extending its apron so that Boeing 747s can be more easily accommodated. To cope with increasing numbers of passengers the airport has provided new departure lounges and new covered walkways were brought into use this year to provide access for passengers direct from the departure lounges to their aircraft. Extra parking space for cars will become available in the near future. Further developments are in the pipeline as more lounge facilities with escalator connections are developed over the winter months in the upper levels of the terminal building.

The increasing levels of air traffic will soon require new and improved local air traffic control facilities. Discussions are already in hand with the air traffic control authorities

[*Mr. Wyn Roberts*]

and new radar installations are expected to be introduced during the winter period. There are also plans for a new hotel development which will serve air travellers.

Therefore, I tend to disagreee with the hon. Gentleman that the prospects for Cardiff airport are not bright. I contradict that. With these developments, the airport's prospects are very good. I am sure that the local authorities that are involved in the running of the airport and with the provision of local roads and improved rail services in the area—they are collaborating with British Rail—will take the airport's prospects and its best interests into account. It is clear that the interests of the airport, which is run by the local authorities, are very much in tune with their own interests. I am sure that they will be safeguarded in the future.

Question put and agreed to.

Adjourned accordingly at twenty-eight minutes past Three o'clock.

House of Commons

Wednesday 14 June 1989

The House met at half-past Two o'clock

PRAYERS

[MR. SPEAKER *in the Chair*]

PRIVATE BUSINESS

BUCKINGHAMSHIRE COUNTY COUNCIL BILL *[Lords]*
Order for consideration, as amended, read.
To be considered tomorrow.

Oral Answers to Questions

FOREIGN AND COMMONWEALTH AFFAIRS

Human Rights

1. **Mr. Atkinson:** To ask the Secretary of State for Foreign and Commonwealth Affairs if he has received any recent representations about human rights abuses in Commonwealth member states; and whether he plans to raise the question of human rights at the forthcoming Commonwealth conference in Malaysia.

The Parliamentary Under-Secretary of State, Foreign and Commonwealth Affairs (Mr. Timothy Eggar): We receive representations about human rights in many countries, including some Commonwealth members. Discussions between Commonwealth Heads of Government are confidential and wide-ranging. It is too early to say what issues my right hon. Friend the Prime Minister will address in her interventions.

Mr. Atkinson: In view of the representations received over the years, can my hon. Friend confirm that basic human rights continue to be denied in at least one quarter to one third of Commonwealth member states, including Malaysia, where to convert from Islam to Christianity is punishable and may render the individual open to persecution? At the forthcoming conference in Malaysia, will my right hon. and learned Friend the Foreign Secretary submit proposals for the establishment of a Commonwealth human rights commission along the lines of the United Nations Commission of Human Rights and the Helsinki process?

Mr. Eggar: My hon. Friend's reference to the state of affairs in Malaysia relates to the laws of the states rather than to federal laws. Within the Commonwealth secretariat there is already a special unit, established in early 1985, to deal with human rights issues. We believe that human rights are universal. Instead of creating another forum for debating them we should concentrate on strengthening the existing United Nations human rights bodies and mechanisms.

Mrs. Mahon: Is the Minister aware that three out of five Tamil refugees who were forcibly returned to Colombo in February 1988 have been tortured? What do the Government intend to do about that?

Mr. Eggar: I am sure that if the hon. Lady can substantiate her assertion we will draw it to the attention of the Sri Lankan Government.

Sir Jim Spicer: My hon. Friend the Minister has rightly said that human rights are universal, and we all accept that. Against that background, will he comment on the persecution, on a major scale, of the Turkish minority in Bulgaria? What representations——

Mr. Speaker: Order. Bulgaria is not in the Commonwealth.

Sir Jim Spicer: With respect, Mr. Speaker, my hon. hon. Friend's reply opened up the discussion by saying that human rights are universal. My question simply followed on from my hon. Friend's answer.

Mr. Eggar: The Government issued a statement this morning on the subject that my hon. Friend raised.

Mr. Anderson: Will the Government be trying to dissuade other Commonwealth premiers from raising the question of human rights in South Africa at the conference? The Government might be less on the defensive if we had joined the Commonwealth Foreign Ministers group and taken a high profile on human rights in South Africa. Will the Government raise the matter of the proposed judicial execution of the Upington 14 next week when the Prime Minister welcomes Mr. F. W. de Klerk to this country?

Mr. Eggar: The hon. Gentleman will be aware that South Africa is no longer a member of the Commonwealth. I imagine that issues of that kind concerning South Africa will be raised at the Commonwealth Heads of Government conference, and certainly we shall do nothing to stop that. As to the Upington 14, it would be inappropriate to make any representations at this stage, when the normal legal processes can still be used.

European Elections

2. **Mr. Fearn:** To ask the Secretary of State for Foreign and Commonwealth Affairs whether he will make a statement on the policy of Her Majesty's Government towards a uniform electoral system for the European elections.

The Minister of State, Foreign and Commonwealth Affairs (Mrs. Lynda Chalker): There are no current proposals for a uniform electoral procedure for European parliamentary elections.

Mr. Fearn: Does the Minister agree that at the forthcoming European elections Britain will be seen as the odd man out in not having a fair voting system?

Mrs. Chalker: No, and the hon. Gentleman ought to know that the right of initiative for a uniform voting procedure lies with the European Parliament and not with individual member Governments or with the Council of Ministers.

Mr. William Powell: Is my right hon. Friend aware that her answer is widely welcomed by Conservative Members and that nothing could be more absurd than trying to dive into a universal system of proportional representation throughout the European Community? Will my right hon. Friend look into the unsatisfactory system of having a separate election day in June so that in future British European elections can be held on the same day as local elections in May?

Mrs. Chalker: Counting of votes in this country for European elections cannot begin until the close of polls in other European countries. It would be inappropriate to have a gap from May to June, which is when the European elections are always likely to be held, before the votes cast in May can be counted.

Mr. Janner: Does the Minister not realise that it makes no difference which electoral procedure is in force tomorrow because Labour will sweep to victory and the population of this country, not least in the marginal seat of Leicestershire, will show the Thatcher Government just what it thinks of them, which is very little indeed?

Mrs. Chalker: I have always had faith in democracy, even when, occasionally, as in 1974, it elects a Government of the wrong colour. We must ensure that democracy prevails in many more countries.

Dame Elaine Kellett-Bowman: Did my right hon. Friend regard it as even remotely fair when the small minority of Liberals in the German Government decided to abandon the Socialists and turn to the Christian Democrats and thus bring about a change of Government without reference to the German electorate?

Mrs. Chalker: My hon. Friend has explained what can happen in some countries as a result of the list system, which gives central control to the parties and allows a change of policy without further reference to the electorate. While it may be liked by some, a list system would not give the current leader of the British Labour group in Strasbourg the chance to be re-elected.

European Commission

3. **Ms. Mowlam:** To ask the Secretary of State for Foreign and Commonwealth Affairs when he next expects to meet the President of the European Commission; and what matters he expects to discuss.

8. **Mrs. Dunwoody:** To ask the Secretary of State for Foreign and Commonwealth Affairs when he next expects to meet the President of the European Commission; and what matters he expects to discuss.

The Secretary of State for Foreign and Commonwealth Affairs (Sir Geoffrey Howe): I next expect to meet the President of the Commission on 26 and 27 June at the meeting of the European Council when discussion will extend to the entire range of business before the Council.

Ms. Mowlam: When the Foreign Secretary meets the President at the European Council meeting, how will he justify the Government's decision this week to veto the EC directive to provide more child care, parental leave and flexible working arrangements for working parents in this country? Does he accept that those improvements are

needed now, and by 1992 they will be essential, or will he follow the Government's usual policy of assuming that if they are in a minority of one they must be right?

Sir Geoffrey Howe: This is one of many issues in which progress can be, should be and has been achieved on the basis of national responsibilities. We must think carefully before we seek to transfer responsibility to the European Community. That is the fulfilment of a principle that the President of the European Community will recognise—the principle of subsidiarity, which leaves it to the nation states to do those things which are best done by them.

Mrs. Dunwoody: When the Foreign Secretary meets his fellow Ministers, will he support the Chancellor's view of our joining the European monetary system or the Prime Minister's view?

Sir Geoffrey Howe: I will support the view expressed by both of them. My right hon. Friend the Chancellor of the Exchequer said at a press conference on Monday:
"It is not a question of whether we join the exchange rate mechanism of the EMS, it is a question of when."
My right hon. Friend the Prime Minister has said many times—I heard her say it at the launching of our manifesto—that:
"The policy is exactly the same as it was. We shall join when the time is right."

Mr. John Marshall: When my right hon. and learned Friend sees the president of the Commission, will he confirm that he disagrees with Dr. Barry Seal's view that Britain should leave the Community?

Sir Geoffrey Howe: I do not know for whom Dr. Seal speaks—he certainly does not speak for the British Government or the British people.

Mr. Wells: Does my right hon. and learned Friend agree that it would be entirely wrong for my right hon. Friend the Prime Minister or for him to discuss the outcome of the Delors report on European monetary union unless a debate had been held in the House before the Prime Minister's attendance at the European Council and her meeting with the Commission?

Sir Geoffrey Howe: There will be a number of opportunities for debate on those matters in the House and in the European Council. It will be for my right hon. Friend the Leader of the House to work out how they can best be reconciled.

Mr. Tony Banks: Would the Foreign Secretary support a move towards greater uniformity in voting practices in Europe? Would it not now be appropriate for him to talk to the Prime Minister and for the Prime Minister to talk to the Leader of the Opposition with a view, for example, to convening a Speakers' Conference to consider proportional representation and fixed-term Parliaments? I think that it is time that we thought about that.

Sir Geoffrey Howe: That is not a matter for a multinational Speakers' Conference. It has been considered by the European Parliament, and its report has been rejected; that is where the matter now rests.

Mr. David Nicholson: Will my right hon. and learned Friend point out to the President of the European Commission that Britain is already showing the way to a real social dimension by generating jobs in their hundreds of thousands through policies of enterprise and growth?

Sir Geoffrey Howe: I have pointed that out to the President and, with my hon. Friends, will continue to do so on every possible occasion. Unemployment in Britain has fallen for 33 consecutive months, and the number of jobs created between June 1983 and June 1987—the last period for which records are available—is larger than that in the whole of the rest of the Community put together, for exactly the reasons that my hon. Friend has given.

Mr. Kaufman: When the Foreign Secretary meets the President of the Commission, will he specify the items in the proposed social charter that have led the Prime Minister to describe it as "Marxist"?

Sir Geoffrey Howe: The right hon. Gentleman will recollect that many provisions in that document provide for substantial increases in the representation of organised trade unions on the boards of companies—an object that the Labour Government were trying to escape 20 years ago. In the past 20 years we have managed to shuffle off many problems and thus enhance the success of our economy. It would be entirely foolish for us to accept such prescriptions and to follow the right hon. Gentleman in the opposite direction.

Middle East

4. **Mr. Andrew MacKay:** To ask the Secretary of State for Foreign and Commonwealth Affairs what is the policy of Her Majesty's Government towards Soviet involvement in the middle east peace process.

The Minister of State, Foreign and Commonwealth Office (Mr. William Waldegrave): We welcome all efforts, including those of the Soviet Union, to build confidence between the parties to the Arab-Israel dispute and to prepare the way for negotiations. Improved Soviet-Israel relations can contribute to this.

Mr. MacKay: As Syria is clearly a major obstacle to the peace process in the middle east, and since no country in the region can bring any influence to bear on it—as the recent Arab League summit in Morocco clearly showed—does my hon. Friend think that the Soviets might have some influence, and might be able to exert some pressure on Syria?

Mr. Waldegrave: My hon. Friend is right. The issue was discussed when my right hon. and learned Friend met Mr. Shevardnadze recently. Soviet influence on Syria should not be exaggerated, but certainly the Soviet contribution must rest on urging Syria to come to the peace table with the other Arab states.

Mr. Bell: We would all welcome the involvement of the Soviet Union in any peace process in the middle east, but is it not a fact that in the past 20-odd years the Soviets have had very little influence in the middle east? What does the Minister believe that they can provide by way of positive input into the peace process?

Mr. Waldegrave: I make two points. First, there is the influence over Syria to which my hon. Friend the Member for Berkshire, East (Mr. MacKay) referred. Secondly, by re-establishing full diplomatic relations with Israel I think that the Soviets would go a long way towards building the confidence in Israel which I consider a necessary part of encouraging Israel to negotiate.

Mr. Latham: Will my hon. Friend confirm that the Soviets have shown considerable interest in Mr. Shamir's proposal for elections on the West Bank and Gaza? Has he discussed those proposals with Soviet diplomats and are they doing what they can to progress this idea further in discussions with the Palestine Liberation Organisation?

Mr. Waldegrave: We believe that one of the influences that has helped to lead the PLO into more moderate paths has been advice from the Soviet Union, because a good many of the groups within the PLO have close relations with Moscow. Certainly our officials have discussed this in Moscow. We hope that the more moderate and pragmatic line will be continued by the Soviet Union.

Ms. Short: Will the Minister discuss with the Soviet Union how to do something about the intransigence of Israel and its absolute breach of international law and of the Geneva convention in the occupied territories? Has not the time now come when the international community ought to exert pressure on Israel so that it will be willing to make peace instead of demanding to hang on to the occupied territories in breach of international law and trying to break the Palestinian people in the process? Is it not time for action and for pressure to be put on Israel to come to the negotiating table?

Mr. Waldegrave: Her Majesty's Government, the Governments of the Twelve, and now the Government of the United States in an excellent speech by Mr. Baker to the American-Israel Public Affairs Committee—in the United States—have made it very clear that we all believe that Israeli policy is leading to a dead end. The most eloquent statement of that position that I have ever read is the extract from Mr. Amos Oz's speech reproduced in *The Daily Telegraph* today.

Sir Dennis Walters: Does my hon. Friend recognise that over the past eight months the PLO, by a series of statements and declarations, has given every possible indication of its desire to make progress towards peace? The Israeli response has been wholly negative. What steps is my hon. Friend considering, with our European partners and the United States, to change the obdurate attitude of Israel?

Mr. Waldegrave: We welcomed the element in Mr. Shamir's proposals which related to elections. We did not believe the proposals as they stood were acceptable to the Palestinians, but they represented a small step forward. We have been urging both sides to take that proposal and to develop it into something which could lead to a full process towards peace. I would not say that there has been no movement on the Israeli side, but I would say that the proposal for elections needs further development, if it is to be acceptable.

European Monetary Union

5. **Mr. Kirkwood:** To ask the Secretary of State for Foreign and Commonwealth Affairs when he last discussed the question of European monetary union with M. Jacques Delors.

Sir Geoffrey Howe: European monetary co-operation was discussed at the Foreign Affairs Council in

Luxembourg on 12-13 June, which M. Delors attended, in the context of preparations for the European Council at Madrid on 26-27 June.

Mr. Kirkwood: Will the Foreign Secretary take it from me that we missed his presence at the Hawick common riding on Friday? I hope that he enjoyed his visit to the Borders, where I can tell him that the Delors report and the details thereof were on everyone's lips. The Government's endless procrastination is not good enough as it is prejudicing London as a financial centre in the longer term. More immediately and urgently, it is prejudicing the interests of millions of young home buyers who are making high mortgage repayments because of high interest rates. Does the Foreign Secretary accept that if there is continuing uncertainty about the currency, whatever the exchange rate, interest rates will always rise and that the only way to end that uncertainty is to join the exchange rate mechanism of the European monetary system?

Sir Geoffrey Howe: I am grateful for the hon. Gentleman's welcome for my visitation to his constituency, where I was delighted to find a growing fund of wisdom determined to return to the European Parliament the excellent Conservative representative. [HON. MEMBERS: "Name him!"] His name is Alasdair Hutton. If I am allowed to do so, I should like to advertise it even more plainly. All prudent voters in the hon. Gentleman's constituency should take the opportunity to vote tomorrow for Alasdair Hutton. I should also add, in answer to the hon. Gentleman's question, that our reaction to the Delors report on economic and monetary union makes a sharp distinction between what is there spelt out for stages 2 and 3 of the process towards economic and monetary union, which involves very far-reaching changes indeed which cannot be contemplated in the foreseeable future. In relation to the first stage, we have already taken many practical steps in that direction. We will need to see how much further we can go. There is a distinction to be drawn, and we strongly support what can be done under stage 1.

Mrs. Currie: Are not the economies of the member states still too different? They have different growth rates, employment patterns, unemployment rates, economic histories and patterns of economic development. Does my right hon. and learned Friend agree that entry into something as rigid and controlled as European monetary union should be a consequence of future closer co-operation between the economies which will come after 1992—and, I hope, before—and not a precursor of it?

Sir Geoffrey Howe: My hon. Friend is right in focusing on one aspect of the many features that are necessary before stages 2 and 3 of EMU can be contemplated. She has drawn attention to the economic factors. Powerful changes in institutional and constitutional arrangements will also have to be made, including transfers of sovereignty to Europe-wide institutions in relation to economic and monetary policy. I am sure that those changes go well beyond those contemplated by the overwhelming majority of hon. Members.

Mr. Spearing: When the Foreign Secretary next meets Mr. Delors and talks about economic and monetary union, will he assure him that the signature of the Governor of the Bank of England on the Delors report

was to show assent to the feasibility of the changes, not their merits or desirability? Will the right hon. and learned Gentleman comment on the particular method used by the Community which may cause misunderstandings about what the signature represents?

Sir Geoffrey Howe: The hon. Gentleman, with his customary insight, has easily overcome any risk of misunderstanding. It has been well known throughout that the Governor participated in that report in a personal capacity, and the report represents the conclusions of a group of experts and others constituted in that way. It is important to recognise that, even in respect of feasibility, the report emphasised the immense sequence of changes that would have to be made over a long period and expressly excluded any commitment to a timetable of any kind—so to that extent as well, it was wise. The least percipient section of the report was paragraph 39, which argued that by taking the first step one was committed to the last. Nothing should be further from the truth.

Cyprus

6. **Mr. Anthony Coombs:** To ask the Secretary of State for Foreign and Commonwealth Affairs when he last met the United Nations Secretary-General to discuss the United Nations initiative for solving the Cyprus problem; and what matters were discussed.

Mrs. Chalker: My right hon. and learned Friend the Secretary of State last discussed the Cyprus problem with the United Nations Secretary-General in Tokyo on 25 February, when they reviewed progress in the intercommunal talks. My right hon. Friend the Prime Minister also discussed the Cyprus problem with the Secretary-General on 18 April and met him again earlier today.

Mr. Coombs: Does my right hon. Friend agree that successful reunification of Cyprus depends upon an improved atmosphere of trust between the two communities, which will be promoted by the kind of intercommunal conference organised under parliamentary auspices in Nicosia this weekend? Given the previous reluctance of the Turkish Cypriot leadership to allow political leaders to attend such conferences, will my right hon. Friend make what representations she can to persuade the leaders that their attendance at these conferences is not an act of political subversion but a constructive commitment to the kind of improvement in relations that will lead to a successful relocation of the army?

Mrs. Chalker: The whole House will accept that the more the two communities and their two leaders—the President of the Republic of Cyprus and the leader from the north—come together, the more likely it is that the efforts of the United Nations Secretary-General will be successful in bringing about a resolution of the problem. That would be further underpinned by a meeting of people from both the communities. As my hon. Friend recognises, that is not being encouraged from the north. One can only hope that by further discussion we will get on top of the problems and that the United Nations Secretary-General's plan will be put into operation.

Mr. John D. Taylor: Arising from the re-equipment and modernisation of the Greek Cypriot guard by French companies during the past year, including the provision of new tanks and missiles, does the Minister think that this militarisation will give an assurance to the Turkish Cypriots about their safety in a united Cyprus? Does she think that it will encourage the Turkish army to reduce its numbers in Cyprus? Does she think that this is helpful to the intercommunal talks with which the Secretary-General is trying to proceed?

Mrs. Chalker: Any increase in tension between the communities, however it may be caused, would be unhelpful. The United Nations force, UNFICYP, has sought to keep the balance between the two communities and it has done a magnificent job, not least Britain's 741 men who form the largest contingent. Both sides need major constraint and a great deal of patience. I am confident that the Secretary-General is prepared to see it through patiently and consistently. We will give whatever help we can to a resolution under his auspices.

Mr. Lawrence: Would it help to speed a solution to the Cyprus problem if the Government followed their more normal pattern of even-handedness and did not give the impression that they were on the side of the Greeks?

Mr. Tony Banks: We are.

Mrs. Chalker: We have supported the United Nations Secretary-General at every turn. We have always tried to be what my hon. and learned Friend described as even-handed. His reference was, perhaps, to our difficulties because the declaration of independence by Rauf Denktas in 1983 was illegal, and nothing can change that. It is crucial to get the timing of further talks right. I sincerely hope that by the end of this month further progress will have been made. We shall continue to be even-handed, as we have been all along.

Mr. Heffer: Everyone welcomes the fact that the Government are trying to be even-handed, but the Minister was right to point out that it was illegal action by the Turks, especially the invasion by Turkish soliders, that led to the division of Cyprus. Should we not be bringing pressure to bear on the Turks? After all, Turkey is a member of NATO. If Britain believes in defending democracy and freedom, should it not tell Turkey that if it wishes to remain a member it should withdraw its troops, thus laying a better basis to bring together the two peoples of Cyprus?

Mrs. Chalker: Britain is absolutely right to continue to support the initiative of the United Nations' Secretary-General. There is no question of trying to resolve such a difficult matter in any other way. However difficult the problem may sometimes appear to be to the President of Cyprus and to Mr. Denktas, it can be resolved only through discussions. It would be to good effect if influence could be brought to bear either by the Turkish or Greek Governments, or by a resolution in line with the Secretary-General's plan.

China

7. **Mr. Winnick:** To ask the Secretary of State for Foreign and Commonwealth Affairs if he will make a statement on current British/Chinese relations.

Mr. Geoffrey Howe: I refer the hon. Gentleman to my statement in the House on 6 June, when I said that under present circumstances there could be no question of continuing normal business with the Chinese authorities.

Mr. Winnick: Will the Foreign Secretary again tell the Chinese authorities, if he has not already done so, of the widespread feeling of revulsion in Britain at the continuing intimidation, brutality and terror tactics that the Chinese authorities are using against anyone considered to be a dissident or a subversive? If they continue their present policy of terror, is there not bound to be a growing feeling among democracies—not just Britain—that effective steps should be taken against that dictatorship?

Will the Foreign Office work closely with the Home Office to ensure that those Chinese students studying in this country who have a well-founded fear of returning home in the present circumstances will receive sympathetic consideration of their requests to stay in this country?

Sir Geoffrey Howe: The first point expressed by the hon. Gentleman was exactly the one expressed at the meeting of European Foreign Ministers on Monday, which I attended. We joined in expressing the clear view that continued repression, such as that being enforced by the authorities in China, following the savagery and brutality of the previous week, is likely to lead to a progressive decline in China's status in the eyes of the rest of the world. We are trying to get that message through as clearly and as plainly as possible. As to Chinese students in Britain and other Community countries, a clear view was expressed that applications to extend their right to stay in their respective host countries should be sympathetically considered in the light of the facts that the hon. Gentleman mentioned.

Mr. Walden: Does my right hon. and learned Friend agree with hon. Members who recently visited Hong Kong that the most honourable approach to the predicament of its people is the most realistic? Does my right hon. and learned Friend further agree that it would be wrong to jettison the Sino-British agreement; that it would be wrong to encourage mass emigration, which would undermine the stability of the colony; and that it would be wrong to encourage the illusion that the swifter introduction of democracy would be any bulwark against a regime that has manifestly taken leave of its senses? Does he agree that there are circumstances in which prudence can be a potent substitute for power?

Sir Geoffrey Howe: I am grateful to my hon. Friend for summarising the chunks of wisdom that we have been able to read in newspaper articles that he has written recently. He is right to urge, above all, a sense of balance and realism. Plainly, as I said in the House last week, if it is possible to make headway by enhancing and consolidating democratic structures within the territory of Hong Kong, it should be considered in the light of the views being expressed there. It would be wrong to do or say anything that would encourage a flood of emigration. Above all, my hon. Friend rightly emphasised the importance of retaining the foundation for the future—the joint declaration. One must ask whether the future would be better or worse in the absence of it. It is clear that a future built on the continuation of the declaration will be far stronger. Our task must be to do all that we can to make the Chinese Government give the declaration the support that their international obligations require.

Mr. Morgan: Having read the press release from the Monday Club last week, which said:

"We should not become the dustbin of Europe"—

Mr. Speaker: Paraphrase, please.

Mr. Morgan: The press release states that the people of Hong Kong are not British but Chinese and that this country should not become the dustbin of Europe. Further to the reply that the right hon. and learned Gentleman gave my hon. Friend the Member for Walsall, North (Mr. Winnick) about the position of mainland Chinese students in Britain, will he say what provision the Foreign Office is making to provide some means of funding for them, because they are funded on a monthly bursary basis by the Chinese Government? How will they survive in Britain if they have a well-founded fear of persecution should they return home?

Sir Geoffrey Howe: It is not possible to address oneself to all the possible implications of what has happened recently in China, save step by step. Our present concern, which was expressed by the hon. Member for Walsall, North (Mr. Winnick), is to secure a minimum assurance about the response that will be given to applications made by Chinese students to extend their stay in Britain. Some of them are here on scholarships financed in this country and some on scholarships financed by their home Government. We shall have to see how the arrangements can best be made. It is most important that the world secures, as soon as it can be achieved, a return to a more reasonable and more restrained style of Government in Peking.

Mr. Adley: I endorse the view put quietly but essentially by my right hon. and learned Friend and by my hon. Friend the Member for Buckingham (Mr. Walden), but does my right hon. and learned Friend agree that the only beneficiaries from the present position are those who, for some time, have been trying to sow mistrust between Britain and China to undermine the joint agreement? Does my right hon. and learned Friend agree that to bring succour to the suffering people of China in their hour of turmoil, and to restore confidence to the people of Hong Kong, it is necessary, however distasteful, to continue to do business with those who are currently in charge of affairs in China?

Sir Geoffrey Howe: I must say to my hon. Friend that it is very difficult, even with the most far-ranging eye, to detect anyone who can be classified as a beneficiary of the tragic brutality of the past few weeks in Beijing. It is certainly right for us to do everything we can to bring about a reversal of those trends. We have moved in that direction by making it plain that neither normal high-level contact nor the continuation of arms contracts can be contemplated in the present circumstances. We have equally made it plain that it is important to retain such contacts as can be built on continuing commercial or personal relationships, for example. Sooner rather than later we must try to achieve a means of getting through to those in authority in Beijing just how deeply the rest of the

world mourns what has happened to the progress that has taken place in the past 10 years and how strongly we urge a return of common sense and sanity to that country.

Mr. Foulkes: Can the Foreign Secretary confirm that what he said in answer to my hon. Friend the Member for Walsall, North (Mr. Winnick) was a clear condemnation of the purge now under way in China? As well as giving sympathetic consideration to applications from Chinese students in the United Kingdom, will he give sympathetic consideration to applications for refugee status from any Chinese democracy activists who feel that they may be in danger in the present purge and who seek refuge in the British embassy in China?

Will the Foreign Secretary tell us his response to the widespread support in Hong Kong for much faster progress towards democracy in that territory? Does he agree that he and his colleagues are on pretty shaky ground when criticising the lack of democracy in China or elsewhere while retaining colonial paternalism in Hong Kong?

Sir Geoffrey Howe: I have already made it very clear that the purge was condemned not only by Her Majesty's Government, but by the other Governments of the European Community last week and again at our meeting this week. I have also explained the extent to which we clearly need to respond sympathetically where possible to the applications about which we have been talking. On Hong Kong, I must tell the hon. Gentleman that the answer is by no means as simple as he thinks. My hon. Friend the Member for Buckingham (Mr. Walden) put a more cautious view of it. It has been discussed at some length in the evidence given by the Governor of Hong Kong to the Select Committee on Foreign Affairs on Monday this week. Obviously, it is prudent to see what more can be done, as I said last week, to advance and consolidate the democratic process as a bulwark for the future of Hong Kong and to do so in the light of the views more recently expressed in Hong Kong. It would not be right to jump to premature, absolutist conclusions.

Sir John Stokes: I have recently been in China and Hong Kong but I hesitate to pontificate on the subject. However, does my right hon. and learned Friend agree that while on one hand we must adopt a very strong attitude to the Chinese Government about their wrongs and our rights, on the other hand it would be wrong to the people of England and Hong Kong to allow the idea to get abroad that we shall be far easier in allowing millions of Chinese to come here from Hong Kong?

Sir Geoffrey Howe: My hon. Friend is right to draw attention to the matter. It was emphasised by a number of hon. Members last week that it would be wrong to give the impression that the House was ready to contemplate offering such an open-ended commitment.

Environment (EC)

9. **Mr. Hardy:** To ask the Secretary of State for Foreign and Commonwealth Affairs if he has reconsidered the suggestion that the Council of Europe's concern for a wide range of environmental matters should be transferred to the European Community; and what assessment he has made of whether the 11 member states not part of the Community will endorse that view.

Mrs. Chalker: I am not aware of any suggestion that the Council of Europe's concern for a wide range of environmental matters should be transferred to the European Community. The Council of Europe is already doing good work on nature conservations. In deciding what new work it should take on, the Council will wish to avoid duplicating work better done elsewhere.

Mr. Hardy: I am grateful to the Minister for that reply. Will the Minister confirm that the environmental role of the Council of Europe should be broad and continuing, not least because it represents a far greater geographical area than the Community and because it embodies, therefore, the genuine interests of the 11 non-member states, as well as the organisation closely involved with local authorities in Europe? Will she make it clear that any suggestion that its interests should be restricted to nature conservation would be absurd and dangerous? Does she agree with the more considered and acceptable view expressed by the Norwegian chairman in office during the assembly last month?

Mrs. Chalker: I assure the hon. Gentleman that the valued work done by the Council of Europe in many environmental areas is something that we hope will continue and perhaps not only among the 23 existing member states. Perhaps it may have influence further afield because so many of these issues know no national boundaries and no Council of Europe boundaries.

I have had long talks with Helga Hernes, the Minister who took the questions at the Assembly and I am sure that we can work well together. However, that is not to undermine in any way the great success that my noble Friend Lord Caithness has had in the Environment Council where good sound decisions were made on ivory, on seals, on strengthening the United Nations institutions for environmental work and on the work on climatic change. Great praise has been given to this country for the work that has been done as a result of the Prime Minister's conference in early March. Everybody should be thoroughly involved.

Sir Geoffrey Finsberg: Does my right hon. Friend agree that much of the duplication that she rightly wishes to avoid comes from the European Parliament, not from the Council of Europe? Does she recognise that the Council of Europe does an immense amount of good work on environmental matters and at a far lower cost to the citizens of Europe?

Mrs. Chalker: I well understand what my hon. Friend is saying. There is no doubt that the Council of Europe was the initiator of many excellent environmental reforms, but we must be careful not to exclude the need for members of the European Community, working together in the creation of the single market, to take the back-up measures that are definitely necessary in matters of trade. I caution against saying that one institution rather than another should be responsible in any specific area and say, as I have said to the hon. Member for Wentworth (Mr. Hardy), that where advances can be made to improve the environment, they should be undertaken without duplication by all the bodies involved.

Mr. Coleman: May I thank the Minister for her attitude to this matter, especially in respect of the way in which the Council of Europe goes about its activities? I hope that she

will agree on the need to ensure that the Council of Europe does not become demoralised over its excellent work on environmental matters.

Mrs. Chalker: I assure the hon. Gentleman that there is no intention and no plan that the Members of the Assembly of the Council of Europe should become demoralised in any way by the actions of others, who want to copy many of the things that they have done. The Council should regard that as a compliment. However, there is no doubt also that there is room for the involvement of more than one forum. Such involvement can be achieved without duplication, and I sincerely hope that it will be.

President Bush

10. **Mr. Andy Stewart:** To ask the Secretary of State for Foreign and Commonwealth Affairs, when he last had discussions with President Bush; and what matters were discussed.

Sir Geoffrey Howe: Together with my right hon. Friend the Prime Minister, I last had discussions with President Bush, and Secretary Baker, on 1 June, during their visit to this country. We discussed East-West relations, the middle east and other regional issues and trade matters.

Mr. Stewart: Did my right hon. and learned Friend have a chance to review the highly successful outcome of the NATO summit with President Bush when he was in London and did President Bush reiterate the position taken by both Governments about the dangers of a denuclearised Europe?

Sir Geoffrey Howe: Yes, that was one of the topics that naturally assumed an important part in our discussions because President Bush's visit to London followed immediately on the successful NATO summit when we agreed on the essential features, not least the circumstances in which negotiations on short-range nuclear weapons should be contemplated.

Mr. Tom Clarke: When the Foreign Secretary next meets President Bush, will he raise with him the denial of fundamental human rights in the apartheid system in South Africa? Does the right hon. and learned Gentleman agree that that would be an appropriate time for both sides to look afresh at the possibility of sanctions?

Sir Geoffrey Howe: The Government and the new American Administration have already expressed their common view of their total condemnation of apartheid and the denial of human rights that that involves. However, we do not draw from that proposition the same conclusion as the hon. Gentleman. We believe that it is most important in the months ahead to keep on course the prospect of the independence of Namibia, in accordance with resolution 435, and to look forward to circumstances in which the South African Government, which will be elected after 7 September, are ready to take the fundamental steps to dismantle apartheid. We do not think that that process would be helped or hastened by any further moves on sanctions.

Sir Peter Blaker: There are now more than 43,000 Vietnamese boat people in Hong Kong. They are arriving at a rate which necessitates the building of two new camps each week to hold them. Will my right hon. and learned

Friend explain to President Bush that there are many people in this country who find it impossible to understand how the American Administration can justify its argument at Geneva that there should not be a policy of compulsory repatriation of economic migrants to Vietnam, with appropriate guarantees from the Government of Vietnam, when it is the policy of the United States for economic migrants from Haiti who arrive in Florida, to be sent back compulsorily and for the same to be done for economic migrants who arrive from Mexico across the American border?

Sir Geoffrey Howe: My right hon. Friend is entirely right. Indeed, the Prime Minister and I impressed on President Bush and Secretary of State Baker the extreme gravity of the situation facing Hong Kong as a result of the continuing inflow of Vietnamese boat people. I had the opportunity to raise the issue of Indo-Chinese refugees again yesterday at the Geneva conference, and I put to the representative of the United States the same arguments as my right hon. Friend has now put to me. It is of crucial importance that, aside from any arrangements to handle those classified as refugees—that is something on which some progress may be made at the Geneva conference— there is a recognition of the need to secure a return flow from Hong Kong to Vietnam of those who are not classified as refugees. I had the opportunity of discussing that also in Geneva with the Vietnamese Foreign Minister, and discussions on that topic will be continuing.

Mr. Kaufman: When the Foreign Secretary next meets President Bush, will he discuss with him the very positive response by President Gorbachev to President Bush's own historic offer on conventional disarmament? Will he discuss, too, with President Bush the historic agreement reached this week in Bonn between the Soviet Union and the Federal Republic of Germany and the statement by the Soviet Foreign Ministry spokesman that an agreement with France is next on the cards—that Paris is the next stop? However, that same Soviet spokesman did not think that an agreement with Britain was possible or that Britain was a willing partner. Why is it that, while the United States, France, West Germany and other western allies speak positively and constructively in discussions with the Soviet Union, this country, and especially this Prime Minister, simply whips up the cold war?

Sir Geoffrey Howe: The right hon. Gentleman can be relied on to have an insight that is fundamentally mistaken. The series of successful visits by President Gorbachev to western European countries commenced with his visit to this country. Our Government—and nobody more than the Prime Minister—have emphasised the extent to which we welcome President Gorbachev's progress on perestroika. We regard the outcome of his visit to the Federal Republic of Germany in the same light. It is not our practice to issue comprehensive joint declarations of the kind recorded in the Federal Republic this week, but a large number of the matters dealt with in that joint declaration have already been the subject of similar agreements between ourselves and the Soviet Union. The right hon. Gentleman need have no fear. The United Kingdom is not lagging in the prudent promotion of better East-West relations.

OECD

11. Mr. Knapman: To ask the Secretary of State for Foreign and Commonwealth Affairs what matters were raised at the most recent summit meeting of the Organisation for Economic Co-operation and Development.

Mrs. Chalker: The OECD Ministerial Council covered a wide range of subjects, including macroeconomic developments and policies, structural reform, trade and debt. Environmental issues also featured prominently.

Mr. Knapman: Does my right hon. Friend agree that Britain is helping Third world countries not only through the quality of its aid programme, but by direct investment in Third world countries and through attempts to open European Community markets to them?

Mrs. Chalker: Indeed I can. Britain has led the way, with the initiative by my right hon. Friend the Chancellor on sub-Saharan debt. We have been cancelling aid debt for the poorest countries—almost £1 billion world-wide. We have led the way in converting loans into grants. We have targeted our aid much better than every before. That is an important help for the developing nations.

The other aspect that my hon. Friend mentioned was direct investment in developing countries. Between 1984 and 1987, the United Kingdom's direct investment was greater than that of the whole of the rest of the European Community put together.

Above all, we believe in open trade, world-wide, in giving opportunities to these countries for trade with the European Community and for avoiding fortress Europe.

Mr. Pike: Can the Minister assure us that urgent consideration will be given to the need for aid for Namibia following independence, especially recognising the debt that it will inherit, which was incurred by the present non-representative Government?

Mrs. Chalker: We are well aware that Namibia will need support and aid further to that which we already give it. We are working hard to ensure, through our representatives with the United Nations force, that the peace plan stays on course, so that free and fair elections will give independence to Namibia in November and we shall be able to work on a further aid programme thereafter.

Angola

12. Mr. Michael Brown: To ask the Secretary of State for Foreign and Commonwealth Affairs what reports has he received on the process towards internal reconciliation in Angola.

Mrs. Chalker: We welcome the security conference of Angola's neighbours in Luanda on 16 May and President Dos Santos' announcement of a peace plan for Angola, including a zone of peace along the line of the Benguela railway. We shall continue to encourage African countries in their mediation efforts.

Mr. Brown: In addition to that answer, does my right hon. Friend agree that the United Nations agreement of last year is most important? Does she not think that we should ensure that the United Nations increases the number of observers in Angola, to make sure that the withdrawal of Cuban troops materialises?

Mrs. Chalker: The Cuban troop withdrawal from Angola is going ahead in accordance with the Geneva protocol. The net withdrawal of 6,885 troops was completed by the end of April. My hon. Friend will probably know that the United Nations has doubled up the monitoring force, because it is by monitoring what is going on that we can assist. I have every confidence that the actions taken by UNAVEM—the United Nations force—will bring about the clear recognition that the plan has been fully executed.

Panama

13. **Mr. Jacques Arnold:** To ask the Secretary of State for Foreign and Commonwealth Affairs if he will make a statement on relations with Panama.

Mr. Eggar: Relations would be improved if General Noriega were to stand down and open the way to democratic government.

Mr. Arnold: Does my hon. Friend feel that Latin America has made considerable progress towards representative democracy in almost all countries? Do not the actions of General Noriega, this ninth-rate villain, do much to tarnish that reputation? Should not our relationship and that of the European countries towards Panama be modified accordingly, until such time as Panama chucks this viper from its nest?

Mr. Eggar: I very much agree with my hon. Friend in welcoming the movement towards democracy in Latin America. If, as we all hope, Chile moves to democracy at the end of this year, that will leave only Nicaragua and Panama as non-democratic states.

Already, together with our European Community partners, we have made a clear statement calling on General Noriega to stand down, to open the way for a peaceful democratic resolution of Panama's problems.

EC Commissioners

15. **Mr. Robertson:** To ask the Secretary of State for Foreign and Commonwealth Affairs when he last met either of Britain's Commissioners in the European Community; and what was discussed.

Mrs. Chalker: Following official calls paid on him by the British members of the Commission in December 1988, my right hon. and learned Friend and I have been in contact with them and other members of the Commission on a range of Community issues, and look forward to continuing such contacts.

Mr. Robertson: When the Minister discusses with the Commissioners the business that is before them, could she read to them part of Herr Genscher's speech to the 40th anniversary meeting of the Deutsch-Englische Gesellschaft in Dusseldorf last week? He said:

"The Community must be a community for all citizens; it therefore needs a social dimension so that it can evolve into a community of social progress."

How does that square with the Government's attitude to the social measures that are being put forward? Specifically, how does it square with the veto on Monday on the equality provisions in the Social Minister's council and the Marxist veto on the social charter that the Christian Democratic Union Minister believed was too bland and needed to be sharpened?

Mrs. Chalker: Of course there is a social dimension to what we do in the Community. Nobody has ever denied that, and that social dimension is the key to improving living standards and working conditions. Getting non-inflationary growth is the way to do that. We shall not achieve that if many of the aspects of the so-called social charter are carried through. We must do everything that we can to continue the fall in unemployment that we have had in this country and throughout the Community. That will be done by deregulation. It is not done by heaping on to business restrictions that are not necessary to improve our economic life.

Foreign Affairs Council

The following Question stood upon the Paper:

18. **Mr. Rowlands:** To ask the Secretary of State for Foreign and Commonwealth Affairs, what was discussed at the last meeting of the Foreign Affairs Council.

3.30 pm

The Secretary of State for Foreign and Commonwealth Affairs (Sir Geoffrey Howe): The Foreign Affairs Council met in Luxembourg on 12 June. My right hon. Friend the Minister of State and I represented the United Kingdom. The Council discussed preparations for the Madrid European Council, which will take place on 26-27 June. The Council agreed the mandate for negotiation with the Soviet Union on a trade and economic co-operation agreement. It also discussed special measures for the French overseas departments, and commissioned further work.

Ministers also met in the framework of political co-operation. They expressed profound concern at the brutal action taken by the Chinese authorities against unarmed civilian demonstrators, and agreed to keep in close touch about the action which member Governments are taking in response. Statements were issued recording the concern of the Twelve at the renewal of the state of emergency in South Africa and their support for the work of the committee of three Arab Heads of State in the Lebanon. Copies have been placed in the Library of the House.

I also briefed our partners fully on the great problems confronting Hong Kong as a result of the growing influx of Vietnamese boat people, and warned that this was creating an intolerable situation. Ministers also had a two-hour meeting with Foreign Ministers of the front-line states covering a wide range of questions concerning southern Africa. My right hon. Friend attended a Co-operation Council with Algeria.

Mr. Rowlands: Is it not disgraceful that we have had to force this statement out of the Secretary of State? Will he give us an assurance that in future he will volunteer such statements, bearing in mind the enormous nature of the issues facing the Foreign Affairs Council? Is he aware that the communities that I represent see 1992 not only as an opportunity for development, but as a potential charter for the exploitation of workers? People know that they are behind on social insurance, maternity benefits and other benefits compared with many of our European partners. In that context, will the Secretary of State try to persuade the rest of the Government to consider their absolutely negative view about the social charter?

Mr. Howe: The first point raised by the hon. Gentleman has generally been a matter for discussion and consultation between Government and Opposition parties. Certainly I am happy to listen to representations about it. There has not been an oral statement for a couple of years. It is important to recognise that Community matters already put substantial pressure on parliamentary time. I think that we have had 13 scrutiny debates in the last five weeks. I shall certainly bear in mind the hon. Gentleman's point. The Council did not have as large an agenda as usual, and it is convenient for me to answer in this way because there is a question about the matter on the Order Paper.

The hon. Gentleman asked about the social charter. There is an important and fundamental point to be understood by the House and more widely. It is that the Government acknowledge the need for social dimension to economic policy. It is our contention that one of the most important social dimensions has been our success in dealing with unemployment. The fact that we have been able to achieve the growth of more jobs in the United Kingdom than in all the other European Community countries put together is a measure of the success of the social dimension of our economic policy.

Regardless of party, hon. Members in all parts of the House would rise up in protest if it was argued that the whole range of matters now on the agenda of the social charter were to be the subject of common Community policies imposed on us by Community legislation and were no longer to be matters for discussion by the House as matters of its national competence.

Mr. Andrew Rowe (Mid-Kent): Will my right hon. And learned Friend confirm that his colleagues in the Council were as well aware as he that the demonstrations in China began with a relatively small-scale demonstration asking for conversations about the future of education? Will he and they use their best endeavours to explain to the Chinese Government that there is no point in sending millions of students to university if, having aroused their intellectual curiosity, they then machine-gun them down in the streets when they ask questions of the Government? Will he and they exert every possible pressure to rescue those students who are at present in danger of their lives for having done no more than ask questions of their Government?

Sir Geoffrey Howe: The insight offered by my hon. Friend is central to the arguments that will be discussed in the Community at the meeting on Monday. We deplore the brutality that is being used, particularly directed at students. We recognise that one of the most important features of what has happened in China in the last decade has been the opening of the minds of Chinese students and of those in Chinese academic institutions. That is why I have told the House this afternoon that we extend special sympathy to Chinese students in this country. The best hope for the future of China may yet spring from the extent to which a generation now rising in that country may be able to re-emerge, championing effective democracy and self-government.

Mr. Merlyn Rees (Morley and Leeds, South): Did any discussions take place for co-ordinated action, limited though it might be, arising out of what has happened in China? For example, one reads that there are queues outside EEC country embassies of Chinese trying to get out. Has there been co-ordinated action in that respect? Is it true that, while some embassy visa sections are open, the British visa section is closed?

Sir Geoffrey Howe: The central question raised by the right hon. Gentleman was referred to in my statement, when I said that we had agreed to keep in close touch about the action that member Governments were taking in response to the matters to which he referred. We were able to express a common view on our attitude towards high-level visits, arms supplies and Chinese students in our countries. We shall seek to co-ordinate our actions, so far as we can, in that way.

The answer to the right hon. Gentleman's question about visas and applications for visas in Peking is that, as the House knows, the size of our mission was reduced at the same time as dependents were withdrawn last week. We are now giving practical consideration to the scale and pace at which that should be restored.

Mr. Teddy Taylor (Southend, East): While I fully support what my right hon. and learned Friend has said about the Socialist nonsenses of the social charter, may I ask him to explain how on earth he can stop them if, as seems to be the case, the majority of member states want them, and the Commission presents them as majority vote issues under the Single European Act?

As we now see a real threat to all the splendid achievements of Her Majesty's Government, will my right hon. and learned Friend be prepared to discuss with our European Community partners the possibility of developing a two-tier Europe, which would be good for us and good for them?

Sir Geoffrey Howe: We shall be challenging any unjustified extension of either the role or the competence of European Community institutions along the lines I have stated. A large number of the topics foreshadowed in the draft of the social charter do not fall within the area covered by majority voting.

We shall be seeking to limit the impact of any possible social charter, so that it does not infringe upon any essential features of our own structure, because it is most important that we do that. We shall be doing that by advancing the arguments that I have been advancing in the Housing this afternoon. However, to believe that it would make sense to do that by consciously espousing the idea of a two-tier Europe, with our country setting itself in some outer tier, would be to set ourselves on a path that has been consistently rejected by the House ever since we joined the European Community in 1976.

Miss Joan Lestor (Eccles): The Foreign and Commonwealth Secretary said that the council regretted the renewal of the state of emergency in South Africa. Bearing in mind the speed with which the British Government condemned the alleged breach by SWAPO, of the United Nation's resolution 435, will the Foreign Secretary say whether, included in that expression of regret, there was any reference to the statements—which I have here—made in Namibia that, should SWAPO win the elections in Namibia, the South African State Security Council plans to sabotage independence in that state?

Sir Geoffrey Howe: I do not know what anonymous statements the hon. Lady may be quoting. The statement that we have tabled in the Library was to reaffirm our condemnation of the system of apartheid, and to call for the liberation of Mandela and other political leaders and the commencement of a dialogue with other political organisations. We also discussed the crucial importance of proceeding with the implementation of resolution 435 and, with the front-line states, emphasised the obligation and interest of all of us to ensure compliance with resolution 435 not merely by SWAPO but by any organisation or body under the control or command of the South African Government. We all have, and emphasise, the same objective—fair and free elections in Namibia at the earliest possible opportunity.

Mr. Neil Thorne (Ilford, South): Was the trade and transit dispute between India and Nepal discussed? Both the European Community and the British Government give substantial aid to both those friendly countries, so it is of considerable concern to us all that such a dispute is continuing, when it is causing wastage of these scarce resources. Is there any hope of an early meeting between those countries with the aim of achieving a satisfactory and honourable resolution of the disputes?

Sir Geoffrey Howe: I understand my hon. Friend's interest in the future relations between Nepal and India, both countries with which we have good and friendly relations. We share his interests in the matters to which he has referred. The topic was not discussed among Foreign Ministers in Luxembourg this week, but I am sure that all would share our interest in looking for an early resolution of these problems in the most friendly and conciliatory fashion.

Mr. Archy Kirkwood (Roxburgh and Berwickshire): Will the Foreign and Commonwealth Secretary expand somewhat on the discussion that took place at the Foreign Affairs Council on the subject of the Vietnamese refugee problem—the boat people—in Hong Kong? Is there any hope of our sister European countries accepting responsibility for this terrible and intractable problem, which is getting worse week by week?

Sir Geoffrey Howe: There was not a great deal of discussion on this in the Foreign Affairs Council, but I took the opportunity to alert my colleagues to the gravity and importance of the problem. It has been more fully discussed at the conference taking place in Geneva yesterday and today. A number of them have taken, are taking and will be taking direct responsibility for the resettlement of additional numbers of refugees. That is one of the categories that the conference has been summoned to consider. I cannot remember the exact number, but some are making additional commitments in that respect. A more difficult category is that of non-refugees— economic migrants—for whom virtually everyone sees the necessity of their being relocated back in their homeland.

Mr. Michael Colvin (Romsey and Waterside): My right hon. and learned Friend will no doubt acknowledge the progress that is being made towards the liberalisation of air transport within Europe. Will he give an undertaking that, when the Foreign Affairs Council next meets, the question of liberalisation within Europe will be on the agenda, as it has implications for air service agreements with third countries—most notably, the United States of America? If it will be given increasing rights to fly within the European Community, it is most important that European countries are given reciprocal rights to fly within America.

Sir Geoffrey Howe: My hon. Friend raises an important set of related points, but they would be more appropriately discussed in due course by the Transport Council rather than by the Foreign Affairs Council. However, I shall certanly bring my hon. Friend's points to the attention of my right hon. Friend the Secretary of State for Transport.

Mr. George Robertson (Hamilton): We are all grateful to whoever is responsible for this rare if limited opportunity to question the Foreign Secretary about the top European Council of Ministers meeting. The last

[*Mr. George Robertson*]

occasion on which the Government offered an oral statement on this, the most important of the European Community's Council of Ministers, despite many requests since by the Opposition, was on 17 December 1986—two and a half years and more than 30 monthly meetings ago, which is clearly unacceptable to the House.

We welcome the discussion on the events in China for which my right hon. Friend the Member for Manchester, Gorton (Mr. Kaufman) asked last week, and the opportunity that all member states had to act in unison and to condemn the cold brutality of the Chinese Government over the past two weeks. We acknowledge that the key business of the Foreign Affairs Council was to fix the agenda for the Madrid summit, but it promises that Britain will once again be on the sidelines—isolated and marginalised by the confusions and divisions in the Government over the European monetary system and by the Government's neanderthal approach to the social dimensions of 1992.

Can the right hon. and learned Gentleman say whether rumours that the Government will accept phase 1 of the Delors plan on European monetary union are true, and whether No. 10 Downing street has yet rubber-stamped that which he and the Chancellor of the Exchequer are clearly cooking up? Why is it that Britain, alone of the 12 Community countries, believes that the social charter is evil, bureacratic and unnecessary—when even the Conservative Right-wing German Minister of Employment, Mr. Norbert Blüm. believes that it is too bland and needs to be toughened up? Is it not the case that, because the Government insist on ignoring the 60 per cent. of British people who, according to this week's poll by the *Daily Telegraph* support the social charter, they well merit the description of themselves in today's editorial in *The Independent*:

"The Conservatives have waged a wretched, negative and dishonest campaign which, far from uniting the party, has embarrassed most of its candidates"?

Does the right hon. and learned Gentleman not agree that *The Times* has it spot on when it comments in an editorial:

"The Labour bandwagon is beginning to gather speed"?

Sir Geoffrey Howe: I am sure that the House is glad to acknowledge the extent to which the hon. Gentleman has broadened his newspaper reading, but we cannot pay tribute to any other aspect of his wisdom. I welcome the hon. Gentleman's comments about the Council's attitude to the events in China. However, when he turns to the Community's immediate agenda, he does not get it very right. As I told the House, there is a sharp distinction to be made between phase 1 as discussed in the Delors report and phases 2 and 3. That distinction has been made by my right hon. Friend the Chancellor of the Exchequer in all the relevant discussions, and it will be made again at Madrid.

As to the social charter, the hon. Gentleman must understand that some of its provisions represent an attempt to reimpose on this country conditions from which some of his predecessors in the Labour party tried to escape. Some of the social charter's provisions would reproduce those features that Barbara Castle and Harold Wilson tried to remove at the time of "In Place of Strife".

It would be totally foolish and negative for the Government of this country, who have achieved substantial economic progress, and record progress on unemployment, to accept obligations of that kind. The position of the Government and of those representing us in the European elections is positive, united and effective —and that unity and effectiveness will be seen when the results of tomorrow's elections are announced at the weekend.

Food Research (Bristol)

3.49 pm

Ms. Dawn Primarolo (Bristol, South): I beg to ask leave to move the Adjournment of the House, under Standing Order No. 20 for the purpose of discussing a specific and important matter that should have urgent consideration, namely,

"the closure announced today of the institute of food research at Bristol, given the continuing rise of food poisoning to near epidemic proportions."

This matter is specific because of the type of research which is conducted at the food laboratories in Bristol. It is important because of the public concern felt by consumers on matters of public health and dietary considerations. It is urgent because the closure was announced this morning at 11 am in Bristol. At the research laboratories in Bristol there are 80 projects—*[Interruption.]* I am sorry. This is an important issue, but it is difficult to concentrate on making my application because I cannot hear myself think for the din from the Conservative Benches.

The projects conducted at Langford in the Bristol food research institute cover listeria, and cook-chill proposals are being investigated. The institute carried out research on salmonella poisoning until that was cancelled and has, in the past, conducted research on botulism. The leading authority in that subject is based at the laboratory.

The institute covers work on food safety and quality. The fat content of food is vital in a society which suffers so much from heart disease. It researches food acceptability and food processing. It is important because of the increasing risk to health from microbial contamination, the emergence of new pathogenic organisms and because consumers prefer fresh foods, which means that the traditional methods of preserving foods cannot be used. Changes in people's dietary patterns means increased hazards associated with increased consumption of some foods. A reliable Government have a duty to ensure that we can consume safe food.

This is urgent, given the context of yet another problem related to food consumption in this country. There are 120 scientists who will lose their jobs by December 1990, and much of the research will not be transferred to other institutions. This is happening at a time when France and Spain are increasing their research and recognising that it is necessary for food safety and the decent health of the consuming public. Our Government are pursuing the trend of making the consumer less safe. The food industry cannot be trusted to ensure that the correct priorities are adopted.

The closure of this institution is foolhardy, callous and, given the current environment, cavalier. It shows scant regard for the best interests of the consumers. I hope that we shall be granted an emergency debate.

Mr. Speaker: The hon. Member for Bristol, South (Ms. Primarolo) asks leave to move the Adjournment of the House under Standing Order No. 20 for the purpose of discussing a specific and important matter that she thinks should have urgent consideration, namely,

"The closure announced today of the institute of food research at Bristol, given the continuing rise of food poisoning to near epidemic proportions."

I have listened with care to what the hon. Lady has said. As she knows, my sole duty in considering an application under Standing Order No. 20 is to decide whether the matter should be given precedence over the business set down for today or tomorrow. I regret that the matter raised does not meet the criteria of Standing Order No. 20; therefore, I cannot submit her application to the House.

Mr. Robin Cook (Livingston): On a point of order, Mr. Speaker. Yesterday, during the exchanges on botulism, I asked the Secretary of State for Health whether the Government would now reverse the cuts in research into food safety that threatened the Bristol laboratory. In his reply the Secretary of State asserted that the laboratory was

"doing no research of any kind relevant to botulism."

This morning I received a letter from the Secretary of State admitting that that was clearly a mistake. I also learned that the Bristol laboratory was one of only two centres in Britain carrying out research into botulism, and that its modelling technique to predict the growth of the organism was relevant to all foodstuffs, not just meat.

In such circumstances, Mr. Speaker, would it not be normal for the Secretary of State to make a personal statement to put the record straight for *Hansard*? It is important that the record on the Bristol laboratory's work should be put straight, in view of this morning's announcement that the centre is to close and its work on botulism is to be dispersed to Reading, which will reduce the food research staff from 560 to 440. The House will want to know how the Government can justify the extraordinary timing of that decision.

The Secretary of State for Health (Mr. Kenneth Clarke): It may be helpful if I share with the House the contents of the letter that I sent to the hon. Member for Livingston (Mr. Cook), with an apology for the mistake that I made on the second occasion on which the subject was raised yesterday, which has caused some confusion.

The question of the research laboratory at Bristol was first raised by the hon. Member for Southport (Mr. Fearn). I answered his question accurately when I said:

"The point about the Bristol research centre to which the hon. Gentleman referred can be answered in more detail by my right hon. Friends with responsibility for that, but I am informed that that research centre is not concerned with any work on food safety relevant to this outbreak."

To the best of my knowledge, that remains accurate.

The question was raised again later by the hon. Member for Livingston. When I reached the relevant part of my reply to him, I began to be interrupted by hon. Members who speak on agricultural matters—first by the hon. Member for South Shields (Dr. Clark) and then, I have to say, by my right hon. Friend the Minister of Agriculture, who was sitting behind me.

The hon. Member for Livingston has taken one phrase from what column 709 of *Hansard* makes it clear was an interrupted and incomplete answer. By the time the interruptions had finished, I had said:

"That must be taken up with the responsible Ministers. My right hon. Friend the Minister of Agriculture, Fisheries and Food will have to deal with that . . . I remain reasonably confident—I look to my right hon. Friend for advice"—
which I was doing—
"that it is doing no research of any kind relevant to botulism."
—[*Official Report,* 13 June 1989; Vol. 154, c. 704-09.]

I said in the letter to the hon. Members for Southport and for Livingston that that was plainly a mistake and that my answer had been incomplete. I had intended to say that the centre was doing no research relevant to this outbreak. Following the restructuring that has been taking place, and on the decision of the Agricultural and Food Research

[*Mr. Kenneth Clarke*]

Council, an autonomous and independent body, work is being transferred from Bristol to Norwich and Reading, and the Bristol expert Terry Roberts is transferring to one of the other centres with his team.

As I made clear yesterday, the Government have no intention of withdrawing funding from the research on botulism, which is to be transferred to one of the institute's other laboratories. On the contrary, we are strengthening and expanding the work on food safety that has hitherto been done at Bristol.

I can only say that I hope that what I have said has cleared up the confusion. Obviously I speak on behalf of the Government, although this is not my departmental responsibility. However, hon. Members who feel strongly that the work would be better done at Bristol than at Norwich or Reading should address their detailed questions either to my right hon. Friend the Secretary of State for Education and Science or to my right hon. Friend the Minister of Agriculture. We are increasing the amount of research being done, and I leave the matter of the location to those who wish to explore the matter further.

Several Hon. Members: On a point of order, Mr. Speaker.

Mr. Speaker: I will take a point of order from the hon. Member for Southport (Mr. Fearn), as he was involved in this matter yesterday.

Mr. Ronnie Fearn (Southport): Thank you, Mr. Speaker. Further to that point of order. The Secretary of State has sent me a letter, for which I thank him. Can he confirm unreservedly that no research or experiments are now being carried out at Bristol on the present outbreak of botulism?

Mr. Clarke: A great number of inquiries are being made about the outbreak. If they throw up the need for further research into how hazelnut puree became infected, I have no doubt that that research will be financed. The decision about Bristol has been taken by the relevant research council. It has decided to transfer the work from Bristol to Norwich or Reading. There will be increased expenditure on some aspects of food safety research. The work on botulism is being transferred. A great expert on botulism, who is based at Bristol, is moving with his team to one of the other two centres. That team will wish to consider the impact on its work of the outbreak that we are suffering at the moment, which I trust will soon be abated.

Mr. Bob Cryer (Bradford, South): On a point of order, Mr. Speaker.

Mr. Speaker: A different point of order?

Mr. Cryer: Yes, a different point of order, Mr. Speaker. It relates to statements made to the House.

The Government are clearly intent on curtailing statements. Today, we have had three instances. The statement on the Foreign Affairs Council was based on an extension of Question Time. Consequently, according to the general rules, you were unable to call the whole range of hon. Members who wished to speak. On a statement, that would have been quite normal. The exchange, therefore, was very limited.

The question that has been raised now—which was raised yesterday by means of a private notice question and

today by means of a Standing Order No. 20 application—has been answered in what can only be described as a very shifty way by the Minister. He ought to have come here and made a statement in order to allow a wide range of cross-examination. You may recall, Mr. Speaker, that all the annunciators in this House carry a message that there is to be a statement by a Minister. Many hon. Members who may not be here would have wished to be here to ask questions. It is a real denial of Members' rights to treat the House in this way.

All that I seek from you, Mr. Speaker, is an assurance that you will keep the matter under review. There is a very real danger that, with their enormous majority of over 100, the Government are treating the processes of democracy with contempt and eroding the conventions of this place, which call for statements at regular intervals from Ministers so that hon. Members can have a proper opportunity—without placing a strain on you, Mr. Speaker, to curtail questions—to cross-examine Ministers, particularly when they are behaving so badly and when their methods of operation are so shoddy.

Ms. Primarolo *rose——*

Mr. Max Madden (Bradford, West) *rose——*

Mr. Speaker: Let me deal with one point of order at a time. I do not think that the hon. Member for Bradford, South (Mr. Cryer) is right about what he called the statement on Question 18. It was a question from one of his hon. Friends, which might well have been reached. The fact that it was taken at the end of questions gave the House a greater opportunity to discuss it. That is a helpful procedure when matters of great importance arise. As to the hon. Gentleman's other point, the Secretary of State has today corrected some information that he gave to the House yesterday. I think that the whole House should applaud that.

Mr. Madden: May I ask for your guidance, Mr. Speaker, as the guardian of the rights of hon. Members? It relates to statements. It is rumoured that tomorrow the Government intend to make a statement about the establishment of a DNA testing scheme. We have been waiting many months for the statement. It is likely to be extremely controversial, because it will dash the hopes of many families who wish to be united and reunited in this country.

I know that this is not a matter for you, Mr. Speaker, but as many hon. Members from all sides of the House will be preoccupied elsewhere tomorrow, I think that it would be quite wrong for the Government to try to slip through a very controversial statement in a House with a very slim attendance. If you are approached by the Government about the matter, could you strongly advise them to hold this statement, which has been on ice for at least nine months, until Monday, so that they can be held accountable on Monday for decisions which they are trying to slip through the House when many hon. Members will be away?

Mr. Patrick McLoughlin (Derbyshire, West): On a point of order, Mr. Speaker. Would you confirm that tomorrow is a normal sitting day for the House of Commons and that it is therefore the right of all hon. Members to attend and to put any questions that they may wish on any statement that is made? If the hon. Member for Bradford, West (Mr. Madden) is skiving off and will not be here to speak up for his constituents, that is a problem for him, not for the Government.

Several Hon. Members *rose——*

Mr. Speaker: I shall deal with one matter at a time. I have no knowledge of the rumours that go around this place. As we approach July, they always seem to accelerate. I do not know anything about that matter. Friday is sometimes said to be a thin day in the House; Thursday usually is a busy day.

Ms. Primarolo: Further to my original point of order arising out of the Minister's comments, Mr. Speaker. I believe that the Minister's statement that all the work from Bristol will be transferred to Norwich or Reading is incorrect. I ask him to take back that statement and reconsider it, to save him having to apologise to the House tomorrow and put the record straight, yet again.

Mr. Kenneth Clarke: Further to the point of order, Mr. Speaker. With great respect, in using points of order, hon. Members are trying to question me about a press notice issued yesterday by the Agricultural and Food Research Council—a body for which I am not responsible, as hon. Members know. In case the hon. Member for Bristol, South (Ms. Primarolo) is in any doubt, I have said, on the advice of those who are responsible for this matter, that the Government have no intention of withdrawing funding from the research on botulism which is being transferred to the institute's other laboratories. Today, the Agricultural and Food Research Council said:
"more will be spent on research into Salmonella and Listeria".

I advise hon. Members, in their interests as well as mine, that if they are seriously interested in questions concerning the laboratory and transfer of work from Bristol to Norwich or Reading, they should direct them to one or other of the Secretaries of State responsible for this matter. All they need do is table a question to whichever Secretary of State they wish.

Dr. David Clark (South Shields): Further to the point of order, Mr. Speaker. As the Secretary of State has acknowledged, there are Ministers who are responsible for the statement which was issued today about the closure of the institute of food research at Bristol. As he said, it is to them that we should address our questions. Given the uncertainty and interest in the House—which is obvious to everyone—because 120 top scientists will lose their jobs, I ask you, Mr. Speaker, to use your good offices to ask the Minister of Agriculture, Fisheries and Food to come to the House later this evening so that we can cross-examine him on this important issue which affects public health and food safety.

Mr. Speaker: That is not a matter for me, but I am sure that the point has been heard.

Mr. Frank Cook (Stockton, North) *rose——*

Mr. Speaker: Final point of order, please.

Mr. Cook: Further to the original point of order, Mr. Speaker. I am afraid that the Secretary of State appears to have heaped confusion upon ignorance. We are now in some difficulty in determining who should answer our questions. In his statement yesterday, the Secretary of State for Health said that the incidence of botulism in this country was significantly less than in other countries. His colleague, however, is issuing statements saying that the food irradiation which occurs in other countries is desirable, so we should adopt it here.

I want the Secretary of State—whichever one is responsible—to bear in mind the fact that clostridium botulinum is not susceptible to irradiation, but that other bacteria—yeasts and moulds—are, and Ministers should know that the bacterium can grow much more virulently without competitors. The Secretary of State for Health should ensure that either he covers this matter or his mate does.

Mr. Speaker: I am sure that that has been heard by those who are responsible.

Creation of Unitary Local Authorities

4.8 pm

Mr. Edward Leigh (Gainsborough and Horncastle): I beg to move,

That leave be given to bring in a Bill to merge regional, county, borough and district councils to create unitary all purpose local authorities in Great Britain and Northern Ireland.

I was reminded of ten-minute Bills when I recently tried to fly a kite with my children. Much anxious preparation was followed by a few minutes of fitful flight. It fell to the ground and no one ever heard of it again. Although I have no illusions about this Bill becoming law at the end of the Session, I am confident that it or something like it will eventually become law.

Continuing the analogy of the kite, if I had left my garden and walked up a hill on top of the Lincolnshire wolds, I would have had a magnificent view and would have understood what lay behind the Bill. From the top of the Lincolnshire wolds there is a fine view of Lincoln cathedral to the south, the Grimsby dock tower to the north and the cooling tower of the Trent valley power stations. There is a fine view also of no fewer than nine local authority areas: three county councils and six district councils. If one of my constituents had been standing alongside me on the top of the Lincolnshire wolds, he would have been confused about the responsibilities of those local authorities. Even had a councillor been standing there with me, I suspect that he would have made a few mistakes. Therefore, reform is timely.

It is not good enough simply to say that local government has enough on its plate with the community charge, competitive tendering and education reform. After all, the Government began the process by creating unitary local authorities in the Greater London area and the metropolitan counties. Reform is needed.

I shall not fall into the trap of trying to impose a uniform structure throughout the country, as happened in 1974, when it was imposed in many areas without prior consultation or local justification. I note that my hon. Friend the Member for Brigg and Cleethorpes (Mr. Brown) is in his place. We know all about the problem in Lincolnshire. One third of it was torn away to form the unloved county of South Humberside. My hon. Friend the Member for East Lindsey (Sir P. Tapsell) reminded me the other day that the boundary of that new county was moved 20 miles to the north following one session with the then Secretary of State, simply to appease local feeling. That is not the right way to deal with local government.

Above all, my Bill proposes consultation and local options, not national uniformity. Let the people decide, if necessary through a referendum. What is right in one part of the United Kingdom is not necessarily right in another. I happen to favour unitary local authorities. They can be justified on the bases of understanding by the people, of stable and good management and, above all, of the concentration of power to create strong local government. As a former councillor, I certainly believe in that.

My area should return to what it was before 1974, when there was the Lindsey county council—there was not South Humberside or East and West Lindsey—and people knew where they stood. My right hon. Friend the Minister for Local Government represents a Suffolk seat, and I am not lecturing him on what should be the case there. Perhaps a two-tier authority is more appropriate. In my part of the world, however, a unitary local authority is needed. My Bill seeks to deal with the problem in terms not of revolution, but of evolution. I should have thought that to be a good Conservative philosophy in which we could all believe.

It is interesting that pressure to create unitary local authorities has come not just from Conservative but from Opposition Members. I read with great interest the reports of the Scottish Labour party, which discussed, I think quite sensibly, the possibility of cutting the number of local authorities in Scotland from 65 to 20 single-tier authorities to which people could relate and which they could understand. My hon. Friend the Member for Pembroke (Mr. Bennett), who is also in his seat today, recently moved a Bill for unitary authorities in Wales. I understand that there is considerable cross-party support in Wales for cutting the number of the 37 existing district councils and merging them with county councils.

Interestingly enough, my Bill also refers to Northern Ireland, which currently has 25 squabbling councils with inadequate powers. Perhaps we could overcome some of the problems of sectarian politics in Northern Ireland if we were to create one unitary local authority for the whole Province, based in Belfast, with real powers.

I repeat that it is essential in matters of local government reorganisation not to repeat past mistakes such as those in the Redcliffe-Maud report, which said that local authorities had to be of a certain size and had to perform certain functions across the entire county. I should like, for example, the re-creation of county boroughs in great cities such as Bristol, which is full of local pride. Why does it not have its own council? That also applies to the great cities of Hull, Lincoln and Portsmouth. The concept of county boroughs was something to be proud of, and it is no accident that the great period of local government prestige was that of the county borough.

My Bill lays open all those interesting proposals. It is on the basis of creating strong and effective local government that people can understand and in which they can take part that I commend it to the House.

Question put and agreed to.

Bill ordered to be brought in by Mr. Edward Leigh, Dame Janet Fookes, Mr. Patrick McLoughlin, Mr. Nicholas Bennett, Dr. Ian Twinn, Mr. Michael Brown, Mr. Greg Knight and Mr. John Marshall.

Creation of Unitary Local Authorities

Mr. Edward Leigh accordingly presented a Bill to merge regional, county, borough and district councils to create unitary all purpose local authorities in Great Britain and Northern Ireland: And the same was read the First time; and ordered to be read a Second time upon Friday 30 June and to be printed [Bill 155.]

STATUTORY INSTRUMENTS, &c.

Mr. Speaker: With the leave of the House, I will put together the two motions relating to statutory instruments.

Ordered,

That the draft Fisheries Act 1981 (Amendment) Regulations 1989 be referred to a Standing Committee on Statutory Instruments,

That the draft Cereals Marketing Act (Application to Oil Seeds) Order 1989 be referred to a Standing Committee on Statutory Instruments, &c.—*[Mr. Alan Howarth.]*

EUROPEAN COMMUNITY DOCUMENTS

Ordered,

That European Community Documents Nos. 8896/84 and the Supplementary Explanatory Memorandum submitted by the Department of Trade and Industry on 3rd December 1987, and 4090/86 and the Department's Supplementary Explanatory Memoranda of 6th November 1987 and 3rd December 1987 on trade marks be referred to a Standing Committee on European Community Documents.—*[Mr. Alan Howarth.]*

Orders of the Day

Local Government and Housing Bill

As amended (in the Standing Committee), further considered.

4.16 pm

Mr. David Blunkett (Sheffield, Brightside): May I seek the permission of the House to expedite business by taking together all the amendments relating to the companies clauses?

Mr. Speaker: Would it be for the convenience of the House to take all the amendments relating to clauses 58 to 64 together?

Mr. Martin Redmond (Don Valley): Object.

Mr. Speaker: If the House does not agree, we shall have to take the amendments separately. Does the hon. Member for Don Valley (Mr. Redmond) mean that?

Mr. Redmond: Object.

Clause 60

COMPANIES SUBJECT TO LOCAL AUTHORITY INFLUENCE

Mr. Blunkett: I beg to move amendment No. 293, in page 67, line 23, at end insert—

'(3A) For the purposes of determining whether any business relationship exists under subsection (3) above, nothing in that subsection shall apply to any single payment by a local authority for a particular purpose where the authority certifies in making the payment that it does not anticipate any recurrence of the type of expenditure concerned.'.

Mr. Speaker: With this it will be convenient to consider amendment No. 294, in page 67, line 23, at end insert—

'(3A) In calculating any aggregate for the purposes of subsections (3)(a) or 3(c) above, the amount of any grant, loan, or other advance shall be disregarded where the payment was made before the coming into force of this section.'

Mr. Blunkett: The amendment deals with the way in which the Bill is formulated in relation to companies. It aims to disentangle what is reasonable and acceptable from what does not make sense to anyone. It further aims to disentangle the position when one-off grants or the allocation of land result in individual companies or trusts being associated with a local authority to such an extent —if more than 20 per cent. of their board members or management committee members are from the local authority or associated with it—that they find themselves designated as influenced companies. If the proportion is more than 50 per cent. they will be regarded as local-authority controlled companies. A one-off grant or a one-off allocation of land should not be treated in that way as it would be reasonable not to infer an association with the local authority in those circumstances.

Labour Members believe that retrospection should not apply to the way in which resources have been allocated to a company, trust or organisation, so that they are not caught by something that has already happened in terms of influenced or controlled company status.

The Parliamentary Under-Secretary of State for the Environment (Mrs. Virginia Bottomley): Amendment No. 293 proposes that the business relationship test will not be satisfied in the case of one-off payments where the local authority concerned has certified that it does not expect a recurrence of the same type of expenditure. The difficulty is that the one-off payment can be for any amount. Indeed, it could be for a sum so large that it more or less covered the entire operation of the company. It is hard to see how such a situation could be regarded as other than a very strong business relationship. Under the terms of the amendment, such a situation would not be caught if the local authority had certified that it did not intend or expect to make further similar payments, although there is no requirement not to make such further payments. In short, we find amendment No. 293 unacceptable.

Amendment No. 294 proposes that grants provided before the legislation came into force should be disregarded when calculating the business association test. Although that may seem superficially attractive, the crucial point in establishing whether the business relationship exists is whether the link is sufficient to provide the authority with influence, not when the link was established. If accepted, the amendment would mean that numerous companies which could clearly be influenced would be exempt from the proposals. I can assure the hon. Member for Sheffield, Brightside (Mr. Blunkett), however, that there can be no requirement to attach such conditions to contracts and such matters awarded before the legislation comes into force.

We have studied the proposals carefully and we have no wish to undermine the useful working of companies which make a valuable contribution. There are cases, such as housing associations, for which we have made exemptions. Our proposals are an important way to ensure that the rules of propriety in local government are adhered to, although it is still possible to use companies, where appropriate, to serve an appropriate end.

Mr. Allen McKay (Barnsley, West and Penistone): Can the hon. Lady confirm the following? In my area, there is an innovation centre which uses European money and local authority money. Some of its directors are also councillors and the chairman of the company is Lord Mason. The centre serves a most useful purpose in acting as a seed-bed workshop, bringing together ideas and promoting jobs and job opportunities. It is doing excellent work.

My second example is a mining museum in the constituency of Wakefield, which would not have been set up but for the consortium of local authorities which provided the incentive and financial arrangements initially. Without local authority backing, that museum would not be there, and without local authority backing it is likely to disappear. Surely that is not right. Can the Minister assure us that those examples will be considered carefully before the proposals are carried out?

Mrs. Virginia Bottomley: I can certainly give that assurance. It is not appropriate to set up a company to undermine the capital rules for local authorities, but we accept, recognise and have encouraged many joint partnerships and a company is often the best way in which to proceed. I will look at the cases to which the hon. Member for Barnsley, West and Penistone (Mr. McKay) has referred.

Question put, That the amendment be made:—
The House divided: Ayes 122, Noes 216.

Division No. 241]　　　　　　　　　　　　　　　**[4.22 pm**

AYES

Abbott, Ms Diane	Howells, Dr. Kim (Pontypridd)
Alton, David	Hughes, John (Coventry NE)
Anderson, Donald	Illsley, Eric
Ashton, Joe	Janner, Greville
Barnes, Mrs Rosie (Greenwich)	Kaufman, Rt Hon Gerald
Battle, John	Kirkwood, Archy
Beckett, Margaret	Leighton, Ron
Beith, A. J.	Lestor, Joan (Eccles)
Bell, Stuart	Lewis, Terry
Bennett, A. F. (D'nt'n & R'dish)	Litherland, Robert
Bidwell, Sydney	Livingstone, Ken
Blunkett, David	Lloyd, Tony (Stretford)
Bradley, Keith	Lofthouse, Geoffrey
Buckley, George J.	McAllion, John
Callaghan, Jim	McKay, Allen (Barnsley West)
Campbell, Ron (Blyth Valley)	McWilliam, John
Campbell-Savours, D. N.	Mahon, Mrs Alice
Cartwright, John	Maxton, John
Clark, Dr David (S Shields)	Meacher, Michael
Clarke, Tom (Monklands W)	Meale, Alan
Clay, Bob	Michael, Alun
Clwyd, Mrs Ann	Michie, Bill (Sheffield Heeley)
Coleman, Donald	Morris, Rt Hon A. (W'shawe)
Cook, Frank (Stockton N)	Mowlam, Marjorie
Cook, Robin (Livingston)	Murphy, Paul
Corbyn, Jeremy	O'Brien, William
Cox, Tom	O'Neill, Martin
Crowther, Stan	Orme, Rt Hon Stanley
Cryer, Bob	Owen, Rt Hon Dr David
Cummings, John	Patchett, Terry
Cunningham, Dr John	Pendry, Tom
Davies, Ron (Caerphilly)	Pike, Peter L.
Davis, Terry (B'ham Hodge H'l)	Powell, Ray (Ogmore)
Dixon, Don	Prescott, John
Dobson, Frank	Primarolo, Dawn
Douglas, Dick	Rees, Rt Hon Merlyn
Dunwoody, Hon Mrs Gwyneth	Richardson, Jo
Eastham, Ken	Robertson, George
Fatchett, Derek	Robinson, Geoffrey
Fearn, Ronald	Rooker, Jeff
Field, Frank (Birkenhead)	Rowlands, Ted
Fields, Terry (L'pool B G'n)	Sheldon, Rt Hon Robert
Fisher, Mark	Skinner, Dennis
Flannery, Martin	Smith, C. (Isl'ton & F'bury)
Flynn, Paul	Smith, J. P. (Vale of Glam)
Foot, Rt Hon Michael	Snape, Peter
Foster, Derek	Soley, Clive
Foulkes, George	Spearing, Nigel
Garrett, John (Norwich South)	Taylor, Mrs Ann (Dewsbury)
George, Bruce	Taylor, Matthew (Truro)
Gordon, Mildred	Wall, Pat
Gould, Bryan	Wallace, James
Griffiths, Win (Bridgend)	Walley, Joan
Grocott, Bruce	Wardell, Gareth (Gower)
Hardy, Peter	Welsh, Andrew (Angus E)
Hattersley, Rt Hon Roy	Williams, Rt Hon Alan
Haynes, Frank	Winnick, David
Heffer, Eric S.	Wise, Mrs Audrey
Hinchliffe, David	Worthington, Tony
Home Robertson, John	
Hood, Jimmy	Tellers for the Ayes:
Howarth, George (Knowsley N)	Mr. Martin Redmond and
Howell, Rt Hon D. (S'heath)	Mr. Harry Barnes.

NOES

Adley, Robert	Bevan, David Gilroy
Alison, Rt Hon Michael	Biffen, Rt Hon John
Allason, Rupert	Blackburn, Dr John G.
Amos, Alan	Blaker, Rt Hon Sir Peter
Arbuthnot, James	Body, Sir Richard
Arnold, Jacques (Gravesham)	Bottomley, Mrs Virginia
Atkinson, David	Bowden, A (Brighton K'pto'n)
Baker, Nicholas (Dorset N)	Bowden, Gerald (Dulwich)
Beaumont-Dark, Anthony	Boyson, Rt Hon Dr Sir Rhodes
Bennett, Nicholas (Pembroke)	Braine, Rt Hon Sir Bernard

Brandon-Bravo, Martin
Brazier, Julian
Brown, Michael *(Brigg & Cl't's)*
Buchanan-Smith, Rt Hon Alick
Buck, Sir Antony
Burns, Simon
Burt, Alistair
Butterfill, John
Carlisle, John, *(Luton N)*
Carrington, Matthew
Carttiss, Michael
Chalker, Rt Hon Mrs Lynda
Channon, Rt Hon Paul
Chapman, Sydney
Chope, Christopher
Churchill, Mr
Clark, Dr Michael *(Rochford)*
Clark, Sir W. *(Croydon S)*
Colvin, Michael
Conway, Derek
Coombs, Anthony *(Wyre F'rest)*
Coombs, Simon *(Swindon)*
Couchman, James
Cran, James
Currie, Mrs Edwina
Davies, Q. *(Stamf'd & Spald'g)*
Day, Stephen
Devlin, Tim
Dickens, Geoffrey
Dorrell, Stephen
Dunn, Bob
Durant, Tony
Dykes, Hugh
Eggar, Tim
Evennett, David
Fairbairn, Sir Nicholas
Favell, Tony
Finsberg, Sir Geoffrey
Fishburn, John Dudley
Fookes, Dame Janet
Forman, Nigel
Forsyth, Michael *(Stirling)*
Forth, Eric
Fox, Sir Marcus
Franks, Cecil
French, Douglas
Fry, Peter
Gale, Roger
Gardiner, George
Garel-Jones, Tristan
Gill, Christopher
Gilmour, Rt Hon Sir Ian
Glyn, Dr Alan
Gorst, John
Gow, Ian
Greenway, Harry *(Ealing N)*
Greenway, John *(Ryedale)*
Gregory, Conal
Griffiths, Peter *(Portsmouth N)*
Grist, Ian
Gummer, Rt Hon John Selwyn
Hague, William
Hamilton, Neil *(Tatton)*
Hampson, Dr Keith
Hanley, Jeremy
Hargreaves, A. *(B'ham H'll Gr')*
Hargreaves, Ken *(Hyndburn)*
Harris, David
Haselhurst, Alan
Hayes, Jerry
Hayhoe, Rt Hon Sir Barney
Hayward, Robert
Heathcoat-Amory, David
Heddle, John
Hicks, Mrs Maureen *(Wolv' NE)*
Hicks, Robert *(Cornwall SE)*
Higgins, Rt Hon Terence L.
Hill, James
Hind, Kenneth
Hordern, Sir Peter

Howard, Michael
Howarth, Alan *(Strat'd-on-A)*
Howarth, G. *(Cannock & B'wd)*
Howe, Rt Hon Sir Geoffrey
Hughes, Robert G. *(Harrow W)*
Hunt, David *(Wirral W)*
Hunter, Andrew
Irvine, Michael
Irving, Charles
Jack, Michael
Jackson, Robert
Janman, Tim
Johnson Smith, Sir Geoffrey
Jones, Gwilym *(Cardiff N)*
Jones, Robert B *(Herts W)*
Jopling, Rt Hon Michael
Kellett-Bowman, Dame Elaine
Kilfedder, James
Knapman, Roger
Knight, Greg *(Derby North)*
Knight, Dame Jill *(Edgbaston)*
Knowles, Michael
Knox, David
Lang, Ian
Latham, Michael
Lawrence, Ivan
Leigh, Edward *(Gainsbor'gh)*
Lennox-Boyd, Hon Mark
Lightbown, David
Lilley, Peter
Lloyd, Sir Ian *(Havant)*
Lloyd, Peter *(Fareham)*
Luce, Rt Hon Richard
MacKay, Andrew *(E Berkshire)*
Maclean, David
McLoughlin, Patrick
McNair-Wilson, Sir Michael
McNair-Wilson, P. *(New Forest)*
Madel, David
Mans, Keith
Marlow, Tony
Marshall, John *(Hendon S)*
Marshall, Michael *(Arundel)*
Martin, David *(Portsmouth S)*
Maxwell-Hyslop, Robin
Mills, Iain
Montgomery, Sir Fergus
Morris, M *(N'hampton S)*
Mudd, David
Nicholls, Patrick
Nicholson, David *(Taunton)*
Norris, Steve
Onslow, Rt Hon Cranley
Page, Richard
Paice, James
Patnick, Irvine
Pawsey, James
Peacock, Mrs Elizabeth
Powell, William *(Corby)*
Price, Sir David
Raison, Rt Hon Timothy
Riddick, Graham
Ridley, Rt Hon Nicholas
Ridsdale, Sir Julian
Rifkind, Rt Hon Malcolm
Rossi, Sir Hugh
Rowe, Andrew
Sackville, Hon Tom
Sainsbury, Hon Tim
Shaw, David *(Dover)*
Shaw, Sir Giles *(Pudsey)*
Shaw, Sir Michael *(Scarb')*
Shelton, Sir William
Shephard, Mrs G. *(Norfolk SW)*
Shepherd, Colin *(Hereford)*
Shepherd, Richard *(Aldridge)*
Shersby, Michael
Sims, Roger
Smith, Sir Dudley *(Warwick)*
Smith, Tim *(Beaconsfield)*

Spicer, Sir Jim *(Dorset W)*
Squire, Robin
Stanbrook, Ivor
Stanley, Rt Hon Sir John
Stevens, Lewis
Stewart, Andy *(Sherwood)*
Stokes, Sir John
Stradling Thomas, Sir John
Summerson, Hugo
Tapsell, Sir Peter
Taylor, Ian *(Esher)*
Taylor, Teddy *(S'end E)*
Temple-Morris, Peter
Thompson, Patrick *(Norwich N)*
Thornton, Malcolm
Thurnham, Peter
Townend, John *(Bridlington)*
Townsend, Cyril D. *(B'heath)*
Tredinnick, David
Trippier, David

Twinn, Dr Ian
Waddington, Rt Hon David
Wakeham, Rt Hon John
Waller, Gary
Walters, Sir Dennis
Ward, John
Wardle, Charles *(Bexhill)*
Watts, John
Wells, Bowen
Wheeler, John
Widdecombe, Ann
Wilkinson, John
Winterton, Nicholas
Woodcock, Dr. Mike
Young, Sir George *(Acton)*

Tellers for the Noes:
   Mr. Kenneth Carlisle and
   Mr. Michael Fallon.

Question accordingly negatived.

Mr. Blunkett: I beg to move amendment No. 297, in page 67, line 31, at end insert

'and holds his position within the company, or voting rights in relation to it, by virtue of an appointment by the authority'

Mr. Speaker: With this it will be convenient to discuss amendment No. 298, in page 67, line 32, at end insert

'and holds his position within the company, or voting rights in relation to it, by virtue of an appointment by the authority.'

Mr. Blunkett: I should like to draw attention to the comments of the Association of British Chambers of Commerce on this part of the Bill. The association has expressed grave anxiety, not about the Government's intention to close what they describe as loopholes—*[Interruption.]*

Mr. Speaker: Order.

Mr. Blunkett: The disturbance was not the fault of the people around me on the Front Bench. I hope that hon. Members will bear with me.

The Association of British Chambers of Commerce is concerned, not about the Government's intention to close loopholes in the ability of local authorities to raise and spend capital outside the restrictions that exist in the form of capital regulations, but about the impact that this and other parts of the Bill relating to companies will have. It believes that one set of restrictions will have a chain reaction in other areas and it is worried that the valuable partnership which has been developing between local authorities and the private sector throughout the country may be damaged.

The association believes that the intentions expressed strongly by the Department of Trade and Industry and less strongly by the Department of the Environment to support this partnership may be undermined by regulations that seek to achieve a goal by what the association describes as

"holding up one's trousers by putting on braces, attaching a belt, tying them up with string and then ensuring that the person cannot move his legs."

In terms of the rupture of this partnership, the association might have mentioned applying a truss, too.

As drafted, the Bill ensures that not only is a loophole to be closed, but a plethora of measures are to be used to prevent local authorities and the private sector from getting together to implement perfectly reasonable regeneration policies that provide jobs for men and women in the most deprived areas of our country—an objective

[*Mr. Blunkett*]

that I believe all hon. Members would applaud. Partnership arrangements ensure that unity of purpose emerges from the work of local authorities with their local business sectors, in the best interests of their communities. The two go together: market forces and reliance on the private sector alone cannot work; nor can a wholly socially owned sector of the economy provide for all our needs. We must recognise that this partnership will enhance the living standards and lives of people. We need unity of purpose in social policy—investing in meeting needs, in training and education and in providing infrastructure and economic regeneration, and in the stimulus to the private sector which will result.

We believe that there is a thrust of policy in local areas across the country which mirrors the progressive and useful policies which have been adopted in places such as the Federal Republic of Germany, France and Italy, where the partnership between the local area and the private sector has yielded considerable fruit. That is why we and the chambers of commerce are worried about how the restrictions will apply to local authorities' capital programmes which are involved in joint companies or trusts, and about the chain reaction that will be touched off between one group of people and another. That is simply because, having been drawn into and having served on the board of management committee of a company, they will, by some sort of guilt by association, affect other such companies.

We recognise that the Government amendments go a little way towards accepting that, in the case of influenced companies which I described earlier, it would be right to restrict the knock-on effect. Our amendment asks the Government to accept the principle, which in Government amendments is partially accepted, that in the case of influenced and controlled companies, serving on one company should not in any way have an effect on one's activities in other areas.

Later in the debate when I hope to avoid making a speech similar to this one, we shall deal with a group of amendments which attempt to ensure that the restrictions promoted by Government amendments Nos. 31 and 281 can be refined still further. That refinement will mean that development by a local authority of a joint company will not result in the people who serve on it disqualifying themselves from independence from the local authority and will ensure that the companies and trusts with which they are associated escape from influenced or controlled status.

By serving on one company—for example, a combined heat and power scheme which might be adjudged to be influenced—people engaging in their normal practice as managers or employees elsewhere should not be placed in a position where anything else they serve on will automatically be judged to be an influenced or controlled company. That is not acceptable and does not make sense in terms of allowing enterprise and innovation to flourish. As the Association of British Chambers of Commerce rightly says, it will make those who are involved wary of taking part in joint ventures. That means that they will be unable to play a part even in normal community activity about which they previously may have had no qualms. Such activity could create influenced or controlled status for the bodies on which such people serve.

As a consequence, any expenditure by a local authority on a company, even if the money is raised in the private sector, will be looked upon as part of the capital credit controls in the Bill. Local authorities and many other bodies will find themselves enmeshed in the maze, in the net that is being woven around this area of activity. That is why our amendments also seek to ensure that the 20 per cent. or above limit on those serving on a company or trust is lifted. That will mean that influence will not start to be designated at that level. Just because one fifth of those on a management board or trust of a company happen to be associated with a local authority should not automatically bring that company within the capital restraints and credit limits of the local authority.

Association and the formulae for influence and control should not apply where more than one local authority is involved. Someone taking part in his own time in the activities of a concern and who works at a senior level in a neighbouring local authority could trigger the machanism for influence or control. That is because that person would breach the 20 or 50 per cent. limit on the number of people on the management board or trust. That is extraordinary and during the debate, sooner rather than later, we hope to be able to put it right.

We recognise the Government's ideological obsession with the market economy and their desire to exclude local authorities from as much as possible of the joint activity that is taking place. They also want to ensure that, while the private sector can raise as much as it likes from the market, the public sector cannot. However, even in the Government's terms, these proposals go too far and that is why we seek to amend them.

4.45 pm

It would be quite wrong if people who genuinely believed that they were excluded suddenly found themselves included. It is not right that just because a company has a contractual arrangement with a local authority someone who works for that company should be affected in any way by the Bill. For example, a cleaner working for a contracting firm should not suddenly find that his presence on a joint body or company triggers the mechanisms that I have described. That is beyond the bounds of reasonableness. The Government amendments would not deal with such a situation but ours would, and that is why we are arguing that common sense should prevail.

No one outside the House engaged in business or commerce or in a local authority of any persuasion is arguing that the restrictions should be as tight as they are or that the levels of direction from the centre should be as great as those that are proposed. Tragically, in the media there is a lack of awareness of what will happen when this part of the Bill becomes law. How many people outside are aware that virtually at a stroke it will destroy the local authority-run public transport sector? It will do that by undermining the ability of local authorities logically to invest in public transport, because any such company that is influenced or controlled will automatically fall within the credit limits. That will wipe out the public expenditure investment in other local authority service areas.

We are asking the Government to be reasonable. I know that the House has much to deal with and that we shall deal with major issues that everybody wishes to debate. I wish that as much attention could be directed to the provisions dealing with the impact on partnerships or those dealing with the impact on rents and the local authority rented sector as will be directed to dog registration. However, that is the way the House works and the way in which the media view things. I hope that, with the assistance of my hon. Friends, I shall be able to keep my later speeches brief.

Mrs. Virginia Bottomley: The speech by the hon. Member for Sheffield, Brightside (Mr. Blunkett) again shows a great deal of misrepresentation of our proposals. It is absolutely clear that the Government must act when a company has been set up in order to undermine the capital rules. The Government must also act when such a company or a local authority company disregards the propriety and standards that a local authority would apply. We have no wish to undermine or to put in jeopardy a great range of useful and productive companies that are based on partnership between public and private sectors.

Consider just one area of misrepresentation. The hon. Gentleman said that he did not think that where only 20 per cent. of the members of a company board were linked with a local authority the company should be treated as influenced by the authority. Nor do we. We are proposing that that should happen only when both that has occurred and when half or more of the company's business is associated with the same local authority, or where there is some other similar test of a close business relationship with the same authority.

It may not be possible to discuss in detail all the amendments that the hon. Gentleman and his hon. Friends have tabled on this issue. Perhaps we should welcome or feel sad about that. But a number of them reveal a misunderstanding about the detail of what we propose and the way in which they will operate. I assure the hon. Gentleman and those who have expressed concern that there are areas where individuals or categories of companies will be exempted either permanently or temporarily. We have discussed a number of specific cases and in virtually every case a solution has been found.

The hon. Member for Barnsley, West and Penistone (Mr. McKay) referred to two companies in his area, the Yorkshire mining museum trust and the Barnsley business innovation centre. I assure him that there have been discussions with both of those companies, which seem satisfied with the outcome. We are prepared to listen. We shall be bringing forward regulations to deal with the detail of many of the proposals.

The hon. Member for Brightside would like to change the association test with a local authority to that of appointment. That may superficially seem attractive, but in many companies which are clearly subject to local authority influence the authority did not appoint anybody to the company.

It is easy for two local authority officers—a chief executive and a treasurer, for example—to form a company with themselves being the two founder members and directors. The articles of association then provide that all future members of the company shall be admitted by the board of directors and that all members of the company shall be directors. The two officers admit a number of councillors, and the two then resign. The membership and board of the company are then composed exclusively of councillors, but the local authority has not

made any of the appointments. I hope the hon. Gentleman will appreciate how important it is that we take the steps that the Government are proposing.

I am grateful to the hon. Member for Brightside for referring to amendments that we shall be moving to address concerns expressed by the British Chamber of Commerce, an issue raised in Committee by my hon. Friend the Member for Taunton (Mr. Nicholson.) They will ensure that people who provide their services voluntarily as directors and secretaries to local authority control companies will not be regarded as associated with the parent authority by virtue of that connection alone.

I hope I have assured the House that these are important measures, that they are necessary and that statements about adverse effects have in some cases been mischievously circulated and have no justification.

Amendment negatived.

Amendments made: No. 31 in page 67, line 33, after 'time' insert

'both an employee and either'.

No. 32 in page 67, line 34, leave out 'or subject to the influence'.

No. 281 in page 67, line 38, leave out 'professional or managerial services' and insert—

'(i) advice with regard to the authority's interest in any company (whether existing or proposed to be formed), or

(ii) advice with regard to the management of an undertaking or the development of land by a company (whether existing or proposed to be formed) with which it is proposed that the authority should enter into any lease, licence or other contract or to which it is proposed that the authority should make any grant or loan, or

(iii) services which facilitate the exercise of the authority's rights in any company (whether by acting as the authority's representative at a meeting of the company or as a director appointed by the authority or otherwise)'.

—[Mrs. Virginia Bottomley.]

Amendment proposed: No. 295 in page 67, line 46, after first 'in', insert

'a branch or constituency section of'.*—[Mr. Blunkett.]*

Question, That the amendment be made, *put and negatived.*

Amendment proposed: No. 296 in page 67, line 46, after 'body', insert

'in the area of the authority'.*—[Mr. Blunkett.]*

Question, That the amendment be made, *put and negatived.*

Clause 61

REQUIREMENTS FOR COMPANIES UNDER CONTROL OR SUBJECT TO INFLUENCE OF LOCAL AUTHORITIES

Amendments made: No. 33 in page 68, line 23, leave out 'The Secretary of State may by order'

and insert

'In order to secure compliance, in relation to companies subject to the influence of local authorities, with provisions made by virtue of subsection (1) above, an order under that subsection may'.

No. 34 in page 68, line 36, leave out from 'may' to 'obtain' in line 37 and insert

'make provision requiring a company or local authority to'.
—[Mrs. Virginia Bottomley.]

New Clause 19

RENT REBATE SUBSIDY

'( ) (1) Each local authority in England and Wales shall receive central Government subsidy to cover the full cost of rent rebates paid out by them in any financial year.

(2) Any rent rebate subsidy payable to a local authority in England and Wales shall be credited to a revenue account which is not the Housing Revenue Account or the Housing Repairs Account.'.—[*Mr. Soley.*]

Brought up, and read the First time.

Mr. Clive Soley (Hammersmith): I beg to move, That the clause be read a Second time.

The new clause would guarantee that local authorities received central Government subsidy to cover the full cost of rent rebates. My hon. Friends and I regard this as an important proposal because it is designed to counter a classic example of the Government trying to get the poor to subsidise the poorest.

The new clause deals with two issues. First, it would mean the reimbursement of local authorities in full as opposed to the present 97 per cent. level of the rents they subsidise. Secondly, it would ensure that rent rebate subsidy remained a separate and distinct form of central Government subsidy. It would involve crediting the subsidy separately to the housing revenue account.

When the Government originally told local authorities to take on responsibility for housing benefit, considerable reservations were expressed about that requirement. Indeed, the way in which the instruction was forced on local authorities caused mayhem in the administration of many authorities, and led to difficulties being experienced by some tenants in attempting to get the subsidy due to them, for which many of them had paid over the years through their taxes.

In addition, the Government gave a commitment that the housing benefit subsidy would be paid in full by the Government. The then Minister responsible for social security matters in 1982 said that housing benefit subsidy, although administered by local authorities, would be refunded to them by central Government. That commitment was undermined when the sum was reduced to 97 per cent., although most people took the view that there was no point in complaining about a reduction of 3 per cent. That was the thin edge of the wedge, however, and today local authorities have to pick up much more of the bill.

We are here discussing the principle that responsibility for the relief of poverty should rest with the taxpayer and not be transferred to local people. Otherwise, the person in one house earning an average or even below the average income may, due to the way in which the new system is structured, be subsidising a next door neighbour receiving full housing benefit because he is unemployed. That must be unfair because, as I said at the outset, it means the poorer sections of society subsidising the very poorest.

The Government are deliberately confusing the funding of housing and the funding of income maintenance. There is a strong case for subsidising housing generally by various means, as we have done in the past—funding revenue, capital, and so on—and there is a strong case for funding people through income maintenance. But there is no case for blurring the distinction between the two so that the one becomes confused with the other.

All other countries of which I am aware pay a decent subsidy for housing, enabling people to rent or buy in a fairer way than we do in Britain. They do not put the burden on to the poorer sections of society to subsidise the very poorest. Not only does no other country do what the Government propose, but it has not been done here for many years. Indeed, one would probably have to go back to the 19th century to find it being done on a major scale.

The story does not end there. What is proposed shows the Government's dislike of council tenants. A bizarre aspect of this provision is that is does not apply to housing associaton tenants or to tenants in the private sector. It applies only to council tenants. Why do the Government expect council tenants to subsidise other council tenants out of their rent payments—as distinct from any taxes that they pay—but do not expect anyone else to do the same?

It is all part of the Government's vitriolic campaign against council tenants. They want them to stop being council tenants. They want to push them into the private sector and they are prepared to adopt any measures to achieve that. If that means bullying them, pushing and shoving them and generally making their lives an economic misery, the Government will do it and they have chosen to do it with this particularly nasty legislation.

5 pm

What would happen if the Government pursued such a policy in other sectors? For example, would they expect the recipients of family credit to fund the benefits of other, less well-off people? That is what would be involved if a similar policy were followed. The Government should discuss with local authorities a fairer system to deal with services, and keep housing benefit separate from other housing subsidies. Let us not underestimate the importance of this subsidy.

Housing benefit is one of the most important sources of income for many people. For example, the average weekly payment for rent rebate in 1988-89 was £15·37. Some 60 per cent. of council tenants are in receipt of housing benefit and about 3·5 million council tenants receive a rent rebate. The majority are pensioners. The Government will recall the mess into which they got themselves a year or so ago when they cut housing benefit for the seventh time. That caused a crisis even in Conservative areas. Pensioners discovered that they were losing £7, £8, £9 or £10 and sometimes even more per week off their incomes. There were desperate scenes, which hon. Members on both sides of the House will remember from their advice surgeries. Elderly people came along and said that they had fought for the country during the war but now could not manage and feared that they might have to go into a hostel. Such scenes make one realise that, although the overall number of people affected is large, it is still a small enough proportion of the population to mean that the Government are prepared to say that they do not care enough to put the problem right.

I brought to the attention of the Minister some time ago a report of a press conference on the effect of the increased rents when housing was transferred from the council sector to a particular organisation. In that case, some pensioners on a joint income of £150 a week with their separate pensions as well as their state pensions were just outside the level at which they would be entitled to housing benefit, but they were being asked to pay a rent of about £40 a week—in other words, 40 per cent. of their net disposable income was going in rent. If any hon. Member were paying 40 per cent. of his net disposable income in housing costs, be it mortgage payments, rent or anything else, it would only be a matter of time before he got into severe economic hardship. Yet, if the couple in my example were in council accommodation—that particular couple were not, but they might be in the future—the Bill would mean that they would be expected to subsidise people on full housing benefit. That is obviously wrong.

Unlike mortgage income tax relief, housing benefit has been repeatedly cut by the Government. In April 1988, 1 million people lost all entitlement to income and 4 million lost some entitlement. There is a strong case for mortgage income tax relief, but there is also a strong case for a decent subsidy for tenants, whether private or public. There is also a case for a system that is fairer between the rented and purchased sectors, as I have spelt out on a number of previous occasions.

We cannot do what the Government have been doing recently—continually cutting housing benefit and continually pushing up rent so that people in both the private and the public sector get into greater economic hardship. Now we have the final humiliating insult that those who are already in difficulties, such as those whom I have described, will be asked to subsidise the poorest, who rely totally on housing benefit for their rent. That must be wrong. That is why we are insisting on the new clause.

Mr. Peter Hardy (Wentworth): I have been looking at this matter in the light of the effects that it is likely to have on my constituency. I have discovered, for example, that retired miners, miners' officials and steelworkers, after a lifetime of hard work and in some cases distinguished military service, are not receiving housing benefit because they have saving levels above the prescribed limit. They are people who live in peace and dignity, but they now face the prospect of having to pay rents that are so high that their savings will rapidly diminish so that they will become recipients of housing benefit. I am glad that my hon. Friend the Member for Hammersmith (Mr. Soley) made the point that the value of housing benefit is being steadily eroded. This will be a cause of division and people will say that there is no point in saving, or in thrift, so that they can provide for a dignified old age, because if they are fortunate enough to be able to save, they will be penalised if they happen to be council tenants.

My hon. Friend is right to point out that this arrangement will not apply to housing association tenants. The Minister may say that people will be able to buy their council houses. What do I say to the chap who spoke to me about this the other day? He is in his 70s and has a reasonable level of savings. Does he use all his savings, which were meant to top up his pension and allow him to have a small holiday every so often, in bearing the burden that the Bill will place on him? The Government have been unwise and unfair. They are not encouraging thrift or dignity, but they will encourage bitterness in the housing estates.

The Minister knows that I have a high regard for him, not least because he has a north of England origin. He may accept the argument that, over the past 10 years, there has been a remarkable increase in division in our society—the division between rich and poor and between the richer areas and the poorer areas. This proposal will compound that division to an extent that I do not believe—I am being generous—the Government have fully perceived. It will not merely cause bitterness in the housing estates as the number of people who pay rents shrinks and the number of people whom the Government will make to feel inferior

grows; it will cause enormous difficulty and enormous additional division between the rich and the poor and between the north and the south because the poorer areas that you and I represent, Mr. Deputy Speaker, will be more adversely affected.

I hope that the Minister will ensure that this matter is looked at again, because I believe that it will have a grossly unfair effect, not least on those who most deserve our consideration.

Mr. Allen McKay: I am a neighbour of my hon. Friend the Member for Wentworth (Mr. Hardy) and we have the same problems because the people we represent work in the same industries, and live in the same type of housing developments and in similar areas. The Bill will add to previous similar Bills, all of which were aimed at a year-in, year-out, step-by-step approach. In doing so, they have split communities and created haves and have-nots.

The Bill will carry that effect into what is probably the most precious part of a person's life, his house. Only council tenants will be affected by this, because under the Bill, if one lives in housing association accommodation, one will not be affected. Therefore, the Government are trying to persuade tenants to become tenants of a housing association by voting for that. Nothing is said about owner-occupiers receiving subsidies or about mortgage relief. The Government are picking only on council tenants. They have nothing against the tenants themselves but are after local authorities. If they want them to exist at all, it is only as enabling bodies.

That is part of the Government's grand strategy to ensure that local government as we know it will disappear. The Government make the mistake of failing to acknowledge public recognition of the advisory role played by local council officers. The public are wondering why officers are no longer available to give advice.

The Bill is a form of ring-fence legislation under which councils cannot subsidise local authority funding from their rates or poll tax funds. However, some local authorities have not done so for years, and mine is one of them. It receives no housing subsidy from the Government. Its housing stock was paid for over 40 or 60 years. Under a housing plan, rents from that stock are put into a rented housing pool whose profits after meeting maintenance costs help subsidise new house construction and rent levels. The Bill is taking that facility from local authorities, because the Secretary of State will be the person who determines each year what rent levels will be, and he will raise them to extremely high levels.

As a consequence, more tenants will rely on housing benefit. However, the Government say that they do not want to meet the cost of that support—the demand for which they created. They say that council tenants should generate profits for a local authority's housing revenue account, and that that should be used to meet the expense of rebates to tenants who cannot afford higher rents. That policy is one of the most disastrous that the Government have ever devised and clearly shows their hatred and vindictiveness towards anything to do with local authorities.

The Bill is designed to dilute the powers of local councils and ultimately to deprive them of their housing stocks. It will compel remaining local authority tenants to subsidise those who cannot afford higher rents, which will create an overall split or divide. That marks a return to the days when townships had a body of governors whose job

[Mr. Allen McKay]

it was to move on any vagrant who turned up because otherwise the vagrant would become the governors' responsibility.

The Bill will produce bitterness among local authority tenants, who will have to pay increased rents to meet the cost of housing rebates for the poorest members of society. As my hon. Friend the Member for Hammersmith (Mr. Soley) remarked, it is a system that makes the poor subsidise the poorest. Once again, the Government are abdicating their responsibilities.

Mr. George Howarth (Knowsley, North): I fully agree with the arguments advanced by my hon. Friends that the Bill is all part of a piece and reflects the Government's vendetta against council tenants. I take that argument further and say that the Government's vendetta is motivated by an attempt to smother their own incompetence.

A number of my right hon. and hon. Friends now in the Chamber sat through the various stages of the Housing Act 1988, which has three central objectives. The first is to break up local authority housing monopolies in certain areas. Part IV gives the Government power to establish housing action trusts or the so-called alternative of tenants' choice, whereby tenants can opt out of council housing into tenancies under approved landlords. The Act's second objective is to encourage by various means the growth of private landlords, and its third is to introduce to some extent private finance to the housing association sector.

5.15 pm

Two months ago, in an attempt to test the success of the Housing Act 1988, I put down a number of questions. The House may be interested to learn the effect so far of that legislation, with its 130 clauses, which took three and a half months to debate in Committee. As to the provision to create HATs and to allow private landlords to take over public sector housing, of the seven original trusts proposed, at least five are unlikely to go ahead, and the other two are tottering along with no clear indication of their future. Up to two months ago, only five organisations had applied to become approved landlords. Clearly there is no great rush to take on that responsibility.

I was also able to establish that, during the lifetime of the present Government, the number of private landlords has decreased from over 11 per cent. of all landlords to less than 8 per cent. Bearing in mind the fact that an increase in private landlords is a central objective of the Act, I asked by what percentage the Government expected the number of private landlords to increase over the next two or three years, but they declined to answer. We all know that when the Government decline to answer a question it is because the answer is not very favourable to them.

Mr. Tony Banks (Newham, North-West): Yes, but how does one know when they are lying?

Mr. Howarth: I shall not repeat my hon. Friend's intervention for fear of incurring your wrath, Mr. Deputy Speaker, but no doubt *Hansard* will pick it up.

I remind the House that the Act's third objective is to introduce private finance into housing associations. I remind the House also that one of the Ministers concerned with the Bill has moved to greener pastures, while another has gone out of the door altogether. The hon. Lady concerned was, I think, a victim of the new eviction regulations, because she was shunted out of her little bolthole at an early stage.

As to that third objective, the Secretary of State for the Environment claimed that the legislation would lead to an explosion in funding for housing associations. I cannot get an answer from the Housing Corporation or from the Minister, but we know for sure that expenditure on that sector will decrease this year because of the mess that the Government made of housing association finance. There will be fewer completions this year than last. Housing associations are in an absolute mess because they cannot work out exactly how to move forward. They have to negotiate each allocation they receive separately with a financial institution. Many of them do not even know whether they can spend that allocation. That was the reality of the Government's policy this time last year.

I had started to explain why the Government have this vendetta against council tenants; it is because they wish to smother their own incompetence. Their policies have totally failed to break up council housing monopolies, as they call them. The inevitable logic of the Government's thinking is that, because their policies are failing, they have to make life so awful, expensive and miserable for council tenants that their only option will be to try to seek an approved landlord because the Government will have weighted the terms so heavily against them.

What a nonsense of a policy for a Government to move from one housing mistake to the next merely to cover up previous mistakes. The Government are in chaos on many fronts, but nowhere is that more true than in their housing policies, which are a mess and utterly disastrous. The sooner we get them out of power, the better.

Mr. John Battle (Leeds, West): I shall focus my comments on housing benefit, which is sometimes referred to as the rebate system. Some people do not realise that the two are the same.

It became clear in Committee that, in the income and costs equation, management, maintenance and debt repayments are on one side, and rents are on the other. In the equation, housing benefit payments will come under expenditure—that is management, maintenance and debt repayments. Some of us would like to press the Government on why housing benefit has been taken out of the income support system, which should be paid in common taxes through the Treasury and passed on to tenants at local level.

At the moment, the poor are being taken out of the national budget and those who are slightly better off, the rent payers, will have to cover them. The national budget in this House should be the place for discussing the relations between pensions, benefits and taxes. We should not push that on to the slightly better-off rent payers.

Before I came to the House, some Opposition Members argued that housing benefit should not have been handed over to local authorities. I have checked the record; it shows that, at that time, it was said that it would become confused with the housing revenue account. It was said that local authorities would become confused with the social security system, and that the Government were determined to ensure that poverty was taken out of the national debate.

It is no surprise that in recent weeks the Secretary of State for Social Security has denied that poverty any longer exists in Britain. His statement was reiterated by the Prime Minister, who said that we no longer had to talk about poverty because we now have only wealth. I should express the argument in slightly less dramatic terms.

The Under-Secretary of State for the Environment speaks for the country on housing. Does he want his hands tied by what happens in the Department of Social Security? In future, what happens to his budget will depend on the level at which income support is set each year. The Minister will have to watch the social security upratings like a hawk, because they will affect every housing revenue account of every local authority in the budget. The Secretary of State for Social Security lost the brief for health and has decided that poverty does not exist. Perhaps he now wants to run the housing department as well. The housing budget should not be run by the DSS.

There have been 14 changes to housing benefit in less than 14 years, which means that there has not been annual budgeting. The budget for housing benefit has not been stuck to each year; transitional arrangements have been put in in between. How on earth can the Minister expect local authorities to put together their budgets and audit them when the figures are changed every few months because the Department of Social Security decides to change its contributions to housing benefit?

The Minister's budget should enable him to improve the housing stock of this country and bring it up to modern standards. Only this last week we have seen another report from the Royal Institute of British Architects suggesting that there is a large job to be done even at this late stage. Why does not the Minister get on with that job instead of making cuts in the benefit system through the back door of the housing revenue account? That is what will happen as long as the rent rebate system remains in the equation.

I press the Minister to assure the House that he understands the sense of the new clause and agrees that we should take housing benefit out of the equation and put it back where it belongs: in the national budget. We could then make decisions in this Chamber about taxes, pensions and benefits, which is where they ought to be made in the context of the national budget, so that the poor are not pushed back on to the limited resources that remain to the rent payers who are not in difficulties.

Mr. Tony Banks: I speak in favour of new clause 19. In a few hours' time the Chamber, certainly the Conservative Benches, will be full of Members who have come in to talk about dog registration, in which there will be much interest, not only on the Floor but probably in the Press Gallery. The Government seem to care less about council tenants than about dogs, and they do not care very much about dogs.

I know that the Minister was in the London borough of Newham last week. Unfortunately, I was unable to be there to go round with him, but I know that my hon. Friend the Member for Newham, North-East (Mr. Leighton), at whose invitation he came, was with him to ensure that he saw what was happening in the borough. I hope that what he saw made some impression on him and that he appreciated the scale of the problems, particularly of housing, in Newham, where 65 per cent. of council tenants receive housing benefit.

It seems scandalous that the London borough of Newham is unable to get back 100 per cent. of the money that it paid out. It is doubly scandalous that, under the

Government's proposals, an additional 3 per cent. will have to come out of the housing revenue account. As my hon. Friend the Member for Hammersmith (Mr. Soley) said, the Government seem to want the poor to pay for the totally impoverished, which seems to fly in the face of decency.

There is very little which is decent left in this Government of second-hand car salesmen, Arthur Daleys and low life generally, which is why we tabled the new clause—*[Interruption.]* My hon. Friend the Member for Leeds, West (Mr. Battle) says that I have been unfair on second-hand car salesmen. I probably have. There are other forms of human existence and activities that would make more apposite comparisons with Conservative Members, but if I went through the list I am sure that I would quickly be brought to order.

The poor are in an extremely onerous position, which is unfair, unjust and typical of the Government. I say, and have done so many times, that I have a slight flicker of hope that one day one of the Ministers will be moved by the experience of coming to a borough such as Newham and seeing how appalling the housing conditions are in terms of demand, need and shortage.

I have not yet had a chance to talk to the Minister, but I should like to know whether he felt that his visit to Newham last week was worth while. Perhaps he can now share some of the experiences of Opposition Members. Week after week in our advice surgeries, we have to confront constituents complaining about the appalling housing conditions in which they live.

This is a reasonable new clause which a reasonable Minister would accept. Will this Minister show himself to be almost alone on the Conservative Front Benches in being a reasonable man with a heart?

5.30 pm

Mr. Jeff Rooker (Birmingham, Perry Barr): I should like to raise a point that is subsidiary to those raised by my hon. Friends.

The Government seem to be saying that local authorities will not be reimbursed directly for payment of housing benefit because those payments will effectively have been made by other tenants. I draw the Minister's attention to a report published by the National Audit Office only a few days ago, on which the Public Accounts Committee will take evidence next Wednesday. It deals with the housing benefit scheme which, according to one headline in today's press, was "botched up" in April 1988. No doubt the PAC will have an interesting session. The report, incidentally, is available in the Vote Office.

Paragraph 3.14 explains that a new system for housing benefit was designed last April under which a high rate of direct subsidy would be paid on most, but not all, housing benefit expenditure. Part of the purpose was to give local authorities an incentive to control some of the costs.

What incentive have local authorities now to control rents, let alone costs? Clearly, if the housing revenue account is to be ring-fenced as the Bill suggests, there will be no incentive for local authorities or for central Government. Rents will go up and up, and the level of housing rebate expenditure will not matter. The cost will be borne by the other tenants, so what the hell—why should there be any need to consider costs and efficiency? Where is the built-in management function to ensure that tenants will not be ripped off more than they are already?

[Mr. Jeff Rooker]

There will now be no incentive for the Government or local authorities to control rents or costs, because the Government will not be part and parcel of the system and the rest of the local authority budget will not pay its share. The responsibility will be on the backs of the tenants. If the Minister can explain that, he will help me to question the Permanent Secretary or accounting officer of the Department of Social Security on Wednesday. The PAC may then obtain better value for money in taking evidence on the report, which is highly relevant to the Bill. The Permanent Secretary will say, "We are going to change the scheme." We know how this scheme is to be changed—we are doing it here tonight—but it would be helpful if the Minister would address himself to paragraph 3.14 of the report.

The Parliamentary Under-Secretary of State for the Environment (Mr. David Trippier): I am bound to suffer from déjà vu, as we discussed this matter so many times during the many weeks of the Committee stage. I thought when we were discussing the details of the housing revenue account that Conservative Members were at a distinct advantage, as it was a rather technical matter. I was quick to point out towards the close of the proceedings that the one Opposition Member who seemed to have got it right was the hon. Member for Leeds, West (Mr. Battle). I said that several times, not merely to damage the hon. Gentleman's chances of reselection but to compliment him genuinely. The hon. Member for Hammersmith (Mr. Soley) and his supporters should, I felt, hang their heads in shame because they had not taken the time and trouble to study the subject and to come to understand it. Now, however, I must claw back every compliment that I paid the hon. Member for Leeds, West.

Mr. Tony Banks: On a point of order, Madam Deputy Speaker. Conservative Members below the Gangway may not be interested in what the Minister is saying, but we are interested. He may not tell us a great deal, but we still want to listen. Can they be brought to order?

Madam Deputy Speaker (Miss Betty Boothroyd): Order. I am sure that the whole House can hear what the Minister is saying.

Mr. Trippier: I said informally to the hon. Member for Hammersmith that we had the advantage not only of excellent briefing from civil servants but of access to diagrams—which are always helpful to Members of Parliament, who may be able to take pictures on board more easily than words. When it was suggested that we might offer Opposition Members the same facility in Committee, I denied them the opportunity so as to retain our advantage. On reflection, I think that I made a great mistake. Had I sent the diagrams across we might have had great fun going through them. No doubt it would have introduced a lighter note to the proceedings, and we might not have encountered the difficulties that we seem to be having today.

I have a simple and straightforward message for the hon. Member for Leeds, West. His speech today got it right in all respects but one—he did not seem to realise that the new housing subsidy is provided by the taxpayer. The subsidy is one side of the equation, supplementing or complementing the amount being made available in the

form of rents, which is the other side. Thus we balance the management and maintenance functions that the hon. Gentleman mentioned with the rent rebate—I think that he is still the only hon. Member to have got the point about rebates being confined to council tenants.

It is nonsense for the hon. Members for Hammersmith, for Barnsley, West and Penistone (Mr. McKay) and for Knowsley, North (Mr. Howarth) to suggest that the Government are anti-tenant. That is so ridiculous that it stretches credulity to breaking point. Which Government introduced the right to buy, which has been so successful? Which Government introduced the priority estates project and Estate Action? Which Government introduced estate management boards to devolve responsibility to tenants whom we wish to have more influence over the running of their affairs? The present Government have done all those things. The Labour party never thought of doing those things when it was last in office.

Mr. Allen McKay: If the Minister will look again at the history of my local authority, he will find that we had tenants associations and organisations on estates long before the present Government came to office.

Mr. Trippier: I think that the hon. Gentleman will regret that intervention. We are not talking about tenants associations, which have been supported for a considerable time—since before the last war, I believe. Having come up through local government, I know what an important rôle they play. But they are not the same as estate management boards. I will send the hon. Gentleman details of estate management boards in the post tonight. They allow tenants to vote some of their number on to a board which runs the estate and has the power to appoint a local government officer in a neighbourhood office serving tenants to their best advantage. There is a link, because we hope that tenants associations will put forward candidates to serve on that body. The schemes are working very well, although they were started only recently. There are now eight in the United Kingdom, and we want to see far more.

As I have said—especially to the hon. Member for Leeds, West—housing subsidy uses taxpayers' money. Under our new policy, rent rebates are taken into the subsidy calculation in full. If there is a surplus from the operating side of the subsidy—the hon. Gentleman will remember that we debated this at length in Committee; I think that that was the term that he rightly used—where will the surplus go?

We must explain to the hon. Member for Wentworth (Mr. Hardy) what we are not trying to do. He can be excused everything, as he did not sit on the Committee. We are not changing the rules on who is eligible for rent rebates or the level of support that people will receive. We are merely looking at how the cost of rent rebates is met. We are not concerned with the cost of anything but the rent rebates granted to a council's own tenants.

Time and again in Committee, Opposition Members claimed that we were bringing into the equation the cost of allowances to private tenants, rate rebates and community charge rebates under the new system. They tried to give the impression that in some way all these extra costs would fall on council tenants. That is absolutely and completely wrong. All rebates and allowances, other than rebates to a council's own tenants, are outside the authority's housing revenue account. The cost is outside the account and will remain outside it. Rebates and allowances to private tenants therefore do not come into the picture.

In the early years of the present system, which we are anxious to change, as well as receiving help with rebate costs most councils also received the general bricks and mortar Government subsidy. They needed Government help to balance their housing revenue accounts. The position today is very different. Councils are providing much less new housing, so the loan charges that they have to pay on capital projects are growing older and being eroded by inflation. The costs falling on housing revenue accounts today are therefore less, in real terms, than they were in the early 1970s. Authorities have enjoyed recently some windfall benefits because of the success of our right-to-buy policy. It is interesting that the hon. Member for Hammersmith suggests that the Government are discriminating against council tenants, but the present system does not discriminate against them. *[Interruption.]* I always know that I am on to a good point when the hon. Member for Hammersmith bursts into peals of laughter because he is so embarrassed. Perhaps if I speak slowly he will be able to take the point on board.

The truth is that we are introducing a system which means that the new housing subsidy will be met by taxpayers' money. Moreover, the windfall profits being made by local authorities will enable them to keep public sector rents down. The same advantage is not available to the private rented sector. That is one of the reasons, as was fairly said by the hon. Member for Knowsley, North for the decline in the private rented sector. However, I would argue strenuously with him, here or anywhere else he wishes, that the reason why it has fallen from 50 per cent. to the present 8 per cent. is principally because of the substantial expansion of public housing and because, due to the Rent Acts, it has not been attractive for people who would normally invest in the private rented sector to do so.

The result of these quite dramatic changes is that, far from needing Government help to balance their housing revenue accounts, many councils are now able to generate surpluses on the account. Nowadays, only about 70 authorities, less than one fifth, claim general housing subsidy, yet throughout this time the Government—or, to be precise, the national taxpayer—have continued to pick up virtually the whole of the local rent rebates bill. An authority might be able to make a very healthy surplus on the account, but this one item alone in the account continues to attract almost the whole subsidy. What began in 1972 as a subsidy directed to authorities which needed help, as most then did, has become an unnecessary subsidy paid to authorities which could quite comfortably meet either the whole or a share of the cost of rent rebates without it.

The general point that I make to the hon. Member for Leeds, West is that the whole purpose of introducing a new housing subsidy along the lines that we discussed at length in Committee is to make a fairer distribution to local authorities, principally in the midlands and the north where the hon. Gentleman and I come from, as recognition of the problems that they face with their housing, particularly in the inner city areas.

The effect of the Opposition's new clause would be to remove the local contribution that the hon. Member for Leeds, West mentioned. I can see what he is driving at. He wants to ensure that tenants will not have to make a contribution, even as little as 3 per cent., to the cost of all

rebates. I can reassure him about that. I hope to make a statement as soon as possible. I trust that the hon. Gentleman will take comfort from what I have said.

I think that I have demonstrated to all those who wanted to listen that the Government are not doing anything devious. The housing finance package provided for in this part of the Bill is specifically designed to meet the concerns that have been expressed by Opposition Members. They do not like the package. They know that it will be successful. For that reason, I hope that my hon. Friends will reject the new clause.

5.45 pm

Mr. Soley: The last few minutes of the Minister's speech demonstrated his best used-car salesman's approach. It would have warned anybody else off. I can now see why he was given pictures to look at to help him to understand. However, one is supposed to fill in the colours on the pictures according to the numbers. That is what the Minister has not understood. He is totally wrong, and he knows it. That is why he did not deal with the fact that the poor are being asked to subsidise the poorest. Any money in the housing revenue account over and above that which allows the account to break even will be used to subsidise the housing benefit system. In addition to their taxes, people will be paying a subsidy to the poorest. That is where the Minister has got the colours wrong in the picture book. I will give him another picture book for his birthday if he will let me know when that is.

The tenants who will be asked to subsidise the system will have to shoulder a double burden. They will pay a subsidy through their taxes and a subsidy through their rents. The Minister has the audacity to say that he expected rents to be kept reasonably low and that the system is designed to help council tenants who will receive additional help. The statements that the Minister made in Committee about council rents varied from one day to the next. On one occasion he said:

"A council's rent policies have not caused distortions in the market that affect people's freedom of choice."

The next thing that he said was:

"We have no preconception about the level to which rents should eventually rise. We have no target for council rents."

Then he said:

"We are not seeking to control rents."

After that, he said:

"The purpose of the subsidy will be to enable efficient authorities to provide a good standard of service at a reasonable and realistic rent."

However, he never told us what a reasonable and realistic rent would be. He then said again:

"We are not seeking to control rents."

In the background has been the Government's constant commitment—much muted, I concede, in the last 12 months—to market rents. Now they are saying that they do not want market rents because, suddenly, they are embarrassed by them. Yet the Government are pushing council rents towards market rents in all these areas. I shall return in due course to some of those areas because of the incredible mess that the Government have made of presenting the Bill on the Floor of the House.

We have to deal with all the amendments and new clauses in two days. It would be absurd to pursue this matter now to the extent to which it deserves to be pursued, and I readily concede that we pursued it in considerable detail in Committee. The basic principle that the Minister constantly avoids—that the poor are being

[*Mr. Soley*]

asked to subsidise the poorest and to do so in addition to what they are already paying through their taxes—leads us to the conclusion that we must press the new clause to a Division.

Question put, That the clause be read a Second time:—
The House divided: Ayes 142, Noes 36.

Division No. 242]   **[5.48 pm**

AYES

Abbott, Ms Diane
Alton, David
Anderson, Donald
Archer, Rt Hon Peter
Ashdown, Rt Hon Paddy
Ashton, Joe
Banks, Tony *(Newham NW)*
Barnes, Harry *(Derbyshire NE)*
Barnes, Mrs Rosie *(Greenwich)*
Barron, Kevin
Battle, John
Beckett, Margaret
Beith, A. J.
Benn, Rt Hon Tony
Bennett, A. F. *(D'nt'n & R'dish)*
Bermingham, Gerald
Bidwell, Sydney
Blunkett, David
Bradley, Keith
Bruce, Malcolm *(Gordon)*
Buckley, George J.
Callaghan, Jim
Campbell, Ron *(Blyth Valley)*
Campbell-Savours, D. N.
Cartwright, John
Clark, Dr David *(S Shields)*
Clarke, Tom *(Monklands W)*
Clay, Bob
Clwyd, Mrs Ann
Cohen, Harry
Coleman, Donald
Cook, Frank *(Stockton N)*
Cook, Robin *(Livingston)*
Corbyn, Jeremy
Cousins, Jim
Cox, Tom
Crowther, Stan
Cryer, Bob
Cummings, John
Cunningham, Dr John
Davies, Rt Hon Denzil *(Llanelli)*
Davies, Ron *(Caerphilly)*
Davis, Terry *(B'ham Hodge H'l)*
Dixon, Don
Dobson, Frank
Dunwoody, Hon Mrs Gwyneth
Eastham, Ken
Fatchett, Derek
Fearn, Ronald
Field, Frank *(Birkenhead)*
Fields, Terry *(L'pool B G'n)*
Fisher, Mark
Flannery, Martin
Flynn, Paul
Foot, Rt Hon Michael
Foster, Derek
Foulkes, George
Fraser, John
Garrett, John *(Norwich South)*
George, Bruce
Gordon, Mildred
Gould, Bryan
Griffiths, Win *(Bridgend)*
Grocott, Bruce
Hardy, Peter
Hattersley, Rt Hon Roy
Heffer, Eric S.

Henderson, Doug
Hinchliffe, David
Home Robertson, John
Howarth, George *(Knowsley N)*
Howell, Rt Hon D. *(S'heath)*
Howells, Dr. Kim (Pontypridd)
Hughes, John *(Coventry NE)*
Hughes, Roy *(Newport E)*
Hughes, Simon *(Southwark)*
Illsley, Eric
Janner, Greville
Jones, Ieuan *(Ynys Môn)*
Kaufman, Rt Hon Gerald
Kirkwood, Archy
Leadbitter, Ted
Leighton, Ron
Lestor, Joan *(Eccles)*
Lewis, Terry
Litherland, Robert
Livingstone, Ken
Lloyd, Tony *(Stretford)*
Lofthouse, Geoffrey
Loyden, Eddie
McAllion, John
McWilliam, John
Madden, Max
Mahon, Mrs Alice
Maxton, John
Meacher, Michael
Meale, Alan
Michael, Alun
Michie, Bill *(Sheffield Heeley)*
Morgan, Rhodri
Morris, Rt Hon A. *(W'shawe)*
Morris, Rt Hon J. *(Aberavon)*
Mowlam, Marjorie
Murphy, Paul
O'Brien, William
Orme, Rt Hon Stanley
Owen, Rt Hon Dr David
Patchett, Terry
Pendry, Tom
Pike, Peter L.
Powell, Ray *(Ogmore)*
Prescott, John
Primarolo, Dawn
Redmond, Martin
Rees, Rt Hon Merlyn
Richardson, Jo
Robertson, George
Robinson, Geoffrey
Rooker, Jeff
Rowlands, Ted
Ruddock, Joan
Sedgemore, Brian
Sheldon, Rt Hon Robert
Shore, Rt Hon Peter
Skinner, Dennis
Smith, C. *(Isl'ton & F'bury)*
Smith, Sir Cyril *(Rochdale)*
Smith, Rt Hon J. *(Monk'ds E)*
Smith, J. P. *(Vale of Glam)*
Snape, Peter
Soley, Clive
Spearing, Nigel
Taylor, Mrs Ann *(Dewsbury)*
Taylor, Matthew *(Truro)*

Wall, Pat
Wallace, James
Walley, Joan
Wardell, Gareth *(Gower)*
Williams, Rt Hon Alan
Winnick, David

Wise, Mrs Audrey
Worthington, Tony

Tellers for the Ayes:
    Mr. Allen McKay and
    Mr. Frank Haynes.

NOES

Adley, Robert
Aitken, Jonathan
Alexander, Richard
Alison, Rt Hon Michael
Allason, Rupert
Amess, David
Amos, Alan
Arbuthnot, James
Arnold, Jacques *(Gravesham)*
Arnold, Tom *(Hazel Grove)*
Ashby, David
Atkinson, David
Baker, Nicholas *(Dorset N)*
Beaumont-Dark, Anthony
Bendall, Vivian
Bennett, Nicholas *(Pembroke)*
Benyon, W.
Biffen, Rt Hon John
Blackburn, Dr John G.
Blaker, Rt Hon Sir Peter
Body, Sir Richard
Bonsor, Sir Nicholas
Bottomley, Peter
Bottomley, Mrs Virginia
Bowden, A *(Brighton K'pto'n)*
Bowden, Gerald *(Dulwich)*
Bowis, John
Boyson, Rt Hon Dr Sir Rhodes
Braine, Rt Hon Sir Bernard
Brandon-Bravo, Martin
Brazier, Julian
Bright, Graham
Brown, Michael *(Brigg & Cl't's)*
Browne, John *(Winchester)*
Buchanan-Smith, Rt Hon Alick
Buck, Sir Antony
Burns, Simon
Burt, Alistair
Butterfill, John
Carlisle, John, *(Luton N)*
Carlisle, Kenneth *(Lincoln)*
Carrington, Matthew
Carttiss, Michael
Channon, Rt Hon Paul
Chapman, Sydney
Chope, Christopher
Churchill, Mr
Clark, Dr Michael *(Rochford)*
Clark, Sir W. *(Croydon S)*
Colvin, Michael
Conway, Derek
Coombs, Anthony *(Wyre F'rest)*
Coombs, Simon *(Swindon)*
Cran, James
Davies, Q. *(Stamf'd & Spald'g)*
Day, Stephen
Devlin, Tim
Dickens, Geoffrey
Douglas-Hamilton, Lord James
Dover, Den
Dunn, Bob
Durant, Tony
Dykes, Hugh
Eggar, Tim
Emery, Sir Peter
Fairbairn, Sir Nicholas
Favell, Tony
Field, Barry *(Isle of Wight)*
Finsberg, Sir Geoffrey
Fishburn, John Dudley
Fookes, Dame Janet
Forman, Nigel

Forsyth, Michael *(Stirling)*
Forth, Eric
Fox, Sir Marcus
Franks, Cecil
Freeman, Roger
Fry, Peter
Gale, Roger
Gardiner, George
Garel-Jones, Tristan
Gill, Christopher
Gilmour, Rt Hon Sir Ian
Glyn, Dr Alan
Gorst, John
Gow, Ian
Greenway, Harry *(Ealing N)*
Greenway, John *(Ryedale)*
Gregory, Conal
Griffiths, Peter *(Portsmouth N)*
Grist, Ian
Gummer, Rt Hon John Selwyn
Hague, William
Hamilton, Neil *(Tatton)*
Hampson, Dr Keith
Hanley, Jeremy
Hannam, John
Hargreaves, A. *(B'ham H'll Gr')*
Hargreaves, Ken *(Hyndburn)*
Harris, David
Haselhurst, Alan
Hayes, Jerry
Hayhoe, Rt Hon Sir Barney
Hayward, Robert
Heddle, John
Hicks, Mrs Maureen *(Wolv' NE)*
Hicks, Robert *(Cornwall SE)*
Higgins, Rt Hon Terence L.
Hind, Kenneth
Hordern, Sir Peter
Howard, Michael
Howarth, Alan *(Strat'd-on-A)*
Howarth, G. *(Cannock & B'wd)*
Hughes, Robert G. *(Harrow W)*
Hunt, David *(Wirral W)*
Hunter, Andrew
Irvine, Michael
Jack, Michael
Janman, Tim
Johnson Smith, Sir Geoffrey
Jones, Gwilym *(Cardiff N)*
Jones, Robert B *(Herts W)*
Jopling, Rt Hon Michael
Kellett-Bowman, Dame Elaine
Key, Robert
Kilfedder, James
Knapman, Roger
Knight, Dame Jill *(Edgbaston)*
Knowles, Michael
Knox, David
Lang, Ian
Latham, Michael
Lawrence, Ivan
Leigh, Edward *(Gainsbor'gh)*
Lennox-Boyd, Hon Mark
Lester, Jim *(Broxtowe)*
Lightbown, David
Lilley, Peter
Lloyd, Sir Ian *(Havant)*
Lloyd, Peter *(Fareham)*
Luce, Rt Hon Richard
Macfarlane, Sir Neil
MacKay, Andrew *(E Berkshire)*
Maclean, David

McLoughlin, Patrick
McNair-Wilson, Sir Michael
McNair-Wilson, P. *(New Forest)*
Madel, David
Mans, Keith
Marlow, Tony
Marshall, John *(Hendon S)*
Marshall, Michael *(Arundel)*
Martin, David *(Portsmouth S)*
Maxwell-Hyslop, Robin
Miller, Sir Hal
Mills, Iain
Mitchell, Andrew *(Gedling)*
Moate, Roger
Montgomery, Sir Fergus
Morris, M *(N'hampton S)*
Mudd, David
Nicholls, Patrick
Nicholson, David *(Taunton)*
Norris, Steve
Onslow, Rt Hon Cranley
Page, Richard
Paice, James
Patnick, Irvine
Pawsey, James
Peacock, Mrs Elizabeth
Powell, William *(Corby)*
Price, Sir David
Raison, Rt Hon Timothy
Riddick, Graham
Ridley, Rt Hon Nicholas
Ridsdale, Sir Julian
Rifkind, Rt Hon Malcolm
Rost, Peter
Rumbold, Mrs Angela
Sackville, Hon Tom
Scott, Nicholas
Shaw, David *(Dover)*
Shaw, Sir Giles *(Pudsey)*
Shaw, Sir Michael *(Scarb')*
Shelton, Sir William
Shephard, Mrs G. *(Norfolk SW)*
Shepherd, Colin *(Hereford)*
Shepherd, Richard *(Aldridge)*
Shersby, Michael
Sims, Roger
Smith, Sir Dudley *(Warwick)*
Smith, Tim *(Beaconsfield)*

Speller, Tony
Spicer, Sir Jim *(Dorset W)*
Squire, Robin
Stanbrook, Ivor
Stanley, Rt Hon Sir John
Steen, Anthony
Stevens, Lewis
Stewart, Andy *(Sherwood)*
Stokes, Sir John
Stradling Thomas, Sir John
Sumberg, David
Summerson, Hugo
Tapsell, Sir Peter
Taylor, Teddy *(S'end E)*
Tebbit, Rt Hon Norman
Temple-Morris, Peter
Thompson, D. *(Calder Valley)*
Thompson, Patrick *(Norwich N)*
Thorne, Neil
Thornton, Malcolm
Thurnham, Peter
Townend, John *(Bridlington)*
Townsend, Cyril D. *(B'heath)*
Trippier, David
Twinn, Dr Ian
Vaughan, Sir Gerard
Waddington, Rt Hon David
Wakeham, Rt Hon John
Waller, Gary
Walters, Sir Dennis
Ward, John
Wardle, Charles *(Bexhill)*
Watts, John
Wells, Bowen
Wheeler, John
Widdecombe, Ann
Wilkinson, John
Winterton, Mrs Ann
Winterton, Nicholas
Wood, Timothy
Woodcock, Dr. Mike
Yeo, Tim
Young, Sir George *(Acton)*
Younger, Rt Hon George

Tellers for the Noes:
Mr. Michael Fallon and
Mr. David Heathcoat-Amory.

Question accordingly negatived.

Schedule 4

THE KEEPING OF THE HOUSING REVENUE ACCOUNT

6 pm

Mr. Matthew Taylor (Truro): I beg to move amendment No. 212, in page 143, line 48, at end insert—
'*Item 1: Percentage of Collectable Rent*
A sum from some other revenue account not greater than 1 per cent. of the Authority's gross annual collectable rent.'.

Madam Deputy Speaker: With this we shall discuss amendment No. 213, in page 143, line 48, at end insert—
'*Item 1: Percentage of Housing Revenue Account Turnover*
A sum from some other revenue account not greater than 0·5 per cent. of the annual turnover of the Authority's Housing Revenue Account.'.

Mr. Taylor: The debate on these amendments directly follows our previous debate and raises very much the same concern about the poor subsidising the very poor. The Minister has failed to resolve an argument that continues to rage and that severely worries tenants of council houses, namely, the effects of the ring-fencing of accounts.

The amendments aim to add to the list of items allowed through the housing revenue account. They would

alleviate the problems caused by the Government's phasing out of rent subsidies and the ring-fencing of the HRA. The arguments for tackling the problems have already been put by the Opposition and I am well aware that the Minister is not prepared to accept what we believe will be the impact of what he is doing. Nevertheless, the people are worried and generally the people are right.

The amendments would break the ring fence and remove the new poverty trap now being created. In fact, they are aimed at helping the Minister out of the pit that he has dug for himself because both impose a cash limit and both, especially No. 212, would reduce to nothing as council-owned homes are sold or transferred to outside management if the Government's policy is successful. It is not an open-ended sum of money; it is directly related to housing held by a council and to the costs that may be involved. Although the amendments break the ring fence, they do so in a precise and limited way.

I hope that the Minister will seize this opportunity to save himself from the difficulties in which he will otherwise find himself. It is almost an act of generosity, and I hope that he will accept the amendments.

Mr. Trippier: I was fascinated with the hon. Gentleman's remark that people were generally worried and that people were generally right. I find that odd. Presumably it is part of the twisted propaganda put out by the SLD. I shall seek to correct the hon. Gentleman in as brief a time as possible. He well knows that the whole purpose of not allowing money from the general rate fund in any way to subsidise the housing revenue account is to draw a clearer correlation between the management efficiency of that housing authority and the tenants that it is meant to serve as its customers.

It is illogical for the hon. Gentleman to table such an amendment. He appears to have plucked a figure out of the air. There is no reason or justification for that figure and, indeed, he did not attempt to give one. I can comfort him by saying that there is no necessity for the amendment, and I hope that he will be good enough to convey that to those who, as he put it, are generally worried.

Mr. George Howarth: During the last debate the Minister said that he would give me an opportunity to intervene, but he did not. He now speaks of plucking figures out of the air. By how much does he expect the private rented sector to grow during the next few years? As yet he has singularly failed to give any information on that.

Mr. Trippier: It would be hazardous for any Minister, of any Government, standing at this Dispath Box to be so reckless as to put a figure on that. It is the same sort of answer that the right hon. Member for Blaenau Gwent (Mr. Foot) gave when he was Leader of the Opposition, when he consistently refused to say what he thought the level of unemployment would be in X years. The hon. Gentleman's question was stupid and unworthy of him.

Mr. Howarth: The difference between the current position and that when my right hon. Friend the Member for Blaenau Gwent (Mr. Foot) was Leader of the Opposition is that last year the Government implemented an Act with the major purpose of expanding the private rented sector. The Minister must have a target in mind because it is clearly a central objective of Government policy.

Mr. Trippier: I do not understand why the Government have to set a target. With the largest public housing stock and the smallest private rented housing stock in the western world, it is clear that the position must be reversed. The balance is out of kilter. Even though this Government are efficient in introducing, developing and pursuing their policies, it is bordering on the ludicrious for the hon. Gentleman to suggest that since the Act took effect on 1 April there must have been such a dramatic incursion into the private rented sector that the results should be shown two months later.

Mr. George Howarth *rose——*

Mr. Trippier: The hon. Gentleman knows that in Committee I was keen to allow him to intervene as many times as he wanted. We have debated these matters in the past and I have no doubt that he will return to them on other amendments. I want to respond to the SLD amendments.

Mr. Howarth: The Minister said that the proportion of private rented sector stock is too small. A few months ago the Government enacted legislation with the specific objective of increasing that proportion. The Minister must have some idea of what he expects that legislation to achieve during the next few years. That is all that I am asking him to tell the House.

Mr. Trippier: Obviously, we can estimate what we want to be developed through the housing association movement——

Mr. Soley: That is the public sector.

Mr. Trippier: I do not want to enter that debate again. The hon. Member for Hammersmith (Mr. Soley) has never accepted that the housing association movement is in the private rented sector. It does not really matter how he defines it; what matters is the way that we define it because we are subject to parliamentary questions. We regard it as being within the private rented sector, but with Government subsidy. If we link the housing association rented sector with the private landlord, it is difficult to predict precisely what the figure might be——

Mr. Soley *rose——*

Mr. Trippier: No.

Mr. Soley: I wish to correct the Minister.

Mr. Trippier: I am sorry, but it is not a correction. The hon. Gentleman well knows that there is a difference of opinion between the Opposition and the Government.

Mr. Soley *rose——*

Mr. Trippier: If the hon. Gentleman would just calm down for a moment, I shall give way to him. There is a difference of opinion between the Government and the Opposition about how to define the housing association movement. In all the statistics that we publish, we make it clear that it is in the private rented sector. The public rented sector covers council houses in the ownership of local authorities.

Mr. Soley: I do not dispute that there is disagreement between us, but when I have tabled questions the Minister has seen fit not to answer them but to ask the Housing Corporation to do so. The Housing Corporation does not share the Minister's view on the definition of a housing association. I want that to be clear, not because I disagree about the differences between us but because it should be understood that not all parliamentary questions give the same answer as the Minister. Answers sent indirectly through the Housing Corporation are different.

Mr. Trippier: I respect the spirit in which the hon. Gentleman made his intervention. I have never been, formally or informally, approached by the Housing Corporation about the matter. If it disagrees with our definition of the private rented sector, I accept that that difference should be ironed out. Perhaps as a result of the hon. Gentleman's intervention the Government and the Housing Corporation will discuss it, but I have received no representations from it thus far.

Mr. George Howarth: It is important that we are given the information for which we are asking. For the purposes of argument, I accept the Minister's definition that the housing association movement can be considered as part of the same parcel as the private rented sector. Will he predict, by his definition, by how much he expects its housing stock to increase over the next few years?

Mr. Trippier: In saying by how much I expect it to rise, I must make it clear that it is my opinion. It is hoped that there will be a net increase in the housing association sector of at least 35,000 houses a year. We shall have to wait and see whether that target is attained. I suspect—my hon. Friends can draw comfort from this—that it might be exceeded, which is precisely the reason why I gave that figure. To have given a higher figure would have been rather reckless, would it not?

Under the budget-making provisions of clause 67, which we introduced in Committee, local authorities will not be required to avoid a deficit on their housing revenue account. We may not have made that clear in Committee, because I cannot remember us specifically dealing with that point.

Clause 67 requires authorities to formulate proposals that, so far as they can foresee, will not result in a deficit, and they must keep them under review, taking reasonably practicable steps throughout the year to avoid a deficit. However, if, despite their best endeavours—perhaps because of outside changes—a deficit arises, it is simply carried over to be cleared in the next financial year. Therefore, the flexibility that the hon. Member for Truro (Mr. Taylor) is seeking is built into the system. There is, therefore, no need for a last-minute balancing contribution from the rate fund. The HRA merely starts the following year showing a deficit.

I hope that I have reassured the hon. Member for Truro and that he will withdraw the amendment.

Mr. Matthew Taylor: The point that the Minister made at the end introduces flexibility, not autonomy, which cannot be a policy of a council. If it were, it would have to disguise it.

We debated the same issue on amendment No. 212. There is no advantage in the House having two votes on the same issue, but put in different ways, so I beg to ask leave to withdraw the amendment.

Amendment, by leave, withdrawn.

Mr. Soley: I beg to move amendment No. 182, in page 145, line 16, at end insert

    'or

(c) expenditure insofar as the Secretary of State determines that it relates solely to the welfare of the occupiers of houses and other property; or

(d) expenditure insofar as the Secretary of State determines that it relates solely or primarily to the provision of a service or services for the benefit of persons who are not occupants of houses and property within the account.'.

The amendment is important and draws attention to the Government's ring-fencing proposals. It is not the amendment that I should have liked to be selected, but there are winners and losers and I did not get the precise wording that I should have liked. Again, because of the way in which the Government have handled the Report stage, I fear that the House will be unable to give sufficient attention to the ring-fencing debate.

The amendment aims to clarify the point that expenditure on the welfare functions of housing and services to the private sector, such as advice to private tenants, improvement grants and agency schemes, will not be debited to the housing revenue account.

The amendment raises the principle and practice of ring fencing. Under their ring-fencing proposals, the Government are saying that the ratepayer or, in future, the poll tax payer must not subsidise rents. The only fair aspect of their proposals is that they are saying that the reverse should not apply. The proposals have serious consequences. They will increase rents and reduce subsidies available to council tenants in some areas. As a consequence, council tenants will feel a further squeeze on their finances.

6.15 pm

We are trying to get the Minister to clarify the Government's housing revenue account policy. Will the HRA be limited to matters relating to buildings or will it include services? Should not the poll tax payer, rather than the council tenant, bear the cost of services that are provided for the benefit of the community? Let me take the example of an advice service to private tenants. Many local authorities are arranging for private tenants to be represented in one form or another, to deal with harassment and such matters. If the charge for such services is to be debited to the HRA, problems will arise. It is logical to allow expenditure on such matters from poll tax revenue as they are a general service to the public. One cannot help suspecting that such costs will be debited to the HRA, which will limit services available to people and, at the same time, increase councils' housing costs.

We believe that the ring-fencing proposals are unfair. The taxpayer generously and properly subsidises people who want to buy houses through grants in the form of income tax relief and grants for houses that they buy from the public sector.

The Minister will remember the slip that he made late at night some months ago when we were debating the squalid Rent Officers (Additional Functions) Order 1989, which reduced a person's housing benefit if he was in a house that was considered to be too large. The Minister said that the taxpayer should not subsidise a spare room. I asked him how many spare rooms he had in his house and how much subsidy he received through mortgage tax relief. He replied, "That does not apply because I do not receive housing benefit." That is how the Minister avoids such questions.

I appreciate that Labour Members are asking the Minister embarrassing and difficult questions, but the reason why we press them is that we know, when proposals such as those on ring fencing are introduced, that a general attack is being made on council housing in an attempt to push up rents. In areas where rents have been subsidised from the rates—soon to be the poll tax—rents have been kept to a reasonable level. I hope that the Minister will not start talking about some rents being unreasonably low. In Committee, he was unable to define the words "unreasonably low". Tory and Labour-controlled authorities charge relatively low rents compared with other areas.

Most people connected with housing, outside the Government, are trying to find some definition of affordability, which is what matters. The Government have got themselves into a crisis on housing because they have never considered that definition. There is a lack of affordable accommodation for rent or sale. That problem is biting most on people who are trying to rent or buy. Under proposals such as ring fencing, councils are being increasingly constrained, thereby increasing rents and worsening the crisis. That is why we shall press the amendment today, although, sadly, it will not receive the attention that it deserves.

Mr. Allen McKay: I did not realise how important the amendment was until it was explained. I read it and reread it and wondered what it was about. It is about matters such as the housing advice centres set up by local authorities. Housing advice centres exist purely and simply because of the housing crisis in certain areas, which is a crisis in people's lives. The benefit for council tenants of having the right to buy, to which the Minister referred, has gone sour for many people who have found that they cannot afford the houses they have bought. Under the Housing Act 1988, local authorities cannot buy back the properties. The only alternative is to put the property on the open market and then to depend again on the local authority for housing.

Houses are not easily available. Local authorities have decided to set up housing advice centres, where advice is available for the residents of the area and people who want to come into the area. They can obtain advice on where houses are available and the waiting time for houses. It would be wrong for such centres to be included in the housing revenue account.

I remember a recent contribution I made. The authority to which I belong decided, quite a while ago, that it no longer wanted to be responsible to the treasurer and the treasurer's department. I suspect that the Minister has the same inclination in his present job. At the same time, the authority wanted nothing from housing, which rightfully belonged to housing, to go back to the treasurer's department. That is where we come to the previous argument.

I have not been convinced by what the Minister said. If the Minister had said that tenants who are now paying rent would not have an increase in their rents, except as a result of increased costs on housing, I would be more than satisfied. However, when we went through that exercise with the treasurer, we had to leave in place matters that, rightfully, belonged to the housing account, such as the various levels of subsidy, but we had to take out such matters as housing advice centres and the cost of grass-cutting in private areas, which at that time were borne by the housing revenue account. If anyone had a grumble, it should have been the council tenants. If the Bill

[*Mr. Allen McKay*]

seeks to bring such matters into the housing revenue account, it is entirely wrong. The Government should accept the amendment.

Mr. Trippier: The hon. Member for Hammersmith (Mr. Soley) seemed to miss the point continually, as he did in Committee. At present, subsidy from the general rate fund bolsters the housing revenue account. I have no doubt that he is embarrassed by the sizeable sums we see in inner-city areas generally, not just in inner London. The general ratepayer, soon to become the community charge payer, is finding that money. The hon. Gentleman never says anything about that and the weight that falls on the shoulders of ratepayers.

With ring-fencing of the housing revenue account, the system will be different. We are talking about new housing subsidy coming, as I have tried to make clear, from the taxpayer. If one strips the cant out of the hon. Gentleman's contribution, he is on to quite a fine point. The examples he gave would be on the margin of the ring fence. The same is true of the interesting examples given by the hon. Member for Barnsley, West and Penistone (Mr. McKay).

The best way to give a simple definition is the way in which I tried to give a definition in Committee. Landlord functions which are provided for local authority tenants —and it might assist the hon. Member for Barnsley, West and Penistone to say that I would not use the example of housing advice centres which are available for a wider audience—would come within the housing revenue account. However, the hon. Member for Hammersmith was on to a good point because it is extremely difficult to say exactly what falls within that definition. He will recall that we took the view in terms of sheltered housing that the warden of sheltered housing provided a welfare function, whereas maintenance—and the only example I could think of at the time was changing light bulbs—would be a landlord function.

We have decided to have negotiations and discussions with local authority associations on all those points and we have also decided that the new regime will begin from 1 April 1990, with the situation as it is. We will run it for a year to see how successful it is. Negotiations with the local authority associations may mean that we are able to change the proposal in another place. I personally doubt it. Opposition Members should welcome the fact that we have decided, because of the complications and the marginal matters on the fringes of the housing revenue account, to deal with the proposal in that way.

Mr. Soley: That is an interesting response. The Department's talks with local authorities have not advanced, but I understand, from what the Minister has said, that he intends to continue with them. He seems to be slightly open-minded on the matter and I welcome that. I am always grateful for small mercies. I beg to ask leave to withdraw the amendment.

Amendment, by leave, withdrawn.

Clause 69

DIRECTIONS TO SECURE PROPER ACCOUNTING

Amendment made: No. 278, in page 74, line 33, leave out subsection (2).—[*Mr. Trippier.*]

Clause 70

HOUSING REVENUE ACCOUNT SUBSIDY

Mr. William O'Brien (Normanton): I beg to move amendment No. 183, in page 75, line 8, at end insert—
> '(4) A local housing authority shall be informed of the result of any determination made under this section or section 71 below not later than 31st December of the year prior to the year to which the determination relates.'.

Madam Deputy Speaker: With this, it will be convenient to consider the following amendments: Government amendment No. 44.

No. 187 in, page 75, line 31, at end insert—
> '(5) The Secretary of State shall serve a notice on each local housing authority informing it of the amount of housing revenue account subsidy (if any) payable to it in any year and of the assumptions he has made in calculating the said amount.
> (6) A local housing authority may appeal against the amount or assumptions referred to in a notice served under subsection (5) above and the appeal shall be determined by an independent person appointed by agreement between the Secretary of State and the said housing authority.'.

Government amendments No. 47 and No. 48.

Mr. O'Brien: Amendment No. 183 is a probing amendment. When we discussed the issue in Committee, the Minister on 18 April said that he would come back on Report with amendments similar to amendment No. 183. I take that as an opportunity to invite the Minister to accept the amendment or to assure us that provisions will be made in the Bill in line with it. If he will not do so, this is an opportunity for him to explain why the local authorities should not be informed about subsidy entitlement for the subsequent financial year by 31 December in the year preceding the point at which the new financial year starts. I ask the Minister either to accept the amendment or to explain why we are not receiving the report that he promised in Committee on 18 April.

Amendment No. 187 introduces two new provisions. In proposed clause 70(6), we are seeking to introduce some democracy into the present system. We ask that, when the Secretary of State decides on the subsidy payable to a local housing authority, it may appeal against the amount or, if no subsidy is to be paid, an appeal may be made and determined by an independent person appointed by agreement between the Secretary of State and the housing authority in dispute. We hear so much from the Government about wanting to apply democracy in many shapes. We are suggesting that the amendment will help to introduce some democracy into housing subsidies.

Each year the Secretary of State will fix the amount of the housing revenue account subsidy for each local authority at the same time as the local authority will be considering its rent increases and management and maintenance costs. The general rent levels will be determined by the rent subsidy, if any is to be paid, and by the rent increases.

The Bill gives the Secretary of State the power to make different assumptions for different authorities. The Government have suggested that they will use that power to give different levels of subsidies to different authorities. Therefore, different rent assumptions could be made for different councils. Because that is so important, I am asking the Secretary of State to give local authorities the opportunity to obtain information where there is to be a reduction in subsidy or where no subsidy is to be paid. Amendment No. 187 would require the Secretary of State to notify an authority of the subsidy determination and of the assumption that he has made in arriving at that determination.

6.30 pm

Under the current system of subsidy fixing, the Government make the same assumption for each authority in relation to, for example, rents. I should like to know whether the Government will stick to that or whether they are going to pick and choose. Will the Government make different assumptions for different councils, or will they apply the same principles across the board? If the former, on what basis will those different assumptions be made?

The Government could make different assumptions for different councils because they think that the rents are too low in certain authorities, because the Bill is leaving the way open for a secret or covert use of that power. That is not in the best interests either of the Government or of the local authorities and it is certainly not in the best interests of the tenants. The Minister has suggested this afternoon that the Government have the tenants' interests at heart. If so, any decision to influence the rent levels that tenants will have to pay should not be secret or arbitrary. The decision should be open and people should be in a position to ask questions about how the Secretary of State has arrived at certain decisions.

Amendment No. 187 seeks to temper the provisions by requiring the Secretary of State to tell the authority concerned why and how he has arrived at his decisions. Will the Minister confirm that that information will be available to local authorities if the Secretary of State uses the powers given by the Bill?

Amendment No. 187 also seeks to give an authority the right of appeal. Does the Minister intend to give individual authorities the right to make representations about the determination of their subsidies?

As I have said, amendment No. 183 is a probing amendment relating to the issue that was raised on 18 April. Amendment No. 187 seeks to obtain assurances from the Minister that, in determining the level of subsidy, housing authorities will have the recourse to request and to obtain information about how the subsidy determination has been made because of the influence of that determination on rents in the local authority's area.

Mr. Trippier: The hon. Member for Normanton (Mr. O'Brien) is absolutely right to say that I gave an undertaking to the Committee that I would return to this issue on Report. I said that we would table an amendment to that effect and was explicit in saying that it would be done by Christmas. If the hon. Gentleman had taken the time and the trouble to read the selection of amendments, he would have seen that we have tabled an amendment to that effect. If he had looked above that, he would have seen that his amendment interprets Christmas as 31 December. In effect, he has given us six days grace. That is incredibly generous and I was tempted to take them, to accept his amendment and to withdraw the Government amendment because probably no one would have noticed. In any case, we have discharged and honoured our responsibilities——

Mr. Rooker: So why is the Minister still speaking?

Mr. Trippier: Because I have to answer amendment No. 187, which the hon. Member for Normanton might just have got right.

The best thing that I can say about amendment No. 187 is that it is a jolly good try and I do not blame the Opposition for having tried. However, it is based on another misconception. I entirely agree that the subsidy formula is a proper matter for consultation, and I gave an undertaking on that several times in Committee, but once the formula has been determined, its application is a matter of arithmetic. The idea behind the amendment appears to be that the proess is like a negotiation, in which an appeals process and the services of an arbitrator may be useful. However, it is not a negotiation at all: it is a simple calculation using the stated formula, and, as such, its outcome is objectively determined.

Therefore, I ask my hon. Friends to reject the Opposition amendments and to support those in the name of my right hon. Friend the Secretary of State.

Mr. O'Brien: If the Minister is saying that he has taken care of our points, and to acknowledge that he promised a Christmas box to the local authority associations on that matter, I am prepared to withdraw amendment No. 183 in favour of his proposals and assurances.

On amendment No. 187, the Minister seems to be seeing things that are not there. We do not want to open up a negotiation process about the application of subsidies. However, because of the powers given to the Secretary of State in determining the level of rent subsidies, we are asking that, where there is doubt and concern and where tenants are questioning their local authorities about the level of rent increases, the housing authorities should have the right to question the Secretary of State about how he has arrived at his decision. If there is still doubt after the Secretary of State's replies, the issue should be submitted to an arbitrator who would decide whether the system was being applied fairly. That is the real purpose of amendment No. 187.

While I do not wish to seek to divide the House on that matter, I still believe that the Minister should take this issue seriously, and I ask him to reconsider the matter carefully.

Amendment negatived.

Clause 71

CALCULATION OF HOUSING REVENUE ACCOUNT
SUBSIDY

Amendment made: No. 44, in page 75, line 12, at end insert

'and for any year the first such determination shall be made before the 25th December immediately preceding that year'. —[*Mr. Trippier.*]

Mr. O'Brien: I beg to move, amendment No. 185 in page 75, line 27, at end insert

'and—

(d) amounts which relate to expenditure in respect of houses, land and other buildings in the account incurred by local authorities prior to 1st April 1990 which was not charged to the account and which was not prescribed expenditure for the purpose of Part VIII of the local Government Planning and Land Act, 1980, and which has been made known to him by local authorities.'.

Madam Deputy Speaker: I must draw the attention of the House to the fact that with, Mr. Speaker's permission, amendment No. 184, which is grouped with amendment No. 185 and 186 on the selection of amendments, is to be debated separately. I want the House to understand that with amendment No. 185 we are now debating only amendment No. 186, in page 75, line 27, at end insert

'and

    (d) the extent to which the authority has and will incur expenditure under Part III of the Housing Act 1985.'.

Mr. O'Brien: Amendment No. 185 relates to expenditure in respect of houses, land and other buildings in the housing revenue account that was incurred by local authorities prior to 1 April 1990, which was not charged to the account, and which was not prescribed expenditure. The operative words in this amendment are "prescribed expenditure" because authorities can currently use the non-prescribed proportion of capital receipts to support certain types of return. That major expenditure is capital repairs. For receipts obtained through selling housing and housing land, the current prescribed proportion is 20 per cent. Both prescribed and non-prescribed receipts can be used for capitalised repairs. The Government do not dispute that the use of both non-prescribed receipts and capitalisation, according to the current regulations, are entirely legal.

In Committee the Minister responsible for housing said:

"There is a real problem here, particularly for authorities that have relied on non-prescribed capital expenditure from receipts to provide a legitimate boost to their repairs programme over a number of years."—[*Official Report, Standing Committee G,* 18 April 1989; c. 927.]

It is accepted, therefore, that the Minister realises that there is a problem with housing repairs.

As the Minister accepts that the new provisions in the Bill will cause problems, why will he not say that he will definitely include past capitalisation, using non-prescribed proportions of receipts within the formula covered by clause 69(1), (2), and (3)?

The Minister has said that, in the first year of the new financial regime, rents will not rise by more than they would have done under the old arrangements. However, unless full account is taken of all capitalised repairs, either rents must rise or there will be a dramatic fall in council repairs programmes for council houses. There has been a dramatic fall in the past 10 years because of the reduction in the HIP programme. If tenants, therefore, are facing a further dramatic fall in council repairs programmes, they will suffer much more than at present. Either way tenants will suffer, and it is the Government's insistence on introducing new capital controls and ring-fencing the housing revenue account that is to blame. Can the Minister say which of the options—rent increases or cuts in repairs—he supports?

In Committee the Minister raised a number of issues concerning non-prescribed receipts and capitalised repairs. The Minister accepts that capitalisation using non-prescribed receipts is a legitimate activity. That has occurred on a large scale and, unless it continues, a large proportion of repairs will not be carried out. The point is not so much from where the resources come, but that the work needs to be done. I underline the fact that repairs to council houses need to be done. The very fact that capitalisation is necessary on such a large scale indicates that allocations are inadequate. Is the Minister saying that capital allocations will be increased to meet all the capitalised repairs funded from the non-prescribed proportion of receipts? If that is the option chosen, will he assure us that the new definition of capital will cover works that it has been accepted would have been capitalised in the past? In other words, there will be no change in what local authorities have been doing to ensure that the necessary repairs to council houses are undertaken and will continue to be undertaken.

I estimate that as much as two-thirds of the current expenditure, using non-prescribed receipts—more than £400 million in England and at least £150 million in London—is devoted to capitalised repairs. Last year local authorities spent a total of £640 million on non-prescribed receipts. The estimated figure for 1988-89 is higher at £688 million, and the HIP returns suggest that in 1987-88 capitalised repairs totalled £812·2 million, with estimates of £878·1 million for 1988-89. Those are high figures. Much money is being used to meet the repairs demands of local authorities. It is not just Labour-controlled authorities that are spending that kind of money to meet council house repairs. Conservative and Democrat-controlled authorities, too, make substantial use of non-prescribed receipts and capitalised repairs.

6.45 pm

The proportion of non-prescribed receipts devoted to capitalised repairs varies with individual authorities. However, for many authorities, virtually all their non-prescribed expenditure has been directed towards capitalised repairs. In Waltham Forest, for example, in 1987-88 the total of non-prescribed receipts was £2·6 million out of £4·1 million on capitalised repairs. Using non-prescribed expenditure, the current estimated expenditure is £6·9 million. That was approved by the district auditor for subsidy purposes. In Greenwich in 1987-88, non-prescribed receipts were £11 million out of £21 million on capitalised repairs; and in 1988-89 non-prescribed receipts were £9 million out of £18 million on capitalised repairs. Current year spending is at the same level as the previous year. That indicates that it is essential that the Government should consider allowing capitalised repairs to continue.

The Government are, however, now changing the rules, both for capital receipts and the housing revenue account. By forcing authorities to devote 75 per cent. of receipts remaining at April 1990 and generated after that date to repayment of debt, they have drastically depleted the available resources generated from sales of local authority assets. In other words, the change in procedure will have a tremendous effect on the local authority's ability to carry out council house repairs.

By changing the rules, the Government have placed in jeopardy a large proportion of expenditure on repairs. By some means that must be replaced. As the system is being introduced at the Government's insistence, it is up to them to replace it. The issue is not so much the method by which the repairs were paid for in the past, but meeting the cost in the future, given the serious reduction in the financial flexibility accorded to local authorities. As has already been recorded, it is an urgent matter that should be discussed between the Department of the Environment and the local authority associations.

It is up to the Minister to decide whether capitalised repairs paid for with non-prescribed receipts will or will not be reflected in future subsidies or capital allocations. The local authority associations have made it clear that those amounts must be picked up, and that the preferred option is through revenue subsidy. Discussions can sort out any detail, for example over the figures, but the only person who can end the uncertainty and decide the matter is the Minister.

I ask the Minister to consider our amendments carefully. They are directed to the level of expenditure that is required to provide facilities for the homeless, and to calculating the necessary subsidy to meet housing need and the debt involved in homelessness. I ask him to accept our proposals.

Mr. Trippier: I got the hon. Gentleman's point at the end of his second paragraph. As much of what he said was superfluous I shall try to convince him briefly that the amendments are, too.

Amendment No. 185 could allow the subsidy formula to refer to authorities' past practice in capitalising repairs expenditure, which is questionable on a number of grounds. I draw the attention of the hon. Member for Normanton (Mr. O'Brien) to clause 71(3), which empowers the Secretary of State to refer to a wide range of factors in the subsidy formula.

First, the formula should not reflect authorities' past practice; it should reflect the needs of local authorities. I do not think the hon. Gentleman disagrees with that. If that were not so, existing inequalities between high and low spenders would be reinforced. If we take account of authorities' spending, it will merely be to ensure a smooth transition to the new regime, and that is all.

Secondly, much of the expenditure that authorities have been undertaking is properly regarded as capital spending. To the extent that that is so, the need for it should be reflected in capital allocations, not in revenue subsidy.

Thirdly—a much more practical point—we do not have the sort of information on capitalised repairs to enable us to build a factor into the subsidy formula even if we wanted to. It is not satisfactory to seek such information now. The scope for authorities to manipulate their housing revenue accounts in order to increase their capitalised repairs, and hence their subsidy entitlements, would be too great. The cynical authorities would gain at the expense of the honest ones, which must be wrong.

I recognise that authorities which have been relying on non-prescribed capital expenditure from receipts to give a legitimate boost to repairs programmes may be concerned about what I have just said, but I in no way demur from what I said in Committee—the hon. Gentleman was right to correct me by reference to the Committee proceedings. The door is not closed. I shall want the Department to discuss this in more detail with the local authority associations. The Bill is perfectly wide enough to permit capitalised repairs to be taken into account if we decide to do that, but the capital allocation route is preferable.

Amendment No. 186 allows the subsidy formula to take account of the costs incurred by an authority under homelessness legislation. I would not rule out the possibility of an element in the management and maintenance allowance to reflect extra management costs for authorities with large numbers of homeless people, if we find that the cost of accommodating homeless people in HRA dwellings is significantly higher than the cost of accommodating other tenants. However, most of the costs related to homelessness arise before homeless people become tenants, not afterwards. These costs do not fall to the housing revenue account, so there is no need to take account of them in the subsidy.

I hope that I have convinced the House that the amendments are superfluous, and the hon. Gentleman that he should withdraw them.

Mr. O'Brien: The Minister says that the Government do not have the statistics that are necessary to provide an idea of past spending. On the contrary, many statistics can be used to obtain that information—the Department has reams of them. The Government can gather the information before 1990, so that some help can be given to local authority organisations which will be holding discussions on this issue with the Department of the Environment.

Let us have some co-operation. We can obtain the information from local authorities. There are statistics that would give some idea of past expenditure and of what future needs might be. The Minister has promised that discussions will continue with local authority associations. If he will give us an assurance that an attempt will be made to obtain the information necessary to allow the people with whom consultations will be held a fair opportunity to resolve the matter, I will be prepared to withdraw the amendment.

Mr. Trippier: I can give that assurance.

Mr. O'Brien: In that case, I beg to ask leave to withdraw the amendment.

Amendment, by leave, withdrawn.

Clause 71

CALCULATION OF HOUSING REVENUE ACCOUNT SUBSIDY

Mr. Soley: I beg to move amendment No. 184, in page 75, line 31 at end insert—

'(5) Notwithstanding the previous provisions of this section, in determining a formula for the purposes of this section and insofar as the said formula includes variables relating to the rents payable by tenants of a local housing authority, the Secretary of State shall assume that the average rent payable by tenants of that authority will change by an amount or factor from the average rent payable in the year prior to that to which the calculation relates and that amount or factor shall be the same for each local housing authority.'.

It may be helpful if I keep my remarks short at this stage because I think the Secretary of State may want to intervene. Perhaps I shall be able to speak again later.

The amendment deals with council rents. We want to try to tie the Secretary of State, when fixing housing revenue account subsidy for each year, to assuming the same level of rent increase, in money or percentage terms, for each local authority. The Secretary of State and other Ministers know that we have been worried for some time because the Government have continually ducked the question of what they believe acceptable levels of rent to be. I and everyone in the housing movement know that no absolute definition can satisfy everyone, but we also know beyond reasonable doubt that rents are becoming increasingly unaffordable for many people, which is why so many have been driven to desperation or homelessness, and why the housing crisis is growing so rapidly. The concept of affordability shuld play at least some part in policy making.

[*Mr. Soley*]

In an earlier debate, I repeated some of the statements that the Minister had made in Committee about rents. I said that they showed an incredible confusion within the Government about what rents should be. In the past 12 months, Ministers have been saying that they do not want market rents, but the Minister is on record as saying—and a number of Government documents show—that not all council rents will rise to market levels. That strongly implies—it necessarily entails—that some council rents will rise to market levels. The Government must deal with this.

Mr. Trippier: Which document?

Mr. Soley: A consultation paper from the summer of 1988 includes the phrase
"would frequently be below market levels".
Various other statements show that rents may at times rise to market levels.

I and my right hon. and hon. Friends have argued for a long time that Britain's housing crisis derives largely from the Government's having driven up rent levels at the same time as house prices inflation has pushed up house prices. As a result, market rents have crept in, thereby approximating to the revenue people could obtain if they sold the houses they owned, invested the money and took the return on it. That is what pushes rents to market rates.

The Government have never addressed this problem, whose complexity I concede, but it is important to realise that a free market in housing, in any serious sense of the term, is impossible. I do not want to debate whether there is such a thing as a free market in other senses—almost certainly there is not, except possibly in fruit and vegetables at the end of the road. But in housing, perhaps more than in anything else, the market is grossly distorted—by the time lag in supply and demand, by land prices and policies, by planning, and above all by the subsidy system, under which we provide a massive and ever-growing subsidy to the purchase sector and a declining subsidy to many people in the rented sector.

We give a dangerously low subsidy to people who rent. Consequently, British people are trapped more than many others and cannot move around the country to seek work or for other reasons, because there is no neutrality in the costs of buying or renting.

Similarly, it is difficult to move, for example, from the south Wales valleys where two-bedroomed houses are sold for about £10,000 to the south-east of England where a similar house costs about £80,000. It is also difficult to move to areas such as mine in the south-east because it is common to pay £60, £70 or £80 a week for a room, never mind a flat or a house. That is the sort of nonsense that the Government have created.

7 pm

I shall not pursue the matter further at this stage, because I know that the Secretary of State wishes to intervene and it may be helpful to hon. Members if that happens. We are trying to tie down the Secretary of State in the way that I have described to a method of assuming the same level of rent increase either in money or percentage terms for each local authority. It is an important amendment and raises the whole issue of rent levels.

As I have said many times during the passage of the Bill, it is grossly unreasonable to have to address such important matters in a debate that has almost become a Committee stage running late into the night on what is supposed to be Report. My hon. Friends, and I think Conservative Members, know that the Bill is virtually out of control in terms of the number of amendments and new clauses.

Mr. Trippier: Come off it.

Mr. Soley: The Minister has no grounds for saying that. He knows that we have been passing on Report legislation that is basically Scottish legislation, which should have gone through the proper procedure.

The Secretary of State for the Environment (Mr. Nicholas Ridley): It is not true to say that council rents have been driven up during the currency of this Government. Throughout the 1980s the guidelines for rent increases have mostly followed increases in earnings, and actual rents have closely followed the guidelines. Before dealing further with the analysis of the housing situation by the hon. Member for Hammersmith (Mr. Soley), with which I do not entirely concur, I thought I would put him right on that.

The amendment is concerned with the assumption that we will make about the rental income of an authority when we set its entitlement to the new housing revenue account subsidy. The point of the new subsidy is to help an authority to balance income and expenditure on the housing revenue account once we have ring-fenced it from the rest of the authority's funds.

In determining how much subsidy authorities need each year, we obviously have to make an assumption about the amount by which they would increase their rents, if at all, from one year to the next. Under the present housing subsidy system we decide each year on a uniform increase in rents for all authorities, to be assumed for subsidy purposes. This year it is £1·95 per week. The amendment would require us to continue to operate the system in this way either by assuming a uniform cash increase for all authorities or a uniform percentage increase.

It is nonsense to assume that every authority should put up its rents by the same amount from levels that have no logical basis. I shall give as an example two pairs of authorities which are similar and neighbouring, and which apparently differ little in their characteristics. I shall give the current average rents in those authorities. In Manchester city the average in rent in 1988 was £15·63 and in Tameside next door it was £19·40. There is no justification for that variation. I shall now look at a different sort of area. In mid-Bedfordshire the average rent last year was £16·22 and in south Bedfordshire next door it was £20·63. Those are big variations.

Mr. Allen McKay: The Minister has given us the differences in rent levels. Could he tell us why they occur? On the reorganisation of local government when 14 authorities came together, there were 14 different rent levels. That was because the authorities had 14 different levels of service and the rent levels depended on the level of service and how repairs were dealt with.

Mr. Ridley: There are many factors that have historically determined local authority rents. Probably the biggest is the historic debt cost. An authority which built most of its houses in the 1920s and 1930s will have a much lower historic debt than an authority which built in the 1970s. That is no fault of the tenant, and there is no reason why those who live in 1930s houses should have a far lower rent than those who live in houses that were built more recently. That is the inequality about which I spoke earlier.

Mr. Tony Banks: Will the Minister give way?

Mr. Ridley: No. I should like to make progress but I shall give way later.

We need a way of accommodating different assumptions for different authorities. We have now reached the stage where I think I can help the House by giving more details about how this would work. The starting point would be a decision each year—as now, there is no change —on the average increase to be assumed. That would produce a new national total of the income from rents. We must remember that it is a hypothetical figure which is used only for subsidy calculation and is not an instruction to councils.

The new national total can be shared between housing authorities according to the number of dwellings that they have and an assessment of their local circumstances. That local assessment is central to our thinking. We want rents to vary geographically, not as they do now in a way which is unfair, discriminatory, haphazard and often based on historical or political bias, but in a way which takes more account of the geographical spread of housing, its type and the demand for it.

I make it plain once again that we are not proposing market values. We are saying that if demand for housing is lower in one part of the country than in another, property values would be seen to be lower there and rents should also be lower. Conversely, where demand is higher it is reflected in property values, and should also be reflected in rents.

A good measure of the variations in the value of property can be found in right-to-buy prices of council houses. In order to assess local circumstances we would look at the prices of council houses and flats that are being sold. To be precise, we would take the average undiscounted valuation for each authority of its right-to-buy sales and other sales of individual properties. We would apply this average price across the whole of the council's remaining housing stock to arrive at an approximation of the total value of the housing stock in each authority.

No one, least of all me, would pretend that that gives a precise valuation of a council's stock, but precision is not needed. We are looking for a convenient and sensible comparison between councils. We would then distribute the assumed new national rent bill pro rata to these local values. For example, if an authority was seen to have one three-hundredth of the national value of council houses, we could reasonably assume that it should raise one hundredth of all the rent that is raised nationally. We would thus reach a new assumption each year about the new total rent bill for each authority which we would use in setting its rent increase guideline.

If the present total rent income of an authority was so far behind the new assumption that a large increase was implied, we would dampen the increase so that no authority was assumed to increase its rents by more than a reasonable amount. The damping factors would be decided each year in the light of prevailing circumstances. Equally, we could dampen the effect of the policy if no rents were assumed to be reduced.

That policy will achieve all three of our main aims. It will encourage rents increasingly to reflect the pattern of house prices around the country, thus to some extent reflecting supply and demand. It will expect those authorities that were furthest behind to catch up more quickly while protecting those who have followed sensible rent policies in the past. Through the damping mechanism the policy will prevent undesirably high increases in individual rent bills from year to year.

As I have stressed, the assumption that we have made about rents is just that. It is a notional assumption which we use for setting subsidy entitlements. It is up to each authority to decide on the basis of its planned expenditure and its other sources of income the level at which to pitch its rents.

Furthermore, the assumption is based on the average rents charged by authorities. Within each authority there will be variation around the average. Rents generally vary according to the size of different properties, but other matters should also affect the spread of rents within an authority. It seems common sense that a three-bedroomed house with a garden should command a relatively higher rent than a similar sized flat halfway up a tower block and that people should pay more for a better location. But that is not always the case in every authority.

Clause 137 of the Bill requires authorities, when setting their rents, to have regard to how rents would vary if the properties were in the private sector. It does not mean that the rents themselves must be pitched at private sector levels, only that they should vary in the same sort of relationship. This will ensure a more sensible distribution of rents within an authority, just as part VI aims to influence the distribution between different authorities. The clause gives authorities a lot of scope in deciding the criteria for their rent structure so long as they have regard, among other things, to this principle.

I have spent some time outlining our proposals on rents because I want to leave no doubt about our intentions. I stress again, as we have done at earlier stages of the Bill's passage, that we have no ultimate target for rents. We are not aiming for market rents and we are not expecting to see large increases result. The decision on the annual guideline will be taken afresh each year. We simply want to see a gradual move towards a more sensible pattern in rents in different areas of the country and within each authority, removing present unfairnesses and reflecting more of the variation in the value of housing rather than the accident of historic cost accounting or the incidence of extra subsidies from rates.

It will remain the responsibility of local authorities, not the Government, to set rents and expenditure taking account of all the circumstances, including their subsidy entitlement. The system is not so different from the present one, except that the calculations currently made are on a uniform basis, but in future will be on a basis taking into account local variations in factors which affect housing in its wider aspects.

It is likely that the drafting of clause 71—the subsidy determination clause—might have to be tightened up in the light of our detailed proposals. If so, we will introduce amendments during the passage of the Bill in another place.

[*Mr. Ridley*]

The Opposition amendment now before the House, however, would prevent the improvements that we aim for. It would treat all authorities the same, irrespective of their individual circumstances or how they have set their rents in the past. It would ensure that local authority housing continued to be insulated from the real world, and I therefore urge the House to reject it.

Mr. John Fraser (Norwood): The voters of Vauxhall will be interested in the announcement that has just been made by the Secretary of State. I have been thinking of comparisons in house values as between one part of the country and another. As the Under-Secretary will be aware, my father-in-law lives in his constituency and I live next door to the Vauxhall constituency. The comparative value of property between the two constituencies is in the region of 3:1.

There are many examples in Rossendale of two-bedroom houses selling for between £10,000 and £20,000. On the other hand, the comparative price of a property of that kind in my constituency, or the adjoining one of Vauxhall, would be between £60,000 and £80,000, and I imagine that the value of comparative properties will be similar as between local authorities.

I appreciate that the Secretary of State said that he would not be forcing local authorities to increase their rents, but the standard from which he will be working, and which he announced, will mean that if the average rent in Rossendale is £15 a week—the figures that the right hon. Gentleman gave for Manchester are not untypical of Rossendale—it would be about £45 in Vauxhall or Norwood.

That would seem to imply an increase in rents in the long-term for council properties in Vauxhall of about £30 a week. The Secretary of State says that he would not for a moment contemplate a rent increase of £30 a week. I also appreciate that it would be subject to damping down and that some discretion would remain with local authorities in terms of rents to be charged. I appreciate all those matters and I assure the right hon. Gentleman that I am not trying to be dramatic or to exaggerate the position by suggesting that immediate rent increases of perhaps £30 a week are in train for council tenants in Vauxhall. Nevertheless, that is the direction in which the Secretary of State's proposals are pointing, if he proposes to follow the formula which he described.

The electors of Vauxhall—indeed, tenants in London and elsewhere—will be grateful for the indication that the right hon. Gentleman has honestly given, immediately before the by-election, of the plans he has in mind.

7.15 pm

Mr. Matthew Taylor (Truro): I listened with interest to the Secretary of State's announcement, which was couched in what one might call friendly terms. He seemed to be saying, "It will not happen in practice" and, "We do not mean this to happen. We want to encourage things to move in a certain direction, though not too much so."

The right hon. Gentleman made a crucial mistake, as I shall show. There is an argument for paying close attention to what happens in the regions, not so much to house prices but to what people can afford, which involves taking account of wage levels and the restraints that lower wages place on people. I come from an area which, because large numbers of people are coming in—to retire or to escape from the pressures in the south-east—is experiencing high house prices, even though the local people are earning low wages.

It seems from the Secretary of State's remarks that his plans do not take account of people's ability to pay as they move from one region to another. In other words, house prices do not reflect people's ability to pay, and my constituency is not the only part of Britain in which house prices are now way above the ability of the local people to pay. In many parts of London and elsewhere the same applies.

Nor has the Secretary of State allowed for the fact that local authority houses which sell are, almost by definition, those of the highest value. Much of the housing stock is too unattractive for people to buy. In my constituency, people seek transfers because they do not want to buy on one estate but want to move and then buy on another. I fear that his proposals could cause a distortion which, in turn, could lead to higher house prices.

There is another distortion in my area which, to an extent, argues against the point that I have made, although it does not justify the Secretary of State's position because it shows that his argument will be distorted once his plans are put into practice. I refer to those cases where council house sales are distorted because of housing defects. In my district council of Carrick and in the borough council of Restormel there are large numbers of Cornish unit properties, the sale value of which is massively reduced because, except in unusual circumstances, they cannot normally be mortgaged. They are classified as defective and accordingly are of less value. I am referring to big estates and to a large proportion of the housing in those areas. While problems such as that could probably be overcome, the Secretary of State seems not to have taken account of those difficulties.

What would the right hon. Gentleman consider to be a reasonable rent increase? That question has been put to Ministers time and again. Today the right hon. Gentleman spoke of "a reasonable increase". He accepts that the implications of what he is doing are large increases, but says, in effect, "We will ensure that that does not happen in practice. In any given year there will not be an increase larger than what we regard as a reasonable increase." If he had said that any increase would be "tied to inflation", we would have understood what he meant. If he had said, "tied to benefit levels", we would have understood and might even have given that commitment a cautious welcome. However, he said only "reasonable", and all politicians know that one person's reasonableness is another person's outrage. I hope that he will be able to clarify his position a little more.

The Secretary of State is seeking to tie rents to the value of properties. I have tabled amendments and my predecessor in this job, my hon. Friend the Member for Southwark and Bermondsey (Mr. Hughes), tabled amendments that would have tied rents to social housing so that those who need such housing could afford to pay for it. There is a justification for saying that different people in different parts of the country can afford to pay different amounts, but people's ability to pay should not be tied to the value of property in the areas in which they live. That is affected by quite different factors, while people come in widely different wage brackets.

Mr. David Winnick (Walsall, North): The Secretary of State's statement will be no consolation to council tenants. Their rents will be substantially increased yet again, as they have so often been through the lifetime of this Government. Rent levels are much too high, but I do not expect the Secretary of State to show any sympathy to those who have to pay them.

The Under-Secretary made the point quite clearly in Committee when he said that the Government were anxious that the councils should play their part in the wider housing market and that the Government felt that an important consideration was that a council's rent policies should not cause distortions in the market. What that means in practice is clear. Although the Secretary of State is denying any wish to bring council rents up to the market level, that remains the Government's objective. It may not be the immediate objective but the whole point of the Government's actions over the past few years is so to increase council rents that there will not be much difference between the public and private sectors.

On Second Reading, my hon. Friend the Member for Newham, North-West (Mr. Banks) intervened in the speech of the Secretary of State with a question about rent levels. In reply, the Secretary of State said:

"First, I hope that the hon. Gentleman has advised such people that they should have exercised the right to buy and they can still do so, avoiding the trap of paying for a lifetime and ending up owning nothing."

What that means is clear. The aim of increasing rents far higher then they should be is to pressure considerably more people to buy their own houses, or to price them out. In effect, the Government are saying, "Why pay these rents? What purpose? What logic?" In the Secretary of State's words, such people would be

"paying for a lifetime and ending up owning nothing."—
[*Official Report*, 14 February 1989; Vol. 147, c. 175.]

That is one of the purposes of substantially increasing rents, apart from considerable savings in central Government expenditure.

The Secretary of State's words on Second Reading are in line with the consultative paper, published before the Bill was brought out, "New Financial Regime—Regime for Local Authority Housing in England and Wales". Paragraph 14 brings to the attention of council tenants their right to exercise an option to buy a property or what is described as "tenants choice". That document, the Secretary of State's words, and what the Under-Secretary said in Committee all add up to the same point— substantial increases in rents, which will put the utmost pressure on council tenants to buy.

The level of subsidy on mortgage relief, which is very much connected with this matter, has increased substantially. Like my right hon. and hon. Friends, I believe that tax relief on mortgages is right and justified, but what cannot be justified is the way that people living on very high incomes are being subsidised through that relief. There are no objections from those on Government Benches about that, but subsidising of council tenants is another matter. We hear from them all kinds of stories about how well off council tenants are, how there are Daimlers and Rolls-Royces outside council houses and other such nonsense. There is a disparity between the way in which council tenants are treated and the way in which rich people who buy their houses are subsidised by the taxpayer.

I have been genuinely shocked by what I have heard in my constituency surgeries about the high rents that people

on incomes as low as £60 or £70 per week have to pay. I can hardly believe it. As one would expect, I write to the local authority, but in nearly every case I am told that that is the right rent level. This happens because of what the Government did last year when they substantially reduced housing benefit and removed the right of local authorities to apply discretion over housing benefit. My constituents are being penalised by an unacceptably high level of rent, and many of them are those least able to afford it. Furthermore, they are hardly able to buy the dwellings in which they live. That is one way in which poorer people have been penalised by the Government in the past few years.

What the Secretary of State has announced today will bring no satisfaction to council tenants. His purpose is to continue increasing rent levels so as to bring them as near as possible in line with the private sector. This is unacceptable, and I hope that my hon. Friend the Member for Hammersmith (Mr. Soley) will press his amendment to a vote.

Mr. Tony Banks: The Secretary of State would have done us a greater courtesy by letting us have this information in Committee. This so-called Report stage is nonsense. As we know, it is like a mini-Committee stage, but it is getting worse and worse. We should go back into Committee to consider the enormous list of amendments and new clauses that the Government have tabled. The Secretary of State now chooses this time to make a major statement on rents. It is no good him saying that it would be helpful to the House to give it the information now. It would have been more helpful if the statement had been made in Committee so that we could have had more detail and longer to consider it.

I have not yet had the opportunity to study the fine print of the statement, but I shall do so—one should always count one's spoons quickly when the Secretary of State is around. I know one thing: the statement will mean that council rents will go up, particularly in inner-city areas, whatever it might mean in Tory areas. Knowing the way in which the Department of the Environment works under this Government, no doubt these proposals will be so manipulated as to bring down rents in Tory areas and to stick them up as hard and as high as possible in Labour areas. That is the prejudiced and partisan way in which the Government operate. Even if I had not heard a word from the Secretary of State, I could draw the conclusion that his statement will result in higher council rents for people in inner London and the people of Newham. If I am proved to be wrong, I will make an abject apology to the Secretary of State, but I suspect that he will not have to call in that promise and I shall not have to make that apology.

We know about the Government strategy on council rents. Perhaps strategy is too grand a word—conspiracy is a much more appropriate word to describe the Government's approach. They are trying to catch council tenants between ever-increasing rents and ever-decreasing subsidies and benefits. As my hon. Friend the Member for Walsall, North (Mr. Winnick) said correctly, this policy is aimed at forcing council tenants into the private market. The Government hate everything in the public sector, and in particular council housing.

The Secretary of State said in so many words that he wants local authorities out of housing provision, other than at a very basic level. The Government's strategy and conspiracy since 1979 indicate that that is so. I refer to the

[*Mr. Tony Banks*]

sale of council houses, massive reductions in housing investment programmes, statutory rent rises, benefit cuts, and, under the Housing Act 1988, the pick-a-landlord and housing action trust schemes. They are geared to forcing local authorities out of the housing market. If the Secretary of State admitted that, he would not earn any plaudits but least one would say that, miserable, cantankerous, surly and ungrateful though he is, the right hon. Gentleman is prepared to speak his mind. We could then go away and hate him with a light heart and with an easy conscience. Nevertheless, I may tell the right hon. Gentleman that my conscience is very easy in my feelings towards him now.

7.30 pm

We need to know what the national assessment will be, because we can then make some calculations. I want to be able to leave the House tonight and when I come to write my local press releases say what the legislation will mean for council rents in Newham. If the Secretary of State did not have some idea what the assessment will be, his civil servants would not have given him the statement that he read this evening.

In his statement, the Secretary of State said that he will reject historic costs when making rent assessments. That is grossly unfair to people who have been living in good houses built by the old London county council in the 1930s for all those years, who paid increased rents, and who have met the historic cost of their homes. They are fairly elderly by now, but if they want to stay in the rented sector they will see their rents continually increasing, knowing that they have already paid for the property in which they live.

I would not like to be in the shoes of any Minister who started arguing the case for rejecting historic costs in respect of mortgage relief. When mortgages increase, that is not because of the increasing value of property but because of the Government's idiotic and lunatic policies on interest rates. What would mortgage payers say if they were told, "Your mortgages must relate not in any way to historic costs but to the existing value of your property. Notwithstanding any interest rate increases that the Government force upon you, you will have to carry on paying a higher and higher mortgage because it must reflect the increased value of your home."? No one would say such a thing because it would be nonsense so to do. Why is it that such a thing can be said to public sector tenants? That is another example of the Government's hypocrisy and double standards, which overlay their intensive, obsessive hatred of people living in public sector housing.

Mr. Winnick: Has my hon. Friend noticed that, while Conservative Members always complain that people receive subsidies when they do not need to do so, not one Conservative Member has stated that because of his various incomes—and some Government Members enjoy very substantial incomes—he is not willing to receive any form of state subsidy and will return his mortgage relief to the Exchequer?

Mr. Banks: I assume that my hon. Friend applies that stricture to all right hon. and hon. Members. I do not see any great rush by right hon. or hon. Members in any part of the House to make such a declaration, and it would be unusual if they did so. In general, we all have much higher

incomes than people living in council houses. I should like to know how many Members of Parliament live in council accommodation. I certainly do not, and I do not particularly want to. I would not want to be continually finding my rent forced up by Government policies and not able to enjoy any great benefit.

If local authorities are left to implement their own policies, they should be able to provide decent, affordable rented accommodation. Many people who are currently owner-occupiers would probably then be willing to leave private housing for the public rented sector. We know that the Government are trying to force people out of public housing. They hate anything being in the public sector. That hatred probably extends to public lavatories. Given that public lavatories are being closed down because public authorities can no longer run them, I suppose that that is another of the problems that will be self-liquidating under Government policies.

Until I read the fine detail of the Secretary of State's comments, I shall not know their full implications. However, I know for certain that his statement will mean higher rents for the people of Newham. I challenge the right hon. Gentleman to tell me that that is not so.

Mr. Rooker: Tonight, we have seen proof that neither the Secretary of State nor the Minister is at all concerned about the seedy aspects of electoral politics. Electoralism passes the Secretary of State by. My hon. Friend the Member for Norwood (Mr. Fraser) went unchallenged when he made it clear that the Secretary of State at least had the courage to come to the House tonight to announce that in reality the target council rents for Vauxhall— though not for this year or for next month—are £45 per week. Today, the House has debated rent rebates, and it is now discussing a massive hike in public sector rents. So far, not one Conservative Member has uttered a word, save for the Secretary of State or the Minister. Not one Conservative Member has spoken about the extra cuts in housing benefit or their effect on poor tenants, who will have to subsidise rebates to the poorest of tenants.

We have now listened to a statement about what I consider to be capital value rents. If it had taken the form of a statement at 3.30 pm, the annunciator would have displayed the caption, "Statement—capital value rents". Never mind the fancy phrases or fancy arithmetic: rents will be targeted and subsidies organised in such a way as to compel local authorities to fix rent levels that reflect the capital value of their properties.

Mr. Ridley: With the leave of the House, I shall respond to the points made by the hon. Gentleman and by his hon. Friends, which are false. As the hon. Member for Birmingham, Perry Barr (Mr. Rooker) has given way, perhaps I may ask him why he opposes capital value rents when his own party is busy advocating capital value rates. We are not advocating capital value rents. How can the hon. Gentleman traduce me over rents and ignore the fact that his own party believes that people should be taxed on the basis of property capital values in paying for local authority services?

Mr. Rooker: It is not as though the Secretary of State has come to the House——

Mr. David Shaw (Dover): Answer.

Mr. Rooker: The otherwise silent hon. Member for Dover (Mr. Shaw) will vote for anything that is put on his plate, not for reality.

The Secretary of State announced a formula for capital value rents tied to the value at which houses and flats can be sold in the market. No matter how it is described, rent —as the Secretary of State freely admitted, and as I would be the first to admit—is money down the drain. Rates or poll tax, however the Government care to describe it, form a community kitty to pay for local services. Nobody denies that, but we are opposed to the way in which it is collected. We have to have local taxation. It cannot be abolished, because it has to provide for our community.

We cannot all have a swimming pool in our back garden, our own fire brigade and a library in our house. We have to pay for them from the community. I will argue until the cows come home—*[Interruption.]* If you, Mr. Deputy Speaker, are prepared to accept a debate on the amendment and alternatives to the poll tax, I will stay all night and all day tomorrow to continue that debate. However, I will not go halfway and then be pulled up by you, Mr. Deputy Speaker, and be unable to complete the rest of my arguments. I want to debate what the Secretary of State has brought to the House tonight: capital value rents.

As I was about to say before the Secretary of State interrupted me again, it is not as though this hike in the rent and the extra money that we will get from it will be used for a certain purpose. We all know what will happen: the money will be creamed off the housing revenue account to subsidise the poll tax. That is the reality.

Rents will be tied to capital value. That is an interesting proposition from the Government because they have always said that they do not want market rents to be fixed by the market of supply and demand and the link between the scarcity of properties and rental values. However, they have found another way of doing the same thing, and the end result of the formula is exactly the same.

It would be interesting if the Government were to do the same for private rents and landlords and, as they moved towards ending the control on private rents, proposed that rents in the private sector should be tied to the capital and market value, at vacant property values. That is what the Secretary of State was talking about, not tenanted values.

Later, I suspect that we shall argue about how the averages are worked out, particularly for local authorities which sell an excess of houses with front and back gardens but in which the majority of properties are tower block flats or deck access flats. That may well be the case in London, in the Lambeth and Vauxhall authority. It is wrong for authorities to fix the rent by applying the average value of the properties they sell to those which they cannot sell, but which people could, if they wished, buy under the right-to-buy scheme.

I understand it when the Secretary of State says that neither he nor the Government will fix the rent. I tell my constituents that and explain that, by manipulating the money that they have taken from local authorities, the Government fix the rent. They use the local authority as their proxy to fix the rent. The Government, not the local authority, will bring in a rental system which is based on the capital value of the property. The House and the Labour party have not asked for that.

7.45 pm

My hon. Friend the Member for Norwood (Mr. Fraser) was right to remind us of the housing tenure mix in the Vauxhall constituency. The long-term consequence of the Secretary of State's statement will be that council house, flat and maisonette rents in Vauxhall will be £45 a week at today's values, and a lot higher in the future. If we also face the prospect of the ring fencing of the housing revenue accounts in respect of rent rebates, that will be appalling. In three or four years, nobody in his right mind will be paying £45 a week rent plus the extra to subsidise the rent rebates for everyone else. They will not do that but will instead buy the deck access and tower block flats. That is what the Government's policy is designed to do.

The Secretary of State deserves our congratulations on having the courage to say, "This is important to the Government. We have a fantastic new rent system I am determined to rush down to the House of Commons on Wednesday 14 June. I don't care what is happening on Thursday 15 June because this is so important that the House of Commons should get it hot off the press. My message is that capital value rents in Vauxhall will hit £45 a week, at 1989 values, at some time in the future".

Mr. Soley: My hon. Friend the Member for Birmingham, Perry Barr (Mr. Rooker) has got it exactly right and my hon. Friend the Member for Norwood (Mr. Fraser) hit the nail on the head: it is incredible.

I have made many allegations about the Ministers being confused about what they want as regards rents, but the Secretary of State is not at all confused. He knows exactly what he wants. I am astounded at his audacity. He emphasised that he did not want market rents, but then described a system which, over a period, would lead to market rents. The system is based on market rent assumptions.

The Secretary of State said that his policy would achieve three goals. First, it would encourage rents increasingly to reflect the pattern of house prices around the country, thus, to some extent, reflecting supply and demand. The important part of that statement was the first part because, as I said earlier, market rents are largely determined by house prices. Therefore, if a system is devised which will, as my hon. Friend the Member for Perry Barr said, have a capital value rent system, inevitably, over a period, prices will move towards those which properties would fetch in the market. That is the other side of the coin that I use as a rule of thumb guide to what a market rent would be—which is the money one would receive if one sold a house, invested the money and drew the interest on it. That is why the private sector continues to decline.

We all know that it pays to buy and sell houses in this country, but it does not pay to rent them. That has nothing to do with the Rent Acts, which are only marginal, but everything to do with the way we subsidise finance for purchasing houses. The Minister has created a system which links that to market values over a period.

My hon. Friend the Member for Norwood, who is astute and quick in such matters, has picked up the figure. My hon. Friend the Member for Perry Barr was exactly right when he said we should thank the Secretary of State for coming here today and telling the electorate that anyone who is in council property can expect to have his rents moving towards market rents over the next few years, because that is what will happen.

[*Mr. Soley*]

Will capitalisation, such as repairs, be included in this system? If it is, the system will be even more incredible and will put up prices even further. My hon. Friend the Member for Perry Barr is right. A great attempt has been made to push people out of the council sector into home ownership or the property of other landlords. However, the reason that the system will not push people into home ownership is that people with the right to buy are increasingly those who cannot exercise it because they cannot afford to do so.

People are trapped in paying rents when, with a little more money, they would be able to buy, but because they cannot afford to pay their rents, even with the assistance of housing benefit, they will not be able to buy. Therefore, their only option is to transfer to another landlord. There is a problem with that as well, because the Secretary of State is also pushing up housing association rents by cutting grant. Some of the examples that I have given recently show how housing association rents have risen and are continuing to rise.

If tenants made the worst choice of all and went to a private landlord, their rents would rise even more rapidly —for we know that private rents rise more rapidly than others. Whatever they do, they are trapped: they will be financially clobbered.

Sooner or later—this has not yet been said today, but the whole tragic situation focuses on it—the Government must take a view on what is an affordable rent. Many people in the housing movement are saying that it should be a maximum of 20 per cent. of net disposable income. That is a common-sense guideline, for we know that those on average or even above-average incomes who spend more than 20 per cent. of their net disposable incomes on housing will get into serious economic difficulties sooner or later—usually sooner. They will find themselves in debt; they will be unable to pay gas or electricity bills.

Under the present Government, more and more people are spending up to 40 per cent. of their net disposable incomes on rent—and, in some cases, mortgages, although I should like to concentrate on rent. As far as I am aware, that has not been the case under any previous Government, Tory or Labour. Those people cannot survive: the facts are as bald as that.

The Government must understand that the crisis is becoming desperate. People are in trouble, whether they are renting or buying. They are trapped at both ends: because of the interest rate policy they cannot buy, or, if they bought recently, they are in trouble because of the dramatic increase in their mortgage rates. If they try to rent, they find that rents are being driven up in the housing association, private and council sectors. This is an extraordinary proposal for the Government to advance now.

Mr. John McAllion (Dundee, East): I am concerned to hear of the massive rent increases that the Tories are imposing on people living in Vauxhall and elsewhere in London. Does my hon. Friend believe that the same will apply in Glasgow—particularly in Glasgow, Central, where voters are also going to the polls?

Mr. Soley: My hon. Friend is right to ask that question. The references that we have made to Vauxhall apply equally to Glasgow, Central, and are also relevant to the European elections. People need to understand that, almost uniquely among western European countries, we are reducing the housing subsidy as a proportion of gross domestic product. Most other countries are increasing it. My hon. Friend the Member for Perry Barr put the electoral message very clearly.

Having spoken twice, I do not wish to delay the House. We cannot vote on the proposal; it is something that the Government intend to do. Let me say this, however: the Minister talks of amending clause 71, and he will probably need to, even with the wide-ranging power that he has given himself with a variety of local government Bills. I assume that that will be done in the House of Lords; but, either there or when the Bill returns to the Commons, we shall want to return to the issue again and again, because the message to those who are renting is desperately serious.

Mr. Ridley: With the leave of the House, I should like to speak briefly to clear up a major and deliberate misinterpretation by many hon. Members.

What I announced today was a new mechanism for local authority rents, in place of an existing mechanism which has been used by the Government for the past 10 years and which is proving more and more defective. As a result—as ·I have already pointed out—we have not increased council house rents, on average, by more than about the level of the increase in earnings over that period. Nothing that I have said today suggests that we will increase them by more than that, or by less, or by any particular amount. All that I have announced is a mechanism: that is my first point.

Mr. Fraser *rose——*

Mr. Ridley: I am coming to the hon. Gentleman's point. He got it completely wrong on two counts. First, he assumed that this was not a mechanism, but a major rent increase, and that rents in Lambeth would in due course rise to £45 a week. He has no right to make such an assumption. When, each year, the annual subsidy is determined, he can come back and say whether he thinks that we have done too much or too little—as he could have done in each of the past 10 years.

Secondly, the hon. Gentleman missed the point that I made earlier—that the adjustments will be from where council rents now lie on the scale to where they would lie under the formula. He assumes that the present base is correct, although I went to some lengths to tell him that I did not consider it fair, equitable or even. If we were to name a percentage of right-to-buy values over a number of years, it might be 50, 40 or 30 per cent.; it might be any percentage. That is not what we are talking about—we are talking about a mechanism—but some authorities are closer to that "x per cent." now than others, and it is right to take into account that inequality within the base.

Mr. Fraser: Surely the Secretary of State understands that—although there will be a revision of base levels— because the average price of a house in Lambeth for a first-time buyer is about £80,000, the base level will if anything go up as a result of market conditions. As for rents, in a borough such as Lambeth they are barely enough to pay maintenance and management charges. Ring-fencing the housing revenue account will inevitably lead to rents being driven up. In future there will be no other source from which to obtain the cost. It cannot be obtained from rate funds.

Mr. Ridley: The hon. Gentleman is entirely wrong. Clearly he has not followed the debates on the new housing subsidy in which we have engaged all afternoon as well as in Committee. The housing subsidy is there to fill that very gap.

I must say that I expect trouble in Lambeth, because the efficiency of its maintenance and management does not give a great deal of satisfaction: I could talk about that at some length. It is, however, within Lambeth's ability to put the matter right, and to adjust that slightly higher rent. In answer to the hon. Member for Truro (Mr. Taylor), who asked what was a reasonable increase, the figure will be determined every year just as it always has been, just as a Labour Government have had to do it before and just as his party would have to do it if it came to office.

I concede—if "concede" is the right word—that the proposals that I have announced bear some relation to right-to-buy values. As hon. Members have rightly pointed out, the best houses tend to be sold under the right to buy, and the inequality that the hon. Member for Norwood (Mr. Fraser) tried to find is present in all authorities, so it will probably work itself out. We feel that the right to buy is a reasonable yardstick, but we are happy to discuss possible modifications with local authorities. We propose only a proportional relationship.

I marvel at the hypocrisy of Opposition Members who are trying to create fuss and indignation just because there are a couple of by-elections tomorrow. They themselves have been going around the country trying to conceal the fact that their system of local taxation is based on capital value rates, not just related to them or a proportion of them. That applies to full capital value rates in Lambeth, Norwood and every other constituency that they have been bleating on about. The hon. Member for Walsall, North (Mr. Winnick) advocates capital value rates for council tenants in Walsall and then he comes here and bleats. He ought to be ashamed of himself for his rank hypocrisy.

The hon. Member for Newham, North-West (Mr. Banks) is the worst of the lot. The Government have been pressed to make a statement about their rent policy. I made a statement. I told the hon. Member for Hammersmith (Mr. Soley) that I intended to do so. What did the hon. Member for Newham, North-West do? He accused me of a conspiracy. I never realised that to say something on the Floor of the House could form part of a conspiracy. The hon. Gentleman is determined to misinterpret. However, I shall tell his constituents that he bases their contribution to local authority services on capital values, whereas we shall only take them into account in determining fair rents.

Amendment negatived.

Clause 73

RESIDUAL DEBT SUBSIDY

8 pm

Mr. O'Brien: I beg to move amendment No. 188, in page 76, line 22, at end insert—

'(4) In making a determination under paragraph (3) above, the Secretary of State shall determine a standard rate of residual debt subsidy applicable to all disposals falling under paragraph (1) above.'.

Mr. Deputy Speaker (Sir Paul Dean): With this, it will be convenient to discuss amendment No. 189, in page 76, line 27, at end insert—

'(5) Where a disposal to which this section applies is made under sections 74 or 104 of the Housing Act 1988 or section 32 or 43 and section 106a and Schedule 3A of the Housing Act 1985, and where the terms of such a disposal include a disposal cost or other payment by the local authority, the Secretary of State shall, in respect of each year to which the cost or payment relates, issue a Supplementary Credit Approval under section 46 above equal to not less than 75 per cent. of the cost or payment in that year.'.

Mr. O'Brien: We have been considering tenant extortion. Now we are considering dowries to people who take over council house estates. Amendment No. 189 continues the debate on dowries. A dowry is a capital payment from a local authority to another landlord when council houses are transferred to a housing action trust, or are dealt with under the change of landlord provisions in the Housing Act 1988, or are the subject of large-scale voluntary transfer. Payment would arise when the transfer took place at negative value.

Where such a dowry is payable, the amendment provides that the capital cost should not come from a council's housing investment programme allocation or basic credit approval. The Government would have to issue a supplementary credit approval to a value of not less than 75 per cent. of the dowry.

The Government have been vacillating on the issue for nearly a year. We want to know when a decision is to be taken. The Government are in a terrible mess. The only formal application for a tenant's choice transfer is in Westminster—a Tory-controlled authority. It seems that that Tory council will have to pay the tenants £30 million, which it does not have. It has embarrassed the Government.

In Committee, we were given a completely unsatisfactory answer by the Under-Secretary of State for the Environment, the hon. Member for Surrey, South-West (Mrs. Bottomley). She said that supplementary credit approvals would be issued in the case of housing action trusts but that a decision had not yet been reached on tenant's choice transfers. She said nothing at all about voluntary transfers. That substantiates my claim that the Government are in difficulties with Westminster city council about the subsidies that will have to be paid under the dowry allocation.

Amendment No. 188 would amend clause 73, which provides for residual debt subsidy to be paid to local authorities for the costs relating to the disposal of houses and other properties. A consultation paper was issued by the Department of the Environment and the Welsh Office in January 1989. It proposes that the rate of residual debt subsidy will vary according to the type of proposal. The consultation paper refers to

"Tenants' Choice and Right to Buy   — 75 per cent.
Voluntary Transfers to Other Landlords— 90 per cent.
Housing Action Trusts   — 100 per cent."

No clear or logical reason was given by the Under-Secretary of State for the Environment in Committee as to why the rate for tenant's choice disposals should be less than for voluntary transfers, or disposals to housing action trusts.

What is the relevance of the different arrangements? Does the Minister not agree that in disposals to a housing action trust and in disposals under tenant's choice a local

[*Mr. O'Brien*]

authority is being forced by the Government to dispose of part of its stock? What possible argument is there for the rates of subsidy to be different?

The Government seem to have accepted the principle that forced disposals should attract a higher rate of subsidy. I refer to the Under-Secretary of State's comments about the Secretary of State's initiative on housing action trusts. Why, therefore, do voluntary transfers attract a higher rate of subsidy—90 per cent. in this case—when another type of forced disposal, tenant's choice, attracts only 75 per cent? In what way are the problems and uncertainties in Wales different from the problems and uncertainties in England? Does the Minister not accept that the cost of a disposal is exactly that, whether it occurs in Wales or in England? What is the outcome of the further considerations?

I ask the Minister to explain why different subsidies are being paid. Would it not be fairer and more just to apply the same subsidy to all houses disposed of?

Mr. Fraser: I am grateful to my hon. Friend the Member for Normanton (Mr. O'Brien) for reminding the House that if houses are transferred under the housing action scheme, the residual debt subsidy will be 100 per cent. under what he described as the dowry—and, I hope, 100 per cent. of the debt, apart from the dowry, under the original loan charges. The Minister knows how important that is in my constituency. Under the housing action trust scheme, the Government propose to do more than was done in the 18th century when the Highlands were cleared —they intend to take out of local authority stock 2,144 homes in two housing action areas.

When I asked the Under-Secretary of State about this, I was told that the maximum cost of the two housing action schemes would be £132 million. That gives some idea of the scale of the meanness of the housing investment programme. Lambeth's housing investment programme amounts to about £20 million per year. That has to cover the massive housing needs of the homeless and those on the waiting list and the improvement of about 48,000 homes. The Minister's own expert's assessment of the cost of improving two estates alone was £132 million. What that expert believes ought to be spent on two estates is about six times more than the annual allocation for the whole of Lambeth's housing requirements.

The cost of essential improvements to a house or flat in a housing action trust area is about £60,000. The maximum that could be obtained under the right-to-buy arrangements would, because of the discount, be about £30,000, but it would probably be much less than that. There would need to be a huge dowry of about £30,000 per house—about £60 million in total—if one took that as the measure of the dowry which would be paid if a housing action trust took over. There is another even more pessimistic way of looking at it. The rents of about £20 per week on that estate would support capital debt of about £10 million, taking a modest 10 per cent. interest rate. The amount to be spent on the estate is £132 million, so the amount needed to service that debt would be much higher. The dowry would be enormous—possibly about £100 million.

I am trying to give an idea of the scale of the dowries. They would be enormous if the housing action trust scheme went ahead. If a dowry adversely affected the minimal housing investment programme in Lambeth, we could forget about doing anything about housing, despite the 20,000 people on the waiting lists and the 1,200 homeless families, about 500 of whom live in expensive bed-and-breakfast accommodation. I ask the Minister to confirm what my hon. Friend the Member for Normanton said by saying that the residual debt subsidy for housing action trust schemes in my constituency will be 100 per cent. I want the hon. Gentleman to give a solemn undertaking that there will be no further diminution in Lambeth's housing investment programme because of any dowry to be paid under the HAT scheme.

I apologise because in a sense this may be a highly theoretical debate as there is no way that my tenants will vote for these measures anyway.

Mr. Trippier: I listened carefully to the hon. Member for Norwood (Mr. Fraser) and I suspect that his last sentence devalued the currency of the rest of his speech. He must realise that his comments are in direct conflict with the statements of his hon. Friend the Member for Normanton (Mr. O'Brien). The hon. Member for Norwood is talking about forced disposals, but he and I know better than that. We know that one of the concessions which was given was that there should be two votes for housing action trust tenants. They can choose, first, whether they should have a housing action trust. They will have a second chance to vote with their feet to opt for various alternatives, for example, a tenants' co-operative, housing association, private landlord or return to local authority control. Let us have no more nonsense about forced disposal. It is equally mad to suggest that tenants' choice is a forced disposal. The choice is placed in the tenants' hands. That is not a forced disposal.

The points raised by the hon. Member for Norwood were rather technical, and I shall deal with them briefly. Another concession that we made with regard to housing action trusts was to say that there would be no further financial penalty on a local authority if it wished to reacquire the houses that had temporarily been in the ownership of the HAT while they were improved. I stand by that statement, as does my right hon. Friend the Secretary of State. We are anxious to get that point across to tenants.

It is a matter for tenants because each tenant will have the opportunity to vote. The consultants are still talking to various tenants on the estates. Because the money about which we are talking is more than that which the local authority would receive in the form of the HIP allocation —which the hon. Member for Norwood said was an enormous sum—I should have thought that it was sensible for that money to be accepted. I have made it clear that, if they wish, many of those tenants can go back to the local authority and it would not be penalised financially. This is an opportunity of a lifetime, and I hope that tenants will be sensible about it.

This money is specifically allocated in a budget within the Department of the Environment for HATs. I have made it clear that if tenants do not want it, that sum of money will be available elsewhere, and I am glad to say that some interest has been sparked in other authorities, not all of which are Conservative-controlled. I do not want that to happen. The money should be targeted in the area that the hon. Member for Norwood represents. I think that deep down he believes that. He knows that that work needs to be done. The local authority can certainly repurchase the properties, and I am delighted to have played a part in discussions on that matter. The hon. Gentleman should help us and make it clear to tenants that this is a good deal.

8.15 pm

I turn to the points made by the hon. Member for Normanton. Recent developments in our policies for new capital and revenue regimes in local government mean that a residual debt subsidy is neither needed nor appropriate from 1 April 1990. From that date, loan charges will be taken 100 per cent. into the subsidy calculation. Sales receipts must be set aside partly for the reduction of debt. Any debt left after that will automatically be taken into account for subsidy.

There is still, however, a case for residual debt subsidy to be paid in this financial year while the housing subsidy arrangements are, I admit, much less generous. We now propose to limit it to those authorities that are not eligible for main housing subsidy. We would limit it also to multiple sales only—the sales of individual properties normally cover the outstanding debt. RDS would therefore be available for tenants' choice and HATs and also for voluntary large-scale transfer. Our new proposals for RDS will not have any permanent effect on main housing subsidy.

I apologise to the hon. Member for Norwood, who asked me a specific question—whether the proposals will in any way affect the HIP allocation that is available for Lambeth. The answer is no. That is another undertaking that I can give him.

There have been persuasive arguments for 100 per cent. RDS. Taking those into account, we have concluded that, for 1989-90, a single rate of subsidy set at 100 per cent. of the loan charges on any residual outstanding debt would be more appropriate and would, moreover, fall into line with the rate of HRA subsidy payable under the new financial regime from April 1990. Suitable amendments reflecting this and the other changes will be made to the Bill in another place. In view of that, I maintain that amendment No. 188 is not necessary and therefore should be withdrawn.

Amendment No. 189 proposes that supplementary credit approvals under the new capital finance system should be issued to cover 75 per cent. of any disposal costs or other payments made in transfers of local authority stock to a HAT, or under the tenants' choice procedures or in respect of voluntary disposal of stock. I am sorry that I cannot give the hon. Member for Normanton all the comfort that he seeks. We are considering how best to deal with problems in funding the disposal costs that may arise because of transfer of local authority stock to the various recipients which I have recently catalogued. We issued a consultation paper earlier this week, so it is obviously premature for me to say more before further comments are received.

In the case of a voluntary transfer, the local authority has full control over the timing of a disposal and can arrange the timing to suit its financial position. Indeed, it is for the local authority to decide whether the disposal takes place at all. As the local authority is in control of timing, there should normally be no reason for it to incur a disposal cost that it had not expected the year before.

In those circumstances, I hope that the hon. Member for Normanton will see fit to withdraw his amendment.

Mr. O'Brien: Some of the Minister's points were interesting. We look forward to the amendments that will be tabled in another place, and obviously we shall consider them carefully.

We are witnessing legislation on the hoof. We have heard about a change in legislation which has never before been presented to the House. What is behind that change in policy on this special issue of housing? The Minister has given an assurance that the HIP allocation will not be affected by residual debt subsidy. We shall carefully watch what happens.

I cannot accept that there would be no compulsory disposal. What the Secretary of State said earlier will, to a large degree, influence compulsory disposal. We shall carefully monitor what happens when we have had time to consider all that has been said by the Secretary of State and the Minister.

Because the Minister has assured us that suitable amendments will be introduced in another place, and because a consultative document is to be released, I beg to ask leave to withdraw the amendment.

Amendment, by leave, withdrawn.

Clause 78

DETERMINATIONS AND DIRECTIONS

Amendments made: No. 47, in page 78, line 16, leave out 'applying' and insert 'relating'.

No. 48, in page 78, line 17, at end insert—

'(3) As soon as practicable after making a determination under this Part, the Secretary of State shall send a copy of the determination to the local housing authority or authorities to which it relates.'.—*[Mr. Trippier.]*

New Clause 8

REBUILDING GRANTS

'(1) In the interests of maintaining stable communities and obtaining value for money in renewal areas designated under Part VII of this Act the Secretary of State shall within one year of the passing of this Act make regulations for the introduction of rebuilding grants.

(2) In Regulations made under the above subsection rebuilding grants will be available to owner occupiers where the local housing authority has made an assessment that it is uneconomic to offer improvement or repair grants.

(3) The Secretary of State after consulting local housing authorities and other appropriate bodies may make regulations as to the numbers of properties, age of properties, payments of rebuilding grant and recovery of such grants as may seem appropriate to meet the needs of the local communities and the Exchequer.'.—*[Mr. Rooker.]*

Brought up, and read the First time.

Mr. Rooker: I beg to move, That the clause be read a Second time.

The new clause is a probing mechanism to test the water, and I shall not attempt to divide the House. No one could deny that some improvement grants have been wasted. Some properties are improved at quite drastic cost, but end up not being worth very much. Indeed, I could name properties in my constituency that have been improved again, again and again. After five years, the owner-occupier obtains the full benefit of any improvement should he wish to put his house on the market. In many ways that has a ratchet effect on house prices.

I am not knocking improvement grant schemes—far from it. They have provided improved housing for thousands of our fellow citizens. However, not all

[*Mr. Rooker*]

improvement grants are economic. Some properties are identified as uneconomic or unsuitable for grant. The cost of improving those properties is so great that it is sometimes argued that instead the owner-occupiers should accept clearance. I shall leave on one side the problems of compulsory purchase orders, compensation and rehousing, and concentrate on the one certain consequence of clearance, which is the destruction of stable communities. Most hon. Members who represent older areas know that to be the case. Only yesterday my hon. Friend the Member for Leicester, South (Mr. Marshall) said that he wanted to speak on the new clause because of the problems in the Spinney Hill area of his constituency. We thought that we would be discussing this matter yesterday, and unfortunately my hon. Friend has to be in Leicester today.

The experts in these matters believe that there is scope for an alternative to traditional improvement grants or clearance compensation. It is important to make far better use of financial and human resources. The cost of the loss of stable communities is incalculable because people are distributed around the four corners of our cities. It affects the quality of life for all concerned.

I take 100 per cent. responsibility for the inadequate drafting of the new clause, which I tabled only because of a telephone conversation about the problems. My aim is to emphasise the importance of making better use of financial resources, helping to maintain stable communities and obtaining value for money. Mechanisms other than clearance should be available for uneconomic properties.

Since I tabled the new clause I have had the benefit of written briefings from the Birmingham environmental services department, the Nationwide Anglia building society and the Rochdale housing department. I wish to draw upon all three briefings as I feel that that would set out matters rather better than the phrasing of my new clause. The basic principle of a rebuilding grant is that it is given to owners of a block of unfit properties, calculated to leave them with the same absolute equity in new equivalent property as they enjoyed in their unfit property. I am referring to new property built on the existing site. I emphasise the phrase "same absolute equity". Any calculation would take account of the existing value, the new build value and the cost of development, together with any outstanding loans on the property. It would also take account of disturbance and temporary rehousing during the development period.

The Minister has probably seen some detailed calculations based on three examples put together by the Nationwide Anglia building society which considered the financing of such an operation. I shall cite just one example provided by the Birmingham environmental services department. The figures are based on a property in a particular part of Birmingham, using a local estate agent's valuation. The current market value of the unfit property would be £35,000; its market value when improved would be £37,000; the cost of improvement would be £20,000; the market value of new build on the same site would be £60,000; and the cost of rebuild on a new site would be £30,000. Under the current policy Birmingham would have compulsorily to purchase the property at a cost of £37,000, which would count against its capital allocation. It would end up owning land worth about £3,000—of which, if it were to sell the land under the proposed rules,

it could use only 25 per cent. for future capital spending. The person whose property was being purchased either would have to buy another property—probably a poorer quality house—or have housing supplied by the city.

The proposal is that the rebuilding grant would be based on the principle that the owner should retain the land throughout and own the same absolute equity in the new house as he did in the old—in this case £35,000. The council would arrange and pay for temporary rehousing and the demolition of the property. It would also arrange for private sector finance—in most cases a building society or a housing association—and build new dwellings on the site at an average cost of £30,000. The new property would then be handed over to the original owner of the site, but with the £30,000 debt attached to it—that is, the cost of rebuild. The owner would have a brand new property worth £60,000, but with a debt of £30,000. The owner's original equity was £35,000—the value of the property in an unfit condition. The council would provide a rebuilding grant of only £5,000 leaving an outstanding debt of £25,000.

It would be a brand new house that allowed the original family to live on the same site in the same street. Obviously, the £25,000 debt would have to be financed. An additional mortgage could be arranged in advance with the building society that adopted the scheme, the owner could find his own money or, most likely, the building society or housing association attached to the scheme could take an equity share in the property. It would retain a 42 per cent. share which either could be funded by charging rent or it could retain its share and reclaim it if and when the property is sold or the owner could afford to buy out the share.

The scheme would depend on the building plot being of sufficient size to allow rebuilding. That would not necessarily be the case in some clearance areas because of the size of properties and the design of dwellings. However, it would still be possible to apply the scheme to the same locality, if not exactly the same site. It would be important to obtain a new-build valuation, and I used the example of £30,000. The example that I gave earlier from Birmingham envisages a scheme for about 50 dwellings. That is not a massive scheme, but it would offer economies of scale for the builder.

8.30 pm

I am told that the current housing market is especially favourable for such schemes, with a relatively high premium on new build property compared with the cost of building.

The example that I have given of a property costing £30,000 to build—I appreciate on land already owned by the owner—subsequently becoming worth £60,000 is incredible. Those figures were provided by local estate agents, not dreamt up by the local council.

The cost of rebuilding compared with rehabilitation is important. In most cases, rehabilitation will clearly be the most economic option. I am putting forward the scheme not as an alternative but as an option where rehabilitation is uneconomic, and as an alternative to clearance and the destruction of a stable community. It is crucial that the social side of the equation is entered on the financial balance sheet. If a cost is not placed on destroying stable communities, a case for rebuilding grants probably cannot be made.

The scheme would enable local rebuilding and would result in a considerable saving for the city of Birmingham on the work that it has done so far. Owners would get a new property at no cost to them and would have a mortgage. Although they would own only a proportion of the property, it would still be their home, they would have the same neighbours and live in the same community from choice, as opposed to being sent elsewhere such as a tower block miles away, having to move their children from school, make new friends and all the other difficulties of breaking up a community. A worse possibility is having their property improved and living through what can be a nightmare for many people, yet in three or four years having to have the property improved yet again, which is a gross waste of money. I am sure that in his tours around the country the Minister will have seen many such examples of waste. I could certainly give him addresses in my constituency where that has happened.

I understand that Rochdale housing department has pursued schemes such as the one that I am proposing but has fallen foul of the Department's financial rigidity. With the best will in the world, it was trying not to waste money on improvement but to maintain stable communities, give owner-occupiers a choice, and ultimately save money. However, it fell foul of the Department's present legal arrangements.

I was quite taken by a couple of paragraphs of the briefing provided to me by Rochdale housing department. It listed some safeguards and said:

"With all aspects of urban renewal, it is important to remember that however attractive a scheme, it is ultimately carried out on the basis that 'The Community is the Client'. Any scheme must be for the benefit of the community and not for the personal satisfaction of officers or councillors."

I pay tribute to whoever drafted that briefing in the Rochdale housing department. I would not lend my name, voice or vote to anything that was dreamt up for the aggrandisement of officers or councillors. The client counts, and in this instance the client is the community. We are debating, by and large, owner-occupiers in run-down inner-city dwellings. The briefing continues:

"Consequently various safeguards must be built into the scheme . . .

1. Properties must be built and sold at the market value for that area. If this requires an additional subsidy it must be applied for from whatever grants are available."

In other words, no new magical money would be dreamt up to make the scheme work. The briefing continues:

2. The scheme should be applied as an option to residents affected by clearance . . . It would be wrong for it to be considered as an alternative to traditional house renovations."

The scheme must be an option for people faced with clearance, otherwise one would not be able to justify the social cost of keeping communities together because, by definition, they would not be sent to various parts of the city.

I tabled the new clause following discussions with my local authority, and I believe that it has some merit. I may not have explained it satisfactorily, but I hope that the Department and the Minister will consider it and do some more work on it. If the scheme saves money, that is important; if it keeps communities together, that is important; and if it prevents us spending improvement grant uneconomically, that is important. I am in favour of money being recycled from where it is spent to the benefit

of the community, hence the mention of value for money to the taxpayer and the Exchequer in the new clause. I am not looking for a new pot of gold to spread around.

The new clause is another way of considering a problem that all hon. Members have experienced and provides another way of tackling it, given the financial and human cost involved. In that spirit I commend it to the House.

Mr. Trippier: I congratulate the hon. Member for Birmingham, Perry Barr (Mr. Rooker) on the amount of research that he has done. I confess that I found much of his speech compelling.

I suspect that the hon. Gentleman was unaware that I was once leader of Rochdale authority. Although I appreciate that it comes up with some innovative schemes, it was a darned sight better when it was Tory controlled. The hon. Gentleman would expect me to say that, but it does not detract from the main thrust of his argument.

I should like to take away and study the hon. Gentleman's proposal. If he is prepared to do so, I am anxious to have a meeting with him. If he will seek leave to withdraw the new clause, we shall ascertain whether it is necessary to introduce further legislation, perhaps in another place.

Mr. Rooker: Had I known that the Minister had served on Rochdale authority, and had I foreseen his response, I might not have made my kind comments about Rochdale.

When I was a Front-Bench spokesman, I said that both Tory and Labour authorities were involved. The client is the community, not the officers or councillors. It is not a question of what we give people. Those days have gone. If people who hold such beliefs are hidden away in little corners of the country, the sooner their beliefs are swept away the better.

I am more than happy to meet the Minister to discuss the scheme in more detail. In that spirit, I beg to ask leave to withdraw the clause.

Motion and clause, by leave, withdrawn.

Clause 83

DUTY TO PUBLISH INFORMATION

Mr. Matthew Taylor: I beg to move amendment No. 215, in page 81, line 29, after 'shall', insert 'provide information, advice and assistance to individual house holders and shall'.

Mr. Deputy Speaker: With this, it will be convenient to consider amendment No. 190, in page 81, line 31, at end insert—

'(3) The Secretary of State shall consult with such representatives of local authorities as he sees fit prior to making any determination under paragraph (2) above.'.

Mr. Taylor: The amendment seeks to provide information, advice and assistance to individual house-holders. In Committee, the Government resisted a similar amendment to include specific mention in the Bill of the provision of free information, advice and assistance for householders in renewal areas wishing to improve their homes. The Government's view then was that in some circumstances local authorities could properly charge "some people" for certain services. They said that clause 83 placed a duty on local authorities to publish information about assistance available for carrying out works in the area and that clause 141 empowered local authorities to provide money, if necessary, to enable others

[*Mr. Taylor*]

such as the National Home Improvement Council to offer advice and assistance to home owners. On that basis, the Government concluded that the amendment was unnecessary. I am not convinced of that, and the National Home Improvement Council also is not convinced. Directly comparable experience in NHIC renewal area projects shows clearly that the provision of free information, advice and assistance is a crucial element in encouraging both the least well off and those ineligible for financial assistance due to means testing to take part in a community-wide improvement project.

Such assistance is not best given by simply producing leaflets, publishing booklets or lodging plans or proposals in town halls or libraries. There is a real need for face-to-face contact on a daily basis and for those responsible for the renewal area to be on hand and readily accessible to the residents, and preferably to be located in the area itself. It is not enough for unrelated parts of the Bill to give powers for such a service to be provided. The requirement for assistance should be clearly stated in the proposals dealing with the renewal areas, with references to those clauses which provide the necessary powers. The provision of advice has to be an integral part of the renewal area concept if it is to work properly. Frankly, I would rather no charges were made, but the suggestion of charging should be considered only in the most extreme circumstances. It should be the exception rather than the rule.

I accept, as the Minister may argue, that Department of the Environment guidance circulars may incorporate those points, but those circulars are subject to change with the passage of time. If the Government's intent is as clear as the Minister suggested in Committee, there is no reason not to incorporate specific provisions in the Bill for local authorities to provide information, advice and assistance, as suggested in the amendment. The amendment is not a radical departure but what the Minister says that he would like to see happening, so it is presumably not an expensive change. The amendment seeks merely to ensure that the Bill will achieve what the Minister says that he hopes will happen anyway. I hope that the Minister will accept the intent of the amendment.

Mr. Trippier: In view of the remarks of the hon. Member for Truro (Mr. Taylor), I am prepared to look at the amendment again. Before I understood what lay behind the amendment, my initial response was that the clause was drafted deliberately so widely and so flexibly that the hon. Gentleman ought to leave the matter wholly to the local authorities themselves to determine how best to inform their tenants. Any Government in these circumstances cannot win. On the one hand, we are accused of interfering too much. On the other hand, we have been accused today by the hon. Gentleman of not interfering enough. So it goes on, and I suppose that it will never end.

I find little to quarrel with in the wording of the amendment, but I wonder whether I can persuade the hon. Gentleman to withdraw it as I am prepared to meet him to see whether we can achieve something. We will give guidance, as the hon. Gentleman suggested. I am always reluctant to include more provisions on the face of the Bill telling local authorities what they should do, but perhaps some form of compromise can be reached.

Mr. Taylor: I welcome the Minister's comments. In view of what he has said, I beg to ask leave to withdraw the amendment.

Amendment, by leave, withdrawn.

Clause 89

PART VIII OF HOUSING ACT 1985

Amendment proposed: No. 163 in page 85, line 28, at end insert—

'(4A) In the application of section 245 of the Housing Act 1985 (contributions by Secretary of State towards expenditure of local housing authorities relating to environmental works in housing action areas) in relation to expenditure—
   (a) which was incurred on or after 14th June 1989, and
   (b) in respect of which no contribution under that section was paid before the appointed day,
for subsection (2) of that section there shall be substituted the following subsection—
     "(2) In the case of any expenditure, the contribution—
       (a) shall be equal to one-half of the amount of the expenditure; and
       (b) shall be payable in one sum or by two or more instalments, according as the Secretary of State may determine."

(4B) In the application of section 259 of the Housing Act 1985 (contributions by Secretary of State towards expenditure of local housing authorities relating to general improvement areas) in relation to expenditure—
   (a) which was incurred on or after 14th June 1989, and
   (b) in respect of which no contribution under that section was paid before the appointed day,
for subsection (2) of that section there shall be substituted the following subsection—
     "(2) In the case of any expenditure, the contribution—
       (a) shall be equal to one-half of the amount of the expenditure; and
       (b) shall be payable in one sum or by two or more instalments, according as the Secretary of State may determine.".'.—[*Mr. Trippier.*]

Mr. Deputy Speaker: With this, it will be convenient to consider Government amendments No. 164 and No. 165.

Mr. Rooker: I want to make a few points about the amendments as they affect clause 89. My only case for raising this is the inter-reaction between the winding-up of housing action areas and the beginning of the housing renewal areas as outlined in clause 89. I want to make a plea about central Handsworth in my constituency. In central Handsworth, in Charles and Turville housing action areas, hundreds of homes remain untouched to this day. They are oases of disrepair and dilapidation surrounded by a sea of improved housing. They have always been left to the end of all the other improvement schemes, because they are the most difficult to improve due to the design and tenure mix. Just as Birmingham city council, through the urban renewal department and with Department of Environment approval, got going on improvements, along came clause 89.

8.45 pm

I am aware that zone 1 of the Charles housing action area will start in a few weeks—or I hope it will. I am told by officials in Birmingham that it is possible to rejig the housing action area into a housing renewal area for central Handsworth. Obviously, it would be done after today's date, as outlined in Government amendment No. 163. I hope that the Minister will answer the key question: if

Birmingham local authority puts in a plan for central Handsworth by 1 April, will the Department of the Environment agree it and fund it?

I want to describe a little of the background to the Minister because it is crucial. I must point out that few Conservative Members of Parliament represent inner cities. They sometimes talk from briefings about the inner cities as though every inner city consisted of council housing and tower blocks. It is not like that, as people discovered four years ago when we had the disturbances in part of central Handsworth. I politely took the Home Secretary and others on one side, and the press less politely, and pointed out that the vast majority of homes in the area were owner-occupied and that the others were owned by bodies other than the local authority.

In Charles action area, owner-occupancy is 47 per cent., housing associations account for 39 per cent., the local authority for less than 5 per cent. and private landlords for 9·5 per cent. In Turville, 48 per cent. of homes are housing association properties. They are almost housing association estates—not the same housing association, because there are two large associations and four or five smaller ones. Some would claim that they are sink estates, such is the extent of the dilapidation. I know that money has been put in, but the properties are not good.

Worse still, one or more housing associations—and I will not give names because I have the information second-hand from the local authority—in inner Birmingham are about to pull out of rehabilitation work, which goes against the grain of the purpose for which the associations were set up, mainly as a result of the new financial regime.

The council could be putting together an alternative to what is presently proposed for central Handsworth but it could not go ahead because of clause 89. There are about 880 homes there. Of those, 43 per cent. are owner-occupied, 42 per cent. are owned by housing associations, 5·3 per cent. by local authorities, only 6 per cent. by private landlords and an odd 3 per cent. floating around which is "others or commercial". Of the homes, 80 per cent. were built before 1919. One of the reasons why the area is always left to the end is not only because the tenure and design mix is all over the place, but because 13·5 per cent. of the properties have rateable value above £225. Many years before I was born, the houses in that part of the city had quarters for servants. Judges used to live there and carriages used to arrive there. The rateable values there are high, compared with the generality. When housing improvement schemes of such a size come up against such rateable value limits, that presents difficulties.

Unemployment in that area is running at 45 per cent. Furthermore, the Minister and I are in the ethnic minority, which comprises 32 per cent. of the population. Pensioner owner-occupiers comprise 18 per cent. of the population of the area.

My constituents in that part of central Handsworth need a copper-bottomed guarantee that their treatment up to now as third-class citizens in relation to housing improvements will cease. When the consequences of the Bill became apparent to them earlier in the year there was much anger in the area. There are unscrupulous people in places such as central Handsworth who seek to exploit for other reasons the fear and the anger of the people that they would not have their houses improved. By and large, I use every opportunity to ensure that my constituents know that their cases can be raised legally and peacefully here in the House of Commons and in the Birmingham city council house and that there is no reason for taking any other action that other people might propose. I promised hundreds of angry constituents that one way or another I would raise their concerns about the Bill and try to put across their case for the equal treatment that is their right. Therefore, I hope that the Minister will give me the assurances that I am seeking.

When, in an Adjournment debate on 14 July 1987—just after the general election—I raised the specific issue of the Charles and Turville housing action areas, the then Minister, the hon. Member for Broxbourne (Mrs. Roe), gave a fairly helpful reply and subsequently agreed to visit the area. However, in the event, the declaration of the Charles housing action area was made and the Minister then saw no useful purpose in the visit.

It is quite clear—this has been notified officially—that because of the provisions of the Bill, the declaration of the Turville housing action area and of the Willmore, Wellington and Wellhead housing action areas which are close by will not be made. Therefore, some time between now and, say, the end of the long recess, I am asking the Minister to pay a short visit to the area to see it for himself. His regional office knows that is a difficult area because of some of the factors that I have explained. It would be useful if the Minister could see it for himself. In view of the Bill's effects on the area and of the fact that there appears to be a setback in the progress of improving those properties, my request for a visit is thoroughly reasonable and justified and I hope that the Minister will accede to that some time later this year.

Mr. Trippier: I am anxious to take up the kind invitation that the hon. Member for Perry Barr has extended to me and to pay an official visit to his constituency. Once again, I congratulate the hon. Gentleman. I genuinely believe that, as a result of his two most recent contributions, he deserves all the local publicity that he can get. I mean that sincerely, because I know that his purpose is to assist those people whom he is so anxious to represent.

However, the straightforward answer is that not only is it possible to transfer from a housing action area to a housing renewal area, but for those that are determined, acceptable and in the pipeline, it would be advantageous for them to do so. Therefore, I do not see any difficulty in giving the hon. Gentleman the assurance that he seeks. If I can pay the so-called official visit sooner rather than later, perhaps we can do whatever we can to improve the situation and the lives of the people living in those areas.

Amendment agreed to.

Amendment made: No. 164, in page 85, line 29, leave out

'subsections (1) to (3) above'
and insert

'the preceding provisions of this section'.—*[Mr. Trippier.]*

Clause 92

GRANTS FOR IMPROVEMENTS AND REPAIRS

Amendments made: No. 39, in page 86, line 26, leave out
'where the improvement, repair or provision is to be by'
and insert

'if the person who would otherwise qualify as the applicant for the grant is'.

No. 40, in page 86, line 42, after 'conversion)', insert

'other than section 523 thereof (assistance for provision of separate service pipe for water supply)'.—[*Mr. Trippier.*]

Schedule 11

ENACTMENTS REPEALED

Amendment made: No. 41, in page 204, line 5, column 3, leave out '526' and insert—

'522.
Sections 524 to 526.'.
—[*Mr. Trippier.*]

Clause 95

THE INTEREST OF THE APPLICANT IN THE PROPERTY

Mr. Paul Murphy (Torfaen): I beg to move amendment No. 191, in page 88, line 4, at end insert

'or

   (d) in the case of an application for a renovation grant to improve a dwelling, the applicant is a tenant to whom Section 79 of the Housing Act 1985 applies.'.

The purpose of this amendment is to ensure that council tenants continue to be eligible for grants to improve their homes. Earlier today, the Minister said that he believed that his Government had done well by tenants. However, that is not the case with this part of the Bill.

The Government's position is indefensible. It was a Conservative Government who introduced the right for council tenants to get grants as part of their "tenants' charter" in 1980. Similarly, that right is now contained in section 463 of the Housing Act 1985. The Minister will remember that his hon. Friend the Member for Surrey, South-West (Mrs. Bottomley) said in Committee that she believed that responsibility for essential repairs and improvements rested with the landlord, not with the tenant. That clearly argues against council tenants having the right to improve, and takes away the individual freedom of council tenants to decide for themselves to what extent they want their property to be improved in a situation when, because of Government cuts, their landlord may not be in a position to help.

Later during the Committee stage, at column 1052, the hon. Member for Surrey, South-West stated:

"No, it is not right . . . It would not be right for council tenants to be eligible for grants".

We know that housing association tenants will be eligible for grants although council tenants will not. The Government are taking away a right that they granted as recently as 1980 and which they confirmed in 1985.

In Committee the Minister also said:

"we have made it abundantly clear that we expect local authorities to make proper provision . . . so there is no difficulty."—[*Official Report, Standing Committee G; 25 April 1989, c. 1052-53.*]

The Minister may say that there is no difficulty, but Exchequer subsidies to local authorities have been cut from £1,393 million in 1980-81 to just £496 million in 1988-89. Local authorities' HIP allocations have been reduced from £5,266 million in 1978-79 to £1,127 million in 1988-89.

If owners can improve and renovate with a grant, council tenants should be able to do exactly the same. The amendment does not extend to essential repairs. This is a debate about principles and about the Government yet again taking away a right that is enjoyed by council tenants.

Mr. Trippier: Although I appreciate the spirit in which the hon. Member for Torfaen (Mr. Murphy) has moved the amendment, we went around that course many times in Committee. The hon. Gentleman quoted my hon. Friend the Under-Secretary of State, the hon. Member for Surrey, South-West (Mrs. Bottomley), accurately although his earlier quote may have been from myself. However, what he said about the Committee stage was absolutely true. If the amendment were to be accepted, it would mean that we would be giving preferential treatment to those in public sector housing as opposed to those in the private sector. That would never do. Even when a Labour Government were in power, they pursued a policy of housing improvement grants available in the private sector.

The whole purpose of the first GIAs that were set up in my own ward by Richard Crossman was to concentrate a considerable amount of funding on private sector stock through housing improvement grants. That is the sort of thing that we are continuing.

The new housing finance regime that we are introducing in the Bill for the public housing sector is expressly designed to tackle the problems that the hon. Gentleman has identified.

Renovation grants are essentially concerned with the repair and improvement of private sector stock. Local authorities and other public sector bodies have other sources of funding with which to meet their responsibilities as landlords. I accept that we could debate that issue at some length on a political platform, because the hon. Member for Torfaen would argue that we have cut the HIP allocation, and we would say that we have increased the amount of capital money available through the increased amount of money made available through the right to buy. That debate would go on endlessly. We have had many opportunities to debate that in the past and no doubt we will again in the future.

In the part of the Bill that we are now discussing, the housing improvement grants are specifically targeted at the private sector. The hon. Member for Birmingham, Perry Barr (Mr. Rooker) wants that to continue, and so do I. I hope that, if the hon. Member for Torfaen will not withdraw the amendment, my hon. Friends will oppose it.

Amendment negatived.

Clause 99

OWNER-OCCUPIERS AND TENANTS

9 pm

Mr. Alfred Morris (Manchester, Wythenshawe): I beg to move amendment No. 317, in page 91, line 2, after 'then', insert

'subject to the exclusions by virtue of subsection (4) below'.

Mr. Deputy Speaker: With this it will be convenient to take the following amendments: No. 193, in page 91, line 23, at end insert—

'(4) This section does not apply where the application for a grant is made—

   (a) by a person over pensionable age; or
   (b) for a disabled facilities grant; or
   (c) by any other person as determined by the Secretary of State.'.

No. 318, in clause 99, page 91, line 23, at end insert—

'(4) No evaluation shall be made of the financial resources of an applicant in respect of a disabled facilities grant or of an applicant for a renovation grant when a member of the applicant's household is a disabled person.'.

No. 195, in clause 104, page 95, line 26, at end insert—

'(3A) If an application for a grant has been approved, the authority is satisfied that, owing to circumstances beyond the control of any person described in section 97(3) their income, assets, needs or outgoings have changed, the authority may increase the amount of the grant.'.

Mr. Morris: As you have indicated, Mr. Deputy Speaker, amendment No. 317, which I now move, is closely linked to amendment No. 318 and other amendments in the group.

The hon. Member for Exeter (Mr. Hannam), my right hon. Friend the Member for Stoke-on-Trent, South (Mr. Ashley) and the hon. Member for Caernarfon (Mr. Wigley) very much wanted to speak in this debate, but cannot do so for unavoidable reasons. Amendments Nos. 317 and 318 have their total backing, which strongly underlines the all-party nature of the amendments. They are very much the amendments, in fact, of the all-party disablement group in the House of which my right hon. Friend the Member for Stoke-on-Trent, South is the chairman and the hon. Member for Exeter, who raised on Second Reading, the problem the two amendments address, is the secretary.

This is a very important series of amendments, well deserving both of maximum public attention and support from both sides of the House. In support of amendments Nos. 317 and 318, the Royal Association for Disability and Rehabilitation has said:

"While we recognise the desirability of directing financial assistance to those in greatest need and agree that the current rateable value limit is an inaccurate means for its achievement, we are not convinced that a test of resources based upon that devised for housing benefit is appropriate for assessing the requirement for a renovation grant."

Housing benefit can be changed as the circumstances of the applicant change, but an assessment of resources for home improvement may lead to considerable long-term financial commitment by the applicant. In many cases a household's circumstances are likely to change as, for example, when it includes a number of single adult children—non-dependants—who may well leave home before a loan for home improvements has been paid off.

The royal association accepts that renovation grants for general house repairs and modernisation of properties occupied by disabled people should be subject to the same test of resources as other households. They strongly insist, however, that any benefits arising from disability, such as mobility and attendance allowances, should be disregarded.

In some cases there may be a temporary accumulation of these benefits. Mobility allowance may be saved to purchase a car or a powered outdoor wheelchair. Attendance allowance may be put on one side to assist with the cost of respite care or back payment of delayed benefits may have been received for which there has been a long-standing need. Such sums should very clearly not be considered along with other savings.

The royal association can see no reason for the complete reversal of the Government's proposal in the November 1987 consultation paper that

". . . for adaptation work, however, applicants will not be subject to a test of resources".

Nor can many other national organisations of and for disabled people that I have heard from in anticipation of the debate see any justification of the Government's volte-face.

Peter Large, CBE, whose work for people with disabilities, in the service of the Disablement Income Group and many other national organisations, is so widely respected on both sides of the House, has also drawn attention to the Government's abandonment of the proposal set out in the consultation paper. He states:

"If disability is acquired during the course of a working life and if it is so great as to require expensive adaptations to a house, the vast majority of those affected will suffer a significant financial loss when they become disabled. The same will be true in the case of a disabled dependant."

It must be remembered that the disabled applicants, or dependants, will probably spend the rest of their lives disabled. Few if any will be able to look forward to employment as a means of making good whatever they are forced to spend on adaptation.

Those with savings at the time when they become disabled can only look forward to seeing any savings they may have steadily depleted, having to spend them on aids and equipment not supplied through the NHS, on all minor and major repairs around the house, on upkeep of the garden, and on helping offset some of the extra costs of daily living as a disabled person. If the disability occurs before a person reaches working age, he or she is unlikely to be adversely affected by a means test, but many with a disabled dependant could be affected.

The recent survey by the Office of Population Censuses and Surveys shows that the incomes of people with disabilities are substantially below those of the rest of the population; that only 31 per cent. of people with disabilities under pension age were in paid work compared with 69 per cent. of the general population; that the earnings of those who have jobs are substantially below those of non-disabled employees and decrease further with increasing severity of disability; that 4·5 million disabled adults live in households in which there are no earners; that three quarters of disabled adults are forced to rely on state benefits as their main source of income, with an average total income of only £65·20 a week; and that the overall average income among all disabled people was only £82·20 a week.

Means testing will, therefore, not save much money but would add to the severe financial stress that accompanies disability for most disabled people, not least owner-occupiers. In the circumstances, means testing hardly seems appropriate or cost-effective. It is particularly inappropriate when the proposed test of means is based on scales established for non-disabled people whose financial position is likely to improve, as opposed to disabled people whose financial position is likely to deteriorate.

While other people are rightly concerned about the greenhouse effect, an increasing number of disabled people have to worry about the "workhouse effect" of the Government's policies for social security, as the facts given by the OPCS so dramatically show.

The purpose of amendment No. 193 is to exempt pensioners, as well as applicants for a disabled facilities grant, from the means-testing provisions of the clause. Exemptions would help target grants where they are most needed. The Government's aim in introducing these changes is better to target grants on those who need them most. Successive house condition surveys have shown that

[*Mr. Morris*]

elderly and disabled people live in the worst conditions, yet are least able to improve them. Exempting these groups of applicants would thus be an effective way of targeting resources on those most in need.

Elderly people see means testing as stigmatising and degrading. Many are put off making applications. They need encouragement and help to improve their property —hence the Government's support for elderly home owners' advice services. The Minister thinks that strong dislike of means testing is a thing of the past. If that is true, why is the take-up of other means-tested benefits by elderly people today so poor?

Amendment No. 195 is about enabling the local housing authority, in its assessment of applicants' grant entitlement, to take account of significant changes in needs or resources.

While recognising the problems of reassessing grants, local authorities need to be able to reassess grant entitlement if the financial circumstances of an applicant worsen significantly. It is easy to envisage circumstances in which a grant level is fixed on the basis of earnings from employment, for example, following which the applicant suffers a permanent disability which requires the end of full-time employment and a signficant and permanent drop in income and yet in which the applicant is unable to escape the financial consequences of the improvement work.

The divide in this debate is not between the Minister and me, or between him and the other sponsors of the amendments on both sides of the House. It is a divide between the Minister and all the major organisations of and for disabled people. We are reflecting their deep concern, and I implore the Minister to give the House a constructive response to these important amendments. It would be utterly wrong to proceed with the clause as drafted.

Sir George Young (Ealing, Acton): I shall speak briefly to emphasise the all-party nature of amendments Nos. 317 and 318 and shall return briefly to some of the debates that we had in Committee when we discussed this subject. I again pay tribute to the Government for introducing new clause 10, as it then was, which went a substantial way towards meeting the anxieties of those who represent disabled people.

I should like to press the Government a little more on some of the issues raised by the right hon. Member for Manchester, Wythenshawe (Mr. Morris). It would be helpful if my hon. Friend the Minister could explain why the Government have changed their mind on what appeared in the original consultation paper. There was a principle there with which most of us could identify, which said that for normal repair or improvement work unrelated to a person's disability people should be exposed to a means test when they apply for an improvement grant. In the case of adaptations which helped people to meet the needs of their disability, they were to be exempt from the test of resources.

That principle was understandable in that it enabled disabled people to come to the starting post at the same time as everyone else, and the rules would be exactly the same. The withdrawal of that proposal in the consultation paper has caused some anxiety and amendments Nos. 317 and 318 refer to that. In his response to the Committee

debate, my hon. Friend the Minister said that he would reflect again on this in the light of letters from George Wilson and Peter Large. Is he now able to move a little towards the position pressed on him by hon. Members in all parts of the House?

Mr. Trippier: One of my difficulties with the amendment is that I do not think that the right hon. Member for Manchester, Wythenshawe (Mr. Morris) is speaking as a representative of the all-party committee of which I was a member before I became a member of the Government. I think that he devalues the currency of what he says because he did not start his speech by making exactly the same comments as my hon. Friend the Member for Ealing, Acton (Sir G. Young).

The whole purpose of the clause is to give additional resources to the disabled. That is what my hon. Friend has just said. The point was effectively made in Committee, but only by him. I have great respect for the right hon. Member for Wythenshawe for the work that he does for the disabled. However, I am surprised at him because he missed a great opportunity to acknowledge how the Government have moved in this direction.

I cannot give my hon. Friend the Member for Ealing, Acton the comfort that he seeks because it is not clear to me what hon. Members would substitute for a test of resources. Perhaps the right hon. Member for Wythenshawe is saying that all pensioners and all disabled people should qualify for 100 per cent. grants irrespective of their ability to afford the cost of the work. I entirely accept that it is perfectly legitimate to hold that view, but I am not at all sure that it would be fair to people who are not in those categories, for example, those on low incomes, nor am I sure that all local authorities would welcome the resource commitment that it would bring. Nobody has mentioned that.

We expect pensioners and the disabled to do well out of the new grants system. If they do not, we have failed in our precise intention. We did not think that the former system was fair. I assure the right hon. Member for Wythenshawe that many of the people that he mentions will qualify for help with the full cost of the work. We have also said that we shall look carefully at the possibility of passporting particular groups of people whose needs have been assessed for other purposes. We shall encourage help for pensioners and others in order to increase their take-up of grant.

I remain of the view that where a pensioner or disabled person has the resources to fund the work either wholly or in part, it is not unreasonable for them to do so, not least because it encourages a degree of independence which many elderly people and others value a great deal.

Amendment No. 195 touches on the issue that we discussed in Committee—the matter of redetermining grant entitlement where the circumstances of the applicant change after grant has been approved. We understand the arguments in favour of that, although I am not sure about why the redetermination should be one way, as the amendment would provide, if an applicant's income increased following grant approval. For instance, why should the grant not be reduced?

There are practical difficulties in providing for the determination which the local authority associations acknowledge, even if Opposition Members do not. We are seeking to keep the test of resources as simple and straightforward as possible. Redetermination will mean placing a duty on applicants to inform the authority whenever their circumstances change. That could happen on a number of occasions—certainly more than once— between the time of approval and even by the time the grant is paid. Would the authority, for example, need to redetermine grant each time or just once? That is not an idle debating point. It must be seriously considered, certainly in terms of legislation. We gave an undertaking in Committee, and I repeat it now, that we are prepared to consider that matter further with the local authority associations. I hope that, in those circumstances and on that understanding, the right hon. Gentleman will withdraw the amendment.

9.15 pm

Mr. Alfred Morris: I assure the Minister that the whole of my submission about amendments Nos. 317 and 318 was based on information made available to me by organisations of and for disabled people which are widely respected on both sides of both Houses. At the same time, I made it clear that the two amendments were those of the all-party disablement group in the House.

What upsets the organisations of and for disabled people is the Government's change of policy since the consultation paper. I heard nothing from the Minister about the change of policy. It is not possible for me now to press the amendments, for reasons the House will understand, but I implore him to try his best between now and the debate in another place to review the Government's policy on this important issue. I hope that there will be significant improvements to the clause before the Bill becomes law.

Amendment negatived.

Clause 102

APPROVAL OF APPLICATIONS TO PROVIDE CERTAIN FACILITIES FOR THE DISABLED

Sir George Young: I beg to move amendment No. 321, in page 93, line 1, leave out 'not'.

Mr. Speaker: It will be convenient to discuss at the same time the following amendments:

No. 322, in page 93, line 2, leave out 'unless' and insert 'if'.

No. 323, in page 93, line 16, leave out paragraph (c) and insert—

'(c) facilitating access by the disabled occupant to, or providing for the disabled occupant, a room used or usable for sleeping.'.

No. 324, in page 93, line 29, leave out from 'dwelling' to end of line 30.

No. 325, in page 93, line 24, leave out paragraph (f) and insert—

'(f) providing or enhancing heating and lighting systems and providing or adapting the controls thereof to make them suitable for the disabled occupant;'.

No. 194, in page 93, line 30, at end insert—

'(h) providing a structure, carport or suitable area for the purpose of parking a motor vehicle used by the disabled occupant which is accessible to him, or facilitating access to and from such a facility by the disabled occupant.
(i) providing a source of power, light, heat, insulation and ventilation for the disabled occupant.

(j) providing suitable accommodation as part of the dwelling for a person living with or regularly attending the disabled occupant for the purpose of caring for him.
(k) providing an additional room or rooms for the purpose of regular medical or associated treatment of the disabled occupant.'.

No. 326, in page 93, line 30, at end add—

'(h) providing adequate thermal insulation, including double-glazing and draftproofing; and
(i) facilitating access to, or providing for the disabled occupant, a garage or covered carport where the disabled occupant is dependent on a road or pavement vehicle for mobility outdoors.'.

Sir George Young: Amendments Nos. 321 and 322 are linked and the Government could concede them without any loss of face. They simply change the emphasis and would require a housing authority to approve an application if it was satisfied, as opposed to asking it not to approve it unless it was satisfied. That would be a more consumer-friendly approach towards processing applications for improvement grants from the disabled, rather than the current wording, which I find somewhat negative.

Amendment No. 323 seeks to push on the generosity already displayed by the Government by making access by the disabled occupant more extensive. Subsection (2)(c) as drafted allows a grant where it would facilitate

"access by the disabled occupant to a room used or usable for sleeping"

In other words, he can get a grant if he changes a sitting room into a bedroom, but he cannot get a grant for adding a new bedroom to the house. Changing a sitting room into a bedroom is likely adversely to affect the whole of the household and should be avoided when it is possible to build an extension to the house which the disabled person could use as a bedroom. I hope that the Minister will look favourable on that amendment.

Likewise, amendment No. 324 deals with subsection (2)(g), which I find somewhat restrictive. It facilitates

"access and movement by the disabled occupant around the dwelling in order to enable him to care for a dependent relative."

Surely the disabled occupant needs access and movement around the dwelling for his or her own sake, not just to look after a dependent relative. Why should it be restricted to

"care for a dependent relative"

when many disabled people have friends whom they look after? Indeed, others have friends who look after them, and they may need to be helped when temporarily unwell. Is it possible to move the boundaries of that provision further and more generously?

Amendment No. 325 affects paragraph (f), which deals with

"facilitating the use by the disabled occupant of a source of power, light or heat by altering the position of one or more means of access to or control of that source".

I am not sure that it is enough merely to facilitate the use of existing heating or lighting systems. For example, partially-sighted people may need a greater intensity of lighting or more directed lighting as well as change of the controls. The need for adequate heating for disabled people with impaired mobility is accepted by everybody, but provision of it is not eligible for a grant under the clause as drafted.

Amendment No. 326 would add some provisions to the end of subsection (2). Extra heating could be provided by paragraph (h), but bearing in mind that in general disabled people have less to live on than non-disabled people, the

[*Sir George Young*]

extra heating could be economically provided by improving standards of insulation. The amendment would provide for this. Paragraph (i) enables access to a garage to be funded through improvement grant. Access to a garage is important to anyone unable, or virtually unable to walk, as evidenced by the fact that they have been subject of rate rebates, and the provision of a cover for a car and/or powered outdoor wheelchair is essential.

Basically, these amendments represent a modest package of improvements in mandatory grants for the disabled, on which I hope that the Government will smile.

Mr. George Howarth: The Minister has already given an undertaking to look again at discretionary grants, particularly those suggested by the Royal Association for Disability and Rehabilitation. We should like the Government to enlarge the existing criteria.

As I understand it, the commitment is only to look at such factors as enabling disabled people to get through their front doors, to have one living room and one bedroom, to build an accessible bathroom or lavatory, to adapt a kitchen so as to be able to reach heating, lighting and other power switches, and to allow access to the home for a dependent relative. We should like to expand the criteria by bringing in such factors as access to car parking and the provision of heating, accommodation for carers, and a special treatment room. These are not dissimilar to the aims of the hon. Member for Ealing, Acton (Sir G. Young). I shall be interested to hear what the Minister says because disabled people are concerned about such matters.

Mr. Trippier: It would be unreasonable not to approach the point made by my hon. Friend the Member for Ealing, Acton (Sir G. Young) about amendments Nos. 321 and 322. I accept that he is suggesting that the wording of this part of the clause appears negative. The difficulty is that the solution that he has come up with—it may be the only one that he could think of or on which he has been advised—goes much further than he intended. The same would happen to me if I did not have the facilities available to me through our super Civil Service. The amendments, if passed, would impose a duty on local authorities to approve all applications for disabled facilities grants, which is not necessarily what my hon. Friend is seeking to achieve.

I shall examine the wording of amendments Nos. 321 and 322. I can give no other undertaking and I cannot promise that I shall find alternative or improved wording. However, in view of the spirit in which my hon. Friend spoke to the amendments, I feel under an obligation to look at them again.

Amendments Nos. 323, 324, 325, 326 and 194 make specific additions or amendments to the purposes for which mandatory grant will be available. The Bill already provides for mandatory grant for an extensive range of works previously available only at the discretion of local authorities. It would be possible to extend that list in a variety of ways, all of which would assist the disabled person to remain in his or her home. However, it is unrealistic to propose that all of them should be requirements on the local housing authority. The resource implications could be large and go far beyond what is necessary.

In any event, subsection (3) enables authorities to provide assistance at their discretion towards the cost of other works that are likely to make the dwelling suitable for the accommodation, welfare or employment of the disabled occupant. They could include all the items listed in the amendments. However, I suppose that there must be a difference between my hon. Friend and me in the end, and the difficulty is that I do not accept that those provisions require mandatory status. I may add that subsection (3)(f) provides mandatory grant where, additionally, specialised adapted heating and lighting controls are necessary. Lighting, heating and ventilation are provided for in the new basic standard of fitness for the property concerned.

I urge the House to resist the amendments and in so doing to support the balance between mandatory and discretionary help for which the Bill already provides.

Sir George Young: I thank my hon. Friend for his characteristically generous reply, and I do not wish to press any of my amendments. My hon. Friend will know that the disabled lobby in another place takes an enormous interest in the parts of the Bill that we have just debated. I have no doubt that my hon. Friend's remarks will be studied and that improvements may be made in another place.

Amendment negatived.

Clause 104

Approval and Refusal of Applications

Sir George Young: I beg to move amendment No. 10, in page 94, line 45, leave out 'twelve' and insert 'six'.

The Committee was unable to come to a decision on the issue to which the amendment relates without the intervention of its Chairman, who used his casting vote in favour of the Government. The amendment relates to the length of time that a local authority can take to process an improvement grant application. The proposition was made in Standing Committee that the authority should have 12 months, but there was a strong feeling that that was a somewhat leisurely period of time and that six months would be more appropriate.

The record of the Division in Standing Committee G states:

"*The Committee divided:* Ayes 112, Noes 11."

As only 25 right hon. and hon. Members served on the Committee, it appears that that is a misprint. The report adds:

"The Chairman: In accordance with precedent, I give my vote to the Noes."—[*Official Report, Standing Committee G, 25 April 1989; c. 1085.*]

I believe that the score was 11 all.

Given the pressure that the Government rightly place on local authorities to process right-to-buy and planning applications more quickly, 12 months is a long time to deal with an improvement grant application. In forcing the matter to a Division in Committee, I hoped to strengthen my hon. Friend's hand in his negotiations with local authorities. I trust that he will be able to tell the House that the period allowed will be only six months.

Mr. Peter Thurnham (Bolton, North-East): I declare an interest as an electrical contractor associated with the subject matter of clause 104. I thank my hon. Friend the Member for Ealing, Acton (Sir G. Young) and my hon. Friend the Minister for covering the point raised in

Committee and agreeing to the amendment. I draw attention to a letter from my hon. Friend the Minister dated 19 May in which he accepts the need for electrical work to be included in the grant provisions. He writes:

"It is often the elderly, living in a home of long standing, who have the most urgent need of assistance with rewiring."

As that need is considered to be urgent, I ask him to consider that a time limit of six months rather than 12 would be better. Nevertheless, I thank him for acknowledging that the previous anomaly needed to be rectified.

Figures for deaths and accidents arising from fires and faulty wiring show the importance of reaching a decision sooner rather than later. Latest statistics show that 3,600 fires in dwellings were directly attributable to faulty electrical wiring, and that they resulted in 22 deaths and 320 non-fatal casualties. The sooner the decisions can be made, the better.

I thank my hon. Friend the Minister for accepting the need for the change to be made, but in practice local authorities are reluctant to accept the need for the grants which are still discretionary rather than mandatory. I should like my hon. Friend to consider the inclusion of the Electrical Contractors Association in the proposed working party which will provide guidance notes on the working of the Act to local authorities. Perhaps my hon. Friend will bear that in mind when he considers whether the period should be reduced from 12 months to six months.

9.30 pm

Mr. Trippier: I shall be happy to look at the last point made by my hon. Friend the Member for Bolton, North-East (Mr. Thurnham).

On a more general point with regard to the powerful advocacy that we have heard both from him and from my hon. Friend the Member for Ealing, Acton (Sir G. Young), to use one of the favourite expressions of my hon. Friend the Member for Ealing, Acton, I am anxious to smile on the amendment and on him, and to be user-friendly. I am therefore prepared to accept the amendment. It may be a lesson to the hon. Member for Newham, North-East that, if he is nice to the Minister who knows what he might get?

Mr. Tony Banks: I am sure that it will be a lesson for my hon. Friend the Member for Newham, North-East (Mr. Leighton), but I happen to come from Newham, North-West.

Amendment agreed to.

Amendment made: No. 125, in page 95, line 15, at end insert—

'(2A) Where an application for a grant is approved, then, except—

(a) with the consent of the Secretary of State, or—*[Mr. Trippier.]*

Clause 109

CONDITION REQUIRING REPAYMENT OF GRANT IN CASE OF CERTAIN DISPOSALS WHERE OWNER-OCCUPATION CERTIFICATE GIVEN

Amendments made: No. 42, in page 98, line 16, leave out 'and (6)' and insert 'to (6A)'.

No. 43, in page 98, line 34, at end insert—

'(6A) In any case where—

(a) within the period referred to in subsection (2) above an owner makes a relevant disposal of the dwelling concerned (not being an exempt disposal), and

(b) the authority having the right to demand payment from the owner as mentioned in that subsection are satisfied that he is elderly or infirm and is making the disposal with the intention of going to live in sheltered housing or a residential care home as his only or main residence.

the authority may determine not to make any demand under subsection (2) above and, on the making of such a determination, any condition under that subsection shall cease to be in force with respect to the dwelling.'.—*[Mr. Trippier.]*

Clause 117

ASSISTANCE FOR PROVISION OF MINOR WORKS TO DWELLINGS

Mr. Battle: I beg to move amendment No. 197, in page 105, line 4, after 'authority', insert—

'(i) shall give assistance as mentioned in subsection (2) below for the provision or improvement of thermal insulation in a dwelling and/or the provision of improvement of draughtproofing to doors and windows, and

(ii)'.

We talked earlier about discretionary and mandatory grants. I wish to draw the Minister's attention to the fact that grants for improving heating installations in existing houses either through the homes installation scheme or through energy grant are at present mandatory, particularly for those on income support, family credit and housing benefit. Rather than making a grant aid discretionary, as the present form of clause 117 would require, will the Minister leave it as a mandatory grant, not least because it is basic to people on low incomes? Making it discretionary would represent a worsening of the current position.

Mr. Trippier: I will try to explain to the hon. Gentleman why that would not be a good idea. The point about the new grant regime and the grant for a range of minor works is to give local authorities some flexibility in the way in which, for example, elderly home owners can be helped to stay in their own homes. It may be that draught-proofing or insulation is the most pressing need and authorities can recognise that by approving a minor works grant, even though more substantial work needs to be done on the property later on. There may, however, be a stronger case for the repair of a gutter or a down pipe, and it may make sense for insulation work to wait until other related work can go ahead. Authorities need that degree of flexibility. Otherwise, we may find ourselves in a position in which insulation work will have to be carried out even though more urgent matters are in need of attention. I hope that the hon. Member will seek leave to withdraw his amendment.

Amendment negatived.

Clause 118

CONTRIBUTIONS BY THE SECRETARY OF STATE

Amendment made: No. 165, in page 106, line 20, at end insert—

'(5) In the application of section 516 of the Housing Act 1985 (contributions by Secretary of State towards expense of grants under Part XV of that Act) in relation to a case where—

(a) an application under section 461 of that Act has been approved by the local housing authority after 14th June 1989, and

(b) the date which is the certified date, as defined in section 499(3) of that Act, in relation to the works to which that application relates falls on or after the day appointed under section 154 below for the coming into force of section 92 above,

for subsection (2) there shall be substituted the following subsection—

"(2) In the case of any grant, the contribution—

(a) shall be equal to a percentage of the amount of the grant determined under subsections (3) and (4) below; and

(b) shall be payable in one sum or by two or more instalments, according as the Secretary of State may determine.".'.

New Clause 29

CONSENT REQUIRED FOR SUBSEQUENT DISPOSALS

'.—(1) Where a dwelling which is for the time being subject to a secure tenancy is transferred under section 143 above to a person as mentioned in subsection (2)(b) of that section (in this section referred to as an "approved person"), that person shall not dispose of it except—

(a) with the consent of the Secretary of State, which may be given either unconditionally or subject to conditions; or

(b) by an exempt disposal, as defined in section 81(8) of the Housing Act 1988;

and any reference in the following provisions of this section to an initial transfer is a reference to the transfer of a dwelling to an approved person under section 143 above.

(2) Where an estate or interest in a dwelling of the approved person who acquired it on the initial transfer has been mortgaged or charged, the prohibition in subsection (1) above applies also to a disposal by the mortgagee or chargee in exercise of a power of sale or leasing, whether or not the disposal is in the name of the approved person; and in any case where—

(a) by operation of law or by virtue of an order of a court, the dwelling which has been acquired on the initial transfer passes or is transferred from the approved person to another person, and

(b) that passing or transfer does not constitute a disposal for which consent is required under this section,

this section (including, where there is more than one such passing or transfer, this subsection) shall apply as if the other person to whom the dwelling passes or is transferred were the approved person.

(3) Where subsection (1) above applies—

(a) the new town corporation by whom the initial transfer is made shall furnish to the approved person a copy of the consent of the Secretary of State under section 143(4) above; and

(b) the instrument by which the initial transfer is effected shall contain a statement in a form approved by the Chief Land Registrar that the requirement of this section as to consent applies to a subsequent disposal of the dwelling by the approved person.

(4) For the purposes of this section the grant of an option to purchase the fee simple or any other interest in a dwelling is a disposal and a consent given to such a disposal extends to a disposal made in pursuance of the option.

(5) Before giving any consent required by virtue of this section, the Secretary of State—

(a) shall satisfy himself that the person who is seeking the consent has taken appropriate steps to consult every tenant of any dwelling proposed to be disposed of; and

(b) shall have regard to the responses of any such tenants to that consultation.

(6) If, apart from subsection (7) below, the consent of the Housing Corporation or Housing for Wales would be required under section 9 of the Housing Associations Act 1985 (control of dispositions of land by housing associations)

for a disposal in respect of which, by virtue of subsection (1) above, the consent of the Secretary of State is required, the Secretary of State shall consult that body before giving his consent for the purposes of this section.

(7) No consent shall be required under the said section 9 for any disposal in respect of which consent is given in accordance with subsection (6) above.

(8) Where the title of the new town corporation to the dwelling which is transferred by the initial transfer is not registered, and the initial transfer is a conveyance, grant or assignment of a description mentioned in section 123 of the Land Registration Act 1925 (compulsory registration of title)—

(a) that section applies in relation to the instrument by which the initial transfer is effected whether or not the dwelling is in an area in which an Order in Council under section 120 of that Act (areas of compulsory registration) is in force;

(b) the corporation shall give the approved person a certificate in a form approved by the Chief Land Registrar stating that the corporation is entitled to make the transfer subject only to such encumbrances, rights and interests as are stated in the instrument by which the initial transfer is effected or summarised in the certificate; and

(c) for the purpose of registration of title, the Chief Land Registrar shall accept such a certificate as evidence of the facts stated in it, but if as a result he has to meet a claim against him under the Land Registration Acts 1925 to 1986 the corporation by whom the initial transfer was made is liable to indemnify him.

(9) On an application being made for registration of a disposition of registered land or, as the case may be, of the title under a disposition of unregistered land, if the instrument by which the initial transfer is effected contains the statement required by subsection (3) above, the Chief Land Registrar shall enter in the register a restriction stating the requirement of this section as to consent to a subsequent disposal.

(10) In this section—

(a) "dwelling" and "new town corporation" have the same meaning as in section 143 above; and

(b) "secure tenancy" has the meaning assigned by section 79 of the Housing Act 1985.'.—[*Mr. Trippier.*]

Brought up, read the First and Second time, and added to the Bill.

New Clause 46

SCOTTISH NON-DOMESTIC RATES: INTERIM PROVISIONS

'(1) For section 3 of the Abolition of Domestic Rates Etc. (Scotland) Act 1987 (determination of non-domestic rates) there shall be substituted the following section—

"Non-domestic rates: interim provisions.

3A.—(1) The Secretary of State shall, in respect of each of the financial years specified in subsection (2) below, prescribe for each local authority a rate which shall be their non-domestic rate in respect of that year.

(2) The financial years referred to in subsection (1) above are those beginning with the financial year 1990-91 and ending with that immediately before the financial year in respect of which the non-domestic rate is first prescribed under section 3B of this Act.

(3) Non-domestic rates shall be levied in accordance with section 7 of the Local Government (Scotland) Act 1975 by each rating authority in respect of lands and heritages—

(a) which are subjects (other than part residential subjects) in respect of which there is an entry in the valuation roll, according to their rateable value; or

(b) which are part residential subjects, according to that part of their rateable value which is shown in the apportionment note as relating to the non residential use of those subjects.

(4) The rates prescribed under subsection (1) above shall be known—

(a) in the case of the regional council, as the non-domestic regional rate;

(b) in the case of the district council, as the non-domestic district rate; and

(c) in the case of the islands council, as the non-domestic islands rate.".'.

(2) Accordingly—

(a) references (however expressed) in any enactment to the non-domestic rate determined by a local authority under section 3 of the Abolition of Domestic Rates Etc (Scotland) Act 1987 shall be construed as references to the non-domestic rate prescribed for the local authority under section 3A of that Act;

(b) in section 109(2) of the Local Government (Scotland) Act 1973 for the words from "non-domestic district rate" onward there shall be substituted the words "information as may reasonably be required for the preparation of demand notes for the purposes of levying the non-domestic district rate";

(c) section 110A(2) of the Local Government (Scotland) Act 1973 and section 128(2) of and paragraph 16 of Schedule 12 to the Local Government Finance Act 1988 shall cease to have effect.'.—*Mr. Lang.]*

Brought up, and read the First time.

The Minister of State, Scottish Office (Mr. Ian Lang): I beg to move, That the clause be read a Second time.

Mr. Speaker: With this we may take the following: Government new clause 47 and Government amendments Nos. 274, 272, 263, 269, 268, 264, 265, 273, 266, 270, 267 and 271.

Mr. Lang: New clauses 46 and 47 replace the existing section 3 in the Abolition of Domestic Rates Etc. (Scotland) Act 1987. Their purpose is to allow us to implement our recently announced policy of moving towards a common non-domestic rate poundage in Scotland. The other amendments in this grouping, including the changes in the grant provisions, are consequential.

The existing section 3 of the 1987 Act provides powers for the Secretary of State to prescribe the maximum annual increase in each local authority's non-domestic rate. The effect of the new clauses is to replace the existing section of the 1987 Act with two new provisions. The first is a transitional provision under which the Secretary of State will be able to prescribe each year the actual rather than the maximum non-domestic rate of each authority. Our intention is to use that power to move the different rate poundages gradually, over the transitional period, towards a common level.

Where the effect is to reduce an authority's rate income by comparison with what it would otherwise have been, the loss in rate income to that authority will be substantially compensated for by grant. By the end of the transitional period it is intended to reach a common rate poundage for all authorities, which will be at the same level as the English uniform business rate. Once that has been achieved, the second new provision will come into force, under which thereafter the Secretary of State will simply prescribe a uniform non-domestic rate each year for the whole of Scotland.

Mr. John Maxton (Glasgow, Cathcart): The Minister says that the uniform business rate will be prescribed by the Secretary of State for the whole of Scotland. Presumably it is prescribed for the whole United Kingdom.

Mr. Lang: No. I am referring to the rate that my right hon. and learned Friend the Secretary of State for Scotland will prescribe, which will be for the whole of Scotland. As our purpose is to achieve a level playing field throughout the United Kingdom, however, the hon. Gentleman is right to suspect that the figure is likely to be identical to that for England.

Amendments Nos. 272 and 274 simplify the provisions of schedule 4 to the 1987 Act, which concern grants distribution, to bring them into line with the new business rate policy and to ensure that grant can be distributed as required to compensate authorities which lose rate income as we move towards a uniform business rate.

The new business rate proposals deliver a commitment specifically announced by my right hon. and learned Friend last month, but we have said consistently for a long time now that we intend to sort out the long-recognised problem of the excessive rate burden on Scottish business. We have already made progress on harmonisation of valuation procedures north and south of the border. That has been a major exercise, the fruits of which will become clear with the 1990 revaluations. We are now completing the picture. Having announced our intentions on poundages on 8 May, we have wasted no time in presenting the proposed legislative changes so that we can begin to implement the new policy in the financial year 1990-91.

Our proposals have been widely welcomed—indeed, I think it would be fair to say that they have been universally welcomed—as proposals that will remedy the long-standing disadvantage under which the business community in Scotland labours. Their rates are too high compared with those of their competitors south of the border.

Mr. Malcolm Bruce (Gordon): Does the Minister expect the 1990 revaluation for businesses in Scotland to be as popular with the business community as the last revaluation?

Mr. Lang: I expect it to be even more popular.

Prominent among those who in recent months urged us to present some proposals was the Convention of Scottish Local Authorities, and it is fair to say that COSLA has also welcomed our announcement. It is a pity that it did not convert to that course sooner—its spending and its present rate poundages might not have been so high and its problem might have been much smaller—but a late conversion is better than none and we shall of course look to local authorities to make their modest contribution to the solution.

My officials and those of COSLA have recently gone over the proposals in some detail. That dialogue will continue between now and the time when—subject to the approval of Parliament—we begin to operate the new proposals with our announcement of the distribution of revenue support grant in the autumn.

With these new clauses and amendments we set in place the coping stone on the archway that we have been building, through which Scottish business can pass to a fairer business rates environment—to the proverbial level playing field that will enable it to operate on level rates terms with other businesses in the rest of the United Kingdom. The problem has developed over many years; the Government have tackled it, and we are now on our way to solving it.

Mr. Maxton: I am aware of the fact that at present there is more interest in rottweiler dogs than in the Scottish non-domestic rating system. When I was canvassing recently during the Glasgow, Central by-election I had the paw of a rottweiler dog put on a very tender part of my anatomy. If any hon. Member ever tries to canvass after having been hit there, he will always thereafter take some interest in rottweiler dogs.

This is an important issue for Scotland. It is an absolute disgrace and a contemptuous act by the Secretary of State for Scotland to put such an important clause at the tail end of the Bill. It will lead to an important change in Scotland's non-domestic rating system. It has been tagged on to a Bill that has nothing whatsoever to do with the subject; it deals largely with English matters. If the Secretary of State had been prepared to say to the Opposition in Scotland that the Government wanted to introduce a small Scottish Bill to deal with the matter, I am sure that he would have had a fair hearing. However, the Scottish Tories are running so scared that they are not prepared to legislate, if they can possibly avoid it, for Scotland by means of a Scottish Bill and to face up to Scottish Members of Parliament. The way in which the Secretary of State now handles Scottish affairs shows both his cowardice and his contempt of the House of Commons.

We welcome the change. I have reservations about the uniform business rate, but if there has to be such a rate, Scottish businesses must not be prejudiced or jeopardised. If the Scottish non-domestic rating system were to be left as it is while England and Wales had a uniform business rate, Scottish businesses would be in trouble with their competitors south of the border. We welcome the change, therefore, on those grounds and look forward to its implementation.

It has taken a lot of pressure from the Opposition, the business community, the Convention of Scottish Local Authorities and local authorities to get the Government to this stage. On 8 May the Secretary of State said that a substantial amount of the money that would be lost to local authorities—£250 million in the longer run—would be made up substantially by the Government in the form of new money. He went on to say that that would have to be found

"from the resources negotiated in the normal way each year for the Scottish expenditure programme . . . I will be assuming that local authorities will be willing to play their part by absorbing a small proportion through modest expenditure reductions or efficiency gains."

The Opposition, local authorities and COSLA want to know exactly what that small proportion is. What proportion of the £250 million will Scottish local authorities have to find?

This will not apply to all Scottish local authorities. If there is to be equalisation, those local authorities with higher non-domestic rate poundages will find that they are reduced, whereas those local authorities with lower domestic rate poundages will not lose revenue during the transitional period. Local authorities where there is the greatest need, because of social deprivation, unemployment and the need to stimulate the growth of industry in the area, will suffer. What proportion will local authorities have to find? If it is a large proportion, two things could happen. Either local authorities would have to cut services to the public, including the poorest people in society, or —this is perhaps more important—there would be an increase in the poll tax in those local authority areas.

We already find in Scotland that the poll tax levels and the poll tax itself are totally abhorrent. It would be absurd if the Government put pressure on local authorities to benefit Scottish business—we accept that it will do that —but poll tax payers, the poor in society, had to pick up the tab. We want a commitment that the Government will pay the whole of the £250 million in grant, preferably in new money, to the Scottish local authorities. That is the fair way to proceed and the way to ensure that the burden is borne not by the people of Scotland but by taxpayers throughout the United Kingdom.

We welcome this measure, but we also expect answers to my questions. I hope that the Minister can provide them.

9.45 pm

Mr. Tony Worthington (Clydebank and Milngavie): The Minister of State has brought a new dimension to the term "brass neck". Only after considerable pressure from all sections of society in Scotland have we been given in the Bill a proposal on the business rate. Unusually, I congratulate the CBI and the chambers of commerce as well as COSLA, the Scottish Trades Union Congress, all sections of society—[*Interruption.*]—and me—on the pressure that has been put on the Government to move some way towards solving this problem. I congratulate Mr. W. M. Mann, who has ceaselessly lobbied people throughout Scotland, pointing out the unfairness involved. I congratulate the *Glasgow Herald* as well on its campaign. The Government have claimed credit for their actions, but 11 months ago the Minister of State said that it was a question not of when but of if there would be equalisation. They cannot claim any credit.

We are talking about a level playing field throughout Europe in 1992, but the Government have found it impossible to allow Scotland to be put on a level playing field in respect of the United Kingdom. They got themselves into an extraordinary muddle. At one stage they said that it would be impossible to have equalisation of rates throughout Great Britain until two complete revaluations had occurred—the revaluation in 1990 and the one in 1995. People inferred, correctly, that there would not be harmonisation of the business rate until the turn of the century.

We remember all the fuss about the substantial piece of legislation to lay down the level of the poll tax. That is the most contentious issue in the Glasgow, Central by-election. That rate is only 21 per cent. of the income for Scottish local government, whereas this issue is concerned with 28 per cent. What have we had? We have had a statement by the Secretary of State for Scotland to an outside body, and this is the first time that we have had a chance to discuss it in the House.

It is extraordinary that the Government introduced the poll tax by arguing that local government caused the shut-down of local industry. They have not followed through their logic but have simply index-linked the local business rate. Using their logic, if business in one area has been treated unfairly, they have perpetuated that unfairness. Why did they do that in Scotland? It was because the Minister's own region would have suffered from the harmonisation of rates.

We have been told that there will be 90 per cent. harmonisation of rating practices in Scotland by 1990. Is it true, however, that some of the most difficult problems will remain? It has been asserted that licensed premises and hotels will be at a considerable disadvantage, with licensed premises paying two and a half times more and some hotels paying five times more in rates than is the case in England and Wales. How quickly will that sort of discrepancy disappear?

Following on from what my hon. Friend the Member for Glasgow, Cathcart (Mr. Maxton) said, I must tell the Minister that it is not good enough simply to say that there will be a contribution from local authorities without specifying the size of that contribution. If harmonisation of the business rate in Scotland is done without an almost total contribution from the Treasury through new money, it will be at the expense of the individual poll tax payer. We do not want to buy a pig in a poke. We want to know the dimensions of the settlement and how much local government will have to contribute.

Mr. James Wallace (Orkney and Shetland): The Government's new clauses are important and I do not agree with the Opposition that to introduce them at this stage is wrong per se. If something is good, the sooner that it is brought in the better. The Opposition's criticism is not strong.

Special provisions were introduced in the 1984 legislation to try to deal with the gross distortions between the Scottish and English valuations. The Government have tried to find some way by which Scottish business could be treated on an equal footing with English business, but it is fair to say that the expectations of the 1984 legislation have not been realised. Obviously some new means must be found.

Although the Government's proposal is generally welcome, I fear that in some important respects it will be at some cost to local government. For example, we should not overlook the reduction in scope for local accountability and decision-making. Although the statutory consultation with non-domestic ratepayers under the 1984 legislation has had mixed success, in my constituency local councillors were expected to account for their expenditure plans in some detail, perhaps in a way that was more successful than is usually the case at a local government election.

The proposal means removing from the determination of local government one of its sources of revenue that has some buoyancy. The only scope left for any local discretion and decision-making will be on the level of the poll tax, which is not a particularly buoyant tax. That will be a real loss for local government.

I want the Minister to consider the problems that will affect my constituency and rural Scotland generally. During questions last Wednesday, the Secretary of State said—and I welcome it—that he was still committed to special arrangements for Orkney and Scotland. He said that his officials would be in touch with local authorities in my constituency to work out the arrangements.

In my constituency, because of the oil terminals, the proportion of local revenue raised from non-domestic rates is high. Anything affecting that could have a considerable impact on local revenue. I welcome the fact that a pooling of Scottish non-domestic rates is not being proposed, but what has the Minister in mind for making special arrangements? He will be aware that for a number of years Shetland Islands council has tried to repay debts that were incurred to build the infrastructure to cope with the oil developments, so that when the through-put of oil

declined the rate burden on the terminals would be less. It is important that non-domestic ratepayers in Shetland, having paid an additional price to store up funds for a rainy day, are not deprived, when that rainy day comes, of an umbrella. I should welcome an assurance on that from the Minister.

It is clear that Government intend to reduce the rate poundage in Scotland to a level equivalent to that in England and Wales. It has been suggested that, throughout Scotland, rates will inevitably come down. The Government have made it clear that they will not fully compensate local authorities for a reduction in revenue, and one fears that any shortfall will have to be met by the poll tax payer.

Do the Government have figures showing which authorities in Scotland have a lower non-domestic rate poundage than the average for authorities in England and Wales? When the Secretary of State made his announcement, the director of finance for Grampian region said that it contained insufficient detail. He said:

"We have the lowest non-domestic rate in Scotland, so fundamentally, we will not get the same degree of benefit as elsewhere. There is also the possibility, depending upon the way the final plans work out, that we could be that little bit worse off."

Will the Minister give some figures so that we can work out what the likely effects of the Secretary of State's announcement will be? If some local authorities gain more than under the present arrangements, does the Scottish Office plan to dock that from revenue support grant? If so, it would further reduce local authorities' decision-making powers.

An attempt to put Scottish business on an equal footing with that in England and Wales is welcome. The Minister must be aware that, in rural areas, not least in my constituency, the Government's proposals may lead to problems, and that we are yet to be satisfied about them.

Mr. Malcolm Bruce: I want to intervene briefly and to follow my hon. Friend the Member for Orkney and Shetland (Mr. Wallace), who mentioned my area.

The Secretary of State proposes to fix a rate before we move to a uniform rate. Will the Minister explain how that will be done? In the present circumstances, the rate set would be different from authority to authority, but what criteria will be applied? Will the Secretary of State penalise authorities that have set low rates or those that have set high rates? Will he try to adjust the rate, possibly by taking money from Grampian and transferring it to Lothian or Strathclyde, as he has done under the poll tax? Given the way in which Grampian region has been clobbered, people in the region would like to know that we shall not be clobbered on the business rate.

What criteria will be applied to the income of local authorities? My hon. Friend the Member for Orkney and Shetland quoted the director of finance for Grampian region, which reflected the director's concern that Grampian may experience a reduction in rate. I suspect that other authorities may suffer further reductions, without having a firm idea where additional grant will come from and when it will be declared so that they can plan and budget ahead.

The third question relates to the implications of the second phase—the uniform business rate. The consequence of the uniform business rate is that there will, inevitably, be winners and losers. I am sure that the Minister will have been harangued on this as frequently as

[*Mr. Malcolm Bruce*]

I and my colleagues have been, especially by the National Federation of Self Employed and Small Businesses. The point that it made, and that I want to make, is that it seems that lower-rated businesses in rural areas, once we move to a uniform business rate, will inevitably be the losers. Will the Minister acknowledge that that is the case? If not, why not? If it is, what other measures does he propose to introduce to ensure that areas——

It being Ten o'clock, the debate stood adjourned.

BUSINESS OF THE HOUSE

Ordered,

That at this day's sitting, the Local Government and Housing Bill and the Police Officers (Central Service) Bill [*Lords*] may be proceeded with, though opposed, until any hour.—[*Mr. Chapman.*]

Local Government and Housing Bill

As amended (in the Standing Committee), again considered.

Mr. Bruce: I would like the Minister to explain clearly how the uniform business rate will apply. If it is likely to lead to losers in areas such as rural Grampian, the Borders and the Highlands and Islands, I hope that he will produce other measures to compensate for that. Those are important points. I am sure that the Minister is well aware that businesses in those areas are extremely concerned about the proposals and that the Government have so far failed to meet those concerns.

Mr. Archy Kirkwood (Roxburgh and Berwickshire): This is an important debate. I can see some quizzical looks coming from the Treasury Bench. I do not intend to speak for more than a few moments, but I want to continue with the point my hon. Friend the Member for Gordon (Mr. Bruce) raised. It is important that those of us who represent areas similar to the Minister's own are given a clear statement by him.

I detected a note of dissent from the Minister when my hon. Friend the Member for Gordon said that currently low-rated rural areas, such as his and my areas, will suffer from the introduction of the new system. I noticed the Minister strike a note of dissent by vigorously shaking his head. If he is of that view, I should be grateful if, when he brings this short debate to a conclusion, he would spell out why he thinks that we are wrong in taking that view.

I have talked widely to people in my own area of the Borders. They cannot see how they can be financially advantaged by the new system, which I appreciate and, for reasons I stated earlier, am prepared to support this evening. It is important that the Minister gives time to these technical matters. We are looking some distance into the future, so it is important that the Government take every opportunity to spell out the proposals.

I have some additional questions. If, in the course of the revaluations in 1990 and 1995, there are big shifts of the non-domestic rate burden between the categories, whether industrial, commercial, offices and shops or factories, that mean there are much heavier burdens on some sectors within those categories, will the Government consider bringing in some relief mechanism? They undertook to do so and I was in favour of the idea. Indeed, I suggested it in 1985, when the last revaluation took place. Will the Government at least keep that option open, as it appears that there are sectors that will be severely prejudiced when the time comes.

I may have missed this point earlier. I am not trying to be clever, but I thought that the Minister said casually that he thought that the two systems of rating and valuation had almost been reconciled. He seemed to be quite satisfied that that would produce no problems. I should be surprised if that were the case, and I should like to hear what evidence the Minister has. Is he prepared to publish the extent to which that reconciliation has been achieved?

There are significant differences between the English and Scottish systems. One is administered and implemented by the Inland Revenue and the other by rating and valuation offices. There is a wide gap there. Some of us fear that, if that reconciliation is not achieved harmoniously and properly and in a considered way, problems will result. Therefore, I hope that the Minister of State will take a moment or two to make sure that some of those real questions and worries are assuaged. I agree with the hon. Member for Clydebank and Milngavie (Mr. Worthington) that this is an important issue and I hope that some of the worries expressed in this short debate can be settled.

Mr. Lang: This has been a valuable debate and it is certainly a very important debate for Scotland. It is worthy of comment that the Scottish National party has not thought fit to be present on this important occasion.

I welcome the grudging support and acceptance for our proposals that has been given by the Labour party—although the hon. Member for Glasgow, Cathcart (Mr. Maxton) complained that we showed a lack of respect in bringing forward this measure at the tail end of this Bill. I suspect that he would like us to put it back for another year. The pretence that the Labour party supports this measure and that it has worked for such harmonisation over a period is absolute nonsense.

I took the opportunity to look up the *Hansard* of the Committee stage of the Abolition of Domestic Rates Etc. (Scotland) Act 1987. The hon. Member for Cathcart then stated:

> "There has been a swing of opinion among Scottish businesses. They increasingly appreciate that local government expenditure is one of their major sources of income. Cuts in rates and Government expenditure make as many businesses less viable and drive as many of them to the wall as increasing their rates does."—[*Official Report, First Scottish Standing Committee;* 20 January 1987, c. 438.]

That is the kind of out-of-touch, self-deceiving approach that the hon. Member for Cathcart demonstrated in that Committee. He said that reform was not needed and that it would not happen. We believe that it was needed, and we have made it happen.

The hon. Member for Cathcart has asked me about the amount of assistance from central Government. I made it clear earlier that the assistance will come substantially from the Government, but that we shall expect a modest contribution from the local authorities. Obviously, the details cannot be announced until the autumn. If I point out that in broad terms we are talking about £250 million as the estimated figure to achieve harmony over a period of five or six years and if I say that local authorities spend over £4·5 billion per year, the matter can easily be seen in perspective.

Mr. Maxton: That does not answer the question. Will the Minister say how much of that £250 million will come from the Exchequer, and how much will have to come from the local authorities?

Mr. Lang: I have already told the hon. Gentleman, both in my opening speech and just now, that the details of the apportionment will be announced in the autumn in the normal way. It would be quite wrong to announce that in advance——

Mr. Worthington *rose*——

Mr. Lang: No, I shall not give way.

I have said that the contribution requested from local authorities will be modest.

The hon. Member for Cathcart also asked me about the position of local authorities that have to make a substantial adjustment while others may be unaffected, because he expected that they would be below the common business rate that we are seeking to achieve. The hon. Member for Gordon also raised that point and asked about winners and losers. I expect that all local authorities will find that their rates are reduced as a result of this measure, with the exception of Orkney and Shetland which I would expect to be the only ones below the common rate.

In answer to the specific points about Orkney and Shetland, we have always recognised that a safety net and grant will have to continue to these islands for a long time. We recognise also their policy to repay debt by 1992. Their grant settlement for this year allowed for and recognised that. We intend to continue to take a sensitive approach to the special circumstances of Orkney and Shetland.

It is natural that, in the apportionment of the criteria that are applied to local authorities when adjusting—a point raised by the hon. Member for Gordon—the higher spenders will be expected to achieve the highest reductions. They are the ones with the most scope for saving, but they are also the ones that are likely to receive larger sums in assistance. Nobody can be in any doubt about the capacity for making modest savings who reflects that the Accounts Commission recently identified a possible saving of £20 million from the school janitor services alone.

I take exception to the claim by the hon. Member for Gordon that Grampian region has been clobbered for the benefit of Strathclyde in the revenue distribution grant for this year. Strathclyde's revenue grant increased by 7·3 per cent., while Grampian's increased by 14·6 per cent.—exactly double.

This is an important measure, which will be of considerable assistance to the business community in Scotland, which will certainly not have been taken in by Labour's protestations. The Labour party did nothing for the business community when it was in office, except through its local authority control, to pile up rate burdens upon it. We have found the solution to its problem. We have announced our plans for implementing it. We shall be bringing it in on the same time scale as the adjustment to the uniform business rate in England. I believe that it will be of considerable advantage to business in Scotland.

Question put and agreed to.

Clause read a Second time, and added to the Bill.

New Clause 47

SCOTTISH NON-DOMESTIC RATE

'(1) For section 3A of the Abolition of Domestic Rates Etc. (Scotland) Act 1987 there shall be substituted the following section—

"Unified non-domestic rate

3B.—(1) The Secretary of State shall, in respect of each of the financial years specified in subsection (2) below, prescribe a rate which shall be the non-domestic rate to be levied throughout Scotland in respect of that financial year.

(2) The financial years referred to in subsection (1) above are those beginning with the first financial year after the coming into force of section *[Scottish non-domestic rate]* of the Local Government and Housing Act 1989.

(3) Subject to subsection (4) below, the non-domestic rate shall be levied in accordance with section 7 of the Local Government (Scotland) Act 1975 by each rating authority in respect of lands and heritages in their area being lands and heritages—

(a) which are subjects (other than part residential subjects) in respect of which there is an entry in the valuation roll, accordingly to their rateable value; or

(b) which are part residential subjects, according to that part of their rateable value which is shown in the apportionment note as relating to the non residential use of those subjects.

(4) In the application of section 7 of the Local Government (Scotland) Act 1975 to the levying of the non-domestic rate prescribed under this section, for the words "to which the rate relates" in each of subsections (1) and (2) of that section there shall be substituted the words "of the rating authority".'.

(2) Accordingly—

(a) references (however expressed) in any enactment to the non-domestic rate determined by or prescribed in relation to a local authority under section 3 of the Abolition of Domestic Rates Etc. (Scotland) Act 1987 shall be construed as references to the non-domestic rate prescribed under section 3B of that Act;

(b) in section 109 of the Local Government (Scotland) Act 1973 rating authorities)—

(i) for paragraphs (a) and (b) of subsection (1) there shall be substituted the following paragraph—

"(a) in the case of the non-domestic rate prescribed under section 3B of the Abolition of Domestic Rates Etc. (Scotland) Act 1987, the regional council and the islands council; and

(ii) in subsection (2) for the words from "non-domestic district rate" onward there shall be substituted the words "information as may reasonably be required for the preparation of demand notes for the purposes of levying the non-domestic rate".

(3) For section 110 of the Local Government (Scotland) Act 1973 (payments by regional councils to district councils in respect of district rates) there shall be substituted the following section—

"*Division between regional and district councils*

110. The Secretary of State may by regulations provide as to the division among the regional council and the councils of the districts within the area of the regional council of the amount collected by way of the non-domestic rate in that area in respect of a financial year.".

(4) Section 111(1)(a), (b) and (d) of the Local Government (Scotland) Act 1973 (power to make regulations as to certain matters connected with non-domestic rates) shall cease to have effect.'.—[*Mr. Lang.*]

Brought up, read the First and Second time, and added to the Bill

New clause 51

RATE SUPPORT GRANT, 1985-86

"The Rate Support Grant Supplementary Report (England) (No. 4) 1985/86 (which was approved by a resolution of the House of Commons on 19th January 1989) shall have effect, and be deemed always to have had effect, as if, in Annex VI (principles for calculating grant-related poundages), for the formula set out in paragraph 4 (grant-related poundages for total expenditure at or above the threshold level) there were substituted—

"GRP = GRP at GRE + 0·69p × threshold amount

$$+0\cdot8625p \times \left(\frac{\text{total expenditure} - \text{GRE}}{\text{population}} - \text{threshold amount}\right) \text{".'}$$

—[*Mrs. Virginia Bottomley.*]

Brought up, read the First and Second time, and added to the Bill.

New clause 1

STANDARD COMMUNITY CHARGE MULTIPLIERS

'(1) In section 10 of the Abolition of Domestic Rates Etc. (Scotland) Act 1987, the following subsections shall be substituted for subsections (6) and (7)—

"(6) The standard community charge due to a local authority in respect of any financial year shall be the product of—

(a) the personal community charge; and

(b) the standard community charge multiplier,

determined in respect of that year by the local authority, provided that if the authority sees fit, different multipliers may be determined for properties of different specified classes.

(6A) A specified class is such class as may be specified in regulations made by the Secretary of State.

(6B) If the Secretary of State so requires by regulations, a multiplier for a specified class of property shall not exceed whichever of the following specifies in the regulations as regards the class, namely, 0, $\frac{1}{2}$, 1, $1\frac{1}{2}$ and 2.

(6C) A class may be specified by reference to such factors as the Secretary of State sees fit.

(6D) Without prejudice to the generality of subsection (6C) above, a class may be specified by reference to one or more of the following factors—

(a) the physical characteristics of properties

(b) the fact that properties are unoccupied or are occupied for prescribed purposes or by persons of prescribed descriptions;

(c) the circumstances of persons subject to standard community charges.

(6E) In determining the annual revenue support grant, the Secretary of State shall take into account the determination by each local authority of the multiplier for each specified class of property.

(7) In subsection (6) above the 'standard community charge multiplier,' means whichever of the following, namely 0, $\frac{1}{2}$, 1, $1\frac{1}{2}$ or 2, as the local authority which determines the personal community charge to which the multiplier is applied shall, before such date in each year as may be prescribed, determine.

2. (1) This section shall come into effect on the day following the passing of this Act.

(2) This section applies to Scotland only".'.—[*Mr. Wallace.*]

Brought up, and read the First time.

Mr. Wallace: I beg to move, That the clause be read a Second time.

Madam Deputy Speaker (Miss Betty Boothroyd): With this it will be convenient to take the following:

New clause 6—*Power of Sheriff to hear evidence in summary appeals under the Abolition of Domestic Rates Etc. (Scotland) Act 1987*—

'(1) After subsection (1) of section 29 of the 1987 Act, there shall be inserted the following subsection—

"(1A) In considering an appeal under this Act the sheriff may hear evidence by or on behalf of any party to the appeal

(1B) In this section the "1987 Act" means the Abolition of Domestic Rates Etc. (Scotland) Act 1987,"

(2) This section shall come into force on the day following the day on which it is passed, and shall extend to Scotland only.'.

New clause 44—*Women's refuges*—

'In section 11 of the Abolition of Domestic Rates Etc. (Scotland) Act 1987, the following subsection shall be added after subsection (2)—

"2A. This section does not apply to premises which are used wholly or mainly for the purpose of providing protected accommodation to women who are or have been threatened with or subjected to violence by their husbands or partners; which premises shall be subject to non domestic rates.".'.

New clause 50

CHARGES FOR SEWAGE SERVICES (SCOTLAND)

'(1) In Part II of Schedule 5 of the Abolition of Domestic Rates Etc. (Scotland) Act, 1987, the following paragraphs shall be inserted after paragraph 18:—

"(18A) A local authority shall separately identify that amount of the community charge which is attributable to the provision of sewage services, which amount shall be the same proportion of the total community charge, as the amount referred to in paragraph 18 above is of the total estimated expenses mentioned in section 9(2) of the Act.

(18B) The liability for personal community charge of any person solely or mainly resident at premises whose drains or private sewers are not connected with public sewers or public sewerage treatment work shall be reduced by a sum equal to one half of the amount of community charge which is identifiable as being attributable to the provision of sewerage services in accordance with paragraph (18A) above.

(18C) Liability for payment of a standard or collective community charge in respect of premises whose drains or private sewers are not connected with public sewers or public sewerage treatment works shall be reduced by an amount equal to the product of—

(a) the personal community charge less a sum equal to one half of the amount of community charge which is identified as being attributable to the provision of sewerage services in accordance with paragraph (18A) above; and

(b)

(i) in the case of premises subject to the standard community charge, the standard community charge multiplier or

(ii) in the case of premises subject to the collective community charge, the community charge multiplier.".'.

New clause 53

REBATE OF WATER CHARGES (SCOTLAND)

' . (1)—(1) The Secretary of State may by order make provision obliging a Scottish region or islands area (hereafter referred to as "a local authority") to grant rebates, of amounts determined as provided in the order in respect of the non-domestic water rate in respect of such financial year as is prescribed in the order, on lands and heritages which qualify under subsection (2) below for such rebate.

(2) The lands and heritages which qualify rebate are lands and heritages in respect of which the non-domestic water rate levied in the financial year are more than one and two thirds times the charge levied in respect of the supply of water to the lands and heritages in the previous financial year.

(3)(a) In subsections (1) and (2) above "the financial year" means the period of twelve months ending with 31st March 1990 or in any year thereafter.

(b) In subsection (2) above "the previous financial year" means the period of twelve months ending with 31st March 1989 or in any year thereafter.

(4) An order under this section may contain incidental and supplemental provisions.

(5) An order under this section can only be made by statutory instrument which shall not have effect until approved by resolution of the House of Commons.'.

Mr. Wallace: I noted that you, Madam Deputy Speaker, included new clause 53, which I believe is listed separately. However, with the consent of both sides, I will take it with the others.

I shall explain to hon. Members who are waiting for what I accept is an important debate on dog registration that this issue might take up some time, because there are a number of points all of which, I believe, even the Minister of State would accept are reasonably substantive.

I would say to those hon. Members from the Scottish National party and who have campaigned for non-payment of the poll tax that the right place to campaign for any changes to this monstrous and unjust system of local government finance is on the Floor of the House. That is why we bring forward these new clauses.

New clause 1 is intended to bring Scotland's poll tax rules for the standard community charge more in line with those that already exist in England and Wales. Clearly, many of us, especially those who represent rural areas, have received many representations about the level of the standard community charge in our constituencies. I, perhaps, am almost unique, because I expect that the Shetland island council is only one of the few councils which has not had a multiplier of two in applying the standard community charge.

Where there has been an amount of dissatisfaction is in those cases where people over the years have had handed down to them family homes and crofts which they have maintained or which they often use for weekend holidays. They are small houses, probably of little monetary value, but, nevertheless, the fact that they have been handed down from generation to generation means that they mean a lot to the families concerned.

Up to now, usually because of the location in remote island communities or in remote areas on the mainland, their rateable value has been relatively low and the amount paid in rates for those properties was very low indeed. Those properties are now landed with a standard community charge two times, in most cases, the personal community charge in any given area. Therefore, people who previously were perhaps paying less than £100 now have to pay more than £500 for the pleasure and for the genuine value that they attach to those homes. That has caused considerable aggravation and annoyance. These are not wealthy people who buy second homes in the country. The people hit are people who usually have modest means, and are now faced with the prospect of having to give up homes which they had gone to or occupied for many years. No doubt, in turn, those properties will be bought up by people to use as second homes who will make no long-term contribution to the community.

There are other anomalies too. In Scotland we are a year ahead of England and Wales and it is only in recent months that we have had to cope with the injustices and anomalies which the poll tax throws up. In some cases, people have taken in elderly relatives to live with them. I am sure that hon. Members on both sides of the House want to encourage the idea of ill or elderly people living with their families rather than being put into institutional care. Often elderly people are naturally reluctant to give up the homes they have long occupied, and in such cases they have been landed with a standard community charge at twice the given amount. A schizophrenic person in my constituency lives with his mother but refuses to give up his house on one of the remoter islands. No amount of rational explanation that it might be in his interests to do so will make him change his mind—and who is to quibble with a person who makes such a choice? He is landed now with a community charge much higher than the rates he had to pay before.

[*Mr. Wallace*]

10.15 pm

What about a person sentenced to prison whose co-habitee or wife no longer stays in the old family home and who has no income at all? His uninhabited home is subject to the standard community charge and he has no income with which to pay it.

Another great injustice is that people do not qualify in the same way for rebates of the standard community charge——

Mr. Worthington: Would the hon. Gentleman add to that list the sheer complexity now emerging on caravan sites, on which some people now pay poll tax and others continue to pay rates? Will he also add the complexities involved in the European Community ruling, which has brought in VAT on rents for the first time, and the fact that people now find that they must also pay an additional VAT levy on the rates they pay? This is all part of the confusion that seems to be spreading from the Scottish Office and the Department of the Environment, in which one hand does not know what the other is doing.

Mr. Wallace: I am grateful to the hon. Gentleman for making that point so eloquently. Within the past seven days I have come across a similar case to do with caravans in my constituency. The hon. Gentleman is right to highlight this confusion.

As I said, a number of anomalies have been thrown up, regarding both property and people. Scotland differs from England and Wales in that under the Scottish legislation the standard community charge must be between one and two times the personal community charge, whereas under section 40 of the Local Government Finance Act 1988, English and Welsh local authorities can apply a multiplier, or indeed a fraction, of zero, 0·5, 1, 1·5 or 2. Part of our new clause would put Scottish local authorities in a position similar to that of those in England and Wales. The other part would empower the Secretary of State to bring forward regulations which would specify the classes of property or persons for which local authorities could set different multipliers. That woud give local authorities the flexibility that is necessary if they are to administer an unjust tax with a lesser degree of injustice.

The Minister of State knows that my hon. Friend the Member for Argyll and Bute (Mrs. Michie) has corresponded copiously with him about this matter, yet he tries to maintain that Scotland is no different from England and Wales and that Scottish local authorities can still exercise considerable discretion about whether to apply a multiplier of one. Although that may be true of one or two cases, many Scottish local authorities have been obliged to set a multiplier of two in the knowledge that if they did not they would lose revenue, because they believe that the revenue support grant that they receive is dictated by the assumption that a multiplier of two will apply. If the Minister of State wishes to deny that that is the underlying assumption in the revenue support grant, I shall give way to him because that would be welcome news.

Mr. Lang: That is the underlying assumption, but it does not necessarily mean that all local authorities would have lost money if the assumption had been different. The assumption is used as a basis for the distribution of a fixed sum of money. Some local authorities on an assumption of a multiplier of one would have had more money and some would have had less.

Mr. Wallace: It is not even very late but arithmetically the Minister's intervention defeats me. He is saying that he takes into account that income is based on the assumption of a multiplier of two, but if there is a multiplier of one the income will be lower. He must explain this further when he replies to the debate. On any rational view there would be net losers. That element of discretion does not exist. [*Interruption.*]

Madam Deputy Speaker: Order. There are a number of conversations going on in the Chamber, which shows great discourtesy to the hon. Gentleman who is moving the new clause. I would be obliged if those who want to hold conversations would do so on the other side of the swing doors.

Mr. Wallace: Our new clause says:
"In determining the annual revenue support grant, the Secretary of State shall take into account the determination by each local authority of the multiplier for each specified class of property."
He will not make an assumption that everyone will go for the highest possible option.

New clause 6 seeks to clarify the powers of a sheriff to hear evidence in summary appeals under the poll tax legislation. I am sure that the Minister is well aware of the points that I intend to make, because we have corresponded about the new clause following a case in my constituency. I can make only brief reference to that case because I think that, technically, it is still subject to a possible appeal to the Court of Session. The sheriff found that he was unable to hear evidence on an appeal about the reasons why my constituent did not give information about the date of birth of his co-habitee. The sheriff took the view that legislation, in particular section 64(5) of the Civic Government (Scotland) Act 1982 and section 39(5) of the Licensing (Scotland) Act 1976, give specific power to the sheriff on summary appeal to hear evidence. The 1987 Act does not.

In that context there is also the opinion of the Lord President in the Court of Session in the case of Cigarro against the City of Glasgow licensing board. In that case the Lord President states:
"The proper starting point for ascertaining the precise limits of a sheriff's powers in dealing with an appeal which is disposed of as in a summary application is a statute which provides for the particular appeal to the sheriff, the statute which enables him to entertain and determine it."
For example, appeals to the sheriff may be made on the reasons for not providing certain information in the registration form. They can also arise in terms of a dispute about the location of a person's sole or main residence. I think that there is legal doubt about the matter and the new clause seeks to put the matter beyond doubt. It would enable those who wish to give evidence to explain why a course of action has been pursued or why they believe themselves to be resident in a specific area, to be allowed to give evidence before the sheriff. It does not in any way strike at the heart of the Government's community charge legislation and I hope that the Minister will be able to give a positive response.

New clause 44 seeks to exempt women's refuges from the scope of the collective community charge. I suspect that my hon. Friend the Member for Gordon (Mr. Bruce) will deal with that matter at great length if he catches your eye, Madam Deputy Speaker. Under the legislation, if a person leaves home the partner is liable for the poll tax. That means that under current legislation a person could be charged the poll tax twice.

Dame Elaine Kellett-Bowman (Lancaster): There is no poll tax.

Mr. Wallace: The hon. Member for Lancaster (Dame E. Kellett-Bowman) says that there is no poll tax.

Dame E. Kellett-Bowman: The hon. Gentleman should describe correctly the legislation passed by the House.

Mr. Wallace: Sellafield or Windscale, poll tax or community charge—it is all the same thing.

New clause 50 deals with charges for sewerage services in Scotland. Aggravation is felt by people who are not connected to the main sewerage but who are nevertheless assessed for full liability to the community charge, a position which is distinct from those who are not connected to a mains water system. In other words, if one is not connected to what is coming in, one does not have to pay the community charge water rate, but if one is not connected to what goes out, one is still fully liable for the charge. It is clear from my postbag that a number of people regard this as an injustice.

I accept the public health argument that as a community as a whole we benefit from the provision of a sewerage service. That is why the new clause does not seek to give a total exemption from any liability to make a contribution towards the provision in a community of sewerage services. It would simply reduce that contribution by 50 per cent.

I anticipate it being said that a similar case could be made for those who do not send their children to a local authority school or those who do not make use of the public library. I repeat that such a distinction is already made by the Government in respect of water charges. Also, when some years ago one of my constituents complained about having to pay for clearing septic tanks, the then Under-Secretary, Michael Ancram, said that while there was a point to the argument, in Scotland the fact that one was not connected to the main sewers could be taken into account by the assessor when determining the rateable value of the premises. With the introduction of the poll tax system, there is now no benefit to be accrued by those who are not connected to the main sewers, and the new clause tries to take account of that.

I regret that the structure of our debates is such that important matters such as this have to be debated late at night. The final point I must raise in dealing with this series of new clauses concerns particularly the business community in Grampian and Highland regions, where metered water charges have placed a considerable burden on local government. Our proposal is a stalking horse to enable us to raise that point, and I will leave my hon. Friend the Member for Gordon to deal with it in more detail.

In addition to non-domestic water rates, the whole issue of metered water charges must be considered. We have chosen an arbitrary figure. We have used the basis of rebates which were set out by the Government in their legislation which followed revaluation in 1985. We cannot, from the Opposition, put forward a provision that any

sums that a local authority is obliged to rebate should be reimbursed by central Government. The rules of the House preclude us from tabling such a provision.

We were anxious to raise the matter on the Floor of the House because the Minister of State is alleged to have said in an informal conversation with the Federation of Small Businesses that there were no legislative possibilities for him to do anything about a problem which hon. Members in all parts of the House accepts exists. We have, as we debate this measure, such a legislative opportunity. The wording of what we propose may be far from perfect, but if the Government wish seriously to address themselves to a problem that is harming the business community in the Grampian and Highland regions they could act now. This debate may prompt them to take that opportunity when the Bill is in another place.

10.30 pm

Mr. Malcolm Bruce: The hon. Member for Lancaster (Dame E. Kellett-Bowman) has told my hon. Friend the Member for Orkney and Shetland (Mr. Wallace) that there is no such thing as a poll tax. When the Government launched an advertising campaign in Scotland to tell people that they could pay the community charge by direct debit, their advertising agency found that nobody knew what the community charge was. The advertisement, paid for by the Government, therefore had to say,

"When you pay your community charge or poll tax, you can do it by direct debit."

Even the Government have been forced to acknowledge that we have a poll tax.

New clause 1 relates to the community charge on holiday homes or second homes, which has caused considerable problems in Scotland. Scotland was a guinea pig because the legislation implementing the poll tax in Scotland went through before that implementing the poll tax for England and Wales. An enormous number of anomalies have cropped up. As a result, the legislation for England and Wales is different from that for Scotland. It seems reasonable that the changes in criteria that it was thought would make the legislation for England and Wales fairer should be applied to Scotland and that is what we are trying to do.

I am not arguing against people who have holiday homes paying community charge on them. That seems reasonable although, as my hon. Friend the Member for Orkney and Shetland said, there are degrees of holiday homes. I have had exchanges with the Minister about the injustice in the fact that a Barrett's timeshare development qualifies for a non-domestic rate, but when a farmer lets out two of his cottages he has to pay double community charge on them, but in Scotland only. That is a monumental injustice and is contrary to the Government's intention to allow farmers and others who live in rural areas to diversify their income. It is a disincentive, and the Government have a duty to ensure that it is put right.

Some tenant farmers have either inherited or bought a croft or cottage for their retirement. One would have thought that the Conservative party would be in favour of people in tied accommodation having somewhere of their own to retire to, but such people are having to pay double poll tax—once on the farmhouse in which they live as a tenant farmer and once on their retirement cottage. Often, such a household would have been paying nothing in rates,

[*Mr. Malcolm Bruce*]

but now has to pay £1,200 to £1,400 out of untaxed income. Is it any wonder that the Tory party is losing support in rural areas?

Mr. Lang: What about your constituency?

Mr. Bruce: I have no qualms. I have just been round my constituency and I did not find many people saying that they would vote for the Tories.

New clause 44 deals with the way in which women's refuges are treated. I have had correspondence with the Minister about this and am waiting for a reply from him. The women's refuges which operate in Aberdeen have been in touch with me, and one operates in my constituency. These provide secure refuges to which women can retreat when they have been battered by their husbands or partners. It is regrettable that this happens —it always has—but it is a positive development that there are now organisations willing to set up and run such refuges, always as charities which rely on voluntary raising of funds.

Until now, such refuges have been treated as hospitals and rated accordingly. Now the Government are saying that they have to be treated as a multiple-occupancy dwelling in which every individual has to pay poll tax. That presents severe practical problems. The women entering those refuges do so at short notice, and may remain there for a very short time or for a longer period. On arrival they are in an emotionally and physically stressed condition. Organisations whose prime objective is to provide such women with support are not in a position to hammer them for money. Yet the Government are saying that that is what refuges must do.

That is an unsympathetic attitude which underestimates the difficulties facing those organisations and the additional stress placed on the women concerned. Worse still, those women will have left homes where they are jointly and severally liable to pay poll tax along with their husbands or partners. The husband or partner may already have paid the woman's share of poll tax and will remain liable to pay it. The Government are in effect pressing for additional revenue by taxing individuals who are already in an extremely distraught and emotional state.

If that is the kind of treatment that the Government want to mete out, it is no wonder that they are seen as heartless philistines—which, in the circumstances that I have described, they are. The number of women involved is relatively small and the circumstances extremely stressful, but still the Government aim to collect double tax. The Minister must make a response which both shows compassion and answers the question of whether women in such circumstances should be pressed to pay the poll tax twice.

My final point relates to new clause 53, which concerns non-domestic water rates, including the general standard and metered rates. I raised that matter in an Adjournment debate, and it has been the subject of considerable correspondence with the Minister. We believe that the Bill presents an opportunity for a legislative change which would ensure that companies currently confronted with draconian increases threatening not only their profitability but in some cases their viability may know that there is a limit to the rates that they will be expected to pay.

The Government may say that they disapprove of such a measure, but they introduced similar legislation at the time of the last property revaluation in Scotland. There was a massive revolt among Conservative supporters in the business community about the revaluation's implications and the extra charges that it would impose.

On that occasion emergency legislation was rushed through the House, with all-party support, to limit the amount of the increase that any business would have to absorb. The purpose of the proposed new clause is to provide similar protection for businesses faced with the same prospect as a consequence of the poll tax or community charge.

I was told by Grampian regional council today that it is very concerned about the implications of the charge. It has taken positive helpful measures, including a series of meetings with businesses at which it sought to offer advice on increasing the efficiency of water operations with a view to reducing waste. The council issued 38 information packs, offered consultancy advice to nine companies, and received one application for grant assistance. That shows a constructive attitude and a positive response.

I hope that the Minister accepts that a 109 per cent. increase in water charges still represents a severe burden. He acknowledges that the scope for manoeuvre was limited and that Grampian complied with the law. The increase in the Highland region was 72 per cent. and in Midlothian and Strathclyde it was 64 to 66 per cent. That sort of increase is a serious burden on companies. So far, the Government's ability to deal with the problem has given no satisfaction. Essentially, they have said, "That is the law. Grampian have interpreted it in one way. It is open to a different interpretation, but on balance that is right because that is what they have to do and the businesses will just have to lump it." Businesses should not have to expect such treatment. Given the Government's previous new clause 47 about the fixing of the new uniform business rate, it goes against the grain that they feel unable to intervene and help in this case.

Given the treatment that has been meted out and the hardship that has been imposed on businesses in the Grampian region, the Minister must understand that there is little willingness to believe that what the Government propose in the form of their new rates measures for businesses will be beneficial. In a previous debate I raised the concerns in the Grampian region, but the Minister did not answer my questions. What we are proposing today shows, as my hon. Friend the Member for Orkney and Shetland said, that we who believe in parliamentary democracy are putting the amendments in the right place —the House of Commons. The Scottish National party Members are conspicuous by their absence. They rarely appear in the House, but stalk the country talking about illegal action, confrontation and extra-parliamentary action. At the end of the day, however, they achieve nothing but failure.

We come here in a constructive spirit to put the arguments to the Government, reflecting the clear representations which have been made to us on behalf of business, and asking for a constructive response. The points that have been raised deserve a serious and, I hope, sympathetic reply from the Minister.

Mr. Lang: I shall certainly respond to the points that have been raised in the debate, which has covered five entirely unrelated subjects. Opposition Members cannot, therefore, be blamed for taking slightly longer than expected. I know that the House wishes to make progress and so I shall stick closely to the amendments which have been tabled.

On new clause 1, the hon. Member for Orkney and Shetland (Mr. Wallace) spoke mainly about the decision of all Scottish local authorities, except Western Isles and Shetland, to choose to impose a multiplier of two, twice as high as they need have done. However, the intention of his new clause is to bring Scotland in line with England and Wales with regard to the standing community charge arrangements, particularly for setting standard community charge multipliers.

However, the new clause is based on a misconception that there are significant differences between the position north and south of the border and that the English and Welsh arrangements are more flexible. That is not so as I shall seek to explain. There are some technical differences between setting the standard charge in Scotland, and doing so in England and Wales. The key point is that in all three countries local authorities have discretion to set the multiplier up to a maximum of twice the community charge for their area.

In Scotland, local authorities' discretion starts at a multiplier of one. They can set a standard community charge multiplier at any point between one and two times the level of the personal community charge, and the multiplier which is determined will apply to any property which may be liable for the standard community charge in a local authority area.

Authorities in England and Wales will be able, subject to certain restrictions, to set multipliers at one of five different specific levels: nought, a half, one, one and a half or two. However, the range of properties liable for the standard charge is smaller in Scotland than in England and Wales. That is because certain Scottish properties do not attract the charge, either by virtue of a specific exemption, such as homes of people who go into hospital on a long-term basis, or by virtue of being retained in rating, for example properties which are not suitable for occupation throughout the year. Equivalent properties in England and Wales will be liable for the standard charge but maximum multipliers will be imposed on them by regulations, for example, nought for the homes of long-term hospital patients and one for planning properties of which the planning conditions do not permit them to be occupied throughout the year.

Mr. Malcolm Bruce: My understanding is that, provided there is no closing order on them, properties which are not occupied throughout the year are levied for the full standard community charge. That is certainly true in my constituency. Is the Minister saying that that is not right?

Mr. Lang: It is not for me to question the decision of the community charge registration officer, but these are matters for appeal if they come into contention.

While the English and Welsh arrangements allow for different multipliers for different classes of property, it is important to realise that the different classes of property are closely defined and that there is no discretion for a local authority to determine its own classes of property for which it will set different multipliers.

In broad terms, the properties in respect of which the English and Welsh local authorities will be able to exercise discretion to set a multiplier of up to two will be comparable to those properties in Scotland, which will be liable for the standard community charge.

I should make it clear that English local authorities have still to determine what multipliers to set on second homes. It is not possible, therefore, to compare outcomes between Scotland and England. If there are differences between Scotland and England in the way in which people are treated in practice, that is more likely to be because local authorities in each country have chosen to use the discretion that is available to them differently rather than because of technical differences in the arrangements for setting the standard charge. This could arise if English authorities decided to set the multiplier at less than the maximum of two, which has been adopted by virtually all Scottish local authorities. In these circumstances I do not consider the new clause to be necessary or desirable.

10.45 pm

New clause 6, which was spoken to by the hon. Member for Orkney and Shetland (Mr. Wallace), relates to a specific interest on which he has expressed concern in the past, which is whether evidence can be heard at community charge appeals before the sheriff. We have given detailed consideration to the hon. Gentleman's proposals. I have already made it clear to him in correspondence that I consider his proposals unnecessary because under summary application procedures, under which community charge appeals are heard, the sheriff can effectively act as he thinks appropriate. The hon. Gentleman will be aware of our concern not to prejudice this general position. We are obviously concerned, however, that there should be no possible doubt that evidence can be heard. In the light of the particular case which has aroused the present concern, I would propose to consider whether we should introduce an amendment in another place along the lines of new clause 6, but making it clear that the power would be without prejudice to the generality of summary application procedures as provided for in the Sheriff Courts Act 1907. On the basis of that undertaking, I hope that the hon. Gentleman will not press his new clause.

New clause 50 relates to sewerage. I listened carefully to the arguments which were advanced but I am not persuaded that payment towards domestic sewerage is any different from payment for other services which are included within the community charge. There are not enough reductions for those who have to maintain private roads, or who do not make use of the education system or who may not have access to a public library. There are many other examples. To concede that special arrangements should be made for sewerage would lead to a proliferation of requests for relief from payment towards services which are not provided or utilised. It would make the community charge register more complex and would introduce additional administrative costs.

Mr. Wallace: I anticipated that the Minister would refer to private roads and public libraries, but surely sewerage provision is most comparable to water supply. The Government have made a distinction between those whose properties are connected to mains water and those whose properties are not. Why make that distinction in respect of what comes in but not in respect of what comes out?

Mr. Lang: That is partly because it was our purpose in making changes to the community charge under the common business rate to minimise the disruption to the existing system. In the past there have been separate arrangements for water, which we have carried forward under a new guise. There were no formal arrangements of that sort for the reasons that I have described.

The hon. Member for Gordon (Mr. Bruce) spoke about women's refuges when he directed himself to new clause 44. I thought that his remarks were wholly intemperate and inappropriate on a matter on which we have shown great concern. We have received a number of representations from Women's Aid about the designation of women's refuges as collective community charge establishments, and the present arrangements were introduced to meet the requirements of Women's Aid. However, we have decided to act upon its subsequent representations and to introduce regulations that will have the effect of moving the refuges back into rating. Officials from my Department met representatives of Women's Aid last week to discuss these proposals. I hope to be in a position to lay regulations before the House quite soon. I think that the hon. Gentleman's remarks were entirely misplaced because we have responded not once but twice, and comprehensively, to the attitude of Women's Aid.

New clause 53 is directed to the non-domestic water rate. Occasionally an amendment or new clause misses the bull's eye, but new clause 53 misses the target altogether. The source of the complaint is the impact of metered water charges. Other water charges, to which the new clause relates, have not increased in the Grampian region. The fact is that they have decreased. Non-metered water charges were 8·16p in the pound last year and they are now 7p in the pound.

The new clause has been tabled on the assumption that non-domestic water ratepayers need some relief, but the hon. Gentleman has failed to take account of the fact that in only two regions do non-domestic water rates amount to more than one and two thirds times last year's domestic water rate, which then applied also to the non-domestic sector. Last year, both regions levied a public water rate which we have now abolished.

If that were taken into account, the increases in those regions would be nowhere near the two thirds limit that the hon. Gentleman seeks to invoke. The new clause is misconceived. It would breach the fairness provisions that we were at pains to introduce in the Abolition of Domestic Rates Etc. Act. Any concessions would have to be paid for by other water users and would introduce additional administrative costs. For those reasons, I cannot accept the new clause.

Mr. Wallace: I am grateful to the Minister for his reply, even though it was fairly short, for understandable reasons.

His reply to new clause 1 was wholly unconvincing. The relevant legislation shows that there are clear differences between Scotland and England. They are not on a par. England can have a multiplier of less than one, but Scotland cannot. The Minister completely failed to respond to the points that were made about holiday cottages and prisoners. The Government have missed an opportunity to rectify some of the injustices in the implementation of the community charge.

As for sewerage, the Minister failed to convince us that water should be treated differently from sewerage. Schedule 5 to the 1987 Act shows that, unlike libraries or private roads, a local authority is obliged to calculate separately its sewerage costs and apportion them between different categories of payers. Sewerage is dealt with in that Act in a way that makes it different from the other services. The Minister's reply—that the charge will not be reduced for supplies to those who are not connected to the main sewerage system—lacked conviction. It is a matter to which we shall return.

As for water charges, if the Minister had listened to what was said he would have realised that we appreciate that the new clause is not drafted as well as it might be. We referred to meter charges. I am always suspicious when Ministers say that the defect lies in the drafting of Opposition amendments. He did not address the issue. The Minister told the business community that there was no legislative opportunity to do anything about this problem. We have proved that he was wrong. He has failed to take that opportunity. I hope that it will be dealt with in another place.

I thank the Minister for having gone some way towards meeting two other points that we raised. I heard what he said about appeals. I welcome the fact that he is giving some thought to the matter and that he intends to ensure that an amendment is tabled in another place to make clear what are the sheriff's powers, while not compromising other legislation.

I welcome also his announcement about women's refuges. It underlines the point that I made at the outset. Those of us who complain about the poll tax and who believe in parliamentary democracy feel that we must make our arguments in this place. There has been some response from the Government tonight, which shows that those who have neither attended nor contributed to the debate and who only bluster have failed the people of Scotland. It is the Social and Liberal Democrats who stand up and tackle the poll tax in the one way that can be effective.

Question put and negatived.

New Clause 13

INDIVIDUAL PRIVACY

'Schedule (Preservation of individual privacy) to this Act (which amends the Local Government Finance Act 1988 and the Abolition of Domestic Rates Etc. (Scotland) Act 1987) shall have effect.'—*[Mr. Cohen.]*

Brought up, and read the First time.

Mr. Harry Cohen (Leyton): I beg to move, That the clause be read a Second time.

Madam Deputy Speaker: With this it will be convenient to discuss amendment No. 7:

'PRESERVATION OF INDIVIDUAL PRIVACY

1. The Local Government Finance Act 1988 and the Abolition of Domestic Rates Etc. (Scotland) Act 1987 shall be amended as mentioned in the following provisions of this Schedule.

2. For the purpose of the Abolition of Domestic Rates Etc. (Scotland) Act 1987 and the Local Government Finance Act 1988, section 26(3) of the Data Protection Act 1984 and Schedule 1, Part II, paragraph 1(2) of the Data Protection Act 1984 (Interpretation of the First Data Protection Principal) shall apply.

3. In Section 20(2)(a) of the Abolition of Domestic Rates Etc. (Scotland) Act 1987 the words "only for a purpose associated with the proper maintenance of a community charge" shall be inserted after the word "inspect".

4. In Schedule 2, at the end of section 17(2) (Inspection etc.) of the Local Government Finance Act 1988, the words "only for a purpose associated with the proper maintenance of a community charge" shall be inserted.

5. Information concerning an individual who is subject to a community charge can only be disclosed by a registration officer or charging authority either:
   (a) with the consent of that individual, or
   (b) to another registration officer or charging authority for a purpose associated with the proper maintenance of a community charge.

6. It shall be an offence for any individual or organisation to hold or process personal data, as defined by the Data Protection Act 1984, that are wholly or in part obtained directly or indirectly from more than one community charges register, except where
   (a) two different charging authorities or registration officers hold personal data for the purpose of the management of community charge when an individual changes his address and becomes subject to a community charge in one of the authorities, or
   (b) an individual is subject to more than one community charge, or
   (c) the individual who is liable to pay a community charge, has consented to the holding or processing of his personal data.

7. Information relating to the date of birth of individuals liable to pay a community charge may only be retained by a registration officer or charging authority if:
   (a) there is more than one individual liable to pay a community charge resident at a specific address, and
   (b) the resident individuals have the same surname and initials, and
   (c) there is no other simple means of identifying the resident individuals.

8. Sections 13, 14 and 15 of Schedule 2 of the Local Government Finance Act 1988 are repealed.

9. Where a department of a charging authority or precepting authority is requested to provide information concerning an individual to a registration officer, the department may refuse that request if the department has reasonable cause to believe that the request for information:
   (a) may cause serious degradation of a service provided by the department to that individual, or
   (b) is unreasonable in terms of the cost to provide the information, or
   (c) will breach an obligation to meet a duty of confidentiality.

10. Section 20(2)(c) of the Abolition of Domestic Rates Etc. (Scotland) Act 1987, and section 29 of the Local Government Finance Act 1988 shall be replaced by:
   "An electoral registration officer shall not sell the electoral register for purposes not associated with the election process if the officer uses any community charges register as a means of improving the accuracy of the electoral register".'.

Mr. Cohen: I shall be brief because hon. Members wish to consider the dog registration scheme, which I support. The amendment is similar to my Poll Tax (Registration of Individual Privacy) Bill which appears at column 162 of *Hansard* on 14 February 1989. I shall not repeat the arguments. The poll tax has a commercial exploitation and police state potential. It presents opportunities for enormous abuse of individual privacy. Until now the Government have handled this aspect very poorly and adopted a couldn't-care-less attitude.

A farrago of misinformation and half-truths has been given to the public, and inadequate and inappropriate information has been given to local authorities by the Government, partly because they have not worked out the details properly. This is causing considerable and increasing consternation to the public. My measures restrict the collection and use of personal information by the community registration officer and the charging authority to purposes associated with the poll tax. This means that the information cannot be passed on for use for junk mail, determining credit ratings or vetting. My measures apply also to the principles and procedures of the Data Protection Act 1984 as they affect the collection and use of poll tax personal information.

There have been some odd questions on the registration forms that have been sent out in the past few weeks. Trafford has asked about the relationship of everyone in the household. Is that ultra vires? Hounslow and Solihull councils have asked who owns the furniture and where it is kept. Is that ultra vires? Croydon council has said that the local authority may use information for other "registered" purposes. That is not right. On 23 February, in an answer to me, the Minister for Local Government said:

"Community charges registration officers and charging authorities have no power to disclose data contained in registers to any third party other than those specified in the Local Government Finance Act 1988 and regulations to be made under it."—*[Official Report, 23 February 1989; Vol. 147, c. 732.]*

That message has not got through to Croydon or, presumably, other local authorities. Will the Minister confirm that the information must not be used other than by community charge registration officers and the charging authority or for any purpose other than the community charge? Will he confirm also that the information must not be used internally by a local authority for any purpose other than the community charge? The Minister must give an unequivocal assurance. Will he confirm that Croydon council is acting ultra vires?

Privacy rights are being seriously eroded by the poll tax. The likelihood that the abuse will worsen is a menace to hundreds of thousands of innocent citizens. It is better that the Government should adopt the protective privacy measures in my amendment and new clause.

The Minister for Local Government (Mr. John Selwyn Gummer): I am happy to confirm my answer to the hon. Gentleman that the information which is requested for the purposes of the community charge may not be used for

[*Mr. John Selwyn Gummer*]

other purposes. We have been particularly concerned to protect people's rights. As the hon. Gentleman knows, a person who fears that he or she may be in some danger can even have his name removed from the list so that it is not available. It can only be shown; it cannot be copied or written down. An individual will, of course, see his or her own details on the list to ensure that it is accurate. The hon. Gentleman need have none of the worries that he has expressed. The law is very particular in the protection that it gives people and it gives community charge officers a restricted ability to gain information. They can gain only specific pieces of information—name and address being two, and age, when that is material to a person coming on to the community charge list at 18.

This is not the time of night to raise a controversial matter, but I hope that the hon. Gentleman will look at his proposals and apply them to the Labour party's proposals to have two taxes, one of which would mean that local income tax information would have to be held in every town hall—which is an incursion into people's freedoms and rights. It would be interesting to see whether people in Leyton appreciate the idea that details of their pay slips and such would have to be held. I wonder whether the hon. Gentleman would like to apply his mind to that. Information on the ownership and value of everybody's home would have to be held also.

Dame Elaine Kellett-Bowman: Will my right hon. Friend confirm that under the Labour proposals one would pay the tax even on a tenanted property that one did not own? [*Interruption.*]

Mr. Gummer: My hon. Friend should not be led astray by the hon. Member for Birmingham, Perry Barr (Mr. Rooker), who rarely speaks other than from a sedentary position. I fear that my hon. Friend is perfectly right in what she says. The tenant would pay on the freehold value of his house, even though he would not gain any benefit from it.

11 pm

Whereas the regulations under the community charge are tightly drawn and present no threat to civil liberty, I could not say the same about the two-tax system that the Labour party is putting forward and which the hon. Member for Leyton (Mr. Cohen) supports— [*Interruption.*] If Opposition Members do not understand that, they should ask to see the letters which show the distinction between the two systems. I think that the country understands.

I hope that the hon. Member for Leyton will now accept that his worries are unfounded and that there is no need for his new clause.

Mr. Cohen: I do not accept what the Minister has said because both a system of rates and a system of income tax are currently in operation. I do not agree that privacy would be more adversely affected. I have already referred to my ten-minute Bill, in which I set out a whole series of invasions of privacy—such as women being hassled under the cohabitation rules. The proof will be in the eating and the Minister will face the consequences.

In the interests of time, I beg to ask leave to withdraw the motion.

Motion and clause, by leave, withdrawn.

New Clause 16

HABITATION (STANDARD)

' .—(1) A local authority may draw up a scheme for the improvement of housing conditions in its area.

(2) Such a scheme may contain reference to a standard (to be known as "The Habitation Standard") to which all dwellings should conform.

(3) The standard referred to in subsection (2) above shall include, but not be restricted to the provisions of Section 604 of the Housing Act 1985.

(4) The standard referred to in subsection (2) above may include the following matters:

(a) any dwelling should be free from substantial or significant disrepair (including electrical, gas and water supply facilities);

(b) any dwelling should be substantially free from damp and not prone to condensation;

(c) any dwelling should have adequate natural and artificial lighting and ventilation in all rooms in circulation areas;

(d) any dwelling shall have adequate space heating;

(e) any dwelling should have an adequate supply of wholesome water within the house;

(f) any dwelling should have within it satisfactory facilities for the preparation and cooking of food, including a sink with a supply of hot and cold water;

(g) any dwelling shall have a wc for the use of the occupants, suitably located within the dwelling;

(h) any dwelling shall have a suitably located fixed bath of shower provided with a satisfactory supply of hot and cold water;

(i) any dwelling shall have a suitably located wash hand basin with an adequate supply of hot and cold water;

(j) any dwelling shall have an effective system for the drainage and disposal of foul, waste and surface water;

(k) any dwelling shall be so arranged internally as to ensure the safety of the occupants;

(l) any dwelling shall have satisfactory thermal insulation, and an adequate overall energy performance;

(m) any dwelling shall have satisfactory sound insulation;

(n) any dwelling shall be free from progressive instability;

(o) any dwelling shall, wherever practicable, have a safe electrical supply and installation;

(p) any dwelling shall be so located that the immediate environmental factors are tolerable;

(q) the habitable rooms of any dwelling shall comprise a minimum size as specified by the Secretary of State for the Environment;

(r) any dwelling shall be free from noxious or hazardous substances.

(5) Before taking action in pursuance of a scheme drawn up under subsection (1) above, the local authority shall seek the consent of the Secretary of State which shall not be unreasonably withheld.'.—[*Mr. Battle.*]

Brought up, and read the First time.

Mr. John Battle (Leeds, West): I beg to move, That the clause be read a Second time.

Parts V, VI, VII and VIII of the Bill refer to housing. If at this late stage of the evening we began to discuss the issue of minimum standards, it might be crowded out of the agenda and not receive a decent debate. I shall not pursue the matter now, but will return to it on Third Reading.

I beg to ask leave to withdraw the motion.

Motion and clause, by leave, withdrawn.

New Clause 22

ENDING OF AUTOMATIC RIGHT OF CERTAIN FUTURE SHARED OWNERS IN RURAL AREAS TO ACQUIRE THE FREEHOLD

Part V of the Housing Act 1985 (the Right to Buy) shall be amended by the inclusion of the following section after Section 153:

"153A—(1) A secure tenant shall not be entitled to exercise the Right to Buy under this Part in respect of a dwelling house in a rural area if he enters into a shared ownership lease of that dwelling house after the 30th June 1989 unless he was a tenant of such house before the shared ownership lease was entered into.

(2) No condition shall be attached by the Secretary of State to the payment of subsidy to a housing association or local housing authority, or to the disposal of land by a local housing authority, which would require such association or authority to grant shared owners a right to acquire the freehold.

(3) For the purposes of this section a rural area means—

  (a) a national park;
  (b) an area designated under section 87 of the National Parks and Access to the Countryside Act 1949 as an area of outstanding natural beauty; or
  (c) an area designated by order of the Secretary of State as a rural area under section 157.".'.—*[Mr. Jopling.]*

Brought up, and read the First time.

Mr. Michael Jopling (Westmorland and Lonsdale): I beg to move, That the clause be read a Second time.

Madam Deputy Speaker (Miss Betty Boothroyd): With this we shall discuss the following amendments to the new clause: (a), in line 1, leave out 'Part V' and insert 'Part II'.

(b), in line 1, leave out '(the Right to Buy)' and insert '(Provision of Housing Accommodation)'.

(c), in line 2, leave out 'Section 153' and insert 'Section 32'.

(d), in line 3, leave out '153A' and insert '32A'.

(e), in line 3, leave out subsection (1).

(f), in line 7, leave out '(2)' and insert '(1) In a rural area'.

(g), in line 9, after 'land', insert 'by a housing association or'.

(h), in line 10, leave out 'the freehold' and insert 'more than a 62½ per cent. share'.

Mr. Jopling: For a long time many hon. Members, especially those who represent rural areas, have felt that more needed to be done to provide greater opportunities for local people to continue to live and work in the rural areas where they were born and brought up. I am not alone in hearing the pleas of my constituents and people throughout Britain's rural areas who are much too frequently priced out by those seeking second or holiday homes. That prevents people from staying in the areas where they have been born and brought up. The House will not be surprised to hear that that is a particular problem in the Lake district, which falls within my constituency, and the same problem can be found in all rural areas.

It is necessary to take new initiatives to make housing in rural areas more easily available to local people.

Dame Elaine Kellett-Bowman: Is there not a substantial effect on schools in rural areas? If properties are purchased for second or holiday homes, there are fewer children to attend those schools, and they might have to close.

Mr. Jopling: My hon. Friend, as usual, is right, but I should get into trouble with you, Madam Deputy Speaker, if I allowed myself to be diverted by her understandable anxieties, which I share, about rural schools.

Last year, I moved a new clause to the Housing Bill, which the Government, in their wisdom, accepted. I believe that it has gone some way to helping local people in rural areas to live where they were born and brought up. This year, I moved new clause 22 on the advice, partly, of the Association of District Councils and the National Federation of Housing Associations. Both bodies strongly feel that it is necessary to change the Bill to embrace the provisions of new clause 22.

I am extremely grateful to the many Conservative Members who have been kind enough to sign my new clause—seven new names were added to it this morning —and a number of others, who have told me that they support it although they have not signed it. I have a wad of copy letters that have been written by various district councils throughout the country to me or my hon. Friends asking us to support the new clause.

Mr. Battle: If the Government do not concede the points that the right hon. Gentleman is making, will he confirm that he will be prepared to press the new clause to a vote?

Mr. Jopling: The hon. Gentleman must allow me to make my own speech. I fully expect the Government to see the sense of my argument. If he had looked at the Order Paper over the past few weeks, he would be aware that enough Conservative Members have supported the new clause to put the fear of God into the Government Chief Whip.

The purpose of the new clause is to create, and, much more important, to maintain, a permanent stock of houses in rural areas for those who are not sufficiently well off to buy more than a share in a house as a first step towards full house ownership. All hon. Members are aware of constituents to whom we have said, "Why don't you buy a house?" only for them to say, "We can't afford to do so." However, they could afford to buy a half share. At present, the law says that people can buy a share in a house—say, 50 per cent.—and then staircase their way up to 100 per cent. Of course that is good, but the downside is that the house is lost for future part owners to take the first step on the lower rungs of the ladder, which is so important in the move to full ownership.

I received a letter within the past few days from an organisation called North Housing, which is signed by Mr. John Sutcliffe, whom many of my colleagues will recall as an hon. Member in the early 1970s. It is interesting to note that the address of North Housing is Ridley house in Newcastle, and I understand that the organisation North Housing was set up by the family of the Secretary of State for the Environment years ago. The letter says:

"It clearly shows that over time, the ethos of shared ownership is being seriously undermined if second and subsequent purchasers are unable to be helped in the same way as first purchasers."

That is a familiar theme that I have heard from the organisations which are so keen on new clause 22.

New clause 22 allows part ownership to rise to a maximum of 62·5 per cent., which is the figure proposed in the amendments tabled by my hon. Friend the Member for Devizes (Sir C. Morrison). I have collaborated with him in those amendments, which I fully support and accept. They

[*Mr. Jopling*]

were drawn up on the recommendation of the organisations which have proposed these measures. The figure of 62·5 per cent. is not sacrosanct, because it is open to discussion. It means that, once the part owner has reached 62·5 per cent. of ownership of the house, he then has two options. He can sit pat and accept that he will never own 100 per cent. of the house. If he is content to continue to own only 62·5 per cent., as we propose, he could do so for as long as he wanted.

The second option is that he could move out of the house, and put the 62·5 per cent. of the value of the house, which is his nest egg, enhanced as it probably would be by the increased value of the house during the time that he had been paying it off, into another house, thus setting off again to move towards 100 per cent. ownership of that second house. The advantage of that arrangement under new clause 22 is that the first house would revert to the ownership of either the local authority or the housing association and it would soon be available for another family to embark on the same process of part ownership, moving eventually to full ownership of a different house.

The Government have recognised already the need to manage the housing market to take account of the problem of rural housing. I very much welcome the Government's announcement in February of their assistance for local people in rural areas. The Government have said that they intend to get over the problem I have explained by allowing part owners of houses to staircase up to 100 per cent. ownership, but then the Government propose to apply an artificial constraint by allowing those owners who have staircased up to 100 per cent. to sell back only to the local authority or housing association from which they originally bought the house.

I believe that that proposal is a move forward. However, it means that the time scale between houses becoming available the second time for part ownership by low-income families will be much more extended than it would be if the new clause was accepted. If we move towards my suggestion of 62·5 per cent., those houses will become available again more quickly for another family to embark on that process. If the new clause is not accepted, the Government's proposal would mean that the pool of houses owned by a local authority or a housing association would be a far less effective means of getting low-income families into the business of home ownership and on to the home ownership ladder.

I hope that the Government will accept the large volume of opinion both inside and outside the House in support of this new clause. I accept that its drafting could be deficient, and I am not prepared to go to the wall on the exact wording of its provisions. However, what I want to hear tonight and what I am determined to hear tonight from the Government is that they accept the principle and are prepared to introduce a professionally drafted amendment in another place to encourage the availability for part ownership of the pool of houses about which I have spoken. In any case, I assure the Government that they will hear a great deal more about this issue when the Bill reaches another place.

11.15 pm

Finally, I am not in the business of creating a device through this new clause whereby local authorities could use the provisions that I am proposing to escape from their responsibilities over the right to buy. I am perfectly content to see a ceiling in the new clause to ensure that the number of houses that can be made available for part ownership is kept under control, so that local authorities cannot totally escape their responsibilities under the right-to-buy legislation.

I hope that, having heard the argument and having heard the large volume of support for the new clause both inside and outside the House, the Government will now be prepared to say that they will move along these lines.

Sir Charles Morrison (Devizes): I wish to take only a few moments of the House's time to speak to my amendments (a) to (h) to new clause 22 and to support wholeheartedly everything that my right hon. Friend the Member for Westmorland and Lonsdale (Mr. Jopling) has said. As he has already said, my amendments have been tabled in agreement with him and amount simply to improvements on the first proposals in new clause 22. Those improvements have been suggested by the Association of District Councils and by the housing associations. I hope that they and the new clause will be accepted.

In face of the support for my right hon. Friend's new clause, his determination and the excellent way in which he moved it, I can only believe that the Government will, with great alacrity, decide to accept the principles. If the new clause were accepted, it would strike a considerable blow for the campaign to improve housing in rural areas.

We know that the National Association of Local Councils supports the new clause, together with the Association of District Councils. The Country Landowners Association has stated:

"It is generally acknowledged that there is an acute shortage of affordable homes for low paid workers in rural areas."

Those of us who represent rural areas echo the words of the Country Landowners Association. However, I sometimes have to admit that I am not yet convinced that the Department of the Environment has fully taken on board the shortage of affordable homes for low-paid workers in rural areas. Tonight the Government have an opportunity not only to allay my doubts but to demonstrate clearly that they are aware of the problem and that they are prepared to take a step forward to do something about it by supporting my right hon. Friend's new clause.

Mr. Ridley: I intervene at this stage to, I hope, reassure my right hon. Friend the Member for Westmorland and Lonsdale (Mr. Jopling) and my hon. Friend the Member for Devizes (Sir C. Morrison) that the arguments that they have been putting are not only shared on this Bench, but have already been dealt with in a way that I hope to convince them they will find more satisfactory than what they have themselves proposed.

I accept the argument of my right hon. Friend the Member for Westmorland and Lonsdale that we should allow shared ownership housing in certain rural areas to be retained as low-cost housing for future generations of local people. At present, local authorities need my consent to dispose of housing, and consent is given for a disposal on shared ownership terms only if the lease entitles the shared owner to staircase to full ownership. Similarly, the Housing Corporation will pay grant on a housing association shared ownership scheme only if the lease provides for full staircasing.

I should mention that the new clause is technically defective. It rests on a misconception. Shared owners will be long leaseholders and long leaseholders are not secure tenants; they therefore do not currently have the right to buy. A shared owner who staircases to full ownership does so under the provisions of the lease, not by exercising the statutory right to buy. Thus, the new clause is wrong.

I am grateful to my hon. Friend the Member for Devizes for his speech. He tried to improve the drafting, but it is still defective. To achieve the objective of my right hon. Friend the Member for Westmorland and Lonsdale and my hon. Friend the Member for Devizes, it is not an amendment that would be needed, but a change of policy. I do not, however, rest my case on that.

My right hon. Friend the Member for Westmorland and Lonsdale explained why some local authorities and housing associations wish to be able to grant shared ownership leases under which there is no right to staircase to full ownership. Their concern is to ensure that, in areas where there is only a limited amount of housing, property continues to be available to people who cannot afford to buy outright. I share that concern.

I am aware of the difficulties facing young people who cannot compete with the prices paid by incomers. I have therefore already done something about it with the local needs planning circular, which should give local authorities a great opportunity to increase the supply of low-cost housing in rural areas. I also agree that we need a way to retain shared ownership housing as low-cost housing once the first beneficiary has moved on. Therefore, we decided, and announced on 7 February, that in rural areas where there could be a real problem—such as those to which my right hon. Friend the Member for Westmorland and Lonsdale referred—in replacing a shared ownership property once the shared owner has moved on, having sold, we will allow a housing association to take a pre-emptive right to buy back the property that it has provided at market prices. We will give the same right where a private landowner in a rural area has originally given land on condition that it is used for low-cost housing.

The proposal meets all the objectives of my right hon. Friend the Member for Westmorland and Lonsdale, but it meets a further objective, too. It not only allows the property to be recycled as low-cost housing to a new shared owner, who might at that stage be ready to ascend the housing ladder, but, importantly, it allows the shared owner to become a full owner—as my right hon. Friend said he would like him to be—and it does not deny him the right to 100 per cent. of the value of his home.

I cannot accept the thinking of my right hon. Friend that 62·5 per cent. of the value of a home is sufficient. I do not know why he should believe that those who engage in the staircasing route, whereby they receive very little, if any, subsidy at all, to home ownership should be put in the position where they can achieve only 62·5 per cent., whereas the council tenant not only receives discount, which can be up to 55 or 60 per cent. in some cases—a huge advantage—but is allowed to progress to 100 per cent. by exercising his right to buy.

The discrimination that my right hon. Friend is suggesting against people who happen to be a little better off and undertake shared ownership as opposed to renting, followed by the right to buy from a council or a housing association, does not appear to me to be worthy of his concern for the welfare of local people of low means in the

rural areas. I do not believe that the House would like to take a step that disadvantages people to this extent. I sincerely commend to the House the proposal that I have put forward, which offers the best of both worlds, in that the tenant or shared owner can become a 100 per cent. owner—and the house can be used a second time for local needs for low-cost ownership.

Mr. W. Benyon (Milton Keynes) *rose*——

Mr. Ridley: Let me anticipate what I think my hon. Friend was going to ask.

If the housing association has to buy back at market value, is not the original shared owner being given a windfall at the community's or generous landowner's expense? The answer is emphatically no. This is a common misconception. The only element of subsidy to the shared owner is in the rent charged, which will decrease as he buys more of the equity. If the shared owner has staircased up to 100 per cent., he will have paid the full market value to the housing association, albeit in stages. That means, for instance, that the benefit of any cheap or free land or initial grant provided by the Housing Corporation remains with the property and is available for the benefit of the next occupier as well.

I have here a sheet of calculations showing all this in a typical case. By coincidence, I think that my hon. Friend the Member for Fylde (Mr. Jack), who is sitting behind me, has a number of copies. Any hon. Member who wishes to see one will find that the figures in the case I have mentioned prove my point. The subsidy is available for the next shared owner.

My right hon. Friend suggested that there would be a quicker turnover if, at 62·5 per cent., the shared owner had to get out if he wished to progress to 100 per cent. The house would indeed be vacated more quickly if he did that; but what a way to achieve——

Mr. Hardy: On a point of order, Madam Deputy Speaker. I am sorry to interrupt the Secretary of State, but it seems that Conservative Members have been supplied with copies of this document, yet the Secretary of State has passed one only to my hon. Friend the Member for Hammersmith (Mr. Soley). Some of us would like to see the document, and believe that we are as entitled as other Members to see it.

Mr. Ridley: I shall make sure that the hon. Gentleman gets a copy as soon as possible.

I reinforce the point that, if a shared owner cannot get past 62·5 per cent., he does not have the resources to go and buy elsewhere. So he will stay in the house at 62·5 per cent. and will not free it for a new occupant.

The related question is: will the housing association be able to afford to buy back? The answer is yes. In the first place, the money paid over in stages by the shared owner will be available. If that is not enough because of the vagaries of changes in house values or inflation, provided there is value for money, the Housing Corporation will top it up. What my right hon. Friend is assured by this scheme, with the added and priceless advantage that the local person is not deprived of the chance to become a full owner and is not discriminated against in the way in which he would be by my right hon. Friend's new clause——

Sir Peter Emery (Honiton): I have been listening closely, and I hope that my right hon. Friend will not have to make a speech to reply to my question. I do

[*Sir Peter Emery*]

understand how, when a house has been disposed of after staircasing to 100 per cent., it will return to being cheap housing once it is at market value. The house will no longer provide cheap housing in an agricultural area: it will remain at market value.

Mr. Ridley: I shall have to give a few illustrative figures to answer my hon. Friend. Let us suppose the subsidy was originally £20,000, through cheap land or a grant, that the house has a market value of £100,000 and that the shared owner has staircased to full ownership. Before he gets there, he will have paid £100,000 for the house. It cost the housing association £80,000 to build the house. It received a grant of £20,000 and will receive back the £100,000 plus the cheap land. The original benefit of the cheap land or the original grant reverts to the housing association when it pre-empts and buys. The figures, which I hope my hon. Friends will study, prove that to be the case.

The new clause is not as good a way of meeting my right hon. Friend's objective as the way that I have outlined. Our way has the advantage of helping the very people we are trying to help—local people in rural areas who find it hard to acquire a house.

11.30 pm

Mr. A. J. Beith (Berwick-upon-Tweed): I want to deal with some of the arguments that the Secretary of State has advanced. However, I cannot do so without first commending the right hon. Member for Westmorland and Lonsdale (Mr. Jopling) for bringing this matter before the House and for taking the trouble to make sure that many other hon. Members were aware of it. He has done rural areas a service by doing so.

The Secretary of State said that the main counter-argument with which he had to deal was that there was a windfall gain. That is not the main counter-argument with which he has to deal, and it is certainly not an argument that I advance as an objection to the way that the Secretary of State proposes to proceed. It would be a long and fruitless occupation to try to wipe windfall gains out of the housing market. The argument is about whether there will continue to be available housing of various kinds and, in this instance, housing which people on relatively low incomes can use as a means to get on to the housing ladder.

It is part of the Secretary of State's argument that 65 or 67 per cent. was not a sufficient objective for people to seek to attain as they went up the staircase. As the right hon. Member for Westmorland and Lonsdale said, people do not stick at 65 or 67 per cent. Indeed, Northumberland community council has suggested that 90 per cent. is appropriate.

All we are trying to do is safeguard the future availability of the house for this particular purpose. At 90 per cent. shared equity, a person's opportunity of buying on the open market is obviously much greater than at 67 per cent.

Mr. Ridley: What about 100 per cent.? That is better still.

Mr. Beith: It is precisely because we wish to get the house back into availability for the purpose of allowing——

Mr. Ridley *rose*——

Mr. Beith: If the Secretary of State will allow me to finish the sentence, I will allow him to intervene.

It is to allow the house to come back into availability so that people in rural areas can become owners of houses.

Mr. Ridley: If the housing association has the right to buy it back, whether at 62, 90 or 100 per cent., it can come back into use as low-cost housing. Why does the hon. Gentleman want to stop at 90 per cent., when the same result is achieved at 100 per cent.—or did he not listen to what I said?

Mr. Beith: It must be obvious that I listened very carefully to the Secretary of State. If he will listen carefully to me, he will understand why I do not accept that argument. I do not accept it because it will mean that there will be no turnover of houses in areas where there are very few. The Secretary of State must realise, because he has been to my constituency and has seen the scale of the project that we are talking about, that in many communities there may be only two or four such houses. One of the ways in which those houses can come back into availability is if someone goes up the staircase and is able to buy a house on the open market. When that happens, that house can come back to the housing association, not at the end of the tenant's life but at a much earlier stage, and be available to someone at the bottom of the ladder. That person can then start to work his way up.

The key to the argument is the few houses that are available. The Secretary of State's answer to that is, "It is all right because I have devised new planning and tax relief procedures which will allow more such houses to be built". That fails to address the central problem in many of the areas that we are talking about which is that additional building is either precluded or difficult. It may be difficult because we are talking about beauty spots, outstanding places and villages in national parks and areas of outstanding natural beauty. In such areas, the cost of new building, taking into account the overwhelming demand that it should be wholly in character with the existing village, can be astronomical.

Sir Geoffrey Johnson Smith (Wealden): The hon. Gentleman need not concern himself only with beauty spots. There are many areas of the south-east which are attractive but would not be described as beauty spots, which suffer considerably from a shortage of land. The people who live there would not want to see more building indiscriminately dotted around the countryside.

Mr. Beith: I accept that, but I wanted to focus the Secretary of State's mind on the problem we face, for example, in some of the beauty spots of the north-east of England, whether in the Lake District, the hon. Gentleman's constituency, or in Northumberland. There is the added problem of high land costs in the south of England.

There is the general planning argument that we will destroy the beauty and attraction of an area if we build more houses there. Hon. Members will be aware of places in the Lake District, or coastal fishing villages tucked into a cleft of rock, in which there is no more room and to which it would be impossible to add by building more houses without destroying the attractions which have led to them being designated areas of natural beauty. Because the Secretary of State has failed to address that problem, he fails to recognise that his solution, although it may help in some areas, will not help in all the places about which we are concerned.

The Secretary of State took the trouble to come to my constituency to open a small housing scheme, where he discovered how high rents can be in such areas. In doing so, he exposed himself to a barrage of advice about rural housing matters. *[Interruption.]* I hope the right hon. Gentleman will listen to what I am saying. He seems to be preoccupied in briefing his junior Minister, the hon. Member for Rossendale and Darwen (Mr. Trippier), on some other matter. I hope he will listen now, as he listened when he came to my area to people of all political persuasions who wanted to ensure that there were adequate opportunities for housing in rural areas for those on low incomes. I do not think that he listened sufficiently to that advice. He must now reconsider the reply that he gave to the right hon. Member for Westmorland and Lonsdale in the light of what I have said and in view of what many hon. Members feel on this issue.

Sir Peter Emery: I intervene again because the point I made earlier was not answered by the Secretary of State. There are many examples to prove that every time a house in an agricultural area becomes available, it is snapped up to become a second home or a place where people spend their vacations. Hence there is a real need to require, where we can, by legislation, a pool of low-cost housing to be kept for first-time buyers and their families.

I will give an example which may show whether we or my right hon. Friend is correct. In my local authority area of east Devon the land for a house is valued at, say, £20,000. The building may cost about £30,000. Thus, the cost of the house into which a person moves is £50,000. Over the period during which that person purchases the house—10 or 12 years—the value of the house will have risen from the original cost of £50,000 to £100,000, an increase in value of 100 per cent. over that period, and that is quite a possibility.

When the housing authority or association repurchases for £100,000, it has had to find £50,000 above the amount it has received in rents over the period. So when it comes back on to the market, it sells at the market value. Or, perhaps one wishes to take the figure of £100,000 less the original £20,000 for the land, costing £80,000. That is no longer cheap housing for first-time buyers.

If that is the case, my right hon. Friend's argument falls to the ground, and for that reason the amendment makes more sense. Even if it is deficient, it might be better to insert it in the Bill and clarify it in another place. That would ensure that the Government accepted the principle of what we want to achieve, and later the drafting could be made perfect. I hope that course will commend itself to the Secretary of State, for those of us who support the amendment fear that the way he is proceeding will not achieve what we wish to achieve.

Mr. Soley: This debate clearly demonstrates the growing concern amongst Tory Members about the drying up of low-cost housing in rural areas. We have been warning them for many years about the crisis in this sector, which is beginning to match the problem in the cities. The blame lies with them. What are we doing even discussing this when the Government cut funding to local authorities and housing associations so massively in the early 1980s that they brought on this crisis?

The hon. Member for Honiton (Sir P. Emery) has done much of my job for me, because he is right. The figures that the Secretary of State has just handed out show what he means by low-cost housing. Tory Members will be interested in this, because it affects them deeply. The first example is of 1 June 1989, and shows a resident buying a 40 per cent. share at £40,000. Two years later, in June 1991, the resident has to buy the remaining share with a new mortgage of £60,000. Who is talking about low-cost housing? Will houses at £100,000 each help to keep the village communities together? Is that how the nurses, the teachers and the postmen will get their houses? Above all, is that how the sons and daughters of those who work in rural areas will be enabled to buy? As we all know only too well, the sons and daughters of people who have been brought up in these areas are unable to rent or buy because of the Government's policies.

The Secretary of State rested his objections to the new clause moved by the right hon. Member for Westmorland and Lonsdale (Mr. Jopling) on the argument that 62 per cent. would be unfair when a council tenant would get more. That argument is an absurdity because it is based on the false assumption that this is a fair subsidy system. What does a tenant in the private sector get if he buys? He does not get anything until he begins to get mortgage income tax relief, which goes to other house owners. A tenant who tries to buy in the private sector will get none of the subsidy that goes to a housing association tenant or to a public tenant, in the council sector.

As we have said before, the Government have introduced a right to buy based on a subsidy system that is unfair within the rented sector. They have then fallen into the deadly trap of not doing what we said they should do, which is to make sure that, in housing stress areas, there is a duty to replace the houses that are sold. Had they done that, they would not have these problems.

The right hon. Member for Westmorland and Lonsdale made a powerful case. He brought forward evidence from housing associations and letters from people to support his case. I have had the same sort of letters, and I am sure that hon. Members who represent rural areas have had them. I noticed the right hon. Gentleman say that he expected the Secretary of State to move towards him and to give him what he wanted. I saw the expression on the Secretary of State's face, and I do not think that the right hon. Gentleman will get everything he wants.

Towards the end of the right hon. Gentleman's speech, I got the distinct impression that his conviction about the needs of the people whom he was trying to help was being drowned out by the knocking of his knees as he thought about going into the Division Lobby. The right hon. Gentleman will not push this to a vote, but we will, because he is being bamboozled by the Secretary of State, who, as the hon. Member for Honiton pointed out, is not talking about low-cost housing or about any significant additional provision for rural areas. We know that there is a real and growing crises in the availability of low-cost housing in rural areas, which is not just hurting individuals but destroying and undermining village communities.

11.45 pm

The problems that emerged in inner cities were largely the consequence of housing difficulties, with some people having the ability to escape from inner cities, whereas others did not, because of the way that housing is financed

[*Mr. Soley*]

and wealth is distributed generally. That inner-city problem is now moving into the rural areas, and it reflects the classic face of Conservatism—private affluence and public squalor. The Government are now paying the price.

My right hon. and hon. Friends want to press the matter to a Division. If the right hon. Member for Westmorland and Lonsdale joins us in the Lobby, he will show those people who wrote to him that his position is that which he claimed in his speech. If he does not join us in the Lobby, what he will get from the other place will be peanuts, and those about whom the hon. Gentleman is worried will not be helped. Above all, the local work force and their sons and daughters will not get the houses they need at prices they can afford.

Mr. John Greenway (Ryedale): I do not for one moment believe that forcing the new clause to a Division will help those people looking for low-cost housing in rural areas or in inner cities. The issues are complex, and balance is required. Over the past two or three decades, and particularly over the 10 years of the present Government, demand for home ownership has been at a level never seen before—but home ownership is meaningless unless it means 100 per cent. ownership. That is what people want.

I have great sympathy for my right hon. Friend's new clause, which I have discussed with him in detail. It is welcome if only because it has produced a packed House of Commons at midnight to debate a matter of considerable interest to the whole country. It is apparent that two separate issues are being confused. My right hon. Friend the Secretary of State took a worthwhile initiative in the planning opportunities he allowed for the development of low-cost housing in rural areas, by suggesting that the provision of such housing could be a material benefit that planning authorities should take into account when considering planning applications.

However, that measure itself creates a difficulty. My understanding is that planning is concerned with the use of land and not with its occupation. The argument for low-cost ownership as the first step on the ladder to full home ownership is just as valid in inner cities and towns as in rural areas. A framework must be established whereby local authorities, housing associations or the private sector can develop opportunities to best effect.

Two fundamental principles must first be balanced. Anyone who purchases a property—whether at 40, 60 or 80 per cent. of its perceived market value initially—ought to have the opportunity to acquire 100 per cent. ownership in due course. In that, I agree entirely with my right hon. Friend the Secretary of State. If such a home owner has to pay for that benefit, the subsidy is not lost to the community because the local authority or housing association will have the funds available to reinvest in social housing.

Secondly, the local authority or housing association must have the right of pre-emption. I urge my right hon. Friend to give the House the assurance that it requires today, that local authorities as well as housing associations can both staircase and have a right of pre-emption within the same scheme. If that is permitted, we can provide social housing for first-time buyers, whether they be young couples in rural areas or 55-year-old couples looking for a retirement home in rural areas, inner cities or market towns.

The key is that we must have a right to staircase for the purchaser and a right of pre-emption for the local authority or housing association. If my right hon. Friend will assure the House today that he will take the Bill away and find a solution to fit those two conflicting objectives, there will be no point in going through the charade of a Division. Instead, we should allow the matter to progress to the other place and bring it back to this House when we consider their Lordships amendments

Mr. Gerald Bermingham (St. Helens, South): I shall be extremely brief. Having listened to the right hon, Gentleman, it occurred to me that £100,000 would buy a nice flat in north London, three semi-detached houses in a good area of Sheffield, or four or five houses in a reasonable suburb of St. Helens. Is that low-cost housing? Is that what the Secretary of State is saying? I looked at his figures and decided that they were those of a cowboy, not of a sensible Department.

Low-cost housing should be a multiple of annual income. For example, if an agricultural worker earns £8,000 or £9,000 a year, low-cost housing should cost two or three times his annual income—about £30,000. The Secretary of State does not seem to live in the world of reality. It is all very nice for those who live in Sussex and Surrey, but an awful lot of people do not live in such places. Many people want to be housed and own their own houses but do not have the income to sustain the Mickey Mouse figures given by the Secretary of State in this first fly leaflet in the House tonight.

In his new clause, the right hon. Member for Westmorland and Lonsdale (Mr. Jopling) is trying to show that people in rural areas have a right to a home and a roof over their heads. I hope that he will have the guts to press the matter to a Division and that the House will have the courage to support him.

Mr. Robert Key (Salisbury): This has been a partial debate on a subject which is close to the hearts of many of my right hon. and hon. Friends. My right hon. Friend the Member for Westmorland and Lonsdale (Mr. Jopling) was at his most understanding and my right hon. Friend the Secretary of State at his most logical.

The hon. Member for Hammersmith (Mr. Soley), however, was spine-chilling—for the 30 seconds or so before one stopped to think about what he was saying. I, for one, will not be lectured about how we in the countryside live by people who dwell in towns and pop out every now and again at weekends. The debate has shown a profound lack of understanding on the part of Opposition Members, who have done nothing but barrack us tonight, about what the countryside is all about. I would take on the chin, however, some of the criticism that my hon. Friends and I will have received in that notable and august publication, *The Field,* which for the past six months has been running a campaign saying that we do not understand the countryside any more. By the same token, it illustrates the appalling lack of understanding of the Opposition.

The debate has been partial because it has only scratched the surface of the problems of rural housing. It has touched on only one point to do with rural housing —a particular aspect of the way in which housing associations are beginning to help. I wish to draw my right hon. and hon. Friends' attention to the remarkable change that has occurred in the past year or two.

Planning policy guidance circulars Nos. 3 and 7, issued by the Department of the Environment, reflect a complete change of tone in the Government's approach to rural development and a change in their approach to planning matters in the countryside. We have been told by the Department—if only people would listen to it—that the days of crowding the countryside with inappropriate, unattractive, badly designed, high-density housing are over. I have taken councillors in my constituency to task because they have not even read the Department's planning circulars.

I congratulate my right hon. Friend the Secretary of State on his policy on rural housing, which allows land to be made available for development which would not be released unless it was to be used for social housing. That is a great step forward. We have only to read the figures relating to the housing associations and the Housing Corporation's budget to realise that my right hon. Friend understands countryside problems. There has been a change of attitude by so many developers. I represent a beautiful constituency which I often describe as being between the devil and the deep blue sea—the devil of Swindon, which is the fastest growing conurbation in Europe, and the deep blue sea of Poole, a beautiful place which is also growing rapidly. My constituency is pincered between those two towns and as a result there are enormous pressures.

The way in which developers view the possibilities of making huge profits has changed, especially in the past six or seven months. There is plenty of evidence to support that statement. I have been approached by builders, who I have put in touch with the district council. They have produced many schemes for low-cost housing, including do-it-yourself housing and bare minimum housing, where the developer buys up the old unprofitable plots such as railway sidings and "Gas lane", for example—the House will know that I mean—and then produces first-time housing. That is a reality. It is a long time since the hon. Member for Hammersmith trotted off into the country. That must be so, or he would understand that what I am saying is the truth.

Farmers and country landowners have shown a deep level of understanding of their responsibility to preserve the fabric of our villages. That is why the Country Landowners Association, for example, is so active in trying to persuade its members to have regard to schemes based on low-cost land which can be developed for social housing. Those are the considerations that should be borne in mind. Despite the astonishing barracking from the Opposition, I urge my right hon. Friends not to be bounced into voting against the Government on this. I urge them instead to take a long-term view and to listen my my right hon. Friend the Secretary of State. We must ensure, of course, that he delivers the goods. That is the right way forward.

Mrs. Teresa Gorman (Billericay): I shall not detain the House because I know that it wishes to make progress. There are two causes of the problem that is outlined in the new clause that have not yet been mentioned in the debate. The first cause is the Rent Acts and the second is planning controls. It is not true that people in rural areas, or anywhere else, all want to buy their own housing. Many

people with low incomes would prefer to rent but there is no rented property market to speak of because we have destroyed it through the Rent Acts. The market will not be restored until we repeal that legislation.

It appears that 85 per cent. of land in the south-east of England, the most crowded part of the country, is held out of housing use. It is held instead for farming or it comes within the green belt. In other areas the amount of land that is held out of use for housing is even greater. There is no real shortage of land but a shortage has been created artificially. Ludicrously high prices are fetched for land that is to be built upon, and that is why the housing supply in rural areas for those on low incomes has almost dried up. I ask my right hon. Friend the Secretary of State to address himself to this problem.

Mr. Christopher Hawkins (High Peak) *rose*——

Mrs. Gorman: Is my hon. Friend on my side?

Mr. Hawkins: I am on my hon. Friend's side of the House. The problem in my constituency, High Peak, and in many others is not a shortage of rented accommodation due to the Rent Acts or to council house sales. The problem is that there is a shortage of housing of all kinds in villages. Houses that are put up for sale are bought as second homes. *[Interruption.]* I do not object to people having second homes. They are bought by people from outside who want the good life. That is fair enough; why should they not be able to buy second homes? However, the planning controls prevent the construction of new homes for local people. Farm workers and the sons and daughters of people who live in villages cannot therefore acquire their own homes in their own villages.

12 midnight

Mrs. Gorman: I am sorry that my hon. Friend persuaded me to give way because I find that he is not on my side at all. He has, however, aired one of the fallacies. People move out of London because they cannot afford to rent or buy homes in London. They have to move into the country, and that creates the shortage. People have to become commuters, which adds to traffic congestion and all the other problems. I hope that my right hon. Friend will deal with the points I have raised.

Mr. Ridley: With the leave of the House, may I make it clear that the figures that I have circulated are purely illustrative. One can use any figure or fraction of a figure that one likes, but sometimes it is useful to use the decimal system, based on 100.

Many hon. Members have referred to the planning constraints. They include the hon. Member for Berwick-upon-Tweed (Mr. Beith) and my right hon. Friend the Member for Westmorland and Lonsdale (Mr. Jopling). They were quite right to point out that the constraint on low-cost housing in the national parks and other areas is largely a planning constraint because of the beauty of those areas. Planning authorities will not grant planning permission to provide sufficient housing. The hon. Member for Hammersmith (Mr. Soley) is wrong. That is not what we are talking about tonight. We are talking about a very limited stock of houses because the policy has been to stop more houses being built by means of a very restrictive planning policy.

[*Mr. Ridley*]

There is a different problem in other parts of the country. We shall not solve the problem in the Lake District, however many houses we can afford to build, because sites will not be made available for them.

As for the example given by my hon. Friend the Member for Honiton (Sir P. Emery), when a resident buys a share of a house he buys a share of the market value of that house. When he pays the last 40 per cent. he pays it at the value of £100,000, the price at which the house was transferred. The housing association that receives the payments at each stage probably puts them into another investment. The improvement in value—my hon. Friend's point—is reflected in the housing association's receipts. Therefore, the problem to which he referred does not arise. If the price of a house goes well above the market price in a particular area, the Housing Corporation will be able to top it up. I do not think that my hon. Friend's arithmetic should deter the House from doing what I have suggested.

The scheme that I have suggested is appropriate where shared ownership is a problem because of the shortage of housing in areas where planning permission cannot come to the rescue. In many rural areas, planning permission through the new low-cost housing needs guidance will come to the rescue and housing associations will be able to come to the rescue, too. We are talking about a limited part of the country where local authorities have the right of pre-emption in national parks, areas of outstanding natural beauty and certain other designated areas. Local authorities or housing associations have the right of pre-emption where planning constraints prevent extra building.

My suggestion has the best of three worlds—it preserves those areas from excessive building; it secures a permanent stock of low-cost housing to enable local people to begin to climb the housing ladder; and it enables people to end up 100 per cent. owners instead of 62·5 per cent. second-class citizens.

Mr. Jopling: I have listened with great care to the arguments of my right hon. Friend the Secretary of State. In his first speech, he sought to shoot down my argument that houses would return more quickly to the housing pool, allowing people to start once more on the first steps of part-ownership, if there were a ceiling of 62·5 per cent. rather than 100 per cent. I am sure that I heard him correctly when he said that a person who reached the stage of owning 62·5 per cent. of a house would not have enough money to buy another one to work up to 100 per cent. I profoundly disagree.

In using figures with many noughts on the end, many hon. Members have been talking about much more valuable houses than those that I envisage in the new clause. They are stratospheric prices compared with prices in some of the villages that I know. Bearing in mind that a person who starts as a part-owner and manages to achieve 62·5 per cent. ownership will take advantage of the general increased value of housing, even with the restrictions of clause 52 arrangements and the insistence that only local people can live in the houses—which would depress prices—he will have more than enough, several tens of thousands of pounds at 62·5 per cent., to move into another house where he is free to achieve 100 per cent.

ownership. The original house will be available to start another family from a low-income group, whom all of us wish to help.

My right hon Friend used another invalid argument. He said that there would be an unfair advantage for council house tenants who could take part in right-to-buy schemes that offer various discounts. Many of these houses, especially those under the management of housing associations, will be available at artificially low levels because of the announcement that my right hon. Friend the Secretary of State made in February. I welcome that extremely good statement. This policy, however, will allow certain land to be made available, but only for local occupancy, on the periphery of villages. The limited availability of land will be reflected in house values, to the advantage of the people who have been involved in part-ownership.

I was also struck by the comments of the hon. Member for Berwick-upon-Tweed (Mr. Beith) about the effect on small villages with a shortage of houses. We cannot continue to keep building new houses. I referred earlier to a letter from John Sutcliffe, who most hon. Members will remember, of North Housing. He is involved with housing associations across the north of England. He referred in his letter to the village of Castleton on the north Yorkshire moors, which many hon. Members will know. He said:

"You can't go on building without ruining villages like Castleton. You must therefore keep a number of houses for locals without large means either to staircase or rent. Since and so long as we can't, we are failing to meet housing need."

That is exactly the excellent point made by the hon. Member for Berwick-upon-Tweed, which I also tried to make earlier.

When I moved an amendment in Committee on the Housing Bill last year, my right hon. Friend the Secretary of State—I hope that he does not mind my saying this —was not terribly keen to accept it, but in the end he did. Since then there has been evidence that, in order to meet the need for better housing opportunities for those on low incomes in rural areas, my right hon. Friend has become much more of an interventionist that I ever thought we could get him to be. I certainly welcome that.

My right hon. Friend's announcements in February were purely interventionism. His suggestion tonight that somebody who staircases from a part ownership up to 100 per cent. ownership can only sell it either to a local authority or a housing association is pure interventionism, which I welcome. I am trying to persuade him to move a little further and deal with a request which, after all, has powerful backing from the Association of District Councils and the National Federation of Housing Associations.

A little earlier the hon. Member for Hammersmith (Mr. Soley) accused me of having knocking knees. I sat in the Whips' seat on the Government Front Bench for far too long to have knocking knees at the prospect of going into one Lobby or another. My knees certainly are not knocking. My concern is that there are not many Opposition Members in the Chamber to support my new clause.

There are few issues in my constituency about which I feel more strongly than the need to provide housing for low-income families in the rural areas where they were born and brought up. My hon. Friend the Member for High Peak (Mr. Hawkins) put his finger on it when he explained that in his constituency local people are more and more being pushed out by people buying second and holiday homes

I did not table the new clause simply to air the problem. If my right hon. Friend the Secretary of State cannot help us, I shall reluctantly go into the Lobby and vote against the Government. I assure them that they will hear a great deal more about this matter in another place.

Question put, That the clause be read a Second time:—
The House divided: Ayes 144, Noes 171.

Division No. 243]   **[12.14 am**

AYES

Abbott, Ms Diane	Griffiths, Win *(Bridgend)*
Aitken, Jonathan	Grocott, Bruce
Alton, David	Hague, William
Anderson, Donald	Hardy, Peter
Archer, Rt Hon Peter	Henderson, Doug
Baker, Nicholas *(Dorset N)*	Hicks, Robert *(Cornwall SE)*
Banks, Tony *(Newham NW)*	Hinchliffe, David
Barnes, Harry *(Derbyshire NE)*	Howarth, George *(Knowsley N)*
Barron, Kevin	Howells, Dr. Kim (Pontypridd)
Battle, John	Hoyle, Doug
Beckett, Margaret	Hughes, John *(Coventry NE)*
Beith, A. J.	Hughes, Roy *(Newport E)*
Benn, Rt Hon Tony	Hughes, Simon *(Southwark)*
Bennett, A. F. *(D'nt'n & R'dish)*	Illsley, Eric
Benyon, W.	Janner, Greville
Bermingham, Gerald	Jones, Ieuan *(Ynys Môn)*
Blunkett, David	Jopling, Rt Hon Michael
Boateng, Paul	Kellett-Bowman, Dame Elaine
Bradley, Keith	Kirkwood, Archy
Bruce, Malcolm *(Gordon)*	Leadbitter, Ted
Buckley, George J.	Leighton, Ron
Callaghan, Jim	Lestor, Joan *(Eccles)*
Campbell, Ron *(Blyth Valley)*	Lewis, Terry
Campbell-Savours, D. N.	Litherland, Robert
Cartwright, John	Livingstone, Ken
Clark, Dr David *(S Shields)*	Lloyd, Tony *(Stretford)*
Clay, Bob	Lofthouse, Geoffrey
Clelland, David	McAllion, John
Clwyd, Mrs Ann	Macdonald, Calum A.
Cohen, Harry	McWilliam, John
Coleman, Donald	Mahon, Mrs Alice
Cook, Frank *(Stockton N)*	Marek, Dr John
Corbyn, Jeremy	Maxwell-Hyslop, Robin
Cousins, Jim	Meacher, Michael
Cox, Tom	Meale, Alan
Crowther, Stan	Michael, Alun
Cryer, Bob	Michie, Bill *(Sheffield Heeley)*
Cummings, John	Morgan, Rhodri
Cunliffe, Lawrence	Morris, Rt Hon A. *(W'shawe)*
Cunningham, Dr John	Morrison, Sir Charles
Davies, Rt Hon Denzil *(Llanelli)*	Murphy, Paul
Davies, Ron *(Caerphilly)*	Nellist, Dave
Davis, Terry *(B'ham Hodge H'l)*	O'Brien, William
Dixon, Don	Patchett, Terry
Dobson, Frank	Pike, Peter L.
Dunwoody, Hon Mrs Gwyneth	Powell, Ray *(Ogmore)*
Eastham, Ken	Primarolo, Dawn
Emery, Sir Peter	Redmond, Martin
Evans, John *(St Helens N)*	Richardson, Jo
Fatchett, Derek	Rogers, Allan
Fearn, Ronald	Rooker, Jeff
Field, Frank *(Birkenhead)*	Rowlands, Ted
Fields, Terry *(L'pool B G'n)*	Ruddock, Joan
Fisher, Mark	Sedgemore, Brian
Flannery, Martin	Shaw, Sir Giles *(Pudsey)*
Flynn, Paul	Shaw, Sir Michael *(Scarb')*
Foot, Rt Hon Michael	Sheerman, Barry
Foster, Derek	Skinner, Dennis
Fraser, John	Smith, C. *(Isl'ton & F'bury)*
Garrett, John *(Norwich South)*	Smith, J. P. *(Vale of Glam)*
George, Bruce	Soley, Clive
Gill, Christopher	Spearing, Nigel
Golding, Mrs Llin	Speller, Tony
Gordon, Mildred	Steen, Anthony
Gould, Bryan	Stradling Thomas, Sir John

Taylor, Mrs Ann *(Dewsbury)*	Williams, Rt Hon Alan
Taylor, Matthew *(Truro)*	Winnick, David
Temple-Morris, Peter	Winterton, Mrs Ann
Turner, Dennis	Winterton, Nicholas
Wall, Pat	Wise, Mrs Audrey
Wallace, James	
Walley, Joan	Tellers for the Ayes:
Wardell, Gareth *(Gower)*	Mr. Frank Haynes and
Wardle, Charles *(Bexhill)*	Mr. Allen McKay.

NOES

Alexander, Richard	Gale, Roger
Alison, Rt Hon Michael	Garel-Jones, Tristan
Allason, Rupert	Glyn, Dr Alan
Amess, David	Gorman, Mrs Teresa
Arbuthnot, James	Gorst, John
Arnold, Jacques *(Gravesham)*	Gow, Ian
Arnold, Tom *(Hazel Grove)*	Greenway, Harry *(Ealing N)*
Ashby, David	Griffiths, Sir Eldon *(Bury St E')*
Atkinson, David	Griffiths, Peter *(Portsmouth N)*
Bendall, Vivian	Grist, Ian
Bennett, Nicholas *(Pembroke)*	Gummer, Rt Hon John Selwyn
Biffen, Rt Hon John	Hamilton, Neil *(Tatton)*
Blackburn, Dr John G.	Hampson, Dr Keith
Blaker, Rt Hon Sir Peter	Hanley, Jeremy
Body, Sir Richard	Hargreaves, A. *(B'ham H'll Gr')*
Bonsor, Sir Nicholas	Hargreaves, Ken *(Hyndburn)*
Boscawen, Hon Robert	Harris, David
Bottomley, Peter	Haselhurst, Alan
Bottomley, Mrs Virginia	Hawkins, Christopher
Bowden, A *(Brighton K'pto'n)*	Hayes, Jerry
Bowden, Gerald *(Dulwich)*	Hayward, Robert
Boyson, Rt Hon Dr Sir Rhodes	Higgins, Rt Hon Terence L.
Braine, Rt Hon Sir Bernard	Hind, Kenneth
Brandon-Bravo, Martin	Hogg, Hon Douglas *(Gr'th'm)*
Bright, Graham	Howard, Michael
Brown, Michael *(Brigg & Cl't's)*	Howarth, Alan *(Strat'd-on-A)*
Budgen, Nicholas	Howarth, G. *(Cannock & B'wd)*
Burns, Simon	Hughes, Robert G. *(Harrow W)*
Burt, Alistair	Hunt, David *(Wirral W)*
Butterfill, John	Hunter, Andrew
Carlisle, John, *(Luton N)*	Irvine, Michael
Carlisle, Kenneth *(Lincoln)*	Irving, Charles
Carrington, Matthew	Jack, Michael
Carttiss, Michael	Janman, Tim
Chapman, Sydney	Jones, Gwilym *(Cardiff N)*
Chope, Christopher	Jones, Robert B *(Herts W)*
Churchill, Mr	Key, Robert
Clark, Dr Michael *(Rochford)*	Kirkhope, Timothy
Clark, Sir W. *(Croydon S)*	Knapman, Roger
Clarke, Rt Hon K. *(Rushcliffe)*	Knight, Dame Jill *(Edgbaston)*
Colvin, Michael	Knowles, Michael
Conway, Derek	Knox, David
Coombs, Anthony *(Wyre F'rest)*	Lang, Ian
Coombs, Simon *(Swindon)*	Lawrence, Ivan
Couchman, James	Lennox-Boyd, Hon Mark
Cran, James	Lightbown, David
Currie, Mrs Edwina	Lilley, Peter
Davies, Q. *(Stamf'd & Spald'g)*	Lloyd, Peter *(Fareham)*
Day, Stephen	Luce, Rt Hon Richard
Devlin, Tim	Macfarlane, Sir Neil
Dorrell, Stephen	MacKay, Andrew *(E Berkshire)*
Douglas-Hamilton, Lord James	Maclean, David
Dover, Den	McLoughlin, Patrick
Dunn, Bob	Mans, Keith
Durant, Tony	Marshall, John *(Hendon S)*
Dykes, Hugh	Marshall, Michael *(Arundel)*
Eggar, Tim	Martin, David *(Portsmouth S)*
Fallon, Michael	Mayhew, Rt Hon Sir Patrick
Favell, Tony	Mellor, David
Finsberg, Sir Geoffrey	Mills, Iain
Fishburn, John Dudley	Mitchell, Andrew *(Gedling)*
Fookes, Dame Janet	Morris, M *(N'hampton S)*
Forman, Nigel	Moynihan, Hon Colin
Forsyth, Michael *(Stirling)*	Onslow, Rt Hon Cranley
Forth, Eric	Page, Richard
Fowler, Rt Hon Norman	Raison, Rt Hon Timothy
Franks, Cecil	Riddick, Graham
Freeman, Roger	Ridley, Rt Hon Nicholas
Fry, Peter	Ryder, Richard

Sainsbury, Hon Tim
Shaw, David *(Dover)*
Shelton, Sir William
Shepherd, Richard *(Aldridge)*
Smith, Sir Dudley *(Warwick)*
Spicer, Sir Jim *(Dorset W)*
Squire, Robin
Stanley, Rt Hon Sir John
Stevens, Lewis
Stewart, Andy *(Sherwood)*
Sumberg, David
Summerson, Hugo
Taylor, Ian *(Esher)*
Taylor, Teddy *(S'end E)*
Tebbit, Rt Hon Norman
Thompson, D. *(Calder Valley)*
Thompson, Patrick *(Norwich N)*
Thornton, Malcolm
Thurnham, Peter

Townend, John *(Bridlington)*
Townsend, Cyril D. *(B'heath)*
Trippier, David
Twinn, Dr Ian
Vaughan, Sir Gerard
Waddington, Rt Hon David
Waller, Gary
Ward, John
Watts, John
Wells, Bowen
Wheeler, John
Widdecombe, Ann
Wilkinson, John
Wood, Timothy

Tellers for the Noes:
Mr. David Heathcoat-Amory
and
Mr. Tom Sackville.

Question accordingly negatived.

Mr. Soley: On a point of order, Madam Deputy Speaker. May I say to the right hon. Member for Westmorland and Lonsdale (Mr. Jopling) that I misjudged——

Mr. Tom Sackville (Bolton, West): That is not a point of order to the Chair.

Mr. Soley: I am making a point of order to the Chair. I misjudged the right hon. Gentleman's character and what I thought—*[Interruption.]*

Madam Deputy Speaker: Order. The hon. Gentleman is raising a point of order with me, and I must listen to it.

Mr. Soley: I misjudged the character of the right hon. Member for Westmorland and Lonsdale and I should like to withdraw my comments about the knocking of his knees because what I thought was the knocking of his knees were the muted chimes of Big Ben. The right hon. Gentleman had mettle and he carried it through and I should like those comments to go on the record.

New Clause 34

DOG REGISTRATION SCHEMES

'(1) In section 37 of the Local Government Act 1988 [Power of Secretary of State to provide for Local Authority dog registration schemes] for the word "may" there shall be substituted the word "shall",
(2) If such regulations have not been made by the first day of January 1990 the Secretary of State shall lay a report before Parliament stating the reasons why not.'.—*[Dame Janet Fookes.]*
Brought up, and read the First time.

Dame Janet Fookes (Plymouth, Drake): I beg to move, That the clause be read a Second time.

Madam Deputy Speaker: With this it will be convenient to take also the following: New clause 43—*Dog registration*—

' .—( ) The following subsection shall be substituted for subsection (1) of section 37 of the Local Government Act 1988—

(1) The Secretary of State shall, by regulations to be laid before Parliament before 1st January 1990, make provision for the establishment and administration of a dog registration scheme by local authorities, or such other organisations as he may, after consulting with them, designate.'.

Amendment No. 262, in Title, line 24, after '1976', insert
'to amend section 37 of the Local Government Act 1988;'.

Dame Janet Fookes: New clause 43 stands in the name of myself, many of my hon. Friends and a number of Opposition Members. In other words, it commands a quite remarkable degree of cross-party support. That feeling is echoed in the country at large. A recent public opinion poll suggested that 92 per cent. of the population questioned was in favour of some form of dog registration scheme. Such a scheme is the purpose of the new clause.

Hon. Members may remember that the Local Government Act 1988 knocked out the dog licence, but that the other place inserted provisions for a dog registration scheme. That gave to the Secretary of State, the power to operate the scheme but did not oblige him to do so. The purpose of the new clause is to impose that obligation upon him. In other words, there would be a compulsory dog registration scheme.

Neither the relevant section of last year's Act nor this new clause lays down details. I think that that is right because I am concerned here to argue the principles in favour of such a scheme. There are many computations and many ways of doing so, in terms of both finance and precise detail. Suffice it to say that several organisations support the principle. It is worth giving a list of them because in themselves they are an interesting reflection of the way in which a dog registration scheme has caught the public imagination. Not surprisingly, the National Farmers Union is strongly in favour of such a scheme. Its members suffer from livestock worrying from stray dogs out of control. It is not surprising either that the postmen's union, the Union of Communication Workers, is very much in favour. It will be able to tell hon. Members better than I could how many thousand bites its postmen receive in a year. I am told that it is a great many.

Mr. Harry Greenway (Ealing, North): I want to confirm my hon. Friend's important point about the interests of the postmen in this matter. On a large estate in my constituency, the postal services have been suspended three times in 18 months due to very severe attacks on postmen.

12.30 am

Dame Janet Fookes: It is also not surprising that animal welfare organisations, such as the Royal Society for the Prevention of Cruelty to Animals, the National Canine Defence League, and the Battersea dogs' home—those who have to deal with stray and difficult dogs in the streets and in the fields—are most keen on such a scheme. Also keen on the scheme are the British Veterinary Association and the Association of District Councils, which is another body that sees the difficulties, quite literally sometimes, on the ground. Dog fouling is something which upsets many members of the public, not only those who love dogs, but those who find this a nuisance and, in some cases, a tragedy where diseases are communicated, especially to children.

It would be helpful if I explained the kind of scheme that I would like to see. However, it is important to bear in mind that there are variations, and that the House could decide at leisure what would be the most suitable, if the principle is adopted tonight. I would envisage a national computer bureau being set up, which would have the names of the owners and the dogs listed. There would be a permanent identification of the dog, which would not simply be by a tag on a collar which could be removed or not put on at all. There are several possibilities, for example, tattooing. Another interesting possibility is a tiny microchip implant under the dog's skin, which could be read off like a bar code at the outlet to a supermarket. It can be done quite painlessly—[*Interruption.*]

Mr. Allan Rogers (Rhondda): On a point of order, Mr. Deputy Speaker. Some of us are extremely concerned to hear the hon. Member for Plymouth, Drake (Dame J. Fookes) put forward her arguments. It is obvious from the attendance in the Chamber that many hon. Members are interested. Could we have a little order so we can understand what the hon. Member says?—[*Interruption.*]

Mr. Deputy Speaker (Sir Paul Dean): Order. I am sure that the House will grant the hon. Lady the courtesy of listening to her quietly.

Dame Janet Fookes: I believe that there is a law still on the statute book requiring animals that are out of control to be muzzled. Perhaps we could do with a few muzzles here tonight.

The RSPCA asked the London School of Economics to report—independent of the RSPCA—various possibilities for schemes and the costings of them. I shall not bore the House with all the details of the report, as it is quite a long document. However, it is worth while anyone with a serious interest in the matter looking at all the information contained in the report. It gives many different figures for the kind of schemes that it might be possible to set up, depending on whether one asked dog owners to foot the entire bill, or whether it was done partly by them and partly by local authorities. What is important is that there should be a dog registration bureau, which, according to this report, could be run quite simply. A famous computer firm was asked to work out the details. So the details are provided by an organisation that knows what it is talking about. That, linked with proper dog wardens introduced everywhere by district councils, would provide the means of enforcement.

Mr. Hardy: The hon. Lady knows that I have a considerable interest in this matter. Does she accept that her view would receive even wider support if she made it clear that any fee that was to be paid as a result of the registration scheme would be centrally determined? I hope that she will reject the Government's longstanding view that responsibility should be passed on to local authorities, and that they should fix the fee. That aspect causes considerable anxiety among many people who are interested in dogs, especially dog owners who know that they would pay whatever fee was charged and that many of those who cause the problem would continue to pay nothing.

Dame Janet Fookes: In this regard it is interesting to note that the number of dog licences rose by 60 per cent. in Northern Ireland when the fee was updated a few years ago under an order that applied only to Northern Ireland. I believe that the scheme I have in mind would have an even higher take-up, for various reasons that might bore the House at this hour.

A colour-coded tag on a dog showing that it has an up-to-date licence enables a dog warden to see at a glance whether the dog is properly registered. Unlike unregistered television sets, unregistered dogs make themselves known. Dog wardens with the power to enforce the law can get on to the problem straight away. It is essential first, however, that the dog be properly registered and linked to its owner.

Dog wardens and RSPCA inspectors tell me that one of their greatest problems is that of trying to prove ownership. It is all too easy for someone to disclaim ownership and to say that a dog belongs to a sister or brother-in-law and is being looked after for two weeks. In a recent court case in Stevenage the charge against a man was dismissed because he claimed that the dogs in question were not his—they belonged to his company. Present or future legislation will not have its full effect as long as that can happen.

I am aware that my right hon. Friend has announced various measures in conjunction with my right hon. Friend the Home Secretary. I have considered them carefully. Some are useful, others less so, but they all fail on this key point: it is essential to be able to identify a dog permanently, and to link it with its owner.

The Association of District Councils has sent in its own plans for a dog registration scheme. I believe they are on my right hon. Friend's desk now. It would be interesting to know whether he has any comments to make on them, but it is instructive that the organisation feels so strongly about the problem that it is prepared to propose its own scheme.

If the Government do not want to take on the ordering of the scheme there is no reason why another body—perhaps voluntary, like the RSPCA, or the Association of District Councils, or even a private firm—should not run the scheme. I hope that my hon. Friends and Opposition Members will join me in the Lobby tonight if the Government cannot concede this point.

I am concerned about stray dogs, and many people who have seen them looking miserably out of dogs' homes share that concern. For the last 15 years I have sought to persuade Governments of both complexions to take some action. The situation does not improve; it gets worse, and now we see the development of a fashion for more aggressive and larger breeds, often kept in unsuitable conditions and often not exercised sufficiently. Some of them are kept in places where there are small children, even though the breeds are not suitable to be in close contact with small children, and it is time to act.

We know that there is the ever-present threat of the spread of rabies through Europe. I am aware, of course, that there are contingency plans , but how much easier it would be if we at least had all dogs registered and knew exactly where we were going.

Mr. Tony Marlow (Northampton, North): My hon. Friend is concerned about people having macho dogs with small children and I think that we all agree with her, but how does a dog registration scheme affect that?

Dame Janet Fookes: If we had the system that I am suggesting whereby every dog was registered on a computer we could have additional information referring, perhaps, to the breed or type of dog. If we had dog wardens whose prime responsibility, in addition to rounding up strays, was the enforcement of the law, it would be easy, using a computer system, to light up where the dogs were and, if necessary, make particular checks on them. That is the key point of that system.

Dogs that were not registered because people had not bothered to do so could be taken in as strays and dealt with. If people did not claim them, one would have an answer. As it is, the requisite powers are not in place and it is high time they were. I hope that the House will show

[Dame Janet Fookes]

decisively that the time has come to take the plunge and go for a compulsory dog registration scheme linked to dog wardens. If my right hon. Friend the Secretary of State is not able to meet me on that, I must force the clause to a Division.

Mr. Matthew Taylor: I should like to address the general question of dog registration, although my hon. Friends and I have tabled a specific amendment. The hon. Member for Plymouth, Drake (Dame J. Fookes) deserves considerable credit for the effort that she has put into campaigning on this subject over many years. Many hon. Members are here to listen and to take part in the debate, and that is a tribute to the public and private concern that the hon. Lady and many others have shown. *[Interruption.]*

Mr. Deputy Speaker: Order. Will hon. Members who are not staying for the debate please leave quietly?

Mr. Taylor: I mentioned public concern because it is clear after attacks over a long period, and especially after the recent attacks by rottweilers, that there is enormous anxiety about the welfare of the animals and the impact on communities of attacks, disease and general pest control. There is also private concern because it is evident from the number of hon. Members who are present that the Secretary of State can be beaten on the issue of his reluctance to take action, although I think that the House will have to press the matter to a Division because he will be reluctant to accept the new clause.

12.45 am

Much has been said in recent weeks about attacks by dogs which have been bred and trained to guard and to attack. Nobody suggests that a dog registration scheme will answer all the problems or that no further attacks will occur, but at least there will be a guarantee that owners can be traced and identified when incidents take place. That will be a strong incentive for them to keep their dogs under proper control.

Mr. Christopher Hawkins: As 60 per cent. of people did not pay the 37½p dog licence, how can the hon. Gentleman guarantee that dog owners will register under the proposed scheme?

Mr. Taylor: The scheme is necessary for other reasons. For example, in addition to attacks, animals cause other nuisances, not least the danger of disease, the concern of farmers over sheep worrying by dogs and car and other accidents caused by strays. Although local authorities have powers to establish their own schemes—no doubt that will form part of the Secretary of State's case against the new clause—they are unlikely to be able to set up effective schemes, even if they could find the cash to do so.

The Secretary of State will probably also argue that there is already a requirement for dogs in public places to wear collars and identity tags. As the hon. Member for High Peak (Mr. Hawkins) pointed out the shortcomings of the previous dog licence system, so a Department of the Environment working party report back in 1976 said that the collar and tag requirement was more honoured in the breach than in the observance. The new clause would ensure that we had an effective scheme in place.

A compulsory scheme would prevent owners from denying ownership. It would be self-financing through the charges that would be levied. Sweden is an example of how effective such a scheme could be. Battersea dogs' home receives about 22,000 strays a year. In Stockholm they have difficulty in filling cages for 50 strays.

The argument used by the hon. Member for High Peak would suggest that when the fee for dog licences was increased in Northern Ireland there would be a dramatic fall even from the low levels registration that there had been before, but that did not happen. In fact, there was an increase in registration, even though the scheme was not on the same scale or basis as the one being argued for today. We are arguing for a scheme in which there is clear identification and enforcement, a scheme that is of benefit to the animals themselves as well as to the public, and one which commands the clear support of the population. If hon. Members have the guts to follow their principles and vote for such a scheme, it will also have the clear support of the House of Commons.

I am not asking for a dramatic change of heart by hon. Members, who have already shown their support for the scheme by signing the early-day motion and by supporting the scheme already set out in legislation, which the Secretary of State has decided not to implement because the Act says "may" rather than "shall". We are asking hon. Members to support just a small change which will compel the Secretary of State to take action. I hope that the House will do so.

Mr. Ridley: I pay tribute to my hon. Friend the Member for Plymouth, Drake (Miss Fookes) for the work that she does for animal welfare, and for the consistency of her campaigns for the registration scheme, about which she spoke so eloquently. Both she and the hon. Member for Truro (Mr. Taylor) spent the majority of their time talking about a dog registration scheme, when the House should first direct itself to the problems and what we should do about them.

Irresponsible owners who fail properly to control their dogs cause three problems of serious concern. The first is attacks by dangerous dogs—a recent phenomenon that has got a lot of publicity. The second problem is fouling in public places, and the third is stray dogs. These are becoming more and more serious in everyday life, particularly in urban areas. Filthy pavements, packs of stray dogs, let alone isolated attacks by uncontrolled dangerous animals, are becoming a major threat to the quality of life, and in some cases to safety and health.

We are determined to do all that is possible to deal with these problems. My hon. Friend said that the time has come to act. I agree with her, and I am happy to announce a package of measures to provide what I believe is the best solution to these important but essentially local problems. I announced in March our intention to require local authorities to tackle these problems. They are local problems and should be tackled by the local authorities. I can now give the House details.

First, on dog fouling, as part of a package of measures to deal with the increasing problem of litter, I propose to place on local authorities a duty to clear up dog messes in public places. This will be enforced through a code of practice to which local authorities will have to adhere. Any member of the public will be entitled to seek an order in the courts if a local authority fails in its duty to do so. This duty will be backed up by the existing powers of local authorities to make byelaws against dog fouling or to restrict dogs from certain public places, particularly where children play.

Secondly, on stray dogs——

Mr. Allan Rogers (Rhondda): Will the right hon Gentleman give way on that point?

Mr. Ridley: No, I will not give way.

Both the police and local authorities have powers to take up, hold and, if necessary, destroy dogs. The police have a duty to hold a stray animal if it is brought in by a member of the public, but no one has the duty to collect up and deal with stray dogs. I propose that that duty should be placed firmly on local authorities, freeing police time for what should be their proper tasks. Local authorities will be able to undertake that duty as they wish.

I do not propose to issue a code of guidance, and many councils will no doubt conclude that a dog warden system on the lines already operated by some 200 local authorities is the best way to fulfil their duties. I see no other way that local authorities will be able to discharge their duties. I claim in aid the Opposition, by quoting from their October 1986 conference declaration:

"We will set up properly financed dog warden services in the interests of people's health and the welfare of domestic pets."

In support of local authorities' general proactive responsibility, I intend giving them powers to charge owners seeking to collect stray dogs from custody and a clear duty to enforce existing requirements in respect of collars and identification tags. Local authorities already have powers, subject to various statutory restrictions, to make byelaws requiring dogs to be held on leads in various public places—on roads, in parks and gardens and on beaches. In other countries such leash laws are used more widely than here. We propose examining the present range of order and byelaw-making powers.

As to dealing with dangerous dogs, we fully share the alarm caused by recent horrific stories concerning rottweilers and the attacks that they made. My right hon. Friend the Home Secretary, who has a responsibility for the control of dangerous dogs and for dog welfare, announced this afternoon a package of measures to tighten up the present controls on dangerous dogs in the Dogs Act 1871.

He proposes, first, to allow the courts to appoint someone other than the owner to destroy a dangerous animal; secondly, to increase to £400 the maximum fine for failure to comply with an order to control or to destroy a dog; thirdly, to give the courts the power to ban from owning or keeping a dog anyone who is the subject of a previous order made under the Act.

Mr. Andrew Bowden (Brighton, Kemptown): I submit that it is neither practicable nor possible to ban an individual from owning a dog. A husband, for example, who is banned from keeping a dog because of cruelty or for any other reason can arrange for his wife or another member of the family to obtain a dog for him. Would it not be possible to ban a dog being kept at a particular residence or under a particular tenancy? When the tenancy changes or when the house or flat is sold, the ban would be cancelled. The problem will never be dealt with if only one member of a family is banned.

Mr. Ridley: I note my hon. Friend's point and shall discuss it with my right hon. Friend the Home Secretary to see whether he believes that such a scheme would be better.

I make the point that nowhere do those effective and straightforward solutions require for their implementation a dog registration scheme. The fact that an owner has paid a registration fee would not have any bearing on the problem of dog fouling. Nor would registration prevent people from allowing their dogs to stray.

In a recent series of advertisements, the Royal Society for the Prevention of Cruelty to Animals declared:

"There is overwhelming evidence that dog registration would help solve the plight of stray dogs in Britain . . . owners could be identified, traced and held responsible for their dogs' actions."

There is already a statutory requirement on owners to put collars and identification tags on their dogs. I agree with my hon. Friend the Member for Drake that identification is essential, and I shall be happy to review the powers currently available to ensure that any modern form of identification can be attached to the dog rather than just to its collar—but that would not involve registration. People can be fined for breaching——

Mr. Rogers *rose*——

Mr. Ridley: I will not give way because I am in the middle of a sentence.

People who breach the law on dogs wearing collars are liable to a fine of—*[Interruption.]*

Mr. Deputy Speaker: Order. The hon. Member for Rhondda (Mr. Rogers) must restrain himself. The Secretary of State has said that he will not give way at the moment.

Mr. Ridley: We shall give local authorities a clear duty to enforce the collar or identification requirement. That is all the powers they need in to order to deal with strays.

The alleged overwhelming evidence rests on the dog registration scheme introduced in Northern Ireland in 1984. The report recently produced on the problem of straying, to which reference has been made, made the following comments on the success of the scheme:

"depending on which figure is accepted for 1984 (of dogs destroyed after straying) the total number of dogs destroyed since the new order was introduced has increased or decreased . . . Longer term evidence will be needed before the new system can be judged fairly."

That is hardly overwhelming evidence.

In none of the recent regrettable rottweiler attacks was there any evidence that identification of the owner was a problem. These owners need the law, albeit reinforced as I have said, to be enforced against them. They do not need registration. The sort of people who would allow their rottweilers to attack pensioners and children in the street will not think twice about buying a dog because of a requirement to register. Therefore, there is no logic in the campaign for a dog registration scheme.

Mr. Marlow: This proposal will obviously be a burden on local government: so be it, that is fine and there is no complaint about that. However, to help local government to discharge that burden, my right hon. Friend suggests that there should be a system of byelaws. At the moment, it is difficult and takes a long time to pass a byelaw. Could my right hon. Friend explain how the byelaws can be made readily available and can be put through the House in a relatively short time?

1 am

Mr. Ridley: I quite agree with my hon. Friend, and my right hon. Friend the Home Secretary and I are reviewing the procedure and the conditions under which byelaws are made to ensure that every local authority can easily apply for the byelaws that it will need. The measures will have to be enacted and will be brought in at the earliest opportunity. There will be time to get the law absolutely right when we come to do that.

Mr. Rogers: Early in his exposition, the Secretary of State mentioned that he was going to charge local authorities with the responsibility to ensure that dogs did not foul pavements, and that that would involve the courts. How will that court process operate in order to prevent dogs from excreting on pavements? What will the process entail for local authorities?

Mr. Ridley: The hon. Gentleman knows that no process of law, administration or registration will prevent dogs from fouling pavements. For the sake of health, it is essential to ensure that someone is responsible for cleaning up the mess. I should have thought that the hon. Gentleman would have wanted that.

There is no logic in the campaign for registration, the real reason for which was that it was a way to raise money. This policy will cost a certain amount of money. Estimates commissioned by the Royal Society for the Prevention of Cruelty to Animals from the London School of Economics suggest that the total annual cost of employing a dog warden, including the cost of holding and dealing with strays, is about £30,000 a year. The city of Bradford, which is widely believed to operate an effective dog warden scheme, and on which the LSE based its estimate, employs five wardens. Therefore, even in a city the size of Bradford, the annual cost will be about £150,000. That is the equivalent of about 40p on the community charge for the city, and that is not counting any revenue support grant which might go towards it.

Is it justifiable to set up a new scheme, with its attendant bureaucracy and the additional costs involved, to collect hypothecated tax from dog owners in order to finance such a small sum, or to chase up the many dog owners who would seek to avoid the tax?

I invite the House to think about the registration scheme. Opposition Members have complained bitterly about the cost and complexity of setting up the community charge registration scheme, and the cost and complexity of a dog registration scheme would be far worse. Every working dog and every old lady's pet dog would have to be registered. Different interest groups would press for exemptions for all sorts of category of owner.

The Royal Society for the Prevention of Cruelty to Animals suggests that the dog registration fee should be £65. That is as much as twice what many people will have to pay as a community charge if they are on full rebate. We cannot expect people to pay twice as much for the registration of their dog as they pay for local authority services. There would have to be a complicated system of rebates for old-age pensioners, for example, the blind, those who own sheepdogs and those who are on income support. The register would have to be kept up to date, and dogs die at a fairly early age and are transferred from one owner to another. New dogs are required at regular

intervals. All these factors would have to be included in the production of a register. It would be the hardest register of all to collect information for and to set up.

The Kennel Club, to which my hon. Friend the Member for Drake did not refer as an organisation concerned with dogs and one which supported her, does not support a dog registration scheme. I shall quote from its letter to me, which I received today. It reads:

"Our data base contains"—

it has its own registration scheme—

"2·3 million dogs and is a voluntary scheme but despite this the change of address of owners and their names does occur with great frequency (10 per cent. a year) and we are seldom notified. The numerous other arguments against a national registration scheme are well known and have been clearly stated".

Mr. Frank Cook (Stockton, North): I ask the Secretary of State to adjust his perspective for about 10 seconds. Does he realise that the registration is of the owner, not of the dog? Responsibility for the behaviour of the dog, including any misdemeanours, and its welfare and care is placed on the owner, and the owner could be traced. Will the Secretary of State consider registration from that angle?

Mr. Ridley: Of course we could not make a dog register itself. We would have to register the owner. The hon. Gentleman states the obvious. The new clause is all about a dog registration scheme. Surely the hon. Gentleman understands that that means registering owners and not dogs.

Mr. Roger Gale (Thanet, North): I am sure that my right hon. Friend did not wish deliberately to mislead the House when he referred to the fee that the RSPCA suggests, but he most certainly has done so. He quoted a flat, one-off fee for life. The annual alternative fee would not be anything like £65. Instead, it would be £15.

Mr. Ridley: I thank my hon. Friend for that elucidation. I do not think that a fee of £15 would be all that popular. Nor do I think that it would be easy to collect that fee instead of £65. I believe that there would be massive problems with evasion if there were fees of that sort.

On the other hand, the community charge mechanism is effective and simple. It would provide a reliable source of income from the local community to deal with a community problem. A dog registration scheme would probably be the worst tax to raise money that it was possible to invent.

We shall of course be consulting local authorities and other interested bodies about the details of what I propose. I believe that the package I have outlined will give local authorities the tools with which to do the necessary job. What the Government propose will tackle the real problems without inventing an expensive and complex bureaucracy and a new tax that many people would find it hard to pay or would wish to evade. I hope that my hon. Friend feels that what we have suggested will meet the real concern of people that the situation should improve and that a dog registration scheme is therefore not necessary.

Dr. John Cunningham (Copeland): I, too, congratulate the hon. Member for Plymouth, Drake (Dame J. Fookes) on her speech, in which she dealt with a series of issues of considerable public significance. The Secretary of State said that we should concentrate on the problems and then try to find effective solutions, and I agree with him. I told my hon. Friend the Member for Sheffield, Brightside (Mr. Blunkett) that I did not care too much whether he was in the Chamber tonight, so long as he made sure that his dog Offa was here and on my side when I spoke.

The recent series of incidents in which people have been savagely mauled by rottweilers has shocked the people of Britain. They want action to be taken now so that safety in public places is improved, with greater control being exercised over dog owners and their animals. In previous years we have endured other such incidents involving other breeds of dog. It just happens that rottweilers are fashionable at the moment. In the past it has been alsatians or doberman pinschers. It is not a new problem.

Unless better protection is provided for the public, and unless better enforcement systems in respect of owners can be used, some of these dogs will, literally, be lethal. A warden scheme and an owner registration scheme represent the best way in which to begin to resolve the problem of dog attacks and the problem of public health and hygiene which is associated with dogs fouling public open spaces and footpaths.

I share the Secretary of State's view that these problems will not be immediately resolved by whatever scheme is finally put in place. It would be unrealistic to suppose otherwise. However, I do not accept that to increase the level of fines and to lay further duties on local authorities without making any specific commitment to provide additional central Government finance to support the administration of the scheme would be right. Apart from public safety and public health and hygiene, the nuisance caused by dogs is often considerable. The number of accidents involving dogs and motor vehicles is also considerable. Taken together, all these things cost a great deal of public money.

Mr. Gary Waller (Keighley): The hon. Gentleman began his speech by referring, quite properly, to the problems caused by dangerous dogs, but does he agree that a dog registration scheme would not deal with the problems caused by dangerous dogs? The RSPCA accepts that a dog registration scheme which tried to identify particular breeds of dogs would be unworkable, particularly if we take into account the fact that many problems are caused not by rottweilers but by other dogs which would also have to be registered.

Dr. Cunningham: I do not agree with any of that. Of course, all owners would be required to register their dogs.

There is a wide range of issues and problems. Although the current anxiety is principally about vicious or violent dogs, there is widespread concern about health, hygiene and accidents. We need a system which can begin to deal with all those issues, not just the recent incidents involving a particular breed. Those incidents which have gained media attention are just a tiny fraction of the incidents involving dogs almost every day.

1.15 am

Perhaps I should declare an interest as a dog owner and dog lover. One of the first points that we should recognise is that not everyone comes into that category. People are often unsure or afraid of dogs, even dogs which are very friendly, like the dog in my family. However we consider these problems, we need to bring more pressure to bear

and exercise more controls over dog owners, and registering them is the beginning of the way to resolve those problems.

According to the latest estimate, there were more than 7 million dogs in the United Kingdom in 1988, 500,000 more than in the previous year. The increase is forecast to continue. The problems will continue to grow. The Secretary of State has said nothing to convince the public that the Government's proposals will resolve the nature or scale of the problems. Of course, we need a system which helps local authorities properly to finance dog warden schemes. I do not believe that that burden should be placed solely on poll tax payers. Surely dog owners have a duty to contribute to the cost of the resolution of these problems. A realistic registration fee is a way of achieving that.

Last year, during the passage of another Local Government Bill, the Government abolished the licence fee, which was a paltry 37p. That fee was out of date and the system was neglected and discredited. It was right that it should go, but it was wrong that it was not replaced by a more effective scheme which addressed the problems. The Government have created a vacuum which they clearly regret, as evidenced by the announcements of the Secretary of State. The House of Lords quite rightly wrote into that Bill provisions for a dog registration scheme. The Secretary of State immediately made clear his intention not to activate those proposals. He should think again. Perhaps the other place will again force him to reconsider, aided by increasing public opinion in support of what the other place and we say.

In 1978, the then Labour Government commissioned a working party on these problems. It reported in 1978, but was overtaken by the 1979 general election. The incoming Conservative Government set the report aside and took no action. We were convinced then and we remain convinced that a registration scheme should be set up, to be administered at local level. I share the view of the Secretary of State that, whatever the system, these problems will be adequately and effectively dealt with only at local level. We cannot resolve them with Ministers and Whitehall having all the powers and local authorities having none.

Mr. Anthony Steen (South Hams): I, too, am a dog owner and a dog lover. I have been trying to understand the arguments of the hon Member for Copeland (Dr. Cunningham) about registration and to relate them to strays. When I was in the north-west, my office was next to the RSPCA home and I saw the horror of all the stray dogs being brought in and put down. It was a terrible sight. How will registration prevent that? How would the hon. Gentleman ensure that owners of dogs which have litters were on some sort of register? The House would be interested to hear how he envisages a system of registration working.

Dr. Cunningham: The best way to tackle a problem is to make a start. Unless we beging to do something, the position will worsen——

Mr. Graham Riddick (Colne Valley): Answer the question.

Dr. Cunningham: Shut up.

Mr. Riddick: Answer.

Dr. Cunningham: I am answering the question, you fathead.

Mr. Marlow: On this side of the House we do not think that you are a fathead, Mr. Deputy Speaker.

Mr. Deputy Speaker: Order. I am in a very tolerant mood tonight.

Dr. Cunningham: No discourtesy to you was intended, Mr. Deputy Speaker.

As the hon. Member for Drake said, we need a system which connects dog owners and animals. Nothing that the Secretary of State has said tonight will bring about that simple connection. Unless there is such a link in identification, which registration would begin to put in place, nothing will begin to resolve the problem of strays. It is no good suggesting that people should pay larger fines to get their dogs out of dog pounds. Only one in 10 stray dogs are collected from the pounds by their owners. If they know that there will be an ever larger financial penalty when they collect their dogs, the percentage being collected will fall, not rise. The right hon. Gentleman's proposals simply do not hang together.

I want to say something about the Secretary of State's dismissal of the proposals in the new clause on grounds of cost and bureaucracy. The RSPCA estimates that the current cost to the public of such a variety of problems is £60 million to £70 million per year and rising. We are already paying a heavy price for our failure to deal with those problems. They can only get worse under the right hon. Gentleman's proposals and the costs will increase.

The right hon. Gentleman said that under the new clause all dogs would have to be registered and he made great play about guide dogs for the blind. Of all the categories that he could have chosen, he could not have been more wrong than he was about guide dogs. Dogs like Offa, who belongs to my hon. Friend the Member for Brightside do not savage people in public parks and they do not foul public places. In any case, they could be exempt because guide dogs are already subject to a registration scheme. The right hon. Gentleman chose a great many nit-picking arguments and rolled them into an argument about cost and bureaucracy to support his claim that the scheme would not work.

The right hon. Gentleman also mentioned the cost of the scheme for pensioners. They, too, could be exempt —*[Interruption.]* The right hon. Gentleman raised the point. Pensioners' house dogs are usually tiny and do not cause the majority of the problems. Exempt or not, with modern technology and management systems it would be quite a simple matter to have a registration scheme which could be effectively administered.

Mr. Rogers: Will my hon. Friend give way?

Dr. Cunningham: I have nearly finished my speech.

The same Secretary of State who opposes dog registration says that he wants to register every person over 18 to pay the poll tax. He says that that will be efficient and will not cost much, but he will not agree to register 7 million animal owners. To use one of his own favourite phrases, he is talking absolute nonsense and he knows it.

Mr. John Marshall (Hendon, South): Interestingly, those who advocate registration are unwilling to talk about its cost. To put forward a scheme that will involve people making a one-off payment of £65 or an annual payment of £15 is unfair to pensioners, one-parent families and other groups in social need.

Mr. Tim Devlin (Stockton, South): Does my hon. Friend have any conception of veterinary fees? Someone who cannot afford to pay £50 or £60 a year should not keep a dog, because every time that their dog is even slightly injured they will pay over £100 for the most elementary treatment. I should welcome a scheme that makes owners pay a proper fee to keep dogs.

Mr. Marshall: As a dog owner, I am well aware of the cost of veterinary fees. There is no reason for placing an additional burden on dog owners, which is what the proponents of the scheme are willing to do.

I do not believe that people would register their dogs. We know that people did not pay the former dog licence. It is perverse logic to suggest that increasing the cost of registration will make people register their dogs. If they did not pay the dog licence, they will not be willing to register.

To say that under a dog registration scheme someone will be able to find out whose dog bit him and who its owner was is absurd in the extreme. If a dog bites someone, will it then stop so that the hon. Member for Plymouth, Drake (Dame J. Fookes) or anyone else can look at its tag to find out who its owner is? Of course it will run away as quickly as possible. It is absurd to suggest that a dog registration scheme will stop dogs biting people, postmen or even Labour party canvassers, if there are any left, or stop dogs fouling the pavement.

I have been shocked by the RSPCA's campaign. Its press advertisement was quite irresponsible because the sight of those dogs was quite unrelated to the abolition of the dog licence. It and every hon. Member knows that that advertisement was quite irresponsible.

If we are to get rid of the problem of strays we need a system of spaying and neutering. In 1939, the RSPCA signed an agreement with the British Veterinary Association that it would not neuter cats or dogs belonging to the general public, except in special circumstances. The RSPCA is a wealthy organisation. I read an article this evening that stated that it has accumulated funds of £40 million. If it wants to deal with the problem of stray dogs it should use that money to set up spaying and neutering centres.

Mr. Peter L. Pike (Burnley): I shall be brief, but I should like strongly to support the new clause. Although I do not believe that it will solve all the problems, it is a move in the right direction. It will deal vigorously with the problems of dogs, which are caused by irresponsible owners. We have to stress that it is not the dogs themselves that cause the problem, but the actions of irresponsible owners, which allow them to become strays or foul the footpath and cause the majority of problems at present.

1.30 am

The proposals outlined by the Secretary of State were some of the greatest nonsense that I have ever heard him utter. That is saying something with that Secretary of State, because he speaks a lot of nonsense at times. He throws another burden on local authorities and assumes that local authorities can solve this problem. He has shifted it from the owners and the Government and has said to local government, "This is your problem. You solve it." Yet he does not give local authorities the resources or the ability to solve the problem. Without a dog registration scheme, his proposal would be totally inoperable and totally ineffective.

I remind the House of what the Secretary of State said last year when we dealt with the Lords amendment. He made it very clear then that, although he was not prepared to disapprove of the Lords amendment, he had no intention of operating it. The only reason that he did not want to disapprove of it at that stage—because it is nonsense to allow a proposal to stand in a Bill if one has no intention of operating it—and the only reason that he did not want to put the Lords amendment to the vote was that he felt that he was in danger of losing. The only reason why he has come forward with his nonsensical proposal is to try to dissuade some of his hon. Friends from standing firmly by the new clause and voting against the Government tonight. He is trying to lead them in a false direction.

I want to echo a point made in an intervention by my hon. Friend the Member for Wentworth (Mr. Hardy). I could say much on the issue of dogs, having had a major problem with dogs being banned from parks in Burnley in the 1970s. My hon. Friend made the point clearly that he hoped that any dog registration scheme would have a nationally fixed fee. We had a saga of problems with banning dogs from certain parks and I could talk for hours on that if it was not so late. The case is strengthened for having a nationally fixed fee.

When the Secretary of State referred to byelaws, he had to recognise the difficulty of bringing in byelaws and he should have done more about it than he has done tonight. When the byelaws were introduced in Burnley under the County Borough Act 1881, they had to be incorporated in the County of Lancashire Act 1984. That Act was blocked in this House and in the other place for about two years solely because of the Burnley dog ban in parks.

If the Secretary of State really believes that his solution can work, he must think again. I ask Conservative Members not to be led astray by what the Secretary of State has said tonight. He has offered a proposal that will not solve the problem. If we want to reduce the incidence of dogs fouling our footpaths, straying and attacking children, old people and postmen, we must support the new clause.

Mr. Gale: I will support my hon. Friend in the Lobby tonight—[HON. MEMBERS: "Which one?"] I will support my hon. Friend the Member for Plymouth, Drake (Dame J. Fookes) and I hope that many of the more than 100 of my hon. Friends who signed the early-day motion will also support the new clause.

I want first to thank my hon. Friend the Member for Surrey, South-West, (Mrs. Bottomley), the Parliamentary Under-Secretary of State for the Environment, for her courtesy on the two occasions when we have met her to discuss the problem and for the attention she has paid to both my hon. Friend the Member for Drake and myself as officers of the all-party group for animal welfare when we have raised the matter with her. It is a sadness to me that after the last occasion on which my hon. Friend and I took a delegation from the RSPCA to meet the Minister, it found it necessary to put out a press release saying that she had been intransigent. She was not. It was neither true nor just. [HON. MEMBERS: "When does the press tell the truth?"] I do not believe that this is a party political issue in any way. There can be no doubt among hon. Members of any party, or on the Front Bench, that there is a problem with stray dogs; with the fact that 1,000 dogs every day of the year—350,000 dogs per year—are being

destroyed; with the damage that is caused by stray animals and with injuries. The difference between us is a genuine one; it is a difference over how the problem should be solved.

I welcome the measures that my right hon. Friend the Home Secretary announced in a written answer earlier today, although I am slightly concerned by the caveat that these measures will be introduced subject to legislative opportunity. As many hon. Members have said, each of those measures is dependent upon the identification of the dog and the owner of the dog in question. Every single measure that my right hon. Friend has announced today, such as taking cases involving dangerous dogs to court, giving courts the power to order the destruction of a dog where the owner is not prepared to do so and ordering the implementation of a fine, is dependent upon an identification system. In a sedentary intervention, my hon. Friend the Member for High Peak (Mr. Hawkins) asked how identification would help. The RSPCA is right to say that although a registration and identification system is not the solution to the problem in itself it is the cornerstone of a series of solutions to what is becoming a national problem.

Other hon. Members have asked how we can make people register and have said, "People did not pay the 7s 6d licence fee." It is true that they did not and that it fell into disrepute——

Mr. John Marshall: People do not always pay the road fund tax.

Mr. Gale: Precisely, as my hon. Friend says, people do not always pay the road fund tax, but there is no suggestion that the Government will abolish the vehicle licensing scheme. There is no suggestion, for the time being at least, that the televison registration scheme or the gun licence scheme will be abolished. The fact that every hon. Member knows that not every dog owner will register immediately is no reason for sitting back and doing nothing.

Mr. Devlin: Will my hon. Friend give way?

Mr. Gale: No, I should prefer not to because other hon. Members wish to speak and I am sure that my hon. Friend will be able to make his own speech in a moment.

My right hon. Friend the Secretary of State has suggested a further set of measures this evening that could be provided through the funding raised as a result of a registration scheme, but he has chosen instead to place that funding burden on the ratepayer.

I believe that a national dog warden scheme is necessary and desirable and that it is necessary locally to ensure that dog owners do not allow their animals to foul public footpaths and playing greens. However, I also believe as a Conservative—although I did say that this was not a party political matter—that the user should pay. I do not see why the ordinary ratepayer, the non-dog owner, should be required to pay for my dogs, the dogs of any of my hon. Friends or of any old-age pensioners. The figures have been given. The RSPCA has stated that the cost of a national registration scheme would be £65 as a flat fee upon the initial registration of a puppy or approximately £15 per year. It has been said that that would place an unfair burden on old-age pensioners but I remind the House that it costs about £200 per year for each and every year of a dog's life to keep a dog fed and properly

[*Mr. Gale*]

maintained in terms of veterinary fees. Frankly, sad though it may be, the person who cannot afford the £15 most certainly could not afford the £200—or more for a larger dog—that it costs to keep an animal per year.

I believe that a national register is practical and possible and that it will help as one ingredient in the solution to the problem. Indeed, I believe that it is essential. However, it need not be unnecessarily bureaucratic. I believe that it needs to be run by the state. It has been said that the Kennel Club already has a regulation scheme. The British Veterinary Association, which backs this proposal, has indicated a willingness to become involved, and so, too, has the RSPCA. For those who would like to see the private sector run the scheme, the Wood Green animal shelter has said that it has the computer capacity and the ability to run such a scheme.

I hope that those more than 100 of my hon. Friends who signed the early-day motion which led to my hon. Friend's new clause will support us in the Lobby tonight.

Mr. McAllion: I do not wish to detain the House at this hour, but, as it was my constituent, an 11-year old girl, Kellie Lynch, who was killed in the attack by a rottweiler dog just two short months ago, I have taken a special interest in the subject. I did not want this debate to pass without making a contribution.

Like the Secretary of State for the Environment, I wish to concentrate on the problems presented to the public by certain breeds of dogs. One problem of which I have been very much aware, but which has not been mentioned so far, is that we do not know the current size of the dog population in this country. In this morning's *The Daily Telegraph,* for example, it was estimated that the population of rottweilers has increased a hundred fold over the past decade—from 1,800 in 1979 to 180,000 currently. In a recent letter to me, the Under-Secretary of State for the Home Department estimated that the rottweiler dog population is 90,000, and the researchers for a BBC programme in which I participated recently estimated it at 50,000.

Estimates varying from 50,000 to 180,000 must show that we do not know the size of the rottweiler population. Until we know that, we cannot begin to understand the seriousness of the threats of certain dogs to human welfare and safety. It is important that we take the first step towards coming to grips with the problem by instituting a national registration scheme, which would at least show the size of the problem.

The Secretary of State admitted that one problem that we have to confront is attacks by dangerous dogs. He appeared to suggest that this was the problem of the owners rather than the dogs. I dispute that argument, because the owner of the dog which killed my constituent was a very respected breeder, who, up to that time, had had a good record for looking after his dogs. I do not believe that the House can get away with laying all the blame at the door of owners.

Certain breeds of dog in this country are sufficiently dangerous in themselves to justify extra control being brought in by the House to ensure that the public are safe from those dogs.

One of our first tasks must be to institute a national registration scheme, and to back that up with an effective dog warden scheme in every part of the country to ensure that those dogs can be kept under proper control.

The law at present is deficient because it does not recognise that there are dogs that are inherently dangerous. As the law stands, an attack must take place before any court will define a dog as dangerous. By the time a dog has been so defined, it is too late, the harm and the pain has already been caused to the people who have been attacked. If we allow the law to remain as it is, we will be responsible for any future attacks, so the House must do something about it.

The Secretary of State announced a whole package of measures, which I believe are too little and already too late for the seriousness of the situation. None of those so-called proper laws on dogs would have saved my young constituent's life when she was attacked by that rottweiler, or prevented a rottweiler dog from dragging a young boy off his bike in a park and severely savaging him. [*Interruption.*] Registration would certainly help; it does not exist now; the House should adopt it to ensure better control of dogs.

The law will deal severely with a dog only after an attack takes place, and less severely with the owner. That is no compensation for the victims of these attacks. We have a responsibility to try to do something to help them.

1.45 am

No one in the House can justify the present unrestricted market in which anyone who wants to can acquire any sort of dog. Anyone can own a rottweiler, which can stand 3 ft high and weigh 15 stones. Anyone can own a pit bull terrier. Only this week on breakfast television an American dog warden reported that pit bull terriers have killed 16 people in the United States in the past two and a half years. Anyone in this country can own an animal that I saw advertised in the *Exchange & Mart* in Scotland a few weeks ago. It was described as a hybrid, 75 per cent. wolf. All one needs to own one of them is money. It does not matter where it is kept, or whether it is allowed to roam free. It does not matter if it is encouraged to be fierce and to attack other people. Dogs are being sold and described as attack dogs and war dogs, and the law will not act until one of them inflicts pain and suffering on someone. That is intolerable.

In an Adjournment debate tomorrow night, I shall make several suggestions about what can be done to control dangerous dogs, but nothing can be done to control them until we have a national registration scheme and know the numbers of dogs and who owns them. That is the essential first step, and the House must not walk away from its responsibilities.

Mr. Hawkins: My hon. Friend the Member for Plymouth, Drake (Dame J. Fookes) spoke on the Jimmy Young show this morning. Throughout the interview her host kept saying how reasonable the dog registration scheme seemed and that he could not see why anyone should object to it. My hon. Friend said in her speech tonight that 92 per cent. of the public would support some form of dog registration scheme. My hon. Friend succeeded in fooling Jimmy Young, and the public have been grossly misled by a campaign by the RSPCA.

On the show, my hon. Friend did not have time to detail exactly what the scheme involves. I want to quote a letter sent to supporters of the RSPCA, of whom I am one. I am also a local vice-president, and a campaigner for animal rights. The RSPCA wrote to supporters as follows:

"Please support our campaign by writing to your MP today. Simply say that you are in favour of dog registration". The people who are in favour of this scheme, while claiming that it will cure rape, famine, pestilence, war, acne, dangerous dogs and everything else, have not told the public that it involves—according to the RSPCA and my hon. Friends the Members for Drake and for Thanet, North (Mr. Gale)—the permanent branding of dogs. The RSPCA has said:

"we need a law that ensures every dog is marked with a unique and permanently applied number".

I do not want that for my dogs, and I should very much like to see the RSPCA conduct a poll among its dog-owning members to discover what proportion of them, when correctly told what the scheme involved, would vote for this permanent branding—

Dame Janet Fookes: First, it is not only the RSPCA which wants a dog registration scheme. Why should the Association of District Councils take the trouble to present a scheme to my right hon. Friend?

Secondly, why are some voluntary schemes using implants? A good many dog owners want their dogs registered so that, if they are lost or stolen, they can get them back easily.

Mr. Hawkins: That is fine if it is voluntary. I am a great believer in freedom of choice. However, we are suggesting not a voluntary scheme but a compulsory one. The Association of District Councils supports such a scheme because it is a method of taxing dog owners to pay for a dog warden service. I am totally in favour of such a service and I understand that it must be paid for. However, it is quite iniquitous to suggest, as my hon. Friend the Member for Thanet, North suggested, that it should be paid for by a tax on dog owners whose dogs commit no offence, behave perfectly normally and are properly looked after and controlled.

It is as absurd to say that dog owners should pay the tax for a dog warden service from which we shall all benefit as it would be to say that only child-bearing parents should pay the tax that is used to finance education. For those reasons I shall oppose the introduction of such a scheme. As I say, I am in favour of dog wardens, but they should be paid for by general taxation, because we will all benefit, or by local taxation.

A dog registration scheme has nothing whatever to do with the problem of dangerous dogs. As my right hon. Friend the Secretary of State has said, most people seem to ignore the fact that in every recent case of rottweilers savaging or damaging people we knew the names of the owners. There was no problem in finding out who they were. The problems arose because of the viciousness of the dogs. That will not solved by an RSPCA scheme for registering dogs, however much such a scheme is supported, and for those reasons I shall oppose it.

Mr. Bob Cryer (Bradford, South): We are not talking about a single scheme but about requiring the Secretary of State for the Environment to produce regulations. He already has powers to do that but he has made it clear that he will not use them. There are 200 dog warden services and he can consult the local authority associations, one of which has already submitted a dog registration scheme to him. We are not resting our case simply on one scheme. We

are saying to the Secretary of State that he is required to produce a scheme and can take into account the objections and benefits put forward in the debate.

Parliament has already required the Secretary of State to produce a scheme, but instead of saying that he "shall" produce one, it said he "may" produce one. This modest new clause does not seek an absolute provision because the second part of it suggests that if the right hon. Gentleman fails to produce a scheme he must produce a statement on 1 January next year and place it before the House so that the House can take a further decision. That is a reasonable request by Parliament.

At a recent meeting of the RSPCA and several other animal organisations, people who face the day-to-day problems posed by stray dogs and problems about the ownership of difficult and savage dogs made it clear that in their day-to-day work they would welcome a dog registration scheme. That day-to-day work is not carried out in the sort of academic fashion in which we work in the House. They said that such a scheme would help them to trace the owners and marry up the stray and difficult dogs with their owners. They said that it would provide some sort of guidance and help for people who often buy dogs and are completely unaware that the soft, cuddly puppies that they buy will grow into dogs that are in some cases completely out of control, even in the families that have helped to bring them up.

I shall give an example of how registration is not only desirable but necessary. One of my constituents, a young girl, was walking through a fair when a dog, apparently under the ownership of a person, set upon her. She suffered severe injuries and complained to the police. The police did nothing. She complained to me, and I took the matter up with the police. Under the Town Police Clauses Act 1847, a person can be prosecuted for having a dangerous dog. In that case, the person in control of the dog at the time simply passed the dog on to its previous owner. The dog was then no longer in the first person's ownership, and the police could not prosecute. They wrote to me saying:

"The contents . . . of the letter . . . are self-explanatory and you will see that unfortunately nothing further can be done. The new owner of the dog, who was also the previous owner, was not present when the attack occurred, and on hearing of the trouble retrieved the dog from Ali. There is no evidence to show that he does not keep the dog under proper control. Nor is there any suggestion that he is unfit to keep the dog. In the circumstances, it was considered inappropriate to take him to court when the owner and person responsible for the dog at the time of the attack was . . . another person. I endorse the views of the Crown Prosecutor that it is unfortunate that no effective proceedings can be instituted against . . . this person . . . for the appalling injury caused by his dog."

With a dog registration scheme, it would be difficult, if not impossible, for such a person to say, "I am terribly sorry. Bad injuries have been caused. I pass the dog to somebody else and I am free from the danger of prosecution." That letter shows that that happens.

A dog registration scheme at one fell swoop would ensure that a long-standing piece of legislation, which has not been amended, would be put into operation. A young girl who has been scarred for life and who has needed plastic surgery would have the satisfaction of knowing that the same fate would not befall other people in the same circumstances.

As has been pointed out, registration would enable strays to be matched to their owners. That is important, for one of the most chilling comments of an RSPCA inspector at last week's meeting was that as circumstances

[*Mr. Bob Cryer*]

such as adverse publicity caused the prices of certain breeds to drop—rottweilers being a good example—more strays were in evidence as people simply tipped their dogs on to the roads. Are we to accept the present situation, with American pit bull terriers being at large, wandering about streets on housing estates, and we cannot do anything about it because we cannot trace their owners? It is not true to say that in all accidents the owners are known. The economics of the situation should appeal to the Government. As prices drop, dogs and puppies are turned out on to the streets, and some of them are potentially highly dangerous breeds.

If the Secretary of State does not like the idea of local authorities raising the money, he can raise it centrally. We are here giving the right hon. Gentleman discretion—not something we would do lightly. On this occasion we are prepared to encourage him in the task. Wardens can educate, inform and help people understand their animals, so that the accidents which have received much publicity recently are not repeated.

In the BBC programme "Face the Facts" on 23 February 1989 a commentator interviewed a Mr. Keith Porter at the Birmingham accident hospital about a horrific accident, the details of which I will not relate. Apparently a rottweiler was being stroked by a small child through a fence. The boy was badly attacked and needed new skin on his damaged legs. The commentator said:

"As well as having to treat more and more victims of vicious dogs, the burden on the National Health Service weighs heavy in terms of cost."

I would have thought the Government would be seeking ways to reduce NHS expenditure.

The commentator continued:

"Last year around five million pounds. The latest figures for injuries show that in 1986 four people died as a result of dog bites, twelve hundred were treated as hospital in-patients, and in one metropolitan hospital surveyed at random, three per cent. of all those who visited the Accident and Emergency Department had been bitten by dogs."

There is a problem, and solving it will involve cost. It will not go away, and it is increasing. My hon. Friend the Member for Copeland (Dr. Cunningham) gave a larger figure because he included all the costs in the use of public services for the problems raised by dogs, and those problems will not go away.

2 am

The Secretary of State said that the Bradford dog warden scheme is good, and employs five people at a modest cost. Let me tell him about the case of a headmaster in a primary school who took a small boy back home because he was ill. Of the three doberman pinschers at the house, one broke its chain and attacked the headmaster, breaking his arm and biting him badly. The dog was put down, but was immediately replaced by a rottweiler, so the family kept three dogs. In an adjacent house lived a young mother with an 18-month-old daughter. Every now and again, by accident or design, or as a result of carelessness, the dogs were released. When they were straying about, she was a prisoner in her house because she dared not go out with the child in case one of the dogss should pounce on them.

The mother would call the dog warden service, but on Sundays it was not staffed sufficiently well to enable it to round up so many dogs. There is no limit on the number of dogs that people can have, and these people chose to have three. Perhaps dog registration would cause them to think about the decisions that they take. They might have thought twice before replacing so rapidly the dog that had to be put down. The Secretary of State praises the Bradford service, but good though it is, it is not adequate to deal with those problems, although they arose from a family who were careless, incompetent and irresponsible in their ownership of dogs. Such situations are repeated elsewhere.

The measures that the Secretary of State has announced do not have any matching facilities. In the example that he used—Bradford—the facilities are not adequate, and more is needed. An important step to start control of these problems and of the growing number of dangerous, ferocious and threatening dogs would be a dog registration scheme. I hope that the Secretary of State can understand that.

Mr. Jeremy Hanley (Richmond and Barnes): I declare an interest as a member of the RSPCA and of the all-party animal welfare group, and as a vice-president of the London Wildlife Trust. I would like to think of myself as a friend of my hon. Friend the Member for Plymouth, Drake (Dame J. Fookes). It pains me to disagree with her as I think that she is one of the most courageous of people in dealing with animal welfare issues, and she has led many campaigns with which I agree. I agree with 99 out of 100 campaigns led by the RSPCA, but I disagree with it in this particular instance. It is sad that in this campaign irresponsibilities and inaccuracies have been made at great expense. When the RSPCA criticised my hon. Friend the Member for Surrey, South-West (Mrs. Bottomley), I felt that that was close to heresy, for she is fragrant. It is also sad that the advertisements with pictures of the large number of dogs that have had to be destroyed by the RSPCA use figures and pictures that have been greatly exaggerated.

All the information that I use will come from a document that has been mentioned by other hon. Members. The hon. Member for Truro (Mr. Taylor) sought honesty and integrity, and I hope to provide him with some, for the document from which I shall quote—and from which a large part of the hon. Gentleman's speech derived—is entitled "A summary of the report commissioned by the RSPCA (1989)" by the London School of Economics and Political Science. Other hon. Members also quoted that document, but not page 3, and those who referred obliquely to page 3, which deals with the cost of the scheme, did not do so accurately.

It is true that in 1988 dog ownership in the United Kingdom totalled 7·3 million—an increase of 500,000 over 1987. It is true also that the figure is likely to continue increasing, and that the LSE stated that compulsory registration and identification is an essential part of any solution. However, no hon. Member mentioned the LSE's finding that

"There are about 500,000 dogs loose in the streets or countryside every day. Evidence from dog wardens shows that less than half of these dogs are lost. Many of the straying dogs are 'latchkey' dogs. These dogs are allowed by their owners to roam the streets, fouling pavements, playing fields and parks, and contributing to many road accidents. Some of them cause injury to humans, or savage other pets and farm livestock. There is at present no law in Great Britain to prevent owners from letting dogs stray."

I hope that no right hon. or hon. Member disagrees with the LSE's other finding:

"About 240,000 stray dogs are taken to the police station each year by wardens and others, and officially recorded with the police as strays."

The summary adds that a further 250,000 strays are identified by wardens and returned directly to their owners without being recorded by the police. That makes a total of 500,000 strays. The summary adds:

"About 60,000 of the recorded strays are claimed by their owners."

Therefore, responsible owners who lose their dogs will bother to claim them, but I wonder how many would do so if their dogs were not registered and they were under an obligation to pay a registration charge as a condition of reclaiming their dogs. The summary continues:

"Others are not traced within the seven days and the dogs must be kept in the pound . . . About 90,000 unclaimed strays are found new homes by the animal shelters."

I wonder whether, with registration, that figure of 90,000 would reduce because of the extra cost involved. It would certainly not increase, because at present there is no registration charge to the new owner, apart from a voluntary payment to the shelter.

The summary continues:

"The remaining 90,000 unclaimed strays have to be destroyed each year to make room in the shelter for new strays."

If those figures are accurate, about 250 dogs are destroyed every day on the basis of a seven-day week, or 280 per day in a six-day week—not the 1,000 per day mentioned by my hon. Friend the Member for Thanet, North (Mr. Gale). In any event, the photograph in the RSPCA advertisement was a collage of the same dogs, as was subsequently admitted.

Mr. Gale: My hon. Friend gives the figure for animal shelters only, whereas the RSPCA's statistics relate to dogs destroyed by the RSPCA, by the police, and by others.

Mr. Hanley: I am merely quoting from the information which has been sent to hon. Members in order that they may balance their arguments.

Sir Michael McNair-Wilson (Newbury): The information given by the RSPCA states that it has to put down 131,000 animals of all kinds per year. The figure of 1,000 per day therefore covers other organisations.

Mr. Hanley: That is most interesting and goes a long way towards confirming what I was saying— [*Interruption.*] The hon. Member for Copeland (Dr. Cunningham) says that it does not. His contribution showed that not only are there dangers normally when he thinks, but that when he thinks on his feet and opens his mouth, he puts his foot right in it. When he talked about guide dogs for the blind he was corrected and told that they were registered anyway. He may have known that —if he did, I will give him credit for it—but he then said that pensioners should be exempt from registration.

Dr. Cunningham: We are asking the Secretary of State. I said that they would be exempt from paying the fee.

Mr. Hanley: The hon. Gentleman said that they would be exempt from registration. [HON. MEMBERS: "No."] When I heard him, I immediately thought that they should be exempt from the fee, which has always been designed within the registration process, but not that they should be exempt from registration. If, when I read the debate tomorrow, I find that I am wrong, I will willingly apologise to the hon. Gentleman.

Dr. Cunningham: We need not argue about it. The point was made by the Patronage Secretary from a sedentary position that pensioners would not be able to afford the cost. I said that they could be exempt from the cost, not the registration.

Mr. Hanley: I will willingly check that in the morning and I will willingly apologise if necessary, but I heard what I heard.

I wish to pose a few questions. How will registration deal with the irresponsible, lazy, ignorant or unaware dog owner, or with the deliberate law breaker—[*Interruption.*] The hon. Member for Bradford, South (Mr. Cryer) says, "You track him down". We track down the dog owners, whose details are on a register only if they have registered their dogs. Those who choose to register their dogs are the responsible ones. I cannot see how this scheme would help the irresponsible, the ignorant, those who are unaware of the legislation or those who deliberately break the law. Those are the people with whom we should be dealing, but we cannot do that by imposing charges which would deter them further.

I wish to place in context the level of charges contained in the document produced by the LSE. The figures of £65 and £15 have been mentioned. When the hon. Member for Truro talked about honesty and integrity, he did not mention the charges. Even my hon. Friend the Member for Drake did not mention the charges set out within the document. I will give them fully because they are important. A one-off payment would be £57, or £66 including a tattoo.

Dame Janet Fookes: I specifically said in my opening speech that the fees and the arrangements could vary depending on the type of scheme in operation but that in the short time available wanted to argue for the principle rather than go into the details of the schemes. It is therefore unfair to suggest that I did not give those details when I explained why I was not doing so.

Mr. Hanley: In no way did I want to give the impression that I believed that my hon. Friend had deliberately left out that information. I hope that she will be pleased that I shall give the information in my speaking time because some of my constituents changed their minds as soon as they heard the figures, which were £57 for the one-off payment or £66 with tattooing, which was regarded by the LSE as essential. It may be tattooing or the permanent fixture of, perhaps, an electrical tag under the skin. In either case, £66 is the figure that we should consider, or a charge of £23, including tattooing, coupled with a £7 annual fee. We have heard that reminders would have to be sent to people which would further increase the cost.

A discount is given for neutered dogs, which are much less of a problem when loose. The registration fee might be £25 for all dogs, with an annual renewal fee of £8 for neutered dogs and £20 for all other dogs. That means that when a dog has a litter the owner will have to register each dog and pay the one-off or first-time charge. If he does not want to do that, he will have to get rid of the dogs, which means finding people prepared to pay £65 or £23 in addition to any charge for the dogs. I would hope that in those circumstances there would be no charge for the dog. It would be extremely difficult to find people prepared to make those payments. The proposed scheme would further persuade people to put down unwanted litters. I

[*Mr. Hanley*]

believe that if the scheme were introduced, there would be mass extermination of dogs whose owners did not wish to register them. That would be wrong.

2.15am

Registration will not curb the bad or natural behaviour of dogs. The hon. Member for Bradford, South referred to a number of instances where dogs have savaged human beings and caused injury, but not once did he say that the owner of the dog could not be identified. Of course individuals should be responsible for the actions of their dogs, but registration will not improve identification of the individual. The hon. Member for Bradford, South said that in each instance to which he referred the owner had been identified. There should be a direct responsibility upon an owner for any injuries caused by his dog, but registration will not achieve that. It will simply introduce an additional inconvenience for responsible dog owners.

Registration will not stop dogs fouling public places. One of the most dangerous and disgusting features of dog ownership—I have been a dog owner for most of my life, but I am not one at present—is the fact that dogs foul public places, and all too often their owners ignore the obvious. We see dog owners with dogs on leads walking along the pavements of domestic side roads with their dogs fouling behind them. The owners look in the opposite direction as if it is not happening, but as soon as the fouling has stopped, they pat their dog and say, "Good dog." They know what has happened and they also know where it has happened. Pavements, grass verges, parks and school playing fields are not dog lavatories, but registration will not end that problem because there will never be enough wardens to police every field, park and playing field.

It is the responsible dog owner who would suffer if the registration scheme were introduced. The irresponsible owner would continue to ignore his responsibilities. The main sufferers would be the dogs that were put down because irresponsible owners refused to identify them. They would refuse to do so in the knowledge that they would be fined as soon as the dog was relocated with them. Irresponsible people would deny the existence of their dogs.

I acknowledge that the RSPCA is a most responsible body, and I understand that the scheme will be supported by the millions who condone the society's actions, but that does not make registration right. If a Government were to introduce a compulsory scheme with charges at the proposed levels, they would pay dearly for so doing. If a Government cannot introduce moderate and reasonable reforms of the National Health Service, what will happen to any Government who introduce the compulsory registration of dogs? Perhaps Opposition Members are so keen that the Government should introduce an unpopular scheme that they are prepared to support the RSPCA's scheme.

Mr. Rogers: I am sorry that this has become a combative debate. I do not accept the suggestion of the hon. Member for Richmond and Barnes (Mr. Hanley) that the Government are on trial. The fact is that a problem exists and that hon. Members on both sides of the House wish to discuss it.

I am sorry that, in a sense, dogs are on trial. I say that as a dog lover. The relationship between a dog and its owner is a long-standing one. We have talked for many years about dogs being man's best friend. The relationship of dogs with a family is important. However, many dogs are out of control, and it is clear that they need to be brought under control.

My hon. Friend the Member for Bradford, South (Mr. Cryer) illustrated the problem in clear terms. He referred to dogs getting into school playgrounds and to the difficulty of identifying the owners of the dogs. Unless the owners of the dogs can be identifed, there will always be a problem.

A dog registration scheme, either national or local, needs to be implemented. The relationship between the owner and the dog must be established. It is not the Government who are on trial. Hon. Members are on trial. We must grow up and tackle the problem. It is not the £60 million or £70 million that my hon. Friend the Member for Copeland (Dr. Cunningham) mentioned that is important. It is the children who are being mutilated by dogs that are not kept under control who are important. Until that relationship between a dog and its owner is established, we shall be failing in our duty.

Mr. Vivian Bendall (Ilford, North): I support the establishment of a dog registration scheme, but it would not solve all the problems that are associated with dogs.

I welcome the announcement tonight by my right hon. Friend the Secretary of State but I want to go into the reasons why there are so many vicious dogs. The public need to be educated about the types of dog that they purchase. Many people do not realise that they may be purchasing a potentially dangerous dog.

There should also be a proper licensing of breeders. For far too long there has been too much interbreeding, especially of vicious dogs. [*Interruption.*] When I talk about interbreeding I am referring to mothers and sons —[*Interruption.*] It is a serious problem. It is one of the reasons why dogs are vicious. Interbreeding causes serious problems.

We should license the breeder. The law stipulates that two or more breeding bitches should be registered, but that does not happen. We should put that right. We should also deal with puppy farms. Thirty or 40 bitches may be breeding at any given time. The puppies are sent to London and to other large conurbations. When people go to pet shops they cannot find the kind of dog they want. Dogs are often incorrectly described. We should license both breeders and the owners of pet shops. We might then stand a chance of controlling the sale of vicious breeds of dogs.

Vicious dogs are to be found in other countries as well. It has been a dramatic problem in the United States of America for some years on account of vicious doberman pinschers, pit bull terriers, other types of bull terriers and rottweilers. Certain individuals want to own a particularly vicious type of dog. The danger is that these individuals deliberately train their dogs to be vicious. That is borne out by the immense increase in illegal dog fighting using Staffordshire bull terriers. Five Staffordshire bull terriers have been stolen in my constituency during the last five weeks. I am convinced, as are the owners and other people, that the dogs were stolen to be trained for dog fighting. A number of British people are participating in this revolting sport.

I declare an interest. For two years, I have had two Staffordshire bull terriers. That kind of dog behaves properly if it is brought up properly. Vicious breeds can be trained to be vicious. Sadly, some breeds are falling into the wrong hands. That is part of the trouble. I should like my right hon. Friend the Secretary of State to ensure that licences are required to import pit bull terriers from America so that we know exactly who has them and where they are going. That would alleviate some of the problems.

The other day, I heard that a pit bull terrier which had been imported from America and lived on an estate in south London had bitten three policemen and generally caused havoc on the estate. Finally, the RSPCA took the dog off the estate, only to have its officers told as they were leaving that the dog had had puppies 10 weeks before which had been given away to people all around the estate.

The problems will be resolved not just by registration but by a combination of measures. There must be dog registration to deal with strays and with the other problems that hon. Members have described.

Mr. Tony Banks: Like others, I pay tribute to the hon. Member for Plymouth, Drake (Dame J. Fookes) for her campaigns on behalf not only of dogs but of animals generally. We owe her a great debt. I shall support new clause 34, but we need to go further. It is only a start. We have argued for a proper licence scheme to enable local authorities to get the funds necessary to run adequate dog warden schemes and help pay for the various "poop" schemes—I cannot think of a better expression—that are run by local authorities. Westminster city council has been running a dog mess clearing scheme. Paris has an effective scheme as well.

Such schemes need substantial resources, which can come only from a substantial dog licence scheme. They could help to pay for education courses in schools and among dog owners. Many responsible owners know little about dog ownership. With a properly funded dog licence scheme, money could be provided for the training of owners so that they looked after their dogs more adequately.

As one who comes from the East End of London, I know that many dogs are kept not as pets but as cheap burglar alarms. Dogs are used as protection against our increasingly violent society. People deliberately opt for the large, exotic and savage dog. If one wants to deter people from breaking into one's house, there is not much point in having a chihuahua, a poodle or a pekinese. One will choose a dog that will frighten people away. These savage dogs are a manifestation of Thatcherism. I was going to say that I could not think of a dog more appropriate to Thatcherism than a rottweiler, but I would not want to insult rottweilers because they are rather nice and loving dogs—the problem is with the owners.

We have been considering the Bill for two days. When we started the debate on new clause 34, the House was packed. When we were talking about the dramatic rent increases that council tenants will have to face in years to come and about housing conditions, there was hardly a Conservative Member here. Yet the House suddenly fills with Members wanting to hear the Secretary of State rambling on like some weird old looney about a scheme that, quite frankly, can be described only as a dog's breakfast.

Yesterday the House was full to hear statements about hazelnut yoghurt. I do not know what this House is coming to; it is far more interested in hazelnut yoghurt and dogs than in people. That is a very sad comment. Although the new clause is to be welcomed, I should like Conservative Members to show a little more interest in the needs of people—especially those on low incomes living on council estates and elsewhere in inner cities—and a little less concern for attention-grabbing debates which do not deal with the real problems of the people of this country.

2.30 am

Mr. James Couchman (Gillingham): In January 1985, the European Parliament addressed itself to the question of tattooing dogs' ears in pursuance of a dog registration scheme. I drew the attention of my right hon. Friend the Prime Minister to that and asked her to confirm that this country would have nothing to do with it. She replied:

"I thought it was absolutely ridiculous. I hope that the European Assembly has something better to do with its time than that."—[*Official Report,* 22 January 1985; Vol. 71, c. 858.]

My right hon. Friend was right then and she would be right now if she were to repeat her contempt for that debate in the European Assembly.

None of us should be surprised that there is such enthusiasm among Opposition Members for a dog registration scheme. It would mean the creation of public sector jobs, something much beloved of Opposition Members. If I thought for one moment that a dog registration scheme would solve the problems that have been enumerated at length this evening, of irresponsible owners with badly trained dogs, I would support it. Whatever sort of registration scheme might be put in place, the responsible owner will register, pay whatever fee is demanded of him, look after his dog and ensure that it does not stray and behave in an irresponsible and anti-social manner. The irresponsible dog owner, however, will continue with his usual stewardship of his dog and allow it to roam free and unregistered, doing what it wants. The attacks during recent weeks have involved dogs of the sort kept by those who simply would not register them, whatever the law. I shall have no difficulty in opposing the new clause.

Mr. Peter Griffiths (Portsmouth, North): The fact that there is no simple solution to the problems posed by dogs in society is not a good reason to reject any components of the complex solution necessary. The measures announced by the Department of the Environment and the Home Department are all welcome, but they will not, by themselves, solve the problems. No one who supports the idea of a dog registration scheme suggests that, even with an adequate fee, it would alone solve the problems. It is part of a complex solution to a complex problem.

The essential component is a national registration scheme to complement the detailed knowledge of local authorities on such matters as areas from which dogs should be excluded, such as playgrounds for very young children, and places where dogs should be kept on leads, such as beaches. Contributions can be made locally, but there needs to be a national registration scheme because dogs are easily transported from one place to another and it is quite wrong to place the burden of dealing with the problems on the local authorities alone.

Any scheme must be adequately financed. If it is not to be entirely financed by dog owners, national funds must be made available to local authorities so that they can operate a proper scheme. It is not reasonable for the House to call

[*Mr. Peter Griffiths*]

for legislation but not provide adequate finance. Hon. Members who are advocating a dog registration scheme must call upon owners to pay a dog licence fee and must accept that there will be a cost to the national or local taxpayer.

The problem is complex, so we must have a range of responses to it. I believe that we should have a national dog registration scheme, and the new clause gives us an opportunity to provide one.

Mr. Richard Page (Hertfordshire, South-West): One of the advantages of speaking down the batting order is that one does not need to go over the ground too deeply for the second or third time.

Sensing the mood of the House, I say at once that I welcome the proposals of my right hon. Friend the Secretary of State, which recognise that solid solutions are necessary to allay the concerns of my constituents, and follow, almost word for word, the leader article in yesterday's *Daily Telegraph*. No doubt the clairvoyant qualities of the reporter will be rewarded by its editor in due course.

Even if my right hon. Friend had not made his proposals, I would have opposed the new clause moved by my hon. Friend the Member for Plymouth, Drake (Dame J. Fookes). I do not doubt her sincerity or the amount of work that she has done on the subject, but she was a little shy about the cost of the scheme. I do not think that my hon. Friend the Member for Thanet, North (Mr. Gale) fully recognised the point about the impact of the scheme on pensioners, the unemployed or the person who needs a dog for company.

I am unhappy about the way in which the RSPCA ran its campaign. It thought that badgering Members would cause them to change their minds because they would receive more and more letters.

A registration scheme would create a layer of bureaucracy, with all the paraphernalia of enforcement, snooping, rights of access and persecution, but for what purpose? It will not make irresponsible owners responsible. Only responsible owners will register, but it is the irresponsible ones we are after. Enforcement is needed, and registration will not make bad owners responsible.

A bite by a dog, whether it is registered or not, will still be painful. The job is to catch that dog and then pursue the legal processes. The Government's proposals, coupled with existing provisions, will provide a positive solution and I hope that the House will support them.

Mr. Devlin: I support the new clause because the ownership of dogs is far too casually entered into. Twenty-eight per cent. of households in Britain own a dog, and the number of dogs increased by 500,000 last year to 7·3 million. About 250,000 people were injured last year by dog bites, which is 700 a day. We cannot permit such a number of vicious dogs.

We should be trying to find a system of controlling the number of dogs, and I believe that registration will do so. Under the new system, any dog that does not have a licence should be destroyed, which would solve the problem.

Mr. Ridley: I will not reply to all the many points raised in this interesting and constructive debate. However, I will study a number of suggestions made by my hon. Friends

and other hon. Members as we prepare the legislation to put my announcement into practice. There has been general agreement, with degrees of enthusiasm, about the three sets of measures I proposed, about the need for local authorities to have wardens and about the vital need for identification of dogs in enforcing the powers we shall give to local authorities.

The dispute has been over how to pay for that service. The speech of my hon. Friend the Member for High Peak (Mr. Hawkins), in which he asked whether it would be right to ask only parents to pay for education, underlined the argument about whether we should have a hypothecated tax or whether the revenue should come from general taxation. It would be nice if we could charge only the irresponsible dog owners for the service, just as it would be nice if we could charge only very bad and dangerous drivers for the cost of road accidents. If we propose to put the cost only on good drivers or only on good dog owners, the case is made for paying for the service out of general revenues. As the dog registration scheme is so complicated, bureaucratic and expensive to administer, the House should conclude that it should adopt my proposals and not proceed to the dog registration scheme.

Dame Janet Fookes: Although I welcome some of the points put forward by my right hon. Friend the Secretary of State, I do not regard them as a substitute for a well-organised dog registration scheme. Most, if not all, of his suggestions depend on being able accurately to pinpoint the owner of the dog. That is where the registration system comes in. The new clause does not insist on a particular form. I described the type of scheme that I should like to see, but if the new clause is passed, it would be left to the Secretary of State to come forward with a scheme after whatever consultations he wishes to make. Nobody is being committed to a particular formula this evening. Having said that, I am anxious to move to a vote. This is an important measure. It is not a panacea for all ills, but a very important step forward.

Question put, That the clause be read a Second time:— *The House divided:* Ayes 146, Noes 159.

Divison No. 244]   **[2.42 am**

AYES

Abbott, Ms Diane	Campbell-Savours, D. N.
Aitken, Jonathan	Cartwright, John
Alexander, Richard	Clark, Dr David *(S Shields)*
Allason, Rupert	Clay, Bob
Alton, David	Clelland, David
Anderson, Donald	Clwyd, Mrs Ann
Archer, Rt Hon Peter	Cohen, Harry
Barnes, Harry *(Derbyshire NE)*	Coleman, Donald
Barron, Kevin	Cook, Frank *(Stockton N)*
Battle, John	Corbyn, Jeremy
Beckett, Margaret	Cousins, Jim
Beith, A. J.	Cox, Tom
Bendall, Vivian	Crowther, Stan
Benn, Rt Hon Tony	Cryer, Bob
Bennett, A. F. *(D'nt'n & R'dish)*	Cummings, John
Bermingham, Gerald	Cunliffe, Lawrence
Biffen, Rt Hon John	Cunningham, Dr John
Blackburn, Dr John G.	Davies, Rt Hon Denzil *(Llanelli)*
Blunkett, David	Davies, Ron *(Caerphilly)*
Boateng, Paul	Davis, Terry *(B'ham Hodge H'l)*
Boyson, Rt Hon Dr Sir Rhodes	Devlin, Tim
Bradley, Keith	Dixon, Don
Bruce, Malcolm *(Gordon)*	Dobson, Frank
Buckley, George J.	Dover, Den
Callaghan, Jim	Eastham, Ken
Campbell, Ron *(Blyth Valley)*	Evans, John *(St Helens N)*

Fatchett, Derek
Fearn, Ronald
Fields, Terry *(L'pool B G'n)*
Fisher, Mark
Flannery, Martin
Flynn, Paul
Fookes, Dame Janet
Foot, Rt Hon Michael
Foster, Derek
Franks, Cecil
Fraser, John
Fry, Peter
Gale, Roger
George, Bruce
Gordon, Mildred
Gould, Bryan
Griffiths, Peter *(Portsmouth N)*
Griffiths, Win *(Bridgend)*
Grocott, Bruce
Hannam, John
Hardy, Peter
Hargreaves, Ken *(Hyndburn)*
Haynes, Frank
Henderson, Doug
Hicks, Robert *(Cornwall SE)*
Hinchliffe, David
Holt, Richard
Howarth, George *(Knowsley N)*
Howells, Dr. Kim (Pontypridd)
Hoyle, Doug
Hughes, John *(Coventry NE)*
Hughes, Roy *(Newport E)*
Hughes, Simon *(Southwark)*
Illsley, Eric
Irving, Charles
Jones, Ieuan *(Ynys Môn)*
Kirkwood, Archy
Leadbitter, Ted
Leighton, Ron
Lestor, Joan *(Eccles)*
Lewis, Terry
Litherland, Robert
Lloyd, Tony *(Stretford)*
Lofthouse, Geoffrey
McAllion, John
McKay, Allen *(Barnsley West)*
McNair-Wilson, Sir Michael
McWilliam, John
Mahon, Mrs Alice

Marek, Dr John
Meale, Alan
Michael, Alun
Michie, Bill *(Sheffield Heeley)*
Mills, Iain
Miscampbell, Norman
Morgan, Rhodri
Murphy, Paul
Nellist, Dave
O'Brien, William
Patchett, Terry
Pike, Peter L.
Powell, Ray *(Ogmore)*
Prescott, John
Primarolo, Dawn
Redmond, Martin
Richardson, Jo
Rogers, Allan
Rooker, Jeff
Rowlands, Ted
Ruddock, Joan
Sedgemore, Brian
Sheerman, Barry
Shepherd, Richard *(Aldridge)*
Skinner, Dennis
Smith, C. *(Isl'ton & F'bury)*
Smith, J. P. *(Vale of Glam)*
Soley, Clive
Spearing, Nigel
Summerson, Hugo
Taylor, Mrs Ann *(Dewsbury)*
Taylor, Matthew *(Truro)*
Taylor, Teddy *(S'end E)*
Temple-Morris, Peter
Thornton, Malcolm
Turner, Dennis
Wall, Pat
Wallace, James
Walley, Joan
Wardell, Gareth *(Gower)*
Watts, John
Williams, Rt Hon Alan
Winterton, Mrs Ann
Winterton, Nicholas
Wise, Mrs Audrey

Tellers for the Ayes:
  Mr. Tony Banks and
  Mrs. Llin Golding.

NOES

Alison, Rt Hon Michael
Amess, David
Arbuthnot, James
Arnold, Jacques *(Gravesham)*
Arnold, Tom *(Hazel Grove)*
Ashby, David
Atkinson, David
Baker, Nicholas *(Dorset N)*
Bennett, Nicholas *(Pembroke)*
Blaker, Rt Hon Sir Peter
Bonsor, Sir Nicholas
Boscawen, Hon Robert
Bottomley, Peter
Bottomley, Mrs Virginia
Bowden, A *(Brighton K'pto'n)*
Bowden, Gerald *(Dulwich)*
Braine, Rt Hon Sir Bernard
Bright, Graham
Brown, Michael *(Brigg & Cl't's)*
Budgen, Nicholas
Burns, Simon
Burt, Alistair
Butterfill, John
Carlisle, John, *(Luton N)*
Carrington, Matthew
Carttiss, Michael
Chapman, Sydney
Chope, Christopher
Churchill, Mr

Clark, Sir W. *(Croydon S)*
Colvin, Michael
Conway, Derek
Coombs, Anthony *(Wyre F'rest)*
Couchman, James
Cran, James
Currie, Mrs Edwina
Davies, Q. *(Stamf'd & Spald'g)*
Day, Stephen
Dorrell, Stephen
Douglas-Hamilton, Lord James
Dunn, Bob
Durant, Tony
Eggar, Tim
Emery, Sir Peter
Fallon, Michael
Favell, Tony
Finsberg, Sir Geoffrey
Fishburn, John Dudley
Forman, Nigel
Forsyth, Michael *(Stirling)*
Forth, Eric
Fowler, Rt Hon Norman
Freeman, Roger
Garel-Jones, Tristan
Gill, Christopher
Glyn, Dr Alan
Gorst, John
Gow, Ian

Greenway, John *(Ryedale)*
Griffiths, Sir Eldon *(Bury St E')*
Grist, Ian
Gummer, Rt Hon John Selwyn
Hague, William
Hamilton, Neil *(Tatton)*
Hanley, Jeremy
Harris, David
Haselhurst, Alan
Hawkins, Christopher
Hayes, Jerry
Hayhoe, Rt Hon Sir Barney
Hayward, Robert
Higgins, Rt Hon Terence L.
Hill, James
Hind, Kenneth
Hogg, Hon Douglas *(Gr'th'm)*
Hordern, Sir Peter
Howard, Michael
Howarth, Alan *(Strat'd-on-A)*
Howarth, G. *(Cannock & B'wd)*
Howell, Rt Hon David *(G'dford)*
Hughes, Robert G. *(Harrow W)*
Hunt, David *(Wirral W)*
Hunter, Andrew
Irvine, Michael
Jack, Michael
Janman, Tim
Johnson Smith, Sir Geoffrey
Jones, Gwilym *(Cardiff N)*
Jones, Robert B *(Herts W)*
Jopling, Rt Hon Michael
Key, Robert
Kirkhope, Timothy
Knapman, Roger
Knight, Dame Jill *(Edgbaston)*
Knowles, Michael
Lang, Ian
Lawrence, Ivan
Lennox-Boyd, Hon Mark
Lightbown, David
Lilley, Peter
Lloyd, Peter *(Fareham)*
Luce, Rt Hon Richard
Maclean, David
McLoughlin, Patrick
McNair-Wilson, P. *(New Forest)*
Mans, Keith
Marshall, John *(Hendon S)*
Marshall, Michael *(Arundel)*
Martin, David *(Portsmouth S)*
Maxwell-Hyslop, Robin
Mayhew, Rt Hon Sir Patrick

Mellor, David
Miller, Sir Hal
Mitchell, Andrew *(Gedling)*
Morris, M *(N'hampton S)*
Morrison, Sir Charles
Morrison, Rt Hon P *(Chester)*
Moss, Malcolm
Moynihan, Hon Colin
Neale, Gerrard
Nicholson, Emma *(Devon West)*
Onslow, Rt Hon Cranley
Page, Richard
Parkinson, Rt Hon Cecil
Patten, Chris *(Bath)*
Patten, John *(Oxford W)*
Raison, Rt Hon Timothy
Riddick, Graham
Ridley, Rt Hon Nicholas
Rumbold, Mrs Angela
Ryder, Richard
Sackville, Hon Tom
Shaw, David *(Dover)*
Shaw, Sir Giles *(Pudsey)*
Shaw, Sir Michael *(Scarb')*
Smith, Sir Dudley *(Warwick)*
Spicer, Sir Jim *(Dorset W)*
Squire, Robin
Stanley, Rt Hon Sir John
Steen, Anthony
Stevens, Lewis
Stewart, Andy *(Sherwood)*
Stradling Thomas, Sir John
Sumberg, David
Taylor, Ian *(Esher)*
Thompson, D. *(Calder Valley)*
Thompson, Patrick *(Norwich N)*
Thurnham, Peter
Townsend, Cyril D. *(B'heath)*
Trippier, David
Twinn, Dr Ian
Waddington, Rt Hon David
Waller, Gary
Ward, John
Wardle, Charles *(Bexhill)*
Wells, Bowen
Wheeler, John
Widdecombe, Ann
Wood, Timothy

Tellers for the Noes:
  Mr. Kenneth Carlisle and
  Mr. David Heathcoat-Amory.

Question accordingly negatived.

New Clause 38

PAYMENTS AND ALLOWANCES TO COUNCILLORS

'Any payments or allowances paid to councillors for duties performed as councillors shall be index linked to gross local government salary and wage scales.'.—*[Mr. Matthew Taylor.]*
Brought up, and read the First time.

Mr. Matthew Taylor: I beg to move, That the clause be read a Second time.

The new clause is designed largely to express anxiety about the Government's intentions to change the method of paying allowances to councillors and to cap funds available for the purpose. It is ironic that the Government's changes will penalise the most hard-working councillors and reward those who are slothful. The vast majority of councillors are hard-working and unrewarded for it, but a few are not. The irony lies in the fact that the Government incessantly talk of incentives for hard work.

[Mr. Matthew Taylor]

The new clause ensures that hard-working councillors who will lose out anyway under the changes will at least be protected against inflation. I hope that the Secretary of State will accept the new clause as a sign of good faith to them.

Mr. Gummer: I cannot possibly agree with the hon. Gentleman's attitude to allowances for councillors. Being a member of a council is a voluntary job, not a paid one. The idea that payment should be organised to reward these people is wholly foreign to the concept that the Government have put forward.

The Government believe it reasonable that there should be some expenses, and we are looking for a form of flat rate allowance to get away from the present system, in which more and more meetings are held so as to claim more and more allowances.

I have no sympathy with the proposal, which betrays a failure to understand how local government should work. We oppose paying councillors, and to link their allowances with the pay increases of local government officers would mean that we were in favour of paid councillors. I hope that the House will reject the proposal.

Mr. Taylor: Nothing that the Minister has said convinces me that he has any intention even of protecting councillors against inflation. He did not answer my point that that rewards sloth. It is therefore difficult to convince me, even at this late hour, that I should withdraw the motion—*[Interruption.]* As Conservative Members say that I should not do so, I shall press the matter.

Question put and negatived.

New Clause 48

PROTECTION FROM EVICTION BY APPROVED LANDLORD

'In section 8 of the Housing Act 1988, the following subsection shall be added after subsection (5)—
"The court shall not make an order for possession on Ground 6 in Schedule 2 to this Act if the landlord is a person approved under section 94 of this Act and the dwelling-house was acquired by the landlord under Part IV of this Act".'.
—*[Mr. Simon Hughes.]*
Brought up, and read the First time.

Mr. Simon Hughes (Southwark and Bermondsey): I beg to move, That the clause be read a Second time.

The new clause would secure protection from eviction in cases in which an approved landlord takes over property under the Housing Act 1988, under what is called tenants' choice. I pursued this suggestion in Committee and on the Floor of the House in the last Session. I continue to pursue it because it is important that tenants whose properties are taken over by private landlords should not be worried that they will be evicted because a landlord wants to develop their homes.

The former Minister with responsibility for housing, the hon. Member for Bristol, West (Mr. Waldegrave), in the last Session described as a "terrifying prospect" the idea that landlords could evict tenants from council properties they had taken over because they wanted to redevelop them. In an answer given me on 9 November 1988, the Under-Secretary of State suggested that the Government would re-examine the matter. He said that although they intended to require the Housing Corporation to require new landlords not to avail

themselves of ground 6 of schedule 2 to the Housing Act 1988 as a method of gaining possession, none the less they might consider that that would be better dealt with by statute than by contract.

3 am

That raises the issue of which would prevail—the contract or the statute. It is important for the matter to be clear beyond doubt in statute so that it stands no risk of being overruled, if in statute, eviction is permitted. Secondly, as Housing Ministers have admitted to me, there is precedent elsewhere in legislation. Section 34 of the 1988 Act makes clear that statute would overrule a contract. Therefore, it is logical to suggest that in this case the same would apply. If the Government want to be consistent they should amend the statute rather than presume that it would have no force.

Tenants remain highly suspicious that the powers of a new landlord who might take over from the council might be excessive and could easily be abused. In areas such as north Southwark and north Lambeth close to central London and the City, there is no doubt that council housing would be of great interest to landlords wishing to redevelop property for up-market renting or sale with little or no regard for existing tenants.

I hope that after reflection over several months the Government can now accept that to amend statute would remove any possibility of landlords exploiting a dangerous possibility under existing legislation. I hope that the Government will take this opportunity to give tenants complete security, which is what the new clause seeks to achieve.

Mr. Trippier: I shall be brief. The hon. Member for Southwark and Bermondsey (Mr. Hughes) has accurately described the undertaking that I gave him and the House in November. As the hon. Gentleman knows, in the past the Government have been reluctant to move an amendment to the former Act because we thought that that was unnecessary. However, on reconsideration and bearing in mind the complexity of the matter that the hon. Gentleman has outlined, he will be pleased to learn that we have concluded that an amendment to deal with it and the point in statute is the best course. If he will withdraw his new clause, the Government will prepare a suitable amendment in another place. Our intention is to provide that ground 6 would not be available where the landlord seeking possession has acquired the dwelling house in question under part IV of the Housing Act 1988, where possession is sought from a tenant who prior to acquisition was under part IV a tenant of a public sector landlord.

Mr. Hughes: I am grateful to the Minister for that answer. Tenants will be greatly relieved to learn that the Government are willing to amend the law. I look forward to the introduction of an appropriate amendment in another place before long. I beg to ask leave to withdraw the motion.

Motion and clause, by leave, withdrawn.

Schedule 5

LOCAL GOVERNMENT FINANCE ACT 1988:
AMENDMENTS

Amendment proposed: No. 60 in, page 150, line 27, at end insert—

'(3A) At the end of paragraph 10(1) (winding up) there shall be added "or, as the case may be, section 221(5)(b) of that Act (winding up of unregistered companies)".'.—[*Mr. Trippier.*]

Question put, That the amendment be made:–
The House divided: Ayes 108, Noes 17.

Division No. 245]   **[3.03 am**

AYES

Alison, Rt Hon Michael
Amess, David
Arbuthnot, James
Arnold, Jacques (*Gravesham*)
Baker, Nicholas (*Dorset N*)
Bennett, Nicholas (*Pembroke*)
Biffen, Rt Hon John
Boscawen, Hon Robert
Bottomley, Mrs Virginia
Bowden, A (*Brighton K'pto'n*)
Bowden, Gerald (*Dulwich*)
Bright, Graham
Brown, Michael (*Brigg & Cl't's*)
Bruce, Malcolm (*Gordon*)
Burns, Simon
Burt, Alistair
Butterfill, John
Carlisle, Kenneth (*Lincoln*)
Carrington, Matthew
Carttiss, Michael
Chapman, Sydney
Chope, Christopher
Conway, Derek
Coombs, Anthony (*Wyre F'rest*)
Couchman, James
Cran, James
Davies, Q. (*Stamf'd & Spald'g*)
Day, Stephen
Devlin, Tim
Dorrell, Stephen
Douglas-Hamilton, Lord James
Dover, Den
Dunn, Bob
Durant, Tony
Emery, Sir Peter
Fallon, Michael
Favell, Tony
Field, Barry (*Isle of Wight*)
Forman, Nigel
Forsyth, Michael (*Stirling*)
Forth, Eric
Franks, Cecil
Freeman, Roger
Gale, Roger
Garel-Jones, Tristan
Gill, Christopher
Gow, Ian
Greenway, John (*Ryedale*)
Griffiths, Peter (*Portsmouth N*)
Grist, Ian
Gummer, Rt Hon John Selwyn
Hague, William
Hamilton, Neil (*Tatton*)
Hanley, Jeremy
Harris, David
Hawkins, Christopher

Hayes, Jerry
Hayward, Robert
Heathcoat-Amory, David
Hind, Kenneth
Hogg, Hon Douglas (*Gr'th'm*)
Howarth, G. (*Cannock & B'wd*)
Hughes, Simon (*Southwark*)
Hunt, David (*Wirral W*)
Irvine, Michael
Jack, Michael
Janman, Tim
Jones, Gwilym (*Cardiff N*)
Knapman, Roger
Knowles, Michael
Lang, Ian
Lennox-Boyd, Hon Mark
Lightbown, David
Lilley, Peter
Lloyd, Peter (*Fareham*)
Maclean, David
McLoughlin, Patrick
Mans, Keith
Martin, David (*Portsmouth S*)
Maxwell-Hyslop, Robin
Mayhew, Rt Hon Sir Patrick
Mills, Iain
Mitchell, Andrew (*Gedling*)
Morrison, Sir Charles
Moynihan, Hon Colin
Ryder, Richard
Shaw, David (*Dover*)
Shaw, Sir Michael (*Scarb'*)
Smith, Sir Dudley (*Warwick*)
Smith, Tim (*Beaconsfield*)
Stanley, Rt Hon Sir John
Stevens, Lewis
Summerson, Hugo
Taylor, Ian (*Esher*)
Taylor, Matthew (*Truro*)
Thompson, Patrick (*Norwich N*)
Thurnham, Peter
Trippier, David
Twinn, Dr Ian
Waddington, Rt Hon David
Wallace, James
Waller, Gary
Wardle, Charles (*Bexhill*)
Watts, John
Wells, Bowen
Wheeler, John
Widdecombe, Ann
Wood, Timothy

Tellers for the Ayes:
    Mr. Alan Howarth and
    Mr. Tim Sackville.

NOES

Barnes, Harry (*Derbyshire NE*)
Buckley, George J.
Cryer, Bob
Cunliffe, Lawrence
Davies, Ron (*Caerphilly*)
Evans, John (*St Helens N*)
Griffiths, Win (*Bridgend*)
Hinchliffe, David
Hughes, John (*Coventry NE*)
Lloyd, Tony (*Stretford*)
Meale, Alan

Michie, Bill (*Sheffield Heeley*)
Nellist, Dave
Patchett, Terry
Powell, Ray (*Ogmore*)
Turner, Dennis
Wise, Mrs Audrey

Tellers for the Noes:
    Mr. Martin Redmond and
    Mr. Eric Illsley.

Question accordingly agreed to.

Amendments made: No. 61, in page 152, leave out line 44 and insert—

'(4) For subsection (4) there shall be substituted the following subsections—

"(4) Where regulations are for the time being in force under this section prescribing a description of non-domestic hereditament in relation to a person designated in the regulations ("the previously designated person"), amending regulations altering the designated person in relation to whom that description of hereditament is prescribed may have effect from a date earlier than that on which the amending regulations are made.

(4A) Where, by virtue of subsection (4) above, the designated person in relation to any description of non-domestic hereditament is changed from a date earlier than the making of the regulations,—

(a) any necessary alteration shall be made with effect from that date to a central non-domestic rating list on which any hereditament concerned is shown; and

(b) an order making the provision referred to in paragraph 3(2) of Schedule 6 below and specifying a description of hereditament by reference to the previously designated person shall be treated, with effect from that date, as referring to the person designated by the amending regulations.".'.

No. 62, in page 152, line 45 leave out from beginning to 'following' and insert—

'15.—(1) Section 55 (alteration of lists) shall be amended as follows.

(2) In subsection (4) (content of regulations)—

(a) in paragraph (b) after "as to the " there shall be inserted "manner and" and at the end there shall be added "and the information to be included in a proposal";

(b) in paragraph (d) for "making" there shall be substituted "and subsequent to the making of"; and

(c) after paragraph (d) there shall be inserted—

"(dd) as to the circumstances within which and the conditions upon which a proposal may be withdrawn".(3) In subsection (5) (regulations about appeals), for the words from "about" to "its alteration" there shall be substituted "between a valuaton officer and another person making a proposal for the alteration of a list—

(a) about the validity of the proposal; or

(b) about the accuracy of the list".

(4) The'.—[*Mr. Gummer.*]

3.15 am

Sir Charles Morrison: I beg to move amendment No. 37, in page 153, line 24, leave out paragraph 18 and insert—

'18.—(1) Schedule 5 paragraph 5(1)(a) shall be amended as follows—

"'After 'livestock' insert 'or the breeding or rearing of horses or ponies.'".'.

Madam Deputy Speaker (Miss Betty Boothroyd): With this it will be convenient to debate amendment No. 3, in page 153, line 30, leave out 'any' and insert 'more than two hectares of'.

Amendment No. 4, in page 153, line 30, leave out 'or agricultural building'.

Amendment No. 5, in page 153, line 36, leave out subsection (a) and insert—

'(a) the proportion of such amount as the area of 500 square metres bears to the total floor area of such building.'.

Amendment No. 6, in page 153, line 42, leave out from beginning to end of line 48.

Sir Charles Morrison: Amendment No. 37 arises from a commitment given by Lord Caithness in another place during the course of the Local Government Finance Bill last year, and from my hon. Friend the Minister living up

[*Sir Charles Morrison*]

to that commitment in Committee on the Bill now before the House. I thank him for allowing time for discussion and correspondence on the derating of horse and pony breeding establishments, which has been a matter for debate for some years.

From the early 1930s until the early 1980s, horse and pony breeding establishments were derated, stemming from a court case in the early 1930s, so for 50 years rating authorities, 13 consecutive Parliaments, Labour, Conservative and coalition Governments and countless Ministers accepted without question that derating existed.

In the early 1980s a rating authority decided to question that belief and gave rise to what became known as the Whitsbury stud case. Ultimately, in the autumn of 1987, the House of Lords decided that for the previous 50 years the law had been misinterpreted and that studs should be rated. Not to put too fine a point on it—the judgment was a good deal more complicated—that was the general effect.

During the progress of that case through the courts, I gained the impression that if it went wrong for horse and pony breeders, the Government would look sympathetically at the possibility of restoring the law as it was thought to be. However, Ministers come and go and my early impression proved to be misguided. None the less, intensive discussion took place and the outcome is schedule 5 as drafted.

Amendment No. 37 aims at restoring the pre-Whitsbury stud case situation to provide exemption from rating for those who breed or rear horses or ponies. Such breeding is an agricultural activity, as it is for the purpose of income tax, corporation tax and capital taxation, and it should qualify for derating. That horse and pony breeding is an agricultural activity is emphasised by the fact that it occurs in conjunction with other agricultural activities such as cattle and sheep grazing.

In an article in *The Times* yesterday, Sir Adam Butler writes that

"three out of four thoroughbreds never get near a racecourse and a good proportion of them and of the half-breds and ponies end up as food."

As a matter of interest, we are the biggest exporter of horseflesh for human consumption in the European Community, and a large proportion of our horsemeat is used in this country for dog and cat food.

The Ministry of Agriculture, Fisheries and Food actively encourages farmers to adopt alternative land use. Horse and pony breeding is a natural alternative, and one that meets the growing interest in horse riding. It would be unfortunate, to put it mildly, if a deterrent to breeding and rearing horses and ponies were constructed. I hope that the Government will accept amendment No. 37, but if not I trust that they will consider instead amendments Nos. 3, 4, 5 and 6.

The Government's objective in their Committee concession was, to quote a letter from my right hon. Friend the Minister to Sir Adam Butler, to

"extend the benefits of a reduction in rateable value to all breeding establishments which meet the agricultural requirements."

To do that, the Government have inserted in lines 32 to 41 on page 153 of the Bill a method of reduction based on rateable value and subject to the introduction of an order by the Secretary of State stating the amount of rateable value to be taken into account when assessing a reduction.

That method seems to have two weaknesses. First, it ensures that there will be continuing uncertainty about rating, both for those involved in the breeding of horses and ponies and, more importantly, for those who may be contemplating going into that business as an alternative land use. Secondly, rateable values will vary in different parts of the country, which will mean not only that a thoroughbred breeder in, for example, Newmarket has a lower overall reduction than the thoroughbred breeder in Yorkshire or the west country, but the small farmer turning partly to horse and pony breeding as an alternative land use in Surrey or Sussex will, in effect, receive less remission than his equivalent in Wales and other lower-rated areas.

My amendments Nos. 3 to 6 aim to avoid those anomalies by reference to a reduction based on a common area of about 500 sq m. That is roughly equal to the area required for two mares and their young stock. I have a suspicion that initially the Government were thinking along the same lines as I was, but they for some unknown reason veered away to the more anomalous proposals.

To sum up—[*Interruption.*] I am grateful to the House for that cheer. It is a great encouragement after working for seven years on this issue. I hope that the Government will be prepared to consider the total exemption, as it was before the Whitsbury stud case. If not, I hope that they will adopt my fallback position in amendments Nos. 3 to 6.

Mr. Gummer: It is reasonable for us to expect every section of the business community to bear its share of the burden of rates. It would not be possible to exempt horse breeding in this way. It was uncharacteristic of my hon. Friend the Member for Devizes (Sir C. Morrison) to speak in the way that he did because the Government have gone a long way and have talked over many months to reach a solution to deal with the de minimis situation. It seemed unfair, for example, that a farmer breeding horses as part of his operation would find a small area of his operation was rated. We tried to reach a compromise to prevent that from happening. I thought that everyone agreed that this was reasonable.

My hon. Friend the Member for Devizes asked, first, that we should get rid of all rating, and then that we should so extend the generous stand that my right hon. Friend in another place initially suggested as to cover a large number of people running a business like any other. It would be difficult to make that distinction. In my view, it would be wrong and unjustifiable. I cannot see the logic of it. My hon. Friend said that it would be more difficult now because there would be more people wishing to buy horses and be involved with horses, but that seems to be an argument on the other side.

It would be good if the interests that my hon. Friend so admirably represents would accept that the Government have gone a long way towards meeting their wishes, and that our proposal is a reasonable and proper compromise which puts the industry at an advantage in relation to others. It is unreasonable to ask for any further compromise from the Government. I therefore hope that my hon. Friend will seek leave to withdraw his amendment and support what the Government have done.

Sir Charles Morrison: My right hon. Friend the Minister entirely ignored the history of the matter, but as the hour is late and I know that right hon. and hon. Members want to get on with the business, I beg to ask leave to withdraw the amendment.

Amendment, by leave, withdrawn.

Amendments made No. 63, in page 153, line 24, at end insert—

'(1A) In paragraph 2, in sub-paragraph (7) after paragraph (c) there shall be inserted—

"(cc) the quantity of refuse or waste material which is brought on to and permanently deposited on the hereditament".'.

No. 225, in page 154, line 5, at end insert—

' .—(1) In Schedule 8 (non-domestic rating: pooling) Part II (non-domestic rating contributions) shall be amended as follows.

(2) In paragraph 5, at the end of sub-paragraph (1) there shall be added "and has effect subject to any provision made by virtue of paragraph 6(2A) below".

(3) In paragraph 6, after sub-paragraph (2) there shall be inserted the following sub-paragraphs—

"(2A) Regulations under paragraph 4 above may incorporate in the rules provision for adjustments to be made in the calculation of the amount of an authority's non-domestic rating contribution under paragraph 5(2) or 5(6) above, being adjustments to take account of relevant changes affecting the amount of the authority's non-domestic rating contribution for an earlier year.

(2B) For the purposes of sub-paragraph (2A) above, a change is a relevant change if it results from a decision, determination or other matter which (whether by reason of the time at which it was taken, made or occurred or otherwise) was not taken into account by the authority in the calculation under paragraph 5(6) above of the amount of its non-domestic rating contribution for the earlier year in question.".'.

No. 64, in page 157, line 21, after 'time', insert 'being'.

No. 65, in page 159, line 33, after 'maintenance', insert 'grant'.—*[Mr. Gummer.]*

Schedule 6

AMENDMENT OF SCOTTISH ENACTMENTS

Amendments made: No. 274, in page 162, line 8, at end insert—

'Revenue support grants

In section 23(2) of that Act, for the words from "a" onward there shall be substituted the words "grants (to be known as "revenue support grants") to local authorities".'.

No. 272, in page 162, line 13, leave out paragraph 7 and insert—

'Revenue support grant

7. For paragraphs 1 to 3 of Schedule 4 to that Act (revenue support grants) there shall be substituted the following paragraphs—

"1.—(1) The local authorities to which revenue support grant is payable in respect of a financial year shall be such local authorities as are specified by order made by the Secretary of State.

(2) The amount of revenue support grant payable in respect of a financial year to a local authority so specified shall be such amount as is determined in relation to the local authority by order made by the Secretary of State.

(3) The Secretary of State may at any time by order amend or revoke any order made under this paragraph and any amount of revenue support grant which has been paid and which, in consequence of anything done under this paragraph, falls to be repaid may be recovered by the Secretary of State whenever and however he thinks fit.

2.—(1) An order under paragraph 1 above shall be made only with the consent of the Treasury.

(2) Before making an order under paragraph 1 above the Secretary of State shall consult such associations of local authorities as appear to him to be appropriate.

(3) An order under paragraph 1 above together with a report of the considerations which led to its provisions shall be laid before the Commons House of Parliament but shall have no effect until approved by a resolution of that House.".'.—*[Mr. Rifkind.]*

Clause 129

POWER TO ALLOW CHARGES

Amendments made: No. 50, in page 112, line 28, leave out 'to be a certain amount, or'.

No. 51, in page 112, line 30, leave out from 'maximum' to end of line 31.

No. 52, in page 112, line 32, leave out from 'provide' to 'amount' in line 33 and insert 'that a charge may not exceed a minimum'.

No. 53, in page 112, leave out lines 38 to 42.—*[Mr. Gummer.]*

Clause 130

POWER TO AMEND PROVISIONS ABOUT CHARGES

Amendments made: No. 54, in page 113, line 38, leave out 'to be a certain amount, or'.

No. 55, in page 113, line 39, leave out from 'maximum' to end of line 40.

No. 56, in page 113, line 41, leave out from 'provide' to 'amount' in line 42 and insert 'that a charge may not exceed a maximum'.

No. 57, in page 114, leave out lines 1 to 5—*[Mr. Gummer.]*

Clause 131

INTERPRETATION, CONSULTATION AND COMMENCEMENT OF SS. 129 AND 130

Amendments made: No. 241, in page 115, line 24, after 'consult', insert—

'(a) as respects England and Wales.'.

No. 242, in page 115, line 25, after 'government', insert 'and (b) as respects Scotland, such associations of local authorities'.—*[Mr. Gummer.]*

Schedule 7

WELSH LANGUAGE NAMES FOR LOCAL AUTHORITIES

Amendments made: No. 106, in page 163, line 19, leave out 'section 21(4)' and insert 'by virtue of a resolution under section 21(5)'.

No. 107, in page 163, line 22, leave out 'section 33(2A)' and insert 'by virtue of a resolution under section 33(2B)'.

No. 108, in page 163, line 23, at end insert—

'6. After section 245 (status of certain districts, parishes and communities) there shall be inserted the following section—

"*Power for borough and town councils in Wales to adopt Welsh language form of their descriptions, etc.*

245A.—(1) If and so long as this subsection is in force in relation to a district in Wales which, by virtue of section 245(1) above, has the status of a borough or for which, by virtue of section 245(4) above, the style of borough may be used—

(a) the council shall bear the name "Cyngor Bwrdeistref" instead of "Council of the Borough" or "Borough Council";

(b) the chairman of the council shall be entitled to the style "maer" instead of "mayor"; and

(c) the vice-chairman of the council shall be entitled to the style "dirprwy maer" instead of "deputy mayor".

(2) Subject to subsection (3) below, subsection (1) above shall come into force in relation to a district which has the status of a borough, or for which the style of borough may be used, three months after the day on which, at a specially convened meeting of the council, it is resolved by a two-thirds majority of the members present and voting that the Welsh language form of the council's description shall be used.

(3) A resolution under subsection (2) above may be passed by the council of a district in Wales notwithstanding that, at the time it is passed, the council does not have the status of a borough; but, if a resolution is passed at such a time, subsection (1) above shall not come into force unless, nor earlier than, the status of a borough is conferred on the district by virtue of section 245(1) above.

(4) Subsection (1) above shall cease to be in force in relation to a district which has the status of a borough, or for which the style of borough may be used, three months after the day on which, at a specially convened meeting of the council, it is resolved by a two-thirds majority of the members present and voting that the Welsh language form of the council's description shall cease to be used.

(5) If and so long as this subsection is in force in relation to a community which, by virtue of section 245(6) above, has the status of a town—

(a) the council shall bear the name "Cyngor Tref" instead of "council of the town" or "town council";

(b) the chairman of the council shall be entitled to the style "maer y dref" instead of "town mayor"; and

(c) the vice-chairman of the council shall be entitled to the style "dirprwy faer y dref" instead of "deputy town mayor".

(6) Subsection (5) above shall come into force in relation to a community which has the status of a town three months after the day on which, at a specially convened meeting of the council, it is resolved by a two-thirds majority of the members present and voting that the Welsh language form of the council's description shall be used.

(7) Subsection (5) above shall cease to be in force in relation to a community which has the status of a town three months after the day on which, at a specially convened meeting of the council, it is resolved by a two-thirds majority of the members present and voting that the Welsh language form of the council's description shall cease to be used.

(8) Subsection (10) of section 245 above has effect in relation to this section as it has effect in relation to the foregoing provisions of that section.".'.—*[Mr. Gummer.]*

Schedule 8

AMENDMENTS OF PARTS VI, IX, XI, XVII AND XVIII OF THE HOUSING ACT 1985

Amendments made: No. 16, in page 166, line 10, leave out from 'is' to 'or' in line 12 and insert 'a protected occupier, within the meaning of the Rent (Agriculture) Act 1976'.

No. 17, in page 175, line 11, leave out from 'entry)' to 'there' in line 13 and insert 'at the end of subsection (3)'.—*[Mr. Gummer.]*

Clause 139

AMENDMENTS RELATING TO DEFECTIVE HOUSING

Amendment made: No. 35, in page 123, line 29, at end insert—

'(6) In section 567 of the 1985 Act (modifications of Part XVI in relation to shared ownership leases) for subsections (1) to (3) there shall be substituted the following subsections—

   "(1) If it appears to a local housing authority that the interest of a person eligible for assistance in respect of a defective dwelling in their area is—

     (a) a shared ownership lease, or

     (b) the freehold acquired under the terms of a shared ownership lease,

the authority shall prepare and submit to the Secretary of State a scheme providing for the provisions of this Part to have effect, in their application to such a case, subject to such modifications as may be specified in the scheme.

   (2) A scheme under subsection (1) above shall not have effect unless approved by the Secretary of State; and any such approval may be made conditional upon compliance with requirements specified by him."

(7) Any power of the Secretary of State to make regulations under subsection (4) of section 567 of the Housing Act 1985 shall cease to have effect; and in paragraph (d) of that section after the word "class" there shall be inserted "or description.".'.—*[Mr. Gummer.]*

Clause 141

POWERS OF LOCAL AUTHORITIES AND SECRETARY OF STATE AS RESPECTS SERVICES ETC. FOR OWNERS AND OCCUPIERS OF HOUSES FOR WORK ON THEM.

Amendments made: No. 301, in page 124, line 5, leave out from 'provide' to second 'or' in line 7 and insert 'professional, technical and administrative services for owners or occupiers of dwellings in connection with their arranging or carrying out relevant works'.

No. 302, in page 124, line 9, leave out 'they' and insert 'the authority'.

No. 303, in page 124, line 9, at end insert—

'( ) Works are relevant works in relation to a dwelling or, as the case may be, a dwelling in any area, if they are works of any of the following descriptions, that is to say—

   (a) works to cause the dwelling to be fit for human habitation,

   (b) where the occupant is disabled, works for any of the purposes specified in section 102(2) or (3) above,

   (c) works for any of the purposes specified in section 103(2) above, and

   (d) works for any of the purposes specified in or under section 117(1) above.'

No. 304, in page 124, line 23, leave out 'houses' and insert 'dwellings'.

No. 305, in page 124, leave out 39 to 44.

No. 306, in page 124, line 49, leave out 'houses' and insert 'dwellings'.

No. 307, in page 125, line 15 leave out from 'charities' to end of line 19.

No. 308, in page 125, leave out 20 to 23.

No. 58, in page 125, line 23, at end insert—

'"housing association" means a housing association within the meaning of section 1(1) of the Housing Associations Act 1985, or a body established by such a housing association for the purpose of, or having among its purposes or objects, those mentioned in section 4(3)(e) of that Act (providing services of any description for owners or occupiers of houses in arranging or carrying out works of maintenance, repair or improvement, or encouraging or facilitating the carrying out of such works);'.

No. 309, in page 125, line 27, leave out 'as respects England and Wales'.

No. 310, in page 125, leave out lines 29 and 30—*[Mr. Gummer.]*

Schedule 10

MINOR AND CONSEQUENTIAL AMENDMENTS

3.30 am

Mr. Gummer: I beg to move amendment No. 12, in page 191, line 6, at end insert—

The Sexual Offences Act 1956

In Schedule 1 to the Sexual Offences Act 1956 (rights of landlord where tenant convicted of permitting use of premises as a brothel) at the end of paragraph 5 there shall be added "Part I of the Housing Act 1988 and Schedule 9 to the Local Government and Housing Act 1989".'

Madam Deputy Speaker: With this it will be convenient to take Government amendments Nos. 13, 166, 14, 15 and 18.

Mr. Gummer: These are drafting amendments.

Mr. Tony Banks: I ask the Minister to give us some more detail to clarify Government amendment No. 18.

Mr. Gummer: Government amendment No. 18 is purely a drafting amendment. It introduces references to the long title to cover provisions that are consequential to parts I and II of the Housing Act 1988. When a house has been acquired or appropriated by a local authority for planning purposes, section 130 provides that the security that is given by the Rent Act to a tenancy of that property does not stop the local authority from obtaining possession.

Mr. Banks: Why parts I and II only of the Housing Act 1988? Why not the whole of the Act?

Mr. Gummer: Because the amendment is more appropriate to parts I and II.

Amendments made: No. 59, in page 191, line 6, at end insert—

'*The Military Lands Act 1892*
In section 8 of the Military Lands Act 1892 (provisions as to disbandment of volunteer corps etc.) subsection (3) shall be omitted.
The Small Holdings and Allotments Act 1908
In section 52 of the Small Holdings and Allotments Act 1908 (borrowing powers and expenses) subsection (3) shall be omitted.'.

No. 13 in page 191, line 21, at end insert—
'*The Leasehold Reform Act 1967*
In section 16 of the Leasehold Reform Act 1967 (exclusion of further rights after extension of lease) after subsection (1A) there shall be inserted the following subsection—
"(1B) A tenancy extended under section 14 above shall not be an assured tenancy or an assured agricultural occupancy, within the meaning of Part I of the Housing Act 1988, and Schedule 9 to the Local Government and Housing Act 1989 shall not apply to a tenancy so extended."'.

No. 66, in page 191, line 24, leave out from 'immunities)' to 'The' in line 25 and insert 'after paragraph 9A there shall be inserted the following paragraph—
"9B'.

No. 166, in page 191, line 37, leave out from beginning to '(scope' and insert—
'5.—(1) In section 130 of the Town and Country Planning Act 1971 (displacement of persons from land acquired or appropriated) in subsection (3) after the words "nothing in" there shall be inserted "Part I of the Housing Act 1988 or".
(2) In section 192 of that Act'.

No. 116, in page 192, line 19, at end insert—
'( ) In sub-paragraphs (1) and (2) of paragraph 41 of Schedule 12 to that Act (recording the minutes of meetings of local authorities), for the word "following" there shall be substituted "suitable"; and after sub-paragraph (3) of that paragraph there shall be inserted the following sub-paragraph—
"(4) For the purposes of sub-paragraphs (1) and (2) above the next suitable meeting of a local authority is their next following meeting or, where standing orders made by the authority in accordance with regulations under section 17 of the Local Government and Housing Act 1989 provide for another meeting of the authority to be regarded as suitable, either the next following meeting or that other meeting.".'.

No. 229, in page 192, line 25, at end insert—
'*Local Government (Scotland) Act 1973*
. In sub-paragraph (1) of paragraph 7 of Schedule 7 to the Local Government (Scotland) Act 1973 (recording the minutes of meetings of local authorities) for the word "following" there shall be substituted the word "suitable"; and after sub-paragraph (2) of that paragraph there shall be inserted the following sub-paragraph—
"(3) For the purposes of sub-paragraph (1) above, the next suitable meeting of a local authority is their next following meeting or, where standing orders made by the authority in accordance with regulations under section 17 of the Local Government and Housing Act 1989 provide for another meeting of the authority to be regarded as suitable, either the next following meeting or that other meeting.".'.

No. 120, in page 192, line 26, at end insert—
' .In section 23(4) of the Local Government Act 1974 (consultation in appointing Local Commissioners), for the words "appropriate representative body," there shall be substituted the words "such persons as appear to the Secretary of State to represent authorities in England or, as the case may be, authorities in Wales to which this Part of this Act applies".
.In section 23(12) of the Local Government Act 1974 (triennial reports to Part III authorities) the words "(through the appropriate representative body designated under section 24 below)" shall be omitted and at the end there shall be inserted the words "and shall send copies of those recommendations or conclusions to the representative persons and authorities concerned".'.

No. 158, in page 193, line 17, leave out from beginning to '(local' in line 18 and insert—
'15.—(1) In section 33 of the Local Government (Miscellaneous Provisions) Act 1976 (restoration or continuation of supply of water, gas or electricity) in subsection (4) for the word "and", where it first occurs, there shall be substituted "the sum so recoverable, together with any interest accrued due, shall, until recovered, be a charge on the premises concerned and if" and at the end of that subsection there shall be inserted the following subsection—
"(4A) A charge under subsection (4) above takes effect from the date when the council makes the payment referred to in that subsection and, for the purposes of enforcing a charge,—
(a) the council shall have the same powers and remedies, under the Law of Property Act 1925 and otherwise, as if it were a mortgagee by deed having powers of sale and lease, of accepting surrenders of leases and, subject to paragraph (b) below of appointing a receiver; and
(b) the power to appoint a receiver shall be exercisable at any time after the expiry of one month from the date when the charge takes effect."

15A. In section 40 of that Act.'.

No. 14, in page 193, line 21, at end insert—
'*The Rent (Agriculture) Act 1976*
In section 33 of the Rent (Agriculture) Act 1976 (suspension of condition attached to planning permission), in subsection (2) after the words "let on or subject to" there shall be inserted "an assured agricultural occupancy, within the meaning of Chapter III of Part I of the Housing Act 1988, or".'.

No. 49, in page 195, line 17, at end insert 'and in this sub-paragraph "year" has the same meaning as in Part XIII of that Act (general financial provisions)'.

No. 312, in page 197, line 9, at end insert—
'*The Local Government Act 1988*
In section 25 of the Local Government Act 1988 (consent required for provision of financial assistance etc.) in subsection (1)(b) after the word "power" there shall be inserted "(whether conferred before or after the passing of this Act)".'.

No. 313, in page 197, line 10, leave out 'the Local Government Act 1988' and insert 'that Act'.

[*Mr. Gummer*]

No. 327, in page 198, line 40, leave out from beginning to '(assistance' and insert—

'(1) In section 21 of the Housing Act 1988 (recovery of possession on expiry or termination of assured shorthold tenancy), in subsection (1)(a) for the words "a statutory periodic tenancy" there shall be substituted "an assured shorthold periodic tenancy (whether statutory or not)".

(2) In section 129(5)(b) of that Act'.

No. 15, in page 198, line 43, at end insert—

'In Schedule 6 to that Act, in paragraph 9 (amendments of section 15 of Housing Associations Act 1985), in sub-paragraph (2) for "(3)" there shall be substituted "(2A)".'

No. 105, in page 198, line 43, at end insert—

'In Schedule 5 to that Act (Housing for Wales), in paragraph 5 (remuneration and allowances), in sub-paragraph (1)—

  (a) for the words "Secretary of State" there shall be substituted "Corporation"; and

  (b) for the word "he" there shall be substituted "Secretary of State".'—[*Mr. Gummer.*]

SCHEDULE 11

Enactments Repealed

Amendments made: No. 99, in page 199, line 7, at end insert—

'45 and 46 Vict. c.50.	The Municipal Corporations Act 1882.	In Part I of Schedule 9, the entry relating to the Local Loans Act 1875.'

No. 100, in page 199, line 9, at end insert—

'51 & 52 Vict. c.25.	The Railway and Canal Traffic Act 1888.	In section 54, subsections (3) and (4).
55 & 56 Vict. c.43.	The Military Lands Act 1892.	Section 8(3).
8 Edw. 7 c.36	The Small Holdings and Allotments Act 1908.	Section 52(3).'

No. 101, in page 199, line 13, at end insert—

'11 & 12 Geo. 6 c.26.	The Local Government Act 1948.	In section 125(2)(d), the words from "section thirty" to "Act) or".'

No. 102, in page 199, line 33, column 3, at end insert—

'Section 123(6).'

No. 103, in page 200, line 2, column 3, at end insert—

'In section 74(5), the words from "(including" to "1875)".'

No. 104, in page 200, line 31, column 3, at beginning insert—

'In section 14(4), the words from "section 34" to "1875 and".'

No. 109, in page 200, line 47, column 3, at beginning insert—

'Section 129(5)(a).'.

No. 263, in page 202, line 6, column 3, at end insert—

'section 110A(2).'.

No. 269, in page 202, line 6, column 3, at end insert—

'In section 111(1), paragraphs (a), (b) and (d).'.

No. 121, in page 202, line 14, column 3, at beginning insert—

'In section 23, in subsections (4), (5) and (6) the word "Local" and in subsection (12), the words "(through the appropriate representative body designated under section 24 below)"'
Section 24.'.

No. 122, in page 202, line 16, column 3, at end insert—

'In section 34(1), the definition of "representative body".'.

No. 36, in page 204, line 5, column 3, at end insert—

'In section 567, in subsection (4), paragraph (c) except for the final "or", in subsection (5), the words "regulations under subsection (4) (c) or" and subsection (6).'.

No. 41, in page 204, line 5, column 3, leave out '526' and insert—

'522.
Sections 524 to 526.'.

No. 279, in page 204, line 49, column 3, leave out 'Section 20' and insert—

'Section 15.
Section 20.
Schedule 3'.

No. 268, in page 204, line 52, at end insert—

'1987 c. 47.	The Abolition of Domestic Rates Etc. (Scotland) Act 1987.	In Schedule 1, paragraph 28(a)(ii) and (iii)'.

No. 264, in page 205, line 18, column 3, at end insert—

'section 128(2).'.

No. 265, in page 205, line 27, column 3, at end insert—

'In Schedule 12, paragraph 16.'.

No. 273, in page 205, line 27, column 3, at end insert—

'In Schedule 12, paragraph 37.'.

No. 280, in page 205, line 28, column 3, at end insert—

'Section 131.'—
[*Mr. Gummer.*]

Clause 154

Short title, commencement and extent

Amendments made: No. 223, in page 133, line 19, after '3', insert ', 9 and 10'.

No. 127, in page 133, line 19, after '17', insert 'and *(Members' interests)'.*

No. 119, in page 133, line 19, at end insert ',' with the exception in Part II of section [Expenses of Commissions for Local Administration]'.

No. 243, in page 133, line 20, after 'sections', insert '126'.

No. 266, in page 133, line 20, after 'sections', insert ' *[Scottish non-domestic rates: interim provisions]'.*

No. 270, in page 133, line 20, after 'sections', insert '*[Scottish non-domestic rate]'.*

No. 226, in page 133, line 29, at beginning insert 'Subject to subsection (4A) below'.

No. 246, in page 133, line 29, after 'sections', insert '29(10)'.

No. 267, in page 133, line 29, after 'sections', insert '*[Scottish non-domestic rates: interim provisions]'.*

No. 271, in page 133, line 29, after 'sections', insert '*[Scottish non-domestic rate]'.*

No. 311, in page 133, line 30, leave out 'to 142' and insert '140, 142,'.

No. 227, in page 133, line 30, leave out 'and 150 onwards' and insert '150, 151, 153(1), 153(4) and this section'.

No. 228, in page 133, line 31, at end insert—

'(4A) Notwithstanding anything in subsection (4) above, any provision of Schedule 10 or Part II of Schedule 11 to this Act which amends or repeals any provision of the following enactments does not extend to Scotland—

(a) the Military Lands Act 1892;

(b) the Local Authorities (Expenditure Powers) Act 1983.'.—*[Mr. Gummer.]*

Title

Amendment made: No. 18, in the title, in line 13, after '1982', insert

'to make amendments of and consequential upon Parts I and II of the Housing Act 1988'.—*[Mr. Gummer.]*

Bill to be read the Third time today, and to be printed. [Bill 159].

POLICE OFFICERS (CENTRAL SERVICE) BILL
[Lords]

Not amended (in the Standing Committee), considered.

Bill read the Third time, and passed, without amendment.

EUROPEAN COMMUNITY DOCUMENTS

Ordered,

That this House takes note of European Community Document No. 10449/88 relating to revision of the Financial Regulation of 21st December 1977 and transfer of appropriations No. 18/88 described in the unnumbered Explanatory Memorandum submitted by the Treasury on 2nd February 1989; and approves the Government's efforts to press for increased value for money in community expenditure.—*[Mr. Chapman.]*

Water Metering Trials (Isle of Wight)

Motion made, and Question proposed, That this House do now adjourn.—*[Mr. Chapman.]*

3.33 am

Mr. Barry Field (Isle of Wight): I am sorry that I have detained my hon. Friend the Under-Secretary of State until such a late hour, but I am sure that he agrees that the fitting of 53,000 water meters in my constituency is a serious matter for my constituents.

The week before the House adjourned for the Whitsun recess, I approached my hon. Friend the Under-Secretary and my hon. and learned Friend the Minister for Water and Planning about my worries about water meterimg trials on the Isle of Wight. After some discussion, both helpfully suggested that they would welcome a debate, although I doubt that they realised the hour at which it would take place. I am pleased that Mr. Speaker generously granted me a debate tonight.

As I said to my hon. Friend the Under-Secretary of State when I met him and his senior officials in the early part of the year, I was worried that the county council elections might lead to a serious deterioration in the presentation of the metering trials on the Isle of Wight and, sadly, my forecast has proved all too accurate. I am sure that my hon. Friend has seen the wholly opportunistic comments by the Liberal party in early-day motion 955. The fact that no member of that party is here to listen to the debate shows the seriousness with which it takes this matter.

On 5 February 1985, almost two and a half years before my election to the House, minute No. 13 of the Isle of Wight water consultative committee said that Mr. Nicholson introduced the paper and explained the possibility of a large-scale pilot scheme on the island for metering domestic premises. Mr Leyton said that he felt that small users of water would welcome such a scheme and Mr. Garth commented that senior citizens would benefit from metering.

I say "opportunistic" because at that time the county, borough and parliamentary seats were all Liberal-controlled. Mr. Leyton was the county's representative on that committee. He has since retired from the county council and one would travel the length and breadth of this country without meeting a nicer man, although I have never agreed with his politics.

The minutes went on to say that the suggestion of using the island for a large-scale trial was given general support. On 30 September 1986, minute No. 9 of the same committee, albeit with some membership changes but still when the island had a Liberal Member of Parliament and a Liberal county and borough council, stated that the committee reiterated its policy that metering would be the best solution for the island.

The House of Commons Library tells me that its records show that my predecessor Steve Ross, now Lord Ross, did not raise this matter in the House in 1985 or 1986. On 22 May this year, in the other place, he said "I agree that if water can be metered"——

Mr. Deputy Speaker (Sir Paul Dean): The hon. Member must paraphrase.

Mr. Field: With respect, Mr. Deputy Speaker, it is a very short quote.

Mr. Deputy Speaker: I am sure that the hon. Member can use his ingenuity to paraphrase.

Mr. Field: Lord Ross indicated that, provided that water can be adequately metered, that was the right way to proceed.

If the noble Lord had not left the Isle of Wight and stepped out of local politics, he would have had something to say to the county council, especially its leader, about pushing the island into the largest metering trial in the country and busily trying to cover its tracks by condemning it.

I shall put these facts behind me, for it will not serve the island's families well simply to return the fire. Indeed, my interest transcends any opportunity for political point scoring. To requote Shakespeare, methinks that a party that has encouraged a means of charging for water when it holds all the local offices but busies itself condemning that when it no longer has borough and parliamentary control "doth protest too much".

I have some questions on behalf of my constituents to which I should like to obtain answers. First, will my hon. Friend the Minister undertake to visit the island to see the trials for himself and visit some of the households affected? Secondly, will he comment on the county council trading standards officer who in last week's county press was reported as saying:

"it was only a matter of time before the meters became inaccurate"?

Thirdly, will my hon. Friend comment on the county secretary's report that a number of meters submitted to the trading standards officer for initial verification have fallen outside tolerance? As the county solicitor states, this has an effect on householders who are keen to be satisfied that the new experiment on the island is conducted accurately and some people are concerned that a credibility gap is appearing. On 8 June 1988, in a circular, the then divisional manager of Southern water authority, Grainger Davies, stated that water meters would be fitted, free of charge, over the next 18 months to measure water supplied to every property on the Isle of Wight and customers would receive bills based on volume for the first time from autumn 1989. Why, then, are householders now receiving bills on a piecemeal basis as and when the meters are installed? That is causing concern and some friction within the community because those still paying on the rateable value method are, in some cases, paying less.

Fifthly, will my hon. Friend reconfirm the undertaking given by Bill Courtney, the chairman of Southern Water, to hon. Members representing constituencies in the Southern Water region during a meeting in one of the Committee Rooms of the House following my question:

"The price of water throughout the company's area will not be subject to cost centre accounting by division?"

As my hon. Friend is aware, more than 24 per cent. of the island's water is imported from the mainland. I doubt whether any of us could afford the true cost of drinking water on the island. My hon. Friend gave me an undertaking on the cost of meter installations in his letter of 13 January 1989 and I am looking for a similar undertaking on the cost of water.

Sixthly, will my hon. Friend set out the mechanism to monitor the total income obtained by Southern Water from the trial? Who will adjust the price if too much has been collected? It must be borne in mind that in some areas more than 25 per cent. of domestic dwellings are holiday homes. How is that loss of revenue to be made up without causing financial hardship to those who pay all the year round—if, indeed, that is the result of the data on the meter trial?

Seventhly, my hon. Friend stated in his letter of 4 October 1988:

"For those families in receipt of income support this payment does not include specific provision for individual amounts payable as was the case under the supplementary benefit."

It is clear that if metered water is more expensive, especially for large young families in low rated property in receipt of income support, that will put them in an unfair position compared with the remainder of the country.

Eighthly, as my hon. Friend knows, the island is to have 30,000 meters fitted externally and 23,000 internally. He knows that I have waged a long campaign to have internal metering dropped now that about 6,000 have been fitted. The whole point of the trial was to determine the cost savings of installing internal meters. There are none; in every area in the country there are none. Why, then, do we have to plough on with that regardless, despite the disruption it causes to householders, their kitchens and the possibility of damage to their effects?

When I wrote to the Home Office about the crime prevention aspects of internal metering with the aim of cutting the number of people required to enter homes to read meters, the Home Office said that I had no reason to worry because, as they were not slot meters, there would be no coins to attract burglars. I wonder what sort of ivory tower would think that we would have to insert 5p for two baths, a shower and a cuppa.

Lest it should be felt that metering on the Isle of Wight has been a story of unprecedented point scoring, I want to pay a special tribute to the county architect who, as a result of his representations to me as early as September 1987 after the original announcement, can take full credit for the reduction of the standing charge to £10 per annum. It is a remarkable indictment of those Liberals who recently waged such as campaign about the cost of metered water that they failed to comment on the draft charges sent to them by Southern Water with its letter of 8 September 1988.

My right hon. Friend the Minister for Local Government visited the Isle of Wight, which has the highest percentage of any county in England and Wales of over-75-years-olds living in their own homes. When my right hon. Friend was asked his views about charging for water in cubic metres, he said that he would not recognise a cubic metre if he tripped over one—I checked with him whether he was content for me to mention that in this debate, so my hon. Friend need not worry—but neither would I or literally thousands of my constituents. Pints, yes; gallons, perhaps; but cubic metres, never.

More questions need to be answered and much more needs to be done. For 53,000 home owners, water metering trials on the Isle of Wight raise genuine concerns. I look to my hon. Friend the Minister for assistance and clarity in response to the questions that I have asked. I hope that he will accede to my request to visit the island and see the meters for himself. In the past he has been most generous with his time when, wearing his other hat as Minister for Sport, he accepted our invitation to the south coast rowing championships on the Isle of Wight. I hope to have an opportunity in the near future of acquainting him with the problems in my constituency so that he can see them for himself.

3.45 am

The Parliamentary Under-Secretary of State for the Environment (Mr. Colin Moynihan): My hon. Friend the Member for Isle of Wight (Mr. Field) is to be congratulated on raising the water metering trial on the Isle of Wight. He has assiduously represented the views of his constituents on the issue through correspondence, direct representation to myself and other Ministers and parliamentary interventions.

The metering trial is one of 12 areas chosen by the water industry around the country. The overall objective of the trials is to obtain information on how to implement effective metering systems and to determine the impact of charging by volume on consumption. They are not intended to show whether metering would be more or less efficient than other non-metering charging systems.

My hon. Friend has asked many questions. Those that I am unable to answer tonight, I undertake to answer in full when I accept his offer to visit the Isle of Wight to consider the problems that he has mentioned and the water metering trial. I shall do so as soon as practicable, but certainly this summer.

As the House will be aware, water charges payable by most domestic customers at present are based on the rateable value of the property. With the abolition of domestic rateable values next year on the introduction of the community charge, new methods of charging need to be found. Metering is one option; another is a flat-rate charge. However, the final decision will rest with each of the privatised water companies. Information gained from the trials will help each company decide whether widespread metering is worthwhile and, if so, how best to go about it with the least inconvenience and at minimum cost to their customers.

The metering trials were set up last year under provisions in the Public Utility Transfers and Water Charges Act 1988. Each metering trial charges scheme had to be approved by my right hon. Friend the Secretary of State under the provisions of the Act. It is worth noting that, as part of the process of considering whether to approve each scheme, my right hon. Friend was required by the Act to have regard to the interests of the customers likely to be affected by the scheme, and a number of other matters, which include the methods and principles on which the tariff was fixed; the reasons for selecting the trial area; the period of the trial; consultation about the proposals; the handling of representations about the trial; and the supply of information to him about the operation of the trial.

As a result of the latter, my Department receives regular reports of progress on each trial and summaries of customer complaints and comments. This monitoring procedure will help my right hon. Friend to ensure that the water undertakers involved in the trials do what they promised to in their original submissions. If the monitoring process shows that the assumptions on which the tariffs were fixed are subsequently proven to be widely out, my right hon. Friend will encourage the water undertakers involved to amend their schemes.

The Isle of Wight trial is the only large-scale trial among the programme of 12 trials announced by the industry. It was chosen by the water industry because it was self-contained, was known to have water-resource problems and contained a wide mix of different types of property in rural and urban areas. The wide mix of

[*Mr. Colin Moynihan*]

properties was a particularly important consideration, as the main objective of the large-scale trial is to establish the practicality, economics and cost of metering on a wide-scale in other areas of England and Wales. The housing had to be represenative if the lessons were to be applied elsewhere.

Within that general objective, the Isle of Wight trial is designed to investigate the advantages of internal versus external metering, and the use of a rising-block tariff. Those objectives contrast with those of the 11 small-scale trials which are designed primarily to assess the impact on demand of various different types of tariffs in tightly controlled areas of similar housing. The results of all of the trials will be made freely available to all of the water industry, including those companies and authorities that are not directly involved. In recognition of that, my Department is contributing up to 50 per cent. of the cost.

My hon. Friend has expressed concern that some of his constituents will face increased bills as a result of being metered. That is an inevitable consequence of the inequity of the present rateable value-based charging system and a move to a fairer system of charging linked to the volume of water supplied to customers. However, I can assure my hon. Friend that the metered tariff to be applied on the Isle of Wight is fair. It contains a number of safeguards designed to protect the interests of customers. Some of those safeguards are worth repeating.

The tariff for the trial area was initially based on regional costs and consumption figures. As such, it did not reflect the additional costs, such as the installation of meters and the processing of data, attributable to the trial. Furthermore, as the average domestic rateable value on the island is lower than that for the whole of Southern Water's area of supply, the tariff was reduced so that the level of income to be recovered from customers on the island did not exceed the income that would otherwise be recovered through regional rateable value-based charges. Southern Water's calculations were based on an average regional consumption figure of 45 cu m per person across the entire region, or about 121 cu m per year for a typical household of 2·5 people on the island. Both those factors favour customers on the Isle of Wight, where average occupancy and rateable value is below the regional average.

As a further safeguard, Southern Water assured my right hon. Friend when he approved its scheme that if consumption in a normal year was found to be above that forecast and income was to rise above the estimate, the tariff for the following years would be adjusted to take that into account. However, the tariff would not be adjusted if income rose from increased consumption caused by abnormally dry weather conditions. That was because consumption in subsequent normal years would revert to lower levels and Southern Water would then suffer an income loss. As I mentioned earlier, my right hon. Friend will monitor all aspects of the trial, including income recovered, and if necessary, the tariff will be adjusted.

Another safeguard is provided by the fact that any future increase in metering trial area tariff will be linked to changes in the regional tariff, so if consumption is less than forecast, Southern Water will not be able to increase the tariff to make up the loss. Once again, that is to the advantage of customers.

As I have already mentioned, customers will be charged for water on the basis of a rising block tariff. Southern Water's lower tariff rate for this year is 30p per cu m for the first 90 cu m of water per year. Consumption above 90 cu m will be charged at 56·5p per cu m. The preferential allowance of 90 cu m represents Southern Water's estimate of the essential water requirements for a typical household of three people. Those essential requirements include water used for food preparation, drinking, hand washing, manual dishwashing, toilet flushing, automatic washing machine use and daily bath or shower. That is a wide interpretation of what constitutes essential use and refutes the suggestions that metering will lead to a decline in health standards.

It is too early to judge how many customers will pay more and how many less. Customers have been paying by measure only for two months and the first bills will not be sent out to customers until the end of September. However, a sample of 1,000 readings taken by Southern Water suggests that the average yearly bill will be around £120. On that basis, Southern Water expects that about 50 per cent. of customers will be paying less than £120 and 90 per cent. paying less than £200 per year. It is encouraging to note that the likely annual charges based on those sample readings are in line with the estimated annual charges that Southern Water set out in its information leaflet which it sent to customers last year. However, I heard what my hon. Friend said earlier, which would appear to vary from the information I have received. I give him an undertaking, therefore, to respond to that point specifically in writing in the very near future.

The trial is being managed on a day-to-day basis by a full-time project manager. He is supported by a large team of technical and supervising staff. The management team's close day-to-day supervision of the contractors has ensured that the equality of work has generally been of a high standard. So far, Southern Water has received only around 50 complaints about poor reinstatement. Of those 34 were for damage to carpets, wallpaper and paintwork when an internal meter was installed, and the remainder related to the level of the meter box lid where the meter was installed in the pavement. Those were all put right by the contractor. Only 10 claims for compensation have been made. Those have been for damage to boundary walls and for grit in taps. All have been resolved.

With over 9,000 external installations and 3,000 internal installations completed so far, I am sure that my hon. Friend will agree that the number of complaints about poor reinstatement and the number of claims for compensation are very small in comparison.

My hon. Friend raised the important issue of internal and external meters. As I have already mentioned, one of the objectives of the Isle of Wight trial is to compare, on a large scale, the costs and benefits of internal and external meter locations. To do that, Southern Water is installing external meters in properties on the more urban, eastern side of the island, whereas those on the more rural western side will have internal meters. Once again, that will generally be to the benefit of customers, as properties in rural areas tend to have longer underground supply pipes and hence are more prone to leakage. Water lost through leakage on supply pipes will not be recorded by internal meters, and customers will therefore not pay for it.

Customers in the trial areas who suspect that they have a leak on their supply pipe can ask their water undertaker to carry out a confidence check of the plumbing system and the accuracy of the meter. This is a service for which customers will not be charged. In addition, we have also agreed with the water industry a code of practice which provides important safeguards for all metered domestic customers where their supply pipe develops an unidentified leak. Essentially, the code provides for water undertakers to reassess metered charges on the basis of past normal consumption when an unidentified leak is located. This reassessment of charges will be a one-off concession and will be conditional on the customer carrying out remedial work within a reasonable period. The code will be one of the licence conditions.

While on the issue of the accuracy of meters, I would like to stress that all meters used in the trials—and generally for domestic purposes since 1 April 1989—have to comply with regulations under the Weights and Measures Act 1986 governing their accuracy and in-service performance. However, as part of the trials, a random sample of meters will be removed at various intervals during the trials and subjected to a detailed accuracy assesment on a test rig. This will provide the industry with further information about the in-service performance of meters to compare with that already done in the laboratory by the water research centre. That research indicated that, in normal conditions, water meters will sustain their accuracy for many years.

I know that my hon. Friend is concerned about the problems that can arise for customers when meters are installed indoors. In such cases, the normal location for a meter would be under the kitchen sink alongside the stoptap. However, in some properties, it has been necessary to install the meter in airing cupboards and in bedrooms. This can cause installation problems, difficulties for the meter reader and privacy problems for customers.

Nevertheless, we should not lose sight of the fact that one of the main purposes of the trials is to investigate the advantages and disadvantages of internal metering. I am sure that the House would agree that it would defeat the purpose of the trials if water undertakers took the easy option every time a problem came along.

We should not forget that internal metering does have a number of advantages for the customer. These include the fact that customers do not have to pay for water lost through repeated leaks on underground supply pipes; it is easier for customers to read the meter; and it is cheaper for water undertakers to install internal meters. The cost is currently averaging £82, whereas for straight forward installations of external meters the average cost is £164. Bearing in mind the fact that about 25 per cent. of customers have so far been identified as having joint supplies, and with the average cost of separation running at £380, the overall cost of installing all external meters is around £260.

It is too early to say whether the obvious disadvantages of internal metering—for example, the problem of gaining access to install and read the meter—outweigh the advantage of generally lower installation costs. That said, let us not forget that most electricity and gas meters are installed internally.

My hon. Friend has previously expressed concern that internal meters could lead to bogus workmen and officials gaining access to customers' properties. He raised this important crime prevention point with my hon. Friend the Minister of State Home Office, the hon. Member for Oxford, West and Abingdon (Mr. Patten). The House will

be pleased to know that Southern Water, in common with all water undertakers involved in the trials, has taken action to ensure that customers, especially the elderly, would not be at risk from bogus workmen or officials.

All employees and contractors requiring access to customers' property have been issued with photopasses. These must be clearly displayed before entering a property. Southern Water has also set up a freephone service to enable any householder to check the authenticity of callers. Even so, not enough people ask to see proof of identity before allowing workmen to enter their homes. In all cases, Southern Water gives advance notice of visits requiring internal access. In addition, all contractors have been asked to give assurances that the workmen engaged on the trials do not have a criminal record.

Because of the size of the Isle of Wight trial, the installation phase will not be complete until April next year. However, customers are being charged on a measured basis from 1 April this year and as meters are installed. Those customers who have paid their rateable value-based charges in advance will receive a rebate for the period when charging by volume commenced.

Meter reading and billing will be every six months, with the first bills being sent out in early October. My hon. Friend suggested that metered billing should be delayed until all customers on the island are metered. Although I appreciate my hon. Friend's concern that all his constituents should be treated equally, such a proposition may not be a practical option with a programme of large-scale metering. For example, if Southern Water decided to meter all its supply area over a 20-year period, it clearly would not wait until the completion of the programme before starting metered billing. All that it would do would be to increase the cost of the exercise and frustrate those customers who are keen to start paying by measure.

My hon. Friend asked about income support. He will be aware that income support does not include separate provision for individual amounts payable, as was the case under supplementary benefit. Instead, when setting the benefit rates, account was taken of the overall amount spent in supplementary benefit on water charges. We feel that, as water charges are among the many elements of a claimant's basic commitments where expenditure varies, there is no reason to make special provision for them to be met separately. Income support claimants are now responsible for paying their charges themselves out of their weekly benefit.

The purpose of income support is to provide help for people whose income, from all sources, is below a minimum level. Benefit is therefore payable on the basis of need. The main components of a person's requirements are the personal allowances and, if appropriate, the premiums. I am certain that my hon. Friend does not want to use our time this evening to discuss the merits or otherwise of individual claims. However, I give him an undertaking that, if he is concerned about specific cases, and if he will write to me with full details, I will ensure that his concerns are answered.

What I can do, very briefly, is give an indication of the level of income support that a typical family could receive. For that purpose, if we consider a typical family to be one with two parents and three children under 11, the parents would initially be entitled to £54·80 per week in income support, and could claim a further £41·75 per week in child benefit—a total of £96·55. However, child benefit would be

[Mr. Colin Moynihan]

considered as part of a reduction in the level of income support paid to the family. The net effect would be that the family would receive benefits totalling £74·80 per week. Such a family could expect to use between 200 and 250 cu m of water a year, which equates to a charge of about £4 to £5 per week.

Clearly, as the trials are still at an early stage, it would be wrong to make any formal impression or draw any firm conclusions about the trials at this particular time. Information is being collected and will continue to be collected on all aspects of the trials. It will be made widely available in a series of reports by the water industry.

The Isle of Wight trial is the one trial that has attracted most attention because of its size and importance to the metering trial programme. It also affects a large number of people. However, I am sure that the House is now far wiser about the developments of the Isle of Wight trial, as well as the other trial areas, from the interesting debate we have had tonight and from the continued excellent and perceptive contribution made by my hon. Friend on this subject. I again congratulate him on bringing this subject to the attention of the House.

The question of the metering trial is usually one of the matters raised by my hon. Friend when we meet, and I probably know more about the trial on the Isle of Wight than about any of the other trial areas. I am also pleased to reiterate that I shall have an opportunity to look at the trial area with my hon. Friend during a visit to the island shortly.

Once again I say to my hon. Friend that I am grateful for his invitation. I apologise for the swiftness of my reply, but that has only been because my hon. Friend has been as assiduous as ever in raising so many subjects.

Question put and agreed to.

Adjourned accordingly at one minute past Four o'clock.

House of Commons

Thursday 15 June 1989

The House met at half-past Two o'clock

PRAYERS

[MR. SPEAKER *in the Chair*]

PRIVATE BUSINESS

ASSOCIATED BRITISH PORTS (NO. 2) BILL *(By Order)*
Order read for resuming adjourned debate on Question
[23 May], That the Bill be now read a Third time.
Debate to be resumed on Thursday 22 June.

BRITISH RAILWAYS (PENALTY FARES) BILL *[Lords]*
(By Order)

LONDON REGIONAL TRANSPORT (PENALTY FARES) BILL
[Lords] (By Order)

BUCKINGHAMSHIRE COUNTY COUNCIL BILL *[Lords]*
Orders for consideration, as amended, read.
To be considered on Thursday 22 June.

HYTHE, KENT, MARINA BILL *(By Order)*

LONDON UNDERGROUND (VICTORIA) BILL *(By Order)*

BRITISH FILM INSTITUTE SOUTHBANK BILL *(By Order)*
Orders for Second Reading read.
To be read a Second time on Thursday 22 June.

Oral Answers to Questions

HOME DEPARTMENT

Teenage Crime

1. **Mr. Gill:** To ask the Secretary of State for the Home Department what representations he has received from the Conservative Family Campaign regarding teenage crime.

The Secretary of State for the Home Department (Mr. Douglas Hurd): I have received two letters from the Conservative Family Campaign about young people's involvement in crime. I greatly welcome the growing interest in the role of the family in steering young children away from crime. The fact that the peak age for offending in this country is 15 underscores the truth that the family is our country's first line of defence. Parents and teachers have a clear responsibility to instil into children habits of self-discipline and respect for others.

Mr. Gill: Will my right hon. Friend undertake to respond positively to the family campaign and say what action he will take in the light of its suggestions and recommendations? In so doing, will he welcome the emphasis that the family campaign puts upon the responsibility of parents in an age when we hear all too much about individuals' rights? Will he furthermore take the opportunity to confirm the Government's commitment to parents and to the concept of the family unit?

Mr. Hurd: Yes, indeed, and I have tried to do that in my earlier answer and on several other occasions. I agree with my hon. Friend. As regards his first point, my hon. Friend the Minister of State, the hon. Member for Oxford, West and Abingdon (Mr. Patten), will be receiving leaders of the campaign shortly to go through with them the specific proposals that they have made.

Mr. Marlow: As the majority of teenage crime arises from bravado, should not retribution be swift, painful and humiliating? Could the Government look again at the possibility of introducing corporal punishment, or alternatively some humiliating punishment like the stocks in modern guise?

Mr. Hurd: The House considered the matter not long ago. I remember the debate and I remember its conclusion. If the matter were put to the House again, I am not sure that it would reach a different conclusion. It is worth noting that as a result of the efforts that have been made the number of juveniles sentenced or cautioned has fallen substantially from 170,000 in 1984 to 140,000 in 1987.

Mr. Sheerman: Is the Secretary of State aware that it is often boredom rather than bravado which leads young people into mischief and crime? Is it not about time that he talked not just to Conservative party committees but to British local authorities which desperately want to supply leisure facilities and the creative leisure that the French are so much better at providing? Is it not about time that we took on an Eté Jeunes programme, which the French have and which has been so successful in reducing crime in French inner cities?

Mr. Hurd: If the hon. Gentleman went up and down the country he would find a number of different organisations in Staffordshire and Humberside, for instance, where the police are putting into effect on the ground precisely the schemes that he wishes to encourage. That is already going on and I hope that the Labour party and Labour local authorities will do their best to encourage it.

Television Licences

2. **Mr. Thurnham:** To ask the Secretary of State for the Home Department how many people were fined for non-payment of television licence fees in each of the last five years; and if he will make a statement.

The Minister of State, Home Office (Mr. Tim Renton): The following information has been supplied by the national TV licence records office and relates to the number of convictions in each of the financial years 1 April to 31 March:

	Number
1984-85	110,042
1985-86	123,122
1986-87	174,509
1987-88	158,182
1988-89	172,604

Mr. Thurnham: Bolton magistrates court tells me that these are by far the most miserable of all the fines that it has to collect as 60 per cent. of those fined are female, many of them single mothers with young children, and there are known cases of women having to resort to prostitution to pay their fines. Is it not high time that my hon. Friend brought in a subscription pay-as-you-view revenue system for the BBC instead of listening to Mr. Hussey saying that people like paying their licence fees to fund a grossly overstaffed BBC?

Mr. Renton: I listened with care to my hon. Friend. We accept that people with limited means may find it hard to pay the BBC licence fee. For that reason, we are doing two things. We are encouraging the BBC to develop other streams of income—for example, through subscription—and, from this September, we will introduce a pay-as-you-go instalment scheme. A successful pilot scheme has been run and, as from September, it will be possible gradually throughout the country for the television licence fee to be paid quarterly.

Mr. Haynes: Is the Minister aware that many pensioners are caught up in this problem? The Government should be ashamed of themselves?[*Interruption.*] The Tories may laugh, but this is a serious matter for pensioners. We have asked regularly for all pensioners to be treated the same and to have a £5 television licence instead of the increase that the Government have introduced. Why do we not have fairness so that pensioners can keep themselves out of court and enjoy their later days? The Government are unfair to the elderly. Let us have the Minister at the Dispatch box saying that he will come my way.

Mr. Renton: The hon. Gentleman has not studied the Labour party policy review with the precise attention that I would have expected. The review says that the BBC licence fee is the core of the BBC's income for the future. To do as the hon. Gentleman suggests would remove £400 million from the BBC. The only way to recoup that would

be to put up the licence fee by about half for everyone else. The hon. Gentleman has not thought his argument through, but that is no surprise.

Mr. Redwood: Does the Minister think that under the pressure of satellite broadcasting and commercial television the BBC's audience share might be so low that this method of financing would no longer be appropriate?

Mr. Renton: Yes, I agree with my hon. Friend. I have no doubt that as we are giving our blessing to a new terrestrial channel—Channel 5—to be financed by advertising and subscription, and in view of the number of satellite channels that are coming and the increasing success of cable, the BBC in its forward planning for the 1990s will be thinking carefully about what it should do if its audience share falls in the way suggested by my hon. Friend so that the continuance of the licence fee would be an intolerable burden on many households who are willing to look at channels other than the BBC.

Police (Leicestershire)

3. **Mr. Janner:** To ask the Secretary of State for the Home Department whether he will make a statement concerning police provision in Leicestershire.

The Parliamentary Under-Secretary of State for the Home Department (Mr. Douglas Hogg): Twenty seven extra police posts were approved for Leicestershire in April so that a total of 54 have been approved since May 1979. In addition, some 130 police officers have been returned to operational duties as a result of civilianisation and other efficiency measures.

The police authority has applied for my right hon. Friend's approval of 75 more posts in 1990-91. Our aim is to announce decisions on this, and applications from other authorities, towards the end of this year.

Mr. Janner: Is the Minister aware that one of the few areas in which the Members of Parliament for Leicestershire agree, with the possible exception of the right hon. Member for Blaby (Mr. Lawson), is that we do not have nearly enough police, that the level of crime, which has doubled since the Conservatives came to office, is insupportable, and that it was wrong to turn down the applications of two successive chief constables for a considerable increase in the number of policemen? Is he aware that all Members of Parliament for the area have expressed in the House their view that it is not safe for people to go out at night in parts of Leicester because there are not enough policemen on the beat and that the Government's continued refusal to accept the recommendations of chief constables is unworthy and wrong?

Mr. Hogg: I have good news for Leicestershire. As I have said, we have increased police posts by 54, a process of civilianisation has freed 130 officers for operational duties and that process is continuing. There is more good news. In 1978-79 expenditure on the Leicestershire constabulary was £15·65 million. In the current year it is £57 million—a huge increase. There is more good news. The hon. and learned Gentleman may have noticed that in 1988 there was a fall of 9·3 per cent. in sexual offences and 5·7 per cent. in burglaries. All that is good news and it is a great pity that the hon. and learned Gentleman did not point out those facts.

Mr. Tredinnick: Is my hon. Friend aware that, contrary to the opinion of the hon. and learned Member for Leicester, West (Mr. Janner), the recent announcement of an increase in police for Leicestershire has been widely welcomed, although it may not be an ideal figure? Will my hon. Friend congratulate the force on the tremendous strides that it has taken towards civilianisation? Is it not a fact that spending on police in England and Wales has been higher than spending on almost any other area of government during this Administration?

Mr Hogg: As one would expect from my hon. Friend, he has given a comprehensive summary of the position. I am sure that the House would like to know that spending this year, compared with the last year of the Labour Government, is 54·9 per cent. up in real terms—a huge increase. We never hear any mention of that from the empty Opposition Benches.

As regards the efficiency of the Leicestershire constabulary, it is a great pity that the hon. and learned Member for Leicester, West (Mr. Janner) did not draw attention to its exceptionally high clear-up rate—42·8 per cent., compared with 35·2 per cent. in England and Wales. I am also glad to say that the county has a much lower crime rate of 5,712 per 100,000 of population, compared with 7,396 in England and Wales, excluding the City and Metropolitan police.

Mr. Speaker: Order. We shall make slow progress if we have long answers.

Child Crime (Parental Responsibility)

4. **Mr. Amess:** To ask the Secretary of State for the Home Department what representations he has received seeking steps to make parents responsible for the criminal activity of their children.

The Minister of State, Home Office (Mr. John Patten): The great majority of the 100 or so letters that we have received in the past few months support the idea. Many specific provisions already existing in law are, however, little used. For example, the power to impose a curfew on juvenile offenders was used by the courts on only eight occasions in 1986 and 1987.

Mr. Amess: Is my hon. Friend aware that his ideas for greater parental involvement in the consequences of children offending has received widespread acclaim throughout Britain? Is it not a tragedy, however, that the powers of curfew have been so seldom used? Will my hon. Friend comment on the suggestion that that is because some probation officers have refused to co-operate in the implementation of such orders?

Mr. Patten: My right hon. Friend the Home Secretary and I greatly welcome the support in the majority of the correspondence that the Home Office has received for our radical and far-reaching new ideas to deal with offending by children. I am advised that there have been problems with some probation officers about co-operating with the courts. In 1985, the National Association of Probation Officers made it its policy not to co-operate with the courts in enforcing and supervising supervision orders. That is extraordinary because probation officers are officers of the court. If they will not fulfil their responsibilities, we may have to look for others who will.

Mr. Tony Banks: Is the Minister aware that attempting to make parents somehow responsible for the criminal activities of their children is entirely superficial and misses the point? Is he further aware that there has been a most alarming upsurge in crime by adolescents in the United States in recent years and that within five to 10 years a similar situation will develop here because Britain is following closely the social and economic policies pursued in the United States? Should not the Minister go for a far deeper study of the causes of crime by adolescents in Britain rather than grasping at the chimeras offered by Conservative Members?

Mr. Patten: During the past year the ministerial group on crime prevention—on which 13 different Government Departments are represented—has been conducting an in-depth study of the causes of crime among children and young people. The hon. Member for Newham, North-West (Mr. Banks) is absolutely right that we must search for those causes. I do not believe, however, that the search would be aided by simply dismissing parental responsibility for the behaviour of children as something of no importance. As my right hon. Friend the Secretary of State has said, the family is the first line of defence against crime by children.

I do not believe that on every occasion trends in the United States are followed 10 or 15 years later in this country. In the past 10 years we have seen a welcome, though slight, reduction in juvenile crime. What alarms my right hon. Friend and myself is that the peak age for offending remains at 15. We are determined to do something about that.

Mr. Patrick Thompson: Bearing in mind that many young children are drawn into crime as a result of addiction to amusement-with-prizes machines in arcades and that many parents, responsible and irresponsible, are involved in such distressing cases, will my hon. Friend seriously reconsider my Bill, which has support on both sides of the House and would give discretion to local authorities to ban under-16s from amusement arcades?

Mr. Patten: I know of my hon. Friend's longstanding interest in this important issue and of the way in which he has dealt with it in the proposals that he has put to Ministers and in his Bill. He is a model of how such a campaign should be conducted. We believe, however, that we should respond to the need for change in the criminal justice system when, to borrow my hon. Friend's phrase, there is clear evidence of a link between addiction and criminality. Independent research carried out by the Home Office's internationally renowned research and planning unit, which is independent in the way in which it conducts its business, supported by the Gaming Board for Great Britain, produced no evidence of such a link. If my hon. Friend and those who support him in his campaign can come forward with firm evidence we shall, of course, reconsider the issue.

Mr. Heffer: May I ask the Minister to take more seriously the point made by my hon. Friend the Member for Newham, North-West (Mr. Banks) about the reasons for child crime? Surely the suggestion that parents are responsible for all the criminal activity of their children is not a serious one, although it is a populist demand on the part of some Conservative Members. [HON. MEMBERS: "Yes"]. There are many Members of Parliament whose children have committed criminal activities. We all know of next-door neighbours and so on whose children have carried out criminal acts. Parents are in no way responsible.

Mr. Tony Banks: It is a superficial suggestion.

Mr. Heffer: Exactly. Of course there is a connection between parents and their children's criminal activity up to a point, but it is a minor one. We must consider this issue much more carefully. I ask the Minister to ignore totally the irresponsible and populist demands that have been made by Conservative Members.

Mr. Patten: I am extremely surprised that the hon. Gentleman, with his well-known upholding of Christian values about which he has told this House on many occasions since I have been here, should feel that parents have no responsibility for their children. As my right hon. Friend the Home Secretary has said, it is critically important to appreciate that the first and best line of defence against offending not just by juveniles, but by children under 10 who commit some 6,000 offences each year, are the parents. I believe that the country appreciates that. I entirely accept that a thuggish, 16-year-old young man may be difficult for a single parent to control, but I do not accept that the parent of an eight, nine or 10-year-old should be exonerated from providing care and attention.

Several Hon. Members *rose*——

Mr. Speaker: Order. We are making extremely slow progress. I ask for brief questions and briefer answers to them.

Mr. Nicholas Bennett: My hon. Friend has already referred to the fact that the peak age for criminal activity is school age. Much of that criminal activity takes place during school hours. Will my hon. Friend have a word with my right hon. Friend the Secretary of State for Education and Science to get schools to check that pupils are attending on a lesson basis rather than on a half-day basis and to ensure that education authorities speed up the process of taking parents to court when children are truanting? The court process should also be speeded up so that it no longer takes between 18 months and two years to bring a truanting child and his parents to court.

Mr. Patten: My hon. Friend makes three important points. Such discussions have taken place between my right hon. Friends the Home Secretary and the Secretary of State for Education and Science in recent months. In addition, we are delighted that my right hon. Friend the Secretary of State for Education and Science has asked the National Curriculum Council to consider the inclusion of lessons on parenthood and responsibility in the national curriculum. That is an important suggestion.

Cross Report

6. **Mr. Holt:** To ask the Secretary of State for the Home Department if any conclusions have yet been reached following the Cross report; and if he will make a statement.

Mr. John Patten: Lord Cross delivered his arbitration on matters of dispute between the Horserace Betting Levy Board and the Horserace Totalisator Board in 1979. We have had no reason to question the acceptance of the arbitration by both boards since then.

Mr. Holt: I am grateful to my hon. Friend, who will realise that 10 years of peace are about to be broken. The proliferation of tote facilities at race courses is now seriously jeopardising on-course bookmakers. Ahead of privatisation, in the not-too-distant future, that proliferation could well result in a problem landing on my hon. Friend's doorstep. I ask him, therefore, to look seriously at the present acceleration in the siting of tote facilities at race courses which is driving away small bookmakers.

Mr. Patten: I have enjoyed more or less a decade of détente with my hon. Friend the Member for Langbaurgh (Mr. Holt) and I hope that hostilities are not about to break out over this of all issues, which we have discussed on several occasions in a variety of settings over the years.

We look to the levy board for advice on this issue, but we have had no such advice from it. However, I believe that the representative bookmakers association has written to the chairman of the levy board, Sir Ian Trethowan, about this and we await his views with interest.

Crime (Greater Manchester)

7. **Mr. Sumberg:** To ask the Secretary of State for the Home Department what progress his Department is making towards reducing the level of crime in the Greater Manchester area.

Mr. Hurd: In the first quarter of 1989, offences recorded by the Greater Manchester police fell by 4·5 per cent. compared with the same period in 1988. The two largest categories—burglary and theft, and handling stolen goods—fell by 14·6 per cent. and 3·1 per cent. respectively.

Mr. Sumberg: Is my right hon. Friend aware that Bury is one of the safest places to live in Greater Manchester, with a fall in recorded crime of 4·5 per cent. compared with last year's figures? Will he join me in saluting that achievement and in thanking the local police, who are obviously part of it, together with all those in the community who are promoting greater involvement—there are now 320 home watch schemes—and the local paper, the *Bury Times,* which has made the public aware of the greater dangers which face the elderly in particular?

Mr. Hurd: I know that Bury, Bolton and several of the old Lancashire towns within the Greater Manchester police area have made great progress and have forged ahead. It is good news that there are now 8,000 home watch schemes in that police area. There must be some connection—a close connection I believe—between all the efforts that my hon. Friend describes and the fall in total recorded crime in the area not just in the first quarter of this year, but with last year's decrease of 8 per cent. compared with 1987.

Mrs. Peacock: I hope that when looking at the great progress that has been made in the Greater Manchester area my right hon. Friend will not be persuaded to go along the lines recently suggested especially in urging parents not to be responsible for their children's criminal activities. Does he agree that it is absolute nonsense not to hold parents responsible? I hope that my right hon. Friend will make that positive move in the rest of his work.

Mr. Hurd: I am obliged to my hon. Friend. Exchanges earlier this afternoon have shown the wide interest and support for the general principle that my hon. Friend the Minister of State has floated.

Drink-related Crime

8. **Mr. Atkinson:** To ask the Secretary of State for the Home Department if he has made any recent studies of methods used in the United States of America in combating drink-related crime; and if he will make a statement.

Mr. Hurd: Experience internationally—the failures as well as the successes—is taken into account as we work out policy. We have done a lot to tackle alcohol misuse here through crime prevention. We have also strengthened the powers of licensing justices and the law on sales to under-age drinkers, and I have approved experimental byelaws in seven areas to ban the consumption of alcohol in public places.

Mr. Atkinson: Can my right hon. Friend confirm that, in response to rising drink-related crime among young people, every American state has now raised its legal drinking age to 21? Will he ensure that the lessons of that experience will be considered not only by his Department but by the ministerial group on alcohol misuse, which is chaired by our right hon. Friend the Lord President of the Council?

Mr. Hurd: I believe that my hon. Friend is right in saying that all the American states have raised the legal drinking age to 21, and I gather that a lively debate about that degree of prohibition is still in progress. I would rather ensure that our own law, under which the legal drinking age is 18, is enforced effectively, and that magistrates and police are reminded of the powers that they already have to deal with disorderly pubs or places where under-age drinking occurs. I agree, however, that we must keep an eye on what happens in the United States as a result of the change.

Mr. Sheerman: The Home Secretary knows that the work of his own research unit shows that disorder and drunkenness go together, not so much in the rural regions as in the non-metropolitan areas. That research was invaluable in pinpointing the sites of such disorder. In the light of what it has shown, will the Home Secretary do two things? First, will he talk to the traditional friends of the Conservative party—the brewers—about their advertising and about helping to enforce our existing drinking laws? Secondly, may I again ask the right hon. Gentleman to give local authorities and others involved in youth work the resources to provide young people with creative leisure, which—whatever the hon. Member for Bournemouth, East (Mr. Atkinson) may say—they do not enjoy at present?

Mr. Hurd: Of course my right hon. Friend the Lord President, as chairman of the ministerial group, is constantly in touch with the drinks industry, and we co-operate closely with the industry in such matters. The

link between drinking and disorder which the hon. Gentleman has accurately described is contrary to the industry's interests, so it is naturally on our side.

I repeat what I said before: a mass of schemes exist to provide leisure facilities, and I do not think that young people in this country have ever had more such facilities. The difficulty is that expectations of excitement are also much greater than they have ever been. The matter cannot be dealt with just as the hon. Gentleman suggests.

Mr. Barry Field: Can my right hon. Friend reassure hon. Members on both sides of the House, as well as the brewing industry, that one of the American methods that he will not be studying is prohibition?

Mr. Hurd: Indeed, Sir.

Licensing Laws

12. **Mr. Knox:** To ask the Secretary of State for the Home Department whether he has any plans to introduce further legislation to liberalise the licensing laws in England.

Mr. Douglas Hogg: No, Sir, but we shall keep the position under review.

Mr. Knox: Following the success of the recent legislation, does my hon. Friend consider that there is a case for taking modest steps towards further liberalisation in the near future?

Mr. Hogg: When we have seen such a case, we have taken steps. We do not see a case for further steps at present.

Mr. Janner: Does the Minister agree that what is needed now is not a further liberalisation of the licensing laws, but a tightening up of efforts to stop people who have been drinking in licensing hours from driving on our roads? Instead of introducing more time in which people can drink, should not more steps be taken to prevent them from endangering the lives of others and killing on the roads after drinking?

Mr. Hogg: That is a very general point, and of course it is correct as far as it goes.

Mr. Allason: Is my hon. Friend taking steps to establish from the police the exact results of the liberalisation of licensing laws? Is he aware that—certainly in the south-west, and in particular in my constituency, where there have been a few moments of disorder at closing time in the past—the liberalising of licensing hours has been of enormous benefit, not only to people who have indulged in recreational drinking but to the police? Will he assure the House that he will report on the police attitude to the liberalisation that has already taken place?

Mr. Hogg: The police attitude has been broadly favourable and along the lines outlined by my hon. Friend. That is also the feeling of the justices, in so far as they are able to make an assessment at present. The Office of Population Censuses and Surveys will be conducting a survey of alcohol consumption and drinking patterns for the Department of Health in the autumn against which to measure the effects of longer opening hours, and I imagine that a summary of its conclusions will be made available to the House in due course.

Crack

15. **Mr. Tredinnick:** To ask the Secretary of State for the Home Department what new initiatives he has taken recently to prevent imports of the drug crack; to what extent organised crime is involved in crack imports; and if he will make a statement.

Mr. Hurd: I take very seriously indeed the threat posed by cocaine and its derivative crack, not only to this country but to the whole of Europe. That is why I called the meeting last month of the Council of Europe's drug co-operation group, the Pompidou group.

The initiatives we have taken include the provision of £1·8 million of drug-related help to Latin American countries over the past three years; posting drug liaison officers to countries on the cocaine trafficking routes; working hard to develop international agreements and bilateral agreements to confiscate the assets of convicted drug traffickers; setting up Customs teams to combat cocaine smuggling; and calling an international conference next year to look at reducing the demand for drugs and, in particular, for cocaine.

Mr. Tredinnick: I welcome that reply. Does my right hon. Friend agree that fighting organised crime before it gets a grip on Britain, particularly from the point of veiw of crack, is of the highest possible priority and that we may have to invest now to avoid serious outbreaks of crime in the future? Is he aware that hon. Members who were in Newark, New Jersey last year during the presidential election campaign were told that they should not leave the hotel for fear of being attacked by crack-crazed youngsters aged under 16?

Mr. Hurd: My hon. Friend is entirely right. The Under-Secretary, who is chairman of the ministerial group on drug misuse, has visited the United States even more recently. All the information that he has come back with and everything that we have heard directly from the enforcement agencies in America confirms the anxiety that my hon. Friend voices. That is why we are taking such energetic action in time.

Mr. Tony Banks: Is the Home Secretary aware that this is yet another example of seeing what was happening in the United States five years ago and projecting it on here? I asked a parliamentary question about crack some four years ago—[*Interruption.*] I am sorry that Conservative Members seem to think that this is a flippant subject. The Home Secretary must make sure that far more study of the problem takes place in the United States to anticipate what will happen in this country. Is the right hon. Gentleman aware that instead of making cuts in the number of Customs and Excise officers, he should increase the numbers of enforcement officers at the ports of entry to try to intercept this evil drug before it takes over our youth?

Mr. Hurd: The hon. Gentleman knows perfectly well that the number of Customs officers employed in this work —and he is right about their importance—has been substantially increased.

Mr. Wheeler: My right hon. Friend will be aware that the Home Affairs Committee will be visiting Washington and the United States next week to investigate this very subject. The members of that committee dare to go where others fear to tread, to see for themselves how the drugs menace has impacted on American society. Does my right

hon. Friend agree that our defences in this country are well prepared at airports and seaports, that our police and Customs are working well together and that while so far the seizures of crack have been low, we are preparing a plan to deal with the future?

Mr. Hurd: That is exactly the position. We must, and we do, keep in touch with experience in the United States. Our defences must be in advance, beyond our shores, in America and in Europe on the cocaine and heroin smuggling routes. They must be at our ports and airports, and that is important in the discussion of 1992. They must be in our cities, with our police, and they must be in our schools and in our homes in persuading parents and children that these are routes not to happiness and power but to disgrace and misery.

Prison Building

18. **Mr. David Nicholson:** To ask the Secretary of State for the Home Department if he will make a statement on the progress of the Government's prison building programme.

Mr. Douglas Hogg: Eight new prisons have been opened since 1985, seven are under construction and one, which has been converted from existing buildings at Banstead in Surrey, will open shortly. Five more are planned to start on site this year, and eight are at various stages of planning and design. The building programme also covers the expansion and improvement of existing establishments. By the end of this year nearly 2,000 new places will have been added to existing establishments in a period of less then two years. By the mid-1990s we will have added about 25,000 places to the system. The prison department directorate of works has also begun a five-year programme to provide over 6,500 cells with access to sanitation in addition to its ongoing programme of maintenance, improvement and renovation.

Mr. Nicholson: Is my hon. Friend aware that I recently received representations, which I forwarded to him, from some of my constituents and those of my hon. Friend the Member for Devon, North (Mr. Speller)? They included one from a former prison chaplain who preaches at my local parish church and they concerned the serious problem of overcrowding in prisons. Does my hon. Friend recognise that such overcrowding is not tolerable in a civilised country such as we consider ours to be? The figures that he has given in his answer are most welcome. Will he continue these operations and consider alternatives to imprisonment for those convicted, and particularly for those on remand?

Mr. Hogg: There are two important points here. Yes, there is overcrowding in the prison system, but it is very confined. There are about 50,000 people in the prison system, and 20,000 of them in the local and remand centres are overcrowded. The balance of 30,000 are not in any sense overcrowded in the circumstances in which they are living. The overcrowding of the 20,000 is a serious matter, but we have a whole range of policies designed to address that problem. Most specifically, we are building new places —25,000 between 1979 and the mid-1990s. I hope that we will have substantially eradicated the problem by the mid-1990s.

Mr. Harry Greenway: While congratulating my hon. Friend on the substantial number of new places in prisons, may I ask him if he will do all that he can to expand prison education, especially for people on remand, some of whom spend three years on remand and are then not convicted of anything? Secondly, is he not concerned about the large number of people in prison dormitories? Is not that a threat to security?

Mr. Hogg: My hon. Friend raises a number of matters. I agree that some people have been on remand for far too long and we are taking urgent measures to reduce the number. My hon. Friend is right about dormitories. Broadly speaking, they are not a secure way of keeping prisoners and we are in the process of eliminating them. We are seeking to improve the provision of education in the prisons, and I am glad to say that the fresh start procedures that we put in place have greatly enhanced the provision of education in the prison system.

Crime Prevention (Norfolk)

24. **Mr. Patrick Thompson:** To ask the Secretary of State for the Home Department what steps his Department is taking to encourage crime prevention in Norfolk; and if he will make a statement.

Mr. John Patten: I congratulate my hon. Friend on his attendance and on his question. The answer to his question is that crime reduction forms part of a strategy that applies to all of England and Wales. Police manpower and resources have been substantially increased, crime concern was launched with Government support in May 1988 to stimulate support and develop local crime prevention activity, and the largest-ever crime prevention publicity campaign was launched last year. My right hon. Friend approved a further 24 police posts for the Norfolk force from 1 April. We give encouragement to the growth and development of neighbourhood watch schemes and crime prevention panels, and I am pleased to note that there are now 472 neighbourhood watch schemes in Norfolk, together with five crime prevention panels and three junior crime prevention panels.

Mr. Thompson: Will my hon. Friend join me in congratulating the police and all others in Norfolk who were involved in the very encouraging recent reduction in crime in that area and in Norwich? Will my hon. Friend confirm that there has been a serious and continuing increase in violent crime? Will he do all that he can in discussions with the police and others in Norfolk to take further action to deal with that disturbing trend?

Mr. Patten: I certainly congratulate the Norfolk constabulary on its sterling efforts to reduce crime. My right hon. Friend the Home Secretary has introduced a lot of very original ideas and thinking about how to reduce violent crime. Indeed, most of my hon. Friends recognise that all the original thinking about crime prevention is coming from these Benches. Nothing is coming from the Opposition Benches and in particular from the right hon. Member for Birmingham, Sparkbrook (Mr. Hattersley), who did not ask a question the last time we had Home Office questions and has not got on his feet once during this session either.

Crime (Humberside)

25. **Mr. Cran:** To ask the Secretary of State for the Home Department what are the latest available figures for the number of criminal offences recorded by police as having been committed in Humberside; and if he will make a statement.

Mr. John Patten: In 1988 the Humberside police recorded 85,113 notifiable offences. This was a very welcome 4 per cent. fall from the previous year's figures.

Mr. Cran: Is my hon. Friend aware that the only category of crime that increased on Humberside last year was violence related to the consumption of alcohol? That being the case, will his Department encourage a whole range of schemes to tackle the problem of under-age drinking, which is endemic in many parts of this country?

Mr. Patten: We will certainly do all we possibly can and the whole Government, and I am sure the whole Conservative party, will support the efforts of my right hon. Friend the Lord President of the Council and his ministerial group on this issue.

PRIME MINISTER

Engagements

Q1. **Mrs. Gorman:** To ask the Prime Minister if she will list her official engagements for Thursday 15 June.

The Prime Minister (Mrs. Margaret Thatcher): This morning I presided at a meeting of the Cabinet and had meetings with ministerial colleagues and others. In addition to my duties in the House, I shall be having further meetings later today.

Mrs. Gorman: Will my right hon. Friend find time in her busy day to remind people of the importance of today's Euro-elections? Will she note the growing support by people in Northern Ireland for the Conservative party? Today they will have a chance to vote for Dr. Laurence Kennedy, our first-ever Conservative Euro-candidate in Ulster? Will she include him in her greetings to our candidates?

The Prime Minister: I have already sent the message of greeting and support which my hon. Friend seeks to our Euro-candidates. I agree that it is a very important election and a very important day and I hope that people will turn out in strength and vote. I note what my hon. Friend says about matters in Northern Ireland. I know her strong views about parties there, and I note what she says.

Mr. Kinnock: Why cannot the Prime Minister simply answer yes to the question, "Is the Chancellor going to retain his job after the forthcoming reshuffle?"

The Prime Minister: I answer on precisely what the Chancellor said on Wednesday of last week in the economic debate. The Chancellor set out the Government's position clearly and in some detail. he said:
"Our overriding"
—I repeat "overriding"—
"objective is to bring inflation back down."
We shall not be diverted from that course.

Mr. Kinnock: Is that "gladly, joyfully, generously, fully, fully, fully" a refusal to guarantee the future of the Chancellor of the Exchequer?

The Prime Minister: I repeat what I said last week. If the right hon. Gentleman would like a little longer lecture I will read out the entire speech.

Sir Peter Tapsell: While the Leader of the Opposition regards all this as a joke, is it not about time that we all began to take the sterling situation rather seriously and that the Leader of the Opposition ceased to try twice a week to talk sterling down?

The Prime Minister: I entirely agree with my hon. Friend. The Leader of the Opposition is normally trying to help the speculators and talks sterling down in the most unBritish way.

Q2. Ms. Primarolo: To ask the Prime Minister if she will list her official engagements for Thursday 15 June.

The Prime Minister: I refer the hon. Lady to the reply that I gave some moments ago.

Ms. Primarolo: Will the Prime Minister confirm that her policy of keeping interest rates as high as necessary for as long as necessary means that she will be prepared to tolerate a further increase in mortgage interest rates?

The Prime Minister: I repeat what the Chancellor said in his most excellent speech in the economic debate giving his policy very fully. He set out the Government's position and said:
"Our overriding"
—I repeat "overriding"—
"objective is to bring inflation back down."
The Chancellor said:
"the policies that have successfully brought inflation down in the past . . . will do so again."—[*Official Report,* 7 June 1989; Vol. 154, c. 264.]
We have had an extremely successful economic policy.

Q3. Mrs. Peacock: To ask the Prime Minister if she will list her official engagements for Thursday 15 June.

The Prime Minister: I refer my hon. Friend to the reply that I gave some moments ago.

Mrs. Peacock: Will my right hon. Friend confirm that the Government's main priority is to reduce inflation? Will she also condemn members of the Opposition, including the Leader of the Opposition, for continually trying to talk the pound down?

The Prime Minister: Yes, I confirm once again that that is the Government's overriding priority, as my right hon. Friend the Chancellor said in the economic debate. We shall not be deflected from that course of action. I agree that the Opposition try to talk down the pound, which is a great tragedy.

Mr. Shore: Apart from the obvious and damaging effect that high interest rates have on the competitiveness of British industry, is it not a fact that the main effect of high interest rates, far from reducing aggregate demand, is simply to redistribute demand away from hard-pressed first-time mortgagors and other borrowers to people who are savers and creditors? If that is so, is this not an extremely unfair and ineffective way to reduce demand and counter inflation?

The Prime Minister: The right hon. Gentleman is aware that inflation is a monetary phenomenon, and short-term interest rates are the main instrument for dealing with it.

Q4. Mr. Patrick McNair-Wilson: To ask the Prime Minister if she will list her official engagements for Thursday 15 June.

The Prime Minister: I refer my hon. Friend to the reply that I gave some moments ago.

Mr. McNair-Wilson: Does my right hon. Friend agree that those both inside and outside Parliament who continually delight in rubbishing the achievements of this country fail to grasp the inherent strength of the British economy? Do we not now have a record level of new job creation in Europe, enjoy a record high standard of living, and have a record repayment of the debts piled up by the Labour party when it last had muddled control of our economy?

The Prime Minister: Yes, I agree with my hon. Friend. We have a record high standard of living and a record high standard of social services.

Mr. Tony Banks: And inflation.

The Prime Minister: No, the Labour party has the record on inflation this century, with a rate of 27 per cent. As well as the record high standards of living and of social services, we have record repayment of debt, and record standards of investment in manufacturing industry and of business investment. I could go on with record after record of good things for the British people—an excellent record.

Dr. Kim Howells: How do the Government intend to clean up our rivers and beaches if they refuse to give the National Rivers Authority the powers to prosecute the regional water companies after they have been privatised?

The Prime Minister: Both our rivers and our beaches are being cleaned up, contrary to what happened during the time of the Labour Government. The directive from Europe came out in 1975, and it asked Governments to identify beaches that did not come up to standard. By 1979, the Labour Government had not identified one. It was left to us to identify them all. We have done so. Two thirds have already been dealt with and the other one third will soon be dealt with. As to rivers, 95 per cent. are classified, on European standards, as good or fair, which is the best record in the Community.

European Commission

Q5. Mr. Leigh: To ask the Prime Minister if she has received representations regarding the European Commission.

The Prime Minister: I receive a number of such representations.

Mr. Leigh: Whatever else divides the two major parties, is not one thing crystal clear, and comes out in representations concerning the European Community? It is that the overwhelming majority of the House insists that this House, representing the people as it does, must retain its untrammelled power over taxation. Were we to subscribe to a central European bank or a common currency, the House would lose the right, uniquely sustained over many centuries, democratically to control economic policy. Is that not why public opinion in this country is so different from that in other parts of the Community?

The Prime Minister: I agree with my hon. Friend that the ability to run monetary, economic and fiscal policy lies at the heart of what constitutes a sovereign state. I very much agree with him that the rights and powers of national Governments and Parliaments in these matters must be preserved. That is what this Parliament is for. We must resist the constant centralising tendency of the European Community.

Mr. Spearing: Is the Prime Minister aware that the House has made representations to the Government about the Commission's proposals for all-European television rules? Is she aware also that at 3 am on Tuesday the House debated those rules, when it became clear that the decision whether a certain pornographic television channel which is transmitted in a member state, which I shall not name, becomes a legal transmission in Britain will be made by a majority vote? When the Prime Minister placed the Single European Act before the House, was she misled by others about its possible effects and potential? Was the right hon. Lady misled by the Commission or the Foreign Office, or is there some other explanation for this extraordinary state of affairs?

The Prime Minister: The hon. Gentleman knows full well that there is nothing misleading about the Single European Act. Greater majority voting in some spheres was clearly on the face of the Act, and he knows that. There is a question about interpretation with regard to one or two matters. Unanimous voting on certain matters was also clearly on the face of the Act. The hon. Gentleman knows that full well.

The hon. Gentleman knows that the Government have done more than any other to try to raise television quality standards, and hitherto we have had precious little help from the Opposition in so doing.

Sir Ian Lloyd: On 27 June nearly 40 years ago, the then Leader of the Opposition, in his matchless prose, made a declaration on behalf of the Conservative and Liberal parties that

"national sovereignty is not inviolable, and that it may be resolutely diminished for the sake of all the men in all the lands finding their way home together."—[*Official Report*, 27 June 1950; Vol. 476, c. 2159.]

When my right hon. Friend discusses these extremely important matters with her colleagues in the Community, will she consider not the unregenerate idealism of someone such as myself, who matters little, but the important idealism of the young people of Britain and elsewhere in Europe, who should be inspired by the idealism of the founding fathers, who have far to travel and who have not yet found their way home?

The Prime Minister: Every time we sign a treaty of international agreement we are voluntarily engaging in a certain pooling of sovereignty. That has been so almost ever since Parliament began and the first treaty was signed. When we went into the Common Market we agreed to pool our sovereignty on such things as the common

agricultural policy. Hitherto it was negotiated completely through Europe. We agreed to pool all our rights in trading with other nations and henceforth the Community conducted our trading negotiations through the Community and the Commission. There are other occasions where one pools one's sovereignty. To revert to what I was asked about earlier, taxation policy, economic policy and monetary policy go to the heart of the rights of this place, to the heart of representations by the people and to control of the Executive, and that is one of the reasons why the House exists.

Mr. Tony Banks: What pathetic, miserable and whingeing excuses is the Prime Minister going to offer the country for her party's humiliation in the Euro polls today?

The Prime Minister: I know that all our supporters will come out and vote strongly for our sort of Europe. I note that Opposition Members were not sufficiently confident in the results to come and question me in the House this afternoon. They had to run away. They felt that if they did not do so their supporters might not come out.

Engagements

Q7. Mr. Thurnham: To ask the Prime Minister if she will list her official engagements for Thursday 15 June.

The Prime Minister: I refer my hon. Friend to the reply that I gave some moments ago.

Mr. Thurnham: If any members of Tonge Moor Conservative club have not heeded Mr. George Handley's excellent advice to be sure to vote today, will my right hon. Friend the Prime Minister remind them that the students in Peking are dying for democracy and that we should all go out and vote for the winning party, the party with more jobs, more exports, more productivity and more investment?

The Prime Minister: I absolutely agree with my hon. Friend. This Conservative Government have created a strong Britain whose reputation rides high because we have put the economy in order. Voting Conservative today will help to create a strong Europe, and a strong Britain in a strong Europe, which pursues the same policies that have been so successful in this country.

Mr. Geoffrey Robinson: Is the Prime Minister aware that nothing so clearly reveals the dead trouble that she is in over sterling than the pathetically orchestrated series of questions about the Leader of the Opposition talking down sterling? Is she not aware that the persistent bickering between her and the Chancellor of the Exchequer and her pathetic record on inflation and the balance of payments are driving down sterling? The Prime Minister's policies and her failure to deal with that situation in the markets in Europe are on trial.

The Prime Minister: The hon. Gentleman has provided evidence of what we were complaining about earlier. The Opposition are out to write sterling down. Once again, he is at it, and his hon. Friends cannot leave it alone.

Rose Theatre

3.32 pm

Mr. Clive Soley (Hammersmith) *(by private notice)*: To ask the Secretary of State for the Environment if he will make a statement on the future of the Rose theatre site.

The Secretary of State for the Environment (Mr. Nicholas Ridley): My announcement on 15 May that Imry Merchant Developers had agreed to delay work on the site of the Rose theatre for up to one month, gave a valuable breathing space. Imry recently announced a new design at an extra cost to them of £10 million.

English Heritage has advised me that the new design will, if it receives planning permission from the London borough of Southwark, both protect the remains and allow their proper evaluation and display. Scheduling is not necessary at this stage.

I have decided, after consideration, to accept that advice. I would reconsider my decision if that became necessary. I hope that all parties will now work together to make a success of a thoroughly sensible deal.

Mr. Soley: Does the Secretary of State recognise that there is an overwhelming demand in this country and overseas that the site should be scheduled? Virtually everyone wants that. The way in which we are treating our heritage is becoming a major item on overseas news broadcasts. The site fully qualifies for scheduling under the National Heritage Act 1983, as the Secretary of State is aware. English Heritage confirms that the site should be scheduled. Building an office block on top of the site is an act of vandalism and incredibly short-sighted, even from a commercial point of view. If the site was properly developed and enhanced it would bring in far more money as a tourist attraction than half a dozen office blocks on the land. Does not the Secretary of State also realise that if he persists in this course and if he does not change his mind, because of the National Heritage Act 1983 and other legislation, he is likely to face a challenge in the courts sooner or later?

Mr. Ridley: The hon. Gentleman clearly comes new to this subject. The demand, with which I have every sympathy, is that the site should be protected and conserved for future public inspection and remain for all time available for people to see. The demand is not for it to be scheduled. The hon. Gentleman is wrong to say that English Heritage has recommended scheduling. It has not done that. The criterion for scheduling is that I should feel that the site is threatened in some way. As a result of advice from English Heritage, I do not feel that. The scheme put forward by Imry Merchant is probably the best way of protecting and putting these very important remains on public display. Instead of always griping in the way that he does, I hope that the hon. Gentleman will pay tribute to the developers for their enormous contribution and co-operation.

Mr. Gerald Bowden (Dulwich): May I say how pleased I am that my right hon. Friend has come forward with a scheme that is practical and that brings together the parties —the developers, the London borough of Southwark, English Heritage, the museum of London and those of us who wish the site to be made available and accessible and preserved for posterity. If there is any further delay, the site may deteriorate. What is there now may be lost to future generations.

I recognise that the proposed solution will not satisfy everybody. There are those who feel that this is holy ground and that nothing should overshadow it. However, those who appreciate the necessity of recognising that we are in the 20th century but who nevertheless wish to preserve these elements of the past feel that this solution, which Imry has further considered and to which it is making a contribution of some £10 million, is one that we should support.

Mr. Ridley: I agree with my hon. Friend that we should pay tribute to all concerned for the wonderful co-operation that they have shown in finding this solution. In the previous plan, 11 of the piles might have interfered with the foundations or other relics that were known to be there. The new design provides that the 11 piles will be moved to locations beyond the outer wall of the theatre. That shows remarkable co-operation. If this is holy ground—I would be too demure to express a view on such an important matter—holy ground needs to be protected. I believe that this is the best way to protect it. The wind, the rain, the frost and the sunlight will not do the ruins any good. They need to be protected.

Mr. Simon Hughes (Southwark and Bermondsey): Does the Secretary of State recognise that I appreciate the efforts that he, his Under-Secretary of State and Imry have made so far? However, the proposal is still a completely hit and miss approach to archaeology and to the rescue of our national heritage. Does he not accept that the logical way forward is to complete the excavation of the site and then to decide what building can be built on, near or around it that will not do any damage?

English Heritage has already agreed that the present proposals—to excavate in the area of the piles—may do damage and has said that as and when anything is found there may well be a request to the developers to move their piles yet again. There could be a series of requests and a series of altered designs. There have already been three. Would it not be far better to say, "Let's get the design right but only after the archaeology has been completed."

The Secretary of State concedes that this is a monument of national importance. English Heritage has admitted that it is a schedulable monument. Is it not crazy for the Secretary of State to say, "I may schedule it later and thereby give it the protection of the criminal law"? At the moment he is relying on a deal with the developer—and it could be a new developer if Imry were to sell tomorrow —which has no statutory force. At the time that the site needs most protection, which is now, the Secretary of State says that he does not intend to use his legal powers to intervene.

Mr. Ridley: I am grateful to the tribute that the hon. Gentleman paid to the Under-Secretary of State who has, I believe, worked wonders in getting this deal through. The heat wave of the last month has created a risk of serious damage to the remains. It is now essential to provide protection for them. A membrane of Terram, followed by 40 cm of clean washed sand, is being placed on the remains for their best preservation. I do not believe that we should expose the remains to the risk of further damage from wind, weather and sunlight. That, therefore, is the correct procedure. If the hon. Gentleman would like to find the cost of deferring the building, I leave it to him individually to do so——

Mr. Hughes: People are willing to do so.

Mr. Ridley: I do not think that the people who own the site are willing to sell it, so the hon. Gentleman has to take both sides of the bargain into account. I do not believe that the monument is under threat, unless we fail to cover it up now. It is only if I believed that the monument was under threat that I should be justified in scheduling it. That is why I have left the position open. If it is under threat, I shall reconsider the position.

Mr. Michael Marshall (Arundel): My right hon. Friend will be aware of my interest as a member of the Theatres Trust, which sought to exert a moderating influence in arguments that at one stage were getting a bit frenzied. I am most grateful for my right hon. Friend's remarks and for putting down a certain backstop. I acknowledge the points made by the hon. Member for Southwark and Bermondsey (Mr. Hughes), but a reasonable compromise has been reached. Does my right hon. Friend agree that if we are in future to encourage other developers to take a responsible attitude there should be some recognition of the developer's role and that we should be seen to suport the work of English Heritage in difficult circumstances?

Mr. Ridley: I am grateful to my hon. Friend's for his remarks. The one-month delay that I intervened to secure, at some cost to public funds, was necessary in the unique circumstances of this important case. I am extremely happy that the result is that English Heritage, the developers, the voluntary sector and others co-operated to produce the correct solution. I echo my hon. Friend's tribute to Imry, whose costs were not inconsiderable. The outcome is a strong endorsement of the system of voluntary preservation and action that the Department has developed to preserve such remains. The whole House ought to be pleased at today's result, which strikes the right balance between the need for development and the need for preservation.

Mr. Mark Fisher (Stoke-on-Trent, Central): I urge the Secretary of State to reconsider four points. First, English Heritage said that the site is of schedulable quality. Secondly, will he look again at his responsibilities under the 1983 Act? Contrary to the right hon. Gentleman's description of them in respect of vulnerability, that legislation defines three criteria and sub-criteria, and the Rose is generally considered to meet them all. Thirdly, archaeologists, the acting world and the public demand scheduling. The Secretary of State misrepresented that aspect. If he does not schedule the site, I suspect that an effort will be made to seek a judicial review or an appeal to judicial process. Fourthly, the right hon. Gentleman is

correct to say that Terram and sand cover the site but I believe that Imry intends concreting on top of that sand, if it has not already done so. If the Secretary of State does not urgently reconsider his decision not to reschedule, he will preserve a 10-storey office block but he will not preserve the Rose.

Mr. Ridley: I am not arguing whether the site is of schedulable quality. The question is whether it is under threat. I am certain that I am correct in thinking that it is not. The hon. Gentleman said that he had four points to make but he only asked in four different ways whether I will reschedule. The hon. Gentleman drew attention to the fact that a skin of concrete is to be laid over the washed sand. that is being done on the recommendation of English Heritage to preserve the monument. The hon. Gentleman does not seem to want to preserve the monument. He takes his case much further than is justified.

Mr. Patrick Cormack (Staffordshire, South): Is my right hon. Friend aware that those right hon. and hon. Members who know the people who run English Heritage have great confidence in their judgment, and believe that their advice to date was wise and balanced and that the solution in prospect is sensible? My right hon. Friend is wise to retain an open mind. I ask him to take a personal interest along with my hon. Friend the Under-Secretary of State for the Environment, who played an extremely constructive and helpful role during a rather difficult period. I ask him also to keep in touch with Southwark borough council. It is important that the remains are displayed in a proper and attractive manner and that the building erected over the site is worthy of its setting.

Mr. Ridley: There is no way that I could avoid taking a personal interest—not only because I want to do so but there is intense public and parliamentary interest. I took a considerable amount of interest in events as they unfolded. I believe that the Government's action in this matter has resulted in an extremely satisfactory position. I am not saying that that will always be the case, but so far the result is extremely good.

I certainly agree that Southwark borough council has an extremely important role to play as it will be necessary to accommodate the new solution with planning consent —I must not prejudice whether that would be right or wrong—and there are various other ways in which Southwark can play a major part in contributing to the success of this operation. I am optimistic that it will work out.

Several Hon. Members *rose*——

Mr. Speaker: Order. I remind the House that it will be possible to raise this matter in the debate which we are about to have on the arts. Some hon. Members now rising have already expressed their interest.

Business of the House

3.45 pm

Mr. Frank Dobson (Holborn and St. Pancras): Will the Leader of the House kindly tell us the business for next week?

The Lord President of the Council and Leader of the House of Commons (Mr. John Wakeham): The business for next week will be as follows:

MONDAY 19 JUNE—Opposition Day (13th Allotted Day). Until about seven o'clock there will be a debate entitled "Investment in Transport", afterwards there will be a debate entitled "Civil Liberties and a Bill of Rights". Both debates will arise on motions in the name of the Social and Liberal Democrats.

Remaining stages of the Pesticides (Fees and Enforcement) Bill.

TUESDAY 20 JUNE—Remaining stages of the Self-Governing Schools etc. (Scotland) Bill.

Motion relating to the statement of changes in immigration rules (HC 388).

WEDNESDAY 21 JUNE—Opposition Day (14th Allotted Day, 1st half), until seven o'clock there will be a debate on an Opposition motion entitled "Food Safety, Research and the Nation's Health".

Third Reading of the Local Government and Housing Bill.

Ways and Means resolutions relating to the Finance Bill.

Motions relating to Scottish social security and community charges regulations. Details will be given in the *Official Report*.

THURSDAY 22 JUNE—Until seven o'clock motion on the Northern Ireland Act 1974 (Interim Period Extension) Order.

Afterwards motion on the appropriation (No. 2) (Northern Ireland) Order.

FRIDAY 23 JUNE—Private Members' motions.

MONDAY 26 JUNE—Opposition Day (15th Allotted Day). There will be a debate on an Opposition motion. Subject for debate to be announced.

[Debate on Wednesday 21 June

Housing Benefit (Community Charge Rebates) (Scotland) Amendment Regulations 1989 (S.I., 1989, No. 361)

Community Charges (Information concerning Social Security) (Scotland) Regulations 1989 (S.I., 1989, No. 476)

Community Charges (Deductions from Income Support), (Scotland) Regulations 1989 (S.I., 1989, No. 507).]

Mr. Dobson: I thank the Leader of the House for his statement. Does he accept that it is intolerable that the new immigration regulations should be debated next Tuesday when they were made available in the House only yesterday? That has caused especial difficulty because of the European elections, and many hon. Members who are closely interested in the subject will not have an opportunity to study the new arrangements that are proposed before next Tuesday, the day of the debate. Will he consider postponing the debate to enable hon. Members on all sides of the House to study the detailed regulations and the Home Secretary's related announcements about DNA testing, and find an opportunity to debate them the following week?

In view of fresh evidence today from the Policy Review Institute that the YTS is failing young people, will the Government provide time for an early debate on their policy for training our young people, so that some improvements can be made before 1992 and our young people do not fall even further behind the training offered by our European competitors?

Returning to two old themes, it is now 15 months since the Government received the Griffiths report on care in the community. When are we likely to hear their response, and when shall we have the oportunity to debate that very important matter? On the other matter, which I have been raising for a long time, what progress or otherwise have the Government made towards establishing a scheme to substitute student loans for student grants? That has been promised for a long time and the Secretary of State for Education and Science does not seem to be making very much progress, even with the Tory bankers with whom he is discussing the matter.

Mr. Wakeham: The hon. Member for Holborn and St. Pancras (Mr. Dobson) asked me four questions about the business for next week. First, he complained about the time and the date that I have allocated for the debate on immigration issues. I agree that it is not the most convenient time in view of other matters, but it enables us to raise the subject. I believe that the time provided is adequate. In view of the hon. Gentleman's request, I shall see whether the matter can be pursued through the usual channels.

The Government fully recognise the importance of training and we are spending £3 billion on training provision now, as opposed to the £500 million spent in 1979. These matters were relevant to a Bill we were discussing a short time ago. I cannot promise a debate in the near future but I am sure that it is a subject to which we shall return when an opportunity presents itself.

I am not sorry that the hon. Gentleman asked about the Griffiths report because the subjects he mentions are up to him. However, he has raised the subject several times before and I can assure him that we attach great importance to the Griffiths report and the Wagner report. Work is ongoing on our proposals, which we shall bring forward in the near future. Given the complexities of the matter, we must give full consideration to the subject so that we reach the right answers. I am sure that the time for a debate will be when we have announced our proposals.

On top-up loans for students, as I said last week, my right hon. Friend the Secretary of State for Education and Science hopes to be able to report his conclusions on the administration of the scheme quite soon now. The right time for a debate will be after that.

Mr. Tony Marlow (Northampton, North): As someone who for a great length of time has been concerned that measures should be introduced to cope with dog nuisance, may I say how delighted I am that the Government have given a commitment to introduce legislation. Can my right hon. Friend say when that legislation will be introduced? For example, will it be introduced in the other place during progress on the Local Government and Housing Bill? If so, will it also cover the new system for introducing byelaws swiftly and effectively.

Mr. Wakeham: I am grateful to my hon. Friend for his welcome of the announcement made by my right hon.

Friend the Secretary of State for the Environment. I cannot give him any further information now, but I shall bear in mind the points he makes.

Mr. James Wallace (Orkney and Shetland): It is known that the Secretary of State for the Environment is considering the issue of strategic planning guidance for London and that an announcement is expected before the summer recess. Undoubtedly, the debate on transport on Monday will provide an opportunity to raise some of the issues about traffic congestion in the capital city. Will the Leader of the House acknowledge the genuine concern of hon. Members who represent seats throughout the country, not just in London, about the strategic planning of our capital city? The need for integrated planning is important and it will be an opportunity for a debate before the Secretary of State makes the announcement.

Mr. Wakeham: I recognise that these matters raise important considerations and that some of my hon. Friends have been asking me to find time for a debate. I have promised that I will consider the matter but, at this stage in the parliamentary year, I cannot promise absolutely that there will be time for a debate.

Mr. Nicholas Baker (Dorset, North): Will my right hon. Friend accept thanks for what he has just said about future development plans, which I understand was included in his previous answer? Will he tell us when he will find time to discuss the Green Papers on the future of the legal profession?

Mr. Wakeham: I have been asked before about providing time for a debate on those matters. We had a short debate rather late at night on the Lord Chancellor's salary order during which the subject was raised. I wish I could find time for further discussion but I have a feeling that we shall return to it before too long.

Mr. Nigel Spearing (Newham, South): Is the Leader of the House aware that on Tuesday and Wednesday week the Prime Minister and, no doubt others, will be going to the European Council Heads of Government meeting? Has he not received a letter from me in my capacity as Chairman of the Scrutiny Committee recommending a debate prior to that meeting? Is he not aware that the Treasury and Civil Service Committee has heard evidence from the Chancellor of the Exchequer and the Governor of the Bank of England and will be issuing a report early next week? Surely a debate on this matter should come within the terms of the resolution of 30 October 1980. The fact that the Leader of the House has not announced a debate next week shows that the Government are not contemplating one. Will he reconsider the timetable and urgently schedule a debate of these important matters for next week, before the Prime Minister goes to Madrid?

Mr. Wakeham: The hon. Gentleman takes a deep interest in these matters and is extremely knowledgeable. I will always reconsider any matter that he raises at Business Question Time. However, as he said, my right hon. Friend the Chancellor of the Exchequer has recently given evidence to the Treasury and Civil Service Select Committee and I regret that as things stand now, I am unable to find time for a debate before the Madrid summit.

Mr. Harry Greenway (Ealing, North): Notwithstanding what you, Mr. Speaker, have just said about today's debate on the arts and heritage, will my right hon. Friend

arrange for a statement on the Rose theatre as soon as there is any change, next week if necessary? Will my right hon. Friend bear in mind the beautiful story by Oscar Wilde called "The Nightingale and the Rose" in which a nightingale thought it right to bleed its breast into the thorn of a rose which was fading, in order to save it. The rose bloomed beautifully but at dawn the nightingale fell dead. No one wishes to see anyone fall dead in this episode, but to save the Rose is worth a sacrifice.

Mr. Wakeham: My right hon. Friend the Secretary of State was neither wilting nor likely to fall dead. He gave a good account of the Government's position on the matter. The best plan would be to have today's debate on the arts and heritage and to watch the developments, but I shall certainly bear in mind what my hon. Friend has suggested.

Mr. Kevin Barron (Rother Valley): When will the Government find time to debate the British coal mining industry? Is the Leader of the House aware that yesterday the Department of Energy announced another 15,000 job losses in that industry this year and that that is on top of the loss of some 140,000 jobs in the industry in the past four and a half years? When the industry has improved productivity by 75 per cent. in the past three years it deserves more protection from the Government than it is getting.

Mr. Wakeham: The hon. Gentleman asks when I can arrange a debate on the coal industry, and the answer to that is tomorrow, Sir.

Mr. Michael Colvin (Romsey and Waterside): My right hon. Friend will recall that on Tuesday Parliament was lobbied by more than 100 workers in the electricity industry, representing the staff of Marchwood engineering laboratories in my constituency which undertakes work for the Central Electricity Generating Board. I have been struck by the response from parliamentary colleagues who support the workers' case, represented on the Order Paper by early-day motion 983:

[That, recognising that 80 per cent. of the electricity research work carried out by Marchwood Engineering Laboratories relates to nuclear power generation, this House calls upon Her Majesty's Government to allocate Marchwood Engineering Laboratories to the National Power Co., rather than, as proposed by the Central Electricity Generating Board, to Power Gen; but as a preferred alternative suggests that the principal Central Electricity Generating Board research facilities including Berkeley, Leatherhead and Marchwood should be combined to form an electricity research and development company which would bid for Rand D contracts from the power generating companies once the electricity industry was privatised.]

That calls upon Her Majesty's Government to reconsider their decision to allocate Marchwood engineering laboratories to Power Gen while 80 per cent. of its research and development work is nuclear-related. There has been a more sensible suggestion that the research and development capability of the CEGB should be incorporated into a single independent company to contract research and development work to the industry once privatised and that proposal is now gaining support. I am sorry to bounce this on my right hon. Friend, but will he consult my right hon. Friend the Secretary of State for

[*Mr. Michael Colvin*]

Energy, who is at present considering the position, and suggest to him that the House should have an opportunity to debate that matter before he reaches a conclusion?

Mr. Wakeham: I have already consulted my right hon. Friend the Secretary of State for Energy, as I do on every early-day motion on the Order Paper as a matter of routine every week so that I come prepared. My right hon. Friend has received detailed representations on the matter from my hon. Friend and from representatives of the Marchwood employees. He is considering the matter most carefully and hopes to give a decision on the allocation of Marchwood shortly.

Mr. Tony Banks (Newham, North-West): Will the Leader of the House please arrange an early debate on advertising standards? We have just been talking about the Rose theatre, but has the right hon. Gentleman seen the advertisements—I have photographs of them—in various streets in London put out by Flowers brewery which say:
"Not all flowers are pansies".
Is he aware that everyone knows that the slang word pansy refers to gay men and that that advertisement is causing a great deal of offence? I have received a number of complaints from my constituents. Those advertisements appear to have gone up in what one can only describe as the hard-drinking macho areas of London, where they are clearly calculated to try to stimulate homophobic attitudes among people. If the Leader of the House is not prepared to have a debate on that, will he make representations to his Cabinet colleague who is responsible for the Advertising Standards Authority to have those offensive advertisements taken down forthwith?

Mr. Wakeham: I do not know whether that is necessarily an appropriate matter for me to deal with in business questions. Whether the hon. Gentleman will be able to make the speech that he might want to make in the debate next Wednesday will depend, to an extent, on you, Mr. Speaker, and on his ingenuity, but it is just possible.

With regard to advertising standards and the drinks industry, I have talks with advertisers from time to time in my capacity as chairman of the Government committee on alcohol misuse. I find their representatives helpful and constructive in their approach to high and proper standards in advertising. I shall certainly see whether it is appropriate to discuss with them the matter raised by the hon. Gentleman.

Mr. Jonathan Aitken (Thanet, South): May I complain to my right hon. Friend about his apparent policy of allowing late debates or, even worse, no debates on EC issues of great importance? Is he aware that the absence of a debate before the Madrid summit is regretted in all parts of the House? Is he also aware that to tackle as important an EC directive as the one on broadcasting, as we did this week at 2 o'clock in the morning, is a matter of regret not just to individual members, but is now, apparently, the subject of an official rebuke from the Select Committee on European Legislation? Since that directive has now to come back to the House as a result of a decision in Europe, will he please guarantee that we shall consider it at an appropriate hour?

Mr. Wakeham: I have an enormous amount of sympathy with my hon. Friend and I entirely agree that our arrangements for dealing with the scrutiny of European matters is not satisfactory. I have done my best to try to encourage further consideration as to how we might improve such scrutiny. I have given evidence to the Procedure Committee and I am glad that it is considering this matter. I have had meetings with the Chairman of the Scrutiny Committee and I hope to have another meeting with him fairly soon. I have had discussions with right hon. and hon. Members from all sides of the House on how best we can deal with what is clearly a problem. If my hon. Friend would like to come to talk to me about how he thinks we could improve matters I should be delighted to see him.

Heads of Government Meeting, Madrid

4.1 pm

Mr. Nigel Spearing (Newham, South): I beg to ask leave to move the Adjournment of the House, under Standing Order No. 20, for the purpose of discussing a specific and important national matter that should have urgent consideration, namely,

"the agenda of the Heads of Government meeting, European Council, in Madrid on 27 and 28 June next".

You will have heard the exchanges, Mr. Speaker, immediately preceding this application and the courtesy of the Leader of the House who said that he is attempting to improve debates on matters of scrutiny. On this occasion, however, I am afraid that he has not provided the opportunity for such a debate.

The matter is specific in so far as some important items on the agenda are concerned, particularly the report of the Delors committee, commissioned at the last Heads of Government meeting, on full economic and monetary union within the European Community. I need not emphasise the importance and significance of that report and its recommendations for the future of the nation and its potential consequences for virtually all our future economic, political and social life.

Two Select Committees of this House will have reports available early next week and the Governor of the Bank of England and the Chancellor of the Exchequer have given evidence to the Select Committee on the Treasury and Civil Service. The Select Committee on European Legislation has reported that the Delors report should be debated within the terms of the resolution of the House on 30 October 1980, which appears to have been discounted or overlooked in the statement that we have just heard from the Lord President in reply to my question.

If the House is to have any influence on those of Her Majesty's Ministers who will be attending this important meeting, where decisions of principle could be taken, it is essential that the matter be debated in time—I refer to the Standing Orders. I submit, therefore, that bearing in mind the ancient privileges of this House, particularly those concerning consultation prior to decisions, and prior to legislation, you, Mr. Speaker, as the protector of the rights and liberties of the House and thus of all the subjects, should place the application before the House.

Mr. Speaker: The hon. Member for Newham, South (Mr. Spearing) asks leave to move the Adjournment of the House for the purpose of discussing a specific and important matter that he believes should have urgent consideration, namely,

"the forthcoming meeting of the Heads of Government in the European Council in Madrid on 27 and 28 June next."

I have listened with great care to what the hon. Gentleman has said about his matter. As he knows, my sole duty in considering an application under Standing Order No. 20 is to decide whether it should be given priority over the business set down for today——

Mr. Spearing: Or for Monday, Mr. Speaker.

Mr. Speaker: On Monday.

I regret that the matter that the hon. Gentleman has raised does not meet the requirements of the Standing Order and I cannot therefore submit his application to the House, but I hope that he will find other methods of raising it.

Arts and Heritage

Motion made, and Question proposed, That this House do now adjourn.—[*Mr. Dorrell.*]

4.4 pm

The Minister for the Arts (Mr. Richard Luce): I welcome the opportunity to open this debate on the arts and heritage. I intend to concentrate on the broad themes of the Government's arts policy. My hon. Friend the Member for Surrey, South-West (Mrs. Bottomley) will answer the debate and dwell in more detail on the heritage.

This House has debated the arts every year since I became Minister for the Arts in 1985. This is the third year running that we have debated the subject in Government time.

There are many heartening signs that an increasing number of people are concerned about issues that will affect the quality of life, not only of themselves but their children and grandchildren. The public interest is becoming all-embracing. The natural desire for a pollution-free environment is matched by a growing interest in our architecture—and in the importance of attractive surroundings. There is an increasing ability to turn away from the mundane aspects of daily life to enjoy a range of recreation. The arts fit within this pattern. The criteria are quite clear: that more people want to enjoy leisure and to educate themselves through museums, galleries, theatres, concerts, opera and jazz or by trying out their own creative talents, through crafts, photography or painting. For deep down we know, as Dostoevsky echoed,

"Man does not live by bread alone".

We need something deeper to turn to.

As we witness the last lashings of the tail of the dying crocodile of Communism in so many parts of the world, the challenge to genuine democracies lies in demonstrating that we offer real political and economic freedom and the best means of improving our quality of life.

We cannot achieve this unless the culture of wealth creation is deeply embedded in our life. This has become the case under this Government. The search for a higher standard of wealth must be tireless, but now is the time to focus our attention upon how to make the best use of this new climate for the quality of our lives. As we look forward to the turn of the century, we must open up even further the opportunity for individuals to extend their horizons and to enrich their daily lives. We have every reason to be proud of our artistic achievements in this country.

It is an important Government job to create the climate whereby we can achieve the highest standards of excellence and creativity. We want to ensure that all those who wish to do so have the opportunity to enjoy the fruits of this or to participate and use their own talents. We best achieve this in a democratic society where the freedom of artistic expression is a central principle. We will best inspire genius and talent by the greatest possible delegation of decision-making from the centre, by encouraging art in our schools and by encouraging financial support from a variety of sources.

The most potent challenge that we face today is the need to ensure that the best our our arts is accessible to all those who have the potential to enjoy it. That is a central part of my strategy and I shall now take a few moments to describe how I am attempting to achieve it.

[*Mr. Richard Luce*]

It is against that background that I reaffirm the importance I attach to a policy of maximum arm's length so that it is not the Minister and his officials in Whitehall who make the day-to-day decisions about artistic standards and management. The arm's-length principle has been totally supported by successive Governments of both parties since the war. I hope that the hon. Member for Stoke-on-Trent, Central (Mr. Fisher) will take the opportunity of this debate to reaffirm his party's support for that principle.

It is important to strengthen and preserve artistic freedom. The arm's-length policy, working for example through the Arts Council and other bodies, is a way to achieve this. I know that the council shares my concern to foster the highest standards of artistic excellence and access to the arts by maintaining and developing centres of excellence throughout the country.

In the context of the arm's-length principle, I am concerned to strengthen the accountability of the arts organisations for the taxpayers' money that they receive and I want to see whether the funding structure which we have, through the Arts Council and the regional arts associations, can be improved, so that they are as coherent and efficient as possible. I have therefore commissioned a review, which is now being conducted by Mr. Richard Wilding—formerly permanent head of the Office of Arts and Libraries—who will report to me by 31 October this year. I regard the review as extremely important.

Let me take this opportunity to tell the House about some of the measures that I am taking, along with the arts world, to promote both excellence and access.

Mr. Nicholas Baker (Dorset, North): My right hon. Friend has referred to access to the past and to the need to develop centres of excellence. Our right hon. Friend's decision about the Rose site is particularly welcome, because access to the past will be provided.

Those who are interested—particularly members of the acting profession, who have shown a commendable concern about the need for access to the past—should be encouraged now to direct their attention to a nearby potential centre of excellence. I refer to the site of the Globe theatre, literally yards from the Rose site. The interests of those people, and of my right hon. Friend, in "living stones" can thus provide a forum for excellence in the future rather than access to the past.

Mr. Luce: My hon. Friend has made an important point, not only about the Rose theatre but about the plans for the Globe, which I believe will lead to considerable public support and interest. I am glad to note the progress that has been made in raising funds, and I hope that the construction of the proposed Globe theatre will start soon. I think that it has every prospect of becoming a great centre of excellence, and my hon. Friend is right to draw attention to it.

I had begun to focus on the question of excellence, and that of accessibility to it. Let me illustrate that further. The national museums and galleries are in the forefront. For example, the Tate gallery opened the new "Tate in Liverpool" in 1988, and has already attracted nearly half a million visitors in its first six months. The National Portrait Gallery has put an important part of its reserve collection on display in no fewer than four country houses

—in Somerset, Yorkshire, Lancashire and North Wales. The British Film Institute's new museum of the moving image has had more than 250,000 visitors since it opened in September 1988, well above the number expected. The Victoria and Albert museum has announced plans to open an outstation in Bradford to house part of its great Indian collection. There are other examples: for instance the imperial war museum and the science museum also have plans.

We have extended the principle to loans and exhibitions, to which considerable importance is attached, not only by me but by many other hon. Members, as they house our greatest objects of art and our greatest collections. The British museum, for example, consistently lends more objects than any other institution in the world —2,500 in 1987. In 1987-88 the Tate gallery, which houses more contemporary works, lent 556, 303 within the United Kingdom and the rest abroad.

The Government help the process through their indemnity scheme. In the last financial year, objects valued at £1 billion were indemnified for exhibition. In April 1988 I established the travelling exhibition unit at the Museums and Galleries Commission, and it promoted 10 projects during its first year. I hope that as it expands it will facilitate many other exhibitions around the country.

I also attach great importance to touring. It was in the interests of excellence and access that I gave the Arts Council extra money for its budget, to be earmarked for increased touring. It allocated £1·5 million for the purpose in 1988-89, financing more than 60 weeks of extra touring, including 38 for drama.

By contrast, I was glad, too, to be able to make a contribution of £150,000 to the fund set up by the Carnegie Trust to help make arts venues more accessible to disabled people.

In areas such as inner cities, and in the rural arts, a great deal is being done to open up the prospects of more access to the arts to people who live in those areas. It would be wrong not to mention in particular the city of Glasgow, which has done outstanding work in promoting its arts, using them to bring great benefits to the city and the country. I was glad to be able to make a contribution of £500,000 towards the city's preparations for its role as European city of culture in 1990.

There are other areas as well. For example, in broadcasting I welcome the fact that the Arts Council is doing work on improving access to the arts through broadcasting, and it is developing some proposals in that context.

I regard investment in education as almost the biggest for the longer term. The Education Reform Act ensures a central place for the arts and heritage in the core curriculum and the GCSE examinations. That is why the Secretary of State for Education and Science and I announced in May a joint initiative to emphasise the importance of the arts in the school curriculum.

The public today expect art to be an integral part of the environment In response to that, many local authorities and private companies are initiating imaginative public arts projects. Birmingham leads the way in that, and the British library has some exciting schemes for its new building.

In that connection, there is no finer example of the Government's commitment to these joint objectives of excellence and access than the new British library. For the first time, we are giving the library a purpose-built home, bringing together under one roof the majority of its London-based collections in a properly controlled, pollution-free environment. The whole building is due to be completed and fully in use by 1996. Costing well over £400 million in cash terms, it is the Government's largest single civil project. It will be one of Britain's greatest cultural achievements and a significant addition to our heritage.

The project shows the importance we attach to the work of scholarship and my concern to marry the best work of our scholars to public access and enjoyment. In this context, I am making a point of visiting national museums and galleries to meet the staff. I have recently been to the V and A and to the national maritime museum, and I have several more visits of that kind planned. I have been impressed by the dedication and hard work that I have seen.

In connection with the heritage, I appreciate that there are particular problems and pressures posed by the constant and high price rises in the art market. I am reviewing some of the mechanisms in this sphere to see where I can help, and I will mention a few.

Recently there was considerable criticism that the price of Turner's "Seascape, Folkestone" was not published when I announced my recommendation to defer a decision on the export licence application. The reason for the withholding of the Turner price was the option given to owners not to disclose. I shared the concern that was expressed and I am rectifying this anomaly. From now on, if an object is placed under deferral, following consideration by the Reviewing Committee on the Export of Works of Art, the price will be published. Owners will be told this in the letter they receive from the Department of Trade and Industry informing them of an objection to export. I hope that this change will help public collections in their fund-raising, especially where they launch a public appeal.

Acknowledging, as I do, this increase in prices, I have decided to revise the limits for export licences very soon. This is in accordance with the recommendations put to me by the export reviewing committee. The Secretary of State for Trade and Industry and I are also well aware of the problems posed by the withdrawal of what is known as the indefinite stop procedure. We are giving urgent attention to finding a solution to that problem.

To give priority to the housing and conservation of existing collections, as the museums and galleries have asked us to do, the Government have been obliged to keep purchase grants at a constant cash level since 1985-86. I am well aware of the problems that this poses and I have already announced that I am considering how to deal with them.

I also conducted a consultation exercise last year on what discretionary powers, if any, museums and galleries should have to dispose of items from their collections. Bearing in mind the responses that I have received, my aim will be to ensure that any relevant powers are, as far as possible, tailor-made to meet the specific requirements of each institution. I hope that it is helpful to the House for me to reaffirm that principle. As I have said, my hon. Friend the Member for Surrey, South-West will cover other important heritage themes, and the House has already had a brief chance today to discuss the latest developments on the Rose theatre.

I shall now deal with the matter of funding. In order to provide excellence for as many people as possible, the arts need financial support, and the more sources that they have to draw on the healthier and freer they will be. However, I fully accept that, for the foreseeable future, the taxpayer's role is also important. Let me put Government art funding in perspective. Some people like to suggest that 10, 20, or 30 years ago, and especially 20 years ago, saw the great golden age of the arts. It is important to put that in perspective.

It is interesting to note that, in real terms, the Arts Council receives three times as much from the Government today as it did in the late 1960s. Since its creation by the Goverment in 1980 the national heritage memorial fund has received over £105 million from the taxpayer. The budgets of our national museums and galleries are also at record levels and central Government spending on them has risen by 25 per cent. in real terms since 1979-80. Funding for their building programmes has increased by about 50 per cent. in real terms over the same period.

Let us make no mistake about the achievement of the Government. There has been an overall increase in arts funding of 39 per cent., in real terms, including abolition money, since 1979, and that is a strong achievement. I am especially pleased that I was able to announce in November 1987 a new departure in arts funding in which firm figures were set for the next three years. The object of that is to give arts bodies a firm basis on which to plan their future activities and their various sources of funding, and to encourage greater self-reliance. We are already seeing its results in some excellent forward thinking—for example, in the Arts Council's three-year business plan and in the corporate plans of the museums and galleries.

Mr. Mark Fisher (Stoke-on-Trent, Central): The Minister will be aware that I have often congratulated him on the achievement of finding a three-year funding formula of which the whole art world approves and has been seeking for a long time. Does he accept that the second and third years of the formula are at rates well below the rate of inflation, and that any advantages arising from the security of planning are more than offset by the fact that in those two years all arts clients will have a cut in real terms?

Mr. Luce: I shall shortly deal with inflation and respond to the hon. Gentleman's question. I again acknowledge that I am fully aware of the pressures and problems faced by the arts. As the hon. Gentleman has said, first among these is the effect of inflation. The Government's absolute priority is and must be the conquest of inflation. We must continue the battle against it, for the arts as well as for all other areas of activity. We are thinking, as we should in the arts world, of three-year funding in many areas, and the amount of money that we make available must be seen in the context of the three-year total. For the first year, I increased the Arts Council's funding by 10 per cent. It is true that the amount was lower in the second and third years.

Creative funding partnerships are seen throughout the arts, and business sponsorship is a marvellous success story. It has been considerably helped by the Government's business sponsorship incentive scheme administered for me by the Association for Business Sponsorship of the Arts. Since its introduction in 1984, it has produced almost £25 million of new money—£2·40 from the private sector for every £1 from the taxpayer.

[*Mr. Luce*]

The first-class management of arts bodies is now being recognised and awarded through the incentive funding scheme. I gave the Arts Council money for that in the 1987 settlement—£12·5 million over three years—and 48 awards have already been made to organisations throughout the country. The Arts Council expects the scheme to produce £3 of private sector money for every £1 from the taxpayer.

I am extending this incentive approach into all areas of my reponsibility. There is a new incentive scheme for the conservation of manuscripts, and the public library incentive scheme is in its second year.

The contribution of local authorities to arts funding is invaluable. To take just one example, Birmingham city council gives an annual grant of just under £800,000 to the City of Birmingham symphony orchestra, showing its total commitment to this outstanding centre of excellence.

The arts are also immeasurably enriched by many outstanding examples of private generosity. We all know of the Sainsbury family contribution for the new wing at the national gallery. We should refer to the Clore Foundation, which contributed no less than £6 million to the cost of the new gallery for the Turner collection at the Tate, and to the remarkable contribution of Mr. John Paul Getty II, who plans to give £50 million as an endowment fund for the national gallery. He is also a leading private donor to funding for the British Film Institute's highly successful museum of the moving image, which was built for £11 million without a penny from the Government.

A private donation is enabling the Victoria and Albert museum to open a new Chinese gallery and the museum has just received generous donations from the Hinduja foundation and from Jenson and Nicholson for its new gallery of Indian art. It should also be mentioned that, in the past five years the British museum has raised nearly £12 million of private money for building and gallery work. The library and services of the British Theatre Association, which were threatened with closure earlier this year, were saved through the outstanding generosity of Mr. Robert Holmes à Court.

Mr. Eric S. Heffer (Liverpool, Walton): This is a genuine question. Can the right hon. Gentleman tell us what efforts are being made to get local business sponsorship and support, because much of what he has said has been in relation to national sponsorship? We no longer have the great shipping magnates in Liverpool and other such cities, where we depended very much on their support. Obviously, we cannot raise all the money at local level through local authorities. This is an important matter and I would like to know how much thought has been given to it and what has been done in that direction.

Mr. Luce: I fully acknowledge the validity of the hon. Gentleman's point. He puts his finger on the problem, which I think is gradually being solved through the business sponsorship incentive scheme. The evidence is that the scheme is successful as a national scheme, not just a London scheme. I have been just as anxious as the hon. Gentleman to encourage sponsorship in Merseyside and Scotland, for example. There is increasing evidence that the scheme is being taken up, sometimes on a modest basis, but that does not matter; once the thing starts, other businesses come in and I believe that the incentive scheme has done a great deal to encourage that.

In this context, I am delighted to tell the House about another noticeable development. The Arts Council has decided to establish an endowment fund to support new and experimental work. It has been launched with a £1·1 million gift to the council from an anonymous legacy. The council is now working on plans to expand the size of the fund to a target of £20 million.

Indeed, great effort from many sources goes into our arts and heritage: into their creation, production and preservation and into funding, supporting and enjoying them.

Mr. Tim Rathbone (Lewes): It seems appropriate here to raise the question of value added tax on new works of art. Whereas VAT is designed to encourage exports of everything else, it also encourages exports of works of art. If they are sold abroad, they are sold at a discount of 15 per cent. or at the price for which the artist is asking rather than being sold in this country, presumably under the scheme that my right hon. Friend has just announced, with a bare 15 per cent. VAT addition. Would he have a word with the Chancellor of the Exchequer to see if that cannot be changed?

Mr. Luce: I know of my hon. Friend's interest in this subject and of course I will raise the point with the Chancellor. There is now a great deal of discussion within the Community of the implications of 1992 for the art trade. But I will, of course, bear the point in mind and raise it with my right hon. Friend.

I am delighted to have this opportunity to blow the trumpet for our marvellous arts organisations and their leadership.

The test of all this is our ability to produce art of lasting quality. As Henry Austin Dobson said:

"All passes; art alone, enduring, stays to us."

There is no reason why we should not be producing the same talent today as we have in previous generations. Just as Shakespeare, Bacon, Gainsborough, Turner, T. S. Eliot, Elgar, Kipling and Byron have endured, so I believe that there are artists of genius today who will be remembered and enjoyed in centuries to come.

Our artistic quality is a true test of the level of our civilisation. Any Arts Minister has the duty to ensure that the outlet for genius and creativity is as strong as ever in the last part of this century. That is the duty which I try to fulfil.

4.29 pm

Mr. Mark Fisher (Stoke-on-Trent, Central): Any congratulations that are due to the Government for this debate on the arts are dwarfed by the timing of the debate. We had an arts debate five years ago on European election day and, by an extraordinary coincidence, once again, on a European election day when hon. Members on both sides of the House wish to be helping in European constituencies, we have another arts debate.

Mr. Toby Jessel (Twickenham): Has the hon. Gentleman thought of that word "dwarfed" in relation to a comparison between the different numbers on the two sides of the House? Despite the difficulties of being present, there are three times as many on Conservative Benches as there are on Opposition Benches.

Mr. Michael Foot (Blaenau Gwent): It is the quality that is important.

Mr. Fisher: As my right hon. Friend has said, by the end of the debate, we shall be able to judge the quality of the contributions. It is hardly surprising that the hon. Gentleman made that point. There is a simple answer. Tory Members know that they will be thrashed in the European elections, so there is no point in them being in the constituencies. They are better cowering here than facing the electorate. We know that we shall have a triumph in the polls today and my right hon. and hon. Friends are out celebrating in advance the enormous vote of confidence that the electorate are giving us. The difference in enthusiasm in getting out and facing the electorate is hardly surprising. It is interesting that Tory Members are here rather than doing that.

It is not good enough to have the debate on this day. I do not blame the Minister for this. It is the usual channels, or the Chief Whip, or the Leader of the House. *[Interruption.]* An hon. Member who is not supposed to speak has said that I am not sure who is to blame and that is probably true. The timing of the debate reflects the interest in art and culture among senior members of the Cabinet. In their view, these are unimportant issues that can be debated on what are, in parliamentary terms, non-days. Our contention is that the arts and heritage are vital to the democratic and cultural life, to community identity and cohesion, to employment and the economy. I wish that the Government—I exclude the Minister from this—placed the same importance on the arts and culture as we do. If they did, we would be having this debate in prime time.

I welcome the debate and the chance to respond to the Minister's interesting speech. It gives us an opportunity both to examine the cultural balance sheet in the arts and heritage after 10 years of the Government and to look at it in the light of this European election day and compare our policies and practice with those of our European partners. Statistics are difficult to compare because they are arranged in different definitions in different countries and with different regional and central Government balances. I welcome the fact that the Office of Arts and Libraries is funding a Policy Studies Institute study to look at those comparative statistics. I hope that it will be finished soon and that we can see the published results.

The Minister will not be surprised to learn that I suspect that those results will show that other European countries spend a great deal more on their arts and heritage than we do. The figures available from the Arts Council and others show that France and West Germany spend 0·8 per cent. of total central Government expenditure on the arts when we spend about 0·25 per cent. We spend less than half the level of other countries. On a per capita basis, we spend between £7 and £9 a head—there are different figures in different parts of the United Kingdom—Germany spends about £15 to £16, France about £17 and Sweden about £24. That is an interesting reflection on the relative importance that other countries give to the arts. I welcome the evidence that the Minister is attempting to ascertain the facts. I hope that he will use that material well in getting more money from the Treasury. Currently we are limping behind our European counterparts.

If central Government are not yet responding, local authorities are. The authorities recognise that there is a real demand from audience and artists in the local community and they have been increasing their expenditure enormously, and probably at a faster rate than any other set of local authorities in the European Community. I hope that the Government will recognise that local message. The Minister's remarks today about Glasgow and other local communities suggest that he may be aware of it and recognises it. It seems, unfortunately, that the local message is something to which the Government are fairly deaf. I hope that they will listen more attentively.

Let us consider the 10-year balance sheet that sets out the Government's record. The Minister has set out some of the criteria that he thinks we should be examining. I have paid tribute already to the fact that he secured three-year funding. He has made attempts with the Arts Council to devolve more to the regions. I welcome, for example, the move of Sadler's Wells to Birmingham, Tate in the north and other initiatives, on which I congratulate the Minister. However, the Government's record overall is a poor one. I welcome the things that are happening but the Government's response to initiatives has been poor.

Over the past 10 years we have done well in museum terms. We have seen the expansion of industrial museums, but the Government's response has been to allow a real crisis to develop in repairs to and maintenance of our national museums. There has been an exciting increase in the interest of audiences in dance. The Government commissioned, through the Arts Council, the Devlin report, which does not take the French Government's view that we should invest to reflect the increased interest of audiences in dance. The premise of the Devlin report was that there should be no more funding. That is why it came to the conclusion that the Northern Ballet Theatre should be axed. We welcome the fact that it has a two-year breathing space. It is unfortunate that the Government are not responding to exciting developments.

There is a range of opera touring companies, including Opera North and Kent Opera. Unfortunately, there are severe question marks over Kent Opera's future. Given the good work that it is doing, it would be a tragedy if it were to be axed.

In local authorities, whatever the political persuasion, we are seeing an increase in the number of arts officers and the development of arts policy. There is an increase in expenditure in both Conservative and Labour-controlled authorities. This is apparent in shire counties and metropolitan areas. It is taking place in spite of the fact that the Government have taken £28 billion from local authorities through the rate support grant over the past 10 years. The RSG has been cut from 61 per cent. of funding to 45 per cent. The enormously exciting increase in expenditure on the arts by local authorities and local communities has not been taken up by the Government. On the contrary, they have done their best to inhibit it. The Government's role has been shortsighted. At a time of unprecedented interest by audiences and extremely high quality of work by artists and writers throughout the country, the Government's record is a miserable one of neglect, underfunding and missed opportunities.

The Government are out of touch and out of sympathy with what is going on in the arts around the country. That is extremely sad.

Both libraries and museums should be enjoying a golden age. I pay tribute to the Government's GCSE syllabus, which put a terrific and new emphasis on children working from primary sources. The opportunities for

[*Mr. Fisher*]

working in libraries and in museums with primary sources is enormous and should mean an expansion of audiences and activities in libraries and museums. We find, however, that, after 10 years of care for libraries by the present Government, fewer public libraries are open. Those that are open are open for fewer hours, and the spending on book funds has fallen.

Everyone agrees that information is the key element in the development of our economy. Our public libraries are the main source of important industrial and community information on patents, standards and legal and tariff barriers. Ten years ago there were 22,000 requests for information at Birmingham central library. Last year, there were 579,000 requests. That is a 163 per cent. increase, showing an explosion of interest and involvement in the public libraries' information services. However, the Government have been cutting the funding of public libraries.

As a result of the GCSE, there is a need for more library facilities as most schools are struggling to keep up their book funds. Very few schools have professional chartered librarians. My four children have now been through the state system and none of them attended a high school or primary school which had a chartered librarian. In school, they had virtually no experience of professional libraries. That is a wasted opportunity and a tragedy.

There has been a general collapse in national and regional libraries. Over the past year there have been reports from the Museums and Galleries Commission, the National Audit Office and the Public Accounts Committee which all tell the Minister the same story. The Select Committee on Education, Science and Arts is hearing evidence from the directors of our major national museums. Mr. Neil MacGregor recently explained to that Select Committee the problems facing his gallery.

When will the Government recognise the crisis? When will they recognise that the Tate gallery needs £27 million for repairs and maintenance of basics like wiring, safety procedures and security? The Victoria and Albert museum has a £50 million backlog of repairs and maintenance and anticipates that it will need £120 million over the next five years. The National Maritime museum needs £19 million for repairs and maintenance. How much more evidence must be put in front of the Minister before he does something about the fabric of our great national museums?

Mr. Luce: The hon. Gentleman takes no notice when we announce positive decisions. He is either deaf or does not want to listen. Does he acknowledge that, as a result of representations about the structure of our important national institutions, I have decided to shift resources to building and maintenance to the tune of an extra 55 per cent. over a four-year period in acknowledgment of that very problem? It is very difficult to take the hon. Gentleman seriously if he does not acknowledge that the Government are trying to do something about it.

Mr. Fisher: Of course we acknowledge that the Government are trying to do something. However, the Minister must understand that the initiative which he has announced, in comparison to the evidence before him, is completely inadequate. Even after the Minister's initiative, the museums are going backwards. He should ask himself why those major museums, 15 months after they were given the opportunity to take over the running of their properties from the Property Services Agency, are still reluctant to take on that responsibility. Instead of being given an opportunity by the Government, they know that they are being handed a load of debt and problems.

In welcoming any small moves which the Minister has made, he must understand that he has made an inadequate response to what is becoming a national scandal about the state of the fabric of our national museums. That point is highlighted particularly by the problems facing the Victoria and Albert museum over the past few months, but the problems are not confined to that museum.

The problems in libraries and museums have been increasing over the past few years. However, this year, the tenth year of the Prime Minister's reign, has been the worst. The Minister has spent the whole year fire-fighting problems which all stem from the problems that have developed over the past 10 years. He should not have had to do that.

For example, the British Theatre Association library was saved by a benefactor, no thanks to the Minister or the Government. We cannot rely on people like Mr. Holmes à Court to come along and bale out the Government, who have a public and national responsibility for a unique archive and resource.

Mr. John Bowis (Battersea): I have been looking at the figures because the hon. Gentleman painted an abysmal picture of libraries. I cannot reconcile what he said with the facts. The number of service points for libraries has increased from 14,000 to 18,000. There has been no fall in the number of books purchased and 11 million books are purchased every year. Library book stocks have increased from 110 million to 116 million and library staffing is at its highest level for 10 years.

Mr. Fisher: The hon. Gentleman should try to understand the figures that he has quoted or with which the Office of Arts and Libraries has provided him. He is not quoting the number of public libraries; he is quoting public book stocks in hospitals and old people's homes. There are not 14,000 or 20,000 public libraries in this country. There are actually——

Mr. Bowis: No, service points.

Mr. Fisher: Service points are not the important thing. The important thing is that there are 4,000 public libraries in this country. There has been a drop of 200 libraries. No one disputes that, with an aging population, there are more service points in old people's homes and hospitals. However, the number of libraries open to the public has fallen. The hon. Member for Battersea (Mr. Bowis), who I am sure looks at these matters fairly, should recognise that.

This year there was a missed opportunity with the British Theatre Association library. A similar opportunity was missed with the Northern Ballet Theatre. The Theatre Upstairs at the Royal Court and the Studio Theatre at the Theatre Royal in Bristol—the Bristol Old Vic—have had to close. Children's theatres such as the Polka and the Unicorn are facing real problems as a result of new regulations which inhibit children and prevent them leaving schools in organised parties to visit theatre performances.

My hon. Friend the Member for Newham, North-West (Mr. Banks) will consider heritage later. The problems at Huggin Hill have matched those of the Rose theatre. We will also have problems very soon about the archaeological remains at the King's Cross site. We shall have similar problems along the route of the Channel tunnel. The problems are stacking up.

This tenth year of Thatcherism has been a very bad year for the Government quite apart from the missed opportunities at Covent Garden, King's Cross, in Docklands and on the South Bank where there are major international opportunities for the Government to make a formidable statement about how much we care about our culture. However, the Government are standing idly by and letting the private sector get on with it.

The Minister made an interesting speech this afternoon. I have often berated him about his lack of policy and vision. I recognise that this afternoon he attempted to address those problems. Many of his aspirations on more opportunities for all, on audience participation, on pride in arts achievements in this country, on arts in schools, devolution, access and excellence were all fine aspirations and fine words which hon. Members on both sides of the House would share and applaud in full.

The Minister asked me to respond in particular to his remarks about the arm's-length principle and the future of the Arts Council. This Government and other Governments have considered the arm's-length principle to involve what is at the end of the arm. The fact that the arm is extended does not mean to say that the Government do not control, at the end of the arm, the Arts Council through Government funding limits. That has become true over the past few years when the arts world has considered that the Arts Council is moving closer to the Government.

We believe that a truly independent Arts Council is one that can speak for the arts world to the Government instead of to the arts world on behalf of the Government as, on occasion, the Arts Council appears to have done over the past few years. There are exceptions to that. It took an honourable, principled and brave stand on clause 28 last year and told the Government that they were wrong. However, too often companies in the arts world feel that the Arts Council must, because of its funding relationship with the Government, speak too much on behalf of the Government instead of to the Government. We would seek to reduce the patronage of the Arts Council to have an independent Arts Council which spoke for, and on behalf of, the arts world. We shall submit evidence to Mr. Wilding's inquiry which we welcome. No doubt we will debate those matters at greater length in future.

I welcome the Minister's announcement about the innovation endowment fund. The need for innovation is great. However, I doubt whether that, of itself, is an adequate or sufficient solution and whether money solely dispensed by the Arts Council from the centre—from London, from the top—is the best way to stimulate innovation in all forms of arts and culture. Innovation is best developed at regional and local level. However, I welcome the initiative, as far as it goes.

Innovation is not simply a question of providing £1 million and thinking that that will suffice. Companies ought to be sufficiently well funded to feel that they have the right to fail. Recently the National Theatre bravely staged a play called "Ghetto". A lot of money was spent on it. It was unlikely to be a box office success. If the reviews had been bad and if audiences had not turned up,

the whole season at the National Theatre would have been put at risk. Theatre companies should not have to risk a whole season in that way. The right to fail and to experiment must be built into their budgets.

The very brave work that Annie Castledine has been doing at the Derby Playhouse does not easily attract audiences, but audiences are being built up for it. The critical appreciation is enormous. Local audiences are responding, so work of that sort needs to be backed. A theatre that has no room for the sort of work that Annie Castledine is doing at Derby is not a theatre which is in good shape.

Mr. Peter Thurnham (Bolton, North-East): Does the hon. Gentleman agree that the way to guarantee box office success is to reduce income tax? It has been reduced from 83 per cent. to 40 per cent. People now have some money to spend on the arts.

Mr. Fisher: The Government are always telling us that people now have very much more money in their pockets, but spending on the arts by audiences is not necessarily the answer to the problem. Most of the companies that I am talking about, which play to large audiences, cannot increase their box office revenue. The Royal Opera House is playing to 96 to 97 per cent. capacity audiences.

Mr. Terry Dicks (Hayes and Harlington): Of course it plays to 96 per cent. capacity audiences. That is because 30 per cent. or 40 per cent. of the seat price is paid for by the rest of us.

Mr. Fisher: I should have thought that the hon. Gentleman would want there to be success at the box office, and 96 per cent. or 97 per cent. at the box office is a good indication of how popular the Royal Opera House and English National Opera programmes are. I should have thought that the hon. Gentleman would welcome popular success, but it seems that he is never satisfied.

The real reason for these problems is that the Government are hoist on their policy of relying on the private sector and market forces. I remind the Minister yet again about his statement to the conference at Newcastle of the Council of Regional Arts Associations. I hope that he will take this opportunity to say that he has changed his mind and that that statement is no longer Government policy. He said:

"The objective of this Government is to reduce the role of the state."

Is that still the Government's objective? If so, I suspect that he has had great success, because most companies reckon that they are getting less state support. However, that is not in the interests of innovation or quality, or of widening access to the arts, even though that is his ambition.

The Minister went on to say:

"Too many in the arts world have yet to be weaned away from the welfare state mentality."

I do not believe that they ever had such a mentality. People in the arts world have always fought for audiences. They are very keen to increase their audiences. Performing artistes want as many people as possible to see their work. I think that they found that remark deeply offensive and deeply insulting.

Is it still the Government's view that a welfare state mentality still exists in the arts? I hope that the Minister will rise to his feet and say that that is not so—that he recognises that the arts are very good at marketing

[*Mr. Fisher*]

themselves and selling themselves to audiences. The Minister seems to be reluctant to take the opportunity I have offered to him to take back a remark that does him no credit. I regret that he does not intend to do so. The arts world will regret it, too, and note the reality of the Government's attitude, beneath all their fine words.

As for funding, the Minister said that three times as much money is devoted now to the arts as in the 1960s. Of course it is, but the demand is much greater and there are many more Arts Council and regional arts association clients. The expansion of the arts has been enormous. However, can the Minister name one arts client who is getting more money now and who feels that the opportunities are greater as a result of central Government policy and funding? Can he name a single company—the Royal Shakespeare theatre or the National theatre, perhaps—that is prepared to go on record and say that it is better off now than it was before, thanks to the Government; that it is able to mount more programmes; that it is able to do more interesting and innovative work and that it is able to employ better designers and expand its activities?

Mr. Michael Colvin (Romsey and Waterside): The hon. Gentleman seems to be coming round to making the case for a centralised arts policy. He has not yet answered the question that my right hon. Friend put to him earlier: whether the Labour party is still committed to an arm's-length policy. Does he still believe in the policy, advocated by his predecessor, of a centralised system, on the basis that he who pays the piper calls the tune? That appears to be the policy that the Labour party advocates. It would pay for the arts and determine what is done by the arts.

Mr. Fisher: The hon. Gentleman should know what Labour policy is because he has been taking part in these debates for a long time. Labour party policy is that there should be an expansion of the arts at local authority level, in response to what local communities, local audiences and local artists want. There should be real devolution. The arts should be encouraged at local authority level by making the arts, for the first time ever, a statutory responsibility of local authorities. The arts are just as important as housing, social services or libraries. That is the way to expand the arts. That is a genuine devolution. It is not centralisation. However, the Government want to control the arts through the Arts Council. They want to control the arts from the centre.

Mr. Tim Devlin (Stockton, South): The hon. Gentleman is arguing against himself now. He said earlier that companies should have the right to put on whatever productions they want, that they should have the right to fail and that we should subsidise them, even if nobody wants to see their productions. Now he is saying that he wants the arts to be funded at local level so that people can be given what they want. If people want something, they will go and see it. If they do not want it, they will not go and see it. Which way does he want it to be?

Mr. Fisher: I thought that I had made the Labour party's policy quite clear. We believe in expansion at local authority level by placing on local authorities a statutory responsibility for the arts and by funding the arts through

the rate support grant. There would then be a flowering of activity in response to local needs. That would be genuine devolution. The response would be different, because different communities would have different arts needs. The needs in Gloucester, Cheltenham, Glasgow—even in Grantham—will be different. That would be a truly local policy which would be welcomed by the arts world.

It is interesting to note that neither the Minister nor any of his Back Benchers can name a single company that believes that it is better off after 10 years of Conservative Government. That says it all. The Minister always talks about sponsorship and makes great play of it. He refers to the admirable gifts of people such as Lord Sainsbury, Mr. Clore and Mr. Getty. He should also pay tribute perhaps to Mr. Annenberg at the National gallery.

The Minister has missed the point about sponsorship. In France, private sector sponsorship is far greater than it is here. The reason is that the French Government believe in an arts policy. They are prepared to fund the arts. That attracts individual sponsors. Why should the corporate sector fund the arts when the Government do not have confidence in the importance of an arts policy? When he calculates his European figures, in the Policy Studies Institute study, I hope that they will include sponsorship. That would prove my point that private sector funding of the arts is much greater in those countries where the Government take a lead and say that they believe in funding the arts. That gives confidence to the private sector and a context within which the private sector can work.

The Government are totally at odds with audiences, with what is happening at local authority level and with what is happening in Europe and further afield. The Prime Minister is apparently taking an interest now in the arts. She has not yet exhibited her interest, but I am told that her speeches are beginning to include little phrases, written for her by other people, about how good and important the arts are. I welcome that. I hope that she will go to the theatre or to a concert—even a pop concert. It would be very interesting to see her there. Until she shows a personal interest in the arts, people will treat her statements with some scepticism. The Prime Minister and the Government display a grudging attitude to the arts. They say, "Let somebody else do it." We applaud what is happening in the arts, but the Government appear to be saying that they want somebody else to be responsible for the arts. The Minister commented in his infamous Newcastle speech:

"The arts world must accept the economic and political climate in which we operate."

The arts world does not accept it. It does not like it, and I suspect that people throughout the arts are casting their votes against the Government at the polls today because of their poor policies.

I conclude by referring the Minister to a quote from Bernard Shaw's "Back to Methuselah", in which, in act 1, the serpent says to Adam,

"You see things and you say why? But I dream things that never were and I say why not?"

The Government ask themselves why they should fund the arts, but we—and the country will show that it is with us —ask: why not? The arts are a vital part of our local and national life and identity and deserve to be funded. The Government should recognise the success that is our country's arts and heritage, and should acknowledge the country's mood and back them.

Several Hon. Members *rose——*

Mr. Deputy Speaker (Sir Paul Dean): Order. I remind the House that the debate must finish at 7 o'clock. As many right hon. and hon. Members wish to speak, I hope that contributions will be brief.

5 pm

Sir Hugh Rossi (Hornsey and Wood Green): My right hon. Friend the Minister will forgive me if I do not follow him in his opening the debate on the arts but instead open the second subject for debate, our heritage. In that respect, the first report from the Environment Select Committee, "Historic Buildings and Ancient Monuments", is relevant, and I regret that it has taken two and half years since publication for it to come before the House in today's debate. A year after that report's publication, a response by the Department of the Environment was published on 20 January 1988, including replies from the standing conference of deans and provosts of English cathedrals and from the dean and chapter of Ely cathedral.

Generally speaking, the Select Committee report was warmly welcomed. In a letter to me, my right hon. Friend the Secretary of State for the Environment, as well as indicating his approval of much of the contents of the report, commented:

"On those matters where we have not felt able to follow your suggestions you should not feel that the door is necessarily closed for all time. We shall naturally keep our legislative and administrative procedures under review and will remain receptive to imaginative, new ideas for the conservation and preservation of our heritage."

I take this opportunity to ask my hon. Friend the Under-Secretary of State for the Environment what progress has been made in the past two and a half years with matters which have remained outstanding since the Select Committee report and the Government's response.

The Select Committee raised three main issues, as well as a number of miscellaneous matters. Those main issues were the multiplicity of agencies responsible for heritage, the listing and scheduling system for buildings and monuments, and the allocation of financial resources for heritage purposes. The Committee found that the existing multiplicity of agencies with overlapping responsibilities resulted in a dissipation of energies. That was among the matters that we said should be examined, and we recommended that more powers and responsibilities— and, it follows, more resources—should be devolved to English Heritage.

The Committee concluded, and the Government agreed, that too little weight was placed on tourism relating to historic buildings and ancient monuments. In his letter to me, my right hon. Friend the Secretary of State remarked:

"Better public access and increased numbers of tourists can . . . make a significant contribution to the upkeep and preservation of the heritage by providing income and enhanced public awareness. But if the longer term effects are to be positive, it is important that tourism is properly managed and controlled. This requires a degree of expertise and close liaison between the various agencies involved, both nationally and locally. The Government is pursuing these objectives . . ."

In the 18 months since that letter was written, how far have the Government progressed in pursuing those objectives on which the Select Committee and the Government were wholly in agreement?

The Select Committee found that the listing of historic buildings was basically sound, but recommended that that responsibility be transferred to English Heritage together

with the power to serve building preservation notices— which it already has in respect of London. I regret that, so far, the Government have not thought it right to adopt that particular recommendation, on the ground of political accountability. Nevertheless, we could still raise such matters in the House even though, in the view of the Select Committee, English Heritage should be given prime responsibility.

As to the scheduling of ancient monuments, in the light of very recent experience, the Committee's recommendations are even more relevant today. Earlier this afternoon there was a private notice question on the subject of the Rose theatre. The Committee suggested that the Government should ensure that areas of archaeological importance were extended. Where such areas are declared under an arrangement between local and central Government, prior notice would be required for any operation which disturbed the ground in the area concerned—including flooding and tipping as well as development. Thereafter, a team could be appointed with the power to enter and investigate, and to excavate the site for up to four months. Alternatively, the team could hold a watching brief while the development progressed.

It is possible that in the case of the Rose theatre such an arrangement would have been unnecessary, because we and the country were fortunate that the developers involved took a very responsible attitude to the discovery, and my right hon. Friend the Secretary of State for the Environment moved in with £1 million to enable the developers to investigate what measures were necessary to preserve the Rose, which they did with very satisfactory results, having regard to the special situation.

What would have been the outcome if a responsible developer had not been involved in that case? As city centres are redeveloped as part of inner city regeneration, it is likely that many other important remains will be uncovered. What is the Government's current view both of funding to rescue archaeology and of the protection of sites of outstanding historical importance? I emphasise again that we cannot always be sure that redevelopment will be in the hands of responsible developers.

The Select Committee's third major point concerned the financing of our heritage. We were critical of the fact that grants could be applied only when the building qualified as "outstanding". We feel that all grade I buildings without exception should qualify for grant automatically, or they should not be grade I in the first place.

The matter which caused the greatest controversy and which the media enjoyed more than anything else was the suggestion that cathedrals which are not subject to grant should become subject to grant once they had shown that they had done everything in their power to raise the necessary funds for the maintenance, repair and restoration of their buildings. We had the temerity to suggest that perhaps for tourists, as distinct from worshippers—they can readily be defined—there should be a charge of at least £1 per person. In putting forward that suggestion, we realised that we were touching a sensitive area as some people say that there should not be a charge to enter the House of God. As one who likes to attend church regularly, I understand that sentiment. However, we are not talking about people from the locality of the cathedral, for whom a part can always be set aside, but about chara-trippers who arrive in multitudes and by the mere weight of their feet and the probing of

[*Sir Hugh Rossi*]

their fingers cause perhaps as much erosion of the fabric of the cathedral as the exterior suffers through acid rain, which is the subject of another report upon which I shall not dwell now.

Mr. Fisher: Hon. Members on both sides of the House will be extremely apprehensive to hear the hon. Gentleman talking about a charge for tourists. How on earth can one distinguish between tourists and residents? Have not tourists the right to worship and pray in cathedrals? When considering funding, did his Committee look at the experience of Germany and other European countries where the state provides some funding through the taxation system and gets around the problem of making a totally impossible distinction between those who wish to pray and those who wish to look at a museum?

Sir Hugh Rossi: Clearly, the hon. Gentleman has not had the advantage of studying the report, although it has been in the Library for two and a half years. We went to Germany to look at the German experience, which involves one third funding from central Government, one third from local government and one third from voluntary subscriptions. If the hon. Gentleman had read the reasons that we received from the deans and provosts of English cathedrals and from the dean and chapter of Ely cathedral, he might have thought a little before leaping in with the question that he has just asked. The dean and chapter of Ely cathedral wrote:

"It is not our experience, after nearly two years of weekday admission charges at Ely, that an entrance charge militates against the character of a Cathedral as a House of God. On the contrary, the prayer board at the far end of the charging area upon which visitors are encouraged to leave intercessions to be used at daily Evensong, has been so full of prayers during the past summer that it has been an embarrassment to recite them adequately at the Service.

Moreover, our experience of charging is that visitors stay far longer in the cathedral having come for a deliberate visit rather than using the buildings as a wet weather call. Problems of noisy parties rushing through the building in ten minutes and of misconduct of bored visitors have practically disappeared."

That is the experience of one cathedral that has followed the advice given by the Select Committee. The practice predated the Committee. That experience prompted us to include the suggestion and recommendation in our report.

The consequence is that Ely cathedral, although it is not on the usual tourist route as York and Durham are, now has an annual fund available to follow a programme of proper maintenance and repair to its building and a surplus which it sends to the diocesan fund. The Select Committee recommendation was that if the popular cathedrals—in tourist terms—were to adopt that policy, the surplus could then be used to set up a national fund for the preservation of those cathedrals which are off the tourist beaten track.

I realise that that view is not shared by every dean and chapter of every cathedral. The pious hope expressed by the provosts is:

"it is the pastoral task of a cathedral to turn tourists into visitors, visitors into guests, guests into pilgrims, and pilgrims into worshippers."

That is a laudable ambition, but whether it has much relation to the way in which tourists react today is open to question. We rely very much on the experience of one cathedral which has had the courage to follow that course

and has solved its financial problems without in any way detracting from the nature of the cathedral or causing any disturbance whatsoever to the worshippers.

Mr. Heffer: I find what the hon. Gentleman said fascinating. As a member of the Church, I would strongly object to anyone having to pay to enter our cathedrals. As the hon. Gentleman knows, I visit Italy regularly. Perhaps he knows more about this than I do, but I can think of no cathedral or church that I have visited—I go to as many as I can—in Venice or anywhere else in Italy where one has to pay. Perhaps the hon. Gentleman can point one out to me.

Sir Hugh Rossi: One in Venice immediately comes to mind—Santa Maria Maggiore, Vergine, or some similar name—and I have a photograph of a plaque outside saying that visitors are requested to put 1,500 lire in the box on entering.

Mr. Heffer: It must have been the one I missed.

Sir Hugh Rossi: Perhaps it was.

Mr. Heffer: Is it on the island?

Sir Hugh Rossi: If the hon. Gentleman would be kind enough to arrange the funds for a visit, I would be happy to join him and point the church out to him.

I shall leave that point as it is not strictly a matter for the Government. It is a matter for the church authorities, who must decide for themselves what to do. I raised the matter because the question has crossed my mind more than once in relation to the problems faced by Hereford cathedral, which has refused to follow Ely and impose a charge. The money needed for repairs could not be raised by appeal. It then went through the dreadful experience over Mappa Mundi and failed to raise money. Its appeal has failed and it is now in dire straits financially. It does not know which way to turn, but perhaps Ely has pointed the way.

5.19 pm

Mr. Michael Foot (Blaenau Gwent): The Minister spoke not with complacency but with astonishing insensitivity for the feelings of many people in the arts world and beyond. It is strange that he should have spoken in that tone, because he referred to the general background in which a Minister for the Arts has to operate. He is concerned not only with artistic matters but with the cultural background of the country. It is astonishing that a Minister in that position should speak in such a tone. He has only to use his eyes, ears and intelligence—I am sure he has all three—to find out what is being said in many different circles.

The Minister referred to the universities and the new examination. I am sure that I meet a different type of person at universities from the right hon. Gentleman and others. My experience is that there is more depression and lower morale in the universities than at any time I can remember, except when the Government were pushing through their Bill affecting universities and threatening action against them. Those threats were partly withdrawn at the last moment. Even the universities with the best funding are complaining about depression and low morale.

Fewer people will be recruited as history teachers in universities. The brain drain is happening. If anybody cares to read the details, there was another report in *The Guardian* yesterday. Anyone who does not understand the depression in the universities does not understand the real mood among academics in this country.

A more obvious example, to which the Minister also referred, is broadcasting. Does the right hon. Gentleman really think that there is confidence within those circles, that morale is high and that they are sharing in the supposed great fruits of 10 years of wonderful industrial and economic progress? There is no such mood. There is a mood of fright and alarm. If the Minister cared to open the newspapers, he could read about that almost every day.

There is also the strike at the BBC. There was a much bigger response to strike action than most people had calculated. It is just one expression of the feeling inside the BBC. The morale within the BBC is even worse than that in private companies. It is alarmed at what the Government intend to do, and it has every right to be alarmed. An excellent article in *The Independent* described the widespread, corrosive fears of privatisation within the BBC and how it thinks it is being pushed in that direction. If the Minister does not think that that is the mood, he should talk to some of the people in charge. He should also talk to those who manage his financial affairs. He is supposed to be one of the great experts because of the way in which he responds to questions by my right hon. and hon. Friends.

The BBC overseas service is one of the finest institutions in the country. It has to grapple with the Government's refusal and failure year after year to match the inflation rate with the money they provide. If the Minister disputes the figures, he has not listened to the people who do the job. The overseas service is magnificent: hon. Members on both sides of the House say that constantly whenever we debate it.

Those who run the overseas service make the best possible use of the small resources available. I am not criticising the people who run it. However, the Government, by implication, are constantly criticising because they are constantly squeezing the amount available to spend. Therefore, in the past few years the overseas service has had to be restricted in many ways. There has been a good example of that in the past week. I am sure that millions of people across China would have been eager to hear the BBC reports on the circumstances there. However, fewer people in China are able to hear those reports than some years ago. That is partly because of the financial squeeze. The BBC has hardly enough money to place telephone calls to China, let alone to provide a broadcast service in that part of the world.

It is not a laughing matter. The Government should be considering a major expansion of the money allocated to the BBC overseas service and the BBC generally so that it can overcome the shockingly low morale that exists. The BBC is one of the best institutions in the country. The Prime Minister cannot bear to see an organisation that has performed well for the nation over the years. She has always got to see whether she can shake it up or change it. She has already shown what a catastrophe such action can cause by the changes in the National Health Service. The same thing has happened with the universities and broadcasting. In the face of all that, it is wrong for the Minister to be so complacent.

I seek to reply to those general arguments because they were raised by the Minister. Usually in such debates my hon. Friend the Member for Paisley, South (Mr. Buchan) is present to put his arguments. He is not here today because of illness, so he cannot give us his assistance. However, he has done the next best thing by producing a book on the subject. I am sure that it has been read by all Opposition Members but some Conservative Members may not have completed their education. I recommend it most strongly. It is entitled "Glasnost in Britain". It is published by Macmillan and edited by Norman Buchan and Tricia Sumner. It is a fine book and gives a clearer picture of what has happened in the past 10 years than anything we have heard from the Minister.

The articles in the book cover the many different themes that are relevant to the debate, but I shall quote a sentence prophylactically. It is from an article by the Earl of Stockton. I know that his grandfather is not regarded favourably by the Government but I hope that they will not visit the sins of the grandfather on the grandson, particularly when he has written an excellent and witty article. He has inherited his grandfather's gift in that respect. The Earl of Stockton warns about VAT on books and says that that issue has not yet been settled. He wants to ensure that it is settled. I should like an absolute assurance from the Government that there will be no retreat on VAT on books.

The excellent article says:
"There is a certain Orwellian irony that the last time we defended the printed word was in 1984."
He was referring to the campaign in 1984 to fend off the imposition of VAT on books. He goes on to say:
"There are those who say that the book trade is unduly alarmist. Well, I am not a hysteric, but nor am I an ostrich. The threat of taxation on the printed word is not only unnecessary, uneconomic and essentially illiberal, but the mechanisms of its impositions are, I suspect, probably corrupt and tyrannical in the most insidious fashion".
The article elaborates that case.

I hope that the Government will now give us an absolute assurance that, whatever happens and whatever the dispute is about, whether or not it is about how the new Common Market is to be dealt with, there will be no departure from the absolute undertaking that there will be no VAT on books and that the Government are not prepared to allow that to go through.

That article should be circulated to every Government Member. I am sure that, on that matter at least, the Minister for the Arts will agree with what I am saying and he is the best person to know how many of his Cabinet colleagues need educating on the subject.

Let me come now to a more major matter that concerns the right hon. Gentleman. About a year ago, in a debate on the arts, we discussed whether the amounts of money that the museums had to spend had been properly increased over the previous few years, whatever might be the promise for the next year or two. As I recall, at that time we had just had the report from the independent committee which had investigated those matters. It showed that, just as there has been a squeeze on the BBC, the universities and others, so a squeeze had been put on the museums. By not making up their money to cover inflation, the Government were, in effect, imposing a cut. I am sure that the right hon. Gentleman will not deny that that report discussed how museum staff throughout Britain were having to bear the burden of the Government's failure to deal with such matters.

In case the right hon. Gentleman thinks that he does not have any special responsibility in such matters, let me

[Mr. Michael Foot]

make the point even more directly. He referred to the Victoria and Albert museum. In a year when there has been such a crisis in that institution, the right hon. Gentleman's references to the subject were derisory. He did not even attempt to discuss the major questions. It is no good him saying that he has mentioned them on other occasions so that there is no need to do so again. He made one reference to the museum, but he did not make any reference to the crisis there. Does he deny that there is a crisis? If he does, he should study the debate that took place in the other place on 22 and 23 March on that subject initiated by Lord Annan. I am sure that he has done so already, but I invite other hon. Members to do so.

The noble Lord Annan is not a scaremonger, but he was outraged by what had happened at the Victoria and Albert museum, and he used many pertinent and potent phrases to describe it. He said that the way in which some of the people had been sacked was vulgar and brutal. He used a series of further words to describe the situation—charges with which I should have thought the right hon. Gentleman would have had some sympathy. I cannot believe that the right hon. Gentleman, or any civilised hon. Member, could think that to sack people in the way that they were was the proper way in which to act.

But the background to the matter affects the right hon. Gentleman even more directly. The noble Lord Annan gave details of the Victoria and Albert museum's finances, which showed that its crisis was largely provoked by the lack of money. If the right hon. Gentleman questions what I say, he need only read what the noble Lord Annan said. He did not just give his own figures. He said:

"However, there is a far more serious charge for the Government to face. The deputy chairman of the trustees, Sir Michael Butler, tells us that the finances of the Victoria and Albert have been cut each year for the past 13 years by 3 per cent. Now the Government are not honouring the pay awards to which they are a party . . . By 1992, so I understand, the V & A will be in deficit unless it gets rid of staff. Is that one reason why eight curatorial staff have been asked to take voluntary retirement?"

He went on:

"I call this policy dishonest and dishonourable".

Those charges are serious and they were sustained by many others who spoke in the debate. No one need take my word for that; they can read the speeches of the noble Lords who supported the noble Lord Annan.

At least the Government's policy towards the Victoria and Albert has made a great contribution to Britain's anthology of invective. The mastery of invective shown in the other place to describe what had happened in the Victoria and Albert was considerable. As I have said, the noble Lord Annan presented the case strongly, but I think that the prize should go to the noble Lord Goodman, who certainly knows something about these matters, and neither the right hon. Gentleman nor anybody else should try to push aside what he had to say. He described what had happened in a paragraph which must have caused a shudder throughout the other place. I shall not quote it now, but anyone who says that I am exaggerating should read that debate. I promise that they will not have any difficulty in doing so because the case against what was done was stated by masters of the English language.

The Government had two replies and two spokesmen in that debate. Neither replied on the question of the money, the one that affects the right hon. Gentleman. Neither

replied to the charge made by the noble Lord Annan, and sustained by others, that the real money that can be spent on maintaining the museum—some of its money goes on repairs, and so on—has been cut and cut, and that, under the prospective plans, there will be still further cuts. The Government made no consistent or reputable reply to that charge, despite the fact that they answered in two different ways. On one happily occasion—again, if anyone thinks that I am exaggerating he can read the debate—the two Government spokesmen found themselves repudiating each other because they got mixed up about who had given the orders to the trustees and those who run the Victoria and Albert to sack the people involved.

Even at the end of the debate, there was no agreement between the noble Lord Armstrong and the other Government spokesmen about who had given the instructions. The noble Lord Armstrong is an interesting spokesman on the subject. He has a reputation of being, in that famous phrase, economical with the truth. I do not wish to make any such platitudinous reference. He almost has a taste for extravagant platitude as well. Explaining the situation, Lord Armstrong said:

"There is some suggestion that we are all appointed with some undisclosed and sinister mandate from the Prime Minister. We are of course all appointed by the Prime Minister because that is how Parliament said that we should be appointed in the National Heritage Act".—[*Official Report, House of Lords,* 22 March 1989; Vol. 505, c. 766–97.]

It is perfectly true that a decision was made along those lines, but nobody then thought that the Prime Minister's power of appointment would be used so swiftly in such a critical case as this to appoint someone such as Lord Armstrong. He is certainly one of them—in that sense, he has great qualifications—but his appointment was bound to give rise to anxieties among the people who run the museum.

If the right hon. Gentleman thinks that that is nonsense and that I am exaggerating the importance of the matter, he should have taken the opportunity to say what will happen at the Victoria and Albert. Is the right hon. Gentleman merely going to accept the fait accompli imposed by Lord Armstrong and others with the approval, concurrence and incitement of the Prime Minister?

If anyone questions what I say, I invite them to read the article written on this subject by someone who knows far more about the Victoria and Albert museum than anyone in this House, or in the other place, and far more than Lord Armstrong, Lord Carrington and the others who were appointed for a year or two. That article was written for the *New York Review of Books* and I am glad to say that *The Guardian* republished it in this country. That article on what has happened to one of our greatest museums represents the most serious discussion on it that has been published in the whole of the controversy.

I am sure that the right hon. Gentleman is familiar with the article and I am sure that his civil servants gave it to him. If that is so, what is the Minister's answer to it? The article is entitled "The Fall of a Great Museum" and it was written by John Pope-Hennessy. He had great experience at that museum and at other museums since. I have not heard anyone—not even a Government Whip—try to blacken the reputation of John Pope-Hennessy and his right to speak on such matters.

Anyone who reads that article will see that it adds up to an appalling indictment of the Government's misuse of power. It outlines the extremely serious consequences for the future of the museum. I shall give one quote from many. He talks of the danger of sacking people of such qualification and says:

"If the dismissals are persisted the Victoria"——

Mr. Dicks: On a point of order, Mr. Deputy Speaker. With great respect to the right hon. Gentleman, I appreciate his interest in this matter, but he has been speaking for 20 mintues. This is a short debate and, through you, Mr. Deputy Speaker, I ask the right hon. Gentleman to remember that many of us still want to speak.

Mr. Foot: I do not believe that that is a point of order, and I hope that the hon. Gentleman will let me proceed.

The serious charge in the article reads:

"If the dismissals are persisted the Victoria and Albert will be more ignorant than at any other period in this century." The museum relies on the advice of its experts. The article concludes:

"When universities are starved of funds there is no means by which members of the public can assess the consequences, but when a vast museum with an international reputation is reduced to an object of ridicule, the result is all too evident. To repair the damage and to get the museum once more into decent working order, some form of special grant may be required, but it will be justified because in its future not only the fate of a magnificent collection, but national self-respect is inescapably involved."

The Minister is as directly responsible as anyone in government and he should give us the reassurances and the funds required so that this appalling catastrophe—the fall of a great museum—is remedied.

I happened to go to Paris last week and I saw what has been done at the new musée d'Orsay. We have some magnificent museums, but anyone who has seen what has been done in France in the past four years could not quarrel too much about the extra money that would be required to bring our museums up to the French standard. The President has some understanding of such matters and the French have created a magnificent new museum in which some of the greatest treasures of French art will be displayed. The French Government are wise enough to know that no single investment since 1945 compares with their investment in that museum.

The Victoria and Albert museum has every right and claim to be a wonderful organisation. In this tenth year of the Prime Minister's operations, the Government should compare what has happened this year to the Victoria and Albert with the new museum in France; they should take that comparison to heart.

I apologise to other hon. Members, but I want to say something further about a matter that is still of great importance to this House and which should be watched with great care—the Rose theatre. I congratulate my hon. Friend the Member for Stoke-on-Trent, Central (Mr. Fisher) on his vigilance in this matter. I do not believe that the question is settled yet. The Secretary of State for the Environment today seemed uncertain about whether it was an importance matter after all. He demurred from making such a claim. He does not normally show such bashfulness or parade his humility, but today he said that he did not wish to be too assertive about whether the Rose theatre was such a treasure after all.

I am sure that the Minister is aware of the appeals that have been made for that theatre. I know that the Under-Secretary of State for the Environment has visited the site and has heard the direct appeals from people such as Dame Peggy Ashcroft and others who have spoken so eloquently upon the matter. I assure Ministers that those people will continue to campaign until the matter is settled properly.

If Ministers have any doubts about the theatre, I commend to them the last paragraph of the article on this subject that appeared in *The Times Literary Supplement* of last week:

"The Rose is a unique phenomenon. Its dates put it, and the changes Henslowe made to it, at the height of the evolution of the Elizabethan playhouse design, neatly disposed between the Theatre of 1576 in Shoreditch, which gave up its timber frame to make the original Globe, and the Swan and Globe alongside the Rose in 1595 and 1599. It gave Marlowe his early chance, and he gave it the first great stage successes of the London theatre. It may well have been Shakespeare's own training ground. In the last three months"——

I stress, three months—

"theatre historians have been given more fresh and utterly reliable information about the design of the Shakespearean stage than they have managed to scrape together from written-sources in the past three centuries. To lose it would be a new kind of Shakespearean tragedy."

It is our business in this House to ensure that that tragedy does not occur. We have not had such assurance from the right hon. Gentleman yet. I am sure that people in all constituencies and the leaders of the theatre world, Dame Peggy Ashcroft at their head, will make certain that that new Shakespearean tragedy shall not be permitted.

5.48 pm

Mr. Timothy Raison (Aylesbury): The right hon. Member for Blaenau Gwent (Mr. Foot) has just referred to the creation of the musée d'Orsay in Paris. Anyone who has seen it would agree that it is a fantastic museum. The right hon. Gentleman's contribution was characteristic of the Opposition as it showed a total lack of appreciation of the outstanding successes being achieved in the arts and the current strength of the British arts.

I, too, was in Paris just a few days ago when the Select Committee on Education, Science and Arts, of which I am lucky enough to be Chairman, was considering the French museums. We saw the great achievements, but we also heard that the position regarding acquisitions is worse for the great French museums than it is for the great British museums. There are also other respects in which the French look to us rather wistfully, one of them being the amount of private support and private patronage that we have been able to generate in our system.

If we recognise the greatness of the musée d'Orsay and dwell with fascination upon the pyramid at the Louvre —both great achievements—we can also talk enthusiastically of what is about to happen to the National gallery and the arrival of the Tate in Liverpool. We can also talk about the Burrell collection and the Clore gallery. We have many things in this country of which we can be proud and in relation to which the Government have played a full part.

Obviously, I do not accept the point of view of the hon. Member for Stoke-on-Trent, Central (Mr. Fisher) who talked about a cultural balance sheet but then made it clear that he was interested only in public expenditure. Although that is not right, I believe profoundly that the state is a crucial provider of the arts and would not accept for one moment that any other argument makes sense. We have achieved a good balance between public and private provision. That strategy has been developed effectively in recent years and long may it continue.

[*Mr. Timothy Raison*]

One cannot help thinking of the enormous contributions made by people who are not essentially part of the state apparatus. One such person was Robin Howard, who died a day or two ago and who made a unique contribution to British contemporary dance. Those who knew him knew that he was a buccaneer, not a bureaucrat. A system that allows for that while also providing a national theatre of the present quality is well founded.

In the last couple of years, we in London have been privileged to see more great paintings than I imagine have ever been open to view in our history. We have had a succession of marvellous exhibitions, covering many different types of works of art. Often they have appeared in places such as the National gallery or the Hayward, to which I pay tribute, but such exhibitions have also been sponsored by our large industrial companies.

Such partnerships seem to work also for the good of those people who are lucky enough to be able to see the things that we can see in London. My right hon. Friend the Minister rightly emphasised what is happening in other parts of the country. Indeed, that was an important element in the Art Council's famous policy document of a year or two ago.

The wonderful developments in touring opera in this country have already been mentioned. The hon. Member for Stoke-on-Trent, Central talked about the difficulties encountered by Kent Opera. Today, as throughout the past, a feature of supporting the arts is that one encounters ups and downs. We shall never have—I certainly hope that we do not—a position in which one can simply collect a cheque from the powers that be without anybody discussing it.

Against that, we have an array of astonishingly good opera companies. I have been lucky enough to see two of them in the past few days. One was Opera 80 which did an absolutely magnificent production of "Figaro" and the other was Pavilion Opera, which has just had a coup in performing in Versailles and, unusually, with an orchestra rather than with the gifted pianist who normally accompanies the company. I gather that all Paris thought that that was the cat's whiskers, or whatever the French equivalent may be. That shows the strength and diversity of what we can see in this country at present.

At the local level I am engaged in an exercise to upgrade Buckinghamshire's county museum. The local county council is taking a sympathetic view. Again, good things are happening in other parts of the country as well as in the capital.

The Government's funding policy is not directed at supporting only the classical and traditional arts. It is genuinely designed to allow the avant garde to flourish, even if occasionally that may cause some slight embarrassment to Ministers. Indeed, such occurrences are very good for Ministers. We are in a strong position.

The Arts Council very much appreciates its three-year funding, although there is a problem with inflation. We all know perfectly well that inflation is now running at a higher rate than any of us would have wished. When the Select Committee of which I am Chairman looked at that matter, we decided that the possibility of inflation was a price worth paying for the certainty, security and ability to plan. We felt that the benefits of the three-year funding scheme outweighed the risks of inflation. However, we also stated that if things got out of hand we hoped that the scheme could be reconsidered. My right hon. Friend is absolutely right to have a three-year funding policy and to stick to it.

As another sign of the Government's support for the arts, I must add that as a vice-chairman of the British Council I am delighted that this year the council is receiving an extra £6 million of new money. That is welcome in our work to present the excellence of British arts in other parts of the world. The picture is encouraging in many ways.

I should like to draw the attention of the Labour party to what happened with the abolition of the Greater London council and of the metropolitan county councils. Those who sat through the prolonged debates and listened to the saga of grief, horror and angst that was portrayed by the opponents of our provisions, who said that we would be destroying the arts in London and in the other great metropolitan areas, must now face the fact that the record shows that, far from arts funding declining following abolition, it has increased. That is clearly the view of the Arts Council and can be seen from the statistics given in evidence to the Select Committee. I confess that over time it will become harder to tell what the real picture is because those statistics cannot be used for ever. However, it is clear that there has been an increase rather than a decrease in support for the arts.

I am happy to note that the credit for that lies with local government in particular. As one had always believed would happen, the successor local authorities have not said, "We are not interested in the arts and will do nothing about them"; with help from central Government they have picked up the shortfall that would otherwise have occurred. Again, that supports the premise that the Labour party is too interested in alarmism and is not sufficiently willing to look at the facts.

The right hon. Member for Blaenau Gwent referred to the importance of broadcasting to the life of the arts. We know perfectly well that the BBC is a major and fundamental provider of the arts in this country. Although like any institution it has its ups and downs, nevertheless we accept that it has generally been devoted to quality. Important reassurances have recently been given by the Government that the crucial instruments will remain as they are. We have now had the announcement about the future of Channel 4, which seems a fairly good safeguard to ensure the quality of that important station. It is clear that the review of broadcasting will not leave the BBC as a whole in a weakened position. There is every reason to believe that Channel 2 will continue to be a major provider of the arts. We must watch carefully to see what happens in relation to radio. However, I believe that the Government's decisions on broadcasting will ensure that our heritage in broadcasting presentation of the arts will be preserved.

My right hon. Friend the Minister for the Arts rightly paid tribute to the way in which the Secretary of State for Education and Science has brought forward the national curriculum. I am sure that all hon. Members welcome the fact that art and music are clearly specified as being among the guaranteed subjects in the national curriculum. However, I accept that there is a problem with music because the shortage of music teachers looks like being serious. The Select Committee on Education, Science and Arts is considering the issue of supply teachers in the 1990s at the moment and I hope that we shall be able to make some constructive and useful comments. If my right hon. Friend the Minister for the Arts knows of any ways in which he can support my right hon. Friend the Secretary of State for Education and Science in this matter, I hope that he will do so. It is absolutely right to spread music through the curriculum and I hope and believe that we can make a success of that.

What we are seeing today in the arts is a richness previously unparalleled in this country. Last summer I visited Siena. In the cathedral museum I read an account of how, when Duccio had finished painting the Maesta, that supreme work of art, it was carried in triumph through the streets of Siena and the whole town had three days' holiday. That is the desirable ultimate objective that I hope that my right hon. Friend will be able to achieve. In the meanwhile, and even if it takes a year or two to bring about, I congratulate my right hon. Friend on what he is doing and wish him all power to his elbow.

5.59 pm

Mr. Simon Hughes (Southwark and Bermondsey): The theme of what I want—briefly—to say concerns tension between culture and commerce, which has been exercising my mind for some weeks.

I do not think that anyone would have put much money on the likelihood of the Rose theatre being the subject of an Adjournment debate and two statements in the House within a couple of months, nor was it predictable that our cultural heritage would be the lead item on the national news for several days. Thankfully, however, that has happened—at the same time, interestingly, as the struggle not hundreds of miles away to find a way of preserving the Mappa Mundi for the people of Hereford. I have an interest in that issue too, because my family comes from the area and I occasionally slip back to involve myself in that struggle as a change from concentrating exclusively on matters on the south side of the Thames.

The bit of north Southwark which has been in the news recently is, of course, an enormously important part of our national cultural heritage. Not only is it the origin of the pilgrims' journey in "The Canterbury Tales" and the place where Shakespearean England had its most glorious flowering, but it later became the centre of Dickens' world and has been home to many other important authors and artists.

It is interesting to reflect that the current issue of whether the Rose theatre should be scheduled, and how it should be preserved, began with the archaeologists. Academics and authors had predicted that the Rose theatre might be found—as well as the Hope, Swan and Globe—but it took the archaeologists to produce the goods. Archaeology in Britain is considerably under-funded, including rescue archaeology, which should be a preliminary to all development. Of course all that is found cannot always be preserved in this capital city or anywhere else, but we need the mechanism to discover what is there and then to evaluate its importance, which requires well-funded archaeological services. My plea is for better funding in the future.

We have come a long way. Without the Greater London archaeology service we probably would not have found the remains of the Rose. Thirty years ago, in the 1950s, when a previous office block was built in Park street, archaeological investigation did not happen and the Rose was not discovered. The progress that has been made

should encourage us, and it should also encourage the Government. The warm response elicited by the excavation and by many others recently should lead the Government to believe that funding such activities more generously from the public purse would be a good investment.

In paragraph 139 of its report on historic buildings and ancient monuments, which is one of the documents informing our debate, the Environment Select Committee recommended that

"the Secretary of State should initiate consultations with local authorities with a view to establishing further AAIs"—

that is, areas of archaeological importance. The report is dated January 1987, and the Government response was published in January 1988. The Government were not convinced then—a year and a half ago—that further designations would be justified. They said that they were undertaking a survey of the five areas already so designated. Significantly, those areas—Canterbury, York, Chester, Exeter and Hereford—are five of our most splendid cities and are of enormous archaeological interest.

I have corresponded with the Parliamentary Under-Secretary of State and her predecessor about this and I plead with the Government not to give up the mechanism provided in the Act, so that areas of archaeological importance can continue to be designated. We have areas of listed buildings and conservation areas; areas above ground are marked out as being of particular significance, and logic dictates that the same should apply to areas that are to be unearthed. I hope that the Department's laborious researches finish soon, and that we shall receive confirmation that other areas can be designated. I include north Southwark in that hope, as I would be expected to.

I wish to deal with one or two issues relating specifically to the Rose. The Rose was, is and will continue to be a classic example of the conflict between the rights of the property owner—in this case Postel, the Post Office pensions board—along with those of the developers, Imry, and the wider interest. It was known that the Rose might be there. A 1971 report had warned that there might be a national and international outcry if, when it was discovered, it was not protected. The developers did not embark on the work in ignorance. We cannot say, "Poor developer—fancy turning up something like that unexpectedly in a car park or basement with no foreknowledge."

As evidenced by the history of the discovery of the Rose, it seems that we are still suffering from a lack of intelligent, strategic planning. Surely the logic of events should be this—first excavate, then decide what can be put on top. As the Under-Secretary of State knows, we are now in a crazy, illogical position. Imry submits its first plans and is given planning permission; the Rose theatre is subsequently discovered, and eventually Imry is persuaded not to go ahead. Ministers and English Heritage are very influential. Imry eventually submits its revised and second plans. Even after that—a week or so ago—Imry knows that some of the areas that it intends to pile are too near the theatre, and it still does not take account of the parts that we have not yet had a chance to see.

Only this week a statement was made by the chief archaeologist of English Heritage, saying that if the archaeological work to be done in the next few weeks finds more of the theatre we shall have to go back to Southwark borough council, which must then go back to the

[*Mr. Simon Hughes*]

developers to ask them to alter their plans again. It is ludicrous to dig and, if something is found, change the plans, and then dig a bit more and perhaps need to change them again.

The reason why there is such a demand for scheduling is that it would give complete protection at law to the site as now excavated, and would give it the status that it clearly deserves. I hope that the Government will change their mind, because I believe that their fear that the cost would be millions or tens of millions of pounds is not justified. There may be some further delay, and that will certainly involve some cost, but I think that a way can be found to meet the cost, and that it will not be enormous. Perhaps the Under-Secretary of State will be able to tell us the rate of any compensation that might be payable.

Nothing in either the Ancient Monuments and Archaeological Areas Act 1979 or the National Heritage Act 1983 suggests that cost—or, indeed, competing commercial pressures—should be a consideration in the decision whether a site should be scheduled as a national monument. Since the ancestor of a previous colleague of mine, Lord Avebury, campaigned in the 19th century for a list of national monuments, the logic has been the same. Monuments of national importance should be scheduled so that the protection that they deserve will follow as a consequence of their appearing in that list.

The other conflict to which I referred at the outset between culture and commerce is that which has been manifesting itself in Hereford between the cathedral authorities wanting money to look after their cathedral and the commercial pressures militating in favour of selling articles of great value so as to acquire those funds.

I listened with interest to the remarks of the Chairman of the Environment Select Committee, the hon. Member for Hornsey and Wood Green (Sir H. Rossi), about the evidence he had received from Ely cathedral. As the Minister will appreciate, many people still regard it as inappropriate for cathedrals to be among those places which one must pay to visit. I share that view, but I hope we shall not hold up the Mappa Mundi story so far as an example of how it is impossible to raise money in the private sector or from voluntary subscription for the protection of our heritage, ecclesiastical or otherwise.

I think that the Hereford cathedral authorities or their advisers—I say this respectfully, as I have said it to them personally—made a mess of it. Had they asked the public to contribute £100, rather than £1,000, they would have got far more in than they did. Had they taken up the offers of substantial gifts that had been made, they would have been well on their way to raising the money that they wanted. There is of course a national responsibility also to look after our ecclesiastical heritage through taxpayers' money, but there is also an opportunity for private sector contribution, which does not override but is consistent with those other aesthetic, religious and cultural requirements.

I hope that the end of this year's struggles between culture and commerce will be that we shall find ways of protecting the arts in a more logical and far-sighted way.

6.12 pm

Mr. Toby Jessel (Twickenham): I refuse to be obsessed by the Rose theatre. My hon. Friend the Member for Dulwich (Mr. Bowden) has made strong and effective representations about it, as no doubt has the hon. Member for Southwark and Bermondsey (Mr. Hughes). A satisfactory scheme was announced this afternoon—[HON. MEMBERS: "No."]—by which what is left of that important relic will be preserved for future generations. It will be shielded by the umbrella of a building, which will protect it from rain, snow, frost and sunshine. Some of those who have been jumping up and down about it have been going over the top, and I believe that Shakespeare would have cared more about the live theatre, to which I shall refer later.

In his excellent speech, the Minister referred to the high standards of art in Britain. I wish to draw the attention of the House to the splendid programme of summer concerts at the Royal Military School of Music, Kneller Hall, where standards remain as high as ever. British Army bands remain one of our finest traditions. They lift the spirits of the nation. Who does not feel uplifted by the sound and sight of a British Army band? They enhance morale, promote recruitment and, from an artistic point of view, provide a first-class training in the playing of musical instruments and, from an economic point of view, military bands help to attract to our shores visitors whose spending generates employment and income. That point applies to all of the arts and heritage; hence its relevance. Visitors to Britain spend not only on the arts and heritage. They also spend on shopping, hotels, restaurants and internal transport. They thereby create jobs and increase incomes. All that provides a tax yield to the Government.

It is for the arts and heritage that the visitors come. They come to our theatres, operas, ballet, concerts, museums, art galleries, art auctions, historic houses, cathedrals, abbeys, churches and to visit our countryside. They come for our history and traditions and in particular they come because of our royal family. They come to see our processions and parades and our Army bands.

They certainly do not come to Britain for the weather and, if the hon. Member for Liverpool, Walton (Mr. Heffer) were still in his place, I would have said that they certainly do not come to see our footballers. They come for our arts and heritage and they bring substantial economic benefit to our country, a point which my hon. Friend the Member for Hayes and Harlington (Mr. Dicks) should address if he is fortunate enough to be called to take part in the debate, for he has not previously done so.

Not that economic benefit is the only reason to support the arts, because of course there are many reasons. The arts are a tremendous asset to the nation. We should build on our strengths, and that is what the Minister has done. He is doing a superb job, and the arts in Britain are flourishing as never before. Consider, for example, the London theatre. It is well patronised. It is going like a bomb. For the best plays, it is often difficult to get seats. In Britain as a whole, more people go to the theatre every week than go to football matches. The number going to the theatre is increasing steadily. But I want to raise some specific matters. One is ticket touts. Ticket touting is an unpleasant and greedy trade. It gives a bad impression to foreign visitors and I urge the Government to consider action to deal with it.

The Dominion theatre is an important theatre with 2,000 seats. It could be threatened by a planning application for development on the site. Its loss would be serious, both from an entertainment and planning point of view. I shall be writing to the Under-Secretary who will be responding to this debate, since she deals with planning matters. I realise that she will be unable to give any undertaking at this stage, but I trust that she will consider my points carefully when I have put them in writing to her.

Mr. Bowis: I agree with my hon. Friend about the importance of the Dominion theatre in the London scene. At present, the theatre is the home of the London Festival Ballet, the English national ballet, and it and the English National Opera have another crucial problem to face— that of funding, with the change of local government finance affecting Westminster council.

My hon. Friend will be aware of the sensible arrangement that existed between the Department of the Environment and Westminster council on the abolition of the GLC, so that funding could be arranged by and continued through that council. That is no longer possible. I hope that my hon. Friend will ask the Under-Secretary to give an assurance that she will make sure that appropriate funding is carried on so that those two excellent companies can plan ahead with some confidence.

Mr. Jessel: My hon. Friend is right, and I hope that the Under-Secretary will confirm, when she replies to the debate, that she has taken note of that important point, that she will consult the Minister for the Arts and the Minister for Local Government and will try to obtain a solution to a problem which has arisen through no fault of the English National Opera and of the Dominion theatre, both of which are great assets to London and the nation. As for the National theatre, as other hon. Members want to speak, may I express the hope that the Government will continue to look sympathetically at the points raised in his Adjournment last month by my hon. Friend the Member for Eddisbury (Mr. Goodlad).

We enjoy a vast range of concerts in London. Attendances at them are increasing steadily. The hon. Member for Stoke-on-Trent, Central (Mr. Fisher) said that more subsidy was available in Paris. That may be so, but there are fewer concerts in Paris. What on earth is the point of having more subsidy and fewer concerts? I hope that the Government will give a fair wind to the excellent proposals of the South Bank board to develop the facilities available there.

With the Secretary of State, the Under-Secretary is responsible for royal parks, such as Bushy park, which is next to Hampton Court in my constituency, where there is a magnificent avenue of chestnut trees. Those trees are greatly cherished by my constituents in Teddington, Hampton, Hampton Wick and Hampton Hill. They are greatly loved and admired. Most of them are sound, although a few were damaged in the 1987 hurricane, and a few others are diseased.

There has been a rumour that there might be a clean sweep, with a large replanting and a new start made. The Under-Secretary was kind enought to see me last month, when I put to her the strong views of my constituents that, except for stunted and badly diseased or badly damaged trees, the whole of the avenue should be retained. I ask her again to note the strong feeling that exists about the matter and I urge her to spare this beautiful avenue of magnificent chestnut trees.

6.19 pm

Mr. Frank Haynes (Ashfield): I shall be brief. I am the last Opposition speaker except for my hon. Friend the Member for Stoke-on-Trent, Central (Mr. Fisher) who is on the Opposition Front Bench, and I shall give Conservative Members an opportunity to take part in the debate. If they keep their speeches brief, they will all get in because the winding-up speeches are to start at 20 minutes to 7.

I congratulate my hon. Friend the Member for Stoke-on-Trent, Central on his contribution. I know of his genuine interest in the arts and in our heritage. I also appreciate the interest of the Minister for the Arts, and he knows that I am interested because I am always here when I can be for arts and heritage debates and regularly ask questions. However, I am never satisfied with the right hon. Gentleman's answers about the arts. I also compliment the right hon. Gentleman's parliamentary private secretary, the Member for Richmond and Barnes (Mr. Hanley), who also has a particular interest. We have one massive interest between us in the arts, and that is in the cinema industry. There is much marvellous acting in the cinema and I and the hon. Gentleman frequently talk about it. Of course, I recognise his family connections in the industry and when I meet him I always ask him how his beautiful mother is getting on.

Although the Minister wants to do much, he is pinned down by public expenditure restrictions. The hon. Member for Hayes and Harlington (Mr. Dicks) is always criticising local authorities about their expenditure. He does not realise that local authorities have to spend the money because of Government cuts. My hon. Friend the Member for Stoke-on-Trent, Central made that clear in the debate.

We in the beautiful county of Nottinghamshire have a real interest in the arts and in our heritage. It has some beautiful buildings and many people are interested in their preservation and in the activities that go on in the county. Nottinghamshire county council does a first-class finance job and Nottingham city council also contributes. When the beautiful theatre was built in Nottingham the Tories on the city council criticised it. Now they all make good use of it. The Tories in Nottingham always criticise Labour policies, but they make good use of the facilities that are provided.

Everything in the birthplace of D. H. Lawrence in my constituency has been preserved. It is beautiful and people come from all over the world to see it. The local authority is responsible for the upkeep because the Government do not want to know about such expenditure. However, they encourage people to come from abroad because that puts money into the Treasury. But when we ask for help to provide and preserve the proper facilities, the Government do not want to know. I know that the Minister would like to do much more than he is doing. I appeal to him to keep banging on the Treasury door, to keep getting stuck in. Let us have the money to do the things that need to be done. If the Government continue to cut the money to local authorities, we shall really suffer.

I shall finish by speaking about the Byron society in Nottinghamshire. Newstead abbey is a beautiful building.

[*Mr. Frank Haynes*]

I am a member of the Byron society, as is my right hon. Friend the Member for Blaenau Gwent (Mr. Foot). I had a letter this week from the society's marvellous secretary, Maureen Crisp, appealing to me to buy a society tie. I reminded my right hon. Friend to send his £6·50 for his tie. I have sent for one, and I appeal to hon. Members to send for them as well. That will enable them to contribute to our heritage, and wearing it in this place will show their support for a worthy cause. At the same time they will realise that they are contributing to the preservation of our heritage, as Nottingham city council and Broxtowe borough council are doing.

6.25 pm

Mr. Terry Dicks (Hayes and Harlington): I am the only authentic opposition voice in the Chamber, bearing in mind the middle-class Opposition Members who are present. I have not been to any wonderful artistic place abroad, although I got my feet wet in the Pacific about a fortnight ago.

The subsidy to the arts is approaching £500 million per annum, and the Arts Council grant increased by 10 per cent. last year to £150 million. It will approach £200 million by the end of next year. The subsidy for two people going to the theatre is almost £60, more than we pay to an unemployed man and his wife to keep themselves. They receive £56 but the middle-class couples and the arty types who want to go to the ballet and the opera receive £60 from public sources. That is a disgrace. The inflation rate last year was about 5 per cent., but we increased the arts grant by 10 per cent. We tell pensioners that pensions can only increase in line with inflation, but for so-called arts lovers the subsidy is increased by more than that so that they can indulge in personal pleasure. That is also a disgrace.

Who benefits from the subsidy? It is certainly not the poor. Those who benefit are the effective arts lobby, the professionals who milk the system, Sir Peter Hall, who got not only a knighthood but a small fortune from public sector funds, and the arts lovers who want to enjoy their pleasures—provided the rest of us subsidise them.

Why should there be subsidies? As I said before, it is said that we are subsidising our heritage. Is a fat Italian singing in his own language supposed to be part of my background? Is the ballet dancer in his female tights and cricket box supposed to be part of my heritage, the heritage of my constituents or of the average person in Britain?

People say that such performances should take place. If they are important enough to be preserved, why do people not want to pay the full price? We are told that the arts are special, but nobody has told me why that is so, or why the commercial theatre is thought to be so ordinary. Commercial entertainment is thought by arts lovers to be ordinary, yet theatres are full. Andrew Lloyd Webber's musicals are packed to the doors. The difference between them and the 96 per cent. of subsidised theatres that the Opposition mentioned is that people are prepared to pay the full commercial price to see Webber's shows, while people who go to the ballet and the opera are subsidised.

Why does football have to meet the cost of crowd control while we provide survival grants for the arts? I keep asking what is the difference between the ordinary man in the street who wants to watch professional football, which to him is an art form, and the man who watches opera and ballet? What is so unusual or special about opera and the ballet? The opera recently survived at Earls Court and it has leading singers for about three of the different positions or whatever they are called. It survived because people going to it were asked to pay a price that was economically related to the cost of production. If that can be done and can enable opera to survive at Earls Court, why can it not be done at the Royal Opera House?

The arts subsidy is unnecessary because professionals earn their living and do not need to be subsidised. Subsidy harms the arts, because the Government want control and the performing bodies become institutionalised. Who needs a national theatre building? Are there not enough empty theatres around? It is bound to fail, because public accountability cannot be satisfied. Subsidy is a distortion because it perpetuates the status quo, while encouraging that which is unappealing and abstruse, and it stifles true creativity. It is politically inept and seen to be financially burdensome. Of course Gresham's law applies, which says that spending on the unnecessary drives out spending on the essential.

It is alienating most of the population and it is unpopular per se. It is expensive. Demand is by definition infinite and there are no agreed measures of value for money. It is misapplied because the target, if any, should be amateurs at local level, and training. I have some sympathy with the need to develop locally but none at all with subsidising at the national level. And of course it is completely incompatible with the generality of Government and Conservative philosophy. Avant garde usually means "'aven't a bean".

Heritage is something that I have not touched on before. When we talk about this issue we get pomposity, to say the least. I am sure that the great and good sitting around me at the moment will say that museums and art galleries are vital to the nation. Of course they are, provided that those who do not enjoy them subsidise those who do. What a good way to talk about essential needs to say that museums, art galleries, historic houses, churches and old theatre sites must be preserved for future generations. Yet, when Hereford cathedral tried to raise money to keep the Mappa Mundi—or Tuesday, or Wednesday, whatever it was—it could not be raised. The Church of England has pounds running out of its ears; why does it not itself fund the repair of churches and cathedrals? That is the question that we should be asking, but none of the great and good here bother to do so.

The Rose theatre is a thorn in the side of the Government—a sweet-smelling pile of bricks and rubble. Heritage addicts claim that the rubble must be preserved —provided the rest of us pay for its preservation. They have all been there on site—this well-known actor, that world-acclaimed actress, Sir Richard this, Sir Michael that, the has-beens, the "never-was's". Even the hon. Member for Newham, North-West (Mr. Banks) was there, a man whose contribution to the arts is about the same as Bluebeard's contribution to the institution of marriage. As I understand it, the only VIP not there was Dr. Who with the Tardis.

I understand—although I am open to correction—that when all the people I have mentioned were at the site, a whip-round was suggested towards keeping the Rose theatre in being. All the millionaires who have made a fortune from the public sector got together and whipped up the miserly sum of £200—a major contribution to the effort to preserve the Rose theatre. Obviously, they did not want to devote too much of their millions to this, but they are quick to turn to the public purse when they think something should be done.

Last year the Government saved £450 million on housing benefit to reduce public expenditure. Then they gave £450 million to the art lovers to increase public expenditure. What nonsense! What a stupid way to spend Government money! The people in this country need many things; what they do not need is the subsidising of the arts.

I wrote to the Financial Secretary to the Treasury asking why it was that the arts were the only area of public activity that had a three-year settlement. I asked why the same did not apply to education, the Health Service or local authorities, for example. I was told that the amount of money was only small and that security must be given to their arts friends over a three-year period. If there is one group in our society that does not need security of income and should not have any financial support at all, it is the arts group. We should be telling them that they must survive on their own income like everybody else and will certainly not get a Government subsidy.

The arts must be self-financing. There is nothing special about them. We must ensure that the Peter Halls of this world can never again make a fortune or get a gong because they have milked the public sector. Museums and art galleries must become cost-effective, and if people do not want to pay the full economic price, they will have to do something else about it. The heritage addicts must fund the full cost of restoration and preservation of such things as the Rose theatre. We cannot continue to fund the pleasures of a few art-loving trendies and other pompous twits who operate in the twilight world of Government subsidy while treating the old and the infirm so dreadfully.

The needs of my constituents reflect such things as housing benefit and increased old-age pensions. If I told them that they must contain their spending in line with inflation but if they want to go to the theatre they will get £60, they would give me a very peculiar look. They want money in their pockets. They are not concerned about the Rose theatre, the arts and ballet. They are concerned with living in a reasonable way, here and now.

6.34 pm

Mr. Patrick Cormack (Staffordshire, South): It is quite an experience to follow Alf Garnett's vicar on earth——

Mr. Dicks: It is better than being a pompous twit.

Mr. Cormack: If ignorance is bliss, my hon. Friend must be an extremely happy man. What his constituents need most of all is a civilised Member of Parliament and perhaps one day they will get one.

On behalf of those of my hon. Friends who, like me, have travelled many hundreds of miles to be here today because of the elections, I think it is most unfortunate that this is such a short debate. There is no reason at all why it should not have been open-ended. We could then have gone on until 8 o'clock or 8.30 and every hon. Member could have had a chance to contribute. Those who arrange these things ought to feel rebuked because they have kept out of the debate a number of hon. Members who have extremely valuable contributions to make.

Mr. Deputy Speaker (Mr. Harold Walker): Order. I remind the hon. Gentleman that I am responsible for the setting down of private business for 7 o'clock. I hope that he is not reproaching me.

Mr. Cormack: I am very sorry, Mr. Deputy Speaker. I thought that the usual channels were responsible and obviously I withdraw any criticism of you. But it would have been possible to resume this debate after a certain time.

We are, I think, debating the arts and heritage jointly for the first time. It underlines a point that many of us have made for a very long time, that these two subjects should be taken together.

We have two admirable Ministers at the moment, my right hon. Friend and my hon. Friend the Under-Secretary, both of whom show that they have their hearts very much in the right place. But I hope that at some stage the Prime Minister or one of her successors will do as the Select Committee recommended in 1981 and create one Ministry which deals with the arts and heritage. With such a Ministry and with two Ministers such as we have today we would be even better served because the voice of the arts and heritage would be heard much more loudly and in higher places. That is no criticism of or reflection on the two Ministers.

We have spoken before about the Victoria and Albert museum. I was able to make a rather longer speech on another occasion on that. I am deeply disturbed that there is still a real crisis of morale in that great national institution. I am still in regular touch with members of the staff and I have seen Lord Armstrong. I impugn no one's integrity or good faith but it really is important that that crisis of confidence to which the right hon. Member for Blaenau Gwent (Mr. Foot) referred—I might say at inordinate length—this afternoon is resolved. I hope that my right hon. Friend the Minister for the Arts is keeping his eye on that.

I talked about the Mappa Mundi and cathedrals before Christmas and my hon. Friend will have a chance to refer to this matter when she replies. It is high time that the Government recognised that there is a responsibility for making a contribution towards the preservation of the fabric of these, our greatest national buildings. The cathedrals of this country constitute our most important single group of great buildings and it is most regrettable that they alone have no direct access to public funds. I am not advocating the French solution, where the fabric becomes the responsibility of the state. I am not suggesting that cathedrals should not make a proper contribution through appeals and other means. If they wish to charge I have no objection as a churchgoer and I believe that the Ely experiment works very well. Nevertheless, there is a real residual responsibility for the maintenance of these great and glorious buildings and it is time the Government faced up to that.

I would like my hon. Friend the Under-Secretary, when she replies, to refer to the very real prolem that has been created because of the judgment of the Court of Referees concerning the Kings Cross Railways Bill. To say that English Heritage, which has been quoted with such approbation by the Secretary of State in the House today, has no standing, no locus, when it comes to appealing in the Kings Cross Railway Bill raises serious questions and it is important that the situation be corrected. I hope that

[*Mr. Cormack*]

the pledges given by my hon. Friend the Minister for Roads and Traffic in a debate not long ago will be quickly fulfilled.

We have already dealt with the Rose theatre, but another matter that is causing concern is the decision made last week by my right hon. Friend the Secretary of State for the Environment that Mr. Palumbo's scheme should go ahead on the basis that the inspector said that it might be a masterpiece. Whether or not it is a masterpiece, it is clear that a number of important listed buildings and a medieval street pattern will be destroyed for ever. I hope, even at this late stage, there will be some further reflection on that.

Time and time again, when people talk about money for the arts and heritage, they say some extreme things. My hon. Friend the Member for Hayes and Harlington (Mr. Dicks) was particularly scathing. Let us remember what the arts and heritage bring to this country. I read an article this morning which said that it has been calculated that the "Gold of the Pharaohs" exhibition in Edinburgh brought in £3·3 million to the city of Edinburgh because of the people who came specifically to see that exhibition. Indirectly, this seven-week exhibition brought in £6·5 million. The arts and heritage bring people in and raise money. They are not a drain on the public purse. Because there happens to be some public responsibility, it does not mean that the Government are being asked to pour money into unproductive effort. Even if one's view is purely economic and even if one is hard-headed to the point of being philistine, one has to recognise that there is a return on investment.

I hope that my hon. Friend the Under-Secretary will reply briefly to the points that I have made and I hope that she and my right hon. Friend the Minister for the Arts will continue, as I know that they have done, indefatigably to hammer on the Treasury door, as the hon. Member for Ashfield (Mr. Haynes) put it so eloquently.

6.43 pm

Mr. Tony Banks (Newham, North-West): I have considerable sympathy with the hon. Member for Staffordshire, South (Mr. Cormack) and those hon. Members who were not able to make a speech. We should stop meeting like this, every five years on a European election day, to discuss arts and heritage. It is the intention of the impending Labour Government to include both arts and heritage in a single Ministry.

I am sorry that the unreconstructed hon. Member for Hayes and Harlington (Mr. Dicks) has left the Chamber. He has probably gone to vandalise a few paintings somewhere. He is to the arts what Vlad the Impaler was to origami. He gives us a laugh, and all he needs is a pig's bladder on a stick to complete his costume.

I shall devote most of my speech to the heritage because this year archaeologists in London have unearthed two priceless gems, the Roman baths complex at Huggin Hill and the Rose theatre. They have also laid bare the appalling lack of protection under existing laws for sites of archaeological influence. The campaigns surrounding Huggin Hill and the Rose have had a partial success in that neither will be totally destroyed, which was the original intention of their respective developers. However, in the case of the Roman baths, access has been lost, as tonnes of

sand have now reburied what one senior archaeologist has described as one of the best preserved and most extensive Roman baths complexes in northern Europe.

I have a few questions to ask the Minister about the Rose theatre, which was mentioned by my right hon. Friend the Member for Blaenau Gwent (Mr. Foot) and the hon. Member for Southwark and Bermondsey (Mr. Hughes). Any Government truly wedded to the positive promotion of arts and the heritage would have scheduled the Rose theatre site under the relevant Act. How can the Government allow a speculative office block, an excrescence, to be built over the Rose theatre site? The adapted plans put forward to date are wholly unacceptable and I have two questions for the Minister. First, why were the museum of London archaeologists moved off site by English Heritage? Is it because English Heritage felt that the museum of London staff would stand too much by their principles and that English Heritage was in a better position to do a cosy deal with Imry Merchant, the developers? Secondly, why are the excavations of the pile sites going ahead before planning permission has been given by Southwark council or before a possible judicial review has been held?

The facts surrounding the Roman site at Huggin Hill present an unbelievable combination of ineptitude, confusion and vacillation. The facts show clearly that within the span of a few months a Roman site nearly 2,000 years old, described in September 1988 as of "national importance" by English Heritage, was, by February 1989, facing total destruction. It is difficult to exonerate English Heritage from a charge of gross incompetence. One can only assume that, since it is a quango headed up by Thatcherist nominees, advice is given on the basis of what it is believed that political masters want, rather than on what archaeology needs.

No other country in Europe would have allowed its archaeological heritage to be treated in such a shameful and purblind fashion as the Government have treated these two important sites. If property developers were interested in anything other than short-term profits, they might realise that heritage can serve mammon and the muse. The political and media campaigns might have secured a partial victory at Huggin Hill and the Rose, but no one can seriously believe that this piecemeal approach to the preservation of archaeological sites is either efficient or acceptable. The next significant site might be uncovered outside of easy walking distance of London and the press offices. What chance then of salvation?

We can and must learn a number of lessons from recent events. English Heritage as it is organised is incapable of properly serving the interests of archaeological preservation. It is too obviously in the pockets of Ministers and there is no serious money in those pockets for archaeology. We need a wholly independent commission, equipped with legislative teeth and a budget, substantially larger than the miserable £7·2 million, allocated for archaeological investigation and recording. Secondly, the 1986 voluntary code of practice between the British Property Federation and the Standing Conference of Archaeological Managers is highly unsatisfactory. The code is an agreement struck between unequals. It places archaeologists in the position of supplicants, relying almost entirely on the good will of property developers—a group not noted for altruism and selflessness.

The Minister for the Arts said that big business gives millions of pounds a year for archaeological restoration and rescue work. Such sums are pocket change in comparison with the profits made by city developers, and small compensation for the destruction being inflicted on archaeological remains in London and elsewhere. A voluntary code is no substitute for statutory regulations backed up by fines and gaol sentences for those who demolish first and try to avoid awkward questions afterwards. I support the call made by the hon. Member for Southwark and Bermondsey and others that any developer wanting to develop in an area of archaeological significance as determined by part II of the Ancient Monuments and Archaeological Areas Act 1979 should be required to carry out at his own expense a full survey before preliminary planning consent is given.

We want to make sure that part II of that Act is immediately extended to the City of London as it has been to the town centres of York, Chester, Hereford, Exeter and Canterbury. It is ironic that the 1979 Act, which was carried through by the Labour Government, started off as a private Member's Bill introduced by the chairman of the Tory party, who is also the Member of Parliament for the constituency in which Huggin Hill Roman baths are located. As far as I am aware, the right hon. Member for City of London and Westminster, South (Mr. Brooke) has not yet found the time to visit the site, nor has he publicly commented on it. One can only assume that the failure to bring the City within part II of the 1979 Act owes much to the cosy relations between Guildhall and the property developers allied to the pusillanimous attitude of English Heritage.

We have to do more for our archaeological heritage. The sign erected over the Rose theatre site reads, "Revealing today's heritage, building tomorrow's". When will it be realised that ugly and short-lived speculative office blocks are no more an acceptable replacement for the past than they are a worthy legacy for the future? The arts and heritage are not safe in the hands of the Government, driven as they are by the do-it-on-the-cheap approach to the arts required by probably the most philistine Prime Minister since the days of Lord Liverpool. It is hardly the mark of a truly civilised society to provide funds galore for defence and then to make the arts rely more and more on the begging bowl and on the good will of big business and the whims of rich men.

We can have no finer role in the world than to become a nation where the artistic skills and creativity of our people are given the maximum encouragement, a nation of craftsmen and craftswomen, painters, writers, poets and sculptors—a Mount Olympus of artistic creativity and excellence. What a prospect. What a vision we can offer the British people. Instead, we are all too often regarded these days as a nation of lager louts with the values of market spivs. I look forward to the vision of a new society, but I know that it will not become a reality until we have a Socialist Government. We shall have a separate Arts Department that will be under the guidance and control of my hon. Friend the Member for Stoke-on-Trent, Central (Mr. Fisher).

6.50 pm

The Parliamentary Under-Secretary of State for the Environment (Mrs. Virginia Bottomley): Hon. Members on both sides of the House have raised a range of important and interesting issues during the debate that has reflected the importance that we all attach to our heritage and the

strength of passion that it can generate. I only feel sad, with others, that so many of my hon. Friends who have been in their places throughout the debate, and who had knowledgeable and detailed contributions to make, have not been able to participate in the debate. To have a debate during which the Chairmen of two Select Committees are able to present their views to the House is, in itself, a mark of distinction.

No arts or heritage debate would be the same without the particularly distinctive contribution of my hon. Friend the Member for Hayes and Harlington (Mr. Dicks). He is good at helping us to keep the subject in perspective.

I shall say little about the contribution of the hon. Member for Stoke-on-Trent, Central (Mr. Fisher). I thought that he was mean-spirited not to recognise the remarkable contribution that has been made by my right hon. Friend the Minister for the Arts, who is universally respected and admired. He has done so much to develop and promote business sponsorship of the arts. His efforts have led to a 39 per cent. increase in real terms in arts funding since 1979. My tributes are as nothing compared with those of my right hon. Friend the Member for Aylesbury (Mr. Raison), who in a particularly lucid contribution made only too clear the standing, quality and diversity of British art and the arts generally.

My hon. Friend the Member for Hornsey and Wood Green (Sir H. Rossi) and I normally debate more toxic subjects than the topic of our debate today. My hon. Friend raised a number of detailed matters that I should like to take the opportunity of writing to him about. English Heritage, our adviser, whose work we greatly trust and value, has made significant strides forward since my right hon. Friend the Secretary of State replied to the report of the Select Committee on the Environment, which is chaired by my hon. Friend. There are further matters, however, that I would appreciate discussing with my hon. Friend.

My hon. Friend the Member for Hornsey and Wood Green referred interestingly to the link between tourism and heritage. I do not take the view that tourism is a form of pollution. My hon. Friend had some important comments to make about the way tourism can be channelled and handled. We have direct responsibility for the royal parks and palaces and we are making strides forward in trying to ensure that the interpretation, handling and management of such magnificent palaces are to the highest standard, especially as we move forward to the establishment of an agency. English Heritage, with its properties in care, is working hard to ensure that the best practices are used and deployed. Its chairman, Lord Montagu of Beaulieu, has made a special contribution in that area of work.

Various hon. Members, including my hon. Friend the Member for Hornsey and Wood Green, the hon. Member for Southwark and Bermondsey (Mr. Hughes) and my hon. Friend the Member for Staffordshire, South (Mr. Cormack), have referred to the funding of cathedrals. The debate on the future of the Mappa Mundi has generated great interest and has caused the issue to be reconsidered. There is no statutory provision preventing English Heritage or the national heritage memorial fund giving grants to cathedrals. It is entirely for them to determine their priorities in the allocation of their funds. If, in future, English Heritage and the Church of England decide that some measure of assistance should be made available to cathedrals and that additional funds from Government are

[*Mrs. Virginia Bottomley*]

necessary for the purpose, we would give full consideration to that view. It has always been the view that grant-in-aid should be left for parish churches because they are less well placed to raise money on their own behalf.

My hon. Friend the Member for Twickenham (Mr. Jessel) made a special reference to the British Army band. If some of us did not realise that it is a vital part of our national heritage, I am sure that coexistence with my hon. Friend in this place has taught us all to mend our ways. My hon. Friend has a special and close interest in Hampton Court and in Bushy park. He and I have had discussions about the magnificent chestnut avenue. I am able to give him an absolute assurance that the trees are being fully examined and that no tree in the avenue will be removed unless it is a clear danger to the public.

My hon. Friend the Member for Battersea (Mr. Bowis) talked about the English National Ballet and international ballet. I give him the assurance that his concern is shared and that discussions are taking place with the London boroughs to determine how best to meet the concern.

I have not strayed into the remarks of the right hon. Member for Blaenau Gwent (Mr. Foot). I think that they were contentious and provocative, save that he spoke at some length about the Victoria and Albert museum. The developments there are making good progress and there is a clear commitment to improving the quality of the museum. My right hon. Friend the Minister for the Arts will be replying in more detail to the points raised by the right hon. Gentleman and my hon. Friend the Member for Staffordshire, South.

Many hon. Members have talked about the developments at the Rose theatre. We have already had a statement about the theatre. The hon. Member for Newham, North-West (Mr. Banks) has spoken about Huggin Hill on many occasions. We believe that a constructive solution has been achieved for the Rose. I wish to pay tribute to all those who have worked so hard to secure its preservation. The developer of the site in which it was discovered, Imry Merchant, has co-operated in the pursuit of a practical and sensible scheme for preserving the remains of the theatre underneath the new building. It will be possible to prepare the site for public display when the construction works are complete. It is outrageous for Opposition Members to seek to denigrate what by any definition is a significant achievement. The developer has committed itself to providing £10 million in resources towards preserving a wonderful site. It is essential when seeking to secure archaeological remains that effective and realistic proposals are brought forward. The hon. Member for Stoke-on-Trent, Central, who seeks frequently to interrupt when this issue is discussed, makes it only too clear that he thinks that the answer to every problem is to write cheques so long as someone else signs them.

The fragile remains of the Rose theatre are not now under threat. The developers propose to preserve them without piling through them. The redesigned scheme allows public access. That is what my right hon. Friend the Secretary of State for the Environment sought when he called for a month's delay on 15 May, and that is what the developers now propose. There were previously about 11 piles that potentially might damage the site, and all of these are to be removed to the outer perimeter of the theatre.

Mr. Fisher: Will the Minister give way?

Mrs. Bottomley: I will not.
Much has been achieved. There has been great interest in scheduling, but, as my right hon. Friend informed the House earlier, we do not propose to take that course at this stage. The detailed reason is set out in the letter to the solicitors for the Rose theatre campaign, a copy of which is in the Library.

There is no suggestion that there is any substance in the allegations made by Opposition Members. This is a good and achievable solution. It means that sites will be preserved and fragile ruins protected. The remains of the Rose theatre are already in a vulnerable state as they have been subjected to the elements. That is why English Heritage has worked so hard to secure their preservation and protection. It is essential now that people work together to look to the way forward. They should not seek constantly for means of conflict and confrontation. Instead, they should look for means of co-operation to find ways to ensure that the site—together with the many other sites which commemorate Shakespeare in the area of the constituency of the hon. Member for Southwark and Bermondsey—is given proper protection.

I hope that the actors who have done so much will not let the curtain fall now. I hope that in years to come they will continue to come back and participate and give us the benefit of their performances as that site in the constituency of the hon. Member for Southwark and Bermondsey becomes what all of us hope it will be, an area in which many of us can commemorate the magnificent Shakespearean legacy which has always been so important to our British heritage.

It being Seven o'clock, the motion for the Adjournment of the House lapsed, without Question put, pursuant to the order [19 June].

NEW SOUTHGATE CEMETERY AND CREMATORIUM LIMITED BILL *(By Order)*

As amended, considered.
To be read the Third time.

ASSOCIATED BRITISH PORTS (HULL) BILL *(By Order)*

Order for Third Reading read.—[Queen's Consent, on behalf of the Crown, signified.]
Bill read the Third time, and passed.

Tees (Newport) Bridge Bill *[Lords] (By Order)*

Order for Third Reading read.

7 pm

Mr. Frank Cook (Stockton, North): I beg to move, That the Bill be now read the Third time.

The Bill is promoted by Cleveland county council, of which my constituency forms part. Its purpose is to remove the statutory obligation on that council to provide for the Tees-Newport bridge to be raised whenever a vessel wishes to pass beneath it.

The bridge was opened in 1934 and has a central roadway span which can be lifted vertically by approximately 100 ft in the space of two minutes or less. The machinery and other equipment required to facilitate the raising of the bridge is very expensive to maintain and given the fact that the bridge has not had to be raised for a commercial vessel since 1984, and is unlikely to be raised again, the financial burden imposed on the county council is considerable and can no longer by justified. If the statutory obligation to raise the bridge can be repealed, the council estimates that it will save approximately £1 million over the next 10 years.

I assure the House that, even with the bridge in its lowered position, there is approximately 6 m clearance for vessels at high water. That compares with a clearance of 5 m for the Victoria bridge up river at Stockton and a minimum clearance of 5·5 m for the proposed new road bridge which would be constructed if and when the River Tees Barrage and Crossing Bill is enacted. I commend this Bill unreservedly to the House.

Bill read the Third time, and passed, without amendment.

Tyne and Wear Passenger Transport Bill (*By Order*)

Order for Third Reading read.

7.3 pm

Mr. Frank Cook (Stockton, North): I beg to move, That the Bill be now read the Third time.

The Bill is promoted by the Tyne and Wear passenger transport executive which operates the Tyne and Wear metro system. I have been asked to move this Third Reading by my hon. Friend the Member for Jarrow (Mr. Dixon) who is the Opposition Deputy Chief Whip and who cannot carry out this important task because of his position. However, he has been most helpful in ensuring that the Bill has reached this stage.

The Bill will extend the metro system from the present terminus of the Bankfoot branch to the Newcastle international airport. As well as serving the airport, the extension will provide park and ride facilities with a bus interchange which will increase the use of the metro system and reduce traffic congestion in Newcastle.

Since its opening a decade ago, the metro system has been most successful in meeting the transport requirements of the area and has contributed to the revitalisation of the local economy. This metro extension is essential to local and regional communications in the north-east and will provide the missing link between our air bridge to Europe and other parts of the United Kingdom and overseas, and a modern urban rail network serving the area directly and via connections at Newcastle Central station with British Rail's local and InterCity networks. The creation of the single European market and the opening of the Channel tunnel both emphasise the need for the highest possible quality of transport for our region.

As vice-chairman of the northern group of Labour Members, it gives me considerable pride to move this Third Reading, which I commend to the House.

Bill read the Third time, and passed.

Isle of Wight Bill (*By Order*)

Order for Third Reading read.
Bill read the Third time, and passed.

PETITION

Football Spectators Bill

7.4 pm

Mr. Jim Lester (Broxtowe): I beg to ask leave to present a petition to the House on behalf of my constituents and Nottingham Forest football club and the Nottingham Forest football club's supporters' association. There are 8,500 signatures on the petition which begs the Government to think again about the Football Spectators Bill and the requirement to carry identity cards to gain entry to football matches.

My supporters who have signed the petition believe that the identity cards Bill is complicated, costly and bureaucratic. They therefore pray that this House will think very carefully before proceeding with the Third Reading of that Bill in the House of Lords.

To lie upon the Table.

Dangerous Dogs

Motion made, and Question proposed, That this House do now adjourn.—*[Mr. Fallon.]*

7.5 pm

Mr. John McAllion (Dundee, East): I am very grateful for the opportunity to raise this matter in a debate on the Adjournment of the House. I stress at the outset that I do not mean this debate to be a re-run of last night's debate. This debate will focus on a problem which was not at the centre of last night's debate—the threat that dangerous dogs and dangerous breeds of dog pose to human safety in this country today.

I readily acknowledge that we are dealing with what can only be a relatively small section of the dog population. The vast majority of dogs are properly looked after and present no real problems, but that in no way diminishes the importance of this subject. Many people, including children, have been seriously savaged and mauled—some have even been killed—by dogs of dangerous breeds. The House must do whatever is practical, reasonable and responsible to try to reduce the danger of such attacks to an absolute minimum.

We must first try to understand the nature of the problem. I do not believe that Ministers have yet been able to do that. We must consider the problem of guard dogs, which are now being kept as domestic pets. The Minister wrote to me recently estimating that there are as many as 500,000 such dogs in homes across the country. Under the Guard Dogs Act 1975, any guard dog used to protect premises must be under the control of a trained handler at all times or it should be tied up. Any failure to comply with that requirement is an offence which is punishable in law, but no such requirement applies to the 500,000 guard dogs being kept as domestic pets.

I wrote to the Library research department asking for the legal position in respect of dogs kept as domestic pets in Scotland. I received a long answer, which was summed up as follows:

"In plain language, what this all means is that dogs are classified as domesticated animals and are therefore not regarded as being inherently dangerous. In normal circumstances, the owner or keeper is expected . . . to ensure that the dog is kept under proper control, but no more than that. It is only if the dog is known to be dangerous either to people or to other animals that the owner is strictly liable to keep it under control at all times."

I assume that that means that the owner is strictly liable in the same way that owners of guard dogs are strictly liable under the Guard Dogs Act 1975.

I do not believe that that is right. It cannot be right that guard dogs such as rottweilers, pit bull terriers or bull mastiffs should be regarded as so dangerous as to require strict control at all times, but are then considered to be so innocuous at home as to require only the same kind of reasonable care as is necessary for a poodle or a pekinese. In that respect, the law is completely inconsistent and indefensible. The law must be tightened up to take account of the inherently dangerous nature of a number of the new guard dog breeds that increasingly are being brought into this country and kept as pets.

I am not alone in being concerned about the danger posed to human safety by certain breeds of dog rather than by individual dogs that the courts have defined as dangerous because of incidents in which they were involved. The *Daily Record,* Scotland's national newspaper, has been running a very effective campaign calling for tighter control of some of the new breeds of dogs. In a special edition on 1 June the *Daily Record* said:

"Today, we list five breeds—named by RSPCA experts —which are potential killers. Danger is deliberately bred into them. And people buy them precisely because they are ferocious, naturally aggressive and frightening—to others."

The dogs to which the *Daily Record* referred were rottweilers, American pit bull terriers, doberman pinschers, German shepherd dogs and Neapolitan mastiffs. It is not just a question of a campaign in a paper such as the *Daily Record* drawing our attention to particular breeds of dogs that it believes to be inherently dangerous and that the RSPCA's own experts believe to be inherently dangerous.

The publication *Dog World*—which is very pro-dog— commented on the incident that led to the death of my own constituent, 11-year-old Kellie Lynch. On 21 April it wrote:

"there are a number of general points which have to be made. Firstly, young children, however mature and apparently responsible, should never be left alone with any breed other than the most docile, and especially not with the big guarding breeds. Ninety-nine per cent. of the time there will be no problem, but the consequence of an unforeseeable accident are so appalling that the risk, however well trained the dog is, is not worth taking."

The article then went on to deal with children being allowed to take dogs for walks. It said:

"Again, the dogs themselves may appear well-tempered, but it needs only for them to be distracted by, for example, another dog running free, then things can go terribly wrong . . . And it is asking for trouble to take out two dogs at a time . . . The dogs may not be intentionally violent; it only needs the child to trip and fall over for the dog's attitude to it to change immediately."

That description—by people whom, I assume, know what they are talking about and who know what are the characteristics of big guard dogs—is quite chilling. I regard such phrases as

"the consequences of unforeseeable accidents are so appalling"

and

"it needs only for them to be distracted . . . then things can go terribly wrong"

and

"it only needs the child to trip and fall over for the dog's attitude to it to change immediately"

as making an unassailable case for the Government to take steps to restrict the ownership of potentially lethal dogs of that kind. However, Ministers have made it absolutely clear that they are prepared to allow a completely free and unrestricted market in the ownership of dogs which have an awesome potential for creating havoc and injury among the population at large.

It is not just the rottweiler breed, which has received so much attention recently, that is a problem. There is the new phenomenon of the American pit bull terrier. That breed of dog is now beginning to appear in this country. According to one television report earlier this week, American pit bull terriers have killed 16 people in the United States of America in just two and a half years. Is that the kind of tragedy that the Minister wants to be repeated in this country, or does he intend to do something about it?

In the same edition of the *Daily Record* on 1 June Mr. Martin Sinnatt, the secretary of the Kennel Club, which is no opponent of dogs in general, issued the following chilling warning to anyone thinking about owning a rottweiler. He said:

"It's like buying a gun without realising that it might go off one day."

He referred then to the American pit bull terrier, and said that the Kennel Club is now

"advising members not to deal with or own them. There is encouragement of the fighting characteristics of this dog by some people. In view of this, we have ruled that no recognition should be accorded to it under any circumstances and that activities involving such dogs should be actively discouraged."

We have to assume that the Kennel Club knows what it is talking about. When it advises its members to have nothing to do with the American pit bull terrier, it really is beyond me that the Government have consistently refused to try to bring the growth in the ownership of American pit bull terriers under control.

When I first raised this matter in the period immediately following the incident in which young Kellie Lynch was killed, the Leader of the House told me that

"there has long been legislation to control dangerous dogs, and remedies are available once it is clear that a particular dog is dangerous."

He was referring to dogs that have been proven by the courts to be dangerous—dogs that have already attacked human beings and savaged or possibly killed them. When dogs have attacked human beings, the law can get tough. The Leader of the House then said:

"We are therefore not contemplating legislation to control a particular breed or type of dog. However, I shall refer the matter to my right hon. Friend."

By "right hon. Friend" the Leader of the House meant the Home Secretary.

The matter was referred to the Home Secretary, who considered the position in the light of what had happened in Dunoon to my constituent. His answer was published yesterday in the form of a written answer. He simply confirmed the position that had been taken by the Leader of the House on 18 April. Having considered the problem for some time, the Home Secretary agreed with the Leader of the House that the penalties for individual dogs which have been proven to be dangerous would be toughened up. By that time it is too late to get tough with the dog. By then it has already created mayhem and attacked people. The Home Secretary went on to say that no action would be taken to control the ownership or the handling of increasingly fierce breeds of dogs which are now becoming more and more fashionable.

It is not good enough for the Minister to say that this is not a new problem. Of course it is not a new problem. It can be traced back to alsatians, the German shepherd dogs first introduced into this country in the aftermath of the first world war. There are fashions in dogs as there are fashions in everything else that people own. At one time it was alsatians. They have now gone out of fashion. For a while, the alsatian was overtaken by the doberman pinscher, but that breed has now become unfashionable and has given way to the rottweiler. The rottweiler will eventually become unfashionable and give way to another breed of dog—the American pit bull terrier. And who knows what the next might be? There have already been advertisements in this country for animals described as wolf hybrids—they are 75 per cent. wolf—which can be openly bought on the market without any restriction. In America people are free to own pure wolves. Is that the direction in which the Minister suggests that we should go?

Should we allow a completely unrestricted market to develop? Should we allow the unrestricted ownership of any kind of lethal and potentially dangerous animal? I hope that that is not the position. Something will have to be done. The Government's response so far has not been good enough. A growing body of informed opinion is calling for the Government to introduce checks and controls over a problem that is now fast accelerating out of control.

The League for the Introduction of Canine Control publishes newsletters. In newsletter No. 27 it referred to a programme on BBC Radio 4—"Face the Facts"—on 23 February. It said:

"the growth of one-man backstreet breeder trainers and thriving businesses selling large guard dogs; these 'security dogs' or 'attacker dogs' sell at £1,000 or more to anyone who can pay. One firm offers already trained Dobermanns, German Shepherds, 15 stone Rottweilers and also Pit-Bull terriers which are bred to bring down even a horse and 'not to give up till it's dead.' The danger of ordinary people owning such dogs is obvious and as Police Inspector Alan Clarke of Keston, said, 'a trained dog is as dangerous as a loaded gun'."

We should compare what was said in that BBC Radio 4 programme about individuals in back streets selling dogs of that kind, which present a lethal threat to other people in society, at high prices with what the Leader of the House said about the sale of such dogs. He said that the breeding of dogs for commercial sale is already controlled by legislation, but that legislation does not necessarily apply to back street sales. He added:

"We do not think it sensible to try to extend these controls to private individuals who wish to sell the offspring of pets."
—[*Official Report,* 18 April 1989; Vol. 151, c. 182.]

Is the Minister saying that it is not sensible to bring under control the kind of situation reported in "Face the Facts" and that he sanctions any individual selling American pit bull terriers regardless of the consequences? If so, that is totally unreasonable, and it is time that the Government took action.

It is not just the occasional radio programme, RSPCA inspector's report, or *Daily Record* survey that adds to the chorus of demand for Government action. Even people associated with some of the breeds involved, such as rottweilers, are themselves concerned. In a recent article in *Dog World,* rottweiler breeder Mary MacPhail stressed the need to socialise and train them, to enable them to fit into society. She commented:

"Breeders must realise that they have a special responsibility to screen rigorously in order to ensure the proper placement of puppies in homes with owners who are able to understand their character and who have the time and inclination to train and exercise them."

The people who know rottweilers best acknowledge that not just anyone can own such dogs but only those who understand the responsibilities involved and who can ensure that their dogs live safely among us.

On the Saturday after my constituent was killed, the *Exchange and Mart* carried 20 advertisements for rottweillers. Only two suggested that ownership involved any special responsibility. The others said, in effect, "If you have the money, come along and we will hand one of these dogs over to you." Nothing done by the Government so far begins to confront the accelerating ownership of potentially dangerous dogs by people who cannot look after them responsibly. It is not good enough for the Government to say that they will act only when dogs get out of control. Steps should be taken before that happens to prevent pain and suffering being inflicted on totally innocent people.

[*Mr. John McAllion*]

Recently, I asked the Home Secretary whether he would establish a review committee to consider what could be done to bring the situation under control. He replied that he considers that there is no need for such a body. Perhaps the Minister will explain tonight why there is no need for a professional body to make recommendations to Parliament in respect of a dramatically changing situation. A host of ideas exists for the Government to explore, but that should not be done behind closed doors, between Ministers and civil servants. Those ideas should also be explored openly by public representatives so that they can be properly tested in the public arena.

One proposal, promoted by the RSPCA, is for a compulsory third party insurance scheme covering all dog owners, involving only a small premium for ordinary dogs and domestic pets of the kind that the majority of people own, but higher premiums in respect of rottweilers, alsatians and doberman pinschers, which might discourage casual ownership of certain breeds. Last night, the Secretary of State for the Environment ruled out a national registration scheme, but demand for one will not go away and eventually the Government will have to concede. Meanwhile, they should consider whether specific breeds ought to be subject to a special licence which only certain people would be allowed to hold. The Home Secretary could also consider whether certain breeds should be muzzled in public. Strict regulations should also apply to breeders to catch back-street sales by people knowing nothing about potentially dangerous dogs to others who know even less. Sales of dogs such as rottweilers should also be restricted to one per owner. If the Home Secretary reads about the history of rottweilers, he will learn that they are pack dogs, so if the leader turns on an individual, the others will follow.

The Home Secretary already imposes a requirement on local authorities to license the owners of kestrels or buzzards. Special permission is required to build an aviary for those breeds and to keep them in built-up areas. Yet, there is no restriction on owning a Neapolitan mastiff or a rottweiler, even though they pose a far greater threat to public safety than kestrels or buzzards.

My constituents Mr. and Mrs. Lynch are so concerned that they are organising a national petition to be presented to the Prime Minister. They wrote to the right hon. Lady asking whether she would receive the petition personally. One appreciates that the Prime Minister cannot accept every petition, but she replied that it could certainly be presented at No. 10. Her letter stated, in relation to the Lynch tragedy, that

"if it were possible to prevent such an incident from ever occurring again simply by changing the law, I would not hesitate."

It may not be possible to prevent a similar incident, but steps can be taken to minimise the risk. It is incumbent on Ministers to encourage an open and comprehensive debate on methods of bringing the situation under control. Dog registration is a difficult subject, but there should be informed discussion and positive action.

7.26 pm

The Parliamentary Under-Secretary of State for the Home Department (Mr. Douglas Hogg): I fully understand the reasons why the hon. Member for Dundee, East (Mr. McAllion) has chosen to raise the subject of dogs tonight.

The whole country was shocked by the attack that two rottweiler dogs made on Kellie Lynch on 14 April. She lived in the hon. Gentleman's constituency, and I ask the hon. Gentleman to take back to her parents the sympathy of the House. I know that my right hon. Friend the Prime Minister has already written to express her sympathy to Kellie's mother and grandmother.

My right hon. Friend asked for a review of legislation relating to dangerous dogs within a very short time of learning of Kellie's death. That review was quickly conducted, and the hon. Gentleman knows that my right hon. Friend the Home Secretary made a statement yesterday as to his conclusions, to which I shall refer shortly.

First, I shall respond to the hon. Gentleman's points concerning the Guard Dogs Act 1975, because he may be under a slight misapprehension as to that statute's nature and purpose. That Act is primarily aimed at the use of guard dogs on commercial premises. It specifically excludes farms and domestic dwellings and is framed in terms of the function of the dog rather than, for example, the breed of the dog.

The Act is concerned solely with working dogs that are carrying out the functions of a "guard dog": that is, a dog being used to protect premises, property or, in very narrowly defined circumstances, a person. The Act ensures that those dogs are securely held. It does not control dogs while they are being kept as family pets.

Mr. McAllion: I am grateful to the Minister for trying to explain the difference. Does he accept that there is an increasing fashion, particularly in inner cities such as London and peripheral estates in Scotland where people fear burglary and attack because of the lack of law and order, for keeping dogs specifically to guard their houses and themselves? In those circumstances, would the Guard Dogs Act apply to those dogs?

Mr. Hogg: It is a matter of interpretation. It might be of assistance to the House if I were to go through the Act at some length. That would enable the hon. Gentleman to form a view.

The primary section of the Guard Dogs Act is section 1. It might be helpful if I refresh the memory of the House as to the terms of that section. Section 1(1) of the Guard Dogs Act 1975 provides:

"A person shall not use or permit the use of a guard dog at any premises unless a person ("the handler") who is capable of controlling the dog is present on the premises and the dog is under the control of the handler at all times while it is being so used except while it is secured so that it is not at liberty to go freely about the premises."

Section 1(2) continues:

"The handler of a guard dog shall keep the dog under his control at all times while it is being used as a guard dog at any premises except—(a) while another handler has control over the dog; or (b) while the dog is secured so that it is not at liberty to go freely about the premises."

Subsection (3) provides:

"A person shall not use or permit the use of a guard dog in any premises unless a notice containing a warning that a guard dog is present is clearly exhibited at each entrance to the premises."

It is important to bear in mind that a guard dog has a narrow definition for the purposes of the Act. That definition is to be found in section 7:

"'Guard dog' means a dog which is being used to protect—
(a) premises; or
(b) property kept on the premises; or
(c) person guarding the premises or such property;".

The hon. Gentleman asked me whether the Guard Dogs Act would apply to a dog which is used to guard domestic premises. That is a matter of interpretation, but my initial response—I do not pretend that I am expressing more than a layman's view—is that it could do. If a person was using a dog for any of the purposes set out in the interpretation section of the Act, it might well be that, notwithstanding the fact that the premises being guarded were domestic rather than commercial, the dog would be a guard dog for the purposes of the Act. Ultimately, that is a matter for the courts. I can only give a not particularly well informed view, but that is my view. It is a matter for the House to reflect upon, and it may be that the Guard Dogs Act 1975 would apply.

Mr. McAllion: I realise that neither the Minister nor myself is a legal expert, but is the Minister seriously suggesting that the 500,000 guard dog types which are being kept as domestic pets should be individually tested through the courts to see whether they come under the auspices of the Guard Dogs Act 1975? That is not a realistic proposition.

Mr. Hogg: The hon. Gentleman does me a considerable injustice. I was not suggesting that the matter should be adjudicated in the instance of every single dog which might or might not be a guard dog. That is not the question. The question is whether any old dog is capable of being a guard dog when being used as a guard dog for the purposes of guarding domestic premises.

The answer to that question, at first blush, is yes. If a dog is being used to guard premises that fall within the scope of the 1975 Act—and that does not appear to be confined to commercial premises, subject to what I have already said regarding the interpretation of section 1(1) —it is possible that the dog is a guard dog. But that is subject to one important proviso, which is that the Act expressly excludes farms and domestic dwellings. That proviso limits the scope and the application of section 1, so I ought to modify the opinion that I have previously expressed.

The Act would not apply to most flats, which are clearly domestic premises. It would depend on the flat and on the circumstances in each case. The Act would not apply to domestic premises, and flats are domestic premises, but it might apply to other premises.

As I have said, the Act is concerned solely with working dogs that are carrying out the functions of a "guard dog": that is, a dog being used to protect premises, property or, in very narrowly defined circumstances, a person. The Act ensures that those dogs are securely held. It does not control dogs while they are being kept as family pets.

Pausing to make a point which must be self-evident, any dog is capable of being a guard dog. I suppose a pekinese is capable of being a guard dog. I had an extremely attractive Welsh springer spaniel, not the kind of dog that one would contemplate as a guard dog, yet he performed most admirably in that role, whereas my rather nice black labrador, which looks formidable, is probably not the kind of dog that one would choose as a guard dog. The definition of a guard dog has nothing to do with the breed but relates to the function that is being performed by the dog at the relevant time.

I foresee many difficulties in following the path which the hon. Gentleman suggests. There is a very great difficulty in defining a guard dog once one has departed from the simple definition used in the Guard Dogs Act, which I have endeavoured to summarise. The Act is not concerned with breeds or type of dog.

Breeds and types of dog have no status in law. The reasons for that are probably self-evident. The evidential problems are great, and cross-breeds are extremely difficult to define and identify. In any case, the evidence of the last few weeks and the tragic attacks which have occurred suggest that dogs of a whole variety of breeds can be dangerous.

We have seen attacks by rottweilers, dobermans and alsatians. We must bear in mind that many alsatians are used as guide dogs. However, I must come back to the fact that spaniels, of which I am particularly fond, are sometimes rather vicious animals. I had a pleasant Welsh springer spaniel of which I was very fond. However, that does not alter the fact that, from time to time, he could be extremely vicious. I am ashamed to say that on one occasion he caught a postman. Worst of all are the Jacks —Jack Russells. My father has had many Jack Russells and they have all been nasty. One Jack Russell—I forget its name—bit my mother three times. The last time was its last bite because it was put down. My point is that Jack Russells can be nasty. My daughter had the misfortune to be caught by another Jack Russell and her face was rather badly bitten.

So there are problems with dogs of all kinds. One must not suppose that the problems are confined to the big and obviously dangerous dogs. I had the misfortune to be bitten twice last year by the same dog on the same evening. It was not a rottweiler, a doberman or an alsatian but a bad-tempered old cross-breed which probably had some terrier and some labrador in it. That dog was very disagreeable. It was guarding a garage. It bit me when I got out of the car and when I went to the garage mechanic's back door, it bit me again. Therefore, one cannot define dangerous dogs by any definition known to the law. Indeed, it was difficult to recognise that dog. One could speculate as to its breed, but one could do no more than that. It certainly could not have been defined in law.

We have to face the fact that there have been attacks by terriers, collies and mongrels and that such attacks are very commonplace. We do not know how many occur. I have heard estimates of 250,000 a year—about 700 a day —or even 1 million a year: nobody really knows. Most dogs present no risk at all. I do not think that there is anything to be gained by trying to define dangerous breeds.

Mr. McAllion: The Minister is missing my point. I am not suggesting that we can define comprehensively what constitutes a dangerous dog. Some dogs will always be dangerous. I am suggesting that some breeds, which have become much more common in recent years, present an entirely different degree of threat to human safety. I do not believe that a Jack Russell is capable of bringing down a horse and killing it but an American pit bull terrier is. Is the Minister seriously arguing that the American pit bull terrier is not a qualitatively more dangerous and different type of dog from the dogs we traditionally have in this country?

Mr. Hogg: I shall finish my point about the Guard Dogs Act 1975 and then I shall deal specifically with the points raised by the hon. Gentleman, because they require serious and considered attention.

[*Mr. Hogg*]

There is another problem with the restricted nature of the Guard Dogs Act. It applies only at the premises on which the dog is held and used. A guard dog outside those premises ceases to be a guard dog within the meaning of the Act. It is a guard dog only when it is employed in that capacity. It is for that reason and the others I have outlined that I do not think that the hon. Gentleman's ingenious solution is the right one.

The hon. Gentleman made two suggestions that are capable of sitting together or of being seen as alternative approaches. His first proposition was that certain classes of dog can be identified and prohibited. His second proposition is that one could set up a licensing system whereby some individuals are authorised to possess dogs which are deemed to be dangerous and some are not. Those two separate propositions need attention, and I shall deal with both.

The hon. Gentleman's first proposition, that some dogs can be defined and prohibited, does not run, for a variety of reasons. Who will determine and by what criteria whether dogs are so dangerous that they should be prohibited? One could say that Parliament should do that, but somebody would have to advise Parliament. What does one do about changing dogs? One of the facts of life which people do not like to remember is that all dogs are man-made; they are no longer natural. If we were to pass a prohibition order on, for example, the American pit bull terrier, it would not be long before somebody developed a dog which had all the characteristics of an American pit bull terrier but which was something different. Therefore, we would have to have an extraordinarily precise and quickly responding system for identifying and translating into the prohibited classes dogs which are manufactured —I make no apology for using that word.

There is another problem associated with the policy of prohibition. What does one do about cross-breeds and half breeds? One might take the view that a dog with one American pit bull terrier parent is an American pit bull terrier, but there would be many problems of identification. Would it be defined by temperament or appearance? What would happen if one parent was an American pit bull terrier and the other was a Newfoundland? At what point would the definitional test bite—if I may put it that way? Should a dog that is one quarter American pit bull terrier fall within the prohibited category?

Mr. McAllion: Is the Minister suggesting that, because it is possible to cross-breed the terrier, he is happy to allow into the country dogs with a record of killing 16 people in two and a half years? Is he prepared to tolerate that simply because it might be difficult to define that dog? It would be possible to say that any American pit bull terrier or any dog sired by an American pit bull terrier should be prohibited in this country.

Mr. Hogg: I am against nonsense. I am trying to explain why the hon. Gentleman's proposition is manifest nonsense. It sounds splendid to say that one should prohibit the American pit bull terrier. Standing by itself, that proposition has appeal. However, when one begins to examine it, one sees that it is nonsense. When does an American pit bull terrier cease to be an American pit bull terrier? A dog with one American pit bull terrier parent is partly an American pit bull terrier. However, would it fit that definition for the purposes of the prohibition orders?

Mr. McAllion: It might.

Mr. Hogg: Of course it might, but we have to have a legal system that is capable of identifying and prohibiting an animal and enforcing the law against it.

Mr. McAllion: A national registration system.

Mr. Hogg: That is a different point. I shall deal with registration if the hon. Gentleman wishes me to do so. It might be a good thing if I did.

But just for the moment let us focus on the question of the half American pit bull terrier. Is it an American pit bull terrier for the purposes of a prohibition order? What happens if a parent mated with a particularly docile breed of dog, so that the puppy had no aggressive characteristics? Is it then an American pit bull terrier? What happens if it has but one eighth in it? Is it an American pit bull terrier? The hon. Gentleman must work such points out before he commends the prohibition order to the House.

Mr. McAllion: The Minister must realise that it is not justifiable to sit back and do nothing because it is difficult to do everything. Just because it is difficult to identify cross-breeds does not mean that pure bred American pit bull terriers should not be prohibited. It may not solve the problem entirely, but it would be a significant step towards solving it, and it may save a number of lives in Britain. Is that not worth trying for?

Mr. Hogg: Yes, of course it is worth trying for. As I shall explain to the House, my right hon. Friend the Home Secretary has brought forward a range of proposals which will do quite a lot and upon which I hope the House will legislate in due course. But we must not pass nonsense simply because we have a problem. Problems must be confronted in a sensible and rational way, not in a silly way. I hope that I have persuaded the hon. Gentleman —I rather think that I have—that the idea of simply prohibiting an American pit bull terrier is a non-runner.

Mr. McAllion: The Minister has in no way persuaded me that to prohibit one breed of dog is a non-runner. It may not be possible to prohibit every dog in the country with a strain of that breed in it, but it is possible to prohibit the pure breed itself. I am suggesting that, although it would not solve the problem entirely, it may be of some significance and it may save the occasional life, and for that reason it would be worth trying.

Mr. Hogg: The hon. Gentleman has just explained clearly why such a prohibition would be rubbish. He said it may not be possible to prohibit the cross-breed; it may be possible only to prohibit the pure breed. At that point, no pure breed will be imported, only cross-breeds, which are not caught by the prohibition. Therefore, the hon. Gentleman will have achieved a prohibition which applies only to pure breeds and has no relevance to cross-breeds simply because cross-breeds are not capable of definition in law. That is the problem.

Let me embark upon a consideration of the other interesting argument advanced by the hon. Gentleman:that we should set up some licensing system which would enable somebody—I shall explore who in a moment—to give or to deny specific individuals the right to own certain classes of dog. That is another proposition to which the hon. Gentleman referred obliquely, which, on occasion, has been canvassed publicly by others.

Let us contemplate what is being discussed. First, let us come back to the old question of, which dog? Presumably the licensing system will not apply to all dogs. Or are we to have a licensing system that applies to all dogs, so that a person has to go to somebody before he can buy a pekinese? I do not suppose that the hon. Gentleman is recommending that. Therefore, we start from the proposition that the licensing scheme which the hon. Gentleman is considering applies only to some classes of dogs. What classes? We are back to where we started. What is to be done about cross-breeds, half-breeds and quarter-breeds? The answer is that dogs cannot be defined in such a way that they are capable of identification in statutory terms. If the parentage is altered to some degree, a different animal will be created. Therefore, that approach is clearly unsustainable.

The next question—although one does not need to deal with it because the premise is unsound—is, who will be responsible for the licensing? I sincerely hope that the hon. Gentleman will not tell me that the overworked police force should be responsible for licensing. Goodness knows how many hundreds of thousands of people would apply to possess a variety of dogs—for example, alsatians, dobermans, collies or mongrels. Who will grant the licence? Will it be the police, the local authority, the Royal Society for the Prevention of Cruelty to Animals, or you, Madam Deputy Speaker, in your spare time? Those are the kinds of questions that one must ask oneself before advancing such a policy.

What about the criteria? Let us assume that dogs to which the licensing procedures apply can be defined and that somehow some long-suffering village constable can be prevailed upon to issue licences in his village. What standards is he to apply? Are they to have regard to the comfort of the dog or the comfort of the house where the dog is to live, to the character of the owner or to the purpose of use?

Mr. McAllion: One of the criteria to which they could have regard would be whether the owner was capable of keeping the dog in a safe pen or stockade at night, and if he was not capable of providing such a facility, he would be denied the right to own that dog. The Minister is arguing for completely free and unrestricted ownership of any kind of animal. Is he suggesting that, because a wolf hybrid is a cross-breed, he would encourage people to own them and use them in public in Britain?

Mr. Hogg: The hon. Gentleman has once again demonstrated why the proposition will not run. He has suggested that one criterion—not the only one—should be the ability of the dog's owner, or its prospective owner, to keep the dog in secure circumstances at night. That means that the licensing authority, whoever that might be, will have to go along at night, or some other convenient time, to see the accommodation, to look at the fences and see how secure they are, what the locks are like, where the dog will be, and what will happen when the owners go out for a drink at the pub.

We heard yesterday that there were about 7·5 million dogs.

Mr. McAllion: That was an estimate.

Mr. Hogg: The hon. Gentleman fairly reminds me that it was an estimate. I do not think that the hon. Gentleman wants to extend the licensing system to all 7·5 million dogs, but let us assume that he wants to extend it to, say, half.

Mr. McAllion: The Minister is being offensive in the light manner in which he is dealing with this serious subject. If he had listened to my contribution to begin with, which most of the time he did not, he would have heard me say that RSPCA experts had defined five breeds of dogs which are particularly dangerous and to which such a system could apply.

Mr. Hogg: The RSPCA is not the final arbiter on the matter. If we are to have a licensing authority and a licensing system, it must be just and the House must decide to which dogs it applies. We would probably all agree that it should apply to a rottweiler. We are told that there are between 90,000 and 180,000 of those. We would probably agree that is should apply to dobermans. I suspect that people would probably urge us to apply it to alsatians. If I judge correctly, there are several hundred thousand of those. I am sure that a Staffordshire bull terrier would be caught in the net. I remember that my housemaster at school had a particularly beastly one called a hog dog; it was an extremely fierce animal which certainly could not be excluded from the licensing system. Many other dogs would have to be subject to control if one went down that road.

One cannot say that control would apply to three or four well known breeds, because that would not rub. One must enlarge the category for licensing so that a lot of dogs are caught by it; otherwise, it is not reasonable. Once one has gone down that road, one is faced with an absurdity because one is regulating the possession of certainly hundreds of thousands, probably millions, of creatures. One simply cannot impose on any central authority the burden of that type of licensing role.

You may recall, Madam Deputy Speaker, that last year I had the responsibility of dealing with firearms. That was a serious issue and we had to consider whether it was possible for the local constabulary to carry out proper inquiries into the ownership and safe keeping of, for example, large-magazine self-loading shotguns. Many people told me that we were putting an impossible burden on to the police. I never accepted that, but it was said by many, including Opposition Members. If it was considered impossible to have control over a few tens of thousands of shotguns, surely we are talking about a total impossibility in respect of the many hundreds of thousands, not to say millions, of dogs that fall into the category we are currently discussing.

Mr. McAllion: It would not necessarily be the police who were given this responsibility. Many hon. Members have been trying to press the Government to establish a properly funded registration scheme. That would mean that dog wardens could be employed by local authorities to take on the responsibility for operating the system.

Mr. Hogg: I am perfectly prepared to contemplate that possibility. Last night, the hon. Gentleman commended to us a dog registration scheme, but let us consider what the hon. Gentleman has just said.

What he is proposing as a possibility is that a dog warden employed under the scheme should have the responsibility to determine whether particular individuals

[*Mr. Hogg*]

should or should not have the right to own a particular class of dog. All right, but what kind of person will be employed as a dog warden? To whom is that dog warden to be accountable? Would most people want to have their right to possess a particular animal determined by the kind of person who is likely to be employed as a dog warden? That is a serious question to ask.

We would have to have an appeal system, because, once one decides to refuse someone the right to have a dog, one must set up an appeal system. After all, that is what we do in the case of firearms. You will bear in mind from your intimate knowledge of the firearms system, Madam Deputy Speaker, that, when one is refused a section 1 certificate, or in certain circumstances a shotgun certificate, one has the right to go to the Crown court to appeal. One could not do less in respect of a person who had been refused ownership of a dog. That person would have to have the right to appeal to the Crown court, with all the paraphernalia that that would entail.

Mr. McAllion: I referred to this, but obviously the Minister was not listening. Local authorities already have the right to refuse to let someone keep a kestrel in a built-up area. That person, however, can appeal to the elected members of the authority. There would be no need for anyone to go to the Crown court or anything else. If we had a properly run, effective dog warden scheme at local authority level with funds provided by a proper licensing system, none of this would be a problem.

Mr. Hogg: Come, come. If a person was denied the right by a dog warden to possess a dog, that could hardly be the final decision. One could hardly allow a dog warden, whoever that person may be, to have the final say-so as to whether another individual should possess a dog.

Mr. McAllion: The Minister has totally missed the point. This House would lay down the guidelines that dog wardens would be asked to apply locally. The House would set down the criteria that would have to be met before someone could own a dog. It would not be the decision of the dog warden, but the decision of the House, after a proper informed debate, as to what criteria could be applied. I plead with the Minister to get this matter sorted out in the open rather than in an obscure Adjournment debate when no one is here.

Mr. Hogg: A most bizarre proposition is coming from the Labour party. It is suggested that we should lay down a code of practice, or at least guidance, for the instruction of a dog warden, who would then be able to interpret that guidance or code of practice as he thought fit, without being subject to any external intervention. That is a form of tyranny.

Mr. McAllion: No, it is not.

Mr. Hogg: Of course it is. If one allows some official —I regret to say that he is unlikely to be highly paid or particularly well qualified—to interpret a range of rules without a right to appeal, one has set up a tyranny.

Mr. McAllion: That is absolute nonsense. The Minister is blethering a load of rubbish. The Minister knows that local authorities undertake a series of activities, and if individuals feel that they have been in any way tyrannised by any local authority official, they can appeal to the

ombudsman system for justice. That prevents such tyranny, and the same could apply in relation to dogs. There is no question of tyranny.

Mr. Hogg: We are now getting rather close to the true voice of Socialism. In this connection, some official, probably not a senior official, should have the right, without any appeal or redress, to tell ordinary people that they can or cannot possess a dog. If one does it in respect of dogs, why not do it in respect of everything else? One could decide that certain people should not have a car or that someone should not have a firearm because Mr. Bloggins down at the county council thinks they should not. Once one starts to look at that proposition slowly and carefully, one sees that it is rubbish. The proposition that the hon. Gentleman must grasp is that if one gives to a dog warden the ability to refuse or grant a licence, that must be the subject of some appeal mechanism.

Mr. McAllion: Various mechanisms could be applied short of going to the highest court in the land to sustain an appeal. The Minister is talking nonsense. Yesterday, the Home Secretary said that he would take the power to ban certain individuals from having the right to own a dog. The same applies to people's right to own a car if people have shown that they are not capable of accepting the responsibility of that ownership. The Minister is defending the right of individuals to own whatever animal they want, but what about the rights of parents? Surely they have the right to know that their children are safe when they play in the parks. Does the Minister want to give them certain rights—for example, the right to life?

Mr. Hogg: Of course, and I shall tell the House of the propositions that the Home Secretary has in mind. First, however, we must dispose of the nonsense that we have heard tonight. Incidentally, I do not want to rub it in, but the Crown court is not the highest court in the land. It is the court that is frequently used for the purpose of appeals in circumstances such as this. That is why I selected it. It is the court, for example, that deals with appeals in the case of firearms, with which there is an analogy. Under section 1 of the Firearms Act 1968, as amended by the Firearms (Amendment) Act 1988, a person must establish a good reason to possess a rifle or pistol. If the certificate is not issued, that person has the right to appeal to the Crown court. That bears a close analogy to what we are discussing now.

We are contemplating a dog warden, not a police constable I note—the hon. Gentleman does not want to involve the police, but dog wardens, whoever they may be for that purpose—granting licences. The least the hon. Gentleman could do is to accept that there should be a proper right of appeal. I hasten to add, however, that I am reasonably content that the appeal should be to the justices. For the purposes of consistency of approach I was referring to the Crown court, but I am perfectly willing to use the justices.

The most difficult issue that faces the hon. Gentleman is the number of dog wardens who must be employed. He and I remember the debates of last night about the cost of a registration scheme. I remember one figure, given at about 2.30 in the morning, of a one-off payment of £60 to £65 in respect of each dog registered. The other approach was an annual charge of £15, again in respect of each dog registered.

However, that assumed that the sole function of dog wardens would be to collect strays. If, as we are told, one of the important functions of a dog warden would be the licensing of the many thousands—probably tens of thousands—of eligible dogs within the area of that district council, we will not be talking about one warden, 50 wardens or even 300 wardens; we will be talking about needing thousands of dog wardens, especiallyif they have to work at night looking at the safe-keeping arrangements that the applicants are proposing to put in place.

Mr. McAllion: There would be no need for thousands of wardens. My suggestion was simply a possibility. The licensing committees of the local authorities could decide whether such licences should be issued, just as they decide about other licences for other purposes. There are millions of cars in this country, but we do not need thousands of wardens to check whether everyone has a licence. There are ways of making sure that a licence system operates effectively without involving thousands of wardens.

Surely it is not beyond the wit of the Minister or his civil servants to come up with something along those lines. They should be looking at that. I am simply suggesting that the Government should acknowledge that further action is required. They must look closely at how they can bring the ownership of such dogs under some control, because if they do not, other people will be killed.

Mr. Hogg: I have noticed that the hon. Gentleman's approach to this matter is to put up a suggestion and then, when I have knocked it down and destroyed it, to say, "I didn't mean that. Perhaps something else could be thought up." Then we go through the same procedure all over again. That approach is nonsense.

Mr. McAllion *rose——*

Mr. Hogg: Perhaps the hon. Gentleman will allow me to continue for a moment with the issue of dog wardens.

About 1,000 dog wardens could be needed in the south Keston district area, especially if they have to visit the home of every applicant. Let us be generous and say 500. In that instance, we would certainly not be talking about £60 in respect of each dog as a one-off charge or about £15 per year. We would be talking about hundreds of pounds.

Mr. McAllion: The Minister is setting up coconuts on stalls just to knock them down. Nobody is suggesting anything of the kind. The Minister has no evidence or data to sustain his argument. He is simply saying that if he says it, it must be the case and that the argument follows from that and that is nonsense. The hon. Gentleman is the Minister responsible for something that is causing a lot of pain and suffering to people outside this House. He should get rid of the flippant attitude that he has shown throughout this debate and start to tackle the problem seriously. He should stop setting up Aunt Sallies just to knock them down and talk about what he can do to bring the problem under control.

Mr. Hogg: I have simply been responding to points made by the hon. Gentleman. I never suggested, in the first instance, that dog wardens should be the licensing authority. That was the hon. Gentleman's suggestion. Similarly, it was his suggestion that there should be a licensing authority. The hon. Gentleman has made a proposition, and I have had the courtesy to examine it. He must not blame me for making the status of dog wardens

an essential part of the debate when he raised that point in the first place. I should never have been so silly as to think of that idea.

The hon. Gentleman thought that there was an analogy between cars and dogs and that these licences could be granted on the nod. However, the hon. Gentleman has forgotten two things. First, one has to pass a test to have a car. Is the hon. Gentleman suggesting that there should be tests for the ownership of certain classes of dogs?

Mr. McAllion: The Minister has argued throughout on the basis that there will be tests for the ownership of some dogs. Deciding whether the applicant meets the criteria is in itself a kind of test. Although the Minister has made that assumption throughout, he is now treating it as if it were a revolutionary idea that has just been thought up. The Minister is not suggesting that, because we have tests for cars, we need thousands of instructors in every city. The people who carry out the tests are small in number, but they seem to cope.

Mr. Hogg: Let us look at the criteria. Car tests comprise a test in skill in driving. There are not all that many driving test applicants each year. However, we are talking about potentially 2 million to 3 million dogs being the subject of the licensing and about somebody having to apply and monitor the criteria and then having to grant a licence.

Mr. McAllion: The Minister is assuming that there will be between 2 million and 3 million dogs. My only suggestion was that made by the RSPCA's experts, who identified five specific breeds. The Minister is spreading the argument beyond those five breeds simply for the convenience of his own argument and so that he can produce a figure of between 2 and 3 million dogs. Neither the Minister nor I knows what the number is because nobody in this country knows the true number of dogs. However, whatever the number, the initial licensing process will occur only once.

This issue should be examined in detail and not be the subject of a flippant exchange between the Minister and myself. There should be expert committees. However, when I asked the Home Secretary whether he would set up such a committee to consider the problems and the suggestions, he said that he did not see any need for it. Why does the Minister think that there is not a need to examine these things in detail, and why does he treat them as a matter for light debate in this place?

Mr. Hogg: I am not treating these issues lightly. I am responding to specific suggestions made by the hon. Gentleman. The hon. Gentleman has rightly said that the RSPCA has identified a number of breeds, but it has certainly not identified all the dangerous breeds, and it has not even begun to address the question of cross-breeds or quarter-breeds, because it cannot.

Is the hon. Gentleman considering a one-off licensing system or an annual licensing system? In the nature of things, people's circumstances and conditions change. Would a person who moves house have to apply for a new licence? The hon. Gentleman has himself told us that one important criterion—indeed, the only one that he mentioned—is the ability of an applicant to keep his or her animal securely at night. The ability of a person to do so will clearly depend on the conditions in which he or she is living. When someone moves house, those conditions change, so would a further application be necessary?

Mr. McAllion: Why does the Minister always find a reason or excuse for taking no action in this matter when, in relation to the poll tax, for which local authorities will find thousands of people's circumstances changing every week, local authorities are expected not only to register the changes but to send out notices to the individuals concerned about those changes in their circumstances? I have discovered today that, in Tayside region, 5,000 changes will be made to the poll tax register every week. If the Minister does not find that a problem, why does he think that there will be a problem with notifying changes in a system for trying to keep dangerous breeds of dogs under control?

Mr. Hogg: The hon. Gentleman has made two points. I am not commending that we do nothing; I am commending—as I shall outline when the hon. Gentleman permits me to do so—that we do what the Home Secretary says that we should do. My right hon. Friend has made his statement in a written answer.

There is no analogy between what the hon. Gentleman has been forced to consider—an annual licensing system for dogs—and the community charge. Of course, when somebody moves house, they notify their change of address to the authorities. That is the beginning and the end of it. However, in the context of the licensing scheme that the hon. Gentleman is considering for a number of dogs that are incapable of definition, the criteria have to be re-examined when the change of address occurs, because the applicant's circumstances then become different. If one moves from, for example, a house in rural Lincolnshire to the middle of Grantham, one's circumstances change. Although one could very well keep a range of big dogs in rural Lincolnshire, that might not be possible in the centre of Grantham in a block of flats.

The point that I am putting to the hon. Gentleman, and which he is so unwilling to grasp, is that under his scheme, when there is a change of circumstances, an inquiry would have to be made about the ability of the applicant, whose circumstances had changed, securely to house the dog at night in those new circumstances. What happens if the authority decides that the applicant cannot house the dog securely at night in those new circumstances? Is it to be put down? I wonder what the RSPCA would have to say about that.

Mr. McAllion: I am not speaking on behalf of the RSPCA; I am simply trying to press the Minister to take some sort of action to control a problem that is becoming ever more dangerous. His alternative is to do nothing—to let dogs be kept by entirely unsuitable owners who do not keep them under control but let them loose in the community, putting others at risk. That is not good enough.

Mr. Hogg: The hon. Gentleman was here last night, and I assume that he reads *Hansard*——

Mr. McAllion: I was here until 2.45 this morning, but I have been in Dundee since then to vote and to make sure that Mr. James Provan is not re-elected as Conservative MEP.

Mr. Hogg: The hon. Gentleman is rather confused. I understand that: most members of the Labour party are normally fairly confused. The hon. Gentleman is merely confused in particular, whereas they are confused in general. That, however, is not an excuse for not remembering what my right hon. Friend the Secretary of State for the Environment said at some length last night, what my right hon. Friend the Home Secretary said yesterday in a parliamentary answer and what—when the hon. Gentleman permits me—I am going to say this evening.

The intellectual quality of the hon. Gentleman's stance —I trust that I am putting this gently and courteously—is not terribly appealing. He is really saying that it is better to do nonsense than to do nothing. When driven into a corner he admits, at least implicitly, that what he has been saying is nonsense. When pressed on a specific point, he will say, "I did not really mean that; I had something rather different in mind."

Let us move on to what I suggest should be done. We should consider with some care how we are to control dangerous dogs. A number of statutes provide protection against dogs: I shall deal primarily with England and Wales, because, as the hon. Gentleman will appreciate, I do not answer for Scotland, and Scottish legislation in this regard is different.

In England and Wales there are three primary statutes. The Town Police Clauses Act 1847 makes it an offence to have an unmuzzled ferocious dog at large—that is, off a lead—in a street, park or open place in most urban areas. Thus, if a dog is ferocious and does not have a muzzle, its owner commits a criminal offence, for which the penalty is a fine of up to £400.

Let me pause there to make a serious point. I think that it is at least possible that some classes of dog would be deemed by the courts to be ferocious without the necessity to prove any particular propensity to violence in a particular dog. I suggest—this is just an idea, not a legal opinion—that in the case of the American pit bull terrier, which was pure-bred and manifested all the characteristics of that breed, the court might be prepared to treat it as a ferocious animal even if there was no evidence that that animal had threatened or injured anyone. The 1847 Act, where it applies—which is primarily in urban areas—may be a remedy that is already available in respect of the dog to which the hon. Gentleman drew attention.

Obviously, if a rottweiler had threatened or injured a person, it would then become a ferocious animal for the purposes of the 1847 Act. I do not think that a rottweiler per se—that is, without proof of some previous injury or propensity to injure—would be treated as a ferocious animal, but once there was some reason to think that it was dangerous or likely to injure someone it would, I think, become one.

Mr. McAllion: Why should there be a distinction between a rottweiler and an American pit bull terrier?

Mr. Hogg: The reasons for the distinction are those that the hon. Gentleman has himself advanced in his many interesting interventions. I think that an American pit bull terrier is essentially a fighting dog, bred for that purpose. No one would say that that was true of a rottweiler: rottweilers are guard dogs.

I had the pleasure of meeting representatives of the Council of Docked Breeds recently, one of whom was the secretary or chairman of the Rottweiler Society. There are 90,000, and although some may be fierce and clearly are, it would be wrong to regard the majority of the breed in that way. That is probably not true of the American pit bull terrier, although it is probably fair to say that the majority of that breed have a propensity to violence, which might well classify them as ferocious animals within the meaning of the 1847 Act. It is at least quite likely that the 1847 Act would prohibit someone from keeping unmuzzled in a public place an American pit bull terrier —or, for that matter, any dog that could be properly regarded as ferocious by reason either of its breed or its past record or present circumstances.

Allowing a ferocious dog off the lead without a muzzle is a serious matter which I do not think that people fully appreciate. They should know that the courts already have powers to deal with them severely. The hon. Gentleman will be pleased to know that, in Scotland, similar powers exist—although expressed in a more modern form—in the Civic Government (Scotland) Act 1982.

Civil liability in respect of injury or damage caused by dogs in Scotland is regulated by the Animals (Scotland) Act 1987. In England and Wales it is regulated by the Animals Act 1971, which provides that the keeper of an animal is liable for any damage that it causes if he knew that the animal was likely to cause such damage or injury if unrestrained. The two Acts allow those who have been attacked and injured to claim damages.

It will, of course, depend on proof of knowledge on the part of the defendant, and that knowledge flows from the defendant's knowledge of a particular dog and of the way that it is likely to respond in specific circumstances. I fully appreciate that no amount of compensation could make good the loss of the daughter of the hon. Gentleman's constituents, but those Acts apply in a number of cases of injury.

I wish, however, to focus on a third piece of legislation, which is of critical importance. It is legislation that my right hon. Friend the Home Secretary is hoping that the House will amend, preferably soon. I refer to the Dogs Act 1871, which applies throughout Great Britain. Under that Act, anyone can complain to a court——

Madam Deputy Speaker (Miss Betty Boothroyd): Order. I hope that the Minister will not refer to future legislation in an Adjournment debate. I was a little concerned about that: I am listening very carefully.

Mr. Hogg: I am grateful to you, Madam Deputy Speaker, for that indication. With your permission, I have it in mind to outline not very detailed proposals of the legislative kind but broad trends of policy.

Madam Deputy Speaker: Order. I hope the Minister will not do that. That would be in breach of our Standing Orders, and I could not allow him to do that.

Mr. Hogg: May we see how far I can go, Madam Deputy Speaker? I should like to give an indication of what we have in mind, without in any way breaching the rules of order. Perhaps we can inch along on this matter, and you will tell me if I have gone too far.

Madam Deputy Speaker: Order. I have listened carefully to all that has been said throughout the debate and I shall continue to do that. The Minister can rest assured that I will call him to order immediately he gets close to the mark.

Mr. Hogg: You are, as ever, most gracious in these matters, Madam Deputy Speaker, and I shall do my best not to go too far.

Let us examine the foundations of the statute. The principal legislation is the Dogs Act 1871. Under that measure, anyone can complain to a court that a dog is dangerous, or simply report the matter to the police. If the court is satisfied that the dog is dangerous and not kept under proper control, it can make an order for the dog to be controlled or destroyed. So far so good, Madam Deputy Speaker, because that is descriptive only of the present legislation.

Madam Deputy Speaker: It is the future that I am concerned with.

Mr. Hogg: I, too, am concerned with that, Madam Deputy Speaker, so I hope that we can proceed in a state of accord.

As the House knows, the Home Secretary has decided that the powers available to the court on a complaint under the Dogs Act should perhaps be extended and the penalties enhanced. That is a general statement of intent. The problem is that, as the Act stands, if a dog is to be destroyed, that must be carried out by the owner, who may decline to carry out the order. The only penalty currently available for that is a fine of £1 a day. In 1871, that fine was considerable. It is manifestly not considerable today.

One could take the view that that was a gap in the law. The Home Secretary is also minded to think that it is a gap in the law and, speaking generally and without, as it were, expressing a precise view on how the legislation should be changed, one way to deal with such a problem might be to give the court power to designate a third party as the person to carry out the destruction order.

Thus it would be possible under such an approach—not that I am proposing legislation on this occasion—for a court to designate, say, an officer of police to carry out the destruction order. That would avoid the problem that can arise under the present legislation. If one were to adopt that approach, it would ensure that dogs which needed to be put down were put down.

I have mentioned that the fine is a problem. There is clearly a case for the House to consider whether we should change the law to a degree so that failure to comply with an order to control a dog or hand it over to be destroyed should be an offence carrying a significant penalty, certainly a penalty greater than £1 a day. A figure that might occur to you, Madam Deputy Speaker, would be a fine of up to level 3 in the standard scale, which is £400. That is a thought that might occur to the House in considering possible approaches to legislation of this kind. If one wanted to do that, a penalty under the 1871 Act would make prosecution under the Act more worth while and greatly enhance the enforcement of the Act.

There is another possibility which I think would attract the hon. Member for Dundee, East. It is that there is no power under the 1871 Act for the court to prohibit a person from owning a dog in future for a specified period. Plainly, where there has been a finding under section 2 of the 1871 Act, there is a case for saying that a court should have the additional power to make an order disqualifying an owner from having custody of a dog for such a period as the court thinks fit. One would need to refer to the parliamentary answer by my right hon. Friend the Home Secretary to see exactly what he had in mind, because I must not say in the course of the debate what he had in mind. If that is what he had in mind, it would be a

[*Mr. Hogg*]

completely new power under the Act. Its effect would be to ensure that dangerous dogs which are not or cannot be controlled are destroyed.

Owners who failed to observe an order of the court would receive a substantial fine and the court would have the additional ability to ban such a person from having custody of a dog. If at some stage the House gave the court the ability to ban a person from possessing a dog in future, the House would have to consider what penalties should be imposed in the event of the person failing to comply with the disqualification order. I propose no legislation, because I am not permitted to do so. However, the House might well think that a level 5 penalty, which is presently set at a maximum of £2,000, might be appropriate.

Somebody who refuses to comply with an order to control his dog or hand it over for destruction may be banned. It follows that anybody who tries in such circumstances to resist the operation of the Act would, if the court so decided, become liable for the £2,000 fine or whatever the level 5 fine might be at the time. That would be a considerable extension of the court's powers under the 1871 Act.

In future, the House might well consider giving to the courts the power to ban somebody from possessing a dog, and it might also give the court a power to designate a third party to carry out a destruction order. The House might well decide that it wanted to increase the fine for findings under section 2 of the 1871 Act to a scale 3 fine. If the House decided on such a course of action it would undoubtedly constitute an important enhancement of the legislative powers that are available. If the House wanted to make the changes that I have contemplated in respect of the Dogs Act 1871, there would be a similar desire for a change in the legislation in Scotland. I suspect that my right hon. and learned Friend the Secretary of State for Scotland would wish to see that, and no doubt other hon. Members would also like to see it.

I had hoped that the hon. Member for Dundee, East and the whole House would come to the view that the simple and effective changes to the Dogs Act that I have contemplated would be an appropriate response to the problem. I hope that, if this approach proves attractive to the hon. Member for Dundee, East and to the House, changes could be implemented as speedily as the House can manage. It would be good if a suitable legislative opportunity could be found to give the House an opportunity to contemplate the kind of changes that I have envisaged.

I cannot pretend to the House that the tragic circumstances which have brought about the debate and which helped to bring about our view of the dog legislation can be prevented by changes in legislation, however sweeping. If there is one lesson to be learned from our review of the legislation in England and Wales it is that the responsibility for the control of dogs rests much more on their owners than upon the framework of law.

The House can take legislative steps to control dogs, like anything else, but the effectiveness of those steps in practice depends very largely on how people respond to their responsibilities. It is therefore important to ensure that any legislative changes which we make this time are measured, sensible and well aimed. That is why I was quarrelling with the hon. Gentleman. It is not that I think

that this matter is unimportant; it is that I am concerned that we should introduce only changes which are viable and not pomote changes which are simply unsustainable.

Mr. McAllion: What I fail to understand is that the Minister qualified many of the other suggestions that have been made by people outside the House as unviable, and particularly suggested that the prohibition of certain species was unviable because of the cross-breed problem. How does that apply to the suggestion that American pit bull terriers should be muzzled in public? How does that come into the problem of the cross-breeds in that respect?

Mr. Hogg: This is a slightly different point. If one is to have a prohibition order, one has in statutory terms to define the dog to which that order applies. For the purpose of an importation prohibition order, or for that matter a possession prohibition order, one cannot define the dog other than by reference to breed. One cannot simply say that everybody is prohibited from possessing a ferocious dog. One can say that, when a ferocious dog is kept in particular circumstances, an offence is committed. One cannot say that no ferocious dog shall be imported into the United Kingdom, because that is an unenforceable piece of legislation. One can say that Latin American pit bull terriers cannot be imported into the United Kingdom.

I do not want to go back to what I was doing previously with regard to the hon. Gentleman, but what is an American pit bull terrier? That is a serious question. Obviously, a pure-bred American pit bull terrier is an American pit bull terrier, but what about a half-breed or a cross-breed? How does one recognise a dog which has in it a sufficient quantity of Amerian pit bull terrier genes to give it the characteristics of an American pit bull terrier but also has different parentage? It loses the definitional character, and therefore the prohibition cannot operate because it is nonsense if one focuses on breeds.

It is the point about the 1847 Act that is troubling the hon. Gentleman. That Act provides in effect that where one has a ferocious animal one has to do certain things: for example, keep it on a leash and keep a muzzle on it. The question is: what is a ferocious animal? That is not a definitional question; that is a question of fact.

I think it is possible, although I do not express a definite view on this, that the courts would be prepared to say that an American pit bull terrier, having regard to its pedigree and essential characteristics, was per se a ferocious animal. I do not think that such a finding would be applied to many dogs, but it might be applied to an American pit bull terrier.

With that exception, one has to apply the test in the context of any dog that is capable of falling within it. Any dog is capable of being ferocious. Therefore, under the 1847 Act, I think it is true that a very small number of a breed may per se be ferocious, otherwise one is looking at the characteristics of the particular dog in respect of which the summons is issued.

If the hon. Gentleman will reflect on it he will see why, on the one hand, it is impossible to prohibit possession and importation by way of breed, while on the other it is possible to express the view that perhaps American pit bull terriers would per se fall within the 1847 legislation.

The point that I am making, therefore, is that it is essential that any legislative changes we make should be measured, sensible and well aimed. They must also, incidentally, command the support of the public and not act against the large numbers of dog owners whose animals present no nuisance and therefore no threat. We think that the kind of changes—not going into detail, Madam Deputy Speaker——

Madam Deputy Speaker: Order. The Minister is sailing very close to the wind.

Mr. Hogg: I know, but fortunately I am tacking, so I am not getting that close.

We think that the proposals which my right hon. Friend outlined yesterday meet these criteria. Courts are familiar with the 1871 Act, and it may well be that the House will wish to give the courts the powers and discretion that they require. I recommend that approach to the House. Those who have a dog which is uncontrolled and has become dangerous, whether it be a rottweiler, a doberman, an alsatian, a terrier or the indefinable mongrel that bit me twice last year, should be in no doubt that they will be dealt with by the courts. In such circumstances their dog could be destroyed and they could be banned from owning another.

I very much hope, Madam Deputy Speaker, that you will feel that this is the proper way forward.

Itinerants

8.46 pm

Miss Ann Widdecombe (Maidstone): I am very grateful to have the opportunity to raise in the House tonight the subject of the control of itinerants as it is one of major importance not only to my own constituents but to the constituents of many hon. Members. It comes up time and time again in the House.

I am also very grateful to my hon. Friend the Minister for being available to reply to this debate. I listened with increasing admiration to the very thorough and comprehensive reply which he gave to the previous debate. I am indeed most grateful to him that after such a magnificent coverage of just about every aspect of the dog problem he should now turn his attention so willingly and readily to a completely different problem. He will, I hope, not suffer from a feeling of déjà vu if I turn briefly to the subject of dogs later in this speech because, unbelievably, since it has come up so often in our deliberations this week, there are also considerable implications concerning the control of dogs and illegal acts connected with them in respect of itinerants.

In looking at the problem of gipsies I should like to look first at the existing state of legislation. I would not dream of proposing any changes to legislation or even of speculating on possible changes since I am quite sure that I could not tack as subtly as my hon. Friend the Minister. But existing legislation is extremely relevant because it is one of the sources of frustration on the part of law-abiding residents who see a situation in which one law appears to apply to the settled population and another to the itinerant population.

I am also fully aware that my hon. Friend the Minister will not be able to respond in any detail to some of the criticisms that I will make, not only of existing legislation but of the way that it is enforced, because this is more properly the concern of his right hon. Friend the Secretary of State for the Environment. But, although the Minister will not be able to respond to that part of my speech which strictly concerns planning legislation and enforcement, I hope that he will be able to pass on the concerns that I express to his right hon. Friend. I would ask him if he would deal with the points that I shall be raising on public order, which more nearly concern him.

The problems of public order and the problem of frustration among the law-abiding community would not arise at all if we had a proper system of planning and enforcement and a proper set of planning rules which would make it possible to control the itinerant population.

First, we have to look at the size of the problem. I have attended many debates in which hon. Members on both sides of the House have raised the problem of those who choose an itinerant way of life or who settle for long periods in illegal encampments and move on only when obliged to do so, or for reasons of their own. A count of gipsy caravans was carried out by the environmental health officer in Maidstone—on whose behalf I am largely raising this thorny problem—in January, so it is already out of date. Even then, there were 14 unauthorised caravans in the borough, 11 of which were in my constituency. In all those cases, the borough council was, and is still, taking action to resolve the breach of control.

[*Miss Ann Widdecombe*]

There are in addition 35 caravans in authorised council-operated sites in the borough and 76 caravans on privately operated authorised sites.

Of those authorised council encampments, 21 are at the village of Marden, and a further 14 at Ulcombe. That is a large count for a geographically small constituency. Marden parish council is now updating its figures, together with other parish councils, with a view to being able to assess the problem more accurately. The recent outbreak of illegal encampments at Marden has caused considerable problems of enforcement and public order. Planning enforcement is a lengthy process. Before taking enforcement action, the local authority is encouraged by the Secretary of State to resolve the problem by negotiation or at least to invite planning applications to be submitted. If this does not resolve the problem, an enforcement notice can be issued. Not only is it a long time before the notices can be issued, but if an appeal is exercised, it can easily be several years before the notice becomes effective, even if the appeal is ultimately dismissed.

Residents at Marden will be told that it could be several years before enforcement can be carried out. If my hon. Friend the Minister were to visit Marden to see the incredible situation that has developed, he would not find it easy to say that it is just and right, even if it is normal legal practice, for it to take several years to rectify such a situation.

Stop notice procedure is available where a local planning authority feels that the normal time scale embodied in an enforcement action is unacceptable, but such a procedure is not permissible or applicable in connection with a caravan that is used solely as a place of residence. The normal problems of enforcement action are compounded when dealing with gipsies, simply because Government advice is quite clear: the gipsies who have resided in the local area should receive planning permission unless there are compelling planning objections. Normal policy objections to the development of the countryside that would be applied to non-gipsies are seldom sufficient to resist proposals for gipsy caravans. Parallel action under the Caravan Sites and Control of Development Act 1960 provides a more expeditious way to deal with the problem in that immediate prosecution for the stationing of the caravan without a site licence is possible, but it seldom provides an effective solution as magistrates will inevitably dismiss a case or impose a minimum fine pending resolution of the planning permission. The will of the police to interfere where there are public order problems at gipsy sites and the will of the magistrates to enforce planning procedures and impose the necessarily deterrent fines are minimal. Therefore, at least part of the planning problem spills over into the responsibilities of my hon. Friend the Minister.

In layman's language, the planning situation is simple. Anybody can encamp himself illegally on any available land. He can then, unbelievable though it is, get himself connected up to local services—electricity and water—and can have his rubbish collected. When the council then tries to evict him, it is faced with a lengthy process of inordinate delay. As a result, resentment builds up in the law-abiding community and this is much intensified where there is continued and blatant bad behaviour, lawlessness and acts of public disorder by the itinerants. In the village of Marden, some of my constituents have been assaulted.

We have a rather romantic view of gipsies. We think of people travelling in a painted caravan, telling fortunes and selling heather. The reality of the people encamped illegally is that they do not use their caravans purely for residential purposes. They are also carrying out a trade, quite often an illegal one, in the area surrounding the encampment. Breaking up of metal, tinkers' business and other such trades are frequently practised. They all cause a great deal of mess, particularly where there are no proper arrangements for disposal of sewage from the caravans or proper rubbish disposal. There is no proper arrangement for disposal of trade waste, which builds up and is extremely detrimental to the environment, particularly to a beautiful part of Kent.

Even where they are not directly responsible for assaults on the population, the behaviour of itinerants is a problem. Dogs and cats regularly disappear from nearby areas to these encampments. My distinguished predecessor, Sir John Wells, lost a pair of much-loved and valuable dogs about a year ago. They were not discovered by the police, who are alleged not to have shown a great deal of interest, nor by any official of the local council calling in to check up on planning procedures, because they do not do much of that. They were seen by a particularly alert constituent, who, walking past the encampment one day, noticed two dogs that were cleaner and fitter not only than the other dogs but the occupants. He decided that a discordant note was being struck and reported the matter to the police. I am pleased to say that the police took action and managed to restore the dogs to their owner. Others are not so lucky.

Thefts of caravans often occur when these people move in, and it is not difficult to make the connection. This causes a great deal of resentment and that is where the question of order and control arises. Itinerancy in our society appears to be rising and more and more designated sites are being made available. There are obviously considerable social arguments about allowing itinerancy to escalate to too great a scale. It is bad for the education of the children of itinerants, which is greatly disrupted. It is bad for good social order because, on the whole, itinerants are resented by the law-abiding population. It is bad for law enforcement, because these people are seen to be blatantly getting away with it, as it were. It is extremely bad in promoting civil obedience in terms of planning orders when it is obvious that one section of the population appears to be especially favourably treated and appears also to be immune from lawful procedures.

Nevertheless, itinerancy is growing, and as it grows so we are having problems of public order and control. We have assaults in Marden. We have assaults elsewhere. We have reported threats in Hunton. We have mess and blatant disregard of the law in Shenley Park. For how long does my hon. Friend the Minister expect the law-abiding and settled population to continue tolerating this behaviour without being led to feel that they must take the law into their own hands or that the law is letting them down so entirely badly that it is not worth obeying and that instead it is worth trying to find some way round it?

I have never yet heard of an illegal encampment being moved on swiftly and legally. The two actions do not go together. If an encampment is to be moved legally, the move will take years before it is completed. If it is to be moved swiftly, assuredly the pressure will not be legal. That is not a happy situation. Indeed, I believe it to be an extremely dangerous one, and one that could develop further. Meanwhile, even if my law-abiding constituents, and my extremely law-abiding villagers of Marden, are prepared patiently to wait for the law to sort out this problem, is it fair that they should have to do so? Surely it is time, even under the existing law, for us to find a way of controlling the menace before it becomes a greater one, when it will no longer be so easy to bring it within the laws that apply to the rest of civilised Britain.

9.1 pm

The Parliamentary Under-Secretary of State for the Home Department (Mr. Douglas Hogg): My hon. Friend the Member for Maidstone (Miss Widdecombe) has made a powerful case for the position of her constituents in Marden. Essentially she has raised two matters. The first is the application of section 39 of the Public Order Act 1986. Secondly, she has raised the more general question of itinerants. I shall deal first with section 39. I think that it will be helpful if I summarise the legislation that is currently in place.

Broadly speaking, if a senior police officer present at the scene has reason to believe that two or more people have entered land as trespassers and are intending to reside there and that the occupier of the land has taken reasonable steps to ask them to leave, he may direct the trespassers to leave the land in any of the following circumstances: where damage has been caused to the property on the land, where the trespassers have used threatening, abusive or insulting words or behaviour towards the occupier or his representative, or where—I suspect that this is commonplace in the circumstances described by my hon. Friend—12 or more vehicles have been brought on to the land. For the purposes of this part of the 1986 Act, a caravan is deemed to be a vehicle.

Section 39 was introduced into the 1986 legislation while it was passing through Parliament to provide criminal sanctions against a type of aggravated trespass that landowners suffered in the Stonehenge area at the time of the summer solstice. It has undoubtedly been used by the police when they have been dealing with gipsies. It was not intended to be used against gipsies, but if gipsies fall within the circumstances described in section 39 they can be dealt with under the Act. The Act provides the police with a power but it does not impose a duty. When we come to operational decisions, we are talking about the duties of the chief constable and those of his officers who are accountable to him.

If my hon. Friend's constituents believe that the provisions under section 39 of the Public Order Act 1986 are not being used in the way that she wishes them to be used, they should make representations to the chief constable for a more expeditious use of the powers that currently exist. We intend shortly to undertake a review of a number of sections of the Public Order Act 1986, including section 39, to evaluate how they are working. Inevitably we will consider the remarks which my hon. Friend has made so clearly in this debate. In essence, the legislation in place is sufficient to meet the problem.

My hon. Friend the Member for Maidstone is troubled by the fact that the police officers concerned do not act sufficiently expeditiously. If she will forgive me saying this, that is an operational matter for the police in her county, rather than for the Home Office.

Miss Widdecombe: I accept what my hon. Friend has said. The local police force has made excellent efforts and I in no way want to criticise it. However, the problems which occur happen on the spur of the moment. The police must then come back after some time to sort out exactly what has happened. It is not like a public order offence or a demonstration where there is a static situation. These are isolated incidents which are very difficult to police.

Mr. Hogg: I entirely agree with my hon. Friend's analysis of the difficulties. She is right. However, I must re-emphasise that there is a distinction between the function of the Home Office and that of the police. We are considering an operational policing matter which is not within the authority of the Home Office. Consequently my hon. Friend must make it plain to her local police officers —and knowing my hon. Friend I rather suspect that she has done this—and in particular to the chief constable, that the matter is a very serious social problem and that the present legislation is appropriate to be used in those circumstances and should be invoked expeditiously.

I accept the point that the policing consequences are difficult in the sense that the incidents are isolated and may give rise to public disorder problems. Therefore, the police face implementation problems. However, that does not alter the fact that it is essentially a policing problem. I am afraid that I do not think that I can usefully go much further than that.

My hon. Friend the Member for Maidstone has been very generous to me—quite unusually so perhaps. She recognises my shortcomings in the sense that the broader issues which could have been debated are more particularly matters for my right hon. Friend the Secretary of State for the Environment. She has given me the opportunity, for which I am much indebted, to reply exclusively on section 39 of the Public Order Act 1986. I hope that she does not think that I am discourteous when I say that she might feel that I would not bring a great deal of expert knowledge to bear on the rest of the points that she so helpfully raised. However, I promise that I will ensure that her comments about Marden and her constituents are brought to the attention of my right hon. Friend the Secretary of State for the Environment.

Madrid Summit

9.9 pm

Mr. Nigel Spearing (Newham, South): In this Adjournment debate I want to raise the subject of the scrutiny of European Community business and the Madrid summit. It is a little ironic that I am raising this subject today of all days. The polling booths in the European elections are just about coming to the end of their day's business to elect to the European Parliament Members who will have an influence on legislation from the European Community.

This Parliament also has influence on such legislation through the Council of Ministers and the Ministers we send to Brussels to comment on the Commission's proposals and finally decide what those legislative proposals should be either through unanimity or by qualified majority. The debate is taking place at relatively short notice—only an hour or so. I thank the Economic Secretary to the Treasury for coming here at some personal inconvenience. I know that he will relay to the Lord President of the Council and Leader of the House my concerns that have arisen exactly today.

I regret very much the need for the debate. The Select Committee on European Legislation and other people have held discussions with the Lord President on the matter. However, in view of the Lord President's statement on next week's business, I was obliged to ask for a debate. I emphasise that I had the support of the Chairman of the Treasury and Civil Service Committee in my questions to the Lord President earlier today—also, I hope, when I raised the matter under Standing Order No. 20 and in this rare third Adjournment debate.

The Treasury and Civil Service Committee had been considering the matter in some detail in the expectation that there would be a debate before the Madrid summit the week after next, particularly on the Delors report on economic and monetary union. I had been confident that after pressure from two Committees and the precedents that have been set there would be a debate before that very important meeting of the European Council. However, at approximately 3.45 this afternoon the Leader of the House said that there would not be a debate—that no business next week related to that particularly important meeting.

Parliament provides procedures such as Standing Order 20 and Adjournment debates for the raising of grievances. I have therefore used those procedures. They are, as it were, fire extinguishers or alarm bells that are used when other people light a fire. The Government have certainly lit a fire today, not perhaps by an act of commission but by an act of omission in not arranging for a debate to take place next week on this very important matter. Some eyebrows may be raised when the Chairman of a Select Committee says that he finds it necessary to use these procedures, but I am sure that the Treasury and Civil Service Committee will agree with what I hope is a measured comment: there was every expectation that such a debate would take place.

I notice that the Lord President of the Council has arrived. I was not necessarily expecting him to be here. He could have read what I intend to say. Nevertheless, in view of his presence, I have to thank him for coming and I hope that what I have to say to him will not be too unexpected. I know that he has certain considerations to bear in mind, but the considerations that I intend to put to him tonight

relate to the Parliament of which he is the Leader and not necessarily to him in his role as Lord President of the Council. I have pointed out on many occasions in the past that I am not sure that the habit of successive Governments in combining those posts is the happiest of habits. Sometimes it means that the same person has to balance conflicting interests. In our democracy, although it is a matter of contention on some occasions, split interests or conflicting interests should be avoided as far as possible.

There are many points of view about the European Economic Community. There are different points of view about the merits of our membership of the EEC, about the conditions under which we joined it, about whether we joined it correctly, the holding of referendums, and all the rest. On one thing, however, there is absolute agreement: that this Parliament must play some part in EEC legislation. This country is subject by treaty to EEC legislation, particularly legislation that is brought about by a weighted majority vote, perhaps against the inclinations of any British Government or the House. There is no doubt whatsoever about that. There is no difference in principle between the right hon. Members for Old Bexley and Sidcup (Mr. Heath) and for Finchley (Mrs. Thatcher), and the hon. Member for Harrow, East (Mr. Dykes) and myself.

How is that influence to be wielded? How should draft legislation be considered, and how will influence be exerted on those who will ultimately decide it? Those questions have echoed down the ages, from the 16th century and Simon de Montfort, and along the corridor between the other place and this House. At the heart of our country's democracy is the extent to which there shall be consultation prior to legislation.

In the Standing Order that gives my Committee its marching orders, the word that is used is "consideration". That provision is contained in a resolution passed by the House on 30 October 1980 after several years' consideration, which regularised the way in which it should operate. That is becoming increasingly important in the public gaze and in the media—and no doubt it will become increasingly important after the Madrid conference and with all that follows from it. Therefore, I shall read the resolution into the record:

"That, in the opinion of this House, no Minister of the Crown should give agreement in the Council of Ministers to any proposal for European legislation which has been recommended by the Select Committee on European Legislation, &c., for consideration by the House before the House has given it that consideration unless—

  (a) that Committee has indicated that agreement need not be withheld, or

  (b) the Minister concerned decides that for special reasons agreement should not be withheld;

and in the latter case the Minister should, at the first opportunity thereafter, explain the reasons for his decision to the House."—[*Official Report*, 30 October 1980; Vol. 991, c. 838.]

In general, the operation of that resolution is relatively smooth. The problems of timing are neither the making of the Government nor of the House. However, problems occasionally arise and administrative slips occur in the best-run offices. Usually they are recognised as such and are smoothed out.

However, I regret to say that—subject to any subsequent correspondence—the spirit of that resolution has been breached. I refer to the Government reply to the "First Special Report, Session 1983-84", HC 527, when the then Leader of the House wrote, on page xxv of HC 400:

"It is the Government's practice that debates on European documents should be held as far in advance as is practicable of the expected adoption of the proposal concerned. It is desirable that this should be at the point when the voice of the House can be most influential. As a general rule, this will normally be early rather than late in the life of a proposal. The Committee rightly notes that the selection of an optimum time for debates is very much a matter of judgment. The Government fully accept the Committee's view that, when making this judgment, it should be the rule always to err on the side of an early debate, and Departments will be instructed accordingly."

I am glad that the Leader of the House reinforced that general sentiment in correspondence with the Committee.

In principle, there is no dissent from that general point. Therefore, the question must be asked whether there is any reason why the spirit of the resolution, and the spirit and terms of that letter and of a subsequent letter from the Leader of the House, should not apply to the particularly important document that will be tabled at the Madrid summit—the Delors report on European monetary union.

I wish for a moment to be a devil's advocate and express what I would say if I were the Lord President or the Economic Secretary. I would say that it is not yet a matter for legislation. It is a report about feasibility—a very important matter. On the other hand, that report suggests that future legislation and future treaty change will be possible. There may not be a decision on Monday, Tuesday or on Wednesday week, but there will certainly be consideration, conceivably in principle. I might also ask whether the document comes within the ambit of the strict legality of the wording of the resolution on 30 October. One could argue that it does not. But if we are concerned about the principle of consultation before legislation and before important meetings which we all know will take place, it surely must, bearing in mind the words of the former Leader of the House and the confirmation of at least the principle by the present Leader of the House in current circumstances.

I also sent a letter to the Leader of the House—which I do not think he was surprised to receive—saying that there must have been some specific decision not to have this debate. It was not a matter of forgetful omission but an absolute decision not to do so.

I now turn to the question of timetable recommendation. The Scrutiny Committee usually produces a report once a week. We sat on 10 May, and what a bumper meeting it was. We dealt with broadcasting; procurement by water, energy and transport; foreign language training—the Lingua programme; freedom of movement and rights of residence; economic and monetary union; and irradiation of foodstuffs. That was rather a heavy week. I shall quote the final paragraph on the Delors document on economic and monetary union which we considered raises questions of legal and political importance and recommended it for further consideration by the House. I shall read out the last paragraph on page xii of that report. I had better read the lot. It states:

"The Committee notes that the Committee for the Study of Economic and Monetary Union"

—that is Mr. Delors' committee—

"was entrusted by the European Council with the task of studying and proposing stages leading towards an economic and monetary union and that its report concluded that Treaty amendment would be necessary to effect the transfer of decision-making powers from Member States to new or existing Community institutions to implement the latter two stages of its conception of economic and monetary union. It also notes that the Prime Minister has stated that the United Kingdom cannot accept the transfer of sovereignty that is implied in the report since economic and monetary union as spelt out in the report would in effect require political union, a United States of Europe, which is not, in her view, on the agenda now or for the foreseeable future, and that the Prime Minister has also stated that the Government does not believe that there should be further Treaty amendment as proposed by the report. Accordingly, in view of the evident legal and political importance of the report and the clear conflict between its proposals and the Government's views, the Committee recommends it for further consideration by the House. It considers that this debate should be held in good time before the European Council on 26-27 June, when the report is expected to be discussed by the Heads of Government."

We know from the press that many Heads of Government may go along with Mr. Delors' proposals. There may be changes in the last few days and it may be that there will not be a consensus. However, some people will go along with the statement made by the Government and the Prime Minister. Others—I will not name them since we know who they are and they have been expressing their views in print recently—may not go along with the statement. However, it is right and proper for the Government to seek to obtain support or otherwise—I am sure that they would receive support—for their view and expose it to debate. In that way when the Prime Minister, the Foreign Secretary, the Chancellor of the Exchequer or the Paymaster General go to subsequent meetings they would have the view of the House. Surely that would strengthen their arm—or weaken it—and at least there would have been some consultation and consideration.

Such consultation was expected by the Treasury and Civil Service Committee. Last week it had before it the Governor of the Bank of England who is a signatory to the report. We are not sure whether he was signing on the principles of the mechanics or the objectives. However, he and the Chancellor of the Exchequer were both witnesses before the Committee. I have been told by the Chairman of the Committee that it is preparing a manuscript report to be available early next week in the expectation that a debate will take place.

Some people may say that we can find out what was said by reading the press. However, surely the idea of Select Committees—certainly departmental Select Committees—is that they are able to sort out and set out for the House in a reasonable and readable way the views and evidence provided by prestigious and well-informed persons. Unless one has had an opportunity to listen to what is going on, one will not know because no papers will be available for information other than through the Committee.

It is no use having material if it cannot be used in time for the deliberations that will take place. A great deal has been written and discussed recently about the departmental Select Committees. However, they are unable to be effective prior to the debate in Madrid.

The debate in Madrid is not public. That is not a criticism. I simply want to place that on record. In fact, its agenda is not known. During Question Time yesterday the Foreign Secretary was not very forthcoming on its full extent. We know that the Delors report will be discussed; as will matters relating to an equally contentious document on the social charter, on which there are different views. We are not having a debate on that but it is different from the document commisioned by the Heads of Government.

Matters may be raised by the Presidency about which we know nothing. I am not suggesting that the Leader of

[*Mr. Nigel Spearing*]

the House should hold a debate on a speculative basis but I am throwing in some of the other problems we have in respect of scrutiny. The Presidency has an entire department within the EEC and is able to select matters at will. A great deal of initiative is left to the Presidency. We may hear from the Prime Minister on her return that this, that or the other has been discussed and that decisions of principle have been taken. We may not know that such matters were being discussed and, therefore, could not debate them even if we wanted to.

Another general point that has arisen in the past week relates to the time and the period of debate. Exactly a week ago I asked the Leader of the House to consider an exemption to the one-and-a-half hour rule in respect of a debate due to take place on Tuesday on broadcasting rules for television, which the Commission proposes should apply to the EC—rules that will be resolved in the end by majority vote. I anticipated that many people would wish to speak in that debate. It started just after one o'clock early on Wednesday morning and lasted until 2.37 am.

Despite the late hour and the fact that the speeches were relatively brief and to the point, there was no time for the Minister to reply. Various matters were raised in the course of the debate on which the Minister could not comment. I do not complain about the choice of day because the matter is being discussed at this minute, so it had to be dealt with when it was. But the House was constrained by the fact that the debate was limited to an hour and a half. I put it to the House and to the Leader of the House—he has heard it before but I cannot over-emphasise it—the one-and-a-half hour limit was originally the time designated for the consideration of British secondary statutory instruments. We are talking about super-primary legislation.

The Prime Minister and the Leader of the House talk about the need for greater scrutiny and better procedures, a matter with which many people are now grappling. The Procedure Committee is having a go at it, the Leader of the House and I are having fruitful conversations on it and there is proper correspondence between the Scrutiny Committee and the Leader of the House. All that is helpful, but there are certain things that should and could happen now which need no change in the Standing Orders, simply the use of the Government's powers and responsibilities to Parliament.

We do not just have a Government to produce legislation on the basis of one philosophy or another, and I hope that I am making a constitutional rather than a party speech. Every Government have a responsibility to parliamentary democracy. We know just how much the Prime Minister is wedded to that. She is always telling us how important it is, particularly in relation to the European Community. There is a moral and a constitutional obligation on the Government, as well as on the Leader of the House, who has particular concerns in this matter, not only to see that parliamentary democracy and representative government go on, but are seen to go on. But in respect of EC legislation, alas, that is not yet the case.

That matter does not relate simply to this Government. My esteemed predecessor, Mr. John Davies, a Cabinet Member and the first Chairman of the Select Committee of which I have the honour to be Chairman, got into dead trouble with the Labour Government of the day, or they got into dead trouble because of what he was doing. On one occasion, he had to get all the members of his Committee to put down an early-day motion, headed by a former Cabinet Minister and well-respected gentleman who had strong views in one direction about the European Community—perfectly honourable and right ones. He had clashes with the Government, I think in good spirit, but in the spirit of parliamentary democracy.

I hope that I have not gone over the top today but rather have used those procedures which parliamentary democracy provides—which have ancient origins and which are there to be used on occasions—to draw attention to the matter, particularly to those who will read what we say, as well as the Leader of the House, whom I am glad to see here, and the Economic Secretary, who has been put to some personal inconvenience to be present.

I do not expect a long reply because the Minister has had only short notice, but the debate has illustrated the profound dilemmas that now confront Parliament and Government in the practice of representative democracy and in making sure that conversations on major matters, such as economic and monetary union, can be read about in the press in yards of articles, or in the form of speculation, argument or debate on the radio, of which we have heard quite a lot and will hear even more after the election results on Sunday. It may have some influence on what appears in the papers on the summit. But for Parliament not to be able to discuss such matters even on Adjournment debates—I am not asking for a substantive or amendable motion—would be seen as something strange by people outside.

As the former Leader of the House, Lord St. John of Fawsley, often told us, it is not this place that is the mother of Parliaments, but Britain. That this Parliament is unable to discuss major matters of European and constitutional issue prior to our representatives going to Europe to speak on our behalf would be judged by any constitutional textbook as something that should not be tolerated—I fear that history will judge it so.

I know that the Economic Secretary to the Treasury will make a short reply; I do not expect a long one. The Lord President has been present and I know that he will draw this speech to the attention of others. There is yet time for something to be done. It has been known for business to be changed and there are other people who may exercise an influence—sometimes they are described as "the usual channels".

I hope that I have used the procedures of the House correctly. Unfortunately, it has been necessary for such a person as myself, with the backing of the Chairman of the Treasury and Civil Service Select Committee, to exercise those procedures. I believe that I have done so in the spirit of parliamentary democracy and I look for a response in exactly the same fashion.

9.36 pm

The Economic Secretary of the Treasury (Mr. Peter Lilley): First, I thank the hon. Member for Newham, South (Mr. Spearing) for his characteristic courtesy in giving me the maximum possible notice of his intention to raise this matter in the third Adjournment debate.

I congratulate the hon. Gentleman and his Committee on the vigilance with which they pursue the scrutiny of the legislation that comes before this House or is in prospect and on the diligence with which they seek to ensure the House can scrutinise such legislation.

I was intending to assure the hon. Gentleman that I would convey to my right hon. Friend the Leader of the House the contents of his speech. As it is, I can assure him that my right hon. Friend has heard the cogent and powerful arguments that he has deployed. He knows that my right hon. Friend will consider them seriously. The fact that my right hon. Friend is here tonight is an indication of the importance he attaches to the hon. Gentleman, to his Committee and to the Treasury and Civil Service Select Committee and its Chairman who, I understand, joined with the hon. Gentleman in the points he raised tonight.

I hope that the hon. Gentleman will excuse me for not giving a fuller and more substantive reply, but I believe that it is more important that such matters are considered by the Leader of the House and those associated with him.

Question put and agreed to.

Adjourned accordingly at twenty-three minutes to Ten o'clock.

House of Commons

Friday 16 June 1989

The House met at half-past Nine o'clock

PRAYERS

[MR. SPEAKER *in the Chair*]

PETITION

Nazi War Criminals

Mr. John Marshall (Hendon, South): I beg leave to present a petition signed by more than 6,000 people. It is appropriate that it should be presented on the day that my right hon. Friend the Home Secretary is likely to receive the report of Sir Thomas Hetherington's inquiry into suspected Nazi war criminals.

In October 1986 my right hon. Friend the Prime Minister was sent a list of 17 individuals suspected of war crimes and resident in the United Kingdom. Currently, the British Government have no jurisdiction to try in the United Kingdom individuals who committed a crime outside the United Kingdom before they became British citizens. Other countries, such as Canada and Australia, have recently altered their laws to allow the prosecution of war criminals.

Anyone who has read the history of the holocaust or who has visited Yad Vashem realise how heinous was the nature of Nazi war crimes. For Nazis, no activity was too vile, no degradation too cruel.

Mr. Speaker: Order. The hon. Gentleman must read or summarise the petition, not make a speech about it.

Mr. Marshall: I apologise, Mr. Speaker. I have never before presented a petition. My error can be blamed on my innocence and good nature. I thank you, Mr. Speaker, for your tolerance.

The petition is as follows:

"To the Honourable the Commons of the United Kingdom and Northern Ireland in Parliament assembled. The Humble Petition of the residents of the United Kingdom sheweth:

That up to 250 alleged Nazi war criminals are living in the United Kingdom today.

That the Governments of Australia, Canada and the United States have recently changed their law to bring such persons to justice.

Wherefore your Petitioners pray that your honourable House will take appropriate measures to ensure that those accused persons in the United Kingdom are brought to justice swiftly. And your Petitioners, as in duty bound, will ever pray, &c."

To lie upon the Table.

Coal Mining Subsidence

9.36 am

Mr. Alan Meale (Mansfield): I beg to call attention to coal mining subsidence damage and its effects on properties, business and services; and to move,

That this House believes that the owners of houses, land, buildings, services and other constructions which have suffered any damage due to subsidence, resulting from the working and getting of coal or of coal and other minerals adjacent to or under their properties shall have the right to full repair and equitable compensation for any damage caused by such activities.

First, I want to place on record my thanks to hon. Members on both sides of the Chamber for the help they have given me in trying to sort out the problem of coal mining subsidence damage, particularly in the north Nottinghamshire and Derbyshire areas. I particularly want to mention my hon. Friends the Members for Ashfield (Mr. Haynes), for Bolsover (Mr. Skinner) and for Bassetlaw (Mr. Ashton) and the hon. Member for Sherwood (Mr. Stewart), who have greatly supported the efforts being made to secure justice for homeowners, businesses and service industries in the constituencies that they and I represent.

I thank also the Under-Secretary of State for Energy for his action arising from a debate on the subject 12 months ago. During my speech, I hope to show that, although he, as the Minister responsible, attempted to be helpful, little has been achieved despite all his efforts, and much still needs to be done.

I draw the Minister's attention to a survey undertaken by district councils in the north Nottinghamshire and Derbyshire areas. I shall explain in detail who were responsible for that survey and then dwell on its findings. It was undertaken by the staff of Trent polytechnic independently of the councils of Amber Valley, Bassetlaw, Ashfield, Mansfield, Bolsover, Chesterfield, Gedling, Newark and Sherwood, although they paid for it. I see that my hon. Friend the Member for Derbyshire, North-East (Mr. Barnes) is here. He has a great interest in the matter. He represents parts of the Chesterfield and Amber Valley district council areas.

If the Minister doubts the value of the report, I should explain to him that it was compiled by a multidisciplinary team organised by Trent polytechnic. Its membership consisted of Professor P. L. Clark, who was the project leader, Mr. W. G. Carter, a senior surveyor, Mr. P. Ramsay-Dawber, a senior surveyor, Mr. M. J. Saunt, another senior surveyor, Dr. R. H. Oldham, a mining engineer, Dr. A. C. Waltham, a geologist, Dr. M. Roberts, a research fellow and Pamela Burke, a research assistant.

The aims of the survey were many. The first was to obtain information relating to subsidence damage in the district council areas concerned. That is not surprising when one knows about the damage levels in those areas. I have often spoken in the House about damage to homes in particular, businesses—small, medium and large— schools, some of which have been either partially or wholly closed, and hospitals. I have also referred to cuts in services, such as water, gas and electricity.

The survey aimed, secondly, at establishing what were the most common concerns about the way in which damage problems were being dealt with at local level by British Coal. I hope to give many examples later.

[*Mr. Alan Meale*]

The third aim was to gain evidence for the Department of energy that would help it to deal with subsidence damage. The Minister will remember that I raised the matter after his responses 18 and 12 months ago about the evidence that his Department was compiling. He said that he hoped to let the House know about a series of decisions on how to alleviate the problem. I managed to gain from him on a number of occasions an assurance that his Department would accept evidence from the district councils. I am grateful to him for that assurance.

A fourth aim of the survey was to offer local authority help to the Department. Local authorities are responsible for planning, building regulations and various services. It would be difficult for anything to be sorted out without their help. They hope that their evidence will influence any legislation that the Government may introduce.

I emphasise that Opposition Members and all hon. Members who are trying to obtain justice for people who have suffered from the effects of subsidence, particularly in areas where coal mining takes place on a large scale, are not against British Coal. Our attitude is quite the reverse. The pressures that these communities experience are also being experienced by British Coal.

The chief executive of Mansfield district, Mr. Richard Goad, aptly described it in the report that is to be presented next Tuesday to the Minister. He says:

"The aim is not to smash British Coal around the head but to obtain equity for people suffering subsidence damage."

That is a very laudable aim. In no way could the council's attitude be construed as being against British Coal.

Everybody who is concerned about this problem recognises that the major factor is old damage, not new. New mining techniques have been introduced by British Coal in recent years. It is old damage that is causing the problem. The statistical evidence in the report provides an impartial information base for any future action that may be taken by the participating authorities.

The questionnaire that was used in the survey was specifically designed to provide information about a number of matters: first, the nature of any compensation that claimants may have received—for example, cash in kind; secondly, any compensation that they expected to receive; thirdly, the parties involved in the claims process —solicitors, estate agents, British Coal, subsidence agents, etc.; fourthly, the degree of statisfaction expressed by claimants in respect of remedial works by the contractors supplied by British Coal; fifthly, the number of subsidence claims outstanding, and many other factors.

Having decided to carry out the survey, local authorities were asked to distribute 160,000 leaflets, restricted to target areas that were known to have coal mining subsidence problems. Local businesses were also contacted by letter. The returned questionnaires were then sorted into two categories—affected and non-affected properties. Different distribution methods were used by each authority. It was thought that, if as wide a variety of methods as possible were used, it would help to reinforce the argument. I shall describe the different methods of distribution.

The questionnaires were distributed in Amber Valley with electoral registration forms and they were returned with the electoral registration forms by the occupiers. They were distributed only where there were known to be subsidence problems. The questionnaires were distributed by hand in Ashfield by council staff—with an addressed, unstamped envelope for return—to all areas in the district. In Bassetlaw, the questionnaire was distributed by means of the local authority's own newspaper and delivered to every house in the district. It was distributed in Bolsover by means of the local free newspaper and by using local newsagents, post offices and libraries in the area.

The questionnaires were distributed in Chesterfield in pre-paid envelopes with the electoral registration forms. Distribution was limited to areas that were likely to have experienced coal mining subsidence. In Gedling, the questionnaires were delivered by hand with the electoral registration forms and there was a pre-paid envelope. It was delivered only in areas that were known to have experienced mine working subsidence within the last 15 years.

The questionnaire was distributed by hand in Mansfield to every householder on the electoral register and it was collected, together with the filled-in electoral forms, by canvassers. In Newark and Sherwood, there was limited distribution of the questionnaire. It was delivered to people in areas where there were known to be underground mine workings. It was hand-delivered and part-collected by canvassers. The others were returned directly by householders.

In order to assess the views of those who responded, particularly concerning the quality of the repairs carried out by British Coal, a random sample of properties affected by mining subsidence were inspected by consultants. The sample included equal numbers of satisfied and dissatisfied claimants in each area. The Minister knows that the background to the debate is the Coal-Mining (Subsidence) Act 1950, which allows the owners of small dwelling houses the right to be compensated for repairs. The Act also covers those who have no rights to compensation under title deed. Another provision relates to a time limit for notice of damage to be given. The Act also provides that British Coal—then the National Coal Board—should be able to serve notice to the effect that repairs can be postponed until the likelihood of further damage has passed. It came to be known as a stop notice. The Minister will correct me if I am wrong, but I understand that the 1957 Act extended the statutory right of compensation to the owners of practically all land, buildings and works damaged by subsidence. The Act stated that British Coal was responsible for making damaged property reasonably fit for its normal use or making a payment equal to the loss in value of the property if the cost of remedial work was in excess of that sum. The Act also contained provision for a time limit from the date when damage was first noticed within which the claimant must have given written notice to British Coal. It also contained four provisions for temporary accommodation which had to be made available by British Coal if a dwelling was uninhabitable due to coal mining subsidence damage.

The Coal Industry Act 1975 extended and made clear British Coal's right to withdraw support in certain situations. The Act requires British Coal either to pay proper compensation or, with the claimant's consent, to make good the damage satisfactorily. Section 2 states that British Coal must give three months' notice of its intention to withdraw support in the few locations where it did not previously have the right to mine coal. Unlike the 1957 Act, the 1975 Act contains no provisions about the onus of proof of liability for any damage.

The Minister is aware that in 1976, as a response to calls for an improvement to the compensation system, a code of practice was introduced which set out five types of claim for which compensation could be given in addition to that already available under legislation: first, damage to chattels; secondly, home loss payments; thirdly, depreciation of crops; fourthly, farm loss payments; fifthly, additional payments to tenant farmers when compensation has been paid to landowners.

The final point is very important, as in my constituency it relates not to tenant farmers but to tenants and owners of properties. I have hundreds of cases, as do hon. Members on both sides of the House, in which small amounts of subsidence compensation were paid to previous owners or landlords, yet the damage has continued and, because of the cosmetic nature of the repair or the small amount of money which was paid, the present occupiers are now being denied any help, as they are being told that British Coal had covered its liability by previous payment or action.

The code also permitted any disputes between British Coal and claimants to be referred to independent arbitration. The coal board, as it was then, gave an undertaking to relieve hardship by dealing with claims sympathetically and allowing special discretionary payments in certain circumstances.

Those changes were made because of evidence gathered which pointed to a number of anomalies in methods which were causing problems. I shall list the problems in the evidence that was given at the time.

Case (a) was dissatisfaction over communications with British Coal by claimants, including complaints about the attitude of its officers, difficulty in contacting officers and the length of time taken, to deal with inquiries. Case (b) was resurgence of damage, often with British Coal denying liability. Case (c) was rejected claims. The reasons often given were that the last workings were too old, compensation had already been paid to the last owner or that damage was due to general dilapidation—or, simply, no reason was given. Case (d) was lack of information from British Coal, such as information regarding possible damage occurrence, how to claim, or claimants' rights. Case (e) was dissatisfaction with services provided by professional advisers. Case (f) was dissatisfaction with repairs, mainly quality of work, the attitude of contractors, the length of time to complete work. Case (g) was dissatisfaction with temporary accommodation provided by British Coal, with complaints about the length of time complainants had to spend away from their own homes and the standard of temporary accommodation provided. Case (h) was complaints about the lack of compensation for financial losses suffered through damage to furniture and fittings, loss of earnings and expenditure on repairs which was not compensated for by British Coal. Case (i) was stress and strain caused by damage disturbance during repairs or simply difficulty in gaining full restitution. Case (j) was loss of property value. Case (k) was difficulty in selling damaged properties. Case (l) was lack of follow-up by British Coal. Case (m) was houses which had to be demolished by British Coal. Case (n) was dissatisfaction with compensation payouts and lack of knowledge of what the amounts were supposed to cover.

On that last point, I agree entirely with the Minister that some of the problems we are now experiencing relate to compensation payments made in previous years. I

wholly agree that damage by coal mining subsidence requires not compensation but repair, and that we should proceed on that principle.

I regret to inform the Minister that, despite his efforts —I know that he has tried to sort them out—many complaints in the recent study mirror the complaints made in 1976 and those given later to the Waddilove inquiry. In my constituency of Mansfield, many of the same complaints are made.

During the last full debate on the issue, I raised a number of cases on which I could not get any sense out of British Coal. I promised the Minister that I intended to deal with those cases personally and that I would not discuss them during the debate. However, I raise the matter again because, when I raised them with the Minister, it appeared that those people were clearly being denied their rights. In certain instances, the position was so clear that I thought that it was simply a matter of the Minister contacting British Coal to review those cases for some action to be taken. I regret to inform the Minister that, despite his efforts in contacting British Coal, the reverse has happened.

I have a letter from British Coal dated 17 August 1988 concerning one of the cases which, after the debate on the matter, the Minister asked British Coal to review.

The letter is from the chairman of British Coal, who denied any movement whatsoever in respect of all the cases. It referred to Mr. G. Johnson of 22 Bosworth Street, Mansfield and stated:

"The last mineworkings in the vicinity of this particular property took place in 1974. Any damage arising from those workings would have become apparent soon afterwards, but it was not until July 1983 that the Corporation received a claim on behalf of Mr. Johnson, through his Agent, Alan Brentnall. An inspection of the property did not reveal any recent damage for which the Corporation has a liability. The Area confirm that subsidence damage exists in the property, but this is in their view considerably more than six years old and is therefore, out of time."

I find that absolutely amazing, as I have visited the home of my constituent many times. The property is so badly damaged that, until the repairs are done, I feel that my constituent should not stay there. The walls are leaning, the ceiling is displaced and there are cracks and small fissures in the footpaths and garden area.

My constituent works all night as a care attendant for the social services. When I originally contacted British Coal, it was not about whether British Coal would sort out the matter, but whether it would either pay an amount to my constituent so that, because he worked permanent nights, he could have those repairs done for him, or that it would quickly get him temporary accommodation.

What is amazing about that incident is that the records that I have clearly confirm that the inquiry about Mr. Johnson's property was earlier than the date stated in the review. Also, it is a semi-detached house and the adjoining semi-detached house has been completely repaired by British Coal. It has carried out repairs almost exactly similar to those of which Mr. Johnson's property is in dire need. The agent and Mr. Johnson have supplied evidence that, some years ago, British Coal sent out its so-called independent arbiters, British Mining Consultants, or whoever it was at that time, who agreed on site that this was recent coal mining subsidence damage.

Having gone back to British Coal and reminded it of all those facts, the only letter I received back from it was to say that the evidence, advice and ruling on site or off site

[*Mr. Alan Meale*]

by British Mining Consultants had been reviewed, and the ruling was subsequently found to be wrong. Mr. Johnson was then denied liability, because, as British Coal pointed out, it was not bound to accept the evidence. It just had to put in place the mechanism to have that property inspected. That is a silly and completely unindependent attitude.

The second case concerns a Mr. and Mrs. Lilley of 37 Harropwhite road, Mansfield. British Coal states:

"The last mineworkings in the vicinity of Mrs. Lilley's property took place in 1978 and a claim was received seven years after the last mining took place and at least six years after any damage would have become apparent."

That again is an amazing reply, because the dates which I have confirm what the chairman of British Coal is saying about this property. It is unbelievable that British Coal could say there is no new damage to the property, because I have seen further deterioration of the property due to subsidence during the 12 to 18 months in which I have been visiting it. The fissures are larger in the garden area and the walls have undoubtedly moved. They have been moved not by a crowbar, but by ground movement. The evidence is clearly not correct.

Another property is 42 Southwell road east, about which British Coal states:

"The last mining to take place in the vicinity of this property arose from Rufford colliery in 1983-84. A claim received from the Agent"——

again Alan Brentnall——

"was considered by Nottinghamshire area".

British Coal went on to say that an amount of money was offered in recompense for subsidence damage to this property.

The property is a bungalow situated on the Southwell road, towards Rainworth in Mansfield. I raise this case because the amount offered would probably not buy a fairly elderly detached property in Mansfield. The property concerned is, in fact, a detached bungalow with considerable ground space. British Coal's offer for the property is completely ridiculous.

British Coal went on to say that it has agreed that the case should go to the Lands Tribunal. That disturbs me, because eventually any independent tribunal or civil court would rule in my constituent's favour. British Coal has accepted that the damage to the bungalow has been caused by coal mining subsidence. It is clearly in desperate need of either demolition or repair. If one goes in the bedroom of the property, one can see the outside world through the walls. There are cracks from one end of the wall to the other and from the ceiling to the floor, windows are displaced and the outside walls and the pavements are cracked. It is in a seriously damaged state.

It is amazing that, as part of the remedy to the problem, the Government have suggested the use of the Lands Tribunal system. It will cost at least £120,000 for that case to go through the Lands Tribunal system, but at present that is the way in which it is heading. As British Coal's offer is ludicrous, that tribunal will undoubtedly rule in favour of the full repair of the property, restitution and compensation payments. I believe that the Lands Tribunal is being abused by British Coal. It is being used as a mechanism to get the people who own the property to take a lesser amount, and one which could not in any way replace the type of property that they have at present. It

has been used to slow up the negotiating process, and British Coal is attempting to get a settlement prior to the tribunal.

The next property is at 24 Williamson street, Mansfield and is owned by Mr. and Mrs. Sharman. Again, British Coal is saying that the claim was received seven years after mining took place. Mr. Sharman worked all his working life in Sherwood colliery. He was a deputy responsible for the safety of those cutting coal underground. On the day of his retirement, he was to finish work at 4 o'clock, but he had to be more or less dragged from the coal face to the top of the colliery to be informed that he was now retired. He gave all his working life to the industry, and he knows when mining took place. He also knows that every house surrounding his has been accepted for damage repair and those repairs have been carried out.

Why is Mr. Sharman's case different? I put it to the Minister that his case is little different from many of those in my area. Mr. Sharman's property is a semi-detached house in a crescent. It was a council house that he bought from the council. British Coal says in its reply:

"I understand that Mr. and Mrs. Sharman as sitting tenants, purchased the property from Mansfield District Council in its damaged condition during 1983 and this was presumably taken into account in the purchase price agreed."

That was not taken into account. Mansfield district council sold that council house under the conditions which normally apply, with the price taking into account the number of years that the tenant has lived in that property, which in Mr. Sharmer's case was considerable. The price was based on the price of housing in that area, less the discount that he was allowed as a sitting tenant. No adjustment of the price was made because of damage to the property. It is cheeky of British Coal to talk about the price that people pay for their council houses. That has nothing to do with British Coal. All that British Coal has to consider is the cost of a similar house in a similar area. It is about time that it stopped using that argument.

The next affected property is 45 High street, Mansfield Woodhouse, Nottinghamshire. There is no joke in the fact that the owners of the property are Mr. and Mrs. Swindell. The Chamber is not the right place in which to have a conversation with the Minister about the swindles that have occurred in coal mining areas, but I am prepared to do so privately. Mr. and Mrs. Swindell are absolutely honest in their determination to try to get their property repaired. They live in a small stone cottage in Mansfield Woodhouse High street and it is seriously damaged. It is not a council house but a listed property, and it must be repaired. British Coal has said that the claim is out of time and that there are no new defects arising out of coal mining subsidence problems. That is wholly misleading. There is clear evidence that the movement and subsequent defects in the property are worsening all the time. Properties in the near vicinity, almost adjacent to the cottage, have moved and claims have been lodged and accepted, but the claims for this property have not been accepted.

It is totally misleading to claim that mining has not occurred. About eight weeks ago I received plans of the current and intended coal mine workings in the Mansfield Woodhouse area. There were three separate plans, one showing the area that is being worked and has been worked for about 18 months for the Shirebrook pit. The other plans showed the workings that would be undertaken in October of this year and in the next 18 months after that. To my mind the coal that has been cut for the past 18 months—it is scheduled to finish in November—has been worked directly adjacent to the cottage. Unbeknown to the chairman of British Coal, who signed the letter to Mr. and Mrs. Swindell, a review had been carried out by the Nottinghamshire or central division of British Coal. The information it collected was incorrect. The plans I received were produced not by builders on the district council, but by the estates department for central area. It is clear that workings have been undertaken near to the cottage and that workings are planned to proceed close to it.

The cottage is listed, and I am not sure whether it could survive any further damage. After all, the new workings will be undertaken almost underneath it. If the worst happens, what then? Will the central division of British Coal say that the damages were old, and that therefore they should not be repaired? That is ludicrous. If the current damage is out of time, it will be considerably worsened by the effects of new mining. That does not mean that British Coal is liable for part repair only, it means that it has considerably worsened the existing damage. The Minister should write to the chairman of British Coal to see whether his officers in the various areas can investigate the properties I have mentioned.

I receive hundreds of complaints from constituents who cannot get any sense from British Coal. Things have improved, but people still ring for days and they are rarely able to get through. When they do, they are often told that the person they want is not there. Many have taken it upon themselves to visit the Nottingham headquarters of British Coal at Edwinstowe. Edwinstowe is a considerable distance from my constituency and many of the people about whom we are talking are elderly and many have given their lives to the coal industry. Those people have to go by car, get a lift from someone or make a series of bus journeys to get to Edwinstowe. When they get there, they are usually given exactly the same response as that given on the telephone: they are told that the person they want is unavailable, but that their details will be noted.

People are extremely anxious about their homes—they are not council houses, but their own homes. Because of their fears and the stress that that causes, those people are pesistent and they eventually get through to the necessary people at British Coal. Their success is a result of having written a series of letters or made God knows how many telephone calls. In some circumstances, people have pressured British Coal so much that it is more fed up with them than they are with British Coal. Once they make contact, people are given all kinds of promises. They are told that inspectors will be sent out, that British Coal will deal with a person's agent or whatever. The way in which British Coal handles this matter must be improved considerably.

Many of my constituents complain about the attitude of some officers employed by British Coal who visit their homes. Many say that they are "offhand" and show little compassion or sympathy with their problem. That problem must be resolved. I appreciate the difficulties and stress encountered by the staff of British Coal in the Nottinghamshire area. They are overworked and stretched, resources are limited and they face a growing number of complaints. What has happened is not the fault of the staff; it is the scale of the damage that has caused the problems. I cannot condone the current situation nor can the Minister. We need action to try to help British Coal's staff and the people suffering damage to their homes.

Why does British Coal say that recurrence of damage is not its liability? That defeats me. If damage recurs it is because the original damage was not properly repaired or because the damage was greater than initially judged. In common with other hon. Members on both sides of the Chamber, I have hundreds of cases on file where further help has been refused, but when British Coal carried out the initial repairs, the contract price was so low that it enabled only cosmetic repairs to be done. The work involved little more than papering cracks and in-filling plaster or paint into cracked walls. It is only common sense to realise that such repairs will last only a short time. British Coal cannot morally argue that it has fulfilled its responsibilities with such repairs. If it believes that, it is conning itself as well as those people with damaged properties.

A better system of communication on rejected claims must be established. At present, British Coal can use the compensation agents hired by property owners to their detriment. The large amounts of financial compensation, as opposed to repair work, that was paid by British Coal and the use and growth of agents have caused problems to the coal-mining areas. Some years ago, there was a compensation bonanza, when large amounts were paid out on claims. We are still living with the effects of that bonanza. My area has suffered massive damage, and many claims were made. From the evidence that I have collected, it appears that anyone who could use a slide rule put himself forward as a compensation agent. Considerable amounts of money were involved.

Earlier, I talked about swindles and frauds. Some arrests occurred of people who work for British Coal in the Nottinghamshire area. Some of them are still on charges awaiting trial, people have gone to gaol and staff have been sacked. We have to think about some of the problems in that area. Many agents, as they call themselves, were interviewed by police. In many cases the use of compensation agents is a deterrent to trying to solve the problem. One agent has so many cases on his file that it is unlikely that anybody will be able to get a settlement.

Little or no communication takes place between home owners and British Coal. British Coal is changing the system and no longer maintains contact with property owners, but a second-class stamp is all that it needs to keep in touch with an owner. Some of my constituents have had to wait months for letters, so it seems that not many second-class stamps are being used.

Agents are used as a mechanism to create a barrier between the home owner and British Coal. Because agents are exerting pressure in order to get settlements and chasing tens or hundreds of cases, they cannot contact people as often as they should. They are trying to cut their costs by not making contact with the home owners or people in British Coal. The people who suffer are the property owners; sometimes it is months before they know about offers or rejections.

The Minister should ask himself why agents are being used at all, because that question is fundamental to the debate. I can tell him that it is basically because home owners in coal mining areas do not trust British Coal to do a fair deal. The evidence in the report shows that people who deal directly with British Coal get a better deal more swiftly. Coal mining is the major industry in some areas and many people have given their lives to it or to one of the industries that serves it. It is sad that an industry which has completely dominated an area is now thoroughly

[*Mr. Alan Meale*]

distrusted by the people living there. The National Coal Board was always regarded as a caring employer, but British Coal has lost that trust.

Bearing in mind the amount of money that is still in the fund, can the Minister say whether he would consider funding, on a trial basis, an experimental, independent legal centre to deal with subsidence claims? The money required to do that would be minimal—peanuts compared to the amount in the fund. A centre could be set up in Nottinghamshire or Derbyshire for both areas. Three or four people could operate the centre and concern themselves only with coal mining subsidence. That would be helpful and the centre would be financially viable. It would enable claimants to get expert advice and representation, especially in areas such as north Nottinghamshire.

Subsidence money is already in the bank waiting to be used. Because of the age of many of the people involved, many of the cases would be legally aided and, with the correct legal advice, people would not be conned or shoved up alleyways. Some people are being told by agents that they should get £50,000, £60,000 or £70,000. They find out that Mrs. Smith down the street got £24,000 or Mr. White round the corner got £14,000, or they are told that they should not take the compensation but should have the house repaired. If we had a proper legal centre, people would be able to determine their exact rights.

For a small additional amount, such a legal centre would be able to liaise with another body which I shall propose. That might take some of the pressure off British Coal, and that is a key factor. The small amount of money required is already there and it is not British Coal or Government money. It has been deducted from the sale of coal and set aside for subsidence grants. Such a scheme would save money because to take a case through the Lands Tribunal can cost six-figure sums. There are thousands of cases and, as I shall later show, many of them could go in that direction if that is the only option. If there was another option, it would be helpful all round.

Fourthly, of major concern to many of my constituents is the lack of information. I accept that British Coal has improved its distribution of information, but much more needs to be done. A central register for damage and property repairs for each district, kept up to date weekly or monthly by the local authority, needs to be available. That is important in areas where, because of coal mining, damage has occurred to properties.

The Conservative party is the party of business and urges people to be entrepreneurial and to stand on their own two feet. We are talking about my constituents and the constituents of my hon. Friends the Members for Ashfield and for Derbyshire, North-East and the hon. Member for Sherwood. Anybody who wants to buy a house goes to an estate agent and asks for a search to be carried out. He receives a piece of paper containing about three sentences and it costs £14·50. It says on the bottom of the piece of paper that if more information is required it will cost another £32. Sometimes it takes weeks to get such information. Who will trust information supplied in that way?

Prospective home buyers are investors and should be able to pop down to the local authority to have a look at a damage register. They could locate the street and check

to see whether there has been any damage or compensation paid or whether repairs have been carried out. When people are investing tens of thousands of pounds in a house or business it is common sense that they should have access to such a register. The documents that I have here are registers from eight local authorities. They are a considerable size, but when the Minister gets his copy it will be smaller.

The registers contain the addresses of damaged properties and the names of the occupants. They will be presented in an indexed form in a booklet. Each of the areas has been surveyed and the results lodged with a local authority, so that anybody who wants to buy a house can see if the property has been damaged or if a claim has been lodged or paid. It is not hard to do, and it would help everybody concerned.

The fifth factor is dissatisfaction with professional advisers, something that I have already mentioned. The Minister should seriously examine the independence of the so-called independent mining consultants being used by British Coal, about which I have great doubts. It was largely through the Minister that we got these independent consultants, because he pushed the case for them and got British Coal to respond by using them more than it had done. In my constituency and that of other hon. Members, the independence of these consultants has been questioned. In every case where they have ruled that subsidence damage clearly exists, even going so far as to talk about what kind of settlement or schedule should be reached, when British Coal has asked for reconsideration of the case, the agents have stood on their heads and changed their decisions. This has happened in hundreds of cases, and there must be something wrong about that. There must be doubt about the independence of such people.

Mr. Frank Haynes (Ashfield): My hon. Friend has hit an important point. My experience, over many years of representing my constituents in Ashfield who have had the problem of mining subsidence, has been similar. For many years we had a fair deal from the National Coal Board and then, suddenly, there was a change and, following the appointment of Ian MacGregor as chairman of the NCB, which became British Coal, it took on an independent body of mining consultants. These people were turning down claims willy-nilly, despite the fact that serious damage had been caused to property. I agree with my hon. Friend, and the Minister should be aware that we shall look seriously at these independent consultants to see what is going on, because of the unfairness of the decisions that affect the people whom we represent.

Mr. Meale: I agree with my hon. Friend. I have been told by people qualified in this sector that such changes of decision are not surprising. The work of these so-called independent consultants is on such a small scale that, if they started to stamp their feet and refuse to change their decisions, other consultants would be used and business would be lost. I should like the Minister to consider this point. If there are to be independent consultants, as there are in industrial relations—we are aware that the Government are arguing the case over rail strikes and miners' strikes and God knows what else—there should also be binding arbitration so that we can see the real value of the independent side of the consultation.

There is dissatisfaction with repairs, which mainly concerns the quality of work and the attitude of contractors. Many hundreds of complaints about the quality of finished work and the appropriateness of the work carried out have been received. The Minister should have this investigated. The prices offered for many repair jobs are so low that many builders will not do them until the winter, when other contracts are slack. Furthermore, many builders use British Coal repair contracts as fill-in jobs, because the prices are so low, so many jobs take weeks to complete.

Many constituents complain to me that in their homes, all their furniture has been moved into one room and is covered in sheets and that they are having to live in that one room while the damage is being repaired. For example, somebody has come round and put a bit of plaster on the wall, but it is taking weeks for them to come back to paint it or put on wallpaper. This is all wrong. It is mainly a result of the prices paid. I have spoken to many builders, from large, medium and small building firms, and they say that, if they could get enough work, they would not bother with British Coal work because of the low prices and because workmen get hassled; it is not a viable exercise for them.

There is dissatisfaction about temporary accommodation. Many complaints are received about the length of time spent in temporary rooms, while at the same time there are lengthy waiting lists for people to be given such accommodation while their homes are being repaired. Twelve months ago, the situation was disgraceful. Hundreds of people were waiting to have their homes repaired but could not have the work done because of the lack of temporary accommodation. There has been movement as a result of the Minister's actions following the debate 12 months ago, and I thank him for that. However, more needs to be done and I hope that the Minister will keep up the pressure to take the strain off the people waiting for repairs.

I have received many complaints about compensation for financial loss. Again, since the last debate, British Coal is helpful whenever possible. One difficulty has been losses accrued through loss of working days while inspections and repairs are carried out. Since the Minister put pressure on British Coal, there has been a better relationship with it, and in a number of cases it has spent quite a lot of time and effort, in difficult circumstances, sorting things out. However, when repairs and inspections are carried out on property, people have to be there to inspect it. They cannot leave the key and say, Inspect it and I will accept your judgment." Inspectors miss damage sometimes. Furthermore, British Coal inspectors find it helpful to have present the person who owns the house because they can explain what is old and what is new and what needs to be done.

The Government encourage people to buy their own homes, and therefore to have a mortgage. Growing interest rates put an increasing burden on home owners, so they are anxious not to lose money by taking days off work. They want to keep up with the bills so that their houses will not be repossessed and they can keep the financial wheels turning. Some 120,000 people live in my district council area and they do not have well-paid jobs like people who live in Westminster, Pimlico, Hampstead and the like. Many of my people are unemployed, but those who are in employment are not on high wages, and cannot afford to lose money.

There is no doubt that worries over repairs, particularly of homes, causes stress and strain. Many cases on my files involve elderly and infirm people and the unemployed, who suffer serious stress through lack of action or even acceptance of liability by British Coal of its responsibility for damage. It is sad that this is happening. I understand, of course, that Department of Health Ministers are directly concerned, and that the Under-Secretary of State is not. I know of two cases where, without any shadow of doubt, the stress and strain that has followed the denial of liability for repairs has led to serious illnesses.

The stress that I see in people's faces, especially those of the elderly, who come regularly to my surgery to see whether they can get help, is proof to me that the stress and strain can cause illness, and sometimes serious illness. I hope that the Minister will take this factor into account in his determination of these matters and in his final recommendations. I hope also that he will try to ensure that British Coal acts more swiftly.

The 10th area of concern is loss of property value. Without any proper guarantee of acceptance of liability, property values have been affected. Property values in north Nottinghamshire, an area of coal mines, demonstrate the effect of subsidence on house prices. Mansfield is one of the cheapest housing areas in Britain. The problems that have come to light over recent years have been reflected in property values, and people in the areas that have been affected are having to sell their properties at lower values than those which prevail in other parts of the country. If anyone wants to sell his home or purchase a home, he will have searches carried out on the property. Sometimes the process takes many weeks to complete. This obviously delays movement within the property market.

British Coal regards the head of claim as extremely important when it comes to determine whether the claim is in time under the six-year rule. A claim is made, and sometimes, after years of waiting for a determination, the owner moves on. When that happens the new owner will have to make a new claim. I ask the Minister to consider whether that is fair. I have met people who were told on buying a property that a claim had already been made and that they would be able to have various repairs carried out. That is not the position. British Coal is saying that, if the head of claim—the owner of the property—changes, all bets are off.

That is a nifty device under the six-year rule. British Coal has only to wait for owners to get so fed up with the delay before repairs are carried out that they decide to move on. When that happens, it is no longer liable. Under the six-year rule, the claim founders. I ask the Minister to intervene. If a property is damaged and a claim is made within time, surely the claim remains in time even if there is a change of ownership. The fact is that many claims have been denied because of a change in the head of claim. It is ludicrous to deny that the properties concerned need repairing.

The 11th area of concern is dissatisfaction with compensation payments and lack of knowledge of what the payments are supposed to cover. This concern is linked undoubtedly with dissatisfaction with the standard of repairs that are carried out. Many people who are not builders do not understand the difference between cosmetic repairs and major repairs. If a builder comes to someone's home to repair damage and says that skimming is all that is required, the owner will be willing to accept

[*Mr. Meale*]

that. He will be pleased that repairs are being done. There is a difference, as I have said, between cosmetic repair and cosmetic damage, and full repair and serious damage.

Many owners are unaware that by signing an agreement to have cosmetic repairs carried out, they are thereby losing any right to full repair. This has happened many times. British Coal has applied pressure and has stated that cosmetic repairs only are needed. It has said, "This or nothing. If you do not accept the scheduled cosmetic repairs that we are offering, you will get no further response from us. We shall delay matters. You will have to go to court, and that will take a considerable time." Presumably these decisions are reached behind closed doors between the so-called agents and members of British Coal's estates department staff.

In many instances, people accept cosmetic repairs because they are fed up with their houses being undecorated. It is pointless decorating a house when it is known that plastering, rewiring, reflooring and the fitting of new doors are required. People are told not to redecorate while their claim is being determined, but sometimes the process takes three, four or five years. How would the Minister like it if he could not carry out any redecorations in his house for three, four or five years? The reality is that many property owners have had enough. If it is a question of cosmetic rather than full repairs, they accept the cosmetic approach because they want to live in a normal home environment.

I refer again to the Nottinghamshire-Derbyshire district council survey. I have stated already that 160,000 questionnaires were distributed to households by various methods. More than 50,000 completed questionnaires were returned. More than 33,000 respondents—64 per cent.—claimed that their residences had suffered damage as a result of coal mine workings. It can be argued that some of these claims are wrong, that some of them might be misleading, and that others might be deliberately misleading. That could be said of three, 33 or 330, but not of more than 33,000

A random selection of properties was carried out in each area covered by the survey and subsequently the properties were inspected by qualified members of the survey team. There were reports of damage throughout the areas covered by the survey where coal mining had taken place. Bearing in mind the many occasions on which my hon. Friend the Member for Ashfield and I have raised the matter with the Minister, he will not be surprised when I tell him that 70 per cent. of the allegedly damaged houses were found to be in the Mansfield and Ashfield district council areas.

Bolsover district council sent out 27,900 questionnaires and received 3,077 returns. That was a response of 11 per cent. There were 2,127 claims of subsidence damage. Of the 3,077 returns, 939 reported no subsidence damage. Chesterfield district council sent out 6,500 questionnaires. There were 1,957 returns. That was a response of 30·1 per cent. Of the 6,500 questionnaires, 1,927 reported subsidence damage. Only 28 per cent. reported no subsidence damage. Gedling district council sent out 6,034 questionnaires and received back 3,792. That was a response of 62·8 per cent. There were 2,970 claims of subsidence damage. There were 775 reports of no subsidence damage.

In Bassetlaw, 16,000 questionnaires were delivered and only 751, or 5 per cent., were returned. They showed 180 cases of subsidence damage and 564 cases of no damage. In the Amber Valley area, 12,000 questionnaires were sent out. Of those 7,589, 63 per cent., were returned. They showed that there were 2,747 cases of damage and 4,842 cases of no damage. In the Newark and Sherwood area 13,000 questionnaires were distributed and 3,252—25 per cent.—were returned. The returns showed that 1,132 properties sustained damage, while 1,963 were undamaged.

The high figure of over 70 per cent. arose in Ashfield, where 41,952 questionnaires were distributed and 12,050 were returned. That was 30 per cent. of the total. Subsidence damage was reported in 9,730 properties and no subsidence damage in 2,320. In Mansfield, 40,787 questionnaires were distributed and 17,744—43·5 per cent. —were returned. Of those, 12,321 reported damage and 4,994 showed no damage.

Those figures show that there were claims that 33,134 properties had been damageed. Those claims have been ratified by the checks made by a qualified survey team. They also show that 16,425 properties were unaffected. In simple terms, those figures show that only 20·7 per cent. of questionnaires were returned. They also show that 66.8 per cent. of returns indicated subsidence damage. In real terms, the figure is much higher, as many people did not bother to fill in the forms, as the percentage of returns shows. In particular, very little public or private rented accommodation replied to the survey.

It is also important to note that the business community, apart from small businesses, was not included in the survey. The Minister has agreed to hold a meeting next Tuesday with interested parties. A senior official of the Severn-Trent water authority will be present at that meeting and he will refer to the millions of pounds worth of damage in the public industry sector. There are difficulties in the gas and electricity industries. The county council also has difficulties with roads and sewers. The business community is very deeply concerned. I hope that the Minister will accept that we are today talking only about privately owned houses and that the problem is really far worse than that.

Other factors also emerged from the survey. It showed that the claims procedure differed throughout the research areas. It also showed that claims were protracted where an agent was appointed by the householder, as I stressed earlier. Claims made directly by the householder to British Coal generally proceeded satisfactorily, as I also stressed earlier.

The survey also showed that few householders received a schedule of work. A schedule was generally prepared when an agent had been appointed and was used as a basis for claims from British Coal. That is amazing. I have seen some of the schedules. I know that negotiations continue between agents and British Coal, as I have received hundreds of the damned schedules. It is amazing that people are not generally given a schedule of damage.

The impression gained from the survey was that many householders did not know when work would commence or by whom. Because the builder usually did not provide a programme of work, householders' homes were worked on without consideration to the occupants' usual needs. For example, in certain circumstances, all rooms were worked upon simultaneously, householders were given insufficient time to prepare for the work and there was a lack of continuity of work by the builder.

The survey also showed that quality control was at the discretion of the householder. As no schedule of work was usually available, quality control generally proved difficult for householders to undertake. Quality control by British Coal has been more in evidence in recent years and I have no doubt that that has happened because of complaints that were sent to the Minister.

The survey showed that householders had little control over the quality of the finished work. I could quote many instances to the Minister of people who have said to the builder as he was about to walk through the door, "What about that?" The builder would reply, "That's got nothing to do with us. It's Friday afternoon, we'll be back on Monday morning. That's not in the schedule. Where's the schedule?" The builder simply has a sheet of paper telling him what work to do. In hundreds of cases, people have waited years for a contractor or someone from British Coal to turn up to repair the last piece of damage in the programme. Those people continue to live in unrepaired accommodation.

The survey showed that dissatisfied householders were concerned about what was and what was not claimable. The allowances given for decorating—for example the rate for wallpaper—were felt to be inadequate in some cases. If this was not so sad, it would be ludicrous. People have shown me an example of a certain quality of wallpaper on their walls. However, they complain that the amount of money allowed by British Coal for wall covering provides for only very basic coverings. If wallpaper or paint is required, it should be of an acceptable standard. British Coal should not have to indulge in piddling and peripheral negotiations.

The survey also showed that there were complaints about the general lack of care and protection of personal possessions and the use of householders' equipment and facilities without permission. The builders do not actually go in and cook sausages and chips on a householders cooker. However, once they have placed coverings on the furnishings, they sit down and lounge about the house. They usually, ruin the kitchen sink because they stick buckets, plaster and paint in it. The Minister may smile at this, but he knows that it is true. He would not have it in his home. Would he like that to happen to him? We are not talking about people who can nip off to the south of France. We are talking about people who want to go to work in the mornings.

There are also complaints about irregular attendance of builders. Some builders disappear for weeks, months or years. That is a bit of a bind, and people are worried because they never quite know when the builder will come back through the door. Sometimes it is so bad that, when the builder comes up the path, he is greeted like a Littlewoods or Vernons pools officer, his appearance is so rare.

There were complaints that householders did not receive formal notification of the completion of work. The builder, as he walks through the door, often says, "That has nothing to do with me."

There seemed to be a disparity between amounts claimable within the same locality. That applied to Mr. Johnson's case. People in one house might be given wallpaper, while those in the neighbouring houses were not. Some houses would have their drains or footpaths

repaired and others would not. In many instances, the state of the houses denied such services would be worse than that of those that received them.

There was a lack of information about what work would be undertaken, when and how. The impression gained was that householders who had been or were currently employed by British Coal expected preferential treatment. My colleagues and I hear that argument time and again. People tell us, "I gave my life to the coal industry. I did not miss a shift in God knows how many years." In Nottinghamshire, they say, "I stood four square with the present Government during the miners' strike. I went to work in opposition to my colleagues. It has caused rifts within my family. Yet I am being treated in this way."

Some householders reported that the builders had a "don't care" attitude to the work. As I told the Minister earlier, I think that that attitude is connected with what builders are paid. They will be in and out as quickly as they can, because the job is probably a "fill-in" and they want to get it over with.

When householders were informed that there would be a delay in handling claims or undertaking work, they generally accepted that. Not knowing was the factor that caused them distress. Householders have come to me with stories of having spoken to the agent three years ago, having received a letter from British Coal and another from the agent a year ago, and having heard nothing since. Surely there is some way of letting people know that the matter is still being dealt with, even if it is only a standard letter with a second class stamp.

The administrative procedure used by British Coal appears to have been inconsistent. Some officers issued claim forms, whereas others relied on receiving letters or telephone calls from householders. In one village—I believe that it is in the constituency of the hon. Member for Sherwood—a public meeting was organised by British Coal, and in another village British Coal undertook door-to-door inquiries.

I do not think that that is a bad idea. Public relations are important, particularly with people who work or worked in the industry or in its service sectors. It is part of the style of a caring employer and a caring industry. It might not be a bad idea either, given the traumas that the industry has been through in recent years, for British Coal to do that more often: it used to do it in the past, and it is good practice in any community.

The public relations aspect of British Coal was perceived by householders to be rather poor. Householders assumed that schedules produced by agents would be the exact list of work to be undertaken when that was not the case. They have been presented with a dilemma. One or two agents will come into the house and look around. They will say, "Oh, yes, I will put that down on the list." Before an agent has left the back kitchen, there will be enough down on his list to make the householder think that he will have a fitted kitchen with quarry tiles and the whole works, and that each room will undergo similar improvements. People are conned into believing that they will get the whole world. By the time the agents are out of the front door, it seems that, if all that has been promised were to come to fruition, the accumulated cost would be such that it would be better to give the householder a house twice the value of the current one.

There is also the problem of independent consultants. They give schedules for what needs to be done; then people who expected to have their repairs done at a cost of

[*Mr. Meale*]

£15,000 or £16,000 suddenly receive an offer of £2,200 through the letterbox. It frightens the living daylights out of them, because of all the problems that have been pointed out to them.

No written guidelines appear to have been prepared to assist in the process of deciding marginal cases, such decisions being made only by British Coal's surveyors. That is rather sad. Where is the independence there? Why could not a local authority send out an inspector? After all, many of the houses used to be owned by local authorities. The inspectors would not say, "Right, we think that you should have everything." They are qualified, understanding people, and they are not going to start abusing their position and indenting for new front doors and walls. If their budgets are controlled, they will respond appropriately.

Some householders were not made aware that significant changes to their homes would occur during and after building work. That, too, is an important point. Like other hon. Members, I have come across such cases. The building work is carried out, and it looks wonderful. It takes away the stress and strain and the householder looks forward to the future. Then he trips on the way into the living room, because the floor is as much as 4 in higher and there is a step there. The way may be in a slightly different position; doors may have been moved. There seems to be no understanding of the effect that that will have on someone who has lived in the same property for years—in some cases, generations.

Each property had repairs which could be regarded as "cosmetic": substantial damage has been repaired, but there was also a good deal of botching up and covering up. All the evidence from the surveyors points to that. The surveyors were not made aware by the householders of any guarantees for other repair work. Householders may believe that something has been repaired and that if there are any more problems they can get back on to British Coal, but, as I have told the Minister, that is not the case. If they do that, they will be told, "Hang on, in 1985 you signed a form and that ended our liability"—although British Coal must have known in its heart of hearts that, without the shadow of a doubt, the damage was more considerable than was being implied.

Many householders had found that claiming for damage and the execution of repairs was a process that caused them considerable distress. In some cases, the stress was the apparent result of genuine grievance about the inconvenience; in others, it appeared to have been caused either by inability to understand the process of building work generally, or by a lack of knowledge of what might be regarded as genuine damage due to subsidence and what is an acceptable standard of repair.

The House is well aware of my concern about coal mining subsidence damage. According to a report that entirely supports the arguments that I have advanced since the last general election, my community has been and continues to be damaged by the effects of coal mining. Let me now discuss with the Minister what is to be done.

In response to a number of questions that I asked on 18 May this year, the Minister said:

"Administration of the subsidence compensation and repair system, including making the necessary provisions in the accounts, is a matter for British Coal."—[*Official Report*, 23 May 1989; Vol. 153, c. *445*.]

I do not think that that is a very helpful answer. Whatever the Minister may think about the responsibilities of British Coal or any other public sector industry, ultimately the responsibility is his: he is in charge of such matters in his Department. He is the person who has to take public responsibility for sorting out the matter, and I shall try to help him.

The Minister also answered a question that I tabled on 15 May 1989 asking him to give possible solutions to some of the dilemmas. He said:

"At the end of 1987-88 repair of and compensation for subsidence damage cost the corporation almost £50 million." —[*Official Report*, 15 May 1989; Vol. 153, c. *102*.]

It would help him greatly if he could find out over how many years that sum was accrued, how much of it was spent in repair and compensation, how much on administration of staff, how much on outside advisory costs, how much on legal costs and how much was paid to the claimants' agents.

I do not expect an answer today, but I think the Minister will find that a low proportion of the money was spent on the purpose for which it was intended: repairing damaged property. If my analysis is wrong, I shall gladly apologise to the Minister either in the Chamber or publicly, but I doubt that I am. However, even if I am, it is still the case that more than £200 million is left in the account which could be used to settle this problem. Presumably, it accrued because it was added to the budget for coal production and was set aside to solve the problems of coal mining subsidence damage.

Some of the money could also be used to set up in the coalfield areas, particularly those which provided the evidence, some form of trust made up of senior figures from local authorities, the legal profession and the mining industry, which could review cases for damage when liability was denied. I am sure that all hon. Members would be grateful if that could be set up on a trial basis for two or three years. If that were done, it would help the Minister because he would no longer keep receiving letters from hon. Members as these could be referred to the regional coalfield trust. I should like to think that local authorities would be represented on the trust because, after all, they have to sort out the problems. Such a trust could look at the major problem of old damage.

New mining techniques have largely solved the major problems. The trust would be appreciated not only by the owners of damaged properties, but by British Coal, which needs help with a problem that is draining a considerable amount of its energy and placing an enormous financial burden on its production activities and pits. It would help to take the pressure off British Coal and the huge number of staff it employs, and help it to meet its advisory costs.

The evidence given to me shows clearly that, before all hell broke loose at the end of the 1970s and early 1980s, the size of the estates department in Nottinghamshire was modest. However, events since then now mean that, if there is any trimming and rethinking to be done on management and design to help solve this problem, that is where it must be done. My hon. Friend the Member for Ashfield has frequently pointed out to me that merely half a dozen people, with some secretarial support, were employed in that department in Nottinghamshire in the 1970s. That number is now close to 50, with fairly high numbers of outside consultants to back them up. The process has gone too far. There is an amazing administrative bottleneck in the coal industry. A coalfield area trust, with a legal department to help it, could look at the old damage problems and review cases.

I wish to thank the Minister for expressing his willingness to meet the chief officers of the district councils next Tuesday morning. I hope that he will reconsider the invitation sent to him to visit the north Nottinghamshire area. This November, the district councils, Coalfield Communities Campaign representatives and county councils are holding a one-day seminar. The Minister has already been asked whether he can come, and has said that he will consider the proposal sympathetically, but that the date is too far off and that it is highly unlikely that he could attend.

I understand that some members of the Department of Energy have since said that they would like to attend. Nottinghamshire is of special interest to Conservative Members, and if the Minister came along we could show him some of the properties. Alternatively, he could stick a pin in the report that I have shown him today, of which he will receive copies, to see which properties to visit. I would be willing to give him the pin with which to do so. Even if he will not stick in the pin and burst the balloon, perhaps he will attend the seminar to give the Government's view. The problems are harrowing, and we need some direction. I hope that this debate has helped the Minister to decide what action he must take.

My hon. Friends the shadow Secretary of State for Energy and his shadow junior Minister, my hon. Friend the Member for Rother Valley (Mr. Barron), have agreed to attend the seminar, and it would be a shame if only one political voice was there to represent Nottinghamshire and Derbyshire. I understand that, on such occasions, the Minister often asks a local Member to represent him. On this occasion, I would go along with that, provided that the Minister will assure us that he will accept whatever his representative says and carry out his findings.

Once the Minister has read the excellent report, which he could do on his holidays or before, he will appreciate the full scale of the damage. Perhaps he will also consider, with his Parliamentary Private Secretary, other Conservative Members present, and even the Whips, that at 2.30 pm when the private Members' Bills are considered, when my Coal Mining Subsidence (Damage, Arbitration, Prevention and Public Awareness) Bill, which has support from both sides of the Chamber, is announced, instead of shouting, "Object," to allow it to proceed. A few Conservative Members smile, but I am prepared to accept that, if my Bill were allowed to proceed to Committee, where the Minister has an inbuilt majority, he could change it. The Government have the built-in numbers to do exactly that and I ask the Minister and the Whips to do it. It would form the basis for a solution to the problem.

I have said that this solution would be wholly self-financing and that £200 million or more is in the accounts for this purpose. I have mentioned a couple of ways in which help could be given to home owners, to British Coal, to the Minister, to businesses and to hon. Members. They would be cost-effective; the money has already been deducted. It exists precisely for this purpose and should be used for it.

We should also remember that the chairman of British Coal has just announced massive profits for this financial year, of £500 million. That money has been derived from the communities which are suffering damage and which will continue to suffer it in the future. Nottinghamshire

contributed £65 million to this profit, of which only a tiny amount need be used to try to find a solution to this problem——

The Parliamentary Under-Secretary of State for Energy (Mr. Michael Spicer): I had not meant to intervene, but it is important to set this point right for the record. The hon. Member for Mansfield (Mr. Meale) is correct to say that there was a notional operating profit, as defined by British Coal, but that was before many other costs had been incorporated in the calculations—in particular, the cost of borrowing, which is a cost usually associated with any business, and the costs of restructuring and redundancies. When British Coal has included those costs, it has to return to Parliament the whole time to ask for more money. The hon. Gentleman must not mislead the House on that point, which is central to a balanced discussion of the subject.

Mr. Meale: I thank the Minister. We should take into account certain costs that have to be deducted. Nevertheless, British Coal is a profitable business now— the chairman has said as much.

These are areas which have been seriously damaged by the effects of a major industry. Elderly, infirm and unemployed people have, directly or indirectly, given their lives to that industry. They do not live in Bermuda or the south of France: they live in the backbone of Britain, in coal mining communities which produce wealth and energy for the nation. I ask all hon. Members and the Minister to help us begin some movement—not subsidence —towards a solution to the problem.

11.23 am

Sir Hugh Rossi (Hornsey and Wood Green): Having listened to the difficult constituency cases which the hon. Member for Mansfield (Mr. Meale) has detailed at some length, I can understand his anxiety and desire to raise all the problems related to coal mining subsidence this morning. I am relieved not to have such problems in my constituency, although I have troubles enough.

I take an abiding interest in compensation and environmental issues and I want to address the House on the broader aspects of the tribulations of the hon. Gentleman's constituents. I have long held the view that when persons or communities are disadvantaged in the public interest they should be fully and adequately compensated for that disadvantage. It matters not whether it takes the form of the building of a motorway, new railway line, or nuclear power station beside their homes, or the digging of a mine underneath them. If people's homes are affected by public works in the national interest, their loss should be fully compensated in every case.

The ideas that I have propounded met with some success in the Land Compensation Act 1973, although it was a compromise in respect of the views that some hon. Members, myself included, proposed in those years. The Act provides for the purchase at full market price of homes directly affected by public works, and for grants for those indirectly affected by them.

For historical reasons the coal industry was isolated from the legislation. It has always enjoyed a privileged-position vis-à-vis the communities which worked for it to provide cheap fuel for the rest of us. So I can understand the feelings of the hon. Member for Mansfield when he speaks on behalf of his constituents. On their behalf, he

[*Sir Hugh Rossi*]

said that he would rather they had a right to sell to British Coal than that British Coal should repair the properties damaged by subsidence.

I also agree with the hon. Gentleman's remark that it is an insult to be offered, not the full market price, but a discounted price if the occupants happen to have bought under the right-to-buy provisions. That is offensive but typical of the cheese-paring attitude of the public sector whenever it deals with compensation matters. The private sector would never be allowed to get away with it. The individual would be entitled to claim through the courts and would often reach a settlement, before the case came to court, granting him full and proper compensation—but the public sector has never operated like that.

I have said before in the House that our railway system, which everyone values and wants to protect, would never have been built by private companies in the Victorian era if the owners of the properties in the way of the new lines had not been paid not merely the full market price but 110 per cent. of the value of their property.

Since nationalisation and the clawing in of so much to the public sector, a different attitude has arisen. In part it dictates that people who suffer for the public good must put up with it. I do not accept that philosophy. The person who gives something to the nation should receive full and adequate compensation for it.

Instead, in the public sector the first thing to happen is a public inquiry. Compulsory purchase procedures are followed when necessary. Protracted negotiations take place with district valuers. We go before the Lands Tribunal. All this is a long and wearisome process which is constructed as much as anything else to wear down the will of the individual so that in the end he will get only what the public sector is prepared to pay him. That is not just, and I see no reason why the Government, or Government bodies, should treat those to whom they have a duty any differently from how we would expect a private company or industry to treat them.

When I was in office, I often asked Ministers and civil servants whether anyone had ever worked out how much cheaper it would be to establish a more generous compensation system in place of the bureaucratic machine we had developed to discourage people from resisting the will of the state.

The hon. Member for Mansfield mentioned management and estate divisions of the coal board that do exactly that. If we did away with all the paraphernalia that supports the operations of the coal board and of Government departments, the savings might allow us to pay adequate compensation quickly. If people felt that they were being dealt with fairly, they would be much more ready and willing to co-operate with the public sector. I leave those thoughts with my hon. Friend the Minister and wish him more success with those ideas than I did when I had an opportunity to press them.

Mr. Dick Douglas (Dunfermline, West): But the Government intend to eliminate his whole Department.

Sir Hugh Rossi: The Minister is currently responsible for legislation affecting the coal industry and the coal board. When it is next amended, it should not be beyond the ingenuity of parliamentary draftsmen to include clauses to give effect to the thoughts I have expressed.

The coal industry developed in a climate in which there was very little regard, if any, for the environmental impact of industrial operations. We all know of the continuing debate about the mere burning of fossil fuel and its impact on the environment—the greenhouse effect and acid rain. Such matters have received attention only in recent years. Mines were dug and have been abandoned with little regard for the effect on the surface above them or on anything built there. Slag heaps disfigure our countryside, and Durham is appallingly polluted by mine residues that have been dumped along the coastline.

Members of the Environment Select Committee visited the north-east and saw for themselves the extent of that pollution, which has continued for many years under many Administrations, and were very disturbed by what they saw. From the evidence they heard, it was clear that the Coal Board wanted to do very little about that situation. The new energy industries are not allowed to get away with anything similar. Radioactive waste will be deposited deep underground, and the industry will have to find the right sites and then, with the benefit of the right scientific advice and proper engineering, construct the necessary safe depositories.

Under other Government measures, the industry will meet the large cost of decommissioning nuclear power stations at the end of their useful life. The coal industry has never been under an obligation to deal with the decommissioning of its mines or slag heaps, or to deal with the mounds that it has left littering the north-east coastline.

The coal industry must be dragged kicking and screaming into this century of the environment and live up to its responsibilities. Although the hon. Member for Mansfield has made a plea on behalf of his constituents because of the direct consequences of subsidence for them, there is wider general interest in what should be done with abandoned coal mines. Should they be allowed to rot and collapse, or is there a way of backfilling and compacting them? Is it possible to use the railway tracks that brought the coal out to return the slag to the mines and ram it back into them to prevent future subsidence? Has the Department of Energy discussed with the Department of the Environment the possibility of using disused coal mines having the right geology and in the right locations to dispose of much of the waste created by our civilisation and for which apparently there is no home at present?

The Environment Select Committee's toxic waste and contaminated land inquiries address the problems of what can be done with such residues. They can be chemically treated or incinerated, but after the mass is made inert, heavy metals and other substances are left that must be disposed of somewhere. At present, the remedy is either to dump them at sea or to use them for landfill. I ask the two Departments jointly to undertake a survey of mines that are disused or are about to be closed to see whether they can be utilised for waste disposal and in such a way that future subsidence will be avoided.

I have thrown out a few thoughts, and have taken the opportunity provided by the hon. Gentleman's description of his constituents' tribulations to express the concern about the way in which we deal with compensation and fail to require the coal industry to live up to its responsibilities to the nation in respect of the impact of its operations on our environment.

11.37 am

Mr. Harry Barnes (Derbyshire, North-East): I congratulate my hon. Friend the Member for Mansfield (Mr. Meale) on his good fortune in coming first in the ballot and on his choice of subject. I know of the frustrations of coming second in the ballot, because I did so on Monday, which denied me an opportunity to participate in the debate. If my hon. Friend did not exist to raise this debate and to present his Bill to the House later today, we would have to invent him, because there is need for such a person and for such a measure.

Given the length of my hon. Friend's speech, it is difficult to imagine that there is anything more to be said, but I wish to raise one or two points in respect of my constituency. I thank my hon. Friend for his kind comments about me, though he is wrong in thinking that Amber valley is part of my constituency. We have no imperialist ambitions to take it over. We believe that at the next general election Labour will be able to take it without the need for any imperialist actions.

The area of Chesterfield affected by mining subsidence is Staveley, which is a separate township. Staveley's southern half falls into the Chesterfield constituency, while its northern part is in mine. My comments and conclusions will relate to the experiences of north Staveley and of developments in south Staveley.

I am worried about what by the hon. Member for Hornsey and Wood Green (Sir H. Rossi) said about backfilling pits. Backfilling is desirable, but to backfill pits with nuclear and toxic waste in areas such as Staveley would be counterproductive. To add to the problems that they face over coal mining subsidence the thought that they would be living on top of dumps of hazardous nuclear waste would be unacceptable. It would be a greater environmental danger than subsidence and would be on top of other hazardous activities, such as those carried on by Staveley Chemicals.

The people in my area are faced with two types of problem. The first is the consequence of mining subsidence in the Hartington road area of Staveley in 1984. Lessons for the future can be drawn from that experience, but they will be of no use to residents who are living there now. Action needs to be taken on their behalf so that their compensation problems can be resolved. I hope that the Minister will be able to persuade British Coal to provide more money in an attempt to resolve numerous outstanding problems, including those in the Hartington road area.

The second type of problem with which people in my constituency are faced is the prospect of coal mining during the next five years from thick seams elsewhere in the Staveley area, including the Lowgates area. In the unlikely event of a Conservative victory at the next general election, following yesterday's European results, there would be the added problem of coal extraction, leading to subsidence, by private coal companies. Subsidence claims would be dealt with first by British Coal and, later, by private firms. People making compensation claims might then have to negotiate with two bodies or companies, which would result in the inadequate funding of compensation claims.

I have received letters from constituents who live in the Hartington road and Hartington view area of Stavely. I shall not mention their names, but I want to refer to some of the problems that were highlighted by my hon. Friend the Member for Mansfield because they affect my area, too. I shall use the words of those who have been affected and will comment on what they say as I do so. Constituent A wrote to me and said:

"I vacated my house for a total of 17 weeks."

That is quite a short period. Some people have to move out of their homes for much longer. That fact needs to be taken into account when compensation claims are made. It causes disturbance to people's lives while their houses are being repaired. The compensation takes no account of that disturbance, but provision ought to be made for it. Constituent A then said:

"Since then the new sills, door frameworks, skirting and ceilings have all pulled away from the walls and have cracked. The Coal Board came to inspect the new damage and offered an inadequate amount to put this right. . .there is also a problem regarding tilt, my neighbour has been informed that he has tilt and is being paid accordingly. Whilst I have been told I have none."

That highlights a number of points that were made by my hon. Friend the Member for Mansfield. The compensation that is paid for tilt varies greatly. That creates a feeling of injustice, because tilt can often be observed with the naked eye. The shoddy work that is done by contractors also causes problems. British Coal uses poor contractors. The role played by British Coal is inadequate. Its inspections are below par. British Coal does not insist on the application of correct standards before a person moves back into his home.

Constituent B wrote:

"We've had six inch nails knocked into door frames to straighten them, and then painted over. Twisted doors have been left on. . .we've had carpets left uncovered during the repair work, yet neither British Coal, nor the building firm concerned, wish to compensate the damage. The out-buildings are in a terrible state. . .brickwork is bulged and twisted, and being left in that condition, broken sewerage pipes have been left under the building. . .we don't feel we are being fairly treated."

There are continuing problems over contractors, the role of British Coal and the difficulty about obtaining fair compensation. People feel that it is inadequate. British Coal's agents are also thought to be inadequate. People resent being bounced between British Coal and its agents. No adequate action is taken, and people end up by bringing their problems to hon. Members and others in an effort to obtain assistance.

Constituent C wrote:

"From my observations and talking to people, I would say that British Coal are exerting people to settle by keeping people waiting and not corresponding, also by their attitude of take-it or leave it. My own property has not yet been repaired."

There is the double problem of incompetence and manipulation. The two seem to go hand in hand. There may be another way of describing it, but incompetence leads to manipulation. If something is not done, an excuse will be found later to get round it.

Constituent D wrote:

"Our chief concern has been the outhouse building . . . when the initial repairs began it was declared that the damaged side needed rebuilding, this did not materialize. Incidentally some three others to our knowledge were similarly neglected. We were out of our home for eleven and a half months, as you can appreciate an exacting time to us all, beyond all sense and reason."

Those people were out of their home for considerably longer than the 17 weeks that were mentioned by constituent A. That led to protracted problems and difficulties.

Constituent E complained about the inconvenience and discomfort that he suffered

[*Mr. Harry Barnes*]

"when old and infirm by having to be out of his home for a considerable period."

Sometimes there is conflict because tilt is taken into account in some cases but not in others, but there is also a great deal of co-operation when people suffer the same inconvenience. They are concerned not just about their own well-being but about the well-being of their neighbours, and they push claims on their behalf.

Constituent F says:

"My main complaint is the decorating. There is no room in my house decorated as I asked . . . I had the kitchen repainted myself paying someone to do it . . . I cannot do much myself in the way of re-decorating (due to age and illness) and cannot afford to pay to have it done."

My hon. Friend the Member for Mansfield referred to wallpaper not having been put up correctly. My constituent refers here to other redecorating problems. These difficulties come on top of the many other burdens that people carry. They will soon have to pay the poll tax. That will cause great problems because of their limited resources. These burdens worry them and nag at them all the time. They create stress, as my hon. Friend the Member for Mansfield said. We are discussing issues relating to shelter and to people's homes. That is one of the three basic provisions—food, clothing and shelter—that bother people.

I sometimes wonder whether the Minister fully appreciates the difficulties. Although he receives plenty of literature, information and representation about issues that affect the coal industry, I believe that his personal experience is limited. I understand that he stood twice as the Conservative candidate for Easington, which may lead him to believe that he understands the problems. Of course, the pit at Easington goes out under the sea so that the subsidence problems are created for passing seamen rather than elsewhere, although there are problems nearby. The hon. Member for Hornsey and Wood Green talked about the dereliction of coastal areas, and I believe that the Committee visited Easington. I am interested in Easington as I come from that area and my parents still live there.

Constituent G wrote:

"When I moved back into my home I discovered several repairs that I can only describe as 'shoddy' and several problems which were listed on the work schedule that had been completely overlooked. To top all this, my attic, which was insulated before the 'repairs' is no longer insulated . . . Now I find new problems, windows leaving walls, new cracks everywhere."

Such issues are quite difficult to resolve. People could pursue various legal rights through litigation and other means, which is entirely inadequate. There should be provision for local consultation, adequate involvement by the board and some local arbitration to resolve matters through avenues similar to the small claims courts.

Constituent H stated:

"I am completely dissatisfied with the general attitude and approach of both British Coal and the contractor's senior staff who are generally arrogant, belligerent and patronising in the extreme and the quality and manner of the work being done is of a very low standard . . . work . . . proceeded in fits and starts."

Contractors move into the Hartington road area, they move out into an entirely different area, and then they come back again, and people are very frustrated by what takes place. The letter continues:

"The list of omissions etc. is too long to include here; a list is attached."—

eleven detailed points were attached to the letter.

"It seems apparent that unless the contractors are continuously supervised one has little chance of satisfactory repairs being made."

That creates another problem because if people are moved out of their homes, in one case for eleven and a half months, they cannot supervise the work themselves and they feel that the board does not provide adequate supervision on their behalf. In some cases walls have been plastered and the occupants of the house do not believe that the repair work underneath has been done. When they challenge the contractors, they tell them that they will break open the wall but the owners will have to pay for replastering. People do not have the money and do not take the chance, although in some cases it would be advisable because the long-term problems might be considerable.

Constituent I stated:

"The path was laid too high covering our damp course and there are no slants to the drains causing the conservatory to flood when it rains. When the path was laid, they disturbed the drains and ever since then the drains keep getting blocked up . . . very little of the plastering was done, because when we moved in we did most of our own plastering."

People face practical difficulties that disrupt their homes and their lives.

I shall quote two more cases. Constituent J complained about the board sending a cheque for a settlement when none had been agreed. My constituent is paying for an independent survey showing $6\frac{1}{4}$ in when the agent was informed by the board that it would recognise only a 4 in tilt.

Finally, one constituent has been involved in putting pressure on the coal board by writing regularly—
[*Interruption.*]

Mr. Deputy Speaker (Mr. Harold Walker): Order. We cannot have a sub-debate or sub-committee meeting.

Mr. Barnes: The hon. Member for Watford (Mr. Garel-Jones) and other Conservative Members involved in the discussion are probably discussing the Coal Mining Subsidence (Damage, Arbitration, Prevention and Public Awareness) Bill, which is sixth on the Order Paper, and trying to persuade the Minister not to shout "Object" to it.

Alternatively, I suspect that they are discussing the same activities that were being discussed on Monday, and that is to stop the second motion on the Order Paper, being discussed as it relates to the poll tax, which is fantastically embarrassing to Conservative Members.

Mr. David Tredinnick (Bosworth): The hon. Gentleman is mistaken. Some Members, like me, have mining decline problems and serious subsidence in our constituencies, and are here to debate that important issue. I resent the hon. Gentleman's imputation.

Mr. Barnes: I am pleased to hear that the hon. Gentlemen were discussing the present motion, were concerned about advancing it, and are attempting to influence the hon. Member for Watford, who may not be as aware of the problem as are hon. Members who have these problems in their constituencies.

Mr. Roger Knapman (Stroud): In the event that we reach the poll tax motion, how many Opposition Members are prepared to contribute to that debate by being present today?

Mr. Douglas: On a point of order, Mr. Deputy Speaker. In view of the remarks of the hon. Member for Stroud (Mr. Knapman), have you had any intimation that if we should reach the motion in my name about the poll tax, a Scottish Minister will be available to respond to the debate? If not we shall be in severe difficulties, as you well know. It appears that the Government are reluctant——

Mr. Deputy Speaker: Order. We have gone far enough along that line. We should get back to the subject of coal mining subsidence.

Mr. Barnes: I shall be very keen to join my hon. Friend in his debate later today.

The last letter from which I shall quote states:

"We have sent numerous letters to the Chairman of British Coal, Robert Haslam, and he just does not want to know. Our complaints are of unsatisfactory work, outstanding repairs and the way in which British Coal conducts itself, their manner towards the people who are affected, we feel that they are fully irresponsible."

I have quoted those letters at length because they concern important issues affecting my constituents. I have not identified any of the writers as members of the community may want to check up on other people's business. There is common concern in the community. I have read out some of their feelings, but all told there are 108 cases and I do not intend to refer to them all. They demonstrate the recurring problems about the board, the sub-contractors, the agents and the inadequate cowboy work that is carried out in many areas.

A number of lessons can be learned. There needs to be negotiation long before the subsidence problems emerge rather than trying to pick up the pieces later. Planning authorities should make plans available and the matters should be fully understood by the community. The Department of the Environment also has a role to play, as has the Department of Energy, in that local authorities need to be advised of their role.

For instance, council housing and other services should become their responsibility so that the money—which should be more readily available through central grants —will begin to be put in funds that are directed towards those services rather than being just estimates contained in general funds. As greater pressure is applied, sometimes those amounts begin to be squeezed and the full amount is not spent on solving the coal mining subsidence problems. There can be difficulties because more than one authority is involved. In Staveley the town council is taking action about future developments and is co-ordinating with the districts and the county council. In difficult funding circumstances, there can be problems for all those authorities unless they have considered fully the discussions and plans concerning their area. The town councillors in Staveley are now in direct negotiation with the board prior to coal extraction in that area.

Considerable sums need to be spent by authorities on preparations within the area. Action has been taken in the Chesterfield constituency to ensure that provision is made for strengthening primary and special school buildings in the Inkersall area of Staveley. If, however, in the end they do not become affected by coal mining subsidence, those structural improvements will benefit the community. There needs to be that kind of planning. Obviously the funding for such matters needs to be considered.

The National Audit Office could have a function and a role in these matters. I wrote to the National Audit Office to see whether there was any chance of it carrying out a survey of the books on coal mining subsidence. I received the type of reply that I expected. It said:

"As I am sure you are aware, the day to day control and management of this scheme rests with the British Coal Corporation and, since there are no specific grants from the Department of Energy to fund coal mining subsidence, the scheme's costs are met by the industry. Unfortunately I have no rights of access to the books and records of the BCC and I am not therefore able to examine the administration of the scheme".

I believe that it would be fruitful if directives or primary legislation were passed by the House to allow the National Audit Office to have such powers. Some of the problems raised by my hon. Friend the Member for Mansfield about the funding available from the now more profitable board could then be solved.

Under section 2 of the Competition Act 1980 there is a provision to order an independent investigation of a nationalised industry under the Monopolies and Mergers Commission to be undertaken by the Secretary of State for Trade and Industry. It might be worth considering whether there should be a similar order specifically directed to coal mining subsidence.

I have been able to deal with only some of the lessons which arise from the difficulties in the Staveley area. I hope that the Minister will propose some serious measures, first, for primary legislation in those areas on the lines of the proposals contained in the Bill of my hon. Friend the Member for Mansfield, which will come before us later and which is a combination of two Bills that he produced to the House last year. Secondly, he has an opportunity to take action without the requirements of primary legislation in areas such as the availability of plans for planning departments. I am sure that there are many other matters that do not require primary legislation, and measures could be pushed forward quickly, however important it is that we get that primary legislation.

12.5 pm

Dr. Mike Woodcock (Ellesmere Port and Neston): I congratulate the hon. Member for Mansfield (Mr. Meale) on raising this important matter. It is not the first time that he has raised it in the House and it is regrettable that he has to continue to raise it. The Government should have acted before now on what they have been told on many occasions by hon. Members on both sides of the House. Similarly, the hon. Member for Ashfield (Mr. Haynes) has raised the matter in the House on a number of occasions. He has campaigned long and hard for his constituents.

Mr. Andy Stewart (Sherwood): Without success.

Dr. Woodcock: Yes, without success, but perhaps we will have success this morning.

I understand that the hon. Member for Ashfield has recently announced his intention not to seek re-election. I had the privilege of serving on the magisterial bench with the hon. Gentleman for many years. I remember that he was greatly missed when he left the bench, and he will be greatly missed in this place, too, for his down-to-earth and forthright contributions. We all hope that before he departs this place he will see at long last some progress on the subsidence issue on which he has campaigned for so long.

Similarly, my hon. Friend the Member for Sherwood (Mr. Stewart), who seeks to catch your eye in this debate, Mr. Deputy Speaker, has campaigned tirelessly for six

[Dr. Woodcock]

years to bring about a different approach not only from the Government, but from British Coal. His constituents, along with those of other hon. Members, have suffered from defective legislation and from unfair practices on the part of British Coal.

I know those three constituencies quite well. I was born and lived for many years in Mansfield and I now have a home in the Sherwood constituency. Many of my family and friends live in Mansfield, Ashfield and Sherwood. I have extensive interests in all three constituencies and many of my family and friends have worked in the coal industry as coal miners. I can say, therefore, that I am not entirely without experience of the effects of mining subsidence and the disruption, inconvenience and hardship that it can cause.

Coal reserves can be both a blessing and a curse in any community. On the one hand, they bring employment and prosperity, but, on the other, the effect of subsidence, as the law stands, can be devastating. I believe that we all recognise that a balance must be struck—one which is fair between British Coal's need to mine coal in the nation's interest and the legitimate interests of home owners, tenants and the business community. It is important that it is a fair balance. It should, in particular, protect the interests of the individual against the abuses of power and the financial strength and monopoly position of British Coal. I have to say from my experience that, for a number of reasons, that fair balance has not been achieved.

As the hon. Member for Mansfield has reminded us, there are vast amounts of subsidence damage which are neither repaired nor compensated for by British Coal for a variety of reasons—British Coal has failed to notify property owners that mining has taken place, tenants have failed to report damage, ignorance as to how subsidence manifests itself, a fear of forms, changes of policy by British Coal without notice, and the infamous so-called six-year rule, which is no more than an excuse for British Coal to avoid its moral responsibilities. All of those items have contributed to the problem. British Coal is denying liability for millions of pounds' worth of damage. It is not that there is disagreement about whether the cause of the damage is coal mining subsidence, but that British Coal is denying liability for it and that legislation allows it to do so. It cannot be right for British Coal to damage property and then to walk away, leaving other people to pick up its bill.

The balance between British Coal and the claimant is unfair because British Coal does not always deal fairly. For example, although the Coal Industry Act 1975 is more favourable to the claimant, British Coal does not point that out to the unsuspecting claimant. It sends out damage notices and, in each case, it invites claimants to claim under the Coal Mining (Subsidence) Act 1957. The unsuspecting claimant fills in the form and so deprives himself of the valuable rights that he could have had under the 1975 Act.

There are many questions that lead one to suspect that British Coal does not act fairly. Why is British Coal so unwilling to let members of the public or hon. Members see its so-called "subsidence manual"? If it has nothing to hide, why does it want to keep it secret? Why does British Coal refuse independent adjudication on the extent of damage or independent adjudication on whether damage

has been caused by subsidence? Why does it refuse independent adjudication on delay or on consequential losses? Why does it refuse adjudication on whether repairs or compensation is appropriate? It now claims that independent adjudication is widely available, but why can it give no figures as to where it is available, when it has been available and how many people have been granted or refused such independent adjudication? Why does British Coal refuse adjudication for loss of income or loss of profit arising from subsidence damage or from its failure to act in reasonable time? Why will it not supply a list of contractors who are prepared to work for British Coal rates?

When British Coal sells properties from its ex-estates, why does it limit liability to
"claims for new damage under the 1957 Act"?
Why does it seek to exclude claims made under the 1975 Act when selling its properties?

The balance between British Coal and claimants is also unfair because British Coal administration is often so appalling. Sometimes it takes months, even years, for British Coal to answer letters. Sometimes it does not answer such letters and sometimes it even loses them. Sometimes British Coal ignores letters that have been written to complain that it has ignored other letters already sent.

I shall quote one case—a claim that was submitted on 2 January 1985. A damage notice was sent in on that date, but it met with no response from the corporation. A year and a half later the owners sent a reminder letter to British Coal on 9 July 1986. Again that letter was ignored. On 27 August 1986 the owners wrote again asking when they might receive a response. The letter was ignored. On 9 October 1986 the owners wrote again and said:
"Could we please have a reply to our letter of 27 August 1986 which asked for a reply to our letter of 2 January 1985?"
Again the letter was ignored. On 15 December 1986 the owners wrote again to British Coal and said:
"Can we please have a reply to our letter of 9 October 1986, which asked for a reply to our letter of 27 August 1986, which asked for a reply to our letter of 2 January 1985?"
This time British Coal responded—nine months later. On 21 August 1987, two and a half years after the claimant had first submitted his claim, British Coal replied and said that it regretted the delay in replying, which had been due to a change in proposed future workings. That was after two and a half years. A letter from the area estates department, however, said that the claim would be dealt with expeditiously. After that letter it took a further eight months to send the next communication.

Mr. Gerald Howarth (Cannock and Burntwood): Does my hon. Friend agree that that correspondence has all the hallmarks of service to the nation by a nationalised industry?

Dr. Woodcock: Yes, and later in my speech I shall make a strong case for moving forward quickly to the denationalisation of the coal industry.

Today, four and a half years after the claim was first submitted on 2 January 1985, it has not been settled, even though the claimant sent a personal letter to the area estates manager which was ignored.

We could all quote such examples all day long, but I shall quote just one more. In this case subsidence damage was reported on 14 April 1986 by way of a damage notice. On 30 July 1986 the owner wrote inquiring whether any progress had been made. The letter was ignored. On 23

June 1987 the owner wrote again. The letter was ignored. On 24 August 1988, two and a half years after the damage notice had been submitted, the owner sent a further reminder to British Coal. His letter was again ignored. In February 1989 British Coal eventually got around to acknowledging that claim when it wrote back to say that it was sorry for the delay and that it had been due to "microfilming currently taking place." It appears that it took two and a half years to microfilm a letter.

Mr. Gerald Howarth: It is a nationalised industry.

Dr. Woodcock: Yes; and such is the incompetence with which claimants must deal regularly and for which they receive no compensation.

Mr. Kevin Barron (Rother Valley): Have all the examples quoted taken place in one particular area of British Coal's operation?

Dr. Woodcock: The first example came from the constituency of the hon. Member for Mansfield and the second from the constituency of the hon. Member for Ashfield. I should be glad to make the details of those cases available to either of those hon. Gentlemen if they so wish.

Although British Coal is so slow and dilatory, the claimant is told that he must submit his claim within two months and that if he does not, technically, he cannot proceed under the 1957 Act. British Coal cannot get round to sending out damage notices within two months, but the claimant is required to complete it and send it back in less than two months.

The present balance between British Coal and the claimant is also unfair because of the time scale operated by British Coal even when it accepts a claim. That time scale is unrealistic. It takes months, sometimes years, for British Caol to get on with the claim——

Mr. Barron: In north Nottinghamshire?

Dr. Woodcock: Yes.

Mr. Barron: The hon. Gentleman should say so.

Dr. Woodcock: I can speak only from my experience, and it is about cases in the three constituencies which I have mentioned that I am speaking.

It often takes a long time for British Coal to deal with claims. British Coal is also the sole arbiter of whether repairs should be effected or whether compensation should be paid. The claimant has no such choice. Even if the claimant has good reason to want either repairs or compensation, British Coal decides what is best for him. British Coal will make that decision on the basis not of what is best for the claimant or what is best for both parties, but of what is best for British Coal, irrespective of the claimant's wishes.

The present balance between British Coal and the claimant is also unfair because the individual householder is no match for the vast legal and financial resources of British Coal. If a claimant wants to challenge British Coal's decision, his only option is to risk what may be his life savings in a costly battle in the Lands Tribunal. The large legal costs of British Coal are paid by the taxpayer. I ask the Minister, is that justice? Even if the claimant is successful and British Coal agrees with his claim he is still out of pocket as he has to pay for the information as to whether mining has taken place near his home. If a man wants to know when mining took place under his home, he must pay a fee to British Coal to obtain that information. How can that be reasonable? The claimant has no right to compensation for consequential losses and no recompense for the time and trouble taken even though he may have spent days arguing his case, drawing up schedules, meeting British Coal and so on. All of that is unfair.

One of the greatest injustices is that there is no system of independent adjudication. I have often heard it said that British Coal acts as judge and jury. Not only is it the judge and jury; it is the offender, judge and jury. What kind of justice is it when the offender is the judge and jury in his own case? The only response for the claimant is to engage in expensive litigation.

We have regulatory organisations for many of our industries—for electricity, telecommunications, financial services, the Post Office, the police force and many other bodies and industries. We even have them for coal consumers because there is the Domestic Coal Consumers council. However, we have no independent complaints procedure for the victims of subsidence damage. Those are just some of the reasons why the present system is unfair to claimants.

What have the government been doing in the last few years about this massive injustice, this appalling situation? Regrettably, some people claim that the Government have just been supporting British Coal by refusing to take any action. I give the Minister credit for the fact that he has made some effort. He regularly forwards letters to the chairman of British Coal and tries to respond to questions from hon. Members.

In 1983 the Government appointed the Waddilove inquiry. A year later, in 1984, the inquiry reported to the Government. That was over five years ago. How can it take five years to take action if, as they say, the Government are taking this matter seriously? The Government published their response to Waddilove in 1987. It took Waddilove just one year to take evidence all over the country, look at thousands of cases and hear hundreds of submissions. However, it took three years for the Government to respond to the report of their own inquiry. It is now six years since the Government set up the Waddilove inquiry and five years since the inquiry reported. How could anyone seriously form the impression that the Government are taking the matter seriously? A few days ago the Secretary of State for the Environment floated the idea of a tax on fossil fuels to encourage the use of cleaner fuels.

Mr. Haynes: He has dropped the idea.

Dr. Woodcock: He may have dropped it, but are home owners who have suffered damage to continue to subsidise British Coal operations to make coal cheaper only to see the Government increase the price of coal by taxation? That would be rather a strange way to proceed.

Of course the Government will argue that British Coal has implemented some of the Waddilove recommendations. They are largely fooling themselves. For example, it is claimed that British Coal responds very quickly to reports of subsidence damage. That is often untrue, and I can cite instances of responses taking years. It is claimed that damage notices are sent by return, but that is untrue because it often takes months to send out a simple damage notice.

It is said that claimants in active mining areas are visited within one month. That is often untrue and I can

[*Dr. Woodcock*]

supply examples of cases where it has taken a year. It is claimed that fully-costed schedules are now provided, but that is largely untrue. It is also claimed that independent adjudication is widely available, but British Coal refuses to offer adjudication in the most important areas of dispute. It continually ignores requests for such adjudication, and many of its inspectors do not even know that such adjudication is supposed to exist. If the Minister is in doubt, I shall be happy to supply examples of all the instances that I have quoted—provided that the Minister will agree to look into them or to have them looked into independently and not merely send them to the chairman of British Coal, who simply sends them to his officials who caused the problems in the first place.

I am afraid that there is a growing view that claimants are battling not only against British Coal but against the Government, who refuse to take action to put matters right. I came to this place to support a Government who prize individual rights and freedoms and who are determined to bridle the power of bureaucracy and state monopoly. In many respects the Government have been highly successful, and I have been delighted to support them. However, in the matter of British Coal subsidence they are failing. People ask why the Government are so reluctant to act positively and quickly. Some people even say that the Government wish to present British Coal as less of a liability in the run-up to privatisation. Some say that they expect the householder to subsidise the privatisation of British Coal.

I disagree with Opposition Members on one aspect of the matter because I want to see British Coal privatised as quickly as possible. Nationalisation of the industry has been a disaster for the nation. British Coal has not served the interests of the consumer and continues to operate wastefully and inefficiently. It stifles the private mining industry with artificially high royalty demands, abuses its monopoly power and even today it continues back-door nationalisation, apparently with the Government's approval, by buying up sectors of the private coal trade. Far from managing the nation's coal assets in the interests of the British people, it has largely managed them against their interests. Privatisation cannot come a moment too soon, but it should not be at the expense of those who have suffered subsidence damage. Subsidence matters must be put on a fair footing before privatisation.

Hon. Members who are taking part in the debate are not the only people concerned about the matter. Many representative bodies, local authorities, health authorities, companies and individuals also look to the Government for action. A couple of weeks ago I took a delegation to see the Secretary of State and the Minister about this subject. The delegation consisted of representatives of the Country Landowners' Association, the National Farmers Union, the Building Societies Association, the Confederation of British Industry, the Association of British Insurers, the Law Society and the British Property Federation. Those are august and, I hope, influential bodies and they are worried about the present state of the law and the practices of British Coal. They have formed what they call a united industry working party. It describes the behaviour of British Coal as "scandalous". It says:

"Clearly, the Government are not taking the matter seriously."

At the meeting those representatives made many of the points made by the hon. Members in the debate. After the meeting the Minister wrote to me and said he hoped that we recognised that the Government were determined to make progress on this important issue. I certainly hope that they are, but I came away from the meeting not convinced that the Government are taking the matter seriously.

It is five years since Waddilove reported and we have seen precious little action. I hope that I am mistaken and that when the Minister responds he will commit the Government to appropriate legislation. I hope that he will put pressure on British Coal to meet not only its legal but its moral obligations.

As far as I am aware, the statute of limitations does not prevent British Coal from meeting its moral obligations. It merely allows it to avoid them if it chooses to do so. British Coal chooses to avoid them. No responsible nationalised industry would wish to avoid liability for the damage that it knows that it has caused, and no Government who prize the rights of the individual above those of a nationalised monopoly should let it avoid its moral obligations. I hope that my hon. Friend the Minister will tell us that he will introduce legislation at the earliest opportunity to do a number of things.

Mr. Harry Barnes: The hon. Gentleman and I have different ideological views about the ownership of the industry. However, if the industry is privatised, it will move from one monopoly to another, so that involves a difficulty that has to be dealt with in legislation so as to ensure that the duties imposed on British Coal are transferred. The hon. Gentleman mentioned the British Property Federation as one of the bodies concerned in the consortium. In the evidence that it gave to the Minister before the deputation saw him, it said:

"While the British Coal Corporation as a national institution may in certain circumstances be regarded as operating in the public interest, the same could not be said of a private company undertaking coal mining for the profit of its shareholders."

Therefore, the federation, which is deep into property itself, recognises that private bodies have to follow that principle.

Mr. Deputy Speaker: Order. The hon. Gentleman has already addressed the House.

Dr. Woodcock: My hon. Friend the Minister should introduce legislation to deal with the vast amount of damage for which British Coal chooses to avoid liability. We should set up a system of local arbitration to adjudicate on claims, without cost to the claimant, where the claimant wishes. We should require British Coal to restore damaged property to a pre-damage condition. We should allow claimants to employ a contractor of their choice, not of British Coal's choice. We should require British Coal to compensate for consequential losses and the cost to individuals of pursuing the claim, and to answer without charge questions about how mining has, or will, affect property. Where there is a dispute on onus of proof, it should lie with British Coal and British Coal should notify property owners or occupiers of future mining plans and of mining that has taken place in previous last year. Above all, we should set up an independent ombudsman system to which claimants could refer cases of delay and administrative failure and which would have the power to require British Coal to pay the costs of losses that arise from unreasonable delay and administrative failure. The seriousness with which the Government treat this issue will be measured not merely by words but by deeds.

I have made a contribution to the debate but not because I have a major constituency interest in coal mining —it finished many years ago in my constituency. However, I have lived most of my life in coal mining areas. I am happy to place on record the fact that I have business interests that include property in mining subsidence areas. My home has been affected by coal mining subsidence, as have those of many of my friends. I speak because I have lived in mining areas all my life and because I know the hardships that can be caused by subsidence damage. People like me and businesses can usually represent themselves, but thousands of home owners in coal mining areas who are affected by subsidence find it difficult to do that against the might of British Coal.

Not only hon. Members here today but thousands of householders and many public and private bodies will be anxious to hear what my hon. Friend the Minister has to say. It is five years since Waddilove reported, and it is high time that the Government took firm action.

12.32 pm

Mr. Kevin Barron (Rother Valley): I do not disagree with much that the hon. Member for Ellesmere Port and Neston (Dr. Woodcock) said about British Coal and its attitude to compensation and damage, but the idea that privatisation of the coal industry would be a green light for the improvement of Britain's environment is far from the truth. Mining areas still bear the scars of the private coal industry. Privatisation of the coal industry is not the answer to the problems of mining and the environment, which were also mentioned by the hon. Member for Hornsey and Wood Green (Sir H. Rossi). Labour Members do not need reminding about the effect of mining on the environment because we have lived with such problems all our lives.

We could be forgiven for thinking that British Coal has a bad track record, but it would be wrong to say that that is the case throughout the areas in which it mines. As a member of the Select Committee on Energy, I took part in a preliminary investigation into coal mining subsidence damage in north Nottinghamshire. My hon. Friend the Member for Mansfield (Mr. Meale) should be congratulated on his tour de force in describing the problems in that area, which stem from bad engineering decisions at coal extraction workings. Bad decisions were taken at the beginning and subsequent bad decisions have been taken to try to tidy up the mess on the surface. An accumulation of shortcomings has left thousands of homes in a damaged condition. I accept, of course, that not all the damage is the making of British Coal. As my hon. Friends have said, some of those who were directly involved are now in prison and others are awaiting trial. A free market was set up in north Nottinghamshire and so-called entrepreneurs established themselves in towns such as Mansfield. We were told that some of those people were further exploiting those living in the area with money paid by British Coal. Some employees of British Coal were involved in the operation. We are having to live with the legacy of that. Many hon. Members have major constituency problems as a result of the operations of the private sector in north Nottinghamshire.

I represent an area in which there has been intensive coal mining for many years, but during my six years as a Member of Parliament I have had brought to my attention fewer than five problems. I can only assume that properties are suffering subsidence damage in my constituency but that British Coal is responding satisfactorily. It should not be thought that what is happening in north Nottinghamshire is happening everywhere else.

The Waddilove committee was set up in 1984 and its remit was specifically to examine subsidence and the damage caused by it. Everyone hoped that improved arrangements would stem from that report. A White Paper was published by the Government in 1987 and we were led to believe that legislation would be introduced and that some of the affected areas would be cleaned up. There are many areas which suffer apart from north Nottinghamshire. The White Paper was followed by the Department of Energy's consultation paper. I understand that there were to be no more responses to the paper after July 1988. It has been said by hon. Members on both sides of the House that there have been no proposals from the Government.

We are faced with the six-year rule and the issue of exactly what damage is or is not caused to property by deep mining. The Waddilove report recommended in paragraph 192 that

"there should be no limit on time for claims for subsidence damage compensation. The onus of proof of the cause of damage should switch to the claimant after three years from the date when the damage should have reasonably become apparent."

That is a contentious issue.

The 1957 legislation allowed only two months for applications to be made for compensation for any damage that was caused to property by coal mining. On any interpretation, British Coal has not followed that line for many years. In most areas compensation is arranged to ensure that people do not fall victim to those hard rules. The Government believe that they should stick with the six-year rule which applies to other forms of compensation under current legislation. That is the rule which British Coal is operating. The six-year rule was not developed by geological experts or experts in deep mining. The experts know that earth moves over a period of time and many people are suspicious about this six-year rule. It seems that because the six-year rule exists in legislation at the moment, it is to be applied in this case. The six-year rule may apply in most cases in future, but there must be flexibility.

My hon. Friend the Member for Stoke-on-Trent, North (Ms. Walley) could not be present today, but she has told me that she has problems with subsidence in her constituency. Her problems are considerably worse than mine. She has had correspondence with her city council about some houses in Riley avenue in Burslem. The council quoted a classic distinction; apparently because of the length of time that mining has gone on beneath that road, British Coal denies that subsidence damage is attributable to deep mining. It claims that compensation is statute-barred because of the length of time that the mining has continued.

A geological fault runs beneath Riley avenue in the constituency of my hon. Friend the Member for Stoke-on-Trent, North. The presence of that fault has been known for many years, presumably even before mining commenced. Obviously mining coal from below such a

[*Mr. Kevin Barron*]

fault is a problem. I have worked beneath geological faults in mines, and I know that faults are very unstable and unpredictable and it is not very nice to work underneath them. Where those faults exist, people are not convinced that long-term mining below a thin crust is satisfactory. I hope that we shall consider the need for flexibility and a re-interpretation with regard to specific cases where compensation claims arise.

I do not want to speak for long because I know that other hon. Members wish to speak. I am sure that my hon. Friend the Member for Mansfield would be happy to see local adjudication so that people do not feel that bureaucracy is preventing them from making claims. Ordinary people cannot afford six-figure fees to go to a land tribunal over a dispute.

I received a letter from a constituent of mine in January. Prior to this I had corresponded with him, with the local parish council and British Coal, at area and national level. I have been trying to get some compensation for damage in the village of Woodall near Harthill in the south of my constituency. The letter is from a Mr. H. Taylor who, although only an ordinary resident, has become something of an expert on coal mining subsidence law—or rather the lack of it—over the past three and a half years. Mr. Taylor lives in South Cottage, Woodall. His letter, written in January, gives a brief outline of what happened in his village:

"Six of us, householders in Dowcarr Lane Woodall, applied in the summer of 1986 to British Coal for compensation for subsidence damage to our houses from the Highmoor Drift mine"—

which is in the constituency of my hon. Friend the Member for Derbyshire, North-East (Mr. Barnes)—

"the main gallery of which runs under our houses in Dowcarr Lane. We got nowhere. A young technician visited and took a very cursory look and BC"—

that is, British Coal—

said 'No' to our claims. I had used a Subsidence Consultant who was in no doubt about the merits of my claim; he was on the basis of 'No payment, no fee' ".

When British Coal said no, the consultant cleared off, as he could see that there was no money to be made—although payment was made in Mansfield, just half an hour's drive from my constituency.

When their claims were turned down, the residents of Dowcarr lane collectively asked Harthill and Woodall parish councils for help. They also had problems with drainage because the road had tilted—a clear sign that subsidence was most likely to have caused the damage. The tilt was also causing problems in nearby fields.

The borough engineers then went into litigation with British Coal to try to obtain compensation. There has been no outcome so far, although the case has been in progress for a considerable time. Mr. Taylor and many other residents are very upset. They have found that British Coal, while denying any responsibility for problems on the roads and in residents' homes, has been negotiating not only with residents collectively—through me or through the parish council—but with individual residents. It came to the attention of Mr. Taylor and his associates that British Coal has decided, without prejudice—a phrase that is often used—to pay compensation to one of the residents of the village. I hope that I am not misquoting British Coal.

A letter written to the clerk of the council stated—referring to a house on a road in which all the other residents had applied for compensation, individually and collectively—

"this property has suffered recent movement but we are still of the opinion, after taking all factors into account that it is not due to the effects of mining subsidence for which we would have a current liability."

Presumably that is an interpretation of the six-year rule that British Coal now uses. The letter continues:

"Completely without prejudice we are however prepared to investigate the matter further and the claimant has been informed of the action proposed."

Mr. Taylor's letter includes a handwritten note, which reads

"A 7th person claimed when we did and that claim was allowed—because, I think, the claimant could get legal aid and therefore dodge the huge expense of the Land Tribunal (High Court) which would require us to use Solicitors and Barristers, at a cost in the region of ten times the size of our claims."

That sums up the householders' problems. British Coal now appears to be prepared, "without prejudice", to pay some compensation on one house in this small village, but is denying it to all the others.

Dr. Woodcock: I understand that no case settled by the land tribunal has not involved legal aid. No one can afford to risk such high costs without it.

Mr. Barron: That is absolutely right. The irony is that if legal aid is granted a massive amount of public money may be payable. People may have interests to declare. Massive legal expenditure may be paid out of the public purse which, as Mr. Taylor pointed out would be far in excess of the compensation claimed for the damage done to the property. That is nonsense.

British Coal thought that it was helping, but in reality it has made matters worse, in that village. I do not for one moment want British Coal to stop paying compensation to the owner of that house, but many other people are caught in a pincer movement and will have to remortgage their homes if they are to have any chance of obtaining justice.

Mr. Meale: Has my hon. Friend considered another danger facing the coal industry? It does not take a genius to realise that the scale of the claims submitted means that as this country is a member of the European Community someone could take to the European court of Human Rights the right to have his home repaired. If that were to happen, implementation of the court's decision might actually rule out the financial viability of the coal industry.

Mr. Barron: My hon. Friend is right to point that out. I hope that the Government will introduce legislation to sort out the mess before we are forced to obtain judgments from elsewhere.

My constituents in Woodhall are not helped by the absence of any form of independent adjudication in which they and British Coal could have faith. Such a body could decide whether and how much compensation should be granted. The Waddilove report states:

"There is a place for local independent adjudication by persons who have appropriate skills and are drawn from an approved list. The Department of Energy should invite nominations for such a list of adjudicators to be available throughout the coalmining areas."

It then described in detail how that should operate.

One of the most disappointing aspects of the consultation paper put out by the Government in April 1988 was that it did not propose that the legislation would deal with the referral to local adjudication. In those circumstances, how are Mr. Taylor and my constituents to receive any form of justice if they cannot receive some money to allow them to go to the land tribunal to fight their case? That is totally and utterly wrong. Conservative Members have said that in other areas of dispute there are consumer protection organisations and arbitration organisations, as well as Government Departments or Government-sponsored agencies, to which consumers can go for some form of arbitration. Yet the Government say that they are not prepared to bring in local adjudication for this matter.

If the legislation as proposed in April 1988 is brought in before the next general election, I assume that the Minister will be in charge of it and the Opposition will strongly oppose it if it does not contain the Waddilove recommendations. It would be the answer to many people's problems if they could have confidence in a local adjudication system which would decide whether it was mining damage, instead of having to rely on the present arbitrary lottery. Under such a system Members could advise their constituents as to whether they would receive compensation.

Until such time as we can get help to the people who have to live with the environmental excesses of coal mining, we shall continue to argue strongly against what is currently being done. I hope that the Minister can tell us when legislation is to be introduced. He must know that people are not happy about the Government's proposals for legislation.

12.54 pm

Mr. Andy Stewart (Sherwood): Today's debate gives hon. Members another opportunity to bring to the attention of the House and the Government the serious and often distressing circumstances that our constituents must endure as a result of damage to their properties from subsidence. I begin by thanking the hon. Member for Mansfield (Mr. Meale) who, knowing at first hand the enormous problems faced by residents of coal mining areas, used his good fortune in winning the ballot for private Members' motions to choose this subject again for debate. The hon. Gentleman may recall that just over a year ago he introduced another important debate on the consequences of subsidence damage.

Some may question the relevance of this debate, but for hon. Members who represent mining areas it is the only way in which we can demonstrate to the Government and to British Coal that the law on subsidence damage must be changed. Under the present regulations British Coal is judge and jury. It decides whether compensation is due and how much it will be, leaving people with two choices —take it or forget it. Since last year's debate, progress on change has been nil, although a constructive meeting was held with my right hon. Friend the Secretary of State for Energy.

Two important milestones, however, have been reached. First, the united district council authorities, covering north Nottinghamshire and north Derbyshire and working in conjunction with Trent polytechnic, have ascertained the depth of the problem facing people who live in their districts. The hon. Member for Mansfield gave a full account of these activities, and I shall not bore the House with repetition. Suffice it to say that I fully support the endeavours of the united local authorities.

Secondly, the united industry working party has been formed, comprising the Association of British Insurers, the British Property Federation, the Building Societies Association, the CBI, the Country Landowners Association, the Law Society, the National Farmers Union and the Royal Institution of Chartered Surveyors. Why have these powerful professional organisations come together? That is easily answered: they are incensed by the scandalous behaviour of British Coal in respect of its members' claims for mining subsidence damage. These bodies have pledged to lobby hard and long for national justice to be seen to be done to the affected property owners.

My hon. Friend the Member for Gedling (Mr. Mitchell) has asked me to apologise to the hon. Member for Mansfield and the House for his absence today—he has eight long-standing engagements in his constituency. I assure the House that he wholly supports our cause on behalf of his constituents.

Since I was first elected to Parliament more than six years ago I have received more than 2,000 letters from, and a similar number of visits to my surgeries by, constituents complaining about British Coal's attitude to, lack of progress on and outright rejection of their subsidence claims. However, we must also bear in mind that British Coal has satisfactorily settled many claims.

One of the principal problems faced by my constituents is that British Coal has moved the goalposts in Nottinghamshire when it has been in its interests to do so. A prime example of that was the reduction, in 1985, of the time limit for claims to be submitted from 12 to six years. If a claim had been lodged but had not yet been processed, that was my constituent's bad luck. If claimants did not accept British Coal's meagre offer, offers were withdrawn.

That change was brought about after serious financial irregularities were uncovered in British Coal's estates office in Nottinghamshire in 1983-84. As a result of a lack of proper supervision by British Coal of its subsidence inspectors, and in the absence of a proper audit, innocent people were made to suffer. At present, their only redress is the right to appeal to the Lands Tribunal. That system may have been satisfactory when first introduced many years ago, but in recent years the cost of bringing a case has, as was mentioned by the hon. Member for Mansfield, varied between £15,000 and £100,000. That does not give claimants much incentive to rush to justice.

A change to a cheap and simple system of recourse for claimants is long overdue. During last year's debate on the subject, I welcomed the White Paper published in response to the Waddilove report in which the Government made clear their determination to alleviate the hardship and distress suffered by property owners affected by subsidence. Action to implement that ideal is also long overdue.

No one can afford to be complacent—least of all British Coal, as many of its employees live in areas prone to subsidence. The Union of Democratic Mineworkers recognises that substantial claims in any one area could place a colliery in jeopardy. Nevertheless, it believes in the principle of fair and just settlements, not only for its own members but for everyone affected by subsidence.

I share the UDM's view that the cost of providing compensation should be met from a national fund and not be set against individual collieries. The cost of meeting compensation claims adds approximately £1 to every tonne of coal that the industry sells. Although that sum

[*Mr. Andy Stewart*]

may be small, it can be crucial to a pit's viability when added to its total costs. I was delighted to read in British Coal's annual report that claims charged to collieries dropped substantially, from £245 million in 1983-84 to £50 million last year, particularly bearing in mind that some related to earlier years. British Coal currently has £270 million set aside for latent liabilities arising from subsidence.

How can justice for claimants be ensured? Improvements could be made by adopting five administrative measures. First, British Coal should publish each year in local newspapers a map of sufficient size and detail showing coal workings in that locality for the past 12 months, currently, and for the next 12 months. Secondly, the Department of Energy's guide to claimants' rights should be corrected and rewritten in a more user-friendly style and be made more freely available. British Coal leaflets should be consolidated and should incorporate all extra current statutory concessions. Thirdly, British Coal should provide claimants with a claim form under the Coal Industry Act 1975, a basic summary of the differences in entitlement from those provided in the Coal-Mining (Subsidence) Act 1957, a copy of the Department of the Environment's revised and updated guide to claimants' rights, and a copy of other British Coal leaflets.

Fourthly, British Coal should acknowledge that claims may be submitted within six years of damage occurring. Fifthly, the Department of Energy should establish an independent user group consultative committee review board to monitor the system's operation and to recommend improvements. As the Government's sponsoring Department for coal, the Department itself cannot function independently of that role.

I should also like to suggest to the Minister that there is a need for interim legislative reform. Interim measures could be included in any forthcoming Coal Bill. There could be local arbitration. All disputes in respect of private dwellings and up to £50,000 in respect of other property should, at the election of the claimant, be resolved by a local arbitration panel. As for the standard of repair, British Coal should be under a duty to restore damaged property, so far as is reasonably practicable, to the condition that is was in when the damage occurred. Compensation should be paid for any shortfall in valuation to the pre-damaged condition equivalent to the residential loss of market value.

As for own contractors, a claimant—unless, in all the circumstances, it was unreasonable to do so—should be entitled to employ a contractor of his own choice to make good the damage after preparation of a proper schedule of repair and competitive estimates. After inspection of completed work, or stages, British Coal should pay the cost of the work, including that of any technical or professional assistance, properly incurred by the claimant in respect of the work and for recording the condition of the property at the time of notification. In all disputes as to whether damage resulted from subsidence caused by coal mining the onus should be on British Coal to prove that it is not subsidence damage. These measures will not solve all the existing problems. They should be looked upon only as interim measures until full legislation can be implemented.

The White paper, in response to Waddilove, said that simple arbitration would be available as an alternative. Unfortunately, 18 months after the White Paper was published that is clearly not happening, even though British Coal has accepted liability. All my submissions on behalf of constituents have been rejected. One constituent has made 20 separate claims for arbitration on differing aspects. All have gone unanswered. Perhaps the Minister will confirm that to date British Coal has not accepted any cases for simple arbitration.

To whom, therefore, do we look when seeking immediate help for our constituents, bearing in mind British Coal's intransigence? Under the existing legislation, it can only be to the Lands Tribunal. In the past, the huge cost precluded that course as an option for hard-pressed claimants. However, the White Paper stated that British Coal would not ask for costs if individuals made their own representations to the tribunal instead of employing a battery of expert witnesses and barristers. Having taken nine months to clarify the position, I am pleased to inform the House that two of my constituents, Mr. and Mrs. Harold Goodwin of 112 Shortwood Avenue, Hucknall, have made a submission to the registrar of the Lands Tribunal for arbitration to determine their claim. On behalf of the many people who need help in my constituency, I have personally thanked Mr. and Mrs. Goodwin for being the front runners on this course. Time will tell whether we have done the right thing. However, I believe in the old adage "Nothing ventured, nothing gained." If the Goodwins' case is successful, the Lands Tribunal will require a substantial increase in staff to cope with the number of applications that it will receive, or it might just dawn on British Coal that it should behave in a civilised way, thus saving everybody time and energy.

During last year's debate I highlighted a number of outstanding cases in my constituency. It will come as no surprise to those of us who have to deal with British Coal estates department to know that they are still outstanding. Today I could relate many further cases in my constituency which could take the debate to 5 o'clock were I not sure that the cases already highlighted by Opposition Members and by my hon. Friend the Member for Ellesmere Port and Neston (Dr. Woodcock) had made it clear that there was still a long way to go.

One of the most traumatic effects of coal mining subsidence is that which lengthy and time-consuming negotiations with British Coal have on human beings. Many people involved have had their lives, health and businesses severely affected by their experiences. There is constant disruption to their daily life and work as people strive for justice and for an equitable solution, and in doing so receive no recompense for the expense and time involved.

Speaking on behalf of my constituents, I do not request the Government to take action. Our patience has run out and we now demand a promise today from the Minister that legislation will be introduced and enacted.

1.10 pm

Mr. Frank Haynes (Ashfield): First, I congratulate my hon. Friend the Member for Mansfield (Mr. Meale) on choosing this subject for debate because of the serious problem in mining constituencies such as his, mine and those of Conservative Members. I recognise the fight that has been put up in the House on behalf of our constituents in mining areas over mining subsidence. Secondly, I sincerely thank the hon. Member for Ellesmere Port and Neston (Dr. Woodcock) for his comments about me. As he said, we had a close association for a number of years on the magistrates' bench at Mansfield. The hon. Gentleman was a fair magistrate and is a fair Member of Parliament. This morning he severely criticised the Government for not having taken action on behalf of our constituents, many of whom have had a raw deal. It is time that the Government took some action about this problem.

I have seized every opportunity to fight in the House on behalf of those people, and it has been an uphill struggle, but I feel that we are over the top now and we are coming down the hill. Whenever I have had the opportunity I have tried to knock the Minister out with one fair blow, but it seems that we will win the battle on points. I am looking forward to the Minister's reply to the debate and I hope that he will respond to the points that we put to him.

The hon. Member for Bolton, West (Mr. Sackville) is sitting in the Minister's place while the Minister nips out to have a bite, no doubt, and I do not deny him that. He cannot sit here all day without a drink or a bite, but I am a little disappointed that the Minister is not here to listen to my speech as I wanted to say one or two things to him before turning to the real problem—mining subsidence. I believe that the Minister is a fair Minister. We often talk outside this place and he says very nice things to me and comes my way on the problems. But when I speak to him in the House he is really vicious to me. I am only speaking on behalf of those whom I represent in my constituency who have problems.

I do not altogether blame the Minister. I blame the present Chancellor of the Exchequer, because not all that long ago he was the Secretary of State for Energy. When we put the problems to him, he did not want to know. Then following on from him, as Secretary of State for Energy, was the present Secretary of State for Social Security. He did not help us either. They just did not want to know. I got the distinct impression, when they were Secretaries of State for Energy, that they were just letting the National Coal Board, as it was known at that time, do as it liked. It could walk all over those people whom we represent—those complainants who are not and have not been getting a fair deal with their mining subsidence claims.

However, the situation has changed. We had two years of MacGregor, and look at the mess he made of the mining industry. People have subsidence problems because of the mining industry. I was lucky enough to be selected to initiate an Adjournment debate only three or four weeks ago, when, once again, I chose the subject of mining subsidence. My hon. Friend the Member for Mansfield also spoke in that debate. The Minister was going our way that night. I could see a light in the tunnel. I am hoping that we will see a massive light today in the interests of our constituents. We need help back in the mining areas.

The Government encourage people to own their own properties, and that has happened. However, many people in our mining areas have problems with their properties because of the damage caused by the mining industry. The Government have a responsibility. I am sick to death of seeing the Minister about the problem. The Minister just passes it back to the mining industry—British Coal and the National Coal Board before that. Many Nottinghamshire hon. Members, for example, went to see the chairman of the board. He told us that we had to go back to the area

where the problems are. He passed the buck back to the areas. We then go to see the area director, but we get no change there either. We are in the same boat—no one wants to do anything. We go to the Minister and he passes it back. We go to the chairman of the board and he passes it back, because he says that it is a matter for legislation. What we are appealing for this morning is a change in that legislation in the interests of those people whom we represent.

I shall carry on with what I have to say now that the appropriate Minister has taken his place.

Mr. Andy Stewart: Start again.

Mr. Haynes: No, I shall not start again; that would take too much time. Other hon. Members who have problems in their areas want to speak. The hon. Member for Bosworth (Mr. Tredinnick), for example, has a pit in his area. Before he was elected to the House, there were a number of pits there. No doubt he has subsidence problems in his constituency, because he is here this morning and is obviously interested in the debate. I hope that he will put up as good an argument as his colleagues before him.

Before you came into the Chair, Mr. Deputy Speaker, I was a little disappointed that the hon. Member for Hornsey and Wood Green (Sir H. Rossi) was slipped into the debate. I thought to myself, "What will he talk about? How many pits are there in Hornsey?" He happens, however, to be the Chairman of the Select Committee on the Environment. I thought to myself that he would be on our side—and, by God, he was. He spoke about the unfairness of some of the public bodies, who walk all over everybody instead of giving fair treatment. He was right. I hope that people outside will read the hon. Member's contribution because it was made by a senior Conservative. The Minister is faced with a real problem today—or is he? I do not think he has a problem because he can get up at the Dispatch Box to tell us what he will do.

I shall cite two examples only, but they are really bad ones. The first concerns an 82-year-old lady whose husband worked at the pit. They saved and saved. They did not go into an elderly people's bungalow supplied by the local authority; they bought their own out of the savings made from the husband's life-long work at the pit. What happened? The property was seriously damaged so they made a claim to, at that time, the National Coal Board for that damage to be repaired or for compensation to be given. But what happened? The poor fellow died and left a widow on her own. She came crying to me at my Saturday morning surgery because she had made a claim to the NCB, but it had told her that it was out of time. That is scandalous. The industry did the damage and it has every cause to put it right by repair or through compensation. When that old lady made her claim the board said that it was going to go under her house again with a different seam. It said that it would not pay out twice and that it would do the necessary little repairs and would do the real jobs later. Nine and a half years later the board said that she was out of time. That is scandalous. She had a genuine claim on a genuine property and yet those—I nearly called them something then, but I just managed to hold it back in time. At that time the NCB continued to reject her claim in line with the legislation. That shows just how stupid the industry is.

[*Mr. Haynes*]

That legislation must be changed in the interests of the people and that is why we are here giving the Minister a rough ride, I hope, so that he will come our way and put matters right.

Currently some people can accept compensation instead of British Coal calling in an outside contractor to do the repairs. In my second example the people said, "We will take the compensation"; but that compensation covered nowhere near the repairs to be done to the property. Who the hell do the people at Hobart house and in the various areas think that they are kidding? It is time that the Minister got on his bike and travelled around and told the area directors and the bloke at Hobart house where to get off. The Minister should tell them to get something done in the interests of the people who have had a real raw deal.

My hon. Friend the Member for Rother Valley (Mr. Barron) mentioned how, under the NCB regime, officials were on the fiddle—I know that it is history, but it damn well happened. They went down the line for it, and quite right too. The result, however, is that the people we represent have suffered. Those officials should be locked up in a cell because of what they have done. They fiddled from the taxpayer and they should be ashamed of themselves, it is the people we represent who have done the suffering.

I hope that the Minister will take on board what I have said as it is a serious matter. Before he came in I said that he was a fair Minister. In my Adjournment debate he started to come our way. I am convinced that the Minister is concerned about what has happened out there over the years. I do not blame him for it; I blame the people before him. He is, however, coming our way as he has talked sensibly about the problem and I hope that he will do so again today.

There are all manner of things happening. I went to look at two bungalows in my constituency that were advertised. I knew that it was an area in which properties have been damaged by mining subsidence. Because of the serious damage to the two bungalows, British Coal bought them from the owners so that they could move on and buy other properties. That shows how much money it would have cost to repair them. British Coal then put the bungalows on the market to "flog" them, and they did it through an estate agent. In the advertisements for those properties it was not mentioned that they were affected by mining subsidence. Somebody could have bought a pig in a poke and found out about it afterwards. That is the sort of thing that is going on in British Coal. It is damned well deceitful, and it should be checked by the Minister.

Some of my constituents have had to wait for a very long time. The hon. Member for Ellesmere Port and Neston talked about the Waddilove report. The previous Secretary of State sat on that report and was not prepared to do anything about it. It was two years before it got to the House and before we knew exactly what Waddilove had said. When we did receive it, we realised why the Secretary of State had sat on it. It was clearly in favour of the complainants. No wonder the Secretary of State sat on it. The matter is now wide open and we know what the Waddilove report says and how the complainants are suffering. We know how British Coal is treating people and it is high time that something was done.

The first question that I ask people who come to see me about a subsidence problem is whether they have an agent to represent them to British Coal. Nine times out of ten they say yes. However, hon. Members have found that they are doing the agent's flipping job, and that is wrong because it is not our responsibility. When the complainant talks to the agent, the agent quietly says, "Go and have a word with your Member of Parliament." It lands on our doorstep and people come to us. Hon. Members have talked about the thousands of claims that drop on our doorstep and for which we are not responsible. Our responsibility is to see that the Minister and the Government do something about the problem.

Mr. Andy Stewart: The hon. Member touches on a topical subject. I recently wrote to an agent and received from him a letter on A4 paper. In the last paragraph he said that he had written to me as a favour because he is not paid to write to Members of Parliament.

Mr. Haynes: That is a shocking state of affairs. There is a great amount of fiddling going on as well.

Mr. Gerald Howarth: Will the hon. Gentleman give way?

Mr. Haynes: No, because I have not yet answered the question asked by the hon. Member for Sherwood (Mr. Stewart). I am really drawing the Conservative Members who are trying to get in. The hon. Member for Sherwood is correct.

Agents get a percentage rake-off on the compensation settlement. I visited a property for which British Coal had offered £6,500. It was the gable end house of five very old properties and the gable wall was falling. The agent wrote to me and said that the compensation offered by British Coal was not enough and that the claim was worth £32,000. That speaks for itself. The chappie wanted to accept the £6,500 but the agent said no, thinking, "I will get 5 per cent. of this lot and if it is a large figure I will get a large amount." That has been going on along with the fiddling by British Coal. Blokes in British Coal were getting a large percentage rake-off as well. That is why they have been sent to Lincoln prison and they will be there a long time.

When British Coal is not prepared to move and the agent gets into difficulties, he suggests taking British Coal to court. He puts it in writing, but finishes off by saying, "It will cost you £5,000." Who will write out a cheque for that amount? Will that elderly widow, for example? Such a figure is scandalous. Big businesses do not have a problem. The Mansfield brewery was affected by subsidence, and British Coal rejected its claim. The brewery had an agent, who told it to take British Coal to court. The brewery is rolling in money. It makes masses of profits. It even has a big advertisement using ex-President Reagan drinking a pint of Mansfield bitter, so it must make a nice profit. Because it is a big business that can afford to take British Coal to court, when it threatened to do so British Coal coughed up. The ordinary person cannot do that because he cannot put his hands on such amounts of money.

I have had enough of the buck passing. The buck stops at that Dispatch Box in front of the Minister. I hope that the Minister will pick up that buck. If he wants, I will put a buck on the Dispatch Box so that, when he gets up to grab it, he will tell us what he proposes to do.

We have had a flipping good debate and hon. Members have expressed themselves well. I congratulate Conservative Members on the way in which they have conducted themselves. They have an incentive to do so. There were some elections yesterday, so no wonder the beggars are coming in here today to support an Opposition motion. They are looking after their backs. I do not mind that. They are entitled to do that, especially when, at the same time, they are speaking out on behalf of people who have had a raw deal.

I was a little disappointed by one thing. I do not want to bring in the National Union of Mineworkers or the Union of Democratic Mineworkers, but the hon. Member for Sherwood did when there was no need for it. He used a political argument, just as the Minister did when, from a sedentary position, he accused the hon. Member for Ellesmere Port and Neston—the hon. Gentleman may not have heard this, but I did—of having a financial interest. The hon. Gentleman might have, but in the properties that he owns in my constituency live people who are affected by mining subsidence. I will back the hon. Gentleman to the hilt because he is speaking in the interests of those people, so he has every right to clobber the Government for what they have not been doing about mining subsidence. I have cleared the air for the hon. Gentleman, who made a first-class contribution. The Minister could only make snide remarks which were uncalled for, because the hon. Gentleman was right.

My hon. Friend the Member for Mansfield and I have been criticised by the UDM for raising the issue of mining subsidence. It said that by bawling our heads off in the House of Commons about mining subsidence, we were closing pits. However, I remember that the general secretary of the UDM in Nottinghamshire had his property seen to and done beautifully because he had a claim against British Coal. He does not own the property —it belongs to the union. It cost a fortune to put the house right and now he has the neck to criticise my hon. Friend and I for raising, on behalf of thousands of constituents, the problem of subsidence. It was nasty to say that after his own property had been repaired.

I have tried so often to deliver the knock-out blow to the Minister but I have not yet been able to hit him. We talk nicely to each other outside the Chamber. We do not talk as I am talking now. On this occasion we are really mounting an action in the interests of our constituents. I think that we are winning on points, and I think that we shall win the battle. British Coal—and the National Coal Board before it—has not given a fair deal to those who made claims. I feel within my bones that the Minister will do something about the problem for he is a sincere chap. He has told me privately that he does not like unfairness. I know that I am giving away secrets, but he is prepared to take action to eradicate unfairness.

We have had unfairness for a long time. At long last people have brought themselves together and, in effect, have said, "It is going to stop. The buck stops here." There is no doubt that the Minister will get the message when a meeting takes place next Tuesday. We who represent our constituents back home will come to Westminster to put the case to the Minister, and it is a good one.

I congratulate my hon. Friend the Member for Mansfield on picking coal mining subsidence as the topic of his motion. It is a beauty. He could have selected another topic, but instead he chose the right one. I believe that the Minister has got the message. If he does not tell us

what we all want to hear, he is in for a rough ride next Tuesday. He will not buy me off with a cup of coffee and biscuit in the Department. He will have to listen to what is said as he has had to listen to us today.

I hope that the Minister will come our way and that we shall sort out all the problems so that our consitutents can say, "That Minister is a first-class chap. He has given us what we want. Our representatives did a good job on Friday morning and afternoon in the House of Commons. The result is that the Minister—a wonderful young fellow —stood at the Dispatch Box and gave us what we wanted. He gave us something for which we have been fighting for a long time."

I hope that the battle has been won. I hope that it is all over and that we shall be working together in the interests of our people back home.

1.38 pm

Mr. David Tredinnick (Bosworth): I represent a declining mining area, so I am especially grateful to catch your eye, Mr. Deputy Speaker. I declare an interest, although it is perhaps not necessary to do so. My family was involved in tin mining in Cornwall for many generations and I feel the sadness that is felt by my constituents that only one pit is left in Bosworth. Desford has gone, Merrilees deep drift mine has gone, and Bagworth is soon to close.

It is clear from the remarks of my hon. Friends the Members for Sherwood (Mr. Stewart) and for Ellesmere Port and Neston (Mr. Woodcock) and those of the hon. Members for Rother Valley (Mr. Barron) and for Ashfield (Mr. Haynes) that there is still great concern about compensation arrangements. I apologise to the hon. Member for Mansfield (Mr. Meale). I was unable to be present to hear his speech as I was detained on other duties earlier in the day.

My hon. Friend the Member for Leicestershire, North-West (Mr. Ashby) had hoped to be in his place, but unfortunately, for pressing reasons, he has been unable to attend. In his constituency, in an area part of which was part of my constituency until the boundary changes, there are I understand problems near former pits around Ellistown, the Nailstone mine which is still working, Snibstone where the new mining museum has been opened and is such a success, Whitwick and Lount.

Subsidence can be fast, slow and unexpected. The Dolcoath mine between Redruth and Camborne in Cornwall, where my family came from, is famous for the enormous extent of its underground workings. A rather unusual case of subsidence occurred at that mine in 1828. A book from the time states:

"The movement—which continued for several weeks— was so slow that the miners who at its commencement were employed at deep levels, by climbing uncrushed portions of the ladders in some places and waiting their opportunity and creeping through crevices between moving rocks in others, managed to reach surface at the west part of the mine in safety."

I am sure that we are all pleased that miners would never be placed in that predicament today. However, mine subsidence still occurs. The point of my little story is that it can occur long after mines have been sunk. That is the problem that we are finding in my constituency.

The motion implies that British Coal and its predecessor, the National Coal Board, have done next to nothing to compensate those suffering from the effects of mining subsidence. I cannot accept that. Something has

[*Mr. David Tredinnick*]

been done. Similarly, I cannot accept that the Government have taken no action. We must recognise that the Government have acted. I want to refer to some of the problems which have affected my constituency.

I welcome the clear undertaking given by the Minister earlier this year that he was aware of the real problems associated with subsidence. He said that

> "The question . . . is how to ensure that those affected by subsidence get a fair deal."—[*Official Report,* 11 May 1989; Vol. 152, c. 1104].

I suggest that the Government have acted to ensure that those affected by subsidence get a fair deal, but they have not done enough. Many of the people affected in my constituency will, like others today, be looking to the Minister for new initiatives to deal with the problem. We have already heard about the important recommendations in the Waddilove report which was based on the 1981 report of the commission on energy and the environment.

The Waddilove committee made 65 recommendations, but it did not recommend a radical revision or overhaul of the system. One principal recommendation involved improvement of public notification procedures. That recommendation, which has been accepted, has had a very beneficial effect. I shall illustrate that by referring to discussions that I had yesterday with council officers from Hinckley and Bosworth borough council. On 20 June, the council's planning committee will consider a report based on a report provided by British Coal about the workings around Bagworth, Nailstone and Markfield. I am pleased to say that the Coal Board's report covers the problems in some detail, for example, outlining the difficulties faced in the areas east of Wigg Farm, south of Bagworth colliery and north of Fox Covert Farm. The report does not skimp and it has had helpful and useful results—I was going to say "meaningful", but I am sure that my hon. Friend the Member for Stroud (Mr. Knapman) would agree that that is a terribly abused word.

As a result of other Waddilove recommendations, British Coal is at least committed to good standards of repair in all cases of subsidence. We have already heard why that commitment may not have been fulfilled in all circumstances, but the fact that claimants can now use their own contractors for repairs, for instance, is significant, as is the fact that British Coal provides the Secretary of State for Energy with an annual report on the administration of subsidence claims. I understand that, so far, British Coal has implemented more than half the committee's recommendations, although I agree with the hon. Member for Ashfield that the presentation of the report may have been a slow process.

Another helpful development has been the publication of a new Department of Energy leaflet offering advice on handling subsidence problems, which is a credit to my hon. Friend the Minister. The inclusion of the address of the area surveyor and minerals manager will make it easier for people to contact British Coal officials. British Coal's new procedures, the annual report to the Secretary of State and the report of mining activities to councils are three steps in the right direction.

There is some evidence that the impact of subsidence problems on householders has been reduced. Both the number of new claims and the total number of claims outstanding have fallen. I believe that in 1983-84 some 50,000 claims were outstanding, but in 1986-87 the figure was down to 36,000, and last year saw a further fall of 14 per cent. to 31,000.

Mr. Meale: Part of the reason for that is that so many claims are being denied because of the implementation of the six-year rule.

Mr. Tredinnick: I accept that. In my constituency, certainly, the six-year rule presents claimants with considerable problems. I hope that my hon. Friend the Minister will consider that point sympathetically.

British Coal now takes more account of subsidence in its planning; it also includes it in the costing of all proposed workings. There has been progress, although the pace may be that not of the hare but of a somewhat smaller creature.

There are serious problems in my constituency of which I hope the Minister will take note. We have heard about the problems facing individuals, but businesses also face tremendous problems. In my constituency, the Bagworth to Merrylees road was closed for more than a month—due to subsidence outside the main gate of the old Desford colliery. The Merrylees mine area is now an industrial complex offering employment to many of my constituents. When the road was closed it posed an enormous burden on the businesses which had to make a long detour. There is a good case for those companies receiving some compensation. The companies include major employers such as Butterley Buick and Hercock Simpson, which receive nothing from British Coal although their businesses have suffered seriously as a result of this problem.

It is no good British Coal saying that the problems are minimal. Not long ago in my constituency we had the case of the disappearing digger. I am referring not to an Australian who had too many "triple Xs", although when we consider the result of the recent Test match some of us might wish that Alan Border were a disappearing digger, but to a disappearing JCB which popped into a hole and could not be found. It simply sank overnight in an area that is supposed to be fairly safe, the site of the old Merrylees deep drift mine.

Sporting facilities in the Bosworth area face problems. The Bosworth parliamentary division has a long tradition of bowling and cricket, which I support at a time when sport seems in decline in this country. It is a credit to my constituents that they have such tremendous sporting interests. It was tough on the Barlestone mining institute when its bowling green suffered subsidence and the club received nothing for it. Barlestone football club pitch suffered movement too. In this House we are familiar with moving goalposts and tilting pitches because we play on them all the time, but I do not see why my constituents should have to suffer that.

The National Coal Board sells off houses and, in the small print of the contract, exempts itself from responsibility for any future problem. What is the use of a beautiful ex-Coal Board house which might make a lovely home when who knows what rabbit warrens of mining passages may run underneath? I say, "Who knows?" because none of us knows and none of us can find out because the information is not available. That is probably because it is a nationalised industry. If it were privatised it might have kept proper records.

We could all give cases, and I know of many of them. The subsidence problems faced by a family business in my constituency should go on the record. A. E. Statham and Sons process and distribute potatoes. Mr. Statham built a factory on land above old mine workings. Very soon subsidence occurred which necessitated repairs to the floors and foundations of the main storage area and the walls. The problem was first raised by my predecessor, Sir Adam Butler, who served his constituents so well. He started work on the case in 1980, and I have followed his work since then. The Coal Board accepted liability and arranged for the work to be carried out.

The beginning of the necessary repairs was also the start of a long saga of frustration about the standard of repairs. Another big problem that my constituent faced was that British Coal was not prepared to carry out the repairs outside usual working hours. My constituent was trying to run a business facing this enormous hurdle. The specifications for the work were poorly drawn up and the job was not properly supervised. Fortunately, Mr. Statham managed to continue in business and, to cut a long story short—think of the parliamentary time which has gone into this long case—he received some, albeit inadequate, compensation.

I know that other hon. Members wish to speak in the debate, so I will finish without giving the House the summary that I had planned to give. I hope that the Minister will respond positively and I look forward to hearing his speech.

1.55 pm

Mr. Dick Douglas (Dunfermline, West): I had not originally intended to take part in this important debate, initiated by my hon. Friend the Member for Mansfield (Mr. Meale). At one time in a previous incarnation I almost became secretary of the Co-operative movement's education committee in Mansfield but, perhaps wisely, it chose not to employ me. In any case, I know the area reasonably well——

Mr. Haynes: I served on the Co-operative board.

Mr. Douglas: Now I know what happened.

I represent what used to be a coal mining constituency, although now there are no active pits within its boundaries. Some of the few remaining miners in my constituency are employed in the Longannet complex. I shall allude to it again in a moment.

We are discussing the impact of mining on the environment and the consensus is that those who disrupt or pollute the environment should pay for the social and economic disruption that they cause. Having established this basic principle, we need to find a way to put it into practice. I have received many letters from constituents about subsidence caused by British Coal, not below but above ground—by the number of lorries that pass through a small village in my constituency called Cairneyhill, driving from opencast mining operations in Fife.

How we enforce the principle that the polluter pays is what counts. My hon. Friends have made a good case for saying that the enforcement procedures bear too heavily on those who cannot afford to go to court and are weighted too much in favour of the big corporations, such as British Coal, which can afford to put off the inconvenienced individual who suffers damage and disruption to his property.

We must take national action. It is not only public corporations that mishandle the individual: private corporations can do the same. We need a scheme that can help these people, and the scheme that we have is legal aid. However, because of the requirement for a reasonable chance of success in the courts, legal aid is difficult to obtain. There is a case for someone such as an independent ombudsman to assist the aggrieved individual.

There is increasing public worry about pollution, and there is some indication of that in the likely results of the European elections, with the exit polls suggesting that the Green party achieved 2 million votes. That illustrates the underlying concern of people in Europe as a whole about the environment. The Coal Board is sensitive to criticism in respect of acid rain and is anxious to prove its claim that it is not as great a polluter as has been suggested.

The Longannet complex is closely linked to a power station and produces coal having a very slow sulphur content. As the Minister knows, important negotiations are under way between the South of Scotland electricity board and British Coal over a reasonably long-term contract for the supply of 2 million tonnes of power station coal. If Longannet does not win that contract, there will be considerable subsidence in central Scotland because a coal mine there dedicated to a power station will no longer be utilised. The social cost of that will be borne by the community as a whole and by the Coal Board, whose £400 million operating profit would be substantially reduced.

Concern has been expressed about the effect of subsidence on property. Under the old rating system, such damage would be reflected in lower rates, but under the change to poll tax property owners will have to pay the full sum regardless of the state of their property.

Because I want to be fair to Conservative Members who have massive constituency interests, I bring my remarks to a conclusion with this observation. I do not know what is the practice now between the usual channels, but when I entered the House in 1970, if an understanding was reached between right hon. and hon. Members as to the allocation of time available for a debate, their respective Whips would get together and reach an understanding. That was done to protect the interests of Back Benchers. Today is for Back Benchers, not for members of the Government or Opposition Front Benchers. Nevertheless, I understand that the type of friendly understanding to which I referred has broken down. Mr. Speaker can do very little about it, but Back Benchers ought to put down some markers. They should reach a harmonious understanding on the timetabling—I use that term loosely —of motions. The usual channels ought to take account of it. The dreary procedure of talking out motions would not then be needed.

Some, though not many, of my constituents have suffered from the effects of mining subsidence. However, we ought to look after the interests of all Back Benchers, particularly when they are successful in the ballot.

2.5 pm

Mr. Roger Knapman (Stroud): I do not represent a constituency with a coal mining interest, but I take a particular interest in the law relating to compulsory purchase and compensation. The steady and logical arguments that are always pursued by my hon. Friends the Members for Sherwood (Mr. Stewart) and for Gedling (Mr. Mitchell) have been of great benefit to the mining

[*Mr. Roger Knapman*]

industry for some years. They are of considerably more benefit than the erratic outpourings of one trade union leader.

The Minister's career is rapidly recovering from the flattering remarks that were made about him by the hon. Member for Ashfield (Mr. Haynes). He will, I believe, have to introduce at some time a Bill to cover compulsory purchase and compensation. It is not just a question of subsidence within the mining industry. It is a complex and complicated issue. It began in the middle of the 19th century. I apologise to *Hansard* for using the Latin phrase "quicquid plantatur solo, solo cedit"—that whatsoever is planted in or attached to the soil remains with the soil.

It was rather hard luck for any farmer who died on 28 September: the landlord automatically took his crop on 29 September. Gradual progress was made towards the end of the 19th century. Further progress was made in 1919 under the Acquisition of Land (Assessment of Compensation) Act. Yet more of the customs of the country were covered in McCartney *v.* Metropolitan Board of Works, a major decision affecting the law on compensation. In 1946—not a particularly good year for legislation—there was the Acquisition of Land (Authorisation Procedure) Act which led to a number of additional complications. By 1947, things were getting even more desperate. Under the Town and Country Planning Act the Labour Government tried to nationalise all development land values. That did not last for very long. There have been town and country planning Acts in almost every year since then. There was also the Land Compensation Act 1973.

The legislative programme of the last 100 to 150 years has led to great complexities. I ask my hon. Friend not to go down the same road. I sat for many hours in the Committee that considered the Water Bill. The Minister recognised that a new compulsory purchase code for land held by water companies would be needed. Many similar matters are covered by the Acts covering electricity and gas supplies. Will every statutory undertaking need a separate code? A comprehensive Bill dealing with compulsory purchase compensation must be introduced, but it must be sufficiently flexible to take account of the needs of different industries, including subsidence in the mining industry.

The hon. Member for Mansfield (Mr. Meale) drew attention to many problems, but many of them have been created because the nationalised industries do not have flexibility to look after people in a reasonable way. Now that at long last the mining industry is becoming increasingly profitable, we can surely afford to address compulsory purchase and compensation in a more flexible way.

2.9 pm

Mr. Gerald Howarth (Cannock and Burntwood): I join my colleagues in congratulating the hon. Member for Mansfield (Mr. Meale) on choosing this subject for debate and for so eloquently, if in a marathon speech, giving us the benefit of his detailed knowledge. I also congratulate my hon. Friend the Member for Sherwood (Mr. Stewart), who has been an equally assiduous proponent of these matters on behalf of his constituents and all our constituents generally.

Today I have moved Bench to indicate that I am speaking in the capacity not of parliamentary private secretary to my hon. Friend the Minister but as a constituency member with coal mining interests as my constituents are very much affected by the problem of coal mining subsidence.

Cannock is well known for its association with the coal industry. In 1945 there were 22 pits in my constituency and today there is not one, although there are two just outside it. I pay tribute to my constituents in the coal industry who have produced a tremendous turnaround in the fortunes of the industry and, I am glad to say, are making money for themselves, for our local economy and for the nation at large.

Like many hon. Members who have spoken, since I was elected in 1983 I have found subsidence to be one of the most difficult problems affecting my constituency. As everyone has pointed out, the villain of the piece is British Coal, which has not dealt with the problem satisfactorily. As my hon. Friend the Member for Hornsey and Wood Green (Sir H. Rossi) said, this is not unassociated with the fact that British Coal is a nationalised industry. Private sector industries simply cannot afford to be so overbearing and churlish about the anxieties of people affected by their operations.

The hon. Member for Mansfield said that home owners simply do not trust British Coal, and that is a widespread feeling throughout the parts of the country where coal mining has been or is being carried on. The sooner that the British coal industry can move into the private sector, the sooner it will have to conform to the disciplines of the private sector. In these modern times the private sector cannot put up with so many dissatisfied customers who will only speak ill of the business. There will be further advantage in competition.

Mr. Douglas: What about British Airways?

Mr. Howarth: My kinsman, the hon. Member for Dunfermline, West (Mr. Douglas), says that I should refer to British Airways, and I am happy to do so. British Airways enjoys superb competition from British Midland and as a result the travelling public get a better deal.

Two issues are involved here. The first is that the problems caused by subsidence are not confined to damage. Blight is a major problem. A crack in one house in my constituency on the new estate sent metaphorical shock waves through the entire housing market, affecting neighbouring houses and streets. Confidence in housing in that area was seriously shaken. Local surveyors simply reported to purchasers that subsidence had taken place and building societies would not lend and people could not sell their houses, they could not move jobs and they could not raise funds on their properties for business or pleasure purposes. As a result of getting together with some of the local and professional interests involved, we were able to dampen that down. I pay tribute to one estate agent in my constituency, Mr. Graham Morris, who did a tremendous amount to take the heat out of the problem.

The second issue is the damage. In my constituency the difficulties are faced by the owners of older properties. The problem is well illustrated by one particular area, the Church hill area of Hednesford, which is well known to those who did national service in the Royal Air Force as one of the bleakest, most inhospitable and horrid places in the land on which to do their square bashing. By the time that I arrived as Member of Parliament for Cannock and Burntwood in 1983, St. Peter's church, a very fine Victorian church, was falling apart, but already negotiations with British Coal were at an advanced stage for compensation of about £250,000 to be paid. Further down the hill is the Hednesford Victoria working men's club. The bottom literally fell out of that club. I went there a couple of days ago and saw a gaping hole underneath the club. The day after, British Coal sent round a JCB, on a no-prejudice basis, to fill up the hole. There is even a road sign on the hill which says, "Road liable to subsidence". In 1978 a sewer collapsed and the board elected to make a payment to the local authority.

If, however, one draws a line on the map between the club and the church—both properties which have been bailed out by British Coal—it is a completely different story for the private houses on that line which have suffered damage. My constituent, Mrs. Flinn, of 128 Church hill has suffered damage to her property and so, too, has Mr. Walker of 140 Church hill—but can they get any joy out of British Coal? They cannot, because they are not a working men's club or a church. They have found it impossible to get any satisfaction. Mrs. Flinn sent me a letter which I believe sums up the position. She said:

"Public places, i.e. St. Peter's church and Church hill working men's club, seem to be top priority, but, when it comes to people's homes, they are right at the bottom of the list."

It is intolerable that British Coal should seek to take advantage of its massive underwriting by the public purse to do selective deals with people who they feel they need to bail out and to ignore the poor private house owners who cannot, as hon. Members on both sides of the House have said, afford to go through the long-winded procedures of the Lands Tribunal and all the rest of it to establish their rights.

British Coal has told me that in this case it is natural movement in the earth's surface that has caused the problem, because mining activity ceased 20 years ago. I went to see a splendid mining engineering consultant who told me that there is no such thing as natural movement in the earth's surface in the United Kingdom. It is significant, too, that the only places in my constituency where there are problems are in areas where there has been mining activity. I do not see how British Coal can have the continuing gall to pay out on some properties but not to pay out to poor householders who do not have the resources to take on Goliath.

I believe that I am in the best position to know that my hon. Friend the Minister has done more than anybody to try to improve the situation. As long as he is at the Department of Energy, I am sure that we shall have a worthy champion of our concerns about mining subsidence. We look forward to hearing what my hon. Friend will say. Ultimately, however, I am sure that the answer lies in the privatisation of the coal industry.

2.18 pm

The Parliamentary Under-Secretary of State for Energy (Mr. Michael Spicer): As has been said already, the hon. Member for Mansfield (Mr. Meale) has raised an important matter. As my hon. Friend the Member for Cannock and Burntwood (Mr. Howarth) stated, this subject has been pursued by a number of hon. Members on both sides of the House. My hon. Friend the Member for

Sherwood (Mr. Stewart), for instance, has represented this cause assiduously during the period in which he has been in Parliament.

In view of the intervention by the hon. Member for Ashfield (Mr. Haynes), I must say that I in no way would denigrate the contributions that have been made over a period by my hon. Friend the Member for Ellesmere Port and Neston (Dr. Woodcock). The fact that he has not a constituency interest, and that perhaps he has some business interest in the matter, which he has always declared, does not mean that he should not be deeply involved in the matter. I do not want the hon. Gentleman ever to cast any implied aspersions on what my hon. Friend may say on this matter.

I came to the House with a 39-page speech in which I intended to outline in great detail what the Government plan to do on this subject. However, so eloquent have been the speeches on both sides of the House, notably that of the hon. Member for Mansfield, who spoke for two hours, that, far from giving a speech of 39 pages, I have time only to give various indications to the House of the principles by which the Government will govern their actions in this regard.

I am very much of the view that subsidence causes both material difficulties and mental anguish to the people affected. That come out strongly from the debate and anyone in British Coal or anyone else who was unaware of such problems will be much more aware of them after this debate, in which some excellent speeches have been made.

I am sure that the House recognises that subsidence is an inevitable consequence of modern, deep-mining techniques. The problems associated with subsidence will therefore remain as long as there is a coal industry, and I certainly predict—I suspect that the Opposition Front Bench spokesmen agree with me—that that industry will be with us for a long time and will undertake deep mining for many years to come.

I intervened in the speech of the hon. Member for Mansfield because it is important to remember that the industry is under considerable financial pressure—far greater than was implied in the hon. Gentleman's speech. There is no question but that the industry is still suffering considerable losses. No doubt I shall return to that aspect when I come to the House some time in the future to ask for more assistance for it.

Currently, the coal industry is under great pressure from the environmental lobby, and in some respects that pressure is not entirely fair. No doubt the industry will address those problems in the future, but it will cost money. It is important to put this debate in context and to point out that the industry is not flush with cash but is still under considerable pressure. However, I completely accept, on behalf of the Government, that there is a problem with subsidence. How are those affected by subsidence to get a fair deal?

Mention has been made of the Waddilove committee report of 1984 and about the lapse of time between that committee publishing its report and the response to it. It is important to remember that one of the committee's conclusions was that the system for compensation and repair had its shortcomings—undoubtedly it took that view—but it did not call for a radical revision or overhaul of the system. Hon. Members have pointed out, however, that the report identified a number of areas in which improvement could be made. The process of implementation—perhaps not fully recognised—has already begun.

[*Mr. Michael Spicer*]

As I stated to my hon. Friend the Member for Ellesmere Port and Neston in a written answer on 12 January 1989. British Coal has already implemented more than half the Waddilove committee's 65 recommendations.

A number of important changes are therefore in place. British Coal has, for example, improved its public notification procedures. It now publishes in local newspapers mining locations for the previous and next 12 months. I appreciate that it is important to ask how effective those notifications are. That is why we are currently conducting a review of how these procedures are operated. We shall then be able to see whether they have been effective.

One of the Waddilove committee recommendations on which it is important to focus—there were lots of them, but I do not have time to go through them all—concerns the necessity for the Secretary of State for Energy to be supplied with an annual report of the administration of the subsidence compensation and repair system in the previous year. I remind the House that the first of those reports was placed in the Library towards the end of last year. It shows that the numbers of new claims and the total number of claims outstanding are on their way down. They may not be coming down quickly enough, but in 1983-84 there were 52,000 claims outstanding, while in 1986-87 there were 37,000. The report shows that by last year the figure had fallen to 31,000. Some hon. Members have suggested that this reduction has been achieved by British Coal simply rejecting claims, but that is not true. In 1987-88, the last full year for which figures are available, British Coal settled more claims than it received.

Last year, British Coal spent £49 million on compensation and repairs. The hon. Member for Mansfield asked for a breakdown of the figure, and perhaps I can supply him with detailed figures in writing. The main point is that the £49 million does not contain a large element of administrative costs as he feared. It is the amount of compensation that was paid. That money has been spent by an industry which, as I have said, has serious financial problems. In addition, it currently makes provision of £260 million in its accounts for subsidence compensation.

It is a distortion—I have to use such a strong word —to say that in some way or other the industry is specifically gearing itself not to make settlements. British Coal has a substantial amount in its accounts for the payment of compensation and pays out almost £50 million a year in compensation settlements. That is indicative not of an industry unwilling to make settlements, but of one that has all sorts of bureaucratic problems.

My hon. Friend the Member for Cannock and Burntwood (Mr. Howarth) and other hon. Members have said that we are talking about a nationalised industry and that it may well be that it operates differently from the way in which a private industry would have to operate. However, much money is set aside and paid out in subsidence compensation. The Government accept many of the recommendations in the Waddilove report for tightening up procedures. I would have gone through that matter in greater detail if I had had the time.

Mr. Barron: Why do the Government think that there should not be any form of the local adjudication that is specifically mentioned in the Waddilove report?

Mr. Spicer: I had intended to deal later with the question of the adjudication review, but I shall deal with it now in some detail as the hon. Member for Rother Valley (Mr. Barron) has quite properly raised it. I know that it is at the root of many of the problems raised by hon. Members. At present the Lands Tribunal procedure can be used, and local independent arbitration is also available. The issue is about what matters can be dealt with by each form of adjudication.

British Coal says that if a matter is not sufficiently simple to be dealt with through local and independent arbitration it should be put to the Lands Tribunal. That is where the controversy arises because it has been said that the Lands Tribunal procedure is expensive. We are reviewing this matter as part of our total appraisal of Waddilove and we have said that we will look at it again before 1990. We shall bring forward the review of the way in which adjudication is conducted and shall review the criteria by which the distinction between the two types of arbitration is made. We shall look at the matter to see whether there is room for improvement.

Mr. Meale: I know that the Minister will not have time to answer all my points, but will he respond to one or two of them?

Mr. Spicer: I shall not have time to deal with the details, but the hon. Gentleman's idea of what he calls an independent legal centre, as part of the review procedure, is interesting, and we shall look at it in the context of what I have just announced to the House. We shall also look at the general circumstances in which arbitration takes place.

We accept the spirit of this motion and of the debate and attach great importance to it. We intend to legislate——

It being half-past Two o'clock, the debate stood adjourned.

Orders of the Day

RE-ENFRANCHISEMENT OF THE PEOPLE BILL

Order for Second Reading read.

Hon. Members: Object.
Second Reading deferred till Friday 23 June.

COAL MINING SUBSIDENCE (DAMAGE, ARBITRATION, PREVENTION AND PUBLIC AWARENESS) BILL

Order for Second Reading read.

Hon. Members: Object.
Second Reading deferred till Friday 23 June.

BRITISH RACING COMMISSION BILL

Order for Second Reading read.

Hon. Members: Object.
Second Reading deferred till Friday 23 June.

FOOTBALL SPECTATORS (No. 2) BILL

Order for Second Reading read.

Hon. Members: Object.
Second Reading deferred till Friday 23 June.

RIDERS OF EQUINE ANIMALS BILL

Order for Second Reading read.

Mr. Gerald Howarth (Cannock and Burntwood): On behalf of the promoter, I beg to move, That the Bill be now read a Second time.

Hon. Members: Object.
Second Reading deferred till Friday 7 July.

BUSINESS OF THE HOUSE

Ordered,
That, at the sitting on Wednesday 21st June, Motions in the name of Mr. Neil Kinnock relating to Social Security and Community Charges (Scotland) may be proceeded with, though opposed, for one and a half hours after the first of them has been entered upon; and if proceedings thereon have not been previously disposed of, Mr. Speaker shall then put the Question already proposed from the Chair.—[*Mr. Heathcoat-Amory.*]

Ordered,
That, at the sitting on Thursday 22nd June, notwithstanding the provisions of paragraph (1)(b) of Standing Order No. 14 (Exempted business), if proceedings on the Motion in the name of Mr. Secretary King relating to the draft Northern Ireland Act 1974 (Interim Period Extension) Order 1989 have not been previously disposed of, Mr. Speaker shall at Seven o'clock, or one and a half hours after the proceedings were entered upon, whichever is the later, put the Question thereon. —[*Mr. Heathcoat-Amory.*]

RAF Biggin Hill (Selection Centre)

Motion made, and Question proposed, That this House do now adjourn.—[*Mr. Heathcoat-Amory.*]

2.31 pm

Mr. John Hunt (Ravensbourne): I am grateful to have the opportunity to raise a matter that is of great concern to my constituents and many people well beyond the boundaries of Bromley. I am particularly pleased to see a number of hon. Members supporting me in the debate, in particular my hon. Friends the Members for Orpington (Mr. Stanbrook) and for Chislehurst (Mr. Sims), my Bromley colleagues, and my hon. Friend the Member for Tayside, North (Mr. Walker), who I think is hoping to catch your eye, Mr. Deputy Speaker. I am referring to the proposed transfer of the RAF office and air crew selection centre from Biggin Hill to Cranwell. This came as a bolt from the blue last October and immediately aroused a wave of protest and indignation, not only from my constituents but from a wide range of groups associated with the RAF.

For many people in Britain and far beyond, there are strong emotional and historic ties with RAF Biggin Hill. It was, after all, the RAF's most famous war-time base and played a decisive role at a crucial stage in the second world war. As a young schoolboy in south-east London, I can remember the pride and excitement of seeing the Spitfires and Hurricanes valiantly defending our capital from the German bombers. I am told that some 1,600 enemy aircraft were shot down by pilots operating from Biggin Hill. We owe it to those men to ensure that an effective and meaningful RAF presence remains at Biggin Hill, and I hope that my hon. Friend the Minister will have noted that I am today wearing the RAF Biggin Hill tie as a mark of my commitment to the cause.

My hon. Friend the Minister has close links with Biggin Hill. He is a former distinguished mayor of the London borough of Bromley and I recall that his parents lived for many years at Leaves Green, just a stone's throw from the airfield. Therefore, like me, he knows of the important role that RAF Biggin Hill plays in the life of the local community. For example, it gives generous help and support to the Spitfire youth club in Biggin Hill and it involves itself in many other community projects within the borough. It is for this reason, among others, that the RAF station was given the freedom of the London borough of Bromley some time ago. It is for this reason also that the proposed closure has caused such distress and dismay in all parts of the borough.

We are told that on cost and service grounds there would be considerable advantages in moving the centre to RAF Cranwell. What are those advantages? I hope, for example, that my hon. Friend the Minister will be able to quantify the cost advantages rather more convincingly than he has so far been able to do. His written answers to my questions on 24 January were somewhat vague. Real doubts have been raised about the projected savings of £10 million over 10 years. It seems that that figure would depend in part upon the cost of additional accommodation required at Cranwell. My hon. Friend has provided an estimate of £5·5 million at current prices for that. In four or five years, however, the figure could well be nearer £10 million. We must remember also that the RAF works services budget is already severely over-stretched.

[*Mr. John Hunt*]

A crucial matter is the capital receipts that are likely to accrue from any disposal of the site. The local Biggin Hill ward representative, Councillor David Haslam, who has considerable professional expertise in such matters, has calculated that the maximum likely to be raised in this way is £16 million, but many think that it would be a substantially smaller sum than that. We must remember that it is a green belt site, so the development potential is necessarily strictly limited.

In his written answer to me on 24 January my hon. Friend the Minister declined to give an estimate of the likely capital receipts, pleading what he called "commercial confidentiality". I hope that he will be a little more forthcoming this afternoon.

What about what are called service grounds? The accessibility of Cranwell is clearly inferior to that of Biggin Hill. My hon. Friend will know that Bromley South station is only a 15-minute train journey from Victoria, and that there is a regular bus service from Bromley to the camp gate at Biggin Hill. Cranwell cannot rival that and by comparison is a remote location.

Currently, 70 civilian personnel are employed at Biggin Hill. In the main, they are locally engaged civil servants who have considerable experience of the special skills that are involved in the selection process. As I understand it, none of them is prepared to move to Cranwell. Is the Minister seriously telling us that suitably experienced replacements will be readily available in Lincolnshire? If not, presumably RAF personnel will have to be recruited to fill the gap, and that means more expenditure. In addition, there will be redundancy payments for the civilians at Biggin Hill.

We cannot overestimate the importance to the RAF of a strong and flourishing air training corps. We have the Minister's assurance that the Biggin Hill squadron of the ATC will remain in its present buildings, and we all welcome that. It seems, however, that that misses the point that RAF Biggin Hill provides a support base for about 135 squadrons of the ATC and cadet forces throughout London and the south-east. If RAF Biggin Hill goes, one is bound to ask where they are to be located. I am sure that my hon. Friend will acknowledge that the continued existence of the ATC squadrons is vital to continued recruitment for the RAF as a whole. The question of recruitment is directly bound up with the location of the officers and aircrew selection centre. I understand that recruitment to the RAF is becoming progressively more difficult as a result of the declining numbers of school and university leavers. At the same time, the RAF is facing greater competition for the reducing number of available technically qualified youngsters.

As I have shown, the Biggin Hill officers and aircrew selection centre is well located within easy reach of London. Its buildings are tailor-made for its important job. In addition, the buildings are bought and paid for and still have plenty of useful life left in them. Incidentally, those buildings are also used for aircrew testing by the Army and the Navy flying arms to carry out aptitude and medical tests. If that facility is no longer available, the Army and Navy presumably would have to build their own facilities and that would be an additional cost to be placed on the debit side of the Minister's balance sheet.

For those reasons, many of us fail to understand the sense or logic in the Minister's proposal. May I therefore make a special request to the Minister this afternoon: while allowing the planning for the move to continue for the time being, will he also ensure that there is a ministerial review of the costs involved before any irrevocable decision is taken? It would also be greatly appreciated if he could find time to visit RAF Biggin Hill to see the splendid spirit there and the efficiency and effectiveness of the centre.

As the Minister will know, his predecessor visited the centre to announce the transfer proposal last October. In fact, it was his first visit there. My feeling was that he was immensely impressed by what he saw and that if he had come a little earlier he might not quite so readily have endorsed the closure plan.

I fully recognise that the Minister has undertaken to retain the chapel and the gate guardians on the site. That undertaking raises more questions and worries. In his letter to me on 12 October, my hon. Friend the Minister's predecessor said:

"The Chapel will be retained as a lasting symbol of the Station's historical role in the Battle of Britain and continue to be accessible to the many visitors it attracts."

However, my understanding is that, without an RAF presence, there could be no chapel. Without regular services, I contend that the chapel would soon become a very sad and sorry symbol. I would welcome any reassurances that my hon. Friend can offer on that point.

More than 11 years ago the selection centre was under a similar threat of closure. In November 1977, my hon. Friend the Member for Orpington (Mr. Stanbrook), whose constituency at the time included Biggin Hill, initiated an Adjournment debate. In those days, the intention was to transfer the officers and aircrew selection centre from Biggin Hill to the RAF station at Bentley Priory. On reading the record, it is interesting to see that the move was justified on the basis of so-called cost-effective benefits to defence expenditure. Apparently however, those benefits were subsequently in doubt because the transfer plan was eventually abandoned. I hope today that I can match the dramatically successful eloquence of my hon. Friend the Member for Orpington on that occasion. I look to my hon. Friend the Minister to maintain my local reputation in that respect.

The station crest of RAF Biggin Hill bears a chain with the motto "The Strongest Link." It seems to me that we owe it to the brave fighter pilots of the Battle of Britain, as well as to future RAF generations, to ensure that that link is not broken by a foolish and short-sighted decision aimed at achieving financial savings which, in the end, could prove illusory and highly damaging.

2.44 pm

Mr. Ivor Stanbrook (Orpington): With the leave of my hon. Friend and neighbour the Member for Ravensbourne (Mr. Hunt) and that of the Minister, I rise briefly to support my hon. Friend's powerful plea for the retention of an RAF presence at Biggin Hill.

I must declare a special interest. I am a graduate of the 1942 class of the aircrew selection centre, which was then based at St. John's Wood. It was a great pleasure and honour subsequently to be elected Member for Parliament for the constituency in which Biggin Hill was then sited.

As my hon. Friend has said, we survived an attempt by the Labour Government in 1977 to transfer Biggin Hill on grounds of cost, and I am surprised and ashamed today that a Conservative Government should see fit, on the same grounds, to abandon the RAF presence there. The very name of Biggin Hill evokes the spirit of patriotism and endeavour in the British nation, and I should have thought that when considering such a move the Minister would take into account more carefully than he has in the past the effect that it would have on morale and recruitment.

Biggin Hill is of great importance to both the RAF and the surrounding population, and I plead earnestly with the Minister not to take this action.

2.46 pm

Mr. Bill Walker (Tayside, North): I thank my hon. Friend the Member for Ravensbourne (Mr. Hunt) for giving me the opportunity to speak. The House is aware of my interest in the Royal Air Force, and I will not go into that. Let me simply say that my hon. Friend the Minister should remember that Biggin Hill is the centre of excellence in selection. The world at large talks about Biggin Hill; it does not talk about the Royal Air Force officer and aircrew selection centre.

Biggin Hill is the brand name of excellence, and no commercial organisation would throw that away. Next year is the 50th anniversary of the Battle of Britain, and to throw away the brand name of excellence in the run-up to that anniversary would make no sense to me or to many others who have spent a lifetime supporting the RAF.

2.47 pm

The Parliamentary Under-Secretary of State for the Armed Forces (Mr. Michael Neubert): It is a mark of the characteristic zeal of my hon. Friend the Member for Ravensbourne (Mr. Hunt) that he should raise the question of Biggin Hill. I know that he has been seeking the opportunity to do so for a long time, and I congratulate him on his success in initiating this short debate. I have known him for longer than anyone else in politics, and I can say that his reputation as a campaigning constituency Member of Parliament is unrivalled and thoroughly deserved.

I thank my hon. Friend the Member for Ravensbourne for raising this issue today. The name of RAF Biggin Hill occupies a lasting and memorable place in the annals of our recent history, reflecting the brave spirit of defiance shown by members of the Royal Air Force who, facing great odds, fought and won for us the Battle of Britain in the dark days of 1940. I know that many people in my hon. Friend's constituency, Members of the House and former service men from both this country and abroad who have been in one way or another associated with RAF Biggin Hill, feel a great deal of sadness that the station is finally to close as an active Royal Air Force location, particularly —as my hon. Friend the Member for Tayside, North (Mr. Walker) mentioned—as we prepare to celebrate the 50th anniversary of the Battle of Britain next year.

As a former mayor of Bromley and leader of the council, and having spent my boyhood at Leaves Green very close to RAF Biggin Hill, I share those feelings of regret, but it is important that we look to the future as well as the past. I am grateful for the opportunity to set out, in response to the excellent case made by my hon. Friend,

some of the reasons why the RAF officer and air crew selection centre is to move—in about four years' time— from Biggin Hill to RAF Cranwell in Lincolnshire.

It would be helpful, to put the matter in full perspective, if I were to give the House some of the wider history of RAF Biggin Hill. This really began in 1917 when it was established as part of the inner patrol zone of the London defence area. During both world wars it played a major part in the defence of London. Originally the station was a base for Bristol fighters which operated at night against German air raids in the last year of the first world war. During 1918, the station was used for experimental work on wireless communication between the ground and aircraft in flight, and by the end of the war movements of the home defence squadrons in the air were being controlled through the transmitter at Biggin Hill.

In 1938, the station was again used for experimental work, in connection with the interception of hostile aircraft, under the direction of Air Marshal Sir Hugh Dowding and Professor Watson Watt. At the outbreak of the second world war, Biggin Hill was home to Nos. 32 and 79 squadrons, both equipped with Hurricanes, and No. 601 squadron equipped with Blenheims. On 29 November 1939, aircraft from 601 squadron, together with others from 25 squadrons, attacked the Borkum seaplane base. However, it was during the Battle of Britain, when its squadrons were engaged in some of the fiercest fighting of those critical three months, that the name of the station became famous. It shared with RAF Hornchurch the doubtful distinction of being the most frequently bombed airfield in Fighter Command.

Most famous squadrons operated from Biggin Hill during the Battle of Britain. Amongst the many famous pilots who flew with them were Group Captain Rankin, Group Captain Green, Wing Commander Kent, Wing Commander Stanford Tuck and Squadron Leader Neville Duke, later to become the well-known test pilot. In 1944, squadrons in the Biggin Hill sector began to escort light bombers of the Tactical Air Force to bomb the French railway system in preparation for the forthcoming landings in Normandy. Later that year, Spitfires of different squadrons provided air cover for Lancasters bombing the dykes on Walcheren Island, the key to the port of Antwerp.

After the second world war RAF Biggin Hill continued as a fighter station, and Nos. 600 and 615 Royal Auxiliary Air Force squadrons, and later a regular squadron, No. 41 squadron, operated from there. But in January 1958 RAF Biggin Hill became non-operational, although the University of London Air Squadron remained there, and No. 61 Group Communications Flight moved there in March 1958. However, on 7 February 1959, more than 30 years ago, all Royal Air Force flying from the station finally ceased.

While the RAF retained some working and domestic accommodation, the actual airfield at RAF Biggin Hill was transferred from the RAF to the Ministry of Aviation in 1964, and later sold to the London borough of Bromley in 1974. I remember, as mayor, presiding over the council meeting which decided to purchase Biggin Hill. Since then, civil flying has continued very successfully from the airfield, and this weekend the annual international air show, which has become a prominent part of flying activities from Biggin Hill, is to be held, with the planned participation of the RAF's Red Arrows. I am sure that this important and prestigious event will once again prove to

[*Mr. Michael Neubert*]

be a resounding success, and will continue well into the future, keeping the name of Biggin Hill before an appreciative public.

In April 1959 with the cessation of flying operations the Ground Officers Selection Centre was transferred to Biggin Hill from Uxbridge, and in April 1962 the officers and aircrew selection centre formed at RAF Biggin Hill and took on the tasks previously performed by the ground officers' selection centre at Biggin Hill and the aircrew selection centre at RAF Hornchurch, thus illustrating the nature of change over the years. Since it was established, the selection centre has done an excellent job in helping the Royal Air Force to choose young men and women to join its ranks, and I would like to pay tribute to all those who have worked and continue to work at the OASC. However, after more than 20 years it has become increasingly apparent that with the changes which the Royal Air Force is facing to keep abreast of modern developments, and the introduction of major new aircraft types such as Tornado and the European fighter aircraft, the centre not only needs to be part of a larger establishment than Biggin Hill can provide, but also needs to share in the spirit and atmosphere of the modern Air Force, to provide potential recruits with a realistic flavour of life in the service today. We have therefore decided that it should move to RAF Cranwell, where it will become a part of the wider activities of the RAF college in an environment that is well suited to its task, alongside an active military airfield.

Various alternative locations for the selection centre were considered before RAF Cranwell was chosen as the most appropriate new site. Apart from financial aspects, a range of other factors was taken into account, including accessibility and ease of travel to the centre for candidates. Examination of the points of origin of candidates showed that a more northerly location than Biggin Hill would be fully justified, and good transport links to Cranwell, which is easily reached by road, bus or train, will make travelling to the centre after relocation simple and convenient. The RAF is prepared to provide a transport service to the nearest railway station, at Grantham. There are of course already many visitors to the RAF college at Cranwell.

This decision has been taken as part of a wider and continuing initiative to keep under review the estate holdings and deployment of the Royal Air Force, and to ensure that the most cost-effective use is made of the resources available to the service. The selection centre is now the only unit based at Biggin Hill, and to maintain its presence it requires a considerable administrative "tail" in supporting functions such as catering, motor transport and supply. By transferring the selection centre to the much larger station at RAF Cranwell, where the administration wing alone is larger than Biggin Hill's total complement, we shall reap economies of scale to correct that imbalance. Cranwell will be able to absorb the OASC with only a small increase in its own support establishment. We will thus be able to save about 113 service and 19 civilian posts and secure running cost savings of more than £2 million a year once the move is complete. Some new building will be required at RAF Cranwell, but income from disposing of most of the existing real estate at Biggin Hill, including a large number of married quarters, will be more than adequate to

compensate for the new facilities needed. I shall keep these factors under review in the years ahead, but I can offer my hon. Friends no prospect of the equation changing in their favour. Indeed, we expect an ample margin of funds from disposal to be available for investment elsewhere, assisting in the process of adjusting the size and shape of the defence estate to meet the challenges that the services must face into the next century.

To revert to this century and the earlier history of the station, to commemorate all the aircrew who died while serving in the Biggin Hill sector during the war, St. George's chapel of remembrance was established at the station. The present chapel is the second on the site, the first having been dedicated on 19 September 1943, some months after the sector had received confirmation of the destruction of its 1,000th enemy aircraft. Unfortunately, the first chapel was completely destroyed by fire in 1946. An appeal was then launched with the endorsement of Sir Winston Churchill to erect a permanent shrine of remembrance at the station. Air Chief Marshal Lord Dowding laid the foundation stone of a new building in July 1951, and the Lord Bishop of Rochester dedicated the chapel on 10 November 1951, since when it has been in full use as a Royal Air Force church.

In recognition of the historical importance of Biggin Hill, we intend to retain and maintain, as a Royal Air Force responsibility, St. George's memorial chapel, along with Hurricane and Spitfire gate guardians, which reflect the past activities of the station. Arrangements will be made to ensure the chapel will be accessible to members of the public, and available for services as appropriate. This will ensure that a lasting memorial of the distinguished history of the station and the famous part it played in the Battle of Britain remains available both to those with a personal memory of, or connection with, those events and to subsequent generations, for whom that epic struggle would otherwise be only a formal entry in their history books.

Mr. John Hunt: Can my hon. Friend add to that by giving an assurance that a chaplain will be appointed?

Mr. Neubert: I shall certainly consider that point in response to my hon. Friend's plea.

I refer now to discussions with Bromley borough council concerning disposal of that part of the site that we shall not retain. Consultants have been appointed to undertake planning. My officials will continue to work closely with the borough council over the future use of Biggin Hill, and we shall be prepared to consider any suggestions for possible development, including aviation use.

The selection centre employs 89 service and 40 civilian personnel. For those civilians without an obligation to move with the centre, every endeavour will be made between now and the time that the move takes place to find them alternative employment, whether in the Ministry of Defence or in other Government Departments. However, at this stage the possibility of some redundancies cannot be ruled out. All staff in both mobile and non-mobile grades will be interviewed at an appropriate time by civilian management authorities to consider the possibility of future employment. Should redundancies eventually prove necessary, I shall ensure that all staff involved are given appropriate periods of notice. As to recruiting new staff needed at Cranwell, our studies have shown that the relatively small numbers involved will not present any difficulty.

As my hon. Friend said, there is an active and thriving air training corps squadron at Biggin Hill, and my predecessor, the hon. Member for Kettering (Mr. Freeman), made it clear that that squadron will be able to continue providing training for local young people, which fosters a practical interest in aviation and develops qualities of leadership and of good citizenship. A planning group is currently considering in detail how the squadron's needs will best be met following the move of the selection centre. I assure the House that we consider it very important to preserve the ability of the squadron to discharge its constructive and worthwhile task and that appropriate arrangements will be made to ensure that that continues.

Biggin Hill also provides support or parenting to a number of other ATC squadrons and combined cadet force sections in the south-east. That function will be transferred to other RAF stations in the area, and arrangements are already in hand for RAF Uxbridge to take responsibility for CCF sections.

In addition to selection procedures for potential RAF officer and aircrew recruits, the centre undertakes aptitude testing of aircrew candidates for the two other services and medical examinations of Army candidates. Following the centre's transfer, facilities will continue to be offered to the other two services who have been fully involved in preparations for the move.

As I said, I personally feel deeply the regret shared by many others that RAF Biggin Hill is soon to close after such an illustrious history, but there have been many far-reaching changes since those early days of 1917. Today, the RAF operates aircraft that would be unrecognisable to pioneers of military aviation. I am sure that the officer and aircrew selection centre will continue to uphold the very best traditions of the RAF following its move—and what better place than the Royal Air Force college, Cranwell, the home and heart of the RAF, for it to carry on its work. Similarly, I am sure that the name Biggin Hill——

The motion having been made after half-past Two o'clock, and the debate having continued for half an hour, MR. DEPUTY SPEAKER *adjourned the House without Question put, pursuant to Standing Order.*

Adjourned at one minute past Three o'clock.

Written Answers to Questions

Tuesday 6 June 1989

ATTORNEY-GENERAL

Listening Devices

Mr. Cran: To ask the Attorney-General whether electronic surveillance listening devices are used by the Lord Chancellor's Department or by any organisation or agency acting on its behalf; and if he will make a statement.

The Attorney-General: Such devices are not used by the Lord Chancellor's Department or by any organisation or agency acting on its behalf.

Legal Reform

Mr. Latham: To ask the Attorney-General whether he will list the meetings which the Law Officers and the Lord Chancellor have had with representatives of the legal profession to discuss the Green Papers; and what further meetings are planned.

The Attorney-General: The Lord Chancellor and the Law Officers have frequent meetings with representatives of the legal profession at which a variety of topics, which may include the Green Papers, are discussed.

Liverpool Law Circuit

Mr. Terry Fields: To ask the Attorney-General what action is being taken to deal with complaints about the Liverpool law circuit; if he will undertake an investigation into procedures on the Liverpool circuit; if he will consider suspending the circuit administrator; and if he will make a statement.

The Attorney-General: A number of complaints about delays in the county court at both Birkenhead and Liverpool have been made. The position at Birkenhead has improved over the past few months and a more satisfactory service is now being provided. At Liverpool difficulties have been experienced, due in part to shortages at junior staff levels and extra staffing resources are being made available in order to provide some immediate relief. A thorough appraisal is also being carried out with a view to strengthening the management structure. There is no intention to suspend the circuit administrator.

WALES

Mid Wales Development Board

Mr. Geraint Howells: To ask the Secretary of State for Wales if he will give the total expenditure of the Mid Wales Development Board in each of the years June 1978 to June 1988 inclusive.

Mr. Peter Walker: It is not possible to provide the information in the form requested. I refer the hon. Gentleman to the reply given by my predecessor to the hon. Member for Meirionnydd Nant Conwy (Dr. Thomas) on 23 February 1987 at columns 8-10 and to the recently published Welsh Office "Commentary on Public Expenditure in Wales 1989-90 to 1991-92" (Table 23), which provides details of the Development Board for Rural Wales' gross expenditure for the financial years 1977-78 onwards.

General Practitioners

Mr. Geraint Howells: To ask the Secretary of State for Wales what representations he has received from general practitioners in Wales about the proposed changes in the National Health Service; and if he will make a statement.

Mr. Grist: We have received a number of representations from GPs and their representatives. We shall be considering them, along with the views expressed during a series of meetings which we and our senior officials are holding with a wide range of interested bodies, before finalising the proposals.

Inward Investment

Mr. Livsey: To ask the Secretary of State for Wales what action he is taking to ensure that inward investment in Wales is evenly spread between all regions of Wales.

Mr. Peter Walker: Potential inward investors are encouraged to consider all parts of Wales for their projects. Welsh Development International has regional executives to effect this policy and liaise with local authorities and other bodies to ensure a co-ordinated response to inquiries. In Mid Wales, the co-ordinating role is undertaken by an official of Mid Wales Development who also acts as the area's direct contact point with Welsh Development International. In addition, initiatives have been taken, or are under consideration, for promoting particular areas such as Swansea bay and Gwynedd.

I am confident that the stronger framework provided by the launch of Welsh Development International will ensure that all of Wales benefits from the inward investment drive, though the choice of location for each project will ultimately always reflect the commercial judgment of the enterprise concerned.

Airports

Mr. Livsey: To ask the Secretary of State for Wales what is his policy on bringing into operation local airports in *(a)* Aberystwyth, *(b)* Anglesey, RAF Valley and *(c)* RAF Brawdy in order to facilitate quick access to European business centres via Birmingham, Cardiff, Manchester and London.

Mr. Wyn Roberts: Airport facilities serving south-west and north-west Wales already exist at Haverfordwest (Withybush) and Caernarfon. There is also a helicopter facility at Aberporth. A privately owned airstrip will soon be in operation at Welshpool. Proposals to develop these facilities or open further airports would be matters for the civil aviation industry in the first instance.

North-South Road

Mr. Livsey: To ask the Secretary of State for Wales what plans he has for constructing a new north-south Wales road before the end of the century.

Mr. Wyn Roberts: My plans for selective improvements to north-south routes in Wales are set out in "Roads in Wales 1989".

Roads (Expenditure)

Mr. Livsey: To ask the Secretary of State for Wales what the inflation-adjusted expenditure on different categories of roads in Wales has been for each year between 1975 and 1988.

Mr. Wyn Roberts: The information is as follows:

	Motorways and trunk roads £'000	Local authority roads £'000
1975-76	146,670	208,378
1976-77	204,977	241,529
1977-78	138,451	226,250
1978-79	128,906	215,970
1979-80	125,938	192,138
1980-81	120,841	169,451
1981-82	150,923	216,530
1982-83	160,826	227,418
1983-84	197,264	222,545
1984-85	138,420	215,794
1985-86	125,646	219,762
1986-87	133,051	214,577
1987-88	145,333	[1]230,468
1988-89	[3]153,895	[2]195,935

[1] Estimate.
[2] Budget.
[3] Does not include EC receipts of £9.0 million.

Note: All figures at 1988 prices, up-dated using the road construction price index.

M54

Mr. Livsey: To ask the Secretary of State for Wales whether he has any plans to extend the M54 to Welshpool or Newtown.

Mr. Wyn Roberts: No, but there are substantial improvements in preparation to trunk roads on both sides of the border as indicated in "Roads in Wales 1989" and in "Policy for Roads in England 1987".

North, Central and South Rail Link

Mr. Livsey: To ask the Secretary of State for Wales whether he has made any representations to British Rail about the case for constructing a new railway linking north, central and south Wales.

Mr. Wyn Roberts: No.

Railway Electrification

Mr. Livsey: To ask the Secretary of State for Wales whether he will make representations to British Rail about the case for electrifying railways from England to *(a)* Holyhead, *(b)* Aberystwyth and *(c)* Pembroke and Fishguard harbour.

Mr. Wyn Roberts: This is a matter for British Rail.

Community Charge

Mr. Roy Hughes: To ask the Secretary of State for Wales if he will now consider reimbursing local authorities with an additional £3 million to meet the cost of introducing the poll tax.

Mr. Grist: My right hon. Friend made it clear at the time that the terms of the 1989-90 RSG settlement were fixed, and that remains the position. Under the settlement, the total revenue provision made in 1989-90 for the implementation of the community charge in Wales was £9 million. Local authorities are budgeting to spend £10·9 million. Capital allocations of £10·3 million were given and local authorities are budgeting to spend £9·1 million. These are budget estimates and it is too early to form a judgment on the level of actual expenditure which might be incurred. I have made it clear to local authorities in Wales that overall spending should not exceed the Government's plans.

Hospital Waiting Lists

Mr. Roy Hughes: To ask the Secretary of State for Wales what are the latest available figures for people waiting for urgent in-patient treatment in *(a)* Wales, *(b)* Gwent and *(c)* Newport; and what were the figures in 1979.

Mr. Grist: The available information is given in the following table.

	People waiting for urgent in-patient treatment as at 30 September	
	1980[1]	1988
Wales	4,240	2,887
Gwent	1,212	855
Newport[2]	778	428

[1] Reliable information in this form is not available prior to this date.
[2] People waiting for treatment at royal Gwent and St. Woolos hospitals.

I welcome the substantial improvement and hope it will continue.

Mr. Roy Hughes: To ask the Secretary of State for Wales (1) what are the latest available figures for non-urgent cases waiting for one month or more in each of the Welsh health authorities; and what were the figures for 1979;

(2) what are the latest available figures for urgent cases waiting one month or more in each of the Welsh health authorities; and what were the figures for 1979.

Mr. Grist: The available information on in-patient waiting lists is given in the following table. Information on non-urgent cases is collected on the basis of the number waiting for one year or more.

	Urgent cases waiting one month or more as at 30 September		Non-urgent cases waiting one year or more as at 30 September	
	1980[1]	1988	1980[1]	1988
Clwyd	108	—	680	440
East Dyfed	—	—	111	236
Pembrokeshire	101	283	708	1,470
Gwent	848	553	1,958	2,207
Gwynedd	160	95	427	341
Mid Glamorgan	417	250	3,942	2,077
Powys	9	3	—	—
South Glamorgan	842	466	1,666	1,767
West Glamorgan	350	181	790	988

[1] Reliable information in this form is not available prior to this date.

Mr. Roy Hughes: To ask the Secretary of State for Wales what proposals he has to reduce the non-urgent hospital waiting lists in Gwent.

Mr. Grist: Responsibility for the management of waiting lists in Wales rests with district health authorities, within their allocated financial resources. The recurrent revenue provision for Gwent health authority for 1989-90 is some £127 million which represents a growth of 34 per cent. over 1978-79 after taking account of inflation. In order to reduce waiting times £1 million of additional moneys were allocated to health authorities by the Welsh Office in each of the last three years to enable them to tackle specific problem lists. A further £1·1 million has recently been made available for 1989-90 of which Gwent's share is £220,000 to fund a scheme to reduce trauma and orthopaedics waiting times in south Gwent. In addition, all health authorities have produced action plans for reducing waiting times and officials of the Welsh Office will be kept in touch with the position through six-monthly reports from authorities.

AGRICULTURE, FISHERIES AND FOOD

Nerds

Mr. Frank Field: To ask the Minister of Agriculture, Fisheries and Food what action he intends to take following the finding of glass in Nerds sweets; and if he will make a statement.

Mr. Ryder: Reports reached Government Departments in the afternoon of 23 May. Following discussions and the receipt of more information, the company decided in the interests of consumers to withdraw stocks of the product from sale on the following day.

Agricultural Development Programmes

Mr. Redmond: To ask the Minister of Agriculture, Fisheries and Food how many agricultural development programmes are operating in *(a)* the three counties of Yorkshire, and *(b)* Humberside; where are the locations; what is the total value of grants made to farmers under these schemes; and what is the source of these funds.

Mr. Ryder: Agricultural development programmes may be part funded by the Commission of the European Communities under article 18 of Regulation 797/85, the balance of the costs being found from national and local resources. There are none in operation in England and Wales.

New rules established at the end of 1988 enabled the Commission to designate "rural areas" the development of which need promotion and may be assisted financially under all three of the Community's structural funds. The Commission announced the first list of such areas on 10 May: none were in Yorkshire or Humberside.

Fishing (Aid)

Mr. Redmond: To ask the Minister of Agriculture, Fisheries and Food (1) how many grants have been given to members of *(a)* the Yorkshire, and *(b)* the Humberside fishing industry under the European agriculture guidance and guarantee fund scheme from May 1979 to May 1989; and how many new vessels were built with those grants;

(2) how much financial aid has been given to the fishing industry in *(a)* Yorkshire, and *(b)* Humberside under the European agriculture guidance and guarantee fund scheme since May 1979 to date;

(3) if he will list the projects in the fish processing industry for *(a)* Yorkshire and *(b)* Humberside, which received European Community grant aid in the period May 1979 to May 1989 and the total value of grants given to each product;

(4) in the period May 1979 to May 1989 *(a)* how many owners of fishing vessels in (i) Yorkshire and (ii) Humberside, received grant aid or the modernisation programme; and what was the total value of these grants, and *(b)* what was the total value of grand aid give to (i) the Yorkshire, and (ii) the Humberside fishing industry for building of new fishing vessels.

Mr. Donald Thompson: The financial aid available to these regions consists of national and EC grants for fishing vessel construction and modernisation and grants for processing and marketing schemes under EEC regulation 355/77.

EAGGF Aid for Fishing Vessels 1979-1989

| Year | Humberside | | | | Yorkshire | | | |
| | Vessel Construction | | Vessel Modernisation | | Vessel Construction | | Vessel Modernisation | |
	Number of Awards	Amount (£)	Number of Awards	Amount (£)	Number of Awards	Amount (£)	Number of Awards	Amount (£)
1979	—	—	—	—	—	—	—	—
1980	—	—	—	—	2	169,915	—	—
1981	1	85,470	8	131,880	—	—	—	—
1982	2	168,014	5	103,472	1	87,562	—	—
1983	4	367,860	3	55,199	3	54,798	—	—
1984	3	291,209	8	69,114	—	—	1	8,874
1985	—	—	14	174,763	—	—	6	55,815
1986	6	1,305,515	13	183,968	1	105,856	5	40,492
¹1987	3	1,134,316	2	8,719	—	—	—	—
1988	—	—	4	65,818	—	—	3	23,413
Total	19	3,352,384	57	792,933	7	418,131	15	128,594

¹ From 1987 awards are made from Fisheries Budget and not from the Agricultural Guidance and Guarantee Fund.

The following organisations have received EC awards for projects involving fish processing under the EC processing and marketing regulation 355/77.

	£
(a) Yorkshire	
1984: Selltop Ltd. Scarborough	25,223

		£
(b) Humberside		
1979: William Hobson Ltd.	Grimsby	31,982
1981: Cawoods Fishcurers Ltd.	Hull	11,329
1982: L. Williamson (Shetland) Ltd.	Hull	38,200
1982: The Grimsby Exchange Ltd.	Grimsby	30,001
1983: Youngs Seafoods Ltd.	Grimsby	215,687
1984: Marr Frozen Foods Ltd.	Hull	18,788
1985: Marr Frozen Foods Ltd.	Hull	10,741
1985: Seataste (International) Ltd.	Bridlington	54,229
1985: The Grimsby Exchange	Grimsby	19,109
1986: Maconochie Seafoods Ltd.	Hull	104,488
1986: Marr Frozen Foods Ltd.	Hull	30,259
1986: Glenrose (Fish Merchants) Ltd.	Hull	47,250
1986: Schooner Seafoods	Hull	44,250
1986: Bluecrest Foods Ltd.	Grimsby	133,017
1987: Marr Frozen Foods Ltd.	Hull	55,745

Note: Total for Yorkshire and Humberside—16 awards totalling £870,298 (May 1979 to May 1989).

Mr. Redmond: To ask the Minister of Agriculture, Fisheries and Food what is the total value of loans made to *(a)* the Yorkshire, and *(b)* the Humberside fishing industry from the Sea Fish Industry Authority in the period May 1979 to May 1989; and how many vessels these loans covered.

Mr. Donald Thompson: The information requested is as follows:

SFIA Loans 1979-1989

	Number of Vessels	Amount £
Yorkshire	12	597,194
Humberside	Nil	Nil

Note: SFIA loans ceased to be available after June 1986.

Farmers (Payments)

Mr. Redmond: To ask the Minister of Agriculture, Fisheries and Food what are the total values of payments made to farmers in *(a)* the three counties of Yorkshire and *(b)* Humberside for the sheepmeat regime since 1979; and how much of this was from *(a)* the European Community and *(b)* central Government in the period May 1979 to May 1989.

Mr. Donald Thompson: Farmers in Great Britain have received support since 1980 under the EC sheepmeat regime through both the sheep variable premium and the annual ewe premium. Both schemes are 100 per cent. financed from European Community funds. A breakdown of payments since 1979 is not available in the form requested by the hon. Member.

Mr. Redmond: To ask the Minister of Agriculture, Fisheries and Food what are the total values of payments made to farmers in *(a)* the three counties of Yorkshire and *(b)* Humberside for the beef premium in the period from May 1979 to May 1989; and how much of this was funded (i) from the European Community and (ii) from central Government.

Mr. Donald Thompson: The beef variable premium scheme operated throughout the period mentioned until it ceased at the beginning of April 1989. Funding from the European Community was at 25 per cent. until 19 May 1982 and at 40 per cent. thereafter.

The beef suckler cow premium was introduced in 1980 and continues. It was fully funded by the European Community for the first two years and has been partly funded at varying rates since then.

Statistics are not maintained in a form to provide the information on a county basis as requested by the hon. Member.

Fishing Vessels

Mr. Redmond: To ask the Minister of Agriculture, Fisheries and Food what is the total complement of *(a)* the Yorkshire and *(b)* the Humberside fishing fleets; what are the categories of vessels; how many fishermen are employed in the industry; where are the home ports of the vessels, for the latest year for which figures are available, and what were the figures 10 years ago.

Mr. Donald Thompson: The information is as follows:

Number of fishing vessels[1]

Port	Under 40 ft		40—79·9 ft		80—109·9 ft		110—139·9 ft		140 ft+		Total	
(a) Yorkshire	[2]1977	[2]1987	1977	1987	1977	1987	1977	1987	1977	1987	1977	1987
Staithes, Port Mulgrove and Runswick Bay	5	22	—	—	—	—	—	—	—	—	5	22
Whitby	15	53	22	20	—	—	—	—	—	—	37	73
Scarborough	20	34	33	27	—	—	—	—	—	—	53	61
Filey	16	25	—	—	—	—	—	—	—	—	16	25
Other	n/a	10	n/a	—	n/a	—	n/a	—	n/a	—	n/a	10
Total	56	144	55	47	—	—	—	—	—	—	111	191
(b) Humberside												
Flamborough	2	4	—	—	—	—	—	—	—	—	2	4
Bridlington	13	26	35	28	—	—	—	—	—	—	48	54
Hull	—	1	11	—	—	1	—	5	58	4	69	11
Grimsby	11	13	162	105	5	—	40	3	30	—	248	121
Other	n/a	26	n/a	—	n/a	—	n/a	—	n/a	—	n/a	26
Total	26	70	208	133	5	1	40	8	88	4	367	216

n/a = not available.

| Numbers of Fishermen | | | | | | |
| | Regularly Employed | | Partially Employed | | Total | |
	[2]1977	[2]1987	1977	1988	1977	1987
(a) Yorkshire	425	586	110	354	535	940
(b) Humberside	2,773	951	333	472	3,106	1,423
Total	3,198	1,537	443	826	3,641	2,363

[1] Changes in the number of vessels under 40ft are due partly to changes in the definitions used for this sector of the fleet.

[2] 1977 = Figures as at 31 December 1977.
1987 = Figures as at 31 December 1987.

Fish Landings

Mr. Redmond: To ask the Minister of Agriculture, Fisheries and Food what were the total values of all fish landings in Yorkshire and Humberside for each year for the last 10 years to date for the current year.

Mr. Donald Thompson: The total values of all fish landings by United Kingdom and foreign vessels in Yorkshire and Humberside for the last 10 years and for January to April 1989 are as follows:

	[1]*Yorkshire* (£'000)	[2]*Humberside* (£'000)
1979	7,577	73,733
1980	6,269	60,623
1981	7,582	46,002
1982	8,886	54,104
1983	10,477	48,206
1984	9,542	41,362
1985	11,519	39,333
1986	12,412	37,237
1987	13,556	37,193
1988[3]	13,305	34,030
1989[3] [4]	2,967	9,320

[1] Landings at the ports of Whitby, Scarborough, Bridlington and Filey.
[2] Landings at the ports of Hull, Grimsby, Immingham and Goole.
[3] Based on provisional landing statistics.
[4] January—April.
Source: MAFF fisheries statistical retrieval system.

Artificial Insemination

Mr. Boswell: To ask the Minister of Agriculture, Fisheries and Food if he will confine restrictions on artificial insemination services exclusively to those required for reasons of animal health.

Mr. Donald Thompson: Yes, subject to the constraints of Community zootechnical legislation.

Salmonella

Mr. David Porter: To ask the Minister of Agriculture, Fisheries and Food (1) how many poultry flocks and how many birds, have been slaughtered since the signing of the Zoonoses Order 1989;

(2) what compensation has been paid to poultry farmers affected by the slaughter of their flocks subsequent to the signing of the Zoonoses Order 1989.

Mr. Donald Thompson: Since the introduction of the Zoonoses order on 1 March, 25 poultry flocks and 338,963 birds have been slaughtered at a cost of £261,163·76p. In addition 6,333 diagnostic samples have been taken from 45 flocks at a cost of £10,459·79p.

Mr. David Porter: To ask the Minister of Agriculture, Fisheries and Food (1) how many random inspections have been carried out by his Department to ensure that the terms of the Testing of Poultry Flocks Order 1989 are being fully and correctly complied with;

(2) on how many occasions poultry farmers have been detected failing to comply fully and correctly with the provisions of the Testing of Poultry Flocks Order 1989; and what action his Department has taken;

(3) what evidence his Department had uncovered of the falsification of specified samples as required under the provisions of the Testing of Poultry Flocks Order 1989; on how many occasions; and what action his Department has taken;

(4) what system of checks his Department has put in place to verify that poultry farmers are supplying full and accurate information in compliance with the Testing of Poultry Flocks Order 1989; and if he will make a statement.

Mr. Donald Thompson: Responsibility for enforcement of the Testing of Poultry Flocks Order 1989 lies with local authorities. As the measure has been in force only since 16 March, and as measures for the registration of poultry flocks are not yet in place, it would be premature to reach a judgment on the extent of compliance. At this early stage, poultry farmers and enforcement authorities are still in the process of introducing the necessary procedures and my Department is providing advice and guidance as necessary.

Mr. David Porter: To ask the Minister of Agriculture, Fisheries and Food if he will list the evidence available on the extent of salmonella infection in the laying flocks of the United Kingdom and other EEC countries.

Mr. Donald Thompson: There have been 35 reports of isolation of salmonella enteritidis in table egg-laying flocks in the United Kingdom so far this year. We have no information on the number of cases reported in other EC countries but know that salmonella infection has been identified in Spain, Portugal, France, the Netherlands, Belgium, West Germany and Denmark.

Mr. David Porter: To ask the Minister of Agriculture, Fisheries and Food what discussions he has had with his European colleagues to ensure standard checking for salmonella infection in eggs.

Mr. Donald Thompson: I refer the hon. Member to the replies given to the hon. Member for Caerphilly (Mr. Davies) on 4 April at column *51,* the hon. Member for Angus, East (Mr. Welsh) on 20 April at column *280* and my hon. Friend the Member for Norfolk, North (Mr. Howell) on 25 April at column *492.*

Mr. David Porter: To ask the Minister of Agriculture, Fisheries and Food what steps he has taken to ensure that all eggs imported into the United Kingdom are subject to the same examination for salmonella infection as those produced in the United Kingdom.

Mr. Donald Thompson: I refer my hon. Friend to the answer I gave to the hon. Member for Angus, East (Mr. Welsh) on 20 April at column *280*.

Flood Defences (Thames Estuary)

Sir Bernard Braine: To ask the Minister of Agriculture, Fisheries and Food what detailed information he has on the maintenance work done by the Anglian Water Authority on the flood barriers and flood gates in the Thames estuary, with particular reference to the area from Southend-on-Sea to Purfleet in each of the last five years; and whether he is satisfied with the authority's standards of maintenance.

Mr. Ryder: Maintenance of the flood gates and barriers in the Southend-on-Sea to Purfleet areas of the Thames estuary is a matter for the National Rivers Authority unit of Anglian water authority. Anglian gives high priority to effective and reliable operation of these gates and barriers and sets standards of maintenance accordingly. The gates and barriers are in any case of "fail safe" design and current overhaul work on barrier machinery is to be completed before the surge tide season commences next autumn.

I am satisfied that the authority's arrangements are satisfactory.

BSE

Mr. Ron Davies: To ask the Minister of Agriculture, Fisheries and Food if any tests exist to diagnose the presence of scrapie or bovine spongiform encephalopathy infected material in animal feed.

Mr. Donald Thompson: There is no test available.

Mr. Ron Davies: To ask the Minister of Agriculture, Fisheries and Food, pursuant to his answer of 22 May, *Official Report*, column *375*, when he first introduced recording procedures in respect of the progeny of bovine spongiform encephalopathy-infected cattle; how such recording takes place; and how many such progeny have so far been recorded in each year of the scheme's operation.

Mr. Donald Thompson: The collection and recording of data from all affected herds commenced in June 1987 and included details of all previously known cases. The Ministry's central veterinary laboratory holds computerised records of female progeny born up to six months before or at any time after the onset of clinical symptoms of bovine spongiform encephalopathy in the dam and which are being retained in their herds of origin. Up to 9 May 1989 details of 562 such progeny had been recorded. Details of the years in which they were recorded are not held as the information is of no epidemiological value.

Mr. Ron Davies: To ask the Minister of Agriculture, Fisheries and Food, pursuant to his answer of 22 May, *Official Report*, column *375*, under what provision he has taken power to control the movement of progeny from bovine spongiform encephalopathy infected cattle.

Mr. Donald Thompson: Powers to control the movement of progeny are provided by article 7 of the Bovine Spongiform Encephalopathy (No. 2) Order 1988, which is made under section 8 of the Animal Health Act 1981.

Mr. Ron Davies: To ask the Minister of Agriculture, Fisheries and Food what evidence his Department has concerning the relative concentration level of the bovine spongiform encephalopathy agent in the brains, spinal columns and thymus of infected animals.

Mr. Donald Thompson: Proposals for research into this area are currently being considered by Dr. Tyrrell's research consultative committee.

Animal Test Certificate (Pharmaceutical Products)

Mr. Ron Davies: To ask the Minister of Agriculture, Fisheries and Food if he will list those pharmaceutical products being tested in 1988 under an animal test certificate under the Medicines Act which were subject to conditions banning the ultimate animal product from sale to the public.

Mr. Donald Thompson: Animal test certificates granted under the Medicines Act 1968 authorise field trials to be carried for the purpose of medicinal tests on animals. Such certificates are granted for two years and are renewable. Trials may not be in progress under all certificates at any one time and it would not be possible to identify products undergoing testing during any specific period.

Mr. Ron Davies: To ask the Minister of Agriculture, Fisheries and Food under what circumstances he bans from sale for human consumption products from animals subject to trials of pharmaceutical products under an animal test certificate.

Mr. Donald Thompson: Before an animal test certificate is granted all aspects relating to the safety of the product to be tested are rigorously assessed. In this assessment consideration is given to the safety to consumers of produce from treated animals. If this cannot be assured by a suitable withdrawal period then it would be made a condition of the certificate that treated animals or produce from treated animals should not be sold or supplied for human consumption.

Nitrate-sensitive Areas

Mr. Ron Davies: To ask the Minister of Agriculture, Fisheries and Food if he will state the area in hectacres which he assesses merits consideration for inclusion in a nitrate-sensitive areas scheme, and the level of funding he intends to allocate to the scheme in its first year.

Mr. Ryder: I am seeking the views of interested parties on all aspects of the nitrate-sensitive areas scheme including potential areas and compensation arrangements and I will make a further announcement when those consultations have been completed. I reassure the hon. Member that the Government have undertaken to pay compensation in the event of substantial restrictions going beyond good agricultural practice.

Hydatid Disease

Mr. Ron Davies: To ask the Minister of Agriculture, Fisheries and Food what information he has concerning the incidence of hydatid diseases; what action he is currently taking to monitor the disease; and what research his Department is conducting or funding into it.

Mr. Donald Thompson: Hydatid (tapeworm) infestation is not notifiable but slaughterhouse monitoring suggests that, nationally, about 3 per cent. of sheep may be affected, although the problem is greater in Wales, particularly in Powys. The condition results from the ingestion by sheep of the eggs of the dog tapeworm by direct transfer from dog faeces or through contaminated food or water. The Ministry, in conjunction with the Welsh Office Agriculture Department, has undertaken a six-year control programme in Powys in which all dogs have been de-wormed at six-week intervals free of charge. This has resulted in a significant reduction of hydatid infestation. The Department is not currently funding research into hydatid.

Sheepmeat Regime

Sir John Farr: To ask the Minister of Agriculture, Fisheries and Food if he will indicate his timetable for the introduction of a new sheepmeat regime; and what prior discussions with farmers he will be having in this connection.

Mr. Ryder: Discussions on the EC Commission's proposals for changes to the sheepmeat regime have made little progress. Negotiations may therefore continue for some time. My officials and I shall continue to maintain regular contacts with representatives of farmers throughout these negotiations.

Agricultural Statistics Act 1979

Sir John Farr: To ask the Minister of Agriculture, Fisheries and Food if, in view of the repetitious nature of the information required from farmers and horticulturalists by virtue of the Agricultural Statistics Act 1979, he will arrange for such returns in future to be on an annual or biennial basis.

Mr. Ryder: Most of the information required under the Agricultural Statistics Act 1979 is collected annually, in the June agricultural census. This covers farm holdings above a specified threshold size and results in a wide range of statistical data which are necessary for Government purposes and are also much valued by the industry. Twenty per cent. of holdings are smaller, and are enumerated only every five years or so.

Information on some items is also collected at other points in the year, to meet particular needs, but normally only from a sample of farmers. The need for statistical surveys, their content and their frequency are kept under regular review.

Untreated Milk

Mr. Waller: To ask the Minister of Agriculture, Fisheries and Food what information is available to him about the legal position relating to the supply of untreated milk in each European Community member state.

Mr. MacGregor: Detailed information is not readily available but I am aware that other member states impose various restrictions on the sale of untreated milk and I understand that in Denmark sales are prohibited with the exception of sales from one small family dairy in North Zealand.

Mr. Malcolm Bruce: To ask the Minister of Agriculture, Fisheries and Food, pursuant to his answer to the hon. Member for Derby, North (Mr. Knight) of 25 May, *Official Report,* column *1111* if he will make it his policy to extend consumer freedom of choice by abandoning plans to outlaw the sale of green top milk to the general public.

Mr. MacGregor: I have nothing to add to the reply given to my hon. Friend the Member for Keighley (Mr. Waller) on 25 May at columns *735-36.*

Milk (Bovine Somatotropin)

Mr. Malcolm Bruce: To ask the Minister of Agriculture, Fisheries and Food, pursuant to his reply to the hon. Member for Derby, North (Mr. Knight) on 25 May, *Official Report,* column *1111,* whether he will also make it his policy to require milk treated with bovine somatotropin to be labelled before going on sale to the general public.

Mr. Ryder: No. I fully recognise the need for consumers to be given adequate information to enable them to make an informed choice. However, the BST hormone occurs naturally in milk and it is not possible to distinguish between the natural hormone in the milk and that induced by the treatment of the cow with BST, since the detectable levels of the hormone in the milk are within the same range in both cases.

Food Quality and Safety

Mr. Malcolm Bruce: To ask the Minister of Agriculture, Fisheries and Food what representations he has received urging that the responsibility for food quality and safety be removed from the auspices of the Ministry of Agriculture; what has been his response; and if he will make a statement.

Mr. Ryder: There is a firm link between agricultural production and the rest of the food chain, and therefore sense and logic in having the whole of the food chain within the Ministry of Agriculture, Fisheries and Food. This enables policy changes to be assessed for the whole of the food chain rather than just part of it for which it might have direct responsibility. I do not think that there is any evidence to suggest that the Ministry does not give sufficient emphasis to the health implications of food. Indeed our overriding concern is that the food supply should be safe, wholesome and properly labelled.

EDUCATION AND SCIENCE

Regional Pay

13. **Mr. John Marshall:** To ask the Secretary of Education and Science whether he will make a statement about the introduction of regional pay in schools.

Mr. Kenneth Baker: I shall shortly be holding further meetings with the employers and the teaching unions to discuss future pay determination arrangements.

Teachers (Recruitment)

15. **Mrs. Gillian Shephard:** To ask the Secretary of State for Education and Science what steps he is taking to encourage the recruitment of former teachers back to the classroom.

Mrs. Rumbold: We are already very successful in recruiting former teachers: over 50 per cent. of new appointments in the four years up to March 1987 were taken up by former teachers. But we are increasing our efforts and have recently announced a new £2 million education support grant programme to support measures to support returners. I look to authorities to come up with imaginative schemes aimed at women in particular, which might include child care facilities and more flexible employment arrangements, such as part-time working and job sharing.

26. **Mr. Irvine:** To ask the Secretary of State for Education and Science what are the latest figures he has available as regards science and mathematics graduates going into teaching; and what are the corresponding figures for five years ago.

Mr. Butcher: In the year ending March 1986 (the latest for which figures are available) the numbers of new entrants to teaching in maintained nursery, primary and secondary schools in England with degrees (including B Eds) in science and mathematics were 1,710 and 860 respectively. The corresponding figures for the year ending March 1981 were 2,040 and 800.

37. **Mr. Hague:** To ask the Secretary of State for Education and Science what progress he is making in meeting the problem of potential teacher shortages in certain subject areas.

Mr. Butcher: Since our action programme was launched nearly three years ago the decline in recruitment to teaching in the shortage subjects which we witnessed up to 1986 has been reversed. We shall continue and reinforce our action programme to ensure that we have the well-qualified teachers that we shall need in our schools in the 1990s.

Student Unions

16. **Mr. Fishburn:** To ask the Secretary of State for Education and Science what representations he has received recently on the funding of student unions.

Mr. Jackson: Since April 1988 we have received 44 letters commenting on the funding of institutional student unions. Thirty two questioned the present system.

Mr. Amess: To ask the Secretary of State for Education and Science if he will make a statement on the progress of his Department's review of student unions.

Mr. Jackson: We plan shortly to publish the factual analysis of the Department's survey of student unions. We are considering separately what action might best be taken and in due course will consult all those concerned on our conclusions.

Mr. Amess: To ask the Secretary of State for Education and Science what recent representations he has received *(a)* supporting and *(b)* opposing automatic membership of student unions; what percentage the latter represents of the former; and if he will make a statement.

Mr. Jackson: Since April 1988 we have received 55 letters expressing a view on automatic membership of institutional student unions. Of these, 20 (36·4 per cent.) supported and 35 (63·6 per cent.) were against automatic membership.

National Curriculum

17. **Mr. Andrew Mitchell:** To ask the Secretary of State for Education and Science if he will make a statement on the state of preparations for the introduction of the national core curriculum.

Mrs. Rumbold: Preparations are well in hand. Statutory orders for mathematics, science and English have been laid; the National Curriculum Council has distributed guidance and training materials free; and LEAs' training programmes, supported by Government specific grants, are under way.

30. **Mr. Janner:** To ask the Secretary of State for Education and Science whether he will make a statement concerning the provision of mother tongue teaching under the national curriculum.

Mrs. Rumbold: My right hon. Friend laid on 19 May the Education (National Curriculum) (Modern Foreign Languages) Order 1989 which specifies those languages eligible to be taught as the national curriculum foundation subject. The order includes the mother tongue languages of some ethnic communities in this country. A school would be able to offer any of these languages towards the national curriculum requirements, provided that it also offered at least one of the European Community working languages. Pupils would choose one modern foreign language from those offered by the school.

38. **Mr. George Howarth:** To ask the Secretary of State for Education and Science what plans he has to ensure that teachers are fully prepared to implement the national curriculum in primary schools next term.

Mrs. Rumbold: I refer the hon. Member to the reply I gave earlier today to the hon. Member for Halifax (Mrs. Mahon).

42. **Ms. Mowlam:** To ask the Secretary of State for Education and Science what steps his Department is taking to ensure that adequate resources will be available to ensure full access to the national curriculum for children with special educational needs, where appropriate.

Mr. Butcher: The Government are making specific grants available to local education authorities to support the introduction of the national curriculum. In this financial year, there will be support for over £100 million expenditure. It is for authorities to decide how much to spend within this total in order to ensure full access to the national curriculum for children with special educational needs, where appropriate.

Careers Education

14. **Mr. Skinner:** To ask the Secretary of State for Education and Science whether he has any discussions with local authority associations with regard to careers education; and if he will make a statement.

Mr. Butcher: My right hon. Friend has not done so recently but he and my right hon. Friends the Secretaries of State for Employment and for Wales have promoted the widest collaboration in careers education and guidance through the "Working Together" initiative which they launched two years ago.

18. **Mr. Turner:** To ask the Secretary of State for Education and Science what advice he has given in the current year to secondary schools with regard to careers education.

Mr. Butcher: I refer the hon. Member to the reply I gave earlier today to the hon. Member for Sheffield, Hillsborough (Mr. Flannery).

Higher Education

19. **Mr. Yeo:** To ask the Secretary of State for Education and Science what representations he has received regarding the case for widening access to higher education.

Mr. Jackson: Many of the large number of representations we receive on higher education matters explicitly favour wider access, as do the Government.

Dyslexia

20. **Mr. Teddy Taylor:** To ask the Secretary of State for Education and Science if he will take steps to review the identification and educational treatment of dyslexia in school pupils; and if he will make a statement.

Mr. Butcher: It is for individual local education authorities in the exercise of their statutory duties under the 1981 Education Act to make provision for the identification of children with special educational needs and the provision of appropriate education to meet their needs. My right hon. Friend has no plans at present to amend these statutory procedures.

Pupil Testing

21. **Mr. Morley:** To ask the Secretary of State for Education and Science what progress he has to report on his plans for testing at age seven; and if he will make a statement.

Mrs. Rumbold: Contracts have been let for the development of standard assessment tasks in the core subjects and technology for seven-year-old pupils. Work has already begun to develop, trial and pilot these SATs in preparation for the first unreported assessments in summer 1991. The first reported assessments will take place in summer 1992. Assessment arrangements for other foundation subjects will be phased in later.

45. **Mr. Amos:** To ask the Secretary of State for Education and Science if he will make a statement on his progress in implementing a system of testing for pupils at ages seven, 11 and 14 years.

Mrs. Rumbold: The national curriculum system of testing rests on the establishment, for each foundation subject, of programmes of study and attainment targets. These will be introduced for mathematics and science for five and 11-year-olds, and for English for five-year-olds, this autumn. Those pupils will be assessed in these subjects on a trial basis when they reach the ages of seven and 14 respectively in 1991 and 1992, and on a reported basis in subsequent years. Contracts have already been let for the development of standard assessment tasks for seven-year-olds and bids for SATs for 14-year-olds are under consideration. Assessment arrangements in these subjects for 11 and 16-year-olds and in other subjects at each age will be phased in over succeeding years.

Committee of Vice-Chancellors and Principals

22. **Mr. Burns:** To ask the Secretary of State for Education and Science when he last met the Committee of Vice-Chancellors and Principals; and what he discussed.

Mr. Jackson: My right hon. Friend and I meet representatives of the Committee of Vice-Chancellors and Principals from time to time in the course of normal business.

Student Loans

23. **Mr. Menzies Campbell:** To ask the Secretary of State for Education and Science if he will make a statement about his plans to introduce top-up loans for students.

28. **Mr. Pike:** To ask the Secretary of State for Education and Science what recent representations he has received on his proposal to introduce student loans.

41. **Dr. Moonie:** To ask the Secretary of State for Education and Science if he will make a statement on the response of the financial institutions to his White Paper on student loans.

44. **Mr. Fisher:** To ask the Secretary of State for Education and Science if he will make a statement on the implementation of his White Paper on student loans.

48. **Mr. Radice:** To ask the Secretary of State for Education and Science if he will make a statement on the implementation of his White Paper on student loans.

Mr. Jackson: I refer the hon. Member to the answer I gave earlier to the hon. Member for Birkenhead (Mr. Field) and my hon. Friend the Member for Ealing, North (Mr. Greenway).

31. **Mr. Doran:** To ask the Secretary of State for Education and Science if he will make a statement on the representations he has received from Scottish universities regarding his White Paper on student loans.

46. **Mr. Darling:** To ask the Secretary of State for Education and Science if he will make a statement on the representations he has received from Scottish universities regarding his White Paper on student loans.

Mr. Jackson: We have received responses to the White Paper from each of the Scottish universities or their student bodies, and from the Standing Conference of the Universities of Scotland. They are being taken into account, along with all other responses, as we proceed to develop a scheme for the introduction of top-up loans.

Careers Education

24. **Mr. Nicholas Brown:** To ask the Secretary of State for Education and Science whether his Department has issued advice to careers departments in secondary schools in the past year; and if he will make a statement.

Mr. Butcher: Her Majesty's Inspectorate published "Careers education and guidance from 5 to 16" in its "Curriculum Matters" series last year. This has informed local education authorities and schools, and authorities drew upon it when preparing the statements of future policy which they submitted recently to my right hon. Friend and my right hon. Friend the Secretary of State for Employment.

Language Study

25. **Mr. Stott:** To ask the Secretary of State for Education and Science if he has any proposals to increase the number of Russian language assistants currently in secondary schools.

Mr. Jackson: The programme of co-operation in the scientific, educational and cultural fields between the United Kingdom and the USSR for 1989-1991 provides for the number of Russian language assistants currently in the United Kingdom to be increased to a maximum of six a year from academic year 1989-90.

29. **Mr. Jim Marshall:** To ask the Secretary of State for Education and Science what plans he has to enable schools to take advantage of opportunities provided by the European Community of other member nations in assisting the teaching in their schools of languages that are currently unavailable to schools in England and Wales.

35. **Mr. Michael:** To ask the Secretary of State for Education and Science what proposals he has to enable schools to take advantage of opportunities provided by the European Community for other member nations in assisting the teaching in their schools of languages that are presently unavailable to schools in England and Wales.

Mr. Jackson: My right hon. Friend is not aware that there are opportunities relating to the teaching of languages in schools provided by the European Community that are available to schools in the other members states but not in England and Wales. He informed the House on 24 May of the agreement on 22 May over the terms of the Community's Lingua programme. The programme is concerned with the support for the improvement of foreign language competence through initial and continuing vocational education. This includes the training of foreign language teachers in schools in the United Kingdom as in other member states and our schools will benefit in equal measure.

47. **Mr. Sean Hughes:** To ask the Secretary of State for Education and Science what steps he is taking to encourage secondary school pupils to study two modern languages.

Mrs. Rumbold: The national curriculum will include a modern foreign language as a foundation subject at secondary level to be studied by all pupils between the ages of 11 and 16. From this autumn, pupils will have to study a modern foreign language for a reasonable time in the first three years of secondary schooling. This requirement will be extended to the last two years of compulsory schooling later. Schools will be free to offer a second foreign language during the 11-16 phase or in the sixth form, in addition to meeting the national curriculum requirements. This reflects the Government's policy on modern foreign languages in the school curriculum which was set out in my right hon. Friend's policy statement "Modern Languages in the School Curriculum" published in January 1988.

Morris Report

33. **Dr. Bray:** To ask the Secretary of State for Education and Science if he will make a statement on the Morris report on research councils' responsibilities for biological sciences.

Mr. Jackson: This report was commissioned by the Advisory Board for the Research Councils in June 1988 and Mr. Morris presented his report to the board at the end of April. The board is now seeking the views of the research councils on the report before submitting detailed advice to my right hon. Friend later in the year. In the meantime the chairman of the board has sent the report to my right hon. Friend and a copy has been placed in the Library. He would not wish to comment on the report until he has had the opportunity to consider the board's advice.

School Governors

34. **Mr. Patnick:** To ask the Secretary of State for Education and Science what progress his Department has made in encouraging parents to become school governors.

36. **Mr. Hind:** To ask the Secretary of State for Education and Science if he will make a statement on the number of schools which have established governing bodies containing parent governors as required by the Education Reform Act.

Mrs. Rumbold: A recent survey for the Department suggests that more than 99 per cent. of parent governor places at county and maintained special schools have been filled.

Parents

39. **Mr. Rowe:** To ask the Secretary of State for Education and Science if he has any plans for providing education or training for parents; and if he will make a statement.

Mr. Jackson: The committee of inquiry into discipline in schools has recommended that the Government should develop a post-school education strategy aimed at promoting socially responsible parenthood. I am considering this recommendation.

Teacher Training

40. **Mr. Morgan:** To ask the Secretary of State for Education and Science what representations he has received concerning the initial teacher training course at the faculty of education at University College, Cardiff.

Mrs. Rumbold: My right hon. Friend has received several representations at the faculty of education at what is now the University of Wales College of Cardiff.

Capital Programme (Cornwall)

43. **Mr. Matthew Taylor:** To ask the Secretary of State for Education and Science what representations he has received regarding the capital programme for schools in Cornwall.

Mr. Butcher: My hon. Friend the Minister of State discussed the 1989-90 capital allocation with a deputation from the Cornwall education committee whom she saw during her visit to the county on 12 April. A number of hon. Members, the chief education officer of the authority and members of the public have written to Ministers on this subject.

City and Guilds Institute

49. Mr. Holt: To ask the Secretary of State for Education and Science when the Secretary of State last met the general secretary of the City and Guilds Institute; and what was discussed.

Mr. Jackson: My right hon. Friend last met the Director General of the City and Guilds of London Institute on 17 November 1987. A range of vocational education issues were discussed with the chairman and senior members of CGLI. Opportunities have arisen since that time for a number of informal discussions with both the Secretary of State and myself.

My right hon. Friend has a meeting arranged with the chairman and Director General of CGLI for 14 June when he intends both to review the achievements of CGLI and discuss the initiatives suggested in his speech to the Association for Colleges of Further and Higher Education on 15 February 1989.

Zidovudine

Mr. Alfred Morris: To ask the Secretary of State for Education and Science if he will update the figures of participants in the MRC/INSERM trial of zidovudine given in reply to the right hon. Member for Manchester, Wythenshawe on 22 February, *Official Report*, column *636*.

Mr. Jackson: The number of participants enrolled in the MRC/INSERM trial of zidovudine up to 26 May 1989 was 382 in the United Kingdom and 384 in France.

Creches

Mr. Harry Barnes: To ask the Secretary of State for Education and Science what plans he has to encourage the provision of creches to attract experienced teachers with their own children back into the profession.

Mrs. Rumbold: Our education support grant programme for 1990-91 includes support for expenditure of £2 million on local recruitment of returners and mature new entrants to the teaching profession. We are looking for imaginative proposals from local authorities which we can support, and which might include the provision of childcare facilities for teachers' children.

Listening Devices

Mr. Cran: To ask the Secretary of State for Education and Science whether electronic surveillance listening devices are used by his Department or by any organisation or agency acting on its behalf; and if he will make a statement.

Mrs. Rumbold: Electronic surveillance listening devices are not used by the Department of Education and Science, nor by any organisation or agency acting on its behalf.

Teachers' Pay

Mr. Alison: To ask the Secretary of State for Education and Science if he will express the salary received by a primary school teacher at the top of scale 2 in 1973-74 in current day's prices; and what salary a primary school deputy head receives at the present day.

Mrs. Rumbold: A teacher with a good honours degree at the top of scale two in 1973-74 would have received a basic salary of £2,699. This is equal to £13,358 at April 1989 prices. The salaries of deputy head teachers vary acording to the size of the school. The deputy head of a typical (group 4) primary school now earns £16,809.

School Milk

Mr. Morley: To ask the Secretary of State for Education and Science what steps he is taking to ensure that all state nurseries are made aware of their right to claim reimbursement for school milk supplied to their children under the Welfare Food Regulations 1988.

Mr. Butcher: My right hon. Friend has no plans for an initiative of this kind.

Medical Research

Mr. Nicholas Winterton: To ask the Secretary of State for Education and Science (1) what Government funding is currently available for research into the causes and treatment of retinal conditions;

(2) what information he has concerning current research projects studying the detection and alleviation of retinal conditions.

Mr. Jackson: The Medical Research Council which receives a grant-in-aid from this Department, is the main agency through which the Government fund medical research in the United Kingdom. The council determines its own priorities for the support of research, with advice from its expert boards and committees. In 1987-88, the last year for which figures are available, the MRC spent £134,000 on research relevant to retinal conditions.

I understand from the MRC that one of the major current interests in research on retinal conditions, and particularly in connection with retinitis pigmentosa, relates to the genetic basis of such diseases. This is the focus of work generally at the MRC human genetics unit which is located at the western general hospital, Edinburgh. Specifically, the unit is undertaking the following studies concerning retinitis pigmentosa:

    i. DNA sequence markers in single gene disorders;
    ii. Mapping the x-linked retinitis pigmentosa gene with a view to the development of clinically useful probes.

Some support for research on retinal conditions may also be provided by this Department through UFC block grants to universities and medical schools.

Mr. Amess: To ask the Secretary of State for Education and Science (1) whether any public funded current or proposed research project into genetic handicap involves the use of the human embryo; and if he will make a statement;

(2) whether the Medical Research Council is involved in any research project into genetic handicap which necessitates the use of the human embryo; and if he will make a statement.

Mr. Jackson: I understand that the Medical Research Council is involved in research at the Hammersmith hospital on the pre-implantation diagnosis of genetic disease; and at Edinburgh and Oxford, on the development of techniques for the diagnosis of genetic handicap. There is other research concerning pre-implantation diagnosis at Bourn hall, Cambridge, on sexing of human embryos; at Hammersmith hospital, for prevention of genetic diseases; and at Oxford by the

Cancer Research Campaign on derivation of cell lines from the human conceptus to investigate the growth regulation of embryonic and tumour cells.

Staff Dispersal

Mr. Blair: To ask the Secretary of State for Education and Science what plans he has to disperse staff from his Department in London to Darlington; how many staff are involved, and in what grade; and if he will make a statement.

Mrs. Rumbold: Government policy requires Departments to review the location of their work with a view to relocation where advantageous. The Department is accordingly considering whether there is scope for relocation of any of its headquarters based activities and, if so, where such activities would be best placed. Relocation of work to Darlington is amongst the options under consideration.

SCOTLAND

Actions for Debt

Mrs. Margaret Ewing: To ask the Secretary of State for Scotland whether he will implement the recommendation of the Grant committee, Cmnd. 3248, that both actions of adjudication in implement and actions of adjudication for debt should be competent in the sheriff court.

Lord James Douglas-Hamilton: As part of its second programme of law reform, the Scottish Law Commission has inititated consultations on proposals for the reform of the law on adjudications for debt and related matters. Its report is awaited.

Electricity Privatisation

Mr. Flynn: To ask the Secretary of State for Scotland what information he has on the amounts of nuclear wastes, spent fuel and plutonium which will be inherited by Scottish Nuclear Ltd. from the South of Scotland Electricity Board after privatisation.

Mr. Lang: I refer the hon. Member to the reply I gave to the hon. Member for Meirionnydd Nant Conwy (Dr. Thomas) on 11 May 1989 at column *429*.

Alcohol Misuse

Mr. Robin Cook: To ask the Secretary of State for Scotland if he intends to issue a circular on alcohol misuse similar to circular (89)4 issued by the Department of Health on 20 February.

Mr. Michael Forsyth: The circular was issued in draft on 25 May to a range of bodies who have been invited to submit comments to the Scottish Home and Health Department by 30 June.

Liver Transplants

Mr. Robin Cook: To ask the Secretary of State for Scotland what is his policy on the funding of a unit for liver transplants in Scotland; and what recent discussions have been held on such a proposal.

Mr. Michael Forsyth: The national specialist services advisory committee is currently considering the need for liver transplant facilities in Scotland. Members of the committee have visited existing transplant units at Birmingham and Leeds. They have also had recent discussions with clinicians who have an interest in the provision of a liver transplant service in Scotland. When I have received the committee's advice I shall look at what needs to be done.

Cancer Screening

Mr. Robin Cook: To ask the Secretary of State for Scotland when he expects the remaining seven health boards to operate a computerised cervical cytology call/recall scheme for women aged 20 to 65 years at three-yearly intervals.

Mr. Rifkind: We asked health boards to establish a computerised call/recall cervical cancer screening service for all women in Scotland aged between 20 and 60 years of age at five yearly intervals. Of the five health boards which have not yet introduced a computerised system, Grampian and Shetland health boards intend to do so during July, Orkney health board during August, Dumfries and Galloway health board during September and Lothian health board during December 1989.

Hospital Consultants (Study Leave)

Mr. Galbraith: To ask the Secretary of State for Scotland (1) if he will give for each health board for each of the past three yars the amount spent on study leave for consultants;
(2) what information he has on the number of consultants in each health board who take their full allocation of study leave.

Mr. Michael Forsyth: This information is not held centrally.

Mr. Galbraith: To ask the Secretary of State for Scotland what measures are taken by health boards to encourage consultants to take their full allocation of study leave.

Mr. Michael Forsyth: Health boards provide financial resources to enable consultants to take study leave and boards also provide staff with information on suitable courses. The question of what study is appropriate is essentially a professional matter for the individual consultant to decide.

Planning Appeals

Mr. Galbraith: To ask the Secretary of State for Scotland if he will give for each of the last five years for which figures are available the amount paid to individuals in expenses for local planning appeals.

Lord James Douglas-Hamilton: This information is not held centrally.

Forestry

Mr. Allen: To ask the Secretary of State for Scotland what representations he has received from forest tree nurserymen and other forestry interests concerning the effects which the ending of schedule D reliefs for investment in forestry is having on the sale of young trees for planting.

Lord James Douglas-Hamilton: Representations on this subject have been received by my right hon. and learned Friend and by other Ministers from the Horticultural Trades Association, from six hon. Members on behalf of four nursery managers and from one nursery manager directly.

Student Fees

Mr. Allan Stewart: To ask the Secretary of State for Scotland whether he will announce the fees to be charged to students attending Scottish institutions other than universities in the academic year 1989-90.

Mr. Michael Forsyth: For the academic year 1989-90, my right hon. and learned Friend has prescribed the following fee levels for home students and for students from other European Community (EC) countries on full-time advanced courses in the central institutions and colleges of education (fees for 1988-89 are shown in brackets):

	£	£
Postgraduate courses	1,890	(1,800)
Undergraduate and equivalent courses	607	(578)

My right hon. and learned Friend has decided that with effect from the academic year 1990-91 the fee levels he will prescribe will relate only to the maximum amounts for the reimbursement of fees through the awards system, so that the colleges will be free in practice to set fees above this level if they so wish.

For non-advanced courses, the central institutions and colleges of education will be invited to set their own fees, having regard to fees charged for comparable courses at local authority further education colleges.

Fees for home and other EC students on courses at local authority colleges are the responsibility of the local authorities. I understand that the Convention of Scottish Local Authorities has decided to recommend fees for such students as follows:

	£	£
Advanced full-time courses	610	(578)
Non-advanced full-time courses	502	(440)

For overseas students the Government's policy is that students should pay fees that cover the cost of their education. Local authorities and institutions are free to determine the fees to be charged in accordance with that policy, and in the light of their own circumstances. I understand that COSLA has decided to recommend to local authorities the following fees for students at local authority colleges paying the overseas rate:

	£	£
Advanced courses	4,145	(3,890)
Non-advanced courses	2,285	(2,145)

Plastic Flowers (Lennox Castle Hospital)

Mr. Galbraith: To ask the Secretary of State for Scotland how much Greater Glasgow health board spent on plastic flowers for Lennox castle hospital in the financial year 1988-89.

Mr. Michael Forsyth: In the financial year 1988-89 Greater Glasgow health board spent £300 on plastic flowers. The board has committed funds to improving the appearance of the wards at Lennox castle, of which I note that the hon. Member has been critical.

Dental Practice Board

Mr. Sean Hughes: To ask the Secretary of State for Scotland (1) what additional costs have been incurred in the change in organisation from the Dental Estimates Board for Scotland to the Dental Practice Board; and whether he will itemise the main headings of expense;

(2) whether the change from the Dental Estimates Board for Scotland to the Dental Practice Board has been accompanied by any additional employment of personnel;

(3) whether he will list the main administrative categories of personnel in the Dental Practice Board for Scotland.

Mr. Michael Forsyth: The change in the board's name to reflect its functions more accurately has not resulted in additional costs or personnel. The main administrative categories of personnel are set out below.

Whitley Council Grade	Numbers as at 1 June 1989
Grade 18	1
Grade 14	1
Grade 4	3
Executive Officer (2)	2
Grade 1	11
Higher Clerical Officer	46
Clerical Officer	75
Machine operator-typist	31
Part-time Clerical Officer	·5
Total	171·5

Dental Practitioners

Mr. Sean Hughes: To ask the Secretary of State for Scotland what plans he has for maintaining a continuous supply of high calibre dental practitioners in Scotland.

Mr. Michael Forsyth: A working party was set up in October last year to consider changes in the current provision of dental education in Scotland. The working party, as part of its remit, is examining the needs of the NHS in Scotland for an adequate supply and distribution of dentists, and for effective and high quality programmes of postgraduate and continuing education. I expect its report shortly.

Community Care

Mrs. Ray Michie: To ask the Secretary of State for Scotland what his Department is doing to improve community care provision in Scotland.

Mr. Michael Forsyth: Since taking office we have increased the planning figure for local authority spending on social work services by 67 per cent. in real terms. In the current year the planning figure is £461·7 million, 13 per cent. higher than last year and 6 per cent. higher than authorities' own budgets for last year. Within these resources it is primarily for local authorities in consultation as necessary with health boards and other interests to provide levels of community care provision appropriate to their area. More specifically, the Government are studying the report by Sir Roy Griffiths on community care and will bring forward proposals in due course.

Concessionary Travel

Mrs. Ray Michie: To ask the Secretary of State for Scotland whether he intends to encourage all local authorities in Scotland to introduce or extend a travel concessionary scheme to include people with mental health problems.

Lord James Douglas-Hamilton: Under the terms of the Concessionary Travel for Handicapped Persons (Scotland) Act 1980 any local authority may make arrangements for the granting of travel concessions to persons suffering from mental disorders. It is, however, for the local authorities to decide what type of scheme is appropriate to their areas.

Self-governing Schools

Mr. Wray: To ask the Secretary of State for Scotland if he will detail the information gathered on the likely change of teacher numbers resulting from his proposals for opting-out schools and their devolved budgetary power.

Mr. Michael Forsyth: The recurrent grant to a self-governing school will be determined so that the school will be neither better nor worse off than it could reasonably have expected if it had remained under local authority management. The grant will thus reflect the education authority's spending on salaries, superannuation and national insurance for teachers. It will be for the board of management of each self-governing school to decide how to spend this grant and how many teachers it wishes to employ in that school.

Scottish Enterprise

Mr. Wray: To ask the Secretary of State for Scotland what response he has given to the Scottish section of the Civil Engineering Contractors regarding its objections to his paper on Scottish Enterprise.

Mr. Lang: We are currently reassessing the proposals in the Scottish Enterprise White Paper in the light of all the responses received, and shall announce our detailed decisions in due course.

Community Charge

Mrs. Ray Michie: To ask the Secretary of State for Scotland what representations he has received regarding payment of commercial rates and the community charge by guest-house owners and bed-and-breakfast landladies in Scotland catering for more than six guests.

Mr. Lang: A number of representations have been received about the liability to non-domestic rates of properties which provide accommodation for tourists and which are also used in part as a sole or main residence. Decisions as to the value on which non-domestic rates are levied are for the assessor, subject to the appropriate appeal procedures.

Severe Weather Payments

Mr. Andrew Welsh: To ask the Secretary of State for Scotland if he will list the regulations covering severe weather cash aid to local authorities.

Mr. Rifkind: Special financial assistance to local authorities has been offered on an extra-statutory basis with the approval of the Treasury. Any payments due once claims have been assessed will be presented for the approval of Parliament in the form of a supplementary estimate in due course. The terms of the assistance made available were sent to every local authority in a Scottish Office circular (Finance Circular No. 6/89) dated 28 April 1989.

Bellwin Scheme

Mr. Andrew Welsh: To ask the Secretary of State for Scotland whether he will consider abolishing the minimum level for claims of £120,000 from individual local authorities under the Bellwin scheme.

Mr. Rifkind: There is no minimum level of £120,000 for claims under the Bellwin scheme of special financial assistance to local authorities. However, on all occasions when assistance under the scheme has been made available, authorities have been expected to meet an initial tranche of emergency expenditure up to a threshold set to reflect the fact that authorities have statutory powers to deal with emergencies and are expected to plan accordingly. Thresholds, based on a proportion of their penny rate, ensure that the smaller the authority the lower the threshold.

Woodland Grant Scheme

Mr. Ron Davies: To ask the Secretary of State for Scotland how many hectares of coniferous and deciduous wasteland, respectively, were planted under the new woodland grant scheme in the first 12 months of its operation.

Lord James Douglas-Hamilton: Grants are available under the new woodland grant scheme for the rehabilitation of neglected woodlands under 20 years of age, provided they contain an adequate stocking of suitable species and have not been previously grant-aided. In the nine months of 31 March 1989, the Forestry Commission had paid such grants under the scheme in respect of four hectares of conifer woodland and 26 hectares of broadleaved woodland.

Mr. and Mrs. Gilchrist

Mr. Wilson: To ask the Secretary of State for Scotland which media outlets were notified by the Scottish Information Office of the home visit of Mr. and Mrs. Gilchrist by the Parliamentary Under-Secretary of State the hon. Member for Stirling (Mr. Forsyth) on Sunday 14 May; and what advance notice of press involvement was given to Mr. and Mrs. Gilchrist.

Mr. Rifkind: My hon. Friend the Minister responsible for education and health did not visit the home of anyone called Gilchrist on May 14.

Electoral Registers

Mr. McFall: To ask the Secretary of State for Scotland if he will list the percentage change in the numbers of local government electoral registers between 1988 and 1989 in the Dumbarton district.

Lord James Douglas-Hamilton: I refer the hon. Member to table 1 in the Office of Population Censuses and Surveys Monitor EL 89-1, from which the percentage change may be derived. A copy of the monitor is in the Library.

Single Market

Mr. McFall: To ask the Secretary of State for Scotland what preparations are being made by his Department to improve communications with the continent via the south-east of England in preparation for the introduction of the single European market on 1 January 1993.

Lord James Douglas-Hamilton: My right hon. and learned Friend the Secretary of State has had meetings with the Chairman of the British Rail Board on how to ensure that Scotland benefits fully from rail links to the Channel tunnel. Section 40 of the Channel Tunnel Act requires British Rail to publish a plan by the end of 1989 setting out its proposals for international rail services through the Tunnel. British Rail are consulting widely with interested parties in the regions over the preparation of this plan. With regard to trunk roads, the A74 is being upgraded to motorway, thus linking the central Scotland motorway network to the M6/M1/M25 route, Scotland's essential link to the south and Europe. In addition, a major study into routes south of Edinburgh is nearing completion.

EC Funds

Mr. Bill Walker: To ask the Secretary of State for Scotland if he will indicate the nature of all funds granted to Scotland from the European Community in the period May 1979 to May 1989; and if he will give headings of the European fund titles and list the total value under each heading of funds granted to Scotland.

Mr. Ian Lang *[holding answer 9 May 1989]:* Scotland has been awarded some £1,400 million in grants during the period 1979-88 from the European Community's structural funds—the European regional development fund, the European social fund and the agricultural guidance fund. In addition, some £1,500 million has been awarded to Scotland from other Community sources, principally in the form of loans from the European Coal and Steel Community and the European Investment Bank. Details of the main funding sources are set out in the table below.

Awards 1979-88

	£ million
European Regional Development Fund	736
European Social Fund[1]	246
Agricultural Guidance Fund[2]	385
European Coal and Steel Community[3]	82
European Investment Bank	1,384

Notes:
[1] Figures available only for 1982-88. Previously figures were not broken down into regions.
[2] Excludes Scottish share of market support expenditure incurred by the Intervention Board for Agricultural produce.
[3] Figure relates to article 56 reconversion loans. Regional breakdown of other ECSC assistance is not available.

Prisons (Lawyers' Visits)

Mr. Dalyell: To ask the Secretary of State for Scotland if he will arrange for the Lord Advocate to make a study of the claims made by a random selection of legal firms in Scotland for visits to prisoners in Barlinnie, Saughton, Perth, Shots and Peterhead prisons, using the legal aid system; and if he will set out the findings against the actual entries made in the official visitors' records of those prisons of lawyers and other personnel from the firms studied.

Lord James Douglas-Hamilton *[holding answer 17 May 1989]:* No. The administration of legal aid, including the settlement of solicitors' accounts, is the responsibility of the Scottish Legal Aid Board. Claims from solicitors are subject to examination, and the board's audit and investigation section would report any cases of possible fraud to the procurator fiscal. If the hon. Member has information which is relevant to the board's assessment of legal aid accounts, he should pass that to the board for consideration.

FOREIGN AND COMMONWEALTH AFFAIRS

Iraq

Mr. Wigley: To ask the Secretary of State for Foreign and Commonwealth Affairs how much the United Kingdom has given by way of *(a)* grants and *(b)* loans to Iraq during each of the last five years.

Mr. Waldegrave: Government grants to Iraq over the past five years have been exclusively for training of Iraqi students. The DTI has disbursed:

	£
1987-88	60,000
1988-89	60,000

The three other principal schemes are: The Foreign and Commonwealth Office scholarships and awards scheme, the British Council fellowship scheme and the Department of Education and Science—overseas research students award scheme, for which the figures are:

	£
1984-85	86,400
1985-86	51,200
1986-87	72,600
1987-88	73,800
1988-89	92,000

Under the United Kingdom-Iraq financial protocols, the Government have negotiated the following Export Credit Guarantee Department-backed credits during the past five years:

	£
1984	300 million
1987	175 million
1988	340 million

Kurds

Mr. Wigley: To ask the Secretary of State for Foreign and Commonwealth Affairs if he will ask the United Nations to investigate allegations of human rights violations, torture and genocide by the Iraqi Government against the Kurds.

Mr. Waldegrave: We have repeatedly made clear to the Iraqi authorities our concern at their failure to respect human rights, particularly those of the Kurdish community. We play a leading role in discussion of Iraqi human rights violations at the United Nations Commission on Human Rights. A strongly-worded British-sponsored resolution in March was blocked by an Iraqi procedural motion.

Mr. John McCarthey

Mr. Wigley: To ask the Secretary of State for Foreign and Commonwealth Affairs what steps have been taken this year to secure the release of Mr. John McCarthey, a hostage in Beirut; and if he will make a statement.

Mr. Waldegrave: Before the break in relations with Iran, we raised the issue frequently with the Iranians. We have also raised the matter with other Governments and groups who might have influence on the hostage holders. Her Majesty's Ambassdor in Beirut remains active in a difficult and dangerous environment in following up all available information. We will continue to do the maximum possible.

Nelson Mandela

Mr. Anderson: To ask the Secretary of State for Foreign and Commonwealth Affairs what reply has been received to the request by the British ambassador to South Africa to visit Nelson Mandela.

Mrs. Chalker: Our main concern is to see Mr. Mandela freed unconditionally. Our efforts are devoted to that end. In response to a letter from Mr. Mandela, the ambassador said that he would welcome a fact-to-face discussion. We understand that it would be for Mr. Mandela formally to notify the South African authorities if he wishes to pursue this.

Refuseniks

Mr. Lawrence: To ask the Secretary of State for Foreign and Commonwealth Affairs if he will raise with the Soviet authorities the case of the long-term refuseniks Emanuel and Judith Lurie who have recently been refused an exit visa.

Mr. Waldegrave: We have raised the Lurie's case with the Soviet authorities on numerous occasions—most recently during Mr. Gorbachev's visit to Britain in April. The latest Soviet response was that their application to emigrate is currently under consideration by a Supreme Soviet commission. We shall not let up until they are allowed to leave.

George Belitsky

Mr. John L. Marshall: To ask the Secretary of State for Foreign and Commonwealth Affairs what representations have been made to the Russians about their continued failure to grant an exit visa to George Belitsky.

Mr. Waldegrave: We have made repeated representations to the Soviet authorities about Dr. Belitsky, most recently during Mr. Gorbachev's visit to Britain in April, and we will continue to press them until he is allowed to emigrate.

Partial Test Ban Treaty

Mr. Flynn: To ask the Secretary of State for Foreign and Commonwealth Affairs when and where the initial discussions on the amendment conference for the 1963 partial test ban treaty took place; and when and where he expects the trilateral discussions between the partial test ban treaty depository states to take place.

Mr. Waldegrave: Initial discussions between the depository Governments have taken place over the last two months in London, Washington, Moscow and Geneva. We expect that the depository Governments will meet trilaterally later this month, probably in Geneva.

Mr. Douglas Forsyth

Sir Geoffrey Johnson Smith: To ask the Secretary of State for Foreign and Commonwealth Affairs what further representations have been made and when by his Department to the Egyptian Government to hasten the determination of the case brought by Mr. Douglas Forsyth in the Egyptian courts to recover the control and possession of his villa.

Mr. Waldegrave: No representations have been made on this matter since the Egyptian Court of Appeal announced its determination on 22 June 1988. Mr. Forsyth subsequently appealed to the Supreme Court (Court of Cassation) in Cairo. He has been warned by his legal advisers that it may take four or five years for a decision.

Sir Geoffrey Johnson Smith: To ask the Secretary of State for Foreign and Commonwealth Affairs what representations have been made by his Department to the Egyptian Government concerning the payment of a tax refund owing to Mr. Douglas Forsyth by the Egyptian Government.

Mr. Waldegrave: A letter from Her Majesty's consul in Cairo to the general director of taxes in the appropriate tax office was given to Mr. Forsyth's legal advisers on 9 May. This asked for payment of the refund to be expedited. On 16 May Mr. Forsyth's legal adviser informed the consul that a cheque had been issued and passed to the Central bank. This has now been credited to Mr. Forsyth's account.

Nuclear Weapons

Dr. Thomas: To ask the Secretary of State for Foreign and Commonwealth Affairs if he will set out Her Majesty's Government's policy in regard to the future continued requirement for United Kingdom retention of nuclear weapons in the light of threshold and aspirant nuclear weapons states capacity to develop or obtain nuclear weapons.

Mr. Waldegrave: We continue to subscribe to the NATO policy that our security will depend for the foreseeable future on an appropriate mix of nuclear and conventional weapons. We fully observe our obligations under the 1968 non-proliferation treaty including those relating to the non-transferral of nuclear weapons technology.

Environmental Protection

Dr. Thomas: To ask the Secretary of State for Foreign and Commonwealth Affairs if the United Kingdom ambassador to the United Nations has made any recent representations at the United Nations to promote environmental protection and global initiatives to achieve this.

Mr. Jack: To ask the Secretary of State for Foreign and Commonwealth Affairs what specific environmental initiatives the United Kingdom representative at the United Nations supported during 1989.

Mr. Eggar: The United Kingdom permanent representative to the United Nations recently proposed the early negotiation of a convention on climate change and the strengthening of existing United Nations institutions concerned with environmental matters, especially the United Nations environment programme.

Missiles

Dr. Thomas: To ask the Secretary of State for Foreign and Commonwealth Affairs, pursuant to the reply to the hon. Member for Linlithgow (Mr. Dalyell), *Official Report,* 13 April, columns *646-47,* what assessment has been made of the SAAD-16 contract; what contacts have been made with the ambassadors of Egypt, Iraq and Argentina, or their diplomatic representatives in the United Kingdom arising from the Condor-2 missile development; and if he will make a statement.

Mr. Waldegrave: We have no reason to doubt the recent media speculation that the SAAD-16 project is connected to Iraq's missile development programme. I made clear to the Iraqi ambassador on 19 April our serious concern over ballistic missile proliferation.

Falkland Fisheries

Mr. Butler: To ask the Secretary of State for Foreign and Commonwealth Affairs if he will make a statement on progress within the Falklands fisheries.

Mr. Waldegrave: The Falklands fishery is in its third successful year. The number of licences issued is regulated to meet conservation targets recommended by the renewable resources assessment group, Imperial college. Accordingly, the Falkland Islands Government reduced the number available for the 1989 second season. Revenue in 1989 is estimated to be £29 million.

Hong Kong

Mr. Atkinson: To ask the Secretary of State for Foreign and Commonwealth Affairs if he has any plans to introduce a Bill to incorporate the United Nations declaration of human rights into the law applicable to Hong Kong citizens; and if he will make a statement.

Mr. Waldegrave: We are considering with the Hong Kong Government as a matter of priority whether to enact a human rights ordinance in Hong Kong and, if so, what form it should take.

Namibia

Mr. Vaz: To ask the Secretary of State for Foreign and Commonwealth Affairs if he will make a further statement on the South African withdrawal from Namibia.

Mr. Waldegrave: South African forces in Namibia are restricted to base and their phased withdrawal in accordance with the United Nations plan is in progress.

Israel

Mr. Latham: To ask the Secretary of State for Foreign and Commonwealth Affairs whether he will make a statement on his meeting with the Prime Minister of the state of Israel on 23 May.

Mr. Waldegrave: My right hon. and learned Friend the Secretary of State and I had a frank and friendly exchange of views on middle eastern issues with Mr. Shamir. We welcomed his proposals for elections in the occupied territories as a useful step forward, but emphasised the need for progress towards a solution based on territory for peace.

Spying

Dr. Thomas: To ask the Secretary of State for Foreign and Commonwealth Affairs how many *(a)* accredited diplomats and *(b)* other foreign nationals given official working permits have been expelled or deported from the United Kingdom in each year since 1979 for activities deemed to be incompatible with their status; and if he will list them by countries.

Mr. Waldegrave: As the information is not readily available, I will write to the hon. Member once it is to hand.

Vietnamese Refugees

Mr. Andrew Smith: To ask the Secretary of State for Foreign and Commonwealth Affairs if he will make representations to other Governments to take Vietnamese refugees from Hong Kong.

Mr. Waldegrave: We are working for a successful outcome to the international conference on Indo-Chinese refugees in Geneva on 13 and 14 June, which we hope will result in a major international effort to resettle all the remaining Indo-Chinese refugees in the region, including the 14,300 in Hong Kong, as part of a comprehensive solution to this problem.

Mr. Andrew Smith: To ask the Secretary of State for Foreign and Commonwealth Affairs what undertakings he has received from the Chinese Government regarding the treatment and status of Vietnamese refugees in Hong Kong after the transfer of sovereignty.

Mr. Waldegrave: The matter has not arisen. It is our firm intention to ensure that the problem of Vietnamese refugees in Hong Kong is resolved well before the transfer of sovereignty in 1997.

Listening Devices

Mr. Cran: To ask the Secretary of State for Foreign and Commonwealth Affairs whether electronic surveillance listening devices are used by his Department or by any organisation or agency acting on its behalf; and if he will make a statement.

Mr. Waldegrave: It is not the practice to comment on matters of this sort.

Chemical Weapons

Mr. Menzies Campbell: To ask the Secretary of State for Foreign and Commonwealth Affairs if he will make a statement on the progress of the Geneva talks on chemical weapons.

Mr. Waldegrave: I refer the hon. Member to the reply I gave to my hon. Friend, the Member for Chelmsford (Mr. Burns) on 9 May. The next round of the negotiations begins on 13 June.

Ivory

Mr. Tony Banks: To ask the Secretary of State for Foreign and Commonwealth Affairs how many seizures of ivory have been made by the Hong Kong authorities from organisations and premises owned by the Poon family.

Mr. Waldegrave: None.

Mr. Tony Banks: To ask the Secretary of State for Foreign and Commonwealth Affairs if CITES certificates are attached to the export of worked ivory from Hong Kong.

Mr. Waldegrave: CITES certificates are normally attached to exports of worked ivory from Hong Kong because most importing countries require them, although this is not a legal requirement of the Hong Kong Government.

Mr. Tony Banks: To ask the Secretary of State for Foreign and Commonwealth Affairs what value of worked ivory was imported from the United Arab Emirates into Hong Kong in October 1988; how many CITES permits were issued for the United Arab Emirates in 1988; and if he will make a statement.

Mr. Waldegrave: No worked ivory was imported from the United Arab Emirates in October 1988. Hong Kong extended its import licence control to cover all forms of ivory on 5 August 1988, and since then no licences have been issued for import of worked ivory from the United Arab Emirates.

Military Aid

Mr. Vaz: To ask the Secretary of State for Foreign and Commonwealth Affairs how much military aid has been granted by Her Majesty's Government in the current financial year.

Mr. Waldegrave: We expect to spend £3 million on supplies of non-lethal military equipment during the current financial year. In addition, £23 million will be spent on foreign and Commonwealth military training in the United Kingdom and overseas.

Belize

Mr. Livsey: To ask the Secretary of State for Foreign and Commonwealth Affairs if he will make it his policy to maintain the military presence of Britain in Belize as long as the people and government of Belize wish it.

Mr. Waldegrave: Our policy is to maintain the British garrison in Belize for an appropriate period.

ENERGY

Coal Industry (Yorkshire)

Mr. Redmond: To ask the Secretary of State for Energy what estimate he has made of the total number of jobs directly and indirectly dependent on the coal industry of *(a)* South Yorkshire and *(b)* North Yorkshire; what were these figures for five years and 10 years ago; and if he will make a statement.

Mr. Michael Spicer: Figures for the number of jobs indirectly dependent on the coal industry are not available and could be provided only at disproportionate cost.

Information on jobs directly dependent on the coal industry for the areas and dates requested, is as follows:

	North Yorkshire	*South Yorkshire*
March 1979	36,856	38,803
March 1984	31,710	31,840
March 1989	14,705	14,724

The data refer to men associated with British Coal's North and South Yorkshire areas.

Nuclear Safeguards

Mr. Flynn: To ask the Secretary of State for Energy if, pursuant to his reply to the hon. Member for Meirionnydd Nant Conwy (Dr. Thomas), *Official Report,* 15 May, column *109,* the United Kingdom has any continuing interest in the imposition of bilateral nuclear safeguards implemented before May 1979 on plutonium exported for use in the Rapsodie test fast reactor in France since November 1964.

Mr. Michael Spicer: The plutonium was exported under the terms of the United Kingdom Euratom agreement 1959 which emphasised the peaceful nature of the co-operation. As far as the Department is aware it remains subject to Euratom safeguards.

Harwell Nuclear Plant

Mr. Andrew Smith: To ask the Secretary of State for Energy how far the refurbishment of the Harwell reactor has progressed following the July 1987 plan set out for refurbishment.

Mr. Michael Spicer: The United Kingdom Atomic Energy Authority informs me that the refurbishment programme for the nuclear research reactors at Harwell is reviewed annually. The current programme has been amended to take account of the closure of the PLUTO reactor in March 1990. This amended programme has been approved by Harwell's reactor safety committee and will be discussed with the Health and Safety Executive's nuclear installations inspectorate.

Mr. Andrew Smith: To ask the Secretary of State for Energy how long it is proposed to store Harwell reactors sea dump barrels containing intermediate level waste in their present condition; and what plans there are to make them safer.

Mr. Michael Spicer: Drums of radioactive wastes prepared for the 1983 sea disposal operation will continue to be stored in a safe condition and will be prepared for eventual disposal in the deep facility for low and intermediate level wastes which Nirex has been asked to develop.

Mr. Andrew Smith: To ask the Secretary of State for Energy (1) how many workers at Harwell reactors exceeded the radiation dosages of *(a)* 15mSv and *(b)* 50mSv; and what was the average dose of those working in the reactor area alone;

(2) what measures are being taken to ensure that doses received by the Harwell work force and local population are as low as reasonably possible; and what dose levels Harwell is working towards achieving.

Mr. Michael Spicer: Details of the radiation exposures incurred by Harwell staff are published annually in the UKAEA report on radiological protection and occupational health.

The UKAEA seeks to keep doses to the lowest reasonably practicable level. From 1 January 1988 it set an upper limit on individual dose of 30mSv per year, which is not normally to be exceeded except in cases of extreme occupational necessity. No one on the Harwell reactor site exceeded this level in 1988.

Exposure of the public to discharges of radioactive wastes from Harwell is monitored routinely and the monitoring results and dose estimates published annually in the Harwell laboratory report on radioactive discharges and environmental monitoring. I am arranging for copies of this report and the report on radiological protection and occupational health to be placed in the Library of the House.

Mr. Andrew Smith: To ask the Secretary of State for Energy (1) if there are any plans to improve the current state of the effluent treatment works at Harwell; and what mechanisms exist to shut down the flow of effluent into the Thames in the event of it exceeding waste safety levels;

(2) what measures have been taken to ensure that discharges and waste from the Harwell reactors in the river Thames are below the new general derived limits in the NRPB document GS-8.

Mr. Michael Spicer: The liquid effluent treatment plant is maintained in a condition which enables it to meet the requirements imposed by the relevant discharge consents issued by the Department of the Environment and the Ministry of Agriculture, Fisheries and Food. The measured effect of these discharges is typically between 5 per cent. and 10 per cent. of NRPB general derived limits. Treated effluent is stored for analysis and is not discharged unless it complies with the requirements of the consents.

Mr. Andrew Smith: To ask the Secretary of State for Energy when a detailed inventory of the Harwell reactor core will be made available to the public.

Mr. Michael Spicer: This information has already been made available in a letter to Dr. P. Taylor of the political ecology research group associated with Oxford city council, a copy of which is being placed in the Library of the House.

Mr. Andrew Smith: To ask the Secretary of State for Energy when he plans to publish the Nuclear Installations Inspectorate safety audit of Harwell.

Mr. Michael Spicer: I refer the hon. Member to the answer that I gave him on 31 January at column *156*.

Mr. Andrew Smith: To ask the Secretary of State for Energy when the route of the waste pipelines from the Harwell reactors to the Thames will be made public.

Mr. Michael Spicer: I understand that information about the route of the pipeline is made available upon request, by the United Kingdom Atomic Energy Authority as required to avoid accidental damage to the pipeline.

Listening Devices

Mr. Cran: To ask the Secretary of State for Energy whether electronic surveillance listening devices are used by his Department or by any organisation or agency acting on its behalf; and if he will make a statement.

Mr. Parkinson: No.

Nuclear Reactors (Safety)

Mr. Malcolm Bruce: To ask the Secretary of State for Energy, in view of the fact that the proposed pressurised water reactors at Sizewell B and Hinkley C will be the first to depend for their reactor safety solely on computer systems *(a)* what assessment he has made of the safety implications of and *(b)* what discussions he has had with the Central Electricity Generating Board about the advisability of relying solely on these computer systems; and if he has any plans to extend the new defence standard (Defstan 00-55) to those reactors.

Mr. Michael Spicer: The Sizewell B and the Hinkley Point C pressurised water reactors (PWRs) will have a computer based primary protection system designed to protect against all faults, and a non-computerised secondary system which will provide protection against the less unlikely faults. Both systems are at the design and development stage. The approval of the Health and Safety Executive's nuclear installations inspectorate will be required before the reactors are allowed to operate. The Ministry of Defence computer software standard "Defstan 00-55" is still in the process of development. It is for the Central Electricity Generating Board to decide if it wishes to use this standard. Its decision would be considered by the NII as part of the safety case.

NORTHERN IRELAND

Natural Gas

Mr. Ashdown: To ask the Secretary of State for Northern Ireland what plans the Government is considering to pipe natural gas from the South of Ireland to the North; what implications there are for those plans of the current state of repair of the gas works in the North; and if he will make a statement.

Mr. Viggers: The Government have no such plans.

Carrick House Hostel

Mr. Jim Marshall: To ask the Secretary of State for Northern Ireland if he will investigate the alleged intimidation of residents by Northern Ireland Housing Executive staff to prevent them from taking their grievances and fears about the future of the Carrick House hostel to the media; and if he will make a statement.

Mr. Needham: I am advised by the chairman of the Northern Ireland Housing Executive that the residents of Carrick House hostel have not been intimidated in any way by staff of the Housing Executive. While residents have access on a daily basis to Housing Executive management on matters of concern to them they are, of course, free as private individuals to approach the media at any time about their concerns which have been given considerable publicity in Northern Ireland.

Mr. Jim Marshall: To ask the Secretary of State for Northern Ireland if he will make a statement on the short-term and long-term future of Carrick House hostel for homeless men, Belfast.

Mr. Needham: This is a matter for the Northern Ireland Housing Executive and I am advised by the chairman that no changes will be made in the day-to-day running of the hostel until 1 April 1990 at the earliest. In the meantime the future of the hostel in its present form will be the subject of a strategic review. No plans for Carrick House will be finalised without prior consultation with the residents.

Mr. Jim Marshall: To ask the Secretary of State for Northern Ireland what steps have been taken to consult the residents, staff and other interested bodies about both the short and long-term future of Carrick House; and what steps it is intended to take in the future to carry out such consultations.

Mr. Needham: This is a matter for the Northern Ireland Housing Executive and I am advised by the chairman that staff of the Carrick House hostel have been made fully aware of the review of the hostel's role which will be undertaken by Housing Executive management. Regular meetings are taking place between residents' representatives and hostel management at which issues of mutual interest are discussed. These will shortly be supported by a regular newsletter to all residents aimed at reinforcing the consultative process.

Mr. Jim Marshall: To ask the Secretary of State for Northern Ireland what steps have been taken to ensure that adequate health and safety standards, medical facilities, hygiene facilities, social counselling facilities and staffing levels exist for the residents of Carrick House.

Mr. Needham: This is a matter for the Northern Ireland Executive and I am advised by the chairman that Carrick House hostel has for many years provided basic facilities and support services for residents. There has been no diminution of existing standards and services since the hostel came under the Housing Executive management. The prospects for enhanced facilities and services commensurate with the needs of residents will be addressed as part of a forthcoming strategic review of the future of the hostel.

Dental Examinations

Mr. Sean Hughes: To ask the Secretary of State for Northern Ireland how much money has been refunded as a consequence of the illegal charges for dental examinations between 1 and 16 January.

Mr. Needham: The total amount refunded to patients was £16,455·60.

Mr. Sean Hughes: To ask the Secretary of State for Northern Ireland what additional use of personnel was incurred and what was the time element involved in rectifying the error relating to illegal dental examination charges between 1 and 16 January.

Mr. Needham: No additional personnel were used. As the work involved was undertaken by existing staff as part of their normal duties, it is not possible to assess the time element involved in rectifying the error.

Mr. Sean Hughes: To ask the Secretary of State for Northern Ireland what costs were incurred in rectifying the errors relating to the illegal charges for dental examinations between 1 and 16 January.

Mr. Needham: The administrative cost of arranging for dentists to refund charges paid by patients for dental examinations carried out during the period 1 to 16 January was £2,612.

Grey Squirrels

Mr. Ron Davies: To ask the Secretary of State for Northern Ireland what measures are in force to control grey squirrels in Northern Ireland; and if he will make a statement.

Mr. Needham: Under article 15(1) of The Wildlife (Northern Ireland) Order 1985 it is an offence to release grey squirrels into the wild. Grey squirrels may be killed or taken, other than by prohibited methods, by owners or occupiers, or persons authorised by them on their own land. The present population of these animals does not constitute a threat.

Health Board Assets

Mr. Robin Cook: To ask the Secretary of State for Northern Ireland if he will give details of assets disposed of by each health board during 1987-88; and what was the total value of those assets.

Mr. Needham *[holding answer 24 April 1989]:* Monies received in respect of assets disposed of by each Health and Social Service board for 1987-88 are as shown in the table:

	Equipment and Vehicles £	Land and Buildings £
Northern Board	14,256	125,894
Southern Board	15,787	145,265
Eastern Board	nil	529,887
Western Board	40,637	195,077
	70,680	996,123

Publicity

Mr. Dobson: To ask the Secretary of State for Northern Ireland if he will place in the Library details of each major publicity campaign mounted by his Department in 1985-86 and each successive year, including in each case the objectives of the campaign, the intended audience and the outcome of the monitoring of the achievement of the intended objectives, and national research conducted for him by the Central Office of Information together with a note of the intended objectives in the campaigns in 1989-90.

Dr. Mawhinney *[holding answer 2 May 1989]:* The information has been placed in the Library.

Police Posts

Mr. Beggs: To ask the Secretary of State for Northern Ireland (1) how many incidents requiring Royal Ulster Constabulary action have occurred in the area formerly served by each limited opening Royal Ulster Constabulary sub-station in east Antrim since these limited opening stations were closed;

(2) whether he will discuss with the new Chief Constable as a matter of priority the impact of closure of limited opening stations in east Antrim.

Mr. Ian Stewart *[holding answer 2 May 1989]:* The Chief Constable tells me that no limited opening police stations have been closed in East Antrim. There were however three police posts closed in the area—Craigyhill (Larne), Sunnylands (Carrickfergus) and Knockfergus

(Greenisland). Since their closure in November 1988 the number of reports received for these areas which required some form of police action was 529, 346 and 169, respectively. The deployment of police resources is an operational matter for the judgment of the Chief Constable in which I do not propose to intervene.

Mr. Beggs: To ask the Secretary of State for Northern Ireland whether there has been any change in levels of crime reported in each of the areas formerly covered by limited opening Royal Ulster Constabulary stations in east

Antrim since they were closed; and if he will publish details of available statistics for a comparable period in the two years prior to closure.

Mr. Ian Stewart *[holding answer 2 May 1989]:* The total number of reported burglaries and thefts in the areas formerly covered by police posts (not limited opening stations) in Craigyhill (Larne), Sunnylands (Carrickfergus) and Knockfergus (Greenisland), which were closed in November 1988 in comparable periods over the last three years was as follows:

Period	Craigyhill burglary	theft	Sunnylands burglary	theft	Knockfergus burglary	theft
26 November 1986 to 28 April 1987	20	7	33	27	71	67
26 November 1987 to 28 April 1988	20	13	28	15	56	45
26 November 1988 to 28 April 1989	25	7	19	17	45	58

It is considered too early to reach a judgment as to the overall trend in the level of crime in these areas since the closure of the police posts.

Telephone System

Rev. Martin Smyth: To ask the Secretary of State for Northern Ireland if he will make a statement about the Department of Economic Development's plans to upgrade the telephone system in Northern Ireland; what role is envisaged for Mecury Communications in this; and what measures his Department plans to ensure competition.

Mr. Atkins: I have been asked to reply.

Plans to upgrade telecommunications systems in the United Kingdom are normally a matter for the telecommunications operators to make in the light of commercial considerations and any relevant obligations in their operating licences. The Telecommunications Act 1984 has already established the framework in which competing companies operate. We have no plans to change the present framework of telecommunications competition in Northern Ireland.

Exceptionally, Northern Ireland qualifies for support under the European Community STAR programme, under which the European Commission made funding available for the economic development of certain less-favoured regions. I understand the Department of Economic Development discussed the STAR programme with both British Telecom and Mercury and subsequently selected BT to provide the infrastructure funded under the programme.

HOME DEPARTMENT

Alcohol Misuse

Sir Bernard Braine: To ask the Secretary of State for the Home Department what progress has been made by the ministerial group on alcohol misuse.

Mr. Hurd: The group, chaired by my right hon. Friend the Lord President of the Council has made good progress. A report of action taken during the group's first year is published today. This gives an account of work in progress and takes a forward look at issues to be considered in the coming months.

Crime Prevention

Dr. Kim Howells: To ask the Secretary of State for the Home Department what proportion of his Department's budget is currently being devoted to crime prevention.

Mr. Hurd: Expenditure on crime prevention is met from Class XI, Vote 3, Home Office administration, immigration and police support services, England and Wales. In the current year, 2·8 per cent. of the total provision for this Vote is devoted to crime prevention.

Vote Tracing

Mr. Andrew F. Bennett: To ask the Secretary of State for the Home Department how many complaints have been received following the recent local elections with regard to the possibility of vote tracing.

Mr. Douglas Hogg: Since the county council elections on 4 May we have received five letters from hon. Members forwarding correspondence from constituents and two letters from members of the public on the procedure whereby a voter's electoral registration number is written on the ballot paper counterfoil when he or she votes.

Passport Checks (Airports)

Mr. David Marshall: To ask the Secretary of State for the Home Department if he will give reasons for the abolition of channels designated for British passport holders at airports for passengers returning to the United Kingdom; and if he will make a statement.

Mr. Renton: I refer the hon. Member to the reply given to a question from my hon. Friend the Member for Warwick and Leamington (Sir D. Smith) on 27 April 1989 at column *637*.

Crime Prevention (Surrey)

Mr. Ian Taylor: To ask the Secretary of State for the Home Department what steps his Department is taking to encourage crime prevention in Surrey.

Mr. John Patten: Our strategy for crime prevention applies to all parts of England and Wales. Police manpower and resources have been substantially increased, Crime Concern was launched with Government support in May 1988 to stimulate, support and develop local crime prevention activity and the largest ever national crime prevention publicity campaign was launched last year.

My right hon. Friend approved a further 10 police posts for the force from 1 April bringing the authorised establishment up to 1,649, and I understand there are now 389 watch schemes covering approximately 20,000 households throughout Surrey, together with nine panels and four junior panels. The Surrey constabulary is one of 10 south east forces involved, with Home Office support, in an ambitious scheme "Secured By Design" which aims to encourage the construction industry to incorporate security measures as standard in new homes; the scheme will be launched on 7 June.

Prison Officers (Relocation)

Mr. Vaz: To ask the Secretary of State for the Home Department what financial assistance is given to officers who are relocated in the prison system since the transfer grant for members of the prison service was stopped in 1984.

Mr. Douglas Hogg: Established prison officers qualify for financial assistance in accordance with the Civil Service pay and conditions of service code unless they are transferred at their own request. This covers, for example, the cost of a preliminary visit to search for new accommodation, night subsistence and lodging allowance, legal expenses of house purchase and sale, reimbursement of interest charges on bridging finance, interest free advance of salary for house purchase, removal and storage expenses, additional housing costs allowance and transfer grant.

This financial assistance is not generally available to civil servants including prison officers when taking up their first appointment.

Asylum

Mr. Vaz: To ask the Secretary of State for the Home Department whether he has any plans to set up a major independent review of Home Office policy and practice with regard to asylum seekers.

Mr. Renton: No.

Mr. Wigley: To ask the Secretary of State for the Home Department on which date he received notification from the independent adjudicator that he had acted wrongly in relation to the cases of five Tamils, Mr. S. Sivakumaran, Mr. N. Vathanan, Mr. V. Rasalingam, Mr. V. Skandarajah and Mr. N. Vilvarajah, who had applied for asylum in the United Kingdom; on what date an application was made by Her Majesty's Government to the immigration appeal tribunal to hear an appeal against the adjudication; and on what date an application was made to the High Court for a judicial review of the tribunal's refusal to hear the appeal.

Mr. Renton: On 13 March 1989 an adjudicator upheld appeals against refusal of leave to enter in these five cases. My right hon. Friend sought leave to appeal to the tribunal on 22 March but on 19 April the tribunal decided that it had no jurisdiction to consider this appeal because of a clerical error in the service of the papers. On 12 May my right hon. Friend sought leave to move for judicial review of the tribunal's decision and leave was granted on 17 May.

Youth Custody

Mr. Devlin: To ask the Secretary of State for the Home Department if he will make a statement about the regime in youth custody institutions, and on any representations thereon which he has received.

Mr. Douglas Hogg: Youth custody centres and detention centres were replaced by young offender institutions when the new unified custodial sentence was introduced last October. Revised guidance on regimes for young offenders was issued then, emphasising the need to prepare young offenders for their return to the community, and recognising the importance for juveniles and short-sentenced young adults of participating from the outset in brisk, modular regimes built on experience gained in detention and youth custody centres.

In general, the guidance was well received and regimes for the new sentence are working well. Representations have been received about one or two establishments which have experienced some difficulties and every effort is being made to resolve these problems.

Popplewell Report

Mr. Lester: To ask the Secretary of State for the Home Department how many recommendations of the Popplewell report which bear on the responsibilities of his Department have not been implemented; what were those recommendations; and, in each case, what are the reasons they have not been acted upon.

Mr. John Patten: Four recommendations of the final report of the Popplewell inquiry which bear on the responsibility of my right hon. Friend have not been wholly implemented.

Recommendation 9(i) and (iii): as set out in the consultative document published in June 1986 the Government took the view that as safety certificates are instruments of continuing control it would not be appropriate to renew them annually or for local authorities to have powers to revoke them. The Safety of Sports Grounds Act 1975 provides for offences for a breach of any term or condition in a safety certificate and gives a separate power to local authorities to prohibit or restrict the admission of spectators to any part of a sports ground if there is judged to be a serious risk to their safety.

Recommendation 11: the Government considered that it would be wrong to provide a power of search which went further than existing statutory powers based on reasonable suspicion. A club may refuse admission to its ground to persons unwilling to be searched.

Recommendation 12: section 5 of the Public Order Act 1986 provides an offence of disorderly conduct which is applicable in all public places, with the qualification that someone within hearing or sight of the conduct in question is likely to be caused alarm, distress or harassment. The Government is not persuaded that this qualification should be dispensed with.

Recommendation 13: section 5 of the Public Order Act 1936 has recently been re-enacted in the Public Order Act 1986 and is supplemented by the wide general powers of arrest in the Police and Criminal Evidence Act 1984. The Government are not convinced that it is necessary to broaden these provisions further.

Police (Video Surveillance Equipment)

Mr. Vaz: To ask the Secretary of State for the Home Department if he will make a statement regarding the use by police forces in the United Kingdom of video surveillance equipment in the community as a means of crime detection and prevention.

Mr. Hurd: The use of surveillance equipment is a matter for the operational judgment of the police acting in accordance with guidelines issued by the Home Office on 19 December 1984.

Turkish Nationals

Mr. Colvin: To ask the Secretary of State for the Home Department whether he intends to impose a visa requirement on Turkish nationals who wish to enter the United Kingdom.

Mr. Hurd: I will shortly lay before Parliament a statement of changes in the immigration rules which will include provisions requiring Turkish nationals to obtain visas before travelling to the United Kingdom. The necessary written notice of one month under the 1960 agreement for the abolition of visas (Cmnd. 1043) was given to the Turkish Government on 23 May. The new visa regime will come into effect on 23 June.

As part of the increasingly close co-operation between the member states of the European Community on immigration matters EC interior Ministers have for some time been discussing a proposal that visa requirements should be harmonised, and in this context that Turkish nationals should have to obtain visas to enter any European Community country. Most member states already require visas of Turkish nationals. Operational reasons now make it necessary for us to do the same.

For many years, the proportion of Turkish nationals arriving in the United Kingdom who were refused admission and removed has been growing. Between 1985 and 1988 it rose from less than 1·5 per cent. to 3 per cent. The number of Turkish nationals against whom action was started for breaches of the immigration law increased from 136 in 1985 to 401 in 1988. A growing number of Turks have claimed asylum on arrival in the United Kingdom. Whereas there were only about 60 such applications in 1987, during May alone this year there were more than 1,500. We are observing the meticulous procedures for examining each application which are necessary under the 1951 United Nations convention, and they necessarily take time. Many of those who have been interviewed are young men who have admitted to making their claim because of employment difficulties in Turkey. During May 106 applicants for asylum withdrew their applications and returned to Turkey.

These developments have placed strains on the immigration control, creating long delays on occasion and inconvenience for the main body of passengers. We have no wish to detain more Turkish asylum applicants than is necessary. But it is often not possible to grant temporary admission, where those involved have no connections in the United Kingdom, have been unable to support or accommodate themselves without help, and may be tempted to abscond. The accommodation which we have for detaining immigrants is being fully used, but because of the large numbers we have also had to use prisons in the south-west. We are grateful to the churches and other organisations and individuals who have undertaken to provide emergency shelter and food for those who can properly be granted temporary admission. We have made it clear that we will consider reimbursing specific costs which community groups have incurred. My officials are also in contact with the British Refugee Council about the establishment of a short-term hostel in Tower Hamlets.

It will be several months before the cases of those who have already arrived can be processed. All claims to asylum by Turkish nationals will continue to be carefully considered. Priority is being given to interviewing those in detention.

Unless we take action now the situation is likely to deteriorate through the summer. That is why we have decided to impose a visa requirement on Turkish nationals who wish to enter the United Kingdom. The new visa regime will inevitably take a little time to settle down but the introduction of a visa requirement should benefit all bona fide travellers including business visitors who will be less likely to encounter delays on arrival in this country. Regular visitors to this country will be eligible for multiple-entry visas.

Passports

Mr. David Young: To ask the Secretary of State for the Home Department what emergency action he intends to take for those who require full passports; and if he will issue guidance for those requiring group passports.

Mr. Hurd: Delays which had been occurring in some areas during the peak season have been made worse by the recent industrial action in the passport offices. I very much regret the inconvenience that this has caused and will continue to cause to the public.

Following a ballot held by the Civil and Public Services Association (CPSA), 84 out of 295 staff in the Liverpool office came out on indefinite strike on 30 May. Following ballots at all other offices, members of the CPSA staged a one-day sympathy strike on 2 June in favour of the Liverpool action, when a total of 219 failed to report for work. A ballot held by the National Union of Civil and Public Servants (NUCPS) obtained no majority for a sympathy strike and, as a result, there has so far been no official action by NUCPS members.

All passport offices have remained open and counter services are being maintained, with priority being given to urgent cases. I am asking my right hon. and learned Friend the Foreign and Commonwealth Secretary to contact certain other Governments to see whether, in the special circumstances in which we find ourselves, they would consider accepting expired British passports or (where they do not do so already) British visitor passports (BVPs).

Travellers should be given the best possible advice and I am urgently considering ways of improving this. Those with an urgent need to travel in western Europe may apply for a BVP to any main post office in England, Scotland or Wales. BVPs are now available on Mondays to Fridays, and on Saturday mornings. Where a standard passport has been applied for in good time and has not been processed, BVP fees will be refunded on application. For countries where a BVP is not acceptable, travellers who have an urgent requirement (including for group passports) are advised to call in person at the most convenient passport office, where every effort will be made to ensure that a suitable travel document is provided.

We shall seek to bring this dispute to a satisfactory end. Management and unions are meeting tomorrow and I hope that they will be able urgently to identify means of resolving the dispute.

The unions' principal demand is for an increase of 381 staff on the permanent complement of 1,000. The demand for passports is partly seasonal. Demand rises in the new year, reaches its peak in early summer and falls away in the autumn. It makes sense to deal with the busy period partly by employing temporary staff and using overtime. At present, for example, a total of 1,420 staff are employed. The unions are not asking for any increase in this total but that the permanent proportion be increased.

It is common ground that there have been changes in the pattern of demand. There is now a smaller difference between the peaks and the troughs. We therefore looked again at the case for a higher proportion of permanent staff. The National Audit Office has recently pointed out that it is not acceptable to staff troughs relatively more favourably than peaks. Nor would it be sensible to pre-empt the findings of the staffing review which both sides have already agreed should be undertaken once we

know of the effects of the present computerisation programme so far implemented only in Glasgow and Liverpool.

But as a result of this examination, the Home Office concluded that the present justifiable maximum addition to the permanent complement was 158, subject to the impending staffing review. We began to recruit these extra permanent staff some weeks ago and propose to complete the process by the end of July.

We have always been ready to provide in total— whether permanent or temporary—as many staff as can be justified by the workload and accommodated in the offices concerned. But we would not be justified in employing on a permanent basis staff who would have little or nothing to do during the slack period in the autumn and early winter.

We have begun the computerisation of offices with the new passport. This must be the right long term solution. There have been teething problems with the introduction of computerisation in Glasgow and Liverpool, but we must see these through with the help of the staff.

We intend to give the passport office the status of an executive agency, and are discussing the timing and details of the change. We believe that this will free the energies of staff and management to give better service to the public.

Mr. Maxwell-Hyslop: To ask the Secretary of State for the Home Department what is the current delay in *(a)* acknowledging receipt of applications to renew passports, *(b)* acknowledging receipt of applications for new passports, *(c)* issuing renewed passports and *(d)* issuing new passports in respect of the Newport passport office; and what specific advice he has given applicants by way of newspaper advertisements as to the lead-time for the two classes of applications.

Mr. Renton: Straightforward non-urgent postal applications of all types are being processed at the Newport passport office within a maximum of 46 working days. Urgent applications are given priority and are processed in accordance with travellers' requirements. Applications are not normally acknowledged. Information about current delay times is frequently given in response to enquiries from the news media, and in the recorded telephone message facility for callers to the Newport office, which is extensively used and updated weekly.

Mr. Speller: To ask the Secretary of State for the Home Department if he will consider appointing major sub-post offices as agents for the issue of British visitors passports; what size of local population would be suitable for such an appointment; and if he will make a statement.

Mr. Renton: The issuing of British visitors passports is generally limited to the 1500 Crown post offices for reasons of security and economy. By agreement with the passport department, the facility is being retained by those Crown offices which are regraded to sub-office status under the Post Office's current restructuring plans, but we would not wish to extend this arrangement to other sub-offices.

Mr. Straw: To ask the Secretary of State for the Home Department what steps he intends to take to deal with the inadequacies of the telephone system and inquiry service at the Liverpool passport office.

Mr. Jack: To ask the Secretary of State for the Home Department what steps he is taking to improve the Liverpool passport office telephone inquiry service.

Mr. Renton: The Liverpool passport office has a 24 exchange line switchboard. A recorded message facility offering an additional 26 telephone lines was installed in April, and further improvements are planned which will route incoming calls directly to the inquiry section. Efforts are being made to reduce the backlog of passport applications which is the reason for most of the telephone enquiries received, but the situation has been adversely affected by the current industrial action at Liverpool.

Mr. Straw: To ask the Secretary of State for the Home Department how many passport applications are awaiting process in *(a)* Liverpool and *(b)* London passport offices; what is the current average delay, in weeks; and what reasons there are for this backlog.

Mr. Renton: The information for the week ended 28 May is shown in the table:

Passport office	¹ *Application*	² *Maximum processing times*
Liverpool	215,469	15 weeks
London	22,622	5 weeks

¹ Shows the estimated number of applications at the various stages of processing.
² Shows the maximum processing time in weeks (averages are not recorded).

Normally most applications are processed well within the maximum period, with priority being given to urgent cases, but a sharp increase in demand early this year has led to an increase in processing times, and staff at Liverpool are also having to adapt to a new computerised system of passport issuing. Additional staff have been employed to help deal with the backlogs, and a system of free two-year extensions to the life of certain expired passports submitted for replacement has been introduced at Liverpool to help relieve the immediate problem there. The situation at Liverpool has recently been made more serious as a result of industrial action by some members of staff.

Mr. Darling: To ask the Secretary of State for the Home Department what is the average time taken to process passport applications at *(a)* Liverpool and *(b)* Glasgow; and what he expects the position to be by 1990.

Mr. Renton: Passport applications are processed according to the applicant's travel requirements, with priority being given to urgent cases. As a result, processing times in a given period vary considerably, and averages are not recorded.

The current maximum processing time for straight-forward non-urgent postal applications at the Liverpool Passport Office is 73 working days, and at Glasgow 50 working days. Most applications are processed well within these maximum periods.

Processing time should be reduced next year when the new computer system is fully established, and staff have become fully conversant with its operation.

Mr. Darling: To ask the Secretary of State for the Home Department if he will estimate loss of revenue to be incurred as a result of his decision to allow a two-year extension to passports without charge.

Mr. Renton: I take it that the hon. Member is referring to the special arrangement at the Liverpool passport office announced by my right hon. Friend on 11 May at column *978*.

We estimate that the measure will cost in the region of £1·3 million in the current financial year. Since, however, the great majority of the applications concerned are likely to be renewed on or before expiry of the two year extension period, the overall loss in passport fee receipts is likely to be small.

Listening Devices

Mr. Cran: To ask the Secretary of State for the Home Department on how many occasions since the introduction of the guidelines on the use of equipment in police surveillance operations authorisation to use electronic surveillance listening and visual devices in each of the provincial police forces has been given by officers other than the chief officer.

Mr. Hurd: I refer to my reply to my hon. Friend's questions on 26 May at columns *756-7*.

Mr. Cran: To ask the Secretary of State for the Home Department what control he exercises over the Metropolitan police use of electronic surveillance listening and visual devices other than that exercised by the force inspectorate.

Mr. Hurd: I refer to my reply to my hon. Friend's questions on 26 May at columns *756-7*.

Vietnamese Refugees

Mr. Andrew Smith: To ask the Secretary of State for the Home Department how many Vietnamese refugees there are currently in Hong Kong; how many he estimates will apply to settle in the United Kingdom; on what criteria their applications will be judged; and how many it is proposed to admit.

Mr. Renton: On 25 May, there were 14,200 Vietnamese refugees in Hong Kong. A further 19,243 Vietnamese were awaiting examination of their claim for asylum. It had been decided that 1,410 did not qualify for refugee status.

On 23 February 1989 the Government confirmed its intention to admit a further 1,000 Vietnamese refugees from Hong Kong for settlement in the United Kingdom. The 1,000 will include relatives of Vietnamese already here and others with the potential quickly to become self-sufficient in the United Kingdom, together with some who have been in the camps for a long time and have not been accepted elsewhere.

Mr. Mullin: To ask the Secretary of State for the Home Department how many Vietnamese refugees have had their travel documents confiscated for using those documents to travel to Vietnam.

Mr. Renton: Refugee status is accorded to those who have a well-founded fear of persecution in their own country. Although withdrawal of status is not automatic, travel to that country may put into question a continuing claim to refugee status and eligibility for refugeee travel documents. Following visits to Vietnam, 39 refugee travel documents have been impounded on return. So far, seven holders have been required to surrender their documents and decisions about the remainder will be made shortly, after careful consideration of the individual circumstances. In all cases, the persons concerned retain indefinite leave to remain in the United Kingdom. It would be open to them to apply for discretionary travel documents.

Visa Applications

Mr. Darling: To ask the Secretary of State for the Home Department (1) if he will indicate the reason for the delay in processing visa applications by his Department; what he proposes to do about it; and if he will make a statement;

(2) on which date those applications for visas to enter the United Kingdom now being completed were submitted to his Department;

(3) what is the average length of time taken to decide visa applications made by non United Kingdom nationals.

Mr. Renton: The reasons for the time taken to complete visa applications and the steps in train or already taken to reduce unnecessary delay were explained in my reply of 23 March to the hon. Member for Stretford (Mr. Lloyd) at column *809* in respect of all entry clearance applications.

The way in which visa applications are allocated within the immigration department means that it is not possible to give a common date on which those applications now being completed were first referred to the department. Visa applications are dealt with according to, first, their perceived priority and, second, the date on which the application was first received within the department.

Information about the average length of time taken to decide visa applications is not readily available and could be obtained only at disproportionate cost.

Remand (Leeds)

Mr. Battle: To ask the Secretary of State for the Home Department if he has any plans to introduce time limits on periods of remand imposed on young people by magistrates in the Leeds area; and if he will make a statement.

Mr. John Patten: Custody time limits were introduced in West Yorkshire on 1 June. They apply to all those of whatever age remanded in prison department custody.

Prison Service (Recruits)

Mr. Vaz: To ask the Secretary of State for the Home Department how many new recruits to the prison service resign in the first 12 months of service due to unacceptable postings, according to the latest available figures.

Mr. Douglas Hogg: Between 3 May 1988 and 30 April 1989, 73 basic grade prison officers resigned from the prison service within 12 months of joining. Information about their reasons for doing so is not available.

Incest

Mr. Nicholas Winterton: To ask the Secretary of State for the Home Department whether he has any plans to introduce legislation to decriminalise incest between brothers and sisters aged over 21 years.

Mr. John Patten: No.

Prison Staff

Mr. Vaz: To ask the Secretary of State for the Home Department if he has any plans to improve working conditions for administrative staff in prisons.

Mr. Douglas Hogg: Proposals to improve working conditions for staff in existing establishments are considered on an individual basis according to the needs of the establishment and competing demands on the building programme. The improved provision which is to be made for administrative staff in new training prisons is described in the prison design brief which was published in March, 1989. Copies have been placed in the Library. Work is in hand on the adaptation of the brief to the requirements of local, female and young offender establishments.

Mr. Vaz: To ask the Secretary of State for the Home Department how many administrative staff are employed in Her Majesty's prisons in England and Wales.

Mr. Douglas Hogg: On 1 May, there were 1,942 members of the administrative group (including part-time staff) employed in prison service out-stations.

Her Majesty's Prison, Leicester

Mr. Vaz: To ask the Secretary of State for the Home Department if he will make a statement about the use and cost effectiveness of agency staff in the hospital wing of Her Majesty's prison, Leicester.

Mr. Douglas Hogg: Nurses employed by agencies have been used at Leicester prison from time to time to meet short-term needs. The director of prison medical services considers this to be a medically and financially acceptable means of filling temporary gaps in health care services.

Mr. Vaz: To ask the Secretary of State for the Home Department if he will make a statement on the introduction of female prison officers at Her Majesty's prison, Leicester.

Mr. Douglas Hogg: Four female officers have now been posted to Leicester. In the governor's view they have settled in well and are making a useful contribution to the work of the establishment.

Mr. Vaz: To ask the Secretary of State for the Home Department why certain petitions from Her Majesty's prison, Leicester to his Department have not been acknowledged, and others have remained unanswered; and if he will make a statement.

Mr. Douglas Hogg: All petitions addressed to the Secretary of State received from prisoners at Leicester and which were handed in prior to 2 April have either been acknowledged or a reply has been sent. All petitions received since that date have been acknowledged.

As a local prison, Leicester has a rapid turnover of inmates. Most of the men whose petitions were recorded as outstanding in the Leicester petitions register have been transferred, and replies have been sent to their current establishment. Arrangements are being made to bring Leicester's records up to date.

Mr. Vaz: To ask the Secretary of State for the Home Department what measures are being taken to end the overcrowding of Her Majesty's prison, Leicester.

Mr. Douglas Hogg: Her Majesty's prison, Leicester, in common with other overcrowded local prisons, will benefit from the delivery of substantial numbers of places under the prison building programme. The greatest measure of relief will be provided by the opening of a new local prison at Milton Keynes in 1992.

Mr. Vaz: To ask the Secretary of State for the Home Department what measures are taken to put non-smoking prisoners in cells with other non-smokers if they so wish at Her Majesty's prison, Leicester.

Mr. Douglas Hogg: Arrangements are made, as far as is practicable, to meet requests from inmates who ask to be located with other non-smokers in circumstances where they are required to share a cell with others.

Mr. Vaz: To ask the Secretary of State for the Home Department what steps are being taken to increase the availability of workshops for prisoners in Her Majesty's prison, Leicester.

Mr. Douglas Hogg: There are no plans to increase the number of workshop places at Leicester but efforts are continuing to ensure the full utilisation of existing places.

Mr. Vaz: To ask the Secretary of State for the Home Department why modernisation of the kitchen at Her Majesty's prison, Leicester is behind schedule.

Mr. Douglas Hogg: A new kitchen was to have been provided at Her Majesty's prison Leicester by late 1994. Design work on this scheme has however recently been suspended, as part of an effort to focus resources on schemes in the prison building programme which are either under way, or where work has to start on site in the next two financial years.

Alcoholic Prisoners

Mr. Vaz: To ask the Secretary of State for the Home Department what help has been given to alcoholic prisoners since the pre-release scheme was abolished.

Mr. Douglas Hogg: I am not aware of the pre-release scheme to which the hon. Member refers.

The number of pre-release courses, which will often include advice on the dangers of alcohol abuse, is increasing steadily. It has long been the prison department's policy to seek to educate prisoners about these dangers. In addition, there is now a branch of Alcoholics Anonymous within most adult establishments, and prisoners nearing the end of their sentence can be put in touch with the local Alcoholics Anonymous group near their home address should they wish to take advantage of the counselling service provided.

Eames Report

Mr. Battle: To ask the Secretary of State for the Home Department if he will make available the Eames report into suicides in Armley prison, Leeds, to the prison officers' representatives on the Whitley council negotiating body.

Mr. Douglas Hogg: No, but the trade union side on the departmental Whitley council has been made aware of its main conclusions and recommendations.

Police Vehicles

Mr. Vaz: To ask the Secretary of State for the Home Department if he has plans to streamline police vehicle fleet management as set out in the third police paper "A Report by the Audit Commission".

Mr. Douglas Hogg: It is for individual chief officers and their police authorities to determine how best to manage their vehicle fleets. I understand that forces are now reviewing their arrangements in the light of the Audit Commission report. Her Majesty's inspectorate of constabulary will be examining these arrangements in the course of their annual inspection. The Home Office intends to issue guidance to forces on best practice.

OVERSEAS DEVELOPMENT

Disaster and Refugee Units

Mr. Harry Barnes: To ask the Secretary of State for Foreign and Commonwealth Affairs how many staff have been employed in each year since 1979 by the disaster and refugee units of the Overseas Development Administration.

Mr. Chris Patten: The information is as follows:

Year	Disaster unit[1]	Refugee unit[2]
1980	4·0	—
1981	3·0	—
1982	3·0	—
1983	3·0	—
1984	2·5	2·5
1985	2·5	2·5
1986	2·5	2·5
1987	2·5	2·5
1988	2·5	2·5
1989	2·5	2·5

[1] Temporary additional staff are assigned to the disaster unit during major and prolonged disasters.
[2] The refugee unit was set up in 1984.

The total number of permanent posts in the disaster and refugee units will shortly increase from five to seven.

Disaster Relief

Mr. Harry Barnes: To ask the Secretary of State for Foreign and Commonwealth Affairs what discussions have taken place between the Overseas Development Administration and non-Government agencies concerned with arrangements for disaster relief since the time of the Armenian earthquake; and if he will make a statement.

Mr. Chris Patten: Regular meetings, some of which I chair, are held between the Overseas Development Administration and those non-Government organisations concerned with providing disaster and refugee relief. I am planning a review of disaster relief arrangements with non-Government organisations before the summer.

Mr. Harry Barnes: To ask the Secretary of State for Foreign and Commonwealth Affairs what information he has on the progress that has been made by the United Nations disaster relief organisation in drawing up a register of the assistance available by donor nations to countries facing major disasters.

Mr. Chris Patten: United Nations disaster relief organisation is in the process of drawing up such a register and I understand is in contact with donor Governments.

Mr. Harry Barnes: To ask the Secretary of State for Foreign and Commonwealth Affairs whether he has any plans to provide further assistance to the United Nations disaster relief organisation in order to improve its effectiveness.

Mr. Chris Patten: We have already provided financial assistance to United Nations disaster relief organisation for its important disaster prevention and preparedness activities. I am planning to increase this assistance in the context of the forthcoming United Nations international decade for natural disaster reduction.

Renewable Energy

Mr. Menzies Campbell: To ask the Secretary of State for Foreign and Commonwealth Affairs if he has any plans to assist developing countries in the development of renewable energy sources; and if he will make a statement.

Mr. Chris Patten: Over the last decade the Overseas Development Administration has promoted the use of renewable energy sources in developing countries through funding research and development for a wide range of technologies, including efficient wood-fuelled cooking stoves, efficient charcoal manufacture, biogas production, windpumps, microhydro turbines, solar crop drying and the use of waste materials for process heating.

Aid funds have also been used to implement projects aimed at utilising geothermal energy, wind-powered electricity generation, and solar-powered water pumping. They have also been used to help finance the manufacture of efficient wood-fuelled stoves, as well as for building and rehabilitating substantial hydropower installations.

We continue to seek ways of helping to carry forward developments in renewable energy which carry real promise of being effective.

Energy Conservation

Mr. Menzies Campbell: To ask the Secretary of State for Foreign and Commonwealth Affairs if he has any plans to assist developing countries with measures for energy conservation; and if he will make a statement.

Mr. Chris Patten: Through our aid programmes we have been assisting developing countries for some years with measures aimed at improving the efficiency of their energy sectors. The provision of British equipment, skills and training has been financed to improve generating efficiency, reduce transmission losses and improve distribution networks. In conjunction with other donors we have also encouraged Governments to adopt appropriate pricing policies for power to ensure that it is used effectively and economically. Against the background of our environmental concerns, we shall continue to give high priority to this kind of assistance in the energy sector.

Mozambique

Sir John Farr: To ask the Secretary of State for Foreign and Commonwealth Affairs what is the current situation relating to the development by the Commonwealth Development Corporation of schemes in Mozambique; and if he will give details of proposals relating to their financing.

Mr. Chris Patten: I authorised the Commonwealth Development Corporation to operate in Mozambique in November 1987.

The CDC is discussing a draft operating conditions agreement with the Government of the People's Republic of Mozambique which we hope will be signed shortly. The CDC are investigating a number of investment possibilities including projects for the development of tea, sugar, forestry, cashew nuts and citrus.

Fiji

Mr. Vaz: To ask the Secretary of State for Foreign and Commonwealth Affairs what amount of grant aid has been allocated to Fiji by Her Majesty's Government; and if he will list it by category.

Mr. Chris Patten: The latest provisional figure for our bilateral aid to Fiji is £1,595,000 in 1988. £39,000 of this total represents expenditure under grant financial aid agreed in 1981. About £1,555,000 was spent on technical co-operation (the provision of expert manpower and advice from the United Kingdom and the training of Fijians). I envisage that technical co-operation will continue at around this level. These figures exclude expenditure by the Commonwealth Development Corporation.

CIVIL SERVICE

Civil Service College

Mr. Baldry: To ask the Minister for the Civil Service what progress has been made towards establishing the Civil Service college as an executive agency.

Mr. Luce: I am pleased to announce that the Civil Service college will today become an executive agency of the Cabinet Office (OMCS). The college is the chief central provider of training for civil servants. It charges for its courses and government departments are free to go elsewhere. Agency status will add to the managerial freedoms which the college has enjoyed for some time and will enable it to compete more effectively for its business. It will provide a sharper focus for the college's operations and a clearer relationship with my Department. I have set demanding targets against which its performance will be measured in future. Copies of the framework document are being placed in the Library of the House.

EMPLOYMENT

Departmental Staff (Relocation)

Mr. Butler: To ask the Secretary of State for Employment whether he has any plans to relocate staff of his Department to Runcorn; and if he will make a statement.

Mr. Cope: The Employment Department, in common with other Departments, has been conducting a study into the potential for moving posts out of London and the south east. The study is nearing completion and we expect to announce its conclusions and our decisions to the House shortly. At present 27 per cent. of Employment Department head office staff are located in Runcorn.

Strikes (Statistics)

Mr. Meacher: To ask the Secretary of State for Employment what information he has as to the number of strike days lost per 100,000 workers for each year since 1975 in *(a)* the United Kingdom, *(b)* France, *(c)* West Germany, *(d)* Italy, *(e)* the EEC average, *(f)* the United States of America, *(g)* Sweden and *(h)* Japan.

Mr. Nicholls: The available information for the years 1977 to 1986 is given in the article "International comparisons of industrial stoppages for 1986" published in the *Employment Gazette*, June 1988, page 335, a copy of which is in the Library. This article also gives a description of the different coverage of the statistics in the various countries. For the data for 1987, the latest available, I refer the hon. Gentleman to the reply I gave to my hon. Friend the Member for Pembroke (Mr. Bennett) on 4 May 1989, *Official Report*, column *241*. Figures for 1975 and 1976 are given in the article "International comparisons of industrial stoppages for 1984" published in the *Employment Gazette*, July 1986, page 266, a copy of which is in the Library.

EEC average figures would not be meaningful because of the wide variation in the coverage of the industrial dispute figures in member states.

International Agreements (ILO)

Mr. Wray: To ask the Secretary of State for Employment if he will list all the occasions on which Britain has been found guilty of breaking international agreements by the United Nations International Labour Organisation.

Mr. Cope: The Government are convinced that United Kingdom law and practice fully conform with ILO obligations.

Construction Industry Training Board

Mr. Heddle: To ask the Secretary of State for Employment if he will make a statement on the outcome of his meeting with the chairman of the construction industry training board in early April.

Mr. Nicholls: I am holding a series of meetings with the chairman of the construction industry training board to discuss plans for training within the construction industry as envisaged in the White Paper, "Employment for the 1990s" (cmd 540).

I have asked the chairman to put forward proposals agreed by the industry for future training arrangements.

Unemployment Benefit

Mr. Harry Barnes: To ask the Secretary of State for Employment in the last year for which figures are available how many people in the Chesterfield area have had their unemployment benefit payment reduced; by what average amount; and for what average period.

Mr. Lee: No figures are kept on the number of people who have their unemployment benefit payments reduced.

Listening Devices

Mr. Cran: To ask the Secretary of State for Employment whether electronic surveillance listening devices are used by his Department or by any organisation or agency acting on its behalf; and if he will make a statement.

Mr. Cope: No electronic surveillance listening devices are used by the Department of Employment or by any organisations or agency acting on its behalf.

Disablement Advisory Service

Mr. McCrindle: To ask the Secretary of State for Employment how many people the Disablement Advisory Service employs; and if he will make a statement.

Mr. Lee: There were 190 Disablement Advisory Service (DAS) staff in post on 31 March 1989. I believe that the Disablement Advisory Service performs an invaluable role in encouraging and assisting employers to apply good policies and practices in the employment of people with disabilities.

Mr. McCrindle: To ask the Secretary of State for Employment how the Disablement Advisory Service is resourced; and if he will make a statement.

Mr. Lee: The Disablement Advisory Service consists of specially trained employment service staff. They are organised in 68 teams, covering all parts of the country, and can be contacted through local jobcentres. For very large employing organisations, there is a special head office advisory service, the major organisations development unit, based in London, but available nationwide.

Mr. McCrindle: To ask the Secretary of State for Employment if the Disablement Advisory Service distributes leaflets concerning its activities to general practitioners' surgeries; and if he will make a statement.

Mr. Lee: No. The Disablement Advisory Service's main role is to help employers to adopt and implement good policies and practices in the employment of people with disabilities. It is not directed towards general practitioners or their patients. A new booklet, "Job Hunting for People with Disabilities", appropriate to disabled jobseekers and their advisers, will be issued shortly for distribution to local points of contact, including surgeries, at disablement resettlement officers' discretion.

Mr. McCrindle: To ask the Secretary of State for Employment if there are any plans to expand the Disablement Advisory Service's activities; and if he will make a statement.

Mr. Lee: There are no current plans to expand the Disablement Advisory Service's (DAS) activities. However, DAS activities are being considered as part of my Department's internal review of its policies and services for people with disabilities.

Non-EEC Workers

Mr. Gregory: To ask the Secretary of State for Employment if he will take action against the restaurant chain Garfunkels over the employment of illegal non-EEC workers; and if he will make a statement.

Mr. Renton: I have been asked to reply.

Action has been taken in the past to deal with illegal entrants and other immigration offenders employed by the restaurant chain Garfunkels. However, there was insufficient evidence available to act against their employer. I will, of course, consider any such evidence which my hon. Friend may wish to provide.

Labour Statistics

Mr. David Nicholson: To ask the Secretary of State for Employment how many new jobs have been created since May 1979.

Mr. Lee: There are no figures for job gains and job losses. Between June 1979 (there are no estimates for May) and December 1988, the latest date for which figures are available, there was a net increase of 1,148,000 in the work force in employment in the United Kingdom. The figures have been adjusted for the effects of seasonal variation. The work force in employment is the sum of employees in employment, the self-employed, Her Majesty's forces and participants in work-related Government training programmes.

Mr. David Nicholson: To ask the Secretary of State for Employment what estimates he has of the average number of people employed by companies with turnovers of *(a)* less than £250,000, *(b)* £250,000 to £500,000, *(c)* £500,000 to £1,000,000, *(d)* £1,000,000 to £2,000,000, *(e)* £2,000,000 to £5,000,000 and *(f)* £5,000,000 and above.

Mr. Cope: The information requested is not available. The Department's employment estimates are taken from short term surveys and censuses of employment which do not relate employee numbers to company turnover.

Mr. Battle: To ask the Secretary of State for Employment (1) how many *(a)* part-time and *(b)* temporary employees there were in the Leeds metropolitan district for each of the years 1979 to 1989 shown by (i) gender and (ii) as a percentage of all employees (1) in manufacturing industries (2) in the service sector;

(2) how many employees were in employment in manufacturing in the Leeds metropolitan district in each of the years 1979 to 1989;

(3) how many manufacturing and non-manufacturing employees there were in employment in the Leeds metropolitan district for each of the years 1979 to 1989.

Mr. Lee: The available employee estimates for the area are from censuses of employment taken in September 1981 and September 1984 and are given in the table. More up-to-date employee estimates for local areas, from the September 1987 census of employment, will become available later this year.

Employees in employment[1] in the Leeds metropolitan district[2]

Standard Industrial Classification (SIC) 1980	Division of SIC	September 1981 Number (thousand)	Per cent.	September 1984 Number (thousand)	Per cent.
Manufacturing industries of which:	2-4	85·5	100·0	71·8	100·0
Male part-time	—	0·9	1·0	0·7	1·0
Female part-time	—	5·5	6·5	4·3	6·0
Service industries of which:	6-9	187·4	100·0	196·1	100·0
Male part-time	—	7·7	4·1	9·4	4·8
Female part-time	—	47·0	25·1	49·8	25·4
Non-manufacturing industries	0,1, 5-9	216·3	—	223·0	—
All industries and services	0-9	301·7	—	294·7	—

[1] Excludes the self-employed and members of Her Majesty's forces; employees in temporary employment are included but are not separately identified; part-time workers are defined as those working not more than 30 hours a week.
[2] The district is defined in terms of ward boundaries as at 1981.

Mr. Battle: To ask the Secretary of State for Employment how many people were self-employed in the Leeds metropolitan district for each of the years 1979 to 1989.

Mr. Lee: The information is available only for Census Day in April 1981. In the census returns 24,601 people living in the Leeds district said that they were self-employed.

This information is available in the Library.

Mr. McLeish: To ask the Secretary of State for Employment what were the unemployment rates by highest qualification held for men and women in each of the standard regions and for Wales for each of the years 1983 to 1988.

Mr. Lee *[holding answer 19 May 1989]:* Estimates from labour force surveys are as shown in the following table:

Unemployment rates for persons of working age[2] by highest qualification and region

	1983 Men	1983 Women	1984 Men	1984 Women	1985 Men	1985 Women	1986 Men	1986 Women	1987 Men	1987 Women	1988[3] Men	1988[3] Women
Northern region												
'A' level or higher	10·1	[1]—	10·9	10·3	11·3	9·3	10·0	8·9	9·1	[1]—	9·1	[1]—
'O' level or equivalent	15·7	12·8	17·8	10·8	14·2	11·3	16·2	13·1	11·8	12·5	[1]—	10·9
Below 'O' level	24·3	15·4	19·6	28·1	23·8	18·2	20·5	[1]—	28·7	16·6	16·9	16·2
No qualification	22·5	11·5	24·6	15·0	21·5	13·2	23·9	13·3	21·1	11·9	26·0	14·5
Yorks and Humberside region												
'A' level or higher	8·3	7·2	7·1	9·0	7·0	7·9	7·5	6·7	6·8	5·1	6·1	8·5
'O' level or equivalent	11·4	11·3	13·4	11·5	14·0	11·0	11·9	9·4	9·4	10·3	9·2	8·1
Below 'O' level	18·9	14·2	17·3	15·3	15·1	13·6	17·8	16·8	15·6	11·0	14·6	[1]—
No qualification	18·8	10·9	17·4	11·8	19·9	12·2	18·2	11·4	21·5	11·8	20·4	11·8
East Midlands region												
'A' level or higher	5·4	[1]—	4·8	[1]—	5·7	6·9	6·1	7·6	6·0	6·1	3·6	6·3
'O' level or equivalent	[1]—	10·2	11·2	9·8	[1]—	6·4	10·1	8·9	9·6	7·9	[1]—	9·2
Below 'O' level	12·9	[1]—	15·7	13·5	16·1	13·0	12·7	14·6	9·9	11·2	11·3	[1]—

	1983		1984		1985		1986		1987		1988[3]	
	Men	Women	Men	Women	Men	Women	Men	Women	Men	Women	Men	Women
No qualification	12·3	10·1	15·0	10·0	15·5	11·9	13·5	9·8	17·2	13·5	13·1	8·4
East Anglia region												
'A' level or higher	6·3	[1]—	4·6	[1]—	4·5	[1]—	4·5	[1]—	6·2	[1]—	[1]—	[1]—
'O' level or equivalent	[1]—	[1]—	[1]—	[1]—	[1]—	[1]—	[1]—	[1]—	[1]—	[1]—	[1]—	[1]—
Below 'O' level	[1]—	[1]—	[1]—	[1]—	[1]—	[1]—	[1]—	[1]—	[1]—	[1]—	[1]—	[1]—
No qualification	12·4	8·2	9·3	7·8	10·4	11·8	10·3	9·6	8·7	10·9	6·2	7·0
South East region												
'A' level or higher	5·3	6·9	4·8	6·9	4·6	6·9	5·1	7·1	5·2	6·0	3·2	4·5
'O' level or equivalent	8·5	7·4	7·0	7·9	6·8	6·7	7·3	7·8	6·0	7·5	5·0	5·2
Below 'O' level	11·9	11·4	11·4	10·3	11·8	11·3	11·2	9·9	8·4	8·5	6·6	7·8
No qualification	12·4	9·6	12·6	10·0	12·3	9·9	13·5	9·5	13·1	8·9	10·7	8·2
Greater London												
'A' level or higher	6·6	6·8	5·9	7·7	5·3	7·0	7·1	8·1	6·6	6·0	4·5	5·6
'O' level or equivalent	10·0	8·3	8·1	9·3	8·3	8·0	9·2	8·1	8·6	8·0	6·8	5·3
Below 'O' level	11·9	11·9	12·4	13·0	14·1	13·3	14·4	11·3	9·6	7·5	8·2	9·6
No qualification	14·3	10·0	14·7	12·3	14·8	12·4	16·5	11·4	16·7	9·6	15·4	10·7
South West region												
'A' level or higher	6·0	6·7	5·2	8·7	5·0	6·7	5·7	7·6	4·6	6·8	3·8	3·9
'O' level or equivalent	9·1	8·0	8·6	9·1	[1]	9·2	8·8	7·8	6·2	9·9	5·6	7·1
Below 'O' level	10·9	13·6	14·2	11·4	12·4	9·2	10·3	11·3	8·7	9·9	6·8	8·1
No qualification	12·1	8·9	11·2	9·2	10·4	8·7	12·9	9·1	14·1	10·1	9·2	9·0
West Midlands region												
'A' level or higher	7·7	7·4	7·9	9·7	6·5	8·2	6·0	7·3	6·6	5·2	4·9	4·1
'O' level or equivalent	13·0	12·3	15·2	12·4	13·5	12·8	13·3	10·4	15·3	12·9	7·2	8·2
Below 'O' level	17·7	17·1	19·4	17·8	21·5	15·3	15·6	16·1	14·7	13·2	10·8	9·8
No qualification	21·2	13·2	20·4	11·7	21·6	13·9	18·5	11·8	20·5	11·4	13·3	9·8
North West region												
'A' level or higher	8·7	7·9	9·7	9·1	8·6	6·9	8·0	8·0	7·8	7·4	6·9	6·8
'O' level or equivalent	13·8	11·1	12·4	10·5	12·5	11·1	11·7	12·3	9·6	11·0	8·3	8·0
Below 'O' level	19·8	14·2	20·6	17·5	18·2	15·4	21·5	18·1	18·8	14·4	14·1	14·4
No qualification	21·7	13·6	23·9	14·0	21·7	13·7	22·9	12·4	21·1	15·1	22·2	12·9
Wales												
'A' level or higher	10·1	[1]	9·3	10·9	8·7	[1]	8·4	8·5	8·4	8·2	7·8	[1]
'O' level or equivalent	15·4	11·6	[1]	12·4	[1]	[1]	13·2	13·0	11·2	10·5	[1]	10·2
Below 'O' level	16·6	[1]	[1]	[1]	19·1	[1]	28·0	21·8	17·6	[1]	17·0	[1]
No qualification	20·9	13·3	20·7	14·5	20·2	14·9	21·9	13·5	21·8	13·7	17·1	14·5

[1] Sample size too small for a reliable estimate.
[2] Men aged 16-64, women aged 16-59.
[3] Preliminary results (1988 only).
Source: Labour Force Surveys.

Wages Councils

Mr. Nellist: To ask the Secretary of State for Employment if, pursuant to his reply of 23 May, *Official Report*, columns *506-7*, he will provide the references to any published evidence from employers in wages council trades that they are more ready to offer young people employment; if he will place in the Library copies of any written but unpublished evidence available to him; and if he will make a statement.

Mr. Nicholls: The evidence consists of comments made by certain organisations in their responses to the consultation document on wages councils and in other correspondence. It is not the Department's practice to ascribe particular comments to individuals or organisations.

Employment Training

Mr. Roy Hughes: To ask the Secretary of State for Employment if he will consider introducing a gardening and caretaking scheme under employment training.

Mr. Nicholls: Training in both gardening and caretaking occupations is already offered under employment training where there is a demand for such training from long-term unemployed people and where there are suitable employment opportunities following training.

TRADE AND INDUSTRY

Sprint Programme

Mr. Cousins: To ask the Chancellor of the Duchy of Lancaster what proportion of the spending of the EEC Sprint programme was spent in Britain in each year of the programme's existence; and if he will list the projects and agencies supported by Sprint in Britain since the programme started.

Mr. Forth: The detailed breakdown of funding requested by the hon. Gentleman is unavailable. However, during the 1984-88 Sprint pilot phase, it is possible to attribute at least 2·3 million ecu to United Kingdom beneficiaries out of Sprint funding of 18·63 million ecu.

Excluding funding of 2·73 million ecu for EC groups and associations (eg EuroTechAlert) the United Kingdom proportion of the Sprint budget amounted to 14·5 per cent.

The list indicates that 80 United Kingdom contractors received support for 123 projects under Sprint since the programme began.

Contractors supported under Sprint

Contractors	Projects
Smida Herts	2
Mackintosh Beds	1
British Executive Overseas London	1
Newtech Clwyd	3
Worldtech Ventures Ltd. London	1
I.C.O.M Yorks	2
Scottish Development Agency Lanarks	7
New Products-EC Gloucester	3
Nesda Aberdeen	1
Europa Industrial Products Berks	2
Wintech Cardiff	2
Shekell-Mooring Herts	2
Shekell Mooring International Licensing Herts	1
North of England Development Council Newcastle-upon-Tyne	1
Kelvington International London	1
C.T.A. (Cosgrove) Berks	2
QMC-Wolfson Fire and Materials CNT London	1
PIRA Surrey	1
University of Bath Bath	1
Macro Group London	1
Mari Advanced Microelectronics Ltd. Gateshead	1
Institute of Physics London	2
P.T.R.C. London	1

Contractors	Projects
Scottish Development and Industry Edinburgh	1
BSRIA Berkshire	3
Licensing Executives Society (Britain and Ireland) London	1
Newcastle-upon-Tyne University (Centre for Urban and Regional Development Studies) Tyne and Wear	2
Peat Marwick McLintock London	1
United Kingdom Science Park Association Birmingham	1
BHRA, The Fluid Engineering Centre Bedford	1
City University London London	1
SATRA Footwear Technology Centre Northamptonshire	1
Institution of Mechanical Engineers London	1
Glasgow Business School Glasgow	1
C.T.A. Economic and Export Analysis Berkshire	1
Technology Exchange (Ex GLEB) London	1
The Technology Exchange Bedford	1
P.E. Consulting Ltd. Surrey	3
Metropolitan Borough of Calderdale Yorkshire	4
Purvis and Company St. Andrews	1
Life Business Development Agency Lanarkshire	1
Heriot-Watt University Edinburgh	3
Lanarkshire Industrial Field Executive Ltd. Lanarkshire	1
Worldtech Ventures Ltd. London	1
Scottish Enterprise Foundation Stirling	1
Pax Technology Transfer London	3
Deloitte Haskins and Sells (UK) London	1
Capital Partners International London	1
Technology International Exchange London	2

Contractors	Projects
March Technologies Limited Manchester	2
Sallingbury Casey Ltd. London	1
European Technology Entrepreneurs Centre Belfast	2
TRC-Education and Research Services Ltd London	1
University of Surrey Surrey	1
Design Council London	2
TWA-The Welding Institute Cambridge	2
Building Research Establishment Hertfordshire	1
Production Engineering Research Association Leicestershire	2
Trada-Timber Research and Development Association Buckinghamshire	4
Satra Footwear Technology Centre Northamptonshire	3
Warrington Fire Research Centre Cheshire	2
B.C.S.A. London	1
Shirley Institute Manchester	2
BCIRA Birmingham	1
B.C.R. Ltd Staffordshire	1
Paint Research Association Middlesex	2
Campden Food Preservation Research Association Wiltshire	1
British Food Manufacturing Industries Research Association Surrey	1
ERA Technology Surrey	2
British Textile Technology Group Leeds	1
Leatherhead Food Research Association Surrey	2
British Maritime Technology Ltd Tyne and Wear	1
Technology Policy Unit Aston Birmingham	1
NRDC London	1

Contractors	Projects
Sheffield City Council Sheffield	2
Cleveland County Council Cleveland	1
PE Inbucon West Midlands	1
Mr. McMullan Antrim	2
Total	123

Innovation and Technology Transfer

Mr. Cousins: To ask the Chancellor of the Duchy of Lancaster if he will name the British members of the consultative committee on innovation and technology transfer; and what proportion of the total EEC membership they comprise.

Mr. Forth: There are two members of my Department on the committee for innovation and technology transfer out of a total membership of twenty four. They are Mr. J. Niblett and Mr. M. Porter.

Manufacturing Industry

Mr. Austin Mitchell: To ask the Chancellor of the Duchy of Lancaster, further to his reply of 27 April, *Official Report,* columns *614-5,* concerning gross output of finished manufactures and imports of semi-manufactures, intermediate products and basic materials, whether he will provide comparable figures for clothing; and if he will add figures for 1973 and for exports.

Mr. Alan Clark: The available figures for gross output of finished manufactures for clothing follow. A split of trade into semi-manufactures, intermediate finished manufactures and basic materials is not appropriate as clothing is a finished manufacture for consumer use.

Gross output of finished manufactures: clothing[1] 1985 prices

	£ million
1970	5,023
1973	5,627
1979	5,844
1988	5,654

[1] Finished clothing is defined as clothing, hats and gloves, hosiery and other weft knitted goods (SIC[80] group 453 and activity 4,363).

Trade Statistics

Mr. Sillars: To ask the Chancellor of the Duchy of Lancaster if he will list the top 20 trading countries for the United Kingdom in each of the past 10 years.

Mr. Alan Clark: The information is in the following tables:
United Kingdom top 20 trading partners

1979
1. Germany
2. United States of America
3. France
4. Netherlands
5. Switzerland
6. Belgium/Luxembourg

7. Ireland
8. Italy
9. Sweden
10. Norway
11. Japan
12. Denmark
13. Canada
14. Saudi Arabia
15. Spain
16. Australia
17. South Africa
18. Soviet Union
19. Finland
20. Hong Kong

1980
1. Germany
2. United States of America
3. France
4. Netherlands
5. Switzerland
6. Belgium/Luxembourg
7. Ireland
8. Italy
9. Sweden
10. Saudi Arabia
11. Japan
12. Norway
13. Canada
14. Denmark
15. South Africa
16. Spain
17. Hong Kong
18. Nigeria
19. Finland
20. Australia

1981
1. United States of America
2. Germany
3. Netherlands
4. France
5. Ireland
6. Belgium/Luxembourg
7. Italy
8. Switzerland
9. Sweden
10. Saudi Arabia
11. Norway
12. Japan
13. Canada
14. Denmark
15. South Africa
16. Spain
17. Nigeria
18. Hong Kong
19. Finland
20. Australia

1982
1. United States of America
2. Germany
3. Netherlands
4. France
5. Belgium/Luxembourg
6. Ireland
7. Italy
8. Sweden
9. Japan
10. Norway
11. Switzerland
12. Denmark
13. Canada
14. South Africa
15. Spain
16. Hong Kong
17. Nigeria
18. Austrialia
19. Finland
20. Saudi Arabia

1983
1. United States of America
2. Germany
3. France
4. Netherlands
5. Belgium/Luxembourg
6. Italy
7. Ireland
8. Sweden
9. Japan
10. Norway
11. Switzerland
12. Denmark
13. Canada
14. Spain
15. South Africa
16. Hong Kong
17. Finland
18. Australia
19. Saudi Arabia
20. Nigeria

1984
1. United States of America
2. Germany
3. France
4. Netherlands
5. Belgium/Luxembourg
6. Italy
7. Ireland
8. Sweden
9. Norway
10. Japan
11. Switzerland
12. Spain
13. Denmark
14. Canada
15. Hong Kong
16. South Africa
17. Finland
18. Australia
19. Soviet Union
20. Saudi Arabia

1985
1. United States of America
2. Germany
3. France
4. Netherlands
5. Italy
6. Belgium/Luxembourg
7. Ireland
8. Norway
9. Sweden
10. Japan
11. Switzerland
12. Spain
13. Canada
14. Denmark
15. Hong Kong
16. Australia
17. Finland
18. South Africa
19. Nigeria
20. India

1986
1. Germany
2. United States of America
3. France
4. Netherlands
5. Belgium/Luxembourg
6. Italy
7. Ireland
8. Japan
9. Sweden
10. Switzerland
11. Norway
12. Spain

13. Canada
14. Denmark
15. Hong Kong
16. Finland
17. Australia
18. South Africa
19. Saudi Arabia
20. India

1987
 1. Germany
 2. United States of America
 3. France
 4. Netherlands
 5. Italy
 6. Belgium/Luxembourg
 7. Ireland
 8. Japan
 9. Sweden
10. Switzerland
11. Norway
12. Spain
13. Canada
14. Denmark
15. Hong Kong
16. Finland
17. Saudi Arabia
18. Australia
19. India
20. South Africa

1988
 1. Germany
 2. United States of America
 3. France
 4. Netherlands
 5. Italy
 6. Belgium/Luxembourg
 7. Japan
 8. Ireland
 9. Switzerland
10. Sweden
11. Spain
12. Norway
13. Canada
14. Denmark
15. Hong Kong
16. Finland
17. Australia
18. South Africa
19. Portugal
20. Saudi Arabia

Note: In descending order, based on value of exports plus imports.

Source: OECD Series A.

Iraq

Mr. Wigley: To ask the Chancellor of the Duchy of Lancaster what was the value of *(a)* United Kingdom exports to Iraq, and *(b)* United Kingdom imports from Iraq in the last year for which information is available.

Mr. Alan Clark: The provisional figures for 1988 are *(a)* United Kingdom exports to Iraq £412·1 million; *(b)* United Kingdom imports from Iraq £43·4 million.

Textile Products

Mr. Vaz: To ask the Chancellor of the Duchy of Lancaster what proportion of the United Kingdom's trade deficit relates to trade in textile products; and if he will make a statement on the extent of import penetration in this sector of the economy.

Mr. Alan Clark: The crude deficit on trade in textiles in 1987 was £1,816·3 million compared with an overall crude deficit of £24,177·5 million. Comparable figures for 1988

show crude deficits of £1,921·4 million and £24,936·7 million. Import penetration for textiles in 1987—the latest year for which figures are available—was 48 per cent.

Manufacturing Investment (North-East)

Mr. Mullin: To ask the Chancellor of the Duchy of Lancaster what has been the level of manufacturing investment in the north-east for each of the last 10 years, giving 1979 as 100.

Mr. Atkins: No regional breakdown of manufacturing investment for 1988 is yet available. The required information for the period 1979 to 1987 is shown in the following table:

Manufacturing investment[1] in the North-East[2], at, constant prices, as a percentage of 1979 level

	North-East
1979	100
1980	66
1981	42
1982	41
1983	41
1984	47
1985	59
1986	50
1987	53

[1] Excluding expenditure on assets leased from the financial industries.

[2] The North-East is not a standard region of the United Kingdom but can be defined as the North less Cumbria. It comprises Cleveland, Durham, Northumberland and Tyne and Wear.

Source: Annual census of production.

Listening Devices

Mr. Cran: To ask the Chancellor of the Duchy of Lancaster whether electronic surveillance listening devices are used by his Department or by any organisation or agency acting on its behalf; and if he will make a statement.

Mr. Forth: My Department's radiocommunications division regularly monitors the radio spectrum to establish patterns of use, to trace radio interference and to assist in the management of radio services, in keeping with its licensing function under the Wireless Telegraphy Acts. Commercially available radio receivers are used for monitoring purposes.

EC (Footwear Imports)

Mr. Henderson: To ask the Chancellor of the Duchy of Lancaster if he will take steps to initiate talks at European Community level between non-European Community producers and European Community members on the regulation of footwear imports to the European Community; and if he will seek to establish an agreement for footwear similar to the multi-fibre arrangement in textiles and clothing.

Mr. Alan Clark: The United Kingdom already operates a range of quantitative restrictions on imports of footwear from Eastern Europe and China. EC member states will need to consider the findings of the Commission's Community-wide investigation into imports of footwear from Taiwan and South Korea before deciding what further action might be appropriate. We have asked the

Commission to look in particular at the effect of imports into the United Kingdom from Taiwan of women's made-to-order footwear.

Mr. Henderson: To ask the Chancellor of the Duchy of Lancaster what steps he has taken to seek an early decision from the European Commission arising out of its investigations into the injury caused to the United Kingdom footwear industry by excessive imports from Korea and Taiwan.

Mr. Clark: I have written to Commissioner Andriessen seeking an early decision on the need for safeguard action on imports into the United Kingdom of women's made-to-order footwear from Taiwan. The Commission is anxious, however, not to pre-judge the outcome of the Community-wide investigation into imports of footwear from South Korea and Taiwan. Commissioner Andriessen has assured me that the Commission will conclude their investigation as quickly as possible. I will of course consider what action is appropriate once the Commission's recommendations are known.

Post Office Users National Council

Mr. Bowis: To ask the Chancellor of the Duchy of Lancaster if he has received the latest report of the Post Office Users National Council; and if he will make a statement.

Mr. Forth: I receive all Post Office Users National Council reports. My right hon. Friend the Chancellor of the Duchy of Lancaster referred to its latest joint announcement with Royal Mail Letters in his reply to my hon. Friend the Member for Gedling (Mr. Mitchell) on 25 May (*Official Report,* column *651*).

Institute of Logistics and Distribution Management

Mr. Bowis: To ask the Chancellor of the Duchy of Lancaster if he has received a copy of the most recent report of the Institute of Logistics and Distribution Management ; and if he will make a statement.

Mr. Forth: I believe the question refers to the report prepared by the Institute of Logistics and Distribution Management on "The Market for Express Goods Services between the UK and Europe, North America and the Far East". The British Overseas Trade Board decided that there were good reasons to examine in detail aspects of the fast growing express freight market for manufactured goods and so funded this study. My Department is considering the report and views on it from interested parties but has not yet reached conclusions on it or on follow-up action.

Postal Monopoly (LSE Report)

Mr. Bowis: To ask the Chancellor of the Duchy of Lancaster if he has received a copy of the report on the postal monopoly, published in September 1988 by the London School of Economics; and if he will make a statement.

Mr. Forth: My Department has received the report on the Post Office's letter monopoly by Saul Estrin and David de Meza of the London School of Economics. We keep all the options for change in the letter monopoly under review, including those put forward in the LSE report.

Post Office Counters

Mr. Bowis: To ask the Chancellor of the Duchy of Lancaster if he will announce the timetable for the privatisation of Post Office Counters.

Mr. Forth: We have no present plans for the sale of Post Office Counters Ltd. The Post Office has, however, announced plans for regrading 250 Crown post offices to sub-offices, which will mean increased private investment in the post office network. Sub-offices already make up most of the counters network.

Post Office Parcels

Mr. Bowis: To ask the Chancellor of the Duchy of Lancaster if he will announce the timetable for the privatisation of Post Office Parcels.

Mr. Forth: We have no present plans for privatisation of Royal Mail Parcels.

Post Office Board

Mr. Bowis: To ask the Chancellor of the Duchy of Lancaster if he will list the salaries and review dates of each member of the Post Office Board, with the date and length of his appointment.

Mr. Forth: The Post Office annual report and accounts lists the names of the members of the Post Office Board and the years of their appointment, and also gives the number in different ranges of remuneration. Their remuneration is revised with effect from 1 April of each year. Appointments are made for periods of up to five years.

CEPT (EC Paper)

Mr. Bowis: To ask the Chancellor of the Duchy of Lancaster if he will place in the Library a copy of the paper submitted to the European Commission by members of the CEPT, as mentioned in his oral reply to the hon. Member for Battersea of 17 May, *Official Report,* column 313.

Mr. Forth: No, CEPT working papers are restricted to the membership. The rules of the CEPT do not allow such documents to be disseminated and I am therefore unable to place them in the Library.

Post Office

Mr. Bowis: To ask the Chancellor of the Duchy of Lancaster to what extent the Post Office subsidises its competitive services by its monopoly services.

Mr. Forth: There is no subsidy from the Post Office's monopoly services to its competitive services.

Remail

Mr. Bowis: To ask the Chancellor of the Duchy of Lancaster what action he has taken to support international express carriers regarding Remail.

Mr. Forth: None. I am, however, aware that the EC is investigating a complaint by courier services about postal administrations.

Postal Service

Mr. Bowis: To ask the Chancellor of the Duchy of Lancaster what aspects of the postal service have been investigated by the Monopolies and Mergers Commission in each year from 1979.

Mr. Forth: Since 1979 the Monopolies and Mergers Commission has published four reports on aspects of the postal service. These were:

1979 Inner London letter post.
1984 The Post Office letter post service.
1986 Post Office procurement activities.
1988 Post Office counters services.

Mr. Bowis: To ask the Chancellor of the Duchy of Lancaster what evidence he has submitted to the European Commission on European postal services from 1992.

Mr. Forth: None.

Courier Services (Anti-competitive Practices)

Mr. Bowis: To ask the Chancellor of the Duchy of Lancaster what evidence he has submitted to the European Commission on the formal complaint made by private courier services about anti-competitive practices by postal administrations.

Mr. Forth: None. It is for the Post Office to reply to questions put to it by the European Commission.

Letter Deliveries

Mr. Bowis: To ask the Chancellor of the Duchy of Lancaster what information he has as to how many letters and what percentage of letters, posted first class, fail to arrive the following delivery day.

Mr. Forth: The Post Office's new end to end monitoring system, which records results separately for each district by destination, shows that for 1988-89 the percentage of first class letters not delivered the day after posting varied widely between districts. The range was:

	per cent.
Delivery within district of posting	6-36
Delivery to neighbouring districts	8-41
Delivery to distant districts (excluding Belfast)	20-50

The detailed figures for each district, which were published by the Post Office on 25 May, have been placed in the Libraries.

Public and Private Postal Services Working Group

Mr. Bowis: To ask the Chancellor of the Duchy of Lancaster when his Department last chaired a meeting of the public and private postal services working group; what was discussed; when it will next meet; and whether representatives of the Institute of Logistics and Distribution Management will attend.

Mr. Forth: The working group chaired by my Department to which I believe my hon. Friend refers is a technical working party of officials and representatives of the industries concerned with Her Majesty's Customs" treatment of express consignments. Its meetings are private and it would be inappropriate to publish details. The Institute of Logistics and Distribution Management is not represented.

Postal Officials (New Zealand)

Mr. Bowis: To ask the Chancellor of the Duchy of Lancaster when his Department last met postal officials from New Zealand; what matters were discussed; and if he will make a statement.

Mr. Forth: My officials last met postal representatives from New Zealand at the Executive Council meeting of the Universal Postal Union (UPU) in April of this year. A wide range of postal topics was disccussed between the representatives of about 40 postal administrations.

Hearing Aids

Mr. Vaz: To ask the Chancellor of the Duchy of Lancaster if he will refer to the Director-General of Fair Trading claims made in advertisements by RRR Ltd. that one of its products can regain crystal clear hearing; and if he will make a statement.

Mr. Forth: Advertisements for hearing aids are covered by specific provisions in the British code of advertising practice, which is administered by the Advertising Standards Authority. False statements in advertisements are covered by the provisions of the Trade Descriptions Act 1968. The Control of Misleading Advertisements Regulations 1988 enable the Director-General of Fair Trading to seek a court injunction to prevent the publication of a misleading advertisement, where other means of control have failed.

I have no powers to intervene in the way in which the director-general performs his functions under the regulations. The hon. Member may wish to write to the Advertising Standards Authority or, if he prefers, to the Director-General of Fair Trading.

Mr. Vaz: To ask the Chancellor of the Duchy of Lancaster whether he has any plans to implement stricter regulations for the dispensing of hearing aids in the private sector to protect the consumer.

Mr. Forth: The Hearing Aid Council (Amendment) Bill sponsored by the hon. Member for Ynys Môn (Mr. Jones), which the Government supports, would achieve stricter controls over the dispensing of hearing aids for the benefit of hearing-impaired consumers.

Ivory

Mr. Tony Banks: To ask the Chancellor of the Duchy of Lancaster how much worked and raw ivory has been exported to Dubai in each of the last five years.

Mr. Alan Clark: There has been no export of worked or raw ivory to Dubai in any of the last five years.

Finished Manufactures

Mr. Austin Mitchell: To ask the Chancellor of the Duchy of Lancaster, further to his reply to the hon. Member for Great Grimsby of 27 April, *Official Report,* columns *615-16,* concerning trade in finished manufactures with the United States of America, whether he will provide the correlation co-efficient between the change in the United States of America share of United Kingdom exports lagged by one year after the change in relative export unit values in United States dollars.

Mr. Alan Clark: The correlation coefficient is negative with a value of 0·2.

Mr. Austin Mitchell: To ask the Chancellor of the Duchy of Lancaster, pursuant to his reply to the hon. Member for Great Grimsby of 27 April, *Official Report,* columns 614-5, concerning gross output of finished manufactures and imports of semi-manufactures, intermediate products and basic materials, whether he will provide comparable figures for finished textiles, including man-made fibres with other fibres as basic materials; and if he will add figures for 1973 and for exports.

Mr. Alan Clark: The available figures are given in the tables. Trade figures at 1985 prices are not available at the required level of detail. Current price data are shown instead.

Gross output of finished manufactures: textiles[1] 1985 prices

	£ million
1970	[2]—
1973	2,039
1979	1,833
1988	2,011

[1] Finished textiles is defined as carpets and other textile floor coverings, household and made-up textiles (SIC[80] groups 438 and 455).

[2] Not available.

Exports and imports: textiles OTS basis, current prices

	[1]Semi-manufactures		[2]Intermediate finished manufactures		[3]Basic materials	
	exports £ million	imports £ million	exports £ million	imports £ million	exports £ million	imports £ million
1970	335·9	217·5	—	—	96·5	183·7
1973	485·4	431·5	—	—	172·1	322·2
1979	1,093·0	1,413·4	—	—	315·7	475·5
1988	1,615·2	2,965·5	—	—	439·5	688·4

[1] Semi-manufactured textiles are defined as division 65 of SITC less made-up articles (658) and floor coverings (659).

[2] Intermediate finished manufactures are not appropriate to textiles.

[3] Basic materials for textiles are defined as division 26 of SITC (textile fibres).

Hand-held Video Cameras

Mr. Oppenheim: To ask the Chancellor of the Duchy of Lancaster what action the Government are taking concerning the European Commission's proposal to increase the tariff on compact hand-held video cameras from 4·9 per cent. to 14 per cent.

Mr. Alan Clark: Neither the United Kingdom nor any other member state, supported the Commission proposal. It has therefore been withdrawn.

Tariffs

Mr. Oppenheim: To ask the Chancellor of the Duchy of Lancaster whether *(a)* the United Kingdom or *(b)* the EEC maintain tariffs on any products where there are no idigenous industries to protect.

Mr. Alan Clark: The United Kingdom applies the common Customs tariff of the European Community. This includes duties on goods not produced in the Community.

Iron and Steel Imports

Mr. Caborn: To ask the Chancellor of the Duchy of Lancaster how many applications the Department of Trade and Industry import licensing board received from traders wishing to exclude existing contracts from the import prohibition on iron and steel from South Africa set out in NTI2097; how many applications were approved; what was the total value of approved applications; what were the dates of entry into such contracts; and how long they will run.

Mr. Alan Clark *[holding answer 26 May 1989]:* Records are kept of licences issued, not of applications. Since 1 January 1987, 377 licences have been issued. Allowing for licences returned unused, the total quantity licensed was 66,187 tonnes. Details for 1986 could be provided only at disproportionate expense.

Information relating to contract terms is provided in confidence by applicants.

Mr. Caborn: To ask the Chancellor of the Duchy of Lancaster what quantity and value of iron and steel goods in each of the commodity categories described in Notice to Importers 2097 and 2180 were imported in each month (i) from all sources and (ii) from South Africa, in the period since September 1986; and what was South Africa's ranking among all sources.

Mr. Alan Clark *[holding answer 26 May 1989]:* The information requested is not readily available, and could be provided only at disproportionate cost.

SOCIAL SECURITY

State Pension Age

Mr. Steel: To ask the Secretary of State for Social Security if he will make a statement on the progress of negotiations with the European Commission and other member states on the state pension age.

Mr. Peter Lloyd: The proposal for a Council directive "completing the implementation of equal treatment for men and women in statutory and occupational social security schemes" was first tabled in October 1987. Since March 1989 there have been three working group meetings of officials from member states in Brussels and the draft directive was also discussed at the informal meeting of Ministers at Toledo on 28 April which I attended. While progress has been made there still remain a number of outstanding problems. Negotiations are continuing to see how these might best be resolved so as to ensure unanimous agreement by member states.

Deaf-blind People

Mr. Hannam: To ask the Secretary of State for Social Security (1) how many deaf-blind people are currently in receipt of the mobility allowance; how many have appealed after an initial refusal; and how many have succeeded on appeal.

(2) what is the estimated cost of extending the mobility allowance to *(a)* all deaf-blind people, and *(b)* deaf-blind people between the age of five and 75 years.

Mr. Scott: I regret that we do not collect information about the number of deaf-blind people who have claimed or who are in receipt of mobility allowance. In view of this and the lack of information about the number of deaf-blind people in the population, it is not possible to provide a reliable estimate of the cost of making the allowance available specifically for deaf-blind people.

Community Care Grants

Mr. Snape: To ask the Secretary of State for Social Security if he will list in the *Official Report* the community care grants expenditure in respect of the Department of Social Security offices in Smethwick and West Bromwich for the year 1988-89; what percentage these figures are of the total amount of community care grants allocations for those offices in Smethwick and West Bromwich for the year 1988-89; and what arrangements are made so far as the disposal of the surplus expenditure for 1988-89 is concerned.

Mr. Peter Lloyd: The 1988-89 outturn data for individual local offices will be placed in the Library shortly.

Local office allocations are made for a financial year. Unspent balances at the end of a financial year are not available for expenditure in the following year.

Income Support Claimants

Mr. Robin Cook: To ask the Secretary of State for Social Security if he will list the number of income support claimants for each Department of Social Security office.

Mr. Peter Lloyd: The latest information available, for 28 February 1989, has been placed in the Library. The source of the information, which is provisional and subject to amendment, is the quarterly count of cases in action which may include some cases not actually in receipt of benefit.

Community Charge

Mr. David Marshall: To ask the Secretary of State for Social Security if he will extend the period of time in which people can apply for a poll tax rebate; and if he will make a statement.

Mr. Peter Lloyd: There are no plans to extend the 56-day limit. The regulations provide that people who claimed community charge benefit within 56 days of 1 April 1989, or who claim within 56 days of receiving their first community charge demand notice if this is later, will have their claim treated as if it had been made on 1 April 1989 provided that they were liable for the charge from that date and the appropriate authority is satisfied that any delay in issuing the demand notice was not caused by the claimant's attempts to evade payment of the charge. The 56-day period was arrived at following discussion with the Convention of Scottish Local Authorities. It has been extensively publicised. It represents a real concession to the

concerns expressed and is a significant departure from the principle that benefit cannot normally be awarded until it has been claimed. The 56 days allow reasonable time for the making of claims, even where people may not have claimed benefit before.

Mr. Blunkett: To ask the Secretary of State for Social Security if he will publish *(a)* his latest estimates of how many people in England and Wales will be entitled to community charge rebate, and *(b)* the expected level of take-up.

Mr. Peter Lloyd: I regret that no estimates are available of the numbers of people who might be entitled to community charge rebate if they were to claim it, so it is not possible to derive an estimated level of take up. Estimates of the numbers of people expected to receive it were given in my hon. Friend's reply to the hon. Member for Sunderland, North (Mr. Clay) on 19 October 1988 at columns *897-8*. Revised estimates will be available in due course.

AIDS

Mr. Alfred Morris: To ask the Secretary of State for Social Security what reply he has sent to the letter from ACT-UP delivered to him on 18 May; what action he is taking to ensure that all people with AIDS or ARC are able to afford the food recommended to them by their doctors; and if he will make a statement.

Mr. Scott: A copy of my reply to the letter from ACT-UP which was handed to their representative on 22 May has been forwarded to the right hon. Member. We will be giving careful consideration to the implications for benefits of the results of all the OPCS surveys. We welcome the views of interested groups such as ACT-UP on those results and their implications.

Listening Devices

Mr. Cran: To ask the Secretary of State for Social Security whether electronic surveillance listening devices are used by his Department or by any organisation or agency acting on its behalf; and if he will make a statement.

Mr. Peter Lloyd: No.

"Our Business is Service"

Mrs. Beckett: To ask the Secretary of State for Social Security what was the cost of publishing the leaflet entitled "Our Business is Service".

Mr. Peter Lloyd: I refer the hon. Member to my reply to the hon. Member for Newham, South (Mr. Spearing) on 26 May at columns *749-50*.

Budgeting Loans and Community Care Grants

Mr. Allen: To ask the Secretary of State for Social Security what percentage of *(a)* budgeting loans and *(b)* community care grants were awarded to each of the 15 client groups defined by his Department for (i) the East Midlands region and (ii) each of the offices serving the Nottingham, North constituency.

Mr. Peter Lloyd: I regret that the information can be obtained only at disproportionate cost.

Family Credit

Mr. Battle: To ask the Secretary of State for Social Security whether the revised estimate for family credit take-up by caseload included the estimated number of families entitled to family credit due to the freeze in the child benefit rate.

Mr. Peter Lloyd: The latest estimate relates to 1988 only. It is based on an examination of family expenditure survey returns for April to December 1988 and therefore has regard to the child benefit rates applicable at that time.

Benefits

Mr. Chris Smith: To ask the Secretary of State for Social Security how many *(a)* families and *(b)* children are in receipt of means tested benefits broken down into family credit, income support and housing benefit as a result of the freeze in child benefit, taking into account the new estimates of the take-up of family credit.

Mr. Peter Lloyd *[holding answer 9 May 1989]:* Estimates are only available on the caseload assumptions in the Public Expenditure White Paper (Cm. 615). They are based on combined 1985 and 1986 family expenditure survey data uprated to reflect the position in 1989-90. Estimates of this kind are particularly uncertain because of small sample sizes. Bearing these factors in mind, it is possible that an extra 15,000 families (with perhaps 30,000 children) are now claiming family credit because child benefit was not uprated in April 1989. The number of extra families receiving income support and housing benefit are likely to have increased by about 5,000 (with perhaps 10,000 children).

ENVIRONMENT

Archaeological Investigations

Ms. Walley: To ask the Secretary of State for the Environment if he will introduce statutory controls to require developers to undertake archaeological investigations.

Mrs. Virginia Bottomley: Many developers already contribute voluntarily to archaeological investigations before development. Where a site is scheduled, archaeological evaluations may be required before an application for scheduled monument consent can be determined, or an opportunity for excavation may be required as a condition of consent. Local planning authorities may in some circumstances require further information about the archaeological implications of development proposals before they determine a planning application. I refer the hon. Member to the answer I gave to my hon. Friend the Member for Dulwich (Mr. Bowden) on 24 May at column *602* about our proposals to issue guidance on such matters.

Water Undertakings

Mr. Austin Mitchell: To ask the Secretary of State for the Environment, further to his reply of 27 April, *Official Report,* column *522,* concerning installing water treatment plant to meet EEC standards, whether he will publish in the *Official Report* the sum of the initial projections together with his view of what constitutes a reasonable return capital on capital invested in water undertakings.

Mr. Howard: Projections of costs are still under discussion with individual water undertakers. We are also still considering the rate of return appropriate for water and sewerage undertakers.

Historic Buildings

Mr. Faulds: To ask the Secretary of State for the Environment whether lists of historic buildings have yet been fully compiled.

Mrs. Virginia Bottomley: The national resurvey of listed buildings, which began in 1970, is virtually complete. Three areas have still to be resurveyed: Isle of Lundy; the parishes of Bracebridge Heath, Canwick, Heighinton, Washingborough in Lincolnshire; and the parish of Southwell in Nottinghamshire, and six areas are in the process of being resurveyed. A further 50 lists are being prepared for publication. To date a total of 1,757 resurvey lists have been published. Some of the lists produced during the early years of the resurvey have been found to be deficient in various respects. English Heritage will be reviewing them over the next few years.

Commercial Premises

Mr. Fraser: To ask the Secretary of State for the Environment whether, in the light of the alteration of valuation lists for commercial premises, he intends to make regulations revising the basis of calculation for compensation to tenants under part 2 of the Landlord and Tenant Act 1954.

Mr. Chope: Yes.

Planning

Mr. Heddle: To ask the Secretary of State for the Environment if he will make a statement on the matter of B1 planning consents in general following the recent High Court case, London borough of Camden *v.* Department of the Environment, and on local authorities' powers to attach conditions to such consents in particular.

Mr. Howard: I refer my hon. Friend to the reply I gave to my hon. Friend the Member for Erith and Crayford (Mr. Evennett) on 11 May at column *521.* I do not believe the recent High Court judgment is inconsistent with the Government's policy in relation to the "business" use class.

South Yorkshire Valuation and Community Charge Tribunal (Members)

Mr. Redmond: To ask the Secretary of State for the Environment if he will list by name and nominating body the current serving members of the South Yorkshire valuation and community charge tribunal.

Mr. Gummer: The following people are all members of the South Yorkshire valuation and community charge tribunal.

Members appointed by Barnsley metropolitan borough council:
Mrs. A. Bailey; Mrs. N. Collett; Councillor T. Dixon; Mr. P. Doyle; Councillor Mrs. C. Evans; Councillor B. G. Goodard; Mr. M. Harper; Councillor Mrs. M. Harrison; Mr. S. Hepworth JP; Mr. F. Hollins; Mrs. N. Hollins JP; Mr. J. Marsden; Mr. D. Roberts; Mrs. P. Smith; Mr. A. Tucker; Mr. A. Vodden.

Members appointed by Doncaster metropolitan borough council:

Mr. M. Burns; Councillor B. Cassley JP; Mr. M. Collins; Mr. H. Dutton; Councillor G. Gallimore JP; Mr. H. Gladders; Mr. A. Greening; Mr. C. Griggs; Councillor A. Grimson JP; Councillor K. S. Judge; Councillor A. Lanaghan; Mr. M. McCoy; Councillor G. M. McDade JP; Miss E. Plumb; Councillor C. W. Verrill; Mr. C. Wedd.

Members appointed by Rotherham metropolitan borough council:

Mr. D. W. Dale; Mr. A. M. Davies JP; Mr. J. P. Dolbon; Mrs. I. Farren; Mrs. A. Jarvis; Mr. A. Kiddy; Mr. R. H. Noble; Mr. R. S. Russell; Councillor Miss M. Sides; Mr. P. Thirlwall; Mr. V. M. Thornes; Councillor B. Walker; Councillor S. Walker; Councillor G. Whelbourn; Mr. B. Williams; Councillor W. Winder.

Members appointed by Sheffield metropolitan district council:

Mr. F. W. Adams; Mrs. M. Burrow; Councillor J. A. Butler; Mr. J. M. Davey; Mr. J. G. Marshall; Mr. M. Nicholson; Mr. C. Oates; Mrs. D. Podlesny; Mrs. G. L. Randell; Councillor Mrs. E. Smith; Mr. M. E. Smith; Mr. G. A. Winter; Mr. P. E. Wood.

Waste Disposal

Mr. Redmond: To ask the Secretary of State for the Environment if he will list the sites in the three counties of Yorkshire, and in Humberside which are licensed to dispose of *(a)* radioactive waste, *(b)* special waste, and *(c)* clinical waste.

Mrs. Virginia Bottomley: I refer the hon. Member to the Department's "List of premises in England and Wales currently authorised under the Radioactive Substances Act 1960 to dispose of radioactive waste" which includes premises in the three counties of Yorkshire and Humberside. A copy of this list is in the Library of the House. The numbers of sites in these counties licensed for the disposal of other wastes are listed below. Information on the types of waste licensed for disposal is held by the appropriate waste disposal authority, which is required to maintain a public register.

	Number
North Yorkshire	118
South Yorkshire	257
West Yorkshire	443
Humberside	154

Steel-framed Houses

Mr. Allen: To ask the Secretary of State for the Environment if he will list those constituencies where he has information that there are steel-framed houses.

Mr. Trippier: Locations of steel-framed houses built in England, and reported to the Building Research Establishment, are listed in its 1987 report "Steel-framed and steel-clad houses: inspection and assessment". A copy is in the Library.

Capital Accounting

Mr. Mills: To ask the Secretary of State for the Environment when he plans to implement the proposals contained in the consultative document on capital accounting requiring local authorities to maintain a comprehensive inventory of assets.

Mr. Gummer: I assume that my hon. Friend is referring to the consultative implementation manual, "Capital Accounting in Local Authorities—The Way Forward", published by the Chartered Institute of Public Finance and Accountancy, the Association of County Councils, the Association of District Councils, and the Association of Metropolitan Authorities. This document is the responsibility of the bodies by which it was published and its implementation is a matter for the local authorities to whom its recommendations are addressed. I am sympathetic to the general approach set out in the manual.

Popplewell Report

Mr. Lester: To ask the Secretary of State for the Environment how many recommendations of the Popplewell report which bear on the responsibilities of his Department have not been implemented; what were those recommendations; and, in each case, what are the reasons they have not been acted upon.

Mr. Moynihan: None. In December 1986, the Home Office issued a revised version of the guide to safety at sports grounds. Chapter 11 of the document—"Fire Safety"—dealt, among other fire-related issues, with recommendation 10 of the Popplewell report. The technical content of the building regulations continues to be under review. Later this year, the Department will issue a consultation document covering all aspects of the building regulations as they relate to fire.

The Government's proposals for a football membership scheme (recommendation 15 of the Popplewell report) are contained in the Football Spectators Bill.

Water Pollution

Mr. Vaz: To ask the Secretary of State for the Environment how many times between 1985 and 1987 water sources in England and Wales were shown to exceed maximum admissible concentrations of pollutants.

Mr. Howard: This information is not held centrally.

Mr. Vaz: To ask the Secretary of State for the Environment on how many occasions in the period from May 1988 to May 1989 maximum admissible concentration levels have been exceeded in water supplies for Leicestershire.

Mr. Howard: I understand that water supplies for Leicestershire regularly complied with the EC drinking water directive in the period May 1988 to May 1989 except for water supplies serving a small part of north-west Leicestershire, which marginally exceeded the standard for magnesium. There were occasional breaches of the pesticide standard set in the EC directive. However, all were within levels considered acceptable by medical advisers.

Nature Conservancy Council

Mr. Vaz: To ask the Secretary of State for the Environment if he will make a further statement on proposals to privatise certain functions of the Nature Conservancy Council.

Mrs. Virginia Bottomley: I refer the hon. Member to the reply which I have given to the hon. Member for Wentworth (Mr. Hardy) today.

Riso Conference

Mr. Flynn: To ask the Secretary of State for the Environment what Ministers or officials of his Department will *(a)* be present, *(b)* present papers and *(c)* be involved in round-table discussion sessions at the Riso international conference on environmental models; emissions and consequences, to be held on 22 to 25 May in Denmark.

Mrs. Virginia Bottomley: One of the Department's principal scientific contractors, an expert on environment modelling, attended parts of the Riso meeting. He gave a paper and participated in discussions.

Ozone Layer

Mr. Flynn: To ask the Secretary of State for the Environment what was his Department's participation at the conference on protecting the ozone layer held in Finland on 2 May; what papers were presented by it; and if he will make a statement on the outcome of the conference.

Mrs. Virginia Bottomley: My right hon. Friend the Secretary of State attended the first meeting of the parties to the Montreal protocol in Helsinki. Copies of the United Kingdom national statement, and of the message from the London "Saving the Ozone Layer" conference, which he presented to the meeting, are available in the Library. The European Community's call, made in response to a United Kingdom initiative, for CFCs to be eliminated by the end of the century, was endorsed by the Governments attending the Helsinki meeting. We shall work towards amendment of the protocol to this effect at next year's second meeting of the parties in London.

"Health for All By The Year 2000"

Mr. Leighton: To ask the Secretary of State for the Environment whether he will ensure that rate support grant reflects the call for local authorities to invest in programmes to achieve the targets set in the "Health For All By The Year 2000" programme.

Mrs. Virginia Bottomley: It is for local authorities to decide to what extent the targets outlined in the WHO "Health For All By The Year 2000" programme should be reflected in their plans and priorities. Rate support grant is unhypothecated and provides support for local authority spending on all services.

Corby New Town

Mr. William Powell: To ask the Secretary of State for the Environment if he will list in the *Official Report* the total sum realised by sale of assets by the Commission for the New Towns in Corby for each year since 1979-80.

Mr. Trippier: The information is as follows:

Sums realised by the Commission for the New Towns for the sale of assets

Year	£ million	Corby
1979-80	6·43	—
1980-81	29·61	·952
1981-82	61·85	·580
1982-83	51·18	5·840
1983-84	55·25	2·517
1984-85	57·59	1·506
1985-86	78·67	1·826
1986-87	169·31	4·464
1987-88	216·66	10·564
[1]1988-89	334·00	17·414
	1,060·55	45·663

[1] Provisional.

Notes:

1. Figures do not include sums realised by development corporations prior to wind-up.

2. Figures are gross, before deduction of selling expenses.

Air Quality

Dr. Thomas: To ask the Secretary of State for the Environment (1) if he will be introducing measures to protect public health based on the World Health Organisation air quality guidelines for Europe 1987;

(2) whether his Department has assessed the World Health Organisation air quality guidelines for Europe 1987;

(3) whether the Government intend to introduce air quality standards for particulates and tropospheric ozone based on the World Health Organisation air quality guidelines for Europe 1987;

(4) whether the Government intend to introduce air quality standards for Britain for sodium dioxide and nitrous dioxide which are more stringent than EEC standards.

Mrs. Virginia Bottomley: Warren Spring Laboratory published a report—LR650 (AP)—in January 1988 comparing the available United Kingdom air quality data with the World Health Organisation guide values. WHO emphasises that these are not limit values but rather targets for improved air quality, to be considered in the context of prevailing exposure and environmental, social, economic and cultural conditions.

We continue to keep air quality under review in relation to the WHO guidelines and other environmental information. At present we see no reason to set more stringent limits in the United Kingdom than are generally applicable in the EC for sulphur dioxide, particulates and nitrogen dioxide. Nor do we have plans to set a standard for tropospheric ozone.

Acid Rain

Mr. Hoyle: To ask the Secretary of State for the Environment what are the most recent figures on the levels of acidification in rainfall *(a)* in Warrington, *(b)* the north-west and *(c)* the average for Britain as a whole.

Mrs. Virginia Bottomley: The data requested are provided for 1988 in the table. The United Kingdom average has been computed from 60 stations in the Department's acid rain network, the north-west average from seven stations and the Warrington value has been interpolated from nearby stations.

Annual mean precipitation weighted acidity in rainfall

Data region	u eq H+/litre	pH
United Kingdom	25	4·6
North-West	31	4·5
Warrington	33	4·5

Simplified Planning Zones

Mr. Cartwright: To ask the Secretary of State for the Environment how many applications for the establishment of simplified planning zones have been *(a)* received and *(b)* approved in (i) England and Wales and (ii) Greater London.

Mr. Chope: The adoption of simplified planning zones is handled locally. At present, two simplified planning zones have been adopted in England, none in Wales and none in Greater London.

Ports (Rating)

Mr. Neil Hamilton: To ask the Secretary of State for the Environment if he has completed his review of rating procedure for statutory and non-statutory ports; if he will publish the conclusions of the review; and if he will make a statement.

Mr. Gummer: Discussions with representatives of the ports about rating are continuing and we shall be making proposals later in the year.

Water Use

Mr. Hayward: To ask the Secretary of State for the Environment if there are any water use restrictions currently in operation.

Mr. Howard: This information is not held centrally.

Mr. Hayward: To ask the Secretary of State for the Environment what advice he is giving to water authorities and water users during the current dry spell.

Mr. Howard: Responsibility for action, including advising consumers, rests with the water undertakers. We are, however, monitoring water resources closely.

Water Stocks

Mr. Hayward: To ask the Secretary of State for the Environment in what regions of the United Kingdom impounded water stocks are below average.

Mr. Howard: Only in the Southern water authority's area are some impounded water stocks below normal.

Housing Associations

Mr. Soley: To ask the Secretary of State for the Environment what are his plans for full implementation of recommendations from the Public Accounts Committee on the control and funding of housing associations, in its 16th report of Session 1985-86, HC 108.

Mr. Trippier: Action taken and in hand on the Committee's recommendations is described in the report No. 312 by the Comptroller and Auditor General "Department of the Environment: Housing Association Grant", published on 13 April 1989.

Management and Maintenance

Mr. Soley: To ask the Secretary of State for the Environment if he will give the latest comparable information on the average level of spending on management and maintenance by *(a)* local authorities and *(b)* housing associations, in (i) Greater London, (ii) metropolitan districts and (iii) non-metropolitan districts in England and Wales.

Mr. Trippier: The latest available study comparing the management costs of local authorities and housing associations is in section 2 of "The Nature and Effectiveness of Housing Management in England" produced by the Centre for Housing Research at the university of Glasgow. This distinguishes metropolitan authorities including London boroughs from non-metropolitan authorities and national or regional housing associations from local housing associations. Copies of the report, which was published earlier this year, are in the Library.

Mr. Soley: To ask the Secretary of State for the Environment if he will give the latest estimates of the levels of expenditure on management and maintenance by local authorities that will take place in 1989-90, 1990-91 and 1991-92.

Mr. Trippier: I assume this is a reference to management and maintenance of local authority housing. This is a matter for the councils concerned.

Listening Devices

Mr. Cran: To ask the Secretary of State for the Environment whether electronic surveillance listening devices are used by his Department or by any organisation or agency acting on its behalf; and if he will make a statement.

Mr. Ridley: The Department does not possess or use any listening equipment for surveillance of its telephone network.

Community Charge

Mr. Blunkett: To ask the Secretary of State for the Environment if he will list all those newspapers contacted by his Department in connection with the Minister for Local Government's community charge articles.

Mr. Nellist: To ask the Secretary of State for the Environment if, further to his reply of 23 May to the hon. Member for Coventry, South-East, (Mr. Nellist) *Official Report,* column *488,* he will list the newspapers to which more than 500 articles were sent.

Mr. Gummer: I will write to the hon. Members with this information.

Mr. Madden: To ask the Secretary of State for the Environment how many local authorities have indicated that they will incorporate the whole or part of the contents of the leaflet, "The Community Charge: The So-Called Poll Tax: How It Will Work For You" in material they are to distribute; and if he will list them.

Mr. John Gummer *[holding answer 15 May 1989]:* The leaflet was not intended for incorporation into other information material although some local authorities have expressed an interest in using it in this way. However, it stands on its own as a concise, accurate and factual introduction to the community charge.

Nene Washes Site

Mr. Morley: To ask the Secretary of State for the Environment what conditions were attached to the offer of a grant by the Nature Conservancy Council to the Royal Society for the Protection of Birds for the purchase of 16·5 acres of lowland damp grassland within the Nene Washes site of special scientific interest near Whittlesey, Cambridgeshire to extend the existing Nene Washes Royal Society for the Protection of Birds reserve.

Mrs. Virginia Bottomley: After careful consideration the NCC decided that no offer of grant should be made in this instance.

Sewage Sludge (Dumping)

Mr. Colvin: To ask the Secretary of State for the Environment if he will make a statement about the blockade by the Greenpeace ship Moby Dick of the tanker Mancunium, due to be loaded with sewage sludge for dumping at sea, at the Slowhill Copse sewage works at Marchwood and about Her Majesty's Government's policy on the dumping of sewage sludge at sea.

Mr. Howard: On 23 May 1989, a vessel operated by Greenpeace UK Ltd. obstructed the departure of a vessel loaded with sewage sludge from Slowhill Copse sewage works of the Southern water authority for disposal at sea. Following an application to the High Court, an injunction was granted to the Southern water authority restraining Greenpeace from this or similar action.

I deplore action of this sort which in this case could itself have caused significant environmental problems. At present the United Kingdom disposes at sea each year of about 30 per cent. of a total of 1·2 million dry tonnes of sewage sludge. The basis of our policy in this area, as for other wastes, is to select the best practicable environmental option for each waste stream.

In the case of sea disposal, dumping operations require approval from my right hon. Friend the Minister for Agriculture, Fisheries and Food and his colleagues in Scotland and Northern Ireland and a licence is granted only where it is clear that no practicable alternative on land is available and it can be shown that there is no risk to the marine environment.

Community Charge (Nottingham)

Mr. Allen: To ask the Secretary of State for the Environment is he yet in receipt of information necessary to give the national community charge for the city of Nottingham for the year 1989-90.

Mr. Gummer: I refer the hon. Member to my reply to him on 9 May at column *386* and to the hon. Member for Sheffield Brightside (Mr. Blunkett) on 25 April at column *532.*

Severn Estuary

Mr. Stern: To ask the Secretary of State for the Environment what plans he has for safeguarding the outstanding natural interest of the Severn estuary, in the light of current development pressures; whether he plans further designations and safeguards in the wider Severn estuary; and if he will make a statement.

Mrs. Virginia Bottomley: The Severn estuary has been notified by the Nature Conservancy Council as a site of special scientific interest under section 28 of the Wildlife and Countryside Act 1981. This notification provides the site with legal protection from activities likely to harm its nature conservation interests and ensures that the views of the NCC are taken into account when development proposals affecting the site are being considered.

Two parts of the estuary, Bridgewater Bay and the upper Severn have been designated as special protection areas for birds under the European Communities directive 79/409/EEC and/or as wetlands of international importance under the Ramsar convention. The whole estuary has also been indentified by NCC as having the potential for designation under the directive and the convention but no formal case for further designations has yet been submitted.

Classification as an SPA imposes stringent criteria, above and beyond those related to SSSI notification, that must be applied when development proposals are being considered; these criteria are set out in detail in DOE circular 27/87—"Nature Conservation". The circular makes it clear that, for planning purposes, potential SPAs should be treated in the same manner as formally designated sites.

Beaches

Mr. John Garrett: To ask the Secretary of State for the Environment (1) if he will list in the *Official Report* the names and locations of all United Kingdom beaches which in 1988 failed to comply with the EEC bathing water directive 76/160 for enteroviruses and salmonella;

(2) if he will list in the *Official Report,* all United Kingdom beaches which were tested in 1988 for compliance with the EEC bathing water directive 76/160 for enteroviruses and salmonella.

Mr. Howard: I refer the hon. Member to the answer I gave him on 18 May at column *265.*

Mr. Speller: To ask the Secretary of State for the Environment how many sources of pollution into the Bristol channel he can identify; and if he will set a target date of 1 January 1993 for the adjacent beaches to meet European Community bathing water standards.

Mr. Howard *[holding answer 25 May 1989]:* This information is not held centrally in the Department but information on consented discharges is available on the public registers held by water authorities. We are currently discussing with water authorities, programmes for improving bathing waters; however, individual schemes necessarily take up a number of years from initial feasibility studies to completion, and may involve major engineering work. Consequently, I am unable to set a target date of 1 January for all the waters along the Bristol channel to meet EC standards.

North West Water (Land Development Officer)

Mr. Pike: To ask the Secretary of State for the Environment what consideration he has given to the implications of the advertisement by North West Water for a senior management post for a land development officer; and if he will make a statement.

Mr. Howard: The notice was an internal staff circular related to the making permanent of a temporary post concerned with disposal of surplus land. The disposal of surplus land by public bodies is well-established Government policy. I would expect the future water plc to pursue the disposal of surplus land. As I have recently announced, provision is being made through the Water Bill for the benefit of proceeds of land disposals to be shared between customers and shareholders.

Housing Costs

Mr. David Nicholson: To ask the Secretary of State for the Environment if he will list, in the *Official Report,* the permitted expenditure limits for house building, repair, renovation and maintenance and the actual expenditure, for each of the Somerset district councils, in the years 1986-87, 1987-88 and 1988-89.

Mr. Trippier *[holding answer 25 May 1989]:* It is for each local authority to decide how its resources should be targeted; the actual expenditure figures are as follows:

Table 1
Somerset—1986-87 outturn £'000

	New build (including land)	Repair and maintenance	Renovation
Mendip	2,218	2,545	2,926
Sedgemoor	2,114	2,061	1,263
Taunton Deane	822	3,190	1,893
West Somerset	806	737	443
South Somerset	2,046	2,493	1,424

Table 2
Somerset—1987-88 provisional outturn £'000

	New build (including land)	Repair and maintenance	Renovation
Mendip	1,005	1,872	1,435
Sedgemoor	1,682	2,452	2,066
Taunton Deane	718	3,033	2,079
West Somerset	894	425	492
South Somerset	2,065	3,818	1,377

Table 3
Somerset—1988-89 estimated outturn £'000

	New build (including land)	Repair and maintenance	Renovation
Mendip	1,010	3,004	1,239
Sedgemoor	3,621	4,078	2,379
Taunton Deane	2,848	4,742	4,085
West Somerset	1,050	650	770
South Somerset	1,732	4,571	3,834

Gipsies

Mr. Wolfson: To ask the Secretary of State for the Environment if he will provide comparative figures for the number of gipsy families known to be in England and Wales at present, five years and 10 years ago.

Mr. Trippier *[holding answer 25 May 1989]:* Accurate information on the numbers of gipsy families is not available. The numbers of gipsy caravans in England as recorded by the twice-yearly counts carried out by the Department for the periods in question were:

	Number
January 1989	11,321
January 1984	9,929
January 1979	8,358

The Welsh Office has its own arrangements for monitoring numbers of gipsies in Wales.

Endangered Species

Mr. Hardy: To ask the Secretary of State for the Environment what action he is taking to prevent trade in endangered species in the United Kingdom; and if he has any plans for new initiatives.

Mrs. Virginia Bottomley *[holding answer 25 May 1989]:* The United Kingdom complies fully with the requirements of EC regulation 3626 which implements the convention on international trade in endangered species within the European Community. Our most recent initiative is to call for concerted European support for a total ban on trade in new ivory. We shall do this at the next Council meeting of Environment Ministers on 8 June.

Mr. Hardy: To ask the Secretary of State for the Environment what quantity of ivory from the African elephant is currently held or has recently been held at Heathrow airport awaiting retrospective import clearance; what information he has as to whether this ivory was obtained in breach of the convention on international trade on endangered species; and what action he proposes to take.

Mrs. Virginia Bottomley *[holding answer 25 May 1989]:* I understand from Her Majesty's Customs and Excise that details of individual consignments cannot be released where Customs action is not yet completed.

Mr. Hardy: To ask the Secretary of State for the Environment why he recently allowed the delivery to the United Kingdom of several tons of African elephant tusks originally obtained in contravention of the convention on international trade on endangered species.

Mrs. Virginia Bottomley *[holding answer 25 May 1989]:* The Department has allowed no such delivery.

Under the convention on international trade in endangered species it is the Department's responsibility to issue import and export permits for ivory. We do so only with the agreement of the CITES secretariat ivory unit in Lausanne, Switzerland and when we are satisfied that the requirements of EC regulation 3226/82 have been met.

Nature Reserves

Mr. Hardy: To ask the Secretary of State for the Environment when he proposes to secure the sale of nationally owned nature reserves; which reserves may be sold during the next two years; and what evidence he has of public support for such disposal.

Mrs. Virginia Bottomley *[holding answer 25 May 1989]:* The Nature Conservancy Council is reviewing policy for NNRs. In response to the council's preliminary report published on 3 May, the Government welcomed the suggestion of increased participation by the voluntary and private sectors in reserve ownership and management. We also recognised that there would be a need for some reserves to be held in the NCC's ownership, and assurances that the ownership and management of sites could only be transferred on condition that there continued to be adequate safeguards to ensure the conservation of their wildlife or geological interest. I understand that the council is planning to submit proposals later this year.

The majority of national nature reserves are already owned and managed for conservation by private landowners or voluntary bodies.

Radioactive Waste

Mr. John Evans: To ask the Secretary of State for the Environment, regarding storage of radioactive waste for which there is presently no disposal site available, whether it is Government policy that radioactive waste shall be stored at the site at which the waste is created in the case of Crown-exempt nuclear operators including the Ministry of Defence.

Mrs. Virginia Bottomley: Waste should be safely stored in an appropriate place where it is created or elsewhere. This Department has no statutory control over the storage by Crown-exempt operators such as the Ministry of Defence. However, they have agreed to observe practices no less stringent than those subject to statutory control.

Mr. John Evans: To ask the Secretary of State for the Environment (1) regarding storage of radioactive waste for which there is presently no disposal site available, whether it is Government policy that radioactive waste shall be stored at the site at which the waste is created;

(2) regarding storage of radioactive waste for which there is presently no disposal site available, whether Government policy allows for the transfer of radioactive waste from one storage facility to another;

(3) what is the Government's policy on the storage of radioactive nuclear waste for which there is, at present, no disposal facility available.

Mrs. Virginia Bottomley *[holding answer 25 May 1989]:* The Government's policy is that wherever such waste is stored it must be safe. This may be at the site where it is created or elsewhere. The safe transport from one storage facility to another is not precluded.

Tributyl Tin (Pollution)

Mr. Onslow: To ask the Secretary of State for the Environment what rivers in England and Wales are known to have been polluted by the use of tributyl tin by boat owners.

Mr. Howard *[holding answer 26 May 1989]:* The main freshwater rivers affected have been those carrying large numbers of pleasure craft, which were treated with tributyl tin antifouling paints before the Government banned their sale and supply in 1987. We have direct evidence of contamination of the Rivers Bure, Yare, Great Ouse, Thames, Aire and Medway. It is too soon to detect the effect of the ban in reducing tributyl tin concentrations in rivers.

Drought Forecasts

Mr. Onslow: To ask the Secretary of State for the Environment what are the latest forecasts available to him; and if he will make a statement.

Mr. Howard *[holding answer 26 May 1989]:* On latest information, areas at risk due to low levels of water resources are confined to limited parts of the south-east and east Devon. Elsewhere, resources are in a healthy state. We are monitoring the position closely.

Rents

Mr. Cohen: To ask the Secretary of State for the Environment, pursuant to his answer of 9 May, *Official Report,* column *386,* to the hon. Member for Bow and Poplar (Ms. Gordon) what steps he proposes to take to ensure that tenants outside the protection of the Rent Acts are not charged rents inclusive of rates after the introduction of the poll tax; and if he will make a statement.

Mr. John Gummer *[holding answer 26 May 1989]:* The Housing Act 1988 will apply to most tenancies entered into after 15 January 1989 and any rents determined by the rent assessment committee under that Act will be exclusive of rates. Any reductions in inclusive rents arising from the introduction of community charge should be settled on the basis of individual contracts.

General Anaesthetic (Minors)

Mr. Amess: To ask the Secretary of State for the Environment if he will list in the *Official Report* the occasions on which a parent or guardian of a minor does not need to sign the consent form for general anaesthetic; and if he will make a statement.

Mr. Freeman: I have been asked to reply.

Parental consent to examination or treatment of a minor is not required in the following circumstances:
1. Where the child has reached age 16;
2. Where there is a medical emergency and parental consent is not obtainable;
3. Where a child has sufficient understanding of the treatment proposed to give consent on his or her own behalf. (It will be a matter of medical judgment as to whether any particular child has sufficient understanding).

HEALTH

Food Poisoning

Mr. Wray: To ask the Secretary of State for Health what specific proposals is he preparing to tackle the problem of food poisoning in airline meals.

Mr. Freeman: It is the responsibility of the airlines and the airline caterers to ensure that their food does not cause food poisoning.

Local authorities are responsible for the enforcement of the food legislation where applicable and this is currently under review.

We are shortly to issue reviewed guidelines on cook-chill preparation and airline caterers using the cook-chill system should follow the recommendations.

Mr. David Nicholson: To ask the Secretary of State for Health how many cases of food poisoning associated with untreated milk occurred in England and Wales in each of the years from 1983 to 1987.

Mr. Freeman: The information requested is as follows:

Year	Number of cases
1983	285
1984	406
1985	233
1986	347
1987	366

Dentists

Mr. Sean Hughes: To ask the Secretary of State for Health if he has received the report of Professor Dawid's study on measurement of the work load of dentists; if he will place a copy in the Library; and if he will make a statement.

Mr. Freeman: The report, "Measurement of Dentists' Workload" by Professor A. P. Dawid, of the department of statistical science, University College, London, was commissioned jointly by the Department and the British Dental Association to advise on the principles on which the measurement of work load in the general dental services should be based. Officials from the Department and the association have studied the report and agree that it is a useful starting point for a programme of further work designed to achieve an agreed position on work load measurement for the purposes of the dental rates study group and the preparation of evidence for the doctors and dentists review body. Initial discussions on how to take this programme forward are already under way. A copy of the report has been placed in the Library.

Mr. Sean Hughes: To ask the Secretary of State for Health what additional costs have been incurred in the change in organisation from the Dental Estimates Board to the Dental Practice Board; and whether he will itemise the main headings of expenditure.

Mr. Freeman: There have been no costs associated with the change of name from the Dental Estimates Board to the Dental Practice Board.

Mr. Sean Hughes: To ask the Secretary of State for Health (1) what discussions are currently being undertaken with the object of improving emergency dental services; and when he anticipates being able to report progress;

(2) what provision he intends to make to enable patients in the community dental service to have access to emergency dental services.

Mr. Freeman: Arrangements for the provision of local emergency dental services are a matter for the relevant family practitioner committee and any such services are also available to persons who have been treated by the community dental service. Discussions, with representatives of the dental profession, on the terms of a new contract for general dental practitioners will cover emergency treatment provision but we cannot say when we shall be able to report on the discussions.

Mr. Sean Hughes: To ask the Secretary of State for Health what progress is being made in computerising the remuneration of general dental practitioners in England and Wales; and whether he will make a statement.

Mr. Freeman: The translation of returns from dentists to the Dental Practice Board into schedules of payments for family practitioner committees to make to them is already fully computerised. A pilot trial to test the feasibility and value of electronic data transmission between dentists and the Dental Practice Board is currently in progress, involving 60 dentists in 26 practices in England and Wales. A full report on the trial is expected in July.

Mr. Sean Hughes: To ask the Secretary of State for Health whether he has held an internal inquiry into the late arrival of form FPN 472 relating to dental charges; and what redress is available through departmental machinery for the general dental practitioners in the event of subsequent under-remuneration.

Mr. Freeman: Family practitioner notice 472 advised dentists of changes in dental charges as from 1 April 1989. The department distributed the notice to family practitioner committees (FPCs) in time for them to deliver to dentists before the changes came into effect. In a very small number of cases there was a delay of a few days in the transmission of the notice from FPCs to dentists. There is no reason why this should lead to any under-remuneration.

Abortions

Mr. Amess: To ask the Secretary of State for Health how many (a) consultants and (b) nurses have taken a conscientious objection to abortion under section 4 of the Abortion Act 1967; and what have been the comparable figures each since 1968.

Mr. Freeman: This information is not collected centrally.

Mr. Amess: To ask the Secretary of State for Health if he will give a breakdown by regional health authority of the total number of abortions performed in England and Wales under the Abortion Act 1967; in each region, how many of these abortions were performed to save the life of the mother; and what percentage the latter represents of the former.

Mr. Freeman: The exact information requested could be provided only at disproportionate cost; the nearest readily available information, covering the years 1970 to 1987, is shown in the table.

Number of notifications of (a) total abortions, (b) abortions performed under grounds of 5 or 6 [1] of the 1967 Abortion Act, by area of usual residence, [2] England and Wales 1970 to 1987.

Area of usual residence	A	B	Percentage B of A
England and Wales	2,137,120	251	0·012
Wales	101,393	15	0·015
Northern	98,905	21	0·021
Yorkshire	120,448	12	0·010
Trent	159,398	28	0·018
East Anglia	64,424	8	0·012
North West Thames	258,054	24	0·009
North East Thames	229,278	15	0·007
South East Thames	184,154	11	0·006
South West Thames	156,905	14	0·009
Wessex	89,641	24	0·027
Oxford	90,772	7	0·008
South Western	108,272	14	0·013
West Midlands	230,402	18	0·008
Mersey	91,559	13	0·014
North Western	153,515	27	0·018

Note: A = Total abortions 1970-87 inclusive.

B = Performed under grounds 5 or 6.

[1] The Act allows abortions to be performed in emergency to savey the life of the pregnant woman (ground 5) or to prevent grave permanent injury to the physical or mental health of the pregnant woman (ground 6).

[2] 1970-73: Hospital regions.

1974-87: Regional health authorities.

Mr. Amess: To ask the Secretary of State for Health what is the total number of abortions that have so far been performed in the United Kingdom under the Abortion Act 1967; how many of these abortions were performed in emergency to save the life of the mother; and what percentage this latter figure represents of the former.

Mr. Freeman: The total number of notifications of legal terminations, to resident and non-resident women, carried out in the United Kingdom under the terms of the Abortion Act 1967 from 27 April 1968 to 31 December 1987 is 2,960,234. Of these 142 (0·005 per cent.) were performed under ground 5 of the Act, in emergency to save the life of the pregnant woman.

Complete United Kingdom data for 1988 are not yet available; currently available data, which are provisional, are as follows:

	Total	Ground 5
England and Wales (1 January to 30 September 1988)	137,103	[1]4
Scotland (1 January to 31 December 1988)	10,003	0

[1] (0·003 per cent. of total).

Note The Abortion Act 1967 does not apply in Northern Ireland.

Mr. Amess: To ask the Secretary of State for Health what percentage of abortions performed on girls under the age of 16 years have been carried out in (a) non-National Health Service premises and (b) pay beds in National Health Service hospitals in each of the last five years for which figures are available.

Mr. Freeman: No data on the number of terminations performed in pay beds in National Health Service hospitals are collected centrally. The other data requested are shown in the table.

Number of notifications of (a) total abortions and (b) those performed in non-NHS premises, on girls under 16 years of age, England and Wales, 1983-87

Year	A Total number	B Performed in non-NHS premises	Percentage B of A
1983	4,566	1,898	41·6
1984	4,609	1,971	42·8
1985	4,427	1,874	42·3
1986	4,240	1,734	40·9
1987	4,075	1,747	42·9

Mr. Amess: To ask the Secretary of State for Health what representations he has received *(a)* supporting and *(b)* opposing a reduction in the upper time limit for abortions to 20 weeks; what percentage the latter represents of the former; and if he will make a statement.

Mr. Freeman: Since March 1989 we have received 25 representations; 14 supported a reduction in the time limit. None referred specifically to a 20-week limit.

Seat Belts

Mr. Amess: To ask the Secretary of State for Health what is his estimate of the saving to the National Health Service as a result of the compulsory wearing of front seat belts, in each year since 1983; and if he will make a statement.

Mr. Freeman: No precise estimate has been made. The introduction of compulsory wearing of front seat belts has undoubtedly saved the lives of some of those involved in road traffic accidents. However, many of those whose lives have been saved have instead received injuries with consequent costs to the National Health Service which would not previously have been incurred.

Mental Health

Mr. Andrew Smith: To ask the Secretary of State for Health how many staffed hostels for discharged psychiatric patients provided by *(a)* local authorities and *(b)* voluntary bodies are available for (i) short-term accommodation andd (ii) long-term accommodation.

Mr. Freeman: The information is not collected centrally in the form requested. The numbers of homes, hostels and residential places for mentally ill people in each local authority in England is published in "Homes and Hostels for Mentally Ill and Mentally Handicapped People (A/F 11)". A copy of the 1986 publication is in the Library; and a copy of the 1987 publication, which it is hoped will be available shortly, will also be placed in the Library.

Mr. Andrew Smith: To ask the Secretary of State for Health if he will list the health districts which have care registers for patients with special mental health needs; and when he plans to direct other districts to establish such registers as recommended in the report of the inquiry into the care and after-care of Miss Sharon Campbell.

Mr. Freeman: This information is not collected centrally. Planning guidance, issued to health and local authorities in July 1988, requires each district to have developed by 1991 a "care programme" to provide a system of co-ordinated continuing care for people chronically disabled by mental illness. Further guidance being prepared by the Department will include the need for a register of patients.

Mr. Andrew Smith: To ask the Secretary of State for Health what plans he has to implement the recommendations of the inquiry into the care and after-care of Miss Sharon Campbell that he issue a written summary, classifying their statutory duties to provide after-care for former mentally disordered patients, to health and local authorities.

Mr. Freeman: This recommendation is under consideration.

Mr. Andrew Smith: To ask the Secretary of State for Health what steps he has taken to ensure that employing authorities have issued guidelines to staff in respect of violence from clients, and the reporting of such incidents of violence, as recommended in the report of the inquiry into the care and after-care of Miss Sharon Campbell.

Mr. Freeman: The Health and Safety at Work legislation places a statutory duty on employers to provide a safe working environment for their staff and the Health and Safety Executive published "Preventing Violence to Staff" with general guidance on this subject last year.

Complementing this for the health and personal social services are: The report, "Violence to Staff, DHSS Advisory Committee on Violence to Staff", chaired by Lord Skelmersdale, which was issued at the same time as the Sharon Campbell report to directors of social services and NHS general managers and the report of the Association of Directors of Social Services, "Guidelines and Recommendations to Employers on Violence Against Employees" which was sent to local authorities in 1987. Last February we issued a video on violence to staff to directors of social services and to general managers. When issuing the video we said the aim was that authorities should use the Skelmersdale report and the video to stimulate constructive discussions amongst members, managers at all levels, staff and their representatives about the development of strategies and the other recommendations in the Skelmersdale report, which included the need for staff to report violent incidents. We said also this material should be useful in training courses to increase the awareness among the staff and managers of the problem of violence and what might be done to counteract it.

At law it is for local authorities and health authorities, as the employers of the staff in these services, to take appropriate action and this was generally considered to be the best level at which action should be taken.

Mr. Andrew Smith: To ask the Secretary of State for Health when he plans to issue the guidelines about psychiatric case management and community care reviews, as recommended in the report of inquiry into the care and after care of Miss Sharon Campbell; and to whom these guidelines will be made available.

Mr. Freeman: Further guidance to health and local authorities is being prepared on the components of "care programmes".

Doctors and Nurses (Derbyshire)

Mr. McLoughlin: To ask the Secretary of State for Health what were the numbers of doctors and nurses in Derbyshire in 1979; and in the latest year for which figures are available.

Mr. Mellor: The available information is given in the tables. Due to the 1982 NHS re-organisation, consistent data is not available for earlier years for these Districts.

NHS Staff in post in North Derbyshire and South Derbyshire District Health Authorities

At 30 September			Whole time equivalents	
District health authority	Medical and Dental		Nursing and Midwife	
	1982	1987	1982	1987
	[1]WTE		[1]WTE	
North Derbyshire	84	88	1,875	2,161
Southern Derbyshire	202	184	3,939	3,947

Source: D of H (SM13) Annual Censuses of NHS Medical and Non-Medical Manpower.

[1] All figures independently rounded to nearest whole time equivalent (WTE).

[2] Figures includes permanent paid, honorary and locum staff and exclude all consultants and senior registrars whose contracts are held by the regional health authority. The district health authority where those staff work cannot be identified centrally. There will therefore be more doctors and dentists actually working in North Derbyshire and Southern Derbyshire district health authorities than are accounted for in the table.

[3] Includes agency nursing and midwifery staff.

FPC staff in post

	Number of all practitioners	Number of nurses	Whole-time equivalent
1982	452	52	28
1987	507	103	56

Note: The number of doctors include all general medical practitioners (unrestricted and restricted principals, assistants and trainees) for which Derbyshire family practitioner committee was responsible. Also the number of nurses employed by those doctors, and their whole-time equivalent.

Grading Returns (Derbyshire)

Mrs. Beckett: To ask the Secretary of State for Health if he will make available the grading returns received from the Southern Derbyshire district health authority.

Mr. Mellor: The grading returns specified the number of nursing and midwifery staff in each old grade that were assimilated to each of the new clinical grades. This information is given in the table.

The new clinical grading structure for nursing, midwifery and health visitor staff
Numbers of old clinical grades assimilated to each of the new clinical grades on the basis of duties and responsibilities on 1 April 1988: South Derbyshire

Previous grade	Staff[3] (Whole time Equivalents)	Numbers transferred to each new clinical grade								
		A	B	C	D	E	F	[2]G	H	I
Nursing Auxiliary	941·53	853·73	79·80	8·00	—	—	—	—	—	—
Staff Nursery Nurse	18·10	—	11·70	6·40	—	—	—	—	—	—
Enrolled Nurse[1]	603·21	—	—	307·44	275·59	20·18	—	—	—	—
Enrolled District Nurse[1]	10·44	—	—	—	10·44	—	—	—	—	—
Senior Enrolled Nurse[1]	40·60	—	—	—	27·50	11·39	1·71	—	—	—
Staff Nurse[1]	657·48	—	—	—	169·07	451·03	37·38	—	—	—
Staff Midwife[1]	50·00	—	—	—	16·89	33·11	—	—	—	—
Deputy Sister[1]	18·37	—	—	—	—	—	17·33	1·00	—	—
Nursing Sister II[1]	451·92	—	—	—	—	—	264·02	174·22	13·69	—
Midwifery Sister II[1]	106·13	—	—	—	—	—	40·95	65·28	—	—
District Nurse (Sister II)[1]	94·33	—	—	—	—	—	94·33	—	—	—
Nursing Sister I	5·00	—	—	—	—	—	—	2·00	2·00	1·00
Midwifery Sister I	2·00	—	—	—	—	—	—	2·00	—	—
Health Visitor	94·53	—	—	—	—	—	—	94·53	—	—
Senior Nurse 9	53·00	—	—	—	—	—	—	11·00	34·00	8·00
Senior Nurse 8 (Midwife)	11·00	—	—	—	—	—	—	5·00	5·00	1·00
Senior Nurse 7	33·60	—	—	—	—	—	—	—	15·60	15·00
Senior Nurse 7 (Midwife)	1·00	—	—	—	—	—	—	—	1·00	—
Clinical Teacher	22·16	—	—	—	—	—	—	—	22·16	—
Fieldwork Teacher	10·75	—	—	—	—	—	—	—	10·75	—
Practical Work Teacher	32·00	—	—	—	—	—	—	3·00	29·00	—
Tutor	19·53	—	—	—	—	—	—	—	—	19·53
Tutor Midwife	6·00	—	—	—	—	—	—	—	—	6·00
Post basic students										
Enrolled	23·00	—	—	23·00	—	—	—	—	—	—
Staff Nurse	56·00	—	—	—	40·00	16·00	—	—	—	—
Deputy Sister	—	—	—	—	—	—	—	—	—	—
Sister II	—	—	—	—	—	—	—	—	—	—
Others	4·21	2·21	—	—	—	—	—	—	—	2·09
Totals	3,365·89	855·94	91·50	344·84	539·49	531·71	361·29	452·36	133·23	55·53

[1] Excludes post basic students

[2] Excludes some additional '6' posts which health authorities have indicated they intend to create in future on existing two-sister wards.

[3] Staff in post plus vacancies.

Listening Devices

Mr. Cran: To ask the Secretary of State for Health whether electronic surveillance listening devices are used by any organisation or agency acting on its behalf; and if he will make a statement.

Mr. Freeman: As referred to in the Younger report on privacy, electronic listening devices are sometimes used in the observation of patients in hospitals.

Hospitals (Policy Decisions)

Mr. Wray: To ask the Secretary of State for Health whether prior to his proposals in the White Paper "Working for Patients", he gathered information on the amount of time necessary to make decisions on general policy for the management of hospitals, and specifically on *(a)* organisation of services for in-patients and out-patients, *(b)* co-ordination of time-tables for staff-rotas and *(c)* organisation and control of funding exercises required for (i) adequate pay rewards for the medical, nursing and auxiliary staff, (ii) demands for changes in numbers of hospital staff and (iii) adequate provisions for the good operation of the different hospital units.

Mr. Kenneth Clarke: We undertook a comprehensive review of all relevant aspects of the NHS before bringing forward our proposals for change.

Hearing Loss

Mr. Vaz: To ask the Secretary of State for Health, if he plans to provide to the public more information and a wider education programme on the facts surrounding loss of hearing.

Mr. Freeman: The Department publishes the booklet "How to use your hearing aid" which is issued free to all NHS hearing aid users. It gives useful general advice and includes reference to other services which may be of help to hearing impaired people. The Department of Social Security publishes leaflet NI 207 on occupational deafness which explains how industrial injuries disablement benefit may be claimed. There are no plans to issue any additional guidance at present. The Royal National Institute for the Deaf has however, referred to the need for better information for consumers in their "Fair Hearing" campaign document "Hearing Aids—The Case for Change", and we shall be considering this along with the other proposals that it has put forward.

Mr. Vaz: To ask the Secretary of State for Health (1) if he has any plans to implement the Royal National Institute for the Deaf proposal, set out in the document "Hearing Aids—a Case for Change", for a new system of dispensing hearing aids, and helping the deaf or hard of hearing to obtain help;

(2) if he will make a statement on his Department's review of its policy on hearing aid provision and services; what proposals he has to improve counselling to those who are deaf or hard of hearing; and if he will make a statement.

Mr. Mellor: We are grateful to the Royal National Institute for the Deaf for their comprehensive package of proposals relating to the provision of hearing aids. We have now received their refined proposals which take into account the comments they have received from other interested organisations. The issues involved are complex and because of the wide-ranging implications of any change in the present system of provision, we shall need to take time to consider them, in the light of the views of all concerned. We shall of course bear fully in mind the need for rehabilitation and after-care services for those who are deaf or hard of hearing.

Mr. Vaz: To ask the Secretary of State for Health if he will take steps to widen the range of hearing aids available on the National Health Service to cover cosmetically designed hearing aids.

Mr. Mellor: The National Health Service range of hearing aids is provided to ameliorate loss of hearing rather than for cosmetic reasons. In-the-ear hearing aids, which are sometimes regarded as more cosmetically acceptable, can be provided where an NHS consultant can see clear clinical reasons for doing so. Skin tone hearing aids are available in each of the NHS series of behind-the-ear aids.

Mr. Vaz: To ask the Secretary of State for Health (1) if he will implement stricter regulations concerning compensation and maintenance cover for users of hearing aids;

(2) what is his policy towards free maintenance of hearing aids in the public and private sectors.

Mr. Mellor: Routine maintenance of all hearing aids issued under National Health Service arrangements is free. However, the cost of repair or replacement of a hearing aid may be recovered in cases of repeated loss or damage from patients or parents of children who are patients. Hearing aids provided by the private sector are the responsibility of my right hon. and noble Friend the Secretary of State for Trade and Industry.

Retinal Conditions

Mr. Nicholas Winterton: To ask the Secretary of State for Health if he will list those centres within the National Health Service which currently specialise in the treatment of retinal conditions.

Mr. Freeman: All district health authorities have access to ophthalmology departments which treat retinal conditions, although some may have a particular interest in certain retinal conditions.

Mr. Nicholas Winterton: To ask the Secretary of State for Health what information he has concerning centres currently undertaking research into retinal conditions.

Mr. Freeman: The Department is currently funding research for the screening of diabetic patients for diabetic retinopathy at Oxford, Sheffield and Exeter. A report of this work will be submitted later this year.

We are aware that work in this area is also being funded by some medical research charities.

Cryptosporidia

Mr. Robin Cook: To ask the Secretary of State for Health what is his Department's officials' involvement in investigations of the incidence of cryptosporidia in the water supply.

Mr. Freeman: An official of the Department is medical secretary to the expert group on cryptosporidium in water supplies, which was announced on 2 March by my hon. and learned Friend the Minister of State for Water and Planning at column 286; another attends its meetings as an observer. The Department monitors other outbreaks of cryptosporidiosis, irrespective of source, in association with the communicable disease surveillance centre which collects data on this disease.

Higher Diploma Examinations

Ms. Harman: To ask the Secretary of State for Health if he will raise with the relevant professional bodies the recommendation of the Hoffenberg committee that questions about brain stem death organ transplantation and related matters should be asked from time to time in higher diploma examinations in medicine, surgery and anaesthesia.

Mr. Freeman: The medical royal colleges are responsible for deciding the content of their examinations. However, officials wrote to the Conference of medical royal colleges on 10 November 1988, drawing attention to the relevant recommendation of the Hoffenberg report.

Body Scanners

Mr. Dave Nellist: To ask the Secretary of State for Health if, pursuant to his answer to my hon. Friend the Member for Don Valley (Mr. Redwood) of 10 May, *Official Report*, column *450*, and the hon. Member for Coventry, South-East, 23 May, *Official Report*, column *488*, he will take steps to obtain the information on whole body scanners in the West Midlands regional health authority; and if he will make a statement.

Mr. Freeman: The information requested is given in the table.

Type of Whole Scanner in use	Location in West Midlands	Installation date	Main source of funding
CT	Birmingham Childrens Hospital	1986	Public Appeal/Health Authority
CT	Birmingham General Hospital	1988	Health Authority
CT	Corbett Hospital Dudley (District Consortium includes Kidderminster and Bromsgrove)	1985	Public Appeal/Health Authority
CT	Coventry, Walsgrave Hospital	1976	Public Appeal
CT	Coventry, Walsgrave Hospital	1988	Health Authority
MRI[1]	Coventry, Walsgrave Hospital	1988	Public Appeal/Health Authority
CT	Good Hope Hospital, North Birmingham	1987	Public Appeal
CT	Midland Centre for Neurosurgery, Sandwell	1976	Health Authority/DoH
CT	Midlands Centre for Neurosurgery, Sandwell	1984	Health Authority
CT	Mobile Unit, serving Hereford/West and East Birmingham/Burton/Walsall	1985	Health Authority
CT	New Cross, Wolverhampton	1987	Health Authority
CT	North Staffs Royal Infirmary	1983	Public Appeal
CT	North Staff Royal Infirmary	1987	Health Authority
CT	North Staffs Royal Infirmary	1987	Health Authority
CT	Q E Medical Centre, Central Birmingham	1984	Health Authority
CT	Robert Jones and Agnes Hunt, Oswestry, Shropshire	1986	Health Authority
CT	Ronkswood, Worcester	1989	Public Appeal
CT	Sandwell D G Hospital	1985	Public Appeal
CT	Walsall	1989	Health Authority

[1] Magnetic Resonance Imager

In the next 12 months, new CT scanners are planned at Dudley road hospital, West Birmingham, and Selly Oak hospital, South Birmingham, both to be funded from health authority sources.

Creutzfeldt Jakob Dementia

Mr. Ron Davies: To ask the Secretary of State for Health, pursuant to his answer of 18 May, *Official Report*, column *289*, what alternative methods of monitoring Creutzfeldt Jakob dementia he is considering.

Mr. Freeman: We are seeking to establish a national register of all cases of Creutzfeldt-Jakob disease, validated by experts in this field. A similar methodology has been used with success in the past: details can be found in the Journal of Neurology, Neurosurgery and Psychiatry (1975) Vol. 38, pages 210-13 and (1988) Vol. 51, 1113-19.

Mr. Ron Davies: To ask the Secretary of State for Health what information his Department now possesses about the incidence of Creutzfeldt Jakob dementia.

Mr. Freeman: The mean annual mortality rate of Creutzfeldt-Jakob disease in England and Wales for the last period studied in detail (1980-84 inclusive) was 0·49 million. Currently, Creutzfeldt-Jakob disease is given on death certificates as the underlying cause of death in about 30 deaths a year.

Wakefield Family Practitioner Committee

Mr. O'Brien: To ask the Secretary of State for Health if he has issued guidelines on the number of members of the Wakefield family practitioner committee that should be appointed to meet hon. Members representing local constituencies; and if he will make a statement.

Mr. Mellor: We have issued no such guidelines. It is a matter for individual FPCs to decide the level of representation at particular meetings.

Mr. O'Brien: To ask the Secretary of State for Health if he issued guidelines to the Wakefield family practitioner committee on when the White Paper "Working for Patients" should be considered and discussed; and if he will make a statement.

Mr. Mellor: We have issued no such guidelines. I welcome discussion by FPCs on the implications for implementing locally the proposals contained in the White Paper.

Mr. O'Brien: To ask the Secretary of State for Health whether the chairman of the Wakefield family practitioner committee has been appointed an agent on behalf of the Secretary of State; and if he will make a statement.

Mr. Mellor: FPCs are the Secretary of State's agents responsible for administering and managing family practitioner services. Chairmen and members are appointed by the Secretary of State and are accountable to him for the discharge of these duties.

Anaesthetics (Consent)

Mr. Amess: To ask the Secretary of State for Health if he will seek to introduce legislation to require that the parent or guardian of a minor signs the consent form for general anaesthetic; and if he will make a statement.

Mr. Freeman: Arrangements for ensuring that patients (and parents or guardians where appropriate) are informed about proposed treatments and for obtaining their consent are under review. Revised guidance will be issued as soon as the review has been concluded. The Government has no plans to introduce legislation.

Population Statistics

Mr. Robin Cook: To ask the Secretary of State for Health what is the population of each district health authority, the mortality rate for those aged under 75 years in each district health authority and the number of people aged over 85 years in each district health authority.

Mr. Freeman: Estimates of resident population for district health authorities in England at mid-1987 are given in the tables. Mortality rates for particular age groups in each area can be provided only at disproportionate cost.

Estimated resident population at mid-1987

Regional and District Health Authorities in England	All ages	Aged 85+
		Thousands
Northern	3,076·8	36·8
Hartlepool	89·8	0·9
North Tees	175·9	1·5
South Tees	288·8	2·6
East Cumbria	177·7	2·5
South Cumbria	172·2	2·8
West Cumbria	136·9	1·4
Darlington	124·0	1·6
Durham	235·2	2·6
North West Durham	86·3	1·1
South West Durham	153·2	1·7
Northumberland	300·9	3·8
Gateshead	206·9	2·5
Newcastle	282·7	4·3
North Tyneside	192·9	2·4
South Tyneside	156·3	2·0
Sunderland	297·1	2·9
Yorkshire	3,604·7	49·1
Hull	301·9	3·9
East Yorks	192·2	2·9
Grimsby	158·8	1·8
Scunthorpe	193·7	2·1
Northallerton	113·9	1·5
York	263·4	3·5
Scarborough	144·4	3·0
Harrogate	135·4	2·3
Bradford	337·2	4·1
Airedale	173·9	2·9
Calderdale	194·8	2·9
Huddersfield	212·1	2·9
Dewsbury	163·7	1·7

Regional and District Health Authorities in England	All ages	Aged 85+
Leeds Western	362·3	5·7
Leeds Eastern	346·7	4·7
Wakefield	144·1	1·5
Pontefract	166·2	1·7
Trent	4,646·3	57·2
North Derbyshire	362·0	4·6
South Derbyshire	527·0	6·4
Leicestershire	879·4	10·8
North Lincolnshire	270·6	3·2
South Lincolnshire	304·0	4·4
Bassetlaw	104·9	1·1
Central Nottinghamshire	288·5	3·2
Nottingham	614·4	7·8
Barnsley	221·5	2·3
Doncaster	290·1	3·0
Rotherham	251·7	2·5
Sheffield	532·3	7·8
East Anglian	2,013·7	28·9
Cambridge	273·0	3·9
Peterborough	205·0	2·0
West Suffolk	226·8	2·7
East Suffolk	321·3	5·2
Norwich	468·9	8·1
Great Yarmouth and Waveney	197·6	3·2
West Norfolk and Wisbech	187·9	2·8
Huntingdon	133·3	1·2
North West Thames	3,488·3	44·6
North Bedfordshire	249·6	2·6
South Bedfordshire	276·4	2·5
North Hertfordshire	185·6	1·9
East Hertfordshire	295·6	3·4
North West Hertfordshire	261·1	3·1
South West Hertfordshire	244·6	3·4
Barnet	305·9	4·6
Harrow	200·1	3·3
Hillingdon	231·0	3·1
Hounslow and Spelthorne	281·1	3·8
Ealing	296·9	3·8
Brent	256·6	2·9
Paddington and North Kensington	120·6	1·5
Riverside	283·4	4·6
North East Thames	3,771·5	52·6
Basildon and Thurrock	281·5	2·4
Mid Essex	289·9	3·2
North East Essex	304·5	5·5
East Essex	252·0	2·5
Southend	323·3	5·5
Barking, Havering and Brentwood	455·8	5·6
Hampstead	109·8	2·0
Bloomsbury	128·8	2·3
Islington	168·7	2·3
City and Hackney	192·1	2·4
Newham	206·5	2·5
Tower Hamlets	159·0	2·1
Enfield	261·5	4·3
Haringey	193·7	2·7
Redbridge	230·1	3·6
Waltham Forest	214·5	3·6
South East Thames	3,635·4	60·8
Brighton	299·0	6·8
Eastbourne	232·5	6·8
Hastings	166·6	5·0
South East Kent	266·6	4·7
Canterbury and Thanet	303·0	6·5
Dartford and Gravesham	219·6	2·2
Maidstone	197·1	2·2
Medway	328·5	3·3
Tunbridge Wells	195·8	3·3
Bexley	220·6	2·7
Greenwich	216·6	2·8
Bromley	298·2	4·4
West Lambeth	161·7	2·5

Regional and District Health Authorities in England	All ages	Aged 85+
Camberwell	212·3	2·8
Lewisham and North Southwark	317·6	4·8
South West Thames	2,959·6	50·1
North West Surrey	206·4	2·9
West Surrey and North East Hampshire	275·1	2·7
South West Surrey	181·3	3·2
Mid Surrey	165·2	2·6
East Surrey	182·8	2·7
Chichester	180·2	4·1
Mid Downs	276·3	3·5
Worthing	243·5	8·0
Croydon	319·2	4·3
Kingston and Esher	175·9	3·1
Richmond, Twickenham and Roehampton	231·9	4·3
Wandsworth	189·2	2·8
Merton and Sutton	332·6	5·9
Wessex	2,905·6	46·5
East Dorset	448·1	10·6
West Dorset	200·5	3·8
Portsmouth and South East Hampshire	529·7	7·2
Southampton and South West Hampshire	418·8	6·4
Winchester	210·4	2·7
Basingstoke and North Hampshire	217·2	2·2
Salisbury	121·1	2·0
Swindon	230·2	2·5
Bath	402·7	6·3
Isle of Wight	126·9	2·8
Oxford	2,501·8	82·1
East Berkshire	359·7	3·6
West Berkshire	451·7	4·7
Aylesbury Vale	144·3	1·5
Wycombe	269·8	3·2
Milton Keynes	170·8	1·2
Kettering	255·0	3·2
Northampton	306·8	3·6
Oxfordshire	543·6	6·4
South Western	3,205·5	54·7
Bristol and Weston	367·2	6·1
Frenchay	220·6	3·1
Southmead	232·4	3·1
Cornwall and Isles of Scilly	453·1	7·5
Exeter	306·1	6·4
North Devon	133·4	2·6
Plymouth	329·9	5·0
Torbay	240·5	6·3
Cheltenham and District	210·6	3·5
Gloucester	311·6	4·1
Somerset	399·9	7·0
West Midlands	5,197·7	57·3
Bromsgrove and Redditch	166·9	1·2
Herefordshire	156·0	2·4
Kidderminster and District	101·7	1·2
Worcester and District	240·6	3·2
Shropshire	396·5	4·7
Mid Staffordshire	311·3	2·9
North Staffordshire	461·1	5·4
South East Staffordshire	255·1	2·1
Rugby	85·2	0·9
North Warwickshire	174·0	1·7
South Warwickshire	255·0	2·8
Central Birmingham	180·7	2·5
East Birmingham	197·6	2·2
North Birmingham	163·7	1·9
South Birmingham	246·3	3·1
West Birmingham	209·9	2·0
Coventry	308·9	3·3
Dudley	302·6	3·1
Sandwell	298·4	3·7
Solihull	203·9	1·9
Walsall	261·8	2·1
Wolverhampton	250·5	2·9

Regional and District Health Authorities in England	All ages	Aged 85+
Mersey	2,408·7	30·3
Chester	177·0	2·1
Crewe	247·8	2·7
Halton	143·1	1·2
Macclesfield	179·3	2·4
Warrington	185·4	1·7
Liverpool	476·0	7·0
St. Helens and Knowsley	348·7	3·1
Southport and Formby	118·7	2·6
South Sefton	178·5	2·2
Wirral	354·1	5·3
North Western	3,991·1	51·4
Lancaster	130·4	2·6
Blackpool, Wyre and Fylde	318·8	6·6
Preston	126·7	1·8
Blackburn, Hyndburn and Ribble Valley	268·6	3·3
Burnley, Pendle and Rossendale	227·8	2·9
West Lancashire	106·7	0·7
Chorley and South Ribble	194·7	1·8
Bolton	262·3	3·1
Bury	173·7	2·2
North Manchester	142·9	1·8
Central Manchester	125·0	1·6
South Manchester	182·1	2·4
Oldham	219·5	2·5
Rochdale	214·2	2·4
Salford	237·7	3·2
Stockport	291·1	3·6
Tameside and Glossop	245·7	2·8
Trafford	216·1	2·9
Wigan	307·2	3·1

Source: OPCS 1987 mid-year estimates

Speech Therapists

Mr. Janner: To ask the Secretary of State for Health how many speech therapists are employed by the Leicestershire health authority with special responsibility for work in schools; how many vacancies the Leicestershire health authority has for such speech therapists and for how long these vacancies have been open; what recruitment efforts are being made to fill these positions and whether these efforts include salary incentives; and if he will make a statement.

Mr. Mellor: We do not hold the information centrally in the form requested. The hon. Member may care to write to the chairman of Leicestershire health authority for the information he seeks.

Medical and Dental Education

Mr. Knox: To ask the Secretary of State for Health what progress has been made by the steering group on undergraduate medical and dental education.

Mr. Kenneth Clarke: The steering group, which contains representatives of all the major bodies concerned with undergraduate medical and dental education, was set up in November 1987 following a conference called by the permanent secretaries of my Department and the Department of Education and Science (*Hansard*, column 577-8, 18 November 1987). The steering group has now produced an interim report which clarifies the roles and responsibilities of the bodies concerned and makes recommendations relating to the principles underlying undergraduate medical and dental education, and to improved planning, management and information. I have today placed copies of the report in the Library.

Paragraph 4.30 of "Working for Patients" emphasised the Government's continuing commitment to maintaining the quality of medical education and research, and said that the steering group would develop its work and make recommendations in the light of the proposals in the White Paper.

The group began this second phase of its work by considering arrangements for the payment of the service increment for teaching (SIFT) which is designed to offset the excess service costs associated with medical education. The group has recommended that SIFT should continue to be paid through NHS channels and according to the following four principles which I have accepted.

  (i) SIFT should be allocated to regions, pro-rata to student numbers;

  (ii) Regions or Districts, as appropriate to local curcumstances, taking advice from medical and dental schools, should contract with hospitals (including self-governing hospitals) to provide service facilities for teaching in return for SIFT payments;

  (iii) SIFT payments should be made in consultation with medical and dental schools and reflect the teaching activity in each hospital—if the number of students increased or decreased, the allocation of SIFT should be reconsidered;

  (iv) while in the past sub-regional allocation of SIFT had been unspecific in many cases, in future payments from regions should be clearly identifiable to all parties as a recognition of the service costs of teaching.

The group has further work in hand and will offer recommendations as soon as they reach conclusions on the issues they must address.

Sight Tests

Mr. Knox: To ask the Secretary of State for Health when he will lay regulations relating to consumer safeguards on sight tests; and if he will make a statement.

Mr. Kenneth Clarke: I intend shortly to lay before the House the Sight Testing (Examination and Prescription) Regulations. I have considered carefully comments made in the course of consultation on these regulations and I have decided in the light of those received that all sight tests, whether National Health Service or private must include a refraction, an eye examination and other tests appropriate for individual patients. In addition all patients will be given a copy of their optical prescription to enable them to shop around for spectacles in order to ensure that the competition which has developed in the optical market continues to grow. The regulations will not apply to people having sight tests for employment or insurance purposes or who are resident in hospital or who are referred to their general practitioner for further investigations or treatment. These will be the only exceptions.

In reaching my decision I noted with interest the intention of the General Optical Council to carry out within the next 12 months a wide-ranging programme of investigations in connection with my consultation document on sight tests. I have made it clear that I shall reconsider the sight test regulations in the light of the council's report.

TRANSPORT

Roads (London)

Mr. Spearing: To ask the Secretary of State for Transport if any of the new roads being considered by his London assessment studies, or the extension of the North Circular road across the east London river crossing are included in the list of projects for consideration as part of his toll road proposals.

Mr. Channon: The consultants reports on the assessment studies are expected in the summer. It is too early to say what road schemes may flow from the studies and whether any will involve tolls.

I refer the hon. Member to my answer of 16 May on the East London River Crossing at column *113*.

Listening Devices

Mr. Cran: To ask the Secretary of State for Transport whether electronic surveillance listening devices are used by his Department or by any organisation or agency acting on its behalf; and if he will make a statement.

Mr. Peter Bottomley: No.

Traffic Flows (Popham—M27)

Mr. John Browne: To ask the Secretary of State for Transport if he will list the latest available summer and winter five-day and seven-day traffic flows for the M3/A33 route between Popham and the M27, for the following sections *(a)* Popham-Easton Lane, *(b)* Easton Lane-Bar End, *(c)* Bar End-Hockley, *(d)* Hockley-Compton, *(e)* Compton-Chandlers Ford and *(f)* Chandlers Ford-M27; and if he will list the peak hour flows for each direction separately for each section.

Mr. Peter Bottomley: Information is not available on summer and winter traffic flows.

The estimated Annual Average Daily Flows (24 hours) for all motor vehicles for 1987 are as follows:

	All days	Weekdays
Popham-Easton Lane M3	19,300	20,500
Popham-Easton Lane A33	26,700	27,400
Easton Lane-Bar End A33	41,800	42,700
Bar End-Hockley A33	54,600	55,500
Hockley-Compton A33	54,500	56,100
Compton-Chandlers Ford A33	46,500	46,800
Chandlers Ford-M27 A33	25,600	25,700

There are limited data on peak flows. The information relates to May 1987 and is for combined directions, as follows.

	AM peak	PM peak
Popham-Easton Lane M3	2,948	2,954
Easton Lane A33	918	924
Bar End Road A33	1,204	1,119
Morestone Road A33	835	783
Compton-Chandlers Ford A33	5,116	4,777

Mr. John Browne: To ask the Secretary of State for Transport what length of the M3-A33 between Popham and the M27 is currently equipped with sensors in the carriageway lanes to detect queues and incidents; what is the spacing of these sensors; whether they indicate speeds of traffic; and for what length of road CCTV can be used to verify queueing or incidents.

Mr. Peter Bottomley: Three queue detectors are provided at 500 m intervals on the southbound carriageway of the A33 between Bar End and Hockley. They are connected to a "Queue Ahead" sign 1·3 km north of Hockley traffic lights and a speed detector 2 km north of the traffic lights, which detects speeds above 50 mph.

CCTV cameras are sited at junction 9 on the M3 with an approximate viewing distance of 2 km north and south, and at A33 Hockley traffic lights viewing 1 km north and 300-400 m south. The camera at Hockley can also view traffic approaching A33 on the A333 (Ghost Corner) and B3335 Twyford with a viewing distance on the side roads of about 75 m.

Traffic Flows (A33-M3)

Mr. John Browne: To ask the Secretary of State for Transport if he will list the present daily and peak-hour flows entering and leaving the A33-M3 at the following junctions: *(a)* M3/A34 interchange, Easton Lane, *(b)* Bar End, *(c)* Hockley, all movements, *(d)* Compton, northfacing slip roads, *(e)* Shawford, A31 junction, *(f)* Chandlers Ford and *(g)* M27 and A35 (northbound flows on to A33).

Mr. Peter Bottomley: The information requested is not available.

Winchester Bypass

Mr. John Browne: To ask the Secretary of State for Transport what is the average lane occupancy in vehicles per mile of the A33 Winchester bypass in each direction in *(a)* offpeak and *(b)* peak hours; and what is the average speed recorded for each situation.

Mr. Peter Bottomley: The information requested is not available.

A33 (Bar End-Compton)

Mr. John Browne: To ask the Secretary of State for Transport if he will list the minor schemes and expenditure undertaken on the A33 between Bar End and Compton since the decision letter on the 1976-77 inquiry was issued in 1979.

Mr. Peter Bottomley: A33 Hockley crossroads £500,000.

Mr. John Browne: To ask the Secretary of State for Transport what is the average number of incidents per week significantly affecting traffic flow on the A33 between Bar End and Compton; and what is the average response time between an incident occurring on this length of dual carriageway and a recovery vehicle removing the vehicle or vehicles immobilised.

Mr. Peter Bottomley: This information is not held by the Department.

SS Ave

Mr. Mullin: To ask the Secretary of State for Transport what steps he took to ascertain that the wages and conditions of the crew on the SS Ave, which recently called at Teesport and Immingham, conform to international regulations.

Mr. Portillo: The Ave was not visited by Department of Transport marine surveyors at Imingham or Teesport. A

port state control inspection had been conducted in Rotterdam on 2 May 1989 and a valid inspection form issued.

Mr. Mullin: To ask the Secretary of State for Transport what information he has about the movements of the SS Ave which recently discharged a cargo of South African coal at Teesport.

Mr. Portillo: The Ave is believed to have arrived in Rotterdam from Maputo, Mozambique, and to have sailed from Rotterdam on 3 May. She arrived in Immingham later the same day, remaining there until 7 May when she sailed for Teesport. The Ave was in Teesport from 7 May until 13 May when she sailed bound for Hamburg.

Vehicles (Silencer Kits)

Mr. Nicholas Winterton: To ask the Secretary of State for Transport (1) what information he has concerning the safety implication of fitting air brake silencer kits to heavy goods vehicles;

(2) what recent representations he has received concerning the requirement that in order to qualify for a permit under the London area lorry scheme vehicles must be fitted with air brake silencer kits;

(3) when he last met the London boroughs transport scheme to discuss the issue of air brake silencer kits; and if he will make a statement;

(4) whether he has had any consultations with representatives of the insurance industry concerning the invalidation of policies by the fitting of air brake silencer kits.

Mr. Peter Bottomley: The Secretary of State has not met the London boroughs transport scheme to discuss the issue of air brake silencer kits. A vehicle's braking system needs to ensure efficient responsive braking. It is for vehicle manufacturers to ensure that this is done. The possible use of air brake silencers should therefore be considered at design stage. If air brake silencers are fitted retrospectively, then as with any other modification, care must be taken. The air brake silencer must be carefully positioned and the manufacturer of the vehicle should be consulted before it is fitted. Good maintenance is essential.

We have not consulted the insurance industry. It is for vehicle operators to ensure that their insurance policies are not invalidated by any modifications they make to their vehicles.

Representations have been received on the issue of air brake silencers from the Freight Transport Association, the Road Haulage Association and the Society of Motor Manufacturers and Traders. We have also received a number of individual representations. The Freight Transport Association has challenged in the courts the requirements by the London boroughs transport scheme to fit brake silencer kits. The matter is currently the subject of a judicial review.

Birmingham cross-city Railway

Mr. Snape: To ask the Secretary of State for Transport if his Department has seen and commented upon a draft proposal from British Rail to electrify the Birmingham cross-city railway line; on how many occasions the matter has been discussed between his Department and British

Rail; which points of clarification have been sought by his Department; and when he expects British Rail to submit a formal investment proposal.

Mr. Portillo: Department of Transport officials have seen and commented upon a draft proposal from British Rail to electrify the Birmingham cross-city railway line and have had two meetings with British Rail to discuss it. The Department is currently awaiting clarification of various issues concerning the forecast net benefit of electrification costs. I expect British Rail to submit a formal investment proposal shortly.

Mr. Snape: To ask the Secretary of State for Transport on what date discussions took place between his Department and British Rail about the proposed electrification of the Birmingham cross-city railway line; whether such discussions are likely to lead to a formal investment proposal; whether any further work which British Rail has to do on the proposals arose as a result of informal discussion between the two parties; and what information he has on the extent of local interest in the possibility of converting the cross-city line into a Metro line.

Mr. Portillo: Informal discussions between Department of Transport officials and British Rail about the proposed electrification of the Birmingham cross-city railway line took place on 5 January 1989 and 21 April 1989. British Rail has further work to do on the proposal as a result of these discussions and is planning to make a formal investment proposal. Although the possibility of converting the cross-city line into a Metro line was raised in connection with the Birmingham integrated transportation study, I understand that it is not now being pursued as part of that study.

Mr. Snape: To ask the Secretary of State for Transport what criteria he expects British Rail to set out when submitting an investment proposal to him regarding the electrification of the Birmingham cross-city railway line.

Mr. Portillo: We expect British Rail to demonstrate that the proposed electrification would represent better value for money than other options, in particular providing a modern diesel service.

Mr. Nellist: To ask the Secretary of State for Transport when his Department intends to take the decision on approval of the electrification of the cross-city line; and if he will make a statement.

Mr. Portillo: We can decide only when we have received a formal investment proposal from British Rail.

Vehicles (M6)

Mrs. Dunwoody: To ask the Secretary of State for Transport if he will assess the effectiveness of the exercise by Staffordshire county constabulary in surveying vehicles on the M6 to discover how many were unfit for use; and if he will take steps to encourage chief constables to undertake similar exercises.

Mr. Peter Bottomley: The types of vehicle check carried out by Staffordshire police are effective both in enforcing the law and increasing inter-agency co-operation. The Department's enforcement staff will continue to assist the police in similar exercises on the M6 and elsewhere.

M4 Motorway

Mr. Roger King: To ask the Secretary of State for Transport if he will give for the M6 motorway between junctions 4 and 10A *(a)* the designed hourly capacity, *(b)* the daily traffic flow, *(c)* the peak time hourly traffic flow, *(d)* the hourly peak time through traffic, *(e)* the total traffic flow between the hours of 8 pm and 8 am and *(f)* the number of heavy goods vehicles per day, in each case: (i) at present and (ii) estimated for 1995 and 2005.

Mr. Peter Bottomley *[holding answer Thursday 25 May 1989]:* The Department uses design reference flows rather than traffic flow standards when designing motorways. These indicate only the starting point for detailed operational and economic assessment of options. The Department's design reference flows for a dual three-lane motorway—which describes the M6 between junctions 4 and 10A—range from 50,000 to 79,000 vehicles per annual average day in the design year (15 years after the year in which the road opens). However, the maximum capacity of any road in terms of throughput is considerably more than its "design flow" and will vary with the vehicle mix, road layout, time of day, time of year, and driving conditions.

The latest estimates of the annual average daily flow (AADF) for the M6 between junctions 4 and 10A relate to 1987. The figures are given in the following table.

Estimated annual average daily flow[1] of all vehicles and of heavy goods vehicles on specified links of the M6: 1987

Junction	All motor vehicles	HGVs
4-5	71,000	14,200
5-6	77,200	13,810
6-7	98,300	18,580
7-8	115,000	24,850
8-9	111,500	21,930
9-10	110,300	21,540
10-10A	n.a.	n.a.

[1] Both directions of travel.
n.a. = not available.

Counts for peak flows and for flows between 8 pm and 8 am are available for only some of these links. The information is in the following table:

Average weekday peak hour and 8 pm and 8 am flows on specified links and for specified dates on the M6

Junction	Date	Peak hour	Average weekday: Peak flow	8 pm-8 am
4A-5 North	February 1989	8 am-9 am	5,700	14,200
4A-5 South	February 1989	5 pm-6 pm	6,000	14,000
5-6 South	February 1989	5 pm-6 pm	5,300	12,500
6-7 North	September 1988	3 pm-4 pm	3,700	15,800
8W-9 South	March 1989	4 pm-5 pm	6,700	17,000
9-10 North	March 1989	5 pm-6 pm	5,900	17,700
9-10 South	March 1989	4 pm-5 pm	5,800	18,000

Note: Separate data for goods vehicles are not available.

Estimates of through traffic were made for two links of this section of the M6 in 1984 and are given in the table.

Proportion of 12 hour daytime flow estimated as through traffic by type of vehicle and for specified junctions on the M6: 1984

Junction	All vehicles	Heavy vehicles
	Per cent.	Per cent.
4A-5	35	45
10-10A	50	57

The Department prepares forecasts of national traffic. Where specific trunk road improvements are being assessed local traffic forecasts are prepared. Projections are not otherwise made for specific roads.

Dursban

Mr. Onslow: To ask the Secretary of State for Transport what restrictions are placed on the transport of the chemical Dursban; and what steps he is taking to ensure that the appropriate regulations are being observed.

Mr. Peter Bottomley *[holding answer Friday 26 May 1989]:* Dursban is not listed as a dangerous substance in transport legislation. It is an organo-phosphate insecticide, approved under the Control of Pesticides Regulations 1986. These regulations make general provisions requiring any person selling, supplying or storing pesticides to take all reasonable precautions, particularly with regard to storage and transport, to protect human health, fauna and flora and the environment.

NATIONAL FINANCE

Balance of Payments

Mr. Morgan: To ask the Chancellor of the Exchequer what is his latest forecast for the United Kingdom balance of payments for 1989.

Mr. Major: The "Financial Statement and Budget Report" for 1989-90 shows a forecast deficit for the current account of the balance of payments in 1989 of £14½ billion.

Balance of Trade

Mr. Tony Lloyd: To ask the Chancellor of the Exchequer what is his latest forecast of the balance of trade in visible goods in 1989.

Mr. Harry Barnes: To ask the Chancellor of the Exchequer what is his latest forecast of the balance of trade in visible goods in 1989.

Mr. Grocott: To ask the Chancellor of the Exchequer what is his latest forecast of the balance of trade in visible goods in 1989.

Mr. Major: The "Financial Statement and Budget Report" for 1989-90 shows a forecast deficit for visible trade in 1989 of £21½ billion.

Prices and Taxes Indexes

Mr. Morgan: To ask the Chancellor of the Exchequer what changes he proposes to make to the release dates for the retail index and the tax and price index, on his assumption of responsibility for their publication.

Mr. Lilley: None.

Inflation

Mr. Macdonald: To ask the Chancellor of the Exchequer what is the current inflation rate in the United Kingdom; and what it was one year ago.

Mr. Lilley: The all-items RPI annual inflation rate in April 1989 was 8 per cent., and was 3·9 per cent. in April 1988. The underlying rate of inflation, as measured by the RPI excluding mortgage interest payments, was 5·9 per cent. in April 1988.

Married Man's Tax Allowance

Mr. Knapman: To ask the Chancellor of the Exchequer what recent consideration he has given to the married man's tax allowance.

Mr. Norman Lamont: When independent taxation begins in April 1990 the present structure of income tax allowances will be replaced by the personal allowance and the married couple's allowance. A husband and wife will each have their own personal allowance and the new system will continue to recognise marriage through the married couple's allowance. This will be given in the first instance to the husband. The personal allowance and the married couple's allowance will together be equivalent to the present married man's allowance.

Public Sector Debt

Mr. Allen: To ask the Chancellor of the Exchequer if he will make a statement on the repayment of the public sector debt held by foreign-owned institutions.

Mr. Lilley: It is not possible to provide the information requested. However, table 8 of the Bank of England *Quarterly Bulletin* and table 2·6 of *Financial Statistics* show transactions in marketable Government debt by the overseas sector.

Exports

Mr. Butterfill: To ask the Chancellor of the Exchequer what estimate he has made for the growth of exports for 1989 as against 1988.

Mr. Major: I refer my hon. Friend to the reply that I gave to the hon. Member for Bootle (Mr. Roberts) on 4 May at columns *203-4*.

Tax Reform

Mr. Speller: To ask the Chancellor of the Exchequer if he will make a statement setting out Government policy on tax reform.

Mr. Norman Lamont: The Government's programme of tax reform has sought to create a climate in which businesses can thrive and individual initiative and risk taking are rewarded. A major objective has been to leave people more of their own money, so that they can choose for themselves what to do with it. In particular the Government have reduced marginal tax rates so that an extra pound of earnings or profits is really worth having. We have reduced the basic rate of income tax from 33 to 25 per cent. and set a target of 20 per cent. Business taxation has been radically restructured, leaving the main United Kingdom corporation tax rate at 35 per cent. one of the lowest in the industrialised world. Five major taxes have been abolished completely.

We have also tried to ensure that, as a general rule, people's choices are distorted by the tax system as little as reasonably possible. In general the objective is to charge lower rates on a broader base; thereby improving incentives and reducing distortions. However the Government have also been prepared, when it it sensible, to promote well-targeted tax reliefs which will help to make the economy work better. Other important objectives have been to provide a fair deal for married women and to simplify the tax system.

Taxation

Mr. Allen: To ask the Chancellor of the Exchequer what was *(a)* the percentage of average wages paid in tax in all kinds, *(b)* the percentage paid in income tax and *(c)* the percentage paid in indirect taxes for each year since 1979.

Mr. Norman Lamont: I refer the hon. Member to the estimates placed in the Library of the House in reply to the hon. Member for Edinburgh, South (Mr. Griffiths) on 13 April at column *624.*

Manufacturing Investment

Mr. Pike: To ask the Chancellor of the Exchequer what was the level of manufacturing investment in the United Kingdom in 1979 and 1988.

Mr. Major: The level of manufacturing investment in the United Kingdom in 1985 prices was £11,157 million in 1979 and £11,586 million in 1988.

Sterling M3

Mr. Cousins: To ask the Chancellor of the Exchequer (1) what is the cumulative growth in sterling M3 from 1979 to the present;

(2) what was the cumulative growth in sterling M3 from May 1979 to 1984 and from 1984 to the present;

(3) what was the average growth of sterling M3 in the years 1970 to 1974, 1974 to 1979, 1979 to 1983 onwards;

(4) what was the percentage growth of sterling M3 in each year since 1970.

Mr. Lilley: Sterling M3 was retitled M3 in 1987. Figures from M3 from 1963 to 1988 were published in the January 1989 volume of *Financial Statistics;* more recent data are available in subsequent numbers of *Financial Statistics* or in Bank of England *Quarterly Bulletin.* Annex 7 of "Breaks in Monetary Series" (Bank of England discussion paper No. 23) discusses the calculation of growth rates of monetary series.

Petrol

Mr. Michael Marshall: To ask the Chancellor of the Exchequer what representations he has received regarding the withdrawal of two-star leaded petrol by the major oil companies; and what assessment his Department has made of the difficulties created for drivers of older vehicles by the suggested use instead of four-star leaded petrol.

Mr. Lilley: My right hon. Friend has received a number of representations about the withdrawal of two-star leaded

petrol by some major oil companies. Many engines which formerly ran on two-star petrol can use unleaded fuel. Those which cannot are able to use four-star leaded petrol without difficulty.

Taxation (EEC)

Mr. Spearing: To ask the Chancellor of the Exchequer if he will tabulate in a similar manner to his written answer of 24 March 1988, *Official Report,* columns 195-6, the likely effects on tax rates and yields in the United Kingdom of the latest proposals from the Commission of the European Communities for harmonising value added tax, showing net and gross yields, respectively.

Mr. Lilley: The Commission's latest proposals are not specific either on the level of the suggested minimum standard rate of VAT or on the scope of future zero rates. I regret, therefore, that it is not possible to update the previous tables.

Mr. Spearing: To ask the Chancellor of the Exchequer if he will tabulate in the *Official Report* in a manner similar to that of his written answer of 23 March 1988, *Official Report* columns 124-26, the effect on excise duties of adoption of the latest proposals of the Commission of the European Economic Community for harmonising national taxes on alcohol, tobacco and hydrocarbon oils and fuels.

Mr. Lilley: The latest Commission proposals contain no suggested rates for excise duties. I regret, therefore, that it is not possible at this stage to provide the information requested.

Ivory

Mr. Tony Banks: To ask the Chancellor of the Exchequer why were a quantity of African elephant tusks detained by Customs and Excise in the Flying Tigers customs shed at Heathrow airport on 20 April 1989; for whom and where the tusks were to be delivered; and what was the total weight of ivory involved.

Mr. Lilley: Five consignments of raw ivory are currently held at the airport at Heathrow. Two have been seized and three were detained on 12 April. The validity of the export permits produced for this ivory is being checked by the international ivory trade monitoring unit. No further details can be given at this stage.

Mr. Tony Banks: To ask the Chancellor of the Exchequer if he will provide full details of all shipments of ivory by nature, value, country of origin and documentation discrepancy currently being detained at British ports of entry.

Mr. Lilley *[holding answer 25 May 1989]:* Details of individual consignments where Customs action is not yet completed cannot be disclosed.

Mr. Tony Banks: To ask the Chancellor of the Exchequer how many cargoes of ivory are currently at British ports of entry in transit to other destinations; and what are those destinations.

Mr. Lilley *[holding answer 25 May 1989]:* Information on such cargoes is not held centrally and could be obtained only at disproportionate cost.

Scottish Bank Notes

Mr. Canavan: To ask the Chancellor of the Exchequer whether the Treasury has had any recent communications with Scottish banks about the issue of Scottish bank notes; and if he will make a statement.

Mr. Lilley: No.

Quangos

Mr. Grocott: To ask the Chancellor of the Exchequer if he will list the people appointed to quasi-autonomous non-governmental organisations whose services were secured by executive search and selection agencies.

Mr. Luce: I have been asked to reply.

This information is not held centrally and could be obtained only at disproportionate cost.

Mr. Grocott: To ask the Chancellor of the Exchequer what was the total cost of running the Government's quasi-autonomous non-governmental organisations in each of the last 10 years.

Mr. Luce: I have been asked to reply.

The figures for the years 1979 to 1988, at current prices, are as follows:

£ million

	Amount of gross expenditure provided by Government	Other associated expenditure by sponsoring Departments
1979	2,970	70
1980	3,080	72
1981	3,860	94
1982	3,910	87
1983	5,120	94
1984	5,160	115
1985	5,100	111
1986	5,330	116
1987	5,690	112
1988	5,930	118

Figures for 1989 will be published in "Public Bodies" later this year.

Mr. Grocott: To ask the Chancellor of the Exchequer whether it is his policy to use the services of executive search and selection agencies to recruit people for quasi-autonomous non-governmental organisations.

Mr. Luce: I have been asked to reply.

The procedures adopted for identifying and selecting candidates for public appointments are the responsibility of the Minister making the appointment. The use by Government of executive search and selection agencies is limited.

Mr. Grocott: To ask the Chancellor of the Exchequer which executive search and selection agencies have been used to recruit people for quasi-autonomous non-govern-mental organisations.

Mr. Luce: I have been asked to eply.

This information is not held centrally and could be obtained only at disproportionate cost.

Capital Gains Tax

Mr. Anthony Coombs: To ask the Chancellor of the Exchequer what is the revenue yield from capital gains tax for the fiscal year ended April 1989; and what it was in the year ended April 1988.

Mr. Norman Lamont *[holding answer 22 May 1989]*: Receipts from capital gains tax in the financial years 1987-88 and 1988-89 were respectively £1,379 million and £2,323 million. These figures exclude receipts from capital gains of companies and taxed within corporation tax.

YTS

Mrs. Margaret Ewing: To ask the Chancellor of the Exchequer if he will list the regulations covering tax liability on YTS earnings with regard to partial refunds of travel or lodging costs necessarily incurred in taking part in YTS.

Mr. Norman Lamont *[holding answer 23 May 1989]*: Payments in respect of costs incurred on travelling and accommodation are only made to YTS trainees who are not employees. These payments are not liable to income tax.

Mrs. Margaret Ewing: To ask the Chancellor of the Exchequer what guidelines have been issued to employers, sponsors and managing agents on the position of young people on YTS in relation to PAYE and NIC.

Mr. Norman Lamont *[holding answer 23 May 1989]*: No special guidance on the position of young people on YTS who are taken on as employees is needed. Employers apply the same PAYE and NIC rules as for all other employees. However, the YTS allowances are below the tax and NIC thresholds, so that no tax or NIC will be payable if the employee's only income is the basic allowance.

As regards trainees who are not employees, the basic allowance is not taxable. Nor are these trainees taxed on payments to which they are also entitled in respect of travel and accommodation costs. The Training Agency's "Managing Agent's Handbook" advises YTS providers to seek advice from the local tax or DSS office if they propose to make payments over and above the basic allowance.

Charitable Gifts (Tax Relief)

Sir John Stanley: To ask the Chancellor of the Exchequer whether he will amend the give-as-you-earn scheme to enable the tax relief to accrue to the benefit of the donor's designated charity.

Mr. Lawson *[holding answer 25 May 1989]*: No. Charities already benefit from the tax relief given to employees on their donations under the payroll giving scheme. Every £1 a basic rate taxpayer gives costs him only 75p.

Tax Fraud

Mr. Barry Jones: To ask the Chancellor of the Exchequer if he will publish the number of prosecutions for tax fraud, the total number of people involved and the amount of money involved in Wales; and if he will make a statement.

Mr. Norman Lamont *[holding answer 25 May 1989]*: The Inland Revenue keeps aggregate figures for prosecutions in England and Wales. Separate figures for Wales could be provided only at disproportionate cost.

Tax Statistics

Mr. Nigel Griffiths: To ask the Chancellor of the Exchequer what is the proportion of gross income paid in income tax, national insurance contributions and value added tax by *(a)* a married man with a non-earning wife and two children and *(b)* a married man with an earning wife and two children at one half, one and a half, two, three, five and 10 times national average earnings in 1989-90; and what were the comparable figures in 1978-79.

Mr. Norman Lamont *[pursuant to his reply, 12 May 1989, c. 560]:* I regret that the original tables contained an error. The amended tables are as follows:

Married man with non-earning wife and two children

Proportion of gross earnings	Multiples of average male earnings						
	$\frac{1}{2}$	1	$1\frac{1}{2}$	2	3	5	10
1978-79							
Income tax	−4·1	14·4	20·6	23·6	32·0	47·1	64·7
NICs	6·5	6·5	5·6	4·2	2·8	1·7	0·8
VAT	—	2·7	2·7	—	—	—	—
1989-90							
Income tax	−1·0	12·0	16·4	20·2	26·8	32·1	36·1
NICs	7·9	8·4	6·8	5·1	3·4	2·0	1·0
VAT	—	5·0	5·7	—	—	—	—

Married man with earning wife and two children

Proportion of gross earnings	Multiples of average male earnings						
	$\frac{1}{2}$	1	$1\frac{1}{2}$	2	3	5	10
1978-79							
Income tax	−11·1	6·4	15·2	19·7	25·9	32·9	50·6
NICs	6·5	6·5	6·5	6·5	5·4	3·4	1·7
VAT	—	3·4	3·4	—	—	—	—
1989-90							
Income tax	−10·6	7·1	13·1	16·3	20·7	27·0	33·6
NICs	5·4	7·5	8·3	8·4	6·8	4·1	2·0
VAT	—	5·9	6·0	—	—	—	—

Notes:

1. Average male earnings in 1989-90 are assumed to be £273·10 per week, $7\frac{1}{2}$ per cent. higher than in 1988-89. This represents a real increase of over 30 per cent. since 1978-79.
2. Child benefit is treated as a negative income tax.
3. Earners, including working wives, are assumed to pay class 1 National Insurance contributions at the contracted in rate. The figures for National Insurance contributions are financial year averages.
4. The two earner couple is assumed to have joint earnings equal to the various multiples of average earnings, split between husband and wife in the ratio 60:40.
5. The estimates of VAT are derived from the 1985 family expenditure survey and are based on the illustrative assumption that 10 per cent. of disposable income is saved. Estimates cannot reliably be made outside the range of 75 per cent. to 150 per cent. of average male earnings.

DEFENCE

Radiation

Mr. George Howarth: To ask the Secretary of State for Defence when he expects to announce new compensation arrangements for British ex-servicemen who have suffered radiation ailments arising from their duties.

Mr. Sainsbury: We have no plans to change the present arrangements.

Trident

Dr. Thomas: To ask the Secretary of State for Defence if he will make a statement on present progress in the development of the new Trident nuclear warhead at the atomic weapons research establishment, Aldermaston.

Mr. Sainsbury: The development of the Trident warhead is progressing satisfactorily towards the Trident submarine in-service date of the mid-1990s.

Helicopters (Forced Landing)

Mr. Rogers: To ask the Secretary of State for Defence why five British military helicopters were forced to land by the actions of other military aircraft in West Germany on Friday 19 May; and if he will make a statement.

Mr. Neubert: The aircraft were taking part in a pre-planned training manoeuvre.

Royal Arsenal, Woolwich

Mr. Cartwright: To ask the Secretary of State for Defence if he will make a statement on the progress of the redevelopment of that part of the Royal Arsenal, Woolwich which has been declared surplus to his Department's requirements.

Mr. Neubert: Following the announcement by my hon. Friend the Member for Hove (Mr. Sainsbury) on 9 March 1989 of our intention to relocate the director general of defence quality assurance to Teesside, discussions with the London borough of Greenwich have now been held to consider arrangements for the release of the entire Woolwich Arsenal west site. The Crown estate commissioners, part owners of the site, were also present and a useful exchange of views took place.

Further meetings are planned to continue this dialogue from which we would expect detailed proposals for the redevelopment of the site to emerge.

F111 Aircraft (Upper Heyford)

Mr. Baldry: To ask the Secretary of State for Defence what information he has concerning the number of *(a)* engine failures, *(b)* engine shutdowns and *(c)* pieces of aircraft falling from planes on F111 aircraft from RAF Upper Heyford in the last five years.

Mr. Neubert: I understand that it is not the practice of the United States Air Force to release this information.

Nuclear Test Veterans

Mr. Ashley: To ask the Secretary of State for Defence, pursuant to his answer to the right hon. Member for Stoke on Trent, South of 23 May, what were the differences in the United States of America and British nuclear test objectives, and in the doses of radiation received by American and British service men, and in the protective measures taken.

Mr. Sainsbury: I have nothing to add to the answer that I gave to the right hon. Member on 23 May at column *464*.

Listening Devices

Mr. Cran: To ask the Secretary of State for Defence whether electronic surveillance listening devices are used by his Department or by any organisation or agency acting on its behalf; and if he will make a statement.

Mr. Neubert: There are many weapons systems and other items of defence equipment in service which use electronic surveillance techniques.

Ministry of Defence Police

Mr. Menzies Campbell: To ask the Secretary of State for Defence if he has any plans to reduce the strength of the Ministry of Defence police force over the next five years; and if he will make a statement.

Mr. Sainsbury: I have nothing to add to the reply which I gave to the hon. and learned member on 27 February at column *43*.

Mr. Menzies Campbell: To ask the Secretary of State for Defence what was *(a)* the establishment and *(b)* the strength of the Ministry of Defence police force in each of the last five years for which information is available.

Mr. Sainsbury: The information requested is as follows:

	Complement	Strength
September 1984	4,229	4,003
September 1985	4,563	4,255
September 1986	4,990	4,681
December 1987	5,001	4,841
December 1988	4,962	4,706

The details are taken from the chief constable's annual reports, which from 1987 relate to calendar years.

CSCE Talks

Mr. Menzies Campbell: To ask the Secretary of State for Defence if he has commissioned any studies on the minimum strength of forces necessary to defend Western Europe in the event that the CSCE talks in Vienna achieve parity between the North Atlantic Treaty Organisation and Warsaw pact forces.

Mr. Neubert: The NATO proposals tabled in Vienna were undepinned by studies which showed that they provided sufficient forces to maintain the forward defence of western Europe. The studies indicated that further significant reductions in tanks, artillery, etc., could have serious implications for NATO's ability to maintain forward defence, as it is currently understood.

Procurement Executive

Mr. Menzies Campbell: To ask the Secretary of State for Defence what action is being taken to eradicate shortages of staff in the procurement executive of his Department; and if he will make a statement.

Mr. Sainsbury: Management action is already in hand to alleviate the problems identified in the recently published House of Commons Defence Committee report. These measures include the application of new and more flexible long term Civil Service pay agreements, the proposed relocation of a substantial part of the procurement executive to parts of the country where it is easier to recruit and retain staff, and the next steps initiative. The shortages tend to be concentrated in disciplines such as electronics and information technology, and in certain geographical areas especially London and the south-east. To a large extent they are a reflection of shortages from which other major employers suffer in these areas.

Type 23 Frigate

Mr. Menzies Campbell: To ask the Secretary of State for Defence (1) what assessment he has made of the proposals by Ferranti Computer Systems for a command and control system for the type 23 frigate; and if he will make a statement;

(2) what consideration he has given to the use of penalty clauses in the contracts for the command and control system for the type 23 frigate;

(3) what measures he is taking to ensure that production difficulties are minimised in the development and manufacture of the command control system for the type 23 frigate.

Mr. Sainsbury: I refer the hon. and learned Member to the statement that I made to the House during this year's Navy debate on 28 February at columns 166-67.

Mr. Menzies Campbell: To ask the Secretary of State for Defence when he next intends to invite tenders for additional type 23 frigates; and to which companies he will extend that invitation.

Mr. Sainsbury: I refer the hon. and learned Member to the answer that I gave on 28 April at column *686*.

War Service Pensions

Mr. David Howell: To ask the Secretary of State for Defence what is the current policy of Her Majesty's Government in relation to service during the Korean war counting towards war service pensions; and whether he has any plans to review it.

Mr. Neubert: Pensions awarded under the scheme for the armed forces do not distinguish between war service and other periods of service. For those personnel of the armed forces who qualify for an award of pension based on length of service given, any service during the Korean war would count on an equal footing with other periods.

There are no plans for a review. Those suffering disability as a result of injury received during the Korean war may, however, be eligible for the award of pension under the war pensions scheme administered by the Department of Social Security, without regard to the length of service given.

Royal Naval Personnel (School Boarding Allowances)

Mr. Brazier: To ask the Secretary of State for Defence how much it would cost to allow seagoing Royal Naval personnel, on shore postings, to claim boarding school allowances, irrespective of the locations of their families.

Mr. Neubert: The total cost of boarding school allowance for Royal Navy personnel is estimated at £24 million for the financial year 1989-90, based on the number of personnel who have drawn the allowance in the past. No reduction has been assumed for the future since it is expected that the great majority of claimants, including those on shore postings, will comply with the new family mobility conditions.

Royal Naval Officers (Travel)

Mr. Brazier: To ask the Secretary of State for Defence how much it would cost to restore first class travel warrants to Royal Naval officers on the scale prevailing before the 1988 review of allowances.

Mr. Neubert: Since facilities for first class duty travel remain unaltered, it is assumed that my hon. Friend is concerned with first class leave travel. The restoration of this facility to eligible officers of the armed forces as a whole would cost an estimated £820,000 of which the Royal Navy's share is approximately £165,000.

"Who Framed Colin Wallace"

Mr. Livingstone: To ask the Secretary of State for Defence if he will establish an inquiry into the evidence presented in the book entitled "Who Framed Colin Wallace", by Mr. Paul Foot, that members of the Army information services *(a)* planted hoax bombs, *(b)* masqueraded as members of paramilitary groups and *(c)* carried and possessed captured terrorist weapons and explosives.

Mr. Neubert: No.

Mr. Livingstone: To ask the Secretary of State for Defence if he has anything to add to his answer to the hon. Member for Keighley (Mr. Waller), *Official Report,* column *707,* 20 July 1988, in the light of information in the book, "Who Framed Colin Wallace", regarding the address to which the alleged information policy document was delivered.

Mr. Neubert: The answer referred to by the hon. Member stated that a classified document was delivered by Mr. Wallace to the London home of a journalist on *The Times.* The document was in fact left by Mr. Wallace at the Northern Ireland address of the journalist.

Exercise Wintex-Cimex

Mr. Redmond: To ask the Secretary of State for Defence what lessons have been learned from the North Atlantic Treaty Organisation exercise, Wintex-Cimex; how many British service personnel took part and of what ranks; and if he will make a statement.

Mr. Neubert: Exercise Wintex-Cimex was the tenth in a series of NATO-wide command post exercises conducted by Alliance members. The exercise took place from 24 February to 9 March 1989. Its objective was to test command, control and consultation plans and procedures and to exercise the appropriate crisis management machinery which would be used in the defence of NATO countries in times of international tension or war. This was successfully achieved. Detailed assessment and evaluation of all aspects of the exercise are currently being carried out.

Though it is not our practice to comment in detail on such matters, all the indications are that useful lessons will have been learnt and that considerable value and experience was gained by those taking part. There was widespread military participation from the chiefs of staff downwards, but information on the numbers of British service participants in total or by rank is not available and could be obtained only at disproportionate cost.

Clayton (Overflying)

Mr. Redmond: To ask the Secretary of State for Defence why, on 23 May, there was a continuous day-long succession of military jet aircraft overflying the village of Clayton in the constituency of Don Valley; and if he will make a statement.

Mr. Neubert: The amount of flying activity in particular areas is influenced by several factors, some of which are unpredictable. These include the weather, the location of major exercises and the availability of range and other facilities. On this occasion however, there is no indication that there was an unusual level of activity in the relevant area. As far as low flying is concerned, the aim remains to spread the training as widely and evenly as possible throughout the entire country to ensure that, as far as practicable, no area receives an undue share.

Army Quarters, Hampshire

Mr. Colvin: To ask the Secretary of State for Defence how many dwellings in Hampshire owned by his Department for use as army quarters have been offered for sale; and, of these, how many have been sold.

Mr Neubert: A total of 105 Army married quarters in Hampshire were offered for sale in the financial year 1987-88 and two in 1988-89. All have now been sold. Since 1 April 1989 one further Army married quarter has been offered for sale.

Mr. Colvin: To ask the Secretary of State for Defence how many dwellings owned by his Department for use as army quarters are currently unoccupied and surplus to requirements *(a)* in Hampshire and *(b)* in the Romsey and Waterside constituency.

Mr. Neubert: *(a)* In Hampshire, as at 31 March 1989, the latest date for which figures are available, out of a total stock of 4,622 Army married quarters 620 were unoccupied, of which 154 have been identified as surplus to requirements. These figures exclude the Tidworth estates, where the county boundary runs through the camp and a split by county is not readily available.

(b) In the Romsey and Waterside constituency, as at 31 March 1989, out of a total stock of 349 Army married quarters 77 were unoccupied, of which 10 had been identified as surplus to requirements.

Plessey plc

Mr. Thorne: To ask the Secretary of State for Defence how he proposes to ensure continued effective competition among defence suppliers in the event that, following the proposed acquisition of the Plessey company by GEC/Siemens, these Plessey business areas become wholly-owned subsidiaries of the German company, Siemens.

Mr. Sainsbury: The MOD's procurement policy will continue to be based on the maximum possible use of competition, involving not only the companies that would result from a merger if it took place, but other defence suppliers. Where the Monopolies and Mergers Commission report has identified specific adverse effects resulting from the proposed merger, it has recommended undertakings to secure a remedy. These are currently under negotiation.

Mr. Thorne: To ask the Secretary of State for Defence what measures are being sought to satisfy United Kingdom national security requirements in the event that, following the acquisition of Plessey by GEC and Siemens, Plessey radar and Plessey defence systems become wholly-owned subsidiaries of the German company, Siemens.

Mr. Sainsbury: The Ministry of Defence gave evidence to the Monopolies and Mergers Commission inquiry on the security issues raised by the proposed merger. The MMC recognised the MOD's concerns in their recommendation that national security undertakings as to the ownership and management of certain activities had to be secured to remedy the adverse effect of the merger. My right hon. and noble Friend the Secretary of State for Trade and Industry placed responsibility on the MOD to secure these undertakings. Negotiations are proceeding, and it would be inappropriate to comment further at this stage.

Mr. Thorne: To ask the Secretary of State for Defence what steps he is taking, in view of the highly integrated nature of Plessey's research facilities, to ensure that GEC does not exercise influence over Plessey's radar and defence systems businesses in the event that they succeed in acquiring the Plessey company.

Mr. Sainsbury: The Monopolies and Mergers Commission report recommended, inter alia, that GEC should undertake not to acquire any interest in or influence or control over the management of the Plessey radar and defence systems businesses. The Office of Fair Trading is currently negotiating to this end, consulting the Ministry of Defence as necessary.

Belize

Mr. Livsey: To ask the Secretary of State for Defence what benefit in training British forces obtain from being stationed in Belize; and what is his assessment of their value.

Mr. Archie Hamilton: The commitment to Belize provides an opportunity for units and equipment to be tested in a demanding environment. Advantage is taken of the possibilities for jungle and adventure training, and field firing practice, whenever possible. Training is conducted jointly by ground, air and naval forces, and with the Belize defence force. These facilities are a valuable by-product of the Belize commitment.

Mr. Livsey: To ask the Secretary of State for Defence whether he has any plans to make changes in the commitment of British forces to Belize.

Mr. Archie Hamilton: British forces are in Belize at the request of the Belize Government, and will remain for an appropriate period to assist with that country's external defence and the training of the Belize defence force. This remains the basis of the Belize commitment.

Headquarter Contracts

Mr. Nellist: To ask the Secretary of State for Defence if he will outline the reasons for the sevenfold increase in the level of payments for headquarter contracts awarded by his Department to British Telecommunications plc in the two years to 31 March 1988.

Mr. Sainsbury *[holding answer 17 May 1989]:* There has not been the significant increase in the actual level of payments to British Telecommunications plc which the answers to the hon. Member's previous questions might imply.

During the period covered by the replies, changes were introduced into Departmental accounting arrangements which brought more payments to British Telecommunications plc into the ambit of the headquarters payment process. On a comparable basis payments in 1985-86 would have been some £50 million.

Nuclear Waste

Mr. John Evans: To ask the Secretary of State for the Environment, regarding storage of radioactive waste for which there is presently no disposal site available, whether the nuclear installations inspectorate is required to licence storage sites operated by the Ministry of Defence or by sub-contractors to the Ministry of Defence.

Mr. Sainsbury *[holding answer 25 May 1989]:* I have been asked to reply.

A site owned and operated by the Ministry of Defence requires no licensing (although, as in all these matters, Ministers are able to give assurances that such a site would be constructed and operated under conditions no less stringent than those imposed on licensed sites). If a site is operated by contractors to MoD, whether or not it is owned by MoD, licensing is required.

PRIME MINISTER

Overseas Aid

Q13. **Mr. Tom Clarke:** To ask the Prime Minister when Her Majesty's Government expect to achieve the United Nations target of 0·7 per cent. gross national product for overseas aid.

The Prime Minister: The Government accept this target in principle but like previous Administrations and many other donors are not able to set a date for achieving it. Progress towards it must depend upon developments in the economy and other claims on our resources. The aid programme is now growing in real terms and its quality is high.

Single European Act

Q55. **Mr. Teddy Taylor:** To ask the Prime Minister if she will present proposals to the Madrid European Council about the volume and nature of the directives stemming from the Single European Act.

The Prime Minister: I have no plans to do so, but I do expect the European Council in Madrid to review progress on completion of the single market.

Nicaraguan President

Dr. Thomas: To ask the Prime Minister if, during her recent meeting with President Ortega of Nicaragua, she discussed the role to be played by the non-aligned movement in strengthening the nuclear non-proliferation treaty at its fourth review conference in 1990.

The Prime Minister: No.

Nigerian President

Dr. Thomas: To ask the Prime Minister if, during the recent visit of the President of Nigeria, she discussed the ways in which the nuclear non-proliferation treaty can be strengthened at its fourth review conference in 1990.

The Prime Minister: No.

Israeli Prime Minister

Dr. Thomas: To ask the Prime Minister if, during the visit of the Prime Minister of Israel to the United Kingdom on 21-22 May, she raised the questions of *(a)* the possibility of Israel signing the nuclear non-proliferation treaty and *(b)* the danger of nuclear weapons proliferation in the middle east.

The Prime Minister: No, but we have raised this issue regularly with the Government of Israel.

Mr. Latham: To ask the Prime Minister whether she will make a statement on her meeting with the Prime Minister of the state of Israel on 22 May.

The Prime Minister: My meeting with Mr. Shamir was held in a friendly spirit reflecting the good relations between Britain and Israel. We discussed Arab-Israel matters, other regional issues and bilateral questions. I welcomed his proposals for elections in the occupied territories as a useful step forward but emphasised the need for an understanding on a solution based on territory for peace.

London Traffic

Mr. Tebbit: To ask the Prime Minister who has overall responsibility for the expedition of London's traffic.

The Prime Minister: Responsibility rests with the Secretary of State for Transport, the London local authorities and the police.

The Secretary of State is the highway authority for trunk roads in London. At the request of the London local authorities he is also responsible for London's urban traffic control systems and all London's traffic lights. The local authorities are the highway and traffic authorities for local roads in their areas. The Metropolitan and City of London police are responsible for the enforcement of traffic and parking laws, and deal with incidents arising from traffic control.

War Widows (Housing Benefit)

Sir George Young: To ask the Prime Minister whether the arrangements for disregarding war widows' pensions for housing benefit purposes are the same in England, Wales, Scotland and Northern Ireland.

The Prime Minister: No. The housing benefit scheme for England, Scotland and Wales has a statutory disregard, currently set at £5 a week, of any war disablement or war widow's pension, and local authorities have discretion to enhance this disregard. The separate housing benefit scheme in Northern Ireland has a statutory disregard of all such pensions.

Political Clubs

Mr. Coleman: To ask the Prime Minister what is the policy of Her Majesty's Government concerning the use by Government agencies of premises located in political clubs; and if she will make a statement.

The Prime Minister: Government Departments should not use premises located in political clubs for official purposes unless no suitable alternative is available. Non-departmental public bodies and Government contractors are responsible for their own operational arrangements.

Disabled Persons (Employment)

Mr. Wareing: To ask the Prime Minister what is the number of disabled persons employed by *(a)* the Cabinet Office, and *(b)* at 10 Downing street; what these figure are as a percentage of the total work force; and if she will make a statement.

The Prime Minister: There are 16 registered disabled persons employed by the Cabinet Office, which represents approximately 1 per cent. of the total work force, and none at 10 Downing street. The Cabinet Office is an equal opportunities employer, and continually seeks to encourage the employment of disabled people.

Green Issues

Mr. Malcolm Bruce: To ask the Prime Minister what assessment she has made of the need to set up a new department concerned with green issues; what discussions she has had on this matter; and when they were held.

The Prime Minister: The Department of Environment has lead responsibility for environmental issues. I have no present plans to set up a new department to deal with such issues.

Engagements

Mr. Harry Greenway: To ask the Prime Minister if she will list her official engagements for Tuesday 6 June.

Mr. Eastham: To ask the Prime Minister if she will list her official engagements for Tuesday 6 June.

Mr. Grocott: To ask the Prime Minister if she will list her official engagements for Tuesday 6 June.

Mr. Stern: To ask the Prime Minister if she will list her official engagements for Tuesday 6 June.

Mr. Livingstone: To ask the Prime Minister if she will list her official engagements for Tuesday 6 June.

The Prime Minister: This morning I had meetings with ministerial colleagues and others. In addition to my duties in the House I shall be having further meetings later today. This evening I hope to have an audience of Her Majesty the Queen.

HOUSE OF COMMONS

Petitions

Mr. Amess: To ask the Lord President of the Council if he will publish in the *Official Report* a table showing the number of public petitions presented in each session since 1970.

Mr. Wakeham: The information requested is as follows:

Session	Number of petitions
1970–71	8
1971–72	21
1972–73	25
1973–74	6
1974	27
1974–75	12
1975–76	46
1976–77	61
1977–78	24
1978–79	6
1979–80	7
1980–81	29
1981–82	27
1982–83	29
1983–84	732
1984–85	1,059
1985–86	516
1986–87	108
1987–88	356
[1]1988–89	94

[1] To 26 May 1989.

Private Members' Bills

Mr. Amess: To ask the Lord President of the Council if he will publish in the *Official Report* a list of private Members' Bills where a Division took place on Second Reading, and where the Bill subsequently did not receive Royal Assent in each Session since 1970.

Mr. Wakeham: The information requested is as follows:

1971-72
Care of the Elderly Bill[1]

1972-73
Penalties for Murder Bill[2]
Council House (Tenant's Representation) Bill

1974
Companies Bill[1]

1974-75
Abortion (Amendment) Bill

1976-77
Abortion (Amendment) Bill
Council Tenants' Charter Bill[2]
Pre-Release Hostels for Prisoners Bill[2]

1977-78
Employment Protection Bill
Employment Protection (Amendment) Bill
Post Office Workers (Industrial Action) Bill

1978-79
Employment Opportunities (Small Businesses) Bill

1979-80
Abortion (Amendment) Bill
Road Traffic (Seat Belts) Bill

1982-83
Shops Bill[2]

1983-84
Sex Equality Bill[2]
House Buyers Bill

1984-85
Unborn Children (Protection) Bill

1985-86
Obscene Publications (Protection of Children Etc.) (Amendment) Bill

1986-87
Free Television Licences for Pensioners Bill[2]
Obscene Publications Bill

1988-89
Protection of Official Information Bill[2]
Abortion (Amendment) Bill

[1] fewer than 40 Members voting
[2] negatived on a Division.

Hand-delivered Items

Mr. Bowis: To ask the Lord President of the Council if he will end the practice whereby hand-delivered items to the Palace of Westminster have to bear postage stamps.

Mr. Wakeham: Under the existing regulations one unstamped letter may be accepted from a Stranger, on a sitting day, for delivery to a right hon. or hon. Member. I have no plans to change these arrangements at present. However, if my hon. Friend has any proposals in mind, may I suggest that, in the first instance, he contacts the Accommodation and Administration Sub-Committee.

EDUCATION AND SCIENCE

Grant-Maintained Schools

27. **Mr. Brandon-Bravo:** To ask the Secretary of State for Education and Science if he will make a statement on the number of schools which have opted for grant-maintained status.

32. **Mr. Dunn:** To ask the Secretary of State for Education and Science how many applications have been received by his Department from schools wishing to become grant-maintained; and if he will make a statement.

Mrs. Rumbold: I refer my hon. Friends to the reply my right hon. Friend gave earlier today to my hon. Friend the Member for Rugby and Kenilworth (Mr. Pawsey).

Written Answers to Questions

Wednesday 7 June 1989

HOME DEPARTMENT

Television Licences (Pensioners)

Mr. Skinner: To ask the Secretary of State for the Home Department what representations he has received seeking the introduction of free television licences for retirement pensioners; and if he will make a statement.

Mr. Renton: Since 1 January this year, we have received five letters—in four cases referred to us by hon. Members —seeking the introduction of free television licences for retirement pensioners.

Television Licences

Mr. Gareth Wardell: To ask the Secretary of State for the Home Department if he has any plans to permit war widows the same concession with regard to television licences as residents in sheltered accommodation.

Mr. Renton: The concessionary TV licence is available to retirement pensioners and disabled people who live in residential or nursing homes, or in equivalent sheltered housing provided by a local authority or a housing association. There are no plans to extend the concession.

Barrow Borough Transport Ltd.

Mr. Franks: To ask the Secretary of State for the Home Department if he will call for a report from the chief constable of Cumbria as to any investigations being undertaken into the activities of former directors and executives of Barrow Borough Transport Ltd. arising from the finding of the administrators appointed to oversee the company.

Mr. Douglas Hogg: I understand that the police are not conducting any inquiries into this case.

Radio Tara

Mr. Tredinnick: To ask the Secretary of State for the Home Department what action he has taken since receiving a request from the Independent Broadcasting Authority that representations be made to the Irish Government seeking alteration to the Radio Tara, Atlantic 252, aerial siting or its configuration.

Mr. Renton: We have made representations to the Irish authorities and await their reply.

Her Majesty's Prison, Leicester

Mr. Vaz: To ask the Secretary of State for the Home Department how many rule 43 prisoners are held in the segregational unit at Her Majesty's prison, Leicester; and what proposals he has for improving the conditions in this unit.

Mr. Douglas Hogg *[holding answer 6 June 1989]:* On 5 June 1989, one prisoner was held in the segregation unit at Leicester prison under rule 43 for the maintenance of good order or discipline. There are no proposals for improving the conditions in that unit.

Mr. Vaz: To ask the Secretary of State for the Home Department what is the extent and effect on the running of gym, exercise and education periods of staff shortages at Her Majesty's prison Leicester; and if he has any plans to reverse this situation.

Mr. Douglas Hogg *[holding answer 6 June 1989]:* The PE department currently has a full complement of four full-time PE officers and the PE programme does not suffer from staff shortages. However, for the 12 months prior to 15 May 1989 the department did run with one PE officer short. This caused 90 classes to be cancelled. Nevertheless, the inmates spent some 29,248 hours on physical education from May 1988 to May 1989.

FOREIGN AND COMMONWEALTH AFFAIRS

Vienna Convention

Mr. Sillars: To ask the Secretary of State for Foreign and Commonwealth Affairs if he will list the 82 states which voted for the adoption of the 1978 Vienna convention on succession of states in respect of treaties; and if he will indicate which of those countries have moved to ratification.

Mr. Eggar: According to the official records of the conference, the Vienna convention on succession of states in respect of treaties was adopted on 22 August 1978 by 76 votes in favour (including the United Kingdom) to none against with four abstentions. Subsequently two of those countries which had abstained informed the UN Secretariat that they had received authorisation to support the convention. This was not a roll call vote and the records do not list who among the 94 participating countries voted in favour.

As at 31 December 1988 the following countries had ratified the convention: Dominica, Egypt, Ethiopia, Iraq, Morocco, Seychelles, Tunisia and Yugoslavia.

Katyn Massacre

Mr. Atkinson: To ask the Secretary of State for Foreign and Commonwealth Affairs if he will make a statement on the progress of his Department's studies of Soviet involvement in the Katyn massacre taking account of the recent statement by the Polish Government on this matter.

Mr. Waldegrave: We are following developments closely. There is substantial circumstantial evidence pointing to Soviet responsibility for the massacre. We urge the Soviet authorities to help establish the facts once and for all.

Cambodia

Mr. Battle: To ask the Secretary of State for Foreign and Commonwealth Affairs what information he has on Vietnamese troop withdrawals from Kampuchea; and what development he envisages in Her Majesty's Government's policies on recognition of *(a)* the coalition Government of democratic Kampuchea or *(b)* the state of Cambodia PRK.

Mr. Eggar: Vietnam has withdrawn some troops from Cambodia, but significant numbers remain. We welcome Vietnam's stated intention of withdrawing fully by September.

We recognise states, not Governments, and have dealings with neither the CGDK nor the PRK. We currently for see no change in this policy.

Egypt

Mr. Tony Lloyd: To ask the Secretary of State for Foreign and Commonwealth Affairs what discussion Her Majesty's Government have had with the Egyptian authorities about the use of torture of political detainees in Egypt.

Mr. Waldegrave: None.

Hong Kong (Ivory Trade)

Mr. Tredinnick: To ask the Secretary of State for Foreign and Commonwealth Affairs what discussions he has had with the Hong Kong Government concerning the trade in ivory in Hong Kong.

Mr. Eggar: We have informed the Hong Kong Government about our decision to support a ban on trade in new ivory. They are now urgently reviewing their position.

Abduction

Mr. David Nicholson: To ask the Secretary of State for Foreign and Commonwealth Affairs what representations he has received during the present Parliament about the abduction and taking abroad by their foreign-born fathers of the children of United Kingdom citizen mothers; what information he has of the numbers of such children and the countries where they are now believed to reside; and if he will make a statement.

Mr. Eggar [pursuant to the reply, 23 May 1989, c. 455]: Foreign and Commonwealth consular records are kept on an individual case-by-case basis. However, it has been possible to identify 56 cases in which Foreign and Commonwealth Office Ministers have received, during the present Parliament, representations about British children who have been taken overseas or are being kept overseas against the wishes of their mothers in the United Kingdom.

The following table gives details of the number of cases together with the countries to which the children have been taken or in which they are believed to be being kept.

In five of these cases—one in Cyprus, two in the United States of America, one in Yemen Arab Republic and one in Yugoslavia—custody of one or more of the children concerned has now been restored to their mothers in the United Kingdom.

Country	Number of cases
Afghanistan	1
Algeria	3
Chile	1
Cyprus	3
France	1
India	1
Iran	3
Libya	1

Country	Number of cases
Malaysia	1
Morocco	2
Netherlands	1
New Zealand	2
Pakistan	9
Saudi Arabia	4
Singapore	1
Spain	3
Sri Lanka	1
Thailand	1
United Arab Emirates	3
United States of America	9
Yemen Arab Republic	3
Yugoslavia	2

TRANSPORT

Lichfield—Redditch Railway Line

Mr. Heddle: To ask the Secretary of State for Transport if he has now received British Rail's submission for the electrification of the cross city line from Lichfield to Redditch via Birmingham New Street.

Mr. Portillo: Not yet.

Heavy Vehicles

Mr. Adley: To ask the Secretary of State for Transport how many motor car axle-load movements of 12-cwt could be undertaken to equate with the equivalent damage caused by 1,000 12-ton axle-load lorries.

Mr. Peter Bottomley: Except for special vehicles, 12-ton axle loads are not allowed. The road wear from 1,000 12-ton axle-load movements would be about the same as from 160 million 12-cwt axle loads.

Speed Limits

Mr. Adley: To ask the Secretary of State for Transport what assessment he has made of how much the kinetic energy as affecting road surfaces has increased through the raising of speed limits (a) of lorries from 50 to 60 mph and (b) of coaches from 60 to 70 mph.

Mr. Peter Bottomley: Detailed research into this aspect of road wear is still in progress. The interplay of the different vehicle forces and suspension types is complex, and the effect on the road surface varies according to speed and loading. Current indications are that, at higher speeds, dynamic effects increase the loading on road surfaces. The increases are small and are countered by the improved load spreading properties of most roads at such speeds. The research programme is aimed at determining where the balance between these opposing effects lies.

Barrow Borough Transport Ltd.

Mr. Franks: To ask the Secretary of State for Transport on what date Barrow-in-Furness borough council applied to him for approval for the council to guarantee with National Westminster bank plc the overdraft facilities of Barrow Borough Transport Ltd.; and what was his reply.

Mr. Portillo: Barrow-in-Furness borough council applied to the Secretary of State for Transport for approval to guarantee an overdraft facility on 12 August 1988 and submitted further information in support of this application on 16 September and 13 October. The application was, however, overtaken by subsequent events leading up to the appointment of administrators on 21 December.

Mr. Franks: To ask the Secretary of State for Transport (1) on what date Barrow-in-Furness borough council applied to him to make loans to Barrow Borough Transport Ltd.; and what was his reply;

(2) what information he has as to the total amount of loans made by the Barrow-in-Furness borough council to Barrow Borough Transport Ltd. and as to between what dates these loans were made; and whether he gave his prior consent to the making of such loans under section 79 of the Transport Act 1985.

Mr. Portillo: We were informed in December 1988 by the council that it had made certain payments on behalf of the company between October 1986 and March 1987 and were asked whether consent was needed. We indicated that retrospective consent was not possible. Otherwise no application for consent to loans has been received and I have no information on loans made by the council to the company. The council does not need the Secretary of State's consent to make loans in connection with the provision or improvement of assets, provided that such loans are on terms no more favourable than those on which the authority can itself borrow.

Mr. Franks: To ask the Secretary of State for Transport what information he has as to *(a)* how many directors were appointed at any one time to the board of directors of Barrow Borough Transport Ltd., *(b)* how many of these directors were also councillors on Barrow-in-Furness borough council and *(c)* the financial status of such appointees.

Mr. Portillo: We have no specific knowledge on these points.

Mr. Franks: To ask the Secretary of State for Transport what information he has as to *(a)* on what date administrators were appointed by Barrow Borough Transport Ltd. and *(b)* what the total amount of indebtedness by Barrow Borough Transport Ltd. to Barrow-in-Furness borough council was at the date of the appointment of the administrators; and whether he gave his consent to the appointment of these administrators.

Mr. Portillo: Administrators were appointed on 21 December. We understand from the council that £628,000 was owed to them by the company. The Secretary of State's consent was not required to the appointment of administrators, which was made by the courts following an application by the directors of the company under the Insolvency Act 1986. The Secretary of State was, however, kept informed by the council and made clear that he had no objection to the council's action in connection with the appointment of administrators.

Mr. Franks: To ask the Secretary of State for Transport what information he has as to the amounts Barrow-in-Furness borough council transferred to Barrow Borough Transport Ltd. between 6 October 1988 and 10 November 1988; and whether his prior consent was sought for such transfers.

Mr. Portillo: We have no information about any such transfers.

Mr. Franks: To ask the Secretary of State for Transport whether his consent was sought for the National Westminster Bank plc to obtain a legal mortgage over Barrow Borough Transport Ltd. property.

Mr. Portillo: No, and we have no information about any such mortgage. Public transport companies are, however, entitled to borrow from banks by way of temporary loans or overdrafts without the Secretary of State's consent, and may offer property as security for such borrowing.

Fuel Duty Rebate

Mrs. Margaret Ewing: To ask the Secretary of State for Transport by how much revenue to the Exchequer would increase if the fuel duty rebate was abolished.

Mr. Portillo: In 1988-89 some £158 million of fuel duty rebate was paid to local bus operators.

Mrs. Margaret Ewing: To ask the Secretary of State for Transport what assessment he has made of the effect of the abolition of fuel duty rebate on *(a)* bus fares and *(b)* bus services in sparsely populated rural areas.

Mr. Portillo: We have estimated in 1988 that, assuming all else stayed the same in the local bus industry, the abolition of fuel duty rebate would result in either an increase in fares of some 13 per cent., supposing the whole effect was on fares, or a decrease in bus miles of some 12 per cent., supposing the whole effect was on bus miles. In practice it is likely that there would be some combination of these two effects. No separate estimate has been made of the effect on bus services in sparsely populated rural areas.

Motorcycle Test

Mr. Roger King: To ask the Secretary of State for Transport when he expects to introduce the new accompanied motor cycle test; and what will the fee be for the test.

Mr. Peter Bottomley: We intend to introduce the new accompanied motor cycle riding test, for both motor cycles and mopeds, throughout Great Britain on Monday 2 October 1989. The examiner, instead of conducting the test on foot, will accompany the candidate on another motor cycle (or sometimes in a car) giving directions by radio link. This will make the test more rigorous. It will cover more ground. The examiner will see the entirety of the candidate's performance in the prevailing road and traffic conditions. The change in the test has been generally welcomed.

The test will be available from 212 driving test centres throughout the country.

Because of the extra costs involved in providing an accompanied test (provision of examiners' motor cycles, protective clothing and mobile radio equipment) it is proposed that the current test fee of £16·50 be increased to £24, compared with £18, with effect from 5 June for a car test. We are consulting all interested organisations on the change in regulations to effect this increase.

Taunton Bypass

Mr. David Nicholson: To ask the Secretary of State for Transport what plans he has for repairing the Taunton bypass section of the M5; and if he will make a statement.

Mr. Peter Bottomley: Four major maintenance schemes will be carried out over the next few years to renew completely the southbound carriageway to enable it to carry the traffic expected well into the next century.

The first of these contracts has recently been completed to the north of junction 26.

Every effort will be made to minimise inconvenience to road users during the works, which will be programmed to avoid peak holiday periods.

The decision to do the work following a study of the long-term maintenance needs of this length of M5 which was commissioned by Somerset county council at the Department's request.

Unleaded Petrol

Sir Hal Miller: To ask the Secretary of State for Transport what progress has been made on the availability of unleaded petrol at motorway petrol service areas since the hon. Member's reply from the Minister for Roads and Traffic of 16 February, *Official Report,* column *294.*

Mr. Peter Bottomley: My hon. Friend the Parliamentary Under-Secretary of State for the Environment and I are pleased that unleaded petrol is now available at all motorway service areas. The number of unleaded petrol pumps at sites is being increased to meet demand.

British Rail (Investment)

Mr. Nicholas Bennett: To ask the Secretary of State for Transport if he will uprate to 1989-90 prices the figures for investment by British Rail in the reply given to the hon. Member for Pembroke on 6 April, *Official Report,* columns *263-64.*

Mr. Portillo: The figures are as follows:

	£ million cash	£ million 1989-90 prices
1948	40	603
1949	44	640
1950	43	624
1951	41	548
1952	38	468
1953	56	666
1954	63	749
1955	68	771
1956	90	966
1957	120	1,235
1958	134	1,324
1959	154	1,512
1960	147	1,427
1961	130	1,220
1962	94	855
1963	73	646
1964	83	710
1965	92	748
1966	81	632
1967	65	488
1968	58	423
1969	39	267
1970	48	305
1971	59	346
1972	73	397

	£ million cash	£ million 1989-90 prices
1973	81	410
1974	103	456
1975	157	546
1976	176	534
1977	193	511
1978	208	494
1979	248	518
1980	304	529
1981	277	433
1982	243	352
1983	252	347
1984[1]	280	368
1985-86	399	491
1986-87	399	475
1987-88	526	594
1988-89	596	[2]629

[1] 1984-5 was a 15 month financial period. The figure shown for 1984 is the 12 month internally reported result.
[2] forecast outturn.

The figures include investment in Freightliners, BRML and BREL but exclude the laying of continuous welded track which BR do not now classify as investment.

Indicative figures for BR's plans for future investment (excluding investment in BREL, which is being sold, and in the proposed high speed link to the Channel tunnel) are:

	£ million
1989-90	781
1990-91	865
1991-92	928
1992-93	865

In order to show the most consistent picture the figures in the table include some elements of "corporate" as well as "railway" investment. BR's standard definitions of these have changed over the years. The figures have been adjusted to current values by the most recent indices. They show that there was a high level of investment during the modernisation programme of the late 1950s and early 1960s. BR's route mileage now is 45 per cent. less than it was in the peak investment year of 1959, but passenger mileage is currently at broadly the same levels as in 1959.

EC Transport Ministers' Council

Mr. Amos: To ask the Secretary of State for Transport what was the outcome of the recent European Council of Transport Ministers meeting in Luxembourg; and if he will make a statement.

Mr. Channon: I successfully negotiated a satisfactory end-date for the United Kingdom derogations from the Community maximum lorry weight limits. Against a Commission proposal that our derogation should end in 1996 I insisted that we needed more time to bring sufficient of our bridges up to suitable strength. It was a major achievement that the 40 tonne gross and 11·5 tonne drive axle weight limits will not apply in the United Kingdom until 1 January 1999.

The Council also agreed to an improved inter-regional air services directive; a regulation to improve the working of air transport computer reservation systems, but with suitable data protection; a directive on road haulage statistics; a Resolution highlighting the need for improved co-operation in air traffic control; and conclusions reaffirming the need to make progress in the Community's transit negotiations with Austria, Switzerland and Yugoslavia. The Commission's proposal on charging infrastructure costs to heavy goods vehicles was referred to Finance ministers. Against the United Kingdom's wishes, but on qualified majority voting, the Council agreed to increase the maximum permitted length of articulated vehicles from 15·5 to 16·5 metres; and to adopt a measure requiring a minimum tyre tread depth of 1·6 millimetres over three quarters of tyres' width.

There was discussion but no agreement on a proposed short-term road haulage cabotage experiment; blood alcohol levels for drivers; the wearing of seat belts; and west Africa shipping.

The Commission presented a proposal on shipping "positive measures" and a revised proposal for Community spending on transport infrastructure. There was some general discussion on the environment and transport under "any other business".

Heavy Lorries

Mr. Teddy Taylor: To ask the Secretary of State for Transport what was the outcome of the Council meeting on heavier lorries on 5 June; and what are the implications for the United Kingdom and roads and bridge expenditure.

Mr. Peter Bottomley: We agreed that 40-tonne lorries will not reach British roads until 1999. We succeeded in persuading other member states that an earlier end-date would be premature.

This date will give us the time needed for our bridges to be adequately strengthened. The strengthening pro-gramme is already underway. There are no new expenditure implications on trunk roads. We shall be talking further to local authorities to consider any implications for their programme.

The Council also agreed on a work programme for improving lorries so that by the late 1990s they should be fitted with road-friendly suspensions which will be less damaging to roads and bridges, safer, quieter and better for the environment.

EDUCATION AND SCIENCE

Teachers' Pay

Mr. Ian Taylor: To ask the Secretary of State for Education and Science when he next intends to meet the teaching unions to discuss the introduction of localised pay agreements.

Mrs. Rumbold: I refer my hon. Friend to the reply given by my right hon. Friend to the hon. Member for Hendon, South (Mr. Marshall) on 6 June 1989 at column *14*.

CIVIL SERVICE

Interchange with Outside Organisations

Mr. Tim Smith: To ask the Minister for the Civil Service what was the level of interchange between the Civil Service and outside organisations in 1988.

Mr. Luce: My Department's report on the interchange of staff between the Civil Service and other organisations in 1988 shows that the number of long-term secondments

—that is, those of at least three months' duration—between the Civil Service and industrial or commercial organisations increased by 7 per cent. in 1988 to 505. There was a slight decrease—of some 3 per cent.—in the number of long-term secondments between the Civil Service and other organisations, of which there were 499 in 1988.

On 1 March 1989, my right hon. and noble Friend the Secretary of State for Trade and Industry and I launched the Bridge programme to increase contact between Government and business. I am confident that, building on the substantial level of interchange achieved in recent years, this programme will provide a valuable boost to secondments and lead to even higher numbers of people being seconded between the Civil Service and other organisations.

A copy of the 1988 interchange report has been placed in the Library of the House.

NATIONAL FINANCE

Interest Charges

Mr. Teddy Taylor: To ask the Chancellor of the Exchequer if he will make a statement setting out his forecast of the effect of current levels of interest charges on inflation.

Mr. Lilley: Current levels of interest rates will, in due course, lead to a reduction in inflation.

Exchange Rates

Mr. Teddy Taylor: To ask the Chancellor of the Exchequer if he will make a statement setting out the considerations he takes into account in establishing whether the pound is overvalued or undervalued against *(a)* the deutschmark and *(b)* other principal currencies.

Mr. Lilley: The considerations the Government take into account in formulating their monetary policy, in which the exchange rate plays a key role, were set out in my right hon. Friend the Chancellor of the Exchequer's Budget speech on 14 March, at columns 294-309.

Mr. Teddy Taylor: To ask the Chancellor of the Exchequer if he will make a statement setting out the considerations which govern his policy in relation to the level of the pound sterling against other currencies.

Mr. Lilley: I refer my hon. Friend to my right hon. Friend the Chancellor of the Exchequer's Budget speech on 14 March, at columns 294-309.

Exchange Rate Mechanism

Mr. Teddy Taylor: To ask the Chancellor of the Exchequer if he will now specify the considerations which would make the time appropriate to join the exchange rate mechanism of the European monetary system.

Mr. Lilley: I refer my hon. Friend to the speech my right hon. Friend the Chancellor of the Exchequer made to the Royal Institute of International Affairs on 25 January.

Payroll Giving

Mr. Hoyle: To ask the Chancellor of the Exchequer what arrangements have been made to introduce chargeable payroll deductions in the Civil Service and associated non-departmental public bodies.

Mr. Brooke: Where appropriate a collection charge of $2\frac{1}{2}$ per cent. of the amount of the deduction is made.

Customs Officers

Mr. Denzil Davies: To ask the Chancellor of the Exchequer how many Customs officers were in post at the ports of *(a)* Fishguard, *(b)* Pembroke Dock and *(c)* Holyhead as at (i) 5 April 1979 (ii) 5 April 1984 and (iii) 5 April 1989.

Mr. Lawson *[holding answer 6 June 1989]:* The numbers of Customs officers in post at the ports of Fishguard, Pembroke Dock and Holyhead at 5 April in the years 1979, 1984 and 1989 were as follows:

	1979	1984	1989
Fishguard	21	22	21
Pembroke	17	[1]18	[2]20
Holyhead	45	39	67

[1] excludes four mobile staff not solely engaged in port duties.
[2] excludes 14 mobile staff.

Mr. Denzil Davies: To ask the Chancellor of the Exchequer how many Customs officers were in post in Britain as of *(a)* 5 April 1979 and *(b)* 5 April 1989.

Mr. Lawson *[holding answer 6 June 1989]:* On 5 April 1979 there were 7,600 Customs officers in post at ports, airports and inland premises. The figure for 5 April 1989 was 8,000.

Value Added Tax Registrations

Sir Anthony Meyer: To ask the Chancellor of the Exchequer what were the numbers of new value added tax registrations for businesses with registered addresses in Wales for the calendar years 1987, 1988 and for 1989 to date.

Mr. Lilley *[holding answer 6 June 1989]:* The local VAT offices that cover Wales also cover parts of England along the Welsh border. These offices are at Chester, Cardiff, Swansea, Carmarthen, Shrewsbury and Colwyn Bay.

The numbers of VAT registrations processed by these officers for the years in question were:

Year	New registrations
1987	11,577
1988	14,748
1989—to 31 March	4,061

TRADE AND INDUSTRY

Small Businesses

Mr. David Nicholson: To ask the Chancellor of the Duchy of Lancaster what estimates he has of the number of small businesses with a turnover of less than £1 million which went into liquidation in *(a)* 1986, *(b)* 1987 and *(c)* 1988; and if he will make a statement.

Mr. Maude: I regret that the information requested is not available.

North East Shipbuilders Ltd

Mr. Trotter: To ask the Chancellor of the Duchy of Lancaster what arrangements he envisages for the disposal of the assets at NESL.

Mr. Newton: I made it clear earlier this year, following the announcement that British Shipbuilders was to close NESL, that the remaining work on ferries originally ordered by Danish interests would take some months to complete, and that no action would be taken to break up the assets in the yard before the end of June.

In the intervening period, there have been several expressions of interest in some or all of the yards for a number of purposes including shiprepair, shipbuilding and general engineering.

I have therefore asked British Shipbuilders and its financial advisers carefully to evaluate all such proposals with a view to advising me by the end of this month whether one or more of them provides a basis for detailed negotiation for the disposal of some or all of the assets. As with the evaluation of bids for NESL prior to the announcement of closure particular weight will be given to the security of resulting employment. In judging viability it will be necessary to allow for the fact that subsidy from the intervention fund would not be available.

In making its judgment on the advice offered by British Shipbuilders on any possible disposal, the Government will need also to take appropriate account of its acceptability under the EC sixth directive on shipbuilding of the balance of advantage by comparison with the alternative of acquisition by the Tyne and Wear development corporation for clearance and development; of the extent to which any form of Government financial assistance was envisaged.

Should such a disposal take place, the Government would also have to decide whether measures to assist the creation of employment to replace that in the yards continued to be necessary. Pending a decision, elements of the proposed remedial package not yet implemented, including designation of an enterprise zone, will be held in abeyance.

Companies Investigation Branch

Mr. Cousins: To ask the Chancellor of the Duchy of Lancaster what is the establishment and staff in post in each grade of the companies investigation branch of the Department of Trade and Industry in each year since 1984.

Mr. Forth: The following table shows the posts allocated by grade to the companies investigation branch on 1 April in each of the years in question. Staff in post tends to change in the course of a year. The table, there,fore also lists the staff in post on 1 April.

Grade	1 April 1984 Allocation	1 April 1984 Staff in Post	1 April 1985 Allocation	1 April 1985 Staff in Post	1 April 1986 Allocation	1 April 1986 Staff in Post	1 April 1987 Allocation	1 April 1987 Staff in Post	1 April 1988 Allocation	1 April 1988 Staff in Post	1 April 1989 Allocation	1 April 1989 Staff in Post
E/DIR/L	1	1	1	1	1	1	1	1	1	1	1	1
INS/GD/A	1	1	1	1	1	1	1	1	2	2	3	3
INS/GD/B	5	5	6	5	7	6	7	8	8	7	12	12

Grade	1 April 1984		1 April 1985		1 April 1986		1 April 1987		1 April 1988		1 April 1989	
	Allocation	Staff in Post	Allocation	Staff in Post	Allocation	Staff in Post	Allocation	Staff in Post	Allocation	Staff in Post	Allocation	Staff in Post
INS/GD/C	14	14	14	14	14	14	20	18	25	25	25	22
G7	—	—	—	—	—	—	—	—	—	—	1	1
HEO	—	—	—	—	1	—	1	1	1	1	2	2
EO	1	1	1	1	1	—	1	1	1	1	2	1
INS/GD/D & E	4	4	5	3	5	5	8	8	7	5	7	4
AO	4	4	5	4	5	3	5	5	5	5	6	7
AA	1	1	1	1	1	1	1	1	2	2	3	3
PS	1	1	1	1	2	1	2	2	3	2	4	3·5
TYP	—	—	—	—	—	—	—	—	—	1	·1	1
Total	32	32	35	31	38	32	47	46	55	52	67	60·5

Private Limited Companies

Mr. Evennett: To ask the Chancellor of the Duchy of Lancaster (1) how many private limited companies registered in England and Wales have a paid-up share capital of greater than £100,000;

(2) how many private limited companies registered in England and Wales have paid-up share capital in each of the bands *(a)* £25,000 to £50,000, *(b)* £50,000 to £75,000 and *(c)* £75,000 to £100,000.

Mr. Maude: This information is not currently available for all private limited companies on the companies' register. However, work is in hand to compile data on the lines requested for companies formed since May 1987 and this is expected to be available from Companies house in a few weeks' time.

Mr. Evennett: To ask the Chancellor of the Duchy of Lancaster what information he has regarding the minimum share capital required by private limited companies seeking authorisation under the Financial Services Act 1986 from the Securities and Investments Board or any self-regulatory organisation; and if he will make a statement.

Mr. Maude: The financial resources requirements for persons authorised by the Securities and Investments Board or by self-regulating organisations recognised under the Financial Services Act are matters for the board and the organisation concerned. As far as I am aware, none of these regulatory bodies expresses its requirements in terms of minimum share capital.

Barlow Clowes

Mr. Hardy: To ask the Chancellor of the Duchy of Lancaster what is the sum recovered so far from the Barlow Clowes international fund; and how much has been returned to investors.

Mr. Maude: I understand the gross realisations, including bank interest, made by the receivers of funds promoted by Barlow Clowes International Limited amount so far to approximately £20 million.

No distribution has yet been made to BCI investors pending the outcome of three court cases, two of which have already been heard with judgment reserved. The third case, to be heard in late June, will determine the basis upon which each individual investor's entitlement to any distribution will be calculated. I understand that it is hoped that after judgment of the three cases an interim distribution to investors in BCI may be made in the late summer or autumn this year.

Bankruptcy (Scotland) Act

Mrs. Margaret Ewing: To ask the Chancellor of the Duchy of Lancaster if he will list regulations made under section 74(7) of the Bankruptcy (Scotland) Act 1985; and what plans he has to extend such definition.

Mr. Maude: Regulations made under section 74(7) of the Bankruptcy (Scotland) Act 1985 are set out in regulation 11 of the Bankruptcy (Scotland) Regulations 1985 (SI 1985 No. 1925 (s147)). There are no current plans to extend the definition.

Mrs. Margaret Ewing: To ask the Chancellor of the Duchy of Lancaster if he will consider legislation to introduce one period applicable to gratuitous alienation to an associate of the debtor or other parties in terms of section 34(3) of the Bankruptcy (Scotland) Act 1985.

Mr. Maude: No such legislation is considered necessary at present.

An associate of a person who has subsequently been bankrupt would have been in a better position than any other person to judge the bankrupt's financial circumstances when the alienation took place. To be fair and just, an alienation in favour of an associate should continue to be challengeable if it was effected five years before the date of sequestration of the bankrupt's estate while an alienation in favour of any other person should be challengeable if it was effected two years before the date of sequestration.

Tourism

Mr. Redmond: To ask the Chancellor of the Duchy of Lancaster what was the total value of tourism in Yorkshire and Humberside at current prices in each of the years from May 1979 to May 1989.

Mr. John Lee: I have been asked to reply.

The available information relates to expenditure by international and domestic visitors staying at least one night in Yorkshire and Humberside in each calendar year from 1979 to 1988. Figures for expenditure by United Kingdom residents on day-trips within Yorkshire and Humberside are not available.

Expenditure by tourists in the Yorkshire and Humberside region
£ millions

	British residents[1]	Overseas residents[2]	Total
1979	255	60	315
1980	275	65	340
1981	300	80	380
1982	295	85	380
1983	335	110	445

	British residents[1]	Overseas residents[2]	Total
1984	385	115	500
1984	[3]405	—	[3]520
1985	[3]375	145	[3]520
1986	[3]435	125	[3]560
1987	[3]420	150	[3]570
1988	[3]500	[4]	[4]

[1] Source: British Tourist Survey Monthly.
[2] Source: International Passenger Survey.
[3] From 1984, an improved method of estimation was introduced, therefore, figures from 1984 to 1988 are not strictly comparable with earlier years.
[4] Not available.

WALES

Agricultural Department

Mr. Geraint Howells: To ask the Secretary of State for Wales whether he has any plans to restructure his agriculture department in Wales; and if he will make a statement.

Mr. Peter Walker: Agriculture Department staff presently located at Plas Crug are in the process of moving to Trawsgoed. This relocation will produce worthwhile savings in accommodation costs and some staff economies. There will be no redundancies.

Heart and Lung Transplants

Mr. Geraint Howells: To ask the Secretary of State for Wales how many people in Wales are on the waiting list for *(a)* heart and *(b)* lung transplants for each of the last five years; and if he will make a statement.

Mr. Grist: Heart and lung transplants are carried out at supra-regional centres in England and the information requested is not held by the Welsh Office.

Disabled People (Housing)

Mr. Alfred Morris: To ask the Secretary of State for Wales what action he is taking to ensure a sufficient supply of wheelchair housing for people with disabilities who wish to leave residential care or to set up home on their own; and if he will make a statement.

Mr. Grist: It is for local authorities and housing associations in conjunction with Housing for Wales to assess housing need in their area and to make appropriate provision for people with special needs including those with disabilities.

Mr. Alfred Morris: To ask the Secretary of State for Wales if he will list the number of completions of *(a)* wheelchair housing and *(b)* mobility housing by (i) local authorities, (ii) housing associations and (iii) the private sector in each of the last 10 years for which figures are available.

Mr. Grist: Returns from local authorities indicate the number of dwellings built for the disabled to be as follows. Reliable estimates as regards the private sector are not available.

	Completions of Wheelchair Housing		Completions of Mobility Housing	
	Local authority and New Towns	Housing association	Local authority and New Towns	Housing association
1979	16	—	14	—
1980	16	—	17	—
1981	8	—	37	—
1982	9	—	72	—
1983	16	—	147	—
1984	31	2	159	—
1985	46	—	9	4
1986	1	27	39	1
1987	29	10	64	175
1988[1]	9	5	49	26

[1] provisional.

East Glamorgan General Hospital

Dr. Kim Howells: To ask the Secretary of State for Wales if he will list the major obstacles remaining in the way of an announcement by him of the start-up date for the construction of a replacement for East Glamorgan general hospital.

Mr. Grist: It is for the Mid Glamorgan DHA to indicate when construction of a replacement for this hospital might commence.

Purolite Factory, Talbot Green

Dr. Kim Howells: To ask the Secretary of State for Wales what action he is taking in response to the messages received by the Welsh Office from people in the Talbot Green area expressing concern about the operation of the Purolite factory in that village.

Mr. Grist: I refer the hon. Gentleman to the reply sent to him on 6 June by my right hon. Friend.

Higher and Further Education

Dr. Kim Howells: To ask the Secretary of State for Wales what assessment he has made of the adequacy of the increase in the current year of 3 per cent. in expenditure on institutions of higher and further education in Wales, in the light of the current inflation levels.

Mr. Wyn Roberts: The higher education quantum for 1989-90 is based on a figure 8·75 per cent. higher than last year's allocation. Some LEAs may provide further resources for higher education in addition to their share of the quantum to meet local priorities. Recurrent expenditure on further education is supported from the overall provision for local authority current expenditure on education, which rose by 6·3 per cent. between 1988-89 and the current year. Capital expenditure on higher and further education institutions in 1989-90 is expected to exceed last year's figure of £10·7 million by a substantial factor.

Young People (Qualifications)

Dr. Kim Howells: To ask the Secretary of State for Wales what he intends to do to overcome the shortage of young people in Wales with the higher education qualifications and training required by industry and the financial services.

Mr. Wyn Roberts: The reform of college governing bodies under the Education Reform Act, the priorities adopted by the Wales Advisory Body in formulating its advice on the distribution of the higher education quantum and the establishment of a transbinary Wales access unit to encourage and support the development of access courses will all assist higher education institutions to meet the demands of industry for highly skilled manpower. We have been encouraging employers to prepare for potential labour shortages by retraining existing workers, and drawing on the unemployed and other adults entering or re-entering the labour market. Our own training programmes are designed to facilitate this. We are particularly aware of the needs of the financial services sector in Wales and my right hon. Friend is discussing with interested parties measures to strengthen the skill base. He will be making an announcement on this shortly.

Stone Quarrying (Taff Ely)

Dr. Kim Howells: To ask the Secretary of State for Wales what is his policy towards a physical expansion of stone quarrying in and around the borough of Taff Ely.

Mr. Grist: Responsibility for mineral planning in Taff Ely lies with the mineral planning authority, Mid Glamorgan county council.

Litter

Dr. Kim Howells: To ask the Secretary of State for Wales what measures he intends to take to combat the problems of litter on and around the streets of the valleys communities.

Mr. Peter Walker: We are considering placing a duty on local authorities to clean public areas, having regard to codes of practice which the Government would issue. We are also looking at ways of enabling local authorities to enforce the Litter Act more effectively.

Sewage Disposal

Dr. Kim Howells: To ask the Secretary of State for Wales, what measures he intends to take to ensure that the Welsh water authority reduces the volume of sewage which it releases into the rivers of south Wales during periods of high rainfall.

Mr. Grist: None. The operation of storm sewage overflows during periods of high rainfall is a necessary practice to prevent the surcharging of sewers and the likely consequent flooding of properties with sewage.

Research and Development (New Industries)

Dr. Kim Howells: To ask the Secretary of State for Wales what measures he intends to take to promote the business of research and development in the new industries of south Wales.

Mr. Peter Walker: My Department actively promotes a wide range of measures aimed at stimulating industrial research and development. Financial assistance is available for collaborative research and for exploring key technologies. The Link scheme encourages companies to work jointly with universities and polytechnics, while small firms can benefit from the SMART competition and the regional enterprise grants for innovation. WINtech, a division of the WDA, has been established specifically to advance the development and use of new technology in Welsh industry. It provides quality advice on technology transfer and product development, and access to seed capital. Welsh Development International complements this broader effort by working hard to encourage inward investors to establish research and development facilities in Wales.

Welsh Water Authority (Headquarters)

Dr. Kim Howells: To ask the Secretary of State for Wales what proportion of the bill for the current construction of the reinforced concrete monitoring building at the Welsh water authority's area headquarters at Nelson, Mid Glamorgan, will be written off under the Government's write-off of water authority debts.

Mr. Grist: Recent Government statements on debt write-off relate only to water authority borrowings from the national loans fund. The Government will not be seeking to identify notional borrowings against specific projects.

Out-patient Waiting Lists

Dr. Kim Howells: To ask the Secretary of State for Wales what information he has on the reasons for the differences in the time it takes to clear out-patient waiting lists in Glamorgan general hospital, Cardiff royal infirmary and the average for all hospitals in Wales.

Mr. Grist: As the introduction to Welsh Hospital Waiting List Bulletin 1989: No. 1 makes clear, for a variety of reasons care is needed in interpreting the data given in the bulletin, thus making meaningful comparisons difficult. In the case of Cardiff royal infirmary the hospital provides a range of specialties which are particularly to it and may be different from those found in other hospitals, notably East Glamorgan hospital. There are further differences between individual specialties, notably in the case of Cardiff royal infirmary trauma and orthopaedics. The East Glamorgan general hospital is understood to have had staffing problems at consultant level which will have affected the notional waiting time figures there, at least in the short term. Detailed information on the explanation for waiting list performance by particular hospitals may be obtained direct from the relevant health authorities, upon which the responsibility to achieve the right balance of services and resources in serving their patients in the light of local circumstances and needs.

Channel Tunnel

Dr. Howells: To ask the Secretary of State for Wales if he will takes steps to ensure that south Wales rail passengers and freight will enjoy direct access to the continent via the Channel tunnel as soon as any other region of the United Kingdom.

Mr. Wyn Roberts: I am keen for British Rail to provide Wales with an appropriate level of service to meet identified needs. It is for British Rail to determine the level and nature of such services in the light of available forecasts of traffic.

Cash Limits

Mr. Gwilym Jones: To ask the Secretary of State for Wales if he proposes to make any changes to the 1989-90 cash limits for class XVII, vote 5 and WO/UA1.

Mr. Peter Walker: Yes. Subject to parliamentary approval of the necessary Supplementary Estimate for class XVII, vote 6, I propose to increase the WO/UA1 urban aid non voted cash limit by £7,000,000, from £58,646,000 to £65,646,000. This will permit enhanced land acquisition this year by the Cardiff Bay development corporation.

This increase will be offset by reductions elsewhere within my expenditure programmes and will not therefore add to the planned total of public expenditure.

These savings are being found from the roads and transport section of class XVII, vote 5. Accordingly, the cash limit for this vote is being reduced by £7,000,000, from £273,711,000 to £266,711,000.

DEFENCE

Nuclear Weapons

Mr. Harry Barnes: To ask the Secretary of State for Defence what proposals exist for the multiple launch rocket system to be capable of firing short-range nuclear weapons.

Mr. Grocott: To ask the Secretary of State for Defence what proposals exist for the multiple launch rocket system to be capable of firing short-range nuclear weapons.

Mr. Archie Hamilton: I refer the hon. Members to the reply I gave to the hon. Member for Newport, West (Mr. Flynn) on 20 February 1989, at column 445.

Mr. Andrew F. Bennett: To ask the Secretary of State for Defence, pursuant to his oral reply to my hon. Friend the Member for Oldham, Central and Royton (Mr. Lamond) of 7 March, *Official Report,* column 738, what distinction he makes between (i) a warhead and (ii) a system when comparing the North Atlantic Treaty Organisation and Soviet reductions in nuclear weaponry.

Mr. Archie Hamilton: A warhead is that part of a missile, projectile, torpedo, rocket or other munition which contains either the nuclear, thermo-nuclear or high explosive device, the chemical or biological agents, or the inert materials intended to inflict damage. A weapon system is the means of delivering the warheads.

Mr. Redmond: To ask the Secretary of State for Defence how many nuclear missiles have been removed from the United Kingdom since the United States/Soviet intermediate nuclear forces treaty; and if he will make a statement.

Mr. Archie Hamilton: By the end of 1988, 16 operational missiles had been removed.

Mr. Redmond: To ask the Secretary of State for Defence if he will make a statement on the North Atlantic Treaty Organisation general political guidelines for use of nuclear weapons; and how many times they have been followed.

Mr. Archie Hamilton: The general political guidelines were agreed by Ministers at the Gleneagles NPG meeting in October 1986. The purpose of the document is to provide political guidelines for the employment of nuclear weapons in defence of NATO within the framework of NATO's strategy of flexible response and forward defence.

These guidelines are the basis for both peacetime planning by political and military authorities and a guide for carrying out their respective responsibilities in times of tension or conflict. They are consulted regularly.

Nuclear Deterrent

Mr. John Marshall: To ask the Secretary of State for Defence what recent representations he has received about the case for modernising the nuclear deterrent.

Mr. Archie Hamilton: My right hon. Friend has received a number of letters from individuals and organisations.

F111G Aircraft

Mr. Redmond: To ask the Secretary of State for Defence how many United States Air Force F111G aircraft are based in the United Kingdom; and if he will make a statement.

Mr. Archie Hamilton: None.

NATO (Scotland)

Dr. Godman: To ask the Secretary of State for Defence what is the estimated total value to the economy for *(a)* Strathclyde and *(b)* Scotland as a whole of the presence of military establishments of the North Atlantic Treaty Organisation armed forces in various locations in the region and the country.

Mr. Archie Hamilton: No such estimate has been made for Strathclyde or for Scotland.

Type 23 Frigates

Mr. Menzies Campbell: To ask the Secretary of State for Defence what is his programme for ordering Type 23 frigates for 1990, 1991 and 1992.

Mr. Sainsbury: Tenders have recently been invited for a batch of up to four type 23s. Decisions will be taken on the precise size and timing of the order after the tenders have been received, evaluated and fully analysed. In the longer term, we have plans to place sufficient orders to maintain a force of about 50 destroyers and frigates.

Procurement Staff

Mr. Menzies Campbell: To ask the Secretary of State for Defence what is the average time in post of each of the grades in the procurement executives of his Department.

Mr. Sainsbury: Information about average time in post, by grade, is not compiled in the form requested, and could be provided only at disproportionate cost.

ATTORNEY-GENERAL

CPS (Pay)

Mr. Allen: To ask the Attorney-General what recent discussions he has had on the pay levels within the Crown prosecution service; and what was the outcome of his discussions.

The Attorney-General: Pay for lawyers in the Crown prosecution service at grade 7 and above was settled in July 1988, setting levels until the new review date of 1 August 1989.

It is not my practice to disclose matters relating to any discussions of the nature of those referred to by the hon. Member.

Serious Fraud Office

Mr. Cousins: To ask the Attorney General, what is the establishment and staff in post in each grade of the Serious Fraud Office in each year of its existence, together with the number of cases referred to it.

The Attorney-General: The Serious Fraud Office was established on 6 April 1989. On 31 March 1989, the final day of the financial year 1988-89, the position was as follows:

Grade	Establishment	Staff in post
2	1	1
3	2	2
5	10	9
6	18	13
7	5	5
Senior Executive Officer	5	6
Higher Executive Officer	10	8
Executive Officer	8	7
Administrative Officer	3	1
Administrative Assistant	2	0
Senior Personal Secretary	1	1
Personal Secretary	4	5
Typing Manager	0	1
Typist	6	0
Support Manager 3	1	1
Support Grade 2	3	0

Of those staff in post, one higher executive officer was on loan from the Crown prosecution service. There were in addition to the figures shown 29 agency staff employed on a temporary basis.

The position to 1 June 1989 in the financial year 1989-90 was follows:

Grade	Complement	Staff in Post
2	1	1
3	2	2
5	10	10
6	18	13
7	5	5
Senior Executive Officer	6	6
Higher Executive Officer	11	8
Executive Officer	9	8
Administrative Officer	3	2
Administrative Assistant	2	0
Senior Personal Secretary	1	1
Personal Secretary	6	5
Typing Manager	1	1
Typist	12	0
Support Manager 3	1	1
Support Grade 2	4	1
Total	92	64

Of those staff in post, one higher executive officer was still on loan from the Crown prosecution service. Three of the four grade 5 accountants currently in post are seconded from private practice. There are in addition 29 agency staff employed on a temporary basis.

In the period 6 April 1988, when the Serious Fraud Office was established, to 31 December 1988, 109 separate cases were referred to it for consideration. This number includes some matters which have previously been dealt with by the Crown prosecution service. From 1 January 1989 to date 28 separate cases have been referred.

ENERGY

Pacific Sandpiper

Mr. Flynn: To ask the Secretary of State for Energy why, pursuant to his reply to the hon. Member for Newport, West, *Official Report,* 11 May, column *481,* on the Pacific Sandpiper, a consignment of spent irradiated nuclear fuel was transported into and out of the United Kingdom without it being reprocessed; and on how many occassions such a stop-off has taken place since May 1979.

Mr. Michael Spicer: The irradiated fuel was from an overseas research reactor and was being returned to its country of origin. The material was subject to international safeguards. It came to the United Kingdom as part of a cargo of irradiated fuel the balance of which was for reprocessing at Sellafield. Since May 1979 there has been an average of about one such shipment a year.

World Association of Nuclear Operators

Dr. Thomas: To ask the Secretary of State for Energy what departmental representation was made at the launch of the World Association of Nuclear Operators in Moscow on 15 May.

Mr. Michael Spicer: None. The World Association of Nuclear Operators comprises representatives of every organisation that operates electrical power producing nuclear reactors. It is independent of Government. However, I welcome its establishment and support its aims.

Pressurised Water Reactor, Wylfa

Mr. Martyn Jones: To ask the Secretary of State for Energy if he has considered the terms of reference for the public inquiry into the proposed pressurised water reactor at Wylfa in Anglesey; and if he will make a statement.

Mr. Michael Spicer: My right hon. Friend received an application from the CEGB on 18 April 1989 for his consent to construct a PWR nuclear power station to be known as Wylfa B. He directed the board to advertise its application and allowed a period of up to 31 July 1989 for objections to be made to him.

Until the response to the advertisements is known and the views of the relevant local planning authorities are received, it is too early to speculate whether a public inquiry will be necessary or, if a public inquiry is held, what matters my right hon. Friend will ask the inquiry inspector to consider.

Berkeley Nuclear Power Station

Mr. Martyn Jones: To ask the Secretary of State for Energy if he will give a timetable for the decommissioning of Berkeley nuclear power station over the next 14 years; and if he will make a statement.

Mr. Michael Spicer: This is a matter for the Central Electricity Generating Board. I will ask the chairman to write to the hon. Member.

Trawsfynydd Power Station

Mr. Martyn Jones: To ask the Secretary of State for Energy if the Central Electricity Generating Board has any plans to reschedule the natural circulation test at Trawsfynydd nuclear power station that was cancelled due to public concern; and if he will make a statement.

Mr. Michael Spicer: I understand from the Central Electricity Generating Board that it has no immediate plans to carry out a natural circulation test at Trawsfynydd nuclear power station. However, if the board should decide to undertake such a test it will publicise its plans in advance. No test can go ahead unless the Health and Safety Executive's nuclear installations inspectorate is satisfied that it is safe.

Miners' Pension Scheme

Mr. Skinner: To ask the Secretary of State for Energy when he intends to introduce the amending order with regard to the retired mineworkers pension scheme benefits lost by former mineworkers due to changes in the availability for work procedures.

Mr. Michael Spicer: The draft Redundant Mineworkers and Concessionary Coal (Payments Schemes) order 1989 will be introduced shortly.

EMPLOYMENT

Birkenhead Jobcentre

Mr. Frank Field: To ask the Secretary of State for Employment if Birkenhead jobcentre has sufficient staff to answer claimants' inquiries about possible job opportunities; and if he will make a statement.

Mr. Lee: Birkenhead jobcentre has sufficient staff to deal with the range of functions and activities offered by an office of its size. There have been no reports of queues or delays from either staff or members of the public.

Disabled People

Mr. Ashley: To ask the Secretary of State for Employment on what date he plans to publish his Department's internal review of employment services for disabled people commissioned in March 1988; and if he will make a statement.

Mr. Lee: I have nothing to add to the reply I gave my hon. Friend the Member for Exeter (Mr. Hannam) on 8 November 1988, at column *54.*

Mr. Ashley: To ask the Secretary of State for Employment what consultations his Department has had with disability organisations and disabled people on the review of employment services for disabled people.

Mr. Lee: I have nothing to add to the reply I gave to my hon. Friend the Member for Exeter (Mr. Hannam) on 7 November 1988, at columns *54-55.*

Employment Protection (Consolidation) Act

Mr. Norris: To ask the Secretary of State for Employment what plans he has to implement section 131 of the Employment Protection (Consolidation) Act 1978.

Mr. Cope: My Department has published a consultation paper today seeking views on the desirability of extending the jurisdiction of industrial tribunals to cases

involving breach of employment contract in certain circumstances. The consultation paper, a copy of which has been placed in the Libraries of both Houses, has been sent to a number of interested organisations. The deadline for receipt of comments is 4 August.

PRIME MINISTER

Gross Domestic Product (Defence)

Mr. Austin Mitchell: To ask the Prime Minister if she will publish in the *Official Report* a table showing the information she has on the percentage of gross domestic product spent on defence in *(a)* Russia and *(b)* North Atlantic Treaty Organisation countries, together with figures showing (i) gross domestic product and (ii) gross domestic product per head in dollar terms.

The Prime Minister: The table sets out the information requested for NATO countries for 1987, the latest year for which complete figures are available. Provisional figures for 1988 defence expenditure as a percentage of GDP in each NATO country were included in the 1989 Statement on the Defence Estimates, Cm. 675-I, page 39. The Soviet Union has recently stated that its defence expenditure for 1989 will be 77·3 billion roubles. We do not know how this figure has been compiled and assess that, when compiled according to the definitions common to NATO countries, outlays should be roughly twice this level. As such, they would constitute an estimated 15 to 17 per cent. of Soviet GDP. No accurate estimates can be given of Soviet GDP or GDP per capita in dollar terms; conversion of rouble data into dollars using commercial exchange rates is likely to prove highly misleading.

	Defence expenditure as a percentage of GDP	GDP million US $[1]	GDP per capita US $[1]
Belgium	3·0	138,526	14,030
Canada	2·1	414,244	16,050
Denmark	2·1	101,315	19,750
France	4·0	879,879	15,710
Federal Republic of Germany	3·1	1,118,839	18,270
Greece	6·2	47,179	4,720
Iceland	—	5,326	21,740
Italy	2·4	751,261	13,090
Luxembourg	1·2	6,061	16,290
Netherlands	3·1	214,641	14,630
Norway	3·4	82,661	19,770
Portugal	3·1	36,312	3,530
Spain	2·4	288,098	7,420
Turkey	4·4	65,044	1,250
United Kingdom	4·7	665,732	11,730
United States	6·5	4,436,018	18,190

[1] Based on 1987 average market exchange rates.

Russia—Nato (Military Advantage)

Mr. Austin Mitchell: To ask the Prime Minister if she will publish in the *Official Report* a table showing the Government's assessment of the change in the balance of military advantage between Russia and the North Atlantic Treaty Organisation countries in 1959, 1968, 1978 and 1988 respectively.

The Prime Minister: Information on the balance between NATO and the Warsaw pact forces for 1978 and 1988 is available in the relevant tables in the Statements on

Defence Estimates for those years, Cmnd. 7099 and Cm. 344–I. Similar information for 1959 and 1968 is not available.

Self-governing Hospitals

Mr. Austin Mitchell: To ask the Prime Minister in what ways the costs of self-governing hospitals can be expected to be reduced.

The Prime Minister: Self-governing hospitals are not being established as a cost saving exercise. They will help to improve the choice and quality of the services offered to the public and the efficiency with which these services are delivered.

Council for Mutual Economic Assistance (Troops)

Mr. Austin Mitchell: To ask the Prime Minister what assumptions about the proportion of the Council for Mutual Economic Assistance nations' troops which would be supplied to take part in an invasion of Europe underlie Her Majesty's Government's defence policy.

The Prime Minister: The Council for Mutual Economic Assistance is not a military organisation. Details of the forces available to the Warsaw pact are set out in chapter six of the Statement of the Defence Estimates 1989, Cm. 675–I.

Patient Care (GPs' Budgets)

Mr. Austin Mitchell: To ask the Prime Minister what will be the effects on patient care of the Government's proposal that overspending by a group of general practitioners in one year will result in a reduction in their budget in the following year.

The Prime Minister: None. If a practice budget becomes overspent, it will be open to the budget holders to seek a budgetary review. Should the review find that a higher level of spending was justified by virtue of changed circumstances since the initial budget was set, there will be no compensatory reduction in the following year. In any event, practice budgets will always be set at levels which safeguard the interests of patients and no changes will be made to budgets which would jeopardise this fundamental principle.

Nuclear Weapons

Mr. Austin Mitchell: To ask the Prime Minister (1) whether any nuclear weapons sited in Britain may be used for defensive purposes without the consent of Her Majesty's Government;

(2) whether nuclear weapons sited in West Germany can be used for defensive purposes without the consent of the Government of the Federal Republic of Germany.

The Prime Minister: At the North Atlantic Council meeting at Athens in 1962, both the United Kingdom and the United States specifically committed themselves to consult their allies, time and circumstances permitting, before releasing their nuclear weapons for use. The Council also adopted guidelines on the degree to which political consultation on such use might be possible. Subsequently the nuclear planning group, meeting in The Hague in 1968, agreed that special weight should be given to the views of the NATO countries most directly affected. It would not be in the public interest to reveal the precise details of the arrangements.

The separate arrangements for joint decision over the use of United States bases in the United Kingdom were set out in the reply of my right hon. Friend the Member for Tonbridge and Malling (Sir J. Stanley) to the hon. Member for Edinburgh, East (Mr. Strang) on 24 February 1987, at column 222.

Mr. Allen: To ask the Prime Minister whether she is prepared to use nuclear weapons first.

The Prime Minister: The possibility of first use of nuclear weapons in response to a conventional attack is central to NATO's strategy of deterrence to which I fully subscribe.

Mr. Austin Mitchell: To ask the Prime Minister what are Her Majesty's Government's policies on the use of available nuclear weapons in the event of a Soviet breakthrough to the Channel ports using conventional weapons.

The Prime Minister: It would undermine our strategy of deterrence to spell out in advance the precise way in which nuclear weapons would or might be used in any given circumstance.

European Community (Benefits)

Mr. Allen: To ask the Prime Minister what benefits have been brought to Nottingham and Nottinghamshire arising *(a)* from membership of the European Community *(b)* the consequences of the Single European Act.

The Prime Minister: Membership of the EC has contributed, with the policies of the present Government, to faster growth and greater prosperity in which Nottinghamshire has shared, and which has reduced unemployment in the Nottingham travel-to-work area from 12·8 per cent. to 8·3 per cent. in the two years to April 1989—a reduction of 35 per cent.

The Single European Act will facilitate the creation of the single European market which will enhance these opportunities still further, particularly in view of the United Kingdom's proven attraction as a location for inward investment projects such as Toyota's, which will create new business and employment opportunities throughout the east midlands.

Nottinghamshire is likely to benefit substantially from the EC's recent decision to make new areas of the county, including Mansfield and Worksop, eligible for help from the European regional development fund.

Kincora Boys' Home

Mr. Livingstone: To ask the Prime Minister if she will establish a further inquiry into events at the Kincora boys' home following the publication of the book "Who Framed Colin Wallace?" by Paul Foot which gives evidence of doubt concerning the validity of information supplied to the Hughes inquiry by the Royal Ulster Constabulary.

The Prime Minister: No. The matter has been fully and carefully investigated by successive inquiries. Any new evidence should be presented to the appropriate authorities.

"Forward Area" (Definition)

Ms. Ruddock: To ask the Prime Minister, pursuant to her oral reply to the hon. Member for Banbury (Mr. Baldry) of 11 April, *Official Report*, column 738, what precise area is covered by the term "forward area".

The Prime Minister: The area referred to in my reply covers territory of the German Democratic Republic, Poland, Czechoslovakia and Hungary.

Taxation

Mr. Austin Mitchell: To ask the Prime Minister if Her Majesty's Government will bring forward proposals to amend section 2 of the European Communities Act 1972 to enable Parliament to decide the level of taxation.

The Prime Minister: We have no plans to amend section 2 of the European Communities Act 1972.

EEC (Harmonisation)

Mr. Austin Mitchell: To ask the Prime Minister if she will make it her policy that Her Majesty's Government will not agree to any form of harmonisation within the European Economic Community of monetary, fiscal or exchange rate policy under the treaty of Rome or the Single European Act.

The Prime Minister: I refer the hon. Member to the exchange between myself and my hon. Friend the Member for Thanet, South (Mr. Aitken) on 18 May at column 1474 and to the answer I gave to my hon. Friend, the Member for Crawley (Mr. Soames) on 2 May at columns 13-14.

Monetary Union and Fiscal Harmonisation

Mr. Austin Mitchell: To ask the Prime Minister what assessment has been made of the disadvantages for the United Kingdom, France, West Germany, Benelux and Spain agreeing to monetary union and fiscal harmonisation.

The Prime Minister: I refer the hon. Member to the speech I made to the College of Europe at Bruges, Belgium on 20 September last year and to the speech my right hon. Friend the Chancellor of the Exchequer made to the Royal Institute of International Affairs on 25 January.

Labour Statistics

Mr. Austin Mitchell: To ask the Prime Minister what is the Government's estimate of the number of jobs which will be lost in United Kingdom manufacturing as a result of the completion of the internal market.

The Prime Minister: Completion of the single market should result in job gains over a number of years: whether or not these potential gains are achieved will depend on how employers and employees respond to the opportunities that the single market will present.

European Community (Integration)

Mr. Austin Mitchell: To ask the Prime Minister whether Her Majesy's Government will commission a survey of public opinion to measure the proportion of voters which want the United Kingdom to be more integrated into the European Community.

The Prime Minister: No.

Germany (Reunification)

Mr. Austin Mitchell: To ask the Prime Minister whether Her Majesty's Government will promote the reunification of Germany and a political settlement between Germany and the East European states on terms acceptable to the Federal Republic of Germany.

The Prime Minister: I remind the hon. Gentleman of article 7 of the convention on relations in the Bonn-Paris conventions of 1955:

"Pending the Peace Settlement the signatory states will co-operate to achieve, by peaceful means, the common aim of a reunified Germany enjoying a liberal-democratic constitution, like that of the Federal Republic."

This long-standing commitment enjoys our continuing support.

EEC (Social Policy)

Mr. Austin Mitchell: To ask the Prime Minister whether she will publish in the *Official Report* a table showing which of the proposals put forward by the European Economic Commission in the social field could not be enacted by the British Parliament on its own account.

The Prime Minister: Parliament can enact legislation in all of the areas proposed in the social field. However, in framing any legislation, the Government will of course have regard to our international obligations, including our obligations under Community law.

NORTHERN IRELAND

Disabled People (Housing)

Mr. Alfred Morris: To ask the Secretary of State for Northern Ireland what action he is taking to ensure a sufficient supply of wheelchair housing for people with disabilities who wish to leave residential care or to set up home on their own; and if he will make a statement.

Mr. Needham: The Department of the Environment (NI) funds the provision of special needs housing in response to proposals by the Housing Executive and by registered housing associations. It is a matter for the Housing Executive and individual associations in consultation with statutory bodies and voluntary agencies to determine the numbers and locations of units to be provided to wheelchair standard. In practice the supply of wheelchair accommodation has, I believe, kept broadly in line with the needs of physically handicapped people who wish to leave residential care or to set up home on their own.

Mr. Alfred Morris: To ask the Secretary of State for Northern Ireland if he will list the number of completions of *(a)* wheelchair housing and *(b)* mobility housing by (i) local authorities, (ii) housing associations and (iii) the private sector in each of the last 10 years for which figures are available.

Mr. Needham: i. I am advised by the chairman of the Northern Ireland Housing Executive that information in the form requested is not readily available and could be compiled only at disproportionate cost. However during the period 1976 to 1 April 1989 102 dwellings were built for use by tenants confined to a wheelchair and 6,044 dwellings were built to mobility standard.

ii. The number of wheelchair units completed by registered housing associations in Northern Ireland in each of the last 10 financial years is as follows:

Year	Number of units completed
1979-80	10
1980-81	11
1981-82	11
1982-83	15
1983-84	53
1984-85	29
1985-86	39
1986-87	10
1987-88	41
1988-89	79
Total	298

No separate record is kept of units built by registered housing associations to mobility standard. However, most sheltered housing for the elderly is built to mobility standard and the number of such units completed in each of the last 10 years is as follows:

Year	Number of units completed
1979-80	181
1980-81	285
1981-82	97
1982-83	448
1983-84	356
1984-85	448
1985-86	497
1986-87	227
1987-88	364
1988-89	421
Total	3,324

iii. Further units to mobility standard were provided for client groups other than the elderly but specific numbers are not readily available.

There are no statistics available for the provision of facilities for the wheelchair disabled within the private housing sector.

Short Bros. plc.

Sir Michael McNair-Wilson: To ask the Secretary of State for Northern Ireland what progress he is making towards the privatisation of Short Bros. plc.

Mr. Tom King: I refer my hon. Friend to the statement that I made this afternoon, a copy of which has been placed in the Library.

ENVIRONMENT

Rating Reform

Sir William Shelton: To ask the Secretary of State for the Environment what would a *(a)* single person on half average earnings, *(b)* single person on average earnings and *(c)* typical ward sister pay in capital value rates and local income tax combined, assuming an 80/20 capital rate to local income tax split if he or she lived in a property in Lambeth worth (i) £65,000, (ii) £75,000, (iii) £85,000, (iv) £100,000 and (v) £150,000.

Mr. Gummer: The information requested is provided in the table.

Illustrative annual liability in Lambeth under a system of capital value rates combined with local income tax, 1988-89

Property value	(a) single person[1] earning £6,360	(b) single person[2] earning £12,725	(c) typical[3] ward sister
£	£	£	£
65,000	1,220	1,400	1,415
75,000	1,395	1,570	1,585
85,000	1,656	1,745	1,755
100,000	1,825	2,000	2,015
150,000	2,685	2,860	2,875

Notes:
[1] Assuming taxable income of £3,755 per year.
[2] Assuming taxable income of £10,120 per year.
[3] Assuming taxable income of £10,595 per year.

The figures are based on the illustrative tax rates placed in the Library on 23 June 1988 and are for 1988-89. No allowance has been made for rebates for those on low income. They assume that the person lives alone, in each case.

Departmental Policy

Dr. Thomas: To ask the Secretary of State for the Environment if he will list *(a)* the failures of implementation of policy and *(b)* the successes in the implementation of policy by his Department since May 1979.

Mr. Ridley: I refer the hon. Member to the answer given by my right hon. Friend the Prime Minister to my hon. Friend the Member for Pembroke (Mr. Bennett) on 25 May (*Official Report* columns 695-719). Columns *706-08* list the major achievements for which my Department is responsible. There have been no failures.

Community Charge

Mr. Cohen: To ask the Secretary of State for the Environment if he will list the circumstances in which a carer, as a consequence of their caring, may become subject to paying more than one poll tax; and if he will take steps to introduce legislation to remove all such circumstances.

Mr. Gummer: The Government have no plans to introduce a poll tax. By the act of caring no one becomes responsible for anyone else's community charge.

Development Grant

Mr. Redmond: To ask the Secretary of State for the Environment what was the total budget for the Yorkshire and Humberside region in grant-in-aid for development for the years May 1979 to May 1989; how much central Government gave towards the budget; and how much was obtained from other sources.

Mr. Trippier: Comprehensive figures for Yorkshire and Humberside are not available, but as a measure of the contribution made by Government the three main Departments concerned with encouraging development —Environment, Employment and Trade and Industry— contributed £489 million in 1988-89 alone.

Housing Grants

Mr. Ken Hargreaves: To ask the Secretary of State for the Environment what is his Department's policy on the timing of announcements as to who will receive grants under *(a)* section 16 of the Housing and Planning Act 1986 and *(b)* section 73 of the Housing Act 1985 in relation to the beginning of the relevant financial year; and how many times this target has been achieved in the last five years, for each grant.

Mr. Trippier: It is the Department's policy now to announce the award of grants under section 73 of the Housing Act 1985 and under section 16 of the Housing and Planning Act 1986 where possible before the start of the financial year to which they apply. Applications may be considered (and grants awarded) at any time during the year.

Section 73 grants

Over the last five years, awards of grants were notified in each July or August with the exception of 1987-88 when grants were not announced until September.

Section 16 grants

This grant regime started in May 1987. Awards for the latter half of that year were made in October 1987. For 1988-89 and 1989-90, all recipients of grant were notified before or at the start of the financial year.

Housing (Grants)

Mr. Knox: To ask the Secretary of State for the Environment whether the grants which are made by his Department under section 16 of the Housing and Planning Act 1986 and under section 73 of the Housing Act 1985 are normally made on an annual basis; and for what periods grants have been made under those powers for the current financial year.

Mr. Trippier: The grants made by my Department under section 16 of the Housing and Planning Act 1986 and under section 73 of the Housing Act 1985 are normally made on an annual basis. This year has been no exception for grants made under section 16. Section 73 grants have been offered for six months pending the outcome of the review of the section 73 grant regime.

Community Charge

Mr. Allen: To ask the Secretary of State for the Environment, pursuant to his reply to the hon. Member for Nottingham, North of 16 May, *Official Report,* column 183, what was the exact amount of the city of Nottingham expenditure on the setting up costs of the community charge which has been supported through the rate support grant.

Mr Gummer: The grant-related expenditure assessment for Nottingham for 1989-90 included £307,000 in respect of community charge preparation costs. This is the level of expenditure which is supported through rate support grant. As I explained in my answer to the hon. Member on 16 May, there will in addition be a specific grant of £306,864 made available to Nottingham in 1989-90 for these purposes.

Housing (Kirklees)

Mr. Reddick: To ask the Secretary of State for the Environment how many new dwellings have been built in the area covered by Kirklees council in total since 1979 and in each of the last five years for which figures are available by *(a)* private builders, *(b)* Kirklees council and *(c)* housing associations.

Mr. Trippier: The reported housebuilding completions in 1979 and 1988 for the borough of Kirklees are published in issues 59 and 89, respectively, of "Local Housing Statistics". Annual figures for intervening years appear in "Housebuilding in England by local authority areas: 1980 to 1987."

Copies of these publications are in the Library.

Mr. Riddick: To ask the Secretary of State for the Environment how many tenants of Kirklees council have exercised their right to buy their council house or flat in each of the last 10 years for which figures are available.

Mr. Trippier: I refer my hon. Friend to the "Statistics on Right to Buy and Other Council House Sales" tables which have been placed in the Library giving available information up to December 1988. The tables show year by year information since 1979-80 together with cumulative figures since April 1979. No returns of sales to sitting tenants have been received by the Department from Kirklees district council since December 1986.

Mr. Riddick: To ask the Secretary of State for the Environment what is the latest figure for the number of council houses in the Kirklees council area which are empty.

Mr. Trippier: The information was provided by Kirklees metropolitan district council in its April 1988 housing investment programme return (HIP 1), a copy of which is in the Library.

Housing Statistics

Mr. Riddick: To ask the Secretary of State for the Environment what was the total number of dwellings in the United Kingdom in 1979; and what is the equivalent figure today.

Mr. Trippier: It is estimated that there were 21·3 million dwellings in the United Kingdom at the end of December 1979 and 23·0 million at the end of December 1988.

Housing Needs (National Forum)

Mr. Wray: To ask the Secretary of State for the Environment what response he is giving to the report of the national forum on housing needs in the nineties; and if he will make a statement.

Mr. Trippier: My right hon. Friend has received no such report. If he does, no doubt he will consider it carefully.

Renovation Grants

Mr. Hannam: To ask the Secretary of State for the Environment what are the proposed lower thresholds for a renovation grant contained in the consultation paper "Renovation Grants: Proposed Test of Resources", for *(a)* a single disabled person with a disability premium, *(b)* a single disabled person with a severe disability premium, *(c)* a married couple, one of whom is in receipt of the disability premium, and *(d)* a married couple with two children one of whom is in receipt of the disability premium.

Mr. Trippier: The consultation paper proposes that the lower income threshold for the new renovation grants should be related to each household's circumstances. It would be calculated using weekly allowances and premiums broadly similar to those used in the calculation of housing and community charge benefits, with the addition of a £20 per week "renovation grant premium". Using the allowances and premiums currently in force under the housing benefit regulations, the lower income thresholds would be as follows:

- *(a)* Single disabled person: £68·60 (£3,567 pa)
- *(b)* Single severely disabled person: £94·80 (£4,930 pa)
- *(c)* Married couple, one disabled: £94·30 (£4,904 pa)
- *(d)* Married couple, two children, one disabled: £122·50 (£6,370 pa)

In each case the applicant is assumed to be between 25 and 59 years old and any children are 11 to 15. Where the applicant is younger a different personal allowance would apply, and there will be a scale of allowances for children of different age groups. There will also be different premiums for people aged 60 or over. The lower threshold will therefore depend upon the precise composition of the household.

Mr. Hannam: To ask the Secretary of State for the Environment what are the proposed upper income thresholds for a grant for eligible works contained in the consultation paper "Renovation Grants: Proposed Test of Resources, amounting to *(a)* £5,000, *(b)* £10,000, *(c)* £15,000 and *(d)* £20,000 in each of the following cases *(a)* a single disabled person with a severe disability premium, *(b)* a single disabled person with a severe disability premium, *(c)* a married couple, one of whom is in receipt of the disability premium and *(d)* a married couple with two children one of whom is in receipt of the disability premium.

Mr. Trippier: The upper income threshold for renovation grant eligibility depends upon the cost of eligible works and the composition of the applicant's household. Net income would be assessed according to rules broadly the same as those applicable to housing and community charge benefit and be subject to similar disregards. Using the rules currently in force for housing benefit, the upper income threshold for renovation grant eligibility in each of the cases cited would be as follows:

case	Upper net income threshold for renovation grant eligibility—£pw (£pa) by cost of eligible works			
	£	£	£	£
Works costing	5,000	10,000	15,000	20,000
(a) Single, disabled	170·48	257·35	344·23	431·10
	(8,865)	(13,382)	(17,900)	(22,417)
(b) Single, severely disabled	196·68	283·55	370·43	457·30
	(10,227)	(14,745)	(19,262)	(23,780)
(c) Married couple, one disabled	196·18	283·05	369·93	456·80
	(10,201)	(14,719)	(19,236)	(23,754)
(d) Married couple, two children, one disabled	219·38	306·25	393·13	480·00
	(11,408)	(15,925)	(20,443)	(24,960)

These figures assume that the applicant is earning, and take into account the appropriate earnings disregards (£15 per week in cases *(a)* to *(c)*, £10 per week in case *(d)*. In each case it is assumed that the claimant is between 25 and 59 years old, any children are aged 11 to 15, and that capital after any appropriate disregard is £5,000 or less.

Disability Premium

Mr. Hannam: To ask the Secretary of State for the Environment what is the maximum proposed level of grant contained in the consultation paper "Renovation Grants: proposed test of resources" in each of the following cases *(a)* a single disabled person with a disability premium, *(b)* a single disabled person with a severe disability premium, *(c)* a married couple, one of whom is in receipt of the disability premium, and *(d)* a married couple with two children one of whom is in receipt of the disability premium for a person with savings of (i) nil, (ii) £3,000, (iii) £5,000, (iv) £8,000 and (v) £10,000.

Mr. Trippier: The amount of grant will depend upon the cost of eligible works, the composition of the applicant's household and the financial resources of the applicant. There is no grant maximum.

Rating Reform

Mr. Tony Lloyd: To ask the Secretary of State for the Environment (1) if he intends to seek powers to rectify the position where local authorities have sought information on poll tax registration forms in excess of his recommendation; and if he will seek powers to determine what information local authorities are able to seek in future years;

(2) what guidance he issued to local authorities about the information they should seek on the poll tax registration form; which information he has concerning local authorities which have asked for information in excess of his recommendation; what communications he has had with those authorities; and what advice he has given to them concerning rectification.

Mr. Gummer: The Government have no plans to introduce a poll tax.

It is for community charges registration officers to ensure that any request for information made for the purpose of compiling registers falls within their statutory powers. Guidance on these matters is contained in Community Charge Practice Note No. 8 pubished in November 1988. Copies of all practice notes are in the Library.

Mr. Cohen: To ask the Secretary of State for the Environment what information he has on the progress in the establishment of local arrangements to cover payment by student nurses of the poll tax; and if he will make a statement.

Mr. Gummer *[holding answer 26 May 1989]:* The Government have no plans to introduce a poll tax.

Most student nurses training under the existing arrangements are salaried and will pay the full personal community charge reduced by any community charge benefit to which they may be entitled. Nursing students training under the proposed Project 2000 scheme will pay only 20 per cent. of the personal community charge like other full time students.

Home Improvement (Document)

Mr. Hannam: To ask the Secretary of State for the Environment if he will list the disability organisations which responded to the consultation document entitled "Home Improvement Policy: Proposed Test of Resources".

Mr. Trippier: The following disability organisations responded to the consultation paper "Renovation Grants: Proposed Test of Resources":

Association of Disabled Professionals;
Derbyshire Centre for Integrated Living;
Disabled Living Foundation;
Disablement Information Centre and Advice Line, Wakefield;
Royal Association for Disability and Rehabilitation (RADAR);
Royal Society for Mentally Handicapped Children and Adults (MENCAP)

Mr. Hannam: To ask the Secretary of State for the Environment if, in light of responses from disability organisations to the consultation document entitled "Home Improvement Policy: Proposed Test of Resources", he plans to review his decision to impose a test of resources on disabled facilities grants; and if he will make a statement.

Mr. Trippier: The proposed test of resources is intended to ensure that those least able to afford the costs of adaptations receive the grants that they need. We do not propose to abandon the principle of the test, but we are not committed to the precise details proposed in the consultation paper. We shall announce our decisions in due course.

Rural Development (Leicestershire)

Sir John Farr: To ask the Secretary of State for the Environment if any of the expenditure for 1989-90 by the Rural Development Commission will be for rural development programmes in the county of Leicester.

Mrs. Virginia Bottomley: There is no rural development programme as such in Leicestershire. The Rural Development Commission makes grants under other headings in the county, as well as providing advice and loans to small rural businesses.

Steel-framed Homes

Mr. Allen: To ask the Secretary of State for the Environment if he will meet a delegation in July from the National Steel-Framed Home Owners Association and their local members to discuss the problems of steel-framed homes.

Mr. Trippier: No.

BISF Estate, Nottingham

Mr. Allen: To ask the Secretary of State for the Environment on what grounds the Nottingham city council's estate action application for the BISF estate in Nottingham was rejected; and if he will make a statement.

Mr. Trippier: The Nottingham city's application for Estate Action resources for the BISF houses was turned down because the scheme did not meet the main Estate Action criterion which is to promote innovation in the way local authorities manage and refurbish their estates.

Mr. Allen: To ask the Secretary of State for the Environment what offers of estates action assistance were made to the deputation on Nottingham BISF properties.

Mr. Trippier: Nottingham city council was invited to make an application for funding improvements to the Bilborough estate which would meet the Department's Estate Action criteria.

Council Tenants (House Purchase)

Mr. Battle: To ask the Secretary of State for the Environment if he will list each local authority which has applied to his Department under the Housing Act 1988, section 129, for approval for a scheme providing cash incentives for their existing tenants to purchase homes elsewhere; and if he will list for each such scheme submitted to his Department for approval *(a)* the total amount of cash which would be made available per annum for the scheme, *(b)* the total number of households which would be eligible each year for assistance, *(c)* the minimum level of assistance which the scheme would provide per household, *(d)* the maximum level of assistance which the scheme would provide per household, *(e)* the criteria which would be used to select which households would be assisted and *(f)* the criteria which would be used to select which properties they would be assisted to buy.

Mr. Trippier: The table sets out the local authorities which have sought approval for schemes in 1989-90, the maximum expenditure to be incurred, and the grants to be made available to households. Most of the schemes are limited to tenants of family houses, and in some cases the grant to be paid varies according to the size of the property vacated; it will be for each authority to determine which tenants to assist if the number of eligible applicants exceeds the funds available. The choice of a new home is left to the recipient of the grant, subject to a price limit.

Local authority	Maximum expenditure £	Maximum number of households assisted	Grant for each household £
Adur	80,000	8	10,000
Arun[1]	50,000	5	10,000
Bromley[1]	1,000,000	100	10–13,000
Carrick[1]	100,000	20	5,000
Colchester[1]	150,000	20	10,000
Croydon[1]	650,000	50	13,000
Ealing	1,500,000	70	15,000
Hammersmith/Fulham	200,000	30	5–10,000
Haringey[1]	500,000	38	13,000
Harrow[1]	200,000	16	12,500
Hart[1]	100,000	12	8,000
Havering	350,000	35	10,000
Hillingdon	250,000	16	15,000
Leominster	Details awaited		
Mendip[1]	80,000	21	10,000
New Forest[1]	250,000	30	7–9,000
North Beds	100,000	13	7,000
North Cornwall[1]	70,000	13	7,500
Rochester[1]	200,000	15	6–8,000
Rushmoor[1]	50,000	6	7–8,000
Shepway[1]	100,000	8	13,000
Slough[1]	500,000	30	18,000
South Bucks[1]	66,000	6	9–11,000
St. Albans	150,000	12	13,000
Taunton Deane[1]	275,000	35	10,000
Test Valley[1]	250,000	25	10,000
Tunbridge Wells[1]	200,000	20	10,000
Wandsworth[1]	2,000,000	150	13,000
Wealden[1]	60,000	10	6,000
Westminster	1,500,000	100	15,000

[1] Approved schemes.

Rent Officers (Guidance)

Mr. Battle: To ask the Secretary of State for the Environment if he will place in the Library a copy of his Department's guidance to rent officers in carrying out their new role under the Housing Act 1988, Part V, as from 1 April 1989.

Mr. Trippier: The detailed basis on which rent officers assess the rent paid by, and accommodation occupied by, private tenants claiming housing benefit is set out in the Rent Officers (Additional Functions) Order 1989. Advice on how rent officers might approach their new task— particularly in circumstances where no direct market evidence is available—was included in a study of the private rented housing market commissioned by the Department from the consultants Price Waterhouse. Copies of that report were circulated to rent officers and were placed in the Library in February.

Homelessness

Mr. Battle: To ask the Secretary of State for the Environment what are his Department's plans to monitor the impact of the Housing Act 1988, Part I, on *(a)* the number of homeless households accepted by local authorities in England and *(b)* the ability of local authorities in England to secure housing for homeless households.

Mr. Trippier: Part I of the Housing Act 1988 should improve the supply of rented accommodation and therefore reduce homelessness. Research into its effects will be carried out in due course, as part of the Department's research programme.

Housing Revenue Accounts

Mr. Battle: To ask the Secretary of State for the Environment what was *(a)* the level of central Government housing subsidy, and *(b)* the level of discretionary rate fund contributions to local authority housing revenue accounts *(a)* in inner London, *(b)* in outer London, *(c)* in the south-east outside London, *(d)* in metropolitan areas outside London, *(e)* in non-metropolitan areas outside the south-east, and *(f)* in England as a whole in each year from 1981-82 to 1987-88; and if he will give this information at constant 1987-88 prices.

Mr. Trippier: The information requested is shown in the table. The rate fund contribution figures (RFCs) are net amounts (the balance between contributions to housing revenue accounts and transfers the other way to general rate funds). For completeness, the information for the GLC/LRB is shown also. The main housing subsidy figures will differ from those published previously because they include subsequent adjustments to the original claims received by the Department and are expressed at 1987-88 prices.

Main housing subsidy (MHS) claimed and net rate fund contributions (RFCs) made

(£0·0 million, 1987-88 prices)

Area	1981-82 MHS	1981-82 RFCs	1982-83 MHS	1982-83 RFCs	1983-84 MHS	1983-84 RFCs	1984-85 MHS	1984-85 RFCs	1985-86 MHS	1985-86 RFCs	1986-87 MHS	1986-87 RFCs	1987-88 MHS	1987-88 RFCs
(a) Inner London boroughs and Corporation of London	466·0	287·0	367·6	252·7	321·0	283·7	318·2	217·0	359·8	211·8	328·8	234·2	287·1	227·4
(b) Outer London boroughs	226·2	89·1	122·4	68·2	84·4	67·6	81·8	40·1	93·3	21·7	80·8	22·9	66·0	11·1
(c) GLC/LRB	105·2	122·3	47·8	126·3	37·8	142·1	30·5	130·5	17·5	144·4	—	—	—	—
(d) South-East—outside London	127·6	−3·6	32·3	0·4	16·6	−2·2	16·3	−3·1	23·2	−7·9	18·0	−8·6	15·9	−15·3
(e) Metropolitan areas —outside London	327·9	195·6	68·6	167·5	19·7	154·9	25·0	103·6	34·5	65·1	35·1	45·2	30·2	65·4
(f) Non-Metropolitan areas —outside the South East	344·1	38·8	51·5	33·6	21·4	28·9	22·0	19·5	66·9	13·2	44·2	−0·9	37·4	−8·4
(g) All England	1,597·0	729·2	690·2	648·7	500·9	675·0	493·8	507·6	595·2	488·3	506·9	292·8	436·6	280·2

Notes:
1. The LRB ceased to operate a Housing Revenue Account after 1985-86.
2. The main housing subsidy figures are entitlements for each financial year and not payments made in that year.
3. The rate fund contributions may not be the final figure for each year but are based on information received by the Department in connection with housing subsidy claims.

Disabled People (Water Bill)

Mr. Hannam: To ask the Secretary of State for the Environment what provision he is proposing to include in the Water Bill to protect disabled people on dialysis machines from disconnection.

Mr. Howard: Water undertakers already take special precautions to ensure continuity of supplies to customers who use dialysis machines. Further safeguards against disconnection of domestic customers will be included in the conditions of appointment of the new water undertakers. Disconnection will not normally be allowed without prior application to the county court for debt recovery, nor where the local social security or social services office has requested a delay to examine the customer's circumstances. No Bill amendment is needed.

Rural Development

Sir John Farr: To ask the Secretary of State for the Environment what criteria are used in reaching decisions on rural development programmes in *(a)* the county of Leicester and *(b)* Northamptonshire.

Mrs. Virginia Bottomley: Rural development programmes are drawn up for the rural development areas designated in 1984 by the rural development commission. The criteria which the Department laid down for the selection of such areas were:
- *(a)* above average unemployment;
- *(b)* an inadequate or unsatisfactory range of employment opportunities;
- *(c)* adverse effects from population decline or sparsity of population;
- *(d)* net outward migration of population;
- *(e)* disproportionate number of elderly people;
- *(f)* poor access to services and facilities.

Disabled People (Housing)

Mr. Alfred Morris: To ask the Secretary of State for the Environment what action he is taking to ensure a sufficient supply of wheelchair housing for people with disabilities who wish to leave residential care or to set up home on their own; and if he will make a statement.

Mr. Trippier: It is for housing authorities to analyse needs locally and to bid for resources through the housing investment programme system to enable provision to be made—in collaboration with voluntary and private agencies.

My Department will be sponsoring a research project this year to assess what proportion of disabled and elderly people need special accommodation and to examine the most cost-effective methods of provision.

Mr. Alfred Morris: To ask the Secretary of State for the Environment if he will list the number of completions of *(a)* wheelchair housing and *(b)* mobility housing by (i) local authorities, (ii) housing associations and (iii) the private sector in each of the last 10 years for which figures are available.

Mr. Trippier: Numbers of new completions of wheelchair and mobility dwellings for local authorities and new towns and for housing associations in 1988 appear in table 1.6(b) of "Housing and Construction Statistics", part 1 No. 36; figures for earlier years appear in table 6.7(b) of "Housing and Construction Statistics 1977-87"; copies of both publications are in the Library. No reliable estimates of private sector completions are available.

Bottle Re-use Schemes

Mr. Menzies Campbell: To ask the Secretary of State for the Environment if he has commissioned any studies on the operation of bottle re-use schemes, with standard specification bottles, in other countries.

Mrs. Virginia Bottomley: The former Waste Management Advisory Council published a study in 1981 of returnable and non-returnable containers, based on a review of overseas practice. The Government believe that the council's recommendations against mandatory re-use schemes are still valid.

Discharge Consents (South West Water)

Mr. Matthew Taylor: To ask the Secretary of State for the Environment what ministerial permission has *(a)* been requested and *(b)* been granted for relaxation of STW discharge consents for South West Water; and what period of time they are to cover.

Mr. Howard *[holding answer 6 June 1989]:* On 7 December (*Official Report,* column *199*) I announced a capital programme costing around £1 billion to bring sewage treatment works into compliance with their discharge consents by March 1992. Water authorities may apply for time limited consents for those works to regularise current performance and maintain the current river water quality while improvements take place.

Eighty three applications for such consents have been received from South West Water. A list of those sewage works for which these applications have been made has been placed in the Library of the House. None has yet been granted. The capital works will generally be completed by March 1992. The time limited consents for any individual works will cover the period up until commissioning of the upgraded works. Thereafter consent conditions no less stringent than those which currently apply will be imposed.

EC Habitats Directive

Mrs. Margaret Ewing: To ask the Secretary of State for the Environment what progress is being made on discussions about the EEC habitats directive; and when he expects an agreement to be reached.

Mrs. Virginia Bottomley *[holding answer 6 June 1989]:* Discussions on the proposal for an EC directive on habitat protection have continued at three working group meetings called by the Spanish Presidency. A technical and scientific working group has been set up to prepare four of the annexes omitted from the Commission's draft. Many of the points which led member states unanimously to reject the Commission's proposals at the Environment Council on 24 November 1988 remain to be resolved.

Grants

Mr. Knox: To ask the Secretary of State for the Environment what system his Department operates to ensure that recipients of grant aid under section 16 of the Housing and Planning Act 1986, and section 73 of the Housing Act 1985 are accountable to his Department for expenditure and performance; and whether that system takes into account such factors as the size of the grant made by the Department, and the administrative capacity of small organisations in receipt of such grants.

Mr. Trippier *[holding answer 26 May 1989]:* The formal conditions of grant for organisations contain the expenditure and performance targets and rules designed to secure the necessary accountability for the proper and effective use of funds. Any organisation unable to meet these vital terms would not receive grant aid. Monitoring by my Department is through audited claims and accounts, general and specific reports and through visits and meetings with the organisations concerned.

Land Register (Statistics)

Mr. Steen: To ask the Secretary of State for the Environment how many sites are currently on the land register; and what is the total acreage owned by local authorities.

Mr. Trippier *[holding answer 6 June 1989]:* There were 7,900 sites on the land register at 31 May 1989. The total acreage owned by local authorities is 49,900.

Barrow Borough Transport Ltd.

Mr. Franks: To ask the Secretary of State for the Environment if he will exercise his powers under section 22(2) of the Local Government Finance Act 1982 to require the Audit Commission to order an extraordinary audit into loans made by the Barrow-in-Furness borough council to Barrow Borough Transport Ltd.

Mr. Gummer: These are matters which the auditor would normally examine in the course of the audit and on which he could take such action as he thought necessary.

Mr. Franks: To ask the Secretary of State for the Environment if he will seek to obtain a copy of the report by the chief executive of Barrow-in-Furness borough council dated 20 April and entitled "Inquiry into the Formation of Barrow Borough Transport Ltd. and the Borough Council's Investment in the Company".

Mr. Gummer: This is a matter for the local authority and its auditor.

SOCIAL SECURITY

Housing Benefit

53. **Mr. Darling:** To ask the Secretary of State for Social Security how many people in Scotland are in receipt of housing benefit in the private and public sectors, respectively.

Mr. Peter Lloyd: The estimated number of recipients in 1988-89 in Scotland is:

	Persons
Rent rebate (public sector)	490,000
Rent allowance (private sector)	75,000

Disabled Persons (Partial Incapacity Benefit)

Mr. Hannam: To ask the Secretary of State for Social Security if, in light of the Social Security Advisory Committee's report entitled, "Benefits for Disabled People: a Strategy for Change," he is examining ways in which a partial incapacity benefit for disabled people could be introduced.

Mr. Scott: I have noted the views of the Social Security advisory committee. We shall look at the need for a partial incapacity benefit when we examine existing benefit provision against the findings of the OPCS surveys.

Disabled Persons Act

Mr. Ashley: To ask the Secretary of State for Social Security (1) what is his latest estimate of the costs of implementing section 7 of the Disabled Persons Act 1986;

(2) when he plans to conclude discussions with local authority associations on the implementation of section 7 of the Disabled Persons Act 1986;

(3) when he plans to implement section 7 of the Disabled Persons Act 1986.

Mr. Scott: We cannot at present indicate when we will implement section 7 as we are still in discussion about the costs, which the local authority associations estimate at more than £100 million a year. We hope to reach firm conclusions later in the year.

Fraud

Dr. Godman: To ask the Secretary of State for Social Security if he will publish the number of prosecutions and convictions for social security frauds in Scotland in each of the past ten years, giving the sums of money and the number of people involved; and if he will make a statement.

Mr. Peter Lloyd: The number of people prosecuted at the instigation of the Department and convicted for social security frauds in Scotland are detailed in the table. Information relating to the sums of money involved is not held centrally and could be obtained only at disproportionate cost. Statistics prior to 1984-85 are not available.

	Total	*Benefit fraud*	*Instrument of payment fraud*
Prosecutions			
1984-85	463	306	157
1985-86	541	327	214
1985-87	791	578	213
1987-88	769	430	339
1988-89	986	566	420
Convictions			
1984-85	444	301	143
1985-86	529	320	209
1986-87	777	569	208
1987-88	754	424	330
1988-89	950	550	400

Dr. Godman: To ask the Secretary of State for Social Security how much money he estimates has been lost in each year since 1979 as a result of fraudulent social security claims and how many persons have been successfully prosecuted in *(a)* England and Wales, *(b)* Scotland, *(c)* Strathclyde and *(d)* Greenock and Port Glasgow.

Mr. Peter Lloyd *[pursuant to his reply, 10 February 1989, columns 857-58]:* I regret an inaccuracy has been discovered and the corrected information is as follows:

The numbers of successful prosecutions instigated by the Department in respect of fraudulent social security claims is as follows:

	Great Britain[1]	*Scotland*[2]	*Strathclyde*[2]	*Greenock and Port Glasgow*[2]
1979-80	16,236	—	—	—
1980-81	18,369	—	—	—
1981-82	13,856	—	—	—
1982-83	11,312	—	—	—
1983-84	5,987	—	—	—
1984-85	6,550	301	—	—
1985-86	6,586	320	176	3
1986-87	6,203	569	147	9
1987-88	6,931	424	181	3

[1] Includes both fraudulent benefit claims and fraudulent instrument of payment encashment. Separation of figures not available.
[2] Relates only to fraudulent benefit claims. Earlier information is not available.

SCOTLAND

Local Authority Tenants

14. **Mr. Gow:** To ask the Secretary of State for Scotland how many houses and flats are owned by local authorities in Scotland; and what proposals he has to give to their tenants the opportunities to become owner occupiers.

Lord James Douglas-Hamilton: Returns by local authorities indicate that, at 30 September 1988, local authorities in Scotland owned some 808,000 houses and flats.

In the light of the continuing success of the Government's right-to-buy policy, we have no plans at present to change the current statutory arrangements.

Bus Services

15. **Dr. Bray:** To ask the Secretary of State for Scotland if he will make a statement on his plans for the privatisation of bus services in Lanarkshire.

25. **Mr. Ingram:** To ask the Secretary of State for Scotland if he will make a statement on his plans for the privatisation of buses within Lanarkshire.

Lord James Douglas-Hamilton: Legislation to provide powers for the privatisation of the Scottish Bus Group, including its operations in Lanarkshire, is currently before Parliament. The Government welcome the interest shown by management and employees of the Scottish Bus Group in Lanarkshire in the opportunities provided by privatisation. The Government are encouraging local authorities to dispose of their bus undertakings and welcome Strathclyde regional council's plans to privatise its undertaking including its operations in Lanarkshire.

European Community

16. **Mr. Salmond:** To ask the Secretary of State for Scotland what direct input Scottish Office Ministers and officials have on the European Commission and the Council of Ministers.

33. **Mr. Andrew Welsh:** To ask the Secretary of State for Scotland what direct input Scottish Office Ministers and officials have on the European Commission and the Council of Ministers.

39. **Mrs. Margaret Ewing:** To ask the Secretary of State for Scotland what direct input Scottish Office Ministers and officials have on the European Commission and the Council of Ministers.

Mr. Sillars: To ask the Secretary of State for Scotland what direct input Scottish Office ministers and officials have on the European Commission and the Council of Ministers.

Mr. Rifkind: The Scottish Office is represented at meetings of the Agriculture and Fisheries Councils by Ministers and/or senior officials. There are also frequent meetings between the Scottish Office and the EC Commission on a wide range of policy issues.

20. **Mr. Maclennan:** To ask the Secretary of State for Scotland what considerations he has given to the future representation of Scottish interests within the European Community; and if he will make a statement.

Mr. Rifkind: Ministers and officials will continue to represent Scottish interests through attendance at Agriculture and Fisheries Councils. Officials will also continue to ensure that particular Scottish interests in other Councils are identified and taken into account in the most appropriate way.

41. **Mr. Marlow:** To ask the Secretary of State for Scotland what estimate he has of the proportion of *(a)* primary and *(b)* secondary legislation relating to Scotland in the last 12 months which originally emanated from institutions of the European Community.

Mr. Rifkind: The only item of primary legislation concerns the adoption of the EC directive requiring member states to recognise professional qualifications obtained elsewhere in the Community, as it applies to teachers. This is included in the provisions of the Self-Governing Schools Etc. (Scotland) Bill. So far as secondary legislation is concerned, my Departments have implemented 16 regulations or statutory instruments ranging over agriculture and fisheries, environmental protection, planning and health.

National Health Service

17. **Mr. Redwood:** To ask the Secretary of State for Scotland what representations he has received from general practitioners about the proposed changes in the National Health Service.

Mr. Michael Forsyth: About 1,650 letters from GPs and members of the public have been received about the White Paper on the Health Service "Working for Patients", and/or the new contract for general practitioners. Agreement on all the major outstanding contract issues was reached with the profession's negotiators on 4 May.

22. **Mr. Alan Stewart:** To ask the Secretary of State for Scotland what progress has been made in implementing policies of competitive budgeting in the National Health Service in Scotland; and if he will make a statement.

Mr. Michael Forsyth: Since the last general election savings from competitive tendering have increased from £600,000 to £25 million on 74 contracts. This represents substantial additional resources for patient care in Scotland's health service over the next three to four years. Boards will continue to make progress in both the scope and range of services to put to competitive tender and are much encouraged by their success to date.

44. **Mr. Ernie Ross:** To ask the Secretary of State for Scotland how many representations he has received supporting his proposals for the National Health Service in Scotland.

Mr. Michael Forsyth: Most correspondence on the White Paper has shown support for some proposals and criticism of others. It is not therefore appropriate to categorise the responses in the manner requested.

Mr. Steel: To ask the Secretary of State for Scotland what further representations he has received from doctors in the Borders about the proposals in the White Paper "Working for Patients" since his reply of 5 April, *Official Report*, column *231*, to the hon. Member for Kilmarnock and Loudoun (Mr. McKelvey).

Mr. Rifkind: It is not possible to supply the information in the form requested. About 30 letters have been received from doctors in the Borders region since 5 April 1989, either direct or through hon. Members about the White Papers "Promoting Better Health" and/or "Working for Patients" and/or the new contract for GPs.

Mr. Wallace: To ask the Secretary of State for Scotland how many replies have been received to the letter sent to general practitioners in Scotland by the Parliamentary Under-Secretary of State, the hon. Member for Stirling (Mr. Forsyth) on 12 April.

Mr. Michael Forsyth: About 762 letters have been received from GPs since I wrote on 12 April, but it is not possible to identify which of these are specifically in response to my letter. Agreement on all the major outstanding contract issues was reached with the profession's negotiators on 4 May.

Freedom of Speech

18. **Mr. David Shaw:** To ask the Secretary of State for Scotland what representations he has received seeking the extension of section 43 (Freedom of speech in universities, polytechnics and colleges) of the Education (No. 2) Act 1986 to Scotland.

29. **Mr. McLoughlin:** To ask the Secretary of State for Scotland what representations he has received seeking the extension of section 43 (Freedom of speech in universities, polytechnics and colleges) of the Education (No. 2) Act 1986 to Scotland.

31. **Mr. Bowis:** To ask the Secretary of State for Scotland what representations he has received seeking the extension of section 43 (Freedom of speech in universities, polytechnics and colleges) of the Education (No. 2) Act 1986 to Scotland.

37. **Mr. Nicholas Bennett:** To ask the Secretary of State for Scotland whether he will consider extending section 43 (Freedom of speech in universities, polytechnics and colleges) of the Education (No. 2) Act 1986 to Scotland.

38. **Mr. Devlin:** To ask the Secretary of State for Scotland whether he will consider extending section 43 (Freedom of speech in universities, polytechnics and colleges) of the Education (No. 2) Act 1986 to Scotland.

42. **Mr. Janman:** To ask the Secretary of State for Scotland whether he will consider extending section 43 (Freedom of speech in universities, polytechnics and colleges) of the Education (No. 2) Act 1986 to Scotland.

Mr. Michael Forsyth: I refer my hon. Friends to the answer given earlier today to my hon. Friends the Members for Hexham (Mr. Amos) and Sherwood (Mr. Stewart).

Secondary Schools (Expenditure)

19. **Mr. Knox:** To ask the Secretary of State for Scotland how much was spent per pupil in secondary schools in Scotland in the most recent year for which figures are available; and what was the comparable figure in 1978-79 at constant prices.

Mr. Michael Forsyth: In 1987-88 net current expenditure per pupil in secondary schools in Scotland at outturn prices was £2,000. This is 36 per cent. more in real terms than the comparable figure in 1978-79 which at 1987-88 prices was £1,469.

Schools

21. **Mr. Riddick:** To ask the Secretary of State for Scotland what representations he has received arguing that schools in Scotland should be allowed to opt out of local authority control; and if he will make a statement.

Mr. Michael Forsyth: I have received a number of representations from individuals and groups of parents expressing interest in the possibility of self-governing status for schools. I expect that when the Self-Governing

Schools Etc. (Scotland) Bill reaches the statute book parents associated with individual schools will begin to assess seriously the benefits of self-governing status for their schools.

Community Charge

23. **Mr. Douglas:** To ask the Secretary of State for Scotland when he now expects to be able to make a statement on the numbers who have not paid the poll tax for April.

Mr. Lang: I refer the hon. Member to the reply I gave him on 3 May 1989, at column *166*.

27. **Mr. Canavan:** To ask the Secretary of State for Scotland what estimate he has of the number of people in Scotland who are on poll tax registers but who have not yet paid at least the first instalment of the poll tax; and whether he will express this figure as a percentage of all the people in Scotland who are on poll tax registers.

Mr. Lang: Local authorities are continuing to receive initial payments of the community charge. However the information required from local authorities to enable an estimate to be made of the numbers of people throughout Scotland who are liable for the community charge but have not made a payment will not become available for some months.

43. **Mr. McAllion:** To ask the Secretary of State for Scotland what has been the cost of publicising the implementation of the poll tax in Scotland.

Mr. Lang: Expenditure to date on the public information campaign on the community charge has been in the region of £950,000.

46. **Dr. Reid:** To ask the Secretary of State for Scotland what plans he has to modify the poll tax regulations.

Mr. Lang: The Government are monitoring the present community charge arrangements in Scotland. If experience shows that there is a need for any changes to the regulations or to statute we will take appropriate action.

Ayr Bypass

24. **Mr. Dunnachie:** To ask the Secretary of State for Scotland if he will make a statement on his plans for the Ayr bypass.

Lord James Douglas-Hamilton: I assume the hon. Member is referring to the section of new road planned between Drumbreck road and Glasgow city boundary which is the responsibility of Strathclyde regional council, and the new trunk road from the city boundary to Malletsheugh which together constitute the Ayr road route.

My right hon. and learned Friend is considering the report of the public local inquiry in respect of this project. The works are at present programmed to start in late 1990 but achieving this will depend upon the outcome of the inquiry.

Criminal Injuries Compensation Board

26. **Mr. Worthington:** To ask the Secretary of State for Scotland how long it takes the Criminal Injuries Compensation Board in Scotland to deal with a typical application.

Lord James Douglas-Hamilton: Since the criminal injuries compensation scheme operates on a Great Britain basis, information in this form is not available. Details of the time taken by the board to resolve cases were provided in the reply given to my hon. Friend the Member for Isle of Wight (Mr. Field) on 20 January 1989, at column *350,* by my right hon. Friend the Minister of State, Home Office.

Hospitals (Opting Out)

28. **Mr. David Marshall:** To ask the Secretary of State for Scotland what discussions he has had with health organisations in Scotland about the possibility of hospitals opting out under the Government's proposals for the National Health Service.

Mr. Michael Forsyth: I am currently giving consideration to this matter.

Economic Growth

30. **Mr. Oppenheim:** To ask the Secretary of State for Scotland what was the rate of economic growth in Scotland in the latest year for which figures are available.

Mr. Lang: The output-based estimates of Scotland's gross domestic product show that between 1986 and 1987 Scotland's economy grew by 2·4 per cent. Later information is available only for the output of the production and construction industries which grew by 5·8 per cent. between 1987 and 1988, the fastest rate of growth since 1973.

Single European Market

32. **Mr. Nigel Griffiths:** To ask the Secretary of State for Scotland if he has any plans to alter regional development policy in Scotland in the light of the forthcoming single European market.

Mr. Lang: The Government made a number of changes to regional policy in 1988 which took into account the single European market. In addition, through the Government's "Europe Open for Business" campaign information, advice and assistance is provided to all United Kingdom businesses in an effort to increase understanding during this run-up period.

Regional Policy

34. **Mr. McFall:** To ask the Secretary of State for Scotland if he has any plans to make regional policy for Scotland more effective.

Mr. Lang: The Government already have an effective regional policy. Provision for regional assistance in Scotland this year is approximately £120 million and we do not expect any underspend. This level of provision is broadly maintained for the following three years.

Fishing Policy

35. **Mr. Harris:** To ask the Secretary of State for Scotland what steps he takes to co-ordinate fishing policy in Scotland.

Mr. Michael Forsyth: Officials of the Department of Agricultural and Fisheries for Scotland are in regular contact with their colleagues in the other United Kingdom fisheries Departments and representatives of the fishing industry. and they participate in EC meetings and working groups as appropriate. My noble Friend the Minister of State, Scottish Office is regularly in touch with the other United Kingdom fisheries Ministers and attends meetings of the European Council of Fisheries Ministers as a member of the United Kingdom delegation.

Development Agency

36. **Mr. Martin:** To ask the Secretary of State for Scotland when he will next be meeting the chief executive of the Scottish Development Agency to discuss attracting industry to areas of high unemployment.

Mr. Lang: My right hon. and learned Friend and I met the Agency Board, including the chief executive, on 22 May and discussed a range of issues of mutual interest.

40. **Mr. Foulkes:** To ask the Secretary of State for Scotland when he next expects to meet the chairman of the Scottish Development Agency; and what matters he intends to discuss.

Mr. Lang: My right hon. and learned Friend and I met the Agency Board on 22 May and discussed a range of issues of mutual interest.

Farmers

45. **Sir Hector Monro:** To ask the Secretary of State for Scotland when he now expects to meet the president of the National Farmers Union of Scotland.

Mr. Rifkind: My noble Friend and I have regular meetings with the union to discuss current issues affecting the farming industry in Scotland. My noble Friend met the president on 19 May and expects to meet him again at the Royal Highland show later this month.

GPs (Seniority Payments)

47. **Mr. Kirkwood:** To ask the Secretary of State for Scotland what representations he has received from Scottish general practitioners about the changes to seniority payments.

Mr. Michael Forsyth: A number of the letters which have been received from general practitioners referred to the proposal to replace seniority allowances and redistribute the released income through other payments. At the meeting on 4 May with the profession's negotiators it was agreed that seniority payments would be retained but reduced by the value of the new postgraduate education allowance.

"Working for Patients"

48. **Mr. Hind:** To ask the Secretary of State for Scotland how many representations he has received on the White Paper "Working for Patients" and if he will make a statement.

Mr. Michael Forsyth: Some 1,900 letters have been received, offering comments and suggestions in relation to various aspects of the White Paper.

New Towns

49. **Mr. Norman Hogg:** To ask the Secretary of State for Scotland if he will make a statement on the future of the new towns.

Mr. Lang: It is intended that the Government's proposals for the future of the Scottish new towns will be announced before long.

Electorates

50. **Mr. Holt:** To ask the Secretary of State for Scotland what is the average electorate in each Scottish constituency.

Lord James Douglas-Hamilton: The average electorate of the constituencies in Scotland on publication of the 1989 electoral registers in February was 54,624.

Bathing Waters

51. **Mr. Malcolm Bruce:** To ask the Secretary of State for Scotland what action he intends to take to ensure that Scotland's bathing waters conform to standards set by European Economic Community directives.

Lord James Douglas-Hamilton: I refer the hon. Member to the answer which I gave to my hon. Friend the Member for Dumfries (Sir H. Monro) on 13 April 1989, at columns *682-83*, and in particular to the paper placed in the Library on that day which sets out the results of monitoring in 1988 and the plans to improve bathing waters where necessary.

Dogs

52. **Mr. Buchanan-Smith:** To ask the Secretary of State for Scotland if he will carry out a review of measures for control of dogs in Scotland and, in particular, of the powers and financial resources of local authorities in this respect; and if he will make a statement.

Lord James Douglas-Hamilton: Such an exercise is already in hand as part of a general review of the provisions of the Civic Government (Scotland) Act 1982 upon which we intend to consult later this year. There is, however, a range of powers relating to the control of dogs already available to local authorities.

Mr. Sillars: To ask the Secretary of State for Scotland if he will set out the statutory powers under which local authorities have power to control dogs; and if he will indicate which authorities are empowered to act.

Lord James Douglas-Hamilton: The information is as follows.

The Dogs Act 1906, as amended by the Civic Government (Scotland) Act 1982, empowers the police and proper officers of district and islands councils to seize, detain and dispose of stray dogs, and prescribes procedures for dealing with dogs so detained. The Control of Dogs Order 1930, made under powers consolidated in the Animal Health Act 1981, requires dogs to wear identity discs bearing the name and address of their owner when in a public place and enables district or islands councils to make curfew regulations to control dogs. The Pet Animals Act 1951 provides for the inspection and licensing by district or islands councils of pet shops and the attachment of conditions to the licence. The Animal Boarding Establishments Act 1963 provides for the inspection and licensing of boarding establishments for dogs and cats by district or islands councils and for the attachment of conditions to the licence. The Road Traffic Act 1972 makes it an offence for a dog to be on a designated road without being held on a lead. The regulations prescribing the procedure involved in designation by regional or islands councils are contained in the Control of Dogs on Roads Order (Procedure) (Scotland) Regulations 1962. The Breeding of Dogs Act 1973 provides for the inspection and licensing by district or islands councils of dog breeding establishments and for the attachment of conditions to the licence. The Guard Dogs Act 1975 lays down requirements for the supervision of guard dogs and the licensing of guard dog kennels by district or islands councils.

There are, in addition, indirect powers such as the power conferred by section 112 of the Civic Government (Scotland) Act 1982, whereby any local authority may make management rules which could include rules relating to dogs while on land or premises owned, occupied or managed by the authority.

Mr. Sillars: To ask the Secretary of State for Scotland what representations he has received from community groups or statutory organisations about the problems posed by lack of control of dogs; what replies he has sent; and if he will make a statement.

Lord James Douglas-Hamilton: My right hon. and learned Friend has received representations from the

Royal Society for the Prevention of Cruelty to Animals, the Scottish Society for the Prevention of Cruelty to Animals, the Convention of Scottish Local Authorities, the National Farmers Union, Scotland as well as from hon. Members and individuals about the problems posed by dogs. Most of these have urged tighter legislative controls and the introduction of a dog registration scheme. Replies to these representations have indicated that we are not convinced that registration would be an effective answer to the range of problems associated with dogs but that we intend to publish later this year a consultation paper in which other options for improving existing measures for more effective control of dogs will be explored.

Prescription and Residential Charges

Mrs. Ray Michie: To ask the Secretary of State for Scotland (1) whether he has any plans to extend exemption from prescription charges in Scotland to people requiring long-term medication related to mental illness;

(2) whether he has any plans to introduce a sliding scale of charges for residents with mental health problems in special accommodation schemes in Scotland who have other sources of income.

Mr. Michael Forsyth: When the existing list of specified medical conditions for which exemption from prescription charges is given was drawn up it was suggested by the medical profession that it should include only readily identifiable conditions which called for prolonged medical treatment, in most cases replacement therapy. The list has been reviewed on a number of occasions by successive Governments, but on each occasion it was decided no change could be made. There are no plans to extend the list at this time or to introduce sliding scales of charges relating to patients' circumstances.

Disabled People (Housing)

Mr. Alfred Morris: To ask the Secretary of State for Scotland what action he is taking to ensure a sufficient supply of wheelchair housing for people with disabilities who wish to leave residential care or to set up home on their own; and if he will make a statement.

Lord James Douglas-Hamilton: The Government attach high priority to the provision of all types of special needs housing. It is for housing authorities to assess local needs. Scottish Homes has been asked in determining its expenditure programme for housing associations for 1989-90 to place more emphasis on housing provision for the disabled. I am pleased to note that the number of sheltered wheelchair and wheelchair houses provided by public agencies in Scotland has increased from 636 in 1979 to 2,586 in 1988.

Mr. Alfred Morris: To ask the Secretary of State for Scotland if he will list the numbers of completions of *(a)* wheelchair housing and *(b)* mobility housing by (i) local authorities, (ii) housing associations and (iii) the private sector in each of the last 10 years for which figures are available.

Lord James Douglas-Hamilton: This information is not available. Information on housebuilding by user category has been collected centrally for authorities on a quarterly basis since 1986 but not for the breakdown required.

Leaflets

Dr. Godman: To ask the Secretary of State for Scotland how many information leaflets were published by the Scottish Office in each of the past five years: and what was the total cost each year.

Mr. Rifkind: Leaflets have been produced in a wide range of circumstances, and central records do not make it possible to provide the information requested without incurring disproportionate cost. If the hon. Member has a particular subject area in mind, perhaps he could write to me about it.

Midwives

Dr. Godman: To ask the Secretary of State for Scotland how many midwives there are in Scotland; how many claims for regrading he has received; and if he will make a statement.

Mr. Michael Forsyth: In the current year 4,119 midwives have been indexed to practise in Scotland. Claims for regrading are for health boards to deal with. Information on such claims is not held centrally.

Health Budget (Research)

Dr. Godman: To ask the Secretary of State for Scotland how much of his current health budget is spent on research in Scotland as a percentage and as a cash sum; and if he will make a statement.

Mr. Michael Forsyth: The provision for research expenditure in the current year is £5,144,000, or 0·2 per cent. of the total health budget. The cash figure represents an increase of nearly 12 per cent. over estimated expenditure in 1988-89.

Water

Mrs. Ray Michie: To ask the Secretary of State for Scotland what long-term funding his Department will be apportioning to upgrade water treatment plants in Strathclyde region.

Lord James Douglas-Hamilton: The Scottish Development Department has asked all regional and islands authorities to provide information about improvements necessary to achieve compliance with drinking water quality standards. When this information has been fully assessed Strathclyde regional council's needs will be taken into account, along with those of other authorities, in reviewing the capital expenditure allocations for water and sewerage services in Scotland.

Mrs. Ray Michie: To ask the Secretary of State for Scotland what representations he has received regarding the reduction in capital allocation to Strathclyde regional water authority for the next financial year.

Lord James Douglas-Hamilton: None. Allocations for water supply services are not issued separately. The provisional allocation for Strathclyde region's water and sewerage programme in 1990-91 was first set in 1988 at £41 million but was increased in February 1989 to £44 million, a rise of £3 million. While this increased provisional allocation is £1 million less than the capital allocation for the present year, it is still provisional and subject to review before final allocations for 1990-91 are set.

Mrs. Ray Michie: To ask the Secretary of State for Scotland whether he has any plans to reduce the proposed time of 20 years given to Strathclyde regional water authority to satisfy European Community requirements for drinking water.

Lord James Douglas-Hamilton: A time period has not yet been agreed with Strathclyde regional council for achieving full compliance with European Community drinking water standards. Water quality improvement schemes currently programmed are due for completion not later than the end of 1995.

Sheepmeat Regime

Sir Russell Johnston: To ask the Secretary of State for Scotland what information he has about the current negotiations on the EEC sheepmeat regime and its implications for Scottish farmers.

Mr. Rifkind: At last week's meeting of the Council of Agriculture Ministers member states once again made it clear that they had difficulties with the Commission's current proposals for reform of the sheepmeat regime. The Council agreed, however, that it should seek to make early progress in the first instance through discussions at official level.

Energy Sources

Mr. Speller: To ask the Secretary of State for Scotland what steps he is taking to promote alternative and renewable energy sources including wind, wave, water and solar technology.

Mr. Lang: Scotland already enjoys the large-scale development of our hydro-electric resources. In addition, a comprehensive research and development programme is under way which incorporates a number of major projects based in Scotland.

Local Health Councils

Mr. Andrew Welsh: To ask the Secretary of State for Scotland what representations he has received regarding local health council funding; and if he will make a statement.

Mr. Michael Forsyth *[holding answer 6 June 1989]:* I have received a number of representations and I am currently considering the most effective means of representing consumers interest in the NHS.

Mr. Andrew Welsh: To ask the Secretary of State for Scotland what funds, in cash and in real terms, his Department has allocated to local health councils since 1979.

Mr. Michael Forsyth *[holding answer 6 June 1989]:* The information is as follows:

Year	Local health council expenditure on a cash basis £'000	Local health council expenditure at 1989-90 prices[1] £'000
1979-80	430	852
1980-81	505	844
1981-82	556	847

Year	Local health council expenditure on a cash basis £'000	Local health council expenditure at 1989-90 prices[1] £'000
1982-83	596	848
1983-84	605	823
1984-85	661	856
1985-86	705	866
1986-87	760	903
1987-88	820	928
1988-89	867	915
1989-90[2]	909	909

[1] Using GDP deflator.
[2] Estimate.

Village and Community Halls (Grant Aid)

Mrs. Margaret Ewing: To ask the Secretary of State for Scotland what level of grant aid was approved by the Scottish Education Department in 1988-89 for village and community halls in Scotland; what is the anticipated level for 1989-90; and if he will make a statement.

Mr. Michael Forsyth *[holding answer 6 June 1989]:* In 1988-89 the Scottish Education Department approved projects for the building and improvement of youth, village and community halls in Scotland to the value of £2·35 million (on which a grant of £1·14 million will become payable over the next few years assuming the projects proceed as planned). In the same year the total amount actually paid in grants in respect of these, and projects approved in earlier years, was £950,000. Provision has been made for the payment of up to £1·045 million in grant aid in 1989-90 and I am at present considering how to allocate this amount, having regard to commitments in respect of previously approved projects.

Fishing

Mr. Salmond: To ask the Secretary of State for Scotland what is his assessment of the current financial position of the Scottish fishing industry; and if he will make a statement.

Mr. Michael Forsyth *[holding answer 23 May 1989]:* The value of landings reached a record high in 1987 but declined during 1988 and there are indications that this trend will continue in 1989. This is mainly because of reductions in quotas for North sea cod and haddock, but we have accepted the need for these reductions based on scientific advice to be made to secure the long-term fishing opportunities and the future prosperity of the industry.

Children (Dumbarton)

Mr. McFall: To ask the Secretary of State for Scotland how many children in Dumbarton constituency are dependent upon *(a)* supplementary benefit or income support, and *(b)* family income supplement or family credit in each year since 1978-79 (i) in total and (ii) as a percentage of all children in Scotland.

Mr. Peter Lloyd: I have been asked to reply.
I regret that this information is not available.

HEALTH

Deaf-Blind People

Mr. Hannam: To ask the Secretary of State for Health how many people are deaf-blind; and how many are aged between five and 65 years.

Mr. Freeman: I refer my hon. Friend to my reply to the right hon. Member for Stoke-on-Trent, South (Mr. Ashley) on 15 March 1989 at column *235*.

Abortions

Mr. Amess: To ask the Secretary of State for Health (1) if he will list the number of women resident in the United Kingdom who had an abortion in 1987 who already had *(a)* one, *(b)* two, *(c)* three, *(d)* four and *(e)* five previous abortions;

(2) if he will list the number of women in the Basildon area health authority who had an abortion in 1987 who already had *(a)* one, *(b)* two, *(c)* three, *(d)* four or *(e)* five previous abortions.

Mr. Freeman: The notification form for abortions carried out under the Abortion Act 1967 requires information about previous abortions to the woman concerned to be recorded, distinguishing between spontaneous miscarriages and legal terminations.

The table shows the information requested for abortions performed in England and Wales in 1987 for those women having had one or more previous spontaneous miscarriages or legal terminations.

Notifications having at least one previous spontaneous miscarriage and also at least one previous legal termination, and women having more than one abortion under the Act in 1987 will be counted more than once in the statistics.

Numbers of abortions performed to usual residents of (a) United Kingdom and (b) Basildon District Health Authority where the woman had had 1, 2, 3, 4 or 5 previous abortions, England and Wales, 1987

	United Kingdom	Basildon DHA
Previous spontaneous miscarriages		
1	9,269	881
2	1,592	85
3/4/5	626	11
Previous legal terminations		
1	26,466	173
2	3,703	17
3/4/5	832	3

Mr. Amess: To ask the Secretary of State for Health how many abortions have been performed in England and Wales under the Abortion Act 1967; how many of these abortions were performed in an emergency to save the life of a mother; and what percentage this latter figure represents of the lower, in each year since 1968.

Mr. Freeman: The information is shown in the table.

Number of abortions performed in England and Wales, under the Abortion Act 1967, and number performed under ground 5 of the Act[3], 27 April 1968 to September 1988[1]

Year	Total abortions	Number under ground 5	Per cent.
	A	B	B of A
1968	23,641	16	·068
1969	54,819	14	·026
1970	86,565	10	·012
1971	126,777	10	·008
1972	159,884	10	·006
1973	167,149	7	·004
1974	162,940	3	·002
1975	139,702	6	·004
1976	129,673	1	·001
1977	133,004	3	·002
1978	141,558	5	·004
1979	149,746	3	·002
1980	160,903	4	·002
1981	162,480	5	·003
1982	163,045	7	·004
1983	162,161	3	·002
1984	169,993	9	·005
1985	171,873	5	·003
1986	172,286	2	·001
1987	174,276	3	·002
1988[1]	137,103	4	·003
Total[2]	2,949,578	130	·004

[1] 1988 data are provisional.
[2] Total from 27 April 1968 to 30 September 1988.
[3] In emergency, to save the life of the pregnant women.

Mr. Amess: To ask the Secretary of State for Health (1) how many abortions have been performed on girls under the age of 16 years; and what percentage this represents of abortions performed, in each year since 1968;

(2) how many abortions were performed on girls in the Basildon area health authority, under the age of 16 years; and what percentage this represents of abortions performed, in each year since 1968.

Mr. Freeman: The information is shown in the table.

Number of abortions performed in England and Wales, and to usual residents of Basildon and Thurrock[2], all ages and to those under 16 years, 27 April 1968 to 31 December 1987.

Year	England and Wales Total under 16		Per cent.	Basildon and Thurrock[2] Total under 16		Per cent.
	A	B	B of A	A	B	B of A
1968	23,641	553	2·3	151	4	2·6
1969	54,819	1,231	2·2	287	9	3·1
1970	86,565	1,822	2·1	427	10	2·3
1971	126,777	2,618	2·1	435	6	1·4
1972	159,884	3,320	2·1	592	16	2·7
1973	167,149	3,660	2·2	541	10	1·8
1974	162,940	3,948	2·4	620	23	3·7
1975	139,702	4,006	2·9	628	24	3·8
1976	129,673	3,835	3·0	635	21	3·3
1977	133,004	4,067	3·1	626	29	4·6
1978	141,558	3,724	2·6	624	21	3·4
1979	149,746	3,856	2·6	614	22	3·6
1980	160,903	4,143	2·6	549	17	3·1
1981	162,480	3,949	2·4	586	20	3·4
1982	163,045	4,343	2·7	687	22	3·2
1983	162,161	4,566	2·8	602	26	4·3
1984	169,993	4,609	2·7	779	21	2·7
1985	171,873	4,427	2·6	840	25	3·0
1986	172,286	4,240	2·5	958	30	3·1
1987	174,276	4,075	2·3	998	27	2·7
TOTAL[1]	2,812,475	70,992	2·5	12,179	383	3·1

[1] Total from 27 April 1968 to 31 December 1987.
[2] 1968-1974: Basildon and Thurrock non-metropolitan counties.
1975-1982: Basildon and Thurrock Health District.
1983-1987: Basildon and Thurrock District Health Authority.

Mr. Amess: To ask the Secretary of State for Health how many abortions were performed on girls aged 10, 11, 12, 13, 14, 15, 16 and 17 years of age in each year since 1968; and how many were performed to save the life of a pregnant woman.

Mr. Freeman: The information on the total number of abortions performed in England and Wales to the requested ages could be provided only at disproportionate cost. However, the readily available data is shown in the table, which relates to abortions performed on usual residents of England and Wales. Information on the number of these which were performed under ground 5 of the Abortion Act cannot be released for reasons of maintaining confidentiality.

Number of abortions performed in England and Wales to usual residents of England and Wales by single year of age, 10 to 17 years, 1968 to 1987

Year	Age of mother							
	10	*11*	*12*	*13*	*14*	*15*	*16*	*17*
1968	n/a	3	6	21	150	363	559	693
1969	n/a	2	7	38	279	848	1,445	1,816
1970	n/a	3	20	85	391	1,233	2,530	3,188
1971	n/a	3	16	77	529	1,671	3,465	4,426
1972	n/a	0	7	98	586	2,113	4,318	5,395
1973	1	4	14	108	693	2,270	5,082	5,775
1974	0	1	9	117	718	2,490	5,348	6,225
1975	0	0	12	120	747	2,691	5,411	6,394
1976	0	6	14	122	738	2,545	5,429	6,285
1977	0	1	13	105	805	2,701	5,510	6,367
1978	0	3	20	113	708	2,454	5,675	6,733
1979	0	9	18	116	698	2,693	6,030	7,412
1980	0	5	17	141	770	2,717	6,370	8,108
1981	——————— 830[1] ———————					2,701	n/a	n/a
1982	——————— 931[1] ———————					2,921	n/a	n/a
1983	——————— 1,029[1] ———————					3,058	n/a	n/a
1984	0	1	9	111	898	3,139	6,802	8,406
1985	0	0	7	118	899	2,978	6,648	8,432
1986	0	0	5	77	842	2,970	6,175	8,309
1987	1	1	10	114	781	2,858	6,251	8,252

n/a = Data not readily available.
[1] These data relate to "under 15 years of age".

Mr. Amess: To ask the Secretary of State for Health what information he has as to the medical circumstances which created the need for abortions to be performed in emergency to save the life of the mother in those cases which have arisen since 1967; and if he will indicate the number of times each of those conditions has been a relevant factor.

Mr. Freeman: The information could be provided only at disproportionate cost.

Special Hospitals

Mr. Ashton: To ask the Secretary of State for Health (1) what compensation he is offering to nurses at special hospitals for their loss of civil servant status;

(2) what consultations he has had with representatives of the Prison Officers Association concerning the recommendations of the Olliff report; when he next expects to meet them; and whether he will list the organisations with whom he has discussed the report;

(3) what is his policy regarding the future negotiations, with the Prison Officers Association on promotion procedures, uniforms, assisted travel, grievances, disciplinary procedure and security if the Olliff report is implemented; and whether the Prison Officers Association will still be able to negotiate locally at each special hospital;

(4) whether he will pay an official visit to Broadmoor, Rampton, Park Lane and Moss Side special hospitals to discuss the Olliff report with nurses who are members of the Prison Officers Association;

(5) whether it is his policy to act on the Olliff report recommendation that the influence of the Prison Officers Association in special hospitals must be eroded and its assessment that attitudes within the special hospitals concentrate more on the secure control of patients than their treatment;

(6) why the future conditions of service and negotiations with the Prison Officers Association at special hospitals is being transferred to the Whitley council; what date he expects this transfer to be implemented; and whether legislation is required for this and for the transfer of direct responsibility for the admission of patients from the Secretary of State to the Special Hospitals health authority;

(7) why the Olliff report on the future of special hospitals was not distributed to the Prison Officers Association.

Mr. Freeman *[holding answer 26 May 1989]:* The Government are setting up the Special Hospitals Service Authority (SHSA) to take over the management functions presently exercised by my Department and the three local hospital boards, which are to be abolished later this year. These changes were announced in a ministerial statement in May 1988. Later in 1988 the Government specified the following six main national objectives for the service:

  (i) to continue to ensure the protection of the public;
  (ii) to ensure the provision of appropriate treatment for patients;
  (iii) to provide a good quality of life for patients, and a good working environment for staff;
  (iv) to develop closer working relationships with local and regional psychiatric services;
  (v) to promote the hospitals as centres of excellence for the training of staff of all disciplines, in forensic and other branches of psychiatry;

(vi) to promote research into forensic psychiatry, and related conditions.

The statements referred to are in the Library.

Statutory instruments have been laid before Parliament which will establish the SHSA from 1 July 1989, and render it fully operational from 1 October 1989. From that date the SHSA will assume all functions, including the admission of patients.

There has already been extensive discussion and consultation on these important changes with staff, management and unions. I have myself visited all the four special hospitals where I met a cross section of staff and patients. Department of Health officials have also been engaged in a programme of visits to all the hospitals where they have had wide ranging discussions with all groups of staff. We are producing full briefing packs to explain the rationale for and effects of the changes. These packs will be sent to all staff and patients before 1 October, when the SHSA becomes the new employing authority for all but administrative staff.

There have been exchanges with staff side interests, including the POA. Indeed, at a meeting with my officials on 18 May the General Secretary of the POA and his colleagues were assured that their members and other non-administrative staff will suffer no material loss through the removal of Civil Service status and will remain on existing NHS terms and conditions. As pay and superannuation will not be affected, the question of compensation does not arise. The POA was also assured that it will continue to be recognised as representing its members in the special hospitals locally (in the hospitals) and centrally (with the new special health authority) in the new arrangements.

It will be for the SHS authority to consider the appropriateness of existing staff procedures in the new arrangements, and in reviewing such procedures we would expect it to talk with the relevant staff interests, including the POA. The Olliff report was a confidential, internal working document about the future operations of the Department's HQ branch responsible for the special hospitals.

Written Answers to Questions

Thursday 8 June 1989

NATIONAL FINANCE

Public Debt

8. Mr. Allan Stewart: To ask the Chancellor of the Exchequer what is his estimate of the proportion of the public debt which will have been repaid in the three years to 1989-90.

36. Mr. Neil Hamilton: To ask the Chancellor of the Exchequer what is his estimate of the proportion of the public debt which will have been repaid in the three years to 1989-90.

120. Mr. Ian Taylor: To ask the Chancellor of the Exchequer what is his estimate of the proportion of the public debt which will have been repaid in the three years to 1989-90.

Mr. Major: It is estimated that roughly one sixth of net public sector debt will have been repaid in the three years to 1989-90.

Company Cars

13. Mr. Riddick: To ask the Chancellor of the Exchequer how many tax-payers will be affected by the increased company-car tax rates *(a)* in total and *(b)* those driving more than 18,000 business miles per annum.

Mr. Norman Lamont: The increase in company car scale charges for 1989-90 will affect about 1·4 million car drivers, of which about 0·3 million drive more than 18,000 business miles per year.

Income Tax

21. Mr. Hind: To ask the Chancellor of the Exchequer what would be the increased income tax payable by a married man on average earnings if the basic rate of income tax were restored to 33 per cent.

45. Mr. Ian Bruce: To ask the Chancellor of the Exchequer what would be the increased income tax payable by a married man on average earnings if the basic rate of income tax were restored to 33 per cent.

Mr. Greg Knight: To ask the Chancellor of the Exchequer what would be the increased income tax payable by a married man on average earnings if the basic rate of income tax were restored to 33 per cent.

Mr. Norman Lamont: If the basic rate of income tax were increased to 33 per cent. a married man on average male earnings would pay an additional £15·12 per week in income tax in 1989-90.

60. Mr. Brandon-Bravo: To ask the Chancellor of the Exchequer if he will make a statement setting out the Government's objective for the basic rate of income tax.

81. Mr. David Shaw: To ask the Chancellor of the Exchequer if he will make a statement setting out the Government's objective for the basic rate of income tax.

83. Mr. Gwilym Jones: To ask the Chancellor of the Exchequer if he will make a statement setting out the Government's objective for the basic rate of income tax.

Mr. Norman Lamont: It remains the Government's aim, as my right hon. Friend announced in his 1988 Budget Statement, to reduce the basic rate of income tax to 20p in the pound as soon as it is prudent and sensible to do so.

79. Mr. John Greenway: To ask the Chancellor of the Exchequer what changes were made in the basic rate of income tax from 1974 to 1979; and what changes have been made since 1979.

96. Mr. Franks: To ask the Chancellor of the Exchequer what changes were made in the basic rate of income tax from 1974 to 1979; and what changes have been made since 1979.

118. Miss Widdecombe: To ask the Chancellor of the Exchequer what changes were made in the basic rate of income tax from 1974 to 1979; and what changes have been made since 1979.

Mr. Norman Lamont: Information is given in the table.

Year	Basic rate of income tax per cent.
1974-75	33
1975-76 to 1976-77	35
1977-78	34
1978-79	33
1979-80 to 1985-86	30
1986-87	29
1987-88	27
1988-89 to 1989-90	25

88. Mr. Page: To ask the Chancellor of the Exchequer what was the highest marginal rate of tax on income paid during the period 1974 to 1979; and what is the equivalent rate in 1989-90.

102. Mrs. Currie: To ask the Chancellor of the Exchequer what was the highest marginal rate of tax on income paid during the period 1974 to 1979; and what is the equivalent rate in 1989-90.

128. Mr. Mans: To ask the Chancellor of the Exchequer what was the highest marginal rate of tax on income paid during the period 1974 to 1979; and what is the equivalent rate in 1989-90.

Mr. Norman Lamont: In each of the years 1974-75 to 1978-79 the highest marginal rate of income tax was 83 per cent. on earned income and 98 per cent. on investment income. For 1989-90 the highest marginal rate of income tax is 40 per cent.

Mr. Hunter: To ask the Chancellor of the Exchequer what proportion of total income tax revenue was paid by higher rate taxpayers in 1978-79; and what proportion was paid by them in 1988-89.

Mr. Norman Lamont: In 1978-79 higher rate taxpayers were liable to pay 20 per cent. of total income tax due. By 1988-89 their share had increased to 32 per cent.

Labour Statistics

52. Mr. Couchman: To ask the Chancellor of the Exchequer by how much employment in the United Kingdom has risen since 1983.

56. Mr. Charles Wardle: To ask the Chancellor of the Exchequer by how much employment in the United Kingdom has risen since 1983.

58. Mr. Summerson: To ask the Chancellor of the Exchequer by how much employment in the United Kingdom has risen since 1983.

76. Mr. Cash: To ask the Chancellor of the Exchequer by how much employment in the United Kingdom has risen since 1983.

Mr. Major: Total employment in the United Kingdom has increased by 2,951,000 since March 1983.

64. Mr. Stevens: To ask the Chancellor of the Exchequer how many people are now registered as self-employed; and what was the comparable figure in 1979.

106. Mr. Andrew Mitchell: To ask the Chancellor of the Exchequer how many people are now registered as self-employed; and what was the comparable figure in 1979.

Mr. Major: In December 1988 3,048,000 people were self-employed in the United Kingdom compared with 1,906,000 in June 1979, an increase of 60 per cent.

82. Mr. Thorne: To ask the Chancellor of the Exchequer for how many months adult unemployment has fallen continuously in the United Kingdom.

Mr. Major: Unemployment in the United Kingdom has fallen for 33 months in succession.

Manufacturing Output

22. Mrs. Peacock: To ask the Chancellor of the Exchequer what has been the annual rate of growth of manufacturing output over the last two years.

69. Mr. William Powell: To ask the Chancellor of the Exchequer what has been the annual rate of growth of manufacturing output over the last two years.

Mr. Major: In the two years to the first quarter of this year, manufacturing output grew at an average annual rate of 7·1 per cent.

Manufacturing Investment

23. Mr. Mills: To ask the Chancellor of the Exchequer what is the latest official projection for the growth of manufacturing investment in 1989.

Mr. Major: I refer my hon. Friend to the reply my right hon. Friend the Chancellor of the Exchequer gave earlier today to my hon. Friend the Member for Wanstead and Woodford (Mr. Arbuthnot).

30. Mr. Hoyle: To ask the Exchequer what was the level of manufacturing investment in the United Kingdom in 1979 and 1988.

91. Mr. Lewis: To ask the Chancellor of the Exchequer what was the level of manufacturing investment in the United Kingdom in 1979 and 1988.

104. Mr. Loyden: To ask the Chancellor of the Exchequer what was the level of manufacturing investment in the United Kingdom in 1979 and 1988.

Mr. Major: The level of manufacturing investment in the United Kingdom in 1985 prices was £11,157 million in 1979 and £11,586 million in 1988.

Corporation Tax

24. Mr. Gill: To ask the Chancellor of the Exchequer what proportion of the total amount raised by corporation tax came from private companies, and what was the amount for the most recently available fiscal year.

Mr. Norman Lamont: I regret that information is not available about the amount of corporation tax paid by private companies. Broadly speaking, the largest 1,000 companies and building societies account for roughly three quarters of the corporation tax collected. The estimated total yield for 1988-89 was £18·4 billion.

Excise Duties

25. Dr. Godman: To ask the Chancellor of the Exchequer what is the estimated reduction in inflation caused by a decision not to index excise duties.

66. Mr. Dunnachie: To ask the Chancellor of the Exchequer what is the estimated reduction in inflation caused by a decision not to index excise duties.

77. Mr. Doran: To ask the Chancellor of the Exchequer what is the estimated reduction in inflation caused by a decision not to index excise duties.

124. Mr. Graham: To ask the Chancellor of the Exchequer what is the estimated reduction in inflation caused by a decision not to index excise duties.

Mr. Lilley: Indexation of excise duties would have increased the RPI by nearly half a per cent.

Investment (GDP)

26. Mr. Turner: To ask the Chancellor of the Exchequer how many countries in the EEC spend a greater proportion of their gross domestic product on investment than the United Kingdom.

35. Mr. Morley: To ask the Chancellor of the Exchequer how many countries in the European Economic Community spend a greater proportion of their gross domestic product on investment than the United Kingdom.

72. Mr. Buckley: To ask the Chancellor of the Exchequer how many countries in the European Economic Community spend a greater proportion of their gross domestic product on investment than the United Kingdom.

92. Mr. Meale: To ask the Chancellor of the Exchequer how many countries in the European Economic Community spend a greater proportion of their gross domestic product on investment than the United Kingdom.

Mr. Brooke: On the basis of estimates for 1987, eight.

Balance of Payments

27. **Mr. Wall:** To ask the Chancellor of the Exchequer if he will forecast the balance of payments in each year until 1992.

34. **Ms. Abbott:** To ask the Chancellor of the Exchequer if he will forecast the balance of payments in each year until 1992.

57. **Mr. O'Brien:** To ask the Chancellor of the Exchequer if he will forecast the balance of payments in each year until 1992.

63. **Mrs. Mahon:** To ask the Chancellor of the Exchequer if he will forecast the balance of payments in each year until 1992.

Mr. Major: The Financial Statement and Budget Report for 1989-90 provides a forecast for the current account of the balance of payments for 1989 and the first half of 1990. Forecasts for later years are not published.

29. **Mr. Win Griffiths:** To ask the Chancellor of the Exchequer what was the balance of payments for the first quarter of 1989.

31. **Mr. Flynn:** To ask the Chancellor of the Exchequer what was the balance of payments for the first quarter of 1989.

Mr. Major: I refer the hon. Members to the reply my right hon. Friend the Financial Secretary gave earlier today to the hon. Member for Clwyd, South-West (Mr. Jones).

110. **Mr. Gareth Wardell:** To ask the Chancellor of the Exchequer what is his latest forecast for the United Kingdom balance of payments for 1989.

116. **Dr. Kim Howells:** To ask the Chancellor of the Exchequer what is his latest forecast for the United Kingdom balance of payments for 1989.

119. **Mr. Rogers:** To ask the Chancellor of the Exchequer what is his latest forecast for the United Kingdom balance of payments for 1989.

Mr. Major: I refer the hon. Members to the reply I gave to the hon. Member for Cardiff, West (Mr. Morgan) on 6 June.

Tax Harmonisation

28. **Mr. Ted Garrett:** To ask the Chancellor of the Exchequer what recent submissions he has received on the tax harmonisation.

93. **Mr. Clelland:** To ask the Chancellor of the Exchequer, what recent submissions he has received on tax harmonisation.

95. **Mr. Cummings:** To ask the Chancellor of the Exchequer what recent submissions he has received on tax harmonisation.

Mr. Lilley: My ministerial colleagues and I have received a number of submissions from a variety of sources.

Foreign Investment

32. **Mr. Battle:** To ask the Chancellor of the Exchequer what was the net flow of foreign direct and portfolio investment into the United Kingdom in 1988.

Mr. Major: Direct and portfolio investment in the United Kingdom by overseas residents (net of disinvestment) is provisionally estimated at £11·2 billion in 1988.

Workplace Nurseries

14. **Mr. Martlew:** To ask the Chancellor of the Exchequer if he will make a statement on his policy in relation to the tax on workplace nurseries.

17. **Mr. Jack Thompson:** To ask the Chancellor of the Exchequer if he will make a statement on his policy in relation to the tax on workplace nurseries.

Mr. Steinberg: To ask the Chancellor of the Exchequer if he will make a statement on his policy in relation to the tax on workplace nurseries.

Mr. Norman Lamont: There is no special tax on workplace nurseries. A subsidised place in a workplace nursery is a benefit in kind and benefits in kind are subject to income tax.

Mr. Vaz: To ask the Chancellor of the Exchequer if he will make a statement on his policy towards the tax treatment of workplace nurseries.

Mr. Norman Lamont: In principle, employees should pay income tax on the whole of their earnings whether received in cash or in kind. A subsidised place in a workplace nursery is a benefit in kind and any subsidy is a proper subject for tax.

Government Debt

53. **Mr. Gow:** To ask the Chancellor of the Exchequer what is the latest estimate of the interest payable on Government debt during the current financial year, and what was the comparable figure, adjusted for inflation, for the year ended 31 March 1979.

Mr. Lilley: The latest forecast of general Government gross debt interest payments in 1989-90 is £17·1 billion as published in the 1989 Financial Statement and Budget Report. In 1987-88 prices, general Government gross debt interest is £15·1 billion in both 1978-79 and 1989-90. As a percentage of GDP, general Government gross debt interests is $4\frac{1}{4}$ per cent. in 1978-79 and $3\frac{1}{4}$ per cent. in 1989-90.

Interest Rates

18. **Mr. Cryer:** To ask the Chancellor of the Exchequer if he will make a statement on the impact of current level of interest rates on the development of manufacturing industry.

Mr. Major: Manufacturing investment reached a record level in 1988 and the outlook is for continued strong growth.

55. **Mr. Knox:** To ask the Chancellor of the Exchequer if he will make a statement about the current level of interest rates.

Mr. Lilley: Bank base rates are 14 per cent.

98. **Mr. Darling:** To ask the Chancellor of the Exchequer what are the current interest rates in *(a)* the United Kingdom, and *(b)* the rest of the G7.

Mr. Lilley: I refer the hon. Member to the answer my right hon. Friend the Chancellor gave earlier today to the hon. Member for Monklands, West (Mr. Clarke).

117. **Mr. Tony Lloyd:** To ask the Chancellor of the Exchequer what is his policy in respect of establishing stable interest rates.

Mr. Lilley: Interest rates are set at the appropriate level to maintain downward pressure on inflation.

Tax and Prices Index

19. **Mr. Nigel Griffiths:** To ask the Chancellor of the Exchequer what is the most recent estimate for the tax and prices index.

37. **Mr. Bell:** To ask the Chancellor of the Exchequer what is the most recent estimate for the tax and prices index.

127. **Mr. McAllion:** To ask the Chancellor of the Exchequer what is the most recent estimate for the tax and prices index.

Mr. Brooke: The tax and prices index increased by 8·3 per cent. over the year to April.

Directors (Salaries)

20. **Mr. George Howarth:** To ask the Chancellor of the Exchequer what was the average salary increase amongst the highest paid directors of the biggest 50 companies in the last year.

33. **Mr. Bradley:** To ask the Chancellor of the Exchequer what was the average salary increase amongst the highest paid directors of the biggest 50 companies in the last year.

39. **Mr. Nellist:** To ask the Chancellor of the Exchequer what was the average salary increase amongst the highest paid directors of the biggest 50 companies in the last year.

54. **Mr. McCartney:** To ask the Chancellor of the Exchequer what was the average salary increase amongst the highest paid directors of the biggest 50 companies in the last year.

Mr. Brooke: Pay is for the parties involved to agree and it is not for the Government to intervene.

51. **Mr. Tony Banks:** To ask the Chancellor of the Exchequer what is the estimated yield to the Exchequer in 1989-90 from income tax from company directors' emoluments.

Mr. Norman Lamont: The income tax liability on company directors' emoluments is estimated to have been about £3 billion in 1985-86. Estimates for later years are not yet available.

Business Start-ups

38. **Mr. Burt:** To ask the Chancellor of the Exchequer what is his latest estimate of the number of business start-ups in 1988-89.

42. **Dr. Twinn:** To ask the Chancellor of the Exchequer what is his latest estimate of the number of business start-ups in 1988-89.

126. **Dr. Goodson-Wickes:** To ask the Chancellor of the Exchequer what is his latest estimate of the number of business start-ups in 1988-89.

Mr. Major: In the calendar year 1987, the latest for which figures have been published by the Department of Employment, the net increase in the number of businesses registered for VAT was 45,000, an average of nearly 900 a week. Indications are that the rate of increase since 1987 has been even faster, and may have amounted to over 1,300 per week. The figures for 1988 will be available later in the summer.

Government Expenditure

40. **Mr. David Evans:** To ask the Chancellor of the Exchequer what was the amount of central Government expenditure in 1988-89 expressed as a percentage of money gross domestic product; and what were the comparable figures for the previous five years.

Mr. Major: The latest available information on the percentage of money GDP at market prices accounted for by central Government expenditure is given in the table. The central Government figures on which the percentages are based exclude privatisation proceeds and grants to local authorities but include debt interest payments.

	Per cent.
1983-84	34·00
1984-85	34·50
1985-86	33·50
1986-87	33·00
1987-88	31·25
[1]1988-89	29·00

[1] April-December only.

41. **Mr. David Davis:** To ask the Chancellor of the Exchequer what has been the fall in general Government expenditure as a share of gross domestic product since 1982-83.

44. **Mr. Jacques Arnold:** To ask the Chancellor of the Exchequer what has been the fall in general Government expenditure as a share of gross domestic product since 1982-83.

48. **Mr. Redwood:** To ask the Chancellor of the Exchequer what has been the fall in general Government expenditure as a share of gross domestic product since 1982-83.

Mr. Major: The 1989 Financial Statement and Budget Report gave a figure of $39\frac{1}{2}$ per cent. for the ratio of general Government expenditure (excluding privatisation proceeds) to gross domestic product in 1988-89. The corresponding figure for 1982-83 was $46\frac{1}{4}$ per cent.

Inflation

43. **Mr. Matthew Taylor:** To ask the Chancellor of the Exchequer what was the rate of inflation in the last month for which figures are available; and what was the rate of inflation in West Germany, France, Italy and the Netherlands in the last month for which figures are available.

Mr. Lilley: The current 12-month inflation rates for the countries in question are given in the weekly OECD publication "Current Economic Indicators", a copy of which is available in the House of Commons Library.

47. **Mr. McAvoy:** To ask the Chancellor of the Exchequer what is the current inflation rate in the United Kingdom; and what it was one year ago.

97. **Mr. McLeish:** To ask the Chancellor of the Exchequer what is the current inflation rate in the United Kingdom; and what it was one year ago.

125. **Mr. McFall:** To ask the Chancellor of the Exchequer what is the current inflation rate in the United Kingdom; and what it was one year ago.

Mr. Lilley: I refer the hon. Members to the reply I gave to the hon. Member for Western Isles (Mr. Macdonald) on 6 June.

87. **Mr. Ashley:** To ask the Chancellor of the Exchequer what is the present level of inflation.

Mr. Lawson: I refer the hon. Member to the reply given by my hon. Friend the Economic Secretary to the hon. Member for Western Isles (Mr. Macdonald) on 6 June.

North Sea Oil

46. **Mr. Flannery:** To ask the Chancellor of the Exchequer what is the total amount of money received by the Exchequer from North sea oil since May 1979.

Mr. Major: Total tax revenues and royalties to United Kingdom oil and gas production over the fiscal years 1979-80 to 1988-89 are estimated at £65·2 billion. Receipts from the gas levy over the same period amounted to a further £3·8 billion. Further details are contained in the report by the Secretary of State for Energy to Parliament of April 1989 (the Brown Book).

Public Expenditure Survey

49. **Mr. Worthington:** To ask the Chancellor of the Exchequer what are his priorities in the forthcoming public expenditure survey.

100. **Dr. Moonie:** To ask the Chancellor of the Exchequer what are his priorities in the forthcoming public expenditure survey.

113. **Dr. Reid:** To ask the Chancellor of the Exchequer what are his priorities in the forthcoming public expenditure survey.

Mr. Major: The public expenditure survey will be carried out within the framework of the Government's objective for public expenditure. This is to maintain a downward trend over the medium term in the ratio of general Government expenditure to GDP.

Balanced Budget

50. **Mr. Patnick:** To ask the Chancellor of the Exchequer when, on present trends, a balanced Budget will be achieved; and when was the last occasion a balanced Budget was achieved.

Mr. Major: The Government intend to move gradually from the present surplus towards a balanced budget over the medium term. The PSBR has been in surplus in each of the last two years, something achieved in only one previous year since the beginning of the 1950s. In all other years, the PSBR has been in deficit.

Balance of Trade (Manufactures)

59. **Mr. Fatchett:** To ask the Chancellor of the Exchequer what is his latest forecast of the balance of trade in manufactures in 1989.

71. **Mr. Barron:** To ask the Chancellor of the Exchequer what is his latest forecast of the balance of trade in manufactures in 1989.

75. **Mr. Vaz:** To ask the Chancellor of the Exchequer what is his latest forecast of the balance of trade in manufactures in 1989.

80. **Mr. Allen McKay:** To ask the Chancellor of the Exchequer what is his latest forecast of the balance of trade in manufactures in 1989.

Mr. Major: The Financial Statement and Budget Report for 1989-90 shows a forecast deficit for trade in manufactures in 1989 of £15$\frac{1}{2}$ billion.

Rateable Values

61. **Mr. Rooker:** To ask the Chancellor of the Exchequer when he expects the Inland Revenue valuation officer to be able to inform businesses of the new rateable values following re-valuation.

Mr. Norman Lamont: Inland Revenue valuation officers are to complete the revaluation and send each charging authority a copy of the proposed list for its area by 31 December 1989. The authority is then to deposit the copy at its principal office and give notice of its availability for public inspection. The list comes into force from 1 April 1990.

Personal Disposable Income

62. **Sir Fergus Montgomery:** To ask the Chancellor of the Exchequer what was the growth of real personal disposable income for the latest full year for which figures are available.

86. **Mr. Waller:** To ask the Chancellor of the Exchequer what was the growth of real personal disposable income for the latest full year for which figures are available.

103. **Mr. Marlow:** To ask the Chancellor of the Exchequer what was the growth of real personal disposable income for the latest full year for which figures are available.

Mr. Norman Lamont: Real personal disposable income is estimated to have grown by 5 per cent. in 1988.

Business Investment

65. **Mr. Quentin Davies:** To ask the Chancellor of the Exchequer what was the share of gross domestic product represented by business investment in 1988.

121. **Mr. Michael Brown:** To ask the Chancellor of the Exchequer what was the share of gross domestic product represented by business investment in 1988.

Mr. Major: Business investment as a share of GDP was 14·6 per cent. in 1988, the highest level recorded.

Poverty

67. **Mr. Henderson:** To ask the Chancellor of the Exchequer when he last met representatives of the Low Pay Unit to discuss the numbers of people in poverty.

73. **Ms. Mowlam:** To ask the Chancellor of the Exchequer when he last met representatives of the Low Pay Unit to discuss the numbers of people in poverty.

89. **Ms. Quin:** To ask the Chancellor of the Exchequer when he last met representatives of the Low Pay Unit to discuss the numbers of people in poverty.

Mr. Major: My right hon. Friend has not met representatives of the Low Pay Unit recently.

Credit Cards

68. **Dr. Michael Clark:** To ask the Chancellor of the Exchequer when he last met representatives of the credit card companies; and what subjects were discussed.

Mr. Lilley: My right hon. Friend often meets representatives of financial insitutions to discuss a variety of issues.

Gross Domestic Product

70. **Mr. Hanley:** To ask the Chancellor of the Exchequer what was the growth of gross domestic product in 1987 and 1988.

131. **Mr. Andy Stewart:** To ask the Chancellor of the Exchequer what was the growth of gross domestic product in 1987 and 1988.

Mr. Major: Gross domestic product is estimated to have grown by 4½ per cent. in both 1987 and 1988.

Governor of the Bank of England

74. **Mr. Cousins:** To ask the Chancellor of the Exchequer when he next expects to meet the Governor of the Bank of England; and what matters he proposes to discuss.

101. **Mr. Illsley:** To ask the Chancellor of the Exchequer what was discussed when he last met the Governor of the Bank of England.

105. **Mr. Hinchliffe:** To ask the Chancellor of the Exchequer what was discussed when he last met the Governor of the Bank of England.

107. **Mr. Caborn:** To ask the Chancellor of the Exchequer what was discussed when he last met the Governor of the Bank of England.

Mr. Lilley: My right hon. Friend meets the Governor from time to time to discuss a variety of matters.

International Debt

78. **Mr. Skinner:** To ask the Chancellor of the Exchequer when he next intends to meet other Finance Ministers to discuss international debt; and if he will make a statement.

Mr. Lilley: My right hon. Friend the Chancellor of the Exchequer met other Finance Ministers on June 1 in the ministerial Council of the OECD. International debt was discussed among other issues.

Balance of Trade

84. **Ms. Walley:** To ask the Chancellor of the Exchequer what is his latest forecast of the balance of trade in visible goods in 1989.

Mr. Major: I refer the hon. Member to the reply I gave to the hon. Member for Stretford (Mr. Lloyd) on 6 June.

Mr. Teddy Taylor: To ask the Chancellor of the Exchequer what importance he attaches to the balance of trade *(a)* with the rest of the EEC and *(b)* with the rest of the world; and what account he takes of the EEC deficit when framing his economic policies.

Mr. Major: The overall current account is one indicator among many that are assessed within the framework of the Government's financial strategy. Movements in trade balances with individual economies or groups of economies will reflect, among other developments, changes in the United Kingdom's commercial and trading arrangements with them.

Value Added Tax

85. **Ms. Armstrong:** To ask the Chancellor of the Exchequer what proportion of gross earnings a one-earner family with two children on average earnings pays in value added tax in *(a)* 1979 and *(b)* now.

111. **Mr. Ronnie Campbell:** To ask the Chancellor of the Exchequer what proportion of gross earnings a one-earner family with two children on average earnings pays in value added tax in *(a)* 1979 and *(b)* now.

Mr. Lilley: I refer the hon. Member to the reply given by my right hon. Friend the Financial Secretary to the hon. Member for Edinburgh, South (Mr. Griffiths) on 6 June.

Higher Rate Taxpayers

90. **Mr. Boswell:** To ask the Chancellor of the Exchequer what proportion of total income tax revenue was paid by higher rate taxpayers in 1978-79; and what proportion was paid by them in 1988-89.

108. **Mr. Andrew MacKay:** To ask the Chancellor of the Exchequer what proportion of total income tax revenue was paid by higher rate taxpayers in 1978-79; and what proportion was paid by them in 1988-89.

122. **Mr. Paice:** To ask the Chancellor of the Exchequer what proportion of total income tax revenue was paid by higher rate taxpayers in 1978-79; and what proportion was paid by them in 1988-89.

Mr. Norman Lamont: In 1978-79 higher rate taxpayers were liable to pay 20 per cent. of total income tax due. By 1988-89 their share had increased to 32 per cent.

Output Statistics

94. **Mr. Janman:** To ask the Chancellor of the Exchequer what are his latest figures for output per hour worked in the United Kingdom.

Mr. Major: The April 1989 edition of the "Economic Progress Report" presented estimates by a leading academic which show that output per hour worked in the United Kingdom economy as a whole in 1986 was about 50 per cent. higher than in Japan and only 5 per cent. lower than Germany.

Tax Reform

99. **Mr. Devlin:** To ask the Chancellor of the Exchequer if he will make a statement setting out Government policy on tax reform.

123. **Mr. Carrington:** To ask the Chancellor of the Exchequer if he will make a statement setting out Government policy on tax reform.

Mr. Norman Lamont: The Government's programme of tax reform has sought to create a climate in which businesses can thrive and individual initiative and risk-taking are rewarded. A major objective has been to leave people more of their own money, so that they can choose for themselves what to do with it. In particular the Government have reduced marginal tax rates so that an extra pound of earnings or profits is really worth having. We have reduced the basic rate of income tax from 33 to 25 per cent. and set a target of 20 per cent. Business taxation has been radically restructured, leaving the main United Kingdom corporation tax rate at 35 per cent., one of the lowest in the industrialised world. Five major taxes have been abolished completely.

We have also tried to ensure that, as a general rule, people's choices are distorted by the tax system as little as reasonably possible. In general, the aim is to charge lower rates on a broader base; thereby improving incentives and reducing distortions. However, the Government has also been prepared, when it is sensible, to promote well-targeted tax reliefs which will help to make the economy work better. Other important objectives have been to provide a fair deal for married women and to simplify the tax system.

Bank Rate

109. **Mr. Mullin:** To ask the Chancellor of the Exchequer what was the bank rate on *(a)* 8 June 1988 and *(b)* 8 June 1989.

Mr. Lilley: The bank base rates stood at $8\frac{1}{2}$ per cent. on 8 June 1988 and 14 per cent. on 8 June 1989.

European Monetary System

112. **Mr. Beith:** To ask the Chancellor of the Exchequer what recent representations he has received on his policy on the European monetary system.

Mr. Lilley: My right hon. Friend has received a number of representations on that subject.

132. **Mr. Denzil Davies:** To ask the Chancellor of the Exchequer what are the major disadvantages he has identified of including the pound sterling in the exhange rate mechanism of the European monetary system.

Mr. Lawson: I refer the right hon. Member to the speech I made to the Royal Institute of International Affairs on 25 January.

Married Man's Allowance

114. **Mr. Wood:** To ask the Chancellor of the Exchequer what recent consideration he has given to phasing out the married man's tax allowance.

Mr. Lamont: When independent taxation begins in April 1990 the present structure of income tax allowances will be replaced by the personal allowance and the married couple's allowance. A husband and wife will each have their own personal allowance and the new system will continue to recognise marriage through the married couple's allowance. This will be given in the first instance to the husband. The personal allowance and the married couple's allowance will together be equivalent to the present married man's allowance.

Group of Seven

115. **Mr. Patrick Thompson:** To ask the Chancellor of the Exchequer when he next intends to meet his counterparts in the Group of Seven finance Ministers; and what matters he intends to discuss.

Mr. Lilley: At the economic summit in Paris in July.

Delors Report

129. **Mr. Simon Hughes:** To ask the Chancellor of the Exchequer what representations he has received on his response to the Delors committee report on economic and monetary union in the European Community.

Mr. Lilley: My right hon. Friend has received a number of representations on the Government's response to the Delors committee report.

Overseas Assets

130. **Mr. Curry:** To ask the Chancellor of the Exchequer what are the latest figures for the identified stock of United Kingdom net overseas assets; and what these represent as a share of gross domestic product.

Mr. Major: An estimate of the value of the stock of United Kingdom overseas assets identified at end-1988 will be included in the Pink Book in August. The latest estimate is of the order of £115 billion to £120 billion, which represents about one quarter of money GDP.

Payroll Giving

Mr. Hoyle: To ask the Chancellor of the Exchequer what steps are being taken to ensure that organisations funded by the Treasury introduce chargeable payroll deductions for charities.

Mr. Brooke: There are no plans to change the present practice of deducting donations to charities free of charge.

Indirect Taxation (EC Proposals)

Mr. Vaz: To ask the Chancellor of the Exchequer if he will make a statement about the European Commission's proposals for indirect taxation and the related issue of the definition of foodstuffs.

Mr. Lilley: I refer the hon. Member to the answer I gave to my hon. Friend the Member for Southend, East (Mr. Taylor) on 23 May 1989 at column *440*. The Commission has yet to define "foodstuffs" for the purposes of its proposals.

EEC (Net Contribution)

Mr. Teddy Taylor: To ask the Chancellor of the Exchequer what estimate he has made of the net contribution to the European Economic Community in the calendar year 1989.

Mr. Brooke: The Government's latest estimate of the United Kingdom's net contribution to the Community budget in 1989 is £1,966 million, which was published in the "Statement on the 1989 Community Budget", Cm 680, in April this year.

Net Overseas Assets

Mr. Yeo: To ask the Chancellor of the Exchequer what are the latest figures for the identified stock of United Kingdom net overseas assets; and what these represent as a share of gross domestic product.

Mr. Major: An estimate of the value of the stock of United Kingdom net overseas assets identified at end-1988 will be included in the Pink Book in August. The latest estimate is of the order of £115 billion to £120 billion, which represents about one quarter of money GDP.

Gross Domestic Product (Business Investment)

Mr. Watts: To ask the Chancellor of the Exchequer what was the share of gross domestic product represented by business investment in 1988.

Mr. Major: Business investment as a share of GDP was 14·6 per cent. in 1988, the highest level recorded.

Mr. Strang: To ask the Chancellor of the Exchequer whether he has made any study of the likely effect of a further increase in interest rates on the level of manufacturing investments in the current year.

Mr. Major: Developments in the economy are constantly monitored. Manufacturing investment is growing strongly and the outlook remains good.

Civil Servants

Mr. Baldry: To ask the Chancellor of the Exchequer what plans he has further to improve the skills and professionalism of civil servants.

Mr. Brooke: Her Majesty's Treasury is today issuing guidance to Departments on improved personnel management arrangements for two key groups, information technology staff and purchasing and supply staff. In future, most entrants to these groups will be recruited for these specific areas of work, and developed and promoted primarily on the basis of their specialised skills rather than those required for general administration. To meet their needs for specialised expertise, Departments will have the facility to recruit staff at more senior levels on a permanent basis. They will also be able to recruit, if required, on a short-term basis. There will be a greater emphasis on professional training and development for both groups. I am confident that the new arrangements will allow Departments to develop rounded professional expertise and thus further improve value for money in their IT and purchasing work.

Premium Bonds

Mr. Jack: To ask the Chancellor of the Exchequer if he will list in the *Official Report* the value of and percentage of premium savings bonds sales made in denominations of £10, £20, £30, £40, £50, £60, £70, £80, £90 and £100 for each of the last five years.

Mr. Lilley *[holding answer 25 May 1989]:* Premium savings bonds are no longer issued in denominations of £60, £70, £80 or £90. The estimated value and percentage of premium savings bond sales made in denominations of £10, £20, £30, £40, £50 and £100 for the financial years 1984-85, 1985-86, 1986-87, 1987-88 and 1988-89 are shown in the attached table.

Ending March	1985	1986	1987	1988	1989
£10					
£ million	10·3	11·0	10·3	10·1	9·8
Percentage of total value of sales	5·0	5·9	4·8	3·4	3·2
£20					
£ million	1·3	2·3	3·1	3·4	3·6
Percentage of total value of sales	0·6	1·2	1·5	1·1	1·2
£30					
£ million	1·5	1·9	2·2	2·3	2·4
Percentage of total value of sales	0·7	1·0	1·0	0·8	0·8
£40					
£ million	1·4	1·6	1·7	1·8	2·0
Percentage of total value of sales	0·7	0·8	0·8	0·6	0·6
£50					
£ million	11·8	13·3	14·4	14·8	16·2
Percentage of total value of sales	5·7	7·2	6·7	5·0	5·2
£100					
£ million	17·3	16·0	16·5	17·1	17·5
Percentage of total value of sales	8·3	8·7	7·6	5·8	5·6

HEALTH

Births

Mr. Wigley: To ask the Secretary of State for Health what information he has as to how many sets of *(a)* twins, *(b)* triplets, *(c)* quadruplets, *(d)* quintuplets and *(e)* sextuplets were born in England and Wales in 1988; and what was the total number of maternities in that year.

Mr. Freeman: In 1988, there were 689,153 maternities in England and Wales. These included:

	Number
Twins	7,452
Triplets	157
Quadruplets	12
Quintuplets	1
Sextuplets or over	0
Total number of maternities with multiple births	7,622

Schoolchildren's Diets

Mr. Norris: To ask the Secretary of State for Health when he expects to publish the final report on the survey of schoolchildren's diets undertaken in 1983.

Mr. Mellor: The report "The Diets of British Schoolchildren" from the chief medical officer's committee on medical aspects of food policy (COMA), giving the final results of the 1983 survey of schoolchildren's diets, is being published today. I welcome this highly detailed scientific document which confirms the findings that we published in the 1986 preliminary report of the survey and copies have been placed in the Library.

The information in these reports has been and continues to be an invaluable guide for the preparation of the health education messages that our children need if they are to benefit from a healthy diet. It shows beyond doubt that although our schoolchildren in all social classes were well nourished and thriving as never before, they ate far too much fat and that many of the older children, especially the girls, needed more detailed advice about their choice of foods and about spending their lunch money more wisely. The Government are continuing to encourage local education authorities and the Health Education Authority in their efforts to inform children and parents about healthy eating and to persuade them to choose a healthy diet.

Dog Attacks

Mr. Alfred Morris: To ask the Secretary of State for Health what recent information he has on the approximate annual cost to the National Health Service of serious attacks on children and others by dogs; and if he will make a statement.

Mr. Freeman: None. No information is collected centrally.

Automated Cleaning Processes

Mr. Gould: To ask the Secretary of State for Health what information he has on the use by district health authorities of automated cleaning processes which emit considerable quantities of CFCs; and what steps are being taken to find alternatives.

Mr. Freeman: A minority of DHAs use automated cleaning and drying equipment in their sterile supplies departments for use prior to sterilisation of surgical equipment. Some of the older equipment will emit levels of CFCs within the statutory limit for operator safety and newer equipment involves solvent reclamation systems which considerably reduce the CFC emission levels. The three United Kingdom manufacturers of such equipment are all in the process of seeking alternative processes.

Health Service Pay

Mr. Hoyle: To ask the Secretary of State for Health if he will publish details of the new package on pay and structure offered on 16 May to staff side representatives of Committee E; and what this will mean for operating department assistants.

Mr. Mellor *[holding answer 7 June 1989]:* Details of the proposals, including the effect on operating department assistants, are contained in the professional and technical staffs B Whitley council documents PTB/J320. A copy has been placed in the Library.

SOCIAL SECURITY

Income Support

Mr. Andrew Bowden: To ask the Secretary of State for Social Security how many men aged 70 to 75 years receive income support; and what is this figure as a proportion of the total number of men aged 70 to 75 years.

Mr. Peter Lloyd: The latest estimate is that there are some 82,000 men aged 70 to 74 (inclusive) dependent on income support. This represents 9 per cent. of all men in this age group.

Loans and Grants

Mr. Allen: To ask the Secretary of State for Social Security what was the total value of *(a)* applications and payments for (i) budgetary loans, (ii) cash loans (iii) community care grants from the social fund for the 1988-89 financial year expressed in money terms and as a percentage of the available budget in respect of Department of Social Security offices covering the Nottingham, North constituency.

Mr. Fatchett: To ask the Secretary of State for Social Security if he will list for each Leeds social security office the funds allocated in 1988-89, and in 1989-90 for social fund *(a)* loans and *(b)* grants and the total expenditure in 1988-89 for (i) loans and (ii) grants.

Mr. Peter Lloyd: The information requested can be obtained from the Library.

However, social fund data for March 1989 are not yet available as a check of the figures has revealed some inaccuracies which have resulted from a new method of calculating the month end balances. The necessary adjustments are being made and the tables will be placed in the Library shortly.

In addition, the value of applications processed during December 1988 remains unavailable because of an earlier computer malfunction.

Attendance Allowance Board

Mr. Frank Field: To ask the Secretary of State for Social Security on what dates in the current year the attendance allowance board has met.

Mr. Scott: The requested information is as follows:

Attendance Allowance Board
Dates of meetings in 1989 (to 6 June 1989)

10 January 1989[1]	30 March 1989[1]
17 January 1989[1]	4 April 1989[1]
24 January 1989[1]	11 April 1989[1]
31 January 1989[1]	20 April 1989[1]
7 February 1989[1]	25 April 1989[1] (am)
14 February 1989[1]	25 April 1989[2] (pm)
16 February 1989[1]	27 April 1989[1]
21 February 1989[1]	4 May 1989[1]
23 February 1989[1]	9 May 1989[1]
28 February 1989[2]	16 May 1989[1]
7 March 1989[1]	23 May 1989[1]
14 March 1989[1]	6 June 1989[1]
21 March 1989[1]	

[1] "Small board" case work meeting attended by the chairman or deputy chairman and two other members.

[2] Formal meeting of the full attendance allowance board.

Visual Handicap

Mr. Favell: To ask the Secretary of State for Social Security when he will be able to publish the report of the working group on inter-agency collaboration on visual handicap.

Mr. Scott: I am pleased to announce that this report, which was commissioned in 1987 by the then Minister for the Disabled, is now available in book form (through Her Majesty's Stationery Office). Versions in braille, large print and on tape are available from the Department of Health. I am very grateful to the members of the working group, and I hope that the report will be carefully studied by all involved in statutory and voluntary services to visually handicapped people. I know that the detailed recommendations will be carefully considered by Ministers in the Department of Health and the Welsh Office.

Disability

Mr. Ashley: To ask the Secretary of State for Social Security on what date he plans to publish the fourth report from the Office of Population Censuses and Surveys on disability.

Mr. Scott *[holding answer 7 June 1989]:* The Office of Population Censuses and Surveys has today published the fourth report on the findings of the surveys of disability in Great Britain carried out between 1985 and 1988. The report covers all the remaining aspects of circumstances of disabled adults which were not included in reports 1 and 2, which were published last year. It provides information on a wide range of topics, including the use of services; equipment and adaptations; mobility and transport; employment; social and leisure activities; and, for those in private households, the informal help and care received. For those in communal establishments, some aspects of residents' finances are described.

The large quantity of detailed and complex information contained in the report has been provided by disabled people themselves or their carers. It therefore reflects their own perception of their activities and experiences, including the type of services they receive and the disability equipment they use.

Taken together, the OPCS reports will provide the most comprehensive and detailed information ever collected about the circumstances of disabled people in this country.

We welcome comments on this report, as we have on the three already published.

HOME DEPARTMENT

Spain (Secretary of State's Visit)

Mr. Dalyell: To ask the Secretary of State for the Home Department if he will make a statement on the follow-up action resulting from his visit to Spain, to discuss matters of mutual concern.

Mr. Hurd: I announced on 17 May the outcome of the meetings of European Community Immigration Ministers and Trevi Ministers, which I attended in Madrid on 12 May, in reply to a question from my hon. Friend the Member for Portsmouth, South (Mr. Martin) at column *208*. Suitable steps are being taken to give effect to these decisions.

Dogs

Mr. Spearing: To ask the Secretary of State for the Home Department what recent representations he has received concerning legislation for control of dogs; what replies he has sent; and what action he proposes to take.

Mr. Alfred Morris: To ask the Secretary of State for the Home Department if there is any action he will be taking in response to the increasingly frequent reports of serious attacks on children and others by dogs; and if he will make a statement.

Mr. David Young: To ask the Secretary of State for the Home Department what immediate action he is taking to deal with attacks by Rottweilers on people and animals.

Mr. Dunnachie: To ask the Secretary of State for the Home Department (1) if he will introduce measures to ensure that dogs with inborn aggressive tendencies must wear muzzles when in public places;

(2) if he will introduce measures to ensure that all dogs must be kept on a lead when in public places.

Mr. Alfred Morris: To ask the Secretary of State for the Home Department if there is any action he will be taking in response to the increasingly frequent reports of serious attacks on children and others by dogs; if he intends to use the statutory powers that may alleviate the problem; and if he will make a statement.

Mr. Douglas Hogg: We have received about 55 representations and are examining the possibility of strengthening the legislation on dangerous dogs.

Mr. David Young: To ask the Secretary of State for the Home Department if he will ban Rottweilers as domestic pets or from being held on domestic premises.

Mr. Douglas Hogg: I am not persuaded that a ban would be the right answer, but we are examining the possibility of strengthening the legislation on dangerous dogs.

Mr. David Young: To ask the Secretary of State for the Home Department (1) if he will make it his policy to ban Rottweilers and other dogs bred for fighting from being kept in domestic premises or as domestic pets, without the express permission of the police;

(2) what action he intends to take to deal with the problem of violent dogs and the environmental problems caused by neglected dogs.

Mr. Douglas Hogg *[holding answer 6 June 1989]:* The Government are examining the possibility of strengthening the legislation on dangerous dogs.

Terrestrial Broadcasting Transmission Networks (Study)

Sir Geoffrey Johnson Smith: To ask the Secretary of State for the Home Department if he will publish the study of privatisation options for the terrestrial broadcasting transmission networks which his Department commissioned from Price Waterhouse.

Mr. Hurd: I have today placed a copy of this report in the Library. Further copies are available from HMSO bookshops at a cost of £3·95.

War Criminals

Mr. Winnick: To ask the Secretary of State for the Home Department when he now expects to make a statement on the position of those persons in the United Kingdom who are alleged to have committed Nazi war crimes.

Mr. John Patten: I refer the hon. Member for the answer given to him on 11 May. I understand that the inquiry still expects to report this month.

Crime (Essex)

Mr. Janman: To ask the Secretary of State for the Home Department what steps he is taking in relation to crime in Essex; and if he will make a statement.

Mr. John Patten: I refer my hon. Friend to the reply that I gave to a question from my hon. Friend the Member for Harlow (Mr. Hayes) on 11 May at column *539*.

Deportation Orders

Mr. Darling: To ask the Secretary of State for the Home Department how many deportation orders were signed by immigration officers in each of the last five years; and how many of those were signed by officers at inspector level or above in each month since August 1988.

Mr. Renton *[holding answer 6 June 1989]:* Deportation orders are always signed by Ministers, normally by my right hon. Friend the Home Secretary.

In the five years from 1984-88, the numbers of notices of intention to deport under section 3(5)(a) of the Immigration Act 1971, against which there is a right of appeal to the independent appellate authorities, signed by members of the immigration and nationality department were as follows:

	Number
1984	2,278
1985	1,578
1986	661
1987	794
1988	1,751

Information about the number of notices of intention to deport signed by an immigration officer in this period on the authority of a responsible official in the deportation section of IND is not readily available and could be provided only at disproportionate cost.

Since 1 August 1988, notices of intention to deport under section 3(5)(a) may be authorised by a member of the immigration service at not less than inspector level. The number so authorised (and signed by an immigration officer) since 1988 is as follows:

	Number
1988	
August	82
September	114
October	121
November	208
December	159
1989	
January	226
February	224
March	252
April	171

THE ARTS

Horniman Museum and Library

Mr. Fraser: To ask the Minister for the Arts if he will publish a timetable for establishing the independence of the Horniman museum and library in Forest Hill.

Mr. Luce: It is intended that the museum will be governed by an independent charitable trust following the abolition of the Inner London education authority. The necessary steps are being taken to put in place as quickly as possible an appropriate charitable trust framework for the museum.

ENVIRONMENT

Rates

Mr. Andrew Bowden: To ask the Secretary of State for the Environment what is the average domestic rates bill in England and Wales for 1989-90 of people in receipt of income support.

Mr. Gummer: The information requested is not available.

Housing Action Trusts

Ms. Harman: To ask the Secretary of State for the Environment (1) how and when he intends to conduct a ballot of the tenants of the Gloucester grove and North Peckham estates in Southwark in relation to a housing action trust;

(2) whether the housing action trust ballot will be on the basis of one vote per tenancy;

(3) who will be entitled to cast the vote in a housing action trust ballot when the tenancy is in joint names.

Mr. Trippier: I refer the hon. Member to the replies that I gave to her on 30 January (*Official Report*, columns *20* and *30*) and to the hon. Member for Norwood on 24 May (*Official Report*, column *592*).

Ms. Harman: To ask the Secretary of State for the Environment how many tenants in Southwark, living on the Gloucester grove and North Peckham estates proposed for the setting up of housing action trusts, were interviewed by the consultants Peat Marwick McLintock in preparing their report on the suitability of these estates for housing action trusts.

Mr. Trippier: The consultants' report acknowledges that they were unable to interview more than a small proportion of tenants living on the North Peckham and Gloucester grove estates. Nevertheless, they held in-depth interviews with 31 tenants and a similar number of people closely connected with the estates, and they used a variety of published sources to produce a good report of housing conditions in the area, with recommendations for improvements. Tenants and tenants associations on both estates are discussing the reports with the consultants as part of the current consultation exercise.

Ms. Harman: To ask the Secretary of State for the Environment if he will give an estimate of the amount of Government support necessary for improvements to the Gloucester grove and North Peckham estates along the lines of those recommended by the consultants in their report on the suitability of these estates for housing action trusts.

Mr. Trippier: The consultants produced an illustrative scheme for costing purposes which estimated the costs of improving the Southwark housing action trust area at around £112 million. We have allocated substantial resources to the housing action trust programme and are committed to pay for the improvements to be carried out by housing action trusts. The amount of resources for any particular trust will depend on the programme of work, to be decided in consultation with residents.

Ms. Harman: To ask the Secretary of State for the Environment if he will make a statement on the future of existing and planned estate action schemes for the Gloucester grove and North Peckham estates in Southwark.

Mr. Trippier: Southwark council has received previous estate action allocations amounting to some £3·75 million for the Gloucester grove and North Peckham estates. The council bid unsuccessfully for Estate Action support towards housing and environmental improvements there in 1989-90, but their request for Estate Action support for the conversion of garages into local estate offices is being considered by the Department.

If Southwark submits Estate Action bids for the Gloucester grove and North Peckham estates in future years, their applications, like all Estate Action bids, will be assessed on their merits.

Ms. Harman: To ask the Secretary of State for the Environment what estimates he has received of the cost of rehabilitation of Gloucester grove and North Peckham estates from his consultants on housing action trusts.

Mr. Trippier: The consultants produced an illustrative scheme for costing purposes which estimated the costs of improving the Southwark Housing Action Trust area at around £112 million—£68 million for North Peckham and £44 million for Gloucester grove. Local residents are now being consulted about the proposals for their estates.

Ms. Harman: To ask the Secretary of State for the Environment what has been the *(a)* total cost of monies paid to consultants and *(b)* the cost to his Department in relation to proposed housing action trusts for the Gloucester grove and North Peckham estates in Southwark.

Mr. Trippier: We expect that the costs in relation to the proposed Southwark housing action trust will amount to around £192,000, including VAT, when all bills have been paid. This figure covers consultants' fees and other costs involved in producing reports and leaflets about the proposals, but excludes consultants' fees under the current consultation exercise. The cost of this contract will remain commercially confidential until it has been completed.

Ms. Harman: To ask the Secretary of State for the Environment whether he intends to implement the consultants' conclusion that more money needs to be invested in the areas designated for housing action trusts in Southwark.

Mr. Trippier: We have accepted our consultants advice that substantial resources should be allocated to a housing action trust in Southwark and have made public expenditure provision accordingly.

Genetically Manipulated Organisms

Mr. Janman: To ask the Secretary of State for the Environment what proposals he has for additional legislation on the intentional release of genetically manipulated organisms.

Mrs. Virginia Bottomley: The Department of the Environment together with the Welsh and Scottish Offices, have today published a consultation paper on proposals for additional legislation on the intentional release of genetically manipulated organisms. Copies have been placed in the Libraries of both Houses.

Existing legislation provides comprehensive protection for the safety of persons against such organisms, but does not provide complete coverage for the environment. The aim is to have a parallel system to protect the environment and so ensure an adequate framework against which biotechnology can be properly developed and its full economic potential realised.

We are proposing to augment the existing legislation to provide a comprehensive system for environmental protection with four main elements:

    a general duty of care to protect the environment on those releasing GMOs;

    notification to Ministers by those proposing to release GMOs;

    authorisation by Ministers of proposed releases;

    appropriate enforcement of the provisions;

Interested organisations and individuals are invited to send their views to the Department by 25 August 1989.

Community Charge

Mr. Blunkett: To ask the Secretary of State for the Environment (1) if he will publish his best estimates of the numbers of staff involved in *(a)* the production and distribution of the Minister for Local Government's articles on the community charge, and *(b)* the direct contact made with local newspapers in connection with these articles;

(2) if he will publish his best estimates of the total cost of *(a)* the production and distribution of the Minister for Local Government's articles on the community charge, and *(b)* the direct contact made with local newspapers in connection with those articles.

Mr. Gummer *[holding answer 6 June 1989]:* As is customary with ministerial articles, several officials made suggestions or contributions. Information officers in London and each of the seven regions helped to contact local newspapers. In all cases, these activities constituted only a small part of the duties of the officials concerned. The precise costs are therefore not readily identifiable.

TRANSPORT

Computer Reservation Systems

Mr. Colvin: To ask the Secretary of State for Transport (1) what are the principal differences between the codes of conduct for computer reservation systems prepared by the European Civil Aviation Conference and the European Commission;

(2) what plans he has for extending the scope of the EEC code of conduct for computer reservation systems to cover non-scheduled passenger air services;

(3) what steps he will be taking to reconcile the two codes of conduct for computer reservation systems prepared by the European Civil Aviation Conference and the European Commission;

(4) when he expects to see agreement on the EEC code of conduct for computer reservation systems; and if he will make a statement on the timetable for its introduction.

Mr. Peter Bottomley: A regulation governing the operation of computerised reservation systems (CRSs) within the European Community was adopted by the Council of Ministers on 5 June 1989. It will come into force on 1 August, subject to certain transitional arrangements for CRSs already established in the Community.

This regulation constitutes binding and directly applicable Community law and therefore takes precedence over the ECAC code of conduct within the member states of the Community. The two codes are consistent in all essential respects. The Community code contains enforcement provisions and lays down additional requirements concerning the disclosure of personal information, displays which are not comprehensive and the provision of a display based on arrival times.

The Council of Ministers invited the Commission to examine the need for a regulation governing CRSs used for non-scheduled passenger air services and for air freight and to bring forward any necessary proposals by 31 December 1990 at the latest.

Highway Investment (North-West)

Mr. Pike: To ask the Secretary of State for Transport if he has yet had time to study the report "Highway Investment Needs Review: North West Region".

Mr. Peter Bottomley: Yes. The massive increase in trunk roads spending announced on 18 May largely meets the needs identified in the report.

Severn Crossing

Mr. Stern: To ask the Secretary of State for Transport what representations he has received in respect of the proposed revisions to the routes of the link roads to the second Severn crossing.

Mr. Peter Bottomley: No formal representations have been received although further information has been sought.

Public exhibitions of approach roads will be held shortly. They will be well publicised and the public will be invited to comment.

PRIME MINISTER

Economy

Q86. **Sir Hugh Rossi:** To ask the Prime Minister if she has received recent representations regarding the state of the economy.

Q137. **Mr. Cash:** To ask the Prime Minister if she has received recent representations regarding the state of the economy.

Q153. **Mr. Malins:** To ask the Prime Minister if she has received recent representations regarding the state of the economy.

The Prime Minister: I have received a number of such representations. Thanks to the policies that we have pursued for the past 10 years, and will continue to pursue, the economy is performing very well.

Low Moor, Bradford

Q104. **Mr. Cryer:** To ask the Prime Minister when she next expects to pay an official visit to Low Moor in Bradford.

The Prime Minister: I have at present no such plans to do so.

EEC (Trade)

Mr. Austin Mitchell: To ask the Prime Minister whether she will make it her policy that Her Majesty's Government will veto any proposals by the European Economic Community in the health, education, housing and social security field except insofar as this is necessary to remove impediments to trade.

The Prime Minister: The Government will continue to examine carefully all proposals for Community legislation to ensure that they are necessary to achieve the objectives of the Treaty of Rome as amended by the Single European Act and that they are appropriate to the Community's competence.

Engagements

Mr. Harry Greenway: To ask the Prime Minister if she will list her official engagements for Thursday 8 June.

Mr. Stern: To ask the Prime Minister if she will list her official engagements for Thursday 8 June.

Mr. Pike: To ask the Prime Minister if she will list her official engagements for Thursday 8 June.

Mr. Grocott: To ask the Prime Minister if she will list her official engagements for Thursday 8 June.

Mr. Robert G. Hughes: To ask the Prime Minister if she will list her official engagements for Thursday 8 June.

Mr. David Shaw: To ask the Prime Minister if she will list her official engagements for Thursday 8 June.

The Prime Minister: This morning I presided at a meeting of the Cabinet and had meetings with ministerial colleagues and others. In addition to my duties in the House, I shall be having further meetings later today.

SCOTLAND

Community Charge

Mr. Sillars: To ask the Secretary of State for Scotland what guidelines he has issued to regional councils about registration for poll tax purposes of Royal Navy ratings who are stationed outwith Scotland.

Mr. Lang: None. It is for community charges registration officers to decide in the light of all the facts and circumstances relating to individual cases where a person, including a Royal Navy rating, is solely or mainly resident in their area and thus liable to be registered there for community charge purposes. I understand that, in the interests of achieving a measure of consistency in the treatment of service personnel, community charges registration officers have agreed with the Ministry of Defence working arrangements for their registration. However, this does not affect any individual's right of appeal against any registration decision.

Skill Shortages

Mr. McLeish: To ask the Secretary of State for Scotland if he will give details of reports commissioned by his Department on (i) skill shortages and (ii) skill shortages and the anticipated impact of 1992 on sections of Scottish industry.

Mr. Lang *[holding answer 19 May 1989]:* My Department is associated with a study commissioned by the SDA which will identify the commercial opportunities and challenges for firms in Scotland arising from the 1992 proposals.

As regards skill shortages, the Department does keep the labour market situation under review. Although no specific studies of skill shortages have been commissioned recently, a report was published last year (December 1988) on new entrants to the labour market in Scotland in the 1990s. In addition the Training Agency in Scotland conducts regular surveys of Scottish industry as part of the routine process of local labour market information gathering which collect, among other things, information on skill shortages. More specifically the Training Agency in Scotland in conjunction with the SDA has recently completed a report (April 1989) on skill shortages on the engineering and oil industries in Tayside.

WALES

Health Research

Mr. Barry Jones: To ask the Secretary of State for Wales how much of his health budget is spent on research in Wales as a percentage and as a cash sum; and if he will make a statement.

Mr. Grist *[holding answer 25 May 1989]:* The 1989-90 health and personal social services research and development budget of my right hon. Friend the Secretary of State for Health, which includes projects for England and Wales, has been increased to £19·02 million. Expenditure by my Department in 1989-90 will exceed £1 million and amount to approximately 0·08 per cent. of provision for the National Health Service in Wales.

FOREIGN AND COMMONWEALTH AFFAIRS

Hong Kong (Refugees)

Mr. Alfred Morris: To ask the Secretary of State for Foreign and Commonwealth Affairs if he will make a statement on the refugee problem in Hong Kong.

Mr. Eggar: There are now some 41,000 Vietnamese boat people in Hong Kong. Over 12,000 have arrived in the past month. The Government are doing everything possible to help the Hong Kong authorities to cope with the influx. We are working for a successful outcome to the international conference on indo-Chinese refugees in Geneva on 13-14 June and for a comprehensive and durable solution to the problem.

Mexico (Illicit Drugs)

Mr. John Marshall: To ask the Secretary of State for Foreign and Commonwealth Affairs what information he has received about measures being taken by the Government of Mexico to combat the illicit drugs problem.

Mr. Eggar: During my recent visit to Mexico I was impressed with the commitment of the new Government of President Salinas to the fight against drugs. Despite economic constraints, the Mexican Government are devoting increasing resources to drug interdiction and eradication. The recent arrest of an alleged major drug trafficker and the government drive to root out corruption are indications of their resolve.

China (British Nationals)

Mr. Kirkhope: To ask the Secretary of State for Foreign and Commonwealth Affairs what steps his Department is taking to protect British nationals in China in the light of recent events; and if he will make a statement.

Mr. Eggar: Our paramount concern at the present time is the safety and well-being of British nationals. Everything that can be done is being done and these efforts will continue until we know that all British nationals who wish to leave China have done so. Her Majesty's embassy in Peking and Consulate-General in Shanghai are, however, working under extremely difficult conditions. The embassy has assisted in arrangements for the evacuation by commercial means of several hundred students, business-men and others with whom they have been in contact. It is important to emphasise that all airports are open and international commercial flights are operating normally.

We understand the deep anxiety of relatives of Britons in China. Firm information may not always be available or indeed possible to obtain. We are in touch with the Association of British Travel Agents (ABTA) about group tours that may still be in China. Inquiries should be made to the consular emergency unit in the Foreign and Commonwealth Office—Telephone No.: 01-270 2700—which opened on 7 June 1989.

ENERGY

Carbon Dioxide

Mr. Flynn: To ask the Secretary of State for Energy if, during the Downing street seminar on 26 April on the greenhouse effect and energy policy options, any representations were made on the contribution to CO_2 pollution made in the processing cycle for nuclear fuel.

Mr. Parkinson: No; the contribution to CO_2 pollution from the processing cycle of nuclear fuel is very small and depends on the sources of energy supply used to run the individual processes involved.

Mr. Alan W. Williams: To ask the Secretary of State for Energy, pursuant to his reply to the hon. Member for

Clwyd, South-West (Mr. Jones), *Official Report,* 15 May, column *105,* what assessment the Government have made of the possibility of reducing carbon dioxide emissions from the use of oil and gas.

Mr. Michael Spicer: Carbon dioxide emissions are an inevitable consequence of the use of any particular fuel containing carbon, although the CO_2 release per unit of useful energy varies according to the fuel and the design of the installation. Studies are planned to investigate the possibilities of removing CO^2 from flue gas, but these are aimed more at large coal-firing plant which produce more CO_2 per unit generated than do gas and oil fired plant.

Cost-effective energy efficiency measures which lead to fuel saving, rather than substitution, can of course reduce CO_2 emissions from any fuel source.

Magnox Power Stations

Mr. Cohen: To ask the Secretary of State for Energy if the Central Electricity Generating Board still retains the original construction plans for each individual magnox-type nuclear power station; and if he will make a statement.

Mr. Michael Spicer: I am advised that the CEGB has retained the construction plans for all of its magnox stations.

Agricultural Crops

Mr. Malcolm Bruce: To ask the Secretary of State for Energy what steps the Government have taken and intend to take to utilise agricultural crops to substitute for fossil fuels in industries.

Mr. Michael Spicer: Fuels derived from agricultural crops are covered by the Biofuels programme, the broad aim of which was described in Energy Paper No. 55 "Renewable Energy in the UK: The Way Forward".

This programme is intended to encourage the widespread commecial exploitation of biofuels by first identifying and then demonstrating where they can be both economically competitive and environmentally acceptable.

Specific agricultural crops which have been investigated within the biofuels research, development and demonstration programme include:

Straw. The development and evaluation of low cost systems for processing and burning baled straw, followed by demonstration of the best systems;

Energy forestry plantations, both coppice and single stem crops. The assessment of likely yields, costs and returns resulting from the establishment of short rotation energy forestry plantation; the investigation of mechanical energy forestry; studies of its environmental impact.

Oscillating Water Columns

Mr. Malcolm Bruce: To ask the Secretary of State for Energy what steps the Government are taking to investigate and promote the use of oscillating water columns for electricity generation, and how much money has been spent on this area to date.

Mr. Michael Spicer: A major element of the Department of Energy's programme of research and development into small scale wave energy is the development of an oscillating water column—Wells turbine shoreline rock gully device invented by Queen's

University, Belfast. At a cost of £308,000 my Department has funded research and construction of an experimental prototype on the island of Islay. I announced to the House on 23 March that the next phase of the project, to install an air driven power turbine and generator, will now proceed, subject to contract, on the basis of the data acquired so far.

AGRICULTURE, FISHERIES AND FOOD

Fur Farming

Mr. Vaz: To ask the Minister of Agriculture, Fisheries and Food if he intends to set up an independent inquiry into the conditions under which fox and mink are farmed for their fur.

Mr. Donald Thompson: No. The Farm Animal Welfare Council is an independent body which has only recently concluded an examination of fur farming and published a statement about it.

Dolphins

Mr. Alan W. Williams: To ask the Minister of Agriculture, Fisheries and Food if he will give an estimate of the number of dolphins around Britain's coasts and their estimated numbers for any year from 1959 onwards for which figures are available.

Mrs. Virginia Bottomley: I have been asked to reply.

It is not at present possible to give reliable estimates of the numbers of small cetacean species, including dolphins, even for relatively small areas of coastal waters. Useful information has been derived from records of strandings and from the voluntary sightings scheme run by the United Kingdom cetacean group of the Mammals Society. Further projects are being considered by the relevant Departments and agencies.

Food Irradiation

Dr. David Clark: To ask the Minister of Agriculture, Fisheries and Food if he will place a copy of his working party's report into control framework and safeguards for food irradiation in the Library.

Mr. Ryder: A copy will be placed in the Library as soon as it is published.

Rabies

Mr. David Young: To ask the Minister of Agriculture, Fisheries and Food what proposals he has to monitor the canine population for rabies.

Mr. Donald Thompson: It is not possible to test an animal for the presence of the disease before clinical signs appear. The disease is in any case not present in the United Kingdom.

Straw

Mr. Malcolm Bruce: To ask the Minister of Agriculture, Fisheries and Food what quantity of straw is *(a)* burnt, *(b)* buried and *(c)* used to supply materials required for paper making and hardboard on average in each year.

Mr. Ryder: My Department's annual sample straw survey indicates the following breakdown for England and Wales:

Percentage of hectarage	1983	1984	1985	1986	1987	1988
Burned in field percentage	37·7	36·7	27·7	27·1	27·2	23·8
Incorporated or cultivated percentage	1·8	7·1	10·4	12·4	17·6	17·6
Baled and removed percentage	60·5	56·2	61·9	60·5	55·2	58·6
Total area ('000 hectares)	3,367·8	3,431·9	3,414·6	3,416·9	3,336·5	3,305·4

No significant quantities of straw are currently used for paper making, but an estimated 1 per cent. of the total has been used for hardboard manufacture in recent years.

Desiccated Liver Powder

Mr. Gould: To ask the Minister of Agriculture, Fisheries and Food if he will designate desiccated liver powder as a food product rather than a pharmaceutical product, so that it requires a health check.

Mr. Donald Thompson: No. However, when the Imported Food Regulations 1984 are reviewed we will ensure that there is no room for doubt about the need for a health mark on imported desiccated liver except where consignments are solely for use in a licensed medicinal product.

Veterinary Surgeons

Mr. Paice: To ask the Minister of Agriculture, Fisheries and Food what action he is proposing to take to consider the supply and demand for veterinary surgeons, particularly in the light of the Riley report.

Mr. MacGregor *[pursuant to his reply, 11 April]:* On behalf of United Kingdom Agriculture Ministers and my right hon. Friend the Secretary of State for Education and Science I have appointed Dr. E. S. Page, MA, BSc as chairman of a committee to review veterinary manpower needs and demand for veterinary education. Professor K. J. Thomson, MSc Lond., MS Iowa, MA (Agric. Econ) and Mr. B. D. Hoskin, BVM & S, MRCVS, have been appointed as members of this committee.

The terms of reference of the committee are:

To assess:

(a) the need for veterinary manpower in the UK, both for the public service and the private sector; and

(b) the demand for veterinary education from home and overseas students;

and, in the light of this, to consider and make recommendations on:

(c) how any increased manpower requirement might be met having regard to constraints on public funding and to the potential funding from the UFC and other sources;

(d) what future arrangements should be developed to assess the demand for veterinary manpower and determine the number of student places.

The Universities Funding Council has decided to postpone consideration of the Riley report until the review is complete.

TRADE AND INDUSTRY

Balance of Trade (West Germany)

133. **Mr. Alan W. Williams:** To ask the Chancellor of the Duchy of Lancaster what was the United Kingdom's balance of trade with West Germany in 1979 and 1988.

134. **Mr. Ron Davies:** To ask the Chancellor of the Duchy of Lancaster what was the United Kingdom's balance of trade with West Germany in 1979 and 1988.

135. **Mr. Boateng:** To ask the Chancellor of the Duchy of Lancaster what was the United Kingdom's balance of trade with West Germany in 1979 and 1988.

Mr. Alan Clark: The crude balance of trade with West Germany in 1979 was £1,566 million in deficit and in 1988 was, provisionally, £8,145 million in deficit.

Alcoholic Drinks

Mr. Sims: To ask the Chancellor of the Duchy of Lancaster following the Greek Government's removal of the regulatory and other discriminatory taxes on spirits as scheduled on 1 January, what subsequent action Her Majesty's Government have taken to press for the elimination of the remaining discrimination against, inter alia, Scotch whisky as compared with ouzo and brandy.

Mr. Alan Clark: The European Commission's infringement proceedings against the Greek Government are still in progress in the European Court of Justice and, as before, we are keeping a close watch on developments. In addition the Government took steps earlier this year to re-register with Greek authorities the United Kingdom's continued concern about VAT discrimination against, inter alia, whisky along with the United Kingdom's general dissatisfaction with the current taxation structure applied to spirituous beverages in Greece.

Mr. Sims: To ask the Chancellor of the Duchy of Lancaster what was the outcome of the recent talks in Lisbon between the European Community Commission and the Portuguese Government concerning the discrimination in rates of alcohol tax and value added tax on spirits; and what further steps Her Majesty's Government are taking to press for the removal of the discrimination.

Mr. Alan Clark: At Her Majesty's Government's request infraction proceedings have been initiated against the Portuguese by the Commission who are still awaiting a formal response. As a result of talks held in November between the Portuguese authorities and Commission services, however, the Portuguese have taken steps to equalise tax on all alcohol, both imported and domestically produced, at 500 escudos per litre.

Mr. Sims: To ask the Chancellor of the Duchy of Lancaster whether the Italian Government's proposed requirement with effect from 1 July for all bottled alcoholic beverages include on their label an anti-litter statement and identification of the container's raw material is compatible with the European Community Commission proposal currently under discussion which would prescribe two mandatory European Community symbols for refillable and recyclable beverage containers, respectively; if he will seek suspension or postponement of the requirement for United Kingdom alcoholic beverages exports to Italy pending agreement on the European Community directive; and if he will make a statement.

Mr. Alan Clark: If introduced, the Italian Government's requirement would pre-empt the discussions which are currently taking place between member states and the Commission on the Commission's proposed amendment to the Beverage Containers Directive EC 185/339, which would require labelling as to material, recyclability and refillability. I understand that Italy has declared its intention formally to notify the Commission of the proposed new law. My Department is keeping in touch with the Commission to ensure that the notification procedure, which would allow member states' observations during a standstill period, is gone through before the law can be introduced. The United Kingdom's position is that new national legislation in this area is inappropriate while discussions are continuing on a Community regime.

Manufactures

Mr. Austin Mitchell: To ask the Chancellor of the Duchy of Lancaster whether he will publish in the *Official Report*, a table showing for the years 1970 to date for the European Economic Community 12 and for the rest of the world, imports and exports of manufactures less erratics, at current and at 1988 prices, together with an index of relative export prices based on 1970 = 100.

Mr. Alan Clark: Taking the EC and the rest of the world as two blocks, and disregarding intra trade within them, EC exports may be considered equal to the rest of the world's imports and vice versa. Similarly relative export prices of EC to the rest of the world will be equivalent to EC's export prices relative to import prices. Because figures for a consistent configuration of the EC are not readily available for the period, a volume index is provided rather than a constant price series. It is not practical to identify and exclude erratic items for these trading blocks.

The available figures are as follows:

EC trade in manufactures[1] with rest of world

	Value[2]		Volume[3] (1980 = 100)		Terms of trade[4] (1980 = 100)
	Exports	*Imports*	*Exports*	*Imports*	
1970	46·9	26·5	n/a	n/a	n/a
1971	51·5	26·9	n/a	n/a	n/a
1972	55·3	29·3	n/a	n/a	n/a
1973	67·2	37·7	n/a	n/a	n/a
1974	94·8	49·6	n/a	n/a	n/a
1975	101·8	49·3	n/a	n/a	n/a
1976	118·6	64·4	n/a	n/a	n/a
1977	137·4	72·6	n/a	n/a	n/a
1978	145·6	82·8	n/a	n/a	n/a
1979	158·7	98·7	99·8	93·2	98·6
1980	180·7	118·3	100·0	100·0	100·0
1981	205·6	120·7	106·7	97·2	97·0
1982	222·2	130·5	104·1	96·4	98·4
1983	234·9	144·8	102·3	99·2	98·1
1984	272·8	174·9	110·6	108·1	95·2
1985	299·9	182·7	115·6	111·1	94·8
1986	277·9	185·7	107·5	120·2	100·4
1987	275·9	198·6	104·5	131·1	103·6

n/a Not available.
[1] SITC 5-8.
[2] Billions of European Currency Units; 1970-84 EC10, 1985 onwards EC12.
[3] 1979-80 EC9, 1981-1985 EC10, 1986 onwards EC12.
[4] EC export unit value as percentage of EC import unit value; 1979-80 EC9, 1981-1985 EC10, 1986 onwards EC12.
Source: Eurostat.

Buses

Mr. Hanley: To ask the Chancellor of the Duchy of Lancaster when the Monopolies and Mergers Commission report on Ulsterbus Ltd. and Citybus Ltd. will be published.

Mr. Maude: The report is published today. The Commission concluded that Ulsterbus and Citybus ran a very efficient operation in spite of the severe problems presented by civil disorder.

The Commission say that the companies have had to cope with a high level of civil disorder which has presented many severe problems, not least the destruction of over 1,100 buses since 1969 and many more damaged. Nevertheless, they found an efficient, low-cost, lean organisation with short chains of command, supported by loyal, hard-working and frequently courageous staff.

They also found that there was little scope for the companies to reduce costs without affecting the quality of service provided and that:
- *(a)* manpower and vehicles were efficiently used and maintenance procedures were effective;
- *(b)* methods of determining the nature, amount and timing of capital expenditure would benefit from the use of systematic appraisal techniques and of whole-life costing;
- *(c)* further studies and experimentation were needed to refine the relationship between fares and costs; and
- *(d)* the companies' efforts to take more account of the impact of quality of service on demand and to make greater use of minibuses were worthy of support.

They also make recommendations on the financial framework and management information systems, comment on the competition from the Black Taxis and discuss the question of fares evasion.

In terms of priorities for action they first endorse and make recommendations about implementing the companies' new market-led approach and its emphasis on the needs of the customer and, secondly, recommend a clear financial framework in line with the 1978 White Paper on nationalised industries.

The Commission found that neither company was pursuing a course of conduct which operated against the public interest. They were more than impressed by the dedication of the companies' staff at all levels to maintaining their services to the public in the face of severe harassment.

Ulsterbus Limited and Citybus Limited will be producing a preliminary response to the Commission's findings within 3-4 months, in the light of which my right hon. Friend the Secretary of State for Northern Ireland will make a statement.

Imports

Mr. Teddy Taylor: To ask the Chancellor of the Duchy of Lancaster what amount of imports came to the United Kingdom in 1988 for each £100 of exports; and what was the comparable figure in 1970.

Mr. Alan Clark: Imports into the United Kingdom in 1988 were estimated to be £126 for each £100 of exports on a balance of payments basis. The comparable figure for 1970 was £100.

Balance of Trade (EEC)

Mr. Teddy Taylor: To ask the Chancellor of the Duchy of Lancaster what estimate he has made of the balance of trade with the EEC in 1989; and if he will make a statement.

Mr. Alan Clark: My Department has made no estimate of the 1989 United Kingdom trade balance with the rest of the European Community.

Alcoholic Drinks

Sir Anthony Grant: To ask the Chancellor of the Duchy of Lancaster what representations he has received from regional and local brewers about the consequences of the Monopolies and Mergers Commission report on the supply of beer; and if he will make a statement.

Mr. Maude: I am aware that there has been considerable speculation in recent weeks about the discussions taking place with the Brewers Society and other interested parties.

The principal concern, both of the MMC and the Government, is the dominant market position of the national brewers, who account for 75 per cent. of United Kingdom beer production, 74 per cent. of the brewer-owned tied estate, and 86 per cent. of loan ties. We have no intention of introducing measures which might adversely affect the competitive position of regional and local brewers. Their continued success is vital to achieving the objective of a freer market with wider choice which was behind the MMC's recommendations.

The MMC's principal proposal, which we are still considering, was to limit pub ownership to a maximum of 2,000—a proposal which of its nature applies only to the national brewers. I can say that our intention is that certain measures, in particular the requirement to allow tenants to choose a cask conditioned guest beer; the abolition of the tie on low alcohol and non alcoholic beers, ciders, wines and spirits and soft drinks; and any measures to reduce local monopoly, should apply to the national brewers but not to other brewers.

There is general agreement that greater security should be provided for tenants. There appears to be a consensus that while it would be appropriate to amend the Landlord and Tenant Act 1954 to remove the present exception for licensed premises, it would not be right to go further and require additional provisions for tenants' protection in a mandatory brewers code of practice.

DEFENCE

Federal Republic of Germany

Mr. Greg Knight: To ask the Secretary of State for Defence if he will outline the United Kingdom military contribution to the defence of the Federal Republic of Germany.

Mr. Archie Hamilton: The British Army of the Rhine and RAF Germany are important parts of the overall United Kingdom contribution to NATO and they have an essential role to play in the defence of the European mainland. Full details of their composition and roles are contained in the 1989 Statement on the Defence Estimates (Com. 675-I).

Nuclear Submarines

Mr. John Evans: To ask the Secretary of State for Defence what is the most serious accident that has taken place in or near dock in British waters of a British or American nuclear-powered submarine.

Mr. Archie Hamilton: Comprehensive records of accidents involving nuclear submarines since the start of the nuclear submarine programme are not readily available. The most serious accident in terms of harm resulting to people is believed to be the death of a Royal Navy officer who fell from HMS Dreadnought while in dock at Chatham in 1976. There has never been any accident involving a Royal Navy submarine which has led to a radiological hazard to service personnel or members of the public.

The United States would be obliged under a bilateral agreement to inform Her Majesty's Government immediately in the event of an accident involving the reactor of a nuclear-powered warship visiting the United Kingdom; no such accident has been reported to us.

Radiation

Mr. Lewis: To ask the Secretary of State for Defence what further radiation checks have been carried out on Royal Navy sailors and personnel exposed to nuclear weapons and reactors; and what were the findings.

Mr. Archie Hamilton: Medical records of all naval personnel are analysed annually, and any health trends are identified. There have been no special surveys to determine whether there is any evidence of medical disorders arising from exposure of Royal Navy nuclear submarine personnel to radiation. However, routine medical surveillance is carried out for those Royal Naval personnel designated as radiation workers in accordance with the Ionising Radiations Regulations 1985.

Radiation dose records are kept for RN radiation workers, and statistics of doses received were published in the replies I gave to the hon. Member for St. Helens, North (Mr. Evans) on 20 March at columns *477-8* and on 2 May at columns *61-2* this year.

Regular radiation surveys are carried out on board nuclear-powered submarines to ensure that personnel not designated as radiation workers do not receive any significant radiation doses.

Lance Missiles

Mr. Andrew F. Bennett: To ask the Secretary of State for Defence when the North Atlantic Treaty Organisation first deployed the short-range nuclear Lance MGM-52C missile in West Germany.

Mr. Archie Hamilton: NATO first deployed the Lance missile system in West Germany in 1972.

Plessey Takeover

Mr. Churchill: To ask the Secretary of State for Defence how he proposes to ensure continued competition for defence-related research and development work between the wholly-owned laboratories of GEC and those in which they will have a 50 per cent. share following the acquisition of the Plessey Company by GEC Siemens.

Mr. Sainsbury: If the merger were to proceed, the Ministry of Defence would expect to retain competition for research contracts and would involve GEC, GEC/Siemens and other companies, whenever it was appropriate.

Mr. Churchill: To ask the Secretary of State for Defence what measures are being taken by his Department to safeguard the national interest in the event that, following their acquisition of the company, GEC and Siemens will jointly own Plessey's research and technology facilities.

Mr. Sainsbury: The Monopolies and Mergers Commission report accepted that if the merger were to go ahead it would be necessary for GEC and Siemens to give certain undertakings to meet the requirements of national security. These are currently under negotiation. Because of their nature, they were not made public in the MMC report and I cannot elaborate further.

Mr. Thorne: To ask the Secretary of State for Defence what measures he proposes to ensure that competition continues for the supply to the United Kingdom of the JTIDs system in the event that GEC and Siemens succeed in acquiring the Plessey Company.

Mr. Sainsbury: The Monopolies and Mergers Commission recommended that GEC and Siemens should undertake to ensure that access to the technology and the licences for production of JTIDS equipment be available on terms satisfactory to the MOD, to competing companies designated by the MOD. Negotiations are continuing to secure such an undertaking.

Mr. Thorne: To ask the Secretary of State for Defence what measures he proposes to ensure that national security is safeguarded when JTIDS information is more widely disseminated in order to maintain competition for the supply of the system to the United Kingdom.

Mr. Sainsbury: There are well established procedures for safeguarding national security when sensitive classified information is released to companies. These procedures will, of course, apply in this case.

Mr. Thorne: To ask the Secretary of State for Defence (1) what safeguards are being sought from GEC for the supply to the United Kingdom of the JTIDS system in the event that GEC and Siemens succeed in acquiring the Plessey Company;

(2) what safeguards are being sought from GEC/ Siemens for the supply to the United Kingdom of the JTIDS system in the event that GEC and Siemens succeed in acquiring the Plessey Company;

(3) what safeguards are being sought from Siemens for the supply to the United Kingdom of the JTIDS system in the event that GEC and Siemens succeed in acquiring the Plessey Company.

Mr. Sainsbury: The Monopolies and Mergers Commission recommended that GEC and Siemens should undertake to ensure that access to the technology and the licences for production of JTIDS equipment be made available on terms acceptable to the MOD. An undertaking is being sought from GEC and Siemens to this end. Negotiations are continuing and it would be inappropriate to comment further.

Bristol Channel (Survey)

Mr. Stern: To ask the Secretary of State for Defence when the hydrographic surveys of the outer Bristol

channel between Ilfracombe and the Gower peninsula were carried out; whether those surveys showed changes in sedimentation patterns in the estuary since the previous surveys of 1965 to 1972; what hydrographic surveys were conducted in 1988; what hydrographic surveys are being conducted in 1989; and when it is intended that the inner Bristol channel should be re-surveyed.

Mr. Sainsbury: The latest hydrographic survey of the area between the Gower peninsula and Ilfracombe was carried out between September 1987 and June 1988 by HMS Beagle. This survey did not show any major change in the general form of the seabed since the previous survey, which dates mainly from 1949.

No additional survey was conducted in this area in 1988. In 1989 work is in hand to survey the area between Port Talbot and Porthcawl by HMS Fawn. In addition, a contract has been placed by the Ministry of Defence for a further survey of an area along the southern coast of the Bristol channel from Lynmouth to Watchet and thence extending northeastward to the approaches to Cardiff and Newport. This work will complete the re-survey of the Bristol channel from the Gower peninsula to Newport with the exception of a small area in the approaches to Bridgwater. The remaining areas of the Bristol Channel are the responsibility of the port authorities of Bridgwater, Bristol, Cardiff and Newport.

Tornado Aircraft

Mr. Stern: To ask the Secretary of State for Defence if he will make a statement on the extent to which the effectiveness of the Tornado in European defence is enhanced by its nuclear weapons capability.

Mr. Archie Hamilton: Dual-capable Tornado aircraft constitute a vital component in NATO's theatre nuclear force posture in Europe.

Armed Forces Personnel (Other Paid Employment)

Mr. Hinchliffe: To ask the Secretary of State for Defence what is his policy towards serving members of the armed forces also being engaged in other paid employment.

Mr. Neubert: In accordance with Queen's Regulations a member of the regular forces may not, without Ministry of Defence approval, accept any continuous employment of profit during his full-time service. This includes carrying on a profession, engaging in trade or acceptance of any form of profitable employment with a corporation, company, partnership etc. Subject to certain conditions and the approval of his commanding officer, a member of the regular forces may accept temporary employment during normal leave or part-time employment during off-duty hours.

Nuclear Weapons

Mr. Speller: To ask the Secretary of State for Defence if he will list those countries in addition to the United States of America, Union of Soviet Socialist Republics, China, France and the United Kingdom which he assesses as having a nuclear weapon capacity, a ballistic weapons delivery capacity or both nuclear capacity and ballistic delivery capacity.

Mr. Waldegrave: I have been asked to reply.

No other country has declared itself to have a nuclear weapon capacity, although certain other countries may have the technological capability to produce nuclear weapons. We strongly support the principle of non-proliferation of nuclear weapons, and as a depositary power, we work actively for the widest adherence to the nuclear non-proliferation treaty. It is not possible to draw up a precise list of countries possessing a ballistic weapon delivery capacity, since different weapons programmes are at different stages. However, the spread of ballistic missiles is a subject of increasing concern. The problem is widespread and as a founder member of the missile technology control regime (MTCR) the United Kingdom urges all countries to adopt the guidelines formulated by the seven governments to control the transfer of equipment and technology which could make a contribution to any missile system capable of delivering a nuclear weapon.

Written Answers to Questions

Friday 9 June 1989

TRANSPORT

Leeds-Bradford Airport

Mr. Sheerman: To ask the Secretary of State for Transport when he will give a decision on whether to permit an extension of operating hours at Leeds-Bradford airport.

Mr. Peter Bottomley: A joint decision by my right hon. Friends the Secretaries of State for Transport and for the Environment will be made as soon as possible.

Motorway Service Areas

Mr. Gregory: To ask the Secretary of State for Transport what facilities motorway service areas offer to heavy goods vehicles and other professional drivers.

Mr. Peter Bottomley: MSAs provide for all motorway users. They provide a minimum stipulated and increasingly widely known level of service. This includes free parking for all classes of vehicle for at least two hours; free toilets; hot and cold drinks; cold food 24 hours a day throughout the year.

Parking areas for HGVs, coaches, and cars are apportioned in relation to traffic demand.

At all but one existing MSA, HGV drivers can stay overnight for a small charge which often includes a meal voucher. Many service areas provide separate eating facilities for commercial drivers and showers and shaving points. Provision of showers and shaving points will be the norm at new MSAs.

Journalists (Coach Trip)

Mr. Nicholas Bennett: To ask the Secretary of State for Transport what was the purpose of his Department's coach trip in London for journalists on 2 June; how many journalists accepted the Department's invitation; and if he will make a statement.

Mr. Peter Bottomley: The purpose of the visit was twofold; to show at first hand the environmental benefits to residents along and around Rochester way from the new relief road, which has reduced accidents by 30 per cent. in six months and to contrast this with the road congestion problems currently afflicting the Archway area. The Department's proposals for a new western environmental improvement route (the only major road proposal in inner London made by the Department in the past three years) would relieve the many transport problems in the area around the Earl's Court one-way system and improve conditions for residents and shoppers.

The visit was organised following a series of press reports in publications as diverse as *The Observer* (Section 5, 28 May) and *City Limits* magazine (11-18 May) criticising the four London assessment studies commissioned by the Department. These unbalanced reports seemed to indicate that the Department's explanations of the aims and objectives of the studies were not being understood or published.

The objectives of the studies are:

    To promote accessiblity
    To support employment, economic growth and regeneration
    To develop an efficient transport system
    To improve the environment
    To enhance safety for travellers, including pedestrians

The following was the media's response to the coach trip invitation:

    No radio journalists attended
    No television journalists attended
    No national newspaper journalists attended
    Only one journalist attended, from a transport newsletter

We shall offer the coach trip again. It is most important for the media and those who rely on it for their information to understand that the assessment studies are about improving conditions for Londoners, and to appreciate that the Department will put forward only solutions which offer net benefits.

Motorway Service Areas (M25)

Mr. Wood: To ask the Secretary of State for Transport if he will make a statement on the provision of motorway service areas on the M25.

Mr. Peter Bottomley: The strategy for provision of MSAs on the M25 was developed following public consultation in 1983. Decisions in principle were made in 1984 to promote four MSAs, at the compass cardinal points and at very roughly 30 mile intervals, the interval used on the motorway network as a whole.

The then Minister of State agreed in August 1985 that the MSA for the northern sector at South Mimms would be developed by BP. This was an exceptional arrangement. The other three sites, at Clacket lane, Thurrock and Iver, were to be developed following competitive tender, in conformity with Government policy for marketing MSAs announced by the then Secretary of State on 4 August 1980. Current policy has been reaffirmed in this House on 17 March this year at columns *372-73*.

South Mimms opened for cars and coaches in 1987 and is due to provide facilities for HGVs at this end of the year.

Public inquiries into the Department's proposals for Clacket lane near Westerham, together with two competing private proposals, were held in 1986 and 1987. A further site visit was made in May 1988 by the inspector who conducted the inquiries to examine the impact of the October 1987 storm. The Secretary of State for the Environment announced on 15 December 1988 his decision to allow the Department's proposals to go ahead but refusing the two competing proposals. The Department is ready to go to tender but now has to delay because of a legal challenge into the planning decisions by one of the parties.

We estimate that over 300,000 vehicles per month would wish to use an MSA in the area had it been open, but will not be able to do so until the challenge is resolved and an MSA built.

At Thurrock outline planning clearance has been obtained, the compulsory purchase order made and the developer appointed. Preliminary ground treatment work on the site has been underway by agreement since 1988. The local planning authority has objected to the proposed design of the buildings. That objection has been referred to the Secretary of State for the Environment under DoE circular 18/84 procedures. Subject to an early resolution this should allow opening in 1990.

The position at Iver is more problematic. This is a particularly heavy trafficked part of the motorway where widening proposals are likely to have a significant impact. A further statement will be made as soon as possible.

EDUCATION AND SCIENCE

Chinese Students

Mr. Andrew Smith: To ask the Secretary of State for Education and Science how many Chinese students are studying full or part-time in the United Kingdom.

Mr. Jackson: In 1987-88 there were 1,200 full-time and part-time students in further and higher education in the United Kingdom from the People's Republic of China.

Institute of Arable Crops Research

Mr. Hoyle: To ask the Secretary of State for Education and Science what representations he has received on why the Institute of Arable Crops Research has not introduced chargeable payroll deductions for charities; and what information he has on whether the payroll computer system it is introducing would be able to make such deductions.

Mr. Jackson: This Department has received no such representations. The new payroll computer system, which is currently under consideration for use in the agricultural and food research service, would enable all staff, including those at the Institute of Arable Crops Research to participate in the payroll giving scheme, if they wished to do so.

Private Schools

Sir Michael McNair-Wilson: To ask the Secretary of State for Education and Science how many inspections of private schools there have been by Her Majesty's Inspectorate in the past five years; and what steps were taken to follow-up recommendations about necessary improvements either in the teaching or the quality of the school buildings subsequent to the publishing of a report on a school.

Mr. Kenneth Baker: Her Majesty's inspectorate of schools operates a continuing programme of visits to independent schools which do not necessarily result in full inspection reports. Nevertheless, the inspectorate has issued 34 reports on independent schools other than those which serve children with special educational needs since June 1984. In each case, the recommendations made in the report were drawn to the proprietor's attention in an accompanying official letter. In certain cases, the proprietor may also have been asked to provide a report on progress within a specified timescale. In subsequent visits, the inspectorate takes particular note of failure to implement the recommendations made. Such failure may lead me to serve a notice of complaint against the proprietor. Between January, 1984, and December 1988, 16 notices of complaint were served following full inspections; a further five were served where fire precautions were found to be deficient and three were served where a proprietor or teacher was not considered a proper person.

Sir Michael McNair-Wilson: To ask the Secretary of State for Education and Science if he will introduce legislation to provide that all private schools should have a board of governors; and if he has any plans to seek to amend the legal structure covering such establishments so as to give parents adequate opportunities for consultation and representation about the staffing and welfare provision.

Mr. Kenneth Baker: I have no plans to do so. However, I would certainly encourage individual schools to establish a broadly based governing structure, where they do not already have one, and to involve parents closely in all aspects of its activity. Parents are well placed to demand a voice.

Pupils (Welfare Assessment)

Sir Michael McNair-Wilson: To ask the Secretary of State for Education and Science what measures are taken by Her Majesty's inspectorate to assess the social welfare of pupils; whether any of his inspection staff have any training in matters relating to child abuse.

Mr. Kenneth Baker: Her Majesty's Inspectorate assesses the quality of pastoral care provision in schools as well as assessing teaching and learning in all subjects. This range of activities includes tutorial arrangements, the social structures devised by the schools and the quality of pupils' responses to these. More generally, Her Majesty's Inspectorate pays attention to children's attendance and behaviour, to relationships both within lessons and about the school, and to teachers' records on pupils' development and progress. Inspectors also have regard during inspection to the qualifications and experience of teachers at the school.

In schools where residential accommodation is provided, Her Majesty's Inspectorate pays attention to the nature and suitability of the accommodation, and to the daily routines of pupils both during school time and at evenings and weekends in order to assess the contributions that these make to the pupils' overall education.

Her Majesty's inspectorate has designated inspectors with national responsibility for child abuse and for counselling. A number of Her Majesty's inspectors have dealt with child abuse cases before joining the inspectorate; others have worked as educational psychologists and therefore also have experience of case-work relating to child abuse. In addition, Her Majesty's inspectorate runs internal training courses on child protection, and is currently running a course for "named persons" in LEAs who have responsibility for child protection. In December, Her Majesty's inspectorate will run a course for representatives from each LEA for those involved in training for child protection. The training programme therefore extends beyond the inspectorate itself.

Castle Hill School, Shropshire

Mr. Ken Hargreaves: To ask the Secretary of State for Education and Science whether he has completed his consideration of the registration and approval of Castle Hill school, Shropshire.

Mrs. Rumbold: Nearly all its pupils are being withdrawn from the school. My right hon. Friend is accordingly seeking confirmation from the proprietor that he is taking steps to close it.

I am placing in the Library copies of the letters to the school and to local education authorities informing them of this action.

PRIME MINISTER

Single Market

Mr. Speller: To ask the Prime Minister which sector of European Community negotiations she will control personally in the run-up to 1992.

The Prime Minister: The Government as a whole are responsible for policy towards the European Community.

EC Directives

Mr. Allen: To ask the Prime Minister if she will list those European Community directives currently not fully implemented; which topics they relate to; and when Her Majesty's Government will implement each of them.

The Prime Minister: The *Official Journal of the European Communities,* c310, volume 31 of 5 December 1988, which is available in the Library, shows that at 31 December 1987 the United Kingdom had not fully implemented 148 of 784 applicable directives. Detailed information on the topics to which these relate and the projected date of enactment of United Kingdom legislation could be provided only at disproportionate cost.

Written Answer (Cost)

Mr. Redmond: To ask the Prime Minister what was the cost to public funds of supplying the answer to the hon. Member for Pembroke (Mr. Bennett) of 25 May, *Official Report,* columns *695-719.*

The Prime Minister: The reply was assembled from material provided by a wide range of Departments. The total cost of time of those who contributed, including secretarial staff, measured by salary, overheads and other costs, including printing, is estimated at £4,600.

HOME DEPARTMENT

Overseas Residents (Voting Rights)

Mr. Ian Taylor: To ask the Secretary of State for the Home Department what representations he has received in the past two years supporting an extension of eligibility for voting rights of United Kingdom citizens living abroad; and when he expects to be able to make an announcement concerning possible legislation on the subject.

Mr. John L. Marshall: To ask the Secretary of State for the Home Department when he intends making a statement about the reform of the franchise qualifications for Britons living abroad.

Mr. Douglas Hogg: Between January 1987 and May 1989, we received eight parliamentary questions and 47 letters from hon. and right hon. Members and 70 representations on this subject directly from members of the general public and organisations representing Britons abroad. We hope shortly to be in a position to announce our plans to extend the franchise for British citizens living overseas.

Remand

Mr. Pike: To ask the Secretary of State for the Home Department what is the average time spent on remand in custody awaiting trial at the latest date for which figures are available; and what was the comparable figure 12 months previously.

Mr. Douglas Hogg: In 1987 the average time spent on remand in custody awaiting trial was 56 days for men and 45 days for women, compared with 57 days for men and 44 days for women in 1986 (Table 2.1 of "Prison statistics England and Wales 1987" (Cm. 547), a copy of which is in the Library). Provisional data for 1988 indicate very little change for males but a further increase for females.

Mr. Sheerman: To ask the Secretary of State for the Home Department what is the present male and female prison remand population for England and Wales; and how many of those remand prisoners belong to an ethnic minority group.

Mr. Douglas Hogg: The latest readily available information is given in the table.

Untried and convicted unsentenced population[1] of prison service establishments in England and Wales on 31 December 1988: by type of prisoner and ethnic origin

	Untried	Convicted unsentenced
White	6,600	1,190
West Indian, Guyanese, African	1,200	140
Indian, Pakistani, Bangladeshi	220	30
Chinese, Arab, Mixed origin	180	30
Other, not recorded (including refusals)	610	100
Total	8,800	1,490

[1] Provisional figures.

Mr. Ieuan Wyn Jones: To ask the Secretary of State for the Home Department how many persons were remanded in custody in England and Wales during 1987 for an offence of criminal damage involving less than £2,000.

Mr. John Patten: The available information on those proceeded against for an indictable offence of criminal damage who were remanded in custody, which may be incomplete, is published in tables 8.8 and 8.10 of "Criminal statistics, England and Wales, 1987". Such figures will not include proceedings for single offences involving criminal damage of value £400 or less.

Female Police Officers

Mr. Redmond: To ask the Secretary of State for the Home Department if, pursuant to his answer of 23 May, *Official Report,* column 499, to the hon. Member for Don Valley in respect of female police officers and firearms, he will publish such information on this subject as is either held centrally or could be obtained without disproportionate cost.

Mr. Hurd: No information on this subject is held centrally, and no statistical information could be obtained at this time without disproportionate cost. Female police officers are, however, fully entitled to volunteer to become authorised firearms officers and are subject to the same selection and training procedures as male officers.

Privacy

Mr. Waller: To ask the Secretary of State for the Home Department (1) when he expects to announce the composition of the inquiry into privacy and related matters;

(2) whether the terms of reference of the inquiry into privacy and related matters will include aspects of the law of defamation.

Mr. Renton: Consideration is still being given to the composition and terms of reference of the review of privacy and related matters. My right hon. Friend expects to make an announcement shortly.

Immigration Detainees

Mr. Sheerman: To ask the Secretary of State for the Home Department how many immigration detainees have escaped from Harmondsworth immigration detention centre in each of the last 10 years.

Mr. Renton: Full records are not available for the period before 1986. The number of absconders in each year since 1986 was:

	Number
1986	38
1987	64
1988	76
1989[1]	15

[1] to 31 May

Fine Defaulters

Mr. Sheerman: To ask the Secretary of State for the Home Department how many people were received into prison as fine defaulters in the latest year for which figures are available.

Mr. Douglas Hogg: The latest readily available information was published in table 7.2 of "Prison statistics England and Wales 1987" (Cm. 547), a copy of which is in the Library.

Prison Visitors

Mr. Sheerman: To ask the Secretary of State for the Home Department what regulations cover the searching of prison visitors.

Mr. Douglas Hogg: Rule 86(1) of the prison rules 1964 and rule 70(1) of the young offender institution rules 1988 provide that any person entering or leaving an establishment may be searched.

Cash-point Thefts

Mr. Vaz: To ask the Secretary of State for the Home Department how many representations he has received, and from whom, regarding cash-point theft.

Mr. John Patten: None.

Missing Persons

Mr. Janner: To ask the Secretary of State for the Home Department whether he has now concluded his consultation with the Central Conference of Chief Constables on its recommendations regarding the proposed register for missing persons; and whether he will make a statement.

Mr. Douglas Hogg: No. My right hon. Friend is now considering the implications of the ACPO report.

Bail Statistics

Dr. Thomas: To ask the Secretary of State for the Home Department how many persons were remanded in custody and subsequently bailed and failed to surrender to court on the date of their trial in England and Wales for the latest year for which statistics are available.

Mr. Ieuan Wyn Jones: To ask the Secretary of State for the Home Department how many persons were bailed and subsequently failed to surrender to court on the date of their trial in England and Wales for the latest year for which statistics are available.

Mr. John Patten: The available information, which may be incomplete, relates to those who failed to appear having been bailed at magistrates' courts or the Crown court and is published annually in "Criminal statistics, England and Wales, 1987" (table 8.12 and paragraph 8.16 of the issue for 1987, Cm. 498).

Mr. Ieuan Wyn Jones: To ask the Secretary of State for the Home Department how many persons were bailed by the court in England and Wales and subsequently committed a further offence before the date of their trial in the latest year for which figures are available.

Mr. John Patten: The most recent figures available on offending while on bail relate to 1978 and were published in Home Office Statistical Department Bulletin 22/81, "Estimates of Offending of those on Bail".

Prison Population

Mr. Ieuan Wyn Jones: To ask the Secretary of State for the Home Department what was the remand and convicted and unsentenced prison population in England and Wales for the latest available date.

Mr. Douglas Hogg: According to records held centrally on 30 April 1989 there were about 8,780 untried and 1,780 convicted unsentenced prisoners in prison service establishments in England and Wales. A further 55 untried prisoners were held in police cells.

Passports

Mr. Nicholas Bennett: To ask the Secretary of State for the Home Department if he will give the following information in respect of each passport office for each of the past five years, the *(a)* number of staff, *(b)* number of passport applications, *(c)* number issued, *(d)* number of applications per member of staff employed and *(e)* number of passports issued per member of staff.

Mr. Renton: The information as to numbers of staff employed and passports issued is given in the tables. The figures for staff employed include headquarters, management and support staff, who are not directly involved in the examination of passport applications. The daily output of examining staff varies according to the volume of applications being dealt with in a particular period, and yearly averages are not calculated. During the present

seasonal peak, staff in the six United Kingdom passport offices are examining, on average, around 90 applications each day.

1.—Permanent staff numbers (authorised complement) (+ maximum number of casuals)

	1984	1985	1986	1987	1988
London¹	300 (+52)	301 (+35)	296 (+47)	301 (+50)	244 (+62)
Liverpool	206 (+27)	206 (+14)	206 (+32)	206 (+49)	206 (+62)
Peterborough	169 (+23)	169 (+28)	169 (+34)	169 (+43)	169 (+60)
Newport	170 (+20)	170 (+24)	169 (+31)	169 (+51)	168 (+53)
Glasgow	83 (+12)	83 (+13)	83 (+18)	83 (+26)	143 (+39)
Belfast	15 (+6)	15 (+6)	15 (+6)	15 (+5)	15 (+8)

¹Includes Headquarters staff but excludes staff at the records unit at Hayes.

2. Annual total of new passports issued and amendments made to existing passports

	1984	1985	1986	1987	1988
London	456,329	444,925	465,986	378,820	437,218
Liverpool	510,492	479,140	592,740	582,588	698,106
Peterborough	444,060	417,709	514,378	509,536	594,713
Newport	421,876	387,453	446,629	453,350	570,860
Glasgow	156,485	146,748	171,541	170,765	175,113
Belfast	35,253	36,192	47,503	53,626	62,706
Total	2,024,495	1,912,167	2,238,777	2,148,685	2,538,716

Public Order Act 1986

Mr. Key: To ask the Secretary of State for the Home Department whether he has received from Salisbury district council an application under section 13 of the Public Order Act 1986, to make an order prohibiting processions; and if he will make a statement.

Mr. Hurd: Salisbury district council, in response to an application from the chief constable of Wiltshire, sought my consent on 23 May to an order under section 13 of the Public Order Act 1986. This was based on the chief constable's assessment that other powers available to him would not be sufficient to prevent the holding of certain classes of public procession in the vicinity of Stonehenge from resulting in serious public disorder. I have therefore given my consent to an order prohibiting the holding of all public processions within a radius of four miles from the monument at Stonehenge, moving in the direction of Stonehenge, other than normal funeral processions, from Saturday 10 June until Sunday 25 June.

Waste Transport (Smuggling)

Mr. Butler: To ask the Secretary of State for the Home Department what measures his Department implements to police large-scale wastes transported internationally, and used as a medium for smuggling.

Mr. Lilley: I have been asked to reply.
The importation of special and hazardous waste is regulated by the Control of Pollution (Special Waste) Regulations 1980 and the Transfrontier Shipment of Hazardous Waste Regulations 1988. Consignments of such wastes must be accompanied by consignment notes, copies of which are sent to the waste disposal authority for the area in which the waste enters the United Kingdom and the area of final disposal. Customs retain the power to regulate importations and exportations of goods, and to search all vessels in United Kingdom territorial waters. Waste is subject to normal customs checks which are based on local knowledge, risk assessment and intelligence.

TRADE AND INDUSTRY

Funeral Costs (Report)

Mr. Andrew Bowden: To ask the Chancellor of the Duchy of Lancaster what response has been received from the National Association of Funeral Directors to the report on funeral costs by the Office of Fair Trading published in January.

Mr. Forth: This is a matter for the Director General of Fair Trading. I shall ask him to write to my hon. Friend.

Departmental Press Briefings

Mr. Grocott: To ask the Chancellor of the Duchy of Lancaster what guidelines he follows in determining which journalists are invited to press briefings by his Department.

Mr. Forth: This depends upon the matter under discussion.

WALES

Eye Tests

Mr. Alan Williams: To ask the Secretary of State for Wales what is the fall in the number of people coming forward for eye tests since April 1989 in *(a)* West Glamorgan and *(b)* Wales.

Mr. Grist: The information is not available centrally.

Welsh Development Agency

Mr. Nicholas Bennett: To ask the Secretary of State for Wales if he will give the total expenditure of the Welsh Development Agency in each parliamentary constituency in each year since 1983-84.

Mr. Peter Walker: The Welsh Development Agency does not maintain details of expenditure in the form requested.

EC Funding

Mr. Win Griffiths: To ask the Secretary of State for Wales if he will list on a district council basis the amount of funding received from the European Community's regional fund, social fund and agricultural guidance and guarantee fund since 1 January 1980.

Mr. Peter Walker: The information as requested is given in the following tables:

European Regional Development Fund—Quota

District Authority Area[1]	Commitment since 1 January 1980 £
Aberconwy	4,022,698
Afan	138,500
Alyn and Deeside	20,350,568
Arfon	2,589,660
Blaenau Gwent	17,592,050
Brecknock	781,631
Cardiff	51,870,420
Carmathen	9,171,480
Ceredigion	3,649,961
Colwyn	27,798
Cynon Valley	4,798,012
Delyn	15,110,049
Dinefwr	678,870
Dwyfor	3,243,710
Glyndwr	740,163
Islwyn	3,036,570
Llanelli	13,732,034
Lliw Valley	1,404,037
Meirionydd	1,985,307
Merthyr Tydfil	17,340,750
Monmouth	9,817,492
Montgomeryshire	3,188,992
Neath	440,059
Newport	27,225,158
Ogwr	6,037,610
Port Talbot	2,749,717
Preseli	3,334,731
Radnor	1,103,624
Rhondda	5,078,642
Rhuddlan	8,040,132
Rhymney Valley	2,790,820
South Pembrokeshire	3,237,909
Swansea	28,644,199
Taff Ely	4,678,416
Torfaen	21,408,140
Vale of Glamorgan	7,575,853
Wrexham Maelor	42,826,240
Ynys Môn	5,135,213
Not Disaggregated by District	26,197,961
Total	381,775,176

[1] Includes commitment for all schemes undertaken by eligible authorities and bodies which are located within a district authority area.

European regional development fund—non quota

Eligible Zone	Commitment since 1 January 1980 £
Clwyd	5,146,000
Dyfed	723,000
Gwent	5,523,000
South Glamorgan	3,376,000
West Glamorgan	4,741,000
Total	19,509,000

Commitments are allocated to the zones, not on a district authority area basis.

European social fund

County	Allocation since 1 January 1980 £
Clwyd	2,232,000
Dyfed	2,706,000
Gwent	2,956,000
Gwynedd	540,000
Mid Glamorgan	4,937,000
Powys	829,000
South Glamorgan	3,263,000
West Glamorgan	3,208,000
Not Disaggregated	38,728,000
Total	59,399,000

Information is not kept on a district authority area basis.

European agricultural guidance and guarantee fund

	Wales (£)
Identifiable receipts since 1 January 1980	395,700,000

Information cannot be disaggregated below the all-Wales level. The grant allocation does not include the 1988 figure as this is not yet available.

NATIONAL FINANCE

South African Coal (Teesport)

Mr. Mullin: To ask the Chancellor of the Exchequer how much South African coal was discharged by the SS Ave during its recent visit to Teesport.

Mr. Lilley [*holding answer 6 June 1989*]: It is not normal practice to disclose information about the nature or quantities in specific importations.

Mr. Mullin: To ask the Chancellor of the Exchequer what dues and other taxes were paid by the owners of the SS Ave which recently discharged a cargo of South African coal at Teesport.

Mr. Lilley [*holding answer 6 June 1989*]: Imported coal is free of customs duties and zero-rated for VAT purposes. Port authority dues are usually payable on a ship and its cargo.

Premium Bonds

Mr. Teddy Taylor: To ask the Chancellor of the Exchequer why the National Savings Department has decided to increase the minimum purchase of premium bonds to £100 on 1 July; and if he will make a statement.

Mr. Lilley [*holding answer 8 June 1989*]: I refer my hon. Friend to the reply that my right hon. Friend the Chancellor of the Exchequer gave to the right hon. Member for Tweeddale, Ettrick and Lauderdale (Mr. Steel) on 5 May at column *255*.

AGRICULTURE, FISHERIES AND FOOD

Factory-Farmed Animals

Dr. Glyn: To ask the Minister of Agriculture, Fisheries and Food whether he will consider making it compulsory for all factory-farmed animals to be labelled as such.

Mr. Ryder: No, Sir. While I fully recognise the importance of informative food labelling I see no need for a statutory labelling requirement for factory farmed products. There would, in any case, be serious enforcement difficulties as it is not possible to distinguish analytically between free range and factory farmed products. There is, of course, nothing to prevent voluntary labelling to indicate when meat is not from factory farmed products.

NORTHERN IRELAND

Female Police Officers (Firearms)

Mr. Redmond: To ask the Secretary of State for Northern Ireland (1) how many female police officers are currently qualified to carry firearms; what were the figures five and 10 years ago; and if he will make a statement;

(2) if he will list by year for the last 10 years *(a)* in how many operations firearms were issued to female police officers and *(b)* in how many of these operations shots were fired by female police officers; and if he will make a statement.

Mr. Ian Stewart: The information is not available in the form requested. However I understand from the chief constable that female officers in the RUC do not normally carry firearms, nor are firearms normally issued to officers in respect of specific operations.

Press Briefings

Mr. Grocott: To ask the Secretary of State for Northern Ireland what guidelines he follows in determining which journalists are invited to press briefings by his Department.

Dr. Mawhinney: This depends on the matter under discussion.

EMPLOYMENT

Small Businesses

Mr. David Nicholson: To ask the Secretary of State for Employment what advice his Department gives to small companies seeking specialist financial assistance with regard to further business development *(a)* when approached directly, *(b)* in general promotional literature and *(c)* at exhibitions attended by his Department.

Mr. Cope: The Department's small firms service provides advice on financial management and control, and the presentation of a case to potential lenders or investors. It also gives information on sources and methods of raising finance, including the loan guarantee scheme (LGS), which enables banks to lend to small firms without security or a track record.

Publications by the small firms service and the Department include free leaflets giving advice on trade credit, accounting, prompt payment and the LGS.

Radiation

Sir John Farr: To ask the Secretary of State for Employment what further steps he is taking to reduce the exposure to occupational radiation of workers in the nuclear industry; and by how much the present exposure level has been reduced from earlier levels.

Mr. Nicholls *[holding answer 6 June 1989]:* Under the Ionising Radiations Regulations 1985 which are enforced by the Health and Safety Executive, all employers are required to ensure that, amongst other matters, doses of ionising radiations received by employees are kept as low as reasonably practicable and not merely below the relevant statutory limits. In the light of recent international advice and continuing revision of risk estimates for ionising radiations, HSE inspectors are ensuring that greater attention is paid to this requirement. Dosimetric information published by the principal employers in the industry indicate an overall long term downward trend in exposure levels.

Bridging Allowance

Ms. Short: To ask the Secretary of State for Employment, by region, how many 16 and 17-year-olds were in receipt of bridging allowance for each of the latest available three months.

Mr. Cope: Figures for the number of young people in receipt of bridging allowance by region are provided in the table:

Region	Bridging Allowance		
	March (9 March 1989)	*April* (13 April 1989)	*May* (11 May 1989)
East Midlands	1,380	1,170	1,075
West Midlands	1,507	1,298	1,202
Wales	774	671	569
London and South East	1,812	1,617	1,427
South West	760	630	538
Northern	1,124	1,021	885
Yorkshire and Humberside	1,816	1,487	1,376
Scotland	2,182	1,912	1,978
North West	2,600	2,235	1,934
TOTAL	13,955	12,041	10,984

Strikes

Mr. Greg Knight: To ask the Secretary of State for Employment if he will introduce legislation to permit a legal strike without a ballot amongst the strikers; and if he will make a statement.

Mr. Nicholls: No. It is not illegal for a union to call a strike without a ballot of its members. However, if a union chose to do so, it would render itself liable to legal action for damages from the employers at whom the action is directed, or from the suppliers of customers of those employers, and to an action in restraint from any of those parties or from any of the union's members which it had induced to take action.

Labour Statistics

Mr. Battle: To ask the Secretary of State for Employment what was the total number of registered vacancies as a percentage of the unemployment figure in the Leeds metropolitan district for each of the years April 1979 to 1989; and what was the average number of vacancies in the Leeds area for the years 1979 to 1989.

Mr. Lee: The following is the available information which is also in the Library. The table shows the monthly average numbers of unfilled vacancies at jobcentres covering an area closely corresponding to the Leeds metropolitan district, together with the monthly average number of unemployed claimants in Leeds, for the years 1983 to 1988. Unemployment figures will be slightly affected by changes to the count.

It is not valid to compare ratios of unfilled vacancies to numbers of unemployed claimants since only about a third of vacancies in the economy are reported to jobcentres and this proportion will tend to vary over time and between regions.

Monthly average figures of unfilled vacancies and unemployment in the Leeds area for the calendar years 1983 to 1988[1]

Calendar year	Vacancies	Unemployment
[2]1983	1,792	40,602
1984	1,664	41,301
1985	1,615	43,517
1986	2,270	41,826
1987	2,824	38,904
1988	2,651	30,982

[1] Comprising the jobcentres of Crossgates, Harefills, Horsforth, Hunslet, Leeds, Leeds Commercial, Morley, Oitley, Rothwell, Seacroft, Wetherby and Yeadon for vacancy figures and the Leeds local authority area for unemployment figures.
[2] The requested information is only available on a comparable basis for vacancies from April 1983 and unemployment from June 1983. The averages for 1983 are compiled using data for June to December, for the sake of consistency.

Council for Social Aid, Manchester

Mr. Leighton: To ask the Secretary of State for Employment what information he has as to why the Council for Social Aid in Manchester, and training manager for employment training, has gone into liquidation.

Mr. Nicholls: I understand that the directors of Manchester Diocesan Church of England Council for Social Aid Ltd. felt that they were unable to meet their financial obligations and for this reason, and in accordance with the provisions of the Companies Act and the Insolvency Act, decided to cease trading and to place the company into voluntary liquidation.

Mr. Tony Lloyd: To ask the Secretary of State for Employment (1) what is the number of workers who will be made redundant as a result of the failure of the Council for Social Aid, Manchester; what is the number of workers who will be or are being offered alternative employment; what guarantees were given to staff in terms of redundancy payments and outstanding earnings; and if he will make a statement;

(2) what was the total number of trainees on the scheme run by the Council for Social Aid, Manchester, at the time of liquidation; what was the number of trainees who will be offered training places on other ET schemes; what guarantees were made to trainees in respect of the training allowance and child care payments; what is the amount of the debt; and if he will make a statement.

Mr. Nicholls: I understand that approximately 200 people have been made redundant following the closure of Manchester Diocesan Church of England Council for Social Aid Ltd.

Any redundancy payments or outstanding earnings are a matter for the company's liquidators who will deal with these matters in the normal way in such cases.

The number of employees who are offered alternative employment will depend on the local demand for their services.

At the time Diocesan Church of England Council for Social Aid Ltd. ceased trading there were 1,011 ET trainees in training. All of these have been, or will shortly be, offered a training place with an alternative training manager. In the meantime all trainees remain on their training allowance.

In addition, until trainees are found alternative training managers, child care costs will be met where this is necessary.

The total amount of the company's debt is not known to my Department and is a matter for the liquidators.

My major concern now is to ensure that everything possible is being done to minimise the disruption for trainees so that they can carry on developing their skills and improving their job prospects.

HEALTH

Clinical Cytogeneticists

Mr. Ted Garrett: To ask the Secretary of State for Health if he will make a statement on the salary negotiations for clinical cytogeneticists.

Mr. Mellor: The pay of clinical cytogeneticists is a matter for negotiation between the management side of the Scientific and Professional Staffs Council and the staff side representing scientists employed in the National Health Service. Negotiations are continuing on the staff side pay claim for 1989-90.

Water Supplies (Fluoridation)

Mr. Churchill: To ask the Secretary of State for Health which countries, having undertaken the fluoridation of their water supplies, have since abandoned it and on what grounds.

Mr. Freeman: Although no specific legislative power was provided, fluoridation was introduced experimentally in the Netherlands in the 1950s. It was discontinued in 1973 when the Amsterdam Supreme Court decreed that there was no legal basis for fluoridation.

In the late 1977 the Highland regional council decided that water fluoridation should not be pursued in its region and the operation in Wick, Scotland, which had provided fluoridated water since 1969, was discontinued in 1979 to bring it into line with the rest of the region.

Water fluoridation was introduced in Chile in 1968 but was discontinued in 1975 partly because of adverse publicity at the time, and partly due to costs. It is understood that fluoridation has since been re-introduced in that country.

Information on the position in other countries is not held.

Mr. Churchill: To ask the Secretary of State for Health what studies his Department has made of dental fluorosis; what evidence it has received on whether fluoridation of the water supplies has had any harmful effect on those consuming fluoridated water and, in particular, on children; and if he will now reconsider his advice to local and water authorities on the subject.

Mr. Freeman: The Department has not carried out any studies on dental fluorosis, but a study by Levine et al; (British Dental Journal 1989; 166/249), confirmed that although significantly more children had higher levels of enamel fluorosis in fluoridated areas the levels were not aesthetically unacceptable.

The Government remain of the opinion that the fluoridation of water constitutes a safe and effective means of reducing tooth decay. We will of course continue to monitor any relevant evidence on the safety and effectiveness of fluoridation and will bring any significant new developments to the attention of health authorities.

National Health Service Reform

Mr. Robert G. Hughes: To ask the Secretary of State for Health what plans he has for a new contract for general practitioners if the medical profession do not accept the agreement reached between him and their negotiators on 4 May.

Mr. Kenneth Clarke: The agreement was a package deal, and it involved a good deal of compromise by both parties. It is for the profession to decide whether or not to endorse the agreement reached by their negotiators. But if they do not, I would feel bound to ensure that the Government's objectives were still achieved. I would therefore have to re-examine the various elements of the agreement before laying regulations before Parliament and determining the contents of the statement of fees and allowances. Between them these documents will secure better services for patients, relate pay to performance

(ensuring that capitation-based payments account for 60 per cent. of the total) and achieve a more cost-effective contract.

Soviet Union (Disaster)

Mr. Knox: To ask the Secretary of State for Health what medical help the Government are providing for the victims of the oil gas pipeline-train disaster in the Soviet Union.

Mr. Kenneth Clarke: The British Government have both offered, and responded to requests for assistance from the Soviet Union. We have already dispatched £64,000 worth of medical equipment.

In addition, an official request was received yesterday from the Soviet embassy in London and the Soviet Ministry of Health for a team of British specialists to fly out to the Soviet Union to advise and help with the treatment of the patients.

A British team of three burns and plastic surgery specialists, together with a renal dialysis expert, a nurse and technician with dialysis equipment is on its way today to the Soviet Union.

We have offered to take a number of burns cases, but no request has so far been received from the Soviet authorities. Voluntary organisations in Britain are also offering their assistance.

SOCIAL SECURITY

Budgeting Loans and Community Care Grants

Mr. Cohen: To ask the Secretary of State for Social Security what amounts and what percentages of *(a)* budgeting loans and *(b)* community care grants were awarded to each of the 15 client groups defined by his Department for each of the three offices serving the Leyton constituency for the financial year 1988-89.

Mr. Peter Lloyd: Estimates based on the data on client groups for the period June 1988 to March 1989 are shown in the table. The totals of the amounts awarded are provisional estimates for 1988-89.

Amounts and percentages of budget loans and community care grants by client groups

	(00)	*(01)*	*(02)*	*(03)*	*(04)*	*(05)*	*(06)*	*(07)*	*(08)*	*(09)*	*(10)*	*(11)*	*(12)*	*(13)*	*(14)*	*(15)*[1]	*Total awarded*
LEYTONSTONE ILO:																	
Community care grants																	
Percentage	0·1	6·23	0·61	10·51	0·00	5·26	5·66	32·59	0·66	0·29	5·56	16·21	6·45	7·95	0·00	0·95	
Amount (£)	108	6,438	631	10,856	0·00	5,433	5,850	33,663	682	299	5,741	16,746	6,659	8,215	0·00	982	£102,303
Budgeting loans																	
Percentage	0·24	0·48	0·1	1·68	0·28	6·13	1·66	56·65	0·05	1·11	10·6	16·04	2·88	2·09	0·00	n/a	
Amount (£)	494	974	206	3,444	578	12,536	3,398	115,863	103	2,279	21,686	32,798	5,893	4,280	0·00	n/a	£204,532
WALTHAMSTOW ILO:																	
Community care grants																	
Percentage	0·56	8·96	5·77	9·27	1·78	4·07	7·64	30·47	0·00	0·17	5·77	16·48	1·18	6·76	0·00	1·10	
Amount (£)	569	9,067	5,837	9,384	1,805	4,121	7,734	30,835	0·00	170	5,835	16,675	1,193	6,837	0·00	1,115	£101,177
Budgeting loans																	
Percentage	0·74	0·52	0·89	3·04	0·26	3·18	2·44	53·5	0·23	1·0	19·04	11·47	1·81	1·89	0·00	n/a	
Amount (£)	1,643	1,163	2,004	6,832	591	7,133	5,484	120,186	516	2,254	42,769	25,759	4,068	4,243	0·00	n/a	£224,645
WOODGRANGE PARK ILO:																	
Community care grants																	
Percentage	0·27	5·7	2·57	20·92	0·81	5·38	8·97	23·4	1·42	0·83	7·5	10·35	2·46	8·5	0·00	0·94	
Amount (£)	500	10,602	4,775	38,919	1,500	10,005	16,686	43,543	2,647	1,540	13,961	19,250	4,569	15,824	0·00	1,751	£186,072

	(00)	(01)	(02)	(03)	(04)	(05)	(06)	(07)	(08)	(09)	(10)	(11)	(12)	(13)	(14)	(15)[1]	Total awarded
Budgeting loans																	
Percentage	0·39	0·27	0·28	2·92	0·10	8·78	1·69	41·57	1·59	1·41	17·88	13·29	3·47	6·36	0·00	n/a	
Amount (£)	2,009	1,407	1,465	15,230	519	45,778	8,810	216,640	8,300	7,351	93,189	69,263	18,061	33,171	0·00	n/a	£521,193

[1] Key to client groups

Code Meaning
00 Unallocated or unidentified.
01 Over 80—with Income Support higher pensioner premium.
02 Aged 60 to 79—disabled with higher pensioner premium.
03 Aged 60 to 79—with ordinary pensioner premium, or over 60 without pensioner premium.
04 Lone parent with Income Support disability premium.
05 Family with disability premium.
06 Other with disability premium.
07 Lone parent without disability premium.
08 Signs at UBO quarterly with Income Support family premium.
09 Signs at UBO quarterly without family premium.
10 Signing unemployed or with training allowance with family premium.
11 Signing unemployed or with training allowance without family premium.
12 Others with family premium.
13 Others without family premium.
14 Involved in trade dispute.
15 Applicant not in receipt of Income Support—not applicable for budgeting loans.

Social Fund

Ms. Mowlam: To ask the Secretary of State for Social Security if he will list the social fund monthly budget profiles in respect of loans and grants as a percentage of the total annual budget in respect of his local offices at Eston, Hartlepool, Middlesborough and Stockton.

Mr. Peter Lloyd: Details showing the monthly anticipated level of expenditure for the period April 1989 to March 1990 as a percentage of the total annual budget for each of the offices are given in the table.

Details of the national anticipated level of expenditure are available in the Library.

Budgetary Profiles for Loans and Community Care Grants in Eston, Hartlepool, Middlesbrough, Redcar and Stockton ILOs.

Per cent.

Office		April	May	June	July	Aug	Sept	Oct	Nov	Dec	Jan	Feb	March
Eston	Loans	8·30	8·30	8·30	8·30	8·30	8·30	8·30	8·30	7·75	7·75	8·80	9·30
	Grants	8·30	8·30	8·30	8·30	8·30	8·30	8·30	8·30	7·75	7·75	8·80	9·30
Hartlepool	Loans	9·17	8·33	8·33	8·33	8·33	8·02	8·58	8·60	7·75	7·38	8·62	8·56
	Grants	8·67	8·33	8·33	8·33	8·33	8·02	8·88	8·89	7·75	7·38	8·62	8·47
Middlesbrough	Loans	8·50	8·50	9·00	8·50	7·50	8·00	8·50	9·00	7·00	7·50	9·00	9·00
	Grants	8·50	8·50	9·00	8·50	7·50	8·00	8·50	9·00	7·00	7·50	9·00	9·00
Redcar	Loans	7·60	7·80	7·80	8·30	6·70	7·00	8·90	12·50	9·00	6·60	8·60	9·20
	Grants	7·60	7·80	7·80	8·30	6·70	7·00	8·90	12·50	9·00	6·60	8·60	9·20
Stockton	Loans	8·32	8·32	8·32	8·32	8·32	8·21	8·95	8·96	7·45	7·82	8·69	8·32
	Grants	8·32	8·32	8·32	8·32	8·32	8·21	8·95	8·96	7·45	7·82	8·69	8·32

Benefits Claimants

Ms. Mowlam: To ask the Secretary of State for Social Security (1) if he will publish a table showing (a) the numbers of claimants of all supplementary benefits, (b) the numbers of claimants of supplementary pensions, (c) the numbers of claimants of supplementary allowances and (d) the numbers of claimants of supplementary benefits required to be available for work, in respect of his Department's local offices at Eston, Hartlepool, Middlesbrough, Redcar and Stockton each April 1979, 1981, 1983, 1985 and 1987;

(2) if he will publish a table showing (a) the total numbers of claimants receiving income support, (b) claimants of income support receiving pensioner premiums and (c) the number of claimants of income support required to be available for work, in respect of his Department's local offices at Eston, Hartlepool, Middlesbrough, Redcar and Stockton each April in 1988 and 1989.

Mr. Peter Lloyd: The information is as follows:

Number of claimants receiving Supplementary Benefit/Income Support by statistical category

Local Office	[1]	May 1979	May 1981	May 1983	May 1985	May 1987	[2] May 1988	February 1989
Eston ILO	E	1,101	2,308	3,909	4,462	3,762	3,106	3,178
	A	1,143	1,167	1,771	2,499	2,752	2,444	2,581
	P	2,266	2,070	1,903	2,161	2,053	2,022	1,985
Total		4,510	5,545	7,583	9,122	8,567	7,572	7,744
Hartlepool ILO	E	2,511	3,674	5,761	6,260	5,188	4,245	4,405
	A	1,616	1,809	2,766	3,627	3,980	3,297	3,514
	P	3,859	3,758	3,380	3,724	3,576	3,541	3,395
Total		7,986	9,241	11,907	13,611	12,744	11,083	11,314

Local Office	[1]	May 1979	May 1981	May 1983	May 1985	May 1987	[2] May 1988	February 1989
Middlesbrough ILO	E	3,508	6,958	10,417	12,013	10,471	8,578	8,607
	A	3,181	3,365	4,931	6,973	7,818	6,935	7,114
	P	5,126	4,935	4,906	5,408	5,390	5,341	5,095
Total		11,815	15,258	20,254	24,394	23,679	20,854	20,816
Redcar ILO	E	970	2,165	3,977	4,724	3,980	3,378	3,437
	A	1,194	1,188	1,717	2,450	2,843	2,531	2,681
	P	2,729	2,561	2,494	2,630	2,547	2,565	2,539
Total		4,893	5,914	8,188	9,804	9,370	8,474	8,657
Stockton ILO	E	2,828	5,867	8,775	10,059	8,851	6,873	6,803
	A	2,562	2,825	4,154	5,689	6,476	5,596	5,880
	P	5,043	4,973	4,425	4,978	5,048	5,128	4,989
Total		10,433	13,665	17,354	20,726	20,375	17,597	17,672

Note:
[1] E = claimants required to be available for work.
A = claimants not required to register for work.
P = pensioners.
[2] 1988 and 1989 data are provisional and subject to amendment.
Source: 100 per cent. count of cases in action, which include a number of cases where benefit payment has ceased but other action is continuing.

Family Income Supplement

Ms. Mowlam: To ask the Secretary of State for Social Security if he will publish information relating to the estimated numbers of claimants of family income supplement in Cleveland in 1979, 1981, 1983, 1985 and 1987, along with any estimates of families entitled to but not claiming family income supplement in Cleveland during those years.

Mr. Peter Lloyd: We do not collect such information on a local basis.

ATTORNEY-GENERAL

Immigration

Mr. Winnick: To ask the Attorney-General what documentation and advice has been recently sent to adjudicators and members of the immigration appeals tribunal by the Lord Chancellor's Department or any other branch of the Laws Officers Departments arising from judgments on cases involving marriage; and if he will make a statement.

The Attorney-General: The Treasury Solicitor acts as solicitor to the independent immigration appellate authorities established under the Immigration Act 1971 and represents the immigration appeal tribunal when its decisions are challenged on judicial review.

In December 1988 the Treasury Solicitor so acted for the immigration appeal tribunal in a case, *R. v Immigration Appeal Tribunal ex parte Mohammed Khatab,* in which the decision of the tribunal refusing the applicant leave to appeal to the tribunal from a decision of an adjudicator was quashed by Mr. Justice Henry. The transcript of the judgment was received at the end of January 1989 and on 6 February the Treasury Solicitor wrote to the president of the tribunal enclosing a copy of the judgment pointing out its importance, and suggesting that it be drawn to the attention of the adjudicators. The Treasury Solicitor did not suggest that any document other than the transcript be circulated and took no steps to secure any such further circulation. It is the Treasury Solicitor's standard practice after any judicial review proceedings to report back to the client, which in this case was the tribunal, with a note of the decision and its implications for the client. In tendering any such advice the Treasury Solicitor acts independently as a solicitor giving advice to a client.

On 7 March the chief adjudicator wrote to all adjudicators enclosing two documents: a copy of the Treasury Solicitor's letter dated 6 February (already referred to) and a copy of standard briefing material prepared by the Treasury Solicitor in December 1988 to be supplied to counsel for the tribunal on applications for judicial review. This briefing material had been sent to the president of the tribunal at an earlier date for information.

Consultations about the role of the tribunal in judicial review proceedings have been going on for some time following an initiative by the Treasury Solicitor's department in 1988, and it has now been agreed that the immigration appeal tribunal should no longer be represented in judicial review proceedings; in future, the Secretary of State or the immigration service will be the respondents in all such cases. Consequently it will no longer be necessary for the Treasury Solicitor to advise the tribunal on the outcome of judicial review proceedings.

Endangered Species

Mr. Allen: To ask the Attorney-General if the Lord Chancellor will have inquires made into the background to the recent proceedings involving endangered species legislation and consider the implications of the judge's comments.

The Attorney-General: This would not be an appropriate course of action for the Lord Chancellor to take.

DEFENCE

Front Line Forces

Mr. Tony Lloyd: To ask the Secretary of State for Defence what consideration he has given to the defence implications of the Soviet proposal to thin out front line forces in Europe.

Mr. Archie Hamilton: Reductions in the Warsaw pact's massive concentrations of forces in Europe would be very welcome. However, their current zonal proposals would make it very difficult to sustain NATO's strategy of forward defence. Nevertheless, we are studying them with care.

Main Battle Tank (Equipment)

Mr. Rogers: To ask the Secretary of State for Defence what is the extent in the delay of the contract awarded to AVIMO for the procurement of the TOGS sighting system for main battle tanks; and if any penalty clauses have been put into operation.

Mr. Sainsbury: Deliveries are some months behind schedule and we shall be seeking redress under the terms of the contract.

Schools (Approval)

Sir Michael McNair-Wilson: To ask the Secretary of State for Defence (1) how many schools have been removed from the list of those approved for the education of service personnel on his Department's grant within the last five years; and if he will give reasons for these decisions in each case;

(2) how often officials from his Department visit independent schools where children of service personnel are educated with the assistance of his Department's grants; what criteria are used before including such a school on the approved list; how often further visits are made to ensure the school is providing a proper academic education and the right moral and social guidance; and what store is placed on the result of any of Her Majesty's inspectors reports on such schools;

(3) what steps his Department takes to satisfy itself that a private school is a fit place for the children of service men to be sent under grant; how many schools are on the approved list; and if he will list them.

Mr. Neubert: Boarding school allowance is payable to service parents who are eligible for all schools which are registered with the Department of Education and which offer a standard of education which is comparable to that obtainable within the state system. In addition, the school authority or local education authority must manage, control and wholly maintain the boarding facilities.

Although the Ministry of Defence maintains an internal record of those boarding schools which parents are currently using, and which satisfy the above criteria, this is not a comprehensive list of approved schools for BSA purposes. All schools which satisfy the basic criteria may qualify for BSA. Schools fail to qualify for BSA purposes only if they no longer meet the criteria or when they close. There is no centrally kept record of the changes in the pattern of usage over the last five years but indications are that these would have been almost entirely as a result of schools closing or ceasing to offer the necessary general education, or, conversely, as a result of the appearance of newly established or expanded schools. The choice of a particular school is a matter for the parents. However, the Service Children's Education Authority will on request assist parents in making their decisions. The SCEA visits many boarding schools on an ad hoc basis in order to be able to advise parents on matters of school facilities and curriculum. In giving such advice SCEA also takes account of any relevant Her Majesty's inspector's reports.

Alternatively, service parents like any others are free to consult local education authorities, ISIS or any other appropriate advisory body.

ENVIRONMENT

Ordnance Survey (Outdoor Leisure Maps)

Mr. Andrew F. Bennett: To ask the Secretary of State for the Environment what information he has as to what plans the Ordnance Survey has *(a)* to extend the outdoor leisure map series, *(b)* to issue a second series of outdoor leisure map of Snowdonia, Conwy valley and *(c)* to use water resistant paper for any other sheets in the series beyond the one for Ben Nevis.

Mr. Ridley: Ordnance Survey is continually reviewing its range of maps and services to ensure that the needs of the market are met within the resources available and that the required return on investment is achieved. The outdoor leisure map series is no exception to this and any change in specification on coverage will be dictated by these marketing principles.

At the moment there are no firm plans to extend the range of outdoor leisure maps but a number of new opportunities are under active consideration. These include the option for publication of a combined Snowdon-Conwy valley map and publishing more Mountainmaster maps of popular climbing areas.

Press Briefings

Mr. Grocott: To ask the Secretary of State for the Environment what guidelines he follows in determining which journalists are invited to press briefings by his Department.

Mr. Ridley: This depends upon the matter under discussion.

Endangered Species

Mr. Allen: To ask the Secretary of State for the Environment if he will take steps to strengthen the law and penalties relating to trade in endangered species following the United Kingdom's first case under the convention; and if he will make a statement.

Mrs. Virginia Bottomley: Trade in endangered species is already strictly controlled within the United Kingdom under EC Regulations 3626/82 and 3418/83, which implement the convention on international trade in endangered species of wild fauna and flora throughout the European Community. Adequate provisions for enforcing the EC regulations already exist under the Customs and Excise Management Act 1979 and The Control of Trade in Endangered Species (Enforcement) Regulations 1985 (SI 1985 No. 1155). There have been many prosecutions for import-export offences under the 1979 Act, most of which have been successful.

Orchids

Mr. Allen: To ask the Secretary of State for the Environment what action his Department is taking to protect rare species of orchids from extinction by smuggling activities based in the United Kingdom.

Mrs. Virginia Bottomley: The Department complies fully with the requirements of EC Regulations (3626/82 and 3418/83) implementing the convention on international trade in endangered species of wild fauna and flora within the United Kingdom when considering applications for import/export permits. Enforcement of the import/export controls at the points of entry is the responsibility of Her Majesty's Customs and Excise.

Mr. Allen: To ask the Secretary of State for the Environment what international co-operation exists between Governments on the protection of endangered species of orchids; and what steps he is taking to improve this.

Mrs. Virginia Bottomley: International trade in orchids is strictly controlled under the convention on international trade in endangered species of wild fauna and flora, to which the United Kingdom and over 100 other countries are party. The EC Regulations (3626/82 and 3418/83) implementing CITES within the European Community already impose more stringent controls on many species of orchids than the convention requires.

Green Belt

Mr. Wolfson: To ask the Secretary of State for the Environment whether his Department's advice to local authorities on the provision of low cost housing in rural areas is related to such areas located within the green belt.

Mr. Howard *[holding answer 25 May 1989]:* My February statement on 3 February at column 433 did not alter the general presumption against inappropriate development in the green belts. Green belt policy remains as stated in planning policy guidance note 2.

Most green belt areas are by their nature close to the main conurbations, and conditions are not typical of the generality of rural areas to which the statement was addressed. Special considerations may, however, arise in some of the more extensive areas of green belt away from the urban fringe, particularly in areas where there are many small settlements and it may not be practicable or appropriate to define green belt boundaries around each one.

In some of these areas local planning policies already recognise that very limited development within existing settlements may be acceptable and consistent with the function of the green belt. It is for local planning authorities to judge whether low-cost housing development for local community needs would fall within the scope of such policies.

The release, exceptionally, for small-scale, low-cost housing schemes of other sites, within existing settlements which would not normally be considered for development under such policies would again be a matter for the judgment of the planning authority, having regard to all material considerations, including the objectives of green belt policy and the evidence of local need. As I made clear in my previous statement, where sites are released for low cost housing as an exception to normal policies of restraint, it will be essential for the planning authority to satisfy itself as to the adequacy of arrangements to reserve the housing in question for local needs, both initially and on subsequent change of occupant.

FOREIGN AND COMMONWEALTH AFFAIRS

Gibraltar (Incident)

Mr. Dalyell: To ask the Secretary of State for Foreign and Commonwealth Affairs what information he has on statements made by Spanish Government officials concerning conflicts between British and Spanish police accounts of circumstances surrounding the Gibraltar shootings; and if he will make a statement.

Mr. Waldegrave: The Spanish Government have assured us that the only authentic account by a Spanish official of the events in question is that of Inspector Rayo of 8 August 1988, a copy of which was placed in the Library of the House of Commons on 9 May. No other statement by an official has any validity.

Soviet Union

Mr. Canavan: To ask the Secretary of State for Foreign and Commonwealth Affairs whether he will make a statement about relationships between the Governments of the United Kingdom and the Union of Soviet Socialist Republics.

Mr. Waldegrave: In the last four years there has been a major improvement in Anglo-Soviet relations. We have developed a worthwhile and substantive high-level political dialogue. Contacts of all sorts have expanded rapidly, helping to break down the barriers of misunderstanding and distrust. But the recent expulsions have shown that there is still a long way to go before our relations with the Soviet Union reach the level of stability and mutual trust to which we aspire.

Consular Assistance (Spain)

Mr. Baldry: To ask the Secretary of State for Foreign and Commonwealth Affairs how many United Kingdom citizens were helped in Spain last year by consular officials.

Mr. Eggar: In 1988, Her Majesty's diplomatic and consular posts in Spain received over 119,000 visitors and received and made over 189,000 telephone calls. A large proportion of the visits and telephone calls were in connection with consular work.

Our records, which do not fully reflect all the assistance given to British citizens, show the following:

	Number
Registrations	17,695
Passports issued	6,728
Passports renewed/exended	1,876
Emergency passports issued	5,619
Thefts reported by Britons	5,061
Births/deaths registered	1,042
Repatriations	26
Official assistance with self-help	695
War Pensioners assisted	232
British prisoners visited at least once	849
Birth/death certificates issued	476

East Germany

Mr. Thurnham: To ask the Secretary of State for Foreign and Commonwealth Affairs if he will make a statement about relations with East Germany.

Mr. Waldegrave: We would like to develop fuller relations with the German Democratic Republic, but this would depend greatly upon progress in that country's fulfilment of its CSCE commitments, particularly on human rights. We shall continue to encourage such progress.

Nelson Mandela

Mr. John Evans: To ask the Secretary of State for Foreign and Commonwealth Affairs if he will make a statement on any diplomatic efforts his Department are pursuing to secure the release of Nelson Mandela.

Mrs. Chalker: We continue to urge the South African Government to release, immediately and unconditionally, Mr. Nelson Mandela and other political prisoners.

BBC World Service

Mr. Sheerman: To ask the Secretary of State for Foreign and Commonwealth Affairs what level of funding the British Broadcasting Corporation world service has received in real terms in each of the last 15 years.

Mr. Eggar: The total grants-in-aid of the BBC world service in the last 15 years, expressed in cash terms and at 1988-89 prices were as follows:

	Cash terms £ million	1988-89 prices £ million
1975-76	27·1	84·9
1976-77	30·8	85·1
1977-78	34·0	82·7
1978-79	37·2	81·4
1979-80	42·9	80·7
1980-81	54·9	87·1
1981-82	62·8	90·7
1982-83	70·9	95·5
1983-84	77·6	100·0
1984-85	81·0	99·5
1985-86	90·0	104·8
1986-87	98·9	111·4
1987-88	97·9	105·0
1988-89	114·5	114·5
1989-90	[1]120·1	[1]113·9

[1] Estimate.
Note: Figures for 1988-89 and 1989-90 exclude provision for FCO-BBC relay stations contract previously funded separately from grants-in-aid: £5·6 million in 1988-89, £5·9 million in 1989-90.

Egypt

Mr. Tony Lloyd: To ask the Secretary of State for Foreign and Commonwealth Affairs whether he has received any reports of human rights violations by law enforcement officials in Egypt; and if he will make a statement.

Mr. Waldegrave: We are aware of the allegations in Amnesty International's recent report; and are naturally concerned at any alleged abuses of human rights, wherever they occur.

Nuclear Arms

Mr. Menzies Campbell: To ask the Secretary of State for Foreign and Commonwealth Affairs what is his policy towards the proliferation of ballistic missiles in Third world countries; and if he will make a statement.

Mr. Waldegrave: We believe that the proliferation of ballistic missiles in Third world countries can have a

seriously destabilising effect, particularly in areas of regional tension. As a founder member of the missile technology control region (MTCR), we have adopted guidelines to control the transfer of equipment and technology. When the MTCR was established in April 1987, the partners urged all states to adopt the guidelines of the regime.

Iran

Mr. Teddy Taylor: To ask the Secretary of State for Foreign and Commonwealth Affairs if Her Majesty's Government will express sympathy to the people of Iran on the death of their nation's spiritual leader; and if Her Majesty's Government sought to be represented at the funeral.

Mr. Waldegrave: No, in both cases.

China

Mr. Teddy Taylor: To ask the Secretary of State for Foreign and Commonwealth Affairs if he will protest to the Government of China about the killing of civilians; and if he will make a statement.

Mr. Eggar: I refer my hon. Friend to the statement that my right hon. and learned Friend the Secretary of State made in the House on 6 June about developments in China.

Katyn Massacre

Mr. Harry Greenway: To ask the Secretary of State for Foreign and Commonwealth Affairs if he will initiate talks with Polish and Soviet Governments on the Katyn massacre; and if he will make a statement.

Mr. Waldegrave: We see no need to initiate talks. We are following developments closely. We urge the Soviet Union to help establish the facts.

British Travellers Abroad

Mr. Greg Knight: To ask the Secretary of State for Foreign and Commonwealth Affairs what services are made available by his Department to British travellers abroad.

Mr. Eggar: Her Majesty's embassies, high commissions and consulates around the world make available a range of statutory and non-statutory consular services to British travellers. Statutory functions include:
>the registration of births and deaths
>the solemnisation and registration of marriages
>the performance of notarial acts
>the servicing of documents and taking of evidence
>duties under the Merchant Shipping Acts.

Non-Statutory functions include:
>the protection of British nationals and British institutions, including assistance in cases of death, illness, arrest, proposed deportation, etc.
>the relief and repatriation of distressed British nationals, as a last resort
>the maintenance of close and good relations with the British community
>the issue of passports.

Lee Chuk Yan

Mr. Soley: To ask the Secretary of State for Foreign and Commonwealth Affairs what representations he has made to the Chinese Government about the detention of Lee Chuk Yan.

Mr. Eggar: Following Lee Chuk Yan's detention by police at Peking airport on 5 June, our embassy in Peking lodged an immediate inquiry with the Chinese Ministry of Foreign Affairs and made considerable efforts to trace his whereabouts. The embassy subsequently established that he was unharmed in a hotel room in Peking and kept in close contact with him. We have now had confirmation that Lee Chuk Yan was evacuated safely from Peking on 8 June.

Members of Parliament (Blackmail)

Mr. Winnick: To ask the Secretary of State for Foreign and Commonwealth Affairs on what criteria he selected *(a)* the means and *(b)* the timing to let it be known that the possible blackmail of hon. Members had not been in any way associated with the recent expulsion of Soviet citizens.

Sir Geoffrey Howe: The story appeared in newspapers on Friday 26 May. The Leader of the Opposition wrote to me on 26 May to seek a statement of the Government's views. I replied on 26 May, making clear that I should have no objection if the right hon. Member for Islwyn (Mr. Kinnock) wished to publish our exchange. He did so on 27 May.

Mr. Winnick: To ask the Secretary of State for Foreign and Commonwealth Affairs what recent statements were made by the Minister of State in his Department, the hon. Member for Bristol West (Mr. Waldegrave) to a BBC correspondent regarding possible blackmail of hon. Members by Soviet agents; and if he will make a statement.

Sir Geoffrey Howe: I have nothing to add to the statement issued by my hon. Friend on 2 June.

Eastern Europe and Soviet Union

Mr. Boswell: To ask the Secretary of State for Foreign and Commonwealth Affairs when he expects to respond to the report of the Select Committee on Foreign Affairs on Eastern Europe and the Soviet Union.

Mr. Waldegrave: The Government's response to the Select Committee report was published today in the form of a Command Paper.

Written Answers to Questions

Monday 12 June 1989

PRIME MINISTER

War Widows' Pensions

Sir George Young: To ask the Prime Minister whether the arrangements for disregarding war widows' pensions for housing benefit purposes are the same in England, Wales, Scotland and Northern Ireland.

The Prime Minister: No. The housing benefit scheme for England, Scotland and Wales has a statutory disregard, currently set at £5 a week, of any war disablement or war widow's pension, and local authorities have discretion to enhance this disregard. The separate housing benefit scheme in Northern Ireland has a statutory disregard of all such pensions.

Electoral Register (Publicity)

Mr. Harry Barnes: To ask the Prime Minister in the period of her premiership for which the latest figures are available, what percentage of Government expenditure on publicity has been spent to encourage people to register to vote.

The Prime Minister: Total expenditure over this period on Government publicity to encourage people to register to vote could be provided only at disproportionate cost. Expenditure on electoral registration advertising as a percentage of all Government advertising has been as follows:

Year	Percent	Year	Percent
1979-80	[1]n.a.	1984-85	0·57
1980-81	0·03	1985-86	0·59
1981-82	[1]n.a.	1986-87	0·30
1982-83	0·46	1987-88	0·29
1983-84	0·53	1988-89	0·31

[1] Not available.

ENERGY

World Association of Nuclear Operators

Dr. Thomas: To ask the Secretary of State for Energy if his Department has placed any restrictions on any category of information that may be disclosed by nuclear power station operators to the World Association of Nuclear Operators established in May.

Mr. Michael Spicer: The World Association of Nuclear Operators is an association of nuclear power plant operators established to facilitate the exchange of information relating purely to nuclear power plant safety. The United Kingdom's members are free to exchange such information.

Magnox Power Stations

Mr. Cohen: To ask the Secretary of State for Energy if he will list how many natural circulation tests have been carried out in the United Kingdom's Magnox nuclear power stations giving their locations; and if he will make a statement.

Mr. Michael Spicer: This is an operational matter for the Central Electricity Generating Board, and British Nuclear Fuels plc. They are responsible for the operation of Magnox power stations in England and Wales. I will ask their respective chairmen to write to the hon. Member.

Mr. Cohen: To ask the Secretary of State for Energy if the Central Electricity Generating Board has indicated to him how it intends to deal with the Wigner energy problem at Berkeley nuclear power station now that both reactors have been closed down; and if he will make a statement.

Mr. Michael Spicer: I am advised by the CEGB that Wigner energy does not present a problem in the decommissioning of Berkeley power station. The board will have to satisfy the Health and Safety Executive's nuclear installations inspectorate before undertaking each stage of decommissioning.

Mr. Cohen: To ask the Secretary of State for Energy if the Central Electricity Generating Board has any plans to carry out natural circulation tests at any of the operational Magnox power stations to further research into understanding the Wigner energy problem; and if he will make a statement.

Mr. Michael Spicer: I am advised that natural circulation tests on nuclear plant have no connection with research into understanding the Wigner energy phenomenon. Any natural circulation tests would be subject to the agreement of the Health and Safety Executive's nuclear installations inspectorate.

Disabled People (Electricity Supply)

Mr. Hannam: To ask the Secretary of State for Energy (1) if he will bring forward provisions in the Electricity Bill to enable electricity meters to be repositioned so that they are accessible for disabled people and to ensure that any charges for this service will be borne by the supplier;

(2) what provision he is proposing for the Electricity Bill to enable electricity meters to be adapted for use by disabled people;

(3) what provision he is proposing for the Electricity Bill to enable electricity meters to be installed in places that are accessible for disabled people.

Mr. Michael Spicer: The draft public electricity supply licence requires the licensee to produce a code of practice specifically aimed at the elderly and disabled. This code would cover special services available to these groups including such matters as the provision of special controls and adaptors for electrical appliances and meters and the placement of meters for convenient access. Where a meter is repositioned, the supplier would have the right to recover from the consumer any costs reasonably incurred. Community care grants are available from the social fund to those in receipt of income support to help with the cost of resiting meters to allow disabled people easier access.

Mr. Hannam: To ask the Secretary of State for Energy what provision he is proposing for the Electricity Bill to protect disabled people on life support systems from disconnection.

Mr. Michael Spicer: The electricity industry currently operates a voluntary code of practice which offers a number of protections against disconnection for consumers in difficulty, and makes special provision for the blind, severely sick and the disabled. The draft public electricity supply licence requires the licensee to produce a similar code to ensure that this approach continues after privatisation.

Severn Barrage

Mr. Stern: To ask the Secretary of State for Energy (1) how much of the tonnage of rock likely to be required for a Severn tidal barrage will come from the limestone quarries of the Mendips and south Wales; whether studies are proceeding as to the likely social effects of such quarrying; and whether studies are proceeding as to the likely effects of such quarrying on road and rail links;

(2) what are his latest estimates of the overall capital cost of a Severn tidal barrage at current prices;

(3) what assessment he has made of the implications of electricity privatisation on *(a)* the programme studies into the effect of the proposed Severn tidal barrage, *(b)* the consideration in committee of these studies, *(c)* consultation with the public and *(d)* the consultation process with the European Community;

(4) what substantive decisions have been made with regard to a Severn tidal barrage since November 1987; and if he will make a statement;

(5) when he expects the results of the further studies into the feasibility of a Severn tidal barrage to be available; and what form their publication will take;

(6) whether longer-term studies into potential damage to sensitive wildfowl species including wildlife and waders arising from the building of the proposed Severn tidal barrage will be undertaken before a decision is reached on the building of the barrage;

(7) which organisations will be represented on the committee to evaluate the information generated by the studies into a Severn tidal barrage; who will be the members; how significant environmental interests will be represented; and how regional industrial and service interests will be represented.

Mr. Michael Spicer: Studies of a Severn tidal energy barrage are nearing completion and I expect to receive a report in the next few months. A summary document of the work will be published in the energy paper series, and supporting reports by the Severn tidal power group will also be published. It is premature at this stage for me to comment on the results of the study or any further work which may be necessary. Whilst the current work includes a study of regional aspects of the barrage project, financial and related issues will be examined in the time-scale of the privatisation of the electricity supply industry.

Press Briefings

Mr. Grocott: To ask the Secretary of State for Energy what guidelines he follows in determining which journalists are invited to press briefings by his Department.

Mr. Parkinson: My Department's contacts with journalists are based on requests for information from the media generally, and on regular contact with relevant specialist correspondents. My Department has contact also with a wider spectrum of newspapers, broadcasting organisations, and specialist journals, as appropriate.

Eastern Electricity Board

Mr. Neil Hamilton: To ask the Secretary of State for Energy if he will list in the *Official Report* the representations he has received regarding alleged anti-competitive practices by the Eastern electricity board.

Mr. Michael Spicer: My right hon. Friend has received two such representations.

Electricity Boards

Mr. Neil Hamilton: To ask the Secretary of State for Energy what action he intends to take regarding cross-subsidisation by the electricity boards of electricity supply through retail promotion.

Mr. Michael Spicer: The public electricity supply licence, which, subject to passage of the Electricity Bill, will be granted to the successors of the area boards, will prohibit cross subsidies between a licensee's separate businesses.

Mr. Neil Hamilton: To ask the Secretary of State for Energy what investigations he has conducted into the retail promotion activities of electricity boards.

Mr. Michael Spicer: The Monopolies and Mergers Commission investigated and reported (Cmnd. 8812) on the direction and management by the London electricity board of its business of retailing domestic electrical goods, spare parts and ancillary goods. The Monopolies and Mergers Commission also considered retailing activities in its reports on some other area boards.

Offshore Installations (Safety)

Mr. Greg Knight: To ask the Secretary of State for Energy what progress has been made regarding proposals for the application off shore of regulations dealing with safety representatives and safety committees.

Mr. Parkinson *[pursuant to the reply, 31 January 1989, c. 156]:* I have today laid before each House the Offshore Installations (Safety Representatives and Safety Committees) Regulations 1989.

Prior to the making of these regulations extensive consultations were carried out with organisations representing those persons likely to be affected by them including Government bodies, employers and trade unions. They have been made on the advice of the Health and Safety Commission under the Mineral Workings (Offshore Installations) Act 1971. The effect of the regulations will be that every offshore worker, including contractors' employees, can make a positive contribution to promoting health and safety on offshore installations through elected safety representatives and safety committees.

EDUCATION AND SCIENCE

St. Benedict's School, Birkenhead

Mr. Frank Field: To ask the Secretary of State for Education and Science how much was allotted for internal redecoration when approving the new St. Benedict's school in Birkenhead.

Mr. Butcher: The proposal to establish St. Benedict's school was approved by the Secretary of State on 2 April 1987. The total cost of the building project to extend and adapt the school premises is £1·8 million. A total of £1·4 million of this will be met by the governors, who will receive 85 per cent. grant from the Department on that expenditure. The local education authority intends to meet the remaining costs of approximately £400,000, including the cost of necessary internal redecoration, and this was taken into account in determining its prescribed capital expenditure allocation for 1989-90.

Student Loans

Mr. Dalyell: To ask the Secretary of State for Education and Science if he will place in the *Official Report* a full account of the objections to his proposals for student loans from banks.

Mr. Jackson: The White Paper "Top-up Loans for Students" (Cm 520) contained, in annex G, a discussion of possible objections which had been expressed in evidence to the review of student support. The potential participation by the banks and other financial institutions in the administration of the scheme is under consideration; my right hon. Friend will announce his conclusions in due course.

Mr. Dalyell: To ask the Secretary of State for Education and Science what is the estimated cost to public funds over the next 10 years of his proposals for student loans.

Mr. Jackson: The estimated costs to public funds of the Government's proposals of top-up loans were set out in annex E of the White Paper "Top-up Loans for Students" (Cm 520). That estimate excluded administrative costs, which have yet to be determined.

Special Needs

Mrs. Mahon: To ask the Secretary of State for Education and Science what plans he has to provide the extra specialist training and resources necessary to enable children with special needs to have access to the national curriculum.

Mr. Butcher: I refer the hon. Member to the replies I gave to the hon. Member for Durham, North-West (Ms. Armstrong) on 15 May at column *2* and the hon. Member for Redcar (Ms. Mowlam) on 6 June at column *16*.

Under-fives (Curriculum)

Ms. Armstrong: To ask the Secretary of State for Education and Science if he will appoint a nursery teacher to the group examining a curriculum for the under-fives, chaired by the hon. Member for Mitcham and Morden (Mrs. Rumbold).

Mrs. Rumbold: Miss L. M. Grundy, the head teacher of Grandpont nursery school, Oxford, has been appointed to serve on the committee.

Teachers (Pay and Conditions)

Mr. Fatchett: To ask the Secretary of State for Education and Science when he expects to announce his proposals for the restoration of collective bargaining for the determination of teachers' pay and conditions.

Mrs. Rumbold: I refer the hon. Member to the reply given by my right hon. Friend to my hon. Friend the Member for Hendon, South (Mr. Marshall) on Tuesday 6 June at column *14*.

ATTORNEY-GENERAL

Crown Prosecution Service

Mr. Cousins: To ask the Attorney-General if he will give the total numbers of staff employed by the Crown Prosecution Service in the year prior to the Prosecution of Offences Act 1985, and for each subsequent year stating whether such staff are qualified or unqualified; and if he will give also *(a)* the number of cases reviewed and *(b)* the number of cases conducted by the Crown Prosecution Service in each such year.

The Attorney-General: The Crown Prosecution Service did not employ any staff prior to its formation on 1 April 1986. The total numbers of staff employed by the Crown Prosecution Service since April 1986 are:

	Total staff	Total lawyers included
1 April 1986	1,360	585
1 April 1987	3,374	1,245
1 April 1988	3,864	1,311
1 April 1989	4,322	1,398

The figures for the year of its formation reflect the fact that until 1 October 1986 the service was established only in the metropolitan counties excluding Greater London; elsewhere it operated in parallel with county prosecuting solicitors' departments. In addition to the lawyers in post on 1 April 1989, 133 unestablished lawyers were also employed, reducing the shortfall to 261 or 15 per cent.

The Crown Prosecution Service does not collect statistics on the number of cases received or conducted, but does collect statistics on the number of defendants. The available figures, based on the number of defendants, are:

	Received by Crown Prosecution Service	Prosecuted in Magistrates Courts	Prosecuted in Crown Courts
1 October 1986-31 March 1987	824,000	611,000	40,000
1 April 1987-31 March 1988	1,548,000	1,335,000	135,000
1 April 1988-31 March 1989	1,574,000	1,328,000	143,000

NATIONAL FINANCE

Press Briefings

Mr. Grocott: To ask the Chancellor of the Exchequer what guidelines he follows in determining which journalists are invited to press briefings by his Department.

Mr. Brooke: There are no formal guidelines. It depends on the matter under discussion.

Married Couple's Allowance

Mr. Chris Smith: To ask the Chancellor of the Exchequer if he intends to make any arrangements in order to enable those married couples who wish to share the benefits of the married couple's allowance equally between them from 1990 to do so.

Mr. Norman Lamont: No. The married couple's allowance which will be introduced under independent taxation in April 1990 will be given in the first instance to the husband. If he has insufficient income to use part or all of the allowance himself he will be able to transfer the surplus to his wife. Allowing married couples generally to share the married couple's allowance between them would add considerably to the complexity of independent taxation and would delay its introduction. Fewer than one in 300 couples would gain any financial advantage from this additional complexity.

Fishing Licences

Mr. McWilliam: To ask the Chancellor of the Exchequer if he has any intention of levying value added tax on angling rod licences; and if he will make a statement.

Mr. Lilley: Fishing licences, which are issued by water authorities, are not liable to VAT. It is proposed that the National Rivers Authority will take over responsibility for the issue of these licences. Their correct VAT treatment, when this happens, is currently being discussed by Customs and Excise, the Department of the Environment and MAFF.

Taxation

Mr. Ron Davies: To ask the Chancellor of the Exchequer how much revenue was accrued to the Exchequer from Wales, for the last year for which figures are available in *(a)* income tax, *(b)* corporation tax, *(c)* value added tax and *(d)* Customs and Excise duty.

Mr. Norman Lamont: Information is available only in respect of income tax.

In 1986-87, the income tax liabilities of residents of Wales were estimated to be about £1,500 million.

Dr. Marek: To ask the Chancellor of the Exchequer if he will obtain a copy in English for his departmental library of the speech by Commissioner Scrivener with regard to the harmonisation of value added tax.

Mr. Lilley: I assume that the hon. Member is referring to Commissioner Scrivener's draft communication to the Council of 17 May. I am making arrangements for the final English version of the communication to be placed in the House Library as soon as it is available.

Inflation

Mr. Chris Smith: To ask the Chancellor of the Exchequer what information he has in respect of the figures given by him to the House on 7 June of comparative inflation rates in the United Kingdom and in Italy on the precise components in each of the two calculations of housing costs.

Mr. Lilley: The inflation rate given for the United Kingdom was for the increase over the year to April in the all items RPI excluding mortgage interest payments. In the quoted Italian index of consumer prices owner-occupier housing costs are not included.

ECOFIN Meeting (S'Agaro)

Mr. Marlow: To ask the Chancellor of the Exchequer if he will make a statement on the conclusions reached at the recent ECOFIN meeting at S'Agaro.

Mr. Brooke *[holding answer 6 June 1989]*: My right hon. Friend the Chancellor of the Exchequer attended the informal meeting of European Community Finance Ministers in S'Agaro, Spain on 19 to 21 May. Ministers examined the report on economic and monetary union in the European Community as requested by the European Council at its meeting on 27 and 28 June 1988. It was not the intention of the discussion to reach conclusions. Ministers also had a further discussion of the approximation of indirect taxation and of proposals on taxation of savings including mutual assistance, which will be discussed again at a future ECOFIN Council.

Deeds of Covenant

Mr. Wallace: To ask the Chancellor of the Exchequer (1) what estimate he has made of the cost to the Exchequer of accepting, as effective, non-charitable deeds of covenant executed prior to 15 March 1988, but not notified to the Inland Revenue before 30 June 1988, for which repayments have been made in respect of convenanted payments due prior to 15 March 1988;

(2) in respect of how many deeds of covenant executed prior to 15 March 1988, but not notified to the Inland Revenue before 30 June 1988, a repayment has been made in respect of a covenant payment due before 15 March 1988;

(3) what information he has regarding the number of non-charitable deeds of covenant executed prior to March 15 1988 but not notified to the Inland Revenue before 30 June 1988.

Mr. Norman Lamont *[holding answer 9 June 1989]:* I regret that this information is not available centrally.

OVERSEAS DEVELOPMENT

India and Nepal

46. **Mr. Worthington:** To ask the Secretary of State for Foreign and Commonwealth Affairs whether he has any proposals to increase funding for population-related projects in India and Nepal.

Mr. Chris Patten: We hope to discuss with the Government of India in the next few months what further help we can give to supplement the substantial family planning assistance being provided through our primary health and slum improvement projects. There will be a family planning component in the primary health care project we are preparing in eastern Nepal.

Overseas Charities

47. **Mr. Thurnham:** To ask the Secretary of State for Foreign and Commonwealth Affairs whether he has received any representations about his Department's support for charities overseas; and if he will make a statement.

Mr. Chris Patten: I regularly meet representatives of many of the British non-governmental organisations. My Department has a productive relationship with them; and they play a distinct and valuable role in developing countries.

I have increased substantially the money allocated for jointly funded development projects and for British volunteers overseas. In 1987-88 aid expenditure of all kinds through British non-governmental organisations exceeded £42 million.

Zimbabwe

52. **Mr. John Marshall:** To ask the Secretary of State for Foreign and Commonwealth Affairs if he will make a statement about the level of British aid to Zimbabwe.

Mr. Chris Patten: Zimbabwe is an important recipent of British aid. We have provided over £200 million in development assistance since independence. In recent months, my right hon. Friend the Prime Minister has pledged a further £25 million in capital aid for agreed development projects.

Aid Projects

53. **Mr. Harry Greenway:** To ask the Secretary of State for Foreign and Commonwealth Affairs how many officials in his Department dealt with how many aid projects *(a)* in the past year and *(b)* 10 years ago; what was the cost of the project in each case; and if he will make a statement.

Mr. Chris Patten: Information in respect of individual projects could be provided only at disproportionate cost,

but in 1978 gross expenditure on aid was £752 million and the number of officials employed in the headquarters of the Overseas Development Administration (as at 1 April) was 1,411. In 1988 the equivalent figures were £1,637 million and 1,196 officials.

Aid

54. **Mr. Tom Clarke:** To ask the Secretary of State for Foreign and Commonwealth Affairs what was the combined percentage of gross national products given in overseas aid by members of the development committee of the OECD, except the United Kingdom, in 1988 or the latest available year.

Mr. Chris Patten: In 1987, the latest year for which figures are available, the combined percentage of GNP devoted to official development assistance by development assistance committee members of the OECD, excluding the United Kingdom, was 0·35 per cent.

56. **Mr. Tony Lloyd:** To ask the Secretary of State for Foreign and Commonwealth Affairs when the development assistance committee of the OECD will next review the United Kingdom aid programme.

Mr. Chris Patten: The next review is scheduled for 1991.

58. **Ms. Armstrong:** To ask the Secretary of State for Foreign and Commonwealth Affairs what proportion of gross national product was given in overseas aid by the United Kingdom Government in 1988.

59. **Miss Lestor:** To ask the Secretary of State for Foreign and Commonwealth Affairs what proportion of gross national product was given in overseas aid by the United Kingdom Government in 1988.

Mr. Chris Patten: Net official development assistance as a proportion of gross national product is estimated at 0·32 per cent. in 1988.

61. **Ms. Mowlam:** To ask the Secretary of State for Foreign and Commonwealth Affairs what proportion of public expenditure was devoted to overseas aid in 1979 and in 1988 or the latest available year.

Mr. Chris Patten: Net public expenditure on overseas aid as a percentage of general Government expenditure was 1·01 per cent. in 1979 and is estimated at 0·85 per cent. in 1988.

Lesotho

55. **Mr. Barry Field:** To ask the Secretary of State for Foreign and Commonwealth Affairs if he will make a statement on British aid to Lesotho.

Mr. Chris Patten: Lesotho has long been an important recipient of British development assistance. Gross bilateral aid disbursements are estimated at almost £5 million in 1988.

In October 1988 we offered a new grant of £10 million for expenditure on agreed development projects over the next few years.

Aid Linkage

57. **Mr. Cohen:** To ask the Secretary of State for Foreign and Commonwealth Affairs what is Her Majesty's Government's policy towards the linkage of aid and other deals.

Mr. Chris Patten: United Kingdom aid is provided in support of sustainable development and to alleviate poverty in developing countries. There is no question of linking aid and "deals".

US Treasury Secretary

60. **Mr. Cousins:** To ask the Secretary of State for Foreign and Commonwealth Affairs when he next expects to meet the United States Treasury Secretary; and what subjects he expects to discuss.

Mr. Chris Patten: Both the United States Treasury Secretary and my right hon. and learned Friend will be at the economic summit in Paris on 14 to 16 July. The summit will be an opportunity to discuss a number of important economic issues.

Rain Forests

Mr. Dalyell: To ask the Secretary of State for Foreign and Commonwealth Affairs what consequences have flowed from the meetings held by officials of the hon. Member for Bath (Mr. Patten) with Megadon and Pa-ikan Amer-Indian chiefs from the rain forest.

Mr. Chris Patten: At my meeting on 28 April with Chief Raoni, Chief Payakan and representatives of the Rainforest Foundation, I invited the Rainforest Foundation to apply for joint funding by the Overseas Development Administration of a project to enforce demarcation of the protected area of the rain forest. When a proposal comes forward, I shall consider it sympathetically.

Mr. Malcolm Bruce: To ask the Secretary of State for Foreign and Commonwealth Affairs what steps the Government are taking to halt the destruction of tropical rain forests; and what he is doing to promote the concept of sustainable yield in timber management in tropical rain forests.

Mr. Chris Patten: The Overseas Development Administration is implementing a forestry initiative aimed at increasing our aid for the sector in an effort to combat forest destruction. We are using the aid programme to promote the concept of sustainable yield in timber management, for example through a £3·7 million forestry inventory and management project in Ghana. We also promote the concept through participation in tropical forestry action plan sector reviews and in the International Tropical Timber Organisation. The recent sixth session of the ITTO council decided to request the executive director to propose ways of implementing policies to promote sustainable management of natural forests and woodlands.

NORTHERN IRELAND

Search Operation, Ards Peninsula

62. **Mr. Mallon:** To ask the Secretary of State for Northern Ireland what firearms and explosives were recovered at the home of a member of the Territorial Army in a search operation in the Ards peninsula, Co. Down, in February; what action has been taken against the person and any associates who are members of the Territorial Army; and whether effective security measures are now in

place to guard against the activities of Loyalist paramilitary groups or their sympathisers in the Territorial Army.

Mr. Ian Stewart: On 24 February, six hand grenades, three handguns and a quantity of ammunition were recovered at the home of a member of the Territorial Army, following an RUC search operation in the Ards peninsula. The individual concerned has been charged with firearms and explosives offences and is now in custody. He has been discharged from the Territorial Army.

No other present of former member of the Territorial Army has been charged by the police following his arrest. Questions about the Territorial Army in Northern Ireland (which has no security role in the Province) are for my right hon. Friend the Secretary of State for Defence.

Short Bros.

Mr. John D. Taylor: To ask the Secretary of State for Northern Ireland, in the heads of agreement for the sale of Short Brothers plc to Bombardier, what commitments there are in relation to the Shorts plants in Newtownards; and if he will make a statement on the future of Shorts in Newtownards.

Mr. Viggers: The heads of agreement are commercially confidential. However, in its public statements Bombardier has made it clear that assurances have been given that the manufacturing, and R and D facilities of Shorts, as well as the company headquarters, will remain in Northern Ireland. While the company has not made specific reference to any single manufacturing operation it has, nevertheless indicated that it plans to examine the potential for expansion for all areas of the business.

Firearms

Mr. William Ross: To ask the Secretary of State for Northern Ireland if he will publish a table in the *Official Report* to show how many *(a)* handguns, *(b)* shotguns, *(c)* semi-automatic and fully-automatic rifles, *(d)* machine guns, *(e)* ammunition and *(f)* explosives by weight have been recovered from the possession of terrorist organisations in Northern Ireland in each year since 1976 to the latest available date.

Mr. Ian Stewart *[holding answer 23 March 1989]:* Such information as is readily available is contained in the following tables. The tables relate to the number of munitions found by the security forces during the period 1976 to 30 April 1989:

Firearms found

Year	Pistols/ Revolvers	Shotguns	Rifles	MG/ SMGs	Total
1976	340	80	275	41	736
1977	209	63	259	32	563
1978	126	46	188	33	393
1979	127	38	104	31	300
1980	89	27	82	25	203
1981	139	44	136	38	357
1982	111	34	118	25	288
1983	87	17	47	15	166
1984	70	28	69	20	187
1985	76	44	47	6	173
1986	61	45	57	11	174
1987	78	58	53	17	206
1988	153	62	215	59	489
1989[1]	38	11	42	27	118

[1] To 30 April
Note: MG/SMGs refers to machine guns/sub-machine guns.

Year	Rounds of ammunition found	Explosives found (tons)
1976	70,306	9·7
1977	52,091	1·7
1978	43,512	0·9
1979	46,280	0·9
1980	28,078	0·8
1981	47,127	3·4
1982	41,452	2·3
1983	32,451	1·7
1984	27,211	3·8
1985	13,748	3·3
1986	29,061	2·4
1987	19,796	5·8
1988	105,052	4·7
1989[1]	17,534	0·2

[1] To 30 April.

HEALTH

Prescription Payments

Mr. Pike: To ask the Secretary of State for Health (1) what was the cost of the available scale margin with respect to prescription payments in the last year of its existence;

(2) how much money has been saved by the abolition of the available scale margin;

(3) on how many occasions were available scale margin payments made during the last year of that payment's existence.

Mr. Mellor: I understand that the hon. Member's questions relate to the tolerance margin which was included in the assessment of claimants' requirements under the scheme for claiming exemption from prescription charges on low income grounds which was in force prior to 11 April 1988. I regret that we have no information about the number of cases in which the existence of this margin affected a claimant's entitlement to exemption from prescription charges; nor is it possible to distinguish between the effects of the abolition of the tolerance margin and those of the other changes which took place at the same time.

NHS Reform

Mrs. Dunwoody: To ask the Secretary of State for Health how he proposes to ensure that self-governing hospitals offer a full range of services to their local community.

Mr. Mellor: District health authorities will continue to be responsible for ensuring that a comprehensive range of health care services is available to their residents through contracts placed with self-governing or directly managed NHS hospitals or the private sector.

Midwives

Mrs. Dunwoody: To ask the Secretary of State for Health what action he expects to respond to the recommendations of the Social Services Select Committee report on midwives' regrading; and if he will make a statement.

Mr. Mellor: I refer the hon. Member to my reply to the hon. Member for Wallsend (Mr. Garrett) and my hon. Friend the Member for Batley and Spen (Mrs. Peacock) on 10 May 1989, at columns *450-51.*

Press Briefings

Mr. Grocott: To ask the Secretary of State for Health what guidelines he follows in determining which journalists are invited to press briefings by his Department.

Mr. Mellor: This depends upon the matter under discussion.

Nurses (Regrading)

Mr. McWilliam: To ask the Secretary of State for Health if he will place in the Library all instructions he and his officials have issued to regional and district health authorities in connection with the nurses' regrading scheme.

Mr. Mellor: Copies of the guidance issued are in the Library.

Medical Education and Research

Mr. Wray: To ask the Secretary of State for Health if he will list the specific studies made by his Department regarding the financial and regional requirements for *(a)* staff time and attention, *(b)* hospital beds, *(c)* laboratory monitoring, *(d)* extra out-patient attention, *(e)* resources for epidemiological controls and care and *(f)* other medical services demanded by medical research in the United Kingdom, during the next 10 years.

Mr. Freeman: The Department has not undertaken any such specific studies.

Mr. Wray: To ask the Secretary of State for Health what are the specific funds to be allocated for medical *(a)* education and *(b)* research for each of the next five years.

Mr. Freeman: Responsibilities for the funding of medical education and research are vested in a number of bodies. We intend to ensure, through an appropriate funding mechanism, that hospitals which incur extra costs in future through their support of teaching and research, are not put at a disadvantage by comparison with others.

Mr. Wray: To ask the Secretary of State for Health what steps he is taking to ensure that the proposals contained in the White Paper, "Working for Patients", will avoid the fragmentation of medical research and making the dissemination of the application of research results throughout the country more difficult.

Mr. Freeman: The Government have stated in their White Paper "Working for Patients" that they are firmly committed to maintaining the quality of research in the NHS. A range of measures will be taken to fulfil this pledge. These include the necessary legislative framework, provision for the service costs of research, and accommodation in the merit award system for consultants engaged in research.

Mr. Wray: To ask the Secretary of State for Health when he responded to the comments and observations made by the Medical Research Council to his White Paper "Working for Patients".

Mr. Freeman: A response to the comments and observations of the Medical Research Council will be made in due course. Officials have discussed these matters with the Medical Research Council and these contacts will be maintained.

Rejected Imported Food

Dr. David Clark: To ask the Secretary of State for Health if, further to his answer to the hon. Member for South Shields of 26 May, *Official Report,* column *788,* he will list the whereabouts of records of rejected imported food consignments.

Mr. Freeman: This information is held by the port health authority of the port of importation.

Chlorinated Water

Mr. Wallace: To ask the Secretary of State for Heath what information his Department has on the effects of drinking chlorinated water.

Mr. Freeman: Nearly all public water supplies in England and Wales are treated with chlorine by the water undertakers in order to kill pathogenic micro-organisms. This leads to the production of chlorination by-products, at a level of a few parts per billion. Some of the chemicals formed cause cancer when administered in large doses for long periods to laboratory animals.

The Government sought advice from the Department of Health's independent expert advisory committee on medical aspects of the contamination of air, soil and water. It said:

"We have found no sound reason to conclude that the consumption of the by-products of chlorination, in drinking water which has been treated and chlorinated according to current practices, increases the risk of cancer in humans.

The effective disinfection of water supplies is clearly of great importance in maintaining public health. In our opinion, modification of chlorination processes which have proved effective over many years, or the replacement of chlorination by other disinfectants, is not required by the available data on cancer epidemiology, animal carcinogenicity, and mutagenicity in relation to chlorination by-products in drinking water."

This advice was conveyed to water authorities and water companies in England and Wales in the Department of the Environment/Welsh Office letter WP 12/1986.

Cystic Fibrosis

Mr. Kirkwood: To ask the Secretary of State for Health what steps he proposes to ensure that opted-out hospitals under his proposals for reform of the National Health Service will finance the necessary care of brain dead organ donors prior to transplant operations including heart-lung transplants for cystic fibrosis patients; and if he will make a statement.

Mr. Freeman: We are awaiting the report of a study, commissioned by the Department of the costs incurred by hospitals which provide donor organs for transplant. We shall be examining future financial arrangements in the light of the results of this study.

NHS (Pay and Prices)

Mr. Dobson: To ask the Secretary of State for Health if he will give for each year since 1979 *(a)* the assumed movement of National Health Service pay and prices for the following financial year at the time of the publication of the public expenditure White Paper and *(b)* the actual movement of National Health Service pay and prices over that year; and if he will give the scale of cash uplift and efficiency savings required to cover (i) the assumed inflation rate and (ii) the actual inflation rate in each year.

Mr. Freeman: The information requested is not available. NHS expenditure plans are made in cash and the Department does not produce projections of a price index for its aggregate programme. Generally, when measuring the effects of inflation on NHS expenditure, the GDP deflator is used as this gives the best picture of the costs of the resources spent on the NHS to the economy as a whole. By this measure gross expenditure on the NHS has increased by more than 40 per cent. over and above retail price inflation since 1978-79, or an average of over 3 per cent. a year. In addition to these extra funds, the Health Service has also benefited from the effects of health authorities' cost improvement programmes.

NHS Review

Mr. Frank Dobson: To ask the Secretary of State for Health (1) what assessment has been made by *(a)* his Department and *(b)* the Central Office of Information of the National Health Service review launch in early 1989;

(2) what is the estimated cost of the campaign to promote the National Health Service review relaunched on 7 June; and how those cost are made up;

(3) which agency or agencies were involved in the relaunch of the National Health Service review publicity campaign.

Mr. Kenneth Clarke: The NHS review launch in early 1989 achieved its objectives of informing the public in general and NHS staff in particular about the Government's proposals. The Central Office of Information was not involved in this communications exercise.

There has been no relaunch of the White Paper proposals.

The second stage of the communication effort will provide information for staff at hospitals and units which have expressed interest in self-governing status and for the general public in the areas concerned.

NML Presentations Ltd has been contracted to provide organisation, production, design and print services in connection with this communication programme.

The cost of this stage of the programme is of the order of £750,000.

Cot Deaths

Mr. Fearn: To ask the Secretary of State for Health if he has any plans to increase the allocation for research into the cause of cot deaths; and if he will make a statement.

Mr. Freeman: The main Government agency for the promotion of medical research is the Medical Research Council, which receives grant-in-aid from the Department of Education and Science. The MRC has funded a number of projects related to sudden infant deaths and respiratory distress in the newborn, details of which were given in a reply to my hon. Friend the Member for Rutland and Melton (Mr. Latham) on 20 February, at columns *524-25.* As a matter of urgency, we are discussing with the MRC what further avenues of research might next be most fruitfully pursued.

Air Ambulances

Mr. Dalyell: To ask the Secretary of State for Health if he will make a statement on the cost of air ambulances; and what proposals he has to improve the service.

Mr. Freeman: Emergency flights by the RAF and the air-sea rescue service are undertaken free of charge. The current costs to the NHS of non-emergency flights are £1,015 per flying hour. Several ambulance authorities within the United Kingdom now use dedicated air ambulance helicopters. No information on costs is held centrally, but running costs of the Cornwall service are reported to be around £250,000 per annum.

It is for health authorities to decide whether local circumstances justify the cost of operating a helicopter ambulance.

Blood Transfusions

Mr. Dalyell: To ask the Secretary of State for Health if he will make a statement on the shortages of blood for blood transfusion in the National Health Service.

Mr. Freeman: There was a temporary reduction in blood supplies following the bank holidays. There has been an excellent response from donors, and stock levels are returning to normal.

Childline

Sir Michael McNair-Wilson: To ask the Secretary of State for Health what assistance is provided by his Department to Childline; what training he requires its counsellors to have; and to what extent its action and inquiries are co-ordinated by his Department.

Mr. Mellor *[holding answer 9 June 1989]:* We made a grant of £50,000 towards the launching of Childline in October 1986 and £100,000 for the financial year 1988-89, and we are considering a further application for grant aid. Childline has developed its own training programme, which all its counsellors are required to successfully complete. The Department maintains a close link with Childline and is represented on its council.

Eye Tests

Mr. Alan Williams: To ask the Secretary of State for Health what is the percentage fall in the number of people coming forward for routine eye tests since April 1989 in England.

Mr. Mellor *[holding answer 9 June 1989]:* We do not yet have information on the number of people receiving sight tests since April 1989. We expect to commission a survey in the autumn into the number of private sight tests being carried out although the precise details for this survey have yet to be worked out.

SOCIAL SECURITY

Severe Disablement Allowance (Leicestershire)

Mr. Vaz: To ask the Secretary of State for Social Security how many people in Leicestershire receive severe disablement allowance.

Mr. Scott: The numbers of people receiving severe disablement allowance from the Department's local social security offices in Leicestershire as at 30 April 1989 are as follows:

	Number
Leicester (Burleys Way)	476
Leicester (Lower Hill Street)	1,054
Leicester (Norton Street)	499
Leicester (Yeoman Street)	838
Loughborough	654

Source: 100 per cent. count of cases in action.

Disabled People

Mr. Vaz: To ask the Secretary of State for Social Security whether the allowances paid to disabled people will be increased to take into account the extra expense of the community charge, also known as the poll tax.

Mr. Peter Lloyd: All community chargepayers on low income, including those who are disabled, will be helped through the community charge rebate scheme which provides rebates of up to 80 per cent. of liability. The special element built into income-related benefit levels will provide help with the 20 per cent. of liability that all chargepayers will have to make from their own resources.

Benefits

Mr. Loyden: To ask the Secretary of State for Social Security if he will list all the grounds of refusal of unemployment-related benefits in a manner consistent with the reports of the chief adjudication officer, and if he will give the number of claims disallowed on each ground in 1988.

Mr Peter Lloyd: The information requested is in the table.

Disallowances of Unemployment-Related Benefits made by Department of Employment Adjudication Officers in 1988

	Numbers
Normal idle day/Full extent normal	1,678
Leaving employment voluntarily	261,029
Misconduct	80,412
Payment in lieu of notice or remuneration	140,362
Delayed claim	136,496
Whether unemployed	45,154
Dependency	1,898
Availability	73,842
Engaged in employment	21,530
Restricted availability	21,424
Refusal of suitable employment	5,373
Premature termination of training	3,881
Recognised or customary holiday	6,754
Seasonal worker	5,125
Other	64,933
Total disallowances	869,891

Loans and Grants

Mr. Nellist: To ask the Secretary of State for Social Security what would be the cost of providing the information on budgeting loans and community care grants sought by the hon. Member for Coventry, South-East, *Official Report,* 25 May, column *683*; what was the the cost of providing similar information in his answers of 24 May, *Official Report,* columns *547-52;* on what criteria he decided in each case as to whether the cost was disproportionate; and if he will make a statement.

Mr. Peter Lloyd: The cost of providing the information on budgeting loans and community care grants sought by the hon. Member was approximately £285. Similarly the cost of providing equivalent information in the replies on 24 May was £180 and £112 respectively. There is a long-standing convention that Ministers may decline to answer a question when the cost of preparing the reply is likely to be in excess of £250.

Family Credit (Advertising Campaign)

Mr. Dobson: To ask the Secretary of State for Social Security if he will place in the Library any assessment of the family credit advertising campaign of April to June 1988 made *(a)* by his Department or its predecessor or *(b)* the Central Office of Information.

Mr. Peter Lloyd: Yes.

Mr. Dobson: To ask the Secretary of State for Social Security what information on the April to June 1988 family credit advertising campaign was provided to those planning and mounting the current family credit publicity campaign.

Mr. Peter Lloyd: The advertising agency concerned did not request any specific information relating to the earlier campaign and none was provided.

Mr. Dobson: To ask the Secretary of State for Social Security which agency or agencies were involved in the family credit advertising campaign mounted in April to June 1988; and what fee or fees they received.

Mr. Peter Lloyd: One agency, BSB Dorland, was involved in the campaign. It did not receive a specific fee for the campaign. The sums involved are commercial in confidence.

Lodgings

Mr. Darling: To ask the Secretary of State for Social Security how many people in local authority supported lodgings in *(a)* Scotland, *(b)* England and *(c)* Wales lost the £17·50 addition in April when the payment of their benefit was divided between income support and housing benefit; what representations he has received about the removal of this addition; if he intends to review it; and if he will make a statement.

Mr. Peter Lloyd: People in supported lodgings should not have seen any reduction in their total benefit income when the new arrangements were introduced in April. Many will have received more benefit overall, because they gained access for the first time to normal income support allowances and premiums which recognise the special needs of the elderly and the disabled. The remainder were entitled to transitional protection which will continue for as long as they remain in supported lodgings.

We have received no recent representations on this issue and have no plans to change the current arrangements.

Income Support

Mr. Robin Cook: To ask the Secretary of State for Social Security what was the value of supplementary benefit income support expressed as a proportion of the appropriate level of average net male earnings, in each year since 1974, for each of the following categories of claimants *(a)* a married couple, plus one child, aged under five years, *(b)* a married couple, plus two children, aged under five years, and *(c)* a married couple, plus three children, two aged under five years, and one aged five to 10 years.

Mr. Peter Lloyd: The latest available information is at tables 6.4b and 6.5b of the 1988 edition of the "Abstract of Statistics for Index of Retail Prices, Average Earnings, Social Security Benefits and Contributions", a copy of which is in the Library. These tables do not include information relating to income support in 1988 for families in category (iii), but the figure requested is 51·5 per cent.

The income support and supplementary benefit figures are not strictly comparable as the latter included an allowance for rent.

LORD PRESIDENT OF THE COUNCIL

Capital Sentences (Jamaica)

Mr. Tony Lloyd: To ask the Lord President of the Council what consideration has been given by the Privy Council to capital sentences passed by Jamaican courts in the last 10 years; and if he will make a statement.

Mr. Wakeham: The following numbers of appeals and petitions for special leave in capital cases from Jamaica have been referred to the Judicial Committee of the Privy Council since 1980.

	Petitions	*Appeals*
1980	1	0
1981	3	2
1982	3	1
1983	4	0
1984	6	0
1985	4	1
1986	8	0
1987	15	1
1988	16	0
1989 (to date)	6	2

It would not be appropriate for me to make any statement regarding the exercise of this judicial function.

HOUSE OF COMMONS

Stationery

Mr. Macdonald: To ask the Lord President of the Council how much House of Commons stationery has been used in each of the last five years; and what was the total cost of such stationery in each of the years for which figures are available.

Mr. Wakeham: The quantity of House of Commons die-stamped stationery which has been ordered by Her Majesty's Stationery Office in each of the last five years, together with the total value, is as follows:

Financial year	*Envelopes*	*Letterheads*	*Value*
			£
1984-85	4,118,000	5,929,000	n/a
1985-86	3,112,000	4,477,000	311,880
1986-87	7,662,000	5,718,000	422,809

Financial year	Envelopes	Letterheads	Value £
1987-88	4,457,000	5,353,000	351,237
1988-89	3,259,000	4,808,000	367,815

EMPLOYMENT

Employment Training

Ms. Short: To ask the Secretary of State for Employment what organisations have been granted ET training agent contracts; what were the planned volumes of trainees between September 1988 and March 1989; what are the planned volumes between April 1989 and August 1989; how many trainees have been referred to ET training agents; and how many action plans had been agreed at the end of each month since September 1988, for each Training Agency area.

Mr. Nicholls: The names and addresses of training agents are in the employment training directory of training agents and training managers, a copy of which is held in the House of Commons Library. Information on the profiles of training agent volumes is for internal management information purposes only. The numbers of employment service referrals to training agents are only available for the 77 employment service areas and are given in table 1. The number of action plans agreed at training agents are given for the 57 Training Agency areas in table 2.

Table 1
Employment service referrals to training agents: September 1988 to March 1989

Employment service area office	Employment service referrals to training agents						
	September 1988	October 1988	November 1988	December 1988	January 1989	February 1989	March 1989
London and South East Region							
London North West	1,241	947	899	783	959	986	887
London East	615	820	921	789	897	826	908
Inner London Central	824	1,217	1,030	889	1,305	1,431	1,641
Essex	1,469	1,530	1,178	832	1,352	1,331	1,539
London North	931	1,111	972	808	1,085	1,085	986
Inner London East	669	923	1,013	841	1,033	1,024	1,160
Inner London West	1,299	1,080	1,243	983	1,350	1,513	1,441
London South East	591	725	534	329	503	629	573
London South	848	715	820	713	859	841	852
North and East Kent	1,604	1,187	1,104	905	1,247	1,146	1,169
London South West	813	631	568	394	519	582	656
Inner London West	1,049	817	727	672	1,022	1,123	827
London West	924	592	689	1,193	755	757	667
East Sussex and West Kent	940	974	876	698	875	784	832
Hampshire and Isle of Wight	1,925	1,686	1,583	1,184	1,842	1,566	1,579
West Sussex and Surrey	1,179	822	736	582	756	773	735
Hertfordshire	936	684	691	464	632	688	802
Bedfordshire and Buckinghamshire	1,392	731	602	508	574	501	647
Berkshire and Oxfordshire	1,476	722	630	536	670	629	762
South West Region							
Avon	817	897	883	718	1,165	976	948
Devon	808	632	633	532	715	614	710
Cornwall/Plymouth	1,425	1,266	1,332	1,028	1,366	1,355	1,513
Gloucestershire/Wiltshire	957	727	611	482	735	932	1,014
Somerset/Dorset	1,124	858	414	715	970	970	983
West Midlands Region							
Birmingham and Solihulll	2,165	2,272	2,857	2,697	3,585	3,682	3,592
Coventry and Warwickshire	1,294	1,046	1,108	1,042	1,204	1,205	1,346
Hereford/Worcester	646	561	556	542	690	634	757
Wolverhampton/Walsall	1,622	1,465	1,264	1,121	1,392	1,346	1,551
Dudley and Sandwell	1,332	1,039	1,214	874	1,018	1,184	1,100
Shropshire	1,035	970	757	555	824	725	771
Staffordshire	2,253	1,299	1,355	1,328	1,799	1,604	1,621
East Midlands and Eastern Region							
Northamptonshire/Cambridgeshire	950	945	928	705	983	1,010	811
Derbyshire	1,752	1,306	1,258	705	1,304	1,208	1,277
Leicestershire	834	879	1,011	739	769	899	815
Lincolnshire	875	807	426	524	695	595	621
Suffolk	696	467	499	370	504	462	499
Nottingham	1,571	1,485	1,403	1,042	1,574	1,606	1,754
Norfolk	855	798	753	557	825	830	821
Yorkshire and Humberside region							
North Yorkshire	640	621	590	541	676	581	631
Wakefield	2,006	1,542	1,599	1,451	2,094	1,927	2,026
Bradford	1,365	1,163	1,216	999	1,226	1,247	1,301
North Humberside	1,183	1,266	1,196	907	1,282	1,063	1,305
South Humberside	1,689	1,777	1,563	1,355	1,982	1,704	2,013
Leeds	1,214	911	915	950	1,174	1,076	1,392
Sheffield	2,023	1,800	1,861	1,349	1,680	1,324	1,312

| Employment service area office | Employment service referrals to training agents | | | | | | |
	September 1988	October 1988	November 1988	December 1988	January 1989	February 1989	March 1989
North West region							
Cheshire	1,664	1,177	1,079	844	1,080	1,009	1,063
Lancashire North	1,126	1,122	983	764	1,230	1,018	1,104
Lancashire South	1,042	875	815	776	1,122	1,154	1,145
Manchester West	709	628	526	475	733	762	1,067
Manchester South	1,007	824	832	648	831	829	985
Manchester City	1,242	1,040	936	858	1,197	1,142	1,485
Manchester North West	750	847	911	664	1,100	1,038	1,229
Manchester North West	1,068	873	928	765	1,030	929	1,092
Cumbria	836	554	496	418	755	566	609
Merseyside North	888	891	1,068	847	1,524	1,346	1,349
Merseyside South	1,297	1,365	1,386	1,160	1,551	1,791	2,201
Liverpool Central/Wirral	1,103	1,206	1,172	931	1,527	1,311	1,345
Northern region							
Northumberland	1,443	898	853	672	1,022	1,074	1,019
South Tyne and Wear	2,970	1,643	1,556	1,366	1,990	2,042	1,950
Cleveland	3,497	2,391	1,585	1,379	2,142	1,657	1,676
Newcastle and Gateshead	2,464	1,364	1,267	1,094	1,406	1,295	1,395
County Durham	2,079	1,394	1,173	1,150	1,689	1,721	1,722
Wales							
Gwent	597	720	848	758	1,114	1,182	1,154
Gwynedd	547	362	390	331	393	305	358
West Glamorgan/Dyfed	1,043	1,520	1,607	1,512	1,654	1,686	1,711
Mid Glamorgan	1,186	1,242	1,136	837	1,294	1,281	1,366
South Glamorgan	1,090	875	943	944	1,060	1,169	1,099
Clwyd/Powys	762	664	773	710	629	607	668
Scotland							
Glasgow North	1,300	1,614	1,763	1,578	2,055	2,512	2,862
Glasgow South	878	1,103	1,122	911	1,503	1,513	1,712
Lanarkshire	1,262	1,098	1,160	1,150	1,371	1,421	2,089
Highlands and Islands	960	639	714	640	703	670	633
Renfrew, Dumbarton and Argyll	1,500	1,628	1,542	1,432	1,734	2,101	2,254
Ayrshire, Dumfries and Galloway	1,128	1,294	1,320	1,141	1,388	1,300	1,287
Lothian and Borders	1,883	1,773	1,866	1,213	1,247	1,513	1,769
Tayside and Grampian	1,997	1,602	1,467	1,259	1,415	1,513	1,771
Central and Fife	1,351	927	1,172	1,148	1,651	1,432	1,449

Table 2
Action plans completed by ET training agents: September 1988 to March 1989

| Area office | Agreed action plans | | | | | | |
	September 1988	October 1988	November 1988	December 1988	January 1989	February 1989	March 1989
South East Region							
Berkshire and Oxfordshire	242	798	0	922	514	450	418
Buckinghamshire and Hertfordshire	219	294	763	411	429	520	500
Essex	227	550	525	1,051	632	748	989
Hampshire and Isle of Wight	411	487	679	409	717	670	772
Kent	32	610	1,159	488	714	652	596
Surrey	102	223	174	615	190	0	196
Sussex	0	682	900	470	555	652	695
London Region							
Inner London North	505	1,196	1,545	1,606	1,651	1,799	2,090
Inner London South	510	655	616	539	645	718	736
London East	793	735	805	670	972	1,117	1,092
London North	732	857	935	846	858	970	996
London South	280	320	479	340	423	542	543
London West	591	867	811	676	900	912	952
South West Region							
Avon	238	361	411	327	453	506	489
Devon and Cornwall	665	692	1,244	795	1,294	615	1,192
Dorset and Somerset	418	478	386	332	342	516	471
Gloucestershire and Wiltshire	357	546	560	433	390	479	536
West Midlands Region							
Birmingham and Solihull	935	1,026	1,201	756	1,553	1,685	1,382
Coventry and Warwickshire	378	617	576	322	638	812	748
Dudley and Sandwell	818	769	899	1,021	978	1,059	1,416
Staffordshire	541	906	434	1,145	1,128	929	1,192

Area office				Agreed action plans			
	September 1988	*October 1988*	*November 1988*	*December 1988*	*January 1989*	*February 1989*	*March 1989*
The Marches, Hereford/Worcester	0	710	677	954	406	613	1,330
Wolverhampton and Walsall	0	1,055	1,913	308	706	821	754
East Midlands and Eastern Region							
Bedfordshire and Cambridgeshire	502	484	520	331	400	426	362
Derbyshire	704	742	743	501	582	677	743
Leicestershire and Northamptonshire	499	607	604	551	718	719	736
Lincolnshire	192	251	267	154	296	359	313
Norfolk and Suffolk	586	625	652	426	753	641	961
Nottinghamshire	602	909	853	669	937	923	851
Yorkshire and Humberside Region							
Bradford, Calderdale and Kirklees	758	944	1,439	911	1,123	1,186	1,316
Humberside	858	821	791	847	949	970	938
North Yorkshire and Leeds	621	826	752	743	777	1,035	1,002
Sheffield and Rotherham	1,078	1,387	1,382	961	1,459	1,236	1,043
Wakefield, Doncaster and Barnsley	861	1,154	1,296	990	1,501	1,547	1,265
North West Region							
Cheshire	809	826	901	588	773	951	699
Cumbria	267	280	406	269	315	377	373
Lancashire	937	1,050	955	943	1,090	1,164	1,279
Central Manchester	597	685	945	936	954	984	837
Greater Manchester North	395	699	711	423	821	834	894
Greater Manchester East	484	904	784	488	604	875	913
Merseyside	630	1,386	1,715	1,504	1,995	2,315	2,220
Northern Region							
Cleveland	1,404	2,633	3,774	4,573	6,197	7,961	9,464
County Durham	1,027	1,921	2,818	3,439	4,453	5,707	6,767
Northumberland, North Tyneside and Newcastle	602	1,564	2,668	3,517	5,861	7,136	13,114
Sunderland, South Tyneside and Gateshead	1,356	2,779	4,170	5,753	6,829	8,474	10,080
Wales							
Dyfed and West Glamorgan	524	759	922	749	909	930	949
Gwent	268	348	536	282	747	779	681
Gwynned, Clwyd and Powys	309	458	545	546	573	679	497
Mid Glamorgan and South Glamorgan	826	935	1,073	856	951	1,302	1,301
Scotland							
Ayrshire, Dumfries and Galloway	550	706	895	832	802	1,003	826
Central and Fife	429	459	710	603	594	832	573
Glasgow City	828	958	1,263	1,160	1,198	1,463	1,915
Grampian and Tayside	937	817	825	726	918	1,018	1,267
Highlands and Islands	158	207	301	351	397	400	308
Lanarkshire	301	649	710	480	639	800	803
Lothian and Borders	604	766	1,269	757	805	824	940
Renfrew, Dumbarton and Argyll	339	397	607	576	770	1,000	1,122

Note: Some months show no agreed action plans because of computer difficulties. Action plans agreed in these months are recorded in subsequent months.

Mr. Loyden: To ask the Secretary of State for Employment if he will produce figures showing the duration of stay for participants on employment training on *(a)* a national and *(b)* a Merseyside basis.

Mr. Nicholls: Information about duration of stay of employment training participants is not yet available.

Mr. Loyden: To ask the Secretary of State for Employment if there have been any cases where an unemployed claimant has had his benefits or credits stopped for refusing the offer of a place on employment training or for leaving the scheme before completion.

Mr. Lee: I am aware of only one case where an unemployed person had credits withheld because of a refusal to accept employment training. This decision was the result of an administrative error and I am satisfied that the case has now been rectified.

Because employment training is voluntary it is not training approved by the Secretary of State for the purposes of the Social Security Act. The right to unemployment benefit and credits is not, therefore, affected by a refusal of employment training or leaving an employment training course early.

Mr. Clelland: To ask the Secretary of State for Employment what were the target numbers of employment training places in September 1988 for the south Tyne and north Tyne areas, for the first year of operation of the employment training scheme.

Mr. Nicholls: Profiles nationally and for area offices for the numbers of filled employment training places are for internal management purposes only.

Mr. Roy Hughes: To ask the Secretary of State for Employment if he will consider providing gardening assistance for elderly and infirm people under employment training.

Mr. Nicholls: Employment training is a training programme designed to meet the needs of individual trainees and to help them get jobs when they finish their training. Gardening training is available where there is a local demand from employers for people with gardening skills and a demand from trainees for this sort of training. In these circumstances, employment training trainees very often provide considerable gardening assistance to elderly and infirm people.

Mr. Meacher: To ask the Secretary of State for Employment if he will list the 50 largest companies participating in the employment training programme, in each case stating the number of places they contracted for, the number of places so far filled, the latter as a percentage of the former and the level of expenditure so far on employment training advertising by each of these companies.

Mr. Nicholls: The table lists the information requested for those companies which have national employment training contracts through the large contractors unit. Other large companies have local contracts. However, for these organisations the information requested is not readily available and could be obtained only at disproportionate costs. There are other large companies who are participating in employment training as placement providers.

Information concerning company expenditure on employment training advertising is the commercial information of the companies involved and thus is unavailable.

Large companies with Training Managers contracts through ET large contractors unit

	Contracted places	Places filled at 28 April 1989	Places filled as a percentage of contracted places
Amarc	1,380	879	64
Comet	354	35	10
Dixons	229	6	3
Habitat	200	0	0
Heron Service Stations	81	1	1
J. Jarvis and Sons Ltd.	2,468	971	39
Kalamazoo	200	89	45
John Laing Construction	2,208	1,045	47
Lloyds British Training Services	2,595	1,950	75
Remploy	456	0	0
Mothercare	50	0	0
Mowlem	405	103	25
Wimpey	472	189	40

It should be noted that several of these companies have only recently signed employment training, training managing contracts and therefore their occupancy figures have not yet built up.

New Businesses

Mr. David Nicholson: To ask the Secretary of State for Employment how many new businesses have started up in each of the last six months for which figures are available, and in the years 1985, 1986, 1987 and 1988; and what estimate he has of the average number of persons employed by each firm.

Mr. Cope: The table gives the date for 1985, 1986 and 1987, the latest year for which figures have been published. Early indications are that the figure for 1988 was greater. Monthly figures are not available. There are no estimates of the numbers employed by these new businesses.

VAT registrations in the United Kingdom: 1985-87

Registrations	Thousand
1985	182
1986	191
1987	205

Labour Statistics

Mr. Andrew F. Bennett: To ask the Secretary of State for Employment how many people have been unemployed for 12 months or more in the Denton and Reddish constituency.

Mr. Lee: The information is available from the Library. In April 1989 there were, 1,148 claimants who had been unemployed for 12 months or more in the Denton and Reddish parliamentary constituency.

Mr. Anthony Coombs: To ask the Secretary of State for Employment by how much long-term unemployment has fallen over the last two years; and if he will make a statement.

Mr. Lee: The information is available from the Library. In April 1989, the number of unemployed claimants in the United Kingdom who had been unemployed for one year or more was 744,120 compared with 1,295,146 in April 1987, a fall of 551,026 or 42·6 per cent. The comparison is slightly affected by the change in the count from September 1988 due to new benefit regulations affecting those people aged under 18 years.

Small Businesses

Mr. David Nicholson: To ask the Secretary of State for Employment how many small businesses have been set up since May 1979; and what is his estimate of the number which have survived.

Mr. Cope: During the eight years from the end of 1979 to the end of 1987, there were an estimated 1,416,000 new registrations for VAT. The percentage of new businesses still registered for VAT after two years is estimated to be 74 per cent.

Mr. David Nicholson: To ask the Secretary of State for Employment whether he has any estimates of the number of jobs created by the factoring business in respect of the role in financing small businesses throughout the United Kingdom; and what advice his Department is able to give to companies seeking guidance on the merits of factoring as distinct from bank loans.

Mr. Cope: We have no estimate of the number of jobs which may have been created or supported by the factoring business. Our small firms service gives advice on all matters affecting small businesses, including where applicable the possibility of factoring. Basic advice on the possibilities of factoring as a method of improving cash flow is also given in the booklet "Prompt Payment Please". The appropriate method of raising finance including factoring, bank loans, or overdrafts, depends on the circumstances of the individual small business.

Press Briefings

Mr. Grocott: To ask the Secretary of State for Employment what guidelines he follows in determining which journalists are invited to press briefings by his Department.

Mr. Cope: This depends on the matter under discussion.

Enterprise Allowance Scheme

Mr. Evennett: To ask the Secretary of State for Employment how many new businesses were established by participants of the enterprise allowance scheme in the last year for which figures are available.

Mr. Cope: The information is not available in the form requested. Over 98,500 previously unemployed people set up a business through the enterprise allowance scheme in the year to 31 March 1989. Latest surveys indicate that around 80 per cent. of participants are sole traders, and nearly all others are in partnerships.

Enterprise Allowance (Northamptonshire)

Mr. William Powell: To ask the Secretary of State for Employment how many people have been in receipt of the enterprise allowance in Northamptonshire in each year since 1983-84.

Mr. Cope: The information is set out in the table. figures for 1988-89 include people joining the scheme in Cambridgeshire. All previous years show figures for Northamptonshire only. Numbers in each year to March 1986 are not available separately.

Financial year	Total number joined in that financial year
1988-89	1,227
1987-88	888
1986-87	446
1985-86 ⎫ 1984-85 ⎬ 1983-84 ⎭	1,226

Co-operative Development Agency

Mr. McFall: To ask the Secretary of State for Employment if he will make it his policy to accept the Co-operative movement's proposals on the future of the Co-operative Development Agency.

Mr. Cope: A number of co-operative organisations have expressed varying views on the merits of the proposal to wind up the CDA. These representations are being given careful consideration. We will announce our conclusions and intentions in due course.

Jobcentre Vacancies (Edinburgh)

Mr. Nigel Griffiths: To ask the Secretary of State for Employment whether the following five vacancies advertised by his Department's jobcentre in Edinburgh are offering rates of pay which fall below wages council rates in their sector: *(a)* Ref: 2761 E, *(b)* Ref: 1965 H, *(c)* Ref: 1985 R, *(d)* Ref: 1507 Q, and *(e)* Ref: 2752 K; and if he will make a statement.

Mr. Lee: Of the vacancies quoted, vacancy *(d)* Ref: 1507 Q is offering rates of pay which fall below wages council rates in the relevant sector. This error is regretted and my staff are now taking appropriate action to rectify it.

The subject of wages council rates is quite complex and in a service dealing with, on average, over 2·7 million vacancies a year, there is always the possibility that a few vacancies with wages below the minimum will slip through.

AGRICULTURE, FISHERIES AND FOOD

Press Briefings

Mr. Grocott: To ask the Minister of Agriculture, Fisheries and Food what guidelines he follows in determining which journalists are invited to press briefings by his Department.

Mr. Donald Thompson: The matter under discussion would determine which journalists are invited to press briefings.

Spanish-owned Fishing Vessels

Mr. Austin Mitchell: To ask the Minister of Agriculture, Fisheries and Food if he will give the total catch by value for 1988 of the Spanish fishing vessels registered as British.

Mr. Donald Thompson: The total catch by value of stocks subject to quota landed into Spain by such vessels during 1988 is estimated to be approximately £19 million.

Mr. Austin Mitchell: To ask the Minister of Agriculture, Fisheries and Food how many Spanish-owned vessels are listed on the British fishing register, giving the number at each fishing port and the numbers who have ceased fishing or left the register since the Merchant Shipping Act was passed.

Mr. Donald Thompson: Since 1 April 1989, only vessels which are largely (at least 75 per cent.) beneficially owned, managed and controlled by British citizens resident in this country are eligible to be registered as British fishing vessels. As a result of the introduction of these new registration rules, some 150 vessels believed to be foreign have been refused registration as British fishing vessels.

Beef

Sir John Farr: To ask the Minister of Agriculture, Fisheries and Food what has been the effect on the cost of beef in the shops of the underspending by £54 million in 1988 on beef support to producers.

Mr. Donald Thompson: The cost of beef in the shops depends on a range of factors including supplies of beef and other competing meats, and consumer demand and preferences. Consumers are already benefiting from the fact that the new beef support arrangements include a much reduced role for intervention thereby leaving greater supplies on the market for consumers. Moreover, the estimated change in expenditure on variable premium and special premium payments to producers between 1988/89 and 1989/90 would be only one of the elements affecting the beef market: in addition to those already noted payments to producers in the coming year will also reflect the 42 per cent. increase in the suckler cow premium which was recently announced.

Coast Protection (Arun)

Mr. Michael Marshall: To ask the Minister of Agriculture, Fisheries and Food what representations he has received regarding delays in allocation for coast protection schemes by the Arun district council; and if he will make a statement.

Mr. Ryder: My Department has received two letters recently from Arun district council setting out its needs for capital allocation for coast protection schemes. Coast protection authorities have been notified that allocation is likely to be in short supply this year. Authorities have been asked for an indication of their needs for capital allocation and I expect the first distribution to take place shortly.

Coastal Protection

Mr. Ron Davies: To ask the Minister of Agriculture, Fisheries and Food what information he has on measures undertaken to protect the coastline of each relevant European Economic Community country, whether by Government action or voluntary agencies.

Mr. Ryder: In England, works are carried out by drainage authorities—water authorities, local authorities and internal drainage boards—under the Land Drainage Act 1976 to protect against flooding from the sea and tidal rivers, and by maritime district councils under the Coast Protection Act 1949 to protect the coastline against erosion. Since 1980 more than £320 million has been spent with Government support on capital works to protect the coastline. Recent increases in such support mean that by 1991-92 Government's annual provision will be almost £46 million for flood and coastal defences, of which over two thirds will be spent to protect the coast. Coastal works also attract higher grant rates. As well as major capital works, support is also provided towards comprehensive studies, such as that on the Anglian coastline, with a view to identifying the best techniques of protection for the future.

With regard to the other members of the European Economic Community, my Department has limited information on the measures undertaken to protect coastlines. This information is primarily of a technical nature and arises from liaison with the responsible authorities with the aim of ensuring that we are fully conversant with latest developments in protection.

Fishery Products (EC Proposal)

Mr. Kirkwood: To ask the Minister of Agriculture, Fisheries and Food when he expects to be able to place in the Library a copy of the final version of the draft European Community Commission proposal on health conditions affecting the production and the placing in the market of fishery products; what consultations he has planned with the fish processing industry relating to the introduction of the changes proposed in the Commission's document; when the proposal is expected to become law; and what financial assistance will be available to the processors to comply with any new requirements.

Mr. Donald Thompson: The timing of this proposal to Council is uncertain, but I understand that the European Commission expects it to be issued during Sepember; thereafter it will be deposited in the House within the usual time scale. We have consulted widely on the early working drafts, and there will be full consultation, including with processors, once the proposal emerges. I cannot yet say when the new fish hygiene requirements will become law; this will need to be determined once the precise nature and scope of the new measures become clearer. Financial assistance through Community and national schemes under EC regulation 355/77 is currently available to processors to improve their facilities. While this regulation terminates for new applications in October 1990, the Commission has recently submitted proposals to the Council for a successor scheme.

Intervention Food Store

Mr. Cryer: To ask the Minister of Agriculture, Fisheries and Food if he will publish in the *Official Report* a list of food stores under the control of the Intervention Board and indicate the type of food stored at each.

Mr. Donald Thompson: Stores used by the Intervention Board and the commodities stored are as follows. The grain stores at Chichester, Clifton, Dumfries, Gainsborough, Kidderminster, Louth, North Humberside and Whitchurch are Government owned; all the others are commercial stores in which the board has hired space.

As the monthly notes deposited in the Library of the House indicate, there has been a very substantial reduction since 1985-86 in the volume of stocks of agricultural commodities held in intervention in this country.

Intervention store locations and commodities held as at 31 May 1989

Location	Commodities
Aberdeen	Beef
Antrim	Beef
Ballymena	Beef
Banbridge	Butter
Banbury	Butter
Belfast	Beef, Butter
Birmingham	Feedwheat
Blackburn	Beef
Bristol	Butter
Cardiff	Beef, Butter
Chichester	Feedwheat
Cleethorpes	Beef
Clifton, Yorks	Barley
Coleraine	Beef, Butter
Colnbrook	Beef
Coventry	Barley
Craigavon	Beef, Butter
Cullompton	Beef, Butter
Dumfries	Barley
Dungannon	Beef
Duns	Barley
Dysart	Barley
Ely	Barley
Exeter	Beef, Butter
Felixstowe	Barley
Fleetwood	Butter
Gainsborough	Feedwheat

Location	Commodities
Glasgow	Beef, Butter
Glenrothes	Barley, Beef, Butter
Goole	Butter
Grantham	Beef
Halesworth	Feedwheat
Haresfield	Barley
Heywood	Butter
Hull	Beef, Butter
Huntingdon	Feedwheat
Kidderminster	Feedwheat, Barley
Leeds	Beef
Lisburn	Beef
Liverpool	Beef, Butter
Londonderry	Beef
Louth	Feedwheat
Maldon	Feedwheat
Manchester	Beef
Market Drayton	Barley
Market Rasen	Barley
Newmarket	Feedwheat
Newport	Butter
Newry	Beef
Newton Abbey	Beef, Butter
North Humberside	Feedwheat, Barley
Omagh	Beef
Ormiston	Barley
Penicuick	Barley
Peterborough	Beef, Butter
Plymouth	Beef
Portadown	Beef, Butter
Preston	Butter
Salisbury	Barley
Scunthorpe	Beef, Butter
Sherborne	Butter
Shrewsbury	Beef
Staughton	Barley
Strabane	Beef, Butter
Stracathro	Barley
Swansea	Butter
Tamworth	Beef, Butter
Telford	Barley
Tranent	Barley
Truro	Beef, Butter
Turriff	Barley
Whitchurch	Barley
Whittlesey	Barley
Wigan	Beef
Wimblington	Feedwheat
Wolverhampton	Butter

Nerds

Mr. Lofthouse: To ask the Minister of Agriculture, Fisheries and Food what information he has received from the United States authorities relating to the contamination of the sweets known as Nerds.

Mr. Ryder: None. I have, however, been informed that there was a contamination threat in the United States last year involving these sweets.

Brewery Sites

Mr. David Porter: To ask the Minister of Agriculture, Fisheries and Food how many breweries have closed down and their sites used for other purposes in the past 10 years.

Mr. Ryder: The information requested by my hon. Friend is not available. Customs and Excise statistics indicate that there are currently 260 working breweries in the United Kingdom compared with 191 on 1 January 1980. These figures reflect both closures and newly established breweries over this period. Further information may be obtained from the Brewers' Society's statistical handbook.

Bovine Spongiform Encephalopathy

Mr. Ron Davies: To ask the Minister of Agriculture, Fisheries and Food whether his Department is sponsoring research into the incidence of bovine spongiform encephalopathy in cattle which consumed, as calves, infected animal feed as part of a herd of which other members have subsequently been confirmed as bovine spongiform encephalopathy infected.

Mr. Donald Thompson: Yes, as part of the epidemiological study being carried out by the Ministry's central veterinary laboratory.

Mr. Ron Davies: To ask the Minister of Agriculture, Fisheries and Food whether heat treatment of 80°C for 30 minutes is proven to be sufficient to inactivate the infective agent responsible for bovine spongiform encephalopathy.

Mr. Donald Thompson: Inactivation experiments are being considered by the Tyrrell committee.

Mr. Ron Davies: To ask the Minister of Agriculture, Fisheries and Food what was the age of the youngest bovine confirmed as suffering bovine spongiform encepalophathy in 1988.

Mr. Donald Thompson: Two years, eight months.

Mr. Ron Davies: To ask the Minister of Agriculture, Fisheries and Food what measures he is taking to record the movements of the offspring of bovine spongiform encephalopathy infected cattle.

Mr. Donald Thompson: I refer the hon. Member to the reply given to him on 22 May, at column *375.* Record keeping is also required under the Movement of Animals (Records) Order 1960.

Mr. Ron Davies: To ask the Minister of Agriculture, Fisheries and Food what is the age of the youngest bovine to be confirmed as suffering from bovine spongiform encephalopathy to date.

Mr. Donald Thompson: Two years, four months.

Mr. Ron Davies: To ask the Minister of Agriculture, Fisheries and Food what action his Department has taken to identify those suppliers of ruminant-based protein for cattle rations whose supplies were originally responsible for the outbreak of bovine spongiform encephalopathy.

Mr. Donald Thompson: Epidemiological studies into the cause of BSE indicate that it was not due to a few specific sources or suppliers.

Cattle (Ante-mortem Inspections)

Mr. Ron Davies: To ask the Minister of Agriculture, Fisheries and Food, pursuant to his answer of 8 May, *Official Report,* column *340,* if he has now collected the information about ante-mortem inspections of cattle.

Mr. Donald Thompson: In the first quarter of this year 16 suspected cases were reported from markets and 26 from slaughterhouses. Of these eight and 16 respectively were confirmed.

Royal Botanic Gardens, Kew

Mr. Ron Davies: To ask the Minister of Agriculture, Fisheries and Food what representations he has received regarding the cut in funding for the royal botanic gardens at Kew.

Mr. Ryder: None.

Mr. Ron Davies: To ask the Minister of Agriculture, Fisheries and Food what are the arrangements whereby his Department funds the royal botanic gardens at Kew; and what are the funding levels from his Department for the last three years and for the next two years.

Mr. Ryder: My Department provides funds for the royal botanic gardens, Kew by means of an annual grant in aid. This grant in each of the last three years amounted to:

	£
[1]1987-88	11,387,000
[1]1988-89	[2]10,987,000
[1]1989-90	[3]10,598,000

[1] The downward trend in funding over this period reflects the completion of a major capital works programme.
[2] Provisional outturn.
[3] Estimated outturn.

Present plans for provision of grant in aid over the next two years are for expenditure of £11 million in 1990-91 and £11·2 million in 1991-92, but these will need to be considered, together with other priorities, in the course of the public expenditure surveys.

Mr. Ron Davies: To ask the Minister of Agriculture, Fisheries and Food what are his projections of staffing levels at the royal botanic gardens, Kew.

Mr. Ryder: Manpower planning at the royal botanic gardens, Kew is a matter for the board of trustees.

Dr. Hugh Fraser

Mr. Ron Davies: To ask the Minister of Agriculture, Fisheries and Food in what capacity and on what subjects his Department is advised by Dr. Hugh Fraser.

Mr. Donald Thompson: My Department works in close collaboration with a number of research establishments. This includes, in relation to research into scrapie and bovine spongiform encephalopathy, the MRC/AFRC's neuropathogenesis unit in Edinburgh.

"Mammal and Bird Pests 1983"

Mr. Ron Davies: To ask the Minister of Agriculture, Fisheries and Food if he will place in the Library a copy of the agricultural development advisory service research and development report, "Mammal and Bird Pests 1983".

Mr. Ryder: A copy of the report to which the hon. Member refers has already been placed in the Library of the House.

Deer

Mr. Ron Davies: To ask the Minister of Agriculture, Fisheries and Food (1) if he will introduce a compulsory slaughter and compensation scheme for deer with tuberculosis;

(2) what is his Department's definition of *(a)* farmed deer, *(b)* parkland deer, and *(c)* wild deer;

(3) what is his estimate of the extent of bovine tuberculosis in deer in the United Kingdom;

(4) what steps his Ministry is taking to combat tuberculosis in deer.

Mr. Donald Thompson: Legislation has been introduced making tuberculosis in deer notifiable, together with marking and movement record requirements. A slaughter with compensation scheme is being urgently considered, as is the introduction of a voluntary health scheme based on herd testing. A blood test has been developed to support the intradermal tuberculin test and surveys are being conducted to assess the extent of tuberculosis in wild deer. Since 1971 only eight wild deer have been found to be infected. A total of eight deer herds are known to be infected and this compares to some 250 farmed deer herds in this country. Article 13(4)(b) of the Tuberculosis (Deer) Order 1989 defines farmed deer; parkland deer and wild deer are not similarly defined.

Lowestoft Fish Market

Mr. David Porter: To ask the Minister of Agriculture, Fisheries and Food if he will now determine a date for a visit by the Parliamentary Under-Secretary to Lowestoft fish market.

Mr. Donald Thompson: I very much hope to visit Lowestoft as soon as my other commitments allow.

Hepatitis

Dr. David Clark: To ask the Minister of Agriculture, Fisheries and Food if, further to his answer of 26 May, *Official Report,* column *806,* he will list the other treatments available in eliminating hepatitis A; and if he will make a statement.

Mr. Ryder: Hepatitis A is effectively eliminated from food by heat treatment. An additional treatment in the case of certain shellfish is maintenance in clean water for a suitable period.

Advisory Committees

Dr. David Clark: To ask the Minister of Agriculture, Fisheries and Food if he will make a statement about the relationship of *(a)* the food advisory committee, *(b)* the veterinary products committee and *(c)* the advisory committee on pesticides to the committee on food safety.

Mr. Ryder: The committee under the chairmanship of Sir Mark Richmond has been given the remit of advising me and my right hon. Friends on the microbiological safety of food. This committee will make recommendations as it sees fit on what further measures may be necessary to deal with food poisoning. We expect it to complete its work by mid-1990. The other three committees are permanent advisory committees with different terms of reference. There is therefore no formal relationship between them and Sir Mark Richmond's committee although the secretaries of the various committees will ensure that there is systematic contact on all matters of mutual interest.

Dr. David Clark: To ask the Minister of Agriculture, Fisheries and Food if he will make a statement about the relationship of *(a)* the food advisory committee, *(b)* the veterinary products committee and *(c)* the advisory committee on pesticides to the steering group on food surveillance.

Mr. Ryder: The steering group on food surveillance (SGFS) is a Government advisory committee which monitors the nutritional value and safety of the United Kingdom food supply. Its primary function is to identify and evaluate potential problems and to propose practical solutions, and it carries this out via a system of 10 working parties covering all the major areas relevant to its work.

The food advisory committee (FAC) is an independent expert advisory committee which advises Ministers on the composition, labelling and advertising of food and on additives, contaminants and other substances that are, or may be, present in food or used in its preparation. The FAC is normally invited to comment on draft SGFS reports and may be asked to advise on any action required as a result of the findings of the SGFS.

The veterinary products committee (VPC), an independent committee of experts in both human and veterinary health established under section 4 of the Medicines Act 1968, advises the licensing authority on the licensing of veterinary medicines. The advisory committee on pesticides (ACP), which is also an independent statutory body, advises Ministers on approvals for pesticides.

The SGFS keeps in close touch with the FAC, VPC and ACP and also specifically monitors pesticide residues and veterinary residues in food via its working party on pesticide residues and its working party on veterinary residues in animal products.

Dr. David Clark: To ask the Minister of Agriculture, Fisheries and Food if he will list the dates of meetings of the advisory committee on pesticides and the items discussed at each meeting over the last 12 months; and if he will make a statement.

Mr. Ryder: The advisory committee on pesticides met eight times and discussed a number of applications for approval of new active ingredients, reviews of older pesticides and a wide variety of related questions. A report on its work in 1988 will be published later this year.

Dr. David Clark: To ask the Minister of Agriculture, Fisheries and Food if he will list the dates of meetings of the veterinary products committee and the items discussed at each meeting over the last 12 months; and if he will make a statement.

Mr. Donald Thompson: In the last 12 months the veterinary products committee met on the following dates:

23 June 1988
20-21 July 1988
21-22 September 1988
20 October 1988
17 November 1988
14 December 1988
19 January 1989
15-16 February 1989
15-16 March 1989
19-20 April 1989
17-18 May 1989

A summary of the VPC's discussions is contained within the "Annual Report for the Medicines Commission and Section 4 Committees", copies of which are available in the Library of the House. The 1988 annual report is due to be published in the next few weeks and I shall ensure that a copy is made available in the Library.

Dr. David Clark: To ask the Minister of Agriculture, Fisheries and Food if he will list all the products for which product licences were *(a)* granted and *(b)* refused by the veterinary products committee in the last 12 months; and if he will make a statement.

Mr. Donald Thompson: Product licences are granted by the licensing authority on the advice of the veterinary products committee. Details of all newly licensed products are published regularly in the London, Edinburgh and Belfast Gazettes. It would be a breach of the commercially confidential nature of the veterinary products committee's discussions to list those applications where the committee was minded to advise the licensing authority that a licence ought not to be granted.

Food Labelling

Dr. David Clark: To ask the Minister of Agriculture, Fisheries and Food if he will list *(a)* the members and *(b)* the observers of the United Kingdom delegation at the Codex Alimentarius meeting on food labelling in Ottawa in April 1989 and the organisations for whom they worked.

Mr. Ryder: The head of food standards division (Mr. C. A. Cockbill) and the head of nutrition branch (Dr. D. H. Buss) from my Department represented the United Kingdom at this year's meeting of the Codex committee on food labelling. There were no observers in the United Kingdom delegation.

Advisory Committees (Publications)

Dr. David Clark: To ask the Minister of Agriculture, Fisheries and Food if he will list any publications of *(a)* the food advisory committee, *(b)* the veterinary products committee and *(c)* the advisory committee on pesticides that were produced in the last 12 months; and if he will make a statement.

Mr. Ryder: There have been no publications from the food advisory committee in the last 12 months, but Ministers have made the following announcements as a result of advice received from the committee:

—use of the term 'low alcohol' in the labelling of alcoholic drinks (MAFF Press Release 358/88
—use of nutritional claims in food labelling and advertising (MAFF Press Release 253/88)
—a proposal to ban the use of Mineral Hydrocarbons in Food (MAFF Press Release 53/89)
—a proposal to ban the sale of certain pills intended as slimming aids (MAFF Press Release 388/88).

In addition, the committee's comments on the report of the working party on pesticide residues 1985-88, published on 13 March 1988 in the food surveillance series, were appended to that report.

During this same period, the 1987 annual report of the veterinary products committee was published within the 1987 report of the Medicines Commission. In addition, the advisory committee on pesticides' annual report for 1986 and its report on aerial applications of pesticides in 1987 were published.

Ministers also announced the results of seven evaluations of new pesticides by the committee (press release 333/88) changes to, or revocation of, the approvals of four pesticides (press releases 312/88, 433/88, 450/88 and 204/88) and issued a paper reporting the results of routine reviews of other, currently permitted pesticides (press release 117/89). Five other pesticide approvals have been included in the Department's pesticide register.

All the publications and press releases have been deposited in the Library of the House.

Pesticides

Dr. David Clark: To ask the Minister of Agriculture, Fisheries and Food if he will list all the pesticides for which approvals were *(a)* given and *(b)* rejected in the last 12 months; and if he will make a statement.

Mr. Ryder: During 1988 my Department received 1,324 applications in relation to pesticide products and rejected 347 of them. In the same period we issued 1,371 approvals. These figures cover a variety of changes to existing products as well as new products. The latest annual listing of approved products is in "Pesticides 1989", which is available in the Library of the House.

Abattoirs

Dr. David Clark: To ask the Minister of Agriculture, Fisheries and Food if he will give a hygiene report for each of the abattoirs in the United Kingdom which received suspensions of their export licences under the Fresh Meat (Hygiene and Inspections) Regulations in 1987.

Mr. Donald Thompson: Reports on individual premises must remain confidential to the operator of those premises, the Ministry and the local authority.

Alar

Dr. David Clark: To ask the Minister of Agriculture, Fisheries and Food how many people in his Department have been working, and how many man hours have been spent, on testing the pesticide Alar; and if he will make a statement.

Mr. Ryder: As indicated in my reply to the hon. Member on 25 May at column *745,* the review of the pesticide Alar was carried out by members of the advisory committee on pesticides. The detailed information available referred to in my response was assembled by scientisits in pesticides safety division at Harpenden. In addition four scientists at the ADAS central science laboratory at Harpenden have spent some 750 man hours on work relating to residues of Alar including the establishment of a reliable method of detecting the small traces of residue that may be found in foodstuffs.

WALES

Mr. Grocott: To ask the Secretary of State for Wales what guidelines he follows in determining which journalists are invited to press briefings by his Department.

Mr. Peter Walker: I follow no guidelines other than common sense considerations in determining which journalists are invited to press briefings by my Department; these may suggest different journalists for different briefings according to specialist subjects and geography.

Rating

Mr. Barry Jones: To ask the Secretary of State for Wales (1) what each district council in Wales for the financial year 1989-90, without safety net, would have charged a household with two adults in 1989-90;

(2) what was the average domestic rate bill per household for the financial year 1989-90 for each district council in Wales;

(3) what, for each district council in Wales for the financial year 1989-90, the notional community charge per adult without safety net would have been if community charge had been in force in 1989-90;

(4) what, for each district council in Wales for the financial year 1989-90, the notional community charge per adult, with safety net would have been if the community charge had been in force in 1989-90.

Mr. Grist: Illustrative figures, based on 1989-90 rate precepts and grant levels, are given in the table. Community charge figures have been calculated using present needs assessments which are under review. The average domestic rate bills given are on a basis consistent with the community charge figures.

	Total community charges for a 2-adult household (without safety net) £	Average domestic rate bill per household £	Community charge without safety net £	Community charge with safety net £
Alyn and Deeside	373	429	187	216
Colwyn	383	405	192	224
Delyn	391	416	196	215
Glyndwr	386	345	193	185
Rhyddlan	378	399	189	201
Wrexham Maelor	382	380	191	196
Carmarthen	336	267	168	135
Ceredigion	319	280	160	146
Dinfwr	310	233	155	119
Llanelli	362	284	181	150
Preseli Pembrokeshire	310	255	155	136
South Pembrokeshire	318	311	159	166
Blaenau Gwent	351	235	175	124
Islwyn	332	265	166	135
Monmouth	310	388	155	187
Newport	331	383	165	204
Torfaen	336	325	168	168
Aberconwy	319	364	160	193
Arfon	315	254	158	145
Dwyfor	318	282	159	182

	Total community charges for a 2-adult household (without safety net)	Average domestic rate bill per household	Community charge without safety net	Community charge with safety net
	£	£	£	£
Meirionnydd	366	278	183	182
Ynys Mon	326	324	163	178
Cynon Valley	319	213	160	114
Merthyr Tydfil	352	249	176	131
Ogwr	362	334	181	162
Rhondda	351	175	176	95
Rhymney Valley	367	295	183	148
Taff Ely	336	324	168	166
Brecknock	290	274	145	143
Montgomeryshire	261	263	130	142
Radnor	274	254	137	144
Cardiff	273	391	136	200
Vale of Glamorgan	294	367	147	176
Port Talbot	406	285	203	151
Lliw Valley	387	283	193	147
Neath	411	298	206	154
Swansea	414	423	207	215
Wales	342	328	171	171

Mr. Ron Davies: To ask the Secretary of State for Wales how much was raised by local authorities in rates in Wales in the last year for which figures are available.

Mr. Grist: The amount budgeted to be raised in rates in 1989-90 by the local authorities in Wales is £786·7 million.

Planning (Completion Notices)

Mr. Nicholas Bennett: To ask the Secretary of State for Wales how many completion notices have been issued by each Welsh local authority in each of the past three years in respect of part-implemented planning consents; and if he will make a statement.

Mr. Grist: Three completion notices have been issued by Welsh local authorities in the past three years; by Delyn borough council and Port Talbot borough council in 1988 and Carmarthen district council in 1989. The Port Talbot and Carmarthen notices were confirmed by the Secretary of State and the Delyn one rejected.

Labour Statistics

Mr. Nicholas Bennett: To ask the Secretary of State for Wales if he will give the figures for *(a)* all unemployed and *(b)* youth unemployment (16 to 24) for the Pembroke constituency in January 1987, January 1988, January 1989 and at the latest available date both in number and percentage terms.

Mr. Peter Walker: The number of unemployed claimants in the Pembroke constituency is as follows:

	January 1987	January 1988	January[2] 1989	April[2] 1989
All unemployed claimants	7,381	6,232	4,899	4,088
Youth unemployed[1]	2,337	1,966	1,416	1,153

[1] Unemployed claimants aged up to and including 24 years.
[2] These figures have been affected by the new benefit regulations for under 18 year olds introduced in September 1988.

Unemployment rates are not calculated for parliamentary constituencies.

Sewage

Mr. Ron Davies: To ask the Secretary of State for Wales if he will list those applications made to him in the current year by water authorities for the lowering of effluent standards.

Mr. Win Griffiths: To ask the Secretary of State for Wales what applications have been made by the Welsh water authority for approval of relaxations and amendments to existing consent standards for the discharge of effluent from sewage treatment works; and if he will list the relaxations and amendments requested.

Mr. Grist: The information is given in the table. I have received applications from Welsh Water for variations of existing discharge consents, which will reflect the current performance of individual works in respect of the following sewage treatment works.

Rhodesmor
Sesswick
Sychdyn
Tyddyn Hywel
Tremeirchion
Caernarfon
Chester
Chirk Rhosywaun
Sarnau
Chirk Bank
Drury
Five Fords
Flint
Glasfryn
Gwalchmai
Groes Bronallt
Hanmer Arrowy
Llan Penmachno
Glynceiriog
Eryrys
Llanbrynmair
Gates Heath
Llaniestyn
Llynfaes
Llanarmon-yn-Yal
Llanbedr DC
Nant Glyn
Overton
Bettws GG
Bryn Crug
Betwys Yn Rhos
Bithawia

Burton
Llangaffo
Llanfrothen
LLanfaes B
Llangefni
Queensferry
Pentre Halkyn
Rhoslefain
Llanddoget
Broughall
Penegoes
Llanybri
Llanddarag
Rhandirmwyn
Capel Iwan
Lyls y Fran
Llanybydder
Llangybi
Cross Inn
Rosemarket
Llanfair Cydogau
New Chapel
Llanddeni Brefi
Ynys Las
Ambleston
Llangewdeirne
Devils Bridge
Hermon
Carway
Trimgaraw
Fountain
Cwmgwrach
Ystradgynlais
Raydypandy
Lampeter Velfrey
Cilycwm
Kidwelly
St. Twynwells
Pembrey
Burry Port
Glwyswrw
Aberdaron
Verwig
Llanwarne
Sparrington
Ruardean Woodside
Acton Green
Kenderchurch
Llandei Rhydderch
Much Dewchurch
Llanyre
Llanyaply
Llangarron (Herberts Hill)
Llangamarch
Llanbister
Llanbedr
Llyswen
Lyonshall
Presteigne
St. Arvans
Gross Gates
Clyro
Edwyn Ralph
Glan Valley (Village)
Garway
Penward
Rockfield
Gardisley
Much Cowarne
Walford (Coughton Place)
Weston Under Penyard
Little Denchurch
Stoke Edith
Pipe and Lyde
Stanford Bishop
Weycock
Rudry
Pen coed Cae
Draethen
Droop

Ocle Pychard
Llanelli

Details of the relaxations and amendments are still under consideration by Her Majesty's inspectorate of pollution.

EC (Financial Support)

Mr. Ron Davies: To ask the Secretary of State for Wales how much financial support Wales received from the European Community in the last year for which figures are available.

Mr. Peter Walker: Details of financial support from the European Community in 1987 are as follows:—

1987

Sources	£ million
European Regional Development Fund—Quota	[1]—
	63·658
European Investment Bank	28·900
European Coal and Steel Community	[1]—
European Social Fund	5·558
European Agricultural Guidance and Guarantee Fund	67·100

[1]Information for 1987 not yet available.

Water Quality

Mr. Win Griffiths: To ask the Secretary of State for Wales if he will publish the current water quality clarifications of rivers in Wales and any changes being recommended to these clarifications by the Welsh water authority and any changes in water quality objectives that may be involved in these reclarifications.

Mr. Grist: The current water authority classifications of rivers in Wales are contained within the 1985 river quality survey, a copy of which is available in the Library of the House. Any changes will be incorporated in the next survey, which is due to be carried out in 1990.

Polytechnic of Wales

Dr. Kim Howells: To ask the Secretary of State for Wales if he will make a statement as to the alleged deficiencies in the financial accounts of the Polytechnic of Wales.

Mr. Wyn Roberts: No. This is a matter for the Polytechnic of Wales' maintaining authority (Mid Glamorgan county council).

Dr. Kim Howells: To ask the Secretary of State for Wales what information he has on the most recent resignations of members of staff at the Polytechnic of Wales.

Mr. Wyn Roberts: Mid Glamorgan county council has informed officials that two members of the Polytechnic of Wales' staff have resigned following an investigation by the authority's internal audit department.

FOREIGN AND COMMONWEALTH AFFAIRS

International Debt

Mr. Skinner: To ask the Secretary of State for Foreign and Commonwealth Affairs when he next intends to meet other Foreign Ministers to discuss international debt; and if he will make a statement.

Mrs. Chalker: I refer the hon. Member to the written reply given him on 8 February 1989 at column *739*.

Falkland Islands

Mr. Stern: To ask the Secretary of State for Foreign and Commonwealth Affairs what is his assessment of the effect on the security of the Falkland Islands of the recent election in Argentina.

Mr. Eggar: We are satisfied that the garrison remains adequate for the present, but we keep force levels in the Falklands under constant review, particularly since Argentina has not yet declared a cessation of hostilities. We would not hesitate to increase the garrison if necessary.

Press Briefings

Mr. Grocott: To ask the Secretary of State for Foreign and Commonwealth Affairs what guidelines he follows in determining which journalists are invited to press briefings by his Department.

Mr. Eggar: The FCO has a daily press conference at 12.30 open to any bona fide journalist. We decide which journalists to invite to other press briefings in the light of the matter under discussion.

Bulgaria (Turkish Ethnic Minorities)

Mr. Atkinson: To ask the Secretary of State for Foreign and Commonwealth Affairs what representation Her Majesty's Government have made at the current CSCE human rights conference in Paris about the treatment of the Turkish ethnic minorities in Bulgaria; and if he will make a statement.

Mr. Waldegrave: Our long-standing concern about Bulgaria's treatment of its Turkish minority has been heightened recently by the harsh reaction of the Bulgarian authorities to demonstrations in the north-east and south of the country.

I raised this question with the Bulgarian ambassador on 1 June, and the leader of our delegation to the Paris conference referred to it in his opening statement on 31 May. Our concern is shared by our EC partners, and the presidency is making representations to the Bulgarian authorities on behalf of the Twelve.

Rain Forests

Mr. Dalyell: To ask the Secretary of State for Foreign and Commonwealth Affairs what proposals are being considered by the European Commission for a tax on energy consumption to finance recovery of the disappearing tropical rain forests of the third world; and if he will make a statement.

Mrs. Chalker: The European Commission has not tabled any proposals for action to conserve rain forests.

Hong Kong

Mr. Andrew Smith: To ask the Secretary of State for Foreign and Commonwealth Affairs if he will explain the differences in the categories of Hong Kong residents referred to in Government replies on 6 June as *(a)* 3·6 million, *Official Report,* column 16, *(b)* 3·5 million, *Official Report,* column 16 and *(c)* 3·25 million, *Official Report,* column 31.

Mr. Eggar: There is no exact figure for the number of British dependent territories citizens in Hong Kong. The figures quoted are all estimates.

China (British Students)

Mr. Andrew Smith: To ask the Secretary of State for Foreign and Commonwealth Affairs how many British students are studying full or part-time in China; and what measures are being taken to ensure their safety.

Mr. Eggar: The exact number of British students in China, either full-time or part-time is not known. Prior to the outbreak of the present troubles, the British Council was aware of 135 full-time students at Chinese universities; but there were probably more, some in the provinces.

In recent days, the British embassy in Peking, the British consulate-general in Shanghai and the British Council offices in these cities have sought to contact all those students registered with them and with others whose names were subsequently provided. They have been given the same advice as that given to other British nationals, that is, if they are in areas where there has been trouble and if they feel concerned for their safety, they should leave China as soon as possible by normal commercial means such as scheduled air services.

Many students were given refuge in the British embassy. At least 70 have left for Hong Kong, some of whom are now back in the United Kingdom.

Minister of State (Lunch)

Mr. Dalyell: To ask the Secretary of State for Foreign and Commonwealth Affairs for what reason the lunch between Mr. John Sergeant, chief political correspondent of the BBC, and the Minister of State, Foreign and Commonwealth Office at the Mijanou restaurant on Thursday 25 May was brought forward at short notice.

Mr. Waldegrave: Two lunches with journalists, which had been long requested, were brought forward following the postponement at short notice of my visit to Hungary, originally scheduled for 24 and 25 May.

Entry Clearance

Mr. Madden: To ask the Secretary of State for Foreign and Commonwealth Affairs (1) when Mr. Afzal Khan, whose date of birth is 18 November 1969, and whose reference is IMM 92807, applied for entry clearance to the United Kingdom at her Majesty's embassy in Islamabad; when his application was refused; and when an explanatory statement setting out the detailed grounds of refusal was despatched to Mr. Khan or his representation;

(2) when instructions were sent to the British embassy in Islamabad to issue a visa to Mr. Zahood Ahmed to enter the United Kingdom; when Mr. Ahmed, whose date of birth is 22 July 1967 and whose Home Office reference is A412361, first applied for entry clearance; when Mr. Ahmed's appeal against refusal to grant him a visa was upheld; and if he will make a statement.

Mr. Eggar: The information is not readily available as the embassy in Islamabad is closed for the Moslem weekend. I will reply to the hon. Member in due course.

TRADE AND INDUSTRY

Trading Partners

Mr. Austin Mitchell: To ask the Chancellor of the Duchy of Lancaster if he will list Britain's top 20 trading partners for *(a)* 1979 and *(b)* 1988 with the value and percentage shown of exports to and imports from each.

Mr. Alan Clark: The information is in the table:

United Kingdom's top 20 trading partners

Country	Imports £ billion	Imports percentage	Exports £ billion	Exports percentage
1979				
1. Germany	5·8	12·0	4·2	9·9
2. USA	4·9	10·1	4·0	9·5
3. France	4·1	8·4	3·1	7·2
4. Netherlands	3·4	7·1	3·1	7·2
5. Switzerland	2·6	5·3	2·4	5·6
6. Belgium-Luxembourg	2·3	4·8	2·5	5·8
7. Ireland	1·7	3·5	2·6	6·0
8. Italy	2·5	5·1	1·5	3·4
9. Sweden	1·6	3·3	1·5	3·6
10. Norway	1·3	2·7	0·8	1·8
11. Japan	1·5	3·1	0·6	1·4
12. Denmark	1·1	2·2	1·0	2·4
13. Canada	1·3	2·6	0·8	1·8
14. Saudi Arabia	1·1	2·3	0·9	2·1
15. Spain	0·7	1·5	0·6	1·3
16. Australia	0·5	1·0	0·8	2·0
17. South Africa	0·5	1·1	0·7	1·7
18. Soviet Union	0·8	1·7	0·4	1·0
19. Finland	0·8	1·6	0·4	1·0
20. Hong Kong	0·7	1·4	0·4	1·0
1988				
1. Germany	17·7	16·6	9·5	11·7
2. USA	10·8	10·1	10·5	13·0
3. France	9·4	8·8	8·3	10·2
4. Netherlands	8·3	7·8	5·6	6·9
5. Italy	5·8	5·5	4·1	5·0
6. Belgium-Luxembourg	5·0	4·7	4·3	5·2
7. Japan	6·6	6·1	1·7	2·1
8. Ireland	3·9	3·6	4·1	5·0
9. Switzerland	3·8	3·6	1·9	2·3
10. Sweden	3·4	3·2	2·2	2·7
11. Spain	2·5	2·3	2·7	3·3
12. Norway	3·1	2·9	1·1	1·3
13. Canada	2·0	1·9	2·0	2·5
14. Denmark	2·0	1·9	1·2	1·4
15. Hong Kong	1·8	1·7	1·0	1·3
16. Finland	1·8	1·7	0·8	1·0
17. Australia	0·7	0·7	1·4	1·7
18. South Africa	0·8	0·8	1·1	1·0
19. Portugal	0·9	0·9	0·8	1·0
20. Saudi Arabia	0·6	0·6	1·7	2·1

Source: United Kingdom Overseas Trade Statistics.

Central America (Trade)

Mr. Pawsey: To ask the Chancellor of the Duchy of Lancaster what is the amount of trade in each direction between central America and the United Kingdom for each year since 1985.

Mr. Alan Clark: The information is given in the table:

United Kingdom trade with Central America from 1985-1988

Year	Imports	Exports
1985	315·7	378·3
1986	193·8	319·1
1987	316·8	344·2
1988	247·7	315·4

Source: Overseas Trade Statistics, Table 1B
Notes:
[1] 1988 figures are provisional.

[2] Exports fob; imports cif.
Central America: Belize, Cuba, Guatemala, El Salvador, Honduras, Nicaragua, Costa Rica, Panama, Mexico.

Mail Users Association (Publication)

Mr. Bowis: To ask the Chancellor of the Duchy of Lancaster if he has received the May 1989 publication from the Mail Users Association entitled "Deliver us from the Post Office"; and if he will make a statement.

Mr. Forth: I was interested to see a copy of the Mail Users Association-Association of Mail Order Publishers report. The report's recommendations mainly cover operational matters, and so fall within the responsibility of the Post Office. The Post Office has no present plans to implement its recommendations, but keeps the situation under review.

Television Technology

Mr. Wray: To ask the Chancellor of the Duchy of Lancaster what assessment Her Majesty's Government have made of the combined initiatives by the *(a)* Japanese Government and business community and *(b)* United States Government and business community, with regard to research and commercial development of high-definition display television technology at the level of (i) their internal and (ii) international markets; and if he will make a statement regarding the United Kingdom's competitiveness, internal and international, in this technology.

Mr. Forth: The Japanese have been developing high-definition television technology for the last 18 years at a cost of some $700 million and are able to offer professional studio products to customers. In 1988 the state-owned broadcasting company established a demonstration satellite link feeding coverage of the Seoul Olympics to 200 high-definition displays at 50 sites including shopping malls, railway stations and leisure centres.

Until recently the United States supported the Japanese high-definition television system and had no development programme of its own, but it has now indicated its intention to develop a system more suited to its own particular requirements. The United States Defence Department has announced a $30 million programme to fund research on high-definition television related technology. A number of United States companies have presented a plan for a $1·35 billion national collaborative high-definition television project to Congress. One recent United States industry estimate has suggested that the worldwide market for high-definition television could total $40 billion by the year 2010.

The development of high-definition television for Europe is a collaborative activity under the EUREKA programme to which the United Kingdom is firmly committed. Leading organisations in the United television industry are at the forefront of many aspects of European high-definition television technology, and with Government support are making significant contributions to the EUREKA project. Equipment developed in the project was successfully demonstrated at the international broadcasting convention last September. The United Kingdom is also fully involved in European efforts to gain international acceptance for the European system.

Mr. Wray: To ask the Chancellor of the Duchy of Lancaster which Government Departments are assisting with research and sponsorship for the high-definition display television technology.

Mr. Forth: This is the responsibility of my Department.

EEC (Burden Sharing)

Mr. Cryer: To ask the Chancellor of the Duchy of Lancaster what discussions have been held with EEC Ministers regarding any burden-sharing arrangement applying to the import of textiles after 1992; and if he will make a statement.

Mr. Alan Clark: I refer the hon. Member to the reply given to him by my hon. Friend the Parliamentary Under-Secretary of State for Corporate Affairs on 9 March 1989 at column *595*. There has so far been no detailed Community discussion of future arrangements, including burden-sharing arrangements, for EC quotas on textiles and clothing.

Multi-fibre Arrangement

Mr. Madden: To ask the Chancellor of the Duchy of Lancaster what representations he has received in the current year, to date, urging the renewal of the multi-fibre arrangement.

Mr. Alan Clark: Support for the renewal of the multi-fibre arrangement was expressed by representatives of the Apparel Knitwear and Textiles Alliance and by a delegation from the all-party group for textiles and the textile industry support campaign when I met them on 11 April and 18 May respectively. In addition I have received seven letters in this sense from hon. Members and the United Kingdom industry.

Selective Investment Brokers Ltd.

Sir Charles Morrison: To ask the Chancellor of the Duchy of Lancaster (1) pursuant to his answer of 7 March, *Official Report,* column *480,* why his Department did not undertake an investigation into the affairs of Selective Investment Brokers Ltd. in December 1986, or earlier following letters to the company from Companies house, Cardiff, in 1984 and 1985 attempting to obtain information regarding the company's trading status;

(2) what action was taken by his Department to initiate an investigation into the affairs of Selective Investment Brokers Ltd., using powers under section 447 of the 1985 Companies Act, or any other relevant powers, following the submission of the Wiltshire constabulary to the Director of Public Prosecutions and his opinion that the report did not disclose sufficient evidence to justify criminal proceedings; and if he will make a statement.

Mr. Maude *[holding answer 6 June 1989]:* The purpose of the letters sent out by Companies house to Selective Investment Brokers Ltd. was to discover whether it was trading and whether dissolution action against it should be taken. Many such letters are sent out routinely every year. They do not in themselves indicate that investigations of the companies to which they are addressed are merited.

In December 1986 my Department received a complaint made on behalf of an investor in the company. The Bank of England was informed of this complaint in January 1987. Subsequently, there was liaison between the DTI, the Bank of England, and the Wiltshire police who made inquiries. A report was submitted by the police to the Director of Public Prosecutions who concluded that the evidence was insufficient to warrant a criminal investigation. The DPP did not refer the matter to my Department which did not receive any further information from any source concerning the company until after it was placed in voluntary liquidation in June 1988.

ENVIRONMENT

Rates

Mr. Andrew Bowden: To ask the Secretary of State for the Environment what is the average domestic rates bill in England and Wales for 1989-90.

Mr. Gummer: £502.

Water and Sewage Charges

Mr. Andrew Bowden: To ask the Secretary of State for the Environment (1) what is the average water rate and sewage charge made in England and Wales in 1989-90;

(2) what is the average water rate and sewage charge made to people on income support in England and Wales for 1989-90.

Mr. Howard: The average domestic bill for water authority customers in England and Wales in 1989-90 is £2·29 per week. Information is not separately available for customers on income support.

Aquatic Flora and Fauna

Mr. Austin Mitchell: To ask the Secretary of State for the Environment, pursuant to his reply of 4 May to the hon. Member for Great Grimsby, *Official Report*, column *245*, whether he will estimate the extent of *(a)* short-term and *(b)* long-term damage to aquatic flora and fauna in inland waters and estuaries caused by pollution incidents.

Mrs. Virginia Bottomley: Specific information concerning the impact of pollution incidents is not available centrally. Water authorities make their own detailed assessments in individual cases: these are to enable management to ensure that appropriate remedial measures can be carried out. The cumulative impact of all sources of pollution is assessed through routine river quality monitoring, the results of which are published comprehensively in the regular national river quality surveys. The most recent survey was carried out in 1985. In future this work will be carried out by the National Rivers Authority, which will also wish to review monitoring procedures. Work on the next river quality survey will commence in 1990.

Waste Disposal Authorities

Sir Eldon Griffiths: To ask the Secretary of State for the Environment what representations he has received from Suffolk county council on his consultation paper regarding the role and function of waste disposal authorities; and what steps he is taking to avoid a hiatus in the search for and acquisition of new disposal sites as foreshadowed by the county council between the date of issuance of his Green Paper and the anticipated date of his implementing his proposed changes.

Mrs. Virginia Bottomley: I have received from Suffolk county council detailed comments about the consultation paper on the role and functions of waste disposal authorities. These comments, along with many others, are being given careful consideration.

Until any changes are implemented, waste disposal authorities will retain their duties under present legislation to arrange, through public or private sector facilities, for the disposal of waste collected by the waste collection authorities. Under the arrangements proposed in the consultation paper public facilities would be provided by local authority waste disposal companies. On the due date all the waste disposal assets of a disposal authority would be transferred to the company which will be under the authority's control as shareholder and board member. There is no reason why a hiatus need develop in the search for and acquisition of new disposal sites.

Water Privatisation

Mrs. Ann Taylor: To ask the Secretary of State for the Environment whether he proposes to introduce provisions by which a privatised water industry could impose a price surcharge to discourage the use of water during a period of drought.

Mr. Howard: No.

Local Government (Miscellaneous Provisions) Act 1976

Mr. Redmond: To ask the Secretary of State for the Environment, pursuant to his answer of 2 March, *Official Report,* column *283,* to the hon. Member for Don Valley, what have been the results of his deliberations in respect of changes to section 19 of the Local Government (Miscellaneous Provisions) Act 1976.

Mrs. Virginia Bottomley: We have not yet reached any decisions on this matter. We shall report to the House as soon as we have done so.

Nitrate Pollution

Mr. Boswell: To ask the Secretary of State for the Environment what evidence he has of additional nitrate pollution in water induced by run-off through the use of urea to clear frost from highways and runways.

Mr. Howard: We have no evidence to suggest that the use of urea to clear frost from highways and runways contributes significantly to nitrate pollution of water.

Housing Statistics

Mr. Cousins: To ask the Secretary of State for the Environment if he will publish a table showing housing starts in each region in the quarter to March showing the percentage change in starts from the quarter ending February 1989 and the quarter ending March 1988.

Mr. Trippier: Housebuilding starts for regions in England in the March quarter of 1989 and the corresponding period a year earlier are given in the table.

	Housebuilding starts in thousands		
	March quarter 1988	*March quarter 1989*	*Percentage change*
North	2·1	2·6	+23
Yorkshire and Humberside	4·3	4·4	+4
East Midlands	5·2	4·7	−9
East Anglia	3·9	3·3	−15
South East:			
Greater London	4·0	4·3	+8
Rest of South East	14·6	12·2	−17
South West	7·3	5·4	−26
West Midlands	5·2	4·4	−16
North West	4·5	5·0	+12
England	50·9	46·2	−9

Provisional estimates of housebuilding starts in the three months to February 1989 were given in my answer to the hon. Member on 4 May 1989.

Seal Pups

Mr. Wallace: To ask the Secretary of State for the Environment how many representations have been received by his Department seeking a continuation of the European Community ban on the import of harp and hooded seal pup skins and products; and if he will make a statement.

Mrs. Virginia Bottomley: The Department has received a number of representations seeking a continuation of the EC ban. The United Kingdom fully supported the European Commission's proposal for an indefinite extension of the ban and we were successful in securing our European partners' agreement to this at the EC Environment Council meeting on 8 June.

Water Supplies (Chlorine)

Mr. Wallace: To ask the Secretary of State for the Environment what information he has on the levels of chlorine in water supplies in England and Wales.

Mr. Howard: This information is not held centrally. It is for individual water undertakers with their knowledge of local conditions to determine the level of chlorine necessary to disinfect the water supply and to maintain bacterial quality of the water during distribution.

Peregrine Falcons

Mr. Ron Davies: To ask the Secretary of State for the Environment what steps he has taken to ensure the safety of peregrine falcons in Wales under the provisions of the Wildlife and Countryside Act 1981.

Mrs. Virginia Bottomley: The peregrine falcon is listed on schedule 1 to the Wildlife and Countryside Act 1981 as a species protected by special penalties. The Act makes it an offence to kill, injure or take a peregrine; destroy or take its eggs or damage or destroy its nest. Anyone found guilty of such an offence is liable to a fine of up to £2,000. Enforcement of these provisions is a matter for the police authorities and the courts.

Wolf Hybrid Dogs

Mr. Kirkwood: To ask the Secretary of State for the Environment if he will now halt the sale of wolf hybrid dogs as pets and have them registered as wild animals.

Mrs. Virginia Bottomley: No. The Dangerous Wild Animals Act 1976 provides controls over the keeping of wild animals by requiring people who wish to do so to obtain a licence from the appropriate local authority. These licences are issued only if stringent conditions concerning safety and welfare have been met. The term "dangerous wild animal" is not defined in the Act, other than by reference to a list of species, which includes wolves, in the schedule to the Act. Mammal hybrids (arising from cross breeding of domestic and wild animals) are covered by the Act if at least one parent is of a species listed in the schedule to the Act.

Separate legislation, the Dogs Act 1871, exists to control dangerous dogs, and empowers the police to take action against anyone failing to control a dangerous dog.

Birchfield Estate, Handsworth

Mr. Rooker: To ask the Secretary of State for the Environment on what date Birmingham city council submitted a proposal for a security project on the Birchfield estate, Handsworth, Birmingham; and when he expects a decision to be made.

Mr. Trippier: The idea was first suggested in December 1987. An urban programme scheme proposal was received from Birmingham city council on 7 September 1988 and approval in principle was issued on 29 September 1988. Detailed costs and plans allowing the go-ahead to spend have not been received to date.

Birds

Mr. Malcolm Bruce: To ask the Secretary of State for the Environment what steps the Government are taking to ensure the continued survival within the United Kingdom of the following species of bird: *(a)* the bittern, *(b)* the red-backed shrike, *(c)* the corncrake, *(d)* the red kite, *(e)* the white-tailed sea eagle and *(f)* the marsh-warbler.

Mrs. Virginia Bottomley: All these species are listed in schedule 1 to the Wildlife and Countryside Act 1981 as being protected by special penalties. Anyone attempting, in contravention of the Act, to kill, injure or take such a bird or to destroy its eggs or nests is liable on conviction to a fine of up to £2,000. In addition, important habitats are safeguarded through the Act's provisions for the notification of sites of special scientific interest. Where appropriate, further action is taken through the classification of special protection areas under article 4 of EC directive 79/409/EEC.

Nene Washes (Bird Reserve)

Mr. Morley: To ask the Secretary of State for the Environment whether it was a condition of the grant application recently discussed between the Nature Conservancy Council and the Royal Society for the Protection of Birds to extend the existing Royal Society for the Protection of Birds reserve on the Nene Washes, near Whittlesey, Cambridgeshire, by the purchase of 16·5 acres of adjoining land within the existence site of special scientific interest, that no grant would be given unless the Royal Society for the Protection of Birds allowed shooting over it.

Mrs. Virginia Bottomley: I understand that the NCC considered the application by RSPB for the purchase of land to extend their existing Nene Washes reserve strictly in the light of the policy agreed with my right hon. Friend that traditional country rights and uses should not be interfered with wherever they are not in direct conflict with conservation interests. Since there was no evidence that the continuation of sporting rights over the site was incompatible with conservation interests the NCC felt unable to offer grant assistance to RSPB if the extinguishment of those rights formed an integral part of the purchase objectives.

Chlorofluorocarbons

Sir Michael McNair-Wilson: To ask the Secretary of State for the Environment whether restrictions relating to products using chlorofluorocarbons will include inhalers used for medicinal purposes.

Mrs. Virginia Bottomley: Members of the British Aerosol Manufacturers Association have agreed to end all non-essential use of chlorofluorocarbons in their products by the end of this year. The industry is actively researching alternatives to chlorofluorocarbons in medical equipment and we expect these to be introduced as soon as they are commercially available and have been approved by the appropriate authorities.

Community Charge

Mr. Kirkwood: To ask the Secretary of State for the Environment (1) whether the community charge regulations allow for delivery of community charge registration forms by registration officers in England to addresses in Scotland;

(2) whether the community charge regulations allow registration officers in England to take action against occupiers of houses in Scotland for non-registration for community charge purposes.

Mr. Gummer *[holding answer 6 June 1987]:* A community charge registration officer may request information from anyone he reasonably believes is, or has been, or will be subject to a community charge in his area. Anyone failing without reasonable excuse to supply the information, or knowingly supplying wrong information, may be subject to a penalty. Nothing in the legislation precludes requests being made to an address in Scotland, or penalties being imposed on individuals with an address in Scotland, in connection with a community charge arising in England or Wales.

Mr. Blunkett: To ask the Secretary of State for the Environment if he will make a statement on *(a)* the progress being made in making fully operational the valuation and community charge tribunals, *(b)* the additional costs involved and *(c)* the role of his Department's staff in this process.

Mr. Gummer *[holding answer 9 June 1989]:* The Department's staff are working closely with members and clerks of the valuation and community charge tribunals to ensure that they have the resources to carry out their functions. Good progress has been made in designing and installing computer systems, in providing enlarged accommodation, and in recruiting and training the staff needed for this task. The cost of running the tribunals in England in 1989-90 is expected to exceed the cost of the old local valuation panels in 1988-89 by about £4 million.

Effluent

Mr. Ron Davies: To ask the Secretary of State for the Environment if he will list those applications which have been sent to his Department in the current year for the lowering of effluent standards by water authorities.

Mr. Howard: No. On 11 May, my right hon. Friend the Secretary of State announced at column *520* that a list of those sewage works for which applications for time-limited consents had been made had been placed in the Library of the House. These consents will regularise current performance while improvement work is undertaken as part of the £1 billion capital programme to bring sewage treatment works up to standard by March 1992. On completion, long-term consent conditions for these works, no less stringent than those which presently apply, will be imposed. The overall programme will result in significant improvements to river quality.

DEFENCE

MARILYN

Mr. Baldry: To ask the Secretary of State for Defence if he will make a statement on progress with MARILYN.

Mr. Archie Hamilton: I refer my hon. Friend to the statement I made in the House on 8 June at columns 388-90, in which I announced that copies of an abridged version of the MARILYN report, which will underpin much of the Ministry of Defence's future work on the problems of army manpower supply in the years ahead, had been placed in the Library of the House.

Nuclear Missiles

Mr. Redmond: To ask the Secretary of State for Defence how many nuclear missiles have been stationed in the United Kingdom since the United States-Soviet intermediate nuclear forces treaty came into effect; and if he will make a statement.

Mr. Archie Hamilton: At the time the INF treaty came into effect last summer there were 96 operational United States group-launched cruise missiles (GLCMs) at RAF Greenham Common and 16 at RAF Molesworth. Since then RAF Molesworth has been closed as a GLCM forward operating base and all the missiles removed.

Half the missiles from RAF Greenham Common will be withdrawn in late 1989; the rest will return to the United States in the first half of 1991.

US Air Force Aircraft (Missiles)

Mr. Redmond: To ask the Secretary of State for Defence, how many United States Air Force aircraft based in the United Kingdom are equipped with *(a)* AGM-69A short-range attack missiles and *(b)* air-launched cruise missiles; if he will name the types of aircraft that would be used to deploy these weapons, and if he will make a statement.

Mr. Archie Hamilton: None.

"Who Framed Colin Wallace"

Mr. Livingstone: To ask the Secretary of State for Defence if he will make a statement on the allegations concerning the activities of the information policy unit of the Army information services reported during the 1970s made by former serving army officers and civil servants reported in the book, "Who Framed Colin Wallace" by Mr. Paul Foot.

Mr. Archie Hamilton: No.

Destroyers and Frigates

Mr. Menzies Campbell: To ask the Secretary of State for Defence how many destroyers and frigates of the surface fleet were available for service at 24 hours notice on 1 June 1988, 1 January 1989 and 1 June 1989.

Mr. Archie Hamilton: Details of ships available for operations at precise periods of notice are classified. However, the table shows the total number of destroyers and frigates in service together with those that were available for operational deployment immediately or within a short period for each of the dates requested.

Number of DD/FF available for operational deployment immediately or within a short period

	Total DD/FF in service	Number
1 June 1988	47	40
1 January 1989	48	40
1 June 1989	47	40

Press Briefings

Mr. Grocott: To ask the Secretary of State for Defence what guidelines he follows in determining which journalists are invited to press briefings by his Department.

Mr. Archie Hamilton: Invitations to press briefings depend very much on the subject under discussion.

NATO (Binational Divisions)

Mr. Menzies Campbell: To ask the Secretary of State for Defence what is his policy towards the creation of binational divisions within NATO, on the model of the Anglo-Dutch marine force.

Mr. Archie Hamilton: The United Kingdom/Netherlands amphibious force has an important part to play in NATO's plans for reinforcement of the northern region. We welcome such practical bilateral co-operation within the Alliance where it serves to enhance overall defence capabilities.

Service Personnel (Children's Education)

Sir Michael McNair-Wilson: To ask the Secretary of State for Defence how many children of service men are being educated in the private sector on Ministry of Defence grants; and how many of these children are being educated at Crookham Court school, Newbury, Berkshire.

Mr. Sainsbury: As at March 1989, the latest date for which figures are available, there were some 22,400 children of service personnel for whom boarding school allowance was being claimed; this figure includes those attending state boarding schools. At Crookham Court school, there are at present 32 children of service parents.

Rosyth Dockyard (Share Sales)

Mr. Gordon Brown: To ask the Secretary of State for Defence what action he intends to take to prevent a foreign sale of shares in Rosyth dockyard.

Mr. Sainsbury: The term contract requires that the prior approval of the Secretary of State must be sought to any change in the ownership or structure of the management company, and the parent companies FKI, Babcock and Thorn EMI are required to ensure that any foreign shareholding in the dockyard management company is less than 30 per cent.

Mr. Gordon Brown: To ask the Secretary of State for Defence what consultations he had before 7 June with Thorn EMI over the sale of its stake in Rosyth dockyard.

Mr. Sainsbury: None.

Mr. Gordon Brown: To ask the Secretary of State for Defence which companies have indicated an interest in purchasing the Thorn EMI stake in Rosyth dockyard.

Mr. Sainsbury: My Department is not aware of any expressions of interest.

HMS Southampton

Mr. Gordon Brown: To ask the Secretary of State for Defence when he expects to make an announcement on HMS Southampton.

Mr. Sainsbury: Shortly.

Rosyth Dockyard

Mr. Gordon Brown: To ask the Secretary of State for Defence when he proposes to meet Thorn EMI to discuss the future of Rosyth dockyard.

Mr. Sainsbury: I have no plans to do so at present. My officials are however in touch with Thorn EMI and also with FKI Babcock, the majority partner in management company at Rosyth (BTL).

Royal Dockyard Management

Mr. Gordon Brown: To ask the Secretary of State for defence whether he will review the contract for royal dockyard management as a result of the uncertainty created from company takeovers.

Mr. Sainsbury: No. The term contract requires that the prior approval of the Secretary of State must be sought to any change in the ownership of, or structure of the management company.

Nuclear Weapons (Germany)

Mr. Menzies Campbell: To ask the Secretary of State for Defence what is his policy towards the Palme commission proposal to negotiate a 150 km nuclear weapon free zone on either side of the inter-German border.

Mr. Archie Hamilton: This Government oppose the creation of a nuclear weapon free zone in Europe, which we believe would not increase but reduce security and stability. The territory of such a zone would still be under threat from weapons positioned outside the zone but targeted on it. Verification would be difficult, if not impossible, since the small size and mobility of many nuclear weapons means that they could be rapidly deployed back into the zone at a time of tension, thus increasing rather than reducing the risk of war. Such a zone would also undermine NATO's strategy of forward defence.

Mr. Colin Wallace

Mr. Dalyell: To ask the Secretary of State for Defence when, pursuant to the undertaking given by the hon. Member for Romford (Mr. Neubert) on 8 June during the debate on the Army the hon. Member for Linlithgow may expect a detailed reply to points raised during the debate on former officer Colin Wallace and the role of Army intelligence in BBC statements relating to alleged blackmail of Labour hon. Members.

Mr. Archie Hamilton: I will write to the hon. Member in due course.

HOME DEPARTMENT

Prisoners

Mr. Tony Lloyd: To ask the Secretary of State for the Home Department (1) what mechanism exists to allow for reconsideration of the allocation of a prisoner to a particular prison;

(2) what weighting is given to the needs of a prisoner when the allocation to a particular prison is made; and at what stage in the process of allocation an assessment takes place.

Mr. Douglas Hogg: The allocation decision is made as soon as possible after the prisoner is received under sentence, and takes account, inter alia, of an assessment of the prisoner's needs which is based on information from records and from interview. The weight which it is possible to give to this factor varies according to circumstances and each case is considered on its merits. Prison service procedures require the allocation decision to be reviewed at least annually following reassessment of the prisoner's security category. It is open to any prisoner to apply at any time to be reallocated.

Police Car Chases

Mrs. Maureen Hicks: To ask the Secretary of State for the Home Department how many deaths there have been during the current year as a result of police car chases *(a)* in the United Kingdom and *(b)* in the west midlands.

Mr. Douglas Hogg: Full information will not be available until returns are submitted by individual forces to Her Majesty's Chief Inspector of Constabulary after the end of the year. However, I am aware of 12 specific accidents which have occurred since 1 March 1989 in cases where the police were pursuing a vehicle, or responding to emergency calls, which have resulted in a total of 15 fatalities. Two of these accidents occurred in the west midlands police area. I understand that there was one other fatal accident in the west midlands police area in February 1989.

Press Briefings

Mr. Grocott: To ask the Secretary of State for the Home Department what guidelines he follows in determining which journalists are invited to press briefings by his Department.

Mr. Douglas Hogg: Media representatives are invited to press briefings according to the nature of the subject to be discussed.

Street Robbery

Mr. Marlow: To ask the Secretary of State for the Home Department what steps his Department is taking against street robbery; and if he will make a statement.

Mr. John Patten: The police give high priority to dealing with street robbery. In 1988 robbery, including mugging, fell by 4 per cent. Certain high-crime urban areas will benefit from our safer cities programme, and we have produced a crime prevention handbook which contains advice on how to reduce the risk of being attacked; nearly 2·5 million copies have been distributed.

Passports

Mr. Speller: To ask the Secretary of State for the Home Department if he will make a statement on the speed and efficiency of the passport issuing offices; and if he will consider instituting regional offices for this purpose.

Mr. Renton: I refer my hon. Friend to the reply given on 6 June to a question from the hon. Member for Bolton, South-East (Mr. Young) at column *47.* There are at present six regional passport offices in the United Kingdom. Since the great majority of passport applications are usually dealt with by post, the location of the issuing office is not normally a significant factor in determining the speed of service. We shall, however, be reviewing the location and number of offices later this year.

Democracy

Mr. Allen: To ask the Secretary of State for the Home Department what research he has undertaken on increasing the levels of participation in the democratic process.

Mr. Douglas Hogg: None directly, though the numbers of people registered to vote in each constituency or electoral area, and the numbers voting, are published after each parliamentary or European parliamentary general election, and following the local government elections in May each year. I understand that an opinion poll carried out by NOP in February/March 1988 found that nearly a quarter of those surveyed said that they would be more likely to vote in local elections when the community charge is introduced.

Hillsborough Stadium Disaster

Mr. Cohen: To ask the Secretary of State for the Home Department who compiled the video of the Hillsborough tragedy which was shown to the inquiry on 19 May; who supervised the editing of it; what steps he is taking to ensure that the edited-out film was not relevant to the policing of the event; and if he will make a statement.

Mr. Douglas Hogg: These are matters for Lord Justice Taylor, but I understand that the video tape shown on 19 May to his inquiry into the Hillsborough stadium disaster was compiled by the west midlands police inquiry team and the Treasury Solicitor's Department from material supplied to the inquiry by the BBC, South Yorkshire police and Sheffield Wednesday football club. Further material was subsequently shown to the inquiry.

A catalogue of all the video material available to the inquiry has been given to counsel for all the parties represented, who may see any of it if they wish to do so.

Lollipop Persons

Mr. Harry Greenway: To ask the Secretary of State for the Home Department, pursuant to his answer to the hon. Member for Ealing, North of 20 April, *Official Report,* columns *289-90,* what progress has been made with the review of the pay of lollipop ladies and gentlemen; and if he will make a statement.

Mr. Douglas Hogg: Authority has recently been given for an increase averaging 4·5 per cent. in the basic rates payable to school crossing patrols with effect from 1 September 1988. I understand from the Commissioner of Police of the Metropolis that the new rates of pay (including the arrears) will be paid from the middle of this month.

Children's Television

Mrs. Dunwoody: To ask the Secretary of State for the Home Department what consideration he gave to children's television programmes provision in drawing up his White Paper on broadcasting; if he will take steps to ensure adequate funding for specific high-quality British material for children's television; and what steps he will take to ensure a minimum adequate level of income for children's programmes on channels 3 and 5.

Mr. Renton: There is at present no specific requirement on the broadcasting authorities to provide children's television programmes, other than schools broadcasts and educational programming—and we see no case for creating such a new requirement in the future.

The general approach of the White Paper on broadcasting is that regulatory bodies should no longer seek to lay down in detail what programmes are shown and when. The White Paper makes it clear that the BBC will continue to be expected to provide high-quality programming across the full range of public tastes and interests. The existing remit of channel 4 is also to be fully sustained. As regards channels 3 and 5, the White Paper proposes that licensees should be subject to a series of quality tests including requirements to provide a diverse programme service calculated to appeal to a variety of tastes and interests.

We see no reason why high-quality children's programmes, sustained by viewer demand, should not continue to flourish on British television after 1992.

Mrs. Dunwoody: To ask the Secretary of State for the Home Department what studies his Department has undertaken into the needs of children for high-quality British programmes other than educational programmes on television.

Mr. Renton: None. Market research into the level and nature of the demand for children's television programmes is a matter for the broadcasters.

Suicides (Prisoners)

Mr. Sheerman: To ask the Secretary of State for the Home Department how many of the prisoners who committed suicide whilst on remand in 1987 and 1988 had been remanded for psychiatric reports.

Mr. Douglas Hogg: Three in 1987 and three in 1988.

Television Licences

Mr. Sheerman: To ask the Secretary of State for the Home Department how many people were imprisoned for failing to pay fines imposed for using a television set without a licence in the latest year for which figures are available.

Mr. Douglas Hogg: The information requested could be provided only at disproportionate cost.

Slopping Out

Mr. Sheerman: To ask the Secretary of State for the Home Department what is *(a)* the number of and *(b)* the proportion of inmates of young offender institutions who have to slop out.

Mr. Douglas Hogg: On 31 March 1989, the latest date for which figures are available, there were something over 3,100 young offenders having to slop out. The proportion of inmates in young offender institutions having to slop out on that date was approximately 46 per cent.

European Prison Rules

Mr. Sheerman: To ask the Secretary of State for the Home Department which rules of the European prison rules are not yet complied with by the prison service; which rules the service does not currently have plans to comply with; and what are the estimated dates for compliance with those rules which the prison service intends to comply with but has not yet done so.

Mr. Douglas Hogg: The European prison rules are intended to guide member states of the Council of Europe in their internal legislation and practice. Her Majesty's prison service in England and Wales complies fully or partially with all of them. Those which are partially complied with are: 1, 14, 15, 16, 17, 19, 25, 39, 42, 65, 67, 71, 94, 96 and 99. There are at present no plans to comply fully with some aspects of rules 14, 39, 67, 96 and 99. The remainder will be complied with as soon as practicable, but it is not possible to give estimated dates.

Electronic Surveillance

Mr. Allen: To ask the Secretary of State for the Home Department if electronic surveillance schemes will be used in court areas in England and Wales which have bail information schemes.

Mr. John Patten: No bail information schemes, as normally defined, are operating within the three electronic monitoring areas.

Mr. Allen: To ask the Secretary of State for the Home Department if it will be possible for participants in the electronic surveillance schemes in England and Wales to remove the equipment during the course of the pilot project.

Mr. John Patten: Yes, but any removal of the equipment will be readily detectable.

Mr. Allen: To ask the Secretary of State for the Home Department if telephones will be installed, or homes provided in appropriate cases, for participants in electronic surveillance schemes.

Mr. John Patten: If a participant who is otherwise suitable does not have a telephone, one will be installed, free of charge. But it will not be possible for him to use it in the normal way: it will provide solely for communication with the central monitoring station through electronic barring at the telephone exchange. The trials will proceed on the basis that participants must be resident in the petty sessional division concerned or be able to make suitable arrangements for such residence during any period of electronic monitoring.

Mr. Allen: To ask the Secretary of State for the Home Department what will be the maximum length of time that a participant can expect to spend tagged in an electronic surveillance scheme in England and Wales.

Mr. John Patten: The information is not available in the form requested. The period for which a participant may be monitored will depend on a number of factors, including whether the case is committed for trial to the Crown court. In such a case the average waiting time from first appearance to completion at magistrates' courts in 1988 was eight weeks. The average time from committal to a Crown court to the start of the case was 12·2 weeks.

Cashpoint Thefts

Mr. Vaz: To ask the Secretary of State for the Home Department if he will set up a public inquiry into the banks' handling of cashpoint thefts in the United Kingdom.

Mr. John Patten: No. The working group on commercial robbery set up by the standing conference on crime prevention reported in 1986 and did not identify this as a notable problem.

Metropolitan Police Officers (Firearms)

Mr. Dobson: To ask the Secretary of State for the Home Department if he will place in the Library a copy of the code of conduct concerning the use of firearms by police officers of the Metropolitan police.

Mr. Douglas Hurd: The guidelines on the issue and use of firearms, which apply to all police forces in England and Wales, were revised in December 1986 by the Association of Chief Police Officers in conjunction with the Home Office working group on the police use of firearms.

A copy of these guidelines was placed in the Library on 3 February 1987, as part of a summary of the working group's 1986 report.

Chinese Students (Political Refugees)

Mr. Andrew Smith: To ask the Secretary of State for the Home Department if he will make it his policy to accept applications for political asylum from Chinese students presently studying in the United Kingdom, who fear for their safety if they return to China.

Mr. Renton: Any application for asylum will be considered in accordance with the UN 1951 convention relating to the status of refugees.

In addition, while the situation in China remains uncertain, we shall look sympathetically at any application by a Chinese national to extend their stay, depending on their individual circumstances.

Isle of Man (Police Action)

Mr. Foulkes: To ask the Secretary of State for the Home Department what information he has sought or received from the Isle of Man authorities regarding police action against Transport and General Workers Union officials, Bernard Moffat and David Quirk, following allegations regarding leaked information; if he has received representations that such action contravenes the European convention on human rights; what action he has taken or proposes to take; and if he will make a statement.

Mr. Douglas Hogg: My right hon. Friend has received no representations on the matters referred to. Having ascertained the facts from the Isle of Man authorities, he is satisfied that the matters are the responsibility of the Isle of Man Government. He has received no indication in this connection of a possible contravention of the European convention on human rights.

Police Forces (Training Manuals)

Mr. Chris Smith: To ask the Secretary of State for the Home Department what information he has as to the content of training manuals used in police forces in relation to HIV infection, AIDS, hepatitis B, and other similar issues; and whether copies of such manuals can be placed in the Library.

Mr. Douglas Hogg: Individual police force training manuals are not held centrally. However, Home Office circulars have been issued to all police forces in England and Wales giving guidance on AIDS (No. 72/1988 on 12 August 1988) and on hepatitis B (No. 48/1989 on 9 June 1989). Copies were sent to the Library.

Lieutenant Colonel Michael Aquino

Mr. Dickens: To ask the Secretary of State for the Home Department if in view of investigations taking place in the United States of America by the criminal investigation division of the Federal Bureau of Investigation, the United States Army, chief of police of the state of Utah and the Attorney-General of County Medolino in northern California of Lieutenant Colonel Michael Aquino of the United States Army involving allegations of serious sexual offences against children, he will take steps to deny him entry into the United Kingdom until such time as all allegations have been tested in a court of law in the United States of America; and if he will make a statement.

Mr. Renton: It is unlikely that action under the immigration rules could be taken on the basis of untested allegations alone, but should Colonel Aquino either come here or apply for an entry clearance to do so, a decision about his eligibility under the immigration rules would be taken in the light of all the information available at the time.

TRANSPORT

Rail Investment

10. **Mr. John Evans:** To ask the Secretary of State for Transport if he has any plans to increase the amount of money available for investment in the railway system.

Mr. Channon: Yes. I expect investment by BR in the railway to be some £781 million this financial year, the highest in real terms since 1962. BR plans to increase its investment by a further 19 per cent. by 1991-92.

Motorway Congestion

12. **Mr. Ian Taylor:** To ask the Secretary of State for Transport what measures he is taking to relieve congestion on the motorways.

Mr. Peter Bottomley: The measures announced by my right hon. Friend on 18 May in "Roads for Prosperity", more than doubling the trunk road programme to over £12 billion, are aimed at relieving congestion on motorways and trunk roads.

Road Safety

13. **Mr. Thurnham:** To ask the Secretary of State for Transport what further measures he is taking to improve road safety.

Mr. Channon: We are now saving 560 lives a year, compared with the position two years ago when I set our overall target.

We have today launched a new campaign against drinking and driving, using fresh TV commercials and publicity material. The basic message remains that "drinking and driving wrecks lives".

British Rail Branch Line Services

15. **Mr. Livsey:** To ask the Secretary of State for Transport what representations he has received regarding the future of British Rail branch line services.

Mr. Portillo: We receive a variety of representations about such services.

Channel Tunnel

17. **Ms. Harman:** To ask the Secretary of State for Transport what representations he has received about the carriage of freight on the rail link from the Channel tunnel through London.

Mr. Portillo: We have received many representations about the importance of rail freight traffic through the Channel tunnel. We have also received representations about the railway lines which British Rail proposes to use to carry this traffic. This is a matter for the board. It is not its current intention to use the proposed new rail link between London and the tunnel for heavy freight trains.

33. **Ms. Armstrong:** To ask the Secretary of State for Transport what representations he has received about the carriage of freight on the rail link from the Channel tunnel through London.

Mr. Portillo: We have received many representations about the importance of rail freight traffic through the Channel tunnel. We have also received representations about the railway lines which British Rail proposes to use to carry this traffic. This is a matter for the board. It is not its current intention to use the proposed rail link between London and the tunnel for heavy freight trains.

Drink-Driving

19. **Mr. Curry:** To ask the Secretary of State for Transport if he will give figures showing the months of the year with the highest incidence of drinking and driving; and if he will explain the reasons underlying the Department of Transport's campaign strategy.

Mr. Peter Bottomley: A good indicator of drink-driving patterns is the number of death and injury accidents involving drivers over the legal limit. These tend to peak in the summer as the monthly figures for 1987 (the latest complete year available) show.

That is why we are today launching a summer drink-drive campaign with two new TV commercials, to complement the regular Christmas campaigns.

The monthly figures are as follows:

Accidents involving death or personal injury where the driver or rider had a blood or alcohol level above the legal limit—1987

	Number
January	680
February	740
March	880
April	890
May	1,140
June	1,050
July	1,060
August	1,100
September	970
October	1,030
November	1,020
December	970

23. **Mr. Tredinnick:** To ask the Secretary of State for Transport what assessment he has made of the role low and non-alcoholic drinks have to play in the campaign against drinking and driving.

Mr. Peter Bottomley: The continuing rapid growth in the demand for non-alcoholic and low-alcoholic drinks (NABLABS) show that they are attractive alternatives for the driver as well as others. This sector of the drinks industry has doubled each year over the last two years. NABLABS mean that no driver has any excuse at all for drinking and driving. There is always an attractive alternative drink available in pubs and clubs. These should be in restaurants, too. Private hosts should ensure the same is true when they entertain.

"Roads for Prosperity"

20. **Mr. Yeo:** To ask the Secretary of State for Transport what representations he has received regarding his White Paper, "Roads for Prosperity".

Mr. Channon: I have received many representations about "Roads for Prosperity". Most express strong support.

London Underground (Automatic Barriers)

21. **Mr. Cohen:** To ask the Secretary of State for Transport when he last discussed with the chairman of London Underground Ltd., the current installation of automatic ticket barriers.

Mr. Portillo: My right hon. Friend met Mr. Newton on 18 May, when the Underground ticketing system was discussed, among other matters.

East Coast Infrastructure

22. **Mr. Cran:** To ask the Secretary of State for Transport whether he has made an assessment of the transport infrastructure requirements of the east coast of England; and if he will make a statement.

Mr. Peter Bottomley: My right hon. Friend announced in "Roads for Prosperity" major improvements to the A1 and other trunk roads in eastern England resulting from our detailed assessment of trunk road needs. It is respectively for British Rail, local authorities and port authorities to assess the need for investment in rail, local roads, airports and ports.

Transport Policy (Environmental Considerations)

24. **Mrs. Mahon:** To ask the Secretary of State for Transport if he will take steps to promote environmental considerations in transport policy.

Mr. Channon: Environmental considerations figure prominently in the development of transport policy. We have recently produced a booklet "Transport and the Environment", which describes our action in this area.

In the key area of vehicle emission standards, my noble Friend the Minister for Housing, Environment and Countryside reached agreement last week with our European partners on much stricter limits for small cars. These will take mandatory effect from 1992.

Volunteer Drivers

25. **Mr. Teddy Taylor:** To ask the Secretary of State for Transport what progress is being made on the EEC directive proposing to restrict the use of volunteer drivers in the use of vehicles for disabled people owned by charities; and if he will make a statement.

Mr. Peter Bottomley: We are continuing to press the European Commission at every level to avoid placing unnecessary restrictions on the drivers of minibuses. Formal discussion of the directive among member states is not expected to start before the autumn. The proposal would have the effect of reducing mobility without improving safety.

Pollution

26. **Ms. Ruddock:** To ask the Secretary of State for Transport what further steps he will take to reduce pollution from motor vehicles.

Mr. Peter Bottomley: We shall be consulting soon on draft regulations to implement the standards which were agreed last year in the European Community for cars, buses and goods vehicles.

My noble Friend the Minister for Housing, Environment and Countryside reached agreement last week with our European partners on much stricter limits for small cars. These will take mandatory effect from 1992.

Roads Programme

27. **Mrs. Dunwoody:** To ask the Secretary of State for Transport what detailed studies of the comparative cost advantages of road and rail access to major cities he carried out before announcing his latest roads programme.

Mr. Peter Bottomley: The relative market shares of road and rail mean that even a 50 per cent. increase in rail travel would be equivalent to less than 5 per cent. of road traffic. Against this background, the Government concluded that the way to tackle congestion on inter-urban roads is by widening existing roads and building new roads, as proposed in "Roads for Prosperity".

37. **Mr. Greg Knight:** To ask the Secretary of State for Transport by how much expenditure will have been increased since 1979 on the trunk road and motorway network when his new expanded roads programme is completed.

Mr. Peter Bottomley: The Government are committed to the greatly expanded road programme announced in "Roads for Prosperity". This will require increased annual expenditure which will be determined in future public expenditure surveys. Capital expenditure on roads has increasd by some 60 per cent. in real terms between 1978-79 and 1989-90.

Mr. Higgins: To ask the Secretary of State for Transport if he will give details of the planned current and capital spending on national and local roads for the next three years, at 1987-88 prices.

Mr. Peter Bottomley: Figures for current and capital expenditure on national and local roads in Great Britain for the period sought, at 1987-88 prices as shown in the table.

£ million in 1987-88 prices			
	1989-90	1990-91	1991-92
National roads			
Current	117	105	112
Capital	1,138	1,384	1,384
Local roads			
Current	1,639	1,627	1,628
Capital	778	738	750

Structural maintenance on national roads is classified as capital expenditure, but on local roads local authorities treat it largely as current expenditure.

British Rail (Privatisation)

28. **Mr. Prescott:** To ask the Secretary of State for Transport if he will place in the Library a copy of the report prepared for his Department by Deloitte, Haskins and Sells, entitled, "Study of Structural Options for Railway Privatisation."

Mr. Channon: No. Deloitte, Haskins and Sells was not asked to make recommendations or reach conclusions: its study for the Department and British Rail consists of a set of working papers which will form a basis for further studies. They contain commercially confidential information and would be unsuitable for publication.

If a decision is taken to privatise British Rail, I shall publish the Government's conclusions in due course.

Rail Transport

29. **Mr. Blunkett:** To ask the Secretary of State for Transport what plans he has to encourage the use of rail transport.

Mr. Portillo: We consider that travellers and freight consigners should generally be free to make their own choices between different means of transport, in the light of their relative cost and quality. The Government's chief concern is to ensure that each means of transport can operate efficiently, provide services linked closely to customer demand, and compete on equal terms.

Safety Inspections

30. **Mr. Barry Field:** To ask the Secretary of State for Transport what progress he has made in transferring safety inspections to regulatory bodies such as Lloyd's.

Mr. Portillo: Most statutory survey work has already been delegated to approved classification societies. The issue of delegation is kept under continuous review.

Railways (Select Committee Report)

31. **Mr. Simon Hughes:** To ask the Secretary of State for Transport what representations he has received urging him to seek a debate on the report of the Transport Select Committee on the future of the railways.

Mr. Portillo: The last report of the Transport Select Committee concerned with railways was on the financing of rail services, to which the Government responded in March 1988. We have received no representations for a debate on this report.

East London Assessment Study

32. **Mr. Corbyn:** To ask the Secretary of State for Transport what representations he has received concerning the east London assessment study; and when he plans to publish the consultants' report.

Mr. Peter Bottomley: We have received representations on various aspects of this assessment study from the London local authority associations, the London planning advisory committee, individual local authorities, national organisations with an interest in transport matters, amenity groups, residents associations, various other bodies, and members of the public.

The consultants are expected to report in the summer. Their report will be published as soon as possible.

South-East Wales (Road Link)

34. **Mr. Roy Hughes:** To ask the Secretary of State for Transport if he will discuss with the chairman of British Rail the possibility of using the former Severn tunnel junction site to provide a road-rail link to south-east Wales.

Mr. Portillo: British Rail is currently examining, in consultation with local interests, possible sites for road-rail freight terminals in planning for future channel tunnel freight services. Its proposals will be set out in the plan which it has to produce by the end of this year under section 40 of the Channel Tunnel Act.

Streetworks (Horne Report)

35. **Mr. Lofthouse:** To ask the Secretary of State for Transport when he intends to introduce legislation on the Horne report on streetworks.

Mr. Peter Bottomley: As soon as there is a suitable opportunity. Detailed proposals have been prepared and an opportunity is currently being given to interested parties to comment on them.

Street Lighting

36. **Mr. Cousins:** To ask the Secretary of State for Transport what was the expenditure in real terms on local authority street lighting in the last three financial years.

Mr. Peter Bottomley: Figures for current and capital expenditure by local authorities in Great Britain on public highways lighting at current prices are estimated to have been as follows:

	£ million
1986-87	235
1987-88	230

Figures for expenditure in 1988-89 are not yet available.

British Rail

38. **Mr. David Marshall:** To ask the Secretary of State for Transport when he next intends to meet the chairman and the board of British Rail.

Mr. Portillo: My right hon. Friend next plans to meet the chairman of British Rail on 11 July.

London Underground (Cabling)

Mr. Cohen: To ask the Secretary of State for Transport (1) if he will call for a report from the chairman of London Regional Transport ascertaining when it is planned that all PVC cable on the London Underground will be replaced by low smoke zero halogen cable; and if he will provide a special grant from Her Majesty's Government to speed up this replacement programme; and if he will make a statement;

(2) if he will call for a report from the chairman of London Regional Transport to ascertain how many electricians are employed on the London Underground; how many are involved in fitting and maintaining cable underground; how many are fully working on the LSZH programme; and if he will provide a special grant from Her Majesty's Government to London Underground Ltd. for the employment of more electricians; and if he will make a statement;

(3) what assessment he has made of the implications for safety of potential toxicity and thick smoke resulting from a fire of *(a)* PVC cabling and *(b)* arcing cables, on the London Underground.

Mr Portillo: The assessment of safety on the Underground is in the first instance a matter for London Underground Ltd. I understand that the Underground stopped installing PVC cable some five years ago and that a replacement programme is under way.

London Underground Ltd. and its consultants are now reconsidering the priorities within this programme, using hazard analysis techniques. The railway inspectorate is being kept fully informed.

Arcing occurs when the cable insulation fails. The risk can be reduced by ensuring that the circuit breakers provided to detect arcing and switch off the power are maintained in the correct setting.

The numbers and deployment of electricians are management matters for London Underground Ltd. It is for LUL to determine appropriate staffing levels in the light of LRT's statutory duty to have due regard to efficiency, economy and safety of operation. The costs involved will be taken into account in the annual discussions of LRT's financing requirements.

Seat Belts (Children)

Mr. Colvin: To ask the Secretary of State for Transport whether he is proposing that children aged one to three years should be required to use adult seat belts where no more suitable restraint is available; and if he will make a statement.

Mr. Peter Bottomley: This issue was discussed in our consultation document "Rear Seat Belt Wearing by Children". Most experts were against making it a legal requirement that very young children must be restrained in adult belts when appropriate child restraints are not available. We will take this into account in preparing the regulations which we plan to bring before Parliament for approval very shortly.

No responsible parents should wait for the law before properly restraining their children in the car.

Commercial Vehicles (Emissions)

Sir Peter Emery: To ask the Secretary of State for Transport if he will introduce new statutory standards based on the mass of emissions from commercial vehicles and backed by regular roadside checks.

Mr. Peter Bottomley: We shall consult interested parties shortly on draft regulations to introduce the limits on the mass of gaseous emissions as set by Community directive 88/77/EEC. The Commission is expected to propose a second stage of limits later this year, which will also include a mass emission limit for particulates.

The Department has over the past two years substantially increased its programme of roadside checks on the condition of heavy goods vehicles. This includes a check on smoke emissions. We are considering how future emission standards might most effectively be enforced.

Air Safety

Mr. Andrew F. Bennett: To ask the Secretary of State for Transport if he will meet the chairman of the Civil Aviation Authority to discuss the implementation of the recommendations made following the Manchester aircraft disaster in 1985 that seats in rows adjacent to the overwing emergency exit should be removed, and that the width in the gap in the forward galley partition should be increased; and if he will make a statement.

Mr. Peter Bottomley: The statutory responsibility for the regulation of air transport safety lies with the Civil Aviation Authority. I have drawn the hon. Member's question to the attention of the chairman of the CAA and have asked him to write to the hon. Member direct.

Press Briefings

Mr. Grocott: To ask the Secretary of State for Transport what guidelines he follows in determining which journalists are invited to press briefings by his Department.

Mr. Peter Bottomley: This depends upon matters under discussion.

Offshore Supply Vessels

Sir David Price: To ask the Secretary of State for Transport what steps he intends to take to ensure that all offshore supply vessels operating in the British zone of the North sea under foreign flags are manned to levels compatible with those laid down by his Department for United Kingdom registered vessels; and if he will make a statement.

Mr. Portillo Manning levels on foreign flag offshore supply vessels are checked in the course of port state control inspections and confirmed to be in accordance with the safe manning certificate issued by the flag state.

London Underground (Safety Management)

Mr. Wray: To ask the Secretary of State for Transport what proposals he has to tackle urgently the problem of lack of effective leadership in safety management of the London Underground.

Mr. Portillo: I refer the hon. Member to the answer my right hon. Friend gave to my hon. Friend the Member for Westminster, North (Mr. Wheeler) on 23 May at columns *502-3*.

Roads (Suffolk and Norfolk)

Mr. David Porter: To ask the Secretary of State for Transport what representations he has received about roads in Suffolk and Norfolk following publication of the White Paper, "Roads for Prosperity".

Mr. Peter Bottomley: My right hon. Friend has received a number of generally favourable representations, including some from my hon. Friend.

A12 (Lowestoft-Ipswich)

Mr. David Porter: To ask the Secretary of State for Transport what timetable he envisages for workings on the A12 Lowestoft-Ipswich, following publication of the White Paper, "Roads for Prosperity".

Mr. Peter Bottomley: We have not yet set a timetable for these improvements. The first step is to appoint design agents. This will be done in the coming months. A roads report will be issued later this year, setting out the expanded road programme in detail.

Teesport (Coal Discharge)

Mr. Mullin: To ask the Secretary of State for Transport what was the country of origin of the coal discharged at Teesport by the MM Ave between 7 and 13 May; and at which port it was loaded.

Mr. Portillo: The origin of the Ave's cargo is not known, but I understand it was loaded at Maputo, Mozambique. The country of origin of a cargo is not a matter which is relevant to the responsibilities of the Department.

Shetland (Fishing Boat-Submarine Collision)

Mr. Foulkes: To ask the Secretary of State for Transport what information he has about a collision between a Norwegian fishing boat and a French Agousta class submarine off Shetland on Monday 22 May; what inquiries have been carried out into the collision; and if he will make a statement.

Mr. Portillo: During the afternoon of 22 May Her Majesty's Coastguard rescue centre in Aberdeen received a report that the nets of the Norwegian trawler Strand Senior had been fouled by a French submarine. The Coastguard established that the trawler was in no danger.

The reported position of the incident was 40 miles north north west of Unst and thus well outside United Kingdom territorial waters. Any further investigation is therefore for the French and Norwegian authorities.

Fylde Coast (Easterly Bypass)

Mr. Jack: To ask the Secretary of State for Transport when he expects to receive the consulting engineer's report on the proposed Fylde coast easterly bypass; and if he will make a statement.

Mr. Peter Bottomley: The Fylde coast easterly bypass is one of the options being considered for linking the M55 to the A585 at Norcross. We expect to receive the consultant's report in the autumn.

Air Traffic Control

Mr. Colvin: To ask the Secretary of State for Transport what is the Government's total capital investment in air traffic control for the next decade.

Mr. Channon: The Civil Aviation Authority has said that it plans to invest approximately £600 million in air traffic control-related projects over the next decade.

Vale of Rheidol Railway

Dr. Marek: To ask the Secretary of State for Transport if he will now give the net price received by British Rail for the sale of the Vale of Rheidol railway to the Brecon Mountain Railway Company.

Mr. Portillo: The price paid to British Rail for the sale of the Vale of Rheidol railway to the Brecon Mountain Railway Company was £306,500.

Vehicle Excise Reminder Forms

Mr. Prescott: To ask the Secretary of State for Transport if there are any plans to include private advertising material with the V11 vehicle excise duty forms issued by the DVLC in Swansea; and if he will make a statement.

Mr. Channon: This is an idea that has been considered on a number of occasions. There are no present plans to take it further.

Road Bridges (Strengthening)

Mr. Prescott: To ask the Secretary of State for Transport who will be responsible for meeting the full costs incurred in strengthening Britain's road bridges in order to cope with the introduction of 40-tonne lorries.

Mr. Channon: The relevant highway authority.

Exeter (Northern Bypass)

Mr. Maxwell-Hyslop: To ask the Secretary of State for Transport (1) whether the proposal to construct a northern bypass for Exeter from the M5 originated in a proposal put to his Department by Devon county council as the highway authority;

(2) whether the proposal to construct a northern bypass for Exeter from the M5 is a scheme originating in his Department, without consultation with, or the approval of, Devon county council.

Mr. Peter Bottomley: A northern bypass of Exeter was first mooted when alternative routes for the M5 were under investigation in the mid-1960s. This work was updated before my right hon. Friend decided to include the scheme in "Roads for Prosperity". Devon county council passed a resolution last year requesting the addition of an Exeter northern bypass to the programme.

Air Transport (Safety of Materials)

Mr. Prescott: To ask the Secretary of State for Transport what evaluation his Department has made of the safety of air transport of *(a)* plutonium metal, *(b)* plutonium dioxide powder, *(c)* isotopes of enriched uranium and *(d)* radio isotopes for nuclear and industrial uses.

Mr. Channon: The transport of such materials has been studied by the advisory committee on the safe transport of radioactive materials (ACTRAM). The results have been published in two reports: "The Transport of Radioactive Materials for Medical and Industrial Use" and "The Transport of Civil Plutonium by Air". Copies of both reports have been placed in the Library.

Enriched uranium, being potentially less hazardous than plutonium, does not call for a separate study.

SCOTLAND

Southern General Hospital (X-ray Department)

Mr. Sillars: To ask the Secretary of State for Scotland how many members of staff of the X-ray department at the Southern general hospital have suffered health problems as a result of excessive chemical fumes arising out of the X-ray process.

Mr. Michael Forsyth: This is a matter for the Greater Glasgow health board, but I understand from the board that following health screening, three members of staff were identified as having allergic sensitivity to the chemicals used in the X-ray processing.

Mr. Sillars: To ask the Secretary of State for Scotland what investigations have been carried out to determine whether an excess of chemical fumes exists or existed in the X-ray department of the Southern general hospital; what were the findings; when they were made known to management; what recommendations were made; and what remedial action has been taken.

Mr. Michael Forsyth: This is a matter for the Greater Glasgow health board, but I understand from the board that in May and December 1988 two reports on the emission of chemical fumes in X-ray departments were produced by the board's occupational health department and by the Health and Safety Executive respectively. On both occasions the concentrations in the atmosphere of the substances measured were found to be well within the current occupational exposure limits. As a result of its own investigations and the recommendations of the Health and Safety Executive, a number of measures including better ventilation have been introduced by the health board to improve the working conditions in the departments concerned.

Medical Education and Research

Mr. Wray: To ask the Secretary of State for Scotland what response he has given to the observations and criticisms of the Medical Research Council on the White Paper, "Working for Patients", regarding medical *(a)* education and *(b)* research in Scotland.

Mr. Michael Forsyth: The comments of the Medical Research Council on the White Paper have been acknowledged and are being considered along with the many responses received from other bodies. They will be taken into account in the implementation of the White Paper proposals in Scotland.

Chlorine

Mr. Wallace: To ask the Secretary of State for Scotland what information he has regarding levels of chlorine in public water supplies in Scotland.

Lord James Douglas-Hamilton: Detailed information on levels of chlorine in public water supplies in Scotland is not held centrally. Water put into supply normally has a level of residual chlorine of 0·1–0·5 mg per litre according to circumstances.

Effluent Standards

Mr. Ron Davies: To ask the Secretary of State for Scotland if he will list those applications made to him in the current year by water authorities for the lowering of effluent standards.

Lord James Douglas-Hamilton: My right hon. and learned Friend has received no applications from the islands councils for a lowering of standards for their discharges during the current year. On the mainland, standards are set by the river purification boards which are responsible for giving consents to discharge effluent in their areas.

Guest Houses (Rating)

Mrs. Ray Michie: To ask the Secretary of State for Scotland how many guest houses in *(a)* Scotland and *(b)* Argyll and Bute will be liable to pay both non-domestic rates and the personal community charge for everyone who lives on the premises.

Mr. Lang: This information is not held centrally. Where, however a person is solely or mainly resident in premises which are subject to non-domestic rates, there is a reduction in the valuation for rating of the property to take account of this.

Mrs. Ray Michie: To ask the Secretary of State for Scotland what is his Department's estimate of the average difference for owners of guest houses in Scotland between the previous rating system and the current system whereby owners of guest houses catering for more than six people are liable to pay both non-domestic rates and the personal community charge for everyone living on the premises.

Mr. Lang: The information that would be required to carry out an estimate of the kind envisaged by the hon. Member is not held centrally.

Community Charge

Mrs. Ray Michie: To ask the Secretary of State for Scotland whether he will consider exempting from liability for the standard community charge accommodation which is unoccupied and where the person who would otherwise be liable for payment is registered elsewhere for the purpose of undertaking a full-time course of education.

Mr. Lang: No. Students in this position and who cannot reasonably be expected to give up their homes on moving to another area for educational purposes may be eligible for a two homes allowance which is payable by the Scottish Education Department as an addition to the student grant.

Mr. Malcolm Bruce : To ask the Secretary of State for Scotland if he will publish a table for each district council in Scotland of the total yield of the community charge payment by the districts to the region in the current financial year.

Mr. Lang: The figures given in the table are the estimated yield in 1989-90 to the relevant regional councils of community charge payments made by residents and standard community charge payers within each of the districts of Scotland.

Estimated Yield of Regional Community Charge

Districts	£000
Berwickshire	2,565
Ettrick and Lauderdale	4,428
Roxburgh	4,780
Tweeddale	2,026
Clackmannan	6,825
Falkirk	20,974
Stirling	11,695
Annandale and Eskdale	4,981
Nithsdale	7,778
Stewartry	3,368
Wigtown	4,177
Dunfermline	20,924
Kirkcaldy	24,190
North East Fife	11,119
Aberdeen City	30,134
Banff and Buchan	11,702
Gordon	9,702
Kincardine and Deeside	6,588
Moray	12,083
Badenoch and Strathspey	1,677
Caithness	3,589
Inverness	8,164
Lochaber	2,630
Nairn	1,371
Ross and Cromarty	6,377
Skye and Lochalsh	1,711
Sutherland	1,958
East Lothian	18,304
Edinburgh City	95,541
Midlothian	17,236
West Lothian	29,143
Argyll and Bute	10,267
Bearsden and Milngavie	6,057
Clydebank	7,314
Clydesdale	8,585
Cumbernauld and Kilsyth	8,862
Cumnock and Doon Valley	6,425
Cunninghame	20,697
Dumbarton	11,597
East Kilbride	12,258
Eastwood	8,565
Glasgow City	106,491
Hamilton	15,505
Inverclyde	14,334
Kilmarnock and Loudoun	11,935
Kyle and Carrick	17,250
Monklands	15,027
Motherwell	21,616
Renfrew	29,652
Strathkelvin	12,857
Angus	15,427
Dundee City	28,484
Perth and Kinross	20,975
Total District	797,922

Note: The estimated figures do not take account of Community Water Charges.

Fishing Fleet

Mr. Salmond: To ask the Secretary of State for Scotland if, further to his answer of 23 May, *Official Report,* column *515,* he will seek and evaluate estimates from the Scottish Fishermen's Federation and the Scottish Fishermen's Organisation on the impact on Scottish fleet costs in a full year of a 5 per cent. interest rate rise.

Mr. Michael Forsyth: I have already noted the estimate of £7·5 million which the hon. Member has quoted and which may have been provided by the Scottish Fishermen's Federation. As I indicated previously, many elements affect the impact of individual cost charges on overall profitability. My noble Friend the Minister of State will meet representatives of the Scottish Fishermen's Federation tomorrow to discuss a paper which the federation submitted to him.

Mrs. Sinclair (Ministerial Visit)

Mr. Wilson: To ask the Secretary of State for Scotland which media outlets were notified by the Scottish Office of the home visit by the hon. Member for Stirling (Mr. Forsyth) to Mrs. Sinclair on Sunday 14 May; what advance notice of press involvement was given to Mrs. Sinclair; and what were the costs to public funds.

Mr. Rifkind: The Scottish information office arranged for media representatives to be told of the visit of my hon. Friend the Parliamentary Under-Secretary of State responsible for health and education to the home of Mrs. Margaret Sinclair and issued a press statement on my hon. Friend's behalf. The statement was sent to the *Glasgow Herald, Scotsman,* the *Daily Record,* the *Scottish Daily Express,* the *Aberdeen Press and Journal,* the *Dundee Courier,* Scottish Television, the BBC, Radio Forth and Radio Clyde.

No advance notice of press involvement was given to Mrs. Sinclair.

The total cost to public funds is estimated at approximately £40.

Correspondence

Mr. Kennedy: To ask the Secretary of State for Scotland when he expects to be in a position to respond to the letter of 19 April from the hon. Member for Ross, Cromarty and Skye on matters of concern to shellfish growers.

Mr. Michael Forsyth: My noble Friend the Minister of State responded on 5 June to the letter of 19 April from the hon. Member on matters of concern to shellfish growers.

Property Services Agency

Mr. Dunnachie: To ask the Secretary of State for Scotland if he will extend the Property Services Agency policy whereby 1 per cent. of the capital expenditure on major building projects is devoted to an arts involvement to include the capital programmes of local authorities.

Mr. Lang: No. It is for local authorities to determine their expenditure priorities within the resources my right hon. and learned Friend makes available to them.

Regions (Rates)

Mr. Malcolm Bruce: To ask the Secretary of State for Scotland if he will publish a table showing the total yield from the rate payment to the regions for the last financial year.

Mr. Lang: The information is set out in the table.

Estimated total rate income 1988-89

	£ million
Borders	22·7
Central	86·1
Dumfries and Galloway	35·9
Fife	124·8
Grampian	156·9
Highland	60·0
Lothian	290·4
Strathclyde	740·0
Tayside	114·2
Islands Councils	
Orkney	9·1
Shetland	50·4
Western Isles	6·7
Total regions and islands	1,697·2

Notes:

1. Rate income is less Domestic Rate Relief.
2. Estimated figures calculated using actual penny rate products, rateable values and rate poundages from "Rating Review".
3. Figures exclude rates collected by the Regions on behalf of the District Councils.

NHS Reform

Mr. Kirkwood: To ask the Secretary of State for Scotland when he intends publishing a list of hospitals and other medical units that have expressed an interest in becoming self governing; and if he will make a statement.

Mr. Michael Forsyth: Health boards in Scotland have not yet been asked to invite from hospitals and other units expressions of interest in self-governing status. I shall be discussing this with health board chairmen later this month. I then intend to make rapid progress in identifying those hospitals and so on that wish to consider becoming self-governing. In the meantime, I have received a number of informal expressions of interest.

Written Answers to Questions

Tuesday 13 June 1989

EDUCATION AND SCIENCE

"Working for Patients"

Mr. Kirkwood: To ask the Secretary of State for Education and Science if he will make a statement on his Department's role in proposals in the White Paper "Working for Patients" as they affect *(a)* teaching hospitals, *(b)* academic research, *(c)* student teaching and *(d)* academic departments of general practice.

Mr. Jackson: Development of the proposals in the Cm 555 is for my right hon. and learned Friend the Secretary of State for Health. However, the inter-relationship with education provision is recognised by close working between our two Departments, particularly through a steering group which also includes representatives of the Committee of Vice-Chancellors and Principals and other bodies with an interest in medical and dental education.

Medical Curriculum

Mr. Kirkwood: To ask the Secretary of State for Education and Science whether he intends to make health promotion a mandatory part of the medical curriculum.

Mr. Jackson: This topic is already covered by the recommendations on basic medical education made by the education committee of the General Medical Council in the light of which medical schools determine the content of their courses.

Voluntary Schools

Ms. Armstrong: To ask the Secretary of State for Education and Science how many bids for funding were received from voluntary schools in the latest year for which figures are available.

Mr. Kenneth Baker: A total of 365 bids for major capital projects were received in respect of voluntary schools during the financial year 1988-89 for approval to start in 1989-90.

Ms. Armstrong: To ask the Secretary of State for Education and Science how many bids from voluntary schools were successful in the latest year for which figures are available.

Mr. Kenneth Baker: A total of 53 projects were approved for a 1989-90 start.

Ms. Armstrong: To ask the Secretary of State for Education and Science what was the total amount of money allocated to voluntary schools in the latest year for which figures are available.

Mr. Kenneth Baker: A total of £86·1 million for 1989-90.

Ms. Armstrong: To ask the Secretary of State for Education and Science what was the total amount of money bid for by the voluntary schools in the latest year for which figures are available.

Mr. Kenneth Baker: The 365 bids for capital projects submitted in respect of voluntary schools in 1988-89 totalled £164,889,000, of which £85,841,000 was for expenditure in 1989-90.

Under-Fives (Curriculum)

Ms. Armstrong: To ask the Secretary of State for Education and Science if he will list the organisations invited to submit evidence to the committee examining the curriculum for the under-fives.

Mrs. Rumbold: When the committee inquiring into the content of the educational experience of under-fives was established, I issued a general invitation to any interested party to submit written evidence or opinion.

Ms. Armstrong: To ask the Secretary of State for Education and Science if he will place the submissions made to the committees considering the curriculum for under-fives in the Library.

Mrs. Rumbold: Most organisations submitting evidence are making their submissions public. I shall ask the committee to consider whether any additional measures to keep the House informed would be desirable.

Hazel Court School, Eastbourne

Mr. Gow: To ask the Secretary of State for Education and Science what are the responsibilities of the East Sussex county council to provide speech therapy and physio-therapy for those children who need those services at Hazel Court school, Eastbourne.

Mr. Kenneth Baker: Responsibility for the provision of speech therapy and physiotherapy services has rested with health authorities since the reorganisation of the National Health Service in 1974. Although an amendment to the Education Act 1981 contained in the Education Reform Act 1988 enables local education authorities, such as East Sussex, to provide non-educational provision, (which includes speech therapy and physiotherapy) for children with statements of special educational needs, this has not affected health authorities' general responsibilities.

Local education authorities will be aware that the recent High Court case of R *v* Lancashire county council ex parte CM ruled that speech therapy could be considered as either educational or non-educational provision.

Student Awards

Mr. Simon Hughes: To ask the Secretary of State for Education and Science how many students pursuing degree courses in nursing in the current academic year are in receipt of local education authority mandatory awards.

Mr. Jackson: This information is not collected centrally.

Nursing (Degree Courses)

Mr. Simon Hughes: To ask the Secretary of State for Education and Science if he will list those educational establishments offering degree courses in nursing, giving the number of such places offered by each for the current academic year.

Mr. Jackson: I will write to the hon. Member.

Top-up Loans

Mr. Simon Hughes: To ask the Secretary of State for Education and Science if he will publish in the *Official Report* the data used to construct chart 7 on page 11 of "Top-up Loans for Students" (Cm. 520).

Mr. Jackson: The data underlying the chart were as follows:

Average gross annual earnings of working males aged 30-39

Year	Earnings of male graduates £	Earnings of all working males £
1979	7,909	5,728
1980	9,119	6,931
1981	10,876	7,867
1982	11,822	8,264
1983	13,374	9,220
1984	14,589	9,814
1985	13,864	10,575

Source: General Household Surveys 1979-1985.

Institute of Food Research

Mr. Ron Davies: To ask the Secretary of State for Education and Science what projections he has made for staffing levels in the Institute of Food Research.

Mr. Jackson: None. This is a matter for the Agricultural and Food Research Council which has responsibility for the Institute of Food Research.

Mr. Ron Davies: To ask the Secretary of State for Education and Science when he expects to be able to announce his decision on the future of the Institute of Food Research laboratories at Bristol.

Mr. Jackson: The management of the Institute of Food Research and the timing of any announcement is a matter for the Agricultural and Food Research Council.

ATTORNEY-GENERAL

Legal Reform

Mr. Lawrence: To ask the Attorney-General what assessment he has made of the cost to the public purse of implementing the Green Papers on the legal profession.

The Attorney-General: The Green Papers set out proposals for the elimination of rules in the legal profession which may not be necessary in order to ensure standards of competence and conduct. The question, therefore, in relation to any particular rule is whether it is necessary for this purpose. If a rule is not necessary for this purpose its elimination is not likely to increase cost.

Mr. Lawrence: To ask the Attorney-General what response he is making to the Coopers and Lybrand report assessing the increase of the cost to the Exchequer of extending rights of audience in the high courts to solicitors in standard fee legal aid cases from £9·8 million to £17·7 million.

The Attorney-General: All the submissions made to the Lord Chancellor on the Green Papers are now being carefully considered, with a view to a response being made before the summer recess. The Lord Chancellor has, however, received a supplementary response from the Law Society which suggests that, contrary to the contentions in the Coopers and Lybrand report, for many straightforward Crown court cases it would be cheaper if a solicitor carried out the advocacy personally rather than employing a barrister.

TRADE AND INDUSTRY

Securities and Investment Board

Mr. Tim Smith: To ask the Chancellor of the Duchy of Lancaster when he expects to receive the annual report of the Securities and Investments board for the year ended 31 March 1989; and if he will take steps to bring forward a motion for the House to take note of the report.

Mr. Maude: My right hon. and noble Friend received the Securities and Investments board's annual report for the year ended 31 March 1989 on 5 June and copies of it were laid before Parliament on 6 June. The question of a debate on a motion taking note of the report is a matter for my right hon. Friend the Lord President of the Council and Leader of the House.

Timber (European Parliament Scheme)

Mr. Malcolm Bruce: To ask the Chancellor of the Duchy of Lancaster what is his policy towards the scheme approved by the European Parliament which would help nations producing tropical timber to move towards sustainable forest management within five years.

Mr. Atkins *[holding answer 12 June 1989]:* I refer the hon. Gentleman to the reply given by the Prime Minister to the hon. Member for Linlithgow (Mr. Dalyell) on 8 June at column *368*.

WALES

Hospitals (Self-Government)

Mr. Geraint Howells: To ask the Secretary of State for Wales when he intends publishing a list of medical units that have expressed an interest in becoming self-governing; and if he will make a statement.

Mr. Grist: I have asked the chairmen of Welsh health authorities to inform me of discussions that they are having on this subject with the hospitals.

Mr. Michael: To ask the Secretary of State for Wales how many hospitals in Wales have so far expressed interest in self-governing status.

Mr. Grist: None so far, but I have asked the chairmen of Welsh health authorities to inform me of any discussions that they have with hospitals on this subject.

General Practice Budgets

Mr. Michael: To ask the Secretary of State for Wales how many general practitioner practices in Wales have expressed interest to date in establishing their own practice budgets.

Mr. Grist: No practice has yet made a formal approach. This is what I would expect since I and Welsh Office officials have yet to complete our discussions with a range of interested parties in Wales, on the implementation of the proposals set out in the White Paper "Working for Patients".

ENERGY

"Climate in Crisis"

Mr. Flynn: To ask the Secretary of State for Energy if his Department will seek to obtain a video cassette and transcript of the BBC2 nature series special programme "Climate in Crisis" broadcast on 5 June.

Mr. Parkinson: My Department has a copy of the BBC2 programme "Climate in Crisis".

Nuclear Reactors

Dr. Thomas: To ask the Secretary of State for Energy when the United Kingdom Atomic Energy Authority reactors Dido and Lido at the Atomic Energy Research Establishment were *(a)* nominated on the facilities list of nuclear plants open to safeguards and *(b)* first visited by safeguards inspectors; and if the reactors have ever been withdrawn from safeguards.

Mr. Parkinson: The DIDO reactor at AERE Harwell has never been nominated for the facilities list. The LIDO reactor was shut down in 1974 and therefore never included on the United Kingdom facilities list.

Thorp Project

Mr. Alan W. Williams: To ask the Secretary of State for Energy if, in view of the lack of confidence expressed by the Central Electricity Generating Board in reprocessing spent fuel from advanced gas cooled reactors at Sellafield, and of the Central Electricity Generating Board's plans to build alternative dry storage facilities at Heysham, he will reconsider the Thorp project; and whether, if cancellation costs are not prohibitive, he will take a decision now to cancel Thorp.

Mr. Michael Spicer: The future of THORP is already assured. British Nuclear Fuels plc has contracts valued at some £4 billion and is negotiating with utilities in the Federal Republic of Germany for additional contracts, worth some £1·6 billion, which will help to guarantee the future of the plant well into the next century. The decision on whether to submit a planning application for a dry buffer store at Heysham is a matter for the CEGB.

AGRICULTURE, FISHERIES AND FOOD

Agricultural Credit Corporation

Mr. Boswell: To ask the Minister of Agriculture, Fisheries and Food if he will make a statement on the future of the Agricultural Credit Corporation.

Mr. Donald Thompson: Decisions on the future of the Agricultural Credit Corporation, which is a private company limited by guarantee, are for the board of the corporation.

Under the provisions of section 64 of the Agriculture Act 1967 Government support was provided in respect of guarantees given by the corporation on bank loans for agricultural and horticultural businesses. These powers expired on 31 March 1989.

I have been reviewing the need for a continuation of such powers and have concluded that it is no longer appropriate for the Government to continue making special provision for this sector.

The Government take the view that public funds for bank loan guarantees should be targeted at those who do not have the necessary security or track record to obtain bank loans through the commercial market and yet have the potential for increasing national prosperity and the generation of additional employment. The Government are, however, considering the feasibility of whether the loan guarantee scheme operated by the Department of Employment, which helps small firms which would otherwise not be able to obtain finance, can be extended to include small firms in agriculture and horticulture.

Slaughterhouses

Mr. Redmond: To ask the Minister of Agriculture, Fisheries and Food if he will review the procedure for slaughterhouses catering solely for the domestic meat market, to have a pre-veterinery inspection, as for export-licensed slaughterhouses; and if he will make a statement.

Mr. Donald Thompson: I have already announced my intention to introduce ante-mortem inspection in non-exporting abattoirs by 1 January 1991 to the hon. Member for South Shields (Dr. Clark) on 13 March 1989 at column *84*. I have also decided that we should move towards a single set of rules for all slaughterhouses producing meat for human consumption. Discussions with the Commission and other member states on the arrangements which are to operate in the single market after 1992 will have a bearing on the implementation of this decision and its timing. I shall be discussing the issues with those in this country who have an interest.

Food Research Projects

Mr. Ron Davies: To ask the Minister of Agriculture, Fisheries and Food if he will list those food research projects which are financed by his Ministry.

Mr. Ryder: Last year the Ministry funded 436 research projects on food. Details can be found in the draft "National Programme of Food R & D 1988/89", a copy of which I am placing in the Library of the House.

Agriculture and Food Research Council

Mr. Ron Davies: To ask the Minister of Agriculture, Fisheries and Food what discussions he has had concerning the research priorities of the Agriculture and Food Research Council.

Mr. Ryder: My Department is in regular contact with the Agricultural and Food Research Council (AFRC) at all levels. Moreover, my chief scientific adviser and the Secretary of the AFRC are both members of the Priorities Board for Research and Development in Agriculture and Food which advises United Kingdom Agriculture Ministers and the chairman of the AFRC on priorities in research and development in agriculture and food.

BSE

Mr. Boswell: To ask the Minister of Agriculture, Fisheries and Food whether he proposes to take any further action in the light of the Southwood report on bovine spongiform encephalopathy.

Mr. MacGregor: The Government have already taken wide-ranging action to deal with this new disease problem and has acted on all the recommendations made by the Southwood working party which was set up to look at all aspects of the disease, including any human health implications.

Although the Southwood working party regarded the risk to humans as remote, the Government acted on its recommendation that, as a precautionary measure, all cattle suspected as having BSE should be slaughtered and destroyed to take them out of the food chain.

As a matter of extreme prudence, the Southwood working party also suggested that certain offals should not be used in the manufacture of baby foods. We established in February that these offals are not in fact currently used by baby food manufacturers. In order to provide even more reassurance to the public, I indicated then that we would bring forward regulations to ensure that there is no possibility of their use in the future.

In working out the details, I have concluded that a better way of dealing with this would be to ensure that the relevant types of bovine offals should be rejected at slaughterhouses for all cattle so that they cannot be used for human consumption in any way. These offals, which include brain, spinal cord, thymus, spleen and tonsils, will have to be stained in the slaughterhouse and disposed of under conditions similar to those applying to unfit meat. This approach also deals with a separate problem, namely, ensuring that if there is any risk that there are cattle incubating the disease but not showing clinical symptoms which are not being slaughtered and destroyed, their offals do not enter the food chain either.

Detailed proposals for regulations under the Food Act implementing this change will be issued for consultation, as required by the Act, very shortly.

Untreated Milk

Mr. Gill: To ask the Minister of Agriculture, Fisheries and Food if he is now able to announce his decision on future sales of untreated milk.

Mr. MacGregor: My right hon. Friends the Secretaries of State for Health and for Wales and I are grateful to the very large number of individuals and organisations—over 1,200 in all—who responded to our consultation paper on untreated milk.

The proposal for a ban on sales of untreated milk was supported by the enforcement authorities and by a number of other organisations, mainly those concerned with public health. Organisations and individuals representing producer interests were opposed to a ban. But the main volume of correspondence came from organisations and individuals representing consumers, the overwhelming majority of whom were also opposed to a ban. Their arguments were:

—they preferred to drink untreated milk, in spite of the additional health risks which this might involve; and
—in accordance with the Government's general philosophy, they should be allowed to decide for themselves whether or not to continue drinking untreated milk.

Having carefully considered the representations which have been made—and in particular the large number received from individuals—my right hon. Friends and I have concluded that the consumer view should prevail. We therefore propose to continue to allow sales of untreated milk. But we recognise that this would continue to present a degree of public health risk, which we are anxious to do what we reasonably can to minimise. We are accordingly proposing that in future:

—untreated milk should be more fully labelled, so that the consumer knows that it has not been heat-treated and may contain harmful organisms;
—it should be subject to more sophisticated tests, which will have to be reflected in higher milk and dairies charges for producers; and
—the procedure under regulation 20 of the Milk and Dairies (General) Regulations 1959 should be simplified to facilitate the issue of heat treatment orders in cases where untreated milk constitutes a threat to health.

Proposals for regulations will be issued shortly to interested parties in the usual way and will indicate the time scale for the various changes proposed. I recognise that new labelling requirements in particular cannot be introduced overnight.

The consultation document also sought views on untreated cream and on cheese made from untreated milk. In both cases there appears to be a need for more informative labelling and I shall be considering this in the light of our Community obligations. Action on goat and sheep milk must await the necessary primary legislation, but prima facie there is a case for making these milks subject to the same rules as cows milk.

OVERSEAS DEVELOPMENT

Central America

Mr. Pawsey: To ask the Secretary of State for Foreign and Commonwealth Affairs how much aid is provided by the United Kingdom to Central America; and what form it takes, giving figures for each year since 1985 and drawing a distinction between aid provided for reconstruction following the recent hurricane, and other aid.

Mr. Chris Patten: The latest figures for Central America are as follows. They include investment by the Commonwealth Development Corporation but do not take account of joint funding provided to non-governmental organisations.

Gross bilateral aid to Central America 1985-88 in current prices.

£ thousands

	1985	1986	1987	[1]1988
Costa Rica	12,685	10,038	2,584	991
El Salvador	103	239	411	154
Guatemala	0	10	1	4
Honduras	3,653	1,258	811	1,201
Nicaragua	116	86	0	180
Panama	67	70	72	988

[1] Provisional.

This aid is in the form of technical cooperation, apart from *(a)* investment by the Commonwealth Development Corporation, which was as follows:

£ thousands

	1985	1986	1987	1988
Costa Rica	12,389	9,516	2,228	258
El Salvador	—	—	—	—
Guatemala	—	—	—	—
Honduras	2,967	500	—	—
Nicaragua	—	—	—	—
Panama	—	—	—	—

(b) £20,000 provided to Costa Rica and £180,000 to Nicaragua in 1988 for relief measures following Hurricane Joan; further relief aid was provided in 1989.

(c) Capital aid to the following countries:

£ thousands

	1985	1986	1987	1988
Honduras	164	271	241	615
Panama	—	—	—	854

The capital aid to Panama was provided under the aid and trade provision.

Oxfam

Mr. Pawsey: To ask the Secretary of State for Foreign and Commonwealth Affairs what is the amount of grant provided by Her Majesty's Government to Oxfam each year since 1985.

Mr. Chris Patten: This information is maintained by financial year rather than calendar year. Our total financial support to Oxfam for the past four financial years, including disaster and refugee aid as well as long-term development projects, was:

	£
1985-86	6,642,014
1986-87	3,951,154
1987-88	5,741,378
1988-89	8,553,027

Cambodia and Nicaragua

Mr. Pawsey: To ask the Secretary of State for Foreign and Commonwealth Affairs what is the attitude of Her Majesty's Government to Cambodia and Nicaragua so far as Oxfam funding is concerned; and if pound for pound funding applies to these two countries.

Mr. Chris Patten: We are prepared to consider, under the joint funding scheme, proposals from Oxfam and other agencies for co-funding specific development projects in Nicaragua and specific projects with humanitarian goals in Cambodia.

Falkland Islands

Mr. Nicholas Winterton: To ask the Secretary of State for Foreign and Commonwealth Affairs what funds have so far been made available under the European Community's regional or other initiatives to encourage the economic development of the Falkland Islands.

Mr. Chris Patten: The Falkland Islands have been allocated project aid under the last three European development funds totalling 1·578 million ecu. They have also been allocated nearly 0·5 million ecu in the form of emergency aid, Stabex transfers and risk capital.

PRIME MINISTER

Teesside (Visit)

Q25. **Mr. Holt:** To ask the Prime Minister if, on a future Friday or Monday, she will accompany the Secretary of State for Transport and the hon. Member for Langbaurgh by normal family car on an official journey from London to Teesside.

The Prime Minister: I have no plans to do so, but I know that the proposals announced in the White Paper "Roads for Prosperity" will do much to improve such a journey.

EC Commission (Powers)

Q184. **Mr. Teddy Taylor:** To ask the Prime Minister if she will raise at the next meeting of the European Council the issue of the Commission submitting proposals which empower officers of the Commission to enter business premises to demand information and to impose fines; and if she will make a statement.

The Prime Minister: I am not aware of any such new proposals which are currently under consideration.

Defence

Q198. **Mr. Bowis:** To ask the Prime Minister if she has received representations regarding the defence of the nation.

Q199. **Mr. Leigh:** To ask the Prime Minister if she has received representations regarding the defence of the nation.

Q200. **Mr. Cash:** To ask the Prime Minister if she has received representations regarding the defence of the nation.

The Prime Minister: I have received a number of representations from individuals and organisations.

Conventional Arms Reductions

Mr. Allen: To ask the Prime Minister if she is prepared to include British land-based aircraft in the negotiations for conventional arms reductions in Europe.

The Prime Minister: Yes.

Mr. Allen: To ask the Prime Minister what is Her Majesty's Government's policy on a timetable for a conventional arms agreement.

The Prime Minister: I refer the hon. Member to paragraph 17 of the declaration of the Heads of State and Government participating in the meeting of the North Atlantic Council in Brussels, 29-30 May 1989, a copy of which is in the Library of the House.

Short-range Nuclear Weapons

Mr. Allen: To ask the Prime Minister when she expects negotiations on reductions in short-range nuclear weapons in Europe to begin.

The Prime Minister: I refer the hon. Member to my statement to the House on Tuesday 6 June 1989 at column 20.

Disarmament

Mr. Allen: To ask the Prime Minister what contribution Her Majesty's Government are prepared to make to the achievement of common security and negotiated disarmament.

The Prime Minister: The two documents issued by last month's NATO summit meeting (the summit declaration and the comprehensive concept paper, both of which have been placed in the Library of the House) set out NATO's objectives for improving our security through arms control. As I made clear in my statement to the House on 6 June, we played a full part in drawing up these documents, and will continue to play a full part in pursuing the objectives set out in them.

Publicity

Mr. Dalyell: To ask the Prime Minister where responsibility will lie for ensuring that the terms of the new guidance on conventions on Government publicity issued by the Cabinet Office will be fully observed; what disciplinary system has been put in place to ensure that any breaches of the guidance are effectively punished; and whether any grades of official or specific post-holders are exempt from the requirements of the new guidance.

The Prime Minister: Responsibility for ensuring that the conventions on Government publicity are fully observed rests with individual Ministers and their Departments. Ministers are answerable to the House for the actions of their Departments in relation to publicity as to other matters. Officials are subject to the general principles of conduct governing civil servants.

Engagements

Mr. Pike: To ask the Prime Minister if she will list her official engagements for Tuesday 13 June.

Mr. Hind: To ask the Prime Minister if she will list her official engagements for Tuesday 13 June.

Mr. Harry Greenway: To ask the Prime Minister if she will list her official engagements for Tuesday 13 June.

Mr. Tony Lloyd: To ask the Prime Minister if she will list her official engagements for Tuesday 13 June.

Mr. David Shaw: To ask the Prime Minister if she will list her official engagements for Tuesday 13 June.

Mr. Stern: To ask the Prime Minister if she will list her official engagements for Tuesday 13 June.

The Prime Minister: This morning I had meetings with ministerial colleagues and others. In addition to my duties in the House I shall be having further meetings later today including one with former President Reagan.

FOREIGN AND COMMONWEALTH AFFAIRS

NATO Summit

92. **Ms. Ruddock:** To ask the Secretary of State for Foreign and Commonwealth Affairs if he will make a statement about the North Atlantic Treaty Organisation summit in Brussels on 29 and 30 May.

93. **Mr. Lamond:** To ask the Secretary of State for Foreign and Commonwealth Affairs if he will make a statement about the North Atlantic Treaty Organisation summit in Brussels on 29 and 30 May.

94. **Mr. Heffer:** To ask the Secretary of State for Foreign and Commonwealth Affairs if he will make a statement about the North Atlantic Treaty Organisation summit in Brussels on 29 and 30 May.

Mr. Waldegrave: I refer the hon. Members to my right hon. Friend the Prime Minister's statement to the House on 6 June.

Gibraltar

Mr. Dalyell: To ask the Secretary of State for Foreign and Commonwealth Affairs if he will place in the Library his recent correspondence with the hon. Member for Linlithgow about the Gibraltar shootings.

Mr. Waldegrave: With his permission, I have today placed in the Library of the House a copy of my written reply of 25 May to the hon. Member for Linlithgow and also copies of other correspondence between us on the Gibraltar shootings. Hon. Members may wish to note that, in addition to these letters, the Library now has copies of the Spanish police officer's statement of 8 August 1988 on Spanish surveillance activities prior to the shootings on 6 March 1988; the attestation before a Malaga court on 9 August of the Spanish police officer's signature; and the attestation before a Malaga court on 22 August of the Gibraltar coroner's officer's signature on that statement. There is also a copy of the English translation of the Spanish police officer's statement prepared by the Gibraltar coroner's officer and a professional commentary on that translation prepared by the Foreign and Commonwealth Office's own translators.

Refugee Camps (Cambodia)

Mr. Pawsey: To ask the Secretary of State for Foreign and Commonwealth Affairs if he is satisfied that all refugee camps in Cambodia are open to free inspection by the United Nations authorities.

Mr. Eggar: The relevant United Nations agencies do not have proper access to camps administered by the Khmer Rouge. We have taken a leading role with the Thai Government and with the United Nations agencies in attempting to secure such access. The agencies have good access to other camps.

Nicaragua (Drugs)

Mr. Pawsey: To ask the Secretary of State for Foreign and Commonwealth Affairs what evidence exists to show a link between drug-growing and trafficking and the civil administration in Nicaragua.

Mr. Eggar: The Nicaraguan Government have denied allegations of high level Government involvement in trafficking.

Cambodia

Mr. Pawsey: To ask the Secretary of State for Foreign and Commonwealth Affairs what representations Her Majesty's Government have made to the United Nations about the United Nations seat for Cambodia, currently occupied by a representative of the Pol Pot regime.

Mr. Eggar: I refer my hon. Friend to the reply my hon. Friend the Minister of State gave the hon. Member for Kirkcaldy (Dr. Moonie) on 5 December 1988 at column *40.*

Falkland Islands

Mr. Nicholas Winterton: To ask the Secretary of State for Foreign and Commonwealth Affairs if he will make a statement outlining the implications for the Falkland Islands of the Single European Act and related European agreements.

Mr. Eggar: The relationship between the Falkland Islands and the European Economic Community is governed by part four of the Treaty of Rome and Council decision 86/283/EEC on the association of overseas countries and territories with the EEC. These provisions are not affected by the Single European Act.

Mr. Nicholas Winterton: To ask the Secretary of State for Foreign and Commonwealth Affairs when he next intends to visit the Falkland Islands.

Mr. Eggar: My right hon. and learned Friend has no immediate plans to do so.

Mr. Nicholas Winterton: To ask the Secretary of State for Foreign and Commonwealth Affairs whether he has had any meetings with representatives of the Falkland Islands administration concerning the impact upon the islands of the single European market in 1992.

Mr. Eggar: No.

Grants and Research

Dr. Thomas: To ask the Secretary of State for Foreign and Commonwealth Affairs what levels of grant-in-aid or research contract have been awarded in 1988-89 to (i) the Royal Institute of International Affairs, (ii) the Royal United Services Institute, (iii) the United Nation Association, (iv) Peace through NATO, (v) the Trilateral Commission, (vi) the British Atlantic Committee, (vii) the North Atlantic Assembly, (viii) the Arms Control Association, (ix) the Verification Technology Information Centre and (x) the European Proliferation Information Centre, from departmental funds.

Mr. Eggar: In the 1988-89 financial year the Foreign and Commonwealth Office gave the following amounts in either grants-in-aid or research contracts to the organisations listed:

		£
(i)	Royal Institute for International Affairs	45,390
(ii)	The Royal United Services Institute	Nil
(iii)	The United Nations Association	24,000
(iv)	Peace Through NATO	113,000
(v)	The Trilateral Commission	2,250
(vi)	The British Atlantic Committee	59,000
(vii)	The North Atlantic Assembly	432,569
(viii)	The Arms Control Association	Nil
(ix)	The Verification Technology Information Centre	Nil
(x)	The European Proliferation Information Centre	Nil

Non-Governmental Organisations (Grants)

Dr. Thomas: To ask the Secretary of State for Foreign and Commonwealth Affairs which non-governmental organisations have received grants-in-aid in regard to their work done to explain arms control and defence issues; how much funding each from his Department such non-governmental organisation received in 1987-88 and 1988-89; and if he will make a statement on the reasons for allocating departmental funds to these organisations.

Mr. Eggar: In 1987-88 and 1988-89 the following organisations received grants-in-aid from the Foreign and Commonwealth Office specifically in regard to their work done to explain arms control and defence issues:

| | 1987-88 | 1988-89 |
	£	£
(i) British Atlantic Committee	57,500	59,000
(ii) Peace Through NATO	110,000	113,000
(iii) The Atlantic Treaty Association	Nil	2,000
(iv) North Atlantic Assembly	271,000	432,569

The grants are paid to the above organisations to assist their work of fostering a greater public understanding of defence and arms control issues.

Nuclear Non-proliferation Treaty

Dr. Thomas: To ask the Secretary of State for Foreign and Commonwealth Affairs whether he has plans to develop a public information programme to highlight issues relevant to the 1990 fourth review conference of the nuclear non-proliferation treaty, in the year leading up to the conference.

Mr. Waldegrave: Issues relevant to the review conference are widely discussed in the media and we make our views known as appropriate. We are of course working for a successful outcome to the conference.

Dr. Thomas: To ask the Secretary of State for Foreign and Commonwealth Affairs why it is not his Department's policy to subsidise the attendance of non-governmental organisations at the 1990 fourth review conference of the nuclear non-proliferation treaty.

Mr. Waldegrave: The amount of money available to the Foreign and Commonwealth Office to assist non-governmental organisations is inevitably limited, and requests for funds exceed the total amount available. We therefore face difficult decisions on allocations every year. It has not been our policy in the past to finance the attendance of non-governmental organisations at NPT review conferences and, in the light of other commitments and our overall policy objectives, we are unable to make new funds available for this purpose in 1990.

Visas

Mr. Madden: To ask the Secretary of State for Foreign and Commonwealth Affairs how many staff are available at the British post in Dusseldorf to interview those applying for visas to visit the United Kingdom; and whether he proposes to increase staffing at the post to reduce current waiting times for interview.

Mr. Eggar: The consulate-general at Dusseldorf normally has four entry clearance officers, of whom three are used to conduct interviews and one to deal with postal applications. In addition, two relief entry clearance officers have recently arrived to assist with the normal increase in applications during the summer months and the expected demand for visas from Turkish nationals resident in the Federal Republic. It is known that the posts are under considerable pressure and the question of deploying further entry clearance staff at Dusseldorf is being kept under review.

Immigration

Mr. Madden: To ask the Secretary of State for Foreign and Commonwealth Affairs when Mr. Mohammad Asif Gill, whose date of birth is 30 September 1964 and whose serial number is SN 65460, applied to the post in Islamabad to enter the United Kingdom; and when a decision on his application is to be taken.

Mr. Eggar: In accordance with the recent guidelines on the handling of representations by Members of Parliament in immigration cases, issued to Members on 14 December 1988, I have referred the question to the correspondence unit of the migration and visa department of the Foreign and Commonwealth Office. The hon. Member will receive a reply from the unit in due course.

HOUSE OF COMMONS

Select Committee Reports

Mr. Allen: To ask the Lord President of the Council how many reports have been published by departmental select committees since 1979; and how many have been debated on a substantive motion.

Mr. Wakeham: Since 1979, 504 reports and 193 special reports have been published by departmentally-related Select Committees. Seven have been debated in the House on substantive motions. Numerous other reports have been debated on other occasions, including debates on motions for the adjournment of the House, and on Estimates days.

ENVIRONMENT

Kirklees (Earnings)

Mr. Riddick: To ask the Secretary of State for the Environment what would be the estimated payment in the area covered by Kirklees council for *(a)* a man on average male earnings and *(b)* a woman on average female earnings in 1990-91 under a system of local income tax.

Mr. Gummer: The level of bills under a system of local income tax would depend primarily on the level of expenditure undertaken by Kirklees council and the amount of support available from Government grants and business rates. Such figures for 1990-91 are not known. However, figures were placed in the Library on 23 June 1988 showing the level of income tax needed to fund local authority expenditure in 1988-89. On this basis the figures sought by my hon. Friend are estimated as follows. a man on average male earnings would pay £775 and woman £445.

Housing Act (Right-to-buy Provisions)

Mr. Allen: To ask the Secretary of State for the Environment what assessment he has made of the implications for the operation of the right-to-buy provisions of the Housing Act of the purchase by Trent Valley Housing Company from elderly council tenants of their recently purchased council houses.

Mr. Trippier: I understand that Trent Valley Housing is in certain cases willing to finance the exercise of the right to buy by tenants aged 55 or over on condition that the former tenant sells to the company after three years, retaining the right to remain in the home rent-free for life. The company recommends prospective clients to take independent legal advice. Tenants may finance a purchase under the right to buy from whatever source they choose and, once they have bought, may sell their home to whomever they choose, subject to the requirement to repay discount in the event of early disposal.

Housing Stock (Northamptonshire)

Mr. William Powell: To ask the Secretary of State for the Environment if he will give the numbers of local authority housing stock in *(a)* Corby and *(b)* East Northamptonshire as at 1 April 1979 and the latest convenient date.

Mr. Trippier: The information for April 1979 and April 1988 was reported by local authorities in their annual housing investment programme returns (HIP1) and appears in column B11 of "HIP1 All Items Print (1979)" and column A11 of "HIP1 All Items Print (1988)".

Copies of both documents are in the Library.

Correspondence

Mr. Steen: To ask the Secretary of State for the Environment why it has taken 11 weeks for him to reply to the letter from the hon. Member for South Hams of 22 March about the boundary fence around HMS Cambridge at Wembury, South Devon; what further information is he awaiting before he can give a substantive reply; and if he will make a statement.

Mr. Chope: I regret that I have not been able to send my hon. Friend a substantive reply to his letter of 22 March 1989. The PSA, which is acting as agent for the erection of the proposed fence, await instructions from the Ministry of Defence. I am told that these will be issued shortly; I will then write to my hon. Friend.

Bristol UDC

Mr. O'Brien: To ask the Secretary of State for the Environment (1) if he has received any request from the Bristol urban development corporation for powers to take land at St. Anne's road, Brislington, Bristol, which is currently in the ownership of the Bristol city council, into the area of the urban development corporation; and if he will make a statement;

(2) if he will take steps to prevent land gifted to Bristol city council to be retained as a children's play area from being vested in the urban development corporation; and if he will make a statement;

(3) on what date the meeting of the Bristol urban development corporation was held at which the decision was made to request that land at St. Anne's road, Brislington be included in the area of the urban development corporation;

(4) what information he has received on the use the Bristol urban development corporation proposes for the land it wishes to have vested from the Bristol city council at St. Anne's road, Brislington; and if he will make a statement;

(5) what procedure has been adopted by the Bristol urban development corporation to obtain land at St. Anne's road, Brislington, from the Bristol city council; if he has approved the procedure; and if he will make a statement.

Mr. Trippier: The land in question is already within the Bristol urban development area as designated by The Bristol Development Corporation (Area and Constitution) Order 1988 dated 10 May 1988 and the amendment order dated 8 December 1988. The corporation decided at its first meeting on 2 February 1989 to ask my right hon. Friend to vest 0·63 Ha of open land at St. Anne's road, Bristol which they anticipate will be needed for a road junction improvement scheme. The timing of any scheme has yet to be determined. My right hon. Friend has decided not to include this site in the vesting orders he will shortly be laying before the House, but to allow an opportunity for further negotiation to see whether the land can be acquired by agreement from Bristol city council.

Mr. O'Brien: To ask the Secretary of State for the Environment on what date the Bristol urban development corporation was formally established; when and where the first meeting was held; and if he will make a statement.

Mr. Trippier: Bristol development corporation was established on 19 January 1989. The board held its first meeting on 2 February 1989 in Tollgate house, Bristol.

Tenants' Choice Transfer

Mr. Patnick: To ask the Secretary of State for the Environment what assistance he can give to local authorities who have to pay large disposal costs on a tenants' choice transfer.

Mr. Trippier: The Department has today issued a consultation paper to the local authority associations proposing ways in which these disposal costs might be phased in certain particular circumstances. Subject to the responses to that, we will come forward with the necessary amendment to the Local Government and Housing Bill.

EC Environment Council

Mr. Patnick: To ask the Secretary of State for the Environment what was the outcome of the European Community Environmental Council in Luxembourg on 8-9 June.

Mrs. Virginia Bottomley: My noble Friend the Minister for Housing, Environment and Countryside represented the United Kingdom at this meeting.

I am delighted to report that, after exhaustive negotiations in which the United Kingdom played a leading role, the Council agreed a directive on the second stage of exhaust emission standards for small cars. This now produces clear guidelines for the motor industry to follow in planning its future car production.

The agreement contains strict standards requiring under present technology three-way catalysts to be introduced on 1 July 1992 for new models and on 31 December 1992 for all new registrations. These are tough targets and the challenge they present to industry should not be underestimated. Nevertheless we believe them to be attainable. They are greatly to the advantage of the European environment, but do not control all the emissions from cars that cause concern. Thus, at United Kingdom insistence the Commission has undertaken to come forward with proposals to reduce these, not least of which is carbon dioxide, the most important greenhouse gas. The present agreement does not limit the emission of this gas and if any will tend to increase it.

The unity of the market will be protected by an article in the directive which circumscribes the fiscal incentives that can be introduced by member states and requires all proposed incentives to be notified to the Commission.

As the House knows, the United Kingdom urged an indefinite ban on the import of harp and hooded seal pup skins and their products in 1985, when EC directive 23/129 was extended for four years. Now I am delighted to announce that the Council has unanimously agreed that the directive should be extended indefinitely. This is a significant step towards ensuring the conservation of these species.

The Community will support the case for listing the African elephant on appendix I of the convention on trade in endangered species, but of course recognises the need to listen to the arguments from all sides on the best long-term measures to protect this species. Meanwhile, as a precautionary measure I am also pleased to report that the Council strongly supported the United Kingdom proposal for an immediate ban on the import into the Community of raw and worked ivory. The Commission will now bring forward proposals to impose a ban throughout the Community. Member states were invited to take their own action in advance of these proposals, and we have immediately imposed a ban on imports of ivory into the United Kingdom.

The Council adopted a resolution on the greenhouse effect which recognises the importance of the issue and the importance of the Community and all member states contributing fully to the wider international efforts to improve the understanding of climate change and develop policy responses to it.

I am pleased to report that agreement was reached on a directive requiring the up-grading of existing municipal waste incinerators according to specific timetables. The Council also adopted a directive setting standards for new municipal waste incineration plants, following the agreement which was reached on 2 March.

The Council agreed an amendment to directive 80/779 on air pollution from smoke and sulphur dioxide. The amendment concerns short-term methods of measurement which do not affect the United Kingdom. It also provides for a general review of the directive in which we shall be closely involved.

Agreement was reached on a directive which establishes a regulatory structure for laboratory and industrial processes working with genetically modified micro-organisms within containment. The directive lays down certain procedures for the notification of work and standards to be followed to protect human and environmental safety, which procedures are broadly compatible with existing domestic safety arrangements. The Council voted unanimously to change the legal base from article 100A to article 130S, recognising that the predominant objective of the directive is one of environmental protection.

The Council adopted a directive leading to the elimination of pollution caused by wastes from the titanium dioxide industry and agreed unanimously that the legal base should be article 130S.

A proposal to introduce controls over discharges of four dangerous substances of water was also discussed.

The Commission presented progress reports on a proposal concerning the protection of waters pollution by nitrates and on a proposal concerning the protection of natural and semi-natural habitats and of wild fauna and flora.

NORTHERN IRELAND

Carrick House Hostel

Mr. Jim Marshall: To ask the Secretary of State for Northern Ireland what changes have taken place in the process of admission to Carrick House since it became the responsibility of the Northern Ireland Housing Executive; why such changes have taken place; and what have been the effects on the hostel of the changes.

Mr. Needham: This is a matter for the Northern Ireland Housing Executive and I am advised by the chairman that the Executive has decided not to accept new admissions other than former residents who left the hostel within the last 12 months. This is because the Housing Executive in carrying out its responsibilities under the Housing Order (NI) 1988 considers that the hostel which had become, under previous management, a long-stay hostel for homeless men is unsuitable to meet the short-term requirements of the homeless. This policy which has been in operation since 1 April has had little effect on the hostel to date.

Tourism

Mr. Fearn: To ask the Secretary of State for Northern Ireland how many new jobs were created in tourism-related development projects in Northern Ireland in the years 1977, 1978, 1987 and 1988.

Mr. Viggers: The information requested is not readily available and could be compiled only at disproportionate cost.

Short Brothers plc

Mr. John D. Taylor: To ask the Secretary of State for Northern Ireland on how many occasions in the current year he has answered questions from the right hon. Member for Strangford relating to the future of Short Brothers plc.

Mr. Viggers: Two written questions, including one that I answered yesterday.

Effluent Standards

Mr. Ron Davies: To ask the Secretary of State for Northern Ireland if he will list those applications made to him in the current year by water authorities for the lowering of effluent standards.

Mr. Needham *[holding answer 12 June 1989]:* The water service of the Department of the Environment for Northern Ireland is the sole water authority in Northern Ireland. Another division of the Department—the Environmental Protection division (EPD)—is responsible for setting standards for discharges from water and sewage treatment works. In the current year EPD will be reviewing the discharge standards of 100 sewage treatment works in a continuing programme of review of all significant discharges from sewage works.

Medical Laboratory Scientific Officers

Rev. Martin Smyth: To ask the Secretary of State for Northern Ireland at what level within health and social services boards responsibility for the grading of medical laboratory scientific officers lies.

Mr. Needham *[holding answer 12 June 1989]:* The Professional and Technical Staffs joint council agreement, under which the grading of medical laboratory scientific officers is currently being reviewed, does not specify the management level at which the review should be conducted. This is a matter for each health and social services board to decide.

Income Support

Rev. Martin Smyth: To ask the Secretary of State for Northern Ireland if he will commission independent research to ascertain the extent to which income support levels are adequate to meet the needs of elderly people in residential and nursing homes in Northern Ireland and to gather information on the practices of using personal expenses allowances to augment income support and other state provision in meeting the costs of staying in such accommodation; and if he will make a statement.

Mr. Needham *[holding answer 12 June 1989].* No such research is proposed. As the hon. Member will know, income support levels in Northern Ireland are kept in line with those applying generally in Great Britain. The Government are currently considering the arrangements for assisting people in residential care in the light of the Griffiths report.

Health (Grading Review Teams)

Rev. Martin Smyth: To ask the Secretary of State for Northern Ireland when he expects area health and social services boards to begin work on grading review teams.

Mr. Needham *[holding answer 12 June 1989]:* All the health and social services boards are already working on the grading of medical laboratory scientific officers. It is up to each board to decide how it carries out the grading exercise and whether or not it sets up a specific grading review team.

Clinical Regrading

Rev. Martin Smyth: To ask the Secretary of State for Northern Ireland whether he will instruct area boards to adhere to the job descriptions outlined in paragraphs 3 and 4 of annex B of the national agreement on clinical regrading; and if he will make a statement.

Mr. Needham *[holding answer 12 June 1989]:* The paragraphs referred to by the hon. Member do not outline job descriptions. They refer to the use of job descriptions and set out the factors to be considered when grading a post. This guidance has already been issued to the health and social services boards.

School Buses (Accidents)

Mr. Hume: To ask the Secretary of State for Northern Ireland what possible measures have been considered to help reduce road traffic accidents involving children disembarking from school buses; whether a cost-benefit analysis was conducted of each possible measure; and what decisions have been made as a result of such appraisals.

Mr. Needham *[holding answer 16 May 1989]:* The following measures have been considered and implemented to help reduce road traffic accidents involving children disembarking from school buses:

(a) Rule 24 of the current edition of the Northern Ireland Highway Code sets out the safety rules for getting on or off buses.
(b) Rule 53 of the Highway Code warns drivers to look out for children getting on or off buses.
(c) Every year since 1973 the Department of the Environment has provided a free copy of a road safety teaching calendar to every primary school teacher in Northern Ireland. This teaching aid always has at least one road safety lesson about getting on and off school buses safely.
(d) In conjunction with the Education and Library boards the Department's road safety education branch produced a leaflet for parents about safety of children on school buses which has been distributed with bus passes.
(e) In consultation with road safety education branch the transport officers of the Education and Library boards have issued a safety manual to all board drivers, which includes instructions about the safety of children entering and leaving school buses.

Suggestions about Education boards employing bus wardens and about traffic being required to stop in rural areas when the school bus stops and a flashing roof light is operating, have been examined but were considered to be impractical or unlikely to be effective.

No cost benefit analyses have been conducted on any of these measures.

HOME DEPARTMENT

Passports

Mr. Buchanan-Smith: To ask the Secretary of State for the Home Department how many applications for passports at the Glasgow passport office are currently outstanding; and if he will make a statement.

Mr. Renton: There are about 80,000 applications for passport services at the various states of processing within the Glasgow passport office. Applications are being processed at a rate of around 8,500 a week, according to the applicant's travel requirements, with priority being given to urgent cases. My right hon. Friend announced on 6 June in reply to a question from my hon. Friend the Member for Bolton, South-East (Mr. Young) at columns *47-48,* a number of measures which are being taken to ease the present problem of delays at the passport offices.

Mr. Gareth Wardell: To ask the Secretary of State for the Home Department if he will publish in the *Official Report,* for each passport office *(a)* the number of telephonists manning the switchboard, *(b)* the number of telephone calls handled per day and *(c)* the average waiting time for callers before the call is answered.

Mr. Renton: Details of the number of staff engaged on telephone answering duties at the six United Kingdom passport offices during May this year, together with the average number of calls dealt with daily, are shown in the table below.

| Passport office | Daily average number of | | |
	Staff on telephone answering duties	Calls dealt with personally	Calls dealt with by recorded message
London	5	465	2,913
Glasgow	5·5	567	1,895
Peterborough	8	817	2,068
Newport	6	311	3,148
Liverpool	¹10	449	4,172
Belfast	1	166	355

¹ Since the start of industrial action at Liverpool on 30 May it has not been possible to staff all the telephone inquiry points.

Waiting times for responses to telephone calls are not recorded at all passport offices. The available information shows that at Peterborough and Belfast all connected calls were answered in under five minutes, while at London, on average, all but 10 connected calls a day were so answered.

Improved telephone facilities to enable more calls to be handled are due to be installed at Newport later this month and at Liverpool during next month.

Education Schemes

Mr. Cartwright: To ask the Secretary of State for the Home Department whether local authorities who claim grant for education schemes under section 11 of the Local Government Act 1966 will be able to continue to do so under local management schemes without having to resubmit their schemes for further approval; and whether there are any plans to alter the mechanism which operates under section 11.

Mr. John Patten: The introduction of local management schemes under the Education Reform Act 1988 will not require local authorities to resubmit posts already approved for grant under section 11 of the Local Government Act 1966 to the Home Office for reapproval unless the duties of the posts concerned change. The Government are at present considering the report of an efficiency scrutiny of the section 11 grant scheme.

Breath Tests

Mr. Home Robertson: To ask the Secretary of State for the Home Department how many of the responses to his consultation on possible changes to the breath testing legislation favoured *(a)* random breath testing or highly

visible mass testing at a roadside checkpoint aimed principally at deterring excess alcohol offenders and *(b)* unfettered police powers; and if he will make a statement.

Mr. Douglas Hogg: I refer the hon. Member to the reply given to his question on 8 May 1989, at column *284.*

Chinese Nationals

Mr. Marlow: To ask the Secretary of State for the Home Department if he will make it his policy to advise Chinese nationals resident in the United Kingdom that activity antagonistic to the Chinese Government within the United Kingdom will not enhance or effect their potential entitlement to refugee status.

Mr. Renton: No. Any applications for asylum will be considered in accordance with our obligations under the 1951 convention and 1967 protocol relating to the status of refugees; and all relevant circumstances will be taken into account.

Police Complaints Authority

Mr. John Marshall: To ask the Secretary of State for the Home Department whether any new appointment has been made to the Police Complaints Authority.

Mr. Hurd: Mr. Gordon Marsh, who has recently retired from his post as Deputy Health Service Commissioner with the office and the Health Service Commissioner for England, has accepted my invitation to serve as a member of the authority. He will take up his post on 3 July. The appointment is being made in order to fill an existing vacancy.

Broadcasting

Mr. Robert G. Hughes: To ask the Secretary of State for the Home Department whether he envisages, under his broadcasting proposals, that applicants will be permitted to bid for more than one Channel 3 licence.

Mr. Hurd: Under the ownership proposals which I announced on 19 May in answer to a written question from my hon. Friend at columns *317-19,* an individual licensee will be able to own two Channel 3 licences provided they are not both large or contiguous. The definition of large will be given in subordinate legislation. Applicants for Channel 3 licences will be permitted to apply for any number of licences provided they make clear their order of preference. Those who are successful in the bidding for more than the two licences to which they are entitled will be awarded the relevant licence or licences on the basis of their declared preference.

Asylum

Mr. Cohen: To ask the Secretary of State for the Home Department how many people are currently seeking asylum.

Mr. Renton: Information on the number of persons applying for refugee status and whose applications were awaiting a decision at the end of a year is published annually in Home Office statistical bulletin "Refugee Statistics United Kingdom". The latest, issue 16/88 relates to 1987, a copy of which is in the Library; that for 1988 will be published within the next month.

May Bank Holidays

Mr. Hayward: To ask the Secretary of State for the Home Department whether he has considered the possibility of moving one of the May bank holidays to September or October.

Mr. Nicholls: I have been asked to reply.

I refer my hon. Friend to the answer I gave on 16 May at columns *160–61,* to my hon. Friend the Member for York (Mr. Gregory).

Night Sanitation (Prisons)

Mr. Sheerman: To ask the Secretary of State for the Home Department (1) how many places in each prison in England and Wales *(a)* do and *(b)* do not have access to night sanitation;

(2) how many places in each prison in England and Wales *(a)* will and *(b)* will not have access to night sanitation by 1995.

Mr. Douglas Hogg: The current position is set out in the table. Equivalent figures cannot be given for individual establishments in 1995 because specific building plans are not approved more than two years ahead and may be subject to change. The total number of places without access to night sanitation will, however, be substantially reduced by 1995 on the lines described by my right hon. Friend in response to a question from my hon. Friend the Member for Boothferry (Mr. Davis) on 20 February 1989 at column *61.*

Access to night sanitation

Establishment	A Number of places with access now	B Number of places without access now
Acklington	448	0
Albany	0	389
Aldington	100	0
Ashford	0	348
Ashwell	404	0
Askham Grange	134	0
Aylesbury	0	286
Bedford	0	167
Birmingham	0	592
Blantyre House	87	0
Blundeston	192	214
Bristol	192	360
Brixton	0	729
Brockhill	14	144
Buckley Hall	100	0
Bullwood Hall	0	120
Camp Hill	24	437
Campsfield House	70	0
Canterbury	0	213
Cardiff	0	338
Castington	300	0
Channings Wood	538	0
Chelmsford	0	242
Coldingley	296	0
Cookham Wood	120	0
Dartmoor	8	643
Deerbolt	240	180
Dorchester	0	145
Dover	0	246
Drake Hall	288	0
Durham	0	715
East Sutton Park	84	0
Eastwood Park	146	0
Erlestoke	218	0
Everthorpe	6	294
Exeter	0	312

Establishment	A Number of places with access now	B Number of places without access now
Featherstone	509	0
Feltham	846	0
Ford	536	0
Frankland	447	0
Full Sutton	432	0
Garth	512	0
Gartree	0	320
Glen Parva	600	0
Gloucester	0	200
Grendon	64	185
Guys Marsh	180	0
Haslar	100	0
Hatfield	180	0
Haverigg	325	0
Hewell Grange	136	0
Highpoint	821	0
Hindley	0	308
Hollesley Bay Colony	569	0
Holloway	515	0
Hull	20	386
Huntercombe-Finnamore Wood	176	122
Kingston	0	150
Kirkham	632	0
Kirklevington	150	0
Lancaster	103	83
Latchmere House	0	121
Leeds	0	604
Leicester	5	199
Lewes	0	369
Leyhill	410	0
Lincoln	0	382
Lindholme	901	0
Littlehey	484	0
Liverpool	282	686
Long Lartin	417	0
Low Newton	92	103
Lowdham Grange	304	0
Maidstone	0	549
Manchester	0	896
Morton Hall	192	0
Mount	484	0
New Hall	36	86
North Sea Camp	202	0
Northallerton	15	112
Northeye	233	0
Norwich	60	421
Nottingham	4	239
Onley	0	420
Oxford	6	120
Parkhurst	0	261
Pentonville	8	645
Portland	0	527
Prescoed	110	0
Preston	8	420
Pucklechurch	0	159
Ranby	365	0
Reading	0	178
Risley	0	486
Rochester	0	374
Rudgate	378	0
Send	101	0
Shepton Mallet	6	161
Shrewsbury	12	152
Spring Hill	210	0
Stafford	270	179
Standford Hill	500	0
Stocken	300	0
Stoke Heath	60	300
Styal	237	0
Sudbury	625	0
Swaleside	504	0
Swansea	0	225
Swinfen Hall	8	152
Thorn Cross	300	0

Establishment	A Number of places with access now	B Number of places without access now
Thorp Arch	72	84
Usk	0	128
Verne	595	0
Wakefield	30	718
Wandsworth	8	1,226
Wayland	484	0
Wellingborough	120	224
Werrington	110	0
Wetherby	0	196
Whatton	84	145
Winchester	0	471
Wormwood Scrubs	0	1,206
Wymott	816	0
Totals	22,310	22,792

Cash-point Thefts

Mr. Vaz: To ask the Secretary of State for the Home Department how many cash-point thefts there have been in the United Kingdom for each year since 1979 and for 1989 to date.

Mr. John Patten: The information requested is not available centrally and could be obtained only at disproportionate cost.

Hong Kong

Mr. Marlow: To ask the Secretary of State for the Home Department what is his assessment of the readiness of the British people to accept a significant level of net migration from Hong Kong.

Mr. Renton: Any substantial increase in immigration to this country would of course present major problems. However, the uncertainties facing the people of Hong Kong are well known. In the light of the recent events in China, we are therefore considering what changes are called for in the immigration arrangements as they relate to British dependent territory citizens in Hong Kong. We shall bring forward proposals in due course.

Prisons (Dormitory Accommodation)

Mr. Harry Greenway: To ask the Secretary of State for the Home Department (1) how many prisoners on remand awaiting trial or sentence are confined in dormitory accommodition;
(2) in how many prisons in each security category prisoners are confined in dormitory accommodation; and how many prisoners are so confined in each prison.

Mr. Douglas Hogg *[holding answer 6 June 1989]:* The available information relates to prisoners held in rooms defined as
"any unit of accommodation whether secure or otherwise designed for 2 or more persons excluding accommodation defined as a double cell".
This definition encompasses accommodation conventionally known as dormitories. The available information does not distinguish between classes of occupant but unsentenced prisoners are not normally held in dormitories.

Prisoners accommodated in rooms/dormitories on 9 April 1989

Establishment	Number of inmates
LOCAL PRISONS AND REMAND CENTRES	
Ashford	11
Bedford	10
Birmingham	73
Bristol	106
Brixton	73
Canterbury	14
Cardiff	4
Dorchester	8
Durham	0
Exeter	3
Feltham[1]	64
Hindley	0
Hull	210
Leeds	0
Leicester	15
Lincoln	22
Liverpool	45
Norwich	18
Oxford	13
Pentonville	4
Rochester	0
Shrewsbury	0
Swansea	30
Wandsworth	160
Winchester	26
CLOSED TRAINING PRISONS	
Category B	
Blundeston	105
Grendon	9
Maidstone	0
Nottingham	14
Category C	
Aldington	58
Blantyre House	24
Camp Hill	126
Featherstone	73
Haverigg	308
Highpoint	454
Lancaster	107
Lindholme	661
Northeye	215
Norwich	196
Ranby	165
Send	72
Shepton Mallet	0
The Verne	106
OPEN TRAINING PRISONS	
Ford	383
Highpoint	61
Kirkham	573
Leyhill	371
Morton Hall	174
North Sea Camp	92
Rudgate	339
Spring Hill	80
Standford Hill	427
Sudbury	426
YOUNG OFFENDER INSTITUTIONS	
Buckley Hall	87
Campsfield House	49
Eastwood Park	0
Feltham	32
Finnamore Wood	8
Glen Parva	55
Haslar	54
Hewell Grange	101
Hollesley Bay	38
Huntercombe	0
Kirklevington	105

Establishment	Number of inmates
Lowdham Grange	116
Swinfen Hall	6
Thorn Cross	0
Usk (Prescoed)	12
Werrington	89
Wetherby	0
Whatton	131

Establishment	Number of inmates
FEMALE PRISONS	
Askham Grange	96
Drake Hall	185
East Sutton Park	79
Holloway	146
New Hall	18
Risley	38

[1] Also functions as Young Offenders Institution.

SCOTLAND

Food Poisoning (Untreated Milk)

Mr. David Nicholson: To ask the Secretary of State for Scotland how many cases of food poisoning associated with untreated milk occurred in Scotland in each of the years from 1978 to 1982; and how many have occurred in each year since the ban on commercial sales of untreated milk introduced in August 1983.

Mr. Michael Forsyth: The numbers of reported cases of food poisoning associated with the consumption of untreated milk for each year since 1978 are as follows:

Year	Number of cases
1978	[1]251
1979	[1]155
1980	103
1981	782
1982	539
1983	29
1984	27
1985	74
1986	10
1987	26
1988	5

[1] Figures for salmonellosis only. Figures for other diseases not available.

Press Briefings

Mr. Grocott: To ask the Secretary of State for Scotland what guidelines he follows in determining which journalists are invited to press briefings by his Department.

Mr. Rifkind: This depends upon the matter under discussion.

Dornie Bridge

Mr. Kennedy: To ask the Secretary of State for Scotland when he anticipates the construction work on the new Dornie bridge, Ross-shire, to commence; and if he will make a statement.

Lord James Douglas-Hamilton: The work on the new Dornie bridge carrying the A87 trunk road to the Skye ferry terminal at Kyle of Lochalsh will start on 10 July 1989 following the award of tender to Harbour and General Works Ltd. on 16 May 1989

New Towns

Mr. Ingram: To ask the Secretary of State for Scotland if he can now give a date for the expected publication of the White Paper on the future of the Scottish new towns.

Mr. Lang: The White Paper detailing the Government's firm policy proposals on the future of the Scottish new towns will be published shortly.

Fire Civil Defence

Mr. Bill Michie: To ask the Secretary of State for Scotland if he will list for each fire authority *(a)* the date of first appointment of a brigade emergency planning officer and *(b)* the expenditure incurred on fire civil defence activities and the amount of grant aid paid towards that expenditure for each year from 1979.

Lord James Douglas-Hamilton: The dates of first appointments of brigade emergency planning staff officers are as shown. Figures for the expenditure incurred by each fire authority on civil defence activities and the amount of grant aid paid towards that expenditure for each year since 1979 could be provided only at disproportionate cost. Amounts for 1987-88, the last year for which all audited claims have been received, are as follows:

Expenditure claimed for Grant Aid in 1987-88

Fire Authority	Date of first appointment	Total expenditure reported £	Grant aid paid £
Central	21 June 1985	27,317	27,317
Dumfries and Galloway	1 July 1987	33,393	33,393
Fife	4 July 1986	21,450	21,450
Grampian	15 May 1985	20,694	20,694
Highland and Islands	4 July 1985	36,249	36,249
Lothian and Borders	3 February 1985	46,870	46,870
Strathclyde	30 November 1987	16,714	16,714
Tayside	19 March 1985	32,677	32,677

Mr. Ingram: To ask the Secretary of State for Scotland when he last met the chairman and chief executives of the Scottish new towns; and if he will make a statement on the items discussed at the meeting.

Mr. Lang: I met the chairman and chief executives of the Scottish new town development corporations on Thursday 1 June 1989, when we discussed a range of matters concerning the new towns.

Scottish Homes

Mr. Ingram: To ask the Secretary of State for Scotland if he will give the capital programme for Scottish Homes for the current financial year.

Lord James Douglas-Hamilton: The gross capital programme figure is dependent on Scottish Homes achieving the projected capital receipts figure for this year. Assuming that figure is achieved, the gross capital programme will be £299 million.

Mr. Ingram: To ask the Secretary of State for Scotland if he will give the projected capital receipts from the sale of houses for the current financial year for Scottish Homes.

Lord James Douglas-Hamilton: The projected net capital receipts figure, which has been agreed with Scottish Homes, is £110 million. This sum is expected to be made up largely from receipts from the sale of Scottish Homes' own stock but also includes receipts expected from the sale of housing association property and a small amount from repayments of grant or bridging finance.

Council House Sales

Mr. Home Robertson: To ask the Secretary of State for Scotland if he will list the number and total value of council houses sold by each district council since the start of the current financial year.

Lord James Douglas-Hamilton: Information on the sale of council houses is collected centrally from local authorities on a quarterly basis. Information relating to the current financial year is not yet available.

Nature Reserves

Mr. Ron Davies: To ask the Secretary of State for Scotland if he will make a statement on the Forestry Commission's proposals to designate sites as nature reserves; and if he will list the sites proposed for such designation.

Lord James Douglas-Hamilton: The Forestry Commission has chosen 46 forest nature reserves from the hundreds of conservation sites on its land. They have been managed by the Commission for conservation purposes for many years, and are accessible and open to everyone. They are listed in the Commission's leaflet entitled "Forest Nature Reserves", which is available in the Library.

Nature Conservation

Mr. Ron Davies: To ask the Secretary of State for Scotland what advice he has received from the Nature Conservancy Council concerning the practice of blocking of badger sets and digging of fox-earths by fox hunters on Forestry Commission land.

Lord James Douglas-Hamilton: My right hon. and learned Friend has not received any recent advice from the Nature Conservancy Council on this subject.

EMPLOYMENT

Employment Schemes

Ms. Short: To ask the Secretary of State for Employment, for each of the Training Agency's areas within Greater London, Merseyside, Greater Manchester, Glasgow, Sheffield, Birmingham and Solihull, Coventry and Warwickshire, and for each of the latest four three monthly periods available, how many unemployed people have *(a)* been called in for a restart interview, *(b)* attended a restart interview, *(c)* been referred to unemployment benefit offices for failing to attend their interview, *(d)* had their benefit or national insurance credits disallowed for failing to attend their interview, *(e)* been called in for a restart follow up interview, *(f)* attended a restart follow up interview, *(g)* been referred to unemployment benefit offices for failing to attend their follow up interview and *(h)* had their benefit or national insurance credits disallowed for failing to attend their follow-up interview.

Mr. Lee: The information as requested is not available. however, the following table gives the information for the relevant employment service areas.

Restart counselling—numbers interviewed and failure to attend outcomes

	Greater London Areas[1]	Merseyside Areas[2]	Greater Manchester Areas[3]	Glasgow Areas[4]	Sheffield Areas[5]	Birmingham and Solihull Areas[6]	Coventry and Warwickshire Areas[7]
April-June 1988							
All Restart Interviews							
(a) Called for Restart interview	91,071	35,468	42,934	19,371	14,194	20,883	9,015
(b) Attended a Restart interview	66,747	30,743	33,594	16,051	10,490	15,312	7,191
(c) Referred to UBO for failing to attend interview	19,568	5,881	5,973	1,796	989	2,502	577
(d) Disallowed				Figures not available			
Restart follow-up interviews (also included in figures above)							
(e) Called for Restart follow-up interview	3,307	468	1,052	59	263	160	0
(f) Attended Restart follow-up interview	1,703	246	753	28	251	61	0
(g) Referred to UBO for failing to attend follow-up interview	723	55	125	0	25	0	0
(h) Disallowed				Figures not available			
July-September 1988							
All Restart Interviews							
(a) Called for Restart interview	106,809	43,251	45,784	15,956	18,934	29,740	9,657
(b) Attended a Restart interview	68,293	33,034	36,712	15,034	14,056	16,914	7,242
(c) Referred to UBO for failing to attend interview	19,072	5,038	6,505	1,565	1,526	1,408	555
(d) Disallowed				Figures not available			
Restart follow-up interviews (also included in figures above)							
(e) Called for Restart follow-up interview	5,980	1,608	3,144	156	784	2,451	1,494
(f) Attended Restart follow-up interview	3,371	795	1,724	144	578	1,823	696

	Greater London Areas[1]	Merseyside Areas[2]	Greater Manchester Areas[3]	Glasgow Areas[4]	Sheffield Areas[5]	Birmingham and Solihull Areas[6]	Coventry and Warwickshire Areas[7]
(g) Referred to UBO for failing to attend follow-up interview	996	90	340	0	54	7	9
(h) Disallowed				Figures not available			
October-December 1988							
All Restart interviews							
(a) Called for Restart interview	121,454	45,519	48,896	27,792	21,415	32,971	11,693
(b) Attended a Restart interview	76,389	31,761	33,315	19,768	14,337	20,520	7,897
(c) Referred to UBO for failing to attend interview	22,172	5,751	6,266	2,130	1,265	1,099	387
(d) Disallowed				Figures not available			
Restart follow-up interviews (also included in figures above)							
(e) Called for Restart follow-up interview	9,280	3,485	3,384	842	1,232	4,997	2,516
(f) Attended Restart follow-up interview	5,211	2,128	1,991	570	1,066	4,462	1,646
(g) Referred to UBO for failing to attend follow-up interview	1,212	366	441	79	144	13	41
(h) Disallowed				Figures not available			
January-March 1989							
All Restart Interviews							
(a) Called for Restart interview	83,811	44,621	45,398	29,755	18,082	32,714	11,823
(b) Attended a Restart interview	78,161	33,420	33,838	22,616	12,461	26,688	8,352
(c) Referred to UBO for failing to attend interview	18,714	5,270	6,097	2,524	972	2,222	754
(d) Disallowed				Figures not available			
Restart follow-up interviews (also included in figures above)							
(e) Called for Restart follow-up interview	17,304	3,383	2,870	2,344	1,077	10,470	3,565
(f) Attended Restart follow-up interview	10,486	2,951	2,264	1,662	1,463	9,563	2,555
(g) Referred to UBO for failing to attend follow-up interview	2,649	513	548	265	149	45	125
(h) Disallowed				Figures not available			

[1] London South East, Inner London South, Inner London East, Inner London Central, Inner London West, London North West, London East, London South, London South West, London West.
[2] Liverpool and Wirral, Merseyside North, Merseyside South.
[3] Manchester City, Manchester North East, Manchester North West, Manchester South, Manchester West.
[4] Glasgow North, Glasgow South.
[5] Sheffield.
[6] Birmingham (including Solihull).
[7] Coventry/Warwickshire.

Ms. Short: To ask the Secretary of State for Employment, for Great Britain and each standard training region, and for each of the latest four three monthly periods available, how many unemployed people have (a) been called in for a restart interview, (b) attended a restart interview, (c) been referred to unemployment benefit offices for failing to attend their interview, (d) had their benefit or national insurance credits disallowed for failing to attend their interview, (e) been called in for a restart follow up interview, (f) attended a restart follow-up interview, (g) been referred to unemployment benefit offices for failing to attend their follow up interview and (h) had their benefit or national insurance credits disallowed for failing to attend their follow up interview.

Mr. Lee: The information as requested is not available. however information for Great Britain and the relevant employment service regions is given in the following tables.

Restart Counselling—Numbers interviewed and failure to attend outcomes

	Northern	Yorkshire and Humberside	East Midland and Eastern	London and South East	South West	Wales	West Midlands	North West	Scotland	Great Britain
April-June 1988										
All restart interviews										
(a) Called for Restart interview	46,432	67,007	60,405	160,641	39,496	39,909	68,667	113,418	83,641	679,616
(b) Attended Restart interview	38,818	50,986	47,314	116,983	26,932	30,919	53,275	89,906	68,516	523,649

	Northern	Yorkshire and Humberside	East Midland and Eastern	London and South East	South West	Wales	West Midlands	North West	Scotland	Great Britain
(c) Referred to UBO for failing to attend interview	4,478	4,442	6,327	28,586	4,500	4,308	6,323	14,887	6,793	80,644
(d) Disallowed for failing to attend	283	342	482	2,197	278	282	483	856	552	5,755

Restart follow-up interviews (figures also included in totals above)

	Northern	Yorkshire and Humberside	East Midland and Eastern	London and South East	South West	Wales	West Midlands	North West	Scotland	Great Britain
(e) Called for Restart interview	1,468	3,196	2,382	8,454	943	2,128	1,298	2,691	792	23,352
(f) Attended Restart interview	1,085	2,545	1,468	4,219	530	1,518	561	1,706	438	14,070
(g) Referred to UBO for failing to attend interview	103	316	134	1,136	52	44	37	272	26	2,120
(h) Disallowed for failing to attend	Not available in form requested included in *(d)* above									

July-September 1988
All restart interviews

	Northern	Yorkshire and Humberside	East Midland and Eastern	London and South East	South West	Wales	West Midlands	North West	Scotland	Great Britain
(a) Called for Restart interview	59,984	81,131	73,102	187,388	36,988	40,500	89,663	121,751	78,135	768,642
(b) Attended Restart interview	45,212	59,424	51,230	129,230	25,396	30,135	61,282	95,760	65,167	562,836
(c) Referred tio UBO for failing to attend interview	4,691	5,448	6,441	30,694	4,085	5,029	5,810	14,741	6,067	83,006
(d) Disallowed for failing to attend	292	428	499	2,295	242	296	413	1,030	505	6,000

Restart follow-up interviews (figures also included in totals above)

	Northern	Yorkshire and Humberside	East Midland and Eastern	London and South East	South West	Wales	West Midlands	North West	Scotland	Great Britain
(e) Called for Restart interview	3,218	4,376	6,689	20,338	1,194	6,794	11,335	6,689	1,610	62,243
(f) Attended Restart interview	2,428	3,226	4,029	12,521	721	5,518	7,027	3,946	1,146	40,562
(g) Referred to UBO for failing to attend interview	295	376	289	2,467	158	344	223	626	48	4,826
(h) Disallowed for failing to attend	Not available in form requested included in *(d)* above									

October-December 1988
All restart interviews

	Northern	Yorkshire and Humberside	East Midland and Eastern	London and South East	South West	Wales	West Midlands	North West	Scotland	Great Britain
(a) Called for Restart interview	54,604	85,627	69,492	176,428	43,417	45,715	100,086	126,956	105,594	807,919
(b) Attended Restart interview	40,492	58,659	50,712	125,934	27,480	34,089	66,062	90,184	73,306	566,918
(c) Referred to UBO for failing to attend interview	4,174	5,713	6,467	29,136	4,122	5,277	6,085	15,234	7,222	83,432
(d) Disallowed for failing to attend	360	462	416	1,941	241	460	537	1,165	690	6,272

Restart follow-up interviews (figures also included in totals above)

	Northern	Yorkshire and Humberside	East Midland and Eastern	London and South East	South West	Wales	West Midlands	North West	Scotland	Great Britain
(e) Called for Restart interview	4,910	7,361	11,955	31,013	2,708	6,001	15,922	9,623	3,017	92,510
(f) Attended Restart interview	3,257	4,745	8,068	20,293	1,484	5,112	13,657	6,905	2,149	65,670
(g) Referred to UBO for failing to attend interview	348	491	585	3,281	149	554	385	1,252	205	7,250
(h) Disallowed for failing to attend	Not available in form requested included in *(d)* above									

January-March 1989
All restart interviews

	Northern	Yorkshire and Humberside	East Midland and Eastern	London and South East	South West	Wales	West Midlands	North West	Scotland	Great Britain
(a) Called for Restart interview	58,769	76,508	73,693	178,648	41,278	46,605	93,470	121,360	114,048	804,379
(b) Attended Restart interview	41,890	57,055	49,052	131,882	28,834	36,314	72,439	89,602	84,208	591,276
(c) Referred to UBO for failing to attend interview	3,810	5,387	5,917	25,979	3,549	4,651	6,893	14,027	8,252	78,465
(d) Disallowed for failing to attend	365	519	623	2,370	311	468	719	1,177	808	7,360

Restart follow-up interviews (figures also included in totals above)

	Northern	Yorkshire and Humberside	East Midland and Eastern	London and South East	South West	Wales	West Midlands	North West	Scotland	Great Britain
(e) Called for Restart interview	5,023	8,886	12,812	40,604	6,523	8,217	21,030	8,177	11,711	122,983
(f) Attended Restart interview	4,591	7,179	9,801	28,577	4,867	6,816	22,397	6,947	8,730	99,905
(g) Referred to UBO for failing to attend interview	453	828	1,172	4,875	309	714	1,200	1,301	667	11,519
(h) Disallowed for failing to attend				Not available in form requested included in *(d)* above						

Ms. Short: To ask the Secretary of State for Employment, for Great Britain and each training Agency area, how many individual child care allowances are being received by lone parent ET participants; and how many were granted or refused for each of the latest available three months.

Mr Nicholls: I refer the hon. Member to my reply of 16 May 1989, at columns *177-79,* which is the latest information available. Information about lone parents receiving child care allowances before April and those refused the allowance is not available and can be provided only at disproportionate cost.

Dockers

Mr. Ian Bruce: To ask the Secretary of State for Employment how many dockers are employed in non-dock labour scheme ports and in dock labour scheme ports currently; how many were employed in 1979; and if he will make a statement.

Mr. Nicholls: The number of dock workers in scheme ports has fallen from 25,770 in 1979 (NDLB annual report) to 9,280 on 30 May 1989 (NDLB figures). There are no comparable figures for the number of dock workers in non-scheme ports in 1979 and currently. The most recent available figures show that in 1987 there were 3,900 dock workers in non-scheme ports, 10 per cent. more than in 1983.

Scheme ports are continuing to lose business and jobs to ports outside the scheme, free from its restrictions. The abolition of the scheme will enable all our ports to compete on equal terms.

Dock Labour Scheme

Mr. Barry Field: To ask the Secretary of State for Employment to how many acres of land in the ports of London, Glasgow, Liverpool and Hull the dock labour scheme applies; and if he will make a statement.

Mr. Nicholls: Questions about authorities' landholdings are for them to answer. The Department of Employment does not have this information.

The dock labour scheme has acted as a disincentive to investment and has caused a decline in employment both in the ports in which it operates, and in the surrounding areas. This has affected not only registered dock workers but those people living near the docks who could otherwise have been employed by companies investing in the port area.

Prices and Costs

Mr. Leighton: To ask the Secretary of State for Employment how his Department monitors movements in the prices and costs of particular goods and services purchased; and how such movements in prices and costs have differed from the gross domestic product deflator.

Mr. Cope: The Department began to introduce a computerised management information system designed to record all purchases at the beginning of 1988. This database makes possible more detailed comparative analysis of spending patterns, but so far insufficient data has been collected to compare the change in the cost and prices of goods and services purchased by this Department with the gross domestic product deflator.

North-West Tourist Board

Mr. Fearn: To ask the Secretary of State for Employment what grants were made to the north-west tourist board from the English tourist board in the years 1987 and 1988.

Mr. Nicholls: The English tourist board has made the following subventions from its grant in aid provision to the north-west tourist board:

Financial year	Total subvention £
1986-87	198,000
1987-88	214,154
1988-89	227,500

Training Schemes

Mr. John Evans: To ask the Secretary of State for Employment how many people have passed through Government employment training schemes in the last 10 years.

Mr. Nicholls: Just over 5 million people started Government employment training schemes funded through the Training Agency (formerly Training Commission, formerly Manpower Services Commission) in the 10 years from April 1979 to March 1989.

Security Guards

Mr. Dalyell: To ask the Secretary of State for Employment if he will propose a code of practice for employers of security guards.

Mr. Nicholls: No. However, I understand that my right hon. Friend the Secretary of State for the Home Department has asked officials to consider with the police and the private security industry ways in which self-regulation of the industry might be improved.

Service Industries

Mr. Greg Knight: To ask the Secretary of State for Employment how many people are currently employed in service industries including tourism in the United Kingdom.

Mr. Nicholls: In December 1988, the latest date for which estimates are available, there were 15,661,000 employees in employment in the service industries including tourism in the United Kingdom.

Tourism-related Projects (Jobs)

Mr. Fearn: To ask the Secretary of State for Employment how many new jobs were created in tourism-related development projects in the inner cities of England and Wales in the years 1987 and 1988.

Mr. Nicholls: This information is not available.

Mr. Fearn: To ask the Secretary of State for Employment how many new jobs were created in tourism-related development projects in north-west England in the years 1977, 1978, 1987 and 1988.

Mr. Nicholls: This information is not available. The number of hotel and catering employees in employment in the north west in each of the years requested is shown in the following table.

Employees in employment in Hotels and Catering
North West England

	thousands
June 1977	96
June 1978	97
June 1987	133
June 1988	140

Mr. Fearn: To ask the Secretary of State for Employment how many new jobs were created in tourism-related development projects in rural areas of England and Wales in the years 1977, 1978, 1987 and 1988.

Mr. Nicholls: This information is not available.

Tourist Attractions

Mr. Fearn: To ask the Secretary of State for Employment what are the top 20 tourist attractions in numbers of tourists attending or visiting in England and Wales.

Mr. Nicholls: The following table gives the information:

Top twenty tourist attractions in England and Wales in 1988

	Attraction	Number of visits (millions)
1	Blackpool Pleasure Beach	[1]6·50
2	British Museum, London	[1]3·84
3	Albert Dock, Liverpool	[1]3·50
4	Westminster Abbey, London	[1]3·25
5	National Gallery, London	[1]3·23
6	Madame Tussaud's, London	2·70
7	Alton Towers, Staffs.	2·51
8	St. Pauls Cathedral, London	[1]2·50
9	Science Museum, London	[1]2·44
10	Pleasure Beach, Great Yarmouth	[1]2·25
11	Tower of London	2·18
12	Canterbury Cathedral	[1]2·13
13	York Minster	[1]2·10
14	Tate Gallery, London	[1]1·58
15	Pleasureland, Southport	[1]1·50
16	Blackpool Tower	1·48
17	Natural History Museum, London	1·37
18	London Zoo	1·33
19	Bradgate Park, Leicestershire	[1]1·20
20	Kew Gardens	1·18

[1] Free admission (visitor numbers estimated).
Sources:
Visits to Tourist Attractions in 1988 (British Tourist Authority).
English Heritage Monitor (English Tourist Board).

Tourism

Mr. Fearn: To ask the Secretary of State for Employment what were the earnings for England from tourism in 1987, 1988, 1977 and 1978.

Mr. Nicholls: The available information relates to expenditure by international and domestic visitors staying at least one night in England. Figures for expenditure by United Kingdom residents on day-trips within England are not available.

Expenditure by tourists in England at current prices
£ millions

	British residents[1]	Overseas residents[2]	Total
1977	2,000	2,120	4,120
1978	2,400	2,250	4,650
1987	[3]5,550	5,645	[3]11,195
1988	[3]6,275	5,495	[3]11,770

[1] British Tourist Authority
[2] International Passenger Survey
[3] From 1984, an improved method of estimation was introduced, therefore, figures after 1984 are not strictly comparable with earlier years.

English Tourist Board

Mr. Fearn: To ask the Secretary of State for Employment what Government grants were made to the English tourist board in the years 1987 and 1988.

Mr. Nicholls: Payments made by my Department to the English tourist board were as follows:

Financial year	Grant-in-Aid £	Section 4 £	Total £
1986-87	10,764,000	9,500,413	20,264,413
1987-88	11,435,000	12,000,000	23,435,000
1988-89	12,576,100	13,200,000	25,776,000

Labour Statistics

Mr. Speller: To ask the Secretary of State for Employment if he will make a statement on the number of people in employment in the United Kingdom.

Mr. Nicholls: Between March 1983 and December 1988 the work force in employment in the United Kingdom increased by 2,951,000 to 26,513,000, the highest level on record. This rising trend has now continued for more than five years. The figures have been adjusted for the effects of seasonal variations. The work force in employment is the sum of employees in employment, the self employed, Her Majesty's Forces and participants in work-related Government training programmes.

Mr. Meacher: To ask the Secretary of State for Employment if he will publish in the *Official Report* the percentage of *(a)* people of working age, *(b)* men of working age, and *(c)* women of working age, who are (1) economically active, (2) in employment, (3) in full-time employment and (4) in part-time employment for the latest available year in each of the European Community's member states.

Mr. Nicholls: International sources do not differentiate full-time workers from part-time. The latest information which is readily available relates to 1986 (except where otherwise stated), and is as follows:

| | Percentage of those aged 15 to 64 | | | | | |
| | In the labour force | | | In employment | | |
	People	Men	Women	People	Men	Women
Belgium	63	75	51	56	69	43
Denmark	83	88	76	78	85	71
Federal Republic of Germany[1]	65	80	50	60	74	46
Greece[1]	60	78	42	55	73	37
Spain	56	78	34	44	63	25
France	66	76	55	59	70	48
Ireland	61	85	37	51	69	32
Italy	61	79	42	54	74	35
Luxembourg	65	86	44	64	85	43
Netherlands	58	75	41	52	68	36
Portugal	71	86	56	65	81	50
United Kingdom	75	89	62	66	77	56

[1] 1985 figures.

Sources:
United Kingdom: Department of Employment.
Other countries: OECD Labour Force Statistics 1966 to 1986.

SOCIAL SECURITY

Family Credit

Mr. William Powell: To ask the Secretary of State for Social Security what is the number of families now in receipt of family credit living in areas covered by *(a)* the Corby Department of Social Security office and *(b)* Wellingborough.

Mr. Peter Lloyd: The latest information relates to the beginning of April 1989. At that time the number of families receiving family credit who, at the time their award was made, were living in the areas covered by the two local Social Security offices was as follows:

	Number
Corby	462
Wellingborough	836

Attendance Allowance

Mr. Ashley: To ask the Secretary of State for Social Security in each of the past five years for which figures are available *(a)* how many people have been receiving attendance allowance, *(b)* how many were awarded the attendance allowance in that year and *(c)* how many lost the allowance because of death or recovery.

Mr. Scott: Reliable information about the termination of attendance allowance awards is not available. The information which is available is as follows:

Attendance allowance: Estimated number of allowances in payment and number of awards made 1984-88

Year	Estimated number of allowances in payment at 31 March	Number of awards made
1984	470,000	181,770
1985	544,000	184,599
1986	585,000	174,064
1987	641,000	208,693
1988	713,000	207,853

Mr. Ashley: To ask the Secretary of State for Social Security what is the estimated cost of reducing the qualifying period for the attendance allowance from six to three months.

Mr. Scott: About £110 million in a full year.

Vocational Rehabilitation

Mr. Alfred Morris: To ask the Secretary of State for Social Security (1) if he is satisfied with the integration of vocational rehabilitation with both the structure and administration of social security; what action he is taking to improve co-ordination; and if he will make a statement;

(2) if he is satisfied with the integration of vocational rehabilitation with both the structure and administration of social security in Wales; what action he is taking to improve co-ordination; and if he will make a statement;

(3) if he is satisfied with the integration of vocational rehabilitation with both the structure and administration of social security in Scotland; what action he is taking to improve co-ordination; and if he will make a statement.

Mr. Scott: As the right hon. Member is aware, the benefits provided for disabled people by this Department are currently subject to review. As part of this process, we and the Department of Employment will consider the relation between the two Departments' provisions.

I understand that the right hon. Member's question has been prompted by a recent report in *The Observer* alleging plans to withdraw benefits from disabled people completing employment training (ET). I am glad to have this opportunity to say that these allegations are completely without foundation. The rules which govern disabled people's entitlement both during and after ET will continue as they have been from the beginning of the programme. People entering ET will be paid in training allowance at the rate of their previous benefits with an additional premium of £10 per week and, if they still fulfil the entitlement criteria for those benefits on completion of training, will be able to resume payment thereafter.

Personal Pensions

Mrs. Beckett: To ask the Secretary of State for Social Security how many people have taken out a personal pension since July 1988.

Mr. Scott: Just over $3\frac{1}{4}$ million people.

Child Benefit (Prisoners)

Mr. Gregory: To ask the Secretary of State for Social Security if child benefit is paid to mothers serving prison sentences; and if he will make a statement.

Mr. Scott: Child benefit can be paid to mothers in custody who have a child living with them in prison. Child benefit is intended to help people responsible for bringing up children. A mother who is looking after her child in prison has a significant responsibility for its welfare.

Mr. Matthew Taylor: To ask the Secretary of State for Social Security what would be the cost of ceasing to treat *(a)* child benefit and *(b)* one parent benefit as a resource for income support, assuming unemployment levels of *(a)* 1,000,000, *(b)* 1,250,000, *(c)* 1,500,000, *(d)* 1,750,000 and *(e)* 2,000,000.

Mr. Peter Lloyd *[holding answer 9 June 1989]:* Using the May 1987 annual statistical enquiry, which is the latest statistical data available, and the level of unemployment (2·86 million) existing at that time, the annual cost of disregarding child benefit and one parent benefit in income support would be £870 million and £160 million respectively at the current rates in payment. It is not possible to estimate the costs for the requested unemployment levels because the number of families entitled to these benefits and their composition do not alter in proportion to the changes in the number of unemployed people.

HEALTH

Self-Governing Status

Mr. Hinchliffe: To ask the Secretary of State for Health (1) what discussion has taken place regarding the proposal for the Wakefield health authority's mental health unit to have self-governing status; and when;

(2) what he regards as constituting an expression of interest in self-governing status for hospitals and National Health Service units;

(3) what response has been received from *(a)* Wakefield community health council, *(b)* Wakefield branch of MIND, *(c)* Wakefield branch of MENCAP, *(d)* West Yorkshire branch of the National Schizophrenia Fellowship and *(e)* Wakefield family practitioner committee to the proposal for Wakefield health authority's mental health unit to have self-governing status.

(4) who has been consulted regarding the proposal for Wakefield health authority's mental health unit to have self-governing status.

Mr. Mellor: Expressions of interest in self-governing status are no more than that. These range from detailed proposals to brief letters registering interest. It would be unrealistic to require consultation at this stage, before people have enough information to make an informed decision. Those with an interest will have an opportunity to express their views at a later stage if those expressing interest decide to proceed with an application.

Hazel Court School, Eastbourne

Mr. Gow: To ask the Secretary of State for Health what are the responsibilities of the Eastbourne health authority to provide speech therapy and physiotherapy for the children who need those services at Hazel Court school, Eastbourne, being a school owned by the East Sussex county council.

Mr. Freeman: Eastbourne health authority has a general responsibility to provide speech therapy and physiotherapy services for its resident population. It is for the authority itself to decide what resources within the total available for speech therapy and physiotherapy services to devote to providing services for children at Hazel Court school.

Hospital Building Projects

Mr. Jack: To ask the Secretary of State for Health if he will list in the *Official Report* the cost and names of all the hospital building projects costing in excess of £500,000 which are being built or have been completed since 1979.

Mr. Freeman: Information held centrally on health building schemes, each costing over £1 million, in England shows that 401 have been completed since 1 January 1979 and that a further 144 are under construction. In view of the length of the lists, I have arranged for the information to be placed in the Library. Information is not held centrally on schemes costing less than £1 million.

Nursing Homes

Ms. Harman: To ask the Secretary of State for Health (1) how much was spent by district health authorities on inspection of registered nursing homes in each of the last five years;

(2) how much was received in nursing home registration fees by district health authorities in each of the past five years.

Mr. Mellor: The total income from fees recorded in the annual accounts of health authorities in England for the registration and inspection of private nursing homes and private hospitals since 1984-85 was as follows:

	£ million
1984-85	0·24
1985-86	0·52
1986-87	1·39
1987-88	1·97

Fees are set at a level which covers the full costs incurred in providing this service. Figures for earlier years are not available and provisional ones for 1988-89 will not be available until the autumn.

Asthma

Mr. Dunnachie: To ask the Secretary of State for Health if, under the new Health Service proposals, sufferers from a stoma will continue to receive free prescriptions.

Mr. Mellor: Yes.

Guy's Evelina Children's Hospital Appeal

Mr. Anthony Coombs: To ask the Secretary of State for Health if he will make a statement on the contribution made by the Guy's Evelina children's hospital appeal to sponsor a cot to supporting cots in that unit.

Mr. Kenneth Clarke: This appeal has been running since 1983 and helps to support additional nurses for the unit's intensive care cots which are always in great demand because of its high reputation. Contrary to recent misleading publicity, Guy's hospital management board has stated that there is no financial crisis in the allocation of National Health Service resources to the unit. The Government fully appreciate, however, the contributions made by individuals and organisations to the support of additional health facilities.

Mental Disorder

Mr. Vaz: To ask the Secretary of State for Health how many persons from which countries of origin, have been refused leave to enter the United Kingdom on the grounds of mental disorder in 1984, 1985, 1986, 1987 and 1988.

Mr. Renton: I have been asked to reply.

The available information is given in the following table.

Passengers who were refused leave to enter and removed from the United Kingdom at a port of entry because of a mental disorder by nationality

Geographical region and Nationality	Number				
	1984	1985	1986	1987	1988
Europe					
Austria	3	3	—	1	—
Belgium	3	—	2	5	7
Cyprus	—	—	1	—	—
Denmark	5	3	3	1	—
Finland	2	—	—	1	1
France	12	9	9	13	12
GDR	1	3	1	—	—
German Federal Republic	12	7	6	10	11
Greece	1	2	2	—	3
Italy	2	4	10	5	4
Netherlands	6	11	18	12	6
Norway	1	2	2	3	2
Poland	—	1	—	—	—
Portugal	1	1	—	1	1
Spain	9	4	6	1	2
Sweden	7	4	3	3	5
Switzerland	1	1	5	4	5
Yugoslavia	—	2	—	1	—
Total	66	57	68	61	57
Americas					
Argentina	1	—	—	—	—
Brazil	1	—	1	—	—
Canada	2	3	5	6	8
Chile	—	1	—	—	—
Jamaica	—	—	2	—	3
Trinidad & Tobago	—	1	—	—	—
USA	31	36	39	43	51

Geographical region and Nationality	Number				
	1984	1985	1986	1987	1988
Uruguay	—	—	—	—	1
Total	35	41	47	49	63
Africa					
Algeria	—	—	—	1	—
Ghana	1	1	3	1	—
Kenya	—	—	—	1	—
Mauritius	—	1	—	—	—
Morocco	—	1	—	2	—
Nigeria	1	1	3	1	—
Sierra Leone	1	—	—	—	—
South Africa	—	1	1	1	1
Sudan	—	1	—	—	—
Tunisia	—	1	—	—	—
Uganda	—	—	—	—	1
Zimbabwe	—	—	—	1	—
	3	7	7	8	2
Asia					
Bangladesh	—	1	1	2	—
Hong Kong	—	—	—	1	1
India	3	2	1	—	—
Israel	—	—	2	2	—
Japan	1	—	2	—	2
Lebanon	—	1	—	—	—
Malaysia	1	1	1	—	—
Pakistan	2	2	—	—	—
Philippines	—	—	—	—	1
Saudi Arabia	1	—	—	—	—
Syria	—	1	—	—	—
Turkey	1	1	—	—	—
	9	9	7	5	4
Australasia					
Australia	1	3	3	1	1
New Zealand	—	—	—	5	1
	1	3	3	6	2
Others					
UKPH	—	1	—	—	—
Other countries not elsewhere specified	4	—	5	2	1
Stateless	5	7	6	5	6
All Nationalities	123	125	143	136	135

Cystic Fibrosis

Mr. Andrew F. Bennett: To ask the Secretary of State for Health if he will take steps to ensure that all cystic fibrosis units in hospitals are retained if individual hospitals decide to opt out.

Mr. Wray: To ask the Secretary of State for Health what specific response he has given to the Association of Cystic Fibrosis Adults regarding the impact of the proposals in his White Paper "Working for Patients" on the care of cystic fibrosis patients.

Mr. Kirkwood: To ask the Secretary of State for Health (1) if a self-governing hospital which provides a specialist service to cystic fibrosis patients will be allowed to discontinue the service solely on the grounds that the service is unprofitable;

(2) if district authorities will be given special dispensation to enable them to refer cystic fibrosis patients to specialist centres for treatment without having regard to cost or contractual arrangements;

(3) what estimate he has made of the future of specialist hospital centres which currently provide a service to cystic fibrosis patients under the new system of acute care proposed in the White Paper "Working for Patients".

Mr. Mellor *[holding answer 12 June 1989]:* A detailed response will be sent to the letter from the Association of Cystic Fibrosis Adults which has only just been received.

Following the implementation of "Working for Patients", cystic fibrosis adults can expect to continue to receive a high quality service. The responsibility for ensuring that a comprehensive range of services is available will remain with the district health authority. The needs of patients requiring unusually expensive medicines or treatments will be taken fully into account when contracts are being placed and when prescribing budgets are being assigned to GP practices.

Every patient will receive the treatment and drugs he or she needs.

Mr. Kirkwood: To ask the Secretary of State for Health what estimate he has made of the effect on treatment of cystic fibrosis patients on long-term drug therapy of the general practitioner budget arrangements proposed in the White Paper "Working for Patients".

Mr. Mellor *[holding answer 12 June 1989]:* Every cystic fibrosis patient will continue to get all the drugs and treatment they require.

Mr. Kirkwood: To ask the Secretary of State for Health what steps he will take to ensure that cystic fibrosis patients will not be refused admission to a general practitioner's list solely because of the potentially high cost of treating the disease under the new general practitioner system of indicative budgets proposed in the White Paper "Working for Patients".

Mr. Mellor *[holding answer 12 June 1989]:* The scheme will be structured to take full account of the fact that some patients, such as those with cystic fibrosis, may need potentially high cost treatment. Indicative prescribing budgets will fully reflect these costs and there will be no disincentive to GPs to accept such patients on their lists.

Medical Education and Research

Mr. Wray: To ask the Secretary of State for Health if he will detail the specific ways in which the Government intend to *(a)* maintain and *(b)* help to further improve the quality of medical education and research.

Mr. Mellor *[holding answer 12 June 1989]:* Paragraph 4.30 of "Working for Patients" affirmed the Government's commitment to maintaining the quality of education and research and recognised the special needs in this area. The steering group on undergraduate medical and dental education, whose interim report was published on 6 June will consider how the current arrangements can best be improved to ensure that the policies and programmes of the bodies concerned are properly co-ordinated and managed; and make recommendations. The group has already made recommendations, which we have endorsed, on support for the higher service costs associated with teaching.

Mr. Wray: To ask the Secretary of State for Health if he will list all the institutions and experts which he consulted about the medical education and research aspects of the White Paper "Working for Patients".

Mr. Mellor *[holding answer 12 June 1989]:* We have received representations from various groups including the Committee on Vice Chancellors and Principals (CVCP), the Joint Medical Advisory Committee (JMAC) and the Joint Committee of Metropolitan and Provincial Deans (JCMPD), which represents the deans of United Kingdom medical schools and clinical facilities. These representations were primarily about education. In addition we have received representations on research from the Medical Research Council (MRC) and the Association of Medical Research Charities and other interested parties. All of these bodies have welcomed the commitment in "Working for Patients" to maintaining the quality of medical education and research.

Nurses (Examinations)

Mr. Kirkwood: To ask the Secretary of State for Health when he plans to introduce the UKCC recommended rule change to allow nurses entered on the roll, or the relevant second level part of the UKCC register, as a result of failing their first level exams the maximum permitted number of times, a further three attempts at passing.

Mr. Mellor *[holding answer 12 June 1989]:* Work on the statutory instrument to introduce this change is in hand and the new rule will be in operation in the near future.

NHS Reform

Mr. Frank Field: To ask the Secretary of State for Health if he will list by family practitioner committee area the numbers of doctors' practices that are eligible to become practice budget holders under the conditions described in "Working for Patients."

Mr. Mellor *[holding answer 12 June 1989]:* I refer the hon. Member to the reply I gave to the hon. Member for Peckham (Ms. Harman) on 4 April at column *93*. In addition, as working paper No. 3 makes clear, practices may group together in order to opt for practice budgets.

Childhood Cancers

Mr. Woodcock: To ask the Secretary of State for Health what steps are being taken to encourage work on early detection of childhood cancers and, in particular, the type called neuroblastoma.

Mr. Freeman *[holding answer 12 June 1989]:* The Department provides research funds to the Childhood Cancer Research group, which maintains a national registry of childhood tumours and carries out studies of the causes and treatment of childhood cancers. The Department also supports the cancer screening evaluation unit, which provides advice on existing and possible future schemes of screening for cancer, including neuroblastoma.

Pharmacies

Sir Michael McNair-Wilson: To ask the Secretary of State for Health whether the reasons for a decision on the location of a pharmacy are *(a)* made public by the rural dispensing committee and *(b)* usually made available to interested parties.

Mr. Mellor *[holding answer 12 June 1989]:* Regulations require the rural dispensing committee (RDC) to give written notice of such decisions to my right hon. and learned Friend the Secretary of State, the applicant, the family practitioner committees concerned, the local medical and pharmaceutical committees for the areas of those committees and to any other person who has submitted written or oral evidence to the RDC.

Disabled People

Mr. Alfred Morris: To ask the Secretary of State for Health if he will make it his policy to take full account of the urgent resource implications of the fourth report of the Office of Population Censuses and Surveys, "Disabled Adults: Services, Transport and Employment", in formulating the Government's response to the Griffiths report on community care; and if he will make a statement.

Mr. Mellor *[holding answer 12 June 1989]:* We are pleased to have available the wealth of information on the circumstances of disabled people provided by the four reports published to date from the OPCS surveys of disability. We will take careful account of their findings in drawing up our proposals on community care and in our consideration of other policies for disabled people.

Mr. Dunnachie: To ask the Secretary of State for Health if he will ensure that, under the new Health Service proposals, the present range and quality of ostomy appliances will be maintained.

Mr. Mellor: Yes.

DEFENCE

Nuclear Weapons

3. **Mr. Dunnachie:** To ask the Secretary of State for Defence whether more United States or North Atlantic Treaty Organisation nuclear-capable forces are proposed to be based in the United Kingdom.

51. **Mr. Wray:** To ask the Secretary of State for Defence whether more United States or North Atlantic Treaty Organisation nuclear-capable forces are proposed to be based in the United Kingdom.

72. **Ms. Primarolo:** To ask the Secretary of State for Defence whether more United States or North Atlantic Treaty Organisation nuclear-capable forces are proposed to be based in the United Kingdom.

Mr. Archie Hamilton: NATO allies are still considering a number of options for adjusting remaining nuclear forces following the INF agreement. Amongst these options is the possible deployment to Europe, including the United Kingdom, of additional longer-range dual-capable aircraft from the United States. However, no decision have yet been taken.

24. **Ms. Abbott:** To ask the Secretary of State for Defence what proposals have been made for additional nuclear weapons to be based in the United Kingdom.

37. **Mrs. Clwyd:** To ask the Secretary of State for Defence what proposals have been made for additional nuclear weapons to be based in the United Kingdom.

71. **Mr. Wareing:** To ask the Secretary of State for Defence what proposals have been made for additional nuclear weapons to be based in the United Kingdom.

Mr. Archie Hamilton: The proposals for restructuring and modernising NATO's nuclear forces which are under consideration within the Alliance would create scope for further significant overall reductions in NATO's European stockpile of land-based nuclear weapons.

Naval Rules of Engagement

5. **Mr. Galloway:** To ask the Secretary of State for Defence what consultations he has had with his United States counterpart regarding possible changes to naval rules of engagement.

Mr. Cohen: To ask the Secretary of State for Defence what consultations he has had with his United States counterpart regarding possible changes to naval rules of engagement.

33. **Mr. Allen McKay:** To ask the Secretary of State for Defence what consultations he has had with his United States counterpart regarding possible changes to naval rules of engagement.

Mr. Younger: I have not had any discussions with Mr. Cheney regarding possible changes to naval rules of engagement, although I have had some with his predecessor, Mr. Carlucci and other NATO Allies. The Alliance naturally reviews and updates its rules of engagement from time to time, but it is not our practice to comment on the detail of such matters.

Lance Missile

11. **Mrs. Fyfe:** To ask the Secretary of State for Defence what is the current number of Lance missiles deployed by the North Atlantic Treaty Organisation in West Germany.

Mr. Archie Hamilton: There are currently 88 Lance missile launchers deployed in Europe by NATO, compared with some 1,500 Warsaw pact nuclear-capable short-range missile launchers. Detailed deployment information is classified.

57. **Dr. Kim Howells:** To ask the Secretary of State for Defence what is the current number of Lance missiles deployed by the North Atlantic Treaty Organisation in West Germany.

59. **Mr. Ray Powell:** To ask the Secretary of State for Defence what is the current number of Lance missiles deployed by the North Atlantic Treaty Organisation in West Germany.

Mr. Archie Hamilton: I refer the hon. Members to the answer I gave earlier today to the hon. Member for Glasgow, Maryhill (Mrs. Fyfe).

Warsaw Pact (Dissolution)

14. **Mrs. Gorman:** To ask the Secretary of State for Defence what recent assessment he has made of the prospects for dissolution of the Warsaw pact.

Mr. Younger: There is no evidence that an early dissolution of the Warsaw pact military alliance is likely.

Nuclear Weapons (First Use)

19. **Mr. Ron Davies:** To ask the Secretary of State for Defence in what circumstances Her Majesty's Government's policy encompasses the first use of nuclear weapons.

Mr. Allen: To ask the Secretary of State for Defence in what circumstances Her Majesty's Government's policy encompasses the first use of nuclear weapons.

87. **Mr. Flannery:** To ask the Secretary of State for Defence in what circumstances Her Majesty's Government's policy encompasses the first use of nuclear weapons.

88. **Mr. Turner:** To ask the Secretary of State for Defence in what circumstances Her Majesty's Government's policy encompasses the first use of nuclear weapons.

Mr. Younger: The possibility of first use of nuclear weapons in response to a conventional attack is central to NATO's strategy of deterrence. However, it would undermine deterrence to spell out in advance the precise circumstances in which nuclear weapons would or might be used.

75. **Mr. Paice:** To ask the Secretary of State for Defence what assessment he has made of the consequences for NATO's strategy of the adoption of a policy of no-first use of nuclear weapons.

Mr. Archie Hamilton: A policy of "no first use" would be fundamentally incompatible with NATO's strategy of flexible response.

NATO (Nuclear Weapons)

21. **Mr. Galbraith:** To ask the Secretary of State for Defence what consultations he has had with his Italian counterpart regarding the modernisation of the North Atlantic Treaty Organisation's short-range nuclear forces.

47. **Ms. Short:** To ask the Secretary of State for Defence what consultations he has had with his Italian counterpart regarding the modernisation of the North Atlantic Treaty Organisation short-range nuclear forces.

77. **Mr. Buckley:** To ask the Secretary of State for Defence what consultations he has had with his Italian counterpart regarding the modernisation of North Atlantic Treaty Organisation short-range nuclear forces.

Mr. Younger: I last met the Italian Defence Minister at the meeting of the defence planning committee last week when we discussed a range of defence and security matters affecting the Alliance.

Staff Relocation (Cleveland)

22. **Mr. Holt:** To ask the Secretary of State for Defence whether it remains his policy to relocate Ministry of Defence staff to Cleveland; what representations he has received from the unions with regard to the move; and what consideration he gave to the adequacy of road transport links with Cleveland when deciding his policy.

Mr. Sainsbury: Yes. It remains our intention to relocate the directorate general of defence quality assurance to Preston farm, Teesside. The trades unions have asked for further information and clarification of a number of points and consultation with them continues. Road transport links with Teesside are recognised as excellent.

Low-flying Aircraft

23. **Mr. Canavan:** To ask the Secretary of State for Defence how many complaints he has received so far this year about low-flying military aircraft.

Mr. Neubert: Between 1 January 1989 and 30 april 1989 the Ministry of Defence received 1,912 inquiries and complaints about military low-flying training in the United Kingdom.

Women (Recruitment)

25. **Mrs. Gillian Shephard:** To ask the Secretary of State for Defence what further steps he is taking to recruit women to the armed services.

Mr. Neubert: We are seeking to widen the opportunities for the employment of women in the armed forces and we expect the number of service women to increase over the next few years. In 1988-89 the number of women recruited into the armed forces rose by 15 per cent. to 3,001. We plan a further increase in the number of female recruits this year.

West German Defence Minister

26. **Mr. Denzil Davies:** To ask the Secretary of State for Defence whether he has any plans to meet in the near future the Defence Minister of the Federal Republic of Germany; and what matters he proposes to discuss.

53. **Mr. Dykes:** To ask the Secretary of State for Defence when he next plans to hold talks with his counterpart in the Federal Republic of Germany on mutual defence subjects.

Mr. Younger: I met Dr. Stoltenberg at the meeting of NATO's defence planning committee on 8-9 June, and we also met in London on 26 May for substantive discussions on a wide range of subjects of mutual defence interest. I have no immediate plans for a further bilateral meeting, but I expect to see Dr. Stoltenberg when the independent European programme group meets at ministerial level later this month.

Takeovers (National Interest)

28. **Mr. Barry Field:** To ask the Secretary of State for Defence what criteria he uses to define the national interest when a United Kingdom defence contractor is the subject of a takeover bid from a non-United Kingdom company.

Mr. Sainsbury: Any factors which could affect the supply to the armed forces of the equipment they need to operate effectively would be taken into account. These factors could be judged only in the context of any specific takeover proposal.

Soviet Union (Force Reductions)

29. **Mr. Parry:** To ask the Secretary of State for Defence what assessment he has made of the Soviet Union's latest planned cutbacks in its European conventional forces as announced during the recent visit of United States Secretary of State, James Baker.

55. **Mr. Clay:** To ask the Secretary of State for Defence what assessment he has made of the Soviet Union's latest planned cutbacks in its European conventional forces, as announced during the recent visit of United States Secretary of State, James Baker.

56. **Mr. Martlew:** To ask the Secretary of State for Defence what assessment he has made of the Soviet

Union's latest planned cutbacks in its European conventional forces as announced during the recent visit of United States Secretary of State, James Barker.

Mr. Younger: I refer the hon. Members to the answer I gave earlier today, to the hon. Member for Sheffield, Heeley (Mr. Michie).

39. **Mr. Battle:** To ask the Secretary of State for Defence what consideration he has given to the defence implications of the Soviet proposal to thin out front-line forces in Europe.

Mr. Archie Hamilton: Reductions in the Warsaw pact's massive concentrations of forces in Europe would be very welcome. However, their current zonal proposals would make it very difficult to sustain NATO's strategy of forward defence. Nevertheless, we are studying them with care.

BAOR (Nuclear Weapons)

30. **Mr. Andrew Mitchell:** To ask the Secretary of State for Defence what assessment he has made of the consequences for the British Army of the Rhine of having no nuclear weapons.

43. **Mr. David Nicholson:** To ask the Secretary of State for Defence what assessment he has made of the implications for the British Army of the Rhine capacity for defence of the removal from its armoury of short-range nuclear weapons.

Mr. Archie Hamilton: NATO's strategy of deterrence and defence requires a mix of conventional, theatre nuclear and strategic nuclear forces. Removal of the theatre nuclear component would undermine deterrence and leave our conventional forces very vulnerable to attack.

Soviet Union (Nuclear Weapons)

31. **Mr. John Greenway:** To ask the Secretary of State for Defence whether his Department will be responding to the Soviet proposal to withdraw 500 nuclear warheads from eastern Europe.

Mr. Archie Hamilton: We welcome the Soviet announcement that they will withdraw 500 nuclear warheads from eastern Europe, but believe that this probably represents as little as 5 per cent. of the total number of Soviet nuclear warheads deployed within the European theatre. In contrast, since 1979 NATO has withdrawn 2,400 nuclear weapons from Europe, leaving only approximately 4,600 within the theatre. The Soviet Union will, therefore, have to make further very substantial reductions if they are to come down to the size of NATO's nuclear stockpile in Europe.

Malaysia

32. **Miss Lestor:** To ask the Secretary of State for Defence whether there was any reference in any of the correspondence concerning the sale of arms to Malaysia that preceded the signing of the memorandum of understanding in 1988, to United Kingdom overseas aid to Malaysia.

Mr. Sainsbury: Following the expression of Malaysian interest in United Kingdom overseas aid in early exchanges, my right hon. Friend the Secretary of State for Defence made it clear to the Malaysian Finance Minister that it would not be acceptable to Her Majesty's Government to link aid with the defence sales package. As I stated at column *191* on 17 May, the memorandum of understanding makes no mention of overseas aid to Malaysia.

Royal Naval Personnel (Radiation)

Dr. Moonie: To ask the Secretary of State for Defence what further radiation checks have been carried out on Royal Navy sailors and personnel exposed to nuclear weapons and reactors; and what were the findings.

Mr. Archie Hamilton: Medical records of all naval personnel are analysed annually, and any health trends are identified. There have been no special surveys to determine whether there is any evidence of medical disorders arising from exposure of Royal Navy nuclear submarine personnel to radiation. However, routine medical surveillance is carried out for those Royal Naval personnel designated as radiation workers in accordance with the Ionising Radiations Regulations 1985.

Radiation dose records are kept for Royal Naval radiation workers, and statistics of doses received were published in the replies I gave to the hon. Member for St. Helens North (Mr. Evans) on 20 March at columns *477-478* and on 2 May at columns *61-62* this year.

Regular radiation surveys are carried out on board nuclear-powered submarines to ensure that personnel not designated as radiation workers do not receive any significant radiation doses.

Deterrent Strategy (Training)

35. **Miss Widdecombe:** To ask the Secretary of State for Defence what training is given at staff college level on the components of an effective deterrent strategy.

Mr. Neubert: The concept of deterrence pervades all Service officers' staff training. The staff colleges' syllabi require students to be conversant with the current threat, the principles of nuclear and conventional deterrence and the defence strategies and military capabilities of NATO and the United Kingdom. Possible alternative strategies, the effects of arms control and the influence of political will are also studied.

Z-Berths

36. **Ms. Gordon:** To ask the Secretary of State for Defence if he has any plans to revise the system of allocating Z-berths.

Mr. Archie Hamilton: No.

Nuclear Deterrent

Mr. Carrington: To ask the Secretary of State for Defence what steps he has taken to ensure that the United Kingdom nuclear deterrent is credible.

Mr. Younger: I refer my hon. Friend to the answer I gave earlier today, to my hon. Friend the Member for Colne Valley (Mr. Riddick).

Short-Range Nuclear Weapons

40. Mr. Cash: To ask the Secretary of State for Defence what is Her Majesty's Government's response to the policy of the West German Government to the modernisation of short-range nuclear weapons.

Mr. Archie Hamilton: At the recent summit all NATO countries, including West Germany, agreed that for the foreseeable future there would need to be deployed in Europe land, sea and air-based nuclear systems, including ground-launched missiles. They also agreed that to remain effective these systems would have to be kept up to date where necessary.

Short Bros.

41. Mr. Colvin: To ask the Secretary of State for Defence if he will make a statement on the defence implications of the privatisation of Short Bros.

Mr. Sainsbury: The MOD welcomes the return of Short Bros. to the private sector. We look forward to dealing with Shorts under its new owners on the same commercial basis as with our other suppliers of defence equipment.

Trident

42. Mr. Madden: To ask the Secretary of State for Defence if he will make a further statement about penalty costs associated with the Trident programme.

Mr. Sainsbury: The Trident programme includes a wide range of contracts. In accordance with MOD policy, all provide where applicable for payment of liquidated damages by the contractor to compensate MOD for the consequences of late delivery of equipment. Equally, provision is made for the prime contractor to recover incurred expenditure and additional costs arising if the MOD cancels a contract. The level of recovery possible will vary, and will depend on a number of factors, including the timing and circumstances of the cancellation.

West Germany

44. Mr. Beaumont-Dark: To ask the Secretary of State for Defence if he will outline the United Kingdom military contribution to the defence of the Federal Republic of Germany.

Mr. Archie Hamilton: The British Army of the Rhine and RAF Germany are important parts of the overall United Kingdom contribution to NATO and they have an essential role to play in the defence of the European mainland. Full details of their composition and roles are contained in the 1989 Statement on the Defence Estimates (Cm. 675-I).

Mr. Kirkwood: To ask the Secretary of State for Defence when he last met his counterpart in the Federal Republic of Germany; and what matters were discussed.

Mr. Younger: I last met Dr. Stoltenberg at the meeting of NATO's Defence Planning committee in Brussels on 8-9 June. We also met bilaterally in London on 26 May for substantive discussions on a wide range of subjects of mutual defence interest.

Flexible Response

45. Mr. Quentin Davies: To ask the Secretary of State for Defence what assessment he has made of the consequences for the strategy of flexible response of a third zero.

48. Mr. Hague: To ask the Secretary of State for Defence what assessment he has made of the consequences for the strategy of flexible response of a third zero.

54. Mr. Patrick Thompson: To ask the Secretary of State for Defence what assessment he has made of the consequences for the strategy of flexible response of a third zero.

Mr. Archie Hamilton: I share the assessment made by NATO Heads of Government at their recent summit that for the foreseeable future there is no alternative to the Alliance strategy of deterrence and that this strategy requires a mix of nuclear forces, including Europe-based ground-launched missiles. I therefore welcome the summit's rejection of a third zero.

78. Mr. Neil Hamilton: To ask the Secretary of State for Defence what assessment he has made of the strategy of flexible response in the light of recent proposals on short-range nuclear weapons.

Mr. Archie Hamilton: I share the assessment made by NATO Heads of Government at their recent summit that for the foreseeable future there is no alternative to the Alliance strategy of deterrence and that this strategy requires a mix of nuclear forces, including Europe-based ground-launched missiles. I therefore welcome the summit's rejection of a third zero.

Eastern Atlantic (Naval Defence)

46. Mr. Evennett: To ask the Secretary of State for Defence if he will outline the United Kingdom's contribution to the North Atlantic Treaty Organisation naval defence of the eastern Atlantic.

Mr. Archie Hamilton: I refer my hon. Friend to paragraph 302 of volume 1 of the Statement on the Defence Estimates 1989 (Cm. 675-I).

Nuclear Weapons and Reactors

49. Mr. Haynes: To ask the Secretary of State for Defence if he will provide an estimate of the number of nuclear weapons and defence reactors currently on sea and ocean floors.

50. Mr. Steinberg: To ask the Secretary of State for Defence if he will provide an estimate of the number of nuclear weapons and defence reactors currently on sea and ocean floors.

74. Ms. Walley: To ask the Secretary of State for Defence if he will provide an estimate of the number of nuclear weapons and defence reactors currently on sea and ocean floors.

Mr. Archie Hamilton: We can be confident that there are no nuclear weapons or nuclear reactors on the sea floor within United Kingdom territorial waters. There are no United Kingdom nuclear weapons or reactors on the sea floor anywhere in the world. Nuclear weapons or reactors which belong to other nations and which present no significant threat to the United Kingdom are not the responsibility of the United Kingdom Government.

United States Secretary of State for Defence

52. **Mr. Menzies Campbell:** To ask the Secretary of State for Defence when he last met the United States Secretary for Defence; and what matters were discussed.

Mr. Younger: I met the United States Secretary for Defence at the ministerial meeting of the NATO defence planning committee last week when we discussed a wide range of matters of mutual interest.

Expenditure

58. **Mr. McCartney:** To ask the Secretary of State for Defence what is the total amount of defence spending proposed in his defence White Paper; and what will be the cumulative defence expenditure from 1979.

66. **Mrs. Beckett:** To ask the Secretary of State for Defence what is the total amount of defence spending proposed in his defence White Paper; and what will be the cumulative defence expenditure from 1979.

76. **Mr. Skinner:** To ask the Secretary of State for Defence what is the total amount of defence spending proposed in his defence White Paper; and what will be the cumulative defence expenditure from 1979.

86. **Mr. John Hughes:** To ask the Secretary of State for Defence what is the total amount of defence spending proposed in his defence White Paper; and what will be the cumulative defence expenditure from 1979.

Mr. Archie Hamilton: The Defence budget for 1989-90 is £20,143 million. Total expenditure on defence between 1979-80 and 1988-89 has amounted to some £154,000 million.

NATO Secretary General

60. **Sir Russell Johnston:** To ask the Secretary of State for Defence when he last met the Secretary General of the North Atlantic Treaty Organisation; and what matters were discussed.

Mr. Younger: I last met Dr. Woerner at the meeting of NATO's Defence Planning committee on 8-9 June. We discussed a range of matters of mutual interest.

CND

61. **Mr. Burns:** To ask the Secretary of State for Defence what representations he has recently received from the Campaign for Nuclear Disarmament; and whether he will make a statement.

69. **Dame Jill Knight:** To ask the Secretary of State for Defence what representations he has recently received from the Campaign for Nuclear Disarmament; and whether he will make a statement.

70. **Mr. Knapman:** To ask the Secretary of State for Defence what representations he has recently received from the Campaign for Nuclear Disarmament; and whether he will make a statement.

Mr. Archie Hamilton: Since my right hon. Friend last replied to this question on 7 March, at column 737, he has received less than a dozen letters from CND which reflects, no doubt, the continuing decline in support for that organisation.

Equestrian Activities

62. **Mr. Marlow:** To ask the Secretary of State for Defence if he will make a statement on the cost of support provided by his Department to equestrian activities, excluding those associated with parades.

Mr. Neubert: Public funds are used only to support official equestrian activities. However support costs, such as training, stabling and veterinary services, are an integral part of the expenditure on horses participating in ceremonial and public duties.

Submarines

63. **Mr. Douglas:** To ask the Secretary of State for Defence if he will make a statement on the progress of the ordering programme for both conventional and nuclear submarines.

Mr. Sainsbury: This Government have ordered five nuclear powered fleet submarines, of which three have already been accepted into service, and four of the new Upholder class of conventional submarines. We envisage further orders for both nuclear and conventional powered submarines, but no decisions have yet been taken.

Nuclear Tests

64. **Mr. Ashley:** To ask the Secretary of State for Defence with which individuals or organisations he has had discussions in the last year about possible hazards from nuclear tests.

Mr. Sainsbury: It is impractical to list all individuals with whom my Department has had discussions concerning the British nuclear tests within the last year except at disproportionate cost.

However, I can confirm that a number of organisations have been consulted during the normal course of business. These include the National Radiological Protection board (NRPB), the Imperial Cancer Research fund (ICRF), the Medical Research council (MRC), the International Commission for Radiological Protection (ICRP), the National Health Service central register, the Office of Population Censuses and Surveys (OPCS), the Defence Radiological Protection service (DRPS) together with a number of overseas individuals representing United States and Australian authorities and organisations. We have also received representations from a number of individuals, including right hon. and hon. Members.

Exercise Wintex

65. **Mr. Tony Banks:** To ask the Secretary of State for Defence what was the extent of United Kingdom involvement in simulated nuclear war fighting in the recent Wintex staff exercise.

83. **Mr. Corbyn:** To ask the Secretary of State for Defence what was the extent of United Kingdom involvement in simulated nuclear war fighting in the recent Wintex staff exercise.

90. Mr. Bernie Grant: To ask the Secretary of State for Defence what was the extent of United Kingdom involvement in simulated nuclear war fighting in the recent Wintex staff exercise.

Mr. Archie Hamilton: Exercise Wintex-Cimex is a NATO-wide command post-exercise conducted by Alliance members. Its objective is to test command, control and consultation plans and procedures and to exercise the appropriate crisis management machinery which would be used in the defence of NATO countries in times of international tension and war, including a nuclear phase. Details of the scenario and the precise involvement of individual participants are classified.

Weapon-Free Corridors

67. Mr. Franks: To ask the Secretary of State for Defence what assessment he has made of the consequences for the North Atlantic Treaty Organisation of adopting a policy of troop, tank and artillery-free corridors.

Mr. Archie Hamilton: We believe that such a policy would be undesirable on both political and military grounds.

Nuclear-Free Zones

68. Mr. Hayward: To ask the Secretary of State for Defence if he will assess the consequences for the security of the United Kingdom of the adoption of nuclear-free zones in Western Europe.

Mr. Archie Hamilton: This Government are against the adoption of nuclear free zones in Western Europe, where we believe they would not increase but reduce security and stability. The territory of a zone would still be under threat from weapons outside the zone but targeted on it. Moreover, the mobility of many ground-launched and air-delivered nuclear weapons means that they could be rapidly deployed back into a nuclear-free zone at a time of tension, thus heightening rather than reducing the risk of war.

HMS Southampton

73. Mr. Robert Hicks: To ask the Secretary of State for Defence when he expects to make an announcement about the re-fit contract for HMS Southampton.

Mr. Sainsbury: Shortly.

Horseshoe Barracks, Shoeburyness

79. Mr. Teddy Taylor: To ask the Secretary of State for Defence if he will make a further statement on his plans to dispose of the Horseshoe barracks in Shoeburyness, Essex.

Mr. Neubert: It remains our intention to dispose of Horseshoe barracks on the open market, once existing facilities have been reprovided elsewhere. We have retained independent consultants to advise on the development potential of the site and we await their definitive recommendations.

Nuclear Test Veterans

80. Mr. Hinchliffe: To ask the Secretary of State for Defence what is the latest information available to his Department on the terms of the recent judgment in the Australian courts regarding compensation for nuclear test veterans; and what are the implications for his policy on British nuclear test veterans.

Mr. Sainsbury: My Department has not yet received a copy of the judgment and until we have had an opportunity to study its content, we will not be able to say what implications, if any, there are for the British nuclear test veterans.

89. Mr. Ted Garrett: To ask the Secretary of State for Defence when he expects to announce new compensation arrangements for British ex-servicemen who have suffered radiation ailments arising from their duties.

Mr. Sainsbury: I refer the hon. Member to the answer I gave the hon. Member for Knowsley, North (Mr. Howell) on 6 June 1989, at column *121*.

Ceremonial Duties

81. Mr. Cyril D. Townsend: To ask the Secretary of State for Defence how many regular service men in *(a)* Greater London and *(b)* Windsor are required on an average day to carry out ceremonial duties as sentries; and how many such sentries are posted in each location.

Mr. Neubert: The number of regular service men required on an average day to carry out ceremonial duties as sentries in London and Windsor depends on whether or not Her Majesty the Queen is in residence. Three service men are required to man each post on a 24 hour basis. The numbers at each location are:

	Her Majesty the Queen in residence	Her Majesty the Queen out of residence
Buckingham Palace	15 service men to man 5 posts	9 service men to man 3 posts
St. James's Palace	15 service men to man 5 posts	9 service men to man 3 posts
Tower of London	6 service men to man 2 posts	
Windsor Castle	21 service men to man 7 posts	15 service men to man 5 posts

Ceremonial sentry duties are mainly undertaken by the Army, but the Royal Navy and the Royal Air Force also provide personnel.

F111

82. Mr. Eastham: To ask the Secretary of State for Defence if he will make a statement on future deployment plans for the F111 in the United Kingdom.

Mr. Archie Hamilton: I refer the hon. Member to the answer that I gave earlier today to the hon. Member for Leeds, Central (Mr. Fatchett).

Soviet Union (Fighting Vehicles)

84. Mr. Janman: To ask the Secretary of State for Defence what evidence his Department has as to whether the Soviets are dismantling their most modern armoured fighting vehicles.

Mr. Archie Hamilton: There is as yet no evidence that the Soviets are dismantling their most modern armoured fighting vehicles.

Anti-satellite Weapons

85. **Mr. Atkinson:** To ask the Secretary of State for Defence if he has any plans to meet his North Atlantic Treaty Organisation counterparts to discuss the deployment of anti-satellite weapons.

Mr. Younger: I have no plans to do so.

European Fighter Aircraft (Radar)

91. **Mr. Graham:** To ask the Secretary of State for Defence when he expects to announce an order for the development of a radar for the European fighter aircraft.

Mr. Sainsbury: I have nothing to add at present to the answer that I gave on 9 May 1989 at column *426* to the hon. Member for Fylde (Mr. Jack).

Type 42 Destroyer

Mr. Harry Greenway: To ask the Secretary of State for Defence how many miles on average type 42 destroyers have travelled over the past 10 years; how many they were designed to travel and over what period; and what steps he is taking to ensure that they are capable of operating for their full service lives.

Mr. Sainsbury: Type 42 destroyers have travelled approximately 31,000 nautical miles per ship per year over the last 10 years. Mileage is not used as a design and operating criterion; ship life is measured in years and experience has shown this to be a good criterion, which takes account of the variety of factors which affect life such as sea states, operational conditions and ship speed. A refitting and maintenance cycle is in operation which ensures that the ships will be fully capable throughout their service life.

Mr. Harry Greenway: To ask the Secretary of State for Defence if the replacement for the type 42 destroyer will be given the same length of trials periods as the type 22 frigates.

Mr. Sainsbury: The acceptance trials of the vessel to replace the type 42 destroyer are expected to take a similar amount of time to those for earlier classes of ships of a similar technical complexity.

Mr. Harry Greenway: To ask the Secretary of State for Defence what plans his Department has to replace the type 42 destroyers when they begin to leave service in 1998.

Mr. Sainsbury: The Government are continuing to participate in the NFR 90 project, which could eventually meet the Royal Navy's requirement for an anti-air warfare escort to replace the type 42 destroyers.

Aegis Air Defence System

Mr. Harry Greenway: To ask the Secretary of State for Defence if he envisages future procurement of the American Aegis air defence system.

Mr. Sainsbury: No.

HMS Bristol

Mr. Harry Greenway: To ask the Secretary of State for Defence if he plans to replace HMS Bristol with an air defence ship of similar capabilities.

Mr. Sainsbury: No decisions have yet been taken on how long HMS Bristol, which was commissioned in 1973, will remain in service. There are no plans to replace her with another type 82 destroyer.

Sea Dart

Mr. Harry Greenway: To ask the Secretary of State for Defence if he will make a statement on the efficiency of the Sea Dart missile system.

Mr. Sainsbury: The Sea Dart missile system meets or surpasses the performance and reliability criteria specified in the naval staff requirement (NSR 6502).

Mr. Harry Greenway: To ask the Secretary of State for Defence if the Royal Navy will be entirely reliant upon the Sea Wolf system for air defence when the Sea Dart system is withdrawn from service; and how area defence will be provided.

Mr. Sainsbury: The Sea Dart system is expected to remain in service into the next century.

Mr. Harry Greenway: To ask the Secretary of State for Defence what assessment he has made of the likelihood of the Sea Dart system becoming obsolete before the end of the service lives of the type 42 destroyers that carry it.

Mr. Sainsbury: As a result of assessments already undertaken, action is in hand to ensure the Sea Dart system continues to be effective and supportable until the ships in which it is fitted are phased out of service.

Sea King

Mr. Harry Greenway: To ask the Secretary of State for Defence if there are any plans to replace the Sea King AEW with a purpose-built aircraft.

Mr. Sainsbury: There are no plans to do so at present. The Sea King, equipped with Searchwater radar, will continue to provide airborne early warning for the Royal Navy into the next century.

Air Search Surveillance

Mr. Harry Greenway: To ask the Secretary of State for Defence what information he has on which NATO services operate three dimensional air search surveillance radars for their ships; and when the Royal Navy will obtain such a capacity.

Mr. Sainsbury: It is not our policy to comment in detail on the operational capabilities of NATO allies. Her Majesty's ships are equipped with a number of air defence radars which provide the capabilities judged to be necessary to satisfy the Royal Navy's operational requirements. Details of the equipments deployed are classified.

Fleet Missile Systems

Mr. Harry Greenway: To ask the Secretary of State for Defence what missile system is planned to defend the fleet from aerial attack at medium and long ranges in the 1990s and into the next century.

Mr. Sainsbury: The United Kingdom is currently engaged in two parallel projects aimed at meeting this requirement, the NATO anti-air warfare system (NAAWS) and the European family of anti-air missile systems (FAMS). We are pleased with the progress of both these projects, but are not yet in a position to indicate a preference between the two.

Type 21 Frigate

Mr. Harry Greenway: To ask the Secretary of State for Defence what plans his Department has to replace the six type 21 frigates which will be at least 20 years old by 1997.

Mr. Sainsbury: We have plans for sufficient orders of new type 23 frigates to ensure that the strength of the destroyer and frigate force remains at about 50 as older ships are progressively paid off in the next decade. No decisions have yet been taken on when the type 21 frigates will be paid off.

Clothing and Vehicles

Mr. Austin Mitchell: To ask the Secretary of State for Defence whether Her Majesty's Government are planning to rely on external sources of supply to equip the armed services with clothing and vehicles in the event of a conventional war.

Mr. Neubert: No. Availability of clothing and vehicles from internal sources of supply is generally deemed sufficient to meet the needs of the armed services in the event of a conventional war.

Personal Injury Claims

Mr. Ashley: To ask the Secretary of State for Defence how many claims for compensation because of personal injury due to alleged negligence have been made by members of the forces in each year since they were entitled to do so; and how many have been successful.

Mr. Archie Hamilton: A total of 139 claims were received in 1987, a further 265 in 1988 and another 204 have been received so far this year. Of these claims, 60 have been successfully concluded and 425 have yet to be finalised. These figures include claims arising from incidents occurring during the six months immediately prior to the repeal of section 10 of the Crown Proceedings Act 1947, which are being dealt with exceptionally on an ex-gratia basis.

Section 10 Certificates

Mr. Ashley: To ask the Secretary of State for Defence how many section 10 certificates have been issued since 1947 in respect of service men/women who were not nuclear test veterans.

Mr. Neubert: The information could not be provided without disproportionate cost.

Vehicle Insurance

Mr. Ashley: To ask the Secretary of State for Defence if he will give details of the insurance policy which the services are required to have for their vehicles by the Road Traffic Acts and whether it covers tracked armoured cars.

Mr. Neubert: The legislation relating to insurance in respect of third-party risks does not apply to vehicles or persons acting in the service of the Crown. Nevertheless, my Department does hold an insurance policy with Guardian Royal Exchange for third-party claims arising out of road traffic accidents involving all its vehicles, including tracked armoured vehicles.

Contractors (Payments)

Mr. Nellist: To ask the Secretary of State for Defence if he will list in the *Official Report* the precise amounts paid to each of the following contractors by his Department in respect of headquarter contracts in the year ended 31 March 1988 *(a)* Jaguar plc, *(b)* Dunlop Ltd. aviation division, *(c)* Rolls-Royce plc supply group and *(d)* Rolls-Royce plc industrial and marine division.

Mr. Sainsbury: Records of payments made to divisions or other sub-groups within companies are not generally kept. Such information is in any event regarded as commercially confidential. We have no record of any payments made to Jaguar plc.

Woolwich Arsenal West Site

Mr. Cartwright: To ask the Secretary of State for Defence what is the total area of the Woolwich arsenal west site which is to be released by his Department; and what is its estimated current market value.

Mr. Sainsbury: I refer the hon. Member to the reply that I gave to him on 11 April 1989 at column *516*. The total area of the Woolwich arsenal west site to be released following the move of the director general of defence quality assurance, a proposal at present the subject of consultation with the trade unions, is approximately 79 acres.

As the site will be sold on the open market by competitive tender, it would not be appropriate to disclose our estimate of current market value.

RAVC, Melton Mowbray

Mr. Latham: To ask the Secretary of State for Defence whether he is now able to announce his decision on the future of the Royal Army Veterinary Corps, Melton Mowbray.

Mr. Archie Hamilton: No. As my hon. Friend, the Under-Secretary of State for the Armed Forces told my hon. Friend on 9 May 1989 at column *427,* consideration of the review into future arrangements for service animal training will be completed this month. We will then be in a position to make a decision.

Written Answers to Questions

Wednesday 14 June 1989

AGRICULTURE, FISHERIES AND FOOD

Fraud

68. **Mr. Gill:** To ask the Minister of Agriculture, Fisheries and Food what further steps have now been taken to prevent fraud in intervention stocks and export refunds following the latest Court of Auditors report.

Mr. MacGregor: As my hon. Friend knows, I have been taking the initiative in the Council of Ministers on many occasions to press for further action to deal with fraud in the common agricultural policy. I am glad to say that the Commission has undertaken to present to Council later this month a report on follow-up action to the recent Court of Auditors report. This will include a proposal to require member states to carry out an annual check on intervention stocks, to ensure that actual quantities present tally with storekeepers' accounts, and a revised proposal on monitoring export refunds, which would require member states to carry out a minimum level of controls. I will again be pressing Council to take speedy action on these proposals. The Commission has also this month introduced a simplification of the system for beef export refunds designed to reduce opportunities for fraud.

Potato Marketing Board

Mr. Kirkwood: To ask the Minister of Agriculture, Fisheries and Food whether he is yet in a position to make a statement on the future of the Potato Marketing Board.

Mr. Ryder: I am still considering this.

Hill Livestock Compensatory Allowances

Mr. Amos: To ask the Minister of Agriculture, Fisheries and Food if he will make it his policy to oppose any European Economic Community proposals to impose headage limitations on its contributions to hill livestock compensatory allowances; and if he will make a statement.

Mr. Donald Thompson: The European Commission has recently made proposals for amendments to the EC legislation governing hill livestock compensatory allowances, as part of a package relating to reform of the structural funds. The proposals are currently being studied. I can assure my hon. Friend that we shall be seeking to preserve the United Kingdom interests in the forthcoming negotiations. In particular, I remain firmly opposed to the principle of ceilings based on farm size and other measures which would discriminate against the United Kingdom.

Confusion Marks

Mr. Boswell: To ask the Minister of Agriculture, Fisheries and Food what have been for each of the last five years, the administration costs of maintaining a register of confusion marks for the purposes of the sheep variable premium scheme; and how many animals were so registered in each of these years.

Mr. Donald Thompson *[holding reply 13 June 1989]:* The cost of administering the confusion mark procedures are not separately recorded. Nor are the number of animals registered under the system noted centrally. Those figures could be extracted only at disproportionate cost.

Fishing Industry

Mr. David Porter: To ask the Minister of Agriculture, Fisheries and Food how many meetings he has had so far in the current year with representatives of the fishing industry in the United Kingdom; and what has been discussed.

Mr. Donald Thompson *[holding reply 12 June 1989]:* I am regularly in touch with the fishing industry. This year I met industry representatives when I visited Hastings and Newhaven on 1 February, the Fish Council in Brussels on 23 February, Billingsgate on 21 March, the Fishing '89 exhibition in Glasgow on 14 April and at the National Federation of Fisheries Organisations' annual general meeting on 10 June. I have discussed a wide range of issues, of both local and national interest, including total allowable catches, vessel licensing, enforcement, management of the Channel cod fishery, quota hopping, beam trawl restrictions, decommissioning, SFIA grants, structure of the fleet and light dues.

TRANSPORT

Bridge Design (East London River Crossing)

Mr. Spearing: To ask the Secretary of State for Transport if, pursuant to his reply to the hon. Member for Newham, South, on 23 March, *Official Report,* columns 708-9, on the studies of bridge design for the proposed east London river crossing, he will state the date when the consultant's report was, or is expected to be received; and if he will make a statement covering its conclusion.

Mr. Channon: I have nothing to add to my reply of 23 March to the hon. Member.

Birmingham Northern Relief Road

Mr. Heddle: To ask the Secretary of State for Transport if, pursuant to his answer to the hon. Member for Mid-Staffordshire, on 12 May, *Official Report,* column *548,* he can indicate when he will announce his decision following the public inquiry held in May 1988 on his Department's proposals for the Birmingham northern relief road.

Mr. Peter Bottomley: My right hon. Friend announced on 22 May his intention to arrange a competition relating to the design, financing and construction of a new highway which would serve broadly the same purpose as the proposed Birmingham northern relief road. A decision on the Department's proposals for BNRR will be made when the outcome of the competition is known.

Davenham Bypass

Mr. Goodlad: To ask the Secretary of State for Transport when he expects work to commence on the Davenham bypass.

Mr. Peter Bottomley: This is a Cheshire county council proposal. I understand that it hopes to start work in 1992.

M66/A664 Interchange

Mr. Tom Arnold: To ask the Secretary of State for Transport what representations he has received about his new draft order for the M66 line order at the M66/A664 interchange; and if he will make a statement.

Mr. Peter Bottomley: We expect to publish a connecting roads order for the M66/A664 junction next year. A period will be allowed for objection and comment.

Semtex (Testing Kits)

Mr. Churchill: To ask the Secretary of State for Transport what information his Department has on the availability of explosive testing kits capable of detecting Semtex; and what steps he has taken to acquire these kits for United Kingdom airports or to recommend them to their operators.

Mr. Peter Bottomley: The Department has a programme for testing—and, where appropriate, assisting with the development of—equipment designed to detect explosives hidden in items carried on aircraft. Several techniques and individual items of equipment have shown promising results in the laboratory, but we have not yet found any system which will perform satisfactorily under operational conditions at airports.

M11 and M25

Mr. Cohen: To ask the Secretary of State for Transport if he will indicate his estimates of repairs and maintenance for each of the M11 and M25 for each of the next five years.

Mr. Peter Bottomley: The need for repairs and maintenance of motorways is reviewed each year in the light of condition surveys. Major maintenance work for the M11 and M25 has been planned for 1989-90, as follows:

Location	Works	Cost £ million
M11		
Junctions 12-14	Overlay	1·0
South of Junction 5 (Northbound)	Overlay	2·6
South of Junction 5 (Southbound)	Overlay	2·9
North of Junction 5 (Northbound)	Overlay	1·3
North of Junction 5 (Southbound)	Overlay	1·2
Total cost		9·0
M25		
Junction 24	Reconstruction	2·9
Junctions 11-13	Reconstruction	0·9
Total cost		3·8

Heavy Lorries

Mr. Cohen: To ask the Secretary of State for Transport whether his route signing in London proposals for change will fully allow for a London-made heavy lorry ban to be enforced; and if he will make a statement.

Mr. Peter Bottomley: The review of signing in London relates to directional signs on the primary route network. Drivers need simple and logical direction signing if they are to reach unfamiliar destinations safely and quickly. It would not be appropriate to include detailed information on lorry restrictions on such signs.

Mr. Allen McKay: To ask the Secretary of State for Transport if full compensation will be paid to local authorities for strengthening of bridges and roads in their areas should 40-tonne lorries be allowed on British roads.

Mr. Peter Bottomley: It is for highway authorities to maintain to the appropriate standards the bridges for which they are responsible. The provision of resources for this is considered in the annual public expenditure round. We shall shortly be discussing with local authority associations the implications of the recent decision that the United Kingdom's derogation from the EC lorry weights will end on 31 December 1998.

Tow-away Zones (London)

Mr. Amos: To ask the Secretary of State for Transport what studies have been made by his Department into the introduction of tow-away zones in selected areas in London; and if he will make a statement.

Mr. Peter Bottomley: The Metropolitan police have powers throughout London to remove any illegally parked vehicle. It is for them to decide how these powers are exercised. The Department has commissioned studies of the effects of vehicle removal in parts of central London as one method of parking enforcement. The studies are not yet complete.

Level Crossings

Mr. William Ross: To ask the Secretary of State for Transport how many deaths and injuries there have been at level crossings, by type of crossing in Great Britain in each of the last five years; whether there are any limits on the speed of trains at each such type of level crossing; and how many of the incidents in each year resulting in death and injury involved collision with road vehicles.

Mr. Portillo: Table A shows the number of deaths and injuries from accidents at level crossings, by type of crossing, in Great Britain during the period 1984-88. Table B shows the number of incidents involving death and/or injury during those years which resulted from collision between rail and road vehicles. The Department's published requirements for level crossings prescribe limits for train speeds at open, automatic open and automatic half-barrier crossings. The criteria for automatic open crossings have been revised following a review of safety at these crossings by Professor P. F. Stott after the accident at Lockington level crossing on 26 July 1986.

Table A: Deaths and injuries in level crossing accidents

Crossing type	1984		1985		1986		1987		[1]1988	
	Deaths	*Injuries*	*Deaths*	*Injuries*	*Deaths*	*Injuries*	*Deaths*	*Injuries*	*Deaths*	*Injuries*
Manned Gates	—	3	3	3	—	4	—	—	1	5
Manned Barriers	—	7	—	—	—	2	—	—	1	6
Manned Barriers with CCTV	—	—	—	—	—	—	—	—	—	12
Automatic Half-barriers	3	4	3	11	5	4	2	1	5	4
Automatic Open (locally monitored)	1	8	2	12	—	9	5	9	1	9
Automatic Open (remotely controlled)	—	1	—	3	11	38	—	1	1	1
Open Crossing	—	4	—	1	—	10	—	6	—	—
User-Worked Crossing	4	9	3	9	9	6	—	6	3	8
User-Worked Crossing with miniature warning lights	—	1	1	—	—	—	2	1	1	1
Footpath	3	2	2	1	2	5	5	—	5	3
Total	11	39	14	40	27	78	14	24	18	49

Table B: Incidents involving deaths and injuries resulting from collisions at level crossings

Year	Number
1984	18
1985	24
1986	24
1987	26
1988[1]	25

[1] Provision

Roads (Chelmsford)

Mr. Burns: To ask the Secretary of State for Transport if he will specify the proposed route of the new motorway from the M25 to Chelmsford as announced in the White paper "Roads for Prosperity."

Mr. Peter Bottomley: The first step is for the Department to appoint design agents to investigate possible schemes. Only then shall we have an indication of practicable routes.

Mr. Burns: To ask the Secretary of State for Transport (1) what timetable he envisages for the building of the new motorway from the M25 to Chelmsford as announced in the White Paper "Roads for Prosperity";

(2) what timetable he envisages for the widening of the Chelmsford A12 by-pass following publication of the White Paper "Roads for Prosperity."

Mr. Peter Bottomley: We shall seek to complete work on these schemes as quickly as possible. Details about timetable will be contained in a roads report to be issued later in the year.

WALES

Iwan Edgar (Letters)

Mr. Wigley: To ask the Secretary of State for Wales when the Transport Policy Division of the Welsh Office received letters from county councillor Iwan Edgar, of Pwllheli, dated 21 November 1988, 2 February 1989, and 10 April 1989, and on what dates each of these letters was answered.

Mr. Wyn Roberts: I regret that due to an error a reply to the first letter was not sent. The subsequent letters were repeats of the first letter. A reply has now been sent.

Drinking Water

Mrs. Ann Taylor: To ask the Secretary of State for Wales if he will give details of which of the standards set in the European Community drinking water directive are regularly exceeded by each of the water supplies in Wales which have been granted derogations.

Mr. Grist: The information is as follows.

The Welsh water authority has been granted derogations under the terms of article 9 of the EC drinking water directive (80/778/EEC) as listed in the following table. Information regarding the monitoring of those supplies is not held by the Department.

Name	Derogated parameter (1 = colour: 6 = pH unit; 15 = aluminium: 33 = iron; 34 = manganese)
Nantybwch	34
Garw Levels	33
Strata Florida	34
Ystradfellte	34
Nantymoel	34
Wern Ddu	6
Afon Cwm-y-Llan	15
Penygoyallt	6
Llanfynydd	6, 34
Alwen	1, 34
Georgetown	6, 34
Cwmsymlog	15
Betws-y-coed	34
Garreglwyd	33, 34
Gryn Goch	33
Nantmor	15, 34
Rhyd-Ddu	34
Portis	34
Penyfan	33
Upper Wenallt Springs	33
Cwm Cegr Springs	33
Llanbedr Springs	33
Caerau	34
Llan Penmachno	15, 34
Crai Reservoir	34
Croesor	34
Rhyd	15, 33, 34
Rhydyronen	33
Tir-Gawen	33
Elan	1, 6, 33, 34
Pendinas	34

ENVIRONMENT

Water Purity

66. **Mr. Matthew Taylor:** To ask the Secretary of State for the Environment when he last discussed with a member of the European Commission the question of British compliance with European Community directives on water purity.

Mr. Howard: Last month my noble Friend, the Minister for Housing, Environment and Countryside satisfactorily concluded discussions with the Commission on the enforcement provisions in the Water Bill. A copy of a letter from Commissioner Ripa confirming this was placed in the Library.

Mrs. Ann Taylor: To ask the Secretary of State for the Environment whether he has responded to the reasoned opinion of 14 April about the failure of the United Kingdom to transpose and its failure to apply correctly Council directive 80/778/EC on the quality of drinking water.

Mr. Howard: A response will be made to the Commission this week.

Planning Appeals (Windsor and Maidenhead)

Mr. Andrew McKay: To ask the Secretary of State for the Environment what percentage of planning appeals in the Royal borough of Windsor and Maidenhead he has approved in each of the last five years.

Mr. Chope: The information requested is in the table.

Year	Appeals decided	Appeals allowed	Percentage allowed
1984-85	90	28	31·1
1985-86	85	44	51·8
1986-87	109	54	49·5
1987-88	149	80	53·7
1988-89	130	55	42·3

Wargrave Sewage Works

Mr. Redwood: To ask the Secretary of State for the Environment (1) if he will make it his policy to take into account the results of the investment being made before considering a relaxation of consent levels at the Wargrave sewage works;

(2) what the discharge levels will be from the Wargrave sewage works when the current round of investment is completed in November;

(3) what were the consent levels for discharges from the Wargrave sewage works in *(a)* 1980 and *(b)* 1983.

Mr. Howard: The consent levels for the works for 1980 and from 1983 up to the present time are set out in milligrammes per litre.

	Suspended Solids	Biochemical Oxygen Demand	Ammonical Nitrogen
1980	30	15	5
1983 to date	45	18	15

The authority has recently undertaken some remedial work at Wargrave and is proposing to undertake further improvements as part of its major programme for upgrading sewage treatment works. In connection with this, the authority has submitted an application for a time-limited consent in accordance with the arrangements set out in my announcement on 7 December 1988 at column *199*—to cover the period up to completion of the works. This is being considered by Her Majesty's inspectorate of pollution who will take into account all relevant factors, including the effects of previous investment together with any representations which are received, before reaching a decision.

Cemetery Clauses Act 1847

Mr. Ken Hargreaves: To ask the Secretary of State for the Environment what plans he has to amend the Cemetery Clauses Act 1847 to require local authorities to give details of the number of burial spaces available in each grave sold by the authority.

Mrs. Virginia Bottomley: None, as the Cemetery Clauses Act 1847 no longer applies to local authority cemeteries. A complete code of administration for local authority cemeteries is now provided by the Local Authorities Cemeteries Order 1977 (SI 1977 No. 204) as amended.

Sewage Treatment Works

Dr. Cunningham: To ask the Secretary of State for the Environment, pursuant to his answer to the hon. Member for Copeland of 11 May, *Official Report,* column *520,* if he will place in the Library an analysis of those sewage treatment works in respect of which applications have been made for revised sewage discharge consents, showing for each works *(a)* its eight-figure national grid reference, *(b)* the parliamentary constituency in which it is situated, and *(c)* the local authority area in which it is situated.

Mr. Ridley: The question can be answered only at disproportionate cost. The grid reference for each sewage treatment works is included on the application form submitted to Her Majesty's inspectorate of pollution. These forms are available for public inspection at each water authority. The applications themselves, including grid references, have been advertised locally in the press. The other information would have to be specifically compiled and is not relevant to the consideration of the application.

Bristol Channel (Discharges)

Mr. Speller: To ask the Secretary of State for the Environment, pursuant to his reply of 6 June, if he will collate the list of consented discharges into the Bristol channel held by Wessex Water, Welsh Water and South West Water; and if he will publish these.

Mr. Howard: Information on discharge consents is not held by the Department in a form which would allow the identification of discharges in any particular area. Details of consents granted are, however, on the public registers maintained by the water authorities.

New Towns (Land Disposal)

Mr. Heddle: To ask the Secretary of State for the Environment if he will arrange for the new town development corporations to make details of their land disposals available to hon. Members by placing them in the Library on a six-monthly basis.

Mr. Trippier: New town development corporations and the Commission for the New Towns published annual reports which contain summary information about their progress in disposing of assets. These reports are laid before the House under the New Towns Act 1981. Discussion of details of land transactions can often involve considerations of commercial confidentiality.

Mr. Heddle: To ask the Secretary of State for the Environment, if he will introduce procedures to monitor the disposals of land by the new town development corporations.

Mr. Trippier: The Department already monitors new town development corporation land disposals.

Housing (Harassment)

Mr. Cox: To ask the Secretary of State for the Environment how many cases of housing harassment have been reported in each of the London boroughs in each of the last three years.

Mr. Trippier: This information is not collected centrally.

Housing Action Trusts

Mr. Fraser: To ask the Secretary of State for the Environment what is his assessment of how long the tenants on the Angell Town estate will need to consider the consultants' reports on housing action trust areas; what steps he will be taking to ensure that tenants have access to the reports; and what resources will be made available to the tenants for these purposes.

Mr. Trippier: As my right hon. Friend announced in his reply to my hon. Friend the Member for Wyre (Mr. Mans) on 16 March, all residents in the proposed trust area in Lambeth have been sent copies of leaflets explaining the consultants' ideas and translations have been made available on request. We have also sent copies of the consultants' reports to tenants' associations, local libraries and advice centres, Lambeth council and to individuals on request. We hope that tenants will play a full part in discussions led by independent consultants about the proposals in the reports and that they will put forward their own ideas. How long these consultations take will depend on how the discussions develop.

Vacant Properties

Mr. Soley: To ask the Secretary of State for the Environment what percentage of properties owned by his Department in Manchester, Westminster, Suffolk Coastal and the Isles of Scilly are vacant.

Mr. Chope *[holding answer 6 June 1989]:* As at 31 May 1989, the total number of all properties (that is, residential, office, storage and specialised) owned by the Department of the Environment in each of the four areas was:

	Total number	Number vacant	Percentage vacant
Manchester	42	1	2·4
Westminster	191	4	2·1
Suffolk Coastal	25	2	8·0
Isle of Scilly	9	1	11·0

Mr. Soley: To ask the Secretary of State for the Environment what percentage of properties owned by local authorities in Manchester, Westminster, Suffolk Coastal and the Isles of Scilly are vacant.

Mr. Trippier *[holding answer 6 June 1989]:* Based on the information provided by the authorities in their last housing investment programme returns for April 1988, the number of dwellings owned by each of the four authorities was:

	Total number	Number vacant	Percentage vacant
Manchester	98,665	5,166	5·2
Westminster	22,175	893	4·0
Suffolk Coastal	5,678	82	1·4
Isles of Scilly	141	1	0·7

Returnable Bottles

Mr. Menzies Campbell: To ask the Secretary of State for the Environment whether he has any plans to encourage the use of standard specification returnable bottles; and if he will make a statement.

Mr. Forth *[holding answer 12 June 1989]:* I have been asked to reply.

The Government have no such plans. We know of no evidence that the introduction of legislation or regulation of this nature would have significant benefit to the consumer, to trade and commerce or to the environment. However, the European Commission, in its draft amendment to the EC beverage containers directive (EC/85/339), has proposed that packagers should be required to label their beverage containers with common recyclable or refillable symbols. Discussions are continuing but, if implemented, this amendment would encourage consumers to return a greater number of bottles for refilling or recycling than happens at present.

SOCIAL SECURITY

Pensioners in Care

Mr. Rowe: To ask the Secretary of State for Social Security on what basis the personal allowance element of the pensions paid to residents *(a)* in local authority care or in long-term hospital beds and *(b)* in the private or voluntary sector is assessed; and if he will make a statement.

Mr. Peter Lloyd: The personal allowance for hospital in-patients has been increased over the years in line with the increases in benefit rates and is now £8·70, expressed in the relevant regulations as equivalent to 20 per cent. of the basic retirement pension rate. The allowance for those in local authority accommodation is fixed at the same rate as that for hospital in-patients. In respect of residents of independent residential care and nursing homes the addition for personal expenses is £10·05. This is uprated to reflect changes in prices in the same way as other income support applicable amounts.

Press Briefings

Mr. Grocott: To ask the Secretary of State for Social Security what guidelines he follows in determining which journalists are invited to press briefings by his Department.

Mr. Peter Lloyd: Journalists are invited to briefings on the basis of the subject to be discussed.

Social Fund

Mr. Redmond: To ask the Secretary of State for Social Security if he will list for his Department's local offices in Doncaster and Mexborough, what statistical information he has as to the different reasons given to applicants by social fund officers for nil awards in respect of application for community care grants.

Mr. Peter Lloyd: The latest available information is given in my reply to the hon. Member on 26 April 1989 at column *543-45*.

Limited Appointments

Mr. Redmond: To ask the Secretary of State for Social Security if he will list the number of limited appointments for each year since 1979 for each office of his Department in South Yorkshire.

Mr. Peter Lloyd: The table gives the number of limited period staff appointments in social security offices in South Yorkshire from May 1987 to March 1989. This is the only period during which such appointments have been made.

Limited period appointments

	May 1987 to March 1988	April 1988 to March 1989
Barnsley East ILO	13	—
Barnsley West ILO	8	—
Doncaster East ILO	14	—
Doncaster West ILO	5	8
Rotherham South ILO	26	1
Rotherham North ILO	9	1
Sheffield North East ILO	19	—
Sheffield North West ILO	19	—
Sheffield South East ILO	16	5
Sheffield South West ILO	1	—
Wath on Dearne AO	6	—
Goldthorpe NIO	2	—
Mexborough NIO	0	—
Total appointments	138	15

Staff Training

Mr. Redmond: To ask the Secretary of State for Social Security what training is given to the staff in South Yorkshire following the introduction of new legislation by his Department.

Mr. Peter Lloyd: When new legislation is introduced full consideration is given in advance to the training

requirements of all local office staff. Where the change is considered minimal or straightforward, instructions are sent to staff as circulars or amendments to the working manuals. Where the change is more complex or fundamental, additional training and advice material is also provided. This can take a variety of forms ranging from training at a national training centre to local training at the workplace using centrally prepared training material.

Visiting Officers

Mr. Redmond: To ask the Secretary of State for Social Security what was the number of visiting officers employed in each office of his Department in South Yorkshire from 1979 to date.

Mr. Peter Lloyd: We do not collect centrally information on the number of visiting officers employed on visiting work in individual offices. Staffing resources allocated for visiting in the Department's north-eastern region are estimated from available data for the following years.

	Number
1983-84	388
1984-85	517
1985-86	444
1986-87	395
1987-88	345
1988-89	244
1989-90	125

The figures do not include specialist visiting or visiting from contributory benefits.

Staff Turnover

Mr. Redmond: To ask the Secretary of State for Social Security what was the turnover of staff in each year since 1979 for each office of his Department in South Yorkshire.

Mr. Peter Lloyd: The table lists the turnover of staff in social security offices in South Yorkshire. Turnover includes resignations, retirements, dismissals, deaths and transfers to other offices. It also includes promotions within an office. The information is expressed as a percentage of the staffing complement as at 1 April in each year. Figures are not available for periods prior to April 1984.

Staff turnover in the South Yorkshire offices

Office	1 April 1984 to 31 March 1985 Number of leavers	Percentage of complement	1 April 1985 to 31 March 1986 Number of leavers	Percentage of complement	1 April 1986 to 31 March 1987 Number of leavers	Percentage of complement	1 April 1987 to 31 March 1988 Number of leavers	Percentage of complement	1 April 1988 to 31 March 1989 Number of leavers	Percentage of complement
Barnsley East ILO	21	16·41	14·0	10·37	10·5	6·52	12·5	8·44	13·0	9·42
Barnsley West ILO	10	9·61	11·0	10·09	15·5	12·92	12·5	10·96	10·0	9·90
Doncaster East ILO	29	20·71	14·5	10·00	22·0	12·57	13·0	8·44	8·5	6·03
Doncaster West ILO	41	22·40	23·5	12·11	33·5	16·03	22·0	11·52	15·0	8·20
Rotherham North ILO	13	19·12	8·5	11·80	17·5	21·60	25·0	35·21	4·0	5·55
Rotherham South ILO	29	14·95	33·0	16·18	24·5	10·16	35·0	15·62	22·5	10·56
Sheffield North East ILO	35	18·04	39·5	18·81	42·0	17·57	26·0	11·35	33·0	15·42
Sheffield North West ILO	42	22·58	16·0	7·51	44·5	18·31	41·5	19·21	31·0	16·58
Sheffield South East ILO	20	14·18	9·5	6·21	31·0	18·02	28·5	19·00	22·0	16·54
Sheffield South West ILO	26	16·35	30·0	17·14	33·5	16·18	22·0	12·15	20·0	12·50

Office	1 April 1984 to 31 March 1985		1 April 1985 to 31 March 1986		1 April 1986 to 31 March 1987		1 April 1987 to 31 March 1988		1 April 1988 to 31 March 1989	
	Number of leavers	Percent-age of comple-ment	Number of leavers	Percent-age of comple-ment	Number of leavers	Percent-age of comple-ment	Number of leavers	Percent-age of comple-ment	Number of leavers	Percent-age of comple-ment
Wath on Deane AO	15	22·73	12·5	17·86	17·0	20·00	13·0	17·81	5·0	8·06
Goldthorpe NIO	2	12·50	3·0	15·79	3·5	16·67	3·0	15·00	1·0	4·76
Mexborough NIO	3	15·79	2·0	9·52	2·0	9·52	3·0	14·28	3·0	14·28

Therese Devine

Sir Eldon Griffiths: To ask the Secretary of State for Social Services what was the result of the appeal by Therese Devine, of Hargrave Green, Bury St. Edmunds, against his decision in 1986 that she was not entitled to supplementary benefit; and what steps he has taken to make the appropriate payments to her in the light of the tribunal's judgment.

Mr. Peter Lloyd: The local social security office have no record of an appeal being received from Therese Devine in 1986 nor was a decision issued at that time refusing her supplementary benefit. I refer my hon. Friend to the reply to his letter of 1 March and the subsequent reply from my hon. Friend the Parliamentary Under-Secretary of State for Employment, dated 12 April in which these matters are fully explained.

Ilford Park Polish Home

Dr. Michael Clark: To ask the Secretary of State for Social Services if he will make a statement about the future of Ilford Park Polish home.

Mr. Scott: Ilford Park Polish home, located near Newton Abbot, Devon, is the last remaining resettlement camp operated by the Department under the Polish Resettlement Act 1947. Polish people who satisfy the criteria laid down in the Act can be considered for admission. The current residents occupy accommodation which mostly predates the opening of the original camp in 1948. The buildings are situated in the central part of a 42-acre site owned by my right hon. Friend the Secretary of State for the Environment.

In view of the declining resident population and the age of the accommodation the Department has for some time now been considering the future of the home. The average age of the residents is increasing and some of them are becoming frail. The present home has more the characteristics of a residential care home for elderly people rather than its original function as a resettlement camp. The present accommodation, age apart, is unsuitable and does not meet the standards required today for residential care homes.

We have therefore concluded that Ilford Park Polish home should be rebuilt at its present site. The aim is to provide accommodation and facilities that meet the standards required of registered residential care homes and nursing homes. On provisional plans the work will be complete by 1992. There will be full consultation with residents and staff, as the details of the scheme are worked out.

HEALTH

Illegitimate Children

Mr. William Powell: To ask the Secretary of State for Health if he will list in the *Official Report* each parliamentary constituency, together with the proportion, in which the proportion of children born outside marriage in the latest year for which figures are available exceeds 20 per cent.

Mr. Freeman: This statistic is routinely available for local authority districts and for health districts and is published in the annual volume "Key Population and Vital Statistics" for local and health authority areas, which is in the Library. I regret that the statistic is not normally tabulated by parliamentary constituency and so could only be provided at disproportionate cost.

Genito-urinary Clinics

Mr. Butler: To ask the Secretary of State for Health how many cases were seen at genito-urinary medicine clinics in England in each year from 1980 to the latest available year.

Mr. Freeman: The information is given in the table.

New cases seen at NHS genito-urinary medicine clinics, England, 1980 to 1987-88

	Grand Total all conditions		
	Males	Females	Persons
1980	271,614	187,365	458,979
1981	281,189	198,735	479,924
1982	296,675	220,993	517,668
1983	309,040	238,397	547,437
1984	319,483	250,445	569,928
1985	332,840	272,466	605,306
1986	349,190	298,169	647,359
1987	328,467	291,799	620,266
1987-88	310,753	282,972	593,725

Source: DH fors SBH60.

Mr. Cohen: To ask the Secretary of State for Health what indication he has on those district health authorities which are setting as a local priority the provision of a genito-urinary clinic.

Mr. Freeman: In a letter sent to health authorities in February the Department advised them that, as part of the reports required under the AIDS (Control) Act 1987, details should be given of all completed and planned developments in genito-urinary medicine services. District health authorities are due to publish their reports by the end of June.

Health Service Management Board

Mr. Spearing: To ask the Secretary of State for Health if he will list for each of the members of the Health Service management board his or her experience *(a)* in Health Service affairs and *(b)* in the supply of personal services to members of the public for which there is no fee or charge.

Mr. Mellor: The members of the NHS policy board were chosen for their capacity to give high calibre independent advice about the strategic direction of the NHS. A significant proportion have had distinguished careers in the Health Service. Others bring a variety of experience from the business world, and an outstanding record of achievement in giving direction to very large organisations.

Family Practitioner Committees (Chairmen)

Mr. Turner: To ask the Secretary of State for Health if he will publish a list showing for each family practitioner committee whose chairman was not reappointed in March-April 1989, the name of the chairmen not reappointed, their length of service on that family practitioner committee, their status on that committee, namely, as a contractor or lay person, and the name of the person appointed in their place, together with a note of their length of service on that family practitioner committee and their status and, where no reappointment has yet occurred, the date on which he hopes to announce the name of the new chairman and the cause of the hiatus.

Mr. Mellor: The information is contained in the table. We hope to announce names for the two remaining vacancies shortly.

Family practitioner committee	Outgoing chairman	Length of service	Status	New chairman	Length of service	Status
Bedfordshire	Mrs. W. Brothwood	4 (2)[1]	Lay	Dr. A. Wood	—	Lay
Birmingham	Dr. A. Llewellyn-Lloyd	8	Contractor	Mrs. C. Vaughan-Griffiths	—	Lay
Bolton	Mrs. J. Rothwell	4	Contractor	Mr. A. Pettengell	—	Lay
Bury	Dr. A. Burt	15	Contractor	Mr. B. Wood	—	Lay
Camden and Islington	Mr. K. Judge	2	Lay	Mr. H. C. Gilbert	—	Lay
City and East London	Mr. J. Keir	2	Lay	Ms. J. Lait	—	Lay
Croydon	Mr. B. Pringle	15	Lay	Mr. R. Lane	—	Lay
Derbyshire	Mr. B. Ashby	3	Lay	Mr. M. Boissier	—	Lay
Dorset	Mr. B. Gillam	5	Lay	Mrs. K. Mulliner	—	Lay
Durham	Mr. N. Thomas	12	Lay	Mr. I. Bonas	—	Lay
Enfield and Haringey	Mr. B. Whycer	6	Contractor	Vacant	—	—
Greenwich and Bexley	Mr. J. Stickland	5	Lay	Mr. B. Marson-Smith	—	Lay
Kingston and Richmond	Mr. D. Lewis	12	Lay	Mr. D. J. G. Banks	—	Lay
Lancashire	Mr. F. Pethybridge	4	Lay	Mr. C. Jeanes	—	Lay
Liverpool	Mr. R. Clark	5	Lay	Mrs. R. Hawley	—	Lay
North Tyneside	Dr. J. Gordon	7	Contractor	Dr. G. Hetherington	—	Lay
Nottinghamshire	Dr. A. MacLaren	10	Contractor	Mr. M. Dessau	—	Lay
Oxfordshire	Lady Williams	12 (3)[1]	Lay	Mrs. D. Levy	—	Lay
Redbridge and Waltham Forest	Mr. L. Bridgeman	4	Lay	Vacant	—	—
Sefton	Mr. B. Worster-Davies	10	Lay	Mr. C. D. Darley	—	Lay
Trafford	Dr. B. Tennant	8	Contractor	Mr. A. Russell	—	Lay
Walsall	Mr. M. Wolverson	7	Lay	Mr. J. Howell	—	Lay
Warwickshire	Mrs. M. Backhouse	13	Lay	Mr. R. Gardner	—	Lay
Wigan	Mrs. C. Caley	4 (11)[1]	Lay	Mr. J. Lewis	—	Lay
Wolverhampton	Mr. D. Evans	4	Contractor	Ms. T. Evans	—	Lay

[1] Figures in brackets show the length of service as a member before becoming chairman.

Drugs Testing

Mr. Cohen: To ask the Secretary of State for Health what is his policy on the use of patients in the United Kingdom for experimental test purposes for an American drug company provided that the company holds a valid clinical test certificate or clinical trial exemption certificate issued by the United Kingdom licensing authority; what arrangements there are for the patients to be informed that they are to be used for experimental test purposes; and if he will make a statement.

Mr. Mellor: Within the National Health Service all research proposals on human subjects, including drug trials, should be approved by a local research ethics committee before they commence. The committee will want to look at all aspects of the research proposal, including any certificates issued by the United Kingdom Licensing Authority and what arrangements have been made for the information of patients involved, before giving or withholding their approval.

Medical Scientists

Mr. Amos: To ask the Secretary of State for Health if he will make a statement on the level of pay for medical physicists in the National Health Service; and if he has any plans to change the level of retention and recruitment of staff.

Mr. Mellor: The pay of medical physicists is a matter for negotiation between the management side of the scientific and professional staffs council and the staff side representing scientists employed in the NHS. Negotiations are continuing on the staff side pay cliam for 1989/90. I understand that the management side has set up a working party which has been investigating the position with regard to recruitment and retention of scientists.

Mr. Key: To ask the Secretary of State for Health what progress he is making in negotiations to resolve the Whitley council PTAA staff pay claim for 1989, covering health care professionals, including clinical psychologists, biochemists, microbiologists and other scientists, including those at the public health laboratory service, Porton Down; and if he will make a statement.

Mr. Mellor: The pay of clinical psychologists, biochemists, microbiologists and other scientists, including those employed at Porton Down, is a matter for negotiation between the management side of the scientific and professional staffs council and the staff side representing scientists employed in the NHS. Negotiations are continuing on the staff side pay claim for 1989-90.

Health Education Authority

Mr. Andrew Bowden: To ask the Secretary of State for Health if he will set out the current remit of the Health Education Authority.

Mr. Mellor: The remit of the Health Education Authority is set out in its establishment and constitution order. The authority's main tasks are to advise my right hon. and learned Friend the Secretary of State for Health on health education matters and to undertake programmes of health education in England, except for AIDS public education, which is on a United Kingdom-wide basis.

Mr. Andrew Bowden: To ask the Secretary of State for Health (1) what guidance has been given by his Department to the Health Education Authority on strategic and operational planning for health education programmes for elderly people;

(2) what particular responsibility the Health Education Authority has for the promotion and support of health education programmes for elderly people.

Mr. Mellor: The Health Education Authority has no responsibility to provide health education for any specific age group. The planning guidelines issued by the Department of Health to the Health Education Authority ask that the Health education needs of elderly people be taken into account in the authority's forward plans which are currently being developed.

Hospitals

Mr. Amess: To ask the Secretary of State for Health if he will list in the *Official Report* those hospitals which opened in each district health authority in 1988, together with the number of beds.

Mr. Freeman: I regret that this information is not available centrally.

Abortion

Mr. Amess: To ask the Secretary of State for Health if he will list in the *Official Report* those recommendations contained in the Select Committee on the Abortion (Amendment) Bill 1974-75 which have been implemented; and if he will make a statement.

Mr. Freeman: The then Secretary of State announced acceptance in principle of the nine recommendations made by the Select Committee and all of them were subsequently implemented in part or in full.

Mr. Amess: To ask the Secretary of State for Health if he will list in the *Official Report* those recommendations contained in the First and Second Reports of the Select Committee on Abortion 1976 which have not been implemented; and if he will make a statement.

Mr. Freeman: The first report of the Select Committee recommended that the Government should introduce legislation to amend the Abortion Act 1967 in a number of ways. This would, however, have involved departure from the longstanding practice of leaving legislation on abortion to Bills brought forward by private Members as successive Governments have been neutral on abortion legislation. The second report concentrated on research, conscientious objection, disparity in the provision of NHS services, and the cost of abortion in the NHS, and made four recommendations which were not taken forward in the terms in which they were expressed.

Mr. Amess: To ask the Secretary of State for Health (1) if he will list the number of abortions performed on girls aged 10, 11, 12, 13, 14, 15, 16 and 17 years according to the grounds of termination in each year since 1968;

(2) what was the total number of abortions performed on girls aged 10, 11, 12, 13, 14, 15, 16 and 17 years since 1968.

Mr. Freeman: I regret that the information could only be provided at disproportionate cost.

Mr. Amess: To ask the Secretary of State for Health if he will list the number of abortions performed on girls aged 10, 11, 12, 13, 14, 15, 16 and 17 years according to the grounds of termination in 1987 and 1988 for 18 weeks and each week thereafter to 28 weeks.

Mr. Freeman: The exact information requested cannot be released for reasons of maintaining confidentiality. The table shows the data which can be released within these constraints for 1987; data for 1988 are not yet available.

Number of abortions carried out under the Abortion Act 1967 by gestation, statutory grounds and mothers age. Residents and non-residents of England and Wales, 1987.

Statutory grounds Age	*Gestation weeks*			
	17-18	*19-20*	*21-22*	*23+*
All grounds				
Under 15	67	27	35	31
15	204	92	71	38
16-19	1,608	978	539	336
2 (alone)				
Under 15	65	25	35	31
15	201	91	71	38
16-19	1,552	926	520	329
3 (with or without 2)				
Under 20	34	23	9	4

Statutory grounds Age		Gestation weeks		
	17-18	19-20	21-22	23+
4 *(alone)* +4 *(with any other except 1)*				
Under 20	26	30	9	5
Others				
Under 20	1	2	1	0

Mr. Amess: To ask the Secretary of State for Health what percentage of abortions at 21 weeks, 23 weeks and 24 weeks gestation were performed during 1987 and 1988 on girls aged 10, 11, 12, 13, 14, 15, 16 and 17 years to save the life of the pregnant woman.

Mr. Freeman: There were three abortions performed in England and Wales in 1987 with mention of ground 5 of the 1967 Abortion Act (which allows abortions to be performed in order to save the life of the pregnant woman). Further details relating to age or gestation cannot be given for reasons of maintaining confidentiality.

Data for 1988 are not yet available.

Cancer Screening

Mrs. Fyfe: To ask the Secretary of State for Health how far the recently agreed programme of breast screening for women aged over 50 years has been implemented; and whether he has any plans to widen the service.

Mr. Mellor: The table lists those breast screening centres in England which are now operational.

Under the programme, all women aged between 50 and 64 years will be invited to be screened by mammography every three years; older women will be screened on request. The purpose of screening is to detect changes in breast tissue which might be cancerous at an early stage when treatment can be simple and most likely to be effective.

Plans for extending the breast screening programme to cover all district health authorities in England are well advanced; a full nationwide service comprising about 80 centres (including mobile units) is expected to be operational in 1990.

The breast screening programmes in the other parts of the United Kingdom are the responsibilities of my right hon. Friends the Secretaries of State for Wales and for Northern Ireland and of my right hon. and learned Friend the Secretary of State for Scotland.

SCREENING CENTRES OPERATIONAL AS AT JUNE 1989

Region and centres

Northern
  Gateshead
  Newcastle

Yorkshire
  Huddersfield

Trent
  Nottingham
  Leicester
  Lincoln

East Anglian
  King's Lynn
  Suffolk
  Peterborough

North West Thames
  Barnet

North East Thames
  Epping
  Elizabeth Garrett Anderson Hospital

South East Thames
  Camberwell

South West Thames
  Guildford

Wessex
  Southampton
  Isle of Wight
  Portsmouth

Oxford
  Aylesbury
  Northampton
  Wycombe

South Western
  Cornwall
  Avon

West Midlands
  Stoke on Trent
  Coventry
  Dudley
  Walsall

Mersey
  Liverpool

North Western
  Manchester
  Bolton
  Wigan

Midwives

Mr. Canavan: To ask the Secretary of State for Health when he now expects to respond to the Social Services Committee regarding midwives' regrading; and whether he will make a statement.

Mr. Mellor: I refer the hon. Member to my reply to the hon. Member for Wallsend (Mr. Garrett) and my hon. Friend the Member for Batley and Spen (Mrs. Peacock) on 10 May 1989, at columns *450-51.*

NHS Reform

Mr. Kirkwood: To ask the Secretary of State for Health (1) how many of the units expressing interest in self-governing status have complied with paragraph 5.3 of the self-governing hospitals working paper No. 1; and if he will take steps to require the remainder to do so;

(2) if he will list those units contained in his list of medical units expressing interest in becoming self-governing who have consulted staff and patient representatives and have met with their approval;

(3) when considering applications for self-governing status from ambulance services, whether he intends consulting other emergency services; and if he will make a statement;

(4) whether he intends to consult medical staff and patient representatives when making a decision to approve or disapprove applications for self-governing status in light of his commitment to judge whether the changes would be in the interests of the National Health Service, hospitals and patients.

Mr. Mellor *[holding answer 12 June 1989]:* Expressions of interest are no more than that. We are aware that in many cases informal consultation has taken place but it would be unrealistic to engage in formal consultation at this stage, because people may not have enough information to give an informed opinion. All the main interests—including staff and the local community—will have an opportunity to express their views when detailed proposals have been worked up. We will take all responses into account when deciding whether to approve an application.

Mr. Kirkwood: To ask the Secretary of State for Health if he will list those units that are entire hospitals with 250 beds or over contained in his list of units expressing interest in becoming self-governing.

Mr. Mellor *[holding answer 12 June 1989]:* The information is not available in the form requested. The table lists those units which include entire hospitals with 250 beds or over:

Northern Regional Health Authority
Darlington—hospital and community services
Freeman Hospital, Newcastle
Hartlepool District
Mental Illness Services in Gateshead
Newcastle General Hospital
Newcastle Mental Health Unit
Northgate Hospital
North Tyneside District

Yorkshire Regional Health Authority
Bradford—Acute Hospital Trust
Calderdale Hospitals, Calderdale HA

General Infirmary, Leeds and associated Units—Leeds Western
Grimsby DGH and associated services
High Royds Hospital Mental Health Services, Leeds Western
St. James's University Hospital, Leeds Eastern
Seacroft and Killingbeck Hospitals, Leeds Eastern
Wakefield District—Mental Health Unit

Trent Regional Health Authority
Bassetlaw Hospital and associated community services
Doncaster Royal Infirmary and Maxborough Montagu Hospital
Nether Edge Hospital, Sheffield
Northern General Hospital, Sheffield
University Hospital, Nottingham
Royal Hallamshire Hospital, Sheffield

East Anglian Regional Health Authority
East Suffolk Psychiatric Services
Newmarket General Hospital
Peterborough DGH, Edith Cavell DGH, Stamford and Rutland Hospital
Queen Elizabeth Hospital, Kings Lynn and associated services

North West Thames Regional Health Authority
Central Middlesex Hospital
East Hertfordshire Acute Services Unit
North Hertfordshire Hospital and Community Services
North West Hertfordshire Priority Services Unit
Northwich Park Hospital
Mount Vernon/Hillingdon Hospitals with associated Community Services
Westminster and Westminster Children's Hospitals

North East Thames Regional Health Authority
Basildon and Thurrock HA
Central North London Mental Health Unit
London Hospital
Mid Essex Acute Unit
Royal Free Hospital + North Middlesex Hospital
St. Bartholomews, Homerton and St. Marks Hospital Trust
St. Bartholomew's Hospital
St. Margaret's Hospital, Epping
Southend Acute Unit
North East Essex Acute Unit
North East Essex Mental Handicap Unit
North East Essex Mental Health Unit
Waltham Forest Mental Health Unit

South West Thames Regional Health Authority
Croydon HA—Mental Handicap Unit
Croydon HA—Mental Illness Unit
East Surrey HA—Acute and Community Services Unit
Kingston and Esher HA—Kingston Hospital
Mid Downs HA—East Unit
Mid Downs HA—West Unit
Mid Surrey HA—General (Acute) Unit
Mid Surrey HA—Mental Illness Unit
North West Surrey HA—Acute Unit
North West Surrey HA—Mental Handicap and Mental Health Units
St. George's Group Trust, Wandsworth HA
St. Helier and Sutton Hospitals, Merton and Sutton HA
South West Surrey HA—Acute Unit
Worthing and Southlands Hospitals, Worthing HA

South East Thames Regional Health Authority
Brighton HA—main acute hospitals
Bromley HA
Camberwell HA (excluding mental illness services)
Eastbourne Hospitals—Eastbourne HA
Guy's Hospital
Lewisham Hospital Unit
Maidstone DGH
Queen Mary's Hospital, Sidcup + Erith and District Hospital + Community
Queen Victoria Hospital, East Grinstead
St. Thomas' Hospital

Tunbridge Wells Mental Handicap Unit
West Lambeth HA—Priority Care Unit
William Harvey and Buckland Hospitals—South East Kent HA

Wessex Regional Health Authority
Bournemouth Acute Unit, East Dorset HA
Christchurch Hospital, East Dorset HA
Psychiatric Division, Basingstoke HA
Swindon HA—All District Services
West Dorset HA—All District Services comprises 1, 2, or 3 trusts

South Western Regional Health Authority
Bristol Royal Infirmary Acute Services
Cheltenham and District
East Cornwall Acute Services
East Somerset (Yeovil): Acute/Primary Care Services + Yateman Hospital
North Devon DHA
Plymouth DHA
Torbay DHA
West Somerset (Musgrove): Acute Services
Wonford Acute Services, Exeter

West Midlands Regional Health Authority
Alexandra DGH/Acute Services Unit (Bromsgrove and Redditch)
Good Hope DGH/Northcroft/Jaffray/Community (N. Birmingham)
Highcroft, Mental Illness Hospital (N. Birmingham)
Manor DGH/Acute Services Unit (Walsall)
Robert Jones and Agnes Hunt Orthopaedic Hospital (Shropshire)
Royal Shrewsbury Hospital (Shropshire)
Rugby District
St. George's Hospital/Mental Health Unit (Mid Staffordshire)
St. Margaret's, Mental Handicap Hospital, (Walsall)
Walsgrave DGH, Coventry

Mersey Regional Health Authority
Arrowe Park and Clatterbridge Hospitals
Broadgreen Hospital, exc. Mersey Regional Cardio-Thoracic Unit
Cranage Hall, Crewe
Leighton Hospital, Crewe (Acute Services)
Liverpool Mental Health Services
Macclesfield DGH (Acute Services)
Macclesfield Mental Health Services
Royal Liverpool Children's Hospital (Alder Hey)
Royal Liverpool Hospital
Southport DGH (Acute Services)
Southport and Formby Psychiatric/Community Services
Walton and Fazakerley Hospitals, South Sefton
Warrington DGH
Whiston and St. Helen's Hospital

North Western Regional Health Authority
Christie Hospital, South Manchester HA
Manchester Royal Infirmary + St. Mary's Hospital + Royal Eye Hospital
Royal Preston Hospital, Preston HA
Stepping Hill Hospital + Stockport Infirmary, Stockport HA
Wrightington Hospital, West Lancashire HA

Mr. Kirkwood: To ask the Secretary of State for Health if he will provide references for the passages in the White Paper, "Working for Patients" and associated documents, in which the implications of and safeguards required for primary care or ambulance services if they become self-governing are discussed.

Mr. Mellor *[holding answer 12 June 1989]:* The White Paper discusses self-governing trusts in terms of hospitals or other units providing care or services for patients. But self-governing status could be practical for a wide range of

NHS services, and we are considering the implications for particular services in the light of any expressions of interest received.

Mr. Kirkwood: To ask the Secretary of State for Health (1) under what conditions he will approve applications from ambulance services to become self-governing; and if he will make a statement;

(2) under what conditions he will approve applications from primary care services to become self-governing; and if he will make a statement.

Mr. Mellor *[holding answer 12 June 1989]:* We would propose to consider each application on its merits, provided it meets the general criteria outlined in the White Paper.

Mr. Kirkwood: To ask the Secretary of State for Health (1) what is his timetable for approving or disapproving applications for medical units to become self-governing;

(2) whether units other than 250 bed hospitals will have their applications to become self-governing approved in time to begin in April 1991.

Mr. Mellor *[holding answer 12 June 1989]:* We would aim to establish the first NHS hospital trust as soon as possible after the necessary legislation receives Royal Assent, so that they can complete their preparations before April 1991, the earliest sensible time to establish the first self-governing hospitals. We would be prepared to consider a wide variety of units among the first self-governing units.

AIDS

Mr. Cohen: To ask the Secretary of State for Health what is his latest assessment of the possible spread of the HIV infection within prisons and after the prisoner is released; and if he will make a statement.

Mr. Douglas Hogg: I have been asked to reply.

An informed assessment is not possible on the basis of HIV screening and practice.

EMPLOYMENT

Employment Schemes

Ms. Short: To ask the Secretary of State for Employment, at the most recently available date, and for the same months in 1986, 1987 and 1988 how many people of YTS eligible age, registered with jobcentres or the careers service were awaiting an offer of a YTS place; and how many unfilled places on the scheme were available at those dates, broken down for each training agency region and for Great Britain as a whole.

Mr. Cope: The Government guarantee the offer of a suitable YTS place to all under-18-year-olds who want one.

As at 31 May 1989, there were some 141,144 unfilled vacancies on YTS in Great Britain. The numbers for each of the Training Agency regions are as follows:

	Numbers
Scotland	13,770
Northern	8,910
North West	17,822

	Numbers
Yorkshire and Humberside	16,518
West Midlands	24,343
Wales	4,454
East Midlands	16,796
South West	11,500
South East	18,267
London	8,764

These figures far exceed the demand for places. Young people have a good choice of training opportunities. It is not possible to compare the current situation with that in previous years when the YTS guarantee was of the offer of a suitable place by Christmas to any of that year's school leavers who were unemployed.

Departmental Expenditure Plans

Mr. Leighton: To ask the Secretary of State for Employment how much the change in the expenditure plans for his Department for 1989-90 from the 1988-89 estimated outturn will be *(a)* in percentage terms and *(b)* after adjustment for the gross domestic product deflator.

Mr. Cope: The 1988-89 estimated outturn for my Department is 2·8 per cent. lower than the 1987-88 outturn. After adjustment for the gross domestic product deflator, the 1988-89 estimated outturn is £289 million (8·5 per cent.) lower than the 1987-88 outturn.

Rehabilitation Centres

Mr. Alfred Morris: To ask the Secretary of State for Employment if he will list the total numbers of people who completed courses at employment rehabilitation centres in each of the last five years for which figures are available; and what percentage in each year subsequently *(a)* obtained employment or *(b)* entered a course of training.

Mr. Nicholls: The total number of people who completed courses with the employment rehabilitation service in each of the last five years was as follows:

	Number
1984-85	12,000
1985-86	13,440
1986-87	14,790
1987-88	16,000
1988-89	26,000

The percentage in each year who either obtained employment or entered a course of training was as follows:

	Employment/ Community Programme	*Training/YTS*
1984-85	29	9
1985-86	34	10
1986-87	39	10
1987-88	41	10
1988-89[1]	40	17

[1] 1 April—31 August 1988 only.

Mr. Alfred Morris: To ask the Secretary of State for Employment what was the average length of attendance at employment rehabilitation centres in each of the last five years; and what was the average per capita cost to his Department.

Mr. Nicholls: The average length of attendance on courses run by the employment rehabilitation service in each of the last five years and the average per capita cost to the Department was as follows:

	Average length of attendance	*Average per capita cost*
		£
1984-85	35 days	2,287
1985-86	32 days	2,214
1986-87	32 days	2,332
1987-88	30 days	1,250
1988-89[1]	17 days	[2]886

[1] 1 April—31 August 1988 only
[2] Provisional figure.

Mr. Alfred Morris: To ask the Secretary of State for Employment what was the total expenditure on employment rehabilitation centres in each of the last five years for which figures are available; and what percentage in each year was received in grants from the European social fund.

Mr. Nicholls: As far as expenditure figures for the employment rehabilitation service are concerned I refer to the reply given to the hon. Member for Liverpool, West Derby (Mr. Wareing) on Wednesday 24 May 1989 at column *576*.

European social fund claims made in report of the employment rehabilitation service resulted in the following grants to HM Government:

	£
1984	6,144,397
1985	8,358,625
1986	2,710,925
1987	3,193,687
1988	2,667,794

Disabled People

Mr. Alfred Morris: To ask the Secretary of State for Employment what outcome measures of rehabilitation are used by his Department to assess the effectiveness of the employment services for people with disabilities; and if he will make a statement.

Mr. Nicholls: The outcome measures used to assess the effectiveness of the employment rehabilitation service are as follows:
  (i) Total number of courses;
  (ii) Total number of clients attending courses;
  (iii) Clients with disabilities expressed as a percentage of the total client group;
  (iv) The percentage of clients who proceed to rehabilitation following an assessment course;
  (v) Average cost per disabled client;
  (vi) Average cost per week per disabled client;
  (vii) Average resettlement rate into employment or training;
  (viii) Average cost per disabled client resettled into employment or training.

Labour Statistics

Mr. Stern: To ask the Secretary of State for Employment how many job vacancies in information technology industries were registered in the Bristol travel-to-work area at the latest available date, and two years earlier.

Mr. Nicholls: The information is not available.

Benefit Entitlement

Mr. Sedgemore: To ask the Secretary of State for Employment how many persons have been disentitled from receiving unemployment benefit where they have been deemed to be unemployed without just cause since October 1988 *(a)* in England and Wales, and *(b)* in unemployment benefit offices in Hackney; and, in each case, if he will state the percentage of cases of which decisions were taken by adjudicating officers to suspend benefit for less than the maximum 26 weeks.

Mr. Nicholls: Information is not available in the precise form requested.

Figures on the number of persons disqualified for leaving their employment voluntarily without just cause in the unemployment benefit offices in Hackney are not collected separately, and could be obtained only at disproportionate cost.

Information requested on the percentage of claimants disqualified for less than the statutory period of 26 weeks is not collected. However, the Department of Social Security has undertaken a survey to establish the proportion of claims which are disqualified for the maximum period. The results are at present being analysed and will be published shortly.

The number of claimants disqualified from receiving unemployment benefit because they left employment voluntarily without just cause for the period 1 July 1988 to 31 March 1989 in England and Wales was 156,683.

Skills Training Agency

Mr. Hague: To ask the Secretary of State for Employment how he intends to finance the expenditure in connection with the privatisation of the Skills Training Agency.

Mr. Cope: The expenses will be covered by receipts from the sale. Parliamentary approval for the new service will be sought in a new token Supply Estimate (Class VII, Vote 5) for the privatisation of the Skills Training Agency, to be presented in the Summer Supplementary Estimates round, seeking provision for preliminary expenses and token provision for the main expenses. Later in the year parliamentary approval will be sought for the substantive provision for the main expenses of the sale. Pending the necessary approval urgent expenditure on fees for professional advice, the first tranche of which is estimated to be £250,000, will be met by repayable advances from the Contingencies Fund.

Mental Handicap (Vocational Training)

Rev. Martin Smyth: To ask the Secretary of State for Employment if he will make a statement about the first European national conference for vocational training for mental handicap in Maastricht, in April; what official representation attended the conference from the United Kingdom; and if he will place in the Library any papers resulting from the conference.

Mr. Cope *[holding answer 12 June 1989]:* The United Kingdom Government were not invited to send representatives. I understand that two officials from the Northern Ireland Department of Economic Development attended, though not in an official capacity.

Claimants

Mr. Meacher: To ask the Secretary of State for Employment if benefit officers or staff, including fraud officers and claimant advisers, have targets for numbers of claimants who cease to claim or are removed from benefit.

Mr. Nicholls *[holding answer 13 June 1989]:* No.

NORTHERN IRELAND

Level Crossings

Mr. William Ross: To ask the Secretary of State for Northern Ireland how many deaths and injuries there have been at level crossings, by type of crossing, in Northern Ireland in each of the past five years; whether there are any limits on the speed of trains at each such type of level crossing; and how many of the incidents in each year resulting in death and injury involved collision with road vehicles.

Mr. Needham: The information requested is as follows:

| Year | Total number of accidents | Type of Crossing | | | | |
| | | AHB | | AOCL | | Controlled |
		Deaths	Injuries	Deaths	Injuries	Deaths
1984	1	—	1	—	—	—
1985	2	—	—	—	4	—
1986	1	—	—	—	—	2
1987	3	—	—	3	1	—
1988	—	—	—	—	—	—
1989	2	—	—	1	3	—

AOCL = Automatic open crossing locally monitored
AHB = Automatic half-barrier

All these accidents resulted from collision with road vehicles. In all cases the speed of trains was limited. The limit varies according to local conditions.

Vocational Rehabilitation

Mr. Alfred Morris: To ask the Secretary of State for Northern Ireland if he is satisfied with the integration of vocational rehabilitation with both the structure and administration of social security in Northern Ireland; what action he is taking to improve co-ordination; and if he will make a statement.

Mr. Needham *[holding answer 13 June 1989]:* The Department of Health and Social Services and the Department of Economic Development have agreed arrangements whereby people receiving social security benefits may participate in a rehabilitation programme and continue to receive benefit for a period of up to four weeks. If at the end of this initial period a person is considered suitable for full-time training, payment of benefit ceases and is replaced by a training allowance, payable at the rate of the previous benefit plus a premium of £10 a week. On completion of training, payment of benefit will resume if the normal conditions are still satisfied. The rules governing people's entitlement both during and after training will continue as at present.

The need for informal co-ordination between Departments in providing help for the disabled will be examined as part of the Government's consideration of the results of the current survey of the disabled in Northern Ireland.

Glen House

Mr. John D. Taylor: To ask the Secretary of State for Northern Ireland which adjoining property owners have been formally notified of the planning application No. 0339 to develop lands at Glen house, Mountain road-Crawfordsburn road, Newtownards.

Mr. Needham [*holding answer 13 June 1989*]: The following occupiers were neighbour notified in relation to planning application No. 0339—Nos 3, 5, 7 and 9 Mountain road and No. 41 Crawfordsburn road, Newtownards.

Mr. John D. Taylor: To ask the Secretary of State for Northern Ireland which adjoining property owners have been formally notified of the planning application No. 0340 to develop lands at Glen house, Mountain Road-Crawfordsburn road, Newtownards.

Mr. Needham [*holding answer 13 June 1989*]: The following occupiers were neighbour notified in relation to planning application No. 0340—Nos. 7, 9, 11, 13, 15, 17, 41, 43, 45, 47 and 49 Mountain road, Newtownards. The occupiers of Nos. 41 and 49 Crawfordsburn road, Newtownards should also have been notified but, due to an oversight, they were not. However, both these occupiers contacted the Department of Environment (Northern Ireland) about the proposed development and were obviously aware of it despite the lack of neighbour notifications.

Mr. John D. Taylor: To ask the Secretary of State for Northern Ireland which adjoining property owners have been formally notified of the planning application No. 0336 to develop lands at Glen house, Mountain road-Crawfordsburn road, Newtownards.

Mr. Needham [*holding answer 13 June 1989*]: The following occupiers were neighbour notified in relation to planning application No. 0336—Nos. 4, 5, 6, 7, 8, 9, 10, 11, 12, 13, 14, 15, 16, 17, 18 and 19 Mountain road, and No. 55 Crawfordsburn road, Newtownards.

SCOTLAND

Severe Weather Payments

Mr. Kennedy: To ask the Secretary of State for Scotland, if he will detail the total monies so far paid out, to individuals and local authorities, respectively, as a result of the severe weather conditions earlier in the current year; and if he will make a statement.

Mr. Lang: My right hon. and learned Friend announced on 27 April details of the special financial assistance being made available, and invited claims from local authorities and those eligible for the higher rates of agricultural grants which were announced at the same time. To date, my officials have held discussions with several local authorities about the possibility of assistance, and a number of inquiries about agricultural grants have been made by persons affected by the severe weather in February. To date, however, no claims under these measures have been received, and therefore no payments have been made.

Health Screening

Mr. Allan Stewart: To ask the Secretary of State for Scotland what are his Department's current priorities for screening in health care in Scotland; and if he will make a statement.

Mr. Michael Forsyth: Current priorities are the establishment of systematic programmes to screen women aged between 20 and 60 at five-yearly intervals for cervical cancer and women aged between 50 and 64 at three-yearly intervals for breast cancer. Computerised call and recall systems will enable health boards to invite all women in the eligible age groups to attend for a cervical smear test by December 1993 and for a breast screening test by March 1994.

In addition, screening of all pregnant women is carried out for the purpose of detecting fetal abnormalities. Following birth, children are screened for inherited or developmental conditions and this is continued throughout the school years. Since 1 December 1988 screening for HIV infection has been available for all women attending ante-natal clinics in Edinburgh and Dundee.

Publicity Campaigns

Mr. Dobson: To ask the Secretary of State for Scotland if he will list all current publicity campaigns being conducted by or for his Department or campaigns planned for the first three months of 1989-90, indicating those which involve television advertising and the starting and finishing dates of each campaign.

Mr. Lang [*holding answer 19 April 1989*]: My Department was conducting publicity campaigns on school boards and the community charge during April. They were scheduled to run from 9 April to 6 May and from 3 to 28 April respectively. Both involved television advertising. A campaign for road safety was shown on television from 6 March to 8 April.

Planning of publicity campaigns for the whole of the first three months of 1989-90 is not yet complete.

New Towns

Mr. Ingram: To ask the Secretary of State for Scotland if he will publish the findings of the surveys carried out in the Scottish new towns on the question of the residents views on the disposal of the development corporations housing stock; and if he will make a statement.

Mr. Lang *[holding answer 13 June 1989]:* This matter will be covered in the forthcoming White Paper on the Scottish new towns.

TRADE AND INDUSTRY

Plessey plc

Mr. Thorne: To ask the Chancellor of the Duchy of Lancaster how, in the event that GEC/Siemens acquire the Plessey company, he proposes to ensure continued competitive solutions in the research and development field.

Mr. Maude: In its report on the proposed acquitition of Plessey by GEC Siemens, the Monopolies and Mergers Commission concluded that the effect of the proposed acquisition on research and development would not operate against the public interest. In accordance with the Commission's recommendations, however, my right hon. and noble Friend the Secretary of State for Trade and Industry has asked my right hon. Friend the Secretary of State for Defence to seek undertakings, amongst others, that would satisfy United Kingdom national security requirements as to the ownership and management of defence, research and development and semiconductor activities. Negotiations on undertakings continue.

Mr. Barry Field: To ask the Chancellor of the Duchy of Lancaster how, in the event that GEC/Siemens acquire the Plessey company, he plans to ensure that Plessey radar and Plessey defence systems can compete equally with GEC companies.

Mr. Maude: Following publication of the Monopolies and Mergers Commission report on the proposed acquisition of Plessey by GEC Siemens, my right hon. and noble Friend the Secretary of State for Trade and Industry has made it clear that the proposed acquisition should not proceed until satisfactory undertakings have been obtained from GEC and Siemens, including undertakings from GEC that GEC should not acquire any interest in or influence or control over the management of the Plessey radar and defence systems businesses. Negotiations on undertakings continue.

Mr. Barry Field: To ask the Chancellor of the Duchy of Lancaster (1) what measures are being taken to safeguard the position of Britain's base of enabling technology in semiconductors in the event that GEC/Siemens succeed in taking over Plessey;

(2) what measures are being taken to safeguard the position of the United Kingdom as the European leader in application specific integrated circuits in the event that GEC/Siemens succeed in taking over Plessey.

Mr. Maude: In its report on the proposed acquisition of Plessey by GEC Siemens, the Monopolies and Mergers Commission concluded that the effect of the proposed acquisition on electronic components would not operate against the public interest. In accordance with the Commission's recommendations, however, my right hon. and noble Friend the Secretary of State for Trade and Industry has asked my right hon. Friend the Secretary of State for Defence to seek undertakings, amongst others, that would satisfy United Kingdom national security requirements as to the ownership and management of defence, research and development and semiconductor activities. Negotiations on undertakings continue.

"Open for Business"

Mr. Barry Field: To ask the Chancellor of the Duchy of Lancaster what response there has been to his Department's European "Open for Business" campaign.

Mr. Maude: The response has been huge. Our weekly survey indicates that 90 per cent. of business throughout the country is now aware of the single market and around 50 per cent. is taking action or considering steps to prepare for it. DTI has received over 230,000 requests for information on the single market since the campaign was launched in March 1988, including over 132,000 calls to our 1992 hotline. In addition, DTI Ministers and officials have spoken at more than 1,000 single market conferences since the campaign began and are committed to over 130 other single market engagements during the remainder of this year.

Imports (Consumer Goods)

Mr. Butterfill: To ask the Chancellor of the Duchy of Lancaster what percentage of the 1987-88 imports figure was accounted for by consumer goods; and if he will make a statement.

Mr. Alan Clark: Consumer goods (1) accounted for 18 per cent. of United Kingdom imports on an overseas trade statistics basis in each of the years 1987 and 1988.

(1) Part of SITC 7 and 8, based on the United Nations broad economic categories.

Refrigeration Industry

Mr. Thurnham: To ask the Chancellor of the Duchy of Lancaster what discussions he has had with representatives of the refrigeration industry about the effects of restrictions on CFC consumption; and if he will make a statement.

Mr. Maude: My hon. Friend the Parliamentary Under-Secretary of State for Industry held a meeting with my hon. Friend the Member for Bolton, North-East and a delegation from the industry on 7 June.

Additionally, officials have had a number of meetings with the industry during the last two years to discuss the implications of the Montreal protocol on substances that deplete the ozone layer, which control the use of chlorofluorocarbons used by the refrigeration, air conditioning and other industries; the extent to which savings in the use of these substances may be made; and the forseeable effects of a strengthened protocol.

Financial Services Act

Mr. Tim Smith: To ask the Chancellor of the Duchy of Lancaster how many responses he received to the consultative document, "Possible Changes to the Financial Services Act 1986", published on 1 March; how many respondents supported the proposals; and if he will make a statement.

Mr. Maude: My Department received responses to the consultation document entitled "Possible Changes to the Financial Services Act 1986" from 67 organisations, companies and individuals. The document invited comments on a number of possibilities, not all of which were related, and many of the responses were also wide-ranging. It would not therefore be meaningful to analyse them in the way requested.

Eastern Europe

Mr. Stern: To ask the Chancellor of the Duchy of Lancaster to what extent trade with eastern Europe, excluding the USSR, has increased in the last 10 years.

Mr. Alan Clark: United Kingdom trade with eastern Europe, excluding the USSR, is given in the following table:

United Kingdom trade with eastern Europe excluding USSR 1979 to 1988

	Imports	*Exports*	*Balance*
1979	563·7	549·6	− 14·1
1980	492·5	673·4	+ 180·9
1981	398·3	600·1	+ 201·8
1982	484·3	510·2	+ 25·9
1983	571·4	503·8	− 67·6
1984	902·8	572·8	− 330·0
1985	851·7	649·4	− 202·3
1986	827·4	626·2	− 201·2
1987	825·5	625·3	− 200·2
1988	859·3	683·9	− 175·4

Value in £ million

Source: Table 1B of the Overseas Trade Statistics.
Notes: 1. Figures for 1988 are provisional.
2. Imports valued at cif, exports fob.

Paperless Share Transactions

Mr. Charles Wardle: To ask the Chancellor of the Duchy of Lancaster whether he will state the Government's intentions for facilitating paperless transactions and holdings in shares.

Mr. Maude: I announced on 1 December at column *369* that I was considering proposing changes to the law that would, if both the company and the shareholder wished, enable shares to be held on computer, without certificates, and to be transferred without the need for paper transfer forms. This process, sometimes referred to as dematerialisation, is important for London's leading position as an international trading market. Paperless schemes will also offer important benefits for wider share ownership by providing a more efficient service to investors.

I issued a consultative document on the proposed changes and I am grateful to all those individuals and organisations who responded. It is essential that any schemes finally developed meet the legitimate needs of all potential users and I welcome the progress made by the international stock exchange as a result of its recent and continuing consultations.

The moves towards paperless trading are intended to reduce transaction risks and costs. In considering possible changes to legislation it is essential to strike the right balance between the interests of shareholders, of companies and of the financial institutions. I have also borne in mind that schemes will develop over time and that competitors may emerge with different approaches from the nominee-based scheme currently being considered by the stock exchange. Against this background it is clearly important that the framework should be flexible.

I hope to bring forward proposals in the form of amendments to the Companies Bill. These will be intended to ensure that the move towards paperless trading does not alter significantly the effect in practice of current company, investor protection and insolvency law. In order to achieve this the Secretary of State would be empowered to make regulations, subject to affirmative resolution, which would then provide a framework within which authorised systems would operate. The purpose of the regulations would be:

(*a*) to facilitate the introduction and operation of computer based systems for recording the holding of securities (or interests in them) and for their transfer;

(*b*) to ensure that, as far as reasonably practicable, investors, issuers (ie companies) and other are in a corresponding position under such a computer-based system as they are under the present paper-based system.

The regulations will make provisions inter alia for ensuring that authorised systems and their participants are properly regulated. They will also ensure that the speed and ease with which information about the identities of owners of shares is made available is comparable to present arrangements; and that investors continue to enjoy broadly the same rights as they do now.

Electricity Boards

Mr. Neil Hamilton: To ask the Chancellor of the Duchy of Lancaster how many representations he has received regarding alleged abuses of Fair Trading and Competition Acts by electricity boards.

Mr. Maude *[holding answer 12 June 1989]:* Three.

Eastern Electricity Board

Mr. Neil Hamilton: To ask the Chancellor of the Duchy of Lancaster if he will instruct the Director General of Fair Trading to investigate the current retail practices of the Eastern electricity board.

Mr. Maude *[holding answer 12 June 1989]:* It is for the Director General of Fair Trading to decide whether to carry out an investigation to establish whether someone is engaging in an anti-competitive practice. I understand that the Director General is following up complaints from retailers of electrical hardware.

Mr. Neil Hamilton: To ask the Chancellor of the Duchy of Lancaster if he will list those who have made representations regarding alleged anti-competitive practices by the Eastern electricity board; and if he will make a statement.

Mr. Maude *[holding answer 12 June 1989]:* No: I treat such representations in confidence.

Beer (MMC Report)

Mr. Allen: To ask the Chancellor of the Duchy of Lancaster when he expects to announce his decision on implementing the Monopolies and Mergers Commission's report on the supply of beer.

Mr. Maude *[holding answer 12 June 1989]:* I made a preliminary statement about the scope of application of some of the proposed measures on 8 June at column *229*. I am anxious to settle the remaining issues quickly.

THE ARTS

School Parties (Museum Charges)

Mr. Cohen: To ask the Minister for the Arts which national museums impose charges for school parties; and what advice he issues museums in respect of educational charges.

Mr. Luce: The National Maritime museum and Merseyside Maritime museum are the only national museums to levy charges for school parties. Both operate concessionary charge schemes.

The policy on charging educational parties is a matter for the director and trustees of each individual museum.

EDUCATION AND SCIENCE

Inner London Education Authority (Women Employees)

Mr. Cartwright: To ask the Secretary of State for Education and Science what representations he has received suggesting that the draft regulations on redundancy and detriment compensation discriminate against women employees of the Inner London Education Authority; and what has been his response.

Mrs. Rumbold: My right hon. Friend is currently considering representations from the TUC on this point.

Further Education (London)

Mr. Cox: To ask the Secretary of State for Education and Science how many 16-year-olds stay on in education after this age in the Inner London education authority.

Mr. Jackson: In 1987-88 there were approximately 11·5 thousand full-time students (a participation rate of 51 per cent.) and 1·5 thousand part-time students (a participation rate of 7 per cent.).

Scottish Qualifications

Mr. Key: To ask the Secretary of State for Education and Science whether he intends to approve Scottish qualifications for use in maintained schools in England in 1990 and 1991.

Mr. Kenneth Baker: Yes. I intend that qualifications certificated by the Scottish Examination Board should be included in the supplementary list of qualifications approved for use in maintained schools in England in 1990 and 1991 which will be issued later this summer and which was foreshadowed in the Department's 31 May circular (11/89).

ENERGY

Wind Turbines

Mr. Alan W. Williams: To ask the Secretary of State for Energy what is the load factor achieved by the three wind turbines at Carmarthen bay *(a)* for 1988 and *(b)* to date during 1989.

Mr. Michael Spicer: The vertical axis wind turbine machine had a load factor of 13·3 per cent. for 1988 and 17·3 per cent. for the first quarter of 1989. The machine is being used as a test bed to support the VAWT development programme and, since 1987, has been operating in a different mode from that originally intended. Over this period, it has given satisfactory performance with an availability of 93 per cent.

The Howden HWT300 machine has had a number of teething troubles with its control system, and representative operating data are not yet available; it is hoped that

suitable data will be acquired over the next year. The wind energy group MS3 machine is not yet fully commissioned, and load factor data are therefore not yet available.

Energy Industries (Fatalities)

Sir John Farr: To ask the Secretary of State for Energy if he will list in the *Official Report* annual totals of fatalities since 1970 in the United Kingdom energy industries, showing separately the figures for *(a)* coal, *(b)* civil nuclear, and *(c)* offshore oil and gas.

Mr. Parkinson: The figures are as follows:

Fatal injuries to employees in the energy sector
Date of Accident (calendar year except where otherwise indicated)

	[1] *Coal Mining*	[2] *Civil Nuclear*	[3] *Offshore Oil and Gas*
1970	91	—	1
1971	72	—	4
1972	64	—	3
1973	80	—	3
1974	48	—	12
1975	64	—	10
1976	50	2	17
1977	40	1	11
1978	63	2	4
1979	46	—	10
1980	42	2	4
1981	35	2	6
1982	38	2	14
1983	30	2	10
1984	19	—	13
1985	25	1	8
1986	[4]18	1	3
1987	[4]12	—	6
1988	[4]20	—	[5]173

[1] Reported to the Health and Safety Executive's inspectorate of mines and quarries (figures include both British Coal and private licensed mines)
[2] None of the civil nuclear fatalities involved exposure to radiation.
[3] The statistics include all fatalities on or near installations and pipeline works or on attendant vessels in the course of any operation undertaken in connection with an installation. They also include fatalities in respect of pipelines or in the course of pipeline works. Fatalities involving helicopters flying to or from installations are only included if they occur in the vicinity of the installation.
[4] Figures for coal fatalities compiled on a financial year basis since April 1986. There were a further seven fatalities between 1 January 1986 and 31 March 1986.
[5] 167 of these fatalities relate to the Piper Alpha disaster.

Harwell (Laboratories)

Dr. Thomas: To ask the Secretary of State for Energy what new laboratories or existing laboratory upgrading and extensions have been built since 1979 at the Atomic Energy Research Establishment, operated by the United Kingdom Atomic Energy Authority at Harwell; which of these have been paid for from a parliamentary vote; and which paid for by commercial contracts signed by the UKAEA or AEA technology.

Mr. Parkinson: Since 1979 the Harwell laboratory has completed seven major laboratory schemes. Details and information on how they were funded is as follows:

Description	*Funding provided by*
Electron Linear Accelerator facility	Vote
Extension to Environmental and Medical Sciences building	Vote
New and improved facilities for handling radioactive wastes	Vote

Description	Funding provided by
Thoria Pelleting plant	Industrial customer
Refurbishment of Post Irradiation Examination Laboratory	[1]Capital
Improvements to Biochemistry Building	[1]Capital

[1] Since 1986, when the finances of the UKAEA were put on a trading fund basis, capital investment which is intended to serve several research and development customers has been capitalised and is funded corporately within the AEA's external financing limit.

Nuclear Materials (Safeguards)

Dr. Thomas: To ask the Secretary of State for Energy what period of notice the United Kingdom is required to give the safeguards authorities at the International Atomic Energy Agency and the European Atomic Energy Agency, Euratom, if nuclear material under safeguards is to be withdrawn from safeguards.

Mr. Michael Spicer: The United Kingdom is required to give to Euratom and the IAEA 10 days notice of withdrawal of material from the terms of the United Kingdom/Euratom/IAEA agreement unless otherwise specified in the relevant facality attachment.

Sellafield

Dr. Thomas: To ask the Secretary of State for Energy what the basic technical characteristics of the Sellafield reprocessing facilities were submitted to Euratom for the purposes of developing safeguards arrangements for Sellafield.

Mr. Michael Spicer: Basic technical characteristics for different material balance areas at Sellafield have been formally submitted to Euratom at different times in addition to Euratom inspectors obtaining the technical characteristics during inspections. The development of safeguards approaches is mostly influenced by that latter knowledge.

Dr. Thomas: To ask the Secretary of State for Energy when the particular safeguards provisions for the Sellafield reprocessing facility were *(a)* first agreed and *(b)* first implemented; and if he will make a statement on the implementations of the safeguards arrangements at Sellafield.

Mr. Michael Spicer: Four particular safeguards provisions were agreed and came into force in 1988. The others are in an advanced stage of consultation, to come into force progressively.

OVERSEAS DEVELOPMENT

International Fund for Agricultural Development

Mr. Paice: To ask the Secretary of State for Foreign and Commonwealth Affairs what was the outcome of the negotiations to replenish the international fund for agricultural development; and what will be the British contribution.

Mr. Chris Patten: I am glad to say that IFAD members successfully agreed early on 8 June to replenish the fund with at least $523 million so as to cover its operations up to 30 June 1992. The final total, to be fixed by the end of September, will depend on how far the group of non-oil developing countries can raise their pledges towards $75 million, in response to an offer by western donors to match this by 3:1. If that figure is reached, the replenishment will come to $611 million, corresponding to over $730 million for a full three year period. But the level already secured, with reflows to the fund, is enough to allow it to continue operations at a reasonable level.

The British contribution, like that of other western donors, will only be finalised at the end of September. I shall report it to the House thereafter, and it will naturally be subject to parliamentary approval.

NATIONAL FINANCE

Taxation

Mr. Harry Greenway: To ask the Chancellor of the Exchequer what is the anticipated effect on the Exchequer of raising the higher rate of taxation to 50 per cent.; and if he will make a statement.

Mr. Norman Lamont: The yield in a full year at 1989-90 levels of income of increasing the higher rate of income tax to 50 per cent. would be about £2½ billion. The estimate includes the consequential effect on the yield of capital gains tax. It is partly based on a projection of the 1986-87 survey of personal incomes and is provisional.

Pension's (Civil Servants)

Sir Peter Hordern: To ask the Chancellor of the Exchequer if he will publish a table showing the total cost of pensions paid to civil servants in each of the last five years.

Mr. Brooke: Pensions paid to civil servants, along with certain other pension payments (including pensions paid to the dependants of former civil servants), are a charge on the civil superannuation vote. It is not possible to separate out the costs of the other pension payments but, with the exception of pensions paid to the dependants of former civil servants, the costs are small. Total pension costs, as recorded in the Appropriation Accounts for subhead A1 of the vote, in each of the last five years are as follows:

	£'000
1983-84	855,079
1984-85	931,344
1985-86	1,017,876
1986-87	1,112,685
1987-88	1,163,226

Sir Peter Hordern: To ask the Chancellor of the Exchequer what is the average pension and lump sum paid to civil servants in retirement after 40 years service in each grade from grade 6 and above.

Mr. Brooke: A civil servant with 40 years' service and paid at the scale maximum of the respective grade (excluding London weighting where payable) would qualify on retirement for a pension and lump sum as follows:

	Pension £	Lump sum £
Grade 6	14,085	42,255
Grade 5	15,801	47,403
Grade 4	17,707	53,122
Grade 3	19,500	58,500
Grade 2	24,000	72,000
Grade 1A	31,375	94,125
Grade 1	34,250	102,750

Taxation

Mr. Gordon Brown: To ask the Chancellor of the Exchequer what is the reduction in annual liability to *(a)* capital gains tax and *(b)* capital transfer tax in 1988-89, 1989-90 and 1990-91 as against the 1978-79 indexed regime, specifying, in each case, the total and average reduction per taxpayer as well as the number of taxpayers in each year.

Mr. Norman Lamont *[holding answer 15 May 1989]:* Latest estimates for 1988-89 and 1989-90 are as follows:

	Capital gains tax	Capital transfer tax/ Inheritance tax
Reduction, compared with indexed 1978-79 regime, in:		
Total liability (£ million)		
1988-89	1,250	600
1989-90	1,350	670
Average liability[1] (£)		
1988-89	1,900	8,500
1989-90	1,900	9,500
Taxpayer numbers (thousands)		
1978-79 indexed regime		
1988-89	650	70
1989-90	700	70
Present regime		
1988-89	145	24
1989-90	160	24

[1] The reduction in the average liability is calculated using the estimated number of taxpayers under the 1978-79 indexed regime.

The figures for capital gains tax exclude capital gains realised by companies and taxed within corporation tax. For each tax, the 1988-89 and 1989-90 tax bases are taken as given. It is not possible to determine to what extent changes to the taxes between 1978-79 and the present may have affected the levels of transfers and disposals. The comparisons can be regarded as no more than indicative of the orders of magnitude involved.

Public Safety Films

Mr. Nellist: To ask the Chancellor of the Exchequer if he will list the title and topic of those Government public safety films and announcements that have been screened on television in each of the last six months.

Mr. Lilley *[holding answer 8 June 1989]:* Details of Government public safety films and announcements produced through the Central Office of Information on behalf of other Government Departments in each of the last six months for which data are available are as follows:

Public Safety Films Broadcast in October 1988
Crime Prevention—Child Molestation
Children Say No—Brownies
Children Say No—Car
Children Say No—Sweets (10s)
Children Say No—Sweets (5s)

Litter and Safety
Keep Britain Tidy—Excuses (70s)
Keep Britain Tidy—Excuses (40s)
Keep Britain Tidy—Excuses (10s)

Fire Prevention—Children
Welephant—Safe with Matches

Fire Prevention—General
Children Alone
Cigarette Fires
Clothes Fire Presenter
Fat Pan Folly

Fire at Night
Fire Exits
Fire in the Fat Pan
Fire Routine
Furniture Fires
House that Jack Built, The
How to Dial 999
Last Smoke, The
Phone Emergency
Portable Heaters (60s)
Portable Heaters (10s)
Short Fires
Upstairs Fire Escape

Health-General
Clean it up
Collars and Leads
Health Hazard

Rabies Advice
Rabies—Airport

Road Safety—Children
Charley's Tea Party
Child Cyclist—Right Turn
Children Crossing (40s)
Children Crossing (20s)
Pelican Pedestrians

Road Safety—General
Amber Gambler—Twins
Dangerous Diamonds
Don't Dazzle
Driver Fatigue
Elderly Pedestrians
Eyesight when Driving
Flying Motorbikes
Hard Shoulders
'Help'
Horses and Cars
How to Brake
Junction Lanes
Junction Parking
Lane Discipline
Let the Other Fella Know
Look Out for Bikes

Mini Roundabouts
Motorway Repair Sites
Motorway Signals
Overtaking near Junctions
Passing Horses
Pavement Parking
Ply Group
Read the Road
Rear Seat Belts (60s)
Rear Seat Belts (40s)
Rear Seat Belts (10s)
Safe Crossing
Safe on the Motorway
Safe Parking
School Entrance Markings
Separation Distances—Motorways
Traffic Shapes
Tyre Pressures
Tyre Safety
Yellow Box Junction
Zig Zag—Parking

Road safety—Motorbikes and Bicycles
Bright Lights
Helmet Advice
Motorbikes—Stay Back
Motorcycle—Overtaking
Motorcycle Training (40s)
Motorcycle Training (10s)
Pedal Cycle Safety

Road safety—Pedestrians
Bright Aware
Car Wash
Lot on his Mind, A
Road Dog
Road Test Pedestrian
Electricity and building safety
Electricity—Sub-stations
Electricity—Pylon
Electricity—Fishing
Keep Off Building Sites

Safety—General
Bare Wires
BSI Chameleon
Careless Fires
Electricity Hazards
Eye Protection
Farm Machinery
Farm Trailer
Lifting Safely
Slipping Ladders

Safety in the home
Children and Bottles
Children and Bottles—Paint Stripper
Children and Bottles—Anti-Freeze
Children and Bottles—Danger Bottle
Fatal Floor, The
Flexes and Young Children (40s)
Flexes and Young Children (20s)
Flexes and Young Children (5s)
The Right Steps (60s)
The Right Steps (30s)
The Right Steps (10s)
Talking Gas

Water safety—General
Learn to Swim—Missing Out
Swimming Lessons

Winter
Christmas Fire
Driving in Fog
Driving in Rain
Motoway Fog
Rear Fog Lamps
Wet Motorbikes

PUBLIC SAFETY FILMS BROADCAST IN NOVEMBER 1988
Crime Prevention—Child Molestation
Children Say No—Brownies (20s)
Children Say No—Car (10s)
Children Say No—Sweets (10s)
Children Say No—Sweets (5s)

Litter and Safety
Keep Britain Tidy—Excuses (70s)
Keep Britain Tidy—Excuses (40s)
Keep Britain Tidy—Excuses (10s)

Fire Prevention—Children
Welephant—Safety with Matches

Fire Prevention—General
Children Alone
Cigarette Fires
Clothes Fire Presenter
Fat Man Folly
Fire at Night
Fire Exits
Fire in the Fat Pan
Furniture Fires
House that Jack Built, The
How to Dial 999
Last Smoke, The
Phone Emergency
Portable Heaters (60s)
Portable Heaters (10s)
Short Fires
Upstairs Fire Escape
Health—General
Clean it Up
Collars and Leads
Health Hazard

Rabies advice
Rabies—Airport

Road safety—Children
Child Cyclist—Right Turn
Children Crossing (40s)
Children Crossing (20s)
Pelican Pedestrians

Road safety—General
Amber Gambler—Twins
Clear Indication
Dangerous Diamonds
Don't Dazzle
Driver Fatigue
Elderly Pedestrians
Eyesight when Driving
Flying Motorbikes
Hard Shoulders
HGV Turning
Horses and Cars
How to Brake
Junction Parking
Lane Discipline
Let the Other Fella Know
Look out for Bikes
Mini Roundabouts
Motorway Repair Sites
Motorway Signals
Overtaking near Junctions
Pavement Parking
Ply Group
Read the Road
Rear Seat Belts (60s)
Rear Seat Belts (40s)
Rear Seat Belts (10s)
Safe Crossing
Safe on the Motorway
Safe Parking
School Entrance Markings
Separation Distances—Motorways
Traffic Shapes
Tyre Pressures

Tyre Safety
Yellow Box Junction
Zig Zag—Parking

Road Safety—Motorbikes and Bicycles
Bright Lights
Helmet Advice
Motorcycle—Overtaking
Motorcycle Training (40s)
Motorcycle Training (10s)
Pedal Cycle Safety
Pedal Cycle Song

Road Safety—Pedestrians
Bright Aware
Car Wash
Lot on his Mind, A
Road Dog
Road Test Pedestrian
Toddler Safety

Electricity and Building Safety
Electricity—Sub-stations
Electricity—Pylon
Electricity—Fishing
Keep Off Building Sites

Safety—General
Bare Wires
BSI Chameleon
Careless Fires
Electricity Hazards
Eye Protection
Farm Machinery
Lifting Safely
Slipping Ladders

Safety in the Home
Children and Bottles
Children and Bottles—Paint Stripper
Children and Bottles—Anti-Freeze
Children and Bottles—Turpentine
Children and Bottles—Danger Bottle
Fatal Floor, the
Flexes and Young Children (40s)
Flexes and Young Children (20s)
Flexes and Young Children (5s)
Hot Drink Child
Right Steps, The (60s)
Right Steps, The (30s)
Right Steps, The (10s)

Water Safety—General
Learn to Swim—Missing Out
Swimming Lessons

Fireworks Safety
Fireworks—Dummy

Winter
Christmas Fire
Driving in Fog
Driving in Rain
Motorway Fog
Rear Fog Lamps
Wet Motorbikes

PUBLIC SAFETY FILMS BROADCAST IN DECEMBER 1988
Crime Prevention—Child Molestation
Children Say No—Brownies (20s)
Children Say No—Car (10s)
Children Say No—Sweets (10s)
Children Say No—Sweets (5s)

Litter and safety
Keep Britain Tidy—Excuses (70s)
Keep Britain Tidy—Excuses (40s)
Keep Britain Tidy—Excuses (10s)

Fire Prevention—Children
Welephant—Safe with Matches

Fire prevention—General
Children Alone
Cigarette Fires
Clothes Fire Presenter
Fat Pan Folly
Fire at Night
Fire Exits
Fire in the Fat Pan
Fire Routine
Furniture Fires
House that Jack Built, The
How to Dial 999
Last Smoke, The
Phone Emergency
Portable Heaters (60s)
Portable Heaters (10s)
Short Fires
Upstairs Fire Escape

Health—General
Clean it Up
Collars and Leads
Health Hazard

Rabies Advice
Rabies—Airport

Road Safety—Children
Child Cyclist—Right Turn
Children Crossing (40s)
Children Crossing (20s)
Children Watch us Cross
Pelican Pedestrians

Road Safety—General
Amber Gambler—Twins
Clear Indication
Dangerous Diamonds
Don't Dazzle
Driver Fatigue
Elderly Pedestrians
Eyesight when Driving
Flying Motorbikes
Hard Shoulders
'Help'
Horses and Cars
How to Brake
Junction Parking
Lane Discipline
Let the Other Fella Know
Look out for Bikes
Mini Roundabouts
Motorway Repair Sites
Motorway Signals
Motorway Symbol
Overtaking near Junctions
Passing Horses
Pavement Parking
Ply Group
Read the Road
Rear Seat Belts (60s)
Rear Seat Belts (40s)
Rear Seat Belts (10s)
Safe Crossing
Safe on the Motorway
Safe Parking
School Entrance Markings
Separation Distances—Motorways
Steep Hill Warning
Traffic Shapes
Tyre Pressures
Tyre Safety
Yellow Box Junction
Zig Zag—Parking
Zig Zag—Sisters

Road Safety—Motorbikes and Bicycles
Bright Lights
Motorbikes—Stay Back

Motorcycle—Overtaking
Motorcycle Training (40s)
Motorcycle Training (10s)
Pedal Cycle Safety

Road Safety—Pedestrians
Bright Aware
Car Wash
Lot on his Mind, A
Road Dog
Road Test Pedestrian

Electricity and Building Safety
Electricity—Sub-stations
Electricity—Pylon
Electricity—Tree Climbing
Electricity—Fishing
Keep Off Building Sites

Safety—General
BSI Chameleon
Careless Fires
Electricity Hazards
Eye Protection
Farm Machinery
Lifting Safely
Slipping Ladders

Safety in the Home
Children and Bottles
Children and Bottles—Paint Stripper
Children and Bottles—Anti-Freeze
Children and Bottles—Danger Bottle
Fatal Floor, The
Flexes and Young Children (40s)
Flexes and Young Children (20s)
Flexes and Young Children (5s)
Loose Carpet Falls
Right Steps, The (60s)
Right Steps, The (30s)
Talking Gas

Water Safety—General
Learn to Swim—Missing Out
Swimming Lessons
Youngsters Learn to Swim

Winter
Christmas Fire
Driving in Fog
Driving in Rain
Motorway Fog
Rear Fog Lamps
Snow Seen
Wet Motorbikes

PUBLIC SAFETY FILMS BROADCAST IN JANUARY 1989
Crime Prevention—Child Molestation
Charley—Mummy Should Know
Charley—Strangers
Mr. Punch
Children Say No—Brownies
Children Say No—Car
Children Say No—Sweets (10s)
Children Say No.—Sweets (5s)

Litter and Safety
Keep Britain Tidy—Excuses (70s)
Keep Britain Tidy—Excuses (40s)
Keep Britain Tidy—Excuses (10s)

Fire Prevention—Children
Welephant—Safe with Matches

Fire Prevention—General
Children alone
Cigarette Fires
Clothes Fire Presenter
Fat Pan Folly
Fire at Night

Fire Exists
Fire Routine
Furniture Fires
House that Jack Built, The
How to Dial 999
Last Smoke, The
Old Smokers
Overfilled Fat Pans
Overloading Sockets
Phone Emergency
Portable Heaters (60s)
Portable Heaters (10s)
Short Fires
Upstairs Fire Escape

Health—General
Clean it Up
Collars and Leads
This is an Emergency

Road Safety—Children
Pelican Pedestrians

Road Safety—General
Amber Gambler—Twins
Clear Indication
Dangerous Diamonds
Don't Dazzle
Driver Fatigue
Eyesight when Driving
Flying Motorbikes
French Frank
Hard Shoulders
'Help'
HGV Turning
Horses and Cars
How to Brake
Junction Lanes
Junction Parking
Let the Other Fella Know
Look out for Bikes
Mini Roundabouts
Motorway Repair Sites
Motorway Signals
Motorway Symbol
Overtaking near Junctions
Pavement Parking
Ply Group
Read the Road
Rear Seat Belts (60s)
Rear Seat Belts (40s)
Rear Seat Belts (10s)
Safe on the Motorway
Safe Parking
Separation Distances—Motorways
Space Invader
Traffic Shapes
Tyre Pressures
Tyre Safety
Yellow Box Junction
Zig Zag—Parking

Road Safety—Motorbikes and Bicycles
Bright Lights
Motorbikes—Stay Back
Motorcycle—Overtaking
Motorcycle Training (40s)
Motorcycle Training (10s)

Road Safety—Pedestrians
Bright Aware
Car Wash
Lot on his Mind, A
Road Dog
Road Test Pedestrian

Electricity Safety
Electricity—Sub-stations
Electricity—Pylon

Safety—General
Airguns
Airguns—Leaflet
Bare Wires
BSI Chameleon
Careless Fires
Electricity Hazards
Eye Protection
Fagged Out

Safety in the home
Children and Bottles
Children and Bottles—Anti-Freeze
Children and Bottles—Turpentine
Children and Bottles—Danger Bottle
Fatal Floor, The
Flexes and Young Children (20s)
Flexes and Young Children (5s)
Hot Drink Child
Right Steps, The (60s)
Right Steps, The (30s)

Water Safety—General
Children and Ponds
Swimming Lessons

Winter
Driving in Fog
Driving in Rain
Rear Fog Lamps
Snow Control and Spin
Wet Motorbikes

PUBLIC SAFETY FILMS BROADCAST IN FEBRUARY 1989
Crime prevention—Child Molestation
Charley—Mummy Should Know
Charley—Strangers
Mr. Punch
Children Say No—Brownies
Children Say No—Car
Children Say No—Sweets (10s)
Children Say No—Sweets (5s)

Litter and safety
Keep Britain Tidy—Excuses (70s)
Keep Britain Tidy—Excuses (40s)
Keep Britain Tidy—Excuses (10s)

Fire Prevention—Children
Welephant—Safe with Matches

Fire prevention—General
Children Alone
Fat Pan Folly
Fire at Night
Fire Exits
Fire in the Fat Pan
Fire Routine
Furniture Fires
House that Jack Built, The
How to Dial 999
Last Smoke, The
Overfilled Fat Pans
Overloading Sockets
Phone Emergency
Portable Heaters (60s)
Portable Heaters (10s)
Short Fires
Upstairs Fire Escape

Health—General
Clean it Up
Collars and Leads
Health Hazard

Road Safety—Children
Child Cyclist—Right Turn
Children Crossing (20s)
Pelican Pedestrians
Supersafe with Super Ted

Road Safety—General
Amber Gambler—Twins
Clear Indication
Dangerous Diamonds
Dazzling Man
Driver Fatigue
Elderly Pedestrians
Eyesight when Driving
Flying Motorbikes
Hard Shoulders
'Help'
Horses and Cars
How to Brake
If Only
Junction Parking
Lane Discipline
Let the Other Fella Know
Look out for Bikes
Mini Roundabouts
Motorway Repair Sites
Motorway Signals
Motorway Symbol
Passing Horses
Pavement Parking
Ply Group
Read the Road
Rear seat Belts (60s)
Rear Seat Belts (40s)
Rear Seat Belts (10s)
Safe on the Motorway
School Entrance Markings
Separation Distances—Motorways
Steep Hill Warning
Tyre Pressures
Tyre Safety
Yellow Box Junction
Zig Zag—parking

Road Safety—Motorbikes and Bicycles
Bright Lights
Helmet Advice
Motorcycle—Overtaking
Motorcycle Training (40s)
Motorcycle Training (10s)
Pedal Cycle Song

Road Safety—Pedestrians
Bright Aware
Car Wash
Lot on his Mind, A
Road Dog
Road Test Pedestrian
Toddler Safety

Electricity and Building Safety
Electricity—Sub-stations
Electricity—Pylon
Electricity—Tree Climbing
Electricity—Fishing
Keep Off Building Sites

Safety—General
Airguns
Bare Wires
BSI Chameleon
Electricity Hazards
Eye Protection
Fagged Out
Farm Machinery
Slipping Ladders

Safety in the Home
Children and Bottles
Children and Bottles—Paint Stripper
Children and Bottles—Anti-Freeze
Children and Bottles—Danger Bottle
Fatal Floor, The
Flexes and Young Children (40s)
Flexes and Young Children (20s)

Flexes and Young Children (5s)
Right Steps, The (60s)
Right Steps, The (30s)
Right Steps, The (10s)
Talking Gas

Water Safety—General
Children and Ponds

Winter
Driving in Fog
Driving in Rain
Rear Fog Lamps
Wet Motorbikes

PUBLIC SAFETY FILMS BROADCAST IN MARCH 1989
Crime Prevention—Child Molestation
Children Say No—Brownies
Children Say No—Car
Children Say No—Sweets (5s)

Litter and Safety
Keep Britain Tidy—Excuses (70s)
Keep Britain Tidy—Excuses (40s)

Fire Prevention—General
Children Alone
Cigarette Fires
Fat Pan Folly
Fire at Night
Fire in the Fat Pan
Fire Routine
Furniture Fires
House that Jack Built, The
How to Dial 999
Last Smoke, The
Old Smokers
Ovefilled Fat Pans
Overloading Sockets
Phone Emergency
Portable Heaters (60s)
Portable Heaters (10s)
Upstairs Fire Escape

Health—General
Clean It Up
Collars and Leads
Health Hazard

Rabies Advice
Rabies—Airport
Rabies—Landing

Road Safety—Children
Charley's Tea Party
Child Cyclist—Right Turn
Children Crossing (40s)
Children Crossing (20s)
Children Turn
Pelican Pedestrians
Supersafe with Super Ted

Road Safety—General
Dangerous Diamonds
Dazzling Man
Driver Fatigue
Elderly Pedestrians
Eyesight when Driving
French Frank
Horses and Cars
How to Brake
If Only
Junction Parking
Lane Discipline
Let the Other Fella Know
Look out for Bikes
Mini Roundabouts
Motorway Repair Sites
Motorway Signals
Overtaking near Junctions

Passing Horses
Pavement Parking
Ply Group
Rear Seat Belts (60s)
Rear Seat Belts (40s)
Rear Seat Belts (10s)
Safe Crossing
Safe Parking
School Entrance Markings
Steep Hill Warning
Traffic Shapes
Tyre Pressures
Tyre Safety
Yellow Box Junction
Zig Zag—Parking

Road Safety—Motorbikes and Bicycles
Bright Lights
Helmet Advice
Motorbikes—Stay Back
Motorcycle—Overtaking
Motorcycle Training (40s)
Motorcycle Training (10s)
Pedal Cycle Safety
Pedal Cycle Song

Road Safety—Pedestrians
Bright Aware
Car Wash
Extra Careful
Lot on his Mind, A
Road Dog
Road Test Pedestrian
Toddler Safety

Electricity and Building Safety
Electricity—Sub-stations
Electricity—Pylon
Electricity—Tree Climbing
Electricity—Fishing
Keep Off Building Sites

Safety—General
BSI Chameleon
Careless Fires
Farm Machinery
Farm Trailer
Know your Tractor
Slipping Ladders

Safety in the Home
Children and Bottles
Children and Bottles—Paint Stripper
Children and Bottles—Turpentine
Children and Bottles—Danger Cupboard
Children and Bottles—Danger Bottle
Fatal Floor, The
Flexes and Young Children (40s)
Flexes and Young Children (5s)
Hot Drink Child
Right Steps, The (30s)
Right Steps, The (10s)

Water Safety—General
Swim Song
Swimming Lessons
Youngsters Learn to Swim

Holidays
Absent Parents
Bonehead Bather
Coastguard
Drink and Drowning (60s)
Drink and Drowning (3m 20s)
Drink and Drowning (10s)
Lifejackets
Look Out for Trouble
Motorboat Explosion
Rabies Advice
Slipping Kids

Winter
Rear Fog Lamps

VAT

Mr. Battle: To ask the Chancellor of the Exchequer, pursuant to his reply to the hon. Member for Argyll and Bute (Mrs. Michie) on 13 March, *Official Report*, column *61*, if he is yet in a position to inform the House of the outcome of the discussions on European Community proposals for imposing value added tax on goods and clothing sold in charity shops; and if he will make a statement.

Mr. Lilley: No. The Commission announced its revised thinking on indirect taxation in the single market on 17 May. It now accepts that some zero rates may be retained. This is clearly a step forward and in indication of our firm stance and we welcome it. However, the Commission's new proposals need much more clarification before we can take a view on them. Fortunately because changes to EC tax law require the unanimous agreement of the member states, there is no question of the Commission's proposals being forced upon us.

Dr. Marek: To ask the Chancellor of the Exchequer what has been decided to date in the discussions in the Economic and Finance Committee on the approximation of value added tax rates and the harmonisation of customs and excise duties: and if he will make a statement.

Mr. Lilley *[holding answer 12 June 1989]:* The Council of Economic and Finance Ministers have discussed these matters, which will be discussed again at a future ECOFIN Council. No decisions have been taken.

HOME DEPARTMENT

Regional Passport Offices

Dr. Hampson: To ask the Secretary of State for the Home Department if he will consider meeting the seasonal pressure of applications by the establishment of passport office facilities in Leeds for those seeking passports who live east of the Pennines; and if he will make a statement.

Mr. Renton: There are at present six regional passport offices in the United Kingdom. Since the great majority of passport applications are usually dealt with by post, the location of the issuing office is not normally a significant factor in determining the speed of service. We shall, however, be reviewing the location and number of offices later this year. My right hon. Friend announced on 6 June in reply to a question from the hon. Member for Bolton, South-East (Mr. Young) at columns *47-8* a number of measures which are being taken to ease the present problem of delays at the passport offices.

Handel Telephone Line System

Mr. Bill Michie: To ask the Secretary of State for the Home Department what effect problems with the Handel telephone line system will have on the United Kingdom Warning and Monitoring Organisation's ability to activate the national network of air-raid sirens from July of this year; and if he will make a statement.

Mr. John Patten: Improvements which British Telecom are making to the telephone network, which carries links in the warning system, will not affect the United Kingdom Warning and Monitoring Organisation's ability to activate the national network of sirens.

Electronic Surveillance Schemes

Mr. Allen: To ask the Secretary of State for the Home Department if he will take steps to ensure that a refusal to agree to participate in an electronic surveillance scheme will not be held to be a breach of bail conditions.

Mr. John Patten: During the trial schemes electronic monitoring will not be offered to defendants unwilling to participate: the question of subsequent breach of a bail condition should not arise.

Mr. Allen: To ask the Secretary of State for the Home Department what estimate he has made of the impact on the incidence of domestic violence or alcohol consumption of persons participating in electronic surveillance schemes.

Mr. John Patten: None.

AIDS

Mr. William Powell: To ask the Secretary of State for the Home Department (1) how many persons who have been prisoners and subsequently released have been diagnosed as HIV positive;

(2) how many prisoners currently in Her Majesty's prisons have been diagnosed as HIV positive.

Mr. Douglas Hogg: On 12 June 1989 the prison population of England and Wales included 63 prisoners reported as having been identified as HIV antibody positive. A total of 174 such prisoners had been released since reporting began in March 1985.

Colin Wallace

Mr. Livingstone: To ask the Secretary of State for the Home Department whether he has concluded his consideration of the conviction of Mr. Colin Wallace for manslaughter in the light of evidence of a conspiracy to pervert the course of justice set out in the book entitled "Who Framed Colin Wallace" by Mr. Paul Foot, referred to in his written reply to the hon. Member for Brent, East of 15 May, *Official Report,* column *96.*

Mr. John Patten: We are considering the material contained in Mr. Foot's book. When this has been carefully examined we will decide whether any action is called for in respect of Mr. Wallace's conviction.

War Crimes Inquiry

Mr. John Marshall: To ask the Secretary of State for the Home Department when he will make a statement about the Government's response to the war crimes inquiry.

Mr. Hurd: I refer my hon. Friend to the reply given to the hon. Member for Walsall, North (Mr. Winnick) on 8 June 1989 at column *215.*

Police Manpower (Derbyshire)

Mr. Oppenheim: To ask the Secretary of State for the Home Department what was the figure for police manpower in Derbyshire in 1979; and what is the latest figure available.

Mr. Douglas Hogg: The information requested is as follows:

Police strength: Derbyshire

	Numbers
31 December 1979	1,757
30 April 1989	1,798

Immigration

Mr. Burt: To ask the Secretary of State for the Home Department what proposals he has for the use of DNA testing in immigration cases; and if he will make a statement.

Mr. Hurd: I announced in July 1988 that DNA profiling appeared to be the most accurate available method of determining parentage in immigration cases, and that we would continue to accept the results of DNA tests commissioned by applicants themselves. Since then, many hundreds of cases have been satisfactorily determined on that basis. In the light of the experience we have gained from this, my right hon. and learned Friend the Foreign Secretary and I have concluded that there is scope for introducing DNA testing into the entry clearance process more generally as a means of resolving relationship disputes. We have therefore set in hand the necessary arrangements with the view to the implementation of a Government scheme later this year in relation to first-time settlement applicants.

DNA testing will not be offered as a matter of routine. We envisage that entry clearance officers will offer to arrange tests, with the consent of the applicant and sponsor, in cases where the relevant relationships could not easily be demonstrated by other means. If an applicant or his sponsor declines to undergo a test that would not of itself be a ground for refusing the application. But if an entry clearance officer is not satisfied as to relationship on the basis of the evidence before him, these arrangements will provide applicants with an opportunity to resolve the matter by taking a DNA test.

DNA tests will be carried out, as at present, by independent scientific experts on a commercial basis. The level of the fee to be charged for application will need to strike a balance between not imposing too great a burden either on the individual applicant or on the taxpayer. My right hon. Friend and I will work up arrangements for financing a centrally-organised scheme on this basis.

A number of cases have come to light where an applicant previously refused entry as a child (frequently after appeal to the independent appellate authorities), on the ground that there was no satisfactory evidence as to relationship, is now able to establish relationship by means of DNA evidence but is now over 18 and does not satisfy the requirements in the rules relating to the admission of adults.

I do not believe that it would now be right to waive those requirements as a matter of course in all such cases, irrespective of the applicant's present age or circumstances. Previous decisions, including those of the appellate authorities, were taken in good faith on the basis of the information available at the time. There can be no automatic presumption that applicants now established as related after all should be admitted regardless of current circumstances. We have always distinguished between children, who are readily admitted to join parents here, and adults, who will be admitted to join parents or relatives only in certain exceptional circumstances. Someone who was refused admission as a child when DNA was not available but has later established the claimed relationship should not by virtue of that fact automatically qualify for admission if the other qualification, namely childhood, is no longer fulfilled.

I do not propose any change in the rules which would have the effect of blurring this fundamental distinction, which has been a settled feature of our immigration policy for many years. In many cases over-age applicants are likely to have settled into independent adult life and may also have married and established a family of their own overseas and I do not propose to waive the requirements of the rules in these cases.

However, in the context of outstanding and future re-applications I am prepared to consider waiving the requirements of the rules in certain circumstances. To be eligible for such consideration a re-applicant aged 18 or over will have to show:

(a) that he was refused entry clearance as a child on relationship grounds;

(b) that DNA evidence establishes that he was, after all, related as claimed;

(c) that he is still wholly or mainly dependent on his sponsor in the United Kingdom; and

(d) that there are compassionate circumstances in his case.

I shall not regard the fact that a re-applicant was refused entry clearance as a child on relationship grounds on any earlier occasion and was therefore unable to join his sponsor in the United Kingdom as satisfying the requirement that there be compassionate circumstances.

In deciding whether to waive the requirements of the rules in cases which fall into this category I will consider all circumstances of the case including in particular:

(a) the degree and nature of the dependency;

(b) the extent and nature of the compassionate circumstances;

(c) the re-applicant's present age and marital status;

(d) whether other close family members, such as siblings, are already settled in the United Kingdom;

(e) the lapse of time between the original application and the re-application.

In considering the compassionate circumstances of the case, I will attach greater weight to compassionate circumstances relating to the situation of the re-applicant abroad than I will to those relating to the situation of his sponsor in the United Kingdom.

Mr. Nicholas Bennett: To ask the Secretary of State for the Home Department whether he intends to lay before Parliament changes to the immigration rules.

Mr. Hurd: I have today laid before Parliament a statement of changes in the immigration rules in consolidated form. The main changes of content are the introduction of a visa requirement for nationals of Turkey and Haiti; curtailing the ability of visa nationals to switch after arrival from visitor to student status; and a provision relating to the status of husbands of women admitted for employment or business. The changes are due to enter into force with effect from 8 July 1989, except for the visa requirement for Turkish nationals, which takes effect from 23 June 1989. A full explanatory statement listing all the changes of content and the reasons for them is available in the Vote Office.

Dogs

Dame Janet Fookes: To ask the Secretary of State for the Home Department if he has any proposals to strengthen the law on dangerous dogs.

Mr. Hurd: Under the Dogs Act 1871, if a court finds that a dog is dangerous and not kept under proper control it may order the dog to be kept under proper control or destroyed.

My right hon. and learned Friend, the Secretary of State for Scotland and I have concluded that the penalties by which the Act is enforced ought to be strengthened. Subject to there being a legislative opportunity, we have in mind (i) giving the court a new power to order that the dog is destroyed by a person nominated by the court; (ii) substantially increasing the penalties for failing to comply with an order either to keep the dog under proper control or to destroy the dog; and (iii) giving the court a further power to ban the person against whom an order is made from owning or keeping a dog.

Probation

Mr. Vaz: To ask the Secretary of State for the Home Department what plans the Government have for making a more concerted national network of probation service projects for offenders, in place of the current localised system.

Mr. John Patten *[holding answer 6 June 1989]:* Steps are being taken to introduce more consistency in the work of the probation service and to disseminate good practice to all probation areas. National standards for the operation of community service orders were brought into effect in April, and all probation areas have been asked to develop action plans for the supervision of young adult offenders within guidelines issued by the Home Office. Ten probation areas have been invited to set up intensive probation projects which will be monitored centrally. Practice guidelines were issued to the probation service in 1988 on accommodation for offenders and the care for young offenders sentenced to custody.

The Government are considering developments in the probation service in the light of proposals made in the Carlisle report on parole and the Home Office's Green Paper "Punishment, Custody and the Community".

FOREIGN AND COMMONWEALTH AFFAIRS

Eastern Europe

14. **Mr. Redwood:** To ask the Secretary of State for Foreign and Commonwealth Affairs if he will make a statement about British relations with eastern Europe.

Mr. Waldegrave: Our relations with the countries of eastern Europe are as varied as the countries themselves. We naturally have the closest relations with those whose systems and values come closest to our own. We welcome the substantial steps towards freedom and democracy taken recently in Hungary and Poland.

Cocaine

16. **Mrs. Maureen Hicks:** To ask the Secretary of State for Foreign and Commonwealth Affairs what efforts have been made to co-ordinate international action against traffic in cocaine.

Mr. Eggar: We discussed the growing threat from cocaine with our European partners at an extraordinary ministerial meeting of the Council of Europe's Pompidou Group in London on 18-19 May. My right hon. Friend the Home Secretary, announced our willingness to host an international conference in London in 1990 on demand reduction in the context of the threat from cocaine.

Anglo-Soviet Relations

17. **Mr. Ian Taylor:** To ask the Secretary of State for Foreign and Commonwealth Affairs if he will make a statement on Anglo-Soviet relations.

Mr. Waldegrave: In the last four years there has been a major improvement in Anglo-Soviet relations. We have developed a worthwhile political dialogue and many useful lower level contacts. But the recent expulsions have shown that serious problems remain in some areas.

George Samoilovich

19. **Mr. John Marshall:** To ask the Secretary of State for Foreign and Commonwealth Affairs what representations have been made to the Russian Government about their failure to grant an exit visa to the family of George Samoilovich.

Mr. Waldegrave: Her Majesty's embassy in Moscow has asked the Soviet authorities for a full clarification of the Samoilovich family's position.

Kurds (Asylum)

20. **Mr. Corbyn:** To ask the Secretary of State for Foreign and Commonwealth Affairs what representations he has made to the Government of Iraq and Turkey concerning Kurdish asylum seekers.

Mr. Waldegrave: We have made no recent representations to the Iraqi or Turkish Governments concerning specific Kurdish asylum cases though no one can be in any doubt about our concern over human rights and the problem of Kurdish refugees.

Namibia

21. **Mr. Pike:** To ask the Secretary of State for Foreign and Commonwealth Affairs what recent reports he has received with regard to the implementation of United Nations resolution 435 in Namibia.

Mrs. Chalker: We receive regular reports from our diplomatic missions in Southern Africa and are in frequent contact with all those involved in the implementation of the United Nations plan for Namibian independence.

22. **Miss Lestor:** To ask the Secretary of State for Foreign and Commonwealth Affairs what representations he has made to the United Nations and South Africa regarding the timetabled withdrawal of South African troops from Namibia in keeping with United Nations resolution 435 on Namibia.

Mrs. Chalker: The phased withdrawal of South African forces from Namibia is proceeding in accordance with the United Nations plan. We have urged the South African Government to ensure that this remains the case, and fully support the efforts of the United Nations Secretary General and his special representative.

48. Mr. Cousins: To ask the Secretary of State for Foreign and Commonwealth Affairs when he last met the United Nations special representative for Namibia; and what was discussed.

Mrs. Chalker: My right hon. and learned Friend has not recently met the United Nations special representative for Namibia. My right hon. Friend the Prime Minister met Mr Ahtisaari in Windhoek on 1 April and discussed with him the implementation of the United Nations plan for Namibian independence.

53. Mr. Robert G. Hughes: To ask the Secretary of State for Foreign and Commonwealth Affairs what progress has been made on the implementation of the settlement in Namibia.

Mrs. Chalker: We welcome the recent progress on the implementation of the United Nations plan for Namibian independence. Agreement has been reached on the repeal of discriminatory legislation and the declaration of an amnesty. The repatriation of Namibian refugees began on 12 June. South African forces are being withdrawn from Namibia according to the United Nations plan.

M. Jacques Delors

23. Mr. Galloway: To ask the Secretary of State for Foreign and Commonwealth Affairs when he last met M. Jacques Delors and what was discussed.

27. Mr. Alex Carlile: To ask the Secretary of State for Commonwealth Affairs when he last met M. Jacques Delors; and what subjects were discussed.

Mrs. Chalker: My right hon. and learned Friend met M. Delors at the Foreign Affairs Council on 12 June. I refer the hon. Member to my right hon. and learned Friend's reply of today to the hon. Member for Merthyr Tydfil and Rhymney (Mr. Rowlands) reporting the outcome.

Austria

24. Mr. Amos: To ask the Secretary of State for Foreign and Commonwealth Affairs if he will make it his policy to have discussions with the Austrian Foreign Secretary to encourage Austria to submit an application to join the European Economic Community.

Mrs. Chalker: It is for the Austrian Government alone to decide whether to submit an application to join the European Community, taking account of the economic and political obligations of membership.

Middle East

25. Mr. Neale: To ask the Secretary of State for Foreign and Commonwealth Affairs if he will make a statement on the middle east peace process.

32. Mr. Dykes: To ask the Secretary of State for Foreign and Commonwealth Affairs if he will make a statement about the peace process in the middle east.

34. Mr. Adley: To ask the Secretary of State for Foreign and Commonwealth Affairs if he will make a statement on the middle east peace process following the visit of the Israeli Prime Minister to London.

Mr. Waldegrave: Mr. Shamir's election proposals are a step forward. It is now for the Israelis to develop them as part of a process leading to negotiations on the basis of land for peace, and for the PLO to respond constructively.

49. Mr. Hind: To ask the Secretary of State for Foreign and Commonwealth Affairs if he will make a statement about Soviet involvement in the middle east peace process.

Mr. Waldegrave: We welcome all efforts, including those of the Soviet Union, to build confidence between the parties to the Arab/Israel dispute and to prepare the way for negotiations. Improved Soviet/Israeli relations can contribute to this.

63. Mr. Grocott: To ask the Secretary of State for Foreign and Commonwealth Affairs whether he has any plans to meet Mr. Yasser Arafat to assist the peace process in the middle east.

Mr. Waldegrave: We are certainly ready for further meetings with the PLO when they can serve a useful purpose. But my right hon. and learned Friend the Secretary of State has no plans at present for a meeting with Mr. Arafat.

64. Sir Dennis Walters: To ask the Secretary of State for Foreign and Commonwealth Affairs if he will make a statement on progress towards peace in the middle east.

Mr. Waldegrave: Mr. Shamir's election proposals are a step forward. It is now for the Israelis to develop them as part of a process leading to negotiations on the basis of land for peace, and for the PLO to respond constructively.

Human Rights (Romania)

26. Mr. David Nicholson: To ask the Secretary of State for Foreign and Commonwealth Affairs what representations have been made by Her Majesty's Government about the abuse of human rights in Romania; and if he will make a statement.

Mr. Waldegrave: There has been no improvement in the Romanian Government's lamentable human rights practices. My right hon. and learned Friend raised this matter with the Romanian ambassador on 9 May.

The leader of our delegation to the Paris Conference on the human dimension of the CSCE drew attention to Romania's deplorable human rights record in his opening statement on 31 May.

EC Commissioners

28. Mr. Norman Hogg: To ask the Secretary of State for Foreign and Commonwealth Affairs when he next expects to meet the British members of the European Commission; and what issues will be discussed.

Mrs. Chalker: My right hon. and learned Friend has no plans at present to meet the British members of the European Commission, but looks forward to maintaining contact with them and their fellow Commissioners.

Gibraltar

29. Mr. Colvin: To ask the Secretary of State for Foreign and Commonwealth Affairs what consultations are held with the Government of Gibraltar about reforms within the European Community which may affect their future.

Mrs. Chalker: We are in regular contact with the Gibraltar Government over the full range of EC matters which concern Gibraltar.

NATO Summit

30. **Mr. Yeo:** To ask the Secretary of State for Foreign and Commonwealth Affairs if he will report on developments at the North Atlantic Treaty Organisation summit.

Mr. Waldegrave: I refer my hon. Friend to my right hon. Friend the Prime Minister's statement to the House on 6 June.

Palestine

31. **Mr. Marlow:** To ask the Secretary of State for Foreign and Commonwealth Affairs what is the rôle of the United Kingdom with regard to the achievement of Palestinian self-determination.

Mr. Waldegrave: We shall continue to work for a just and durable solution to the Arab/Israel dispute which takes account of the Palestinians' right of self-determination as well as Israel's right to security.

Argentina

33. **Mr. Cyril D. Townsend:** To ask the Secretary of State for Foreign and Commonwealth Affairs if he will make a statement on Britain's relations with Argentina.

Mr. Eggar: We remain committed to seeking more normal relations with Argentina, while upholding our commitment to the Falkland Islanders. We believe it should be possible for both countries to benefit by working together on practical matters such as trade, air and sea links and fisheries conservation, leaving the issue of sovereignty, which most divides us, aside.

Since 1982 we have accordingly taken a series of initiatives, but the Argentine response so far has been disappointing. Nevertheless our offers remain open, and will still be on the table when the new President assumes power.

55. **Mr. Patnick:** To ask the Secretary of State for Foreign and Commonwealth Affairs whether any message has been received by Her Majesty's Government from the new President of Argentina.

Mr. Eggar: No; in any case, the President elect Mr. Menem has not yet taken office.

Foreign Affairs Council

35. **Mr. McAllion:** To ask the Secretary of State for Foreign and Commonwealth Affairs if he will make a statement on the last meeting of the Foreign Affairs Council.

Mrs. Chalker: The main item at the Foreign Affairs Council on 12 June was preparations for the Madrid European Council. A full statement on the Foreign Affairs Council is being deposited in the Library of the House today.

London Information Forum

36. **Mr. Boswell:** To ask the Secretary of State for Foreign and Commonwealth Affairs if he will make a statement on the outcome of the London Information Forum.

Mr. Waldegrave: I refer the hon. Member to the reply I gave my hon. Friend the Member for Bournemouth, East (Mr. Atkinson) on 19 May at column *329*. The view then expressed that the London Information Forum was a success has been borne out by comments received subsequently.

European Foreign Policies

37. **Mr. Knox:** To ask the Secretary of State for Foreign and Commonwealth Affairs when he next proposes to have discussions with his European Community partners concerning the development of common European foreign policies.

Sir Geoffrey Howe: I refer my hon. Friend to the reply I gave today to the hon. Member for Merthyr Tydfil and Rhymney (Mr. Rowlands). I next expect to discuss political co-operation matters with them during the European Council in Madrid on 26-27 June.

Human Rights (Romania)

38. **Mr. Burns:** To ask the Secretary of State for Foreign and Commonwealth Affairs what representations have been made by Her Majesty's Government about human rights abuses in Romania; and if he will make a statement.

Mr. Waldegrave: There has been no improvement in the Romanian Government's lamentable human rights practices. My right hon. and learned Friend raised this matter with the Romanian ambassador on 9 May.

The leader of our delegation to the Paris conference on the human dimension of the CSCE drew attention to Romania's deplorable human rights record in his opening statement on 31 May.

Afghanistan

39. **Mr. Brazier:** To ask the Secretary of State for Foreign and Commonwealth Affairs what representations he has received on the current state of the war in Afghanistan.

Mr. Eggar: It has long been our practice to stay in touch with a wide range of Afghan opinion and with other parties interested in Afghanistan. These contacts have confirmed our view that the resolution of the conflict requires the establishment of a truly representative Government in Kabul.

Cocaine

40. **Dr. Twinn:** To ask the Secretary of State for Foreign and Commonwealth Affairs if he will report on progress in initiatives to curb the international cocaine trade.

Mr. Eggar: On 18 May my right hon. Friend the Home Secretary announced a number of initiatives to help combat the threat from cocaine. These included provision of additional resources to United Nations drugs bodies, establishment of a customs training facility, targeting of overseas assistance on cocaine and the United Kingdom's willingness to host an international conference on demand reduction in the context of the threat from cocaine.

Ethiopia

41. Mr. Brandon Bravo: To ask the Secretary of State for Foreign and Commonwealth Affairs if he will make a statement on the current situation in Ethiopia.

Mrs. Chalker: The Ethiopian Government reasserted control after an attempted coup by military officers on 16-17 May. They announced on 5 June their readiness to enter into unconditional negotiations on the situation in Eritrea. We regard negotiations to resolve internal conflicts, together with respect for human rights and the adoption of sensible economic policies, as pre-requisites for positive developments in Ethiopia.

Syria

42. Mr. Janner: To ask the Secretary of State for Foreign and Commonwealth Affairs if he will make a statement concerning Britain's relations with Syria.

Mr. Waldegrave: We could not consider restoring diplomatic relations without firm evidence that Syria had given up support for international terrorism.

Single European Market

43. Mr. Stott: To ask the Secretary of State for Foreign and Commonwealth Affairs what efforts his Department is making in promoting the single European market.

Mrs. Chalker: The Foreign and Commonwealth Office and our posts abroad are fully involved in promoting the single European market. British embassies lobby and report on single market measures and also provide a range of services to help British exporters make the most of the growing opportunities.

South Africa

45. Mr. Anderson: To ask the Secretary of State for Foreign and Commonwealth Affairs when he next expects to meet his South African counterpart.

Mrs. Chalker: My right hon. and learned Friend the Secretary of State has no current plans to do so.

Anglo-Soviet Relations

46. Mr. Patrick Thompson: To ask the Secretary of State for Foreign and Commonwealth Affairs if he will make a statement about Anglo-Soviet relations.

59. Mr. Amess: To ask the Secretary of State for Foreign and Commonwealth Affairs if he will make a statement about Anglo-Soviet relations.

Mr. Waldegrave: In the last four years there has been a major improvement in Anglo-Soviet relations. We have developed a worthwhile and substantive high-level political dialogue. Contacts of all sorts have expanded rapidly, helping to break down the barriers of misunderstanding and distrust. But the recent expulsions have shown that there is still a long way to go before our relations with the Soviet Union reach the level of stability and mutual trust to which we aspire.

Poland

47. Mr. Sumberg: To ask the Secretary of State for Foreign and Commonwealth Affairs what encouragement and assistance he is giving to the process of Polish economic reconstruction.

50. Miss Widdecombe: To ask the Secretary of State for Foreign and Commonwealth Affairs, what encouragement and assistance he has given to the round table talks in Poland and the process of Polish economic reconstruction.

Mr. Waldegrave: We welcome recent political events in Poland. Economic reform and adjustment are possible only with the full consent of the people. My right hon. Friend the Prime Minister told General Jaruzelski on 10 June of the help we are ready to provide: we will support an IMF programme which underpins effective economic reconstruction; we will support rescheduling of 1989 debt payments in the Paris Club; bilaterally we will contribute £5 million per year over five years to provide training and advice to support progress towards democracy and a market economy.

Decision-making

51. Mr. Wallace: To ask the Secretary of State for Foreign and Commonwealth Affairs whether, at the forthcoming European Council, the British Government will make any proposals for improving the quality of European decision-making.

Mrs. Chalker: No.

Anglo-Israeli Relations

52. Mrs. Gillian Shephard: To ask the Secretary of State for Foreign and Commonwealth Affairs if he will make a statement about Anglo-Israeli relations.

Mr. Waldegrave: Relations with Israel are good. We were glad to welcome Mr. Shamir to London last month and look forward to remaining in close touch with him on Arab-Israeli and other issues.

Arab-Israeli Conflict

54. Mr. Robert Hicks: To ask the Secretary of State for Foreign and Commonwealth Affairs what is the latest position regarding the proposal to hold an international conference to resolve the Israeli-Arab conflict and the Palestinian problem in particular; and if he will make a statement.

Mr. Waldegrave: An international conference remains the most suitable framework for negotiations between the parties to the Arab-Israeli dispute. We are working to help establish the necessary common ground and confidence between the parties to enable negotiations to begin.

Gulf States

56. Mr. Pawsey: To ask the Secretary of State for Foreign and Commonwealth Affairs when he next expects to visit the Gulf states.

Mr. Waldegrave: My right hon. and learned Friend has no plans to do so.

China

57. Mr. Riddick: To ask the Secretary of State for Foreign and Commonwealth Affairs whether he will make a statement on developments in the People's Republic of China.

Mr. Eggar: I refer my hon. Friend to the statement made by my right hon. and learned Friend the Secretary of State in the House on 6 June on developments in the People's Republic of China.

PLO

58. **Mr. Lawrence:** To ask the Secretary of State for Foreign and Commonwealth Affairs what is Her Majesty's Government's policy towards the attempts by the Palestinian Liberation Organisation to obtain a quasi-Governmental recognition by membership of various United Nations Organisations.

Mr. Waldegrave: We have not recognised the "state of Palestine" declared by last November's Palestine National Council. Accordingly, we do not believe that "Palestine" satisfies the criteria for membership of UN agencies. We have advised the PLO against pursuing these applications.

Treaty of Rome

60. **Mr. Spearing:** To ask the Secretary of State for Foreign and Commonwealth Affairs what consideration has been given by the Council of Ministers of the European Economic Communities to the activating of article 236 of the treaty of Rome.

Mrs. Chalker: No proposals under article 236 have been put before the Council since the amendment of the treaty of Rome by the Single European Act.

Council of Ministers

61. **Mr. McFall:** To ask the Secretary of State for Foreign and Commonwealth Affairs, when he next expects to meet his counterparts in the Council of Ministers; and what he expects will be discussed.

44. **Mr. Radice:** To ask the Secretary of State for Foreign and Commonwealth Affairs when he next expects to attend a meeting of the Foreign Affairs Council; and what he hopes will be discussed.

Mrs. Chalker My right hon. and learned Friend the Secretary of State will next meet his EC counterparts at the Madrid European Council on 26/27 June. The next Foreign Affairs Council will take place on 17/18 July. The agenda is unlikely to be set until nearer the time.

62. **Mr. Wood:** To ask the Secretary of State for Foreign and Commonwealth Affairs if he will report on the outcome of his discussions with the Nigerian Foreign Minister.

Mrs. Chalker My right hon. and learned Friend the Secretary of State and I had talks with Foreign Minister Nwachukwu, held during the state visit of President Babangida, that covered bilateral issues and international developments of mutual interest, focussing in particular on Southern Africa. Our discussions were extremely friendly, reflecting the close and cordial nature of our bilateral relations.

Tibet

65. **Mr. Mullin** To ask the Secretary of State for Foreign and Commonwealth Affairs when he last discussed Tibet with a representative of the Chinese Government.

Mr. Eggar I refer the hon. Member to the reply I gave him on 12 April at col 559.

General Wladislaw Sikorski (Remains)

Mr. Frank Field: To ask the Secretary of State for Foreign and Commonwealth Affairs whether the Government have any plans to return the remains of General Wladislaw Sikorski to Poland in the foreseeable future.

Mr. Waldegrave My right hon. Friend the Prime Minister told General Jaruzelski at the weekend that we had reconsidered this question. We felt the time was not yet right. We would continue to review the matter, in the light of the changing situation in Poland.

Russian Diplomats (Expulsion)

Mr David Evans: To ask the Secretary of State for Foreign and Commonwealth Affairs how many members of the Russian diplomatic mission have been expelled from the United Kingdom since 1970 for engaging in activities incompatible with their status.

Mr. Eggar: Ninety nine; a further 69 Soviet citizens who were not accredited as diplomats have been expelled during the same period.

Agni Missile

Mr. Cohen: To ask the Secretary of State for Foreign and Commonwealth Affairs if he will make a statement on the recent test launch by India of its Agni missile; whether the missile is considered to have a nuclear capability; and if he proposes to discuss the matter in his next discussions with the Indian Government.

Mr. Waldegrave: We have noted the successful test launch of the Indian Agni missile. As a founder member of the missile technology control region, we are obviously concerned about the proliferation of ballistic missiles. When the MTCR was established in April 1987, the partners urged all states to adopt the guidelines of the regime.

There have been press reports that Agni is a nuclear —capable missile, although the Indian Prime Minister has stated that it is not a nuclear weapons system. We have no immediate plans for discussions on this matter with the Indian Government but we make our views on non-proliferation clear whenever a suitable opportunity arises.

Immigration Appeals (Bombay)

Mr. Cohen: To ask the Secretary of State for Foreign and Commonwealth Affairs what is he average time from an appeal being submitted to *(a)* the date of it being set and *(b)* it being heard at the post in Bombay.

Mr. Eggar: The average waiting time from receipt of an appeal at the deputy British high commission in Bombay to the despatch of the explanatory statement to the independent appellate authority is 11 weeks. The subsequent wait for an appeal hearing to take place in the United Kingdom (not Bombay) is a matter for the Lord Chancellor's Department.

Disasters (Compensation Rights)

Mr. Cohen: To ask the Secretary of State for Foreign and Commonwealth Affairs whether he will take an initiative to achieve an international agreement under the auspices of the United Nations on safety and compensation rights in the event of such tragedies as the Bhopal disaster; and if he will make a statement.

Mr. Eggar: Issues of safety and compensation for victims of major industrial disasters fall primarily within the competence of national legislatures and, in Europe, of the European Community. However, the UN centre of transnational corporations does work to promote safety and to minimise pollution and environmental damage; and the UN Disaster Relief Organisation has an overall co-ordinating role in respect of both natural and man-made disasters. The United Kingdom participates fully in the work of both these bodies and is currently consulting western partners with a view to putting forward proposals to enhance UNDRO's effectiveness. I see no justification for any further initiative in this field.

WPC Yvonne Fletcher

Mr. Shersby: To ask the Secretary of State for Foreign and Commonwealth Affairs what representations have been made by Her Majesty's Government to the Government of Libya concerning the payment of compensation for the death of the late WPC Yvonne Fletcher in 1984; and if he will make a statement.

Mr. Waldegrave: We continue to take every opportunity to remind the Libyans of our claim for compensation for the life and career of WPC Fletcher.

Daya Bay Nuclear Plant

Mr. Flynn: To ask the Secretary of State for Foreign and Commonwealth Affairs if, in the light of recent events in the People's Republic of China, Her Majesty's Government will withdraw United Kingdom co-operation and export credit guarantees for the Daya bay nuclear plant being built in Guandong.

Mr. Eggar: We have no plans to do so. Contracts for the project were signed by the companies concerned some time ago and work is proceeding. In these circumstances we do not intend to suspend ECGD cover.

Soviet Union (Emigration)

Mr. Dykes: To ask the Secretary of State for Foreign and Commonwealth Affairs if he will seek to clarify with the Soviet authorities whether those wishing to emigrate will in future require permission from relatives remaining in the Soviet Union.

Mr. Waldegrave: We have repeatedly underlined our concern at the so-called "poor relatives clause" in the existing Soviet rules covering emigration. We have pressed the Soviet authorities to ensure that no provision of this sort is included in the new emigration law, which we understand is in preparation.

Nuclear Arms

Dr. Thomas: To ask the Secretary of State for Foreign and Commonwealth Affairs if he has any plans to submit proposals on the full separation of civil and military nuclear facilities and attendant verifiable safeguards to the fourth review conference of the 1968 nuclear non-proliferation treaty, to be held in 1990, following the initiatives made at the third non-proliferation treaty review conference in 1985.

Mr. Waldegrave: The final document of the third review conference of the parties to the treaty on the non-proliferation of nuclear weapons, held in 1985, recommended, inter alia,

"consideration of separation of the Civil and Military facilities in the Nuclear-Weapon States".

We have no plans to submit proposals on this subject to the fourth review conference in 1990. However, the United Kingdom has made significant progress in the direction envisaged. In 1986, we brought to an end the co-processing of civil and non-civil materials at Sellafield. Inspectors of the European Atomic Energy Community have access to all civil material at Sellafield on a continuing basis.

Anglo-Egyptian Relations

Mr. Butler: To ask the Secretary of State for Foreign and Commonwealth Affairs if he will make a statement about Anglo-Egyptian relations.

Mr. Waldegrave: Our relations with Egypt are very close and friendly. The talks with the Egyptian Foreign Minister last week confirmed that our views of current middle east issues are very similar.

Nigeria and Ghana

Mr. Speller: To ask the Secretary of State for Foreign and Commonwealth Affairs if he has any plans to visit Nigeria or Ghana before the end of the current year; and if he will make a statement on his plans for bilateral assistance to each of the states.

Mrs. Chalker: My right hon. and learned Friend the Secretary of State plans to visit Nigeria for the next round of United Kingdom/Nigeria bilateral talks, dates for which we hope will be agreed soon. He has no present plans to visit Ghana. I shall be visiting Nigeria from 25-27 June to lead a delegation from the Energy Industries Council for a DTI-sponsored seminar on the hydrocarbon sector in Nigeria; and I shall be visiting Ghana from 27-30 June.

In addition to our technical co-operation programme for Nigeria, we have pledged this year $100 million balance of payments assistance in support of Nigeria's structural adjustment programme. As part of our substantial programme of development assistance to Ghana, we have offered this year a further £20 million balance of payments finance, in support of Ghana's economic recovery programme.

Cyprus

Mr. John Marshall: To ask the Secretary of State for Foreign and Commonwealth Affairs what representations he will make to secure compensation for those British citizens whose property was expropriated in northern Cyprus in 1974.

Mr. Eggar: We do not recognise the "Turkish Republic of Northern Cyprus" and have no formal dealings with its authorities. The British high commissioner in Nicosia nevertheless has informal contacts with Mr. Denktash and we are thus able to protect the interests of British nationals.

Whilst we are not aware of any instances of the outright expropriation of property by those authorities, we are continuing to press for all outstanding claims for compensation from our citizens to be dealt with expeditiously and for the remaining difficulties facing those attempting to establish their freehold title to property to be resolved.

Diplomatic Staff (Vehicles)

Mr. Barry Field: To ask the Secretary of State for Foreign and Commonwealth Affairs if he will list those British embassies whose ambassadors or consuls do not drive British manufactured motor cars as their official vehicle.

Mr. Eggar: With one exception, the official vehicles provided for heads of mission at British embassies and high commissions overseas are British-manufactured. In Addis Ababa, the ambassador has an EC-manufactured Ford Granada, which was purchased in Britain.

There are five consuls-general/consuls who drive non-British manufactured cars. These are the consulates-general at Montreal (Chrysler), Rio de Janeiro and Sao Paulo (Chevrolet), and the consulates at Cape Town (Vauxhall Carlton) and Durban (Ford Sierra).

It is FCO policy to purchase British manufactured cars where possible. However, for operational reasons, one head of mission and five heads of post around the world drive non-British-manufactured cars.

Chile

Mr. Macdonald: To ask the Secretary of State for Foreign and Commonwealth Affairs what measures he is taking to assist the transition to democracy in Chile before the elections there.

Mr. Eggar: Both we and our partners in the Twelve fully support the continuing transition process in Chile. We welcome the satisfactory progress made this year towards the restoration of a democratic system in Chile. We regularly invite to Britain leading representatives of Chilean political parties.

DEFENCE

Nuclear Weapons

67. **Mr. Denzil Davies:** To ask the Secretary of State for Defence what is the policy of Her Majesty's Government regarding the retention of battlefield and short-range nuclear weapons.

Mr. Archie Hamilton: The Government share the assessment made by NATO at its recent summit that for the foreseeable future there is no alternative to the Alliance strategy of deterrence and that this strategy requires a mix of nuclear forces, including Europe-based ground-launched missiles. The Government therefore welcome the summit's rejection of a third zero.

Protection Vests

Mr. Madden: To ask the Secretary of State for Defence if he will list the dates when personal protection vests for use by armed forces in general war were issued to armed forces in each country belonging to the North Atlantic Treaty Organisation.

Mr. Archie Hamilton: The information requested is not readily available and it would involve disproportionate cost and effort to obtain it.

Alcohol Consumption

Mr. Dalyell: To ask the Secretary of State for Defence what conveniently available figures over a recent convenient period of time he has *(a)* for excessive consumption of alcohol among service personnel and *(b)* for alcohol-related courts martial; and if he will set up an internal departmental committee to consider excessive alcohol consumption in Her Majesty's Forces.

Mr. Archie Hamilton: Figures are not maintained for excessive consumption of alcohol among service personnel. Figures for alcohol-related convictions at courts martial for the years 1986, 1987 and 1988 are given in the table. Figures for 1989 are not yet available.

	1986	1987	1988
Royal Navy/Royal Marines	[1]12	[1]10	[1]21
Army	[1]36	[1]56	[1]45
Royal Air Force	34	52	54

[1] Figures relate to convictions where the charge was directly concerned with drink and exclude cases where the charge was for another offence.

An existing tri-service committee on drug abuse prevention is the appropriate departmental committee for considering excessive alcohol consumption in the armed forces.

Royal Navy Ships (Town Links)

Ms. Short: To ask the Secretary of State for Defence if he will list the Royal Navy ships which have been granted honorary freedom of their affiliated towns or cities.

Mr. Archie Hamilton: Many Royal Navy ships have been granted honorary freedom of their affiliated towns or cities. However, no comprehensive list of such ships is held centrally and one could only be obtained at disproportionate cost and effort.

Ms. Short: To ask the Secretary of State for Defence what links each of the following Royal Navy ships have, or are expected to have with towns or cities in the United Kingdom: (1) HMS Cornwall, (2) HMS Cumberland, (3) HMS Campbeltown, (4) HMS Chatham, (5) HMS Norfolk, (6) HMS Marlborough, (7) HMS Argyll, (8) HMS Lancaster, (9) HMS Vanguard, (10) HMS Victorious, (11) HMS Vengeance, (12) HMS Venerable, (13) RFA Fort Grange, (14) RFA Fort Austin, (15) RFA Resource, (16) RFA Regent, (17) HMS Trafalgar, (18) HMS Turbulent, (19) HMS Tireless, (20) HMS Torbay, (21) HMS Trenchant, (22) HMS Talent, (23) HMS Triumph, (24) HMS Swiftsure, (25) HMS Sovereign, (26) HMS Superb, (27) HMS Sceptre, (28) HMS Spartan, (29) HMS Splendid, (30) HMS Churchill, (31) HMS Courageous, (32) HMS Conqueror, (33) HMS Valiant, and (34) HMS Warspite.

Mr. Archie Hamilton: The ship to town/city links are as follows:

Ship	Town
HMS Cumberland	Cumbria
HMS Campbeltown	Campbeltown
HMS Chatham	Medway
HMS Trafalgar	Lancaster
HMS Turbulent	Warrington
HMS Tireless	Rugby
HMS Torbay	Torbay
HMS Trenchant	Shrewsbury
HMS Swiftsure	Southport
HMS Sovereign	Derby
HMS Superb	Stafford

Ship	Town
HMS Sceptre	Wigan
HMS Spartan	Rothesay
HMS Spendid	Plymouth
HMS Churchill	Redbridge
HMS Courageous	Preston
HMS Conqueror	Congleton
HMS Valiant	Scarborough
HMS Warspite	Hereford

Royal Fleet Auxiliaries are not affiliated to towns or cities. Most of the remaining vessels are under construction and as yet have no affiliation.

Paper Products

Mr. Menzies Campbell: To ask the Secretary of State for Defence how much his Department spends on paper products; how much paper is consumed by his Department in an average month; what steps he plans to take to reduce the quantity of paper consumed; and if he has plans to purchase recycled paper for his Department.

Mr. Sainsbury: The Ministry of Defence, world wide, spends some £7·7 million per year on paper products. This equates to just under 900 tonnes consumption per month.

All demands for paper products are closely scrutinised; in particular, there is a continuing review of forms usage within the MOD which has already reduced the consumption of printed material and will continue to do so.

The MOD is already obtaining many stock ranges with a high recycled content such as envelopes, notebooks, file covers etc. More recycled products will be purchased provided that this does not affect quality, versatility and represents value for money.

Written Answers to Questions

Thursday 15 June 1989

TRADE AND INDUSTRY

Exports (Group of Seven)

Mr. Baldry: To ask the Chancellor of the Duchy of Lancaster if he will publish a table of the volume of exports per head of population of the Group of Seven countries.

Mr. Alan Clark: The information in both value and volume terms is in the following table.

Exports per head of population, 1988

	[1]*Volume* 1985 = 100	*Value* *United States $*
France	110	2,896
Federal Republic of Germany	111	5,273
Italy	110	2,247
United Kingdom	109	2,538
Canada	117	4,316
United States of America	129	1,302
Japan	103	2,160

[1] Export volume index adjusted for population change between 1985 and 1988.
Source: OECD

Post Office Monopoly

Mr. John Marshall: To ask the Chancellor of the Duchy of Lancaster what proposals he has for ending the Post Office monopoly.

Mr. Forth: We keep the options under review, but we have no present plans to end the monopoly. We have, however, made it clear that the Post Office's letter monopoly is a privilege, not a right, and that in the event of a cessation or serious disruption of the letter service, we would consider suspending it.

Liquidators

Mr. Aspinwall: To ask the Chancellor of the Duchy of Lancaster if he will give the figures for the number of certificates issued for licensed liquidators since the Insolvency Act 1986 came into operation.

Mr. Maude: There are currently 1,737 individuals authorised to act as insolvency practitioners under the Insolvency Act 1986.

Telecommunications (Liberalisation)

Mr. Robert G. Hughes: To ask the Chancellor of the Duchy of Lancaster whether any decisions have been made as a result of the recommendations from the Director General of Telecommunications about the further liberalisation of telecommunication services; and if he will make a statement.

Mr. Atkins: My right hon. and noble Friend the Secretary of State has received advice from the Director General of Telecommunications following a major consultation exercise which he undertook earlier this year. We are very grateful to the director general and his staff for the thorough and professional way they carried this out.

We have decided to accept the recommendations the director general has made for changes to the current regime for the provision of telecommunications services using the networks of, or circuits provided by, a fixed-link public telecommunications operator (PTO), that is British Telecommunications plc, Mercury Communications Ltd. or Kingston Communications plc.

The first, and most important, of these is that we have decided to liberalise entirely the use made by companies of private circuits domestic to the United Kingdom leased from a PTO. Until now, companies leasing circuits have not been permitted to resell capacity to others or to share it with them. This prohibition arose from the fact that the price of private circuits leased from BT was historically below cost and provided significant opportunities for the use of leased lines to bypass the public network, to the detriment of the ordinary user. For this reason, the operating licences of the PTOs prohibited until 1 July 1989 the use of leased lines to provide simple resale, that is the routing of a call from the public network, over a leased line and back on to the public network. This was intended to allow for the rebalancing of leased line and network charges.

This rebalancing has now largely taken place within the United Kingdom, and we see no need any longer to prevent companies making use of leased lines however they choose, whether for voice or data services. We therefore intend to issue a licence permitting simple resale of United Kingdom domestic private circuits as well as other forms of resale, bypass and shared use. Those networks connected to the public switched network (PSN) will continue to be subject to the rules on technical quality standards.

Although considerable tariff rebalancing has taken place on circuits within the United Kingdom, international tariffs are still out of line with costs. We have therefore decided to retain the current prohibition on international simple resale for the time being. However, we have accepted the director general's recommendation that he should keep the situation under review and advise us as and when further liberalisation is justified. The new licence will therefore be drafted in such a way as to allow us to liberalise international private circuits on a case-by-case basis as opportunities arise.

The director general has also recommended other major changes to the existing licensing regime. In the light of his experience in administering the fair trading rules in the current value-added and data services licence, he has recommended that they be simplified in operation and more clearly targeted on companies likely to abuse a dominant position. Thus, companies which the director general considers dominant, with large businesses in telecommunications services, will continue to be covered by the present rules against cross-subsidisation, showing undue preference or discrimination and other detailed conditions. However, those rules in the current regime which impose heavy cost and which may deter people because of the difficulty of compliance are to be removed. These include the rule on publication of prices which is in abeyance already. Conversely, rules which are of value to users, such as those on privacy and confidentiality, metering and numbering are to be applied to all operators, rather than just the largest.

We have also accepted the director general's advice that the new licence should include a condition aimed at alleviating the nuisance to the users of the telephone, fax or other telecommunications systems caused by persistent but unsolicited attempts to sell products and services. Sellers by telephone or fax or those acting as their agents, will be required by the new licence to stop making these direct sales calls to any particular user of a telecommunication system when he has given them a written instruction to do so.

Other changes which are to be made include provisions allowing greater flexibility for installers, maintainers and users of call-routing apparatus, the reduction of the minimum period for the termination of maintenance contracts to 42 days and the introduction of a requirement to provide inductive couplers in emergency telephones in lifts.

Although the limit of 200 m for the provision of privately provided circuits between buildings will be retained, service providers will be permitted to run these systems on others' premises and the procedure for permitting exceptions to the 200 m rule (where justified) will be simplified.

We believe these changes will add greatly to the freedom and the flexibility of telecommunications operators in the United Kingdom, and will keep the United Kingdom in the vanguard of telecommunications liberalisation both in Europe and worldwide. We intend to bring these changes about by issuing a new branch systems general licence during July. This will replace both the existing branch systems general licence and that for value-added and data services. My Department and the Office of Telecommunications are currently finalising the details of the new licence, and we shall inform the House when it is to be issued.

NATIONAL FINANCE

Civil Servants (Numbers)

Mr. Amos: To ask the Chancellor of the Exchequer what was the number of staff in post in central Government Departments at 1 April.

Mr. Major: On 1 April 1989, there were 569,215 staff in post in central Government Departments. Of these 499,821 were non-industrials and 69,394 were industrials.

Trustees

Mr. Bowis: To ask the Chancellor of the Exchequer whether he will make a statement about the residence status of trustees for income tax purposes in the light of the recent decision of the House of Lords in the case of Dawson *v* CIR.

Mr. Norman Lamont: We have considered the implications of the House of Lords' recent decision in the case of Dawson *v* CIR, and have decided that the present law does not deal satisfactorily with the residence status for income tax purposes of trustees in cases where the trustees of a settlement include both a United Kingdom resident and a non-resident. We therefore propose to introduce new rules to determine the residence status of

such "mixed residence" trustees. Provided that the settlor was not resident, not ordinarily resident and not domiciled in the United Kingdom at the time he made the settlement (and at any later time when he provided funds), the trustees will be treated as not resident in the United Kingdom. Otherwise "mixed residence" trustees will all be treated as United Kingdom resident.

This proposal will not affect trusts where the trustees are all United Kingdom residents, or all non-resident. In those cases, the existing rules will continue to apply.

There will also be similar rules governing the residence status of personal representatives of a deceased person, where they include both a United Kingdom resident and a non-resident.

There will also be provisions, applying to all trustees and personal representatives, to make it clear that income tax assessments may be made on any one or more of them.

Further details of the proposals are set out in an Inland Revenue press release published today. The necessary provisions have been tabled for Committee stage of the Finance Bill.

Savings

Mr. Butterfill: To ask the Chancellor of the Exchequer what plans he has to increase the personal savings ratio.

Mr. Lilley: We expect many of the factors which led to the fall in the personal savings ratio to reverse themselves over the medium term. In addition, the rise in interest rates over the past year will encourage higher savings and lower borrowing.

Orchids

Mr. Allen: To ask the Chancellor of the Exchequer what steps Her Majesty's Customs and Excise take to prevent the smuggling of rare orchids into Britain.

Mr. Lilley *[holding answer 9 June 1989]*: Customs and Excise makes every effort to prevent the illegal import of listed orchids and other items covered by the convention on international trade in endangered species.

CIVIL SERVICE

Mr. David Morphet

Mr. Andrew F. Bennett: To ask the Minister for the Civil Service whether any conditions have been attached by the advisory committee on business appointments to the employment by Balfour Beatty of Mr. David Morphet, formerly of the Department of Energy; and if he will make a statement.

Mr. Luce: It is not our practice to divulge information about individual applications under the business appointment rules, as to do so would be a breach of confidence and privacy.

ENERGY

AGR Fuel Rods

Mr. Alan W. Williams: To ask the Secretary of State for Energy how many spent AGR fuel rods are expected to be produced in each year from 1989 to 2000 and if advanced gas-cooled reactors produce electricity at their planned output during the 1990s.

Mr. Michael Spicer This is an operational matter for the Central Electricity Generating Board. I have asked the chairman to write to the hon. Member.

Spent Nuclear Fuel

Mr. Alan W. Williams: To ask the Secretary of State for Energy what is the earliest date by which the proposed Heysham AGR dry storage facility could be ready; and whether it will be large enough to store all the spent AGR fuel from all of Britain's AGRs for their planned lifetimes.

Mr. Michael Spicer This is an operational matter for the Central Electricity Generating Board. I have asked the chairman to write to the hon. Member.

Nuclear Materials (Safeguards)

Mr. Flynn: To ask the Secretary of State for Energy if he will set out the details of safeguards inspection for civil nuclear materials and facilities agreed with the European Commission regulation 3227/76; and when such inspections began.

Mr. Michael Spicer: Euratom inspections began in 1973. It is not the custom within Euratom to publish details of the inspection arrangements for any nuclear facility in the Community.

Irradiated Fuel

Mr. Flynn: To ask the Secretary of State for Energy if, pursuant to his answer to the hon. Member for Newport, West, June, he will list the countries of origin and dates on which consignments of irradiated fuel have been returned to their countries of origin since 1979.

Mr. Michael Spicer: The country of origin of the shipments referred to in the answer to the hon. Member on 7 June is included in those listed in the answer given by my hon. Friend the Member for Eddisbury (Mr. Goodlad) on 18 February 1987 at column *635.* Details of individual consignments are confidential.

Plutonium

Mr. Flynn: To ask the Secretary of State for Energy, pursuant to the reply to the hon. Member for Meirionnydd Nant Conwy, (Dr. Thomas) *Official Report,* 8 May column *289,* whether the reports on plutonium production sent by reactor operators to safeguards authorities are detailed routinely to *(a)* single gramme quantities, *(b)* tens of grammes quantities, or *(c)* hundreds of grammes quantities.

Mr. Michael Spicer: Euratom regulation 3227/76 article 21 (a) requires quantities of special nuclear material to be expressed in grammes.

Uranimum (Namibia)

Mr. Flynn: To ask the Secretary of State for Energy, pursuant to the reply to the hon. Member for Newport, West, *Official Report,* 19 May, column *314,* which was the competent authority in Namibia which gave the N obligation code to the consignment of Namibian uranium imported to the United Kingdom since 1979.

Mr. Michael Spicer: The N obligation code was assigned by the Euratom safeguards authorities.

Pollution

Mr. Wray: To ask the Secretary of State for Energy if he will detail all his Department's policies and proposals regarding *(a)* acid rain and *(b)* pollution by nuclear waste; and if he will make a statement.

Mr. Michael Spicer: The Government will ensure that the CEGB and its successor companies contribute to the emission reduction requirements of the European Communities' large combustion plant directive. These are to reduce emissions of sulphur dioxide by 60 per cent. on 1980 levels by 2003 and nitrogen oxides by 30 per cent. on 1980 levels by 1998. We shall encourage the development and application of renewable energy sources wherever they have prospects of being economically competitive and environmentally acceptable. Furthermore, the non-fossil fuel obligation which will be placed on the public electricity suppliers in the privatised electricity industry and the continuing work of the energy efficiency office will help to reduce acid rain.

Policy on radioactive waste is a matter for my right hon. Friend the Secretary of State for the Environment.

Conservation

Mr. Wray: To ask the Secretary of State for Energy if he will detail his Department's specific proposals for energy conservation for each year since 1981.

Mr. Peter Morrison: Details of the Government's proposals on energy efficiency have been published annually in the public expenditure White Paper and in response to reports of the Select Committee on Energy.

Safeguards Agreement

Mr. Flynn: To ask the Secretary of State for Energy how many withdrawals from safeguards, under article 14 of the 1978 tripartite safeguards agreement between United Kingdom—Euratom—International Atomic Energy Authority, have been made since May 1979.

Mr. Michael Spicer *[holding answer 11 May 1989]:* Some temporary withdrawals have been made for technical operational reasons with the material being returned to safeguards after it has been processed in unsafeguarded facilities. Some permanent withdrawals have also been made. It would not be in the public interest to reveal details of these.

WALES

Careers Teachers

Mr. Barry Jones: To ask the Secretary of State for Wales how many schools careers local education authority school teachers there were in Wales in May 1980 and at the latest available date; and if he will make a statement.

Mr. Wyn Roberts: The information is not available in the form requested. However, information from the 1984 secondary school staffing survey indicates that in 1984 there were 473 teachers of careers education. A further staffing survey is currently under way.

Education Reform

Mr. Barry Jones: To ask the Secretary of State for Wales (1) if he has met teachers' organisations to discuss his Department's plans to test children at seven years of age; and if he will make a statement;

(2) if he has met teachers' organisations to discuss his Department's policy of testing pupils at the age of 14 years; and if he will make a statement.

Mr. Wyn Roberts: Welsh Office Ministers and officials have met representatives of teachers' organisations on numerous occasions and the subjects discussed have included assessment and testing of children in accordance with the Education Reform Act.

Dog Registration

Mr. Barry Jones: To ask the Secretary of State for Wales if he has plans for compulsory dog registration in Wales; and if he will make a statement.

Mr. Peter Walker: I have no plans to introduce dog registration in Wales.

Shotton and Connah's Quay Bypass

Mr. Barry Jones: To ask the Secretary of State for Wales if he will meet Alyn and Deeside district council, Clwyd county council and the Deeside town and community councils to discuss how his Department might assist in the building of a Shotton and Connah's Quay bypass, including a new river crossing of the River Dee at Connah's Quay; and if he will make a statement.

Mr. Wyn Roberts: It would not be appropriate: this is a matter for Clwyd county council as the responsible highway authority. However I am fully aware of its proposals and expect to receive a bid for transport supplementary support.

Land Development (Shotton)

Mr. Barry Jones: To ask the Secretary of State for Wales if he will visit Clwyd county council and Alyn and Deeside district council to discuss with them how his Department might assist those local authorities in developing land adjacent to the River Dee which was previously the site of steelmaking activity at Shotton.

Mr. Peter Walker: No. My statutory responsibilities under the Town and Country Planning Act 1971 preclude me from discussing with local authorities the proposals for the development of specific sites. If proposals that emerge for the development of the site demonstrate a need for central Government financial support, my Department's officers will be available to discuss this with the local authorities.

Hill Farms

Mr. Livsey: To ask the Secretary of State for Wales if he will give for hill farms in marginal land areas within the less-favoured areas the *(a)* average size in hectares, *(b)* farm income, *(c)* number of farms, *(d)* number of ewes and *(e)* number of beef cows for the latest period for which figures are available.

Mr. Peter Walker: Figures relating to holdings in the disadvantaged areas of the less-favoured areas in respect of June 1988 are given in the following table:

	Figures
(a) Average size in hectares	41·5
(c) Number of holdings	6,082
(d) Number of breeding ewes	582,024
(e) Number of breeding beef cows	23,859

A figure for *(b)* farm income is not published separately for marginal area farms. However, for all LFA livestock farms net farm income in 1987-88 was £9,453.

Minibus Licensing

Mr. Michael: To ask the Secretary of State for Wales what assessment he has made of the impact of proposed European Economic Community regulations on minibus licensing on voluntary organisations in Wales; and whether he will oppose the proposed regulations.

Mr. Peter Walker: The proposed EC regulation, which would require new minibus drivers to take a second driving test and to meet higher health standards, would have significant social and cost consequences for voluntary and community transport organisations which rely heavily on volunteer drivers. The Government consider there are no road safety reasons for the proposed change, and the European Commission is being pressed to avoid introducing unnecessary restrictions.

Mandatory Repairs Grant

Mr. Nicholas Bennett: To ask the Secretary of State for Wales on what date Welsh local authorities were first informed of changes in the amount of mandatory repairs grant from 75 per cent. to 25 per cent. for landlords under sections 130 and 131 of the Housing Act 1988.

Mr. Grist: Local authorities were consulted about proposals for changes to the rate of repair grant for landlords during the course of 1987 and 1988, and were notified of the change in rate (to 20 per cent.) in advance correspondence which was issued on 10 January this year.

Sewage

Mr. Win Griffiths: To ask the Secretary of State for Wales, pursuant to his answer to the hon. Member for Bridgend on 12 June, *Official Report,* columns *306-308,* concerning the applications from the Welsh water authority for variations of existing discharge consents for sewage treatment works, if he will indicate for which of the works listed requests were made for the discharge standards to be *(a)* relaxed and *(b)* tightened up.

Mr. Grist: I shall write to the hon. Gentleman with full details of the applications as soon as possible and I will place a copy of my reply in the Library of the House.

Local Authority Services

Mr. Ron Davies: To ask the Secretary of State for Wales how much was spent by central and local government in Wales, for the last year for which figures are available, on *(a)* local authority services, including the police, *(b)* health services and *(c)* economic development.

Mr. Peter Walker *[holding answer 12 June 1989]:* Details of expenditure within my responsibility are given in "The Government's Expenditure Plans 1989-90 to

1991-92" (Cm. 617) and in the Welsh Office commentary. The last year for which firm outturn figures are available for local authorities is 1986-87. The net public expenditure figures requested are as follows:

	£ million
	1986-87 outturn
Local authority expenditure in Wales[1]	2,015
National Health Services	989
Industry and Employment	178

[1] Including police and other non-Welsh Office services.

OVERSEAS DEVELOPMENT

Heroin (Crop Substitution)

Mr. Wareing: To ask the Secretary of State for Foreign and Commonwealth Affairs what funds he is currently providing to promote crops substitution in Pakistan to control heroin traffic: how the funds are to be administered and monitored; and if she will make a statement.

Mr. Chris Patten: We have committed £3·4 million to the United Nations fund for drugs abuse control crops substitution and special rural development programme in the Dir district of the North-West Frontier province. The programme is part of the special development and enforcement plan for poppy growing areas. £2·4 million of the grants has been spent so far.

Administrative and monitoring arrangements are to be strengthened by the recruitment of a three-man technical support unit to assist provincial government officials and the UNFDAC field officer.

PRIME MINISTER

European Commission

Q15. **Mr. Bowis:** To ask the Prime Minister if she has received representations regarding the European Commission.

The Prime Minister: I receive a number of such representations.

Rain Forest

Q104. **Mr. Corbyn:** To ask the Prime Minister what communication she has received from the Government of Brazil concerning assistance with preservation of the tropical rain forest.

The Prime Minister: Following discussions with senior representatives of the Brazilian Government, the Secretary-General of the Brazilian Ministry of the Interior has written to my hon. Friend the Minister for Overseas Development inviting Her Majesty's Government to agree on a programme of technical co-operation in the environmental field. A team of British professional experts has this week returned from Brazil where they discussed how we might help; my hon. Friend will take this further when he visits Brazil in July.

European Directives

Q170. **Mr. Teddy Taylor:** To ask the Prime Minister if she will raise at the next meeting of the European Council the scale and pattern of directives emerging from the Commission; and if she will make a statement.

The Prime Minister: I expect the European Council to discuss a number of current Community issues. I also refer my hon. Friend to my reply to him on 6 June at column *129*.

Engagements

Ms. Mowlam: To ask the Prime Minister if she will list her official engagements for Thursday 15 June.

Mr. Michael Brown: To ask the Prime Minister if she will list her official engagements for Thursday 15 June.

Mr. Harry Greenway: To ask the Prime Minister if she will list her official engagements for Thursday 15 June.

Mr. McGrady: To ask the Prime Minister if she will list her official engagements for Thursday 15 June.

Mr. Stern: To ask the Prime Minister if she will list her official engagements for Thursday 15 June.

Mr. Pike: To ask the Prime Minister if she will list her official engagements for Thursday 15 June.

Mr. Hind: To ask the Prime Minister if she will list her official engagements for Thursday 15 June.

Mr. Barry Field: To ask the Prime Minister if she will list her official engagements for Thursday 15 June.

The Prime Minister: This morning I presided at a meeting of the Cabinet and had meetings with ministerial colleagues and others. In addition to my duties in the House, I shall be having further meetings later today.

Government Publicity

Mr. Dalyell: To ask the Prime Minister whether, in the light of paragraph 13 of the guidance on conventions on Government publicity issued by the Cabinet Office, advice on the propriety of methods of releasing official information by officials will be sought from the Cabinet Office prior or subsequently to the receipt of ministerial sanction for express approval for the release of such information.

The Prime Minister: It is for Departments to decide whether and when to seek such advice in the light of paragraph 12 of the guidance.

EDUCATION AND SCIENCE

Press Briefings

Mr. Grocott: To ask the Secretary of State for Education and Science what guidelines he follows in determining which journalists are invited to press briefings by his Department.

Mrs. Rumbold: The journalists invited to press briefings depend upon the matter under discussion.

Medical Research

Mr. Kirkwood: To ask the Secretary of State for Education and Science if he will publish the amount of money spent on medical research in each of the last 10 years broken down into *(a)* the total figure per year, *(b)* the percentage spent on AIDS and *(c)* as a percentage of the total research budget.

Mr. Jackson: The main agency through which the Government support medical research is the Medical Research Council. The following table shows, for each of the last 10 years, the grant in aid to the MRC, the amount of that spent on specific programmes of AIDS research, and the grant in aid to the MRC as a percentage of the total science budget:

	(a) Grant in aid to MRC £ million	(b) Amount of (a) spent on specific programmes of AIDS research £ million	(c) (b) as a percentage of (a) Percentage	(d) Science Budget £ million	(e) (a) as a percentage of (d) Percentage
1979-80	57·2	—	—	333	17·2
1980-81	86·6	—	—	396	21·9
1981-82	101·5	—	—	440	23·1
1982-83	107·5	—	—	469	22·9
1983-84	113·7	—	—	504	22·6
1984-85	117·2	0·1	0·1	535	21·9
1985-86	122·3	0·4	0·3	571	21·4
1986-87	128·3	0·7	0·5	603	21·3
1987-88	139·8	3·7	2·6	658	21·2
1988-89	149·6	5·0	3·3	709	21·1

In addition, universities and medical schools support a range of medical research, including AIDS research, from block grants provided by the Universities Funding Council (formerly the University Grants Committee). Other medical research is supported by the health authorities.

Schools (Fences)

Mr. Janner: To ask the Secretary of State for Education and Science whether he will issue a circular to local authorities, concerning the dangers caused to pupils and teachers through inadequate fencing around primary schools.

Mrs. Rumbold: It is not necessary to issue a circular on the danger caused to pupils and teachers through inadequate fencing around primary schools. Local authorities are already aware of the requirements of the Health and Safety at Work, etc. Act and circular 11/74 issued by the DES following that Act.

Gateshead City Technology College

Mr. Clelland: To ask the Secretary of State for Education and Science how many tenders were received for the development of the Gateshead city technology college; and what were the various tender prices submitted.

Mrs. Rumbold: Five tenders were received. Prices ranged from £6,730,000 to £7,245,000. The price offered by Laing Northern was the lowest, and its design proposals were considered to be the most appropriate of those submitted.

Mr. Clelland: To ask the Secretary of State for Education and Science in the light of the contribution from public funds towards the development costs of the Gateshead city technology college *(a)* who will own the buildings, *(b)* who will own the land which constitutes the site once the project is completed and *(c)* to whom the assets will revert should the school fail to open or close at some future date.

Mrs. Rumbold: The Tyneside city technology college trust will own the land and buildings. The funding

agreement between my right hon. Friend and each individual CTC will specify the conditions under which repayment will be made to him in the event that the school should close.

Mr. Clelland: To ask the Secretary of State for Education and Science on what date John Laing plc became a sponsor of the Gateshead city technology college.

Mrs. Rumbold: John Laing announced its sponsorship of the CTC in Gateshead in October 1988.

Mr. Clelland: To ask the Secretary of State for Education and Science what elements of the national curriculum the Gateshead city technology college will be obliged to adopt.

Mrs. Rumbold: As a condition of grant, all CTCs will be bound to offer the full national curriculum including assessment arrangements throughout the compulsory years of education.

Mr. Clelland: To ask the Secretary of State for Education and Science what investigations were made into possible inner-city sites for the Gateshead city technology college.

Mrs. Rumbold: Investigations were made into other sites in Tyne and Wear, but none was found to be suitable.

Mr. Clelland: To ask the Secretary of State for Education and Science what is the total contribution of the CTC Trust to the development of the Gateshead city technology college to date; for what specific purposes such money has been allocated; and what further advances are planned.

Mrs. Rumbold: The CTC Trust has not itself contributed financially to the development of the Gateshead CTC. It was, however, involved in the negotiations for the acquisition of the site.

Mr. Clelland: To ask the Secretary of State for Education and Science what proportion of the Gateshead city technology college roll must be drawn from the inner-city area in order for the college to comply with the aims and objectives of Her Majesty's Government's policy to develop city technology colleges.

Mrs. Rumbold: The catchment area for the Gateshead CTC is not yet finalised, but it will be drawn so as to include surrounding areas of deprivation, and every effort will be made to ensure that as high a proportion of children as possible come from those areas.

Mr. Clelland: To ask the Secretary of State for Education and Science what were the opening and closing dates for the submission of tenders for the development of the Gateshead city technology college; and what date the tender from Laing Northern was received; and who had access to the tenders submitted prior to the closing date.

Mrs. Rumbold: The date for submission of tenders was 12 May. All tenders, including the tender from Laing Northern, were received under sealed cover on that day. They were opened, stamped, and their contents formally recorded, in the presence of five witnesses. I do not know of any person who had access to the tenders before submission. The DES, and the sponsors (other than John Laing plc), and the members of the panel had no such access.

Mr. Clelland: To ask the Secretary of State for Education and Science which of the sponsors of the Gateshead city technology college were involved in the decision to award the development contract to Laing Northern.

Mrs. Rumbold: The decision upon the award of the development contract was made by an evaluation panel composed of Mr. Peter Vardy, as the principal sponsor, the chief architect of Argyll plc, the chief architect of the DES, the project director, and three independent assessors nominated by my Department. John Laing plc was not represented on the panel and had no part whatsoever in the decision.

Student Loans

Mrs. Wise: To ask the Secretary of State for Education and Science if it is his intention to charge interest on student loans in cases where repayment is deferred because of low earnings after graduation.

Mr. Jackson: As was made clear in the White Paper "Top-up Loans for Students" (Cm. 520), the Government's proposals are for a zero real interest rate on the outstanding balance of the top-up loan; where repayments are deferred because a graduate's income is low, a real interest rate of zero will continue to apply during the period of deferment.

EMPLOYMENT

Dock Labour Scheme

Mr. Nicholas Bennett: To ask the Secretary of State for Employment what representations he has received about the future of the scheme ports once the dock labour scheme is abolished; and if he will make a statement.

Mr. Nicholls: I have received a number of representations supporting the Government's proposals to abolish the dock labour scheme so that scheme ports can become more competitive and attract new investment to provide jobs in the ports themselves and in surrounding areas.

Lifting the barriers to business and jobs imposed by the scheme's damaging and unnecessary controls has been widely welcomed throughout industry.

EC Social Charter

Mr. Simon Hughes: To ask the Secretary of State for Employment what is the policy of Her Majesty's Government towards those clauses of the European Community's draft social charter which would ensure the participation of the work force in decision making within companies.

Mr. Cope: The Government believe firmly that employee involvement in the United Kingdom is best developed on a voluntary basis. We shall therefore continue to oppose attempts to legislate on this subject.

SCOTLAND

Nuclear Accidents

Mr. Redmond: To ask the Secretary of State for Scotland what contingency plans his Department has for dealing with an accident involving *(a)* any seaborne, *(b)* any airborne or *(c)* any landborne nuclear weapons, in the course of non-operational activities, including courtesy calls.

Lord James Douglas-Hamilton: I refer the hon. Member to the reply that my right hon. Friend the Secretary of State for Defence gave today to a similar question from the hon. Member.

Tree Planting

Mr. Allen: To ask the Secretary of State for Scotland, further to his answer of Thursday, 25 May, *Official Report,* column *25,* if he will place those representations on tree planting in the Library.

Lord James Douglas-Hamilton: The representations were contained in private correspondence and it would therefore be inappropriate to place them in the Library.

Rates

Mr. Malcolm Bruce: To ask the Secretary of State for Scotland if he will produce a table for each district council showing the total yield from the rate payment for 1988-89 showing the breakdown of the amount attributed to district and region.

Mr. Lang: The estimated yields from rate payments are set out in the table.

	Total District Rate Income 1988-89	Total Regional Rate Income 1988-89	Total Rate Income 1988-89
Islands Councils			
Orkney	—	9·076	9·076
Shetland	—	50·370	50·370
Western Isles	—	6·656	6·656
District Councils			
Berwickshire	0·765	3·925	4·690
Ettrick and Lauderdale	1·766	8·015	9·781
Roxburgh	1·800	7·345	9·145
Tweedale	0·644	3·426	4·070
Clackmannan	4·617	13·468	18·085
Falkirk	12·819	46·081	58·899
Stirling	11·063	26·574	37·637
Annandale and Eskdale	1·958	8·568	10·526

	Total District Rate Income 1988-89	Total Regional Rate Income 1988-89	Total Rate Income 1988-89
Nithsdale	3·425	15·082	18·507
Stewartry	1·132	5·642	6·774
Wigtown	1·242	6·621	7·863
Dunfermline	11·316	52·843	64·159
Kirkcaldy	13·738	50·716	64·454
North East Fife	5·250	21·294	26·543
Aberdeen City	25·213	86·238	111·451
Banff & Buchan	6·076	23·127	29·203
Gordon	3·009	13·839	16·847
Kincardine & Deeside	1·978	11·195	13·173
Moray	4·970	22·472	27·442
Badenoch & Strathspey	0·516	3·604	4·120
Caithness	1·344	6·002	7·346
Inverness	3·868	22·961	26·829
Lochaber	1·581	6·148	7·729
Nairn	0·339	2·319	2·658
Ross & Cromarty	3·142	14·122	17·264
Skye and Lochalsh	0·510	2·367	2·876
Sutherland	0·425	2·467	2·892
East Lothian	7·637	27·209	34·846
Edinburgh City	54·718	200·989	255·706
Midlothian	5·860	20·778	26·638
West Lothian	10·214	41·445	51·659
Argyll & Bute	5·842	18·518	24·360
Bearsden & Milngavie	3·045	13·810	16·855
Clydebank	4·431	13·784	18·215
Clydesdale	4·031	14·429	18·460
Cumbernauld & Kilsyth	4·980	18·265	23·246
Cumnock & Doon Valley	2·444	8·575	11·019
Cunninghame	14·997	44·444	59·441
Dumbarton	8·424	26·847	35·271
East Kilbride	6·721	28·520	35·241

	Total District Rate Income 1988-89	Total Regional Rate Income 1988-89	Total Rate Income 1988-89
Eastwood	3·022	17·731	20·752
Glasgow City	113·829	262·992	376·820
Hamilton	8·883	29·705	38·588
Inverclyde	6·870	25·781	32·651
Kilmarnock & Loudoun	6·690	21·806	28·495
Kyle & Carrick	10·509	37·274	47·782
Monklands	8·342	27·957	36·298
Motherwell	11·868	44·333	56·201
Renfrew	18·752	62·941	81·692
Strathkelvin	5·981	22·301	28·283
Angus	5·861	24·001	29·862
Dundee City	20·687	53·522	74·209
Perth & Kinross	9·262	36·725	45·988
Scotland	488·401	1,697·242	2,185·644

Notes:

(1). Rate income is less domestic rate relief.
(2). Estimated figures calculated using actual penny rate products, rateable values and rate poundages from "Rating Review".

Community Charge

Mr. Malcolm Bruce: To ask the Secretary of State for Scotland if he will provide a breakdown of the figures given in the table in his written answer of 12 June showing the amount attributable to the district and the region.

Mr. Lang: The figures given in the table are the estimated yields, in 1989-90, of community and water charges in the district, regional and islands councils in Scotland.

£ thousands

	Yield of district community charge	Yield of regional community charge	Yield of water charge	Total yield of community charge
Islands Councils				
Orkney	—	1,812	386	2,198
Shetland	—	1,746	110	1,856
Western Isles	—	3,223	800	4,023
District Council				
Berwickshire	457	2,565	457	3,480
Ettrick and Lauderdale	1,069	4,428	789	6,286
Roxburgh	1,154	4,780	852	6,785
Tweeddale	501	2,026	361	2,888
Clackmannan	2,999	6,825	517	10,340
Falkirk	4,873	20,974	1,589	27,435
Stirling	5,729	11,695	886	18,310
Annandale and Eskdale	1,312	4,981	781	7,074
Nithsdale	1,699	7,778	1,220	10,698
Stewartry	698	3,368	528	4,594
Wigtown	936	4,177	655	5,768
Dunfermline	5,231	20,924	1,712	27,868
Kirkcaldy	6,597	24,190	1,979	32,767
North East Fife	4,144	11,119	910	16,173
Aberdeen City	13,552	30,134	4,783	48,469
Banff and Buchan	3,510	11,702	1,857	17,069
Gordon	2,259	9,702	1,540	13,501
Kincardine and Deeside	1,115	6,588	1,046	8,749
Moray	2,685	12,083	1,918	16,686
Badenoch and Strathspey	326	1,677	186	2,189
Caithness	498	3,589	399	4,486
Inverness	1,179	8,164	907	10,251
Lochaber	541	2,630	292	3,462
Nairn	213	1,371	152	1,737
Ross and Cromarty	1,382	6,377	709	8,468
Skye and Lochalsh	238	1,711	190	2,138
Sutherland	65	1,958	218	2,241
East Lothian	4,401	18,304	1,148	23,853
Edinburgh City	28,962	95,541	5,992	130,495
Midlothian	3,543	17,236	1,081	21,860

	Yield of district community charge	Yield of regional community charge	Yield of water charge	Total yield of community charge
West Lothian	5,483	29,143	1,828	36,454
Argyll and Bute	2,977	10,267	975	14,220
Bearsden and Milngavie	2,392	6,057	575	9,025
Clydebank	2,852	7,314	695	10,861
Clydesdale	3,520	8,585	816	12,920
Cumbernauld and Kilsyth	2,481	8,862	842	12,186
Cumnock and Doon Valley	1,831	6,425	610	8,867
Cunninghame	6,106	20,697	1,966	28,769
Dumbarton	4,581	11,597	1,102	17,280
East Kilbride	6,086	12,258	1,165	19,491
Eastwood	2,698	8,565	814	12,076
Glasgow City	46,323	106,491	10,117	162,931
Hamilton	5,582	15,505	1,473	22,560
Inverclyde	5,160	14,334	1,362	20,856
Kilmarnock and Loudoun	2,984	11,935	1,134	16,052
Kyle and Carrick	7,676	17,250	1,639	26,565
Monklands	5,560	15,027	1,428	22,015
Motherwell	9,295	21,615	2,054	32,964
Renfrew	11,268	29,652	2,817	43,737
Strathkelvin	5,143	12,857	1,221	19,221
Angus	3,646	15,427	1,473	20,546
Dundee City	10,746	28,484	2,719	41,949
Perth and Kinross	5,530	20,975	2,002	28,508

Sir Hector Monro: To ask the Secretary of State for Scotland what arrangements he is proposing to make for relieving owners of unoccupied farm cottages of their liability to pay the standard community charge.

Mr. Lang: I have today laid before Parliament a set of regulations—the Standard and Collective Community Charges (Scotland) Amendment Regulations 1989—which provide that certain unoccupied and unfurnished agricultural dwellinghouses, which fulfil conditions prescribed in those regulations, will be exempt from the standard community charge and the standard community water charge.

Forestry

Mr. Ron Davies: To ask the Secretary of State for Scotland how much land was approved for afforestation in *(a)* Scotland, *(b)* England and *(c)* Wales in the 12 months ending 1 April; of this how much was for (i) coniferous and (ii) deciduous planting; how much was actually planted; and of both approved and planted totals how much was in respect of land on which set-aside payments were being made.

Lord James Douglas-Hamilton: The following areas of land were approved for afforestation under Forestry Commission grant schemes in the year ended 31 March 1989:

		Hectares
Country	Area of planting (including set-aside)	Area under set-aside
Scotland	16,000	120
England	2,100	40
Wales	600	nil
Total	18,700	160

Information is not held centrally on the breakdown of these areas between broadleaves and conifers.

The following were the areas of new planting on which grants were paid under Forestry Commission Grant schemes in the year ended 31 March 1989:

Area of planting

		Hectares
Country	Conifers	Broadleaves
Scotland	20,900	1,550
England	750	900
Wales	700	200
Total	22,350	2,650

No planting grants were paid in respect of land on which set-aside payments are to be made.

It should be noted that (i) areas approved for planting are not necessarily planted and grant aided in the same year, and (ii) the above figures exclude land for which planting grants were approved or paid in association with the farm woodland scheme.

Language Teaching

Mrs. Fyfe: To ask the Secretary of State for Scotland whether Indic language teaching in Scottish schools is given equal status with European languages; and what is done to overcome any lack of availability of such classes for school children of Asian extraction who wish to learn one of the Indic languages.

Mr. Michael Forsyth *[holding answer 14 June 1989]*: Guidance to education authorities on the teaching in schools of languages other than English, issued in SED circular No. 1178 of 12 January 1989, urges that Asian languages and the traditions they represent should be respected and fostered, and confirms that the inclusion of an Asian language within the curriculum from S1 or S2 is appropriate where demand exists and can be met. It is for education authorities to decide whether and when it may be appropriate to include such a language in the curriculum of any school.

AGRICULTURE, FISHERIES AND FOOD

Eggs

Mr. Kirkwood: To ask the Minister of Agriculture, Fisheries and Food what estimate he has made of the shortfall in eggs to meet domestic demand this summer; and whether he has any control over the eggs imported to meet this shortfall.

Mr. Donald Thompson: It is not possible to provide a precise estimate of the likely balance between the supply and demand for eggs this summer. Placings for egg layer production have fallen in recent months, in line with reductions in demand earlier this year, and this will have an effect on the supply situation. On the question of controls on imported eggs, I would refer the hon. Member to the reply given to the hon. Member for Angus, East (Mr. Welsh) on 20 April at column *280*.

Monofilament Nets

Dr. Godman: To ask the Minister of Agriculture, Fisheries and Food what is the depth at which monofilament nets are usually set at *(a)* inshore waters and *(b)* at sea; and if he will list the regulations and byelaws which control the siting and setting of such nets.

Mr. Donald Thompson: Monofilament nets are set at varying depths depending on the location and the species of fish sought. There are no specific national regulations governing the siting and setting of fixed nets within the fishery limits for England and Wales but their use out to six miles may be regulated by local byelaws made by water authorities and sea fisheries committees. Details of such byelaws are available from the offices of these bodies.

Dr. Godman: To ask the Minister of Agriculture, Fisheries and Food whether his fisheries inspectors routinely examine fixed monofilament nets by removing them from the water; if these inspections involved the recording and monitoring of the incidental capture of marine mammals and sea birds; and if he will make a statement.

Mr. Donald Thompson: There are currently no regulations on fixed monofilament nets and consequently no requirement for my fisheries inspectors to examine them. As regards the incidental capture of marine mammals, I refer the hon. Member to the reply I gave him on 20 March 1989 at column *464:* my Department is continuing to develop its plans for the monitoring scheme. We have no plans at present for monitoring the incidental capture of sea birds, although we are keeping the situation under review.

Slaughter and Compensation Schemes

Mr. Ron Davies: To ask the Minister of Agriculture, Fisheries and Food if he will list those notifiable diseases in animals for which a slaughter and compensation scheme operates; and if he will list those notifiable diseases in animals for which a compensation scheme does not operate.

Mr. Donald Thompson: The information is as follows:
(a) Notifiable diseases for which a slaughter and compensation scheme operates are:
    African swine fever
    Aujeszky's disease
    Bovine spongiform encephalopathy
    Brucellosis melitensis in cattle
    Cattle plague in ruminants and swine
    Classical swine fever
    Foot and mouth disease
    Pleuro-pneumonia in cattle
    Rabies
    Swine vesicular disease
    Tuberculosis in cattle

(b) Notifiable diseases for which a slaughter and compensation scheme does not operate are:
    African horse sickness
    Anthrax
    Contagious equine metritis
    Dourine in horses, asses, mules and zebras
    Enzootic bovine leukosis
    Epizootic lymphangitis in horse, asses and mules
    Equine encephalomyelitis
    Equine infectious anaemia
    Fowl pest (fowl plague, Newcastle disease and paramyxovirus) in poultry of any kind
    Glanders and farcy in horses, asses and mules
    Paramyxovirus in pigeons
    Sheep pox
    Sheep scab
    Teschen disease of pigs
    Tuberculosis in deer
    Warble fly

Nitrates

Mr. Ron Davies: To ask the Minister of Agriculture, Fisheries and Food what information he has concerning the leaching of nitrates from land formerly used for nitrogen-fixing crops once that land has been included in the set-aside scheme.

Mr. Ryder: Such information is not yet available from set-aside scheme trials, but it will be provided by experiments currently in progress. Meanwhile, scientific evidence indicates that nitrate leaching from land converted from nitrogen fixing crops to permanent fallow could be relatively high in the first year, but it would fall subsequently.

Mr. Ron Davies: To ask the Minister of Agriculture, Fisheries and Food what provision is made within the set-aside scheme to minimise pollution of ground water and water courses by nitrates.

Mr. Ryder: Under the rules for the management of land set aside to fallow under the scheme, a plant cover must be established and maintained on the land concerned and the use of fertilisers is not generally permitted. Furthermore, advice is available to farmers from my Department on the best practices for the avoidance of pollution by nitrates.

Set-aside Land

Mr. Ron Davies: To ask the Minister of Agriculture, Fisheries and Food when he expects to announce his top-up scheme for enhancing the environmental value of set-aside land.

Mr. Ryder: The top-up scheme, which will be known as the countryside premium for set-aside land, will be administered by the Countryside Commission with advice and assistance from the Nature Conservancy Council, the Department of the Environment and my Department. Details of the scheme are to be announced on 19 June by the chairman of the Countryside Commission.

Bovine Somatatropin

Mr. Ron Davies: To ask the Minister of Agriculture, Fisheries and Food whether cows treated with bovine somatatropin under experiment can subsequently be sold for slaughter for human consumption; and whether his Department imposes any time limit on the period to elapse between the ending of bovine somatatropin treatment and slaughter.

Mr. Donald Thompson: When the animal test certificates for BST products were assessed, the veterinary products committee, following rigorous evaluation of all the available data, was satisfied that it would be safe to eat meat from treated cows when they were culled. Accordingly, such cows may be sold for slaughter for human consumption; no withdrawal period has been specified.

Dogs

Mr. Gale: To ask the Minister of Agriculture, Fisheries and Food (1) for what purpose information is collected on each dog imported into the United Kingdom;

(2) how many American bandogs are presently in quarantine following importation;

(3) if he will make a statement on the powers available to his Department to control the importation of dogs;

(4) if records on the importation of dogs kept by the animal health division of his Department are kept manually in written form, or on computers;

(5) what advice has been issued to members of his Department concerning American bandogs; and if he will make a statement;

(6) what information he has on the origins, purpose, characteristics and temperament of the American bandog; and if he will make a statement;

(7) what is the number of Neopolitan mastiff bitches currently in quarantine in the United Kingdom; and what information he has as to the purposes of their import;

(8) what records his Department keeps on the importation of dogs; and whether these include information as to the breed, sex, age, weight, name, colour, distinguishing marks, exporter and importer of each dog;

(9) what returns of information on the importation of dogs are submitted by the animal health division of his Department to the central statistical unit of his Department.

Mr. Donald Thompson: The Rabies (Importation of Dogs, Cats and Other Mammals) Order 1974 as amended restricts the importation of dogs to licensed animals landed at prescribed ports and airports and requires them to be quarantined for six months. These powers are designed to prevent the introduction of rabies into this country and not to limit the number and breeds of dogs imported. Applicants for import licences must provide information, necessary for identification should it escape during quarantine, concerning the dog's breed, sex, age, weight, name, colour and distinguishing marks, together with details of the owner, authorised carrying agent, quarantine premises and expected date of landing. No information is required as to the purpose of the importation.

All information is retained on a confidential basis by the animal health division in the form of manual records. Summary data by breed are not kept and it is not possible to say how many Neopolitan mastiff bitches or American bandogs are presently in quarantine, as these may not have been described as such in the licence application. I understand that an American bandog is a cross between a pit bull terrier and a Neopolitan bull mastiff bull. No advice has been issued concerning this breed.

Rabies

Mr. Colin Shepherd: To ask the Minister of Agriculture, Fisheries and Food what is the latest information he has on the prevalence of rabies in Europe.

Mr. Donald Thompson: The WHO centre at Tuebingen, West Germany recorded 5,051 European rabies cases for the fourth quarter 1988. The total for the same quarter 1987 was 4,280 cases. A species breakdown for the fourth quarter 1988 reveals:

	Numbers
Wild animals	3,950
of which Red Fox	3,536
Domestic animals	1,100
of which	
Dogs—Europe	75
Dogs—Turkey	100

Urban rabies continues to occur in Turkey, where 77 per cent. of all cases were in dogs, and 99·6 per cent. of all cases occurred in domestic animals. One human case occurred, in Blackburn, England. The disease had been contracted in Pakistan. There are undoubtedly cases of human rabies in Turkey but there is no regular reporting of these cases to the rabies centre. In several countries, a substantial rise in cases has been reported. Although a single quarter's figures must not be taken out of context, it is clear that the progress being made in the control of wildlife rabies in western Europe will be slow.

The yearly total shows a reduction of 3·7 per cent. In West Germany, which has previously recorded dramatic falls in the number of cases, the number recorded was 31 more than in the fourth quarter 1987. A substantial increase in cases (490—53 per cent. of the country's total) occurred in the Bundesland Hessen. All the other Bundeslander registered slight rises or remained stable. However, the total for 1988 in West Germany was 2,628, compared with 791 in 1987. It seems that areas where the oral vaccination of foxes has only been used once are the most vulnerable. Clearly, this form of control has to be repeated regularly. Although expensive, this appears to be a successful method of limiting the number of cases. It is not, however, a procedure which will, without other supporting mechanisms, lead to the eradication of rabies from Europe.

In Belgium, the number of cases continues to increase, taking the year's total to 515 cases; however, in the areas where oral vaccination of foxes has been carried out, the number of cases has reduced by 49 per cent.

In France, there has been no extension of the "rabies front" westwards. A total of 2,223 known cases was recorded in 1988, 155 more than in 1987. Most of the cases are found in the fox.

Italy has recorded 19 cases in the area bordering Yugoslavia. Much surveillance of wild and domestic animal carcases has been carried out, and some foxes were found positive in one Alpine region. Oral vaccination of foxes is planned in the spring, using the Tuebingen vaccine, in conjunction with Yugoslavia and Austria. Vaccination of dogs and grazing animals is also compulsory.

Switzerland recorded only 16 cases, and none were recorded from Ireland, Portugal, Denmark, Greece, Norway and Spain.

Bats found positive to rabies-related virus were recorded in the Netherlands (5) and West Germany (1). The total number of cases in Europe in 1988 was 53, compared to 140 in 1987. Denmark and Spain (affected in 1987) had no new cases. There continues to be no evidence of bat-related rabies virus in terrestrial mammals in Europe. During the quarter, 25 bats were examined in Great Britain, and all were found to be negative.

Confusion Marks

Mr. Boswell: To ask the Minister of Agriculture, Fisheries and Food what were the annual administration costs, for each of the last five years of operation of the beef variable premium scheme and of maintaining the register of confusion marks; and how many animals were so registered in each of these years.

Mr. Donald Thompson [*holding answer 13 June 1989*]: The beef variable premium scheme was administered on behalf of the Intervention Board for Agricultural Produce by the Meat and Livestock Commission in Great Britain and by the Department of Agriculture for Northern Ireland in Northern Ireland. Their costs over the last five years are estimated to have been as follows:

	£ million	
	[1]*MLC*	*DANI*
1984-85	3·8	0·6
1985-86	4·0	0·7
1986-87	4·1	0·7
1987-88	4·4	0·8
1988-89	4·4	0·8

[1]BVPS duties were usually carried out by MLC officers concurrently with their responsibilities under the sheep variable premium scheme. BVPS costs are therefore calculated as a proportion of the total cost of administering both schemes based on the number of presentations under each.

These figures include the costs of administering the confusion mark procedures. These were operated on a local basis and the costs of administration and numbers of animals were not centrally recorded.

NORTHERN IRELAND

Nuclear Accidents

Mr. Redmond: To ask the Secretary of State for Northern Ireland what contingency plans his Department has for dealing with an accident involving *(a)* any seaborne, *(b)* any airborne or *(c)* any landborne nuclear weapon, in the course of non-operational activities, including courtesy calls.

Mr. Ian Stewart: Contingency plans throughout the United Kingdom for accidents involving nuclear weapons are a matter for the Secretary of State for Defence. In the event of any such incident affecting Northern Ireland these would be complemented by local contingency plans.

School Buses (Accidents)

Mr. Hume: To ask the Secretary of State for Northern Ireland what information is available to indicate the incidence by area or district of road traffic accidents involving children disembarking from school buses, indicating the number of such fatalities in the past five years.

Mr. Ian Stewart [*holding answer 15 May 1989*]: Information is not available in the exact form requested. Existing records do not differentiate between types of bus operators and the following information includes buses operated by education and library boards, public service vehicles used solely for transporting children to and from school and buses used by the general public. Details of children, that is, persons under 15 years of age, killed immediately after alighting from buses are as follows:

Location	Year	Number of fatalities
1 Armagh	1984	3
1 Lisburn		
1 Bellaghy		
1 Greyabbey	1985	1
1 Loup	1986	2
1 Ballymoney		
1 Castledawson	1987	1
1 Coleraine	1988	1

HOME DEPARTMENT

Immigrants

5. **Mr. Fraser:** To ask the Secretary of State for the Home Department if he will make a statement about the policy of his Department in treating as illegal immigrants entrants who have been given leave to enter the United Kingdom and who are alleged to have withheld information from an entry certificate officer or immigration officer.

Mr. Renton: A person who deliberately withholds evidence and thereby gains entry to which he would not otherwise be entitled may be treated as an illegal entrant under the Immigration Act 1971 and removed from the country. It is clearly right that people coming to this country should not benefit from deceiving the entry clearance officer or the immigration officer. All such cases are fully and carefully considered before removal is authorised.

Racial Harassment

9. **Mr. Dykes:** To ask the Secretary of State for the Home Department if he has been able to make an assessment of the anti-racial harassment campaign launched by the Metropolitan police at the beginning of the current year and its effect on public opinion and public reaction.

Mr. Douglas Hogg: It is for the commissioner, not the Home Office, to make his assessment of the Metropolitan police campaign, I understand that the commissioner intends that the campaign will be evaluated. The Metropolitan police are determined to meet the needs of the community in this sensitive area, and the campaign is playing a central part in their strategy.

Neighbourhood Watch

10. **Mr. Stern:** To ask the Secretary of State for the Home Department how many neighbourhood watch schemes are known to his Department; and what was the equivalent number five years ago.

Mr. John Patten: At the end of March 1989 there were 66,423 neighbourhood watch schemes in England and Wales, covering approximately 3·25 million households. This compares with 3,669 schemes in January 1985—an increase of 62,754, or 1,710 per cent. over the period.

Prevention of Terrorism Act

11. **Mr. Parry:** To ask the Secretary of State for the Home Department if he will make a statement on the working of the Prevention of Terrorism Act.

Mr. Hurd: During the 12 months ending 31 March 1989 a total of 184 people were detained in Great Britain under the Prevention of Terrorism (Temporary Provisions) Acts 1984 and 1989. A total of 173 of these detentions were in connection with Northern Irish terrorism and 11 were in connection with international terrorism. Twenty seven of those people were charged. During the same period, 17 people were made subject to new exclusion orders.

Jersey (Housing)

13. **Mr. Foulkes:** To ask the Secretary of State for the Home Department what representations he has received concerning housing in Jersey.

Mr. Douglas Hogg: During the last year we have had representations about three such cases.

Burglary (Humberside)

14. **Mr. David Davis:** To ask the Secretary of State for the Home Department what steps his Department is taking to reduce burglary in Humberside.

Mr. John Patten: The Government believe that a high proportion of burglaries are preventable. That is why we have encouraged neighbourhood watch schemes which can do so much to help prevent crime. Five years ago there were no watch schemes in Humberside. There are now over 1,300 such schemes in Humberside, covering some 30,000 households. At the end of April 1989 burglaries from dwellings in Humberside had fallen by 21 per cent. compared to two years ago. Detection of burglaries has increased by 28 per cent. over 1988 figures. Hull has agreed to participate in the Home Office safer cities programme and a project is being set up in the city this year. Its aims are to reduce crime, lessen the fear of crime, and create a safer city within which economic enterprise and community life can flourish.

Prohibited Drugs

16. **Mr. Patnick:** To ask the Secretary of State for the Home Department if he will make a further statement on his plans to ensure that prohibited drugs are not imported into the United Kingdom after 1992.

Mr. Hurd: In our discussions with other member states of the European Community, we are maintaining the position that, given our island geography, frontier checks are, and will continue to be, an indispensible part of the protection for our citizens against the evil of drug trafficking. Sir Leon Brittan confirmed in a speech to the Association of Chief Police Officers' drugs conference on 20 April that the control of drugs trafficking involves, among other things, the ability to conduct checks.

Electoral Registration

17. **Mr. Harry Barnes:** To ask the Secretary of State for the Home Department if he plans to produce new publicity material to encourage people to register to vote, in the light of the recent Office of Population Censuses and Surveys reports on electoral registration.

Mr. Douglas Hogg: We shall, as in previous years, support electoral registration officers in their statutory task with a nationwide advertising campaign during the autumn. We also plan to issue guidance to electoral registration officers on the need for a co-ordinated local publicity strategy.

Community Trusts

19. **Dr. Goodson-Wickes:** To ask the Secretary of State for the Home Department if he has had discussions with the chief charity commissioner regarding the future development of community trusts.

Mr. John Patten: No, but I know that the charity commissioners played an essential part, with my Department, in promoting the community trust movement in this country by, among other things, advising on the development of model trust instruments.

Vagrancy

20. **Mr. Nellist:** To ask the Secretary of State for the Home Department if he will seek to collect more frequent statistics about the numbers of young people charged under section 3 of the Vagrancy Act 1824.

Mr. John Patten: Information is currently collected on all young people proceeded against or cautioned for offences under this Act and summary statistics are published annually.

Time Zones (Harmonisation)

21. **Dr. Michael Clark:** To ask the Secretary of State for the Home Department what response he has received to his consultation document on harmonisation of time zones in Europe.

Mr. Douglas Hogg: The Government plan to publish a Green Paper in the next few weeks. Harmonisation with the central European time zone is one of three options presented for discussion on future summer time arrangements.

Mentally Disordered Prisoners

22. **Mr. Butler:** To ask the Secretary of State for the Home Department what plans he has to reduce the number of mentally disordered offenders in the prison population.

Mr. Douglas Hogg: The guidance in "The Sentence of the Court" is now being revised to encourage courts to avoid sending mentally disturbed people to prison if at all possible, for example by using their powers to remand to hospital under the Mental Health Act 1983, or make attendance at or admission to hospital a condition of bail. We are also preparing a circular to the police and courts on provision for mentally disturbed offenders.

Football Matches (Policing)

23. **Mr. David Evans:** To ask the Secretary of State for the Home Department what estimates he has of the total cost of policing football matches in England and Wales in 1988.

Mr. Douglas Hogg: There is no central record of the costs of policing football matches. This information could be obtained only at dispropotionate cost, but substantial resources are involved. Typically 5,000 officers are deployed, at a total cost of perhaps £200,000 to £300,000, each football Saturday.

China

26. **Mr. Knapman:** To ask the Secretary of State for the Home Department what plans he has to meet the Minister of Justice of the People's Republic of China; and if he will make a statement.

Mr. Hurd: As my right hon. and learned Friend the Secretary of State for Foreign and Commonwealth Affairs informed the House on 6 June, all scheduled ministerial visits have been suspended.

Street Robbery

27. **Mr. Colin Shepherd:** To ask the Secretary of State for the Home Department what steps his Department is taking to combat street robbery; and if he will make a statement.

Mr. John Patten: The police give high priority to dealing with street robbery. We are concentrating resources on certain urban high-crime areas through our safer cities programme, and we have produced a crime prevention handbook which contains advice on how members of the public can reduce the risk of being attacked; nearly 2·5 million copies of it have been distributed.

Processions

28. **Mr. Key:** To ask the Secretary of State for the Home Department how many requests he has received in the past 12 months to make orders under section 13 of the Public Order Act 1986, to prohibit processions; and if he will make a statement.

Mr. Hurd: We have received four such applications during that time.

Broadcasting Reform

29. **Mr. Maclennan:** To ask the Secretary of State for the Home Department what representations he has received concerning the proposals contained in his White Paper, Cm 517 to institute a regionally based privatised transmission system; and if he will make a statement.

Mr. Renton: We received over 3,000 responses to the broadcasting White Paper, a number of which touched on our proposals to privatise the transmission system. We published on 8 June the report commissioned from Price Waterhouse to identify options for privatisation, and we are considering its conclusions in consultation with interested parties.

French Interior Minister

30. **Mr. William Powell:** To ask the Secretary of State for the Home Department if he will make a statement on his recent talks with the French Interior Minister, M. Joxe.

35. **Mr. Oppenheim:** To ask the Secretary of State for the Home Department if he will make a statement on his recent talks with the French Interior Minister, M. Joxe.

Mr. Hurd: M. Joxe and I met on 19 May and had wide-ranging and fruitful discussions on matters of common concern, including immigration policy, action against terrorism, drug trafficking and organised crime, and the measures required to maintain the necessary controls in these areas after 1992. We also signed an arrangement providing for further practical co-operation between the United Kingdom and France on all these matters.

Firearms Committee

31. **Mr. Bellingham:** To ask the Secretary of State for the Home Department when he intends to appoint a chairman of the consultative committee on firearms.

Mr. Douglas Hogg: I refer my hon. Friend to the reply which my right hon. Friend gave to a question by my hon. Friend the Member for Ryedale (Mr. Greenway) on 25 May at columns *637-38*.

Special Constables (Harbours)

32. **Mr. Shersby:** To ask the Secretary of State for the Home Department what assessment he has made of the implications for matters within his responsibility of the use of section 47 of the Harbours, Docks and Piers Clauses Act 1847 to appoint special constables.

Mr. Douglas Hogg: This provision has operated without major difficulty at many ports for many years. However, I am aware of the concern expressed by my hon. Friend, some other hon. Members and the Police Federation following the recent use of this provision by a statutory harbour authority. My right hon. Friend has brought this matter to the attention of my right hon. Friend the Secretary of State for Transport who has primary responsibility for the Harbours, Docks and Piers Clauses Act 1847. We shall jointly be examining the representations which have been made.

Broadcasting (Ownership)

33. **Mr. Harris:** To ask the Secretary of State for the Home Department what steps he has taken to promote diversity of ownership in television and radio broadcasting.

38. **Mr. Hague:** To ask the Secretary of State for the Home Department how he proposes to ensure diversity of ownership in British television and radio.

Mr. Renton: I refer my hon. Friends to the reply my right hon. Friend gave to a question from my hon. Friend the Member for Harrow, West (Mr. Hughes) on 19 May at column *317*.

Juvenile Crime (Parental Responsibility)

34. Mr. Pawsey: To ask the Secretary of State for the Home Department what steps his Department is taking to encourage greater parental responsibility for the prevention of juvenile crime; and if he will make a statement.

50. Mr. Burns: To ask the Secretary of State for the Home Department what steps his Department is taking to encourage greater parental responsibility for the prevention of juvenile crime; and if he will make a statement.

56. Mr. Riddick: To ask the Secretary of State for the Home Department whether he has any plans to make parents of children under 16 years of age responsible for the crimes committed by those children.

Mr. Patten: I refer my hon. Friends to the reply given to questions from my hon. Friends the Members for Warrington, South (Mr. Butler) and for Basingstoke (Mr. Hunter) on 11 May at column 981.

Prisons (Crown Immunity)

36. Mr. Ashley: To ask the Secretary of State for the Home Department if he has any plans to abolish Crown immunity for prisons.

Mr. Douglas Hogg: There are no plans to remove Crown immunity from penal establishments. I am satisfied that the present arrangements are effective in setting and monitoring standards required by the relevant legislation.

Police Cells

37. Mr. Squire: To ask the Secretary of State for the Home Department how many prisoners were held in police cells at the most recent available date.

Mr. Douglas Hogg: A total of 215 on 14 June, of which 182 were held in the north of the country as a consequence of the recent loss of accommodation at Risley remand centre.

Bus Lanes

Mr. Corbyn: To ask the Secretary of State for the Home Department if he will call for a report from the Commissioner of Police of the Metropolis as to what action the Metropolitan police are taking in enforcement of bus lanes.

Mr. Douglas Hogg: The enforcement of bus lanes is undertaken by the Metropolitan police as one of the many and varied demands made on police time by the enforcement of traffic law.

European Police (Co-operation)

40. Mr. Nicholas Bennett: To ask the Secretary of State for the Home Department what progress his Department is making in fostering greater co-operation between British police forces and their counterparts elsewhere in Europe.

Mr. Douglas Hogg: I refer my hon. Friends to the reply given to questions from my hon. Friends the Members for Dover (Mr. Shaw) and for Ludlow (Mr. Gill) on 2 February 1989 at column *384*.

Durham Prison (Transfers)

41. Mr. Cousins: To ask the Secretary of State for the Home Department how many prisoners at Durham prison were awaiting transfer to Thorp Arch prison at the end of the last four months.

Mr. Douglas Hogg: The information requested is available only in respect of 31 May, when 42 prisoners at Her Majesty's prison Durham were awaiting transfer to Her Majesty's prison Thorp Arch.

Car Crime

42. Mr. Devlin: To ask the Secretary of State for the Home Department what steps his Department is taking against car crime; and if he will make a statement.

Mr. John Patten: We are examining, in consultation with other Departments, the car manufacturing industry and other agencies, how best the recommendations of the 1988 Home Office standing conference on crime prevention working group on car crime might be taken forward. We are considering research into the correlation between car theft and road accidents, a car crime prevention video for use in schools, and the inclusion of assessments of car security features in published road tests. Publicity on the prevention of car crime will continue at a high level.

Illegal Drugs

43. Mr. Tony Lloyd: To ask the Secretary of State for the Home Department what assessment he makes of the changes in volume and types of illegal drugs in Britain.

Mr. Douglas Hogg: The Government attach high priority to tackling drug misuse in all its aspects and have developed a comprehensive strategy for that purpose, which is overseen by the ministerial group on the misuse of drugs. The group, which I chair, receives regular assessments of the drug misuse situation as it affects the United Kingdom, based on information from a number of sources.

Prison Building

44. Mr. French: To ask the Secretary of State for the Home Department if he will make a statement on the progress of the Government's prison building and refurbishment programme.

Mr. Douglas Hogg: I refer my hon. Friend to the reply given today to my hon. Friend the Member for Taunton (Mr. Nicholson).

Drug Abuse

45. Mr. Teddy Taylor: To ask the Secretary of State for the Home Department what progress is being made in the campaign against drug abuse; and if he will make a statement.

Mr. Douglas Hogg: The Goernment's strategy is to tackle drug misuse by a number of measures aimed at reducing both the supply of and the demand for drugs.

In furtherance of the strategy, we are working through the United Nations, the Council of Europe's Pompidou group and bilaterally to strengthen international co-operation against drug trafficking. We have given the police and Customs services substantial new resources to enable them to seize increased amounts of drugs. We have passed the Drug Trafficking Offences Act 1986, under which some £11 million of drug traffickers' assets has been ordered to be confiscated. Prevention, publicity and education are being stepped up, while funds for the expansion of drug misuse treatment and rehabilitation services have been increased to some £17·5 million in 1989-90.

European Ministers of Justice

46. **Mr. Baldry:** To ask the Secretary of State for the Home Department if he will make a statement about the meeting of European Ministers of Justice in San Sebastian, Spain on 26 and 27 May.

Mr. John Patten: I represented the United Kingdom at this meeting, which discussed a range of topics of concern to European Community Ministers of Justice. I stressed the need for stronger co-operation to confiscate the assets of drug traffickers and other major criminals. I urged that the arrangements to enforce the payment of maintenance to women whose husbands moved to another Community country were not effective and should be made to work in practice. Similarly, on measures to prevent the abduction of children from one country to another, I stressed the need for practical action to help individual citizens.

Sunday Trading

47. **Mr. Gow:** To ask the Secretary of State for the Home Department what are his present proposals for reform of the Sunday trading laws.

Mr. Renton: The Government are continuing to meet interested parties to try to devise reforms which are both workable and likely to command parliamentary majority. As yet, there is insufficient agreement to support early legislation in this area.

Fire Service (Wage Negotiations)

48. **Mr. Ilsley:** To ask the Secretary of State for the Home Department what representations he has received regarding wage negotiations for fire service employees.

Mr. John Patten: Fire service pay is determined by an agreement of the national joint council for local authorities' fire brigades, under which the rate of pay of qualified firefighters is adjusted in November each year to a level which equates to that for the upper quartile of male manual workers, calculated by reference to the Department of Employment's new earnings survey.

We have received a number of representations from hon. and right hon. Members and from members of the public on conditions of service issues in the fire service. We have explained that my right hon. and noble Friend Earl Ferrers, the Minister of State, has recently had a series of meetings with the member organisations of the national joint council with a view to establishing a working party to address a number of conditions of service-related issues raised by the Audit Commission and to consider whether the current pay formula represents the best way forward for the future.

Crime Prevention

49. **Mr. Boswell:** To ask the Secretary of State for the Home Department what steps his Department is taking to promote effective crime prevention; and if he will make a statement.

Mr. John Patten: The contribution that the public can make towards reducing crime is the theme of a three-year publicity campaign which we started in March 1988; the associated crime prevention handbook, which contains a great deal of practical advice, is now in its second edition and nearly 2·5 million copies of it have been distributed. In May 1988 an independent crime prevention organisation, Crime Concern, was launched with financial support from the Home Office, with the objective of stimulating and developing local crime prevention activity. The development of crime prevention in the inner city is being taken forward through the safer cities programme which was launched in March 1988.

Broadcasting Authorities

51. **Mr. Canavan:** To ask the Secretary of State for the Home Department when he next expects to meet representatives of the British Broadcasting Corporation and the Independent Broadcasting Authority; and what subjects he expects to discuss.

Mr. Renton: My right hon. Friend is in regular touch with the chairmen of the BBC and the IBA on a wide range of broadcasting matters.

Burglary (Suffolk)

52. **Mr. Lord:** To ask the Secretary of State for the Home Department what steps his Department is taking to reduce burglary in central Suffolk; and if he will make a statement.

Mr. John Patten: Neighbourhood watch continues to grow in Suffolk and there are now more than 200 schemes covering over 10,000 households. There are crime prevention panels in Ipswich, Stowmarket and Needham Market and the Mid Suffolk police liaison committee is active in spreading the crime prevention message to the rural community. In the first three months of this year burglary figures were nearly 9 per cent. lower than in the corresponding period for 1988.

Litter

53. **Mr. Sheerman:** To ask the Secretary of State for the Home Department what impact police anti-litter campaigns are having upon crime prevention.

Mr. John Patten: The police deal with litter offences in their routine enforcement of the law. I am not aware of any particular impact which this enforcement has on crime prevention.

Metropolitan Police (Supervisions)

54. **Mr. Tony Banks:** To ask the Secretary of State for the Home Department how many serving Metropolitan police officers have been suspended from duty following allegations of improper conduct in each of the past three years.

Mr. Douglas Hogg: The number of officers suspended from duty pending investigation of alleged misconduct is as follows:

	Number
1986	73
1987	95
1988	74

Drinking and Disorder

55. **Mr. Duffy:** To ask the Secretary of State for the Home Department when he expects to meet representatives of the drinks and fast food industries to discuss problems arising from drinking and disorder.

Mr. Douglas Hogg: My right hon. Friend the Leader of the House in his capacity as chairman of the ministerial group on alcohol misuse, has invited representatives of the drinks, fast food and leisure industries and the licensed trade to discuss these matters. A meeting should take place later this month or early next. My hon. Friend the Parliamentary Secretary to the Ministry of Agriculture, Fisheries and Food and I will also be present.

Mentally Ill Prisoners

57. **Mr. Lofthouse:** To ask the Secretary of State for the Home Department what action he intends to take to safeguard the mentally ill remanded in custody.

Mr. Douglas Hogg: Prison medical officers in examining inmates on reception identify as a priority those who, by reason of their mental state, may require particular attention whether of a medical or general management nature. In such cases, referral to a psychiatrist would be an early course of further action.

The police and prison services are working closely together to ensure similar early identification, and correct follow-up action can be taken in the case of a defendant who, because of overcrowding in local prisons and remand centres, is initially held in a police cell, where this cannot be avoided.

Private Security Industry

58. **Mr. O'Brien:** To ask the Secretary of State for the Home Department what steps he is taking to consider the accountability and regulation of the private security industry.

Mr. John Patten: I would refer the hon. Member to the reply I gave to questions from the hon. Members for Clwyd, South-West (Mr. Jones) and Walsall, South (Mr. George) on 15 December 1988 at column *716*.

Cruel Tethering

Mr. Amess: To ask the Secretary of State for the Home Department how many *(a)* males and *(b)* females have been (i) charged and (ii) convicted under section 1 of the Protection Against Cruel Tethering Act 1988.

Mr. John Patten: Section 1 of the Protection against Cruel Tethering Act 1988 amended the Protection of Animals Act 1911. It is not possible from the information held centrally to isolate such offences from others under the Protection of Animals Act 1911.

Greater Manchester Police

Mr. Andrew F. Bennett: To ask the Secretary of State for the Home Department if he has received a copy of the chief constable's annual report on the policing of Greater Manchester; and if he will make a statement.

Mr. Douglas Hogg: We have received the report; I am glad to see that there was a decrease of nearly 8 per cent. in the total number of crimes recorded during the year in his force area.

Surplus Prison Property

Mr. Barry Field: To ask the Secretary of State for the Home Department what representations he has received about alternative uses for surplus prison property on the Isle of Wight.

Mr. Douglas Hogg: The only representations received have been from my hon. Friend on behalf of the Isle of Wight Youth Trust. Of the 19 surplus prison quarters on the Isle of Wight, 10 are to be demolished—mainly on grounds of prison security—and nine sold.

Hillsborough Inquiry

Mr. Beaumont-Dark: To ask the Secretary of State for Home Department what arrangements are being made to finance the cost of Lord Justice Taylor's inquiry into the Hillsborough stadium disaster.

Mr. Hurd: Parliamentary approval of the expenditure on this inquiry will be sought in a revised Estimate for the Home Office vote for "administration etc." (class XI, vote 3). Pending that approval, urgent expenditure estimated at £100,000 is being met by a repayable advance from the contingencies fund.

Civil Disasters

Mr. Lester: To ask the Secretary of State for Home Department what conclusions he has reached following his Department's review of arrangements for handling major civil disasters in the United Kingdom.

Mr. Hurd: Our emergency services have shown repeatedly how effectively they respond to widely differing disasters, but a number of suggestions have been made as to ways in which central Government could provide better support for those with operational responsibilities.

The whole field of emergency response has therefore been reviewed. Consultations have involved the emergency services, local authorities, professional emergency planners, voluntary bodies and interested individuals, as well as other Government departments. A senior level seminar for those with operational responsibilities was held at the civil defence college, Easingwold, last November.

Our main conclusions are:

(a) prime responsibility for handling particular disasters should remain at the local level. It would not be helped by anything in the nature of a 'national disaster squad';

(b) we need improved arrangements to give national oversight to the development of co-ordinated emergency planning, and to address specific practical issues raised by recent disasters;

(c) more needs to be done to encourage and develop co-ordination of the various services at the local level.

To help meet these objectives I shall be appointing a civil emergencies adviser, charged with oversight of the whole subject and reporting directly to me. I shall announce a name as soon as I can.

The adviser will consider matters of current concern in the field of civil emergency planning in peacetime, with a view to helping those with operational responsibilities to achieve the highest standards of co-ordination and compatibility between their contingency arrangements. He will not have an operational role during an emergency, but will be closely concerned with general questions of planning and training and with drawing out the broad lessons to be learnt from particular incidents. To achieve this he will work closely with senior officers of the emergency services, local authorities, voluntary bodies, safety inspectorates, Government Departments and others directly concerned. He will be supported by a small civil emergencies secretariat within the Home Office, working in association with the Cabinet Office. The secretariat will begin preliminary work immediately.

A number of specific issues have been identified in the course of the review which I shall want the adviser to take forward as a matter of priority. These include the handling of casualty inquiries, psychological damage to survivors and relatives, assistance for foreign disasters, training and exercises. He may wish to draw on the work of existing groups which are already looking at some of the issues, or to convene interdisciplinary expert groups to address detailed questions.

To support the adviser's work I am giving the civil defence college at Easingwold a wider remit and will expect it also to address questions of peacetime emergency planning irrespective of any wartime connections. This will be reflected in a change of name to "emergency planning college".

In the course of the review local authorities argued strongly for a duty to be imposed on them to plan for peacetime emergencies. I have noted their views, but I am not at present convinced of the need for legislation. Much can be done without it. I will, however, keep the position under review as work progresses.

The arrangements I have set out here do not alter the relationships or responsibilities of central Government Departments. The Department with the closest involvement acts as "lead department" co-ordinating the central Government response, organising the necessary executive action and keeping Parliament and the public informed. The lead department is supported by arrangements for collective discussion should that prove necessary. The new arrangements are complementary to existing arrangements and will provide as a new element, a central focus for the shared views and experience of the emergency services, local authorities and voluntary bodies.

I am placing in the Libraries of both Houses a more comprehensive statement about the conduct and outcome of the review.

Bail

Mr. Allen: To ask the Secretary of State for the Home Department (1) if magistrates will be able to impose the condition of participation in electronic surveillance schemes without the defendant's consent;

(2) if the consent of the defendant will be required before a condition of bail is imposed by a magistrates' court in England and Wales.

Mr. John Patten: The defendant's consent to a condition of bail is not required under the Bail Act 1976, and the Government have no plans to alter the Act in this respect. The trials of electronic monitoring will, however, proceed on the basis that in each case the willingness of the defendant to participate in the scheme will be established before the equipment is installed.

Fire Authorities (Grants)

Mr. Bill Michie: To ask the Secretary of State for the Home Department if he will give details for each fire authority of the amounts of grant aid paid towards *(a)* salary costs, *(b)* training costs and *(c)* other costs in respect of each brigade emergency planning staff officer in 1986-87.

Mr. John Patten: The amounts of grant aid paid in respect of each brigade emergency planning staff officer for 1986-87 are given in the table. Training costs are not separately identified in records of grant paid.

Fire authority	Salary costs	Training and other costs
Avon	8,979	—
Bedfordshire	—	—
Berkshire	14,190	1,424
Buckinghamshire	14,255	1,328
Cambridgeshire	16,818	292
Cheshire	19,003	831
Cleveland	14,402	2,129
Clwyd	17,240	1,160
Cornwall	16,446	366
Cumbria	19,181	2,506
Derbyshire	—	—
Devon	14,837	3,206
Dorset	15,194	67
Durham	18,024	1,996
Dyfed	10,454	2,767
Essex	20,127	1,488
Mid-Glamorgan	—	—
South Glamorgan	—	—
West Glamorgan	10,491	948
Gloucestershire	—	—
Gwent	—	—
Gwynedd	18,641	2,553
Hampshire	15,027	3,934
Hereford and Worcester	17,397	1,292
Hertfordshire	11,917	2,294
Humberside	16,100	1,916
Isle of Wight	13,210	1,336
Kent	13,740	3,116
Lancashire	16,999	14
Leicestershire	—	—
Lincolnshire	16,913	—
London	12,012	4,968
Greater Manchester	—	—
Merseyside	—	—
West Midlands	—	—
Norfolk	12,448	2,588
Northamptonshire	15,849	3,116
Northumberland	—	—
Nottinghamshire	16,193	4,428
Oxfordshire	11,746	2,018
Powys	14,144	579
Shropshire	—	—
Somerset	21,157	414
Staffordshire	13,771	1,575
Suffolk	10,833	255
Surrey	16,571	—
East Sussex	—	—
West Sussex	12,342	4,837
Tyne and Wear	17,381	2,563
Warwickshire	10,418	1,987
Wiltshire	15,139	2,966
North Yorkshire	9,825	852

Fire authority	Salary costs	Training and other costs
South Yorkshire	—	—
West Yorkshire	14,626	2,475

Civil Defence College, Easingwold

Mr. Bill Michie: To ask the Secretary of State for the Home Department if he will give details of proposed expenditure in 1989-90, 1990-91 and future years on *(a)* the construction of a new lecture theatre at the civil defence college, Easingwold and *(b)* the refurbishment and upgrading of the bedroom annexes at the civil defence college, Easingwold; and if he will make a statement upon the future programme at the civil defence college.

Mr. John Patten: The information requested is as follows:

			£,000
	1989-90	*1990-91*	*1991-92*
New Lecture Theatre	285	471	452
Bedroom Annex	105	75	NIL

Construction and refurbishment programmes at the college are planned on the basis of need and the availability of funding.

District Authorities (Civil Defence Grants)

Mr. Bill Michie: To ask the Secretary of State for the Home Department if he will list the amounts of Home Office civil defence grant aid paid to each of the district authorities employing emergency planning staff funded by such grant for each year from 1979-80 to the present.

Mr. John Patten: Civil defence grant in respect of expenditure incurred by district authorities is normally claimed on their behalf by the relevant county or fire and civil defence authority. No records are held of the amounts in respect of individual districts.

Regional Fire Advisers

Mr. Bill Michie: To ask the Secretary of State for the Home Department if he will make arrangements to place in the Library of the House the minutes of, and any papers relating to, regional fire advisers meetings since 1979.

Mr. John Patten: No. It is not normal practice for the papers relating to such meetings to be placed in the Library.

TRANSPORT

Midland Main Line

Mr. Tredinnick: To ask the Secretary of State for Transport whether he has the report commissioned by midlands local authorities to consider the electrification of the midland main line; what representations he has received from Leicestershire's Conservative county councillors about its recommendations; and if he will make a statement.

Mr. Portillo: I have not seen the report commissioned by a group of local authorities into the midland main line,

though I receive representations about the line from time to time. Services and journey times along the line have recently been substantially improved, and BR plans to improve them further when rolling stock becomes available from the east coast main line, following my right hon. Friend's announcement on 12 June of additional rolling stock. It is for British Rail to propose electrification schemes where it believes that they would be worthwhile. The midland main line is not presently due for reinvestment.

Taxis

Mr. Nicholas Bennett: To ask the Secretary of State for Transport pursuant to his reply to the hon. Member for Pembroke on 10 April *Official Report,* column *409,* whether he now has plans to bring forward legislation to abolish the power of local authorities to restrict the number of taxis which might be operated in their area.

Mr. Portillo: I refer my hon. Friend to the reply I gave to my hon. Friend the Member for Ilford, North (Mr. Bendall) on 11 May at column *488.*

Marine Radio Navigation

Sir David Price: To ask the Secretary of State for Transport if he will make a statement about the future of marine radio navigation in United Kingdom waters.

Mr. Channon: I am today publishing a consultative document entitled "The Future of Marine Radionavigation in United Kingdom Waters" which seeks the views of the marine community about decisions needed on the land-based system of radio navigation to be provided in United Kingdom waters into the next century. In essence the choice appears to be between continuing with the present Decca navigator system, which is operated by Racal Decca Marine Navigation Ltd. under contract to the general lighthouse authorities, or adopting a system known as Loran C as part of an international co-operative venture. The consultative document sets out the considerations to be weighed and reaches a provisional view favouring participation in the Loran C project. I have, however, not yet reached a firm conclusion and I am inviting views from all interested parties. These should be sent to the Department of Transport not later than 11 September. I expect to take a decision later this year taking account of the responses received and the position reached on the current international discussions on the Loran C option. If my decision were to be in favour of the Loran C system, this would be contingent on a formal memorandum of understanding being concluded between the participating countries.

Copies of the consultative document have been placed in the Library.

London Underground (Exit Gates)

Mr. Bendall: To ask the Secretary of State for Transport whether London Underground Limited has reported to him on progress with work on the Underground ticketing system to ensure that exit gates open automatically in the event of a single phase power failure.

Mr. Portillo: London Underground informs me that the work has been completed some two weeks ahead of schedule and assures me that all the gates will now spring open automatically if there is a power failure of any sort.

A16 (Improvement)

Dr. Cunningham: To ask the Secretary of State for Transport if he will make a statement on progress being made with the A16 Spalding to Sutterton road improvement scheme.

Mr. Peter Bottomley: We intend to publish draft orders for the A16 Spalding to Sutterton improvement this summer. We had hoped to do so earlier.

London Underground (Automatic Barriers)

Mr. Cohen: To ask the Secretary of State for Transport if, further to his answer of 16 May, *Official Report,* column *112,* about the cost of installing automatic ticket barriers at London Underground stations, he will indicate (i) the revised costs when the full cost of the computer is included, and (ii) what proportion of the cost of computers could be attributed to the purpose of running the automatic ticket gates.

Mr. Portillo: Information in the form requested is not held in the Department. May I suggest that the hon. Member writes to the chairman of London Underground.

Lichfield—Redditch Cross-city Line

Mr. Heddle: To ask the Secretary of State for Transport, further to his answer to the hon. Member for Mid-Staffordshire of 7 June, if he will investigate the reasons why he has not yet received British Rail's submission for the electrification of the cross-city line from Lichfield to Redditch via Birmingham New Street; if he will publish in the *Official Report* copies of relevant correspondence between his Department and British Rail; and if he will now make a statement.

Mr. Portillo: The position is described in my replies of 6 June to the hon. Member for West Bromwich, East (Mr. Snape) which included a summary of discussions between British Rail and the Department. Since these meetings, I understand that British Rail carried out further work on engineering and financial matters. I expect a formal submission shortly.

Buses (Exit Mechanisms)

Mr. Cohen: To ask the Secretary of State for Transport what commitment, including provision of finance, Her Majesty's Government have received from London Regional Transport of the extension of its safe centre exit door mechanisms to all buses; what is his estimate of the date when this is likely to be achieved; and if he will make a statement.

Mr. Portillo: We have not received such a proposal from London Regional Transport or London Buses Ltd. However, I understand that London Buses is currently testing a safety mechanism which automatically reopens bus doors if they come into contact with an obstruction when closing.

Safety is the Department's and LRT's highest priority. The Department has recently issued for comment draft regulations which include provisions to reduce the risk of people being trapped in power-operated bus doors. The consultation period ended on 31 May and responses are now being considered.

London Underground (Disabled People)

Mr. Cohen: To ask the Secretary of State for Transport whether he will make representations to the chairman of London Regional Transport to change its policy so that prior permission is not required for individuals confined to a wheelchair to use London Underground provided they are accompanied by an able-bodied person; and if he will make a statement.

Mr. Portillo: Existing regulations are for the protection and convenience of disabled passengers. I understand that passengers in wheelchairs may use the surface and sub-surface Underground lines and need only advise staff at their local station of their wish to travel. Prior notice is necessary so that staff can ensure that there are no local difficulties preventing easy wheelchair access, and can give assistance if required.

Buses (Concessionary Fares)

Mr. Cohen: To ask the Secretary of State for Transport whether his answer to the hon. Member for Leyton of 26 April about concessionary fares on buses, stating that it is for local authorities to decide whether to make any changes in their present arrangements, represents a change from the pledges made by Her Majesty's Government during the passage of the London Regional Transport Act assuring the continuance of the free fares system for pensioners in London; and if he will make a statement.

Mr. Portillo: There has been no change in the Government's stance on concessionary fares for elderly, disabled and blind Londoners. The present concessionary scheme in London is voluntarily agreed between the London boroughs. It is primarily a local authority decision as to what concessions are provided; that is no change from the position prior to the passage of the London Regional Transport Act 1984. However, this is underpinned in law by a reserve scheme which guarantees free travel should the boroughs fail to agree voluntarily upon a uniform Londonwide scheme.

London Underground (Rolling Stock)

Mr. Cohen: To ask the Secretary of State for Transport whether the railway inspectorate has examined any proposal for new Underground rolling stock submitted to them by London Underground Ltd. which would provide for *(a)* fewer seats or *(b)* more people to stand, than the current carriages; and if he will make a statement.

Mr. Portillo: The railway inspectorate is currently considering London Underground Ltd's specification for replacing rolling stock on the Central line. This shows slightly fewer seats per train than existing stock and more space for standing passengers. The capacity of the replacement stock is not directly a matter for the inspectorate, which is principally concerned with its safety of operation.

London Transport (Passenger Attacks)

Mr. Cox: To ask the Secretary of State for Transport how many reported attacks there have been on passengers on London transport *(a)* buses and *(b)* Underground trains in each of the last five years.

Mr. Portillo: Assaults on passengers on buses in London are dealt with by the Metropolitan police. London Regional Transport does not maintain a central statistical record of such assaults. The numbers of recorded assaults on passengers on London Underground in each of the four years were:

Year	Numbers
1985	467
1986	646
1987	635
1988	777

Passenger assaults in the first quarter of 1989 were 185 which represented an 11 per cent. reduction on the figure of 207 for the same period last year. A figure for 1984 is not available.

South London Assessment Study

Mr. Cox: To ask the Secretary of State for Transport when he expects to receive the consultant's reports on the south London assessment study; if he will outline the action that will be followed by his Department after these reports have been considered; and if he will make a statement.

Mr. Peter Bottomley: The consultant's report is expected late this summer. The results of the study will be published. There will be a period for public comment and discussion before decisions are taken. Subsequent action will depend on the measures adopted.

Exeter (Northern Bypass)

Mr. Maxwell-Hyslop: To ask the Secretary of State for Transport (1) whether the proposal to construct a northern bypass for Exeter from the M5 originated in a proposal put to his Department by Devon county council as the highway authority;

(2) whether the proposal to construct a northern bypass for Exeter from the M5 is a scheme originating in his Department, without consulation with, or the approval of Devon county council.

Mr. Peter Bottomley *[pursuant to his reply, 12 June 1989, c. 338]:* When the routes for the M5 were originally investigated the choice lay between a route to the east and south and one to the north and west of Exeter. This was before the advent of public consultation and the then local authorities would have been consulted in confidence. I am sorry if my previous reply was not as full as my hon. Friend would have liked.

M20

Mr. Speed: To ask the Secretary of State for Transport if he will now state when he intends to let the contract for the Charing Heath to Ashford section of the M20 motorway.

Mr. Peter Bottomley: On 14 June.

Birmingham Relief Road

Mr. Richard Shepherd: To ask the Secretary of State for Transport how long, following his recent announcement that the proposed Birmingham relief road will now be subject to a competition for the private sector to finance, design, build and operate, he envisages this process will take; when he expects to publish the report of the inspector to the public inquiries; how much money has already been spent on compensation for the previously announced preferred route; and how many claims for compensation relating to the previously preferred route are currently under negotiation.

Mr. Portillo: The Government want to see the road constructed as quickly as possible, and will announce a timetable for the competition as soon as possible. A decision on the inspector's report will be announced when the competition has taken place.

The compensation provisions do not come into force until the statutory orders for the scheme have been made. The Department has bought a number of properties under planning blight, costing approximately £2·3 million. A further nine cases are currently being processed.

Mr. Richard Shepherd: To ask the Secretary of State for Transport if he will publish his Department's estimate of the cost to date of the work carried out by Sir Owen Williams and Partners and the estimated cost of any further contractual commitments with Sir Owen Williams and Partners relating to the previously preferred route for the Birmingham relief road.

Mr. Portillo: A number of specialist firms and consultants have been employed in the preparation of the Birmingham northern relief road. The total cost so far is about £10 million. The work done is not abortive; the information gathered will be made available to the private sector. The future role of Sir Owen Williams and Partners is still under discussion.

Mr. Richard Shepherd: To ask the Secretary of State for Transport if his Department will consider claims for compensation towards the legal costs of individuals, companies and local authorities represented at the public inquiry relating to the previously preferred route for the Birmingham relief road.

Mr. Portillo: Claims for compensation towards the legal costs of individuals, companies and local authorities represented at the public inquiry for the Birmingham northern relief road will be dealt with in accordance with the normal practice once a decision on the scheme has been announced.

Mr. Richard Shepherd: To ask the Secretary of State for Transport what are his Department's estimated costs to date for the previously preferred route for the Birmingham relief road; what are his Department's estimated costs to date of the various public inquiries relating to the previously preferred route; and if he will estimate his Department's costs in implementing the competition for the road.

Mr. Portillo: I refer my hon. Friend to the answers already given on costs. The Department is unable to disaggregate its own internal running costs to individual schemes. We are not able to give details of the indirect costs of public inquiries, such as departmental staff costs. The direct costs, such as accommodation were about £39,000.

It is too early to estimate what the costs of implementing the competition will be. Much will depend on how many bids are received and the nature of those bids.

Minibus Drivers

Mr. Michael: To ask the Secretary of State for Transport, pursuant to his answer to the hon. Member for Battersea (Mr. Bowis), on 15 May, *Official Report*, columns *10-11*, what progress he has made towards securing the withdrawal of the draft European Community proposals relating to licensing of minibus drivers.

Mr. Peter Bottomley: I would refer the hon. Member to the reply to my hon. Friend the Member for Southend, East (Mr. Taylor) on 12 June at column *331*.

Blackburn Southern Bypass

Mr. Ken Hargreaves: To ask the Secretary of State for Transport what changes have been made in the route of the Blackburn southern bypass of the M65 since the proposal in 1977.

Mr. Peter Bottomley: Since 1977 there have been changes in the route of the bypass at Brindle and Guide and a shift in alignment at Knuzden Brook. Last year we announced that the bypass would be extended westwards to link to the A585 and to Bamber Bridge bypass.

Emergency Routes

Mr. Redmond: To ask the Secretary of State for Transport if he will make a statement in respect of his emergency transport plan "Main Road Route System", and the various major roads in England and Wales designated with military code names Hen, Mole, Moth, Newt, Pig, Tiger, Vole, Worm and Yak.

Mr. Archie Hamilton: I have been asked to reply. No.

FOREIGN AND COMMONWEALTH AFFAIRS

Hong Kong

Mr. Chris Smith: To ask the Secretary of State for Foreign and Commonwealth Affairs if any plans exist in the Hong Kong Administration for enacting a Bill of Rights and incorporating the international covenant on civil and political rights into domestic law during the transitional period to 1997; and if he will make a statement.

Mr. Eggar: The international covenant on civil and political rights was extended to Hong Kong, with certain reservations, in 1976. It is at present implemented in Hong Kong, as in the United Kingdom, through a combination of common law, legislation and administrative rules. We are now considering with the Hong Kong Government as a matter of priority whether to enact a human rights ordinance, and if so, what form it should take.

Mr. Chris Smith: To ask the Secretary of State for Foreign and Commonwealth Affairs what exceptions to aspects of the joint declaration have been excluded from the proposed second draft of the proposed Basic Law for Hong Kong; and if he will make a statement.

Mr. Eggar: The latest draft of the Basic Law repeats many provisions of the joint declaration word for word. However, there are undoubtedly other areas where improvements would be welcome in Hong Kong. Consultation on the draft Basic Law has been temporarily suspended in Hong Kong. When consultation resumes, Hong Kong people will no doubt wish to continue to express their views.

Mr. Chris Smith: To ask the Secretary of State for Foreign and Commonwealth Affairs what requests were received from the People's Republic of China seeking a postponement of direct elections to the Legislative Council in Hong Kong; what information he has as to the view of the People's Republic of China authorities as to the implementation of reforms to the political system in Hong Kong prior to the promulgation of the Basic Law; and if he will make a statement.

Mr. Eggar: The Chinese Government made clear their view that any changes introduced in Hong Kong Government's 1988 White Paper on the development of representative government should be compatible with the Basic Law to be promulgated in 1990.

Mr. Chris Smith: To ask the Secretary of State for Foreign and Commonwealth Affairs what specific measures have been taken to ensure that the high degree of autonomy promised for the special administrative region by the People's Republic of China authorities will be effected; what sanctions exist should that autonomy not be granted; and if he will make a statement.

Mr. Eggar: A high degree of autonomy for Hong Kong is provided for in the Sino-British joint declaration of 1984, an international agreement binding under international law. We have the right to satisfy ourselves that the Basic Law fully and faithfully reflects the provisions of the joint declaration. We intend to live up to our commitments under the joint declaration and we look to the Chinese to do the same.

Mr. Chris Smith: To ask the Secretary of State for Foreign and Commonwealth Affairs whether the power of independent and final adjudication of the Basic Law of the special administrative region of Hong Kong will vest in the territory's courts; and if he will make a statement.

Mr. Eggar: The Sino-British joint declaration on the future of Hong Kong provides that the courts of the future special administrative region shall exercise judicial power independently and free from any interference, and that the power of final judgment shall be vested in the court of final appeal in Hong Kong. These provisions are reflected in articles 81 and 84 of the latest draft of the Basic Law.

Mr. Chris Smith: To ask the Secretary of State for Foreign and Commonwealth Affairs whether, in the light of recent events in the People's Republic of China, he will consider ordering direct elections for the Legislative Council of Hong Kong; if a fully and directly elected legislature will be achieved prior to 1 July 1997; and if he will make a statement.

Mr. Eggar: In the light of recent events in China, and evidence of a change of opinion in Hong Kong, we and the Hong Kong Government are taking a careful look at the programme for advancing and consolidating effective democracy in Hong Kong.

Mr. Chris Smith: To ask the Secretary of State for Foreign and Commonwealth Affairs whether he will suspend all extradition of prisoners to Hong Kong where there is a possibility of the extradited person being handed over to the People's Republic of China authorities on 1 July 1997; and if he will make a statement.

Mr. Eggar: We have no plans to suspend the return of fugitives to Hong Kong. My right hon. Friend the Home Secretary can only order the return of a fugitive when all court proceedings in the United Kingdom have been concluded. If a fugitive offender is returned to Hong Kong under the Fugitive Offenders Act before 1997, that will be for an offence against Hong Kong laws. It will not be for offences against the laws of the PRC. The case will be heard by the Hong Kong courts. Under the joint declaration, Hong Kong will retain its separate legal system after 1997, and will not be relying on the PRC criminal code.

Mr. Ali Ghavami

Mr. Chris Smith: To ask the Secretary of State for Foreign and Commonwealth Affairs whether there is any financial or contractual relationship between Mr. Ali Ghavami, formerly an information officer at the Iranian embassy in London, and his Department in relation to his work in west Africa and elsewhere; and if he will make a statement.

Mrs. Chalker: There is no relationship between Mr. Ghavami and the Foreign and Commonwealth Office.

DEFENCE

Military Command Centres

Mr. Redmond: To ask the Secretary of State for Defence what action is currently being planned or acted upon to update the United Kingdom's redevelopment and replacement of subordinate military command centres; what rank of people and personnel will use them; and if he will make a statement.

Mr. Archie Hamilton: I assume that the surbordinate military command centres to which the hon. Member is referring are the area flag officers' headquarters, the Army district headquarters and the RAF group headquarters in the United Kingdom. There are no plans to replace these. A number of works programmes relating to them are at various stages of planning. It is not our practice to give details of the ranks of personnel stationed at particular locations.

Naval Headquarters

Mr. Redmond: To ask the Secretary of State for Defence what are the plans for the *(a)* Royal Naval headquarters at Northwood and *(b)* Pitreavie castle, Fife; what ranks of personnel and people will be stationed at them; and if he will make a statement.

Mr. Archie Hamilton: Currently, and for the foreseeable future, the functions of these headquarters are as follows:

Northwood is the headquarters of Commander-in-Chief Fleet, who also fills the NATO appointments of Commander-in-Chief Channel and Commander-in-Chief Eastern Atlantic; and of the Air Officer Commanding 18 group, who also fills the NATO appointments of Commander Air Eastern Atlantic and Commander Air Channel.

Pitreavie is the headquarters of Flag Officer Scotland and Northern Ireland, and of Air Officer Scotland and Northern Ireland, who both also fill NATO sub-area appointments relating to the Channel and Eastern Atlantic areas.

It is not our practice to give details of the ranks of personnel stationed at particular locations.

RAF Headquarters

Mr. Redmond: To ask the Secretary of State for Defence what are the plans for the Royal Air Force headquarters at *(a)* High Wycombe, Buckinghamshire and *(b)* Stanmore, Middlesex; what ranks of people and personnel will be stationed there; and if he will make a statement.

Mr. Archie Hamilton: Currently, and for the foreseeable future, the functions of these headquarters are as follows:

High Wycombe is the headquarters of the Air Oficer Commander-in-Chief, RAF Strike Command, who also fills the NATO appointment of Commander-in-Chief UK Air.

RAF Bentley Priory, which I assume the hon. Member has in mind when he refers to Stanmore, is the headquarters of Air Officer Commanding 11 group, and of the Royal Observer Corps.

It is not our practice to give details of the ranks of personnel stationed at particular locations.

Land Forces Headquarters

Mr. Redmond: To ask the Secretary of State for Defence (1) what are the current plans for the war headquarters of the Army's United Kingdom land forces

command at Hawthorn, Wiltshire; what ranks of people and personnel will be stationed there; and if he will make a statement;

(2) what are the plans for the war headquarters of the Army's United Kingdom land forces command at Sopley, Hampshire; and if he will make a statement.

Mr. Archie Hamilton: The headquarters of United Kingdom land forces is at Wilton. It is not our practice to comment on the existence or otherwise of particular contingency plans relating to the outbreak of hostilities.

Nuclear Weapons (Accidents)

Mr. Redmond: To ask the Secretary of State for Defence what contingency plans his Department has for dealing with an accident involving *(a)* any seaborne, *(b)* any airborne or *(c)* any landborne nuclear weapon, in the course of non-operational activities, including courtesy calls in England and Wales.

Mr. Archie Hamilton: The Ministry of Defence has contingency plans to deal with a wide range of possible accidents involving nuclear weapons in the United Kingdom. These are kept continuously under review and are tested regularly in exercises. Other Government Departments, local authorities and the civil emergency services are consulted where appropriate, and participate in exercises.

No. 2 Signals Brigade

Mr. Redmond: To ask the Secretary of State for Defence what is the *(a)* present and *(b)* future role of No. 2 Signals Brigade; how many personnel and of what rank the brigade contains; where it will be stationed during (i) 1989, and (ii) 1990; and if he will make a statement.

Mr. Archie Hamilton: The role of 2 Signals Brigade is the provision of communications. The brigade has its headquarters at Corsham, Wiltshire and is currently stationed at 192 further locations. It is not our practice to give details of the strengths of operational formations.

Combat Body Armour

Mr. Madden: To ask the Secretary of State for Defence if he has invited manufacturers to tender for the supply of combat body armour for general issue; and if combat body armour will be introduced into general service in 1989.

Mr. Sainsbury: Modifications were required to the original design in the light of experience during the troop trials. A further trial of the modified design is now taking place and should be completed shortly.

Manufacturers have not yet been invited to tender for the supply of combat body armour for general issue. Its introduction into general service is now expected to begin in 1990.

Greenham Common

Ms. Richardson: To ask the Secretary of State for Defence whether he will make a statement on the rights of commoners at Greenham common.

Mr. Archie Hamilton: I refer the hon. Member to the statement made by my hon. Friend the Member for Kettering (Mr. Freeman) on 29 April 1988 at columns

310-11. Negotiations are taking place over the extinguishing of rights of common in accordance with the relevant statutory procedures.

Exercises (West Germany)

Mr. Menzies Campbell: To ask the Secretary of State for Defence how many representations have been received from West German local governments in the past year concerning environmental damage by the British Army during exercises; if he will make a statement on the views expressed; and if he will outline the actions taken in the light of these representations.

Mr. Archie Hamilton: During the past year, four representations were received from West German land governments about environmental damage caused by British troops during exercise; all have now been satisfactorily resolved. At lower level, there are frequent exchanges with stadt authorities about matters of mutual concern, and frequent meetings between civil and military authorities at which environmental matters are often discussed.

BAOR takes its obligation to protect the environment very seriously. All representations from local government in Germany are given careful and sympathetic consideration. Environmental issues are taken into account during the planning and conduct of exercises, and exercise play is adapted to meet local concerns where this can be done without unacceptable operational penalties. Some damage is, however, an unavoidable consequence of military training. Specific incidents are always fully investigated and a formal response made to any complaints. Well-established machinery exists for the quick processing of any claims.

Mr. Alan Thomas (Bonus)

Mrs. Mahon: To ask the Secretary of State for Defence pursuant to his reply of 24 April, *Official Report,* column *367,* how the performance bonus of the head of defence export services designate, Mr. Alan Thomas, will be calculated.

Mr. Sainsbury: As with other performance increments at senior levels in the Civil Service, this will be assessed judgmentally. The assessment will be made, within an annual maximum of £25,000, by senior officials, with Treasury representation.

Submarine Crews (Training)

Dr. Godman: To ask the Secretary of State for Defence when the hon. Member for Greenock and Port Glasgow can expect an answer to his letter, dated 12 May on the subject of the training of submarine crews.

Mr. Archie Hamilton: I wrote to the hon. Member on 14 June 1989.

SOCIAL SECURITY

Loans and Grants

Mr. Redmond: To ask the Secretary of State for Social Security what was the total number and percentage of *(a)* budgetary loans and *(b)* community care grants awarded to the 15 client groups defined by his Department for each of the departments of social security serving Doncaster and Mexborough areas in the county of South Yorkshire for the financial year 1988-89.

Mr. Peter Lloyd: The table contains the provisional figures for the period 11 April 1988 to 31 March 1989.

Budgeting loans and community care grants for the Doncaster and Mexborough areas: Numbers and percentages by client group

	Budgeting Loans						Community Care Grants					
	Doncaster East ILO		Doncaster West ILO		Wath on Dearne ILO		Doncaster East ILO		Doncaster West ILO		Wath on Dearne ILO	
	Number	Per cent	Number	Per cent	Number	Per cent	Number	Per cent	Number	Per cent	Number	Per cent
Unallocated or unidentified	7	0·3	5	0·2	7	0·3	0	0·0	3	0·7	1	0·3
Over 80—with Income Support higher pensioner premium	7	0·4	5	0·2	1	0·7	7	2·3	2	0·5	2	0·7
Aged 60-79—disabled with higher pensioner premium	9	0·6	8	0·3	10	2·4	12	3·6	15	3·5	7	2·4
Aged 60-79—with ordinary pensioner premium, or over 60 without pensioner premium	65	4·1	64	2·9	42	7·3	34	10·4	38	9·1	21	7·3
Lone parent with Income Support disability premium	2	0·1	3	0·1	14	3·1	2	0·6	1	0·2	9	3·1
Family with disability premium	33	2·1	35	1·6	100	7·0	13	3·9	7	1·7	20	7·0
Other with disability premium	39	2·4	63	2·9	47	11·5	22	6·8	19	4·4	34	11·5
Lone parent without disability premium	645	40·5	832	38·1	462	23·0	88	26·5	159	37·7	67	23·0
Signs at UBO quarterly with Income Support family premium	5	0·3	13	0·6	16	0·3	2	0·6	5	1·2	1	0·3
Signs at UBO quarterly without family premium	38	2·4	50	2·3	19	1·0	10	2·9	6	1·5	4	1·0
Signing unemployed or with training allowance with family premium	470	29·5	603	27·7	326	18·5	65	19·7	85	20·2	54	18·5
Signing unemployed or with training allowance without family premium	228	14·3	432	19·8	303	18·1	55	16·5	56	13·3	53	18·1
Others with family premium	8	0·5	23	1·0	15	3·1	6	1·9	5	1·2	9	3·1
Others without family premium	41	2·6	48	2·2	62	3·5	12	3·6	17	4·0	10	3·5
Involved in trade dispute	0	0·0	0	0·0	0	0·0	0	0·0	0	0·0	0	0·0
Applicant not in receipt of Income Support—not applicable for budgeting loans	n/a	—	n/a	—	n/a	—	2	0·6	2	0·5	0	0·0

n/a = not applicable.

Mr. Nellist: To ask the Secretary of State for Social Security what percentage of *(a)* budgeting loans and *(b)* community care grants were awarded to each of the 15 client groups defined by his Department for each of his Department's two offices serving the Coventry area for the financial year 1988-89.

Mr. Lloyd *[holding answer 8 June 1989]:* Estimates of the proportions of budgeting loans and community care grants awarded to client groups for the period 11 April 1988 to 31 March 1989 are given in the table.

Budgeting loans and community care grants for Coventry (East) and Coventry (West) percentage by client group 1988-89

Per cent.

Client Group	Budgeting Loans Coventry (East) ILO	Budgeting Loans Coventry (West) ILO	Community Care Grants Coventry (East) ILO	Community Care Grants Coventry (West) ILO
Unallocated or unidentified	0·4	0·4	0·0	1·3
Over 80—with income support higher pensioner premium	0·1	0·4	4·4	4·5
Aged 60-79—disabled with higher pensioner premium	0·5	0·4	2·8	3·1
Aged 60-79—with ordinary pensioner premium, or over 60 without pensioner premium	2·8	4·2	14·0	8·9
Lone parent with income support disability premium	0·3	0·1	0·2	1·3
Family with disability premium	1·6	2·8	1·7	2·2
Other with disability premium	4·3	3·3	12·0	9·4
Lone parent without disability premium	46·3	49·2	33·4	30·8
Signs at UBO quarterly with Income Support family premium	0·6	0·7	0·2	0·4
Signs at UBO quarterly without family premium	2·3	2·1	1·5	2·2
Signing unemployed or with training allowance with family premium	12·5	16·5	2·8	8·5
Signing unemployed or with training allowance without family premium	23·4	16·4	16·6	21·9
Others with family premium	1·0	0·9	1·7	0·9
Others without family premium	4·3	2·6	7·4	3·6
Involved in trade dispute	0·0	0·0	0·0	0·0
Applicant not in receipt of income support—not applicable for budgeting loans	n/a	n/a	1·1	0·9

n/a = not applicable.

Personal Data (Departmental Index)

Mr. Cohen: To ask the Secretary of State for Social Security if he will list the items of personal data held in the new computerised departmental central index, the size of the index, and how many accesses were made to the index over the last two months.

Mr. Peter Lloyd: Each record on the departmental central index holds up to five items of information relating to one person and the index currently holds around 60 million records. The information held is the person's name, date of birth, address, sex and date of death where appropriate. Over the last two months, 1,503,485 trace and inquiry accesses were made of the system.

Community Charge Rebate

Mr. Blunkett: To ask the Secretary of State for Social Security if he will list by each charging authority in Wales the income level at which *(a)* a single person aged under 25 years, *(b)* a single person aged over 25 years, *(c)* a single pensioner, *(d)* a pensioner couple and *(e)* a couple with two children all with no savings would lose entitlement to a community charge rebate, assuming the most recent safety-netted community charge figures.

Mr. Peter Lloyd: The information requested is given in the table.

Community charge benefit: net income at which minimum CCB of 50 pence is payable

Local authority	Annual community charge	Single under 25 working	Single 25 to 59 working	Single pensioner aged 60-74 not working	Pensioner couple aged 60-74 not working	Couple two children under 11 working
Alyn and Deeside	216·00	51·23	58·73	64·93	112·84	135·79
Colwyn	224·00	52·05	59·55	65·75	114·48	137·43
Delyn	215·00	51·13	58·63	64·83	112·63	135·58
Glyndwr	185·00	48·05	55·55	61·75	106·48	129·43
Rhuddlan	201·00	49·70	57·20	63·40	109·76	132·71
Wrexham Maelor	196·00	49·18	56·68	62·88	108·74	131·69
Carmarthen	135·00	42·93	50·43	56·63	96·22	119·17
Ceredigion	146·00	44·05	51·55	57·75	98·48	121·43
Dinefwr	119·00	41·29	48·79	54·99	92·94	115·89
Llanelli	150·00	44·46	51·96	58·16	99·30	122·25
Preseli Pembrokeshire	136·00	43·03	50·53	56·73	96·43	119·38
South Pembrokeshire	166·00	46·11	53·61	59·81	102·58	125·53
Blaenau Gwent	124·00	41·80	49·30	55·50	93·97	116·92
Islwyn	135·00	42·93	50·43	56·63	96·22	119·17
Monmouth	187·00	48·26	55·76	61·96	106·89	129·84
Newport	204·00	50·00	57·50	63·70	110·38	133·33
Torfaen	168·00	46·31	53·81	60·01	102·99	125·94
Aberconwy	193·00	48·87	56·37	62·57	108·12	131·07

Local authority	Annual community charge	Single under 25 working	Single 25 to 59 working	Single pensioner aged 60-74 not working	Pensioner couple aged 60-74 not working	Couple two children under 11 working
Arfon	145·00	43·95	51·45	57·65	98·27	121·22
Dwyfor	182·00	47·75	55·25	61·45	105·86	128·81
Meirionnydd	182·00	47·75	55·25	61·45	105·86	128·81
Ynys Mon	178·00	47·34	54·84	61·04	105·04	127·99
Cynon Valley	114·00	40·77	48·27	54·47	91·91	114·86
Merthyr Tydfil	131·00	42·52	50·02	56·22	95·40	118·35
Ogwr	162·00	45·70	53·20	59·40	101·76	124·71
Rhondda	95·00	38·82	46·32	52·52	88·02	110·97
Rhymney Valley	148·00	44·26	51·76	57·96	98·89	121·84
Taff-Ely	166·00	46·11	53·61	59·81	102·58	125·53
Brecknock	143·00	43·75	51·25	57·45	97·86	120·81
Montgomery	142·00	43·64	51·14	57·34	97·66	120·61
Radnor	144·00	43·85	51·35	57·55	98·07	121·02
Cardiff	200·00	49·59	57·09	63·29	109·56	132·51
Vale of Glamorgan	176·00	47·13	54·63	60·83	104·63	127·58
Port Talbot	151·00	44·57	52·07	58·27	99·50	122·45
Lliw Valley	147·00	44·16	51·66	57·86	98·68	121·63
Neath	154·00	44·87	52·37	58·57	100·12	123·07
Swansea	215·00	51·13	58·63	64·83	112·63	135·58

1. The levels of community charge used are the illustrative safety netted figures for 1989-90 given by my right hon. Friend the Secretary of State for Wales in reply to the hon. Member for Alyn and Deeside (Mr. Jones) on 12 June 1989 at columns *303-6.*

2. The net income levels shown have been derived using the current housing benefit rates and rules for calculating net income and applicable amounts. A maximum rebate of 80 per cent., a taper of 15 per cent., and a minimum weekly rebate of 50 pence per claim have been used.

3. The following assumptions have been made:
   (i) no claimant is disabled;
   (ii) each claimant under pension age is in full-time work;
   (iii) no claimant over pension age is working;
   (iv) each claimant with dependent children is in receipt of child benefit and, where appropriate, family credit;
   (v) each claimant has assessed capital of under £3,000.

HEALTH

Organ Transplants

Mr. Redmond: To ask the Secretary of State for Health of he will list by year for the last 10 years, the number of times a recipient receiving a transplanted organ from a donor has been infected by a disease from the donor that was not diagnosed at the time; if he will show in his answer the type of disease; and if he will make a statement.

Mr. Freeman: Comprehensive information is not collected centrally, but the number of cases of disease transmitted through transplants is believed to be very small.

Hospital Wards (Wirral)

Mr. Frank Field: To ask the Secretary of State for Health how many wards in the Wirral would be classified as deprived under the Jarman formula.

Mr. Freeman: Professor Jarman's index of comparative deprivation for the 22 local authority wards in the Wirral is shown in the table. This is based on a national average of zero with the large positive numbers indicating the most deprived areas and the large negative numbers the least. The index ranges nationally from +72·95 to −62·52.

Jarman Index—Wirral

Ward	[1]UPA 8 Score
Bidstom	+45·33
Birkenhead	+37·62
Tranmere	+32·45
Seacombe	+21·13
Leasoure	+20·20
Upton	+13·29
Liscard	+11·47
New Brighton	+10·00

Ward	[1]UPA 8 Score
Bromborough	+9·81
Egerton	+8·83
Oxton	+5·01
Claughton	+4·68
Moreton	+3·06
Hoylake	−3·24
Preston	−4·56
Bebington	−5·64
Thurstaston	−5·66
Eastham	−6·87
Wallasey	−7·66
Royden	−11·98
Clatterbridge	−14·33
Heswall	−18·06

[1] UPA (Under privileged area) 8 score takes account of eight variable components.

Mental Illness and Handicap

Mr. Robin Cook: To ask the Secretary of State for Health how many patients were discharged to the community from National Health Service mental illness and mental handicap hospitals and units after a stay of one year or more in each year since 1979.

Mr. Freeman: The table shows the number of patients discharged to the community from National Health Service mental illness and mental handicap hospitals and units in England after a stay of one year or more, for the period 1979 to 1986, the last year for which information is currently available. The table excludes death and transfers to other hospitals.

England (1979 to 1986)
Discharges¹ from mental illness and mental handicap hospitals and units

Year	Mental illness	Mental handicap	Total
1979	3,460	1,178	4,638
1980	3,376	1,120	4,496
1981	3,516	1,246	4,762
1982	3,465	1,229	4,694
1983	3,563	1,457	5,020
1984	3,928	1,919	5,847
1985	3,441	2,052	5,493
1986	3,751	2,528	6,279

[1] Excludes deaths and transfers to other hospitals.

Food Safety

Mr. Robin Cook: To ask the Secretary of State for Health how often the expert committee on microbiological safety in food has met; what topics it has discussed; and if he will refer the recent botulism outbreak to it.

Mr. Kenneth Clarke: The microbiological safety of food committee held its first meeting on 14 April, and has met at approximately weekly to fortnightly intervals since then. At the request of Ministers it has been looking at specific questions relating to the increasing incidence of microbiological illnesses of foodborne origin, particularly from salmonella, listeria and campylobacter. The committee has no role in the handling of acute emergencies such as the recent outbreak of botulism. Once the outbreak has been dealt with, the committee will be asked to consider and advise on its implications when formulating its recommendation on microbiological food safety.

Day Care

Mr. Robin Cook: To ask the Secretary of State for Health if he will publish in the *Official Report* a table listing *(a)* the current number of day care places for the elderly per 1,000 of the population aged 65 years and over and *(b)* the number of day care places for the mentally handicapped per 10,000 of the population for each local authority.

Mr. Freeman: "Adult Training Centres for Mentally Handicapped People and Day Centres for Mentally Ill, Mentally Handicapped, Elderly and Younger Physically Handicapped People, at 31 March 1987—England" shows at tables A and C for each local authority, per 1,000 population of the relevant age groups, the most recent numbers of day centre places for the elderly and for the mentally handicapped and of adult training centre places for the mentally handicapped. A copy is in the Library.

Mr. Robin Cook: To ask the Secretary of State for Health what was the number of day care places for mentally ill and mentally handicapped people in each year since 1979.

Mr. Freeman: The table shows the number of day care places provided by local authority social services departments in each of the years specified. In addition, day care places are provided by mental illness and mental handicap hospitals in England, but the number of such places is not centrally collected.

Number of places provided by local authorities

Year	Mental illness¹	Mental handicap
1979	6,984	42,061
1980	7,242	42,337
1981	7,603	43,627
1982	7,887	45,152
1983	8,689	46,558
1984	8,919	47,464
1985	9,308	48,824
1986	9,216	50,374
1987	9,875	51,732

[1] Including places made available to local authorities by voluntary or private organisations and estimates of places for mentally ill people in day centres for mixed client groups. 1987 figures are revised.

Salmonella (Derbyshire)

Mr. Harry Barnes: To ask the Secretary of State for Health if he will make a statement on the cases of salmonella poisoning reported in north Derbyshire during May.

Mr. Freeman *[holding answer 13 June 1989]:* We understand that 61 cases of salmonella poisoning have been reported in Chesterfield, north-east Derbyshire and Mansfield. The health authority is thoroughly investigating the source of the outbreak.

ENVIRONMENT

Housing Kirklees

Mr. Riddick: To ask the Secretary of State for the Environment what would be the estimated total payment of a couple on average earnings living in a house valued at *(a)* £60,000, *(b)* £30,000 in the area covered by Kirklees council in 1990-91 under a system of local income tax and rates based on capital values.

Mr. Gummer: The level of bills under a system of local income tax and rates based on capital values would depend primarily on the level of expenditure undertaken by Kirklees council and the amount of support available from Government grants and business rates. Such figures for 1990-91 are not known. However, figures were placed in the Library on 23 June 1988 showing the tax rates which would have applied in 1988-89. Based on these figures, with capital value rates providing 80 per cent. of the total raised in local domestic taxes, a couple each earning average full-time wages, and with only the minimum tax allowance, would have paid £970 in a £60,000 house and £595 in a £30,000 house.

Historic Buildings and Monuments Commission (Grants)

Mr. Hanley: To ask the Secretary of State for the Environment what grants in aid were received by the Historic Buildings and Monuments Commission for England for the maintenance and running costs of the three former Greater London council properties, Kenwood house, Rangers house and Marble Hill house during the financial years 1986-87; 1987-88; 1988-89 and 1989-90 in cash and real terms; and how these grants were apportioned between the three properties.

Mrs. Virginia Bottomley: The year 1986-87 was the only one in which a separately identifiable allocation of grant-in-aid was paid to the commission in respect of all the ex-GLC functions, including Kenwood house, Rangers house and Marble Hill house, for which it assumed responsibility; this amounted to £7·75 million in total. For subsequent years, provision for these properties was subsumed in the total grant-in-aid provision, the allocation of which is for the commission to decide. I have asked the chairman of the commission to write to my hon. Friend with the details he requests for 1986-87 and subsequent years.

Local Authority Direct Labour Organisations

Mr. Thornton: To ask the Secretary of State for the Environment if he will list for each financial year between 1983-84 and 1988-89 the number of local authority direct labour organisations which have failed to meet the required rate of return under the Local Government, Planning and Land Act 1980 on capital employed when undertaking *(a)* general highway works and works in connection with the construction or maintenance of a sewer, *(b)* new construction, other than general highway or sewer works, the cost of which in the estimation of the authority or development body exceeded £50,000, *(c)* new construction, other than general highway or sewer works, the cost of which in the estimation of the authority or development body did not exceed £50,000 and *(d)* building maintenance within the meaning of the Local Authorities (Goods and Services) Act 1970, other than in connection with highways or the maintenance of a sewer.

Mrs. Virginia Bottomley: The number of DLOs in England on which reports are submitted to the Department and which have failed to meet the required rate of return on capital employed under the Local Government, Planning and Land Act 1980 is indicated in the table.

	I	*II*	*III*	*IV*
1983-84	18	22	21	43
1984-85	20	23	12	44
1985-86	21	18	6	36
1986-87	21	8	5	13

I   Highways.
II   Major Construction (over £50,000).
III Minor Construction (under £50,000).
IV Maintenance.

The Department has not yet completed its examinations of DLO reports for 1987-88 and those for 1988-89 are not required to be received until 31 October 1989.

Valuation and Community Charge Tribunals

Mr. Frank Field: To ask the Secretary of State for the Environment why he intends placing staff of his Department in valuation and community charge tribunal offices; and what assessment he has made as to how these placements will affect the independence of the tribunal system.

Mr. Gummer: A small number of staff with specialised computer skills are to assist the clerks of the valuation and community charge tribunals in the use of new computer systems. The independence of the tribunal system is not affected.

Bed and Breakfast (London)

Mr. Cox: To ask the Secretary of State for the Environment how many families were living in bed and breakfast accommodation in each of the London boroughs on 1 June 1989.

Mr. Trippier: The latest available figures, for the end of March 1989, appear in table 7 of "Local authorities' action under the homelessness provisions of the 1985 Housing Act: England. Results for the first quarter of 1989. Supplementary Tables", which is in the Library.

Rhinoceros Horn and Ivory

Mr. Nicholas Baker: To ask the Secretary of State for the Environment what action he is taking to combat illegal trade in rhinoceros horn and ivory.

Mrs. Virginia Bottomley: The United Kingdom implements the provisions of the convention on international trade in endangered species of wild fauna and flora (CITES) under which commercial trade in rhinoceros and the Indian elephant is already prohibited. The European Council of Environment Ministers agreed on 8 June to support the extension of such a ban to the African elephant. A ban on imports of ivory into the United Kingdom came into force on 9 June. All these measures help prevent illegal trading.

Parliamentary Offices (Heating)

Mr. Cohen: To ask the Secretary of State for the Environment why the heating in the parliamentary offices in which hon. Members' secretaries work is not switched on when Parliament is not sitting; and if he will make a statement.

Mr. Chope: Because members and staff continue to use their offices the heating is not turned off automatically at the start of a recess. This year the heating was first turned off on 8 May during the period of warm weather.

Fauna and Flora

Mr. Malcolm Bruce: To ask the Secretary of State for the Environment (1) if he will reconsider his opposition to the European Community directive on fauna, flora and habitats; what steps he proposes to take or is taking to protect endangered species of fauna and flora; and if he will make a statement;

(2) whether he will make it his policy to support attendance by non-governmental organisations at meetings convened to discuss the implementation and management of the European Community directive 8149/88, when it is adopted.

Mrs. Virginia Bottomley: We are not opposed to the principle of Community action to protect Europe's natural heritage. However the European Commission's proposal for a directive on the protection of natural and semi-natural habitats and of fauna and flora (8149/88) was unanimously rejected by member states at the Environmental Council on 24 November 1988. Instead, there was agreement that Community action could most usefully be focussed on assisting member states, as necessary, to implement fully the existing international conventions. We remain ready to discuss any sensible and practicable proposals to secure this objective.

Local Authority Dwellings

Mr. Meacher: To ask the Secretary of State for the Environment if he will publish the estimated total capital value of dwellings owned by local authorities in England and Wales and the estimated outstanding loan debt on such dwellings.

Mr. Gummer: Total outstanding loan debt on local authority owned dwellings in England and Wales at 31 March 1987 was approximately £25 billion. The Department does not collect information on the capital value of local authority dwellings. However, the 1986 English house condition survey estimated the total capital value of local authority stock in England and Wales at 1 November 1986 to be £123 billion, based on market value with vacant possession.

Offshore Mineral Dredging

Dr. Godman: To ask the Secretary of State for the Environment if he will outline the procedure that will be employed, under the recently announced review of licence applications for mineral dredging offshore to ensure that such activities are not damaging to the fish stocks, sea bird populations and marine mammals; and if he will make a statement.

Mr. Chope: The revised procedures for determining licence applications for minerals dredging issued earlier this year make provision for an environmental assessment (EA) to be undertaken into the application where the Crown Estate Commissioners judge this to be necessary.

Among the criteria used to assess the need for an EA are the potential impact of the dredging area on a marine nature reserve; the inclusion in the dredging areas of an important fish (including shell fish) spawning area or nursery ground; or whether the dredging area is within an area which supports a known important commercial fishery. A copy of the revised procedures is available in the Library.

These new procedures reflect the important role which marine sand and gravel play in maintaining supplies to the construction industry whilst recognising the need to safeguard sea fisheries and the marine environment.

Listed Buildings

Mr. Sedgemore: To ask the Secretary of State for the Environment if he has any plans to introduce new legislation to safeguard listed buildings where redevelopment is proposed.

Mrs. Virginia Bottomley: No. We are satisfied that existing legislation provides an adequate framework for the protection of listed buildings.

Mr. Sedgemore: To ask the Secretary of State for the Environment (1) if he will list those schemes in the City of London which he has approved since June 1987 which would allow developers to pull down listed buildings;

(2) if he will list those schemes which he has approved since June 1987 which would allow developers to pull down five or more grade 2 listed buildings to enable redevelopment to go ahead.

Mrs. Virginia Bottomley: I will write to the hon. Member.

Mr. Sedgemore: To ask the Secretary of State for the Environment (1) if he will set out the criteria he uses to determine whether listed buildings should be retained in applications for redevelopment;

(2) if, in the light of his decision to allow redevelopment of the Mappin and Webb site in the City of London, he will make a statement on his policy as regards preserving listed buildings.

Mrs. Virginia Bottomley: The Government's policy and criteria in respect of the protection of listed buildings are set out in DoE circular 8/87.

Immigrating Birds (Protected Species)

Mr. Ron Davies: To ask the Secretary of State for the Environment what action he is taking to ensure the adequate protection of immigrating birds of protected species.

Mrs. Virginia Bottomley: The Wildlife and Countryside Act provides a statutory framework for the protection of all wild birds in Great Britain including those who migrate here from overseas. Where appropriate, further action is taken through the classification of special protection areas under article 4 of EC directive 79/409 EEC.

Endangered Species

Mr. Ron Davies: To ask the Secretary of State for the Environment what criteria he follows in determining appeals against refusal for import licences under CITES; how many such applications have been made in each of the last three years; and of these how many were approved.

Mrs. Virginia Bottomley: Applications for import licences are decided on their merits, in the light of advice from our scientific advisers and in accordance with the requirements of EC regulation 3626/82 which implements the convention on international Trade in Endangered Species (CITES) within the European Community. There is no statutory right of appeal against the refusal of an import licence, but if new evidence is presented the Department is normally willing to reconsider applications which have been refused. The Department has no record of the number of applications which have been reconsidered.

Submarine Base, Faslane

Mr. Rogers: To ask the Secretary of State for the Environment what is the length of delay in the construction of the ship lift in the Clyde submarine base at Faslane; what penalty clauses exist in the contract; and if any of these clauses have been invoked.

Mr. Chope *[holding answer 9 June 1989]:* I refer the hon. Member to the answer I gave the hon. Member for Dumbarton (Mr. McFall) on Tuesday 23 May at column *497.* The contract does not contain penalty clauses, but liquidated damages may be invoked once a contract completion data has been passed. For commercial reasons it would not be appropriate to comment further at this stage.

Written Answers to Questions

Friday 16 June 1989

SCOTLAND

Gaelic Broadcasting

Mr. Kennedy: To ask the Secretary of State for Scotland what discussions he has had with *(a)* BBC Scotland, and *(b)* STV on the future of Gaelic broadcasting; and if he will make a statement.

Mr. Rifkind: Earlier this year I met the chief executives of Scottish Television, Grampian Television and Border Television to discuss their views on the White Paper "Broadcasting in the '90s: Competition, Choice and Quality" and on the possible future arrangements for broadcasting in Scotland, including the future of Gaelic broadcasting. My officials had similar discussions with staff of BBC Scotland and last December I discussed Gaelic broadcasting with BBC representatives at the offices of Radio Nan Eilean in Stornoway. In April this year, I met representatives of Comunn na Gaidhlig specifically to hear their views on the future of Gaelic broadcasting.

As my right hon. Friend the Home Secretary said during his statement on 13 June, we will make announcements before long on our proposals for Gaelic broadcasting.

Severe Weather (Highlands and Islands)

Mr. Kennedy: To ask the Secretary of State for Scotland when he expects to be in a position to respond to the several letters outstanding from the hon. Member for Ross, Cromarty and Skye concerning specific cases of individual financial losses or commercial damage as a result of the severe weather conditions in the Highlands and Islands earlier in the current year; and if he will make a statement.

Mr. Michael Forsyth: A reply covering all eight cases raised by the hon. Member for Ross, Cromarty and Skye was sent by my noble Friend the Minister of State on 27 April, the day on which my right hon. and learned Friend the Secretary of State announced the Government's package of measures for assisting with storm damage *Hansard,* columns *609-12.*

A follow-up letter from the hon. Member on behalf of one of the cases involved is being considered and a reply will be issued shortly.

Unified Business Rate

Mr. Kirkwood: To ask the Secretary of State for Scotland if he will consider introducing a link between rate poundages in Scotland and the new unified business rate to be applied in England after 1990.

Mr. Lang: We have announced firm proposals to achieve a common rate poundage for Scotland at the same level as for England. We are seeking powers through the current Local Government and Housing Bill to enable us to prescribe the actual non-domestic rate of each local authority for a transitional period beginning in 1990-91. Our intention is that rate poundages in Scotland will generally be reduced relative to the uniform business rate in England and Wales so that, after five years or so, they will be brought into line with the rate in England and Wales.

Mr. Kirkwood To ask the Secretary of State for Scotland if he will consider introducing an extension of the mechanism of industrial derating to commercial premises in Scotland in the period leading up to the introduction of the unified business rate.

Mr. Lang: The future of industrial derating will fall to be considered once the likely effect of the 1990 revaluations on different sides of the Border and on different sectors of property become known later this year.

Mr. Kirkwood: To ask the Secretary of State for Scotland if he will provide for interim relief to business rate payers in Scotland to take account of the discrepancies in rates paid north and south of the English border in the period leading up to the introduction of the unified business rate.

Mr. Lang: The plans I have announced will ensure that the discrepancies are removed on a reasonable timetable which takes account of the likely timetable of changes in England and Wales.

Land Registration (Scotland) Act 1979

Mr. Kirkwood: To ask the Secretary of State for Scotland if he will make a statement on progress being made to implement the provisions of the Land Registration (Scotland) Act 1979.

Lord James Douglas-Hamilton: Progress to date has been as follows:
Operational area and date of implementation
County of Renfrew—6 April 1981.
County of Dumbarton—4 October 1982.
County of Lanark—3 January 1984.
County of the Barony and Regality of Glasgow—30 September 1985.

These four counties contain about 30 per cent. of the housing stock of Scotland.

Further extension of the Land Register will be undertaken once current backlogs in the General Register of Sasines and the Land Register have been substantially reduced.

Local Health Councils

Mr. Kirkwood: To ask the Secretary of State for Scotland if he will make a statement on the future role of local health councils in Scotland.

Mr. Michael Forsyth: I am considering a number of proposals put to me, and I shall make an announcement on this in the near future.

General Register of Sasines

Mr. Kirkwood: To ask the Secretary of State for Scotland if he will publish in the *Official Report* the average length of time it has taken to record a deed in the General Register of Sasines over the last 10 years.

Lord James Douglas-Hamilton: The information is as follows:

Average turnround time in days

Year	Days
1979	63
1980	64
1981	85
1982	79
1983	115
1984	123
1985	110
1986	110
1987	137
1988	158

Note: Turnround time is the number of calendar days between receipt of a writ for recording and its return to the presenter.

Tourism

Mr. Kirkwood: To ask the Secretary of State for Scotland if he will take urgent steps to introduce common methods for use by assessors in Scotland when deciding questions relating to the status of tourist accommodation to include guidance in the assessment of the domestic element in computing the commercial rateable value of hotels and guest houses, the criteria to be used to classify bed-and-breakfast establishments as commercial subjects not subject to the standard community charge and circumstances to be taken into account in deciding whether self-catering cottages are subject to the payment of the full standard community charge.

Mr. Lang: There are no plans to do this. The decisions of assessors and community charges registration officers in matters of this kind are subject to appeal.

Solicitors' Fees and Court Expenses

Mr. Kirkwood: To ask the Secretary of State for Scotland what steps he is taking to ensure that statutory instruments dealing with matters such as solicitors' fees and court expenses are not implemented until after the regulations are made available to the legal profession.

Lord James Douglas-Hamilton: I appreciate the desire of solicitors for adequate notification of forthcoming revisions to solicitors fees and court expenses. The normal arrangements for publishing statutory instruments permit this.

Tourism

Mr. Kirkwood: To ask the Secretary of State for Scotland what steps he is taking to monitor the effect the introduction of the community charge is having on the tourist industry in Scotland; and if he will make a statement.

Mr. Lang: The effects of rating reform on the various sectors of the tourist industry are being looked at in the light of representations which have been received.

Mr. Kirkwood: To ask the Secretary of State for Scotland when he next plans to meet representatives of the Scottish tourist industry to discuss the effects on tourism of the introduction of the community charge in Scotland.

Mr. Lang: My right hon. and learned Friend has no plans to do so.

East Kilbride Development Corporation

Mr. Ingram: To ask the Secretary of State for Scotland if he intends to maintain the existing number of appointees from local authorities to the board of East Kilbride development corporation when appointments fall to be made to the board.

Mr. Lang: In appointing members to new town development corporations, the Secretary of State is required to consult the local authorities and to have regard to the desirability of securing the services of at least one person resident in or having special knowledge of the locality. Both East Kilbride district council and Strathclyde regional council have been invited to offer nominees for vacancies due to arise in the board of East Kilbride development corporation on 1 January 1990. I cannot say at this stage what will be the outcome of that consultation, but all members are appointed because of the contribution their personal qualities enable them to make to the new towns.

Forestry Commission Land

Sir Hector Monro: To ask the Secretary of State for Scotland what plans the Government has with regard to the disposal of Forestry Commission land.

Mr. Rifkind: In answer to a question from the hon. Member for Suffolk, Central (Mr. Lord) on 8 November 1984 (*Official Report*, columns 6-7), my right hon. Friend the Member for Ayr (Mr. Younger) announced that the Forestry Commission's disposals programme would be extended to 31 March 1989, and that its main purpose would be to rationalise the forestry estate thereby improving the commission's efficiency and the commercial effectiveness of the forestry enterprise.

We welcome the important contribution that the rationalisation of the forestry estate has made to the increased efficiency of the forestry enterprise over the past few years. The commission has been able to dispose of a large number of plantations in a way which has assisted the streamlining of its management structure and enabled it to achieve significant improvements in its operational efficiency. The annual net call on Exchequer funds for the enterprise has been greatly reduced. At the same time the commission has been able to make an important contribution to the major new developments which have taken place in the wood-processing industry in recent years. The market for timber is now buoyant, to the great benefit of both public and private sector timber-growers.

My right hon. Friends and I have considered the future extent and purpose of the commission's disposal programme. We have had regard to the needs of the wood-processing industry for a steady and secure source of supply; to the effect of the programme on the use of the commission's forests for public access and recreation; and to environmental considerations. We also accept that the commission must be able to plan ahead without the uncertainty caused by frequent reviews, and that it will continue to make a small but effective contribution towards the fulfilment of our targets for new planting.

We consider that the rationalisation policy has been successful and that there is scope for it to continue to be pursued with vigour. In accordance with the general policy of this Government, we also wish to see some further transfer of forests out of the public sector. This will have the important effect of strengthening and enhancing the role of the private sector, whose proportion of the nation's woodland estate has already risen to over 60 per cent. We also see it as a valuable opportunity to widen interest and participation in British forestry.

We have therefore asked the Forestry Commissioners to proceed with the further disposal of some 100,000 hectares of forestry land and properties in the period up to the end of the century, of which they should seek to dispose of some 50,000 hectares in the first half of the period. The commissioners will continue to be responsible for selecting properties for sale, and in doing so they will have regard to the selection guidelines which forestry Ministers set them in 1981. In particular I have referred to the use of the commission's forests for public access and recreation, which my right hon. Friends and I warmly support and encourage. Forests have a major part to play in the enjoyment and understanding of the countryside and the commission will continue to have an important role in this.

We are concerned, however, that the general public should also continue to enjoy access to those forests to be disposed of by the commission in a way which is compatible with management for forestry and other purposes. We are therefore giving careful consideration to ways of achieving the objective.

It is estimated that, subject to market factors, the programme which we have now asked the commissioners to carry out should realise up to £150 million over the period. By settling this issue for a decade, we intend to put the commissioners in a position to implement the programme so as to consolidate their forestry estate in a rational and orderly manner.

Head Injuries (Rehabilitation Centre)

Mr. Kirkwood: To ask the Secretary of State for Scotland what recent representations he has received on the need to establish a centre in the south of Scotland for the rehabilitation of persons suffering from head injuries; and what progress has been made in funding the necessary resources and possible site for such a centre.

Mr. Michael Forsyth *[holding answer 15 June 1989]:* I have had a number of letters about improving rehabilitation services in Scotland for people suffering from head injuries. I expect to receive a report very shortly, following a study by the Scottish Home and Health Department, on how these services could be improved, and what arrangements for funding and location would be appropriate.

PRIME MINISTER

Falkland Islands

Mr. Dalyell: To ask the Prime Minister if she will meet President-elect Carlos Menem to discuss the future of the Falkland Islands.

The Prime Minister: No.

OVERSEAS DEVELOPMENT

Namibian Refugees

Mr. Atkinson: To ask the Secretary of State for Foreign and Commonwealth Affairs how much money Her Majesty's Government has allocated to assist in the repatriation of Namibian refugees; and how this will be deployed.

Mr. Chris Patten: We have provided £1·15 million— £500,000 to the United Nations High Commissioner for Refugees and £650,000 to the World Food Programme for food for the returnees.

Aid

Sir John Stanley: To ask the Secretary of State for Foreign and Commonwealth Affairs, further to his reply to the hon. Member for Eccles (Miss Lestor) of 12 June, *Official Report,* column *274,* what figures he used for *(a)* net development assistance, and *(b)* gross national product, in calculating the figure of 0·32 per cent.

Mr. Chris Patten: The figures are as follows:

	£ million
Net official development assistance	1,467·84
Gross national product	459,610

Grants

Sir John Stanley: To ask the Secretary of State for Foreign and Commonwealth Affairs if he will list the grants to United Kingdom non-governmental organisations engaged in overseas development made by the European Community in the latest year for which figures are available.

Mr. Chris Patten: Under its NGO programme the European Community co-finances projects in developing countries and development education projects with European NGOs. Normally the Community contributes 50 per cent. of the costs of individual projects. In 1987, the latest year for which figures are available, amounts granted to United Kingdom NGOs were as follows:

1. For projects in developing countries

	£
Accord	384,571
Action Aid	298,789
Africa Now	41,823
Aga Khan Foundation	253,521
Christian Aid	883,272
Commonwealth Trade Union Council	169,086
Concern Universal	30,929
Cooperation for Development	633,954
Friends of Ngora Hospital	91,472
Health Unlimited	68,375
Help the Aged	446,044
International Boys Town Trust	17,767
Intermediate Technology Development Group	84,094
Leonard Cheshire Foundation	74,115
Namibia Refugees	89,060
Order of St. John	165,914
Oxfam	1,310,327
Population Concern	212,666
Population Services	446,373
Richmond Fellowship	158,701
Rufiji Leprosy Trust	57,242
Save the Children Fund	268,308
SOS Sahel International	253,521
Sylvia Wright Trust	28,798
Tear Fund	94,105
Twin	229,640
Voluntary Service Overseas	279,183
World University Service—United Kingdom	26,976
War on Want	140,845

	£
	7,239,471

2. For Development Education

	£
Action for World Development Fund	38,028
Africa Centre	85,241
CAFOD	99,615
Centre for World Development Education	45,634
Christian Aid	49,403
Catholic Institute of International Relations	83,594
Federal Trust	21,127
International Boys Town Trust	10,203
National Association of Developing Education Centres	74,690
Namibia Support Committee	62,639
Oxfam	44,703
Oxford House Trust	18,612
Returned Volunteer Action	65,705
TV Trust for Environment	76,125
Voluntary Service Overseas	19,177
Workers Education Association	32,917
World Development Group	19,471
	846,884

Sir John Stanley: To ask the Secretary of State for Foreign and Commonwealth Affairs which official bodies and organisations outside the United Kingdom make grants to United Kingdom non-governmental organisations engaged in overseas development after either consulting or obtaining the approval of his Department.

Mr. Chris Patten: There are no formal arrangements for organisations outside the United Kingdom to consult my Department or seek its approval before making grants to United Kingdom voluntary agencies engaged in overseas development. But we are happy to put such organisations in touch with British agencies if asked to do so; and we have taken the initiative in encouraging the Japanese to use their grant aid in support of projects undertaken in developing countries by British and other third country NGOs.

NORTHERN IRELAND

Republic of Ireland

Mr. Dennis Canavan: To ask the Secretary of State for Northern Ireland what subjects were discussed at his last meeting with representatives of the Government of the Republic of Ireland.

Mr. Tom King: I last met representatives of the Government of the Republic of Ireland at the meeting of the intergovernmental conference in Belfast on 24 May. At that meeting we completed the review of the working of the conference and copies of the joint statement were placed in the Library.

Mitchell House School for the Handicapped

Mr. John D. Taylor (Stratford): To ask the Secretary of State for Northern Ireland how many pupils are resident at Mitchell House school for the handicapped, Holywood road, Belfast; what proposals he has for them after the closure of this school; and at which other similar schools there is residential accommodation available for these students.

Dr. Mawhinney [*holding answer 15 June 1989*]: Ten pupils are currently attending the boarding department at Mitchell House special school, Belfast. The only other school providing residential accommodation for physically handicapped pupils is Fleming Fulton special school, Belfast. I understand that the Belfast education and library board is currently considering the closure of the boarding department at Mitchell House school but no decision has yet been taken. Should the board decide to close this facility, it would be required to publish a development proposal which would enable objectors to make their views known to the Department of Education within two months. The Department would have the ultimate decision in the matter.

TRADE AND INDUSTRY

Press (Referral)

Mr. Allen: To ask the Chancellor of the Duchy of Lancaster what is the current position of the referral of the press to the Office of Fair Trading and Monopolies and Mergers Commission.

Mr. Maude: I understand that the Director General of Fair Trading is continuing his inquiries into the structure of newspaper publishing, competition between newspapers, and the involvement of newspaper groups in other media. If a full-scale investigation were seen to be necessary it would be likely to take the form of a reference to the Monopolies and Mergers Commission.

Inflation

Mrs. Mahon: To ask the Chancellor of the Duchy of Lancaster what representations he has received on the effects of the level of inflation on industry.

Mr. Forth: A number of representations which I receive refer to inflation. The great majority of these recognise that the control of inflation must remain the prime objective of economic policy.

Manufactures (Trade Deficit)

Mr. Canavan: To ask the Chancellor of the Duchy of Lancaster what is the present trade deficit on manufactured goods.

Mr. Alan Clark: In the first four months of 1989 there was an estimated seasonally adjusted deficit in trade in manufactures of £5·8 billion.

Open University Technology Centre

Mr. Flynn: To ask the Chancellor of the Duchy of Lancaster if he has any plans to visit the newly founded centre for technology strategy at the Open university in Milton Keynes.

Mr. Forth: The Chancellor of the Duchy of Lancaster is aware of the recent formation of the centre for technology strategy at the Open university in Milton Keynes but has no plans for a visit.

NATIONAL FINANCE

Full Funding

Mr. Allen: To ask the Chancellor of the Exchequer what he expects to achieve through the Government's policy of full funding.

Mr. Lilley: The aim of the full fund policy is that the Government should conduct their own financial affairs so as to have a broadly neutral impact on liquidity.

Housing Costs

Mr. Chris Smith: To ask the Chancellor of the Exchequer if, further to the Economic Secretary's answer to the hon. Member for Islington, South and Finsbury on 12 June, *Official Report*, column *272*, he will indicate what other housing costs are included in the Italian index of consumer prices quoted by him on 7 June; and what housing costs other than mortgage interest payments are included in the United Kingdom retail price index figures.

Mr. Lilley *[holding answer 15 June 1989]:* The only housing costs included in the Italian consumer price index are rent, water charges and repairs. The housing group of the United Kingdom RPI includes rent, domestic rates, water and other charges, repair and maintenance charges, do-it-yourself materials and dwelling insurance and ground rents as well as mortgage interest payments.

CIVIL SERVICE

Crown Servants (Business Appointments)

Mr. Cyril D. Townsend: To ask the Minister for the Civil Service whether he will publish a further report on business appointments of former Crown servants.

Mr. Luce: I have today placed copies of a statistical report entitled "Acceptance of Outside Appointments by Crown Servants—1988" in the Libraries of both Houses of Parliament.

TRANSPORT

Lead in Paint

Mr. Andrew Smith: To ask the Secretary of State for Transport when he expects lead to be eliminated from paint used for road markings.

Mr. Peter Bottomley: The constituents of road materials are specified by the British Standards Institution. I understand that the institution has not yet set a timetable for substituting a lead-free pigment in their specification. Work to develop such a pigment of acceptable performance and durability is in progress.

Pervious Road Surfaces

Mr. Amos: To ask the Secretary of State for Transport what conclusions have been drawn from the research into pluvious road surfaces being carried out at the Transport and Road Research Laboratory with regard to *(a)* whether spray-reducing benefit can be applied to the resurfacing of existing roads and *(b)* whether this will be a general specification of new roads as proposed in the White Paper, "Roads for Prosperity"; and if he will make a statement.

Mr. Peter Bottomley: The Transport and Road Research Laboratory has been undertaking a full-scale trial of pervious macadam road surfaces since 1984 on the A38 Burton bypass.

Trials of new materials normally last for five years so that their performance can be compared with conventional materials before they are permitted for general use.

In this case the material appears to be as durable as conventional materials and is effective in reducing vehicle spray.

We are proposing to amend the Department's specification to allow the use of pervious macadam on new or existing trunk roads. The aim is to issue it early in 1990 as soon as the trials have been completed and the results fully assessed. This will depend on those results being satisfactory.

Pervious macadam could prove more expensive than conventional materials and if so its use is more likely to be justified on sections of road where, for example, increased accident savings can be demonstrated.

MV Majestic (Sinking)

Mr. Foulkes: To ask the Secretary of State for Transport what information he has concerning the circumstances in which the fishing vessel MV Majestic was sunk between Shetland and Orkney on 13 June; and if he will make a statement.

Mr. Portillo: The Fraserburgh registered fishing vessel Majestic capsized and sank some 30 miles west of Sumburgh Head at about 1300 on 13 June with the loss of five lives. Two crew survived.

The vessel was pair trawling at the time of the incident when the net snagged on an underwater obstruction. There are no indications at this stage of any involvement by a submarine.

One of the Department's marine surveyors has been appointed to investigate the casualty.

Birmingham Relief Road

Mr. Richard Shepherd: To ask the Secretary of State for Transport what was his Department's latest estimated cost for completion of the previously preferred route for the Birmingham relief road; and if he will estimate the number of man hours his Department has spent on the previously preferred route.

Mr. Portillo *[holding answer 15 June 1989]:* The estimated cost of the Birmingham northern relief road is £219·5 million at May 1989 prices. The Department is unable to disaggregate the number of man hours spent on individual schemes.

ENERGY

Electrical Supply Industry

Mr. Blair: To ask the Secretary of State for Energy what is the current number of people employed in the electrical supply industry by region.

Mr. Parkinson: This is a matter for the electricity supply industry. I shall ask the Chairman of the Electricity Council to write to the hon. Member.

Rexo (Member's Letter)

Mr. Ashton: To ask the Secretary of State for Energy whether he is now in a position to reply and treat as a matter of urgency the letter from the hon. Member for Bassetlaw of 11 April regarding redundancy payments at Rexo which was passed on to him by the Department of Employment on 30 May.

Mr. Michael Spicer: The hon. Member should now have received my reply which was sent on 14 June.

WALES

School-Business Links

Mr. Barry Jones: To ask the Secretary of State for Wales if he will make a statement on his Department's policy of encouraging high schools in Wales to develop links with businesses.

Mr. Peter Walker: It is important that there should be effective links between schools and business so that young people have the opportunity to experience the world of work and learn about the career choices available to them, and business has a workforce better prepared and equipped to meet its needs.

We have a range of activities designed to improve communications between schools and industry and to encourage enterprise activities in schools. The Technical and Vocational Education Initiative has proved successful and is being extended to all schools and colleges. The GCSE examination has an emphasis on learning by experience and the certificate of pre-vocational education also assists in the transition from school to adulthood and the world of work. The new national curriculum has as one of its main aims the preparation of pupils for adult life and work. Businessmen also have the opportunity to become governors of schools and colleges.

Each local education authority in Wales has an officer responsible for education/industry links and there is evidence of increasing interest in organisations at the local level working to develop partnerships between education and industry.

In addition, we now have a network of enterprise and education advisers whose purpose is to market to employers the benefits of links with schools and persuade them to become involved. Also, in the context of my valleys programme, I have met with the chairmen of the education committee and director of education of each of the five valleys LEAs to discuss ways of improving links between schools and industry. Positive action has already been taken and I hope to have further meetings in the near future.

Sewage Works (Pollution Standards)

Mr. Livsey: To ask the Secretary of State for Wales whether he will list sewage works in Wales that are at present failing the established effluent pollution standards.

Mr. Grist: The following Welsh Water Authority sewage treatment works failed to meet their consent standards during 1988:

Ross New (Lower Cleeve)
Kenderchurch
Presteigne
Llanbister
Eardisley
Rockfield
Llanbedr
Ponthir
Bonvilston
Weycock Cross
Acton Green
Stoke Edith
Hereford Rotherwas
St. Owens Cross
Fair View
Llanwarne—Monkton Place
Walford (Caughton Place)
Carnay
Kidwelly
Rhydypandy
Carew
Kilgetty East/Stepaside
Rosemarket
Devils Bridge
Llanybyther
Rhandirmyn
Brithdir
Bryncrug
Dolgellau
Llandwcwyn
Tyddyn Hywel
Cynon
Deinolen (Brynrefail)
Edwin Ralph
Ffeirh
Fountain
Glewstone-Wilson
Groes Bronallt
Gwalchmai
Talybont (Price Bros.)
Llangefni
Llanfaes 'A'
Sarnau
Sesswick
Five Fords
Mold (Filters Plant)
Gresford
Maes Y Groes
Penley
Henllan
Denbigh
Nantglyn
Llanbedr Dyffryn Clwyd
Burton
Flint
Bagillt (East)
Bethesda
Bettws
Brendenbury
Bynea
Capel Iwan
Cefn Mawr
Chwilog
Cilfynydd
Cilgerran
Clyro
Connahs Quay
Coolech
Crossgates
Cwmyoy
Rhoslefain
Rhydymawyn
Spamington
St. Arvans
Tirabad
Weston Beggard
Wolferlow
Ystradgynlais
Kupeck
Kington
Langdon
Llanarmon Yn Ial
Llanddew
Llandegfan (Red)

Llanfechreth
Llanfaes 'B'
Llanfaethlu
Llanfaglan
Llangaffo
LLangyli
Llanrhidian
Llanrug
Llansey
Llanvapley
Llanyre
Llanystumdwy
Llynfaes
Llysuen Village
Melin Y Wig
Pentraeth
Pentre Halkyn
Penygausi

Local Authority Houses

Mr. Livsey: To ask the Secretary of State for Wales if he will list the number of local authority houses to rent by district in Wales in *(a)* 1986, *(b)* 1987 and *(c)* 1988.

Mr. Grist: The information requested is as follows:

Estimates of dwellings owned by local authorities or new towns at 1 April[1]

Welsh Districts	1986	1987	1988
Aberconwy	3,227	3,139	3,060
Alyn and Deeside	5,573	5,503	5,415
Arfon	5,304	5,237	5,194
Blaenau Gwent	11,012	10,871	10,749
Brecknock	3,095	3,019	2,967
Cardiff	22,551	21,776	21,190
Carmarthen	3,740	3,711	3,661
Ceredigion	3,700	3,662	3,631
Colwyn	2,877	2,821	2,746
Cynon Valley	5,699	5,596	5,497
Delyn	5,088	4,992	4,864
Dinefwr	2,795	2,755	2,711
Dwyfor	1,490	1,484	1,478
Glyndwr	3,284	3,217	3,154
Islwyn	6,858	6,667	6,470
Llanelli	7,626	7,529	7,360
Lliw Valley	5,547	5,458	5,351
Meirionnydd	2,259	2,203	2,153
Merthyr Tydfil	7,541	7,357	7,145
Monmouth	5,388	5,351	5,185
Montgomery[2]	4,626	4,503	4,435
Neath	6,190	6,096	5,959
Newport	14,020	13,839	13,699
Ogwr	10,892	10,613	10,333
Port Talbot	7,115	6,834	6,539
Preseli	6,286	6,200	6,117
Radnor	1,268	1,262	1,220
Rhondda	5,234	5,153	5,095
Rhuddlan	2,907	2,905	2,862
Rhymney Valley	10,920	10,641	10,460
South Pembrokeshire	3,112	3,072	3,005
Swansea	18,788	18,554	18,196
Taff-Ely	8,609	8,356	8,030
Torfaen	14,787	14,519	14,222
Vale of Glamorgan	7,105	6,927	6,738
Wrexham Maelor	16,857	16,666	16,533
Ynys Môn	6,087	6,037	5,994
Wales Total	259,457	254,525	249,418

[1] Includes some dwellings unavailable for rent, undergoing repair or improvement, awaiting sale or demolition, etc.
[2] Includes new town dwellings in Newton.

Cottage–Community Hospitals

Mr. Livsey: To ask the Secretary of State for Wales whether he can give for each county in Wales the number of cottage-community hospitals with fewer than 70 beds in *(a)* 1985 and *(b)* 1988, and the percentage these represented of the total number of hospitals in (i) 1985 and (ii) 1988.

Mr. Grist: The total number of hospitals, including psychiatric hospitals, with less than 70 beds are shown in the table:

	Number of hospitals with fewer than 70 beds[1]		Percentage of all hospitals in authority	
Health Authority	1985	1988	1985	1988
Clwyd	15	17	60·0	70·8
East Dyfed	7	7	58·3	58·3
Gwent	8	8	44·4	44·4
Gwynedd	16	18	76·2	81·8
Mid Glamorgan	13	15	41·9	46·9
Pembrokeshire	1	1	33·3	33·3
Powys	11	11	73·3	73·3
South Glamorgan	5	5	31·3	31·3
West Glamorgan	10	8	52·6	50·0

[1] As at 31 December.

Rivers (Pollution Standards)

Mr. Livsey: To ask the Secretary of State for Wales whether he will list those rivers in Wales which in 1988 were graded 3 and lower in pollution standards.

Mr. Grist: This is a matter for the Welsh Water Authority and I will ask the chairman to write to the hon. Gentleman.

Small Businesses

Mr. Nicholas Bennett: To ask the Secretary of State for Wales what is the average time taken to process applications for discretionary grants in respect of capital investments by small businesses; and what action is being taken by his Department to reduce the time taken to process applications and forward grants.

Mr. Peter Walker: The main forms of discretionary grants towards capital investment by small firms are regional enterprise grants (investment) and regional selective assistance. The average times taken to process grant applications and payment claims during the period 1 January—31 May 1989 were as follows:

	Weeks
Regional enterprise grants (investment) applications	3·9
Regional enterprise grants (investment) payment claims	1·2
Regional selective assistance applications	7
Regional selective assistance payment claims	3·1

The Department is continuing its downward pressure on processing times consistent with the proper administration of the scheme.

Botulism

Mr. Michael: To ask the Secretary of State for Wales what consideration was given by officers of his Department to the need to publish advice to the public in Wales prior to the Government's recommendation on Monday 12 June that people should not consume hazelnut yoghurt pending the outcome of investigations into the recent incidents of botulism.

Mr. Peter Walker: My Department became aware of suspected cases of botulism associated with the consumption of hazelnut yoghurt on 12 June. Standard arrangements are that the Department of Health notifies national and regional media interests in such cases, including those in Wales. Copies of the Department of Health's press statement were subsequently sent by my Department to chief environmental health officers and medical officers for environmental health in Wales for information.

Mr. Michael: To ask the Secretary of State for Wales, what information he has available on the cases of botulism in Clwyd referred to in the answer of his right hon. Friend to the private notice question on Tuesday 13 June.

Mr Peter Walker: My officials are in close touch with the chief administrative medical officer/director of public health medicine in Clwyd health authority regarding the four suspected cases of botulism. Investigations are continuing as to the source of the outbreak.

Food Hygiene

Mr. Michael: To ask the Secretary of State for Wales what research projects into food hygiene and food production are currently sponsored by his Department; what resources are allocated to each project and what plans he has for expanding such research in Wales.

Mr. Peter Walker: My Department has no agricultural research funds. Last year the Government funded 436 research projects on food in England and Wales. Details can be found in the draft National Programme of Food R&D 1988-89, a copy of which was placed in the Library of the House on 13 June 1989.

Future plans for Government funded research will be guided by the advice of the Research Consultative Committee on Food Safety and Applied Nutrition which is expected to report at the end of August. This Government are firmly committed to food safety research and will place the work with the most appropriate contractors.

Mr. Michael: To ask the Secretary of State for Wales whether he will make it his policy to increase the resources available to local authorities in Wales to enable them to increase the number of environmental health officers available to inspect food producing and processing establishments in view of fresh public concern over dangers to health.

Mr. Grist: Provision for local authority spending in 1989-90 was announced in the rate support grant report published on 8 December 1988. My officials are presently discussing with the local authority associations their need to spend for 1990-91.

The bulk of resources provided to local authorities are unhypothecated: it is for the individual authority to determine its own spending priorities.

Mr. Michael: To ask the Secretary of State for Wales what steps he is taking to ensure the future security of adequate funding levels with predictable continuity for S4C in the light of the statement on 13 June, by the Home Secretary on the future of commercial television.

Mr. Peter Walker: The White Paper on broadcasting made clear the Government's view that S4C has been a considerable success. At present the Independent Broadcasting Authority determines the channel's level of income. My right hon. Friend the Home Secretary and I envisage that the Independent Television Commission and S4C will make similar arrangements to ensure adequate funding for the channel in the future.

HEALTH

Project 2000

Mr. McLoughlin: To ask the Secretary of State for Health what will be the level of bursaries to be paid to nursing students undertaking the first Project 2000 training courses; and if he will make a statement.

Mr. Kenneth Clarke: The Government have accepted the proposal of the United Kingdom Central Council for Nursing, Midwifery and Health Visiting, made after consultation with the nursing professions, that Project 2000 students should have student, rather than employee, status and receive bursaries rather than salaries. The personal element of these bursaries will not be means-tested.

Project 2000 students in receipt of bursaries will not be liable for income tax or national insurance or superannuation contributions. All Project 2000 students will pay only 20 per cent. of the personal community charge, like other full-time students, and will have the benefit of seven weeks' holiday each year, compared with the four or five weeks for those who continue to be trained under the existing arrangements.

The following basic levels of bursary are to be offered to students undertaking Project 2000 courses. They are broadly comparable with the average net basic salary of existing student nurses.

Under 26 at start of course:

	£
London:	4,700
	£
Elsewhere:	4,000

Age 26 and over at start of course:

	£
London:	5,200
	£
Elsewhere:	4,500

In addition to the above basic/personal levels of bursary, there will be additions for dependents which will be means-tested on the basis of Department of Education and Science mandatory grant rules.

Existing NHS staff who enter Project 2000 training, provided they have been employed at least one year, will retain their current salary rather than receiving a bursary.

Pre-registration nursing students who are not on Project 2000 courses will continue to receive salaries.

Private Patients (Doncaster)

Mr. Redmond: To ask the Secretary of State for Health what was the revenue generated from private patients at hospitals in the Doncaster area in 1988; and what were the comparable figures for each of the last 10 years, at 1989 prices.

Mr. Freeman: The available information is given in the table.

Income from private patients: Doncaster health authority (at 1988-89 prices)

	£
1978-79	17,141
1979-80	19,611
1980-81	27,382
1981-82	50,428
1982-83	53,757
1983-84	46,051
1984-85	52,258
1985-86	71,592
1986-87	79,595
1987-88	[1]65,837

[1] Latest available.

Notes:
1. The figures have been expressed at 1988-89 prices by the use of the gross domestic product deflator.
2. The Doncaster health authority was established on 1 April 1982. The figures used for earlier years are derived from the annual accounts of the former Doncaster area health authority which was broadly comparable to the present district health authority.

Community Charge

Mr. Wigley: To ask the Secretary of State for Health (1) what guidance has been given to registered medical practitioners on issuing certificates for poll tax exemption on the grounds that the individual is severely mentally impaired; and if he will make a statement;

(2) whether he has issued any guidance in relation to the poll tax on the question as to whether those seeking a certificate of exemption from a registered medical practitioner will be required to undergo any examination; who will pay for any such examination; if there will be guidance on any standard scale of charges; how much will be charged for such certificates; and who will be required to make the payment.

Mr. Freeman: I have been asked to reply.

The Government have no plans to introduce a poll tax.

Guidance to registered medical practitioners on issuing certificates of severe mental impairment in connection with applications for exemption from payment of the personal community charge will be issued as soon as possible.

Queen's Park Hospital, Blackburn (Maternity Unit)

Mr. Ken Hargreaves: To ask the Secretary of State for Health what discussions he has had with the North West regional health authority since 14 April regarding provision of a maternity unit at Queen's park hospital, Blackburn; and if he will make a statement.

Mr. Mellor: My hon. Friend the Parliamentary Under-Secretary of State for Health will be meeting the chairman of North Western regional health authority on 19 June to discuss the implications of the extension of maternity services in phase IIIA of Queen's Park hospital, Blackburn, for the region's current review of its capital programme. It is unlikely that the outcome of the review will be known before the autumn of this year.

Miss Claire Johnson

Mr. Cartwright: To ask the Secretary of State for Health when his Department's superannuation branch first received a request to transfer pension rights in respect of Miss Claire Johnson from the National Health Service to the Professional Association of Teachers; why it has failed to reply; and when he expects the transfer to be effected.

Mr. Freeman: National Health Service superannuation branch first received a request to transfer Miss Johnson's pension rights on 30 August 1988 when the Professional Association of Teachers (PAT) wrote. They enclosed a copy of correspondence they had sent to Central Nottinghamshire health authority about the same subject.

No reply, apart from an inquiry of the PAT about their scheme and routine acknowledgements, has yet been sent because the transfer value of the service was not apparently available. The health authority had exceptionally given details of Miss Johnson's final year's salary on 28 April 1988 when giving details about the cessation of her employment. This information was overlooked when the transfer request was received. A standard inquiry was therefore sent to the authority on 23 September 1988. Only when a belated reply was received on 8 May 1989 was attention drawn to the previous information.

Urgent action is being taken to give details of a pension transfer value. Miss Johnson will then have the option of transferring the pension value or leaving it in the National Health Service scheme.

Pharmacists

Mr. Ashley: To ask the Secretary of State for Health, pursuant to his answer of 19 May to the hon. Member for Swansea, East (Mr. Anderson) setting out the amount due to pharmacists from 1978 to 1988, if he will specify the amounts included which are in respect of drug and container cost reimbursement; whether the amounts due for profit are stated on a pre-interest basis; if he will express these as a percentage of turnover; and if he will give estimates of the amount due for costs in £m and the profit in £m and percentage of turnover for 1988-89 and 1989-90.

Mr. Mellor *[holding answer 15 June 1989]:* The figures given in my reply to the hon. Member for Swansea, East (Mr. Anderson) on 18 May at column *284,* excluded the payments made as reimbursement of expenditure on drugs and containers. The amounts due for profit included interest on capital employed. Amounts due for profit expressed as a percentage of amounts paid as reimbursement of expenditure on drugs and containers in England and Wales were as follows:

Year	Percentage
1978	3·57
1979	3·52
1980	4·78
1981	5·48
1982	5·10
1983	4·67
1984	4·62
[1]1985	5·28
1985-86	5·19
1986-87	4·79
1987-88	4·58

[1] 1 January 1985 to 31 March 1985.

Current estimates for 1988-89 are: amount due for costs £437·2 million amount due for profit £70·7 million, profit as a percentage of drug and container costs 3·68 per cent. As from 1 April 1989 amounts due for costs and profit are no longer calculated as separate items of remuneration.

Portable Oxygen Cylinders

Mr. McCartney: To ask the Secretary of State for Health what is the cost of a portable oxygen cylinder; and what guidance he issues to doctors on the provision of portable oxygen cylinders for use in the home and elsewhere by patients with chronic lung disease.

Mr. Mellor *[holding answer 15 June 1989]:* The basic cost of a portable oxygen cylinder is at least £157·00. Such equipment for use in the home and elsewhere may be provided through the hospital service on the prescription of a hospital consultant if he considers it clinically necessary for the treatment of his patient. Guidance on the provision of oxygen and other specialised equipment is contained in the booklet MHM50, "Provision of Medical and Surgical Appliances". A copy is in the Library.

Nebulisers

Mr. McCartney: To ask the Secretary of State for Health whether he will ensure that compressor-driven nebuliser systems are made available to patients when so advised by a consultant with specialist knowledge in thoracic medicine.

Mr. Mellor *[holding answer 15 June 1989]:* It is for health authorities to decide whether to issue compressor-driven nebuliser systems (either permanently or on loan) to patients for whom they are prescribed by hospital consultants. In making these decisions, health authorities will have regard to the costs of the equipment and its potential benefit to patients and the competing claims on available resources.

Benzodiazepines

Mr. Wareing: To ask the Secretary of State for Health on how many occasions, and by what means, his Department has drawn the attention of the medical profession to the dangers of represcribing benzodiazepine drugs; and if he will make a statement.

Mr. Mellor *[holding answer 15 June 1989]:* The Department issues regular advice to doctors on a wide range of topics which from time to time include guidance on the prescribing of benzodiazepines. Examples include:

  (i) Guidance on Good Clinical Practice in the Treatment of Drug Misuse, issued free in 1984 and 1985 to all doctors, includes advice on withdrawal from benzodiazepines. This publication is also issued annually to medical schools for distribution to final year medical students.
  (ii) The Committee on Safety of Medicines reinforced prescribing advice on benzodiazepines in "Current Problems No. 21" issued in January 1988.
  (iii) Up-to-date information on benzodiazepine prescribing is included in the British National Formulary, which is issued twice a year free to all doctors, pharmacists and to all first and final year medical students.
  (iv) The Drug and Therapeutics Bulletin, issued fortnightly and distributed free by the Department has, on occasions, published articles on benzodiazepines.

Mr. Wareing: To ask the Secretary of State for Health what advice he has received from the Committee on the Safety of Medicines on the use and prescribing of benzodiazepine drugs; and if he will make a statement.

Mr. Mellor *[holding answer 15 June 1989]:* The Committee on the Safety of Medicines advice about the use and prescribing of these drugs remains as published in its bulletin "Current Problems No. 21" issued in January 1988. A copy is in the Library.

FOREIGN AND COMMONWEALTH AFFAIRS

China

Mr. Adley: To ask the Secretary of State for Foreign and Commonwealth Affairs if he will make a statement on his latest meeting with the chargé d'affairs at the Chinese embassy in London.

Mr. Eggar: My right hon. and learned Friend's latest meeting with the Chinese chargé d'affaires was on 5 June. He reported this meeting to the House on 6 June. A senior official had a meeting with the Chinese chargé d'affaires on 12 June, at which he further clarified our view of events in Peking, particularly with respect to the prospects and procedures for the implimentation of the joint declarations on Hong Kong. He also raised reports of Chinese embassy harassment of Chinese students here and the case of the Hong Kong resident detained in Shanghai.

Mr. Sims: To ask the Secretary of State for Foreign and Commonwealth Affairs what information he has concerning allegations that Chinese students in this country have received threatening telephone calls from officials at the Chinese embassy; whether he has made representations to the Chinese chargé d'affaires on the matter; and if he will make a statement.

Mr. Eggar: We have noted press reports that the Chinese embassy has been harassing Chinese students in this country. A senior official raised this matter with the Chinese chargé d'affaires on 12 June and reminded him that we expected the Chinese embassy to act in accordance with British law. The Chinese chargé d'affaires said that the reports were a complete fabrication.

Mr. David Young: To ask the Secretary of State for Foreign and Commonwealth Affairs if he will grant to Chinese students studying in the United Kingdom, on completion of their courses, extension of stay until their safety can be guaranteed.

Mr. Renton: I have been asked to reply.
I refer the hon. Member to the reply that I have given today to questions from the hon. Members for Leyton (Mr. Cohen), for Leeds, West (Mr. Battle) and for Tooting (Mr. Cox).

Hong Kong

Mr. David Young: To ask the Secretary of State for Foreign and Commonwealth Affairs if he will seek to amend the treaty with China to exclude the stationing of the Chinese army in Hong Kong after 1997.

Mr. Eggar: The prospect of the stationing of Chinese troops in Hong Kong after 1997 has always been a matter of concern in the territory. Recent events have increased this. We shall be considering how best to meet this concern when we resume our discussions with the Chinese authorities about the future of Hong Kong. But we have no plans to seek to amend the joint declaration, which is a solemn international agreement equally binding both Governments.

Mr. David Young: To ask the Secretary of State for Foreign and Commonwealth Affairs what recent discussions he has had seeking to ensure that a democratic Government are fully in place in Hong Kong before 1997.

Mr. Eggar: In the light of recent events in China, and evidence of a change of opinion in Hong Kong, we and the Hong Kong Government are considering carefully suggestions for advancing and consolidating effective democracy in Hong Kong. My right hon. and learned Friend the Secretary of State discussed this question with the Governor of Hong Kong on his visit to London last week and will be having further discussions with a broad range of Hong Kong opinion when he visits the territory early next month.

Mr. Wajid Mahmood

Mr. Madden: To ask the Secretary of State for Foreign and Commonwealth Affairs when Mr. Wajid Mahmood, whose date of birth is 19 July 1971 and whose reference is IMM/92276, first applied to the post in Islamabad for permission to enter the United Kingdom; and when a decision is to be taken on his application.

Mr. Eggar: In accordance with the recent guidelines on the handling of representations by Members of Parliament in immigration cases, issued to Members on 14 December 1988, I have referred the question to the correspondence unit of migration and visa department of the Foreign and Commonwealth Office. The hon. Member will receive a reply from the unit in due course.

Mr. Abbass Tabbakhi (Execution)

Mr. Tony Banks: To ask the Secretary of State for Foreign and Commonwealth Affairs what information he has regarding the execution without trial in Iran of Mr. Abbass Tabbakhi of Forest Gate, London E7; when Mr Tabbakhi was arrested; when he was executed; and if he will make the stongest representation to the Iranian Government about the execution of Mr. Tabbakhi.

Mr. Waldegrave: We have no information about the case of Mr. Tabbakhi. It is usually impossible to verify reports of individual executions in Iran, given the absence of information about the situation there. We have consistently expressed concern about Iran's human rights record and have taken vigorous action at the UN to try to persuade Iran to allow the UN special rapporteur to visit that country.

Sharks (Slaughter)

Mr. Tony Banks: To ask the Secretary of State for Foreign and Commonwealth Affairs what representations he has made to the Governments of Japan and South Korea regarding the slaughter of sharks in the waters around the Galapagos Islands; and if he will make a statement.

Mr. Eggar: We have asked the Japanese and South Korean Governments for assurances that their fishing fleets around the Galapagos Islands are acting in accordance with their obligations on the protection of endangered species. Sharks are not protected under the Convention on International Trade in Endangered Species of Wild Fauna and Flora (CITES).

Private Education

Sir Michael McNair-Wilson: To ask the Secretary of State for Foreign and Commonwealth Affairs whether the sons and daughters of Foreign Office personnel can receive grants towards the cost of private education; and whether the Foreign and Commonwealth Office keeps a list of schools approved for the education of such young people.

Mr. Eggar: All members of the Diplomatic Service who have an obligation to serve overseas are eligible to apply for an allowance towards the costs of their children's boarding school education. The allowance is paid in order that children may be guaranteed continuity of education in the British system. In certain cases, provided the paramount principle of continuity is observed, it may be possible for an officer to be refunded the cost of private day school fees at a boarding school where the child will be educated when his/her parents are abroad.

The allowance is based on an average of the fees of schools on the Headmasters Conference list, but attendance is not limited to those schools. Any United Kingdom boarding school can be approved, provided that it offers the full range of subjects normally offered by a state day school and in a form generally available in the state system. No attempt is made to keep a comprehensive list of schools which meet those criteria.

Staff whose children are resident with them overseas may reclaim the cost of local private education in countries where the state education system is inadequate or unsuitable. Refunds in such cases are limited to tuition or scholastic activities of a kind which would be provided without cost under the United Kingdom state education services. Each overseas post maintains its own list of authorised schools.

AGRICULTURE, FISHERIES AND FOOD

Salmonella

Mr. Kirkwood: To ask the Minister of Agriculture, Fisheries and Food what assessment he has made of the adequacy of the current checks and controls for salmonella enteritidis undertaken by continental egg producers who export their produce to the United Kingdom.

Mr. Kirkwood: To ask the Minister of Agriculture, Fisheries and Food what plans he has to differentiate between eggs being sold in retail outlets for tested flocks as opposed to untested laying flocks.

Mr. Donald Thompson: It is a legal requirement that all UK flocks selling eggs should be tested. As for imports, I refer the hon. Member to the reply given to the hon. Member for Angus, East (Mr. Welsh) on 20 April at column *280*.

Mr. Nicholas Bennett: To ask the Minister of Agriculture, Fisheries and Food how many representations he has received for and against the continued sale of untreated green top milk; and whether he is now in a position to make a statement on such sales.

Mr. Donald Thompson: I refer my hon. Friend to the reply that my right hon. Friend the Minister gave to the hon. Member for Ludlow (Mr. Gill) on 13 June at column *353*.

Beef

Mr. Nicholas Bennett: To ask the Minister of Agriculture, Fisheries and Food what representations he has received about seasonal variations in the price of beef and consequent shortages; and if he will make a statement about any proposals to alter support arrangements in order to ensure that there is a more even supply of beef throughout the year.

Mr. Donald Thompson: The ending of the beef variable premium has removed from the support regime an element which included seasonal variation. However, in practice the rate of premium remained fixed at its maximum rate for extended periods which limited its impact. Under the present arrangements the EC Commission has at its disposal measures designed to moderate fluctuations in beef supply. It can release beef from intervention stocks onto the market when supplies are short or introduce aids to private storage to hold beef off the market in times of over supply. We and other member states encourage the Commission to make use of these provisions as appropriate to market circumstances.

French Potato Growers (Payments)

Mr. Nicholas Bennett: To ask the Minister of Agriculture, Fisheries and Food what representations he has received about possible retrospective payments being made to French early potato growers in Brittany; and if he will make a statement.

Mr. Ryder: I have received no such representations.

Deer (Slaughter)

Mr. Jopling: To ask the Minister of Agriculture, Fisheries and Food if he will introduce a compulsory slaughter scheme for deer suffering from tuberculosis.

Mr. Donald Thompson: Only a few herds are believed to be infected with tuberculosis, but in the interests of preventing it becoming established the Government have decided to introduce a compulsory slaughter scheme where this is necessary to control disease in deer kept in farms or parks. Compensation will be paid at 50 per cent. of the value of the slaughtered animal, subject to a ceiling. The necessary order under the Animal Health Act 1981 will be introduced as soon as possible. This measure, together with the steps already announced to make tuberculosis in deer a notifiable disease and to introduce movement controls and marking requirements, represent a major initiative by the Government to deal with the disease. I now hope that rapid progress can be made in devising a deer health scheme in co-operation with the industry.

NUVAN Fish 500 EC

Mr. Boswell: To ask the Minister of Agriculture, Fisheries and Food if a product licence under the Medicines Act 1968 has been issued for NUVAN Fish 500 EC; and if he will make a statement.

Mr. Donald Thompson: A product licence for Aquagard sea lice treatment (formerly known as NUVAN Fish 500 EC) was granted yesterday. The product licence was granted in accordance with the provisions of the Medicines Act 1968 following a detailed and thorough assessment of data relating to the safety, quality and efficacy of the product. As part of this assessment very careful consideration was given to the safety of the product to the fish, the consumers of treated fish, those operators administering the product and to the environment.

In reaching their decision to grant a product licence for Aquagard sea lice treatment Ministers were advised by the Veterinary Products Committee, an independent committee of experts in human and animal health. In reaching its recommendation, the Veterinary Products Committee took advice from experts in environmental safety.

SOCIAL SECURITY

Benefits

Mr. Oppenheim: To ask the Secretary of State for Social Security what transitional help the Government give to those people who lose their benefit entitlement due to taking up a full-time job, and thus find themselves financially worse off than previously.

Mr. Peter Lloyd: In most cases, people who decide to accept a full-time job offer should find themselves better-off financially than when they were unemployed. The Department of Employment claimant advisory service helps claimants determine whether particular job offers could prove worthwhile financially. It also provides rapid access family credit facilities for unemployed people with children, so that delays in payment are minimised. People entering lower-paid remunerative work may receive help through the housing benefit and community charge rebate schemes if they are responsible for rent, rates or community charge in Scotland. If they have at least one dependent child they may also be entitled to family credit. Payment of these benefits will continue to be made as long as the qualifying conditions remain satisfied. People on low incomes are also able to claim help with dental, optical and prescription charges, and with the cost of travel to hospital for treatment.

Mr. G. Watterson

Mr. Steen: To ask the Secretary of State for Social Security when he hopes to hold an inquiry into the claim for industrial disablement benefit made by Mr. G. Watterson of North Park holiday centre, Totnes road, Dartmouth, on 23 June 1986, Ref. INS/5999/8057/4; and if he will make a statement.

Mr. Peter Lloyd: Arrangements are in hand for fixing a date for an inquiry and Mr. Watterson should be hearing from the appropriate branch in the next ten days.

The Department will be doing all that it can to process the matter smoothly.

HOME DEPARTMENT

Public Order Act 1986

Mr. Pike: To ask the Secretary of State for the Home Department if he has issued any guidelines for the use of section 39 of the Public Order Act 1986; and if he will make a statement.

Mr. Douglas Hogg: Home Office circular 11/1987 issued on 23 February 1987 gave guidance on those parts of the Public Order Act 1986, including section 39, which came into force on 1 April 1987. A copy is in the Library.

Mr. Pike: To ask the Secretary of State for the Home Department on how many occasions and in what situations section 39 of the Public Order Act has been used; and if he will make a statement.

Mr. Douglas Hogg: This information is not recorded by police forces or otherwise available.

Immigration

Mr. Cohen: To ask the Secretary of State for the Home Department whether, further to his answer to the hon. Member for Islington, North (Mr. Corbyn) *Official Report,* 15 March, column *231,* exceptional and compelling circumstances which would warrant the Minister deferring removal include *(a)* a mistake and *(b)* a misrepresentation of a relevant fact by an immigration officer; and if he will make a statement.

Mr. Renton: As I said in reply to a question by the hon. Member for Islington, North (Mr. Corbyn) on 15 March at column *231,* the examples given in the guidelines introduced on 3 January are not exclusive but are illustrative of the sort of circumstances which would justify deferment of removal. A right hon. or hon. Member may contact my private office (or, out of working hours, the Home Office duty officer) in any case where he believes that the immigration service has wrongly refused to defer removal on the basis of exceptional and compelling circumstances.

Prisoners (Transfer)

Mr. Andrew Smith: To ask the Secretary of State for the Home Department (1) when he anticipates making a decision on the application for transfer to a jail in the North of Ireland from prisioner number 851715, John McComb;

(2) when he anticipates making a decision on the application for transfer to a jail in the North of Ireland from prisoner number 463799, Ronald McCartney;

(3) when he anticipates making a decision on the application for transfer to a jail in the North of Ireland from prisoner number B69204, Thomas Quigley;

(4) when he anticipates making a decision on the application for transfer to a jail in the North of Ireland from prisoner number 119034, Paul Holmes.

Mr. Douglas Hogg: Mr. McCartney's application was answered on 31 May. The applications of Mr. McComb and Mr. Holmes will be answered as soon as possible. To date, there is no outstanding request from Mr. Quigley.

Police Custody (Escapes)

Mr. Alton: To ask the Secretary of State for the Home Department how many prisoners escaped from police custody before being sentenced in each police authority in the most recent period for which such figures are available.

Mr. Douglas Hogg: The information is not held centrally.

Mr. Alton: To ask the Secretary of State for the Home Department if he will make a statement on the escape of five prisoners from police custody in Liverpool on the evening of 12 June.

Mr. Douglas Hogg: I understand from the chief constable of Merseyside police that at about 5.30 pm on 12 June a police bus left the main Bridewell in Liverpool bound for HM prison Hindley with 14 remand prisoners and a police escort on board. Shortly after leaving the Bridewell, a number of the prisoners, who were in individual cells, made a concerted attempt to force off the roof of the vehicle, and four of them managed to escape through a gap in the roof. Two of the prisoners were recaptured immediately, one was caught later the same day, and the other one is still at large. The chief constable is conducting an investigation into the circumstances of the escape.

Mr. Alton: To ask the Secretary of State for the Home Department whether, following a further break-out of five prisoners from a police custody van in Liverpool on the evening of 12 June, he will review the regulations for holding and transporting people held in custody; and if he will make a statement.

Mr. Hurd: I understand that the chief constable of Merseyside is conducting an inquiry into the incident and he will consider whether there are any lessons to be learnt for the future.

Chinese Nationals

Mr. Cohen: To ask the Secretary of State for the Home Department if he will make it his policy for Chinese students in London who feel unable to return to be allowed to remain beyond the expiry of their permit; and if he will make a statement.

Mr. Battle: To ask the Secretary of State for the Home Department if he will extend the entry permits of all Chinese nationals currently in the United Kingdom on the same basis as the Australian Government have done; and if he will make a statement.

Mr. Cox: To ask the Secretary of State for the Home Department (1) if he will ensure that no Chinese students will be forced to leave the United Kingdom to return to China once their student visa has expired, until condition greatly improve in China; and if he will make a statement;

(2) what is the present number of Chinese students studying in the United Kingdom.

Mr. Renton: There are between 6,000 and 6,500 Chinese nationals in the United Kingdom who are subject to immigration conditions and of these some 3,500 are studying here. In view of the current situation in China, we shall look sympathetically at applications for leave to remain here by Chinese nationals who do not wish to return to China at the present time. Any Chinese national therefore whose leave to remain here is due to expire soon, or has already expired, and who does not wish to return should write to the Immigration and Nationality Department, Home Office, Lunar House, Croydon CR9 2BY, and if they do not qualify to remain under the immigration rules, they will nevertheless be allowed to stay for a further six months on an exceptional basis. This is, I understand, a somewhat longer period than the Australian authorities have agreed. I am taking steps to have this advice published as widely as possible in the universities and colleges, and in the Chinese community.

Mr. Garcia (Money)

Mr. Tony Banks: To ask the Secretary of State for the Home Department if he will call for a report from the Commissioner of Police for the Metropolis regarding money taken by Metropolitan Police officers from the home of Mr. Garcia of Stratford, London E15 on 6 February; where the money now is; and why it has not been returned to Mr. Garcia.

Mr. Douglas Hogg: The investigation of alleged criminal offences is an operational matter and, as such, is the responsibility of the commissioner. My right hon. Friend has no authority to intervene in such matters and it would therefore not be fitting for him to call for a report on Mr. Garcia's case.

Mr. Bahadur Singh

Mr. Madden: To ask the Secretary of State for the Home Department further to his letter to the hon. Member for Bradford, West on 23 March concerning Mr. Bahadur Singh; reference IMP S656383/4(S), when he expects to despatch his explanatory statement to the appellate authorities and to Mr. Singh and his representative.

Mr. Renton: The explanatory statement will be despatched to the appellate authorities very shortly. They will make arrangements for it to be forwarded to the appellant's nominated representative.

ENVIRONMENT

City Grants

Mr. Cohen: To ask the Secretary of State for the Environment if he will list (a) all projects and (b) the companies involved and the amounts they are likely to receive, which have been offered a city grant.

Mr. Trippier: The information requested is as follows:

Approved city grant schemes as at 13 June 1989

Local Authority	Project name	Developer's name	Approved city grant
West Midlands			
Coventry	Seven Stars Industrial Estate	Deeley Investments Limited	1·627
Birmingham	Startpoint Industrial Development	English and Overseas Properties Limited	0·283
Birmingham	The Bond	The Bond Limited	0·391
Wrekin	Ketley Business Park, Phase 3	C. J. Pearce & Co. Ltd.	0·230
Dudley	Washington Centre, Dudley	Folkes Properties Ltd.	3·500
Birmingham	Garrison Lane, Ind. Dev. Birmingham	J. A. Elliot (Developments) Ltd.	0·570
Sandwell	Windmill Lane, Smethwick	Tarmac Contract Housing	0·775
Birmingham	Constitution Hill	T. S. Gandhi	0·068
Dudley	Garrick Business Park	Garrick Properties Limited	0·750
Birmingham	Birmingham Factory Centre	Slough Estates	1·260
Sandwell	Sandwell Ski Centre	Glenarn Investments Limited	0·282
		Total	9·736
North West			
Oldham	Park Road Hotel	Florshiem Company (UK) Limited	1·053
Bolton	Prospect Mills Housing	Tay Homes (Northern) Limited	0·650
Bolton	Frederick Street, Farnworth	Allen Homes Limited	0·203
Bolton	Rose Hill, Bolton	Lovell Urban Renewal Ltd.	0·560
Manchester	Carriageway, Manchester	Upton Hunter Estates Ltd.	0·099
Manchester	Every Street Housing Scheme	Tay Homes (North West) Ltd.	0·457
Manchester	Bell Crescent, Manchester	Tay Homes (North West) Ltd.	0·622
Salford	Hazel Avenue and Acme Mill Housing Development	Brackenlea Homes	0·580
Salford	Salford University Tower	Manchester Parc Securities Limited and Amec Regeneration Limited	2·550
Blackburn	Atlantic Mill Site	Hillcrest Homes Limited	0·381
Blackburn	Ice Rink, Blackburn	Arena Associates Ltd.	0·680
Blackburn	Oozebooth Mill	Euro Jeans Ltd.	0·142
		Total	7·977
Northern			
Hartlepool	Hartlepool Business Park	East Mercia Developments Ltd.	0·634
Newcastle	7-19 Mosley Street	Kelburn Holdings Limited	0·413
Stockton	West Row, Stockton	Glynns Estates (Cleveland) Ltd.	0·097
South Tyneside	Boldon Business Park	Washington Developments Ltd.	1·231
Sunderland	Ascot Court, Phase 3, Farringdon	Two Castles Limited	0·101
Hartlepool	Teesbay Business Park	Humberside Properties Ltd.	1·916
Sunderland	Ascot Court, Sunderland, Phase 4	Two Castles Limited	0·055
Sunderland	Gilley Law, Sunderland	Wimpey Homes Holdings Ltd.	1·221
Gateshead	Wellington Road, Dunston	Stannah Lifts Limited	0·201
South Tyneside	Mowbray Court, South Shields	North Country Estates Ltd.	0·101
Newcastle	43-49 Grey Street, Newcastle	City & Northern Properties Ltd.	0·487

Local Authority	Project name	Developer's name	Approved city grant
North Tyneside	Coach Lane, North Shields	Onix Construction Ltd.	0·089
Newcastle	Dean Street, Newcastle	Avatar	0·351
North Tyneside	Grosvenor Mews, North Shields	R. A. Construction Ltd.	0·065
Hartlepool	Owton Manor, Hartlepool	Wimpey Homes Holdings Ltd.	0·570
		Total	7·532
Yorkshire and Humberside			
Kirklees	Site 2, Ringway Industrial Centre	Slough Properties Limited	0·223
Kirklees	Canalside Warehouse	Mr. Marino Belivacoua	0·100
Sheffield	Victoria Buildings	Lynthorpe Properties	0·073
Sheffield	175 Arundel Gate	Manor Developments (Chesterfield) Ltd.	0·246
Leeds	Maxi's Chinese Restaurant	Maxi's (Yorkshire) Co. Ltd.	0·074
Calderdale	Abbey Park	Barrett Leeds Limited	0·365
Bradford	Holroyd Hill/Wibsey Bank	Amex Regeneration Limited	0·700
Sheffield	Huttons Buildings, Sheffield	Crofton Place Estate Co.	0·270
		Total	2·051
London			
Hackney	Ackermans Chocolates Ltd.	Ackermans Chocolates Ltd.	0·070
Tower Hamlets	Atlantis Paper Co.	Atlantis Paper Co.	0·400
Lewisham	Catholic Church Site, Deptford High Street	First Premise Limited	0·158
Tower Hamlets	Alami Import/Export	Alami Import and Export	0·780
Southwark	Alaska Works, SE1	Charterhouse Estates Limited	4·162
		Total	5·570
East Midlands			
Derby	Sir Francis Ley Industrial Park South	J. F. Miller & Company Limited	3·287
Nottingham	20, 20A Fletcher Gate	Garratt Properties	0·160
Nottingham	Players Court, Nottingham	Thomas Long & Sons Ltd.	0·969
Derby	The Former Art Annexe	Michael Goodall Quality Homes Limited	0·120
Nottingham	Pilcher Gate, Nottingham	James McArtney Architects	0·080
Nottingham	Glasshouse Street (Avalon Court)	Avalon Holdings Limited	0·674
Leicester	Arnhem House, Leicester	London & Manchester Assurance Co. Ltd.	0·708
Leicester City	St. Johns Corner	Provident Mutual Life Assurance Assoc.	0·566
Nottingham	The Nottingham Business Design Centre	Local London Group	2·196
Nottingham	3 and 4 Kayes Walk, Nottingham	Spenbeck Ltd.	0·129
Nottingham	Rutland Square Hotel	Wendchoice Limited	0·738
Nottingham	Lamberts Factory Office Development	Pickering Developments Limited	0·796
Nottingham	8 Stanford Street, Nottingham	Emmermoss Limited	0·305
		Total	10·728
Merseyside			
Knowsley	Former Huntley & Palmer Building	Montrose Holdings Limited	0·335
		Total	0·335
South West			
Bristol	Bristol Hawks Gymnastics Centre	Hawkeshyde Motel Limited	0·145
		Total	0·145
		Grand Total	44·074

Dog Registration

Mr. Ron Davies: To ask the Secretary of State for the Environment if he will place in the Library a copy of the dog registration proposal submitted to him by the Association of District Councils in association with the RSPCA, the Institution of Environmental Health Officers and the National Farmers Union.

Mrs. Virginia Bottomley: Yes.

Planning Gain

Mr. Lewis: To ask the Secretary of State for the Environment what directions have been issued by his Department since 1979 with regard to planning gain.

Mr. Chope: My Department's circular 22/83 gives advice to local authorities about the proper scope for "planning gain". That advice is summarised in paragraphs 25-26 of Planning Policy Guidance Note 1, issued in January 1988.

New Parliamentary Building

Mr. Ray Powell: To ask the Secretary of State for the Environment what progress had been made in implementing the recommendation in the Services Committee's report, "New Parliamentary Building Phase 2: The Next Steps", HC561, that the Property Services Agency should undertake a feasibility study for the development of the phase 2 site; and if he will make a statement.

Mr. Chope: Since the House approved the report in December, the agency has undertaken a wide-ranging search to identify an architectural practice with the talent and expertise to undertake the development of this highly sensitive and technically difficult site. Following interviews by a panel chaired by Bryan Jefferson, CBE, past president of RIBA and special advisor to the Secretary of State on architectural matters, a short-list of suitable practices submitted fee bids. I am now able to announce that, with the agreement of the New Building Sub-Committee, Michael Hopkins and Partners have been commissioned by the Department to carry out the studies on the Palace Chambers site, Nos. 1 and 2 Bridge street and the proposed subway in accordance with the Committee's recommendations.

I am grateful to the hon. Member and his colleagues on the New Building Sub-Committee for their advice and support in making this recommendation and look forward to a close working relationship between the Department and the Sub-Committee in developing the proposals for the benefit of Parliament.

I hope to be able to report the results of the studies before the end of the year.

Community Charge

Mr. Cartwright: To ask the Secretary of State for the Environment what representations his Department has received about the impact of the community charge on the residents of almshouses who currently receive the benefit of mandatory or discretionary rate relief; and if he will make a statement.

Mr. Gummer *[holding answer 13 June 1989]:* I continue to receive representations on all aspects of the community charge.

Rate relief for almshouses arises because they are used for charitable purposes. With the introduction of the community charge they will no longer be subject to rating. The community charge is a personal liability which is not linked to the status or value of the property occupied by the chargepayer. Protection for people on low incomes,

including residents of almshouses, will be provided through rebates of up to 80 per cent. of the community charge plus, where appropriate, an amount included in income support in respect of the remaining 20 per cent.

Mr. Vaz: To ask the Secretary of State for the Environment how many representations he has received concering exemption for disabled people from the community charge, also known as the poll tax.

Mr. Gummer *[holding answer 14 June 1989]:* I have received a large number of representations on this subject. People who are severely mentally impaired as defined in schedule 1 of the Local Government Finance Act 1988 are already exempt from the community charge. Others will be liable to pay the community charge, as they now are to pay domestic rates if they are rateable occupiers of domestic properties, and, depending upon their income, would be entitled to rebates. Disabled people with limited means receive particular help under the community charge rebates scheme.

Caravan Sites Act 1968

Dr. Cunningham: To ask the Secretary of State for the Environment if he has any proposals to seek to amend the Caravan Sites Act 1968; and if he will make a statement.

Mr. Ridley: No. I completed a review of the policy just over two years ago and announced the conclusions on 6 February 1987.

EMPLOYMENT

Labour Statistics

Mr. Meacher: To ask the Secretary of State for Employment if he will publish in the *Official Report (a)* the average number, and *(b)* the average percentage of the unemployed who have been unemployed for (i) 0-six months, (ii) over six months, (iii) six months to one year, (iv) over one year, (v) one to two years, (vi) over two years, (vii) two to three years, (viii) over three years, (ix) three to four years, (x) over four years, (xi) four to five years, and (xii) over five years, in each year 1979 to 1988 and April 1989.

Mr. Nicholls *[holding answer 13 June 1989]:* The information is available from the Library. The table shows, for the United Kingdom, the annual average number of unemployed claimants, and these as a percentage of the total in each duration category requested, for the years 1983 to 1988 and the corresponding information for April 1989. Information for the years 1979 to 1982 is only available at disproportionate cost.

Number of unemployed claimants by duration in the United Kingdom

	[1]1983	1984	1985	1986	1987	1988	April 1989
0-6 months	1,303,262	1,318,098	1,341,831	1,352,052	1,206,243	1,004,031	794,075
percentage of total	43·4	41·7	40·9	40·8	40·0	41·4	42·2
Over 6 months	1,696,541	1,840,157	1,939,523	1,960,331	1,809,307	1,421,895	1,098,506
percentage of total	56·6	58·3	59·1	59·2	60·0	58·6	57·8
6-12 months	599,848	610,779	607,263	606,079	549,276	431,006	345,386
percentage of total	20·0	19·3	18·5	18·3	18·2	17·8	18·3
Over 12 months	1,096,693	1,229,378	1,332,260	1,354,252	1,260,030	990,889	744,120
percentage of total	36·6	38·9	40·6	40·9	41·8	40·8	39·5
12-24 months	572,894	557,781	538,746	509,233	463,082	329,301	252,454

	[1]1983	1984	1985	1986	1987	1988	April 1989
percentage of total	19·1	17·7	16·4	15·4	15·4	13·6	13·4
Over 24 months	523,799	671,596	793,514	845,019	796,948	661,587	491,666
percentage of total	17·5	21·3	24·2	25·5	26·4	27·3	26·1
24-36 months	263,665	302,447	299,044	274,968	233,989	181,730	121,382
percentage of total	8·8	9·6	9·1	8·3	7·8	7·5	6·4
Over 36 months	260,133	369,149	494,469	570,050	562,959	479,857	370,284
percentage of total	8·7	11·7	15·1	17·2	18·7	19·8	19·7
36-48 months	143,302	186,590	205,688	194,894	162,775	121,320	89,815
percentage of total	4·8	5·9	6·3	5·9	5·4	5·0	4·8
Over 48 months	116,831	182,559	288,780	375,156	400,183	358,536	280,469
percentage of total	3·9	5·8	8·8	11·3	13·3	14·8	14·9
48-60 months	50,940	92,462	139,600	147,500	128,096	93,523	63,862
percentage of total	1·7	2·9	4·3	4·5	4·2	3·9	3·4
Over 60 months	65,890	90,097	149,180	227,656	272,087	265,013	216,607
percentage of total	2·2	2·9	4·5	6·9	9·0	10·9	11·5

Note: Annual averages are the averages of the four months January, April, July and October. Figures are individually rounded and therefore may not appear to balance.

[1] Average of two months, July and October.

Employment Schemes

Ms. Short: To ask the Secretary of State for Employment what are the monthly statistics since December 1988 for employment training for each standard GB region showing *(a)* entrants in each monthly period, and the number of cumulative entrants since the scheme started, *(b)* a breakdown of entrants which shows how many were male and female, the length of time they had been out of work, their ethnic backgrounds and whether or not they had any disabilities, *(c)* the number of trainees in each monthly period who entered work placements and the cumulative total of how many are in project places at the latest available date, *(d)* trainees who left the scheme in each monthly period, and the number of cumulative leavers since the scheme started, *(e)* for all those trainees who have left the scheme how many found work, failed to attend, went on to another course of training or education, completed the course, left for sickness or went back into umemployment and *(f)* the total number of currently filled places.

Mr. Nicholls: The information is not available in the precise form requested. Information is only available for the eight Training Agency regions in England and for Scotland and Wales. The figures for entrants to employment training are given in table 1. Figures for entrants showing what proportion are men and women, duration of unemployment prior to joining the programme, ethnic background and whether disabled or having a health problem, are given in table 2. Information about trainees entering work placements is not available. The figures for those on project placements are given in table 3. Figures for the number of people who have joined employment training since September and have now left are currently only available for Great Britain as a whole and are estimated; the figures are given in table 4. Information on the breakdowns requested is not available. Information about the number of filled places is given in table 5.

Table 1
Employment training entrants—December 1988 to May 1989

Region	December	January	February	March	April	May	Cumulative since 5 September
South East	1,700	2,300	2,500	2,100	2,300	1,600	18,000
London	2,400	3,800	3,400	3,800	3,100	2,600	27,600
South West	1,700	2,100	2,500	2,300	2,000	1,700	17,100
West Midlands	3,300	4,300	5,000	4,800	4,100	3,200	34,800
East Midlands and Eastern	2,200	3,000	3,600	3,200	3,100	2,400	24,700
Yorkshire and Humberside	4,400	5,500	6,100	5,400	4,900	4,100	43,300
North West	4,100	5,500	7,100	6,500	5,800	4,800	47,300
Northern	2,900	3,600	4,800	4,700	3,800	3,300	32,100
Wales	2,200	2,900	3,600	3,200	2,900	2,300	23,100
Scotland	4,000	3,700	5,400	6,000	4,400	4,000	36,800

Table 2
Employment training characteristics of entrants (September-April)
(all figures are percentages, figures may not total 100 because of rounding)

Region	Men	Women	Unemployment duration (months)				Ethnic Origin[1]					PWD[2]	
			0-6	6-12	13-23	24+	1	2	3	4	5	Yes	No
South East	64	36	25	28	12	34	91	2	2	2	2	15	85
London	58	42	14	32	16	37	51	25	11	7	6	10	90
South West	68	32	24	33	13	30	93	2	1	2	2	15	85
West Midlands	68	32	17	27	13	42	79	9	8	2	2	12	88
East Midlands and Eastern	72	28	12	34	14	39	88	4	5	1	2	14	86
Yorks and Humberside	74	26	20	31	14	35	90	2	4	1	2	10	90

Region	Men	Women	Unemployment duration (months)				Ethnic Origin[1]					PWD[2]	
			0-6	6-12	13-23	24+	1	2	3	4	5	Yes	No
North West	72	28	19	31	14	37	92	2	3	1	2	11	89
Northern	74	26	17	35	15	34	96	1	1	1	2	9	91
Wales	71	29	19	36	14	31	95	1	1	1	3	11	89
Scotland	73	27	12	32	17	39	96	..	..	1	2	11	89
Great Britain total	70	30	18	32	14	36	88	5	4	2	2	12	88

[1] Ethnic origin
 1 — White
 2 — Black/African/Caribbean
 3 — Indian/Pakistan/Bangladeshi/Sri Lankan
 4 — None of these
 5 — I prefer not to say
[2] PWD — People with disabilities. Those trainees answering whether they had a long-term health problem or disability which affected the type of work they could do.
 .. = less than 0·5 per cent.

Table 3
Employment training in training on project placements—May 1989

Region	Number
South East	4,200
London	8,500
South West	5,200
West Midlands	13,000
East Midlands and Eastern	8,700
Yorkshire and Humberside	12,700
North West	12,900
Northern	11,600
Wales	6,500
Scotland	13,800

Table 4
Employment training leavers (estimated)

	Number
December	7,000
January	11,000
February	19,000
March	26,000
April	23,000
Cumulative since 5 September	99,000

Table 5
Employment training filled places at 26 May 1989

Region	Number
South East	10,700
London	17,700
South West	11,500
West Midlands	22,400

Region	Number
East Midlands and Eastern	15,300
Yorkshire and Humberside	24,900
North West	26,400
Northern	21,800
Wales	14,500
Scotland	22,300

Ms. Short: To ask the Secretary of State for Employment, for each of the Training Agency's areas within Greater London, Merseyside, Greater Manchester, Glasgow, Sheffield, Birmingham and Solihull, Coventry and Warwickshire, and for each of the latest four three monthly periods available, how many unemployed people have been referred to the following outcomes as a result of their restart interviews and, for each of the outcomes, how many people started or attended them *(a)* referred to a job, *(b)* allocated to restart courses, *(c)* referred to ET, *(d)* referred to community programme, *(e)* referred to new job training scheme, *(f)* referred to jobclubs, *(g)* referred to EAS, *(h)* referred to voluntary work/VPP, *(i)* referred to ERC, *(j)* referred to a DRO, and *(k)* referred to a claimant adviser.

Mr. Lee: The information is not available in the form requested. However, the attached table gives the information for the relevant Employment Service areas.

We do not know how many of those interviewed ultimately end up in a job or other opportunity as a result of the Restart interview.

Restart counselling: Numbers referred to menu options

	[1]Greater London	[2]Merseyside	[3]Greater Manchester	[4]Glasgow	[5]Sheffield	[6]Birmingham and Solihull	[7]Coventry and Warwickshire
April—June 1988							
(a) Job	5,506	2,828	3,296	1,487	904	1,512	850
(b) Restart course	2,188	801	1,385	669	219	776	113
(c) ET	0	0	0	0	0	0	0
(d) CP	1,322	1,189	1,477	789	554	493	47
(e) New JTS	6,242	2,642	4,548	2,112	1,707	2,141	144
(f) Jobclub	9.076	3,082	3,837	2,232	678	530	193
(g) EAS	5,049	1,259	1,263	310	225	700	52
(h) Voluntary work/VPP	499	374	266	189	169	152	21
(i) ERC	168	43	106	34	29	29	5
(j) DRO	2,466	761	1,093	664	270	428	237
(k) Claimant adviser	5,815	2,737	2,206	1,135	698	1,212	444
July—September 1988							
(a) Job	7,705	2,754	3,329	1,276	1,216	1,212	594
(b) Restart course	2,052	1,073	1,405	568	351	667	321
(c) ET	5,188	1,715	2,527	1,313	1,189	1,152	758

	[1]*Greater London*	[2]*Merseyside*	[3]*Greater Manchester*	[4]*Glasgow*	[5]*Sheffield*	[6]*Birmingham and Solihull*	[7]*Coventry and Warwickshire*
(d) CP	639	879	846	204	302	216	387
(e) New JTS	5,570	2,240	4,310	1,341	1,562	2,023	1,690
(f) Jobclub	8,848	2,722	3,592	1,621	883	1,900	1,286
(g) EAS	5,440	1,305	1,499	260	239	828	414
(h) Voluntary work/VPP	545	302	161	96	109	92	218
(i) ERC	124	34	80	16	45	20	46
(j) DRO	2,677	880	1,077	669	366	461	164
(k) Claimant adviser	6,085	3,180	2,478	1,049	878	1,273	439
October—December 1988							
(a) Job	6,156	2,466	2,587	1,215	810	2,634	505
(b) Restart course	1,663	651	1,302	664	415	747	198
(c) ET	16,467	6,586	6,928	5,454	1,354	4,929	2,306
(d) CP	0	0	0	0	0	0	0
(e) New JTS	0	0	0	0	0	0	0
(f) Jobclub	7,943	2,074	3,543	1,949	717	1,210	700
(g) EAS	5,085	1,309	1,582	313	223	1,036	238
(h) Voluntary work/VPP	0	0	0	0	0	0	0
(i) ERC	0	0	0	0	0	0	0
(j) DRO	2,364	720	1,114	741	306	511	118
(k) Claimant adviser	5,490	2,795	2,462	1,380	689	1,322	527
January—March 1989							
(a) Job	7,766	2,421	2,971	727	717	4,727	756
(b) Restart course	1,976	562	1,135	686	381	613	253
(c) ET	16,648	6,936	6,907	6,409	4,662	5,533	1,951
(d) CP	0	0	0	0	0	0	0
(e) New JTS	0	0	0	0	0	0	0
(f) Jobclub	8,617	2,616	3,723	2,504	726	1,574	727
(g) EAS	5,570	1,330	1,628	365	177	1,289	244
(h) Voluntary work/VPP	0	0	0	0	0	0	0
(i) ERC	0	0	0	0	0	0	0
(j) DRO	2,518	723	1,033	690	220	598	137
(k) Claimant adviser	6,629	2,848	2,554	1,510	716	1,486	443

[1] Areas: London SE; Inner London S; Inner London E; Inner London Central; Inner London W; London N; London NW; London E; London S; London SW; London W.

[2] Areas: Liverpool and Wirral; Merseyside N; Merseyside S.

[3] Areas: Manchester City; Manchester NE; Manchester NW; Manchester S; Manchester W.

[4] Areas: Glasgow N; Glasgow S.

[5] Area: Sheffield.

[6] Area: Birmingham (includes Solihull).

[7] Area: Coventry/Warwickshire.

Ms. Short: To ask the Secretary of State for Employment, for each of the Training Agency's areas within Greater London, Merseyside, Greater Manchester, Glasgow, Sheffield, Birmingham and Solihull, Coventry and Warwickshire, what are the monthly statistics for the latest available three months for employment training showing *(a)* entrants in each monthly period, and the number of cumulative entrants since the scheme started, *(b)* a breakdown of entrants which shows how many were male and female, the length of time they had been out of work, their ethnic backgrounds and whether or not they had any disabilities, *(c)* the total number of currently filled places, *(d)* the number of trainees in each monthly period who entered employer based work placements and the cumulative total of how many are in employer placements at the latest available date, *(e)* the number of trainees in each monthly period who entered project based work placements and the cumulative total of how many are in project based placements at the latest available date, *(f)* trainees who left the scheme in each monthly period, and the number of cumulative leavers since the scheme started, *(g)* for those trainees who have left the scheme how many found work, failed to attend, went on to another course of training or education, completed the course, left for sickness, or went back into unemployment, *(h)* for those trainees who have left the scheme how many have obtained a vocational qualification and *(i)* for those trainees who have left the scheme how many have received a training bonus, giving the average training bonus received.

Mr. Nicholls: The figures for entrants to employment training for each of the last three months are given in table 1. Figures for entrants showing what proportion are men and women, duration of unemployment prior to joining the programme, ethnic background and whether disabled or having a health problem are given in table 2. The number of currently filled places is provided in table 3. Information about trainees entering employer and project placements is not available. The figures for those currently in training on project and employer placements are given in table 4. The numbers of trainees who left the scheme are not available on an area basis. Information on the breakdowns requested and for the number obtaining vocational qualifications is not available. Information on the number of trainees who have left the scheme who have received a training bonus and the average bonus paid is not available.

Table 1
Employment training entrants March—May 1989

Area	March	April	May	Cumulative since September
London North	850	570	580	5,750
London West	280	180	190	2,130
London East	490	380	340	3,590
London South	300	360	220	2,380
Inner London North	1,120	930	770	8,780
Inner London South	760	680	460	4,990
Merseyside	2,030	1,860	1,640	13,810
Manchester East	800	660	550	5,160
Manchester Central	870	920	770	7,220
Manchester North	720	620	520	5,250
Glasgow	1,310	970	800	7,410
Sheffield	1,340	1,140	820	9,390
Birmingham and Solihull	1,580	1,440	960	11,080
Coventry and Warwickshire	570	560	410	3,910

Table 2
Employment training characteristics of entrants (September-April)
(all figures are percentages, figures may not total 100 because of rounding)

Area	Men	Women	Unemployment duration (months)				Ethnic origin[1]					PWD[2]	
			0-6	6-12	13-23	24+	1	2	3	4	5	Yes	No
London North	54	46	19	31	16	35	45	26	14	7	8	10	90
London West	58	42	24	25	16	35	62	11	18	5	4	10	90
London East	63	37	10	36	16	38	61	16	17	2	3	11	89
London South	57	43	20	29	15	37	67	16	8	4	5	12	88
In London North	58	42	15	30	18	37	50	26	9	7	9	9	91
In London South	60	40	12	32	19	37	44	35	5	10	6	7	93
Merseyside	69	31	23	27	13	37	95	2	3	1	2	8	92
Manchester East	68	32	23	31	13	33	94	1	3	1	1	11	89
Manchester Central	70	30	22	31	14	34	83	7	5	2	3	10	90
Manchester North	66	34	25	30	14	31	91	1	5	1	2	9	91
Glasgow	74	26	19	27	14	40	94	2	1	1	2	7	93
Sheffield	76	24	13	33	14	41	90	3	2	3	2	8	92
Birmingham and Solihull	63	37	19	26	12	43	65	17	12	3	3	8	92
Coventry and Warwickshire	65	35	20	25	13	42	82	5	8	3	2	13	87

[1] Ethnic origin: 1—White; 2—Black/African/Caribbean; 3—Indian/Pakistan/Bangladeshi/Sri Lankan; 4—None of these; 5—I prefer not to say.

[2] PWD—People with disabilities. Those trainees answering whether they had a long-term health problem or disability which affected the type of work they could do. Figures to end February.

[3] Less than 0·5 per cent.

Table 3
Employment training filled places at 26 May 1989

Area	Number
London North	3,555
London West	1,176
London East	2,198
London South	1,609
Inner London North	5,794
Inner London South	3,345
Merseyside	8,701
Manchester East	2,626
Manchester Central	4,189
Manchester North	2,622
Glasgow	4,505
Sheffield	5,489
Birmingham and Solihull	7,346

Area	Number
Coventry and Warwickshire	2,662

Table 4
Employment training in training on project and employer placements May 1989

Area	Project placements	Employer placements
London North	1,460	1,000
London West	220	290
London East	750	510
London South	870	240
Inner London North	3,190	700
Inner London South	2,340	130
Merseyside	4,790	1,390

Area	Project place-ments	Employer placements
Manchester East	550	1,420
Manchester Central	1,970	1,220
Manchester North	870	970
Glasgow	3,290	630
Sheffield	2,960	1,100
Birmingham and Solihull	4,920	1,100
Coventry and Warwickshire	1,380	510

Ms. Short: To ask the Secretary of State for Employment, for Great Britain and each standard training agency region, and for each of the latest four three-monthly periods available, how many unemployed people have been referred to the following outcomes as a result of their restart interviews and, for each of the outcomes, how many people started or attended them: *(a)* referred to a job, *(b)* allocated to restart courses, *(c)* referred to ET, *(d)* referred to community programme, *(e)* referred to new job training scheme, *(f)* referred to jobclubs, *(g)* referred to an EAS, *(h)* referred to voluntary work/VPP, *(i)* referred to ERC, *(j)* referred to a DRO, and *(k)* referred to a claimant adviser.

Mr. Lee: The information as requested is not available. However, information for Great Britain and the relevant employment service regions is given on the attached table.

We do not know how many of those interviewed ultimately end up in a job or other opportunity as a result of the Restart interview.

Restart counselling: Numbers referred to menu options

	Northern	Yorkshire and Humberside	East Midlands and Eastern	London and South East	South West	Wales	West Midlands	North West	Scotland	Great Britain
April to June 1988										
(a) Job	3,687	4,362	4,996	11,659	2,338	4,879	6,970	9,266	9,843	58,000
(b) Restart course	2,413	883	1,487	3,683	1,088	1,811	1,964	3,378	3,540	20,247
(c) ET	0	0	0	0	0	0	0	0	0	0
(d) CP	2,364	2,131	1,725	2,607	909	1,663	2,551	3,663	4,074	31,687
(e) New JTS	6,036	8,267	6,353	12,169	2,861	4,115	7,006	10,642	8,542	65,991
(f) Jobclub	4,199	3,788	4,339	14,133	2,347	3,826	5,647	9,938	9,368	57,585
(g) EAS	795	1,464	1,589	7,456	1,607	1,246	2,331	3,412	1,895	21,795
(h) Voluntary work/VPP	336	615	1,010	1,449	446	644	741	1,113	663	7,017
(i) ERC	124	84	195	246	30	109	119	191	152	1,250
(j) DRO	1,235	1,348	1,144	4,396	939	1,002	1,872	2,864	2,461	17,261
(k) Claimant adviser	2,892	3,346	3,223	10,634	2,139	2,459	4,812	7,204	4,395	41,104
July to September 1988										
(a) Job	4,080	5,121	5,257	14,387	2,135	5,311	7,432	9,321	8,186	61,230
(b) Restart course	2,141	1,274	1,717	3,271	1,081	1,814	2,032	3,547	3,305	20,182
(c) ET	4,144	5,104	4,029	9,632	1,694	2,842	5,212	6,307	6,313	45,277
(d) CP	1,755	1,230	954	1,369	346	1,139	1,333	2,117	1,709	11,952
(e) New JTS	4,662	7,230	5,288	10,033	1,961	3,754	6,996	8,976	6,160	55,060
(f) Jobclub	3,746	4,114	4,006	13,425	2,048	3,675	5,023	8,928	7,593	52,558
(g) EAS	996	1,798	1,582	7,987	1,193	1,420	2,775	3,912	1,686	23,349
(h) Voluntary work/VPP	194	341	563	1,124	219	456	412	700	365	4,374
(i) ERC	148	97	131	190	15	80	87	133	105	986
(j) DRO	1,399	1,761	1,278	4,655	968	1,120	2,261	3,039	2,397	18,878
(k) Claimant adviser	3,261	3,914	4,038	11,198	2,243	2,855	5,903	7,664	4,931	46,007
October to December 1988										
(a) Job	2,834	4,179	5,064	13,228	1,758	3,375	8,400	8,184	6,493	53,515
(b) Restart course	1,405	1,532	1,472	2,765	1,310	1,647	1,890	2,955	2,887	17,863
(c) ET	11,034	14,518	10,402	26,940	5,564	9,188	15,748	18,415	19,798	131,607
(d) CP	0	0	0	0	0	0	0	0	0	0
(e) New JTS	0	0	0	0	0	0	0	0	0	0
(f) Jobclub	3,193	4,230	3,961	26,304	2,211	3,451	4,913	8,169	7,776	50,075
(g) EAS	875	1,749	1,506	7,475	1,393	1,305	2,910	3,822	1,717	22,752
(h) Voluntary work/VPP	0	0	0	0	0	0	0	0	0	0
(i) ERC	0	0	0	0	0	0	0	0	0	0
(j) DRO	1,199	1,605	1,174	4,332	1,007	1,079	2,129	2,895	2,472	17,892
(k) Claimant adviser	2,241	3,368	3,529	9,757	2,251	2,504	5,613	7,234	5,505	42,002
January to March 1989										
(a) Job	3,256	4,193	5,657	15,763	2,016	3,960	11,471	8,391	7,808	62,515
(b) Restart course	1,475	1,867	1,288	2,983	1,240	1,557	1,738	2,524	3,173	17,845
(c) ET	11,173	13,032	9,716	25,445	5,255	9,104	15,595	18,117	21,010	128,627
(d) CP	0	0	0	0	0	0	0	0	0	0
(e) New JTS	0	0	0	0	0	0	0	0	0	0
(f) Jobclub	4,093	4,292	3,948	12,719	2,353	3,711	5,325	8,680	9,769	54,890
(g) EAS	899	1,613	1,594	7,909	1,272	1,446	3,090	3,828	1,969	23,620
(h) Voluntary work/VPP	0	0	0	0	0	0	0	0	0	0
(i) ERC	0	0	0	0	0	0	0	0	0	0
(j) DRO	1,132	1,499	1,034	4,325	925	1,065	2,062	2,727	2,428	17,197
(k) Claimant adviser	2,411	3,171	3,403	11,171	2,104	2,621	5,150	7,004	5,593	42,628

Ms. Short: To ask the Secretary of State for Employment, for Great Britain and each standard training agency region, what are the monthly statistics for the latest available three months for employment training showing *(a)* entrants in each monthly period, and the cumulative number of entrants since the scheme started, *(b)* a breakdown of entrants which shows how many were male and female, the length of time they had been out of work, their ethnic backgrounds and whether or not they had any disabilities, *(c)* the total number of currently filled places, *(d)* the number of trainees in each monthly period who entered employer based work placements and the cumulative total of how many are in employer placements at the latest available date, *(e)* the number of trainees in each monthly period who entered project based work placements and the cumulative total of how many are in project based placements at the latest available date, *(f)* trainees who left the scheme in each monthly period, and the number of cumulative leavers since the scheme started, *(g)* for those trainees who have left the scheme how many found work, failed to attend, went on to another course of training or education, completed the course, left for sickness, or went back into unemployment, *(h)* for those trainees who have left the scheme how many have obtained a vocational qualification and *(i)* for those trainees who have left the scheme how many have received a training bonus, giving the average training bonus received.

Mr. Nicholls: The figures for entrants to employment training for each of the last three months are given in table 1. Figures for entrants showing what proportion are men and women, duration of unemployment prior to joining the programme, their ethnic background and whether disabled or having a health problem are given in table 2. The total number of currently filled places is provided in table 3. Information about trainees entering work and project placements is not available. The figures for those on project and work placements are given in table 4. Figures for the number of people who have joined employment training since September and have now left are currently only available for Great Britain as a whole and are estimated; the figures are given in table 5. Information on the breakdowns requested and for the number obtaining vocational qualifications is not available. Information on the number of trainees who have left the scheme who have received a training bonus, and the average bonus paid, is not available.

Table 1
Employment training entrants[1]

Region	March	April	May	Cumulative (since 5 September)
South East	2,100	2,300	1,600	18,000
London	3,800	3,100	2,600	27,600
South West	2,300	2,000	1,700	17,100
West Midlands	4,900	4,100	3,200	34,800
East Midlands and Eastern	3,200	3,100	2,400	24,700
Yorkshire and Humberside	5,400	4,900	4,100	43,300
North West	6,500	5,800	4,800	47,300
Northern	4,700	3,800	3,300	32,100
Wales	3,200	2,900	2,300	23,100
Scotland	6,000	4,400	4,000	36,800
Great Britain total	42,100	36,300	30,000	304,800

[1] Combined regional figures may not equal Great Britain totals because of rounding.

Table 2
Employment training characteristics of entrants (September-April)
(all figures are percentages, figures may not total 100 because of rounding)

Region	Men	Women	Unemployment duration (months)				Ethnic Origin[1]					PWD[2]	
			0-6	6-12	13-23	24+	1	2	3	4	5	Yes	No
South East	64	36	25	28	12	34	91	2	2	2	2	15	85
London	58	42	14	32	16	37	51	25	11	7	6	10	90
South West	68	32	24	33	13	30	93	2	1	2	2	15	85
West Midlands	68	32	17	27	13	42	79	9	8	2	2	12	88
East Midlands and Eastern	72	28	12	34	14	39	88	4	5	1	2	14	86
Yorks and Humberside	74	26	20	31	14	35	90	2	4	1	2	10	90
North West	72	28	19	31	14	37	92	2	3	1	2	11	89
Northern	74	26	17	35	15	34	96	1	1	1	2	9	91
Wales	71	29	19	36	14	31	95	1	1	1	3	11	89
Scotland	73	27	12	32	17	39	96	..	..	1	2	11	89
Great Britain total	70	30	18	32	14	36	88	5	4	2	2	12	88

[1] Ethnic origin
   1 — White
   2 — Black/African/Caribbean
   3 — Indian/Pakistan/Bangladeshi/Sri Lankan
   4 — None of these
   5 — I prefer not to say
[2] PWD — People with disabilities. Those trainees answering whether they had a long-term health problem or disability which affected the type of work they could do.
.. = less than 0·5 per cent.

Table 3
Employment training filled places at 26 May 1989

Region	Number
South East	10,700
London	17,700
South West	11,500
West Midlands	22,400
East Midlands and Eastern	15,300
Yorks and Humberside	24,900
North West	26,400
Northern	21,800
Wales	14,500
Scotland	22,300
Great Britain total	187,000

Employment training in training on project and work placements
May 1989

Region	Project placements	Work placements
South East	4,200	3,300
London	8,500	3,200
South West	5,200	3,000
West Midlands	13,000	4,500
East Midlands and Eastern	8,700	4,100
Yorks and Humberside	12,700	6,200
North West	12,900	7,400
Northern	11,600	5,200
Wales	6,500	3,900
Scotland	13,800	4,700
Great Britain	97,000	45,000

Employment training leavers (estimated)

	Number
February	19,000
March	26,000
April	23,000
Cumulative[1]	99,000

[1] Cumulative leavers since September 1988.

Training and Enterprise Councils

Mr. McAllion: To ask the Secretary of State for Employment what representations he has received from the training and enterprise councils.

Mr. Cope: Twenty two applications for development funding have been received by the national training task force who is reviewing these proposals and will forward its recommendations to me. I will announce which TECs have been awarded development funding shortly after.

Small Businesses

Mr. Patrick Thompson: To ask the Secretary of State for Employment if he will report what the Government are doing to help small businesses; and if he will make a statement.

Mr. Cope: The Government have created an overall economic climate which has helped small firms to flourish and grown. It also supports a wide range of schemes to help new and growing firms gain access to professional advice, to finance and to training. These include the small firms service, the business expansion scheme, the enterprise allowance scheme and the enterprise initiative. In April I announced the extension of the highly successful loan guarantee scheme and I also launched business growth training to help small businesses improve their competitiveness and profits through training.

The Reserve

Mr. Leighton: To ask the Secretary of State for Employment to what extent and for what reasons his Department envisages needing to call on the Reserve over the planning period in Cm. 607; and if the Reserve is likely to be needed to provide for capital spending.

Mr. Cope: The Department is likely to call on the Reserve this year to the extent of £580,000 in support of end year flexibility on capital because of slippage.

Major Capital Projects

Mr. Leighton: To ask the Secretary of State for Employment to what extent major new capital projects are separately indentified in departmental booklets; what major new capital projects have been undertaken since Cm. 288; and what costs will arise from them *(a)* in 1989-90 and *(b)* in future years.

Mr. Cope: Major capital projects are separately indentified in my Department's Supply Estimates published each year. Details of projects costing over £500,000 are contained in table 1 to Votes 1 and 2 and table 2 to vote 4 in "Supply Estimates 1989-90, Class VII Department of Employment", Her Majesty's Treasury March 1989 (231-VII), copies of which are available in the Library.

Long-term projects—Details of capital projects costing over £500,000 and reconciliation with the Estimates (Subheads A2, A4, G2)

£ thousand at 1989-90 prices[3]

Project	Year of start/ original estimate of year of completion[1]	Current estimate of year of completion	Original estimate of expenditure[2]	Total	Current estimate of expenditure Spent in past years	Current estimate of expenditure Estimates provision for 1989-90	Current estimate of expenditure To be spent in future years
Field systems review Subhead A2	1988-89/ 1992-93	1992-93	13,850	13,850	0	750	13,100
Personnel data processing Subhead A4	1987-88/ 1992-93	1992-93	937	937	0	521	416
Local area network Subhead A4	1989-90/ 1995-96	1995-96	2,065	2,065	0	265	1,800
Total						1,536	

Project	Year of start/ original estimate of year of completion[1]	Current estimate of year of completion	Original estimate of expenditure[2]	Total	Current estimate of expenditure		
					Spent in past years	Estimates provision for 1989-90	To be spent in future years
Capital works below £500,000						13,308	
Total subheads A2, A4, G2						14,844	

[1] The dates shown for year of start/completion refer to the main contracts. Only schemes on site during 1989-90 are shown in the table. Schemes which will reach practical complettition before the start of 1989-90 or which are due to start on site after 1989-90 are not shown, though there may be expenditure on these schemes in the form of fees, equipment costs, enabling works etc. Expenditure figures shown include preliminary expenditure prior to the main contract and residual expenditure following completion of the work on site.
[2] Based on budget estimates updated to 1989-90 for inflation.
[3] All projected and outturn cash prices have been brought to 1989-90 prices using GDP deflators.

1989-90, Class VII, Vote 2

Long-term projects—Details of computer and construction projects costing over £500,000 and reconciliation with the Estimates (subheads D2 and L3)

£ thousand at 1989-90 prices[3]

Project	Year of start/ original estimate of year of completion[1]	Current estimate of year of completion	Original estimate of expenditure[2]	Total	Current estimates of expenditure		
					Spent in past years	Estimates provision for 1989-90	To be spent in future years
Refurbishment of Watford HQ—Subhead D2(3)(a)	1987-88/1988-89	1989-90	1,979	2,301	2,223	78	—
Construction UBO Gt. Yarmouth—Subhead D2(3)(a)	1988-89/1989-90	1990-91	433	1,196	614	562	20
Construction UBO Swindon—Subhead D2(3)(a)	1988-89/1989-90	1990-91	1,155	1,738	415	1,082	241
Construction UBO Handsworth—Subhead D2(3)(a)	1986-87/1989-90	1989-90	1,312	1,256	1,248	8	—
Construction UBO Camberwell—Subhead D2(3)(a)	1986-87/1989-90	1989-90	2,131	2,412	2,074	338	—
Extension and Refurbishment Fulham UBO —Subhead D2(3)(a)	1987-88/1989-90	1989-90	1,357	1,849	1,832	17	—
Construction UBO Dartford—Subhead D2(3)(a)	1985-86/1987-88	1989-90	1,321	1,615	1,442	173	—
Extensions and Refurbishment Exeter UBO— Subhead D2(3)(a)	1988-89/1989-90	1990-91	709	1,321	147	1,070	104
Construction new H.Q. Building Sheffield— Subhead D2(3)(b) and D4	1988-89/1990-91	1990-91	12,600	12,600	368	4,200	8,032
Additional Mainframe Peripherals and Resilience Programme—Subhead L(3)(1)	1988-89/1989-90	1990-91	2,835	2,835	840	1,050	945
Refurbishment Nottingham RO—Subhead D2(3)(b)	1987-88/1988-89	1989-90	597	712	693	19	—
Extension and alterations Yeovil UBO— Subhead D2(3)(a)	1988-89/1989-90	1990-91	394	858	436	395	27
Construction UBO Kidderminster—Subhead D2(3)(a)	1985-86/1987-88	1989-90	506	694	685	9	—
Construction UBO Willenhall—Subhead D2(3)(a)	1986-87/1988-89	1989-90	602	564	543	21	—
Construction Failsworth UBO—Subhead D2(3)(a)	1988-89/1989-90	1991-92	708	708	57	187	464
Extension Bedminster UBO—Subhead D2(3)(a)	1987-88/1988-89	1990-91	394	532	431	96	5
Extension and Refurbishment Selly Oak UBO—Subhead D2(3)(a)	1988-89/1988-89	1989-90	1,666	861	81	780	—
Runcorn Services—Subhead L(3)(1)	1987-88/1988-89	1989-90	755	872	857	15	—
Computer Page Printing System Runcorn— Subhead L(3)(1)	1989-90/1989-90	1989-90	630	630	—	630	—
Supervacs—Subhead D2(1)(b)	1988-89/1989-90	1989-90	1,909	2,364	1,276	888	—
Total						11,618	
Capital Works below £500,000						70,050	
Total Subheads D2, L3						81,668	

[1] The dates shown for year of start/completion refer to the main contracts. Only schemes on site during 1989-90 are shown in the table. Schemes which will reach practical completion before the start of 1989-90 or which are due to start on site after 1989-90 are not shown, though there may be expenditure on these schemes in the form of fees, equipment costs, enabling works etc. Expenditure figures shown include preliminary expenditure prior to the main contract and residual expenditure following completion of the work on site.
[2] Based on budget estimates updated to 1989-90 for inflation.
[3] All projected and outturn cash prices have been brought to 1989-90 prices using GDP deflators.

Comparing the above projects with previous years' Estimates tables the trend is:—

	1987-88	1988-89	1989-90
Percentage of projects with later completion dates than original	—	83	75
Percentage of projects with higher current estimate of expenditure than original	—	—	60

Long term projects—Details of capital projects costing over £500,000 and reconciliation with the Estimates (Subhead C)

£ *thousand at 1989-90 prices*[3]

Project	Year of start/ original estimate of year of completion[1]	Current estimate of year of completion	Original estimate of expenditure[2]	Total	Current estimate of expenditure		
					Spent in past years	Estimates provision for 1989-90	To be spent in future years
Office conversion and construction of new laboratory (Subhead C) Works in progress 1 April 1989							
London HQ office conversion	1987-88/ 1990-91	1990-91	1,710	1,710	878	780	52
Sheffield Laboratory	1987-88/ 1993-94	1993-94	12,519	12,519	599	967	10,953
Building projects total (A)			14,229	14,229	1,477	1,747	11,005
Other works costing up to £500,000 total (B)			—	—	—	634	—
Total (A & B) Subhead C			—	—	—	2,381	—

[1] The dates shown for year of start/completion refer to the main contracts. Only schemes on site during 1989-90 are shown in the table. Schemes which will reach practical completion before the start of 1989-90 or which are due to start on site after 1989-90 are not shown, though there may be expenditure on these schemes in the form of fees, equipment costs, enabling works etc. Expenditure figures shown include preliminary expenditure prior to the main contract and residual expenditure following completion of the work on site.

[2] Based on budget estimates updated to 1989-90 for inflation.

[3] All projected and outturn cash prices have been brought to 1989-90 prices using GDP deflators.

Community Charge

Mr. Harry Barnes: To ask the Secretary of State for Employment if he will list the categories of information held by his Department that will be available for use by community charge registration officers.

Mr. Cope: Unemployment benefit offices are required to disclose details of the name and address of any person or their partner, aged 18 or over, to a registration officer for a charging authority. This information may only be disclosed if

    (i) at any time between 22 May 1989 and 31 March 1990 a person is in receipt of income support but is not receiving housing benefit; and

    (ii) from April 1990 where a person is awarded income support but has not made a claim for community charge benefits.

Mr. Leighton: To ask the Secretary of State for Employment if he has received a copy of the comparative training of clothing workers in Britain and West Germany by the National Insitute of Economic and Social Research; and if he will make a statement.

Mr. Cope: My Department has received a copy of the National Institute Economic Review (No. 125, May 1989) in which the article "Productivity, Machinery and Skills: Clothing Manufacture in Britain and Germany" appears.

The article points to long standing differences between the training arrangements adopted in Britain and Germany and warrants careful consideration by the industry. In doing so they will be aware of the considerable progress made in recent years, notably through the introduction of two-year YTS and the "Clothing Skill Awards" accredited by the National Council for Vocational Qualifications in 1988.

YTS (Teachers)

Mr. Harry Greenway: To ask the Secretary of State for Employment how many teachers are involved in full-time YTS and in what capacities; and if he will make a statement.

Mr. Cope: There are no statistics on the full-time involvement of teachers in YTS. Scheme staff frequently have teaching qualifications, and teachers are often employed in delivery of off-the-job training.

To promote closer co-operation and understanding between teachers and trainers, the Training Agency has run two successful pilot schemes under which 78 teachers were seconded to YTS managing agents for periods of up to 16 weeks. Consideration is being given to the introduction of a national scheme of short duration secondments.

Rexo (Member's Letter)

Mr. Ashton: To ask the Secretary of State for Employment why it took from 11 April to 30 May for his Department to decide that a letter from the hon. Member for Bassetlaw regarding redundancy payments at Rexo was the responsibility of the Department of Energy.

Mr. Cope: The hon. Member's letter was received by my Department on 19 April. My Department considered that the issue was the responsibility of the Department of Energy and the letter was forwarded to them on 21 April. Subsequently checks showed that the letter had been lost in transit. Action was taken immediately to despatch a further copy. I apologise for the delay.

Departmental Expenditure Plans

Mr. Leighton: To ask the Secretary of State for Employment how much the change in the expenditure plans for his Department for 1989-90 from the 1988-89 estimated outturn will be *(a)* in percentage terms and *(b)* after adjustment for the gross domestic product deflator.

Mr. Cope: The expenditure plans for my Department for 1989-90 are 2·3 per cent. higher than the 1988-89 estimated outturn. After adjustment for the gross domestic product deflator, the expenditure plans for 1989-90 are £85 million 2·6 per cent. below the 1988-89 estimated outturn.

INDEX TO THE

PARLIAMENTARY DEBATES

OFFICIAL REPORT

SIXTH SERIES

SESSION 1988–89

VOLUME 154

6th June—16th June 1989

SCOPE OF THE INDEX, ARRANGEMENT AND ABBREVIATIONS

This index is derived from the House of Commons Library's Parliamentary On-Line Information System (POLIS), and the subject terms used are based on those used in POLIS. There are often changes in column numbering, etc, between the daily part or weekly Hansard (which simply collects together the daily parts without revision) and the bound volume. The index for the bound volume is revised to take account of these changes.

Scope and arrangement of the Index

Oral and Written Parliamentary Questions are indexed under subject headings and the names of Members asking and Ministers replying to them. Questions are not listed under the names of Departments replying. Departmental listings can be arrived at indirectly by looking under the names of the Minister(s) of that Department. There are, however, the headings 'Northern Ireland', 'Scotland', and 'Wales' under which one can find not only most Questions answered by the Northern Ireland Office, Scottish Office, Welsh Office but also Questions about these areas of the United Kingdom which are answered by other Departments. Ministerial statements are indexed under subject headings, under 'Ministerial statements' and the names of Ministers making them and Members speaking on them. General debates are indexed under broad subject headings and under the names of all Members and Ministers taking part. Debates on legislation (Bills, Orders, Regulations etc.) are indexed under the name of the Bill, Statutory Instrument etc, under subject headings and under the names of those taking part.

Rulings and Statements by Mr. Speaker and his deputies are brought together under the heading Speaker's rulings and statements.

Other contributions by Mr. Speaker and his deputies appear under the heading Speaker.

Opposition Day Debates, Estimates Day Debates and Standing Order No. 10 applications are listed under those respective headings and under subject headings too.

The date of each item except Parliamentary Questions is inserted immediately before the reference.

Members' names are given in the form by which they prefer to be known and are printed in bold italics. Under their names, entries are arranged under one of the two headings *Debates etc* (to include interventions on statements, points of order and so on) or *Questions*.

Abbreviations

Bills 1R=first reading, 2R=second reading, Money res=money resolution, Com=Committee stage, Rep=Report stage, 3R=third reading, amendt/amendts=amendment/amendments, *=matter taken formally, without debate.

Column numbers followed by the letter W refer to Written Questions. These appear at the end of each daily part or volume with their own sequence of column numbers printed in italics.

Flynn, Mr Paul—*continued*
Nuclear fuels, Sea transport 156w
Nuclear safeguards 483w
Nuclear safeguards, Treaties 484w
Nuclear test ban 31-2w
Open University, Science & technology
 policy 546w
Ozone layer, International conferences 83-
 4w
Plutonium, Nuclear safeguards 36w, 483w
Radioactive wastes, Imports 483w
Scottish Nuclear, Radioactive wastes 23w
Uranium, Namibia 483w

Food
AIDS 78w
Research 349w, 553w
Tax harmonisation 208w

Food Advisory Committee
300-3w

Food contamination
Food imports 279w
Sweets 297w

Food hygiene
Eggs 560w
Fish products 295-6w
Slaughterhouses 303w
Wales 553w

Food imports
Eggs 10-1w, 497w
Food contamination 279w

Food inspection
Slaughterhouses 349w
Wales 553w

Food labelling
302w
Factory farming 246-7w
Untreated milk 350-1w

Food poisoning
Airlines 94w
Untreated milk 94w, 373w

Food prices
Beef 294-5w

Food standards
14w
Eggs 10w

Fookes, Dame Janet
Debates etc.
Army (08:06:89) 408-10
Local Government & Housing Bill, Rep
 (14:06:89) 1047-51, 1065, 1070, 1076
Questions
Dogs, Law reform 463w

Foot, Rt Hon Michael
Debates etc.
Arts (15:06:89) 1141, 1152-8

Football
Identity cards (15:06:89) 1178
Public order policing 505w

Football Safety Review
44-5w, 82w

Football Spectators (No 2) Bill 1988/89
Debates etc.
2R order read (09:06:89) 527, (16:06:89)
 1275

Footwear
EC action 70-1w
Imports 70-1w

Foreign aid
International Monetary Fund 355-6
OECD countries 274w

Foreign & Commonwealth Office
560w
Electronic surveillance 34w
Press 309w

Foreign investment in UK
200w
Wales 2w

Foreign languages
8

Foreign policy
Argentina 467w
China 505w, 897-900
East Germany 260-1w
Eastern Europe 463w
Egypt 473-4w
Israel 470w
Panama 905
Syrian Arab Republic 469w
USSR 260w, 464w, 469w

Forest protection
Rain forests 275w

Forestry
495-6w
Road damage 212-3
Set-aside schemes 495-6w

Forestry Commission
Foxes 375-6w
Land acquisition 213, 542w
Nature conservation 212
Nature reserves 375w

Forsyth, Douglas
32w

Forsyth, Mr Michael, *Under-Secretary
of State for Scotland*
Questions
Alcoholism, Departmental circulars 23w
Community care, Scotland 26w
Community health councils, Scotland 540w
Contracts for services, NHS 178w
Dental Practice Board, Scotland 26w
Dentists, Scotland 26w
Family doctors, Contracts of employment
 178w
Family doctors, Scotland 183w
Fisheries, Interest charges 341w
Fisheries, Scotland 182w, 188w
Freedom of expression, Higher education
 179w
Freedom of expression, Universities 210-2
Hospital consultants, Educational leave
 24w
Injuries, Medical rehabilitation 543w
Languages education, India 496w
Lennox Castle Hospital, Artificial flowers
 25-6w
Liver diseases, Transplant surgery 23-4w
Maternity hospitals, Construction 210
Medical research, Scotland 186w
Medical Research Council, NHS Review
 338-9w
Midwives, Scotland 186w
NHS, Contracts for services 214-5
NHS finance, Scotland 187-8w
NHS Review, Family doctors 178w, 225-6
NHS Review, Scotland 178w, 183w, 209
NHS Review, Tayside 224-5
Prescription charges exemptions, Scotland
 185w
Screening, Scotland 438w
Secondary education, Per capita costs 179w
Self-governing hospitals, Scotland 181w,
 342w
Self-governing schools 179w
Self-governing schools, Teachers 27w
Shellfish, Members' correspondence 341w
Southern General Hospital Glasgow, X
 rays 338w
Storms, Government assistance 539w
Students, Tuition fees 25w
Untreated milk, Food poisoning 373w
Village halls, Scotland 188w
Women, Doctors 209-10

Forth, Mr Eric, *Parliamentary Under-
Secretary of State for Industry and
Consumer Affairs*
Debates etc.
Consumer protection (12:06:89) 566, 576-7,
 598-605
Questions
Bottles, Labelling 418w
Company investigations, Civil service
 manpower 146-8w

Forth, Mr Eric—*continued*
Electronic surveillance, Dept of Trade &
 Industry 70w
European Conference of Postal &
 Telecommunications Administration 72w
Funerals, Fees & charges 244w
Hearing aids, Consumer protection 74w
Hearing aids, Trade descriptions 74w
Industry, Inflation 546w
Institute of Logistics & Distribution
 Management 71w
Open University, Science & technology
 policy 546w
Post Office, Monopolies 479w
Post Office, Pay 72w
Post Office Counters, Privatisation 72w
Post Office Users' National Council 71w
Postal deliveries 73w
Postal services 72-3w
Postal services, Courier services 73w
Postal services, EC internal trade 73w
Postal services, Mail Users' Association
 312w
Postal services, Monopolies 71-3w
Postal services, New Zealand 74w
Postal services, Parcels 72w
Press, Dept of Trade & Industry 244w
Strategic programme for innovation &
 technology transfer 62-6w
Television engineering, International
 cooperation 313w
Television engineering, Science &
 technology research 313w

Foster, Mr Derek
Debates etc.
Economic policy (07:06:89) 318

Foulkes, Mr George
Debates etc.
China, Protest movements (06:06:89) 34
Oral question time intervention (07:06:89)
 223
Questions
Hong Kong, Democracy 900
Housing, Jersey 503w
MV Majestic, Shipping accidents 548w
NHS Review, Family doctors 225
Police, Isle of Man 327-8w
Scottish Development Agency 182w
Shipping accidents, Shetland 336w

Foxes
Forestry Commission 375-6w

France
International cooperation 506w
Potatoes 561w

Franks, Mr Cecil
Questions
Barrow Borough Transport, Criminal
 investigation 135w
Barrow Borough Transport, Debts 139w
Barrow Borough Transport, Directors
 139w
Barrow Borough Transport, Loans 138-
 40w
Barrow Borough Transport, Secured loans
 140w
Barrow in Furness Borough Council,
 Loans 174w
Barrow in Furness Borough Council, Local
 government finance 174w
EC social charter 699
Income tax, Tax rates & bands 196w
NATO, Armed forces deployment 403w

Fraser, Mr John
Debates etc.
Local Government & Housing Bill, Rep
 (14:06:89) 963, 972-3, 975-6
Questions
Business premises, Rating revaluations 80w
Horniman Museum, Charitable trusts 216w
Housing action trusts, Angell Town estate
 417w
Illegal immigrants, Immigration rules 502w
Trials 550

Fraud

Handicapped—*continued*
Water supply 171w

Handicapped pupils
Mitchell House School Belfast 545-6w

Hanley, Mr Jeremy
Debates etc.
Employment Bill, Rep & 3R (06:06:89) 130
Local Government & Housing Bill, Rep
(14:06:89) 1068-71
Questions
Bus services, Northern Ireland 228w
Historic buildings, Greater London 534-5w
London Underground, Rolling stock 539
National income 205w

Hannam, Mr John
Questions
Electricity disconnections, Handicapped
267w
Electricity meters, Handicapped 266w
Handicap benefits 175w
"Home Improvement Policy Consultation
Paper", Handicapped 168-9w
House renovation grants, Handicap
benefits 166-8w
Housing & handicapped, Handicap benefits
169w
Mobility allowance, Multiply handicapped
76-7w
Multiply handicapped 189w
Water supply, Dialysis machines 171w

Harbours Docks & Piers Clauses Act 1847
Questions
506w

Hard core unemployed
Denton & Reddish 291w

Hardy, Mr Peter
Debates etc.
Local Government & Housing Bill, Rep
(14:06:89) 933-4, 1034, 1049
Questions
Barlow Clowes, Compensation 147w
Council of Europe, EC Environment
Council 900-1
Ivory, Imports 91-2w
Nature conservation, Overseas trade 91w
Nature reserves, Land acquisition 91-2w

Hargreaves, Mr Ken
Debates etc.
Abortion, Carlisle Hospital (08:06:89) 463-
4
United Nations, Children's rights
(06:06:89) 200-2
Questions
Bypasses, Blackburn 522w
Castle Hill School, School closures 238-9w
Cemeteries, Property transfer 416w
Housing management, Government grants
165w
Lotteries 368
Queen's Park Hospital Blackburn,
Maternity services 555w

Harman, Ms Harriet
Questions
Channel tunnel, Railway freight transport
329w
Housing action trusts, Southwark 216-8w
Housing estates, Southwark 217w
Nursing homes, District health authorities
388w
Transplant surgery, Examinations 103-4w

Harmondsworth Detention Centre
Immigrant detainees 241w

Harmonisation of legislation
EC social policy 162w

Harmonisation of standards
Time zones 504w

Harp seals
317w

Harris, Mr David
Questions
Broadcasting, Ownership 506w
Fisheries, Scotland 182w

Haselhurst, Mr Alan
Questions
Student loans, Deaf 6

Hawkins, Mr Christopher
Debates etc.
Employment Bill, Rep & 3R (06:06:89)
122, 130
Local Government & Housing Bill, Rep
(14:06:89) 1042, 1051, 1064-5

Haynes, Mr Frank
Debates etc.
Arts (15:06:89) 1166-7
Coal mining, Subsidence (16:06:89) 1226,
1248, 1258-64, 1267
Employment Bill, Rep & 3R (06:06:89) 62-
3, 72, 122-4, 126, 129, 133, 171-4, 183-4
Local Government & Housing Bill, Rep
(13:06:89) 729, 733
Questions
Concessionary television licences,
Pensioners 1107-8
Nuclear weapons, Seas & oceans 400w

Hayward, Mr Robert
Debates etc.
Drug abuse (09:06:89) 497-502
Economic policy (07:06:89) 253
Questions
Nuclear free zones, Western Europe 403w
Public holidays 366w
Water conservation 86-7w

Hazardous wastes
Waste disposal 81w

Hazel Court School Eastbourne
Speech therapy 344w, 388w

HBMC
see Historic Buildings & Monuments
Commission for England

Health education
Elderly 425w
Medical education 343w

Health Education Authority
425w

Health for All
85w

Health hazards
Pesticides 303-4w
Sweets 5w

Health service staff
Northern Ireland 363-4w
Pay settlements 424-5w
Pension rights 555-6w

Health services
Rate support grants 85w
Research finance 221w

Health warnings
Benzodiazepines 557w
Botulism 552-3w

Hearing aids
101-2w
Consumer protection 74w
Trade descriptions 74w

Heath School
Public petitions (12:06:89) 676

Heathrow Airport
118w

Heating
House of Commons accommodation 536w

Heddle, Mr John
Questions
Construction Industry Training Board 57w
New towns development corporations,
Property transfer 416-7w
Planning permission, Business premises
80w
Railway electrification, Lichfield-Redditch
railway 138w, 517w

Heddle, Mr John—*continued*
Road construction, Birmingham 410w

Heffer, Mr Eric S
Debates etc.
Army (08:06:89) 386, 391
Arts (15:06:89) 1139, 1152
Questions
Cyprus, Peace negotiations 897
NATO 355w
Unemployment 354-5
USSR, Arms control 690
Young offenders, Parental responsibility
1110-1

Helicopters
Military exercises 121-2w
West Germany 121-2w

Henderson, Mr Doug
Questions
Footwear, Imports 70-1w
Poverty, Low Pay Unit 205w

Hepatitis
Irradiated food 300w

Hereditary diseases
Medical research 22-3w

Hetherington Committee
see War Crimes Inquiry

Hicks, Mrs Maureen
Questions
Botulism 706
Drug crimes, Narcotics 463-4w
Police vehicles, Death 323w

Hicks, Mr Robert
Questions
HMS Southampton 403w
Middle East, Peace negotiations 470w

Higgins, Rt Hon Terence L
Questions
Road works, Greater London 539
Roads, Expenditure 332w

High Wycombe
Armed forces deployment 524-5w

Higher civil servants
Civil service pensions 446-7w

Higher education
Freedom of expression 179w
Student numbers 17w
Wales 150w

Highlands of Scotland
Storms 539w

Hill livestock allowances
409w

Hillsborough Stadium
324w

Hillsborough Stadium Inquiry
Expenditure 512w
Video recordings 324w

Hinchliffe, Mr David
Debates etc.
Snapethorpe Hospital Wakefield, Hospital
closures (07:06:89) 343-7
Questions
Armed forces conditions of service, Dual
jobholding 232w
Bank of England 205w
Nuclear weapons tests, Compensation 403-
4w
Wakefield Health Authority, Self-governing
hospitals 387-8w

Hind, Mr Kenneth
Debates etc.
Economic policy (07:06:89) 254-5, 268, 274,
295-8
Local Government & Housing Bill, Rep
(13:06:89) 752-3, 755
Questions
Income tax 195w

Rangers House
534-5w

Rate fund contributions
172w

Rate support grants
Health services 85w

Rates & rating
204w
Hotels 339w
Local government revenue 305w, 342w,
    492-4w
Ports 86w
Scotland 339w, 342w, 492-4w
Wales 305w

Rathbone, Mr Tim
    Debates etc.
Arts (15:06:89) 1140
Drug abuse (09:06:89) 479-88, 495, 500,
    504, 513, 514

Rating revaluations
Business premises 80w

RAVC
see Royal Army Veterinary Corps

Recognition of states
Cambodia 136-7w
Palestine 471w

Recruitment
Teachers 3-4, 14-5w, 21w

Recycling
Bottles 173w

Redbridge Borough Council
(06:06:89) 79-118

Redbridge London Borough Council Bill
1988/89
    Debates etc.
(06:06:89) 79-118

Redmond, Mr Martin
    Debates etc.
Local Government & Housing Bill, Rep
    (14:06:89) 922
Redbridge London Borough Council Bill,
    2R (06:06:89) 81-2, 85, 90, 91-2, 99, 109-
    11, 113
    Questions
2 Signals Brigade, Army strength 526w
Agriculture, EC grants & loans 5-6w
Armed forces, Buildings 524-5w
Beef premiums, Yorkshire & Humberside
    8w
Coal mining, North Yorkshire 35-6w
Common sheep meat regime, Yorkshire &
    Humberside 7-8w
Dept of Social Security local offices, South
    Yorkshire 419-22w
Exercise Wintex-Cimex 125-6w
Fisheries, EC grants & loans 6-7w
Fisheries, Loans 7w
Fishing catches, Yorkshire & Humberside
    9w
Fishing vessels, Yorkshire & Humberside
    8-10w
High Wycombe, Armed forces deployment
    524-5w
Low flying, Clayton 126w
Military aircraft, USA 154w
Northwood, Armed forces deployment
    525w
Nuclear weapons, Nuclear accidents 492w,
    501w, 526w
Nuclear weapons deployment, INF Treaty
    153w, 320w
Nuclear weapons deployment, US bases
    320w
Nuclear weapons policy, NATO 153-4w
Policewomen, Police firearms 240w, 247w
Private patients, Doncaster 554-5w
Radioactive waste disposal, Yorkshire &
    Humberside 81w
Regional development grants, Yorkshire &
    Humberside 164w

Redmond, Mr Martin—*continued*
Roads, Emergency planning 522w
Slaughterhouses, Food inspection 349w
Social Fund, Community care 419w
Social Fund, Doncaster 528w
Sports facilities, Local authorities 316w
Tourism, Yorkshire & Humberside 148-9w
Transplant surgery 531w
Valuation & community charge tribunals,
    South Yorkshire 80-1w
Wilton, Armed forces deployment 525-6w
Written questions, Government
    achievements 239w

Redundancy
Inner London Education Authority 443w

Redundancy pay
Departmental correspondence 588w
Rexo 549w

Redundant mineworkers' payments scheme
157w

Redwood, Mr John
    Debates etc.
Commercial television (13:06:89) 722
Economic policy (07:06:89) 251
House of Commons broadcasting,
    Television (12:06:89) 619
    Questions
British Rail, Privatisation 547
Eastern Europe, Foreign policy 463w
NHS Review, Family doctors 178w
Public expenditure, Central government
    202w
Sewage, Wargrave 415-6w
Television licences, Income 1108

Re-enfranchisement of the People Bill 1988/
89
    Debates etc.
2R order read (16:06:89) 1275

Rees, Rt Hon Merlyn
    Debates etc.
Commercial television (13:06:89) 715
House of Commons broadcasting,
    Television (12:06:89) 612
    Questions
Business statements 372
EC Foreign Affairs Council 908-9

Refrigeration
Chlorofluorocarbons 440w

Refugee camps
Cambodia 355w

Refugees
Namibia 543-4w

Reg(EURATOM)3227/76
483w

Reg(EEC)3626/82
258-9w

Reg(EEC)3418/83
258-9w

Regional development grants
Yorkshire & Humberside 164w

Regional enterprise grants
552w

Regional planning & development
EC internal trade 181w
Scotland 182w

Regional selective assistance
552w

Register of Sasines
Administrative delays 540-1w

Rehabilitation centres
Employment rehabilitation 433-4w

Reid, Dr John
    Questions
Community charge, Orders & regulations
    180w
NHS, Contracts for services 214

Reid, Dr John—*continued*
Public expenditure 203w

Relocation of employees
Prison staff 43w

Remand in custody
240w
Criminal damage 240w
Leeds 51w
Young offenders 51w

"Renovation Grants Proposed Test of
Resources Consultation Paper"
166-8w

Rent officers
Private rented housing 170w

Rented housing
Community charge 93w

Renton, Mr Tim, Minister of State at
the Home Office
    Debates etc.
Broadcasting controls, EC action (13:06:89)
    858-64, 868-9, 870, 877
    Questions
Administrative delays 324w
Aquino, Michael, Entry clearances 328w
BBC 510w
Broadcasting, Ownership 506w
Broadcasting, Privatisation 505-6w
China, Overseas students 558w
Concessionary television licences,
    Pensioners 135w, 1107-8
Concessionary television licences, War
    widows 135w
Deportation 215-6w
Garfunkel's, Overseas workers 58w
Illegal immigrants, Immigration rules 502w
Immigrant detainees, Harmondsworth
    Detention Centre 241w
Immigration, Hong Kong 369w
Immigration appeals 566w
Immigration controls, Airports 42w
Immigration controls, China 564-5w
Mentally ill, Entry clearances 389-90w
Overseas students, China 327w
Passport Office, Civil service manpower
    242-4w
Passport Office, Glasgow 364-5w
Passport Office, Telephone services 48-9w
Passport Office, Telephone systems 365w
Passports, Administrative delays 48-9w
Passports, Fees & charges 49-50w
Passports, Leeds 459w
Passports, Sub post offices 48w
Political refugees 43w
Political refugees, China 366w
Political refugees, Immigration applications
    366w
Political refugees, Tamils 43-4w, 563w
Privacy & Press Law Review 241w
Radio, Republic of Ireland 135w
Sunday trading 509w
Television licences, Fines 1107
Television licences, Income 1108
Television programmes, Children 325w
Vietnamese refugees, Hong Kong 50w
Vietnamese refugees, Travel requirements
    50w
Visas, Administrative delays 51w

Repairs & maintenance
Public sector housing 87w
St Benedict's School Birkenhead 269w

Republic of Ireland
545w
Radio 135w

Research
Animal diseases 299w
Food 349w, 553w
Parasitic diseases 12-3w

Research councils
Biology 19-20w

Research finance
AIDS 488-9w
Health services 221w

Social security benefits rules—continued
Unemployment benefits 282w

Social security claims
Income support 283-4w
Industrial disablement benefits 562w

Social security recipients
Attendance allowance 385-6w
Child benefit 79w
Dumbarton 188w
Housing benefits 175w
Social security appeals 421w

Social security reform
Board & lodging charges 283w

Social Services Select Committee
277-8w, 429w

Soley, Mr Clive
   Debates etc.
Local Government & Housing Bill, Rep
   (13:06:89) 728, 731-5, 738, 740, 745, 814,
   819, 822, 823, 828-9, 839-40, (14:06:89)
   931-3, 942-3, 947-50, 951, 958-60, 970-2,
   1037-9, 1047
   Questions
China, Police custody 262-3w
Empty property, Dept of the Environment
   418w
Empty property, Local government
   property 417-8w
Housing association grant 87w
Public sector housing, Repairs &
   maintenance 87w
Rose theatre, Archaeological sites 1123

Solicitors
Legal aid 345-6w
Orders & regulations 541w
Prison visits 29-30w

Solihull
10

Somerset
Housing finance 90-1w

Sopley
Armed forces deployment 525-6w

South Africa
469w
Apartheid 902
Coal 246w
Human rights 890
Iron & steel 75-6w
SS Ave 112w

South East region
City technology colleges 11-2

South London
London assessment studies 519w

South of Scotland Electricity Board
23w

South Tyneside
290w

South Wales
Channel tunnel 152w
Industrial research 151-2w
Railway network (13:06:89) 882-8
Sewage 151w

South West Water Authority
Sewage 173w

South Yorkshire
Coal mining 35-6w
Dept of Social Security local offices 419-
   22w
Valuation & community charge tribunals
   80-1w

Southern Derbyshire Health Authority
Nurses 100w

Southern General Hospital Glasgow
X rays 338w

Southwark
Housing action trusts 216-8w
Housing estates 217w

Southwood Committee
see Bovine Spongiform Encephalopathy
   Working Party

Sovereignty
EC integration 1121
West Germany 161-2w

Spain
Diplomatic service 260w
Fishing catches 294w
Fishing vessels 294w

*Speaker and his deputies, For rulings &
statements see separate heading
Speaker's rulings & statements*
   Debates etc.
Amendments & new clauses (06:06:89) 57-
   8, 67, 140, 144, 166, 175, (13:06:89) 746,
   772-3, 782, 790-2, 794, 801, 804, 809, 815,
   818, 825, 827, 829, 837, 838, 842, 844,
   845, 856, 858, (14:06:89) 922-1088 passim
Disallowed questions (12:06:89) 540
Orders & regulations motions (14:06:89)
   920
Private Members' Bills, 2R order read
   (09:06:89) 527-8
Procedure (06:06:89) 152, 155, (07:06:89)
   247, 278, 295, 360, 365, (13:06:89) 687,
   689, 915, (14:06:89) 926, 939, 1049, 1051
Standing Order No 20 applications, Alar
   (07:06:89) 240
Standing Order No 20 applications, Dog
   registration scheme (06:06:89) 50
Standing Order No 20 applications,
   European Council (15:06:89) 1133
Standing Order No 20 applications,
   Institute of Food Research (14:06:89) 913-
   4, 918
Standing Order No 20 applications,
   Passports (06:06:89) 48

Speaker's rulings & statements
Calling of Members (07:06:89) 238,
   (15:06:89) 1126
House of Commons division of time
   (13:06:89) 715, 721, 724, (15:06:89) 1170
House of Commons divisions (06:06:89) 75
House of Commons procedure (08:06:89)
   379, (12:06:89) 607, (13:06:89) 729
Members' conduct (07:06:89) 216, 259, 266,
   314, (14:06:89) 1016, (16:06:89) 1242
Members' interventions (06:06:89) 16, 17,
   (08:06:89) 366, 386, (13:06:89) 755, 757,
   792, 814, (14:06:89) 1047, 1054, (16:06:89)
   1250
Members' speeches (07:06:89) 247,
   (08:06:89) 380, 421, 443, (12:06:89) 584,
   598, 605-6, 631, 638, (14:06:89) 1094-5,
   (15:06:89) 1149
Ministerial statements (07:06:89) 237,
   (09:06:89) 487, (12:06:89) 557, (14:06:89)
   917
New clauses (06:06:89) 57
Oral questions (13:06:89) 687, (14:06:89)
   916, (15:06:89) 1109, 1111
Points of order (06:06:89) 51-2, 53,
   (07:06:89) 247, (13:06:89) 709, 858
Prime Minister's questions (08:06:89) 364
Public petitions (16:06:89) 1215
Scope of debate (06:06:89) 84, 86, 88, 154,
   172, (12:06:89) 589, 595, (15:06:89) 1197-8,
   1201, (16:06:89) 1243
Supplementary questions (08:06:89) 368,
   (12:06:89) 540, 554, (14:06:89) 890, 899
Ten minutes rule (07:06:89) 247
Terminology (08:06:89) 379
Unparliamentary expressions (06:06:89)
   133, (13:06:89) 693, 701-2, (14:06:89) 1059

Spearing, Mr Nigel
   Debates etc.
Broadcasting controls, EC action (13:06:89)
   861, 875-8
EC law (15:06:89) 1207-12
European Council, Standing Order No 20
   applications (15:06:89) 1133
House of Commons broadcasting,
   Television (12:06:89) 611, 617, 641-3
   Questions
Business statements 374, 1129

Spearing, Mr Nigel—continued
Channel tunnel, Railway stations 548
Dogs, Liability for animals 214w
East London river crossing 410w
European monetary union 895-6
NHS Policy Board, Public appointments
   422-3w
Road tolls, Greater London 110w
Schools, Extracurricular activities 4
Tax harmonisation, Excise duties 118w
Tax harmonisation, VAT 118w
Television, EC action 1121
Treaty of Rome 471w

Special constables
Ports 506w

Special education
Curriculum 16w, 269w
Deaf 13-4
Dyslexia 17w

Special hospitals
191-4w

Special Hospitals Service Authority
191-4w

Special protection areas
Severn estuary 89w

Speech therapists
Leicestershire Health Authority 108w

Speech therapy
Deaf 13
Hazel Court School Eastbourne 344w,
   388w

Speed, Mr Keith
   Questions
M20, Road construction 519w

Speed limits
Road damage 138w

Speller, Mr Tony
   Questions
Administrative delays 324w
Alternative energy, Scotland 187w
Bristol Channel, Pollution monitoring 90w
EC internal trade 239w
Employment 384-5w
Nigeria, Overseas aid 474w
Nuclear weapons 232-4w
Passports, Sub post offices 48w
Sea pollution, Bristol Channel 416w
Tax reform 116-7w

Spicer, Sir Jim
   Debates etc.
Army (08:06:89) 384, 421-3
   Questions
Bulgaria, Human rights 890

*Spicer, Mr Michael, Under-Secretary of
State for Energy*
   Debates etc.
Coal mining, Subsidence (16:06:89) 1236,
   1271-4
   Questions
Acid rain, Energy policy 484w
Air pollution control, Carbon dioxide 222-
   3w
Alternative energy, Crops 223w
Atomic Energy Research Establishment,
   Nuclear reactors 37w
Atomic Energy Research Establishment,
   Nuclear safety 37w
Atomic Energy Research Establishment,
   Radiation hazards 37w
Atomic Energy Research Establishment,
   Radioactive waste disposal 37-8w
Berkeley power station, Power station
   closures 156w
Coal mining, North Yorkshire 35-6w
Eastern Electricity Board 268w
Electricity area boards, Retail trade 268w
Electricity disconnections, Handicapped
   267w
Electricity meters, Handicapped 266w
Magnox reactors, Construction 223w